FOURTH EDITION

SCHROEDER'S ANTIQUES PRICE GUIDE

Edited by Sharon & Bob Huxford

COLLECTOR BOOKS
A Division of Schroeder Publishing Co., Inc.

The current values in this book should be used only as a guide. They are not intended to set prices, which vary from one section of the country to another. Auction prices as well as dealer prices vary greatly and are affected by condition as well as demand. Neither the Editor nor the Publisher assumes responsibility for any losses that might be incurred as a result of consulting this guide.

On the cover: Wyandotte coupe toy car, ca. 1940, $25.00; Lone Star or Star of Bethlehem quilt, 1880's, $1,000.00+; Red Wing salt glaze "Success Filter" water cooler, $800.00; Haviland demitasse cup and saucer, $55.00; Art Nouveau butterfly belt buckle, $80.00; Rabbit chocolate mold, $125.00.

Cover items courtesy *American Quilter* magazine; *Red Wing Stoneware; Haviland Collectibles and Object of Art; Art Nouveau, Art Deco Jewelry;* Kay Blackburn Smith; Charles Rayl.

Additional copies of this book may be ordered from:

COLLECTOR BOOKS
P.O. Box 3009
Paducah, Kentucky 42001

@$9.95 Add $1.00 for postage and handling.

ISBN: 0-89145-314-8

Introduction

Our goal for the Fourth Edition of *Schroeder's* has been to give our readers even more useful, comprehensive, and accurate information than ever before. As soon as we had completed the Third Edition, we began photographing new items, adding new information to our files, and compiling listings from dealer ads and auction catalogs. One of our primary aims for 1986 was to increased the size of our Advisory Board. Because our sources are so varied, we realized that within each of our nearly 600 categories we would be in error to assume that each sale that was recorded, or each 'asking price' we included was entirely reflective of realistic market values. We felt that the best way to alleviate this problem was to solicit help from the experts. We recruited authors, researchers, appraisers,and many of the country's top collectors and dealers; 154 people and several nation-wide collectors' organizations covered more than 400 categories. (Last year we had advisors for 68 subjects!) To correspond with that many people was in itself a three-month full-time job for our office manager, but we feel her efforts achieved the results we had hoped for. Our experts went over our computer print-outs line by line, deleting listings that were misleading or too vague to be of merit. Many of them sent us new background information, and corrected errors we were unaware of in our narratives; others sent photos of the more esoteric antiques and collectibles. When they had finished with their editing, we were left with 52,000 lines (by actual count, not an inflated estimation) of useful, accurate evaluations that provide a sound understanding of the dealings in today's market place.

Several new categories have been added this year that have recently sparked collectors' interest, and it will continue to be our policy to stay abreast of any 'new' areas of activity, reporting those to you as soon as warranted judged on recorded sales, dealer exposure, etc.

Our Directory, which you will find in the back of the book, lists each contributor by state. These are people who have allowed us to photograph various examples of merchandise from their show booths, sent us pricing information, or in any way have contributed to this year's book. Feel free to contact them; many will be glad to ship you the merchandise you need. If you happen to be travelling, consult the Directory for shops along your way. We also list clubs who have worked with us, and auction houses who have agreed to permit us the use of photographs from their catalogues.

To be used to your best advantage, this guide should be regarded as a basic tool, a rule of thumb, only one source of the information you need to digest in order to become a knowledgeable dealer or collector. Antique shows, trade papers, collectors' books, and association with others sharing the same interests all contribute toward making you more keenly aware of market trends, and thus educate you toward becoming a wise and confident buyer.

We have organized our topics alphabetically, following the most simple logic, usually either by manufacturer or by type of product. If you have difficulty in locating your subject, consult the index. Our guide is unique in that much more space has been allotted to background information than any other publication of this type, and it is easier to read due to the larger-than-average print. Our readers tell us that these are features they enjoy. To be able to do this, we have adopted a format of one-line listings wherein we describe the items to the fullest extent possible in the allotted space by using several common-sense abbreviations; they will be easy to read and understand if you will first take the time to quickly scan through them.

Listing of Standard Abbreviations

The following is a list of abbreviations that have been used throughout this book in order to provide you with the most accurate descriptions possible in the limited space available. No periods are used after initials or abbreviations. When two dimensions are given, height is noted first. If only one dimension is listed, it will be height, except in the case of bowls, dishes, plates, or platters, when it will be diameter. The standard two-letter state abbreviations apply.

For glass items, when no color is noted, glass is clear. A number following the last comma in a listing indicates how many items are included in the lot price. Teapots and sugar bowls are assumed to be 'with lid,' and butter dishes 'with cover.'

Since condition is extremely important in determining market value, this year each collectible has been evaluated to determine the usual condition in which it is most likely to be offered for sale without the dealer feeling it necessary to mention wear or damage. For instance, advertising items are priced for examples in excellent condition since mint items are scarce enough that when one is offered for sale, the dealer will most likely make mention of the fact. On the other hand, when buying glassware, pottery, and china, the collector trusts that an item is mint (that is without damage), and that if it is not, the dealer will note the damage. A basic rule of thumb is that an item listed as VG (very good) will bring 40% to 60% of its mint price (a first-hand, personal evaluation will enable you to make the final judgement); EX (excellent) is a condition midway between mint and very good, and values would correspond.

American	Am
Attributed to	att
Back	bk
Bisque	bsk
Black and white	b/w
Blue	bl
Brown	brn
Bulbous	bulb
Cardboard	cb
Cast iron	CI
Century	C
Circa	ca
Composition	compo
Copyright	c
Creamer & sugar	cr/sug
Cross	X
Cup & saucer	c/s
Dark	dk
Dated	dtd
Decoration	decor
Diameter	dia
Diamond Quilted	Dia Quilt
Double	dbl
Dovetail	dvtl
Drawer	drw
Each	ea
Embossed	emb
Embroidered	embr
Engraved	eng
Excellent	EX
Exterior	ext
Foot, footed	t, ftd
Framed	fr
Good	G
Graduated	grad
Grain painted	grpt
Green	gr
Hand painted	HP
Handle, handled	hdl, hdld
Impressed	imp
Individual	ind
Interior	int
Iridescent	irid
Large	lg
Lavender	lav
Leaded glass	ldgl
Length	L
Light	lt
Lithograph	litho
Mahogany	mahog
Mark	mk
Mint	M
Mint in box	MIB
Mother of pearl	MOP
Mount, mounted	mt, mtd
Multicolor	mc
Near mint	NM
New England	NE
Opalescent	opal
Original	orig
Otherwise	o/w
Paint	pnt
Pair	pr
Patented	pat
Pedestal	ped
Piece	pc
Pink	pk
Pint	pt
Professional	prof
Porcelain	porc
Refinished	rfn
Regarding	re
Repainted	rpt
Replaced	rpl
Restored	rstr
Reticulated	retic
Reverse painted	rvpt
Round	rnd
Salt & pepper	S&P
Signed	sgn
Silverplated	SP
Size	sz
Small	sm
Square	sq
Standard	std
Straight	str
Thumbprint	t'print
Turned, turning	trn
Turquoise	turq
Upholstered	uphl
Very good	VG
Victorian	Vict
White	wht
Width	W
With	w/
Without	w/o
Yellow	yel

A B C Plates

Children's plates featuring the alphabet as part of the design were popular from as early as 1820 until after the turn of the century. The earliest English creamware plates were decorated with embossed letters and prim moralistic verses; but the later Staffordshire products were conducive to a more relaxed mealtime atmosphere--often depicting playful animals and riddles, or scenes of pleasant leisure-time activities. They were made around the turn of the century by American potters as well. All featured transfer prints, but color was sometimes brushed on by hand to add interest to the design. Braille plates were made for the blind, but are rather scarce, and therefore usually more valuable. You may also find an occasional bowl or mug . . . a matching set is rare.

When no condition is indicated, the items listed below are assumed to be in mint condition.

Teddy bears and children, 7½″, $200.00.

Am Sports, Baseball Striker & Catcher, boys play ball.........150.00
Animated Conundrums, polychrome transfer, bl rim, 5″........50.00
Behold Him Rising, mc w/lustre rim, Meakin, 5½″............65.00
Boy Crossing Stile, Staffordshire..........................80.00
Boy fishing, w/rhyme, Staffordshire, 6″.....................50.00
Bread & milk set, alphabet around ea piece, Germany, 3-pc.....45.00
Campbell Kid..65.00
Candle Fish, 2 Indians in canoe, Staffordshire, 7½″............45.00
Cat & Mouse, 7¼″...75.00
Cats, imp sign-language hands, Staffordshire, scarce, 6½″......150.00
Child fishing, polychrome transfer/verse, imp Elsmore, 5½″.....55.00
Christmas, snowman & children..............................75.00
Creamer, Buster Brown, alphabet...........................95.00
Creamer, kittens & lady bug, alphabet.......................38.00
Creditors Have Better Memories Than Debtors, 5″, EX.........55.00
Crusoe Rescues Friday.....................................98.00
Dish, Baby Bunting & Little Don Bunch......................55.00
Dish, boy & girl 'Campbell Kids,' sgn GG Drayton...........125.00
Dish, teddy bears, china..................................125.00
Dog & bird, mc transfer, 7⅝″, NM..........................60.00
Elephant, 3 figures on howdah wave flag, sgn R&C, rare, 6″...150.00
Elephant fishing w/2 little girls, sgn Staffordshire.............85.00
Finch on limb, brn transfer w/brn/bl/gr, ironstone, 7″..........55.00
Flowers That Never Fade..., boys & girls dancing, 5¾″.........75.00
For Age & Want..., Dr Franklin's Maxims, gr rim, 6½″.........80.00
Geo Washington, brn transfer, Staffordshire, 7¼″, EX..........85.00
Girl on swing, polychrome, 3½″............................30.00
Glass, Arabic & Roman numeral center, clear, 6″.............35.00
Glass, carnival; stork in center w/#s, ABCs, marigold...........55.00
Glass, chicken in relief, clear.............................40.00
Glass, child's head in center, bl, Clay Crystal Works, 8″........35.00
Glass, children/elephants, frosted center, sgn R&C, rare........75.00
Glass, clock face, clear, 7″...............................25.00
Glass, Garfield in center, 6″.............................120.00
Glass, girl's head, beaded rim w/name Emma, Higbee..........85.00
Glass, hen & chicks, 6″...................................40.00
Glass, Independence Hall center, dtd 1776-1876.............150.00
Glass, rabbit/cabbage patch, stippled edge, frosted center.......30.00
Glass, Star Medallion, 6″..................................40.00
Glass, stork, frosted, Iowa City............................95.00
Glass, Westward Ho, 6″....................................46.00
Going to Market, polychrome, Staffordshire..................60.00
Greece..95.00
Harry Baiting His Line, mc, Elsmore, 5½″....................65.00
Harvest Home, mc, 5½″.....................................55.00
He That Hath a Trade Hath an Estate, gr transfer/mc, 6″......50.00
Horse Race, red transfer, Staffordshire......................45.00
I Live Man's Unrelenting Foe, girls playing, 5″, EX............55.00
Industry Needs Not Wish..., Dr Franklin's Maxims, 7½″.......125.00
Like Rest Consumes Faster Than Labor Wears, Staffordshire....80.00
Lincoln, bl transfer bust, 7″..............................240.00
Machinery Hall, 1893 Expo................................85.00
Men fighting on donkeys, Staffordshire, 7″...................28.00
Mug, milk glass w/alphabet................................40.00
N Currier, Lithographer, blk/wht ad, mk Adams, 6½″..........65.00
New Pony, blk transfer/mc, red rim, 6″.....................42.00
Old Mother Hubbard, Staffordshire, NM.....................58.00
Oriental Hotel, Staffordshire..............................80.00
Punch & Judy, bl transfer, mk Allerton's, 7″................100.00
Ready for a Ride, 2 children in wicker stroller, 6″............75.00
Religious transfer, polychrome, sm verse, imp Meakin, 5″.......55.00
Shepherd boy, horn/dog/fence/goat, polychrome, china, 5¼″.....75.00
Silverplate, Hey Diddle Diddle, Wm Rogers, 6″...............18.00
Soldier on horse attacks foot soldiers, Staffordshire, 7½″.......55.00
Steeple Chase, Staffordshire, 7″............................35.00
Teddy bears jump from pier, brn transfer w/mc, 7½″..........100.00
That Girl Wants the Pup Away, 5½″........................85.00
Tin, boy & girl w/hoops, 3″...............................85.00
Tin, cats w/yarn basket, colored litho.......................26.00
Tin, Cock Robin...58.00
Tin, Hey Diddle Diddle, 8½″...............................55.00
Tin, Jumbo in center, good detail, 6″.......................120.00
Tin, Liberty, w/alphabet...................................60.00
Tin, Mary Had a Little Lamb, verse, 8″.....................85.00
Tin, plain center, alphabet edge, dk tin, 6″..................40.00
Tray, animal decor/alphabet, aluminum, 8x15″................18.00
Want of Care..., Dr Franklin's Maxims, 7½″.................125.00
Wash Day, scene, Germany.................................38.00
Wolf & the Crane, Staffordshire, 5⅝″.......................45.00
Young Artist, brn transfer, baby w/palette, 6″................45.00
Zebra Hunt, Staffordshire, 8″..............................28.00

Abingdon

From 1934 until 1950, the Abingdon Pottery Co. of Abingdon, Ill., made a line of art pottery with a white vitrified body, decorated with various glazes in an array of lovely colors--matt as well as glossy, crystalline, and iridescent. Novelties, cookie jars, utility ware, and lamps were made in addition to several lines of simple yet striking artware. Fern Leaf, introduced in 1937 featured molded vertical feathering. La Fleur, in 1939, consisted of flowerpots and flower-arranger bowls with rows of vertical ribbing. Classic, 1939-40, was a line of vases, many with evidence of Chinese influence. Several marks were used, most of which employed the company name. In 1950, the company reverted to the manufacture of sanitary ware that had been their mainstay before the Art Ware Division was formed.

Highly decorated examples and those with black, bronze, or red glaze usually command at least 25% higher prices.

When no condition is indicated, the items listed below are assumed to be in mint condition.

Cookie jar, #471, Black Lady, decorated 85.00
Cookie jar, #471, Little Ol' Lady, undecorated, 7½" dia 55.00
Cookie jar, #495, Fat Boy, red 72.50
Cookie jar, #495, Fat Boy, undecorated, 8¼" 55.00
Cookie jar, #549, Hippo, undecorated, 8" 60.00
Cookie jar, #588, Money Bag, undecorated, 7¼" 55.00
Cookie jar, #611, Jack-in-the-Box, undecorated, 11" 70.00
Cookie jar, #651, Locomotive, undecorated, 7½" 55.00
Cookie jar, #653, Clock, undecorated, 9" 65.00
Cookie jar, #663, Humpty Dumpty, undecorated, 10¼" 55.00
Cookie jar, #664, Pineapple 45.00
Cookie jar, #677, Daisy, undecorated, 8" 25.00
Cookie jar, #694, Bo Peep, undecorated, 12" 60.00
Cookie jar, #695, Mother Goose, undecorated, 12" 65.00
102, vase, Beta, 10" 15.00
105, vase, Classic, Alpha, 8" 20.00
109, vase, Classic, Alpha, 5½" 20.00
118, vase, Classic, 10" 16.50
179, vase, floral, 10" 22.00
301, jar, Ming, undecorated, w/lid, 7¼" 35.00
305, bookends, seagull, undecorated, 6½", pr 40.00
310, jar, Chang, undecorated, w/lid, 10½" 50.00
318, vase, Ring, undecorated, 10¼" 35.00
326, ash tray, Greek, undecorated, 4¼x3" 25.00
347, flowerpot, egg & dart, undecorated, 7½" 8.00
353, vase, Penthouse, 10" 35.00
363, bookends, colt, undecorated, 5¾", pr 60.00

Figurine, Shepherdess and Fawn, black glaze, ca 1939-40, made on special order, 11½", $225.00.

374, bookends, cactus planter, undecorated, 7", pr 30.00
377, wall pocket, lily & morning glory, undecorated, 9" 25.00
378, mask, male & female, undecorated, 4" 35.00
379, wall pocket, daisy, undecorated, 9" 20.00
397, pot, undecorated, 5¾x5¾" 8.00
400, teapot tile, Geisha, undecorated, 5x5" 25.00
401, teapot tile, coolie, undecorated, 5x5" 25.00
407, rose bowl, undecorated, 6" 15.00
417, vase, scroll, undecorated, 8" 35.00
420, vase, fern leaf, undecorated, 7¼" 15.00
423, bowl, fern leaf, undecorated, 7¼" 10.00
431, wall pocket, fern leaf, undecorated, 7½" 15.00
448, window box, sunburst, undecorated, 9½x3" 10.00
449, cornucopia, shell, undecorated, 4½" 15.00
455, vase, asters, undecorated, 12" 15.00
457, wall pocket, Ionic, undecorated, 9" 15.00
461, candle holder, panels, undecorated, 2½" 6.00
463, vase, star, undecorated, 7" 15.00
466, vase, wheel hdl, undecorated, 8" 25.00
489, planter, Dutch boy, wall mt, undecorated, 10" 15.00
490, planter, Dutch girl, wall mt, undecorated, 10" 15.00
496, vase, hollyhock, plain or decorated, 7" 15.00
528, bowl, hibiscus, 15" 35.00
534, vase, Boyne, undecorated, 9" 20.00
582, flower basket, plain or decorated, 8" 25.00
98, upright goose, undecorated, 5" 20.00

Adams

Wm. Adams, whose potting skills were developed under the tutelage of Josiah Wedgwood, founded the Greengates Pottery at Tunstall, England in 1769. Many types of wares including basalt, ironstone, parian, and jasper were produced, and various impressed or printed marks were employed. Until 1800, 'Adams Co.' or 'Adams' impressed in block letters identified the company's earthenwares and a fine type of jasper similar in color and decoration to Wedgwood's. The latter mark was used again from 1845 to 1864 on parian figures. Most examples of their product found on today's market are transfer-printed dinnerwares with ornate backstamps which often include the pattern name and the initials 'W.A. & S.' This type of product was made from 1820 until about 1920. After 1890, the word 'England' was included in the mark; 'Tunstall' was added after 1896. From 1914 through 1940 a printed crown with 'Adams, Estbd 1657, England,' identified their products. From 1900 to 1965 they produced souvenir plates with transfers of American scenes, many of which were marketed in this country by Roth Importers of Peoria, Illinois. In 1965, the company affiliated with Wedgwood. Although there were other Adams potteries in Staffordshire, their marks incorporate either the first name initial or a partner's name and so are easily distinguished from those of this company.

When no condition is indicated, the items listed below are assumed to be in mint condition.

See also Spatter; Staffordshire

Adams Rose, bowl 75.00
Adams Rose, cup & saucer, early 165.00
Adams Rose, plate, early, 10½" 135.00
Adams Rose, plate, early, 8" 70.00
Adams Rose, plate, early, 9½" 110.00
Adams Rose, plate, late, 9½", pr 70.00
Biscuit jar, cream matt w/enamel medallions 65.00
Bowl, porridge; rooster, Save Your Breath..., 7½" 30.00
Bowl, vegetable; rural scene transfer, cobalt, w/lid, 11" 55.00
Butter chip, Cries of London 15.00

Charger, stick spatter, gaudy 3-color floral, sgn, 18″ 300.00
Cookie jar, jasper, bl/wht, hunting scene 140.00
Creamer & sugar bowl, Cries of London 20.00
Creamer & sugar bowl, Titian Ware, Royal Ivory, w/lid 20.00
Cup, Dr Syntax Setting Out on His Tour 20.00
Plaque, lions emb, mc, softpaste, sgn/1818, 8¾x10¾″, NM . . . 1,200.00
Plate, Andalusia, lady & man on horses, pink transfer, 8″ 40.00
Plate, Audubon Bird, ca 1902, 10½″ 28.00
Plate, Caldonia, elk & hunter, blk transfer, 9½″ 45.00
Plate, cows, dk bl transfer, sgn, 9″, VG 50.00
Plate, Cries of London, 8¼″ 35.00
Plate, Currier & Ives, Husking, 10½″ 18.00
Plate, Mr McCawber at Mr Wardles, Christmas, 8 sides, 8″ 35.00
Tankard, jasper, Dominion of Canada crest, Tunstall 65.00
Toddy plate, bl feather edge, minor stains, 4½″, EX 45.00

Advertising

The advertising world has always been a fiercely competitive field. In an effort to present their product to the customer, every imaginable gimmic was put into play. Colorful and artfully decorated signs and posters, thermometers, tape measures, fans, hand mirrors, and attractive tin containers--all with catchy slogans, familiar logos, and often bogus claims--are only a few of the many examples of early advertising memorabilia that are of interest to today's collectors.

Porcelain signs were made as early as 1890 and are highly prized for their artistic portrayal of life as it was then . . . often allowing amusing insights into the tastes, humor and way of life of a bygone era. As a general rule, older signs are made from a heavier gauge metal. Those with three or more fired on colors are expecially desirable.

Tin containers were used to package consumer goods ranging from crackers and coffee to tobacco and talcum. After 1880, can companies began to decorate their containers by the method of lithography. Though colors were still subdued, intricate designs were used to attract the eye of the consumer. False labeling and unfounded claims were curtailed by the Pure Food & Drug Administration in 1906, and the name of the manufacture as well as the brand name of the product had to be printed on the label. By 1910, color was rampant with more than a dozen hues printed on the tin or on paper labels. The tins themselves were often designed with a second use in mind--as canisters, lunch boxes, even toy trains. As a general rule, tobacco related tins are the most desirable, though personal preference may direct the interest of the collector to peanut butter pails with illustrations of children, or talcum tins with irresistible babies or beautiful ladies. Coffee tins are popular, as are those made to contain a particularly successful or well known product.

Perhaps the most visual of the early advertising gimmics were the character logos--the Fairbank Company's Gold Dust Twins, the goose trademark of the Red Goose Shoe Company, Nabisco's Zu Zu Clown and Uneeda Kid, the Campbell Kids, the RCA dog Nipper, and Mr. Peanut, to name only a few. Any example of these brings high prices on the market today.

Our listings are alphabetized by company name, or in lieu of that information, by word content or other pertinent description.

When no condition is indicated, the items listed below are assumed to be in excellent condition.

See also Advertising Dolls; Advertising Cards; Banks; Calendars; Cookbooks; Fans; Paperweights; Posters; Sewing Items, tape measures; Thermometers

Key:

cb—cardboard	ps—porcelain sign
fr—framed	sf—self-framed
lcs—litho on canvas sign	tc—tin container
pp—pre-prohibition	ts—tin sign

A&W Root Beer, mug, 4″, EX 4.00
A-1 Beer, cb sign, Cowboy's Dream, in fr 125.00
Abbott's Ice Cream, porc sign, picture of maid 75.00
Acme Beer, cb sign, wagon wheel & gold pan 120.00
All Nations Tobacco, bin, VG 195.00
Allen Hard Candies, tin container, VG 15.00
Allen's Red Tame Cherry, dispenser, etched glass top, 31″ 950.00
Allis Chalmers, porc sign, 1930s 45.00
Altes Lager Beer, tray, Bohemian waiter, Tivoli Brewery 75.00
American Line, pocket mirror, rnd, w/ship 65.00
American Line, tip tray, w/ship 85.00
Angelus Marshmallows, pocket mirror, 2 cherubs w/product 55.00
Angelus Marshmallows, sample tin, 2½x3½″ 35.00
Anheuser-Busch, corkscrew inside bottle, 1897, 2½″ 25.00
Anheuser-Busch, fr paper litho/Custer, 1890s, 36x47″ 300.00

Anheuser–Busch serving tray, 14″ x 16½″, mint condition, $695.00.

Anheuser-Busch, tray, levee scene, 1914, VG 100.00
Animal Crackers, store display, lion, mechanical, 1930s 750.00
Apollo Marshmallow, tin container 35.00
Apple Blossom Talcum, tin container, floral 6.00
Arbuckles Coffee, thermometer, tin w/lb pkg 185.00
Argonaut Beer, cb bottle display, prospector/mule/bridge 55.00
Armour's Lard-Star Brand, pail, tin 28.00
Atlantic Refining Co, porc sign, pump, X-arrows logo 125.00
Atlas Beer, tray, enamel eagle astride hemisphere, pp 125.00
Aunt Martha Bread, clicker, celluloid 15.00
Austex, wall billhook, celluloid, EX 16.00
Avery, stick pin, bulldog 25.00
AW Faber, tin container, knights jousting 15.00
Azonis Toilet & Nursery Powder, tc, bl & wht stripes, EX 12.00
Azuera Talcum, tin container, floral 6.00
Baby Ruth, change receiver, glass/tin, gum dispenser, EX 90.00
Baby Ruth, tape moistener, porcelain 50.00
Baby's Bottom Tobacco, tin container 35.00
Baird Tobacco, clock, figure-8, orig, 1892 . . . . 900.00
Baker's Chocolate, pencil sharpener, lady figural, iron 40.00
Baker's Chocolate Cocoa, box from salesman's miniature case . . . 45.00
Baker's Extracts, blotter, celluloid backing 25.00
Baker's German Sweet Chocolate, candy bar display, 1906 . . . . . . 75.00
Ballentine & Sons, tip tray, 3 rings, woodgrain background 40.00
Bank Note 5¢ Cigars, cb stand-up sign 60.00

Bath Hotel, clock, lists mealtimes, changes messages........1,760.00
Bavarian Beer, tin sign, w/man, 10x5″......................20.00
Baxter's 5¢ Cigar, tin sign, drum, NM......................40.00
Bee Brand Insect Powder, tc, cylindrical, unopened, EX.........8.00
Beech-Nut Tobacco, sign, fr litho, John & Demijohn, 15x22″....88.00
Bell Roasted Coffee, pocket mirror, rnd, bell.................45.00
Bell System, porc sign, bell w/1921 & letters, rnd, EX........195.00
Bell System, porc sign, rnd, 7″, EX........................50.00
Bell Telephone, toy truck, Hubley, 1930s, NM...............350.00
Bell Telephone of MI, porc sign, early......................95.00
Bell Telephone of PA, porc sign, sm........................125.00
Bell's Soapona, poster, Blk couple, product in horse/wagon....850.00
Ben Hur, stickpin, bicycle................................30.00
Ben Hur Spice, tin container, allspice, EX..................10.00
Berghoff Beer, tin sign, hunting dogs pointing, 13x21″, EX.....65.00
Berkely Knit, sign, cb stand-up, man wearing tie, 8x10″, EX....32.00
Bickmore Shaving Cream, cb sign, man shaving, 1930, 30x21″..20.00
Bickmore's Gall Salve, tin container, full/sealed...............12.00
Big Bee, motor oil can, big red bee........................125.00
Big Ben Tobacco, pocket tin...............................36.00
Billy Baxter, tray, big red bird, 12″, EX....................32.00
Biltrite Heels & Soles, thermometer, emb sole & heel, M.......86.00
Birchola, tin sign, Ice Cold...Sold Here, 2-sided, 10x12″........30.00
BL Johnson Confectioner, clock, EX....................1,300.00
Black Draught Laxative, wall dispenser, porc.................65.00
Black Sambo, tin gameboard...............................60.00
Blackstone Cigars, porc sign, sm...........................60.00
Blank Roasted Coffee, clock, Ingraham, EX...............1,700.00
Blanke's Coffee, coffee pot, wht ironstone, name emb, lg.......75.00
Blanke's Coffee, Saratoga trunk, red & gold, 6¾x4¾x9″, G.....65.00
Blue Seal Grain Products, porc sign, chickens/cow/horse........95.00
Blue Star Coal, tin sign, lg bl star.........................20.00
Bluff City Beer, wall hanging bottle, papier mache.............15.00
Bob's Peanut Butter Sandwiches & Salted Peanuts, store jar....66.00
Bobwhite Tobacco, tin container, VG.......................150.00
Bokar Coffee, bank, tin, EX...............................12.00
Bon Ami, booklet, The Chick That Never Grew Up............10.00
Borax, tin sign, Extract of Soap, 1920s, 7x23″...............25.00
Boraxo, tin container, paper label..........................6.00
Borozin, tin container, baby..............................10.00
Boston Smoker 5¢ Cigar, porc sign.........................65.00
Brazilla, syrup dispenser, orig pump.......................950.00
Breakfast Call Coffee, tin container, 1-lb...................20.00
Breyer's Ice Cream, ash tray, M............................20.00
Briggs', pocket tobacco tin................................10.00
Briggs', tobacco canister..................................15.00
Briggs' Pianos, bookmark, celluloid heart shape...............15.00
Brown's Iron Bitters, fr sign, ¾ view of lady, 21x17″.........240.00
Brown's Mule Tobacco, tin tray, w/16 mules, 12x12″...........38.00
Brownie Peanuts, tin container, 10-lb.......................85.00
BTS Paints, porc sign, flanged, man looks in can, slogan......135.00
Bubble-Up, sign, has pa-ZAZZ!, 12x28″, NM..................20.00
Buckeye, syrup dispenser, orig pump.......................550.00
Buckeye Distillery, jug, stoneware, miniature.................46.00
Buckeye Root Beer, tin sign, Refreshing, 1950s, 24x18″........15.00
Budweiser Beer, Bud Man stein.............................45.00
Budweiser Beer, clock, duck/emblem on reverse, revolves.......80.00
Budweiser Beer, light, revolves...........................650.00
Budweiser Beer, sign w/horse, revolves.....................550.00
Buffalo Vanilla, cb sign, pictures lady, 1930s, 12x10″..........8.00
Buick Motors, thermometer, porcelain......................175.00
Bull Durham, sign, cb w/orig wood fr, 1909, 35x23″..........425.00
Bull Durham, store figure, bull, after Bonheur, 17x23″......1,750.00
Bull Durham Cigars, clock, copper, Louisville, KY, 12″........450.00
Bulwark Tobacco, tc, man w/telescope looking to sea, EX......65.00
Burgemeister Beer, sign, electric, hangs/revolves, 16x12″.......52.00
Burger Beer, tap hdl......................................18.00
Burkhardt Beer, cb sign, lady holds pilsner glass, 24x29″.......16.00
Busch Ginger Ale, porc sign, 1920s, 11x21″..................85.00
Bush & Gerts Pianos, yo-yo, tin...........................45.00
Buster Brown Shoes, pocket watch w/strap & fob.............145.00
Buster Brown Shoes, wax head mannequin, 1910, 38″, VG....600.00
Butte City Leader Union Made 5¢ Cigar, oilcloth banner........25.00
Butter Finger, whistle, tin, Curtiss Candy....................15.00
Butter Nut Bread, emb tin sign, 1930s, 12x26″................35.00

C. D. Kenny

C.D. Kenny was determined to be a successful man, and he was. Between 1890 and 1934, he owned seventy-five groceries in fifteen states. He accomplished this success in two ways: fair business dealings and premium give-aways. These ranged from trade cards and advertising mirrors to tin commemorative plates and kitchen items. There were banks and toys, clocks and tins. Today's collectors are finding hundreds of these items, all carrying Kenny's name.

C.D. Kenny, Mammy's Favorite Brand Coffee, with lid, 10¾″, $85.00.

Chair, beach; folding type, Germany, miniature...............25.00
Fan, Kenny's Tea..3.50
Figurine, poodle, porcelain, Germany.......................24.00
Fish scaler, CI, 19th C...................................20.00
Funnel, metal, w/advertising...............................25.00
Pin-back, elks/turtles/bird, fraternal.......................10.00
Plate, boy & dog, holly edge, Vienna Art....................75.00
Plate, girl w/muff, mk, 10″...............................78.00
Trade card, baby on pillow................................12.00
Tray, girl praying, 4″....................................65.00
Tray, Raising the Flag...................................172.00
Tray, Victorian lady, seated, 4″...........................65.00

Cactus Brand Coffee, tc, faded paper label, w/lid, 9x7½″........15.00
California Peanut Peanut Butter, tin pail....................125.00
Call Again Cigars, emb tin sign, 1930s, 12x32″...............40.00

Calumet Baking Powder, clock, open lettering, EX..........1,300.00
Calumet Baking Powder, clock, Sessions regulator, orig, NM...750.00
Calumet Baking Powder, sample, 4-oz........................6.00
Calumet Baking Powder, tin container......................14.00
Calumet Baking Soda, bank...............................110.00
Calumet Brewing Co, tray, cavalier scene, 12x17"............250.00
Calvert, shot glasses, emb, set of 4, EX....................16.00
Camel Cigarettes, Flat 50s, cb container, EX.................12.00
Camel Cigarettes, paper sign, So Mild, So Good, 23½x42"......20.00
Camel Cigarettes, thermometer, emb pack, 4x12", EX.........42.00
Camel Cigarettes, thermometer, tin, 5½x13"..................35.00
Camel Cigars, pocket tin, EX..............................55.00
Camels, emb tin sign, Need Cigarettes?, 1940s, 12x19".........25.00
Campbell & Woods, tin coffee bin, red/gold/blk, 14x18x17½"...385.00
Canada Dry, clock, light-up, rnd, EX........................30.00
Canada Dry Hi-Spot, tin sign, 1946, 24x7"...................20.00
Canada Dry Sport Cola, clock, 13x18", EX...................26.00
Carling's Ale, tin sign, 9 Pints of the Law, NM...............75.00
Carlsburg Beer, sign, plastic, label, 10x5", EX................16.00
Carta Blanca, tray, lady & man dining.......................75.00
Carter's Inx, thermometer, porcelain, 1915, 7x27", EX........152.00
Cascade Beer, tray, Uncle Sam, EX.........................650.00
Cascarets, cb sign, hobo asleep, 1910, 22x16"...............100.00
Case, stickpin, eagle.....................................30.00
Centlivre Tonic, cb sign, pictures lady w/tonic, 12x22".........60.00
Ceresota Flour, pocket mirror.............................50.00
Ceresota Flour, tin flour bin, Ceresota boy, rare.............675.00
Chair, beach; folding type, Germany, miniature...............25.00
Cherry Blossoms Soda, dexterity puzzle, rnd.................15.00
Cherry Chic, syrup dispenser, complete, ca 1925............1,595.00
Chesterfield Cigarettes, canister, rnd, 50s, EX................25.00
Chesterfield Cigarettes, cuff links, 1930s, pr.................15.00
Chesterfield Cigarettes, die-cut, Monty Irvin/Willy Mays........145.00
Chesterfield Cigarettes, sign, cb, lady/pack, 24x24", EX........32.00
Chesterfield Cigarettes, thermometer........................20.00
Chesterfield Flat 50s, tin container..........................7.00
Chief Oshkosh Beer, tray, top hat, EX......................200.00
Chief Watta Pop, sucker holder............................125.00
Christy's, coffee tin, Blk people picking coffee beans...........90.00
Cinco Cigars, enamel sign, dbl-sided........................40.00
Cinderella Never Fail Stoves, egg separator, tin..............950.00
Cinzano Vermouth, brandy snifter, EX.......................16.00
Clabber Girl Baking Powder, tin sign, 1952, 12x30"...........25.00
Clarke's Pure Rye, wall plate, man pours shot, brn, 11".......125.00
Climax Tobacco, cb sign, woman on terrace, heavy, 17" dia.....85.00
Clover Ice Cream, pop gun, litho cylinder, ca 1915............15.00

Coca-Cola

J.S. Pemberton, creator of Coca-Cola, originated his world-famous drink in 1886. From its inception, the Coca-Cola Company began an incredible advertising campaign which has proved to be one of the most successful promotions in history. The quantity and diversity of advertising material put out by Coca-Cola in the last one hundred years is literally mind-boggling. From the beginning, the company has projected an image of wholesomeness and Americana. Beautiful women in Victorian costumes, teenagers and school children, blue and white collar workers, the men and women of the Armed Forces--even Santa Claus--have appeared in advertisements with a Coke in their hand. Some of the earliest collectibles include trays, syrup dispensers, gum jars, pocket mirrors, and calendars. Many of these items fetch prices in the thousands of dollars. Later examples include radios, signs, lighters, trays, thermometers, playing cards, clocks, and toys--particularly toy trucks.

In 1970, the Coca-Cola Company initiated a multi-million dollar 'image refurbishing campaign,' which introduced the new 'Dynamic Contour' logo, a twisting white ribbon under the Coca-Cola and Coke trademarks. The new logo often serves as a cut-off point to the purist collector. Newer and very ardent collectors, however, relish the myriad of items marketed since that date, as they often cannot afford the high prices that the vintage pieces command.

Caution should be observed by novice collectors--there has been an ever-increasing influx of reproduction and fantasy items. A fantasy item is a novelty made to appear authentic with inscriptions such as 'Tiffany Studios,' 'Trans Pan Expo,' 'World's Fair,' etc. In reality, these items never existed as originals. Of the hundreds of reproductions (designated 'R' in the following examples) and fantasies (designated 'F') on the market today, these are the most deceiving:

Reproductions and Fantasies

Belt buckle, no originals thought to exist, F, up to.............5.00
Cigar cutter belt buckle, nude nun figural, Trans Pan, F.........5.00
Doll, Santa w/Coke bottle, blk, F..........................25.00
Knife, pocket; yel & red, 1933 World's Fair, F................2.00
Push plate, brass, gallons sold, dtd 1901, 10x3¾", F...........3.00
Soda fountain glass, flared/syrup line/shield on bottom, R........3.00
Soda fountain glass holder, word 'Drink' not on orig, R.........5.00
Straight razor, folding; Trans Pan on blade, F.................5.00
Tray, Tarzan, American Artworks only on orig, 1934, R.........5.00
Watch, pocket; often old watch w/new face, R................10.00

Ad, man in tux, color, Messengale, from 'Theatre,' 1907........75.00
Ad, Nordica, color w/coupon, Messengale, 1904, 6½x9¾"......100.00
Almanac, farmer's; Coke ad inside cover, 1901, EX............18.00
Ash tray, aluminum, rests all around edge, ca 1960, EX.........6.00
Ash tray, ruby red, 1940, set of 4, MIB....................200.00
Bank, dispenser, plastic, ca 1960, EX.......................50.00
Bank, dispenser, tin/litho, 1950s, Line Mar, NM..............175.00
Bank, vending machine, ca 1957, 5½", MIB..................65.00
Barrel, syrup; wooden, w/spigot, 5-gal, ca '40, 80% label......100.00
Blotter, policeman on motorcycle w/child, b/w, 1930..........100.00
Blotter, Refresh Yourself, pictures bottle, 1926, M............14.00
Blotter, Tune In, ca 1931, EX............................40.00
Blotter, Western Coca-Cola, w/Gold Seal Ginger Ale, ca '11.....85.00
Blotter, Wholesome Refreshment, Boy Scouts, 1942............6.00
Booklet, shaped like case, plant tour giveaway, ca 1950.........8.00
Bottle, Bear Bryant commemorative, 1982, full.................6.00
Bottle, Cumberland, MD, amber, ca 1905, NM.................75.00
Bottle, display; 1920s, w/cap, X-mas, 20", M................150.00
Bottle, display; 1940s, w/cap, Pat'd, 20", M.................125.00
Bottle, display; 1960s, Mexican ACL, 20", M.................90.00
Bottle, display; 1960s, w/cap, ACL, 20", M..................75.00
Bottle, Erie, PA, logo: block type in circle, amber, '05........175.00
Bottle, Florence, AL, amber, ca 1903.......................75.00
Bottle, Ft Meade, FL, Coca-Cola paper label, EX.............150.00
Bottle, gold, ACL, w/cap, ca 1960, NM.....................18.00
Bottle, gold, embossed Pat'd, ca 1950.......................25.00
Bottle, Goshen, NY, logo at base, amber, rare, EX...........185.00
Bottle, London, all languages, throwaway, ca 1980.............5.00
Bottle, Louisville, KY, circle arrow, cloudy, ca 1908...........35.00
Bottle, New Orleans, LA, logo at base, amber, ca 1905.........65.00
Bottle, perfume; miniature bottle, ca '30, w/stopper, M.........45.00
Bottle, Scranton, PA, very dk amber, logo at base, ca 1908.....75.00
Bottle, water; w/emb ship, bl, cap, ca 1940..................50.00
Bottle opener/can piercer, Have a Coke, folds, ca 1965.........10.00
Bowl, pretzel; aluminum, sits on 3 bottles, ca '35, NM.........65.00
Calendar, 1903, Lillian Nordica, no pad, NM.................500.00
Calendar, 1919, Marion Davis, full pad, 8x14", NM...........400.00
Calendar, 1923, lady w/Coke glass or bottle, full pad, NM......250.00

Coca-Cola figure-8 clock, Baird, 5¢ version, near mint, $4,000.00.

Calendar, 1924, lady holding Coke glass, not full pad, EX.....225.00
Calendar, 1925, lady w/fur, holds Coke, not full pad, VG......100.00
Calendar, 1926, side view of lady sitting holding Coke, EX....295.00
Calendar, 1929, lady sitting holding Coke, NM..............275.00
Calendar, 1951, Party Girl, 6 sheets, M.....................40.00
Calendar, 1960, man & lady w/skis, complete 6 sheets, M.......18.00
Calendar, 1963, lady looks in mirror, complete 6 sheets........20.00
Camera, Coke can, 110, ca 1983, w/box......................25.00
Cardboard cut-out, Fishing Boy/Rockwell, '31, fr, 27", NM.....500.00
Cardboard cut-out/window display, Haden, '34, creased, EX....400.00
Change purse, emb gold straight side bottle, ca 1907..........65.00
Cigar band, pictures Coke bottle, ca 1940, M.................75.00
Cigar band, pictures glass, ca 1940, M......................75.00
Cigarette lighter, 'In Every Language,' ca 1950, EX...........16.00
Clock, Baird, Delicious Refreshing 5¢, 1890s, NM...........4,000.00
Clock, battery op, ¾-size regulator, 12x27", MIB.............150.00
Clock, wood frame, Selecto, ca 1939, 16x16", NM..........150.00
Cooler, airline carry-on, 1940s, 17x12x6½", EX..............65.00
Dart board, Silhouette Girl, 1940, NM......................35.00
Desk set, Scheaffer, pen & base, 1980s, MIB.................12.00
Dictionary, Webster's Lil' Gem, ca 1928.....................35.00
Doll, Buddy Lee, compo, w/Coke uniform, 1940s.............500.00
Doll, Buddy Lee, plastic, w/orig uniform, 1940s..............250.00
Fan, pictures bottle, Drink Coca-Cola, 1940s, NM.............20.00
Figure, policeman on base, porc, for school zone, 1940, EX...300.00
Flashlight, miniature, Coke bottle shape, 1950s, MIB..........10.00
Fly swatter, plastic novelty, 1960s, M.......................9.00
Folder, Toonerville, promotes advertising, color, 1931, M.......10.00
Game, dominos, bottle on ea, complete, MIB..................30.00
Game, dragon checkers, Coca-Cola on ea, 1940s, w/box, NM....35.00
Glass, fountain; 'trademark' under logo, 1940s, 6-oz...........10.00
Glass, fountain; w/holder, orig, EX.........................800.00
Glass, fountain; w/holder, reproduction......................10.00
Glass, Olympic, gold ACL/multi-language, Montreal Expo/'76.....5.00
Glass, R Porter 50th Anniversary, gold ACL, '36, 6-oz........350.00
Jar, gum; Pepsin, w/scalloped lid, 1908, M..................525.00
Key chain & charm, 50th Anniversary, EX......................6.00
Knife, bone hdl, Delicious/Refreshing, Kastor Bros, ca '20.....100.00
Lapel pin, 5 years service, gold w/1 ruby, ca 1950.............35.00
Lock, door; Kam Indore Lock, ca 1920, w/box.................20.00
Match striker, wall mt, porc, ca 1939, EX....................75.00
Menu board, wood & masonite, Silhouette Girl, ca 1939.......150.00
Mug, different languages, ca 1980...........................5.00
Pen/pencil set, cross bottle clip, recent, MIB.................25.00
Pencil, mechanical; bottle clip, ca 1940.....................12.00
Pencil, mechanical; Scripto, NM.............................7.50
Pencil, Things Go Better With Coke, red, ca 1960, M..........1.00
Pencil box, red, ca 1930, box w/9 pcs.......................25.00
Pencil holder, NY 75th Anniversary, ceramic dispenser, '60.....80.00
Pencil sharpener, bottle shape, red metal, 1920s, 1½".........18.00
Photo, delivery truck, b/w, 1908, 8x10"......................100.00
Photo, horse-drawn wagon, kids drink Coke, b/w, ca 1900.....100.00
Pillow, bottle shaped, 1950s, NM...........................50.00
Plate, china, bottle & glass in center, 1930s, 7¼", NM........125.00
Playing cards, 1943, girl w/leaves, Coke bottle, MIB...........35.00
Playing cards, 1943, nurse or operator, MIB..................46.00
Playing cards, 1959, girl in water, MIB......................30.00
Playing cards, 1971, food & Coke bottle on table, MIB..........5.00
Playing cards, 1980s, Coke Is It, MIB.........................5.00
Postcard, Coca-Cola building, Baltimore, MD, early............14.00
Postcard, Coke truck, Ritchfield Oil, b/w, 1930s...............15.00
Radio, Coke bottle, 1930, 30", EX..........................950.00
Radio, cooler form, bakelite, ca 1949, 7x12x9½", EX.........300.00
Radio, vending machine, AM/FM, '82, 7¾x3¼x1⅝", M.........40.00
Safety marker, brass, Drink CC/Safety 1st, ca 1900, 3⅝" dia...150.00
Salesman's sample, cooler, open front, 1939, 8½x11x9", NM...450.00
Sheet music, The Coca-Cola Girl, in fr, ca 1928.............185.00
Sign, cb, cheerleader w/Coke in hand, 1940s, 20x36"..........41.00
Sign, cb, Roadster Girls, w/orig fr w/logo, ca '42, 29x50".....200.00
Sign, cb, Woman Flyer, Thirst Takes Wings, ca 1941, 20x36"...50.00
Sign, cb 3-D/attached glass pc/'6 Oz Glass,' '20s, 11", NM.....375.00
Sign, masonite/wood, Silhouette Girl/Kay display, '40, 36".....125.00
Sign, metal, disk form, red, w/out bottle, 36"..................40.00
Sign, porc, candy/films/Coke logo, 1950s, 16x24", EX..........50.00
Sign, porc, disk form, red, w/bottle, 24"......................65.00
Sign, porc, disk form, wht w/bottle, no logo, ca 1950, 24"......65.00
Sign, porc, Fountain Service, red/yel/gr, ca 1950, 12x20".......75.00
Sign, porc, Fountain Service, shield, red/gr, '40s, 22x26"......150.00
Sign, porc, shows dispenser w/hand, ca 1939, 24x26".........200.00
Sign, tin, Drink Coca-Cola, 1923 bottle ea end, 19x54", NM...150.00
Sign, tin, girl w/bottle, 1927, 8x11"........................500.00
Sign, tin, Take Home A Carton, ca 1930s, 19x54", EX..........85.00
Sign, tin, Things Go Better/shows paper cup, '60s, 28", NM.....50.00
Sign, tin, 2-sided arrow, Ice Cold/Sold Here, ca 1928.........200.00
Straws, full box of 'frozen' straws, 1960......................8.00
Thermometer, 1920s, bottle shape, Dec 25, 1923, 17", NM.....75.00
Thermometer, 1930s, gold bottle on red oval, 7x16", NM.......45.00
Thermometer, 1930s, Silhouette Girl/Delicious/Refresh, 16".....60.00
Thermometer, 1940s, twin bottles, 7x16"......................60.00
Thermometer, 1950s, Refresh Yourself, oval, 30", EX..........35.00
Thimble, aluminum, ca 1930, M..............................20.00
Tie clasp, all-star dealer campaign award, ca 1950, M..........20.00
Tip tray, 1913, Hamilton King girl, 4½x6"....................150.00
Tip tray, 1914, Betty, hat w/long scarf tie, 4½x6", EX........100.00
Tip tray, 1917, Elaine, 4½x6", NM..........................100.00
Tip tray, 1920, lady holding Coke, 4½x6", NM................180.00
Token, 5¢, weight & size of nickel, ca 1930....................5.00
Toy, hamburger stand, tin/litho, ca 1950, w/box...............75.00

Toy, Playtown Coke stand, 1940, MIB....................100.00
Toy train, Am/Flyer, #6073, 13 pieces, w/logo, rare.........1,920.00
Toy train, Am/Flyer, #6073, 13 pieces, w/logo, w/orig box....2,000.00
Toy truck, Budgie, 11 cases, 1950, MIB....................225.00
Toy truck, Dinky, #402, red/wht, 1965, MIB................200.00
Toy truck, Marx, red/yel metal, ca 1940, 20″................100.00
Toy truck, Marx #22, tin/litho, w/24 cases, MIB..............300.00
Toy truck, Matchbox #37, GPW, 1950s, 2″, EX..............20.00
Toy truck, Matchbox Model Y-12, ca 1980, MIB..............25.00
Toy truck, Metalcraft, Deco, long nose, 10 bottles, EX........525.00
Toy truck, Metalcraft, rubber tires, 10 bottles, 1930, EX.......275.00
Toy truck, Metalcraft, sheet iron, w/bottles, 6x11″, VG........180.00
Toy truck, Pyro, plastic, 1950, 5″, M........................40.00
Toy truck, Smith Miller, red, ca 1979, 50 made, MIB.........500.00
Toy truck, 1960 GMC, battery operated, yel/wht, MIB..........75.00
Tray, 1909, lg oval, 13½x16½″, EX........................650.00
Tray, 1910, Hamilton King: girl/wide brim hat, 10x13″, EX....300.00
Tray, 1914, Betty, wearing big hat, 10x13″, EX..............150.00
Tray, 1923, flapper girl, 10x13″, NM.......................145.00
Tray, 1925, girl w/fur, 10x13″, NM........................135.00
Tray, 1927, curb service, 10½x13¼″, NM...................200.00
Tray, 1927, soda jerk, man holds glasses, 10½x13¼″, NM.....175.00
Tray, 1929, lady sitting, w/bottle, 10x13″, EX...............150.00
Tray, 1930, bathing beauty, 10x13″, NM...................125.00
Tray, 1931, Norman Rockwell: boy fishing, 10x13″, NM.......250.00
Tray, 1932, girl in yel bathing suit, 10x13″, NM.............200.00
Tray, 1934, Johnny Weissmuler, 'Tarzan,' 10x13″, NM........325.00
Tray, 1935, Madge Evans, 10x13″, NM.......................80.00
Tray, 1936, The Hostess, 10x13″, NM......................75.00
Tray, 1937, girl running on beach, 10x13″, NM...............75.00
Tray, 1938, French, girl in the afternoon, 10x13″, NM.........75.00
Tray, 1941, ice skater, 10x13″, NM.........................65.00
Tray, 1957, birdhouse, 10x13″, NM.........................75.00
Tray, 1957, French, lady holds umbrella & Coke, 10x13″, NM...85.00
Tray, 1957, French, rooster & Coke bottle, 10x13″, NM.......75.00
Tray, 1957, French, sandwiches/Cokes on table, 10x13″, NM....75.00
Tray, 1958, picnic basket, 10x13″, NM......................20.00
Tray, 1960, fishtail, Drive In For Coke, EX.................165.00
Tray, 1961, French, hand pours Coke into glass, 10x13″, NM...15.00
Tray, 1969, Nordica, 10x13″, EX..........................10.00
Tray, 1970, Santa, orig, not Long John Silver, 10x13″, NM.....25.00
Tray, 1976, Indiana NCAA champions/B Knight inset, rnd, NM..10.00
Tray, 1980, Imperial Gasoline/Coke logo on rim, 10x13″, NM...35.00
Tray, 1982, Delicious/Refreshing, KEG label/5 gal, rnd, NM.....12.00
Tray, 1982, Hawaii's 75th Anniversary, rnd, NM..............10.00
Wallet, blk leather/gold stamping, tri-fold, 1920s, EX..........25.00
Wallet, pigskin, Coke bottle emblem, ca 1950, in box..........15.00
Watch fob, brass w/blk enamel, girl w/bottle, ca 1914, EX.....130.00
Whistle, aluminum, thimble form, Coca-Cola logo, ca 1930......32.00

Colby's Clothing House, mirror, 1876.......................45.00
Columbia Typewriter Ribbon, tin container, twins.............10.00
Congress Beer, tray, label, 12″...........................46.00
Cook's Beer, tin sign, woman in red dress, wood fr...........229.00
Cook's Beer, tin sign, 1940s, 16x24″.......................20.00
Coon Collars, case, oak.................................425.00
Copenhagen Castle Beer, sign, tin, bottle & king, 10x12″.......26.00
Cortez Cigars, tin sign, lady w/cigar box, flakes, 20x16″.......275.00
Cresca Cluster Raisins, tc, odd oblong shape, gr/gold, EX.......40.00
Crescent Beverages, emb tin sign, 1940s, 12x18″.............15.00
Crescent Beverages, tin sign, emb moon & star, 19½x13″.......56.00
Crescent Brewing Factory, tray, Nampa, ID, VG..............450.00
Crescent Flour, cb sign, hanging, Mother's Delight, 5x8″........5.00
Crosley Radio, puppy, papier mache.......................175.00
Crystal Wedding Oats, box, Quaker Co......................20.00
Crystal White Soap, store display, lattice bottom/3-D box......145.00
Cuervo Tequilla, set of 6 barrel-shaped shots on tray...........75.00
Custer's Last Stand, cb sign, fr, Custer/Indians, 1950s..........75.00
Cuticura, change receiver, glass, EX........................36.00
Cuticura Talc, tin container, baby/lady.......................50.00
D-Lish-O Ice Cream, emb tin sign, 1930s, 18x26″.............40.00
Dad's Root Beer, thermometer, 5x27″.......................40.00
Dan Patch Cut Plug Tobacco, tin container, 6x3½″............45.00
Darkie Toothpaste, Blk man on tube & box..................40.00
Davis Baking Powder, pitcher, emb, 8½″....................75.00
Davis Carriage Mfg, tin, carriage/horses/people, 7x20″.........150.00
Dawson's Ale & Lager, tray, lady & man dining...............85.00
DeCoursey's Ice Cream, tray..............................36.00
Deer Run Whiskey, clock, Ingraham, EX..................1,700.00
DeLaval, change tray, tin, scenic, rnd.......................65.00
DeLaval, oak cabinet w/tin inset: Agency for DeLaval, VG......285.00
DeLaval, porc sign, We Use..., 12x16″.......................45.00
DeLaval, tin die-cut, cow/calf.............................50.00
DeLaval, tin sign, girl w/cows, orig sgn fr, 41x30″, VG.......1,050.00
Denver Sandwich Candy, emb tin sign, 1940s, 12x28″.........50.00
Detroit Tivoli Brewing, tin tray, Altes Lager, waiter, EX........95.00
Devilish Good Cigars, tin sign, children smoke stogies, EX.....125.00
Dewer's White Label, sign, emb distillery, 13x20″, EX.........10.00
Dial Smokeless Tobacco, pocket tin.........................17.50
Diamond Dye, cabinet, Evolution of Woman, EX.............850.00
Diamond Dye, tin, 3 all-American girls, 1900, 14x28″.........845.00
Dick Bros Bock Beer, felt pennant.........................60.00
Dill's Best Tobacco, pocket tin, short, lady, EX...............20.00
Dodge, porc sign, 1930s, 15x45″..........................125.00
Doe Wah Jack Stoves, calendar, rnd oak stove...............290.00
Doe Wah Jack Stoves, sgn, 8″ dia.........................225.00
Don Digo Cigars, change receiver, glass, palm trees............20.00
Douglas Corn Meal for Cows, tin sign, shows cow/feed sacks...110.00

Dr Pepper

A young pharmacist, Charles C. Alderton, was hired by W.B. Morrison, owner of Morrison's Old Corner Drug Store in Waco, Texas, around 1884. Alderton, an observant sort, noticed that the drugstore's patrons could never quite make up their minds as to which flavor of extract to order. He concocted a formula that combined many flavors, and Dr. Pepper was born. The name was chosen by Morrison, in honor of a beautiful young girl with whom he had once been in love. The girl's father, a Virginia doctor by the name of Pepper, had discouraged the relationship due to their youth, but Morrison had never forgotten her.

On December 1, 1885, a U.S. patent was issued to the creators of Dr. Pepper.

Bottle, plastic, 1940s, 49x13″............................375.00
Clock, bottle cap shape..................................35.00
Fan pull, Santa w/parachute, NM..........................20.00
Match box holder, gr....................................40.00
Opener, machine; 14x4″..................................45.00
Plate, girl facing left, Vienna Art..........................225.00
Plate, roses, Vienna Art..................................175.00
Postcard, 10¢ coupon, M.................................10.00
Sign, Dick Clark/Am Bandstand Spectacular..................15.00
Sign, man barbecuing, 10/2/4 bottle, 1957...................15.00
Sign, tin, 7x20″, EX......................................20.00

Dr. Pepper tray, late '30s-early '40s, 3″ x 10½″, $125.00.

Watch fob, billiken....50.00
Watch fob, Louisiana Expo....80.00
Wrist watch, zodiac, in case, M....28.00

Dr Daniel's Veterinary Products, store cabinet....576.00
Dr Johnson's Educator Crackers, tin container....35.00
Dr LeGear's Gall Remedy, tin container, red/blk, full, 2-oz....6.50
Dr Palmer's Almoel, tin container, lady....18.00
Dr White's Dandelion Alternative, mirror, gold leaf, 1885....750.00
Droste Chocolate, tin can, Dutch children, 4-oz....25.00
Duck Head Overalls, sign, metal, barn board fr, 21x29″....95.00
Duffy's Malt Liquor, clock....2,000.00
Duffy's Malt Whiskey, pocket mirror, oval, chemist, EX....66.00
Duffy's Malt Whiskey, thermometer, wood, old chemist....126.00
Duke's Mixture, porc sign, shows lg tobacco pouch....165.00
Dupont Gunpowder, tin can, red w/paper label, 1924....35.00
Dupont Powders, sf tin sign, bird dogs, 1903, VG....450.00
Dusseldorfer Beer, tray, baby holding bottle....345.00
Dutch Boy Paints, papier mache figural display box....250.00
Dybala's Beverages, emb tin sign, bottle on right, 10x27″....25.00
Eagle Brewery, Utica, NY, tray, eagle center....150.00
Early Morning Pure Coffee, tc, Dubuisson, 8-oz....3.50
Early Times Whiskey, plaster sign, fr, in relief, 23x27″....345.00
Eastman Kodak, wood sign, Brownie For Her Birthday, 24x30″.250.00
Eastside Old Tap Lager, celluloid sign, 9x20″....36.00
Eclipse, stickpin, bicycle....30.00
Edgeworth Tobacco, pocket tin, EX....16.00
Edgeworth Tobacco, tin sign, gold/bl/red, 32x8″....25.00
El Roi Tan Cigars, tin container....15.00
El Verso Cigars, pocket tobacco tin, sheep/girl, 5x3½x1″....25.00
El Wadora Cigars, tin sign, 1930s, 24x36″....35.00
Electric Fence, tin sign, lightning bolts, little man, M....12.00
Electro Carbon Steel Pens, school motif, wood burnt, 7x4½″....37.50
Electrolux, letter opener....15.00
Emersons, display umbrella, For Clothing Trade w/Emersons...150.00

English Biscuit Tins

Huntley & Palmers, book, Waverly....165.00
Huntley & Palmers, Cecil Alden scenes....100.00
Huntley & Palmers, lantern....125.00
Huntley & Palmers, Oriental design....65.00
Huntley & Palmers, tavern scene....65.00

EP Bosyshell Buggies, die-cut/emb, kids in wagon, 12x16″....100.00
Eskimo Pie, sign, circus scene, 22x7″....10.00
Espanola Cigars, tin plate....28.00
Esso, scissor sharpener....15.00
Eve Tobacco, pocket tin....140.00
Ever Ready, clock, safety razor, EX....2,900.00
Eversharp Pens, trade sign, oversize pen/pencil, brass....450.00
Evinrude Motors, coaster, lady operating outboard, VG....60.00
Ex-Lax, thermometer, porc, horizontal....80.00
Ex-Lax, tin container....10.00
Fab Soap, tape measure, celluloid....23.00
Fairy Soap, change tray....65.00
Falls City Beer, plaster sign, mallard....40.00
Farmers' Produce Exchange, thermometer, 5″, EX....12.00
Fatima Cigarettes, sf tin sign, oval, veiled lady, 21x28″....350.00
Fehr's Brewing Co, poster, fr, 1910, 28x39″....290.00
Fels Naptha, soap shaver....9.00
Ferry Seed, sign, child holds coin, lg graphic letters....350.00
Figaro Liquid Smoke, glass jug, colorful pictures, pt....22.00
Finzer Bros Tobacco, wall regulator/8-day, Seth Thomas, NM.1,695.00
Firestone, porc sign, 1930s....40.00
Five-O Chocolate, tin sign, 1930s, 10x27″....25.00
Fleishmann, paper/glass sign, boy/girl/tree, 19½x13½″....100.00
Floressence Violette Talcum, tc, stylized floral decor, EX....12.00
Fluffy Flour, tc, Mother's Choice Since 1837, 3-lb....45.00
Flystop, dome-top can, traffic cop stops giant fly....20.00
Forest & Stream Tobacco, pocket tin, ducks, NM....30.00
Foster's Peanut Butter, tin pail....75.00
Fowler's Cherry Smash, syrup dispenser, tall base, 15″, NM....550.00
Fox Head Beer, tray, fox head on bl background, 13″, M....65.00
Frances Wilson Cigar, tin sign, box on fancy table/3 men....375.00
Frank Fehr Brewing Co, tray, rnd, dtd 1910, EX....275.00
Frank Jones Ale, tip tray, logo, 5″....52.00
Franklin, cigar tin, old Ben flying kite....125.00
Friedman Keiler & Co Distillers, ts/wood fr, pre-pro....1,250.00
Fry's Choice Chocolates, show case, etched glass/wood, '10....425.00
Gail & Ax Fine Cut, majolica tobacco humidor, M/C logo, NM..195.00
Gail & Ax Tobacco, tin canister, NM....250.00
Game Cut Tobacco, pheasants, tin container....275.00
Ganong's Chocolates, thermometer, porc, 38″, NM....100.00
GE Refrigerator, tape measure, celluloid....18.00
Gem Razors, clock....850.00
General Electric, Big Top Circus set, 1950, 60-pc....45.00
Germania Brewing Co, tray, w/stag....125.00
Gipp's Beer, emb tin sign, Peoria, 1930s, 16x20″....30.00
Globe Tobacco Co, amber barrel jar, tin top, 1882....75.00
Globe Wernicke Bookcases, tin sign, good color, 29x40″....352.00
Goebel's Meats, porc sign, 19″....65.00
Gold Crumb Tobacco, tin sign, w/pouch, 7x11″....42.00
Gold Dust Washing Powder, trolley card, Twins dry dishes....150.00
Gold Seal Champagne, tip tray, mc bottle/country scene....65.00
Golden Knight Shaving Soap, glass mug, emb....12.00
Golden Shred, pin, enamel golliwog....18.00
Goldyrock Birch Beer, emb tin sign, 1930s, 11x22″....25.00
Good Housekeeping, tin sign, anti-smoking....20.00
Good Old Summer Time Tobacco, tin can, Gibson girl label....50.00
Goodrich Silvertowns, porc sign, dbl sided, mc, 18x17″....65.00
Gordon Scotch Whiskey, tape measure, bell shape, plaid....25.00

Grandpa's Wonder Soap, puzzle, colorful, 1910 ... 25.00
Granger Pipe Tobacco, cb sign, w/Alexander Woolcott, NM ... 30.00
Grape Nuts Cereal, tin sign, girl/dog on way to school, M ... 1,250.00
Grapette, elephant bank, clear w/metal slotted lid ... 20.00
Gravely Tobacco Co, folding chair, wooden ... 295.00
Green River Soda, sign, cb, 1940s, 7x10" ... 12.00
Green River Whiskey, Blk man/mule chalkware figural, 36" ... 250.00
Green River Whiskey, cb sign, in fr, 18x22" ... 165.00
Green River Whiskey, folding corkscrew & bottle opener ... 18.00
Green River Whiskey, tin sign, orig fr, 1899, 35x25", EX ... 1,250.00
Greiner's Bread, tin sign, loaf of bread & midget baker ... 85.00
Gretz Beer, tray, comic man riding bicycle, 13", M ... 46.00
Grover's Shoes, litho sign on wood, lady w/shoe, slogan ... 275.00
Gulf Gas, clock, electric ... 125.00
GW Bishop Drugs & Jewelry, clock, EX ... 1,300.00
Half & Half Tobacco, pocket tin, VG ... 5.00
Hallmark Coconut, tin pail, 3½x2¾" ... 35.00
Hambone Cigars, sign, Blk theme, cb circle, 7" ... 25.00
Hamilton Watch Co, ts, blonde girl, RR Timekeeper, 19x13" ... 310.00
Hamm's Beer, moving scenery sign, no clock ... 150.00
Hamm's Beer, moving scenery sign w/clock ... 200.00
Hanford's Balsam, booklet, Noah's Ark Primer ... 12.00
Hanna Paints, emb tin sign, 1940s, 3x12" ... 10.00
Hannis Whiskey, tip tray, red triangle, EX ... 35.00
Hans Wagner Cigars, cigar label, 1909, 4x4" ... 2,500.00
Harmony Tobacco, cb sign, to hold sample tin, 12" ... 8.00
Harris Engine Oils, die-cut porc sign, barrel form, 1916 ... 325.00
Harvest Home, tin container, peanut butter, stenciled ... 40.00
Hauptman's Hand Made Tobacco, tin container, red, 5½" ... 7.50
Heburn House Coal, tip tray, gold eagle atop coal, M ... 30.00
Heckers Flour, sifter ... 20.00
Heinekin Beer, sign, electric, cash register, EX ... 22.00
Heinz, hard plastic bust of man in top hat, EX ... 15.00
Heinz, pickle barrel, wood, orig pnt ... 95.00
Heinz 57, bean warmer, ceramic, brn glaze ... 110.00
Heptol Splits, tip tray, CM Russel cowboy/bronco, 1904 ... 175.00
Hi-Plane Tobacco, pocket tin, 2 engines ... 30.00
Hickory Children's Garters, counter display, die-cut/wood ... 95.00
Hill's Bros Coffee, thermometer, porc, robed man w/coffee ... 115.00

Hires

Bottle, paper label, 1915 ... 80.00
Buckle, Tiffany ... 75.00
Chalk board ... 50.00
Checkerboard ... 125.00
Container, porc, w/pump ... 285.00
Door push, w/foil bottle, 1930s, 3½x11" ... 35.00
Fan, Chinese ... 165.00
Fan, Dutch girl ... 100.00
Mirror, roses on celluloid, minor cracks ... 145.00
Mug, w/child, Mettlach, VG ... 150.00
Sign, pop-eyed soda jerk, 5x13", EX ... 126.00
Stand-up counter display, c 1892 ... 35.00
Straw holder ... 125.00
Tin sign, die-cut tin, w/bottle, 1940s, 13x41" ... 45.00
Trade card, hold-to-light ... 35.00
Tray, Josh Slinger ... 365.00
Watch fob ... 55.00

Hoffman Cigars, tin container, frolicking nudes/satyr ... 37.50
Hoffman Old Time Coffee, clock, Ingraham, EX ... 1,700.00
Hoffman Willis Ice Cream, fan, girls eat ice cream, 1900 ... 15.00
Holeproof Hosiery, pocket mirror, rnd, EX ... 12.00
Holsum Bread, emb tin sign, 1940s, 6x22" ... 20.00
Honeymoon Tobacco, tin sign, emb man/lady/moon, oak fr ... 375.00
Horlick's Milk, mirror, girl under tree w/cow ... 38.00
Hoster Brewery, ts, monks in cellar, oval fr, 1900, 27x23" ... 845.00
Hostetter's Stomach Bitters, clock, EX ... 1,700.00
Humpty Dumpty Shoes, clicker ... 10.00
Hupfels Beer, poster, hunter w/3 Irish Setters, 20x29" ... 165.00
Huxley's Plasma Powder, tc, paper label, floral design, EX ... 10.00
Hyroler Whiskey, LJ Adler, tip tray, man in tuxedo/hat, 4" ... 45.00
Imperial Ginger, tin container, 5x5x1" ... 10.00
Imperial Plows/Harrows/Cultivators; tin sign, farmer/plow ... 225.00
Interstate Coal Co, picture w/thermometer, pretty girl ... 18.00
Invincible Motor Insurance, tin sign, car/ship, 21x10" ... 76.00
Iron Bitters, Brown Chemical, fr sign, lady on anvil, 25" ... 500.00
Iroquois Beer, Indian head figural, store display, early ... 50.00
Irwins' Milk, china pitcher, mc logo, sm ... 15.00
Ivory Soap, wall dispenser ... 30.00
IW Harper Whiskey, sign, dog/cabin/guns, fr, 1900, 20x26" ... 650.00
J&P Coats, cb sign, factory in winter, 1880s ... 225.00
Jackie Coogan Peanut Butter, tin pail ... 200.00
James Bryce, fan pull, VG ... 18.00
Jell-O, booklet, M Parrish illus ... 35.00
Jenney Aero Gasoline, tip tray, 4 Extra Lbs of Fuel, NM ... 60.00
JH Cutter Whiskey, tray, ship, 17", EX ... 250.00
John Deere, bronze medallion, deer jumps plow ... 30.00
John Deere, clock, rnd, electric, 14" ... 60.00
John Deere, stickpin, plow ... 40.00
John Deere, tape measure ... 40.00
Joli Sois Poudre de Toilette, tc, house, flowers, EX ... 16.00
Joys Beverages, clock, electric ... 55.00
JP Coats Thread, oak/glass cabinet, turns/roll top/4-sided ... 575.00
JP Squire, ts, sitting pig, orig paper label, 24x19½", VG ... 600.00
Junket Dessert, pot scrapper ... 150.00
Kato Beer, sign, convex glass, eagle, 15", EX ... 126.00
Kaufmann Bondy Mfg Meerschaum & Briar Pipes, pocket mirror ... 12.00
Keds, sign, die-cut, cb, VG ... 30.00
Keep Kool Use To-Ko-Ku-La, fan hanger, cb, 6x5" ... 5.00
Kellogg's, booklet, Funny Jungleland ... 8.00
King Midas Cigar, tin container ... 45.00
Kinney Shoes, pencil box, baseball bat shaped, rare, 11" ... 50.00
Kis-Me Gum, lamp, flashes, 1900s, rare, EX ... 650.00
Kist Root Beer, emb tin sign, 1940s, 16x26" ... 40.00
Kiwi Boot Polish, counter display, bird on lid, EX ... 15.00
Kleenatub & Wrigley Scouring Soap, clock, EX ... 1,500.00
Knox Gelatin, litho sign, Blk lady makes gelatin for girl ... 375.00
Ko-Pac-Ta Toasted Peanuts 5¢, display canister, w/insert ... 275.00
Kodak, film dispenser, elephant, 12 jumbo prints for 5¢ ... 85.00
Koken Talc, tin container ... 75.00
Kool Cigarettes, tin sign, 1940s ... 15.00
Kool Cigarettes, wall matchbook holder, tin, penguin, EX ... 16.00
Kraft, emb tin sign, I Get the Milk Bank Boost, 11x18" ... 90.00
Lady Mary Tea, tumbler, etched/fluted ... 20.00
Lafayette Life Insurance, tin sign, hanging, 1930s, 15x9" ... 60.00
Laflin & Rand Powder, fr poster, hunter/boy, 1870, 26" ... 745.00
LaPalina Cigars, pocket tin, flat, lady ... 22.00
LaPerfencia Cigars, sign, paper under glass, orig fr ... 245.00
LaReclama Habana Cigars, wood box, metal clasp & hinges ... 16.00
LaReolina Cigars, cigar box ... 12.00
LaResta Cigars, tin container, NM ... 25.00
Larkin Orange Blossom, talcum tin, sample ... 15.00
Leich Electric Co, candlestick phone, Genoa, IL ... 95.00
Leisey Brewing Co, tankard/4 mugs, mc, gr w/gold leaf, EX ... 385.00

Liberty Root Beer, syrup dispenser, 13½"....................550.00
Lifesavers, dispenser, Candy Mint w/the Hole, 13x9x9", EX.....50.00
Lifesavers, store display rack, 1920s........................26.00
Lillian Russel 5¢ Cigars, store lighter/oil lamp w/shade........950.00
Lime Cola, emb tin sign, 1930s, 3x21".......................15.00
Lime Cola, fan, palm trees, NM............................25.00
Lime Cola, tin sign, old bottle, colorful, 28x10"...............55.00
Lime Julep, emb tin sign, 1920s, 6x21"......................25.00
Lion Brewery, mug, ceramic, pp, lions/monogram.............55.00
Lion Brewery, tray, oval, lion pushing barrel, EX..............86.00
Lipschutz '44' Cigars, tin sign, die-cut, flange.................85.00
Lipton Tea, stickpin, leaf...................................35.00
Liquid Gold Beer, tap hdl...................................18.00
Liserated Pepsin Gum, jar, blown glass, rare.................125.00
Loan Co, bank, piggy, metal, no key........................12.00
Loewer's Gambrinus Brew, tin sign, King Gambrinus, 14", EX..126.00

Log Cabin Syrup

Log Cabin Syrup tins have been made since the 1890s, in variations of design that can be attributed to specific years of production. Until about 1914, the log cabin tins were made with paper labels. These are quite rare and highly prized by today's collectors. Tins with colored lithographed designs were made after 1914. When General Foods purchased the Towle Company in 1927, the letters 'GF' were added to the tins.

A cartoon series, illustrated with a mother flipping pancakes in the cabin window and various children and animals declaring their appreciation of the syrup in voice balloons, was introduced in the 1930s. A Frontier Village series followed in the late 1940s. A schoolhouse, jail, trading post, doctor's office, blacksmith shop, inn and private homes were available. Examples of either series are today in the $75 to $100 range.

Bank, glass...20.00
Bank, tin, Towle's, 4x3"....................................40.00
Bottle, Towle's Log Cabin Syrup.............................65.00
Display, picture of cabin, cb...............................375.00
Spoon, demitasse..16.00
Spoon, teaspoon...17.00
Syrup tin, cartoons on 4 sides...............................75.00
Syrup tin, Express Office....................................45.00
Syrup tin, Frontier Inn, NM..................................90.00
Syrup tin, lady flipping pancakes.............................65.00
Syrup tin, 1-pt..22.00
Syrup tin, 5-lb..50.00

Towle's Log Cabin Syrup container, both sides shown, $75.00.

Los Angeles Talcum, tin container...........................21.00
Lowenbrau Beer, sign, plastic w/raised gold lion, 14x16"........12.00
Lowney's Cocoa, tc, paper label, old-fashioned lady, G.........18.00
Lucas Service for Imported Cars, thermometer, 5x18", EX......20.00
Lucky Lager, tip tray, Western Hemisphere/boat, 4x6", EX.....26.00
Lucky Strike Cigarettes, box, flat, EX........................16.00
Lucky Strike Cigarettes, clock, schoolhouse, EX............1,200.00
Lucky Strike Cigarettes, cuff links, 1930s, pr.................15.00
Lucky Strike Cigarettes, pocket tin, sm.......................25.00
Lucky Strike Cigarettes, sample tin, EX.......................45.00
Lusterite Stove Enamel, cb sign, 1920s, 9x8"...................6.00
Lux Fire Extinguishing Equipment, porc sign, 13x28"..........65.00
Luxor Toilet Requisites, Egyptian lady figure chalk display......45.00
Lydia Pinkham's, sewing set, wall hanging.....................35.00
Ma's Root Beer, thermometer, bottle form, 1944...............55.00
Ma's Root Beer, tin sign, 1940s, 13x23"......................25.00
Magnolia Petroleum, porc sign, rnd, 30", VG.................135.00
Mail Pouch, wall thermometer, tin litho, w/2 packages, NM......75.00
Maltby's Coconut, tin container, early........................45.00
Manilla Anchor Brewing, sign, emb tin, mc, 13½x19½"........325.00
Mapa Cuba Cigars, pocket tin, EX............................50.00
Marburg Bros Cigarettes, paperweight.........................32.00
Mark Twain Restaurant, plate, sandwich; shows Mark..........10.00
Marvels Cigarettes, thermometer.............................30.00
Maryland Club Tobacco, pocket tin, flat lid, NM.............250.00
Mason's Root Beer, bottle, boy waiter, amber..................20.00
Master Marine & Rival Tobacco, tin sign, 1920s, 10x13".......20.00
Mastercraft, smoking pipe display model, blk/gold, 36" L......245.00
Masury Paint Co, ts, fr, worker makes paint, 1900, 29x23"....950.00
Mayo Tobacco, tin container, 4x6"...........................30.00
McCall's Patterns, porc sign, 2-sided, 1920s, 9x18"............60.00
Megill's Gauge Pins, tin sign, 1930s, 7x11"..................10.00
Melachrino Cigarettes, cb box, EX............................12.00
Menu Baking Powder, clock, EX.........................1,200.00
Merrick's Spool Cotton, schoolhouse clock, short drop........950.00
Metropolitan Velvet Ice Cream, ts, litho sodas, flowers.........295.00
Miller Brewing, cb sign under glass, brewery, 1930, 30x28"....150.00
Miller High Life Beer, tray, girl on moon, 1950s, 13", EX......52.00
Miller Lite Beer, sign, electric, raised logo w/hops, EX.........15.00
Miller Tire, porc sign, 1930s................................45.00
Minard's Liniment, fold-out window display, men w/skis, EX.....60.00
Minard's Liniment, sign, lg triad, red devils, EX...............16.00
Minneapolis Moline, stickpin, plow man......................40.00
Mission Lime, syrup dispenser, gr glass lid...................95.00
Mission of California, tin sign, 5 bottles, 1946, 29x11".........20.00
Mission Orange, syrup dispenser, emb pink globe............100.00
Mission Orange, tin thermometer, 1950, 17x5"...............20.00
Mobil Oil, porc sign, gargoyle, 24" dia.......................95.00
Mobil Oil, tin container, red horse..........................13.00
Monarch Axle Grease, tin pail, eagles, w/lid, bail hdl...........25.00
Monarch Light of Asia Tea, tin container.....................48.00
Monticello Whiskey, sf tin sign, fox hunt, 1907..............275.00
Morton's Salt, blotter, child/product/bird/worm, EX............10.00
Morton's Salt, potato peeler.................................10.00
Morton's Salt, trivet..10.00
Mother Goose Shoes, papier mache full-bodied figural.........110.00

Moxie

The Moxie Company was organized in 1884 by George Archer of Boston, Massachusetts. It was at first touted as a 'nerve food' to improve the appetite, promote restful sleep and in general to make one 'feel better'! Emphasis was soon shifted, however, to the good taste of the brew, and extensive advertising campaigns rivaling those of such giant competitors as Hires and Coca-Cola resulted in successful marketing through the 1930s. Today the term Moxie has become synonomous with courage and audacity, traits displayed by the company who dared compete with such well-established rivals.

Ad, Moxie Man, Drink Pureoxia, full color, 1931, NM 30.00
Book, court cases when Moxie sued imitating products 48.00
Bottle, Pureoxia, paper label, emb glass, NM 20.00
Bottle, seltzer; Pureoxia, by Moxie, EX 45.00
Bottle holder, cardboard 22.00
Bottle opener, slides into hdl 10.00
Carrying bag, paper, Moxie Kid print 6.50
Counter pad, cardboard 35.00
Fan, girl w/Moxie tumbler, 1924 .... 35.00
Fan, Muriel Ostriche sitting on rock, 1916 .... 35.00
Label, picture of Ted Williams, 1950s 8.00
Match holder, tin, bottle shape 200.00
Menu booklet 22.00
Pin-back, Moxie man 30.00
Plate, early, 9½″ 75.00
Sign, man pointing, die-cut, fr, 23x19″ 350.00
Sign, Nerve Food, printed metal molded in relief, 23x31″ 250.00
Sign, paper, Drink Moxie 5¢, sm 12.00
Soda glass 18.00
Standing wooden figure holds metal ash tray, EX pnt, 28″ 285.00
Thermometer, clerk pointing, bottle 75.00
Thermometer, man pointing, gr 200.00
Tip tray, National Health Beverage, 3½″, NM 110.00

Moxie advertising poster on cardboard, easel back, 28″ x 39″, $125.00.

Munsingware, lcs/orig fr, granny/twins, 1914, 36x28″ 415.00
Murad Cigarettes, sign, paper, Xmas package/lady, 10x20″ 42.00
Murad Tobacco, punchboard sign, 30x40″ 145.00
Murray Hill Coffee, tin container, building 55.00
MW Baldwin Locomotive Builders, poster 2,090.00
Narragansett Lager & Ale, serving tray, rnd 52.00
National Beer, sign, Baltimore Colts, raised helmet 25.00
National Cash Register, bill holder 36.50
National Cigar Stands Co, change tray, rnd 110.00
Nature's Remedy, porc sign/chalkboard/thermometer, EX 225.00
Nature's Remedy, thermometer, 5x25″, EX 126.00
Near's Poultry, emb tin sign, 1940s, 9x12″ 12.00
Nehi, thermometer, pictures bottle, 15″ dia 25.00
Nesbitt's California Orange, dispenser, glass top, VG 30.00
Nesbitt's California Orange, thermometer, 22″ 40.00
Nesbitt's Soda, enamel sign, 12x22″ 40.00
New Idea, stickpin, spreaders 35.00

Honest Scrap, paper sign with original frame, 30″ x 22″, $550.00.

None Such Mincemeat, clock 350.00
North Star, tin container, sq corner, rare, early 350.00
Nu-Grape Soda, sf tin sign, emb bottle, NM 85.00
Nu-Grape Soda, thermometer, odd-shape bottle, tin 65.00
NY Biscuit Co, box, tin/brass w/glass front 85.00
O'Dell Tires, tin sign, flanged 65.00
Odo-Ro-No, cb sign, bottle shape, 26″ 40.00
Oh Boy Gum, tin sign, 1930s, 16x8″ 90.00
Old Boone Distilling Co, sf tin sign, D Boone/cabin, 1904 .... 650.00
Old Charter Whiskey, clock 55.00
Old Colony Tobacco, pocket tin, EX 70.00
Old Crow Whiskey, papier mache figural 275.00
Old Dutch Beer, tray, Eagle Brewery, jolly man w/mug 75.00
Old Dutch Cleansers, stickpin, woman 35.00
Old English Curve Cut Tobacco, tc, 4½x3½x3″ 10.00
Old Gold Leaf Rye, sign, portrait of blonde, 1900 .... 146.00
Old Heidelberg Blatz, plaster sign, barmaid on barrel, 36″ 495.00
Old Manse Syrup, tin container, oblong, farm scene 30.00
Old Overholt Rye, canvas sign, fisherman, 1913, 27x38″ 400.00
Old Reliable Coffee, cb sign, pictures lady, 1920s, 14x9″ 35.00
Old Virginia Cheroots, cigar box, Blk man 18.00
Olixir Motor Oil, tin sign, lg hand pushes '30s car uphill 85.00
Omar Cigarettes, poster, fr, men in tuxedos, 1910, 26x35″ 290.00
Orange Crush, seltzer bottle, 'Sparkling Soda' label 45.00
Orange Crush, thermometer, rnd w/bottle cap, NM 30.00
Orange Julep, cb sign w/fr, cozy couple, NM 38.00
Orient Insurance of Hartford, tin sign, deer head, fr 100.00
Orinco Coffee, canister, rnd, Riley & Wilson Co, MO, G 35.00
Owensboro Wagons, sf tin sign, 1906, 38x26″ 1,100.00
Pabst Blue Ribbon Beer, clock, wood, 11x23″, EX 46.00
Pabst Old Heidelberg, porc sign, emb curved corner, EX 450.00
Pacific Shoes, pocket mirror, rnd, high-button shoe, EX 36.00
Palisade Beer, tray, Union City, oval, w/factory 200.00
Parker Pens, glass sign, hand filling pen, lights up 145.00
Parry Buggies, clock, schoolhouse, EX 1,200.00
Passport Scotch Whiskey, pitcher, EX 10.00
Patterson's Seal Cut Plug Tobacco, tin container, hdld, 6″ 42.50
Peachy Tobacco, pocket tin, EX 35.00
Peanut Kid's Peanut Butter, pail, tin, minor dents 25.00
Peep O'Day Perfume, sign, paper w/metal ends, 11x14″, EX 46.00
Peidmont Cigarettes, porc sign, 12″, EX 76.00
Penn's Tobacco, tin container, EX 40.00
Penzoil, emb tin sign, Safe Lubrication, 1930s, 12x35″ 35.00

Pepsi-Cola

Pepsi-Cola was first served in the early 1890s to customers of Caleb D. Bradham, a young pharmacist who touted his concoction to be medicinal as well as delicious. It was first called 'Brad's Drink,' and renamed Pepsi-Cola in 1898.

Ball, rubber, 3″ 15.00
Blotter, Pepsi & Pete, EX 17.50
Blotter, pink, early 1900s, NM 30.00
Bottle opener, 1924 . . . . . 6.50
Calendar, Sportsman's, 1940, complete 30.00
Change tray, blonde girl's face w/bottle, plastic 16.00
Change tray, Victorian lady/soda fountain, oval, 4x6″, NM 225.00
Cigarette lighter, musical, Be Sociable, Have a Pepsi 22.00
Counter bottle display, figural lady, Sparkling Quality 110.00
Hat, Say Pepsi Please 10.00
Menu, waitress pouring product, NM 25.00
Pen, ink; old, EX 35.00
Poster, attractive girl w/flowers, fr, rare, 1914, 31x36″ 845.00
Radio, dispenser, w/carrying harness, NM 145.00
Radio, PCT-5, looks like cooler, RCA 225.00
Radio, vendor, w/carrying case, M 60.00
Radio, vendor, 3 sections across, EX 80.00
Record, service man's message home, in orig envelope, '43 . . . . . 23.00
Sign, cb w/wood fr mk 'Pepsi-Cola Girl,' Armstrong, 1919 . . . . . 305.00
Sign, tin, early carton & bottles w/paper labels, 1920 . . . . . 295.00
Sign, yel/blk, Ice Cold Pepsi-Cola Sold Here, 19x28″ 235.00
Syrup can, drum motif, w/lid, EX 40.00
Tap knob, musical, chrome & celluloid, 1930s 125.00
Thermometer, girl sipping through straw 125.00
Tip tray, Evervess, Yes, Yes!, parrot, rectangular, NM 20.00
Toy, plastic van w/sign on side, M 15.00
Tray, children singing, 1940s 30.00
Tray, Coney Island, 1950s 25.00
Tray, girl in bar room, 1900s 450.00

Pepsi tray, late '50s-early '60s, $28.00.

Pepsodent, jigsaw puzzle, Molly Goldberg/family, complete 35.00
Permatex Penetrating Car Oil, can, Deco design, full 5.00
Pet Milk, can opener, wooden 10.00
Peter Pan Ice Cream, tin sign, emb Peter, 1940s, 19x28″ 75.00
Peter Rabbit Peanut Butter, tin pail 150.00
Peters' Shoes, alarm clock, Deco, New Haven 50.00
Philip Morris, ash tray, Johnny standing, ceramic, rare 95.00
Philip Morris, tin sign, 15x27″, EX 40.00
Phillip's Milk of Magnesia, letter opener/magnifying glass 15.00
Phoenix, Sparkling & Delicious, emb shield shape sign, 28″ 100.00
Pickaninny Peanut Butter, tin pail 150.00
Picobac, pocket tin 35.00
Piedmont Cigarettes, cb cut-out 3-D sign, boy w/carton, VG 65.00
Piedmont Cigarettes, tin sign, orig fr, 1916 . . . . . 375.00
Pierce's Lignite Floor Varnish, clock, EX 1,500.00
Piff's Beverages, tin sign, pictures bottle, 1940s, 20x28″ 20.00
Pilsener Beer, tin sign, barmaid serves beer, 20x15½″, EX 350.00
Pilsener Beer, tin sign, barmaid serves beer, 20x15½″, VG 200.00
Piper Heid Sieck Chewing Tobacco, tin container 22.50
Piso's Tooth Powder, tin container, floral 13.00

Planters Peanuts

Mr. Peanut, the dashing peanut man with the top hat, spats, monocle and cane, has represented the Planters Peanut Company from 1916 to 1961, when the company was purchased by Standard Brands. He promoted the company's product by appearing on premium give-aways, store displays, jars, scales and in special promotional events. Among the favored treasures of collectors today are the glass display jars. They come in a variety of styles; some are square, some hexagonal, some barrel shaped, and others are round. The earliest, issued in 1926, was octagonal and is usually referred to as the 'pennant' jar. Although later reproduced, these are marked 'Made in Italy' on the bottom. The original is embossed on the back panel 'Sold Only in Printed Planters Red Pennant Bags'; in a second octagonal style this embossed message was replaced with a paper label.

In 1930, a 'fishbowl' jar was introduced, and in 1932 a 'four-corner peanut' jar was issued. The rarest jar of all, the 'football' jar, was also used during the early 1930s. The Planters' square jar followed in the 1930s, and was replaced by the 'barrel' jar. The six-sided jar with Mr. Peanut decals and the 'pickle' jar were later. All in all more than fifteen different styles were developed.

In the late 1930s, premiums such as glass and metal figural paperweights, pens, and pencils were distributed; post-war items were often made of plastic--Mr. Peanut salt and pepper shakers, mugs and banks were popular. Today's collectors find a treasure trove of advertising memorabilia depicting that debonair, tasteful gentleman, Mr. Peanut.

Ash tray, ceramic, Mr Peanut figural w/3 peanuts 65.00
Ash tray, metal, gold, Mr Peanut in center, orig 20.00
Ash tray, metal, silver, Mr Peanut in center, orig 38.00
Bank, vender; w/can of peanuts, dtd 1938, MIB 275.00
Book, coloring; Presidents from Washington to Johnson, '63 . . . . . 10.00
Book, coloring; Presidents of the US, 1953 . . . . . 15.00
Book, paint; USA, 32 pg 20.00
Bookmark, Greetings from Mr Peanut, yel cb 15.00
Bookmark, 1939 World's Fair 25.00
Bowl, counter display, clear plastic 28.00
Box lid, Buy US War Bonds, Mr Peanut in corner 32.50
Can, cashew nuts, 1944, 4-oz 10.00
Can, Old Fashion peanut candy, 14-oz 20.00
Can, Pennant Brand, 10-lb, G 175.00
Can, train, standard gauge, w/lid, in box 25.00
Candy dish, glass, serrated edge, Mr Peanut on base 10.00
Champagne glass, plastic, red/wht/bl, Mr Peanut stem 12.00
Charm bracelet, complete 20.00
Cigarette lighter 55.00
Container, counter; Mr Peanut head, plastic, bl hat 15.00

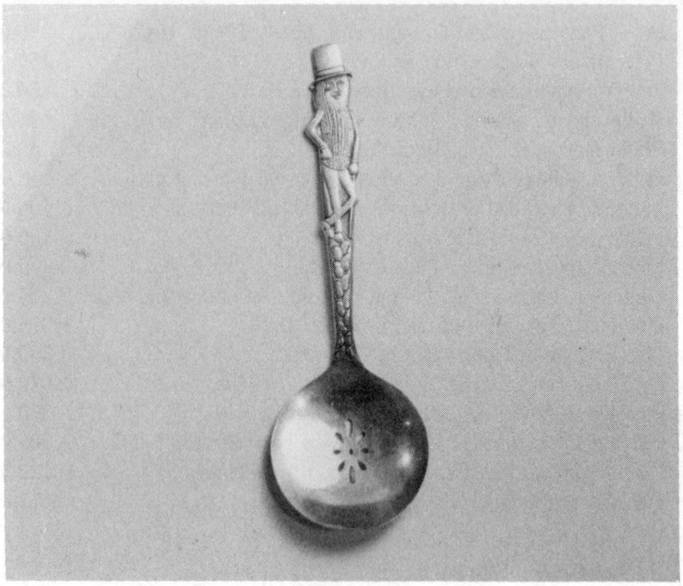

Planter's, Mr. Peanut silverplated nut spoon, 5¼", $22.00.

Container, papier mache, peanut shape, 11" L 55.00
Cookie cutter, plastic, bl 10.00
Die-cut, woman holding peanuts 275.00
Dispenser, peanut; plastic, lg Mr Peanut decor, Sears, 12" 27.50
Display, cardboard fold-out, 2-shelf, Mr Peanut atop 75.00
Jar, Barrel, running peanut man, paper label 200.00
Jar, Clipper, tin lid 60.00
Jar, Fish Bowl, rectangular label 100.00
Jar, Fish Bowl, sq paper label 125.00
Jar, Football, peanut lid finial 200.00
Jar, frosted label, big knob, rnd 45.00
Jar, Leap Year, sm fired-on decal, orig red tin lid 65.00
Jar, octagon, Pennant 5¢, 7 sides embossed 80.00
Jar, octagon, Pennant 5¢, 8 sides embossed 95.00
Jar, Pennant 5¢, T paper label 150.00
Jar, red/wht/bl label, big knob 45.00
Jar, sq, lg blown-out peanut ea corner 185.00
Jar, Streamline, tin lid 50.00
Jar, 6-sided, yel printed label 60.00
Lamp, works, rare 120.00
Marbles, 14 agate, unopened, orig Mr Peanut bag 35.00
Mr Peanut, CI, orig mtd on fence at PA factory, 38" 2,500.00
Mr Peanut, papier mache peanut holder, 12½" 185.00
Mr Peanut, plaster nodder, 6¾" 50.00
Mr Peanut, plaster of paris, eye lights up 2,500.00
Mr Peanut, plastic windup figural walker, red 125.00
Mr Peanut, rag doll 8.00
Mr Peanut, wood, peanut body, 1930, 8½" 75.00
Night light, Mr Peanut figural, glows in dark 50.00
Note book pad, 18", VG 12.50
Nut chopper, tin 28.00
Nut dish, all metal, 4½" Mr Peanut in center 20.00
Nut dish, divided, red plastic w/Mr Peanut in center 20.00
Nut set, 1939 NY Fair, 5-pc 25.00
Peanut bag, 1950s, 3-oz, 12 for 10.00
Peanut butter maker, Mr Peanut 18.00
Peanut oil tin, High Hat, pour spout, full 50.00
Pen, ballpoint, blk/tan 10.00
Pencil, mechanical; Mr Peanut in oil, red/wht 20.00
Pennant 76.00
Pin, metal w/gr stones, Mr Peanut figural 47.50
Pocket knife, Mr Peanut, w/celluloid case 17.50
Punchboard, cocktail can, 5¢ per punch, 9x10" 45.00
Scoop, tin 65.00
Shakers, china Mr Peanut w/rhinestone monocle, 4½", pr 40.00
Shakers, plastic Mr Peanut figurals, blk/tan, 4", pr, M 10.00
Shipping crate, wood 120.00
Shopping bag, patriotic colors, An Am Tradition, 1940s 25.00
Sign, plaster over wood, lg 135.00
Truck, plastic, open bed, bl/yel, 2-pc 37.50
Whistle, Mr Peanut figural 15.00

Players Navy Cut 100 Cigarettes, tin container 48.00
Plow Boy Tobacco, litho paper-wrapped pkg, unopened 20.00
Plow Boy Tobacco, tin pail, rnd, w/paper label 60.00
Polar Bear Flour, rolling pin, Tulsa Feed Store 110.00
Polar Ice Cream, aluminum sign, 1930s 20.00
Pollack Wheeling Stogies, porc thermometer, 39x8", VG 85.00
Popsicle, tin sign, yel/orange/blk, 28x10" 65.00
Possom Cigars, pocket tin, EX 55.00
Prestone Antifreeze, thermometer, porcelain, 8x27" 26.00
Pride of Virginia Tobacco, pocket tin, floral/feathers 16.00
Prince Albert Tobacco, pocket tin, EX 12.00
Prince Albert Tobacco, tin container, in Christmas box 20.00
Prof Field's Worm Powder, ts, girl w/dog, 1880, 9x14" 345.00
Progress Beer, sign, cb, Blk men playing cards, 25x19" 100.00
Providence Washington Insurance Co, ts, fr, 18x24" 752.00
Prudential Has Strength of Gibraltar, oil/canvas, 35x28" 85.00
Prudential Insurance, needle threader, tin litho 10.00
Prudential Insurance, tip tray, oval, Rock of Gibraltar, M 12.00
Public Telephone, porc sign, w/arrow & bell 45.00
Public Telephone, porc sign, 2-sided, 16x18" 50.00
Pure-Pep Gasoline, porc sign 35.00
Purina, pocket knife, 3 blades 12.00
Puritan Tobacco, pocket tin 75.00
Putnam Dyes, cabinet, wood, tin front, Putnam on horse, EX 176.00
Quaker Oats, booklet, Frolie Grasshopper Circus, 1898 ..... 24.00
Quaker Oats, booklet, puzzle pictures, spine rust, 1900 ..... 15.00
Quick Mill Stoves & Ranges, porc sign, hatching chick 465.00

RCA Victor

Nipper, the RCA Victor trademark was the creation of Francis Barraud, an English artist. His pet's intent fascination with the music of the phonograph seemed to him a worthy subject for his canvas. Although he failed to find a publishing house who would buy his work, the Gramaphone Co. saw its potential and adopted Nipper to advertise their product. The company eventually became the Victor Talking Machine Co. and was purchased by RCA in 1929. Nipper's image appeared on packaged accessories, in ads and brochures. If you are very lucky you may find a life-size statue of him--but all are not old, they have been reproduced! Except for the years between 1971 and 1981, Nipper has seen active duty, and with his image spruced up only a bit for the present day, the ageless symbol for RCA still listens intently to 'His Master's Voice.'

Bank, RCA service man, plastic, pnt suit, 1960, 5" 4.00
Book, Rip Discovers Radio, 1939 ..... 10.00
Calendar, Elvis Presley giveaway, w/7 photos, 1963 ..... 35.00
Catalog, Victor Records, 1940-41 ..... 15.00
Catalog, 1917 ..... 3.50
Clock, promotional gold record display 190.00
Clock, shaped like record, Victor, early 700.00
Doll, wood/compo, by Kallus, designed by Parrish, 15" 350.00
Mirror, pocket; shaped like record 75.00

Needle case, full tone, Nipper & phonograph, 2½x 1½″........32.00
Needle tin, bl, Victor, lg........25.00
Nipper, bank, metal........100.00
Nipper, imp Victor, 1904, 4″, MIB........40.00
Nipper, papier mache, 14″........375.00
Nipper, plaster, minor ear rpr, EX orig pnt, sm........125.00
Puzzle, Victor, 1908........65.00
Radio tube, Nipper on tube & box, MIB........15.00
Record album, Nipper emblem, dtd 1918, +10 records........40.00
Record brush, oblong, gold leaf Nipper on bl hdl, 1900s........32.00
Record cleaner, celluloid, shows Nipper........35.00
World globe, tin........40.00

R&H Beer, tray, gold letters on woodgrain background, 12″........66.00
Rainbow Beverage, sign, bottle, bl/wht/orange........25.00
Rainbow Bread, emb tin sign, 1940s, 3x14″........12.00
Raleigh Cigarettes, tin sign, emb, pack w/Sir Walter........85.00
Ralston Purina, bowl, bl, Find the Bottom........50.00
Raptco Wafers, pocket tin, flat, emb leaf on lid, EX........26.00
Rayette Cold Waves, kit, wood rollers/clamps, in wood box........65.00
Red Cross Coffee, tin container, early........55.00
Red Cross Stoves & Ranges, pocket mirror, rnd, EX........26.00
Red Fox Beverages, tin sign, 1940s, 13x4″........9.00
Red Goose Shoes, child's shoe box, children playing........25.00
Red Goose Shoes, clicker, tin........10.00
Red Goose Shoes, happy/sad clown face, 3-D........450.00
Red Goose Shoes, neon sign........850.00
Red Goose Shoes, pencil box, celluloid........75.00
Red Goose Shoes, sign, flanged........80.00
Red Goose Shoes, token, Texas centennial........50.00
Red Goose Shoes, wall bill spindle........20.00
Red Jacket Tobacco, pocket tin........15.00
Red Man Chewing Tobacco, tin sign, Indian........25.00
Red Raven Splits, tip tray, 1904 World's Fair........80.00
Red Raven Splits, tray, pictures man........175.00
Red Star 5¢ Cough Drops, self-strip sign........15.00
Red Wing Flour, pot scraper........125.00
Red Wolf Coffee, tin container, 1-lb........26.00
Reed/Jamaica Ginger, tin container, 4-oz........7.00
Regal Beer, clock, electric........65.00
Remington, sign, banner & rifle........25.00
RG Dun Cigars, pocket tin, pictures man, 5x3½x1″........20.00
Rheingold Beer, sign, cb, Miss Rheingold w/fire engine........12.00
Rhinelander Butter, tin sign, 2 pkgs of butter........75.00
Richardson's Silk, spool cabinet, oak/glass, 32x16″ sq........500.00
Richfield Ethyl Gas, sign, glass, 4x12″, EX........26.00
Richmond Mixture Tobacco, tc, Allen & Ginter, 3x2⅓x2″........16.00
Ricksecker's Perfumes, showcase, etched glass, rnd, 12″........650.00
Ridgway's Tea, tc, emb, says Safe-Tea First, 1836........25.00
Rival Dogfood, bank, tin, can shape........10.00
Rochelle Club Ginger Ale, cb sign, bottle shape, 11x36″........36.00
Rochester Barber's Sterilizer, box, emb metal, early........22.00
Rockford Watches, tip tray, lady sitting on grass, 2x4″, M........56.00

Roly Poly

The Roly Poly tobacco tins were patented on November 5, 1912, by Washington Tuttle and produced by Tindeco of Baltimore, Maryland. There were six characters in all--Satisfied Customer, Storekeeper, Mammy, Dutchman, Singing Waiter and Inspector. Four brands of tobacco were packaged in selected characters; some tins carry a printed tobacco box on the back to identify their contents. Mayo and Dixie Queen Tobacco were packed in all six; Red Indian and U.S. Marine Tobacco in only Mammy, Singing Waiter and Storekeeper.

Of the set, the Inspector is considered the rarest, and in mint condition may fetch as much as $1,000 on today's market.

Dutchman, M........750.00
Dutchman, VG........450.00
Inspector from Scotland Yard, EX........800.00
Mammy........500.00
Satisfied Customer........450.00
Singing Waiter........450.00
Storekeeper........650.00

Rothenberg Handmade Cigars, cb box, elegant man, EX........16.00
Roxo Ice Cream, ash tray, brass........20.00
Royal Baking Powder, litho tin container, 1920s, 26x20″........25.00
Royal Crown Cola, cb sign, Jeanette MacDonald, 26x40″, EX........75.00
Royal Crown Cola, fan, All American, EX........20.00
Ruhstaller's Factory, beer tray, oval, VG........450.00
Rumford Baking Powder, sample tc, emb lid, scarce........15.00
Rummy, emb tin sign, A Grapefruit Mixer, 1940s, 11x18″........25.00
Ruppert's Beer, tip tray, Hans Flato cartoon, M........42.00
Ruppert's Beer, tray, hands holding mug, 13″, EX........66.00
Russell's Chocolates, tin, child w/rose, 1904, 13½x19″........345.00
Safeguard Insurance, tin sign, dog by safe, New York........125.00
Salsbury's Poultry & Livestock Medicines, cb sign/wood fr........75.00
Salvo Pine Healing Oil, sign under glass, horse, 32″........165.00
Sambo Axle Grease, tc, Blk boy, blk & wht, 1-lb, G........65.00
Samoset Chocolates, charger, chalk, Indian in canoe, 16″........325.00
San Felice Cigars, cloth banner, 26x141″........65.00
Sanitol Talcum, tc, Colonial man & woman, EX........16.00
Satin Skin Powder, paper sign, Oriental lady w/fan, early........55.00
Schaefer Beer, foam scraper........7.00
Schinasi Egyptian Cigarettes, tin container........24.00
Schlitz Beer, sign, electric, stained glass/logo, 22x30″........52.00
Schmidt Beer, bank, bottle shape, 24″........18.00
Schoen's Beer, enameled beer glass........15.00
Schrafft's Chocolate, sign, Victorian lady, 29½x23¼″, EX........295.00
Schrauth's Ice Cream, stickpin, boy........30.00
Schwinn Bicycles, sign, lights up........145.00
Seal Cut Plug Tobacco, tin container, tall, sq........60.00

Satan-et, Smooth as Satin, 5¢, double-sided tin sign, 20″ x 12″, $650.00.

Sears Cross Country Motor Oil, can....65.00
Segram Whiskey, clock, electric....30.00
Seilheimer's Ginger Ale, porc sign, wood fr, 11x22″....70.00
Sensible Tobacco, tin container, 4½x3x3½″....15.00
Shaefer Pianos, pocket mirror, oval, upright piano, EX....46.00
Sheehan's Strawberry Syrup, jug, stoneware w/label, NM....85.00
Shell, clock, wood, EX....3,000.00
Shell, porc sign, 1930s....50.00
Sherwood Auto, bob sled, boy sledding downhill....275.00
Silver Spring Ale, tin sign, pop bottle, 1930s, 17x11″....50.00
Silver Spring Brewery, stone litho, Victoria BC, 20x20″....35.00
Simmons' Liver Regulator, brass horseshoe....55.00
Simon Pure Beer, tray, winged hops center....35.00
Sinclair, porc sign, pump, pictures Dino....35.00
Sir Walter Raleigh Tobacco, dummy store canister, lg, EX....50.00
Sir Walter Raleigh Tobacco, pocket tin....15.00
Sir Walter Raleigh Tobacco, tc, in Christmas box....20.00
Smith Brothers' Cough Drops, blotter, 8x2″, EX....6.00
Smith Brothers' Jewelers, clock, rnd....22.00
Snowdrift Coconut, container, 10-lb....22.50
Socony, sign, tin, emb oil can....126.00
Socony Motor Gasoline, pocket mirror, lg....38.00
Souvain Tablets, pocket tin....6.00
Spalding Skates, cb sign, skaters, 1920, 14x22″....125.00
Spanish Segaros, paper ad, in color, 18x22″....85.00
Spark Plug Chewing Tobacco, cb sign, display/pack, 15x14″....40.00
Squirrel Brand Salted Nuts, peanut jar, emb squirrel, 14″....75.00
Squirt, thermometer, emb bottle, Squirt kid, 5x13″....32.00
Squirt, tin sign, w/bottle, 4x17″....17.00
SSS For the Blood, string holder....110.00
St Charles Evaporated Milk, clock....200.00
Standard Paint, sf tin sign, happy painter/product....265.00
Standard Red Crown/White Crown, porc sign, gas pump....45.00
Star Brand Shoes, pull toy race car, 1920s....150.00
Star Soap, porc sign, sm....45.00
Star Tobacco, porc sign, 1930s, some wear....35.00
Stegmaier Beer, change tray, Home of..., tin, oval, 6″....75.00
Stegmaier Beer, emb tin sign, pictures beer bottle, 10x14″....25.00
Stewart Warner Radio, rvpt sign, lighted....345.00
Stillboma Oriental Polish, tc, deer, 5x1½″, EX....16.00
Stroh's Beer, cb sign, man w/top hat, fr, 28x20″....195.00
Sunbeam Bread, door push, Miss Sunbeam....50.00
Sunkist California Dream, tin can, peacocks/castle....25.00
Sunny Monday Soap, shaver, tin, 1900s....17.00
Sunshine Beer, tray, 15″, EX....52.00
Sunshine Biscuits, pen knife, 3 blades, yel....11.00
Sunshine Coffee, tc, Fresh Roasted Since 1867, 1-lb....35.00
Surbrug's Navy Cut Tobacco, pocket tin, rnd....22.00
Swan's Down Cake Flour, pan, tin....10.00
Swan's Down Cake Flour, ts, cake & flour box, 9x6″, G....38.00
Sweet Burley Tobacco, bin, upright, EX....125.00
Sweet Mist Tobacco, store canister, rnd, 10-lb....150.00
Sweetheart Talc, tin container, lady, orig box, EX....26.00
Swisher Soules Whiskey, papier mache owl, 2-sided, VG....35.00
Tampa Nugget Cigars, porc sign....75.00
Target Cigarette Tobacco, cloth sign, mc on yel, 29½x63″....35.00
Tasty Food Products, Dinner Bell Coffee, tc, 1-lb....4.00
Taylor's Cough Syrup, paper banner, early, NM....12.00
Tetley Ice Tea, emb ceramic barrel counter dispenser....95.00
Texaco, porc sign, 1930s....50.00
Texaco Gasoline, salt & peppers, pump figurals, pr....15.00
Thomas the Tailor, paper litho sign, 2 gents playing pool....145.00
Thomas Wilson Cigars, tin sign, 3 men/cigar box, fr, 1900s....325.00
Tiny Tot Talc, tin container....20.00
Tom Moore Cigars, tin container....20.00
Toyland Peanut Butter, tin pail, w/lid, G....75.00
Traiser's Pippins 5¢ Cigar, porc sign, w/apple, 24x33″, NM....100.00
Treasure Coffee, tc, JE Dubuisson & Bros, ca 1936, 1-lb....4.00
Triner's Bitter Wine, cb sign, ca 1920s, sgn....125.00
Triumph Hair Vigor, dog, bisque, Don't Use It on Dog, 3½″....35.00
Tuck's Chewing Tobacco, thermometer, shows package, tin....115.00
Turco Beverages, emb tin sign, 1920s, 10x21″....20.00
Tuxedo Tobacco, oblong canister, EX....100.00
Tuxedo Tobacco, pocket tin, EX....25.00

Vigorator Hair Tonic, tin sign, 9″ x 5″, $35.00.

Tydol, gasoline poster, litho on canvas, 1920s, 55x36″....252.00
Uneeda Graham Crackers, litho, baby in highchair, 8x11″....50.00
Union Leader Cut Plug Tobacco, tin box, 3″....27.50
Union Leader Tobacco, pocket tin, Uncle Sam, EX....45.00
Universal Theatres Concession Co, mirror, celluloid....10.00
Urban's Liberty Flour, Buffalo, NY, pink glass plate, 8″....20.00
Utica Club, West End Brewing Co, tray, w/brewery, ca 1900....400.00
Valentines' Automobile Varnish, thermometer, celluloid/tin....95.00
Valley Forge Beer, tray, Washington's Headquarters, 12″....40.00
Vantage Cigarettes, clock, rnd, battery, EX....22.00
Vantine's Incense, tin container, Deco lady....25.00
Velvet Tobacco, pocket tin, old style pipe....16.00
Velvet Tobacco, porc sign, pictures pocket tin, 48x12″, EX....152.00
Vermont's Household Remedies, clock, New Haven, EX....1,400.00
Vigorola, syrup dispenser, rare, M....1,250.00
Virginia Smoking Tobacco, tc, gold & blk, 4x5″, EX....22.00
Voisin & Co, plate, Vict bldgs, horse-drawn carriage, EX....35.00
Walkover Shoes, tin sign, Victorian lady w/oversize shoe....195.00
Walla Walla Gum, tin sign, 9¼x8½″....60.00
Warrier Cement, porc sign, detailed Indian head....85.00
Washington-Provident Ins, tin sign, color litho of Geo, fr....175.00
Washington's Cabinet Cigars, tin container....65.00
Waverly Motor Oil, emb tin sign, 1920s auto....85.00
Webster's Tobacco, tin container, man's face, flat, 3x4½″....18.00
Weinhard Factory, beer tray, oval, EX....550.00
Welch-Penn Motor Oil, tin sign, 1940s, 9x24″....20.00
Wellsbach Mantels, tip tray, eagle, M....55.00
Westchester County Brewing, sign, wood, few flakes, 24x34″....275.00
Western Union Telegram & Cable Office, porc sign....126.00
Wheat Heart Brand, metal bread box....75.00
Wheaties, Hike-O-Meter....20.00
Whistle Pop, whistle, brass....18.00
White Cat Union Suits, pocket mirror, oval, w/cat, EX....36.00
White Rock Beer, tin sign, girl & tiger, pre-pro, EX....245.00
White Swan Cigars, cb sign, cigar box/swan label, 21x30″....16.00
Whitney Wagonworks, checkerboard....65.00

Wiedemann's, beer tap hdl 18.00
Wilbur's Stock Tonic, paper litho sign, wagon, fr, EX 135.00
Wildroot, emb tin sign, 1940s, 12x36" 35.00
Willy's Knight Autos, sign, w/whippet 125.00
Wilson's Peanut Butter, tin pail 90.00
Winchester Blended Cigarettes, porc sign, mc, 30x18" 65.00
Wings Cigarettes, cb sign, flying airplane, 1941, 26x21" 40.00
Winston, thermometer 20.00
Wise Potato Chip, clock, electric, figural owl 70.00
Woodward Suckers, emb cb stand-up, baby plays w/toes, 1892 . . . 45.00
Wooltex Cloaks, mirror, suits, oval, 14" 25.00
Wren's Basement Shoes, cb sign, giant pencil 25.00
Wrigley's Chewing Gum, tin sign, 3 packs of gum/mints 120.00
Wrigley's Spearmint Gum, oversize display pack 125.00
Wyandotte Clothing House, pocket mirror, oval 16.00
Y-B Cigars, tin tray, woman, jeweled border, 1908, EX 95.00
Yacht Club Beverages, tin & cb sign, 1918, 10x21" 20.00
Yale Mixture Tobacco, tc, Marbrug Bros, 3x2x1" 20.00
Yankee Boy Tobacco, pocket tin, blonde baseball player 175.00
Yankee Girl Tobacco, emb tin sign, 1930s, 6x19" 75.00
Yellow Cab, thermometer, wood 35.00
Yellowstone Whiskey, tin sign, 3 Pleasures of Life, fr 750.00
Ying Mee Tea Co, tc, paper label, birds & flowers 16.00
Yuengling's Beer, pocket mirror 90.00
Yuengling's Beer, thermometer, 12" 35.00
Yuengling's Beer, tray, horse head, NM 60.00
Yuengling's Beer, tray, pretty blonde w/glass 100.00
Zeno Gum, display cabinet, oak, all orig 385.00
Zett's Bavarian Beer, tray, king/banner/beer glass, 13½" 352.00
20-Muleteam Borax, fan, w/Maud, 1905 . . . . . 10.00
3-S Blood Tonic, gypsy pot, iron, miniature 65.00
7-Up, bottle, Zetz, New Orleans, Blk waiter w/tray, EX 65.00
7-Up, clock, plastic, Get Real Action 85.00
7-Up, clock, wood fr 65.00
7-Up, pencil clip 8.50

Advertising Cards

Advertising trade cards enjoyed a heyday during the last quarter of 19th century when the printing process known as chromolithography became refined and put into popular use. The purpose of the trade card was to acquaint the public with a place of business, a product or an available service. Most trade cards range in size from 2" x 3" to 3" x 5", however some are found in both larger and smaller sizes. Four categories of particular interest to collectors are:

Mechanical--those which achieve movement through the use of a pull tab, fold-out side or rotating disk.

Metamorphic--cards that transform a person or a thing from a 'before' to an 'after' condition, which of course represents a marked improvement immediately upon use of the featured product.

Hold-to-light--cards that reveal their design only when viewed before a strong light.

Die-cuts--cards in figural forms such as the Heinz pickle series. Die-cuts are usually in the shape of the advertised product, or a theme-related object.

For a more thorough study of the subject, we recommend *The Advertising Trade Card*, by Kit Barry; his address can be found in the Directory under Vermont.

When no condition is indicated, the items listed below are assumed to be in mint condition.

Allen & Ginter Cigarette Mfg, sea w/coral, shells, & ships 1.50
Arbuckle Bros Coffee, picture of Vienna, Austria, 1891 . . . . . 2.50
Arm & Hammer Brand, Beautiful Birds, sm series 3.00
AST Co Black Tips, mother hen w/babies in boot 1.50
Ayer's Cathartic Pills, 7 nude cherubs load pills 3.00
Brown's Iron Bitters, detailed litho of Victorian room 6.50
BT Babbitt's Best Soap, factory w/pictures of nations 4.50
Capitol Cylinder Oil, blk/wht, dog w/muzzle 2.50
Carter's Little Liver Pills, pallet w/boy & girl sleeping 5.00
CCC Certain Chill Tonic, girl sitting on leather trunk, EX 3.00
Celluloid Collars & Cuffs, shows map of Europe w/flag 3.50
Clark's Thread Co, couple sitting at table w/oil lamp 3.50
Currier & Ives, Blood Will Tell, 1879, VG 60.00
Currier & Ives, Bound to Shine, 1880, EX 60.00
Currier & Ives, High Toned, 1880, EX 60.00
Currier & Ives, Laying Back, 1878, VG 60.00
Currier & Ives, The Crowd that Scooped the Pools, 1878, VG . . . 60.00
Currier & Ives, The Parson's Colt, 1880, VG 60.00
Currier & Ives, The Young Cadets, EX 60.00
Dalley's Magical Pain Extractor, mother churning butter 3.50
Dilworth's Coffee, little girl w/coffee urn beside her 2.00
Dr Jayne's Expectorant, man & woman at well, pretty colors 3.50
Dr Jayne's Tonic Vermifuge, 2-pg foldover, buff/wht 5.50
Dr Schenck's Sea Weed Tonic, boy & girl in Victorian dress 3.50
Dr Warner's Corsets, black flowered corset 3.50
Dr Winchell's Teething Syrup, man holding screaming baby 5.50
Edwin C Burt & Co Fine Shoes, girl picking flowers 3.00
French Villa Soap, boy & girls walking home from church 2.50
Hall's Vegetable Sicilian Hair Renewer, 1886 . . . . . 3.00
Hartshorn's Shade Rollers, 2-pg foldover, maid & baby 6.00
Hills Bros Millinery Good, World's Fair, New Orleans, 1885 . . . . . 4.00
Hires Improved Root Beer, Ruth & Naomi 3.00
Hood's Tooth Powder, girl in pretty blue dress 3.50
Household Sewing Machine Co, Bo-Peep, 3x4½" 2.50
Hoyt's German Cologne, girl holding calendar, 1889 . . . . . 3.50
International Baking Powder, boy playing flute 2.50
JA Bleeker's Book Store, Xmas scene calendar, 1880 . . . . . 2.00
James Pyle Pearline, girl's face w/red turban 2.50
JD Larkin & Co, boy playing w/top 5.00
John Hancock Mutual Life Insurance Co, boy hunting 2.50
Keller's Sure Cure for Diphtheria & Croup, 1881, EX 3.50
Kickapoo Indian Remedies, Indian lying in clump of grass 7.50
Kinney Bros Cigarettes, 5 die-cuts, different ladies 5.00
Lutten's SP Cough Drops, Mary & her lamb at school, 1882 . . . . . 2.50
Lydia Pinkham's Vegetable Compound, sailboats in river, EX 3.00
ME Phelan Hair Restorer, lady in flowered dress, 4x6½" 1.50
Minard's Liniment, bl fancy script logo on wht 7.50

Anheuser-Busch Brewing Association, 4¼" x 6½", $25.00.

Mrs Dinsmore's Great English Cough & Croup Balsam, EX......5.50
Page's Arnica Oil, mama tying tie of uniformed gentleman.......2.50
Peach Sweet Snuff, die-cut can of peach snuff................4.00
Porter's Cough Balsam, 2 scenes, shows Madam herself, EX......3.50
Quacker Bitters Co, girl in wht dress, lg wht hat...............5.00
Risley's Extract Witch Hazel, sm child playing w/top............2.50
Scott's Emulsion, little boy in sailor suit.......................4.50
Shaumut Soap, girl carrying kittens, 1894......................2.50
Singer Sewing Machine, scene of Boston, 10 cards............25.00
St Jacobs Oil, picture of fox hunt, colorful.....................4.00
Sulphur Bitters, portrait of Mrs Grover Cleveland, EX..........12.50
Tennyson Tobacco, sm booklet w/bridge rules..................4.00
Terrant's Seltzer Aperient, girl sitting in velvet basket...........3.50
Thurber's Baked Beans, mc, in cherry fr, 6x8"...............10.00
Vanity Fair Cigarettes, pictures of packages, 2 for.............5.00
WS Nickerson, dealer in patent medicines, 3 for...............3.00

Advertising Dolls

Whether your interest in ad dolls is fueled by nostalgia or strictly because of their amusing, often clever advertising impact, there are several points that should be considered before making your purchases. Condition is of utmost importance; never pay book price for dolls in poor condition, whether they are cloth or of another material. Restoring fabric dolls is usually unsatisfactory and involves a lot of work--seams must be opened, stuffing removed, the doll washed and dried, and then reassembled. Washing old fabrics may prove to be disasterous--colors may fade or run, and most stains are totally resistant to washing. It's usually best to leave the fabric doll as it is.

Watch for new dolls as they become available. Save related advertising literature, extra coupons, etc., and keep these along with the doll to further enhance your collection. Old dolls with no marks are sometimes challenging to identify. While some products may use the same familiar trademark figures for a number of years--the Jolly Green Giant, Pillsbury's Poppin' Fresh, and the Keebler Elf, for example--others appear on the market for a short time only and may be difficult to trace. Most libraries have reference books with trademarks and logos that might provide a clue in tracking down your doll's identity. Children see advertising figures on Saturday morning cartoons that are often unfamiliar to adults, or other ad doll collectors may have the information you seek.

Advertising dolls are still easy to find and relatively inexpensive, ranging in cost from $1.00 to $100.00, with the average price at about $10.00. They are popular with children as well as adults.

For a more thorough study of the subject, we recommend *Advertising Dolls*, by Joleen Robison and Kay Sellers.

When no condition is indicated, the items listed below are assumed to be in excellent condition.

American Airlines, Stewardess, plastic, uniform, 1967, 12".......2.00
Aunt Jemima Pancake Flour, Aunt Jemima, cloth, 1905, 15"....75.00
Babbitt Cleanser, Babbitt Boy, compo, 1916, 15"............175.00
Bazooka Bubble Gum, Bazooka Joe, stuffed cotton, 1973, 18"...6.00
Blatz Beer, Blatz Beer Man, beer-can body, no arms, 10½".....15.00
Borden Company, Elsie, cow, brn plush, yel hooves, 15".......10.00
Chicken of the Sea, Mermaid, cloth, litho, 1974, 15"...........8.00
Chiquita Brand, Inc; Chiquita Banana, fabric, 1944, 10"........20.00
Close-Up Toothpaste, Dumbo, plastic, movable parts, 1974.......6.00
Dunkin' Donuts, Munchkin, plastic, inflatable, 1976, 24"........3.00
Eskimo Pie Corporation, Pie Boy, cloth/brn parka, 15".........4.00
Fels-Naptha Soap, Anty Drudge, dress w/name, 1933, 11"......85.00
Final Touch, snowman, b/w plush, stuffed, 1975, 11"..........12.00
General Mills, Frankenberry, purple/pink monster, 7½"..........6.00
Green Giant Company, Sprout, cloth, 1973, 10"...............8.00
Hamburger Helper, Helping Hand, glove-like, wht, 1976, 14".....6.00

Campbell Kids, cloth, 11½", $8.00 each.

Hawaiian Punch, Punchy, inflatable, unusual headgear..........4.00
Icee Corporation, Icee Bear, bank, bear drinks Icee, 8".........4.00
Irish Spring, leprechaun, gr broadcloth/pnt eyes, '76, 19".......10.00
Jolly Roger Restaurant, Jolly Roger, cloth, pirate w/patch........8.00
Just Rite Restaurant, Li'l Miss Just Rite, vinyl, 1965, 8".........8.00
Keebler Co, Keebler Elf, gr coat, yel pants, 1974, 6½"..........5.00
Kellogg's, Dig 'Em Frog, litho, gr & yel, 1973, 16".............6.00
Kellogg's, Tony the Tiger, cloth face, plush, 1970, 13".........10.00
Kellogg's, Woody Woodpecker, pre-stuffed cloth, 1966, 13"......8.00
Kentucky Fried Chicken, Colonel Sanders, bank, 1965, 12½"....8.00
Levi Strauss & Co, denim rag doll/yel yarn hair, 1974, 14"......6.00
Little Crow Foods, Gretchen, cut-out fabric, 1966, 13".........20.00
Mason Mints, Peppermint Pattie, bean-bag body, 1973, 10"......8.00
Maxwell House Coffee, bear, brn plush, striped shirt, 1971.......8.00
MD Bathroom Toilet Tissue, Maisy & Daisy, cloth, 18", ea.......8.00
Michelin Tires, Michelin Tire Man, inflatable, wht, 25"..........5.00
Mohawk Carpet Company, Mohawk Tommy, Indian, cloth, 16"...8.00
Mountain Dew, Hillbilly, plaid shirt, wht beard, hat, 18"........20.00
Mr Turtle Candy, Mr Turtle, inflatable, formal attire, 20"........5.00
Nestle Co, Nestle Quik Rabbit, brn plush/'Q' on shirt, 24".......8.00
Old Crow Whiskey, Old Crow/plastic/formal attire, 1950, 4"......8.00
Oster Corporation, Super Pan, cloth w/cape, 1972, 19"........15.00
Pan Am Airlines, wooden cylinder w/ball head, no face, 3½".....2.00
Pepperidge Farm, Goldfish, gold, cotton cloth, 16".............6.00
Pepto Bismol, 24-Hour Bug, bank, vinyl, green creature, 7".....12.00
Pillsbury Co, Poppin' Fresh, knit velour, chef hat, 1972..........8.00
Pillsbury Funny Face, Lefty Lemon, hard plastic, 1976, 3½".....5.00
Pine Sol, Pine Sol Bear, fur fabric, sitting, 1978, 15x15".......15.00
Post Cereals, Linus the Lion, plush, gold, 10"..................6.00
Quaker Oats Co, Jean LaFoote, bank, barefoot pirate, 7½"......6.00
Ralston Purina, Meow Mix, vinyl, name on front, 1976, 4½".....2.00
Red Barn Restaurant, Hamburger Hungry, plush/felt, '70, 22"....8.00
Rexall Drug Co, vinyl baby, pnt eyes, bowed legs, 7½"..........6.00
Royal Gelatin, King Royal, bank, vinyl, huge nose, 9½".........6.00
Sambo's Restaurant, Sambo Tiger, fuzzy beard, 1970, 7"........6.00
Scott Paper Co, Scottie Dog, plush, blk or wht, 1976, 7".........3.00
Seiko Watches, Seiko Robot, inflatable, w/date, 21"............8.00
Shakey's Pizza Restaurant, Shakey Chef, wht fabric, 10½".......6.00
Snoboy Apples, Snuggly Snoboy, plush & felt, wht, 12"........10.00
Star-Kist Tuna, Charlie, talking pillow, litho mouth, 15"........15.00
Sunbeam Bread, Miss Sunbeam, open/closed mouth, apron, 17".25.00

Tastee-Freez International, Bear of a Burger, puppet, 1970......6.00
Texaco Cheerleader, plastic, mk T30, 2 outfits, 1978, 11"......10.00
Tillamook Cheese Co, Tillie the Cow, rubber, brn, 1958, 9".....8.00
Tony's Pizza, Mr Tony chef, vinyl squeeze toy, 1972, 8"........4.00
Vermont Maid Syrup, Vermont Maid, braided hair, 1964, 15"...18.00
Victors Eucalyptus Cough Drops, Koala Bears, 17", pr.........13.00
Western Union, Dolly Gram, velvet w/raffia hair, 1975, 6".......4.00
Westinghouse, kangaroo, tan plush fabric, 1976, 18"..........12.00
7-Up, Undeer, hand puppet, plastic horns, rust, 10"............4.00

African Art

These artifacts of the African nation are a unique form of folk art, of interest not only in relation to the craftsman evident in their making but because of the culture they represent.

When no condition is indicated, the items listed below are assumed to be in excellent condition.

Left to right: Mask, animal and vegetable dyes in orange and blue tones, 15", $135.00; Mask, Cowrie shells attached to snake skin, hand carved, 12", $1,000.00; Mask, pierced mouth, eyes, and upper lip, 9", $1,000.00.

Breast ornament, shell, openwork plaque w/bird, Santa Cruz...800.00
Bust, woman, elephant ivory, wood base, Congolese, 4".......185.00
Comb, 4 teeth, seated male figure surmount, Baule, 20th C...1,500.00
Cult hook, openwork hdl, pnt dots/stripes, New Guinea, 36"...300.00
Fetish, female, notched/chevron cicatrice, Bembe, 6".........800.00
Figure, female, kneeling w/shallow bowl on lap, Yoruba, 4"....500.00
Figure, knees bent/arms to side, scarifiction, Mumuye, 27".....750.00
Figure, sanggriyau, exagerated features, New Guinea, 58"......550.00
Figurine, lady kneels w/hands at side, elephant ivory, 5".......225.00
Figurine, man/loincloth, elephant ivory, Congolese, 7½".......350.00
Heddle pulley, sq shoulders, sm head, twisted neck, Baule.....800.00
Heddle pulley, stylized head atop, Guro, 7"..................500.00
Heddle pulley, tapered/incised, lg definied head, Guro, 7"....1,500.00
Mask, animal teeth, sensitive features, Dan, 8½"...........8,000.00
Mask, filed teeth/scarification, wood beads, Chokwe, 8"........600.00
Necklace, hoop of grad brn stone disks joined w/brass tube....300.00
Necklace, 25-strand glass beads, w/tube/rnd beads, Naga.......900.00
Staff, bronze, lattice terminals/hawk surmount, Benin, 10".....375.00
Staff, Voodoo, human head finial, lizard skin bound, Yoruba...800.00
Steering oar, carved head/incised blade, New Guinea, 130".....600.00

Agata

Agata glass is a very rare and expensive type of art glass that was made at the New England Glass Co. in 1887. John Locke developed the method for achieving the characteristic mottled effect which was commonly used on their lovely peachblow glass, although occasionally it was applied to opaque green as well. The procedure involved spraying an alcohol mixture on the surface of the glass while it was still very hot. The results produced a marbelized appearance not unlike the agate stone. Caution--be sure to use only gentle cleaning methods!

When no condition is indicated, the items listed below are assumed to be in mint condition.

Bowl, flared/ruffled, allover gold/raspberry to pink, 3" H.....2,000.00
Mustard, raspberry color, metal top.......................1,150.00
Toothpick, cylindrical, EX color............................950.00
Tumbler, New England, 3¾"...............................600.00

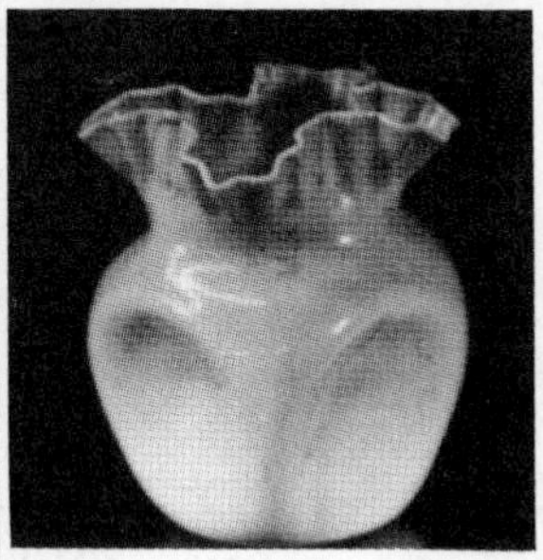

Vase, four-lobed fluted rim, squared shape, very dark oil spots, 4½", $550.00.

Akro Agate

The Akro Agate Company founded in 1914 in Clarksbury, West Va., was primarily a marble factory. Not until 1932 did they start to manufacture their popular lines of children's dishes, novelty items, etc. Although not always marked, much of their ware was made in a distinctive marbled or opaque glass that is easily recognized. Some of the children's pieces were also made of clear colors. In the list that follows, colors not termed opaque or marble are clear. Items that are marked bear the circle seal with AKRO and a flying crow carrying marbles in his talons. The company closed in 1951.

When no condition is indicated, the items listed below are assumed to be in mint condition.

Chiquita

Creamer, baked-on colors, 1½"..............................5.50
Creamer, gr opaque, 1½"...................................4.25
Creamer, transparent cobalt, 1½"...........................9.00
Cup, baked-on colors, 1½"..................................4.50
Cup, gr opaque, 1½".......................................4.00
Cup, transparent cobalt, 1½"...............................5.00
Plate, baked-on colors, 3¾"................................1.75
Plate, gr opaque, 3¾".....................................2.25
Plate, transparent cobalt, 3¾".............................5.50
Saucer, gr opaque, 3⅛"....................................2.00
Saucer, transparent cobalt, 3⅛"............................3.00
Set, 16-pc, baked-on colors................................58.00
Set, 16-pc, gr opaque.....................................55.00
Set, 16-pc, transparent cobalt............................120.00
Set, 22-pc, gr opaque.....................................72.50
Sugar, baked-on colors, no lid, 1½"........................4.50
Sugar, gr opaque, no lid, 1½"..............................4.00
Sugar, transparent cobalt, no lid, 1½"......................9.00
Teapot, baked-on colors, w/lid, 3"........................13.00
Teapot, gr opaque, w/lid, 3"...............................9.00
Teapot, transparent cobalt, w/lid, 3"......................20.00

Concentric Rib

Creamer, gr or wht, 1¼″	4.50
Creamer, opaque colors other than gr or wht, 1¼″	5.50
Cup, gr or wht, 1¼″	3.00
Cup, opaque colors other than gr or wht, 1¼″	3.50
Plate, gr or wht, 3¼″	2.00
Plate, opaque colors other than gr or wht, 3¼″	3.00
Saucer, gr or wht, 2¾″	2.00
Saucer, opaque colors other than gr or wht, 2¾″	2.50
Set, 7-pc, gr or wht, MIB	27.50
Sugar, gr or wht, 1¼″	4.50
Teapot, opaque colors other than gr or wht, w/lid, 3⅜″	8.50

Concentric Ring

Cereal, lg, solid opaque colors, 3⅜″	14.00
Cereal, lg, transparent cobalt, 3⅜″	25.00
Creamer, lg, marbleized bl, 1⅜″	35.00
Creamer, lg, transparent cobalt, 1⅜″	25.00
Creamer, sm, marbleized bl, 1¼″	26.00
Creamer, sm, transparent cobalt, 1¼″	20.00
Cup, lg, marbleized bl, 1⅜″	30.00
Cup, lg, solid opaque colors, 1⅜″	12.00
Cup, sm, marbleized bl, 1¼″	29.00
Cup, sm, transparent cobalt, 1¼″	26.00
Plate, lg, solid opaque colors, 4¼″	7.00
Plate, lg, transparent cobalt, 4¼″	12.00
Plate, sm, marbleized bl, 3¼″	13.00
Plate, sm, solid opaque colors, 3¼″	6.00
Plate, sm, transparent cobalt, 3¼″	12.00
Saucer, lg, marbleized bl, 3⅛″	9.00
Saucer, lg, transparent cobalt, 3⅛″	7.50
Saucer, sm, marbleized bl, 2¾″	10.00
Saucer, sm, solid opaque colors, 2¾″	3.50
Saucer, sm, transparent cobalt, 2¾″	9.50
Set, lg, 21-pc, transparent cobalt	375.00
Set, sm, 16-pc, marbleized bl	320.00
Set, sm, 16-pc, solid opaque colors	115.00
Sugar, lg, marbleized bl, w/lid, 1⅞″	40.00
Sugar, sm, transparent cobalt, 1¼″	20.00
Teapot, lg, solid opaque colors, 3¾″	35.00
Teapot, sm, transparent cobalt, w/lid, 3⅜″	30.00

Interior Panel

Cereal, lg, transparent topaz, 3⅜″	10.00
Creamer, lg, marbleized bl/wht, 1⅜″	22.00
Creamer, sm, azure bl or yel, 1¼″	27.00
Creamer, sm, marbleized red/wht, 1¼″	25.00
Creamer, sm, transparent gr or topaz, 1¼″	10.00
Cup, lg, marbleized red/wht, 1⅜″	21.00
Cup, sm, marbleized bl/wht, 1¼″	20.00
Cup, sm, pink or gr luster, 1¼″	8.00
Cup, sm, transparent gr or topaz, 1¼″	6.50
Plate, lg, marbleized gr/wht, 4¼″	9.00
Plate, sm, azure bl or yel, 3¾″	6.00
Plate, sm, pink or gr luster, 3¾″	4.00
Saucer, lg, marbleized bl/wht, 3⅛″	7.00
Saucer, sm, azure bl or yel, 2⅜″	7.00
Saucer, sm, marbleized red/wht, 2⅜″	7.00
Set, lg, 21-pc, marbleized bl/wht	325.00
Set, lg, 21-pc, marbleized red/wht	350.00
Set, sm, 16-pc, marbleized gr/wht	130.00
Set, sm, 8-pc, transparent gr/topaz	40.00
Sugar, lg, marbleized gr/wht, w/lid, 1⅞″	22.00
Sugar, sm, azure bl or yel, 1¼″	27.00
Sugar, sm, marbleized bl/wht, 1¼″	22.00
Sugar, sm, transparent gr or topaz, 1¼″	10.00
Teapot, lg, marbleized bl/wht, w/lid, 3¾″	37.00
Teapot, lg, marbleized red/wht, w/lid, 3¾″	42.00
Teapot, sm, azure bl or yel, w/lid, 3⅜″	32.00
Teapot, sm, marbleized red/wht, w/lid, 3⅜″	40.00

J.P. (Made for J. Pressman Company)

Cup, transparent cobalt w/ribs, 1½″	4.00
Cup, transparent gr or cobalt, 1½″	13.00
Cup, transparent red or brn, 1½″	18.00
Plate, baked-on colors, 4¼″	2.00
Plate, transparent red or brn, 4¼″	12.50
Saucer, baked-on colors, 3¼″	1.50
Saucer, transparent cobalt w/ribs, 3¼″	2.50
Saucer, transparent red or brn, 3¼″	7.50
Set, 17-pc, transparent red or brn	258.00
Set, 21-pc, baked-on colors	89.00
Sugar, transparent gr or cobalt, w/lid, 1½″	25.00
Sugar, transparent red or brn, w/lid, 1½″	32.50

Miss America

Creamer, wht	27.00
Cup, wht	27.00
Plate, wht	15.00
Saucer, wht	10.00
Set, wht	325.00
Sugar, wht, w/lid	37.00
Teapot, wht, w/lid	55.00

Octagonal

Cereal, lg, pink, yel, or other opaques, 3⅜″	6.00
Creamer, lg, gr, wht, or dk bl, closed hdl, 1½″	3.50
Creamer, lg, pink, yel, or other opaques, closed hdl	5.00
Creamer, sm, dk gr, bl, or wht, 1¼″	12.00
Cup, lg, beige, pumpkin, or lt bl, closed hdl, 1½″	10.00
Pitcher, sm, dk gr, bl, or wht, 1¼″	12.00
Plate, lg, gr, wht, or dk bl, 4¼″	2.00
Plate, lg, pink, yel, or other opaque colors, 4¼″	3.00
Plate, sm, dk gr, bl, or wht, 3⅜″	4.00
Saucer, sm, dk gr, bl, or wht, 2¾″	3.00
Set, lg, 21-pc, gr, wht, or dk bl	300.00
Sugar, lg, pink, yel, or other opaque colors, w/lid	7.00
Sugar, sm, dk gr, bl, or wht, 1¼″	12.00
Teapot, lg, gr, wht, or dk bl, closed hdl, w/lid, 3⅝″	8.00
Teapot, lg, pink, yel, or other opaque colors, w/lid	10.00

Raised Daisy

Creamer, yel, 1¾″	27.00
Cup, bl, 1¾″	27.00
Plate, bl, 3″	11.00
Saucer, beige, 2½″	8.00
Sugar, yel, 1¾″	27.00
Teapot, gr, 2⅜″	22.00

Raised Daisy, Play-Time Tea Set, in box, 19-pc, $325.00; 13-pc, $195.00.

Teapot, yel, 2⅜″ ... 30.00
Tumbler, beige, 2″ ... 18.00
Tumbler, yel, 2″ ... 18.00

Stacked Disc

Creamer, opaque gr or wht, 1¼″ ... 3.00
Cup, opaque gr or wht, 1¼″ ... 2.00
Pitcher, gr, 2⅞″ ... 6.00
Pitcher, opaque colors other than gr or wht, 2⅞″ ... 8.50
Plate, bl, 3¼″ ... 3.00
Plate, opaque colors other than gr or wht, 3¼″ ... 3.00
Saucer, opaque gr or wht, 2¾″ ... 1.75
Set, 21-pc, opaque colors other than gr or wht ... 66.00
Set, 21-pc, opaque gr or wht ... 39.00
Sugar, opaque colors other than gr or wht, 1¼″ ... 6.00
Teapot, opaque gr or wht, 3⅜″ ... 9.00
Tumbler, opaque gr or wht, 2″ ... 4.00

Stacked Disc & Interior Panel

Cereal, lg, marbleized bl, 3⅜″ ... 25.00
Cereal, lg, transparent cobalt, 3⅜″ ... 20.00
Creamer, lg, opaque solid colors, 1⅜″ ... 12.00
Creamer, lg, transparent gr, 1⅜″ ... 15.00
Cup, sm, transparent cobalt, 1¼″ ... 16.00
Pitcher, sm, transparent gr, 2⅞″ ... 12.00
Plate, lg, marbleized bl, 4¾″ ... 10.00
Plate, lg, transparent gr, 4¾″ ... 10.00
Plate, sm, marbleized bl, 3¼″ ... 12.00
Saucer, lg, transparent gr, 3⅛″ ... 7.00
Set, sm, 8-pc, marbleized bl ... 150.00
Set, sm, 8-pc, transparent gr ... 140.00
Sugar, lg, transparent gr, w/lid, 1⅞″ ... 25.00
Sugar, sm, marbleized bl, 1¼″ ... 27.00
Teapot, lg, transparent gr, w/lid, 3¾″ ... 35.00
Tumbler, sm, transparent cobalt, 2″ ... 10.00

Stippled Band

Creamer, lg, transparent gr, 1½″ ... 8.00
Creamer, sm, transparent gr, 1¼″ ... 8.00
Cup, lg, transparent amber, 1½″ ... 10.00
Plate, lg, transparent gr, 4¼″ ... 4.50
Plate, sm, transparent gr, 3¼″ ... 3.00
Saucer, lg, transparent amber, 3¼″ ... 5.00
Saucer, sm, transparent amber, 2¾″ ... 2.00
Set, lg, 17-pc, transparent azure ... 250.00
Set, sm, 8-pc, transparent amber ... 40.00
Sugar, lg, transparent azure, 1⅞″, w/lid ... 30.00
Teapot, lg, transparent amber, 3¾″, w/lid ... 22.00
Tumbler, sm, transparent gr, 1¾″ ... 6.50

Alexandrite

Alexandrite is a type of art glass introduced around the turn of the century by Thomas Webb and Sons, of England. It is recognized by its characteristic shading--pale yellow to rose and blue. It was also produced by other companies.

When no condition is indicated, the items listed below are assumed to be in mint condition.

Bowl, berry; w/underplate, crimped, Webb, bowl: 5″ dia ... 1,000.00
Bowl, honeycomb, ruffled, 2x4½″ ... 750.00
Bowl vase, flared/ruffled, Webb & Sons, 3½x3¼″ ... 585.00
Toothpick holder, Webb, 2½″ ... 945.00
Tumbler, juice; honeycomb, Webb, 3⅝x2⅜″ ... 950.00
Wine, Baby Thumbprint, amber stem & foot, Webb, 4½″ ... 800.00

Alhambra China

Bowl, vegetable; 9″ ... 40.00
Candy dish, 4 shell ft, rectangular, 8½x6″ ... 45.00
Creamer & sugar bowl, w/lid, no mk ... 45.00
Mayonnaise set, Rococo boat-shaped underplate ... 40.00
Pitcher, mc decor, gold trim, sgn, 8½x4¾″ ... 135.00
Pitcher, tankard; w/3 mugs ... 350.00
Plate, pierced hdls, 10½″ ... 50.00
Plate, 6″ ... 20.00
Plate, 7½″ ... 25.00
Plate, 8½″ ... 30.00
Sauce boat, ftd ... 30.00

Almanacs

The earliest evidence indicates that almanacs were used as long ago as Ancient Egypt. Throughout the Dark Ages they were circulated in great volume and were referred to by more people than any other book except the Bible. *The Old Farmer's Almanac* first appeared in 1793 and has been issued yearly since that time. Usually more of a phamphlet than a book (only a few have had hard covers) the almanac provided planting and harvesting information to farmers, weather forecasts for seamen, medical advice, household hints, mathematical tutoring, postal rates, railroad schedules, weights and measures, 'receipts' and jokes.

Before 1800, the information was unscientific and based entirely on astrology and folklore. The first almanac in America was printed in 1639 by William Pierce Mariner; it contained data of this nature. One of the best-known editions, Ben Franklin's *Poor Richard's Almanac* was introduced in 1732 and continued to be printed for twenty-five years.

By the 19th century, merchants saw the advertising potential in a publication so widely distributed, and the advertising almanac evolved. These were distributed free of charge by drugstores and mercantiles, and were usually somewhat lacking in information, containing simply a calendar, a few jokes, and a variety of ads for quick remedies and quack cures.

Today its concept and informative, often amusing text make the almanac a popular collectible that may usually be had at a reasonable price. Because they were printed in such large numbers and often saved from year to year, their prices are still low--most fall within a range of $4 to $15. Those printed before 1860 are especially collectible.

Quite rare and highly prized are the Kate Greenaway 'Almanacks,' printed in London from 1883 to 1897. These are illustrated with her drawings of children, one for each calendar month.

When no condition is indicated, the items listed below are assumed to be in excellent condition.

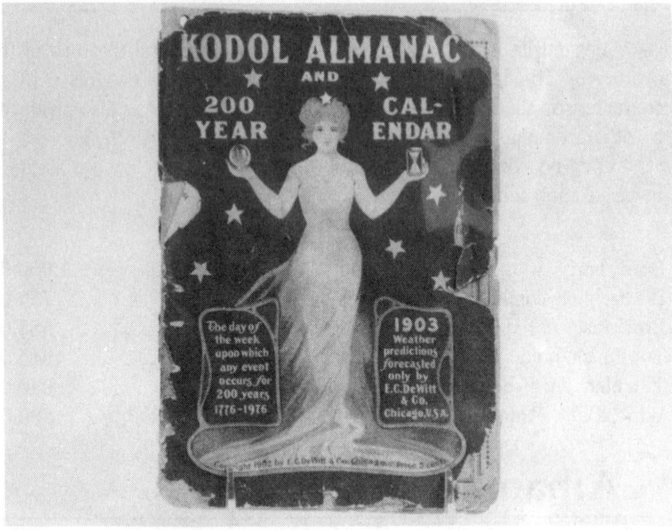

Kodol Almanac, 1903, 200-yr. calendar, price 5¢, 8¼″ x 6″, $6.50.

AT&T, 1935 . . . . . 10.00
Barker's, puzzle pictures, 1902 . . . . . 9.00
Cruikshank's Comic, 1844-1853 . . . . . 40.00
Dr Jayne's Medical, 1912, EX ads, 32 pg 5.00
Dr Pierce, Happiness in the Home, 1928, 32 pg 3.00
Foley's Family, 1921, NM 8.00
German, 1848 . . . . . 12.00
Hazeltines, 1886, miniature 5.00
Hazeltines, 1896, miniature 5.00
Hostetter's, 1882 . . . . . 5.00
Hostetter's, 1900 . . . . . 5.00
International Harvester, 1914 . . . . . 12.00
Kate Greenaway, 1883 . . . . . 80.00
Kate Greenaway, 1885 . . . . . 65.00
Kate Greenaway, 1887, Geo Routledge 65.00
Kate Greenaway, 1888 . . . . . 85.00
Kate Greenaway, 1892 . . . . . 60.00
London, 1845, folding front pocket, tan lining, gilt edges 110.00
Marshall's Cigarettes, 1914 . . . . . 8.00
Old Farmer's, 1856 . . . . . 10.00
Old Farmer's, 1860 . . . . . 9.00
Old Farmer's, 1861 . . . . . 9.00
Rawleigh, 1927, 64 pg 4.00
Seven Wonders of the World, 1886 . . . . . 8.00
Shaker, 1882 . . . . . 22.00
Shaker, 1893 . . . . . 15.00
Simmon's Liver Regulator, 1903 . . . . . 26.00
Telephone Almanac, 1936 . . . . . 8.00
Union, The; 1939, 48 pg 4.00
Vinegar Bitters 15.00
World, The; 1923 . . . . . 4.00

Aluminum

Aluminum, though being the most abundant metal in the earth's crust, always occurs in combination with other elements. Before a practical method for its refinement was developed in the late 19th century, articles made of aluminum were very expensive. After the process for commercial smelting was perfected in 1916, it became profitable to adapt the ductile, non-tarnishing material to many uses.

By the late thirties, novelties, trays, pitchers, and many other tableware items were being produced. They were often hand crafted with elaborate decoration. Russell Wright designed a line of lovely pieces such as lamps, vases, and desk accessories, that are becoming very collectible. Many that crafted the ware marked it with their company logo, and these signed pieces are attracting the most interest. In general, 'spun' aluminum is from the '30s or very early '40s, and 'hammered' aluminum is from the '50s.

When no condition is indicated, the items listed below are assumed to be in mint condition.

Bowl, fruit; floral/fruit in relief, hdls, 11″ 12.00
Cake safe, sgn Russel Wright 40.00
Crumber & brush, hammered, Rodney Kent, #444 . . . . . 20.00
Garden ornament, rabbit, cast, 12″ 55.00
Percolator, fluted/ornate, blk wood hdl, 1920s, 11″ 18.00
Pitcher, water; hammered, no decor, lg 8.00
Relish, hexagonal, fruit decor, scalloped, Cromwell 7.50
Teapot, gooseneck spout, 2½-cup 11.50
Tray, tulips relief, fancy hdls, hammered, w/lid, Kent #440 . . . . . 20.00
Wastebasket, flowers, rivets, sgn Everlast, 11x11″ 20.00

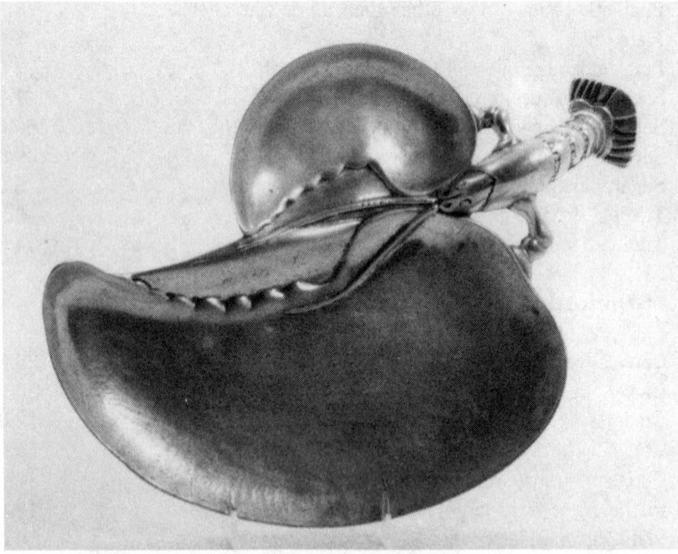

Tray, lobster figural, sgn in script: Bruce Cox, 15½″ x 11″, $65.00.

Amberina

Amberina, one of the earliest types of art glass, was developed in 1883 by Joseph Locke, of the New England Glass Company. The trademark was registered by W.L. Libbey who often signed his name in script within the pontil.

Amberina was made by adding gold powder to the batch which produced glass in the basic amber hue. Part of the item, usually the top, was simply reheated to develop the characteristic deep red or fuchsia shading. Early amberina was mold-blown, but cut and pressed amberina was also produced. The rarest type is plated amberina, made by New England for a short time after 1886.

Other companies, among them Hobbs and Brockunier, Mt. Washington Glass Company, and Sowerby's Ellison Glassworks of England, made their own versions, being careful to change the name of their product to avoid infringing on Libbey's patent.

When no condition is indicated, the items listed below are assumed to be in mint condition.

Bowl, Optic Dia Quilt, EX color, 1½x4½" 145.00
Bowl, waisted, scallop rim, bl tinged/fuchsia, 2¾x5⅜" 175.00
Celery vase, Dia Quilt, Mt Washington, 6½" 250.00
Celery vase, Dia Quilt, sq mouth, New England, 6¼" 225.00
Champagne glass, hollow stem, pontil unground, 6" 185.00
Condiment set, Baby Invt T'print, sgn Pairpoint fr, 3-pc 400.00
Creamer, Dia Quilt, reverse color, sq top, 5" 226.00
Creamer & sugar, plated, squat/ribbed, EX color, 2½", pr 5,500.00
Mug, Inverted Thumbprint, 3" 58.00
Mug, paneled, 2¼" 48.00
Mug, pnt florals, 3¾x2¾" 85.00
Pitcher, florals/jewels, reverse color, 8x5" 245.00
Pitcher, tankard; honeycomb, amber hdl, Webb, 5x3½" 325.00
Pitcher, Thumbprint, reeded hdl, sgn Libbey, w/4 tumblers 595.00
Pitcher, triangle neck, bulbous, reed hdl, 4½" 105.00
Punch cup, Invt T'print, reeded hdl, 2⅝x2½" 110.00
Shakers, Dia Quilt, pr 175.00
Syrup pitcher, honeycomb pattern, w/lid, 8" 395.00
Syrup pitcher, Invt T'print, SP top, att NE, rare, 5⅝" 650.00
Toothpick holder, Baby T'print, ribbon/pleated top 250.00
Tumbler, Dia Quilt, 4½" 58.00
Tumbler, Inverted Thumbprint, 4" 58.00
Tumbler, lemonade; Optic, low hdl, 4" 175.00
Tumbler, lemonade; Optic, low hdl, 5" 225.00
Tumbler, plated, ribbed effect, 3¾" 2,000.00
Tumbler, ribbed, slender waist, NE, 4⅜" 125.00
Tumbler, swirl, ftd, 4" 65.00
Vase, ruffled, gold decor, 12" 270.00
Vase, trumpet form, ruffled, 15" 65.00
Vase, Venetian Diamond, urn shape 175.00

Left to right: Creamer, Inverted Thumbprint, attributed to Boston and Sandwich, rare form, 5½", $275.00; Sugar bowl, Inverted Thumbprint, attributed to Boston and Sandwich, near mint, 4¾", $275.00; Pitcher, Inverted Thumbprint, attributed to Mt. Washington, rare form, 5¾", $350.00.

American Encaustic Tiling Co.

A.E. Tile was organized in 1879 in Zanesville, Ohio. Until its closing in 1935, they produced beautiful ornamental and architectural tile equal to the best European imports. They also made vases, figurines and novelty items with exceptionally fine modeling and glazes.

When no condition is indicated, the items listed below are assumed to be in mint condition.

Bookends, cupid & rabbit, pr 75.00
Card holder, Deco lady figural, caramel over aqua, 7" 60.00
Tile, child's portrait, dtd Dec 25th, 1878, mk Limited 145.00
Tile, Elizabethan man/lady, 2 sets, 3 6x6" tiles in ea, fr 450.00
Tile, floral relief, gr gloss, 6x6" 30.00
Tile, geometric, glossy olive gr, 6x6" 14.00
Tile, knight & sheep, fairy-tale style, 5½" 45.00
Tile, portrait, turq, Garrett Hobart 60.00
Tile, Simple Simon, 6x6" 80.00
Tile, tavern scene, artist Hardwick 32.00
Vase, hdld, dk brn glaze over lt brn, 9" 125.00

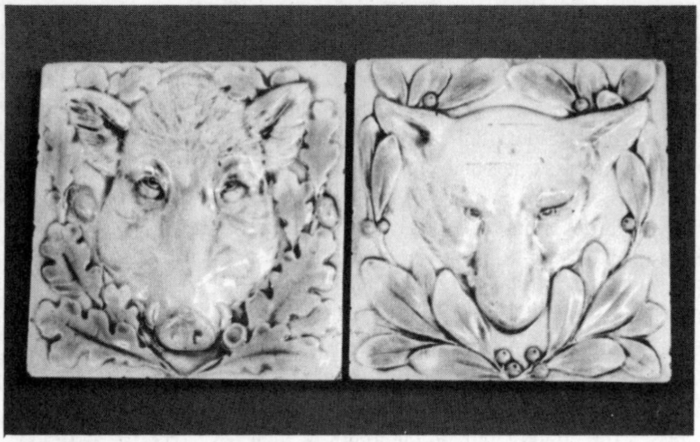

Tile, fox and wild boar, 6", $175.00 for the pair.

American Indian Art

That time when the American Indian was free to practice the crafts and culture that was his heritage has always held a fascination for many. They were a people that appreciated beauty of design and colorful decoration in their furnishings and clothing; and because instruction in their crafts was a routine part of their rearing, they were well accomplished. Several tribes developed areas in which they excelled. The Navajo were weavers and silversmiths, the Zuni lapidaries. Examples of their craftsmanship are very valuable. Today, even the work of contemporary Indian artists--weavers, silversmiths, carvers and others--is highly collectible.

For a more thorough study we recommend *North American Indian Artifacts* by Lar Hothem; you will find his address in the Directory under Ohio. When no condition is indicated, the items listed below are assumed to be in excellent condition. State origin is indicated by two-letter state abbreviations directly preceeding the size.

Key:
bw—beadwork dia—diamond

Apparel and Accessories

Before the white traders brought the Indian women cloth from which to sew their garments and beads to use for decorating them, clothing was made from skins sewn together with sinew, usually made of buffalo tendon. Porcupine quills were dyed bright colors and woven into bags and armbands and used to decorate clothing and mocassins. Examples of early quillwork are scarce today and highly collectible.

Early in the 19th century, beads were being transported via pony pack trains. These 'pony' beads were irregular shapes of opaque glass imported from Venice. Nearly always blue or white, they were twice as large as the later 'seed' bead. By 1870, translucent beads in many sizes and colors had been made available, and Indian beadwork had become become commercialized. Each tribe developed their own distinctive methods and preferred decorations, making it possible for collectors today to determine the origin of many items. Soon after the turn of the century the practice of beadwork began to diminish.

Apparel and Accessories

Arm bands, Blackfoot, 10½x1″ quilled dangles....85.00
Arm bands, Ponca, full bw on trade cloth, 1890, pr....95.00
Arm bands, Sioux, Am flags, mc bw on yel, 1880s, 6x12″, pr..170.00
Belt, Blackfoot, rawhide/leather ends, full bw panel, 1920....100.00
Belt, Nez Perce, buffalo hide w/brass & silver tacks....350.00
Belt, Sioux, full bw, 3x28″....195.00
Belt & drop, woman's; Cheyenne, brass tack geometric, 1900....45.00
Bib, Tlingit, cloth, bw shield w/hawk, 8 bird's beaks, 12″....1,430.00
Bonnet, baby; Sioux, full bw....300.00
Boots, woman's; Cheyenne, hide w/red pigment & bw, 21″....185.00
Boots, Woodlands, bw trim, 7″ bw leg flaps, hard soles, VG....80.00
Breastplate, N Plains, bone hair pipes/brass beads, 1860....500.00
Breastplate, Sioux, celluloid sqs/beads/shell suspensions....25.00
Breastplate, Sioux, leather thongs/bone tubes/lg beads....900.00
Ceremonial outfit, Ojibwa, velvet w/full bw/tassels, 4-pc....400.00
Coat, Cherokee, hide w/bw/ribbon trim, European cut, 37″...3,000.00
Cuffs, Yakima, beaded, pr....50.00
Dance set, woman's; Chippewa, full bw breastplate/crown....65.00
Dress, Crow, trade cloth w/ribbonwork & shell decor, 1910....150.00
Dress, Nez Perce, corduroy/full bw shoulders, shells, 1920....235.00
Dress, Paiute, bw shoulders/sleeves/shield on front/fringe....330.00
Dress, Plateau, bw/fringed hide, openwork sleeves, 45″....900.00
Dress yoke, Chippewa, gr brocade w/fringe/sequins, 1910....24.00
Dress yoke, Chippewa, velvet w/fringe/sequins....22.00
Garters, Winnebago, loom beaded geometrics, ca 1920....210.00
Gauntlets, Nez Perce, buckskin/cloth lined, bw/fringe, 14″....70.00
Gauntlets, Plains, hide w/bw/fringe, cuffs, silk trim, 15″....400.00
Gloves, N Plains-Cree, smoked moose hide/fur border, 1920....85.00
Hair drop, Sioux, quilled, feathers/cones, 1890s, 9″, VG....165.00
Hair ornament, Arapaho, full bw on hide, hair suspensions....60.00
Hat, NW Coast, dbl weave, wear/some rim damage, 5¾x13″....325.00
Hat, Penobscot, made from fur, 1900....15.00
Headband, Cree, loom beaded, ca 1885....35.00
Headband, Plains, woven, full bw w/15 Xs, VG....25.00
Headdress, Crow, Love Medicine, elk hide/horn/bone, 1900....190.00
Leggings, Chippewa, buffalo horn/fur/ribbons/sequins, 1920....45.00
Leggings, Osage, trade cloth w/mc ribbonwork ea side, 1890...250.00
Leggings, Osage, wool w/4-color ribbonwork, 1880s....135.00
Leggings, Sioux, full bw trade cloth/leather tassels, 24″....300.00
Leggings, women's; Sioux, full bw geometrics on wht, 1920....200.00
Moccasins, Algonkian, full bw oval top panel, soft soles....85.00
Moccasins, Arapaho, near full bw, ochre stain, 1890s....165.00
Moccasins, child's; Cheyenne, bw top/sides of cuff, 1895....50.00
Moccasins, child's; Plains, full bw/hard soles, 1880s, NM....250.00
Moccasins, Chippewa, buckskin w/bw & cloth toes, ca 1890....40.00
Moccasins, full bw, beaded sole, mc geometrics, 10″, pr....595.00
Moccasins, Kiowa, pointed toe, bw trim, red pigment....300.00
Moccasins, Plains, bw geometric panels/hard soles, VG....100.00
Moccasins, Plains, hide w/mc quillwork uppers, 9¼″....1,320.00
Moccasins, Plains Sioux, full bw, cuff/tongue/hard sole....200.00
Moccasins, S Arapaho, bw/yel pnt hide, ornate, 1870s....165.00

Squaw's hat, black velvet with heavy beadwork, 4″ x 11½″ , $350.00.

Moccasins, Santee Sioux, mc floral bw, ca 1900....150.00
Moccasins, Sioux, full bw top, minor wear, ca 1900....185.00
Moccasins, Sioux, full bw top & soles, tin cones/horsehair....770.00
Moccasins, Sioux, mc full bw top, EX workmanship, 1800, EX..325.00
Shirt, Plains, fringed hide, cloth lapel, side slits, 28″....165.00
Vest, baby's; Sioux, hide w/fringe/full bw horses, ribbons....770.00
Vest, boy's; Sioux, pictorial on hide/sequins/pearls, '30s....25.00
Vest, Sioux, hide/full bw: Am flags/geometrics, 20″ L....660.00

Arrowheads and Points

Relics of this type usually display characteristics of a general area, tribe, or a particular location. With study, those made by the Plains Indians are easily discerned from those of the West Coast. Because modern man has imitated the art of the Indian by reproducing these artifacts through modern means, use caution before investing your money in 'too good to be authentic' specimens.

Adena, gray & tan, TN, 4¼″....15.00
Archaic, glossy blk flint, corner-notched, serrated, 1½″....10.00
Archaic, gray/brn flint, side-notched, G chipping, 1¾″....8.00
Beveled-edge, shouldered, IA, 2½x1½″....16.00
Birdpoint, late Woodland, EX basal notches, ⅞″....2.50
Clovis type, chert, both sides fluted, MN, 3″....55.00
Clovis type, translucent agate/flint, EX flutes, NM, 2⅞″....195.00
Copper, rattail, tanged, notched at sides of point, 3″....40.00
Dalton, gray, IL, 2⅝″....25.00
Dalton, off wht, serrated, AR, 2¾″....35.00
Dalton, tan, MO, 1⅝″....12.00
Deer antler, hollow base, KY, 2¼″....4.00
Dovetail, St Charles, gray/tan, OH, 5⅜″....350.00
Evans, pink, dbl notches, AR, 3x1¼″....9.00
Frio, pinkish wht stone, TX, 2¼x3/4″....4.00
Gempoint, blk obsidian, corner notch/bifurcated base, 2⅞″....35.00
Godar type, pink flint, side-notched, AR, 2¾x1½″....14.00
Hardin barbed, wht flint, IL, 2¼″....9.00
Hohokam, wht flint, narrow w/3 indents on base side, 2⅞″....60.00
Iron-tipped, Sioux....15.00
Kramer type, wht flint, side-notched, thin, IL, 2¾x1″....8.00
Nebo Hill, gray w/patina, MO, 3¼″....35.00
Nebo Hill, gray w/tan flecks, IL, 4″....25.00
Oregon, petrified wood, red/yel stripe, stemmed/barbed, 1″....13.00
Pedernales, gray, TX, 2¼″....15.00
Pedernales, gray, TX, 3″....30.00
Sandia type, single-shouldered, heavy duty, NM, 2″....75.00
Steuben, gray flint, classic, 2¾x3/8″....7.00

Bags and Cases

The Indians used bags for many purposes and most display excellent form and workmanship. Of the types listed below, many collectors consider the pipe bag to be the most desirable form. Pipe bags were long, narrow leather and bead or quillwork creations made to hold tobacco in a compartment at the bottom and the pipe, with the bowl removed from the stem, in the top. Long buckskin fringe was used as trim, and complemented the quilled and beaded design to make the bags a masterpiece of Indian Art.

Apache, hide/mc geometric bw, fringe, drawstring, 11x6″ 70.00
Bannock, pipe, scallop top/mc floral bw panel/fringe, 23″ 185.00
Cheyenne, awl case, full bw, tin cones/horsehair, 8″ 160.00
Cheyenne, medicine case, bw/quills/tin cones on hide, 1890 . . . . 180.00
Cheyenne/Sioux, belt pouch, mc bw design on buffalo, 1800 . . . . 85.00
Chippewa, shoulder bag, floral bw, beaded tassels, 12x5″ 795.00
Cree, pipe, scallop top, geometric bw panels, fringe, 28″ 200.00
Crow, belt type pouch, full bw Arbitrary Floral, 7x5½″ 85.00
Crow, parfleche case, geometric pnt buffalo hide, 15x27″ 235.00
Drawstring, lacy bw edging/bw geometrics, 1900, 6x8″, VG 100.00
Flathead, coin purse, full bw, ornate, 3x2½″ 30.00
Iroquois, purse, red w/bw florals, bk: Am flag, 1900, 3x4″ 35.00

Pipe bag, Sioux, quilled and fringed hide with multicolor geometrics, tin cones and feather suspensions, 26½″, $1,200.00.

N Plains, Possible bag, hide w/bw/tin cones/horsehair, 12″ 600.00
Nez Perce, cornhusk, commercial dyed designs, 8½x9½″ 60.00
Nez Perce, cornhusk, dbl sided/mc decor, 14½x21″ 300.00
Nez Perce, cornhusk w/mc stars/etc ea side, 1880s, 19x13″ 170.00
Nez Perce, cornhusk/red swastika/mc dia, beads/fringe, 14″ 200.00
Plains, awl case, bw trim 50.00
Plains, flint pouch, buckskin w/bw, 4″ 40.00
Plains, medicine, thin leather w/bird/geometric bw, 1900 . . . . 325.00
Plains, Possible bag, full mc bw, tin cones/horsehair, 18″ 1,100.00
Plains, ration ticket pouch, bw, drawstring, pre-1900 . . . . 125.00
Plains, strike-a-lite, smoke decor, fringed, bw Xs 100.00
Plains, strike-a-lite, soft leather/bw trim, w/striker 85.00
Plains, strike-a-lite, X bw on front/bw bands on flap, 4″ 45.00
Plains, tobacco, buckskin, raindrop design/bw edge trim 75.00
Plains, tobacco, deerskin, full bw, 1890, 4x5″+9″ fringe 160.00
Plains, tobacco, mc geometric bw ea side, 1920, 6x9″ 100.00
Santee Sioux, 3-sided, EX mc bw, minor rpr, 1880, 14″ 225.00
Sioux, awl case, full bw, beaded drops, EX 95.00
Sioux, dbl saddle bag, full bw sides w/butterflies, 66″ L 2,000.00
Sioux, knife case, full bw, drop/feathers/tin cones, 7x2½″ 185.00
Sioux, medicine pouch, buffalo hide/full bw X design, 1890 . . . . . 85.00
Sioux, pipe, bw geometrics, quilled openwork, fringe, 33″ 450.00
Sioux, pipe, full bw sides/quilled slats/yel stain/fringe 750.00
Sioux, pipe, mc quills on 9″ fringe, EX bw top, 1840, 33″ 850.00
Sioux, pipe, quilled: officer/Indian, bw trim, fringe, 38″ 1,600.00
Sioux, pouch, full bw, tin cone/quill-wrapped fringe, 21″ 600.00
Squaw's, suede w/full mc bw ea side, rnd bottom/flap top 75.00
Yakima, pouch, stylized animal, mc bw, ca 1880, 5x8″ 60.00

Baskets

Woven containers of plant fibers go far back into prehistory. Some early groups (like the Basketmakers) are noted for the skill with which they wove and decorated their creations. Dozens of materials, from spruce-root peels to yucca and pine needles, were used. Relatively few of the ancient baskets survive; most of those on the market today are recent and contemporary Southwestern baskets, trays and plaques. Older birch bark and wood-splint baskets from eastern regions are also sought, as are Southeastern examples. Size, condition and decoration are the main value considerations.

Achumawi, utility, twined, arrows/terraced lozenges, 12″ 900.00
Apache, bowl w/2 rows brn radiating arrows, 1900, 14½″ 205.00
Apache, coiled, circle in tondo/checked bands/arrows, 18″ 450.00
Apache, coiled, 5 serrated columns/5 humans below rim, 18″ . . . 600.00
Apache, lg star/sm Xs, willow/devil's claw, coiled, 9″ dia 315.00
Apache, tray, tight weave, checkered triangles at rim, 7″ 300.00
Apache, tray, willow/devil's claw, whirled arrowheads, 15″ 600.00
CA Mission, coiled, mc mtns/echo lines/geometrics, 5x9″ 250.00
CA Mission, coiled, windmill rosette, EX weave, 9″ dia, EX 250.00
CA Mission, tray, coiled mc, checkered/whirling decor, 16″ . . . 1,275.00
Cherokee, carrier, cane, oak hdl, rows of diamonds, 17x16″ 100.00
Cherokee, tray, oval, bundled reed/raffia lashed, 8x6″ 30.00
Havasupai-Apache, waterproof bowl/rattlesnake pattern, 10″ 250.00
Hopi, coiled, bl center star, bl/rust snowflakes, 12″ 120.00
Hopi, wicker, Orabi shallow bowl shape, mc decor, 2¾x10½″ 80.00
Hupa, utility, twined/steel hoop support, zigzags, 24″ 800.00
Hupa-Yurok, squaw's hat, brns/blk overlay stitch, 1900, EX 175.00
Karok, twined geometrics, knob lid finial, 4½″, EX 225.00
Klamath, soft/flexible, root/grass, geometrics, 3½x6″ 75.00
Maidu, blk bud/seed decor, 16 stitches per 1″, 1890s, 9″ 300.00
Maidu, devil's claw/geometrics, EX tight/firm weave, 4½″ 400.00
Maidu, redbud root sunburst, tight weave, 1910, 11″ dia 65.00
Makah, bowl shaped w/mc stripes, 2½x5¾″ 40.00

Makah, cedar bark/bear grass, geometrics, w/lid, 2½″..........40.00
Makah, pad, 2 whales/seabirds, natural/purple/red, 7″.........130.00
Makah, twined geometric bandings, w/lid, 2x2½″ dia...........45.00
Makah, 3 purple dogs, deer, fine weave, w/lid, 2x4¼″.........125.00
Makah-Jurok, twined, faded dyed fiber bands, w/lid, 1¾x2″......35.00
Makah-Nootka, twined, 3-color birds/bands, w/lid, 2x4″ dia......70.00
Mescalero Apache, oval w/deep lid, coiled/mc, 7x14x10″.......300.00
Micmac, birchbark w/scraped pictograph, hdls, 13x12″ dia.....475.00
Navajo, wedding, tight coil/3-color star/spirit trail, 16″.........225.00
NW, beehive, knob on lid, fine coils, red/blk geometrics.......160.00
NW, 15 mc human figures, w/lid, 2″ dia, VG..................40.00
Paiute, bottleneck, red flame/blk bear's claw decor, 4x7″......425.00
Panamint, bowl shape, geometrics, mc, fine weave, 3x5″.......900.00
Panamint, 3 eagles, flower in base, fine weave, 3x7″........1,250.00
Papago, bowl shape w/geometrics, 1890s, 3x12″.............100.00
Papago, coiled fiber on reed core, blk serpent decor, 6″........35.00
Papago, coiled w/brn geometrics, flared, used, 2½x6″..........95.00
Papago, coiled/4 knot whorl, dk/lt grasses, 3x5¾″.............65.00
Papago, cylinder w/yucca & martynia geometric, 5½x7″, EX.....45.00
Papago, flattened form, simple trefoil design, 3x13½″..........55.00
Papago, horse & '+' in martynia & willow, bowl form, 5x7½″...95.00
Papago, lg coils w/meander coyote trail/Xs, 8x10½″...........125.00
Papago, raffia woven spiral, chevron sides, tight, 9″...........40.00
Papago, thick coils w/4 brn dogs, hdls, 7x9″................125.00
Papago, tight coils w/brn swastika/geometrics, 2¾x4¾″........160.00
Papago, tray, coiled willow w/brn geometrics, 6″ dia...........25.00
Papago, willow coils w/3-color terraced band, 4½x7½″.........110.00
Pima, brn human figure band, bundle rod coiled, 3½x6″......250.00
Pima, geometric willow & martynia decor, miniature, 3″ dia.....30.00
Pima, giho, 4 saguaro ribs/lace coiled net agave, EX..........550.00
Pima, pinwheels in dk brn, fine weave, 4½x15½″, EX.........650.00
Pima, storage, willow coils/brn geometrics, early, 8x8″........100.00
Pima, tight coiled reed/grass, meander maze, 12″ dia.........200.00
Pima, tightly wound yucca w/brn grass meander, 2x4″.........125.00
Pima, tray, coiled/flared, w/devil's claw whirlwind, 12″.........700.00
Pima, willow/devil's claw, geometrics, early 1900s, 13″........400.00
Pomo, coil bundle base/1-rod coil sides, brn meander, 3x6″....150.00
Pomo, gift, EX fine 1 rod coils/wht beads/blk/brn pattern......450.00
Pomo, 3-rod coiled gift, terrace triangles/bw/shells, 4½″.......900.00
Pomo, 3-rod woven gift, feathered diamonds/shell disks, 6″....900.00
Salish, box, tight weave on horizontal splint, mc, 9x9x16″.....200.00
Salish, stem/flower/leaf/bud 3-color decor, coiled, 5x7″........250.00
Salish, storage, tight coil w/mc surface patterns, 5x9x7″.......250.00
Shoshoni, conical/disk ft, tight weave, dia/bands, 5x4″.........275.00
Tlingit, covered bottle, tight weave w/mc geometrics, 12″......165.00
Tlingit, rattle finial, aniline zigzags, fragile, 5½x8″............350.00
Tlingit, tightly twined triangles, rattle top lid, 8″ dia..........475.00
Tlingit, tray, twined, geometrics, overlay weave, 7″............85.00
Tlingit, twined spruce root/str sides/faux embroidery, 12″......800.00
Yavapi, starflower w/key border, rpr, 3½x14¾″...............390.00
Yokuts, coiled bottleneck, checkered diagonals, 5″...........190.00
Yokuts, coiled mc bottleneck, rattlesnake bands, 9″..........600.00
Yurok-Hupa, tight coils/1-strand rod, dyed grass, 2½″..........40.00

Blankets

Pueblo Indians first made blankets centuries ago, but today most are made by Navajo Indians. Blankets were still made into the 1800s, when Pendleton and Hudson's Bay blankets became widely available. Around the turn of the century, rugs were developed because tourists were more likely to buy them as floor coverings and wall-hangings. Rugs or blankets are made in various regional styles; an expert can usually identify the area where it was made--sometimes even the individual who made it. The colors of wool are natural (gray-white, brown-black), vegetal (from plant dyes), or artificial (aniline, from synthetic chemicals). Value factors include size, tightness of weave, artistry of design, and condition. Examples by artists whose names are well known command the higher prices.

Chinle Revival, pastel bands/geometric panels, 77x49″.......3,300.00
Navajo, Ganada, 22x12″...................................40.00
Navajo, Germantown, dia/geometric borders, mc, 52x30″.....1,800.00
Navajo, Germantown, Eyedazzler on red, fringe, 55x33″.....2,000.00
Navajo, Germantown, red w/lg mc lozenges, 68x52″.........4,000.00
Navajo, Germantown, Sunday Saddle, red/mc meander, 33x27″.900.00
Navajo, pr terraced wedges flanked by serrated dia, 81x53″....900.00
Navajo, saddle, dbl twill, natural/vegetal/aniline, 32x40″........150.00
Navajo, saddle, hand spun aniline wool on cotton, 26x32″......65.00
Navajo, saddle, twill, dia/linear in red/blk gray, 49x32″........300.00
Navajo, saddle, twilled/woven, handspun/commercial, 61x32″...400.00
Navajo, Sunday Saddle, commercial yarn/7-row wedge, 68x31″..200.00
Navajo, Transitional, aniline/naturals, 8 bands, 56x37″........350.00
Navajo, wearing; Transitional, banded, mc, 62x45″...........750.00
Navajo, Xs w/serrated borders, lazy line weave, 1890, lg.......700.00
Navajo, 2 Gray Hills, 2 lg starbursts+center panel, 96″.......900.00
Navajo, 3rd Phase burial, Saxony/vegetal dye, 1880, VG......2,300.00
Navajo, 3rd Phase Chief's, 4 corners of world Xs, 64x43″....2,000.00
Pendleton trade, mc bands, sgn, 64x58″......................50.00

Crafts and the Arts

Box, birch, quilled chevron/floral, ca 1930, 4¾″ dia, VG.......120.00
Box, birch/allover quilling, relief dia on cover, 1890, 6″........240.00
Box, MicMac, birch/chevron quilling on sides, 5½x8″ dia......275.00
Box, MicMac, line-drawn quilling/spruce-root wrap, 7″, VG.....175.00
Box, MicMac, open quilling, star/geometrics, 4½″ dia, VG......100.00
Box, Ojibwa, quilled strawberry/floral, 1900, 6″ L, EX.........160.00
Box, quill/splint ash coiled w/spruce root, 1840, 2x2″ dia.......50.00
Box, quill/spruce root, geometric, dome lid, 1840s, 2x5x4″.....100.00
Box, quilled, moose head on lid, sweetgrass bound, 2x5x3″....200.00
Box, quilled, puffy crown lid w/tufted ball, '20, 3x3″ dia.......150.00
Box, Woodlands, birch, moosehair floral, 1800s, 5″ L, VG......85.00
Box, Woodlands, completely quilled, X on cover, 1890, 5x4″...200.00
Box, Woodlands, starfish shape/moosehair decor, 3¾″, VG......65.00
Bronze, Indian w/trailing feather, ½ model, sgn West/'13......150.00
Chest, MicMac, birch, allover quilling, 1850s, 6x9″, VG.......300.00
Cushion, velour star w/bw, rooster in center, 1900, 9″ W.......40.00
Cushion, velour top w/allover mc bw, red cloth bottom, 7″......40.00
Horse martingale, Plateau, mc floral bw, 3¼″ W, EX.........295.00
Picture frame, bw on trade cloth, dtd 1903, 9x7″.............80.00
Pillow, Chippewa, floral bw, bw edges, 6½″ sq................50.00
Pin holder, hanging, velvet w/heavy bw, bead tassel, 1910.......30.00
Salt & pepper shakers, silver squash blossoms w/turq, sgn......55.00
Textile, wool, Navajo Reservation, Helen Morgan, 11x12″.......40.00
Totem, Haida, argillite, 7 animals/some w/prey, Moody, 24″...2,000.00
Totem, Kwakiult, spread-wing hawk/elaborate, sgn/1928, 30″..2,200.00
Totem, NW, attached wings, wood w/mc decor, 1930s, 15″....175.00
Totem, NW Coast, mc raven & bear heads, 1900, 13″........145.00
Tray, sweetgrass/birch bark w/floral quilling, 1920s, 9″........100.00
Wallet, Attu, fine weave twine, embroidered, 2-pc, 5″ L.......450.00
Wallet, Sioux, full mc bw, trade cloth bands, 14x11½″........325.00
Watercolor, Zia Pueblo, Buffalo/Antelope dancers, Ma-pewi.....700.00

Dolls

Corn husk face, beaded hair, wrapped in old blanket, 11″.....150.00
Kachina, Bean Dance, mc 1-pc cottonwood/fur/feathers, 13″....150.00
Kachina, Bird Dance, 1-pc cottonwood, well carved, 15″.......175.00
Kachina, God Mother, arrowhead blk face/feather mask, 15″....80.00

Kachina, Kokopelli, 1-pc cottonwood/fur/feathers, sgn, 18″.....300.00
Kachina, Malo, tube snout/1 blossom ear/corn symbols, 9″.....500.00
Kachina, Mountain Sheep, rattle/bow/horns, late, 21″.........300.00
Kachina, Ogre, w/spear, leather cape, pop-eyed, late, 25″......250.00
Kachina, Pahi-ala, pop-eyed, lg ½ rnd ears, 3 horns, 11″......400.00
Kachina, Qoia, gr mask/inverted V mouth, yarn/feathers, 9″....850.00
Kachina, Rasp, mc face/body, mask w/tube snout/lg ears, 9″..1,700.00
Kachina, Sikya-Chantaka, pop-eyes/protruding sq mouth, 12″...300.00
Kachina, Tasaf, brn w/gr mask, kilt/jacla, 1-eared, 15″.......1,900.00
Made from sock, Chippewa, w/cradleboard, ca 1900, 6x14″....125.00
Maiden, hide dress/beads, sgn Carlson, 18″...................35.00
Male, leather/cloth, dressed in fancy beaded clothes, 13″......150.00
Man & woman, Snohomish, basketry, 8″, pr...................90.00
Seminole, palmetto netting, handmade dress, 1900, 14″.........85.00
Sioux, buckskin/bw features/dress, buffalo hair, 1900, 17″......395.00

Kachina doll, Hopi, wooden butterfly maiden, Palhik Mana, 17¾″, $4,000.00.

Domestics

Bowl, burl, spout/ladle notch/relief bosses/mk 1754, 11x8″...1,500.00
Bowl, salt; speckled burl, 2½x4x3½″.......................340.00
Bowl, smooth brn stone, edges somewhat chipped, OR, 2½x5″..35.00
Bowl, Tlingit, wood, seal/octopus on side, inlay rim, 12″.....1,200.00
Bowl, Tlingit, wood, 2 bears at base/rim w/inlay eyes, 16″....1,900.00
Comb, NW Coast, wood, 19 teeth/mask w/vacant eyes hdl, 4″.1,320.00
Cradle, Apache, slat bk, muslin wrappings, 1800s............450.00
Cradle, Cherokee, wicker type, ca 1850s, 38″ L...............250.00
Cradle, Sioux, full bw on hide, finged panel below, 27″......2,750.00
Cradleboard, Plains, hide, bw trim, fringe, 20″...............835.00
Dipper, Nez Perce, horn, bent/shaped, 8¾″..................60.00
Food pulverizer, Sioux, 4″ stone head w/flat base, w/hdl........55.00
Ladle, NW Coast, cedar, totemic: fish/whale head, 1950, 11″....50.00
Ladle, Sioux, wood, horse effigy hdl, 1900, 13″................35.00
Mortar & pestle, stone, from SD...........................125.00
Pestle, wood, pre-1900, 23″................................25.00
Spoon, NW Coast, horn, wide bowl, late 1800s, 7x4″..........65.00
Spoon, serving; Winnebago, walnut, notched hdl, 1800s, 14″....70.00
Spoon, Sioux, horn, hand carved............................25.00

Jewelry

As early as 500 A.D., Indians in the Southwest drilled turquoise nuggets and strung them on cords made of sinew or braided hair. The Spanish introduced them to coral and it became a popular item of jewelry; abalone and clam shells were favored by the Coastal Indians. Not until the last half of the 19th century did the Indians learn to work with silver. Each tribe developed their own distinctive style and preferred design, which until about 1920 made it possible to determine tribal origin with some degree of accuracy. Since that time, because of modern means of communication and travel, motifs have become less distinct.

Quality Indian silver jewelry may be antique or contemporary--age, though certainly to be considered, is not as important a factor as fine workmanship and good stones. Pre-1910 silver will show evidence of hammer marks, and designs are usually simple. Beads have sometimes been shaped from coins; stones tend to be small, and when silver wire was used, it is usually square. To insure your investment, choose a reputable dealer.

Bracelet, silver and turquoise, old pawn, 3″ front medallion, $600.00.

Beads, trade, cranberry glass, 24″..........................35.00
Beads, trade, milk glass, tube shaped, 90″ L.................90.00
Beads, trade, red/yel/bl/blk glass, 20″.......................25.00
Belt, Navajo, 6 repousse oval conchas+5 butterfly slides.....1,800.00
Belt, Navajo, 7 repousse conchas, ornate buckle, 40″ hide...2,000.00
Belt, Navajo, 8 oval conchas, sm openwork stamped buckle...1,200.00
Bow guard, Navajo, turq, German silver mt, contemporary......40.00
Bracelet, Adena, copper, thick top, prehistoric...............125.00
Bracelet, child's; Navajo, silver, cast & stamped, ca 1920.......20.00
Bracelet, child's; Navajo, silver, thunderbird & 2 turq..........25.00
Bracelet, Navajo, five ¾″ turq cabs, dbl shank..............130.00
Bracelet, Navajo, inlay kachina on twisted/etched silver.........60.00
Bracelet, Navajo, lg triangle turq w/in silver orle, heavy........100.00
Bracelet, Navajo, sandcast, lg turq stone, old pawn...........100.00
Bracelet, Navajo, three ¾″ turq, dbl shank...................75.00
Bracelet, Navajo, 2 flowers ea w/4 oval turq/applied beads......400.00
Bracelet, Navajo, 7 grad oval turq plaques w/silver beads......500.00

Bracelet, Navajo, 7 sq turq w/in serrated bezels/beading.......500.00
Bracelet, Zuni, open shoulders, teardrop/rnd turq cluster......500.00
Bracelet, 2 wire/2 band mt w/fine lg #8 oval turq plaque.......700.00
Buckle, rawhide w/full bw, eagle in center, 3¾x2¾″............85.00
Choker, Blackfoot, full bw, orig scalp remains, 14″ L.........170.00
Earrings, Zuni, Knife Wing Dancer, mc inlay.................95.00
Earrings, Zuni, thunderbird, turq channel inlay, 1930s.........70.00
Jaclas, coral bead ends, turq disk beads w/3 pendants, 10″.....300.00
Jaclas, grad turq disk beads+6 shell disks, 13″ L, pr.........600.00
Necklace, bear teeth on hide w/trade beads/buckeyes/acorns....385.00
Necklace, flat turq nuggets, sm turq spacers, old pawn........900.00
Necklace, Navajo, 18 box-bow squash w/turq, 14-turq naja.....800.00
Necklace, Navajo, 2-strand 12-turq squash blossom/dbl naja....275.00
Necklace, Navajo, 2-strand/12-MOP squash blossom/dbl naja....200.00
Necklace, Plains, trade bead/shell/shell pendant, 2-strand.......40.00
Necklace, 5-strand trade beads, various exotic origins........1,200.00
Pendant, beaver, trade silver, solid cast, sgn, 1½″............135.00
Pin, Zuni, mc mosaic butterfly, silver rosettes, 2″ L...........275.00
Ring, Navajo, 1″ triangular turq cab.........................55.00
Ring, Navajo, 1 lg rnd bl turq cab, 1930s....................60.00
Ring, 2 rows of 3 sm turq, old pawn.........................65.00
Trade beads, Venetian, millifiori, ca 1850, 24″ strand..........30.00

Knives and Chipped Blades

The knife was an indispensable tool to the Indian whether he was in battle, hunting game, or doing chores at the campsite. Before the white man's metal blades, all were made of copper, obsidian, flint, or chert. Knife cases fashioned of leather with intricate decorations of quilling or beadwork, were sometimes worn suspended from the neck, and in later years attached to the belt.

Blade, Archaic, duo-beveled, bi-point, flint, TX, 3⅞″...........75.00
Blade, Archaic, slight shouldering, Iowa, 4⅛″................225.00
Blade, bevel edge, E-notched base, blk flint, 2¼″.............15.00
Blade, cache; Adena, Flintridge, rnd base, 3¼″...............85.00
Blade, ceremonial; Hopewell, flint, excurvate, 2⅞″............45.00
Blade, flared, quartzite, dull tip, early, 2⅞″..................4.00
Blade, fossil coral, broad base, rnd edge, Florida.............20.00
Blade, Godar, side-notched, sm serrations, 3½″...............55.00
Blade, micro, gray flint, Alaska, minor chips, ¾″...............4.00
Blade, Osceola, side-notched, WI, 6¼″.....................350.00
Blade, Paleo uniface, high-grade chert, 2½″..................14.00
Blade, Paleo uniface, 1 graver tip, gray flint, 2⅞″.............15.00
Blade, serrated edges, stemmed, heavy duty, blk, 2½″..........25.00
Blade, stemmed, sq base, translucent wht, 4¼″...............25.00
Chert, Hopewell, corner-notched, wht, tip damage, 3⅛″........30.00
Chert, Perkiomen, broad, stemmed, gray, NY, 2½″.............10.00
Chert, 5 sides, rnd tip, corner-notched, pink, 2″...............6.00
Crooked, birch burl w/horseshoe/heart/anchor/star, jeweled.....200.00
Crooked, burl, 3 relief hearts/voided dia, str razor blade.......250.00
Crooked, burl w/Indian head/feathers/bear head atop, 12″......675.00
Crooked, carved burl hdl, honed str razor blade, 10″, VG.....120.00
Crooked, duck body effigy, ca 1850.........................90.00
Crooked, hardwood serpent w/open mouth/body grooves, 9″....225.00
Crooked, maple, thumb rest platform end, str razor blade......200.00
Crooked, walnut burl ram's head w/curled blk horns, 10″......425.00
Crooked, wood w/carved heart, barrel hdl terminus...........150.00
Crooked, wood w/carved heart/X-hatching, bk: tintype.........325.00
Crooked, 3 crescent-form figures/zigzag/X-hatch, str razor......350.00
Knife, angled blade, constricted base, blk flint, 1½″............4.00
Knife, flake; Hopewell, retouched edges, 2″...................6.00
Knife, obsidian, leaf shaped, duo tipped, red, Oregon, 5″.......60.00
Knife, obsidian, stemmed, Mexico, 3½″......................18.00
Knife, serrated edge, blk obsidian, corner-notched, 4″..........30.00
Knife, St Charles dvtl, colorful Flintridge, 4¼″...............375.00
Spear, fish; well tipped, yel flint, 3″........................20.00

Masks, Early Iroquois False Face Society

Blind Man, blank brass eyes, blk w/red horsehair.............450.00
Long Nose, copper eyes, 10″ tree-limb nose, beaver hair......500.00
Masked Whisperer, full mc, nose protrudes/corn-husk braids....500.00
Medicine Man, copper eyes, wht/brn pnt, horse-tail hair.......450.00
Miniature, blk on red w/wht teeth, horsehair hair, 5½″.........75.00
Old Man, realistically carved chieftan, horsehair hair..........900.00
Spoon Mouth, stone studs, metal eyes, horse-tail hair.........500.00
Whistler, grotesque, twisted/braided corn-husk hair...........500.00

Pipes and Ceremonial Items

Pipe bowls were usually carved from soft stone, such as catlinite or pipestone, an argilaceous sedimentary rock composed mainly of clay. Granite was also used. Some ceremonial pipes were simply styled, while others were intricately designed naturalistic figurals, sometimes in bird or frog forms, called effigies. Their stems, made of wood and often covered with leather, were sometimes nearly a yard in length.

Arm band bells, Blackfoot, boot hide, ea w/4 bells.............50.00
Bannerstone, butterfly, slate, grooved, MI, 4¼″..............425.00
Bannerstone, crescent, brn hardstone, 3¾x2½″..............400.00
Bannerstone, geniculate, bl/blk banded slate, IL, 3¼x2″.......300.00
Bannerstone, pink, curved, blk/gray banded slate, 4¼x1″......115.00
Bannerstone, tube/rnd top/flat base, drilled, slate, 2¾″........120.00
Bannerstone, winged, granite-like, polish/undrilled, 3¾″.......195.00
Birdstone, elongated, banded slate, classic, 5⅞x1½″..........995.00
Birdstone, pipe-eyed; hardstone w/EX color.................650.00
Birdstone, slate, good form, 4x1½″........................550.00
Birdstone, slate, sm base type, 4x1″.......................100.00
Canteen, Zuni, stirrup form, mc frog/lizard/etc, 1850, 8″......650.00
Club, ceremonial; dk gray, human head at base of hdl, 4-lb....550.00
Club, Navajo, feather suspensions, stone head, lg..............45.00
Crop wand, Apache medicine man's, horsehair 'rattlesnake'.....75.00
Dance apron, Chippewa, blk cloth w/floral bw, 1910...........85.00
Dance bells, Sioux, legging type, 18 1¼″ hawk bells...........65.00
Drum, Cree, single-headed, pnt decor, ca 1920...............80.00
Drum, Navajo, peyote ceremony, 3-leg kettle, 1800s, 9½x7″.....75.00
Drum, Osage, single-head, hide w/wood fr, pnt decor, 1900....175.00
Drum, Pueblo, dbl-headed, pnt w/buffalo/eagle, 1890..........165.00
Drum, Sioux, hand-held, wood hoop type/hide covers, 11″......55.00
Drum, Sioux, 14″ sq box w/pnt deer/star decor, hide covers....110.00
Drum striker, sinew-sewn leather, maple hdl, 1880s, 14″........20.00
Effigy, lizard, slate, sq head/tail, jutting shoulders, 5″.........550.00
Effigy, Zuni, stone bear w/heishi beads/sinew wrapped, 3″.......75.00
Fetish, Plains, buckskin/bw lizard/tin cone, 1880, 6″..........165.00
Fetish, Plains, umbilical, snake/lizard, tin cone, 12″..........120.00
Fetish, Plains, umbilical, turtle, hide/bw/18 thong ft, 5″........90.00
Fetish, Sioux, bw/hide lizard, tin cones/horsehair, 7″..........300.00
Gorget, concavo-convex, slate, wide ends, 2 holes, 4¼x2¼″....175.00
Gorget, elongated, 2 holes, expanded center, 5½″.............60.00
Gorget, hematite, rectangular, 2 holes, polished, 3½″.........180.00
Gorget, Hopewellian, reel form, polished banded slate, 4½″....260.00
Gorget, humped, slate, 2 holes, G lines, 4¼x1¾″.............105.00
Mask, Seneca, woven/braided corn-husk face, fringed, '30s.....300.00
Medicine bow/feather arrows, Navajo, ca 1900, 10″............70.00
Pendant, Adena, bell shape, lt hole, tally mks, 4″.............80.00
Pendant, anchor type, slate, expanded lower base, 5x1½″.......70.00
Pendant, b/w hardstone, polished, drilled, IL, 2¾x1⅜″........250.00

Pendant, rectangular, banded slate, lg hole, 5″ L. 110.00
Pendant, red hematite, lg drill hole, 3¼x1½″. 135.00
Pendant, shovel shape, slate, VG lines, 4½x1¾″. 60.00
Pipe, barrel, quartzite, hole in center, 2x1¾″. 125.00
Pipe, Blackfoot, carved emblems on blk bowl, wood stem 280.00
Pipe, bowl type, OH pipestone, 1½x1½″. .40.00
Pipe, cloud blower, fancy tube, pottery pipe, 1900, 4½x2″. 75.00
Pipe, E Plains, catlinite, fish stem/horse-head bowl, 12″. 990.00
Pipe, effigy, bird figure, bowl on bk, granite, 3½x1½″. 195.00

Birdstone, 3½″, $1,500.00.

Pipe, elbow type, granite, 2½x4″. 85.00
Pipe, Haida, argillite panel, openwork nautical motif, 8″. 1,250.00
Pipe, NW Coast, wood, seated human, iron bowl atop, 5″. 800.00
Pipe, Plains, catlinite, hardwood/branded stem, 1880, 18″. 185.00
Pipe, Plains, pipe-tomahawk form, red pipestone, 19½″. 295.00
Pipe, platform, pipestone, concave base, polished, 4⅛″. 995.00
Pipe, platform type, steatite, polished, 1½x4″. 100.00
Pipe, raised bowl, flat 3¾″x1″ stem, ridge atop, 1½″. 345.00
Pipe, Sioux, catlinite, snake on 3x8″ bowl/twist wood stem. 350.00
Pipe, squaw; red catlinite, spiral stem/ribbed bowl, 2-pc. 250.00
Pipe, steatite, highly polished, sm 2¾″ stem, 4¼″. 255.00
Pipe, T-shape, redstone, 9″ L. 400.00
Pipe, trade, clay, VA, 1700s. 8.00
Pipe, tube; Diegueno, soapstone, entirely drilled, 5x1″. 230.00
Pipe-tomahawk, authentic wood hdl, brass head EX. 600.00
Pipe-tomahawk, brass, orig head/later undrilled hdl. 410.00
Pipe-tomahawk, iron, British type bowl. .225.00
Pipe-tomahawk, spontoon type, no haft, 9½x3½″. 210.00
Rattle, Iroquois, folded elm bark w/seeds, 11″. 50.00
Rattle, Navajo, gourd, Yie-Bi-Shei Dance, ca 1900. . . . . .30.00
Rattle, Navajo, gourd/cedar hdl, constellation decor, 1900. . . . . . .40.00
Rattle, NW-Salish, red cedar seal/mc, copper pendants, 9″. 325.00
Rattle, red stained hide/fur on wood hdl/feathers, 7″. 45.00
Rattle, Sioux, buffalo testes, sinew wrap/bone hdl, VG. 65.00
Rattle, Tesuque Pueblo, pnt gourd/wood hdl, 1830s. 45.00
Spear, dance staff, pnt head, yarn on hdls, ca 1930, 25″. 22.00

Pottery

Indian pottery is nearly always decorated in such a manner as to indicate the tribe who produced it or the pueblo in which it was made. For instance, the designs of Cochite potters were usually scattered forms from nature or sacred symbols. The Zuni preferred an ornate repetitive decoration of a closer configuration. They often used stylized deer and bird forms, sometimes in dimensional applications.

Bird, Santa Clara, blkware w/incised details, polished, 4″. 55.00
Bowl, brn/rust geometrics on cream, sgn Namoki, 2½x3½″. 40.00
Bowl, Hopi, blk on red pattern w/in, sgn Z Adams, 6″. 40.00
Bowl, Navajo, dk brn geometrics on cream, sgn Lissa, 2¼x4″. . . .45.00
Bowl, Santa Clara, blk on blk, sgn Flora Jaranjo, 2½x4½″. 85.00
Bowl, Santa Clara, blkware, Rosalie & Jon, 1¾x3″ dia. 145.00
Bowl, Santo Domingo, mc scalloped bands/stars, 7¾″. 250.00
Canteen, Hopi, 1700s, 10x7″. 160.00
Effigy pot, bowl w/2 animal head spouts, edge chips, 5″. 255.00
Effigy pot, Pima, owl form, red clay, blk/red decor, 6. . . . . .75.00
Jar, Acoma, mc decor, ca 1930, 7½x5″. .36.00
Jar, Adena Plain, ca 600 BC, miniature. .25.00
Jar, Cochiti, cream/blk frieze of deer/birds/trees, 9½″. 1,000.00
Jar, Hopi, smoked buff w/mc geometrics, Patty Maho, 4⅛″. 90.00
Jar, Santa Clara, carved decor, blk on blk, 4x5″. 250.00
Jar, storage; Acoma, red/decor rim, ca 1900, fancy, 7x9″. 50.00
Jar, storage; Picuris Pueblo, mica ware, ca 1900, 8x9″. 50.00
Olla, Acoma, ornate mc design, 8x8″. 65.00
Olla, Maricopa, red w/blk geometrics, mk w/bear paw, 9x8″. . . .185.00
Plate, Santa Clara, blkware/knife-wing, Cresencia, 5½″. 135.00
Pojaque-Hopi, mc geometrics, V Duwakuku, 2½x5″. 100.00
Pot, Acoma, brn/orange geometrics on wht, thin walls, 3″. 65.00
Pot, redware w/2 etched figures/etc, sgn, 1½x2″ dia. 60.00
Pot, Santa Clara, blk on blk geometrics, sgn John, 3″ dia. 75.00
Pot, Santa Clara, incised blk on blk, sgn Anita Suazo, 3″. 75.00
Pot, Santo Domingo, blk/feather band/sq mouth, Josie M, 4″. . . .90.00
Pot, Sioux, redware w/4 pinched corners, 3″. 30.00
Vase, Sioux, cream w/mottled mc, 1930s, 6″. 30.00
Vessel, Zuni, mc owl effigy w/'pocket,' 10″. 2,000.00
Wedding pitcher, Santa Clara, dbl spout, hdl between, 5½″. 50.00
Wedding pot, Santa Clara, blk on blk, joined dbl neck, 5″. 60.00

Seed jar, Hopi, cream with black and red birds, 6¾″, $1,200.00.

Pottery, San Ildefonso

The pottery of the San Ildefonso pueblo is especially sought after by collectors today. Under the leadership of Maria Martinez and her husband Julian, experiments began about 1918 which led to the development of the 'black-on-black' design achieved through exacting methods of firing the ware. They discovered that by smothering the fire at a specified temperature, the carbon in the smoke that ensued caused the pottery to become blackened. Maria signed her work from the late teens to the 1960s; she died in 1980. Today a piece with her signature may bring prices in the $500 to $3,500 range. Examples listed here are black-on-black unless noted otherwise.

Basket, protruding knobs at rim, shiny blk, 5x6″. 50.00
Bowl, blk, sgn Lipita R Vigil, 3x4½″, EX. 300.00
Bowl, blk, sgn Marie & Julian, 5½x4″. .425.00
Bowl, blk on blk geometric, sgn Anna, 2½x6½″. 250.00
Bowl, blk on blk sunburst/feather motif w/in, used, 4x11″. 150.00
Bowl, design around top, sgn Marie, 5½″. 577.50

Jar, Avanyu water serpent and rain cloud band, signed Maria and Santana, 6¾″, $1,600.00.

Bowl, geometric shoulder decor, 5″, EX....................90.00
Bowl, sienna redware w/incised geometrics, sgn Rose, 9″......325.00
Bowl, triangle decor, blk on blk, abrasions, 3x5″..............60.00
Jar, feather rim frieze over ring band, Marie/Santana, 9″.....2,000.00
Jar, redware w/umber slip geometrics, 3¾″..................40.00
Jar, serrated diagonal wings frieze, Marie/Julian, 5″ W........700.00
Jar, serrated wings/scalloped diagonal band, Marie, 8″.......1,600.00
Pitcher, highly polished, w/hdl, 1940s, 5″....................50.00
Plate, radiating feathers, Marie/Santana, 11″...............1,700.00
Plate, 4 terraced rim hooks, Marie/Julian, 10″...............800.00
Platter, incised decor, sgn Rose, 11½″.....................475.00
Vase, Avanyu/cloud band, teardrop form, Marie, 11″........2,250.00
Vase, center design w/3 rings, bulbous, sgn Blue Fawn, 7″.....577.50
Vase, incised geometrics, gourd shape, att R Gonzales, 10″....300.00
Vessel, 2 necks & openings, w/hdl, 3½″.....................35.00

Rugs, Navajo

Blanket/rug, banded/dia, transitional, 1910, 72x48″, VG.......335.00
Blanket/rug, 2 Grey Hills, Anson Begay, hand spun, 63x41″..1,500.00
Chinle-Crystal, banded, A Carroll (Begay), 31x25″............185.00
Crystal, banded, pastel tones, A Carroll, 30x21″.............150.00
Crystal, banded w/central geometrics, contemporary, 30x21″....150.00
Eye Dazzler, extended serrated dia, 1940, 48x27″.............300.00
Eye Dazzler, Sunday Saddle, Germantown yarn, 1910, 30x25″..550.00
Ganado, red w/3 4-color dia/terrace bands, 1910, 100x38″.....800.00

Two Grey Hills, by Helen White, Navajo, 48″ x 68″, $500.00.

Kayenta, bands/serrated dia, red ground, 1940, 46x31″........165.00
Klaetoh, dia/serrated strips, 1910, 60x29″, EX...............250.00
Lightening/serrated bands, aniline dyes, med weave, 50x25″....100.00
Pictorial, SW scenic, genre scenes/animals, L Nez, 59x40″...3,300.00
Pueblo, blk line dia, red/wht terrace border, 1910, 70x32″.....275.00
Regional, serrated lozenges w/in checkerboard, 90x70″........900.00
Shiprock Yei, 4 females/goddess, A Goodtooth, 36x29″........235.00
Step Mountain, Wide Ruins, brn/blk/gray/wht, 1920, 21x40″....50.00
Storm, gray/blk/wht detailed pattern, 57x30″...............600.00
Teec Nos Pos, dia w/zigzag borders, EX color, J Clani, 38″....225.00
Teec Nos Pos, hand-spun wool, dia/geometrics, 38x35″........250.00
Teec Nos Pos, strong pattern w/abberations, 1870s, 93x45″....650.00
Teec Nos Pos, terrace dia, zigzag border, 1930, 83x44″, VG...450.00
Transitional, serrated/terrace border w/dia/swastika, 107″......650.00
Wide Ruins, banded pattern, mc, Mary Gaddy, 24x40″........110.00
Wide Ruins, mc geometrics, 21x40″........................50.00
Wide Ruins, med weave, 5-band/3-dia, 1930, 58x30″..........175.00
Yei, Cornplanter spirits, Ginse Lewis, 31x18″...............200.00
Yei, Cornplanter spirits w/corn shafts, mc on wht, 28x15″.....175.00
Yei, Lakachukai, 9 feathered females+male, DuPont dye, 99″.2,700.00
Yei, tapestry, spirit release lines in borders, 24x16″...........175.00
2 Grey Hills, L Yazzi, terraced geometrics, 58x30″...........300.00
2 Grey Hills, meander/terrace edge/ornate lozenge, 90x63″...1,500.00
2 Grey Hills, serrated lozenges, feather border, 118x64″.....1,250.00

Tools

Adz, elk horn blade, wood hdl, 12″, VG....................125.00
Adz, hardstone, flat bottom, rnd cutting edge, 4⅞x1⅞″.........35.00
Arrow shaft straightener, TN, 4″..........................15.00
Awl, bone, polished, KY, 4″.............................20.00
Awl, splintered deer bone, prehistoric, NY, 4½″...............13.00
Axe, full groove, blk basaltic rock, polished, AZ, 6″..........125.00
Axe, full groove, unpolished, PA, 8¼x4¾″..................65.00
Axe, full groove, well polished, IL, 3⅛″.....................45.00
Axe, iron belt, rnd eye, early 1800s.......................135.00
Axe, polished stone, ¾ groove, 2½x4″......................35.00
Axe, spike; hand-forged, 10″............................125.00
Axe, stone, ¾ groove, KY, 3½″............................35.00
Axe, stone, ¾ groove, MO, 5¼″............................75.00
Axe, trade, metal, 1700, 7¾x3½″..........................95.00
Axe, ¾ groove, Hohokam, highly polished, 8x3″.............135.00
Celt, Caddoan, dk gray stone, AR, 5x1¾″....................17.00
Celt, copper, flared bit, EX patina, 3¾x3″...................70.00
Celt, flaked, brn flint, MO, 5x3″..........................19.00
Celt, flaked, good shape, AR, 3½″.........................17.00
Celt, flared bit, MO, 6½x2½″............................35.00
Celt, gray stone, 5x2¼″................................25.00
Celt, polished, IL, 7x3¼″...............................120.00
Chisel, blk hardstone, 1 end str/2nd rnd, heavy use, 4½″.......30.00
Drill, gray, IA, 2¾″...................................12.00
Drill, KY Carter Cave flint, wide base, IN, 1⅞″...............15.00
Drill, notched base, off wht, patina, AR, 2½″................12.00
Drill, pin; gray, OH, 3⅛″...............................50.00
Drill, tan, 2″ L...6.50
Engraver, lt gray, 1⅞″...................................8.00
Flesher, Northern Plains, wood/metal, pre-1870...............35.00
Hammer, stone, lg, EX..................................25.00
Hoe, bison shoulder blade, orig hdl.......................115.00
Hoe, blk flint, notched base, polished edge, 5¼x4¼″...........60.00
Hoe, sq bk, pink chert, AR, 5½x2½″........................30.00
Hoe blade, buffalo shoulder blade..........................40.00
Needle, bone; polished, 6½″..............................35.00
Pounder, NW Coast, carved stone, humanoid, stylized detail....950.00

Scraper, rnd-notched, tan, MO, 2″ 8.00
Spade, flared bit, brn Mill Creek tabular flint, 8½x5½″ 100.00
Spade, oval type, good polish, 8¼x5½″, EX 90.00
Spud, granite, well polished/good form, 8x3″ 160.00

Weapons

Arrow, Apache, metal point, wood shaft, 25″ L 45.00
Arrow, Plains, complete, pre-1870 . . . . . 50.00
Bow, Apache, shaped/sinew bk/fibre draw/3 arrows, 1860, 42″ . . 200.00
Bow, NW Coast, carved wood, pre-1870s, 56″ 110.00
Carbine, 1886 Winchester, NW Coast carvings, trade era 1,700.00
Club, Plains, skull-cracker, VG 145.00
Knive, fighting; Tlingit, steel/baleen raven-head hdl, 20″ 1,600.00
Long bow, Gueverra, w/4 cane arrows, fancy foreshafts 110.00
Musket, Plains, trade era, brass-tack trim, VG 350.00
War club, Kiowa, rawhide wrapped, very old 80.00
War club, Pueblo, pnt wood, ca 1830s, 18″ 40.00
War club, Sioux, rawhide wrapped 150.00

Miscellaneous

Booklet, Kickapoo Dr, remedies/medicine, 8x5″, EX 35.00
Broadside, Use Great Sagawa...Indian Medicine, 7¾x5″ 55.00
Carte de visite, Pawnee scout/military coat & squaw, sgn 130.00
Carte de visite, Tokee, Iowa Chief, full costume 80.00
Check, US Indian trader, Blackfoot Reservation, dtd 1899 . . . . . 20.00
Crupper, Yakima, braided horsehair/rosettes/buttons, 16″ 40.00
Fan, Peyote, pheasant feathers w/beaded hdl 45.00
Fishhook, copper, WI, 1½″ 15.00
Fishhook, NW Coast, primitive carved figure, 9¼″ 185.00
Flute, E Sioux, spiral carved cedar/lead soundplate, 1880s 375.00
Hairpin, bone, Xd/dotted decor, polished, 7½″ 65.00
Horse bridle, Santee Sioux, red/navy trade cloth w/florals 250.00
Letter, US Indian service, from Crow Agency, 1892, 2 pg 40.00
Photo, Hudson Bay Trading Post, sepia, interior, 5x7″ 60.00
Photo, surrender of Nez Perce leader, Chief Joseph, 4x6″ 425.00
Photo, wagon train on steep mtn trail, sepia, Fiske, 5x8″ 65.00
Pictograph, Sioux, ledger drawing, Chief Blue Horse, 8x10″ 350.00
Poster, Dr Hailes 'Ole Injun' Tonic, w/Indian head, 20x13″ 40.00
Print, McKenny Hall, Mon-Ka-Ush-Ka, Sioux Chief, 25x30″ 115.00
Robe, carriage; baby muskrat pelts w/wolf border, 76x59″ 900.00
Snowshoes, Woodland, NE Territory, 1914, 10x42″ 175.00
Stakes, captive; Apache, wood w/rawhide lacings, pre-1890 . . . . . 40.00

Amethyst Glass

Amethyst simply describes the rich purple color of this glassware, made by many companies both here and abroad since the 19th century.

When no condition is indicated, the items listed below are assumed to be in mint condition.

Bottle, scent; blown 2-mold, 2 sides sunburst, 2 ribbed 175.00
Candlestick, hexagonal w/stem joined by wafer, 7½″ 270.00
Console set, 9½″ bowl, pr 9½″ candlesticks 45.00
Creamer, Inverted Thumbprint, reed hdl, pontil 40.00
Cuspidor, blown, 19th C, 4¾x8⅜″ 350.00
Flowerpot, blown, attached saucer, folded rim, 2¾″ 95.00
Hair receiver, blown, enamel/brass hinge, ormolu brass ft 85.00
Jug, frosted/glossy, florals, emb pewter top/hdl, 12x5″ 135.00
Lemonade set, enamel floral, 13″ pitcher, 4-pc 145.00
Vase, enamel houses/winter scene, fluted top, 14¼x5″, pr 385.00
Whiskey taster, 8 panels in base, rim flakes, 2½″ 45.00

Amphora

The Amphora Porcelain Works of Teplitz, Austria, produced Art Nouveau styled vases and figurines during the latter part of the 19th century. They marked their wares with various stamps, some incorporating the name and location of the pottery with a crown or a shield.

When no condition is indicated, the items listed below are assumed to be in mint condition.

Basket, bearded man decor, tall/slim shape, sgn, 12″ 165.00
Bowl, bl/wht speckled w/mosaic birds, 6¼″ 45.00
Bowl, enamel sailboat, matt bkground, 2¾x3¾″ 50.00
Centerpiece, water lilies/applied blackberries, 13½″ L 145.00
Figurine, stalking lion climbs down rocky ledge, 10x15″ 285.00
Mug, fox & bear, Austrian crown mk, ca 1891, 5¾″ 95.00
Rose bowl, enamel Deco leaves/flowers, wht w/cobalt trim 70.00
Vase, applied nuts/berries on bl/wht irid, drip mold, 9½″ 170.00
Vase, Art Deco, mosaic lovebirds, 12″ 135.00
Vase, bird on front, shouldered cylinder, 5½″ 75.00
Vase, blown-out flowers, bulbous/leaf hdls, crown mk, 7¾″ 80.00
Vase, branches/leaves w/mc relief floral, #2228, 7″ 110.00
Vase, enamel stork, earth tones, cobalt top/bottom, hdl, 5″ 80.00
Vase, female warrior w/jeweled helmet, mc/gilt, 9½″ 1,100.00
Vase, floral, artist sgn, 4-hdl, 11″ 300.00
Vase, floral/Deco bird, pink/lav, bulbous, 1922, 13x14″ 265.00
Vase, florals, artist sgn, 6″ 165.00
Vase, grapes/leaves applied on bark, hdls, 3¼″ 85.00
Vase, grapes/leaves applied on bark, hdls, 7″ 100.00
Vase, irid gr, gold applied floral, some reticulation, 10″ 185.00
Vase, leaf decor, applied Cosmos, sgn, ftd, hdls, 16″, pr 275.00
Vase, leaves/dandelions on lt/dk bl, gilt rim/hdls, 5½″ 195.00
Vase, mc oval/rnd stones on tan, spider web effect, 5½″ 125.00
Vase, parrots, mc on beige, 6¾x4″ 165.00
Vase, portrait, jeweled, 9″ 1,400.00
Vase, roses & blackberries on cream basketweave, 16¾″ 395.00
Vase, scenic, gr/gold, 6″ 150.00
Vase, yel roses, ball body/can neck, 4-hdl, 7″ 98.00
Vase, 2 children pull on doll, Imperial mk, 13¼″ 425.00

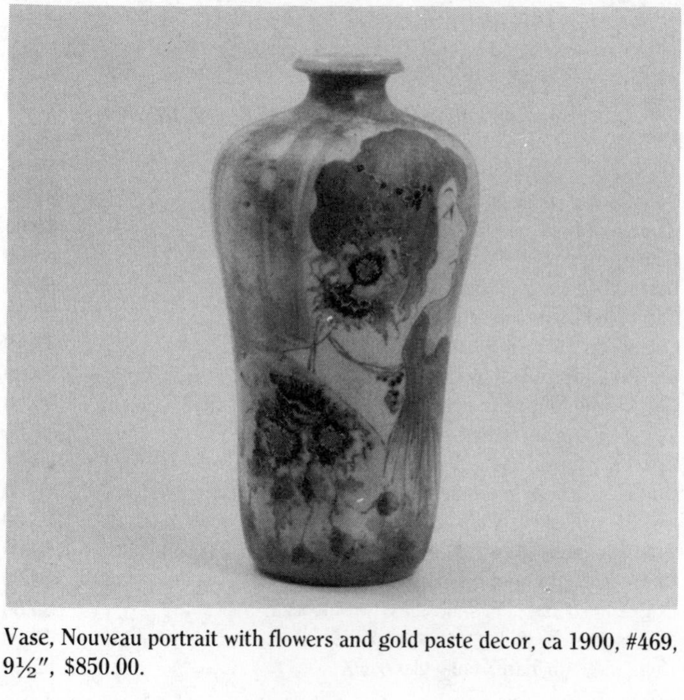

Vase, Nouveau portrait with flowers and gold paste decor, ca 1900, #469, 9½″, $850.00.

Animal Dishes with Covers

Covered animal dishes have been produced for nearly two centuries and are as varied as their manufacturers. They were made in many types of glass--slag, colored, clear, and milk glass--as well as china and pottery. On bases of nests and baskets you will find animals and birds of every sort. The most common was the hen.

Some of the smaller versions made by McKee, Indiana Tumbler and Goblet Company, and Westmorland Glass of Pittsburgh, Pennsylvania, were sold to food processing companies who filled them with prepared mustard, baking powder, etc. Occasionally, one will be found with the paper label identifying the product and processing company still intact.

Many of the glass versions produced during the latter part of the 19th century have been recently reproduced. As late as the 1960s, the Kemple Glass Company made the rooster, fox, lion, cat, lamb, hen, horse, turkey, duck, dove, and rabbit, on split ribbed or basketweave bases. They were made in amethyst, blue, amber, and milk glass, as well as a varigated slag. Careful comparison to known examples of older glass with strict attention to detail is sometimes necessary to recognize reproductions.

When no condition is indicated, the items listed below are assumed to be in mint condition.

Swan on knobbed basket, amber, 6½″, $125.00.

Boar's head, milk glass, w/eyes....950.00
Camel, resting, bl milk glass, 6½″....140.00
Camel, resting, milk glass, 6¼″....85.00
Cat, ribbed base, bl milk glass w/wht head, 5¼″....60.00
Cat, ribbed base, milk glass, base mk #6, 5¼″....25.00
Cat on drum, milk glass, mk Portaeux, VG....45.00
Cat on wide ribbed bottom, milk glass....55.00
Chick emerging from egg on basket, milk glass, 3½″....40.00
Chick in egg on sleigh, milk glass, 5¼″....45.00
Chick on top of mounded eggs, Atterbury, dtd....175.00
Chick on top of mounded eggs, milk glass, Westmoreland....65.00
Chicks in basket, 5 chicks hatching from eggs, milk glass....125.00
Crawfish, milk glass, 4¼″....150.00
Deer, milk glass, sgn Flaccus....250.00
Dog, ribbed base, bl milk glass w/wht head, 5½″....50.00
Dog, setter, bl milk glass, sgn, Vallerysthal....75.00
Dog, wide rib base, milk glass, EX....85.00
Dog w/bone on gr blanket in relief, bisque, 5½x6½x9″....595.00
Dolphin, bl milk glass....75.00
Dove, split-ribbed base, milk glass, sgn McKee, 5½″....150.00
Duck, grass base, milk glass, 5½″....75.00
Duck, no eyes, milk glass, Atterbury, Mar 15, 1887....150.00
Duck, pintail, basket base, milk glass, EX....30.00
Duck, swimming, bl milk glass, 5½″....50.00
Duck, wavy base, w/eyes, milk glass, 8″....90.00
Eagle, 'American Hen,' milk glass, pat applied for, 1898....85.00
Fish, entwined, red eyes, milk glass, Atterbury, Aug, 1889....105.00
Fish, sea base, frosted, 9½″ L....75.00
Fox, ribbed base, no eyes, milk glass, Aug 1889....135.00
Hen, basketweave base, #3, bl milk glass, 5½″....25.00
Hen, basketweave base, bl milk glass, 2⅜″....25.00
Hen, basketweave base, bl milk glass, 3½″....30.00
Hen, basketweave base, bl milk glass w/pnt head, 4″....80.00
Hen, basketweave base, gr milk glass, 2½″....20.00
Hen, basketweave base, mc bisque, Staffordshire, 9x10″....550.00
Hen, basketweave base, milk glass, 2½″....45.00
Hen, basketweave base, transparent gr glass, Greentown....175.00
Hen, lacy base, eyes, milk glass, 7½″....45.00
Hen, w/chicks on base, milk glass, Atterbury, dtd, 6¼″....125.00
Horse, milk glass, sgn base, McKee....200.00
Lion, picket base, milk glass....65.00
Lion, scroll base, milk glass, 6″....45.00
Pig on drum, milk glass, mk Portieux, EX....65.00
Quail, milk glass, 6½″, NM....50.00
Rabbit, chocolate glass, basketweave base, Greentown....375.00
Rabbit, mule-eared, picket base, milk glass, 5½″....65.00
Rabbit, split-ribbed base, milk glass, sgn McKee, 5½″....150.00
Rabbit finial, egg shape, milk glass, lg....58.00
Robin on nest, bl milk glass, Vallerysthal, 5″....50.00
Rooster, ribbed base, milk glass, bl head, mk #1/#4, 5½″....40.00
Rooster, split-rib base, milk glass, sgn McKee, 5½″....135.00
Rooster, standing, blk opaque....75.00
Rooster, standing, milk glass, Westmoreland, 1940....45.00
Squirrel, split-rib base, milk glass, sgn McKee, 5½″, EX....150.00
Swan, bl milk glass, mk Vallerysthal, 5½″....80.00
Swan, closed neck, basket base, milk glass, mk #1, 5½″....30.00
Swan, raised wings, milk glass, 9½x5¾″....150.00
Turkey, split-ribbed base, milk glass....65.00
Turkey, split-ribbed base, milk glass, sgn McKee, 5½″....150.00
Turtle, milk glass, 4¼″, 7¼″ hdl to hdl....275.00

Antiquities

The ancient Egyptians, Romans, and the early craftsmen of India and China have left us with exquisite treasures bearing mute witness of their esthetic convictions that even a water carrier, a knife, or a rug should be created a thing of beauty.

Though time and the elements have taken their toll on the more fragile works of these ancient artisans, it is incredible that many remain intact to this day. The fragile tear and scent bottles, blown by Roman artisans from the 1st century A.D., and examples of the red or black predynastic potteries of Egypt--though understandably quite rare--can yet occasionally be found on the market today. Jewelry, often interred with the dead, has survived the centuries well; figurines of marble and terra cotta, ceremonial masks, earthenware vessels, and other relics such as these offer us of the 20th century the only tangible link possible to the ancient world.

When no condition is indicated, the items listed below are assumed to be in excellent condition.

Key:
tc—terra cotta

Bronze

Bust, Apollo, 200 AD, 3¼″ 770.00
Censer, hemispherical/ftd, openwork, Coptic, 800 AD, 4½″ 450.00
Cheek-piece, horse w/bow-shape body, Luristan, 900 BC, 4½″ . .600.00
Horse, leaping, Parthian, 150 AD, 3½″ 300.00
Horus Falcon, 30th Dynasty Egypt, 650/300 BC, 5¾″ 4,800.00
Horus figural, wearing split crown, Egypt, late period, 4″ 115.00
Nefertum, striding/lotus headdress, 730 BC, rstr, 6¾″ 685.00
Osiris, w/flail & crook, Upper Egypt crown, 600 BC, 5″ 600.00
Pendant, humped bull, pierced eyes, Iranian, 1000 BC, 3″ 700.00
Priestess, missing 1 hand, Iberian, 400 BC, 4″ 190.00

Hardstones and Related Carvings

Aphrodite, elaborate coiffure, marble, Roman, 175 AD, 15″ . .7,200.00
Boy, necklace/amulets/etc, limestone, Cypriot, 400 BC, 12″ . . .1,150.00
Fragment, limestone, deer/acanthus relief, Coptic, 6x12″ 240.00
Good Shepherd, sheep on bk, marble, N Africa, 300 AD, 16″ .3,000.00
Head of youth, limestone/cut-in detail, Coptic, 500 AD, 7″ 550.00
Horse head, bared teeth w/bit, marble, Roman, 150 AD, 3″ 650.00
Jar, Qebusenuf-head lid, slender form, Canopic, 16″ 1,650.00
Limestone relief fragment w/snake/Horus Falcon, 1785 BC . . .1,200.00
Offering table, limestone, relief carved, 450 BC, 10x13″ 300.00
Pacifier, alabaster, w/loop, Egypt, 1200 BC, 1½″ 55.00

Pottery

Amphora, Attic Blk-figure panel, ftd/hdls/lid, 600 BC, 18″ 1,800.00
Amphora, ftd/hdls, bichrome bands/lines, Cypriot, 9″ 600.00
Amphora, turq, bulbous/hdls, Roman, 1st C, rstr, 6½″ 600.00
Bowl, Grisaille, str ft/rnd body, floral, Ilkhanid, 7″ 325.00
Bowl, low ft, underglaze geometrics, Ilkhanid, 1275, 7″ 600.00
Bowl, mc champleve, stylized leopards, Seljuk, 12th C, 13″ 750.00
Bowl, sgraffito/mc splotches, Samanid, 10th C, 13½″ 450.00
Bowl, wht w/streaks/inscription, Samanid, 800 AD, 12¾″ 800.00
Cup, brn/yel sgraffito decor, hdls, Byzantine, 1300, 7″ 700.00
Dish, lustre, couple/fancy garments, Seljuk, 1100, 8″ 750.00
Epichyis, Gnathia, vintage decor, Apulian, 400 BC, 7″ 300.00
Ewer, goddess head body/high hdl, Apulian, 400 BC, 18″ 4,400.00
Isis, seated, holding fragmentary Horus, bl, 700 BC, 2½″ 250.00
Jug, sgraffito/mc glaze, fragmentary, Byzantine, 900, 7″ 600.00
Jug, turq w/incised foliate motif, Seljuk, 1200s, 8½″ 300.00
Krater, Apulian Red-figure, ftd/hdls, 320 BC, 18″ dia 2,200.00
Kylix, Attic Red-figure, sgraffito inscription, 8½″ 1,750.00
Mug, Etruscan Blk-figure, ftd, Pontic Class, 650 BC, 6½″ 700.00
Pendant, ram, fragmentary horns, Iranian, ca 1200 BC, 3½″ . . .165.00
Sack Askos, buffware, foliate decor, Apulian, 300 BC, 9″ 800.00
Tankard, turq faience, birds/animal relief, Roman, 1st C 800.00
Tile, lustre, star form/intricate motif, Seljuk, 1200, 12″ 350.00
Ushabti, w/tools/sack, inscriptions, bl-gr, 375 BC, 6½″ 2,000.00
Vase, turq faience/animal relief, Roman, 1st C, 6¾″ 250.00
Vase, turq w/mc medallions, pyriform, Seljuk, 1200, 10″ 450.00
Vase, 3-color faience, fragmentary neck, Roman, 1st C, 6¾″ . . .400.00

Terra Cotta

Bottle, scent; buff, bulbous w/hdl/ft, Roman, 100 BC 60.00
Bull, ochre w/mc harness, Hellenistic, 300 BC, 4¾″ 185.00
Bust, Dionysos, from banquet scene, Tarnetum, 400 BC, 6½″ . .500.00
Figure, boy riding boar, mc remains, Hellenistic, 4¾″ 350.00
Figure, Maenad, classic stance, mc, Apulian, 300 BC, 8½″ 400.00
Goddess, psi type, braid, stylized, Mycenaenan, 1230 BC 1,350.00
Goddess, seated w/scroll, Greek, 450 BC, 2¾″ 495.00

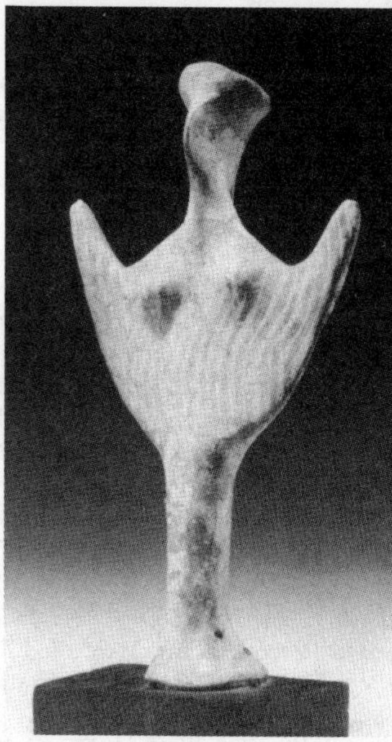

Mycenaenan terra cotta goddess, red-painted garment, ca 1300-1230 B.C., 5″, $1,500.00.

Head, architectural, Manga Graecia, 400 BC, 12″ 700.00
Head of deity, beard/wreath in curled hair, Medma, 500 BC . . .400.00
Horse, leaping, w/harness, bl details, Hellenistic, 7″ 1,000.00
Krater, str sides, plant decor, 4-hdl, Crete, 1150 BC, 16″ 4,125.00
Lady, bl/lav chiton, wreath in hair, Apulia, 300 BC, 18″ 1,200.00
Lamp, oil; simple rim relief, Mediterranean, 500 AD, 3″ 47.50

Miscellaneous

Beaker, glass w/pnt birds/escutcheons, Mamluk, 1200, 7″ 850.00
Bowl, ribbed aquamarine glass, Islamic, 1st C AD, 4¾″ 700.00
Horse bit, split, lg side rings ea w/2 ring loops, 700 BC 160.00
Nail, iron, broad head, Roman, 100 BC-100 AD, 3¾″ 17.50
Necklace, mummy beads, faience, 600 BC, 16″ 25.00
Panel, linen tapestry, portrait medallion, Coptic, 400, 8″ 500.00
Ring, gold w/l.5cm garnet intaglio, carved Athena, 50 AD 500.00
Roundel, tapestry, lg dove, Coptic, 400/500 AD, 11″ 400.00

Appliances, Early Electric

Collectors of America enjoy vintage appliances such as those used in the kitchen--toasters, coffee makers, etc. -- as well as early TV sets, vaccuum cleaners, short-lived innovations, and examples with particularly distinctive Deco styling. Early light bulbs are popular, and can be found in interesting shapes and variations. The Edison-type of the 1800s had a carbon filament; double-looped and self-supporting, it gave off a mellow subdued light. The General Electric 'Mazda' bulbs introduced thirty years later, replaced its golden glow with a brilliant white illumination made possible with the new drawn metal tungsten filament, which was supported by a central glass rod. While most early bulbs had straight sides, a few were pear shaped or round. Nearly all were made with small tips on the top through which air was exhausted.

See also Kitchen Collectibles.

When no condition is indicated, the items listed below are assumed to be in excellent condition.

Coffee pot, Farberware, gooseneck, wood hdl 30.00
Coffee server, chrome over copper, orange hdls 100.00
Fan, brass cage & blade, old style, 12″ 60.00
Fan, Emerson Long Nose 150.00

Fan, Emerson Trojan, all brass, 8″ 100.00
Fan, Trico vaccuum, 4″ 40.00
Fan, Westinghouse, brass cage, 16″ blade 85.00
Fan, Westinghouse, brass frame, six 12″ brass blades 75.00
Hot plate, gr speckled granite 45.00
Iron, Sunbeam, dtd 1925, in orig fireproof case 65.00
Light bulb, carbon w/1900 type Edison base 20.00
Light bulb, Edison carbon, oval label w/Edison, 1901-1907 .... 20.00
Light bulb, manufacturer unknown, cemented base, 1895-1900 .. 30.00
Light bulb, Thomson-Houston bases, manufacturer unknown 25.00
Light bulb, typical carbon, manufacturer unknown, ca 1900s 10.00
Light bulb, typical Mazda, name on side, 1915-1920 .... 10.00
Mix master, Sunbeam, w/gr bowls, 1930s 30.00
Mixer, dough; ad incised lid, metal, pat 1902, 8x13″ 50.00
Razor, Packard, in leather case w/instructions, 1936 .... 25.00
Razor, Vibro-Shave, red hdl, in case 35.00
Server, Chase, bakelite knobs, Pyrex liner, 12″ 65.00
Television, Hallicrafters, projection 300.00
Television, Philco Predica 125.00
Toaster, Reverso Electric Weld Co, EX 22.00
Toaster, Son-Chief, flip down, Deco styling 35.00
Toaster/grill, Westinghouse, 1910 .... 27.50
Vaccuum, Bissel Superba, 1917 .... 45.00
Waffle iron, M Bowman, cut-out stand, brass, pat 1908 .... 15.00
Washer, Speed Queen, 1910 .... 175.00

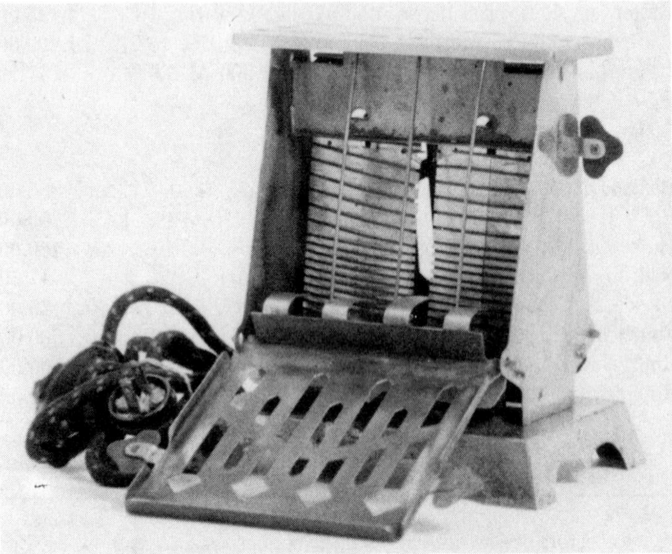

Toaster, ca 1925, 5½″ x 8″, $18.00.

Arc-En-Ciel

The Arc-En-Ciel Pottery Company operated in Zanesville, Ohio, from 1903 until 1907. Artware was produced only until 1905, typically finished in a high lustre gold glaze. Though not always marked, those pieces that are carry the half-circle rainbow logo containing the company name.

Vase, eagle & Washington, gold glaze, 7″ 200.00
Vase, poppy relief, gold irid, waisted, 10″ 250.00

Arequipa

The Arequipa Pottery operated from 1911 until 1918 at a sanitorium near Fairfax, California. Its purpose was two-fold--therapy for the patients and financial support for the institution. Frederick H. Rhead was the originator and director. The ware, made from local clays, was often hand thrown, simply styled and decorated. Marks were varied, but always incorporated the name of the pottery and the state. A circular arrangement encompassing the negative image of a vase beside a tree is most common.

When no condition is indicated, the items listed below are assumed to be in mint condition.

Ash tray, brn w/mixed colors, bowl shape, 2x3¾x4¾″, EX 125.00
Bowl, shell device ea side, cream/orange lustre, 1¾x6″ 200.00
Planter, gr w/diamond design, AP trademk/USA, 3¼x2¾x3¾″ ... 150.00
Vase, bl matt, sgn F/#110, 3½″, NM 150.00
Vase, gr matt, sloping sides, compressed base, 4″ 175.00
Vase, leaves relief, matt lt/dk bl, 7¾″ 350.00
Vase, leaves relief, wht, octagonal, 4¼″ 200.00
Vase, tan, sq pedestal, mk, USA, 4x4″ 150.00

Argy-Rousseau, G.

Gabriel Argy-Rousseau produced both fine art glass and quality commercial ware in 1918, in Paris, France. He favored Art Nouveau as well as Art Deco, and in the twenties produced a line of vases in the Egyptian manner, made popular by the discovery of King Tut's tomb. One of the most important types of glass he made was pate de verre. Most of his work is signed.

When no condition is indicated, the items listed below are assumed to be in mint condition.

Bowl, band of blossoms, violet/purple/raspberry, 4¼″ 550.00
Bowl, grapevine relief, mottled colors, thin sides, 3½″ 2,600.00
Pendant, dahlia, wht & yel on gray, oval, 2⅝″ 550.00
Plate, center; 3 rim sqs w/melons, bl/gray streaked, 12″ 2,750.00
Vase, chevron devices, gray/turq/lav mottle, 7″ 1,850.00
Vase, 2 females kneel before harp, orange on mottle, 9¾″ 7,975.00
Vase, 3 Nordic warriors relief, ochre/orange, 12″ 1,950.00

Art Deco

To the uninformed casual observer, 'Art Deco' evokes thoughts of chrome and glass, streamlined curves and aerodynamic shapes, mirrored prints of pink flamingos, and statues of slender nudes and greyhound dogs. Though the Deco movement began in 1925 at the Paris International Exposition and lasted to some extent into the 1950s, within that period of time the evolution of fashion and taste continued as it always has, resulting in subtle variations.

The French Deco look was one of opulence--exotic inlaid woods, rich material, lush fur and leather. Lines tended toward symmetrical curves. American designers adapted the concept to cover every aspect of fashion and home furnishings from inexpensive picture frames and cigarette lighters, plastic and bakelite jewelry, to high fashion designer clothing and exquisite massive furniture with squared or circular lines. Vinyl was a popular covering and chrome-plated brass was used for chairs, cocktail shakers, lamps and tables. Dinnerware, glassware, theaters, and train stations, were designed to reflect the new 'Modernism.'

The Deco movement made itself apparent into the fifties in wrought iron lamps with stepped pink plastic shades and Venetian blinds. The sheer volume of production during those twenty-five years provides collectors today with fine examples of the period that can be bought for as little as $10 to $20 into the thousands. Chrome items signed 'Chase' are prized by collectors and are available at prices ranging from $15 to $20 for smaller items to $200 to $300 for larger pieces. Blue glass radios and tables with blue glass tops are high on the list of desirability in many areas.

When no condition is indicated, glass and china items in the following listings are assumed to be in mint condition; all others are assumed excellent. See also Aluminum; Bronzes; Frankart; Furniture; Jewelry; Lalique

Desk set, skyscraper motif, airplane letter opener, signed Silver Crest, Decorated Bronze, 6-pc, $400.00.

Ash tray, brass, crimped receiver, rib std, Ruhlmann, 32″......700.00
Ash tray, floor; Belmet Rollador, chrome/brass, 24½″..........95.00
Ash tray, frosted glass/chrome, female head, 7½″.............200.00
Box, powder; onyx w/metal lady finial.........................36.00
Buffet, ebene-de-macassar/burl, Chermayeff, 38x60″...........500.00
Carpet, geometric, wool, Ivan da Silva Bruhns, 128x81″.....3,080.00
Clock, shaped body, pnt parrot in sq reserve, marble, 8½″.....950.00
Door stop, lady w/scarf, CI w/gr pnt, advertising.............120.00
Figure, dancer, plated pewter on amber onyx base, 8″........150.00
Figure, female nude dancer, metal, sgn Fayral, 12½″..........525.00
Figure, hoop dancer, metal/marble, sgn C Charles, 13″........450.00
Figure, nude dancer, metal/marble, sgn Denis, 11½″..........500.00
Figure, nude sits by stork atop books, Fraureth, 5″...........145.00
Fishbowl holder, brass, lady & dog in quarter moon..........125.00
Lamp, alabaster column w/bronze frieze: soldiers/nudes, pr.....300.00
Lamp, Harlequin girl, bronze metal, w/millefiori globe, 9″......375.00
Lamp, La Danseuse, E Movier, mc figure, ivory head, 7½″.....675.00
Lamp, lady on bk holds globe on feet, 3 tier shade, Cheko....165.00
Lamp, metal elephant holds up satin glass globe, vase top.....150.00
Lamp, seated Oriental, gold crackle shade, Ronson............95.00
Lamp, silk parachute shade, ivory/bronze lady base, Lange...6,000.00
Lamp, 2 chrome nudes by frosted cobalt ball on 3 rnd tiers....145.00
Lamp, 3 nudes encircle crackle globe, copper on metal, 12″...175.00
Letter rack, 3-compartment, cut-out flower, brass, ES Gesh.....50.00
Mirror, cheval; rnd w/silver bronze ribbed base, Ruhlmann...2,750.00
Panel, rvpt gilt horse head in frothing wave, J Dupas, 49″....5,500.00
Pretzel stand, man strutting/mirror underplate, chrome, 7″......75.00
Radiator cover, brushed steel/vertical panels, Jean Perzel.....1,500.00
Radio, floor; 2 nudes back to back, Fada.................2,200.00
Sconce, silver bronze w/3 flared alabaster panels, Cheuret.....950.00
Shaving set, traveling; hand blown tube holds brush/razor.......55.00
Tea set, brn cross on beige, gr trim, Suzy Cooper............300.00

Art Glass Baskets

A popular novelty and gift item during the Victorian era, these one-of-a-kind works of art were produced in just about any type of art glass in use at that time. They were never marked, since these were not true production pieces, but 'whimsies' made by glassworkers to relieve the tedium of the long work day, or as special gifts. The more decorative and imaginative the design, the more valuable the basket.

When no condition is indicated, the items listed below are assumed to be in mint condition.

Amber, 6-panel, feathered hdl, scalloped, 8¾x6″..............38.00
Amberina, amber hdl, sgn Libbey, 7½″....................1,500.00
Bl drapery, gr hdl & applied flowers, polished pontil...........68.00
Candy stripes, red/wht, wht w/in, thorn hdl, 6x9¾″...........285.00
Cased, wht/pink, trn-down corners, twisted hdl, 5½x4″........145.00
Cased, wht/yel, clear/mica edge, thorn hdl....................50.00
Diamond Point, bl milk glass, bulbous, ruffled top, 10″.........85.00
Diamond Quilt, apricot MOP.............................365.00
Diamond Quilt, peppermint cased swirl.....................385.00
Diamond Quilt, yel satin w/wht, frosted hdl, 4½x5¾″..........225.00
Fry, wht opal w/bl hdl, no mk, 7½x7″......................285.00
Hobnail, wht w/amber T-shape hdl.........................225.00
Intaglio florals, feathered hdl, scalloped, 7¼x4″...............28.00
Pink, reticulated, clear twisted hdl..........................80.00
Pink w/bl applied hdl & edge, blown, 6″.....................45.00
Purple, ribbed, vaseline wishbone hdl & rim, 7″.............150.00
Rubena, ribbon-candy edge, braided clear hdl, 1880s..........85.00
Spangle, bl w/in, thorn hdl, sm...........................225.00
Spangle, butterscotch, thorn hdl..........................225.00
Spangle, wht w/gold-flecked buff casing, twist hdl, 9″.........150.00
Spangle, wht w/yel int, reeded twist hdl.....................115.00
Spatter, clear casing, thorn hdl, scalloped, 9x6″..............180.00
Spatter, Fluted Fan, cobalt/red/wht, ped base/loop hdl, 7″.....165.00

Diamond Quilted aquamarine casing and handle, 5″ x 7½″, $275.00.

Art Nouveau

From the famous 'L'Art Nouveau' shop in the rue de Provence in Paris, 'New Art' spread across the continent, and belatedly arrived in America in time to add its curvilineal elements and assymetrical ornamentation to the ostentatious remains of the Rococo revival of the 1880s. Nouveau manifested itself in every facet of decorative art. In glassware, Tiffany turned the concept into a commercial success that lasted well into the second decade of this century, and created a style that inspired other American glassmakers for decades. Furniture, lamps, bronzes, jewelry, and automobiles, were designed within the realm of its dictates.

Today's market abounds with lovely examples of Art Nouveau, allowing the collector to choose one or several areas that hold a special interest.

When no condition is noted, glass and china items in the listings that follow are assumed to be in mint condition; all others are assumed excellent.
See also Bronzes; Jewelry; Tiffany

Ash tray, woman's face in relief, pewter.....................20.00
Clothes brush, lady's face in relief/sterling/fully mk, 6″.........57.50
Desk set, box w/calendar/caddy/10″ inkstand, Silvercrest.......150.00
Desk set, water lilies/etc, crystal/brass, 5-pc.................215.00

Desk plateau, bronze, after model by K. Radetzky, early 20th century, lion and lioness at pool, 15″ long, $350.00.

Figurine, nude looks into pond, sgn, silver on copper..........68.00
Knife, pen; sterling, 2-blade..............................35.00
Lamp, desk; lady w/flowing hair, bl slag, 8½x4½″.............195.00
Mirror, cast bronze figural lady holds oval beveled mirror.......70.00
Mirror, hand; blown-out flowers/lady's head w/flowing hair......125.00
Panel, peacock/tail spread, carved/pnt wood, Curtis, 47″.....2,310.00
Paper clip note holder, swan figural relief, brass..............65.00
Plaque, lady & Cupids, chalkware, pastels.....................45.00
Tazza, silver metal female water carrier, glass bowl, 18″.......990.00
Vase, bronze, flori-form, Griffoul, Newark, NJ, 9″, pr.........275.00
Vase, buds/stems, bronze w/sterling overlay, Heinze, 13″......250.00
Vase, pottery w/brass floral overlay, Delaherche, 1900.......1,500.00

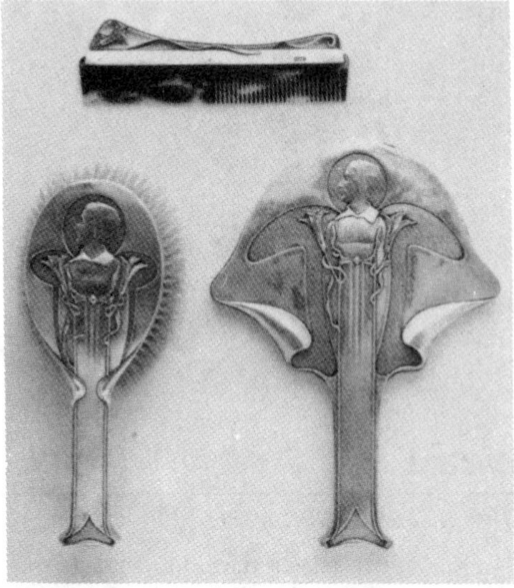

Dresser set, English silver, W. Hutton & Sons, 1899, height of mirror, 11″$1,200.00.

Arts and Crafts

The Arts and Crafts movement began in England during the last quarter of the 19th century and its influence soon was felt in this country. Among its proponents in America were Elbert Hubbard (see Roycrofters) and Gustav Stickley (see Furniture). They rebelled against the mechanized mass production of the industrial revolution, and against the cumulative influence of hundreds of years of man's changing taste. They subscribed to the theory of purification of the styles--that designs be geared strictly to necessity. At the same time, they sought to elevate these basic ideals to the level of accepted 'art.' Simplicity was their virtue; to their critics it was a fault.

The style of furniture they promoted was squarely built of heavy oak, and so simple was its appearance that as a result many began to copy the style, which became known as 'Mission.' Soon factories had geared production toward making cheap copies of their designs. In 1915, Stickley's own operation failed, forced into bankruptcy by the machinery he so despised. Hubbard lost his life that same year on the ill-fated *Lusitania*. Within the decade, the style had lost its popularity.

When no condition is indicated, the items listed below are assumed to be in mint condition. See also Furniture; Roycroft; and specific manufacturers.

Andirons, wrought iron, scroll base/spiral finial, 27″, pr.......500.00
Ash tray, copper, polished, #271, sgn Craftsman, 6¾″.........160.00
Book rack, table top/sliding, G Stickley, red decal, 7x12″......375.00
Bowl, brass, sq w/curving sides, Dirk Van Erp, 3¾x11¼″......125.00
Bowl, hammered sterling, Kalo, 1⅞x7¼x10⅛″...............200.00
Box, oak w/spindle ends, G Stickley, #95, top missing.........700.00
Calendar frame, G Stickley, mk w/compass, 5x8″..............65.00
Candlestick, brass, bulbous bobeche, slender stem, 12″, pr.....140.00
Candlestick, copper w/applied wire scrolls, 14½x7¼″..........125.00
Chafing dish, hammered copper/terra cotta, scroll fr, 15″......250.00
Chamber stick, copper, removable bobeche, G Stickley, 9″.....425.00
Chamber stick, hammered copper, G Stickley, logo, 9″........250.00
Clock, tall case, oak, shelves/door aside, ldgl panel, 67″.....1,210.00
Compote, copper set w/malachite, leaf band, disk ft, 3x7″......150.00
Curtains, linen, applique trees w/sq buds, 46x23″, 7 for.......750.00
Fork, hammered sterling, Kalo, 8¼″.........................65.00
Inkwell, copper, strapwork corners, 4 curl ft, 3½x5″..........110.00
Lamp, iron/slag glass, bent arm on oak base, sq lantern.......225.00
Lamp, pierced brass conical shade, hammered slim std, 20″....265.00
Lamp, silver overlay bronze, mica panels, Heinze Art.........250.00
Lantern, ceiling; copper/glass, taper sq, G Stickley, 8″ W....1,200.00
Lantern, copper fr, cut-out hearts, yel glass cylinder, 9″.......200.00
Lantern, copper/textured glass, G Stickley, #766, 21x12″.....2,200.00
Magazine rack, 3-slat sides, 4 shelves, J&JG Stickley, #46......400.00
Magazine stand, 4-shelf, rnd cut-out on side, Limbert, 37″.....350.00
Magazine stand, 4-shelf, solid sides, Limbert, 19x14″.........350.00
Mirror, wood slat hung w/iron chains, att Roycroft, 23x29″....250.00
Pin, etched brass triangle w/spread-wing eagle, Frost, 3″........30.00
Plaque, copper, 4 indents/emb buttons, sgn Craftsman, 14″....625.00
Sconce, copper, oval, dbl socket branch, mk Craftsman, 15″...800.00
Screen, 3-sectioned oak, G Stickley, unsgn, ea part 22″ W...6,000.00
Screen, 4-panel, emb canvas w/HP florals, ea part 18x71″.....425.00
Silk batik, Pharaonic ships/ibises, CB Hartman, 130″.........770.00
Table runner, emb stylized floral device, fringed, 22x20″.......45.00
Tea set, hammered pewter, sgn Craftsman Sheffield, 5-pc......150.00
Umbrella stand, copper pan removes, G Stickley, #54, label....250.00
Vase, bronze w/sterling pussy willows, Heinze, 4″.............75.00
Wall sconce, brass/copper, dbl, emb interlocked rings, 15″.....450.00
Wastebasket, oak, vertical slats, G Stickley, #94, 14x12″.....1,200.00

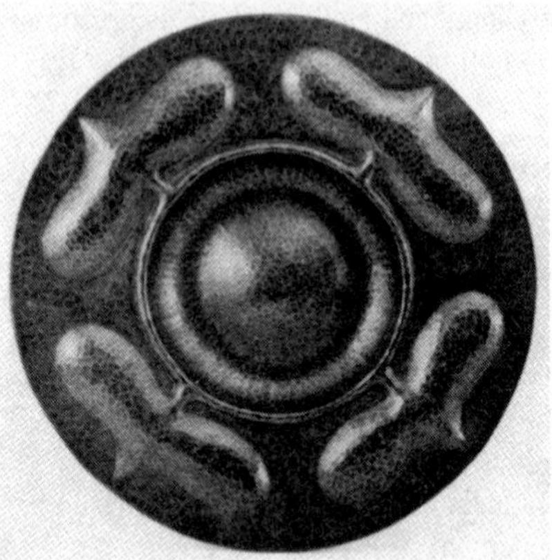

Wall plaque, hammered copper with four stylized spades around recessed center, stamped 'Al ik Kan,' by Gustav Stickley, catalog #344, 15″, $4,600.00 at auction; $800.00 to $1,200.00 estimate.

Aurene

Aurene, developed in 1904 by Frederick Carder of the Steuben Glass Works, is a metallic iridescent glassware similar to some of Tiffany's. Usually a rich lustrous gold, blue is also found, and ocassionally red or green. It was used alone and in combination with calcite, a cream-colored glass with a calcium base, also developed by Carder. Decorated examples are very rare. It is usually marked Aurene or Steuben, sometimes with the factory number added, etched into the glass by hand. Paper labels were also used.

When no condition is indicated, the items listed below are assumed to be in mint condition.

Vase, green with gold swirled decor, 3″, $1,295.00.

Atomizer, gold, slender shape, VG bulb, o/w M, 7½″ . . . 185.00
Bottle, scent; gold w/purple, melon rib, flame stopper . . . 375.00
Bowl, bl, incurvate rim, 3x5⅝″ . . . 900.00
Bowl, centerpiece; lt gr irid/gold int, sgn/#2877, 10½″ . . . 375.00
Candlestick, gold, domed ft, wafer connector, 10x4¾″, pr . . . 800.00
Candlestick, gold, 4-prunt stem, roll top, sgn/#6384, 3½″ . . . 325.00
Candy dish, gold, sgn/#532, 1½x5″ . . . 250.00
Compote, gold, sgn/#2760, . . . 435.00
Creamer & sugar, gold, Dia Quilt, reed hdl, sgn, 3½″; 2½″ . . . 695.00
Cup & saucer, gold, sgn . . . 325.00
Dish, gold, lipped, rope center hdl, #2997 . . . 385.00
Goblet, gold, twist stem, sgn/#2361, 6″ . . . 350.00
Lamp, brn 6x7¼″ intarsia banded shade; harp std, 14″ . . . 650.00
Nut dish, gold, ruffled . . . 200.00
Punch cup, gold, ftd, #2367, set of 6 . . . 1,350.00
Salt cellar, bl, ped ft, sgn/#d, 1½x2⅜″ . . . 225.00
Shade, gr w/platinum leaves & vines, 6½x6″ . . . 950.00
Sweetmeat, bl, SP bail/lid, sgn/#5204, 3½x4″ . . . 450.00
Vase, bl, lily form, ruffled, sgn, 9″ . . . 450.00
Vase, bl, stick neck, sgn/#d, 10″ . . . 395.00
Vase, bl, stick neck, 12″ . . . 525.00
Vase, bl, tree stump, ribbed/prunts, sgn/#2741, 6″ . . . 325.00
Vase, bl, trumpet form, sgn, 9″ . . . 450.00
Vase, bl, urn form, sgn/#2867, 2″ . . . 325.00
Vase, gold, bulbous/wide mouth, sgn/2683, 8″ . . . 650.00
Vase, gold, Jack-in-the-Pulpit, sgn/#202, 6″ . . . 695.00
Vase, gold, sgn/#2648, 2½″ . . . 350.00
Vase, gold, vines/leaves on opal, sgn F Carder, 6½″ . . . 950.00
Vase, gold, 3 hdls on shoulder, dimples, 8¼″ . . . 850.00
Vase, opal w/4 gr peacock eyes/feathers, sgn/#243, 12½″ . . . 2,800.00

Austrian Ware

From the late 1800s until the beginning of WWI, several companies were located in the area known at the turn of the century as Bohemia. They produced hard paste porcelain dinnerware and decorative items, primarily for the American trade. Today, examples bearing the marks of these firms are usually referred by collectors as Austrian ware, indicating simply the country of their origin. Of those various companies, these marks are best known: M.Z. Austria; Victoria, Carlsbad, Austria (Schmidt and Company); and O. & E.G. (Royal) Austria.

Though most of the decoration was achieved through transfer designs which were sometimes signed by the original artist, pieces marked Royal Austria were often hand painted, and so indicated alongside the backstamp.

Of these three companies, Victoria, Carlsbad, Austria, is the most valued by today's collectors.

When no condition is indicated, the items listed below are assumed to be in mint condition.

Basket, lav/pink/rose, much gold, Art Deco, artist sgn . . . 40.00
Bowl, irid, pink w/in, 4 gold hdls, Carlsbad, 3½x6¾″ . . . 125.00
Bowl, sleeping warrior & maid on cobalt, Kauffman, 9½″ . . . 55.00
Box, stamp; HP roses, gold trim, lift-off lid, MZ, 3x1¼″ . . . 35.00
Chocolate pot, pink floral on lt bl/cream, HP, +cr/sug . . . 175.00
Chocolate pot, poppies, HP/emb on satin, gilt, Vienna, 10″ . . . 75.00
Chocolate pot, roses on gr, +4 cups & saucers . . . 110.00
Creamer & sugar bowl, yel floral on lt gr, gold hdls/trim . . . 85.00
Cruet, corn on cob, brn/yel, Vienna, gold hdls/stopper, 9″ . . . 200.00
Dish, child's; child feeding chickens, MZ, 7″ . . . 30.00
Egg caddy, 12-egg, rooster in center, roses in cups, 5x9″ . . . 75.00
Fish set, w/1 lg platter & 12 plates, floral, aqua/gold . . . 375.00
Hair receiver, pink roses, gr/pink on wht/gold, MZ . . . 30.00
Humidor, grotesque animal head atop, rat on rim, Floretta . . . 65.00
Humidor, puffy owl, sm hairline . . . 40.00
Pitcher, bee on bamboo hdl, gold/ivory, Stellmacher, 7″ . . . 75.00
Pitcher, moose head w/rack, open mouth, bl/brn, sgn, 4½″ . . . 45.00
Pitcher, tankard; floral on gr, gold edge, HP, 12½″ . . . 165.00
Plate, bl lattice, gold, Kauffman, Victoria . . . 95.00
Plate, cake; girl w/draped veil, cobalt bl/gold, 10″ . . . 65.00
Plate, fruit center, pastel rim, 7½″, set of 4 . . . 25.00
Plate, sleeping warrior/female, gr, Kauffman, 9″ . . . 84.00

Plate, lady's portrait, signed Monreau below portrait, gilt trim, marked Royal Austria, 9½″, $125.00.

Plate, woman profile, turq dottings & gold tracings on red......75.00
Shakers, shrimp color, mushroom shape, sgn Schuyler, pr......13.00
Sugar shaker, floral, egg shape............................42.00
Vase, brn trees/water on yel pearl, cylinder, MZ, 11"...........70.00
Vase, Dutch scene intaglio, tree hdls, ftd, Dressler, 11"........90.00
Vase, fall flowers on cream, hdls, bl crown mk, 9½"...........75.00
Vase, lady's portrait entire front, sgn, Victoria, 8¾x5"..........85.00
Vase, lt gr w/pink & yel roses, gold hdls, 9x6"................90.00

Autographs

Philography is defined as the practice of collecting autographs, or literally translated, the 'love of writing.' It is estimated that two million Americans own autographs of famous people, and of these at least twenty thousand are serious collectors. In recent years, autograph collecting has grown both from a standpoint of popularity as well as investment. Examples that only fifteen years ago sold for $5 to $10, now command prices in the hundreds. For example, in 1970 a Clark Gable signature was valued at about $15.00; today it would bring approximately ten times that amount. Knowledgeable collectors watch the market for the opportunity of purchasing a rare item that within a few years can be turned over at a substantial gain. In one instance, a collector purchased a handwritten letter of James 'Wild Bill' Hickok for $2,500.00--within five years he had turned down two different offers of $25,000 for the same letter.

The law of supply and demand is the foremost consideration in placing a value on an autograph. In most cases, age is not relevant. The greater the supply, the lower the value; when demand is great, the price goes up. Since the supply of signatures of persons no longer living is obviously stable, as more people become collectors, their values increase. Some celebrities are known to have signed their autographs thousands of times--others only a few, limiting their availability. With less to go around, the cost to the collector would be higher.

The least desirable type of autograph is the simple signature signed on a card. The most desirable and valuable autograph is generally a handwritten letter, signed in full. In between come signed photos, signed documents, typed letters signed, and various other types of autographs. In a letter, the content is important. Those conveying personal thoughts on or indicating involvement in issues of public interest are more highly valued.

The beginning collector can add to his collection by corresponding with current celebrities. Most will respond to a letter when a self-addressed, stamped envelope is included. Because of their willingness to sign, the value of these autographs rarely exceed a few dollars. There are exceptions: Regan's signature is worth around $50; Carter's about $40; and Nixon's about $35. Ford brings in around $25. Even more valuable--simply because they refuse to sign, or letters requesting signatures never reach them--are Greta Garbo, Idi Amin, Muhammar Khadafy, and the Ayatollah Kohmeni, whose mere signature could easily bring $500 on today's autograph market.

Philography can be a fun and rewarding hobby--often all it takes to start is the address of someone you admire.

In the listings below, photos are assumed black and white unless noted color. When not otherwise indicated, items are assumed to be in excellent condition.

Key:

ALS—handwritten letter	LH—letterhead
AQS—autograph quotation signed	LS—signed letter, typed or written by someone else
DS—document signed	PLH—porcelain letterhead
ins—inscription	sig—signature
ISP—inscribed signed photo	SP—signed photo

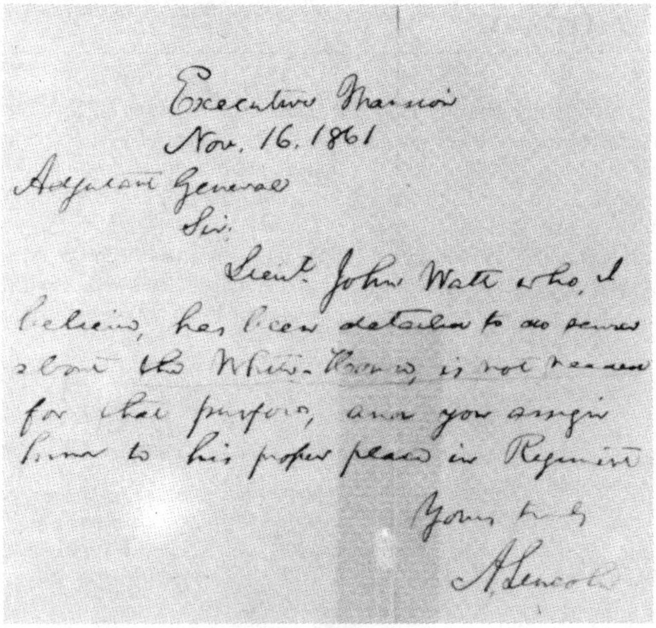
Executive Mansion
Nov. 16, 1861
Adjutant General
Sir:
Lieut. John Watt who, I believe, has been detailed to do service about the White-House, is not needed for that purpose, and you assign him to his proper place in Regiment
Yours truly
A. Lincoln

Autograph letter signed A. Lincoln, Executive Mansion, Nov. 16, 1861, to Adjutant General regarding placement of Lieut. John Watt, cracked and taped, 5½", $1,500.00.

Anslinger, Leopold; sig on postcard picture..................40.00
Armstrong, Louis; ISP, smiling pose w/trumpet, 8x10".........75.00
Armstrong, Neil; ISP, NASA pose in spacesuit, color, 8x10".....45.00
Baldwin, Stanley; sig on 2½x4½" paper, emb seal............15.00
Barnard, Christian; SP, sig above portrait, 5x7"...............20.00
Barnet, Charlie; SP, inscribed to collector, 8x10".............25.00
Barrymore, John; sig on bookplate w/image of lady, 3x6".......75.00
Beecham, Sir Thomas; sig on album leaf, 1946...............15.00
Berlin, Irving; sig on 5x9" blank stationery...................30.00
Bolger, Ray; ISP, Wizard of Oz, sgn by cast, 8x10"...........30.00
Burns, George; ISP, w/wife Gracie, vintage, 8x10", EX.........17.00
Burroughs, Edgar R; LS, PLH, re: Tarzan, March 21, 1924....185.00
Capote, Truman; sig on card, w/unsgn postcard photo..........75.00
Carter, Jimmy; sig on bank check, Georgia, 1960...........650.00
Cole, Nat 'King'; ISP, vintage, 8x10", EX....................75.00
Conlan, John Bertrand; sig on postcard picture...............17.50
Coolidge, Calvin; LS, PLH, March 15, 1930.................165.00
Coolidge, Calvin; sig on bank check, Massachusetts, 1910......150.00
Corcoran, Corky; SP, holding saxophone, 5x7"...............20.00
Cosell, Howard; sig on Brazilian sports cover, 1958............10.00
Crabbe, Buster; ISP, stands in pool, color, 8x10", EX..........35.00
Crawford, Joan; ALS, PLH, 1970..........................65.00
Crawford, Joan; ISP, vintage..............................35.00
Daltrey, Roger; (singer of The Who), SP, 8x10"..............27.50
Dawes, Charles G; sig on stock certificate, 1915, 8x10"........40.00
Dayan, Moshe; sig on title page, Story of My Life...........100.00
Dewey, Thomas E; LS, PLH, re: political speech, 1960.........20.00
Di Maggio, Joe; SP, early shot swinging in game, 8x10", EX....15.00
Dickinson, Jacob M; LS, 1909, 5x7"........................18.50
Dirks, Rudolf; sig on orig ink sketch, April, 1957............57.50
Dorsey, Tommy; ISP.....................................20.00
Douglas, Lloyd C; sig on flyleaf of White Banners, 1936........27.50
Eckstine, Billy; SP, inscribed to collector, 8x10"..............20.00
Edwina, sig on orig ink sketch, signed 'Tippie,' 1947..........20.00
Eisenhower, Dwight D; sig, paper, 2x4", received in person.....60.00
Eisenhower, Mamie Doud; lg blk ink sig on 3x5" card, M......25.00
Falkenhausen, Baron Ludwig; ALS, correspondence card, 1916..20.00
Field, Eugene; ALS, Chicago Daily News, 1892, 5x7"..........75.00

Fields, Jackie; ALS, 2 pgs, 1942, 5x7″....................17.50
Ford, Betty; ISP, March 11, 1980, 8x10″, EX....................25.00
Ford, Gerald R; SP, smiling pose sitting at desk....................115.00
Foreman, Grant; ALS, 1 pg, 1927, 8x10″....................16.00
Gable, Clark; LS, PLH, ca 1939, 5x7″....................125.00
Garner, John; sig on 8x10″ page, 1936....................30.00
Garson, Greer; ISP, vintage, 8x10″....................10.00
Gerry, Ellridge Thomas; LS, LH, 1 pg, 8x10″, 1885....................17.50
Gish, Lillian; ISP, reproduction of film scene, 8x10″....................20.00
Glenn, John; SP, as astronaut....................25.00
Goodman, Benny; sig on first day cover, Los Angeles, 1944....................20.00
Gottfried, Banfield; SP, in Naval uniform, 4½x7″....................50.00
Grable, Betty; ISP, WWII pin-up type, mounted, 8x10″....................55.00
Grange, Red; sgn, Football Hall of Fame, w/uniform, 8x10″....................25.00
Guest, Edgar A; sig on flyleaf, book, A Heap O' Livin'....................35.00
Guiterman, Arthur; SP, sig on back....................16.00
Harding, Florence K; ADS, personal check....................65.00
Holmes, Larry; SP, in boxing pose, 8x10″....................27.50
Howard, Moe; (The Three Stooges), sig on bank check....................20.00
Hughes, Charles Evans; LH, October, 1907, 5x7″....................25.00
Humphrey, Hubert; sig & ins on book, Education of...Man....................65.00
Irwin, James; ISP, stands on moon saluting flag, 8x10″, EX....................12.00
Jacobs, Helen Hull; (tennis star), sig on 6-line note....................16.00
Johnson, Lady Bird; PLH, December, 1978, 5x7″....................20.00
Jolson, Al; ins on theater program, 1932....................75.00
Kennedy, John F; sig, album page, 1953....................250.00
Kennedy, Robert F; AQS, speaker, Cleveland Club's rostrum....................85.00
Ketcham, Hank; sketch sgn Dennis the Mennace, 1953....................35.00
Leigh, Janet; SP, 8x10″....................5.00
Lodge, Henry C; sig in book, Pilgrims of Plymouth, 1921....................90.00
MacArthur, Douglas; sig on first day cover US Army, 1945....................125.00
Manson, Charles; ISP, sig on both sides, ins on bk, 4x5″....................50.00
Mantle, Mickey; SP, shot of dugout, color, 8x10″, EX....................15.00
Marx, Chico; sig in pencil....................30.00
McFarland, George 'Spanky'; ISP, 1958, 5x6″, EX....................20.00
Moses, Grandma; AQS, grandma on album leaf, January 1947....................100.00
Nagel, Charles; sig on card....................15.00
Namath, Joe; ISP, in football uniform, color, 8x10″, EX....................15.00
Natwick, Mildred; SP, Barefoot in the Park scene, 8x10″....................22.50
Nimoy, Leonard; ISP, Dr Spock, 8x10″, EX....................15.00
Nixon, Richard; sig & ins in book, Six Crises, 1962, EX....................75.00
Pavarotti, Luciano; SP, color, 8x10″, EX....................15.00
Power, Tyrone; sig on paper, early form, 1936, 5x7″....................75.00
Presley, Elvis; ISP, Elvis holds lady, 1955, 2½x3½″....................350.00
Queen Victoria, full sig....................70.00
Ray, James E; LS, 1 pg, 1979, 8x10″....................50.00
Reagan, Ronald; LS, PLH, re: campaign plan, February, 1970....................100.00
Rockwell, Norman; LS, PLH, w/sgn Christmas card, 1976....................65.00
Rogers, Ginger; ISP, vintage, 8x10″....................12.00
Rogers, Roy; sig on card....................15.00
Roosevelt, Theodore; LS, LH, cb mount, 1916, 8x10″....................125.00
Rubinstein, Arthur; album leaf inscribed to collector....................18.50
Ruby, Jack; DS, loan agreement for $2500, 1955, 4x7″....................165.00
Russell, Lillian; sig on card....................35.00
Russell, Rosalind; sig on bank check, Beverly Hills, 1947....................20.00
Salk, Jonas; sig on reprint of article from 1977 Science....................15.00
Sandburg, Carl; SP, profile view, 5x6″....................90.00
Sinclair, Upton; ALS, postcard, September, 1902....................20.00
Snead, Sam; ISP, postcard, vintage, EX....................7.00
Sousa, John Philip; PLH, 1929, 5x7″....................65.00
Spillane, Mickey; ISP, as young man, 8x10″....................25.00
Spinner, Frances E; sig on engraved check, 1849....................30.00
Stevenson, Adlai E; sig on flyleaf, book, What I Think....................55.00
Swanson, Gloria; SP, vintage, 8x10″....................20.00
Taft, William H; LS, White House LH, 1910, 5x7″....................225.00
Taft, William H; sig, bank check, December 20, 1920....................275.00
Temple, Shirley; ISP, age 12, unpublished sepia snapshot....................45.00
Tracy, Spencer; sig on 3x3″ paper, ca 1939....................75.00
Truman, Harry S; SP, 11x14″....................275.00
Tucker, Sophie; sig & ins in book, Some of These Days....................35.00
Updike, John; sig & ins on copy of typed poem Cosmic Gall....................12.00
Van Brocklin, Norm; SP, football quarterback, 8x10″....................22.50
Van Cleef, Lee; SP, as cowboy w/revolver in hand, 8x10″....................6.00
Wallace, George; ALS, PLH, w/sgn envelope, 1979, 8x10″....................25.00
Washington, Booker T; LS, LH, 1911, 8x10″....................65.00
Washington, George; signed ship's passport, July 6, 1795....................3,630.00
Whitney, Eli; sig cut from letter....................125.00
Wilder, Thornton N; sig on card....................15.00
Wilkie, Wendell L; sig, book, One World, 1944....................85.00
Williams, Esther; ISP, full length, in swimsuit, 8x10″, EX....................10.00
Wilson, Henry; sig as Vice President....................15.00
Wilson, Woodrow; ISP, 9x12″ portrait w/6x9″ image....................350.00
Wray, Fay; SP of theatre w/King Kong poster, 1930's, sepia....................40.00

Automobilia

While some automobilia buffs are primarily concerned with restoring vintage cars, other concentrate on only one area of collecting. For instance, hood ornaments were often quite spectacular. Made of chrome or nickel plate on brass or bronze, they were designed to represent the 'winged maiden' Victory, flying bats, sleek greyhounds, soaring eagles and a host of other creatures. Today they bring prices in the $75 to $200 range. R. Lalique glass ornaments go much higher!

Horns, radios, clocks, gear shift knobs and key chains with company emblems are other areas of interest. Generally, items pertaining to the classics of the thirties are most in demand. Paper advertising material, manuals and catalogues in excellent condition are also collectible.

License plate collectors search for the early porcelain-on-cast-iron examples. First year plates--e.g., Massachusetts, 1903; Wisconsin, 1905; Indiana, 1913--are especially valuable. The last of the states to issue regulation plates were South Carolina and Texas in 1917, and Florida in 1918. While many northeastern states had registered hundreds of thousands of vehicles by the 1920s making these plates relatively common, those from the southern and western states of that period are considered rare. Naturally, condition is important--a pair in mint condition might sell for as much as $100 to $125, while a pair with the porcelain in poor condition may sometimes be had for as little as $25 to $30.

When no condition is indicated, the items listed below are assumed to be in excellent condition.

Almanac, Mobil Flying Red Horse, 1943....................10.00
Ash tray, Chrysler Corp, World's Fair, copper, 1933....................12.50
Ash tray, Ford plant tour, 1950....................20.00
Ash tray, Goodrich rubber tire, 36x6″ tire....................30.00
Ash tray, Indianapolis Speedway, Clabber Girl Special....................45.00
Badge, chauffeur; New Hampshire, 1921....................12.50
Badge, employee; Crosley Corporation, Richmond plant....................20.00
Badge, employee; Packard....................50.00
Badge, employee; REO Motor Works....................20.00
Badge, inspector; Goodyear G-3....................15.00
Book, Crash Club, by Felsen, paperback....................10.00
Book, facts; Oldsmobile, 1953....................25.00
Book, instruction; Dodge Brothers Eight, 1930....................40.00
Book, instruction; Hercules gas engine, w/repair list....................17.50
Book, instruction; Peerles Model 67....................35.00
Book, Motorcycle Chums in the Adirondacs, hardbound....................10.00
Book, Pontiac, shop manual, 1959....................15.00

Bottle opener, Chevrolet, Sweet, Smooth & Sassy, 1957........15.00
Brake extension, Moto-Lever style, Model A..................65.00
Catalog, Overland Model 4 & 75B, ea........................30.00
Catalog, Plymouth, 1949, sm...............................4.00
China, Ford script, lg plate, pictures Rotunda building.........45.00
Choke holder, Eclipse Model T accessory.....................5.00
Clock, alarm; Auto-Gard, pendulum style, for early auto........20.00
Clock-mirror, New Haven, in orig box......................100.00
Coin, Chrysler, A Century of Progress in a Decade, 1934.......20.00
Coin, Ford, San Diego Expo, 1935..........................45.00
Coin, Ford, 1934, NM....................................25.00
Coin, Oldsmobile Futuramic 88, brass.......................10.00
Coin holder/scraper/keychain, Buick V8 & Riviera..............8.00
Dice, Ford script, pr......................................5.00
Fender skirt medallion, Oldsmobile, 1947-1948................35.00
Gaskets, head & block; Whizzer, pr.........................10.00
Gear & axle, Chevrolet...................................20.00
Gearshift knob, glass, no insert, bl & wht swirl...............15.00
Gearshift knob, pool ball hdl, #10..........................10.00
Grill cover, for front, w/operating slats, MIB..................50.00

Booklet, *Ford Times*, Nov. 1915, 9″ x 6″, $38.00.

Heater, electric, instant manifold, heats intake gas.............15.00
Hood ornament, Armstrong-Siddeley, Sphinx, wood base, '30s...65.00
Hood ornament, Chevy, 1950s.............................20.00
Hood ornament, eagle, soaring, wood base, 1930s.............75.00
Hood ornament, goddess, w/gr insert........................25.00
Hood ornament, jaguar, leaping, wood base, 1930s............85.00
Hood ornament, jockey on horse, wood base, 1930s...........75.00
Hood ornament, Lincoln, leaping Greyhound, 1930s...........85.00
Hood ornament, Packard, Goddess of Speed, 1930s...........75.00
Hood ornament, Pontiac, 1950s...........................20.00
Hood ornament, Spirit of Triumph, winged male w/wheel.......75.00
Hood ornament, Vauxhall Griffin, 1915......................85.00
Horn button, Ford, standard, 1942.........................40.00
Ink blotter, Smooth as a '47 Ford..........................3.50
Innertube tire repair kit, w/vise & patches....................9.00
Key, deck lid; Ford, 1927................................15.00
Keychain, Buick Wildcat...................................6.50
Keychain, Texaco Star & Scotty dog.........................5.00
Keys, Cadillac logo, uncut, pr............................10.00
License plate, Alabama, Heart of Dixie, farm, 1973.............3.00
License plate, Arkansas, Land of Opportunity, 1961............9.00
License plate, Florida, Sunshine State, 1975-1979, EX..........3.00
License plate, Idaho, Famous Potatoes, 1962, EX..............6.00
License plate, Missouri, BF Goodrich, miniature, 1939.........40.00
License plate, motorcycle; Wyoming, in wrapper, 1974..........7.50
License plate, White Motor Co, brass, patent.................20.00
License plate attachment, Am flag, God Bless America.........25.00
License plate attachment, D-X diamond shaped, M............20.00
License plate attachment, Remember Pearl Harbor............40.00
License plate attachment, UMWA, CIO......................20.00
Lighter, cigarette; Prompto Cordless.......................10.00
Magazine, Auto Show issue of Milwaukee Journal, 1951.........6.00
Magazine, Ford service, February & September 1928, ea.......10.00
Matchbook, Gilmore Red Lion.............................10.00
Mirror, Phillips 66 Flite Fuel, 1955........................15.00
Money clip, Pontiac......................................25.00
Motometer, Sunbeam arrow style...........................45.00
Name plate, Fairbanks-Morse, Z-engine, brass..................9.50
Name plate, Kaiser Supercharger..........................15.00
Oil can, Texaco, w/screw top, 1-qt.........................15.00
Paperweight, Henry Ford, centennial, brass..................65.00
Paperweight, Illinois Central, brass, 1951...................25.00
Paperweight, Studebaker, brass/revolves, 100th anniversary......95.00
Pay envelopes, Ford script, used last in 1949..................2.50
Pencil, International Harvester, mechanical..................15.00
Pencil clip, Sterling Oil....................................5.00
Pin, Chevrolet, the Leading Six for '46......................10.00
Pin, Chevrolet, Watch the Leader, 1933.....................12.50
Pin, Chrysler, 10k gold, 30-year service.....................30.00
Pin, Ford, Punt, Pass & Kick...............................5.00
Pin, Ford, We Listen Better.................................6.00
Pin, Lone Scout, brass...................................25.00
Pin, Silvertown Safety League.............................15.00
Pitcher, Cadillac, crystal w/etched emblem on front............25.00
Pliers, Ford, script......................................12.00
Postcard, Buick, color, 1941, set of 3......................10.00
Postcard, Mustang convertible, color, 1967....................2.50
Radio, GM, transportable.................................100.00
Radio microphone, Vogue, in orig box......................10.00
Ruler, Pontiac Rules the Low priced Field for 1938...........15.00
Running lights, kero burner, pr............................50.00
Screwdriver, Marathon Oil, metal..........................15.00
Sign, Ford Tractor, Ferguson..............................20.00
Slides, Plymouth/Chevrolet/Dodge, 1920-30s, set of 20........125.00
Spark plug, AC K-9, set of 6..............................75.00
Spark plug, Hercules Junior...............................18.00
Spark plug, Red Head primer cup..........................55.00
Spoon, Ford script...8.00
Steering control, Ford...................................25.00
Stickpin, Case eagle & globe, brass........................17.50
Stock certificate, Kaiser-Frazer Corporation.................10.00
Switch & ammeter, Ford, 1918-1925, rfn....................50.00
Taillight, Hudson Essex, Type A...........................25.00
Thimble, Buick..3.50
Tie clip, Century of Progress................................6.00
Tie tack, Drott shovel.....................................8.00
Timer, Ford script, CI, w/roller...........................25.00
Timer, Model T, crystal, glass front, visible spark............40.00
Tin box, Dupont blasting caps............................15.00
Tire gauge, Buick, script Schrader.........................40.00
Tire gauge, Moco bicycle dial type.........................25.00
Token, Chrysler Silver Anniversary, 1949....................25.00
Tool check, early Model T era, Des Moines plant, brass........25.00
Toothbrush holder, 2 children w/goggles driving car, 1930s.....38.00

Toy car, Buick, battery operated, tin, ca 1954 .... 25.00
Trouble light, Premier Magnetic 10.00
Uniform crest, Fire Protection, Chrysler 10.00
Watch fob, American Gopher shovel 20.00
Watch fob, Early Touring Car 35.00
Watch fob, Union Central Life of Cincinnati 15.00
Wrench, script; Maytag 8.00

Autumn Leaf

In 1933, the Hall China Company designed a line of dinnerware for the Jewel Tea Company who offered it to their customers as premiums. Although you may hear the ware referred to as 'Jewel Tea,' it was officially named 'Autumn Leaf' in the 1940s. In addition to the dinnerware, frosted Libbey glass tumblers, stemware, and a tilt jug with the orange and gold bittersweet pod were available over the years, as were tablecloths, plastic covers for bowls and mixers, and metal items such as cake safes, hot pads, coasters, waste baskets, and canisters. Even shelf paper and playing cards were made to coordinate. In 1958, the International Silver Company designed silverplated flatware in a pattern they called 'Autumn.' These accessory lines are prized by collectors today. Recent discoveries include a one-pound bud-ray lid butter dish, and a 'morning' tea set made by Hall; a pair of unlisted candlesticks attributed to Hall; and a Libbey frosted tumbler in a 'pilsner' style. Collectors believe the tea set and the tumbler to be sample items that were never distributed.

Hall discontinued the Autumn Leaf line in 1978. At that time the date was added to the backstamp to mark ware still in stock in the Jewel warehouse.

When no condition is indicated, the items listed below are assumed to be in mint condition.

Bake dish, Swirl, 3-pt, 8″ top dia 12.00
Baker, oval, ind 80.00
Bean pot, 1-hdl 200.00
Bean pot, 2¼-qt, 2-hdl 85.00
Blanket, twin size 50.00
Bowl, cereal; 6″ 8.00
Bowl, coupe soup 10.00
Bowl, cream soup; 2-hdl 20.00
Bowl, fruit; 5½″ 4.00
Bowl, mixing; set of 3: 6¼″, 7½″, 9″ 35.00
Bowl, Royal Glas-Bake, set of 4 .... 40.00
Bowl, salad; 3½-pt 15.00
Bowl, stackette; set of 3: 18-oz, 24-oz, 34-oz, w/lid 65.00
Bowl, vegetable; divided, 10½″ 55.00
Bowl, vegetable; oval, 10″, w/lid 35.00
Bowl, vegetable; oval, 10½″ 12.00
Bowl, vegetable; 9″ 55.00
Bowl cover set, plastic, 8-pc: 7 assorted covers in pouch 70.00
Bread box, metal 100.00
Bud vase, crimped edge 150.00
Butter dish, 1-lb 150.00
Butter dish, ¼-lb 135.00
Butter dish, ¼-lb, Square Top 350.00
Butter dish, ¼-lb, Wings 350.00
Cake plate, 9½″ 10.00
Cake safe, metal, motif on top & sides, 5″ 25.00
Cake safe, metal, side decor only, 4½x10½″ 22.00
Canister, metal, round, w/coppertone lid, set of 4 .... 125.00
Canister, metal, round, w/ivory plastic lid 10.00
Canister, metal, round, 6″, w/matching lid 15.00
Canister, metal, round, 7″, w/matching lid 25.00
Canister, metal, round, 8¼″, w/matching lid 35.00
Canister, metal, square, set of 4: 8½″ & 4½″ 100.00

Candy dish, gold pedestal and base, 4¾″, $250.00.

Casserole, Royal Glas-Bake, deep, w/clear glass lid 25.00
Casserole, Royal Glas-Bake, shallow, w/clear glass lid 20.00
Casserole/souffle, 10-oz 10.00
Casserole/souffle, 2-pt 55.00
Cleanser can, metal, square, 6″ 150.00
Clock, original works 350.00
Coaster, metal, 3⅛″ 5.00
Coffee carafe-percolator, Douglas, w/warmer base 85.00
Coffee dispenser/canister, metal, wall-type, 10½x19″ dia 125.00
Coffee maker, 5-cup, all china, w/china insert 195.00
Coffee maker, 9-cup, 8″, w/metal dripper 35.00
Coffee percolator, electric, all china 225.00
Cookie jar, Big Ear 85.00
Cookie jar, Tootsie 85.00
Creamer, New Style 8.00
Creamer, Old Style, 4¼″ 12.00
Cup & saucer 8.00
Cup & saucer, St Denis 22.00
Custard cup 4.00
Fruit cake tin, metal 10.00
Golden Ray base, to be used w/candy dish or cake plate, pr 50.00
Granulator, metal, no decal 35.00
Gravy boat 15.00
Hot pad, metal, red or gr felt-like backing, oval, 10¾″ 12.00
Hurricane lamp 95.00
Kitchen utility chair, metal 350.00
Marmalade jar, 3-pc 40.00
Mixer cover, Mary Dunbar, plastic 25.00
Mug, beverage 55.00
Mug, Irish coffee 85.00
Mustard jar, 3½″ 40.00
Napkin, ecru muslin 15.00
Pickle dish, oval, 9″ 15.00
Picnic thermos, metal 200.00
Pie baker, 9½″ 18.00
Pitcher, beverage jug; 5½-pt 18.00
Pitcher, utility; 2½-pt, 6″ 15.00
Place mat, paper, scalloped 15.00
Plate, 10″ 10.00
Plate, 6″ 4.00
Plate, 7″ 4.00
Plate, 8″ 8.00
Plate, 9″ 7.00

Platter, 11½" 15.00
Platter, 13½" 15.00
Playing cards, regular or Pinochle 100.00
Range set, shakers & covered drippings jar 35.00
Sauce dish, serving; Douglas, bakelite hdl 65.00
Shakers, Casper, pr 16.00
Shakers, range, hdl, pr 22.00
Sifter, metal 125.00
Sugar bowl, New Style 12.00
Sugar bowl, Old Style, 3½" 18.00
Tablecloth, cotton sailcloth w/gold stripe, 54x54" 55.00
Tablecloth, cotton sailcloth w/gold stripe, 54x72" 65.00
Tablecloth, ecru muslin, 56x81" 85.00
Teakettle, metal 55.00
Teapot, Aladdin 32.00
Teapot, long spout, 7" 45.00
Teapot, Newport 100.00
Toaster cover, plastic, fits 2-slice toaster 25.00
Towel, dish; pattern & clock motif 35.00
Towel, tea; cotton, 16x33" 30.00
Trash can, metal, red 65.00
Tray, glass, wood hdl, 19½x11¼" 85.00
Tray, metal, oval 55.00
Tray, red w/allover red & yel design, red border 65.00
Tray, tidbid; 2-tier 45.00
Tray, tidbit; 3-tier 42.00
Tumbler 13.50
Tumbler, frosted, 14-oz, 5½" 11.00
Tumbler, frosted, 9-oz, 3¾" 18.00
Tumbler, gold frost etched, 10-oz, flat 30.00
Tumbler, gold frost etched, 10-oz, ftd 45.00
Tumbler, gold frost etched, 15-oz, flat 45.00
Tumbler, gold frost etched, 6½-oz, ftd 45.00
Warmer base, oval 100.00
Warmer base, round 90.00

Aviation

Aviation buffs are interested in any phase of flying--from early developments with gliders, balloons, airships and flying machines, to more modern innovations. Books, catalogues, photos, patents, lithographs, ad cards, and posters are among the paper ephemera they treasure, alongside models of unlikely flying contraptions, propellers and rudders, insignia and equipment from WW I and II, and memorabilia from the flights of the Wright Brothers, Lindbergh, Earhart and the Zepplins.

Altimeter, Navy, Kolsman, EX 55.00
Ash tray, Air France, w/model of plane, 8x12" 40.00
Ash tray, airplane on side, silver metal, 'Airtray,' 7" 27.00
Ash tray, 2 man bi-plane in flight, etched/oval/brass, 8" 45.00
Badge, hat; WWII CAA, Indian head, pin-bk, sterling, EX 50.00
Badge, Hindenburg Landing Crew, Lakehurst, metal, 1¾" 400.00
Badge, WWII AAF, merit for 500 hours, pin-bk, sterling, EX 20.00
Book, 30 Seconds over Tokyo, 1st WWII edition, EX 12.00
Boots, flying, felt lined/zipper, type A-9, VG 25.00
Box, wood, 1st Aeroplane Flight, Dec 17/1903, Kitty Hawk 85.00
Bracelet, WWII AAF, bombardier, hallmk, sterling, 3", VG 20.00
Cap, officer's overseas, WWII AAF, Lt Col insignia 25.00
Clock, type A-13A, 8-day, w/elapsed timer, EX 50.00
Compass, navigation; WWII AAF, used in B-17, in box, 5" 25.00
Compass, wrist; WWII Aviator, Japanese, w/leather strap 50.00
Encyclopedia, Aircraft Engines & Specifications, 547 pg 40.00
Escape & evasion kit, USAF pilot, Viet Nam, complete 20.00
Flight surgeon wings, WWII, hallmk/pin-bk, gold plated 30.00
Flying pants, WWII, type E-1, OD wool blanket lined 20.00
Flying suit, USAF, Nomex, VG 25.00
Flying suit, USAF, type K-2B, Viet Nam, VG 20.00
Goggles, WWII, Skyway, similar to 6530s, 1930s, VG 60.00
Guide, officer's, orig, customs/procedures, 540 pg, 1943 .....16.00
Handbook, USAF, model T-28A aircraft, complete, 1952, EX 35.00
Hat, Spirit of St Louis/Lindbergh, 1930s 20.00
Helmet, WWII RAF, type C, leather, w/earphones 75.00
Insect repellent, for vest, WWII AAF, type C-1, orig 5.00
Jacket, WWII, Sgt Ike, gunner's wings/AF patch 35.00
Lamp, cockpit; WWII AAF, type B-7, bulb & cord, mk AAF, EX 20.00
Manual, American Air Navigator training, 1944, VG 20.00
Manual, packing parachutes, illustrated, Irving Air Chute 20.00
Manual, Pilot Training for B-26, illustrated, 140 pg, EX 50.00
Microphone, WWII AAF, type T-17, lollipop type, complete 20.00
Mittens, WWII gunner, fits to elbow, thumb/trigger finger 50.00
Model, AAF, P-39, cardboard, 1:72 scale, blk, M 10.00
Model, bi-plane, hand-carved pine/wire, rudder moves, 39" 210.00
Model, Hindenburg, iron w/orig pnt, 27" 145.00
Model, RAF, Wellington, ID model, cardboard, blk 20.00
Model, Spirit of St Louis, celluloid, 5½x6" 55.00
Model, Spirit of St Louis, Metalcraft 150.00
Model, thimble drone/gas powered, Navy, orig box, 1950s 35.00
Model, WWII, Italian Reggianne 200, rubber, blk 55.00
Parachute, chest pack, USAF, w/packed chute, 1966 .....75.00
Parapad kit, WWII, USN, type M-592, empty, VG 10.00
Pencil box, tin, Spirit of St Louis, Lindbergh & plane 40.00
Pencil sharpener, airplane w/removable nose, metal 30.00
Photo, USAF/USN, aircraft pictures, b/w, 8x10", set of 100 .....100.00
Plate, Lindbergh flight, Limoges, 1927, 8½" 35.00
Plotter, WWII AAF, type MK II, envelope/instructions, mk 5.00
Poster, WWII AAF Aircraft ID, mk AAF, EX, set of 10 .....50.00
Radio, survival, USAF pilot, receiver & transmitter, VG 25.00
Sculpture, Spirit of St Louis, commemorative, 1977 .....85.00
Uniform, aviator's, USN, w/wings, cap w/Navy insignia, wht 35.00
Vest, Mae West, WWII AAF, type B-4, horseshoe style, yel 35.00
Visor, helmet, WWII AAF, type A-1, VG 8.00
Whistle, aviator's, WWII AAF, used on A-2 jackets, w/chain 15.00
Wings, navigator's, WWII AAF, hallmk, pin-bk, orig, 3", EX 10.00

Avon

The California Perfume Company, the parent of the Avon Co., was founded in 1886. Although an 'Avon' line was introduced by the company in the mid-20s, not until 1939 did it become known as Avon Products, Inc. Collectible Avon items include not only figural bottles, containers and jars, but jewelry, awards, product samples, magazine ads, and catalogues as well.

See also California Perfume Company. When no condition is indicated, the items listed below are assumed to be in mint condition.

Avon Facial Tissue, 1937-44, turq & wht box, M 20.00
Award, Albee, 1978, porcelain, MIB 125.00
Award, Circle of Excellence Ring, 1971 .....275.00
Award, Currier & Ives Tea Set, 1977-78 .....35.00
Award, Door Knocker Earrings, 1966 .....32.50
Award, Door Knocker Tie Tac, 1970s 60.00
Award, Fashion History Glasses 30.00
Award, Fostoria Coin Plate, MIB 12.00
Award, Heart Stick Pin, 1978, MIB 30.00
Award, President's Celebration Clock, 1976 .....12.00
Award, President's Trophy, 1959-60 .....125.00
Award, Retirement Pin, 1967, CMV 50.00

Award, set: Ultra Crystal Event Glasses, 1981 . . . . .50.00
Award, Team Achievement, 1977, MIB 20.00
Award, Top 10 Division Trophy, 1977 . . . . .40.00
Award, Victory Pin, 1942 . . . . .70.00
Award, 25-Year Service Pin, 1970 . . . . .150.00
Award, 4A Double Stick Pin, 1960-70, MIB 75.00
Bath Blossoms, 1969, sponge & soap 8.00
Bath Salts, 1936, glass jars, 9-oz 30.00
Beauty Dust Demo, 1966-68, boxed 11.00
Beauty Mark Set, 1948 . . . . .40.00
Betsy Ross Decanter, 1976, 4-oz 5.00
Bird of Paradise Bath Brush & Soap, 1970-71 . . . . .8.00
Bird of Paradise Cologne Decanter, 1970-72, 5-oz, 8", MIB 6.00
Candlestick cologne, 1966, 3-oz, MIB 15.00
Cape Cod 1876 Hostess Bell, 6½", MIB .10.00
Checker Cab 1926 Decanter, yel, 5-oz 6.00
Christmas Gift Plate, no box 12.00
Christmas plate, Bringing Home the Tree, 1976, 9", MIB 20.00
Christmas plate, Christmas on the Farm, 1973-75, MIB 80.00
Christmas plate, Skaters on the Pond, 1976-80, MIB 20.00
Cologne Mist, 1971-75, 2-oz 1.00
Cotillion Beauty Dust, 1959-61 . . . . .6.00
Cotillion Talc, 1950-53, MIB 15.00
Country Kitchen Decanter, 1973-75, 6-oz, MIB 5.00
Country Style Coffee Pot Decanter, 1975-76, 10-oz, MIB 5.00
Cream Hair Lotion, 1948-49, 4-oz 20.00
Cream Sachet Jars, 1973-75, .66-oz 1.25
Decorator Soaps (3), 1969, MIB 10.00
Delivery Bag, 1960s, bl & silver, 4A emblem 6.00
Demo bag, 1937, ostrich leather 35.00
Eiffel Tower Cologne, 1970, no box, 3-oz, 9" 5.00
Fluff Puff w/Beauty Dust, 1967 . . . . .20.00
Fostoria Egg Soap Dish w/soap, 1977 . . . . .12.00
Freddie the Frog, 1969-70 . . . . .6.00
Futura Decanter, 1969, silver, 5-oz, 7½", MIB 12.50
Gems in Crystal Set, 1957, MIB 75.00
Golden Thimble, 1972-74, 2-oz, MIB 3.00
Hunter's Stein, 1972, nickle plated, 8-oz, MIB 12.00
Island Lime After Shave, 1969-73, 6-oz, MIB 2.00
Keepsake Cream Sachet, 1971-73, 6½", MIB 5.00
Kwick Foaming Shave Cream, 1955-57, 10-oz 8.00
Liberty Bell, 1976, bronze, 5-oz 4.00
Lily-of-the-Valley Toilet Water, 2-oz, MIB 45.00
Man's World, 1969-70, plastic stand holds globe, 6-oz 6.00
Mascara Compact, 1936-41, turq & gold, MIB 15.00
Men's Travel Kit, 1933-36, blk leather case 100.00
Mount Vernon Sauce Pitcher w/Candle, 1977-79, 5½", MIB 12.00
Oland Gift Set, 1970, soap, talc, 6-oz cologne 15.00
Olympic Set, 1940-46, maroon & ivory box 95.00
On the Avenue Decanter, 1978-79 . . . . .7.00
Pampered Piglet Ceramic Pomander, 1978-79, MIB 8.00
Past & Present Brush & Comb Set, 1972-73, MIB 6.00
Pepperbox Pistol 1850 Decanter, 1976-77, 3-oz, MIB 8.00
Perfection Baking Powder, 1931-41, 1-lb, MIB 30.00
Perfection Furniture Polish, 1941, 12-oz 12.00
Perfume Handkerchief Set, 1933-36 . . . . .85.00
Petti Fleur Cologne, 1969-70, 1-oz, MIB .5.00
Pipe Dream After Shave, dk amber glass, 6-oz 15.00
Queen Elizabeth Cup & Saucer, 1953 . . . . .80.00
Rose Fragrance Jar, 1948-57, 6-oz 32.50
Sheer Mist Face Powder, 1955-57, MIB 5.00
Short Pony Decanter, gr glass, gold cap, 4-oz, MIB 4.00
Slipper Soap & Perfume, 1970-71, ⅛-oz, MIB 9.00
Somewhere Perfume, 1961-63, no box, 1-oz 50.00
Spongaroo Soap & Sponge, 1966-67, 15x5¾", MIB 12.00
Stage Coach Decanter, 1970-77, 5-oz, MIB 5.00
Two Turtledoves Pompander, 1979-80, MIB 9.00
Valet Set, 1949-50 . . . . .40.00
Victorian Manor Cologne Decanter, 1972-73, 5-oz, MIB 7.00
White Milk Glass Candle, 1964-66, MIB .12.00

Baccarat

The Baccarat Glass company was founded in 1765 near Luneville, France, and continues to this day to produce quality crystal tableware, vases, perfume bottles, and figurines. The firm became famous for the high quality millefiori and caned paperweights produced there from 1845 until about 1860. Examples of these range from $300 to as much as a several thousand. Since 1953, they have resumed the production of paperweights on a limited edition basis. These are listed later, in the Paperweight section.

When no condition is indicated, the items listed below are assumed to be in mint condition.

Atomizer, green cut to clear, 5¾, $95.00.

Bottle, cologne; gilt classical scene, 7¾" 55.00
Bottle, scent; Guerlain paper label, 4½" 30.00
Bottle, scent; rose teinte, swirl, 8x3" 75.00
Bowl, rose teinte, swirl, sgn, 2¼x4½" 48.00
Candelabra, ormolu mts, floral branches, 16", pr 1,800.00
Celery, rose & amber swirl, 3½x9½" 49.00
Centerpiece epergne, rose teinte, swirl, scalloped, lg 425.00
Figurine, pelican, sgn, 6½" 125.00

Inkwell, cresting wave, gilt-bronze mermaid atop, double well, 15" long, $2,500.00.

Lamp, sapphire bl, emb sunburst, frosted ball shade, 9½″......175.00
Paperweight, sulphide w/Adlai Stephenson w/bl star-cut bk.....110.00
Ring tree, rose tiente, swirl..............................50.00
Tumble-up, sparkling bl, swirl design, 7½″..................165.00

Badges

The breast badge came into general usage in this country about 1840. Since most are not marked and styles have changed very little to the present day, they are often difficult to date. The most reliable clue is the pin and catch. One of the earliest types, used primarily before the turn of the century, involved a 't-pin' and a 'shell' catch. In a second style, the pin was hinged with a small square of sheet metal, and the clasp was cylindrical. From the late 1800s until about 1940, the pin and clasp were made from one continuous piece of thin metal wire. The same type, with the addition of a flat back plate, was used a little later. There are exceptions to these findings, and other types of clasps were also used. Hallmarks and inscriptions may also help pinpoint an approximate age.

Badges have been made from a variety of materials, usually brass or nickel silver, but even solid silver and gold were used on special order. They are found in many basic shapes and variations--stars with five to seven points, shields, discs, ovals, and octagonals being most often encountered.

Of prime importance to collectors, however, is that the title and/or location appear on the badge. Those with designations of positions no longer existing (City Constable, for example) and names of early western states and towns are most valuable.

When no condition is indicated, the items listed below are assumed to be in mint condition.

Air Police, Dept of Air Force, w/eagle.......................35.00
Armed Forces Police, w/eagle & US flag.....................25.00
Constable, Greene Co, IA, eagle top, silver color, lg..........30.00
Constable, NY, eagle-top shield, no mk, pre-1930............30.00
Constable, Village of Dayton, MN, no mk, 1940s, med sz.......25.00
Constabulary, West Yorkshire, crown top, silver color, lg.......15.00
Deputy Sheriff, Alachua Co, FL, 5-point star, gold color.......40.00
Deputy Sheriff, Brazoria Co, TX, 6-point star, gold color......45.00
Deputy Sheriff, Dallas Co, TX, early pin....................95.00
Deputy Sheriff, Dallas Co, TX, Patrolman, 5-point star.........45.00
Deputy Sheriff, Ellis Co, TX, wallet size, NM................35.00
Deputy Sheriff, Harris Co, TX, 5-point star..................35.00
Deputy Sheriff, NY, shield, pre-1930.......................30.00
Deputy Sheriff, Spokane Co, WA, ornate, 7-point star, lg.......35.00
Deputy Sheriff, Starr Co, TX, 5-point star, wallet size.........35.00
Deputy Sheriff, 6-point star, screw back, brass, lg.............5.00
Detective, Captain, Iowa, gold shield, good wear..............30.00
Detective, Kansas City, MO, shield, silver color...............50.00
Fire Dept, Engine Co, MN, sterling, eagle top, med, 1900......45.00
Highway Patrol Patrolman, TX, cap badge...................10.00
Junior Deputy Sheriff, McLennan Co, TX, German silver........10.00
Justice of Peace, PA, eagle-top shield, no mk, 1940s, sm.......25.00
Lieutenant, CA state seal, sterling, lg eagle..................55.00
Lieutenant, Palestine, TX, nickel w/gold-color plate............50.00
Marshal, Brownsville, TX, circle shaped, gold color, rare........85.00
Patrol Officer, PA, eagle-top shield, no mk, 1940s, med........25.00
Patrolman, PA, eagle top, no mk, 1940s, lg...................25.00
Police, Arkansas Pass, TX, German silver, cap badge, lg........10.00
Police, Ballinger, TX, plated brass shield, early..............70.00
Police, City; San Marcos, TX, German silver, old..............55.00
Police, Laredo, TX, bl/gr/lt bl/wht enamel center shield.........55.00
Police, Palacios, TX, gold plated cap badge..................50.00
Police, RI, eagle-top shield, no mk, 1940s, lg.................25.00
Police, San Antonio, TX, cap badge........................10.00
Police, Sergeant, Gouchester, TX, gold color, w/bl enamel......30.00
Police, Sergeant, MN, eagle-top shield, Hi-Glo, '40s, lg.........25.00
Special Deputy, Saginaw Co, MI, eagle-top shield..............20.00
Special Deputy Sheriff, Douglas Co, NB.....................45.00

Baltimore & Ohio Railroad Railway Police, nickel-finished shield shape, no mark, $95.00.

Banks

Still banks were manufactured from as early as 1800, and were intended to inspire thriftiness through amusing character themes, charming animal figures, and areas of special interests. They were made in virtually every kind of material existant: wood, glass, ceramics, and metal. Among the most prominent manufactures were J. & E. Stevens Company of Cromwell, Connecticut, and A.C. Williams Company of Revanna, Ohio. Stevens was the first company to design and market a mechanical bank in 1890. During the years of the Civil War, people hoarded coins to the extent that silver became scarce. The paper money issued to alleviate this situation was regarded with distrust, and the hoarding continued. This created a natural market for the new mechanical banks, and their complex, often amusing actions made saving money fun. It is estimated that more than 250 designs were patented, some as late as 1935. Others who manufactured mechanical banks were Shephard Hardware of Buffalo, New York; Kilgore Manufacturing Company of Westville, Ohio; Kyser and Rex of Philadelphia, Pennsylvania; and the Mechanical Novelty Works of New Britain, Connecticut. Each attempted to outdo the other in producing the more complex mechanism. Sensitive balances, rotating wheels, springs, and levers interacted one with another to produce animation of every description.

Popular concepts of the day dictated design. Buildings, such as Victorian domes with gingerbread trim, gave way to early 20th century skyscrapers. Comic strip characters were immortalized in cast iron banks, and political and patriotic themes aptly reflected the state of the Union.

Registering banks were designed to divulge the total amount of the money as it was deposited. Some would accomodate only one denomination; others had separate slots for different sized coins.

Advertising banks have a two-fold interest--both bank collectors and those who like antique advertising find them appealing.

Because many old banks are so valuable, reproductions are common. Some of these restrikes were themselves made over forty years ago, so some study is required to be able to recognize the originals.

Condition is judged by the percentage of the remaining original paint, and whether all parts are present, original, and in working order. Rarity is a factor in evaluating worth, but those with an especially popular design may bring the higher prices. Some of the banks listed here are identified by C for Cranmer, G for Griffeth, and W for Whiting, standard references used by many collectors. When no condition is indicated, the items listed below are assumed to be in excellent condition.

Key: NPCI—nickel-plated cast iron EPCI—electroplated cast iron

Advertising

Amherst Stoves, C-178, buffalo, standing, 5″ ... 125.00
Arcade Stoves, C-464, figural kitchen stove, 3¾″ ... 75.00
Campbell Kids, W-45 ... 150.00
General Electric, W-237, refrigerator figural ... 65.00
Goodyear, C-583, Goodyear Zeppelin, duralumin, 7⅜″ L ... 75.00
Inland Security Co, Kansas City, MO, CI, w/key ... 25.00
Magic Chef Stoves, C-463, figural kitchen stove, 3½″ ... 75.00
Marshall Furnace Co, round figural furnace, CI, 3⅞″ ... 75.00
Red Goose School Shoes, W-215 ... 150.00
Worcester Salt, C-163, elephant sitting on base, pot metal ... 25.00

Two Frogs, C-20, one flips coin in mouth of second, $800.00.

Mechanical

Alligator, C-48, 1960, 9″ L ... 35.00
Always Did 'Spise a Mule, G-125, jockey, CI, 10″, VG ... 850.00
Always Did 'Spise a Mule, G-126, bench, 10¼″, EX ... 750.00
Artillery Bank, C-32, soldier w/cannon aimed at fort ... 300.00
Bad Accident, C-24, mule pulls man in cart/child on ground ... 1,200.00
Bear, C-66, arms & legs around narrow stump ... 550.00
Billie Grin, C-33, bust of bald-headed grinning man ... 300.00
Bird, C-46, on church roof ... 650.00
Bird, mother feeding young, mouths open w/lever, CI, 6x8″ ... 225.00
Boy on Trapeze, pnt CI, VG ... 800.00
Boy Scout Camp, G-24, CI, 9¾″, NM ... 3,575.00
Buffalo, C-97 ... 175.00
Butting Buffalo, C-9, butts Blk man on tree trunk ... 2,000.00
Cannon & Tank, C-104, aluminum ... 250.00
Captain Kidd ... 160.00
Cat & Mouse, pnt CI, trap missing, rpl base, VG ... 550.00
Chief Big Moon, G-48, CI, 10″, G ... 450.00
Chief Big Moon, pnt CI, NM ... 1,000.00
Clock, G-48, 4-coin, Kingsbury ... 70.00
Clown, C-85, sits atop globe, round ftd base ... 650.00
Clown, Chein, tin ... 27.00
Coffin, C-353, tin/plastic/orig box, faulty lock, Yone, EX ... 15.00
Creedmore, C-2, pnt CI, orig pnt, NM ... 500.00
Creedmore, C-2, pnt CI, VG ... 300.00
Dancing Bear, C-42, man w/organ grinder next to building ... 300.00
Darkie in Cabin, G-39 ... 450.00
Darktown Battery, G-68, CI, 10″, EX orig ... 1,320.00
Dog, Bulldog, G-30, CI, 8″, EX ... 750.00

Eagle and Eaglets, C-59, painted cast iron, 5¾″, near mint condition, $750.00.

Dog, Speaking Dog, C-83, blue dress, rare, 7″ ... 1,200.00
Dog, Speaking Dog, C-83, red dress, rare, 7″ ... 900.00
Dog, St Bernard, C-17, keg on back, 'I Hear A Call' ... 125.00
Eagle & Eaglets, C-59, EX pnt, 5¾″, NM ... 750.00
Elephant, C-10, howdah ... 225.00
Elephant w/3 Clowns, C-41 ... 1,000.00
Ferris Wheel, Hubley clockwork wheel on bank base, 21½″ ... 525.00
Frog, C-78, on reticulated drum-shape base ... 450.00
Frog, Leap Frog, C-58 ... 1,500.00
Frog on Rock, C-57 ... 250.00
Frog on Stump, C-53 ... 250.00
Globe Savings Fund, W-439, lacks drw, 7″, NM ... 275.00
Grenadier, C-51, soldier aims rifle at tree ... 350.00
Guessing Bank, C-36, Pays 5 for 1 If You Guess Rite Number ... 650.00
Hall's Excelsior, C-105, bank building ... 100.00
Hall's Liliput, C-22, man puts coin in building, 1875, 4½″ ... 400.00
Hen & Chick, G-114, CI, pnt only G, 9¾″ ... 1,500.00
Home Bank, pnt CI, EX ... 800.00
Hoop-La, C-28, dog jumps through hoop held by clown ... 550.00
Horse Race, G-122, CI, 5¼″, NM ... 3,850.00
Humpty Dumpty, C-8, pnt CI, minor pnt flakes, rare ... 750.00
Indian & Bear, pnt CI, wht bear, orig feathers, VG ... 1,200.00
Joe Socko, G-130, prize fighters, tin, 1930s ... 225.00
Jolly Nigger, C-101, w/earring & necklace, iron & lead, M ... 500.00
Jolly Nigger, C-88, sm ... 100.00
Jolly Nigger, C-89, lg ... 100.00
Jolly Nigger w/High Hat, C-87, aluminum ... 175.00
Jonah & the Whale, C-95, long rectangular base ... 1,200.00

Uncle Sam, C-69, excellent original paint and condition, $1,000.00.

Jumbo the Elephant, C-19, on wheels....250.00
Lion, w/2 monkeys....650.00
Lion Hunter, G-151, CI, 10¾″, VG....1,760.00
Little Joe, pnt CI, EX....150.00
Magic, C-102, pnt CI, floral panels/blk door, orig red/yel....725.00
Magician, C-31, orig pnt, rare, 8″....2,600.00
Mailbox, C-455, pnt CI, orig, 3⅝″....60.00
Mammy & Child, G-162, CI w/EX pnt, rpl spoon, 7¾″, NM...2,200.00
Man, C-12, bald head, seated in chair, The Trust Bank....350.00
Mason, C-25, 2 bricklayers at work....1,200.00
Merry-Go-Round, C-62, hexagon w/ped foot, semi-mechanical...175.00
Merry-Go-Round, G-165, CI, 6¼″, EX....12,100.00
Money Moves The World, C-30, figure w/globe 'head'....300.00
Monkey & Coconut, pnt CI, rpr, VG....500.00
Monkey & Lion....400.00
Monkey & Parrot, C-55, tin....250.00
Mule, C-99, entering barn....650.00
Organ Bank, CI w/orig mc pnt, minor wear, 7½″....445.00
Organ Grinder & Monkey, C-52....175.00
Organ Grinder & Performing Bear, G-195, CI, 7″, G....1,320.00
Organ Grinder & Performing Bear, NM....2,000.00
Owl, turns head, CI....300.00
Paddy & Pig, pnt CI, dtd, no trap, o/w NM....1,400.00
Panorama, G-200, CI, paper cylinder NM, 6½″, VG....3,000.00
Peter Pan League, C-34, dog atop rectangular chest, 7″....250.00
Pig, C-106, sitting in highchair....350.00
Pistol, C-37, tin, 1909, 5½″ L....75.00
Plantation Darky Savings Bank, G-289, Weeden, G pnt, 5½″...440.00
Prof Pug Frog's Great Bicycle Feat, G-217, 11¼″....2,000.00
Punch & Judy, pnt CI, mk Buffalo, NY, 1884, 7½″, EX....800.00
Rabbit, C-79, standing on rectangular base, holding nut....650.00
Rabbit, C-80, standing on round base, holding nut....175.00

Indian Shooting Bear, C-26, painted cast iron, brown bear, 7½″ near mint condition, $900.00.

Rabbit in Cabbage, C-11, 4½″....250.00
Reclining Chinaman, C-44....2,000.00
Rooster, G-231, crowing, CI....195.00
Santa by Chimney, original....1,000.00
Squirrel, C-47, sits next to stump, holds nut....350.00
Stollwerck Vendor, C-15, tin....125.00
Stump-Speaker, G-254, Blk man w/carpet bag & top hat....1,200.00
Tammany, C-67, pnt CI, drop coin in politician's pocket....250.00
Teddy & the Bear, pnt CI....900.00
Toad on Stump, pnt CI, VG....200.00
Trick Dog, original....650.00
Trick Pony, C-82....700.00
Tricky Pig, C-76....175.00
Two Frogs, C-20, CI, 1 flips coin in mouth of 2nd, EX pnt....800.00
Uncle Sam, C-69, pnt CI, orig pnt, rare, EX....1,500.00
Uncle Tom, G-282, CI, 5½″, VG....200.00
William Tell, C-3, pnt CI, all orig, NM....1,000.00
William Tell, C-3, pnt CI, VG....600.00
Wireless, C-103, bank building, iron/tin/wood....150.00
World's Fair, G-296, CI, 8¼″, VG....750.00
Zoo, C-4, building w/animals in windows....650.00

Registering

Astronaut Daily Dime....20.00
Automatic Boy & Girl, dime registering....40.00
Bank Building, C-500, 'Recording,' dime registering....100.00
Book of Knowledge, dime registering....10.00
Capital Register Bank, dime registering....25.00
Daily Dime Clown....15.00
Daily Dime Cowboy....15.00
Daily Dime Piggy Bank....15.00
Elves Rolling Coins, dime registering....40.00
Empire State Building, dime registering....10.00
Gem, dime registering....15.00
Honeycomb, C-501, dime registering, 5¼″....100.00
Keene Savings Bank Building, C-507, 'Self Accounting,' tin....100.00
Lucky, dime registering....10.00
Magic Dime....35.00
Marvel, dime registering....10.00
New York World's Fair, dime registering....10.00
Prince Valiant, dime registering....30.00
Prudential....125.00
Sen-Sen....150.00
Snow White, dime registering....35.00
Stag Tobacco, no dial....100.00
Statue of Liberty, dime registering....10.00
Thrifty Elf, dime registering....20.00
Treasury, dime registering....10.00
Trunk, C-499....45.00
Uncle Sam's 3-Coin Bank, earliest model....125.00
Vacation Daily Dime....15.00
World Scope, dime registering....20.00

Still

Airplane, C-293, tin, 8″ L....65.00
Airplane, C-506, 'Spirit Saving'....75.00
Amish Boy, holding pig, sits on bale of hay....65.00
Andy Gump, pnt die cast, no trap, 5½″, VG....175.00
Apple, W-299, yel....750.00
Atlas, C-87, holds world on shoulders, 4¾″....200.00
Auto, C-283, 3½″....400.00
Auto, C-290, 'Armored Bank,' tin, 6¼″ L....35.00
Auto, W-157, pnt CI, 6¼″ L....450.00
Baby, C-535, emerging from eggshell....100.00
Banque de France, C-543, building w/statue atop, lead, 11″....100.00
Barrel on Wheelbarrow, C-431, 4¼″....350.00
Baseball, C-368, supported by 3 bats, 5″....450.00
Battleship Maine, W-142, sm....225.00
Battleship Oregon, C-298, lg, 6¼″ L....250.00
Bear, C-227, standing on hind legs, orig gold/red/blk, 5⅜″....50.00
Bear, C-228, 'Teddy Wants A Penny,' aluminum, 6″....65.00
Beehive, C-471, 2½″....50.00
Beehive, W-169, bear stealing honey, pnt CI, 7¼″....195.00
Beggar Boy, C-8, boy kneels, holding hat, 7″....100.00
Bill-E-Grin, aluminum....65.00
Billiken, C-51, Good Luck, pnt CI, red & gold, 4″....50.00

Hawaiian Statehood Commemorative, dated 1960, mint condition, $135.00.

Billiken on the Throne, 6½"....125.00
Blackpool Tower, C-310, 7½"....150.00
Boot, C-425, 3"....50.00
Boy in Boat, C-73, 'Dolphin' in boat, 4½"....450.00
Buffalo, C-177, CI, gold, pnt worn, rare, 3"....40.00
Buster Brown & Tige, W-83, horseshoe....225.00
Caisse Building, C-313, 5"....75.00
Camel, C-256, recumbent, trunk on back, 2½"....500.00
Camel, C-257, sm....65.00
Camel, W-201, lg....195.00
Cannon, C-534, 7¾" L....500.00
Captain Kidd, W-38....245.00
Carpet Bag, C-352, bronze, 3½"....45.00
Cash Register, Jr....150.00
Castle, C-311, circular tower ea corner, 4"....75.00
Castle, C-515, pnt CI, gold, old, 3½"....50.00
Cat, C-146, standing, tail up, bow at neck, 4½"....75.00
Cat, C-149, sitting on tub, 4"....75.00
Cat, C-172, playing with ball, 2½"....125.00
Cat, C-191, seated, pnt CI, gold, 4⅜", EX....80.00
Cat with Toothache, C-192, face bandaged, die-cast, 4"....35.00
Charlie Chaplin, W-393, by barrel, M....125.00
Chest, C-349....45.00
Child's Block, C-409, octagonal w/alphabet, 3¼"....1,000.00
Church, C-316, sq tower entry, pot metal, 4¾"....35.00
Churchill Bust, C-81, composition, 4¾"....35.00
Clock, C-403, Time is Money, pnt CI, blk, gold traces, 3¾"....70.00
Clock, C-404, A Money Saver, pnt CI, blk w/gold dial, 3½"....70.00
Clown, C-26, standing, pnt CI, orig gold & red, 6"....90.00
Clown Head, C-68, Blk man wears sm top hat, pot metal, 4"....35.00
Clown Head, C-70, long tusk-like nose, pot metal, 3½"....35.00
Coin Purse, C-423, 2¾"....500.00
Columbia Tower, C-414, 7"....150.00
Columbian Expo Administration Building, C-563, 1892, 5"....125.00
Coronation Crown, C-390, 4½"....75.00
Cow, C-263, 3½"....75.00
Deer, C-231, lg antlers, 9"....150.00
Deer, C-232, pnt CI, red, rare, 6"....75.00
Deer, W-195, 6"....75.00
Devil, Two-Faced; C-43, 4¼"....500.00
Dog, C-179, St Bernard, standing, keg at neck, 8x11"....125.00
Dog, C-195, sitting, howling, on oval base, 5½"....300.00
Dog, C-197, aluminum....35.00
Dog, C-197, Setter, pnt CI, bl, 3¼x5½"....40.00
Dog, C-205, seated Bulldog, silver spiked collar, 4¼", EX....45.00
Dog, C-209, Scotties in wicker basket, pot metal, 4½"....25.00
Dog, W-110, Scotty, blk....95.00
Donkey, C-234, wears saddle, brass, silver finish, 4⅜", EX....60.00
Dreadnought, C-382, 6¾"....250.00
Duck on Tub, C-180, w/hat & umbrella, 'Save For Rainy Day'....75.00
Duckling, C-166, wings up, 5"....75.00
Dutch Girl, C-34, 6½"....450.00
Eagle, C-122, w/shield, 4"....500.00
Egg Man, C-13, 4"....250.00
Egyptian Tomb, C-385, 6¼"....100.00
Elephant, C-123, political, 2 faces on side, 2½"....350.00
Elephant, C-131, GOP, trunk up, 4"....75.00
Elephant, C-132, CI, standing/trunk down/saddle seat, 3"....35.00
Elephant, C-140, circus....125.00
Elephant, C-162, w/drum, pot metal, 4¼"....25.00
Elephant, C-240, w/howdah, on wheels, 4"....150.00
Ferry Boat, C-304, 2½"....150.00
Fireman, W-9....165.00
Fireplace w/Mantel, C-557, tin, 4½"....50.00
Football Player, C-15, holds lg ball overhead, 5"....1,000.00
Football Player, C-23, running w/ball, 5¾"....250.00
Fort Dearborn, C-314, 6"....75.00
Gas Pump, C-467, 5¾"....175.00
General Butler, C-9, resembles frog, 6½"....500.00
General Pershing, W-312....100.00
General Sherman, W-88, on horse....575.00
Girl in Boat, C-71, 'Mermaid' on boat, 4½"....450.00
Globe, C-10, pnt CI, w/eagle, Enterprise Mfg, paint wear....35.00
Globe, C-477, Chicago Expo, tin....50.00
Globe, C-478, dog atop, tin....50.00
Globe, C-510, eagle atop, globe sits on ped ft....150.00
Golywog, C-35, 6¼"....200.00
Graf Zeppelin, C-291, w/wheels, 8" L....150.00
Graf Zeppelin, C-292, 6½" L....85.00
Guardhouse, C-407, soldier in doorway, tin, 3½"....45.00
Hand Grenade, C-398, 3¾"....35.00
Happy Fats, C-113....160.00
Hat, Fez; C-493, 1½"....75.00
Hat, WWI Soldier's; W-167....95.00
Hen on Nest, C-217, 3"....500.00
Home Bank, tin brick building w/inset teller, 6", EX....95.00
Horse, C-238, on wheels, 5"....150.00
Horse, C-244, rearing, pnt CI, blk/red, minor wear, 5"....40.00
Horse, C-245, Beauty, rearing, on oval base, 4¾"....75.00
Horse, C-252, rearing, CI, orig blk pnt, 7", EX....60.00
Horse, C-253, rearing, CI, nickel plated, 7", EX....40.00
Horse, W-78, prancing, on base....65.00
House, C-482, CI, silver & bl, 4"....110.00
House, C-483, CI, gr & gold, 3"....95.00
House of Knowledge, C-396, lithographed tin, 6½"....50.00
Humpty Dumpty, C-91, lithographed tin, 5½"....25.00
Ice Cream Freezer, C-366, Save Your Money/Freeze It, 4"....250.00
Independence Hall, C-322, glass, 7½"....100.00
Independence Hall, C-337, inscriptions, CI, 10¼x9½x7½"....500.00
Indian, W-39, pnt CI, 6"....295.00
Indian Brave, C-74, full figure, hand to forehead, 6"....150.00
Indian Chief, bust, pot metal....45.00
Indian Family, C-32, 3¾"....500.00
Jarmulowsky Building, C-315, Where It Is Safe, 8"....75.00
Kewpie, C-3, brass, 6"....75.00
Key, C-461, 5½"....100.00
King Midas, C-42, 5"....500.00

Lighthouse, C-536, hexagonal base 200.00
Lindbergh Bust, C-80, aluminum, 6½" 50.00
Lion, C-215, pnt CI, some rust, 5" 25.00
Lion, C-216, quilted pattern on body, 4" 75.00
Lion, sits on tub, 5½" 110.00
Litchfield Cathedral, C-329, 6½" 100.00
Log Cabin, C-508, 3⅞" 35.00
Mailbox, C-450, 4-legged street-corner type, 5½" 45.00
Mailbox, C-468, Stop & Save, red & gold, 5½", EX 150.00
Mailbox, w/key, gr, 9" 30.00
Mammy, C-67, w/clothes basket under arm, pot metal, 5½" 35.00
Mary & Lamb, C-6, 4½" 350.00
Middy 135.00
Money Bag, C-421, '$100,000,' 3½" 500.00
Monkeys, Three; W-236 .... 225.00
Mourner's Purse, C-509, lead, 4¾" 50.00
Mutt & Jeff, C-22, pnt CI, gold, 5¼" 90.00
Old South Church, C-338, 9½" 500.00
Oriental Fisherman, C-36, seated, 3½" 50.00
Our Kitchener Bank 145.00
Owl, C-184, on sq base, 4¼" 65.00
Owl, C-185, on stump, Be Wise Save Money, 5" 125.00
Padlock, C-532, heart shape, on ped ft, 7" 150.00
Pass the Hat 75.00
Pay Telephone, C-481 .... 150.00
Peaceful Bill, C-72, 4" 350.00
Peoples Life Insurance, w/key 40.00
Peter's Weatherbird, C-14, bird wearing coat, 4¼" 250.00
Picaninny Money Bank, C-96, 5¼" 150.00
Pig, C-267, tail curled up, Invest in Pork, 7" L 100.00
Pig, C-270, seated, pnt CI, gold w/red mouth, 3", EX 85.00
Pig, C-272, standing, w/bow, CI, nickel finish, worn, 2⅞" 40.00
Pig Bust, C-114, USS Pig, w/necktie & top hat, aluminum 75.00
Pinocchio, C-549, coming out of drum, pot metal, 5⅞" 50.00
Pirate, holding pistols, sitting on chest, pot metal 45.00
Plymouth Rock, C-347, '1620,' 2½" 75.00
Possum, Billy; C-119, on 6-sided base, 3" 1,000.00
Possum, C-120, 2½" 250.00
Prof Pug Frog, C-218, 3¼" 150.00
Pumpt, C-392, 4½" 100.00
Puzzle Box, C-418, tin, 3" 25.00
Rabbit, C-124, on oval base, 2¼" 750.00
Rabbit, C-141, begging, 5¼" 75.00
Rabbit, C-143, lying down, ears laid back, 2¼" 350.00
Radio, C-447, Cathedral style, 4¼" 75.00
Railway Saloon Car, C-285, English, 4½" 100.00
Reid Library, C-555, 5½" 75.00
Rocking Chair, C-560, seat is reticulated box, 6½" 500.00
Roosevelt Bust, W-309 .... 175.00
Rooster, C-170, CI, orig pnt, 4¾" 110.00
Rooster, movable head, grassy base, CI w/mc pnt, 6¼" 190.00
Safe, C-355, Pet Safe, 4½" 25.00
Safe, C-357, The Best Kast Iron Clothing, 4" 35.00
Safe, C-553, Washington bust atop, 5½" 150.00
Safe, dog on door, Roman figures on sides, 6", VG 110.00
Safe, Security Safe Deposit, combination lock, 4x4½x5½" 85.00
Santa, C-548, asleep in chair, pot metal, 5½" 50.00
Santa, C-62, carries sack over shoulder 100.00
Santa, C-63, holds tree, 5½" 350.00
Saving Sam, C-5, man in business suit, 5¼" 100.00
Seal, C-262, 3½" 200.00
Share Cropper, C-75, Blk man, hands in pockets, 5½" 75.00
Sheep, C-260, lying on rectangular base, pot metal, 3" 35.00
Shell, C-400, 5¼" 25.00

Independence Hall, 'Liberty Proclaimed July 4, 1776,' cast iron retaining most of its bronze-like finish, in good condition, 10" x 9½", $500.00.

Shell, C-422, Shell Out, 2½" 250.00
Shell, W-385, 1½" 55.00
Shoe, lady's; C-424, 2½" 50.00
Silo, C-344, Indiana Silo, 3½" 350.00
Silo, C-345, 5¾" 350.00
Soldier, WWI, W-40, NM 300.00
Squirrel, C-173, holding nut, 4" 300.00
Statue of Liberty, C-340, 10" 250.00
Statue of Liberty, C-343, 6" 65.00
Steamboat, C-302, Arcade, 7¾" L 150.00
Stoneware, cobalt glaze, covered urn form, 6¼" 125.00
Stork, C-29, carries baby in blanket, Harper, 5½" 500.00
Suitcase, C-351, aluminum, 3x5½" L 35.00
Sundial, C-346, 4¼" 500.00
Tally Ho, C-381, horseshoe w/horse head in center, 4¼" 100.00
Tank, C-295, WWI, pnt CI, gold, 2⅜x4¼" 100.00
Tank, C-296, Tank Bank USA/1918, 3¼" 75.00
Throne, C-410, 3½" 150.00
Tom Tom the Piper's Son, tin 40.00
Traders Bank of Canada, C-339, 'Colborne St,' 8½" 200.00
Trolley Car, C-288, 'Main Street,' w/people, 3" 350.00
Trolley Car, W-265, no wheels 250.00
Turkey, C-181, 3½" 75.00
Turkey, C-182, 4½" 350.00
Two Kids, C-255, goats w/front hooves on stump, 4½" 1,000.00
Washington, tall bust 900.00
Washington Monument, C-324, 7½" 100.00
Water Wheel, C-348, 4½x4" 500.00
Westminster Abbey, C-330, 6¼" 100.00
Westwood Memorial Building, C-556, 5¼" 75.00
White City Puzzle Bank #1, C-417, barrel shape, 4" 75.00
White City Puzzle Bank #2, C-415, bucket shape, 3" 75.00
Windmill, C-394, 3¾" 35.00
Windmill w/Dog, C-393, tin, 3½" 35.00
Woolworth Building, C-308, 8" 100.00
Yellow Cab, W-158 .... 395.00
Young American, CI, 4½", EX 90.00

Barber Shop Collectibles

Even for the stranger in town, the local barber shop was easy to find, its location vividly marked with the traditional red and white striped barber pole that for centuries identified such establishments. As far back as the 12th century, the barber has had a place in recorded history. At one time, he not only groomed the beards and cut the hair of his gentlemen clients, but was known as the 'blood letter' as well--hence the red stripe for blood and the white for the bandages. Many early barbers even pulled teeth! Later, laws were enacted that divided the practices of barbering and surgery.

The Victorian barber shop reflected the charm of that era with fancy barber chairs upholstered in rich wine-colored velvet; rows of bottles made from colored art glass held hair tonics and shaving lotion. Backbars of richly carved oak with bevelled mirrors lined the wall behind the barber's station.

During the late 19th century, the barber pole with a blue stripe added as a patriotic gesture to the standard red and white came into vogue.

Today the barber shop has all but disappeared from the American scene, replaced by modern unisex salons. Collectors search for the barber poles, the fancy chairs, and the tonic bottles of an era gone but not forgotten.

When no condition is indicated, the items listed below are assumed to be in excellent condition. See also Razors; Shaving Mugs

Towel sterlizer, copper sphere on pedestal base, brass handles and hardware, stamped Premier Sterilizer, 39″, $450.00.

Backbar, w/bevelled mirror & mug cabinet, oak, 84x96″, EX . 3,750.00
Blade sharpener, mechanical 9.00
Book, Treatise on Razors, Kingsbury, rare, 59 pg, 1797 . . . . 225.00
Bottle, amber, floral enamel, orange/wht dot pattern 50.00
Bottle, amethyst, gold leaf floral w/wht highlights 175.00
Bottle, bl, wht lily-of-the-valley, enamel, gilt w/stopper 150.00
Bottle, cobalt bl, boy walking in forest, enamel, 7½″, EX 125.00
Bottle, cobalt bl w/silver & enamel design, rare, 7½″, EX 70.00
Bottle, cobalt bl w/wht & orange pnt, porc stopper, 9¼″ 110.00
Bottle, cranberry & wht stripes w/swirls, no stopper, 7″ 80.00
Bottle, cranberry w/wht streaks, metal stopper, 10½″ 200.00
Bottle, deer cameo, wht w/brn, wht flowers/leaves, 8″ 135.00
Bottle, gr satin, paneled, sq 95.00
Bottle, Krank's Luxury Head Rub label under glass, rare 125.00
Bottle, lt bl, floral relief, w/enamel stopper, 7″ 105.00
Bottle, lt bl w/wht enamel floral, orange/yel bead design 45.00
Bottle, lt gr, HP 'Toilet Water,' flowers & leaves 85.00
Bottle, lt gr opaque w/floral spray, 'Hair Tonic' 60.00
Bottle, lt gr w/pnt red & wht floral, wht scroll, 8″, EX 55.00
Bottle, milk glass, windmill enamel, ewer form, 11″ 120.00
Bottle, milk glass w/pnt yel roses, 'Cologne' 125.00
Bottle, octagon neck, 'Witch Hazel,' w/porcelain stopper 40.00

Sign, tin with wood frame, single-sided, red and blue on white, 30″ x 54″, $75.00.

Bottle, vaseline, hobnail, w/stopper, 8½″, VG 100.00
Brush, porcelain bulldog head hdl, sgn Germany, 7½″ 40.00
Brush, shaving; high grade carved bone, rare, 4″ 24.00
Cabinet, 2 shelves, wood w/glass door, label, 12x12x6″, EX 45.00
Chair, carved oak, Koch, EX orig 475.00
Chair, carved oak, rstr & reupholstered 750.00
Chair, carved oak w/tufted leather, prof rstr 1,500.00
Chair, child's; adjustable, porcelain w/leather seat & bk 300.00
Chair, child's; wood horse's head, worn pnt/uphl seat 190.00
Display rack, holds 7 mugs or bottles, quarter moon & star 35.00
Hair clippers, hand operated 5.00
Leather strop 7.00
Mirror/coat & hat rack, oak, refinished, EX 110.00
Mug rack, curved glass/fancy crown, Crystal Case Co, 1897 . . . 1,350.00
Mug rack, revolves, fits between chairs, wood, 22½x19x41″ 100.00
Pole, carved wood, w/mt bracket, HP, 36″, EX 225.00
Pole, carved wood, w/mt bracket, HP red & wht, 28x4″ 109.00
Pole, porcelain, electric cylinder rotates, Koch, 76″, VG 1,750.00
Pole, stained glass, wall model, Koken 475.00
Shaving lamp, Williams, eng brass, shell hdl, rare, 7″ 85.00
Sign, Ask For Wildroot, barber pole, porc/metal, 28x10″ 33.00
Sign, Assoc Barbers of Am, plastic over tin 35.00
Sign, Barber Shop, 2-sided, porcelain/steel, red/wht/bl 67.00
Sign, Gillette logo in gold on blk metal, rare, 8½x4″ 51.00
Sign, Haircut 15¢, 3-sided, cutwork edging, pnt wood, 23″ 200.00
Sign, Indian at left, cb stand-up, red w/gr border 20.00
Sign, Ladies' & Gentlemen's Hairdressing, glass, 20x30″ 175.00
Sign, Stimulate Your Falling Hair, w/tonic bottle, VG 48.00
Towel steamer, nickel-plated copper, porcelain base, VG 350.00

Barometers

Barometers are instruments designed to measure the weight or pressure of the atmosphere in order to anticipate approaching weather changes. Those made around the turn of the century--earlier in England and on the continent--were beautifully housed in period cases of mahogany, rosewood, walnut, or cherry, often with brass trim. These quality pieces bring high prices on today's market.

Alvan Lovejoy, Boston, Weather House, chalk man/lady 150.00
Cantil, Hplwht, mahog w/line/shell/flower inlay, 39″ 1,200.00
Chas Ciuati, inlaid mahog cistern/thermometer, 1820s, 36″ . . . 1,200.00
Chas Wilder, NH, curly walnut case, 38″ 650.00
Dollond, inlaid mahog cistern/thermometer, 1820s, 40″ 1,900.00
TB Matthews, rosewood veneer, eng brass face, 38″, EX 200.00
Vecchio, Geo III, inlaid satinwood/brass urn, 1775, 38″ 3,200.00

Basalt

Basalt is a type of black unglazed pottery developed by Josiah Wedgwood and copied by many other companies during the late 18th and early 19th century. It was also call 'Egyptian Black.'

When no condition is indicated, the items listed below are assumed to be in mint condition. See also Wedgwood.

Bowl, emb stripes & rim design, Wedgwood, 4x9" 300.00
Sugar bowl, floral between gadrooning, imp mk, ear hdls 95.00
Tall pot, basketweave, Widow Warburton finial, no mk, 9" 300.00

Creamer and sugar bowl with lid, marked Wedgwood, Made in England, #42, $125.00.

Baskets

Basket weaving is a craft as old as ancient history. Baskets have been used to harvest crops, for domestic chores, and to contain the catch of fishermen. Materials at hand were utilized, and baskets made in one region are often distinguishable simply by analyzing the natural fibers used in their construction. Early Indian examples were made of corn husks or woven grasses. Willow splints, straw, rope, and paper are only a few of the materials that have been used. Until the invention of the veneering machine in the late 1800s, splint was made by water soaking a split log until the fibers were softened and flexible. Long strips were pulled out by hand, and while still wet and pliable, woven into baskets in either a cross-hatch or hexagonal weave.

Most hand- crafted baskets on the market today were made between 1860 and the early 1900s. Factory baskets, with a thick, wide splint cut by machine, are of little interest to collectors.

The more popular baskets are those designed for a specific purpose, rather than the more commonly found utility baskets that had multiple uses. Among the most costly forms are the Nantucket Lighthouse baskets, which were basically copied from those made there for centuries by Aboriginal Indians. They were designed in the style of whale oil barrels, and named for the South Shoal Nantucket Lightship, where many were made during the last half of the 19th century. Cheese baskets, used to separate curds from whey, herb-gathering baskets, and finely woven Shaker miniatures are other highly-prized examples of the basket weaver's art.

When no condition is indicated the items listed below are assumed to be in excellent condition. Height does not include handle; baskets are splint unless noted otherwise. See also Sewing; Shaker

Apple, curved splint staves, wood bottom, wire bale, 14" dia 95.00
Apple, wood bottom, wire bale, 6x9" dia 115.00
Bushel, staves curve up from wood base, metal band, rim hdl 75.00
Buttocks, applied ft, hinged lid, minor wear, 10½x10x18" 85.00
Buttocks, bentwood hdl, 5½x9½x11" 135.00
Buttocks, G age & color, minor wear, 5½x10¾x11½" 165.00
Buttocks, red faded color, mid-20th C, 3½x4½x6½" 125.00
Buttocks, twist hdl, brn stain, contemporary, 11x18" 70.00
Buttocks, well made, G construction, early 20th C, 6x13" 85.00
Buttocks, well made, 2-batten base, minor wear, 7x12x16" 125.00

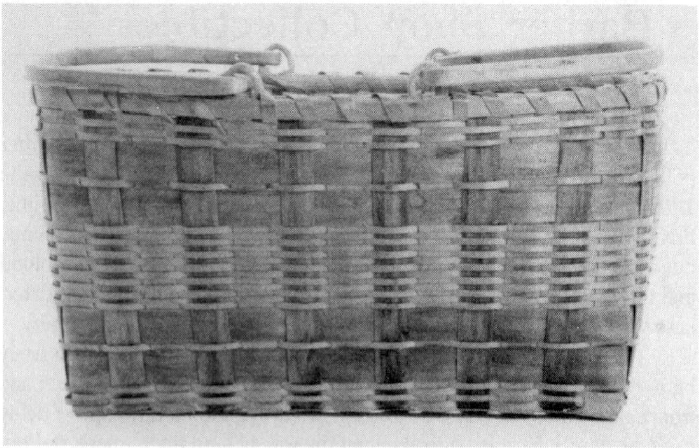

Basket, two-color splint, bentwood swing handles, 8½" x 17" x 9½", $135.00.

Buttocks, well-pronounced shape, 4x7x8", NM 195.00
Buttocks, 3 shades of splint, w/hdl, 6½x12x14" 155.00
Charcoal sieve, splint, NE, 1800s, 24x26" 485.00
Cheese, woven splint, G age & color, minor wear, 18x19" 475.00
Drying, openwork base, #8 on hdl, att Shakers, 18", VG 90.00
Drying, openwork base, wide splint/open rim hdls, 6x11x15" 70.00
Gathering, flower; oak, sides trn up/rnd ft/hdl, 11x12x10" 46.00
Gathering, high bentwood hdl, 3x11" sq 135.00
Grass, brn & natural, 3½" dia 30.00
Half, splint, flat bk, wall hanging, minor wear, 9½" 145.00
Laundry, splint, end hdls, base damage, 17x26½" 60.00
Laundry, splint, minor wear, 19½x30½" 65.00
Laundry, splint, wrapped rim, bentwood hdls, 13x20x33", NM .. 275.00
Loom, bentwood loop hdl, incomplete rim lacing, 13½x15½" ... 154.00
Loom, shades of brn woven design, hanger hdl, 5x7x9", EX ... 105.00
Melon rib, diamonds woven at hdls, copper rivets, 7x14" 165.00
Melon rib, G age, color & condition, 6½x10" dia 150.00
Melon rib, G age & color, 10½x18½x21½", VG 160.00
Melon rib, striped willow, hickory hdl, 1900s, 11x10" 85.00
Melon rib, twist willow hdl, pnt, 1900, 11x10" 70.00
Miniature, Chinese export, HP, lid, hdls, 1860-80, 5x3½" 125.00
Miniature, fine weave, natural, gr stripe, w/hdl, 2¼x3" 30.00
Miniature, melon rib, bentwood hdl, 5½x6¼" 145.00
Miniature, wrapped rim, w/hdl, 1⅝x2¾" 35.00
Nantucket, pocketbook, ivory raccoons on rosewood panel 850.00
Nantucket, shallow, swing hdl, 9¼" dia 650.00
Nantucket, swivel hdl, copper rivets, 5½x8", EX 425.00
Nantucket, w/lid & orig brass hinge, 10" dia, at auction 3,100.00
Nantucket, well woven, 2 sm hdls, 3½x7½" 650.00
Nantucket, well-shaped stationary wood hdl, 4x6½x9", NM 450.00
Pea picker's, vertical splint, bentwood hdl/rim, ft, 11x5" 95.00
Picnic, rice straw, Chinese, swing hdl, HP florals, 10x8" 85.00
Picnic, willow/ash hdls, lift top, tin lined, 20x15x15" 70.00
Potato print, faded, 3-color, w/lid, wear, 13x12x18" 150.00
Potato print, red/bl/gr, wear/fading, 14x12x17½" 90.00
Rye straw, bentwood rim hdls w/chip carving, 3¼x5½" 275.00
Rye straw, oval, w/lid, worn, 17x23" 120.00
Rye straw, rim hdls, minor wear, 6½x12" 110.00
Rye straw, rim hdls, minor wear, 7½x15" 145.00
Sewing, baleen/twisted brass, clover shape, 1880s, 7½" 300.00
Splint, bentwood hdl, 7¾x13½" dia 80.00
Splint, bentwood rim hdls, rnd, minor wear, 12½x18" 105.00
Splint, bentwood rim hdls, rnd, 4½x9 14", EX 95.00
Splint, bentwood rim hdls, sq w/oval rim, 1860, 11x22x24" 175.00
Splint, bentwood rim hdls, 12¾x19½x20½" 135.00

Buttocks basket, twig handle, 7″ x 7″, $130.00.

Splint, bentwood swivel hdl on wire loops, 6x9½″ 90.00
Splint, bl pnt worn, w/hdl, 7x12x13″ 135.00
Splint, built-up rim hdls, G age & color, 8x17x23″ 85.00
Splint, carved wood rim hdls, minor wear, rnd bottom, 6x12″ . . .95.00
Splint, dbl hinged lids, w/hdl, 8½x12x16″ 95.00
Splint, dk gr pnt worn, hdl, rnd, 6½x12″ 185.00
Splint, fine weave, well-made bentwood swivel hdl, 6x10″ 175.00
Splint, natural w/red/bl woven design, rim hdls, 5½x10″ 135.00
Splint, oak w/leather carrying straps, 21x16x13″ 175.00
Splint, old pnt, minor rim damage, w/lid, 13x14½″ dia 150.00
Splint, red/blk woven design faded, w/hdl, 6¾x12x14″ 130.00
Splint, rim hdls, rnd, 10½x21½″ 95.00
Splint, rnd, minor wear, 6x8″ 75.00
Splint, side hdls, peaked lid, wide splint, 24″ 70.00
Splint, splint-wrapped wood rim hdls, 3¾x9″ dia 70.00
Splint, sq w/radiating ribs, brn stripes worn, hdl, 6x14″ 100.00
Splint, sq wood hdl, primitive, 9x13½x15½″ 120.00
Splint, well made, 4 hand holds in rim, 11x17x26″ 180.00
Splint, well-shaped wood hdl, varnished, 10x16″ 105.00
Splint, well-shaped wood swivel hdl, 7x13″, VG 105.00
Splint, wide strands, watercolor decor faded, w/lid, 13x12″ 65.00
Splint, willow; diamond designs, gr pnt, tall sq hdl, 10x7½x5″ . . .75.00
Splint, wood rim hdls, old wht pnt, 5x11″ dia 60.00
Splint, 20x11″ dia 50.00
Splint/cane, well made, w/hdl, 6¾x10x11″ 70.00

Batchelder

Ernest A. Batchelder was a leading exponent of the Arts and Crafts movement in the United States. His influential book, *Design in Theory and Practice*, was originally published in 1910. He is best known, however, for his artistic tiles which he first produced in Pasadena, California, from 1909 to 1916. In 1916 the business was relocated to Los Angeles where it continued until 1932, closing because of the Depression.

In 1938 Batchelder resumed production in Pasadena under the name of 'Kinneola Kiln.' Output of the new pottery consisted of delicately cast bowls and vases in an Oriental style. This business closed in 1951. Tiles carry a die-stamped mark; vases and bowls are hand incised.

When no condition is indicated, the items listed below are assumed to be in mint condition.

Bowl, Batchelder Tiles ad on gray matt, hexagonal, 2x4″ 85.00
Tile, antelope, 4x4″ 50.00
Tile, architectural, 7x12″ 100.00
Tile, facing peacocks relief, unglazed, 12x12″ 225.00
Tile, floral, 4x4″ 45.00
Tile, grapes, bl wash, 3x3″ 25.00
Tile, lion, 4x4″ 50.00

Battersea

Battersea is a term that refers to enameling on copper or other metal. Though originally produced at Battersea, England, in the mid-18th century, the craft was later practiced throughout the Staffordshire district. Boxes are the most common examples--some are figurals, and many bear an inscription.

When no condition is indicated, the items listed below are assumed to have only minimal damage, as is normal.

Box, pair of lovebirds on cover, 'Take This For a Kiss,' outstanding condition except for minor crack on inside of lid, 2″ long, $400.00.

Box, animal head form, minor wear/cracks, 1″ L 95.00
Box, flowerpot shape, florals/scrolls, ca 1800, 1¼″ 285.00
Box, quotation on top, lt bl/wht, oval, 1800 . . . . .295.00
Box, spread wing brn eagle/X stds/laurel/crown on wht 125.00
Box, Who opens this must have kiss, bl/wht/blk, 1½x1½″, EX . .145.00
Box, wreath/crown/eagle on hinged lid, 1⅝″ dia 145.00

Bauer

Originally founded in Paducah, Kentucky, in 1885, the J.A. Bauer Company moved to Los Angeles where it was re-established in 1909. Until the 1920s, their major products were terra cotta gardenware, flowerpots, and stoneware and yellowware bowls. During prohibition, they produced crocks for home use.

A more artful form of product began to develop with the addition of designer Louis Ipsen to the staff in 1915. Some of his work--a line of molded vases, flowerpots, bowls, etc. -- was awarded a bronze medal at the Pacific International Exposition the following year.

In 1930, the first of many dinnerware lines was tested on the market. Their initial pattern, Plain Ware, was well accepted and led the way to the introduction of the most popular dinnerware in their history and with today's collectors--Ringware. It was produced from 1932 into the early 1960s, in solid colors of jade green, royal blue, Chinese yellow, light blue, orange-red, and in very limited quantities, black or white. Its simple pattern was a design of closely spaced concentric ribs, either convex or concave. Over the years more than one hundred shapes were available. Some were made in limited quantities, resulting in rare items to whet the appetites of Bauer buffs today.

Other patterns were La Linda, produced during the 1940s and 1950s, and Monterey Modern, introduced in 1948 and remaining popular into the 1950s. It was made in turquoise, burgandy, orange, yellow, white, rust, green and blue.

After WWII, a flood of foreign imports drastically curtailed their sales, and the pottery began a steady decline that ended in failure in 1962.

For more information, we recommend *The Complete Collector's Guide to Bauer Pottery* by Jack Chipman and Judy Stangler, whose address may be found in the Directory under California. When no condition is indicated, the items listed below are assumed to be in mint condition.

Batter bowl, Ring pattern, 2-quart, $25.00.

Ashtray, cowboy hat, turq....40.00
Bowl, cereal; Ring, orange, 4½″....7.00
Bowl, mixing; Ring, #18, gr....15.00
Bowl, mixing; Ring, #36, gr....8.50
Bowl, mixing; Ring, #9, blk....62.50
Bowl, mixing; Ring, #9, gr....25.00
Bowl, oval veg; LaLinda, pink, 10″ L....24.00
Bowl, salad; Ring, low, gr, 14″....30.00
Bowl, soup plate; LaLinda, gray, 7″....15.00
Bowl, soup plate; Ring, yel, 7″....18.00
Bowl, soup/cereal; LaLinda, gray, 6″....9.00
Butter, Ring, rnd, lt bl....50.00
Cactus jar, orange, M Carlton, 4½″....45.00
Coffee pot, Ring, gr, 8-cup....75.00
Cookie jar, fish, speckled pink....50.00
Cookie jar, Ring, orange....80.00
Cup & saucer, El Chico, any color....45.00
Cup & saucer, LaLinda, yel....10.00
Cup & saucer, Ring, blk....50.00
Dealer sign, chartreuse....200.00
Flowerpot, swirl, blk, 5″....12.00
Garden vase, wht, F Johnson, 13½″....75.00
Gravy boat, LaLinda, hdl, gr....10.00
Honey jar, Ring, bee hdls, orange....200.00
Jug, water; Ring, orange, w/lid....100.00
Oil jar, orange, #129, 20″....350.00
Pickle dish, swirl design, hdl, gr....7.50
Pitcher, ball; Ring, yel, 1½-qt....60.00
Planter, swan figural, matt wht, 12″ L....50.00
Plate, bread; El Chico, any color, 6″....15.00
Plate, bread; LaLinda, ivory, 6″....4.50
Plate, chop; LaLinda, pink, 13″....22.50
Plate, chop; Ring, ivory, 14″....50.00
Plate, dinner; El Chico, any color, 9″....25.00
Plate, dinner; LaLinda, ivory, 9″....9.00
Plate, dinner; Ring, yel, 10½″....30.00
Plate, dinner; Ring, yel, 9″....15.00
Plate, salad; El Chico, any color, 7½″....20.00
Plate, salad; LaLinda, ivory, 7½″....7.50
Plate, salad; Ring, yel, 7½″....12.00
Platter, LaLinda, oval, gray, 12″ L....15.00
Shakers, Ring, barrel, gr, pr....16.00
Shakers, Ring, low, burgundy, pr....24.00
Sherbet, Ring, ped base, lt bl....30.00
Sugar shaker, Ring, blk, 5″....62.50
Teapot, Aladdin, yel, 8-cup....30.00
Teapot, Ring, yel, mk USA, 6-cup....45.00
Tumbler, LaLinda, brn, 8-oz....8.00
Tumbler, Ring, ivory, 12-oz....30.00
Tumbler, Ring, ivory, 6-oz....15.00
Vase, art, matt gr, 8½″....65.00
Vase, bud; Ring, gr, 5″....25.00
Vase, Ring, cylinder, turq, 12″....45.00

Bavaria

Bavaria, Germany, was long the center of that country's pottery industry; in the 1800s, many firms operated in and around the area. Chinaware vases, novelties, and table accessories were decorated with transfer prints as well as by hand by artists who sometimes signed their work. The examples here are marked with 'Bavaria' and the logos of some of the various companies who were located there. When no condition is indicated, the items listed below are assumed to be in mint condition.

Berry set, roses on wht, 9″ master+four 5¼″....30.00
Bowl, florals/reticulated, Schumann, US Zone, 2x8½x12½″....45.00
Bowl, girl w/flower on cobalt & lt bl, 9″....55.00
Bowl, parrots, mc, lav pierced edge, octagonal, 7½″....35.00
Bowl, pastel florals, reticulated sides, 9″....22.00
Cake set, grapes, gr/brn, sgn Charlotte, 7-pc....50.00
Celery dish, Christmas rose, artist sgn, 14″ L....32.00
Celery dish, pink roses, Orleans ZS & Co....30.00
Coffee set, demitasse; lovers in silhouette, mk ZS, 23-pc....150.00
Cracker jar, pink roses/gold trim on wht, MV ZS & Co, 8½″....35.00
Creamer & sugar bowl, gr/bl HP decor on pink....38.00
Dessert set, pink rose garland, gr leaves, lattice border....135.00
Dish, pink roses on gr, 3 gold ft, HP, 5″....25.00
Figurine, child w/2 geese, Gerald & Co, 5½″....45.00
Jar, powder; pearlized w/florals, sgn Esther Gardner....25.00
Mug, Blue Onion, red mk....35.00
Plate, birds of paradise, oval/reticulated, sgn, hdls, 12″....35.00
Plate, cake; lg roses, open hdl, 9″....15.00
Plate, chop; roses, pink/yel on gr/wht, HP, gilt edge, 12″....55.00
Plate, grapes/leaves, HP, Schumann mk, gold rim, 10½″....38.00
Plate, HP roses, ZS & Co, 6½″....20.00
Plate, lady in purple hat w/fan, HP, scalloped, 10½″....65.00
Plate, man on horse/dogs/sheep, lattice edge, Shumann, 8″....50.00
Plate, pheasant, scalloped gold rim, 9½″....45.00
Plate, pink/yel roses at rim, 12″....45.00
Plate, poinsettia, HP, sgn, 8½″....45.00
Plate, veiled lady w/roses, wide gold border, HP, 10½″....100.00
Plate, violets & lg leaves, gold border, 8½″....35.00

Beer Cans

When the flat top can was first introduced in 1934, it came with printed instructions on how to use the triangular punch opener. Cone top cans, which are rare today, were patented in 1935 by the Continental Can Company. By the 1960s, aluminum cans with pull tabs had made both types obsolete.

The hobby of collecting beer cans has been rapidly gaining momentum over the past ten years. Series types such as South African Brewery, Lion, and the Cities Series by Schmit and Tucker are especially popular.

Condition is an important consideration when evaluating market price. Grade 1 must be in like new condition, with no rust. However, the triangular punch hole is acceptable. Grade 2 cans may have slight scratches or dimples, but must be free of rust. For Grade 3, light rust, minor scratching, and some fading may be acceptable. Grade 4 cans have the same defects, but are in much worse condition. Cans in less than excellent condition devaluate sharply.

In the listing that follows, cans are arranged alphabetically by brand name, not by brewery.

Unless noted otherwise, values are for cans in Grade 1 condition.

ABC, flat top, 12-oz 20.00
ACME, flat top, 12-oz 15.00
ACME Gold Label, flat top, 11-oz 25.00
Alpine, pull top, 11-oz 10.00
Ballantine Beer, 32-oz cone top 60.00
Ballantine Extra Fine, flat top, 12-oz 15.00
Bantam Ale, flat top, 7-oz 20.00
Barbarossa, flat top, 12-oz 100.00
Blatz, flat top, 12-oz 8.00
Burgermeister, flat top, 16-oz 12.00
Busch Bavarian, pull top, 16-oz 5.00
Canadian Ace Malt Liquor, flat top, 7-oz 175.00
Cardinal, flat top, 12-oz 7.00
Champagne Velvet, flat top, 12-oz 12.00
Chief Oshkosh, flat top, 12-oz 12.00
Cooks Beer, steamboat, cone top 95.00
Crown Darby, flat top, 12-oz 150.00
Dakota, flat top, 12-oz 40.00
Drewrys Malt Liquor, flat top, 12-oz 200.00
Eastside Old Tap, flat top, 12-oz 12.00

Yuengling Beer, cone top, yellow and white, 5¾″, $58.00.

Falls City, flat top, 12-oz 15.00
Falstaff, flat top, 12-oz 15.00
Fitzgerald's Burgomaster, cone top, 12-oz 200.00
Fort Schuyler Ale, 12-oz cone top 65.00
Fort Schuyler Beer, 12-oz cone top 60.00
Frankenmuth Bock, flat top, 12-oz 100.00
Gettelman Rathskeller, cone top, 12-oz 45.00
Goebel, flat top, 8-oz 20.00
Goebel Bock, EX 115.00
Golden Velvet, flat top, 12-oz 35.00
Gotham, cone top, 12-oz 200.00
Great Falls Select, flat top, 12-oz 15.00
Heidelberg, pull top, 12-oz 8.00
Heidelbrau, flat top, 12-oz 12.00
Highlander, cone top, Montana, EX 125.00
International Frankenmuth, flat top, 12-oz 25.00
Jet Malt Liquor, flat top, 12-oz 15.00
Kingsbury, cone top, 12-oz 30.00
Kingsbury, pull top, 12-oz 4.00
Kruegers Ale, punch top, 1st can, EX 170.00
Kuebler Cream Ale, 32-oz cone top 850.00
London Bobby Ale, cone top, 12-oz 200.00
Lone Star, pull top, 12-oz 7.00
Malt Duck, pull top, 12-oz 30.00
Meister Brau Bock, flat top, 1958, 12-oz 20.00
Michelob, emb letters, pull top, 12-oz 4.00
Miller, flat top, 12-oz 15.00
Milwaukee's Best, pull top, 12-oz 4.00
Neuweiler, flat top, 8-oz 20.00
North Star, flat top, 12-oz 12.00
Old Bohemian Ale, flat top, 12-oz 45.00
Old Dutch Brand, flat top, 12-oz 18.00
Old Milwaukee, 1962, pull top, 12-oz 8.00
Old Style, 1958, flat top, 12-oz 6.00
Old Topper Ale Crowntopper 75.00
Pabst, flat top, 12-oz 10.00
Pabst Blue Ribbon Ale, flat top, 12-oz 75.00
Pfeiffer's, flat top, 12-oz 10.00
Red Top, flat top, 12-oz 30.00
Schlitz, 1954, flat top, 16-oz 15.00
Winchester, pull top, 16-oz 5.00

Belleek, American

From 1883 until 1930, several American potteries located in Trenton, New Jersey, and in Ohio, manufactured a type of china similar to the famous Irish Belleek soft paste porcelain. The American manufacturers identified their porcelain by using 'Belleek' in the marks. American Belleek is considered the highest achievement of the American porcelain industry. Production centered around artistic cabinet pieces and luxury tablewares. Many examples emulated Irish shapes and decor with marine themes and other naturalistic sytles. While all is highly collectible, some companies' products are rarer than others. The best-known companies are Ott & Brewer, Willets, The Ceramic Art Company (CAC), and Lenox. See also these specific categories.

For a more thorough study of the subject, we recommend you refer to *American Belleek*, by Mary Frank Gaston (you will find her address in the Directory under Texas). When no condition is indicated, the items listed below are assumed to be in mint condition.

Cup & saucer, demitasse; Tridacna, gold trim, mk CAP 90.00
Cup & saucer, floral bouquet pattern, mk Gordon 175.00
Ewer, HP roses on bulbous body, branch hdl, mk Belleek 450.00

Loving cup, 3-hdl, sgn A Heidrich, Morris & Wilmore, lg......495.00
Plate, dinner; Victoria pattern, mk Morgan Belleek, 10″.......150.00
Salt, individual; HP leaf decor, gold trim, 3-ftd, mk CHC......135.00
Shell dish, pink lustre int, mk Am Belleek Co, 4x5″..........125.00
Sugar bowl, open; pink flowers, mk American Art China, 2½″..225.00
Teapot, gold trim, mk Perlee, 5″..........................175.00
Tumbler, dtd 1899, Morris & Wilmore......................225.00

Teapot, dragon form, gold paste leaves on cream, sgn Columbian Art Pottery, 7½″ x 9″, $1,000.00.

Belleek, Irish

Belleek is a very thin translucent porcelain that takes its name from the district in Ireland where it originated in 1857. The glaze is a creamy ivory color with a pearl-like lustre. Tablewares, baskets, figurines, and vases have been produced; Shamrock, Tridacna, Echinus and Lotus are but a few of the many patterns.

It is possible to date an example to within twenty to thirty years of manufacture by the mark. Pieces with an early stamp often bring prices nearly triple that of a similar but current item. With some variation, the marks have always incorporated the wolfhound, castle, harp, and shamrock. The first three marks (usually in black) were used from 1863 to 1946. One of a series of three green marks was in use from 1946 until 1980. Since then the mark has been done in gold.

When no condition is indicated, the items listed below are assumed to be in mint condition.

Aberdeen, ewer, 2nd blk mk, lg...........................900.00
Aberdeen, vase, 2nd blk mk, 6″..........................415.00
Aberdeen, vase, 3rd blk mk, scroll hdl, applied floral, 9″......750.00
Aberdeen, vase, 3rd blk mk, 8″..........................590.00
Allingham, candlestick, 2nd blk mk, lt yel lustre trim.........375.00
Bamboo, teapot, 2nd blk mk, much gilt trim................745.00
Basket, 2nd blk mk, purse, basketweave w/floral, pearl, 6″.....450.00
Basket, 3-strand, bird's nest, flowers, mk Fermanagh, 4x4″....850.00
Basket, 3-strand, Sydenham, early, 10″...................1,850.00
Basket, 4-strand, rnd w/hdl & applied flowers, imp mk, 12″...1,100.00
Boat, ash tray, 3rd blk mk...............................90.00
Boat, spoon holder, 1st blk mk, 4½″.......................240.00
Bucket, double; 1st blk mk, 12″ L.........................595.00
Bust, Clyte, 2nd blk mk................................1,000.00
Cake plate, 4-strand basketweave, hexagonal, ca 1926, 10″....550.00
Celtic, creamer, 3rd blk mk, red/gold trim..................190.00
Cleary, salt, open; 2nd blk mk, light green coral..............90.00
Cleary, salt, open; 3rd blk mk.............................55.00
Comport, 1st blk mk, 3-dolphin stem, pink/gr/lav, 7½″.......1,250.00
Cone, cup & saucer, 2nd blk mk, gr trim...................135.00
Cone, teapot, 2nd blk mk, rust/gilt trim....................550.00
Dragon Shell, 1st blk mk, 7″...........................1,250.00
Echinus, cup & saucer, 1st blk mk, pink/gold trim...........165.00
Echinus, dejeuner set, 1st blk mk, pearl..................2,800.00
Echinus, plate, bread; 1st blk mk, pink/gold trim, 9″.........160.00
Echinus, plate, 1st blk mk, pink/gold trim, 7″................85.00
Echinus, tea tray, 1st blk mk, pearl lustre & bisque, oval......750.00
Echinus, teapot, 1st blk mk.............................595.00
Egg cup, 1st blk mk, basketweave.........................135.00
Egg frame, 1st blk mk, basketweave, gold trim...............225.00
Erne, cup & saucer, 2nd blk mk..........................195.00
Erne, teapot, 2nd blk mk, gr trim.........................495.00
Figurine, Affection, 2nd blk mk, glazed & bisque...........1,400.00
Figurine, frog, 2nd blk mk, 4½″..........................475.00
Figurine, pig, 2nd blk mk, 3x2x4″........................375.00
Figurine, pig, 3rd blk mk, 3″............................230.00
Figurine, swan, 1st blk mk, much gilt trim, 6x5″.............420.00
Figurine, swan, 1st blk mk, 6x5″.........................350.00
Figurine, swan, 2nd blk mk, sm............................85.00
Figurine, swan, 2nd blk mk, 4½x4″........................140.00
Font, Angel, 2nd blk mk.................................685.00
Frog spoon warmer, 1st blk mk...........................985.00
Grasses, beehive, pedestal, 1st blk mk.....................990.00
Grasses, cup & saucer, 1st blk mk.........................160.00
Grasses, plate, 1st blk mk, 5″.............................65.00
Grasses, teapot, 1st blk mk, color decor, 8¼″ L.............750.00
Grasses, teapot, 1st blk mk, lg...........................495.00
Grasses, water kettle, 1st blk mk, lg......................950.00
Greek, compote, 2nd blk mk, gold trim, 10″ W...............750.00
Greek, plate, serving; 2nd blk mk, bl/gold trim, 9½″..........350.00
Harp & Shamrock, condiment set, 2nd blk mk, w/holder......500.00
Hawthorne, jardiniere, 2nd blk mk, applied florals, lg........1,600.00
Heart, basket, 3rd blk mk................................200.00
Heart, plate, 2nd blk mk, gr trim..........................98.00
Hexagon, cup & saucer, 2nd blk mk, gr trim.................95.00
Hexagon, dejeuner set, 2nd blk mk, gr trim, 17″ tray.......2,400.00
Hexagon, salt, open; 2nd blk mk...........................30.00
Hexagon, saucers, 2nd blk mk, pink........................15.00
Hexagon, set; teapot, c/s, cr/sug, pink, 2nd blk mk.........1,995.00
Imperial Shell, 2nd blk mk, gr trim, 9″...................1,550.00
Institute, plate, 1st blk mk, pink/gold, monogram, 7¼″........135.00
Jardiniere, 2nd blk mk, coral hdls, applied flowers, 7x9″.....1,100.00
Jardiniere, 2nd blk mk, 3 lg ft, applied florals, 10½″........1,750.00
Lily, cream & sugar, 3rd blk mk, pink......................160.00
Lily, plate, 2nd blk mk, gr trim, 6″........................45.00
Lily, 3-strand, basket, early, 10½″.......................2,000.00
Limpet, bread plate, 3rd blk mk..........................150.00
Limpet, coffee pot, 3rd blk mk...........................570.00
Limpet, creamer, 3rd blk mk..............................50.00
Limpet, cup & saucer, demitasse; 3rd blk mk, pink/gold........85.00
Limpet, cup & saucer, 3rd blk mk.........................115.00
Limpet, salt, open; 2nd blk mk...........................120.00
Limpet, set; teapot, cr/sug, bread plate, c/s, 3rd blk mk......1,990.00
Lotus, cream & sugar, 3rd blk mk.........................120.00
Lotus, creamer, 2nd blk mk, orange hdl.....................80.00
Low Lily, tea set, 2nd blk mk, gr trim, rare...............1,500.00
Muffin dish, 1st blk mk, gr trim/shells, 4½x8½″..............525.00
Mustache cup & saucer, 2nd blk mk, pink & gilt.............145.00

Table centre, applied multi-floral decoration, 1st black mark, 11½″, $1,800.00.

Neptune, creamer, 2nd blk mk, bl trim 75.00
Neptune, cup & saucer, 2nd blk mk, gr trim 65.00
Neptune, cup & saucer, 3rd blk mk, bl trim 65.00
Neptune, dejeuner set, 2nd blk mk 1,685.00
Neptune, dejeuner set, 2nd blk mk, gr trim 1,800.00
Neptune, plate, 3rd blk mk, bl, 10″ 85.00
Neptune, teapot, 2nd blk mk, bl trim 645.00
Neptune, teapot, 2nd blk mk, pink trim 350.00
Neptune, teapot, 3rd blk mk, pink trim 225.00
Night light, Lighthouse, 1st blk mk, 8″ 700.00
Octagon, flowerpot, 2nd blk mk 270.00
Plate, leaf, 2nd blk mk, 8″ 80.00
Plate, leaf, 3rd blk mk, 7″ 50.00
Pot, cauldron, 2nd blk mk 130.00
Prince of Wales, flower holder, open, pearl/biscuit, 1896 .... 2,500.00
Ribbon, creamer & sugar, 3rd blk mk 160.00
Ribbon, jam pot, 1st blk mk, biscuit barrel size, D496 .... 265.00
Shamrock, basket, 4-strand, 5½″ 490.00
Shamrock, basket, 4-strand, 6½″ 545.00
Shamrock, beehive, pedestal, 2nd blk mk 390.00
Shamrock, cup & saucer, 3rd blk mk 50.00
Shamrock, honey pot on pedestal, 2nd blk mk, pink trim 645.00
Shamrock, mug, 2nd blk mk 120.00
Shamrock, plate, 3rd blk mk, 7″ 48.00
Shamrock, salt, open; 3rd blk mk 50.00
Shamrock, sugar bowl, 3rd blk mk 35.00
Shamrock, teacup w/saucer, 3rd blk mk 60.00
Shamrock, vase, 2nd blk mk, harp hdl, pearl/gr, 9½″ 425.00
Shamrock, vase, 3rd blk mk, trunk stump 110.00
Shamrock, 3-strand, basket, tri-lobe, 5½″ 550.00
Shell, biscuit barrel, 2nd blk mk, gr trim, 8″ 1,200.00
Shell, plate, 3rd blk mk, pink & gilt trim, 6½″ 95.00
Shell, table decoration, 1st blk mk/registry mk, 8½″ 350.00
Shell, teapot, 3rd blk mk, wht 570.00
Shell, tray, 1st blk mk, pink trim 1,850.00
Shell, triple menu holder, 2nd blk mk, gr trim 125.00
Soup bowl, 1st blk mk, earthenware, rim pattern, 10¼″ 75.00
Sydney, egg frame, 1st impressed mk, w/cups, 2nd blk mk 1,650.00
Thorn, tea tray, imp 1st registry mk, orange web, sq, 14½″ 1,250.00
Thorn, tray, 1st imp mk, gilt & silver trim 1,500.00
Tridacna, creamer & sugar, 2nd blk mk 120.00
Tridacna, cup & saucer, demitasse; 2nd blk mk, gr trim 95.00
Tridacna, cup & saucer, farmer's; 2nd blk mk, gr trim 135.00
Tridacna, cup & saucer, 2nd blk mk 90.00
Tridacna, plate, 1st blk mk, pink & gilt trim, 6¾″ 110.00
Tridacna, plate, 2nd blk mk, pink trim, 6″ 40.00
Tridacna, salt, open; 2nd blk mk 120.00
Tridacna, salt, open; 3rd blk mk 60.00
Tridacna, teapot, 1st blk mk, pink 690.00
Tridacna, teapot, 2nd blk mk, D356 .... 395.00
Tridacna, teapot, 2nd blk mk, D356, pink trim 395.00
Tridacna, teapot, 2nd blk mk, D477 .... 395.00
Tridacna, tray, tea; 2nd blk mk, pink trim, 16″ 595.00
Tridacna, water kettle, 2nd blk mk 570.00
Tridacna, water kettle, 3rd blk mk 345.00
Vase, Celtic, tan & gold trim, miniature 225.00
Vase, Feather, 3rd blk mk, 6″ 170.00
Vase, Fish, Triple; 1st blk mk, in color, 16″ 2,450.00
Vase, Fish, 1st blk mk, 7½″ 750.00
Vase, Lily, 3-lily, 2nd blk mk, 8″ 975.00
Vase, Marine Center, 1st blk mk, 11″ 2,000.00
Vase, Princess, 2nd blk mk 900.00
Vase, Ribbon, 3rd blk mk, 8″ 395.00
Vase, spill; Lily, 2nd blk mk, lg 150.00
Vase, spill; Lily, 2nd blk mk, sm 125.00
Vase, spill; Rock, 2nd blk mk, pink trim 470.00
Vase, spill; Rock, 3rd blk mk 295.00
Vase, Sunflower; 3rd blk mk, 8″ 270.00
Vase, Triple Cornucopias, 2nd blk mk, 8″ W 350.00
Vase, Victorian, 2nd blk mk, dk gr/gilt trim, 11½″ 1,250.00
Wall pocket, 1st blk mk, swan neck ea side, 9″ 1,450.00

Bells

The earliest form of the bell, the crotal or closed mouth, is most familar to us today as the sleigh bell. Rattles, hollow forms containing stones or seed pods, are also of this type of construction. Gongs, most often associated with the Orient, have no clapper and must be struck to sound. The more common forms of bells are made with a flaring shape and a freely moving interior clapper.

Bells come in many shapes, and serve many uses. They have been used throughout history to sound an alarm, call a congregation, announce dinnertime, or signal a victory. School bells called children in from recess, and cow bells made the herd easier to locate. Bells have been made in brass, glass, china, bronze, and cast iron, in simple as well as elaborately embossed forms, and in amusing figurals.

When no condition is indicated, the items listed below are assumed to be in mint condition.

Lady in hoop skirt, painted brass, 3″, $45.00.

Bell metal, intricate wrought iron hood w/cast floral, 22″......125.00
Brass, herons/nest emb on sides, fish-head hdls, 4¾x4″.........85.00
Cherry burl, 3x7″...50.00
Colonial lady w/tiered skirt & shawl, brass, 6½x3″............110.00
Colonial maid w/tiered skirt, wears cross/cap, brass, 4¾″........60.00
Cow, tin w/orig leather neck strap, late 19th C................24.00
Cut glass, brilliant, deep-cut pinwheel, notch hdl, 5¾″.........295.00
Delft, scenic, German......................................42.00
Dinner, triangle shape.....................................60.00
Elizabeth I, brass figural, 7″...............................85.00
Farm type, w/mounting stanchion, new mt, rpt blk, 8″.........50.00
Girl, bl/wht/gilt, Staffordshire, 6″..........................85.00
Lady in hoop skirt, powdered wig & fan, brass, 5¾x3½″........75.00
Lady in hoop skirt w/muff & hat, brass, 5½x3″...............50.00
Lamasery, brass, head of Asian on hdl, 7¼x3¼″..............95.00
Locomotive, bell metal, CI fr, mt on wood base, 26″..........225.00
Locomotive, bronze, no mt, 12″ dia.........................150.00
Nun, brass figural, 4¾″....................................58.00
Peasant girl w/jug is figural hdl, brass, 6x3″..................75.00
Sheep, brass, strap hdl....................................40.00
Sleigh, nickle on brass, 32 on orig straps....................96.00
Sleigh, 19 sm brass bells on leather strap, 37″...............85.00
Trolley, brass...45.00
Wedding, cranberry, bl/wht ribbon in clear hdl, 11″..........250.00
Wedding, cranberry, lg....................................185.00
Wedding, cranberry, Pairpoint, orig clapper, 9¾″.............225.00
Wedding, lav art glass w/nailsea loops, 1860s, 12″............395.00
Wedding, vaseline w/nailsea loops, 22″.....................400.00

Bennett

The firm of Edwin Bennett was established in 1846 in Baltimore, Maryland. They produced stoneware, majolica, and Rockingham glazed pitchers and teapots in designs such as Rebecca at the Well, an adaptation of an earlier model by S. Alcock & Company, Staffordshire. Underglaze slip decorated artware was attempted in 1895, called Albion Ware. A variety of marks were used; some contained Bennett's full name, but usually only his initials were incorporated.

When no condition is indicated, the items listed below are assumed to be in mint condition.

Mug, Toby; brn, 1850s, 6″................................70.00
Stein, majolica, metal top, dtd 1878, 6″....................100.00
Syrup jug, olive gloss, pewter hinged lid, sgn, 6¾″.............80.00
Syrup picher, majolica, dtd 1878..........................150.00

Plate, Destruction of the Spanish Fleet, marked EBPCo Warranted, Patented, $65.00.

Bennett Faience, New York

Vase, flowers/butterflies, underglaze, 9¾″...................565.00
Vase, mineral floral on bl/bl overglaze, thin neck, 10″........425.00

Bennington

Although the term has become a generic one for the mottled brown ware produced there, Bennington is not a type of pottery, but rather a town in Vermont where two important potteries were located. The Norton Company, founded in 1793, produced mainly redware and salt glazed stoneware; only during a brief partnership with Fenton (1845-47) was any Rockingham attempted. The Norton Company endured until 1894, operated by succeeding generations of the Norton family.

Fenton organized his own pottery in 1847. There he manufactured not only redware and stoneware, but many other artistic types as well--graniteware, scroddled ware, flint enamel, a fine parian, and vast amounts of their famous Rockingham. Though from an esthetic standpoint his work rated highly among the country's finest ceramic achievements, he was unsuccessful economically. His pottery closed in 1858.

It is estimated that only one in five Fenton pieces were marked, and although it has become a common practice to link any fine piece of Rockingham to this area, careful study is vital to distinguish Bennington's from the similar wares of many other American and Staffordshire potteries. Although the practice was without the permission of the proprietor, it was nevertheless a common occurrence for a potter to take his molds with him when moving from one pottery to the next. So particularly well-received designs were often reproduced at several locations. Of eight known Fenton marks, four are variations of the '1849' impressed stamp--'Lyman Fenton Co., Fenton's Enamel Patented, 1849, Bennington, Vermont.' These are generally found on examples of Rockingham and flint enamel. A raised, rectangular scroll with 'Fenton's Works, Bennington, Vermont,' was used on early examples of porcelain. From 1852 to 1858, the company operated under the title of the United States Pottery Company. Three marks--the ribbon mark with the initials USP; the oval with a scrollwork border and the name in full; and the plain oval with the name in full--were used during that period.

Among the more sought-after examples are the bird and animal figurines, novelty pitchers, figural bottles, and all of the more finely modeled items. Recumbent deer, cows, standing lions with one forepaw on a ball, and opposing pairs of poodles with baskets in their mouths and 'coleslaw' fur were made in Rockingham, flint enamel, and occasionally in parian.

When no condition is indicated, the items listed below are assumed to be in mint condition.

Key: c/s—cobalt on salt glaze

Bank, bulb w/birds atop/base w/posts, scroddled, 1886, 8½″....300.00
Bank, chest of drawers, scroddled ware, paw ft, 5½″, EX......165.00
Bottle, Coachman, w/tassels, 1849 mk, 11″.................750.00
Bottle, Coachman, 1849 mk, 10″..........................650.00
Bottle, pretzel; applied pebbles on brn, 5½x3½″...............48.00
Bottle, Toby barrel, Old Tom, Rockingham, 8½″, NM.........650.00
Bowl, Rockingham, ribbed, 4x9″..........................120.00
Candlestick, flint enamel, 9½″...........................575.00
Candlestick, flint enamel, 9⅞″, pr......................1,350.00
Creamer, Ben Franklin Toby, Rockingham, boot hdl, mk, 5¾″.525.00
Creamer, cow, flint enamel, 8″...........................475.00
Creamer, cow, Rockingham, w/lid, 4¼″, EX.................225.00
Croup kettle, Rockingham, 6⅝″, EX.......................275.00
Cuspidor, flint enamel, emb leaf design, 4¾x9¾″..............75.00
Cuspidor, shell pattern, Rockingham.......................125.00

Pitcher, Rockingham glaze, hound handle, ca 1845 to 1855, 9″, in mint condition, $650.00 to $750.00.

Figurine, Rockingham, poodle, seated, 10″ 350.00
Flask, book, flint enamel, Departed Spirits, 1849-1859 .... 600.00
Flowerpot, emb cattails, wht clay, brn-amber glaze, 5″ 45.00
Flowerpot, emb cattails, wht clay, brn-amber glaze, 6½″ 60.00
Flowerpot, imp Bennington Centennial, Aug 16, 1877, 3″ 75.00
Nameplate, Rockingham, 3⅜x6⅜″ 50.00
Paperweight, spaniel, flint enamel, 1849, VG 550.00
Pitcher, flint enamel, paneled str sides, imp 1849, 12″ 450.00
Pitcher, parian, tulip & sunflower, wht, 8″ 175.00
Pitcher, porcelain, Charter Oak, bl/wht, USP mk, 9½″ 475.00
Pitcher, porcelain, Paul & Virginia, bl/wht, USP mk, 10¾″ 450.00
Pitcher, Rockingham, can-form bottom/concave top half, 8½″ 250.00
Pitcher, Rockingham, floral designs in panel, N&F, 8½″ 165.00
Pitcher, Rockingham, hound hdl, 9″, NM 700.00
Snuff jar, Toby, non-flint, 4½″ 575.00
Tobacco jar, flint enamel, alternate rib, 1849 mk, 8¾″ 450.00
Vase, parian, Am eagle, bl/wht, 1850s, 8½″ 175.00
Vase, parian, hand w/corn, 7″ 140.00
Vase, parian, ribbed, bl/wht, 6″ 75.00
Vase, parian, sea shells & grapes, 7¾″ 65.00
Wash bowl, flint enamel, imp 1848 mk, 4½x13½″, VG 300.00

Stoneware

Cake crock, fern, c/s, E&LP Norton, 7″, NM 265.00
Crock, apple butter; floral 'butterfly,' c/s, J&E, 10″ 375.00
Crock, floral spray, c/s, E&LP Norton, 7x8″, EX 260.00
Jar, elaborate floral spray/ribbon tie, c/s, E&LP, 13½″ 250.00
Jar, lion & building, c/s, J&E Norton, stain/flakes 1,200.00
Jar, tulips, ochre on gray, L Norton, ovoid, 2-gal, EX 425.00
Jug, dbl flower, c/s, J&E Norton, 1-gal, 11½″, NM 295.00
Jug, E Norton, spout/flared lip, Albany glaze, 1-gal 190.00
Jug, floral, c/s, E Norton & Co, sm lip flakes, 10½″ 205.00
Jug, floral, rare brn on salt glaze, L Norton, ovoid, 11″ 425.00
Jug, floral spray, c/s, J&E Norton, 4-gal 525.00
Jug, floral/3 lg leaves, c/s, J Norton, 14″, EX 275.00

Pitcher, Charter Oak, blue and white porcelain, ca 1852 to 1858, USP mark, 9½″, $475.00.

Beswick

James Wright Beswick operated a pottery in Longston, England, in the early 1890s, where he produced fine dinnerware as well as ornamental ceramics. Collectors of Beswick today are most interested in the figurines made since 1936 by a later generation Beswick firm, John Beswick, Ltd. They specialize in reproducing authentic breeds of animals in accurate detail in a fine bone china body. Their Fireside Series includes models of dogs, cats, elephants, horses, the Huntsman, and an Indian figure, all of which measure up to 14″ in height. The Connoisseur line is modeled after the likenesses of famous racing horses.

Beatrix Potter's characters, and some of Walt Disney's, are charmingly recreated, and appeal to adults as well as children. Other items, such as character Tobys, have also been produced.

The Beswick name is stamped on each piece. The firm was absorbed by the Doulton group in 1973.

When no condition is indicated, the items listed below are assumed to be in mint condition.

Mr. Jackson, by Beatrix Potter, copyright 1974, F. Warne & Co., Ltd., England, 2¾″, $18.50.

Dinner set, Mickey Mouse 95.00
Figurine, bird on sunflower, #929 .... 36.00
Figurine, Clydesdale horse, 8½x10″ 50.00
Figurine, Indian on horse, 8¼″ 79.00
Figurine, panda, Beatrix Potter, 3½″ 18.00
Figurine, Persian cat, 5x5½″ 19.00
Figurine, Pickles, Beatrix Potter, 4½″ 18.00
Figurine, Tom Kitten, Beatrix Potter 30.00
Figurine, wht pig w/piglet on bk, 7″ 17.00
Jug, Robert Burns, 7½″ 35.00
Jug, Tony Weller, #281 .... 48.00
Platter, Romeo & Juliet 95.00
Teapot, #691 .... 85.00
Teapot, Peggotty, 6″ 85.00
Toby jug, Pickwick, 3″ 35.00
Vase, Naeda, floral w/gold trim, bl sponge, 8½″ 32.00

Big Little Books

The first Big Little Book was published in 1933, and copyrighted in 1932, by the Whitman Publishing Company of Racine, Wisconsin. Its hero was Dick Tracy. The concept was so well accepted that others soon followed Whitman's example, and though the 'Big Little Book' phrase became a trademark of the Whitman Company, the formats of his competitors--Saalfield, Goldsmith, Van Wiseman, Lynn, and World Syndicate--were exact copies. Today's Big Little Book buffs collect them all.

These hand-sized sagas of adventure were illustrated by full-page cartoons on the right-hand page, and the story narration on the left. Colorful cardboard covers contained hundreds of pages, usually totaling over an inch in thickness. Big Little Books originally sold for 10¢ at the dime store; as late as the mid-1950s, when the popularity of comic books caused sales to decline signaling an end to production, their price had risen to a mere 20¢.

Their appeal was directed toward the pre-teens who bought, traded, and hoarded Big Little Books. Because so many were stored in attics and closets, many have survived. Among the super heroes are G-Men, Flash Gordon, Tarzan, the Lone Ranger, and Red Ryder; and in a lighter vein, Blondie and Dagwood, Mickey Mouse, Little Orphan Annie, and Felix the Cat.

In the early to mid-30s, Whitman published several Big Little Books as advertising premiums for the Coco Malt Company, who packed them in boxes of their cereal. These are highly prized by today's collectors, as are Disney stories and super hero adventures.

For specific values, see listings below.

Air Fighters of America, 1941, EX........................12.00
Alice in Wonderland, 1934................................25.00
Allen Pike of the Parachute Squad, 1941, VG...............10.00
Apple Mary, Dennie's Lucky Apples, 1939, VG...............10.00
Arizona Kid, The Bandit Trail, 1936, EX...................10.00
Betty Boop, in Snow White, Whitman, 1934..................35.00
Big Chief Wahoo & the Lost Pioneers, 1942, VG.............12.00
Billy the Kid...12.50
Blaze Brandon with the Foreign Legion, 1938, VG...........15.00
Blondie, Bouncing Baby Dumpling, 1940, NM.................18.00
Blondie, Count Cookie in Too, 1947, NM....................18.00
Bob Stone, The Young Detective, VG........................10.00
Bobby Benson, On the H-Bar-O, 1934, VG....................12.00
Brad Turner, The Transatlantic Flight, 1939, VG...........10.00
Bronco Peeler, The Lone Cowboy, 1937, EX..................15.00
Buck Jones, The Killers of Crooked Butte, 1940, VG........22.00
Buck Jones, The Roaring West, EX..........................15.00
Buck Rogers, Cocomalt giveaway, 1933, VG..................25.00
Buck Rogers, The Adventures of; 1934, rare, G.............85.00
Buck Rogers, The City Below the Sea, 1934, VG.............40.00
Buck Rogers, The Doom Comet, 1935.........................60.00
Buck Rogers, The Planatoid Plot, 1936, NM.................55.00
Buck Rogers, The Planatoid Plot, 1936, VG.................30.00
Buckskin & Bullets, 1938, VG...............................8.00
Buffalo Bill Plays a Lone Hand, 1936, VG...................8.00
Bugs Bunny & His Pals, 1945...............................18.50
Buz Sawyer, Bomber 13, 1946, VG...........................15.00
Captain Frank Hawks Air Ace & the League of 12, 1938, EX...12.00
Charlie Chan of the Honolulu Police, 1939, VG..............15.00
Charlie McCarthy & Edgar Bergen, #1456....................35.00
Chester Gump, Pole to Pole Flight, 1937, NM...............15.00
Chuck Mallory, Railroad Detective on the Streamliner, 1938.....12.00
Dan Dunn, On the Trail of Wu Fang, 1938, VG...............15.00
Dan Dunn & the Underworld Gorillas, 1941, VG..............15.00
Danger Trails in Africa, 1935, VG.........................20.00
Detective Higgins of the Racquet Squad, 1938, M...........12.00
Dick Tracy, The Adventures of; 1st story, rare...........100.00
Dick Tracy, The Hotel Murders, 1937, VG...................20.00
Dick Tracy, The Spider Gang, 1937, VG.....................25.00
Donald Duck, Forgets to Duck, 1939, VG....................18.00
Donald Duck, Ghost Morgan's Treasure, EX..................20.00
Donald Duck, Here Again, 1944, VG.........................15.00
Donald Duck, Sees Stars, 1941, EX.........................35.00
Donald Duck, Such a Life, 1939, EX........................23.00
Draftie of the US Army....................................12.00
Erik Noble & the Forty-Niners.............................10.00
Fighting Heroes Battle for Freedom, 1943, EX..............12.00
Flash Gordon, Forest Kingdom of Mongo, VG.................30.00
Flash Gordon, Monsters of Mongo, ca 1935..................75.00
Flash Gordon, Power of Mongo, 1943, VG....................50.00
Flash Gordon, Red Sword Invaders, VG......................30.00
Flash Gordon, Tournament of Mongo, VG.....................50.00
Flash Gordon, Tyrant of Mongo, 1941, VG...................40.00
Flash Gordon, Water World of Mongo, 1937, VG..............40.00
Flash Gordon, Witch Queen of Mongo, 1936..................75.00
Freckles & the Lost Diamond Mine, 1937, EX................12.00
Freddie Bartholomew, The Story of; 1935, VG...............15.00
G-Man, The Radio Bank Robbers, 1937, VG...................18.00
Gene Autry, Cowboy Detective, 1940, G......................9.00
Gene Autry, Gunsmoke Reckoning, EX........................25.00
Gene Autry, Red Bandit's Ghost, 1959, VG..................18.00
Gene Autry, Riders of Range...............................12.00
Ghost Avengers, 1943, EX..................................18.00
Guns in the Roaring West, 1937, VG.........................8.00
Houdini's Big Little Book of Magic, 1927, VG..............35.00
Inspector Wade Solves Mystery of Red Aces, 1937, NM.......10.00
Jack Armstrong, The Ivory Treasure, 1937, VG..............18.00
Jack Swift & His Rocket Ship, 1934, VG....................20.00
Jane Withers, Keep Smilin', movie edition, 1938, VG.......15.00
Jane Withers, This is the Life, movie edition, 1939.......18.00
Jimmie Allen, Air Mail Robbery, 1936, VG..................10.00
Jimmy Keen & Radio Spies, Calling W-I-X-Y-Z, 1939, VG.......15.00
Joe Louis, The Brown Bomber, 1936, VG.....................50.00
John Carter of Mars, 1940, EX............................125.00
Jungle Jim, #1138, G......................................15.00
Kay Darcy, The Mystery Hideout, 1937, NM..................12.00
Ken Maynard, Strawberry Roan..............................15.00
King of the Royal Mounted, Great Jewel Mystery, 1939........15.00
Kit Carson, 1933, EX......................................25.00
Les Miserables, movie edition, 1935, VG...................15.00
Little Lord Fauntleroy, Freddie Bartholomew, movie edition.....20.00
Little Miss Muffet, 1936, VG..............................10.00
Little Orphan Annie, In the Movies, 1937, VG..............30.00
Little Orphan Annie, Mysterious Shoemaker.................20.00
Little Orphan Annie, The Ghost Gang, 1935, EX.............30.00
Little Orphan Annie, 1933, VG.............................60.00
Lone Ranger, Black Shirt Highwayman, 1939, Vallely art, NM...35.00
Lone Ranger, His Horse Silver, 1935, EX...................40.00
Lone Ranger, Menace of Murder Valley, EX..................18.00
Lone Ranger, Red Renegades, 1939, G.......................10.00
Lone Ranger, Secret Killer, 1937, VG......................22.00
Lone Ranger, Secret of Somber Cavern......................12.00

Lone Ranger, Secret Weapon, #1428, EX....25.00
Mandrake the Magician, The Flame Pearls, 1946, EX....45.00
Mary Lee, Mystery of the Indian Beads, 1937, M....12.00
Maximo the Amazing Superman, The Supermachine, 1941, NM..20.00
Maximo the Amazing Superman, 1940, VG....18.00
Men of the Mounted, 1933, VG....25.00
Men with Wings, movie edition, 1938, NM....15.00
Mickey Mouse, Mickey Runs Newspaper, 1937, VG....16.00
Mickey Mouse, On Cave Man Island, 1944, VG....25.00
Mickey Mouse, 1st Mickey BLB, 1933....65.00
Mickey Mouse & Pluto, 1930s....24.00
Moon Mullins & Kayo, 1933, VG....15.00
Mr District Attorney on the Job, 1941, VG....15.00
Og, Son of Fire, 1936, EX....25.00
Pat Nelson, Ace of Test Pilots, 1937, VG....10.00
Peggy Brown, The Jewel of the Fire, 1943, EX....10.00
Peggy Brown, 1940....10.00
Phantom, The Sign of the Skull, 1939, VG....25.00
Phantom, 1936....35.00
Pluto the Pup, 1938, NM....26.00
Popeye, In Quest of his Poopdeck Pappy, 1937, VG....25.00
Popeye, In Quest of the Rainbird, 1943, VG....20.00
Popeye, Super Fighter, EX....15.00
Radio Patrol, Outwitting the Gang Chief, 1939, EX....15.00
Radio Patrol, 1935, VG....15.00
Ray Land of the Tank Corps, USA, 1942, EX....15.00
Red Barry, Undercoverman, 1939, VG....15.00
Red Ryder, Code of the Range, 1941, G....10.00
Red Ryder, Fighting Westerner, 1940, EX....30.00
Red Ryder, Little Beaver on Hoofs of Thunder, 1939, M....35.00
Red Ryder, Squaw Tooth Rustlers, 1941, VG....15.00
Robinson Crusoe, VG....15.00
Roy Rogers, King of the Cowboys, 1943, EX....19.00
Roy Rogers, Mystery of Howling Mesa, 1948, EX....19.00
Roy Rogers, Robin Hood of the Range, VG....15.00
Roy Rogers, The Dwarf Cattle Ranch, 1947, EX....18.00
Shadow & Master of Evil, w/movie flip pgs....15.00
Shirley Temple, Story of; 1930s....23.00
Shooting Sheriffs, Sheriffs of Wild West, 1936, EX....10.00
Silver Streak, RKO....15.00
Skippy, The Story of; 1929, VG....18.00
Skyroads with Hurricane Hawk, 1936, EX....20.00
Smilin' Jack, The Stratosphere Ascent, 1937, VG....20.00
Smitty, Going Native, 1938, M....18.00
Smitty, Golden Gloves Tournament, 1934, NM....15.00
Speed Douglas & the Mole Gang, 1941, VG....12.00
Story of Charlie McCarthy & Edgar Bergen....15.00
Sybil Jason, in Little Big Shot, movie edition, 1935, EX....18.00
Tailspin Tommy, Famous Payroll Mystery, 1933, VG....15.00
Tailspin Tommy, Great Air Mystery, movie, 1936, VG....25.00
Tailspin Tommy, Hooded Flyer, 1937, NM....22.00
Tailspin Tommy, Sky Bandits, 1938, VG....15.00
Tailspin Tommy, Wings over the Arctic, 1935, VG....15.00
Tarzan, Beasts of; 1937, NM....30.00
Tarzan, Journey of Terror....25.00
Tarzan, Of the Apes, 1933, EX....60.00
Tarzan, Son of; EX....17.00
Tarzan, The Untamed, EX....12.00
Tarzan, Twins, 1935, NM....100.00
Terry & the Pirates, Shipwrecked on a Desert Island, 1938....20.00
Terry & War in the Jungle....15.00
Tex Thorne Comes Out of the West, 1937, VG....9.00
Texas Kid, The; 1937, NM....12.00
Three Musketeers, 1935, VG....16.00
Tim McCoy, The Prescott Kid....15.00
Tim McCoy, The Western....15.00
Tim Tyler's Luck & the Plot of the Exiled King, 1939, NM....15.00
Tom Mix, Circus on the Barbary Coast....15.00
Tom Mix, Fighting Cowboy, 1925, NM....40.00
Tom Mix, Hoard of Montezuma, 1937, VG....25.00
Tom Mix, Range War, 1937, NM....40.00
Tom Mix & Tony, Rider of Death Valley, 5-Star Pub/1934, VG..30.00
Tom Swift & His Giant Telescope, 1939, VG....40.00
Torch is Passed, The....9.00
Treasure Island, 1934, VG....20.00
Uncle Don's Strange Adventure, 1936, VG....12.00
Will Rogers, 1935, VG....12.00
Zip Saunders, King of Speedway....10.00

Bing and Grondahl

In 1853, brothers M.H. and J.H. Bing formed a partnership with Frederick Vilhelm Grondahl in Copenhagen, Denmark. Their early wares were porcelain plaques and figurines, designed by the noted sculptor Thorvaldsen of Denmark. Dinnerware production began in 1863, and by 1889 their underglaze color 'Copenhagen Blue' had earned them worldwide acclaim.

They are perhaps most famous today for their Christmas plates, the first of which were made in 1895. The plate was titled 'Behind the Frozen Window,' and the series has continued to the present with annual editions. A second series commemorating Mother's Day was added in 1969.

When no condition is indicated, the items listed below are assumed to be in mint condition. See also Collector Plates

Left, Cow, #2121C, 15″, $300.00; Right, Vase, Danish landscape with mill, signed L. Negitholm, #5507, 11¾″, $250.00.

Ash tray, seagull....10.00
Figurine, billy goat w/head down biting foreleg, 4x5½″....135.00
Figurine, bird, bl/wht, gray bill, head forward & down, 4″....125.00
Figurine, bird on branch, lt gr w/bl tail, head right, 6″....75.00
Figurine, boy, #1617, 7¾″....110.00
Figurine, boy buttoning bl pants, #1759, 6″....125.00
Figurine, boy looking in pocket, 6″....125.00
Figurine, boy sitting on rock, #1757....125.00
Figurine, cat, #1553....65.00
Figurine, cat, #2256, 7½″....100.00
Figurine, cat, Siamese; #2308, 5½″....65.00
Figurine, girl in long wht gown & cap kisses boy, #1614....150.00

Figurine, girl in wht sits on box, knits, #1656 . . . . . 125.00
Figurine, girl kneels over cat in basket, #2249, 3x4¼″ 110.00
Figurine, girl w/3 geese, sgn Axel Locher, 9¼″ 225.00
Figurine, penguin, #1821/3 . . . . . 45.00
Figurine, reclining nude & baby, sgn Nielsen, 1913, 7″ 185.00
Figurine, seated girl playing guitar, #1684, 9″ 295.00
Figurine, seated mother holding little boy, #1552JC, 11″ 400.00
Ginger jar, reticulated flowering trees, sgn EHL, 9″ 1,650.00
Paperweight, Christian X Silver Jubilee, pyramid shape, 5″ 105.00
Vase, seagulls, gold tips, 8″ 75.00

Birdcages

Birdcages can be found in various architectural styles and in a range of materials--wood, wicker, brass, and gilt metal with ormolu mounts. Those that once belonged to the wealthy are sometimes inlaid with silver or jewels. In the 1800s, it became fashionable to keep birds, and some of the most beautiful examples found today date back to that era. Musical cages that contained automated bird figures became popular--today these bring prices of several thousand dollars. In the latter 1800s wicker styles came into vogue. Collectors still appreciate their graceful lines, and find they adapt easily to modern homes.

When no condition is indicated, the items listed below are assumed to be in excellent condition.

Automaton, 2 birds sing & move, Swiss, 19″, NM 2,300.00
Brass, cut glass sides, Hendrix 185.00
Brass, rnd, polished, Hendrix 68.00
Pottery, cream glaze, wren's, hanging, 11″ 87.50
Wicker, natural, fancy wall bracket 140.00
Wicker, plant stand w/hanging birdcage atop, 63x29x10″ 365.00
Wood, bamboo & reed w/pine baseboards, canister form, 24″ . . . 55.00
Wood, curved peak roof/steps ea side/porch w/railing, 19″ 105.00
Wood, 3-tier castle, directional atop, '20s, 28x15″ 200.00
Wood fr w/wire bars, carved bird atop, 2 drws, fancy, 36″ 450.00

Bisque

Bisque is a term referring to unglazed earthenware or porcelain that has been fired only once. During the Victorian era, bisque figurines became very popular. Most were highly decorated in pastels and gilt, and demonstrated a fine degree of workmanship in the quality of their modeling. Few were marked.

When no condition is indicated, the items listed below are assumed to be in mint condition. See also Heubach; Piano Babies; Snow Babies

Baby, sitting, gr/wht dress, pr: 1 w/saucer, 1 w/cup, 5″ 150.00
Blk boy in top hat w/musical instrument, mc, 6½″ 90.00
Blk boy sits on stump, plays squeak box, Germany, 4½″ 115.00
Blk child & wht child sitting on chamber pots, kissing 135.00
Blonde child by tree trunk, pink coat, 7″ 48.00
Boy & girl in swing, movable, tan/wht, 5½x2x3″ 100.00
Boy & girl w/cats, common base, pastels, 11½x5¾x4″ 245.00
Boy sits in beach chair, orange shorts/turban, 4¾x2¾″ 88.00
Boy w/basket on arm, Victorian, 7¼″ 38.00
Cat, recumbent, wht w/blk spots, pink bow, 4¼x9″ 110.00
Dutch shoe, dancing pigs & shamrocks in relief, 3½x6″ 85.00
Flower arranger, 2 Cupids hold flowers, 8¾x5¼″ 185.00
Frogs, 2 before 2 eggs, color decor, 2¾x3¼″ 75.00
Girl w/long hair, w/ball, Victorian, 8¾″ 70.00
Lady, lies on stomach, turtle body, risque, Germany, 2x4″ 165.00
Little girl playing dress-up, wire glasses, blanket, 7″ 45.00
Man, woman, child on boat, pastels, German, 12x6x13″ 395.00
Man & lady, ea w/baskets, mc, French, anchor mk, 17½″, pr . 1,200.00
Man on bench w/concertina, mc, sgn Gardner, Russian, 6¾″ . . . 495.00
Monk taking snuff, pitcher bk of monk, German, 6¾″ 85.00
Night light, owl, gray w/brn glass eyes, candle cup, 3½″ 145.00
Planter dish, seated child/pine cones/leaves, beaded, 6x3″ 45.00
School boy w/book bag, gold trim, brn/tan, 7¼″ 38.00
School children, lav/cream/gr, 12⅜x3⅝″, pr 298.00
Twin girls standing w/flowers, oval base, 4x2½″ 32.00
Vase, 1 w/Victorian boy & 1 w/girl, gr w/gold, 6x3¾″, pr 55.00
Whippet in racing coat, decorated, 5½x6¼″ 135.00
Wolf, erect, red jacket, bl pants, yel shirt, bow tie, 5″ 45.00

Figurines, pastel costumes, gilt trim, #89, 16″, $350.00 for the pair.

Black Americana

Black memorabilia is without a doubt a field that encompasses the most widely exploited ethnic group in our history. But within this field there are many levels of interest: arts and achievements such as folk music and literature; caricatures in advertising, souvenirs, toys, and fine art; and legitimate research into the days of their enslavement and enduring struggle for equality. The list is endless.

In the listing below are some with a derogatory connotation. Thankfully, these are from a bygone era, and represent the mores of a culture that existed nearly a century ago. They are included only to convey the fact that they are a part of this growing area of collecting interest.

When no condition is indicated, the items listed below are assumed to be in excellent condition. See also Posters, minstrel

Ash tray, Coon Chicken Inn 40.00
Ash tray, glass Mammy's Shanty, '50s, 4¼″ 28.00
Bank, Nash's Jolly Joe, glass, red paper lips, 4¼″ 15.00
Book, History of Long Island, Ross, 3 volumes, illus, 1903 . . . . . 150.00
Book, Life in Phila, comic Blk characterizations, 1829 . . . . . 550.00
Book, Little Brown Koko Has Fun 45.00
Book, Little Jeemes Henry, 45 pg 35.00
Bottle, scent; Golliwog, glass, 2¼″, EX 40.00

Figurines, painted iron, family group, sizes range from 2″ to 3¼″, $250.00 for the set.

Bowl, cereal; Rastus, Spirit of St Louis, Cream of Wheat.......65.00
Box, Aunt Jemima Pancake Flour, 1917.......................85.00
Brush, pnt wood Mammy, skirt is brush, 7″, EX..............25.00
Cabinet photo, Gracie Washburn as Eva, 1890s...............35.00
Chalkware head, Coon Chicken Inn.........................125.00
Clock, Mammy, painted metal, 7½x10½″....................350.00
Clock, pickaninny novelty w/moving eyes & tie, Lux..........500.00
Cocktail towel, forbidden fruit, print, cotton, 5x8½″...........10.00
Cookie jar, Mammy, red lips, blk eyes, NS Company, 10x6½″...85.00
Coupons, Nigger Hair tobacco, framed, 7½x9½″...............18.00
Creamer & sugar w/lid, Aunt Jemima, & Uncle Mose, EX.......40.00
Doll, Blk man, plaid cloth covered body, sock head, 13″.......45.00
Doll, carved apple head Mammy, print cotton dress, 8″.........65.00
Figurine, angel tooting horn, chalkware, mc, 3½x4″...........18.00
Figurine, bronze, Blk baby mermaid on bk of penguin........165.00
Figurine, eats melon on burlap/steel-wrap bale, bisque, 3″......60.00
Figurine, fishing boy lawn ornament, 10-lb, 6x12″.............45.00
Figurine, Louis Armstrong, plaster, grinning, 1970s, 7x18″......35.00
Game, Snake Eyes, complete, 1945..........................65.00
Handkerchief, wht w/pink printed scenes, cotton, 9½x10″.......15.00

Vargas wax figure, Mammy with basket, life-like detail, 7″, $150.00.

Humidor, Blk face, hat lid, majolica, 8½″...................225.00
Label, Caroga cane syrup, bright red/gr/brn, 6½x8″............18.00
Light, jockey, pnt metal, 13″, EX.........................125.00
Match holder, advertising w/racist connatation, '20s............20.00
Menu, Coon Chicken Inn.....................................35.00
Menu, Coon Chicken Inn, child's, mc, 4″.....................45.00
Mug, Occupied Japan, face, 5″..............................38.00
Napkin, Aunt Jemima, paper, folded to 6x6″, G...............15.00
Noisemaker, litho tin w/5 different Blk men, G................18.00
Nut dish, Blk boy figurine, ceramic, 9x6″....................25.00
Picture, Blk Cupid Asleep, brn tin fr, 5x7″..................225.00
Pincushion & tape measure, Mammy w/wood face, Japan, 36″...35.00
Pipe rack, devil & 4 men, plaster, 4x15″.....................38.00
Pipe rack, Sunny Jim, bronze, hangs on wall................150.00
Place mat, Coon Chicken Inn, paper, 13½x16½″, EX..........38.00
Planter, Blk girl eating watermelon, mc, Japan, 5x5″...........45.00

Towel, multicolor print, $25.00.

Planter, Mammy w/knapsack, ceramic, mc, 5½″................18.00
Plaques, Umbrella Kids, chalkware, mc, exaggerated, 8″........30.00
Plate, Coon Chicken Inn, mc, 9½″.........................150.00
Plate, Famous & Dandy, 6″, EX...........................125.00
Pot holder, cloth, Mammy & Pappy faces, comical, 5x6″ pr.....15.00
Pot holder hook, pnt wood chef, mc, exaggerated.............22.00
Print, Far from the Madding Crowd, mc, 11x14″, EX..........24.00
Print, Picking/Weighing Cotton in the South, Harpers, 7x10″...16.00
Print, The Thoroughbred, c 1951, mc, 12x15″................12.00
Puzzle, Jolly Nigger, metal, skill game, 1½″..................25.00
Recipe box, Aunt Jemima, red plastic, 5x3x3″.................65.00
Seal, yel glass, slave kneels, Am I Not...Sister, 1800s..........175.00
Shakers, Blk boy reading, laying on tummy, Japan, 4½″........12.00
Shakers, Blk head & watermelon slice, ceramic, mc, 3″, pr.....18.00
Shakers, chef w/barrels, mc, Japan, 5¼x5¼″.................38.00
Shakers, Mammy, Luzianne, pr.............................38.00
Shakers, Mammy & chef, chalkware, full body, 2½x2½″........12.00
Shakers, Mammy & chef, mc, Pearl Pottery, 4½″, EX, pr.......26.00
Sheet music, Colored Aristocracy, b/w, 1899, 11x14″..........15.00
Sheet music, Turkey in the Straw, 1921.......................25.00
Sign, Ballyhoo's Back, cardboard, mc, 11x21″.................30.00
Sign, Picaninny Freeze, cardboard, 1922, mc, 11x14″..........30.00

Spice jar, Aunt Jemima, nutmeg, 4″, EX....................15.00
Spoon, sterling, boy eating watermelon in bowl, 5½″, EX.......95.00
Spoon rest, nodding chef w/big hat, mc, orig label, 4½″........25.00
Tablecloth, dancing mammys, mc print cotton, 46x52″, EX.....40.00
Tablecloth, kitchen-working Blacks, mc, 43x50″..............45.00
Thermometer, Dapper Dan, shows little boy, 1949, 5½x4″......10.00
Tie rack, Flemish wood art, 3-D effect, smiling boys, 16″.......38.00
Tobacco tag, Happy Nig, fr, tag 1″ oval, 3½x3½″.............35.00
Toothpaste, Darkie, wht & blk tube, w/orig gr/blk/wht box......10.00
Toothpick, Coon Chicken Inn, heavy metal w/copper, 4″.......95.00
Towel, kitchen; singing/washing dishes......................25.00
Towels, set: four linens w/embroidered Blk girl, 17x22″........28.00

Black Cat

The main producer of 'Black Cat' collectibles was the Shafford Company, although occasionally pieces will be found bearing the marks of other firms. Wood & Sons, Ltd., in Burslem, England, produced an 8″ figural teapot as part of a novelty line marketed in this country by Fondeville of New York. Other items have been found marked 'Wales,' 'Empress,' and 'Napco Ceramics, Japan.' Black Cat collectors usually prefer to limit their 'litter' to those kittens with a shiny black glaze and styling similar to the Shafford cats.

When no condition is indicated, the items listed below are assumed to be in mint condition.

Ash tray, cat head, open mouth..............................9.00
Bookends, cat by book, 6¾″, pr..........................18.00
Condiment set, 2 cat heads.............................18.00
Cookie jar...38.00
Creamer, sitting figural.................................15.00
Cruet, dbl, 6″..14.00
Cruet, vinegar & oil, 7½″, pr.............................22.00
Egg cup..17.50
Figurine, arched cat on book by vase, gold trim, 3″...........15.00
Figurine, stack of 7 books w/cat on top, 5″..................22.00
Jar, w/lid, 5½″...35.00
Match holder/ash tray set, 4-pc...........................25.00
Mug..18.00
Pitcher, milk; full figure, Shafford, 6″......................25.00
Planter, sitting cat, 8″....................................9.00

Shakers, 4″, $12.00 for the pair.

Shakers, crouching, rhinestone eyes, 5¾x1½″, pr..............15.00
Shakers, seated, 4″, pr.................................12.00
Shakers, strolling, 3½x2½″, pr.............................9.00
Spice set, wood rack, paper Shafford labels..................75.00
Sugar bowl, wire hdl....................................20.00
Teapot, full figure, Shafford, 7½″..........................35.00
Teapot, twin spout, wicker hdl............................45.00
Teapot, 5″..18.50
Wall pocket...55.00

Black Glass

Black glass is a type of colored glass that when held to strong light usually appears deep purple--though since each glasshouse had its own formula, tones may vary. It was sometimes etched or given a satin finish, and occasionally it was decorated with silver, gold, enamel, coralene, or any of these in combination. The decoration was done either by the glasshouse or by firms that specialized in decorating glassware. Crystal, jade, colored glass or milk glass was sometimes used with the black as an accent.

Black glass has been made by many companies since the 17th century. Contemporary glasshouses produced black glass during the Depression, seldom signing their product. It is still being made today.

When no condition is indicated, the items listed below are in mint condition.

Bowl, silver floral motif, signed 'Sterling,' 4″ x 10″, $65.00.

Ash tray, elephant figure in center, 1930s, 4″ dia.............15.00
Bathroom set, enameled castle scene, 1920s, 7-pc, Czech......130.00
Bean pot, silver daisy design, key-shape finial, 1930s...........35.00
Bookends, rearing horse, 1930s, LE Smith, 8″, pr............25.00
Boot w/spur..40.00
Bowl, Art Deco, 6½x4″....................................24.50
Bowl, candy; hdl, 3-part, 5½″.............................12.00
Bowl, fern; Hobnail, w/flower frog, 7″.......................55.00
Bowl, orange/purple roses, ca 1910, Cambridge, 15″..........90.00
Bowl, ram's head hdls, silver rim, 5¼x8½″..................55.00
Box, cigarette; rectangular, dog finial, 1930s, 5″ L............15.00
Box, cigarette; turtle figural, ca 1948.......................38.00
Box, powder; Hobnail, ca 1930s...........................15.00
Bulb box, classical figures emb, satin finish, 9½″ L...........40.00
Candlestick, child kneels on 1 knee, ca 1931, Cambridge.......55.00
Candlestick, ftd ring shape, 5¾″, pr.......................25.00
Candlestick, Mt Pleasant, 2½″..............................8.00
Candlestick, octagonal bell shape, hdl, 1930s, Federal, 4″......10.00

Candlestick, triangular, stepped base, 2½", pr................16.00
Candy dish, red flowers, gold trim, hdls....................22.00
Candy dish, rnd, w/knob & metal lid, 1½"...................19.50
Card holder, draped motif...............................30.00
Compote, fish stem, shell bowl, 8"........................62.50
Compote, lace edge, ftd, 7¼"............................27.50
Console bowl on stand, 3 gold parrots w/in, satin finish........50.00
Console set, octagonal w/silver floral, 3-pc, Westmoreland.......40.00
Creamer & sugar, open; Fairfax, ftd, 1930s.................18.00
Cup, dotted band, 1930s...................................4.00
Decanter, fox hunt, sterling overlay, Nat'l Silver Co, pr........300.00
Figurine, Chessie Cat, satin finish, US Glass, 11"............100.00
Figurine, Scottish terrier, red collar/brn eyes, 5".............20.00
Flower bowl, bulbous, 3-ftd, crystal flower frog, 1940s..........20.00
Flower frog, owl, 4½".................................35.00
Inkwell, pear-shaped well, fancy base, turns, Deco, w/pen.......85.00
Lady's shoe, bow at front, 1880s English mk.................60.00
Mug, profile in beaded fr & laurel leaves both sides............40.00
Nut bowl, ftd, Mt Pleasant, 9"...........................20.00
Plate, cake; Shaggy Daisy, 1930s, US Glass.................18.00
Plate, Club & Shell border, 9¼".........................25.00
Plate, heart shape w/open hearts forming border, 8"...........29.00
Plate, S-border, triangular, 8"...........................30.00
Plate, skating boy w/dog, wht enamel, lattice edge, 8½"........40.00
Rolling pin...85.00
Shakers, Art Deco, sgn McKee, lg, pr......................30.00
Shakers, Flo, octagonal, ftd, hdl, pr.......................16.00
Sugar bowl, scalloped, dbl hdl, 4"........................10.50
Tray, floral etching, 8-sided, center hdl....................24.50
Vase, Amy, narrow neck, bulbous, flared, scalloped, 9½".......22.00
Vase, cattails, gold on satin, ftd trumpet shape, 8"............20.00
Vase, fan shape, sterling silver decor, ftd, 1930s, 8½"..........65.00
Vase, Grecian dancers, emb, Art Nouveau, 7"................35.00
Vase, HP floral, 10".................................30.00
Vase, iris, emb, 1930s, US Glass Co, 6"....................15.00
Vase, scalloped, 5"....................................8.50
Vase, silver trim, #905, LE Smith, 10½"....................35.00

Blown Glass

Blown glass is rather difficult to date; 18th and 19th century examples vary little as to technique or style--it ranges from the primitive to the sophisticated. But the metallic content of very early glass caused tiny imperfections that are obvious upon examination, and these are often indicative of age.

In America, Stiegel introduced the English technique of using a patterned, part-size mold, a practice which was generally followed by many glasshouses after the Revolution. From 1820 to about 1850, glass was blown into full-size 3-part molds.

When no condition is indicated, the items listed below are assumed to be in mint condition. Glass is assumed clear unless color is mentioned. See also specific manufacturers.

Beaker, bulbous ft, 6"................................30.00
Bottle, bulbous w/narrow neck, olive, 5⅛"..................180.00
Bottle, flattened globe, dk olive-amber, 11"................250.00
Bottle, globular, lt gr, minor wear/scratches, 9"..............130.00
Bottle, high kick-up, tubular pontil, globular, 7½", NM........105.00
Bottle, kick-up, cylindrical w/full neck, olive-amber, 10"........28.00
Bottle, scent; hourglass form, cobalt/blk/wht stripes, 2¼"......140.00
Bottle, scent; tam-o'-shanter stopper, cobalt, 6"..............115.00
Bottle, 24 swirl ribs, globular, brilliant aqua, 7¾"...........225.00
Bottle, 24-rib broken swirl, club shape, cornflower bl, 8"......550.00

Left, Decanter, blown 3-mold, with period sunburst stopper (not original), 11½", $150.00; Right, Decanter, blown 3-mold, 11¾", $325.00.

Bottle, 3-mold, olive-amber, Keene, 7¼"....................260.00
Bowl, opal netting on clear, red rim, 3x4"....................55.00
Bowl, polished base, sapphire bl, 3⅛x4½"....................90.00
Bowl, 16 swirl ribs, applied cobalt rim, ftd, 3¼x4½"..........205.00
Bowl, 16 swirl ribs, puce, folded rim, ftd, 2⅝x4¼"............90.00
Bowl, 3-mold, 3½x4½".................................95.00
Celery vase, blown 3-mold, 7½", M........................700.00
Christmas light, expanded diamond, flared, lt bl, 3½"..........75.00
Christmas light, expanded diamond, flared, lt gr, 3⅝".........125.00
Christmas light, expanded diamond, fold rim, amethyst, 3¼"...105.00
Christmas light, expanded diamond, fold rim, cobalt, 3½".......55.00
Christmas light, expanded diamond, fold rim, cranberry, 3½"....85.00
Christmas light, expanded diamond, fold rim, emerald gr, 3"....85.00
Christmas light, 16-diamond, 16 ribs below, gray-bl, 2¾"......120.00
Christmas light, 16-diamond/ogival pattern, amethyst, 3⅜".....250.00
Christmas light, 24-diamond, folded lip, puce, 3⅝"............90.00
Creamer, hdl w/scrolled base, peacock-gr, 3⅞"...............205.00
Decanter, blown 3-mold, Baroque, Rum, orig stopper, 11".....225.00
Decanter, blown 3-mold, fold rim, French, cobalt-violet, 6"......75.00
Decanter, cobalt w/wht looping, 8¾"........................65.00
Demijohn, in wicker basket, grass gr, 20-gal, 27½"...........225.00
Egg cup, opaque wht w/blk rim, 3¾".........................35.00
Egg cup, wafer stem, wht edge gallery rim on violet-bl, 3"......75.00
Fish bowl, applied flared ft, folded rim, top flared, 11".........75.00
Flask, chestnut; 25 swirl ribs, aqua, 6½", EX.................75.00
Flask, eng heart/foliage/1846, bk: wreath, 6½", EX............75.00
Flask, sunburst, olive-gr, 6¼"............................325.00
Flip, molded rib pattern in base, smokey gr, 5½"..............60.00
Hat, cobalt, 2½"......................................65.00
Hourglass, in wrought iron fr, 8½"........................200.00
Inkwell, blown 3-mold, clear olive-gr, 1¾x2¼"...............170.00
Inkwell, 24-rib w/slight swirl, minor sickness, 1⅞"............130.00
Jar, wide flared lip, olive-amber, some sickness, 13½".........135.00
Jug, sloped collared mouth, burgundy, w/hdl, 8⅜"............260.00
Pan, pinched lip, lt gr w/wide out-folded rim, NY, 3x7¼"......350.00
Pan, 3-mold, folded rim, 6¼"..............................90.00
Pitcher, Baroque, 3-mold, 6", EX..........................375.00
Pitcher, hollow hdl, applied ft, amber, 7"....................450.00
Pitcher, strap hdl, threaded neck/shoulder, aqua, 6", NM......525.00
Pitcher, 12-rib pillar-mold, ground pontil, 9½"...............240.00
Pitkin, ½-post neck, 35-rib broken swirl, gr, 7"..............225.00
Pitkin, 36 swirl ribs, olive, minor wear/residue, 5"............145.00
Pitkin, 36 swirl ribs, olive-amber, 5¼".....................140.00
Pitkin, 36-rib broken swirl, dk olive-gr, 5⅞"................250.00
Pitkin, 36-rib broken swirl, EX impression, amber, 6", EX.....195.00

Salt, applied ft & knop stem, bl-aqua, Lockport, NY, 3½″.....300.00
Salt, 10-diamond mold w/applied petal ft, 3″.....225.00
Salt, 13 vertical ribs swirl at rim, med bl, 1½x3″.....150.00
Sugar bowl, base/lid w/swirl gather, ft, gallery rim, 6½″.....375.00
Syllabub, tooled ft, 3¼″.....60.00
Syrup, blown 3-mold, applied hdl, tin lid, 7½″, EX.....155.00
Tumbler, blown 3-mold, from inkwell mold, aqua, 2⅝″.....625.00
Vase, ribbed, applied ft/baluster stem, lt bl opal, 12″.....400.00
Watch fob, clear w/cotton twist & color spiral, 1¾″.....35.00
Wine, applied ft, thick stem, crude, cobalt, 3½″.....60.00
Wine, applied ring at base of flared bowl, 4¼″.....35.00
Wine, folded rim, teardrop stem, flared, 6″, NM.....95.00
Wine, latticinio gr/yel/wht spiral stem, 4″.....225.00
Wine, wafer stem, eng swags, 3¾″.....85.00

Blue and White Stoneware

Blue and white stoneware, much of which was decorated with such in-mold designs as grazing cows and Dutch children, was made by practically every American pottery from the turn of the century until the mid-1930s. Crocks, pitchers, wash sets, rolling pins, and canisters are only a few of the items that may be found in this type of 'country' pottery that has become one of today's popular collectibles.

Roseville, Brush-McCoy, Uhl Co., and Burley Winter were among those who produced it, but very few pieces were ever signed.

Naturally, condition must be a prime consideration, especially if one is buying for resale; pieces with good, strong color and a fully molded pattern bring premium prices. Normal wear and signs of age are to be expected, since this was utility wear and received heavy use in busy households.

In the listings that follow, crocks and jars are without lids unless noted otherwise.

When no condition is indicated, the items listed below are assumed to be in near mint condition.

Butter crock, Apricot, original lid, excellent condition, $160.00.

Batter jar, Wildflower, w/lid, 8x7″ dia.....150.00
Bean pot, Swirl, Boston Baked Beans, w/lid, 9″.....295.00
Bowl, Apricot, w/bail.....85.00
Bowl, Currants & Diamonds, piecrust rim, 5x9½″ dia.....100.00
Bowl, Diamond Point, set of 4 nesting.....165.00
Bowl, Flying Bird, berry.....95.00

Soap dish, Rose and Fishscale, mint condition, 5″, $135.00.

Bowl, Reverse Pyramids/Reverse Picket Fence, 5x10½″.....55.00
Bowl, Wedding Ring, 10″.....100.00
Bowl, Wedding Ring, 3½x7″.....75.00
Butter crock, Apricot, orig lid.....160.00
Butter crock, Basketweave, orig lid.....170.00
Butter crock, Basketweave & Flower, w/lid & bail.....185.00
Butter crock, Block, w/lid & bail.....145.00
Butter crock, Blue Band, w/lid & bail.....75.00
Butter crock, Butterfly, no lid.....85.00
Butter crock, Butterfly, w/lid & bail.....130.00
Butter crock, Cow, printed, w/bail.....105.00
Butter crock, Cows & Columns.....180.00
Butter crock, Cows & Fence, w/lid & bail.....275.00
Butter crock, Daisy & Trellis, orig lid.....135.00
Butter crock, Dragonfly & Flower, w/lid & bail.....250.00
Butter crock, Dutch stencil, w/bail, no lid.....95.00
Butter crock, Eagle, orig lid, NM.....275.00
Butter crock, Indian & Wigwams, no lid.....225.00
Butter crock, Indian Good Luck, orig lid.....115.00
Butter crock, Peacock, no lid.....225.00
Butter crock, Scroll, orig lid.....110.00
Butter crock, Waffle Weave, no lid.....115.00
Butter crock, Wildflower, no lid.....85.00
Canister, Basketweave, Cinnamon, orig lid, 5½″.....135.00
Canister, Basketweave, Coffee.....175.00
Canister, Basketweave, Nutmeg, 3½″.....110.00
Canister, Basketweave, Raisins, orig lid.....195.00
Canister, Blue Band, Cinnamon, sm.....45.00
Canister, Blue Band, Pepper, sm.....45.00
Canister, Snowflake, Coffee, 6½″.....110.00
Chamber pot, Bow Tie, no lid.....75.00
Coffee pot, Swirl, orig liner.....550.00
Cookie jar, Basketweave, Put Your Fist In, orig lid, 7½″.....200.00
Crock, milk; Apricot, 10″.....125.00
Crock, milk; Daisy & Lattice, 4x8″ dia.....140.00
Cup, Paneled Fir Tree, 3½x3″ dia.....65.00
Grease jar, Flying Bird, orig lid.....250.00
Measuring cup, Spearpoint & Flower.....135.00
Meat tenderizer, Wildflower.....175.00
Mug, Barrel.....48.00
Mug, Basketweave & Apple Blossoms.....75.00

Mug, Bow Tie....50.00
Mug, Felko....115.00
Mug, Flying Bird....145.00
Pedestal, Tulip, 7″....200.00
Pitcher, Alpine, beer, 10½″....400.00
Pitcher, American Beauty Rose, 10x7″....195.00
Pitcher, Apricot, chain medallion, rope hdl, 8″....145.00
Pitcher, Avenue of Trees, lg....235.00
Pitcher, Basketweave & Morning Glory, 9″....160.00
Pitcher, Beaded Panels w/Open Rose, hot water, 10x8″ dia....150.00
Pitcher, Blue Band....135.00
Pitcher, Blue Band Scroll....175.00
Pitcher, Bluebird, 3 birds on side, allover bl....175.00
Pitcher, Bluebird, 3 birds on side, scarce, 9″....215.00
Pitcher, Bow Tie, bird transfer, w/bowl, set....275.00
Pitcher, Butterfly, 4½″....235.00
Pitcher, Butterfly, 9x7″....135.00
Pitcher, Castle & Fishscale, 8″....195.00
Pitcher, Cattail, 7″....135.00
Pitcher, Cattail, 9″....150.00
Pitcher, Cherry Band, 6″....195.00
Pitcher, Cherry Band, 8½″....210.00
Pitcher, Cherry Cluster....185.00
Pitcher, Cosmos....110.00
Pitcher, Cows, rope/bead medallion, rope hdl, 8″....165.00
Pitcher, Dainty Fruit....115.00
Pitcher, Daisy....175.00
Pitcher, Diffused Blue....65.00
Pitcher, Doe & Fawn....195.00
Pitcher, Doe & Fawn, allover bl....145.00
Pitcher, Dutch Boy & Girl....150.00
Pitcher, Dutch Farm, 9″....145.00
Pitcher, Dutch Landscape, tankard style....165.00
Pitcher, Eagle, M....325.00
Pitcher, Edelweiss, bl/gray....175.00
Pitcher, Girl & Dog, sponge trim....300.00
Pitcher, Grape w/Rickrack, 8″....150.00
Pitcher, Indian Boy & Girl....185.00
Pitcher, Indian Good Luck....140.00
Pitcher, Indian Head in War Bonnet, waffle sq body, 8″, EX...195.00
Pitcher, Leaping Deer, 8½″....145.00
Pitcher, Pine Cone, straight sides, 9½x5¾″ dia....175.00
Pitcher, riveted band, 'Seattle Export Co-Chicago,' 7″....175.00
Pitcher, Rose & Fishscale....140.00
Pitcher, rose decal, lg....95.00
Pitcher, Rose on Trellis, bulbous base, 6½″....120.00
Pitcher, Swan, 8″....185.00
Pitcher, Swirl....185.00
Pitcher, Tulip....165.00
Pitcher, Windmill & Bush, 7″....145.00
Pitcher & wash bowl, Feather & Swirl....250.00
Roaster, Swirl, 8x15½″....225.00
Roaster, Wildflower, w/lid, 8½x12″ dia....125.00
Rolling pin, rust band, w/advertisement....175.00
Rolling pin, Swirl, orig wood hdls, 13x3″ dia....225.00
Rolling pin, Wildflower, no advertising....185.00
Rolling pin, Wildflower, w/advertising....225.00
Salt crock, Apricot, orig lid....125.00
Salt crock, Blackberry, 5½x5½″ dia....110.00
Salt crock, Butterfly, orig lid....185.00
Salt crock, Daisy, orig lid....135.00
Salt crock, Flying Bird, no lid....235.00
Salt crock, Flying Bird, orig lid....300.00
Salt crock, Peacock, orig lid....225.00
Salt crock, pointer dog relief, Flemish, 6x5½″....60.00
Salt crock, Wildflower....95.00
Soap dish, Beaded Rose....150.00
Soap dish, Cat's Head....195.00
Soap dish, Indian in War Bonnet, beaded snake rim....175.00
Soap dish, Lion....165.00
Soap dish, rose decal, orig lid....75.00
Spittoon, Peacock, brick foundation design, 9x10″ dia....250.00
Teapot, Swirl, wire bail, 9″....550.00
Toothbrush holder, Bow Tie....40.00
Toothbrush holder, rose decal....50.00
Wash bowl & pitcher, Bluebird....375.00
Water cooler, 'Ice Water,' Apple Blossom, w/lid, 6-gal....800.00
Water cooler, Apple Blossom, 17″....525.00
Water cooler, Polar Bear....475.00

Bluebird China

Made from 1910 to 1934, Bluebird china is lovely ware decorated with bluebirds flying among pink flowering branches. It was inexpensive dinnerware, and reached the height of its popularity in the second decade of this century. Several potteries produced it; shapes differ from one manufacturer to another, but with only minor variations, the decal remains the same.

Among the backstamps, you'll find W.S. George, Cleveland, Carrolton, Homer Laughlin, and Limoges China of Sebring, Ohio . . . and there are others.

Bowl, covered; mk SP Clinchfield, 8½″ dia....85.00
Bowl, fruit; mk Hopewell China, 5″....8.00
Bowl, soup; mk PMC Co, 8″....25.00
Bowl, vegetable; mk National China, 7½x10″....25.00
Butter, 4½″ holder w/in 7″ dia dish, mk Steubenville....85.00
Casserole, covered; mk Ostrow China, 10½″ dia....95.00
Casserole, covered; mk SP Clinchfield, 8½″ dia....85.00
Casserole, open; mk Hopewell China, 7½x11½″....95.00
Creamer & sugar w/lid, Homer Laughlin....45.00
Pitcher, milk; mk Colonial Co, 10½″....120.00
Plate, dessert; mk Limoges, 6″....8.00
Plate, luncheon; mk WS George, 9¾″....15.00
Plate, mk National China, 8″....10.00
Platter, mk Clinchfield, 8½x11½″....50.00
Platter, mk Hopewell, 13x17½″....95.00
Platter, no mk, 7½x10″....35.00
Syrup, no mk, 4½″....25.00
Tea cup, no mk....15.00
Teapot, mk ELP Co, 8½x8½″....125.00

Blue Ridge

Blue Ridge dinnerware was produced by Southern Potteries of Erwin, Tennessee, from the late 1930s until 1956, in eight basic styles and over four hundred different patterns, all of which were hand decorated under the glaze. Vivid colors lit up floral arrangements of seemingly endless variation, fruit of every sort from simple clusters to lush assortments, barnyard fowl, peasant figures, and unpretentious textured patterns.

Although it is these dinnerware lines for which they are best known, collectors prize the artist signed plates from the forties and the limited line of character jugs made during the fifties most highly.

Authority Betty Newbound has compiled a lovely book, *Blue Ridge Dinnerware*, with beautiful color illustrations and current market values. She is listed in the Directory under Michigan.

When no condition is indicated, the items listed below are assumed to be in mint condition.

Apple, Colonial, bowl, cereal....4.00
Apple, Colonial, bowl, fruit....3.00
Apple, Colonial, cup....4.00
Apple, Colonial, plate, 10″....6.00
Apple, Colonial, plate, 7″....4.00
Apple, Colonial, plate, 8″....4.00
Apple, Colonial, plate, 9″....5.00
Apple, Colonial, saucer....3.00
Apple, Skyline, bowl, fruit....3.00
Apple Jack, plate, 10″....7.00
Apple Jack, plate, 9″....5.00
Arlene, plate, yel trim, 10″....4.00
Ash tray, advertising....7.50
Ash tray, individual....3.50
Autumn Apple, cup & saucer....5.00
Autumn Apple, plate, 9½″....4.00
Avon, plate, salad....5.00
Avon, plate, 11½″....10.00
Betty, server, 2-tier....15.00
Big Apple, cup & saucer....6.00
Big Apple, plate, 10″....5.00
Big Apple, saucer....2.00
Big Apple, sugar bowl w/lid, lg....7.00
Blossom Top, shaker, 5″....9.50
Blue Flower, sugar bowl w/lid....7.00
Bluebell Bouquet, Candlewick, plate, 9¼″....5.00
Bluebell Bouquet, Candlewick, saucer....2.00
Carnival, Candlewick, bowl, fruit....3.00
Carnival, Candlewick, bowl, soup; flat, 8″....4.00
Carnival, Candlewick, plate, 6″....3.00
Carnival, Candlewick, plate, 9″....4.00
Caroline, Skyline, bowl, vegetable; oval....9.00
Caroline, Skyline, cup....4.00
Caroline, Skyline, plate, 6″....2.00
Caroline, Skyline, sugar bowl w/lid....6.00
Caroline, Woodcrest, creamer....5.00
Caroline, Woodcrest, cup & saucer....6.00
Caroline, Woodcrest, gravy boat....9.00
Cheerio, plate, 10″....7.00
Cherokee Rose, bowl, cereal; 6″....3.50
Cherokee Rose, bowl, fruit; 5¼″....3.00
Cherokee Rose, creamer....4.00
Cherokee Rose, cup & saucer....5.00
Cherokee Rose, plate, 9½″....5.00
Cherokee Rose, platter....6.00
Chickory, Colonial, plate, 9″....5.75
Child's play set, 16-pc....120.00
Chrysanthemum, cup & saucer....3.50
Colonial Rose, plate, 9½″....3.50
Coreopsis, bowl, 6″....3.00
Coreopsis, plate, dinner....4.00
Country Garden, plate, 9½″....4.00
County Fair, plate, assorted fruit, 8¼″....4.50
Crabapple, bowl, rnd, 9″....8.00
Crabapple, bowl, soup; flat....3.50
Crabapple, bowl, vegetable; oval....9.00
Crabapple, cake plate, 10½″....8.00
Crabapple, cup & saucer....4.00
Crabapple, plate, 6″....3.00
Crabapple, plate, 9¼″....5.00

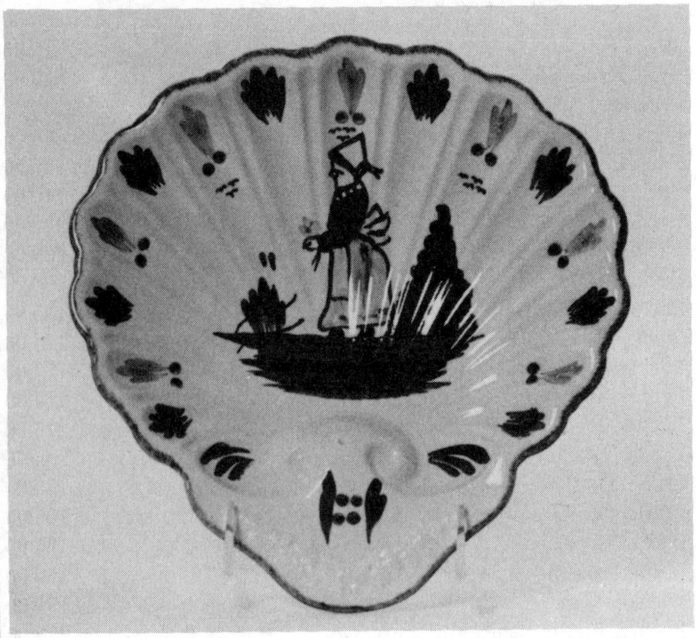

Shell dish, French Peasant, 9¼″, $50.00.

Crabapple, platter, 13½″....6.00
Crabapple, saucer....2.00
Cumberland, Astor, plate, 10″....8.00
Delicious, plate, 9¼″....3.50
Delicious, platter, 11½″....6.00
Desert Flower, Skyline, plate, 9″....4.00
Easter Parade, relish, deep....27.00
Evening Flower, Skyline, bowl, vegetable; oval....8.00
Evening Flower, Skyline, sugar bowl, no lid....4.00
Flower Wreath, Candlewick, plate, 7″....4.00
Foxfire, platter, 13½″....8.00
Fruit Fantasy, bowl, 9¼″....8.00
Fruit Fantasy, relish, leaf shape, 10″....28.00
Fruit Punch, plate, 9½″....3.50
Garden Lane, party plate & cup....6.00
Garden Lane, plate, 9½″....4.00
Gingham Fruit, plate, 9½″....3.50
Green Eyes, Skyline, plate, 10″....6.00
Greenbrier, Piecrust, bowl, fruit....3.00
Greenbrier, Piecrust, bowl, 9½″....9.75
Greenbrier, Piecrust, cup & saucer....7.00
Greenbrier, Piecrust, saucer....3.00
June Bouquet, cup & saucer, demitasse....12.00
Mardi Gras, Colonial, plate, 9″....5.00
Mardi Gras, sugar bowl....4.00
Mayflower, Skyline, bowl, fruit....2.00
Mountain Ivy, platter, 12½″....5.50
Nocturne, Colonial, casserole, w/lid....10.00
Nocturne, Colonial, plate, 10″....6.00
Nocturne, Colonial, plate, 6″....3.00
Nocturne, Colonial, plate, 9″....5.00
Peony, cup & saucer, demitasse....12.00
Petal Point, Skyline, cup....5.00
Petal Point, Skyline, plate, 9″....5.00
Petunia, plate, 10″....7.00
Plantation Ivy, Skyline, cup & saucer....6.00
Plantation Ivy, Skyline, sugar bowl w/lid....7.00
Plate, Christmas....20.00
Plate, Turkey....20.00
Poinsettia, plate, sq, 12″....10.00

Poinsettia, plate, 10″ 8.00
Poinsettia, plate, 7″ 3.00
Red Barn, plate, 6¼″ 4.00
Ridge Daisy, cup & saucer, demitasse 12.00
Ridge Daisy, plate, sq, 7½″ 4.00
Rosalind, Colonial, bowl, fruit 3.00
Rosette, plate, 9″ 3.50
Sculptured Fruit, pitcher 35.00
Shakers, chicken figural, pr 17.50
Southern Camelia, Piecrust, bowl, 9½″ dia 9.00
Southern Camelia, Piecrust, creamer & sugar w/lid 12.00
Southern Camelia, Piecrust, plate, 9½″ 5.50
Spider Web, Skyline, bowl, soup; flat, yel 4.00
Spider Web, Skyline, plate, yel, 7″ 3.00
Spider Web, Skyline, plate, yel, 8″ 4.00
Spider Web, Skyline, shaker, salt; yel 4.00
Spindrift, plate, 9½″ 3.50
Spray, Piecrust, bowl, cereal 4.00
Spray, Piecrust, cup & saucer 6.00
Spray, Piecrust, plate, 6″ 2.00
Spray, Piecrust, plate, 9″ 4.00
Stanhome Ivy, bowl, fruit 3.00
Stanhome Ivy, bowl, rnd, 9″ 5.00
Stanhome Ivy, cup 4.00
Stanhome Ivy, gravy boat 5.00
Stanhome Ivy, plate, 6″ 2.00
Stanhome Ivy, plate, 9″ 4.00
Stanhome Ivy, platter, lg 5.00
Stanhome Ivy, sugar bowl 4.00
Strawberry, bowl, rnd, 9″ 8.00
Strawberry, platter, 12″ 7.50
Summertime, celery tray w/hdl 20.00
Sun Bouquet, platter, 12″ 5.00
Sunny Spray, bowl, vegetable; oval 7.00
Sunny Spray, bowl, vegetable; rnd 6.00
Sunny Spray, cup & saucer 6.00
Sunny Spray, plate, 10″ 6.00
Sunny Spray, plate, 6″ 3.00
Sunny Spray, plate, 7″ 4.00
Sunny Spray, plate, 9″ 5.00
Sunny Spray, platter, oval 5.00
Tic Tack, plate, 9½″ 3.50
Tralee Rose, Spiral, pitcher, 7″ 28.00
Tray, for batter set 25.00
Tray, for chocolate set 75.00
Tulip Trio, plate, dinner 4.00
Vase, hdl, made into lamp 35.00
Wild Strawberry, Colonial, plate, 6″ 3.00
Windflower, Colonial, plate, 9″ 5.00
Winesap, bowl, 6¼″ 3.00
Winesap, platter, oval, 9″ 4.50

Boch Freres

Founded in the early 1840s in La Louviere, Boch Freres Keramos became the foremost producer of art pottery in Belgium. Though primarily they served a localized market, in 1844 they earned world-wide recognition for some of their sculptural works on display at the International Exposition in Paris.

In 1907, Charles Catteau of France was appointed head of the art department. Before that time the firm had concentrated on developing glazes and perfecting elegant forms. The style they pursued was traditional, favoring the re-creation of established 18th century ceramics. Catteau brought with him to Boch Freres the New Wave, or Art Nouveau influence in form and decoration. His designs won him international acclaim at the Exhibition d'Art Decoratif in Paris in 1925, and it is for his work that Boch Freres is so highly regarded today. He occasionally signed his work as well as that of others who, under his direct supervision, carried out his preconceived designs. He was associated with the company until 1950, and lived the remainder of his life in Nice, France, where he died in 1966.

The Boch Freres Keramos factory continues operations today, producing bathroom fixtures and other utilitarian wares.

A variety of marks were used, all incorporating some combination of 'Boch Freres,' 'Keramos,' 'BFK,' or 'Ch Catteau.'

When no condition is indicated, the items listed below are assumed to be in mint condition.

Bowl, yel leaves/gr ribbon/circles, brn, Art Deco, 11x2¼″ 95.00
Plaque, cattle/windmill, floral trim, delft, pierced, 15½″ 68.00
Plaque, man & lady in 1-horse sleigh, delft, pierced, 15½″ 68.00
Vase, bl streaky glaze, metal mts, ovoid, 12″, pr 225.00
Vase, gulls & waves, stylized, ivory, bulbous, sgn, 9″ 260.00

Plates, fisherman, lady with book, flow blue, marked Boch Freres, 11¼″, $55.00 for the pair.

Boehm

Boehm sculptures were the creation of Edward Marshall Boehm, a ceramic artist who coupled his love of the art with his love of nature to produce figurines of birds, animals, and flowers in lovely background settings accurate to the smallest detail. Sculptures of historical figures and those representing the fine arts were also made, and along with many of the bird figurines have established secondary market values many times their original price.

His first pieces were made in the very early 1950s, in Trenton, New Jersey, under the name of Osso Ceramics. Mr. Boehm died in 1969, and the firm has since been managed by his wife. Today, known as Edward Marshall Boehm, Inc., the private family-held corporation produces not only porcelain sculptures, but collector plates as well. Both limited and non-limited editions of their works have been issued.

Examples are marked with various backstamps, all of which have incorporated the Boehm name since 1951. 'Osso Ceramics' in upper case lettering was used in 1950 and 1951.

When no condition is indicated, the items listed below are assumed to be in mint condition.

Alex's Red Rose 1,100.00
Angel, brother, kneeling, no decor, 5¼″ 60.00
Angel Face Rose 300.00
Apollo, wht bsk, rare 450.00

Arabian Stallion ... 1,150.00
Ash tray, clover in center, glazed ... 50.00
Basket, bee, wht bsk ... 400.00
Black Capped Chickadee ... 550.00
Blue Iris on Stem ... 350.00
Blue Moon Rose ... 600.00
Bob White Quail, female, wood base, early, rare ... 800.00
Bob White Quail, wht bsk, rare ... 2,000.00
Bookends, owls, closed 1970, 9″, pr ... 450.00
Box, bunny, glazed ... 275.00
Box, cigarette; celadon ... 65.00
Box, cigarette; clover, glazed/decorated ... 175.00
California Quail ... 2,000.00
Canada Geese, wht bsk, rare ... 1,800.00
Canvasback Duck, male, rare ... 550.00
Cat w/Kittens, early ... 595.00
Catbird ... 1,500.00
Cedar Waxwing w/Cherry ... 600.00
Chick, yel, old ... 200.00
Chipmunk, sitting ... 110.00
Cocker Spaniel, 3-color, old ... 450.00
Colt, w/emerald eyes, gold ... 750.00
Crimson Topaz Hummingbird ... 1,100.00
Dachshund, early ... 400.00
Dalmation, glazed ... 350.00
Eastern Bluebird ... 350.00
Edward Boehm Camellia ... 650.00
Elizabeth of Glamis Rose ... 1,400.00
Emmett Barnes Camellia, Ltd ... 600.00
Everglade Kites ... 5,000.00
Firecrest w/Larch ... 400.00
Fledgling Baby Grouse ... 200.00
Fledgling Barred Owl ... 150.00
Fledgling Blackburnian Warbler, issued 1964-1972 ... 275.00
Fledgling Blue Jay ... 200.00
Fledgling Brown Thrasher ... 435.00
Fledgling Canadian Warbler ... 1,700.00
Fledgling Cardinal II ... 150.00
Fledgling Cuckoo ... 150.00
Fledgling Eastern Bluebird II ... 150.00
Fledgling Little Blue Heron ... 200.00
Fledgling Magpie ... 165.00
Fledgling Pileated Woodpecker ... 175.00
Fledgling Puffin ... 150.00
Fledgling Robin ... 200.00
Fledgling Saw-Whet Owl ... 250.00
Fledgling Western Bluebirds ... 300.00
Fledling Gosling, Ltd ... 90.00
Frog, w/sapphire eyes, gold ... 360.00
Frog on Lily Pad ... 175.00
Giant Panda ... 5,500.00
Goldfinches w/Scottish Thistle ... 1,500.00
Gorilla ... 2,850.00
Gray Wagtail ... 900.00
Helen Boehm Camellia ... 650.00
Helen Boehm Yellow Iris ... 875.00
Hereford Bull ... 650.00
Hooded Merganser ... 2,250.00
Hooded Warbler w/Iris ... 1,600.00
Hunter ... 900.00
Indigo Bunting on inverted flowerpot ... 400.00
Kestrels ... 2,500.00
Kitten, blk/wht ... 95.00
Lamb ... 75.00
Lesser Prairie Chickens, old, pr ... 975.00
Linnet w/Gentians ... 500.00
Lion Cub ... 475.00
Madonna, wht bsk ... 150.00
Magnolia Grandiflora ... 1,650.00
Meadowlark w/Dandelions & Mushrooms ... 1,800.00
Mearns Quail w/Cactus, pr ... 3,000.00
Mercury, bsk, rare ... 450.00
Mute Swans ... 5,500.00
Neptune w/Seahorse, wht bsk ... 450.00
Non Pareil Buntings, limited ... 800.00
Nut dish, shell shape, wht glaze, rare ... 150.00
Orchid w/Hummingbird ... 400.00
Oven Bird ... 1,100.00
Pascali Rose Centerpiece ... 1,200.00
Peach Rose Centerpiece ... 1,600.00
Pink Begonia, Ltd ... 1,000.00
Pink Rainbow Rose ... 125.00
Pitcher, grape, bl glazed/decorated, rare ... 650.00
Pope Pius XII, bust, wht bsk, lg ... 800.00
Pope Pius XII, bust, wht bsk, sm ... 350.00
Purple Martins ... 6,500.00
Rabbits, male & female, 1950s, pr ... 300.00
Raccoons ... 1,400.00
Red Poppies ... 850.00
Red Squirrels w/Oak ... 1,800.00
Rhododendron Centerpiece ... 1,450.00
Robin w/Snowdrops ... 575.00
Rose, w/diamond dewdrop, gold ... 660.00
Ruby Crowned Kinglets ... 1,100.00
Ruffled Grouse ... 3,900.00
Scissor-tail Flycatcher ... 2,400.00
Snow White Rose ... 350.00
Spanish Iris ... 475.00
Squirrels, ltd ... 1,500.00
Supreme Peace Rose ... 1,800.00
Swan Lake Camellia ... 1,600.00
Towhee ... 1,500.00

Hooded Kestrels, #492R, issued 1968, 16″, $800.00 for the pair.

Tree Sparrow, 1953 .... 380.00
Tropicana Rose, Early 900.00
Turtle, w/sapphire eyes, gold 360.00
Western Bluebird, pr 5,500.00
White Dogwood, Old 750.00
Willow Warbler 500.00
Wood Thrush 5,700.00
Yellow Billed Cuckoo 1,800.00
Yellow Rose, on base 300.00
Young Fee Fawns 1,500.00

Bohemian Glass

The term 'Bohemian glass' has come to refer to a type of glass developed in Bohemia in the late 6th century at the Imperial Court of Rudolf II, the Hapsburg Emperor. The popular artistic pursuit of the day was stone carving and it naturally followed to transfer familiar procedures to the glassmaking industry.

During the next century, a formula was discovered that produced a glass with a fine crystal appearance which lent itself well to deep, intricate engraving, and the art was further advanced.

Although many other types of art glass were made there, collectors today use the term 'Bohemian glass' to most often indicate clear glass overlaid with color, through which a design is cut or etched. Red on crystal was used most often, but other colors may also be found. Another type of Bohemian glass involves cutting through and exposing three layers of color in patterns that are often very intricate. Items such as these are sometimes further decorated with enamel work.

When no condition is indicated, the items listed below are assumed to be in mint condition.

Decanters, red overlay, vintage motif, 12″, $195.00 for the pair.

Bottle, ruby, vintage, w/stopper, 7½″ 55.00
Bottle, scent; floradora, cranberry, VG gold, orig stopper 145.00
Bottle, scent; gr, gold motif, orig stopper 125.00
Bottle, scent; ruby, deer scene/circles, cut stopper, 7½″ 135.00
Bowl, ruby, deer & castle, 8″ 65.00
Butter dish, ruby, deer & castle 100.00
Candlesticks, olive gr, deer & castle, scalloped, 9″, pr 105.00
Candy dish, ruby, castle & trees 75.00
Decanter, amber, deer & castle, 16″ 100.00
Decanter, amber, vintage, 15″ 85.00
Decanter, ruby, birds, leaves & flowers, w/stopper, 9¾″ 45.00
Decanter, ruby, deer & castle, #d stopper, 14½″ 100.00
Decanter, ruby, duck in flight/cattails, 17″, pr 175.00
Decanter, ruby, leaf design, #d stopper, EX 85.00
Decanter, ruby, vintage, 10″ 65.00
Decanter, ruby, vintage, 15″ 85.00
Finger bowl, ruby, vintage, 4¼″ 45.00
Goblet, crystal, two deer in woods, octagon form, 7″ 135.00
Stein, amber, building on front, pewter/glass lid, 2¼″ 125.00
Sweetmeat, ruby, dove & castle, 10″ 65.00
Vase, cranberry, 10″ 160.00
Vase, ruby, dove & castle, 6½″ 56.00
Vase, ruby, frosted flower panel, blown, 7½″ 29.00
Wine, ruby, ea w/eng wild animal, set of 6 .... 450.00
Wine, ruby, vintage, 5″ 25.00

Bookends

Though a few were produced before 1880, bookends became a necessary library accessory and a popular commodity after the printing industry was revolutionized by Mergenthaler's invention, the linotype. Books became abundantly available at such affordable prices that almost every home suddenly had need for bookends. They were carved from wood, cast in iron, bronze, or brass, or cut from stone. Today's collectors may find such designs as ships, animals, flowers and children. Patriotic themes, art reproductions, and those with Art Nouveau and Art Deco styling provide a basis for a diverse and interesting collection.

In the listings below, bookends are priced as a pair. When no condition is indicated, they are assumed to be in mint condition.

Acorns & leaves, cluster of 3 upright, CI, 7″ 50.00
American eagles, metal figurals 45.00
Basket of nuts & fruit, CI w/orig gold pnt, early 1900s 30.00
Chas Lindbergh, Our Aviator, CI 90.00
Chas Lindbergh, portrait style, bronzed metal 60.00
Crouching tiger, bronze, c 1930 .... 45.00
Deer, erect, head to side, full rack, CI/pnt, 8″ 35.00
Dying Gladiator, bronzed metal 30.00
Elephant, teak w/ivory tusks/toenails/eyes 125.00
Farmer & wife in field, bronzed metal 30.00
Geo Washington, bronze, sgn John F Dix 40.00
Indian, detailed bust of warrior, bronze 35.00
Innocence, little girl, bronze 75.00
Isadora Duncan, FF Ziegler, bronze, 2 views, 1921, #521 .... 500.00

End of the Trail, marked 'Solid Bronze,' 4½″, $45.00.

Lincoln Memorial, bronzed wht metal........................45.00
Little Egypt, bronzed metal, 7″..............................75.00
Man on bench, book in hand, orange/gold on heavy metal......55.00
Nautical, ship's wheel, compasses...........................55.00
Nude, kneeling, horseshoe base, imp Tinos, bronze, 7½″......165.00
Old man w/book in armchair, gr/gold/wht on metal, Ruhl.......70.00
Oriental scholars, polychromed carved wood/brass mts..........85.00
Owls, Art Deco, solid brass, sgn Art Brass Co, NY, 4″.........55.00
Pointers, facing pr, 7¾″......................................25.00
Sailing ships, bronze...25.00
Shakespeare, metal figural....................................45.00
Shepherd dog & house, bronze, lg..............................35.00
Statue, They that go down to the sea..., Jennings, 8½″.........75.00
Swan, metal figural, blk marble base..........................65.00
Turkey, stylized, French ceramic, cream/silver glaze, 6¾″......150.00

Bootjacks and Bootscrapers

Bootjacks were made from metal or wood - - some were fancy figural shapes, others strictly business! Their purpose was to facilitate the otherwise awkward process of removing one's boots. Bootscrapers were handy gadgets that provided an effective way to clean the soles of mud and such.

When no condition is indicated, the items listed below are assumed to be in excellent condition.

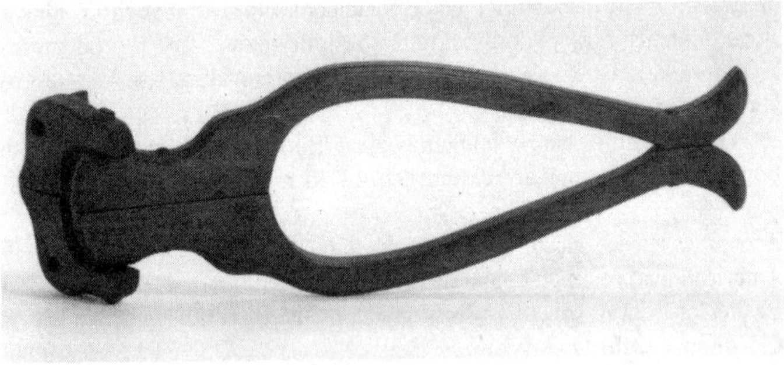

Bootjack, black walnut wood, wall mount, 23″, $80.00.

Bootjack, beetle, sand-cast iron, open heart bk, 10x4½x3″.....135.00
Bootjack, collapsible, iron, rare.............................65.00
Bootjack, cricket, CI, 9¼″....................................35.00
Bootjack, mule's head, CI.....................................38.00
Bootjack, Naughty Nellie, CI, no pnt, 9″......................18.00
Bootjack, Naughty Nellie, CI, orig gold pnt...................55.00
Bootjack, Try Me, lacy CI.....................................57.00
Bootscraper, blade shaped on bottom, wrought iron, 6x12″.....75.00
Bootscraper, dachshund, barking, rnd tail hdl, CI, 22x8″......165.00
Bootscraper, dachshund, pnt CI, Alabama Pipe Co ad, 11″.....85.00
Bootscraper, dog silhouette/tooled, wrought iron, 12″ L.......525.00
Bootscraper, foliage, CI, 12x14½″.............................90.00
Bootscraper, ram horn scrolls, wrought iron/stone, 8x12″......225.00
Bootscraper, Scotty dog, CI...................................65.00
Bootscraper, simple blade/ball-top posts, wrought iron, sm......55.00
Bootscraper, thin scraper/2 supports: C-shape atop, forged......80.00

Boru, Sorcha

Sorcha Boru was the professional name used by California ceramist Claire Stewart. She was a founding member of the Allied Arts Guild of Menlo Park (California) where she maintained a studio from 1932 to 1938. From 1938 until 1955, she operated Sorcha Boru Ceramics, a production studio in San Carlos. Her highly acclaimed output consisted of colorful, slip-decorated figurines, salt and pepper shakers, vases, wall pockets, and flower bowls. Most production work was incised by hand 'S.B.C.'

When no condition is indicated, the items listed below are assumed to be in mint condition.

Figurine, blue jay, 6½″.......................................165.00
Wall pocket, Joan Crawford mask, sgn SBC, 7x6″...............250.00

Chess set, Capitalism vs. Labor, ca 1930, 32 pcs, $3,000.00 at auction.

Bottles and Flasks

As far back as the first century B.C., the Romans preferred blown glass containers for their pills and potions. Though you're not apt to find many of those, you will find bottles of every size, shape and color made to hold perfume, ink, medicine, soda, spirits, vinegar, and many other liquids.

American business firms preferred glass bottles in which to package their commercial products, and used them extensively from the late 18th century on. Bitters bottles contained 'medicine'--actually herb flavored alcohol--and judging from the number of these found today, their contents found favor with many! Because of a heavy tax imposed on the sale of liquor in 17th century England by King George, who hoped to curtail alcohol abuse among his subjects, bottlers simply added 'curative' herbs to their brew and thus avoided taxation. Since gin was taxed in America as well, the practice continued in this country. Scores of brands were sold; among the most popular were Dr. H.S. Flint & Co. Quaker Bitters, Dr. Kaufman's Anti-Cholera Bitters, and Dr. J. Hostetter's Stomach Bitters. Most bitters bottles were made in shades of amber, brown and aquamarine. Clear glass was used, to a lesser extent, as were green tones. Blue, amethyst, red-brown, and milk glass examples are rare.

Perfume or scent bottles were produced abroad by companies all over Europe from the late 16th century on. Perfume making became such a prolific trade that as a result beautifully decorated bottles were fashionable. In America, they were produced in great quantities by Stiegel in 1770, and by Boston and Sandwich in the early 19th century. Cologne bottles were first made in about 1830, and toilet water bottles in the 1880s; Rene Lalique produced fine scent bottles from as early as the turn of the century. The earliest were one-of-a-kind creations with silver casings. He later designed bottles for the Coty Perfume Company, with a different style for each Coty fragrance. (See also Lalique)

Spirit flasks from the 19th century were blown in specially designed molds that produced various motifs including political subjects, railroad trains, and symbolic devices. The most commonly used colors were amber, dark brown and green.

From the 20th century, early pop and beer bottles are very collectible, as are nearly every extinct commercial container.

Bottles may be dated by the methods used in their production. For instance, a rough pontil indicates a date before 1845. The iron pontil, used from then until about 1860, left a metallic residue on the base of the bottle which is evident upon examination. A seam that reaches from base to lip marks a machine-made bottle from after 1903, while an applied or hand finished lip points to an early mold-blown bottle. The Industrial Revolution saw keen competition between manufacturers, and as a result scores of patents were issued. Many concentrated on various types of closures; the crown bottle cap, for instance, was patented in 1892. If a manufacturer's name is present, consulting a book on marks may help you date your bottle.

When no condition is indicated, the items listed below are assumed to be in mint condition. Color is assumed clear unless noted otherwise.

See also Advertising, various brands such as Coca-Cola; Avon; California Perfume Company; Lalique; Medical Collectibles

Key:

am—applied mouth	gp—graphite pontil
bk— back	grd—ground pontil
bt—blob top	GW— Glass Works
cm—collared mouth	ip—iron pontil
fm —flared mouth	ps—pontil scar
gm—ground mouth	sm—sheared mouth
	tm—tooled mouth

Suffolk Bitters, figural pig, double-collared mouth, smooth base, yellow, 10¼″, $575.00.

Bitters Bottles

Andrew Lee Compound Cathartic, sq cm, aqua, stained, 8″.....45.00
Augauer, rectangular, sloping cm, yel-gr, 8⅛″................100.00
Begg's Dandelion, sloping cm, amber, 9⅛″, EX..............45.00
Berkshire, pig, cm, dk gold-amber, 9½″ L.................1,000.00
Boerhaves Holland, dbl cm, aqua, 9″......................60.00
Boker's Stomach, label only (damage), gold-amber, 12¼″.......50.00
Bourbon Whiskey Bitters, barrel, dk strawberry puce, 9⅜″.....200.00
Bow's Cascara, sloping cm, 9⅜″..........................55.00
Brown's Celebrated Indian Herb, Indian queen, amber, 12″....300.00
Brown's Celebrated Indian Herb, Indian queen, gr-yel, 12⅛″...800.00
Cacamoke, sloping cm, yel-amber, 9⅝″.....................80.00
California Fig & Herb, sloping cm w/ring, yel-amber, 9⅞″.......50.00
Canteen, sloping cm w/ring, bl-gr, 9⅞″....................350.00
Carmeliter's Stomach, sloping cm, dk yel-olive, 10″...........100.00
Carter's Liver, sloping cm, gold-amber, minor wear, 8½″........40.00
CH Swain's Bourbon, sloping cm, yel-olive, 9⅛″.............170.00
Cole Bros Vegetable, tm, EX label, aqua, 7¾″................50.00
Covert's Modoc Stomach, sloping cm, gold-amber, 8⅞″.........80.00
Damiana, sloping cm w/ring, aqua, 11½″....................45.00
Doctor Fisch's, fish form, rnd cm, lt gold-amber, 11½″........100.00
Dr Beard's Alterative Tonic & Laxative, aqua, 8½″............60.00
Dr Gillmore's Laxative, Kidney & Liver, red-amber, 10¼″......110.00
Dr GW Roback's Stomach, barrel, cm, gold-amber, 9⅜″.......125.00
Dr Harter's Wild Cherry, base: #1/emb cherries, amber, 7⅜″....75.00
Dr HC Stewart's Tonic, letters on side at base, amber, 7½″.....40.00
Dr Henley's Wild Grape Root, IXL, am w/ring, aqua, 12½″.....75.00
Dr Huntington's Golden Tonic, sloping cm, amber, 9⅜″, EX....50.00
Dr Huntington's Golden Tonic, sloping cm, aqua, 9¼″........110.00
Dr J Hostetter's Stomach, sloping cm, dk olive-amber, 9½″.....50.00
Dr Langley's Root & Herb, sq cm, gold-amber, 8¾″, NM.......40.00
Dr Lawrence's Wild Cherry Family, sloping cm, amber, 8¾″....100.00
Dr MC Ayer Restorative, dbl cm, aqua, 8¼″..................60.00
Dr Petzold's Genuine German, log cabin, amber, 10¼″, EX.....50.00
Dr Petzold's Genuine German, log cabin, lt yel-amber, 10″......85.00
Dr Rattinger's Herb & Root, sloping cm, gold-amber, 9¼″......70.00
Dr Ryder's Clover, fm, gold-amber, inside stain, 7¼″..........50.00
Dr Sawen's Life Invigorating, sloping cm, yel-amber, 9⅞″.......50.00
Dr Sims' Anti-Constipation, sloping cm, gold-amber, 9¼″.......60.00
Dr Sims' Anti-Constipation, sloping cm, red-amber, 9¼″........80.00
Dr Wheeler's Sherry Wine Bitters, aqua, 7¾″.................90.00
Dr Wonser's, sloping cm w/ring, lt bl-gr, 8⅞″...............210.00
Dr Young's Wild Cherry, dbl cm, yel-amber, minor stain, 8″....75.00
Drake's, see also ST Drake's
Drake's Plantation, cabin, arabesque decor, olive-yel, 10″......210.00
Drake's Plantation, cabin, yel-amber, 10⅛″...................60.00
Eureka, sloping cm, dk gold-amber, exterior stain, 9½″.........50.00
Faith Whitcomb's, dbl cm, aqua, inside stain, 9⅜″.............35.00
Ferro Quina Stomach, sq, gold-amber, 9⅛″...................60.00
Fish, The; fish, rnd cm, dk gold-amber, 11½″................140.00
Fish, The; fish, rnd cm, gold-amber, 11⅜″..................110.00
German Balsam, sloping cm, milk glass, 9″..................350.00
Greeley's Bourbon Whiskey, barrel, dk strawberry-puce, 9⅜″...190.00
Greeley's Bourbon Whiskey, barrel, sq cm, puce, 9¼″.........210.00
Green Mountain Cider, dbl cm, aqua, 10⅜″..................125.00
Greer's Eclipse, sloping cm, gold-amber, 8¾″.................60.00
Hall's, barrel, sq cm, lt gold-amber, 9¼″....................80.00
Hall's, barrel, sq cm, yel, 9⅛″..........................110.00
Hibernia, sloping cm w/ring, amber, 10″, EX................175.00
Holtzermann's Stomach, 2-sided roof, yel-amber, 9¼″.........450.00
Holtzermann's Stomach, 4-sided roof, dk gold-amber, 9⅜″.....100.00
Holtzermann's Stomach, 4-sided roof, lt gold-amber, 10″......125.00
Home, sloping cm, amber, minor stains, 9⅛″..................30.00
Home, sloping cm, red-amber, 9⅛″, NM.....................60.00
Hunkidory Stomach, sloping cm, gold-amber, 9¼″..............130.00
Johnson's Calisaya, sloping cm, gold-amber, 10¼″.............50.00
JT Higby Tonic, sloping cm, lt yel-amber, 9½″, NM...........50.00
Kelly's Old Cabin, cabin, cm, dk gold-amber, 9⅛″............380.00
Kelly's Old Cabin, cabin, dk olive-amber/blk, 9″..............470.00
Kimball's Jaundice, sloping collar, ip, olive-amber, 6⅞″........210.00
King Solomon's, sloping cm w/ring, yel-amber, 7¼″............50.00
Lewis Red Jacket, sloping cm w/ring, gold-amber, 11″..........60.00
Litthauer Stomach, cm, milk glass, minor age cracks, 9½″......65.00
Litthauer Stomach, tm, 9⅝″..............................70.00
Lohengrin, case gin type, cm, milk glass, 9″................100.00
Lyman's Dandelion, sq cm, aqua, stained, 10½″...............30.00
Marshall's, sloping cm, yel-amber, 8¾″......................40.00
McConnon's Stomach, sloping cm, amber, inside stain, 9¼″.....50.00
National, ear of corn, sloping cm, gold-amber, 12¼″..........200.00
Niagara (Star), am w/ring, yel-amber, 10″, NM...............175.00
O'Leary's 20th C, sloping cm, gold-amber, minor stain, 8⅝″.....60.00
Old Continental, sq cm, lt gold-amber, minor stain, 10″........70.00
Old Dr Goodhue's Root & Herb, sq cm, aqua, 9″..............40.00
Old Dr Solomon's Indian Wine Bitters, sq cm, aqua, 8½″.......75.00
Old Homestead Wild Cherry, cabin, cm, olive-amber, 9¾″.....310.00
Old Homestead Wild Cherry, cabin, cm, yel-amber, 9¾″.......175.00
Old Sachem, barrel, sq cm, gold-yel, 9⅜″, NM...............170.00
Pepsin Calisaya, cm, lt yel-gr, 8⅛″.........................50.00
Peruvian Tonic, sloping cm, yel-amber, 10″...................80.00
Peychaud's American Aromatic Cordial, amber, 10¾″...........50.00
Peychaud's American Aromatic Cordial, gold-amber, 10⅜″.......30.00
Polo Club Stomach, sloping cm, gold-amber, 9⅛″..............50.00
Records & Goldsborough Morning (Eye) Opener, yel-amber, 9″.325.00
Reed's, lady's leg, sloping cm w/ring, gold-amber, 12¼″.......125.00
Rising Sun, sloping cm, amber, 9¼″........................70.00
Royal Amaranth, sloping cm w/ring, aqua, 11½″, VG..........100.00
Royal Pepsin Stomach, dbl cm, amber, 9″....................40.00

Russ St Domingo, sloping cm, dense amber, 10″ 40.00
Saint Jacob's, sloping cm, amber, exterior stain, 8½″ 50.00
Sanborn's Kidney & Liver Vegetable Laxative, amber, 10″ 30.00
Sarasina Stomach, sloping cm, gold-amber, 9½″ 50.00
SB Rothenberg, Pat Applied For seal, cm, milk glass, 9″ 60.00
Schroeder's, lady's leg, gold-amber, 12¼″ 300.00
ST Drake's Plantation, cabin, amber/blk, 9¾″ 90.00
ST Drake's Plantation, cabin, burgundy/blk, 10″ 130.00
ST Drake's Plantation, cabin, dk gold-amber, 10″ 150.00
ST Drake's Plantation, cabin, lt amber, 10⅛″ 50.00
ST Drake's Plantation, cabin, puce, 9⅞″ 150.00
Star Kidney & Liver, sloping cm, yel-amber, 8¾″ 60.00
Suffolk, pig, dbl cm, yel, 10¼″ L 450.00
Suffolk, pig, gm, gold-amber, 9¾″ L 400.00
Suffolk, pig, gm, yel-amber, mouth chip, 9¾″ L 275.00
Sun Kidney & Liver, sloping c/machined/m, gold-amber, 9⅝″ 45.00
Tippecanoe, mushroom mouth, dk-gold amber, 8⅞″ 60.00
Tonola, sq cm, aqua, 8⅜″ 50.00
Von Koster Stomach, sloping cm, amber, w/product, 9″ 75.00
Waite's Kidney & Liver, sloping cm, gold-amber, 8⅞″ 30.00
Webb's Improved Stomach, sloping cm, gold-amber, 9″ 80.00
WF Serva Stomach, sloping cm, amber, 10″ 50.00
Wheat, sloping cm, gold-amber, 9⅝″ 60.00
Yamara Cordial, fm, 9¼″, EX 300.00
Yerba Buena, flask, sloping cm, gold-amber, qt 70.00
Yerba Buena, sloping cm w/ring, amber, pt, NM 40.00
Zingari, lady's leg, applied mouth w/ring, gold-amber, 12″ 185.00
Zuzu, sloping cm, yel-amber, 8¾″, EX 50.00

Cologne or Scent Bottles

Ambrosia, Hinze Inc, see California Perfume Co
Amethyst, blown 3-mold, fm/ps, att Sandwich, 5⅞″ 460.00
Cobalt, blown in mold, petal ft, w/stopper, 6″ 75.00
Cobalt, free-blown, fm/ps, w/blown stopper, 5½″ 300.00
Cobalt, free-blown, fm/ps, w/pressed stopper, 5¼″ 170.00
Cut glass, gr to clear, 1905, London, 8½x3½″ 175.00
Goetting's, see California Perfume Co
Lion, rectangular, EX label, rm/ps, aqua, 9½″ 100.00
Lithyalin, dk brn, Eggerman, 1830, 2″ sq sides, pr 1,750.00
Lithyalin, dk red, Frederich Eggerman, 1830, 5″ 1,250.00

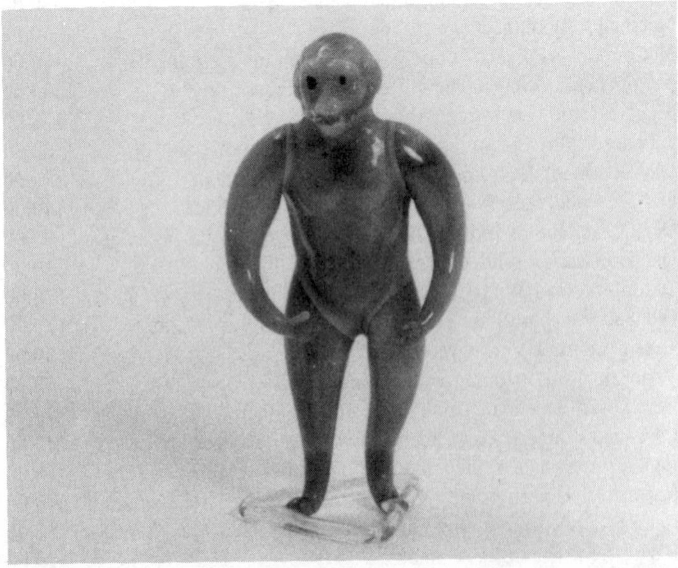

Cologne, ape figural, stopper in tail, round paper label: Made in Germany, 3½″, $40.00.

Opaque bl, tm/ps, rnd, ca 1840-1860, 9″ 90.00
Perfume/tear vial, gilded, Victorian, 6½″ L 35.00
Savoi Et Cie, Paris, see California Perfume Co
Sea horse w/opal spiral, 3″ L, EX 50.00
Toilet water, pillared, flared mouth, gp, cobalt, 12″ 140.00
Yel flower/gr leaves on bl in clear, Chas Kaziun, mini 1,250.00

Figural Bottles

Barrel, horizontal rib relief, amber, w/stopper, 10″ 60.00
Barrel, tm, smooth base, cobalt, 5½″ 50.00
Bull fighter, tooled mouth, milk glass, 6½″ 35.00
Cabin, 3 sides logs, 1 w/6, cm w/ring, dk gold-amber, 10″ 120.00
Fish, cod liver oil, amber, ca 1902, 10″ 26.00
Grandfather clock, milk glass, Europe, 1890s, 12″ 45.00
Grant's Tomb, milk glass w/metal Grant cover, 10″ 175.00
Monk, milk glass, tooled mouth, 9¼″ 130.00
Pig, applied ears, eyes, tail & ft, aqua/amber, 10½″, VG 700.00
Pineapple, cm, dk gold-amber, 9″ 80.00
Statue of Liberty bronze top, mb base, lip flakes, 15¼″ 135.00

Flasks

Adams, bk: Jefferson, GI-114, sm/ps, gold-amber, ½-pt 130.00
Baltimore GW, anchor, bk: Phoenix, GXIII-53, aqua, pt 60.00
C-scroll, GIX-25, sm/ps, dk aqua/pt 80.00
Clasped hands, bk: eagle, GXII-43, dk gold-amber, qt 170.00
Corn for the World, bk: Baltimore, aqua, qt, 8¼″, EX 75.00
Cornucopia, bk: urn, GIII-12, sm/ps, olive-amber, ½-pt 60.00
Cornucopia, bk: urn, GIII-16, Lancaster, sm/ip, aqua, pt 75.00
Cornucopia, bk: urn, GIII-4, sm/ps, bright gr, pt 130.00
Deer & boar, amethyst, late, 5¼″ 750.00
Eagle, bk: cornucopia, olive-amber, pt, 7″ 90.00
Eagle, bk: Drafted, man, GII-140, aqua, pt, EX 250.00
Eagle, bk: Dyottville GW, GII-38, lt gr-aqua, pt, NM 60.00
Eagle, bk: flag, GII-52, aqua, pt 75.00
Eagle, bk: New London GW, anchor, GII-66, aqua, qt 150.00
Eagle, bk: New London GW, anchor, GIII-67, lt gr, ½-pt, NM .. 190.00
Eagle, bk: plain, GII-143, calabash, ip, bright gr, qt, NM 70.00
Eagle, bk: Stag, BII-49, Coffin & Hay, sm/ps, aqua, pt, EX 170.00
Eagle, bk: Success to the Railroad, dk olive-amber, 7″, EX 95.00
Eagle, bk: tree, GII-41, sm/ps, Kensington, aqua, sq 100.00
Eagle, bk: tree, GII-47, aqua, qt, NM 200.00
Eagle, bk: Union & clasped hands, dk amber, pt, 7⅝″, EX 75.00
Eagle, bk: Willington Glass Co, GII-61, dk gold-amber, qt 150.00
Eagle, bk: Willington Glass Co, GII-64, emerald gr, pt, EX 140.00
Eagle, dbl; aqua, qt, 8½″, EX 95.00
Eagle, dbl; aqua, ½-pt, 6⅛″ 35.00
Eagle, dbl; GII-78, sm/ps, olive-amber, qt 90.00
Eagle, dbl; GII-87, sm/ps (chip), olive-gr, ½-pt 75.00
Eagle, dbl; oval & banner, olive-amber, ½-pt, 6″, EX 40.00
Eagle, dbl; Pittsburgh in oval, dk gr, pt, 7½″, NM 95.00
Eagle, dbl; Pittsburgh in oval, dk gr, qt, 8¾″, EX 105.00
Eagle, dbl; Pittsburgh in oval, olive-gr, pt, 7⅞″ 95.00
Eagle, dbl; pontiled, olive-gr, pt, 6⅞″ 70.00
Eagle & Keene, bk: Masonic, olive-amber, pt, 7½″, NM 55.00
Eagle & Liberty, bk: Westford, amber, ½-pt, 6⅜″, NM 60.00
Eagle & Liberty, bk: Willington, dk gr, 8″, NM 75.00
Eagle & monument, bk: Indian shoots bird, GII-42, aqua, qt .. 100.00
Eagle & TWD, bk: ship 'Franklin,' lt yel-gr, pt, 6⅝″, EX 75.00
Eagle & Union Co, bk: bust w/Kensington, lt aqua, 7″, NM 350.00
Eagle & 13 stars, bk: Anchor/Ravenna, ip, emerald gr, 7½″ 800.00
Eagle w/Arsenal Glass Works oval, bk: prospector, 8″, EX 125.00
Flora Temple, bk: plain, GXIII-21, copper, pt, EX 290.00

Flora Temple, bk: plain, GXIII-23, am w/ring, bl-gr, pt........425.00
For Pike's Peak, bk: hunter, aqua, ½-pt, 6", EX.............100.00
Franklin, bk: Franklin, GI-97, sm/ps, Kensington, aqua, qt.....110.00
Franklin & Dyott, aqua, pt, 6¾"..........................145.00
Good Game, stag, bk: willow tree, GX-1, aqua, pt............135.00
Granite Glass Co, bk: Stoddard, GXV-7, aqua, 8", EX..........45.00
Granite Glass Co, bk: Stoddard, GXV-8, olive-amber, pt.......110.00
Horse & rider, bk: dog, aqua, pt, 7¾", NM..................45.00
Hunter, bk: fisherman, GXIII-4, calabash, bl-gr, qt............275.00
Hunter, bk: fisherman, GXIII-5, calabash, aqua, qt.............50.00
Hunter, bk: hound, GXIII-7, dbl cm/ps, aqua, pt, VG..........100.00
Isabella Glass Works, anchor, bk: sheaf of wheat, aqua, pt.....125.00
Jenny Lind, bk: factory, GI-101, sloping cm/ps, aqua, qt........60.00
Jenny Lind, bk: factory, GI-104, calabash, lt bl, qt, NM........260.00
Jenny Lind, bk: factory, GI-99, calabash, emerald.............425.00
Jenny Lind, bk: Kossuth, GI-100, calabash, aqua, qt...........60.00
Jenny Lind, bk: Millfora GW, GI-101, calabash, bl-gr, qt.......160.00
LaFayette, Coventry CT, bk: Liberty cap/S&S, olive-amb, 7"....285.00
LaFayette, Coventry CT, Liberty cap on pole/S&S, aqua, pt...4,150.00
Louis Kossuth, bk: frigate, GI-112, aqua, qt, NM.............120.00
Major Ringgold, bk: Rough & Ready, lt sapphire, 6¾", NM....275.00
Masonic, bk: eagle, dk olive-gr, ½-pt, 6½", VG...............135.00
Masonic, bk: eagle, GIV-17, Keene, olive-amber, pt...........130.00
Masonic, bk: eagle, GIV-42, calabash, aqua, qt, NM............40.00
Masonic, bk: eagle/Shepherds, Zanesville, gold-amber, 7"......450.00
Masonic/star/eye/AD, bk: star/arm/CRFA, pt, 7¼", EX..........65.00
Not for Joe, girl on bicycle, GXIII-2, aqua, pt................110.00
Pike's Peak, bk: eagle, GXI-9, am w/ring, aqua, pt............50.00
Pike's Peak, prospector, bk: eagle, GXI-34, dk bl-aqua, qt......75.00
Pike's Peak, prospector, bk: eagle, GXI-35, lt yel-gr, pt........190.00
Pike's Peak, prospector, bk: eagle, GXI-9, aqua, pt, EX.........50.00
Pike's Peak, prospector, bk: hunter, GXI-50, amber, pt........300.00
Railroad, bk: eagle, olive-gr, pt, 6⅝", EX...................105.00
Roosevelt, bk: TVA, GI-129, calabash, aqua, qt...............50.00
Scroll, GIX-2, sm/ps, aqua, roughness/stain, qt................40.00
Scroll, GIX-2, sm/ps, lt yel-gr w/amber striations, qt.........1,025.00
Scroll, ip, olive-yel, qt, 9", EX...........................350.00
Seeing Eye Masonic, GIV-43, sm/ps, yel-olive, pt..............75.00
Sheaf of Wheat, bk: star, calabash w/hdl, amber, qt, NM......220.00
Sheaf of Wheat, bk: star, GXIII-43, calabash, aqua, qt..........35.00
Sheaf of Wheat, bk: star, GXIII-44, calabash, lt amber, qt......125.00
Sheaf of Wheat, bk: Westford, GXIII-35, olive-amber, pt........75.00
Spring Garden Glass Works, bk: cabin, honey-amber, 7⅝", EX.445.00
Stoddard Flag, GX-27, sm/ps, New Granite, gold-amber, pt...1,800.00
Success to the Railroad, dbl; olive, minor sickness, 6½"........95.00
Summer tree, bk: summer tree, GX-18, deep aqua, qt..........90.00
Sunburst, GVIII-1, Keene, lt gr, pt.........................425.00
Sunburst, GVIII-18, sm/ps, Coventry, olive-yel, ½-pt..........290.00
Sunburst, pontiled, dk aqua, ¾ pt, 6⅞", NM................175.00
Sunburst w/Keen & P&W in ovals, olive-gr, pt, 7½"..........275.00
Traveler's Companion, bk: Railroad Guide, pontil, aqua, 6".....60.00
Traveler's Companion, bk: Ravenna, aqua, pt, 7"...........125.00
Traveler's Companion, bk: Ravenna, GXIV-3, gold-amber, pt...260.00
Traveler's Companion, bk: Ravenna, ip, grass gr, 6½".........900.00
Traveler's Companion, bk: wheat sheaf, dk gold-amber, qt......80.00
Union, dbl; clasped hands, gr-aqua, qt, 8½"..................35.00
Union/clasp hands, bk: eagle/banner, aqua, ½-pt, 6¼", EX......35.00
Union/clasp hands/Frank & Son, bk: cannon/flag, aqua, 7⅞"....70.00
Urn & cornucopia, dk gr, pt, broken blisters/residue, 6¾".....65.00
Urn & cornucopia, olive, some sickness, pt, 7"...............45.00
Urn & cornucopia, olive-amber, minor residue, 6⅞"............65.00
Washington, bk: Baltimore Glass Works, aqua, pt, 6¾", NM....95.00
Washington, bk: Bridgton NJ, aqua, pt, 6⅞", EX..............85.00
Washington, bk: Jackson, olive-amber, ½-pt, 5¼"............125.00
Washington, bk: sailing ship, GI-28, sm/ps, aqua, pt..........140.00
Washington & sheaf, aqua, pt, minor sickness, 7⅜"............35.00
Washington & Taylor, aqua, pt, 7", NM.......................35.00
Washington & Taylor, aqua, ½-pt, 5⅝", EX...................45.00
Washington & Taylor, dk red-puce, lip chips/residue, 7".......445.00
Washington & Taylor, pontiled, lt aqua, pt, 6¾"..............45.00
Will you take a drink/will a (duck) swim, aqua, 6"............225.00

Ink Bottles

Bank of England, building, tm, aqua, 3¾"...................550.00
Black Writing Fluid, Moses Brickett, fm/ps, yel-olive, 4⅜"......150.00
Blake NY, umbrella, octagonal, aqua, 3"....................100.00
Building, gm, ca 1870-1890, 3¼"..........................150.00
Cabin, fm/ps, ca 1830-1850, rpr, 3".......................250.00
Cabin, gm, ca 1860-1880, 3¼"............................510.00
Cabin, tm (flake), 2½"...................................270.00

Ink bottle, cabin figural, tooled mouth, smooth base, aqua, 1860-1880, 2⅝", excellent condition, $100.00.

Cone, rm/ps, dk sapphire, 2½"............................220.00
David's, turtle, sm, gr, minor stain, 1¾"....................130.00
Davis & Miller, sides: 2 emb/3 rib/3 plain, aqua, 2⅝".........170.00
Farley's, octagonal, sm/ps, dk gold-amber, 1⅞"..............280.00
Fine Black Writing/JP Preston, rnd, fm/ps, olive-amber, 5".....100.00
G&R's American Writing Fluid, cone, rm/ps, aqua, 2⅝".......250.00
Hard Cider, Tippecanoe, fm/ps, 1⅞"........................170.00
Harrison's Columbian, fm/pc, 4¾", VG.......................65.00
Hoover Phila, vertical relief, fm/ps, lt gr, 5⅛"...............50.00
Igloo, gm, sapphire bl, 1⅞"................................70.00
J & IEM, domed, gm, electric bl, 1¼", VG....................85.00
J & IEM, turtle, gm (flake), amber, 1⅝"......................60.00
M&P Co, cone, tm (flake), aqua, 2½"........................30.00
Ma Carter, made in Germany, EX............................50.00
Penn Mfg, P Garrett, rnd w/8-sided base, milk glass, VG........40.00
SI Comp, building, tm, milk glass, rpr, 2¾"...................80.00
SI Comp, building, tm (flake), aqua, 2⅝"....................75.00
SI Comp, building, tm (flake), clear, 2⅝"....................75.00
SO Dunbar Taunton, umbrella, rolled mouth/ps, aqua, 2⅜"....180.00
Thompson & Crawford, umbrella, lt gr, minor stain, 2½"......310.00
Umbrella, 12-sided, rm/ps, lt bl-gr, minor stain, 1¾"..........110.00
Umbrella, 8-sided, rm/ps, olive-yel, 2¼"......................65.00
Umbrella, 8-sided, tm, teal-bl, 2½".........................250.00
Weber Waterproof Drawing, turtle, w/label, bright gr, 1¾".....100.00

Medicine Bottles

California Fig Syrup, emb..................................7.00
Cary Gum Tree Cough Syrup, lime-gr, 7½"...................15.00
D Evan's Camomile Pills, pontil, aqua, 3¾"...................25.00
Dr Bell's Pine Tar Honey, emb...............................7.00
Dr Miles' Restorative Nervine, emb..........................10.00

Frog Pond Chill & Fever Tonic, cobalt, 7″ 12.00
Grove's Tasteless Chill Tonic, Paris Co, St Louis, emb 10.00
Hunt's Remedy, Wm E Clarke Pharmacist, Providence, aqua 15.00
John R Dickey's Old Reliable Eye Water, Dickey Drug Co 10.00
Lavender Salts, Goetting & Co, see California Perfume Co
Mrs Allen's World's Hair Restorer, amber, emb, NM 15.00
Royal Gall Remedy, machine made, dk amber, 7″ 10.00
Sarsaparilla, Bristol's Extract of, rm/ps, aqua, 5¼″ 50.00
Sarsaparilla, Dr Guysott's Yellow Dock, ip, 10″, NM 205.00
Sarsaparilla, Turner's, sloping cm, aqua, stained, 12½″ 275.00
Sassafras Eye Lotion, eye cup, cobalt bl, cork top, label 25.00
Scott's Emulsion Cod Liver Oil, emb man w/lg fish 9.00
Sloan's Liniment Kills Pain, emb 8.00
Thompson & Crawford, rm/ps, aqua, 5″ 22.50
United Chemists, emb mortar & pestle, 3¾″ 15.00
Veno's Lightning Cough Cure, aqua, emb 10.00

Mineral Water Bottles

DA Knowlton, dbl cm, dk olive-gr, qt 40.00
Improved, blob top, graphite pontil, bl, 6¼″ 30.00
Missisquoi, olive-gr, 9¾″ 30.00
Saratoga A Spring Co, sloping cm, yel-olive, pt, NM 40.00
Vermont Spring Saxe & Co, gr 14.00

Soda Bottles

Bay City Soda Water Co, star symbol, bl, 7″ 15.00
Chadsey & Bro, bulb lip/minor flake, sapphire bl, 6″ 40.00
Codd, w/marble, ca 1890 . . . . . 18.00
Crystal Springs Bottling Co, Hutchinson type, paper label 65.00
Dearborn, 83 3rd Ave NY, bt, gr, 7″ 30.00
Hires Rootbeer, paper label, NM 30.00
Hutchinson, WW Lake, Jackson MS, aqua, 7″ 12.50
Stolen From Eureka Bottling Works, aqua, 6¾″ 35.00
T Cecil Superior C Mineral Water, pontil, gr 45.00
White Rock Ginger Ale, early paper label, NM 30.00

Soda bottle, Mission Dry, silver metallic with blue label, 12-oz., $25.00.

Spirits Bottles

AM Bininger & Co, cannon-barrel form, gold-amber, 12½″ 325.00
AS/CR, sloping cm/ps, dk olive-amber, 11⅜″ 60.00
Duffy Crescent (Moon) Saloon, pig, gold-amber, 7¾″, EX 750.00

Mohawk Whiskey bottle, figural Indian warrior, rolled collared mouth, smooth base, yellow-amber, 1860-1880, 12″, $475.00.

Eman Coll, sloping cm/ps, olive-amber, sealed, 11¼″ 60.00
H Pharazyn Whiskey, Indian warrior, yel-amber, 12¼″ 625.00
John Winn Jr, sloping cm/ps, dk olive-amber, 9″ 75.00
Kidney shape, tm w/ring/ps, olive-gr, 8″ 290.00
Lediard's Morning Call Whiskey, vertical emb, yel-gr, 10″ 60.00
Lion, sloping cm/ps, dk olive-amber, 10⅝″ 65.00
Mist of the Morning Whiskey, barrel, yel-amber, 10⅛″ 125.00
P Clark Kenwen, 1813; sloping cm/ps, dense olive-amber, 9″ . . . 220.00
PC Brooks Wine, 1820; sloping cm/ps, dk olive-amber, 10¼″ . . . 160.00
Roehling & Schutz, cabin, tm, amber, 9¾″ 60.00
Star Whiskey, jug w/hdl, applied seal, gold-amber, 7½″ 400.00
Wm Uglow Wabstow, 1794, dk olive-amber, 9″, EX 275.00

Miscellaneous

Ambrosia, Hinze Inc., see California Perfume Co
Goofus type, milk glass, floral relief, 15″, VG 140.00
Lavender Salts, Goetting & Co, see California Perfume Co
Ludlow, applied lip, olive-amber, minor sickness, 6¾″ 55.00
Milk, dbl baby face, sgn Baby Top, Brookfield, qt 22.00
Milk, Indian Hill Farm Dairy, Indian chief, 1930s 25.00
Pepper sauce, ER Durkee, pat Feb 1874, med emerald-gr, 7¾″ . . 30.00
Pickle, Goofus type, milk glass, floral relief, 15″, VG 140.00
Pickle, Gothic arch, aqua, minor sickness, 12″, pr 85.00
Sweet 16, Goetting & Co, see California Perfume Co

Boxes

Boxes have been used by civilized man since ancient Egypt and Rome. Down through the centuries, specifically designed containers have been made from every conceivable material. Precious metals, papier mache, battersea, Oriental lacquer, and wood have held riches from the treasuries of kings, snuff for the fashionable set of the last century, China tea, and countless other commodities.

When no condition is indicated, the items listed below are assumed to be in excellent condition. See also Jewelry Boxes

Apple storage, pine, worn pnt w/decor, 10x10¾″ 75.00
Ash, sponge/brush decor, brass hdl atop, 1830s, 17x12x5½″ . . . 235.00
Ballot, pine, 2-drw, chamfered top, orig pnt, 1860s, 8x8″ 110.00
Band, block print wallpaper w/lg squirrels, 12x13½x17½″ 375.00
Band, flowers, orig mc on pine, laced seams, 15½″ L, VG 475.00
Band, orig stencil on dk gr, bentwood, 17″ L, VG 350.00
Band, red/bl, mc floral, decoupage top, sgn, 7x19x12″, EX 525.00
Bentwood, finger built/iron tacks, bl pnt, 5x6″ 405.00
Bentwood, old finish, 3¾x8″ dia 55.00
Bentwood, orig dk gray pnt, 4½x9½″ 115.00
Bentwood, swivel hdl, old gr finish, 6¾x11½″ 75.00
Bentwood, wrought iron nails, rfn, 6¾x16¾x27″ 325.00
Bible, oak, punched decor/initials, butterfly hinges, 22″ 115.00
Bible, oak, stylized carving, trn H-stretcher base, 26x24″ 350.00
Bible, pine, chip-carved edges/compass star/tombstone, lg 1,250.00
Bible, walnut, dvtl, trn ft, edge molding, rfn/rpl, 9½x26″ 425.00
Birch bark & pine, laced seams, old dk finish, oval, 11″ L 85.00
Blanket, walnut, snipe hinges top/base, 1700s, 12x9x17½″ 335.00
Book shape w/drw, inlaid wood, sgn/1896, 5x6″ 55.00
Bride's, bentwood, inscription/rooster & hen, laced, 17″ L 675.00

Fraktur decorated oval wood bride's box, lady and gent above a motto vignette within leafage border, late 18th century, 18½″ x 11½″, $650.00.

Cutlery, mahog w/satinwood inlay, orig fittings, 15″ 1,000.00
Dome top, florals, mc on dk bl, iron lock/hasp, 9⅜″ L 410.00
Dome top, rawhide w/copper tacks, iron escutcheon, 17″ L 125.00
Enamel on copper, harbor scenes & florals, French, EX 485.00
Knife, mahog, Boston, ca 1789, M 225.00
Knife, orig walnut finish, PA, ca 1830 . . . . 225.00
Knife, vase form, satinwood inlay, late 1800s, 26″ 2,000.00
Lacquer, hunting scene on blk, American, 3″ 140.00
Lacquer, shoe form, gilt/butterfly & bird decor, 7″ 70.00
Lead, cast lion head on lid, 3½″ 30.00
Mahog, coffin shape w/brass tack trim, 5½″ L 70.00
Pantry, pine/gr pnt, mk Murdock, wood peg/tin tacks, 3x7″ 115.00
Patch, bone, w/pnt scene of lady & flowers, 2¼″ 70.00
Patch, horse, rider, hounds on pink, sgn Samson, 1⅛x1¾″ 285.00
Pill, coin silver, lion relief on lid, oval, ¾x2″ L 75.00
Pill, pear form, fruit decor, Fr enamel, 1¾″ 350.00
Pill, urn form, Fr enamel, silver gilt mts, 18th C, 1″ 260.00
Pine, dvtl, dome top, orig yel/brn grpt, 24″ L 375.00
Pine, dvtl, panel front, strap hinges, lock, rfn, 10x19x12″ 95.00
Pine, staple hinges, orig bl pnt, 3½x4x16″ 180.00
Pine, storage, grpt, dvtl, brass hdw, 1830s, 8x12″ 100.00
Pipe, hanging; oak, quarter-sawn w/mahog X-banding, 19″ 100.00
Poplar, carved & decorated, mc fruit/foliage, 4½x7x11″ 425.00
Poplar, dome top, blk flame grain on yel, dvtl, 30″ L, VG 200.00
Poplar, dome top, curly maple grpt orig, 10x24x12″ 450.00
Poplar, dome top, dvtl, brn/yel vinegar sponging, 9x18″ 200.00
Poplar, dome top, grpt on red w/blk stripe, no hasp, 28″ L 200.00
Poplar, vinegar graining, dvtl, iron hdls, 10x24″ 250.00
Poplar, vinegar graining, iron lock, 15x13x30″ 400.00
Poplar, vinegar graining, staple hinges, dvtl, 3x4x8″ 200.00
Poplar, vinegar graining on yel, dovetail, 5½x6x11½″ 200.00
Porcelain, floral & geometrics, HP/sgn, 1¼x2x2″ 165.00
Portrait, English enamel, 3″ 180.00
Primitive, made from 1 pc of wood, 2 sliding lids, 5¾″ 40.00
Rosary, silver filigree, rnd, 1″ 35.00
Ruby glass w/wht lining, 16 cuttings, pnt floral, 3x3½″ 385.00
Spice, bentwood, gr w/dk gr eagle stencil, 3x5″, EX 350.00
Stamp, china w/HP roses, gold trim, MZ Austria, 3x1¼″ 35.00
Tortoiseshell, ivory faced/paw ft, Continental, 1800, 8″ L 150.00
Wallpaper on cb, floral, 1854 newspaper w/in, 4¾x6x8½″ 150.00
Wallpaper on cb, lilies, 9x10x14″, VG 95.00
Walnut, dvtl, rpr staple hinges, old finish, 8x19x12½″, VG 175.00

Boyd's Crystal Art Glass

In 1978, Bernard C. Boyd and his son bought the Degenhart factory in Cambridge, Ohio, acquiring fifty of Elizabeth Degenhart's glass molds with the 'D in heart' trademark removed. Many are used by Boyd, who also produces the pony Joey and the elephant Zack. These are issued each month in a new and different color of crystal as well as slag or 'marble' glass. The Louise doll was also produced until September 1984, when it was discontinued.

When no condition is indicated, the items listed below are assumed to be in mint condition.

Chick, 1″, Butterscotch 20.00
Chick, 1″, Candy Swirl 20.00
Chick, 1″, Deep Purple, March 1979 . . . . 20.00
Chick, 1″, Firefly 20.00
Chick, 1″, Ice Green, October 1979 . . . . 15.00
Chick, 1″, John's Surprise, December 1980 . . . . 15.00
Chick, 1″, Marigold 20.00
Chick, 1″, Rubina, May 1979 . . . . 15.00
Chick, 1″, Willow Blue 15.00
Hen, 3″, Heather, January 1980 . . . . 20.00
Hen, 3″, Ice Green, October 1979 . . . . 20.00
Hen, 3″, Old Ivory Slag, April 1981 . . . . 15.00
Hen, 3″, Pink Champagne, August 1979 . . . . 20.00
Hen, 5″, Apricot 20.00
Hen, 5″, Candy Swirl 20.00
Hen, 5″, Dawn, February 1980 . . . . 20.00
Hen, 5″, Delphinium, March 1981 . . . . 20.00
Hen, 5″, Lemon Ice, September 1979 . . . . 20.00
Hen, 5″, Rubina, May 1979 . . . . 20.00
Joey Horse, Chocolate 25.00
Joey Horse, Flame, 1980 . . . . 10.00
Joey Horse, Persimmon 10.00
Joey Horse, Zack Boyd Slag, 1980 . . . . 10.00

Kitten on Pillow, Apricot....15.00
Kitten on Pillow, Cathedral Blue....10.00
Kitten on Pillow, Dawn....10.00
Kitten on Pillow, Magic Marble....20.00
Kitten on Pillow, Pecan....15.00
Kitten on Pillow, Persimmon Slag....15.00
Kitten on Pillow, Purple Variant....10.00
Kitten on Pillow, Royalty Slag Warmed-In....20.00
Kitten on Pillow, Vacation Swirl....15.00
Louise, Chocolate, old mk....15.00
Louise, Dawn, old mk....15.00
Louise, Delphinium, old mk....15.00
Louise, English Yew, old mk....15.00
Louise, Flame, old mk....15.00
Louise, Furr Green, old mk....15.00
Louise, Handpainted Milk White....20.00
Louise, Heather, old mk....15.00
Louise, Ice Green, old mk....15.00
Louise, Impatient, old mk....15.00
Louise, Lemon Ice, old mk....110.00
Louise, Mardi Gras, old mk....15.00
Louise, Mountain Haze, old mk....15.00
Louise, Olde Ivory Slag, old mk....15.00
Louise, Persimmon, old mk....15.00
Louise, Persimmon Slag, old mk....15.00
Louise, Purple Variant, old mk....15.00
Louise, Sandpiper, old mk....15.00
Louise, Sandpiper Slag, old mk....15.00
Louise, Zack Boyd Slag, old mk....15.00
Owl, Black Walnut....10.00
Owl, Cobalt Blue....10.00
Owl, Deep Purple....10.00
Owl, Lavender 'N Lace....10.00
Owl, Lemon Ice....10.00
Owl, Mardi Gras....10.00
Zack Elephant, Cobalt Blue, October 1981....15.00
Zack Elephant, December '82 Swirl, 1985....15.00
Zack Elephant, Furr Green, 1981....15.00
Zack Elephant, Lavender, 1982....15.00
Zack Elephant, Sandpiper, 1981....15.00

Bradley and Hubbard

The Bradley and Hubbard Mfg. Company was a firm who produced metal accessories for the home. They operated from about 1860 until the early part of this century, and their products reflected both the Arts and Crafts and Art Nouveau influence.

Their logo was a device with a triangular arrangement of the company name containing a smaller triangle and an Aladdin lamp.

When no condition is indicated, the items listed below are assumed to be in excellent condition.

Lamps

Banquet, oil burning, all orig, 11″ ball shade....300.00
Base, pnt metal simulates gr patina, Arts & Crafts, 11″....65.00
Etched floral frosted 12″ shade, bulbous brass base, 12″....250.00
Frosted w/4 etched panels Nouveau women, on brass urn, 21″..375.00
Gr & red glass panels in heavy overlay, 15″ shade....325.00
Hanging, brass w/orig lg tin shade....300.00
Ldgl gr/wht shade; brass lily-pad base w/frog ft....800.00
Oil, acid etched globe....250.00
Oil, 8-petal 12″ slag shade, serpent hdl brass std, 19″....485.00
Piano, marble/brass, 11″ raspberry ball+4 gas shades....550.00
Student, lt bl cased swirl shade, sgn, rpr, 20″....225.00
Wall sconce, brass, electric, candle inserts, 10″, 3 for....95.00

Miscellaneous

Andirons, brass, baluster stems, urn finials....150.00
Bookends, columns/vignette of lady at desk, label, 5″....50.00
Bookends, sailing ship on frothy waves, bronze over CI....40.00
Candlesticks, brass/copper, 10″, pr....30.00
Desk set, brass & SP, mk, Art Deco, 5-pc....135.00
Ink stand w/glass well....10.00
Letter holder, sgn....12.00
Match safe, CI, dbl urn w/grapes, dtd 1868....55.00
Plaque, colored metal w/medieval lady/dog/dove, 12x19½″....175.00
Plaque, pnt bronze w/brass trim, courting couple, 7x9″....85.00
Smoking stand, orig glass insert....125.00
Thermometer, on metal fold-up stand, ornate, 11″....100.00

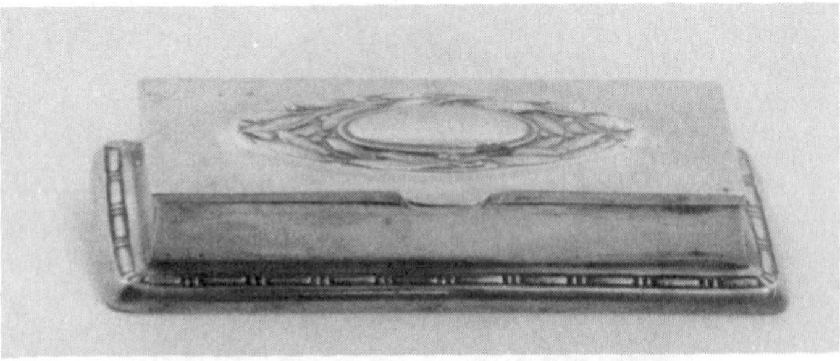

Stamp box, brass, signed, 5″ x 2¼″, $120.00.

Brass

Brass is an alloy consisting essentially of copper and zinc in variable proportions. It is a medium that has been used for both utilitarian items and objects of artistic merit. Today, with the inflated price of copper and the popular use of plastics, almost anything made of brass is collectible.

Authority Mary Frank Gaston has compiled a lovely book, *Antique Brass*, with full-color photos; you will find her address in the Directory under Texas.

When no condition is indicated, the items listed below are assumed to be in mint condition.

Soap dish and sponge holder, 7″ x 6½″, $55.00.

Bowl, spun, tin wash w/in, ring hanger, H Hayden, 4x10".......75.00
Bust, Lincoln, on rnd medallion w/hanging loop, 5"...........20.00
Candlestick, reverse beehive & diamond, push-up, 12"........235.00
Coal scuttle, helmet style, burnished, w/bail.................220.00
Coal scuttle, urn finial, dbl hdls, paw ft, 1800s, 16"..........150.00
Dipper, well-shaped wide hdl, 16"..........................55.00
Dish, Neoclassic design, very lg ear hdls, shallow, 8"...........35.00
Harness buckle, ca 1810, 2¾x3½"..........................15.00
Horse brass, crown motif, pierced, Victorian, 3½x4¼"..........20.00
Horse brass, ornate engraved initials, 6 prongs, 2x2½".........10.00
Ink sander, ca 1800-1850, American, 3"....................100.00
Kettle, cast, w/iron strap hdl, 3½x6"........................30.00
Kettle, shelf, polished, 5½x6x14"..........................55.00
Kettle, shelf, reticulated w/horse & wreath, 8x8" dia...........90.00
Kettle, shelf, scrollwork top w/birds, paw ft, 3¾x10x6"........150.00
Kettle, spun, wrought iron stand, iron bail hdl, 14", EX.......225.00
Kettle stove, reticulated sides/hdl, paw ft, charcoal, 4x6"........90.00
Pail, sheet brass, copper bottom, 5x10"......................45.00
Pail, spun, wire bail, mk HW Hayden's Pat, 5½x9", VG........55.00
Pail, spun, wrought iron bail hdl, polished, 5x12".............60.00
Paperweight, peacock figural, cast, 4¼"......................30.00
Planter, hanging; ribbed beehive, mk Chase...................45.00
Pot, 3 legs, Wescott II, 9½" hdl, 6x6"......................54.00
Scissors wick trimmer, 7½"................................40.00
Skimmer, pierced, copper rivets in iron hdl, 1850s, 17"........85.00
Spittoon, removable top, concave sides, EX..................90.00
Stove cover, pnt w/winter landscape, 12"....................36.00
Teakettle, gooseneck, acorn finial, cast hdl, sgn, 12".........175.00
Teakettle, gooseneck, dtd 1812, lg........................165.00
Teakettle, gooseneck, 3 button ft, swivel hdl, oval, 5".........125.00
Teakettle, melon rib, 4 ball ft, trn wood hdl, 8".............120.00
Teakettle, trn wood hdl, minor dents, 8¼"....................70.00
Teapot, amber glass hdl, Dutch, polished, 8¼"...............135.00
Tray, reticulated sides, almond shape, 3x17x13"..............95.00

Brastoff, Sascha

The son of immigrant parents, Sascha Brastoff was encouraged to develop his artistic talents to their fullest––encouragement that was well taken, as his achievements aptly testify. Though at various times he has been a dancer, sculptor, Hollywood costume designer, jeweler, and painter, it is his ceramics that are today becoming highly regarded collectibles. In a beautiful studio built for him by his friend and mentor, Winthrop Rockefeller, he designed innovative wares that even then were among the most expensive on the market. All designing was done personally by Brastoff; he also supervised the staff which at the height of production numbered approximately 150. Wares signed with his full signature were personally crafted by him, and are valued much more highly than those signed 'Sascha B.,' indicating work done under his supervision. Sascha Brastoff still resides in Los Angeles, California, at present producing 'Sascha Holograms' which are distributed by the Hummelwerk Company.

When no condition is indicated, the items listed below are assumed to be in mint condition.

Ash tray, blk, gold w/in, mk B56A, sgn, 7"..................30.00
Ash tray, gold & silver circus horse, lg......................45.00
Ash tray, orange/blk matt..................................25.00
Bowl, centerpiece; circus horses decor, 14" dia................75.00
Bowl, glossy mc walrus motif, body half out of water, 2x7"......40.00
Candy bowl, yel w/gold streaking, gold mk, 2x6"..............20.00
Cigarette/match holder, pipe shape..........................30.00
Jar, bird decor, egg shape, ftd, w/lid........................48.00
Pitcher, lady, arms form hdls, 3rd hdl in bk, '50s, 13".........80.00
Tea set, Surf Ballet, pot/creamer/sugar/4 cups & saucers........95.00
Wall pocket, Oriental roof top, glossy blk, 24x10"............110.00

Brayton Laguna

Durlin E. Brayton made hand-crafted vases, lamps and dinnerware in a small kiln at his Laguna Beach, California, home in the late 1927s. He soon married, and with his wife, Ellen Webster Grieve as his partner, the small business became a successful commercial venture. They are most famous for their amusing, well-detailed figurines, some of which were commissioned by Walt Disney Studios. Though very successful even through the Depression years, with the influx of imported novelties that deluged the country after WWII, business began to decline. By 1968 the pottery was closed.

When no condition is indicated, the items listed below are assumed to be in mint condition.

Cookie jar, Grandma, arms folded, HP, imp mk, 13".........100.00
Cookie jar, Mammy, HP, ink mk, 13"......................150.00
Cookie jar, Matilda, rotund, HP, imp mk, 11"...............100.00
Figurine, bear, wht crackle, unmk, 6x7" L...................50.00
Figurine, cow/bull/calf, purple, HP, unmk, set.................80.00
Figurine, Donald Duck, Disney, fist up, HP, unmk............350.00
Figurine, Fawn, Disney, pink w/brn spots, unmk, lg............25.00
Figurine, Gay '90s couple, HP, mc, ink mk, 8½"..............35.00
Figurine, hippo, turq, imp mk, 7½" L.......................25.00
Figurine, horse, abstract, matt blk, imp mk, 9"...............65.00
Figurine, monkey couple, wht crackle/brn, imp mk, 12", pr....175.00
Figurine, Peruvian Dancers, mc male & female, unmk, 9", pr..175.00
Figurine, Pluto, Disney, head up, pink/blk, unmk..............65.00
Figurine, Sambo & Petunia, HP, mc, ink mk, 7½", pr.........80.00
Figurine, Snow White/Dwarfs, Disney, HP, mc, unmk, set....1,500.00
Shakers, Chef & Jemima, HP, unmk, 4"......................40.00
Tile, cartoon of tree w/plants, mc, imp mk, 6½"..............65.00
Tile, cats on roof, mc, imp mk, 4½".........................50.00
Vase, organ grinder w/monkey, HP, mc, ink mk, 11"...........35.00

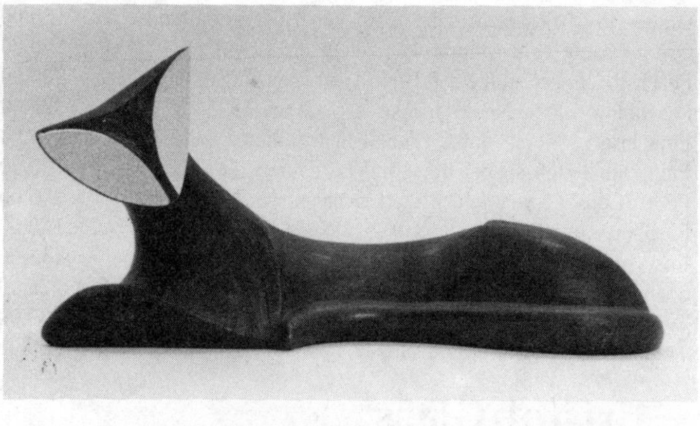

Cat, hand incised, marked W-95, 8" x 16¾", $65.00.

Bride's Baskets

Victorian brides were showered with gifts, as brides have always been; one of the most popular gift items was the bride's basket. Art glass inserts from both European and American glasshouses, some in lovely clear color with dainty enameled florals, others of Peachblow, Vasa Murrhina, satin or cased glass, were cradled in complimentary silverplated holders. While many of these holders were simply engraved or delicately embossed, others such as those from Pairpoint and Wilcox were wonderfully ornate, often with figurals of cherubs or animals. The bride's basket was no longer in fashion after the turn of the century.

When no condition is indicated, the items listed below are assumed to be in mint condition.

Mother of Pearl, Herringbone, 10½", $785.00.

Bl opal, crimped; Biggins-Rodgers fr, ornate....165.00
Bl overlay w/mc butterfly/floral; SP fr, 11½x11¼"....295.00
Bl; ftd Poole holder....175.00
Burmese; SP holder, lg....1,750.00
Cased, apple gr/raspberry enamel floral; SP fr....250.00
Cranberry, Mt Washington; orig Pairpoint fr, 1880....450.00
Cranberry, ruffled opal rim; SP fr....145.00
Cranberry, swirl; figural birds on mk Pairpoint fr....395.00
Cranberry w/custard overlay, ruffled; SP fr, 4x9"....150.00
Lt pink to rose, ruffled; Rogers fr w/lacy ft, appliques....185.00
Orange to wht cable twist bowl; Barker fr w/applied loops....150.00
Overlay satin, gold w/floral, ruffled; SP fr, 11½x13½"....550.00
Peach to apricot, ruffled; ftd fr w/top ornamentation....225.00
Peachblow; SP fr, New Martinsville Glass, ca 1901-'07....325.00
Pink insert w/floral, fluted rim; SP fr w/trimmed bail....225.00
Pink satin, shell shape; ftd, floral Barbour fr....195.00
Pink to dusty rose w/much gold & pnt flowers; Poole fr....295.00
Raspberry to wht, fluted; on 9½" SP ped, 10¾"....150.00
Rose to pink overlay w/florals; in ormolu basket, 7x5x7"....145.00
Spangle glass, mica flecks; fancy SP ftd fr....225.00
Tomato w/yel overlay; Middletown SP ftd fr, 12x11"....350.00
Tree of Life; ornate figural bird fr....195.00

Bristol Glass

Bristol is a type of semi-opaque opaline glass whose name was derived from the area in England where it was first produced. Similar glass was made in France, Germany, and Italy. In this country it was made by the New England Glass Company, and to a lesser extent by its contemporaries. During the 18th and 19th century, Bristol glass was imported in large amounts and sold cheaply, thereby contributing to the demise of the earlier glasshouses here in America. It is very difficult to distinguish the English Bristol from other opaline types. Style, design, and decoration serve as clues to its origin; but often only those well educated in the field can spot these subtle variations.

When no condition is indicated, the items listed below are assumed to be in mint condition.

Biscuit jar, gr opaque w/enamel floral, str sides, 6¾"....95.00
Box, turq w/gold decor, hinged top, 1⅛x1½" dia....95.00
Cake stand, jade, herons & tree, gold trim....95.00
Cruet, bl w/wht floral, gold leaves, ball stopper, 4¾"....88.00
Dresser set, gold butterflies on wht, 3-pc....57.50
Ewer, birds & floral on bl, wht bulbous base, hdl, 12"....160.00
Ewer, lion's head on metal base, bird on hdl, 19", pr....385.00
Jar, biscuit; child's head peeps out from flower....125.00
Pitcher, turq w/gold top bands/flowers/hdl trim, 2⅛"....75.00
Plate, castle & seaside view, HP, ruffled....45.00
Vase, bird/floral/bands, mc on turq, ped ft/flat oval, 10"....175.00
Vase, birds/floral, mc on wht, 24"....450.00
Vase, floral, mc on brn, threaded neck/crimped top, 5"....65.00
Vase, floral, mc on gr, 10"....40.00
Vase, floral, wht w/pink casing, ruffled, 9"....50.00
Vase, floral/ferns, lt tan satin, 12x7", pr....150.00
Vase, floral/leaves, mc on turq, enamel, rough pontil, 11"....85.00
Vase, floral/leaves, pink, ftd, bulbous, cone neck, 12"....75.00
Vase, gold panels of bl jewels/florals on turq, hdls, 7"....98.00
Vase, Grecian design w/portrait medallions, wht, dbl hdl....70.00
Vase, quail, mc on gray, 13¼", pr....295.00
Vase, Wedgwood bl band w/Greek Key pattern, rose-beige, pr..135.00
Vase, 1 w/woman & child; 1 w/winter scene, 11½x5⅜", pr....265.00
Vase, 4 birds chase insect, gold/wht dots, blk hdls, 11¾"....165.00

British Royal Commemoratives

British souvenir items have been made to commemorate coronations as well as other notable occasions involving the royal families for many years. Bells, thimbles, postcards, mugs, plates, and spoons are the most common.

When no condition is indicated, the items listed below are assumed to be in mint condition.

Key: com—commemorative cor—coronation

Ash tray, cor King Geo & Queen Elizabeth, portraits, 1937....14.00
Bank, cor Queen Elizabeth II, crown shape, CI, red & gold....20.00
Beaker, cor Queen Elizabeth, mfg British Pottery, 1953, 4"....15.00
Book, Ceremonies & Pageantry Guide, cor Queen Elizabeth....6.00
Book, Queen Elizabeth & Princess Diana, photos....15.00
Book, Royal Family, color photos....5.00
Book, The Tatler, cor King Geo, color photos, 1937, VG....14.00
Bowl, shield w/Colonial soldiers, inscription, 3½" dia....36.00
Brooch, George V & VI, Edward VIII, Queen Elizabeth, EX....27.00
Busts, Elizabeth & Phillip, basalt, Doulton, orig box, pr....275.00
Calendar, Edward VIII, color portrait, in fr, 1937, 6"....16.00
Calendar, Queen Elizabeth & Duke of Edinburg, photos, 1953..10.00
Candy dish, cor Queen Elizabeth, mfg Meakin, 1953, 6x6"....18.00
Coin, Diamond Jubilee, Royal Family, inscription, EX....35.00
Creamer, Canadian Crest, mfg Royal Winton, gold trim, 3"....12.00
Creamer, com King Geo/Queen Elizabeth, Canada visit, 1939....23.00
Cup & saucer, cor Queen Elizabeth, bone china, 1953....25.00
Dish, cor Queen Elizabeth, portrait, mottled brn, 5½", EX....12.00
Dish, Geo VI 1937 inscription, glass, scalloped edge, 9½"....46.00
Letter holder, cor Queen Elizabeth, w/verse, 1953, 8x10"....20.00
Mug, Britain Prime Minister, Duke of Wellington, portraits....10.00
Mug, cor King Geo & Queen Elizabeth, mfg Bovey, 1937....25.00
Mug, cor King Geo & Queen Mary, color portraits, w/flags....55.00
Mug, Prince Charles & Diana, color portraits, gray-blue....25.00
Mug, Queen Elizabeth, portrait, mfg Royal Doulton, 3¼"....38.00
Mug, Queen Victoria's Jubilee, profile, dates of reign....80.00
Picture, Princess Elizabeth & Margaret, color, fr, 12x16"....23.00
Pin tray, com Queen Elizabeth Silver Jubilee, 1977, 5x4"....20.00

Pin-back button, cor George VI & Elizabeth..................15.00
Pitcher, cor George V, stoneware, Doulton, 1911, 6″.........120.00
Pitcher, cor King Geo VI & Queen Elizabeth, portraits, 5″......40.00
Pitcher, cor Queen Elizabeth, mfg Dartmouth, 4¼″, EX........30.00
Pitcher, Victoria Jubilee 1887, stoneware, Doulton, 7″........135.00
Plaque, Queen Victoria Jubilee, center portrait, 3″, VG.........24.00
Plate, com King Geo & Queen Elizabeth, USA visit, 1939......34.00
Plate, cor King Geo VI & Queen Elizabeth, portraits, 6″.......22.00
Plate, cor Queen Elizabeth, color portrait, gold trim, 7″........12.00
Plate, cor Queen Elizabeth, color portrait, 1953, 8½″..........20.00
Plate, cor Queen Elizabeth, portrait w/lion & unicorn, 10″......26.00
Plate, Queen Elizabeth, portrait, Royal Crest, 10½″...........49.00
Plate, Queen Elizabeth Jubilee, inscription, 10½″.............40.00
Playing cards, triple deck, royal crown picture, color...........24.00
Postcard, Buckingham Palace, London, color, #1023............2.00
Postcard, Duke & Duchess of York walking, b/w, #201N.........2.00
Postcard, King Geo V, b/w, informal, #3997...................2.00
Postcard, Prince & Princess of Wales at Balmoral, #28..........2.00
Postcard, Queen Elizabeth, head & shoulders, #237............2.00
Postcard, Royal Family at Sandringham, color, #16, 1977........2.00
Sheet music, The Windsor Waltz, by Reine & May.............6.00
Spoon, cor Queen Elizabeth, profile on hdl, orig box, 1953.....25.00
Spoon, tea caddy; Silver Jubilee, King Geo/Queen Mary........12.00
Sugar bowl, cor Queen Elizabeth, color portrait, 2-hdl.........22.00
Teapot, cor Queen Elizabeth, portrait/crest/crown, 1953........57.00
Tin, cor Queen Elizabeth, color portrait, 1953.................9.00
Tin, portrait of Royal Family, by Marcus Adams, 7″...........26.00
Tumbler, cor Queen Elizabeth, glass, purple trim, pr...........28.00
Tumbler, cor Queen Elizabeth, Mayfair shape, crystal, 3½″......54.00
Tumbler, Queen Elizabeth & Duke of Edinburg, glass, bl/wht....13.00
Tumbler, Queen Elizabeth motif in red, glass.................11.00

Broadsides

Webster defines the term as simply a large sheet of paper printed on one side. During the 1880s, the broadside was the most practical means of mass communication. By the middle of the century they had become elaborate and lengthy with information, illustrations, portraits, and fancy border designs.

Ad handout, Gunnison Valley Salt Co, 1880s, 11x8″, EX.......20.00
Auction, gives directions, lists merchandise, 1852, 11x12″......30.00

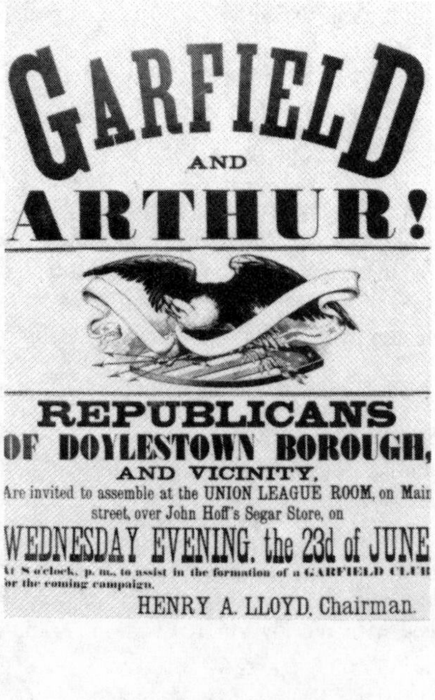
GARFIELD AND ARTHUR!

REPUBLICANS OF DOYLESTOWN BOROUGH, AND VICINITY,
Are invited to assemble at the UNION LEAGUE ROOM, on Main street, over John Hoff's Segar Store, on
WEDNESDAY EVENING, the 23d of JUNE
At 8 o'clock, p. m., to assist in the formation of a GARFIELD CLUB for the coming campaign.
HENRY A. LLOYD, Chairman.

Garfield and Arthur, announcing a Party meeting, matted and framed, 18″ x 23¼″, $110.00.

Auction, horses/cows/etc, NJ, 1827, stains/folds, 13x16″........90.00
Auction, Public Sale of Vermont Sheep, 1865, fr, 15x16″.......95.00
Auction, 22 cows/2 yokes oxen, 1834, by CFS Thomas, 14x11″.275.00
Commemorative, opening show Chicago's Opera House, silk....135.00
Foot race, $200 prize, men on horses woodcut, 1851, 19x13″..150.00
Lyceum, at the Masonic Hall, Natchez, 1833, stains, 10x13″...105.00
Political, Wide Awake Club Torchlight Procession, Lincoln...1,320.00
Sale of Dry Goods, sgn Norris & Brintnall, 1852, 19x24″.......55.00
Showbill, Grand Exhibition by...Indians, woodcut, 15x6″........65.00
Theatre ad, Civil War theme, woodcut w/Davis on bk, 19x6″....40.00

Bronzes

Thomas Ball, George Bessell, and Leonard Volk were some of the earliest American sculptors who produced figures in bronze for home decor during the 1840s. Pieces of historical significance were the most popular, but by the 1880s a more fanciful type of artwork took hold. Some of the fine sculptors of the day were Daniel Chester French, Augustus St. Gaudens, and John Quincy Adams Ward.

Bronzes enjoyed the height of their popularity at the turn of the century. The American West was portrayed to its fullest by Remington, Russell, James Frazier, Hermon MacNeil, and Solon Borglum. Animals of every specie were modeled by A.P. Proctor, Paul Bartlett, and Albert Laellele, to name but a few.

Art Nouveau and Art Deco influenced the medium during the twenties, evidenced by the works of Allen Clark, Harriet Frismuth, E.F. Sanford and Bessie P. Vonnoh.

Be aware that recasts abound, and while often esthetically satisfactory, they are not original and should be priced accordingly. In much the same manner as prints are evaluated, the original castings made under the direction of the artist are the most valuable. Later castings from the original mold are worth less. A recast is not made from the original mold. Instead, a rubber like substance is applied to the bronze, peeled away, and filled with wax. Then, using the same 'lost wax' procedure as the artist uses on completion of his original wax model, a clay-like substance is formed around the wax figure and the whole fired to vitrify the clay. The wax of course melts away, hence the term 'lost wax.' Recast bronzes loose detail and are somewhat smaller than the original due to the shrinkage of the clay mold.

When no condition is indicated, the items listed below are assumed to be in mint condition.

After the Hunt in Scotland, PJ Mene, 29″ L, 65″ pedestal...8,250.00
Allegorical, woman, pen/scroll, G Bareau/Barbedienne, 24″...1,430.00
Almeria, ivory face, IN&JL Paris, sgn Chiparus, 16¾″.......5,000.00
Amazon w/quiver/helmet, Barbedienne, Reduction, 32″......1,430.00
Arab smokes pipe, holds string instrument, Strasser, 25″.....2,750.00
Aram vendor inspects rifle, E Peynot, Salon, 1883, 30″......4,125.00
Archer, reclining nude, Bouraine, 1900, 17½″ L............1,210.00
Bacchnal group, 2 nymphs/satyr/pipes, Clodion, 23″.........2,420.00
Bathers, pr in 1900s costume, polychrome, Austrian, 13″......770.00
Beethoven, as young man, hands to side, imp Berndorf, 16″...800.00
Bellerophon upon horse w/slain beast, Emile Herbert, 30″....4,950.00
Bloodhound, on the scent, J Moizniez, late 19th C, 22″ L...1,650.00
Bronco buster, ivory head/hands, Guiraud Riviere, 17″ L......935.00
Bust, Diana, A Falguiere, marble socle, 24½″..............1,375.00
Bust, Lacordaire, Bonnassieux, 9¼″.......................420.00
Bust, Napoleon, eagle below, R Colombo, 1885, 22½″.......1,210.00
Bust, Salammbo, maid w/ribbon in flowing hair, 10″..........700.00
Bust, Voltaire, after Jean-Antoine Houdon, 18″...............715.00
Bust, woman awakening: Le Matin, Mauer, imp Tiffany, 22″....825.00
Bust, Zerline, after Leon Pilet, 18½″.......................330.00
Caesar Agustus, battle dress/trunk w/Cupid, Boschetti, 20″.....550.00
Child, dancing, drapery about his arms, Wylie, 38″...........935.00

Herme and Eagle of Jupiter, no mark, 26″, $1,695.00.

Cupid on mandolin, Riedel, 9″ . . . 570.00
Dancer, arms out/head back, Ferdinand Liebermann, 12″ . . . 385.00
Dancer, Bayadere, ivory face/hands, Chiparus, minor losses . . . 3,300.00
Dancer, Grecian robe/billowing scarf aloft, A Leonard, 24″ . . . 4,675.00
Dante, Blavier, 27″ . . . 1,950.00
Daphne, nude, sgn Raoul Larche/SIOT, H756, 13″ . . . 600.00
David killing lion w/sabre, Medaille D'or Paris/MD, 22½″ . . . 1,540.00
Donkey & Arab boy, enameled, Austrian, 5x5¼″ . . . 1,250.00
Dromedary, Algerian; standing, oval base, Barye, 10″ L . . . 1,200.00
Egyptian dancer, sgn DH Chiparus, marble plinth, 27″ . . . 2,750.00
Elephant, seated, monkey in trunk, A Vimar, 988A, 8″ . . . 825.00
Exotic dancer in halter costume, French, 20th C, 25½″ . . . 3,300.00
Farm girl w/basket/rooster, Moreau Math hors concours, 16″ . . . 605.00
Fisherman & boy in boat, turbulent sea, LA Jeanette, 22″ . . . 1,650.00
French soldiers at battle, group of 6, banner, Croisy, 26″ . . . 1,540.00
German Shepherd, ears up/recumbent, L Riche, France, 24″ L . 605.00
Gossamer Days, Salmson, 18½″ . . . 800.00
Henri IV Enfant, Bosio, 27″ . . . 2,300.00
Horse & jockey w/reins in hand, I Bonheur, 33½″ L . . . 1,760.00
Horse & spearman, Vordermayer, 17″ . . . 1,300.00
Huntsman w/stalking bloodhound, PJ Mene, 19″ . . . 1,760.00
Indian, Little Soldier, C Kuba, 7½″ . . . 450.00
Javelin thrower, nude warrior, on granite, LeVerrier, 24″ . . . 825.00
La Force Protegeant le Droit, Eugent Marioton, 32″ . . . 2,420.00
La Jeunesse, sgn Antoin Carles, imp A112, 12¾″ . . . 1,000.00
Lamp, Loie Fuller, sgn Raoul Larche, G229, 13″ . . . 7,000.00
Laocoon, ca 1820, 28x21″ . . . 3,200.00
Leda & Swan, sgn Silvestre, foundry mks, 31x13″ . . . 2,750.00
Lion & serpent, Barye, late 19th C, 13″ L . . . 715.00
Lion sur Caimon, E Delabrierre/1892, 27″ L . . . 2,500.00
Louis D'Orleans on horseback, E Fremiet, 20″ . . . 935.00
Man w/sledge, C Meunier, 21″ . . . 1,850.00
Mare & foal, trotting, after Bugatti, Cire/Perdue, 24″ . . . 27,500.00
Mask, female w/flowing hair, cast on angle, Lorski, 7½″ . . . 6,250.00
Mercury in petasus/winged sandals, caduceus, Italian, 37″ . . . 440.00
Mermaid seduces lad w/lyre in upraised arm, Hannaux, 22″ . . . 1,650.00
Mill structure, mechanical, Bergmann/Austria, 13½″ . . . 2,700.00
Nature unveiling before Science, silver/gilt, 1900, 23″ . . . 4,125.00
North African soldier, plaque: Moore Trophy, Debut, 38″ . . . 5,775.00
Nude, drapery suspended from arms, gilded, Bartholome, 9½″ . . 550.00
Nude, seated, bobbed hair, Guiraud Riviere, on marble, 17″ . . 1,650.00
Nude, starburst headdress/sorrowing man, Lamourdedieu, 12″ . 1,650.00
Nymph, nude, playing pipes, Kowalczewski, stone socle, 15″ . . 1,000.00
Nymph, partly clad, before grotto, Math Moreau, 31″ . . . 2,530.00
Nymph, shell tiara, sgn Dumaige, 26½″ . . . 1,100.00
Peasant woman, sgn H Mueller, 19½″ . . . 600.00
Philosopher in Greek toga upon seat, E Drouot, 18″ . . . 900.00
Pierrot, serenading w/lute, w/gilt/soapstone, Gazan, 21″ . . . 2,475.00
Plaque, automobile scene: 3 people ride in '20s car, 6x4″ . . . 4,100.00
Plaque, L'enfer des Luxurieux de Dante, Garnier, 21″ . . . 660.00
Plaque, Paris Welcomes 20th Century, Roine, 15x25″ . . . 680.00
Plaque, Ste Genevieve Veillant, Purvis de Chavannes, 3¼x2″ . . . 375.00
Repentant Magdalene, sgn H Muller, AGG mk, on plinth, 16″ . . 500.00
Retriever, 2 pheasants hide in rocks, E Delabrierre, 18″ L . . . 1,045.00
Satan, seated, melancholy, Jean-Jacques Feuchere, 8¾″ . . . 1,870.00
Satyr, seated, after Claude-Michel, late 19th C, 25″ . . . 825.00
Satyr sits by tree stump w/owl or sparrow, French, 15″, pr . . . 1,210.00
Shepherd boy, F Charpentier, 16½″ . . . 700.00
Shepherds of Arcadia, Aizelin, 25″ . . . 1,650.00
Ski jumper, on onyx jump, ivory face, Jaquemin, 13¾″ . . . 1,650.00
Snake dancer, halter/hip drape, parcel gilt, Austrian, 16″ . . . 825.00
Sorceress, after Jean Boucher, ca 1913, 26½″ . . . 2,640.00
Stag, doe & fawn on leaf base, C Masson/Vrai Bronze, 23½″ . 1,500.00
Venus, partial drape, after Antonio Canova, 33½″ . . . 880.00
Vestal Virgin, Huzel, 14½″ . . . 700.00
Virtutes Civicae Ense et Labore, E Picault, 44½″ . . . 3,190.00
Woman, arms/bust emerge from floral wrap, Bergmann, 11″ . . 1,650.00
Woman, windswept hair/robes, Bolestas/Biegas, 21″ . . . 1,850.00
Woman captive chained to stump, after Belleuse, 29″ . . . 1,870.00
Woman holding dove to breast, ivory/polychrome, Gallo, 8″ . . 1,540.00
Woman w/tambourine & child, Bulio, 16½″ . . . 1,250.00
Women, 2 kneeling ea end of base, EP Seidel, 1930, 20″ L . . 1,980.00

Brownies by Palmer Cox

Created by Palmer Cox in 1883, the Brownies charmed children through the pages of books and magazines, as dolls, on their dinnerware, in advertising material, and on souvenirs. Each had his own personality--among them The Bellhop, The London Bobby, The Chairman, and Uncle Sam--but the oversized, triangular face with the startled expression, the protruding tummy, and the spindle legs were characteristics of them all.

They were inspired by the Scottish legends related to Cox as a child by his parents, who were of English descent. His introduction of the Brownies to the world was accomplished by a poem called *The Brownies Ride*. Books followed in rapid succession--thirteen in the series, all written as well as illustrated by Palmer Cox.

By the late 1890s, the Brownies were active in advertising. They promoted such products as games, coffee, toys, patent medicines, and rubber boots. 'Greenies' were the Brownies' first cousins, created by Cox to charm and to woo through the pages of the advertising almanacs of the G.G. Green Company of New Jersey. Perhaps the best-known endorsement in the Brownies' career was for the Kodak Brownie, which became so popular and sold in such volume that their name became synonomous with this type of camera.

When no condition is indicated, the items listed below are assumed to be in excellent condition.

Ash tray, Brownies decor, RS Germany, 1913 . . . 45.00
Bank, ceramic, head & hat figural, unsgn . . . 65.00
Bank, wooden, Palmer Cox decal . . . 55.00
Book, Brownies, Their Book . . . 50.00
Book, Brownies & Other Stories . . . 35.00
Book, Brownies & the Farmer, 1902 . . . 22.00
Book, Busy Brownies, Brownie Series Weekly Vol 1, #1 . . . 25.00

Book, paint; Whitman #669-10, 1949 . . . 25.00
Book, Queer People, Donohue . . . 28.00
Booklet, shoe store giveaway, illus Cox, E Veale, 1896 . . . 8.00
Bottle, laxative; Brownies Work While You Sleep, boxed . . . 20.00
Bottle, soda; emb figures, rare . . . 45.00
Box, Little Buster Popcorn, pictures Brownies . . . 10.00
Catalog, Brownie cameras . . . 22.00
Doll, cloth . . . 50.00
Game, Auto Race, tin board . . . 38.00
Game, Horseshoes, in orig box, EX . . . 65.00
Game, Prize Ring Toss, litho paper/wood, in 12x18″ box, VG . . 225.00
Game, Ring Toss . . . 45.00
Magazine, Ladies' Home Journal, w/Brownies . . . 22.00
Mustache mug . . . 115.00
Plate, Brownie decor, sgn Fisher, 5″ . . . 55.00
Plate, 2 Brownies & billy goat, Staffordshire . . . 28.00
Poster, Snag-Proof rubber boots, Maryland Litho, 1900s . . . 715.00
Puppet, hand; celluloid head & hands, pnt features, 8″ . . . 40.00
Puzzle, metal; Uncle Sam, Brownies on front, 1920, #1 & #2 . . . 25.00
Puzzle, Scroll, McLoughlin . . . 125.00
Ruler, Mrs Winslow's Soothing Syrup ad, w/Brownies, NM . . . 20.00
Shakers, Brownies decor, Mt Washington, 2¾″, pr . . . 400.00
Sheet music, Dance o/t Brownies, 1895 . . . 30.00
Sheet music, Frolic o/t Brownies, 1896 . . . 30.00
Sign, emb tin, Brownie pours chocolate drink into glass . . . 175.00
Stickpin, Uncle Sam figural . . . 18.00

Picture frame, paper on wood, 8″ x 10″, $32.00.

Brush

George Brush began his career in the pottery industry in 1901, working for the J.B. Owens Pottery Co. in Zanesville, Ohio. He left the company in 1907 to go into business for himself, only to have fire completely destroy his pottery less than one year after it was founded.

Brush became associated with J.W. McCoy in 1909, and for many years served in capacities ranging from General Manager to President. (From 1911 until 1925, the firm was known as The Brush-McCoy Pottery Co; see that section for information.) After McCoy died, the family withdrew their interests, and in 1925 the name of the firm was changed to The Brush Pottery.

The era of hand decorated art pottery had passed for the most part, and would soon be completely replaced by the production of commercial lines. Of all the wares bearing the later Brush script mark, their figural cookie jars are the most collectible.

When no condition is indicated, the items listed below are assumed to be in mint condition. See also Brush-McCoy

Cookie Jars

Antique Touring Car . . . 55.00
Boy w/Balloons . . . 75.00
Chick in Nest . . . 55.00
Cinderella Pumpkin . . . 50.00
Circus Horse . . . 75.00
Clown, yel pants . . . 55.00
Clown Head . . . 55.00
Cookie House . . . 30.00
Covered Wagon . . . 85.00
Cow, w/cat on back . . . 45.00
Davey Crockett . . . 85.00
Dog w/Basket . . . 45.00
Donkey & Cart . . . 75.00
Elephant, w/monkey on back . . . 125.00
Elephant in Baby Bonnet . . . 85.00
Fish . . . 45.00
Formal Pig . . . 55.00
Granny . . . 65.00
Happy Bunny, wht w/pastels . . . 48.00
Hen on Basket . . . 45.00
Hill Billy Frog . . . 200.00
Hobby Horse . . . 65.00
Humpty Dumpty, w/beanie & bow tie . . . 60.00
Humpty Dumpty, w/peaked hat . . . 50.00
Laughing Hippo . . . 70.00
Little Angel . . . 75.00
Little Boy Blue . . . 70.00
Little Girl . . . 65.00
Nite Owl . . . 50.00
Old Clock . . . 55.00
Old Shoe . . . 40.00
Panda . . . 55.00
Pear . . . 55.00
Peter Pan . . . 75.00
Pumpkin . . . 45.00
Puppy Police . . . 65.00
Raggedy Ann . . . 65.00
Red Riding Hood . . . 95.00
Sitting Hippo . . . 75.00
Sitting Pig . . . 65.00
Smiling Bear . . . 65.00
Squirrel in Top Hat . . . 65.00

Old Clock, $55.00.

Squirrel on Log....35.00
Stylized Owl....50.00
Stylized Siamese....65.00
Teddy Bear, feet apart....50.00
Teddy Bear, feet together....42.00
Treasure Chest....55.00

Miscellaneous

Bowl, Bronze Line, 4-toed base, 4½x11½"....9.00
Flowerpot, Rockcraft, 5½"....4.00
Frog, old coloration, 11"....145.00
Frog, old coloration, 8"....90.00
Jardiniere, floral relief on gr, removable yel liner, #692....7.50
Matchbox holder, wall hanging, gr w/'Matches'....22.50
Oil jar, maroon glaze, ca 1930, 19"....45.00
Pitcher, character face, wht w/gold detail, #88A....25.00
Planter, duckling, head to side, #560....7.50
Planter, Red Riding Hood, sitting w/planter basket....22.50
Planter, sitting cat, head to right, HP florals....7.50
Planter, squirrel on log....7.00
Turtle, lawn sprinkler, ca late '20s, 16x8"....200.00
Vase, Bittersweet, ca 1945, 8"....12.00
Vase, Oriental motif, sq w/bamboo corners, gr w/bronze, 8"....7.50
Wall plaque, African masks, mk USA, 10½", pr....30.00
Wall pocket, bucking bronco horse, ca 1952....20.00

Brush McCoy

The Brush-McCoy Pottery was formed in 1911 in Zanesville, Ohio, an alliance between George Brush and J.W. McCoy. Brush's original pottery had been destroyed by fire in 1907; McCoy had operated his own business there since 1899.

After the merger, the company expanded and produced not only their staple commercial wares, but also fine artware. Lines such as Navarre, Venetian, Persian, Oriental, and Sylvan were of a fine quality equal to that of their larger competitors. Because very little of the ware was marked, it is often mistaken for Weller, Roseville, or Peters and Reed.

In the twenties, after a fire in Zanesville had destroyed the manufacturing portion of that plant, all production was contained in their Roseville (Ohio) plant #2. A stoneware type of clay was used there, and as a result, the artware lines of Jewell, Zuniart, King Tut, Florastone, and Panel-Art are so distinctive that they are more easily recognizable. Examples of these lines are unique and very beautiful--also quite rare and highly prized!

The Brush-McCoy Pottery operated under that name until after J.W. McCoy's death, when it became the Brush Pottery. The Brush-Barnett family retained their interest in the pottery until 1981, when it was purchased by the Dearborn Company.

When no condition is indicated, the items listed below are assumed to be in mint condition. See also Brush.

Bowl, Zuniart, 2x7"....45.00
Bud vase, Jewell, #41-12"....165.00
Bud vase, Onyx, dk brn, 10"....35.00
Candlestick, Jetwood, 10¼", pr....185.00
Candlestick, Zuniart, 10¼", pr....150.00
Clock, Wise Birds, w/owl figural....150.00
Jardiniere, Jetwood, 7¼"....125.00
Jardiniere, Stonecraft, wht w/pastel enamel, #241, 6"....20.00
Jardiniere & pedestal, Athenian, 39"....495.00
Lamp, Wise Birds, owl figural, 9"....150.00
Pitcher, Nurock, peacock at fountain, lg....160.00
Umbrella stand, Onyx, bl, 1920s, 20½"....145.00
Vase, Cleo, Nouveau motif, 11"....110.00
Vase, Florastone, 12"....125.00
Vase, Jewell, #055, 2½"....50.00
Vase, King Tut, 10"....325.00
Vase, lg peony incised on textured ground, 1920s, 8"....125.00
Vase, Majolica Amaryllis, bl/brn gloss, incurvate, 6½"....50.00
Vase, Navarre, gr w/wht Nouveau lady, w/hdls, 8½"....245.00
Vase, Onyx, dk brn, 4"....15.00
Vase, Oriental, hand-brushed Landsun-type glaze, 5"....15.00
Vase, Sylvan, dk gr, trees, bulbous top, #08, 10"....45.00
Vase, Vogue, blk/wht Greek Key motif, 10"....35.00

Zuni vase, 8¾", 120.00.

Buffalo Pottery

The founding of the Buffalo Pottery in Buffalo, New York, in 1901, was a direct result of the success achieved by John Larkin through his innovative methods of marketing 'Sweet Home Soap.' Choosing to omit 'middleman' profits, Larkin preferred to deal directly with the consumer, and offered premiums as an enticement for sales. The pottery soon proved a success in its own right and began producing advertising and commemorative items for other companies, as well as commercial tableware.

In 1905 they introduced their Blue Willow line, after extensive experimentation resulted in the development of the first successful underglaze cobalt achieved by an American company.

Between 1905 and 1909, a line of pitchers and jugs were hand decorated in historical, literary, floral, and outdoor themes. Twenty-nine styles are known to have been made. These have been found in a wide array of color variations.

Their most famous line was Deldare Ware, the bulk of which was made from 1908 to 1909. It was hand decorated after illustrations by Cecil Aldin. Views of English life were portrayed in detail through unusual use of color against the natural olive green cast of the body. Today, the 'Fallowfield Hunt' scenes are more difficult to locate than 'Scenes of Village Life in Olden Days.' A Deldare calendar plate was made in 1910. These are very rare and are valued highly by collectors. The line was revived in 1923 and dropped again in 1925. Every piece was marked 'Made at Ye Buffalo Pottery--Deldare Ware Underglaze.' Most are dated, though date has no bearing on the value.

Emerald Deldare, made with the same olive body and on standard Deldare Ware shapes, featured historical scenes and Art Nouveau decorations. Most pieces are found with a 1911 date stamp. Production was very limited due to the intricate, time consuming detail. Needless to say, it is very rare and extremely desirable.

Abino Ware, most of which was made in 1912, also used standard

Deldare shapes, but its colors were earthy and the decorations more delicately applied. Sailboats, windmills, and country scenes were favored motifs. These designs were achieved by overpainting transfer prints, and were often signed by the artist. The ware is marked 'Abino' in hand printed block lettering. Production was limited, and as a result, examples of this line are scarce today. Prices only slightly trail those of Emerald Deldare Ware.

The many uncatalogued items that have been found over the years indicate that Buffalo Pottery decorators were free to use their own ideas and talents to create many beautiful one-of-a-kind pieces.

When no condition is indicated, the items listed below are assumed to be in mint condition.

Deldare

Bowl, Breaking Cover, 9"....450.00
Bowl, Fallowfield Hunt, Breakfast at 3 Pigeons, 12"....585.00
Bowl, Fallowfield Hunt, 9"....395.00
Bowl, fruit; Ye Village Tavern, 9"....385.00
Bowl, soup; Fallowfield, Breaking Cover, 9"....250.00
Candlestick, drilled for electricity, 9½", pr....495.00
Creamer, Scenes of Village Life in Ye Olden Days, 1924....140.00
Creamer & sugar bowl, Scenes of Village Life....350.00
Creamer & sugar bowl, Ye Olden Days....350.00
Cup & saucer, Fallowfield Hunt....195.00
Cup & saucer, Village Scene....175.00
Cup & saucer, Ye Olden Days....185.00
Egg cup, unsgn....250.00
Hair receiver, Ye Village Street....280.00
Humidor, Emerald, Sailor, 8"....700.00
Humidor, Ye Lion Inn, 7"....665.00
Jar, powder; Ye Village Street....280.00
Match holder, Scenes of Village Life in Ye Olden Days....385.00
Mug, Fallowfield Hunt, Breaking Cover, 3½"....225.00
Mug, Fallowfield Hunt, 2½"....370.00
Mug, Fallowfield Hunt, 4½"....295.00
Mug, Scenes of Village Life in Ye Olden Days, 2½"....285.00
Mug, Ye Lion Inn, 3½"....260.00
Mug, Ye Lion Inn, 4¼"....275.00
Pitcher, Fallowfield Hunt, Breaking Cover, 10"....590.00
Pitcher, Fallowfield Hunt, sgn L Striessel, 1908, 6"....475.00
Pitcher, Fallowfield Hunt, The Return, 8"....495.00
Pitcher, Their Manner of Telling Stories, 6"....385.00
Pitcher, To Demand My Annual Rent, 8"....450.00
Pitcher, With a Cane Superior Air, 9"....500.00
Pitcher, Ye Olde English Village, 10"....550.00
Plaque, Emerald, The Garden Trio, 16½"....3,500.00
Plaque, Fallowfield Hunt, Breakfast At 3 Pigeons....475.00
Plaque, Ye Lion Inn, 12"....375.00
Plate, At Ye Lion Inn, 6¼"....70.00
Plate, calendar; 1910, 9½"....1,320.00
Plate, chop; An Evening at Ye Lion Inn, 14"....425.00
Plate, chop; An Evening at Ye Village Inn, 1908, 14"....360.00
Plate, chop; Fallowfield Hunt, The Start, 14"....500.00
Plate, Dr Syntax Soliloquising, 7¼"....250.00
Plate, Emerald, Dr Syntax Soliloquising, 7¼"....450.00
Plate, Emerald, Misfortune at Tulip Hall, 8½"....450.00
Plate, Fallowfield Hunt, Breaking Cover, 10"....185.00
Plate, Fallowfield Hunt, The Death, 8½"....125.00
Plate, Fallowfield Hunt, The Start, 9¼"....175.00
Plate, Misfortune at Tulip Hall, 8½"....450.00
Plate, Ye Olden Days, 9½"....150.00
Plate, Ye Olden Times, 9½"....150.00
Plate, Ye Town Crier, 8¼"....110.00
Punch bowl, Fallowfield Hunt, 14½"....5,000.00
Relish dish, Ye Olden Times, 6½x12"....365.00
Sugar bowl, Emerald, Dr Syntax in the Wrong Lodging House....385.00
Sugar bowl, open; Fallowfield Hunt, 6 sides, 3"....265.00
Tankard, Village Scene, 12½"....900.00
Tea tile, Emerald, Dr Syntax Taking Possession, 6"....550.00
Tea tile, Travelling in Ye Olden Days, 6"....235.00
Teapot, Scenes of Village Life in Ye Olden Days, sm, 3¾"....320.00
Teapot, Scenes of Village Life in Ye Olden Days, 1908, 5¾"....450.00
Tray, card; Fallowfield Hunt, 7¾"....325.00
Tray, card; Ye Lion Inn, 7¾"....290.00
Tray, Dancing Ye Minuet, 9x12"....500.00
Tray, Heirlooms, 12x10½"....540.00
Tray, pin; Emerald, Dr Syntax....535.00
Tray, pin; Ye Olden Days, 6¼x3½"....275.00
Tray, pin; Ye Village Days....185.00
Tray, The Dancing Minuet, 12x9"....540.00
Vase, fashionable men & women, 8"....750.00
Vase, village scene, 9"....350.00
Vase, Ye Village Parson, 8½"....725.00

Deldare Ware, tankard, The Great Controversy, Teach the Dutchman English, dated 1908, 12½", $1,000.00.

Miscellaneous

Creamer, Blue Willow, sq, 15-oz....45.00
Cup & saucer, Blue Willow, 1914....45.00
Egg cup, Blue Willow, dbl....30.00
Fish set, RK Beck, 7-pc....400.00
Jug, Cinderella....400.00
Jug, Gaudy Willow, 50-oz....185.00
Jug, George Washington, bl w/gold trim, 7½"....485.00
Jug, Gloriana, mc, 9¼"....625.00
Jug, Holland, scenes of Dutch children, 6"....325.00
Jug, Hounds & Stag, 6½"....355.00
Jug, Landing of Roger Williams, 6"....490.00
Jug, Pilgrim, 9"....550.00
Jug, Robin Hood....375.00
Jug, Roosevelt Bears, 9"....590.00
Jug, Sailor....500.00
Mug, Anticipation, 4½"....65.00
Mug, child's; boy & girl at play....45.00
Mug, Friar w/stein, 5½"....65.00

Abino Ware plate, sailing ships, dated 1912, 10″, $600.00.

Plate, Blue Willow, 10¼″ 25.00
Plate, Blue Willow, 9¼″ 22.00
Plate, Christmas, 1960 .... 50.00
Plate, Gaudy Willow, 9¼″ 125.00
Plate, Indian hunting buffalo 200.00
Plate, Japan, 10¼″ 42.00
Plate, Mandalay, 10″ 22.50
Plate, Sea Cave Restaurant, Multifleure Lamelle, 8″ 45.00
Plate, Washington's Home, mc, 7½″ 110.00
Platter, Dr Syntax Advertisement for a Wife, bl/wht 225.00
Relish, Blue Willow, shell form, 1915 .... 40.00
Teapot, Argyle, w/tea ball, bl/wht 165.00
Vase, HP roses, 7″ 85.00

Burmese

Burmese glass is opaque, in soft shades of yellow shading to pink. It was patented in 1885 by Frederick Shirley of the Mt. Washington Glass Co. The formula he developed contained gold which reacted with the fire to produce the delicate pink blush. It was made in both a glossy and satin finish. Some pieces were decorated by hand or gilded.

Similar glass was later produced by Webb in England; it was reissued by Gunderson-Pairpoint, and again in 1978 by Bryden at the Sagamore Pairpoint factory.

Creamer, berries & vines, Mt WA, 2¾″ 460.00
Cruet, melon-rib, 2nd-fired yel spout edge, Mt WA, 6½″ 985.00
Cruet, melon-rib body & stopper, 6½″ 885.00
Finger bowl, ruffle, circle sgn: Webb, Queen's, 2½x5″ 500.00
Lamp, table; 10″ satin shade, shiny w/in, att Mt WA, 15″ 1,250.00
Perfume, gold leaves & berries, sgn gilt/silver top, 4¾″ 795.00
Pitcher, Hobnail, sgn Mt WA, 9¾″ 750.00
Pitcher, oak leaves/vines, gold decor & rim, Mt WA, 9″ 1,450.00
Pitcher, prunus blossoms, ball body/ruffled collar, 2½″ 685.00
Rose bowl, berries/leaves, mc, 8-crimp top, unsgn Webb, 2½″ 295.00
Rose bowl, flowers of dots, Queen's Design, Mt WA, 5″ W 1,250.00
Shakers, floral/beading, ribbed barrel, Pairpoint holder 225.00
Sugar shaker, blossoms of wht/rust dots, 4½″ 585.00
Sugar shaker, egg shape, foral/beading, Mt WA 650.00
Syrup, pansies front & bk, SP top & lid, 6″ 1,950.00
Toothpick holder, hat, glossy, Webb, 2¼″ 225.00
Toothpick holder, prunus blossoms, 4-lobed top, wear, 2⅝″ 435.00
Toothpick holder, rigaree center, ruffled 375.00
Toothpick holder, rose bowl shape, hexagon top 350.00

Vase, decorated by Timothy Canty of Mt. Washington, ca 1895, rigaree collar, 3¼″, $845.00.

Toothpick holder, sm Dia Quilt, tricon top, glossy 425.00
Tumbler, whiskey; Dia Quilt, Mt WA, 2⅝″ 325.00
Vase, bottle; ivy decor, sgn Thos Webb, Queen's, 7¾″ 850.00
Vase, bottle; mums, wht/gr decor, Mt WA, 6⅜x3¼″ 850.00
Vase, buds/leaves, unsgn Webb, 8x4″ 750.00
Vase, butterfly/daisy/Montgomery verse, Mt WA, 12″ 2,300.00
Vase, columbines, sgn Webb, 3½″ 350.00
Vase, daisies in 3 shades of gold relief, Mt WA, 9x4¾″ 685.00
Vase, dome shape, Mt WA, 3¾x5¼″ 485.00
Vase, fern over-pnt/bkground: 2 lions/eagle, Mt WA, 8″ 1,250.00
Vase, flared petticoat shape, Mt WA, 8¾x5¼″ 185.00
Vase, floral, gold relief outlines, egg shape, Mt WA, 9x4″ 685.00
Vase, floral, hexagonal, Webb, 2½″ 450.00
Vase, floral & leaves, glossy, 4″ 325.00
Vase, flower petal top, berries decor, unsgn Webb, 3⅜″ 325.00
Vase, ibises fly over oasis, gold relief palms, 12x7″ 2,950.00
Vase, inverted bell, top flared/crimped/pinched, ftd, 4″ 375.00
Vase, Jack-in-Pulpit, pie-crust crimped, Mt WA, 12½″ 645.00
Vase, lily; leaves/berries of bl dots, gilt, Mt WA, 9″ 585.00
Vase, pinecones, ped ft, flower top, Webb, Queen's, 5½″ 595.00
Vase, 7-petal blush top, etched Webb/Queen's/RD 8016, 3¾″ 485.00

Butter Molds and Stamps

The art of decorating butter began in Europe during the reign of Charles II. This practice was continued in America by the farmer's wife who sold her homemade butter at the weekly market to earn extra money during hard times. A mold or stamp with a special design, hand carved either by her husband or a local craftsman, not only made her product more attractive, but helped identify it as hers. The pattern became the trademark of Mrs. Smith, and all who saw it knew that this was her butter, 'for butter or worse.' It was usually the rule that no two farms used the same mold within a certain area, thus the many variations and patterns available to the collector today.

The most valuable of the collectible molds are those which have animals, birds, or odd shapes. The most sought after motifs are the eagle, cow, fish, and rooster. These works of early folk art are quickly disappearing from the market.

Molds

Acorn, 1½″	60.00
Berries, 2 w/leaves, 2½″	65.00
Bird on branch, simple, rnd, 3⅝″	90.00
Circles & leaves, 2″	45.00
Cow, 1½″	190.00
Crocus, lg, 4″	90.00
Flower, miniature, 1½″	35.00
Flower, 6-petal, flanked by stars, sq, 3x5″	70.00
Geometric leaves & flower, 3″	85.00
Heart & leaf, age crack, 3½″	145.00
House, primitive carved detail, 9-pc, 4″	105.00
Maple leaf & fern, knob hdl, 3¾″	47.00
Mountain laurel & leaves, 3½″	45.00
Pineapple, over-ripe, miniature, 1½″	45.00
Rose & bud, 3½″	65.00
Sheaf of wheat, miniature, 1¾″	45.00
Star, 5-point, ornate, 2½″	45.00
Starflower, miniature, 1½″	12.50
Starflower, simple, rnd, 4¾″	55.00
Strawberry & leaves, 3-pc, pewter bands, wood pusher	145.00
Swan, miniature, 1½″	65.00
Thistle, miniature, 1½″	45.00
Thistle, 2″	68.00
Y & leaves, 3″	70.00

Repetitive floral and leaf carving, 1-pc, 3⅜″, $55.00.

Stamps

Acorns, wheel print, 7″	75.00
Acorns & oak leaf, shallow carving, trn hdl, 2¼″	60.00
Acorns & oak leaves, inserted trn hdl, rnd, 4½″	95.00
Acorns in cluster, finely carved, short hdl, 4″	145.00
Basket w/apple & cucumber, no hdl, 4″	295.00
Clover cluster, knob hdl, 4″	80.00
Cow, miniature, 1½″	170.00
Cow, tiny print, long hdl, 1″	140.00
Cow, well carved, 1-pc w/trn hdl, 4″	225.00
Crisscross, primitive, long hdl, 1½″	45.00
Daisy, knob hdl, 4″	85.00
Eagle, EX carving, hdl, 6″	400.00
Eagle, primitive, 1-pc, carved hdl, 3¼x3½″	75.00
Eagle & star, trn hdl, rnd, 3½″	225.00
Eagle w/heart-shaped shield body, rnd, 4″	320.00
Fern, knob hdl, 3½″	45.00
Flower, primitive, short hdl, sq, 2x2″	37.00
Flower, primitive, stylized, 1-pc, lg trn hdl, 5x5″	115.00
Flower, single; trn hdl, 4⅜″	65.00
Flower, 6-petal, primitive, long hdl, 1½″	50.00
Flower & leaves, elliptical, metal bail for strap hdl	375.00
Flower & 2 buds, sm, 2″	43.00
Leaf, hexagonal, 3″	30.00
Leaf, leaf shaped, lg knob hdl, 1½″	175.00
Leaf, simple, on concave almond shape, 3¾x9″	55.00
Leaves, knob hdl, 3½″	40.00
Leaves & initials, 2 of ea in 4-part design, 4½″	50.00
Lollipop, compass star, chip-carved edge, 8″ L	300.00
Pear, dbl, knob hdl, 4″	195.00
Pineapple, early example, knob hdl, 4″	70.00
Pineapple, fully ripened, knob hdl, 3¾″	65.00
Pinwheel, cookie-print shape, 4″	130.00
Pinwheel, PA, chip carving end of lollypop hdl, 9¾″ L	400.00
Sheaf of wheat, EX carving, trn, miniature, 2⅞x1¾″	85.00
Sheaf of wheat, rectangular, 2¾x5″	30.00
Stag w/stylized foliage, 3½″	140.00
Star, star shaped, lg knob hdl, 1½″	175.00
Star, trn inserted hdl, 3″	60.00
Star, 1-pc, carved hdl, 3″	30.00
Starflower, deeply cut, 5″	125.00
Starflower on front, bk: foliage, rnd, 5¼″	415.00
Strawberry, dbl, deep carving, hdl, 3½″	190.00
Sunflower, knob hdl, 3½″	175.00
Swan, miniature, 2″	170.00
Thistle, short hdl, 2½″	65.00
Tulip, deep carving, 1-pc w/5¾″ trn hdl, 3½″ dia	75.00
Tulip, stylized, primitive, 5⅛″	95.00

Button Hooks

Buttonhooks were made from around the mid-1800s, when high-button shoes made of stiff leather became fashionable, and continued to be used to some extent until 1935. They were made of bone, brass, iron, or silver--simple utilitarian no-nonsense styles, fold-up styles with jeweled gold handles, combination styles with built-in gadgets--all designed to ease the struggle of buttoning high top shoes, long kid gloves, and stiffly starched collars.

While most do have a hook end, some were made with a wire loop instead. Study the construction, since quality workmanship is an important worth-assessing factor, in addition to the more obvious elements of material and design.

When no condition is indicated, the items listed below are assumed to be in excellent condition.

Adler & Schact Clothiers, Juster Bros	10.00
Art Nouveau, 9k gold, curlicue hdl, 2¾″	89.00
J Bacon's, Louisville, KY, w/folding shoehorn	15.00
Metal, mk FL George, Derry, NH	10.00
Sterling, turq stone at end of Art Nouveau hdl	48.00
Sterling, Victorian, ornate, lg	21.00
Velvet lined case, 2 hooks, 1 shoehorn, sterling hdl	75.00

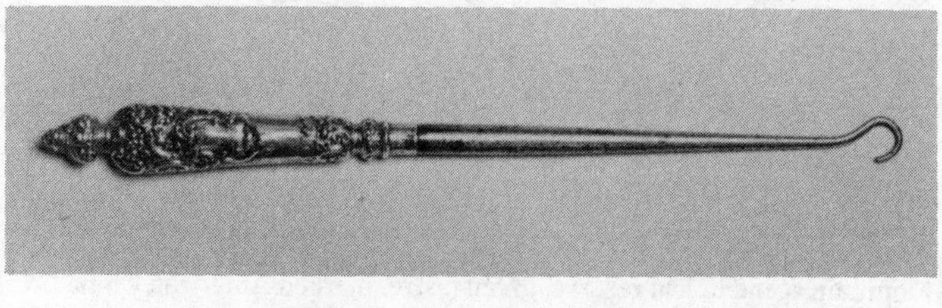

Sterling with floral and scrollwork relief, 7″, $17.50.

Calendar Plates

Calendar plates were popular advertising give-aways most popular from about 1906 until the late twenties. They were decorated with colorful underglaze decals of lovely ladies and handsome men, flowers, animals, and birds--and, of course, the twelve months of the year of their issue.

During the late thirties they came into vogue again, but never to the extent they were originally.

Those with exceptional detailing, or those with scenes of a particular activity are most desirable--so are any from before 1906.

When no condition is indicated, the items listed below are assumed to be in mint condition.

1906, holly & roses, candy store advertisement, rare, 9″........37.50
1908, roses..20.00
1908, Victorian lady driving auto, West End Pottery...........35.00
1909, bird, souvenir MA, 8″...............................20.00
1909, bird in center, MN advertisement.....................25.00
1909, flower girl center, floral border, WI souvenir............32.00
1909, New York State Capitol Building, gr on wht, 9½″........27.50
1909, portrait in center, SD advertisement...................32.00
1910, boxer dog holding calendar banner, 7½″...............35.00
1910, cherubs ringing bell, 8″.............................35.00
1910, hunting scene, 7½″.................................25.00
1910, lg pink roses, dbl gold bands on edge, 10½″............40.00
1910, lovely lady.......................................28.00
1910, ships & windmills..................................22.50
1911, flowers, store advertisement, 7″.......................20.00
1911, flying duck, Taylor, TX.............................35.00
1911, hunter & dog peer at flock of quail, 8¼″...............25.00
1911, Sunbonnet Kids..................................125.00
1911-12, floral, Goodwin Pottery Co, 9½″...................25.00
1912, cherubs & fruit....................................26.00
1912, floral center, MI advertisement.......................22.00
1912, Kewpies/butterflies/lady, MA hotel advertisement.........45.00
1913, bi-plane w/aircraft in bkground, 7½″..................42.00
1919, lg American flag, John J Rutgers Co, 8¼″..............35.00
1920, Victory flags.....................................30.00
1924, game birds & dog, MN..............................32.00
1929, tea caddy, sm bouquet of roses in center, 7″............40.00

Mountain scene in leaf reserve, green lustre, marked American China Co., 1909, 8½″, $35.00.

Calendars

Calendars are collected for their colorful prints, often attributed to a well-recognized artist of the period. Advertising calendars from the turn of the century often have a double appeal when representing a company whose products are themselves collectible.

When no condition is indicated, the items listed below are assumed to be in near mint condition.

1888, Scott's Emulsion, girl holding kitten/puppy..............12.00
1893, Hood's Sarsaparilla, EX.............................32.00
1894, Hood's Sarsaparilla, complete........................50.00
1894, Hood's Sarsaparilla, no pad.........................10.00
1895, Hood's Sarsaparilla, EX.............................32.00
1895, Prang, 4-pg.......................................45.00
1896, Hood's Sarsaparilla, w/envelope.......................30.00
1897, Hood's Sarsaparilla, complete........................50.00
1897, Hood's Sarsaparilla, 1 month only, EX.................30.00
1897, Iroquois Brewing Co, w/Indian, 12x17″................250.00
1897, Winchester Repeating Arms Co.......................600.00
1898, Hood's Sarsaparilla, complete........................50.00
1898, Hood's Sarsaparilla, 2 months only, EX................22.50
1899, Hood's Sarsaparilla, NM............................30.00
1899, 3-section die-cut, w/children.........................35.00
1900, Dupont Powder, ram jumps ravine/hunters w/dogs, 28″...250.00
1900, Hood's Sarsaparilla, incomplete pad....................22.00
1902, Quaker Oats Queens of Home & Nations, 4 pg..........40.00
1903, Fairbank's Fairy Soap..............................145.00
1905, Metropolitan Insurance..............................15.00
1906, Fleishmann's Yeast, horse-drawn wagon in street scene....45.00
1908, Peter's Cartage Co, in fr..........................350.00
1909, Clark Carriage Repository, winter scene................12.00
1911, Swifts Lowell Fertilizer, c WF Powers 1910, 24x15″......50.00
1912, Champion Harvesting Machines........................45.00
1912, Gollings, 2 Wyoming cowboys rope steer, 28x16″, EX....75.00
1912, Western Live Stock, Playing Hooky, 3 kids fishing.......22.00
1913, Hood's Sarsaparilla, complete, NM....................60.00
1915, Hercules Powder Co, eagle in forest, 32½″............150.00
1915, Hercules Powder Co, hunting dog & quail, 32½″.......150.00
1915, Hercules Powder Co, moose in snowy forest, 32½″......150.00
1915, Hercules Powder Co, oil rigger w/Hercules explosives....125.00
1915, Hercules Powder Co, red-headed ducks flying, 32½″.....130.00
1916, Pabst Malt Tonic, beautiful woman, lav dress...........85.00
1917, horse review, champions, records, complete.............70.00
1917, Pompeian Soap, Mary Pickford picture.................47.50
1918, Hood's Sarsaparilla, no pad, EX......................26.00
1918, New England Fertilizer, farm boy/milk maid, 24x15″......32.00
1919, Edison Mazda, Sunrise, M Parrish, 11x8½″, M..........45.00
1920, Brown & Bigelow, Two's Company, by Russel, top only...45.00
1920, girl w/rifle/dogs, die-cut, Atlantic Tea, 17″.............35.00
1923, Hunt-Lasher, Where a Hen's a Man, Goodwin...........65.00
1924, Mt Rainer, Glowing in Rosy Splendor, RA Fox..........60.00
1927, Pompeian Co, The Bride, Rolf Armstrong, 7x26″........40.00
1928, Buster Brown Shoes, B Crandell art, complete, NM......15.00
1928, Skyward, Byrd.....................................8.00
1929, Edison Mazda, Golden Hours, M Parrish, 12½x8½″......45.00
1930, DeLaval Separator, complete.........................28.00
1930, Times Square, night scene, in fr.....................125.00
1932, Belden, cowboy/horse w/Wyoming scenery, b/w, 22x14″...25.00
1932, Solitude, Parrish, M in envelope.....................295.00
1932, Western Cartridge, Champion Mars Guy, top only........75.00
1934, Wrigley's Gum, complete, NM........................15.00
1935-37, DeLaval, historical scenes/factory, 17x9″............25.00

Victorian lady in oval reserve, 1908, 13½" x 9½", $95.00.

1937, Goodwin, Surprised, hunter shoots at moose, 43x21"..... 95.00
1937, Nehi Soda, full pad, good color, NM.................. 105.00
1937, Next Time, Old Gal, sport scenes, 40x30", VG.......... 60.00
1937, Tivoli Mercantile, mc sports litho, 16½x9".............. 27.00
1938, Goodwin, sporting scenes, w/pad/tabs/hangers, 45x21"... 145.00
1938, Shaw-Barton, Law & Order, Wieghorst, 44x29".......... 95.00
1939, Hintermeister, The Flight, hunters shooting, 49x25"...... 88.00
1940, Earl MacPherson, pin-up, 14x9"........................ 18.00
1940, Hansen, The Outlaw, cowboy on horse, 33x16".......... 60.00
1941, Hudson Bay, McLoughlin welcomes Americans, 30x18"... 30.00
1942, Surprised, cowboy on horse startled by bear, 23x14"..... 40.00
1945, Lawson Wood... 18.00
1946, Cloes Real Estate, girl & dog in car, EX............... 12.00
1946, Esquire, Vargas illus.................................. 38.00
1948, Dr Pepper, complete, M................................ 26.00
1948, Wieghorst, hunter/Indian, tabs/pad, Shaw-Barton......... 95.00
1949, Boy Scout, Friend in Need, Rockwell, sm rpr, 16x33".... 75.00
1950, Royal Crown Cola, Wanda Hendrix, EX................... 30.00
1951, 4 Seasons, Rockwell.................................... 35.00
1954, various game birds, by Bishop.......................... 50.00
1957, Hercules Powder, Pheasant Hunting in Oregon.......... 85.00
1957, Marilyn Monroe, complete pad.......................... 25.00
1958, Playboy, EX... 85.00
1959-1960, Playboy, EX...................................... 55.00
1961-1962, Playboy, EX...................................... 25.00

California Faience

'California Faience' was the trade name used by William V. Bragdon and Chauncy R. Thomas on vases, bowls, and other artware produced at their pottery known as 'The Tile Shop' in Berkeley, California, from 1920 to 1930. Faience tile was the principal product of the business during these years and is the favorite with today's collectors. Items in a glossy glaze are rare and therefore more valuable. Tiles were marked 'California Faience' with a die stamp.

When no condition is indicated, the items listed below are assumed to be in mint condition.

Bowl, bright bl, incurvate rim, 4" opening, 2"................ 50.00
Bowl, console; blk matt, aqua w/in, w/flower frog............ 150.00
Bowl, shell, bl over dk brn clay, minor wear, 3x16x13"........ 45.00
Bowl, 2 figural ducks flower frog, bl........................ 175.00
Bowl, 3-color, Chinese, w/figural flower frog, set, 12"......... 275.00
Candlestick, bl-purple high glaze, 7", pr.................... 225.00
Potpourri, matt yel, hat-like lid, incised mk, 4½"............ 225.00
Tile, floral relief, 2-color, 4x4"............................. 75.00
Tile, flowerpot motif, Arts & Crafts, 4x4".................... 75.00
Vase, bl gloss, 4".. 125.00
Vase, bl gloss, 5".. 150.00
Vase, bl textured matt on red clay, bulbous, 5½x6"........... 100.00
Vase, cobalt over turq, 6½"................................ 150.00
Vase, crystalline-like highlights, gourd shape, rare, 11"........ 300.00
Vase, dk pink gloss, full body, sgn, 7"....................... 145.00
Vase, gr semi-gloss, red clay, squat, 4½x7".................. 100.00
Vase, rose, matt finish, 7"................................. 100.00
Vase, stylized leaves, incised, red gloss, 6½"................ 200.00
Vase, yel matt, cylinder, 4x2"............................. 135.00

Tile, six-color floral, 5¼", $295.00.

California Perfume Company

D.H. McConnell, Sr., founded the California Perfume Company (C.P. Company; C.P.C.) in 1886, in New York City. He had previously been a salesman for a book company, which he later purchased. His door-to-door sales usually involved the lady of the house, to whom he presented a complimentary bottle of inexpensive perfume. Upon determining his perfume to be more popular than his books, he decided that the manufacture of perfume might be more lucrative. He bottled toiletries under the name 'California Perfume Company,' and a line of household products called 'Perfection' until 1929, when 'Avon Products, Inc.' appeared on the label. In 1939, the C.P.C. name was entirely removed from the product.

The success of the company is attributed to the door-to-door sales approach and 'money back' guarantee offered by his first 'Depot Agent,' Mrs. P.F.E. Albee, known today as the 'Avon Lady.'

The company's containers are quite collectible today, especially the older, hard-to-find items. Advanced collectors seek bottles and other items labeled Goetting & Co., New York; Goetting's; or Savoi Et Cie, Paris. Such examples date from 1871 to 1896, and were distributed for some time from C.P.C.'s West-Coast branch. The Goetting Company was at one time owned by D.H. McConnel; Savoi Et Cie was a line which they imported to sell through department stores. Also of special interest are packaging and advertising with the Ambrosia or Hinze Ambrosia Company label. This was a subsidiary company whose objective seems to have been to produce a line of face creams, etc., for sale through drugstores and other such commercial outlets. They operated in New York from about 1875 until 1954. Because very little is known about these companies, and since only a few examples of their product containers and advertising material have been found, market values for such items have not yet been established. Other examples of rare items sought by the collector include products marked 'Gertrude Recordon'; Marvel Electric Silver Cleaner; Easy Day Automatic Clothes Washer; pre-1930 catalogs; and California Perfume Company 1909 and 1910 calendars.

There are hundreds of local clubs throughout the world that are supported by the National Association of Avon Collectors Organization and the Western World Avon Collectors Clubs. Those wishing to join (as well as those seeking additional information concerning California Perfume Company and its products) may contact Dick Pardini, listed in the Directory under California.

When no condition is indicated, the items listed below are assumed to be in mint condition.

American Ideal Perfume, 'Introductory Size,' in wood box, M...225.00
Ariel Toilet Water, 2-oz, 1930-1935...100.00
Baby Set, 3-pc, w/box, 1923...200.00
Bandoline Hair Dressing, 1923...65.00
Bay Rum, 4-oz, 1908, M...140.00
Boudoir Manicure Set, 4-pc, w/booklet, 1929...165.00
California Tooth Tablet, 1896-1905...85.00
Carnation Sachet, bottle, 1915...90.00
Catalog, color, w/tabs, 1920s...125.00
CPC Sample Case, basketweave w/label, 1915...100.00
Cut Glass Perfume, 1915...225.00
Daphne Talcum Powder, 4-oz can, 1923...65.00
Depilatory, 1-oz, 1915...90.00
Eau De Quinine, 6-oz, 1923...90.00
Elite Powder, Perfect Foot Powder, sm oval can, 1923...45.00
Elite Powder, Perfect Foot Powder, 1-lb tin can, 1923...75.00
Gentleman's Shaving Set, 7-pc, w/box, 1917...400.00
Gertrude Recordon's Introductory Facial Treatment Set...275.00
Juvenile Set, 1915...425.00
Lavender Salts, green glass, 1910...250.00
Lemonal Cleansing Cream, jar, 1926...65.00
Liquid Shampoo, 6-oz, 1923...85.00
Little Folks Set, 4 bottles, 1937...130.00
Lotus Cream, 12-oz, 1917...150.00
Massage Cream, jar, 1916...125.00
Mission Garden Compact, 1925...40.00
Nail Cream, container w/contents, 1924...20.00
Narcissus Perfume, 1-oz, 1925...110.00
Natoma Rose Perfume, ½-oz, 1916, M...110.00
Natoma Rose Talcum, w/squaw, triangle shape, 1914...80.00
Perfection, Auto Lustre, 1-pt, 1930...65.00
Perfection, Baking Powder, 1-lb can, 1931...25.00
Perfection, Coloring, ½-oz bottle, 1934...17.00
Perfection, Coloring Set, 5 bottles in box, 1920...250.00
Perfection, Coloring Set, 5 bottles in tin box, 1941...70.00
Perfection, Flavoring Set, 5 bottles in tin box, 1941...60.00
Perfection, Furniture Polish, 12-oz, 1936...20.00
Perfection, Kwick Cleaning Polish, 8-oz, 1922...40.00
Perfection, Laundry Crystals, in box, 1931...30.00
Perfection, Liquid Shoe White, sample, ½-oz, 1935...40.00
Perfection, Liquid Shoe White, 4-oz, 1935...30.00
Perfection, Liquid Spots Out, 4-oz, 1925...45.00
Perfection, Machine Oil, 3-oz, ribbed side, 1945...25.00
Perfection, Mending Cement, tube, 1933...10.00
Perfection, Mothicide, 1-lb can, 1925...40.00
Perfection, Olive Oil, 1-pt can, 1931...25.00
Perfection, Powdered Cleaner, 10-oz, 1934...20.00
Perfection, Prepared Starch, 6-oz, 1931...25.00
Perfection, Savoury Coloring, 4-oz, 1941...12.00
Perfection, Silver Cream Polish, ½-lb can, 1931...20.00
Perfume Sample Set, 1931...315.00
Powder Sachets, 1890s...90.00
Powder tin, 2 nude babies playing w/giant rose ea side...75.00
Radiant Nail Powder, 1923...50.00
Rose Pomade, jar, 1914...65.00
Shampoo Cream, 4-oz jar, 1908...75.00
Sweet Sixteen Face Powder, 1916...45.00
Tooth Tablet, 1923...55.00
Tooth Wash, 1915...100.00
Trailing Arbutus Face Powder, 1925...40.00
Trailing Arbutus Talcum, sample can, 1914...85.00
Trailing Arbutus Talcum, 1-lb tin can, 1920...70.00
Vernafleur, powder can, 1925...35.00
Vernafleur Toilet Soap, 3 bars in box, 1936...55.00
Violet Almond Meal, 4-oz tin can, 1923...60.00
Violet Almond Meal, 4-oz tin can, 1923, VG...20.00

Calling Cards, Cases and Receivers

The practice of announcing one's arrival with a calling card, borne by the maid to the mistress of the house, was a social grace of the Victorian era. Different messages were related by turning down one corner or another--condolences, a personal visit, or a goodbye. The custom was forgotten by WWI.

Fashionable ladies and gents carried their personally engraved cards in elaborate cases made of such materials as embossed silver, mother-of-pearl with intricate inlay, tortoiseshell, and ivory. Card receivers held cards left by visitors who called while the mistress was out or 'not receiving.'

Calling cards with fringe, die-cut flaps that cover the name, or an unusual decoration are worth about $3.00 to $4.00, while plain cards usually sell for around $1.00. When no condition is indicated, the items listed below are assumed to be in mint condition.

Cases

Coin silver, eng bird, hinged, in orig box, 1840...110.00
Ivory, deeply carved scene of Wm Tell, German...185.00
Lacquer, Battle of Buena Visto, hand pnt decoupage, 5½"...700.00
MOP, gentleman's...28.00
Tortoiseshell, Victorian...65.00
Wood, allover carved, Oriental people/buildings, 3¼x2¼"...26.00

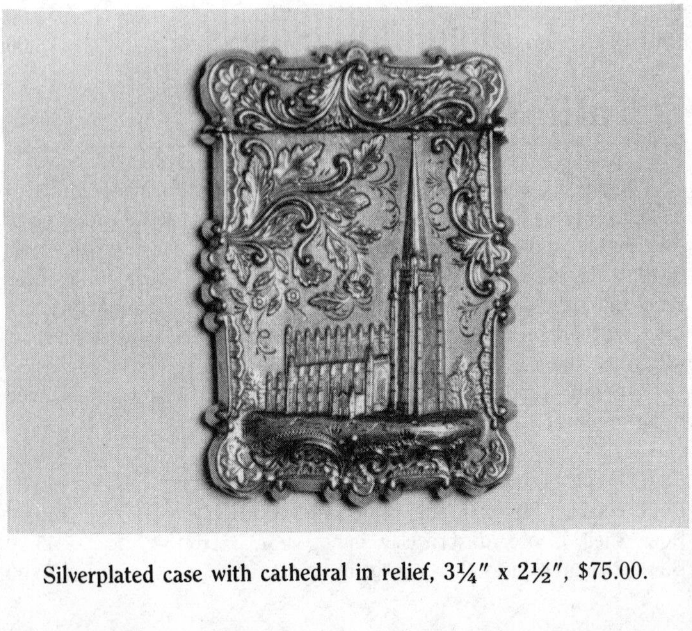

Silverplated case with cathedral in relief, 3¼" x 2½", $75.00.

Receivers

Bronze, faces on hdls/ped ft, sgn Ceres, 8x10″ 125.00
Milk glass, Jewish star motif 22.00
Porcelain, Napoleon decal 36.00
SP, goat figurals, quad plate, Meriden 195.00
SP, tray on stand, boy & dog stand on base, Meriden, 5″ 60.00

Camark

The Camden Art and Tile Company of Camden, Arkansas, was organized in 1926. John Lessell and his wife were associated with the company only briefly before he died that same year. After his death, his wife stayed on and continued to decorate wares very similar to those he had made for Weller. Le-Camark closely resembled Weller LaSa; Lessell was almost a duplication of Marengo. Perhaps the most outstanding was a mirror black line with lustre decoration. Naturally, examples of these lines are very rare.

The company eventually became known as Camark, and began production of commercial ware of the type listed below.

When no condition is indicated, the items listed below are assumed to be in mint condition.

Basket, bl, dbl, #138, 4½x5¾″ 6.00
Basket, cream w/pink & bl flowers, HP, w/hdl 7.00
Basket, high gloss gr, flared rim, 2-hdl, 4½x5″ 6.00
Basket, pale olive, 4½x3¾″ 6.00
Bowl, apple gr, scalloped, tab hdl, 4½″ 3.00
Bowl, turq, dbl shell, 12x5½″ 12.00
Bowl, turq, flaring, orig paper label, 12″ 30.00
Bowl, turq, scalloped, melon rib, 9½x3″ 7.00
Cornucopia, cream, horizontal rib, 8x9″ 12.00
Creamer, high gloss blk, Deco, 4¼″ 4.00
Dealer sign, yel, Arkansas shape, base: 7¼x7¾″ 45.00
Dish, lt gr, 7x4″ rectangle, w/7¾″ crane figure 17.50
Ewer, turq/plum w/out, yel w/in, melon rib, sticker, 10″ 25.00
Pitcher, apple gr, bead & scroll relief, 4¼″ 5.00
Pitcher, relief decor, 3¼″ 4.00
Planter, dbl swan, gr, 7x7″ 10.00
Planter, duck, pink, 3″ 3.00
Planter, elephant w/trunk up, high gloss blk, 6¼x5½″ 9.00
Vase, emb floral, gr/bronze, swirl hdls/scalloped/ftd, 8″ 20.00
Vase, high gloss gr, ftd, leaf-form, flared split top, 5″ 5.00

Vase, pink with deep plum trees, signed Le-Camark, 8½″, $550.00.

Cambridge Glass

The Cambridge Glass Company began operations in 1901, in Cambridge, Ohio. They made primarily crystal dinnerware and well-designed accessory pieces until the 1920s, when they introduced the concept of color that was to become so popular on the American dinnerware market.

Always maintaining high standards of quality and elegance, they produced many lines that became best sellers; through the twenties and thirties they were recognized as the largest manufacturer of this type of glassware in the world.

Of the various marks the company used, the 'C in triangle' is the most familar. Production stopped in 1958.

For a more thorough study of the subject, we recommend *Colors in Cambridge Glass*, by the National Cambridge Collectors, Inc.; their address may be found in the Directory under Clubs. When no condition is indicated, the items listed below are assumed to be in mint condition.

Swan, 6½″ x 8½″, $50.00.

Animals

Bluejay 145.00
Bluejay, peg base 100.00
Eagle, bookend 75.00
Heron, lg 125.00
Heron, sm 75.00
Scottie 65.00
Scottie, frosted 75.00
Seagull 45.00
Swan, blk w/crystal blocks, 10½″, +pr 4½″, set 450.00
Swan, candlesticks, milk glass, 4½″, pr 200.00
Swan, dk gr, 3½″ 40.00
Swan, pink, 10½″ 200.00
Swan, 10½″ 95.00
Swan, 4½″ 25.00
Swan, 6½″ 40.00
Swan, 8″ 50.00

Adam, crystal; compote, #695, 7″ 15.00
Apple Blossom, colors; tumbler, ftd; #3130, 12-oz 20.00

Apple Blossom, crystal; bowl, cereal; 6″ 10.00
Apple Blossom, crystal; candlestick, keyhole, 1-light 12.50
Apple Blossom, crystal; compote, 7″ 25.00
Apple Blossom, crystal; finger bowl w/plate, #3130 .... 18.00
Apple Blossom, crystal; goblet, cordial; #3120, 1½-oz 35.00
Apple Blossom, crystal; goblet, water; #3130, w/gold 22.50
Apple Blossom, crystal; pitcher, #3130, 64-oz 75.00
Apple Blossom, crystal; plate, dinner; 9½″ 25.00
Apple Blossom, crystal; platter, 11½″ 30.00
Apple Blossom, crystal; stem, water; #3135, 8-oz 15.00
Apple Blossom, crystal; tray, server; center hdl, #3400 .... 25.00
Apple Blossom, crystal; tumbler, #3025, 4-oz 10.00
Apple Blossom, crystal; vase, 5″ 17.50
Apple Blossom, mandarin gold; candlestick, keyhole, 5″, pr 50.00
Apple Blossom, mandarin gold; cheese & cracker, #3400 .... 45.00
Apple Blossom, mandarin gold; creamer & sugar, ftd 35.00
Apple Blossom, mandarin gold; mayonnaise, 3-pc 55.00
Apple Blossom, mandarin gold; tray, server; center hdl 45.00
Apple Blossom, mandarin gold; tumbler, ftd, 8-oz, 4¾″ 20.00
Apple Blossom, mandarin gold/gr; bowl, bonbon; 2-hdl, 5½″ 15.00
Apple Blossom, mandarin gold/gr; bowl, 2-hdl, 10″ 30.00
Apple Blossom, mandarin gold/gr; candy box, 4-ftd 85.00
Apple Blossom, mandarin gold/gr; cheese center, #3400 .... 35.00
Apple Blossom, mandarin gold/gr; cup 20.00
Apple Blossom, mandarin gold/gr; goblet, champagne; #3130 .... 20.00
Apple Blossom, mandarin gold/gr; plate, salad; sq 12.00
Apple Blossom, mandarin gold/gr; plate, tea; 7½″ 10.00
Apple Blossom, willow blue; bowl, #3400, 13″ 60.00
Bashful Charlotte, blue frosted, 11″ 500.00
Bashful Charlotte, crystal, 11″ 135.00
Bashful Charlotte, crystal, 6″ 45.00
Bashful Charlotte, green, 11″ 200.00
Bashful Charlotte, green, 6″ 145.00
Bashful Charlotte, pink, 6″ 145.00
Bashful Charlotte, pink frosted, 11″ 225.00
Blossom Time, crystal; compote, 7″ 30.00
Blossom Time, crystal; plate, 12½″ 36.00
Blossom Time, crystal; tray, relish; 3-part, 8¾″ 28.00
Blossom Time, crystal; tumbler, ftd, #1675, 12-oz 15.00
Caprice, blue; ash tray, 4″ 12.00
Caprice, blue; bonbon, sq, ftd, 6″ 25.00
Caprice, blue; bonbon, 4½″ 20.00
Caprice, blue; bottle, bitters; 7-oz 150.00
Caprice, blue; bowl, crimped, 4-ftd, 12½″ 45.00
Caprice, blue; bowl, jelly; 2-hdl, 5″ 20.00
Caprice, blue; bowl, pickle; 9″ 25.00
Caprice, blue; bowl, relish; 3-part, 12″ 125.00
Caprice, blue; bowl, relish; 3-part, 8″ 30.00
Caprice, blue; bowl, 4-toe, oval, #65 .... 45.00
Caprice, blue; candlestick, 3-light 37.50
Caprice, blue; candlestick, 5″ 18.00
Caprice, blue; candy dish, ftd, w/lid, 6″ 67.50
Caprice, blue; celery & relish, 3-part, 8½″ 30.00
Caprice, blue; cigarette box, 3½x2¼″ 30.00
Caprice, blue; cigarette holder, triangle, 3x3″ 22.50
Caprice, blue; coaster 20.00
Caprice, blue; compote, 6″ 40.00
Caprice, blue; cordial, blown, #300, 3-oz 60.00
Caprice, blue; creamer & sugar, lg 35.00
Caprice, blue; creamer & sugar, med 30.00
Caprice, blue; goblet, water; #300 .... 30.00
Caprice, blue; ice bucket 120.00
Caprice, blue; marmalade, w/lid 100.00
Caprice, blue; mustard, w/lid 75.00
Caprice, blue; pitcher, ball shape, 32-oz 150.00
Caprice, blue; pitcher, tall, Daulton style, 90-oz 1,000.00
Caprice, blue; plate, bread & butter; 6½″ 12.50
Caprice, blue; plate, cabaret; 4-ftd, 14″ 45.00
Caprice, blue; plate, dinner; 9½″ 70.00
Caprice, blue; plate, lemon; 6″ 20.00
Caprice, blue; plate, 16″ 95.00
Caprice, blue; plate, 2-hdl, 5″ 18.00
Caprice, blue; plate, 7½″ 15.00
Caprice, blue; shakers, ball, pr 45.00
Caprice, blue; shakers, flat, pr 35.00
Caprice, blue; sherbet, low, blown, #300, 6-oz 20.00
Caprice, blue; sherbet, tall, molded, 7-oz 30.00
Caprice, blue; sugar bowl, ind 15.00
Caprice, blue; tumbler, #184, 12-oz 40.00
Caprice, blue; tumbler, flat, molded, 12-oz 40.00
Caprice, blue; tumbler, ftd, molded, 10-oz 30.00
Caprice, blue; vase, 6″ 80.00
Caprice, blue; vase, 7½″ 75.00
Caprice, blue; wine, molded, 3-oz 60.00
Caprice, crystal; ash tray, 3″ 4.00
Caprice, crystal; ash tray, 3-ftd shell, 2¾″ 5.00
Caprice, crystal; basket, almond; #93, 2½″ 22.00
Caprice, crystal; bowl, crimped, 4-ftd, 10½″ 27.50
Caprice, crystal; bowl, cupped, 4-toe, 10″ 25.00
Caprice, crystal; bowl, ftd, hdl, #66, 13″ 35.00
Caprice, crystal; bowl, relish; 2-part, hdl, 6½″ 12.00
Caprice, crystal; bowl, relish; 3-part, 8″ 16.00
Caprice, crystal; cigarette box, w/4 ash trays, sm 37.50
Caprice, crystal; cigarette box, 3½x2¼″ 15.00
Caprice, crystal; cigarette holder, triangle, 2x2¼″ 15.00
Caprice, crystal; claret, blown, #301, 4½-oz 15.00
Caprice, crystal; compote, 6″ 25.00
Caprice, crystal; compote, 7″ 25.00
Caprice, crystal; cordial, blown, #300, 1-oz 27.50
Caprice, crystal; cup 10.00
Caprice, crystal; goblet, water; 8-oz 15.00
Caprice, crystal; goblet, wine; #300 .... 27.50
Caprice, crystal; jelly dish, 2 hdls, #151 .... 14.00
Caprice, crystal; mustard, w/lid 45.00
Caprice, crystal; pitcher, ball shape, 80-oz 75.00
Caprice, crystal; plate, bread & butter; 6½″ 6.00
Caprice, crystal; plate, cabaret; 4-ftd, 14″ 30.00
Caprice, crystal; plate, dinner; 9½″ 30.00
Caprice, crystal; shakers, ball, pr 27.50
Caprice, crystal; sherbet, low 12.00
Caprice, crystal; stem, water; blown, #301, 9-oz 14.00
Caprice, crystal; tray, oval, 6″ 12.00
Caprice, crystal; tray, relish; 3-part, #125, 12″ 55.00
Caprice, crystal; tumbler, flat, molded, 5-oz 18.00
Caprice, crystal; tumbler, straight side, molded, 12-oz 18.00
Caprice, crystal; vase, ivy bowl; 8″ 50.00
Caprice, crystal; vase, 9½″ 60.00
Caprice, crystal; wine, blown, #301, 2½-oz 15.00
Caprice, emerald green; bowl, #66 .... 55.00
Cascade, crystal; candy dish, w/lid, ftd 35.00
Cascade, crystal; ice tub 30.00
Chantilly, crystal; bottle, oil & vinegar; sterling foot 125.00
Chantilly, crystal; bowl, bonbon; 2-hdl, ftd, 7″ 18.00
Chantilly, crystal; candlestick, 5″ 17.50
Chantilly, crystal; claret, #3625, 4½-oz 35.00
Chantilly, crystal; compote, 5½″ 30.00
Chantilly, crystal; creamer & sugar, #3900 .... 25.00
Chantilly, crystal; creamer & sugar, ind, #253 .... 35.00

Chantilly, crystal; hurricane lamp, candlestick base.............75.00
Chantilly, crystal; pitcher, ball.............................115.00
Chantilly, crystal; plate, dinner; 10½″.......................55.00
Chantilly, crystal; shaker, hdl, sterling silver top, pr...........40.00
Chantilly, crystal; sherbet, low, #3625.......................18.00
Chantilly, crystal; tray, relish; 2-part, #3900, 6¼″.............22.00
Chantilly, crystal; tumbler, iced tea; #3600...................24.50
Chantilly, crystal; tumbler, iced tea; ftd, #3779, 12-oz..........18.00
Chantilly, crystal; vase, bud; 10″............................27.50
Chantilly, crystal; wine, #3779, 2½″..........................25.00
Cleo, all colors; bowl, compote; 4-ftd, 6″.....................27.50
Cleo, all colors; candle holder, 1-light, gr, pr.................40.00
Cleo, all colors; candlestick, 2-light..........................32.50
Cleo, all colors; compote, tall, #3115, 7″.....................35.00
Cleo, all colors; covered candy dish, 3-toe, #864..............50.00
Cleo, all colors; pitcher, 22-oz, w/lid........................125.00
Cleo, all colors; sherbet, tall, #3115, 6-oz....................18.00
Cleo, all colors; tumbler, ftd, #3115, 5-oz....................15.00
Crown Tuscan, ash tray, #33, 4″..............................12.50
Crown Tuscan, bowl, centerpiece, flying nude, enamel, 10″....250.00
Crown Tuscan, bowl, flying nude, lg..........................175.00
Crown Tuscan, bowl, 4-toed, 12″.............................60.00
Crown Tuscan, candy dish, w/lid, 3-part, #3500-57.............45.00
Crown Tuscan, shell compote, nude stem, 8″...................150.00
Crown Tuscan, swan, 3½″.....................................35.00
Crown Tuscan, swan, 8″......................................145.00
Crown Tuscan, tray, relish.....................................45.00
Crown Tuscan, urn, w/lid.....................................250.00
Crown Tuscan, vase, cornucopia, 10″..........................50.00
Crown Tuscan, vase, globe, coral, 6½″.........................45.00
Decagon, cobalt; bowl, berry; 10″.............................25.00
Decagon, cobalt; bowl, cereal; flat rim, 6″....................12.00
Decagon, cobalt; bowl, cream soup w/liner......................22.50
Decagon, cobalt; bowl, flat rim fruit, 5¾″.....................12.00
Decagon, cobalt; bowl, relish; 2-part, 9″.....................18.00
Decagon, cobalt; bowl, vegetable; rnd, 11″....................30.00
Decagon, cobalt; bowl, vegetable; rnd, 9″.....................27.50
Decagon, cobalt; compote, tall, 7″............................35.00
Decagon, cobalt; compote, 5¾″...............................20.00
Decagon, cobalt; creamer, scalloped edge.......................18.00
Decagon, cobalt; creamer, tall, ftd, lg.........................22.00
Decagon, cobalt; cup...10.00
Decagon, cobalt; plate, bread & butter; 6¼″....................5.00
Decagon, cobalt; plate, dinner; 9½″...........................20.00
Decagon, cobalt; plate, service; 10″...........................30.00
Decagon, cobalt; salt dip, ftd, 1½″............................22.00
Decagon, cobalt; sauce boat & plate...........................65.00
Decagon, cobalt; sugar bowl, ftd..............................22.00
Decagon, cobalt; tray, pickle; 2-hdl, flat, 8″..................17.00
Decagon, cobalt; tray, service; oval, 11″......................25.00
Decagon, cobalt; tray, service; oval, 12″......................30.00
Decagon, cobalt; tray, service; oval, 15″......................35.00
Decagon, pastels; basket, 2-hdl, up-turned sides, 7″............12.00
Decagon, pastels; bonbon, 2 hdls, 6¼″.........................10.00
Decagon, pastels; bowl, belled, cranberry, 3½″.................10.00
Decagon, pastels; bowl, bonbon; 2-hdl, 6¼″....................10.00
Decagon, pastels; bowl, cereal; flat rim, 6″....................8.00
Decagon, pastels; bowl, cream soup w/liner.....................15.00
Decagon, pastels; bowl, fruit; flat rim, 5¾″....................7.00
Decagon, pastels; bowl, relish; 2-part, 9″.....................14.00
Decagon, pastels; bowl, vegetable; rnd, 11″....................20.00
Decagon, pastels; bowl, vegetable; rnd, 9″.....................18.00
Decagon, pastels; bowl, 5½″..................................12.50
Decagon, pastels; candlestick, #637, 3½″......................12.00
Decagon, pastels; compote, 5¾″..............................15.00
Decagon, pastels; creamer, scalloped edge......................10.00
Decagon, pastels; creamer, tall, lg ft..........................12.00
Decagon, pastels; cup..6.00
Decagon, pastels; mayonnaise w/liner & ladle...................24.00
Decagon, pastels; plate, bread & butter; 6¼″...................3.00
Decagon, pastels; plate, dinner; 9½″..........................15.00
Decagon, pastels; plate, salad; 8½″............................6.00
Decagon, pastels; plate, service; 10″..........................20.00
Decagon, pastels; plate, 2-hdl, 7″.............................6.00
Decagon, pastels; sauce boat, w/liner..........................50.00
Decagon, pastels; saucer.......................................2.00
Decagon, pastels; sugar bowl, scalloped edge...................10.00
Decagon, pastels; tray, pickle; 9″............................10.00
Decagon, pastels; tray, service; oval, 11″.....................18.00
Decagon, pastels; tray, service; oval, 12″.....................20.00
Decagon, pastels; tray, service; oval, 15″.....................24.00
Decagon, willow blue; goblet, water; #3077....................18.00
Decagon, willow blue; plate, dinner; 10″.......................30.00
Decagon, willow blue; sherbet, low, #3077.....................14.00
Diane, crystal; basket, 2-hdl, ftd, 6″.........................18.00
Diane, crystal; bowl, baker; 10″..............................40.00
Diane, crystal; bowl, berry; 5″...............................16.00
Diane, crystal; bowl, cereal; 6″..............................18.00
Diane, crystal; bowl, 4-ftd, 11″..............................40.00
Diane, crystal; butter, rnd...................................100.00
Diane, crystal; candelabrum, 2-light, keyhole...................22.50
Diane, crystal; candlestick, 5″...............................17.50
Diane, crystal; cigarette urn.................................45.00
Diane, crystal; claret, #3122, 4½-oz..........................30.00
Diane, crystal; compote, #3400/13, 6″.........................25.00
Diane, crystal; creamer......................................15.00
Diane, crystal; creamer & sugar, ftd..........................30.00
Diane, crystal; cup..15.00
Diane, crystal; goblet, #3122, 9-oz...........................20.00
Diane, crystal; hurricane lamp, candlestick base...............90.00
Diane, crystal; pitcher, ball.................................125.00
Diane, crystal; plate, #3400, 8½″.............................15.00
Diane, crystal; plate, dinner; 10½″...........................55.00
Diane, crystal; shakers, flat, pr..............................35.00
Diane, crystal; sherbet, #1066, tall, 7-oz.....................15.00
Diane, crystal; tray, relish; 5-part, #3400/67..................40.00
Diane, crystal; tumbler, ftd, #3135, 5″........................18.00
Diane, crystal; tumbler, iced tea; #3122......................20.00
Diane, crystal; tumbler, sham bottom, 10-oz...................22.00
Diane, crystal; tumbler, tea; #3106, ftd, 12-oz................12.00
Diane, crystal; vase, bud; 10″................................25.00
Diane, crystal; vase, flower; 13″.............................50.00
Draped Lady, amber, 13″.....................................250.00
Draped Lady, amber, 8½″.....................................175.00
Draped Lady, blue, 8½″......................................250.00
Draped Lady, crystal, 13″....................................150.00
Draped Lady, crystal, 8½″.....................................45.00
Draped Lady, crystal frosted, 13″............................150.00
Draped Lady, custard #1, 13″.................................975.00
Draped Lady, green, 8½″.....................................100.00
Draped Lady, green frosted, 8½″..............................115.00
Draped Lady, lt emerald, 13″.................................225.00
Draped Lady, lt emerald frosted, 13″..........................250.00
Draped Lady, lt pink, 8½″....................................100.00
Draped Lady, lt pink 13″.....................................225.00
Draped Lady, mocha, 8½″.....................................175.00
Draped Lady, pink frosted, 13″...............................250.00
Elaine, crystal; bowl, bonbon; ftd, tab hdl, 7″.................22.00

Elaine, crystal; bowl, bonbon; 2-hdl, 5¼″ 16.00
Elaine, crystal; bowl, celery & relish; 5-part, 12″ 35.00
Elaine, crystal; candlestick, 3-light, 6″ 25.00
Elaine, crystal; creamer, #3500-15 .... 12.50
Elaine, crystal; ice pail, #1402-52 .... 65.00
Elaine, crystal; pitcher, ball 100.00
Elaine, crystal; plate, dinner; 10½″ 45.00
Elaine, crystal; plate, salad; 8″ 12.50
Elaine, crystal; sherbet, stemmed, tall, #3035 .... 18.00
Elaine, crystal; stem, water; #3121, 10-oz 20.00
Elaine, crystal; tumbler, water; ftd, #3121, 10-oz 18.00
Elaine, crystal; vase, ftd, 8″ 25.00
Everglades, lt blue; bowl, belled, #8, 12″ 55.00
Farber Ware, amber; candy dish, hdls 15.00
Farber Ware, amber; compote, 5½″ 25.00
Farber Ware, amber; relish, 3-part, #3500/112 .... 15.00
Farber Ware, amethyst; cocktail set, shaker & 6 goblets 75.00
Farber Ware, amethyst; creamer & sugar, w/lid, 4″ 25.00
Farber Ware, amethyst; relish bowl, w/lid 25.00
Geisha, crystal, 1-bun, wood base 250.00
Gloria, colors; bowl, cereal; sq, 6″ 16.00
Gloria, colors; butter dish, 2-hdl 150.00
Gloria, colors; pitcher, w/lid, 64-oz 140.00
Gloria, colors; plate, dinner; sq 35.00
Gloria, colors; syrup, tall, ftd 75.00
Gloria, crystal; basket, 2-hdl, sides up, 6″ 14.00
Gloria, crystal; bowl, 4-ftd, oval, 12″ 45.00
Gloria, crystal; candy box, 4-ftd, tab hdl 55.00
Gloria, crystal; compote, tall, 7″ 40.00
Gloria, crystal; goblet, #3115, 9-oz 20.00
Gloria, crystal; plate, bread & butter; 6″ 6.00
Gloria, crystal; saucer, rnd 3.00
Gyro Optic, amber; tumbler, 13-oz 10.00
Gyro Optic, lt emerald; tumbler, 13-oz 10.00
Laurel Wreath, crystal; plate, #556, 8″ 7.50
Laurel Wreath, crystal; sherbet, high, #3109, 6-oz 10.00
Laurel Wreath, crystal; sherbet, low, #3109, 6-oz 8.00
Laurel Wreath, crystal; tumbler, ftd, #3109, 12-oz 10.00
Laurel Wreath, crystal; tumbler, ftd, #3109, 9-oz 9.00
Lorna, crystal; plate, 2 hdls, w/gold, #972, 11″ 25.00
Lorna, crystal; sugar bowl, #3400-68 .... 10.00
Mandolin Lady, crystal 200.00
Martha, crystal; bowl, high ftd, 9½″ 20.00
Martha Washington, crystal; sherbet 6.00
Martha Washington, crystal; sugar bowl, ftd 8.00
Martha Washington, green; bowl, flared, 9″ 20.00
Minerva, crystal; ash tray, #3500-126, 4″ 16.00
Minerva, crystal; sandwich server, hdl, w/gold, #3400-10 .... 35.00
Nautilus, amethyst; pitcher, jug; 84-oz, 9½″ 60.00
Nude stem, claret, carmen 125.00
Nude stem, cocktail, amethyst 80.00
Nude stem, cocktail, crystal w/ebony ft & stem 70.00
Nude stem cocktail, mandarin gold 80.00
Nude stem, cocktail, mocha 115.00
Nude stem, cocktail, pistachio 115.00
Nude stem, cocktail, royal blue 125.00
Nude stem, ivy bowl, royal blue w/crystal stem 175.00
Portia, crystal; bowl, pickle or relish; 7″ 18.00
Portia, crystal; bowl, 2-hdl, 11″ 35.00
Portia, crystal; candlestick, 5″ 17.50
Portia, crystal; candy box, rnd 45.00
Portia, crystal; champagne, #3122, 6-oz 18.00
Portia, crystal; cheese & cracker, #3400 .... 40.00
Portia, crystal; compote, 5½″ 27.50
Portia, crystal; decanter, w/stopper, #1321 .... 150.00
Portia, crystal; hurricane lamp, candlestick base 95.00
Portia, crystal; plate, dinner; 10½″ 45.00
Portia, crystal; tray, relish; 3-part, #3500-69, 6½″ 22.00
Portia, crystal; tumbler, water; #3126, 10-oz 18.00
Portia, crystal; vase, ftd, 8″ 30.00
Portia, crystal; wine, #3124, 3-oz 20.00
Portia, pink; bowl, rare, #3400-1, 13″ 55.00
Ramshead, bowl, amethyst, #3500/109, 4-toed, 11″ 240.00
Ramshead, bowl, bluerina, ped ft 750.00
Ramshead, bowl, helitrope w/orig gold 250.00
Rose Lady, amber 200.00
Rose Lady, crystal 150.00
Rose Lady, crystal frosted, #1 .... 175.00
Rose Lady, green frosted 225.00
Rose Lady, mocha frosted #1 .... 250.00
Rose Lady, pink 175.00
Rose Point, crystal; ash tray, sq, 2½″ 35.00
Rose Point, crystal; basket, #3500/51, 5″ 150.00
Rose Point, crystal; basket, #3500/55, 2-hdl, ftd, 6″ 25.00
Rose Point, crystal; bowl, #3400, flared, 4-ftd, 12″ 50.00
Rose Point, crystal; bowl, bonbon; #3900, hdld, ftd, 7″ 27.50
Rose Point, crystal; bowl, relish; #3400, 2-part, 6″ 25.00
Rose Point, crystal; bowl, relish; #3900, 3-part, 9″ 40.00
Rose Point, crystal; bowl, serving; 2 hdls, #3900-34, 11″ 60.00
Rose Point, crystal; bowl, tab hdl, #3900, 11″ 55.00
Rose Point, crystal; butter dish, 5″ 150.00
Rose Point, crystal; candlestick, raised drip, 5″ 35.00
Rose Point, crystal; candlestick, 3-tiered light, 6″ 40.00
Rose Point, crystal; candlestick, 5″ 25.00
Rose Point, crystal; candy box, 3-part, 8″ 65.00
Rose Point, crystal; cigarette box 125.00
Rose Point, crystal; claret, #3500, 4½-oz 55.00
Rose Point, crystal; cocktail, #3121, 3-oz 30.00
Rose Point, crystal; cocktail icer, 2-pc 55.00
Rose Point, crystal; cocktail shaker, metal top, 48-oz 125.00
Rose Point, crystal; compote, #1066, blown, 5⅜″ 50.00
Rose Point, crystal; compote, 5″ 30.00
Rose Point, crystal; corn dish, #477 .... 45.00
Rose Point, crystal; creamer, #3500 .... 15.00
Rose Point, crystal; cup 25.00
Rose Point, crystal; goblet, cocktail; #3500 .... 32.00
Rose Point, crystal; goblet, water; w/gold 45.00
Rose Point, crystal; goblet, wine; #3500 .... 55.00
Rose Point, crystal; goblet, wine; w/gold 75.00
Rose Point, crystal; hurricane lamp, candlestick base 175.00
Rose Point, crystal; ice bucket w/chrome hdl 115.00
Rose Point, crystal; juice, low-ftd, #3121, 5-oz 27.50
Rose Point, crystal; pitcher, Daulton, #3400/152 .... 265.00
Rose Point, crystal; pitcher, 20-oz 175.00
Rose Point, crystal; pitcher, 76-oz 150.00
Rose Point, crystal; plate, bread & butter; 6½″ 12.00
Rose Point, crystal; plate, dinner; 10½″ 85.00
Rose Point, crystal; plate, torte; 4-ftd, 13″ 50.00
Rose Point, crystal; plate, 2 hdls, ftd, #3500-161, 8″ 25.00
Rose Point, crystal; plate, 2-hdl, 6″ 20.00
Rose Point, crystal; platter, 2-hdl, rectangular, 12½″ 75.00
Rose Point, crystal; relish; 2 hdls/4-part, #3500-62 .... 65.00
Rose Point, crystal; relish; 3 hdls/3-part, #3900-125 .... 40.00
Rose Point, crystal; saucer 10.00
Rose Point, crystal; shakers, w/chrome tops, ftd, pr 50.00
Rose Point, crystal; sherbet, #3121, tall, 6-oz 20.00
Rose Point, crystal; sherbet, #3500, low ftd, 7-oz 18.00
Rose Point, crystal; stem, wine; #3121, 3½-oz 50.00

Rose Point, crystal; sugar bowl....15.00
Rose Point, crystal; tumbler, #3900, 13-oz....40.00
Rose Point, crystal; tumbler, tea; #3121, 12-oz....25.00
Rose Point, crystal; vase, bud; 10″....40.00
Rose Point, crystal; vase, cornucopia; 10″....110.00
Rose Point, crystal; vase, flower; high ftd, 6″....50.00
Roselyn, crystal; tray, relish; 3-part, #3500-69....25.00
Scotch & Thistle, crystal; liquor dispenser, #1380....50.00
Spiral Optic, amber; tumbler, 12-oz, 5½″....10.00
Spiral Optic, carmen; 12-oz, 5½″....10.00
Swan Punch bowl, #1221, 16″....665.00
Tally Ho, carmen; goblet, #2, 14-oz....32.50
Tally Ho, carmen; tray, relish; #90, 2-part, 6″....18.00
Tally Ho, carmen; tumbler, flat, 12-oz....22.00
Tally Ho, carmen; tumbler, flat, 5-oz....16.00
Vase, cut/etched, bluerina, 10″....150.00
Wildflower, crystal; bowl, bonbon; 2-hdl, 5¼″....15.00
Wildflower, crystal; bowl, relish; 7″....22.50
Wildflower, crystal; bowl, 2-hdl, 11″....35.00
Wildflower, crystal; candlestick, 3-light, pr....55.00
Wildflower, crystal; candy box, 3-part, 3-hdl, 8″....52.50
Wildflower, crystal; cocktail icer, 2-pc....45.00
Wildflower, crystal; creamer....12.50
Wildflower, crystal; cruet, w/rpl stopper, #3900-100, 6-oz....75.00
Wildflower, crystal; cup....16.50
Wildflower, crystal; hurricane lamp, keyhole base & prisms....110.00
Wildflower, crystal; parfait, low, #3121, 5-oz....30.00
Wildflower, crystal; pitcher, ball....125.00
Wildflower, crystal; plate, bread & butter; 6½″....9.00
Wildflower, crystal; plate, salad; 8″....12.00
Wildflower, crystal; saucer....8.00
Wildflower, crystal; shakers, pr....30.00
Wildflower, crystal; sugar bowl....12.50
Wildflower, crystal; tumbler, water; #3121, 10-oz....18.00
Wildflower, crystal; vase, bud; 10″....30.00
Wildflower, crystal; vase, flower; ftd, 6″....27.50
Wildflower, crystal; wine, #3121 3½-oz....30.00

Cambridge Pottery

The Cambridge Art Pottery operated in Cambridge, Ohio, from 1900 until 1909. During that time several lines of artware were developed under the direction of C.B. Upjohn, an established ceramic artist of the period.

Their standard brown-glazed line was Terrhea, examples of which are often found bearing the signature of the artist responsible for the underglaze decoration. Oakwood was a second brown-glazed line, without the slip painting. Other lines were Acorn, introduced in 1904; and Otoe, a matt green ware (introduced in 1907) that utilized already existing shapes from earlier lines. However, their most successful product was a line of cookware called Gurnsey, made from a red-brown clay with a white-glazed interior. Sales proved to be so profitable that by 1908 all artware was discontinued in favor of its exclusive production. By the following year, the firm elected to change the name of their pottery to The Gurnsey Earthenware Company. Marks varied, but all incorporate a device comprised of the letters 'CAP,' with the co-joined 'AP' most often contained within a larger scale 'C.'

When no condition is indicated, the items listed below are assumed to be in mint condition.

Ewer, Terrhea, floral, 4x5″....195.00
Vase, Terrhea, clover, sgn/mk, 6″....125.00
Vase, Terrhea, wild rose on dk brn, disk ft, 5¾″....95.00

Cameo

The technique of glass carving was perfected 2,000 years ago in ancient Rome and Greece. The most famous ancient example of cameo glass is the Portland Vase, made in Rome around 100 A.D. After glass blowing was developed, glassmakers devised a method of casing several layers of colored glass together, often with a light color over a darker base, to enhance the design. Skilled carvers meticulously worked the fragile glass to produce incredibly detailed classic scenes. In the 18th and 19th centuries, Oriental and Near Eastern artisans used the technique more extensively. European glassmakers revived the art during the last quarter of the 19th century. In France, Galle and Daum produced some of the finest examples of modern times, using as many as five layers of glass to develop their designs, usually scenics or subjects from nature. Hand carving was supplemented by the use of copper engraving wheel, and acid was used to cut away the layers more quickly.

In England, Thomas Webb and Sons used modern machinery and technology to eliminate many of the problems that plagued early glass carvers. One of Webb's best known carvers, George Woodall, is credited with producing over four hundred pieces. Woodall was trained in the art by John Northwood, famous for reproducing the Portland Vase in 1876.

Cameo glass became very popular during the late 1800s, resulting in a market that demanded more than could be produced, due to the tedious procedures involved. In an effort to produce greater volume, less elaborate pieces with simple floral or geometric designs were made, often entirely acid etched with little or no hand carving. While very little cameo glass was made in this country, a few pieces were produced by James Gillender, Tiffany, and the Libbey Glass Company. Though some continued to be made on a limited scale into the 1900s, for the most part, inferior products caused a marked reduction in its manufacture by the turn of the century.

When no condition is indicated, the items listed below are assumed to be in mint condition. See also specific manufacturers.

Wall shelf, demilune panel with river landscape within fruitwood frame, signed in cameo Jacques Gruber, ca 1900, 21½″, $1,200.00.

Bowl, elongated leaves, wht on red, SP lid & bail, 5″ dia......550.00
Perfume, bamboo/leaves allover, stick neck, English, 5″.......975.00
Perfume, florals/butterfly, wht on dk bl, English, rnd, 7″.....1,950.00
Perfume, fuchsia, wht on red, silver ball cap, 4″.............450.00
Perfume, lay-down; fern/butterfly, wht/citron, English, 9½″....1,250.00
Perfume, wht floral on lt bl satin, silver cap, 2¾″............550.00
Rose bowl, leaves & berries, 3-color, 2x2½″...............1,000.00
Rose bowl, morning glory, bl/wht, 3-ft, att: Webb, 4″, EX....1,250.00
Vase, berries/foliage, 4-color, English, no mk, 7x4½″........2,450.00
Vase, birds on branches, ped ft, hdls, Deco, Ver-Art, 12½″....300.00
Vase, bleeding hearts, lav on gray, gilded, BS&Co, 3″.........385.00
Vase, floral, violet on martele, gilded, BS&Co, 9″............880.00
Vase, passion flower/butterfly, peachblow, English, 6″........1,750.00
Vase, poppies/butterfly, frost/rose/gilt/red, Pantin, 10½″........800.00
Vase, raspberries/elaborate border, 4-color, English, 7″......2,450.00
Vase, wildflowers, egg & dart border, bun base, BS&Co, 8″....550.00
Vase, yel blooms/leaves, Art Nouveau, Honesdale, 12″, EX.....350.00

Camphor Glass

The term 'camphor glass' refers to a type of acid-finished lusterless glassware, so named for its resemblance to gum camphor.

When no condition is indicated, the items listed below are assumed to be in mint condition.

Basket, pink, flaring, braided hdl, 3½″ W....................16.00
Decanter, HP can-can girl, 'Gin,' Dia Quilt sides, stopper.......22.00
Powder jar, elephant atop...............................40.00
Shaving mug...25.00
Toothpick holder, Baby Mine, Sandwich......................85.00
Vase, wht w/bl floral enameling, 10½″.......................40.00

Canary Lustre

Canary lustre was produced from the late 1700s until about the mid-19th century in the Staffordshire district of England. The body of the ware was of yellow clay, with a yellow overglaze; and, more often than not, copper or silver lustre trim was added. Decorations were usually black-printed transfers, though occasionally hand painted polychrome designs were also used.

When no condition is indicated, the items listed below are assumed to be in mint condition.

Bowl, red flowers, rust line on scalloped rim, 3¼x5¼″.........145.00
Cup & saucer, handleless; gaudy florals in 3 colors, VG.......250.00
Mug, child's; Harp for Elisabeth, 2¼″.....................225.00
Mug, child's; Present for Charles, rpr, 1⅞″..................275.00
Pitcher, Lafayette Crowned in Glory, w/copper lustre, 4″.......450.00
Plate, floral rim, emb/mc, 7½″, EX.........................275.00
Saucer, blk transfer: lady at keyboard, 2 children, 5¼″.........70.00
Waste bowl, floral rim, emb/mc, hairline, 2⅞x5⅜″............220.00

Candle Holders

The earliest type of candlestick, called a pricket, was constructed with a sharp point on which the candle was impaled. The socket type, first used in the 16th century, consisted of the socket and a short stem, with a wide drip pan and base. These were made from sheets of silver or other metal; not until late in the 17th century were candlesticks made by casting. By the 1700s, styles began to vary from the traditional fluted column or baluster form, and became more elaborate. A Rococo style with scrolls, shellwork, and naturalistic leaves and flowers came into vogue that afforded the individual silversmith the opportunity to exhibit his skill and artistry. The last half of the 18th century brought a return to classic fluted columns with neoclassic motifs. Because they were made of thin sheet silver, weighted bases were used to add stability.

The Rococo styles of the Regency period were heavily encrusted with applied figures and flowers. Candelabra with six to nine branches became popular. By the Victorian era, when lamps came into general use, there was less innovation and more adaptation of the earlier styles.

When no condition is indicated, the items listed below are assumed to be in excellent condition.

Cast metal with multicolored protruding 'jewels' and crystal prisms, Victorian era, 10½″, $110.00 for the pair.

Brass, beehive/diamond quilt, push-up, Victorian, 10″, pr......170.00
Brass, beehive/diamond quilt/England, 8¾″, pr.................75.00
Brass, bulbous paneled stem & screw-on rnd base, 4½″........25.00
Brass, hex base/mid drip, tooled/cast rim, early, 11″, pr......1,250.00
Brass, Neo-Classic, 9″.....................................40.00
Brass, Queen Anne, scalloped base, rpr, 6¾″................300.00
Brass, Queen Anne, scalloped base, 8¾″, pr, EX.............980.00
Brass, Queen Anne, scalloped base & lip, 7⅝″...............315.00
Brass, Queen of Diamonds, w/push-up, Victorian, 11″, pr......270.00
Brass, removable bobeche, 8⅛″, pr.........................170.00
Brass, saucer base & push-up, late 1700s, 4½″..............100.00
Brass, spring loaded, emb: Cornelius & Baker, 13″, EX.......100.00
Brass, sq base, VA Metal Crafters, 7″.......................45.00
Brass, twist stem, 11″, pr.................................30.00
Brass, Victorian, miniature, 4″, pr.........................60.00
Brass, w/push-up, mk Diamond Princess, Victorian, 10¾″, pr...200.00
Brass, wide central drip pan, screw joint, early, 20″, pr........850.00
Brass, wide spun domed base, sm mid drip pan, early, 10″.....500.00
Brass, 3 paw ft, French, late 19th C, 10¾″, pr..............200.00
Brass w/SP, push-up, Victorian, worn, 7″, pr................130.00
Bronze, female holds 2 scrolling foliate stems, 22½″, pr.....1,540.00
Candelabra, bronze/gold, French Empire, 18½″, pr...........550.00
Candelabra, 6-arm, gilt/bronze, Chas X, paw ft, 29″, pr......1,210.00
Candelabra, 6-arm, scroll tripod ft, wrought iron, 8″, pr.......350.00
Chamber stick, brass, early 1800s, polished, 3″..............100.00
Chamber stick, brass, rectangle pan/push-up, 5″, pr, EX.......170.00
Chamber stick, brass, w/push-up, minor dents, 4¼″............75.00

Chamber stick, tin, deep saucer base, push-up, 4⅞x7" .50.00
Chamber stick, tin, oblong base, push-up & snuffer, 7x9" .75.00
Chamber stick, tin, push-up telescopes, Rockwell's pat, 5" .125.00
Chamber stick, tin w/brass push-up, ?-shape hdl, 4¼" .65.00
Chandelier, 6-light, Louis XVI style, flame std, 19" dia .2,200.00
Crucifix, cobalt glass, 9¾", pr, EX .325.00
Crucifix, emerald gr glass, 9¾" .425.00
Crucifix, milk glass, att NE, 11⅜", pr .175.00
Flint, loop base & petal socket, mismatched size, 7", pr .150.00
Flint, sq stepped base, columnar stem, petal font, 9", pr .145.00
Gilt bronze, Empire style, acanthus/3 dolphin ft, 13", pr .605.00
Hog scraper, iron, push-up, hanging tab, 6" .95.00
Hog scraper, iron, sgn push-up, lip hanger, 7¼" .105.00
Hog scraper, tin w/push-up, 4", pr .120.00
Pewter, w/bobeche, minor dents, 9¾", pr .140.00
Sconce, brass, dbl scroll arms, 1800s, 13¾", pr .260.00
Sconce, 3-arm, Louis XV style, gilt/bronze, rstr, 31", pr .1,760.00
Sticking Tommy, polished steel, 12" L .30.00
Tin, deep saucer base, push-up, 4x7" .30.00
Wood, poplar w/dk patina, primitive, 6" .35.00

Candlewick

Candlewick crystal was made by the Imperial Glass Corporation, a division of Lenox Inc., Bellaire, Ohio. It was introduced in 1936, and though never marked except for paper labels, is easily recognized by the beaded crystal rims, stems, and handles inspired by the tufted needlework called candlewicking, practiced by our pioneer women.

During its production, more than 741 items were designed and produced. In September 1982, when Imperial closed its doors, thirty-four pieces were still being made.

Identification numbers and mold numbers used by the company help collectors recognize the various styles and shapes. Most of the pieces are from the #400 series, though other series numbers were also used. Stemware was made in eight styles--five from the #400 series made from 1941 to 1962, one from #3400 series made in 1937, another from #3800 series made in 1941, and the eighth style from the #4000 series made in 1947.

In the listing that follows, some #400 items lack the mold number because that information was not found in the company files.

A few pieces have been made in color, or with a gold wash, and at least two lines, Valley Lily and Floral, utilized Candlewick with floral patterns cut into the crystal. These are scarce today. Other rare items include gifts such as the desk calendar, made by the company for its employees and customers; the dresser set comprised of a mirror, clock, puff jar, and cologne; and the chip and dip set.

When no condition is indicated, the items listed below are assumed to be in mint condition.

Ash tray, heart, 4½" .4.00
Ash tray, ind .5.00
Ash tray, sq, 4½" .5.50
Ash tray set, nesting, 3-pc, sq .15.00
Bell, 5" .30.00
Bowl, basket; 1-hdl, 11" .55.00
Bowl, basket; 1-hdl, 6½" .25.00
Bowl, belled, 10½" .22.50
Bowl, butter/jam; 3-part, 10½" .30.00
Bowl, celery boat; oval, 11" .20.00
Bowl, centerpiece; mushroom shape, 13" .30.00
Bowl, cottage cheese; 6" .15.00
Bowl, crimped, ftd, 9" .20.00
Bowl, deep, 2-hdl, 10" .22.00
Bowl, float; incurvate rim, ftd, 11" .18.00
Bowl, fruit; low ftd, 9" .20.00
Bowl, fruit; 2-hdl, 4¾" .11.50
Bowl, fruit; 5" .8.50
Bowl, hdld, 12" .20.00
Bowl, heart shape, hdld, 9" .25.00
Bowl, jelly; 5½", w/lid .20.00
Bowl, mint; 6" .10.00
Bowl, nappy; 3-ftd, 4½" .15.00
Bowl, oval, 14" .30.00
Bowl, oval w/partition, 11" .18.00
Bowl, pickle/celery; 7½" .15.00
Bowl, punch base; belled, 10" .15.00
Bowl, relish; divided, sq, 7" .17.00
Bowl, relish; divided, 2-hdl, 8½" .15.00
Bowl, relish; 3-part, 10" .19.00
Bowl, rnd, divided, 6" .10.00
Bowl, rnd, 2-hdl, 4¾" .12.00
Bowl, rnd, 2-hdl, 7" .15.00
Bowl, rnd, 6" .12.00
Bowl, rnd, 8" .12.00
Bowl, sauce; 5½" .12.00
Bowl, sq, crimped edge, 4-ftd, 9" .22.00
Bowl, 2-hdl, 6½" .14.00
Bowl, 3-ftd, 8½" .15.00
Butter dish, bead top, ¼-lb .16.00
Candle holder, bowled-up base, hdld, 5" .15.00
Candle holder, flat .13.00
Candle holder, rolled edge .12.00
Candle holder, w/finger hold, 3½" .40.00
Candle holder, 3½" .12.00
Candle holder, 6½" .20.00
Candy box, flared, 7" .22.00
Cigarette box .14.00
Coaster, 4" .5.00
Cocktail, seafood; bead-ftd .11.00
Cocktail set, 2-pc: cocktail & plate w/indent .20.00
Compote, beaded stem, flared, 5½" .15.00
Compote, bulbous bead stem, 5" .14.00
Compote, oval, ftd .25.00
Creamer, ind bridge .6.00
Creamer & sugar, w/6" tray .22.00

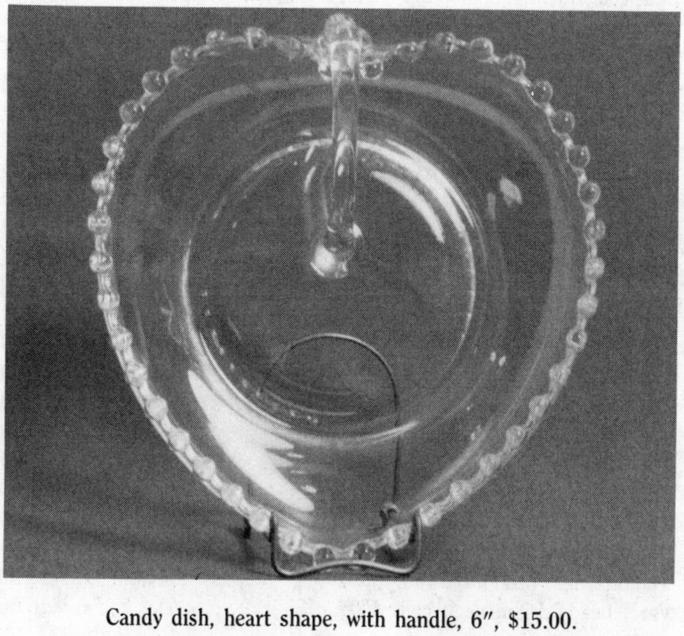

Candy dish, heart shape, with handle, 6", $15.00.

Cup, coffee....7.50
Cup, tea....7.00
Decanter, w/stopper....40.00
Egg cup....13.50
Hurricane lamp, 2-pc, candle base....22.50
Icer, 2-pc, for seafood or fruit cocktail....22.50
Jam set, 5-pc: oval tray w/2 marmalade jars w/ladles....75.00
Knife, butter....20.00
Marmalade set, 3-pc: bead-ftd jar, lid, spoon....18.00
Marmalade set, 4-pc: liner saucer, jar, lid, spoon....32.00
Mayonnaise set, 2-pc: scoop side bowl & spoon....20.00
Mayonnaise set, 4-pc: plate, bowl, 2 ladles....32.50
Mirror, rnd, standing, 4″....50.00
Mustard jar w/spoon....21.50
Oil, bulbous bottom, hdl, 4-oz....22.50
Oil, bulbous bottom, 6-oz....28.00
Oyster cocktail, #3400, 4-oz....15.00
Pitcher, bead hdl, w/lip, 40-oz....100.00
Pitcher, juice/cocktail; 40-oz....85.00
Pitcher, low ftd, 16-oz....75.00
Pitcher, 20-oz....85.00
Plate, birthday cake; w/holes for candles....85.00
Plate, bread & butter; 6″....6.50
Plate, crescent salad; 8¼″....12.00
Plate, crimped, 2-hdl, 10″....17.00
Plate, oval, w/indent....10.00
Plate, oval, 8″....13.00
Plate, salad; 7″....8.00
Plate, service; 14″....20.00
Plate, serving; cupped edge, 13″....24.00
Plate, sides up-turned, 2-hdl, 9″....15.00
Plate, torte; cupped edge, 12½″....22.50
Plate, torte; hdl, 14″....25.00
Plate, triangular, 7½″....9.00
Plate, 2-hdl, 10″....17.00
Plate, 2-hdl, 5½″....6.00
Punch set, family; 8 demi cups, ladle, lid....175.00
Rose bowl, crimped edge, ftd, 7¼″....20.00
Salt spoon, ribbed bowl....3.00
Saucer, tea....3.00
Shakers, bulbous w/bead stem, chrome top, pr....7.50
Shakers, plastic top, pr....8.00
Snack jar, ftd....32.50
Stem, cocktail; #3800....17.50
Stem, cordial; bead-ftd, #400, 1-oz....17.50
Stem, goblet, #3800....17.50
Stem, goblet, #400, 11-oz....12.00
Stem, juice tumbler; bead-ftd, #400, 5-oz....15.00
Stem, parfait; #3400, 6-oz....17.00
Stem, water; #3800, 9-oz....17.50
Stem, wine; #3400, 4-oz....17.00
Stem, wine; #3800....18.00
Sugar bowl, bead hdl, 6-oz....6.00
Tidbit server, 2-tier....40.00
Tray, fruit; center hdl, 10½″....25.00
Tray, hdl, 5½″....12.50
Tray, hdl, 7½″....15.00
Tray, relish; 13″....27.50
Tray, 2-hdl, crimped....27.50
Tumbler, #3800, 9-oz....14.00
Tumbler, bead-ftd, #400, 10-oz....12.00
Tumbler, plain-ftd, #3400, 10-oz....12.00
Tumbler, tea; bead-ftd, #400, 14-oz....16.00
Vase, bead-ftd, sm neck ball, 4″....16.00
Vase, bead-ftd, straight side, 10″....25.00
Vase, fan, 6½″....17.00
Vase, flat, crimped edge, 6″....15.00
Vase, flat, crimped edge, 8″....22.00
Vase, fluted rim, bead hdl, 8″....25.00

Candy Containers

Figural glass candy containers have been made in hundreds of designs from as early as 1876, when Independence Hall and the Liberty Bell inspired patriotic candy containers for our country's centennial year celebration. From then until as late as 1960, hundreds of designs have been made--locomotives, comic characters, suitcases, telephones, submarines, lanterns, and automobiles are only a sampling. When full they held tiny colored candies; empty they became a toy or a bank. While most were made in clear glass, a few from around 1910 were produced in milk glass, sometimes trimmed with gilt. Many early containers were painted, and during the late twenties, some were pressed in green, amber, blue, and pink. Often tin and paper parts were added.

Among the better known manufacturers were West Bros., Cambridge, L.E. Smith, Victory, and Jeanette Glass. The last containers to be made were produced by T.H. Stough. Value is enhanced by excellent paint, original parts and closures.

There are a number of reproductions on the market--the Camera, Rabbit Pushing Wheelbarrow, and Jackie Coogan; soon to be joined by Baby Sweeper, Piano, Safe, Bureau, Show Case, Lawn Swing, and the Express Wagon. These will be produced by Summit Art Glass, and will be advertised as repros.

Papier mache containers were also made in figural form; most are marked 'Made in Germany.' Many of this type were made for special holidays--bunnies and eggs for Easter, turkeys for Thanksgiving, and black cats and jack-o'-lanterns for Halloween.

The numbers in our listings refer to a standard reference series, *An Album of Candy Containers*, Vols 1 and 2, by Jennie Long, one of our advisors for this section.

When no condition is indicated, the items listed below are assumed to be in mint condition. All are assumed with closure.

Airplane, Army Bomber, cardboard closure, #328....20.00
Airplane, Liberty Motor Bi-Plane, #319....475.00
Airplane, Musical Toy Airplanes, many variations, complete....22.00
Airplane, P-38, cardboard closure, #326....125.00
Airplane, P-51, cardboard closure, #327....50.00
Airplane, Passenger Plane, metal nose cone, #323....150.00
Airplane, Spirit of Goodwill, metal nose cone, #320....85.00
Airplane, Spirit of St Louis Mono-Plane, #321....275.00
Amos n' Andy....375.00
Automobile, Air Flow, Victory Glass Co, tin wheels, #369....200.00
Automobile, Auto-Rear Trunk, pnt, w/closure, #367....120.00
Automobile, Coupe, long hood, glass wheels, #359, 5½″ L....75.00
Automobile, Coupe, long hood, tin wheels, #357, 5½″ L....100.00
Automobile, Coupe, Victory Glass, tin wheels, #368, 4½″ L....450.00
Automobile, Electric Coupe, bottom closure, #355....85.00
Automobile, Electric Coupe, top closure, #356....60.00
Automobile, Four Door Sedan, glass wheels, #371....35.00
Automobile, Four Door Sedan, original tin wheels, #370....150.00
Automobile, Hearse type, w/tassels #1, #360, w/closure....120.00
Automobile, Limousine, glass wheels, pnt, w/closure, #349....100.00
Automobile, Limousine, West Bro, original tin wheels, #350....175.00
Automobile, Limousine, West Bro, replaced tin wheels, #350....100.00
Automobile, Miniature Streamline, cardboard closure, #377....25.00
Automobile, Ribbed Top Sedan, complete w/closure, #375....30.00
Automobile, Taxi, 12 vents, pnt, w/closure, #366....75.00

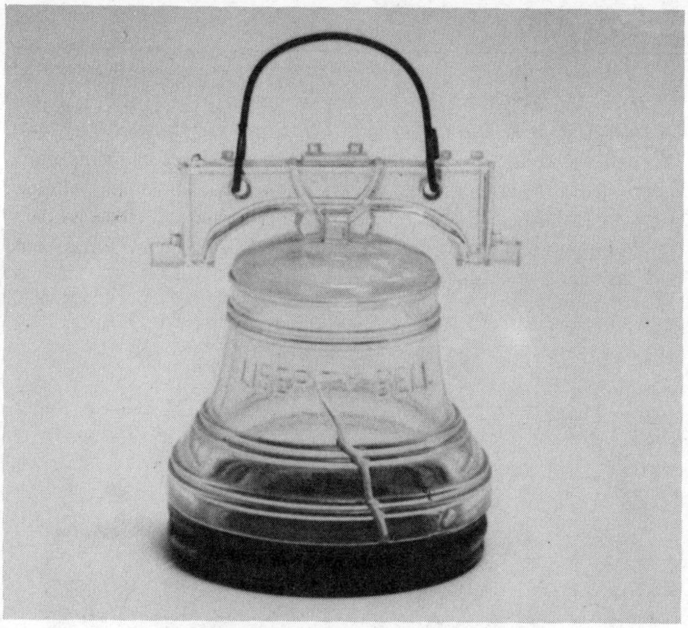

Liberty Bell, 3½", $40.00.

Automobile, Tiny Sedan, pnt, no closure, #374 .... 25.00
Baby Chick, pnt, w/closure, #6 .... 90.00
Baby Jumbo Pencil 45.00
Baby Sucking Bottle, nude, Victory Glass, #94 .... 50.00
Barney Google, by Smith, #79 .... 325.00
Barney Google, on ped, #78 .... 150.00
Battleship, Miniature; Victory Glass Co, #337 .... 20.00
Battleship on Waves, Cambridge, #335 .... 140.00
Bear on Circus Tub 250.00
Bell, gr glass, w/closure, #228 .... 35.00
Bird on Mound, w/pewter whistle, w/closure, #3 .... 400.00
Black Cat for Luck, #4 .... 600.00
Black Cat Sitting, #5 .... 600.00
Bulldog, Stough, cardboard closure, #16 .... 20.00
Bulldog, Victory Glass Co, tin closure, #15 .... 30.00
Bureau, pnt, w/closure, #125 .... 125.00
Charlie Chaplin, pnt, w/slotted closure, #83 .... 175.00
Chicken in Sagging Basket, pnt, w/closure, #8 .... 75.00
Chicken on Oblong Basket, gr, w/closure, #10 .... 75.00
Clock, Alarm; gilded, w/closure, #118 .... 125.00
Clock, pnt, slotted closure, #117 .... 150.00
Colorado Boat, reproduced tin 135.00
Cruiser, cardboard closure 15.00
Dog by Barrel, pnt, w/closure, #13 .... 175.00
Dolly's Milk Bottle 22.00
Duck-Rectangular Basket, aqua, good pnt, w/closure, #27 .... 75.00
Duckling, pnt, w/closure, #30 .... 100.00
Duckling, Ugly; pnt, w/closure, #28 .... 140.00
Electric Iron 35.00
Fire Engine, Little Boiler, pnt, w/closure, #383 .... 50.00
Fire Engine, Stoughs, 1914, #379 .... 75.00
Gun, Rapid Fire, #143 .... 250.00
Gun, Tiny Revolver 35.00
Happifats in Drum, orig pnt & slotted closure 250.00
Hat, milk glass/tin rim, orig paper closure w/slogan, #166 .... 125.00
Hat, Uncle Sam type, milk glass, red/bl pnt, closure, #168 .... 100.00
Horn, Trumpet, milk glass, w/good decals, #280 .... 125.00
Horn, 3-valve, pnt, complete w/closure/mouthpiece, #281 .... 125.00
House, no closure, #75 .... 100.00
House, pnt, w/closure, #75 .... 150.00
Independence Hall, w/closure, #74 .... 250.00
Kewpie, big Barrel, Borgfeldt & Co 85.00
Lamp, w/glass chimney, plastic shade, #569 .... 12.00
Lantern, bevelled glass globe, #175 .... 50.00
Lantern, w/chimney, #573 .... 12.00
Lawn Swing, #135 .... 500.00
Liberty Bell, amber, aqua, or green; orig screw closure 45.00
Locomotive, dbl rectangular windows, w/closure, #413 .... 75.00
Locomotive, dbl sq windows, mk C of C, w/closure, #414 .... 75.00
Locomotive, Man in Window, #408 .... 150.00
Locomotive, Mapather, w/closure, #404 .... 75.00
Locomotive, single oblong window, w/closure, #415 .... 75.00
Locomotive, Stough's #3, no closure, #426 .... 10.00
Locomotive, Stough's #5, no closure, #428 .... 10.00
Locomotive, w/closure, #426 .... 20.00
Los Angeles Dirigible 225.00
Old Oaken Bucket, #237 .... 125.00
Opera Glass, milk glass, gilt decor, w/closure, #261 .... 100.00
Owl 100.00
Phonograph, glass record, w/closure & tin horn, #288 .... 225.00
Pocket Watch, no fob, #122 .... 90.00
Pocket Watch, w/eagle fob, complete, #122 .... 150.00
Pumpkin Head Policeman, #163 .... 600.00
Pumpkin Head Policeman, #165 .... 500.00
Rabbit, Mother; #45 .... 800.00
Rabbit, Mr Rabbit, #39 .... 900.00
Rabbit Begging, pnt, w/closure, #50 .... 50.00
Rabbit Family, #43 .... 700.00
Rabbit Pushing Chick in Cart, orig pnt 250.00
Rabbit Running on Log, orig closure, EX pnt 125.00
Rabbit w/Layed-Back Ears 75.00
Rocking Horse, variation A or B, #58 & #59, ea 275.00
Rocking Horse w/Clown, bl pnt, w/closure, #57 .... 250.00
Rocking Horse w/Clown, clear, #57 .... 165.00
Rolling Pin, 7" 175.00
Santa Claus, banded coat, pnt, w/closure, #97 .... 150.00
Santa Claus, sq chimney, pnt, w/closure, #99 .... 250.00
Santa Claus Leaving Chimney, #102 .... 75.00
Santa Claus w/Dbl Cuff, #101 .... 75.00
Santa's Boot, #233, if complete 30.00
Snowman, Santa's; Sears, #105 .... 8.00
Soldier by Tent 2,500.00
Spark Plug, pnt, w/closure, #109 .... 110.00
Statue of Liberty 1,200.00
Submarine, #338 .... 350.00
Swan Boat, #60 .... 700.00
Tank, Victory Glass, orig cardboard closure 25.00
Telephone, lg, pewter top, crank bell, #294 .... 150.00
Telephone, sm, pewter top, #296 .... 65.00
Telephone, Victory glass, wood receiver, #303 .... 30.00
Toonerville Trolly, #111 .... 700.00
Top #1, lg, w/winder, #271 .... 125.00
Top #1, Spinning Top, #272, sm 75.00
Turkey, traces of pnt, w/closure, #61 .... 75.00
Wheelbarrow, complete w/closure, #273 .... 125.00
Witch, on broom pulling a cart 35.00
World Globe, glass only 65.00
Zeppelin, orig pnt, closure & contents, w/stand 250.00

Papier Mache and Composition

Chick, dressed in formal attire & top hat, 1910, 9" 110.00
Hen, by nest on cylinder, HP, wire legs, German, 4x3" 55.00
Rabbit, glass eyes, 7" L 75.00

Rabbit, playing banjo, nodder, musical....................250.00
Santa Claus, no base, early.............................185.00
Snow White & 7 Dwarfs, hanging, German, orig box, 1936....325.00
Soldier, standing w/rifle, hat askew, 12″..................110.00
Sunbonnet baby, HP, polka-dot dress, egg basket, 6½″.........90.00
Turkey, metal feet, mk Germany, 6″, NM...................55.00

Canes

Fancy canes and walking sticks were once the mark of a gentleman. Hand carved examples are collected and admired as folk art from the past, and the glass canes that never could have been practical, as unique whimseys of the glass blower's profession.

When no condition is indicated, the items listed below are assumed to be in excellent condition.

Canes

Amethyst hdl, coat of arms, gold banded hole w/cord, 39″.....325.00
Blown glass, aqua, swirled, hdl chips, 48″....................85.00
Blown glass, aqua w/wide yel-amber swirls, 39″..............165.00
Blown glass, clear, interior twist of red/wht/bl, 46⅜″...........90.00
Blown glass, clear w/red spirals, gold lines, 56″, EX..........200.00
Blown glass, pale aqua w/int amber stripe, swirled, 38″.........65.00
Blown glass, red/yel/bl spirals, 66″.........................250.00
Carved hickory, man's head in cocked cap hdl, 19th C........145.00
Carved horn, fox in tree hdl, thornewood shaft, inscribed......400.00
Carved ivory, baboons/bamboo shaft, gold end/ferrule, 35½″....400.00
Carved wood, African face hdl...........................150.00
Carved wood, dog's head hdl, glass eyes, delicate, 32″........135.00
Carved wood, snake head hdl end..........................90.00
Ebony, crouching lion, ½″ gold ferrule, horn tip, 36″.........350.00
Horn or bone, horses head hdl, ebony shaft, bone tip, 35″....325.00
Softwood, seated monkey over lizard on carved shaft, 44″.....360.00
Zebra wood, ivory hdl: woman on bear rug, Victorian, 38″.....400.00

Walking Sticks

Carved walnut, man's clenched fist atop, silver band, 37″......250.00
Carved wood, rope twist shank, ball atop, 1-pc...............125.00
Carved wood, vine twist shank, man's head hdl, primitive.......45.00
Folk art, carved snake, turtle, man's head, G detail, 36″.......255.00
Folk art, 4 free-carved balls in cages, ball atop...............95.00
Ivory hand hdl, blk laquered wood stick....................250.00
Knob unscrews, 4 bottles w/in.............................30.00

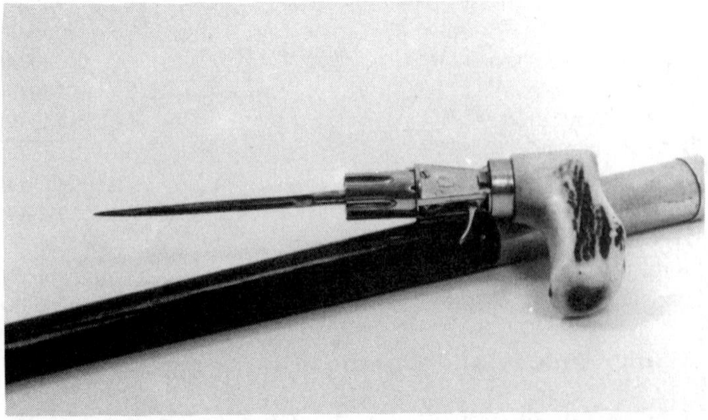

Cane, stag handle removed to show blade and six-shot pistol, French, ca 1880, $1,700.00.

Canton

From the last part of the 18th century until late in the 1900s, dinnerware was made in and around Canton, China, expressly for western export. This pattern, whose name was borrowed from the city of its manufacture, is decorated in blue on a white ground with a scene containing a bridge, willow trees, birds, and a teahouse, all within a rain and cloud border.

When no condition is indicated, the items listed below are assumed to be in mint condition.

Drip tray with drainer, 10″ x 13½″, $800.00; without drainer, $400.00.

Bowl, fruit lid finial, orange peel glaze, 9½″ L...............325.00
Bowl, fruit; oval, reticulated, w/undertray, early, 9x10½″.......850.00
Bowl, open almond shape, orange peel glaze, shallow, 10″ L...150.00
Bowl, oval/canted corners, orange peel glaze, shallow, 12″.....275.00
Bowl, rectangular, 8¾″.....................................125.00
Bowl, salad; canted corners, sq, early, 10″..................750.00
Bowl, scalloped, orange peel glaze, 9½″....................425.00
Bowl, soup; scalloped, very late, 8¾″, set of 4...............150.00
Creamer, 5x3″...100.00
Cup & saucer..75.00
Hot water dish, oblong, octagonal, 1800s, 13½″.............425.00
Plate, 10″...125.00
Plate, 6″...65.00
Plate, 8½″..75.00
Platter, canted corners, early, 14½x11¾″...................250.00
Platter, octagonal, late 1800s, 18½″.......................300.00
Platter, oval, 19th C, 12¾x10½″..........................250.00
Salt, trencher; pr..550.00
Teacup, pomegranate finial, twisted hdl, w/lid................125.00
Teapot, twisted side hdl, dome lid, 9″......................580.00
Tray, canted corners, 11″ L................................125.00

Capo-Di-Monte

Established in 1743 near Naples, and sponsored by Charles II, King of Naples, Capo-Di-Monte produced soft paste porcelain figurines and dinnerware, usually marked with a 'crown over N' device, though a fleur-de-lis was used on occasion. The factory was closed throughout the 1760s, but reopened in 1771 in the city of Naples. There, both hard and soft paste porcelains were made, sometimes decorated with applied florals in high relief.

This technique, and their marks as well, were blatently copied. As a result, this type of encrusted decoration is often referred to today as Capo-Di-Monte. The original factory closed in 1821. Some of their molds were purchased by the Docceia Porcelain factory in Florence, which continues to operate to the present time.

Nearly all wares of this type on the market today are of fairly recent manufacture. Capo-Di-Monte type wares have been made in Hungary and Germany, as well as France and Italy. Many of these pieces continue to bear the 'crown over N' gold stamp.

When no condition is indicated, the items listed below are assumed to be in mint condition.

Bottle, scent; cherub in garden, bl crown mk, 3″ 60.00
Bowl, children in relief, ftd, triangle shape, 7″ 50.00
Cache pot, castle/lady/cherub, sgn Toulan, hdls, 9½″ 175.00
Compote, HP cupids/landscape, cherub lid finial, 8″ 65.00
Cup & saucer, cherubs in relief, oversize 50.00
Cup & saucer, demitasse; floral sprays, cherub w/garlands 45.00
Cup & saucer, demitasse; maidens/dog/tree/mtns, branch hdl 65.00
Cup & saucer, Phaeton, 1860 .... 75.00
Figurine, boy on stump, fishing, orange cap/boots, 5¾″ 75.00
Figurine, Buccaneer, on rnd rock, sgn A Colle, 12x6″ 160.00
Figurine, gypsy lady w/tambourine, parrot on shoulder, 4½″ 55.00
Figurine, lady by tree, gloves/dog, 10″ 75.00
Figurine, man playing trumpet, bl crown mark 125.00
Figurine, man w/jug in wheelbarrow pushed by 2nd, 6x12″ 160.00
Figurine, old lady roasts nuts at stove, child, 7x8x10″ 245.00
Figurine, organ grinder w/cart, Menegheti, 10½x9½″ 350.00
Figurine, 3½″ Hunchback Dwarf Musicians, w/6″ Conductor 275.00

Teapot, signed with the crown over N mark, 8½″, $275.00.

Carlton

Carlton Ware was the product of Wiltshaw and Robinson, who operated in the Staffordshire district of England from about 1890. During the 1920s, they produced ornamental ware with enameled and gilded decorations such as flowers and birds, often on a black background. In 1958, the firm was renamed Carlton Ware Ltd. Their trademark was a crown over a circular stamp with 'W & R, Stoke on Trent' surrounding a swallow. 'Carlton Ware' was sometimes added by hand.

When no condition is indicated, the items listed below are assumed to be in mint condition.

Bowl, chinoiserie, med bl w/heavy enamel scene, 11″ 225.00
Compote, Rouge Royal, spider web/insects, 8½x4½″ 120.00
Pitcher, Rouge Royal, chinoiserie, maroon, 6½″ 85.00
Sugar shaker, cottage figural, yel/orange/brn/gr 60.00
Sugar shaker, gr/orange/gold tree on beige, 4½″ 45.00
Vase, chinoiserie, red/blk w/detailed scene, 10½″ 210.00
Vase, chinoiserie on gr, panels on bottom, 8½″, pr 285.00
Vase, Rouge Royal, gold hdls, 11½x8″ 175.00
Vase, Rouge Royal, helmet shape, 7″ 69.00

Carnival Collectibles

Carnival items from the early part of this century represent the lighter side of an America that was alternately prospering and sophisticated, or devastated by war and domestic conflict. But whatever the country's condition, the carnival's thrilling rides and shooting galleries were a sure way of letting it all go by . . . at least for an evening.

When no condition is indicated, the items listed below are assumed to be in excellent condition.

Banner, tapir exploited, pnt by F Johnson 225.00
Chalkware prize, Geo Washington on horse 20.00
Chalkware prize, seated Kewpie, 1919 .... 24.00
Clown Toss, penny in mouth lights up button, chalkware 150.00
Figure, mechanical fat lady 'Laughling Sal,' 6 ft 3,310.00
Game, jailbird, carved/pnt, legs swing, lens in body, 12″ 245.00
Knock-down doll, canvas, ca 1920s 20.00
Poster, De Kreko Bros Shows, midway scene, ca 1900, 40″ L .. 100.00
Shooting gallery target, CI, duck, pnt poor, 1900s, 7x6x4″ 80.00
Shooting gallery target, CI, moose, early 20th C, 7x5½″ 90.00
Shooting gallery target, CI, running rabbit, pnt, 11″ 80.00
Shooting gallery target, CI, swan, early 20th C, 6x5″ 70.00
Shooting gallery target, CI, turkey, early 20th C, 7x5½″ 85.00
Shooting gallery target, steel, cut-out donkey kicks, 30″ 850.00

Carnival Glass

Carnival glass is pressed glass that has been coated with a sodium solution and fired to give it an exterior lustre.

First made in America in 1905, it was produced until the late 1920s and had great popularity in the average American household; for unlike the costly art glass produced by Tiffany, Carnival glass could be mass produced at a small cost.

Colors most found are marigold, green, blue, and purple, but others exist in lesser quantities and include white, clear, red, aqua opalescent, peach opalescent, ice blue, ice green, amber, lavender, and smoke.

Companies mainly responsible for its production in America include the Fenton Art Glass Company, Williamstown, West Virginia; the Northwood Glass Company, Wheeling, West Virginia; the Imperial Glass Company, Bellaire, Ohio; the Millersburg Glass Company, Millersburg, Ohio; and the Dugan Glass Company (Diamond Glass), Indiana, Pennsylvania.

In addition to these major manufacturers, lesser producers included the U.S. Glass Company, the Cambridge Glass Company, the Westmoreland Glass Company, and the McKee Glass Company.

Carnival glass has been highly collectible since the 1950s, and has been reproduced for the last twenty-five years. Several national and state collector's organizations exist, and many fine books are available on old Carnival glass, including *The Standard Encyclopedia of Carnival Glass* by Bill Edwards.

Values are for items in mint condition.

Acanthus (Imperial), bowl, 8½″, amethyst 80.00
Acanthus (Imperial), plate, 10″, marigold 155.00

Acorn (Fenton), bowl, 7″, marigold . . . 35.00
Acorn (Fenton), plate, scarce, 9″, amethyst . . . 490.00
Acorn Burrs (Northwood), bowl, flat, 10″, marigold . . . 90.00
Acorn Burrs (Northwood), bowl, flat, 5″, marigold . . . 32.00
Acorn Burrs (Northwood), butter dish, amethyst . . . 225.00
Acorn Burrs (Northwood), creamer or spooner, amethyst . . . 120.00
Acorn Burrs (Northwood), punch bowl, w/base, green . . . 650.00

Acorn Burrs (Northwood), punch cup, blue . . . 45.00
Acorn Burrs (Northwood), tumbler, amethyst . . . 75.00
Acorn Burrs (Northwood), whimsey vase, rare, marigold . . . 1,000.00
Advertising Ash Tray, various designs, marigold . . . 375.00
African Shield (English), toothpick holder, marigold . . . 45.00
Age Herald (Fenton), bowl, scarce, 9¼″, amethyst . . . 865.00

Age Herald (Fenton), plate, scarce, 10″, amethyst . . . 910.00
Amaryllis (Northwood), compote, sm, marigold . . . 195.00
Amaryllis (Northwood), whimsey, flattened, amethyst . . . 175.00
American (Fostoria), tumbler, rare, marigold . . . 500.00
Apple Blossom Twigs (Dugan), bowl, marigold . . . 40.00

Apple Blossom Twigs (Dugan), plate, green . . . 120.00
Apple Blossoms (Dugan), bowl, 7½″, amethyst . . . 40.00
Apple Blossoms (Dugan), plate, 8¼″, marigold . . . 95.00

Apple Panels (English), creamer, marigold . . . 30.00
Apple Panels (English), sugar bowl, open; green . . . 36.00
Apple Tree (Fenton), pitcher, water; marigold . . . 160.00
Apple Tree (Fenton), tumbler, marigold . . . 44.00
April Showers (Fenton), vase, marigold . . . 40.00
Arcadia Baskets, plate, 8″, marigold . . . 50.00
Arched Fleur-De-Lis (Higbee), mug, rare, marigold . . . 110.00
Arcs (Imperial), bowl, 8½″, marigold . . . 30.00

Arcs (Imperial), compote, amethyst . . . 50.00
Art Deco (English), bowl, 4″, marigold . . . 25.00
Australian Swan (Crystal), bowl, 5″, marigold . . . 38.00
Australian Swan (Crystal), bowl, 9″, amethyst . . . 95.00
Autumn Acorns (Fenton), bowl, 8¾″, marigold . . . 30.00
Autumn Acorns (Fenton), plate, rare, amethyst . . . 900.00
Aztec (McKee), creamer, marigold . . . 100.00
Aztec (McKee), pitcher, rare, marigold . . . 1,300.00
Aztec (McKee), rose bowl, clambroth . . . 250.00
Baby's Bouquet, child's plate, scarce, marigold . . . 90.00
Ball & Swirl, mug, marigold . . . 90.00
Balloons (Imperial), cake plate, marigold . . . 60.00
Balloons (Imperial), perfume atomizer, smoke . . . 85.00
Bamboo Bird, jar, complete, amethyst . . . 500.00
Banded Diamond & Fan (English), toothpick holder, marigold . . . 65.00
Banded Diamonds (Crystal), bowl, 10″, amethyst . . . 110.00
Banded Diamonds (Crystal), bowl, 5″, marigold . . . 50.00

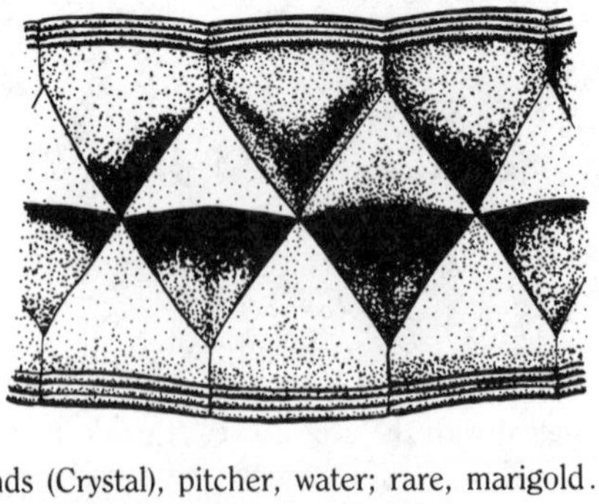

Banded Diamonds (Crystal), pitcher, water; rare, marigold . . . 750.00
Banded Diamonds (Crystal), tumbler, rare, amethyst . . . 350.00
Banded Drape (Fenton), pitcher, water; white . . . 450.00
Banded Drape (Fenton), tumbler, blue . . . 45.00
Banded Grape & Leaf (English), tumbler, rare, marigold . . . 90.00
Banded Panels (Crystal), sugar bowl, open; marigold . . . 35.00
Barber Bottle (Cambridge), complete, marigold . . . 375.00
Basket (Northwood), either shape, ftd, amethyst . . . 85.00
Basketweave (Fenton), open-edge hat, blue . . . 45.00
Basketweave (Fenton), vase whimsey, rare, marigold . . . 250.00
Basketweave & Cable (Westmoreland), creamer, amethyst . . . 70.00
Basketweave & Cable (Westmoreland), sugar bowl, white . . . 110.00
Beaded Acanthus (Imperial), pitcher, milk; green . . . 210.00

Beaded Bull's Eye (Imperial), vase, 8″, amethyst. 40.00
Beaded Cable (Northwood), candy dish, blue. 65.00
Beaded Cable (Northwood), rose bowl, aqua opalescent. 365.00
Beaded Hearts (Northwood), bowl, green. 60.00
Beaded Panels (Westmoreland), compote, amethyst. 50.00
Beaded Shell (Dugan), bowl, ftd, 5″, marigold. 30.00
Beaded Shell (Dugan), mug, amethyst. 85.00
Beaded Shell (Dugan), pitcher, water; marigold. 360.00

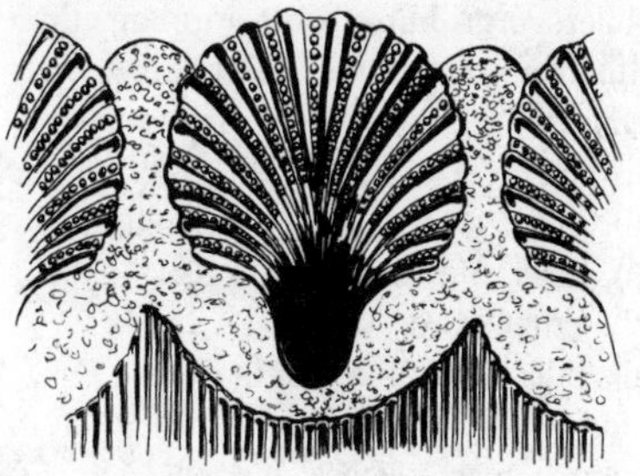

Beaded Shell (Dugan), sugar bowl, amethyst. 120.00
Beaded Shell (Dugan), tumbler, amethyst. 90.00
Beaded Spears (Crystal), pitcher, rare, marigold. 175.00
Beaded Spears (Crystal), tumbler, rare, amethyst. 90.00
Beaded Swirl (English), butter dish, marigold. 60.00
Beaded Swirl (English), compote, marigold. 45.00
Beaded Swirl (English), sugar bowl, open; blue. 45.00
Beads (Northwood), bowl, 8½″, marigold. .40.00
Beauty Bud Vase (Dugan), regular size, marigold. 25.00
Beauty Bud Vase (Dugan), twig size, rare, amethyst. 158.00
Bellaire Souvenir (Imperial), bowl, scarce, marigold. 65.00
Bells & Beads (Dugan), bowl, 7½″, peach opalescent. 60.00
Bells & Beads (Dugan), compote, amethyst. 52.00
Bells & Beads (Dugan), gravy boat, hdld, marigold. 46.00
Bells & Beads (Dugan), plate, 8″, amethyst. 120.00
Big Basketweave (Dugan), basket, sm, marigold. 35.00
Big Basketweave (Dugan), vase, 6″, amethyst. 40.00
Big Fish (Millersburg), banana bowl, rare, green. 1,500.00

Big Fish (Millersburg), bowl, various shapes, green. 500.00
Bird With Grapes (Cockatoo), wall vase, marigold. 55.00
Birds & Cherries (Fenton), bonbon, green. 60.00
Birds & Cherries (Fenton), bowl, rare, 5″, amethyst. 85.00
Birds & Cherries (Fenton), bowl, rare, 9½″, marigold. 200.00
Birds & Cherries (Fenton), compote, marigold. 45.00
Blackberry (Fenton), open-edge hat, amethyst. 45.00
Blackberry (Fenton), plate, rare, blue. 375.00
Blackberry (Fenton), vase whimsey, rare, blue. 325.00
Blackberry (Northwood), bowl, ftd, 9″, amethyst. 60.00
Blackberry (Northwood), compote, marigold. 52.00
Blackberry Banded (Fenton), hat shape, green. 50.00
Blackberry Block (Fenton), pitcher, green. 600.00
Blackberry Block (Fenton), tumbler, blue. .60.00
Blackberry Bramble (Fenton), bowl, blue. .50.00
Blackberry Bramble (Fenton), compote, green. 60.00
Blackberry Spray (Fenton), bonbon, marigold. 30.00
Blackberry Spray (Fenton), compote, blue. 45.00
Blackberry Spray (Fenton), hat shape, green. 40.00
Blackberry Wreath (Millersburg), plate, rare, 6″, amethyst. 600.00
Blocks & Arches (Crystal), pitcher, rare, amethyst. 200.00
Blocks & Arches (Crystal), tumbler, rare, marigold. 70.00
Blossoms & Band (Imperial), bowl, 10″, marigold. 35.00
Blossoms & Band (Imperial), bowl, 5″, amethyst. 28.00
Blossomtime (Northwood), compote, green. 70.00
Blueberry (Fenton), pitcher, scarce, blue. 690.00
Blueberry (Fenton), tumbler, scarce, marigold. 40.00
Border Plants (Dugan), bowl, flat, 8½″, amethyst. 50.00
Bouquet (Fenton), pitcher, blue. 375.00
Bouquet (Fenton), tumbler, white. 65.00
Boutonniere (Millersburg), compote, green. 95.00
Bow & English Hob (English), bowl, nut; blue. 55.00
Brocaded Summer Gardens, cake plate, center hdl, pastel. 75.00
Brocaded Summer Gardens, cake tray, pastel. 80.00
Brocaded Summer Gardens, ice bucket, pastel. 90.00
Brocaded Summer Gardens, vase, pastel. .90.00
Broken Arches (Imperial), bowl, 8½″, marigold. 42.00
Broken Arches (Imperial), punch cup, amethyst. 30.00
Brooklyn Bridge (Dugan), bowl, scarce, marigold. 320.00
Bull's Eye (US Glass), oil lamp, marigold. 185.00
Bull's Eye & Leaves (Northwood), bowl, 8½″, amethyst. 50.00
Butterflies (Fenton), bonbon, green. 65.00
Butterflies (Fenton), card tray, blue. 60.00
Butterfly (Northwood), bonbon, regular, marigold. 45.00
Butterfly & Berry (Fenton), bowl, ftd, 5″, blue. 40.00
Butterfly & Berry (Fenton), butter dish, marigold. 110.00
Butterfly & Berry (Fenton), creamer, w/lid, blue. 150.00
Butterfly & Berry (Fenton), hatpin holder, rare, marigold. 750.00

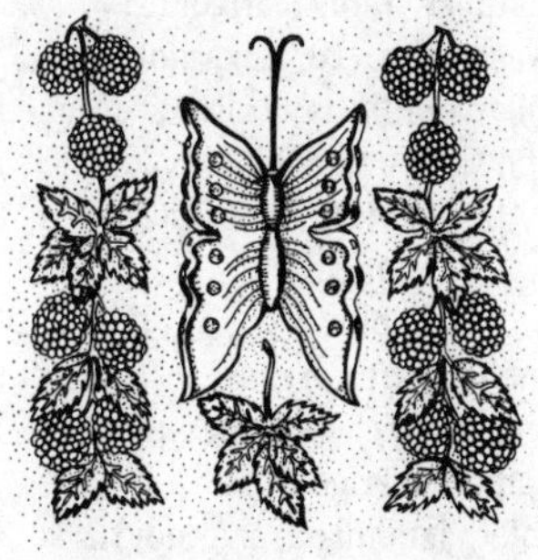

Butterfly & Berry (Fenton), pitcher, marigold. 275.00
Butterfly & Berry (Fenton), tumbler, blue. 60.00
Butterfly & Fern (Fenton), pitcher, marigold. 350.00
Butterfly & Fern (Fenton), tumbler, amethyst. 47.00
Butterfly Bower (Crystal), compote, amethyst. 115.00
Buttermilk, Plain (Fenton), goblet, amethyst. 55.00
Buzz Saw (Cambridge), cruet, lg, rare, 6″, marigold. 380.00
Cane (Imperial), bowl, 10″, marigold. 30.00
Cane (Imperial), pickle dish, marigold. 25.00
Cane & Daisy Cut (Jenkins), basket, hdld, rare, marigold. 175.00
Cane & Scroll (Sea Thistle) (English), creamer, marigold. 45.00
Cane & Scroll (Sea Thistle) (English), rose bowl, marigold. 55.00
Capitol (Westmoreland), bowl, ftd, sm, blue. 65.00
Captive Rose (Fenton), bowl, 8½″, green. 48.00
Captive Rose (Fenton), plate, 7″, blue. 95.00

Carnation (New Martinsville), punch cup, marigold 45.00
Carnival Honeycomb (Imperial), bowl, hdld, 6″, marigold 30.00
Carnival Honeycomb (Imperial), plate, 7″, amethyst 80.00
Carolina Dogwood (Westmoreland), bowl, 8½″, opalescent 125.00
Caroline (Dugan), basket, scarce, peach opalescent 400.00
Caroline (Dugan), bowl, 7″, marigold 52.00
Cathedral, bowl, 10″, blue 50.00
Cathedral, chalice, 7″, marigold 75.00
Cathedral, compote, 2 sizes, marigold 40.00
Cathedral, creamer, ftd, marigold 45.00
Central Shoe Store (Northwood), bowl, 6″, amethyst 210.00
Chain & Star (Fostoria), tumbler, rare, marigold 750.00
Chatelaine (Imperial), tumbler, rare, amethyst 360.00
Checkerboard (Westmoreland), goblet, rare, amethyst 295.00
Checkerboard (Westmoreland), tumbler, rare, amethyst 450.00
Checkerboard Bouquet, plate, 8″, amethyst 50.00
Cherry (Dugan), bowl, flat, 8″, marigold 50.00
Cherry (Dugan), plate, 6″, amethyst 190.00
Cherry (Millersburg), banana compote, rare, amethyst 1,700.00
Cherry (Millersburg), bowl, scarce, 9″, green 100.00
Cherry (Millersburg), bowl, 4″, green 55.00
Cherry (Millersburg), pitcher, scarce, amethyst 670.00
Cherry (Millersburg), tumbler, 2 variations, marigold 250.00
Cherry & Cable (Northwood), bowl, scarce, 9″, marigold 95.00
Cherry & Cable (Northwood), pitcher, rare, marigold 1,350.00
Cherry & Cable (Northwood), tumbler, rare, marigold 400.00
Cherry & Cable Intaglio (Northwood), bowl, 5″, marigold 50.00
Cherry & Daisies (Fenton), banana boat, marigold 700.00
Cherry Blossoms (Fenton), tumbler, blue 28.00
Cherry Circles (Fenton), bowl, 8″, blue 56.00
Cherry Circles (Fenton), compote, marigold 50.00
Cherry Circles (Fenton), plate, rare, 9″, white 175.00
Chrysanthemum (Fenton), bowl, flat, 9″, blue 75.00
Chrysanthemum (Fenton), bowl, ftd, 10″, marigold 60.00
Circle Scroll (Dugan), bowl, 10″, marigold 57.00
Circle Scroll (Dugan), bowl, 5″, marigold 32.00
Circle Scroll (Dugan), butter dish, marigold 250.00
Circle Scroll (Dugan), hat shape, rare, amethyst 120.00
Circle Scroll (Dugan), tumbler, rare, marigold 300.00
Classic Arts (English), vase, rare, 10″, marigold 200.00
Cleveland Memorial (Millersburg), ash tray, rare, amethyst 1,600.00
Cobblestones (Dugan), bowl, 5″, amethyst 40.00
Cobblestones (Imperial), bowl, 8½″, amethyst 70.00
Coin Dot (Fenton), bowl, 6″, amethyst 50.00
Coin Dot (Fenton), rose bowl, blue 70.00
Coin Dot (Fenton), tumbler, rare, green 125.00
Coin Spot (Dugan), compote, peach opalescent 300.00
Colonial (Imperial), creamer, marigold 36.00
Colonial (Imperial), goblet, lemonade; marigold 60.00
Colonial (Imperial), toothpick holder, green 85.00
Colonial Lady (Imperial), vase, rare, marigold 300.00
Columbia (Imperial), compote, green 57.00
Concave Diamonds (Northwood), tumbler, russet 400.00
Concave Flute (Westmoreland), rose bowl, marigold 50.00
Concave Flute (Westmoreland), vase, green 65.00
Concord (Fenton), bowl, scarce, 9″, marigold 60.00
Concord (Fenton), plate, rare, 10″, green 565.00
Cone & Tie (Imperial), tumbler, rare, amethyst 550.00
Constellation (Dugan), compote, peach opalescent 60.00
Coral (Fenton), bowl, 9″, blue 75.00
Coral (Fenton), compote, rare, green 95.00
Coral (Fenton), plate, rare, 9½″, marigold 750.00
Corinth (Westmoreland), bowl, amethyst 50.00
Corinth (Westmoreland), vase, marigold 28.00
Corn Vase (Northwood), regular mold, amethyst 485.00
Corning (Corning), insulator, marigold 20.00
Cosmos & Cane, bowl, 10″, marigold 58.00
Cosmos & Cane, chop plate, rare, white 475.00
Cosmos & Cane, compote, marigold 150.00
Cosmos & Cane, pitcher, rare, marigold 665.00
Cosmos & Cane, spooner, marigold 95.00
Cosmos & Cane, tumbler, rare, white 150.00
Country Kitchen (Millersburg), bowl, rare, 9″, marigold 150.00
Country Kitchen (Millersburg), butter dish, rare, amethyst 500.00
Country Kitchen (Millersburg), spooner, vaseline 500.00
Country Kitchen (Millersburg), vase, rare, amethyst 450.00
Covered Hen (English), one size, blue 110.00
Crab Claw (Imperial), bowl, fruit; w/base, marigold 90.00
Crab Claw (Imperial), bowl, 5″, marigold 25.00
Crab Claw (Imperial), cruet, rare, marigold 650.00
Crab Claw (Imperial), pitcher, scarce, marigold 295.00
Crackle (Imperial), auto vase, amethyst 35.00
Crackle (Imperial), punch bowl, w/base, marigold 48.00
Crackle (Imperial), tumbler, dome base, green 26.00
Crackle (Imperial), window planter, rare, marigold 95.00
Cut Arcs (Fenton), compote, blue 45.00
Cut Cosmos (Millersburg), tumbler, rare, marigold 295.00
Cut Ovals (Fenton), bowl, 7″, marigold 50.00
Dahlia (Dugan), bowl, ftd, 10″, amethyst 130.00
Dahlia (Dugan), sugar bowl, open; white 325.00
Dahlia (Dugan), tumbler, rare, amethyst 135.00
Daisy (Fenton), bonbon, scarce, blue 75.00
Daisy & Drape (Northwood), vase, green 175.00
Daisy & Plume (Northwood), candy dish, green 60.00
Daisy & Plume (Northwood), compote, amethyst 60.00
Daisy & Plume (Northwood), rose bowl, 2 shapes, marigold 55.00
Daisy Block (English), rowboat, scarce, marigold 265.00
Daisy Squares (Millersburg), goblet, rare, pastel 350.00
Daisy Squares (Millersburg), rose bowl, green 185.00
Dandelion (Northwood), mug, marigold 350.00
Dandelion (Northwood), tumbler, green 65.00
Deep Grape (Millersburg), compote, rare, green 850.00
Diamond & Daisy (US Glass), compote, blue 60.00
Diamond & Daisy (US Glass), tumbler, rare, marigold 45.00
Diamond & Rib (Fenton), vase, 7″, blue 32.00
Diamond & Rib (Fenton), vase whimsey, green 600.00
Diamond & Sunburst (Imperial), bowl, 8″, green 48.00
Diamond & Sunburst (Imperial), wine, marigold 40.00
Diamond Band (Crystal), float set, marigold 250.00
Diamond Checkerboard, bowl, 9″, marigold 35.00
Diamond Checkerboard, tumbler, marigold 85.00
Diamond Fountain (Higbee), cruet, rare, marigold 675.00
Diamond Lace (Imperial), bowl, 5″, amethyst 37.00
Diamond Lace (Imperial), tumbler, marigold 65.00
Diamond Ovals (English), creamer, marigold 35.00
Diamond Pinwheel (English), compote, marigold 45.00
Diamond Point Columns (Imperial), compote, marigold 26.00
Diamond Point Columns (Imperial), vase, pastel 40.00
Diamond Ring (Imperial), bowl, 5″, amethyst 28.00
Diamond Top (English), creamer, marigold 32.00
Dogwood Sprays (Dugan), bowl, 9″, amethyst 50.00
Double Dolphins (Fenton), bowl, flat, 8″, pastel 60.00
Double Dolphins (Fenton), compote, pastel 60.00
Double Scroll (Imperial), bowl, marigold 40.00
Double Star (Cambridge), tumbler, scarce, amethyst 85.00
Dragon & Lotus (Fenton), bowl, flat, 9″, aqua opalescent 650.00
Dragon & Strawberry (Fenton), bowl, flat, scarce, 9″, blue 375.00
Dragonfly Lamp, oil lamp, rare, pastel 650.00

Drapery (Northwood), candy dish, amethyst....................67.00
Drapery (Northwood), vase, blue..............................48.00
Dreibus Parfait Sweets (Northwood), plate, 6", amethyst.......175.00
Dugan Fan (Dugan), gravy boat, ftd, amethyst..................60.00
Duncan (National Glass), cruet, marigold....................410.00
Dutch Twins, ash tray, marigold..............................45.00
Elks (Fenton), Parkersburg plate, rare, green................850.00
Elks (Millersburg), paperweight, rare, amethyst.............1,000.00
Embroidered Mums (Northwood), plate, marigold..............145.00
Emu (Crystal), bowl, rare, 10", marigold......................80.00
English Button Band (English), sugar bowl, marigold...........38.00
English Hob & Button (English), bowl, 7", blue................60.00
Engraved Grapes (Fenton), candy jar, w/lid, marigold...........45.00
Engraved Grapes (Fenton), pitcher, tall, marigold..............85.00
Estate (Westmoreland), bud vase, 6", marigold..................40.00
Fanciful (Dugan), bowl, 8½", marigold.........................45.00
Fancy Flowers (Imperial), compote, marigold...................75.00
Garden Mums (Northwood), bowl, 8½", green.....................70.00
Garden Mums (Northwood), plate, 7", handgrip, amethyst......100.00
Garden Path (Dugan), bowl, fruit; 10", marigold................85.00
Garden Path (Dugan), bowl, 8½", amethyst......................70.00
Garden Path (Dugan), plate, 6", rare, peach opalescent........360.00
Garland (Fenton), rose bowl, ftd, blue.........................65.00
Gay 90s (Millersburg), pitcher, rare, green.................8,700.00
Gay 90s (Millersburg), tumbler, rare, marigold..............1,250.00
Georgia Belle (Dugan), card tray, ftd, rare, amethyst...........85.00
Georgia Belle (Dugan), compote, ftd, green.....................80.00
God & Home (Dugan), pitcher, rare, blue......................900.00
God & Home (Dugan), tumbler, rare, blue......................135.00
Goddess of Harvest (Fenton), bowl, 9½", rare, blue.........4,100.00
Golden Cupids (Crystal), bowl, 9", rare, pastel..............165.00
Golden Flowers, vase, 7½", marigold...........................48.00
Golden Grapes (Dugan), bowl, 7", green........................45.00
Golden Grapes (Dugan), rose bowl, collar base, marigold........50.00
Golden Harvest (US Glass), decanter, w/stopper, amethyst......230.00
Golden Honeycomb (Imperial), bonbon, green....................50.00
Golden Honeycomb (Imperial), compote, marigold.................47.00
Golden Honeycomb (Imperial), plate, 7", marigold...............45.00
Good Luck (Northwood), bowl, 8¾", blue.......................175.00
Good Luck (Northwood), plate, 9", amethyst...................285.00
Gooseberry Spray, bowl, 10", blue.............................90.00
Gooseberry Spray, bowl, 5", green............................125.00
Gooseberry Spray, compote, rare, amethyst....................110.00
Graceful (Northwood), vase, blue..............................80.00
Grand Thistle (Swedish), tumbler, rare, blue..................550.00
Grape, Heavy (Dugan); bowl, 5", rare, peach opalescent..........70.00
Grape, Heavy (Imperial); bowl, 9", amethyst....................50.00
Grape, Heavy (Imperial); plate, 11", amethyst.................200.00
Grape, Heavy (Imperial); plate, 8", green......................75.00
Grape, Heavy (Imperial); punch bowl, w/base, green............240.00
Grape (Fenton's Gr & Cable), bowl, 8¾", ftd, green.............67.00
Grape (Fenton's Gr & Cable), orange bowl, ftd, amethyst......185.00
Grape (Fenton's Gr & Cable), plate, 9", ftd, amethyst.........115.00
Grape (Imperial), bowl, fruit; 8¾", marigold...................36.00
Grape (Imperial), bowl, 10", green.............................50.00
Grape (Imperial), cup & saucer, green..........................85.00
Grape (Imperial), decanter, w/stopper, green..................165.00
Grape (Imperial), goblet, rare, green..........................65.00
Grape (Imperial), pitcher, green..............................170.00
Grape (Imperial), pitcher, milk; amethyst.....................225.00
Grape (Imperial), spittoon whimsey, marigold..................975.00
Grape (Imperial), tumbler, amethyst............................38.00
Grape (Northwood's Gr & Cable), banana boat, footed, blue....250.00
Grape (Northwood's Gr & Cable), bonbon, marigold...............35.00

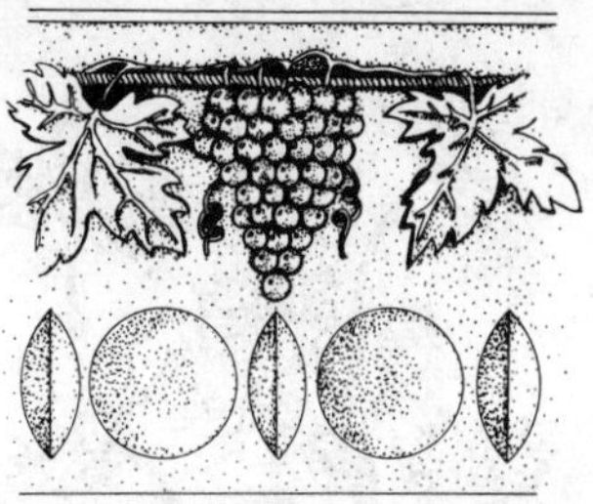

Grape (Northwood's Gr & Cable), bowl, 5½", flat, green........40.00
Grape (Northwood's Gr & Cable), candlesticks, green, pr.......220.00
Grape (Northwood's Gr & Cable), compote, open, marigold.....350.00
Grape (Northwood's Gr & Cable), cup, green.....................40.00
Grape (Northwood's Gr & Cable), dresser tray, amethyst.......180.00
Grape (Northwood's Gr & Cable), ice cream sherbet, green......52.00
Grape (Northwood's Gr & Cable), nappy, amethyst...............58.00
Grape (Northwood's Gr & Cable), orange bowl, ftd, green......195.00
Grape (Northwood's Gr & Cable), pin tray, green..............145.00
Grape (Northwood's Gr & Cable), pitcher, standard, green.....300.00
Grape (Northwood's Gr & Cable), plate, handgrip, green........76.00
Grape (Northwood's Gr & Cable), sugar bowl, amethyst........110.00
Grape (Northwood's Gr & Cable), sweetmeat, amethyst, w/lid...250.00
Grape (Northwood's Gr & Cable), tumbler, regular, green.......70.00
Grape & Cherry (English), bowl, 8½", rare, blue..............150.00
Grape & Gothic Arches (Northwood), bowl, 10", amethyst......55.00
Grape & Gothic Arches (Northwood), bowl, 5", green..........45.00
Grape & Gothic Arches (Northwood), pitcher, marigold........200.00
Grape & Gothic Arches (Northwood), sugar bowl, marigold......60.00
Grape & Gothic Arches (Northwood), tumbler, green...........90.00
Grape Arbor (Dugan), bowl, ftd, 9½", marigold.................50.00
Grape Arbor (Northwood), hat, marigold........................60.00
Grape Arbor (Northwood), pitcher, amethyst...................540.00
Grape Leaves (Millersburg), bowl, rare, 10", marigold.........350.00
Grape Leaves (Northwood), bowl, 8¾", amethyst.................70.00
Grape Wreath (Millersburg), bowl, ice cream; 10", green.......170.00
Grape Wreath (Millersburg), bowl, 5", marigold................38.00
Grapevine Lattice (Dugan), bowl, 5", marigold..................26.00
Grapevine Lattice (Dugan), bowl, 8½", amethyst................57.00
Grapevine Lattice (Fenton), pitcher, rare, amethyst..........480.00
Grapevine Lattice (Fenton), tumbler, rare, amethyst............75.00
Greek Key (Northwood), bowl, 7", green.......................100.00

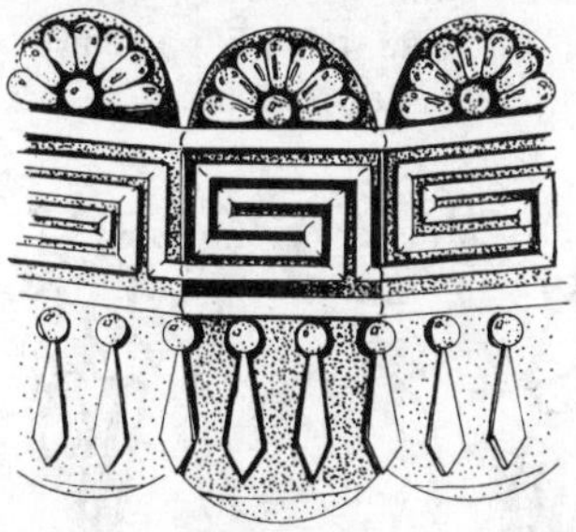

Greek Key (Northwood), pitcher, rare, amethyst...............900.00
Greek Key (Northwood), tumbler, rare, marigold................75.00
Greengard Furniture (Millersburg), bowl, rare, amethyst.......310.00
Ice Crystals, salt, ftd, pastel................................65.00
Imperial #5 (Imperial), bowl, 8", marigold.....................40.00
Imperial #9 (Imperial), compote, marigold......................38.00
Inca (English), vase, 7", rare, marigold......................750.00
Intaglio Daisy (English), bowl, 4½", marigold..................26.00
Inverted Coin Dot (Northwood-Fenton), bowl, amethyst.........45.00
Inverted Coin Dot (Northwood-Fenton), rose bowl, green.......60.00
Inverted Coin Dot (Northwood-Fenton), tumbler, blue..........85.00
Inverted Feather (Cambridge), compote, marigold................45.00
Inverted Feather (Cambridge), cracker jar, amethyst..........375.00

Inverted Strawberry, candlesticks, rare, green, pr............300.00
Inverted Strawberry, compote, lg, rare, amethyst............400.00
Inverted Strawberry, compote whimsey, rare, marigold.........375.00
Inverted Strawberry, pitcher, rare, amethyst................900.00
Inverted Thistle (Cambridge), bowl, 9″, rare, amethyst.........200.00
Inverted Thistle (Cambridge), butter dish, rare, green.........600.00
Inverted Thistle (Cambridge), spooner, rare, marigold.........350.00
Inverted Thistle (Cambridge), tumbler, rare, marigold..........425.00
Iris, Heavy (Dugan); tumbler, green........................85.00
Iris (Fenton), compote, amethyst...........................60.00
Iris (Fenton), goblet, buttermilk; scarce, marigold.............52.00
Jackman, whiskey bottle, marigold..........................30.00
Jewelled Heart (Dugan), bowl, 5″, amethyst..................42.00

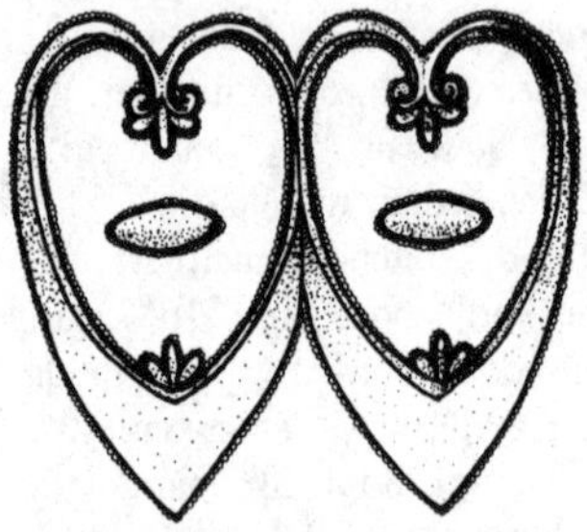

Jewelled Heart (Dugan), plate, 6″, marigold.................125.00
Jewels (Imperial), creamer or sugar, pastel...................70.00
Jewels (Imperial), hat shape, red..........................190.00
Jockey Club (Northwood), bowl, 7″.........................145.00
Kingfisher & Variant (Australian), bowl, 5″, amethyst..........50.00
Kittens (Fenton), bowl, cereal; scarce, blue.................165.00

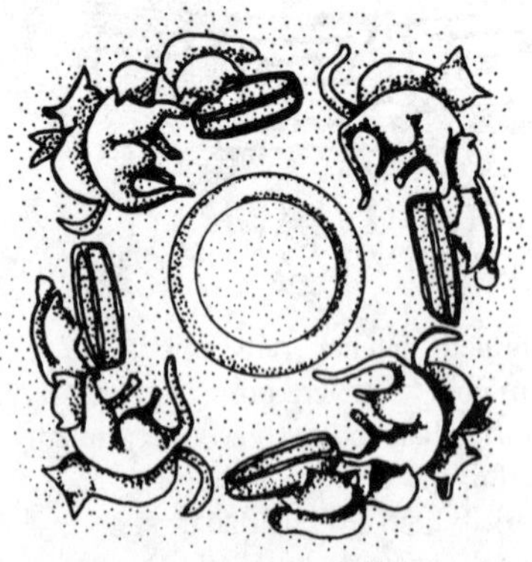

Kittens (Fenton), plate, 4½″, scarce, blue..................170.00
Kittens (Fenton), vase, 3″ tall, marigold....................160.00
Kiwi (Australian), bowl, 10″, rare, amethyst.................175.00
Knotted Beads (Fenton), vase, 4″, blue.....................37.00
Kokomo (English), rose bowl, ftd, marigold...................45.00
Lacy Dewdrop (Westmoreland), banana boat, pastel...........350.00
Lacy Dewdrop (Westmoreland), pitcher, pastel...............585.00
Lacy Dewdrop (Westmoreland), tumbler, pastel...............250.00

Large Kangaroo (Australian), bowl, 10″, amethyst.............85.00
Large Kangaroo (Australian), bowl, 5″, marigold..............40.00
Lattice & Daisy (Dugan), bowl, 9″, marigold..................60.00
Lattice & Daisy (Dugan), pitcher, white.....................220.00
Lattice & Grape (Fenton), pitcher, blue.....................310.00
Lattice & Grape (Fenton), tumbler, marigold..................38.00
Lattice & Leaves, vase, 9½″, blue..........................67.00
Lattice & Points (Dugan), vase, marigold....................35.00
Lattice Heart (English), bowl, 10″, marigold..................50.00
Lattice Heart (English), compote, blue.......................85.00
Laurel Leaves (Imperial), plate, marigold.....................47.00
Leaf & Beads (Northwood-Dugan), bowl, 9″, green............85.00
Leaf & Beads (Northwood-Dugan), candy dish, ftd, green.......52.00
Leaf Chain (Fenton), bonbon, blue..........................46.00
Leaf Chain (Fenton), bowl, 7″, green........................52.00
Leaf Chain (Fenton), plate, 9¼″, marigold...................65.00
Leaf Column (Northwood), vase, peach opalescent.............56.00
Leaf Swirl (Westmoreland), compote, marigold................50.00
Leaf Swirl & Flower (Fenton), vase, white....................65.00
Leaf Tiers (Fenton), banana bowl whimsey, marigold..........190.00
Leaf Tiers (Fenton), bowl, ftd, 10″, marigold.................58.00
Leaf Tiers (Fenton), pitcher, ftd, rare, green................630.00
Leaf Tiers (Fenton), sugar bowl, open; ftd, marigold..........88.00
Lily of the Valley (Fenton), tumbler, rare, blue..............450.00
Lined Lattice (Dugan), vase, 7″, green......................45.00
Lion (Fenton), bowl, scarce, 7″, blue.......................150.00
Little Beads, bowl, 8″, marigold............................18.00
Little Daisies (Fenton), bowl, rare, 8″, marigold.............190.00
Little Fishes (Fenton), bowl, flat or ftd, 10″, green...........90.00
Little Fishes (Fenton), plate, rare, 10½″, blue...............450.00
Little Flowers (Fenton), bowl, 5½″, amethyst.................38.00
Little Flowers (Fenton), bowl, 9¼″, marigold.................48.00

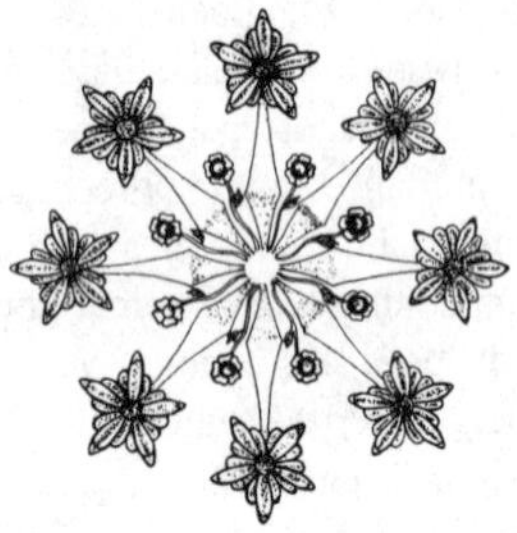

Little Flowers (Fenton), plate, rare, 10″, marigold............750.00
Little Stars (Millersburg), bowl, rare, 10½″, green............750.00
Little Stars (Millersburg), bowl, scarce, 7″, marigold..........65.00
Little Swan, miniature, 2″, pastel..........................75.00
Loganberry (Imperial), vase, scarce, amethyst................185.00
Long Hobstar, bowl, 10½″, marigold.........................56.00
Long Hobstar, punch bowl, w/base, marigold.................125.00
Long Thumbprint (Dugan), bowl, 8¾″, marigold................30.00
Long Thumbprint (Dugan), compote, amethyst..................39.00
Long Thumbprint (Dugan), vase, 7″, marigold..................28.00
Lotus & Grape (Fenton), bonbon, marigold.....................36.00
Lotus & Grape (Fenton), bowl, ftd, 7″, blue...................56.00
Louisa (Westmoreland), candy dish, ftd, marigold..............48.00
Louisa (Westmoreland), plate, ftd, rare, 8″, amethyst.........150.00
Lustre & Clear (Fenton), fan vase, marigold...................40.00
Lustre & Clear (Imperial), bowl, 5″, marigold..................20.00
Lustre & Clear (Imperial), creamer or sugar, amethyst..........65.00
Lustre & Clear (Imperial), rose bowl, marigold.................50.00
Lustre & Clear (Imperial), vase, ftd, 8″, green...............120.00
Lustre Flute (Northwood), bowl, 8″, green....................54.00
Lustre Flute (Northwood), compote, amethyst..................48.00
Lustre Flute (Northwood), punch bowl, w/base, amethyst.......160.00
Lustre Rose (Imperial), bowl, flat, 7″, marigold...............35.00

Lustre Rose (Imperial), plate, 6″, amethyst....70.00
Lustre Rose (Imperial), plate whimsey, ftd, green....58.00
Lustre Rose (Imperial), sugar bowl, open; green....54.00
Lustre Rose (Imperial), tumbler, marigold....25.00
Malaga (Dugan), plate, rare, 10″, amethyst....250.00
Many Fruits (Dugan), cup, marigold....25.00
Maple Leaf (Dugan), bowl, stemmed, 9″, amethyst....110.00

Maple Leaf (Dugan), creamer, blue....62.00
Maple Leaf (Dugan), sugar bowl, open; marigold....65.00
Maple Leaf (Dugan), tumbler, marigold....30.00
Marilyn (Millersburg), pitcher, rare, marigold....500.00
May Basket (English), basket, 7½″, marigold....46.00
Mayan (Millersburg), bowl, rare, 9″, green....125.00
Mayflower, compote, marigold....38.00
Mayflower, hat, peach opalescent....50.00
Melon Rib (Imperial), powder jar, marigold....35.00
Memphis (Northwood), bowl, 10″, marigold....65.00
Memphis (Northwood), bowl, 5″, green....50.00
Memphis (Northwood), cup, marigold....30.00
Milady (Fenton), pitcher, marigold....475.00
Miniature Bell, paperweight, 2½″ tall, marigold....45.00
Mirrored Lotus (Fenton), bonbon, marigold....50.00
Mirrored Lotus (Fenton), rose bowl, rare, blue....145.00
Mirrored Peacocks, tumbler, rare, marigold....90.00
Moonprint (English), banana boat, rare, marigold....135.00
Moonprint (English), bowl, 14″, marigold....80.00
Moonprint (English), candlesticks, rare, marigold, ea....50.00
Moonprint (English), jar, marigold....60.00
Morning Glory (Millersburg), tumbler, rare, marigold....950.00
Multi-Fruits & Flowers (Millersburg), cup, rare, marigold....40.00
Multi-Fruits & Flowers (Millersburg), tumbler, amethyst....850.00
Nell (Higbee), mug, marigold....65.00
Nesting Swan (Millersburg), bowl, tri-cornered, marigold....400.00
Nesting Swan (Millersburg), rose bowl, rare, marigold....1,600.00
Northern Star (Fenton), card tray, 6″, marigold....38.00
Northwood Jester's Cap, vase, marigold....40.00
Northwood's Nearcut, compote, amethyst....130.00
Northwood's Poppy, bowl, 7″, blue....58.00
Northwood's Poppy, pickle dish, oval, amethyst....58.00
Nu-Art Chrysanthemum (Imperial), plate, rare, green....950.00
Number 4 (Imperial), bowl, ftd, marigold....26.00
Octagon (Imperial), butter dish, marigold....85.00
Octagon (Imperial), creamer, marigold....48.00
Octagon (Imperial), decanter, complete, amethyst....250.00
Octagon (Imperial), goblet, marigold....65.00
Octagon (Imperial), pitcher, marigold....120.00
Octagon (Imperial), tumbler, green....44.00
Ohio Star (Millersburg), vase, rare, marigold....600.00
Open Flower (Dugan), bowl, flat or ftd, 7″, green....38.00
Open Rose (Imperial), bowl, flat, 9″, amethyst....40.00
Open Rose (Imperial), bowl, fruit; 7″, green....68.00
Open Rose (Imperial), plate, 9″, marigold....70.00
Optic & Buttons (Imperial), bowl, 5″, marigold....28.00
Optic & Buttons (Imperial), pitcher, sm, rare, marigold....185.00
Optic Flute (Imperial), bowl, 5″, marigold....25.00
Orange Peel (Westmoreland), cup, marigold....20.00
Orange Peel (Westmoreland), punch bowl, w/base, marigold....125.00
Orange Tree (Fenton), bowl, flat, 8″, blue....40.00
Orange Tree (Fenton), bowl, ftd, 5½″, green....30.00
Orange Tree (Fenton), compote, sm, marigold....32.00

Orange Tree (Fenton), plate, 8″, marigold....78.00
Orange Tree (Fenton), punch bowl, w/base, green....325.00
Orange Tree (Fenton), rose bowl, blue....54.00
Orange Tree (Fenton), tumbler, white....75.00
Orange Tree & Scroll (Fenton), pitcher, blue....385.00
Orange Tree Orchard (Fenton), pitcher, blue....400.00
Orange Tree Orchard (Fenton), tumbler, amethyst....48.00
Oriental Poppy (Northwood), pitcher, amethyst....600.00
Ostrich (Australian), cake stand, rare, marigold....160.00
Oval & Round (Imperial), bowl, 7″, amethyst....30.00
Oval & Round (Imperial), plate, 10″, marigold....58.00
Oval Star & Fan (Jenkins), rose bowl, marigold....46.00
Palm Beach (US Glass), banana bowl, marigold....100.00
Palm Beach (US Glass), bowl, 5″, marigold....30.00
Palm Beach (US Glass), pitcher, marigold....450.00
Palm Beach (US Glass), plate, 9″, rare, amethyst....250.00
Panelled Dandelion (Fenton), pitcher, amethyst....525.00
Panelled Hobnail (Dugan), vase, 5″, green....70.00
Panelled Tree Trunk (Dugan), vase, rare, 7″, green....110.00
Panels & Ball (Fenton), bowl, 11″, marigold....48.00
Pansy (Imperial), bowl, 8¾″, amethyst....48.00

Pansy (Imperial), dresser tray, marigold....56.00
Pansy (Imperial), plate, ruffled, rare, amethyst....90.00
Panther (Fenton), bowl, ftd, 10″, green....175.00

Pastel Panels (Imperial), tumbler, pastel . . . 70.00
Peach (Northwood), bowl, 9″, white . . . 210.00
Peach (Northwood), butter dish, white . . . 220.00

Peach (Northwood), spooner, marigold . . . 160.00
Peach & Pear (Dugan), banana bowl, amethyst . . . 95.00
Peacock, Fluffy (Fenton), pitcher, marigold . . . 300.00
Peacock (Millersburg), banana bowl, rare, amethyst . . . 1,350.00
Peacock (Millersburg), bowl, 5″, amethyst . . . 55.00
Peacock (Millersburg), plate, rare, 6″, marigold . . . 500.00
Peacock & Dahlia (Fenton), plate, rare, 8½″, blue . . . 210.00
Peacock & Urn (Fenton), bowl, 8½″, marigold . . . 50.00
Peacock & Urn (Fenton), goblet, rare, blue . . . 75.00
Peacock & Urn (Northwood), bowl, 5″, amethyst . . . 54.00
Peacock & Urn (Northwood), plate, rare, 6″, marigold . . . 250.00
Peacock at the Fountain (Northwood), bowl, 5″, blue . . . 45.00

Peacock at the Fountain (Northwood), butter dish, marigold . . . 125.00
Peacock at the Fountain (Northwood), compote, rare, blue . . . 245.00
Peacock at the Fountain (Northwood), pitcher, marigold . . . 270.00
Peacock Tail (Fenton), bowl, 4″, marigold . . . 28.00
Peacocks on the Fence (Northwood), plate, 9″, marigold . . . 195.00
Perfection (Millersburg), pitcher, rare, marigold . . . 3,800.00
Persian Garden (Dugan), bowl, berry; 10″, marigold . . . 140.00
Persian Garden (Dugan), bowl, fruit; w/base, amethyst . . . 270.00
Persian Garden (Dugan), bowl, ice cream; 11″, amethyst . . . 275.00
Persian Medallion (Fenton), bowl, 8¾″, amethyst . . . 50.00
Persian Medallion (Fenton), compote, blue . . . 68.00
Persian Medallion (Fenton), plate, 7″, amethyst . . . 80.00
Petal & Fan (Dugan), bowl, 5″, amethyst . . . 44.00
Petal & Fan (Dugan), plate, ruffled, 6″, blue . . . 165.00
Petals (Dugan), banana bowl, peach opalescent . . . 110.00
Petals (Dugan), bowl, 8¾″, marigold . . . 40.00
Peter Rabbit (Fenton), bowl, rare, 9″, blue . . . 775.00
Pine Cone (Fenton), bowl, 6″, marigold . . . 38.00
Pine Cone (Fenton), plate, rare, 8″, blue . . . 96.00
Pineapple, Heavy (Fenton); bowl, ftd, rare, 10″, blue . . . 350.00
Pineapple (English), butter dish, marigold . . . 85.00
Pineapple (English), creamer, marigold . . . 40.00
Pinwheel (Dugan), plate, 6½″, marigold . . . 58.00
Pinwheel (English), vase, 8″, marigold . . . 50.00
Plaid (Fenton), plate, rare, 9″, marigold . . . 125.00
Poinsettia (Imperial), pitcher, milk; green . . . 250.00
Pond Lily (Fenton), bonbon, marigold . . . 38.00
Pony (Dugan), bowl, 8½″, amethyst . . . 120.00
Poppy & Fish Net (Imperial), vase, rare, 6″, red . . . 550.00
Poppy Show (Imperial), vase, 12″, green . . . 650.00
Poppy Show (Northwood), bowl, 8½″, amethyst . . . 200.00
Potpourri (Millersburg), pitcher, milk; rare, marigold . . . 1,150.00
Premium (Imperial), bowl, 12″, amethyst . . . 90.00
Premium (Imperial), bowl, 8½″, marigold . . . 45.00
Pretty Panels (Northwood), pitcher, marigold . . . 120.00
Primrose (Millersburg), bowl, ruffled, 8¾″, green . . . 150.00
Princely Plumes, candle holder, amethyst . . . 260.00
Prism & Daisy Band (Imperial), bowl, 8″, marigold . . . 30.00
Prism & Daisy Band (Imperial), sugar bowl, marigold . . . 35.00
Prism Band (Fenton), tumbler, decorated, marigold . . . 32.00
Prisms (Westmoreland), compote, scarce, 5″, amethyst . . . 80.00
Propeller (Imperial), compote, marigold . . . 30.00
Quartered Block, sugar bowl, open; marigold . . . 50.00
Question Marks (Dugan), compote, marigold . . . 40.00
Quill (Dugan), pitcher, rare, marigold . . . 1,200.00
Quill (Dugan), tumbler, rare, amethyst . . . 450.00
Rambler Rose (Dugan), pitcher, marigold . . . 120.00
Ranger (Imperial), butter dish, marigold . . . 90.00
Ranger (Imperial), pitcher, milk; marigold . . . 165.00
Raspberry (Northwood), compote, marigold . . . 48.00
Raspberry (Northwood), pitcher, milk; amethyst . . . 150.00
Rays & Ribbons (Millersburg), plate, rare, amethyst . . . 1,100.00
Rex, pitcher, marigold . . . 365.00
Rib & Panel (Fenton), spittoon whimsey, marigold . . . 90.00
Ribbon & Block, lamp, complete, marigold . . . 500.00
Ribbon & Fern, atomizer, 7″, marigold . . . 75.00
Ribbon Tie (Fenton), plate, ruffled, 9″, blue . . . 140.00
Rising Sun (US Glass), tray, rare, blue . . . 400.00
Rising Sun (US Glass), tumbler, rare, marigold . . . 400.00
Robin (Imperial), pitcher, scarce, marigold . . . 275.00
Rock Crystal (McKee), punch bowl, w/base, amethyst . . . 590.00
Rococo (Imperial), base, 5½″ tall, green . . . 57.00
Rococo (Imperial), bowl, 5″, marigold . . . 26.00
Rood's Chocolates (Northwood), advertising plate, amethyst . . . 245.00
Rosalind (Millersburg), bowl, rare, 5″, green . . . 400.00
Rosalind (Millersburg), compote, ruffled, 8″, marigold . . . 750.00
Rose Columns (Millersburg), vase, rare, amethyst . . . 1,250.00
Rose Garden (Norway), bowl, 8¾″, amethyst . . . 65.00
Rose Garden (Norway), rose bowl, rare, amethyst . . . 175.00
Rose Pinwheel, bowl, rare, blue . . . 900.00
Rose Show (Northwood), bowl, 8¾″, marigold . . . 137.00
Rose Show Varient (Northwood), bowl, 8¾″, amethyst . . . 300.00
Rose Show Varient (Northwood), plate, 9″, blue . . . 350.00
Rose Spray (Fenton), compote, marigold . . . 60.00
Rose Wreath (Northwood), bonbon, rare, amethyst . . . 250.00
Rosettes (Northwood), bowl, ftd, 7″, amethyst . . . 95.00
Round-Up (Dugan), plate, rare, 9″, blue . . . 175.00
Royalty (Imperial), cup, marigold . . . 28.00
Ruffled Rib (Northwood), bowl, 8″, marigold . . . 46.00
S-Band (Australian), compote, amethyst . . . 65.00
S-Repeat (Dugan), cup, rare, amethyst . . . 185.00
S-Repeat (Dugan), toothpick holder, rare, amethyst . . . 40.00
Sailboats (Fenton), compote, marigold . . . 37.00
Sailboats (Fenton), goblet, blue . . . 40.00
Sailboats (Fenton), plate, blue . . . 260.00
Saint (English), candlestick, marigold, ea . . . 275.00
Scale Band (Fenton), pitcher, blue . . . 210.00
Scale Band (Fenton), plate, flat, 6½″, marigold . . . 40.00
Scales (Westmoreland), bonbon, marigold . . . 40.00
Scales (Westmoreland), plate, 6″, amethyst . . . 58.00
Scotch Thistle (Fenton), compote, marigold . . . 46.00
Scroll & Flower Panels (Imperial), vase, 10″, marigold . . . 90.00
Scroll Embossed (Imperial), bowl, 8½″, marigold . . . 36.00
Seacoast (Millersburg), pin tray, rare, green . . . 250.00

Seaweed (Millersburg), bowl, ice cream; 10½", amethyst.......450.00
Seaweed (Millersburg), plate, rare, 10", green................900.00
Shell & Balls, perfume, 2½", marigold.........................48.00
Shell & Jewel (Westmoreland), creamer, w/lid, marigold.........46.00
Sheraton (US Glass), sugar bowl, open; pastel..................80.00
Sheraton (US Glass), tumbler, pastel...........................48.00
Shrine (US Glass), toothpick holder, amethyst.................515.00
Silver & Gold, pitcher, marigold..............................100.00
Singing Birds (Northwood), bowl, 10", marigold.................52.00
Singing Birds (Northwood), pitcher, amethyst..................265.00

Singing Birds (Northwood), sugar bowl, open; green............155.00
Singing Birds (Northwood), tumbler, marigold...................45.00
Single Flower (Dugan), hat, amethyst...........................32.00
Six Petals (Dugan), plate, rare, amethyst.....................120.00
Six-Sided (Imperial), candlestick, marigold, ea...............125.00
Ski-Star (Dugan), bowl, 5", blue...............................50.00
Small Rib (Dugan), compote, marigold...........................35.00
Smooth Panels (Imperial), pitcher, marigold....................85.00
Smooth Panels (Imperial), vase, peach opalescent...............65.00
Smooth Rays (Northwood-Dugan), bowl, 6", amethyst..............48.00
Smooth Rays (Northwood-Dugan), compote, marigold...............36.00
Smooth Rays (Westmoreland), bowl, flat, 7", green..............47.00
Snow Fancy (McKee), creamer, marigold..........................47.00
Soda Gold (Imperial), bowl, 9", marigold.......................45.00
Soda Gold (Imperial), tumbler, marigold........................40.00
Soda Gold Spears (Dugan), bowl, 4½", marigold..................26.00
Soda Gold Spears (Dugan), plate, 9", marigold..................50.00
Soutache (Dugan), bowl, 10", peach opalescent..................85.00
Souvenir Vase (US Glass), rare, 6½", amethyst.................120.00
Spiral (Imperial), candlestick, marigold, ea...................55.00
Split Diamond (English), butter dish, scarce, marigold.........70.00
Split Diamond (English), creamer, sm, marigold.................36.00
Spring Opening (Millersburg), plate, rare, 6½", amethyst......260.00
Springtime (Northwood), bowl, 5", amethyst.....................50.00
Springtime (Northwood), pitcher, rare, green..................950.00
Springtime (Northwood), sugar bowl, marigold..................135.00
Square Diamond (English), vase, rare, blue....................125.00
Stag & Holly (Fenton), bowl, ftd, 9", green...................190.00
Stag & Holly (Fenton), plate, ftd, 9", amethyst...............450.00
Star (English), coaster, marigold..............................35.00
Star & Fan (English), cordial set, marigold...................750.00
Star & File (Imperial), plate, 6", marigold....................65.00
Star & File (Imperial), rose bowl, marigold....................65.00
Star & File (Imperial), tumbler, marigold.....................140.00
Star & File (Imperial), vase, w/hdl, marigold..................50.00
Star Center (Imperial), plate, 9", pastel......................90.00
Star Medallion (Imperial), butter dish, marigold...............85.00
Star Medallion (Imperial), celery tray, marigold...............42.00
Star Medallion (Imperial), custard cup, marigold...............20.00
Star Medallion (Imperial), goblet, marigold....................45.00
Star Spray (Imperial), bowl, 7", marigold......................28.00
Starfish (Dugan), compote, amethyst............................50.00
Stippled Diamond Swag (English), compote, blue.................56.00
Stippled Flower (Dugan), bowl, 8½", peach opalescent...........60.00
Stippled Rambler Rose (Dugan), bowl, nut; ftd, marigold........60.00
Stippled Rays (Fenton), compote, amethyst......................40.00
Stippled Rays (Fenton), creamer, blue..........................35.00
Stippled Rays (Imperial), creamer, stemmed, green..............46.00
Stippled Rays (Northwood), bowl, 8", marigold..................46.00
Stork (Imperial), vase, marigold...............................48.00
Stork & Rushes (Dugan), butter dish, rare, amethyst...........165.00
Stork & Rushes (Dugan), sugar bowl, open; rare, marigold......100.00
Stork & Rushes (Dugan), tumbler, marigold......................30.00
Stork & Rushes (Imperial), basket, hdld, marigold..............40.00
Stork ABC (Imperial), child's plate, 7½", marigold.............67.00
Strawberry (Millersburg), bowl, scarce, 8", marigold..........110.00
Strawberry (Millersburg), compote, rare, amethyst.............175.00
Strawberry (Northwood), plate, 9", green.......................95.00
Strawberry Intaglio (Northwood), bowl, 9½", marigold...........50.00
Sunflower (Northwood), bowl, 8½", amethyst.....................65.00
Sunk Diamond Band (US Glass), pitcher, rare, marigold.........145.00
Sunk Diamond Band (US Glass), tumbler, rare, marigold..........50.00
Superb Drape (Northwood), vase, rare, aqua opalescent.........875.00
Sweetheart (Cambridge), cookie jar, rare, green...............695.00
Swirl (Northwood), pitcher, marigold..........................150.00
Swirl (Northwood), tumbler, green..............................65.00
Swirl Hobnail (Millersburg), rose bowl, rare, amethyst........300.00
Swirl Hobnail (Millersburg), vase, rare, 7", green............250.00
Swirl Variant (Imperial), bowl, 7", marigold...................28.00
Swirl Variant (Imperial), plate, 6", green.....................50.00
Swirled Flute (Fenton), vase, 7", marigold.....................28.00
Taffeta Lustre (Fostoria), candlestick, rare, amethyst, pr....300.00
Tejas Headdress (Westmoreland), punch cup, marigold............40.00
Ten Mums (Fenton), bowl, ftd, rare, 9", marigold..............295.00

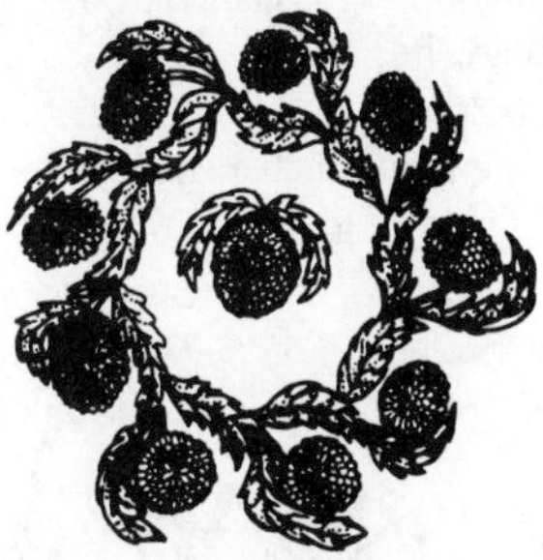

Ten Mums (Fenton), pitcher, rare, blue........................875.00
Ten Mums (Fenton), plate, rare, 10", green....................375.00
Thin Rib (Fenton), candlestick, marigold, pr...................60.00
Thistle (Fenton), compote, marigold............................46.00
Thistle & Lotus (Fenton), bowl, 7", marigold...................40.00
Thistle & Thorn (English), bowl, ftd, 6", marigold.............46.00
Three Diamonds (Dugan), vase, 6", marigold.....................30.00
Three Fruits (Northwood), bowl, 9", blue.......................56.00
Three Fruits (Northwood), plate, round, 9", amethyst..........100.00
Three Row (Imperial), vase, rare, amethyst....................395.00
Three-In-One (Imperial), bowl, 4½", marigold...................18.00
Thunderbird (Australian), bowl, 5", amethyst...................45.00
Tiger Lily (Imperial), pitcher, marigold......................130.00

Tiger Lily (Imperial), tumbler, green........................38.00
Tiny Hobnail, lamp, marigold...............................95.00
Tornado (Northwood), vase, plain, amethyst.................250.00
Tree Bark (Imperial), pickle jar, 7½″, marigold................35.00
Tree Bark (Imperial), pitcher, w/lid, marigold.................70.00
Tree of Life (Imperial), plate, 7½″, marigold..................37.00
Triands (English), celery vase, marigold......................55.00
Triplets (Northwood), bowl, 6″, green.......................42.00
Tulip (Millersburg), compote, rare, 9″, marigold..............650.00
Tulip & Cane (Imperial), goblet, rare, 8-oz, marigold...........62.00
Tumble-Up (Fenton-Imperial), plain, complete, marigold........55.00
Twins (Imperial), bowl, 5″, marigold........................24.00
Two Flowers (Fenton), bowl, ftd, 5″, marigold................28.00
Two Fruits (Fenton), bowl, divided, scarce, 5½″, amethyst......85.00
Two Fruits (Northwood), spooner, rare, blue.................450.00
Urn, vase, 9″, marigold.....................................40.00
US Diamond Block (US Glass), shakers, marigold, pr..........60.00
Valentine (Northwood), bowl, rare, 5″, amethyst..............125.00
Venetian (Cambridge), butter dish, rare, marigold.............600.00
Victorian, bowl, rare, 12″, amethyst.......................175.00
Vineyard (Dugan), tumbler, marigold........................20.00
Vining Twigs (Dugan), hat, marigold........................30.00
Vintage (Fenton), bowl, 8″, blue...........................48.00
Vintage (Fenton), plate, 7″, marigold......................100.00
Vintage (Fenton), rose bowl, blue..........................57.00
Vintage Banded (Dugan), mug, marigold.....................30.00
Vintage Banded (Dugan), pitcher, marigold..................200.00
Waffle Block (Imperial), basket, hdld, 10″, marigold...........47.00
Waffle Block (Imperial), cup, marigold.......................18.00
Waffle Block (Imperial), sugar bowl, open; marigold............60.00
Waffle Block (Imperial), vase, 11″, marigold..................40.00
Water Lily (Fenton), bowl, ftd, 10″, marigold.................40.00
Water Lily & Cattails (Fenton), bowl, 5″, blue................50.00
Water Lily & Cattails (Fenton), pitcher, marigold.............295.00
Water Lily & Cattails (Fenton), toothpick whimsey, marigold.....50.00

Water Lily & Cattails (Fenton), tumbler, marigold.............95.00
Water Lily & Cattails (Northwood), tumbler, amethyst.........165.00
Weeping Cherry (Dugan), bowl, w/flat base, amethyst...........75.00
Western Daisy (Westmoreland), bowl, marigold................35.00
Wheat (Northwood), bowl, w/lid, rare, amethyst............2,000.00
Whirling Hobstar (Imperial), punch bowl, w/base, marigold......90.00
Whirling Star (Imperial), compote, marigold..................55.00
Whirling Star (Imperial), punch bowl, w/base, marigold........135.00
White Oak, tumbler, rare, marigold.........................350.00
Wide Panel (Northwood-Fenton-Imperial), cup, red...........975.00
Wide Panel (Northwood-Fenton-Imperial), goblet, marigold......36.00
Wide Panel (Northwood-Fenton-Imperial), vase, blue...........40.00
Wide Panel (US Glass), salt, marigold.......................38.00
Wide Rib (Dugan), vase, marigold...........................38.00
Wild Fern (Australian), compote, amethyst..................165.00
Wild Loganberry (Westmoreland), wine, marigold..............85.00
Wild Rose (Millersburg), lamp, sm, rare, marigold............600.00
Wild Rose (Northwood), bowl, flat, 8″, green.................42.00
Wild Strawberry (Dugan), plate, rare, 7″, amethyst............285.00
Wildflower (Millersburg), compote, ruffled, rare, marigold......900.00
Windflower (Dugan), bowl, 8½″, marigold....................36.00

Windflower (Dugan), nappy, hdld, peach opalescent...........145.00
Windmill (Imperial), bowl, 9″, green........................37.00
Windmill (Imperial), pickle dish, marigold....................20.00

Windmill (Imperial), pitcher, green.........................150.00
Wine & Roses (Fenton), pitcher, cider; scarce, marigold.......195.00
Wishbone (Northwood), bowl, flat, 8″, marigold...............50.00

Wishbone (Northwood), pitcher, rare, green.................850.00
Wishbone & Spades (Dugan), bowl, 8½″, amethyst............90.00
Wishbone & Spades (Dugan), plate, rare, 10½″, amethyst......750.00
Wisteria (Northwood), bank whimsey, rare, white.............800.00
Wreath of Roses (Dugan), rose bowl, marigold................45.00
Wreath of Roses (Fenton), compote, blue....................42.00
Wreathed Cherry (Dugan), bowl, oval, 10½″, amethyst.........135.00

Wreathed Cherry (Dugan), butter dish, marigold 95.00
Wreathed Cherry (Dugan), pitcher, white 775.00
Zig Zag (Fenton), tumbler, decorated, blue 50.00
Zig Zag (Millersburg), bowl, ruffled, 9½″, amethyst 325.00
Zipper Loop (Imperial), hand lamp, rare, marigold 425.00
Zippered Heart (Imperial), bowl, 5″, marigold 37.00

Carousel Figures

Who can forget the dazzle of the merry-go-round--lights blinking, animals prancing proudly by to the waltzes that bellowed from the band organ . . .

Gustav Dentzel, a German woodworker, created one of the first carousels in America in 1867. By the turn of the century, his animals had evolved from horses with a military bearing to fanciful creatures in various postures with garlands of flowers, exotic saddles, and other adornment. Dentzel was followed in the business by his son, William, and both are noted for the exacting perfection of their carving and painting. The Philadelphia Toboggan Company, established in 1903, is famous today for its superior chariot designs. In 1901, Marcus Charles Illions formed his company, M.C. Illions and Sons. Illions carvings became more intricate with the growth of his company, and those from the twenties are generally valued more highly than those from between 1901 and 1910. The largest carousels were produced by the Artistic Carousel Manufacturers of Brooklyn, Harry Goldstein and Solomon Stein. Charles Carmel and Daniel Muller are both exquisite carvers whose work is today very highly regarded. Other builders whose works are highly valued (though much less intricate) are The Herschell–Spillman Company; American Merry-Go-Round and Novelty Company; Charles Dare of the New York Carousel Manufacturing Company; and Charles Parker.

Until the 1930s, carousels were found in nearly every fair and amusement park in the country. One by one, as they fell into disrepair, many have been dismantled and junked, or sold at auction. Today, these hand carved creatures are respected examples of American folk art, and often bring prices well into the thousands. Price is based on a number of factors, the most important of which are: carver (with Dentzel, Looff, PTC, Carmel, Illions, and Muller the most valued), type of animal (some specie are rarely encountered), and intricacy of carving. Also to be considered are size, wood and paint condition, where the figure was located on the carousel, whether it stands or jumps, and in some cases its age. Because there are so many factors to consider, and since no two figures are identical, exact pricing is difficult. The values listed below are for reference in order to provide a better understanding of the relative dollar value.

Be aware that newly-made copies are being sold as originals, and as the market continues to rise the practice will most likely accelerate. In the listings that follow, condition is graded E for excellent, VG for very good, G for Good, and F for fair. Since all carousel animals have seen many years of use, none can be considered mint. An animal that has been professionally restored or in original paint with very little wear has been graded excellent. Fair condition would indicate one with a good deal of wear, seams separating, and the presence of nails and/or screws and bolts from prior repairs. Condition can affect the price of an animal as much as $3,000 for the more elaborate pieces and up to 50% for the lower priced animals.

Authority Tobin Fraley has compiled a lovely book *The Carousel Animal*, complete with beautiful full-page, full-color illustrations. His address is listed in the Directory under California.

Key:
OR—outside row
PP —park paint
PR—paint removed
PTC— Philadelphia Toboggan Company

Caramel outside row jumper, ca 1914, excellent restored condition, $13,500.00. (Photo by G. Sinick)

Figures from Traveling Rides

These are the types of figures one is most likely to find in an antique store or flea market. Horses for these machines were produced in great numbers, and are generally much more simply designed than those found on the larger carousels. They are usually in worse condition, due to constant use and the dismantling and traveling to which they were subjected.

AH, sm jumper, ca 1925, PP, F 1,100.00
Allan Herschell Co, sm jumper, ca 1925, PP, F 1,100.00
Armitage Herschell Co, med jumper, ca 1890, PP, F 2,400.00
CW Parker Amusement Co, med jumper, ca 1915, PP, F 1,800.00
Herschell-Spillman, sm jumper, ca 1910, PP, G 2,400.00
Mexican, sm jumper, ca 1965, aged pnt, G 1,000.00
Spillman Engineering Corp, med jumper, ca 1925, PP, G 2,600.00

Permanent Location Carousels

Carmel-Borelli, outside row stander, ca 1911, PP, G 13,800.00
Charles Carmel, middle row jumper, ca 1914, PR, VG 7,200.00
Charles Carmel, outside row jumper, ca 1914, rstr, EX 13,500.00
Dentzel, inside row jumper, ca 1912, PP, G 4,600.00
Dentzel, lion w/figure, ca 1915, PP, G 29,000.00
Dentzel, middle row jumper, ca 1912, PR, VG 6,800.00
Dentzel, middle row prancer, ca 1895, PP, G 5,200.00
Dentzel, outside row stander, ca 1895, orig pnt, VG 12,750.00
Dentzel, outside row stander, ca 1922, PR, G 12,500.00
Dentzel, outside row stander w/figure, ca 1905, rstr, EX 21,000.00

Dentzel, rabbit, middle row, ca 1907, PP, G..............14,000.00
Herschell-Spillman, outside row jumper, ca 1912, PP, G.....4,500.00
Herschell-Spillman, rooster, middle row, 1914, rstr, VG......5,400.00
Illions, inside row jumper, ca 1904, PR, VG...............3,400.00
Illions, outside row jumper, ca 1904, PP, G................7,800.00
Illions, outside row jumper, ca 1924, PP, G...............12,250.00
Illions, outside row stander w/figure, ca 1924, rstr, EX......17,500.00
Looff, camel, OR jumper w/figure, ca 1915, orig pnt, VG....14,250.00
Looff, middle row jumper, ca 1915, PR, VG...............6,500.00
Looff, middle row prancer, ca 1890, PR, VG...............4,500.00
Looff, outside row jumper w/figure, ca 1914, PR, G........16,500.00
Muller Brothers, inside row jumper, ca 1912, PP, G.........5,400.00
Muller Brothers, OR stander, military, ca 1910, PR, VG....22,500.00
PTC, inside row jumper, ca 1906, orig pnt, VG............4,400.00
PTC, lion w/eagle & PTC sgn, ca 1909, PP, G............27,500.00
PTC, middle row jumper, ca 1924, PP, G.................6,200.00
PTC, outside row stander, ca 1932, PR, VG..............13,200.00
PTC, outside row stander w/PTC sgn, ca 1926, PP, G......18,000.00
Stein & Goldstein, middle row stander, ca 1912, PR, G......7,200.00
Stein & Goldstein, OR jumper, armored, ca 1914, PP, G....18,500.00

Carpet Balls

Carpet balls are glazed china spheres, decorated with intersecting lines or other simple designs, that were used for indoor games in the British Isles during the early 1800s.

Mint condition examples are rare; listings are for those with minimal damage.

Pink w/pink dots in wht stars, 3¼″.........................70.00
Pink w/wht sponging.....................................85.00
Plaid, blk/red/yel on wht, 3⅛″ dia..........................95.00
Red/wht stick spatter stars, 3½″............................85.00
Wht bull's eye w/in wide bl band w/in 2 bl stripes, 2″..........65.00
Yel w/yel dots in frilly wht reserves, 3¼″, EX.................70.00

Cartoon Art

Collectors of cartoon art are interested in many forms of original art--animation cels; sports, political or editorial cartoons; syndicated comic strip panels; and caricature.

To produce even a short animated cartoon strip, hundreds of original drawings are required, each showing the characters in slightly advancing positions. Called 'cels' because those made prior to the 1950s were made from a celluloid material, collectors often pay hundreds of dollars for a frame from a favorite movie. Background paintings, model sheets, storyboards, and preliminary sketches are also collectible--so are comic book drawings executed in India ink, and signed by the artist. Daily 'funnies' originals, especially the earlier ones portraying super heroes, and Sunday comic strips, the early as well as the later ones, are collected. Cartoon art has become recognized and valued as a novel yet valid form of contemporary art.

When no condition is indicated, items listed below are assumed to be in mint condition.

Key:
ab—airbrushed wc—watercolor

Animation Cel—Full Color

Cinderella, 4 mice w/needle & thread, WDS, 7x8″, EX........385.00
Fantasia, satyrs & unicorns, ab bkground, sgn WD, 11½x8″..1,210.00

Celluloid, from 'The Pointer,' Mickey Mouse & Pluto, Walt Disney, 1939, 10½″ x 8½″, $800.00.

Goofy, threatened by mousetrap, wc, sgn WD, 1940, 12x9″...1,210.00
Ichabod & Mr Toad, 2 men in early auto, WDS, 1949, 2½x3″...82.00
Lady & the Tramp, Lady, cartoon color, WDS, 4x5″, EX......250.00
Peter Pan, Smee nose-to-nose w/pirate, WDS, 7x7½″, EX......363.00
Pinocchio, Jiminy Cricket behind 8-ball, ab, 1939, 10x8″.....1,210.00
Pinocchio, w/Kossack Marionettes, ab bkground, 1939, 8½″....935.00
Sleeping Beauty, Maleficent w/sceptre, WDS, 4x7″, EX........500.00
Snow White, kisses Grumpy, wc bkground, WDE, 1937, 9½x8″.935.00
Snow White, witch in boat, ab bkground, 1937, WDE, 12x10″.880.00
Snow White, 2 sleeping deer, ab bkground, WDE,'37, 9x6½″.1,430.00
Terrytoons, princess/haunted woods, sgn Craig, '40s, 11x8″....165.00

Animation Drawing

Cock o' the Walk, Hick Rooster, pencil, 1935, 5½x5½″, EX....55.00
Donald Duck, pencil, looking over shoulder, '30s, WDS, 4″.....63.00

Comic Books

Conan the Barbarian #140, pg 5-8, ink, J Buscema, 10x15″.....63.00
Felix the Cat #52, pg 3, ink, Otto Messmer, 12x18″, EX.......50.00
Incredible Hulk #250, pg 9 & 26, ink, Buscema, 10x15″, EX...10.00

Daily Newspaper Comic Strip

Barney Google, 12/11/37, ink, Billy De Beck, 4x16″, EX......135.00
Blondie, 11/5/47, ink/shading, Chic Young, 5x18″, EX........105.00
Bringing Up Father, 3/31/38, ink/shading, McManus, 4″, VG....63.00
Dick Tracy, 11/6/68, ink, Chester Gould, 5x16″, EX...........57.00
Donald Duck, 12/3/53, ink/shading, A Taliaferro, 5x19″, EX....82.00
Freckles & Friends, 9/18/56, India ink, Blosser, 5x16″, EX.....16.00
Orphan Annie, 6/21/73, India ink, Blaisdell, 5x17″, EX........17.00
Thimble Theatre, 6/5/35, Toar/Popeye, ink, EC Segar, 5x20″...279.00

Storyboard

Alice in Wonderland, tempera, Rabbit/Cards, WDS, 6x7″, EX..100.00
Bambi, charcoal/litho crayon, Wise Owl, WDS, 4x5″, EX.......55.00
Mickey's Garden, 14 insects (5 sketchy), WDS, 7x11″, EX......44.00
Three Little Pigs, pencil, Practical & others, WDS, 2½x5″......96.00

Sunday Newspaper Comics

Archie, 3/11/51, India ink, Bob Montana, 14½x20½", EX......100.00
Katzenjammer Kids, 3/2/30, India ink, HH Kner, 15x16½", EX.157.00
Tim Tyler's Luck, 5/14/44, India ink, Tim/Spud, Young, EX.....45.00

Cartoon Books

'Books of cartoons' were printed during the first decade of the 20th century, and remained popular until the advent of the modern comic book in the late thirties. Cartoon books, printed in both color and black and white, were merely reprints of current newspaper comic strips. The books, ranging from thirty to seventy pages and in sizes from 3½" x 8" up to 11" x 17", were usually bound with cardboard covers, and were often distributed as premiums in exchange for coupons saved from the daily paper. One of the largest of the companies who printed these books was Cupples and Leon, producers of nearly half of the two hundred titles on record. Among the most popular sellers were Mutt and Jeff, Bringing Up Father, and Little Orphan Annie.

When no condition is indicated, the items listed below are assumed to be in excellent condition.

Barney Google & His Faithful Nag Spark Plug................50.00
Best of Blondie, McKay, 1944.............................15.00
Bringing Up Father, 1st series, 1919.........................50.00
Bringing Up Father, 1917..................................45.00
Bringing Up Father, 2nd series, Cupples & Leon.............45.00
Bringing Up Father, 5th Series, Cupples & Leon, 1921.........35.00
Jazz Era, The; Ding Darling, CW, 1920.....................10.00
Little Orphan Annie, #1, EX................................55.00
Little Orphan Annie in the Circus, #2, Cupples & Leon, EX....50.00
Mutt & Jeff, #15, EX......................................35.00
Mutt & Jeff, #6, 1919, NM..................................55.00
Nebbs, by Sol Hess, Cupples & Leon Co, 1928, EX...........35.00
Popeye, Saalfield, 1934, NM..............................150.00
Reg'lar Fellers, soft cover, Cupples & Leon.................35.00
Tailspin Tommy, 1932......................................75.00
Toonerville Trolley, 1921...................................65.00
Winnie Winkle, #2...20.00

Cash Registers

Cash registers are being restored, rebuilt, and used as they were originally intended, in businesses ranging from eating establishments to antique stores. Their brass and marble construction has made them almost impervious to aging, and with just a bit of polish and shine they bring a bit of the grand Victorian era into modern times.

Antique cash registers are categorized as either restored or unrestored. A restored register is one where the cabinet has been stripped, polished, and lacquered; indicators are free of dust, dirt and visible signs of wear; key stems are rust-free, plated or painted; and key checks and rings are new, used, or originals. The drawer has been stripped and revarnished, and the rails are in good condition. All mechanisms are completely reworked, broken parts are replaced, oiled, and working perfectly.

Prices for registers in unrestored condition vary greatly. Unrestored registers are classed as either working or non-working. Values for those with missing major parts are much lower. In the listings that follow, values are consistent with machines in excellent, unrestored condition.

National #1, brass.......................................1,000.00
National #12, brass..750.00
National #130, w/orig amount purchase sign...................600.00
National #2, brass...500.00
National #211, brass.......................................600.00
National #215, fleur-de-lis w/orig 'Amount Purchased' sign.....650.00
National #216, w/sign.......................................675.00
National #238..375.00
National #247, registers up to $7, brass.....................350.00
National #250, orig...550.00
National #3, brass...500.00
National #310, orig...500.00
National #312; 316; 317....................................500.00
National #313, EX orig condition, w/sign.....................550.00
National #313, good orig condition, w/sign...................450.00
National #313, 100% prof restored condition, w/sign........1,400.00
National #324, 12"..300.00
National #327, EX base.....................................750.00
National #332, EX orig condition, w/sign.....................300.00
National #332, good orig condition, w/sign...................200.00
National #332, 100% prof restored condition, w/sign........1,000.00
National #336, keyed from 1¢ to $3, brass...................250.00
National #347 2-2, 2 drawers...............................500.00
National #349, brass, dolphin design........................300.00
National #35, EX orig condition, w/sign......................400.00
National #35, good orig condition, w/sign....................325.00
National #35, 100% prof restored condition, w/sign.........1,200.00
National #356G, brass......................................300.00
National #4, brass...900.00
National #4, wood..1,750.00
National #40, brass..300.00
National #441, crank.......................................400.00
National #442, crank.......................................400.00
National #452, brass crank..................................400.00
National #452E, brass, electric..............................500.00
National #47¼, wood.......................................950.00
National #5, fleur-de-lis design.............................800.00
National #50, brass..550.00
National #522EL2C, brass...................................750.00
National #542-4..475.00
National #542E, single drawer electric.......................650.00
National #552-5F, floor model, orig sign..................1,200.00
National #592EL9F, floor model............................1,200.00
National #6, wood base, w/orig amount purchase sign.........900.00
National #8, brass...500.00
National #92, bronze.......................................750.00

Cast Iron

In the mid-1800s, the cast iron industry was raging in the United States. It was recognized as a medium extremely adaptable for uses ranging from ornamental architectural filigree to actual building construction. It could be cast into any conceivable design from a mold that could be reproduced over and over, at a relatively small cost. It could be painted to give an entirely versatile appearance. Furniture with openwork designs of grapevines and leaves and intricate lacy scrollwork was cast for gardens, as well as inside use. Figural doorstops of every sort, bootjacks, trivets, and a host of other useful and decorative items were made before the 'ferromania' had run its course.

Items listed below are for examples in excellent condition.

Alligator or salamander, worn gr rpt w/gold beneath, 16".......70.00
Amish man & woman, worn naturalistic pnt, 8", pr...........180.00

Bench, reticulated fern fronds, 1850's, pr. 9,075.00
Bird, stylized flat profile, simple, 5″. 50.00
Bust, Geo Washington in relief, 15¾″. 95.00
Can opener, fish form, ball end, ca 1800s, 5¾″. 60.00
Can opener, stylized cow, curved tail hdl, lower jaw blade. 25.00
Cardinal, rpt, 5½″. 65.00
Cat, recumbent, head raised, good detail, 2¾″. 55.00
Cookie board, swan, oval, 4¾x5⅞″. 135.00
Dog, made in 2 sections, on wood mt, rpr, 30″ L. 325.00
Dog, recumbent, head raised, good detail, on plinth, 7″ L. 60.00
Dog, sitting, perky ears/glass eyes, old worn wht pnt, 23″. . . . 4,500.00
Eagle, wings spread, head low, architectural, 30″ W. 600.00
Eagle, wings spread, on rock: World Freedom, Shonnard, 10″. . . 65.00
Eagle on ball, spread wings/N on breast/architectural, 10″. 115.00
Gate, orig tree trunk poles, branch/foliage motif, 53x43″. 950.00
Heron, worn pnt, late 1800s, 21″. 245.00
Hitching post finial, circus horse head, 13¾″. 325.00
Horse, circular base, 5½″. 20.00
Kettle, gypsy; w/lid, 10¼″. 35.00
Kettle, iron bail, 3 legs, 9x11″. 35.00
Kettle shelf, reticulated w/thistles, 3-leg, rpt, rnd, 10″. 55.00
Lion, open legs, good detail, 9¼″. 85.00
Muffin pan, makes 8 cakes, mk N Waterman, 1859, 17x14¼″. . . 55.00
Muffin pan, 2 ea: hearts/stars/circles/scallops, Dec 1870. . . . . 80.00
Ornament, bull, from butcher shop rack, on rod, 8x5x1″. 125.00
Pan, 3 short legs, rim hdl, 9″ dia. 25.00
Plant stand, 12 disk arms, 19th C, 34″. 5,500.00
Plate, scalloped rim, 9½″. 75.00
Porringer, lacy tab hdl, sgn Kenrick, 4½″ dia. 85.00
Pot, Kenrick, straight hdl, w/lid, 1-qt. 95.00
Pump, pitcher; remains of orig striped decor, Ramsey Co. 35.00
Rabbit, sitting on haunches, rpt, 11½″. 110.00
Rack, butcher's; saw/knife/etc atop 8-hook bar/cow finial. 490.00
Sheaf of grain, old worn pnt, 7½″. 60.00
Shelf, folds, grapevines/leaves/flowers, pat 1868, 12x10″. 120.00
Shelf bracket, scroll & tulip detail, 8x9¾″, pr. 35.00
Spittoon, turtle form, step on head, lid raises. 195.00
Star for building top, open center, 10x10″. 65.00
Stork, old red/wht rpt w/gray on wing tips, rusty, 12½″. 45.00
Stove foot, grotesque face w/wing mask, 8½″. 20.00
Stove plate, 2 stylized tulips, German inscription, 21x23″. 275.00
Tea kettle, fits griddle, KY Stove Co. 30.00
Tea kettle, hdl/hinged lid dtd 1875, 8-lbs. 100.00
Urn, floral/foliage, 2-pc sq base, 31″. 240.00
Urn, foliage, high step base, 4-part, pnt layers, 41x37″. 425.00

Castor Sets

Castor sets became popular during the early years of the 18th century, and continued to be used through the late Victorian era. Their purpose was to hold various condiments for table use. The most common type was a circular arrangement with a center handle on a revolving pedestal base that held matching shakers, a mustard pot, and oil and vinegar bottles. Some had extras; a few were equipped with a bell for calling the servant. Frames were made of silver or plated, and some were of pewter. Though most bottles were of pressed glass, some of the designs were cut, and occasionally colored glass with enameled decorations was used.

To maintain authenticity and value, castor sets should have matching bottles. Prices listed below are for those in frames with plating that is in excellent to near mint condition.

Blown, 5-bottle; glass stand. 150.00
Breakfast, 3 blown Gothic Arch bottles; Rogers fr. 50.00

Daisy and Button, blue, matching bottles and jars in glass stand, $125.00.

Breakfast, 3 cut bottles; ftd SP stand w/ornate hdls. 65.00
Call bell, 6-bottle; floral/butterfly eng skirt, Wilcox. 350.00
Child's, 4 Am Shield bottles; revolving pewter fr, 9″. 165.00
Cut glass bottles; Geo III, Paul Storr silver fr w/leaf ft. 2,200.00
Daisy & Button, 3-bottle/toothpick; pressed glass stand. 95.00
Daisy w/Panel, 4-bottle, amber; amber glass holder. 115.00
Etched decor, 5-bottle; revolving SP holder. 195.00
Revolving, Paneled Dia Cross, 6 bl bottles; Meriden emb fr. . . . 225.00
Revolving, 4 blown Gothic Arch bottles; pewter fr. 115.00
Revolving, 4 floral gray cut bottles; eng skirt, rnd hdl. 110.00
Revolving, 6 blown bottles w/floral etch; sgn Hartford fr. 185.00
Revolving, 6-bottle; fr w/eng skirt, bird motif hdl, 18½″. 225.00
Ribbon stripe, bl satin glass, 5-bottle; SP fr. 245.00
Rubena, 4-bottle; SP fr. 195.00
Tree of Life, 5-bottle; orig stoppers/lids, pewter holder. 150.00
3-bottle, 1 w/glass stopper, 2 w/pewter tops; wire fr. 45.00

Catalina Island

Catalina Island pottery was made on the island of the same name, which is about twenty-six miles off the coast of Los Angeles. The pottery was started in 1927 at Pebbly Beach, by Wm Wrigley, Jr., who was instrumental in developing and using the native clays. Its principal product was brick and tile to be used for construction on the island. It became very popular and was soon being shipped to the mainland as well. Garden pieces were produced, then vases, bookends, lamps, ash trays, novelty items, and finally dinnerware.

Some of the pottery was handmade; some was made in molds. Most pieces are marked Catalina Island or Catalina, with a printed incised stamp, or handwritten with a pointed tool. Cast items were sometimes marked in the mold; a paper label was also used.

The color of the clay can help to identify approximately when a piece was made: 1927 to 1932--brown to red clay; 1931 to 1832--an experimental period with various colors; 1932 to 1937--mainly white clay, but tan to brown were used occasionally.

When no condition is indicated, the items listed below are assumed to be in mint condition.

Key:
C—Catalina
CI—Catalina Island

Charger, orange seahorse on bl, mk C, 12″ 185.00
Mug, bl, red clay, mk C, 5″, VG 25.00
Mug, matt gr, hand thrown, red clay body, early, lg 65.00
Pitcher, wine; bl, imp C, 8″, VG 35.00
Plate, classical lady, wht on bl, brn clay, CI, 14″ 85.00
Urn/oil jar, glossy mottled aqua, incised mk C, 18x12″, VG 250.00
Vase, florist's, wht clay, sgn CI, 7¾″ 40.00
Vase, ringed, Descanso gr, CI, 8″ 46.00

Catalogs

Catalogs are not only intriguing to collect on their own merit, but for the collector with a specific interest, they are often the only remaining source of background information available, and as such offer a wealth of otherwise unrecorded data.

The mail order industry can be traced as far back as the mid-1800s. Even before Aaron Montgomery Ward began his career in 1872, Laacke and Joys of Wisconsin, and the Orvis Company of Vermont, both dealers in sporting goods, had been well established for many years. The E.C. Allen Company sold household necessities and novelties by mail on a broad scale in the 1870s. By the end of the Civil War, sewing machines, garden seed, musical instruments, even medicine, were available from catalogs. In the 1880s, Macy's of New York issued a 127-page catalog; Sears and Spiegel followed suit in about 1890.

Craft and art supply catalogs were first available about 1880, and covered such varied fields as china painting, stenciling, wood burning, brass embossing, hair weaving, and shellcraft. Today, some collectors confine their interests not only to craft catalogs in general, but often to one subject only. Examples may range from $1 to as much as $25 for the larger, color-illustrated versions.

A 20th century enterprise, Johnson, Smith & Company, has published catalogs since 1914. Their merchandise tends toward books and novelties, such as magic tricks, magnetic lodestones, fireworks, and puzzles. By the late twenties their catalogs contained nearly eight hundred pages in both soft and hard cover editions; they retained this large size until late in the forties. The company still exists, and continues to offer novelties similar to those from earlier times. Reproductions of their 1929 catalog are currently available.

For a more thorough study of the subject, we recommend *American Trade Catalogs*, by Don Fredgant, available at your local bookstore and public library. When no condition is indicated, the items listed below are assumed to be in excellent condition.

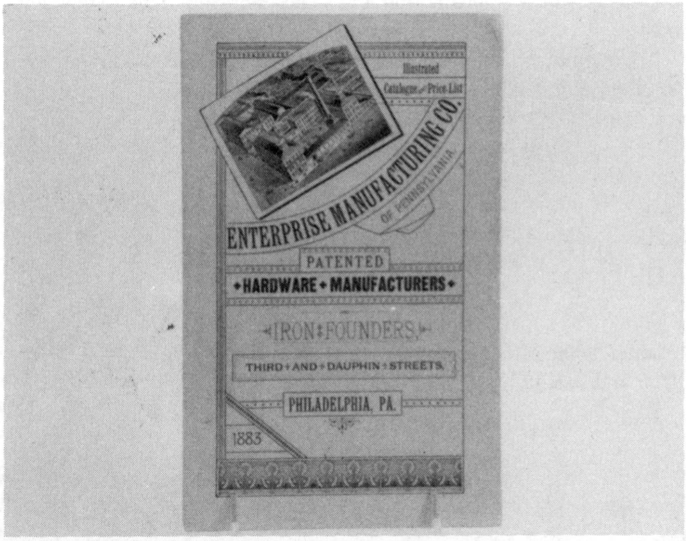

Enterprise Manufacturing, hardware products, 1883, 9″ x 6″, $65.00.

Acme Road Machinery, Frankfort, NY, 1927, illus, 45 pg 16.00
Aladdin, Bay City, MI, housewares, illus, 1916, 151 pg 30.00
American Jewelry, illus, 1880s, 84 pg 32.00
Athletic Shoe, Chicago, IL, 1920s, 24 pg 6.00
Baldwin Refrigerator, Burlington, VT, illus, 1917, 64 pg 25.00
Bausch & Lomb Optical, Rochester, NY, illus, 1900, 185 pg 25.00
Beck & Sons, tools & hardware, illus, 1930 . . . . 11.00
Bennett Homes, New York, NY, color illus, 1926, 104 pg 32.00
Book Supply, Chicago, IL, wrappers, 1930, 352 pg 19.30
Brown & Sharpe, Providence, RI, sm tools, illus, 1916 . . . . 11.50
Cambridge Glass, Cambridge, OH, illus, 1903, 47 pg 65.00
Chalmers Motor Car, autos, illus, 1923, 10 pg 32.00
Chevrolet Automobiles, trucks, illus, 1922, 22 pg 27.00
Covert Saddlery Hardware, leather, 1927, 231 pg 32.00
Crescent Bicycles, illus, 1897, 48 pg 15.00
Detroit Boat, Detroit, MI, launches, illus, 1912, 8 pg 16.00
DM Osborne, Auburn, NY, harvest machinery, illus, 1893 . . . . 15.00
Donnelley's, jewelry, first issue, illus, 1927, 240 pg 75.00
Eastman Kodak, Rochester, NY, cameras, illus, 1899, 60 pg 40.00
Eberhard Faber, school supplies, illus, 1922 . . . . 6.00
Eureka Mower, Utica, NY, illus, 1889-1890, 24 pg 25.00
Federal Telephone & Telegraph, equipment, illus, 1923 . . . . 27.00
Ford Motor, cars, illus, 1911, 24 pg 50.00
General Electric, household devices, illus, 1902, 15 pg 16.00
Greenfield Tap & Die, Greenfield, MA, tools, illus, 1916 . . . . 12.00
Hamilton Garment, New York, NY, illus, 1928-1929, 39 pg 12.00
Harris, New York, NY, mirrors & metals, illus, 1914, 36 pg 32.00
Hartman Furniture, Chicago, IL, illus, 1916, 422 pg 32.00
Haverford Cycle, Philadelphia, PA, illus, 1914, 22 pg 8.00
Herrick Refrigerators, Waterloo, IA, color illus, 1919 . . . . 25.00
Hotpoint, Chicago, IL, electric stoves, color illus, 1935 . . . . 9.00
Hudson Sporting Goods, New York, NY, illus, 1930, 48 pg 15.00
Indian Head Table, Nasua, NH, illus, 1920s, 46 pg 20.00
International Harvester, Chicago, IL, farm, illus, 1920 . . . . 32.00
Jenkins Brothers, Boston, MA, coffins, illus, 1887, 102 pg 75.00
JI Case Supply, farm supplies, 1917 . . . . 12.00
John Wilcox, Milford, NY, school supplies, illus, 1914 . . . . 5.00
Johnson & Son, Goshen, IN, hardware, illus, 1903, 128 pg 50.00
Keating Wheel, Middletown, CT, bicycles, illus, 1899 . . . . 30.00
Kohler, Kohler, WI, plumbing, illus, 1914 . . . . 40.00
Ladies' Home Journal, illus, 1893-1894, 28 pg 15.00
Lamm, Chicago, IL, men's clothes, illus, 1913-1914 . . . . 90.00
LC Smith Gun, Syracuse, NY, firearms guide, 1923 . . . . 16.00
Lloyd & Magnus, toys, fireworks, etc, illus, 1886-87 . . . . 615.00
Lope Fire Alarm, Stonington, CT, illus, 1908, 16 pg 20.00
Louden Machinery, Fairfield, IA, farm supply, illus, 1917 . . . . 20.00
Malleable Range, South Bend, IN, illus, 1906, 64 pg 40.00
Marine Model, New York, NY, models & parts, 1937, 12 pg 6.00
Matador Auto Supply, Chicago, IL, illus, 1913 . . . . 20.00
McCormick Harvesting, 1885 . . . . 100.00
Milton Bradley, Springfield, MA, games, 1920, 14 pg 11.50
Monogram Glass, Evanston, IL, glass gifts, illus, 1944 . . . . 5.00
Montgomery Ward, bicycles, illus, 1895 . . . . 12.00
Myrex Music, New York, NY, sheet music, illus, 1915, 16 pg 6.00
National Cash Register, Dayton, OH, industry, color photos 11.00
National Cloak & Suit, clothing, illus, 1921-1922 . . . . 16.00
Paine Lumber, Oshkosh, WI, illus, 1891, 325 pg 65.00
Peck & Hills Furniture, New York, NY, wholesale, 1915 . . . . 40.00
Pflueger, Akron, OH, fishing tackle, illus, 1938 . . . . 14.00
RCA, New York, NY, RCA records, 1912, 31 pg 14.00
Regal Shoes, men's shoes, illus, ca 1915, 12 pg 5.00
Reliable Locke & Safe, Covington, KY, illus, 1921, 68 pg 32.00
Rochester Optical, Rochester, NY, illus, 1902, 80 pg 40.00
Royal, Detroit, MI, silverware, illus, ca 1903, 88 pg 75.00

Schoenhut, circus toys, illus, 1915 . . . . . 16.00
Sears, Roebuck; general, illus, 1899 . . . . . 200.00
Sears Spring & Summer, Golden Jubilee, 1936 . . . . . 50.00
Sedgewick, New York, NY, elevators, illus, 1920, 52 pg 40.00
Singer Sewing Machine, New York, NY, illus, 1897, 32 pg 25.00
Southern Saddlery, Chattanooga, TN, illus, 1890s, 108 pg 40.00
Spiegel, Chicago, IL, general, illus, 1928 . . . . . 20.00
Studebaker Brothers, South Bend, IN, illus, 1922, 28 pg 50.00
Thalman, Baltimore, MD, stencils & stamps, illus, 1898 . . . . . 14.00
Tinker Toys, toys, color illus, 1920s, 16 pg 14.00
Trenton Potteries, Trenton, NJ, bath, illus, 1921, 321 pg 27.00
United Lighting, light fixtures, illus, ca 1910, 48 pg 40.00
US Buggy & Cart, Cincinnati, OH, illus, 1900s, 45 pg 32.00
Van Dorn Iron Works, Cleveland, OH, illus, 1884, 11 pg 40.00
Vaughan's Seed Store, Chicago, IL, seeds, 1941 . . . . . 5.00
Vega, Boston, MA, banjos, illus, 1920s 27.00
Victor Talking Machine, Camden, NJ, records, 1919 . . . . . 12.00
Vogue, pattern book, 1949 . . . . . 8.00
Weber Lumber & Supply, illus, ca 1909, 73 pg 11.00
Western Electric, New York, NY, illus, 1924, 860 pg 32.00
Wiley & Russell, Greenfield, MA, machinery, illus, 1894 . . . . . 25.00
Wing & Son, New York, NY, pianos, illus, 1913, 135 pg 16.00
Wood Harvesting, 1889 . . . . . 100.00

Caughley Ware

The Caughley Coalport Porcelain Manufactory operated from about 1775 until 1799 in Caughley, near Salop, Shropshire, in England. The owner was Thomas Turner, who gained his potting experience from his association with the Worcester Pottery Company. The wares he manufactured in Caughley are often referred to as 'Salopian.' He is most famous for his blue-printed earthenwares, particularly the Blue Willow pattern, designed for him by Thomas Minton.

For a more detailed history, see Coalport. When no condition is indicated, the items listed below are assumed to be in mint condition.

Bowl, Salopian, soft paste w/brn Britannia/floral, 6½", VG 55.00
Jug, Salopian, bl chinoiserie/tobacco leaf, prof rpr spout 350.00
Saucer, Salopian, deer, blk transfer w/mc leaves, EX 45.00
Set w/crystal bottles/boxes, mk Fr ivory, 10-pc 80.00

Celluloid

Celluloid was patented in 1869 by John W. Hyatt, who developed the formula by mixing pulp from the cotton plant with solvents and camphor. Although others claimed to have made the product earlier, it was ruled that Hyatt's celluloid was different enough to protect his patent rights. Today, celluloid is a generic term for all early plastics. World War II marked the end of its usefulness.

Earlier pieces have a creamy color with striations meant to imitate the texture of ivory or bone. Trademarks were not generally added until the 20th century when the color and weight became lighter, with little or no striations. During the twenties, tints were sometimes added; relief designs and gilding were popular decorative treatments.

The term 'French Ivory' was used until it was outlawed in 1920 by a bill which curtailed the practice of deceptive trademarks and advertising. Items bearing this mark are especially collectible. Other trade names were DuPont Pyralin, Windsor Arch Amerith, and Acwalit.

When no condition is indicated, items listed below are assumed to be in mint condition.

Baby's comb & brush set, pink roses decor, in orig box 20.00
Ball, baby's; ca 1800 . . . . . 85.00
Box, Collar & Cuff, emb lady, w/contents, ca 1890 . . . . . 60.00
Box, powder; in imitation of tortoiseshell, 2x5" dia 10.00
Cane hdl, dog head w/glass eyes, curved 28.00
Frame, 3¾x4½" oval w/in 8x6" outside measurement 20.00
Gavel 25.00
Hair receiver, w/lid 10.00
Letter opener, w/pencil figural on end 22.00
Manicure set, in fold-up case 12.00
Pencil sharpener, airplane shape, pocket size 7.50
Photo album, windmills/boats on cover, metal scroll edge 40.00
Postcard, for birthday 10.00
Purse, orange/amber, X-motif on lid, w/hdls, 4x8" 110.00
Rattle, baby's 19.00
Scissors, buttonhole; Germany, 4½" 15.00
Set, dresser; in lined box, 4-pc 30.00
Set, mirror/tray/2 brushes/clock/3 boxes/nail tools, 12-pc 125.00
Tape measure, picture of 2 kittens 18.00

Dresser set, simple styling, 12-pc, $55.00.

Ceramic Art Company

Jonathan Coxon, Sr., and Walter Scott Lenox established the Ceramic Art Company in 1889, in Trenton, New Jersey, where they produced fine belleek porcelain. Both were experienced in its production, having previously worked for Ott and Brewer. They hired artists to hand paint their wares with portraits, scenes, and lovely florals. Today artist signed examples bring the highest prices. Several marks were used, three of which contain the 'CAC' monogram. A green wreath surrounding the company name in full was used on special order wares, but these are not often encountered. Coxon eventually left the company, and it was later reorganized under the Lenox name.

When no condition is indicated, the items listed below are assumed to be in mint condition. See also Lenox

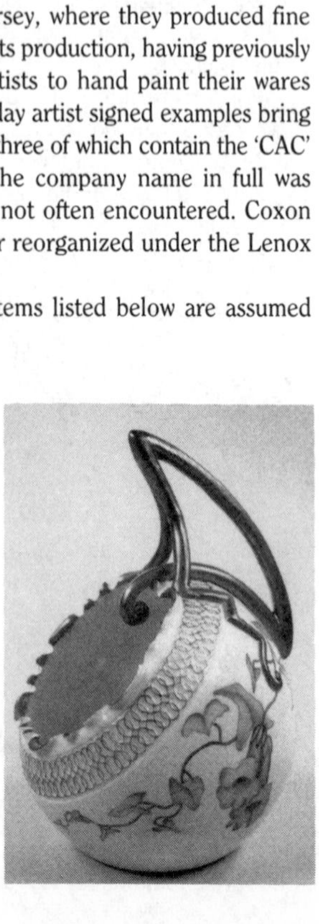

Planter, white with lavender flowers, gold trim and handle, 7½", $325.00.

Cup & saucer, demitasse; scalloped/ftd, jewel trim............. 65.00
Cup & saucer, demitasse; tea roses/gold trim, octagonal........ 45.00
Decanter, Scotch & Rye, sterling stopper/lettering, lg, pr...... 350.00
Jar, perfume; matt w/lily-o/t-valley, metal insert............ 225.00
Mug, chestnuts on shaded ground, sgn/1903, 5¼"............. 55.00
Mug, Indian chief in full headdress, palette mk, lg........... 185.00
Nut dish, ornate decor, Masonic, oval, 5¾"................. 65.00
Pitcher, tankard; mc grapes, gr/gold hdl, 14"................ 190.00
Pitcher, violet motif, HP, ftd, 5¾"........................ 45.00
Salt, individual; HP leaf decor, gold trim, 3-ftd, mk CAC...... 135.00
Salt dip, floral, palette mk............................... 9.00
Salt dip, swan, brushed gold trim, lav palette mk, 2½"......... 35.00
Sugar bowl, cobalt w/sterling overlay....................... 95.00
Tankard, ale; brn w/monk playing mandolin, EA DeLan, 14½".. 400.00
Tea strainer & base, gold & floral decor, lav wreath mk....... 200.00
Vase, full-figure woman, Delft bl, sgn, 12".................. 400.00

Ceramic Arts Studio, Madison

The work of the Ceramic Arts Studio has recently begun to attract a following of fascinated collectors, and for apparent reason. Though sold from 1938 until about 1955 as knick-knacks and novelty items, the workmanship is far superior to most Japanese imports, and the original, often complex designs are distinctively American. Betty Harrington is the designer credited for creating the line of figurines.

Many pieces are marked, but even unmarked items become easily recognizable after only a brief study of their distinctive styling and glaze colors. Those that are marked carry the black ink underglaze stamp: 'Ceramic Arts Studio, Madison, Wisc.' Do not confuse this mark with 'Ceramic Art' or 'Arts Studio,' which have both been used by American and Japanese companies on other novelty ware.

Values are for items in mint condition.

Bank, barber head, gray hair, tan face, 4¾".................. 45.00
Bank, paisley pig, pink & gray, rare, 3"..................... 95.00
Bud vase, Chinese, 7", pr................................. 45.00
Candle holder, bedtime boy & girl, 4¾", pr.................. 35.00
Candle holder, 5" lady kneels w/candle holder cups, pr......... 95.00
Ewer, jasperware, wht raised ballerina, Wedgwood bl, 4"....... 45.00
Figurine, Arabesque & Attitude, dancers, hangs, pr, 9½"....... 25.00
Figurine, Archibald the Dragon, gr/blk/red, 8"................ 45.00
Figurine, Balinese dancers, semi-bisque, 9½", pr.............. 65.00
Figurine, Beth & Bruce, 6", pr............................. 40.00
Figurine, Cinderella's prince holding slipper, 6¼"............ 25.00
Figurine, Collie dog, standing, lt brn, 2½".................. 18.00
Figurine, Collie mother, 5", w/3 sprightly pups, 2", 4-pc........ 45.00
Figurine, Columbine & Harlequin, blk & wht attire, 8", pr...... 60.00
Figurine, Comedy & Tragedy, 10", pr........................ 75.00
Figurine, Dawn w/flowing hair, pastel glaze/Deco, #468, 7"...... 25.00
Figurine, Dutch boy & girl, bl & yel, 3", pr.................. 18.00
Figurine, elephant, 2¼x5"................................ 15.00
Figurine, Fire Woman, dk wine swirled gown, 11½"........... 45.00
Figurine, Gay '90s couple, blue, 6½", pr..................... 65.00
Figurine, Hansel & Gretel on single base, 4½", pr............. 35.00
Figurine, Harem girl, reclining, 6"......................... 18.00
Figurine, Indian boy & girl, yel & bl, 3", pr.................. 25.00
Figurine, Lady Rowena on charger, gr, 8¼".................. 65.00
Figurine, Little Bo Peep, 5½".............................. 25.00
Figurine, Little Boy Blue, 4½".............................. 25.00
Figurine, Little Miss Muffet................................ 30.00
Figurine, man & dog...................................... 30.00
Figurine, monkey family, parents & baby, brn/blk/wht, 3-pc..... 60.00
Figurine, Peter Pan & Wendy, 5¼", pr....................... 65.00
Figurine, Pied Piper, 6", w/3 children, 3½", 4-pc set........... 75.00
Figurine, Polish couple, 5½", pr............................ 45.00
Figurine, rhumba dancers on 1 base, bl/red/gold, 7", pr........ 45.00
Figurine, seahorse & coral, gr & lt gr, 4", pr................. 35.00
Figurine, Southern Bell, by Peggy Porcher, 10½"............. 50.00
Figurine, Southern couple, cobalt & pink, 7", pr.............. 45.00
Figurine, Spanish couple................................... 25.00
Figurine, St George on charger, gr, 8¼".................... 65.00
Figurine, Sultan, 4½", w/2 harem girls, 3-pc set.............. 60.00
Figurine, Sultan on pillow, 5".............................. 18.00
Figurine, wht kitten taking bath, bl bow..................... 18.00
Figurine, Zora & Zorina, bl draped clothing, pr............... 60.00
Planter, Mei-Ling, Oriental girl, bl, 5"....................... 30.00
Plaque, Harlequin & Columbine, blk, palette shape, 9", pr...... 30.00
Shakers, Bavarian couple, 3¼", pr.......................... 12.00
Shakers, Blackamoor, 4¾", pr............................. 45.00
Shakers, boy & circus elephant w/trunk up, pr................ 20.00
Shakers, cheese & mouse, pr............................... 18.00
Shakers, Chirp & Twirp, canaries, pr........................ 16.00
Shakers, cow, pr... 35.00

Figurines, Tragedy and Comedy, gray with blue masks, 10½", $75.00 for the pair.

Shakers, Eskimos, 3¼", pr................................ 18.00
Shakers, fish, yel & gr, 4", pr............................. 16.00
Shakers, kangaroo w/baby in pouch, 5", pr................... 18.00
Shakers, leprechaun & mushroom, pink & bl, pr............... 18.00
Shakers, monkey, pr...................................... 35.00
Shakers, Oriental boy & girl, 3", pr......................... 15.00
Shakers, Oriental boy & girl, 4½", pr........................ 18.00
Shakers, Paul Bunyan & sm tree, pr......................... 25.00
Shakers, pigs, pr... 12.50
Shelf sitters, Chinese boy & girl, pr........................ 20.00
Shelf sitters, Mexican boy & girl, pr........................ 20.00
Shelf sitters, Michelle & Maurice, 7¾", pr................... 20.00
Shelf sitters, Oriental boy & girl, 4", pr..................... 16.00
Shelf sitters, Pierrot & Pierette, 7", pr...................... 55.00
Vase, African Lady/African Man, brn & wht matt, 8" ea, pr..... 60.00
Wall hanger, Shadow Dancers, pr........................... 35.00

Chalkware

Chalkware figures were a popular commodity from approximately 1860 until 1890. They were made from gypsum, or plaster of Paris, formed in a mold and then hand painted in oils or watercolors. Items such as animals and birds, figures, banks, toys, and religious ornaments modeled after more expensive Staffordshire wares, were often sold door to door. Their origin is attributed to Italian immigrants.

Today, regarded as a form of folk art, 19th century American pieces bring prices in the hundreds of dollars. Carnival chalkware from this century is also collectible, especially figures that are personality related.

Values are for examples in excellent condition.

Bank, Boston bulldog, red/blk decor, G color, 1900s, 7⅜″......35.00
Bank, cat smoking pipe, 1900s, 10″........................100.00
Bank, horse w/pnt harness, 20th C, 4½″.....................65.00
Cat, seated, blk, new paint, 9½″...........................50.00
Cat, seated, old brn pnt, blk/red/yel trim, touch-up, 9″........300.00
Cat, seated, wht eyes, ears & mouth pink, blk rpt, 16″........385.00
Cat, sleeping, bl/wht, 7x12″ L.............................75.00
Cat, sleeping, bl/wht collar, late 1800s, 4½″..................15.00
Compote w/fruit, orig mc pnt, wht base, wear minor, 9x8½″....900.00
Compote w/fruit, worn orig mc pnt, 11″, pr..................800.00
Deer, orig olive w/blk stripes, red touches, wear, 5⅜″.........290.00
Deer, recumbent, striped decor, rstr, 8½x10½″..............325.00
Deer, recumbent, wht, 8½x10½″...........................225.00
Dog, seated, wht w/blk ears, red collar w/tag, wear, 6x4″.......85.00
Dog, seated on base, collar w/tag, emb, pnt, wear, 9″..........95.00
Dog, standing, brn ears/tail, bl chain, wear, 1860s, 8″.........120.00
Dog, standing, oval base, red/blk/yel, faded/worn, 4¾″..........70.00
Ewe & lamb, red/blk/yel, worn gr-gold base, 6″..............320.00
Nodder, cat, orig red & blk decor, chips, 6″................325.00
Parrot, on ball, orig decor G, rpr to base 7¾″...............200.00
Parrot, orig gr/yel/red decor, minor wear, 9″................410.00
Rabbit, seated, red & blk decor, 5¼″.....................225.00
Rooster, good orig pnt, red & blk, 6¾″....................425.00
Shepherd boy & lamb, no paint, 11x9½″.....................75.00

Left, Compote with fruit, white base, polychrome decor on fruit, 9″ x 8½″, excellent condition, $900.00; Right, Cat, old brown paint with black, red, and yellow trim, excellent condition, 9″, $300.00.

Champleve

Champleve, enameling on brass, differs from cloisonne in that the design is depressed or incised into the metal, rather than being built up with wire dividers as in the cloisonne procedure. The cells, or depressions, are filled in with color, and the piece is then fired.

When no condition is indicated, the items listed below are assumed to be in mint condition.

Belt buckle, 2-pc, lg.......................................65.00
Box, arabesque decor, florals, ca 1900, 6″ dia...............550.00
Jardiniere, winged horse on turq, foo dog ft, 15x13″..........450.00
Table lamp, turq band w/red, yel & bl flowers, 23″...........125.00
Urn, elephant hdls, w/lid, 9x5¼″..........................150.00
Urn, floral panels, sq base w/paw ft, late 19th C, 7″, pr.......990.00
Vase, elephant hdls, ftd, 10″...............................95.00
Vase, marbleized bulbous onyx center w/ormolu, 7½″.........150.00
Vase, Tao mask, bronze, imp Oriental M King, 4¾″, pr.......125.00

Candlesticks, figural court pages, 8½″, $450.00 for the pair.

Chelsea

The Chelsea Porcelain Works operated in London from the middle of the 18th century, making porcelain of the finest quality. In 1770 it was purchased by the owner of the Derby Pottery and for about twenty years operated as a decorating shop. Production periods are indicated by trademarks: 1745-1750--incised triangle , sometimes with 'Chelsea' and the year added; early 1750s--raised anchor mark on oval pad; 1752-1756--small painted red anchor, only rarely found in blue underglaze; 1756-1769--gold anchor; 1769-84--Chelsea Derby mark, the script 'D' containing a horizontal anchor. Many reproductions have been made; be suspicious of any anchor mark larger than ¼″.

When no condition is indicated, the items listed below are assumed to be in mint condition.

Bodkin, ½ figure lady on ped, holds flowers, 1755, 4½″......1,800.00
Bonbonniere, Cupid w/lamp, Pensez on strap, silver mt, 2″...1,000.00
Bust, set of 4 representing seasons, 1765, ea 4″............2,600.00
Charm, actor, hands on hips, pink jacket, 1765, 1″...........500.00
Charm, lady w/muff, 1765, 1⅛″, NM........................500.00
Cup, landscape by JH O'Neale, relief anchor mk, 2½″.........650.00
Cup & saucer, exotic birds, Trembleuse, gold anchor, 1760....750.00
Dish, Flying Dog, 10-sided, red anchor mk, 1775, 6½″......1,250.00
Dish, Kakiemon tree/pheasant, relief anchor mk, 1750, 6½″....900.00
Figurine, huntsman, rose cape/gr coat/yel pants, 1755, 2″......500.00
Figurine, man/woman/lamb, gr/yel/pink/lav/bl/maroon, pr.......950.00
Figurine, Tithe Pig, clergy/farmer/wife, 1765, 6″, VG..........900.00

Seal, Africa kneeling, Je Brule D'Amour, 1760, EX...........500.00
Seal, blackbird on stump, gr base, gold seal, NM.............500.00
Seal, Cupid as barrister, sardonyx intaglio, 1760, 1¼".........500.00
Seal, Cupid as huntsman, horn on side, no seal, 1760s........500.00
Seal, dancing man, Toujours Gay, 1760s, NM................500.00
Seal, grotesque woman dancing, wht glaze, red anchor, EX....500.00
Seal, harlequin w/domino, gr base, gold rim, no seal, NM......500.00
Seal, partridge, mc, ca 1760, no seal, EX..................500.00
Seal, standing Chinaman by ped w/vase, no seal, 1760s, 1¼"...500.00
Soup plate, vignettes/floral JH O'Neale, silver form, 9½".....1,100.00

Vases, Mazarine Blue with panels of birds and flowers, gilt trim, gold anchor mark, 10", excellent condition, $1,350.00 for the pair.

Chelsea Dinner Ware

Made from about 1830 to 1880 in the Staffordshire district of England, this white dinnerware is decorated with lustre embossings in the grape, thistle, sprig, or fruit and cornucopia patterns. The relief designs vary from lavender to blue, and the body of the ware may be porcelain, ironstone, or earthenware. Because it was not produced in Chelsea as the name would suggest, dealers often prefer to call it 'Grandmother's Ware.'

When no condition is indicated, the items listed below are assumed to be in mint condition.

Plate, white with lavender relief thistles, 6¾", $10.00

Grape, bowl, oval vegetable.................................24.00
Grape, cup & saucer.......................................24.00
Grape, pitcher, 1840s......................................47.50
Grape, plate, bread & butter..................................6.00
Grape, plate, cake...28.00
Grape, plate, 8½"..12.00
Grape, ramekins w/under plate, set...........................20.00
Grape, saucer, demitasse.....................................4.00
Grape, saucer, reg..4.50
Grape, shaving mug..55.00
Grape, tea set, pot/creamer/sugar, 3-pc.....................175.00
Lyre w/Wreath & Shells, plate, 10"..........................10.00
Thistle, cup w/deep saucer, lg...............................25.00

Chelsea Keramic Works

Established in 1872 in Chelsea, Massachusetts, by several members of the Robertson family who later formed the Dedham Pottery, this firm is most noted for its experiments in attempting to re-create the ancient Oriental oxblood-red glaze. They succeeded in this in 1885, and also developed several other outstanding glazes as a result of their perseverance. One was their Oriental crackle glaze which they ultimately used in the manufacture of the very successful Dedham dinnerware.

Though their very early artware utilized a redware body, by the late 1870s it was replaced with yellow or buff burning clay. A line called Bourgla-Reine (underglaze slip-decorated ware with primarily blue and green backgrounds) was produced, though not to any great extent. Other pieces were designed in imitation of metalware, even to the extent that surfaces were 'hammered' to further enhance the effect. Occasionally, live flora were pressed into the damp vessel walls to leave a decorative impression.

The pottery closed in 1889. Early wares were not marked; those made from 1875 to 1880 were marked with either two or three lines containing 'Chelsea Keramic Art Works, Robertson and Son,' or the 'C-KA-W' cipher which was used up to 1889. A paper label was used for a short time on the crackleware.

Values are for examples in mint condition. See also Dedham

Flask, brn/gr mottle, imp mk, 5¼"..........................275.00
Pitcher, bl w/incised plant decor, 7½"......................245.00
Plate, raised pineapple border, mk CKAW, 10"..............495.00
Teapot, gr/bl gloss w/red/yel/blk leaf & berry, sgn, 7".........500.00
Vase, bl flambe, overglaze HP roses, ftd pillow form, 12½".....100.00

Children's Books

Children's books, especially those from the Victorian era, are charming collectibles. Colorful lithographic illustrations that once delighted little boys in long curls, and tiny girls in long stockings and lots of ribbons and lace, have lost none of their appeal.

When no condition is indicated, the items listed below are assumed to be in excellent condition.

A Visit to Grandma, Biffi illus, movable pictures...............50.00
Aesops Fables, Tenniel, 1848..............................66.00
Aladdin, Cupples & Leon, 1915.............................20.00
All Around Town, Flack illus, 1st ed, 1929...................35.00
All the Funny Folks, King Features, 1926, EX.................76.00
Always Jolly! Movable Toybook, L Meggendorfer, VG.........110.00
America's Paul Revere, Ward illus, 1st ed, 1946...............15.00
Animals of the Farm, linen, 1909...........................20.00
Arabian Nights, Bull illus, color plates, no date, G.............25.00

Tim Tyler in the Jungle, pop-up, King Fisher's Syndicate, 1935, $95.00.

Around the Zoo, color illus, 1910 .... 20.00
Book of Games #1, Goldsmith Pub Co, 1916 .... 25.00
Brownyboo, Lapen, color plates, 1908 .... 60.00
Chatterbox, 1879-1880, VG 46.00
Children of Dickens, The; Smith illus, 1926 .... 50.00
Denslow's Animal Fair, Denslow illus, 1st ed, 1904 .... 25.00
Father Tuck's Comic Nursery Rhymes, 1911 .... 25.00
Glinda of Oz, JR Neill illus, 1920 .... 27.50
Golden Staircase, The; poems & verses, Spooner illus 40.00
Goldilocks, pop-up, Blue Ribbon Press, 1934 .... 60.00
Goop Encyclopedia, The; 254 illus by Gelett, 1st ed, 1916 .... 20.00
Hans Andersen's Fairy Tales, Rand McNally, 1928 .... 20.00
How Plants Grow, Gray, botany for young people, 1858 .... 15.00
How the Buffalo Lost His Crown, Russell illus, 1898 .... 30.00
In the Closed Room, Burnett, 1st ed, 1904 .... 50.00
Journeys Through Bookland, Sylvester, 10-volume set, 1922 .... 50.00
Keeping Up with the Joneses, 1st series, 1920 .... 20.00
Land of Oz, The; JR Neill illus, 1939 .... 22.50
Little Lulu at the Seashore, Marge, 1946 .... 15.00
Lucky Bucky in Oz, JR Neill illus, 1st ed, 1942 .... 75.00
Magic Drawing Book of Trains & Ships, 1916 .... 25.00
Mickey Mouse the Miracle Maker, Disney, 1948 .... 15.00
Midnight Folk, The; Hilder illus, color, 1932 .... 30.00
Mother Goose, pop-up, Blue Ribbon Press, 1934 .... 60.00
Mr Munchausen, John Bangs, 1st ed, 1901 .... 35.00
Mrs Wiggs of the Cabbage Patch, Hegan, 1902 .... 6.00
My ABC Book, muslin, in color, Saalfield, 1909 .... 20.00
Nowadays Fairy Book, J Wilcox Smith, 1911, 9x12" 195.00
Old French Fairy Tales, Sterrett illus, 1920 .... 35.00
Old Mother Hubbard, color illus, Samuel Gabriel, 1911 .... 20.00
Overall Boys, The; 1905 .... 70.00
Patriotic Paint Book, Goldsmith Pub Co, 1919 .... 20.00
Pied Piper of Hamelin, The; Dunlap illus, 1910 .... 20.00
Pinocchio, Petersham illus, 1932 .... 20.00
Pinocchio, pop-up, illus Harold Lentz, 1943, w/jacket, EX 60.00
Poor Richard, Daugherty illus, 1941 .... 25.00
Princess and the Goblin, The; Kirk illus, pictorial boards 10.00
Raggedy Ann & Andy, Gruelle, movable illus, 1944 .... 25.00
Railroad Ride, A; color illus, Thos Nelson & Sons, 1910 .... 25.00
Rip Van Winkle, Cooke illus, 1923 .... 8.50
Scrap Basket Sam, story of a rag doll, 1923 .... 18.00
Shoes & Ships & Sealing Wax, Scott illus, 1928 .... 15.00
Soldier Rigdale, Birch illus, 1st ed, 1899 .... 15.00
Story of Dr Dolittle, The; Lofting illus, 1922 .... 10.00
Story of Happy Hooligan, McLoughlin, 1932, 9x12", EX 22.00
Sunbonnet Babies Primer, illus, Corbett, 1902 .... 85.00
Tales from Shakespeare, Rhead illus, 1918 .... 20.00
Tales Told in Holland, Miller, 1926 .... 20.00
Tarzan & Forbidden City, w/dust jacket, 1st edition 125.00
Tatsinda, Haas illus, 1st ed, 1963 .... 15.00
Two Little Pilgrims' Progress, Birch illus, 1st ed, 1895 .... 15.00
Understood Betsy, Williamson illus, 1st ed, 1917 .... 25.00
Wally, His Cartoons o/t AEF; 1919 .... 25.00
Water Babies, The; Goble illus, 1st ed, 1909 .... 85.00
Wild Animal Actors, Little illus, 1st ed, 1935 .... 12.50
Wind in The Willows, The; Barnhart illus, leather binding 16.00
Wise Gray Cat, The; Caroline Hofman, 1918 .... 20.00

Children's Things

Nearly every item devised for adult furnishings has been reduced to child's size--furniture, dishes, sporting goods, even some tools. All are very collectible.

During the late 17th and early 18th centuries, miniature china dinnerware sets were made both in China and in England. They were not intended primarily as children's playthings, however, but instead were made to furnish miniature rooms and cabinets that provided a popular diversion for the adults of that period. By the 19th century, the emphasis had shifted, and most of the small-scaled dinnerware and tea sets were made for children's play.

Late in the 19th century and well into the 20th, toy pressed glass dishes were made, many in the same pattern as full-scale glassware. Today, these toy dishes often fetch prices in the same range as those for the 'grown-ups'! Authorities Margaret and Kenn Whitmyer have compiled a lovely book, *Children's Dishes*, with full-color photos and current market values; you will find their address in the Directory under Ohio. We also recommend *Children's Glass Dishes, China, and Furniture*, by Doris Anderson Lechler, available at your local bookstore or public library.

The earliest cradles made in America were box-shaped structures with crude rockers and very little trim. The idea of 'field' or 'slave' cradles is said to have originated with European peasants. Walkers have been used for about two hundred years, and construction methods have varied, including a round type utilizing a wooden frame on coasters, with a padded ring to support the child under his arms; and a vertical pole model with ball bearings and a padded angle arm that rotated to allow the child to move in circles. Early hobby horses either rocked or jumped via steel-band springs, and were often decked out with leather saddles and reigns. Some were painted, while others had realistic plush coats.

Toy sewing machines, first available in the early 1900s, have become popular collectibles today. One of the companies that made these working machines was Kay-an-EE, located in Germany. Many models were made, all of which, with some variations, were capable of sewing a chain stitch. They were made until after World War II, when plastic began to replace metal as the material used in toy production.

When no condition is indicated, the glass and chinaware listed below are assumed to be in mint condition; furniture and miscellaneous are assumed excellent.

Key:
cs—child size ds—doll size

China

Bowl, soup; Sporting Bears, English 65.00
Bowl, tan lustre, flowers in pots, w/lid, Made in Japan 8.00
Bowl, waste; Old Curiosity Shop scene, bl transfer 30.00
Bowl, waste; Punch & Judy, bl transfer, England, 2⅛" 40.00
Bowl, waste; Water Hen, bl transfer, Caason's England, 2½" 35.00
Casserole, Blue Willow, Made in Japan, 5½" 18.00
Casserole, Dicken's Old Curiosity Shop, bl transfer, w/lid 45.00
Casserole, Maiden Hair Fern, oval, w/lid, Ridgway's, 5¼" 30.00

Cereal set, Little Bo Peep, pink lustre, German, 2-pc..........75.00
Chocolate pot, man & woman in 18th C clothes, German.......20.00
Creamer, ballerina on stage, red rose above, Japan.............4.00
Creamer, blue Dutch children/windmill/trim, Japan..............4.00
Creamer, Blue Willow, Made in Japan, 1½″...................8.00
Creamer, Blue Willow, Made in Japan, 2″.....................8.00
Creamer, Buster Brown & Tige, scalloped base/rim, Germany....35.00
Creamer, chinaman figural, Japan, 2¼″......................30.00
Creamer, dog on ball/goose/clown, gray lustre, Japan............5.00
Creamer, Dutch children scene, tan lustre ground, Japan........4.00
Creamer, Dutch girl w/buckets, windmill bkground, Japan........5.00
Creamer, Gaudy Ironstone, bulbous, ftd, England, 2⅜″.........30.00
Creamer, red Willow pattern, Made in Japan, 1½″.............17.00
Creamer, Santa in dirigible mc scene, pink trim, Germany......35.00

Silhouette Children, signed Victoria Czecho-Slovakia. Cup and saucer, $5.00; Teapot, 3⅝″, $16.00; Creamer, 2⅛″, $6.00.

Creamer, sunset scene, silhouette trees, Made in Japan..........5.00
Creamer, tan & gray lustre, blk trim, mkd Phoenix China........8.00
Creamer, tan lustre, flowers in pots, Made in Japan, 1½″........5.00
Cup, saucer, plate; child/dog/cat, pink/wht, Staffordshire........30.00
Cup & saucer, bear kicks football, advertising, Japan...........17.00
Cup & saucer, bl Dutch children/windmills/trim, Japan...........5.00
Cup & saucer, bluebirds among floral branches, Japan..........4.50
Cup & saucer, clown riding donkey.........................15.00
Cup & saucer, Colonial couple silhouette, Made in Japan........8.00
Cup & saucer, gr lustre trim, Merry Christmas, Germany........17.00
Cup & saucer, hunting scene, pink lustre, Germany............32.00
Cup & saucer, Punch & Judy, bl transfer, England............35.00
Cup & saucer, tan & gray lustre, blk trim, Phoenix China.......7.00
Dinner set, bl acorn pattern, imp RSR, 28-pc, NM...........200.00
Dinner set, Flow Blue, butter, tureen+39 pcs, EX..........2,300.00
Dinner set, orange & ivory w/floral, Japan, 24-pc.............65.00
Dinner set, Rhodesia, Ridgways, 35-pc......................260.00
Feeder, baby; Little Boy Blue, story/scenes, Staffordshire.......65.00
Gravy boat, Dicken's Old Curiosity Shop, bl transfer, 5½″.......35.00
Ice bucket, tan lustre, flowers in pots, Made in Japan..........10.00
Mug, 'S' & 'T' w/representative images, 2⅜″, EX..............55.00
Mug, bear, Buddy Tucker....................................45.00
Mug, bears, dressed, Getting Ready for Walk, 2¾″, VG.........55.00
Mug, cat & zebras, mc on blk transfer, 3½″, VG..............85.00
Mug, girl w/geese, HP, sgn/1913, 3″.........................35.00
Mug, Hot Hand, children spank little girl, soft paste, 2½″.......30.00
Mug, kittens & mother cat personified, Staffordshire, 2¼″.......75.00
Mug, Present for Charles, brn on yel, rare, 1⅞″.............345.00
Mug, Token of Esteem, blk transfer, 2¾″, EX................150.00
Mug, We be loggerheads/point of honour, Staffordshire, 2½″....50.00
Plate, Bashful dwarf, WD Ent, c 1937, Made in Japan, 4⅜″......4.00
Plate, bear w/baseball bat, Made in Japan, 5″..................7.00
Plate, bl Dutch children/windmills/trim, Japan...................2.00
Plate, Blue Willow, Made in Japan, 3¾″.......................4.00
Plate, Brundage Girls, Germany, 6¼″........................20.00
Plate, Buster Brown & Tige, scalloped rim, Germany, 5″.......35.00
Plate, butterflies, floral band at rim, Made in Japan.............3.00
Plate, cake; tan lustre, flowers in pots, Made in Japan..........10.00
Plate, dog on ball/goose/clown, gray lustre, Japan...............3.50
Plate, Dutch girl w/buckets, windmill bkground, Japan...........3.00
Plate, gold 'Merry Christmas' & people, pink lustre, 5″..........9.00
Plate, grill; Blue Willow, Made in Japan, 4¼″.................20.00
Plate, hunting scene, pink lustre, scalloped, Germany..........10.00
Plate, Joseph/Mary/donkey outside inn, 'Merry...,' Germany......10.00
Plate, kite scene, bl transfer, England, 2¾″..................45.00
Plate, Little Bo Peep, ribbed rim, Salem China Co.............6.00
Plate, Little Orphan Annie, tan lustre rim, Made in Japan........8.00
Plate, Mary & lamb, mc, Brentleigh Ware, Staffordshire.........5.00
Plate, Mickey waters flowers, tan lustre, Made in Japan..........7.00
Plate, pink/wht roses, mustard lustre, 17-pc/service for 4.......140.00
Plate, red Willow pattern, Made in Japan, 3¾″.................7.00
Plate, See Saw nursery rhyme & scene, gold rim, Germany.......7.00
Plate, silhouette, girl pushing carriage, Noritake, 4¼″...........7.00
Plate, Sporting Bears, English..............................65.00
Plate, sunset lake scene, silhouette trees, Made in Japan.........3.00
Plate, tan & gray lustre, blk trim, Phoenix China, 3″...........4.00
Plate, This is the House That Jack Built, Germany, 5¼″.........8.00
Plate, Tinkerbell scene, Japan, 3⅞″.........................4.00
Platter, fish center, cobalt & gold trim, Karlsbad, 11″..........55.00
Platter, Little Orphan Annie, tan lustre, oval, Japan, 5″........14.00
Platter, Maiden Hair Fern, oval, Ridgways, 7¼″...............18.00
Reamer, tan lustre, flowers in pots, Made in Japan, 2⅝″........65.00
Salt box, tan lustre, flowers in pots, w/lid, Japan, 2⅛″.........18.00
Saucer, Little Orphan Annie, tan lustre, Made in Japan..........4.00
Shakers, tan lustre, flower in pot, Made in Japan, 1¼″, pr......12.00
Spatula, tan lustre, Made in Japan...........................7.00
Sugar bowl, angel in country scene decal, w/lid, Germany.......30.00
Sugar bowl, ballerina, red rose above, w/lid, Japan.............4.00
Sugar bowl, Gaudy Ironstone, ftd, tab hdls, w/lid, England......45.00
Sugar bowl, Happy dwarf, w/lid, WD Ent, c 1937, Japan.........9.00
Sugar bowl, open; chariot scene, bl transfer, Cauldon, 1½″.....22.00
Sugar bowl, otter scene, w/lid, Noritake.....................50.00
Sugar bowl, tan & gray lustre, blk trim, w/lid, Phoenix..........8.00
Tea set, acorn, brn, Cork Edge & Malkin, 12-pc, NM.........100.00
Tea set, Bittersweet & Royal Blue, Japan #62, 10-pc, EX......500.00
Tea set, children/turkeys/dog/etc, German..................250.00
Tea set, circus clowns & animals, German, 1900s.............225.00
Tea set, orange & bl floral, Germany, in box, 21-pc...........150.00
Tea set, pink roses, German.................................85.00
Teapot, bluebirds among floral branches, w/lid, Japan...........9.00
Teapot, car decal, pink lustre, w/lid, Germany.................75.00
Teapot, cobalt & gold, portrait medallion, w/lid, Germany.......70.00
Teapot, geisha scene, rust trim, Japan.......................30.00
Teapot, gr lustre trim, 'Merry Christmas,' w/lid, Germany.......60.00
Teapot, red Willow pattern, w/lid, Made in Japan, 2⅝″.........50.00
Teapot, Snow White & Doc, w/lid, WD Ent, c 1937, Japan.....22.00
Teapot, tan & gray lustre, blk trim, w/lid, Phoenix China.......20.00
Teapot, tan lustre, flowers in pots, w/lid, Made in Japan........12.00
Teapot, This is the House That Jack Built, w/lid, 5¾″..........50.00
Teapot, 18th C couple, flower border, colorful, Japan..........12.00
Tray, cobalt & gold, woman's portrait center, Germany, 5″......35.00
Tureen, kite scene, bl transfer, w/lid, England, 3¼x4¼″.......140.00
Tureen, Little Orphan Annie, tan lustre, w/lid, Japan...........20.00
Waffle dish, tan lustre, flowers in pots, Made in Japan.........16.00

Furniture

Baby buggy, wicker, Victorian, 40x40″.....................450.00
Bed, brass & iron, 55x30″, EX............................260.00

Bed, folk art, mirror in headboard, 19" L....50.00
Bed, mahog, canopy, trn posts, quilt/canopy/etc, 10x16"....315.00
Bed, trn brass wire, folds, w/mesh mattress, 1800s, 28x17"....75.00
Bed, walnut, Eastlake, applied relief, 1800s, 19x28x16"....200.00
Bed, walnut, Victorian, 1860s, 40x40"....475.00
Bed, walnut, 12x20", EX....45.00
Bed, wrought iron, scrolls, brass finials, late, 18x24"....125.00
Buggy, wood/pnt/stripes, open w/canopy, lg bk wheels, 29"....175.00
Bureau, pine, silvered tin swinging mirror, 3-drw, 24x15"....85.00
Candlestand, trn tripod, band inlay, orig finish, 11½"....170.00
Carriage, oilcloth hood, Joel Ellis, ds....750.00
Carriage, pnt tin, no canopy, Marklin, 1910, 9¼" L....715.00
Carriage, wood, 3½"....18.00
Chair, arm; fumed oak, velvet seat, G Stickley, #344, 26"....385.00
Chair, arm; ladderbk, primitive, splint seat, 25½"....50.00
Chair, arm; ladderbk, 2-slat, rpt, orig rush seat, 18"....105.00
Chair, arm; rocker, ladderbk, G Stickley, #343, unsgn, 25"....325.00
Chair, arrow bk, plank seat, early decor, 30"....100.00
Chair, bamboo turnings, trn plank seat, 1880s, 8"....23.00
Chair, bow bk, centennial, Windsor....150.00
Chair, caned, walnut, Victorian, 30"....100.00
Chair, folding, walnut, 1860s, 28"....190.00
Chair, Gothic Revival, fretwork bk, trn legs/posts, 33"....150.00
Chair, ladderbk, cane seat, 12½"....20.00
Chair, ladderbk, yel/gold stencil, rpl rush seat, 15½"....85.00
Chair, Mission....24.00
Chair, plank seat, bootjack bk, curved crest, rfn, 20"....105.00
Chair, primitive, unfinished, rpl rope seat, 14½"....95.00
Chair, rocker, Boston, some old pnt & stencilling, cs....125.00
Chair, rocker, ladderbk, woven splint seat, 23", EX....40.00
Chair, rocker, orig gr w/stripes/mc florals, rpr arms, 23"....75.00
Chair, rocker, plank seat, oak spindles, orig, 30"....60.00
Chair, rocker, pressed oak back, 29"....80.00
Chair, rocker, pressed oak bk w/carved Santa head, 28"....160.00
Chair, rocker, scroll bk, oak, 30", EX....200.00
Chair, rocker, spindle bk arm, old rpt, 20¼"....40.00
Chair, rocker, wicker, maple fr, 28"....45.00
Chair, spindle bk, old blk finish, 11"....38.00
Chair, spindle bk, slip seat, mahog, Hepplewhite, 24x12"....80.00
Chair, trn legs/posts, stenciled caning on seat, rpr, 17"....110.00
Chair, Windsor, bow bk arm, Nutting copy, 25"....125.00
Chair, Windsor birdcage side, bamboo trn, 27"....400.00
Chair, ½ arrow bk spindles, 13½" high plank seat, cs....105.00
Chest, bow front, 2 over 2 dvtl drawers, mahog, Sheridan....170.00
Chest, dvtl gallery, rare, 1800s, 11x14"....240.00
Chest, French-ftd, 2 over 3 drawers, Hepplewhite, 20x20"....410.00
Chest, strap hinges, till & secret drawer, 11x18"....140.00
Chest, 2 over 2 drawers, pine, old patina, 10x13"....100.00
Chest, 2 over 2 dvtl drawers, pine, porc pulls, 14x14"....150.00
Chest, 2 over 2 dvtl drawers/mustard patina, 12½x13¼"....155.00
Cradle, caned, trn mahog, 1850s, 40x40"....210.00
Cradle, mahog, trn posts, matching head/foot board, 37x41"....230.00
Cradle, pine, hooded, orig finish, 14x20"....110.00
Cradle, pine, old finish, w/rockers, 18"....50.00
Cradle, pine w/buttermilk red, butterfly rockers, PA, 35"....345.00
Cradle, poplar, orig brn pnt/mc decor, touch-up/rpr, 15½"....90.00
Cradle, walnut, dvtl, scalloped sides & rockers, 40"....275.00
Cradle, walnut, Victorian, 12x10x24"....55.00
Cupboard, china; glass doors, metal pulls, mirror, ds....100.00
Cupboard, orig, 26x14"....90.00
Cupboard, poplar, cut-out ft, 2 shelves behind door, 12"....150.00
Cupboard, pressed cardboard w/metal pulls, pnt, O-Joy, ds....85.00
Cupboard, step bk, pine, 7 drw w/wood pulls, sq nails, 24"....300.00
Cupboard, wire nail construction, 1-pc, minor damage, 14"....95.00

Child's oak pedestal table, 15¾", $95.00.

Desk, dvtl construction/2 drawers, pine, ca 1820, 5x12"....160.00
Desk, walnut, Wm & Mary, slat front, ball ft, 1710, 24"....6,875.00
Dresser, pine, fruit pulls, WM Castle, Springfield, O, 23"....125.00
Dresser, swivel mirror/handkerchief drws, Vilas-Harsha, 12"....150.00
Dresser, walnut, 4 drw, mirror, Victorian, rpr/rpl, 19"....75.00
Dresser, wht wood w/tole pnt, brass pulls, 1911, 11"....75.00
Foot stool, primitive, cut-out legs, scrolled, 7x4x9", VG....95.00
Highchair, bentwood cane bk & seat, w/tray, 40"....85.00
Highchair, enamelware, Amsco, 24"....30.00
Highchair, ladderbk arm/trn splay legs/posts/3 curve slats....550.00
Highchair, makes play table, wheels, maple, Victorian, cs....190.00
Highchair, makes rocker, wheels, no tray, Victorian, cs....85.00
Highchair, maple, 3 slat bk, bulb finials, 1720, cs....935.00
Highchair, Mission oak, ds....45.00
Highchair, Windsor bow bk, 6-spindle/plank seat, gr pnt/cs....1,870.00
Ice cream parlor set, wood table w/iron legs/chairs, cs....180.00
Piano stool, trn legs, wood, 8"....25.00
Potty chair, wicker, w/lid, VG....75.00
Settee, armchair, table; bentwood/caned seats, Thonet, ds....1,000.00
Settle bench, blk pnt w/yel stripes & roses, 20th C, 10"....75.00
Stool, piano, screw type, ds....35.00
Stove, gr/cream granite/tin, gas stove styling, 1920s, ds....45.00
Stroller, Victorian, high bk wheels, ds....395.00
Swimming pool, pnt tin, clockwork, rooms/steps, 1900, 17"....880.00
Swing, dowel frame, wire bk, orig box, early 1900s, ds....85.00
Table, cherry, trn/paneled legs/drw/bevel edge, 12x15" W....135.00
Table, dinette; handmade w/drw, w/2 slat bk chairs, 11x7"....85.00
Table, drop leaf, walnut, trn legs, rnd leaves, 15x13x14"....200.00
Table, w/2 chairs, oak, orig decor, 17x24", EX....240.00
Trunk, paper on wood, complete w/till, 12" W....55.00

Glassware

Acorn, spooner, frosted....100.00
Acorn, sugar w/lid, 4¾"....110.00
Amazon, creamer....35.00
Amazon, spooner....35.00
Amazon Variant, spooner....30.00
Arched Panel, pitcher....22.00
Arched Panel, pitcher, cobalt....75.00
Arched Panel, tumbler....12.00
Arched Panel, tumbler, amber....19.00

Austrian, creamer, chocolate, 3¼″ . . . 265.00
Austrian, spooner, canary, 3″ . . . 155.00
Austrian, sugar bowl w/lid, 3¾″ . . . 140.00
Baby Flute, individual berry, 1¾″ dia . . . 15.00
Baby Flute, master berry, 3½″ dia . . . 60.00
Baby Thumbprint, cake stand, 2x2⅝″ dia . . . 70.00
Baby Thumbprint, cake stand, 3x4⅛″ dia . . . 75.00
Baby Thumbprint, compote, w/lid, 3⅞″ . . . 130.00
Basket Weave, cup & saucer, amber . . . 30.00
Bead & Scroll, spooner, red flashed, 2½″ . . . 80.00
Bead & Scroll, sugar bowl w/lid, 4″ . . . 105.00
Beaded Swirl, butter dish, 2½″ . . . 30.00
Beaded Swirl, spooner, 2¼″ . . . 45.00
Block, spooner, 3″ . . . 55.00
Block, sugar bowl w/lid, blue, 4½″ . . . 110.00
Block & Rosette, creamer, 2½″ . . . 48.00
Block & Rosette, sugar bowl w/lid, 4⅞″ . . . 80.00
Braided Belt, butter dish, 2¼″ . . . 120.00
Bucket, spooner, 2½″ . . . 80.00
Bullseye & Fan, individual berry . . . 35.00
Bullseye & Fan, master berry, 4¼″ dia . . . 100.00
Button Arches, creamer . . . 75.00
Button Panel, butter dish, clear, EX gold . . . 90.00
Button Panel, sugar bowl w/lid, 4⅝″ . . . 80.00
Buzz Saw, creamer . . . 20.00
Buzz Saw, spooner . . . 20.00
Buzz Saw, sugar bowl w/lid, 3⅜″ . . . 25.00
Buzz Saw, table set . . . 80.00
Candle holder, Good Night, amber, 4″ W, pr . . . 55.00
Castor, pewter fr, 4 bottles/tin lids/glass stoppers, 7½″ . . . 95.00
Clear & Diamond Panels, butter dish, gr, 5⅝″ dia base . . . 75.00
Clear & Diamond Panels, butter dish, 4½″ dia base . . . 50.00
Clear & Diamond Panels, spooner . . . 30.00
Clear Swirl, cruet . . . 22.00
Cloud Band, butter dish, milk glass . . . 135.00
Cloud Band, spooner . . . 40.00
Colonial, pitcher, 3⅜″ . . . 25.00
Colonial, tumbler, 2″ . . . 6.00
Colonial #2630, butter dish, 2½″ . . . 24.00
Colonial #2630, creamer, gr, 2⅜″ . . . 35.00
Colonial #2630, spooner, cobalt . . . 40.00
Colonial #2630, sugar bowl w/lid, cobalt, 3″ . . . 55.00
Colonial #2630, table set, cobalt, Cambridge, 4-pc . . . 190.00
D&M #42, creamer, 2⅞″ . . . 40.00
D&M #42, honey pitcher, 2½″ . . . 65.00
D&M #42, Mardi Gras, spooner, gold horizontal ribs . . . 45.00
D&M #42, rose bowl, 2⅛″ . . . 70.00
Daisy & Button w/V Ornament, mug, vaseline, 3″ . . . 28.00
Deer & Pine tree, mug, pinpoint rim flakes, 2¾″ . . . 25.00
Dewdrop, creamer, 2¾″ . . . 50.00
Dewdrop, sugar bowl w/lid, bl, 4⅛″ . . . 100.00
Diamond Ridge (D&M #48), spooner, 2¾″ . . . 65.00
Dog Medallion, cup & saucer, 3½″ dia saucer . . . 110.00
Doyle #500, creamer, amber, 2½″ . . . 55.00
Doyle #500, mug, bl, 2″ . . . 45.00
Doyle #500, tray, 6⅝″ dia . . . 45.00
Drum, mug, w/eagle & gold trim . . . 25.00
Dutch Kinder, pitcher, milk glass, 2¼″ . . . 60.00
Dutch Kinder, potty, bl milk glass, 2⅛″ . . . 70.00
English Hobnail, cruet w/stopper & shakers, set . . . 40.00
Fancy Cut, butter dish . . . 32.00
Fernland, butter dish, cobalt . . . 45.00
Flattened Diamond, punch bowl . . . 20.00
Flattened Diamond, punch bowl w/6 cups/hangers . . . 55.00
Flattened Diamond, punch cup . . . 6.00
Flattened Diamond, spooner . . . 20.00
Good Boy, mug, enclosed in wreath, ftd, 3⅜″ . . . 20.00
Good Girl, mug, enclosed in wreath, ftd, 3½″ . . . 20.00
Hawaiian Lei, butter dish . . . 40.00
Hawaiian Lei, spooner . . . 30.00
Heisey Colonial, creamer . . . 32.00
Heisey Colonial, spooner . . . 30.00
Hickman, condiment tray . . . 20.00
Hickman, salt shaker . . . 18.00
Hobnail w/Thumbprint, creamer, amber . . . 20.00
Horse Medallion, spooner, EX . . . 20.00
Inverted Strawberry, punch set . . . 120.00
Lacy Daisy, bowl, berry; lg . . . 10.00
Lacy Daisy, bowl, clear, sm . . . 6.00
Lacy Daisy, bowl, mint gr, sm . . . 15.00
Lacy Daisy, celery . . . 23.00
Lacy Medallion, sugar, open, gr . . . 20.00
Lamb, sugar bowl, w/lid, milk glass . . . 190.00
Lion, butter dish, frosted . . . 135.00
Lion, cup & saucer, crystal . . . 55.00
Lion, sugar bowl, w/lid, crystal . . . 95.00
Lion, table set, crystal, 4-pc . . . 350.00
Mitered Sawtooth, spooner . . . 25.00
Monk, stein set, milk glass, pink on gold . . . 125.00
Mug, robin, amber, 3½″ . . . 22.50
Nursery Rhyme, bowl, sm . . . 22.00
Nursery Rhyme, butter dish . . . 85.00
Nursery Rhyme, tumbler . . . 20.00
Oval Star, creamer . . . 15.00
Oval Star, punch cup . . . 9.00
Patee Cross, berry set, 5-pc . . . 60.00
Patee Cross, bowl, berry; sm . . . 9.00
Patee Cross, pitcher . . . 35.00
Patee Cross, tumbler . . . 10.00
Pillar, mug, smooth hdl, 1½″ . . . 10.00
Rexford, butter dish . . . 17.00
Rexford, creamer . . . 16.00
Sandwich, tumbler, 1¾″ . . . 20.00
Star & Ivy, cup & saucer . . . 46.00
Stippled Dahlia, mug . . . 22.00
Sweetheart, butter dish . . . 36.00
Sweetheart, creamer . . . 25.00
Sweetheart, spooner . . . 30.00
Tappan, butter dish . . . 26.00
Tappan, creamer, crystal . . . 15.00
Tappan, spooner . . . 16.00
Tulip & Honeycomb, bowl, oval . . . 52.00
Tulip & Honeycomb, creamer . . . 15.00

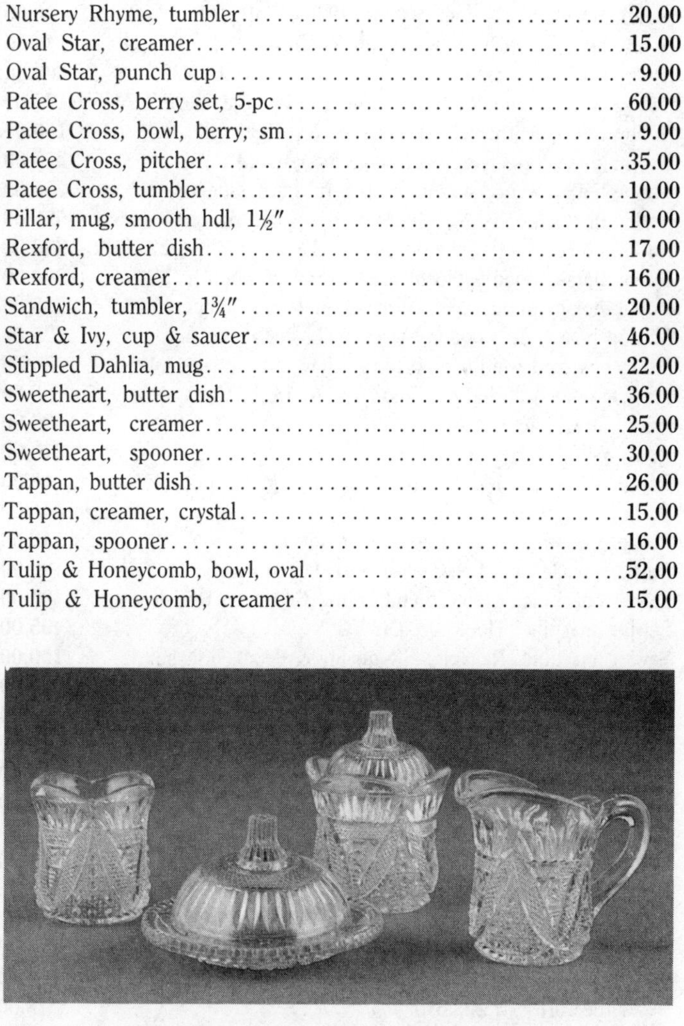

Twin Snowshoes, crystal table set, $245.00.

Tulip & Honeycomb, punch bowl....25.00
Tulip & Honeycomb, punch bowl, 4 cups....75.00
Tulip & Honeycomb, spooner....24.00
Tulip & Honeycomb, sugar bowl....20.00
Twin Snowshoes, creamer....40.00
Twist, butter dish, frosted....75.00
Wee Branches, butter dish, sm....100.00
Wee Branches, cup....15.00
Wee Branches, plate....25.00
Wee Branches, spooner....55.00
Wee Branches, sugar, open....35.00
Wee Branches, table set, 4-pc....425.00
Wheat Sheaf, punch bowl....26.00
Wheat Sheaf, punch cup....9.00
Wild Rose, creamer, milk glass....30.00
Winged Scroll, butter dish, pink....45.00

Miscellaneous

Blocks, 1½" sq, in orig wood box, 1890s, 9½x13"....195.00
Bottle, baby; The Little Papoose....85.00
Chalk board, pressed oak, 45", VG....45.00
Coffee set, litho tin, birds/leaves/gold, Victorian, 6-pc....50.00
Cook set, tin: pan/platter/plate/3 utensils, on orig card....40.00
Cup, tin, birds, flowers, farm scene litho....18.00
Flatware, child's set, pusher/spoon/fork, Georg Jensen....250.00
Golf club, wooden shaft, 26" L....15.00
Grand piano, oak, orig, 14x14"....15.00
Handkerchief, Sunbonnet Babies, 1920s, MIB....20.00
Hobby horse, cloth over wood, on fr, 40x40", VG....140.00
Hobby horse, felt cover, on wheels, Armour's Star, 22"....600.00
Hobby horse, laminated wood, primitive, losses/damage, 27"....175.00
Hobby horse, leather saddle/early decor, 1860s, 32x36", VG...160.00
Hobby horse, primitive, wood, rockers, rstr, 43", EX....275.00
Hobby horse, wood, stationary, rpt, rpl harness/mane, 35"....255.00
Hobby horse, wood pnt, wheels & removable rockers, 35x51"..525.00
Hobby horse, wood w/dapple pnt, rockers, primitive, 22x43"...350.00
Hobby horse, wood w/plush, glass eyes, pnt wood fr, 32"....200.00
Hobby horse, wood w/rpt, harness/saddle rpl, jumper, 35" L...295.00
Ironing board, all wooden, very small....25.00
Music box, rnd w/litho of Victorian boy, 2 tunes, 3¼" W....50.00
Print, mother w/little boy, criss-cross fr, 14x17"....25.00
Print, Stray Lambs, 20x27", VG....75.00
Print, You Dursn't, 20x26", EX....210.00
Rattle, Cat & the Fiddle, bun shape, flat, MOP ring, 1¼"....48.00
Rattle, Good Child, w/whistle, tin....45.00
Rattle, owl w/bells, sterling w/MOP hdl, EX....145.00
Rattle, whistle end, bells, silver/pearl hdl, worn, 5¼"....90.00
Sewing machine, Casige, hand crank, Germany, British zone....35.00
Sewing machine, Hook, Jr; CI, VG....95.00
Sewing machine, Reliable, EX quality & detail, orig box....100.00
Sewing machine, Singer....60.00
Sewing machine, Wilcox & Gibbs....75.00
Skillet, peacock design in base, CI....16.00
Sled, logging; all wood, dbl runners w/iron strips....185.00
Sled, metal, scarlet w/blk trim & runners, 1920s, 21x36"....160.00
Sled, wood runners w/CI eagle heads/rpt stencil decor, 33"....200.00
Sled, wood w/iron runners, orig brn pnt, 20" L....185.00
Sled, wood w/iron runners, orig floral pnt decor, 16" L....305.00
Sleigh, push type, wood w/iron runners, cloth hood, VG....250.00
Spoon & fork, First Love....10.00
Stroller, wicker, needs parasol, 1890s....575.00
Teakettle, brass, rare, 6x5"....28.00
Teakettle, CI, mk Falkirk #1, 7"....35.00

Baby rattle, sterling with decorative embossing, 4", $145.00.

Telephone, wood/orig pnt, bells, crank, 1900s, 11"....65.00
Trunk, steamer; brass tacks, complete w/hangers, 22"....60.00
Trunk, w/lift-out till, orig, 10x10x16"....45.00
Wagon, coaster; wood w/iron wheels, ca 1902....225.00
Wagon, orig pnt/stencil, wood spokes, iron rim wheels, 36"....450.00
Wagon seat, gr pnt w/yel/blk stripe, Studebaker Jr, 20"....155.00
Wash boiler, dk tin, side hdls, w/lid....35.00
Wash set, tin tub/bucket, wood/tin board, wood bench/pins....85.00
Wash set, wooden: tub/wringer/washboard/drying rack....125.00
Washboard, all wood, circle for soap at top....35.00
Washboard, dk tin, 4½x8½"....35.00
Washboard, thick wood, wide dk tin scrub surface, 10x6½"....35.00
Wheelbarrow, tin w/pnt wood hdls, 15x28"....75.00
Wheelbarrow, wood w/solid wood wheel, 1880s, 16x34"....145.00

Christmas Collectibles

Christmas past . . . lovely mementos from long ago attest to the ostentatious Victorian celebrations of the season.

St. Nicholas, better known as Santa, has changed much since 300 A.D. when the good Bishop Nicholas showered needy children with gifts and kindnesses. During the early 18th century, Santa was portrayed as the kind gift giver to well-behaved children, and the stern switch-bearing disciplinarian to those who were bad. In 1822, Clement Clark Moore, a New York poet, wrote his famous 'Night Before Christmas,' and the Santa he described was jolly and jovial--a loveable old elf who was stern with no one. Early Santas wore robes of yellow, brown, blue, green, red, or even purple. But Thomas Nast, who worked as an illustrator for Harper's Weekly, was the first to depict Santa in a red suit instead of the traditional robe, and to locate him the entire yearat the North Pole headquarters. Today's collectors prize early Santa figures, especially those in robes of fur or mohair, or those dressed in an unusual color.

Some early examples of Christmas memorabilia are the pre-1870 ornaments from Dresden, Germany. These cardboard figures--angels, gondolas, umbrellas, dirigibles, and countless others--sparkled with gold and silver trim. Late in the 1870s, blown glass ornaments were imported from Germany. There were over 6,000 recorded designs--carrots and cucumbers, clown faces and angel heads, butterflies and stars--all painted inside with silvery colors. From 1890 through 1910, blown glass spheres were often decorated with beads, tassels, and tinsel rope.

Christmas lights, made by Sandwich and some of their contemporaries, were either pressed or mold-blown glass, shaped into a form similar to a water tumbler. They were filled with water and then hung from the tree by a wire handle; oil floating on the surface of the water served as fuel for the lighted wick.

Kugels are glass ornaments that were made as early as 1820 and as late as 1890. Ball-shaped examples are more common than the fruit and vegetable forms, and have been found in sizes ranging from 1″ to 14″ in diameter. They were made of thick glass with heavy brass caps, in cobalt, green, gold, silver, and occasionally in amethyst.

Although experiments involving the use of electric lightbulbs for the Christmas tree occured before 1900, it was 1903 before the first manufactured socket set was marketed. These were very expensive and often proved a safety hazard. In 1921, safety regulations were established and products were guaranteed safety approved. The early bulbs were smaller replicas of Edison's household bulb. By 1910, G.E. bulbs were rounded with a pointed end, and until 1919 all bulbs were hand blown. The first figural bulbs were made around 1910 in Austria. Japan soon followed, but their product was never of the high quality of Austrian wares. American manufacturers produced their first machine-made figurals after 1919. Today, figural bulbs, especially character-related examples, are very popular collectibles.

Bubble lights were popular from about 1945 to 1960 when miniature lights were introduced. These tiny lamps dampened the public's enthusiasm for the bubblers, and manufacturers stopped providing replacement bulbs.

When no condition is indicated, the items listed below are assumed to be in excellent condition.

Bulbs

Andy Gump w/mustache, VG 25.00
Baby in red stocking, EX 12.00
Ball w/stars, red 10.00
Bell, w/2 Santa faces in relief, 3″, G 12.00
Boy 25.00
Boy Scout, EX 18.00
Choir girl, milk glass 20.00
Clown, balloon style suit/full figure, rare, EX pnt 80.00
Clown, w/mask, milk glass 20.00
Clown head 25.00
Dog, hockey player carrying stick, full figure, G 25.00
Dog, in basket, milk glass 23.00
Doll head 25.00
Dutch girl, milk glass 12.50
Dwarf, 1 of 7 .... 30.00
Ear of corn, gr/yel/pink, 3″, EX 25.00
Elephant, milk glass 65.00
Gazelle, leaping, Art Deco, 8″ 27.50
Girl, milk glass 10.00
House, milk glass 12.00
Humpty Dumpty 35.00
Kewpie 45.00
Lemon, clear glass 17.50
Lion, red tailcoat, bl vest, John Bull, milk glass 12.50
Lion w/tennis racket, EX 20.00
Little Orphan Annie, milk glass 25.00
Little Red Riding Hood 65.00
Log cabin, milk glass 12.00
Mickey & Minnie Mouse, pr 50.00
Moon Mullins, milk glass 45.00
Owl, clear glass 48.50
Parrots in birdcage, milk glass 20.00
Peach, clear glass 10.00
Pig 65.00
Queen of Hearts, w/2 blk birds, EX 55.00
Rabbit playing banjo, winking, 2¾″, EX 60.00
Sailor, 2-faced, w/diving helmet & scarf, milk glass 60.00
Santa, atop chimney, milk glass 12.50
Santa, by Amico, working, 6″ 25.00
Santa, by chimney 20.00
Santa, dbl faced 22.00
Santa, roly-poly, milk glass 22.50
Santa, 2-sided, milk glass 22.50
Snowman holding stick, clear glass, exhaust tip, EX 40.00
Teddy bear, full figure, red w/yel paws & eyes, EX 75.00
Three Men in a Tub 45.00

Ornaments

Airplane, cb w/mica, w/compo faced Santa atop, '30s, 6x4″ 40.00
Airplane, Dresden 180.00
Airship, blown glass, w/scrap cupid, gold pnt, 5″ 60.00
Angel, flesh pnt, spun glass 42.50
Angel, glass, tree top, 10″ 12.50
Angel, papier mache face, cotton batting 17.50
Angel, spun glass wings, wax 52.50

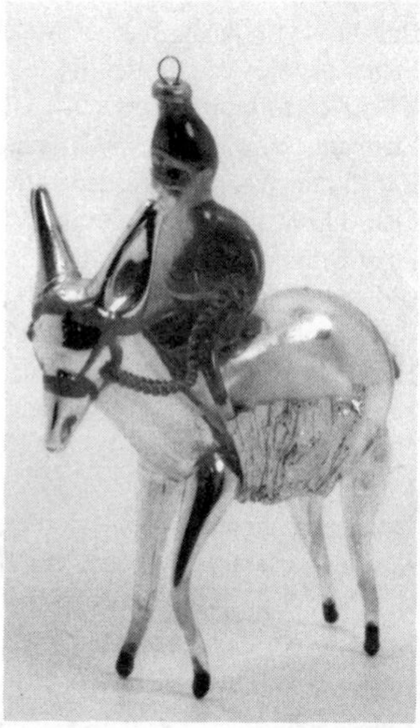

Ornament, Santa on donkey, blown glass, 5″ x 4½″, $165.00.

Angel, wax w/wool pants, no wings or horn, 11″ L, VG 90.00
Automobile, blown glass, silver/gr, rare 85.00
Baby Jesus, head only 72.50
Balloon, blown glass, w/paper scrap cupid, wire trim, 5½″ 70.00
Balloon, blown glass, w/scrap angel, tinsel wrapped 92.00
Balloon, blown glass, w/scrap Santa, all orig, 5″, EX 70.00
Basket, wire, w/paper flowers 25.00
Basket of fruit, blown glass, mc, German, 1900s, 4″ 48.00
Bear, blown glass, frosted finish, 3″ 20.00
Bear w/stick, blown glass, peach/blk, minor wear, 4″ 80.00
Bell, blown glass, gr w/glass clapper, early 20th C, 2″ 6.00
Bell, blown glass, ribbed, leaf decor, early 20th C, 3″ 16.00
Bell, glass ball w/eagle decor atop lg ½ ball, minor wear 35.00
Bird, bisque w/spun glass wings, 4″ 25.00
Bird, blown glass, clip on, pink & bl, old 10.00
Bird cage, blown glass, wht/yel w/mc pnt parrots, early 25.00
Bird on nest, blown glass, tinsel wrapped 45.00
Boat, blown glass, EX pnt, 3″ L 20.00
Candle lantern, blown glass 20.00
Carrot, blown glass, EX emb detail, slightly worn pnt, 4″ 65.00
Cat, blown glass, Germany 45.00
Cat head, Lauschan 150.00
Cat in shoe, blown glass 55.00
Christmas tree, blown, gr sawdust w/in, silver base, 4″ 10.00

Clown, full figure, ½ moon in stomach, blown glass, 5½" 55.00
Clown bust, blown glass, ball/teardrop base, '20s, 6½" 70.00
Clown head, blown glass, sand finish, few pnt chips, 2" 90.00
Clown head, blown glass, 4" 30.00
Clown head, spun glass 67.50
Clown head on cone, blown glass 52.50
Clown w/banjo, sits on stump, blown, German, 1900s, 4½" 38.00
Cockatoo, blown glass, clip on, early 14.00
Cockatoo, blown glass w/feathered tail, clip-on 24.00
Cone w/fruit, blown glass, 7" 22.50
Corn, blown glass, yel 40.00
Cuckoo clock, blown glass, emb & mc pnt face, 3" 25.00
Devil face, pink & silver, old 85.00
Dog, bulldog head, Lauschan 110.00
Dog, Scottie; blown glass, stands on haunches, yel/bl 55.00
Dog, sitting, wearing red shirt/collar & tie, blown, 4" 80.00
Dog in bag, My Darling, blown, silver/pink, 3½", EX 85.00
Doll, bisque, crepe paper dress w/tinsel, mk Germany, 7" 110.00
Doll face in bunch of grapes, blown glass, 4½" 150.00
Doll head, blown glass 45.00
Doll head, ribbon in hair, blown, minor pnt chips, 3" 50.00
Eagle, glass eyes, Dresden, lg 250.00
Ear of corn, blown glass 45.00
Elephant, blown blass, pink drape, 3½" 45.00
Elk, 3-dimensional, Dresden, lg 195.00
Fish, blown glass, mc, German, 1900s, 3" 20.00
Foxy Grandpa, full figure, blown/applied legs, 4½", VG 135.00
Girl, full figure, blown glass, 3" 35.00
Girl's head, blown glass, blown glass eyes, pnt gone, 2½" 22.50
Happy Hooligan, blown glass, applied legs, 4½", VG 145.00
Horse, blown glass, silver 95.00
Horse, Dresden 165.00
Icicle, cotton batting 10.00
Japanese character, paper clothes, plaster face/wool ft 125.00
Japanese character w/paper lantern/clothes, plaster/wool 150.00
Keystone Kop, clip on 140.00
Kugel, gold, emb cap, 4" 25.00
Kugel, gold, fancy CI holder at top, 12" 185.00
Kugel, gold, 8", VG 50.00
Kugel, gr, emb cap, 6" 60.00
Kugel, gr, 3", VG 30.00
Kugel, gr, 7", VG 70.00
Kugel, grapes, gr, brass hanger, 5" L 280.00
Kugel, grapes, gr w/brass cap, 3½" 135.00
Kugel, grapes, silver 125.00
Kugel, royal bl, 1¾" 25.00
Kugel, turnip, silver, in metal holder, 29" dia 65.00
Lantern, blown glass, silver & gold, early 20th C, 3½" 16.00
Lighthouse, blown blass, pink base, G pnt, 3" 20.00
Little Miss Muffet, blown glass, gold pnt, 3½", EX 80.00
Man in Moon, blown glass, devilish grin, gr, 3" 85.00
Man w/beard in moon-shaped pine cone, pk top, 3½" 105.00
Mandolin, blown glass, silver w/gold, early 20th C, 3½" 16.00
Mushroom, blown glass, on clips, 3", pr 10.00
Owl's head, blown glass, pink 150.00
Peach, blown glass, 3" 40.00
Peacock, blown w/spun glass tail, hook in bk, 3½", EX 60.00
Pear, blown glass, yel w/orange spray, 4", EX 40.00
Pear, cotton 20.00
Penguin, blown glass, bl/silver, red beak, emb feet, 1¾" 37.00
Pickle, blown glass, silver 85.00
Pine cone, blown, pink snow covered, early 20th C, 3½" 6.00
Pipe, blown glass, gr, no hanger, 3½" 15.00
Pocket watch, blown, red, paper face/bk: emb flower, 2" 50.00
Purse, blown glass, tinsel wrapped 32.50
Rabbit w/carrot, blown glass, 4" 65.00
Reindeer, blown glass, w/bud vase, Germany 27.50
Reindeer, pulling Santa, scene in a sq, milk glass 12.50
Revolver, blown glass, pink/bl 150.00
Rooster entering chicken coop, blown glass, red 85.00
Rose, open, blown glass, sand finish, clip on 55.00
Round, blown, emb X-d sword/anchor/bleeding heart, 2½", NM ..25.00
Sailboat, blown glass, Czechoslovakian label, silver, old 10.00
Sailboat, blown glass, gold mesh & braid trim 150.00
Santa, blown glass, w/tin clip, rare, 4" 20.00
Santa, carries bag of toys, blown glass, 1930s, 2½" 20.00
Santa, in cb sleigh w/2 celluloid reindeer, fabric 30.00
Santa, in fireplace, blown glass, lg 35.00
Santa, on pine cone, blown glass 25.00
Santa, on tinselled airplane, cotton body w/plaster face 47.50
Santa, on 2-tone bl ball, blown glass 52.50
Santa, papier mache, seated, sgn, Made in Germany 20.00
Santa, w/red sack, cloth 55.00
Santa head, blown glass, sanded beard, 3" 40.00
Santa head, blown glass, stylized emb features, 1930s, 2" 22.00
Santa head, blown glass, 2¼" 20.00
Scallop shell, pearl in center, blown glass, 3" 65.00
Ship, blown glass, hook hanger, Germany 40.00
Snake, coiled, pr 70.00
Snow White & 7 Dwarfs, flocked, w/costumes, 3", set 50.00
Snowman, blown glass, sand finish, clip on, early 47.50
Snowman, w/top hat, glitter on cb, 5" 5.00
Snowman w/broom, blown glass, smiling, early, 3½" 40.00
Spider in web 55.00
Stag, free-blown, gold antlers, orig MIG label, 3" 35.00
Stag, leaping, blown glass, bl 40.00
Stocking, blown glass, Victorian 65.00
Stork, blown glass, clip-on, blk/wht, lg open red bill, EX 40.00
Stork, Dresden 200.00
Sugar bowl, blown, gold w/florals, early 20th C, 3½" 8.00
Swan, blown glass, silver/wht/gold, old 10.00
Swan, blown glass, w/scrap Santa, all orig, 6", EX 40.00
Swan, blown glass, w/scrap Santa, tinsel wrap, 7½", EX 65.00
Teapot, blown glass, pink w/florals, early 20th C, 3½" 8.00
Teddy bear, blown glass, gold pnt, 3½", EX 60.00
Teddy bear on swing w/paper tree, cotton/wool/mica, 5½" 170.00
Tree, blown glass, clip-on 45.00
Tree, w/Santa face, blown glass, 3" 5.00
Turkey, blown glass, on clip, rare, 3" 15.00
Turkey, free-blown, tinsel wings & tail, 5" 12.00
TV Stars of '50s, bells w/decals, King Features, set of 12 ....45.00
Umbrella, wood fringe, wire trim, 6", VG 50.00
Watermelon wedge, blown glass 65.00
Zeppelin, Los Angeles, w/American flag, blown glass 200.00

Miscellaneous

Book, A Christmas Carroll, by Wither, illus Merrill, 1907 ....22.00
Book, pop-up; Christmas Time 12.00
Book, Santa Claus Stories, McLoughlin, c 1898 ....15.00
Candle holder, tin clip-on, early 20th C 3.00
Candy container, feather tree w/candle clips, cb base, 5" 80.00
Candy container, Santa, glass, 5" 30.00
Candy container, Santa, glitter/cb, mk West Germany 8.00
Candy container, Santa, mesh body w/celluloid face 30.00
Candy container, Santa, papier mache, Germany, 8" 40.00
Candy container, Santa in basket, plaster hands, Japan, 5" 70.00
Candy container, Santa w/plaster face in felt shoe, 7" 55.00

Candy container, Santa/feather tree/mica, Bellsnickle, 8½″.....310.00
Father Christmas, compo/fur beard, cb/mica sleigh, '30, 6″......45.00
Father Christmas, cotton batting/papier mache, French, 14″....350.00
Father Christmas w/tree & basket, red robe, die-cut, 10x6″.....85.00
Fence, picket, gr, for tree base, 24 ft L.....................65.00
Hooked rug, Santa in sleigh, 1920s.........................90.00
Lantern, glass paneled sides, tin, 6″.......................18.00
Lights, Disney Silly Symphony, Noma, no shades o/w MIB......75.00
Lights, Mickey Mouse, Noma, 1930s, w/orig box.............150.00
Lights, Popeye, 1930s, w/orig box..........................150.00
Lights, Scrappy & his friends, in orig box, 1930s............125.00
Log cabin, w/picket fence for tree stand, folk art, 24x24″.......50.00
Lunch box, w/Santa, 1900s................................37.50
Mug, Santa hdl, by Morley, 4½″, EX.........................25.00
Print, A Cat's Christmas Dance, Wain, 20x26″.................50.00
Print, Another Stocking..., Thos Nast, matted/fr, 20x27″......100.00
Print, Night Before Christmas, McLoughlin...................20.00
Print, Santa w/reindeer.....................................10.00
Puzzle, Santa & child, in fr, Victorian, 15x20″..............150.00
Reindeer, lead w/orig pnt, German, ea 2½″, set of 6..........125.00
Rudolph the Red Nose Reindeer, tin, Japan, 6x6″..............8.00
Santa, '20s airplane/pkgs/tree, heavy emb paper, 12″...........45.00
Santa, battery operated, bells ring/eyes light, 13″, VG..........80.00
Santa, bends at waist, Electric Automaton, 32″...............65.00
Santa, bisque, Japan, 1930s, 2″............................35.00
Santa, blown glass, w/tree, 4″.............................38.00
Santa, celluloid, sleigh & 3 reindeer, Japan...................40.00
Santa, celluloid & tin, Suzuki, 4″...........................5.00
Santa, celluloid face, keywound, working, 6½″, VG............90.00
Santa, compo face, velour tree, red suit, 1930s, 5″............40.00
Santa, compo w/felt suit, 1930s, 6″.........................45.00
Santa, emb paper, glitter, sgn, Germany.....................25.00
Santa, holding feather tree, compo w/felt coat, 12½″, EX......250.00
Santa, holding sm feather tree, HP, German, 9″..............90.00
Santa, holding tree, scrap art, cotton batting, 17″...........120.00
Santa, holding tree w/back pack, plaster face, Japan, 6″........55.00
Santa, honeycomb folded tissue, cb head/beard, life sz........100.00
Santa, HP cloth face/real hair/compo boots, arms move, 28″...145.00
Santa, in composition sleigh, plaster face, 8″.................30.00
Santa, in sleigh pulled by 2 reindeer, wood/paper, 7x20″.....1,100.00
Santa, in sleigh pulled by 4 reindeer, papier mache, 8x26″.....750.00
Santa, in wood sleigh w/8 reindeer, plaster face, 14″ L.........40.00
Santa, jtd, compo/molded hair/hair/cap, pnt eyes, 19″.........250.00
Santa, molded papier mache, wht coat, 7″, VG.................30.00
Santa, nodder, clockwork, all orig, 28″....................1,550.00
Santa, nodder, sitting, clockwork, papier mache/wool, 16″.....350.00
Santa, on polar bear, papier mache, 9½″, EX.................105.00
Santa, papier mache face, early, 24″.......................350.00
Santa, plaster face, cloth coat, German, 7″...................35.00
Santa, plaster face, paper coat, Japan, 7″...................15.00
Santa, plaster face, wool coat, sack over shoulder, 6″..........45.00
Santa, plaster face/hands/ft, w/sticker: Japan Calient, 9″........55.00
Santa, puppet, hand-carved wood, orig clothes, 18″...........140.00
Santa, riding tricycle, Korea, 4″...........................18.00
Santa, straw stuffed, 22″..................................35.00
Santa, stuffed, fully dressed, rubber face, 24″................10.00
Santa, w/sleigh, CI, Booneville, NY, 6x14″...................330.00
Santa Claus, soap figural, orig box.........................40.00
Sleigh, CI, 14″ L..210.00
Snow children on sleigh, Electric Automaton, 28x30″..........30.00
Teapot, Santa, ¾ figure, made in England, 7½″, EX..........150.00
Tree, bubble gum charms, plays Silent Night as it turns........15.00
Tree, feather, gr, candle clips, rpt rnd base, 37″, VG.........150.00
Tree, feather, gr, candle clips, wood base, 22″, VG...........130.00
Tree, feather, gr, in wooden block, 38″, NM..................310.00
Tree, feather, no stand, w/candle holders, 60″................300.00
Tree, feather, red berry limb tips, MIG, 26″, EX.............135.00
Tree stand, CI, bottom mk IM, gr w/gold pine cones...........45.00
Tree stand, CI, mk Marras, Germany, 6¾″...................45.00
Tree stand, maple, 3 trn tripod ft support holder, 19x17″......85.00
Tree stand, musical, wind-up, plays 2 tunes, Germany, 19″.....135.00
Tree stand, revolves, cylinder music box, Eckardt, 10″........275.00

Chrysanthemum Sprig, Blue

This is the blue opaque version of Northwood's popular pattern, Chrysanthemum Sprig. Though collectors often refer to it as 'blue custard,' in the strictest sense it is not. It was made at the turn of the century, and is today very rare, as its values indicate.

When no condition is indicated, the items listed below are assumed to be in mint condition.

Butter dish...800.00
Celery vase...750.00
Compote, jelly..500.00
Creamer...325.00
Cruet...650.00
Pitcher, water..900.00
Sauce dish..145.00
Spooner...250.00
Sugar bowl, open..200.00
Sugar bowl, w/lid.......................................425.00
Toothpick holder..375.00
Tumbler...200.00

Cincinnati Art Pottery

The Cincinnati Art Pottery was established in 1879 by T.J. Wheatley along with several others, primarily, it is felt, to generate funds to augment his further experimentation with the underglaze decorated Cincinnati Faience. It was this type of ware that was produced there until 1882, when Wheatley withdrew his interests and the firm actually began to utilize the title 'Cincinnati Art Pottery.'

During the years that followed, several other artware lines were successfully developed. Hungarian Faience was a light glazed line depending on its in-mold modeling for decoration. The resulting patterns were painted in contrasting colors, often highlighted with gold tracing. Portland Blue Faience imitated the rich blue of the famous Portland vase, and it, too, was often highlighted with gold.

But their most famous product was an ivory line featuring flowers painted in natural colors and elaborate gold scrollwork. The ware is often marked 'Keyonta,' either in block letters or with a circular device containing a turtle, the Indian translation of the line's name.

When no condition is indicated the items listed below are assumed to be in mint condition.

Vase, Kezonta, floral, bl/gr on yel, gold trim, 16″...........650.00
Vase, Kezonta, snow scene/scrolls, mc, bottle form...........775.00

Circus Collectibles

The 1890s--the Golden Age of the circus. Barnum and Bailey's parades transformed mundane city streets into an exotic never-never land inhabited by trumpeting elephants with gold jeweled headgear, strutting by to the strains of the calliope that issued from a fine red and gilt painted wagon extravagantly decorated with carved wooden animals of every description. It was an exciting experience--is it any wonder that collectors today treasure the mementos of that golden era?

Posters that once whetted interest and stirred imaginations are today avidly sought, and though rarely signed by the artist, often carry the name of the printer or lighographer. Among them, many consider the work of the Strobridge Lithograph Company to be the finest. Other early printing companies were Gibson and Company Litho, Erie Litho, and Enquirer Job Printing Company.

When no condition is indicated, the items listed below are assumed to be in excellent condition.

Key:
lm—linen mount
RR B&B—Ringling Brothers, Barnum & Bailey

Kapt. Wall, printed by Friedlander, linen back, ca 1929, 28" x 38", $450.00 in near mint condition.

Banner, Lionella, Lion-headed Woman, Snap Wyatt, 8x10"....850.00
Bells, elephant's; 3 nickeled brass on 10x50" leather strap.....250.00
Big Top Circus, cut-outs, General Electric premium, unused.....75.00
Helium balloon fixture, Zeppelin shape, CI...................38.00
Lamp, coach; wood, pnt layers over orig stencil, 11", pr.......350.00
Medal, for daring performance of lion tamer, 1911...........660.00
Poster, acrobatic monkeys & chimpanzees, 96x108"..........400.00
Poster, All Girl Revue, w/Little Egypt, canvas, 10x8"..........320.00
Poster, Brown's Shows, men balance girls on poles, 1890s.....150.00
Poster, Daniel & Sohn balancing act, '06, Friedlander, 38"....450.00
Poster, De Marce's Baboon-Circus, 1907, Friedlander, 28"......200.00
Poster, Pin Head Henry, Man From Mars, canvas, 72x96".....270.00
Poster, RB B&B, Col McCoy/Rough Riders, 1935, lm, 28x40"..200.00
Poster, Ringling Bros/Kings of Circus World, 1908, lm, 29"....225.00
Poster, 3 clowns above oval w/animals, stock, Friedlander......400.00
Program, RB B&B, 1937.................................12.50
Program, RB B&B, 1939.................................12.50
Program, Ringling Bros, 1913, 56-pg......................37.50

Clambroth

Clambroth is a term that refers to a type of glass popular during the Victorian period. It was semi-opaque and gray-white in color, said to resemble the broth of the clam.

Unless noted otherwise, values are for examples in mint condition.

Cake stand, base & top joined by wafer, 8x11" dia............75.00
Candlestick, hexagonal, 7", EX..........................55.00
Candlestick, loop base, 6 petal top, 7", EX..................75.00
Candlestick, sq base, fluted std, petal socket, 8¾", EX.........85.00
Jigger, 10 panels, w/hdl, 1⅞"..............................40.00
Pickle dipper, pierced 4½" dia bowl, 9½"....................12.00

Clarice Cliff

Between 1928 and 1935, in Burslem, England, as the director and part owner of Wilkinson and Newport Pottery Companies, Clarice Cliff and her 'paintresses' created a body of hand painted pottery whose influence is felt to the present time.

The name for the oevre was Bizarre Ware, and the predominant sensibility, style, and appearance was Deco. Almost all pieces are signed and include the pattern names. There were over 160 patterns and more than 100 shapes, all of which will be illustrated in *A Bizarre Affair--the Life and Work of Clarice Cliff*, to be published by Harry N. Abrams Inc. in 1986, written by Susan and Louis Meisel and Len Griffen. You will find their address in the Directory under New York.

Clarice Cliff died in 1972, shortly after the Victoria and Albert Museum showed her work in retrospect, and collectors, primarily in England, began seeking and admiring her work. The Metropolitan Museum of Art in New York City, in September of 1982, acquired and has placed on view a selection of six pieces.

When no condition is indicated, the items listed below are assumed to be in mint condition.

Basket, Bizarre, 13"...................................475.00
Bowl, Bizarre, Cottage & Hills, 8"........................150.00
Bowl, Bizarre, Crocus, acorn, 8"..........................85.00
Bowl, Bizarre, Fantasque, 8"............................140.00
Bowl, Bizarre, Gayday, plated rim, 9"......................150.00
Bowl, Fantasque, Canterbury Bells, 9"......................125.00
Bowl, Inspiration, Persian pattern, 7"......................880.00
Bowl, wooded landscape, 3"..............................29.00
Cache pot, Bizarre, 3"..................................60.00
Candle holder, Bizarre, 2¼x3½"..........................85.00
Centerpiece figure, Age of Jazz, musicians/dancers, 7".......3,300.00
Coffee set, Bizarre, Chintz, 15-pc........................150.00
Gravy boat, Bizarre.....................................100.00

Bizarre wash set, $6,000.

Jardiniere, Inspiration, landscape, gr/bl on ivory mat..........220.00
Pitcher, Celtic Harvest, mc fruit & flowers, 10x6″............165.00
Pitcher, Fantasque, landscape & pagoda roof, squat, 5″.......150.00
Pitcher, Fantasque, 11-color, octagonal, 7″...................200.00
Pitcher, lotus; Visceria, bright flowers, 8″...................175.00
Pitcher, Newport.......................................150.00
Plate, Inspiration, turq w/3 russet & mauve flowers...........400.00
Sugar bowl, Bizarre.......................................75.00
Sugar shaker, Bizarre, metal top.........................100.00
Tea set, Rodanthe, 12-pc.................................265.00
Tea set, Solitaire, D-shape, 6-pc..........................250.00
Tea-for-2 service, Fantastique, bl/mauve/pink...............1,320.00
Tray, geometric, bold colors, 11″.........................200.00
Tureen, Bizarre, Canterbury Bells.........................150.00
Vase, Blue Pines, dk bl/mauve trees, disk ft.................820.00
Vase, lotus; center band w/kite forms, w/hdl, 12″...........1,700.00
Vase, lotus; Fantastique, orange circles/animals, 12″.........1,760.00
Vase, lotus; Inspiration, Persian pattern, w/hdl, 12″.........5,000.00
Vase, lotus; Willow Tree, 8″..............................95.00
Vase, parakeet in relief, branch hdl, 8″.....................300.00
Vase, parakeets in high relief on str sides, 12½x4¾″..........300.00
Vase, Yo Yo, Inspiration, 9″.............................935.00
Wall plaque, Fantastique, bl/gr/pink w/bl bands, 10″..........495.00
Wall plaque, Inspiration, free-form abstract, special, 13″.....2,420.00
Wall plaque, lady's head form...........................1,100.00
Wall pocket/mask, woman, rare...........................350.00

Cleminson

A hobby turned to enterprise, Cleminson is one of several California potteries whose clever hand decorated wares are attracting the attention of today's collectors. The Cleminsons started their business at their El Monte home in 1941, and were so successful that eventually they expanded to a modern plant that employed more than 150 workers. They produced not only dinnerware and kitchen items such as cookie jars, canisters and accessories, but novelty wall vases, small trays, plaques, etc., as well. Though nearly always marked, Cleminson wares are easy to spot as you become familiar with their distinctive glaze colors. Their grayed-down blue and green, berry red, and dusty pink say 'Cleminson' as clearly as their trademark.

Unable to compete with foreign imports, the pottery closed in 1953. When no condition is indicated, the items listed below are assumed to be in mint condition.

Wall pocket, red long-johns, 8″, $10.00.

Dish, heart shape, bl/brn floral on ivory, 4″...................6.50
Match holder, rectangular box w/bird decor, ivory w/brn/bl......15.00
Salt box, wall hanging; gray w/pink/bl flowers & butterfly.......65.00
Sprinkler bottle, girl figural, brn/bl/gr/yel/maroon, 6½″.........20.00
Wall pocket, coffee pot, yel/bl decor, metal bail hdl, 9″........30.00
Wall pocket, 3 bells, red glaze, 7″ W........................7.50

Clewell

Charles Walter Clewell was a metal worker who perfected the technique of plating an entire ceramic vessel with a thin layer of copper or bronze treated with an oxidizing agent to produce a natural deterioration of the surface. Through trial and error, he was able to control the degree of patina achieved. In the early stages, the metal darkened, and if allowed to develop further, formed a natural tuquoise blue or green corrosion. He worked alone in his small Akron, Ohio, studio from about 1906, buying undecorated pottery from several Ohio firms, among them Weller, Owens, and Cambridge.

His work is usually marked. Clewell died in 1965, having never revealed his secret process to others.

When no condition is indicated, the items listed below are assumed to be in mint condition.

Tankard and four mugs, riveted copper-clad surface, $900.00.

Bowl, copper w/gr patina, mk, #384-6″......................220.00
Bowl, riveted overlay finish, sgn w/imp copper seal, 1½″.......150.00
Box, hammered copper, riveted, Arts & Crafts, 4¾x6½″ dia....150.00
Bud vase, flares from sm neck, partial rough surface, 10″......225.00
Bud vase, slender w/widened base, gr/rust patina, 6½″........195.00
Ewer, paneled, bronze-clad, 5¾″..........................185.00
Mug, advertising, rivets, porc liner, rare raised mk, 1914......175.00
Pitcher, copper over Owens blank, design on ea side, 5¾″.....150.00
Vase, #3-25, exceptional orange/gr patina, 6x3½″............275.00
Vase, #331-1-6, gr/rust patina, 7″.........................235.00
Vase, bottle form, flared top, dk patina, 6¾″................225.00
Vase, flared top, bulbous, allover patina, 8¾″................200.00
Vase, orig gr patina, 4½x3″..............................180.00
Vase, squat, 2 lg integral loop hdls, EX patina, 5x7¼″........265.00

Clews

Brothers Ralph and James Clews were potters who operated in Cobridge, in the Staffordshire district, from 1817 to 1835. They are best known for their blue and white transfer-printed earthenwares, which included American Views, Moral Maxims, Picturesque Views, and English Views. A series called *Three Tours of Dr. Syntax* contained nearly eighty different scenes, with each piece bearing a descriptive title. Two other popular series were *Don Quixote*, with twenty prints, and *Pictures of Sir David Wilkie*, with twelve.

Both printed and impressed marks were used, often incorporating the pattern name as well as the pottery. When no condition is indicated, the items listed below are assumed to be in mint condition. See also Staffordshire, Historical

Plate, bl feather edge, bl transfer Welcome Lafayette, 10" 425.00
Plate, Moral Maxims, blk transfer, 7" 50.00
Plate, toddy; dk bl transfer: Am & Independence, 4¾" 250.00
Platter, bl feather edge, 17", EX 150.00

Clifton

Clifton Art Pottery, of Clifton, New Jersey, was organized in 1905, and until 1911 when they turned to the production of wall and floor tile, made artware of several varieties.

The founders were Fred Tschirner and William A. Long. Long had developed the method for underglaze slip painting that had been used at the Lonhuda Pottery in Steubenville, Ohio, in the 1890s.

Crystal Patina, the first artware made by the small company, utilized a fine white body and flowing, blended colors, the earliest a green crystalline. Indian Ware, copied from the pottery of the American Indians, was decorated in black geometric designs on red clay. Robin's Egg Blue, pale blue on the white body; and Tirrube, a slip decorated matt ware were also produced.

When no condition is indicated, the items listed below are assumed to be in mint condition.

Bowl, Indian Ware, 8" 85.00
Bowl vase, Indian Ware, sgn Florida, 1¾" H 25.00
Humidor, Indian Ware 60.00
Platter, blackberry, oval, 9¾" 60.00
Pot, Indian Ware, brn w/rust/gray, Chevrun, AZ, #220, 4x6" 90.00
Pot, Indian Ware, cream/blk geometrics, 3½" 50.00
Teapot, Crystal Patina, gold finish, #272, 6½x6¾" 110.00
Teapot, Indian Ware, 7" 55.00
Vase, Crystal Patina, bl/brn/gold flambe, hdls, 4x6" 80.00
Vase, Crystal Patina, brn on wht, curled rim, hdls, 7" 35.00
Vase, Crystal Patina, crystalline gr w/emb decor, 1¾x4¾" 175.00
Vase, Crystal Patina, gr streaks, w/hdl, 1906, 6" 275.00
Vase, Crystal Patina, mk & dtd 1906, 2x3¼" 55.00

Humidor, Indian Ware, 5½", $60.00.

Vase, Indian Ware, red w/beige/brn decor, #230, 5x7" 175.00
Vase, Indian Ware, sgn Four Mile/AZ, 2¾" 30.00
Vase, Indian Ware, sgn Homolobi, 6½" 95.00
Vase, Indian Ware, sgn Homolobi, 7¾" 120.00
Vase, Indian Ware, 3½x5½" 40.00
Vase, Tirrube, floral on red, bulb bottom/thin neck, 8x4" 175.00
Water bottle, Indian Ware, Arkansas, 8½x6½" 125.00

Clocks

In the early days of our country's history, clock makers were influenced by styles imported from Europe and Germany. They copied their cabinets and re-constructed their movements. But needed materials were in short supply; modifications had to be made. Of necessity was born mainspring motive power and spring clocks. Wooden movements were made on a mass-production basis as early as 1808. Before the middle of the century, metal movements had been developed.

Today's collectors prefer clocks from the 18th and 19th centuries, with pendulum regulated movements. Bracket clocks made during this period utilized the shorter pendulum improvised in 1658 by Fromentiel, a prominent English clock maker. These smaller square-face clocks usually were made with a dome top fitted with a handle or a decorative finial. The case was usually walnut or ebony, and was often decorated with pierced brass mountings. Brackets were often mounted on the wall to accommodate the clock, hence the name.

The banjo clock was patented in 1802 by Simon Willard. It derived its descriptive name from its banjo-like shape. A similar but more elaborate style was called the lyre clock.

Twentieth century novelty clocks, such as the animated examples in the listings that follow, are becoming very popular collectibles, as their values indicate.

Key:

esc—escapement	pnd—pendulum
mvt—movement	T&S—time and strike

Aaron Willard, banjo, mahog/giltwood, eagle/rvpt, rpr, 33" 880.00
Aaron Willard, banjo, mahog/giltwood/rvpt, 1825, 41x10½" ... 2,750.00
Abiel Chandler, banjo, mahog w/veneer, pnd, rpl/rpr, 33" 550.00
American Clock & Timepiece Co, CI front 125.00
Animated, cowboy on horse, alarm 135.00
Animated, Hickory Dickory Dock, mouse 900.00
Animated, Roosevelt, Man of Hour, electric 90.00
Animated, Roosevelt, Man of Hour, wind up 140.00
Animated, Steersman of USA, drummer playing on dial 145.00
Animated, Teeter Totter, Hanson Synchron #15, 11" 25.00
Animated, Woody Woodpecker at Cafe, alarm, EX 100.00
Animated, Woody Woodpecker at Cafe, alarm, MIB 160.00
Ansonia, Apex, crystal regulator 1,750.00
Ansonia, Bagdad, oak regulator, weight drive 1,275.00
Ansonia, beehive, 8-day/T&S, rosewood 240.00
Ansonia, Capitol, porc dial, time only, spring 800.00
Ansonia, Capitol, porcelain dial, weight, time only 1,200.00
Ansonia, clock on pole, swinging doll, bsk figures, 1890s 720.00
Ansonia, Envoy, crystal regulator 900.00
Ansonia, Floral, crystal regulator 1,400.00
Ansonia, General 3,400.00
Ansonia, Jupitor, crystal regulator, glass columns 2,100.00
Ansonia, La Rata, outside escapement porcelain 600.00
Ansonia, Lucia, crystal regulator 900.00
Ansonia, Lydia 1,150.00
Ansonia, mantel, 8-day/T&S, blk, CI, 10" 135.00
Ansonia, Marchioness, crystal regulator 950.00

E.N. Welsch, Parisian Model, walnut case (teardrop style) eight-day, bell strike, alarm, stenciled glass in gold or silver, ca 1895, 24″, $375.00.

Ansonia, Marquis, visible escapement, crystal regulator........900.00
Ansonia, Muses, bronze figural, open escapement...........1,200.00
Ansonia, Queen Mary, oak regulator, 8-day/T&S.............800.00
Ansonia, Queen Mary, oak regulator, 8-day/T&S, walnut case...750.00
Ansonia, Queen Mary, time only.........................700.00
Ansonia, Queen Mary, time only, walnut case...............650.00
Ansonia, Regis, crystal regulator.........................475.00
Ansonia, regulator, ormolu mt/beveled glass, pnd/8-day/T&S....850.00
Ansonia, Royal Bonn, porc dial, open escapement, 11x13″.....650.00
Ansonia, shelf, Empire style, 8-day/T&S, mahog..............375.00
Ansonia, Trilby, bronze, statue, porcelain dial...............350.00
Ansonia, Trump, China Rose...............................325.00
Ansonia, Zenith, crystal regulator.........................650.00
Banjo, mahog/giltwood, Fed, rvpt, gilt pendant, rstr, 30″......935.00
Barnes & Bartholomew, shelf, mahog 3-decker, rvpt rpl, 37″...550.00
Birge & Fuller, Empire, 8-day/T&S, 33″....................375.00
Blick, punch clock, oak w/heavy brass trim, 48″.............300.00
Boston, tandem wind, crystal regulator, 8-day/T&S, Delphus....600.00
Brewster & Ingraham, steeple, 8-day/T&S...................325.00
Carriage, floral champleve/bronze, 20th C, 8″...............1,540.00
Carriage, swags/columns/snake hdl, gilt bronze, French, 9″.....600.00
Concord Watch Co, desk, Arabic #s, 8-day, 15-jewel, EX......185.00
Cuckoo, 30-hour, mc bird, gr leaves, German, blonde case......65.00
Cuckoo, 30-hour, 2-weight, Japan, dk case, 18″ bird to pnd.....45.00
Elgin, Art Deco, 7-jewel, 2-door, wht face, brass, 4″...........60.00
Eli Terry, pillar & scroll, mahog on pine, wood works, 32″...2,200.00
EN Welch, Arditi, calendar, 8-day/T&S, walnut shelf case....1,500.00
EN Welch, mantel, iron w/side urns/statue atop, 8-day/T&S....325.00
EN Welch, Sinico, walnut regulator, 8-day/T&S.............1,100.00
English, skeleton, dbl fusee, 1 bell.......................1,450.00
Fashion, #7, dbl blk dials, calendar, walnut case............2,400.00
Fashion, #8, dbl blk dials, calendar, walnut case............2,200.00
Figural, Sambo, Blk man blinks eye, banjo is clock, 1860s...1,200.00
French, Empire style mantel, 3-dolphin support, eagle atop....650.00
French, pinwheel, 14-day/1 weight, oak/porc dial, 2nds, 60″..4,800.00
French, Westminster, Petillot Provins, walnut case, 38″.......375.00
General Electric, Moniter, refrigerator top, Telechron, EX......75.00
German, alarm, 30-hr, winds at 3, alarm winds at 7, 13″.......65.00
German, ardvvark novelty, eyes tell time....................225.00
German, Bim-Bam, 8-day/T&S, balloon shape, pnd, 11″.......185.00
German, camel bk, Westminster chimes, brass ball feet........165.00
German, cuckoo, T&S, EX...................................50.00
German, globe novelty, turns to tell time, metal case..........325.00
German, key wind, fancy face, G Becker, 8″ dial, 48″.........550.00
German, key wind, fancy oak case, box regulator, 38″........275.00
German, key wind, rod chime, Vienna case, Kenzle Uhren, 40″.425.00
German, owl novelty, eyes tell time........................250.00
Gilbert, #10, oak regulator, weight drive, time only..........2,100.00
Gilbert, #11, oak regulator, weight drive, striking...........1,400.00
Gilbert, #14, oak case, weight/time, dead beat esc..........2,000.00
Gilbert, #3, rosewood w/brass, weight drive, dead beat esc....1,400.00
Gilbert, #64, oak regulator, weight drive....................800.00
Gilbert, mantel, blk wood w/ornate columns & ft, 8-day/T&S...125.00
Gilbert, Maranville, 8-day, office calendar..................1,700.00
Gilbert, Tuscan, crystal regulator..........................900.00
Gustav Becker, bracket, mahog, Westminster ¼-hr chime, 16″..475.00
Gustav Becker, bracket, w/strike...........................350.00
Gustav Becker, Vienna, ornate, free swinger.................600.00
Howard, #26, watchman's, walnut........................1,400.00
Howard Miller, different times of the world, rectangular........100.00
Hubbell & Son, ebonized, Reeds Tonic, mini tall case.........900.00
Ingersoll, alarm, Big Bad Wolf, animated, VG...............195.00
Ingraham, beehive style, 8-day/T&S, 16″....................260.00
Ingraham, Cameo S Duplex, T&S...........................45.00
Ingraham, Dew Drop, 8-day/time/chimes.....................400.00
Ingraham, Ionic, rosewood, 8-day/time only, 12″ dial..........400.00
Ingraham, kitchen, golden oak, 8-day/T&S, Ducat model.......250.00
Ingraham, mantel, 8-day/T&S, tambour......................85.00
Ingraham, Nyanza, banjo..................................500.00
Ingraham, Schoolhouse, oak, long drop, time & calendar......450.00
Ingraham, store regulator, oak, calendar....................425.00
Ingraham, Treasure Island, banjo, 8-day/T&S, EX............450.00
Ingraham, Venetian, #2 Extra, 8-day/T&S, mahog, veneer......210.00
Ithaca, #10, dbl dial calendar, 8-day/T&S, farmers............675.00
Ithaca, #11, dbl dial, calendar, 8-day/T&S, walnut, old........800.00
Ithaca, #4, office, dbl dial calendar, 8-day, rosewood........1,250.00
Ithaca, shelf, library, calendar/dbl dial.....................975.00
Japy Freres, mantel, urn atop, elaborate bronze mts, 20″......800.00
JC Brown, steeple, etched lower glass, walnut case...........400.00
Jennings Bros, rear wind/set, porc dial, 8-day, Tonly, 6″........95.00
Jerome & Darrow, shelf, mahog veneer, trn columns/pnd, 33″..250.00
John Harbud, shelf, mahog veneer, rnd top, dvtl, rpl, 12½″....175.00

Seth Thomas, black bakelite, marked on back N+680, eight-day, 5¾″ x 4¾″, $145.00.

Jungham, Venus, 8-day/time only, swinging arm....600.00
Junghans, elephant, 8-day/time only, swinging arm....650.00
Junghans, kitchen, porc, 8-day, 8½x10″....65.00
Keebler & Lux, courthouse novelty, 12½″....400.00
Kundo, enamel dial, 1950s....85.00
Kundo, miniature, anniversary, glass dome....65.00
Lux, animated, man/woman at spinning wheel/dog, red....95.00
Lux, banjo, castle scene in lower panel, 19″....100.00
Lux, bluebird feeding nest, pendulette....45.00
Lux, bobbing bird, pendulette....35.00
Lux, cat pendulette, rpr, 1940s, 7″....250.00
Lux, Christmas wreath, pendulette....150.00
Lux, clown w/original tie, pendulette....375.00
Lux, clown w/seals, 6¼x6″....225.00
Lux, country scene, wall clock....75.00
Lux, cuckoo, hunting scene, T&S, lg, EX....225.00
Lux, Dutch scene, porc face, 8-sided....150.00
Lux, golfer, pendulette....275.00
Lux, Jack & Jill, pendulette....425.00
Lux, lovebirds kissing, pendulette....75.00
Lux, Mary Had A Little Lamb, pendulette....300.00
Lux, Pussy in the Well, pendulette....425.00
Lux, Sally Rand, fan dancer, pendulette....350.00
Lux, scottie dog pendulette, brn w/gr collar, 6″, EX....250.00
Lux, ship's wheel, pendulette....225.00
Lux, shmoo pendulette, bl/wht, 6″....135.00
Lux, steamboat, animated, alarm....75.00
Mage A Paris, mantel, torch/bow/quiver atop, bronze, 15″....880.00
Mantel, CI, polychrome fruit & flowers, 1860s....200.00
Mantel, dolphin corners, paw ft, urn atop, bronze, 20″....1,650.00
Mark Leavenworth, shelf, Fed, mahog/rvpt, rstr, ca 1835....770.00
Mark Leavenworth, shelf, pillar/scroll, wood mvt....1,000.00
New Haven, banjo, T&S, pnd, rfn rvpt glass, 33″....215.00
New Haven, banjo, Westminster chimes, electric, orig....165.00
New Haven, Elbe, walnut, 8-day/T&S....350.00
New Haven, Elfrida, oak regulator, weight drive....1,250.00
New Haven, Lohengrin, music box mantel, ca 1890....275.00
New Haven, mantel, iron/marbleized trim w/gold, 8-day/T&S....175.00
New Haven, tambour, Westminster chimes....160.00
Pagoda, 400-day....100.00
Schoolhouse, English type cable fusee, 14-day, fancy case....450.00
Sempire, #48, Vestibule regulator, fancy, 48″....800.00
Sessions, #5, walnut regulator, weight drive....1,800.00
Sessions, blk panther w/gold accents, Art Deco, 9x12″....75.00
Sessions, mantel, blk, EX....125.00
Sessions, pillar & scroll, 18″....160.00
Sessions, schoolhouse, fancy pnd, 11″ dial....357.00
Seth Thomas, #1, office calendar, rosewood case....2,800.00
Seth Thomas, #11, regulator....3,500.00
Seth Thomas, #2, cherry or walnut case....1,025.00
Seth Thomas, #2, oak....950.00
Seth Thomas, #31, oak regulator, weight drive....3,000.00
Seth Thomas, Adamantine, mantel, marbleized, 8-day/T&S....175.00
Seth Thomas, carved columns, paw feet, wooden....1,175.00
Seth Thomas, Deco, bl mirror glass front....110.00
Seth Thomas, kitchen, walnut, 8-day, Dover model....200.00
Seth Thomas, Lincoln, oak, weight drive....925.00
Seth Thomas, Lincoln, walnut, T&S....775.00
Seth Thomas, mantel, Gothic, walnut, 9½″....110.00
Seth Thomas, mantel, single bar chime, mk Peterborough....60.00
Seth Thomas, Plymouth Hollow, dbl dial calendar, rosewood..1,600.00
Seth Thomas, Plymouth Hollow, octagon dial, rosewood case...450.00
Seth Thomas, Queen Anne, oak, T&S....800.00
Seth Thomas, Queen Anne, walnut, time only....750.00

Ansonia 'Dresden Extra' porcelain shelf clock, eight-day, cathedral gong strike, porcelain dial, $450.00.

Seth Thomas, rosewood veneer/gilt pilasters, 30-hour, 33″....165.00
Seth Thomas, shelf, Empire, 8-day/T&S, bull's eye, sm....350.00
Seth Thomas, Sonora, chime....450.00
Seth Thomas, wall regulator, weight drive, time/2nds pnd....3,200.00
Seth Thomas, World Regulator, 15-day, time only....475.00
Shelf, mohog w/inlay, Gothic, brass side grills/ft, 17″....350.00
Shelf, rosewood, eagle splat/columns, 30-hr wood mvt, T&S....210.00
Simmons, cupola w/3 putti, cloisonne/bronze, 17″....1,100.00
Sohm, electric office regulator, ca 1890....750.00
Standard, schoolmaster, 1930s....750.00
Standard Electric, master, orig, 66″....500.00
Standard Electric, slave, oak, 60″....200.00
Stennes, New Hampshire, mirror, 8-day, weight....800.00
Swiss, regulator, 8-day/time, lyre pnd, walnut, sweep 2nds....1,750.00

Tall Case

A Willard, mahog/inlay, eagle & scroll bonnet, 1804, 91″....3,200.00
Cherry, Hplwht, burl walnut inlay/gooseneck pediment, 94″...1,780.00
Cherry, scallop crest/trn finials/brass works, no pnd, 86″....1,425.00
Eli Bentley, cherry, Fed, flat top, rstr, 1820, 69″....5,000.00
English, bell striker, 12″ dial, early....900.00
English, mahog, simple moldings, brass works, 76″....700.00
German, oak, 2-weight....700.00
Massey, mahog/X-bands, swan neck crest/glaze door, 1830″....990.00
Pine w/orig stencil, cut-out ft, dvtl, chamfer waist, 78″....2,400.00
Scottish, mahog, 2nd hand/calendar, gooseneck bonnet, 84″..1,100.00
Walnut, cherry door/gooseneck/brass finials in bonnet, 95″...4,900.00
Whiting, pine, Country, wood works/2nd hand/calendar, 86″..1,150.00

Tatoo Intermittent, alarm, pat 11/29-1898....75.00
Transition, shelf, 30-hour wood movement, T&S, eagle splat...500.00
Vienna, regulator, 2-weight, porc dial, carved walnut, 46″....900.00
Vienna, 2-weight, walnut/porc dial, strikes hr & ½-hr, 44″....850.00
Wag-on-wall, wood/mc decor, 3 animated men ring bell, 19″...825.00
Waltham, #1500, banjo, 8-day/time only....1,400.00
Waltham, miniature banjo, 8-day/time only....125.00
Waltham, Perry's Victory glasses, weight banjo, mahog case...1,400.00
Warren Telechron, Art Deco, bl mirror/scrolled chrome base....45.00
Waterbury, #3, walnut regulator, weight drive....2,800.00
Waterbury, #42, dbl dial calendar....900.00
Waterbury, #67, wall, 2-weight, 2nd bit, walnut case, 50″....1,400.00
Waterbury, blk mantel, 8-day/T&S....125.00
Waterbury, china, 8-day/T&S....350.00
Waterbury, jewelers regulator, 8-day/time only, golden oak....250.00
Waterbury, mahog veneer, steeple, rvpt, w/key/pnd, 19½″....130.00

Waterbury, meteor, carriage, bevel glass/jewel mvt, 4½″.......300.00
Waterbury, miniature schoolhouse, 5″ dial, 8-day pnd mvt.....175.00
Waterbury, Sambo, 30-hr levers, time only.................1,200.00
Waterbury, Springfield, TSC, oak case, 8-day................800.00
Welch, Arditi, dbl dial..................................1,400.00
Westclox, Big Ben alarm, pat 1906-1919....................50.00
Westclox, Bingo, alarm, MIB..............................35.00
Wilcock, bracket, oak case, separate chime mvt, Canadian.....400.00
Willard, banjo, mahog, rvpt throat/base, rpl/rfn, 34″.........1,250.00
Willard, banjo, rvpt Enterprise & Boxer rstr, 1830, 38″......1,320.00
Wurtemburg, porc enamel, 8-day, spring wind, brass pnd.......85.00

Cloisonne

Cloisonne is a method of decorating metal with enameling. Fine metal wires are are soldered onto the metal body following the lines of a predetermined design. The resulting channels are filled in with enamels of various colors, and the item is fired. The final step is a smoothing process that assures even exposure of the wire pattern.

The art is predominately Oriental, and has been practiced continuously, except during war years, since the 16th century. The most excellent examples date from 1865 until the turn of the century.

The early 20th century export variety is usually lightweight, and the workmanship inferior. Modern wares are of good quality and are produced in Taiwan as well as China.

Several variations of the basic art include plique-a-jour, achieved by removing the metal body after firing, leaving only the transparent enamel work; foil cloisonne, using transparent or semi-translucent enameling over a layer of embossed silver covering the metal body of the vessel; wireless cloisonne, made by removing the wire dividers prior to firing; and cloisonne executed on ceramic, wood, or lacquer rather than metal.

When no condition is indicated, the items listed below are assumed to be in mint condition.

Belt buckle, lotus blossoms on blk, 2¾x1⅝″..................50.00
Bird, atop rnd box, openwork forms elaborate tail, 9″.........800.00
Bowl, birds/peonies on lt gr, scalloped/bl loop rim, 9″.........225.00
Bowl, blk w/mc floral, w/lid, late, 5x7″....................125.00
Bowl, florals, mc, 4″....................................75.00
Bowl, lotus on bl, sm circle cloison clusters, 3½x12″..........395.00
Bowl, mc floral/butterflies on bl, w/lid, 4x8″................350.00
Bowl, mc peonies on wht, cloud scrolls, short ft, 10″.........280.00
Bowl, plique-a-jour, goldfish/seaweed on lt gr, 5″.............695.00
Box, apple form, birds/florals, mc on bl, 5x5″...............110.00
Box, Peking duck, standing, mc scrolls on bl, wing lid, 7″.....140.00
Box, stamp; Chinese, lg, floral............................95.00
Box, stamp; gr w/mc flowering branch, modern, 4½″ L.........55.00
Box, 6 sides, blk, w/floral pattern in colors, 2″..............45.00
Cache pot, bl/pink/yel floral/leaves on blk, mk China, 5″.......395.00
Charger, butterflies, mc on turq, fancy rim band, 12″.........425.00
Charger, Totai, butterflies/birds/trees, ca 1890, 18″...........725.00
Cigarette case, 3 dragons on gr, Chinese...................125.00
Compote, mc florals on bl, scalloped, 5½x9″................250.00
Crane, mc design on bl, 7″...............................200.00
Crane, on rock, candle spike in mouth, yel dragons/mc, 14″...350.00
Eagle, on rock, tan/blk/goldwork feathers, 10″...............550.00
Goblet, mc goldfish/seaweed on bl, 2¾″.....................60.00
Horse, winged; mc dragons/phoenix/etc on bl, 12″............950.00
Incense burner, yel w/mc lotus, dragon hdls/3 ft, 5x3″.........125.00
Jar, dragon, yel on blk, w/lid, late, 6¼″, NM.................90.00
Jar, flowers/butterflies on blk, 3 ft, 1890, w/lid, 4″............225.00
Jar, potpourri; detailed motif, w/lid, late, 6½″, pr.............135.00
Jar, potpourri; flowers/butterfly panels, Japanese, 7x3″........195.00

Vase, cloisonne on pottery with Satsuma inserts, ca 1850, 11½″, $1,350.00.

Jar, scenes on bl/diapering on orange, intricate motif, 8″......850.00
Letter opener, bronze, hdls..............................34.00
Lion, bl w/cloison hair/gold work, ball under foot, 9″.........800.00
Mirror, mc lotus on lt bl, eng mirror, ped ft, 19″............450.00
Napkin ring, dragon theme, openwork.......................45.00
Parrot on mound, cloisons form feathers, bl/brn, 8¼″.........400.00
Pencil pot, mc peonies on bl, cylindrical, Chinese, 6″.........150.00
Plaque, floral/leaves/birds, bl, scalloped, Japanese, 12″........425.00
Plate, cranes/scenes on bl/mc floral border, Japanese, 9¾″.....335.00
Plate, pr of cranes, brn/bl, late, 12″.......................150.00
Salt cellar, ftd, bl, pr....................................18.00
Teapot, bl w/mc dragons/goldstone, ftd, 6¼″................175.00
Teapot, dragon in clouds/mc phoenix bird on red, 7½x5½″....175.00
Teapot, flowers, red & pink on bl, 4½x2½″.................100.00
Teapot, flowers & brush pots, bl on red, rectangular, 7″.......185.00
Teapot, on porcelain, tree bark/dragons, gourd form, 4½″.....365.00
Teapot, 6 butterflies/floral, royal bl base, 2¼x4″.............245.00
Vase, bird & floral, intricate, early, 9x4½″..................385.00
Vase, bird & flowers, mc on bl, 5x3″.......................135.00
Vase, bird in cherry tree, pink/wht blossoms, 18½x7½″......2,200.00
Vase, bl w/pink/yel/red floral, gold base, Chinese mks, 9″......140.00
Vase, bl w/red reserves: mc florals, slim neck/bulbous, 5″......110.00
Vase, brn w/bl dragon, late, 10″..........................100.00
Vase, bush of mc flowers on bl, 5″.........................105.00
Vase, coral w/cranes/floral, late, 13″.......................70.00
Vase, deer & geese in panels, mc floral, bulbous, 7½″........160.00
Vase, Egyptian animals/fish, mc on bl mottle, 1900, 8½″......500.00
Vase, eng floral/birds/gr branches, red enamel, 11¾x7¼″.....1,100.00
Vase, fish & seaweed on gray, 7x2¾″......................265.00
Vase, fishscale w/floral, Japanese, 1915, 1½″.................68.00
Vase, floral on emerald gr, plique-a-jour, 7″................595.00
Vase, floral reserves on bl, Japanese, 5x3″.................100.00
Vase, floral/butterflies, brn/bl/gr, 6-panel, rare, 7½″..........495.00
Vase, floral/butterfly reserves, goldstone, Japanese, 3¾″........125.00
Vase, floral/leaf cloisons, reserves, goldstone, 3¾″............125.00
Vase, florals on front, sm spray on bk, gray ground, 6x3″.....225.00
Vase, flowering prunus/wht flowers on dk bl, baluster, 12″.....225.00
Vase, flowers & woman on red, Japanese, 5″................150.00
Vase, flowers/butterflies, goldstone/bl panels, 1890, 5″.........195.00
Vase, foil ground, bl w/cobalt/lav floral, Japanese, 3½″.........95.00
Vase, foil ground, carp on bl & blk, Japanese, 5½″...........385.00
Vase, foil ground, dk bl w/pk/silver foil flowers, 2½x1½″........70.00

Vase, foil ground, gr w/dragon, 7″ 275.00
Vase, foil ground, pink flowers on yel, Japanese, 5″ 250.00
Vase, foil panels, bl/gr, butterflies w/in, Japanese, 5¼″ 165.00
Vase, lt bl porcelain w/fans/florals/birds, 9½″ 375.00
Vase, on pottery, florals/mc, artist sgn, ped ft, 9x4″ 395.00
Vase, orange-red w/basse taille bamboo, peonies, 8½″ 135.00
Vase, orange-red w/wht mums, late, 13″ 150.00
Vase, panel w/flowers/plants/feathers on beige, 15″ 625.00
Vase, panels of flowers/fruit on bl, dbl gourd, 9½″ 165.00
Vase, panels w/birds/butterflies/florals on bl, 7½x3½″ 225.00
Vase, panels w/flowers/butterflies, goldstone/bl, 1890, 5″ 195.00
Vase, raspberry flowers on blk, late, 7″, pr 90.00
Vase, red w/branches of wht flowers & bird, 6″ 115.00
Vase, 5-claw mc dragons on lime, gold clouds/bl waves, 11″ 275.00

Clothing and Accessories

'Second-hand' or 'vintage'? It's all a matter of opinion. But these days it's considered good taste--downright fashionable--to wear clothing from Victorian to World War II styles. Jackets with padded shoulders from the thirties are 'trendy.' Jewelry from the Art Deco era is just as beautiful and often less expensive than current copies. Victorian blouses on models with Gibson Girl hair styles are pictured in leading fashion magazines--but why settle for new, when the genuine article can be bought for the same price with exquisite lace that no reproduction can rival?

Where once the 'style' of the day of the day was so strictly obeyed, today--in New York and the larger cities of California and Texas, in particular--nothing well designed and constructed is 'out of style.' And though in recent days costumes by such designers as Chanel, Fortuny, and Lanvin may bring four-figure prices at fine auction houses, as a general rule, prices are very modest considering the wonderful fabrics one may find in vintage clothing, many of which are no longer available. Cashmere coats, elegant furs, and sequined or beaded gowns can be bought for only a small fraction of today's retail.

Though some are strictly collectors, many do buy their clothes to wear. Care must be given to alterations, and gentle cleaning methods employed to avoid damage that would detract from their value.

When no condition is indicated, the items listed below are assumed to be in excellent condition.

Key:
cap/s—cap sleeves
embr—embroidery
hs—hand sewn
lgth—length
plt—pleated
s/s—short sleeves
¾/s—three-quarter sleeves
l/s—long sleeves
n/s—no sleeves
ms—machine sewn

Apron, homespun, hs/hm crochet lace on hem & tie ends, 39″ . . 25.00
Apron, Victorian, wht, tucks, wide crochet lace on bottom 23.00
Bathing tunic, blk sateen, 1910 . . . . . 22.00
Bed jacket, bl satin w/lace trim, '40s 12.00
Bed jacket, bl silk, embr 12.00
Bed jacket, rayon, ca 1940 . . . . . 9.00
Bed jacket, silky beige, cut-out/embr work on front 12.00
Blouse, battenburg lace, high neck, 1900 . . . . . 75.00
Blouse, bl sequin, 1950s 20.00
Blouse, blk fishnet, beige net & lace high neck, 1880 . . . . . 75.00
Blouse, button-up w/crochet lapels, l/s, Victorian 17.50
Blouse, crepe, beaded front & neck, 1950s 15.00
Blouse, crepe-de-chine/plt panel fits through slits, Worth 522.00
Blouse, crocheted, Irish, Victorian 210.00
Blouse, openwork eyelet, lined, s/s, peplum style, 1880s 40.00
Bodice, lace/beads/sequins, lined, high collar, 1880s 30.00
Bodice, net on satin w/lace sleeves/beading, V-neck, 1880s 25.00
Bonnet, Amish, blk cotton, 50 yrs old 40.00
Bonnet, baby; ecru loose-weave crochet w/wool liner 17.00
Bonnet, baby; embr/drawn work on ruffle edge, VG 17.50
Bonnet, baby; eyelet 16.00
Bonnet, baby; wht cotton w/lace, embr & ribbon decor 10.00
Bonnet, baby; wht crochet w/ribbon tie 17.00
Bonnet, brn sateen, hs, minor wear, 12″ 25.00
Booties, baby; brn cotton w/blk trim & ties, hm 8.00
Bridal gown, flapper w/tango hem, silk, 1923, EX 225.00
Bridal gown, Georgette, lace, long train, 1940 . . . . . 25.00
Bridal gown, net over satin, embr/pearls, Worth/Paris, '05 . . . . 200.00
Bridal gown, satin/beaded, headpiece/veil/petticoat/etc 98.00
Bridal gown, silk crepe, satin & lace, 1918 . . . . . 110.00
Bridal gown, tiers of lace, satin, long train, 1950 . . . . . 30.00
Camisole, pink satin w/tatting 38.00
Cap, blk lace, boudoir 5.00

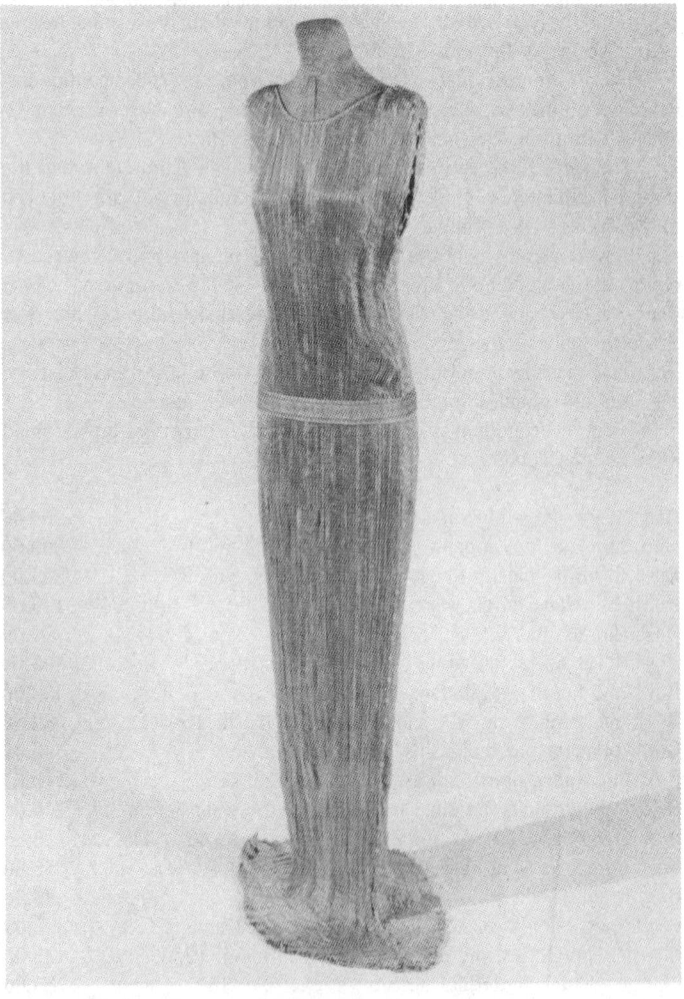

Tea gown, pleated silk, Venetian glass beads down side, with original Fortuny lable, $1,200.00.

Cap, hunting; sm boy's, brn w/blk braid, early 20th C 20.00
Cap, pink crochet & net, boudoir 10.00
Cap, ruffled pink lace, boudoir, Victorian 18.00
Cape, blk velvet, long, 1930s 50.00
Cape, blk wool, theatrical, satin lining, 1940s 95.00
Cape, silk brocade, red silk lining, 1870 . . . . . 55.00
Cape, wool w/monkey fur trim, silk lining, 1880s 85.00
Chemise, chiffon/lace inset & trim/pin tucks, Callot Soeurs 495.00
Chemise, pleats, lace panels, ms, 28″ 25.00

Chemise, silk/lace bands, waist-to-hem plt, Callot Soeurs.......300.00
Chemise, wht cotton, pink ribbon drawstring.................11.00
Christening gown, tucks/lace inserts/ruffles, l/s, 2-pc............85.00
Christening gown w/slip, ornate lace, tucks, embr, 1890s.......90.00
Coat, baby's; corduroy, shawl at top, 32″....................35.00
Coat, beige wool, braided trim, ca 1918......................85.00
Coat, blk velvet, w/hood, full lgth, Victorian..................38.00
Coat, cashmere, blk fox collar/cuffs, gussets, Vionnet..........500.00
Coat, cashmere, nutria collar/puffed cuffs, Callot Soeurs.......250.00
Coat, cashmere, squirrel: collar to hip/cuffs, Vionnet.........1,430.00
Coat, child's; brocade, Victorian, rare, sm....................85.00
Coat, evening; Chinese silk, floor length.....................85.00
Coat, faille, crepe-de-chine lining, shawl collar, Vionnet........935.00
Coat, faille, ermine strips on collar/cuffs, Callot Soeurs........700.00
Coat, frock..20.00
Coat, girl's; bl/wht tweed, taffeta under-dress, Lanvin..........165.00
Coat, girl's; gabardine, crepe-de-chine dress, Lanvin...........465.00
Coat, girl's; velvet, w/dress: n/s, plt skirt, Lanvin............400.00
Coat, girl's; wool, lg embr pockets, Lanvin..................330.00
Coat, mohair, w/silk dress, sailor collar, Chanel.............3,410.00
Coat, ribbed wool, unborn lamb shawl collar, silk lined........200.00
Coat, satin, lined, beaded/tassels, full lgth, 1880s.............100.00
Coat, silk, ermine: collar to hem/cuffs, Molyneux.............350.00
Coat, velours de laine, mink: collar to hem/cuffs, Lanvin.......825.00
Coat, velvet w/gray fur 7″ collar &. cuffs, short in front........ 75.00
Coat, velveteen w/wht fox collar & cuffs, 1920s...............65.00
Coat, wool, fur: shawl collar to hem, Lanvin, 1924...........385.00
Coat, wool gabardine, ermine: flat collar/cuffs, Molyneux.......220.00
Coat & knee pants, little boy's, wool tweed, orig label, M.......35.00
Coat & skirt, faille, ermine cuffs/collar, Lanvin, 1924.........715.00
Collar, Maltese lace, extends to waist, Victorian...............20.00
Collar & cuffs, Honiton lace.............................15.00
Combing sacque, silk w/fagot-sewn lace bands, tassels.........220.00
Dress, afternoon; blk/wht checked cotton, ca 1900............40.00
Dress, baby's; slip & pants, silk w/lace trim, 1920............28.00
Dress, blk chiffon, layered points on sleeves/hem, flapper.......25.00
Dress, blk crepe, beaded bodice & skirt, padded shoulders......30.00
Dress, blk crepe, gored skirt, 1940s........................15.00
Dress, blk satin, steel beading at hem/neckline................45.00
Dress, blk sheer, embr ribbon trim, tucks, 1920s..............22.00
Dress, blk w/netted lace trim, Victorian, 2-pc.................60.00
Dress, brn Coin Dot full skirt, puffy sleeves..................15.00
Dress, brn crushed velvet, 1920s...........................28.00
Dress, chiffon, applied self rosettes collar/hem, Vionnet......1,100.00
Dress, chiffon, pin-tucked zigzag band, w/slip, Chanel........1,980.00
Dress, chiffon l/s underblouse, lace neck/underlay, 1880s.......50.00
Dress, christening gown, lace collar & sleeve trim.............28.00
Dress, christening gown, pleats, front lace panel, ms, 34″.......40.00
Dress, christening; pleats, lace on bodice, l/s, skirt, ms.........45.00
Dress, cocktail; blk crepe, allover sequins, s/s, w/belt...........65.00
Dress, cocktail; satin/gold threaded crepe, low waist, '30........40.00
Dress, country lady's, bl/wht, 3-pc, 1890s...................125.00
Dress, ecru chiffon, 1930s.................................35.00
Dress, evening; allover diagonal chiffon panels, att Chanel.....715.00
Dress, evening; blk pleated net w/ermine trim, '30s, EX.......225.00
Dress, evening; blk w/embr flowers, H Bergdorf, 1930s, EX....165.00
Dress, evening; chiffon, charmeuse/lace slip, Chanel............825.00
Dress, evening; hand beaded/sequined silk, '50s, 3-pc, EX.....375.00
Dress, evening; silk velvet, bias/V-neck/bat sleeves, '30s.........50.00
Dress, evening; yel chiffon, Ginny Lind, 1920s, EX...........125.00
Dress, evening; 3-color gauze/narrow straps, Callot Soeurs.....330.00
Dress, formal; pink net, strapless, floor lgth, 1950s............35.00
Dress, formal; taffeta/chenille waves on net skirt, 1940s.........55.00
Dress, girl's; taffeta panels on tulle, plt skirt, Lanvin..........135.00
Dress, girl's; taffeta/lace hoop skirts+bloomers, Vionnet.......385.00
Dress, high neck, openwork bodice/sleeves/skirt, 1900.........135.00
Dress, jet blk beadwork on both sides, 1920s.................68.00
Dress, l/s/cuffs, train, blk lace trim, boned, 1890, 2-pc........150.00
Dress, layered tunic top, areas of embr eyelet.................45.00
Dress, long, wht w/scalloped over-shirt, Victorian..............45.00
Dress, mauve chiffon/bugle beads, geometric design...........125.00
Dress, mini; gold threaded, Anne Fogarty, 1960s..............35.00
Dress, sheer over pk satin, drop waist, ruffle tiers, 1920........50.00
Dress, steel beads form pointed panels at hem, blk velvet.......85.00
Dress, tiered embr taffeta/lace, beading/tassels, 1917..........200.00
Dress, wht, V-neck, s/s, lacy border, Edwardian...............85.00
Dress, wht organdy, eyelet trim, 1920.......................75.00
Dressing gown, charmeuse, sunburst stitching, 1929, Lanvin....440.00
Dressing gown, charmeuse kimono, l/s w/much embr, Lanvin..1,210.00
Dressing gown, hand crewel embr on gr wool.................65.00
Driving duster, lady's, linen..............................45.00
Fur cape, silver fox, ¾ lgth..............................300.00
Fur coat, Alaskan seal, full lgth, EX.......................400.00
Fur coat, blk bear, full lgth..............................125.00
Fur coat, blk Karacol, fingertip lgth.......................125.00
Fur coat, brn mink, wide shawl collar to hem, cuffs, rpr.......770.00
Fur coat, ermine, full lgth, sable collar/cuffs................600.00
Fur coat, girl's; sheared beaver, faille lined, Paris tag.........200.00
Fur coat, leopard, wide sheared beaver cuffs, 40″ L, EX.......400.00
Fur coat, man's, raccoon, lg..............................175.00
Fur coat, mink tails, brn, full lgth.........................300.00
Fur coat, muskrat w/sable dyed border, 1925-30..............65.00
Fur coat, Persian lamb, 4 wide bands of mink at hem.........220.00
Fur coat, Russian sable, wide collar, silk lined, Ben Kahn....8,800.00
Fur hat, Canadian lynx....................................75.00
Fur hat, cloche, brn beaver...............................15.00
Fur hat, cloche, leopard, lined.............................15.00
Fur hat, pillbox, brn milk.................................15.00
Fur jacket, beaver, mink collar, new lining, short............197.00
Fur jacket, broadtail, short fitted waist......................40.00
Fur jacket, pony fur, mink stencilled, 1940s.................150.00
Fur muff, blk Persian lamb, zipper compartment..............25.00
Fur muff, blk seal, satin lined, gathered pocket w/in, 18″.......12.00
Fur muff, child's..25.00
Fur muff, fake leopard, 1940s..............................16.00
Fur muff, raccoon w/satin shirred zipper purse, 1920s..........60.00
Fur neckpiece, golden fox.................................30.00
Fur neckpiece, mink, 2-skin...............................30.00
Fur stole, mink, gray Cerulean............................250.00
Gloves, crocheted..10.00
Gloves, kid leather.......................................16.00
Gloves, lacy flowers, ruffled edge, crocheted..................35.00
Gloves, over the elbow, pearls/bugle beads, suede, 1905........38.00
Gown, evening; net w/paillettes over satin/feathers, short.......175.00
Gown, tea; pink/wht polka dot, 1880s........................75.00
Gown, tea; plt silk, n/s, Venetian side buttons, Fortuny......1,200.00
Gown, tea; wht w/heavy embr, net trim, 1900................125.00
Gown, Victorian, wht, wide fillet crochet yoke front/bk.........75.00
Gown, wht, low neck, s/s, flounce on bottom, short............20.00
Hat, blk, cloche..12.00
Hat, blk Derby...32.00
Hat, blk velvet, beret type................................15.00
Hat, boy's sailor, 1910...................................14.00
Hat, brn felt tam w/gr feather, 1940s........................10.00
Hat, brn homburg...25.00
Hat, brn textured straw, 1880s.............................35.00
Hat, checked cotton, pioneer bonnet.........................35.00
Hat, little boy's; gr felt, dress style, Henry Roelofs.............35.00

Hat, top hat, folds flat, ca 1890....50.00
Hat, navy bl, Hattie Carnegie....7.00
Hat, straw, lady's riding, 1740s, VG....85.00
Hat, top hat, w/working clock in front....100.00
Jacket, smoking; 1915....35.00
Kimono, lav silk w/hand printed/embr florals, lined....75.00
Kimono, pink silk w/embr....120.00
Knickers, boy's; patterned, 1920s....8.00
Knickers, wht linen, for golfing....10.00
Mantilla, blk lace, 1940s....25.00
Mittens, Amish, med bl, knitted, 10" L, pr....40.00
Muff, quilted ribbon-bk satin, blk satin lined....45.00
Muffler, blk voile, 48x36"....7.00
Nightgown, bib yoke w/Austrian lace, peach, 1940s, M....65.00
Nightgown, lace, Victorian, wht, button-down front, l/s....45.00
Nightgown, peach, rayon, bias cut....33.00
Nightgown, rayon, deep V-neck, lace/cutwork, n/s, long....28.00
Nightgown, silky crepe w/lace, flower bow, long....35.00
Nightgown, viole, short sleeve, 1920s....24.00
Nightie, wht, Nainsook, Philippine embr, long....25.00
Pajamas, lav satin/lace trim, fitted w/cap/s, flared legs....28.00
Pajamas, pink satin, tailored, s/s, flared legs, '30s....20.00
Panties, silky w/embr, button sides....7.00
Pants, evening; blk chiffon w/ruffles, Cardinali....70.00
Parasol, blk lace....65.00
Parasol, blk satin w/lace trim, appliqued 9" butterflies....65.00
Parasol, child's; blk silk, ruffle, folding, VG....55.00
Parasol, satin w/blk lace, tree branch hdl....45.00
Parasol, silk, collapsible hdl, Victorian....50.00
Parasol, Sunday Stroll, Victorian, blk silk, sm....35.00
Petticoat, child's; Victorian....28.00
Petticoat, crocheted, much lace....28.00
Petticoat, ecru & wht, ms w/smocking & lace, 38"....27.50
Petticoat, lady's; eyelet ruffle....60.00
Prayer cap, blk....10.00
Robe, Chinese, blk satin, emb in gold, ¾ lgth, 1900s....150.00
Robe, cotton gauze, bl w/mc animal/bird embr, full lgth....100.00
Robe, Victorian, button-down front, l/s, tucks, lace, wht....115.00
Shawl, blk lace, triangle, lg....30.00
Shawl, Merino wool, fringe, 1875, 60x72"....40.00
Shawl, paisley, Victorian....75.00
Shawl, silk, embr pink Chinese figures/flowers, fringe....140.00
Shawl, silk, embr scarlet roses/silver foliage, fringe....100.00
Shawl, silk crepe-de-chine w/woven gold medallion, Reboux....400.00
Shawl, wool, brn w/brn & cream print border, EX fringe....50.00
Shirt, coarsely woven natural linen, hs....75.00
Shirt, gr wool, WWII, Army issue....10.00
Shirt, man's; wht, no collar, early 20th C....14.00
Shirt, men's dress; wht, celluloid collar, early 20th C....14.00
Shoe buckles, tooled silver on steel, 1½x2½", pr....65.00
Shoes, beige w/leopard vamp & heel....14.00
Shoes, child's; leather w/button strap, wood soles, 1700s....85.00
Shoes, child's; red leather w/velvet scrollwork, high top....32.00
Shoes, gold & silver, rhinestone, gold mesh trim, 1950s....12.00
Shoes, pumps; blk suede, 1940s....28.00
Shoes, tennis; lady's, 1920s, never worn....22.00
Shoes, tennis; man's, hightop, 1920s....22.00
Skirt, bl irid taffeta, Hattie Carnagie, 1930s, EX....125.00
Skirt, felt, 1950s....23.00
Skirt, gr satin, quilted lining, lace hem trim, 1880s....40.00
Skirt, organza, ruffled hem....35.00
Skirt, ribbed velvet w/applique peacock eyes, 1910....95.00
Skirt, sport style, wht, long, 1915....30.00
Skirt, wrap; Chinese, satin, brn w/bl floral embr/stripes....30.00
Slip, blk silk, bone bodice, Victorian, scarce....75.00
Slip, cotton, wht, long....30.00
Slip, wht, 2-tier lace edge, full lgth, Victorian....45.00
Slip, ½; crepe-de-chine/Chantilly inset/plt, Callot Soeurs....195.00
Slip, ½; wht, 4 tiers of lace, VG....25.00
Spats, poplin, pearl buttons, cream....15.00
Stockings, hand knit, Amish, blk, '20s, 14"....65.00
Stockings, hand knit, Amish, purple w/yel band, '20s, 11"....85.00
Suit, girl's; middy, silk plt skirt, w/blazer, Molyneux....465.00
Suit, little boy's sailor; wht linen w/red accents....18.00
Suit, traveling; satin, button-up, l/s jacket, 1875....80.00
Suit, wht linen, 2-pc, ca 1915....85.00
Suit, 2-pc brn velvet, boned waist, taffeta ruffle, 1850s....125.00
Suit, 3-pc charmeuse w/chiffon chrysanthemum, Chanel....7,150.00
Suit, 3-pc wool plaid w/silk piping, Vionnet....825.00
Sweater, blk cashmere, wht beads....45.00
Sweater, lamb's wool, lined, beaded....22.00
Sweater, pink cashmere, intricate pearl & beaded design....35.00
Sweater, wht wool, heavy beaded yoke & sleeves....35.00
Sweater, wht wool, pearls & beading....22.00
Teddy, beige silky material, lace work at hip....22.00
Teddy, coral silk w/beige lace trim, 1920s, never worn....45.00
Teddy, cream silky material, lace trim, V lace-up front....24.00
Teddy, rayon, gr w/pink lacy trim....22.00
Trousers, drop front, wool....50.00
Tuxedo, blk wool, onyx studs, w/vest, 1930s....25.00
Tuxedo, cutaway style, dtd 1914, 3-pc....110.00
Uniform, nurse's; cadet, WWII....35.00
Waist, blk velvet, beige taffeta, shirred sleeves, 1890....35.00
Waist, lav & cream, lace trim, full upper sleeves....35.00
Waist, quilted, blk silk, ca 1940....25.00
Waist & long skirt, wht, heavy elegant lace, 1800s, 2-pc....95.00

Cluthra

The name Cluthra is derived from the Scottish word 'clutha,' meaning cloudy. Glassware by this name was first produced by J. Couper and Sons, England. Frederick Carder developed Cluthra glass while at the Steuben Glass Works. It is found in both solid and shaded colors, and is characterized by a spotty appearance resulting from small air pockets trapped between its two layers.

When no condition is indicated, the items listed below are assumed to be in mint condition.

Bowl, lav, Steuben, 3¼"....125.00
Cologne, pink to white, Steuben, 7"....400.00
Rose bowl, pink/wht mottle, rigaree sides & front, 6x6"....150.00
Vase, amethyst, Steuben, 11x10½"....1,400.00
Vase, bl/orange/brn, Kimball, 4"....185.00

Vase, mottled orange and opaque white, signed 'K, #20142-7', 6¼", $400.00.

Vase, gold, ribbed, 6″ 185.00
Vase, gr to clear, dbl cone, Steuben, 12″ 800.00
Vase, lav, sgn Steuben, #6415, 4½″ 550.00
Vase, strawberry, sgn fleur-de-lys, Steuben, bulbous, 11″ 1,450.00
Vase, wht, bulbous, Steuben, 10½″ 550.00
Vase, wht, gourd form, Kimball, 7¾x11″ 125.00
Vase, wht & gr, Steuben, 6¾″ 275.00
Vase, yel, bulbous, Kimball, 7″ 250.00

Coalport

In 1745 in Caughley, England, Squire Brown began a modest business fashioning crude pots and jugs from clay mined in his own fields. Tom Turner, a young potter who had apprenticed his trade at Worcester, was hired in 1772, to plan and oversee the construction of a 'proper' factory. Three years later he bought the business, which he named Caughley Coalport Porcelain Manufactory. Though the dinnerware he produced was meant to be only everyday china, the hand painted florals, birds, and landscapes used to decorate the ware were done in exquisite detail and in a wide range of colors. In 1780 Turner introduced the Willow pattern, which he produced using a newly perfected method of transfer printing. (Wares from the period between 1775 to 1799 are termed 'Caughley' or 'Salopian'--see section on Caughley.)

John Rose purchased the Caughley factory from Thomas Turner in 1799, adding that holding to his own pottery he had built two years before in Coalport. (It is from this point in the pottery's history that the wares are termed 'Coalport.') The porcelain produced there before 1814 was unmarked, with very few exceptions. After 1820, some examples were marked with a '2' with an oversize top loop. The term 'Coalbrookdale' refers to a fine type of porcelain decorated in floral bas relief, similar to the work of Dresden.

After 1835, highly decorated ware with rich ground colors imitated the work of Sevres and Chelsea, even going so far as to copy their marks. From about 1895 until about 1920, the mark in use was 'Coalport' over a crown, with 'England, A.D. 1750,' indicating the date claimed as the founding, not the date of manufacture. From the 1920s until 1945, 'Made in England' over a crown, and 'Coalport' below, was used. Later, 'Coalport' again got top billing, over a smaller crown, with 'Made in England' in a curve below.

In 1926 the Coalport Company moved to Shelton in Staffordshire, and today belongs to a group headed by the Wedgwood Company.

When no condition is indicated, the items listed below are assumed to be in mint condition.

Box, heart shape, cobalt w/wht roses, scenic reserve, 2½″ 325.00
Box, patch; bl rose/leaf decor, petal top, 1x2½″ 230.00
Cup & saucer, demitasse; pink w/gold, gold w/in, 1891, 3″ 135.00
Figurine, Judith Anne, dress/hat/necklace, mk 1920-45, 7″ 75.00
Loving cup, cobalt bl, gold ornamentation, 9½″ 750.00
Plate, dessert; floral, HP by Thos Dixon, gilt, 1847 . . . . . 175.00
Urn, Loch Achray in reserve, cobalt/ivory, w/lid, 11″ 550.00
Vase, gold w/turq jewels & scenic reserve, 1910, 2½″ 325.00

Cobalt Glass

Cobalt glass is characterized by its deep transparent blue color obtained by mixing cobalt oxide and alumina to the batch. It may be found in free-blown, mold-blown, and pressed glassware.

When no condition is indicated, the items listed below are assumed to be in mint condition.

Biscuit jar, consolidated open heart & arches enamel 145.00
Bottle, scent; blown 3-mold, tam-o'-shanter stopper, 5½″ 160.00
Bottle, toilet water; ribbed, tam-o'-shanter stopper, 5¾″ 165.00
Bowl, loop & petal, ground pontil, 2⅜x8″ 175.00
Box, foliage/floral in cream enamel, hinged/rnd, 1¼x2½″ 95.00
Candlestick, hexagon, minor edge flakes, 9″ 175.00
Candlestick, pressed, rib pattern, 4⅞″, pr 100.00
Castor set, 6-bottle, relief deer heads, revolves, 4 legs 185.00
Flask, blown, half post, broken swirl, 6⅝″ 200.00
Flask, lady's; crackle w/pnt bird/stopper, ½-pt 65.00
Mug, blown, applied ft & hdl, gold wreath w/forget-me-not 20.00
Mustard jar, sterling holder & lid 75.00
Pitcher, blown, applied ft & hdl, 4¼″ 115.00
Pitcher, wht pnt bird/butterfly, cobalt hdl, 2¼x1¼″ 45.00
Plate, silver floral trim, 12″ 65.00
Rolling pin, sgn T Webb 145.00
Sugar bowl, plain w/star base, w/lid, att NE, 7″ 155.00
Tumbler, paneled, 3¼″ 40.00
Vase, bulbous, 10″ 45.00
Vase, HP floral, ruffled, 4½″ 28.00
Vase, octagon w/flare & scallops, 7″ 35.00

Coffee Grinders

The task of preparing coffee has become much easier since the first coffee mill, a simple mortar and pestle, was used to grind the beans two hundred years ago. The first patent was issued in 1790 for a device made solely for grinding coffee. Between 1825 and 1900 the hand-cranked coffee mill was patented and improvements on the original evolved at a very competitive rate. Coffee and coffee-grinding devices became 'big business.' By the 1920s, however, vacuum sealed cans and sealed bags were introduced, and the coffee mill became obsolete. Mills patented before 1920 are very popular with today's collector. Most common old mills are usually sold for $45.00 to $75.00, while the more unusual examples bring a much higher price. Floor model store mills in mint condition can bring as much as $3,500.00. Be cautious of reproductions; if it looks too new, then it probably is!

For a more thorough study of the subject, we recommend you refer to *Coffee Mills*, an illustrated price guide by Terry Friend, whose address can be found in the Directory under Virginia. When no condition is indicated, the items listed below are assumed to be in excellent condition.

Lap mill, iron work by Landers, Frary & Clark, fine box joints, pine, all original, total height 9″, $80.00.

Adam's, lap; pewter hopper, 8x6½" sq....................110.00
Arcade, side; #5, pat 6/1894, CI, orig lid....................50.00
Arcade, table; 1-lb, pat 6/5/1884, w/decal, 12½x7x7", orig......85.00
Arcade, wall; crystal glass canister, orig measuring glass........55.00
Arcade Golden Rule, Citizens Supply Co, Columbus, OH......180.00
Arcade Telephone, pat April 11/1893, wall or shelf mt........250.00
Blacksmith made, funnel hopper, ca 1790-1825..............165.00
Canister, miniature, boy & girl decal, 5½x1½", orig............80.00
Chas Parker, counter; #5000, pat 3/9/97, 12½" wheels, 16"....265.00
Chas Parker, side; #350, pat 4/1876, CI orig top..............55.00
Chas Parker, table; 1-lb, tall, orig..........................90.00
Coles Mfg Co, Phila, PA, pat 1887, 16" wheels, 28", orig.....300.00
Daisy #867, miniature, 4x2½x2½", orig......................80.00
Delmar, table; 1-lb, Simmons Hdwe, St Louis, MO, orig........80.00
Elgin National #44, 15" wheels, 24", orig..................285.00
Enterprise, counter; #1, pat '73, open hopper/11" hdl.........175.00
Enterprise, counter; #3, pat '98, 11" wheels/13½", orig.......275.00
Enterprise, floor; #118½, pat 1873, all orig, 72"............2,000.00
Enterprise #9, pat '98, brass eagle, 19" wheels, 28", orig......350.00
Imperial, lap; CI top w/eagle, 8½x6¾" sq....................85.00
Lap, common, no decals/mk, CI hopper, box joints, 8x6½" sq...45.00
PS&W Co, side; #3500, CI.................................45.00
Table, no decals, 1-lb, 10¾x6½x6½"........................55.00
Table, primitive, dvtl, 14x7½" sq box, 28" board, unique......150.00
Universal #12, canister; pat 2/14/1905......................60.00
W Cross & Son, lap; CI, brass hopper.......................70.00
WW Weaver, lap; primitive, dvtl, tin hopper, ca 1810-1825....140.00

Coin Operated Machines

Slot machines may be the fastest appreciating collectible on the market today. Legal in about half of the states, many are bought, restored, and used for home entertainment. The rate of appreciation has been estimated at 20% per year to 5% monthly. Older machines from the turn of the century, and those with especially elaborate decoration and innovative accessories are most desirable, often bringing prices in excess of $5,000.

Vending machines sold a product or a service. They were already in common usage by 1900, selling gum, cigars, matches, and a host of other commodities. Peanut and gumball machines are especially popular today. The most valuable are those with their original finish and decals. Older machines made of cast iron are especially desirable, while those with plastic globes have little or no collector value. When buying unrestored peanut machines, beware of salt damage.

The coin operated phonograph of the early 1900s paved the way for the juke boxes of the twenties. Seeburg was first on the market with an automatic 8-tune phonograph. By the 1930s, Wurlitzer was the top name in the industry, with dealerships all over the country. As a result of the growing ranks of competitors, the forties produced the most beautiful machines made. Wurlitzers from this era are probably the most popularly sought-after models on the market today. The model 1015 of 1946 is considered the all time classic, and often brings prices in excess of $5,000.

When no condition is indicated, the items listed below are assumed to be in excellent originial condition.

Juke Boxes

AMI Continental II, 1960s..............................550.00
AMI Model B, 1948....................................950.00
AMI Model D-45.......................................350.00
AMI Singing Towers...................................1,700.00
Capehart, radio atop, wood case, 5¢ play, rare............1,500.00
Chicago Coin Band Box.................................700.00
Mills Swing King......................................450.00
Risteaucrat, countertop................................250.00

Wurlitzer Model 81 countertop, walnut case with yellow and red marbleized plastic panels containing twelve-selection 78 rpm mechanism, restored, 23", $4,000 auction estimate.

Rockola #1428....................................2,200.00
Rockola #1464, M orig.............................1,275.00
Scopitone Video, w/36 films..........................650.00
Seeburg #100......................................425.00
Seeburg #100 wall box, VG............................60.00
Seeburg L-100, EX rstr.............................1,200.00
Williams Music Mite................................1,500.00
Wurlitzer, P-10.....................................650.00
Wurlitzer #1015, bubble tubes, M rstr...................7,200.00
Wurlitzer #1015, complete, VG unrstr...................3,250.00
Wurlitzer #1050....................................4,000.00
Wurlitzer #1080, M rstr.............................5,000.00
Wurlitzer #1100, plays orig 78/rpm, 1947, EX orig.........1,700.00
Wurlitzer #1100, revolving lights ea side, 1947, M rstr.......4,500.00
Wurlitzer #1400, G..................................975.00
Wurlitzer #2104.....................................365.00
Wurlitzer #580 speaker, 1942, EX orig..................7,500.00
Wurlitzer #61 countertop, walnut w/plastic panels, rstr.......2,000.00
Wurlitzer #700, M rstr..............................2,500.00
Wurlitzer #71, on #810 stand, M rstr...................5,000.00
Wurlitzer #750, EX orig.............................2,600.00
Wurlitzer #81, countertop, rstr........................4,000.00
Wurlitzer #850A, rfn, rechromed, rare, 1942..............7,500.00
Wurlitzer speaker #240...............................100.00

Slot Machines

Aikens 10¢, extra bell..............................2,000.00
Aikens 5¢, EX orig.................................2,600.00
Bally 25¢ Reliance.................................2,900.00
Bally 5¢ Draw Bell..................................575.00
Bally 5¢/25¢ Double Bells...........................3,000.00
Big Jax 5¢, payout w/5 jackpots, oak case.................400.00
Burnham 5¢, ftd, CI................................6,500.00
Caille Ben Hur.....................................3,000.00
Caille Bull Frog...................................16,000.00
Caille New Century Detroit...........................6,500.00
Caille New Century Detroit, gr, #231....................8,900.00
Caille 10¢ Superior, Dancing Girl front..................1,850.00

Caille 5¢ Victory, center pull w/mint vendor, M orig........6,000.00
Jennings $1 Lite Up w/jackpot........2,200.00
Jennings Century........1,600.00
Jennings Ciga-Rola 5¢........1,450.00
Jennings Console Chief........1,800.00
Jennings Golf Ball........1,800.00
Jennings 1¢ Little Duke, triple jackpot, vendor, EX orig......1,650.00
Jennings 1¢ Little Duke, triple jackpot, vendor, M orig.......2,300.00
Jennings 1¢ Silver Club, EX rstr........1,050.00
Jennings 25¢ Dutch Boy & Girl........1,450.00
Jennings 25¢ Silver Chief........1,400.00
Jennings 25¢ Standard Chief........1,250.00

Left, Jennings 5¢ three-reel slot with jackpot, ca 1935, excellent restored condition, $1,600.00; Center, Watling Treasury 5¢ three-reel slot, top and front cast with cascading coins, single jackpot, ca 1936, restored, 24", $3,500.00; Right, Pace 50¢ Comet three-reel slot, front cast in Art Deco taste, ca 1935, restored, $1,600.00.

Jennings 5¢ Blue Seal........1,400.00
Jennings 5¢ Dutch Boy, EX orig........1,300.00
Jennings 5¢ Dutch Boy, jackpot on 3 lemons, EX rstr.......1,650.00
Jennings 5¢ Silent FOK........1,500.00
Jennings 5¢ Sun Chief........1,500.00
Jennings 5¢ Victoria, mint vendor front........1,500.00
Jennings 5¢ Victoria #7, Deco front........1,450.00
Jennings 5¢ Witch........4,500.00
Jennings 5¢ 4-Star Chief........1,450.00
Keeney Pyramid........2,200.00
Mills Checkboy, 1907........5,500.00
Mills Chicago, musical, EX rstr........11,000.00
Mills Dewey, M rstr........12,000.00
Mills Dewey, orig music mechanism, EX rstr........8,500.00
Mills Diamond Bell........1,495.00
Mills Golden Falls........1,495.00
Mills Gooseneck, EX rstr........1,495.00
Mills OK Bell........1,495.00
Mills 1¢ Jr Bell........1,800.00
Mills 10¢ Black Cherry........1,495.00
Mills 10¢ Extraordinary........1,495.00
Mills 20th Century, M orig........9,200.00
Mills 25¢ Bonus, EX orig........1,500.00
Mills 25¢ Bursting Cherry, w/3rd diamond jackpot........1,450.00
Mills 25¢ Extraordinary........1,495.00
Mills 25¢ High Top........1,450.00
Mills 25¢ QT........1,450.00
Mills 25¢ War Eagle, single jackpot, pay card, EX orig.......1,650.00
Mills 25¢ Wolfe Head........1,450.00
Mills 5¢ Baseball........1,500.00
Mills 5¢ Castle Front, 3-reel, oak fr, 1932, EX orig........1,600.00
Mills 5¢ Diamond Front, EX orig........1,450.00
Mills 5¢ Firebird QT, mint vendor, EX rstr........1,450.00
Mills 5¢ FOK Eagle Front, M orig........2,000.00
Mills 5¢ FOK Skillstops, EX rstr........1,495.00
Mills 5¢ High Top, 3-reel, bl finish, w/jp, 1940s........1,400.00
Mills 5¢ Lion Front, EX orig........1,600.00
Mills 5¢ Operator Bell, 3-reel, copper plate, w/jp, '30s.......1,600.00
Mills 5¢ Silent FOK, EX orig........1,500.00
Mills 5¢ Skyscraper........1,450.00
Mills 5¢ Vest Pocket, NM orig........450.00
Mills 5¢ Watermelon High Top, EX orig........1,495.00
Mills 5¢ 4-Column Front........1,450.00
Pace Rocket........1,400.00
Pace 5¢ Double, w/base stand........1,800.00
Pace 5¢ Fancy Front........1,500.00
Rockola 1¢ 5 Jacks, NM orig........950.00
Watling 25¢ Roll-A-Top, EX rstr........3,500.00
Watling 5¢ Blue Seal, twin jackpot, vendor, EX orig........1,375.00
Watling 5¢ Brownie, jackpot pinwheel countertop, EX orig...2,800.00
Watling 5¢ Treasury........2,200.00

Trade Stimulators

AdLee Try It, VG orig........350.00
American Flags 1¢, gum dispenser........265.00
Bally Baby, 3-reel, mini........250.00
Bally Poker........600.00
Buckley 1¢ Ball Gum, w/gumball dispenser, rstr........400.00
Crystal Gazer, penny activated dice........650.00
Daily Races Jr, 5¢, dice, horserace motif, countertop........300.00
Dandy, 1¢ gumball vendor, EX orig........325.00
Daval Cent-A-Smoke, 3 cigarette reels........400.00
Daval 1¢ American Eagle, token payout........210.00
Garden City Novelty Gem, rfn........250.00
Ginger, 3-reel, token receiver for 1-10 packs, w/63 tokens.....225.00
Griswold 5¢ Wheel of Fortune, rstr........595.00
Groetchen Ball Gum........450.00
Heads or Tails, play 1¢, 5¢, 10¢ or 25¢, match coin shown.....400.00
Hershey's Ball Gum, flat top, w/Hershey bar, rpt........200.00
Hi Fly 5¢ Baseball, flip........265.00
Jennings 1¢ Target Practice, Indian decor........600.00
Mills Perfection........485.00
Penny Pack, VG rstr........265.00
Reel 21 Blackjack, w/gumball dispenser........295.00
Sparks 1¢ Champion........350.00
Spiral, cigar store stimulator, EX orig........1,800.00
2-wheel Bicycle, ca 1893, EX orig........1,900.00

Miscellaneous

Abbey gum machine........75.00
Advance gumball machine........125.00
Advance nut vendor........150.00
Advance 1¢ match machine, dome globe........375.00
American Grip Meter, rstr........250.00
Asco Hot Nut, vendor........125.00
Atlas 1¢ Baseball Game, countertop, EX graphics........600.00
Automatic Games Scoop, rstr........800.00
Baker 1¢ Pik-A-Pak........400.00
Ball Gum 1¢ Baseball, hit gum w/bat, trigger activated........265.00
Bally Champ, pinball, EX orig........225.00
Bally Ho, pinball, 7 balls for 1¢........425.00
Bayer Asprin, dispenser, metal, 1960s........50.00
Bingo, 1¢ pinball, 1931, 25"........400.00

Booz Barometer, 5¢, M orig....175.00
Buckley Point Maker....400.00
Buckley Track Odds....2,000.00
Buckley Treasure Chest Digger, rstr....1,050.00
Cail-O-Scope Peep Show, rstr....950.00
Caille, floor model automatic gum vendor, rare, M rstr....6,500.00
Caille Mascot, grip & lung tester, rstr....1,800.00
Challenger 1¢ Target Shoot....225.00
Chester Pollard, football game....1,200.00
Chester Pollard, golf game, rstr....1,495.00
Climax #10, peanut vendor, CI, VG orig....800.00
Columbus A, vendor....225.00
DD Lewis dispenser, brass nameplate, VG orig....150.00
Derby Lite, countertop horse race....135.00
Disposition Register, 1¢....195.00
Exhibit Photoscope....495.00
Exhibit Supply Ball Lifter....675.00
Exhibit Supply High Striker, rstr....1,050.00
Exhibit Supply Iron Claw, VG orig....950.00
Exhibit Supply Iron Claw digger, 1920s, rstr....1,500.00
Exhibit Supply Lift & Grip machine, CI....600.00
Exhibit Supply Lighthouse Strength Tester....850.00
Exhibit Supply Striking Clock....750.00
Exhibit Supply 1¢ Radio Love Message, w/cards....495.00
Ford, vendor....60.00
Gem Confection Vendor, penny flip/vendor, Indian head....1,000.00
Genco Fortune Teller....1,500.00
Globe Ball Lifter....975.00
Gottlieb 1¢ Grip Tester, metal countertop....200.00
Groetchen 1¢ Skill Jump, guide balls down ramps, 32″....300.00
Heads or Tails Donkey, gambling device....250.00
Hit the Target, penny drop gumball dispenser, 1960s....145.00
Hit-A-Home, 5¢ ping-pong ball flip....175.00
Hot Nut, 5¢, w/cup dispenser....125.00
Jergens Lotion, 1¢ dispenser, Deco styling, CI/glass top....400.00
Jockey Club, pinball, 1930....500.00
Keep 'Em Bombing 1¢ Smak-A-Jap Penny Drop, 1940s....600.00
Kenney's 5¢ Scramball, marbles roll down ramps....145.00
Kiss-O-Meter....750.00
Lighter fluid dispenser....200.00
Little Whirl Wind, 1¢, countertop....350.00
Love Tester, floor model, arcade....450.00
Lucky Lindy, gumball, w/Statue of Liberty, 1929....475.00
Lucky Strike, 1¢ pinball machine, table top, oak, 15½″....550.00
Master 1¢ gumball machine....175.00
Master 1¢/5¢ gumball machine....245.00
Mercury Deluxe Lift & Twist, EX rstr....450.00
Mercury 1¢ Grip Tester....200.00
Mills Firefly 1¢ Electricity Machine....600.00
Mills 1¢ Lollipop Scale, claw feet, fancy head....950.00
Mills 1¢ Lollipop Scale, rstr....750.00
Mills 1¢ Target Practice....295.00
Mills 1¢ Wizard Fortune Teller, wood case....400.00
Miniature Baseball, 1¢, flip ball into circles....600.00
Mutoscope, CI, clamshell, rstr....1,495.00
Mutoscope Career Pilot....775.00
Mutoscope Shoot-A-Matic, prize vending shooting gallery....2,500.00
Mutoscope table-top strip tease....900.00
National Penny Confention gumball vendor, boxing/screen....1,200.00
National Self Service, mint & gum vendor....150.00
National Sidewalk Scales, on pipe w/claw ft, VG orig....975.00
Northwestern, dispenser for boxes of 1¢ matches, 1911....400.00
Northwestern 5¢ gumball, 1949....60.00
Over the Top 1¢ Skill Machine, wall mt....400.00
Papna & Hochrein, 1¢ baseball game/vendor, ca 1918, M orig....950.00
Peerless 1¢ Lolipop Scales....475.00
Penny Nickel Fantail Masters, gumball....375.00
Peppy the Clown, arcade, 1950s....225.00
Pikes Peak....500.00
Pitchem 1¢ Kicker Catcher, basketball graphics....250.00
Premiere, 2¢ gumball & baseball card machine....125.00
Pulver Cop & Robber, rnd edge....550.00
Pulver gumball machine, policeman....350.00
Pulver gumball machine, yellow kid....275.00
Pulver 1¢ gum vendor, thin tab....75.00
Reliable Target Practice, 1¢....275.00
Riverboat, pinball, 1960s....300.00
Roberts 10¢ mint vendor, gooseneck, orig stencil, EX orig....1,250.00
Rockola, 1933 World Series pinball....500.00
Rockola Scales, CI....225.00
Scultoscope, counter stereo card viewer, VG orig....400.00
Sel-Mor 1¢ peanut vendor, CI, decal....165.00
Shake 'Em Up, 5¢ dice game w/gumball vendor....300.00
Silver Comet, 1¢, single cigarette dispenser....250.00
Skill Crane Digger....550.00
Solar Horoscope Fortune Teller....550.00
Stamp vendor, CI....220.00
Stamp vendor, three 25¢ slots, metal, 8x12″....30.00
Superior Pool Game, w/mirror, rstr....500.00
Target Skill, 1¢, load pistol w/penny, gumball consolation....600.00
Trip-L-Jacks, all orig, EX....700.00
Uncle Sam, stamp vendor, porc front....60.00
Wee Gee 1¢ Fortune Teller Penny Drop, wall mt, cast front....500.00
Wilbur Suihard 1¢ Chocolate Vendor, CI w/mirror....300.00
Wrigley Gum, gum vendor, never used....250.00
Zeno Collar Buttons, vendor....350.00
Zeno gum machine, wood & tin, NM orig....550.00
Zipper Skill, 1¢ flip ball....200.00

Collector Plates

After a period of reduced activity in the market of limited edition plates, a renewed enthusiasm, brought on perhaps by full-scale publicity effected through direct mailing, magazines, and national television, has established what many collectors optimistically regard as a solid secondary market. As a result, values of choice issues are steadily appreciating; first editions usually prove the best investment. In the listings that follow, they are indicated by the letters FE.

Two of the earliest manufacturers of Christmas plates were Bing and Grondahl, who issued their first plate in 1895, and the Royal Copenhagen Porcelain Manufactory who followed with their series in 1908. In this country, Frankoma Pottery began producing limited editions plates in 1965. Today they have been joined by well over one hundred manufacturers and marketing organizations world-wide. Only a few are listed here to represent some of the more familiar companies.

There are several specific publications and many other sources of information available to keep today's collector aware of the current market trends. Values are for plates in mint condition.

American Commemorative

1976, Southern Landmarks, Gov Tryon's Palace....70.00
1977, Southern Landmarks, Elmscourt....62.00
1978, Southern Landmarks, Mt Vernon....50.00
1979, Southern Landmarks, Custis Lee....50.00

American Express

1976, American Trees of Christmas, Douglas Fir 60.00
1977, American Trees of Christmas, Scotch Pine 58.00
1978, Birds of North America, Saw-Whet Owls 38.00
1981, Roger Tory Peterson series, Bob-O-Link 55.00

American Heritage Art

1982, Celebrity Clowns/Jon Helland, Judy 50.00
1982, Lil' Critters/Allen A Adams, Chatty 40.00
1983, American Sail/Edward Ries, Down Easter in a Squall 40.00
1983, Kitty Hawk, FE 45.00

American Historical

1972, Aviation, Amelia Earhart 60.00
1973, Bicentennial, Silent Foe 60.00
1973, Natural History, Painted Lady 40.00
1974, Bicentennial, One Nation 58.00

American Rose Society

1975, All-American Rose, Oregold 120.00
1976, All-American Rose, Yankee Doodle 112.00
1979, All-American Rose, Paradise 70.00
1980, All-American Rose, Love 60.00

Anna Perenna

1978, Carol Burgues, June Dream 70.00
1978, Dr Irving Burgues, Chun Li 80.00
1978, Floral Fantasies/Carol Burgues, Empress Gold 95.00
1978, Triptych Series, Byzantine 350.00
1979, Romantic Lovers/Russell-Barrer, Romeo & Juliet 115.00
1979, Uncle Tad's Cats/T Krumeich, Oliver's Birthday 160.00
1980, Romantic Lovers/Russell-Barrer, Lancelot & Guinevere 98.00

Anri

1972, Pipers at Alberobello 135.00
1974, Young Man & Girl 99.00
1975, Christmas in Ireland 103.00
1976, Father's Day, Sailing 105.00
1976, Knitting 65.00
1977, Cliff Gazing 90.00
1977, Heiligenblut 140.00
1979, All Hearts 125.00

Arabia

1973, Commemoration 65.00
1976, Vainamoinen's Sowing 145.00
1977, Aino's Fate 70.00
1978, Inland Village Scene 49.00
1980, Vainamoinen's Rescue 65.00

Artists Of The World

1977, The Clown Also Cries, Don Ruffin 30.00
1979, Children of Aberdeen, Girl with Little Brother 60.00
1979, Game Birds/Larry Toschik, Ring-Necked Pheasant 50.00
1980, Children Series/Don Ruffin, Flowers for Mother 50.00
1980, Sun Kachina, Don Ruffin 50.00
1982, Prowlers of the Clouds/Toschik, Golden Eagle 45.00
1983, Little Satchmo, Anthony Sidoni 30.00

Avondale

1978, Cameos of Childhood, Melissa 60.00
1979, Cameos of Childhood, First Born 70.00
1979, Myths of the Sea, Poseidon 65.00
1979, World of Dance, Prima Ballerina 75.00
1981, Christmas Annual, ...and the Heavens Rejoiced 85.00

Bareuther

1968, Christmas, Kapplkirche 47.00
1969, Christmas, Christkindlemarkt 34.00
1970, Christmas, Chapel in Oberndorf 25.00
1971, Christmas, Toys for Sale 41.00
1971, Father's Day, Castle Heidelberg 27.00
1972, Mother's Day, Mother & Children 25.00
1974, Christmas, Black Forest Church 45.00
1975, Christmas, Snowman 34.00
1976, Christmas, Chapel in Hills 28.00
1976, Mother's Day, Rocking the Cradle 25.00
1980, Father's Day, Castle Cochem 30.00

Berlin

1970, Christmas in Bernkastel 145.00
1971, Christmas in Rothenburg 28.00
1971, Father's Day, Brooklyn Bridge 20.00
1972, Christmas in Michelstadt 45.00
1972, Mother's Day, Fledglings 25.00
1973, Father's Day, Landing of Columbus 40.00
1974, Mother's Day, Squirrels 40.00
1975, Christmas in Dortland 30.00
1975, Mother's Day, Cats 40.00
1975, Washington Crossing the Delaware 40.00
1977, Mother's Day, Storks 35.00
1977, Zeppelin 35.00
1978, Christmas in Berlin 38.00

Bing & Grondahl

1911, Christmas, Angels & Shepherds 95.00
1912, Christmas, Going to Church 90.00
1914, Christmas, Amalienborg Castle 90.00
1916, Christmas, Sparrows 92.00
1916, Easter Plaque 65.00
1917, Christmas, Christmas Boat 100.00
1918, Easter Plaque 65.00
1919, Christmas, Outside Lighted Window 98.00
1920, Christmas, Hare in Snow 80.00
1921, Easter Plaque 65.00
1922, Christmas, Star of Bethlehem 80.00
1923, Christmas, The Hermitage 80.00
1924, Christmas, Lighthouse 75.00
1924, Easter Plaque 72.00
1925, Christmas, Child's Christmas 90.00
1927, Christmas, Skating Couple 105.00
1928, Christmas, Eskimos 80.00
1928, Easter Plaque 160.00
1929, Christmas, Fox Outside 87.00
1930, Christmas, Town Hall 100.00
1932, Easter Plaque 200.00

Bing and Grondahl, Mother's Day, 1976, $150.00.

1938, Christmas, Lighting Candles........125.00
1940, Christmas, Delivering Letters........150.00
1943, Christmas, Ribe Cathedral........175.00
1946, Christmas, Commemoration Cross........90.00
1950, Christmas, Kronborg Castle........155.00
1955, Christmas, Kalunborg Church........110.00
1959, Christmas, Christmas Eve........135.00
1962, Christmas, Winter Night........82.00
1967, Christmas, Sharing Joy........45.00
1970, Christmas, Pheasants in Snow........22.00
1972, Mother's Day, Mare & Foal........20.00
1972, Olympic........23.00
1973, Christmas, Family Reunion........27.00
1974, Mother's Day, Bear & Cubs........25.00
1977, Christmas, Copenhagen Christmas........30.00
1978, Seagull........70.00
1979, Mother's Day, Fox & Cubs........28.00

Carson Mint

1979, Mother's Day/Jan Hagara, Daisies from Mary Beth........85.00
1980, America Has Heart, My Heart's Desire........85.00
1980, Magic Afternoons, Enchanted Garden........40.00
1981, America Has Heart, Hearts and Flowers........40.00

Count Agazzi

1970, Children's Hour, Owl........9.00
1971, Easter, Playing the Violin........10.00
1972, Father's Day........35.00
1973, Christmas........20.00

D'Arceau Limoges

1973, Lafayette Series, The Secret Contract........45.00
1974, Lafayette Series, Battle of Brandywine........55.00
1975, Christmas, Fuite on Egypte........110.00
1976, Ganeau's Women, Colette........30.00
1976, Ganeau's Women, Scarlet en Crinoline........39.00
1977, Christmas, Refus d'Hebergement........30.00
1978, Cambier Four Seasons, La Jeune Fille d'Ete........110.00
1979, Les Tres Riches Heures, Janvier........75.00

Dave Grossman Designs

1977, Looney Tunes Christmas, FE........13.00
1978, Christmas/Barnard, Peace........40.00
1979, Children of the Week/Barnard, Wednesday's Child........26.00
1979, Huckleberry Finn/Rockwell, The Secret........40.00
1979, Rockwell, Young Doctor........50.00
1981, Boy Scout Annual/Rockwell, Can't Wait........30.00

Fairmont

1976, Famous Clowns/Red Skelton, Freddie the Freeloader....410.00
1977, Famous Clowns/Red Skelton, WC Fields........100.00
1977, Spencer Annual, Patient Ones........55.00
1978, Hug Me........95.00
1978, Wieghorst, Sioux Warrior........80.00
1979, Big Beautiful Cats, Sheena........75.00
1979, Early Works/Rockwell, Old Man Winter........20.00

Fleetwood Collection

1980, Annual Christmas/Fritz Wegner, The Magi........75.00
1980, Annual Mother's Day/Don Balke, Cottontails........75.00
1981, Annual Christmas/Fritz Wegner, The Holy Child........58.00
1981, Annual Mother's Day/Don Balke, Raccoons........58.00
1981, Prince Charles & Lady Diana........70.00

Franklin Mint, Crystal

1972, Audubon Society Birds, Goldfinch........115.00
1972, James Wyeth, Brandywine........140.00
1972, Mother's Day/Spencer, Mother & Child........175.00
1973, Audubon Birds, Wood Thrush........125.00
1973, Audubon Society Birds, Cardinal........110.00
1973, Birds, American Bald Eagle........145.00
1975, Four Seasons, Spring Blossoms........210.00
1976, Historical/Roberts, The Liberty Tree........130.00
1977, Annual, Tribute to the Arts........300.00
1977, Christmas, The Skating Party........35.00
1977, Freedom Series, Lafayette Joins Washington........300.00
1977, Mother's Day/Belskie, Infant........250.00

Franklin Mint, Porcelain

1976, Christmas Annual, Silent Night........70.00
1976, Hans Christian Andersen, Ugly Duckling........75.00
1978, Cinderella........55.00
1978, Grimm's Fairy Tales, The Twelve Dancing Princesses....42.00
1979, Hometown Memories/Jo Sickbert, Country Fair........29.00

Ghent Collection

1974, Christmas Wildlife, Cardinals in Snow, FE........50.00
1975, Mother's Day, Cotton Tail........40.00
1976, American Bicentennial Wildlife, American Bald Eagle....300.00
1976, Christmas Wildlife, Partridges & Pear Tree........40.00
1976, Fausett Mural Plates, From Sea to Shining Sea........225.00
1977, Memory Annual........85.00
1978, April Fool Annual/Rockwell........60.00
1978, Israeli Commemorative/Tobey, The Promised Land........85.00
1978, Treasures of Tutankhamun, The Golden Mask........125.00

Gorham

1970, Rockwell, American Family Tree........100.00
1971, Barrymore, Quiet Waters, FE........20.00
1971, Gallery of Masters, Rembrandt, FE........25.00
1972, Barrymore, Little Boatyard........145.00
1973, Remington Western, New Year on the Cimarron........35.00
1974, Rockwell, Golden Rule........30.00

1976, Black Regiment....35.00
1977, Julian Ritter, Christmas Visit....29.00
1977, Santa Fe Railway Collection, Navajo Silversmith....38.00
1980, Four Seasons Landscape/Rockwell, Summer Respite....45.00
1981, Sesame Street Christmas....18.00

Hoyle Products

1977, Norman Rockwell Clowns, The Runaway....75.00
1977, Western, Sharing an Apple....35.00
1978, Norman Rockwell Clowns, It's Your Move....60.00
1978, Wilderness Wings/David Maass, Gliding In....65.00
1979, Norman Rockwell Salesmen, The Horse Trader....40.00

Hutschenreuther

1972, Ruthven Songbirds, Bluebird & Goldfinch, FE....80.00
1977, Allegro Ensemble....140.00
1977, Plates of the Month/Winter, Jan-Dec, 6½", each....27.00
1978, Mother & Child Annual/Ole Winter....65.00
1979, Enchantment/Dolores Valenza, Princess Snowflake....60.00

Incolay Studios

1977, Romantic Poets Volume I/Appleby, She Walks in Beauty.215.00
1979, Great Romances of History, Antony/Cleopatra....65.00
1979, Life's Interludes/JW Roberts, Uncertain Beginning....95.00
1981, Romantic Poets Volume II/Akers, The Kiss....65.00

Kaiser

1970, Christmas, Waiting for Santa....37.00
1971, Mother's Day, Mare & Foal....40.00
1972, Anniversary, Doves in the Park....20.00
1973, Christmas, Holy Night....35.00
1973, Toronto Horse Show....40.00
1975, Anniversary, Tender Moment....25.00
1975, Mother's Day, German Shepherd....34.00
1977, Little Men/L Trester, Come Ride with Me....60.00
1978, People of the Midnight Sun/Peter, Northern Lullaby....70.00

Kern

1976, Mother's Day/E Runci, Mother & Children....40.00
1977, Prince Tatters/L Jansen, Johnny & Duke....48.00
1978, Christmas of Yesterday/M Nye, Christmas Call....45.00
1978, Linda's Little Lovables/L Avey, The Blessing....40.00
1979, Christmas of Yesterday/M Nye, Woodcutter's Christmas....50.00
1980, Great Achievements in Art, The Arabian....170.00

Lake Shore Prints

1973, Rockwell, Butter Girl....140.00
1974, Rockwell, Truth About Santa....75.00
1975, Rockwell, Home from the Fields....60.00
1976, Rockwell, A President's Wife....80.00

Lihs Lindner

1972, Christmas, Little Drummer Boy, FE....70.00
1972, Mother's Day, Mother & Child, FE....90.00
1972, Union Pacific Railroad....25.00
1973, Christmas, Carolers....20.00
1973, Easter, Happy Easter....45.00
1973, Flag....135.00
1973, Mother's Day, Mother & Child....18.00
1974, Mother's Day, Bouquet....30.00
1975, America the Beautiful, Independence Hall....45.00
1975, Mother's Day, Happiness....30.00
1976, Freedom Train....60.00
1976, Playmates, Timmy & Friend....55.00
1978, Child's Christmas, Holy Night....40.00

Lynell

1978, Little Traveler/Malick, On His Way....35.00
1979, Betsy Bates Annual, Olde Country Inn....45.00
1979, Rockwell Legendary Art/Christmas, Snow Queen....30.00
1979, Soap Box Derby, Last Minute Changes....30.00
1980, American Adventure/E Szabo, The Trapper....55.00
1980, Rockwell Legendary Art, Artist's Daughter....65.00
1980, Rockwell Legendary Art/Mother's Day, Cradle of Love....39.00

Pickard

1972, Lockhart Wildlife, Cardinal & Mockingbird....195.00
1973, Presidential, Lincoln....30.00
1975, Lockhart Wildlife, White-Tailed Deer....120.00
1978, Annual Christmas, Rest on the Flight into Egypt....100.00
1979, Children of Renoir, Girl with Hoop....110.00
1981, Children of Mexico/J Sanchez, Maria....190.00

Poole Pottery

1972, Medieval Calendar, January/Drinking Wine by Fire....100.00
1973, Christmas, Adoration of the Magi....125.00
1978, Home at Christmas, Santa's Helpers....38.00
1979, Birds of North America, Great Horned Owl....38.00
1979, Mother's Day, Tenderness....38.00

Porsgrund

1968, Christmas, Church Scene....195.00
1969, Christmas, Three Kings....15.00
1970, Castle, Hamlet....15.00
1970, Christmas Deluxe, Road to Bethlehem, FE....45.00
1970, Jubilee, Femboringer....30.00
1970, Mother's Day, Mare & Foal....15.00
1971, Father's Day, Fishing....10.00
1972, Easter, Ducks....15.00
1973, Father's Day, Sledding....13.00
1973, Mother's Day, Cat & Kittens....12.00
1974, Christmas, The Shepherds....40.00
1974, Easter, Bunnies....20.00
1977, Christmas, Jesus & Fishermen....20.00
1977, Mother's Day, Boy & Chickens....20.00
1979, Father's Day, Father & Daughter....20.00

Reed & Barton

1970, Zodiac....75.00
1971, California Missions, San Diego....75.00
1972, Currier & Ives, Village Blacksmith....85.00
1972, Free Trapper....65.00
1972, Kentucky Derby, Nearing the Finish....85.00
1973, Audubon, Red Cardinal....65.00
1973, Christmas/Altar Art, Adoration of Kings....60.00
1975, Founding Fathers, Thomas Jefferson....65.00

1976, American Christmas, Morning Train....................75.00
1978, Old-Fashioned Christmas, General Store at Christmas.....55.00

Rorstrand

1970, Christmas, Nils with His Geese........................35.00
1971, Father's Day, Father & Child, FE......................20.00
1971, Mother's Day, Mother & Child, FE.....................25.00
1974, Christmas, Vadstena..................................40.00
1976, Father's Day, Plowing................................25.00
1976, Mother's Day, Apple Picking..........................25.00
1980, Christmas, Nils in Holland...........................48.00

Rosenthal

1917, Christmas, Angel of Peace...........................200.00
1924, Christmas, Deer in the Woods........................195.00
1932, Christmas, Christ Child.............................185.00
1940, Christmas, Marien Church in Danzig..................250.00
1944, Christmas, Wood Scape...............................295.00
1953, Christmas, The Holy Light...........................190.00
1963, Christmas, Silent Night.............................195.00
1974, Classic Rose Christmas, Memorial Church in Berlin......125.00
1975, Summertime..95.00
1976, Fantasies & Fables, Oriental Night Music...............50.00
1977, Classic Rose Christmas, Hannover Town Hall..........100.00
1977, Fantasies & Fables, Mandolin Players..................80.00
1978, Wiinblad Crystal, Three Kings.......................260.00
1979, Wiidblad Christmas, Exodus from Egypt...............310.00

Royal Bayreuth

1974, Christmas, The Old Mill.............................20.00
1976, Antique American Art, Farmyard Tranquility............70.00
1976, Sunbonnet Babies Composite..........................75.00
1978, Christmas, Peaceful Interlude........................50.00

Royal Copenhagen

1911, Christmas, Danish Landscape.........................160.00
1913, Christmas, Frederik Church Spire....................150.00

Royal Copenhagen, Christmas 1956, $120.00.

1919, Christmas, The Park.................................95.00
1921, Christmas, Aabenraa Marketplace.....................85.00
1925, Christmas, Christianshavn...........................100.00
1928, Christmas, Vicat's Family...........................90.00
1932, Christmas, Frederiksberg Gardens....................110.00
1938, Christmas, Round Church in Osterlars................290.00
1944, Christmas, Typical Winter Scene.....................200.00
1950, Christmas, Boeslunde Church.........................270.00
1956, Christmas, Rosenborg Castle.........................250.00
1962, Christmas, The Little Mermaid.......................205.00
1966, Christmas, Blackbird................................65.00
1967, Virgin Islands......................................25.00
1969, Danish Flag...25.00
1973, Christmas, Homeward Bound...........................28.00
1975, Historical, Royal Copenhagen Bicentennial..............30.00
1978, Historical, Captain Cook............................35.00
1979, National Parks of America, Shenandoah................75.00

Royal Cornwall

1977, Mingolla Christmas, Winter Wonderland................65.00
1978, Golden Age o/t Cinema, The King & His Ladies.........45.00
1979, Kitten's World, Are You a Flower?...................45.00
1979, Promised Land, Pharoah's Daughter Finds Moses........45.00
1980, Beauty of Bouguereau, Madelaine.....................35.00
1980, Dorothy's Day/Bill Mack, Brand New Day...............55.00
1980, Five Perceptions of Weo Cho, Sense of Taste...........75.00
1980, Memories of America, Bringing in Maple Sugar.........120.00
1980, Most Precious Gifts of Shen Lung, Fire................50.00
1980, Promised Land, Miriam's Song of Thanksgiving..........45.00
1980, The Little People/Seima, Off to the Picnic............35.00
1980, Windows o/t World, Golden Gate of San Francisco.......45.00
1981, Love's Precious Moments, Love's Sweet Vow............55.00

Royal Delft De Porceleyne Fles

1916, Christmas, Cradle with Child, 10″....................370.00
1917, Christmas, Shepherd, 10″.............................450.00
1918, Christmas, Christmas Star, 10″.......................275.00
1920, Christmas, Church Tower..............................388.00
1924, Christmas, Shepherd, 10″.............................400.00
1927, Christmas, Church Tower, 7″..........................300.00
1928, Christmas, Lighthouse, 10″...........................375.00
1931, Christmas, Snow Landscape, 10″.......................375.00
1933, Christmas, Interior Scene, 10″.......................450.00
1940, Christmas, Christmas Tree, 10″.......................438.00
1960, Christmas, Landscape, 7″.............................170.00
1960, Christmas, Street in Delft, 10″......................350.00
1962, Christmas, Town View, 7″.............................160.00
1964, Christmas, Mill in Poelenburg, 7″....................155.00
1964, Christmas, Tower in Hoorn, 10″.......................360.00
1970, Christmas, Cathedral in Veere, 10″...................320.00
1974, Christmas, Kitchen in Hindeloopen, 10″...............375.00
1974, Valentine...135.00
1976, George Washington...................................350.00
1978, Christmas, Christmas Angels, 7″......................140.00

Royal Tettau

1971, Pope Paul VI..175.00
1972, Christmas, Carriage in the Village....................15.00
1972, Pope John XXIII.....................................150.00
1973, Pope Pius XII.......................................125.00

Stumar

1970, Christmas, Angel, FE....35.00
1971, Mother's Day, Amish Mother & Child, FE....35.00
1972, Christmas, Countryside....22.00
1973, Mother's Day, Mother Sewing....21.00
1976, Mother's Day, Reading to the Children....15.00
1977, Christmas, Joyful Expectations....20.00
1977, Egyptian, Ancient Trilogy....45.00
1978, Egyptian, Charioteer....54.00

Veneto Flair

1972, Dogs, German Shepherd....70.00
1972, Mother's Day, Madonna & Child....85.00
1973, Dogs, Poodle....45.00
1973, Easter, Rabbits....90.00
1973, Mosaic, Justinian....75.00
1974, Cats, Persian....55.00
1974, Easter, Chicks....55.00
1975, Christmas Card, Christmas Eve....40.00
1977, Valentine Boy....60.00
1978, Flower Children, Rose....45.00
1979, American Landscape, Hudson Valley....75.00
1979, Children's Christmas, Carolers....60.00

Comic Books

Public acceptance of the cartoon book as an enjoyable form of entertainment caused printing companies to experiment with size and format, and by the early 1930s the comic book as we know it today had evolved--7" x 9" paper back books stapled together and selling for 10¢. Each unfolded a new saga of adventure as experienced by detective extraordinare Dick Tracy; super-heroes like Batman and Robin, Superman and Wonderwoman, Tarzan, and The Lone Ranger; or the science fictional characters Flash Gordon and Captain Midnight.

Today first issues in excellent condition may bring prices as high as $300 or over. Rarity, age, and quality of artwork are prime factors in determining comic book values.

When no condition is indicated, the items listed below are assumed to be in excellent condition.

Abbott & Costello, #1, Nov 1953, 3-D, w/glasses, EX....90.00
Action, #101, nuclear explosion cover, EX....90.00
Action, #76, Sept 1944, EX....100.00
Adventure, #258, EX....14.00
Adventure, #300, EX....90.00
Adventure, #314, M....12.00
Air Fighters, V2#4, Jan 1944, Airboy, Blk Angel, VG....38.00
Airboy, V7#10, origin of the Head, G....10.00
All Select, #7, EX....90.00
All Winners, #17, Winter 1945-46, EX....140.00
All-American, #50, June 1943, EX....120.00
All-Flash, #23, June-July 1946, EX....90.00
All-Star, #27, 1945, Justice Society story, G....40.00
Alley Oop, #2, Argo, NM....30.00
Alley Oop, #3, EX....20.00
Amazing Spider-Man, #10, Mar 1964, M....70.00
Amazing Spider-Man, #13, NM....40.00
Amazing Spider-Man, #2, May 1963, EX....160.00
Amazing Spider-Man, #31-40, 1965-66, M....70.00
Amazing Spider-Man, #7, Dec 1963, Ditko art, EX....50.00
Amazing Spider-Man, #96, M....8.00
Amazing-Man, #22, VG....35.00
America's Best, #3, Nov 1942, EX....60.00
Animal, #7, VG....30.00
Astonishing Tales, #1-36, 1970-76, M....25.00
Atom, #2, EX....20.00
Atomic War, #1, atomic bomb cover, Nov 1952, EX....150.00
Avengers, #1, G....60.00
Avengers, #1, Sept 1963, EX....300.00
Avengers King-Size Special, #1-5, 1967-72, M....30.00
Batman, #100, June 1956, EX....120.00
Batman, #109, EX....25.00
Batman, #119, M....20.00
Batman, #120-125, 1958-59, EX....70.00
Batman, #14, Dec-Jan 1942-1943, Penguin cover, VG....100.00
Batman, #170-200, 1965-68, EX....120.00
Batman, #47, 1st detailed Batman origin, June-July 1948, EX..150.00
Batman, #62, orig of Bat Plane II, VG....30.00
Batman, #78, VG....23.00
Batman Annual, #1, EX....20.00
Batman Annual, #7, EX....8.00
Beware the Creeper, #1-6, 1968-69, EX....15.00
Big Shot, #11, Mar 1941, Skyman, Joe Palooka, EX....20.00
Big Shot, #17, Sept 1941, EX....20.00
Black Cat, #25, EX....25.00
Black Cat, #65, EX....10.00
Black Knight, #1, May 1953, EX....10.00
Blackhawk, #111, EX....7.00
Blackhawk, #27, VG....15.00
Blackhawk, #79, EX....12.00
Blazing Combat, #2, EX....10.00
Blue Beetle, #10, Dec 1941, BB & Gorilla, VG....26.00
Blue Beetle, #2, M....5.00
Blue Beetle, #25, Sept 1943, EX....20.00
Boy, #19, Dec 1944, EX....25.00
Boy Commandos, #27, EX....15.00
Brave & Bold, #24, EX....20.00
Brave & Bold, #30, June-July 1960, EX....50.00
Brave & Bold: Hawkman #43, M....25.00
Brer Rabbit's Sunken Treasure, 1950-51, 32 pg, 7x2½"....8.00
Brothers of the Spear, #1, 1972, EX....10.00
Buck Rogers, #1, G....77.00
Buz Sawyer, #1, June 1948, EX....28.00
Captain America, #33, Dec 1943, Schomburg cover, VG....79.00
Captain Atom, #79, EX....5.00
Captain Atom, #82, EX....8.00
Captain Marvel, #16, Oct 1942, 4 stories, EX....55.00
Captain Marvel, #21, Feb 1943, EX....50.00
Captain Marvel, #25, M....5.00
Captain Marvel, #35, May 1944, EX....25.00
Captain Marvel Jr, #22, Aug 1944, EX....25.00
Captain Midnight, #12, Sept 1943, EX....20.00
Captain Science, #6, EX....22.00
Castle of Frankenstein, #1, blk & wht monster magazine, EX....25.00
Castle of Frankenstein, #5, EX....14.00
Castle of Frankenstein, #7, M....20.00
Cat-Man, #17, Jan 1943, Cat-Man & the Hood, G....21.00
Cat-Man, #2, June 1941, EX....40.00
Cat-Man, #32, Aug 1946, EX....30.00
Chamber of Darkness, #4, M....5.00
Champion, #5, Mar 1940, EX....45.00
Christmas Parade, #5, EX....10.00
Christmas Parade, #5, M....15.00
Cinderella, #272, EX....10.00
Comic Cavalcade, #9, 1944, EX....50.00

Conan, #25-30, 1973-75, EX....45.00
Conan, #4, EX....15.00
Conan, #6, EX....15.00
Conan, #8, M....15.00
Crack, #36, Winter 1944, EX....25.00
Crackajack Funnies, #26, Aug 1940, EX....30.00
Creepy, #1, EX....10.00
Creepy, #3, M....8.00
Crime Machine, The; #1, M....5.00
Daredevil, #1, Apr 1964, orig, Everett, EX....115.00
Daredevil, #181, M....5.00
Daredevil, #2, June 1964, M....50.00
Daredevil, #23, Apr 1944, Daredevil & Claw, Briefer, EX....36.00
Daredevil, #4, Oct 1964, EX....20.00
Daring, #12, Fall 1945, EX....60.00
Dark Shadow, #18, M....5.00
Detective, #141, Nov 1948, EX....25.00
Detective, #183, EX....42.00
Detective, #267, EX....15.00
Detective, #33, Nov 1939, origin of Batman/Spy/Cosmo, VG....275.00
Detective, #60, Feb 1942, Batman vs Joker, Air Wave, EX....108.00
Dick Tracy, #113, VG....15.00
Dick Tracy, #130, EX....16.00
Dick Tracy, #89, EX....15.00
Doll Man, #15, EX....10.00
Doll Man, #30, Sept 1950, EX....20.00
Doll Man, #32, Feb 1951, EX....15.00
Donald & Mickey Merry Christmas, 1947, Firestone, M....148.00
Donald Duck in Indian Country, 1950-51, 32 pg, 7x2½", EX....8.00
Dr Solar, #1, EX....7.00
Dracula V1, #1-12, 1971, EX....24.00
Exciting, #33, June 1944, EX....25.00
Exciting, #49, EX....17.00
Famous Funnies, #76, Nov 1940, EX....25.00
Famous Funnies, #91, EX....15.00
Famous Monsters Yearbook, #1, blk & wht, EX....25.00
Fantastic Comics, #1, Dec 1939, EX....85.00
Fantastic Comics, #6, May 1941, VG....40.00
Fantastic Four, #16, EX....28.00
Fantastic Four, #19, EX....22.00
Fantastic Four, #2, Jan 1962, FF Vs the Scrulls, Kirby, EX....292.00
Fantastic Four, #24, EX....15.00
Fantastic Four, #25, EX....20.00
Fantastic Four, #31-40, 1964-65, M....45.00
Fantastic Four, #5, July 1962, EX....100.00
Fantastic Four, #7, G....10.00
Fantastic Four, #9, Dec 1962, FF Vs Sub-Mariner, EX....38.00
Fantasy Quarterly, #1, Elfquest, EX....25.00
Fawcett Movie Comic, #15, Man from Planet X, rare, G....60.00
Fear, #10-31, 1972-75, M....25.00
Feature Films, #4, EX....25.00
Felix the Cat, #15, 1942, EX....50.00
Fight, #20, Aug 1942, EX....40.00
Fight, #43, EX....35.00
Fight, #46, VG....27.00
Fighting American, #1, EX....10.00
Flash, #217/219/223/226, 1972-74, M....25.00
Flash Annual, #1, M....15.00
Flash Comics, miniature edition, VG....30.00
Flash Gordon, #1-10, 1966-67, M....45.00
Flash Gordon, #12, M....5.00
Flash Gordon, #13, M....5.00
Fly, The; #11, EX....6.00
Flying Saucers, #1, 1950, EX....80.00
Funnies, #45, July 1940, origin of Phantasmo, EX....55.00
Funnies, The; #44, June 1940, EX....30.00
Green Hornet, #3, Apr 1941, EX....50.00
Green Lantern, #12, G....44.00
Green Lantern, #4, EX....15.00
Green Lantern, #85, EX....10.00
Green Lantern, #9, Fall 1943, EX....75.00
Hawkman, #1, EX....20.00
Heroes Inc Presents Cannon, #1, EX....15.00
His Name is Savage, #1, EX....8.00
Hit, #31, Spring 1944, EX....20.00
Hit Comics, #2, Aug 1940, VG....120.00
Horror Monsters, #4, M....10.00
House of Secrets, #92, EX....15.00
House of Terror, #1, 3-D, no glasses, EX....15.00
Human Torch, #38, Aug 1954, EX....35.00
If an A-Bomb Falls, 1951, M....30.00
Illustrated Gags, #16, 1940, single series, EX....25.00
Incredible Hulk, #2, July 1962, 1st series, EX....50.00
Incredible Science Fiction, #30, July-Aug 1955, EX....25.00
Iron Man & Sub-Mariner, #1, M....8.00
Jaguar, The; #1, EX....6.00
Jimmy Olsen, #10, EX....20.00
Joe Palooka, #23, EX....10.00
Journey Into Mystery, #111-120, 1964-65, EX....40.00
Journey Into Mystery, #39, EX....10.00
Journey Into Mystery, #86, Nov 1962, M....30.00
Journey Into Mystery, #97, EX....20.00
Judge Parker, #2, EX....20.00
Jumbo, #34, Dec 1941, Sheena & Lightning, VG....40.00
Jumbo, #40, June 1942, EX....35.00
Jungle, #15, Mar 1941, EX....45.00
Jungle, #78, VG....10.00
Justice League of America, #21, NM....18.00
Justice League of America, #8, EX....10.00
Katzenjammer Kids, #41, feature book, EX....20.00
Kid Eternity, #1, Spring 1946, EX....45.00
Kid Komics, #4, 1944, EX....50.00
King Conan, #1-13, 1980, M....5.00
Korak, #1, EX....10.00
Kull, #1, M....7.00
Lars of Mars, #11, July-Aug 1951, EX....30.00
Leading, #7, Summer 1943, EX....60.00
Little Orphan Annie, #1, Mar-May 1948, Gray reprint, VG....24.00
Lois Lane, #12, EX....20.00
Looney Tunes & Merrie Melodies, #16, Feb 1943, EX....20.00
Looney Tunes & Merrie Melodies, #29, EX....15.00
Mad Comic, #2, Dec-Jan 1953, EX....104.00
Mad Magazine, #29, EX....15.00
Mad Magazine, #35, 5th anniversary issue, EX....10.00
Mad Monsters, #1, magazine, EX....25.00
Mad Monsters, #2, magazine, EX....12.00
Mad Special, #9, magazine, M....8.00
Magnus, Robot Fighter, 1963-77, 34 issues, EX....75.00
March of Comics, #60, Mickey Mouse, NM....44.00
March of Comics, #74, Mickey Mouse, EX....25.00
Marvel Collector's Item Classics, #1-22, 1965-69, reprint, EX....30.00
Marvel Mystery, #22, Aug 1941, EX....75.00
Marvel Preview, #1, M....8.00
Marvel Spotlight, #1-30, 1971-76, M....25.00
Marvel Tales Annual, #1, M....10.00
Master, #75, EX....10.00
Master Comics, #4, 1940....46.00
Mickey Mouse & the Magic Mountain, 1950-51, 32 pg, 7x2½"....8.00

Mickey Mouse & the Pharoh's Curse, 1950s, 32 pg, 7x2½", EX...8.00
Mighty Mouse Album, EX...15.00
Military, #38, Apr 1945, EX...35.00
Minnie Mouse, Girl Explorer, 1950-51, 32 pg, 7x2½", EX...8.00
Mister Miracle, #1-23, 1971-78, M...20.00
Mole People, The; 1964, EX...10.00
Monster Mania, #1, EX...8.00
Monster Mania, #2, M...15.00
Monsters & Heroes, #1, magazine, blk & wht, M...15.00
Monsters Unleashed, #1, magazine, blk & wht, EX...8.00
More Fun Comics, #58, 1940, VG...180.00
More Trash From Mad, #1, magazine, EX...10.00
Mr Magoo & Gerald McBoing Boing, #561/602, EX...30.00
Mystic, #1, Oct 1944, EX...75.00
New Funnies, #99, EX...10.00
Nostalgia Comics, #1, EX...10.00
Not Brand Echh, #1-13, 1967-69, EX...25.00
Nukla, #1, EX...10.00
Our Gang, #14, Banks, Kelly Ant, VG...12.00
Panic, #1, Feb-Mar 1954, EX...30.00
Pep Comics, #9, Nov 1940, VG...40.00
Phantasmagoria, #1, magazine, blk & wht, M...5.00
Phantom, FB #39, VG...50.00
Piracy, #4, EX...15.00
Planet, #38, Sept 1945, EX...60.00
Planet, #49, July 1947, VG...35.00
Planet, #53, Mar 1948, EX...30.00
Plastic Man, #17, May 1949, Jack Cole art, EX...44.00
Plastic Man, #48, EX...15.00
Plastic Man, #58, EX...15.00
Pluto Canine Cowpoke, 1950-51, 32 pg, 7x2½"...8.00
Pluto Saves the Ship, #7, 1942, written by Carl Barks, EX...140.00
Pogo, #12, EX...20.00
Police, #47, Oct 1945, EX...25.00
Police, #98, EX...20.00
Police, #99, EX...25.00
Popeye, FC #113, VG...21.00
Popeye & Wimpy, #17, 1940, 1st Popeye Comic/regular format...55.00
Popular, #38, Apr 1939, EX...40.00
Popular, #49, Mar 1940, Gang Busters/Captain Tornado, EX...28.00
Prize, #42, June 1944, EX...14.00
Rangers, #26/27/29/30, 1945-46, EX...45.00
Rangers, #34, NM...16.00
Red Ryder, #24, Mar-Apr 1945, Captain Easy/Alley Oop, EX...23.00
Red Ryder, #43, EX...15.00
Red Wolf, #1-9, 1972-73, M...8.00
Reg'lar Fellers Heroic, #10, Jan 1942, EX...35.00
Savage Sword of Conan, #2, EX...10.00
Savage Tales, #1, Conan, magazine, blk & wht, M...30.00
Savage Tales, #2, Conan, magazine, blk & wht, EX...10.00
Savage Tales, #3, Conan, magazine, blk & wht, M...7.00
Sea Devils, #3, M...8.00
Secret Origins, #1, EX...12.00
Sensation, #31, July 1944, EX...45.00
Sensation, #44, Aug 1945, EX...20.00
SGT Fury & His Howling Commandos, #3, Sept 1963, EX...20.00
SGT Fury Annual, #1, M...5.00
Shadow, #8, Jan 1941, VG...45.00
Shadow, The; #1-12, 1973-75, M...20.00
Shadow V5, #8, Nov 1945, EX...34.00
Shanna the She-Devil, #1-5, 1972-73, M...10.00
Shield-Wizard, #1, 1940, orig, VG...108.00
Shock Illustrated, #1, EX...16.00
Shock Suspenstories, #2, Apr-May 1952, EX...70.00
Shock Suspenstories, #4, Aug-Sep 1952, VG...30.00
Shock Suspenstories, #7, Feb-Mar 1953, EX...52.00
Showcase, #18, Jan-Feb 1959, 2 Adam Strange stories, VG...38.00
Showcase, #60-80, 1966-69, EX...40.00
Silver Surfer, #1, Aug 1968, EX...50.00
Six Million Dollar Man, #2, EX...5.00
Smash, #41, Mar 1943, EX...30.00
Smash #49, Jan 1944, EX...35.00
Spacemen, #5, NM...15.00
Spirit, #1, EX...10.00
Spirit, #15, 1949, 1st series, EX...44.00
Spirit, #2, 1945, 1st series, EX...60.00
Spirit World, #1, EX...5.00
Sport, #4, Nov 1941, EX...20.00
Spy Smasher, #7, EX...25.00
Star Wars, #1, M...10.00
Startling, #12, Jan 1942, EX...25.00
Steve Canyon, #3, NM...25.00
Steve Canyon, #6, EX...20.00
Story of Silver, Cheerios cereal giveaway, 1954...12.00
Strange Adventures, #1, Aug-Sept 1950, 1st issue, Hamilton...122.00
Strange Adventures, #3, EX...45.00
Strange Adventures, #6, EX...35.00
Strange Tales, #116-120, Jan-May 1964, EX...35.00
Strange Worlds, #3, June 1951, EX...120.00
Sub-Mariner, #2-72, 1968-74, 73 issues, M...50.00
Sub-Mariner, #38, Feb 1955, EX...30.00
Super-Mystery V6, #4, EX...8.00
Superboy, #50, EX...23.00
Superman, #111, EX...15.00
Superman, #120, EX...15.00
Superman, #124, EX...12.00
Superman, #55, Nov-Dec 1948, EX...35.00
Swamp Thing, #1, M...7.00
Swamp Thing, #1-22, 1972-76, M...20.00
Tales From the Crypt, #10, M...8.00
Tales From the Crypt, #32, Oct-Nov 1952, EX...40.00
Tales of Suspense, #40, Apr 1963, EX...60.00
Tales of Terror, #1, EX...7.00
Tales of Terror Annual, #2, 1952, 2nd EC reprint, EX...372.00
Tales to Astonish, #27, Jan 1962, Ant-Man, EX...38.00
Tales to Astonish, #41-44, Mar-June 1963, EX...55.00
Tales to Astonish, #42, M...20.00
Tales to Astonish, #50-59, 1963-64, EX...30.00
Target Comics, #3, April 1940, VG...70.00
Target V3, #8, Oct 1942, EX...50.00
Terror Illustrated, #2, EX...15.00
Terry Toons, #25, EX...10.00
Thor, #151-200, 1968-72, EX...60.00
Thrilling, #32, Jan 1943, EX...20.00
Torchy, #1, Nov 1949, Bill Ward cover, VG...199.00
Uncle Sam Quarterly, #8, Autumn 1943, EX...30.00
Uncle Scroogе, #17, Mar-May 1957, EX...25.00
Uncle Scrooge, #7, EX...15.00
Uncle Scrooge & Money, M...15.00
Vacation Parade, #4, EX...15.00
Vampirella Special, 1972, magazine, blk & wht, M...12.00
Vault of Horror, #29, Feb-Mar 1953, EX...25.00
Vault of Horror, #34, Dec-Jan 1954, EX...35.00
Walt Disney's Comics & Stories, #230-335, 1967-68, EX...25.00
Wambi, #13, EX...10.00
Weird Science-Fantasy, #26, EX...30.00
Weird Tales of the Future, #1, EX...45.00
Werewolves & Vampires, #1, magazine, blk & wht, EX...15.00

Whirlwind, #3, Sept 1940, EX....40.00
Whiz, #81, EX....20.00
Whiz, #91, EX....15.00
Wildest Westerns, #4, M....8.00
Wings, #22, G....10.00
Wings, #49, EX....18.00
Wonder Wart-Hog, #2, underground, EX....8.00
Wonderworld, #11, Mar 1940, EX....60.00
World's Best, #1, 1941, EX....200.00
World's Finest, #7, 1942, Superman, Batman, VG....56.00
X-Men, #3, Jan 1964, EX....35.00
X-Men, #53, EX....10.00
X-Men, #7, VG....15.00
Young Allies, #10, Winter 1943, EX....55.00
Young Allies, #16, 1945, Schomburg cover, VG....66.00
3D Comics, #1, Mighty Mouse, VG....12.00

Compasses

Brass, eng birds/foliage/shells, 3 ft, also sundial, 3"....715.00
Brass, eng w/festoons, base eng in Russian, also sundial....1,320.00
Brass, jar form, mk IGH, Scandinavian Burrwood, 1800, 3-pc....450.00
Chinese, gilt-brass & enamel, 3 ft, case, also sundial....825.00
Chinese, rosewood and brass, table type, also sundial, 5½"....1,000.00
German, wood, Diptych, sgn Deicher, also sundial, 4⅜"....500.00
JE Hands & Sons, US Coastguard, in copper box, 8x6" sq....185.00
Sperry Gyro, nautical, floor style, by Dodge/Chrysler, 52"....500.00
Taylor Usanite, nickel hunting case, Eng Dept USA '18, WWI....35.00
W&LE Gurley, engineer's, Troy, NY, dtd 1918....100.00

Russian brass compass and sundial, engraved with festoons and leaf-tip borders; base engraved in Russian with cities and their latitudes, ca 18th century, 4¾" long, $1,200.00.

Cookbooks

Cookbooks from the 19th century, though often hard to find, are a delight to today's collectors both for their quaint formats and printing methods, as well as for their outmoded, often humorous views on nutrition. Recipes required a 'pinch' of salt, butter 'the size of an egg' or a 'walnut,' or a 'handful' of flour.

Collectors sometimes specialize in cookbooks issued as advertising premiums. Especially desirable are the figurals that were shaped like a jar, a slice of bread, or some other form pertinent to the product. Others with unique features such as illustrations by well-known artists or references to famous people or places are priced in accordance.

Cookbooks written earlier than 1874 are the most valuable, and when found command prices as high as $200; figurals usually sell in the $10 to $15 range. Values are for books in excellent condition.

Key: Cb—Cookbook

Art of Polish Cooking, by Zeranska, 1968, 366 pg, VG....5.00
Astor Cb, Jane, NY....30.00
Baker's Weekly Complete Recipes, Charles A Glabau, 304 pg....10.00
Better Homes & Gardens, 414 pg, 1953....10.00
Blue Sea Cb, by Alberson, 290 pg, VG....5.00
Book of Cookies, Bakers Helper Co, 135 pg....7.50
Cakes & Pastries, Joseph A Lambeth, 1938, 115 pg....10.00
Compendium of Cooking & Knowledge, 1890....15.00
Cook's Book-KC Baking Powder, EX color, 48 pg, 1933....15.00
Cow Brand Baking Soda, 1933....3.00
Czechoslovakian Pastries, 106 pg, 1957....4.00
Dr King's Electric Bitters Cb....18.50
Enterprise Co Cb, 1906....20.00
Everyday Cb, 1892....15.00
Fannie Farmer's Boston Cooking School Cb, scarce, 1897, G....75.00
Fannie Farmer's Cb, 1906....15.00
Farm Journal, 420 pg, 1959....10.00
Gourmets Basic French Cb, by L Diat, 1962, 654 pg, VG....15.00
Household Discoveries & Mrs Curtis' Cb, 1908, 1023 pg, VG....12.50
Malone Cb, New York, 1923....12.00
Miss Parloa's Cb, 1881....15.00
Modern Family, 938 pg, 1942....12.00
National Biscuit Co, boy in slicker, 1921....10.00
Naturopathic-Vegetarian Cb, 1907, 72 pg....24.00
New York World's Fair Cb, 1939....15.00
Pillsbury Cb, illus, 1914, 122 pg, G....25.00
Pillsbury Family Cb, dust jacket, 1960s, 576 pg....6.00
Practical Cb, by Mrs Bliss, 1000 recipes, scarce, 1887....25.00
Practical Cooking & Dinner Giving, 1881....20.00
Sun Maid Raisin Recipes, 1923....7.00
Tonawanda Review Cb, by 500 ladies, scarce, 1883, VG....25.00
Treatise on Cake Making, Standard Brands, 1935, 468 pg....12.50
Universal Cb, Jeanie L Taylor, 1888, 185 pg....10.50
Watkins Cb....5.00
White House Cb, 1900....25.00
White House Cb, 1928....50.00
1000 Ways to Please a Husband, 1917....15.00

Cookie Jars

The appeal of the cookie jar is universal; folks of all ages, both male and female, love to collect 'em! The early thirties heavy stoneware jars of a rather nondescript nature, quickly gave way to figurals of every type imaginable. Those from the mid- to late thirties were often decorated over the glaze with 'cold paint,' but by the early forties underglaze decorating resulted in cheerful, bright, permanent colors and cookie jars that still have a new look forty years later.

The jars listed here were made by companies other than those represented by other sections; see also specific manufacturers. When no condition is noted, items listed below are assumed to be in mint, though used, condition. That is, no chips, cracks or noticeable loss of paint.

Wilma Flintstone, 11¾", $65.00.

Albert Apple, Pee Dee Co....45.00
Aunt Jemima, celluloid, mk F&F Mold & Die Works....125.00
Balloon Lady, Pottery Guild of America....40.00
Bandit, Metlox, Poppytrail....30.00
Bear, Avon, limited edition....56.00
Bear, cookie in paw, eyes open, good color, Am Bisque....25.00
Bear, cookie in paw, fair color, Royalware, EX....25.00
Bear, gr hat is lid, American Bisque....32.00
Bear, Ludowici Celadon, 2-faced....35.00
Bear, Terrace....25.00
Bell, Ring for Cookies, American Bisque....35.00
Blackboard Bum, American Bisque....35.00
Blackboard Clown, American Bisque....35.00
Blackboard Girl, American Bisque....50.00
Blackboard Saddle, American Bisque....40.00
Blackboard School Boy, American Bisque....50.00
Bo-Peep, Napco, Stamped JC....25.00
Boots, American Bisque....45.00
Boy, full figure, bl, 8" fruit basket lid, Pottery Guild....35.00
Bull, American Pottery....25.00
Bunny, Grandma; American Bisque....30.00
Bunny, w/carrot, USA, EX....30.00
Bunny in Hat, American Bisque....25.00
Carousel, American Bisque....32.00
Cat, in basket....20.00
Cat, indented pnt spots, American Bisque....22.00
Chef, Angel; full figure angel, chef hat/mixing bowl, unmk....25.00
Chef, Black Mammy; National Silver....65.00
Chef, French; Cardinal China....30.00
Chick, beret-type hat, indented pnt spots, American Bisque....28.00
Churn, w/red flowers, American Bisque....15.00
Cinderella, w/gold & decals....75.00
Clown, indented pnt dots, American Bisque....26.00
Clown, lg stand-out ruffle at neck, Poppy Trail by Metlox....30.00
Clown, Sad; 'I Want Some Cookies,' Cardinal China....30.00
Clown on Stage, American Bisque, G....30.00
Cookie Flyer, Pfaltzgraff....42.00
Cookie Monster, from Sesame Street, California Originals....25.00
Count, from Sesame Street, California Originals....40.00
Cow, good color, American Bisque, G....25.00
Cup of Hot Chocolate, American Bisque....20.00
Cylinder, w/raised apple, American Bisque....15.00
Cylinder, w/raised daisy in lid, American Bisque....12.00
Disney Cookie Bus, minor wear to character decals....85.00
Dog in Basket, little color, mk 97X, G....20.00
Donald-Jose Turnabout, no pnt....40.00
Donkey & Cart, American Bisque....30.00
Dove, FAP Co....16.00
Duck, baby girl, good color, mk 101X, G....25.00
Dumbo Turnabout, Walt Disney....50.00
Dutch Boy, med color, American Bisque, G....25.00
Dutch Girl, bl skirt, mc lid, Pottery Guild of America....25.00
Elephant, American Bisque....25.00
Elephant, Laughing; Sierra Vista....45.00
Elephant, w/trunk up, wearing scarf, cold pnt....25.00
Farmer in Barrel, Twin Winton....25.00
Flasher Cheerleaders, corner cookie jar....45.00
Flour Sack, American Bisque....20.00
Fluffy, Ludowici Celadon....45.00
Fred Flintstone, American Bisque....75.00
Frog, Holiday, EX....25.00
Garage, Cardinal China....25.00
Gingerbread Christmas Candy House....20.00
Granny, American Bisque, EX....40.00
Hen, brn, chick finial, FAP Co....25.00
Hippo, full figure, dressed, mc, minor ear nick, Doranne....35.00
House, rain/shine scenes, mc decor, DeForrest of CA....25.00
House, yel, w/smiling face, Sierra Vista, lg....25.00
Howdy Doody, inside rim chips on lid....175.00
Jack-in-Box, American Bisque, EX....30.00
Ken-L-Ration Pup, advertising, celluloid, F&F....38.00
Kitten on Beehive, American Bisque, EX....25.00
Lady Pig, American Bisque, EX....25.00
Lamb, brn, Twin Winton....25.00
Lamb, poor color, American Bisque, G....15.00
Liberty Bell, American Bisque....36.00
Lion, Twin Winton....18.00
Lion, w/cowboy hat, excellent color, Belmont, EX....25.00
Majorette, red & gold trim, Regal China....65.00
Mickey & Minnie Turnabout, EX pnt....60.00
Money Sack, American Bisque....15.00
Monk, Twin Winton....25.00
Monkey, Sierra Vista....25.00
Oscar the Grouch, from Sesame Street....20.00

Toby Cookies, Regal China, $175.00.

Owl, Twin Winton....20.00
Owl, winking, w/polka dots....15.00
Pig, 'Go Ahead and Make a Pig of Yourself,' Cardinal China....30.00
Pig, Baby; Regal China....65.00
Pig, gr overalls, 'Goody Bank' across forehead, DeForrest....45.00
Pig with patch on pants, American Bisque, EX....30.00
Pine Cones Coffee Pot, American Bisque, EX....25.00
Poodle, American Bisque, marked USA....30.00
Popeye....225.00
Puppy in Blue Pot, American Bisque, EX....25.00
Quaker Oats, Regal China....40.00
Rooster, Pottery Guild of America....25.00
Rooster, Sierra Vista....25.00
Rose, Metlox, Poppytrail....25.00
R2-D2, from Star Wars movie....40.00
Safe, Cardinal....25.00
Santa, Just Take 1, pop-up, w/shakers, Holt Howard....45.00
Santa Face, winking, plastic....15.00
Schoolhouse, bell in lid, paper label, American Bisque....26.00
Snowman, good color, mk 98X, G....40.00
Snowman, RRP Co....70.00
Soldier, Cardinal #312....40.00
Spaceship, American Bisque....45.00
Squirrel, brn, w/cookie, Twin Winton....20.00
Squirrel, brn w/mc trim, eating cookie, Sierra Vista....25.00
Stagecoach, glass windows, mailbag is hdl, Sierra Vista....40.00
Stella Strawberry, Pee Dee Co....50.00
Strawberry, fair color, Sears, G....15.00
Superman, California Original....40.00
Teepee, w/Indian brave & chief, Twin Winton....45.00
Telephone, old-fashioned wall phone....40.00
Toy Soldier, in guard house, American Bisque....25.00
Train, good paint, American Bisque, EX....30.00
Train, Sierra Vista....25.00
Truck, American Bisque....30.00
Tug Boat, American Bisque, EX....50.00
Turtle, seated, w/flowers, gr....15.00
Windmill, excellent color, FAP Co....25.00
Winnie the Pooh, holds small honey pot, Disney....36.00
Winnie the Pooh, honey pot larger than Winnie, Disney....50.00
Wonder Woman, California Original....50.00
Yarn Doll, American Bisque....35.00
Yogi Bear, Hanna Barbera Productions....50.00

Coors

The firm that became known as Coors Porcelain Company in 1920, was founded in 1908 by John J. Herold, originally of the Roseville Pottery in Zanesville, Ohio. Though still in business today, they are best known for their artware vases and Rosebud dinnerware produced there before 1939.

When no condition is indicated, the items listed below are assumed to be in mint condition.

Bean pot, Rosebud, yel....15.00
Bowl, Rosebud, sm....8.50
Bowl, Rosebud, tab hdl, tan, 6½″....7.50
Casserole, Rosebud, yel, w/lid....12.00
Cookie jar, Rosebud, tab hdl....30.00
Mug, advertising, ivory, 1½″....10.00
Mug, Rosebud....15.00
Pie plate, Rosebud....17.50
Plate, bread & butter; Rosebud....6.00
Plate, dinner; Rosebud....10.00
Platter, Rosebud, maroon, 15″....12.00
Stack set, Rosebud, rose....32.50
Vase, orange, turq w/in, hdls, Coors Beer 1939, St Fair....35.00
Vase, twist rope hdls, bulbous, 8x8″....28.00
Vase, wht, gr w/in, ring hdls, ridged mock hdls, sgn....30.00
Vase, yel, 8″....15.00
Vase, yel/wht, tab hdls, sgn, 12″....35.00
Vase, 1 w/smiling monk; 1 w/sad monk, 5½″, pr....50.00

Rosebud salt and pepper shakers, 4¾″, $20.00 for the pair.

Copper

Hand-crafted copper was made in America from early in the 18th century until about 1850, with the center of its production in Pennsylvania. Examples have been found signed by such notable coppersmiths as Kidd, Buchanan, Babb, Bently, and Harbeson.

Of the many utlitarian items made, teakettles are the most desirable. Early examples from the 18th century were made with a dovetailed joint which was hammered and smoothed to a uniform thickness. Pots from the 19th century were seamed.

Coffee pots were made in many shapes and sizes, and along with mugs, kettles, warming pans, and measures are easiest to find. Stills, ranging in sizes of up to fifty-gallon, are popular with collectors today.

Authority Mary Frank Gaston has compiled a lovely book, *Antique Copper*, with many full-color photos and current market values; you will find her address in the Directory under Texas. When no condition is indicated, items listed below are assumed to be in excellent condition.

Ale warmer, hinged lid w/final, trn wood hdl, 1700s, 6″....175.00
Boiler, fits inside top of wood stove, polished/coated....75.00
Can w/spout, emb plate: Chas Schenck Mfr, 1898, 8″....35.00
Dipper, polished, flattened hdl, 20¾″....85.00
Funnel, oval, handmade, G detail, 4x5½″....35.00
Jar, dvtl, old patina, w/hdl, 7″....40.00
Lid, Irish, tin lined, 5″ steel hdl, sgn Hodges & Sons....40.00
Measure, haystack, block hdl, sgn S Hill, 9″....95.00
Measure, haystack, block-braced hdl, 2-qt....85.00
Mug, handmade & hammered, heavy, 6″....20.00
Pan, bundt; dvtl, tin w/in, brass ring hdl, 4½x10″....140.00
Pan, dvtl bottom, curved hdl, sgn, 3¼x6½″....125.00
Pitcher, mk GWR, ½-pt, pt, qt, minor dents, set of 3....75.00
Pitcher, mk 1-Gal, Liquid, 10″....60.00
Punch set, brass hdls, hooks on side of bowl, 3-gal....250.00
Sauce pan, dvtl, wrought copper hdl w/heart shape, 7¾″ W....165.00

Teakettle, American, signed Eisenhunt, replaced finial, dovetailed construction, 12″ to top of handle, $295.00.

Sauce pan, dvtl, 10″ CI hdl, 7¾″ dia....................145.00
Sauce pan, dvtl, 10″ wrought copper hdl, 5x9″..............150.00
Sauce pan, dvtl, 7½″ CI hdl, 4¼″ dia....................140.00
Skimmer, fancy pierced design..............................45.00
Skimmer, hand-forged iron hdl, PA, 1850s, 26″...............95.00
Teakettle, dvtl, brass finial, dome shape, 10½″..............180.00
Teakettle, dvtl, gooseneck, acorn finial, cast hdl, 11″.........175.00
Teakettle, dvtl, gooseneck, GT Rissler, rpl finial, 7″..........245.00
Teakettle, dvtl, gooseneck, mk Pittsburgh, 9″, VG............150.00
Teakettle, dvtl, gooseneck w/flap, G sm size, 6½″............100.00
Teakettle, dvtl, gooseneck w/hinged flap, G detail, 11″........150.00
Teakettle, dvtl, gooseneck/brass finial, Kidd, 12″.............300.00

Copper Lustre

Copper lustre is a term referring to a type of pottery made in Staffordshire after the turn of the 19th century. It is finished in a metallic rusty-brown glaze resembling true copper. Pitchers are found in abundance, ranging from simple styles with dull bands of color to those with fancy handles and bands of embossed, polychromed flowers. Bowls are common; goblets, mugs, teapots, and sugar bowls much less so. It's easy to find, but not in good condition. Pieces with hand painted decoration and those with historical transfers are the most valuable.

When no condition is indicated, values are for undamaged specimens.

Creamer, canary band w/wht reserves, brn swans w/in, 5″.......65.00
Creamer, yel w/reserves: playing badminton/inscription..........50.00
Cup, bl band w/spray of relief florals, rim beading.............40.00
Cup, bl w/copper leaf, pink inner rim.........................45.00
Goblet, canary band, reserves w/mother & child, 1825, 5″.....135.00
Jug, birds & flowers, 8″....................................180.00
Jug, bl & yel bands, 6″......................................45.00
Jug, bl band decor, 4¼″.....................................24.00
Jug, bl design, 3″...20.00
Jug, faceted enamel diamond design, bulbous, 6½″.............65.00
Jug, florals on 1½″ bl band, 6″..............................45.00
Jug, Gen Jackson, wht reserve on red, reeded neck, 5¾″......950.00
Jug, Gen Jackson commemorative, bl transfer, ca 1828, 7″...1,100.00
Jug, lady/children play badminton, mc/wht reserve, 6″..........75.00
Jug, mulberry couple, Gray's Pottery.........................45.00
Jug, raised figures, bl band, 3½″............................35.00
Jug, schoolhouse on pink, 4″.................................55.00
Jug, souvenir, Old Man/Mtn, lustre w/in & spout, 4½″..........20.00
Jug, wide bl band w/emb child & dog, mask spout, 3½″.........35.00
Jug, wide bl band w/emb child & dog, mask spout, 5½″.........65.00
Jug, yel bands w/pink lustre decor, 5″........................45.00
Jug, 2 bl bands w/lustre sprigs, 5½″.........................55.00
Mug, bl band w/lustre florals, 2½″...........................45.00
Mug, yel band & teal stripes, purple lustre w/in rim, 2¾″.......50.00
Shaving mug, bl w/diagonal copper stripes, pink inner rim......55.00
Toby jug, seated man w/pipe & mug, cobalt coat, 4½″........125.00

Coralene Glass

Coralene is a unique type of art glass easily recognized by the tiny grains of glass that form its decoration. Lacy allover patterns of seaweed, geometrics, and florals were used, as well as solid forms such as fish, plants, and single blossoms. It was made by several glasshouses, both here and abroad.

When no condition is indicated, the items listed below are assumed to be in mint condition.

Pitcher, water; bl satin w/allover coral-like beading...........600.00
Rose bowl, shaded peach, bl flowers, gold leaves, 6 wht ft.....385.00
Toothpick holder, gold to wht w/gold seaweed beading........250.00
Tumble-up, cranberry w/snowflakes..........................195.00
Vase, apricot, hdls, 8″.....................................450.00
Vase, bl to pink to rose w/yel starflower beading, 11″.........650.00
Vase, gold Dia Quilt MOP w/pink seaweed, 6¾″..............485.00
Vase, Jack-in-the-Pulpit, bl seaweed, satin, sgn Webb, 5″......195.00
Vase, lt bl MOP w/seaweed & jewel-center blossoms, 7″.......485.00
Vase, peachblow, 4″..150.00
Vase, pink MOP w/yel snowflakes, wht dot trim, 2¾″.........425.00

Pitcher, allover coralene seaweed on Mother of Pearl, 8¾″, $495.00.

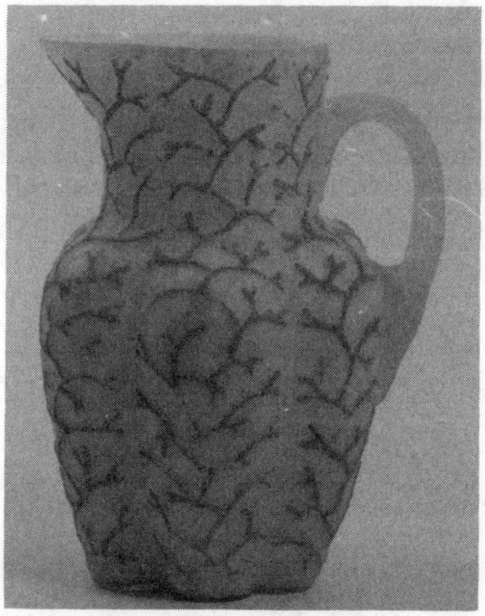

Cordey

The Cordey China Company was founded in Trenton, New Jersey, in 1942 by Boleslaw Cybis. The operation was small, with less than a dozen workers. They produced figurines, vases, lamps, and similar wares, much of which was marketed through gift shops both nationwide and abroad.

Though the earlier wares were made of plaster, Cybis soon developed his own formula for a porcelain composition which he called 'Papka.' Cordey figurines and busts were characterized by old-world charm, Rococo scrolls, delicate floral appliques, ruffles, and real lace which was dipped in liquified clay to add dimension to the work.

Although on rare occasions some items were not numbered or signed, the 'basic' figure was cast both with numbers and the Cordey signature. The molded pieces were then individually decorated, and each marked with their own impressed indentification number, as well as a mark to indicate the artist-decorator. Their numbering system began with 300 and in later years progressed into the 8000s. As can best be established, Cordey continued production until sometime in the mid-1950s. Boleslaw Cybis died in 1957, and his wife in 1958.

For further information we recommend the booklet *Cordey--Past, Present, and Future* by Mary E. Collier; you will find her address in the Directory under California. When no condition is indicated, the items listed below are assumed to be in mint condition.

Key: ff—full figure

Ash tray & cigarette holder, #6002, unusual, set..............55.00
Bottle, scent; #7074, pink roses, w/stopper, scarce, 6″.........75.00
Bottle, scent; #7074, yel roses, w/stopper, scarce, 6″...........75.00
Bowl, #7012, Marcelle lady bust in center, scarce, 13″........165.00
Box, #7060, bluebird & roses on lid, rnd, 7″................125.00
Bust, #8035, Russian peasant, male, scarce, 15″.............200.00
Candlestick, #8048, Cupid/roses/leaves, gold, 7½″, pr.........150.00
Cat, #8060, seated, calico, gr ribbon, pink rose, rare, 8″......215.00
Clock, #908, 2 lg birds/pink roses/leaves, rare, 12″...........200.00
Cookie jar/tea caddy, #627, sm roses on gray-bl, rare, 7″.......90.00
Cup & saucer, #605/#606, bl pnt pattern/applied roses.........75.00
Dbl ff, #5044 P, stump & floral, scrolled base, 11″...........150.00
Godey Lady, #5062, ff, w/brimmed hat, 14″.................150.00
Lady's shoe, #599, high-heel, roses/leaves/scrolls/gr, 14″.......225.00
Lamp, #316, Phoenix bird, wood finial/base/orig shade, 34″....185.00
Lamp, hurricane, lg bluebird/roses, porc/brass base, 16″.......150.00
Man & lady, #300/#301, ff, Colonial bl/pink, hats, 16″, pr.....150.00
Man & lady, #4075/#4076, ff, Colonial, brn base, rare, 14″....315.00
Man & lady, #5099/#5098, ff, 'Mandarin,' blk base, 26″, pr...1,250.00
Man & lady, #5099/#5098, ff, 'Mandarin'/pattern brass base...1,250.00
Man & lady, ff, on rnd self base, he w/ukulele, 10″, pr........175.00
Monsieur & Madame, #5041/#5084, ff/Colonial dress, 11″, pr...200.00
Pheasant, #343, vibrant mc, very early, scarce, 17″...........185.00
Plaque, #7000, ff lady in center, Primrose, scarce, 12″........155.00
Tray, card; #8047, cherub w/pink roses/leaves, 8″.............65.00
Tray, dresser; #7022, roses/gold scrolls/leaves, bl, 9x16″.......125.00
Vase, #7094, 2 ladies in relief, Oriental, rnd, 7″.............100.00

Lamp, large blue Phoenix bird, wooden base and original shade with blue velvet trim, early piece, 24″, $185.00.

Corkscrews

The history of the corkscrew dates back to the mid-1600s, when wine makers concluded that the best-aged wine was that stored in smaller containers, either stoneware or glass. Since plugs left unsealed were often damaged by rodents, corks were cut off flush with the bottle top, and sealed with wax or a metal cover. Removing the cork cleanly with none left to grasp became a problem. The task was found to be relatively simple using the worm on the end of a flintlock gun rod--and the corkscrew evolved.

Endless patents have been issued for mechanized models; handles range from figural ivories (lady's legs are popular) to repousse silver, carved bone, wood and porcelain. When no condition is indicated, the items listed below are assumed to be in excellent condition.

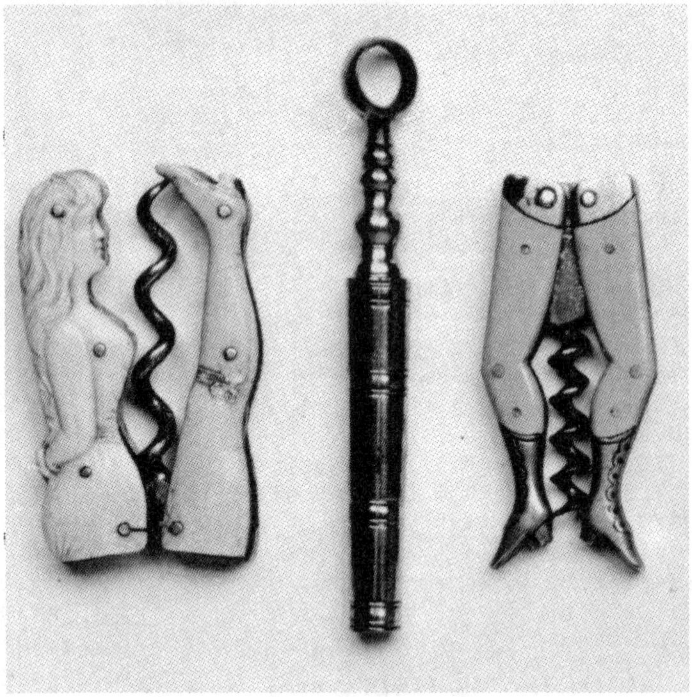

Left to right: Celluloid lady figural with helical worm, marked Ges. Gesch & Germany, mint condition, $450.00; Steel picnic corkscrew, banded sheath, baluster neck, ring handle, helical worm, 19th century, mint condition, $90.00; Lady's legs figural (all flesh colored), Archimedean screw, Gestzlich Geschutzt, mint condition, $275.00.

Archimedean screw, metal, mk Denmark, straight tusk hdl......70.00
Archimedean screw, script mk Club, wooden, dbl hdl..........30.00
Beau Brummel, sterling, mk Tiffany........................195.00
Boar's tusk, silver mt, eng, 2 screws, nickel plated cap........110.00
Boar's tusk, sterling end cap, eng 1903, 5½″.................85.00
Can-Can dancer's legs, German silver, high button shoes.......110.00
Cat, Cheshire; iron, 5″ hdl..............................110.00
Cat, jewelled, cast metal, applied floral decor, 4¼″............20.00
Champagne tap, trn ebony hdl, Archimedean screw, Holborn...110.00
Coney & Co 1904 Pat, mk King, steel/brass fr, trn wood hdl...120.00
Folding, 'harp,' heavy, nickel plating, 1890, 2½x3″............35.00
Folding, steel hdl, liner/wire breaker, German, 1895, 4¼″.......30.00
Folding bow, steel balloon, forms carriage key when folded....200.00
French pearwood, dbl turning hdl, long centre worm, 1890s.....65.00
Georgian button, steel shaft, trn bone hdl, no brush...........70.00
German silver, threaded hollow shaft, dbl hdl spigot, 1900......45.00
HD Armstrong's Pat Concertina, steel cyphered worm..........30.00
Henshall-type, baluster stem, bladed worm, rosewood hdl.......80.00

Henshall-type, incised button, helical worm/bone hdl, 1820.....120.00
Henshall-type, steel stem, w/brush, mahog trn hdl............100.00
Horn hdl, silver mt, dbl action, wax pick, American...........100.00
Jackson-type, brass farrow/steel-bladed worm/butterfly hdl......140.00
James Heeley, pat A1 dbl lever, nickel plated/helical worm......80.00
Key shape, plain sheath, hdl w/scroll design, beaded chain.....100.00
Knife, folding; horn hdl, imp Suze Apertif, Pradel, 3½"........17.50
L'Excelsior, Archimedean screw, baluster ebony hdl/open fr....110.00
Lady figural, German, folding, helical worm, wht celluloid......350.00
Lady's legs, brn/wht stockings, German...................235.00
Lady's legs, flesh-colored legs, German...................250.00
Lemp Brewing Co, St Louis...............................12.00
London Rack, wood hdl, orig brush, 1870..................135.00
Lund's, pat London Rack & Pinion, baluster wood hdl/brush...110.00
Male & female, erotic, brass, steel helical worm..............150.00
Mumford, cylinder sheath, wood barrel hdl, 2 prongs, rare.....280.00
Nude, celluloid, bent at waist............................600.00
Nuts & Wine, stand-up brass, ½ figure of Shakespeare, 7"......85.00
Old Snifter, Congressman Volstead, opener/screw combo.......200.00
Old Snifter, wht metal, removable hat.......................45.00
Peter Schoenhofen Brewing Co, Edelweiss...................10.00
Redfern's pat, wood/brass/steel, Georgian shaft, trn hdl.........80.00
Rodger's, wood/brass/steel, Georgian-style shaft, trn hdl.........70.00
Sea snail shell hdl, silver & jeweled coral cap, 1897, 5½"......110.00
Staghorn hdl, butt end flared, 2" shaft cover.................85.00
Steel, bell moves on wire stem, trn wood hdl, American.......340.00
Surprise, orig copper finish, English, 1884..................45.00
Thomason-type, brass, sgn Dowler Pat, trn wood hdl...........90.00
Waiter, Syroco, 8".......................................25.00
Walker pat 1893, advertising Equinox champagne, barrel hdl....80.00
Whale's tooth hdl, rnd steel shaft, 1880, 3"..................45.00

Cosmos

Cosmos, sometimes called Stemless Daisy, is a patterned glass tableware produced from 1894 through 1915 by Consolidated Lamp and Glass Company. Relief molded flowers on a fine cross-cut background were painted in soft colors of pink, blue, and yellow. Though nearly all were made of milk glass, a few items may be found in clear glass, with the designs painted on. In addition to the tableware, lamps were also made. When no condition is indicated, the items listed below are assumed to be in mint condition.

Pitcher, 9", with six 3¾" tumblers, $475.00.

Bottle, scent...140.00
Butter dish...190.00
Condiment set...250.00
Creamer, w/pink band..................................165.00
Cruet...220.00
Lamp, banquet, kerosene, 24"............................475.00
Lamp, oil; Cosmos variant, mid-size, 8" shade...............275.00
Lamp, pink band, 10"...................................410.00
Pickle castor, trimmed bail, ftd SP fr......................315.00
Pickle castor set, dbl, pink band, rare......................500.00
Pitcher, water...175.00
Shakers, tall, pr..95.00
Spooner, w/pink band...................................165.00
Sugar bowl, w/lid......................................200.00
Sugar shaker, bulbous bottom............................165.00
Syrup...165.00
Table set..275.00
Tumbler..50.00

Coverlets

The Jacquard loom, made in the early 1800s in France, made possible the production of intricately woven coverlets in various designs. They were made of wool, both dyed and natural, from patterns punched into paper cards that indicated the colors of woof and warp necessary to develop the motif.

Soon after 1820, the Jacquard loom was brought to this country, and by 1840 was standard equipment for every professional weaver. Pictorial designs once reserved for the wealthy became available at modest prices. The old geometrics were replaced by florals, eagles, and elaborate medallion patterns. The new process enabled the weaver to sign and date his work, though not all names refer to the artist. It was also a common practice to weave the new owner's name into the corner of the coverlet.

In America the earliest pattern-woven coverlets were made around 1820 at the Colonel Rutger's Works of Brunswick, New Jersey. Often used to cover the dead for burial, they became known as 'corpse coverlets.' Usually buried with the departed, true examples of this type of coverlet are rarely found today.

When no condition is indicated, the items listed below are assumed to be in excellent condition.

Jacquard

Bird & pine tree border, 3-color, 1840, 2-pc dbl, 75x82"......510.00
Bird border, bold pattern, 3-color, 2-pc dbl, EX..............495.00
Bird border, medallions, bl/wht, sgn/1846, 2-pc single.........425.00
Bird medallions, red/wht/olive-gold, 1-pc dbl, 78x91", VG......325.00
Birds feeding young, Christian & heathen border, bl-wht.......550.00
Birds/flowers in pots/side-wheel ship bands, 1845...........1,550.00
Eagles in spandrels, 4-color, 1-pc single, EX................350.00
Eagles w/baskets/stars/cannons/trees, 2-pc dbl, 78x81", EX.....325.00
Floral, big/bold on stripes, 4-color, 1858, 1-pc, 79x92"........425.00
Floral, 3-color, minor fringe wear, 80x88"..................375.00
Floral, 3-color, 1855, 2-pc dbl, 76x83", EX.................450.00
Floral, 3-color, 1865, 1-pc dbl, minor stains................400.00
Floral medallions, eagle border, tan/natural/wht, 1837, VG.....500.00
Floral medallions, vintage border, sgn/1868, 2-pc, NM.........400.00
Floral medallions, 4-color, 1-pc dbl, 1858, EX...............650.00
Foliage scrolls/buildings, bl/wht, 2-pc dbl, EX................310.00
Fruit medallions, floral border, bl/wht, 1-pc dbl, EX..........275.00
Geometric florals, 3-color, 2-pc dbl, minor stains, 82"..........310.00
House border, rnd medallions, 4-color, sgn, 2-pc, EX.........775.00
Medallion center, floral border, bl/wht, 1-pc dbl, 83", EX......300.00

Left, One-piece single-weave jacquard, central medallion with eagles in spandrels, in red, blue, lavender and white, 82″ x 86″, $700.00; Right, Two-piece double-weave jacquard, in blue, red and white, minor edge wear, 72″ x 82″, $495.00.

Medallion center, 4-color, Oswald, 1850, 1-pc single, EX......565.00
Medallion/vines, 'Latest by Stager,' 4-color, VG..............250.00
Roses, bl/wht, 1-pc dbl, minor stains........................175.00
Snowflake, bl/wht, 2-pc, minor stains/wear, 76x96″...........200.00
Snowflake, pine tree border, 3-color, 2-pc dbl, 76x86″, NM....310.00
Star medallion/building bands, 3-color, 2-pc, VG.............200.00
Starflowers/bird bands, 3-color, 1849, 2-pc, VG..............350.00
Stars/flowers, bird borders, bl/wht, Myers, 1842, 2-pc, VG......250.00
4 rose medallions, bl/wht, sgn/1852, 2-pc, 78x86″, EX........350.00
4 rose medallions/bird borders, 3-color, Myers/1842, VG.......500.00

Overshot

Compass stars w/in sqs w/checkered corners, 4-color, 2-pc.....235.00
Interlocking circles, bl/wht, 2-pc, minor wear, 67x92″.........150.00
Intricate optical pattern in indigo/onionskin brn/natural........275.00
Olive gr, tan & natural, woven border w/fringe, 3-pc, 100″.....325.00
Optical sqs & bars, 4-color, label: Plymouth Carding Mill......325.00
Red/natural, 2-pc, wear/worn fringe, 70x84″.................175.00
Squares, bars & circles, gr/wht, 2-pc, 60x78″................200.00
X'd circles & bars, gr/tan/natural, 1-pc, faded, 96x98″.........175.00

Cowan

Guy Cowan opened a small pottery near Cleveland, Ohio, in about 1912, where he made tile and artware on a small scale from the natural red clay available there. He developed distinctive glazes--necessary, he felt, to cover the dark red body. After the war and a temporary halt in production, Cowan moved his pottery to Rocky River, where he made a commercial line of artware utilizing a highly fired white porcelain. Although he acquiesced to the necessity of mass production, every effort was made to insure a product of highest quality. Fine artists, among them Waylande Gregory, Thelma Frazier Winter, and Viktor Schreckengost, molded figurines which were often produced in limited editions, some of which sell today for upwards of $1,000. Most of the ware was marked 'Cowan' or 'Lakewood,' not to be confused with the name of the 1927 mass-produced line called 'Lakeware.' Falling under the crunch of the Great Depression, the pottery closed in 1931.

When no condition is indicated, the items listed below are assumed to be in mint condition.

Ash tray, duck figural, gr.................................25.00
Ash tray, emb deer, brn mottle, oval, 5½″...................65.00
Bookends, elephant figurals, Push/Pull, blk, pr...............395.00
Bowl, bl lustre, low, 8″...................................22.00
Bowl, marigold lustre, 10″.................................50.00
Bowl, paneled, floral decor ends, bl lustre, 11½″ L............75.00
Bowl, seahorse ends, bl/gr ext, gr int, Arabian Night, 16½″....110.00
Candle holder, Byzantine angel figural, guava yel, 9″.........120.00
Candle holder, oval/bulbous, ivory, 3½″, pr...................39.00
Candle holder, rectangular, ivory, base 5½x3″, pr.............20.00
Candle holder, rectangular, matt bl, base 5½x3″, pr...........17.00
Candle holder, rnd, bl lustre, 3″, pr........................59.00
Candle holder, triangle base w/scroll hdls, ivory, pr............32.00
Candle holder, 3-light, curved/vine decor, ivory, 8½x5″, pr......55.00
Candy dish, ftd, gr ext, ivory int, 4″........................45.00
Cigarette holder, seahorse base, gr..........................22.00
Compote, candy; gr ext, ivory int............................30.00
Console set: bowl/pr 3-light candlesticks/nude, ivory...........275.00
Console set: Pterodactyl bowl/pr sticks, Arabian Night.........435.00
Console set: tray/bowl/grid/pr 3-light candlesticks, tan.........125.00
Creamer & sugar bowl, bl lustre, pr..........................95.00
Decanter, King & Queen, Chinese red, pr.................1,000.00
Flower frog, standing nude #698, ivory......................120.00
Flower holder, flamingo, wht matt w/brn speckles, 12½″.......250.00
Jar, strawberry; gr, 12″...................................150.00
Jazz Bowl, gr, 14″, M...................................3,000.00
Lamp, rooster figure, Schreckengost, gr mottle, metal base.....225.00
Tea tile, emb fish decor, ivory.............................150.00
Vase, #583, gray/bl airspray lustre, R in circle, 13″............75.00
Vase, bud; seahorse base, pink (Apple Blossom), 7½″...........50.00
Vase, bulbous, larkspur bl lustre, 9″.........................85.00
Vase, cylindrical, marigold lustre, 10″........................75.00
Vase, emb squirrel, stork & pheasant, bl/wht, 9″.............425.00
Vase, fan shape w/seahorse base, gr, 6″......................35.00
Vase, horizontal ribbing, foliage, narrow top, gr, 12″.........195.00
Vase, horizontal ribbing, plum, 5″...........................75.00
Vase, Logan Award, matt tan, w/hdls, 8″......................40.00
Vase, Oriental red, basic form, 9″..........................150.00
Vase, simple shape, lav lustre, 5″...........................50.00
Vase, slim body, pink lustre, 6″............................32.00
Vase, turned-in top, base design, ftd, gunmetal, 6″...........250.00
Wall pocket, paneled, bl lustre, 10″.........................95.00

Vase, crane, rabbit, squirrel and pheasant in relief, light to medium blue, 9″, $425.00.

Cracker Jacks

Kids have been buying Cracker Jacks since it was first introduced at the Columbian Exposition in 1893. By 1912, it was packaged with a free toy inside. Before the first kernel was crunched, eager fingers had revived the surprise from the depth of the box--actually no easy task, considering the care required to to keep the contents so swiftly displaced from spilling over the side! Though a little older, perhaps, many of those same kids still are looking--just as eagerly--for the Cracker Jack prizes. Point of sale, company collectibles, and the prizes as well, have over the years reflected America's changing culture. Grocer sales and incentives from around the turn of the century--paper dolls, postcards and song books--were often marked Rueckheim Brothers (the inventors of Cracker Jacks) or Reliable Confections. The first loose-packed prizes were toys made of wood, clay, tin, metal, and lithographed paper. Plastic toys were introduced in 1948. Paper wrapped for saftey purposes in 1933, subjects echoed the 'hype' of the day--yoyos, tops, whistles, and sports cards in the simple, peaceful days of our country, propaganda and war toys in the forties, games in the fifties, and space toys in the sixties. Few of the estimated 15 billion prizes were marked.

Advertising items from Angelus Marshmallow and Checker Confections (cousins of the Cracker Jack family) are also collectible. When no condition is indicated, the items listed below are assumed to be in excellent condition.

Cast Metal

Air corps wings, silver or blk, CJ, 3″........................35.00
Dollhouse items: lantern, mug, candlestick, etc, no mk, ea.......4.00
Horse & wagon, Angelus & CJ, 3-D, silver or gold, 2½″........95.00
Inked flats w/base: animals/people, not game pc, no mk, ea......7.00
Miniature animals, shoes, tools, pipe, etc, no mk, 1″, ea.........2.50

Point of sale piece showing older toys.

Presidential coins, 31 pieces to set, aluminum, CJ, ea...........4.00
Stud button, crossed bats & ball, mk: Pitcher, etc; ea..........59.00
Thimble, Angelus & CJ, aluminum w/red pnt fill..............89.00
Tootsie Toy series, boats, cars, animals, CJ, 1-3″, ea............8.25

Paper

Ad, comic book...10.00
Ad, Saturday Evening Post, 1918-1920, ea...................22.00
Baseball cards, 1906 & 1907 series CJ, ea....................19.00
Baseball score counter, CJ.................................63.00
Bear postcards, 1907, series of 16, CJ, ea...................14.00
Book, 'Animals to Color' or 'Birds to Color,' ea...............31.00
Book, drawing; w/tracing paper, to color, early................40.00
Book, Jackie's Friends, mini, early, CJ, ea...................38.00
Book, Riddles, Jack & Dog Bingo on cover, RWB.............28.00
Book, Riddles, Jester on cover, RYBK.......................30.00
Book, Stories of Presidents, series of 6, mini, CJ, ea...........38.00
Book, Uncle Sam's Famous National Songs, CJ...............35.00
Halloween mask, CJ, 10″ or 12″, ea.........................11.00
Hat, overseas paper-type vendor cap, RWB, CJ...............45.00
Movies, pull tab for 2nd picture, CJ, early, about 3″...........48.00
Puzzles, envelope w/metal puzzle, CJ, series of 15, ea..........16.00
Riddle cards, CJ, series of 20, ea.............................7.00
Spinner w/string, round or rectangular, CJ, 1½″, ea............22.00
Stationery, letterheads & envelopes, 1900-1920, CJ............22.00
Toy, jumping frog, early, CJ...............................39.00

Plastic

Baseball players & spacemen, 3-D, CJ, ea.....................4.50
Fobs, alphabet letter, CJ, ea.................................3.00
Nosco, rocking base, animals & people, CJ, ea.................3.50
Nosco, stand-up semi-flat animals & people, CJ, ea.............1.50
Railroad train engine & cars, 3-D, CJ, about 2″, ea.............6.00

Tin

Bank, book shape, Vol 1, red/gr/blk, CJ, 2″ H.................47.00
Bookmarks, bulldog, etc, CJ, ea...............................9.25
CJ band, gold or silver, Hummer, CJ, 1¾″ dia................34.00
CJ shows, circus animals in cage, RBY, 1¾″, ea..............55.00
Clicker, Noisy Cracker Jack, tear shape, CJ, 2″...............17.50
Comic characters, oval stand-ups, CJ, 2″, ea..................47.50
Die cut, boy & dog, complete w/bend-over tabs, CJ............48.00
Die cut, boy & dog, RBW, 2″, tab broken off.................25.00
Doll's dish, silver or gold, CJ, 1¾″.........................25.00
Doll's plate, silver, CJ, 2″.................................25.00
Harmonica, early premium, mk CJ..........................150.00
Horse & wagon, litho & die-cut.............................31.00
Lunch box & thermos, recent, full size......................25.00
Model T Ford, NY 1916 #999, blk & wht, CJ, 2″............100.00
Pocket watch, silver or gold, CJ, 1½″.......................28.00
Sulky, 2 wheels, CJ, 5″ w/stick............................10.00
Top, Fortune Teller, CJ....................................45.00
Top, mk 'Two Toppers,' CJ, ea..............................48.00
Top, of various common types, ea...........................22.00
Train engine & tender, '#512,' RBW, CJ, 2″, ea..............39.00
Tray, pictures package, mini, 2 different sizes, CJ, ea..........49.00
Truck, Angelus, ad on 1 side, CJ on other, 1½″..............31.00
Whistle, 'close end w/fingers,' ID etched, CJ..................37.50
Whistle, 'close end w/fingers,' ID in relief, CJ................22.00
Whistle, enameled twin tune, CJ, 2½″.......................35.00
Whistle, lifesaver shape, CJ, 1¼″ dia.......................42.00

Crackle Glass

Crackle glass (or craquelle) was made during the 1800s in America as well as abroad. The name is derived from the crackled texture of the ware, achieved either by plunging the hot glass into cold water, or by rolling it in small particles of broken glass which fuse to the surface upon reheating. When no condition is indicated, the items listed below are assumed to be in mint condition.

Basket, clear w/vaseline, applied hdl, scalloped, 8x7½" 85.00
Biscuit jar, enameled, ornate plated lid w/fancy finial 150.00
Pitcher, vaseline, w/lid & 2 tumblers 95.00
Pitcher, water; crystal, bulbous, w/lid 50.00
Rose bowl, lt purple, sgn Degue 125.00
Tumbler, cranberry 85.00
Vase, amber, blown, dimpled, 5½" 17.50

Cranberry

Cranberry glass is named for its resemblance to the color of cranberry juice. It was made by many companies, both here and abroad, becoming popular in America soon after the Civil War. It was made in both free-blown ware as well as mold-blown. Today, cranberry glass is being reproduced, and it is sometimes difficult to distinguish the old from the new. Ask a reputable dealer if you are unsure. When no condition is indicated, the items listed below are assumed to be in mint condition.

Bell, Inverted Thumbprint 135.00
Bottle, scent; crackle glass, applied clear decor, 9¾", pr 450.00
Bottle, scent; frosted bottom, orig ball stopper, 5¾x3⅛" 145.00
Bottle, scent; silver panels w/gold scrolls/flowers, 5¼" 110.00
Bowl, enameled flowers, clear rigaree around top, 7½" 125.00
Bowl, 6 berries/3 fan devices/clear scroll ft, 5½x6" 265.00
Creamer & sugar bowl, gold flowers/bl leaves, clear ped ft 135.00
Cruet, cut bevelled neck, star base, bubble stopper, 10x5" 195.00
Decanter, cut to clear, buzz stars/allover cutting 175.00
Finger bowl, paneled, sq top 98.00
Liqueur, floral decor, clear stem & ft, 4¾x1½" 40.00
Liqueur, gold panels w/bl/wht/yel floral, gold leaves, 2¼" 48.00
Mayonnaise jar w/lid, wht enamel flowers w/gold trim 125.00
Pitcher, Baby Inverted Thumbprint, sq top, bulbous, 6x3½" 100.00
Pitcher, melon rib w/diamond effect, clear hdl, 5x5" 85.00
Pitcher, panel optic, clear hdl, 12¾x6" 290.00
Sugar shaker, Drape pattern, hallmk on top, 6½" 78.00
Tumbler, opal 10-Row Hobnail, 3¾" 100.00
Vase, bl/wht flowers at shoulder/base, gold scrolls, 11" 145.00
Vase, branch/cherries in gold, 4 scroll ft, 2 hdls, 7½" 200.00
Vase, buds of wht dots, gold leaves, clear ped ft, 5" 55.00
Vase, crystal leaves/rigaree/ped ft, 9⅜x4¼" 165.00
Vase, florals in wht/gold/pink, ped ft, 12¼x4" 195.00
Vase, gold panel w/mc floral, ruffle fan top/clear ft, 11" 200.00
Vase, gold sanded floral/bands/leaves, ftd, 8¾x4", pr 350.00
Vase, gold sanded w/wht bl floral, bottle form, 10x3¾" 150.00
Vase, Inverted Thumbprint, trefoil fluted top, 7½" 125.00
Vase, lilies-o/t-valley in wht, gold leaves, 7½x3" 70.00
Vase, wht forget-me-nots, ruffled top, 2x2¼" 95.00

Creamware

Creamware was a type of earthenware developed by Wedgwood in the 1760s, and produced by many other Staffordshire potteries, including Leeds. Since it could be potted cheaply, and was light in weight, it became popular abroad as well as in England, due to the lower freight charges involved in exporting the ware. It was revived at Leeds in the late 19th century, and the type most often reproduced was heavily reticulated or molded in high relief. These later wares are easily distinguished from the originals since they are thicker and tend to craze heavily.

When no condition is indicated, the items listed below are assumed to be in mint condition.

Bowl, quatrefoil, emb base, reticulated lid, Leeds, 4¾" 165.00
Caddy, reticulated, center rope loop hdl, 2 sections, 8" 85.00
Cake plate, reticulated, Leeds, 4⅜x9" 80.00
Dish, flower border, serrated rim, Leeds, 6¼" 40.00
Dish, reticulated rim, 5x5¾" 45.00
Jardiniere, duck form w/gr & brn accents, 6¾" L 275.00
Plate, reticulated rim, 9⅞" 60.00
Sweatmeat, reticulated, sm cup on stem, Wedgwood, 7x6½" 180.00
Tray, reticulated rim, emb decor, 8x9¾", EX 35.00
Tureen, applied decor, rope twist hdls, 7½x10" 165.00
Tureen, applied decor, rope twist hdls, 9½x13" 300.00
Tureen, reticulated dome lid, ped ft, 7x8¾" 165.00

Crown Devon and Devon

Crown Devon and Devon were trade names of S. Fielding and Company, Ltd., an English firm founded about 1879. They produced majolica, earthenware, and pottery mugs, vases, and kitchenware. In the 1930s they manufactured an exceptional line of Art Deco vases that have recently been much in demand. When no conditon is indicated, the items listed below are assumed to be in mint condition.

Cheese dish, pink/bl flowers, Spring pattern, 4⅜x5½x7" 70.00
Cheese dish, Windsor, tan w/mc florals, gold trim, 5x7x8" 80.00
Creamer, cobalt w/orange & wht trim, sgn, 1⅛x1x1½" 120.00
Cup, head of bearded man w/crown, mc, mk, 3⅞", EX 80.00
Figurine, bulldog wears Union Jack flag, 6x4" 65.00
Humidor, 2 ships, gr irid, raised enamel work, sgn D Cole 110.00
Jug, John Peel, musical, fox hdl, stopper, 8¼x6½" 250.00

Vase, fantasy flowers and butterflies, gold traced, Art Deco, with handle, 13", $400.00.

Crown Milano

Crown Milano was introduced in 1884 by the Mt. Washington Glass Company. When the company merged with Pairpoint in 1894, it continued to be one of their best sellers. It is an opaque, highly decorated ware, with gold or colored enamels in intricate designs on pale backgrounds, nearly always in a satin finish. Many pieces are marked 'CM' with a crown. Values are given for items in mint condition.

Vase, raised gold enamel roses and leaves, 7″, $1,350.00.

Bowl, autumn leaves, swirl molded, Mt WA, 4x2½″...........385.00
Cracker jar, floral/jewels/beading on mottled burmese, 8″.....1,500.00
Cracker jar, nasturtiums, ribbed, sgn SP lid/bail, 8x7″.........545.00
Creamer & sugar, florals & gold scrolls, #539, pr..........2,850.00
Cup & saucer, handleless; burmese color w/gold decor, #d....1,200.00
Decanter, roses/gold scrolls, glossy, Albertine, 10x6″........1,250.00
Ewer, chrysanthemums/swirls, gold decor, rope hdl, 10″.....2,700.00
Ewer, lady/sheep; bk: roses/birds, lilac/gold decor, 10″.......2,750.00
Ewer, profuse 8-color geometrics, no mk, 13″..............1,750.00
Pickle castor, pansy, SP lid/holder sgn Mt WA, tongs, 10″.....985.00
Pitcher, spider web design, florals, burmese shading, 9″......2,750.00
Rose bowl, burmese-colored ground, pansies decor, #d, M.....375.00
Salt cellar, emb/pnt floral, glossy, gilt, 1½x3¼″..............285.00
Tray, thistles/foliage, glossy, rolled/serrated, 9″...............845.00
Urn, blossoms/foliage, gold relief, crown lid, 16½x8x5½″.....2,950.00
Vase, ducks, 4 on gold wheat, glossy, Guba, Albertine, 17″...3,750.00
Vase, ducks, 8 in all, 2 hdls, Frank Guba, 10x5½″..........4,500.00
Vase, floral, 3 lg/10 sm, cone form, sgn, 8¾″...............875.00
Vase, floral & jewels in gold, stick neck, sgn, 12½″...........850.00
Vase, geometrics decor, sq w/rnd corners, no mk, 8″.........745.00
Vase, oak leaves/acorns allover, gold/mc, 2 hdl, label, 8″......985.00
Vase, snow geese, gold decor on lt pink ground, Guba, 12″..1,600.00

Cruets

Cruets, containers made to hold oil or vinegar, are usually bulbous with tall narrow throats and a stopper. During the 19th century and for several years after, they were produced in abundance, in virtually every type of glassware available. Those listed below are assumed to be with stopper and mint unless noted otherwise.

Acanthus & Scroll, bl opal..................................135.00
Alaska, vaseline opal w/decor.............................200.00
Amber, bl applied hdl & bubble stopper, 4 dimples, 8″.........85.00
Amber, bl fans, lacy wht pnt dots, bulbous rnd mouth, 7″.....120.00
Amber flashed, w/enameling, blown.........................175.00
Amberina, Baby Thumbprint, reed hdl.......................125.00
Beaded Grape (California), emerald gr.........................75.00
Beaded Swirl & Lens, 1890s...............................25.00
Bl, amber hdl & bubble stopper, wht floral, squared, 7¾″......110.00
Broken Column, orig stopper................................55.00
Bull's Eye & Button, gold buttons............................55.00
Burmese, ribbed, yel hdl, Mt WA, 7x3¾″....................800.00
Buzz Saw, gr, NM...325.00
Cane Horseshoes...35.00
Cone, cased glossy yel, Consolidated Glass..................175.00
Cosmos 220.00
Cranberry, opal swirl..165.00
Croesus, emerald gr...200.00
Daisy & Button w/Crossbars, vaseline, lg....................135.00
Daisy & Button X-Bar w/Thumbprint, vaseline, lg.............110.00
Daisy & Fern, bl, clear stopper..............................125.00
Daisy & Fern, clear opal, Northwood..........................65.00
Dewey, amber, Greentown...................................175.00
Double Circle, gr..135.00
Flora, gr, clear stopper.......................................25.00
Forget-Me-Not, gr, Challinor.................................275.00
Frosted Circle..65.00
Fry, opal wht w/cobalt stopper & hdl, unsgn..................285.00
Green, enameled floral.......................................100.00
Green, peach hdl & stopper, wide flat base..................325.00
Guttate, glossy pink, flat, inverted goblet body...............265.00
Herringbone, clear opal, orig stopper........................125.00
Herringbone, emerald gr.....................................125.00
Hidalgo, clear & frosted.......................................65.00
Hobb's Hobnail, vaseline opal................................225.00
Hobnail, bl opal...80.00
Hobnail, clear opal, Hobb's-Brockunier........................75.00
Inverted Thumbprint, amber, enameled floral, lg.............195.00
Inverted Thumbprint, amber, sm...............................95.00
Inverted Thumbprint, bl, amber hdl..........................145.00
Jackson, vaseline...195.00
Lily-of-the-Valley 110.00
Lime green w/wht lacy decor, gold trim, clear stopper, 10″.....110.00
Log & Star, amber, orig stopper...............................70.00
Mary Gregory, amber..265.00

Shoshone, emerald green, 7½″, $75.00.

Melon ribbed, applied hdl, amber/bl, w/bl stopper. 90.00
National Eureka, ruby stained. 180.00
New Jersey, orig stopper. 49.00
Pineapple & Fan, gr w/EX gold. 225.00
Pointed Hobnail, blown, applied hdl. 18.00
Ribbed Thumbprint, bl, enameled floral. 175.00
Ruby, clear cut stopper & applied hdl, tri-lobe top, 5½″. 50.00
Scroll w/Acanthus, bl opal. 135.00
Shoshone, emerald gr. 75.00
Spatter, maroon/wht, clear ft/hdl/stopper, 10″. 65.00
Sprig, cranberry. 155.00
Stars & Bars, bl. 135.00
Thousand Eye, 3-Knob, vaseline. 325.00
Threaded, lime gr to clear, clear ball stopper, 9x3½″. 85.00
Wimpole, ruby & clear, orig stopper, lg. 135.00
Zipper, orig top. 38.00

Cup Plates

Before the middle 1850s, it was socially acceptable to pour hot tea into a deep saucer to cool. The tea was sipped from the saucer rather than the cup, which frequently was handleless and too hot to hold--the cup plate served as a coaster for the cup. It is generally agreed that the first examples of pressed glass cup plates were made about 1826 at the Boston and Sandwich Glass Co. in Sandwich, Cape Cod, Massachusetts. Other glassworks in three major areas--New England, Philadelphia, and the Midwest (especially Pittsburgh)--quickly followed suit.

Antique glass cup plates range in size from 2⅝″ up to 4¼″ in diameter. The earliest plates had simple designs inspired by cut glass patterns, but by 1829 they had become more complex. The span from then until about 1845 is known as the 'Lacy Period,' when cup plate designs and pressing techniques were at their peak. To cover pressing imperfections, the backgrounds of the plates were often covered with fine stippling which endowed them with a glittering brilliance called 'Laciness.' They were made in a multitude of designs--some purely decorative, others commemorative. Subjects include the American eagle, hearts, sunbursts, log cabins, ships, George Washington, the political candidates Clay and Harrison, plows, beehives, etc. Of all the patterns the round George Washington plate is the most rare and valuable--only four are known to exist today.

Authenticity is most important. Collectors must be aware that contemporary plates which have no antique counterparts and fakes modeled after antique patterns have had wide distribution. Condition is also important, though it is the exceptional plate that does not have some rim roughness. More important considerations are scarcity of design and color.

The book *American Glass* by George and Helen McKearin has a section on glass cup plates. A more definitive book is *American Glass Cup Plates*, by Ruth Webb Lee and James H. Rose. Numbers in the listings that follow (computer sorted) refer to the latter. When no condition is indicated, the listings below are assumed to have only minor rim roughness as is normal. See also Staffordshire; Pairpoint

LR-11. . . . . 38.00
LR-124A, VG. 37.00
LR-129, slightly cloudy, EX. 42.00
LR-136A, minor rim flake. 25.00
LR-148, minor flakes, VG. 30.00
LR-149. . . . . 35.00
LR-151, sm chip, minor flakes, VG. 32.00
LR-155. . . . . 35.00
LR-159B. 35.00
LR-160B, rough table rest, VG. 30.00
LR-162A. 35.00
LR-162B, slightly cloudy, VG. 31.00
LR-164B, sm rim nick, VG. 35.00
LR-169A. 30.00
LR-171, amethyst, 1 of 6 existant. 575.00
LR-172A, sm edge nick, slightly cloudy, VG. 31.00
LR-172B, sm edge nick, sm pot stone, VG. 29.00
LR-174, EX. 45.00
LR-176A, sm nick, unbroken bubble, VG. 30.00
LR-177, EX. 40.00
LR-178B. 30.00
LR-180A. 30.00
LR-191B. 25.00
LR-193, lt gr, EX. 150.00

Left, LR-193, light green, one slight nick, $150.00; Right, LR-323, four tiny nicks, $90.00.

LR-198, rim chips, 3⅛″. 30.00
LR-199. . . . . 40.00
LR-200A. 50.00
LR-216, bl, extremely rare, NM. 615.00
LR-216, scallop tipped, minor flakes, VG. 67.00
LR-217A, edge spall, minor flakes, VG. 67.00
LR-22, 3⅜″. 25.00
LR-224, extremely rare, VG. 170.00
LR-226. . . . . 30.00
LR-226A. 40.00
LR-226C. 40.00
LR-229B, scarce, M. 40.00
LR-232. . . . . 55.00
LR-233A. 40.00
LR-235, VG. 35.00
LR-236. . . . . 38.00
LR-242A. 40.00
LR-243. . . . . 36.00
LR-245. . . . . 40.00
LR-246, 3 scallops tipped, VG. 34.00
LR-249, 3 scallops tipped, 1 nicked, VG. 34.00
LR-25, 3½″, EX. 30.00
LR-255A. 40.00
LR-257. . . . . 35.00
LR-257, 2 scallops tipped, VG. 26.00
LR-258. . . . . 30.00
LR-263, cobalt, rim chips, 3¼″. 75.00
LR-265, EX. 65.00
LR-269. . . . . 35.00
LR-269B. 40.00
LR-271A, sm nick on table rest, VG. 32.00
LR-273, rim chips, 3½″. 23.00
LR-276. . . . . 35.00
LR-278. . . . . 40.00
LR-28. . . . . 40.00
LR-285, hairpin, opal, NM. 60.00

LR-29, 3⅝″........25.00
LR-291........35.00
LR-292........40.00
LR-310, rare........85.00
LR-311........30.00
LR-311, opal, NM........50.00
LR-313........20.00
LR-315, EA & SR Filley, St Louis, rare, rim chips, 3½″........40.00
LR-323, red-amber........90.00
LR-324........20.00
LR-331, butterfly, rim chips, 3¼″........15.00
LR-333........16.00
LR-335, scarce........65.00
LR-339........16.00
LR-342........20.00
LR-343B........40.00
LR-345........12.00
LR-36, slightly underfilled, o/w M........50.00
LR-364........18.00
LR-365........20.00
LR-388........15.00
LR-389........15.00
LR-39........30.00
LR-390A........14.00
LR-391........14.00
LR-392........12.00
LR-393........12.00
LR-396........12.00
LR-402, sm scallop spall, minor flakes, VG........14.00
LR-412........20.00
LR-415........20.00
LR-426, scarce, EX........40.00
LR-436A, scarce, VG........40.00
LR-439B........35.00
LR-440B........35.00
LR-440B, hearts & arrow, dk bl, NM........125.00
LR-440B, hearts & arrow, 3½″........40.00
LR-441........45.00
LR-445, very rare, rim chips, 3½″........75.00
LR-465A, fiery opal, VG........50.00
LR-465F, 13 hearts, rim chips, 3⅜″........3.00
LR-465J........25.00
LR-465J, opal, EX........60.00
LR-465L, VG........20.00
LR-465L, violet bl, several scallops missing........75.00
LR-465O, opal, EX........50.00
LR-47........30.00
LR-476........20.00
LR-477........20.00
LR-479........16.00
LR-48........40.00
LR-49........35.00
LR-522........10.00
LR-522, opal........25.00
LR-538........25.00
LR-550........40.00
LR-56, minor edge flakes, scarce, VG........50.00
LR-563, bust, minor rim flakes, 3⅝″, pr........35.00
LR-564........35.00
LR-564, Henry Clay, opal, NM........200.00
LR-565A, Henry Clay, 3⅝″, EX........40.00
LR-565B, Henry Clay, peacock bl, scarce........175.00
LR-569........50.00
LR-575, Victoria, fire polished, scarce, 3½″........65.00
LR-576........85.00
LR-585C, Ringgold, clear........550.00
LR-590........40.00
LR-593, cabin, scarce, 3⅛″, EX........55.00
LR-594........40.00
LR-595, cabin, scarce, sm rim flakes, 3¼″, VG........35.00
LR-596, cabin, 3⅝″, EX........40.00
LR-605A, octagonal w/boats, scarce, sm rim chips, 3½″, VG........125.00
LR-61, NM........60.00
LR-610A........40.00
LR-612A, octagonal w/boat, rare, rim chips, 3½″, EX........200.00
LR-619, Ben Franklin........50.00
LR-628, Chancellor Livingston, med bl, very rare, NM........425.00
LR-629, Chancellor Livingston ship, scarce, 3½″, VG........55.00
LR-632........50.00
LR-641, Bunker Hill, minor rim flakes, 3⅝″, pr, VG........30.00
LR-641A........25.00
LR-643, Bunker Hill, 3⅝″, EX........25.00
LR-654A, sm edge & table rest nicks, slightly cloudy, rare........255.00
LR-655, rare, minor rim flakes, 3⅛″........225.00
LR-66, NM........75.00
LR-660, EX........60.00
LR-661, sm rim flakes, 3½″........30.00
LR-662, eagle........45.00
LR-665A........40.00
LR-666, 3 scallops tipped, unbroken bubble, VG........36.00
LR-666A, bubbly glass, scarce, EX........55.00
LR-667A, eagle, minor rim flakes, 3″........35.00
LR-670........60.00
LR-670A, sm edge flakes, 3½″........40.00
LR-672, eagle, scarce, minor rim flakes, 3½″........60.00
LR-675A, eagle, rim flakes, 3¼″........35.00
LR-676C, eagle w/Fort Pitt, scarce, minor rim flakes, 3¾″........50.00
LR-677........40.00
LR-679........30.00
LR-680, good imprint........30.00
LR-686, rare........170.00
LR-69, rare, minor rim flakes, 3½″........75.00
LR-691........65.00
LR-692, lyre, scarce, rim flakes, 3″........50.00
LR-694A, beehive, scarce, 3″........90.00
LR-77, rare, VG........300.00
LR-78........65.00
LR-84, opaque bl, 1 of 5 existant........1,100.00
LR-97........50.00

Custard

As early as the 1880s, custard glass was produced in England. Migrating glassmakers brought the formula for the creamy ivory ware to America. One of them was Harry Northwood, who in 1898 founded his company in Indiana, Pennsylvania, and introduced the glassware to the American market. Soon other companies were producing custard, among them Heisey, Tarentum, Fenton, and McKee. Not only dinnerware patterns, but souvenir items were made. Today, custard is the most expensive of the colored pressed glassware patterns. The formula for producing the luminous glass contains uranium salts which imparts the cream color to the batch and causes it to glow when it is examined under a black light.

When no condition is indicated, the items listed below are assumed to be in mint condition.

Argonaut Shell, bowl, master berry........165.00
Argonaut Shell, bowl, sauce; ftd, 3x5¼″........65.00

Argonaut Shell, butter dish....250.00
Argonaut Shell, compote, jelly....125.00
Argonaut Shell, creamer....110.00
Argonaut Shell, cruet....350.00
Argonaut Shell, pitcher, water; EX gold....325.00
Argonaut Shell, spooner....96.00
Argonaut Shell, sugar bowl....145.00
Argonaut Shell, tumbler....80.00
Beaded Cable, rose bowl, EX nutmeg stain....85.00
Beaded Circle, butter dish....235.00
Beaded Circle, creamer....120.00
Beaded Circle, pitcher, water....350.00
Beaded Circle, shakers, pr....250.00
Beaded Circle, spooner....115.00
Beaded Swag, goblet....62.00
Beaded Swag, toothpick....150.00
Butterfly & Berry, vase, gr stain, 7½"....35.00
Cherry & Scale, butter dish, nutmeg stain....225.00
Cherry & Scale, creamer, nutmeg stain....112.00
Cherry & Scale, pitcher....325.00
Cherry & Scale, sugar bowl, w/lid....126.00
Chrysanthemum Sprig, bowl, berry; oval, 10½"....195.00
Chrysanthemum Sprig, butter dish, gold decor....265.00
Chrysanthemum Sprig, celery vase, rare....600.00
Chrysanthemum Sprig, compote, jelly....95.00
Chrysanthemum Sprig, creamer....100.00
Chrysanthemum Sprig, cruet....250.00
Chrysanthemum Sprig, pitcher, water....345.00
Chrysanthemum Sprig, sauce dish....55.00
Chrysanthemum Sprig, shakers, pr....185.00
Chrysanthemum Sprig, spooner....90.00
Chrysanthemum Sprig, sugar bowl....120.00
Chrysanthemum Sprig, toothpick....250.00
Chrysanthemum Sprig, tumbler, gold decor....55.00
Chrysanthemum Sprig, water set, 7-pc....650.00
Delaware, sauce dish, rose decor....48.00
Delaware, tray, pin; bl decor....52.00
Delaware, tray, ring; bl decor....60.00
Delaware, tumbler....50.00
Diamond w/Peg, bowl, master berry....165.00
Diamond w/Peg, butter dish....200.00
Diamond w/Peg, creamer....75.00
Diamond w/Peg, creamer, souvenir, miniature....45.00
Diamond w/Peg, mug, souvenir....70.00
Diamond w/Peg, napkin ring, rare....150.00
Diamond w/Peg, shakers, Coney Island, souvenir, pr....95.00
Diamond w/Peg, sugar bowl, w/lid....140.00
Diamond w/Peg, toothpick....50.00
Diamond w/Peg, tumbler....45.00
Diamond w/Peg, water set, souvenir, 7-pc....500.00
Diamond w/Peg, wine....50.00
Fine Cut & Roses, rose bowl....95.00
Geneva, banana boat, gr/red decor, ftd, 11x7½"....150.00
Geneva, berry set, oval, 7-pc, EX....340.00
Geneva, bowl, master berry; rnd, EX decor....126.00
Geneva, compote, jelly....65.00
Geneva, creamer, EX decor....75.00
Geneva, pitcher, water; no decor....200.00
Geneva, sauce, rnd, EX decor....40.00
Geneva, spooner, EX decor....68.00
Geneva, sugar bowl, w/lid, EX decor....110.00
Geneva, syrup....250.00
Geneva, tumbler....50.00
Georgia Gem, bowl, berry; gilt trim, sm....25.00

Argonaut Shell, master berry bowl, with green and gold decor, 5" x 10" x 7", $165.00.

Georgia Gem, bowl, master berry, gilt trim....75.00
Georgia Gem, butter dish, enamel floral....210.00
Georgia Gem, butter dish, gilt trim....145.00
Georgia Gem, creamer, enamel floral....80.00
Georgia Gem, creamer, no decor....40.00
Georgia Gem, cruet, enamel floral....280.00
Georgia Gem, spooner, enamel floral....70.00
Georgia Gem, sugar bowl, w/lid, enamel floral....90.00
Georgia Gem, sugar bowl, w/lid, gilt trim....70.00
Georgia Gem, table set, gilt trim, 4-pc....375.00
Georgia Gem, tumbler....48.00
Grape & Cable, bottle, scent; w/stopper, nutmeg stain....465.00
Grape & Cable, bowl, fruit; ped ft, nutmeg stain, sm....45.00
Grape & Cable, butter dish, nutmeg stain....250.00
Grape & Cable, compote, jelly; nutmeg stain....75.00
Grape & Cable, creamer & sugar, breakfast; nutmeg stain....145.00
Grape & Cable, humidor, VG nutmeg stain, NM....500.00
Grape & Cable, nappy, 2-hdl....45.00
Grape & Cable, plate, 7"....40.00
Grape & Cable, plate, 8"....55.00
Grape & Cable, powder jar, VG nutmeg stain....295.00
Grape & Cable, punch bowl....800.00
Grape & Cable, spooner, nutmeg stain....95.00
Grape & Cable, sugar bowl, w/lid, nutmeg stain....125.00
Grape & Cable, tray, dresser; nutmeg stain, lg....225.00
Grape & Cable, tray, pin....115.00
Grape & Cable, tumbler....75.00
Grape & Gothic Arches, bowl, master berry....175.00
Grape & Gothic Arches, butter dish....165.00
Grape & Gothic Arches, creamer, pearl finish....90.00
Grape & Gothic Arches, goblet....50.00
Grape & Gothic Arches, pitcher, water....250.00
Grape & Gothic Arches, rose bowl....70.00
Grape & Gothic Arches, spooner....80.00
Grape & Gothic Arches, sugar bowl, w/lid, pearl finish....125.00
Grape & Gothic Arches, tumbler....50.00
Harvard, toothpick holder, souvenir....40.00
Harvard, wine....100.00
Honeycomb, wine....60.00
Horse Medallion, bowl, gr stain, 7"....77.00
Intaglio, bowl, fruit; ftd, w/decor, 7½"....220.00
Intaglio, butter dish, w/decor....200.00
Intaglio, compote, jelly; w/decor....100.00
Intaglio, creamer, w/decor....80.00

Intaglio, cruet, w/decor....275.00
Intaglio, sauce dish/berry, w/decor....52.00
Intaglio, shakers, w/decor, pr....150.00
Intaglio, spooner, w/decor....90.00
Intaglio, sugar bowl w/lid, w/decor....120.00
Intaglio, table set, w/decor, 4-pc....500.00
Intaglio, tumbler, w/decor....64.00
Inverted Fan & Feather, berry set, 7-pc....540.00
Inverted Fan & Feather, bowl, master berry....195.00
Inverted Fan & Feather, butter dish....290.00
Inverted Fan & Feather, cruet, orig stopper....630.00
Inverted Fan & Feather, shakers, old tops, pr....365.00
Inverted Fan & Feather, spooner....100.00
Inverted Fan & Feather, tumbler....85.00
Ivorina Verte, spooner, gold decor....75.00
Jackson, creamer....50.00
Jackson, pitcher....200.00
Jackson, sauce dish....40.00
Jackson, shakers, pr....125.00
Jackson, spooner....55.00
Jackson, tumbler....40.00
Lion, plate, gr traces....100.00
Lotus & Grape, bonbon, hdls, pink stain....30.00
Louis XV, berry set, 7-pc....375.00
Louis XV, bowl, master berry....125.00
Louis XV, butter dish....165.00
Louis XV, creamer....80.00
Louis XV, cruet, M gold....145.00
Louis XV, pitcher, water....220.00
Louis XV, sauce....35.00
Louis XV, spooner....75.00
Louis XV, sugar bowl w/lid....120.00
Louis XV, table set, 4-pc....450.00
Louis XV, tumbler....55.00
Louis XV, water set, 7-pc....550.00
Maple Leaf, banana bowl....200.00
Maple Leaf, bowl, master berry....350.00
Maple Leaf, butter dish, EX decor....235.00
Maple Leaf, compote, jelly....395.00
Maple Leaf, creamer, EX decor....85.00
Maple Leaf, cruet....1,000.00
Maple Leaf, pitcher, water....335.00
Maple Leaf, shakers, EX decor, pr....475.00
Maple Leaf, spooner, EX decor....85.00
Maple Leaf, sugar bowl, open....45.00
Maple Leaf, sugar bowl, w/lid....135.00
Maple Leaf, tumbler....85.00
Peacock & Urn, ice cream dish, ind; w/nutmeg....65.00
Peacock & Urn, ice cream dish, master; w/nutmeg....265.00
Persian Medallion, rose bowl....65.00
Pineapple & Fan, creamer, miniature, McPherson, Kansas....45.00
Pineapple & Fan, pitcher, tankard; pink decor....130.00
Poinsettia Lattice, bowl, ftd, nutmeg stain....75.00
Poppy, pickle dish, nutmeg stain....50.00
Punty Band, creamer, souvenir, miniature....40.00
Punty Band, mug, souvenir, 3¼″....35.00
Punty Band, shakers, souvenir, pr....75.00
Ribbed Drape, butter dish....235.00
Ribbed Drape, compote, jelly....175.00
Ribbed Drape, cruet....300.00
Ribbed Drape, pitcher, water....325.00
Ribbed Drape, sauce dish....40.00
Ribbed Drape, shakers, pr....185.00
Ribbed Drape, spooner....75.00
Ribbed Drape, tumbler....50.00
Ring & Beads, mug, souvenir, 3″....28.00
Ring Band, bowl, master berry; w/rose....120.00
Ring Band, butter dish....225.00
Ring Band, celery vase, w/rose....280.00
Ring Band, condiment tray, w/rose....175.00
Ring Band, creamer, w/rose....75.00
Ring Band, cruet, w/rose....300.00
Ring Band, cup, White Rock, SD, w/rose, 2½″....50.00
Ring Band, pitcher, water; St Fair, 1906, w/rose....215.00
Ring Band, sauce dish, w/rose....40.00
Ring Band, shakers, w/rose, pr....115.00
Ring Band, spooner, red dots, w/gold....100.00
Ring Band, toothpick holder, w/rose....70.00
Singing Birds, bowl, berry; ftd, sm....75.00
Vermont, creamer, gr & pink flowers....70.00
Victoria, pitcher, milk; Tarentum, gilt decor, 6¼″....165.00
Victoria, spooner, pnt & gilt decor, Tarentum....85.00
Wild Bouquet, butter dish, EX decor....325.00
Wild Bouquet, spooner, no decor....65.00
Winged Scroll, bowl, master berry; lg....140.00
Winged Scroll, butter dish, EX gold....145.00
Winged Scroll, creamer, EX gold....80.00
Winged Scroll, cup....45.00
Winged Scroll, dish, olive; sides folded up, EX gold, 5½″....40.00
Winged Scroll, hair receiver, M gold....120.00
Winged Scroll, sauce dish, gr decor....30.00
Winged Scroll, shakers, EX gold, pr....165.00
Winged Scroll, spooner, EX gold....80.00
Winged Scroll, toothpick holder, M gold....120.00
Winged Scroll, tumbler, gold....90.00
Winged Scroll, water set, 7-pc....575.00

Winged Scroll, creamer and open sugar bowl, $160.00.

Cut Glass

The earliest documented evidence of commercial glass cutting in the United States was in 1810; the producers were Bakewell and Page of Pittsburgh. These first efforts resulted in simple patterns with only a moderate amount of cutting. By the middle of the century, glass cutters began experimenting with a thicker glass which enabled them to use deeper cuttings, though patterns remained much the same. This period is usually referred to as Rich Cut. Using three types of wheels––a flat edge, a mitered edge, and a convex edge––facets, mitres, and depressions were combined to produce various designs.

In the late 1870s, a curved mitre was developed which greatly expanded design potential. Patterns became more elaborate, often covering the entire surface.

The Brilliant Period of cut glass covered a span from about 1880 until 1915. Because of the pressure necessary to achieve the deeply cut patterns, only glass containing a high grade of metal could withstand the process. For this reason, and the amount of hand work involved, cut glass has always been expensive.

When no condition is indicated, the items listed below are assumed to be in mint condition.

Key:
dia—diamonds x-cut—cross-cut
straw—strawberry x-hatch—crosshatch

Basket, notched hdl, 6″....300.00
Bell, dinner; sgn Fry, 6″....110.00
Bottle, barber; vertical bull's eyes & notching....110.00
Bottle, scent; Aurora Borealis, sgn Pitkin & Brooks, 7″....295.00
Bottle, scent; bulbous, honeycomb stopper, 6½″....165.00
Bottle, scent; flowers, sterling stopper, 5″....40.00
Bottle, scent; laydown, 8-panel, vermeil ends, dbl, 5″ L....115.00
Bowl, daisy & butterflies, Mt Washington, 1909, 2¼x8½″....200.00
Bowl, expanded Harvard, lg base hobstar, scalloped, 3¾x8″....140.00
Bowl, fans/cane/etc overall, lg hobstar base, 3¾x9″....140.00
Bowl, hobstar & cane, scalloped top, 8x2¾″....150.00
Bowl, hobstars, pointed hobnail, semi-whirls, Clark, 8″....265.00
Bowl, muti-cut, feathered pinwheel hobstar center, 3x8″....75.00
Bowl, Nassau pattern, fans, sgn J Hoare, 8″....200.00
Bowl, sawtooth edge & base, vase shape, deep cut, 11″....400.00
Bowl, strawberry diamond/fans/stars, Niagara, sgn, 8½″....250.00
Box, handkerchief; intaglio flowers, hinged lid, 7″ sq....325.00
Box, hobstar chains top & sides, hinged, rnd, 6″....395.00
Box, intaglio & eng floral w/3 birds, rnd, w/lid, 6″....225.00
Box, jewelry; flower & leaf, hinged lid, rnd, lg....185.00
Box, jewelry; ormolu fittings, flashed gr, 4x3½x5½″....400.00
Box, puff; intaglio flowers/leaves, SP collar, 3x5½″ dia....135.00
Bud vase, swirl/comet, att Hoare, 7⅝″....150.00
Butter dish, allover geometric cutting....225.00
Candle holder, notched flute/lapidary knob, prism, 10″, pr....550.00
Candy, 4-part, hobstars/pinwheels/diamonds/arcs, hdls, 11″....175.00
Candy, 4-part, split vesica, hobstars, etc, 12″....235.00
Carafe, brilliant, squatty, 7″....135.00
Carafe, water; strawberry & fan....50.00
Carafe, water; X-hatching, bull's eye, allover cut....65.00
Celery boat, Russian/strawberry hobs/intaglio floral, 13″....125.00
Cheese dish w/underplate, hobstars/cane/dia/star & fan....400.00
Compote, cane/strawberry hobs/intaglio floral panels, 9x7″....135.00
Compote, Cornflower, flashed star base, sgn Clark, 3x7¼″....200.00
Compote, hobstar & saw, 6-sided stem/16-point bottom, 6½″....300.00
Compote, hobstars, X-hatching, teardrop stem, 8¾x7⅜″....375.00
Compote, hobstars & fan, skirted base w/teardrop, 7x8″....200.00
Compote, jelly; ped std, oval bowl....250.00
Compote, petticoat ped, 7″....325.00
Compote, scalloped, 4 various cuttings, heavy, 9½x7″....235.00
Condiment jar w/underplate, prism/hobstars, w/lid....135.00
Cordial, hobstar, faceted knob on stem, sgn Egginton....100.00
Cordial, Persian Button, teardrop in stem, 4″....125.00
Creamer & sugar, buzz stars & vesicas, flat star on base....120.00
Creamer & sugar, hobstars/diamond/fan, miniature....90.00
Cruet, Harvard band, intaglio floral, faceted stopper, 11″....150.00
Cruet, Russian....200.00
Cruet, strawberry diamond fan, X-hatch, trefoil spout, 7″....65.00
Cruet, tankard style, deep cutting, 10″....145.00
Decanter, buzz star, variants, w/hdl, 11″....235.00
Decanter, Harvard, hobstars at bottom/in base, no hdl, 15″....350.00
Decanter, Harvard, 15″....375.00
Decanter, Harvard/floral/leaves, hollow stopper, 15″....250.00
Decanter, straw dia, panels/disk ft, teardrop stopper, 13″....250.00
Decanter, X-cut diamond, +6 stemmed cordials....325.00

Cake stand, pinwheel, deeply cut and frosted roses, three-footed, 12½″, $275.00.

Dish, diamond hobstars/strawberry diamond, scalloped, 6″....65.00
Dish, Russian, oval, 10x7″....245.00
Finger bowl w/underplate, strawberry diamond, lotus style....150.00
Flask, lady's; geometric lines & stars, repousse top, 4x3″....95.00
Flask, lady's; panels & notched prisms, sterling top, 4″....100.00
Flask, oval panels ea side w/cane, sterling top, 4¾x3″....150.00
Flower center, allover cut, gigantic hobstar buzz base, 8″....295.00
Flower center, brilliant cut, sgn Strauss, 7½x10″ dia....575.00
Flowerpot, pinwheel hobstars/notch fan/strawberry diamond....110.00
Goblet, Brunswick variation, 6x3¾″....90.00
Goblet, ruby cut to clear, gold decor, continental, for 4....150.00
Goblet, Russian, cranberry bowl/clear stem, hobstar base....250.00
Goblet, Venetia pattern, 6⅜x3⅛″....115.00
Goblet, zipper-edge panels w/oval t'print, ray base, 6x3¼″....20.00
Hair receiver, cane & notched prism, Art Nouveau top....100.00
Humidor, honeycomb, hobstar base, sterling top....250.00
Ice bucket, cornflower....250.00
Ice bucket, hobstars, fans, diamonds, w/tab hdls, 7¼″ dia....110.00
Ice cream set, straw diamond, shell fans, 7-pc....350.00
Inkwell, convex corners, star ea side, repousse top....95.00
Inkwell, Pineapple & Fan, bl cut to clear, brass lid....60.00
Jar, dresser; repousse sterling top, 14 panels, 2⅞x2¾″....125.00
Jar, horseradish; hollow stopper, Elmira, #33, 5½″....295.00
Jar, powder; hobstars, sterling Art Nouveau top....125.00
Jar, powder; Sultana, glass lid, Blackmer....275.00
Jar, puff; pineapple & fan, multi-rayed base, 4½x3¼″....135.00
Jar, rnd, cutting top & bottom, rare, 4¾x6¾″....350.00
Jar w/underplate/lid, allover verticle notch prisms, 4½″....135.00
Jug, whiskey; hobstar & bull's eye, teardrop & cut stopper....450.00
Jug, whiskey; strap hdls, att Fry, 8x5″....450.00
Knife rest, heavy, lapidary cutting, EX lg....40.00
Knife rest, notched panel shaft/faceted ball ends, 5½″....40.00
Knife rest, notched prism, 4″....30.00
Ladle, hdl w/hobstars/fan, 13½″....325.00
Loving cup, prism cut, sterling rim, 3-hdl, rare, 3″....135.00
Mayonnaise w/underplate, hobstars/etc, ped ft, Maple City....290.00
Mayonnaise w/underplate, hobstars/etc, serrated/scalloped....145.00
Muffineer, sterling top....145.00
Nappy, clusters of hobstars, hdl....58.00
Pitcher, allover hobstars w/intersecting cane, 4½x5″....175.00

Pitcher, champagne; hobstar/cane/bull's eye/straw dia, 11″.....295.00
Pitcher, hobstar diamond, cut lip/hdl, heavy, 9″..............275.00
Pitcher, hobstar row top/base, puntie/X-hatch columns........300.00
Pitcher, hobstars, 11½″......................................275.00
Pitcher, pinwheel, ray bottom, feathered fans/notches, 10″......70.00
Pitcher, pinwheels, cut lip/hdl, heavy........................130.00
Pitcher, sterling rim, Egginton Glenville, 11½″, VG...........450.00
Pitcher, tankard; hobstars, X-hatching, cut hdl, 8½″..........165.00
Pitcher, tankard; notched prism, sterling hdl, 7¾″............375.00
Pitcher, 2 cane-cut panels, 3 w/hobstars/X-hatch/etc, 9″.......245.00
Plate, butterfly & flowers, Mt Washington Glass, 1909, 8″.....125.00
Plate, notched prism fans/X-hatching/hobstars, 10″...........250.00
Plate, sterling rim, Gorham, 10″..........................350.00
Plate, strawberry diamonds/flat hobs/shell fans, 7″.............50.00
Punch cup, diamonds/fans/canes, set of 6....................180.00
Punch set, St Louis Diamond, w/12 cups, rare, 28-lb........1,100.00

Punch bowl and stand, hobstars, cane, and cross-cut diamond, early 1900s, T.B. Clark & Co., 14″ x 12″, $900.00.

Relish, vertical notched prism w/in 24-pt hobstars, 8x4¾″......110.00
Rose bowl, diamond/fan/hobnail, 6½″ dia....................125.00
Rose bowl, huge roses, cane, 3-ftd, heavy crystal..............50.00
Rose bowl, X-cut diamond & fan, miniature, 3½x3¾″..........95.00
Rose bowl, X-cut diamond & fan border/notch rim, 5x5¾″.....130.00
Server, allover checkered dia/fans, deep form, 6½x9½″........160.00
Shakers, allover cut, bulbous, repousse silver tops, 2½″........38.00
Spittoon, lady's; beaded sterling rim, hobnail/straw dia........395.00
Spooner, hobstars/hobnail/diamond points, hdls, 4¾″.........300.00
Stem, wine; emerald cut, panels/fans/notched.................40.00
String holder, notched prism, cut-out Gorham sterling top.....185.00
Syrup, hobstars, beaded, SP hdl & top, 7″....................165.00
Syrup, notched prisms, ornate lid/hdl........................110.00
Tazza, hobstars, 8½″.......................................325.00
Toothpick holder, ped ft, 3¼″..............................75.00
Tray, dresser; Russian w/X-hatch buttons, 11¼x6¼″..........295.00
Tray, ice cream; deep cutting, oval, 14″.....................235.00
Tumble-up, panels/relief dia, wafer ped base, mid-flare.........175.00
Tumbler, hobstars/strawberry diamond, sgn....................28.00
Tumbler, Heart, sgn Hoare, 3⅞″............................75.00
Tumbler, hobstar & fan....................................25.00
Tumbler, lemonade; strawberry diamond, heavy................40.00
Tumbler, pinwheel, heavy..................................18.00
Tumbler, Pluto, Hoare, 3¾″...............................135.00
Vase, challice, geometric cut, scallop hobstar ft, 12½″.........375.00
Vase, floral & geometric cut, yel overlay, flared, 11″..........595.00
Vase, floriform, hobstars/cane/allover cut, teardrop, 12″.......250.00
Vase, hobstar, 10″..110.00
Vase, hobstars/diamonds of pyramidal stars/X-hatched, 11⅝″...125.00
Vase, hobstars/strawberry diamond/notched/bull's eye, 11¾″....170.00
Vase, paperweight w/teardrop base/trumpet top, Hoare, 10″....225.00
Vase, pineapple scalloped top, fans/miters, bulbous, 12″.......350.00
Vase, strawberry diamond, notched, 3⅛″......................32.00
Vase, trumpet; hobstars, notch panels, ray/notch ft, 16″.......325.00

Cut Velvet

Cut Velvet glassware was made during the late 1800s. It is characterized by the effect achieved through the application of relief molded patterns, often ribbing or diamond quilting, which allows its white inner casing to show through the outer pastel layer. When no condition is indicated, the items listed below are assumed to be in mint condition.

Ewer, Dia Quilt, bl, wht w/in, frosted hdl, 4¾x3½″...........135.00
Ewer, Herringbone, apricot/pk, frosted thorn hdl, 11″.........375.00
Finger bowl, Dia Quilt, bl, wht w/in, 2½x4½″................118.00
Pitcher, Honeycomb, rose/pink/wht, amber hdl, 4½x5″........325.00
Rose bowl, Dia Quilt, bl, 3⅜x3⅝″..........................165.00
Rose bowl, Dia Quilt, rose, wht w/in, crimped top, 3¾″.......185.00
Vase, Dia Quilt, bl, bottle form, 7¼″.......................115.00
Vase, Dia Quilt, bl, ruffled top, 7″..........................145.00
Vase, Dia Quilt, gr, bulbous body, shaped neck, 6¼″.........110.00
Vase, Dia Quilt, gr, wht w/in, bottle form, 5⅞x3¼″............95.00
Vase, Dia Quilt, rose, bottle form, 7″.......................145.00
Vase, Dia Quilt, rose, ruffled, 7x3″.........................175.00
Vase, Dia Quilt, 4-corner pinched mouth, bl, 4¼″............185.00
Vase, ribbed, bl, slim neck/bulbous, 8x3¾″..................125.00
Vase, ribbed, mauve, 8½x4″...............................150.00

Cybis

Boleslaw Cybis was a graduate of the Academy of Fine Arts in Warsaw, Poland, and was well recognized as a fine artist by the time he was commissioned by his government to paint murals in the Polish Pavillion's Hall of Honor at the 1939 World's Fair. With the outbreak of World War II, the Cybises found themselves stranded in the United States, and founded an artists' studio, first in Astoria, New York, and later in Trenton, New Jersey, where they made fine figurines and plaques with exacting artistry and craftsmanship entailing extensive hand work. The studio still operates today producing exquisite porcelains on a limited edition basis.

When no condition is indicated, the items listed below are assumed to be in mint condition.

Abigail Adams...950.00
Alexander Elephant......................................330.00
Alice in Wonderland.....................................800.00
American White Buffalo................................1,900.00

Appaloosa Colt . . . 215.00
Apple Blossoms . . . 395.00
Baby Boy & Girl Heads, pr . . . 1,400.00
Baby Owl . . . 75.00
Ballerina, wht, red shoes . . . 1,100.00
Ballerina on Cue, color . . . 800.00
Berengaria . . . 2,000.00
Blue Gray Gnatcatchers . . . 1,500.00
Blue Vireo w/Lilac, pr . . . 1,500.00
Buffalo . . . 90.00
Burro, Fitzgerald . . . 195.00
Cat, w/bl ribbon . . . 350.00
Cheerful Dragon . . . 300.00
Christmas Bell, 1950s . . . 350.00
Cinderella, old . . . 800.00
Clown head, boy w/funny face . . . 325.00
Colts, Darby & Joan . . . 375.00
Columbine . . . 1,700.00
Court Jester . . . 1,500.00
Crucifix, Redeemer, wht bisque & glaze, 13″ . . . 1,800.00
Desdemona, #90 . . . 1,650.00
Duckling, Baby Brother . . . 110.00
Edward . . . 300.00
Elizabeth Ann . . . 200.00
Eros Bust, wood base, 6½″ . . . 235.00
Eskimo Child Head . . . 200.00
Exodus . . . 1,100.00
First Flight . . . 130.00
Folk Singer . . . 750.00
Funny Face, boy clown head . . . 325.00
Goldilocks . . . 275.00
Great White Heron . . . 1,650.00
Gretel . . . 300.00
Hamlet . . . 1,300.00
Hansel & Gretel . . . 500.00
Harlequin . . . 1,600.00
Heidi . . . 300.00
Hiawatha . . . 1,650.00
Holiday Child, 1980 . . . 150.00
Holy Child, glaze decor, lace, 5″ . . . 560.00
Holy Water Font, 1940s . . . 800.00
Indian Girl, Running Deer . . . 425.00
Jayne Eyre . . . 1,050.00
Kwan Yin . . . 2,200.00
Lady Bug . . . 95.00
Lady McBeth . . . 1,075.00
Little Blue Heron . . . 700.00
Little Eagle . . . 475.00
Little Princess . . . 600.00
Little Red Riding Hood . . . 250.00
Lotus Blossom . . . 300.00
Madonna, Queen of Angels, wht . . . 175.00
Madonna w/Lace Veil . . . 175.00
Magnolia . . . 300.00
Mary, Mary . . . 350.00
Melissa . . . 390.00
Minnehaha . . . 1,650.00
Mr Snowball . . . 40.00
Mural, Shepherd w/Flock . . . 1,000.00
Mural, 3 Wise Men . . . 1,000.00
Mushroom . . . 300.00
Neferititi . . . 1,900.00
Noah . . . 1,600.00
Orphelia . . . 2,400.00

Philioa, #300, 13¾″, $600.00.

Panda Bears . . . 175.00
Pandora . . . 200.00
Pansy, China Maid . . . 200.00
Persephone . . . 2,400.00
Peter Pan . . . 350.00
Pink Rose . . . 375.00
Pollyanna . . . 340.00
Priscilla . . . 950.00
Queen Anne . . . 850.00
Queen Esther . . . 1,400.00
Queen of Angels . . . 200.00
Queen Titania . . . 1,425.00
Raffles the Raccoon . . . 225.00
Rapunzel . . . 550.00
Running Deer . . . 400.00
Satin . . . 1,750.00
Scarlett . . . 1,750.00
Shepherd w/Flock . . . 1,100.00
Sleeping Beauty . . . 550.00
Snail . . . 200.00
Springtime . . . 585.00
St Francis, wht/gold w/pink rose at feet, rare, 1950s, 11″ . . . 350.00
St Patrick, coin gold & glaze decor, 13″ . . . 3,500.00
Stallion, #226 . . . 550.00
Suzanne w/Kitten . . . 250.00
Tiffin . . . 200.00
Tinkerbell, 1959 . . . 750.00
Turtle Doves . . . 3,500.00
Unicorn . . . 1,800.00
Unicorns, Gambol & Frolic . . . 750.00

Vireo Building Nest, 1950s....1,100.00
Wendy....200.00
White Buffalo....2,100.00
Wild Turkey, mc....2,000.00
Wildflower....250.00
Wind Flower....275.00
Yankee Doodle Dandy....350.00
Yellow Rose....375.00
Young Boy & Girl Heads, pr....1,100.00

Czechoslovakian Collectibles

Czechoslovakia came into being as a country in 1918. Located in the heart of Europe, it was a land with the natural resources necessary to support a glass industry that dates back to the mid-14th century. This ware has recently captured the attention of today's collectors, and for good reason. There are beautiful vases--cased, ruffled, applied with rigaree or silver overlay--fine enough to rival those of the best glasshouses. Czechoslovakian art glass baskets are quite as attractive as Victorian America's, and the elegant cut glass perfumes made in colors as well as clear crystal are unrivaled. There are also pressed glass perfumes, molded in lovely Deco shapes, of various types of art glass. Some are overlaid with gold filigree set with 'jewels.' Jewelry, lamps, porcelains and fine art pottery are also included in the field.

More than thirty-five marks have been recorded, including those in the mold, ink stamped, acid etched, or on a small metal name plate. The newer marks are incised, stamped 'Royal Dux made in Czechoslovakia' (see Royal Dux), or simply a paper label which reads 'Bohemian Glass made in Czechoslovakia.'

For a more thorough study of the subject, we recommend you refer to the book *Made in Czechoslovakia*, by Ruth A. Forsythe; she is listed in the Directory under Ohio. When no condition is indicated, the items listed below are assumed to be in mint condition. See also Erphila

Basket, glass, mottled colors, blk rim & hdl, 7"....120.00
Basket, glass, turq, blk hdl....75.00
Basket, pottery, Deco motif, red/wht/bl/gr, 4x5½"....45.00
Basket, spangled, mc, clear twisted thorn hdl....65.00
Biscuit jar, HP country scene, ceramic, SP lid/bail, 6"....85.00
Bottle, scent; amber, engraved, frosted flower stopper, 5"....24.00
Bottle, scent; bl, cut glass, fan shape, w/stopper....50.00
Bottle, scent; clear w/enamel daisy....35.00
Bottle, scent; cut bottle & stopper, 6"....55.00
Bottle, scent; gr, frosted squirrel top, bead stopper, 6"....150.00
Bottle, scent; opaque blk, clear stopper, 4"....110.00
Bottle, scent; orange/blk/brass lid, long glass dauber, 6"....45.00
Bottle, scent; pink, cut bottle & stopper, 6"....85.00
Bowl, lustre w/Oriental bird, 9"....30.00
Bowl, Peasant Art, 8"....35.00
Bowl, stylized yel chick, porc, w/lid....25.00
Box, cigarette; horse finial....22.00
Bud vase, yel cased, blk enamel decor, 8"....20.00
Candle holders, fish, Amphora, pr....95.00
Candy dish, amethyst glass w/HP grapes, w/lid, 10"....65.00
Canister set, orange flowers on top half, 15-pc....200.00
Cocktail, lt pumpkin color, crystal overlay w/ebony....15.00
Creamer, parrot figural, mc....38.00
Creamer, sitting cow, orange lustre, 6"....55.00
Decanter, cased, wht cut to gr panels, florals, 14", pr....150.00
Decanter, crystal w/cobalt teardrops/stopper, 15x5½"....70.00
Decanter (2) & liqueur (5) set, cranberry, HP, sgn....750.00
Dispenser, liquor; overshot, barrel shape, legs, 8-pc....40.00
Dresser set, lav glass w/HP floral, jar w/lid & bottle....35.00
Epergne, 1-lily, wht opaline w/fluted ruby rim, 10½", pr....145.00

Figurine, nude in flower, peach and white, signed and numbered, 5½", $65.00.

Figurine, dog, bl glass, miniature....25.00
Figurine, monkey, amethyst glass, miniature....25.00
Flower arranger, birds on tree trunks, 4¾"....15.00
Ice bucket, overshot....28.00
Jardiniere, flying bird border, 6"....35.00
Lamp, beaded basket w/fruit cover....350.00
Lamp, brass/crystal bead basket, fruit cover, 10½"....245.00
Lamp, perfume; bl cut frosted flowers....35.00
Lamp, pottery w/Dutch scene, orig HP cloth shade, 24"....235.00
Lamp, ram head urn, glass fruit cover, bronze, 15½"....470.00
Necklace, faceted mc crystal beads, hand knotted, 58"....20.00
Pitcher, cat hdl, lustre, 4½"....20.00
Pitcher, orange w/5 red/bl stripes, 'X' w/in, bulbous, 6½"....18.00
Plate, orchids & roses, mk Epiag Pirkenhann, Czech....20.00
Powder jar, amber, cut glass....90.00
Rose bowl, mercury glass, sgn....35.00
Rose bowl, spatter, ruby, flat top, 4½", pr....68.00
Salt cellar, clear Flute, w/4 spoons, Iris label & box....20.00
Shakers, desert scene w/camel, 2½", pr....25.00
Tea set, blk w/wht int, 21-pc....52.00
Vase, bl satin glass, mottled colors, 6", pr....45.00
Vase, cobalt glass w/silver rose decor, ruffled lip, 8"....40.00
Vase, cranes & foliage on orange, silver decor, 9¾", pr....65.00
Vase, desert scene w/camel, 8½"....75.00
Vase, enamel floral, cased crystal, matt finish, 8½"....48.00
Vase, orange, applied bl/crystal trimming, no mk, 10½"....18.00
Vase, orange w/zigzag enamel design, Deco, 7"....85.00
Vase, peacock feathering, triple overlay, 10½"....125.00
Vase, silver bird, blk amethyst, 10½"....55.00
Vase, wht w/pink overlay top, 7"....55.00
Wall pocket, bird beside nest....18.00
Wall pocket, birdhouse figural....18.00
Wall pocket, pineapple w/bird....28.00

D'Argental

D'Argental cameo glass was produced in France from the 1870s until about 1920, in the Art Nouveau style. Browns and tans were favored colors used to compliment florals and scenic designs developed through acid cuttings.

When no condition is indicated, the items listed below are assumed to be in mint condition.

Lamp, sealing wax; sgn, complete/orig, 7¼″ 750.00
Vase, chateau on hill, 3 cuts, sgn, 6¾″ 650.00
Vase, houses, scenes in 3 panels, 3 cuts, sgn, 9½″ 750.00
Vase, pastoral scene, shepherd/dog, multi-layered, 14″ 2,500.00
Vase, ruins/gorge/waterfall, pink/ochre on yel, 14″ 1,540.00
Vase, scene w/boats, rust/sienna, sgn, 18″ 2,090.00
Vase, scenic, EX art, brn tones, 12½″ 1,100.00
Vase, thistles/leaves, bl/yel, bulbous, 1″ neck, sgn, 3½″ 348.00
Vase, tree landscape, bl/rose, sgn, 9½″ 950.00
Vase, Venice/boats/statue, purple/frosted, sgn, 13″ 1,295.00

Daum Nancy

Daum was an important producer of French cameo glass, operating from the late 1800s until after the turn of the century. They used various techniques--acid cutting, wheel engraving, and handwork--to create beautiful scenic designs and nature subjects in the Art Nouveau manner. Marked examples are much in demand and command very high prices.

When no condition is indicated, the items listed below are assumed to be in mint condition.

Cameo

Bowl, ferns/trees, 3 curled ft, X-Lorraine, 6″ W 975.00
Bowl, maple leaves, 2 applied cabochons, 3″ 600.00
Bowl, oak leaves, applied acorns/beetles, 5¾″ 770.00
Bowl, pate-de-verre snail hdls, cameo grapes w/in, 5x10″ 2,750.00
Bowl, summer scene, enamel detail, X-Lorraine, 2½x6″ 875.00
Bowl, 3 trees, 3 applied ft, mc, trefoil top, 6″ W 650.00
Decanter, thistles in cameo & silver, inscribed band, 13½″ . . . 1,500.00
Jar, primrose, partial polish, silver mt, lid, 4½″ 440.00
Lamp, landscape, brn on yel/orange, 9″ helmet shade, 16½″ . . 2,750.00
Lamp, landscape, yel/brn, helmet form 9¾″ shade, 20½″ 3,300.00
Lamp, lilies, red on lt orange, 7½″ dome shade, 13″ 2,400.00
Lamp, river scene, 6½″ dia conical shade, 17″ 2,750.00
Lamp, trees in foreground w/bay scene, bell shade, 15″ 2,600.00
Liqueur, winter scenic, barrel shape, 1⅞″ 400.00
Perfume, floral on gold stripe, silver mts, 4¾″ 495.00
Rose bowl, winter scene, 1 cut/pnt, oval, 4x5x6″ 1,100.00
Salt dish, floral, 1 cut, sgn, 1⅛x1¼x2″ 300.00
Salt dish, rain on trees, 1 cut, tab hdls, sgn, 1½″ 650.00
Salt dish, trees, 1 cut/enamel, sgn, oval, 2″ W 500.00

Vase, red and black cameo orchid on frosted ground, signed, 6″, $1,600.00.

Salt dish, winter, 1 cut/enamel, sgn, oval, 2″ W 550.00
Tumbler, meadow scenic on wht frost, barrel shape, 5″ 650.00
Tumbler, sailboats on gold to yel frost, barrel shape, 5″ 650.00
Vase, bellflowers, tri-corner, disk ft, 4¾″ 550.00
Vase, berried branches, shaded w/gr/orange/blk, 14″ 880.00
Vase, irreg etched stripes w/polished circles, topaz, 15″ 880.00
Vase, jewel pine cones applique, gr/yel/pink, 5″ 750.00
Vase, mold-blown forest w/village, X-Lorraine, 12″ 2,900.00
Vase, mold-blown lg trees, gr on yel/violet, 11″ 2,800.00
Vase, olive branches, gr/brn on salmon/gray, 8½″ 750.00
Vase, orchids, waisted ft, flat shoulder, 7″ 1,600.00
Vase, prunus blossoms, wht/lav, irregular rim, ftd, 6½″ 1,200.00
Vase, roses, sm applied disks, gilt on bun ft, 15″ 1,210.00
Vase, sailing boats/trees/mtns, salmon on bl, 12½″ 1,200.00
Vase, summer scenic, 1 cut/enamel, flat oval, 3½x2¾″ 495.00
Vase, summer scenic, 1 cut/enamel, flat oval, 4x4½″ 795.00
Vase, summer scenic, 1 cut/enamel, 6½x3″ 695.00
Vase, vines/berries, applied berries, 7″ W 850.00
Vase, wildflowers, cone neck/ball body, polished, 5″ 750.00

Miscellaneous

Paperweight, mouse w/in leaves, pate-de-verre, 3¼″ L 1,500.00
Vase, enameled, winter forest scene, brn/wht, 16″ 650.00

Davenport

W. Davenport and Company were Staffordshire potters operating in that area from 1793 to 1887, producing earthenware, creamware, porcelain, and ironstone. Many different stamps, all with 'Davenport,' were used to mark the various types of ware.

When no condition is indicated, the items listed below are assumed to be in mint condition.

Cup & saucer, pink lustre, imp mk, set of 6 . . . . 250.00
Pitcher, Winchester, lustre, purple/blk, 8½″ 300.00
Plate, Legend of Montrose, anchor mk, 7″ 40.00
Plate, Waverly-Scott's Illustration, dtd 1852, 10¼″ 70.00
Pot, wht clay w/mottled glaze, emb hunt scenes, 6¾″, EX 65.00
Sauce boat, bl feather edge, very minor stains, 3⅝″ 80.00
Vase, lion's head in gold ea side, gr/pink w/florals, 6½″ 245.00

De Vez

De Vez was a type of acid-cut French cameo glass produced by Cristallerie de Pantin in Paris around the turn of the century.

When no condition is indicated, the items listed below are assumed to be in mint condition.

Cameo

Light fixture, children in orchard, 3 panels, iron fr, 12″ 850.00
Vase, dog w/bird in mouth, 3 cuts, sgn, 6x3″ 750.00
Vase, harbor scene w/boats/men, 3 cuts, sgn, 9¾″ 850.00
Vase, house/mtns, bl/rose on gold, 3 cuts, 12x3½″ 950.00
Vase, man in boat/mtns/tree, leaf/berry trim, 10½″ 850.00
Vase, men in boat/house, leaf fr, 3 cuts, bottle neck, 12″ 950.00
Vase, mtn scenic on pink ground, 3 cuts, 6½x2⅞″ 600.00
Vase, palms/shoreline/mosque, 5″ 750.00
Vase, sailboat/house/mtns, bl/yel on pink, sgn, 8⅛″ 800.00
Vase, sailboats/clouds/shore, gr/maroon, sgn, 9⅝″ 795.00

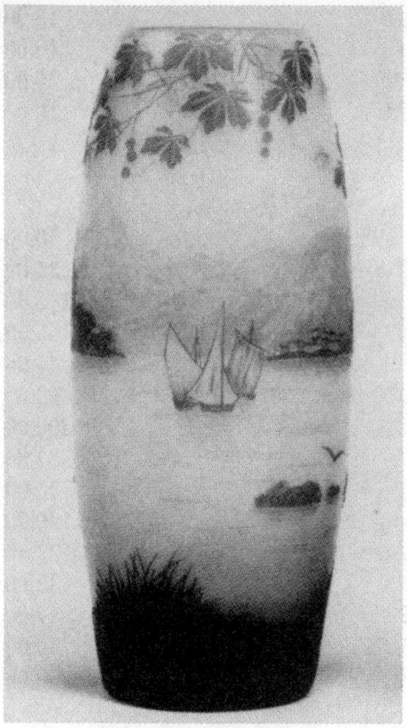

Vase, village nestled in mountain cove, sailing boats and trees in foreground, blue with salmon and green, signed, 12⅜″, $1,500.00.

Vase, swans/lake/vine, gr/rose, 9⅝x3½″....................850.00
Vase, water/mtns/trees, gold/gr/rose, sgn, 9¾″..............650.00
Vase, water/mtns/trees, gold/rose opal, sgn, 10¼x2⅛″.........695.00
Vase, 3 towers on island, pine cone trim, bl/rose, 8¼″........750.00
Vase, 4 carved birds, tails form pattern, sgn, 7½″...........675.00

De Vilbiss

Perfume bottles, atomizers, and dresser accessories marketed by the De Vilbiss Company are appreciated by collectors today for the various types of lovely glassware used in their manufacture, as well as for their pleasing shapes. Those most preferred are marked with the etched De Vilbiss signature.

When no condition is indicated, the items listed below are assumed to be in mint condition.

Atomizer, amber lace motif, lg............................40.00
Atomizer, bl w/blk butterflies, 7″.........................47.50
Atomizer, bl w/blk Deco enamel design on base...............38.00
Atomizer, Coin Spot, bl opal, paper label...................28.00

Atomizers, left to right: Gold crackle glaze, paper label, 3″, $10.00; Opalescent swirl on clear glass, 4¾″, $17.50; Gold with floral etching, 4¾″, $25.00.

Atomizer, crystal top, bottom half gold crackle...............25.00
Atomizer, gold crackle w/blk Deco trim, sgn, lg..............55.00
Atomizer, jade gr, gr bulb, sgn............................75.00
Atomizer, orange/blk/gold, Nouveau shape, in orig box, 19″....115.00
Atomizer, rabbit, Lenox, sgn..............................75.00
Atomizer, wht satin glass.................................35.00
Bottle, scent; feathered wht opal..........................40.00
Bottle, scent; pink opal, Fenton...........................35.00
Bottle, scent; turq, long dauber/enamel lid, sgn..............55.00
Catalog, trade; perfume bottles, Art Deco, 48 pg, 9x12″........20.00
Dresser set, enamel flowers on gold, sgn, rare, 7-pc..........595.00
Powder jar, amber lace motif..............................30.00

Decanters

Ceramic whiskey decanters were brought into prominence in 1955 by the James Beam Distilling Company. Few other companies besides Beam produced these decanters during the next ten years or so; however, other companies did eventually follow suit, so that today there are at least twenty prominent companies and several on a lesser scale that make these decanters.

We have tried to list those brands that are the most popular with collectors. Likewise, individual decanters listed are the ones, or representative of the ones, most commonly found. These are a small fraction of the several thousand different decanters that have been produced.

These decanters come from all over the world. While Jim Beam owns its own china factory in the U.S., some of the others import from Mexico, Taiwan, Japan and elsewhere. They vary in size from miniatures (approximately 2 oz.) to gallons. Values range from a few dollars to more than $3,000 per decanter. A mint condition decanter is one with no chips or cracks and all labels intact. Whether a decanter is full or not has no bearing on the value, nor does a missing federal tax stamp. It is advisable to empty the contents of a ceramic decanter, otherwise the thin inner glaze could crack, allowing the contents to seep through the porous body, thus ruining the decanter.

An (m) behind a listing indicates a miniature. All others are fifth or 750 ml size. When no condition is indicated, the items listed below are assumed to be in mint condition.

Beam

Centennial Series, Civil War, North, 1961...................25.00
Centennial Series, Civil War, South, 1961...................55.00
Centennial Series, Colorado Centennial, 1976.................14.00
Centennial Series, St Louis Arch, 1966......................18.00
Centennial Series, Washington Bicentennial, 1976.............12.00
Clubs & Organizations, Elks, 1977..........................15.00
Clubs & Organizations, Marine Corps, 1975..................45.00
Clubs & Organizations, Pearl Harbor, 1972...................20.00
Executive Series, Charisma, 1970..........................10.00
Executive Series, Flower Basket, 1962......................45.00
Executive Series, Majestic, 1966...........................30.00
Executive Series, Presidental, 1968.........................7.00
Executive Series, Yellow Rose, 1978........................15.00
People Series, Charlie McCarthy, 1976......................25.00
People Series, Hatfield, 1973..............................18.00
People Series, Martha Washington, 1976.....................10.00
People Series, McCoy, 1973................................25.00
People Series, Mortimer Snerd, 1976........................25.00
People Series, Paul Bunyan, 1970............................6.00
Regal China Series, Bell Scotch, 1969.......................8.00
Sport Series, Bing Crosby 30th, 1971.......................10.00
Sport Series, Hawaiian Open Pineapple, 1972.................10.00
Sport Series, Kentucky Derby 100th, 1974.....................8.00
Sport Series, Kentucky Derby 97th, 1971......................6.00

State Series, Colorado, 1959 ... 35.00
State Series, Hawaii, 1959-60 ... 40.00
State Series, Idaho, 1962 ... 65.00
State Series, Kansas, 1960 ... 50.00
State Series, Montana, 1963 ... 75.00
State Series, Nevada, 1963 ... 45.00
State Series, Ohio, 1966 ... 10.00
State Series, Pennsylvania, 1967 ... 6.00
State Series, West Viriginia, 1963 ... 200.00
Trophy Series, Cats, Burmese, Tabby or Siamese, 1967 ... 10.00
Trophy Series, Dog, 1959 ... 55.00
Trophy Series, Duck or Fish, 1957 ... 28.00
Trophy Series, Female Cardinal, 1973 ... 18.00
Trophy Series, Fox, gr, 1965 ... 30.00
Trophy Series, Horses, 1962 ... 20.00
Trophy Series, Owls, 1979 ... 15.00
Trophy Series, Pheasant, 1960-61 ... 18.00
Trophy Series, Poodles, gray or wht, 1970 ... 10.00
Trophy Series, Ram, 1958 ... 110.00
Trophy Series, Red Cardinal, 1968 ... 45.00
Trophy Series, Woodpecker, 1969 ... 6.00
Wheel Series, Cable Car, 1958 ... 5.00
Wheel Series, Circus Wagon, 1979 ... 38.00
Wheel Series, Duesenberg, 1981, 1982 ... 65.00
Wheel Series, Ford Model A, blk, 1978 ... 36.00
Wheel Series, Harold's Club Covered Wagon, 1974 ... 22.00
Wheel Series, Jewel Tea Van, 1976 ... 85.00
Wheel Series, Mack Fire Truck, 1982 ... 65.00
Wheel Series, Model T Ford, 1974 ... 50.00
Wheel Series, Olsonite Eagle Racer, 1975 ... 45.00
Wheel Series, Thomas Flyer, bl, 1977 ... 75.00
Wheel Series, Volkswagen, 1973 ... 30.00
Wheel Series, 1904 Oldsmobile, 1972 ... 75.00
Wheel Series, 1929 Ford, 1982 ... 55.00

Brooks

Animal Series, Charolais, 1972 ... 14.00
Animal Series, Man O'War, 1969 ... 12.00
Animal Series, Tiger, Bengal, 1979 ... 30.00
Automotive & Transportation Series, Cable Car, 1968 ... 7.00
Automotive & Transportation Series, Corvette Mako Shark ... 20.00
Automotive & Transportation Series, Stagecoach, Overland ... 10.00
Automotive & Transportation Series, Train, Casey Jones ... 35.00
Bird Series, Eagle, gold, 1971 ... 15.00
Bird Series, Macaw, 1980 ... 35.00
Bird Series, Owl #1, Ol' Ez, 1977 ... 55.00
Bird Series, Owl #2, Eagle, 1978 ... 75.00
Bird Series, Owl #4, Scops, 1980 ... 30.00
Bird Series, Phoenix, 1971 ... 24.00
Heritage China Series, Dueling Pistol, 1968 ... 12.00
Heritage China Series, Phonograph, 1970 ... 20.00
Heritage China Series, Totem Pole #1, 1972 ... 12.00
People Series, Betsy Ross, 1975 ... 15.00
People Series, Clown #1, Smiley, 1979 ... 40.00
People Series, Clown #2, Cowboy, 1979 ... 35.00
People Series, Clown #3, Pagliacci, 1979 ... 20.00
People Series, Clown #4, Keystone Cop, 1980 ... 25.00
People Series, Clown #5, Cuddles, 1980 ... 20.00
People Series, Clown #6, Tramp, 1980 ... 20.00
People Series, Clown w/Accordian, 1971 ... 16.00
People Series, Clown w/Balloons, 1973 ... 22.00
People Series, Minuteman, 1975 ... 16.00
People Series, Oliver Hardy, 1976 ... 18.00

Sport Series, Badger #1, Boxer, 1973 ... 15.00
Sport Series, Casey at Bat, 1973 ... 16.00
Sport Series, Razorback Hog, 1969 ... 20.00
Sport Series, Tennis Player, 1973 ... 10.00

Cyrus Noble

Birds of the Forest Series, Owl, 1980 ... 40.00
Dancers South of the Border, 1978 ... 35.00
Mine Series, Assayer, 1972 ... 165.00
Mine Series, Bartender, 1971 ... 165.00
Mine Series, Gambler, 1974 ... 45.00
Mine Series, Gambler's Lady, 1976 ... 38.00
Mine Series, Gold Miner, 1970 ... 500.00
Mine Series, Land Lady, 1977 ... 28.00
Mine Series, Miner's Daughter, 1975 ... 45.00
Mine Series, Snowshoe Thompson, 1972 ... 190.00
Mine Series, The Mine, 1978 ... 32.00
Mine Series, Violinist, 1976 ... 35.00
Sea Animal Series, Dolphin, 1979 ... 40.00
Sea Animal Series, Sea Turtle, 1979 ... 50.00
Sea Animal Series, Walrus Family, 1978 ... 50.00

Hoffman

Animal Series, Cats, 6 different, 1981, 50 ml, ea ... 12.00
Animal Series, Dogs, 6 different, 1981, 50 ml, ea ... 12.00
Duck Decoy Series, Golden Eye, 1978, (m), pr ... 15.00
Mr Lucky Series, Barber, 1980 ... 32.00
Mr Lucky Series, Bartender, 1975 ... 40.00
Mr Lucky Series, Carpenter, 1979 ... 42.00
Mr Lucky Series, Fiddler, 1974 ... 28.00
Mr Lucky Series, Mr Lucky, 1973 ... 50.00
Mr Lucky Series, Mr Lucky & Rockwell ... 50.00
Mr Lucky Series, Mrs Lucky, 1974 ... 28.00
Mr Lucky Series, Railroad Engineer, 1980 ... 32.00
Mr Lucky Series, School Teacher, 1976 ... 30.00
No-Hunting Series, Bear & Cub, 1978 ... 35.00
No-Hunting Series, Setter, 1979 ... 50.00
Sports Series, Big Red Machine, 1973 ... 30.00
Sports Series, Dallas Cheerleader, 1979, 8-oz ... 25.00

Lionstone

Bird Series, Bluebird, Western, 1972 ... 22.00
Bird Series, Canadian Goose, 1980 ... 60.00
Bird Series, Goldfinch, 1972 ... 26.00
Bird Series, Meadowlark, 1969 ... 22.00
Bird Series, Roadrunner, 1969 ... 30.00
Circus Clowns Series, #1-#6, 1978-1979, (m), ea ... 14.00
Circus Clowns Series, #1-#6, 1978-1979, ea ... 35.00
Firefighter Series, #1, w/Hose, 1972 ... 110.00
Firefighter Series, #2, w/Child, 1974 ... 95.00
Firefighter Series, #3, Down Pole, 1975 ... 65.00
Firefighter Series, #4, Emblem, 1978 ... 28.00
Firefighter Series, #5, Emblem, 1979 ... 28.00
Old West Series, Gambler, 1970 ... 12.00
Old West Series, Sheriff, 1969 ... 12.00
Sports Series, Football or Basketball Players, 1974 ... 24.00

McCormick

Bicentennial Series, Benjamin Franklin, 1975 ... 24.00
Confederate Series, Jefferson Davis, 1976 ... 20.00

Entertainer Series, Elvis #1, 1978 .... 70.00
Entertainer Series, Elvis #1, 1979, (m) 26.00
Entertainer Series, Elvis #2, 1979 .... 35.00
Entertainer Series, Elvis #2, 1980, (m) 20.00
Entertainer Series, Elvis #3, 1980 .... 38.00
Entertainer Series, Elvis #3, 1980, (m) 20.00
Entertainer Series, Elvis Gold, 1979 .... 200.00
Entertainer Series, Elvis Silver, 1980 .... 95.00
Entertainer Series, Hank Williams, Jr, 1980 .... 65.00
Entertainer Series, Tom T Hall, 1980 .... 35.00
Football Mascots Series, Baylor Bears, 1972 .... 25.00
Football Mascots Series, Indian Hoosiers, 1974 .... 20.00
Great American Series, Ulyssis S Grant, 1976 .... 20.00
Gunfighter Series, Wyatt Earp, 1972 .... 30.00
King Arthur Series, Sir Lancelot, 1979 .... 20.00
Warrior Series, Napoleon, 1969 .... 20.00

Old Bardstown

Bulldog, 1980 .... 60.00
Bulldog, 1980, 1.75 liter 200.00
Citation, 1979 .... 100.00
Delta Queen, 1980 .... 35.00
Stanley Steamer, 1978 .... 45.00
Tiger, 1979 .... 35.00
Wildcat, #3, 1980 .... 190.00

Old Commonwealth

Elusive Leprechaun, 1980 .... 35.00
Heroic Volunteer #4, 1981 .... 60.00
Miner #1, 1975 .... 100.00
Miner #1, 1980, (m) 32.00
Miner #2, 1976 .... 45.00
Miner #2, 1982, (m) 25.00
Octoberfest, 1983 .... 55.00
Volunteer Fireman #2, 1978 .... 55.00
Waterfowler #1, 1978 .... 50.00
Waterfowler #2, 1980 .... 40.00

Ski Country

Bicentennial Series, Eagle-on-Drum, 1976 .... 130.00
Christmas Series, Mrs Cratchit, 1978 .... 48.00
Circus Series, Jenny Lind, bl, 1976 .... 75.00
Circus Series, Palomino Horse, 1975 .... 45.00
Circus Series, Ringmaster, 1975 .... 25.00
Customer Specialties Series, Idaho Snake River Stampede 65.00
Customer Specialties Series, US Ski Team, 1980, (m) 15.00
Domestic Animal Series, Labrador Dog w/Pheasant, 1976 .... 75.00
Fish Series, Muskie, 1977 .... 25.00
Fish Series, Rainbow Trout, 1976 .... 40.00
Indian Series, Eagle Dancer, 1979 .... 200.00
Indian Series, North American Indians, 1977, set of 6 .... 160.00
Indian Series, Warrior #2 w/Lance, 1979 .... 125.00
State Bird Series, Cardinal, 1976 .... 50.00
Waterfowl Series, Pelican, 1976 .... 45.00
Wild Life Series, Falcon, Peregrine, 1980 .... 65.00
Wild Life Series, Fox on a Log, 1973 .... 110.00
Wild Life Series, Koala, 1973 .... 25.00
Wild Life Series, Owl, Spectacled, 1975 .... 90.00
Wild Life Series, Partridge, Chucker, 1979 .... 35.00
Wild Life Series, Ram, Bighorn, 1973 .... 70.00
Wild Life Series, Wild Turkey, 1976 .... 140.00

Wild Turkey

Lore Series, #1, 1979 .... 45.00
Lore Series, #2, 1980 .... 30.00
Lore Series, #3, 1981 .... 35.00
Lore Series, #4, 1982 .... 45.00
Series I, #1, 1971 .... 300.00
Series I, #2, 1972 .... 200.00
Series I, #3, 1973 .... 95.00
Series I, #4, 1974 .... 95.00
Series I, #5, 1975 .... 35.00
Series I, #6, 1976 .... 25.00
Series I, #7, 1977 .... 22.00
Series I, #8, 1978 .... 38.00
Series I, Mini #1, 2, 3, or 4, 1981-1982, ea 12.00
Series I, Mini #5, 6, 7, or 8, 1983, ea 20.00
Series III, Turkey & Bobcat, 1983 .... 110.00
Series III, Turkey & Eagle, 1984 .... 85.00
Series III, Turkey & Eagle, 1984, (m) 45.00
Series III, Turkey & Fox, 1985 .... 85.00
Series III, Turkey & Fox, 1985, (m) 40.00
Series III, Turkey & Poults, 1984 .... 85.00
Series III, Turkey & Poults, 1984, (m) 40.00
Series III, Turkey & Raccoon, 1984 .... 85.00
Series III, Turkey & Raccoon, 1984, (m) 40.00
Series III, Turkey in Flight, 1983 .... 110.00
Series III, Turkey in Flight, 1984, (m) 40.00
Series III, Turkeys Fighting, 1983 .... 110.00

Decoys

American colonists learned the craft of decoy making from the Indians who used them to lure birds out of the sky as an important food source. Early models were carved from wood such as pine, cedar, balsa, etc., and a few were made of canvas or papier mache. There are two basic types of decoys: water floaters and shorebirds (also called 'stick-ups'). Within each type are many different species, ducks being the most plentiful since they migrated along all four of America's great waterways. Market hunting became big business around 1880, resulting in large scale commercial production of decoys which continued until about 1910, when such hunting was outlawed by the Migratory Bird Treaty.

Today, decoys are one of the most collectible types of American folk art. The most valuable are those carved by such artists as Laing, Crowell, Ward, and Wheeler, to name only a few.

Each area, such as Massachusetts, Connecticut, Maine, the Illinois River, and the Delaware River produces decoys with distinctive regional characteristics. Examples of commercial decoys produced by well-known factories--among them Mason, Stevens, and Dodge--are also prized by collectors. Though mass produced, these nevertheless required a certain amount of hand carving and decorating.

Well-carved examples, especially those of rare species, are appreciating rapidly, and those with original paint are more desirable.

Authority Carl F. Luckey has compiled a fully-illustrated identification and value guide, *Collecting Antique Bird Decoys*; you will find his address in the Directory under Alabama. When no condition is indicated, the items listed below are assumed to be in excellent condition.

Key:

RP—repaint	OP—original paint
WOP—worn original paint	OWP—original working paint
ORP—old repaint	WRP—working repaint

Black Duck, Elmer Crowell, G OP 1,210.00
Black Duck, Elmer Crowell, EX OP 2,145.00

Blue-Winged Teal Drake, by H.A. Stevens Decoy Factory, Weedsport, N.Y., stencil signature on bottom, near mint original paint, $6,000.00.

Black Duck, Mason's, glass eyes, worn RP, age cracks, 16″....185.00
Black Duck, Mason's, tack eye, NM....375.00
Black Duck, Mason's Challenge, sm tail chip, o/w NM....450.00
Black Duck, Mason's Premiere, EX OP, minor wear, prof rstr..650.00
Black Duck, Mason's Standard, pristine....275.00
Black Duck, Nathan Cobb, carved split tail, EX OP....18,000.00
Black Duck, tin stick-up, 1930s, 9x16″....30.00
Black Duck, Ward Bros, balsa body, ca 1948....1,650.00
Black-Bellied Plover, att Cobb family, ca 1900....3,300.00
Black-Bellied Plover, Dr Hill, M....225.00
Black-Bellied Plover, Geo Boyd, EX OP, minor shot scars....4,000.00
Blue Heron, NJ, hollow cedar, aggressive, OP, age crack....220.00
Blue-Winged Teal, Frank Hass, tin eyes/tack pupils, OP, 13″....85.00
Blue-Winged Teal, Mark Whipple, ca 1930, EX....500.00
Blue-Winged Teal, Wm Shaw, male/female pr....2,750.00
Blue-Winged Teal drake, Mason's Standard, glass eyes/EX OP..300.00
Blue-Winged Teal drake, Stevens, NM OP....6,000.00
Bluebill, dvtl head, flange tail, glass eyes, OP, 12½″....125.00
Bluebill, MI, incised wing lines, glass eyes, combed pnt....85.00
Bluebill, Mike Frisque, WRP, 1930s....75.00
Bluebill, Stevens, OP, average wear, stamp....1,430.00
Bluebill drake, Stevens, humpbk, VG OP....500.00
Bluebill drake sleeper, Susquehanna Flats, WOP, 1930, 11″....75.00
Bluebill hen, Herter's, printed canvas bobtail, pine head....65.00
Bluebill hen, J Baker, glass eyes, swing keel, WOP, 13½″....50.00
Bluebill hen, Mason's Standard, rpl eyes, scars, RP, 13½″....125.00
Bluebills, Ward Bros, ca 1930s, male/female pr....4,620.00
Brant, att Pitman, EX OP, average wear, age splits, chip....425.00
Brant, Chauncey Wheeler, NM....3,300.00
Brant, Ira Hudson, WOP....600.00
Brant, J Lincoln, RP removed to OP, fine crack....1,430.00
Brant, John Holloway, hollow, EX OP....175.00
Brant, Madison Mitchell, solid body, EX OP....300.00
Bufflehead drake, A Meekins, tack eyes, OP, 10″, EX....145.00
Bufflehead hen, A Meekins, tack eyes, primitive, OP, 10½″....140.00
Canada Geese, watcher/feeder, silhouette/Horicon Marsh, pr....45.00
Canada Goose, balsa w/carved wood head/glass eyes, RP, 22″..115.00
Canada Goose, canvas/wire fr body, wood head/base, WOP, 26″.45.00
Canada Goose, sheet metal stick-up, folding head, worn, 21″....35.00
Canada Goose, VA shore, stick-up, carved eyes, agressive....850.00
Canada Goose, Walker, tin silhouette, WRP, 1910s....75.00
Canada Goose, Ward Bros, balsa body, ca 1948....2,145.00
Canvasback, Ira Hudson, WOP....300.00
Canvasback, Mason's Challenge, WOP, scars/crack, 15¾″....260.00
Canvasback, Toby Sherburne, OP, 1930s....85.00
Canvasback drake, Chesapeake Bay, WOP, 15½″....45.00
Canvasback drake, Dodge, tack eyes, partial RP, 13¾″....60.00
Canvasback drake, H Lohr, cork/wood, glass eyes, RP, 16″....25.00
Canvasback drake, J Dodge, glass eyes, WOP, ca 1890, 14″....105.00
Canvasback drake, WI, pegged-on head, glass eyes, OP, 17″...185.00
Canvasbacks, Tom Schroeder, on pnt wood mt, M, pr....600.00
Coot, AJ Buchmann, contemporary, glass eyes, sgn, OP, 12″....90.00
Coot, Herter's, balsa, OP, 1930s....65.00
Coot, IL River, hollow, glass eyes, WOP, bill damage, 12½″....45.00
Crow, IL, silhouette stick-up, orig blk pnt, 1930s....48.00
Curlew, J Winslow, EX OP, average wear, rpl bill....2,750.00
Curlew, Thos Gelston, ca 1900, rpl bill....900.00
Dowitcher, running; Mason, tack eyes, orig wood bill....2,400.00
Eider drake, Capt GB Smith, carved bill, NM....375.00
Folding, tin, blk/wht pnt, 9¾″....55.00
Golden Plover, AE Crowell, miniature, EX....975.00
Golden Plover, Coffin, OP w/minor wear, rpl bill....400.00
Golden Plover, John Dilley....3,300.00
Golden Plover, MA, pnt eyes, beetle head, all orig, NM....650.00
Golden Plover, Mason's, tack eyes, average wear....1,100.00
Golden Plover, Nantucket, Geo Dyer rpt....150.00
Goldeneye drake, Alexandria Bay, glass eyes, scars, OP, 14″....95.00
Goldeneye drake, Keyes Chadwick, worn RP....300.00
Goose, tin stick-up, OP, 3 colors, '20s, 32x22″....65.00
Great Blackbacked Gull, L Reineri, hollow body, OP, 27″....150.00
Gull, Miles Smith, glass eyes, working decoy, OP, 18″....95.00
Herring Gull, AE Crowell, miniature, EX....800.00
Hooded Merganser drake, Mark McNair....900.00
Magnum Black Mallard, Herter's, balsa wood....55.00
Mallard, Carrylite Decoy Co, salesman's sample....15.00
Mallard drake, Evans, glass eyes, WOP, shot/scars, 15″....65.00
Mallard drake, Hec Whittington, OP....550.00
Mallard drake, IL, hollow, tack eyes, EX carving/pnt, 16″....115.00
Mallard drake, Perry Willcoxen, hollow, glass eyes, WOP....110.00
Mallard hen, Bert Graves, hollow, EX OP, minor wear/split....650.00
Mallard hen, Hec Whittington, OP....770.00
Mallard hen, IL, OP, 18″....135.00
Mallard hen, JRW, hollow, all orig, sgn....1,000.00
Mallards, Mason's Standard, glass eyes, sm split o/w M, pr....400.00

Merganser drake, Ben Smith, EX OP w/in-use wear.........1,600.00
Merganser hen, Mason's Challenge grade, snaky head, NM...3,850.00
Morning Dove, IL, sgn Marvin S, brn/blk/gray, 1940s, 13"......60.00
Pintail, Ira Hudson, banjo tail, minor touch-up.............2,585.00
Pintail drake, RL Janson, glass eyes, RP, ca 1920, 17"........135.00
Pintail hen, Fresh-Air Dick, neck rpr, new RP, 16¼".........150.00
Plover, Chas Thomas, balsa/carved wings, EX OP, minor scar..350.00
Red-Breasted Merganser, Ira Hudson, unused..............7,700.00
Redhead drake, Chris Smith, hollow/glass eyes, WOP, 16".....175.00
Redhead drake, F Baumgartner, glass eyes, RP, 11½"........110.00
Redhead drake, G Weir, hollow, glass eyes, WOP, 1835, 15"....75.00
Redhead drake, Keyes Chadwick, EX OP, minor wear.......2,700.00
Redhead drake, Otto Misch, hollow/glass eyes, WOP, 15".......95.00
Robin Snipe, Mason's, shorebird, 1890s, prof rpr.............375.00
Ruddy Duck, J Hayman, rstr bill, minor pnt damage, 1920...1,760.00
Ruddy Duck, Ned Burgess, WRP........................1,320.00
Ruddy Turnstone, Dodge, ca 1890, NM...................1,870.00
Ruddy Turnstone, Obediah Vertiy, 1890..................5,775.00
Snipe, carved wings, WOP..............................375.00
Squaw drake, Hurley Conklin, branded mk, carved wings, EX..375.00
Swan, JP Hand, hollow cedar, OP..........................935.00
White-Winged Scooter, early Maine, primitive, ORP, 19½"......75.00
Widgeon drake, Mason's Standard, WRP, damage, 16"........110.00
Willett shorebird, Mason's, glass eyes, OP, EX...............240.00
Willett shorebird, Mason's, tack eyes/fall plumage, all orig....1,900.00
Wood Duck, Hurley Conklin, pr...........................950.00
Yellowlegs, Geo Boyd, orig, M..........................3,500.00
Yellowlegs, Geo Hinckley, oversize feeder, 1900............2,500.00

Dedham

Originally founded in Morrisville, Pennsylvania, as the Chelsea Keramic Works, the name was changed to Dedham Pottery in 1895, after the firm relocated in Dedham, near Boston, Massachusetts. The move was effected to make use of the native clay deemed more suitable for the production of the popular dinnerware designed by Hugh Robinson, founder of the company. The ware utilized a gray stoneware body with a crackle glaze and simple cobalt border designs of flowers, birds, and animals. Decorations were brushed on by hand using an ancient Chinese method which suspended the cobalt within the overall glaze. There were thirteen standard patterns, among them Magnolia, Iris, Butterfly, Duck, Polar Bear, and the Rabbit, the latter of which was chosen to represent the company on their logo. On the very early pieces the rabbits face left; decorators soon found the reverse position easier to paint, and the rabbits were turned to the right.

In addition to the standard patterns, other designs were produced for special orders. These and artist signed pieces are highly valued by collectors today.

The firm was operated by succeeding generations of the Robertson family until it closed in 1943.

When no condition is indicated, the items listed below are assumed to be in mint condition. See also Chelsea Keramic Works

Bowl, Azalea, shallow, base chip, 7¼"......................100.00
Bowl, Rabbit, sq serving, 8½" W..........................150.00
Bowl, soup; Rabbit, sgn NG 5/4/10, 9⅛"...................200.00
Bowl, whip cream; Rabbit, 7½"...........................225.00
Charger, Elephant, minor glaze imperfections, 12"...........900.00
Creamer, Rabbit...150.00
Cup & saucer, Rabbit....................................150.00
Cup & saucer, Rabbit, oversize, cup: 4" dia.................175.00
Figurine, rabbit, 2¾"....................................325.00
Marmalade jar, Grape, bulbous, 5"........................300.00
Mug, Rabbit..250.00
Pitcher, Azalea, 7"......................................425.00

Left, Plate, central coat-of-arms, rabbit border, stamped and dated 1931, 8¾", $1,600.00; Right, Fairbanks house, rabbit border, stamped registered, early 1900s, 8½", $2,200.00.

Pitcher, Day-Night, 5"...................................450.00
Pitcher, Oak Block, stamped registered, 5¾"................900.00
Plate, butterfly border, dk bl ground, 6½"..................245.00
Plate, central lily, 6" dia.................................550.00
Plate, crab/waves, bl/wht crackle, post-1929, 6¼".............310.00
Plate, Elephant, in-the-making chip, 7½"...................125.00
Plate, Elephant, 6¼"....................................300.00
Plate, fish/scrolling waves, bl/wht crackle, pre-1929, 8½".....1,100.00
Plate, French Mushroom, minor flake, 8½".................150.00
Plate, Grapes, border motif, bl/wht crackle, 6"...............125.00
Plate, Lobster, dtd 1931, 7½"............................300.00
Plate, Lobster, 2 mks, rare, 6½"..........................185.00
Plate, Poppy, 8½".......................................385.00
Plate, poppy/leaves, bl/wht crackle, pre-1929, 8½"............500.00
Plate, poppy/leaves in center, pod border, bl/wht, 8½", NM....400.00
Plate, Rabbit, Dedham tercentenary, 1636-1936, 8½".........220.00
Plate, Rabbit, post-1929, 8½"............................125.00
Plate, Rabbit, pre-1929, 9½".............................145.00
Plate, Rabbit, 6½".......................................95.00
Plate, Snowtree, 10"....................................150.00
Plate, Turtle, minor factory flaw, 6"........................125.00
Plate, Water Lily, imp rabbit ears & bl registry mk, 6"........125.00
Plate, Water Lily, 8½"...................................145.00
Plate, Woodcock in flight, bl/wht crackle, pre-1929, 8½".....1,430.00
Tray, bacon; Rabbit, pre-1929, 9¾x6¼"....................250.00
Trivet, Turkey, 6" dia....................................400.00

Dedham Art Pottery

Planter, blocked mirror, DPCO in hexagon, sgn, 8¾x5¼x3¾"..350.00
Planter; gr circular mirror design, JHR/HCR, 6x3¼x3¼", EX...200.00
Planter, leaf design, pedestal, short rabbit mk, 8¾" L.........300.00
Vase, dogwood, rabbit, 'I' in oval, crackleware/spongeware.....450.00
Vase, gr w/bl drip, mk Dedham, sgn HR, base chip, 7½"......250.00
Vase, gr w/highlights, sgn HCR, 6"........................200.00
Vase, hand thrown, gr w/highlights, sgn HR, 5¾"............275.00
Vase, mottle brn to gr flambe, Chinese form, HCR, 9x5½".....350.00
Vase, oxblood, base-swell cylinder, mk Dedham, 6½"........1,200.00
Vase, oxblood/blk, tapered bulb, DP96G, 7¼x6⅜"..........1,200.00
Vase, red/orange/blk, yel rabbit mk, BHR/volcano shape, 8"..1,000.00
Vase, Volcanic bl/blk/gr glaze, hairline, 10"................550.00
Vase, Volcanic brns/taupe/tan runs, Robertson/BW, 9", NM....385.00
Vase, Volcanic red/wht drips, 7¼", EX.....................770.00

Degenhart

The Crystal Art Glass factory in Cambridge, Ohio, opened in 1947 under the private ownership of John and Elizabeth Degenhart. John had previously worked for the Cambridge Glass Company, and was well known for his superior paperweights. After his death in 1964, Elizabeth took over management of the factory, hiring several workers from the defunct Cambridge Company, including Zack Boyd. Boyd was responsible for many unique colors, some of which were named for him. From 1964 to 1974, more than twenty-seven different moulds were created, most of them resulting from Elizabeth Degenhart's work and creativity, and over 145 official colors were developed. Elizabeth died in 1978, requesting that the ten moulds she had built while operating the factory were to be turned over to the Degenhart Museum. The remaining moulds were to be held by the Island Mould and Machine Company, who, complying with her request, removed the familiar 'D in heart' trademark.

The factory was eventually bought by Zack's son, Bernard Boyd. He also acquired the remaining Degenhart moulds, to which he added his own logo. When no condition is indicated, the items listed below are assumed to be in mint condition.

Baby Shoe Toothpick, Milk Blue 15.00
Basket Toothpick, Cobalt 15.00
Beaded Oval Toothpick, Amber 15.00
Beaded Oval Toothpick, Lemon Custard 25.00
Beaded Oval Toothpick, Milk Blue 20.00
Beaded Oval Toothpick, Pink 20.00
Bell, Amethyst 12.00
Bell, Bernard Boyd's Ebony 25.00
Bell, Canary 12.00
Bell, Persimmon 12.00
Bird Salt, Amberina 25.00
Bird Salt, Milk Blue 20.00
Bird Salt, Persimmon 25.00
Bow Slipper, Milk Blue 20.00
Buzz Saw Wine, Amberina 35.00
Buzz Saw Wine, Amethyst 15.00
Buzz Saw Wine, Carnival Cobalt 35.00
Buzz Saw Wine, Cobalt 40.00
Buzz Saw Wine, Crystal 15.00
Buzz Saw Wine, Emerald Green 25.00
Buzz Saw Wine, Honey Amber 15.00
Buzz Saw Wine, Opal 25.00

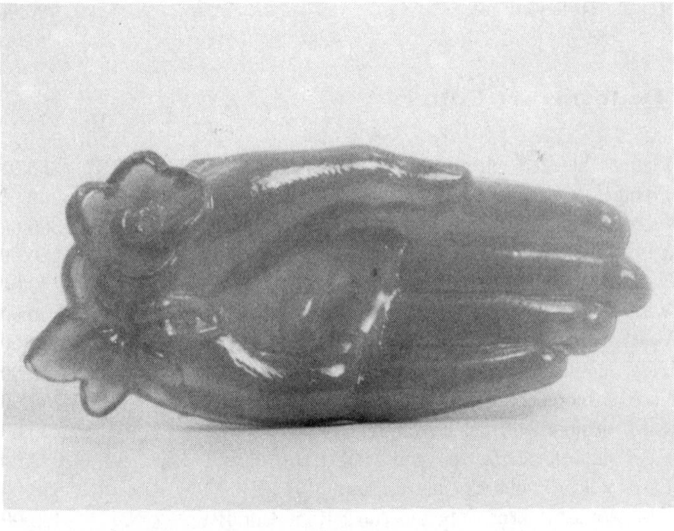

Hand, Tomato, signed on bottom, 5", $50.00.

Buzz Saw Wine, Pink 25.00
Buzz Saw Wine, Sapphire Blue 20.00
Buzz Saw Wine, Vaseline 20.00
Coaster, Amber 8.00
Coaster, Persimmon 8.00
Colonial Drape Toothpick, Crystal 15.00
Daisy & Button Salt, Amethyst 12.00
Daisy & Button Salt, Cobalt 20.00
Daisy & Button Salt, Crown Tuscan 25.00
Daisy & Button Salt, Milk Blue 15.00
Dog, April Green 15.00
Dog, Bittersweet 18.00
Dog, Bittersweet Slag 25.00
Dog, Blue Marble Slag 20.00
Dog, Buttercup 18.00
Dog, Buttercup Slag 18.00
Dog, Caramel Custard Slag 20.00
Dog, Caramel Slag 15.00
Dog, Charcoal 20.00
Dog, Daffodil 18.00
Dog, Ebony 18.00
Dog, Fantastic 30.00
Dog, Fawn 20.00
Dog, Green Marble 20.00
Dog, Gun Metal 20.00
Dog, Heatherbloom 20.00
Dog, Ivory Slag 22.00
Dog, Lite Toffee 20.00
Dog, Mauve #2 . . . . . 15.00
Dog, Periwinkle 15.00
Dog, Persimmon 60.00
Dog, Pink 20.00
Dog, Red 20.00
Dog, Smoky Blue 15.00
Dog, Toffee Slag 15.00
Dog, Tomato 25.00
Dog, Vaseline 15.00
Forget-Me-Not Toothpick, Amethyst 15.00
Forget-Me-Not Toothpick, Canary 15.00
Forget-Me-Not Toothpick, Cobalt 15.00
Forget-Me-Not Toothpick, Crown Tuscan 20.00
Forget-Me-Not Toothpick, Milk Blue 15.00
Forget-Me-Not Toothpick, Periwinkle 15.00
Forget-Me-Not Toothpick, Persimmon 15.00
Gypsy Pot Toothpick, Bluebird #2 . . . . . 25.00
Gypsy Pot Toothpick, Canary 20.00
Gypsy Pot Toothpick, Crown Tuscan 25.00
Gypsy Pot Toothpick, Crystal 15.00
Gypsy Pot Toothpick, Honey Amber 20.00
Gypsy Pot Toothpick, Milk Blue 25.00
Gypsy Pot Toothpick, Persimmon 20.00
Gypsy Pot Toothpick, Sapphire Blue 20.00
Hand, Canary 6.00
Hand, Honey Amber 6.00
Hand, Persimmon 8.00
Heart Toothpick, Amethyst 15.00
Heart Toothpick, Bernard Boyd's Ebony 35.00
Heart Toothpick, Milk Blue 20.00
Hen Covered Dish, Canary 25.00
High Boot, Crystal 15.00
Lamb Covered Dish, Vaseline 45.00
Mini-Pitcher, Sapphire Blue 15.00
Owl, Amberina 25.00
Owl, Amethyst 30.00

Owl, Antique Blue....35.00
Owl, Apple Green....15.00
Owl, Bittersweet....50.00
Owl, Bloody Mary....85.00
Owl, Blue & White Slag....50.00
Owl, Bluebird (dark)....50.00
Owl, Bluebird (light)....50.00
Owl, Canary....35.00
Owl, Caramel....75.00
Owl, Charcoal....40.00
Owl, Chartreuse....40.00
Owl, Cobalt....15.00
Owl, Crown Tuscan....40.00
Owl, Crystal....15.00
Owl, Custard....40.00
Owl, Dark Amber....35.00
Owl, Degenhart Green....15.00
Owl, Dickie Bird Opalescent....100.00
Owl, Dk Caramel....50.00
Owl, Elizabeth's Gift....15.00
Owl, Emerald Green....15.00
Owl, Forest Green....15.00
Owl, Frosty Jade....45.00
Owl, Heatherbloom....50.00
Owl, Heliotrope....75.00
Owl, Honey....20.00
Owl, Ivorene....35.00
Owl, Jade....35.00
Owl, January Blizzard....75.00
Owl, Lemon Chiffon....25.00
Owl, Lemon Opalescent....45.00
Owl, Lemonade....25.00
Owl, Mauve....35.00
Owl, Midnight Sun....25.00
Owl, Milk Blue....20.00
Owl, Misty Green....30.00
Owl, Mystery Surprise....125.00
Owl, Opal Variant....35.00
Owl, Pink Lady....30.00
Owl, Rose Marie....15.00
Owl, Sapphire....15.00
Owl, Seafoam....35.00
Owl, Shell....35.00
Owl, Smokey....40.00
Owl, Spicy Brown....35.00
Owl, Sunset....25.00
Owl, Tangerine....100.00
Owl, Tiger....40.00
Owl, Tomato....50.00
Owl, Vaseline....15.00
Owl, Wanda Blue....35.00
Owl, Wanda Blue Opalescent....35.00
Owl, Willow Blue....40.00
Portrait Plate, Crystal....35.00
Priscilla, Amber....75.00
Priscilla, Amethyst....85.00
Priscilla, April Green....100.00
Priscilla, Baby Green....95.00
Priscilla, Bittersweet Slag....125.00
Priscilla, Blue & White....180.00
Priscilla, Blue Lady....95.00
Priscilla, Crown Tuscan....100.00
Priscilla, Crystal....75.00
Priscilla, Daffodil....95.00
Priscilla, Degenhart Green....100.00
Priscilla, Delft....95.00
Priscilla, Ebony....100.00
Priscilla, End of Day....120.00
Priscilla, Fawn....85.00
Priscilla, Green Lavender Slag....100.00
Priscilla, Heather....100.00
Priscilla, Ice Blue Carnival....75.00
Priscilla, Ivory....85.00
Priscilla, Jade....100.00
Priscilla, Jade Green....100.00
Priscilla, Light Amethyst....85.00
Priscilla, Light Lavender....95.00
Priscilla, Milk Blue....65.00
Priscilla, Milk Blue Opalescent....95.00
Priscilla, Orchid....85.00
Priscilla, Orchid #2....125.00
Priscilla, Peach....75.00
Priscilla, Periwinkle....85.00
Priscilla, Powder Blue....100.00
Priscilla, Smokey....75.00
Priscilla, Smokey Blue....95.00
Priscilla, Snow White....75.00
Priscilla, Willow Blue....85.00
Star & Dewdrop Salt, Amethyst....15.00
Star & Dewdrop Salt, Opalescent....15.00
Star & Dewdrop Salt, Sapphire....15.00
Texas Boot, Amethyst....15.00
Texas Boot, Milk White....15.00
Wildflower Candy Dish, Pink....25.00
Wildflower Candy Dish, Twilight Blue....35.00

Delatte

Delatte was a manufacturer of French cameo glass. Founded in 1921, their style reflected the influence of the Art Deco era, with strong color contrasts and bold design.

When no condition is indicated, the items listed below are assumed to be in mint condition.

Cameo

Sweetmeat, fern/mushrooms, silver rim/hdl & lid, 2¼x4″....700.00
Vase, floral, wht w/blues, ped ft, EX work, 7″....750.00
Vase, floral/leaves, lav on bl, 8⅝″....675.00
Vase, magnolia, purple on gray mottle, bulbous, 13″....1,000.00
Vase, peacock in reserve, feathers, gold/bl/navy, 9″....850.00
Vase, trumpet flowers, maroon on gray, rnd body, 7″....550.00

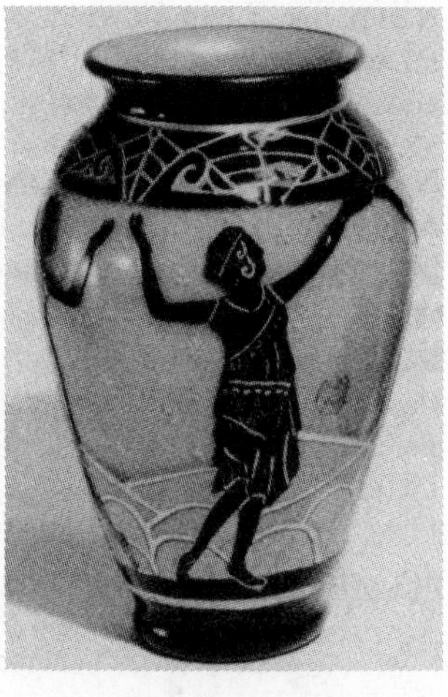

Vase, abstract landscape with dancing Grecian maidens, cameo with enameling, signed, ca 1925, 12″, $1,200.00.

Delft

Old Delftware, made as early as the 16th century, was originally a low-fired earthenware coated with a thin opaque tin glaze with painted-on polychrome designs. It was not until the last half of the 19th century, however, that the ware became commonly referred to as Delft, acquiring the name from the Dutch village that had become the major center of its production.

English potters also produced Delft, though with noticeable differences, both in shape and decorative theme.

In the early part of the 18th century, the German potter, Bottger, developed a formula for porcelain; in England, Wedgwood began producing creamware--both of which were much more durable. Unable to compete, one by one the Delft potteries failed. Soon, only one remained. In 1876, De Porcelyne Fles reintroduced Delftware on a hard white body with blue and white decorative themes reflecting the Dutch countryside, windmills by the sea, and Dutch children. This type continues to be produced and can be found today in nearly any gift shop.

When no condition is indicated, the items listed below are assumed to be in mint condition.

Parlor set, signed Germany, 3″ x 4″ sofa, 3″ side chair, and 3¼″ armchair, $375.00 for the set.

Bowl, floral, mc, sgn, late, 6x12¾″, EX 175.00
Butter tub, Dutch, harbor scenes, mc, mk VA, rpr, 4½″ 350.00
Candlestick, mc, ca 1790, 9″ 90.00
Candlestick, 3-color, ca 1850, 10″ 65.00
Charger, French, mc w/bl underglaze, 1700s, 13″ 300.00
Charger, London, geometrics, 2 shades of bl, 1700s, 14″ 175.00
Charger, mc florals, minor edge chips, 13″ 225.00
Charger, Rembrandt portrait, Thooft/Labouchere, 16″ 180.00
Charger, tavern scene, sgn, Dutch, very early, 24″ 750.00
Funnel, bl/wht, 20th C 85.00
Inkwell, windmills & boats, bl/wht, sq, 2¾″ 65.00
Measuring cups, bl/wht, 20th C, set 95.00
Mug, Holland, floral w/windmill/house in reserve, 4¾″ 14.00
Pastille burner, castle w/sign: Inde Rokende Moor, 5¼″ 200.00
Plaque, WWII Peace 125.00
Plate, bianca sopra border, Oriental decor, lt bl, 9″, EX 230.00
Plate, bird motif, mc, edge wear, 9″ 155.00
Plate, Bristol, Chinese figure in pagoda, scalloped, 12″ 400.00
Plate, circles & petals, 'worm' bands, dk bl, 18th C, 7″ 225.00
Plate, Dutch, bird center, mc, no ft rim, ca 1670, 8½″ 325.00
Plate, Dutch, bird center, 3-color, no foot rim, 8½″ 325.00
Plate, English, floral w/floral border, bl, 1700s, 10″ 285.00
Tile, animals/birds/trees/flowers, 4-color, late, 5½x11″ 25.00
Vase, Holland, stylized bl/wht floral, bulbous, sgn SP, 8″ 95.00
Vase, pagodas, gold trim, fluted, 1875, 13″ 150.00

Depression Glass

Other than coins and stamps, colored glassware produced during the Depression era is probably the most sought-after collectible in the field today. There are literally thousands of collectors in the United States and Canada buying, selling, and trading 'Depression Glass' on today's market.

Depression Glass is defined by Gene Florence, author of several best-selling books on the subject, as 'the inexpensive glassware made primarily during the Depression era in the colors of amber, green, pink, blue, red, yellow, white, and crystal.' This glass was mass produced and sold through five-and-dime stores and mail-order catalogs, and given away as premiums with gas and food products.

The listings in this book are far from being complete. If you want a more thorough presentation of this fascinating glassware, we recommend *The Collector's Encyclopedia of Depression Glass* by Gene Florence, whose address is listed in the Directory under Kentucky. This beautiful full-color volume contains thousands of descriptions and prices. It is available at your favorite bookstore or public library.

When no condition is indicated, the items listed below are assumed to be in mint condition.

Adam, Jeannette Glass Co., 1932-1934

Bowl, dessert; green, 4¾″ 9.50
Bowl, pink, 7¾″ 14.00
Butter dish, pink 70.00
Candlesticks, pink, 4″, pr 52.50
Coaster, pink, 3¾″ 14.50
Creamer, green 13.00
Pitcher, green, 32-oz, 8″ 32.50

Plate, grill; pink, 9″ 11.50
Plate, sherbet; green, 6″ 4.00
Shakers, green, 4″, pr 72.50
Sugar bowl, pink 10.00
Tumbler, pink, 4½″ 17.50
Vase, green, 7½″ 32.50

American Pioneer, Liberty Works, 1931-1934

Bowl, green, hdl, 5″ 10.00
Bowl, pink, hdl, 9″ 12.00
Coaster, pink, 3½″ 13.50
Creamer, pink, 3½″ 15.00
Cup, green 8.00
Goblet, water; green, 8-oz, 6″ 27.50
Pitcher, covered urn, green, 7″ 160.00
Plate, pink, 6″ 4.00
Sherbet, pink, 4¾″ 15.00
Sugar bowl, pink, 2¾″ 14.00
Tumbler, green, 12-oz, 5″ 30.00

American Sweetheart, Macbeth Evans, 1930-1934

Bowl, vegetable; oval, pink, 11″ 30.00
Pitcher, pink, 80-oz, 8″ 350.00
Plate, salad; monax, 8″ 6.00
Plate, salver; pink, 12″ 9.50
Saucer, pink 2.50

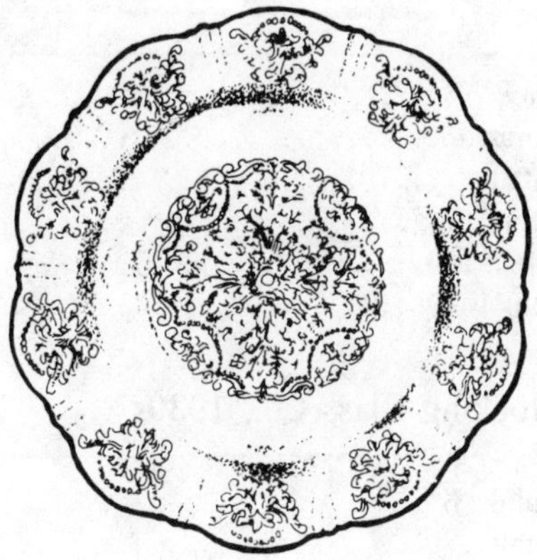

Sherbet, footed, monax, 4¼″ 13.50
Sugar bowl, open; footed, monax 6.50
Sugar cover, monax 145.00
Tumbler, pink, 5-oz, 3½″ 32.50

Anniversary, Jeannette Glass Company, 1947-1949

Bowl, fruit; crystal, 9″ 7.00
Butter dish, crystal 22.50
Cake plate, pink, 12½″ 8.50

Creamer, footed, pink 6.50
Pickle dish, crystal, 9″ 3.50
Plate, sherbet; crystal, 6¼″ 1.25
Sugar bowl, open; crystal 2.00
Sugar cover, crystal 3.00
Vase, crystal, 6½″ 6.00
Wine glass, pink, 2½-oz 9.00

Aunt Polly, U.S. Glass Co., Late 1920s

Bowl, oval, blue, 8⅜″ 30.00
Butter dish, green 200.00
Creamer, blue 25.00
Plate, sherbet; green, 6″ 3.00
Sherbet, green 7.50
Tumbler, blue, 8-oz, 3⅝″ 13.50
Vase, footed, green, 6½″ 22.50

Avocado "Sweet Pear," No. 601, Indiana Glass Co., 1923-1933

Bowl, preserve; 1-hdl, green, 7″ 15.00
Bowl, 2-hdl, pink, 5¼″ 20.00
Creamer, footed, pink 27.50

Cup, footed, green 28.00
Plate, luncheon; pink, 8¼″ 12.50
Saucer, pink 20.00
Sugar bowl, open; footed, green 29.00
Tumbler, pink 72.50

Beaded Block, Imperial Glass Co., 1927-1930s

Bowl, jelly; 2-hdl, green, 4½″ 5.50
Bowl, round, flared, opalescent, 7¼″ 14.50
Bowl, round, green, 6¼″ 6.50

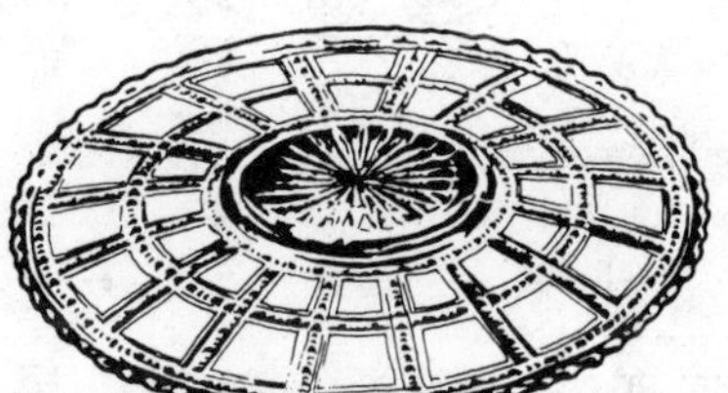

Bowl, square, opalescent, 5½″ 7.50
Creamer, opalescent 16.50
Pitcher, pint jug; green, 5¼″ 100.00
Plate, round, opalescent, 8¾″ 10.00
Plate, square, green, 7¾″ 5.00
Sugar bowl, open; green 9.50
Vase, opalescent, 6″ 16.00

"Bubble," "Bullseye," "Provincial," Anchor Hocking Glass Co., 1934-1965

Bowl, berry; blue, 4″ 8.50
Bowl, cereal; crystal, 5¼″ 3.00

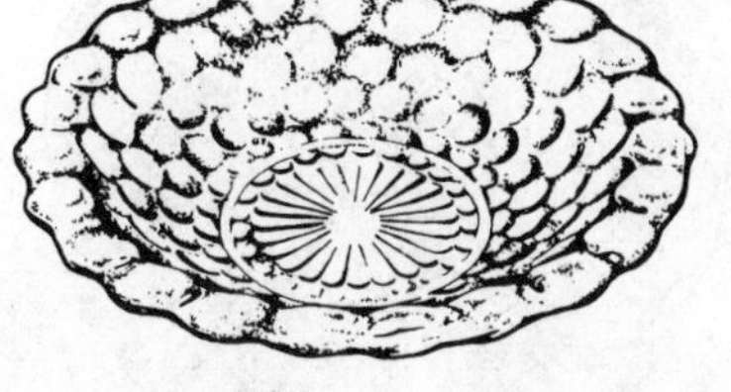

Bowl, fruit; blue, 4½″ 6.00
Cup, blue 3.00

Plate, dinner; crystal, 9⅜" 3.00
Platter, oval, blue, 12" 9.00
Sugar bowl, open; blue 12.50
Tumbler, iced tea; blue, 12-oz 8.50
Tumbler, juice; blue, 6-oz 6.00

Cameo, "Ballerina" or "Dancing Girl," Hocking Glass Co., 1930-1934

Bowl, cream soup; green, 4¾" 45.00
Bowl, soup; rimmed, green, 9" 32.50
Cake plate, 3-legs, green, 10" 14.00
Candy jar, green, 6½" tall, w/lid 92.50
Compote, mayonnaise; green, 4" wide 21.50
Decanter, green, 10", w/stopper 90.00
Goblet, wine; green, 3½" 147.50
Pitcher, syrup or milk; 20-oz, 5¾" 137.50
Plate, grill; yellow, 10½" 6.00
Plate, sandwich; green, 10" 9.50

Platter, closed hdl, green, 12" 14.50
Saucer, green, w/cup ring 87.50
Shakers, footed, green, pr 50.00
Sherbet, yellow, 3⅛" 19.50
Sugar bowl, open; green, 4¼" 17.50
Tumbler, flat, yellow, 11-oz, 5" 27.50
Tumbler, juice; footed, green, 3-oz 45.00
Tumbler, water; green, 9-oz, 4" 19.00
Vase, green, 5¾" 95.00

Cherry Blossom, Jeannette Glass Co., 1930-1939

Bowl, berry; green, 4¾" 12.50
Bowl, cereal; pink, 5¾" 22.00
Butter dish, pink 65.00
Coaster, green 10.00
Mug, pink, 7-oz 155.00

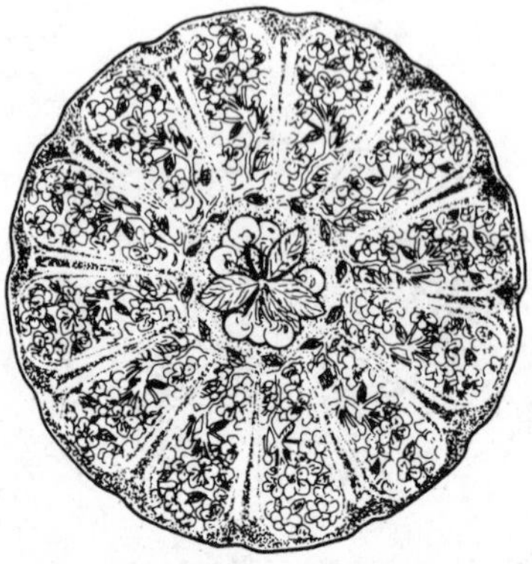

Pitcher, pattern at the top, flat, 42-oz, 8" 35.00
Plate, salad; green, 7" 15.00
Platter, oval, green, 11" 25.00
Shakers, scalloped bottom, green, pr 750.00
Tumbler, allover pattern, round foot, green, 9-oz, 4½" 28.00
Tumbler, pattern at the top, flat, pink, 12-oz, 5" 31.50

Chinex Classic, Macbeth-Evans, Late 1930s-Early 1940s

Bowl, cereal; ivory, 5¾" 3.50
Butter dish, decorated 60.00
Creamer, decorated 7.00
Plate, sherbet; ivory, 6¼" 2.00
Sherbet, low footed, ivory 6.50
Sugar bowl, open; ivory 4.00

Circle, Hocking Glass Co., 1930s

Bowl, green or pink, 8" 5.50
Cup, green or pink 2.00
Decanter, hdl, green or pink 20.00
Goblet, water; green or pink, 8-oz 6.50
Plate, sherbet; green or pink, 6" 2.00
Sherbet, green or pink, 3⅛" 3.50
Sugar bowl, green or pink 4.50
Tumbler, juice; green or pink, 4-oz 3.50
Vase, hat shape, green or pink 17.50

Cloverleaf, Hazel Atlas Glass Co., 1930-1936

Bowl, cereal; yellow, 5" 20.00
Bowl, salad; yellow, 7" 35.00
Candy dish, green, w/lid 37.50
Creamer, footed, yellow, 3⅝" 12.50
Plate, sherbet; green, 6" 3.50

Shakers, yellow, pr 80.00
Sugar, footed, yellow, 3⅝" 10.00
Tumbler, flat, 10-oz, 3¾" 30.00

Colonial, "Knife and Fork," Hocking Glass Co., 1934-1936

Bowl, cereal; green, 5½" 39.50
Bowl, low soup; pink, 7" 27.50
Butter dish, green 45.00
Goblet, cocktail, green, 3-oz, 4" 20.00
Goblet, wine; green, 2½-oz, 4½" 20.00
Mug, pink, 12-oz, 4½" 150.00

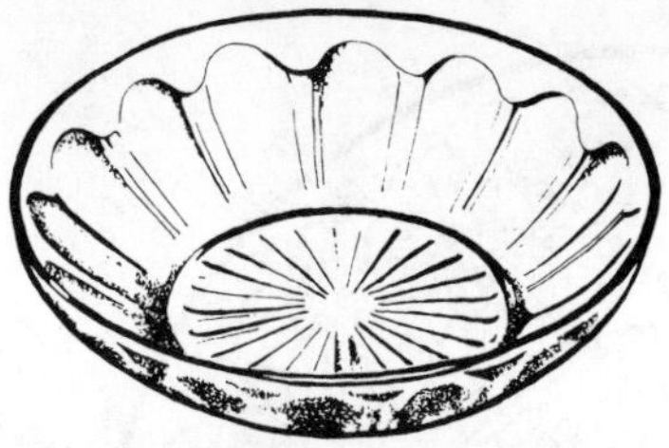

Pitcher, ice lip or no ice lip, pink, 54-oz, 7″ 150.00
Platter, oval, pink, 12″ 13.50
Sherbet, pink 6.00
Tumbler, footed, pink, 3-oz, 3¼″ 10.00
Tumbler, green, 10-oz 20.00

Colonial Fluted, "Rope," Federal Glass Co., 1928-1933

Bowl, cereal; green, 6″ 5.00
Bowl, salad; deep, green, 6½″ 10.00
Cup, green 3.50
Plate, luncheon; green, 8″ 3.00
Sherbet, green 4.50
Sugar bowl, open; green 3.50
Sugar cover, green 7.50

Columbia, Federal Glass Co., 1938-1942

Bowl, cereal; crystal, 5″ 8.00
Bowl, soup; low, crystal, 8″ 9.00
Butter dish, crystal 15.50

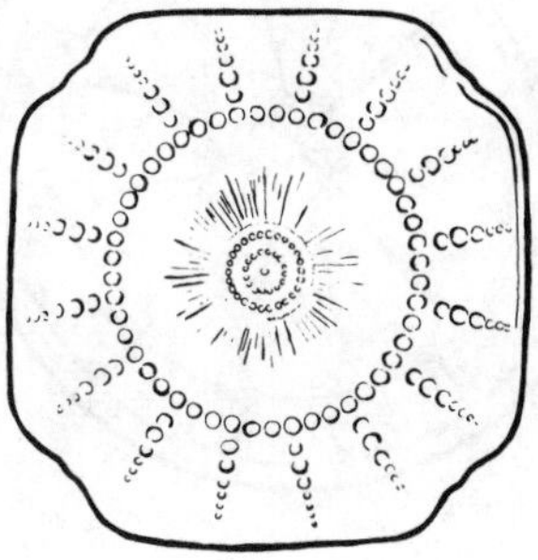

Cup, pink 8.00
Plate, bread & butter; pink, 6″ 4.00
Saucer, pink 5.00
Tumbler, crystal 8.00

Coronation, "Banded Rib," "Saxon," Hocking Glass Co., 1936-1940

Bowl, nappy; red, 6½″ 6.50
Cup, red 4.50
Pitcher, pink, 68-oz, 7¾″ 135.00
Plate, sherbet; pink, 6″ 1.50
Sherbet, pink 3.50
Tumbler, footed, pink, 10-oz, 5″ 8.50

Cube, "Cubist," Jeannette Glass Co., 1929-1933

Bowl, deep, pink, 4½″ 4.50
Bowl, dessert; pink, 4½″ 4.00
Butter dish, green 50.00
Coaster, pink, 3¼″ 3.50
Creamer, green, 3″ 6.00
Plate, luncheon, green, 8″ 4.50

Sherbet, footed, green 6.00
Sugar bowl, pink, 3″ 3.50
Tumbler, pink, 9-oz, 4″ 22.00

"Cupid," Paden City Glass Co., 1930s

Bowl, center hdl, green or pink, 9¼″ 35.00
Bowl, fruit; footed, green or pink, 9¼″ 30.00
Cake plate, green or pink, 11¾″ 37.50
Candy, 3-part, green or pink, w/lid 47.50

Creamer, footed, green or pink, 4½″ 25.00
Ice bucket, green or pink 50.00
Plate, green or pink, 10½″ 22.50
Tray, oval, footed, green or pink, 10⅞″ 40.00
Vase, elliptical, green or pink, 8¼″ 67.50

"Daisy," No. 620, Indiana Glass Co., crystal, 1933; amber, 1940; green & milk, 1960-80s

Bowl, berry; amber, 4½″ 6.50
Bowl, vegetable; oval, crystal, 10″ 5.50
Plate, dinner; crystal, 9⅜″ 3.00

Plate, luncheon; amber, 8⅜″ 5.50
Plate, sherbet; amber, 6″ 2.00
Platter, amber, 10¾″ 9.50
Relish dish, 3-part, amber, 8⅜″ 15.00
Sugar bowl, open; footed, crystal 4.00
Tumbler, footed, amber, 12-oz 30.00

Diamond Quilted, "Flat Diamond,"
Imperial Glass Co., Late 1920s-Early 1930s

Bowl, cereal; blue, 5″ 7.50
Bowl, 1-hdl, green, 5½″ 5.50
Candlesticks, green, pr 8.50
Creamer, green 5.50
Goblet, champagne; green, 9-oz, 6″ 7.50
Goblet, wine; green, 2-oz 5.00

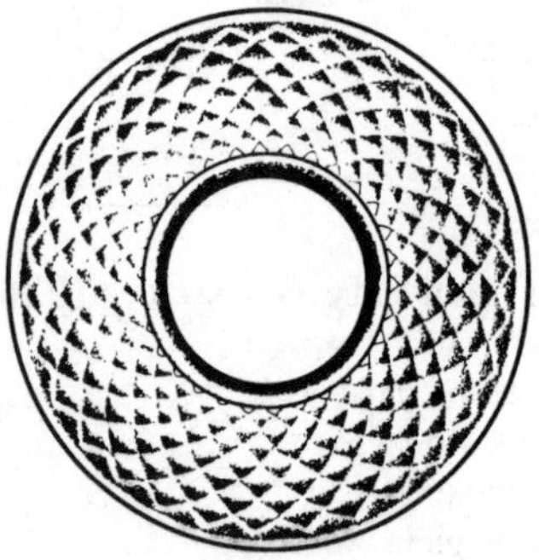

Mayonnaise set, ladle, plate, 3-footed dish, green 25.00
Plate, salad; blue, 7″ 5.50
Plate, sherbet; green, 6″ 2.00
Sandwich server, center hdl, green 17.50
Tumbler, footed, green, 6-oz 5.00
Tumbler, footed, green, 9-oz 8.50
Whiskey, green, 1½-oz 6.00

Diana, Federal Glass Co., 1937-1941

Ash tray, pink, 3½″ 3.00
Bowl, cereal; amber, 5″ 3.50
Bowl, salad; pink, 9″ 6.50
Cup, amber 4.00
Plate, bread & butter; pink, 6″ 1.50

Plate, sandwich; amber, 11¾″ 6.00
Platter, oval, pink, 12″ 6.50
Shakers, amber, pr 62.50
Tumbler, pink, 9-oz, 4⅛″ 10.00

Dogwood, "Apple Blossom," "Wild Rose," Macbeth Evans, 1929-1932

Bowl, fruit; green, 10¼″ 100.00
Cake plate, heavy, solid foot, green, 13″ 55.00
Creamer, thin, pink, 2½″ 12.00
Pitcher, decorated, green, 80-oz, 8″ 450.00

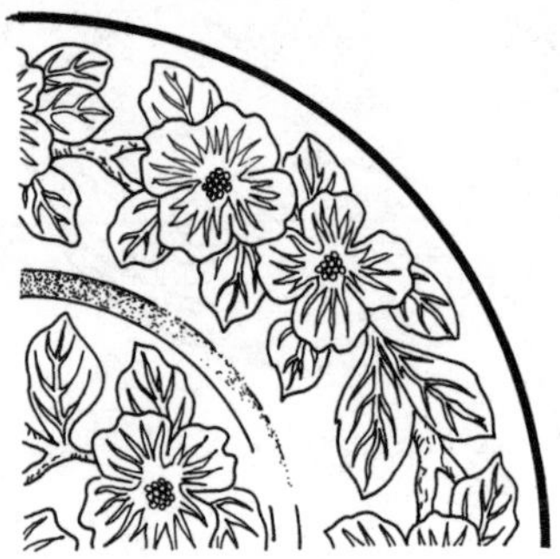

Plate, dinner; pink, 9¼″ 18.00
Plate, luncheon; pink, 8″ 4.75
Sugar bowl, open; thin, green, 2½″ 37.50
Tumbler, decorated, pink, 11-oz, 4¾″ 30.00
Tumbler, decorated, pink, 5-oz, 3½″ 125.00

Doric, Jeannette Glass Co., 1935-1938

Bowl, berry; pink, 8¼″ 9.50
Bowl, cream soup; green, 5″ 130.00
Bowl, 2-hdl, pink, 9″ 9.50
Butter dish, green 67.50
Candy dish, pink, 8″, w/lid 25.00
Coaster, pink, 3″ 10.00
Pitcher, footed, green, 48-oz, 7½″ 600.00
Plate, dinner; pink, 9″ 7.50

Shakers, green, pr 27.50
Tray, serving; pink, 8x8″ 7.50
Tumbler, flat, pink, 9-oz, 4½″ 30.00
Tumbler, footed, green, 12-oz, 5″ 45.00

Doric & Pansy, Jeannette Glass Co., 1937-1938

Bowl, berry; ultramarine, 4½″ 9.50
Bowl, hdl, ultramarine, 9″ 27.50

Creamer, ultramarine....167.50
Plate, dinner; ultramarine, 9″....18.00
Shakers, ultramarine, pr....400.00
Tumbler, ultramarine, 9-oz, 4½″....35.00

English Hobnail, Westmoreland Glass Co., 1920s-1970s

Bowl, footed, 2-hdl, green or pink, 8″....40.00
Bowl, relish; oval, green or pink, 12″....16.50
Candlesticks, green or pink, 8½″, pr....45.00
Candy dish, cone shaped, green or pink, ½-lb....45.00
Celery dish, green or pink, 12″....20.00
Cigarette box, green or pink....22.50
Cologne bottle, green or pink....25.00
Cup, green or pink....12.00
Egg cup, green or pink....32.50
Goblet, cocktail; green or pink, 3-oz....15.00
Grapefruit, flange rim, green or pink, 6½″....14.00
Lamp, electric, green or pink, 6¼″....60.00
Pitcher, green or pink, 60-oz....175.00
Plate, dinner; green or pink, 10″....20.00
Tumbler, footed, green or pink, 7-oz....13.50
Tumbler, footed, green or pink, 9-oz....15.00
Whiskey, green or pink, 1½-oz & 3-oz....20.00

Fire-King Dinnerware, "Philbe," Hocking Glass Co., 1937-1938

Bowl, vegetable; oval, all colors, 10″....37.50
Goblet, thin, all colors, 9-oz, 7¼″....125.00
Plate, grill; all colors, 10½″....25.00
Plate, luncheon; all colors, 8″....25.00
Plate, sandwich; heavy, all colors, 10″....27.50
Tumbler, footed, all colors, 10-oz, 5¼″....37.50
Tumbler, water; flat, all colors, 9-oz, 4″....100.00

Fire-King Oven Glass, Anchor Hocking Glass Corporation, 1941-1950s

Baker, blue, 1½-qt....8.50
Baker, round or square, blue, 1-pt....3.00
Casserole, knob hdl lid, blue, 1½-qt....12.50
Casserole, pie plate lid, blue, 2-qt....18.00
Custard cup, blue, 5-oz....2.50
Nurser, blue, 8-oz....15.00
Percolator top, blue, 2⅛″....3.50
Pie plate, blue, 8⅜″....7.00
Pie plate, deep dish, blue, 5⅜″....7.00
Roaster, blue, 10⅜″....42.50
Utility bowl, blue, 8⅜″....9.00

Floragold, "Louisa," Jeannette Glass Co., 1950s

Bowl, fruit; ruffled, iridescent, 5½″....3.50
Bowl, square, iridescent, 4½″....4.25
Butter dish, oblong, iridescent, ¼-lb....17.50
Creamer, iridescent....6.00
Cup, iridescent....4.50
Plate, sherbet; iridescent, 5¾″....6.00
Shakers, plastic tops, iridescent, pr....35.00
Sherbet, low footed, iridescent....8.00

Sugar bowl, open; iridescent....5.00
Tumbler, footed, iridescent, 10-oz....11.50
Vase, iridescent....87.50

Floral, "Poinsettia," Jeannette Glass Co., 1931-1935

Bowl, cream soup; green, 5½″....250.00
Bowl, vegetable; pink, w/lid, 8″....25.00
Butter dish, green....72.50
Candy jar, pink, w/lid....27.50
Compote, pink, 9″....300.00
Pitcher, flat, green, 23-oz or 24-oz, 5½″....500.00
Plate, salad; green, 8″....7.50
Plate, sherbet; pink, 6″....3.50
Platter, oval, pink, 10¾″....11.00

Relish dish, oval, 2-part, pink....10.00
Saucer, pink....6.00
Tumbler, juice; footed, 5-oz, 4″....12.00
Tumbler, lemonade; footed, green, 9-oz, 5¼″....30.00
Vase, 8-sided, green, 6⅞″....450.00

Floral and Diamond Band, U.S. Glass Co., Late 1920s

Bowl, nappy; hdl, green, 5¾″....7.00

Plate, luncheon; pink, 8″ 12.00
Sugar bowl, open; pink, 5¼″ 7.50
Sugar cover, pink 25.00
Tumbler, iced tea; green, 5″ 17.50

Florentine No. 1, "Old Florentine," "Poppy No. 1," Hazel Atlas Glass Co., 1932-1935

Ash tray, yellow, 5½″ 25.00
Bowl, cereal; green, 6″ 13.00
Creamer, green 7.50

Pitcher, flat, ice lip or none, green, 54-oz, 7½″ 40.00
Plate, dinner; yellow, 10″ 13.00
Plate, salad; green, 8½″ 5.00
Saucer, yellow 3.50
Shakers, footed, yellow, pr 42.50
Sugar bowl, open; yellow 9.50
Sugar cover, yellow 14.00
Tumbler, iced tea; footed, green, 12-oz, 5¼″ 16.00

Florentine No. 2, "Poppy No. 2," Hazel Atlas Glass Co., 1934-1937

Bowl, berry; large, green, 8″ 15.00
Bowl, green, 5¼″ 20.00
Butter dish, yellow 125.00
Coaster, yellow, 3¾″ 22.50
Cup, green 6.00
Pitcher, yellow, 54-oz, 7½″ 142.50
Plate, sherbet; yellow, 6″ 3.50
Platter, for gravy boat, yellow, 11½″ 32.50
Shakers, yellow, pr 40.00
Sherbet, footed, green 7.00
Sugar bowl, open; green 6.50
Sugar cover, green 10.00
Tumbler, footed, green, 9-oz, 4½″ 15.00
Tumbler, footed, yellow, 5-oz, 4″ 11.00
Vase, yellow, 6″ 55.00

Forest Green, Anchor Hocking Glass Co. Corporation, 1950-1957

Ash tray, green 3.00
Bowl, dessert; green, 4¾″ 6.00
Bowl, salad; green, 7⅜″ 6.50
Creamer, flat, green 4.50
Pitcher, round, green, 3-qt 17.50
Plate, luncheon; green, 8⅜″ 4.00
Platter, rectangular, green 10.00
Saucer, green 1.00
Tumbler, green, 10-oz 4.00

Fortune, Hocking Glass Co., 1937-1938

Bowl, dessert; pink, 4½″ 3.50
Bowl, hdl, pink, 4½″ 3.50
Candy dish, flat, pink, w/lid 14.00

Plate, sherbet; pink, 6″ 2.00
Saucer, pink 2.00
Tumbler, juice; pink, 5-oz, 3½″ 3.50

"Fruits," Hazel Atlas and other glass companies, 1931-1933

Bowl, berry; green or pink, 8″ 32.50
Saucer, green or pink 2.00
Sherbet, green or pink 7.00
Tumbler, combination of fruits, green or pink, 4″ 8.50
Tumbler, 1 fruit, green or pink, 4″ 7.50

Georgian, "Lovebirds," Federal Glass Co., 1931-1936

Bowl, berry; green, 4½″ 5.00
Bowl, vegetable; oval, green, 9″ 47.50
Creamer, footed, green, 3″ 8.50
Hot plate, center design, green, 5″ 32.50
Plate, luncheon; green, 8″ 6.25
Saucer, green 3.00
Sugar bowl, open; footed, green, 3″ 10.00
Sugar cover, green, 3″ 20.00
Tumbler, flat, green, 12-oz, 5¼″ 62.50

Harp, Jeannette Glass Co., 1954-1957

Ash tray, crystal 3.50
Cake stand, crystal, 9″ 16.50
Coaster, crystal 2.00
Plate, crystal, 7″ 4.00
Tray, rectangular, crystal 20.00

Heritage, Federal Glass Co., Late 1930s-1960s

Bowl, berry; crystal, 5″ 4.50
Creamer, footed, crystal 11.50
Cup, crystal 3.50
Plate, luncheon; crystal, 8″ 5.00
Plate, sandwich; crystal, 12″ 8.50
Saucer, crystal 2.00

Hex Optic, "Honeycomb," Jeannette Glass Co., 1928-1932

Bowl, berry; ruffled, green or pink, 4¼″ 2.50
Bucket reamer, green or pink 37.50
Pitcher, footed, green or pink, 48-oz, 9″ 27.50
Platter, round, green or pink, 11″ 5.00

Refrigerator dish, green or pink, 4x4″ 7.00
Saucer, green or pink 1.50
Shakers, green or pink, pr 17.50
Tumbler, footed, green or pink, 7″ 5.50
Tumbler, green or pink, 9-oz, 3¾″ 3.50

Hobnail, Hocking Glass Co., 1934-1936

Bowl, cereal; crystal, 5½″ 2.50
Goblet, iced tea; crystal, 13-oz 5.00
Pitcher, crystal, 67-oz 20.00
Plate, sherbet; crystal, 6″ 1.00
Sherbet, crystal 2.00

Sugar bowl, footed, crystal 2.50
Tumbler, juice; crystal, 5-oz 3.00
Tumbler, wine; footed, 3-oz 5.00

Holiday, "Buttons and Bows," Jeannette Glass Co., 1947-1949

Bowl, console; pink, 10¾″ 67.50
Bowl, soup; pink, 7¾″ 27.50
Candlesticks, pink, 3″, pr 50.00
Pitcher, milk; pink, 16-oz, 4¾″ 40.00
Plate, dinner; pink, 9″ 9.50
Sandwich tray, pink, 10½″ 9.00
Sherbet, pink 5.00
Sugar bowl, open; pink 5.00
Sugar cover, pink 7.50
Tumbler, footed, pink, 6″ 60.00

Homespun, "Fine Rib," Jeannette Glass Co., 1939-1940

Bowl, cereal; crystal or pink, 5″ 7.50
Butter dish, crystal or pink 42.50
Plate, dinner; crystal or pink, 9¼″ 8.50
Saucer, crystal or pink 2.00
Sherbet, low, flat, crystal or pink 6.00
Tumbler, footed, crystal or pink, 5-oz, 4″ 7.00
Tumbler, water; crystal or pink, 9-oz, 4″ 7.00

Indiana Custard, "Flower and Leaf Band," Indiana Glass Co., 1930s & 1950s

Bowl, soup; flat, ivory, 7½″ 16.50
Bowl, vegetable; oval, ivory, 9½″ 20.00
Plate, bread & butter; ivory, 5¾″ 4.50
Plate, dinner; ivory, 9¾″ 13.50

Platter, oval, ivory, 11½″ 22.50
Sherbet, ivory 67.50
Sugar bowl, open; ivory 8.50
Sugar cover, ivory 15.00

Iris, "Iris and Herringbone," Jeannette Glass Co., 1928-1932, 1950s, 1970s

Bowl, cereal; crystal, 5″ 30.00
Bowl, fruit; crystal, 11″ 30.00
Candlesticks, crystal, pr 17.50
Coaster, crystal 32.00
Cup, demitasse, iridescent 50.00
Goblet, crystal, 4-oz, 5¾″ 15.00
Goblet, wine; crystal, 4½″ 13.00

Pitcher, footed, iridescent, 9½″ 26.50
Plate, luncheon; crystal, 8″ 32.50
Plate, sandwich; crystal, 11¾″ 12.00
Sherbet, footed, crystal, 4″ 11.00
Sugar bowl, open; iridescent 6.50
Sugar cover, iridescent 7.00
Tumbler, footed, crystal, 7″ 15.00
Vase, iridescent, 9″ 14.00

Jubilee, Lancaster Glass Co., Early 1930s

Bowl, fruit; hdl, topaz, 9″ 32.50
Cheese & cracker set, topaz 35.00

Goblet, topaz, 10-oz, 6″ 22.50
Mayonnaise, plate, ladle, topaz 85.00
Plate, salad; topaz, 7″ 6.50
Saucer, topaz 3.50
Tray, sandwich; center hdl, topaz 29.50

Lace Edge, "Open Lace," Hocking Glass Co., 1935-1938

Bowl, cereal; pink, 6⅜″ 12.50
Bowl, 3-leg, pink, 10½″ 127.50
Candlesticks, pink, pr 127.50
Compote, pink, 7″ 15.00

Flower bowl, crystal frog, pink 17.50
Plate, grill; pink, 10½″ 11.50
Plate, salad; pink, 7¼″ 12.50
Platter, 5-part, pink, 12¾″ 17.50
Relish dish, 3-part, pink, 7½″ deep 40.00
Sherbet, footed, pink 47.50
Tumbler, footed, pink, 10½-oz, 5″ 40.00
Vase, pink, 7″ 225.00

Lake Como, Hocking Glass Co., 1934-1937

Bowl, berry; white w/blue scene 5.00
Bowl, soup; flat, white w/blue scene 12.50
Creamer, footed, white w/blue scene 8.50
Plate, dinner; white w/blue scene, 9¼″ 10.00
Plate, salad; white w/blue scene, 7¼″ 5.00
Platter, white w/blue scene, 11″ 17.50
Shakers, white w/blue scene, pr 25.00

Laurel, McKee Glass Co., 1930s

Bowl, cereal; ivory, 6″ 4.50
Bowl, 3-leg, green, 10½″ 25.00
Cheese dish, green, w/lid 40.00
Creamer, tall, ivory 8.50
Plate, grill; ivory, 9⅛″ 6.00
Platter, oval, ivory, 10¾″ 16.50
Sherbet, ivory 9.50
Tumbler, flat, ivory, 12-oz, 5″ 27.50

Lincoln Inn, Fenton Glass Co., Late 1920s

Ash tray, red or blue, ... 10.00
Bowl, cereal; red or blue, 6″ 7.50
Bowl, finger; red or blue 10.00

Cup, red or blue 10.00
Goblet, water; colors other than red or blue 11.00
Nut dish, footed, colors other than red or blue 6.50
Plate, red or blue, 12″ 14.50
Plate, red or blue, 8″ 6.50
Tumbler, footed, colors other than red or blue, 9-oz 9.50

Lorain, "Basket," No. 615, Indiana Glass Co.

Bowl, cereal; green, 6″ 25.00
Bowl, vegetable; oval, yellow, 9¾″ 37.50
Cup, yellow 11.00

Plate, luncheon; green, 8⅜″ ... 13.00
Plate, salad; yellow, 7¾″ ... 11.00
Plate, sherbet; green, 5½″ ... 4.00
Platter, yellow, 11½″ ... 29.00
Relish, 4-part, green, 8″ ... 13.50
Sherbet, footed, green ... 13.50
Tumbler, footed, green, 9-oz, 4¾″ ... 13.50

Manhattan, "Horizontal Ribbed," Anchor Hocking Glass Co., 1938-1941

Bowl, berry; hdl, crystal, 5⅜″ ... 5.50
Bowl, salad; crystal, 9″ ... 9.50
Bowl, sauce; pink, 4½″ ... 6.00
Candy dish, 3-leg, pink ... 6.50
Creamer, oval, crystal ... 4.00
Plate, dinner; crystal, 10¼″ ... 7.50
Relish tray, 4-part, crystal, 14″ ... 10.00
Sherbet, pink ... 6.00
Vase, crystal, 8″ ... 8.50

Mayfair, Federal Glass Co., 1934

Bowl, cereal; amber, 6″ ... 12.00
Bowl, sauce; green, 5″ ... 6.00
Creamer, footed, green ... 8.50

Cup, green ... 6.50
Plate, salad; green, 6¾″ ... 5.50
Platter, oval, green, 12″ ... 4.50
Saucer, green ... 2.50
Tumbler, amber, 9-oz, 4½″ ... 11.50

Mayfair, "Open Rose," Hocking Glass Co., 1931-1937

Bowl, fruit; scalloped, deep, pink, 12″ ... 38.00
Bowl, vegetable; pink, 7″ ... 17.50
Cake plate, footed, blue, 10″ ... 40.00
Goblet, water; pink, 9-oz, 5¾″ ... 40.00
Pitcher, blue, 60-oz, 8″ ... 97.50
Plate, dinner; pink, 9½″ ... 39.50
Plate, grill; blue, 9½″ ... 24.00
Platter, oval, open hdl, blue, 12″ ... 35.00
Sugar bowl, open; footed, pink ... 15.00
Sugar cover, pink ... 850.00
Tumbler, iced tea; pink, 13½-oz, 5¼″ ... 30.00
Tumbler, juice; blue, 5-oz, 3½″ ... 72.50
Whiskey, pink, 1½-oz, 2¼″ ... 57.50

Miss America, Diamond Pattern, Hocking Glass Co., 1935-1937

Bowl, vegetable; oval, crystal, 10″ ... 10.00
Candy jar, pink, 11½″, w/lid ... 97.50
Goblet, water; pink, 10-oz, 5½″ ... 35.00

Plate, grill; pink, 10¼″ ... 13.00
Plate, sherbet; crystal, 5¾″ ... 3.00
Relish, 4-part, pink, 8¾″ ... 13.50
Tumbler, iced tea; pink, 14-oz, 6¾″ ... 47.50
Tumbler, juice; crystal, 5-oz, 4″ ... 12.50

Moondrops, New Martinsville, 1932-40

Bowl, berry; red or blue, 5¼″ ... 6.00
Bowl, divided relish, 3-footed, red or blue, 8½″ ... 12.50
Bowl, console; round, 3-footed, red or blue, 12″ ... 35.00
Candlesticks, triple light, red or blue, 5¼″, pr ... 65.00
Candy dish, ruffled, colors other than red or blue, 8″ ... 12.50
Compote, colors other than red or blue, 4″ ... 7.50
Decanter, large, red or blue, 11¼″ ... 70.00
Goblet, liquor; red or blue, ¾-oz, 2⅞″ ... 25.00
Goblet, wine; metal stem, red or blue, 5⅛″ ... 12.00

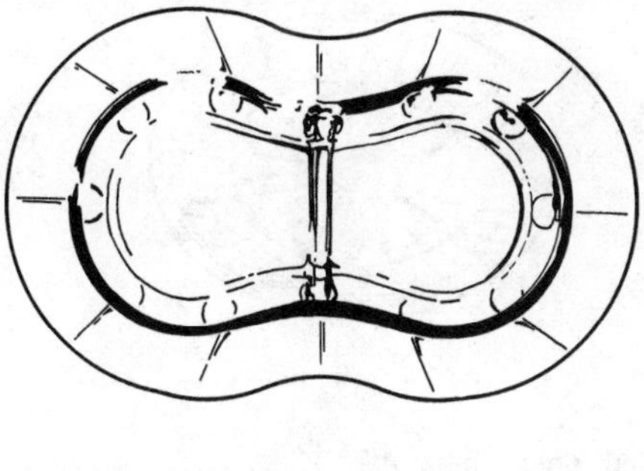

Pitcher, red or blue, w/ice lip, 50-oz, 8″ ... 147.50
Plate, luncheon; colors other than red or blue, 8½″ ... 4.50
Plate, sandwich; round, red or blue, 15″ ... 25.00
Plate, sherbet; colors other than red or blue, 6⅛″ ... 2.50
Tumbler, colors other than red or blue, 9-oz, 4⅞″ ... 10.00
Tumbler, red or blue, 8-oz, 4⅜″ ... 12.00
Vase, ruffled top, flat, red or blue, 7¾″ ... 50.00

Moonstone, Anchor Hocking Glass Corporation, 1941-1946

Bowl, dessert; crimped, opalescent, 5½″ ... 6.00
Bowl, relish; divided, opalescent, 7¾″ ... 7.50
Candle holder, opalescent, pr ... 15.00
Creamer, opalescent ... 6.00
Goblet, opalescent, 10-oz ... 14.50

Plate, sandwich; opalescent, 10″ . . . 15.00
Plate, sherbet; opalescent, 6¼″ . . . 3.00
Sherbet, footed, opalescent . . . 6.00
Sugar bowl, open; footed, opalescent . . . 6.00
Vase, bud; opalescent, 5½″ . . . 8.50

Mt. Pleasant, "Double Shield," L.E. Smith Co., 1920s-1934

Bowl, scalloped, 2-hdl, cobalt, 8″ . . . 16.50
Bowl, 3-footed, rolled-in edges, as rose bowl, black . . . 12.50
Candlesticks, double stem, black, pr . . . 25.00
Cup, black . . . 7.00
Plate, scalloped or square, cobalt, 8″ . . . 7.50
Plate, solid hdl, black, 8″ . . . 8.50
Sherbet, scalloped, cobalt . . . 11.00

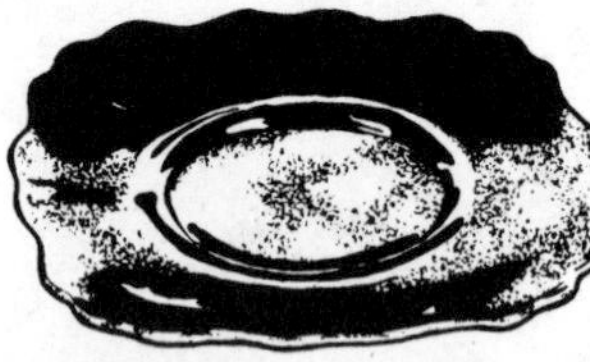

New Century, incorrectly, "Lydia Ray," Hazel Atlas Glass Co., 1930-1935

Bowl, berry; green, 4½″ . . . 5.00
Bowl, casserole; green, 9″, w/lid . . . 45.00
Creamer, green . . . 6.00
Cup, green . . . 5.00
Goblet, cocktail; green, 3¼-oz . . . 12.50
Pitcher, green, 80-oz, 8″ . . . 27.50
Plate, dinner; green, 10″ . . . 10.00
Plate, sherbet; green, 6″ . . . 2.50

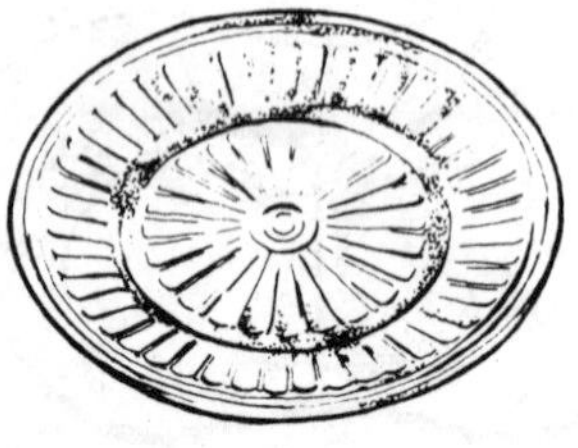

Shakers, green, pr . . . 25.00
Sherbet, green, 3″ . . . 6.00
Tumbler, footed, green, 5-oz, 4″ . . . 9.00
Tumbler, green, 10-oz, 5″ . . . 10.00
Tumbler, green, 5-oz, 3½″ . . . 8.00
Whiskey, green, 1½-oz, 2½″ . . . 6.50

Newport, "Hairpin," Hazel Atlas Glass Co., 1936-1940

Bowl, berry; cobalt, 4¼″ . . . 9.00
Bowl, cereal; amethyst, 5¼″ . . . 15.00

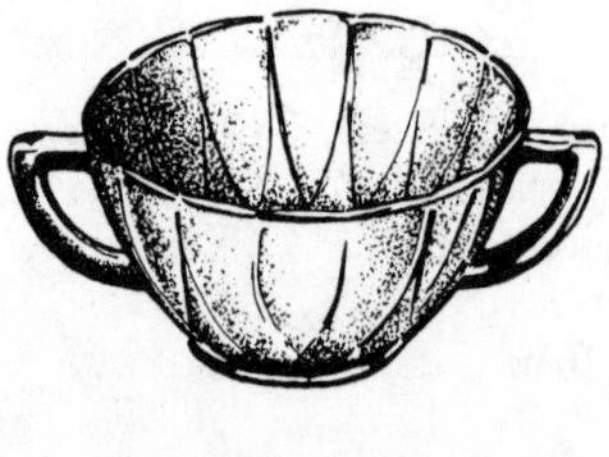

Creamer, cobalt . . . 10.00
Plate, sandwich; cobalt, 11½″ . . . 20.00
Plate, sherbet; amethyst, 6″ . . . 3.50
Platter, oval, cobalt, 11¾″ . . . 23.00
Sherbet, cobalt . . . 9.00
Tumbler, amethyst, 9-oz, 4½″ . . . 18.00

Normandie, "Bouquet and Lattice," Federal Glass Co., 1933-1940

Bowl, berry; amber, 5″ . . . 4.00
Bowl, vegetable; oval, pink, 10″ . . . 20.00
Cup, pink . . . 6.50
Plate, dinner; amber, 11″ . . . 14.00
Plate, salad; pink, 8″ . . . 7.50
Platter, amber, 11¾″ . . . 10.00
Shakers, amber, pr . . . 35.00
Sherbet, pink . . . 6.00
Tumbler, iced tea; pink, 12-oz, 5″ . . . 32.50
Tumbler, water; amber, 9-oz, 4¼″ . . . 11.00

No. 610, "Pyramid," Indiana Glass Co., 1928-1932

Bowl, berry; yellow, 4¾″ . . . 23.50
Bowl, pickle; pink, 9½″ . . . 25.00
Ice tub, yellow . . . 167.50

Pitcher, pink . . . 150.00
Relish tray, 4-part, hdl, yellow . . . 50.00
Sugar bowl, pink . . . 17.50
Tumbler, footed, pink, 8-oz . . . 17.50

No. 612, "Horseshoe," Indiana Glass Co., 1930-1933

Bowl, berry; green, 4½″ . . . 17.50
Bowl, vegetable; oval, yellow, 10½″ . . . 16.00
Cup, green . . . 7.00
Pitcher, green, 64-oz, 8½″ . . . 185.00

Plate, grill; yellow, 10⅜″ 20.00
Plate, salad; green, 8⅜″ 6.00
Relish, footed, 3-part, green 15.00
Saucer, yellow 3.50
Tumbler, footed, yellow, 12-oz 75.00
Tumbler, green, 9-oz, 4¼″ 70.00

No. 618, "Pineapple and Floral," Indiana Glass Co., 1932-1937

Bowl, amber, 4¾″ 14.00
Bowl, cream soup; amber 17.50
Bowl, salad; crystal, 7″ 5.00
Compote, diamond shaped, amber 6.50
Plate, salad; crystal, 8⅜″ 5.00
Platter, closed hdl, amber, 11″ 12.00
Saucer, crystal 3.00
Tumbler, crystal, 8-oz, 4¼″ 22.50
Vase, cone-shaped, large, crystal 27.50

Old Cafe, Hocking Glass Co., 1936-1938, 1940

Bowl, berry; red, 3¾″ 4.00
Bowl, 1 or 2 hdls, pink, 5″ 3.00
Candy dish, low, red, 8″ 10.00
Plate, sherbet; pink, 6″ 1.50
Tumbler, water; red, 4″ 7.00
Vase, pink, 7¼″ 8.50

Old English, "Threading," Indiana Glass Co., Late 1920s

Bowl, fruit; footed, all colors, 9″ 20.00
Candy jar, footed, all colors, w/lid 37.50
Creamer, all colors 12.00
Pitcher, all colors 50.00
Plate, indent for compote, all colors 17.50
Sandwich server, center hdl, all colors 30.00

Sherbet, all colors 15.00
Tumbler, footed, all colors, 5½″ 20.00
Vase, all colors, 13″ 35.00

Ovide, incorrectly, "New Century," Hazel Atlas Glass Co., 1930-1935

Bowl, cereal; black, 5½″ 7.00
Cocktail, fruit; footed, black 6.50
Plate, sherbet; black, 6″ 2.50
Shakers, green, pr 7.50
Sherbet, black 6.50

Oyster and Pearl, Anchor Hocking Glass Corporation, 1938-1940

Bowl, fruit; deep, red, 10½″ 30.00
Bowl, pink, 5¼″ 5.00
Plate, sandwich; pink, 13½″ 10.00
Relish dish, oblong, pink, 10¼″ 6.50

"Parrot," Sylvan, Federal Glass Co., 1931-1932

Bowl, berry; amber, 5″ 10.00
Bowl, vegetable; oval, green, 10″ 35.00
Hot plate, green, 5″ 375.00
Jam dish, amber, 7″ 25.00
Plate, grill; round, green, 10½″ 20.00
Plate, salad; green, 7½″ 15.00
Plate, sherbet; amber, 5¾″ 10.00
Platter, oblong, amber, 11¼″ 40.00
Sugar bowl, open; amber 16.50
Sugar cover, amber 150.00
Tumbler, amber, 12-oz, 5½″ 100.00
Tumbler, green, 10-oz, 4¼″ 80.00

Patrician, "Spoke," Federal Glass Co., 1933-1937

Bowl, berry; green, 5″ 8.00
Bowl, cereal; amber, 6″ 16.00
Bowl, vegetable; oval, green, 12″ 18.00
Creamer, footed, amber 7.00

Pitcher, amber, 75-oz, 8¼″ 80.00
Plate, grill; green, 10½″ 10.00
Plate, salad; green, 7½″ 9.75
Platter, oval, amber, 11½″ 16.50
Sherbet, green 10.00
Tumbler, amber, 14-oz, 5½″ 27.50
Tumbler, green, 5-oz, 4″ 25.00

"Peacock Reverse," Line 412, Paden City Glass Co., 1930s

Bowl, square, hdl, red or blue, 8¾″ 52.50
Bowl, square, red or blue, 4⅞″ 20.00
Candy dish, square, red or blue, 6½″ 50.00
Creamer, flat, red or blue, 2¾″ 47.50
Plate, sherbet; red or blue, 5¾″ 16.50
Sherbet, red or blue, 4⅞″ high, 3⅝″ base 32.50
Tumbler, flat, red or blue, 10-oz, 4″ 42.50

Petalware, Macbeth-Evans Glass Co., 1930-1940

Bowl, cereal; monax, 5¾″ 4.50
Bowl, cream soup; pink, 4½″ 4.50
Cup, pink 2.50
Lamp shade, many sizes, monax 7.50
Plate, salver; pink, 11″ 4.00
Plate, sherbet; monax, 6″ 2.00
Sherbet, footed, low, monax 4.50
Sugar bowl, open; footed, pink 2.50

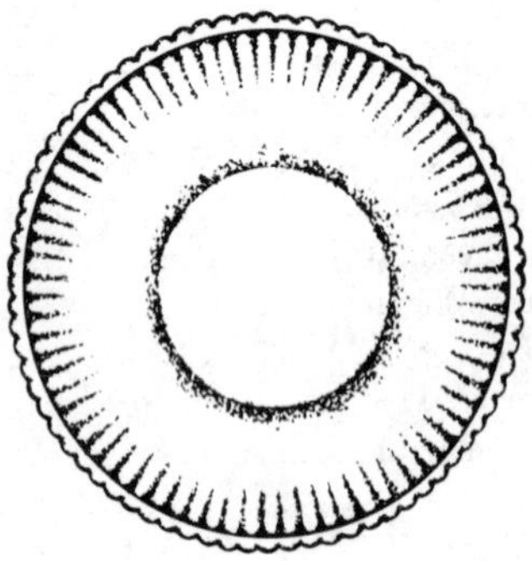

Princess, Hocking Glass Co., 1931-1935

Ash tray, pink, 4½″ 57.50
Bowl, cereal or oatmeal; green, 5″ 20.00
Bowl, vegetable; oval, pink, 10″ 15.00
Cake stand, green, 10″ 15.00
Coaster, pink 52.50
Cup, green 9.00
Pitcher, footed, pink, 24-oz, 7⅜″ 425.00

Plate, salad; pink, 8″ 7.00
Plate, sandwich; hdl, pink, 11½″ 7.50
Plate, sherbet; green, 5½″ 5.50
Platter, closed hdl, pink, 12″ 12.00
Relish, plain, green, 7½″ 60.00
Shakers, pink, 4½″, pr 30.00
Sherbet, footed, pink 11.00
Tumbler, footed, pink, 12½-oz, 6½″ 30.00
Tumbler, water; pink, 9-oz, 4″ 12.50
Vase, green, 8″ 22.50

Queen Mary (Prismatic Line), "Vertical Ribbed," Hocking Glass Co., 1936-1940

Ash tray, oval, crystal, 2x3¾″ 3.50
Bowl, berry; crystal, 5″ 3.50
Bowl, cereal; crystal, 6″ 3.50
Candy dish, pink, w/lid 15.00

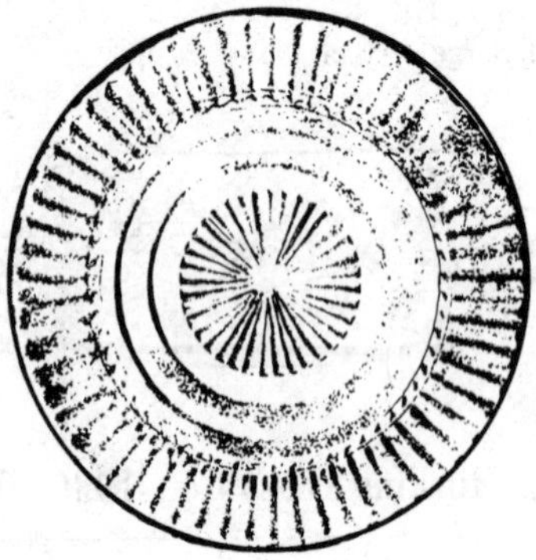

Celery dish/pickle dish, pink, 5x10″ 2.50
Coaster, crystal, 3½″ 2.50
Creamer, oval, crystal 4.50
Cup, crystal 5.00
Plate, crystal, 6″ & 6⅝″ 2.50
Plate, salad; pink, 8½″ 3.50
Plate, serving tray; crystal, 14″ 10.00
Relish tray, 3-part, crystal, 12″ 8.50
Shakers, pink, pr 85.00
Tumbler, footed, crystal, 10-oz, 5″ 15.00
Tumbler, juice; pink, 5-oz, 3½″ 2.50

Raindrops, "Optic Design," Federal Glass Co., 1929-1933

Bowl, cereal; green, 6″ 3.50
Cup, green 4.00
Plate, luncheon; green, 8″ 3.00
Plate, sherbet; green, 6″ 1.50
Saucer, green 1.50
Tumbler, green, 4-oz, 3″ 3.50
Whiskey, green, 1⅞″ 4.00

"Ribbon," Hazel Atlas Glass Co., Early 1930s

Bowl, berry; large, green, 8″ 13.50
Creamer, footed, green 4.50
Shakers, black, pr 30.00

Sherbet, footed, green 4.00
Sugar bowl, open; footed, black 19.00
Tumbler, green, 10-oz, 5½″ 10.00

Ring, "Banded Rings," Hocking Glass Co., 1927-1933

Bowl, soup; crystal, 7″ 6.00
Cocktail shaker, green w/decoration 15.00
Cup, green w/decoration 3.50
Ice tub, crystal 12.00
Plate, sherbet; crystal, 6¼″ 1.25
Sandwich server, center hdl, green w/decoration 20.00

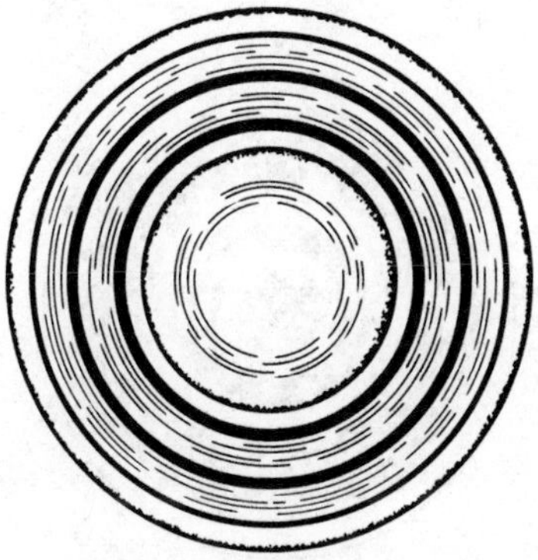

Tumbler, green w/decoration, 12-oz, 5⅛″ 4.50
Tumbler, green w/decoration, 5-oz, 3½″ 3.50
Tumbler, iced tea; footed, crystal, 6½″ 5.00
Whiskey, crystal, 1½-oz, 2″ 3.00

Rock Crystal, "Early American Rock Crystal," McKee Glass Co., 1920s & 1930s

Bowl, celery; oblong, pink, 12″ 27.50
Bowl, relish; 6-part, pink, 14″ 37.50
Cake stand, footed, crystal, 2¾x11″ 20.00
Candelabra, 3-light, pr 60.00
Candlesticks, low, crystal, 5½″, pr 27.50
Compote, pink, 7″ 37.50
Creamer, footed, crystal, 9-oz 15.00
Goblet, iced tea; low footed, crystal, 11-oz 15.00
Pickle tray, crystal, 7″ 15.00
Pitcher, large, pink 175.00
Plate, bread & butter; scalloped edge, pink, 6″ 6.50
Roll tray, crystal, 13″ 22.50
Salt dip, crystal 20.00
Saucer, pink 4.50
Stemware, champagne; footed, crystal, 6-oz 11.00
Stemware, cocktail; footed, pink, 3½-oz 17.50

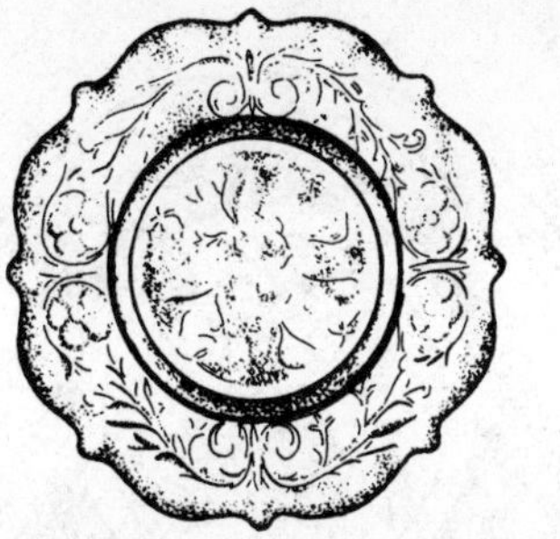

Sundae, low footed, pink, 6-oz 17.50
Tumbler, concave or straight, pink, 12-oz 27.50
Tumbler, juice; crystal, 5-oz 12.00

Rosemary, "Dutch Rose," Federal Glass Co., 1935-1937

Bowl, cream soup; amber, 5″ 8.00
Bowl, vegetable; oval, amber, 10″ 9.00
Cup, green 7.00
Plate, grill; green 9.00
Plate, salad; amber, 6¾″ 4.00
Saucer, green 2.50
Tumbler, green, 9-oz, 4¼″ 14.00

Roulette, "Many Windows," Hocking Glass Co., 1935-1939

Bowl, fruit; green, 9″ 9.00
Plate, luncheon; green, 8½″ 4.00
Plate, sherbet; green, 6″ 2.25
Sherbet, green 4.50
Tumbler, iced tea; green, 12-oz, 5⅛″ 12.00
Tumbler, water; pink, 9-oz, 4⅛″ 6.00
Whiskey, pink, 1½-oz, 2½″ 6.00

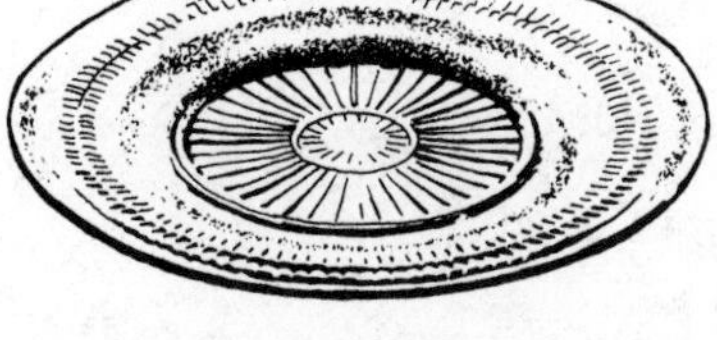

Royal Lace, Hazel Atlas Glass Co., 1934-1941

Bowl, berry; pink, 5″ 13.00
Bowl, 3-leg, straight edge, blue, 10″ 42.50
Butter dish, pink 100.00
Candlestick, ruffled edge, blue, pr 92.50
Cookie jar, blue, w/lid 235.00

Creamer, footed, pink 12.00
Pitcher, blue, 68-oz, 8″ 120.00
Pitcher, pink, 96-oz, 8½″ 65.00
Plate, grill; pink, 9⅞″ 9.00
Shakers, pink, pr 40.00
Sugar bowl, open; pink 9.00
Sugar cover, pink 22.50
Tumbler, blue, 5-oz, 3½″ 28.00
Tumbler, pink, 12-oz, 5⅜″ 20.00

Royal Ruby, Anchor Hocking Glass Co., 1938-1960s, 1977

Ash tray, square, red, 4½″ 2.50
Bowl, vegetable; oval, red, 8″ 15.00
Creamer, flat, red 6.00
Lamp, red 20.00
Pitcher, tilted or upright, red, 3-qt 27.50
Plate, salad; red, 7″ 3.00
Plate, sherbet; red, 6½″ 2.00
Punch bowl, red, w/stand 35.00
Punch cup, red 2.00
Sugar bowl, open; flat, red 6.00

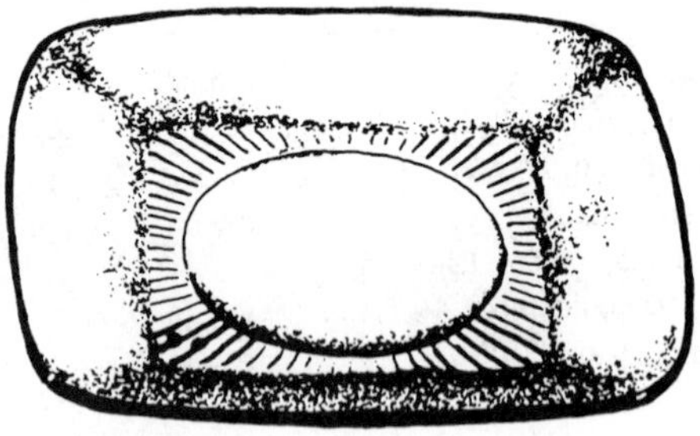

Tumbler, iced tea; red, 13-oz 8.50
Tumbler, water; red, 10-oz 5.00
Vase, bulbous, tall, red, 6½″ 7.50
Vase, large, red 10.00

'S' Pattern, "Stippled Rose Band," Macbeth Evans, 1930-1933

Bowl, berry; large, crystal, 8½″ 6.50
Pitcher, amber, 80-oz 67.50
Plate, dinner; amber, 9¼″ 4.50
Plate, sherbet; amber, 6″ 2.00
Sherbet, low footed, amber 4.50
Tumbler, amber, 9-oz, 4″ 5.50
Tumbler, crystal, 12-oz, 5″ 4.50

Sandwich, Hocking Glass Co., 1939-1964, 1977

Bowl, berry; crystal, 4⅞″ 3.00
Bowl, smooth or scalloped, green, 6½″ 20.00
Bowl, smooth or scalloped, green, 8″ 35.00
Creamer, green 15.00
Custard cup, crystal 3.50
Pitcher, juice; crystal, 6″ 45.00
Plate, dessert; crystal, 7″ 6.00
Plate, dinner; green, 9″ 32.00

Plate, sandwich; crystal, 12″ 7.50
Saucer, green 4.00
Tumbler, juice; crystal, 5-oz 5.00

Sandwich, Indiana Glass Co., 1920s-1980s

Bowl, berry; pink, 4¼″ 3.00
Bowl, console; crystal, 9″ 10.00
Bowl, console; pink, 10″ 18.00
Candlesticks, pink, 7″, pr 35.00
Cruet, crystal, w/stopper, 6½-oz 37.50
Cup, pink 4.00
Goblet, pink, 9-oz 12.00
Plate, bread & butter; pink, 7″ 3.00
Plate, sandwich; crystal, 13″ 6.00
Plate, sherbet; pink, 6″ 2.50
Tumbler, water; footed, crystal, 8-oz 10.00
Wine, crystal, 4-oz, 3″ 7.00

Sharon, "Cabbage Rose," Federal Glass Co., 1935-1939

Bowl, cereal; amber, 6″ 10.00
Bowl, fruit; pink, 10½″ 25.00

Bowl, vegetable; oval, pink, 9½″ 16.00
Cake plate, footed, pink, 11½″ 25.00
Cheese dish, amber, w/lid 150.00
Cup, pink 10.00
Plate, bread & butter; pink, 6″ 4.00
Plate, salad; amber, 7½″ 10.00
Shakers, amber, pr 32.50
Sherbet, footed, pink 10.00
Tumbler, footed, amber, 15-oz, 6½″ 52.50
Tumbler, thick or thin, amber, 9-oz, 4⅛″ 20.00

Sierra, "Pinwheel," Jeannette Glass Co., 1931-1933

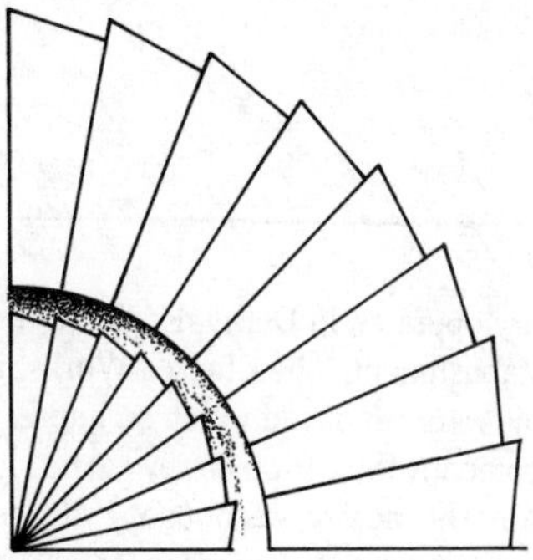

Bowl, berry; large, green, 8½″ 15.00
Pitcher, pink, 32-oz, 6½″ 40.00
Plate, dinner; pink, 9″ 10.00
Saucer, pink 3.50
Serving tray, 2-hdl, green 10.00
Tumbler, footed, green, 9-oz, 4½″ 30.00

Spiral, Hocking Glass Co., 1928-1930

Bowl, berry; green, 4¾″ 4.00
Bowl, mixing; green, 7″ 4.50
Creamer, flat or footed, green 4.00
Ice or butter tub, green 13.50
Plate, sherbet; green, 6″ 1.00
Shakers, green, pr 16.00
Sherbet, green 2.50
Tumbler, juice; green, 5-oz, 3″ 2.75

Starlight, Hazel Atlas Glass Co., 1938-1940

Bowl, closed hdl, pink, 8½″ 8.50
Creamer, oval, crystal 3.00
Plate, bread & butter; pink, 6″ 3.00
Plate, dinner; pink, 9″ 6.00

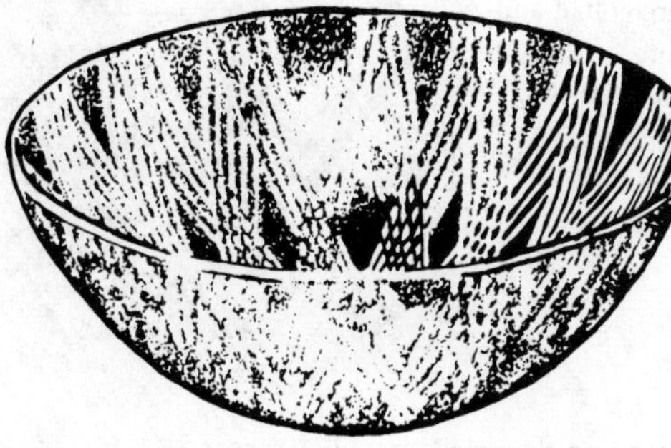

Plate, sandwich; pink, 13″ 7.50
Saucer, pink 2.00
Shakers, crystal, pr 15.00

Strawberry, "Cherryberry," U.S. Glass Co., Early 1930s

Bowl, berry; deep, pink or green, 7½″ 14.00
Bowl, berry; pink or green, 4″ 7.00
Compote, pink or green, 5¾″ 13.00
Olive dish, 1-hdl, pink or green, 5″ 10.00
Pitcher, pink or green, 7¾″ 132.50
Plate, sherbet; pink or green, 6″ 5.00
Sugar bowl, open; large, pink or green 14.00
Tumbler, pink or green, 9-oz, 3⅝″ 20.00

Swirl, "Petal Swirl," Jeannette Glass Co., 1937-1938

Bowl, console; footed, pink, 10½″ 15.00
Bowl, salad; ultramarine, 9″ 15.00
Butter dish, ultramarine 200.00
Candy dish, open, 3-leg, ultramarine 8.50

Cup, ultramarine 7.50
Plate, salad; ultramarine, 8″ 9.50
Plate, sandwich; pink, 12½″ 7.50
Plate, sherbet; ultramarine, 6½″ 3.50
Tumbler, ultramarine, 9-oz, 4″ 13.00
Vase, footed, ultramarine, 8½″ 17.50

Tea Room, Indiana Glass Co., 1926-1931

Bowl, celery; green, 8½″ 22.50
Bowl, salad; deep, pink, 8¾″ 36.50
Creamer, green, 4″ 12.00
Goblet, pink, 9-oz 42.50
Ice bucket, pink 32.50
Lamp, electric, green, 9″ 32.50
Parfait, pink 35.00
Plate, sherbet; pink, 6½″ 12.00
Plate, 2-hdl, green, 10½″ 32.50

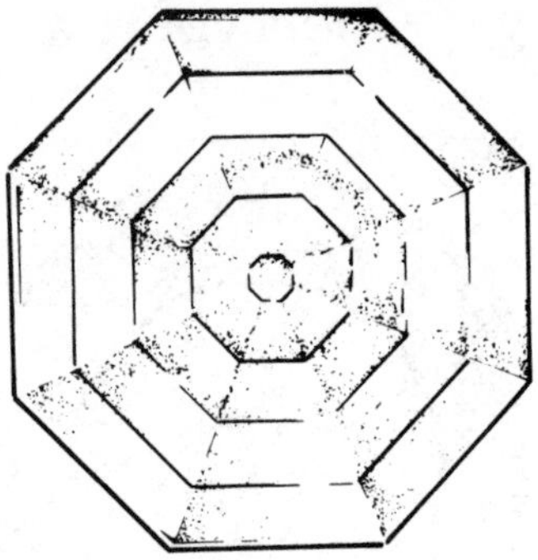

Tumbler, footed, green, 9-oz	20.00
Tumbler, footed, pink, 12-oz	28.00
Vase, pink, 9″	30.00

Twisted Optic, Imperial Glass Co., 1927-1930

Bowl, cereal; pink or green, 5″	2.00
Bowl, salad or soup; pink or green, 7″	5.50
Candlesticks, pink or green, 3″, pr	10.00
Creamer, pink or green	4.50
Cup, pink or green	2.50
Plate, oval, pink or green, 7½x9″	3.50
Plate, sherbet; pink or green, 6″	1.50
Sandwich server, 2-hdl, flat, pink or green	14.00

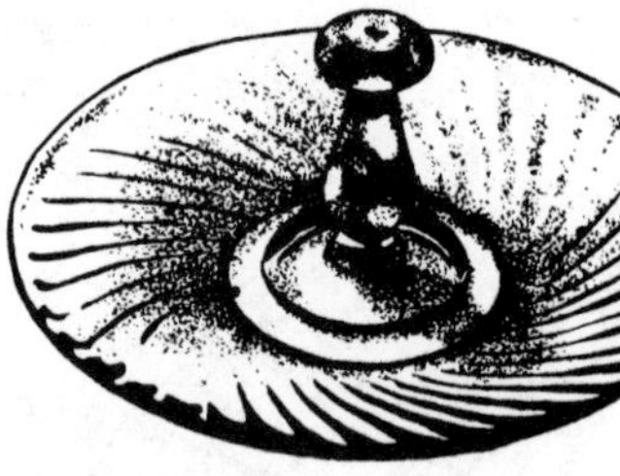

Sherbet, pink or green	4.00
Sugar bowl, open; pink or green	4.50
Tumbler, pink or green, 12-oz, 5¼″	6.50

Vitrock, "Flower Rim," Hocking Glass Co., 1934-1937

Bowl, vegetable; white	5.00
Cup, white	2.00
Plate, dinner; white, 10″	3.50
Plate, soup; white, 9″	5.00
Platter, white, 11½″	12.50

Waterford, "Waffle," Hocking Glass Co., 1938-1944

Bowl, berry; crystal, 4¾″	3.50
Bowl, cereal; pink, 5½″	12.00
Coaster, pink, 4″	4.00
Goblet, crystal, 5¼″ or 5⅝″	10.00
Plate, cake; hdl, pink, 10¼″	9.00
Plate, sherbet; pink, 6″	3.50
Saucer, pink	3.50
Sherbet, footed, pink	7.00
Tumbler, footed, pink, 10-oz, 4⅞″	12.00
Vase, crystal, 6¾″	8.50

Windsor, "Windsor Diamond," Jeannette Glass Co., 1936-1946

Bowl, berry; large, pink, 8½″	9.00
Bowl, cream soup; pink, 5″	10.50
Bowl, fruit; console, crystal, 12½″	10.00
Butter dish, pink	35.00
Coaster, pink, 3¼″	4.50
Plate, salad; pink, 7″	9.00
Plate, sandwich; hdl, pink, 10¼″	9.00
Platter, oval, pink, 11½″	8.50
Tray, square, pink, 4″	6.50
Tumbler, crystal, 12-oz, 5″	5.50
Tumbler, pink, 5-oz, 3¼″	9.50

Derby

William Duesbury operated in Derby, England, from about 1755, purchasing a second establishment, The Chelsea Works, in 1769. During this period fine porcelains were produced which so impressed the King that in 1773 he issued the company the Crown Derby patent. In 1810, several years after Duesbury's death, the factory was bought by Robert Bloor. The quality of the ware suffered under the new management, and the main Derby pottery closed in 1848. Within a short time the work was revived by a dedicated number of former employees who established their own works on King Street, in Derby.

The earliest known Derby mark was the crown over a script 'D'; however this mark is rarely found today. Soon after 1782, that mark was augmented with a device of crossed batons and six dots, usually applied in underglaze blue. During the Bloor period the crown was centered within a ring containing the words 'Bloor' above and 'Derby' below the crown, or with a red printed stamp--the crowned Gothic 'D.' The King Street plant produced figurines that may be distinguished from their earlier counterparts by the presence of an 'S' and 'H' on either side of the crown and crossed batons.

In 1876, a new pottery was constructed in Derby, and the owners revived the earlier company's former standard of excellence. The Queen bestowed the firm the title Royal Crown Derby in 1890; it still operates under that name today.

When no condition is indicated, the items listed below are assumed to be in mint condition.

See also Royal Crown Derby

Watering can, cobalt and rust on white with gilt trim, ca 1790-1820, 3½″, $650.00.

Figurine, canary on flowering tree, 1789, rpr, 2½″	425.00
Figurine, Dr Syntax Treed by Bull, HS Hancock, 7″, EX	600.00
Figurine, pug, sits on scroll base, gr/turq/gold, 2¼″	600.00
House, elaborate moss & shrubbery, 1820, 6″, EX	1,250.00

Pickle stand, 4 shell bowls, 1 w/pickle, insects, 1775, 9″.....1,500.00
Plate, bird in tree, red underglaze mk, ca 1785-1800, 8½″.....150.00
Tureen, floral bouquets, floral finial, w/hdls, Bloor, 7½″.......385.00
Vase, cream w/stylized bl/orange flowers, gold trim/lid.........275.00

Documents

Although the word 'document' is defined in the general sense as 'anything printed or written, etc., relied upon to record or prove something . . .,' in the collectible market, the term is more refined, with broadsides, billheads, checks, invoices, letters and letterheads, lands grants, receipts and waybills some of the most sought after. Some documents in demand are those related to a specific subject such as advertising, mining, railroads, military, politics, banking, slavery, nautical or legal (deeds, mortgages, etc.). Other collectors look for examples representing a specific period of time such as colonial documents, Revolutionary, or Civil War documents, early western documents or those from a specific region, state or city.

Aside from supply and demand, there are five major factors which determine the collector value of a document. These are:

1) Age--Documents from the eastern half of the country can be found that date back to the 1700s. Most documents sought by collectors usually date from 1800 to 1900. Those with twentieth century dates are still abundant and not in demand unless of special significance or beauty.

2) Region of origin--depending on age, documents from rural and less-populated areas are harder to find than those from major cities and heavily populated states. The colonization of the West and Mid-West did not begin until after 1850, so while an 1870s billhead from New York or Chicago is fairly common, one from Albuquerque or Phoenix is not, since most of the Southwest was still unsettled.

3) Attractiveness--while some documents are plain and unadorned, collectors prefer colorful, profusely illustrated letterheads. Additional artwork and engravings add to the value.

4) Historical content--unusual or interesting content, such as a letter written by a Civil War soldier giving an eye-witness account of the Battle of Gettysburg, or a western territorial billhead listing numerous animal hides purchased from a trapper will sell for more than one with mundane information.

5) Condition--through neglect or environmental conditions, over many decades paper articles can become stained, torn, or deteriorated. Heavily damaged or stained documents are generally avoided altogether,while those with minor problems are more acceptable although their value will decrease anywhere from 20% to 50% depending upon the extent of damage. Avoid attempting to repair tears with scotch tape--sell 'as is' so that the collector can take proper steps toward restoration.

Foreign documents are plentiful, and though some are very attractive, resale may be difficult. The listings that follow are generalized; prices are variable depending entirely upon the five points noted above. Values here are based upon examples with no major damage.

Key: illus—illustrated

Appointment for postmaster, Baltimore, 1840..................30.00
Billhead, Ellis & Co, Butchers, Chicago, illus, 1902.............5.00
Billhead, Levi Strauss & Co, San Francisco, 1878.............15.00
Billhead, Mosler Safe Co, New York, illus, 1888................8.00
Billhead, Peaslee Brewery, Des Moines, Iowa, 1884, illus.......12.00
Check, First Ntn'l Bank of Boulder, CO Terr, illus, 1874.......30.00
Check, People's Bank of Portland, Maine, illus, 1855..........15.00
Check, State Bank of Louisville, KY, illus w/stamp, 1869........9.00
Check, Wells Fargo & Co, Virginia City, Nevada, 1878.........15.00
Ft Benton, Montana Territory merchandise waybill, 1876.......25.00
Ft Craig, New Mexico Territory forage voucher, 1868..........25.00
Invoice, Baltimore & Ohio Railroad Co, 1858..................15.00
Invoice, Central Pacific Railroad Co, San Francisco, 1879.......15.00
Invoice, Golden Treasure Mining Co, Boise, ID, illus, 1890......12.00
Land grant from Ohio, dated 1856.............................25.00
Land grant from Utah Territory, dated 1873....................30.00
Land grant from Wisconsin, dated 1895........................15.00
Lawyer's certification to practice law, Kansas City, 1892........25.00
Legal deed to house in Nashville, Tennessee, 1855.............25.00
Legal deed to land in Texas, dated 1881, 2 pg.................12.00
Legal deed to mining claims in Arizona Territory, 1893.........20.00
Legal deed to saloon in Laramie, Wyoming Territory, 1877.....40.00
Letterhead, Boston First National Bank, 1857..................20.00
Letterhead, Central Georgia Railroad Co, Atlanta, 1875........15.00
Letterhead, Espuela Cattle Co, Ft Worth, Texas, 1880.........20.00
Letterhead, Pacific Timber Co, Portland, Oregon, 1886........15.00
Military Commission, Civil War, illus, 1864....................40.00
Mining Assay Report, Silver Bar Mng Co, Eureka, NV, 1868....25.00
Promissory note on financial loan, Boston, MA, 1848..........25.00
Promissory note on oil lands, Tulsa, Oklahoma, 1908..........10.00
Revolutionary War pay order to soldier, Boston, 1814..........75.00
Slavery document listing slaves sold, New Orleans, 1855........35.00
Stagecoach waybill, Oregon Stage Co, Salem, OR, 1866........25.00
Steamboat bill of lading on Miss River, Memphis, 1870..........20.00

Dollhouses and Furnishings

Dollhouses were introduced commercially in this country late in the 1700s by Dutch craftsmen who settled in the East. By the middle of the 1800s, they had become meticulously detailed, divided into separate rooms, and lavishly furnished to reflect the opulence of the day. Originally intended for the amusement of adults of the household, by the latter 1800s their status had changed to that of a child's toy. Though many early dollhouses were lovingly hand fashioned for a special little girl, those made commercially by such companies as Bliss and Schoenhut are highly valued.

Furniture and furnishings in the Biedermeir style featuring stenciled Victorian decorations often sell for several hundred dollars each. Other early pieces made of pewter, porcelain, or papier mache are also quite valuable. Certainly less expensive, but very collectible none-the-less, is the quality hallmarked plastic furniture produced during the forties by Renwal and Acme, and the 1960s Petite Princess line produced by Ideal.

When no condition is indicated, the items listed below are assumed to be in excellent condition.

Aluminum and white metal, signed Fairy Furniture by Adrin Cooke, five pieces, excellent condition, $175.00.

Furniture

Bathinette, Renwal...12.00
Bathroom set, pink, Renwal, 4-pc............................20.00
Bathroom set, Renwal, 3-pc..................................10.00
Bathtub, metal faucets, old fashioned ft, porc................30.00
Bed, twin size, Renwal...5.00
Bird cage, silver..185.00

Buffet, Royal; Petite Princess, MIB 18.00
Candlestick, trn brass, Queen Anne, pr, ⅝", EX 10.00
Chair, arm; Tootsie Toy 12.00
Chair, corner; ball/claw ft, needlepoint seat, walnut, 2½" 70.00
Chair, host dining; pr, MIB 12.00
Chair, overstuffed, Renwal 8.00
Chair, side; uphl seats, pr, clock & mirror, litho on wood 330.00
Clock, Grandfather; Petite Princess, w/screen 28.00
Coal skuttle, tin 40.00
Couch/4 chairs/table w/checkerboard top/piano, Bliss ABC 245.00
Cupboard, kitchen; Petite Princess 45.00
Desk, drop front, 4 drw, Beidermier style, 4¼" 250.00
Doll, father, Petite Princess 14.00
Dresser, baby's; Renwal 4.00
Dresser, drws open, Renwal 9.00
Fireplace, Petite Princess 15.00
Hamper, Renwal 4.00
Hutch, kitchen; Petite Princess 45.00
Hutch, Renwal 6.00
Ice box, tin 145.00
Kitchen appliance, 3-pc, +table & 4 chairs, Renwal 35.00
Magazine rack, w/drw, mahog, 1¾x1¾x1¼", EX 40.00
Night table, baby's; Renwal 2.00
Nursery set, CI, bl, 4-pc 150.00
Phonograph, Renwal 8.00
Piano, grand; Petite Princess 20.00
Piano, Tootsie Toy 40.00
Piano & bench, Renwal 12.00
Potty chair, Renwal 5.00
Radio, Renwal 5.00
Radio, w/pull-out phonograph, Renwal 30.00
Radio, walnut, Strombecker 10.00
Rocker, blk w/flowers, Renwal 12.00
Settee, 2 chairs, table, wicker, 5" 56.00
Sewing stand, Queen Anne, EX 17.50
Sink, kitchen; w/accessories, Petite Princess 50.00
Sofa, gr, Petite Princess, MIB 23.00
Table, dining; Petite Princess 17.00
Table, dining; 8-sided w/leaf, +4 chairs, Beidermier style 735.00
Table, folding type, gold, w/2 chairs, Renwal 20.00
Table, rnd, Tootsie Toy 20.00
Table, tea; candle pull-outs, mahogany, Queen Anne, 2¼" 50.00
Table & chair, porcelain 75.00
Table w/lamp, Renwal 8.00
Tea caddy, 3 compartments, 2 w/lids, ebony, 1x1½x⅝" 30.00
Tea cart, Tootsie Toy 25.00
Tea set, china, Germany, in orig box 125.00
Television, Petite Princess 60.00
Vanity, Renwal 7.00
Victrola 20.00
Washing machine 13.00
Weathervane, rooster, spins 15.00

Houses

Babyland nursery set, tin litho, w/all accessories, MIB 150.00
Bungalow, German litho, 'glass' windows/orig curtains, 10" 195.00
Dolly's Playhouse, McLaughlin, 2-story Victorian, orig box 350.00
Folding table-top house, McLaughlin, ca 1894, VG 275.00
Grocery store, w/counter/scale/accessories, German, 25" W 275.00
Litho, 2-room, front opens, red roof, German, 9x5½" 75.00
Litho, 2-story, 'glass' windows down, w/3-pc lr suite, 14" 360.00
Litho, 2-story, yel w/gr roof, orig wallpaper, 10", VG 350.00
Litho, 2-story w/porch, 'glass' windows, red/yel, 13", NM 395.00

Dollhouse, lithographed paper on wood, Bliss, 17½"x 11"x21", excellent condition, $1,800.00.

Norstar Foldamatic, cb 28.00
Row houses, litho paper on wood, steps missing, 25" L, VG . . . 200.00
Schoenhut, 6-room, front opens, orig furniture, lighted 550.00
Stable, groom's apartment atop, pnt/litho, 3 stalls, 10" 245.00
Stable, 3 stalls & carriage house, German 475.00
Tudor, printed paper over wood, English, 28x38" 160.00
Tudor, wood, w/metal windows, 17x24" 90.00
Twig siding, sgn, dtd Nov 1896 . . . . . 785.00
Victorian, side porch, frame/brick base, paper/wood, 21x18" . . 1,500.00
Victorian country, wood/pnt brick/4 fireplaces, 25x21" 700.00
Wood, 5 glass windows, chimney, stoop, handmade, 8x8" 70.00
2-story, wood, 2 sides open, wht w/bl shutters, 1940s, lg 175.00
3-story, picket fence, glass windows, brick paper, 32x22" 450.00

Dolls

Collecting dolls of any sort is one of the most rewarding hobbies in the United States. The rewards are in the fun, the search and the finds--plus there is a built-in factor of investment. No hobby, be it dolls, glass, or anything else, should be based completely on investment, but any collector should ask: 'Can I get my money back out of this item if I should ever have to sell it?' Many times we buy on impulse, rather than with logic, which is understandable; but by asking this question we can save ourselves a lot of 'buyer's remorse,' which we have all experienced at one time or another.

Since we want to learn to invest our money wisely while we are having fun, we must become aware of defects which may devaluate a doll. In bisque, watch for eye chips, hairline cracks and chips, or breaks on any part of the head. Composition should be clean, not crazed or cracked. Vinyl and plastic should be clean, with no pen or crayon marks. Though a quality replacement wig is acceptable for bisque dolls, composition and hard plastics should have their originals, in uncut condition. Original clothing is a must, except in bisque dolls, since it is unusual to find one in its original costume. However, they should be well-dressed and ready for your collection.

A price guide is only that--a guide. It suggests the average price for each doll. Bargains can be found for less than suggested values; and 'unplayed-with' dolls in their original boxes may cost more. Dealers must become aware of condition so that they do not over-pay and therefore over-price their dolls--a common occurence across the country. Quantity does not replace quality, as most find out in time. A faster turnover of sales with a smaller margin of profit is far better than being stuck with an item that does not sell because it is over-priced. It is important to remember that prices are based on condition and rarity. When no condition is noted, dolls are assumed to be in excellent condition, with the exceptions of Armand Marseille, Madame Alexander and Effanbee dolls which are priced in mint condition. In relation to bisque dolls, excellent means having no cracks, chips or hairlines, being nicely dressed, shoed and wigged, and ready to to be placed into a collection.

For a more thorough study of the subject, we recommend you refer to the many lovely doll books written by authority Pat Smith, available at your favorite bookstore or public library.

Key:
bjtd—ball-jointed
blb—bent limb body
bsk—bisque
c/m—closed mouth
hh—human hair
hp—hard plastic
jtd—jointed
MIG—Made In Germany
NC—no clothes
o/c—open closed
OC—original clothes
P/E—pierced ears
ptd—painted
pwt—paperweight eyes
RpC—replaced clothes
ShHd—shoulderhead
ShPl—shoulderplate
SkHd—sockethead
str—straight
trn—turned

Armand Marseille

A 0½ M, Armand Marseille, 300n, Germany, SkHd, 15½″......185.00
A 10/0 M, 324, Germany, Armand Marseille, pnt eyes, 7″......495.00
A 10/0 M, 390, 1900, SkHd, 18″......275.00
A 11 M, DRGM, Germany, SkHd, 26″......450.00
A 11 M, DRGM 276/1, Germany, SkHd, 26″......450.00
A 11 M, G 327 B, Germany, SkHd, 1914, 20″......400.00
A 11 M, 1894, ShPl, 26″......550.00
A 11/0 M, 255, DRGM, Germany, SkHd, intaglio eye, 7½″......485.00
A 11/0 M, 323, Germany, SkHd, glass eyes, 7½″......625.00
A 11/0 M, 395, Germany, SkHd, Heidi, 1920, 9″......165.00
A 11/0 M, 500, MIG, molded hair, Infant Berry, 1908, 5″......165.00
A 12 M, 390n, Germany, SkHd, Louisa, 1915, 27″......465.00
A 12/0 M, MIG, SkHd, sleep eyes, 7″......95.00
A 2/0 M, DRGM 201013, Germany, trn ShHd, talks, 16″......350.00
A 2/0 M, G 329 B, Germany, SkHd, girl, 9″......185.00
A 2/0 M, 500, DRGM, molded hair, Infant Berry, 1908, 10″...475.00
A 3/0 M, 990, SkHd, baby, 8″......125.00
A 30/0 M, MH, Germany, SkHd, c/m, lady, dimples, 1913, 10″.625.00
A 4 M, 347, Germany, SkHd, Bumble Puppy, 1909, 16″......325.00
A 4/0 M, 320, Germany, SkHd, c/m, pnt eyes, 6½″......245.00
A 4/0 M, 323, Germany, SkHd, 11″......850.00
A 450 M, 1½, Germany, SkHd, c/m, provincial attire, 19″......950.00
A 5 M, 590, DRGM, Germany, o/c, Hoopla Girl, 16″......1,000.00
A 5/0 M, 402, Germany, SkHd, pnt bsk, 14″......325.00
A 6 M, 550, DRGM, Germany, SkHd, c/m, 16″......1,200.00
A 6/0 M, G 327B, DRGM 259, Germany, SkHd, 1914, 12″....265.00
A 7 M, Germany, SkHd, 17″......295.00
A 7 M, 257, Germany, SkHd, baby, 1914, 22″......450.00
A 7 M, 390, MIG, SkHd, 23″......395.00
A 7/0 M, MIG, ShHd, boy, 14″......165.00
A 7/0 M, 390, MIG, SkHd, 9½″......125.00
A 9 M, CM Bergmann, MIG, SkHd, 24″......400.00
A 985 M, 3, Germany, SkHd, baby, 13½″......265.00
Alma 10/0/Germany, ShHd, 26″......450.00
Alma 14/0, ShHd, 26″......450.00
Alma 3/0, ShHd, 12″......110.00
Alma 9/0, ShHd, 15″......165.00
AM Darling Baby, 1906, 12″......275.00
AM DEP, MIG, SkHd, 16″......225.00
AM DEP, 3/0, 1894, MIG, SkHd, 14″......195.00
AM DEP, 3200, ShHd, some trn, 1898, 16″......250.00
AM G 327B, DRGM, SkHd, baby, fur hair, 1914, 12″......250.00
AM G 327B, Germany, SkHd, baby, 12″......250.00
AM G 328 B, Germany, SkHd, closed dome, 1922, 14″......285.00
AM 0½ DEP, 3200, MIG, ShHd, 1898, 14″......225.00
AM 1½, DEP, 1894, SkHd, wht, 16½″......225.00
AM 11 DEP, 3200, ShHd, some trn, 26″......550.00
AM 12, Germany, flange neck, 1907, 16″......450.00
AM 1894, DEP, Germany, SkHd, blk, 12″......250.00
AM 2½k, Germany, SkHd, open mouth, blk, 12″......295.00
AM 2/0, DEP, 3500, MIG, ShHd, 17″......325.00
AM 2/0 DEP, 370, MIG, ShHd, 19½″......225.00
AM 20/0, Germany, SkHd, o/c, Indian, 1890s, 8″......350.00
AM 3 DEP, 370, MIG, ShHd, fur eyebrows, 22½″......325.00
AM 3k, 362, Germany, SkHd, closed dome, baby, wht, 15″....325.00
AM 341 7, Germany, flange, c/m, My Dream Baby, 18″......525.00
AM 341/Ok, Germany, SkHd, c/m, My Dream Baby, 16″......450.00
AM 341/10, Germany, flange, c/m, My Dream Baby, 21″......600.00
AM 341/3, Germany, socket & flange, c/m, baby, wht, 8″......165.00
AM 341/4, Germany, flange, c/m, My Dream Baby, 15″......425.00
AM 351 10/0, Germany, w/rubber body, Wee One, 7″......165.00
AM 351 17/0, Germany, socket & flange, open mouth, 6″......135.00
AM 351/4k, Germany, socket & flange, open mouth, wht, 22″..625.00
AM 351/6, Germany, flange & socket, open mouth, 26″......825.00
AM 352 10, Germany, flange, Baby Love, 1914, 19″......450.00
AM 3524, 7, Germany, flange neck, baby, Baby Gloria, 18″....550.00
AM 390, MIG, SkHd, My Dearie, 1908-1922, 18½″......300.00
AM 4/0x DEP, 370, MIG, ShHd, 16½″......250.00
AM 4/0x DEP, 370, ShHd, 16½″......250.00
AM 5 DEP, 3200, ShHd, some trn, 15″......325.00
AM 5/0x, 370, MIG, ShHd, c/m, 15½″......200.00
AM 500, DRGM, Germany, Infant Berry, 1908, 8″......300.00
AM 6/0 DEP, 370, ShHd, 15″......225.00
AM 600, DRGM, Germany, flange, SkHd, c/m, 1910, 10″......350.00
AM 7/0 DEP, 1894, MIG, SkHd, 12″......165.00
AM 8 DEP, 3200, trn ShHd, 22″......495.00
AM 800, 'Mama,' talker in head, Baby Sunshine, 1925, 16″....485.00
AM 83115, SkHd, 8″......145.00
AM 917, Germany, SkHd, baby, Mobi, 1921, 16″......500.00
AM 95 6 DEP, Armand Marseille, trn ShHd, 20″......325.00
AM 966 3, MIG, SkHd, baby, flirty eye, 14″......300.00
AM 980, Germany, SkHd, baby, 14″......300.00
Armand Marseille, A 0½ M, 990, Germany, SkHd, 13″......300.00
Armand Marseille, A 1 M, 390, SkHd, 16″......250.00
Armand Marseille, A 11 M, 990, SkHd, Happy Tot, 1910, 21″..525.00
Armand Marseille, A 11/0 M, 390, Germany, o/c mouth, 7½″....95.00
Armand Marseille, A 2 M, 390n, Germany, Patrice, SkHd, 18″.400.00
Armand Marseille, A 2/0 M, 995, Germany, SkHd, 12″......275.00
Armand Marseille, A 2/0 M, 996, Germany, SkHd, baby, 15″...300.00
Armand Marseille, A 4½ M, 990, Germany, SkHd, 1910, 16″...325.00
Armand Marseille, A 4/0x M, 390n, Germany, SkHd, 1915, 11″.165.00
Armand Marseille, A 6 M, 390, MIG, SkHd, walks, 22″......350.00
Armand Marseille, A 6 M, 390, SkHd, 21″......325.00
Armand Marseille, A 7 M, 390, Germany, SkHd, 22″......325.00
Armand Marseille, A 7 M, 992, Germany, SkHd, 1914, 22″....525.00
Armand Marseille, A 9 M, 390, SkHd, pnt bsk, 9″......125.00
Armand Marseille, A 975 M, 13, Germany, SkHd, 1914, 24″...600.00
Armand Marseille, A 975 M, 2/0, Germany, SkHd, 1914, 9″....150.00
Armand Marseille, AM 10/0 DEP, 370, MIG, ShHd, 12″......135.00
Armand Marseille, AM 7/0 DEP, 370n, MIG, ShHd, 12″......135.00
Armand Marseille, Germany, SkHd, c/m, 14″......550.00
Armand Marseille, 390, MIG, SkHd, 24″......400.00
Armand Marseille, 560a, DRGM 232, Dorothy, 1912, 15″......375.00
Columbia, MIG, ShHd, 1904, 24″......500.00
DRGM 377439, MIG, SkHd, fur eyebrows/Wonderful Alice, 26″.550.00
Fany, A 11 M, 231, DRGM 248/1, baby, c/m, 1913, 25″......3,200.00
Floradora, A 0 M, MIG, SkHd, 17″......325.00

Florodora, A 11 M, MIG, SkHd, 27″ 525.00
Florodora, A 3 M, MIG, ShHd, 23″ 400.00
Florodora, A 4 M, SkHd, 23″ 400.00
Florodora, A 5 M, Germany, ShHd, 24″ 425.00
Florodora, A 77 M, MIG, SkHd, 15″ 225.00
Florodora, A 9/0 M, MIG, SkHd, 12″ 165.00
Florodora, 1347, ShHd, fur eyebrows, 21″ 365.00
Florodora, 3740, 30, 1374, ShHd, 21″ 350.00
GB, A 5/0 M, DRGM 248/1, SkHd, open mouth, 1912, 10″ 125.00
GB 250, A 1 M, Germany, SkHd, c/m, molded hair, 10½″ 795.00
Googly, A 11/0 M, 254, SkHd, molded hair, 8″ 650.00
Googly, A 12/0 M, 210, Germany, SkHd, pnt eyes, 6″ 225.00
Googly, A 253 M, 5/0, DRGM, Germany, SkHd, 1915, 16″ 1,400.00
Googly, A 3/0 M, G 252 B, DRGM, Germany/SkHd, 1915, 9½″ 795.00
Googly, A 3/0 M, 200, DRGM 213, SkHd, 11½″ 995.00
Googly, A 6/0 M, SB 252, DRGM, Germany, SkHd, 10″ 795.00
Googly, AM, 353, 5/0, SkHd, 6½″ 285.00
Googly, AOM, 253 SB, DRGM, Germany, SkHd, 8″ 650.00
Kiddiejoy, A 3 M, 997, Germany, SkHd, 14″ 350.00
Kiddiejoy, AM, 991, Germany, SkHd, 14″ 350.00
Kiddiejoy, AOM, Germany, ShHd, 9″ 200.00
Kiddiejoy, 3/0, Germany, ShHd, cloth body, c/m, girl, 20″ 950.00
Kiddiejoy, 372, Germany, ShHd, molded hair, 1926, 9″ 285.00
Kiddiejoy, 375 6, Germany, c/m, molded hair, girl, 20″ 950.00
Lily, 4/0, MIG, ShHd, 1913, 17″ 395.00
Mabel, 131, Germany, ShHd, 1898, 17″ 375.00
Mabel, 3/0, Germany, ShHd, 1898, 15″ 325.00
My Dearie, A 2M, DRGM 246/1, SkHd, 1908, 14″ 295.00
My Playmate (Body), AM Germany, closed dome & mouth, 18″ 950.00
Otto Gans, A 5 M, 970, Germany, Lady Marie, 1916, 20″ 400.00
Otto Gans, A 7 M, 975, Germany, SkHd, Sadie, 1914, 17″ 425.00
Queen Louise, Germany, SkHd, 1910, 22″ 475.00
Queen Louise, 100, Germany, SkHd, 1910, 12″ 195.00
Queen Louise, 100, SkHd, 1910, 18½″ 400.00
Queen Louise, 315, Germany 12, SkHd, 27″ 625.00
Rosebud, A 4/0 M, MIG, ShHd, 1902, 15″ 265.00
Roseland, AOM, 1910, 18″ 400.00
Sunshine, 1910, Germany, ShHd, 24″ 500.00

Armand Marseille, incised A.18M., with brown sleep eyes and open mouth with four teeth, on a ball-jointed composition body, 37″, $1,200.00.

Barbie Dolls and Related Dolls

When no condition is indicated, the items listed below are assumed to be nude and in excellent condition unless otherwise specified. For further information, we recommend *An Illustrated Price Guide to Collectible Barbie Dolls* by Paris, Susan and Carol Manos; and *The Collectors Encyclopedia of Barbie Dolls and Collectibles* by Sibyl DeWein and Joan Ashabraner.

Allan, 1964, straight legs, red pnt hair 15.00
Allan, 1965, bendable legs, bl trunks, red jacket, MIB 200.00
Barbie, 1959, #1, blonde, holes in feet 800.00
Barbie, 1959, #1, blonde, swimsuit, holes in feet, MIB 1,500.00
Barbie, 1959, #2, blonde, no holes in feet 800.00
Barbie, 1959, #2, brunette, holes in feet for holder, MIB 1,250.00
Barbie, 1960, #3, bl irises & curved eyebrows, ivory skin 150.00
Barbie, 1960, #3, bl irises & curved eyebrows, MIB 300.00
Barbie, 1960, #4, striped swimsuit, sunglasses, MIB 250.00
Barbie, 1960, #4, vinyl plastic, tan skin 125.00
Barbie, 1961, Bubble Cut 20.00
Barbie, 1961, Bubble Cut, MIB 125.00
Barbie, 1961, Ponytail, striped swimsuit, red lips, MIB 175.00
Barbie, 1963, Fashion Queen, w/3 wigs 15.00
Barbie, 1963, Fashion Queen, w/3 wigs, swimsuit, MIB 150.00
Barbie, 1964, Ponytail Swirl, no curly bangs 35.00
Barbie, 1964, Ponytail Swirl, no curly bangs, MIB 200.00
Barbie, 1965, Color 'N Curl, 2 heads & accessories, MIB 300.00
Barbie, 1965, Legs, bendable legs, MIB 200.00
Barbie, 1966, Color Magic, bendable legs, w/swimsuit, MIB 200.00
Barbie, 1967, Hair Fair Set, w/hair accessories, MIB 50.00
Barbie, 1967, standard, straight legs, pnt lashes 15.00
Barbie, 1967, Twist 'N Turn, bendable knees, pnt lashes 15.00
Barbie, 1968, Spanish Talking 20.00
Barbie, 1968, Spanish Talking, MIB 100.00
Barbie, 1968, Talking, undivided fingers, w/plastic box 20.00
Barbie, 1969, Twist 'N Turn 50.00
Barbie, 1970, Living, bendable knees, straight hair 15.00
Barbie, 1970, Living, bendable knees, swimsuit, MIB 50.00
Barbie, 1971, Growin' Pretty Hair, bendable knees 35.00
Barbie, 1971, Growin' Pretty Hair, bendable knees, MIB 85.00
Barbie, 1971, Hair Happenin's, w/3 hairpieces 100.00
Barbie, 1971, Hair Happenin's, w/3 hairpieces, MIB 350.00
Barbie, 1971, Live Action, wild clothes, headband, MIB 65.00
Barbie, 1972, Busy, long blonde hair 25.00
Barbie, 1972, Busy, long blonde hair, denim top, MIB 85.00
Barbie, 1972, Busy Talking, short blonde hair w/bangs 35.00
Barbie, 1972, Walk Lively, blonde, red jumpsuit, MIB 75.00
Barbie, 1972, Ward's Anniversary, 100th Anniversary 150.00
Barbie, 1973, Baggie, MIB 35.00
Barbie, 1973, Quick Curl, blonde, bendable knees 5.00
Barbie, 1973, Quick Curl, blonde, bendable knees, MIB 30.00
Barbie, 1974, Newport, w/sailing accessories 4.00
Barbie, 1974, Newport, w/sailing accessories, MIB 75.00
Barbie, 1974, Sun Valley, w/ski accessories, MIB 45.00
Barbie, 1974, Sweet Sixteen, Barbie's birthday, MIB 35.00
Barbie, 1975, Free Moving, blonde, MIB 45.00
Barbie, 1975, Free Moving, blonde, 1-piece play suit 10.00
Barbie, 1975, Funtime, bendable knees, twist waist, MIB 45.00
Barbie, 1975, Gold Medal, w/gold medal & patch 4.00
Barbie, 1975, Gold Medal Skater, w/skates & stand 4.00
Barbie, 1975, Gold Medal Skier, w/Olympic ski clothes, MIB 45.00
Barbie, 1975, Hawaiian, straight hair, grass skirt, MIB 35.00
Barbie, 1975, Malibu, long blonde hair, red swimsuit, MIB 15.00
Barbie, 1976, Ballerina, blonde ponytail, wht tutu, MIB 35.00

Barbie, 1976, Ballerina on Tour....6.00
Barbie, 1976, Ballerina on Tour, w/3 outfits, MIB....45.00
Barbie, 1976, Beautiful Bride, bendable knees, twist waist....25.00
Barbie, 1976, Beautiful Bride, bendable knees, w/gown, MIB....65.00
Barbie, 1976, Deluxe Quick Curl, w/Jergen's Beauty Kit....6.00
Black Francie, 1967, 1st issue, lt brn eyes/red oxidized hair....200.00
Black Francie, 1967, 2nd issue, dark eyes/dk brn hair....175.00
Brad, 1970, bendable legs, Black, pnt hair, MIB....50.00
Brad, 1970, Talking, Black, pnt hair, MIB....50.00
Buffy, 1968, Family Affair TV show, pigtails & freckles....20.00
Cara, 1975, Free Moving, Black, long hair w/bows, MIB....35.00
Cara, 1975, Free Moving, Black, long hair w/orange bows....8.00
Cara, 1976, Ballerina, Black, swivel head & arms, blk hair....5.00
Cara, 1976, Deluxe Quick Curl....25.00
Cara, 1976, Deluxe Quick Curl, Black, yel outfit....5.00
Carla, 1965, Black, blk ponytail w/wht ribbon, MIB....35.00
Casey, 1967, blonde or brunette, bendable knees....30.00
Casey, 1975, Baggie, blonde, swimsuit, straight legs, MIB....15.00
Chris, 1967, blonde or brunette w/barrette & 2 bows, MIB....100.00
Christie, 1969, Talking, Black....20.00
Christie, 1969, Talking, Black, clothes match Brad's....20.00
Christie, 1970, Twist 'N Turn, Black, swimsuit, MIB....65.00
Christie, 1971, Live Action, Black, bendable knees, MIB....75.00
Christie, 1973, Malibu, Black....4.00
Christie, 1973, Malibu, Black, MIB....20.00
Curtis, 1975, Free Moving, Black, pnt hair....25.00
Francie, 1966, bendable legs....15.00
Francie, 1966, bendable legs, swimsuit, MIB....75.00
Francie, 1966, straight legs, pnt lashes, swimsuit....25.00
Francie, 1967, Twist 'N Turn, bendable legs....15.00
Francie, 1970, Growin' Pretty Hair, pull to lengthen hair....25.00
Francie, 1970, Hair Happenin's, 4 blonde hairpieces, MIB....100.00
Francie, 1971, Malibu, swimsuit, pnt lashes, MIB....25.00
Francie, 1972, Busy, blonde, blue jeans & gr tank top, MIB....100.00
Francie, 1973, Quick Curl, Black, bendable knees....8.00
Ginger, 1976, Growing Up Ginger, brunette....25.00
Ginger, 1976, Growing Up Ginger, brunette, bl outfit, MIB....75.00
Jamie, 1970, Walking, bendable knees, mini dress, MIB....175.00
Julia, 1969, Talking, fancy jumpsuit, MIB....45.00
Julia, 1969, Twist 'N Turn, 2-pc nurse's uniform, MIB....75.00
Kelley, 1973, Quick Curl, bendable knees, red hair....10.00
Kelley, 1974, Yellowstone, bendable knees, red hair....50.00
Kelley, 1974, Yellowstone, bendable knees, red hair, MIB....150.00
Ken, 1961, Flocked Hair, movable head, arms, & legs....35.00
Ken, 1965, bendable legs....50.00
Ken, 1965, bendable legs, red trunks & bl jacket, MIB....200.00
Ken, 1969, Talking....45.00
Ken, 1969, Talking, bendable knees, jacket & shorts, MIB....75.00
Ken, 1970, Spanish Talking....15.00
Ken, 1970, Spanish Talking, bl & orange outfit, MIB....75.00
Ken, 1971, Live Action, bendable knees, wild clothes, MIB....65.00
Ken, 1971, Live Action on Stage, bendable knees....20.00
Ken, 1971, Malibu, orange-red trunks, MIB....20.00
Ken, 1972, Busy, bendable elbows, jeans & tank top, MIB....85.00
Ken, 1972, Busy Talking, brn hair, red pants, MIB....175.00
Ken, 1972, Walk Lively, pnt hair....15.00
Ken, 1972, Walk Lively, pnt hair, MIB....75.00
Ken, 1973, Mod Hair, bendable knees, 4 brn hairpieces....8.00
Ken, 1974, Sun Valley, ski accessories, MIB....45.00
Ken, 1974, Ward's Dressed, bl & blk tuxedo, mod hair, MIB....100.00
Ken, 1974, Ward's Dressed, mod hair....8.00
Ken, 1975, Free Moving....10.00
Ken, 1975, Gold Medal Skier, w/ski accessories, MIB....45.00
Ken, 1976, Funtime, bl trunks, MIB....45.00
Ken, 1976, New Look, longer blk hair....8.00
Midge, 1963, straight legs....15.00
Midge, 1963, straight legs, MIB....75.00
Midge, 1965, bendable legs, bouffant hair....45.00
Midge, 1965, bendable legs, bouffant hair, 1-pc suit, MIB....200.00
Midge, 1965, Color 'N Curl, head w/4 wigs, MIB....300.00
Midge, 1965, Wig Wardrobe, MIB....100.00
Miss America, 1972, Kellogg's Walk Lively, wht gown, MIB....75.00
Miss America, 1973, Quick Curl, brunette....35.00
Miss America, 1973, Quick Curl, brunette, wht gown, MIB....150.00
Miss America, 1974, Kellogg's Blonde Quick Curl....5.00
Miss America, 1974, Kellogg's Blonde Quick Curl, MIB....50.00
Miss America, 1974, Kellogg's Brunette Quick Curl....35.00
Miss America, 1974, Quick Curl, blonde, wht gown, MIB....25.00
PJ, 1969, Talking, blonde....20.00
PJ, 1970, Twist 'N Turn, blonde....15.00
PJ, 1970, Twist 'N Turn, blonde, pink swimsuit, MIB....100.00
PJ, 1971, Live Action, blonde, wild clothes, MIB....65.00
PJ, 1971, Live Action on Stage, blonde, wild clothes, MIB....75.00
PJ, 1971, Live Action PJ on Stage....75.00
PJ, 1972, Malibu, blonde....4.00
PJ, 1972, Malibu, blonde, lav swimsuit, MIB....20.00
PJ, 1975, Free Moving, blonde, MIB....45.00
PJ, 1975, Gold Medal Gymnast, w/balance beam....4.00
PJ, 1975, Gold Medal Gymnast, w/balance beam, MIB....45.00
PJ, 1976, Deluxe Quick Curl, blonde, extra hairpiece, MIB....25.00
Ricky, 1965, straight legs, red hair, freckles....25.00
Skipper, 1964, straight legs, movable limbs, 9¼"....8.00
Skipper, 1965, bendable legs, 1-pc bl suit w/wht trim, MIB....65.00
Skipper, 1967, blonde, bendable knees, swimsuit, MIB....45.00
Skipper, 1967, Deluxe Quick Curl, blonde, w/fall, MIB....100.00
Skipper, 1967, Funtime, blonde, bendable knees....15.00
Skipper, 1968, Twist 'N Turn....15.00
Skipper, 1968, Twist 'N Turn, swimsuit, headband, MIB....75.00
Skipper, 1970, Living, blonde, bendable knees....5.00
Skipper, 1970, Pose 'N Play, MIB....20.00
Skipper, 1971, Malibu, blonde, orange swimsuit, MIB....20.00
Skipper, 1972, Pose 'N Play, w/gym, swing-free arms....20.00
Skipper, 1972, Pose 'N Play, w/gym, swing-free arms, MIB....200.00
Skipper, 1973, Malibu, blonde....4.00
Skipper, 1973, Malibu, blonde, orange swimsuit, MIB....15.00
Skipper, 1973, Quick Curl, blonde, w/hair accessories, MIB....30.00
Skipper, 1975, Growing Up, turn arm to grow ¾" taller....5.00
Skooter, 1965, straight legs, pigtails & freckles....20.00
Skooter, 1966, bendable legs, swimsuit, MIB....200.00
Skooter, 1967, Funtime, bendable knees, twist waist....50.00
Skooter, 1967, Funtime, bendable knees, twist waist, MIB....150.00
Stacey, 1968, Talking, British accent, w/plastic box....20.00
Stacey, 1968, Talking, British accent, w/plastic box, MIB....100.00
Stacey, 1968, Twist 'N Turn, bendable knees, swimsuit, MIB....100.00
Stacey, 1969, Talking, British accent....20.00
Steffie, 1972, Busy, brunette, long dress, MIB....100.00
Steffie, 1972, Busy Talking, blonde....50.00
Steffie, 1972, Busy Talking, blonde, hot pants, MIB....250.00
Steffie, 1972, Walk Lively, brunette, jumpsuit, MIB....85.00
Steffie, 1974, Babs, in plastic bag, MIB....100.00
Tangie, 1970, blonde....30.00
Tiff, 1972, Pose 'N Play, swing-free arms....50.00
Todd, 1966, Sundae Treat, w/Tutti....30.00
Todd, 1966, Sundae Treat, w/Tutti, MIB....200.00
Todd, 1966, w/Tutti, in brn box, MIB....150.00
Truly Scrumptious, 1969, straight legs, fancy hat, MIB....400.00
Truly Scrumptious, 1969, Talking, bendable legs....150.00
Tutti, w/Todd, in brn box, MIB....150.00

Tutti, 1966, Me & My Dog, set....25.00
Tutti, 1966, Me & My Dog, set, MIB....275.00
Tutti, 1966, Melody in Pink, set....25.00
Tutti, 1966, Night-Night Sleep Tight, set, MIB....100.00
Tutti, 1966, Walkin' My Dolly, set....25.00
Tutti, 1967, Cookin' Goodies, set, MIB....150.00
Tutti, 1967, Swing-A-Ling, set, MIB....200.00
Twiggy, 1967, blonde, bendable knees, mini dress, MIB....75.00

Barbie Gifts Sets and Related Accessories

When no condition is indicated, the items listed below are assumed to be mint and in box.

Barbie, Ken & Midge on Parade Gift Set, #1014 (1964 booklet)....400.00
Barbie, Living Barbie Action Accents Gift Set, #1585, 1970....275.00
Barbie, Talking Barbie Perfectly Plaid Set, #1193, 1971....275.00
Barbie, World of Barbie House, #1048, M....25.00
Barbie & Me Play Jewelry Set, M....10.00
Barbie & Midge Queen Size Chifferobe, M....50.00
Barbie & Skipper Living Room Furniture Group....50.00
Barbie Beauty Kit, 1961, M....15.00
Barbie Chair, Ottoman & End Table....20.00
Barbie Chaise Lounge....30.00
Barbie Cookin' Fun Kitchen....25.00
Barbie Country Living House, #8862, M....15.00
Barbie Doll Case, 1963, M....5.00
Barbie Electric Wristwatch Wall Clock, M....30.00
Barbie Fan Club Bracelet, M....15.00
Barbie Fan Club Promotional Wristwatch, M....40.00
Barbie Fashion Shop, #817, (1962 booklet)....50.00
Barbie Goes to State College, #4093, (1964 booklet)....75.00
Barbie Good Grooming Manicure Set, M....15.00
Barbie Heirloom Service, 1961....30.00
Barbie Icebreaker Set, #942....150.00
Barbie Knitting Kit....10.00
Barbie Mattel-A-Phone, M....15.00
Barbie Regal Bed, M....40.00
Barbie Sings Album, 45 rpm, 1961, M....15.00
Barbie Sofa, Bed & Coffee Table....30.00
Clothes, American Airlines Captain, #1779, (1964 booklet)....40.00
Clothes, Ballerina, #689, (1961 booklet)....20.00
Clothes, Best Man, #1425, (1965 booklet)....50.00
Clothes, Cheerful Chef....20.00
Clothes, Fashion Luncheon, #1656, (1965 booklet)....40.00
Clothes, Flower Girl, #1904, (1962 booklet), MIB....20.00
Clothes, Fraternity Dance, #1638, (1964 booklet)....40.00
Clothes, Fun at the Fair, #1624, (1964 booklet)....30.00
Clothes, Goin' Huntin', #1409, (1963 booklet)....25.00
Clothes, Ken in Hawaii, #1404, (1963 booklet)....35.00
Clothes, King Arthur, #0773, (1963 booklet)....40.00
Clothes, Land & Sea, #1917, (1964 booklet)....25.00
Clothes, Midnight Blue, #1617, (1964 booklet)....50.00
Clothes, Mr Astronaut, #1415, (1964 booklet)....100.00
Clothes, New Disco-Dater, #1807....25.00
Clothes, Outdoor Life, #1637, (1964 booklet)....20.00
Clothes, Patio Party, #1692, (1966 booklet)....35.00
Clothes, Picnic Set, #967, (#2 1958 booklet)....50.00
Clothes, Sailor, #0796, (1963 booklet)....25.00
Clothes, Sporting Casuals, #1671, (1965 booklet)....20.00
Clothes, The Yachtsman, #0789, (1963 booklet)....45.00
Francie & Casey Studio House, #1026, M....20.00
Francie House, #3302, (1966 booklet), M....20.00
Francie Mod a Go-Go Bedroom Furniture, by Suzy Goose, M....150.00
Francie Rise 'N Shine Gift Set, #1194, (1971 booklet)....275.00

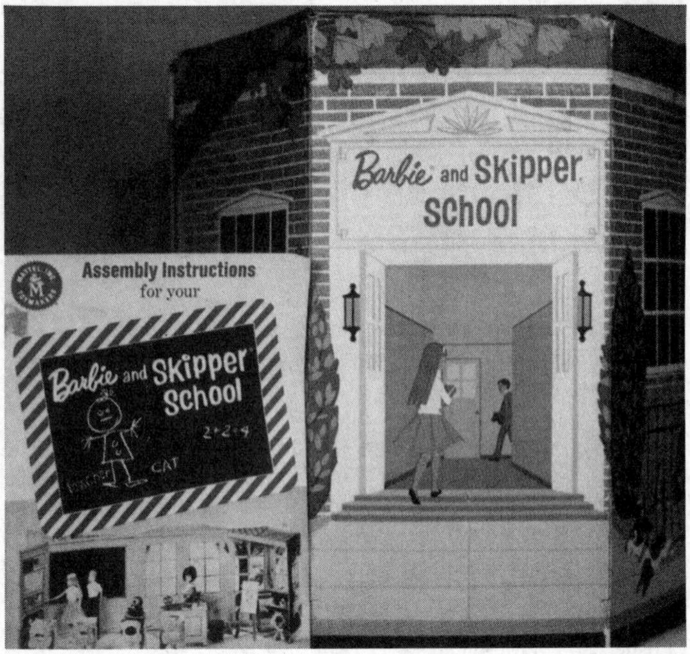

Barbie and Skipper's Schoolroom, 1965 Sears Christmas catalog, rare, $150.00, mint in box.

Malibu Ken Surf's Up Set, #1248, Sears Special, 1971....200.00
Miss Barbie Carrying Case, M....30.00
Skipper 'N Skooter Double Bunk Beds & Ladder....45.00
Skooter Cut 'N Button Gift Set, 1967 Sears Christmas catalog....175.00
Tutti & Chris Patio Picnic Case, M....15.00
Walking Jamie Strollin' in Style Gift Set, #1247, 1972....275.00

Bisque, Unmarked

#3 incised on head, brn o/c eyes, EX OC, 7″....700.00
#370, cloth body, bsk hands, glass eyes, o/m, 18″....300.00
Baby in gown, movable arms/legs, all orig, 5″....25.00
Boy, bsk head, fixed eyes, open mouth, orig clothes, 7″ L....110.00
French fashion, c/m, P/E, pwt eyes, hh, kid body, 15½″....2,000.00
French fashion, c/m, P/E, pwt eyes, hh, long bsk arms, 16″....1,850.00
Frozen Charlotte boy, 2¾″....30.00
Glass eyes, c/m, mohair wig, possibly Fr, EX costume, 6¼″....770.00
Immobiles, Japan, 1930s, orig box, set of 6, 3″....65.00
O/c eyes, o/m, bjtd, 21″....300.00
SkHd, w/fixed eyes, 9″....65.00

French Fashion Doll, bisque shoulderhead, hands and lower legs, with cloth and wire body, stationary eyes, closed mouth, red wig in purple velvet Victorian dress, hat and purse, 21″, $2,300.00.

Bru

Closed mouth, all kid body, bisque lower arms; Bru, 16″.....6,500.00
Closed mouth, all kid body, bisque lower arms; Bru, 18″.....7,400.00
Closed mouth, all kid body, bisque lower arms; Bru, 21″.....8,300.00
Closed mouth, all kid body, bisque lower arms; Bru, 26″.....9,500.00
Closed mouth, kid/wood body, bsk lower arms; Bru Jne, 12″..6,000.00
Closed mouth, kid/wood body, bsk lower arms; Bru Jne, 14″..6,600.00
Closed mouth, kid/wood body, bsk lower arms; Bru Jne, 16″..8,500.00
Closed mouth, kid/wood body, bsk lower arms; Bru Jne, 20″.10,000.00
Closed mouth, kid/wood body, bsk lower arms; Bru Jne, 25″.14,500.00
Closed mouth, kid/wood body, bsk lower arms; Bru Jne, 28″.15,500.00
Closed mouth, kid/wood body, bsk lower arms; Bru Jne, 32″.17,500.00
Closed mouth, kid/wood body, bsk lower arms; Bru Jne, 36″.22,000.00
Closed mouth, mkd Bru, circle dot, 16″..................7,400.00
Closed mouth, mkd Bru, circle dot, 19″.................11,500.00
Closed mouth, mkd Bru, circle dot, 23″.................14,500.00
Closed mouth, mkd Bru, circle dot, 26″.................16,000.00
Closed mouth, mkd Bru, circle dot, 28″.................17,300.00
Open mouth, comp walker's body, throws kisses, 18″........4,000.00
Open mouth, comp walker's body, throws kisses, 22″........4,500.00
Open mouth, comp walker's body, throws kisses, 26″........6,000.00
Open mouth, nursing (Bebe), high color, late SFBJ, 12″.....1,800.00
Open mouth, nursing (Bebe), high color, late SFBJ, 15″.....2,800.00
Open mouth, nursing (Bebe), high color, late SFBJ, 18″.....3,500.00
Open mouth, nursing Bru (Bebe), early, EX bsk, 12″........4,500.00
Open mouth, nursing Bru (Bebe), early, EX bsk, 15″........7,500.00
Open mouth, nursing Bru (Bebe), early, EX bsk, 18″........8,500.00
Open mouth, socket head on compo body; Bru, R, 14″......4,000.00
Open mouth, socket head on compo body; Bru, R, 17″......5,500.00
Open mouth, socket head on compo body; Bru, R, 22″......6,000.00
Open mouth, socket head on compo body; Bru, R, 25″......7,000.00
Open mouth, socket head on compo body; Bru, R, 28″......8,000.00
Open mouth, socket head on compo body; Bru, R, 32″......7,200.00

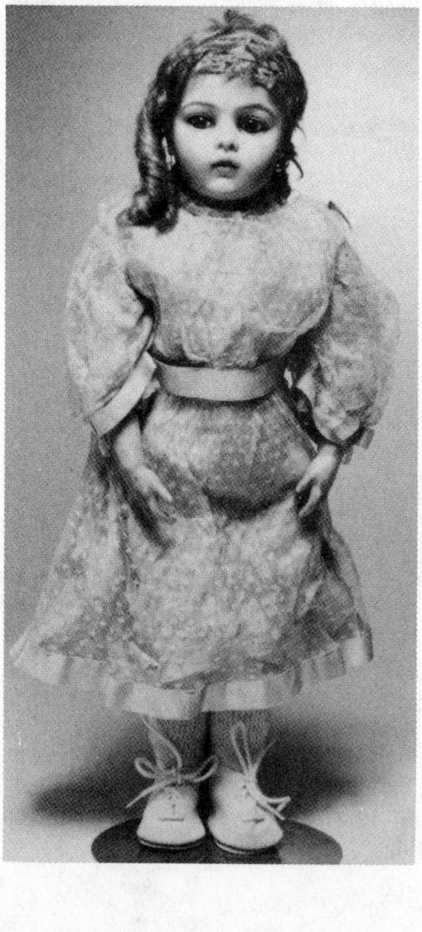

French bisque-head Bebe, incised Bru Jne, 6, brown paperweight eyes, pierced ears, closed mouth; kid body with paper label, bisque lower arms and wooden lower legs, in period dress with F.A.O. Schwarz label, 18½″, $8,500.00.

Bye-Lo

Kestner-type, 13″ head, OC, 11″ sgn body..................650.00
Molded bl shoes/wht socks, molded hair, OC, in carriage, 5″...650.00
Putnam, Grace; o/c eyes, cloth body, celluloid hands, 11″.....575.00

China, Unmarked

Blk, Blk features, OC, 9″..................................300.00
Blk molded hair, orig body, china limbs, dressed, 20″.........295.00
Blonde, low brow, molded eye lids, kid w/gussets, OC, 12″.....150.00
Blonde boy, EX details, exposed ears, cloth body, 23″........500.00
Blonde boy, exposed ears, Steuber body, pink tint, 14″.......375.00
Child, brush mkd, bsk arms/hands, china ft, EX dress, 14″....475.00
China hands & feet, undies only, early, 18½″, VG............350.00
Dotter, rpl body, china hands & ft, 23″......................495.00
Greiner-type, pnt lower lashes, exposed ears, 19″...........1,200.00
Molded necklace, glazed limbs/boots, 16″....................450.00
Pink lustre, wood body, china limbs, 6″.....................695.00
Ring box statue, mk Germany, 6″, EX.........................65.00
ShHd, 9 curls/pnt eyes, china/jtd wood body, OC, 1875, 5″....600.00
Smiling, kid body/rpl china hands, old clothes, early, 19″......325.00
Snood ShHd, OC, 14″...475.00
Steuber-type body, flat top, EX detail, leather limbs, 28″......950.00

Cloth

Amish girl, denim/wht cotton, dressed, Hazleton, Iowa, 19″....180.00
Art Fabric Mills, dtd Feb 13, 1900, as found, 22″, VG........140.00
Babyland Rag, all orig, 16″, EX............................495.00
Blk girl, embroidered features, yarn pigtails, 12½″, VG.........45.00
Blk girl, jtd arms/legs, yarn hair, handmade, 1930s, 16″........90.00
Cat, printed gray/wht, turn of C, 10½″.......................90.00
Embroidered face, old calico dress, late 1800s, 15″...........125.00
Jtd body, sewn-on features, yarn pigtails, 1930s, 15″..........40.00
Primitive, embroidered face, bl bead eyes, jumpsuit, 21″.......125.00
Red Cross nurse, in uniform w/scissors/symbols, 1900, 15″.....145.00
Shaker lady w/blk cape, print blouse, etc, embroidered, 13″.....65.00
Tom & Jerry, lithographed faces, 1940s, 19″, 8″, pr..........225.00

Composition, Unmarked

Indian lady, orig dress, 1930s, 25″ L, VG....................200.00
Negro, Southern woman, orig costume, 24″.................225.00
Negro, w/orig clothes, 14″.................................95.00
Nun, early, VG...40.00
Threaded pwt eyes, c/m, cloth body, Fr, 1870s, 16″..........550.00

Effanbee

Absolutely Abigail, 1952....................................65.00
Afternoon Tea, 1982..65.00
Alice, 1958, 15″..135.00
Alice Lee, 1924, 23″......................................200.00
Amanda, 1958..55.00
America's Children, 1936-1940, 21″.........................750.00
American Beauty Collection, 1979, ea........................50.00
Autumn, 1976-1980, ea......................................70.00
Baby Beauties, 1973, ea....................................55.00
Baby Bodkins, 1915, 11″...................................100.00
Baby Buds, 1919-1920, 7″...................................95.00
Baby Catherine, 1918, 20″..................................195.00
Baby Dainty, 1912-1925, 15″................................95.00
Baby Effanbee, 1925, 12″...................................125.00

Baby Evelyn, 1925, 18″ 165.00
Baby Huggins, 1913-1925, 9″ 50.00
Baby Snowball, 1915, 12″ 145.00
Baby-kin, 1940-1949, 9″ 135.00
Baroness, 1976-1977 .... 85.00
Bettina, 1960-1961, 1968, 16″ 95.00
Betty Ann, 1938, 15″ 185.00
Billy Bum, 1982-1983 .... 95.00
Bobbsey Twins, 1982-1983, ea 50.00
Bottle Tot, 1934, 16″ 125.00
Boudoir Doll, 1938, 24″ 125.00
Brigette, 1980 .... 70.00
Bubbles, Charlotte, 1924, 20″ 176.00
Bubbles, Dolly, 1924, 14″ 165.00
Bubbles, Walking, 1926, 14″ 178.00
Bud, 1960, 24″ 175.00
Buttons Monk, 1923, 12″ 95.00
Candy Kid, 1946, 13″ 150.00
Candy Walker, 1954-1956, 12″ 55.00
Caroline, 1976, 1978-1979 .... 55.00
Celeste, 1967, 18″ 125.00
Chantilly, 1981 .... 75.00
Charming Cheeks, 1974, ea 55.00
Chipper, 1965-1980, 15″ 55.00
Chris, 1969, 18″ 85.00
Civil War Lady, 1978-1979 .... 65.00
Cleopatra, 1978 .... 85.00
Coco, 1980 .... 95.00
Cookie, 1968-1969, 16″ 50.00
Cotton Candy Collection, 1980, ea 55.00
Country Look, 1973, ea 55.00
Crown Princess, 1976-1978 .... 85.00
Crystal Palace, 1979-1980 .... 75.00
Daphne, 1981 .... 75.00
Denise, 1981 .... 70.00
Downing Square, 1978-1979 .... 75.00
DyDee Educational Doll, 1971-1979, 20″ 115.00
DyDee Ellen, 1940, 15″ 85.00
Elizabeth, 1938, 29″ 175.00
Fairy Princess, 1935, 9″ 185.00
Florence Nightengale, 1977-1978 .... 85.00
Fluffy, 1954-1965, 8″ 35.00
Francoise, 1981 .... 55.00
Friday, 1980-1983 .... 50.00
Genevieve, 1981 .... 70.00
Gramercy Park, 1981 .... 75.00
Grandma, 1934, 10″ 175.00
Greece Soldier, 1980 .... 100.00
Grumpy, 1913-1930, 12″ 150.00
Gumdrop, 1962-1977, 16″ 55.00
Happy Boy, 1959-1965, 11″ 75.00
Hattie Holiday, 1981-1983 .... 95.00
Hearth Witch, 1981-1983 .... 60.00
Her Royal Highness, 1976-1978 .... 85.00
Honey Ann, 1952, 24″ 150.00
Honeybunch, 1923, 16″ 125.00
Hyde Park, 1980 .... 95.00
Jambo, 1940, 14″ 125.00
Jezebel, 1980 .... 95.00
John Wayne, Cowboy, 1981 .... 95.00
Jumbo Infant, 1915-1920, 20″ 200.00
Katherine, 1982, 1983 .... 60.00
Katie Kroose, 1918, 15″ 225.00
Lady Ashley, 1977 .... 85.00
Lady Grey, 1978 .... 80.00
Laughing Marietta, 1912, 12″ 110.00
Little Boy Blue, 1912, 12″ 100.00
Little Lady, Black, 1943, 21″ 265.00
Little Luv, 1970-1977, 14″ 45.00
Lovey Mary, 1926, 14″ 95.00
Lucifer, 1937, 14″ 145.00
Macawful The Scot, 1948, 14″ 110.00
Mae West, 1982 .... 95.00
Mama, 1979-1980 .... 65.00
Margie, 1921, 16″ 125.00
Marilee, 1924, 24″ 200.00
Mary Ann, 1923-1937, 18″ 175.00
Mary Jane, 1917-1923, 20″ 145.00
Mary Jane Toddler, 1963, 13″ 55.00
Mary Poppins, 1982 .... 50.00
Melodie, 1953-1956, 30″ 250.00
Memories, 1978, ea 65.00
Mimi, 1980 .... 55.00
Miss Chips, 1965-1980, 18″ 85.00
Miss France, 1976-1978 .... 65.00
Miss Israel, 1980-1981 .... 70.00
Miss Russia, 1978-1981 .... 65.00
Monday, 1980-1982 .... 55.00
Monique, 1980 .... 70.00
My Baby, 1963-1965, 14″ 40.00
My Friend, 1980 .... 50.00
Nanette, 1981 .... 70.00
Nap Time Gal, 1959, 13″ 45.00
Nast Santa, 1982-1983 .... 65.00
New Born Baby, 1925, 12″ 125.00
Nicole, 1978-1979 .... 95.00
Olivia, 1982-1983 .... 55.00
Pajama Baby, 1913, 14″ 95.00
Party Boy & Girl, 1979-1980, ea 60.00
Patricia, 1932, 14″ 185.00
Patricia Walker, 1954, 14″ 85.00
Patsy, 1926, 15″ 185.00
Patsy Ann, 1929, 19″ 225.00
Patsy Babyette, 1932-1947, 10″ 150.00
Patsy Joan, 1930, 1946, 16″ 200.00
Paul Revere, 1976-1977 .... 80.00
Peddler Woman, 1981-1983 .... 65.00
Pennsylvania Dutch, 1936, 1939, 9″ 125.00
Plains Couple, 1939, 9″ 145.00
Plymouth Landing, 1978-1980 .... 75.00
Popeye, 1933, 16″ 200.00
Precious Baby, 1962-1975, 24″ 65.00
Prince, 1978 .... 80.00
Puss 'N Boots, 1931, 11″ 200.00
Rabbit, 1931, 11″ 200.00
Red Cross Nurse, 1918, 12″ 110.00
River Brethern, 1936-1939, 7″ 90.00
Riverboat Gambler, 1981 .... 100.00
Rootie Kazootie, 1954, 12″ 95.00
Rosemary, 1925, 14″ 150.00
Ruth Ann, 1936-1939, 21″ 300.00
Saratoga, 1981 .... 55.00
Saturday, 1980-1983 .... 50.00
School Girl, 1913, 11″ 95.00
Shauna, 1981 .... 75.00
Sherry, 1955, 19″ 150.00
Sleeping Beauty, Disney, 1977-1978 .... 125.00
Snow White, Disney, 1977-1978 .... 125.00

Sonja on Skates, 1938, 16″ . . . 165.00
Spain Boy, 1980 . . . 100.00
Spring in Yellow, 1976 . . . 100.00
Sugar Baby, 1936-1940, 20″ . . . 165.00
Sugar Plum, 1963-1980, 20″ . . . 65.00
Sunday Best, 1982-1983 . . . 95.00
Suzette, 1939, 11″ . . . 125.00
Suzie Sunshine, Black, 18″ . . . 75.00
Sweetie, 1976, 16″ . . . 45.00
Tango Kiddies, 1914, 12″ . . . 95.00
Thursday, 1980-1983 . . . 55.00
Tinkerbelle, 1978 . . . 85.00
Today's Girl, 1943, 18″ . . . 145.00
Toonga, 1940, 14″ . . . 145.00
Tousle Tot, 1939-1941, 16″ . . . 125.00
Touslehead, Black, 1943, 15″ . . . 200.00
Trottie Trulife, 1921, 20″ . . . 165.00
Tuesday, 1976-1983 . . . 55.00
Turquoise, 1981 . . . 75.00
Twinkie, 1952-1980, 15″ . . . 65.00
Vanilla Fudge Collection, 1977, ea . . . 55.00
Violette, 1977 . . . 80.00
Wayside Inn, 1978-1979 . . . 70.00
WC Fields, 1980 . . . 250.00
Winkie, 1963, 16″ . . . 45.00
Winter, 1976-1980, ea . . . 70.00
Wolf, 1934, 10″ . . . 175.00

Germany

Bsk, movable arms, sgn, 5″ . . . 65.00
Bsk, orig clothes, kid body, o/m, o/c eyes, 21″ . . . 375.00
Mk 'My Sweet Baby,' bsk, 24½″ . . . 1,400.00
Tin head, leather hands, as found, mk, 10″ . . . 25.00
121, bsk, Skhd, fixed glass eyes, compo arms/legs, 8″ . . . 95.00
130/13, o/c eyes, o/m, jtd shoulders/hips, all bsk, 10½″ . . . 600.00
159/6, 2-faced: o/c mouth/eyes; o/c mouth pouter, 15″ . . . 1,210.00
165/1, o/c googly eyes-to-side character, bjtd compo, 13″ . . . 1,540.00
4/0, rpl wig, o/w orig, 12″ . . . 350.00

Half Dolls

Arms on chest & waist, yel ribbon in hair, Germany, 6″ . . . 65.00
Bald, molded corset, arms bent, Germany . . . 85.00
Blk bob hair, gold earrings, arms above, w/legs, in box . . . 325.00
Blonde, sitting, china legs, OC, hands away, 1 w/rose, 5″ . . . 145.00
Child, blonde curls, arms bent, Germany . . . 75.00
Court lady, 1 hand to hair, 1 away, Goebel, lg . . . 375.00
Elaborate costume & hair, hand to face/bodice, Goebel, 6″ . . . 600.00
Elaborate hairdo, draped neckline, posey held to chest, 6″ . . . 185.00
Flapper, hat & arms away, beads/blouse, legs on stand, 4″ . . . 300.00
Flapper, pink bodice & hat, w/pink flower, 2″ . . . 105.00
Flapper, purple dress, 2⅛″ legs w/gold slippers, 2¼″ . . . 170.00
Flapper, 1 bl & 1 gold bracelet, Germany, #5848, 1¾″ . . . 48.00
Gr bonnet & tie, hands to bonnet strings, Germany, #8030 . . . 100.00
Gray fancy hair-do, arms free, w/orig dress, legs, in box . . . 250.00
Hand touches gray hair, wht bodice, yel bow, Germany, 3¾″ . . . 75.00
Lady in evening dress, Germany, #6717, 3½″ . . . 125.00
Lady w/fan, arms away, #1202/3, Goebel, Crown mk, 5″ . . . 700.00
Mannequin, blonde w/ribbons/roses, arms away, Goebel, 6″ . . . 700.00
Nude bsk, applied roses in fancy hair, arms away, 4¾″ . . . 500.00
Nude bsk bust, hands out, roses in gray hair, 4¾x3″ . . . 300.00
Nude china bust, flower in hand, arms away, hairdo, 4¾″ . . . 500.00
Old fashioned lady, brn hair, Germany, #17243, 3⅜″ . . . 125.00

Half Doll brush, blonde hair, German, 8″ overall, $100.00.

Old fashioned lady, pink dress, brn hair, 5″ . . . 85.00
Old fashioned lady, very pretty, Germany, #5580, 3″ . . . 95.00
Pierrette head as powder puff in orig French box, Art Deco . . . 200.00
Pincushion, Carmen, china, 4½″ . . . 120.00
Pincushion, Flapper, blonde, china, 1920s, 3¼″ . . . 110.00
Pincushion, Isadora Duncan, china, 4¼″ . . . 300.00
Pincushion, lady w/yel silk crinoline, china, 7¼″ . . . 95.00
Pincushion, Marie Antoinette, china, #12903, 6″ . . . 95.00
Powder box, holds bouquet of flowers, mk Bavaria, 4½″, M . . . 125.00
Spanish dancer, comb, earrings, arms/castanets away, 11″ . . . 900.00
Tea cosy cover, baby in bonnet, hands outstretched . . . 300.00
Tea cosy cover, Jenny Lind, modeled bodice . . . 450.00
Tea cosy cover, little girl serving tea . . . 320.00
Tea cosy cover, Little Lottie . . . 425.00
Tea cosy cover, Marie Antoinette, modeled bodice . . . 200.00
Turban, arms away, no clothes, D&K, 4½″ . . . 300.00
2-faced, bust only, D&K . . . 450.00

Handwerck

#109, bl o/c eyes, P/E, brn wig, EX clothes, ca 1899, 20″ . . . 450.00
Bebe Cosmopolite, all orig, orig box . . . 1,200.00
GK, all orig, 7″ . . . 325.00
Goebel 720, bsk head, bl o/c eyes, 5-pc compo body, 4½″ . . . 250.00
Heinrich 119, P/E, brn o/c eyes, hh wig, old clothes, 26″ . . . 700.00
O/c eyes, all orig, sgn, 7″ . . . 400.00

Heubach

Boy, whistler, intaglio eyes, molded hair, all orig, 11½″ . . . 750.00
Boy, 5/6896, molded hair, intaglio eyes, o/c mouth, 17½″ . . . 1,200.00
Boy, 76/23, molded/pnt hair, intagio eyes, o/c mouth, 18″ . . . 1,200.00
Cat, sq mk, all orig, 6½″ . . . 1,250.00
Character, #11702, c/m, cloth body, o/c eyes, 20″ . . . 1,475.00
Character, #8192, o/c eyes, orig body, 9″ . . . 250.00
Character baby, #7608, 10½″ . . . 495.00
Character boy, molded hair, #7622, fan mk, 16½″ . . . 1,500.00
Character boy, o/c mouth, intaglio eyes w/teeth, 11″, EX . . . 650.00
Character boy, open mouth/bsk, 2 teeth, mk Sunburst, 12″ . . . 550.00
Coquette, c/m, leather body, 10″ . . . 775.00
Googlie, intaglio eyes to side, jtd limbs, all bsk, 4½″ . . . 200.00
Pouty, commercial baby clothes, #6894, 13″ . . . 750.00
Toddler, character face, o/c eyes/lashes, all jtd, 18½″ . . . 895.00

Heubach-Koppelsdorf

#250, pwt eyes, 5-pc mache body, German costume, 10″......225.00
#250.4, bl o/c eyes w/lashes, bjtd body, orig pnt, hh, 23″......475.00
#267.3 toddler, all jtd, orig wig, dimples, o/c eyes, 20½″.......895.00
Bent limb baby, #300, 16″...............................225.00
Bl o/c eyes, o/m, all orig, 14½″..........................250.00
Breather, brn o/c eyes/lashes, 5-pc bent limb baby, 12″.......425.00
O/c eyes, celluloid hands/orig christening gown, #339, 15″.....600.00
Toddler, #342, flirty eyes, wobbly tongue, 15-pc body, 23″.....850.00
98/12, o/c eyes, pierced nostrils, o/m/teeth, 5-pc, 22″.........365.00

Horsman

Campbell Kid, compo, w/tag, 12″.........................125.00
Chubby Baby Ruthie, cloth w/vinyl head/limbs, cryer, 20″.......35.00
Gold Medal Doll, 1-pc vinyl body/legs, o/c eyes, 1953, 26″.....165.00
Mary Poppins, vinyl, carpet bag outfit+2 extras, box, 11″......85.00

Ideal

Evel Knievel & rescue set, 7″............................20.00
Mortimer Snerd, all orig, 12½″...........................250.00
Saucy Walker, hp, auburn saran pigtails, RpC, 22″, VG........55.00
Superman, wood, jointed, 1940s, no cape, 13″...............345.00

Jumeau

Closed mouth, mkd EJ (incised) Jumeau, 10″..............3,500.00
Closed mouth, mkd EJ (incised) Jumeau, 14″..............4,800.00
Closed mouth, mkd EJ (incised) Jumeau, 16″..............5,200.00
Closed mouth, mkd EJ (incised) Jumeau, 19″..............5,600.00
Closed mouth, mkd EJ (incised) Jumeau, 21″..............6,000.00
Closed mouth, mkd Tete Jumeau, 10″....................2,200.00
Closed mouth, mkd Tete Jumeau, 14″....................2,600.00
Closed mouth, mkd Tete Jumeau, 16″....................2,800.00
Closed mouth, mkd Tete Jumeau, 19″....................3,300.00
Closed mouth, mkd Tete Jumeau, 21″....................3,600.00
Closed mouth, mkd Tete Jumeau, 23″....................3,700.00
Closed mouth, mkd Tete Jumeau, 25″....................4,100.00
Closed mouth, mkd Tete Jumeau, 28″....................5,200.00
Closed mouth, mkd Tete Jumeau, 30″....................5,500.00
Depose/Tete Jumeau, swivel head, earrings, long curls, 18″...3,700.00
Depose/Tete Jumeau, swivel head, earrings, long curls, 28″...5,000.00
E 6 J/Jumeau, swivel head, inset eyes, kid body, 16″........5,200.00
E 6 J/Jumeau, swivel head, inset eyes, kid body, 20″........5,600.00
EJ/Depose Brevete, swivel head, inset eyes, 'mama/papa,' 16″.5,200.00
Jumeau 1907, SkHd, applied ears, o/m, 18″ head, 32″......3,200.00
Jumeau 1907, swivel head, o/m, o/c eyes, pierced ears, 18″...1,600.00
Jumeau 1907, swivel head, o/m, o/c eyes, pierced ears, 23″...2,000.00
Jumeau 1909, swivel head, o/m, inset eyes, pierced ears, 21″.1,800.00
Long face, closed mouth, 21″..........................10,000.00
Long face, closed mouth, 25″..........................12,000.00
Long face, closed mouth, 30″..........................14,000.00
Open mouth, mkd Tete Jumeau, 10″.....................1,000.00
Open mouth, mkd Tete Jumeau, 14″.....................1,400.00
Open mouth, mkd Tete Jumeau, 16″.....................1,600.00
Open mouth, mkd Tete Jumeau, 19″.....................1,900.00
Open mouth, mkd Tete Jumeau, 21″.....................2,100.00
Open mouth, mkd Tete Jumeau, 23″.....................2,300.00
Open mouth, mkd Tete Jumeau, 25″.....................2,500.00
Open mouth, mkd Tete Jumeau, 28″.....................2,800.00
Open mouth, mkd Tete Jumeau, 30″.....................3,000.00
Open mouth, mkd 1907 Jumeau, 14″......................950.00
Open mouth, mkd 1907 Jumeau, 17″.....................1,500.00
Open mouth, mkd 1907 Jumeau, 20″.....................1,800.00
Open mouth, mkd 1907 Jumeau, 25″.....................2,300.00
Open mouth, mkd 1907 Jumeau, 28″.....................2,600.00
Open mouth, mkd 1907 Jumeau, 32″.....................3,000.00
Phonograph in body, o/m, 20″.........................2,600.00
Phonograph in body, o/m, 25″.........................3,000.00
Portrait Jumeau, closed mouth, 16″....................4,800.00
Portrait Jumeau, closed mouth, 20″....................5,500.00
211/Jumeau, swivel head, o/m, inset eyes, screamer, 17″....12,000.00

Bebe, incised 1907, 5, stamped in red: Tete Jumeau, paperweight eyes, brushed eyelids, pierced ears, open mouth with four teeth, 14″, $1,300.00.

Kammer and Reinhardt

#101, boy or girl w/glass eyes, 12″......................2,000.00
#101, boy or girl w/glass eyes, 16″......................3,800.00
#101, boy or girl w/glass eyes, 20″......................4,500.00
#101, boy or girl w/glass eyes, 9″.......................1,300.00
#101, boy or girl w/painted eyes, 12″....................1,500.00
#101, boy or girl w/painted eyes, 16″....................1,900.00
#101, boy or girl w/painted eyes, 20″....................2,850.00
#101, boy or girl w/painted eyes, 9″.....................1,000.00
#109, rare, w/glass eyes, 15″...........................7,500.00
#109, rare, w/glass eyes, 18″..........................12,000.00
#109, rare, 15″.......................................6,500.00
#109, rare, 18″......................................10,000.00
#112, rare, w/glass eyes, 15″...........................7,500.00
#112, rare, w/glass eyes, 18″..........................12,000.00
#112, rare, 15″.......................................7,200.00
#112, rare, 18″.......................................9,500.00
#114, rare, w/glass eyes, 15″...........................5,200.00
#114, rare, w/glass eyes, 18″...........................6,500.00
#114, rare, 15″.......................................3,600.00
#114, rare, 18″.......................................4,200.00
#115, closed mouth, 15″................................2,500.00
#115, closed mouth, 18″................................3,000.00
#115, closed mouth, 22″................................3,400.00

#115, open mouth, 15″ 1,400.00
#115, open mouth, 18″ 2,000.00
#115, open mouth, 22″ 2,500.00
#115a, closed mouth, 15″ 2,500.00
#115a, closed mouth, 18″ 3,000.00
#115a, closed mouth, 22″ 3,400.00
#115a, open mouth, 15″ 1,400.00
#115a, open mouth, 18″ 2,000.00
#115a, open mouth, 22″ 2,500.00
#116, closed mouth, 15″ 2,000.00
#116, closed mouth, 18″ 2,500.00
#116, closed mouth, 22″ 3,200.00
#116, open mouth, 15″ 1,000.00
#116, open mouth, 18″ 1,900.00
#116, open mouth, 22″ 2,300.00
#116a, closed mouth, 15″ 2,000.00
#116a, closed mouth, 18″ 2,500.00
#116a, closed mouth, 22″ 3,200.00
#116a, open mouth, 15″ 1,000.00
#116a, open mouth, 18″ 1,900.00
#116a, open mouth, 22″ 2,300.00
#117, closed mouth, 18″ 3,800.00
#117, closed mouth, 24″ 5,000.00
#117, closed mouth, 30″ 6,200.00
#117a, closed mouth, 18″ 3,800.00
#117a, closed mouth, 24″ 5,000.00
#117a, closed mouth, 30″ 6,200.00
Dolly face, open mouth, mold #400-403-109, etc, 16″ 425.00
Dolly face, open mouth, mold #400-403-109, etc, 20″ 500.00
Dolly face, open mouth, mold #400-403-109, etc, 24″ 625.00
Dolly face, open mouth, mold #400-403-109, etc, 28″ 725.00
Dolly face, open mouth, mold #400-403-109, etc, 38″ 1,450.00
Dolly face, open mouth, mold #400-403-109, etc, 40″ 2,000.00

Kestner

A, ShHd, o/m, MIG/Kestner, 19″ 358.00
A/5, ShHd, o/c mouth, 23″ 1,200.00
B, SkHd, o/m, 1896; MIG/Excelsior; DRP #70686/G, 22″ 425.00
B/6, ShHd, kid w/bsk ½ arms, o/c eyes, o/m w/teeth, 19″ 395.00
B/6, SkHd, jtd compo, o/m 2 teeth, set eyes, 22″ 425.00
Bergmann, SkHd, made for CM Bergmann, o/m; JDK/CM, 14″ 300.00
Bergmann, SkHd, made for CM Bergmann, o/m; JDK/CM, 17″ 375.00
Bergmann, SkHd, made for CM Bergmann, o/m; JDK/CM, 20″ 395.00
Century Doll Co, flanged closed dome, c/m, 15″ 700.00
D/8, SkHd & ShHd, kid w/bsk ½ arms, c/m, 15″ 800.00
E/9, ShHd, o/m, MIG, 26″ 565.00
E/9, SkHd, o/m, 1892, 26″ 565.00
G/11, SkHd, brn, o/m, 16″ 600.00
G/8, TrnShHd, o/m; MI/JDK, 19″ 395.00
Grace Putnam, bsk, 1-pc, pnt eyes; 10/10/COPR, 6″ 325.00
Grace Putnam, bsk, 1-pc body & head, 1923, 1/copy, 6″ 365.00
Grace Putnam, Bye-Lo baby, 1927, 6 12/Copr, 16″ 600.00
H 1/2, ShHd, o/m, 23″ 450.00
H/12, SkHd, o/c mouth, 1892, JDK, 23″ 1,500.00
Handwerck, SkHd, made for Handwerck, o/m; JDK/H/12, 23″ 425.00
Handwerck, SkHd, made for Handwerck, o/m; JDK/H/12, 27″ 600.00
I/13, SkHd, o/m, JDK, 1892, 16″ 350.00
I/13, SkHd, o/m, JDK, 1892, 26″ 525.00
J/13, SkHd, o/m, 1896, 27″ 600.00
JDK, bsk head on celluloid, R Gummi Co, turtlemark, 18″ 695.00
K/12, ShHd, made for Century, o/c mouth, molded hair, 21″ 1,350.00
Kewpie, bsk, Rose O'Neill/10 945G, 1913, 8″ 350.00
L/15, SkHd, c/m, 21″ 1,400.00
L/15, SkHd, swivel, ShPl, c/m, 21″ 1,400.00
L/3, ShHd, o/c mouth molded teeth, 23″ 1,300.00
N/17, SkHd, o/m, 1892, 17″ 375.00
SkHd, oriental, o/m; JDK/Kestner, 14″ 1,850.00
SkHd, pnt eyes, JDK/3 4/0, 8″ 295.00
TrnShHd, Kidoline w/bsk ½ arms, o/c eyes, G/MIG, 16″ 350.00
10, SkHd, bsk ShPl, c/m, 21″ 1,700.00
10 SkHd, o/c mouth 2 teeth; JDK/MIG, 12″ 350.00
10/G, SkHd, c/m, 1912; JDK, 12″ 695.00
1070, SkHd, o/m; G11/237 15/JDK Jr 1914 HILDA/GES, 16″ 2,550.00
11, SkHd, o/c mouth, pnt eyes to side; JDK/MIG, 11″ 800.00
12, SkHd, 5-pc baby, o/c eyes, o/m 2 teeth, JDK/MIG, 15″ 595.00
13, SkHd, o/m; JDK/MIG, 18″ 425.00
143, ShHd, kid w/bsk ½ arms, o/m, 17″ 650.00
145, ShHd, kid w/bsk ½ arms, o/c mouth, 15″ 850.00
145, SkHd, c/m; MI/O/G/18, 14″ 700.00
145, SkHd, c/m; 143/4/0/JDK, 11″ 750.00
147, TrnShHd, o/m; JDK, 25″ 495.00
148, ShHd, kid w/bsk ½ arms, o/m, 7½, 18″ 450.00
148, ShHd, kid w/bsk ½ arms, o/m, 7½, 21″ 495.00
150.1, bsk, Kestner seal on body, 8″ 375.00
151, SkHd, 5-pc baby, intaglio eyes, o/m/teeth, MIG/5, 12″ 400.00
151, SkHd, 5-pc baby, intaglio eyes, o/m/teeth, MIG/5, 16″ 525.00
151, SkHd, 5-pc baby, intaglio eyes, o/m/teeth, MIG/5, 20″ 700.00
152, SkHd, made for Wolf, 1916, o/m; LW & CO 12, 20″ 495.00
154, SkHd/ShHd, kid w/bsk ½ arms, o/m/teeth, DEP, 14″ 350.00
154, SkHd/ShHd, kid w/bsk ½ arms, o/m/teeth, DEP, 17″ 425.00
154, SkHd/ShHd, kid w/bsk ½ arms, o/m/teeth, DEP, 20″ 495.00
154, SkHd/ShHd, kid w/bsk ½ arms, o/m/teeth, DEP, 26″ 625.00
16, SkHd, o/m; JDK/MIG, 21″ 475.00
16/GES#1, ShHd, o/c mouth, molded boy's hair, 16″ 1,550.00
168, SkHd, o/m; MID/G7, 26″ 650.00
171, SkHd, jtd compo, o/m o/c eyes, 'Daisy'; F/M110, 15″ 350.00
171, SkHd, jtd compo, o/m o/c eyes, 'Daisy'; F/M110, 18″ 425.00
171, SkHd, jtd compo, o/m o/c eyes, 'Daisy'; F/M110, 22″ 495.00
172, ShHd, ball, kid fashion, bsk arms, c/m, earrings, 14″ 1,400.00
180 12/Ox/Crown seal, SkHd, o/m, 16″ 375.00
201, ShHd, celluloid on kid, set eyes/lashes, o/m JDK, 19″ 350.00
211, SkHd, 5-pc baby, o/c mouth, o/c eyes, MI10/G/JDK, 12″ 400.00
211, SkHd, 5-pc baby, o/c mouth, o/c eyes, MI10/G/JDK, 15″ 450.00
215, SkHd, jtd compo, fur eyebrows, o/m; MI9/GJDK, 21″ 475.00
217A/Kestner, bsk, c/m smile, googly pnt eyes, 12″ 2,750.00
221/GES/GESCH, SkHd, c/m smile, googly eyes; G/JDK, 21″ 6,500.00
245, SkHd, 5-pc baby, G/MIG/11/JDK Jr/1914 Hilda, 14″ 2,395.00
245, SkHd, 5-pc baby, G/MIG/11/JDK Jr/1914 Hilda, 17″ 2,750.00
257, SkHd, 5-pc baby, o/m, G/JDK, 10″ 350.00
257, SkHd, 5-pc baby, o/m, G/JDK, 16″ 500.00
257, SkHd, 5-pc baby, o/m, G/JDK, 20″ 685.00
257, SkHd, 5-pc baby, o/m, G/JDK, 24″ 825.00
26, K & Co/JDK/MIG/81, 16″ 375.00
270, SkHd, o/m, made for Carl Trautman; CP/39, 38″ 1,500.00
639, TrnShHd, closed dome, c/m; G/6, 18″ 995.00

Lenci

#109, organdy dress, sgn on ft, all orig, 22″, NM 1,800.00
American Indian, 17½″, NM 1,600.00
Chinaman, w/opium pipe, 1920s, 12½″, M 2,000.00
Dutch boy, pnt bl eyes, 17″ 550.00
Eastern European boy w/whip, brn pnt eyes, paper tag, 17″ 550.00
Hard plastic, tag inside foreign costume, '50s, in box, 9″ 65.00
Lady, EX silk & felt costume, ostrich feathers, '30s, 15½″ 850.00
Mascotte, w/tags, 9″ 225.00
Oriental, 25″, NM 2,800.00

Left, Rudolph Valentino as the Sheik, in striped caftan and leather boots with spurs, felt construction, Lenci, 29″, $1,500.00; Right, Lady; with brown painted eyes and curly blonde, possibly redressed in wine velvet robe with felt appliques, felt construction, Lenci, in doll's overstuffed chair, 29″, $1,000.00.

Russian boy, pnt gr eyes, 16½″ 550.00
Scandinavian boy, pnt brn eyes, 16″ 880.00
Scottish boy, pnt bl eyes, 16½″ 990.00
Turkish boy, pnt bl eyes, 16″ 575.00
Vinyl, o/c eyes, tag in orig dress, orig stand, '50s, 13½″ 125.00

Madame Alexander

Active Miss, hp, Violet/Cissy, 1954, 18″ 450.00
African, hp, 1966-1971, 8″ 575.00
Agatha, hp, Me & My Shadow series, Cissy, 1954, 18″ 750.00
Agatha Portrait, Jacqueline, 1975, 21″ 650.00
Alexander-kins, bend knee, walker, Wendy Ann, 1956-64, 8″ ... 200.00
Alice, hp, Maggie, 1951, 18″ 350.00
Alice in Wonderland, compo, Margaret, 21″ 575.00
Alice in Wonderland, compo, Wendy Ann, 11″ 350.00
American Child, compo, Tiny Betty, 1938, 7″ 185.00
American Tots, cloth, dressed in child's fashions 225.00
Antoinette, compo, 1946, 21″ 950.00
Apple Annie, hp, Americana Group, Wendy Ann, 1954, 8″ ... 1,400.00
Argentine Girl, hp, straight legs, mk Alex, 1973-1976, 8″ 65.00
Arlene Dahl, hp, Maggie, 1950-1951, 18″ 1,200.00
Aunt Agatha, hp, Wendy Ann, 1957, 8″ 1,200.00
Aunt Betsy, cloth/felt, 1930's 365.00
Aunt Pitty Pat, compo, 1939, 14″ 1,900.00
Babs, hp, Maggie, 1949, 20″ 400.00
Babsie Skater, Prince Elizabeth, 1941, 15″ 365.00
Baby Ellen, Black Sweet Tears, 1965-1972, 14″ 175.00
Baby Genius, cloth, 1930's, 11″ 365.00
Baby McGuffey, compo, 1937, 22″ 225.00
Baby Precious, cloth/vinyl, 1975, 14″ 150.00
Ballerina, hp, Wendy Ann, 1953-1956, 8″ 375.00
Beau Brummel, cloth 400.00
Beauty Queen, hp, Cissette, 1961 .... 325.00
Best Man, hp, Wendy Ann, 1955, 8″ 600.00
Betsy Ross, hp, bend knees, Wendy Ann, 1967-1972, 8″ 150.00
Betty, compo, Tiny, 1935-1937, 7″ 185.00
Binnie, hp, Ballerina, Cissy, 1956, 14″ 250.00
Binnie Walker, hp, Skater, 1955, 15″ 250.00
Bliss, Betty Taylor, 1979, 1980, 1981 .... 225.00
Blue Danube, hp, Margaret, 1953-1954, 18″ 700.00
Bo Peep, Little; hp, bend knees, Wendy Ann, 1962-1972, 8″ ... 165.00
Bonnie Baby, vinyl, 1954-1955, 16″ 125.00
Brazil, compo, Tiny Betty, 1937, 7″ 185.00
Brenda Starr, hp, 1964, 12″ 200.00
Bride, hp, Cissy, 1956, 25″ 475.00
Bride, hp, Margaret, in pink, 1950, 17″ 375.00
Bride, plastic/vinyl, 1973-1976, 14″ 225.00
Bridesmaid, compo, Little Betty, 1937-1939, 9″ 225.00
Bridesmaid, hp, Cissy, 1955, 20″ 400.00
Buck Rabbit, cloth/felt, 1930's 375.00
Bunny, plastic/vinyl, Melinda, 1962, 18″ 400.00
Butch, compo/cloth, 11″ 125.00
Camille, compo, Wendy Ann, 1938, 21″ 950.00
Canada, hp, bend knees, Wendy Ann, 1968-1972, 8″ 145.00
Carmen Portrait, compo, Tiny Betty, 7″ 225.00
Caroline, vinyl, w/dresses, 1961, 15″ 385.00
Carrot Top, cloth, 1967, 21″ 150.00
Chatterbox, plastic/vinyl, 1961, 24″ 350.00
Christening Baby, cloth/vinyl, 1951-1954, 11″ 175.00
Cinderella, compo, Betty, 1935-1937, 15″ 295.00
Cinderella, hp, Wendy Ann, 1955, 8″ 500.00
Cissette, hp, w/ballgowns, 10″ 350.00
Cissy, hp, trunk & wardrobe, 1955-1959, 20″ 1,200.00
Civil War, hp, Margaret, 1953, 18″ 700.00
Clarabell Clown, 1951, 19″ 225.00
Cornelia, Portrait Series, 1972, 21″ 575.00
Country Cousins, cloth, 10″ 150.00
Cry Dollie, vinyl, 1963, 14″ 225.00
Cynthia, hp, Black Margaret, 1952, 15″ 625.00
Danish, compo, Tiny Betty, 1937, 7″ 185.00
Davy Crockett Girl, hp, Wendy Ann, 1955, 8″ 650.00
Denmark, hp, Cissette, 1962, 11″ 1,200.00
Dilly Dally Sally, compo, Tiny Betty, 1937, 7″ 185.00
Ding Dong Dell, compo, Tiny Betty, 1937, 7″ 185.00
Dionne Quints, compo, toddlers, wigs & sleep eyes, 11″, ea ... 275.00
Dionne Quints, compo, toddlers, 19″, ea 475.00
Dottie Dumbunnie, cloth/felt, 1930s 450.00
Drum Majorette, hp, Wendy Ann, 1955, 7½″ 1,000.00
Dumplin' Baby, 1957, 23½″ 165.00
Dutch, compo, Tiny Betty, 1935-1939, 7″ 185.00
Edith, The Lonely Doll; plastic/vinyl, 1958, 16″ 300.00
Elise, hp/vinyl arms, in street clothes, 1957-1960, 16½″ 300.00
Elise, hp/vinyl arms, w/Marybel head, 1962, 16½″ 325.00
Evangeline, cloth, 18″ 350.00
Fairy Princess, compo, Tiny Betty, 1940, 7″ 185.00
Fairy Queen, compo, Wendy Ann, 1940, 14½″ 350.00
Faith, Americana Group, hp, Wendy Ann, 1961, 8″ 1,400.00
Findlay, Jane; 1979, 1980, 1981 .... 225.00
Finnish, compo, Tiny Betty, 1935-1937, 7″ 185.00
Five Little Peppers, compo, 1936, 13″ 250.00
France, compo, Tiny Betty, 1936, 7″ 185.00
French, hp, bend knees, Wendy Ann, 1961-1972, 8″ 145.00
Frou-Frou, cloth, in ballerina dress, 1951, 40″ 475.00
Gainsbourgh, Jacqueline, 1973, 21″ 500.00
Genius Baby, plastic/vinyl, 21″ 200.00
Gidget, plastic/vinyl, Mary Ann, 1966, 14″ 600.00
Girl on Flying Trapeze, cloth, pink satin tu-tu, 1951, 40″ 475.00
Godey, Jacqueline, 1965, 21″ 850.00
Godey Bride, hp, Margaret, 14″ 700.00
Godey Lady, hp, Margaret, 14″ 700.00
Goes Visiting, hp, Wendy Ann, 1955, 8″ 300.00
Goldilocks, cloth, 1930s, 18″ 450.00

Goya, hp, Wendy Ann, 1953, 8″........................1,200.00
Graduation, hp, Wendy Ann, 1957, 8″....................1,200.00
Grandma Jane, plastic/vinyl, Mary Ann, 1970, 14″...........325.00
Hansel, compo, Tiny Betty, 1937, 7″......................185.00
Happy, cloth/vinyl, 1970, 20″...........................250.00
Hedy LaMarr, hp, Margaret, 1949, 17″....................700.00
Honeybea, vinyl, 1963, 12″............................225.00
Hungarian, hp, bend knees, Wendy Ann, 1962-1972, 8″.......145.00
Ice Capades, Jacqueline.................................1,700.00
India, hp, bend knees, Wendy Ann, 1965-1972, 8″...........145.00
Indonesia, hp, bend knees, Wendy Ann, 1970-1972, 8″.......145.00
Italy, hp, bend knees, Wendy Ann, 1961-1972, 8″...........145.00
Jack & Jill, compo, Tiny Betty, 1938-1939, 7″..............185.00
Jacqueline, hp/vinyl arms, 1961-1962, 21″.................985.00
Jane Withers, compo, 1937, 20″.........................900.00
Janie, plastic/vinyl, 1960, 36″..........................400.00
Jeannie Walker, compo, 13″............................325.00
Joanie, plastic/vinyl, 1960, 36″.........................400.00
Judy, compo, Wendy Ann, 1945, 21″.....................950.00
Juliet, compo, Wendy Ann, 21″..........................950.00
June Bride, compo, 21″.................................525.00
Karen, hp, Margaret, 1948-1949, 15″.....................300.00
Kathleen, vinyl, rigid, 1959, 23″........................250.00
Kathy Baby, vinyl, molded hair, 11″.......................95.00
Kitten, cloth/vinyl, 1962, 14″...........................125.00
Kitten Kries, cloth/vinyl, 1967, 20″......................275.00
Lady Churchill, hp, Margaret, 1953, 18″..................800.00
Lady in Waiting, hp, Wendy Ann, 1955, 8″...............1,600.00
Lady Lovelace, cloth/felt, 1930s........................400.00
Lazy Mary, compo, Tiny Betty, 1936, 7″...................185.00
Lila Bridesmaid, compo, Tiny Betty, 1938, 7″..............185.00
Little Betty, compo, 9″..................................225.00
Little Butch, cloth/vinyl, 1967, 9″........................125.00
Little Dorrit, cloth, Dicken's character, 16″...............400.00
Little Genius, compo/cloth, 1937, 12″.....................165.00
Little Jack Horner, compo, Tiny Betty, 1937, 7″............185.00
Little Minister, hp, Wendy Ann, 1957, 8″................1,600.00
Little Shaver, cloth, 1940, 10″...........................275.00
Little Women, hp, bend knees, Wendy Ann, 1956-1959, 8″, ea.175.00
Lively Kitten, 1962, 14″...............................125.00
Lollie Baby, rubber/compo, 1941........................125.00
Lollie Bridesmaid, compo, Tiny Betty, 1938, 7″............185.00
Lucinda, plastic/vinyl, Janie, 1969, 12″..................350.00
Lucy, Americana Group, hp, Wendy Ann, 1961, 8″..........600.00
Madame Pompadour, hp/vinyl arms, Jacqueline, 1970, 21″...1,200.00
Madelaine, compo, Wendy Ann, 1940, 14″.................325.00
Madison, Dolly; President's Ladies, 1976..................275.00
Magnolia, 1977..585.00
March Hatter, cloth/felt.................................400.00
Marine, compo, 14″....................................325.00
Marlo Thomas, plastic/vinyl, Polly, 1967, 17″.............495.00
Mary Ann, plastic/vinyl, 1965, 14″.......................350.00
Mary Ellen Playmate, plastic/vinyl, Mary Ann, 14″..........475.00
Mary Martin, hp, Margaret, 1949, 14″....................600.00
Mary Muslin, cloth, pansy eyes, 1951, 19″.................300.00
Mary Sunshine, plastic/vinyl, 1961, 15″...................300.00
McGuffey Ana, cloth/vinyl, Barbara Jane, 1952, 29″.........400.00
McGuffey Ana, compo, Wendy Ann, 1938, 13″..............350.00
Melaine, compo, Wendy Ann, 1945, 21″...................750.00
Melinda, hp, Cissette, 1969, 11″.........................585.00
Mimi, plastic/vinyl, 1961, 30″...........................500.00
Miss America, compo, holding flag, 1940, 14″..............300.00
Mistress Mary, compo, Tiny Betty, 1937, 7″................185.00
Mommy & Me, hp, Margaret, 14″.........................600.00

Mrs Buck Rabbit, cloth/felt.............................400.00
Mrs Snoopie, cloth/felt.................................400.00
Muffin, cloth, 1966, 19″...............................175.00
Nan McDare, cloth/felt.................................400.00
Nancy Drew, plastic/vinyl, 1967, 12″....................325.00
Nina Ballerina, compo, Tiny Betty, 7″....................185.00
Nurse, compo, Tiny Betty, 7″...........................185.00
Orchard Princess, compo, Wendy Ann, 21″................950.00
Orphan Annie, plastic/vinyl, Mary Ann, 1965, 14″...........350.00
Parlour Maid, hp, Wendy Ann, 1956, 8″..................1,800.00
Patchity Pam & Pepper, cloth, 1965, 15″..................150.00
Peasant, compo, Tiny Betty, 1936, 7″....................185.00
Pinky, cloth, 16″......................................350.00
Piper Laurie, hp, Margaret, 1950, 14″....................700.00
Pitty Pat, cloth, 16″...................................375.00
Playing on the Beach, hp, Wendy Ann, 1955, 8″............325.00
Polish, compo, Tiny Betty, 1935-1936, 7″..................185.00
Polly Pigtails, hp, Maggie, 14½″.........................295.00
Pollyana, rigid vinyl, 1960, 16″.........................300.00
Poodles, standing or sitting, 14″.........................300.00
Precious, compo/cloth baby, 1937, 12″....................150.00
Prince Phillip, hp, Margaret, 1953, 17″...................500.00
Princess Alexandria, cloth/compo, 1937, 24″...............175.00
Princess Elizabeth, compo, Tiny Betty, 7″.................250.00
Princess Margaret Rose, compo, 1937-1938, 21″............395.00
Priscilla, cloth, 18″....................................400.00
Pumkin', rooted hair, 1976, 24″.........................225.00
Queen, hp, Margaret, 1953, 18″.........................600.00
Quiz-kins, hp, Wendy Ann, 1953, 8″...................1,200.00
Randolph, Martha; President's Ladies, 1976................275.00
Red Boy, hp, bend knees, Wendy Ann, 1972, 8″.............185.00
Red Cross Nurse, compo, Tiny Betty, 1937, 7″..............185.00
Red Riding Hood, compo, Tiny Betty, 1936, 7″..............185.00
Renoir, compo, Wendy Ann, 1945, 21″....................950.00
Riding Hood, cloth/felt, 1930s...........................400.00
Rodeo, hp, Wendy Ann, 1955, 8″.......................1,800.00
Roller Skating, Wendy Ann, 1953-1955, 8″.................650.00
Rose Fairy, hp, Wendy Ann, 8″........................2,000.00
Rosey Posey, cloth/vinyl, 1976, 14″......................250.00
Royal Wedding, compo, 21″.............................950.00
Ruffles Clown, 1954, 21″...............................400.00
Sally Bride, compo, Wendy Ann, 1938, 14″................250.00
Scarlett O'Hara, compo, Wendy Ann, 1945, 21″.............750.00
Scarlett O'Hara, w/white gown, 1965, 8″..................600.00
School Girl, compo, Tiny Betty, 7″.......................185.00
School Visitor's Day, hp, Wendy Ann, 1955, 8″.............325.00
Scotch, compo, Tiny Betty, 7″...........................185.00
Scottish, hp, bend knees, Wendy Ann, 1964-1972, 8″.........145.00
Seven Dwarfs, compo, 1937, ea..........................450.00
Sir Lapin Hare, cloth/felt, 1930s.........................400.00
Sleeping Beauty, compo, Little Betty, 1941, 9″..............225.00
Smarty, plastic/vinyl, 1962, 12″.........................325.00
Snow White, compo, Princess Elizabeth, 12″................300.00
Snow White, hp, Margaret, 21″..........................500.00
Soldier, compo, Wendy Ann, 14″........................325.00
Sonja Henie, compo, Wendy Ann, 1939, 11″................325.00
Sound of Music, dressed in sailor suit & tagged, Fredrich......275.00
Sound of Music, large set, Louisa, 14″....................295.00
Southern Belle, hp, Wendy Ann, 1954-1956, 8″...........1,000.00
Spanish, compo, Tiny Betty, 1935-1939, 7″.................185.00
Sugar Darlin', cloth/vinyl, 1964, 14″......................200.00
Summer Morning, hp, Wendy Ann, 1955, 8″.................325.00
Sunbeam, newborn infant, 1951, 11″......................165.00
Sunflower, clown, flower eyes, 1951, 40″..................450.00

Superior Quints, compo, 8″, ea....85.00
Susie Q, cloth, 1940....600.00
Sweet Baby, cloth/laytex, 1948, 18½″....200.00
Sweetie Baby, 1962, 22″....200.00
Tea Party, hp, Wendy Ann, 1955, 8″....325.00
Tennis, hp, Wendy Ann, 8″....400.00
Three Pigs & Wolf, compo, 1938, ea....425.00
Tiny Tim, compo, Wendy Ann, 1938, 14″....425.00
Tommy, hp, Lissy, 1962, 12″....1,400.00
Tyler, Julia; 1979-1981....275.00
Tyrolean Boy or Girl, became Austria 1974, 1962-1973, ea....145.00
Victoria, compo, Wendy Ann, 1938, 21″....950.00
Virginia Dare, compo, Little Betty, 1940, 9″....185.00
Wendy Ann, compo, 11″....350.00
Wendy Bride, compo, Wendy Ann, 14″....250.00
Wendy Bridesmaid, hp, Wendy Ann, 1955, 8″....800.00
Winnie Walker, hp, Cissy, 1953, 15″....250.00
Yolanda, Brenda Starr, 1965, 12″....225.00

Papier Mache

Jtd arms/legs, o/c eyes, c/m, 22″....250.00
Milliner's model, OC, 9½″....550.00
Molded hat/nape curls, wood hands/ft, 15½″....600.00
ShPl/hands/ft, orig pnt/wig, straw filled, 32″....495.00

Schoenhut

Baby w/wardrobe, 14″....500.00
Boy, baby-faced, pnt hair, rpt, 16″....550.00
Dolly face girl, RpC, 19″....445.00
Girl, pouty, brn mohair, rpt hair, 22″....695.00
Toddler, baby face, 12″, NM....425.00

SFBJ

Bebe Parisiana, 1902, bsk head, c/m, inset eyes, 16″....1,800.00
Celestine, bsk SkHd on mache, o/m, inset eyes, 18″....900.00
SkHd, fully jtd mache/wood body, o/m, o/c eyes, 30″....2,200.00
Tete Jumeau, pierced ears, o/c eyes/lashes, o/m, 18″....1,600.00
11, compo w/bsk swivel head, c/m, inset eyes, 16″....700.00
20, molded ptd shoes & eyes, 5-pc body, Paris/12, 10″....350.00
203, 1900 bsk head on compo, o/c mouth, inset eyes, 20″....2,000.00
215, bsk swivel on compo, c/m, inset eyes, 15″....1,600.00
227, brown swivel closed dome head, animal skin wig, 15″....2,200.00
227, brown swivel closed dome head, animal skin wig, 18″....2,600.00
227, closed dome, o/m, inset eyes, ptd hair, 15″....1,800.00
228, toddler, c/m, inset eyes, mache body, 16″....1,900.00
229, swivel head, o/c mouth, inset eyes, compo, 18″....2,200.00
229, wood walker, o/c mouth, inset eyes, 18″....1,850.00
230, pierced ears, compo walker, o/m, inset eyes, 16″....1,200.00
230, SkHd, pierced ears, o/m, o/c eyes, 23″....1,700.00
235, closed dome, molded hair, o/c mouth & eyes, 16″....1,700.00
235, closed dome, molded hair, o/c mouth & eyes, 8″....750.00
236, laughing Jumeau, o/m, o/c eyes, double chin, 12″....900.00
236, laughing Jumeau, o/m, o/c eyes, double chin, 20″....1,600.00
238, swivel head, o/m, inset eyes, compo body, Paris 6, 15″....3,500.00
239, Poulbot, c/m, street urchin, red wig, 14″....3,900.00
239, Poulbot, c/m, street urchin, red wig, 17″....4,500.00
247, toddler, o/c mouth/2 inset teeth, 16″....2,200.00
247, toddler, o/c mouth/2 inset teeth, 20″....3,000.00
247, toddler, o/c mouth/2 inset teeth, 24″....3,400.00
247, twirp, o/c eyes & mouth/2 teeth, SkHd, 21″....2,800.00
251, 1099 character baby, o/c mouth, eyes, hair lashes, 16″....1,500.00
251, 1099 character baby, o/c mouth, eyes, hair lashes, 18″....1,800.00
252, character, pouty, c/m, inset eyes, mache body, 18″....3,000.00
252, character, pouty, c/m, inset eyes, mache body, 22″....5,500.00
257, 1900 toddler, o/c mouth, inset eyes, 16″....1,600.00
266, bsk head, closed dome, o/c mouth, character, 20″....1,800.00
301, bsk SkHd on compo, o/m, inset eyes, 16″....595.00
301, bsk SkHd on compo, o/m, inset eyes, 22″....895.00
301, bsk SkHd on compo, o/m, inset eyes, 30″....1,300.00
60, French WWI nurse, 5-pc body, SFBJ/13/0, 8½″....250.00
60, Kiss-Blower, cryer walker, 22″....1,650.00
60, SkHd, compo w/straight legs, o/m, curved arms, 15″....650.00
60, SkHd, mache/compo 1-pc body, plunger cryer, o/m, 11″....450.00

Shirley Temple

Compo, 11″, cowboy outfit, orig pin, EX....675.00
Compo, 11″, in trunk, EX....700.00
Compo, 11″, orig dress, wig, undies, flirty eyes, EX....595.00
Compo, 13″, all orig, in Shirley trunk....500.00
Compo, 13″, Curly Top, orig dress, M....400.00
Compo, 13″, dress not tagged....275.00
Compo, 13″, EX orig....310.00
Compo, 13″, Stand Up & Cheer, all orig....300.00
Compo, 13″, tagged bl/wht dress w/pin, 1930s, all orig....360.00
Compo, 15″, Capt January, bl suit, w/label, EX....445.00
Compo, 16″, Our Little Girl, w/pin, all orig, tagged, M....500.00
Compo, 16″, red dotted dress, velvet coat/hat, all orig....500.00
Compo, 17″, copy of Curly Top, EX....575.00
Compo, 18″, w/pin, all orig....565.00
Compo, 20″, all orig, tagged dress, orig box....600.00
Compo, 22″, sailor, w/pin & label, all orig....600.00
Compo, 22″, tagged pink dance dress, all orig, Ideal, VG....600.00
Compo, 25″, flirty, redressed....585.00
Compo, 25″, sailor suit, EX....725.00
Compo, 27″, flirty eyes, orig, EX....675.00
Compo, 27″, flirty eyes, sailor dress, w/pin, in box, EX....795.00
Compo, 28″, orig wig, EX....1,200.00
Compo, 7″, Japan, M....100.00
Dress, for 13″ compo, tagged....50.00
Dress, for 18″ compo, tagged....100.00
Vinyl, 12″, 1950s, MIB....200.00
Vinyl, 12″, 1957, script pin, pocketbook, 1957, M....140.00
Vinyl, 15″, RpC, Ideal....150.00
Vinyl, 16″, Rebecca, Ideal, 1972....150.00
Vinyl, 17″, OC, 1950s, M....210.00
Vinyl, 18″, OC, Ideal, M....235.00
Vinyl, 19″, flirty eyes, all orig, 1957....250.00
Vinyl, 8″, Stowaway, Ideal, 1982....35.00
Wig, for 20″ doll....85.00

Simon and Halbig

AW, SkHd, o/m; SH/13, 21″....450.00
Baby Blanche, SkHd, o/m baby; S&H, 16″....495.00
Baby Blanche, SkHd, o/m baby; S&H, 21″....695.00
CM Bergmann, SkHd, o/m, 1895; Halbig/S&H5, 30″....850.00
CM Bergmann, SkHd, o/m, 1897; S&H6, 12″....175.00
CM Bergmann, SkHd, o/m; Simon & Halbig, 3½, 18″....450.00
Elenore, SkHd, o/m; CMB/Simon & Halbig, 18″....550.00
G68, SkHd, flirty eyes, 1908; S&H/K*R, 16″....500.00
Handwerck, SkHd, o/m, 1893; 16″....375.00
Handwerck, SkHd, o/m, 1895; G/S&H/1, 16″....375.00
Handwerck, SkHd, o/m; G/Halbig, 4, 26″....600.00
S&H3, all bisque, c/m, inset eyes, molded on shoes, 6″....285.00

SkHd, 2 teeth, tongue; K*R/Simon & Halbig, 116a-38, 17″...1,800.00
10, SkHd, o/m; G/Halbig/S&H, 16″....400.00
10, SkHd, o/m; G/Halbig/S&H, 19″....475.00
10, SkHd, o/m; G/Halbig/S&H, 22″....500.00
10½, SkHd, o/m, flirty o/c eyes; S&H, 18″....950.00
100, SkHd, o/m; Simon & Halbig/S&C/G, 15″....395.00
100, SkHd, o/m; Simon & Halbig/S&C/G, 22″....500.00
101, SkHd, c/m; Simon & Halbig/K*R, 16″....1,900.00
1059, SkHd, swivel on ShPl, wood w/kid fashion, o/m, 19″...1,400.00
109, SkHd, o/m, 1895; Handwerck/G/Halbig, 23″....500.00
114, SkHd, c/m; Simon & Halbig K*R/L, 14″....3,000.00
114, SkHd, c/m; Simon & Halbig K*R/L, 20″....4,400.00
114, SkHd, c/m; Simon & Halbig K*R/L, 9″....1,500.00
115, SkHd, c/m, 1912; K*R, Simon & Halbig, 16″....2,400.00
115a, SkHd, c/m pouty; K*R/Simon & Halbig, 15″....2,500.00
1159, SkHd, adult body, 1905; G/Simon & Halbig/S&H7, 14″..750.00
1159, SkHd, adult body, 1905; G/Simon & Halbig/S&H7, 18″.1,200.00
1159, SkHd, adult body, 1905; G/Simon & Halbig/S&H7, 24″.1,600.00
116a, SkHd, c/m; K*R/Simon Halbig, 17″....2,500.00
117, SkHd, c/m, 1919; Simon & Halbig/K*R, 16″....3,300.00
117, SkHd, c/m, 1919; Simon & Halbig/K*R, 20″....4,200.00
117a, SkHd, c/m; K*R/Simon & Halbig, 16″....3,300.00
117a, SkHd, c/m; K*R/Simon & Halbig, 20″....4,200.00
117n, SkHd, c/m; Simon & Halbig/K*R, 20″....3,900.00
119, SkHd, o/m; 13/Handwerck 5/Halbig, 16″....400.00
120, SkHd, o/m; SH, 28″....2,500.00
121, SkHd, o/c mouth/teeth, flirty o/c eyes, 1920; K*R, 16″..1,200.00
121, SkHd, o/c toddler, 16″....1,400.00
121, SkHd, o/m, 1920; K*R/Simon & Halbig, 14″....400.00
121, SkHd, o/m, 1920; K*R/Simon & Halbig, 19″....525.00
122, SkHd, 1920; K*R/Simon & Halbig, 14″....450.00
126, SkHd, o/c mouth; SH, 23″....1,500.00
126, SkHd, o/m; Simon & Halbig/K*R, 14″....425.00
126, SkHd, o/m; Simon & Halbig/K*R, 19″....575.00
127, SkHd, o/m; K*R, Simon & Halbig, 18″....425.00
128, SkHd, o/m; K*R/Simon & Halbig, 14″....425.00
128, SkHd, o/m; K*R/Simon & Halbig, 19″....575.00
1296, SkHd, 1911; FS&Co/Simon & Halbig, 14″....475.00
1329, SkHd, o/m, olive; G/Simon & Halbig/SH, 14″....1,600.00
151, SkHd, o/c mouth, ptd eyes; S&H/1, 16″....4,000.00
156, SkHd, 1925; S&H, 18″....450.00
156, SkHd, 1925; S&H, 22″....500.00
159, SkHd, o/m; Simon & Halbig, 16″....400.00
179, SkHd, o/m; Simon & Halbig S11H DEP, 20″....2,100.00
1848, SkHd, o/m; Jutta Simon & Halbig, 16″....485.00
191, SkHd, o/m; Bergmann/CB, 18″....450.00
1923, SkHd, o/m; SH Sp 53/4/G, 14″....325.00
1923, SkHd, o/m; SH Sp 53/4/G, 21″....475.00
1923, SkHd, o/m; SH Sp 53/4/G, 26″....650.00
246, SkHd, o/m, 1900; K*R/Simon & Halbig, 18″....450.00
282, SkHd, o/m; S H, 14″....375.00
282, SkHd, o/m; S H, 18″....450.00
282, SkHd, o/m; S H, 22″....500.00
383, SkHd, flapper body; S H, 14″....900.00
402, SkHd, o/m; K*R SH, 16″....400.00
403, SkHd, o/c mouth; K*R, Simon & Halbig, 20″....1,200.00
403, SkHd, o/m, walker; K*R SH, 21″....750.00
409, SkHd, o/m; S&H, 24″....550.00
409, SkHd, o/m; S&H, 26″....650.00
409, SkHd, o/m; S&H, 30″....800.00
48m SkHd, o/m, 1905; Simon & Halbig/K*R, 27″....650.00
50, SkHd, c/m; Simon & Halbig, 16″....950.00
50, SkHd, o/m, 1900; K*R/Simon & Halbig, 14″....375.00
53, SkHd, c/m, brown bsk; Simon & Halbig/K*R, 16″....1,200.00
530, SkHd, o/m; G/Simon & Halbig, 21″....450.00
540, SkHd, o/m; G/Halbig/S&H, 16″....1,000.00
550, SkHd, o/m; Simon & Halbig/S&H, 16″....400.00
570, SkHd, o/m, walking, head turns; G/Halbig S&H, 18″....700.00
570, SkHd, o/m; Halbig S&H/G, 18″....475.00
576, SkHd, o/m; Simon & Halbig, 16″....400.00
612, SkHd, o/m; MIG/S&H/CM Bergmann, 16″....400.00
670, SkHd, o/m; Simon & Halbig, 16″....400.00
70, SkHd, o/m, 1896; Halbig/K*R, 26″....650.00
719, SkHd, c/m; S&H DEP, 16″....1,800.00
739, SkHd, c/m, brown; S 5 H DEP, 14″....1,400.00
739, SkHd, c/m, brown; S 5 H DEP, 18″....2,000.00
759, SkHd, o/m, brown; S 10 H DEP, 20″....850.00
769, SkHd, S&H DEP, 17″....1,600.00
929, SkHd, c/m; S&H, DEP, 20″....1,800.00
929, SkHd, c/m; S&H, DEP, 25″....2,800.00
939, o/c eyes, o/m; S16H, 30″....3,200.00
939, SkHd, c/m; S 11H DEP, 17″....2,000.00
939, SkHd, c/m; S 11H DEP, 23″....2,800.00
940, SkHd, closed dome, o/c mouth; S 2 H, 26″....2,900.00
945, SkHd, c/m; S 2 H DEP, 16″....2,000.00
99, SkHd, o/m, 1899; 11½ Handwerck/Halbig, 16″....400.00

Steiner

A series, Bte SBGD FRE-9, pwt eyes, mohair, jtd, 17″....3,400.00
Bourgoin, bl eyes, c/m, French clothes, rpl wig, 16″....4,200.00
C/m, wired glass eyes, P/E, hh, bjtd, str wrists, 29″....6,000.00
Mechanical, orig clothes, rpl wig, 20″....2,500.00
Phoenix, *88, close mouth, pwt eyes, hh, bjtd, 16″....2,400.00
Ste C 3/0, Bourgoin, threaded eyes, c/m, h/h, 9¾″....990.00
Wire eyes, c/m, bjtd body, old clothes, 33″....6,400.00
Wire eyes w/lever, jtd wrists, P/E, orig sgn body, 23″....5,200.00
12, pwt eyes/brushed lids, P/E, c/m, bjtd compo, 27½″....4,600.00

Bebe, Jules Steiner, incised 12, with paperweight eyes, brushed eyelids, pierced ears and closed mouth, on ball-jointed composition body, 27½″, $4,200.00.

Vogue

Ginny, Far Away Lands, Austrian Boy, pnt eyes, MIB..........50.00
Ginny, Far Away Lands, Jamaica, upsweep, pnt eyes, MIB.......50.00
Ginny, Far Away Lands, Spain, lace/velvet gown, MIB..........50.00
Ginny, hp, str leg, jtd knees..............................100.00
Ginny, hp, str leg, molded lashes..........................125.00
Ginny, hp, str leg, pnt eyes...............................175.00
Ginny, hp, str leg, pnt lashes.............................175.00
Ginny, o/c eyes, blonde, gr overalls, 1978, MIB...............20.00
Ginny student desk, MIB......................................20.00
Ginny wardrobe, MIB..35.00
Nicole, long brn hair, bl o/c eyes, bl dress...................32.00
Toodles, blonde wig, gown, jacket, slip, teddie, shoes, 8″......175.00

Wax, Poured Wax

Bl glass eyes, orig clothes, 12″...........................175.00
Over compo, glass eyes, 1840 provenance, all orig, 13″.......500.00
Poured, bl eyes, rooted hair, old clothes, EX rstr, 16″........950.00
Poured, glass eyes, inserted hair, OC, ca 1790, 10″..........575.00

Miscellaneous

ABG, #1361, bl o/c eyes, lashes, 22″......................695.00
ABG, character, o/m/teeth, bjtd compo, jtd wrists, 29″.......1,200.00
American Character, Sweet Sue Bride, hp/vinyl, '50s, 20″.......95.00
Amish, girl, dressed, Clark Co, MO, 1930s, 20″..............170.00
Amish, girl, dressed w/cape, stocky, Hazelton, IA, 18½″.......185.00
Averill, Georgene; Bonnie Babe, 4½″.......................950.00
Baby Barry Tag, NYC, Emmett Kelly, rubber hands/ft, 20″.....125.00
Billiken, OC, sgn, 12″...................................275.00
Borgfeldt, George, baby, 17½″ head, 5-pc compo, hh, 26″...1,250.00
Borgfeldt, My Girlie, hh lashes/braids, o/c eyes, jtd, 26″.......695.00
CB, 3-face: smiles/sleeps/cries; bsk/cloth/compo, 11″..........650.00
Chad Valley, girl, w/tag, 15″..............................245.00
Chase, bobbed hair, old clothes (orig?), 16″.................950.00
Chase, hospital baby, weighted body, 20″, M.................450.00
Chase, orig cloth body w/bent legs & arms, 1903, 28″.......1,200.00
Chase, orig sateen torso, jtd limbs, bobbed hair, 16″.........950.00
Demalcol, googlie eyes, orig body, 11″.....................895.00
DEP, brn bsk, o/m w/upper teeth, glass eyes, P/E, hh, 12″....595.00
Dolly Mine, bsk head, jtd, orig box, 20″ L..................450.00
ED, P/E, pwt eyes, hh, bjtd/jtd wrists, 17″.................2,200.00
ED 9 D, o/m, set eyes, bsk bjtd/jtd wrists, hh, P/E, 21″......2,600.00
Eden Bebe, o/m, pwt eyes, orig body, antique clothes, 30″...3,200.00
EJ, sgn dress, 11½″.....................................3,600.00
F&B, Baby Tinyette, brn molded hair, brn eyes, 7½″, EX......125.00
FG, F 11 G, child, pwt eyes, c/m, applied ears, 28″..........3,900.00
FG, French fashion, P/E, pwt eyes, hh, head swivels, 16″....1,495.00
FG, Harlequin, orig silk clothes, gold metal trim, 12″.......1,495.00
French Limoges, Cherie, pwt jeweled eyes, bjtd body, 20″.....950.00
Gerber Baby, red/wht romper, Anniversary, 1979, 17″, MIB.....45.00
Gibbs, Ruth: Godey's Little Lady, OC, pink china, 7″, EX......45.00
Greiner, old clothes, 1858 label, 20″, EX...................950.00
H, French fashion, molded eyelids, fat face, OC, 17″........3,200.00
Hummel, Our Hero, jtd cloth body/compo head, all orig, 16″.1,200.00
Jullian, French, open mouth, pwt eyes, hh, bjtd, OC, 30″....3,800.00
Kley & Hahn, brn o/c eyes/lashes/lg curls, bjtd, rpt, 34″.....1,850.00
Kley & Hahn, character baby #158, c/m/teeth, o/c eyes, 19″..2,200.00
Kley & Hahn, toddler, solid dome, o/c mouth, 5-pc, 17″.......875.00
Kley & Hahn, 520/8½, pnt eyes, c/m, bjtd compo body, 21″..2,400.00
Kley & Hahn, 525/S ½, molded pnt hair, intaglio eyes, 19½″.2,300.00
Kruse, Kathe; boy, no clothes, EX pnt, 16″..............1,200.00
Kruse, Kathe; Puppe I, ca 1911-20, 16″, NM..............1,600.00
Kruse, Kathe; 5-seam leg, stuffed head, ft sgn, OC, 17″......1,250.00
Leopold Lambert, musical automaton, girl w/bird, 19″........3,800.00
LPS, mk on head, bjtd, str wrists, OC, Germany, 10½″........600.00
Lyon, French, wood w/glass eyes, hh, worn OC, in box, 20″..5,500.00
Morimura Bros, Japan, bent limb baby, o/c eyes, 13½″........375.00
Munich Art, oil-pnt compo head, jtd body, old clothes, 15″...1,200.00
Nippon, A3/RE, bsk w/compo body, o/m, 10″..................225.00
Pandora, wood, rpl strips, 1700s, 19″.....................1,500.00
Penwiper, sleep-eyes, 1½″ head incised 203/3.................325.00
Rabery & Delphieu, R3D, pwt eyes, P/E, o/c mouth, 23″.....2,600.00
RD, c/m, glass eyes, P/E, hh, bjtd/jtd wrists, 19″...........2,200.00
Regal, Barbara Ann Scott, very minor crazing, 15½″..........200.00
Reliable, Hiawatha, mohair braids, OC, tag, 12½″..............85.00
Reliable, Highland Laddie, compo, all orig, w/tag, 12½″........85.00
S&Co, o/c eyes, o/c mouth, bsk head, 5-pc compo baby, 15″...625.00
Superior #2015, cloth body, rpt leather arms, 25″, EX........850.00
Turtlemark, Dutch boy, jtd celluloid, glass eyes, OC, 12″......125.00
UFDC Convention, Miami Sunshine, smocked dress...........165.00
UFDC Convention, Milwaukee, the clown...................145.00
UFDC Convention, NYC Little Apple, w/highchair............125.00
Wood, articulated, detailed face/fingers/toes, worn, 11½″.......125.00
Wood, Queen Anne, horsehair wig, antique clothes, 20″, EX...650.00
WPA, lady & man, made for work projects, 12″, pr..........225.00

Door Knockers

Door knockers, those charming precursors of the door bell, come in an intriguing array of shapes and styles--the very rare ones come from England. Cast iron examples made in this country were often produced in forms similar to the more familiar doorstop figures.

When no condition is indicated, the items listed below are assumed to be in excellent condition.

Acanthus leaf design, CI, 7″..............................25.00
Arm & Hammer advertising, brass..........................35.00
Bat finial, CI, 9½″......................................25.00
Bear standing by tree trunk, brass, 3½″......................35.00
Cat, body hunched, menacing, brass, oval bk, 5″ L............25.00
Cat, high arched back, bronze, English, 1900, 3½″.............25.00
Flower basket, knocks against openwork patterned plate, CI.....35.00
Foliage detail, CI, 8½″...................................10.00

Brass, Empire style, lady's head, stamped England, 4″ x 2¾″, $20.00.

Fox head, w/knocking ring in mouth, CI, EX detail, 5½" 65.00
Genie w/lamp, brass 40.00
Lady's head, CI, 1840s, 8" 75.00
Owl, knocks against grooved plate, CI, orig colors 35.00
Parrot, CI, colorful 25.00
Simple Scroll/no bkplate, brass, Victorian, 9½" 25.00
Victorian, ornate, CI, mk Akedrick & Sons, Eng reg mk, 9½" ...15.00
Warrior's head, brass, 1920s, lg 30.00
Wm Wadsworth bust, bronze, mk England, 3¼x1¼" 30.00
Woodpecker, brass 25.00
Woodpecker, wooden, VG pnt 49.00

Doorknobs

Decorative doorknobs are found in Bennington-type pottery, fancy Victorian brass, glass, and hand painted porcelain. Just about any interesting old knob is collectible.

When no condition is indicated, the items listed below are assumed to be in excellent condition.

Bennington type, pr 25.00
Brass, relief decor, pr 18.00
Cut glass, 2", pr 45.00
Mercury glass, grape design, pr 45.00
Porc, HP rose, orig box & ad 22.00

Doorstops

Although introduced in England in the mid-1800s, cast iron doorstops were not made to any great extent in this country until after the Civil War. Once called 'door porters,' their function was to keep doors open to provide better ventilation. They have been produced in many shapes and sizes, both dimensional and flat backed, and in the past few years have become a popular yet affordable collectible. While cast iron examples are the most common, brass, wood, and chalk were also used. An average price is in the $40 to $50 range, though some are valued at more than $100. Doorstops retained their usefulness and appeal well into the thirties.

When no condition is indicated, the items listed below are assumed to be in excellent condition.

Basket of flowers, bow atop, basketweave, mc rpt, 10½" 50.00
Basket of flowers, high arched hdl, CI, rpt, 9½" 45.00
Basket of flowers, loop hdl, rnd stepped base, CI, rpt, 8" 30.00
Basket of flowers, low hdl, CI, mc pnt worn, 5¾" 30.00
Basket of flowers, ribbon atop, CI, rust, 15½" 85.00
Basket of flowers, twist hdl, sq ft, CI, rpt, 9⅝" 45.00
Basket of flowers, very full, no hdl, CI, rpt, 7" 30.00
Basket of fruit & foliage, CI, worn pnt, 4⅞" 45.00
Bird drinking from ewer, CI, rpt, 10⅞" 95.00
Bouquet of flowers, sm 3-step base, CI, rpt, 9" 20.00
Camel, full figure, striding, CI, rpt, 5¾" 110.00
Cat, angora; CI w/orig wht pnt, mk Hubley, 10¾" 110.00
Cat, Halloween, arched bk, gr eyes, CI 135.00
Cat, pr kittens in clothes, rpt, 7" 135.00
Cat, recumbent, CI, orig wht pnt, sgn Hubley, 10¾" 90.00
Cat, seated, bow at neck, head to left, CI, rpt, 8¾" 60.00
Cat, seated, full figure, CI, orig pnt, 7½" 110.00
Cat, seated, head to right, CI, worn pnt, 10¾" 125.00
Cat, seated, mk Angora Pat, c 1929, polychrome pnt, 8" 68.00
Cat, seated, sleeping, CI, rpt, 8" 105.00
Cat, Siamese, sitting, full figure, CI, worn pnt, 10" 115.00
Coach, drawn by 2 horses, closed, rare, yel/gr, 6½x8½" 95.00
Coach, London Royal Mail, orig pnt, 12x7½", 7-lb, EX 85.00
Cockatoo, sitting upright, CI, rpt, 14" 155.00
Cottage, shrubbery/flowers, CI, orig pnt, 6x8¾" 70.00
Dog, Airdale, rhinestone eyes, leather collar, rpt, 8½" 45.00
Dog, Boston Bull, head to right, worn orig pnt, 10¼" 70.00
Dog, English Pointer, old blk/wht pnt, CI, 15½" L 125.00
Dog, Greyhound, mk Col Nerths Fullerton, CI, rpt, 8⅜" 65.00
Dog, Pointer, CI 85.00
Dog, pr of Scotties, sitting, ears up, CI, mc pnt worn, 6" 55.00
Dog, puppy, seated, mk Iron Rain, CI, worn pnt, 12¾" 150.00
Dog, Russian Wolfhound, CI w/G orig pnt, 12x8x3" 110.00
Dog, Scotty, CI 55.00
Dog, Spaniel, stoneware, cobalt highlights, 1850s, 10" 265.00
Dutch boy & girl, standing, 5¾" 85.00
Dwarf, standing, full figure, CI w/EX orig pnt, 11" 125.00
Dwarf, w/lantern & keys, 10" 135.00
Eagle, standing, spread wings, orig gold pnt, 15x4x2½" 115.00
Elephant, trunk over head, full figure, gray-blk, 9½x8" 75.00
Elephant & palm tree, CI, rpt, 13¼" 125.00
Elf, CI, orig pnt, 11" 125.00
Fireman's hat, CI, 6" 70.00

Prairie Schooner, cast iron with original paint, ca 1860s, $75.00.

Flowerpot, nasturtiums, CI 45.00
Flowers in urn, hexagonal base, CI, rpt, rust, 7" 35.00
Girl in hoop skirt, holds out bl dress, worn pnt, 6⅝" 65.00
Golfer, club raised, CI w/worn mc pnt, 10¼" 385.00
Golfer, putting, CI w/worn mc pnt, 8⅜" 350.00
Horse, front leg raised, CI w/worn pnt, 8" 135.00
Horse, grazing, w/saddle, copper plated CI, 9x10" 60.00
Horse's head, CI/worn orig blk pnt, 6¾x5¾x2" 36.00
Jack, replica of one used in game, wht, orig pnt, 5x6" 105.00
Lady w/scarf, CI w/gr pnt, advertising, 7" 120.00
Lion, blk pnt, St Blazey Foundry, England, 1850s, 15x10x3" ...125.00
Lion, in foliage, raised tail hdl, CI, worn pnt, 11½" 125.00
Lion, old orange rpt w/blk/brn/red, CI, 9½" 100.00
Lion, standing, orig gold pnt, 11½x8½x4" 130.00
Lion, tail curled on bk, open legs, head right, CI, 10¾" 135.00
Monkey, seated; full figure, CI, worn rpt, 6¾" 85.00
Old Man of the Sea, G 70.00
Olive Picker, walks behind donkey, w/Mexican hat, 7½x7" 175.00
Palm tree w/coconuts, wht metal, rpt, 7", EX 70.00
Parrot, flat back, orig mc pnt, early 1900s, 7x5½x2½" 85.00
Parrot on ring, rectangle base, mc, EX detail, 7x7x4" 85.00
Parrot on rock, CI, rpt, 11" 85.00

Parrot on stump, old gold pnt, 8½x4x4" 85.00
Parrot w/cockatoo, on stump, bl crest/yel head, 12", VG 85.00
Peacock, full spread tail, orig mc pnt G, 7x7x3" 85.00
Punch w/dog, comic figure, 12", EX 260.00
Rabbit, wht w/pink ears, CI 125.00
Ram, oval base, looking ahead, CI, worn pnt, rust, 7x9¾" 110.00
Ry station, pnt tin, red roof/yel towers, Germany, 9x23" 225.00
Squirrel, sitting on log eating nut, National Foundry, 11" 165.00
Stork, head retracted to shoulders, CI, rpt, 7½" 65.00
Tombstone, garland of flowers around stone, orig pnt, 4½" 38.00
Windmill, solid brass, 9-lb, 7½x7" 42.00
Witch on broomstick, brass 125.00

Dorflinger

C. Dorflinger and Sons, Inc., was a glass company that operated in White Plains, Pennsylvania, from the 1880s until about 1921.

When no condition is indicated, the items listed below are assumed to be in mint condition.

Bowl, ambrosia; Prince of Wales knobbed stem, 7x9" 375.00
Bud vase, asters, 12" 70.00
Cruet, pyramid shape, 24-star base, 7½" 40.00
Jar, powder; Middlesex, puffy top w/hobstars 350.00
Pitcher, Colonial, 7½" 185.00
Plate, Essex, 9" 225.00
Tumbler, Old Colony, 3¾", sm underside chips 125.00
Tumbler, poppy 35.00
Vase, bud; asters, cut glass, 12" 78.50
Vase, gr cut to clear, gold over sterling base, 10½" 1,500.00
Wine, w/enamelled roosters 20.00

Doulton and Royal Doulton

The range of wares produced by the Doulton Company since its inception in 1815 has been vast and varied. Their earliest wares produced in the tiny pottery in Lambeth, England, were salt glaze pitchers, plain and fancy figural bottles--all utility type stoneware geared to the practical need of everyday living.

The original partners, John Doulton and John Watts, saw the potential for success in the manufacture of drain and sewage pipes, and during the 1840s concentrated on this highly lucrative type of commercial ware. Watts retired from the company in 1854, and Doulton began experimenting with a more decorative style of product. As time went by, many glazes and decorative effects were developed, among them Faience, Impasto, Silicon, Carrara, Marqueterie, Chine, and Rouge Flambe. Tiles and architectural terra cotta were an important part of their manufacture. Late in the 19th century, at the original Lambeth location, fine artware was decorated by such notable artists as Hannah and Arthur Barlow, George Tinworth, and J.H. McLennan. Stoneware vases with incised animal drawings, gracefully shaped urns with painted scenes, and cleverly modeled figurines rivaled the best of any competitor.

In 1882 a second factory was built in Burslem, which continues even yet to produce the famous figurines, character jugs, series ware, and table services so popular with collectors today. Their Kingsware line, made from 1899 to 1946, featured flasks and flagons with drinking scenes, usually on a brown glazed ground, some of which were limited editions, while others were commemorative and advertising items.

The Gibson Girl series, twenty-four plates in all, was introduced in 1901. It was drawn by Charles Dana Gibson, and is recognized by its blue and white borders and central illustrations, each scene depicting a humorous or poignant episode in the life of 'The Widow and Her Friends.' Dickensware, produced from 1911 through the early 1940s, featured illustrations by Charles Dickens, with many of his famous characters.

The Robin Hood series was introduced in 1914, and the Shakespeare series #1, portraying scenes from the Bard's plays, was made from 1914 until World War II. The Shakespeare series #2 ran from 1906 until 1974, and was decorated with featured characters.

The Nursery Rhymes series was produced first in earthenware in 1903, and later in bone china. In 1933 a line of decorated children's ware, the Bunnykins series, was introduced and continues to be made to the present day. About 150 'bunny' scenes have been devised, the earliest and most desirable being those signed by the artist Barbara Vernon.

The value of a figurine is appreciated by age, because of a limited production run, or by exceptional color and detail. Those signed by the artist, marked 'Potted' (indicating pre-1939 origin), or those bearing the title of the figure and date of production, are also more valuable. After 1920, wares were marked with a lion--with or without a crown--over a circular 'Royal Doulton.'

When no condition is indicated, the items listed below are assumed to be in mint condition.

Animals

Dog, Airedale, #1023 .... 90.00
Dog, Airedale, med 50.00
Dog, Alsatian, Benign of Picardy, lg 295.00
Dog, Boxer, #2643, old, med 65.00
Dog, Bulldog, #1044 .... 125.00
Dog, Bulldog, English, #1047, brn, 3" 40.00
Dog, Bulldog w/flag, lg 250.00
Dog, Cairn, Charming Eyes, med 100.00
Dog, Cairn, sm 33.00
Dog, Cocker Spaniel, #1021, blk, sm 70.00
Dog, Cocker Spaniel, #1037 .... 115.00
Dog, Cocker Spaniel, #2516 .... 65.00
Dog, Cocker Spaniel, blk/wht, lg 200.00
Dog, Cocker Spaniel, K-9 .... 35.00
Dog, Cocker Spaniel w/Pheasant, blk/wht, lg 195.00
Dog, Collie, #1058 .... 50.00
Dog, Collie, #1059 .... 105.00
Dog, Corgi, #2557 .... 55.00
Dog, Dachshund, blk, med 50.00
Dog, Dachshund, K series, miniature 45.00
Dog, Dachshund, lg 200.00
Dog, Dalmation, #113, med 50.00
Dog, Dalmation, sm 85.00
Dog, Doberman, med 50.00
Dog, English Setter, #1051, sm 105.00
Dog, Foxhound, K series, miniature 45.00
Dog, Greyhound, brn, sm 100.00
Dog, Irish Setter, #1049 .... 275.00
Dog, Irish Setter, #1056, sm 95.00
Dog, Labrador, med 50.00
Dog, Pekinese, sm 45.00
Dog, Poodle, #2631, med 75.00
Dog, Scottish Terrier, #1016 .... 45.00
Dog, Scottish Terrier, med 100.00
Dog, Sealyham, Scotia Stylist, sm 85.00
Dog, St Bernard, D-19 .... 40.00
Dog, St Bernard, K series, miniature 45.00
Dog, Terrier, #1101 .... 75.00
Dog, Terrier w/plate, #1158 .... 50.00
Duck, #806, miniature 25.00
Horse, Gude Gray Mare & Foal, #2530 .... 215.00
Kitten, Tammy, licking paw, #2589 .... 30.00

Kitten, Tammy, sitting on all 4 paws, #2590 30.00
Kitten, Tammy, sitting up, #2582 30.00
Kitten, Tammy, sleeping on side, #2579 30.00
Koala bears 30.00
Lizard, stoneware, Tinworth, 5″ 150.00
Rabbit, K37 35.00
Rabbit, K39 35.00

Character Jugs

Apothecary, lg 52.00
Arriet, lg 185.00
Arriet, miniature 75.00
Arry, lg 136.00
Arry, miniature 70.00
Arry, sm 85.00
Auld Mac, lg 50.00
Auld Mac, sm, A 30.00
Ben Franklin, sm 32.00
Blacksmith, lg 50.00
Bootmaker, lg 52.00
Captain Cuttle, sm 125.00
Captain Hook, lg 300.00
Captain Hook, sm 200.00
Captain Morgan, lg 62.00
Captain Morgan, miniature 30.00
Captain Morgan, sm 30.00
Cardinal, lg 115.00
Cardinal, miniature 40.00
Cardinal, sm 50.00
Cardinal, tiny 200.00
Cavalier, lg 110.00
Cavalier, sm 50.00
Clark Gable, lg 1,000.00
Cliff Cornell, bl, lg 300.00
Cliff Cornell, bl, sm 400.00
Clown, wht hair, lg 1,000.00
D'Artagnon, lg 50.00
Dick Turpin, gun hdl, lg 105.00
Dick Turpin, gun hdl, miniature 40.00
Dick Turpin, horse hdl, mask down, lg 65.00
Dick Turpin, horse hdl, mask down, miniature 32.00
Dick Whittington, lg 395.00
Drake, lg 135.00
Drake, sm 60.00
Falconer, sm 22.00
Farmer John, lg 175.00
Farmer John, sm 76.00
Fat Boy, miniature 45.00
Fat Boy, sm 55.00
Fat Boy, tiny 95.00
Fireman, lg 45.00
Fortune Teller, lg 400.00
Fortune Teller, miniature 250.00
Fortune Teller, sm 265.00
Friar Tuck 325.00
Gardener, lg 50.00
Gardener, miniature 25.00
Gardener, sm 32.00
George Washington, lg 50.00
Gladiator, lg 575.00
Gladiator, minature 340.00
Gladiator, sm 295.00
Gondolier, lg 400.00
Gondolier, miniature 300.00
Gone Away, lg 60.00
Gone Away, miniature 30.00
Gone Away, sm 30.00
Granny, lg, A 60.00
Granny, sm 25.00
Guardsman, lg 50.00
Gulliver, sm 350.00
Hamlet, lg 50.00
Hatless Drake 5,000.00
Henry VIII, lg 45.00
Isaac Walton, old, lg 90.00
Jarge, sm 162.00
Jester, sm 80.00
Jimmy Durante, lg 53.00
Jockey, lg 188.00
John Barleycorn, lg 110.00
John Barleycorn, miniature 45.00
John Barleycorn, sm 55.00
John Peel, lg 115.00
John Peel, miniature 38.00
John Peel, sm 40.00
Johnny Appleseed, lg 276.00
Long John Silver, lg 50.00
Long John Silver, miniature 26.00
Long John Silver, sm 25.00
Lord Nelson, lg 275.00
Louis Armstrong, lg 54.00
Lumberjack, lg 60.00
Mad Hatter, sm 32.00
Mae West, lg 53.00
Mark Twain, sgn, lg 70.00
Mephistopheles, lg 3,000.00
Mikado, lg 395.00
Mine Host, lg 60.00
Mine Host, sm 30.00
Mr Micawber, miniature 40.00
Mr Pickwick, lg 110.00
Mr Pickwick, miniature 40.00
Night Watchman, sm 30.00
Old Charley, lg, A 60.00
Old Charley, miniature 22.00
Old Charley, sm, A 30.00
Old Curiosity Shop, square pitcher 140.00
Old King Cole, lg 175.00
Old King Cole, sm 110.00
Oliver Twist, square pitcher 115.00
Othello, lg 50.00
Paddy, lg 100.00
Paddy, tiny 95.00
Parson Brown, lg 110.00
Parson Brown, sm, A 40.00
Pied Piper, lg 65.00
Pied Piper, miniature 22.00
Poacher, miniature 20.00
Punch & Judy, miniature 350.00
Punch & Judy, sm 225.00
Red Haired Clown 3,500.00
Regency Beau, lg 600.00
Rip Van Winkle, lg 42.00
Robin Hood, lg 125.00
Robin Hood, miniature 50.00
Robin Hood, sm 50.00
Robinson Crusoe, sm 36.00

Sairey Gamp, miniature, A....25.00
Sairey Gamp, sm, A....30.00
Sairey Gamp, tiny....85.00
Sam Johnson, lg....165.00
Sam Johnson, sm....150.00
Sam Weller, miniature....45.00
Sancho Panza, lg....55.00
Sancho Panza, miniature....25.00
Scaramouche, lg....545.00
SGT Buz Fuz, sm....100.00
Simon the Cellarer, lg....110.00
Simon the Cellarer, sm....40.00
Simple Simon, lg....400.00
Sir Francis Drake, lg....135.00
Sleuth, sm....22.00
Smuggler, lg....60.00
Smuggler, sm....30.00
Smuts, lg....1,800.00
St George, lg....120.00
St Georgia, sm....50.00
Tam O'Shanter, lg....65.00
Tam O'Shanter, sm....32.00
Toby Philpots, lg....110.00
Toby Philpots, miniature....35.00
Toby Philpots, sm, A....40.00
Tony Weller, lg....125.00
Tony Weller, sm....40.00
Touchstone, lg....175.00
Town Crier, lg....140.00
Town Crier, miniature....100.00
Town Crier, sm....100.00
Trapper, lg....66.00
Ugly Duchess, lg....275.00
Ugly Duchess, miniature....250.00
Ugly Duchess, sm....250.00
Uncle Tom Cobbleigh, lg....325.00
Vicar of Bray, lg....175.00
Viking, lg....125.00
Viking, miniature, rare....150.00
Viking, sm....40.00
Walrus & Carpenter, lg....75.00
Walrus & Carpenter, miniature....35.00
Walrus & Carpenter, sm....32.00
WC Fields, lg....54.00
Whittington, only comes in lg....400.00
Yachtsman, lg....86.00

Figurines

A La Mode, #2544....135.00
A'Courting, #2004....480.00
Abdullah, #2104....540.00
Affection....95.00
Afternoon Tea, #2164....200.00
Alexandra....95.00
Alice, #2158....90.00
Anna, #2802....70.00
Anthea, #1527....450.00
Antoinette, #2326....100.00
Apple Maid....350.00
Arab, #33....1,200.00
Ascot, #2356....130.00
At Ease....155.00
Autumn, #2087....300.00

Left to right: Her Ladyship #1977, 7½", $265.00; Orange Lady, #1953, 8½", $155.00; Adrienne, #2304, 7½", $90.00.

Autumn Breezes, #1911, pink....155.00
Autumn Breezes, #1913, gr....176.00
Babie, #1679....52.00
Bachelor....175.00
Ballerina....175.00
Balloon Man....126.00
Balloon Seller, #583....300.00
Beachcomber....120.00
Beat You To It....175.00
Bedtime, #1978....45.00
Belle-of-the-Ball....182.00
Bernice, #2071....750.00
Bess....225.00
Biddy, #1513....150.00
Biddy, gr, #1445....175.00
Biddy, no balloons, model #1088, prototype, 1940....400.00
Blacksmith of Williamsburg....100.00
Blithe Morning, #2021....165.00
Bluebeard, #2105....220.00
Bluebird, #1280....695.00
Bo Peep, M-82....300.00
Boatman, #2417....115.00
Bon Appetit....125.00
Bonnie Lassie, #1626....315.00
Boy of Williamsburg, #2183....76.00
Bride, #2166....180.00
Bridesmaid, #2196....84.00
Bridget....226.00
Broken Lance....350.00
Buddies....130.00
Butterfly, #720....700.00
Calumet, #1689....650.00
Camellia, #2222....190.00
Captain MacHeath....500.00
Carmen, #1267....600.00
Carpet Seller....205.00
Carrie, #2800....72.00
Cassim, #1231....450.00
Cavalier, #2176....145.00
Celeste, #2237....220.00
Celia, #1727....700.00
Cellist, #2226....380.00
Centurion, #2726....135.00

Charley's Aunt, #1703 .... 450.00
Cherie 185.00
Chief, #2892 .... 130.00
Child of Williamsburg, #2154 .... 76.00
Chloe, M-9 .... 155.00
Chloe, pink, #1767 .... 175.00
Choir Boy, #2141 .... 100.00
Christine, #2792 .... 125.00
Christmas Morn, #1992 .... 100.00
Christmas Parcels 125.00
Cicely, #1516 .... 800.00
Cissie, #1809 .... 65.00
Claire, #2793 .... 170.00
Clarinda, #2724 .... 126.00
Clockmaker, #2219 .... 200.00
Coachman, #2282 .... 410.00
Cobbler, #1706 .... 216.00
Collinette, bl, #1998 .... 575.00
Coppelia, #2115 .... 550.00
Coralie, #2307 .... 100.00
Country Lass, #1991 .... 152.00
Cup of Tea, #2322 .... 92.00
Cymbals, #2699 .... 650.00
Cynthia, #1586 .... 500.00
Daffy Down Dilly, #1712 .... 225.00
Dancers of the World, Balinese 450.00
Dancers of the World, Breton 450.00
Dancers of the World, Chinese 450.00
Dancers of the World, Mexican 450.00
Dancers of the World, North American Indian 450.00
Dancers of the World, Philippine, #2439 .... 450.00
Dancers of the World, Polish 450.00
Dancers of the World, Scottish Highland, #2436 .... 450.00
Dancers of the World, West Indian 450.00
Dancing Years 275.00
Daphne 135.00
Darby, #2024 .... 150.00
Darling, #1985 .... 60.00
Darling, potted, #1319 .... 110.00
Daydreams, #1731 .... 100.00
Debbie, #2385 .... 72.00
Dectective, #2359 .... 105.00
Delphine 200.00
Denise, #2273 .... 225.00
Derrick 400.00
Diana, #1986 .... 80.00
Dimity 316.00
Doctor, #2858 .... 145.00
Dog of Foo 152.00
Dreamweaver, #2283 .... 150.00
Drummer Boy, #2679 .... 210.00
Easter Day 250.00
Elegance 110.00
Eliza 180.00
Elsie Maynard 535.00
Emma, #2834 .... 72.00
Enchantment, #2178 .... 125.00
Ermine Coat, #1981 .... 190.00
Fair Lady, #2193, gr 120.00
Fair Maiden, #2211 .... 60.00
Fairy, #1379 .... 225.00
Falstaff, #2054 .... 95.00
Faraway 175.00
Fat Boy, #2096 .... 215.00
Fat Boy, #555 .... 210.00
Fiddler, #2171 .... 575.00
Fiona, #1933 .... 750.00
Fiona, #2694 .... 120.00
First Steps, #2242 .... 300.00
First Waltz, #2862 .... 150.00
Fleur 116.00
Fleurette 350.00
Flower Seller's Children, #1342 .... 326.00
Foaming Quart 125.00
Fortune Teller, #2159 .... 400.00
Forty Winks, #1974 .... 215.00
Francine, #2422 .... 70.00
French Peasant, #2075 .... 480.00
Friar Tuck 450.00
Gay Morning, #2135 .... 210.00
Genevieve, #1962 .... 190.00
Gentleman of Williamsburg, #2227 .... 100.00
Geraldine 125.00
Giselle, #2139 .... 300.00
Golden Days 150.00
Golliwog, #2040 .... 235.00
Good King Wenceslas 200.00
Good Morning 125.00
Gossips 350.00
Grace, #2318 .... 110.00
Grand Manner, #2723 .... 130.00
Grandma 276.00
Granny's Shawl, #1647 .... 295.00
Greta 135.00
Griselda 450.00
Grizel, #1629 .... 500.00
Grossmith's Tibetian Girl, #582 .... 400.00
Guy Fawkes 850.00
Gwynneth 175.00
Gypsy Dance, #2230 .... 230.00
Harlequinade, #1400 .... 1,000.00
Harp, musician, limited edition 650.00
He Loves Me & She Loves Me Not, #2046 & #2045, pr 250.00
Helen of Troy 695.00
Henrietta Maria 365.00
Here a Little Child 250.00
Herminia, #1704 .... 750.00
Hilary, #2335 .... 112.00
Hinged Parasol, #1579 .... 225.00
Honey 325.00
Hornpipe, #2161 .... 545.00
Hostess of Williamsburg, #2209 .... 100.00
HRH Prince of Wales, #2883 .... 350.00
Huntsman 166.00
Innocence, #2842 .... 95.00
Invitation 115.00
Irene, #1621 .... 310.00
Ivy 64.00
Jack & Jill, pr 240.00
Janet, #1916 .... 250.00
Janice, #2165, blk 375.00
Jean, #2032 .... 252.00
Jennifer, #2392 .... 100.00
Jester, face mask 255.00
Joan, #2023 .... 150.00
Jolly Sailor, #2172 .... 525.00
Jovial Monk 150.00
Judith, #2189 .... 250.00

June, #1691 250.00
Kate Hardcastle, pink & gr 470.00
Katrina 225.00
Ko Ko, #1266 450.00
La Sylphide, #2138 325.00
Lady Charmain, #1948 222.00
Lady Clare, #1465 650.00
Lady Diana Spencer, #2885 250.00
Lady Fayre 320.00
Lady Fayre w/lamp 355.00
Lady of Williamsburg, #2228 140.00
Lady Pamela 152.00
Lambing Time 116.00
Laurianne, #2719 125.00
Lavina, #1955 85.00
Leading Lady, #2269 145.00
Lights Out 155.00
Lilac Time 250.00
Linda, #2106 120.00
Lisa, #2310 122.00
Lisette 500.00
Little Boy Blue, #2062 120.00
Little Bridesmaid, #2148 115.00
Little Bridesmaid, M-30 165.00
Little Mistress 190.00
Long John Silver 390.00
Lord Nelson, stoneware 220.00
Loretta, #2337 105.00
Love Letter, #2149 275.00
Lucy Lockett, #524 425.00
Lunchtime 156.00
Madonna of Square, #326 1,200.00
Maisie, #1619 325.00
Mantilla, #2712 150.00
Margaret, #1989 215.00
Margaret of Anjou, #2012 500.00
Marguerite, #1928 310.00
Marie 60.00
Mary Had a Little Lamb 70.00
Mary Mary, #2044 142.00
Mask Seller, #2103 120.00
Mask Seller, red, #1361 600.00
Masquerade, #599 350.00
Masquerade, #600 450.00
Master Sweep 550.00
Matilda 450.00
Maureen, #1770 225.00
Maureen, #1771, blue 425.00
Mayor 252.00
Maytime, #2113 256.00
Melanie, #2271 112.00
Memories 320.00
Mendicant 180.00
Mermaid 550.00
Micawber 200.00
Michele 100.00
Midinette, #2090 260.00
Midsummer Noon 375.00
Milkmaid, #2057 112.00
Minuet, #2019 200.00
Miranda, #1818 1,000.00
Miss Demure 200.00
Miss Fortune, #1897 515.00
Miss Muffet, #1936 152.00
Modena, #1846 1,000.00
Mother Hubbard, #2314 200.00
Mr Pickwick, #556 190.00
My Pet, #2238 95.00
Nana, #1766 175.00
Negligee, #1219 900.00
Nell Gwynn 415.00
Newsboy 490.00
Nina 140.00
Noelle, #2179 315.00
Officer of Line, #2733 105.00
Old Meg 186.00
Olga, #2463 115.00
Omar Khayyam, #2247 95.00
Organ Grinder, #2173 560.00
Owd Willum, #2042 175.00
Paisley Shawl, #1988 100.00
Paisley Shawl, M4 175.00
Pamela, #1469 450.00
Pantalettes, M-15 160.00
Parisian 136.00
Parson's Daughter, #564 225.00
Past Glory 156.00
Patchwork Quilt 250.00
Patricia, M-8 225.00
Pearly Boy, #1547 300.00
Pearly Boy, #2035 190.00
Pearly Girl, #2036 190.00
Peggy 80.00
Penelope, #1901 270.00
Pickwick, 4″ 20.00
Pied Piper, #2102 180.00
Pillow Fight, #2270 175.00
Piper, The; #2907 170.00
Pirouette, #2216 222.00
Poacher, #2043 245.00
Polka, #2156 200.00
Polly Peachum, #463 350.00
Polly Peachum, #549 190.00
Premiere, #2343 116.00
Primroses, #1617 500.00
Priscilla 165.00
Professor 126.00
Prue, #1996 225.00
Queen Elizabeth, #2502 1,000.00
Queen Elizabeth, #2878 270.00
Queen of Sheba, #2328 650.00
Red, #2065 166.00
Regal Lady, #2709 142.00
Rendevous, #2212 310.00
Repose, #2272 135.00
River Boy, #2128 150.00
Robin 275.00
Romance 130.00
Rosabell, #1620 660.00
Rose, #1368 72.00
Roseanna 270.00
Rosebud, #1983 375.00
Royal Govenor Cook of Williamsburg, #2233 142.00
Sabbath Morn 200.00
Sailor's Holiday 146.00
Sairey Gamp, #1896 250.00
Schoolmarm 156.00
Scribe, #305 850.00

Sea Harvest, #2257....170.00
Sea Sprite, #1261....400.00
Seashore, #2265....125.00
Shepherd, #1975....150.00
Shore Leave, #2254....152.00
Shy Anne, #60....1,000.00
Silversmith of Williamsburg, #2208....110.00
Simone, #2378....136.00
Sir Walter Raleigh....530.00
Skater, #2117....295.00
Sleepy Darline, #2953....152.00
Soiree....100.00
Solitude, #2810....160.00
Spring Flowers....275.00
Spring Morning....190.00
Springtime, #1971....600.00
Stayed at Home, #2207....160.00
Stephanie, #2807....136.00
Stitch in Time, #2352....122.00
Stop Press, #2683....152.00
Suitor, #2132....250.00
Summer, #2086....250.00
Summers Day, #2181....350.00
Suzette, #2026....275.00
Sweet & Twenty, #1298....135.00
Sweet & Twenty, #1589....180.00
Sweet Anne, #1318....175.00
Sweet Anne, #1331....175.00
Sweet Anne, M-27....160.00
Sweet April, #2215....275.00
Sweet Maid, #2092....320.00
Sweet 16....155.00
Swimmer, #1326....600.00
Symphony....275.00
Tall Story, #2248....125.00
Tess, #2865....72.00
Tete a Tete....1,000.00
Thank You, #2732....80.00
Thanks Doc, #2731....125.00
This Little Pig....69.00
Tinkle Bell, #1677....75.00
To Bed....125.00
Tootles....77.00
Town Crier, #2119....220.00
Toymaker, #1836....325.00
Treasure Island, #1961....135.00
Twilight, #2256....146.00
Uncle Ned & Forty Winks, #2094 & #1974, pr....400.00
Under the Gooseberry Bush, #49....1,300.00
Uriah Heep, #1897....276.00
Valerie, #2107....60.00
Vanity....88.00
Veneta, #2722....120.00
Veronica....155.00
Victoria, #2471....120.00
Victorian Lady....155.00
Viola D'Amore....500.00
Vivienne....220.00
Votes for Women, #2816....192.00
Wardrobe Mistress....376.00
Wayfarer, #2362....140.00
Wee Willie Winkie, #2050....210.00
Wigmaker of Williamsburg, #2239....142.00
Winter....275.00
Wistful, #2396....170.00
Wizard, #2877....145.00
Wood Nymph....190.00
Yeoman, #2122....455.00
Young Love, #2735....250.00

Flambe

Dragon, #2058, Veined Sung....400.00
Duck, #112....35.00
Duck, #395....35.00
Elephant, #489A, 5½″....120.00
Elephant, 4½″....90.00
Elephant w/Howdah, 3½″....150.00
Fat Mouse, 2″....125.00
Jar, elephant knob, Sung....300.00
Penguin, #84....45.00
Rabbit, #1157....40.00
Rabbit, #656A....45.00
Vase, bullet, 2″....45.00
Vase, camel, w/rider, woodcut, 3″....70.00
Vase, deer, woodcut, 11″....69.00
Vase, English country scene in blk, sgn, 6″....80.00
Vase, landscape w/deer, bullet shape, sgn FM & OCK, 7″....80.00
Vase, red, bulbous w/3″ can neck, sgn/1618, 10″....140.00
Vase, Sung, brass rim & base, 5″....175.00
Vase, Veined Sung, fish decor, sgn FM, 8½″....250.00
Vase, Veined Sung, pumpkin shape, sgn FM, 6x10″....275.00

Series Ware

Biscuit barrel, Dutch Series, all-around nautical scene....100.00
Bowl, child's; Bunnykins, To the Hunt Ball, sgn Vernon, 6″....18.50
Bowl, Coaching Days, 6″....42.00
Bowl, Coaching Days, 7½″....65.00
Bowl, Dickensware, Mr Pickwick, sq, 2x8¾″....85.00
Bowl, Dickensware, 7½″....85.00
Bowl, Gallant Fishers, 3 fishermen, ped ft, 8″....70.00
Bowl, Old Moreton Hall, 7½″....42.00
Bowl, Rustic England, farmer, cows & sheep, ped, 7½″....75.00
Bowl, Rustic England, hounds, octagonal, 8½″....65.00
Candle holders, Dickensware, Fagin & Sam Weller, pr....160.00
Candlestick, Old Moreton Hall, Squire in entrance, 6½″....50.00
Creamer, Arabian Knights, The Councillors....40.00
Creamer, Kingsware, old woman at hearth, sgn Noke....65.00
Creamer & sugar, Coaching Days, pursued by highwaymen....50.00
Creamer & sugar, Teatime Sayings, men at best....40.00
Cup & saucer, Coaching Days....42.00
Cup & saucer, demitasse; Kingsware, Pied Piper....85.00
Cup & saucer, Gaffers....50.00
Cup & saucer, Nursery Rhymes, Hey Diddle Diddle....40.00
Cup & saucer, Old Moreton Hall....45.00
Hat pin stand, Countryside, view of Lincoln Cathedral....70.00
Jar, jam; Gaffers, w/lid....65.00
Jardiniere, Shakespeare, Ophelia/Hamlet, 8½x10″....150.00
Jug, Baron, Eastern Figures, 2 costumed women w/trellis, 7″....80.00
Jug, Comical Hunt, runaway horses, 5½x4¼″....95.00
Jug, Concord; Gondoliers, boating on Venetian canal, 7″....65.00
Jug, Dutch, girls & mother w/child on nautical ground, 6″....50.00
Jug, Old Sea Dogs, Jack's the Boy for Play, 6½″....75.00
Jug, Tavern; The Stirrup Cup, Speed the Parting Guest....75.00
Loving cup, Dickensware, Mark Tapley, 6½″....110.00
Loving cup, Kingsware, sterling silver rim, miniature....75.00
Loving cup, Welsh Ladies, miniature, 1½″....40.00

Mug, Fisherfolk, Breton women w/children, hdld, silver rim.....60.00
Pitcher, Chaucer Series, Chaucer Ye Tabard, 7¼″.............95.00
Pitcher, Dickens relief, Oliver Twist, jug type, sq.............145.00
Pitcher, Dickensware, Fagin, sgn Noke, tankard style, 7″.......85.00
Pitcher, Dickensware, Oliver Twist, 8″.....................125.00
Pitcher, Dickensware, Tony Weller, 6″.....................100.00
Pitcher, Hunting Scenes, horsemen tip hats, ice lip, 9″.........85.00
Pitcher, Jackdaw of Rheims.............................100.00
Pitcher, Kingsware, Ben Johnson, jug type, 6″................85.00
Pitcher, Kingsware, Parson Brown, 7″......................80.00
Pitcher, Kingsware, Watchman, Enough Is As Good..., 6x5″....140.00
Pitcher, Sports Series, raised figures playing bowls............140.00
Plate, An Old Jarvey, coachmen discussing document, 10″......40.00
Plate, Athens Series, scene of Greek procession...............40.00
Plate, Automobile, Itch Yer on Guvenor, w/old auto, 10½″.....150.00
Plate, Bayeux Tapestry, ship at sea, 10″.....................70.00
Plate, Canadian Centennial, Centennial map of Canada, 10″.....25.00
Plate, Canadian Centennial, The Peace Tower & Parliament.....25.00
Plate, Canadian Centennial, View of Old Quebec, 10″..........25.00
Plate, Castles & Churches, Hurstmonceaux Castle, 10″.........30.00
Plate, Castles & Churches, Rochester Castle, early version......30.00
Plate, chop; African Series, lion, 13″.......................75.00
Plate, chop; Jackdaw of Rheims, 13″.......................95.00
Plate, Coaching Days, coach pursued by highwaymen, 10″......65.00
Plate, Coaching Days, coach stopped w/broken harness, 10″....65.00
Plate, Dickensware, Bill Sykes, early version..................75.00
Plate, Dickensware, Little Nell, early version, 10″............75.00
Plate, Dickensware, Little Nell, 7½″.......................35.00
Plate, Dickensware, Tony Weller, early version, 10″...........70.00
Plate, Eglington Tournament, knights in sword combat.........50.00
Plate, Egyptian Series, Egyptian pottery.....................30.00
Plate, Gaffers, old man/gate/house, 8½″.....................35.00
Plate, Gibson Widow Series, A Quiet Dinner w/Dr Bottles.......80.00
Plate, Gibson Widow Series, And Here, Winning New Friends...80.00
Plate, Gibson Widow Series, Mrs Diggs Is Alarmed...........80.00
Plate, Gibson Widow Series, She Becomes a Trained Nurse.....80.00
Plate, Gibson Widow Series, She Contemplates the Cloister.....80.00
Plate, Gibson Widow Series, They All Go Skating.............80.00
Plate, Gleaners & Gypsies, campfire scene..................40.00
Plate, Gleaners & Gypsies, man leading donkey w/family........30.00
Plate, Gnomes, 10″....................................100.00
Plate, Golfers w/Proverbs, Fine Feathers Make Fine Birds......165.00
Plate, Greenaway Children Scenes, kids playing at house.......75.00
Plate, Greenaway Children Scenes, playing w/kite in field.......75.00
Plate, Historic England, Charles II at Chelsea Hospital.........40.00
Plate, Historic England, Dr Johnson at Temple Bar, 10″.......40.00
Plate, Historic England, Sir Francis Drake at Plymouth Hoe....40.00
Plate, Home Waters, unloading sailboat on far side of pier......50.00
Plate, Home Waters, 2 sailboats inside stone harbour..........50.00
Plate, Hunting Scenes, mounted horsemen tip hat to ladies.....50.00
Plate, Hunting Scenes, 2 huntsmen w/horses, 10″.............50.00
Plate, Jackdaw of Rheims, Off That Terrible Curse He Took....65.00
Plate, King Arthur's Knights, knights on horseback, 10″........50.00
Plate, Maple Tree, maple tree w/roses, shamrock & thistles.....35.00
Plate, Nautical History, Sir Francis Drake, 10″...............45.00
Plate, Old English Coaching Scenes, coach outside inn.........65.00
Plate, Old English Inns, The Kings Head, Chigwell, 10″........30.00
Plate, Old English Scenes, cobbler w/townspeople, 10″.........30.00
Plate, Old Moreton Hall, squire taking Queen's hand, 10″......30.00
Plate, Robert Burns, Scotsman w/glass aloft, pipe on table......40.00
Plate, Rochester Castle, 10″.............................25.00
Plate, Rustic England, man & child in front of cottage.........35.00
Plate, Shakespeare Portrait, bust w/character border, 10″.......50.00
Plate, Shakespeare's Plays, As You Like It, 10″...............60.00
Plate, Shakespearean Characters, Katherine..................60.00
Plate, Shakespearean Characters, Shylock, 10″...............60.00
Plate, Sir Roger de Coverly, playing bowls, 10″...............40.00
Plate, Skating Series, skater w/3 observers, 10″...............50.00
Plate, Sketches from Teniers, men at table in tavern, 10″......50.00
Plate, Sporting Scenes, The Benevolent Sportsman, 10″........70.00
Plate, Squire, 10″......................................40.00
Plate, St George, on horseback, brandishing his sword, 10″.....70.00
Plate, Teatime Sayings, profile old lady drinking tea, 10″.......70.00
Plate, The Professionals, The Admiral, earthenware............40.00
Plate, The Professionals, The Falconer, earthenware, 10″.......40.00
Plate, The Professionals, The Jester, earthenware.............40.00
Plate, The Professionals, The Mayor, earthenware, 10″.........40.00
Plate, The Professionals, The Parson, earthenware............40.00
Plate, The Professionals, The Squire, earthenware, 10″.........40.00
Tea set, Kingsware, Don Quixote & Sancho Panza, 36-pc......700.00
Tea set, Robin Hood, 3-pc...............................70.00
Tea stand, Gallant Fishers, man fishing off wall, 6½″..........65.00
Teapot, Castles & Churches, Cawdor Castle, Westcott shape.....75.00
Teapot, Coaching Days, coach going up hill/attendants walk....110.00
Teapot, Dickensware, Bill Sykes, rectangular, 6x4½x6″........150.00
Teapot, Old Moreton Hall, Squire, lady & daughter, w/stand....125.00
Toothpick holder, Kingsware, sterling silver rim..............65.00
Tray, Harlequin Series, w/5 sandwich plates: 5¾″; 6⅛x13″.....118.00
Tray, Minstrels, border of ribbons & lanterns, 7x8″............55.00
Tray, Rustic England, hounds leaping at fence, 5x10½″........35.00
Tray, Rustic England, 12″...............................60.00
Tray, sandwich; man's head, Zunday Zmocks, sgn Noke, 5x11″..88.00
Vase, Babes in Woods, flow blue, girls w/dog, hdls, 5¼″.......110.00
Vase, Babes in Woods, flow blue, lady plays w/girl, 10x4½″....165.00
Vase, Babes in Woods, flow blue, mother & girl, 13″..........175.00
Vase, Babes in Woods, flow blue, 2 girls w/pixie, 5x3½″.......125.00
Vase, Babes in Woods, flow blue, 3 girls by forest, 7″........150.00
Vase, Coaching Days, barrel shape, sgn, 8¾x4½″.............145.00
Vase, Coaching Days, innkeeper & driver, hdls, 6½″...........95.00
Vase, Dickensware, Barnaby Rudge, hdls, 8″................100.00
Vase, Dickensware, bud; The Fat Boy, hdls, 5½″..............85.00
Vase, Dickensware, Sergeant Buz Fuz, hdls, 9½x3″...........165.00
Vase, Dickensware, The Artful Dodger, hdls, 6½″.............115.00
Vase, Gaffers, sq, 7½″..................................75.00
Vase, Gleaners & Gypsies, woman holding boy's hand, 2″.......35.00
Vase, Kingsware, Dutchman, miniature, 4″...................60.00

Stoneware

Ash tray, lg bird w/lg beak on rock, mc, 4⅛x4¼″............165.00
Beaker, hunting relief, silver rim, 10-oz....................35.00
Beaker, hunting relief, silver rim, 12-oz....................40.00
Candlestick, Silicon, rugby football, silver rim...............65.00
Flask, Duke of York, 1830..............................300.00
Flask, Lord Brougham, Doulton-Watts, 1830.................275.00
Flask, spirit; brn salt glaze, Lord Balfour figural, 7″..........300.00
Flask, spirit; Mrs Caudle, mk Doulton & Watts, rare, 7″.......350.00
Humidor, gr/tan/brn, 3 monks, imp lion, mk crown, Lambeth...115.00
Jug, Alexandra portrait, brn/tan, 1902, 8″..................145.00
Jug, brn w/applied cherubs, salt glaze, imp mk, 3½″...........35.00
Jug, brn/tan, applied figures, Ye Olde Cheshire Cheese, 2″......25.00
Jug, Queen Victoria 1887 Jubilee, tan w/emb decor, 6″........135.00
Jug, tan/brn, applied 'Highland Whiskey,' 7″.................70.00
Loving cup, brn/beige, applied motto, 3-hdl, 7″..............125.00
Mug, blk leatherware, silver rim, 6″.......................35.00
Mug, brn/tan, applied wht figures, miniature, 1½″.............30.00
Pitcher, cows, sgn Hannah Barlow, 9¼″....................350.00
Pitcher, Silicon, geometrics, hinged lid, 1881, 6″.............65.00

Pitcher, tankard; Silicon, geometric bands, 1884, 8¾″ 85.00
Plate, Queen Alexandria/King Edward VII, coronation, 1902 ..... 75.00
Salt glaze, Hunting Ware, hunting scenes/dogs/men 175.00
Soap dish, dragonfly, Wright's Coaltar 60.00
Teapot, tapestry, floral, gold trim, Slater's pat, 5″ 50.00
Vase, Art Nouveau inspired panels, mc, 1910, #736/F, 13″ 150.00
Vase, chrysanthemums in gold, sgn LH, Faience, 11x5″ 140.00
Vase, circus horses, Hannah Barlow, 12¾″ 450.00
Vase, crackleware, amber, 9″ 30.00
Vase, floral on bl, Kate Rogers, Faience mk, 9½″ 135.00
Vase, flowers on gr, sgn CMB & AC, ped ft, mk Lambeth, 14″ . 125.00
Vase, horses, incised, Hannah Barlow, 12″ 425.00
Vase, Impasto, 8″ 30.00
Vase, incised birds, carved foliage, 1869, 16″ 165.00
Vase, scrolling plants, Frank Butler, 11″ 120.00
Vase, sheep frieze, Hannah Barlow, 12″ 285.00
Vase, tapestry, florals, feather bands, Slater's pat, 10″ 85.00

Doulton Lambeth vase, Silicon, Persian motif, reticulated rim, ca 1880, signed EDL, 14″, $150.00.

Toby Jugs

Churchill, lg 60.00
Falstaff, old, sm 40.00
Happy John, lg 60.00
Honest Measure, sm 25.00
Huntsman, lg 60.00
Miss Nostrum 25.00
Mr Furrow 25.00
Mr Litigate 25.00
Old Charley, 5½″ 125.00
Sam Weller, 4½″ 135.00

Miscellaneous

Ash pot, Sir Roger De Coverly 45.00
Ash tray, Dickensware, Fat Boy 35.00
Biscuit jar, bird/animal panels on band, ribbed, 7½″ 160.00
Biscuit jar, gr/bl base/top trim, pk/rust/gold foliage, 7″ 110.00
Biscuit jar, mc HP flowers/gold leaf, Burslem, SP lid, EX 150.00
Bowl, Art Deco, blk/yel lustre, enamel decor, 11″ 35.00
Bowl, bird/leaf, ped ft, orig paper label, Titanian, 3½″ 75.00
Chocolate pot, roses in line reserves, scroll hdl, Burslem 150.00
Cup & saucer, cobalt w/gold relief, made for Tiffany 40.00
Figurine, Queen Victoria sits on fancy chair, parian, 7½″ 325.00
Hatpin stand, rural scene/castle, rare 105.00
Honey pot, Victoria Jubilee, 1887 .... 135.00
Loving cup, Queen Elizabeth II portrait, ltd ed, detailed 250.00
Pitcher, ladies/fence/roses, Art Nouveau, Morrisian, 7¼″ 100.00
Pitcher, Queen Elizabeth II portrait, emb decor, 6″ 145.00
Plate, fish; ea w/different species, C Hart, 9½″, 12 for 1,500.00
Plate, villa on inlet w/mtns scene, sgn Boulton, 10″ 145.00
Tray, florals, pnt decor, irregular shape, 6″ L 45.00
Vase, castle scene, griffin hdls, bl, Burslem, 9″ 100.00
Vase, Faience, w/flowers, Mary Butterton, 11x9″ 225.00
Vase, Japanese irises, flow blue, gold trim, 14¼″ 165.00

Dresden

Today, the term Dresden is used to indicate the porcelains that were produced in Meissen and Dresden, Germany, from the very early 18th century, well into the next. John Bottger, a young alchemist, discovered the formula for the first true porcelain in 1708, while being held a virtual prisoner at the palace in Dresden because of the King's determination to produce a superior ware. Two years later, a factory was erected in nearby Meissen, with Bottger as director. There, fine tableware, elaborate centerpieces, and exquisite figurines with applied details were produced. In 1731, to distinguish their product from the wares of such potters as Sevres, Worcester, Chelsea, and Derby, Meissen adopted their famous crossed swords trademark. During the next century, several potteries were producing porcelain in the 'Meissen style' in Dresden itself. Their wares were marked with their own logo and the Dresden indication. Those listed here are from that era. See the Meissen section for examples with the crossed swords marking.

When no condition is indicated, the items listed below are assumed to be in mint condition.

Bowl, mc floral/gilt, pierced rim, hdls, Schumann, 6x10″ 56.00
Carriage, horse drawn, HP/gold trim, relief flowers, 45″ L 3,500.00
Compote, lattice bowl on rib ped ft, mc florals, 5x8¼″ 250.00
Console set, basket: 13″ w/flowers; candelabra: 8x11″ 675.00

Compote, three figural cherubs, applied flowers, 18″, $800.00.

Cup & saucer, Egyptian scenes, dk bl on yel, ca 1905, 2″.....235.00
Cup & saucer, gold/gr w/oval medallions, KP.................55.00
Cup & saucer, mustache; flowers...........................37.00
Figurine, boy on sled, girl standing, sgn, late, 5x3x4″.........150.00
Figurine, child sitting in lace dress, 2½″....................65.00
Figurine, clown in striped pants/floral vest, Thieme, 8½″.......160.00
Figurine, colonial couple dancing, sgn N/Crown, 7″...........130.00
Figurine, colonial lady holds basket w/flowers, sgn, 6½″........70.00
Figurine, colonial lady holds baskets w/flowers, 8″............125.00
Figurine, colonial lady w/parasol, pink, sgn, 8″..............115.00
Figurine, Dame de La Courde Francois I, Carl Thieme, 8″.....450.00
Figurine, dancer in pink dress w/red rose/bl bodice, 6¼″......160.00
Figurine, dancing couple, crinoline dress w/roses, 6″..........250.00
Figurine, farm girl feeding chickens, 7½″...................125.00
Figurine, man playing piano/lady w/bass, lace dress, 9x14″.....400.00
Figurine, semi-nude Art Deco Siamese dancer, N/Crown, 14″...195.00
Ink stand, floral/Oriental man, w/2 porc ink pots, 14″.........495.00
Loving cup, nymphs in woods on red, 3 gold hdls, 5″.........500.00
Plate, Dutch, reticulated border, port scene, late, 9″..........700.00
Plate, Sight Seeing, sgn Christy, gold border, 1908, 6½″.......50.00
Urn, acanthus leaf/florals, hdls & lid, crown mk, 20″..........125.00
Urn, cupids, HP panels/gold reserves, w/lid, 1900, 21″........500.00
Vase, lady in garden scene, heavy gold, sgn, 8½″............360.00
Vase, portrait, artist sgn, 19″.............................595.00
Vase, scene from opera, sgn Klemm, bottle form, 10″.........450.00

Dresser Accessories

Dresser sets, ring trees, figural or satin pincushions, manicure sets--all those lovely items that graced milady's dressing table--were at the same time decorative as well as functional. Today they appeal to collectors for many reasons. The Victorian era is well represented by repousse silver-backed mirrors and brushes, and pincushions that were used to display ornamental pins for the hair, hats, and scarves. The hair receiver--similar to a powder jar, but with an opening in the lid--was used to hold the lovely strands of hair retrieved from the comb or brush. These were wound around the finger and tucked in the opening to be used later for hair jewelry and pictures, many of which survive to the present day. (See Hair Weaving)

Celluloid dresser sets were popular during the late 1800s and early 1900s. Some included manicure tools, pill boxes, and button hooks, as well as the basic items. Because celluloid tends to break rather easily, a whole set may be hard to find today. (See Celluloid)

With the current interest in anything Art Deco, sets from the thirties and forties are especially collectible. These may be made of crystal, bakelight, or silver, and the original boxes just as lavishly appointed as their contents.

When no condition is indicated, the items listed below are assumed to be in excellent condition.

Box, full figural Art Deco lady, clown hat, porcelain, 9½″......195.00
Brush, clothes; Art Nouveau design, sterling, 7″..............22.00
Brush, hair; lav Jasper bk w/wht lady & cherub...............85.00
Centerpiece, ruffled bowl/mirror, bl/wht spatter, 18x13¾″......395.00
Curling iron, hand forged, decorated, scissors form, 1800s......35.00
Curling iron, Nouveau hdl, SP, 7″.........................28.00
Curling iron, Nouveau hdl, sterling, 7½″....................50.00
Jar, aqua glass w/HP decor, hinged lid, 3x2½″................55.00
Jar, Fr enamel, 8-side base w/star, bl w/basket of flowers......270.00
Jar, powder; HP, clown w/mandolin, pink frosted glass.........40.00
Jar, sgn Jensen sterling lid w/figural dolphin.................250.00
Mirror, blown-out daisy, Art Nouveau, sterling, hand size.......95.00
Mirror, repousse flowers, Art Nouveau, w/brush, hand size.....125.00
Set, amber bull's eye on clear, tray/jar/pr bottles, Paris........150.00
Set, pink satin glass, 1920s-30s, 4-pc.......................65.00

Sterling silver clothes brush and hair brush, relief cherubs and roses, $250.00 for the pair.

Set, shoehorn/button hook/glove stretcher, hdls, hallmk.......145.00
Set, sterling silver, w/initial, Wallace Carmel, 16-pc..........1,195.00
Tray, lace w/center medallion under glass, brass trim, 15″......40.00

Duncan and Miller

The firm that became known as the Duncan and Miller Glass Company in 1900, was organized in 1874, a partnership between George Duncan, his sons Harry and James, and his son-in-law Augustus Heisey, in Pittsburgh, Pennsylvania. John Ernest Miller was hired as their designer. He is credited with creating the most famous of all Duncan's glassware lines, Three Face. (See Pattern Glass) The George Duncan and Sons Glass Company, as it was titled, was only one of eighteen companies that merged in 1891 with U.S. Glass. Soon after the Pittsburgh factory burned in 1892, the association was dissolved and Heisey left the firm to set up his own factory in Newark, Ohio. Duncan built his new plant in Washington, Pennsylvania, where he continued to make pressed glassware in such notable patterns as Bagware, Amberette, Duncan Flute, Button Arches, and Zippered Slash.

The firm was eventually sold to U.S. Glass in Tiffin, Ohio and officially closed in August, 1955.

In addition to the early pressed dinnerware patterns, today's Duncan and Miller collectors enjoy searching for opalescent vases in many patterns and colors, frosted 'Satintone' glassware, acid-etched designs, and lovely stemware such as the Rock Crystal cuttings. Milk glass was made in limited quantity and is considered a good investment.

Ruby glass, Ebony (a lovely opaque black glass popular during the twenties and thirties), and of course the glass animal and bird figurines are all highly valued examples of the art of Duncan and Miller.

When no condition is indicated, the items listed below are assumed to be in mint condition. Expect to pay at least 25% more than values listed for 'color' for ruby and cobalt, and as much as 50% more in the Georgian, Pall Mall and Sandwich lines. Pink, green and amber Sandwich is worth approximately 30% more than the same items in crystal. Milk glass examples of American Way are valued up to 30% higher than color, 50% higher in Pall Mall. Add approximately 40% to listed prices for opalescent items. Etchings, cuttings and other decorations will increase values by about 50%. For further study, we recommend *The Encyclopedia of Duncan Glass*, by Gail Krause; she is listed in the Directory under Pennsylvania.

American Way #71, bowl, oval, crystal, 12½″................40.00
American Way #71, candlestick, crystal, 2″, pr...............27.50
American Way #71, compote, flared, low ftd, crystal, 7½″.......27.50
American Way #71, plate, rolled edge, crystal, 14″...........45.00
American Way #71, vase, flared, satintone, 8″................65.00
Astaire #22, champagne, saucer shape, crystal.................8.50

Astaire #22, goblet, crystal 9.50
Astaire #22, iced tea, cobalt, 12-oz 12.50
Astaire #22, plate, satintone, 8½″ 11.50
Canterbury #115, ash tray, crystal, 3″ 5.50
Canterbury #115, bowl, salad; crystal, 10″ 27.50
Canterbury #115, candlestick, 3-light, crystal, 6x10″ 25.00
Canterbury #115, candy box & cover, opal, 7″ 50.00
Canterbury #115, compote, ftd, color, 6″ H 25.00
Canterbury #115, ice bucket, color, 5″ 24.00
Canterbury #115, mayonnaise, crystal 12.50
Canterbury #115, nappy, 2-hdl, color, 6″ 17.50
Canterbury #115, plate, crystal, 8″ 11.50
Canterbury #115, plate, 2-hdl, crystal, 11″ 20.00
Canterbury #115, rose bowl, crystal, 4½″ 25.00
Canterbury #115, sugar bowl, crystal, 7-oz 12.50
Canterbury #115, vase, opal, 8″ 45.00
Caribbean #112, bowl, oval, color, 5½″ H 35.00
Caribbean #112, punch cup, color 10.00
Caribbean #112, relish tray, crystal 17.50
Colonial #54, creamer, crystal, 11-oz 9.75
Colonial #54, goblet, crystal, 9-oz 9.00
Colonial #54, mustard, w/lid, crystal, 3½-oz 10.50
Colonial #54, nappy, crystal, 4½″ 6.50
Colonial #54, pitcher, crystal, pint 12.50
Colonial #54, pitcher, crystal, quart 15.00
Colonial #54, shakers, crystal, 1-oz, pr 13.00
Colonial #54, sugar bowl, ind; crystal, 3-oz 7.50
Colonial #54, vase, sweet pea; crystal, 9″ 18.50
Diamond #75, bowl, crimped, amber, 8″ 22.00
Diamond #75, bowl, salad; pink, 9″ H 25.00
Diamond #75, candy box & cover, crystal, 6″ 25.00
Diamond #75, flower arranger, pink, 5″ 19.50
Diamond #75, muffin tray, 2-hdl, crystal, 11″ 20.00
Diamond #75, pickle, 2-hdl, oval, amber, 7″ 20.00
Diamond #75, plate, rolled edge, crystal, 13″ 27.50
Diamond #75, sweetmeat, crimped, 2-hdl, pink, 7″ 17.50
Diamond #75, wine, crystal, 3½-oz 12.50
First Love, ash tray, club, color, #12, 5″ 32.50
First Love, bowl, salad; color, #111, 9″ H 55.00
First Love, bowl, scalloped, ftd, color, #126, 10″ 75.00
First Love, bud vase, ftd, color, #506, 9″ 31.00
First Love, candlestick, 2-light, color, #41, 5″, ea 50.00
First Love, creamer & sugar bowl, ftd, color, #111, pr 55.00
First Love, finger bowl, color, #5111½ 35.00
First Love, goblet, tall, color, #5111½, 10-oz 27.50
First Love, ice cream, color, #5111½, 5-oz 25.00
First Love, iced tea, ftd, color, #5111½, 12-oz 27.50
First Love, jug, ice lip, color, #5202, 80-oz 165.00
First Love, mayonnaise, ftd, hdld, color, w/plate & ladle 75.00
First Love, plate, salad; color, #111, 7½″ sq 28.50
First Love, plate, torte; flat edge, color, #111, 13″ 85.00
First Love, relish, 4-compartment, 2-hdl, color, #111, 9″ 75.00
First Love, vase, cornucopia; color, #117, 4″ 35.00
First Love, vase, ftd, trumpet shape, color, #507, 8″ 55.00
Georgian, creamer, berry; oval, crystal 8.50
Georgian, cup & saucer, tea; crystal 12.50
Georgian, goblet, crystal, 9-oz 12.50
Georgian, ice bucket & hdl, color, 6″ 37.50
Georgian, parfait, color 17.50
Georgian, plate, color, 9½″ 35.00
Georgian, plate, crystal, 7½″ 9.50
Georgian, whiskey, color, 5-oz 17.50
Grecian, bowl, sq-ftd, color, #556, 6x8½″ dia 75.00
Grecian, cigarette holder, sq-ftd, crystal, #538, 3½″ 17.50
Grecian, urn, swan-hdld, sq-ftd, crystal, #550, 10″ 70.00
Grecian, vase, sq-ftd, color, #529, 7″ 60.00
Grecian, vase, sq-ftd, crystal, #527, 5½″ 25.00
Hobnail #118, ash tray, color, 3″ 9.50
Hobnail #118, basket, hdld, color, 7″ 35.00
Hobnail #118, bonbon, ftd, hdld, diamond shape, color, 6″ 27.50
Hobnail #118, bowl, fruit; sq, color, 10″ 45.00
Hobnail #118, candlestick, crystal, 4″ 14.25
Hobnail #118, candy jar & lid, ftd, color, ½-lb 55.00
Hobnail #118, cheese & cracker set, 2-hdl, color, 11″ 55.00
Hobnail #118, coaster, crystal, 3″ 6.50
Hobnail #118, cocktail, color, 3½-oz 15.00
Hobnail #118, cologne, crystal, w/stopper, 8-oz 20.00
Hobnail #118, compote, crimped, tall, color, 6″ 30.00
Hobnail #118, compote, low, crystal, 8″ 24.00
Hobnail #118, cup & saucer, tea; color or crystal 16.50
Hobnail #118, flip jug, crystal, 1½-gal 34.00
Hobnail #118, ivy ball, ftd, crystal, 5″ 27.00
Hobnail #118, nappy, 2-hdl, crystal, 9″ 14.00
Hobnail #118, plate, sandwich; 2-hdl, color, 11″ 42.00
Hobnail #118, relish, 2-compartment, hdld, color, 6″ 12.50
Hobnail #118, table tumbler, crystal, 10-oz 12.00
Hobnail #118, top hat, crystal, 6″ 17.00
Hobnail #118, tray, ftd, crystal, 6½″ 14.00
Laguna, candy box & cover, crystal, #154/48, 6½″ 9.00
Laguna, cocktail, crystal, #154/E, 3½-oz 6.50
Laguna, plate, oblong, color, #154/29, 17″ 20.00
Laguna, relish, 3-compartment, crystal, #154/28, 14″ 18.50
Laguna, sugar bowl, color, #154/42, 7-oz 12.50
Laguna, vase, color, #154/51, 12″ 18.50
Language of Flowers, candlestick, crystal, #115, 3″ 22.50
Language of Flowers, cordial, crystal, #5331, 1-oz, 4½″ 25.00
Language of Flowers, iced tea, ftd, crystal, #5331, 13-oz 20.00
Language of Flowers, juice, ftd, crystal, #5331, 5-oz, 5½″ 20.00
Language of Flowers, plate, crystal, #115, 14″ 55.00
Murano #127, bowl, crimped, crystal, 5x10″ dia 35.00
Murano #127, plate, color, 14″ 45.00
Murano #127, vase, flared, color, 7″ 45.00
Murano #127, vase, flared, crystal, 7″ 26.00
Pall Mall #30, bowl, flower; flared, crystal, 3½x12″ dia 23.50
Pall Mall #30, bowl, oval, crystal, 11″ 22.00

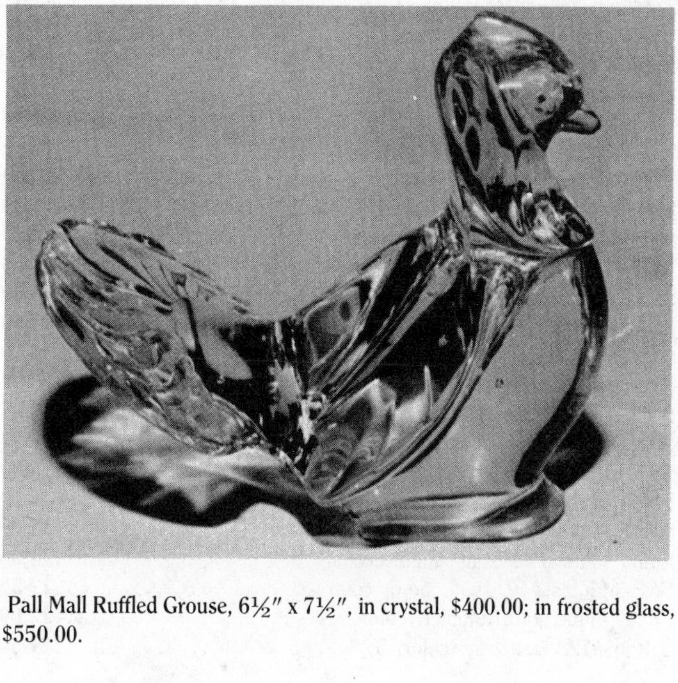

Pall Mall Ruffled Grouse, 6½″ x 7½″, in crystal, $400.00; in frosted glass, $550.00.

Pall Mall #30, mayonnaise set, oval, crystal, 3-pc..............32.50
Pall Mall #30, mint tray, oval, crystal, 7″....................12.50
Pall Mall #30, plate, oval, crystal, 8½″......................13.50
Pall Mall #30, salad dressing boat, crystal, 2¼x4″ W...........18.00
Plaza #21, bowl, color, 10″...............................38.50
Plaza #21, candlestick, 2-light, crystal.......................38.00
Plaza #21, flip pitcher, crystal.............................35.00
Plaza #21, goblet, color..................................15.00
Plaza #21, mustard & cover, color..........................27.50
Plaza #21, parfait, crystal.................................9.00
Plaza #21, plate, color, 7½″...............................17.50
Plaza #21, plate, hdld, crystal, 10½″.......................16.00
Plaza #21, shakers, crystal, pr.............................25.00
Plaza #21, table tumbler, crystal............................7.25
Plaza #21, wine, color...................................15.00
Radiance #113, ash tray, color, 6″.........................17.50
Radiance #113, candlestick, crystal, 4″, pr...................23.00
Radiance #113, creamer, color, 6-oz.........................22.50
Radiance #113, plate, crystal, 14″..........................42.50
Radiance #113, vase, crystal, 8″............................12.00
Ripple, celery tray, crystal, #100, 11″.......................12.00
Ripple, cocktail, color, 3-oz..............................13.50
Ripple, finger bowl, color, #100............................10.00
Ripple, goblet, luncheon; crystal, 9-oz.......................9.50
Ripple, pitcher, color, #100, ½-gal..........................45.00
Ripple, plate, color, #100, 8″..............................12.50
Ripple, tumbler, ftd, color, #101, 11-oz......................12.50
Ripple, water bottle, color, #100...........................35.00
Sandwich #41, ash tray, individual, crystal....................8.50
Sandwich #41, bonbon, heart shape, hdld, crystal, 6″..........20.00
Sandwich #41, bowl, oblong, crystal, 12″.....................45.00
Sandwich #41, candlestick, crystal, 4″, pr....................27.50
Sandwich #41, candy box & cover, crystal, 5″.................35.00
Sandwich #41, celery tray, crystal, 10″......................20.00
Sandwich #41, cheese & cracker set, 2-pc, crystal, 12″.........45.00
Sandwich #41, compote, crystal, 5½″ H.......................27.50
Sandwich #41, creamer, crystal, 7-oz........................12.50
Sandwich #41, cup & saucer, tea; crystal.....................16.50
Sandwich #41, goblet, crystal, 9-oz.........................13.50
Sandwich #41, ivy bowl, ftd, crystal, 5″......................32.50
Sandwich #41, nappy, 2-compartment, crystal, 6″..............17.50
Sandwich #41, plate, chop; flat edge, crystal, 12″.............45.00
Sandwich #41, plate, crystal, 12″...........................25.00
Sandwich #41, relish, 3-compartment, crystal, 12″.............45.00
Sandwich #41, sugar bowl, crystal, 8-oz......................12.50
Sandwich #41, tray, mint; hdld, crystal, 6″...................16.50
Sandwich #41, tray, oval, crystal, 8″........................11.50
Sandwich #41, vase, fan shape, ftd, crystal, 3″................15.00
Sanibel #130, ash tray, tropical fish form, color, 3½″..........45.00
Sanibel #130, bowl, flower; crimped, color, 2¾x14x13″.........75.00
Sanibel #130, bowl, fruit; oval, crystal, 5½x9½″ W............37.50
Sanibel #130, muffin tray, color, 13″........................65.00
Sanibel #130, plate, hors d'oeuvre; crystal, 14″...............40.00
Sanibel #130, relish, 2-compartment, crystal, 8½″.............30.00
Sanibel #130, sweetmeat, color, 8″..........................45.00
Sanibel #130, vase, ftd, oval, crystal, 5½x8x5″...............50.00
Spiral Flutes #40, candlestick, crystal........................9.00
Spiral Flutes #40, cup & saucer, crystal.....................15.00
Spiral Flutes #40, nappy, color.............................9.00
Spiral Flutes #40, plate, dinner; color.......................15.00
Spiral Flutes #40, soup, hdld, crystal........................11.00
Spiral Flutes #40, sugar bowl, color.........................12.50
Spiral Flutes #40, tumbler, color...........................12.00
Sylvan #122, ash tray, color, 5½″..........................27.50
Sylvan #122, bonbon, hdld, crystal, 5½″......................18.50
Sylvan #122, bowl, fruit; crystal, 11″........................35.00
Sylvan #122, candy box & cover, color, 7½″...................50.00
Sylvan #122, plate, salad; crystal, 7½″.......................21.00
Sylvan #122, swan, crystal, 7½″............................55.00
Tavern #83, finger bowl, crystal, 4½″........................6.25
Tavern #83, goblet, flared, crystal, 9-oz......................9.50
Tavern #83, parfait, crystal, 5-oz...........................7.50
Tavern #83, pitcher, crystal, ½-gal..........................25.00
Tavern #83, plate, crystal, 5½″.............................7.00
Tavern #83, sugar bowl w/lid, crystal, 16-oz...................9.50
Tavern #83, table tumbler, crystal, 9-oz......................6.00
Tavern #83, water bottle, crystal, 48-oz......................25.00
Teardrop, bonbon, 4-hdl, crystal, 6″.........................12.00
Teardrop, goblet, crystal, 9-oz.............................14.50
Teardrop #301, ash tray, crystal, 5″.........................10.50
Teardrop #301, candlestick, crystal, 4″.......................15.00
Teardrop #301, candy box & cover, crystal....................55.00
Teardrop #301, cheese stand, crystal........................17.00
Teardrop #301, compote, low, crystal, 6″.....................14.00
Teardrop #301, creamer, crystal............................12.50
Teardrop #301, cup & saucer, demitasse; crystal...............17.50
Teardrop #301, ice bucket, crystal, 6″.......................55.00
Teardrop #301, nappy, hdld, crystal, 5″.......................8.50
Teardrop #301, plate, crystal, 10½″.........................45.00
Teardrop #301, plate, hdld, crystal, 11″......................35.00
Teardrop #301, relish, hdld, 3-compartment, crystal, 11″.......25.00
Teardrop #301, shakers, crystal, glass top, 5″, pr.............37.50
Teardrop #301, sweetmeat, hdld, crystal, 6½″.................17.50
Teardrop #301, urn & cover, crystal, 9″......................40.00
Teardrop #301, vase, fan-shape, crystal, 9″...................27.50
Teardrop #5300, pitcher, ice-guard lip, crystal, ½-gal..........65.00
Teardrop #5300, tumbler, ftd, crystal, 9-oz...................10.50
Teardrop #5301, goblet, ale; crystal, 8-oz....................14.50
Teardrop #5301, sherry, crystal, 1¾-oz......................17.50
Terrace #111, bowl, salad; crystal, 9″.......................27.50
Terrace #111, mayonnaise, 2-compartment, crystal.............27.50
Terrace #111, plate, torte; rolled edge, color, 18″.............58.00
Three Face, celery, crystal...............................200.00
Three Face, compote, crystal, 7″..........................165.00
Three Face, creamer, crystal..............................165.00
Three Face, goblet, crystal...............................125.00
Three Face, pitcher, water; crystal.........................350.00
Three Face, salver, crystal, 9″............................275.00
Three Feathers #117, bowl, oval, crystal, 4x12x7½″............65.00
Three Feathers #117, candle holder, color, 4″.................35.00
Venetian #126, bowl, oval, crystal, 14″......................23.00
Venetian #126, bowl, ruby, sq, 10″.........................58.00
Venetian #126, vase, crystal, 9″............................21.00
Venetian #126, vase, ruby, 9″..............................45.00
Victorian, finger bowl & plate, color.........................22.00
Victorian, goblet, crystal, 9-oz.............................10.00
Victorian, iced tea, ftd, crystal, 12-oz........................9.75
Victorian, nappy, crystal, 5″...............................9.50
Victorian, plate, color, 7½″...............................13.00
Victorian, sugar bowl, color, 8-oz...........................13.00

Durand

Durand Art Glass was a division of Vineland Glass Works, in Vineland, New Jersey. Created in 1924, it was geared specifically toward the manufacture of fine handcrafted artware. Iridescent, opalescent, and cased glass was used to create such patterns as King Tut, reminiscent of Tiffany and Steuben.

Production halted in 1931, after the death of Victor Durand.

When no condition is indicated, the items listed below are assumed to be in mint condition.

Bowl, Bridgeton Rose, ftd, 6″ dia 275.00
Box, bl irid w/King Tut pattern on lid, bulbous, 3½x5½″ 875.00
Candle holder/vase, King Tut, gold, sgn, 10″ 550.00
Candlestick, pink tulip cups/gr leaf bobeches, 7½″, pr 125.00
Compote, gold irid, sgn/#d, 6¾x7″ 350.00
Compote, King Tut, bl on gold, gold w/in, sgn, 6″ 450.00
Goblet, gold ruby 100.00
Lamp, threaded/pulled feather shade/bronze lily pad base 575.00
Lamp base, heart leaves/allover threading, wrought iron mt 350.00
Lamp base, pulled feather, gold/bl, Lyon Co fixture 625.00
Parfait, pulled feather, opal on bl w/yel ft, pr 425.00
Plate, bl, 10-sided/paneled, 8½″ 100.00
Plate, cobalt, opaque rim, paneled, 6¾″ 75.00
Plate, flashed ruby w/wht feathers, eng rose by Link, 8″ 300.00
Plate, ruby w/wht pulled feathers, eng Bridgeton Rose, 8″ 300.00
Rose bowl, Bridgeton Rose, 3-ftd 400.00
Shade, gas; bl/gold leaves on wht, scalloped edge, 5½″ 120.00
Shade, red w/gold lining, ribbed, minor fitter chips, 9½″ 625.00
Sherbet, pulled feather, bl/wht 225.00
Sherbet, pulled feather, opal on ruby & gold 275.00
Vase, abstract swirls, gold/bl/yel on wht, sgn/#1707, 9″ 1,800.00
Vase, amethyst, bl rim & ft applique, paneled, Larson, 6¾″ 200.00
Vase, bl/wht, gold w/in, crackle finish, 9½″ 395.00
Vase, cut overlay, bl to clear, 4⅛″ 400.00
Vase, gold, bulbous, sgn/#1710-8, 8½″ 500.00
Vase, gold, sgn/#1812-8, 7⅜″ 300.00
Vase, gr & opal decor, silver lustre, Amergris, 6¾″ 285.00
Vase, gr/brn translucent, sgn, 5½″, pr 425.00
Vase, gr/brn/purple/yel translucent, bulbous, 7″ 225.00
Vase, heart leaves/veins, wht on bl, sgn/#1812-6, 6½″ 650.00
Vase, heart leaves/veins, wht on bl, sgn/#1990-8, 7¾″ 800.00
Vase, irid gold, baluster, sgn, 10″ 550.00
Vase, King Tut, gold on deep gr w/pink/lav irid, sgn, 12½″ . . . 1,200.00
Vase, King Tut, gold on lt gr, 8½″ 700.00
Vase, King Tut, gold/platinum on med gr, sgn, 10″ 800.00
Vase, marbled, bl/wht, slim/concave sides, sgn/#32, 8″ 300.00
Vase, pulled feather, stringing, applied hdls, sgn, 8″ 850.00
Vase, satin amber crackle, 10⅛″, pr 250.00
Vase, scrolls/pulled devices, wht/gold/orange, no mk, 10½″ . . . 1,200.00

Table lamp, threaded and pulled feather shade, painted bronze base in the form of a leaf and bulrush, 14″, $585.00.

Vielleuse, gold drag loop on calcite, De Vilbiss base, 7½″ 625.00
Wine, King Tut, gold w/in 385.00
Wine, peacock feather, ruby, 5½″ 425.00
Wine glass, dk raspberry on vaseline stem, ribbed, unsgn 100.00

Durant Kilns

The Durant Pottery Company operated in Bedford Village, New York, in the early 1900s. Its founder was Mrs. Clarence Rice, who was aided by L. Volkmar to whom she assigned the task of technical direction. (See also Volkmar) The artware and tableware they produced was simple in form, relying on the unique glaze treatments developed by Volkmar. The creative aspects of the work were carried on almost entirely by Volkmar himself, with only a minimal crew to help with production. After Mrs. Rice's death in 1919, the pottery was purchased by Volkmar, who chose to drop the Durant name by 1930.

The ware was marked simply 'Durant' and dated prior to 1919, after which a stylized 'V' was added.

When no condition is indicated, the items listed below are assumed to be in mint condition.

Bowl, bl/purple, ftd, 3x6″ 135.00
Bowl, Chinese bl, ftd/flared, mk V/1920, 2x7″ 225.00
Bowl, leathery semi-gloss aubergine, sgn V/1919, 3½x7½″ 325.00

Easter

Eggs, bunnies, chicks and baskets have all become basic elements of our Easter celebrations; and the older, more interesting examples are being collected, often for nostalgic reasons, and displayed during the holidays to make the festivities brighter.

When no condition is indicated, the items listed below are assumed to be in excellent condition.

Bunny w/basket on bk, papier mache, 8″ 20.00
Candy container, satin egg w/picture mother & child, 1900 . . . . . 45.00
Egg, blown glass, frosted, HP floral & 'Easter Joys' 18.00
Egg, compo, Japanese boy & chick peek thru crack, 4″ 105.00
Egg, milk glass, chick in egg 30.00
Egg, milk glass, HP birds/flowers/gold horseshoe, 4½″ 22.00
Rabbit w/basket, papier mache 15.00

Elfinware

Made in Germany, these miniature vases, boxes, salt cellars, and miscellaneous novelty items are characterized by the tiny applied flowers that often cover their entire surface. Pieces with animals and birds are the most valuable, followed by the more interesting examples such as diminutive grand pianos, candle holders, etc.

When no condition is indicated, the items listed below are assumed to be in mint condition.

Covered dish, chick on nest, 2½″, $75.00.

Basket, bl lustre, mk, miniature....25.00
Box, floral lid, 1½x2½"....30.00
Coffee pot, miniature....26.00
Inkwell, 3x3¾"....35.00
Perfumes, lilies-o/t-valley, 3½", pr....25.00
Shoe, miniature....18.00
Toothpick holder, wht rose decor....23.00
Wheelbarrow salt....45.00

Epergnes

A popular item during the Victorian era, epergnes were fancy centerpieces often consisting of several tiers of vases (called lilies), candle holders, or dishes, or a combination of components. They were made in all types or art glass, and some were set in ornate plated frames.

When no condition is indicated, it is assumed that all glass parts are mint, and that silverplated frames are in excellent to near mint condition.

Bl ruffled edge, 4-lily, spiraling rigaree, 9" bowl, 16"....260.00
Bl satin glass, 1-lily, HP birds/florals, 18"....250.00
Burmese, 1-lily, gr applied vine/leaves, in 8" dish....400.00
Cranberry, 1-lily, eng floral, ruffled/scalloped, 18"....350.00
Cranberry, 1-lily, trn down flower, clear rim, 12x8"....195.00
Cranberry opalescent, 3-lily, clear rigaree, ruffled rim....290.00
Cranberry/vaseline, 4-lily, applied crimp work, 15"....239.00
DQ MOP, 3 stem bowls, glass leaves, mirror base, Webb, 9"..1,800.00
Orange-amber, 1-lily, clear lower stem/rigaree, 14½"....135.00
Pink glass, 1-lily, ftd base, 14½x12"....75.00
Ruffled lily w/pnt florals in 12" bowl, WMF SP/copper base....795.00
Shaded bl satin w/HP birds & floral, 1-lily, 18"....250.00
Squirrel perched on SP base w/3 crystal vases, Wilcox....100.00
Vaseline opal, 1-lily....95.00
Yel, 1-lily, ruffled bowl, applied rigaree....260.00

Cut glass and gilt-bronze, central vase plus twelve in clear glass with diaper-cut ground; scrolling arms, four lion-paw feet, signed Osler, in excellent condition, 22½", $900.00.

Erickson

Carl Erickson of Bremen, Ohio, produced hand-formed glassware from 1943 until 1960, in artistic shapes, no two of which were identical. One of the characteristics of his work were the air bubbles that were captured within the glass. Though most examples are clear, colored items were also made. Rather than to risk compromising his high standards by selling the factory, when Erickson retired, the plant was dismantled and sold.

When no condition is indicated, the items listed below are assumed to be in mint condition.

Ash tray, red, crystal casing, spaced bubbles, 5" W....40.00
Bowl, free-form, rounded bottom, 4 flared ends....70.00
Bud vase, red, solid paperweight base, sgn, 9"....65.00
Candle holder, purple, bubble designs, 2", pr....90.00
Compote, red, spaced bubbles, paperweight base, 9" dia....135.00
Cruet, crystal, ground stopper, 9½"....60.00
Goblet, crystal base w/lg teardrop bubble, 7"....30.00
Nut dish, leaf shape, gr & crystal, 9" L....35.00
Perfume, gr, clear stopper, 7"....55.00
Pitcher, smoke, applied hdl, heavy bottom, 13"....95.00
Plate, cake; gr/flattened bubbles, irregular edge, 15" dia....75.00
Relish, red & crystal, oblong, 13"....45.00
Tumblers, aqua, set of 4, 3¼"....90.00

Erphila

Rather difficult to find, these fine porcelain novelty items were made for only a short time in Czechoslovakia and Germany. They are marked with a stamp 'Erphila,' and the country of origin.

When no condition is indicated, the items listed below are assumed to be in mint condition.

Cracker jar, orange poppy....35.00
Dresser doll, Madame Pompadour....65.00
Figurine, boy artist paints bird on ped, mc, sgn....95.00
Figurine, Colonial couple, airbrush decor, sgn, 5½"....50.00
Figurine, Deco lady, sgn Germany, 10"....48.00
Figurine, German shepherd dogs, 2 on base, 4½x4½"....45.00
Figurine, Victorian couple, orig paper seals, 5", pr....45.00
Match set, Colonial man between holder & ash tray....20.00
Pitcher, poppies decor, w/lid, 5"....15.00
Pitcher, poppies decor, w/lid, 8"....20.00
Planter, girl, goat & child, pnt decor....68.00
Teapot, dachshund figural, 8¼"....48.00
Teapot, elephant figural....45.00
Tray, relish; roses/leaves on pearl, open hdls, 9x4"....28.00

Eskimo Artifacts

While ivory carvings made from walrus tusks or whale teeth have been the most emphasized articles of the Eskimo art, basketry and woodworking are other areas in which these Alaskan Indians excell. Their designs are effected through the application of simple yet dramatic lines and almost stark decorative devices. Though not pursued to the extent of American Indian art, the unique work of this northern tribe is beginning to attract the serious attention of today's collectors.

When no condition is indicated, the items listed below are assumed to be in excellent condition.

Basket, Attu, twined cylinder w/faux embroidery, 5½" dia....900.00
Basket, beehive, lid w/knob, coiled, red/gr worm decor, 6"....100.00

Box, carved wood, human face in sunk relief, ivory details, 4″ diameter, $600.00 at auction.

Basket, beehive, lid w/knob, 2-color ascending terrace, 5″......70.00
Basket, coiled dyed grasses, simple decor, w/lid, 6x7″ dia......140.00
Basket, coiled over bundled rods, flared, red Xs, 9x10″.......135.00
Basket, flared oval, ped base, side hdls, ca 1920, 3x9x13″......65.00
Basket, Haida, twined cylinder w/pigment totem, 4½″.........230.00
Basket, whale baleen, ivory walrus head surmount, 3″ dia......650.00
Basket tray, coiled, gr/pink butterflies, 11x9″................50.00
Bear point, chipped chert, stemmed, rnd shoulders, 3¾″.......30.00
Chisel, ivory, ground-down tooth in bone hdl...............180.00
Cup, made from jaw of walrus...............................60.00
Effigy, ivory, hand holds tusk: bear engulfing seal, inlay.......400.00
Effigy, upright walrus ivory bear w/inlay claws, 1800s, 5″......500.00
Fetish, ivory, bear, drilled for cord, 1⅜″....................80.00
Figure, playing seals, under-cut, ivory/polychrome, 2″, pr......290.00
Figure, walrus w/baby, simple carving, walrus ivory, 6″........100.00
Goggles, snow; carved ivory w/eye slits, early, 4½x1½″.........400.00
Halibut hook, sea mammal carving, iron barb, 11″..........120.00
Harpoon socket, made from horn, pre-1900, 7½″.............25.00
Ivory, eng tusk, hunting/trapping/fishing/genre, 23″..........400.00
Kayak, whale ivory, Eskimo w/in, +paddles/harpoon, 7″ L.....225.00
Mask, wood, seal spirit in 2 hoops, feathers attached, 10″.....800.00
Meat hook, bone w/ivory holding barb, 14½″................215.00
Moccasins, mc beads on hide, fur cuffs, 1910, 10″ L..........200.00
Model, dog sled, wood, laced & pin-built, 3 dolls, 18″ L........95.00
Net toggle, walrus ivory carved as seal, 2″..................25.00
Pipe, carved wood w/inlay pewter decor....................575.00
Polar bear, walrus ivory, ears extend/incised features, 2″........85.00
Polar bear, walrus ivory, incised/darkened detail, '30, 3″.......125.00
Shovel, snow; bone blade, ca 1900, 48″....................150.00
Sled, walrus ivory, standing dog attached w/sinew, 6″ L.......150.00
Story board, 7 steatite figures portray seal hunt, 1910.........165.00
Wedding spoon, caribou, scrimshaw, ornate hdl, 1840, 5¾″....200.00

Fans

The Japanese are said to have invented the fan. From there it went to China, and Portuguese traders took the idea to Europe. Though usually considered milady's accessory, even the gentlemen in 17th century England carried fans! More fashionable than practical, some were of feathers and lovely hand-painted silks with carved ivory or tortoise sticks. Some French fans had peepholes. There are mourning fans, calendar fans, and those with advertising. All are collectible!

When no condition is indicated, the items listed below are assumed to be in excellent condition.

Advertising, Purox Punch, Horlacher Cereal Beverages.........30.00
Cardboard, Victorian lady's portrait: Olivia, 1911...............7.50
Celluloid, HP swans, 11″...................................40.00
Celluloid, lacy, blk w/gold trim.............................15.00
Fabric, embroidered, wood sticks w/silver HP floral............25.00
Fabric, printed w/Victorian lady, velvet hdls..................32.00
Folding, Love's Greetings, red roses/couple, Germany..........38.00
Lace HP inserts, MOP sticks, enamel flowers, French..........85.00
Mourning, carved sticks.....................................20.00
Ostrich, ivory celluloid sticks, lg............................45.00
Ostrich, pnt Japanese figures...............................32.00
Paper on bone sticks, Hamburg Am Ship Lines, French........65.00
Satin, embroidered, HP, 25″...............................125.00
Silk, pierced ivory sticks, ca 1890...........................28.00
Venetian lace, celluloid sticks..............................125.00
Voile & lace, HP floral/butterflies, opens to 25″...............50.00
Wedding, wht silk w/lace trim, HP flowers, sequins, in fr.......45.00

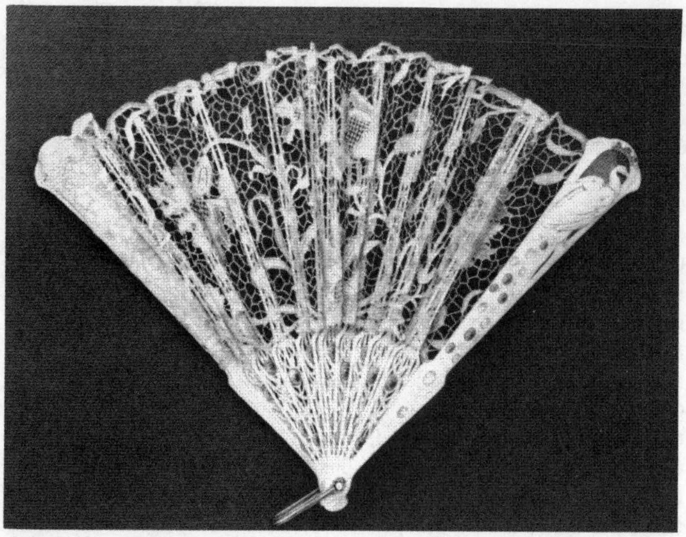

Ivory with one shaped stick carved with a peacock, the tail mounted with enamel 'eyes' on plique-a-jour ground, the crest set with diamonds and emeralds, two-color gold loop handle with diamond-set hinges, signed Phillipe Wolfers, ca 1900, 17″ long when open, $1,300.00.

Farm Collectibles

Country living in the 19th century entailed plowing, planting, and harvesting; gathering eggs and milking; making soap from lard rendered on butchering day; and numerous other tasks performed with primitive tools of which we in the 20th century have had little first-hand knowledge.

For more information on this subject, we recommend *Collecting Farm Antiques*, an identification and value guide by Lar Hothem; his address is listed in the Directory under Ohio. When no condition is indicated, the items listed below are assumed to be in excellent condition.

Apple butter stirring stick, 36″.............................12.50
Ax head, Kansas City, MO, Pioneer, Ericharn 1857............22.50
Barbed wire, 4-point, dbl duo-tipped, 18″ strand...............8.50
Barn lantern, tin, Embury Manufacturing Co.................17.50
Bee smoker, fabric bellows, sheet copper, copper spout........50.00
Bell, goat or sheep; attached to leather strap, 3½″............16.50
Bell, goat; iron, 4 slant sides, sm, 2½″.....................14.50
Bridle rosette, w/horse's head, fancy brass edge...............7.50
Bull nose key, used to lead bull..............................8.00
Chick feeder, pine, homemade..............................14.00
Chicken waterer & buttermilk feeder, Stoneware, Westko.......42.00
Chicken weighing bucket, w/hanging chain...................24.50
Corn dryer, 10-prong, iron.................................15.00
Corn dryer, 24-prong, heavy twist wire, early 1900s, 30″........12.00

Corn sheller, Pat Feb 28, 1875, cast iron, $75.00.

Corn grader, dbl, original red pnt 40.00
Corn grinder, heavy iron, lg wheel, resembles coffee mill 28.00
Corn planter, Deere & Mansur Co, Moline, IL, July 28, 1895 . . . . 20.00
Corn planter, hand type, original natural finish 19.50
Corn sheller, wood/carved-out hdls, sq nails form grater 125.00
Corn sheller, wood/hand forged sq iron teeth, red, 2-part 220.00
Corn sheller scraping plate, mk TJ Hoover, iron, oblong 55.00
Cow kickers, iron & chain, used at milking time 8.00
Crowbar, to straighten buggy axles, smithy touchmk, 53″ 45.00
Egg case, tin, cardboard fillers, 2-doz, 13x9½x3½″ 32.00
Egg case, w/lid & fillers, Humpty Dumpty, 6-doz 38.00
Feed sack, burlap, Great Northern Beans, red & bl, 100-lb 8.50
Feed sack, cloth, red & bl letters, hen on nest, 100-lb 6.50
Gate hook, iron, lg 2.00
Grain measure, round, bentwood, w/metal bands, peck size 40.00
Grain palette, hand hewn, finger/thumb holes, 6x17″ 75.00
Grain sieve, handmade, wood box/wire bottom, old pnt, 11″ 75.00
Grappling hook, iron, 3-prong 17.50
Harness, brass trim 2.50
Hay saw, 2 wooden hdls 20.00
Hog hanging stick, wooden, notched & curved, 35½″ 22.50
Hog scraper, lg wood hdl, w/rounded iron cup bottom 8.50
Hog scraper, wood hdl, heavy tin cup on bottom 10.00
Horse bit, rings on each end 5.00
Horse collar hook, iron, lg, 10″ L 14.50
Horse food measure, dk tin, emb Pratts...for Horses/Cattle 18.00
Horse muzzle, oval, fancy design, all wire 12.50
Horseshoe, salesman's sample 8.00
Implement seat, Adriance Buckeye, iron, fancy cut-outs 50.00
Implement seat, Hapgood 185.00
Implement seat, Oliver Chilled Plow Works 90.00
Implement seat, Stoddard, iron, fancy cut-outs 50.00
Meal grinder, heavy iron, funnel-shaped top, crank hdl 28.50
Meat hook, iron, 1″ 18.00
Meat hook, iron, 2-prong, V-shaped top 12.50
Milk can, tin, sm hand type w/lid, tinner made 22.50
Milk strainer, tin, screen bottom, w/wire stand, sm 14.00
Milking stool, 3-legged, seat 2″ thick 38.50
Nest egg, blown milk glass, lg 16.00
Nose ring, for bull, polished, copper, 3″ 6.50
Ox yoke, single, scrubbed wht finish, age cracks/wear, 35″ 65.00
Oxen shoes, mk Pat 1882, pr 12.00
Pail, cream; tin, dk, w/lid & hdl, 1-gal 17.50
Pail, cream; tin, dk, w/lid & hdl, 2-gal 20.00
Pitch fork, wrought iron, 2 tines, long wood hdl, 80″ 20.00
Rope winder, wooden, lg 30.00
Rug/sack sewing tool, wooden, w/metal needle 12.00
Scales, dairy; round, hanging 30.00
Scales, steelyard, w/hooks & weight, Whitmore, #52 . . . . . 26.00
Scoop, cherry, open D-hdl, 1-pc 195.00
Scythe, hay; mortised wood rack, orig pnt, G detail, 46″ 55.00
Seed corn bag, Pioneer, cloth, wht w/red & blue letters 4.50
Seed sower, w/canvas bag, Horn Trademark Seed Sower 15.00
Shucking peg, long metal peg on leather, fits over fingers 2.50
Shucking peg, The Boss, on orig sgn leather strap 15.00
Shucking peg, wooden, w/leather strap 12.50
Sickle, barley; thin curved blade, sgn Long, 1700s 35.00
Sickle, hand; wood hdl, long curved blade 18.00
Spigot, for wooden barrel, lg 12.00
Stirrup, wooden, lg 16.00
Stirrup, wooden, sm 14.00
Tool, wood, T-shape w/pointed end, used to tie stock 55.00
Trap, fly; wire & wood, never used, w/instructions, 1930s 22.50
Trap, mole; wire, pat October, 1916 . . . . . 11.00
Trap, mouse; wire, oval 18.50
Trap, rat; wire, oval 21.00
Whetstone carrier, wooden, old 33.00

Fenton

Frank and John Fenton were brothers who founded the Fenton Art Glass Company in 1906 in Martin's Ferry, Ohio. The venture, at first only a decorating shop, began operations in July of 1905, using blanks purchased from other companies. This operation soon proved unsatisfactory, and by 1907 they had constructed their own glass factory in Williamstown, West Virginia. John left the company in 1909, and organized his own firm in Millersburg, Ohio.

The Fenton Company produced over 130 patterns of carnival glass. They also made custard, chocolate, opalescent, and stretch glass. This company has always been noted for its various colors of glass and have continually changed its production so as to satisfy the decorating vogue of the times. In 1925 they produced a line of 'handmade' items that incorporated the techniques of threading and mosaic work. Because the process proved to be unprofitable, the line was discontinued by 1927.

Even their glassware made in the past twenty-five years is already regarded as collectible. Various paper labels have been used since the 1920s; only since 1970 has the logo been stamped into the glass.

When no condition is indicated, the items listed below are assumed to be in mint condition. See also Carnival Glass; Collector Plates; Custard Glass

Amber Crest, vase, flared, 6″ 28.00
Apple Blossom, compote, 7″ 28.00
Aqua Crest, bowl, cereal 12.75
Aqua Crest, bowl, 8½″ 35.00
Aqua Crest, candle holder, cornucopia, pr 25.00
Aqua Crest, candy dish, ped ft, 3x6″ 19.75
Aqua Crest, compote, ftd, 8″ 20.00
Aqua Crest, epergne, lily insert, 6″ 15.00
Aqua Crest, plate, 8½″ 20.00
Aqua Crest, vase, triangular, #835, 5½″ 30.00
Aqua Crest, vase, 10″ 45.00
Aqua Crest, vase, 4″ 14.00
Aqua Crest, vase, 7″ 28.00
Beaded Melon, bowl, milk glass, gr w/in, 7″ 32.00
Beaded Melon, pitcher, ivy gr, 6″ 55.00
Beaded Melon, vase, bl overlay, rnd, 4″ 38.00
Beaded Melon, vase, Jack-in-the-Pulpit, gr, 7″ 30.00
Bicentennial, compote, Jefferson, Patriot Red 100.00
Bicentennial, paperweight, w/eagle, Patriot Red 35.00
Bicentennial, plate, Patriot Red 35.00
Block & Star, shaker, wht milk glass, orig lid, 3¼″, pr 15.00

Bottle, scent; De Vilbiss, pink opal....35.00
Bowl, flower form, royal bl....30.00
Bowl, Mandarin Red on blk base....80.00
Bowl, swan, sq, pink, #6, 11½"....65.00
Bubble Optic, vase, honey amber, #1359, 11½"....135.00
Burmese, bowl, maple leaf, #7422, 8"....55.00
Burmese, cruet vase, #7262....30.00
Burmese, epergne, 4-lily, 500 limited ed....350.00
Burmese, vase, #7253, 7"....35.00
Burmese, vase, Mandarin....200.00
Cactus, compote, stemmed, wht milk glass, 5½"....10.00
Candy dish, lt gr cased, swirled, w/lid, 6"....110.00
Candy jar, red-cased milk glass, w/lid, 7"....100.00
Chessie, box, Rosalene....200.00
Chessie, compote, carnival, w/lid, 1970....175.00
Coin Dot, basket, cranberry opal, #1353, 12"....198.00
Coin Dot, bottle, scent; bl opal, #92....45.00
Coin Dot, bowl, crimped, cranberry opal, 6"....45.00
Coin Dot, cruet, cranberry opal, #814, 8"....70.00
Coin Dot, decanter w/stopper, cranberry opal....175.00
Coin Dot, hat, cranberry opal, 3⅛"....45.00
Coin Dot, jug, cranberry opal, #201, squat....140.00
Coin Dot, jug, wht, 5"....55.00
Coin Dot, rose bowl, cranberry opal, 3¾"....40.00
Coin Dot, student lamp, honey amber opal, 21"....250.00
Coin Dot, tumbler, cranberry opal, 4⅛"....35.00
Coin Dot, vase, cranberry opal, #1455, 3¾"....40.00
Coin Dot, vase, cranberry opal, #1456, 6½"....50.00
Coin Dot, vase, cranberry opal, #1457, 7"....55.00
Coin Dot, vase, cranberry opal, #1459, 6½"....40.00
Coin Dot, vase, French opal, #1925, 6"....25.00
Coin Dot, vase, honeysuckle opal, 8"....75.00
Coin Dot, vase, yel opal top, 6x7"....65.00
Coin Spot, pitcher, ice lip, gr opal....115.00
Crystal Crest, basket, 7½"....150.00
Crystal Crest, vase, 4"....14.00
Crystal Crest, vase, 8½"....20.00
Daisy & Button, ash tray, horseshoe, aqua, 8"....12.25
Daisy & Button, candlesticks, milk glass, ca 1953, pr....18.00
Daisy & Button, creamer, vaseline....15.75
Daisy & Button, cup & saucer, amber....32.50
Diamond Lace, bowl, French opal, 9½"....35.00
Diamond Lace, candlestick, clear opal, pr....22.50
Diamond Lace, candlestick, cornucopia, bl opal, pr....45.00
Diamond Lace, epergne, bl opal, #4808, 12"....145.00
Diamond Optic, basket, blk, chrome hdl, 8"....220.00
Diamond Optic, basket, pink, chrome hdl, 7"....28.00
Diamond Optic, basket, ruby overlay, 7"....65.00
Diamond Optic, candlestick, orchid, 3", pr....35.00
Diamond Optic, creamer & sugar, ftd, orchid, #1502....35.00
Diamond Optic, hat, cranberry, 4"....55.00
Diamond Optic, pitcher, cranberry, 6"....75.00
Diamond Optic, shakers, amber, pr....40.00
Diamond Optic, shakers, ruby, pr....85.00
Diamond Optic, vase, lime opal, 12"....40.00
Diamond Optic, vase, transparent gr, #1502, 8¼"....20.00
Diamond Quilted, vase, ring neck, cranberry, #192, 7¼"....30.00
Dolphin, bonbon, Cameo, opal, old, 6"....48.00
Dolphin, bonbon, ftd, hdl, jade, 6"....25.00
Dolphin, bonbon, topaz stretch, 6"....58.00
Dolphin, bowl, Florentine, gr stretch, #1608, 10"....95.00
Dolphin, bowl, ftd, 2-hdl, jade, 11"....80.00
Dolphin, bowl, oval, ftd, 2-hdl, jade, 6"....35.00
Dolphin, bowl, 2-hdl, gr, 6½"....27.00
Dolphin, candlestick, red, 3½"....35.00
Dolphin, compote, ftd, 2-hdl, ruby....75.00
Dolphin, compote, oval, 2-hdl, jade....40.00
Dolphin, compote, ruffled, 2-hdl, jade....40.00
Dolphin, vase, fan shape, bl opal....90.00
Dolphin, vase, fan shape, stretch glass, Dolphin hdl, pink....20.00
Dolphin, vase, fan shape, topaz stretch, 5"....58.00
Dot Optic, basket, cranberry opal, 7"....80.00
Dot Optic, bowl, bl, 6½"....35.00
Dot Optic, lamp, table; yel opal, 21½"....95.00
Dot Optic, lamp base, frosted bl, G-70....45.00
Dot Optic, pitcher, cranberry opal, #352, 80-oz....110.00
Dot Optic, pitcher, ice lip, lime opal, 70-oz....90.00
Dot Optic, pitcher, squat, cranberry opal, 4"....57.00
Dot Optic, tumbler, cranberry opal, #1353, 4"....16.00
Dot Optic, vase, cranberry opal, #192, 8"....85.00
Emerald Crest, compote, 7"....35.00
Emerald Crest, cup & saucer....26.00
Emerald Crest, plate, 8¼"....24.00
Figurine, Happiness Bird, lav satin....22.50
Georgian, goblet, cocktail; ruby....10.00
Georgian, goblet, pink, 5⅝"....17.00
Georgian, shakers, amber, pr....45.00
Green Crest, bowl, #7329, 4"....25.00
Heart & Vine, candlesticks, irid, 1920s, 12", pr....295.00
Hobnail, ash tray, fan shape, bl opal, w/label, 5½"....22.50
Hobnail, ash tray, French opal, oval....10.00
Hobnail, basket, bl opal, #389, 8"....50.00
Hobnail, basket, bl opal, 4¾"....25.00
Hobnail, basket, cranberry opal, #248, 6½"....65.00
Hobnail, basket, cranberry opal, 10½"....110.00
Hobnail, basket, gr pastel, 7"....48.00
Hobnail, bonbon, crimped, topaz opal, 6"....15.00
Hobnail, bonbon, oval, cranberry opal, 6"....16.00
Hobnail, bonbon, oval, 2-hdl, bl opal, #389, 6½"....14.00
Hobnail, bowl, bl opal, 11"....50.00
Hobnail, bowl, crimped, bl opal, 9"....30.00
Hobnail, bowl, fruit; crimped, ftd, gr opal, 6½x11"....80.00
Hobnail, bowl, nappy, bl opal, 6"....14.00
Hobnail, bowl, oval, French opal, #389, 7"....15.00
Hobnail, bowl, yel opal, 8½"....55.00
Hobnail, bowl, 2-hdl, bl opal, #389, 4"....12.00
Hobnail, cake stand, crystal, 13"....25.00
Hobnail, candlestick, bl opal, #839, 3", pr....24.00
Hobnail, candlestick, cranberry opal, #3470....37.00
Hobnail, candy dish, w/lid, bl opal, 7"....45.00
Hobnail, candy dish, w/lid, French opal, #3980....24.00
Hobnail, compote, crimped, plum opal....55.00
Hobnail, compote, yel opal, 6¾"....35.00
Hobnail, creamer & sugar, bl opal, crimped top, #3906....65.00
Hobnail, creamer & sugar, bl opal, individual....11.50
Hobnail, creamer & sugar, French opal, #3901....12.00
Hobnail, cruet, oil; w/stopper, bl opal, 5-oz....22.00
Hobnail, cruet, oil; w/stopper, cranberry opal, 5-oz....65.00
Hobnail, cruet, oil; w/stopper, French opal, 5"....15.00
Hobnail, epergne, bl opal, #3801, 4-pc....80.00
Hobnail, goblet, bl opal, #3845....22.00
Hobnail, goblet, French opal....12.75
Hobnail, hat, bl opal, 2¼"....18.50
Hobnail, mayonnaise, bl opal, #3803, 3-pc....35.00
Hobnail, mayonnaise, w/liner, cranberry....40.00
Hobnail, mustard, bl opal, w/lid....25.00
Hobnail, mustard, French opal, 3-pc....16.50
Hobnail, pitcher, cranberry opal, 80-oz....200.00

Hobnail, pitcher, French opal, #3967, 80-oz.................125.00
Hobnail, pitcher, juice; bl opal, #3965.......................40.00
Hobnail, pitcher, juice; cranberry opal, 4½″..................40.00
Hobnail, pitcher, juice; French opal, #3965...................25.00
Hobnail, pitcher, juice; honey amber, threaded hdl, 6″.........45.00
Hobnail, pitcher, juice; plum opal, 4½″.......................65.00
Hobnail, plate, cake; ftd, bl opal, 13″.......................60.00
Hobnail, plate, cake; ftd, milk glass, 13″....................12.00
Hobnail, plate, crimped, French opal, 8½″.....................12.50
Hobnail, powder jar, bl opal..................................38.00
Hobnail, rose bowl, cupped, bl opal, 2¾″......................30.00
Hobnail, shakers, bl opal, pr.................................32.00
Hobnail, shakers, flat, cranberry, pr.........................55.00
Hobnail, toothpick, ftd, vaseline..............................9.00
Hobnail, tumbler, bl opal, #3985, 5-oz........................10.00
Hobnail, tumbler, French opal, #3945, 5-oz....................10.00
Hobnail, tumbler, French opal, #3946, 16-oz...................20.00
Hobnail, tumbler, French opal, #3949, 12-oz...................12.50
Hobnail, tumbler, iced tea; topaz opal........................22.00
Hobnail, vanity lamp, French opal, 7″.........................22.00
Hobnail, vanity set, w/lid & stopper, French opal, 3-pc.......40.00
Hobnail, vase, crimped, bl opal, 5½″..........................20.00
Hobnail, vase, cupped, bl opal, 3½″...........................15.00
Hobnail, vase, dbl crimped, bl opal, 5″.......................40.00
Hobnail, vase, fan shape, bl opal, ftd, 4″....................15.00
Hobnail, vase, fan shape, bl opal, 5¾″........................35.00
Hobnail, vase, fan shape, French opal, #281, 8″...............30.00
Hobnail, vase, fan shape, French opal, 7″.....................12.00
Hobnail, vase, fan shape, yel opal, 4″........................22.50
Hobnail, vase, ftd, crimped, French opal, 5¼″.................22.00
Hobnail, vase, miniature, crimped, cranberry, 4″..............29.00
Hobnail, vase, miniature, triangle, cranberry, 4″.............29.00
Hobnail, vase, ruffled, bl opal, 3″...........................10.00
Hobnail, vase, sq, bl opal, 4½″...............................25.00
Ivory Crest, bowl, 10″..45.00
Ivory Crest, candlestick, 6½″, pr.............................80.00
Jacqueline, pitcher, apple gr................................150.00

Shakers, Jacqueline, apple green, 2¾″, $60.00 for the pair.

Jacqueline, shakers, apple gr, pr.............................60.00
Lincoln Inn, champagne, gr....................................10.00
Lincoln Inn, goblet, pink.....................................13.50
Lincoln Inn, plate, cobalt, 8″................................12.00
Lincoln Inn, shakers, jade, pr...............................225.00
Lincoln Inn, shakers, red, pr................................250.00
Lincoln Inn, sherbet, cobalt, 4½″.............................16.00
Lincoln Inn, sherbet, crystal, 4½″............................12.00
Lincoln Inn, tumbler, ftd, cobalt, 6″.........................22.00
Lincoln Inn, tumbler, iced tea; ftd, ruby.....................25.00
Lincoln Inn, wine, cobalt.....................................25.00
Lincoln Inn, wine, crystal....................................12.75
Lotus, candlestick, 3-toe, ebony, pr..........................12.50
Mandarin Red, basket, #1684...................................95.00
Mandarin Red, candlestick, 6¾″................................75.00
Mandarin Red, vase, fan form, 8″..............................95.00
Ming, basket, gr..95.00
Ming, bonbon, 3-toe, pink, 7″.................................25.00
Ming, bowl, deep, 3-toe, pink, 6″.............................34.00
Ming, candlesticks, cornucopia; gr, 5½″, pr...................45.00
Ming, jar, macaroon; reed hdl, gr............................125.00
Ming, plate, 3-ftd, pink, 8″..................................25.00
Ming, tidbit, 3-toe, pink, 7″.................................30.00
Ming, vase, crystal, #621, 8″.................................25.00
Ming, vase, crystal, 6½″......................................20.00
Ming, vase, crystal, 7″.......................................22.00
Mongolian, jar, macaroon; gr, 6½″.............................95.00
Moonstone, basket, hdl, red decor, 9½″, VG....................55.00
Moonstone, bottle, scent; w/stopper...........................55.00
Peach Crest, basket, #192, 10″...............................125.00
Peach Crest, basket, 8″.......................................85.00
Peach Crest, bowl, crimped, 6¼″...............................24.00
Peach Crest, hat, 3¼″...32.00
Peach Crest, jug, #192, 8″....................................67.00
Peach Crest, top hat, crimped, 5″.............................55.00
Peach Crest, top hat, 3¼″.....................................27.50
Peach Crest, vase, tulip, 9″..................................35.00
Peachblow, vase, smooth top, 8″...............................20.00
Pink Crest, bowl, fruit; ftd, sq..............................47.00
Plated amberina, jar w/lid, 7″...............................125.00
Polka Dot, shakers, cranberry, #2206, pr......................87.00
Polka Dot, vase, cranberry, #2251, 8″.........................75.00
Rib Optic, barber bottle, wht sleeve, bl opal.................45.00
Rib Optic, shakers, cranberry, salt: 5″/pepper: 4″, pr........85.00
Rope Twist, candlestick, jade, 10″, pr.......................120.00
Rosalene, bonbon, butterfly, hdls.............................35.00
Rosalene, compote w/lid.......................................55.00
Rosalene, light, owl..25.00
Rose, basket, hdl, blk, #7237, 7″............................195.00
Rose, cake stand, pastel, #3513, 13″..........................42.50
Rose, shakers, swirl rib, pastel, pr..........................37.50
Rose, student lamp, amber, 19″...............................145.00
Rose Crest, basket, 10″......................................125.00
Rose Crest, bowl, 7″..60.00
Rose Crest, candlestick, 5″, pr...............................45.00
Rose Crest, candlestick, 6″, pr...............................60.00
Rose Crest, plate, 12″..35.00
Rose Crest, vase, crimped, 6″.................................25.00
Rose Overlay, vase, #192, 4¾″.................................18.00
September Morn, flower frog, blk opaque......................170.00
September Morn, flower frog, Chinese yellow, jade base.......275.00
September Morn, flower frog, crystal, star base...............65.00
September Morn, flower frog, jade opaque.....................120.00
September Morn, flower frog, lt bl transparent...............160.00
September Morn, flower frog, lt gr, blk base.................120.00
September Morn, flower frog, med gr transparent..............135.00
September Morn, flower frog, pink transparent.................85.00
September Morn, flower frog, red transparent.................175.00
Sheffield, candy container, w/lid, crystal, 3-part............30.00
Silver Crest, banana stand.....................................25.00
Silver Crest, basket, low, 8″.................................18.00
Silver Crest, basket, Spanish lace emb, crimped hdl, 10¼″.....50.00
Silver Crest, basket, 7″......................................18.00
Silver Crest, bottle, scent; melon rib, w/stopper, 7″.........22.00

Silver Crest, bowl, fruit; ftd, sq.......45.00
Silver Crest, bowl, 12½″.......25.00
Silver Crest, cake stand, Holly Sprig pattern.......28.00
Silver Crest, cake stand, 13″.......32.00
Silver Crest, candle holder, 6″, pr.......28.00
Silver Crest, compote, ftd, 7″.......11.00
Silver Crest, compote, w/lid, 6¾″.......25.00
Silver Crest, compote, 6″.......9.00
Silver Crest, creamer & sugar bowl.......20.00
Silver Crest, cup & saucer.......15.00
Silver Crest, pitcher, 6½″.......40.00
Silver Crest, plate, dessert; 6½″.......14.00
Silver Crest, plate, dinner; 10½″.......20.00
Silver Crest, plate, luncheon; 8¼″.......15.00
Silver Crest, plate, torte; 15¼″.......65.00
Silver Crest, plate, 11½″.......22.00
Silver Crest, plate, 12¾″.......27.00
Silver Crest, punch set, bowl/base/24 cups.......200.00
Silver Crest, server, center hdl, 12½″.......25.00
Silver Crest, sherbet.......9.00
Silver Crest, tidbit, 2-tier.......32.50
Silver Crest, tidbit, 3-tier.......36.00
Silver Crest, vase, fan shape, 13″.......32.00
Silvertone, bowl, flared, 3-toe, amethyst, #1005, 6½″.......18.00
Silvertone, bowl, 3-toe, amber.......5.00
Snow Crest, hat, emerald gr, #1921, 7″.......35.00
Snow Crest, vase, amber, #3005, 7½″.......45.00
Snow Crest, vase, bl, 6″.......35.00
Snow Crest, vase, emerald gr, rnd, 4″.......40.00
Spiral Optic, bottle, bitters; cranberry opal, 9″.......110.00
Spiral Optic, vase, cranberry opal, #183, 9½″.......90.00
Spiral Optic, vase, lime opal, #186, 8″.......37.50
Stretch, bonbon, gr, #363.......35.00
Stretch, fan vase, bl, 9½″.......70.00
Stretch, lemon server, topaz.......25.00
Stretch, plate, topaz, 6″.......20.00
Stretch, vase, fan shape, Florent, gr.......30.00
Vasa Murrhina, basket, bl/gr, 11″.......100.00
Vasa Murrhina, vase, autumn orange, #6451, 10″.......135.00
Vase, cranberry overlay, crimped, 5x5½″.......65.00
Vase, Dancing Girl, gr.......150.00
Vase, Dancing Girl, periwinkle bl, ped ft.......190.00
Vase, Empress, milk glass.......65.00
Vase, flip, jade, #1668.......30.00
Vase, Karnak Red, 9½″.......525.00
Vase, Milady, ming crystal, 11″.......135.00
Vase, mosaic, red/yel on irid bl, threaded, ca 1926, 10″.......250.00
Vase, Peacock, bl satin.......35.00
Vase, Sophisticated Ladies, D Ellington tribute, blk, 10⅝″.......118.00
Vase, Venetian Red, #857, 1920s.......110.00
Vase, Vessel of Gems, orange, Verlys mold.......95.00
Water Lily & Cattails, bowl, crimped, amethyst opal, 8¾″.......45.00
Wine, Sailboats, marigold carnival, rare.......135.00

Ferrandiz

Artist Juan Ferrandiz designs the figurines, ornaments, music boxes, and bells that are sculpted by carvers at the world's most renowned wood-carving workshop, Anri, in St. Ulrich, Italy. Discontinued or retired editions often bring many times their original price on the secondary market.

When no condition is indicated, the items listed below are assumed to be in mint condition. See also Collector Plates

Adoration, sgn by Ferrandiz, 6″.......500.00
Bell, Signs of Spring, brass.......70.00
Bouquet, 6″.......179.00
Creche set, w/camel & driver, 13-pc.......1,349.00
Duet w/Bagpipes, 5″.......97.00
Friends, 6″.......150.00
Girl w/Rooster, 3″.......99.00
Have You Heard?, 6″.......115.00
Hurdy Gurdy, 6″.......179.00
Inspector, 6″.......225.00
Introduction, 6″.......135.00
Jolly Piper, dtd, 6″.......105.00
Lighting the Way, 6″.......105.00
Love Letter, 3″.......99.00
Melody for Two, 6″.......150.00
Riding in the Rain, 10″.......450.00
Rock-A-Bye, 6″.......145.00
Spreading the Word, 1978, 6″.......260.00
Trumpeter, 3″.......109.00

Fiesta

Fiesta is a line of dinnerware produced by the Homer Laughlin China Company of Newell, West Virginia, from 1936 until 1973. It was made in eleven different solid colors, with over fifty pieces in the assortment. The pattern was developed by Frederic Rhead, an English Stoke-on-Trent potter who was an important contributor to the art pottery movement in this country during the early part of the century. The design was carried out through the use of a simple band of rings device near the rim. Fiesta Red, a strong red-orange glaze color, was made with depleted uranium oxide. It was more expensive to produce than the other colors, and sold at higher prices. Today's collectors still pay premium prices for Fiesta Red pieces.

During the fifties the color assortment was gray, rose, chartreuse, and dark green. These colors are relatively harder to find, and along with Fiesta Red and medium green (new in 1959) command the higher prices.

Fiesta Kitchen Kraft was introduced in 1939; it consisted of seventeen pieces of kitchenware such as pie plates, refrigerator sets, mixing bowls, and covered jars, in four popular Fiesta colors.

As a final attempt to adapt production to modern-day techniques and methods, Fiesta was restyled in 1969. Of the original colors, only Fiesta Red remained. This line, called Fiesta Ironstone, was discontinued in 1973.

Two types of marks were used, an ink stamp on machine-jiggered pieces, and an indented mark molded into the hollow-ware pieces.

In the listings below, 'original colors' indicates only five of the original six--ivory, light green, cobalt, turquoise, and yellow. Red values are listed separately.

When no condition is indicated, the items listed below are assumed to be in mint condition.

Dinnerware and Accessories

Ash tray, original colors.......22.00
Ash tray, red & '50s colors.......28.00
Bowl, dessert; '50s colors, 6″.......16.00
Bowl, dessert; original colors, 6″.......12.50
Bowl, dessert; red, 6″.......20.00
Bowl, fruit; '50s colors, 4¾″.......10.00
Bowl, fruit; medium green, 4¾″.......30.00
Bowl, fruit; medium green, 5½″.......18.00
Bowl, fruit; original colors, 4¾″.......8.00
Bowl, fruit; original colors, 5½″.......9.00
Bowl, fruit; red, 4¾″.......12.00

Bowl, fruit; red & '50s colors, 5½" 13.00
Bowl, fruit; 11½" 80.00
Bowl, ftd salad; original colors 100.00
Bowl, ftd salad; red 135.00
Bowl, ind salad; medium green 40.00
Bowl, ind salad; yel, red, & aqua 35.00
Bowl, unlisted; yellow 35.00
Candle holders, bulb; original colors, pr 30.00
Candle holders, bulb; red, pr 40.00
Candle holders, tripod; original colors 95.00
Candle holders, tripod; red 125.00
Carafe, original colors 62.00
Carafe, red 90.00
Casserole, French; yellow 120.00
Casserole, medium green 85.00
Casserole, original colors 42.00
Casserole, red & '50s colors 58.00
Coffee pot, '50s colors 70.00
Coffee pot, demitasse; original colors 85.00
Coffee pot, demitasse; red 100.00
Coffee pot, original colors 45.00
Coffee pot, red 58.00
Compote, original colors, 12" 42.00
Compote, red, 12" 60.00
Compote, sweets; original colors 20.00
Compote, sweets; red 32.00
Creamer, ind; red 50.00
Creamer, ind; yellow 27.50
Creamer, original colors 6.50
Creamer, red, medium green & '50s colors 12.00
Creamer, stick hdl; orig colors 12.00
Creamer, stick hdl; red 15.00
Cup & saucer, demitasse; '50s colors 75.00
Cup & saucer, demitasse; original colors 24.00
Cup & saucer, red & '50s colors 18.50
Egg cup, '50s colors 40.00
Egg cup, original colors 20.00
Egg cup, red 30.00
Gravy boat, original colors 16.00
Gravy boat, red & '50s colors 20.00
Marmalade, original colors 70.00
Marmalade, red 85.00
Metal hdl for 13" chop plate 25.00
Metal holder for marmalade 25.00
Mixing bowl, #1, original colors 25.00
Mixing bowl, #2, original colors 23.00
Mixing bowl, #3, original colors 27.00
Mixing bowl, #4, original colors 29.00
Mixing bowl, #5, original colors 40.00
Mixing bowl, #6, original colors 45.00
Mixing bowl, #7, any color 85.00
Mug, original colors 22.50
Mug, red, medium green & '50s colors 45.00
Mustard, original colors 50.00
Mustard, red 80.00
Nappy, original colors, 8½" 13.00
Nappy, original colors, 9½" 18.00
Nappy, red, 9½" 23.00
Nappy, red & '50s colors, 8½" 18.50
Pitcher, disc; chartreuse 65.00
Pitcher, disc; orig colors 32.00
Pitcher, disc; red 38.00
Pitcher, disc; rose, dk gr & gray 55.00
Pitcher, ice lip; original colors 32.00

Left, Carafe, original colors, $62.00; Right, Ice pitcher, red, $50.00.

Pitcher, ice lip; red 50.00
Pitcher, jug, 2-pt; original colors 23.00
Pitcher, jug, 2-pt; red & '50s colors 42.00
Plate, chop; '50s colors, 13" 22.00
Plate, chop; '50s colors, 15" 26.00
Plate, chop; original colors, 13" 12.50
Plate, chop; original colors, 15" 15.00
Plate, chop; red, 13" 16.00
Plate, chop; red, 15" 20.00
Plate, compartment; '50s colors, 10½" 20.00
Plate, compartment; original colors, 10½" 14.00
Plate, compartment; red, 10½" 17.50
Plate, compartment; 11½" 22.00
Plate, deep; original colors 11.50
Plate, deep; red or '50s colors 18.00
Plate, medium green, 10" 22.00
Plate, original colors, 10" 9.50
Plate, original colors, 6" 3.00
Plate, original colors, 7" 4.50
Plate, original colors, 9" 6.00
Plate, red, medium green & '50s colors, 6" 4.50
Plate, red, medium green & '50s colors, 7" 6.00
Plate, red, medium green & '50s colors, 9" 10.00
Plate, red & '50s colors, 10" 14.00
Platter, original colors 11.50
Platter, red & '50s colors 20.00
Relish, mc 65.00
Shakers, original colors 10.00
Shakers, red & '50s colors 16.00
Soup, cream; '50s colors 22.00
Soup, cream; original colors 15.00
Soup, cream; red 20.00
Soup, onion; original colors 130.00
Soup, onion; red 150.00
Sta Brite tableware, 6 place settings 45.00
Sugar bowl, '50s colors 14.50
Sugar bowl, original colors 9.50
Sugar bowl, red & medium green 20.00
Syrup, original colors 80.00
Syrup, red 110.00
Teapot, large; original colors 50.00
Teapot, large; red & '50s colors 70.00
Teapot, medium; medium green 125.00
Teapot, medium; original colors 40.00
Teapot, medium; red & '50s colors 56.00
Tom & Jerry, wht w/lettering 13.50

Tray, figure-8; cobalt....30.00
Tray, figure-8; turquoise....50.00
Tray, figure-8; yellow....65.00
Tray, utility; original colors....13.00
Tray, utility; red....20.00
Tumbler, juice; original colors....13.50
Tumbler, juice; rose & red....15.00
Tumbler, red, 10-oz....28.00
Tumbler, regular colors, 10-oz....21.50
Vase, bud; original colors....24.00
Vase, bud; red....35.00
Vase, original colors, 10″....175.00
Vase, original colors, 12″....190.00
Vase, original colors, 8″....150.00
Vase, red, 10″....225.00
Vase, red, 12″....250.00
Vase, red, 8″....200.00

Kitchen Kraft

Cake plate, other than red....22.00
Cake plate, red....25.00
Casserole, ind; other than red....50.00
Casserole, ind; red....65.00
Casserole, other than red, 7½″....55.00
Casserole, other than red, 8½″....60.00
Casserole, red, 7½″....65.00
Casserole, red, 8½″....70.00
Fork....30.00
Jar, large; other than red....125.00
Jar, large; red....135.00
Jar, medium; other than red....110.00
Jar, medium; red....130.00
Jar, small; other than red....100.00
Jar, small; red....125.00
Jug....135.00
Pie plate, in frame, 10″....50.00
Pie plate, other than red, 10″....28.00
Pie plate, other than red, 9″....25.00
Pie plate, red, 10″....35.00
Pie plate, red, 9″....32.00
Platter, in frame....70.00
Platter, without frame....50.00
Server....38.00
Shakers, other than red, pr....40.00
Shakers, red, pr....50.00
Spoon, other than red....30.00
Spoon, red....38.00
Stack set....80.00
Stack set, lid only....25.00

Finch, Kay

Kay Finch and her husband Braden operated a small pottery in Corona Del Mar, California, from 1939 to 1963. The company remained small, employing from twenty to forty local residents who Kay trained in all but the most requiring tasks, which she herself performed. The company produced animal and bird figurines most notably dogs, Kay's favorites. Figures of 'Godey' type couples were also made, as were dinnerware and tiles. Most pieces were marked.

When no condition is indicated, the items listed below are assumed to be in mint condition.

Ash tray, dog head, any breed, HP, ink mk....15.00
Christmas plate, Santa, 1st ed, 1950, imp mk, 6½″....100.00
Figurine, baby's block w/teddy bear, HP, ink mk, 6½″....35.00
Figurine, Chanticleer, HP, mc, imp mk, 10½″....100.00
Figurine, Chinese boy & girl, mc, HP, ink mk, 7½″, pr....50.00
Figurine, Cocker, blk/wht, HP, imp mk, 11½x15″ L....150.00
Figurine, elephant, mc, HP, imp mk, 17″....200.00
Figurine, Godey man & lady, mc, HP, ink mk, 7½″, pr....50.00
Figurine, Grumpy & Smiley Pig, flowers, HP, ink mk, 6″, pr....75.00
Figurine, horse, prancing, gray/gr/blk, HP, ink mk, 4″....15.00
Figurine, Persian cat, pink/wht/blk, HP, imp mk, 10½″....75.00
Figurine, quail, matt wht, unmk, 7″....12.00
Figurine, Yorkshire Terrier, mc, HP, imp mk, 11x15″ L....150.00
Figurine, Yorky pup, pink/wht/blk, HP, ink mk, 5½″....35.00
Wall masks, Grecian man/woman, lustre pink w/gold, 10″, pr....100.00
Wall plaque, seahorse, matt pink, unmk, 16″....25.00

Findlay Onyx

Findlay, Ohio, was the location of the Dalzell, Gilmore, and Leighton Glass Company, one of at least sixteen companies that flourished there between 1886 and 1901. Their most famous ware, Onyx, is very rare. It was produced in 1889, in several colors--cream, raspberry, and amber among them--developed by layering two or three compatible shades together. Lustre trapped between the layers accented the dainty pattern. Heavy losses were incurred in the manufacturing process, and it was made for only a short time.

When no condition is indicated, the items listed below are assumed to be in mint condition.

Bowl, custard, 8″, NM....575.00
Celery, custard w/silver motif....525.00
Jam jar, raspberry, open, 3⅞x4¼″; ¾″ collar....785.00
Jar w/lid, custard w/silver motif, 6″....450.00
Pitcher, water; custard w/silver motif, fluted top....800.00
Salt shaker, bl-gr w/gold motif, 2¾″....250.00
Salt shaker, custard w/silver motif, 2¾″....125.00
Spooner, custard w/silver motif, 6″....350.00
Sugar shaker, custard w/silver motif....375.00
Vase, custard w/silver motif, 4½″....200.00

Fire Fighting Collectibles

Fire fighting collectibles from the early 19th century reflect the feeling of pride the men had in their brigades and in their roll as volunteer fire fighters. Dress uniforms and fancy helmets recall the charisma of the unit on parade. The leather buckets; blown glass, liquid-filled fire extinguishers; and brass hatchets serve as reminders of their heroism and dedication to their calling.

In the 1860s, volunteer units were replaced by municipal fire departments. Equipment evolved from horse-drawn wagons and bucket brigades to fire engines and water wagons with hoses. Today, many collectors find a fascination with these fire fighting relics of the past.

When no condition is indicated, the items listed below are assumed to be in excellent condition.

Alarm bell, New Haven Clock Co, 1886....350.00
Alarm box, Gamewell, CI, 17″....140.00
Alarm box, SAFA, rpt, no key, EX....135.00
Alarm system, register/take-up reel/bell, Gamewell....500.00
Ash tray, iron, fireman figural, advertising....35.00
Axe, parade; very ornate....250.00
Axe, parade; Viking style, ca 1880....160.00

Badge, Dayton OH Junior Fire Chiefs, maltese X-shape, EX.....10.00
Badge, Engineer 1; clasp helmet/horns on top, shield type......30.00
Badge, Lockport PA, helmet/Xd trumpet, clasp, shield type.....35.00
Badge, Woodport MA, sterling silver.........................50.00
Belt, blk patent w/wht trim, NP buckle, Cairns & Bros.........35.00
Belt, Flatbush Volunteer Co Washington......................40.00
Belt, Washington on belt, VG...............................55.00
Book, As You Pass By, Ken Dunshee, c 1952, EX............30.00
Book, Complete Book of Fire Engines, illus, c 1892, EX.......18.00
Book, Fire, Thos Dougherty, 1931, 245 pg, 6x9″.............25.00
Book, Fire Engines/Firefighters, P Ditzel, illus, 1976, EX.......23.00
Book, General Alarm, dramatic account of fires, Haywood......12.50
Book, History of Hartford Fire Insurance Co, 1810-1910, EX....25.00
Book, MD Firemen Volunteers' Assoc, 1897, hard bk, 64 pg....25.00
Book, Our Fire Laddies, JF Kernan, NY, 1885, 903, 7x10″....150.00
Book, Our Firemen, Baltimore, 1898, 400+ pgs, 8x10″.......125.00
Book, Our Firemen, NY, EX...........................185.00
Book, Pictorial History of Fire Fighting, Masters, c 1950.......10.00
Book, Volunteer Fire Dept of Old NY 1790-1866, c 1962, EX....5.00
Book, 100 Yrs of America's Fire Fighting Apparatus/1863-63....18.00
Bucket, leather, mc coat of arms, English, 20th C, 15½″......100.00
Bucket, leather w/blk pnt, wht label: BO VIs, #5, 11″..........95.00
Bucket, red pnt metal, w/blk 'Fire,' wire bail, ca 1890..........85.00
Cap, navy wool, blk patent leather bill, gold braid/button.......65.00
Certificate, eagles/hose/Xd ladder/1879, NY, 26x24″ fr.........95.00
Certificate, etched: hoses/helmets/etc, Union City, oak fr........90.00
Certificate, inscribed w/eagle/axes/hose, May 14, 1879..........95.00
Certificate, Veteran Exempt/Vol Firemen, 1905...............35.00
Coat, dress; navy wool, dbl breasted, gilt buttons, 1900........150.00
Extinguisher, barrel w/quilted band, cobalt, 1800s, 7″.........210.00
Extinguisher, Canteen, amber..........................200.00
Extinguisher, Comet, red...............................35.00
Extinguisher, Hardens, aqua, pat 1871.....................20.00
Extinguisher, Hardens Star, clear.........................45.00
Extinguisher, Hardens Star, ribs, cobalt, 6½″...............120.00
Extinguisher, Haywards, clear, pleated....................110.00
Extinguisher, Haywards, cobalt, pleated...................185.00
Extinguisher, Imperial Grenade, yel-gr, partial full, 6½″........180.00
Extinguisher, London Fire Appliance, Coy, yel-gold, 9″........170.00
Extinguisher, Manville, tin, filled, 22″......................18.00
Extinguisher, Spong & Cos, tubular, gold-yel, 13½″..........120.00
Extinguisher, tin canister type, cylindrical shape..............22.00
Fire rattle, used in hotels to warn patrons, early.............35.00
Gong, for firehouse, Gamewell, 10″......................135.00
Grave marker, ornate CI, 1897...........................90.00
Graveyard flag stand, CI, fire hat/horn, Association, 1894.......75.00
Hat, eagle & trim in gold, Cairns & Bros, 1847, rpt/rpl........150.00
Helmet, aluminum, AFD on front, w/eagle holder/shield, EX....200.00
Helmet, fox holder, Redwood VIII Newport on front, Horsham..475.00
Helmet, hi-eagle, aluminum, blk w/red/wht/brn, Cairns.........150.00
Helmet, hi-eagle, aluminum, mk Chief ECFD, pat 1897.........65.00
Helmet, hi-eagle, Brooklyn NYC, Flatbush Volunteer..........185.00
Helmet, hi-eagle, front: Astoria 1 from NYC; brim: Wilson.....175.00
Helmet, hi-eagle, mk H Beck, wire rim missing, rare...........55.00
Helmet, hi-eagle, no front, Wilson, EX....................85.00
Helmet, hi-eagle, VFA Jamaica FD on front, 64 combs, VG....120.00
Helmet, hi-eagle, Xd ladder/hook, Olson, VG................185.00
Helmet, leather w/8 seams, brass eagle, Cairns, 1900..........200.00
Helmet, low front, new style, EX.........................40.00
Insurance policy, NH Underwriters Assoc, Aug 9, 1889, EX.....15.00
Lantern, Dietz King, tin w/copper base, pat Aug 7, G.........100.00
Lantern, mk Boston Wovenhose & Rubber Co, brass, no cage...95.00
Letter head, condolence letter to member, Prospect Park NJ.....5.00
Litho, fire engines/flames, Cole Bros ad, 1870, fr, 27x33″....2,100.00

Fire helmet, solid brass, marked N.S.W.F.B., minor dents, $275.00.

Magazine, Harper's Weekly, life of NY fireman, 10/1877, EX....20.00
Medal, In Memory of the Volunteer Fireman, 1891............25.00
Multi-versa-deluge set, 3-wag, lt weight, Akron, #501..........875.00
Nozzle, brass, deck pipe, Morse Invincible, McIntire..........385.00
Nozzle, brass, 12″ L...................................15.00
Nozzle, NYFD, Navy type, chrome over brass, 2½″............25.00
Photo, cabinet; fireman in parade coat & helmet, 4x6½″.......40.00
Photo, cabinet; fireman w/belt holds helmet, 2½x4″............30.00
Photo, ladder team racing, firemen pull up boots, 18x22″......40.00
Photo album, dept souvenir, 1913, 80 pg, 9x12″..............25.00
Pole, brass, Veteran, 240x2″............................250.00
Tintype, 2 firemen w/flowers in bib shirts & parade belts.......85.00
Trumpet, eng bird/helmet w/Xd axes/ladder, w/o mouthpiece....475.00
Trumpet, eng engine/ladder/dog heads, 9″ flared speaker......950.00
Trumpet, eng presentation, brass, 12½″...................550.00
Trumpet, machine eng w/hand eng Xd hatchet/etc, brass, 15″..300.00
Trumpet, SP, eng floral/ladders/presentation, 1870, 21″.......525.00
Trumpet, SP, eng Foreman/Hose Co, dtd 1862, 17″..........495.00
Uniform, parade; leather helmet/cap/belt/shirt/coat, 1890s......325.00

Fire Marks

During the early 18th century, insurance companies used fire marks--signs of insurance--to indicate to the volunteer fire fighters which homes were covered by their company. Handsome rewards were promised to the brigade that successfully extinguished the blaze, so competition was fierce between rivals, and sometimes resulted in an altercation at the scene to settle the matter of which brigade would be the one to fight the fire!

Fire marks were originally made of cast iron or lead; later examples were sometimes tin or zinc. They were used abroad as well as in this country, and those from England tended to be much more elaborate.

When municipal fire departments were organized in the mid- to late 1860s, volunteer departments and fire marks became obsolete.

When no condition is indicated, the items listed below are assumed to be in excellent condition.

Aetna, tin, United States.................................145.00
Fire Association of Philadelphia, CI, 7½x11″................125.00

Guardian Assurance Co of London, copper....110.00
Legal Ins Co....140.00
Mutual Assurance & Fire Association of Phila, lead, 3x2¼″....55.00
Protector, copper, fireman w/hose, building burning, 1825....190.00

Fireplace Implements

In the colonial days of our country, fireplaces provided heat in the winter, and were used year round to cook food in the kitchen. The implements that were a necessary part of these functions were varied and have become treasured collectibles today, many put to new use in modern homes as decorative accessories. Gypsy pots may hold magazines; copper and brass kettles, newly polished and gleaming, contain dried flowers or green plants. Firebacks, highly ornamental iron panels that once reflected heat and protected masonry walls, are now sometimes used as wall decorations.

By Victorian times, the cookstove had replaced the kitchen fireplace, and many of these early utensils were already obsolete. But as a source of heat and comfort, the fireplace continued to be used for several more decades.

When no condition is indicated, the items listed below are assumed to be in excellent condition.

Andirons, brass, ball/claw ft, twist flame dbl finial, 25″....275.00
Andirons, brass, urns w/floral garland, French, 1800s, 14″....125.00
Andirons, brass, 18th C, 14½″....250.00
Andirons, bronze, woman w/flowers in hair terminals, 27″....1,980.00
Andirons, CI, Hessian soldier w/sword, 19x18″....165.00
Andirons, CI, Indians, full figure, EX detail, 19″....550.00
Andirons, CI, lady's head & torso, scalloped skirt, 12½″....230.00
Andirons, hammered iron, Arts & Crafts, 18″....350.00
Andirons, knife blade/penny ft/EX details, brass urns, 17″....900.00
Andirons, wrought iron, gooseneck/penny ft, 20¾″....100.00
Andirons, wrought iron, knob finials, primitive, 17″, VG....55.00
Andirons, wrought steel/brass finials/scrolls, 18″....175.00
Bellows, turtle bk, brass nozzle, stencil/HP decor, 17″, VG....75.00
Bellows, turtle bk, brass nozzle, mc floral, 18½″, VG....125.00
Broiler, wrought iron, hdl mk: anchor/CF, 10x18¾″....60.00
Broiler, wrought iron, rotary, rnd grill/str rods, 22″....85.00
Broiler, wrought iron, 14x30″....95.00

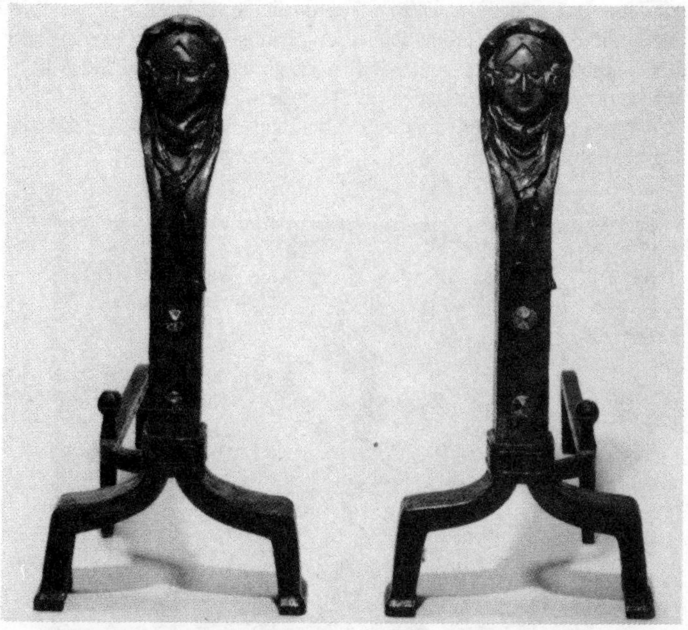

Andirons, bronze and patinated metal, Art Nouveau woman with flowers in hair, French, ca 1900, 27″, $1,800.00.

Coal hod, Neo-Classic, brass, Edwardian, inner liner, 16″....95.00
Crane, wrought iron, 14¾x45″....45.00
Fender, brass, floral reticulation, paw ft, ca 1840, 51″ L....250.00
Fender, brass, paw ft, reticulated, 36″....85.00
Fender, brass, reticulated, grayhounds & urn, serpentine....400.00
Fender, brass, reticulated leaves, rib ft, 10x54″....375.00
Fender, iron w/twist wire grill, bulb brass ft/finial, 36″....300.00
Fender, wire grill & brass rail, 6x28″....135.00
Fender, wrought & CI, horizontal knife bars, urn finials....170.00
Fender, wrought iron, twists/spindles/scroll ft, 11x41x12″....225.00
Fireplace fan, brass, reticulated, folding, late, 27½″....300.00
Griddle, CI, forged overhead hdl w/loop, 3 ft, early 1800s....115.00
Grill, CI, 3 legs, hdl w/cut-out heart, 10″ hdl, 13½″....35.00
Hearth block, marble, carved to hold tools, 6x6x2″....30.00
Insert, brass & iron, detailed columns & finials, 32x45″....170.00
Kettle holder, wrought iron, decorative scrollwork, 15x21″....95.00
Mantel, marble, Rococo style, 19th C, 46x72″....1,320.00
Oven, roasting; tin can w/side door, ftd, w/spit, 22x25″....200.00
Peel, wrought iron, ram's horn finial, 39″....105.00
Roaster, wrought iron, tripod w/penny ft, G detail, 29″....500.00
Shelf, warming; wrought iron, hooks fit grate, 20″ L....45.00
Spider, brass/wrought iron, 15″ well shaped hdl, 9″....60.00
Toaster, hearth; sheet iron w/2 wire arches, wood hdl, ftd....120.00
Toaster, wrought iron, swivel rack, 17½x15″....85.00
Tongs, wrought iron, accordion type, 20″ L....65.00
Tongs, wrought iron, G detail, 27″....75.00
Tongs, wrought iron, spring grip hdl, curved, 19½″....200.00
Trammel, wrought iron, twist detail/tooled, 3-hook, 64x45″....85.00

Fischer

Fine porcelain has been produced in the Herend area of Hungary since the late 18th century. In 1839 Moritz Fischer founded a pottery that continues today to produce hard-paste porcelain dinnerware, vases, and figurines similar to those of Sevres and Meissen.

When no condition is indicated, the items listed below are assumed to be in mint condition.

Candy dish, mums/butterflies, gr on wht, gilt, w/lid, 6½″....95.00
Figurine, bear w/honey pot....135.00
Jar, allover mc florals, reticulated, gold traced, 9½″....275.00
Pitcher, reticulated, helmet form, cobalt w/reserves/gilt....450.00
Tray, reticulated, shell shape, polychrome/gold, 8½x13½″....240.00
Urn, gold, sgn, Budapest, 11x8x15″....250.00
Vase, Chinese Bouquet, pilgrim form, gilt, 13″....165.00
Vase, vine/flower reticulated long neck, bulbous body, 18″....295.00

Fishing Collectibles

Although some people have been interested in old fishing tackle for over twenty-five years, it is only in the last decade that it has become a very popular collectible. Because of this, many dealers and collectors are still unsure of themselves concerning rarity as well as pricing. Old wood lures seem to be among the most popular items; reels are second, followed by bamboo rods, steel rods, metal lures, and miscellaneous items such as fish decoys, nets, and minnow buckets. Paper goods--tackle catalogs and cardboard advertising signs, for example--are also starting to show a real gain in value. As with most collectibles, prices for old fishing tackle depend more on rarity and condition than age, though any item should be more than twenty-five years old to be considered a bonafide collectible.

The following prices represent a nationwide average and should be used only as a guide, since prices may vary from one region to another. Values listed here are for examples in excellent condition.

Catalog, Creek Chub, 1940 .... 45.00
Catalog, Heddon, 1927 .... 80.00
Catalog, South Bend, 1931 .... 20.00
Decoy, Creek Chub, wood body/metal fins, glass eyes 250.00
Decoy, primitive, wood body/metal fins, tack eyes, 7¾" 10.00
Lure, Al Foss, Oriental Wiggler, glass eyes, plastic 10.00
Lure, Arbogast, Jitterbug, pnt eyes, plastic body & lip 6.00
Lure, Arbogast, Jitterbug, pnt eyes, wood 10.00
Lure, Creek Chub, Castrola, glass eyes, wood 75.00
Lure, Creek Chub, Ding Bat, glass eyes, wood 15.00
Lure, Creek Chub, Gar Minnow, glass eyes, wood 200.00
Lure, Creek Chub, Pikie, glass eyes, wood 5.00
Lure, Creek Chub, Plunker, glass eyes, wood 5.00
Lure, Creek Chub, Wiggle Fish, glass eyes, wood 30.00
Lure, Fenner Weedless Bait, no eyes, plastic 25.00
Lure, Garland Cork Head Minnow, tack eyes, wood 100.00
Lure, Heddon, Game Fisher, no eyes, wood 15.00
Lure, Heddon, Near Surface Wiggler, glass eyes, wood 75.00
Lure, Heddon, Underwater Minnow, glass eyes, wood 65.00
Lure, Heddon, Wiggle King, no eyes, wood 40.00
Lure, Heddon, Zig Wag, glass eyes, wood 15.00
Lure, Helga Devil, no eyes, plastic 8.00
Lure, Mermaid, plastic replica of mermaid w/hooks 8.00
Lure, Paw Paw, Trout Caster, tack eyes, wood 15.00
Lure, Paw Paw, Watta Frog, tack eyes, wood 20.00
Lure, Pflueger, Neverfail, glass eyes, wood 35.00
Lure, Pflueger, Palomine, glass eyes, wood 10.00
Lure, Pflueger, Wizard, glass eyes, wood 30.00
Lure, Rush Tango, no eyes, wood 50.00
Lure, Shakespeare, River Pup, carved eyes, wood 5.00
Lure, Shakespeare, Swimming Mouse, glass eyes, wood 10.00
Lure, Shakespeare, Tantalizer, glass eyes, wood 75.00
Lure, South Bend, Bass Oreno, glass eyes, wood 5.00
Lure, South Bend, Min Oreno, tack eyes, wood 30.00
Lure, South Bend, Surf Oreno, glass eyes, wood 15.00
Lure, South Bend, Vacuum Bait, glass eyes, wood 75.00
Lure, Winchester, 2-hook model, glass eyes, wood 125.00
Lure, Winchester, 3-hook model, glass eyes, wood 300.00
Lure, Winchester, 5-hook model, glass eyes, wood 250.00
Reel, Gentleman Streamliner, with rod, level wind 75.00
Reel, Heddon, 3-15, non-level wind 100.00
Reel, Langley, Lure Cast, level wind 6.00
Reel, Pflueger, Skilcast, level wind 12.00
Reel, Pflueger, Summit, level wind 15.00
Reel, Pflueger, Supreme, level wind 25.00
Reel, Shakespeare, Marhoff, level wind 12.00
Reel, Shakespeare, True Blue, level wind 5.00
Reel, Shakespeare, Wonderreel, level wind 5.00
Reel, South Bend, Free Cast, level wind 5.00
Reel, Talbot, #3 Nevada, non-level wind 300.00
Reel, Winchester, #4253, 80-yard 80.00
Rod, Winchester, Bamboo, fly rod 75.00
Rod, Winchester, Steel, casting rod 25.00

Flag

One of the earliest American flags was displayed in 1775. Called 'Continental Colors,' it consisted of a red field with a 'Union Jack' and six white stripes. During the Revolution other designs and mottos, such as the rattle snake 'don't tread on me' flag, made symbolic statements pertinent to the times.

Soon after the United States was declared an independent nation, the Union Jack was replaced by stars, representing the free states. Since then, as our country expanded, so did the number of stars, with various arrangements of circles and rows having been used. Of most interest to serious collectors of American flags are those with thirty-seven stars or less, and those which are hand stitched. Design, size, construction, scarcity, and condition are factors to be considered in arriving at a fair market price. Reproductions or commemorative flags have little or no value.

Larger American Flags of All Sewn Construction (4-ft. fly and up; ordinary star patterns)

49-48 star—5.00-25.00
46-44 star—25.00-55.00
43 star, rare—Negotiable
42-38 star—55.00-100.00
37-34 star—100.00-200.00
33 stars or less—200.00 and up

Larger All Printed American Flags (over 2x3 ft.; silk most preferred)—50%-75% of above listing.

Smaller All Printed American Flags (up to 2x3 ft.; silk most preferred)—20%-50% of above listing.

Printed 'Flaglets' (5"x7" or less). Most have 37 stars or less, usually printed on glazed muslin, and are latter day commemoratives—1.00-5.00

American Flags of Unusual or Special Design ('great star' patterns, wreath patterns, etc.)—150%-200% of above prices for ordinary patterns.

American Flags of Proven Historical Significance (military, political, etc.)—Negotiable—some priced just slightly above the norm, but potentially the highest priced category of American flags.

13 Star American Flags/Naval Ensigns—Priced according to above listings, by age.

Florence Ceramics

Figurines marked 'Florence Ceramics' were produced in the forties and fifties in Pasadena, California. The quality of the ware and the attention given to detail are prompting a growing interest among today's collectors. These lovely ladies, gents, and figural groups are nearly always identified by the name ink stamped on the base.

When no condition is indicated, the items listed below are assumed to be in mint condition.

Story Book House, $150.00.

Abigail....95.00
Beth....40.00
Camille....55.00
Clarissa....55.00
Douglas....55.00
Irene....40.00
Kay....48.00
Louis XV & Madame Pompadour, 12″, pr....250.00
Matilda....95.00
Melanie....65.00
Oriental boy & girl, pr....95.00
Oriental man playing musical instrument, 10½″....65.00
Scarlett....95.00
Sue....40.00
Victor & Charmaine, 9″, pr....118.00

Flow Blue

Flow Blue ware was produced by many Staffordshire potters, among the most familiar were Meigh, Podmore and Walker, Samuel Alcock, Ridgway, John Wedge Wood (who often signed his work Wedgwood), and Davenport. It was popular from about 1825 through 1860, and again from 1880 until the turn of the century. The name describes the blurred or flowing affect of the cobalt decoration, achieved through the introduction of a chemical vapor into the kiln. The body of the ware is ironstone, and Oriental motifs were favored. Later issues were on a lighter body, and often decorated with gilt.

Authority Mary Frank Gaston has compiled a lovely book, *The Collector's Encyclopedia of Flow Blue China*, with full-color illustrations and current market values; you will find her address in the Directory under Texas. When no condition is indicated, the items listed below are assumed to be in mint condition.

Abbey, bowl, fruit; 13″....170.00
Abbey, bowl, ftd, 8″....152.00
Abbey, bowl, w/lid, 5½″....100.00
Abbey, cake plate, 9½″....50.00
Abbey, chocolate pot, 6″....85.00
Abbey, cup & saucer....40.00
Abbey, trivet, 5″....50.00
Acantha, pitcher, 2-qt....100.00
Alaska, bowl, rnd, Grindley, 1891, 10″, EX....50.00
Alaska, bowl, soup; Grindley, 1891, 8″, EX....30.00
Alaska, plate, 8″....27.00
Alaska, plate, 9″....40.00
Albany, plate, dessert; Grindley....14.00
Albany, plate, 9″....48.00
Amoy, cup....60.00
Amoy, honey dish, 5⅛″....56.00
Amoy, plate, 10⅝″....105.00
Amoy, plate, 7¼″....66.00
Amoy, plate, 8¼″....76.00
Amoy, soup plate, minor hairline, 10½″....75.00
Amoy, sugar bowl, no lid, Davenport, 1840....95.00
Andorra, gravy boat....76.00
Anemone, plate, 10¼″....56.00
Anemone, sauce tureen, oval, Minton, 1880, 7½x4″, EX....95.00
Arcadia, bowl, soup....36.00
Arcadia, cake plate....85.00
Arcadia, plate, 10″....40.00
Argyle, plate, luncheon; w/cup & saucer, Grindley, set....75.00
Argyle, platter, Grindley, 15½″....135.00
Argyle, sauce dish, Johnson....25.00
Argyle, tureen, sauce; underplate/ladle/lid, Ford & Son....175.00
Argyle, tureen, vegetable; w/lid, Ford & Son....165.00
Ashburton, cup & saucer, demitasse....45.00
Ashburton, gravy boat, Grindley, 1891....68.00
Ashburton, plate, Grindley, 1891, 8″....34.00
Ashburton, plate, Grindley, 1891, 9″....38.00
Ashburton, plate, Grindley, 6¾″....30.00
Ashburton, tureen, w/lid....195.00
Athens, plate, 7″....35.00
Athens, soap dish....115.00
Ayr, bowl, vegetable; 8½″....50.00
Baltic, bowl, soup....35.00
Baltic, plate, 10″....40.00
Beaufort, creamer....65.00
Beauty Roses, creamer, Grindley....65.00
Beauty Roses, plate, dinner; Grindley....50.00
Beauty Roses, waste bowl, Grindley....52.00
Bentick, plate, 8½″....45.00

Touraine, relish dish, by Henry Alcock, 8¾″ x 4¾″, $95.00.

Blue Rose, plate, 7″....18.00
Bombay, cup, demitasse; Furnival, 1876, EX....75.00
Brazil, soup plate....40.00
Brunswick, plate, NWP, 9″....45.00
Brunswick, plate, Wood & Son, 1891, 9¼″, glaze wear....20.00
Candia, cake plate....60.00
Canton, cup & saucer, oriental scene....115.00
Canton, plate, wildflower center, daisy border, 9″....34.00
Carlton, gravy boat....150.00
Carlton, plate, 9½″....60.00
Cashmere, creamer....190.00
Celtic, bone dish, Grindley....46.00
Celtic, gravy boat, Grindley....42.00
Celtic, platter, 19″....135.00
Chapoo, butter dish....215.00
Chapoo, plate, Wedgwood, 1850, 10″, EX....95.00
Chapoo, plate, Wedgwood, 1850, 6½″....60.00
Chapoo, plate, Wedgwood, 1850, 9¼″....85.00
Chapoo, soup plate, Wedgwood, 1850, 10½″....110.00
Chapoo, waste bowl, Wedgwood, 1850, sm hairline....135.00
Chatsworth, plate, Ford & Sons, 1893, 10¼″....40.00
Chen-si, cup plate, unmk....125.00
Chen-si, plate, Maddock, ca 1835, 7½″....65.00
Chen-si, plate, 9″, EX....85.00
Cheswick, cup & saucer, Ridgway....46.00
Chrysanthemum, pitcher, 7″....136.00
Chusan, cup....50.00

Chusan, plate, Clementson, 1840s, 7¼″ 65.00
Chusan, plate, Clementson, 9¼″ 90.00
Claremont, platter, Johnson, 7x11″ 42.00
Clarence, bowl, soup 35.00
Clarence, plate, 6″ 25.00
Clarissa, bone dish 46.00
Clarissa, service for 6, Johnson Brothers, 55-pc 875.00
Clover, plate, dinner 50.00
Clover, platter, 13″ 85.00
Clover, platter, 16″ 100.00
Coburg, plate, Edwards, 1869, 9¼″, EX 70.00
Coburg, plate, 7″ 40.00
Columbia, sugar bowl, Clementson, prof rpr 85.00
Constance, saucer 20.00
Conway, bowl, New Wharf Pottery, 1891, 9″, EX 50.00
Conway, plate, 10″ 50.00
Conway, plate, 9″ 32.00
Conway, platter, 10″ 88.00
Countess, plate, 8″ 32.00
Dahlia, plate, 6¾″ 20.00
Dahlia, plate, 8½″ 65.00
Dainty, bowl, vegetable; oval, Maddock, 9¾x7½″ 65.00
Dainty, cake plate, shaped hdl, 10″ 88.00
Dainty, tureen, vegetable; oval, w/lid, Maddock 195.00
Dainty, tureen, vegetable; rnd, w/lid, Maddock, ca 1896 . . . . . 195.00
Daisy, creamer & sugar, B&L 150.00
Delaware, plate, Alcock, 7¾″ 35.00
Delft, egg cup, Minton 40.00
Delft, sauce boat, Minton 75.00
Devon, bone dish 45.00
Dorothy, bone dish, Upper Hanley 25.00
Douglas, bowl, vegetable; rectangular, w/lid, 8x11″, EX 125.00
Dover, plate, 5⅞″ 20.00
Dresden, sauce tureen, w/undertray & lid, B&L 155.00
Duchess, bowl, hdl lid, 5½x11″ 126.00
Duchess, bowl, scalloped, 9½″ 60.00
Duchess, gravy boat, w/underplate, Grindley, 4x9½″ 95.00
Duchess, plate, dinner; Grindley, 10″ 45.00
Duchess, plate, salad; Grindley, 7″, G 30.00
Duchess, platter, Grindley, 10x14″, G 88.00
Duchess, sauce dish, Grindley, 5″ 25.00
Dudley, platter, 12″ 75.00
Dundee, cup & saucer, demitasse; Ridgway 66.00
Ebor, creamer, Ridgway, lg 145.00
Fairy Villas, bowl, flowers on rim & center, 10x2½″ 75.00
Fairy Villas, butter pat, Adams, 1891, 3″, EX 18.00
Fairy Villas, creamer 75.00
Fairy Villas, plate, 10″ 50.00
Fairy Villas, plate, 8½″ 40.00
Fairy Villas, soup tureen, Adams, 1891, 7x12″, sm flake 295.00
Fairy Villas, vegetable, ind; Adams, 1891, EX 35.00
Florence, gravy boat, w/liner 110.00
Florida, sauce dish, Johnson Brothers 30.00
Formosa, plate, Mayer, 10½″ 150.00
France, soup plate, Brown, Westhead & Moore, 1868, 10¼″ 45.00
Geisha, plate, Meakin, 9″ 40.00
Geisha, tray, relish; Meakin 40.00
Genevese, plate, Malkin, 1873, sm flake, 9¼″ 45.00
Georgia, plate, Johnson Brothers, 7″ 30.00
Georgia, plate, 10″ 56.00
Gironde, bone dish 30.00
Gironde, bowl, soup 35.00
Gironde, butter pat 20.00
Gironde, pitcher 150.00
Gironde, platter, Grindley, 1891, 10x15″, EX 125.00
Gironde, platter, 19x13½″ 150.00
Gladys, bowl, 9½″ 40.00
Gladys, cup & saucer 45.00
Glenmore, plate, Grindley, 9″ 25.00
Gothic, soup plate, Furnival, 1850s, 10½″ 96.00
Grosvenor, cake plate, Moyott & Son 60.00
Haddon, butter pat, Grindley, 1891, EX 18.00
Haddon, cup & saucer, Grindley 45.00
Haddon, plate, Grindley, 9″ 45.00
Haddon, platter, Grindley, 14″ 135.00
Hindustan, biscuit jar, floral, pumpkin shape 175.00
Hindustan, plate, Maddock, 1855, 7¾″, EX 45.00
Hindustan, plate, 9½″ 80.00
Hindustan, platter, 13½″ 165.00
Hindustan, salt box, w/wood lid 125.00
Holland, bone dish 35.00
Holland, bowl, vegetable; w/lid 125.00
Holland, gravy boat 95.00
Holland, plate, Johnson, 10″ 50.00
Holland, sugar bowl 116.00
Hong Kong, cup plate 65.00
Hong Kong, honey dish 65.00
Hong Kong, plate, 10″ 80.00
Hong Kong, tray, relish 125.00
Imperial, platter, Grindley, 12x16½″ 136.00
Imperial, platter, Grindley, 9x12″ 80.00
Indian, bowl, soup; Pratt, 1840, 10¾″, EX 85.00
Indian, bowl, vegetable; w/lid 150.00
Indian, cake plate 180.00
Indian, plate, Pratt, 1840, 10½″, EX 90.00
Indian, platter, 15½″ 200.00
Indian, saucer, Pratt, 1840, EX 40.00
Indian, sugar bowl, Pratt, 1840, rpl finial 125.00
Indian, teapot 265.00
Indian Jar, cup & saucer, Furnival, 1843, hairline 60.00
Indian Jar, platter, Furnival, 1844, 18x14″, EX 295.00
Iris, plate, 10″ 30.00
Italia, cup & saucer 66.00
Ivanhoe, plate, 10″ 76.00
Jewel, platter, 14″ 85.00
Kaolin, platter, Podmore Walker, 13x10¼″ 165.00
Keele, butter dish 115.00
Kelvin, bowl, 7″ 30.00
Kelvin, plate, wild roses on border & center, 9″ 40.00
Keswick, platter, Wood & Son 100.00
Kin Shan, cup & saucer, EC & Co, 1855, prof rpr 70.00
Kirkee, platter, 12x15½″ 200.00
Kyber, bowl, vegetable 90.00
Kyber, plate, Adams, 10″ 65.00
Kyber, plate, 9″ 45.00
Kyber, platter, 10x7½″ 100.00
Kyber, platter, 17″ 300.00
Kyber, waste bowl 65.00
La Francaise, platter, bl border w/gold trim, 11½x9″, G 45.00
LaBelle, bowl, vegetable; sq 126.00
LaBelle, butter pat 22.00
LaBelle, cake plate 80.00
LaBelle, creamer & sugar 230.00
LaBelle, plate, mk LaBelle, 9½″ 50.00
LaBelle, platter, 8¼x11½″ 125.00
LaBelle, sugar bowl, w/lid 126.00
LaBelle, syrup 150.00
LaBelle, tray, relish 66.00

LaBelle, vase, celery....72.00
Ladas, pitcher, Ridgway, 6″....125.00
Lancaster, plate, 10″....55.00
Lancaster, plate, 9″....35.00
Leicester, plate, 7¾″....45.00
Leighton, bowl, vegetable; w/lid....155.00
Leipsic, bowl, vegetable; Clementson, 8x10½″, EX....110.00
Leister, plate, 7¾″....50.00
Lily, vase....125.00
Lois, bowl, New Wharf Pottery, 1891, 9″, EX....55.00
Lonsdale, bowl, vegetable; open....60.00
Lonsdale, bowl, vegetable; Ridgway, rough edge, w/lid....135.00
Lorne, tray, relish....75.00
Lotus, bowl, 10½″....110.00
Lotus, saucer, Grindley....20.00
Lusitania, bowl....60.00
Madras, cake plate, open hdld....190.00
Madras, pitcher, 7″....180.00
Madras, pitcher, 8½″....170.00
Madras, plate, 7″....35.00
Manilla, plate, Walker, 1845, 9½″, EX....90.00
Marechal Neil, butter pat....18.00
Marguerite, bowl, Grindley, 1891, 6″....20.00
Marguerite, sugar bowl....95.00
Marquis, plate, Grindley, 1906, 8″, EX....40.00
Mattean, soup tureen, octagonal, scenic, 1909, w/lid....180.00
Melbourne, bowl, berry; 5″....25.00
Melbourne, bowl, fruit; master....145.00
Melbourne, bowl, soup; flat....35.00
Melbourne, bowl, vegetable; oval, 10″....70.00
Melbourne, bowl, vegetable; oval, 9″....60.00
Melbourne, bowl, vegetable; w/lid....150.00
Melbourne, butter dish, no lid....60.00
Melbourne, butter pat....20.00
Melbourne, gravy boat....95.00
Melbourne, plate, 6¾″....35.00
Melbourne, plate, 7¾″....45.00
Melbourne, plate, 8¾″....55.00
Melbourne, platter, 10″....90.00
Melbourne, platter, 12″....130.00
Melbourne, platter, 16″....160.00
Melbourne, soup plate....35.00
Melbourne, sugar bowl....95.00
Melbourne, tray, relish....76.00
Melbourne, waste bowl....75.00
Melrose, plate, 9¼″....40.00
Melrose, platter, 18″....175.00
Melrose, sauce tureen, w/base plate....125.00
Mikado, tureen, open hdl, oval, w/lid, Furnival, 10½″....200.00
Monarch, creamer, Myott, 5″....75.00
Morning Glory, plate, 1860, 9¼″, EX....55.00
Morning Glory Variant, waste bowl....125.00
Ning Po, plate, Hall, 1845, 8½″....75.00
Non Pareil, bone dish, Burgess & Leigh, 1891....45.00
Non Pareil, butter pat, Burgess & Leigh....20.00
Non Pareil, cup & saucer, Burgess & Leigh, 1891....60.00
Non Pareil, cup & saucer, demitasse; Burgess & Leigh, EX....60.00
Non Pareil, plate, Burgess & Leigh, 1891, 8¾″....45.00
Non Pareil, plate, Burgess & Leigh, 9¾″....60.00
Non Pareil, platter, Burgess & Leigh, 13x15″, EX....195.00
Non Pareil, saucer, Burgess & Leigh, 1891, 6½″, EX....25.00
Non Pareil, saucer, demitasse; Burgess & Leigh, 1891, EX....25.00
Non Pareil, waste bowl, Burgess & Leigh, 1891....60.00
Normandy, bowl, gold trim, 7½x10″....55.00
Normandy, bowl, gold trim, 8″....45.00
Normandy, bowl, gold trim, 9″....55.00
Normandy, bowl, soup; gold trim, 8″....35.00
Normandy, cup, gold trim....45.00
Normandy, plate, gold trim, 10″....35.00
Normandy, plate, gold trim, 7″....20.00
Normandy, plate, gold trim, 8″....60.00
Normandy, platter, gold trim, 10x14″....90.00
Normandy, platter, gold trim, 12x16″....160.00
Normandy, saucer, gold trim....14.00
Normandy, tray, relish; gold trim....40.00
Normandy, tureen, vegetable; w/lid, gold trim....150.00
Old Curiosity Shop, undertray, Ridgway, 1900, w/hdls....40.00
Ophir, plate, 10″....45.00
Oregon, pitcher, water; 13″....400.00
Oregon, plate, Mayer, 1845, 7½″, EX....55.00
Oregon, plate, 9⅝″....90.00
Oregon, platter, Mayer, 1845, 14x18″, EX....325.00
Oregon, teapot, sm spout damage....250.00
Ormode, cup & saucer, Meakin....50.00
Ormond, platter, Meakin, 1891, 15x18″, EX....160.00
Osborne, bone dish, Ridgway....30.00
Osborne, bowl, covered vegetable; 4-leaf clover shape....185.00
Oyama, pitcher, Doulton, 1902, 6½″....150.00
Paisley, cup & saucer, Mercer, 1890, EX....50.00
Paisley, gravy boat, w/undertray, Mercer, 1890, EX....95.00
Pansy, bowl, 10″....50.00
Peach, bone dish....46.00
Peach Royal, plate, 10″....50.00
Pekin, gravy boat & underplate....75.00
Pelew, cup & saucer, handleless; Challinor, 1840....95.00
Pelew, plate, Challinor, 1840, 8½″....75.00
Pelew, plate, Challinor, 1840, 9½″....95.00
Pelew, plate, soup; Challinor, 10½″....110.00
Pelew, platter, 13¼x10¼″....190.00
Pelew, sauce dish....40.00
Penang, plate, Ridgway, 7″....35.00
Persian, bone dish, Johnson....42.00
Persian, bowl, applied hdls, Johnson Bros, 9½x7″....95.00
Persian, bowl, ftd, hdls, oval, 11½″....135.00
Plymouth, creamer & sugar....140.00
Plymouth, tray, relish....40.00
Poppy, cup & saucer....45.00
Portman, bowl, ftd....75.00
Portman, pitcher, Grindley, 2-qt....75.00
Portman, sauce dish....22.00
Portsmouth, cup & saucer, New Wharf....35.00
Princeton, plate, Johnson, 1900, 9″....40.00
Princeton, sauce dish....20.00
Quebec, saucer, 1891, EX....15.00
Regout's Flower, cup & saucer, Maastricht, 1900....55.00
Regout's Flower, saucer, Maastricht, paneled, 1900....25.00
Richmond, platter, serving; Alfred Meakin, 11½x16″....150.00
Rock, platter, 14x10″....160.00
Rock, saucer, Challinor, 1850, prof rpr....20.00
Rose, bowl, vegetable; w/lid, oval....95.00
Rose, creamer, Grindley....60.00
Rose, plate, Grindley, 7″....20.00
Rose, plate, Grindley, 9″....35.00
Rose, plate, soup; Grindley....40.00
Roseville, plate, Hughes, 1891, 7″....35.00
Rosyln, plate, AC Tunstall, 1909, 10″....50.00
Royal Blue, tureen....215.00
Scinde, bowl, vegetable; Alcock....225.00

Persian, soup tureen with lid, by Johnson Bros., dated 1902, $250.00.

Scinde, creamer & sugar, w/hdls, Alcock....200.00
Scinde, plate, soup; Alcock, 10½″....95.00
Scinde, plate, 7¼″....50.00
Scinde, sugar bowl, no lid....70.00
Scinde, teapot, Alcock....295.00
Seaweed Variant, creamer, elegant ft....190.00
Sefton, plate, Ridgway, 1905, 8″....35.00
Seville, bowl, vegetable; oval, Wood, 1891....80.00
Shanghae, plate, Furnival, 1860, 10″....95.00
Shanghae, plate, Furnival, 1860, 9¼″....80.00
Shanghae, platter, Furnival, 1860, 15½x12″....175.00
Shanghae, saucer, Furnival, 1860, 6½″....40.00
Shanghai, cup & saucer, Corn, 1900....60.00
Shanghai, plate, Adams, 1878, 9¼″....60.00
Shanghai, plate, Grindley, 1891, 9¾″....65.00
Shapoo, creamer & sugar, T&R Boote....200.00
Shapoo, cup, T&R Boote....75.00
Shapoo, plate, soup; T&R Boote, 9½″....110.00
Shapoo, plate, T&R Boote, ca 1842, 10¼″....95.00
Shapoo, plate, T&R Boote, 7½″....60.00
Shapoo, plate, T&R Boote, 9¼″....85.00
Shapoo, platter, T&R Boote, 12½x9½″....225.00
Shell, plate, Challinor, 1860, 9½″....80.00
Shell, sauce dish, Challinor, 1860, 5″....40.00
Singan, bowl, vegetable; 10″....70.00
Sobraon, saucer, 1850, EX....35.00
Spinach, bean pot....75.00
Spinach, bowl, 8″....40.00
Spinach, mush bowl....46.00
Spinach, plate, Libertas, 1900, 8″, EX....50.00
Spinach, plate, 7″....42.00
Spinach, saucer....25.00
Splendid, bowl, 9″....40.00
St Louis, bone dish, Johnson....46.00
St Louis, bowl, scalloped edge, 10x7½″....50.00
Sydney, sauce dish....24.00
Temple, chamber pot, Walker....450.00
Temple, cup & saucer, handleless, dk bl....100.00
Temple, plate, Podmore Walker, 1850s, 8¾″....85.00
Temple, plate, 9⅞″....100.00
Togo, bowl, 8″....35.00
Togo, plate, Stone, England, 9″....38.00
Togo, platter, 16″....150.00
Tonquin, plate, Adams, 10″....80.00
Tonquin, plate, Adams, 8½″....70.00
Tonquin, sauce dish, Adams....55.00
Touraine, bacon dish....40.00
Touraine, bone dish....45.00
Touraine, bowl, dessert; 5¼″....26.00
Touraine, bowl, soup....40.00
Touraine, bowl, vegetable; oblong, 9″....76.00
Touraine, bowl, vegetable; oval, w/lid, 11¾″....190.00
Touraine, bowl, vegetable; w/lid, 9″....200.00
Touraine, butter dish....60.00
Touraine, butter pat....35.00
Touraine, creamer, lg....150.00
Touraine, creamer, sm....135.00
Touraine, cup, lg....45.00
Touraine, cup & saucer, lg....60.00
Touraine, cup & saucer, reg....55.00
Touraine, gravy boat....105.00
Touraine, pitcher, water....400.00
Touraine, plate, bread & butter....25.00
Touraine, plate, dinner....60.00
Touraine, plate, luncheon; 8¾″....50.00
Touraine, plate, salad....35.00
Touraine, platter, 10½″....125.00
Touraine, platter, 12½″....150.00
Touraine, platter, 15″....175.00
Touraine, platter, 8½″....100.00
Touraine, sauce dish, Stanley, 1898, 5¼″....32.00
Touraine, saucer, Alcock....26.00
Touraine, soup plate....45.00
Touraine, sugar bowl, no lid....80.00
Touraine, sugar bowl, w/lid....126.00
Touraine, waste bowl....75.00
Triumph, pitcher, milk; Maddock, 7″....145.00
Troy, plate, Meigh, 1840, 7¼″....50.00
Turin, plate, dinner....55.00
Venice, gravy boat....65.00
Vermont, bowl, vegetable; w/lid, oval, B&L....125.00
Vermont, platter, 12″....125.00
Vermont, teapot, 8″....215.00
Verona, plate, Wood & Son, 8″....60.00
Verona, platter, 17″....175.00
Verona, sauce tureen, w/liner, 8″....150.00
Versailles, creamer....47.00
Virginia, bowl, vegetable; oval, Maddock, 7x9½″....60.00
Virginia, plate, Maddock, 1891, 9¾″....35.00
Virginia, saucer, Maddock, 1891, 6″....20.00
Wagon Wheel, shaving mug, Brush Stroke....135.00
Waldorf, bowl, New Wharf, 9″....70.00
Waldorf, cup & saucer....55.00
Waldorf, plate, 10″....55.00
Waldorf, platter, New Wharf Pottery, 10½″....135.00
Warwick, platter, 10½″....65.00
Warwick, sauce boat, pour from either end....75.00
Watteau, bowl, soup....70.00
Watteau, bowl, vegetable; 9½″....90.00
Watteau, butter pat....15.00
Watteau, loving cup....152.00
Whampoa, cup & saucer, Mellor & Venables, 1835....65.00
Whampoa, plate, Mellor & Venables, 1835, 7½″....55.00
Yeddo, plate, 9½″....50.00

Flue Covers

When spring house cleaning started and the heating stove was taken down for the warm weather season, the unsightly hole where the stovepipe joined the chimney was hidden with an attractive flue cover. They were made with a colorful litho print behind glass with a chain for hanging. Although scarce today, some scenes were actually reverse painted on the glass itself. The most popular motifs were florals, children, and lovely ladies. Square, rectangular, or diamond shapes are more valuable than oval or round covers, especially when Victorian ladies or children are pictured. Occasionally flue covers were made in sets of three––one served a functional purpose, while the other two were added to provide a more attractive wall arrangement. They range in size from 7″-8″ to 13″-14″, but 9″ is the average.

When no condition is indicated, the items listed below are assumed to be in excellent condition.

Flue cover with basket of violets, 9¾″, $38.00.

Cameo insert of child, floral, gem stones for November..........35.00
Cherub on bl center, gold to dk bl surround, punched tin......48.50
Female bust, sgn Andre..45.00
Girl & boy, Victorian, 9″.......................................32.00
Girl in red w/dog, Germany......................................35.00
God Bless Our Home, chain fr....................................25.00
Pug dog oil painting, beaded around rim, brass, 12″ dia........58.00
Victorian child, no chain, 6″...................................18.00
Victorian girl, litho print, German.............................22.00
Victorian interior scene, 9¼″...................................40.00
Winter landscape w/house/etc, HP, brass, late 19th C, 12″......35.00

Folk Art

That the creative energies of the mind ever spark innovations in functional utilitarian channels as well as toward playful frivolity is well documented in the study of American folk art. While the average early settler rarely had free time to pursue art for its own sake, his creative energy exemplified itself in fashioning useful objects carved or otherwise ornamented beyond the scope of pure practicality. After the advent of the Industrial Revolution, the pace of everyday living became more leisurely, and country folk found they had extra time. Not accustomed to sitting idle, many turned to carving, painting, or weaving. Whirligigs, imaginative toys for the children, and whimsies of all types resulted. Though often rather crude, this type of early art represents a segment of our heritage, and as such has become a valued collectible.

Baskets, decoys, frakturs, samplers, trade signs, weathervanes, and wood carvings are specialized areas of folk art dealt with in other sections; see those specific headings. Values are given for items in excellent condition.

Calligraphy, militia guard & prancing horse/scrolls, 7x8″.......100.00
Calligraphy, scrollwork eagle atop ovals/scrolls, 7x8″...........50.00
Calligraphy, Wellington on horse, EX detail, 7x8″................80.00
Doll, apple-head bride, lace dress, hat, turn of C, 11″..........95.00
Drawing, ink, humorous wharf scene w/couple, W Slinn, 1890..130.00
Eagle, sheet metal w/red/wht/bl pnt, rust/damage, 27″...........75.00
Foot stool, turtle w/carved ft & head, uphl top, 17½″.........150.00
Jumping Jack, well carved, 1800s, 15″..........................225.00
Log cabin, made of sticks, chimney on front, 1920s, 11x9½″....65.00
Painting on tin, bird on cherry tree branch, PA, 12x16″......115.00
Paper cutting, peacock in flowering tree, 5x7″..................65.00
Paper cutting, various farming scenes, 18x21½″, VG..........250.00
Paper cutting, wreath w/birds/name, gilded fr, 18x22″..........95.00
Picture, charcoal/chalk/sandpaper, Niagara, 1853, 21x29″......825.00
Pin-prick eagle w/hearts/tulips/banner, 1858, old fr, 12″.......125.00
Sun dial, wood/sheet iron, dated 1880, 10x9½x4″ top.........125.00
Theorem on paper, vase of flowers, 3-color, stains, 18x21″.....250.00
Theorem on velvet, flower baskets/butterfly, 13x17″............325.00
Theorem on velvet, melon/peaches/etc, 1840, EX fr, 41x50″..1,760.00
Theorem on velvet, wild roses, matt/fr, 9x9″...................175.00
Whirligig, bearded farmer milking blk/wht cow, 16x12″.........115.00
Whirligig, Blk man in suit/tie, lg arms, EX detail, 16½″.......850.00
Whirligig, man w/beard/cap, curved root arms, rpr/rpl, 25″...1,650.00
Whirligig, open-side house, tin roof, 4 metal columns, 24″.....185.00
Whirligig, prop animates 2 figures & ferris wheel, 30″.........675.00
Whirligig, sailor in whts w/flags, 20th C, rpt/rpl, 16″..........210.00
Yard ornament, robin on stump cut-out, worn orig pnt, 14″.....70.00

Watercolor theorem painting, American, 18th century, in frame, 10″ x 12½″, $700.00.

Fostoria

The Fostoria Glass Company was built in 1887 at Fostoria, Ohio, but by 1891 it had moved to Moundsville, West Virginia. During the next two decades they produced many lines of pressed patterned tableware and lamps. Their most famous pattern, American, was introduced in 1915, and has been produced continuously since that time, in well over two hundred different pieces. From 1920 to 1925, top artists designed tablewares in colored glass--canary (vaseline), amber, blue, orchid, green, and ebony--in pressed patterns as well as etched designs. By the late thirties Fostoria was recognized as the largest producer of handmade glassware in the world. The company continues in operation today, making the same quality glassware for which it became famous.

When no condition is indicated, the items listed below are assumed to be in mint condition.

Animals

Chanticleer....195.00
Colts, sitting....35.00
Colts, standing....32.00
Deer, sitting....35.00
Deer, standing....35.00
Eagle, bookend....95.00
Mermaid....100.00
Seahorse 75.00
Seal 85.00

Acanthus, amber; plate, 7¼″....6.00
Acanthus, green; goblet....30.00
American, ash tray, oval, 5½″....9.00
American, ash tray, sq, 5″....17.50
American, basket, wicker, hdls....135.00
American, beer mug....40.00
American, bottle, bitters; w/tube, 4½-oz, 5¾″....45.00
American, bottle, scent; w/stopper, 4½-oz....40.00
American, bottle, scent; w/stopper, 8-oz....47.50
American, bowl, boat, 2-part, 9″....18.00
American, bowl, boat, 8½″....7.50
American, bowl, bonbon....12.00
American, bowl, centerpiece, tri-corner, 11″....20.00
American, bowl, centerpiece; hat shape, 15″....125.00
American, bowl, cream soup, 2-hdl....27.50
American, bowl, cupped, 7″....35.00
American, bowl, deep, 8″....40.00
American, bowl, float; 10″....30.00
American, bowl, fruit; flat, ped ft, 16″....95.00
American, bowl, fruit; rolled edge, 11½″....45.00
American, bowl, jelly; w/lid, 6¾″....16.00
American, bowl, lily; 12″....60.00
American, bowl, master almond; oval, 4½″....32.50
American, bowl, nappy; 4½″....8.00
American, bowl, nappy; 6″....10.00
American, bowl, olive; oblong, 6″....6.50
American, bowl, oval, 4½″....7.00
American, bowl, pickle; oblong, 8″....10.00
American, bowl, relish; 3-part, 9½″....37.50
American, bowl, rolled edge, 11½″....37.50
American, bowl, sauce; oval, 6¾″....10.00
American, bowl, shallow, 13″....27.50
American, bowl, sm punch; ped ft/Tom & Jerry/flares to 12″....90.00
American, bowl, vegetable; divided, oval, 10¼″....32.50
American, bowl, vegetable; oval, 9″....32.50
American, bowl, vegetable; 2-hdl, 9″....10.00
American, bowl, w/lid, 5″....25.00
American, bowl, wedding; sq, ped ft, 6½″....40.00
American, bowl, 4¼″....13.50
American, bowl, 4¾″....11.00
American, box, candy; 6-sided, w/lid, 3-part....65.00
American, box, cigarette....25.00
American, box, hairpin; 3½x1¾″....75.00
American, box, handkerchief; 5⅝x4⅝″....85.00
American, box, jewel; 5¼x2¼″....75.00
American, butter dish, rnd, plate 7¼″....95.00
American, butter dish, ¼-lb....20.00
American, candle lamp w/chimney, 8½″....175.00
American, candlestick, rnd ft, 3″....15.00
American, candlestick, 2-light, bell base, 6½″....50.00
American, candlestick, 3-toe, tricorne, 6½″....35.00
American, candy dish, ped ft....17.50
American, cheese & cracker....37.50
American, cocktail, cone shape, ftd, #2056, 3-oz, 2⅞″....13.00
American, compote, jelly; 4½″....13.00
American, compote, w/lid, 5″....18.00
American, compote, w/lid, 9″....38.00
American, cordial, plain bowl, #5056, 1-oz....25.00
American, creamer, tea; 2¼″....7.50
American, creamer & sugar, hdl, lg....35.00
American, creamer & sugar, w/lg rnd tray, med....39.50
American, cruet, w/stopper, 5-oz, 6¼″....25.00
American, crushed fruit w/lid & spoon....175.00
American, cup, punch; flared rim....10.00
American, cup, sherbet; ftd, 4½-oz, 3½″....11.00
American, cup & saucer....15.00
American, decanter, cordial; w/stopper, 10-oz....125.00
American, decanter, w/stopper, labeled, 24-oz....95.00
American, dresser set, powder boxes w/covers & tray....200.00
American, finger bowl, 4½″....15.00
American, flowerpot, w/perforated lid, 9½″ dia....125.00
American, goblet, rnd bottom, short stem, 9-oz....10.00
American, goblet, water; hexagon bottom, 10-oz....12.50
American, hair receiver....50.00
American, hat, 3″....22.50
American, hat, 4″....35.00
American, hurricane lamp....125.00
American, hurricane lamp base....90.00
American, ice bucket, w/tongs....50.00
American, ice bucket, 2-hdl....75.00
American, ice tub, w/special bent underplate, 6″....110.00
American, ice tub, 6″....60.00
American, ice tub w/liner, 6½″....45.00
American, icer, w/juice insert....42.00
American, icer, w/shrimp insert....42.00
American, jam pot, w/lid....40.00
American, jar, pickle; pointed lid, 6″....200.00
American, lemon dish, w/lid....26.00
American, marmalade, w/lid & chrome spoon....35.00
American, mayonnaise, divided w/2 ladles....37.50
American, mayonnaise, ftd, w/ladle....50.00
American, mayonnaise, w/liner & ladle....35.00
American, molasses can, hdl, 11-oz, 6¾″....95.00
American, mug, beer; 12-oz....30.00
American, mustard, w/lid & spoon....30.00
American, napkin ring....4.00
American, oyster cocktail, #2056, 4½-oz....11.00
American, oyster cocktail, plain bowl, #5056, 4-oz....10.00
American, pitcher, ftd, 1-pt, 5⅜″....32.00
American, pitcher, ftd, ½-gal, 8″....62.50
American, pitcher, ftd, 3-pt, 8″....40.00
American, pitcher, w/ice lip, flat bottom, ½-gal, 8¼″....40.00
American, pitcher, water; no ice lip, 3-pt....65.00

American, plate, bread & butter; 6″ 6.00
American, plate, cake; 2-hdl, 10″ 16.00
American, plate, cake; 3-toe, 12″ 35.00
American, plate, cream soup/liner 8.00
American, plate, crescent salad; 7½″ 27.50
American, plate, dinner; 9½″ 14.50
American, plate, sandwich; 9″ 14.00
American, plate, torte; rnd, cupped, 14″ 22.50
American, plate, torte; ruby, 14″ 50.00
American, plate, torte; 18″ 125.00
American, platter, oval, 10½″ 27.50
American, punch bowl, w/high ftd base, 14″ 175.00
American, rose bowl, 3½″ 15.00
American, rose bowl, 5″ 20.00
American, salver, cake; rnd pedestal 80.00
American, salver, rnd, ped ft, 10″ 35.00
American, salver, sq ped, 10″ 74.50
American, sauce boat 50.00
American, saucer 5.00
American, set: toddler, w/baby tumbler & bowl 40.00
American, set: 2 jam pots w/tray 95.00
American, shaker, 3½″ 5.00
American, sherbet, #2056½, 4½-oz 10.00
American, sherbet, flared, #2056, 4½-oz 10.00
American, spooner, 3¾″ 32.50
American, straw holder, w/lid 195.00
American, sugar bowl, no hdl, lg 12.00
American, sugar bowl, open; hdld, 3¼″ 10.00
American, sugar bowl, 2-hdl 17.00
American, sugar shaker 125.00
American, sundae, low ftd, #2056, 6-oz 10.00
American, syrup, non-pour screw top, 6-oz, 5¼″ 85.00
American, syrup, w/glass cover & 6″ liner plate, 10-oz 85.00
American, tidbit, rnd, 3-toe, crystal, 7″ 25.00
American, tomato liner, blown, 5-oz 4.00
American, toothpick 17.50
American, tray, celery; canoe, 12″ 20.00
American, tray, comb & brush; oval, 10¼″ 70.00
American, tray, for creamer & sugar, tab hdld, 6¾″ 9.00
American, tray, ice cream; oval, 13½″ 50.00
American, tray, oval, hdld, 10½x5″ 50.00
American, tray, oval, hdld, 6″ 30.00
American, tray, rectangular, 10½″ 65.00
American, tray, rectangular, 5x2½″ 15.00
American, tray, relish; oval, 10½″ 40.00
American, tray, sandwich; center hdl, 12″ 37.50
American, tray, sq, 10″ 40.00
American, tumbler, iced tea; ftd, crystal, 12-oz 15.00
American, tumbler, juice; ftd, plain bowl, #2056, 5-oz 12.00
American, tumbler, old fashioned, flat, #2056, 6-oz 12.00
American, tumbler, water; flared, flat 15.00
American, tumbler, water; ftd, 9-oz, #2056, 4⅜″ 12.00
American, tumbler, water; straight side, #2056½, 8-oz 12.00
American, urn, sq, ped ft, 6″ 25.00
American, vase, bud; cupped, 6″ 10.00
American, vase, bud; cupped, 8½″ 14.00
American, vase, bud; flared, 6″ 18.00
American, vase, flared, 7″ 35.00
American, vase, flared, 8″ 30.00
American, vase, flat, sterling rim, 10″ 140.00
American, vase, sq ped ft, 9″ 40.00
American, vase, straight sides, 12″ 85.00
American, vase, sweet pea; 4½″ 85.00
American, whiskey, #2056, 2-oz, 2½″ 12.50
American, wine, crystal 12.50
Baroque, blue; ash tray 14.50
Baroque, blue; bowl, flared, 12″ 48.00
Baroque, blue; bowl, hdld, 4″ 15.00
Baroque, blue; bowl, jelly; w/lid, 7½″ 37.50
Baroque, blue; bowl, relish; 3-part, 10″ 27.50
Baroque, blue; bowl, sq, 6″ 14.00
Baroque, blue; candelabra, 2-light, w/bob & prisms, pr 180.00
Baroque, blue; candlestick, 4″ 15.00
Baroque, blue; compote, 6½″ 22.00
Baroque, blue; creamer & sugar, w/tray, ind 50.00
Baroque, blue; ice bucket 95.00
Baroque, blue; plate, cake; 2-hdl 40.00
Baroque, blue; plate, torte 48.00
Baroque, blue; plate, torte; 14″ 27.50
Baroque, blue; plate, 8″ 11.00
Baroque, blue; sweetmeat, sq, 6″ 18.00
Baroque, blue; tray, relish; 3-part 40.00
Baroque, blue; tumbler, old fashioned; 6½-oz 20.00
Baroque, crystal; bowl, cereal; 6″ 10.00
Baroque, crystal; bowl, hdl, 4⅜″ 9.50
Baroque, crystal; bowl, pickle; 8″ 8.00
Baroque, crystal; bowl, rolled edge, 11″ 20.00
Baroque, crystal; candelabra, dbl, pr 55.00
Baroque, crystal; candelabrum, 3-light, 24-lustre, 9½″ 75.00
Baroque, crystal; candle holder, 4″, pr 20.00
Baroque, crystal; candlestick, 3-light, 6″ 15.00
Baroque, crystal; cheese & cracker 45.00
Baroque, crystal; compote, ftd, #2496, 4½″ 15.00
Baroque, crystal; compote, jelly; no lid 25.00
Baroque, crystal; compote, jelly; w/lid 25.00
Baroque, crystal; cup & saucer 14.00
Baroque, crystal; grapefruit, blown, w/insert 49.00
Baroque, crystal; ice bucket 45.00
Baroque, crystal; mayonnaise, w/underplate & ladle 35.00
Baroque, crystal; nappy, flared, hdl 12.00
Baroque, crystal; pitcher, 6½″ 150.00
Baroque, crystal; plate, dinner 15.00
Baroque, crystal; rose bowl, 3¾″ 18.00
Baroque, crystal; shakers, pr 25.00
Baroque, crystal; tray, oval, 11″ 10.00
Baroque, crystal; tumbler, tea; 14-oz, 5¾″ 15.00
Baroque, crystal; tumbler, water; flat, 4¼″ 22.50
Baroque, gold tint; bowl, hdld, 10″ 30.00
Baroque, gold tint; bowl, 2-hdl, 8″ 26.00
Baroque, gold tint; bowl, 2-part, 6½″ 12.50
Baroque, gold tint; candlestick, 5½″ 15.00
Baroque, gold tint; compote, 5″ 20.00
Baroque, gold tint; creamer & sugar, w/tray, ind 40.00
Baroque, gold tint; cruet & stopper 350.00
Baroque, gold tint; plate, cake; 10″ 20.00
Baroque, gold tint; plate, 6″ 4.00
Baroque, gold tint; saucer 4.00
Baroque, gold tint; sugar bowl, ind; 3″ 10.00
Baroque, gold tint; tray, relish; 3-part, 10½″ 27.50
Baroque, gold tint; tray, relish; 3-part, 12″ 20.00
Baroque, gold tint; tumbler, juice; 5-oz, 3¾″ 18.00
Baroque, gold tint; vase, 7″ 37.50
Beverly, amber; plate, rolled edge, 14½″ 40.00
Beverly, green; bowl, cereal; 6″ 13.00
Beverly, green; bowl, cream soup; ftd, w/underplate 25.00
Beverly, green; creamer, ftd 18.00
Beverly, green; finger bowl, w/underplate 19.00
Beverly, green; plate, 8¾″ 8.00

Buttercup, crystal; candlestick, 1-light, #2594, 5½″ 22.50
Buttercup, crystal; goblet, #6030, 10-oz 18.00
Buttercup, crystal; plate, dinner; 9½″ 35.00
Century, crystal; bowl, crescent salad 35.00
Century, crystal; bowl, vegetable; oval 32.50
Century, crystal; bowl, 2-hdl, 8¼″ 27.50
Century, crystal; candlestick, dbl, pr 45.00
Century, crystal; candlestick, triple, pr 60.00
Century, crystal; condiment set, 3-pc 75.00
Century, crystal; creamer & sugar, w/tray, 3-pc 37.50
Century, crystal; cruet w/stopper 45.00
Century, crystal; ice bucket 35.00
Century, crystal; mayonnaise, 3-pc 37.50
Century, crystal; pitcher, lg 95.00
Century, crystal; preserve, ftd, w/lid 29.00
Century, crystal; server, sandwich; center hdl 36.00
Century, crystal; sherbet, 4½″ 15.00
Century, crystal; tray, muffin 27.50
Century, crystal; tray, relish; 3-part, 11″ 27.50
Century, crystal; tumbler, iced tea 16.00
Chintz, crystal; bowl, dessert; 2-hdl, 8½″ 50.00
Chintz, crystal; bowl, oval, 9½″ 30.00
Chintz, crystal; bowl, 4-toe, 2-hdl, 10½″ 45.00
Chintz, crystal; candle holder, dbl, pr 46.75
Chintz, crystal; candlestick, 1-light, 4″, pr 30.00
Chintz, crystal; claret, wine 28.00
Chintz, crystal; cocktail, sherry; 3½-oz 22.50
Chintz, crystal; cocktail, 4-oz, 5″ 22.00
Chintz, crystal; compote, 4⅝″ 25.00
Chintz, crystal; cream soup, 7¼″ 7.00
Chintz, crystal; cruet, w/stopper 57.50
Chintz, crystal; dinner bell 45.00
Chintz, crystal; goblet, low, 6¼″ 24.00
Chintz, crystal; goblet, water; 7¾″ 24.50
Chintz, crystal; goblet, water; 9-oz 25.00
Chintz, crystal; plate, dinner 37.50
Chintz, crystal; plate, 7¼″ 15.00
Chintz, crystal; sherbet, 4⅜″ 19.00
Chintz, crystal; tray, hdl, 10¼″ 29.50
Chintz, crystal; tray, sandwich; center hdl 35.00
Chintz, crystal; tumbler, iced tea; ftd, 12-oz 22.50
Coin Glass, amber; creamer 12.50
Coin Glass, amber; jelly dish, ftd 14.00
Coin Glass, crystal; vase 15.00
Coin Glass, green; compote, wedding, w/lid 30.00
Colony, crystal; bowl, almond, ftd 4.50
Colony, crystal; bowl, celery; 11½″ 12.50
Colony, crystal; bowl, hdld, 8″ 15.00
Colony, crystal; bowl, low ft, 9″ 15.00
Colony, crystal; bowl, olive; oblong, 7″ 8.00
Colony, crystal; bowl, pickle; 9½″ 12.00
Colony, crystal; bowl, sq, 5½″ 5.50
Colony, crystal; bowl, 3-toe, 5¾″ 18.00
Colony, crystal; candlestick, dbl, pr 42.00
Colony, crystal; candlestick, w/prisms, 14½″ 150.00
Colony, crystal; candlestick, w/8 prisms, 7½″ 25.00
Colony, crystal; candlestick, 3″, pr 35.00
Colony, crystal; candlestick, 9¾″ 14.00
Colony, crystal; candy dish w/lid, 6½″ 25.00
Colony, crystal; cheese compote w/cracker plate 24.50
Colony, crystal; compote, cheese 12.50
Colony, crystal; compote, jelly; w/lid 32.50
Colony, crystal; compote, 4″ 11.00
Colony, crystal; cream soup, ftd 8.00
Colony, crystal; cup, ftd 5.00
Colony, crystal; finger bowl, 4¾″ 7.00
Colony, crystal; goblet, cocktail 10.00
Colony, crystal; goblet, 5¼″ 13.00
Colony, crystal; jam pot, w/lid 32.50
Colony, crystal; mayonnaise, w/liner 15.00
Colony, crystal; oyster cocktail, 3⅜″ 9.00
Colony, crystal; pitcher, 64-oz 40.00
Colony, crystal; plate, hdl, 9½″ 25.00
Colony, crystal; plate, salver; ftd, 12″ 20.00
Colony, crystal; plate, 7″ 3.00
Colony, crystal; plate, 9″ 4.50
Colony, crystal; saucer 1.50
Colony, crystal; shakers, orig label, w/tray, pr 30.00
Colony, crystal; shakers, pr 12.50
Colony, crystal; sugar bowl, open; 3½″ 7.50
Colony, crystal; tumbler, ftd, 12-oz, 5¾″ 12.00
Colony, crystal; tumbler, 5-oz 8.00
Colony, crystal; urn, ftd, w/lid 65.00
Colony, crystal; vase, 8″ 20.00
Colony, crystal; wine, 4¼″ 12.50
Corsage, crystal; cordial, #6014, 1-oz 25.00
Corsage, crystal; tumbler, ftd, #6014, 12-oz, 6″ 19.00
Cupid, black; bowl, console; 3-pc 85.00
Eilene, blue; goblet, water 17.50
Eilene, blue; pitcher 350.00
Fairfax, amber; ash tray 13.00
Fairfax, amber; baker, oval, 9″ 22.50
Fairfax, amber; bonbon 8.00
Fairfax, amber; bouillon, ftd 7.00
Fairfax, amber; bowl, cereal; 6″ 8.00
Fairfax, amber; bowl, fruit; 5″ 8.00
Fairfax, amber; bowl, nappy; rnd, 8″ 12.00
Fairfax, amber; bowl, 12″ 15.00
Fairfax, amber; butter dish 80.00
Fairfax, amber; candlestick, oval base, 3-toed, #2299, pr 29.00
Fairfax, amber; candlestick, 1-light, #2470½, 5½″, pr 55.00
Fairfax, amber; candlestick, 3″, pr 22.00
Fairfax, amber; candy dish, w/lid, 3-part 32.00
Fairfax, amber; cheese & cracker, #2368, 2-pc, 11½″ 22.00
Fairfax, amber; compote, salver; #2327, 7″ 28.00
Fairfax, amber; creamer, flat 10.00
Fairfax, amber; creamer, ftd 9.00
Fairfax, amber; creamer & sugar, flat 26.00
Fairfax, amber; cup, demitasse 10.00
Fairfax, amber; goblet, water; #5097 . . . . . 18.00
Fairfax, amber; mayonnaise 9.00
Fairfax, amber; pickle, 8½″ 7.00
Fairfax, amber; pitcher 110.00
Fairfax, amber; plate, cake; 10″ 13.00
Fairfax, amber; plate, lemon; 2-hdl 10.00
Fairfax, amber; plate, salad; 7″ 3.00
Fairfax, amber; platter, oval, 15″ 20.00
Fairfax, amber; shakers, #2111, 2½″, pr 10.00
Fairfax, amber; sugar bowl, ftd 6.00
Fairfax, amber; sugar cover 20.00
Fairfax, amber; vase, Tut, hdls, 8½″ 15.00
Fairfax, blue; baker, oval, 10½″ 30.00
Fairfax, blue; bowl, fruit; 5″ 8.00
Fairfax, blue; bowl, master almond; #2375 . . . . . 35.00
Fairfax, blue; bowl, 12″ 20.00
Fairfax, blue; bowl, 3-toe, #2375, 12″ 40.00
Fairfax, blue; candlestick, 3″ 11.50
Fairfax, blue; candy dish, on pedestal, #2380 . . . . . 85.00

Fairfax, blue; candy dish, w/lid, 3-part....43.00
Fairfax, blue; cheese dish, ftd, scarce, #2368....22.00
Fairfax, blue; compote, #2400, 6″....15.00
Fairfax, blue; compote, blown, #5099....42.50
Fairfax, blue; compote, 7″....15.00
Fairfax, blue; creamer, tea....11.00
Fairfax, blue; cup, demitasse....15.00
Fairfax, blue; cup, ftd....8.00
Fairfax, blue; cup & saucer....11.00
Fairfax, blue; goblet, water; #5082....20.00
Fairfax, blue; goblet, water; #5098....25.00
Fairfax, blue; mayonnaise ladle....12.00
Fairfax, blue; oil, ftd....75.00
Fairfax, blue; parfait, #5298....32.50
Fairfax, blue; pitcher....135.00
Fairfax, blue; plate, bread; 12″....14.00
Fairfax, blue; plate, canape....5.00
Fairfax, blue; plate, dinner; 10¼″....17.50
Fairfax, blue; plate, luncheon; 9½″....8.00
Fairfax, blue; plate, salad; 8″....6.00
Fairfax, blue; plate, 7⅜″....6.00
Fairfax, blue; platter, oval, 10½″....20.00
Fairfax, blue; relish, 11½″....15.00
Fairfax, blue; sauce boat liner....12.00
Fairfax, blue; saucer....4.00
Fairfax, blue; shakers, ftd, pr....50.00
Fairfax, blue; sugar bowl, ftd....10.00
Fairfax, blue; sugar pail....47.50
Fairfax, blue; sweetmeat....11.00
Fairfax, blue; tray, center hdl, 11″....20.00
Fairfax, blue; tray, lunch; hdl, #2375....32.00
Fairfax, crystal; ice bucket, w/tongs, liner w/orig label....35.00
Fairfax, green; ash tray....17.50
Fairfax, green; baker, oval, 9″....20.00
Fairfax, green; bonbon....9.00
Fairfax, green; bouillon, ftd....7.75
Fairfax, green; bowl, cereal; 6″....10.00
Fairfax, green; bowl, cream soup....15.00
Fairfax, green; bowl, dessert; 2-hdl, 8½″....25.00
Fairfax, green; bowl, fruit; 5″....6.00
Fairfax, green; bowl, nappy; rnd, 8″....13.50
Fairfax, green; bowl, 12″....18.00
Fairfax, green; candlestick, #2402, pr....25.00
Fairfax, green; cheese, ftd....25.00
Fairfax, green; compote, 7″....12.00
Fairfax, green; cream soup, ftd....8.00
Fairfax, green; creamer, tea....9.00
Fairfax, green; creamer & sugar, flat....26.00
Fairfax, green; cup, demitasse....12.50
Fairfax, green; cup & saucer, demitasse; ftd....26.00
Fairfax, green; flower holder, oval....10.00
Fairfax, green; ice bucket, w/tongs....25.00
Fairfax, green; icer, w/insert, #945½....30.00
Fairfax, green; mayonnaise....10.00
Fairfax, green; mayonnaise liner, 7″....3.50
Fairfax, green; plate, bread & butter; 6″....2.50
Fairfax, green; plate, bread; 12″....12.00
Fairfax, green; plate, dinner; 10¼″....13.50
Fairfax, green; plate, grill; 10¼″....10.00
Fairfax, green; plate, salad; 7″....3.50
Fairfax, green; plate, salad; 8″....5.00
Fairfax, green; plate, torte; 14″....15.00
Fairfax, green; platter, oval, 10½″....17.50
Fairfax, green; platter, oval, 15″....25.00
Fairfax, green; relish, 11½″....12.00
Fairfax, green; sauce boat....25.00
Fairfax, green; saucer....3.00
Fairfax, green; saucer, demitasse....5.00
Fairfax, green; shakers, ftd, pr....35.00
Fairfax, green; sherbet, tall, #5298....18.00
Fairfax, green; sugar bowl, flat....12.00
Fairfax, green; sugar bowl, tea....8.00
Fairfax, green; sugar cover....22.50
Fairfax, green; sweetmeat....9.00
Fairfax, green; tankard, water; #5000....130.00
Fairfax, green; tray, center hdl, 11″....15.00
Fairfax, orchid; ash tray....14.00
Fairfax, orchid; bowl, soup; 7″....15.00
Fairfax, orchid; compote, w/cutting, #2327, 7″....35.00
Fairfax, orchid; console, mushroom, oval....35.00
Fairfax, orchid; cream soup, ftd....12.00
Fairfax, orchid; creamer & sugar....30.00
Fairfax, orchid; cup, ftd....8.00
Fairfax, orchid; ice bucket....40.00
Fairfax, orchid; mayonnaise ladle....12.00
Fairfax, orchid; mint dish....25.00
Fairfax, orchid; plate, dinner; 10¼″....17.50
Fairfax, orchid; plate, salad; 7″....5.00
Fairfax, orchid; platter, oval, 10½″....20.00
Fairfax, orchid; relish, 8½″....10.00
Fairfax, orchid; sauce boat....30.00
Fairfax, orchid; saucer....4.00
Fairfax, orchid; tumbler, water; #5000....20.00
Fairfax, rose; baker, oval, 9″....25.00
Fairfax, rose; butter dish, w/lid....85.00
Fairfax, rose; candlestick, 3″....10.00
Fairfax, rose; candy dish, w/lid, ½-lb, #2394....40.00
Fairfax, rose; compote, blown, #5098....45.00
Fairfax, rose; compote, tall, #2375....30.00
Fairfax, rose; compote, 5¼″....25.00
Fairfax, rose; creamer, flat....12.00
Fairfax, rose; cup, ftd....7.00
Fairfax, rose; cup & saucer, demitasse....22.00
Fairfax, rose; mayonnaise....10.00
Fairfax, rose; oil, ftd....90.00
Fairfax, rose; pitcher....120.00
Fairfax, rose; plate, bread & butter; 6″....2.50
Fairfax, rose; plate, cake; 10″....15.00
Fairfax, rose; plate, dinner; 10¼″....13.50
Fairfax, rose; plate, salad; 8″....5.00
Fairfax, rose; plate, torte; 13″....27.50
Fairfax, rose; plate, torte; 14″....15.00
Fairfax, rose; platter, 12″....29.50
Fairfax, rose; relish, 11½″....12.00
Fairfax, rose; sauce boat....20.00
Fairfax, rose; saucer, demitasse....5.00
Fairfax, rose; shakers, ind, ftd, pr....25.00
Fairfax, rose; sugar bowl, flat....12.00
Fairfax, rose; sugar bowl, ftd....8.00
Fairfax, rose; sugar cover....22.50
Fairfax, rose; sweetmeat....9.00
Fairfax, rose; tray, center hdl, 11″....15.00
Fairfax, rose; tray, service....75.00
Fairfax, rose; vase, loop optic, w/orig brn label, 8″....30.00
Fairfax, yellow; ash tray....13.00
Fairfax, yellow; baker, oval, 10½″....20.00
Fairfax, yellow; bowl, fruit; 5″....5.00
Fairfax, yellow; bowl, nappy, rnd, 8″....12.00

Fairfax, yellow; candlestick, #2394, pr........................25.00
Fairfax, yellow; candlestick, scroll, 5″, pr....................34.00
Fairfax, yellow; claret, #5298, 6″..........................25.00
Fairfax, yellow; cup & saucer, demitasse......................23.00
Fairfax, yellow; decanter, cloudy, w/stopper, #4220............70.00
Fairfax, yellow; goblet, #5299..............................22.00
Fairfax, yellow; goblet, water; #6017.........................15.00
Fairfax, yellow; goblet, wine; #6017, 2½-oz...................18.00
Fairfax, yellow; ice bucket................................30.00
Fairfax, yellow; lemon insert, scarce........................35.00
Fairfax, yellow; parfait, #5098.............................15.00
Fairfax, yellow; pitcher, jug; ftd, #5000....................175.00
Fairfax, yellow; plate, luncheon; 9½″.........................5.00
Fairfax, yellow; plate, salad; 7″.............................3.00
Fairfax, yellow; relish, 8½″.................................7.00
Fairfax, yellow; sauce boat................................20.00
Fairfax, yellow; saucer....................................2.50
Fairfax, yellow; shaker, ftd, w/lid..........................45.00
Fairfax, yellow; sherbet, tall, #5299.........................15.00
Fairfax, yellow; sugar bowl, ftd.............................6.00
Fairfax, yellow; sugar cover...............................20.00
Fairfax, yellow; tray, lemon; 2-hdl.........................12.00
Fairfax, yellow; tray, service...............................40.00
Fern, ebony; candlestick, scroll, 5″, pr.....................39.00
Heather, crystal; bowl, vegetable; oval, 9½″.................22.50
Heather, crystal; cruet, w/stopper..........................47.50
Heather, crystal; goblet, claret; 6″.........................27.50
Heather, crystal; pitcher, milk.............................95.00
Heather, crystal; plate, dinner; 9½″........................35.00
Heather, crystal; shakers, orig label, pr....................30.00
Heather, crystal; tray, cheese; 11″.........................29.50
Heather, crystal; wine.....................................35.00
Heirloom, yellow opal; pitcher/vase, #2728/807, 9″............38.00
Hermitage, blue; goblet, water.............................25.00
Hermitage, crystal; cruet, w/stopper........................27.50
Hermitage, green; cocktail, cone, 3½-oz.....................11.50
Hermitage, green; creamer.................................22.50
Hermitage, topaz; ice tub, #2449............................37.50
Hermitage, topaz; plate, 8¼″...............................10.00
Hermitage, topaz; sherbet, low.............................12.00
Hermitage, topaz; tumbler, iced tea; flat, 6″..................25.00
Jamestown, amethyst; shakers, pr...........................24.00
Jamestown, blue; goblet, water.............................15.00
Jamestown, cinnamon; tumbler, iced tea; ftd..................10.00
Jamestown, crystal; tray, muffin............................20.00
June, blue; ash tray......................................35.00
June, blue; bowl, bonbon..................................20.00
June, blue; bowl, centerpiece; 11″..........................50.00
June, blue; bowl, cereal; 6″...............................27.50
June, blue; bowl, lemon...................................25.00
June, blue; bowl, soup; 7″................................35.00
June, blue; candlestick, 2″................................20.00
June, blue; candlestick, 5″................................22.50
June, blue; candy dish, w/lid, ½-lb........................110.00
June, blue; compote, 5″...................................32.50
June, blue; compote, 7″...................................45.00
June, blue; creamer, ftd...................................20.00
June, blue; cup, ftd......................................27.50
June, blue; goblet, water; 10-oz, 8¼″........................33.00
June, blue; goblet, wine; 3-oz, 5½″..........................52.50
June, blue; plate, salad; 7½″..............................10.00
June, blue; plate, sm dinner; 9½″...........................16.00
June, blue; saucer, demitasse..............................25.00
June, blue; tumbler, 2½-oz................................37.50
June, blue; tumbler, 9-oz, 5¼″.............................27.50
June, blue; vase, 8″.....................................125.00
June, crystal; ash tray, 2½″...............................35.00
June, crystal; bowl, nappy; 7″.............................15.00
June, crystal; candlestick, #2394...........................25.00
June, crystal; cruet, w/stopper............................250.00
June, crystal; cup, demitasse..............................27.50
June, crystal; finger bowl, w/liner..........................32.50
June, crystal; goblet, claret...............................37.50
June, crystal; goblet, cocktail; 5¼″.........................27.00
June, crystal; goblet, water; 10-oz, 8¼″.....................21.00
June, crystal; goblet, wine; 5½″............................21.75
June, crystal; plate, dinner; 10¼″..........................20.00
June, crystal; plate, salad; 7½″.............................5.00
June, crystal; sugar bowl, ftd..............................17.00
June, crystal; tumbler, 9-oz, 5¼″...........................15.00
June, crystal; vase, fan ftd, 8½″...........................50.00
June, crystal; wine, 5½″..................................35.00
June, rose; ash tray......................................30.00
June, rose; bowl, mint; 3-ftd..............................15.00
June, rose; bowl, nappy; ftd...............................18.00
June, rose; bowl, salad; hdl, 11″...........................55.00
June, rose; bowl, 10″....................................35.00
June, rose; candlestick, mushroom..........................25.00
June, rose; candlestick, 3″................................17.50
June, rose; compote, 6″...................................26.00
June, rose; creamer, tea..................................30.00
June, rose; cup, ftd......................................22.00
June, rose; cup & saucer..................................35.00
June, rose; goblet, water; 10-oz, 8¼″........................28.00
June, rose; goblet, wine; 3-oz, 5½″..........................45.00
June, rose; ladle, mayonnaise..............................35.00
June, rose; pitcher......................................335.00
June, rose; plate, bread & butter; 6″.........................5.00
June, rose; plate, chop; 13″...............................35.00
June, rose; plate, luncheon; 8¾″...........................10.00
June, rose; sugar bowl, tea................................30.00
June, rose; tumbler, 9-oz, 5¼″.............................21.50
June, topaz; bouillon, w/liner..............................25.00
June, topaz; bowl, bonbon.................................17.50
June, topaz; bowl, cereal; 6″...............................25.00
June, topaz; bowl, soup; 7″................................25.00
June, topaz; bowl, whip cream..............................20.00
June, topaz; candlestick, 5″...............................20.00
June, topaz; candy base, low, rare, #2394...................150.00
June, topaz; cheese & cracker set...........................40.00
June, topaz; compote, 7″..................................27.50
June, topaz; cup & saucer.................................32.50
June, topaz; goblet, iced tea; ftd...........................27.50
June, topaz; goblet, water.................................30.00
June, topaz; goblet, wine; 3-oz, 5½″.........................45.00
June, topaz; grapefruit liner...............................40.00
June, topaz; oil, ftd, w/stopper............................395.00
June, topaz; pitcher.....................................335.00
June, topaz; plate, dinner; 10¼″...........................32.50
June, topaz; plate, luncheon...............................15.00
June, topaz; plate, salad; 7½″..............................8.00
June, topaz; plate, sm dinner; 9½″..........................15.00
June, topaz; relish, 8½″..................................20.00
June, topaz; salt shaker..................................65.00
June, topaz; sauce boat...................................60.00
June, topaz; saucer.......................................5.00
June, topaz; sherbet, high, 6-oz, 6″.........................25.00
June, topaz; sugar bowl, ftd...............................22.00

June, topaz; sugar bowl, ind . . . 47.50
June, topaz; tray, center hdl, 11" . . . 35.00
June, topaz; tray, relish; 11" . . . 32.50
June, topaz; tumbler, iced tea; 6" . . . 32.50
June, topaz; tumbler, 9-oz, 5¼" . . . 21.50
June, topaz; vase, 8" . . . 110.00
Kashmir, green; candlestick, 5" . . . 22.50
Kashmir, green; plate, dinner; 10" . . . 30.00
Kashmir, green; stem, high sherbet; 6-oz . . . 17.50
Kashmir, yellow; bowl, cereal; 6" . . . 20.00
Kashmir, yellow; plate, salad; rnd, 7" . . . 6.00
Kashmir, yellow; stem, wine; 2½-oz . . . 30.00
Lafayette, green; bonbon, 5" . . . 15.00
Lafayette, ruby; bowl, mayonnaise; 2-pt . . . 30.00
Lafayette, topaz; tray, relish; rnd, 2-hdl, 6" . . . 15.00
Lafayette, wisteria; cup & saucer . . . 17.50
Lido, crystal; goblet, water . . . 17.50
Lido, crystal; ice bucket . . . 65.00
Lido, crystal; tumbler, iced tea . . . 17.50
Manor, topaz; bowl, 6" . . . 12.00
Mayfair, green; creamer & sugar, for tea . . . 15.00
Mayfair, green; cruet, no stopper . . . 25.00
Mayfair, pink; cup . . . 10.00
Mayfair, topaz; cruet, w/stopper . . . 65.00
Mayfair, topaz; plate, dinner . . . 10.00
Mayflower, crystal; bowl, flared, 4-toe, #2496, 11" . . . 37.50
Mayflower, crystal; candlestick, 1-light, #2545, 4½", pr . . . 35.00
Mayflower, crystal; goblet, water; 7¼" . . . 19.50
Mayflower, crystal; parfait, rare . . . 25.00
Mayflower, crystal; shakers, pr . . . 75.00
Mayflower, crystal; sherbet, high . . . 25.00
Mayflower, crystal; tumbler, 5¾" . . . 25.00
Meadow Rose, blue; cup, coffee . . . 25.00
Meadow Rose, crystal; cocktail . . . 25.00
Meadow Rose, crystal; compote, jelly; w/lid . . . 50.00
Meadow Rose, crystal; creamer & sugar . . . 25.00
Meadow Rose, crystal; cup & saucer . . . 25.00
Meadow Rose, crystal; goblet, water . . . 26.00
Meadow Rose, crystal; plate, torte; 13" . . . 45.00
Meadow Rose, crystal; plate, 2-hdl, 10½" . . . 36.00
Meadow Rose, crystal; sherbet, #6016, 6-oz, 4⅜" . . . 16.00
Midnight Rose, crystal; pickle dish, oval, 8½" . . . 16.00
Minuet, topaz; candlestick, 3-legged, 2", pr . . . 27.00
Morning Glory, crystal; pickle dish, oval, 8½" . . . 14.00
Navarre, blue; claret, 6" . . . 35.00
Navarre, blue; goblet . . . 35.00
Navarre, crystal; candy dish, w/lid, 3-part . . . 55.00
Navarre, crystal; creamer & sugar, lg, pr . . . 42.00
Navarre, crystal; cup, coffee . . . 20.00
Navarre, crystal; goblet, claret; 4½-oz, 6" . . . 25.00
Navarre, crystal; goblet, water; 7¾" . . . 27.50
Navarre, crystal; ice bucket, w/bail, #2375 . . . 60.00
Navarre, crystal; shakers, ftd, pr . . . 95.00
Navarre, crystal; tumbler, ftd, 10-oz . . . 30.00
Navarre, crystal; tumbler, high-ball; 5" . . . 25.00
Navarre, crystal; wine, 3-oz, 5¼" . . . 29.00
New Garland, topaz; tumbler, ftd, #4220, 16-oz . . . 22.50
Oak Leaf, green; candlestick, 3-toe, #2394, 2" . . . 20.00
Oak Leaf, green; plate, 8½" . . . 15.00
Oak Leaf, pink; bowl, #2394 . . . 38.00
Oakwood, blue; bowl, dessert; 2-hdl, #2375, 8½" . . . 60.00
Oakwood, blue; bowl, 3-toe, #2394, 12" . . . 60.00
Oakwood, blue; compote, #2400, 8" . . . 120.00
Oakwood, blue; mayonnaise, ftd, #2350 . . . 45.00
Oakwood, orchid; bowl, 3-toe, #2394, 12" . . . 45.00
Oakwood, orchid; ice bucket, #2378 . . . 110.00
Oakwood, orchid; parfait, #877 . . . 30.00
Oakwood, orchid; sherbet, low, #877 . . . 25.00
Paradise, crystal; bowl, rolled edge, ftd, #2315 . . . 67.50
Paradise, crystal; compote, #2350, 8" . . . 46.00
Paradise, crystal; compote, low ftd, MOP wash, 8" . . . 28.00
Paradise, green; bowl, rolled edge, #2329, 11" . . . 36.00
Pioneer, amber; butter dish . . . 55.00
Pioneer, amber; sauce boat, w/underplate, VG . . . 22.00
Pioneer, green; candlestick, 4", pr . . . 17.00
Pioneer, green; compote, cheese . . . 12.00
Pioneer, green; egg cup . . . 7.00
Priscilla, green; bouillon . . . 7.50
Priscilla, green; tumbler, hdl . . . 13.00
Richmond, crystal; wine, 5" . . . 15.00
Romance, crystal; creamer & sugar, lg, pr . . . 25.00
Romance, crystal; cup & saucer . . . 22.50
Romance, crystal; goblet, claret . . . 30.00
Romance, crystal; plate, dinner; 9½" . . . 35.00
Romance, crystal; tumbler, iced tea; 6" . . . 22.50
Royal, green; plate, 8½" . . . 8.00
Royal, green; server, sandwich; center hdl . . . 24.00
Seascape, blue opal; preserve, hdl, orig brn paper label . . . 28.00
Seascape, pink opal; tray, relish; 3-part . . . 35.00
Seville, crystal; goblet, cordial . . . 25.00
Seville, crystal; goblet, water . . . 17.50
Shirley, crystal; nappy, hdl, sq, 5" . . . 20.00
Shirley, crystal; tray, relish; 2-hdl, 3-part, 10" . . . 36.00
Spiral, amber; ice bucket . . . 40.00
Spiral, green; whip cream pail . . . 40.00
Springtime, topaz; tray, relish; 2-hdl, 4-part, #2419 . . . 40.00
Strawflower, crystal; plate, 10½" . . . 22.00
Sunray, crystal; bonbon, 3-toe . . . 22.00
Sunray, crystal; bowl, oval, 2-hdl, 11½" . . . 35.00
Sunray, crystal; creamer & sugar . . . 22.50
Sunray, crystal; creamer & sugar, ind . . . 15.00
Sunray, crystal; cruet, oil; w/stopper . . . 25.00
Sunray, crystal; cup & saucer . . . 14.00
Sunray, crystal; mayonnaise, 3-pc . . . 42.50
Sunray, crystal; nappy, hdl, sq, 5" . . . 11.00
Sunray, crystal; pitcher, water; w/ice lip . . . 75.00
Sunray, crystal; sherbet . . . 10.00
Sunray, crystal; tray, relish; 3-part . . . 15.00
Sunray, crystal; tray, 2-hdl, 9" . . . 22.00
Trojan, rose; ash tray, lg . . . 27.50
Trojan, rose; bowl, cream soup; ftd . . . 17.50
Trojan, rose; bowl, mint . . . 15.00
Trojan, rose; bowl, soup; 7" . . . 22.50
Trojan, rose; candlestick, 3" . . . 15.00
Trojan, rose; creamer, tea . . . 35.00
Trojan, rose; cruet, w/stopper . . . 350.00
Trojan, rose; goblet, claret; 6" . . . 35.00
Trojan, rose; pitcher . . . 265.00
Trojan, rose; plate, dinner; 10¼" . . . 32.50
Trojan, rose; plate, sm dinner; 9½" . . . 16.00
Trojan, rose; platter, 12" . . . 32.50
Trojan, rose; relish, 8½" . . . 15.00
Trojan, rose; sugar, tea . . . 35.00
Trojan, rose; tray, service . . . 27.50
Trojan, rose; tumbler, ftd, 9-oz, 5¼" . . . 15.50
Trojan, rose; vase, 8" . . . 95.00
Trojan, topaz; bowl, bonbon . . . 12.50
Trojan, topaz; bowl, cereal . . . 26.50

New Century, mayonnaise with underplate, clear, 3½″ tall, $20.00.

Trojan, topaz; bowl, dessert; hdl, lg, #2375 ... 38.00
Trojan, topaz; bowl, mint ... 15.00
Trojan, topaz; bowl, soup; 7″ ... 22.50
Trojan, topaz; candy dish, w/lid, #2394 ... 150.00
Trojan, topaz; compote, 6″ ... 27.50
Trojan, topaz; compote, 7″ ... 35.00
Trojan, topaz; console, 3-ftd, 12″ ... 25.00
Trojan, topaz; cup, demitasse ... 27.50
Trojan, topaz; goblet, water; 8¼″ ... 27.50
Trojan, topaz; pitcher, jug; ftd, #5000 ... 325.00
Trojan, topaz; plate, bread & butter; 6″ ... 5.00
Trojan, topaz; plate, dinner; 10¼″ ... 32.50
Trojan, topaz; plate, sm dinner; 9½″ ... 16.00
Trojan, topaz; plate, torte; 13″ ... 55.00
Trojan, topaz; platter, 12″ ... 32.50
Trojan, topaz; sauce boat ... 40.00
Trojan, topaz; shakers, pr ... 95.00
Trojan, topaz; sweetmeat ... 13.50
Trojan, topaz; tray, service ... 225.00
Trojan, topaz; tumbler, ftd, 12-oz, 6″ ... 20.00
Vernon, amber; baker, 9″ ... 30.00
Vernon, amber; mayonnaise, ftd ... 26.00
Vernon, amber; server, sandwich; center hdl ... 37.50
Vernon, orchid; candy dish, w/lid, #2331 ... 150.00
Vernon, orchid; champagne ... 27.50
Vernon, orchid; compote, tall ... 29.00
Vernon, orchid; cup & saucer ... 29.50
Verona, green; wine ... 35.00
Versailles, blue; ash tray ... 30.00
Versailles, blue; bowl, centerpiece; oval, 13″ ... 47.50
Versailles, blue; bowl, cereal; 6″ ... 25.00
Versailles, blue; bowl, cream soup; ftd ... 24.00
Versailles, blue; candlestick, #2375, 3″, pr ... 55.00
Versailles, blue; candlestick, 5″ ... 25.00
Versailles, blue; cheese & cracker set ... 60.00
Versailles, blue; compote, 6″ ... 32.00
Versailles, blue; cup, demitasse ... 40.00
Versailles, blue; goblet, claret; 4-oz, 6″ ... 65.00
Versailles, blue; goblet, wine; 3-oz, 5½″ ... 50.00
Versailles, blue; pitcher ... 400.00
Versailles, blue; plate, dinner; 10¼″ ... 42.00
Versailles, blue; plate, sm dinner; 9½″ ... 17.50
Versailles, blue; tray, service ... 40.00
Versailles, green; baker, oval, 9″ ... 75.00
Versailles, green; bowl, centerpiece; rolled edge ... 35.00
Versailles, green; bowl, dessert; hdl, 9″ ... 65.00
Versailles, green; bowl, fruit; 5″ ... 20.00
Versailles, green; bowl, soup; 7″ ... 25.00
Versailles, green; candy dish, w/lid, ½-lb ... 55.00
Versailles, green; creamer, lg ... 18.00
Versailles, green; cruet, w/stopper, scarce ... 575.00
Versailles, green; finger bowl, w/underplate ... 38.00
Versailles, green; goblet, cordial; rare ... 85.00
Versailles, green; goblet, water; 10-oz, 8¼″ ... 27.50
Versailles, green; grapefruit, w/insert ... 110.00
Versailles, green; ice bucket, w/tongs ... 95.00
Versailles, green; plate, bread & butter; 6″ ... 4.00
Versailles, green; plate, cake; 2-hdl, 10″ ... 26.00
Versailles, green; plate, dinner; 10¼″ ... 32.00
Versailles, green; plate, luncheon; 8¾″ ... 8.00
Versailles, green; plate, 7½″ ... 6.00
Versailles, green; sherbet, high, 6″ ... 20.00
Versailles, green; sugar lid, rare ... 150.00
Versailles, green; sugar pail ... 150.00
Versailles, green; tray, service ... 30.00
Versailles, green; tumbler, ftd, 12-oz, 6″ ... 22.50
Versailles, green; tumbler, ftd, 5¼″ ... 20.00
Versailles, pink; baker, oval, 9″ ... 65.00
Versailles, pink; bowl, #2375, 12″ ... 35.00
Versailles, pink; bowl, bouillon; ftd ... 16.00
Versailles, pink; bowl, centerpiece; 11″ ... 30.00
Versailles, pink; bowl, mint ... 14.00
Versailles, pink; candlestick, 3″ ... 16.00
Versailles, pink; compote, 7″ ... 45.00
Versailles, pink; creamer, tea ... 27.50
Versailles, pink; cruet, w/stopper ... 325.00
Versailles, pink; cup & saucer, demitasse ... 45.00
Versailles, pink; finger bowl ... 25.00
Versailles, pink; goblet, water; 8¼″ ... 27.50
Versailles, pink; grapefruit ... 75.00
Versailles, pink; ice bucket ... 75.00
Versailles, pink; mayonnaise, w/liner ... 35.00
Versailles, pink; pitcher, jug; ftd, #5000 ... 325.00
Versailles, pink; plate, cake; hdl, 10″ ... 29.25
Versailles, pink; plate, chop; 13″ ... 30.00
Versailles, pink; plate, salad; 7½″ ... 6.00
Versailles, pink; sauce boat ... 40.00
Versailles, pink; shakers, ftd, pr ... 80.00
Versailles, pink; sherbet, low ... 18.00
Versailles, pink; sugar lid ... 75.00
Versailles, pink; sugar pail ... 150.00
Versailles, pink; sweetmeat ... 12.00
Versailles, pink; tray, service & lemon ... 32.50
Versailles, pink; tumbler, ftd, 5-oz, 4½″ ... 20.00
Versailles, pink; vase, 8″ ... 85.00
Versailles, pink; whip cream pail ... 95.00
Versailles, pink; wine, 5½″ ... 45.00
Versailles, yellow; baker, oval, 9″ ... 65.00
Versailles, yellow; bowl, cream soup; ftd ... 20.00
Versailles, yellow; bowl, dessert; 2-hdl, 8½″ ... 40.00
Versailles, yellow; bowl, mint ... 16.00
Versailles, yellow; bowl, mint; 3-toe, #2394 ... 35.00
Versailles, yellow; bowl, sweetmeat; 2-hdl ... 19.00
Versailles, yellow; bowl, 10″ ... 32.00
Versailles, yellow; candlestick, scroll, 5″, pr ... 55.00
Versailles, yellow; candlestick, 2″ ... 16.00
Versailles, yellow; candy base, #2394 ... 100.00
Versailles, yellow; claret, 6″ ... 45.00

Versailles, yellow; cocktail 25.00
Versailles, yellow; creamer, ftd 15.00
Versailles, yellow; cup, demitasse 30.00
Versailles, yellow; goblet, cocktail 35.00
Versailles, yellow; goblet, water; 10-oz, 8¼" 30.00
Versailles, yellow; grapefruit 40.00
Versailles, yellow; ice bucket 75.00
Versailles, yellow; icer, no insert, #5082½ 42.00
Versailles, yellow; mayonnaise, w/liner 40.00
Versailles, yellow; oyster cocktail 22.00
Versailles, yellow; pitcher 300.00
Versailles, yellow; plate, bread & butter; 6" 4.00
Versailles, yellow; plate, chop-torte; 13¾" 55.00
Versailles, yellow; plate, dinner; 10¼" 37.50
Versailles, yellow; plate, sm dinner; 9½" 15.00
Versailles, yellow; platter, 15" 50.00
Versailles, yellow; sauce plate 15.00
Versailles, yellow; saucer 5.00
Versailles, yellow; sherbet, low, 4¼" 22.00
Versailles, yellow; sugar bowl 23.00
Versailles, yellow; tray, celery; oval, 11½" 32.50
Versailles, yellow; tray, sandwich; center hdl 40.00
Versailles, yellow; tumbler, ftd, 12-oz 25.00
Versailles, yellow; tumbler, ftd, 9-oz, 5¼" 21.50
Versailles, yellow; vase, 8" 110.00
Versailles, yellow; wine, 5½" 45.00
Vesper, amber; bowl, cereal; 6½" 24.00
Vesper, amber; bowl, soup; deep, 8" 18.50
Vesper, amber; bowl, 9" 27.50
Vesper, amber; butter dish 150.00
Vesper, amber; candlestick, 9" 17.50
Vesper, amber; candy dish, w/lid, #2331 .... 125.00
Vesper, amber; compote, 7½" 45.00
Vesper, amber; cordial 85.00
Vesper, amber; creamer & sugar, ftd 35.00
Vesper, amber; ice bucket 75.00
Vesper, amber; pitcher, ftd 295.00
Vesper, amber; plate, dinner; 10½" 27.50
Vesper, amber; wine, 2¾-oz 25.00
Vesper, blue; bowl, soup; shallow, 7¾" 25.00
Vesper, blue; candlestick, 4" 30.00
Vesper, blue; compote, 7" 40.00
Vesper, blue; urn, lg 80.00
Vesper, green; bowl, cereal; 6½" 14.00
Vesper, green; finger bowl 15.00
Vesper, green; ice bucket, w/tongs 75.00
Vesper, green; pitcher, water 295.00
Vesper, green; plate, dinner; 10½" 27.50
Vesper, green; plate, sm dinner; 9½" 10.00
Vesper, green; tumbler, ftd, 9-oz 15.00
Vesper, green; vase, 8" 60.00
Westchester, gr w/crystal; goblet, cordial 12.00
Westchester, ruby w/crystal; goblet, water; #6012 .... 20.00
Willow, crystal; goblet, tall 20.00
Willow, crystal; ice tub 56.00
Willowmere, crystal; plate, torte 25.00
Wistar, crystal; creamer & sugar, lg 26.00
Woodland, crystal; pitcher, squat jug 75.00
Woodland, crystal; tankard, tall 75.00

Fraktur

Fraktur is a German style of black letter text type. To collectors, the fraktur is a type of hand-lettered document used by the people of German decent who settled in the area of Pennsylvania and New Jersey. These documents recorded births, baptisms, and marriages, and were used as bookplates and as certificates of honor. They were elaborately decorated with colorful folk art borders of hearts, birds, angels, and flowers. Examples by recognized artists, and those with an unusual decorative motif, bring prices well into the thousands of dollars. Frakturs made in the late 1800s, after the invention of the printing press, provided the writer with a prepared text that he needed only to fill in at his own discretion. The next step in the evolution of machine-printed frakturs combined woodblock-printed decorations along with the text which the 'artist' sometimes enhanced with color. By the late 1800s, even the coloring was done by machine.

The vorschrift was a handwritten example prepared by a fraktur teacher to demonstrate his skill in lettering and decorating. These are often considered to be the finest of frakturs. Those dated before 1820 are most valuable.

The practice of fraktur art began to diminish after 1830, but hung on even to the early years of this century among the Pennsylvania Germans ingrained with such customs.

When no condition is indicated, the items listed below are assumed to be in excellent condition.

Key:
hc—hand colored
p/i—pen and ink
p/wc—printed and watercolored
wc—watercolored

Birth Record

Oil colors, 2 angels ea side, 1832, 13x15" 225.00
P/i/wc, att Mt Pleasant artist, 1824, 9x11" 775.00
P/i/wc, floral standards by verse, X-corner fr w/birds, sm 250.00

Fraktur, watercolor on laid paper, four-color florals, central chandelier and grapevines, dated 1788, 16" x 12", $800.00.

P/i/wc, flowers/hearts/vines, Ohio, 1844, prof rpr, 15″.........400.00
P/i/wc, heart/tulip/zigzag, 1829, 8x9½″, EX..................400.00
P/i/wc, red/blk/tulip in yel, 1811, in fr, 16x12″, VG...........250.00
P/i/wc, shields/hearts/floral, G colors, M Brechall, 1797........900.00
P/i/wc, vines/tulips/hearts, 1781, 11x16″, EX................475.00
P/wc, angels/birds, A&W Blumer, 1841 Ohio birth, 15x15″.....55.00

Miscellaneous

Bookplate, p/i, simple trees ea side, 1823, stained, 5x8″.......150.00
Bookplate, p/i nameplate, mc wc, cut-out tree, 1811, 6½x9″....460.00
Christmas greeting, p/i/wc, German verse, 1811, 10x12″.......140.00
Drawing, p/i birds/flowers, mc, 1864, 10x16″................460.00
Drawing, p/i/wc, compass design/hearts/birds/trees, 12x10″.....325.00
Drawing, wc, compass star w/2 birds/tulip, stains, 10x15″......325.00
Family register, p/i, compass flowers/faces, 1780-1829, fr.......650.00
House blessing, freehand parrots, pencil/wc, 1860, 15″, VG....150.00
Memorial, p/i/wc, tomb/mourners/willow, 1811, 11x15″, EX...1,525.00
P/i/wc, floral tree in 4 colors, faded/torn, no fr, 4x7″..........70.00
P/i/wc, horse/2 ornate letters w/birds/tulips, 1798, 19x15″......800.00
P/i/wc, tulip, unfinished inscription, 1822, 11x11″, EX........150.00
Vorschrift, birds/flowers/inscription, 5-color, 9½x10″..........750.00
Vorschrift, p/i/wc, inscription, dtd 1783, 10x13″..............750.00
Vorschrift, p/i/wc, 1807, minor stains, 8x13″.................550.00
Writing exercise, p/i, 3-color ink, 1826, 3½x5½″, EX..........50.00

Frames

Styles in picture frames have changed with the fashion of the day, but those that especially interest today's collectors are the deep shadow boxes made of fine woods such as walnut or cherry, those with Art Nouveau influence, and the oak frames decorated with molded gesso and gilt from the Victorian era.

When no condition is indicated, the items listed below are assumed to be in excellent condition.

Bird's eye, maple, 2¼″ W, 24x28″........................150.00
Bird's eye veneer, gilt liner, 1⅞″ W, 13¾x16½″..............85.00
Bird's eye veneer, ogee, 2½″ W, 30x39″...................190.00
Bird's eye veneer, 2″ W, 28½x33″........................160.00
Cherry, from a country 2-part mirror, 11¼x27½″.............120.00
Cherry, scrollwork, hinged glass door, rpr, 18¼x21¾″.........600.00
Curly maple, turned corner blocks, 2½″ W, 17x20¾″.........445.00
Curly maple grpt w/gray liner, 2½″ W, 15x19″, VG............97.50
Folk art, carved oval ring mt, red/wht/bl pnt, 4½x5″..........300.00
Gesso, gilt, 2½″ W, 14½x16¾″...........................35.00
Grpt striped, beveled, 2½″ W, 14x18″.....................175.00
Mahogany veneer, blk ebonized edge stripe, 1″ W, 6⅝x8⅝″.....45.00
Oak, worn blk velvet liner, 5½″ W, 52x70″.................105.00
Pine, beveled, blk pnt w/yel stripe, 1½″ W, 10¾x13¼″.........95.00
Pine, beveled, old bl pnt w/smoked decor, 1⅜″ W, 10x12″....265.00
Pine, beveled, old red, 1½″ W, 11½x14½″...................45.00
Pine, beveled, old yel pnt, 2⅞″ W, 15¼x17¼″..............115.00
Pine, beveled, orig brn red sponging, 1¾″ W, 8¼x9⅞″.........95.00
Pine, brn sponging w/fingerprint border, 2″ W, 13x17″.......175.00
Pine, carved, old dk brn patina, 11¼x13⅞″.................115.00
Pine, carved, worn red-brn finish, 1″ W, 6½x6¾″.............50.00
Pine, molded, dk natural finish w/yel liner, 2″ W, 14x17⅝″....105.00
Pine, molded, old blk & tan pnt, 1⅛″ W, 11½x15½″..........55.00
Pine, reeded, old brn pnt, 1⅞″ W, 8⅛x10″..................50.00
Pine, reeded w/curly maple corner blocks, 3″ W, 17⅜x21½″...695.00
Pine, X-corner, chip carved, gilt trim, 2″ W, 17x23″...........65.00
Poplar, beveled, old blk pnt, 2⅜″ W, 17x20″, pr.............140.00

Black enamel with Mother-of-Pearl inlay, easel type, 14½″ x 9″, $28.00.

Poplar, beveled, old red-brn finish, 1¾″ W, 12⅝x16¾″........160.00
Poplar, beveled, orig blk pnt, yel stencil, 1¾″ W, 13x17″......135.00
Poplar, molded edge, orig red grpt, 1¾″ W, 15x17″..........100.00
Poplar, orig red flame graining, beveled, 1¾″ W, 15x17″......125.00
Poplar, primitive yel designs on red, 2″ W, 11¼x13⅜″.........70.00
Poplar, reeded, old blk pnt, 1⅜″ W, 12½x16⅜″.............185.00
Poplar, 4 carved hearts, brn patina, 2-part, 1¼″ W, 9x13″.....275.00
Vinegar pnt, beveled, red-brn, 2″ W, 17x20″................450.00
Walnut, primitive, mortised/pinned corners, ⅞″ W, 7x8⅛″.....105.00
Walnut, reeded, old dk finish, 1″ W, 7¾x9¾″................85.00
Walnut, shadow box, old finish, 1⅞″ W, 15½x18½″...........30.00
Wood, oval w/emb brass facade, 4x4¾″.......................55.00

Franciscan

Franciscan is a trade name used by Gladding McBean and Co., founded in northern California in 1875. In 1923 they purchased the Tropico plant in Glendale, where they produced sewer pipe, gardenware, and tile. By 1934 the first of their dinnerware lines, El Patio, was produced. It was a plain design, but made in bright, attractive colors. El Patio Nouveau followed in 1935, glazed in two colors--one tone on the inside, a contrasting hue on the outside. Coronado, a favorite of today's collectors, was introduced in 1936. It was styled with a wide swirled border, and was made in pastels in both a satin and glossy finish.

Before 1940, fifteen patterns had been produced. The first hand-decorated lines were introduced in 1937; the ever-popular embossed, hand-decorated Apple pattern in 1940; Desert Rose in 1941; and Ivy in 1948. Many other hand-decorated and decaled patterns have been produced from 1934 to the present.

Dinnerware marks before 1940 include: (1) GMcB in an oval; (2) 'F' within a square; and (3) 'Franciscan' with 'pottery' underneath--which was later changed to 'ware.' A circular arrangement of 'Franciscan' with 'Made in California USA' in the center was used from 1940 until 1949. At least forty marks were used before 1975, several more were introduced after that, and at one time, a paper label was used.

The company merged with Lock Joint Pipe Company in 1963, becoming part of the Interspace Corporation. In July of 1979, Franciscan merged with Wedgwood Limited of England, and the Glendale plant closed in October, 1984.

Authority Delleen Enge has compiled an informative book, *Franciscan Ware*, with current values. You will find her address in the Directory under California. When no condition is indicated, the items listed below are assumed to be in mint condition. See also Gladding McBean

Coronado

Bowl, cereal....8.50
Bowl, cream soup....12.00
Bowl, vegetable; oval....20.00
Bowl, vegetable; rnd....12.00
Candlestick, pr....24.00
Creamer....9.50
Cup & saucer....10.00
Cup & saucer, demitasse....20.00
Demitasse pot....37.50
Gravy....22.50
Plate, chop; 12"....15.00
Plate, chop; 14"....20.00
Plate, 10½"....14.00
Plate, 6½"....5.50
Plate, 7½"....7.00

Coronado, cup and saucer, demitasse; cup: 2¼", $20.00.

Plate, 8½"....9.50
Plate, 9½"....9.00
Saucer, cream soup....4.00
Shakers, pr....12.50
Sherbet....8.00
Sugar bowl, w/lid....11.00
Teapot....35.00

El Patio

Bowl, cereal....8.00
Bowl, fruit....6.00
Bowl, oval vegetable....14.00
Bowl, salad; 3-qt....20.00
Butter dish, w/cover....25.00
Creamer....8.00
Cup....7.00
Cup, jumbo....15.00
Gravy w/attached underplate....23.00
Plate, bread & butter....6.00
Plate, 10½"....12.00
Plate, 8½"....10.00
Saucer....3.00
Saucer, jumbo....5.00
Sherbet....8.00
Sugar bowl w/lid....14.00
Teapot, w/lid, 6-cup....25.00

Hand Painted Earthenware

Values listed here apply to these patterns: Apple, Desert Rose, Ivy, Meadow Rose and Forget-Me-Not.

Bowl, batter....35.00
Bowl, cereal/soup....8.00
Bowl, fruit; 5½"....8.00
Bowl, soup; flat....14.00
Bowl, vegetable; divided....25.00
Butter dish, w/lid, ¼-lb....28.00
Casserole, stick hdls, 12-oz....20.00
Clock, electric....135.00
Coaster, 3¾"....8.00
Compote, ftd....24.00
Creamer....14.00
Cup & saucer....10.00
Cup & saucer, lg....18.00
Egg cup....8.00
Goblet....16.00
Gravy boat, w/attached stand....28.00
Mug....15.00
Pickle dish, 10½"....16.00
Pitcher, water....32.00
Pitcher, 14-oz....10.00
Plate, bread & butter....7.00
Plate, chop; lg....22.00
Plate, dinner; 10½"....14.00
Plate, luncheon, 9½"....12.00
Plate, salad; 8"....9.00
Platter, oval, 12"....30.00
Platter, oval, 14"....35.00
Relish, 3-part, 11"....20.00
Shakers, Rosebud, pr....10.50
Shakers, tall, pr....18.00
Sugar bowl, w/lid, sm....18.00
Tray, 3-tier....35.00
Tumbler, 5⅛"....15.00

Montecito

Cream soup w/saucer, gr....22.00
Cup & saucer, demitasse, gray satin....20.00
Demitasse pot, turq gloss....35.00
Gravy, coral gloss....20.00
Sugar bowl w/lid, coral satin....22.00

Padua

Bowl, tab hdl....10.00
Plate, 6½"....5.00
Plate, 9½"....10.00
Teapot....25.00

Francisware

Francisware, produced in the 1880s by Hobbs, Brockunier and Company of Wheeling, West Virginia, is a clear or frosted tableware with amber stained rim bands. The most often found pattern is Hobnail, but Swirl was also made.

When no condition is indicated, the items listed below are assumed to be in mint condition.

Hobnail, clear; barber bottle, spout........................135.00
Hobnail, clear; pitcher, water..............................95.00
Hobnail, clear; spooner, amber rim..........................55.00
Hobnail, clear; tumbler.....................................35.00
Hobnail, frosted; butter dish..............................110.00
Hobnail, frosted; celery vase, amber rim....................70.00
Hobnail, frosted; creamer...................................60.00
Hobnail, frosted; ice cream set, scarce....................350.00
Hobnail, frosted; pitcher, lemonade........................175.00
Hobnail, frosted; pitcher, milk; rare size, 5⅜"............180.00
Hobnail, frosted; pitcher, water; amber rim................185.00
Hobnail, frosted; plate, sq, 5¾"............................55.00
Hobnail, frosted; sauce, sq.................................25.00
Hobnail, frosted; shakers, pr...............................75.00
Hobnail, frosted; spooner...................................60.00
Hobnail, frosted; sugar bowl w/lid, amber rim/knob..........75.00
Hobnail, frosted; syrup....................................125.00
Hobnail, frosted; table set, amber rim, 4-pc...............300.00
Hobnail, frosted; tumbler...................................50.00
Hobnail, frosted; waste bowl................................65.00
Swirl, frosted; finger bowl.................................25.00
Swirl, frosted; finger bowl, amber rim......................25.00
Swirl, frosted; sugar bowl w/lid............................85.00
Swirl, frosted; toothpick holder............................85.00

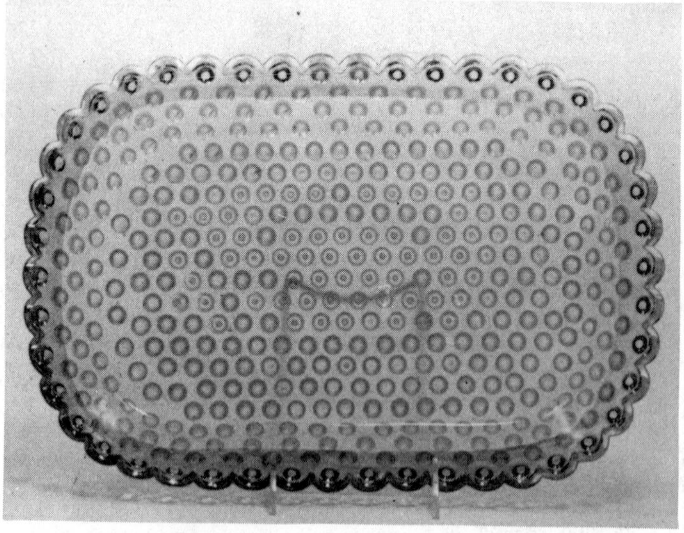

Tray, Hobnail, frosted with amber rim, 14" x 9½", $135.00.

Frankart

During the 1920's Frankart, Inc., of New York City produced a line of accessories that included nude figural lamps, bookends, ash trays, etc. These white metal composition items were offered in several finishes including verde green, jap black and gunmetal gray. The company also produced a line of caricatured animals, but the stylized nude figurals have proved to be the most collectible today. With few exceptions all pieces were marked 'Frankart, Inc.' with a patent number or 'pat. appl. for.'

When no condition is indicated, the items listed below are assumed to be in near mint condition.

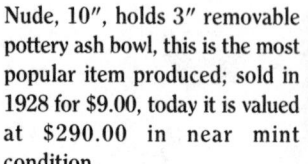

Nude, 10", holds 3" removable pottery ash bowl, this is the most popular item produced; sold in 1928 for $9.00, today it is valued at $290.00 in near mint condition.

Ash tray, acrobatic nude balances 3" ball on toes, 12", NM....285.00
Ash tray, bulldog guards 3" sq tray, insert missing, 4", G.......25.00
Ash tray, dachshund spans 4½" sq tray, w/insert, rpt, 5".......48.00
Ash tray, monkey w/curled tail, insert missing, rpt, 8¾", G......47.00
Ash tray, nude dancer holds 3" pottery bowl aside, 10", VG...260.00
Bookends, cowboy in chaps/hat, w/cigarette, on horse, 7", pr...150.00
Bookends, golfers (caricature) putting, pnt gone, 7½", pr.......75.00
Bookends, modernistic female heads, 6", pr, NM.............170.00
Bookends, stylized dolphins, 6½", pr, VG....................85.00
Lamp, nude, leg raised, embraces 11" crackle tube, 13", VG...480.00
Lamp, nude kneels before 4" crystal bubble ball, 8", VG......475.00
Lamp, standing nude holds 8½" rnd frosted disc, 15", VG.....425.00
Lamp, 2 inverted nudes hold 8" crackle globe on toes, 18"....610.00
Lamp, 2 nudes kneel bk to bk, arms hold 8" glass globe, 9"...450.00
Lamp, 2 nudes stand bk to bk, horizontal cylinder, 12", VG...525.00
Vase, nude w/upraised leg holds 10" vase to side, 12½", VG...575.00

Frankoma

The Frank Pottery, founded in 1933 by John Frank, became known as Frankoma in 1934. The company produced decorative figurals, vases, and such, marking their ware from 1936-38 with a pacing leopard 'Frankoma' mark. These pieces are highly sought. The entire operation was destroyed by fire in 1938 and new molds were cast--some from surviving pieces--and a similar line of production was pursued.

The body of the ware was changed in 1954 from a honey tan to a red brick clay, and this, along with the color of the glazes (over forty have been used) helps determine the period of production.

A Southwestern theme has always been favored in design as well as in color selection. In 1965 they began to produce a limited edition series of Christmas plates, followed by a bottle vase series in 1969. Considered very collectible are their political mugs, bicentennial plates, Teenagers of the Bible plates, and the Wildfire series. Their ceramic Christmas cards are also very popular items with today's collectors.

Frankoma celebrated their 50th Anniversary in 1983. On September 26, of that same year, Frankoma was again destroyed by fire. Because of a fire-proof wall, master molds of all 1983 production items were saved, allowing plans for rebuilding to begin immediately. 'Grand Opening' was celebrated in July, 1984.

For a more thorough study of the subject, we recommend you refer to *Frankoma Treasures*, by Phyllis and Tom Bess; you will find their address in the Directory under Oklahoma. When no condition is indicated, the items listed below are assumed to be in mint condition.

Bowl Maker, Osage Brown, 5½″, $70.00.

Ash tray, Aztec, gr, #470 .... 7.50
Ash tray, Bronze Gr, #456 .... 6.00
Ash tray, clover shape, Flame, Sapulpa clay, #513 .... 2.00
Ash tray, Deco, Prairie Gr, #456 .... 10.00
Ash tray, dogwood, Flame, #477 .... 2.00
Ash tray, fish shape, Flame, #468 .... 7.50
Ash tray, fish shape, Flame, wht, blk, or gold, #78, ea 6.00
Ash tray, freeform, Peach Glow, #467 .... 5.00
Ash tray, leaf shape, Peach Glow, Sapulpa clay, #512 .... 5.00
Ash tray, Spaniel, Onyx, #460 .... 45.00
Baker, bean; Barrel, brn, Ada clay, #97V, 8 sm bakers, set 65.00
Baker/bean pot, Flame, #5V 6.00
Bank, cowboy boot, Flame 10.00
Bank, long-eared puppy, doorstop size, yel 30.00
Bean pot, eared hdls, w/lid, Prairie Gr, 8½″ 18.00
Bookend, charger, Desert Gold 52.00
Bookend, Irish Setter, Ada clay, Desert Gold, #430 .... 75.00
Bookend, seated figure, ivory, #425, leopard mk 175.00
Bookends, bronco, gr, pr 135.00
Bowl, gr, 'Frank Potteries,' 8″ 95.00
Bowl, leaf, Redbud, Ada clay, #226 .... 7.00
Bowl, mint; Desert Gold, #34, 1936 .... 25.00
Bowl, mint; w/panther mk, 9″ 50.00
Bowl, swan, Desert Gold, #288 .... 25.00
Candle holder, Oral Roberts, Desert Gold, pr 10.00
Candle holder/ash tray, Wagon Wheel, Ada clay, #454 .... 18.00
Christmas card, 1953 .... 65.00
Christmas card, 1957 .... 65.00
Christmas card, 1964 .... 45.00
Christmas card, 1972, 3 vases 15.00
Christmas card, 1974, butterfly 25.00
Christmas card, 1975, Year of the Potter 20.00
Christmas card, 1976, Bicentennial 15.00
Christmas card, 1978, Baby Jesus, wht, Grace Lee 75.00
Cornucopia, Desert Gold, #56 .... 25.00
Creamer, Guernsey, Desert Gold, #93A 15.00
Creamer & sugar, Wagon Wheel, gr, 4″ 8.00
Donkey mug, 1975, yel 15.00
Donkey mug, 1976, Centennial Red 15.00
Donkey mug, 1977, Carter & Mondale, Dusty Pink 15.00
Donkey mug, 1978, Woodland Moss 12.00
Donkey mug, 1979, Brn Satin 12.00
Elephant mug, 1968, Wht Sand 85.00
Elephant mug, 1969, Nixon & Agnew, Flame 65.00
Elephant mug, 1970, bl 45.00
Elephant mug, 1971, blk 60.00
Elephant mug, 1972, Prairie Gr 30.00
Elephant mug, 1973, Nixon & Agnew, Desert Gold 40.00
Elephant mug, 1974, Coffee 25.00
Elephant mug, 1975, Autumn Yel 20.00
Elephant mug, 1976, Centennial Red 15.00
Elephant mug, 1977, Dusty Pink 15.00
Elephant mug, 1978, Woodland Moss 12.00
Elephant mug, 1979, Brn Satin 12.00
Elephant mug, 1983, Wisteria 8.00
Flowerabrum, Prairie Gr, 1942 only 50.00
Flowerpot, Prairie Gr, fluted, #45 .... 16.00
Indian head, miniature, Autumn Yellow, #135 .... 7.50
Jar, Prairie Gr, #70 .... 35.00
Jug, Indian Bl, w/stopper, 1934-35, 3-cup 45.00
Jug, miniature, brn, Ada clay, #559S 5.00
Jug, Uncle Slug, brn 15.00
Lamp base, charger, Onyx 65.00
Mask, African woman/man, gunmetal, #124-25, leopard mk, pr .. 125.00
Mask, Indian head, Fawn Brn, #135, miniature 35.00
Mask, Indian head, Fawn Brn, 4½″ 50.00
Mask, Indian maid in headdress, 3-color, leopard mk, 4⅛″ 100.00
Medallion, turq, cowboy motif, 'Texas, 1936,' rpr, 1¾x2″ 110.00
Mug, US Postal Service ad on side, wht 6.50
Pansy ring, Onyx, Ada clay, 12″ 12.00
Pitcher, Aztec, gr, #551 .... 7.50
Pitcher, emb eagle, Clay Bl, #555 .... 12.00
Pitcher, emb eagle, Red Bud, #555 .... 12.00
Pitcher, juice; Guernsey, bl, #93, w/6 tumblers 50.00
Pitcher, juice; Guernsey, Red Bud, #93 .... 25.00
Pitcher, snail, blk, Ada clay, miniature 2.00
Pitcher, snail, Jade Bl, miniature 7.00
Pitcher, tea; w/lid, ivory, #94 .... 85.00
Pitcher, Wagon Wheel, Onyx, miniature 7.50
Pitcher, Wagon Wheel, Wht Sand, #94D 20.00
Planter, log; Prairie Gr, Ada clay, #9L 7.50
Plaque, Wiley Post, w/border, gr 175.00
Plaque, Will Rogers, Ada clay, borderless 45.00
Plaque, Will Rogers, w/border, gr 30.00
Plate, Bicentennial, 1973, wht 15.00
Plate, Bicentennial, 1975, wht 15.00
Plate, Bicentennial, 1976, wht 15.00
Plate, Christmas, 1965, wht 235.00
Plate, Christmas, 1966, wht 90.00
Plate, Christmas, 1967, wht 75.00
Plate, Christmas, 1983 .... 22.50
Plate, Easter, 1972, Oral Roberts, wht, 7½″ 10.00
Plate, Grace Madonna, brn, #1, 1977 .... 30.00
Plate, Madonna of Love, brn, #2, 1978 .... 30.00
Plate, Rose Madonna, brn, #3, 1981 .... 20.00
Plate, 50th Anniversary, Desert Gold, 1983 .... 35.00
Rose bowl, banana shape, Terra Cotta, Ada clay, #211 .... 18.00
Sculpture, Billiken, for Jester's Day, 1954 .... 75.00
Sculpture, coyote, Rubbed Bisque 20.00

Sculpture, Fan Dancer, Onyx, Ada clay, early 185.00
Sculpture, Fan Dancer, red clay, 1972 ....100.00
Sculpture, Gardner Boy & Girl, very early, set 150.00
Sculpture, Indian Chief, Brn Satin 15.00
Sculpture, Indian Maiden, Brn Satin 15.00
Sculpture, mare & colt, Rubbed Bisque 20.00
Sculpture, Peter Pan, flat back 45.00
Sculpture, squirrel, Rubbed Bisque 15.00
Sculpture, squirrel, wht 20.00
Shaker, teepee, Prairie Gr, #47, pr 10.00
Shakers, Barrel, Onyx, Ada clay, #92H, pr 15.00
Shakers, bull, gr, pr 45.00
Shakers, Guernsey, gr, pr 20.00
Shakers, puma, Desert Gold, pr 35.00
Starred boot, Royal Bl, Ada clay, #507, miniature 15.00
Sugar bowl, Wagon Wheel, #560 ....6.00
Swan, turq, open tail, #229, 9" L 50.00
Syrup pitcher, Desert Gold, #87D 15.00
Teapot, Aztec, Desert Gold or Prairie Gr, #7T, 1948-1971 ....15.00
Teapot, Plainsman, Brn Satin, lg 30.00
Teapot, Wagon Wheel, gr, 4¾" 12.00
Trivet, Bicentennial Flag, gr or blk, ea 8.00
Trivet, Cattlebrands, Flame 8.00
Trivet, Cherokee alphabet 8.00
Trivet, Mont Co Legal Secretaries, 1974, 6½" 25.00
Trivet, Will Rogers, Desert Gold 15.00
Vase, ball form, Silver Sage w/blk ft, #55 ....15.00
Vase, Bl-gr Jade, #500, leopard mk 35.00
Vase, bud; blk, Ada clay, #505 ....10.00
Vase, bud; Crocus, Prairie Gr, #43 ....10.00
Vase, bud; 4-lobe top, drapery, Cherokee Red, #29, 1930s 40.00
Vase, Cactus, Desert Gold, Ada clay, #206 ....22.00
Vase, Cactus, Prairie Gr, ftd disk w/relief scenic, #4 ....20.00
Vase, Cactus bloom, Prairie Gr, #5 ....35.00
Vase, carved jar, Desert Gold, #70 ....35.00
Vase, Chinese bottle, Royal Bl, #14 ....30.00
Vase, collector; V-1, Prairie Gr, 1969, 15" 65.00
Vase, collector; V-11-C, Coffee, wht w/in, 1979, 11½" 30.00
Vase, collector; V-13, blk w/Terra Cotta, 1981, 13" 30.00
Vase, collector; V-15, Flame & blk, 1983 ....35.00
Vase, collector; V-2, turq, 1970, 12" 50.00
Vase, collector; V-3, red & blk, 1971, 12" 65.00
Vase, collector; V-4, blk & Terra Cotta, 1972 ....60.00
Vase, collector; V-5, Flame, 1973, 13" 60.00
Vase, collector; V-6, Celadon, 1974, 13" 70.00
Vase, collector; V-7, Desert Gold & Coffee, 1975, 13" 50.00
Vase, collector; V-8, Freedom Red & Wht, 1976 ....60.00
Vase, collector; V-9, wht w/blk base & stopper, 1977 ....50.00
Vase, cross, wht, #804 ....15.00
Vase, Fawn Brn, #501, leopard mk 35.00
Vase, flying goose, Desert Gold, Ada clay, #60B 12.00
Vase, flying goose, Red Bud, #60B 15.00
Vase, Gracetone, Orbit pattern, w/pedestal, pink, #106P 15.00
Vase, Gracetone, sq pillow, brn, #68 ....5.00
Vase, leaf hdl, bl, #71 ....48.00
Vase, modeled wheat, Prairie Gr, Ada Clay, #74 ....22.00
Vase, Peach Glow, 9½" 8.00
Vase, ram's head, Desert Gold, #38, sm 25.00
Vase, ram's head, Prairie Gr, #38, sm 25.00
Vase, spiral carved, Prairie Gr, #73 ....45.00
Vase, thunderbird canteen, Flame, #59 ....8.00
Vase, Wagon Wheel, blk, #94 ....15.00
Vase, Wagon Wheel, Clay Bl, Ada clay, #510 ....10.00
Vase, Wagon Wheel, gold or gr, #510, ea 7.50
Vase, Wagon Wheel, mottled turq, Ada clay, #94 ....15.00
Wall pocket, Acorn, gr, Ada clay, #190 ....15.00
Wall pocket, Acorn, gr, Sapulpa clay, #190 ....6.00
Wall pocket, Boot, Woodland Moss, #133 ....9.00
Wall pocket, Phoebe, Desert Gold, #130 ....35.00
Wall pocket, Phoebe, Prairie Gr, #730 ....45.00
Wall pocket, Wagon Wheel, Prairie Gr, #94Y 20.00

Fraternal Organizations

Fraternal memorabilia is a vast and varied field. Emblems representing the various organizations have been used to decorate cups, shaving mugs, plates, and glassware. Medals, swords, documents, and other ceremonial paraphernalia from the 1800s and early 1900s are especially prized.

When no condition is indicated, the items listed below are assumed to be in excellent condition.

Elks

Cigar cutter & match safe 20.00
Fob, dbl elks tooth, w/elk 35.00
Lap robe, 51x71" 150.00
Mug, BPOE, Koken, name in gold 95.00
Pin-back, elks/turtles/bird, CD Kenny 10.00
Pin-back, w/celluloid elk on ribbon, 1916, 2x2" 15.00
Plate, elk, porcelain, 10" 12.00
Plate, Grand Lodge Reunion, Philadelphia, tin, July 1907 ....50.00
Stein, beige/gr, BPOE, Detroit, Elk's Temple Court House 60.00

Masons

Masonic apron, white silk printed with trumpeting angels and figures of two gentlemen in green waistcoats and Masonic medals, ca 1815, in 18" x 14" frame, $1,600.00.

Apron, HP doeskin, 1800s....110.00
Champagne, alligators, Neptune, New Orleans, 1910....45.00
Cuff link, 10k gold....12.50
Cup, Niagara Falls, raised gold beading, 3 saber hdls, 4″....75.00
Cup plate, lt bl transfer w/gilt rim, lists names, 1870....65.00
Fob, carnelian eng w/emblem, bk: eng bloodstone, 9k fr....135.00
Knife, pocket; 10k gold....85.00
Locket, gold color w/eng designs, dtd 1896, 1¼″....25.00
Mug, creamware w/mc 'Delft' woman, sponged trees, 1805, 9″..350.00
Mug, Indian head in relief, mk Saratoga, 1903, glass....95.00
Plate, camels/desert scene, Shenango....45.00
Pocket knife, pewter....35.00
Sign, wood w/applied letters: Masonic Hall, ½-circle, 72″....275.00
Spoon, combination, sterling, scarce....68.00
Square & compass, carved wood, 6x6″....35.00
Walking stick, compass/sq/G symbol carving, folk art, 27″....85.00
Wine glass, ruby, St Paul in relief, 2 gold saber hdls....70.00

Shrine

Champagne, alligator hdls, Pittsburgh/New Orleans, 1910....50.00
Cup, orange, in crystal saucer, Los Angeles, 1906....35.00
Cup, sword hdl, Niagara Falls, 1915....45.00
Loving cup, 3 scimitars, hdl, Niagara Falls, 1905....40.00
Mug, Indian, Saratoga, 1903....35.00
Pin, sm diamonds, mk by jeweler, dtd, 1¾″....75.00
Toothpick holder, Pittsburgh Syria Temple, clear, pink base....85.00

Miscellaneous

Eastern Star, teaspoon....25.00
Odd Fellows, graveside flag holder, CI, Pat 1901, 28½″....115.00
Odd Fellows, shovel, emb scales, hand emblem, brass, sm....15.00
Pythias, goblet, gr, 1900....28.00

Fraunfelter

Charles Fraunfelter organized his company in Zanesville, Ohio, in 1915. It was known as the Ohio Pottery Company until 1923. During this period their main product was a line of utilitarian articles for chemical laboratories made of hard paste porcelain. In 1918 they used the same body to produce a brown and white line called 'Petrascan.' By 1920 a line of hotel ware was added. The company organized in 1923 and became known as the Fraunfelter China Company; but after the death of Fraunfelter in 1925, the business fell into hard times and eventually closed altogether in 1939.

When no condition is indicated, the items listed below are assumed to be in mint condition.

Pitcher, jug; cream & yel w/silver bands, hdl, 7-cup....40.00
Teapot, gr/wht, flat lid, 3″....15.00

Fruit Jars

As early as 1829, canning jars were being manufactured for use in the home preservation of foodstuffs. For the past fifteen years, they have been sought as popular collectibles. At the last estimate, over four thousand fruit jars and variations were known to exist. Some are very rare, perhaps one-of-a-kind examples, known to have survived to the present day. Among the most valuable are the black glass jars, the amber Van Vliet, and the cobalt Millville. These often bring prices in excess of $1,500.00 when they can be found. Aside from condition, values are based on age, rarity, and special features.

When no condition is indicated, the items listed below are assumed to be in mint condition.

Atlas, Mason Fruit Jar, aqua, qt....6.00
Atlas, Mason Improved Patented, lt bl, pt....8.00
Atlas, Mason's Patent Nov 30, 1858, sky bl, ½-gal....19.00
Atlas, Strong Shoulder Mason, lt bl, pt....8.00
Atlas E-Z Seal, smooth lip, olive, no bail, qt....19.00
Atlas Strong Shoulder Mason, gr, ½-gal....15.00
Atlas Strong Shoulder Mason, lt bl, qt....19.00
Atlas Strong Shoulder Mason, olive, pt....20.00
Ball, block letters, aqua, pt....10.00
Ball (script), pat apl'd for, no lid, aqua, qt....50.00
Ball (script) Mason's Patent 1858, aqua, qt....5.00
Ball (script) Mason's Patent 1858, aqua, ½-gal....11.00
Ball Perfect Mason, Ball underlined, amber, ½-gal....25.00
Ball Sure Seal, Ball underlined, clear, pt....5.00
BBGM Co, monogram variation, aqua, qt....30.00
BBGM Co, monogram variation, aqua, ½-gal....40.00
Best (script) Fruit Keeper, aqua, lip chip/no clamp, qt....35.00
Clark's Peerless, aqua, pt....12.00
Clarke Fruit Jar Co Fruit Jar, orig closure, aqua, qt....50.00
Cohansey, aqua, ½-gal....25.00
Crown, crown emblem, aqua, qt....5.00
Crown, crown emblem, clear, pt....12.00
Crown, Made in Canada, crown emblem, clear, pt....5.00
Crown Cordial & Extract Co, New York, clear, ½-gal....12.00
Crystal Jar, clear, qt....30.00
Daisy, FE Ward & Co in circle, aqua, pt....10.00
Double Safety, clear, qt....5.00
Double Safety, Smalley, Kivlan & Onthank, clear, pt....5.00
Drey Perfect Mason, clear, pt....5.00
EG Co Imperial, crown, aqua, ½-gal....18.00
Empire, within stippled cross in fr, clear, pt....10.00
Everlasting Jar, word 'Jar' in flag, aqua, pt....20.00
Flaccus Bros Steers Head Fruit Jar, no lid, clear, pt....50.00
Gem, w/cross, aqua, midget....20.00
Gem, w/cross, aqua, qt....10.00
Genuine Boyd's Mason, aqua, qt....6.00
Globe, aqua, qt....15.00
Green Mountain CA Co, in circle, no bail, aqua, pt....15.00
Haines' #3 Patent March 1st 1870, w/closure, gr-aqua, qt....80.00
Haserot Co, Mason Patent, Cleveland, aqua, qt....15.00
Hazel Atlas E-Z Seal, w/ghost 'lightning,' aqua, qt....10.00
Hero, name above cross, wire bail, aqua, pt....35.00
HGW, monogram on bk, aqua, qt....12.00
Hom-Pak Mason, clear, qt....4.00
Honest Mason Jar, Patent 1858, clear, qt....15.00
HW Pettit, base: Westville, NJ, aqua, ½-gal....12.00
King, on stippled banner below crown, clear, pt....12.00
King, on stippled banner below crown, clear, qt....12.00
Legrand Ideal Vacuum Jar, repro closure, aqua, qt....80.00
Leotric, aqua, pt....10.00
Leotric, name in circle, aqua, qt....8.00
Lockport Mason Improved, aqua, pt....6.00
Magic (star) Fruit Jar, no clamp, aqua, qt....100.00
Marion Jar, Mason's Patent Nov 30 1858, aqua, pt....35.00
Marion Jar, Mason's Patent Nov 30 1858, aqua, ½-gal....12.00
Mason, Keystone in circle, aqua, qt....10.00
Mason, Keystone in circle, aqua, ½-gal....10.00
Mason, script, underlined, clear, qt....6.00
Mason, w/sq shepherd's crook, underlined, aqua, qt....6.00
Mason Fruit Jar, Keystone, pat Nov 30 1858, aqua, qt....12.00
Mason's CFJ Co Improved, aqua, midget....15.00

Mason's CFJ Co Improved, Clyde, NY on bk, aqua, midget......30.00
Mason's CFJ Co Patent Nov 30 1858, no lid, aqua, midget......10.00
Mason's Crystal Jar, clear, qt.............................30.00
Mason's Improved, shield emblem on bk, aqua, qt..............8.00
Mason's Improved Patented, aqua, pt........................8.00
Mason's Improved Trade Mark, CFJ Co on bk, aqua, midget....18.00
Mason's Patent Nov 30 1858, Christmas Mason, aqua, pt.......50.00
Mason's Patent Nov 30 1858, Crescent Moon/Star, aqua, ½-gal..70.00
Mason's Patent Nov 30 1858, cross on bk, aqua, midget........15.00
Mason's Patent Nov 30 1858, Crowleytown seal, aqua, qt, M...150.00
Mason's Patent Nov 30 1858, w/reversed Ns, aqua, qt..........15.00
Mason's SG Co Patent Nov 30 1858, aqua, qt.................8.00
Mason's 2 Patent Nov 30 1858, aqua, ½-gal..................10.00
Mason's 5 Patent Nov 30 1858, aqua, qt.....................10.00
Mason's 8 Patent Nov 30 1858, aqua, qt.....................12.00
Millville Atmospheric Fruit Jar, aqua, no lid/clamp, ½-gal.......25.00
Millville Atmospheric Fruit Jar, aqua, qt......................25.00
Moore's Patent Fruit Jar, no clamp, aqua, qt.................35.00
P Lorillard Co, name on base, amber, qt.....................15.00
Pearl, aqua, qt..30.00
Pearl, aqua, ½-gal.......................................35.00
Protector, no lid, aqua, qt................................40.00
Queen, circle: Pat Dec 28 1858 Pat June 16 1868, aqua, qt.....35.00
Queen, Queen Jar Patented Nov 2 1869, no band, aqua, qt.....18.00
RE Tongue & Bros Co Inc, aqua lustre, qt...................10.00
Red (over key) Mason's Patent Nov 30 1858, aqua, qt..........10.00
Red (superimposed over key) Mason, aqua, pt.................8.00
Root Mason, olive, ½-gal...................................48.00
Royal (below crown) Trade Mark Full Measure Reg Qt, amber...64.00
Royal (superimposed on crown) Trade Mark, clear, pt...........6.00
Safety, wide mouth, Mason, Salem Glass Works, aqua, qt.......15.00
Safety Valve Pat May 21 1895, over triangle, clear, ½-pt........15.00
Schram Automatic Sealer, script, clear, pt....................10.00
Schram Automatic Sealer, script, no wire, clear, qt...........10.00
Simplex, name within diamond on front, clear, pt.............12.00
SKO Queen, wide mouth adjustable, smooth lip, clear, qt........5.00
Smalley Full Measure AGS, clear, qt.........................10.00
Smalley's Nu-Seal Trade Mark, name in diamonds, clear, pt.....10.00
Standard, W McCully & Co on bk, sky bl, lip chips, qt........100.00
Telephone Jar, Trade Mk Reg Whitney Glass Works, aqua, qt...10.00
Trade Mark Banner, WM Warranted in circle, aqua, qt..........8.00
Trade Mark Banner Reg US Pat Office, widemouth, aqua, qt....10.00
Trade Mark Bee Hive, emb bees & hive, clear, midget........300.00
Trade Mark Keystone Registered, clear, qt...................10.00
Trade Mark Lightning, lt yel-amber, qt......................50.00
Trade Mark Lightning, Putnam on base, amber, pt.............75.00
Trade Mark The Dandy, clear, qt.........................35.00
Union #1, Beaver Falls Glass Co, lip chip, aqua, qt............40.00
Victory in shield, The Victory Jar on lid, clear, qt.............10.00
Wears Jar, name in circle, w/Improved on neck, clear, qt.......12.00
White Crown Mason, within fr, aqua, ½-gal....................8.00
Whitney Mason Patented 1858, 3 dots below Mason, aqua, qt....8.00
Whitney Mason Patented 1858, 4 dots below Mason, aqua, pt...12.00

Fry

Henry Fry established his glassworks in 1901 in Rochester, Pennsylvania. There, until 1933 when it was sold to the Libbey Company, he produced glassware of the finest quality. In the early years they produced beautiful cut glass, and when it began to wane in popularity, Fry turned to the manufacture of occasional pieces and oven glassware. He is perhaps most famous for the opalescent pearl glass called 'Foval.' It was made in combination with crystal or colored trim, and because it was in production for only a short time in 1926 and 1927, it is hard to find.

Collectors of depression era glassware look for the opalescent reamers and opaque green kitchenware made during the early thirties.

When no condition is indicated, the items listed below are assumed to be in mint condition.

Basket, Foval, cobalt bl hdl, no mk, 7½x7″..................285.00
Candy dish, opal swirl, ring stem, 12″......................135.00
Casserole, Foval, w/lid, May 27, 1919, 1½-qt..................30.00
Compote, daisy/button cuttings, ped ft, oval, 8x12x8½″........180.00
Cruet, Foval, cobalt stopper & hdl, unsgn...................285.00
Cup & saucer, Foval, gr.................................85.00
Juicer, heat resistant, 6½″...............................15.00
Luncheon set, Foval, Delft bl trim, rare, 16-pc...............495.00
Pitcher, clear craquelle w/gr hdl, ground pontil, water sz.......85.00
Pitcher, Foval, cobalt hdl, w/lid, lemonade, 10½″.............150.00
Rose bowl, brilliant cut on standard, sgn, 6x7″..............250.00
Vase, crackle glass, applied bl rosettes, flared, 8½″...........135.00
Vase, Foval, blk amethyst stem, ftd, ovoid, 11½″.............250.00
Vase, Foval, cone shape, jade base, 10″....................175.00
Vase, Jack-in-Pulpit, bl spiral w/bl band on rim, sgn, 11″......150.00

Fulper

The Fulper Pottery was founded in 1899 after nearly a century of producing utilitarian stoneware under various titles and managements. Not until 1909 did Fulper venture into the art pottery field. Vasekraft, their first art line, utilized the same heavy clay body used for their utility ware. Shapes were severe, unadorned, and rather ungraceful. But the glazes they developed were used with such flair and imagination, alone and in unexpected combined harmony, that each piece was truly a work of art. In contrast to the Vasekraft line, graceful Oriental shapes were produced to compliment the important 'famille rose' glaze developed by W.H. Fulper, Jr. Other designs were developed with an Art Deco influence.

During WWI, doll's heads and Kewpies were made as a substitute for imports. Figural perfume lamps and powder boxes were made both in bisque and glazed ware. Although the plant was in operation until 1935, the most prized examples pre-date 1930. Much of the ware was marked with a vertical 'Fulper' in line reserve, although a horizontal mark as well as a 'Vasekraft' paper label was also used.

When no condition is indicated, the items listed below are assumed to be in mint condition.

Ash tray, lava gr...50.00
Bottle, music, olive w/silver overlay sport views, 3-sided........120.00
Bottle, pinch sides, dk bl/silver gray flambe, 7¾″.............85.00

Powder jar, figural top, 6¾″, $125.00.

Bowl, bl flambe/ivory, ftd, 3x7″ 100.00
Bowl, bl/gr lustre w/brn, cream flambe w/in, Prang, 3x6″ 65.00
Bowl, copper gr flambe on gr matt, brn w/in, line band, 9″ 95.00
Bowl, effigy; 3-figure support, bl/brn, 7¾x10½″ 350.00
Bowl, gr/bl/yel crystalline on mustard, 3½x10″ 225.00
Bowl, ivory/yel/brn/bl crystalline drip on mustard, 4x10″ 225.00
Bowl, matt bl w/bl & gr crystalline drip, 3x6½″ 50.00
Bowl, olive-gr crystalline, 16″ 115.00
Bowl, purple drip over rose, flambe w/in, 2x9½″ 45.00
Bowl, rolled edge, drip glaze trim, tan/bl, 2½x7½″ 48.00
Bowl, wht matt w/bl/brn-gr crystalline drip, 3x7½″ 60.00
Bowl vase, famille rose, 5½″ 85.00
Bud vase, bl crystalline, stick body/wide ft, 8″ 38.00
Bud vase, brn over bl, 4-ftd, 8″ 55.00
Bud vase, gr matt w/crystalline drip, 4-point base, 8¾″ 50.00
Bud vase, purple w/gr & cream crystalline, sq, 8½″ 50.00
Bud vase, verte antique gr matt, 5¾x2¼″ 45.00
Candle holder, aqua, 7x2″, pr 45.00
Candle holder, brn gloss/rust/bl touches/pointed hdl, 2½″ 30.00
Chamberstick, pink matt, shield bk w/hdl, 7½″ 70.00
Flower frog, bl crystalline, tulip form, 8x6″ at top 40.00
Flower jar, crystalline olive, 3½″ 40.00
Frog, lily pad, blk/gr 18.00
Jar, bl/gr, #452 .... 65.00
Jardiniere, caramel/blk gloss, 3 hdls above rim, 4″ 85.00
Jug, feathered gr to dk gr matt/semi-gloss, Vasekraft, 12″ 550.00
Jug, grapevine, silver deposit on bl, w/music box, 15½″ 190.00
Jug, metallic glaze, w/music box 150.00
Lamp, perfume; ballerina, M 125.00
Lamp, perfume; Dutch girl w/hat holds skirt out, 7¾″ 225.00
Lamp base, famille rose, 4 hdls, ringed, 11x6″ 120.00
Mug, cucumber glaze, pr 82.00
Mug, semi-gloss purple/rose glaze, squat, lg hdls, mk 95.00
Mug, speckled mustard matt 40.00
Planter, bl-gr streaks/wht drip on tan mirror, belted, 4x7″ 55.00
Stein, metal top, brn/gray/yel flambe 140.00
Tankard, wht crystalline flambe over famille rose base 225.00
Vase, bl, 2¾″ 25.00
Vase, bl crystalline glaze, rim hdls, rare, 3″ 78.00
Vase, bl crystalline over brn, ovoid, 5¼″ 145.00
Vase, bl flambe, ovoid, 5″ 75.00
Vase, bl flambe over gr, swelled cylinder, 10½″ 300.00
Vase, bl flambe w/brn at top/neck, ovoid, 6″ 90.00
Vase, bl gloss on brn, emb brn bosses at shoulder, 7″ 150.00
Vase, bl gloss on chocolate brn, #017, 4″ 55.00
Vase, bl gloss w/gr matt top & on sides, 5″ 40.00
Vase, bl matt w/heavy dripping, rnd, 3 rim hdls, 6½″ 60.00
Vase, bl semi-matt w/brn touches, sq Deco hdls, 4½x6″ 35.00
Vase, bl wisteria crystalline, lion's head hdls, 6″ 95.00
Vase, bl/brn flambe w/gr in middle section, 10″ 325.00
Vase, bl/gr crystalline, bulbous w/rim-to-width hdls, 6x7″ 480.00
Vase, bl/gr crystalline on wht/lt gr, collar rings, 8¾″ 225.00
Vase, bl/gr crystalline, 4 Nouveau motifs, bulb base, 8″ 225.00
Vase, bl/gr flambe/bl crystalline, Arts & Crafts, 7½x10½″ 395.00
Vase, bl/gray crystalline drip on pink, bottle form, 8″ 100.00
Vase, blk gloss, 4 molded drips down sides, 4½″ 85.00
Vase, blk mottle over gr, hand-thrown, w/hdls, 8¾″ 100.00
Vase, blk to copper flambe, incised mk, 11x10″ 550.00
Vase, blk/brn/caramel flambe, 4″ 45.00
Vase, brn through bl, rnd w/sq rim-to-width hdls, 6½x7″ 120.00
Vase, brn w/gr/blk splotches, hand-thrown, 3-hdl, 6″ 45.00
Vase, caramel/rust crystalline, 4 hdls under rim, 6½″ 350.00
Vase, copper dust, #572A, 9½″ 275.00
Vase, dk bl crystalline, sq stick w/sq base, 12″ 90.00
Vase, dk bl/lt bl/cream to brn, 3 hdls, 6¾″ 225.00
Vase, famille rose top over gr matt w/brn flecks, hdls, 6″ 120.00
Vase, famille rose w/gr/bl/red crystalline, 6¾″ 175.00
Vase, fan; butterscotch mirror/flambe blk crystalline top 175.00
Vase, gr crystalline, melon shape, incurvate top, 4¼″ 125.00
Vase, gr crystalline texture, hdld urn form, 12x11″ 300.00
Vase, gr crystalline w/heavy crystals, ogee w/hdls, 5¾″ 95.00
Vase, gr crystalline w/heavy crystals, 7¾″ 125.00
Vase, gr crystalline/yel touches, bar hdls under rim, 6¾″ 145.00
Vase, gr flambe w/brn, rolled quatralobe top, 6¾″ 80.00
Vase, gr flambe w/brn drip, 4″ 40.00
Vase, gr flambe w/mirror blk over-drip, 5″ 125.00
Vase, gr flambe/drip, vertical relief, compressed base, 8″ 155.00
Vase, gr gloss w/brn/blk 'stripes,' concave sides, 9½″ 100.00
Vase, gr gloss w/lav/gray drip, bulbous, sm rim hdls, 7″ 185.00
Vase, gr matt crystalline on lt gr gloss, 12½″ 135.00
Vase, gr matt w/brn/bl flecks, sq w/flare at bottom, 8″ 85.00
Vase, gr w/blk drip, bulbous, rim-to-shoulder hdls, 7½″ 175.00
Vase, gr/blk/brn glaze/stripe effect, trumpet form, 9½″ 120.00
Vase, gr/brn/lt yel mirror finish, 6″ 145.00
Vase, gun metal blk, 6½″ 265.00
Vase, ivory flambe on bl/brn, short collar/full body, 9″ 165.00
Vase, ivory flambe w/dk brn, 7-sided cylinder, 8¾″ 90.00
Vase, leopard skin, 6½″ 175.00
Vase, leopard skin w/blk/silver crystals on gr, hdls, 5x6″ 185.00
Vase, lt gr/gold crystalline, 4-panel, 8½″ 100.00
Vase, maroon, spiral form, ft ring, 3-hdls, sgn, 6x8″ 65.00
Vase, matt gr w/dk gunmetal spotting, full body, 9½″ 160.00
Vase, med bl flambe, cobalt crystals, 6½″ 110.00
Vase, metallic lustre, brn/purple on cream, 7-sided, 9″ 150.00
Vase, mirror bl/gr flambe, 7″ 225.00
Vase, mirror blk, bulbous Chinese form, collar neck, 9½″ 400.00
Vase, mission matt brn, 3-ftd, 5″ 90.00
Vase, moss to rose, Chinese, 10x8¾″ 225.00
Vase, orchid, 12½″ 75.00
Vase, purple blend, Chinese, hdls, 5″ 65.00
Vase, red matt, waisted top w/str hdls, angle shoulder, 7″ 90.00
Vase, red w/bl/purple drip, flared, incurvate sides, 6″ 40.00
Vase, red w/gray/bl touches, 8″ 100.00
Vase, rose, bulbous, sm hdls, 7″ 225.00
Vase, rust/dk bl w/purple base, wht overall drip, 6¾″ 85.00
Vase, tan/grn/gunmetal crystalline, w/hdls, 3x3¾″ 75.00
Vase, volcanic bl, #642 .... 65.00
Vase, yel flambe w/blk/brn top, slim/flared, sq hdls, 11″ 180.00
Vase, yel w/brn runs, bl touches, str sides, 9″ 195.00
Vase, yel/pink/gr w/blk drip, sm sqs at neck, 8 sides, 7½″ 195.00
Wall pocket, bl flecked matt, 6 tubes meet at base, 10¾″ 160.00

Furniture

From the cabinetmaker's shop of the early 1800s, with apprentices and journeymen who learned every phase of the craft at the side of the master carpenter, the trade had evolved by the mid-century to one with steam-powered saws and turning lathes and workers who specialized in only one operation.

By 1870 the Industrial Revolution was in progress and large factories in the East and Midwest turned out increasingly elaborate styles, ornately machine carved and heavily inlaid. Rococo, Egyptian, and Renaissance Revival furniture lent themselves well to factory production. Eastlake offered a welcome respite from Victorian frumpery, and a return to quality handcrafting. All of these styles remained popular until the turn of the century.

As early as 1880, factories began using oak; early mail-order catalogs offered oak funiture, simply styled and lighter in weight, since long distance shipping was often a factor. Mission, or Craftsman, a style introduced around 1890, was simple to the extreme. Stickley and Hubbard were two of its leading designers. Other popular Victorian styles were Colonial Revival, Cottage, Bentwood, and Windsor. Prices are as variable as the styles.

When no condition is indicated, the items listed below are assumed to be in excellent condition.

Key:

Am—American	grpt—grainpaint
brd—board	hdbd—headboard
c&b—claw and ball	hdw—hardware
Chpndl—Chippendale	Hplwht—Hepplewhite
Co—Country	NE—New England
do—door	ped—pediment
drw—drawer	pt—part
Emp—Empire	QA—Queen Anne
Fr—French	trn—turning
ftbd—footboard	Vict—Victorian
Geo—Georgian	W/M—William and Mary

/—over (example: 1 do/2 drw—one door over two drawers)

Bed

Brass, tester, spindles, medallions, 108″....................1,320.00
Co, sq posts, cut-out finials, peaked hdbd, rpl rails, 38″.......550.00
Curly maple, Fed, sq hd posts/reed ft posts, 1815, 64″......2,600.00
Curly maple, Fed, trn ft/hd posts, shaped hdbd, 1830, 60″...1,550.00
Iron & brass, ½-rnd hd/ftbd w/ornate scrolls, 70x68″.........1,200.00
Mahog, Chpndl, pineapple finials/reeded posts, 1775, 89″ H..8,000.00
Rope, curly maple/walnut/poplar, cannon balls, rfn, 52″.......700.00
Rope, maple/pine, trn ftpost, sq hdposts, not period..........450.00
Rope, old red, trn posts/ft/finials on ftbd, 32x54x68″.........580.00
Rope, poplar, tall trn posts/urn finials, mattress: 68x53″.......675.00
Rope, youth, poplar, sq chamfered posts, scrolled hd/ftbd......350.00
Stickley, G; #923, twin, arch crest rail/3 slats, decal.........1,500.00
Stickley, G; inlaid oak, arch hd/ftbd, tapered posts, 58″.....20,000.00
Walnut, Jenny Lind style, spindle hdbd, scalloped ftbd........175.00

Bench

Co Emp, trn legs/ball ft/plank seat/arrow bk, rpt, 75″.........325.00
Hardwood, shoe ft, mortised, cut-out ends, rpr/crack, 68″......255.00
Kneeling, birch, 4 short trn legs, primitive, rfn, 41″ L.........45.00
Mammy's, trn legs/spindles, curved arms, baby guard, 61″.....650.00
Orig bl pnt, NY, 1870s, 9½x43″..........................150.00
Pine, cut-out ends w/star, renailed, rpt, 17½x10x24″..........115.00
Pine, cut-out ft, 4 diagonal braces, gr pnt worn, 17x64″.......125.00
Pine, cut-out legs mortised through top, 18½x90x11″.........110.00
Pine, mortised, rake legs, PA, 1820-30, 16x12x48″...........325.00
Pine, mortised cut-out ft, old worn pnt, rpr/rpl, 19x84″........95.00
Pine, primitive, weathered rpt, 17x60″......................55.00
Poplar, low scallop apron, panel front, head rest end, 73″.....375.00
Primitive, plank seat, splay whittled legs, pnt, 21x27″..........30.00
Rocking, ½-arrow spindles, stencil decor, w/arms, 58″.........635.00
Settle, Co Emp, arrow bk, bulbous arm support, rpt, 76″......375.00
Settle, trn legs/plank seat/scroll arms/vase splats, 82″.........400.00
Stickley, G; #205, 6 bk slats, spring cushion, decal, 56″.....1,500.00
Stickley, G; #222, settle, red decal, 79″...................4,500.00
Stickley, G; piano, cut-out hdls on solid sides, #217..........950.00
Stickley, L&JG; #220, settle, wide flat arms & crest rail......6,500.00
Stickley, L&JG; #275, panel-side settle, unsgn, rst, 84″......1,600.00
Water, poplar, single brd ends/shelves/curve crest, 31x26″.....350.00
Water, poplar, worn gray pnt/weathered, 24x28″.............150.00
Water, primitive, cut-out ends/inset shelf, weathered, 33″......115.00
Windsor, bow bk, scroll arms/trn supports/stretcher, 68″ L...1,650.00
Windsor, fan bk, early 20th C reproduction, 79″ L...........850.00
Windsor, removable baby rail, orig floral/stripes, 35″ L......1,200.00

Bookcase

Mahog, gilt mt, Emp style, 3 arched mullioned do, 55x75″...1,200.00
Quaint, earred crest on rectangle, 2 glass do, 60x62″.........375.00
Stickley, G; 12 glazed panel do, lg red decal, 56x48″.........3,500.00
Stickley, L&JG; gallery/2 mullioned do, #645, decal sgn......1,800.00
Stickley, L&JG; 2 sliding do/glass panel/arch apron, 54x36″..1,200.00

Bureau

Bachelor's, walnut, Chpndl, writing slide, 1770, 32x32″......7,500.00
Bird's eye maple/cherry, Country Fed, NE, ca 1815............440.00
Cherry, Chpndl, 3 short/2 med/5 grad drw, orig hdw, 73″....3,500.00
Cherry, Chpndl, 4 grad drw, fluted ¼-columns, rfn/rpr, 32″...1,800.00
Cherry, Hplwht, line inlay, 4 drw, scallop apron, rfn/rpl........650.00
Curly maple/inlay, Chpndl, bracket ft, 1790, rpr, 48x36″.....2,500.00
Figured maple, Fed, oblong top bow front, ca 1815/NE, 38″..1,320.00
Mahog, Chpndl, 4 cockbead/grad drw, 1785/NY, 38x43″.....1,210.00
Mahog, Emp, bow front, rope/leaf pilasters, 3 sm top drw/4...1,250.00

Bureau, late Empire, mahogany with carved panel document drawer over two longer drawers, curved stiles above base drawer, bracket feet, 48″ x 44″ x 20″, $450.00.

Mahog, Fed, bow front, 4 drw, splay bracket ft, 1800, 38″...1,760.00
Mahog veneer, Fed, bow front, rope pilasters, rfn/rpr, 38″.....925.00
Mahog/cherry inlay, Fed, bow front/4 drw, 1800, 40x39″.....2,090.00
Mahog/flame veneer, Emp, overhang drw/leaf pilasters, 40″.....225.00
Maple w/orig red, 5 drw, bracket ft, rpl hdw, 44x40″........2,525.00
Stickely, G; #906, vertical strap hdw & ring hdls, 42″.........800.00
Walnut, Chpndl, cornice projects, 2 short/5 drw, rstr, 60″....1,980.00
Walnut, Chpndl, fluted ¼-columns, shell/c/b ft, rpl, 42″......2,090.00

Cabinet

Bar, walnut, German, marble lined, marble slide, 48x51″......525.00
China, oak, bent glass, claw ft, 5 shelves, 70x30″............450.00

Corner, scroll bamboo & lacquer, triangle base shelf, 66"......385.00
Curio, gilt bronze mt, Vernis Martin, ca 1900, 54x25"........770.00
Curio, gilt wood, Louis XV style, oval top/glass, 42"..........660.00
Curio, maple, Regency style, marble top/brass gallery, 55".....850.00
Curio, Vernis Martin type, dbl do w/HP, serpentine, 55".......750.00
Lacquered, Fr, cylinder w/mirror atop, 1 do, 32x15"..........700.00
Mahog, 3 levels, 3 do+open shelving, Mercier Freres, 65"...3,740.00
Side, gilt/bronze mt ebony/tulipwood inlay, Napoleon III.......935.00
Wright, Frank L; mahog, 2 do w/applied sqs, low stand, 26"...715.00

Candlestand

Cherry/poplar, Co, tilt top, cut-out X base, trn column........225.00
Mahog, tilt top, 2-pc column, 18" 1-brd top w/edge inlay......250.00
Maple top: 15" dia, various hardwood parts, trn splay legs.....150.00
Primitive, tripod w/cut-out legs, 12x17" hex top, red pnt......925.00
Windsor, all wood, 2-socket candle arm, rpt/rpr, 32"..........375.00
Windsor, 16" dia top, octagon base w/trn tripod & std, pnt....700.00

Chair

Arm, Co Hplwht wingbk, mahog legs, uphl, rpr..................300.00
Arm, curly maple, QA, trn/carved, rush seat, 1740/PA, rstr.....935.00
Arm, lady's; Louis XV-style, chintz uphl, EX..................450.00
Arm, mahog, Chpndl, acanthus crest/beaker splat, ca 1780...1,430.00
Arm, mahog, Chpndl, pierced splat/volute hand holds, c/b ft..3,960.00
Arm, mahog, fancy urn w/plumed foliage bk, Victorian.........335.00
Arm, mahog, Fed, swag/tassel crest, uphl scroll arms, rstr....4,000.00
Arm, mahog, Geo-style, ornate carving, EX needlepoint seat....400.00
Arm, mahog, Hplwht, open splat/carved drapery, ornate.......500.00
Arm, mahog, Sheraton Transition, scroll arms, EX............225.00
Arm, oak w/inlay seagull panel/leather seat, Arts & Crafts......275.00
Arm, QA style, Centennial, orig seat/finish..................175.00
Arm, Sheraton style, cane seats/bks, blk/gold putti............500.00
Bannister bk, walnut/sausage trn/scroll arms, Centennial........135.00
Bannister bk side, curly maple posts, rfn/rpl rush seat.........275.00
Bannister bk side, maple, G trn, ornate crest, rpl seat.......1,950.00
Bannister bk side, split trn splats, sausage legs, rfn...........250.00
Bannister bk side, trn posts, split trn slats, rpt...............225.00
Captain's, Co, bentwood arms, rfn..........................40.00

Side chair, walnut, Queen Anne, Rhode Island, ca 1750s, $1,850.00.

Corner, mahog, Chpndl, pierced splats, 1770, rpr...........2,500.00
Corner, mahog, pierced splat sides/leaf carve knees, 1700s...1,900.00
Highchair, Co, 3 tapered dowel bk/thick seat, rpt/rpr, 33"......85.00
Highchair, ladderbk, trn arms/supports/finials, rush seat.......650.00
Ladderbk arm, Co, 4 slats, worn splint seat, arm rpr..........200.00
Ladderbk arm, G trn, leather seat, rpr/rpt...................100.00
Ladderbk arm, maple, pnt/trn, rockers removed, 1760..........110.00
Ladderbk arm, sausage trn/wide rpl rush seat/4 slats, rpr.....1,600.00
Ladderbk arm rocker, EX trn legs/posts/supports, 4 slat.......700.00
Ladderbk arm rocker, trn posts/arms, 4 slats, splint seat.......135.00
Ladderbk arm rocker, trn posts/mushroom arm finals, rpr......300.00
Ladderbk rocker, trn legs/posts, 6 slats, rpl rush seat.........425.00
Ladderbk side, worn rpt w/stencil, rpl splint seat..............65.00
Ladderbk side, 4 grad slats, trn finials, orig finish............175.00
Limbert, #1656, slat-side arm, branded, 41"..................300.00
Limbert, #517, adjustable, open arms, branded..............575.00
Maple, Co QA, Spanish ft/trn legs/shaped crest/rush seat.......650.00
Moravian, side, walnut, shaped bk w/cut-out hand hold, 36"....165.00
Potty, arms, orig red/blk graining w/yel decor, oversize........250.00
Rocker, bamboo trn, orig bamboo decor, new paper rush seat..135.00
Rocker, Boston, w/arms, brn pnt w/gold decor, worn...........85.00
Rocker, brn w/yel striping, freehand crest decor..............175.00
Rocker, oak, 5 vertical slats, open arms, att Stickley..........125.00
Rocker, red/blk grpt/stencil worn, writing arm, rpl rocker......300.00
Rocker, spindle bk rabbit ear, re-decor fruit/flowers, EX.......100.00
Side, arrow bk, orig mc decor on crest & seat, pr..............250.00
Side, birch, Co QA, trn legs/Spanish ft/rush seat, rpr/rfn.......540.00
Side, cherry, Co Chpndl, EX pierced splat/carved ears, EX...1,050.00
Side, cherry, Co QA, unusual stylized details, Spanish ft.....2,000.00
Side, Chinese Chpndl, uphl on mahog fr, fretwork brackets...1,400.00
Side, Co, arrow bk, rfn, pr................................170.00
Side, Co QA, trn legs/stretcher, carve ear crest, rpl seat.......425.00
Side, Co QA, trn posts/worn orig rush seat/vase splat, rfn......145.00
Side, curly maple, classical revival, rpl cane seat, rfn..........200.00
Side, decor PA, plank seat/trn legs/vase splat/wing crest.......150.00
Side, giltwood, Louis XVI style, pr.........................605.00
Side, mahog, Chpndl, Gothic splats, scroll head rail, pr......1,000.00
Side, mahog, Chpndl, ribbon bk, rpr........................200.00
Side, mahog, Duncan Phyfe type, carved slat, rpr, no seat.....250.00
Side, mahog, Geo, shield bk, late 18th C, rfn/re-uphl, pr......400.00
Side, mahog, QA, simple crest, cabriole legs/duck ft, rpr........350.00
Side, maple, Country QA, bulb trn legs, shaped crest.........500.00
Side, maple, QA, trn/carved, Spanish ft, rush seat, 1740.......700.00
Side, spindle bk, orig grpt w/floral decor, mk Kilburn.........355.00
Side, walnut, QA, cabriole legs/duck ft, trn stretcher..........800.00
Side, Wm/Mary, walnut, trn legs/stretcher/3-slat bk............375.00
Side, ½-spindle, grpt/stencil, Haskell label..................125.00
Stickley, G; #306½, ladderbk side, label/decal, pr.............200.00
Stickley, G; #321, billiard, leather seat, label, 46"............650.00
Stickley, G; #339, sewing rocker, rush seat, sm decal, rfn......185.00
Stickley, G; #361, office, leather bk/seat, on ped, decal......1,200.00
Stickley, G; #369, adjust bk, w/bent arm/5 slats, decal.......2,000.00
Stickley, G; #387, rocker, tall bk, slat sides, label............550.00
Stickley, L&JG; #408, 6-slat side, arms, cushions, unsgn.....1,000.00
Stickley, L&JG; #471, adjustable bk armchair, 6-slat sides......500.00
Windsor, arm, 9-spindle bk w/central medallion, re-grpt......1,175.00
Windsor, birdcage side, bamboo trn/blk rpt..................175.00
Windsor, bow bk, shaped arms, trn legs/arm supports, rpt....1,100.00
Windsor, bow bk arm, bulb trn base/H stretcher, G rfn........800.00
Windsor, bow bk arm, saddle seat, slim trn, sm rpr/rpt......1,000.00
Windsor, bow bk knuckle arm, chip-carve saddle seat, rpt....1,200.00
Windsor, bow bk side, bamboo/saddle seat/9-spindle, rfn.......525.00
Windsor, bow bk side, bulb leg trn, saddle seat, rfn/rpl........375.00
Windsor, brace bk/continuous arm/bulb trn/saddle seat, rpl.....725.00

Windsor, cage bk side, bamboo, rpt, 18″ seat height..........175.00
Windsor, comb bk, EX style/shaped crest/carved ears, rpl....1,075.00
Windsor, comb bk arm, saddle seat, 9-spindle, EX, pr.......1,000.00
Windsor, comb bk arm, shaped crest, G rpr/rfn, seat: 16″ H...800.00
Windsor, comb bk arm, 7-spindle, shaped crest..............400.00
Windsor, comb bk arm rocker, bamboo trn, rpt..............600.00
Windsor, comb bk side, early 20th C reproduction...........400.00
Windsor, continuous arm, bulb trn/shaped seat, rpr/rpl/rpt.....450.00
Windsor, fan back arm, 'Nutting' copy w/brand, rfn.........1,225.00
Windsor, fan bk, G trn/saddle seat/shape crest, sgn, 19″.......750.00
Windsor, fan bk, sm seat, shaped crest, old grpt, sm..........650.00
Windsor, fan bk/writing arm, shaped seat/drw, 1785, rpr.....3,600.00
Windsor, highchair, bamboo, rfn/rpr, 38″...................125.00
Windsor, rabbit ear spindle bk rocker, worn decor/cracks......150.00
Windsor, sack bk, bow crest/7-spindle, shaped arms/seat.......770.00
Windsor, side, bamboo, rfn................................200.00
Windsor, step down side, bamboo base/spindle bk, stencil......275.00
Windsor, 7-spindle, shaped seat, rfn.......................250.00
Wing bk arm, cabriole mahog legs/pad ft, uphl, 1700s.......4,500.00
Wing bk arm, cherry/uphl, Fed, ft rpr, 1880...............1,200.00
Wing bk arm, mahog/EX needlepoint uphl, Geo style.........800.00

Chair Set

Arrow bk, decor, worn pnt/rpr, 4 for........................440.00
Co European, trn legs/duck ft/scallop apron/ladderbk, 6 for....360.00
Curly maple, Fed, cane seat, concave crest, 1820, 8 for......2,750.00
Fruit/flowers decor, bold trn legs/posts, 4 for................260.00
Mahog, Chpndl, pierced beaker splat, c/b ft, 1770, pr.......3,575.00
Mahog, Geo, urn-form bk splat/spade ft, EX rfn, 8 for.......3,500.00
Maple, pnt/decor, rush seat/hoof ft, att Gragg, 1815, 10 for...2,500.00
Pnt/decor, plank seat, lyre splat/trn legs, 1840/PA, 6 for.......825.00
Roycroft, 1 vertical slat, leather seat, 4 for..................900.00
Stickley, G; #383, 3 bk slats, arched seat rail, 8 for.........1,400.00
Walnut, Chpndl, shell/flower crest/pierce splat, c/b ft, 4 for...2,640.00

Chest

Apothecary, pine, scallop base, 12 drw, sq nails, rfn, 19″......250.00
Blanket, cherry & poplar, trn applique & ft, grpt, 27x45″......375.00
Blanket, pine, dvtl, 2 drw & till w/2 drw, orig hdw, rpt........450.00
Blanket, pine, dvtl/trn ft/till, dtd 1846, rpr/rfn, 22x32″........250.00
Blanket, pine, 6-brd, bracket ft, orig pnt, 22x43″, EX..........355.00
Blanket, pine, 6-brd, rose nails, stamp design/1694, 52″ W....800.00
Blanket, pine w/harlequin decor, 3 base drw, PA, 30x53x23″.3,700.00
Blanket, pine/orig smoke decor, dvtl/trn ft, Ohio, 42″ W......950.00
Blanket, poplar, dvtl, grpt, blk ft, sgn, 21x20x41″.............750.00
Blanket, poplar, grpt, paneled, trn ft, 1880, 18x21x16″......1,250.00
Blanket, poplar, orig pnt/tulip decor, panels, trn ft, VG......1,050.00
Blanket, poplar, rpt w/3 arched panels w/flowers/unicorns......700.00
Blanket, poplar, yel w/gr brush strokes, w/till, 28x50″..........400.00
Blanket, poplar, 3-color fan-like graining, Ohio, 46″ W......3,100.00
Blanket, poplar, 6-brd, base molding, old red, sgn Budlong....205.00
Blanket, poplar w/grpt, dvtl, trn ft, lg till, rpr, 50″ W..........250.00
Butler's, Wm/Mary, pull-out shelf, 4 mahog veneer drw, rpl....155.00
Cherry, Co Sheraton, 4 dvtl cockbead drw, rpr/rpl, 43x40″.....400.00
Cherry, Hplwht, band inlay, 6 dvtl cockbead drw, rfn, 54″....2,025.00
Cherry, Hplwht, 4 grad dvtl drw w/cockbeading/inlay, orig....1,800.00
Cherry, Sheraton, 4 veneer bow front drw, trn ft, rpr/rpl.......550.00
Cherry/butternut, Fed, recessed panel ends, PA, 1810, rfn.....715.00
Cherry/curly maple, Co Emp, 2 short drw/4 grad/trn ft, 52″....600.00
Cherry/inlay/mahog bands/fancy veneer, Sheraton bow front...4,000.00
Curly maple/mix, Co Emp, 7 drw, trn ft/pilasters, 48″.........650.00
Immigrant's, orig rosemalling, dvtl pine, 1853, 46″ W, VG.....650.00
Mahog veneer facade, Hplwht, rpl high ft/apron, rpr/rfn.......550.00
Mule, pine, dvtl ft/2 overlapping+3 false drw, rpl, 44″........450.00
Mule, pine, 6-brd, cut-out ft, 2 nailed drw, rfn, 40x41″........350.00
On frame, mahog, Chpndl, 2-part, 2 short/3 long drw, rpl......880.00
Pine, Co Chpndl, 4 dvtl drw/cut-out bracket ft, rfn/rpl.........550.00
Pine, molded cornice/4 grad drw/bracket ft, rpl/rfn, 40″......1,100.00
Pine/poplar, Co, 2 step-bk drw/3, trn pulls, rfn/rpr, 44″.......295.00
Spice, curly maple, Co Hplwht/Fr ft/8 drw, rpr/rfn, 18x20″.....750.00
Spice, walnut, QA, 2-part/molded cornice/11 drw, 1760, 49″.10,725.00
Sugar, cherry, high trn ft/sq posts, rfn, 26x16x36″............325.00
Walnut, Co, scallop base, 2 sm set-bk drw/3, rfn/rpr, 45″......175.00
Walnut, Co Hplwht, 4 drw/reed posts, rpl hdw/rfn, 49x43″.....550.00

Commode

Blk lacquer/bronze mts, Louis XV style, 39x54″............2,200.00
Fruitwood, Fr, 4 drw, ormolu mts, canted corners, 31″ W.....400.00
Fruitwood, 4 drw, panel sides, rpl ft, rfn, 44″ W..............425.00
Kingwood/bronze mtd, Louis XV style, 36x48″.............1,760.00
Mahog, Fr, shaped marble top/2 do/scroll ft, mirror, '30s.....1,540.00
Parquetry inlay, Louis XVI style, 2 drw, marble top, 24″ W....325.00
Tulipwood/inlay, Louis XVI style, marble top, 25x50″.........450.00
Walnut, Louis XVI style, 2 drw, trn legs, orig hdw, 35x43″....350.00

Commode, bombe form, Louis XV, marquetry inlaid fruitwood with marble top, 46″ wide, $800.00.

Cupboard

Butternut, cut-out ft, panel do, gallery top, 33x27″............210.00
Butternut, primitive, 2-brd do/3 shelves w/in, rfn, 79x31″......265.00
Butternut, 2 4-panel do/step-bk/2 drw/2 do, rfn/rpl, 85″.......900.00
Cherry, base: trn legs/2 dvtl drw; 2 glazed do top, 57x54″.....650.00
Cherry, scroll base, glaze do/2 drw/2 do, rfn, 85x48″........1,100.00
Chimney, pine, built-in, molding, panel do, rpt, 32x28″.......215.00
Chimney, pine/poplar w/dk pnt & yel stripes, 68x15″..........850.00
China, Mission oak, corbeled supports, 2 glass do, 59x47″.....450.00
Corner, cherry, arch/glaze/mullion do/3 drw/do, 78″.........3,600.00
Corner, maple, Fed, 2 glaze do/2 drw/cupbrd do, rpr, 82″....1,430.00
Corner, pine, barrel bk, 3 curve shelves/panel do, rfn, 71″...2,000.00
Corner, pine, barrel front, 2-parts w/convex do, 78x40″......2,750.00
Corner, pine, Chpndl, much rope carving, mullioned do, 87″.3,850.00
Corner, walnut, Fed, swan neck w/urn crest/mullion do, 84″..3,080.00
Curly cherry, Ohio, step-bk, punch tin do/drw/2 do, 75x39″..2,300.00
Hanging, walnut, panel do, openwork frieze, rfn, 39x27x11″...200.00
Jelly, pine, diagonal panel do/scallop bracket ft, 52x36″.......330.00

Cupboard, Shaker, original mustard wash over pine, Tailor Shop Case, Handcock, 86″ x 39″, $8,500.00.

Jelly, pine, 1-brd ends w/cut-out ft, brd/batten do, 49″........265.00
Monk's, walnut, Gothic do, dvtl case........................200.00
Pine, front/sides/2 drw/2 do paneled, rosehead nails, 58″......950.00
Pine, molded cornice/4 open compartments/high ft, rpr, 44″...360.00
Pine, orig flame grain, 2 panel do/beaded fr, rpr/rpl, 82″......700.00
Pine, pr 3 panel do, carved apron/dentilated cornice, 65″......950.00
Pine, primitive, board/batten do, nailed, rpr/rfn, 75x35″......800.00
Pine, red/blk/yel, grpt, glaze do/fancy arch/step-bk, 88″......3,600.00
Pine, rosemalled floral on brd/batten do, 29x23x12″, EX......900.00
Poplar, Co Emp, trn/reed pilasters/step-bk/2 do/2 drw/2 do.....800.00
Poplar, cornice/2 panel do/step-bk/2 panel do/grpt, 76x48″.....700.00
Poplar, raised panel do/molded cornice, rpr/rfn, 72x48″.......325.00
Walnut, corner; cove molding/2 glaze do/2 panel do, 80x52″...975.00
Welsh, pine, English Co, open shelf/3 drw, rfn, 76x60″......1,400.00

Desk

Birch/ash, Co Chpndl, slant lid/4 drw, orig hdw, rpr/rfn......1,600.00
Bureau plat, gilt bronze mt kingwood/leather top, Louis XV..3,800.00
Bureau plat, tulipwood inlay/kingwood/bronze mtd, 60″ W...3,850.00
Butler's; mahog, w/mirror, Duncan Phyfe, ca 1810, 76″.......1,300.00
Cherry, Chpndl, slant top/4 grad drw/ogee ft, rpl hdw, 37″...6,000.00
Cherry, Hplwht, slant top, orig hdw, losses, as found, 44″....2,000.00
Cherry/inlay, Hplwht, tambour do fitted w/in, fold-out top....2,600.00
Davenport, Renaissance, gilt incised/porcelain mtd, 40x26″.....450.00
Davenport, rosewood, Rococo, acanthus front legs, 38x23″.....800.00
Limbert, drop front/drw/2 do, branded, 46x36x14″..........550.00
Mahog, block front, slant lid, handmade, 1700s, 33x44″.....4,500.00
Mahog, Chpndl, slant front/4 drw, c/b ft, rpr, 43x42″........2,500.00
Mahog, dbl ped, emb leather top, 48″ W...................400.00
Mahog veneer, Chpndl oxbow, c/b ft, slant lid, 4 drw, rstr....1,000.00
Maple, slant front/curly lid, 4 dvtl drw, fitted w/in, rpl.......1,800.00
Pine, table top, dvtl, slat top, 10x25″, VG...................165.00
Stickley, G; #708, flat top, letter holder, 2 drw, branded......500.00
Stickley, G; #720, lady's, red decal, 36½x38″................650.00
Stickley, G; #732, drop lid, 2 half drw/2, branded, 44x32″.....900.00
Stickley, G; chalet, trestle ft, unsgn, rst, 45x24″ dia.........650.00
Stickley, L&JG; #604, sm version, 36x34x20″...............375.00
Walnut, Chpndl, slant front/4 drw, fluted ¼-columns, 44″....2,500.00
Walnut, Chpndl, slant front/4 drw/bracket ft, rstr, 42x37″....3,600.00
Walnut, Co, 2 panel do/fall front, fitted w/in, rfn, 71″.........800.00
Wooton, Rockefeller Extra Grade.........................15,000.00
Wooton, roll top.......................................4,500.00
Wooton, Standard Grade, Wells Fargo....................6,500.00
Wooton, walnut, dbl ped.................................3,500.00

Desk, Georgian style, walnut with leather inset top, acanthus leaf-capped feet, late 19th century, 54″ wide, $1,600.00.

Dresser

Oak, Geo II, 2 pt, 2 shelves/arched apron w/3 drw, 70x74″...3,500.00
Oak, Welsh Provincial, 2 shelves/3 drw/3 do, 75x59″.........2,500.00
Satinwood, Geo III, 3 frieze drw/3 drw ea side, arch apron..14,000.00
Walnut, Louis XVI style/serpentine top/4 drw/EX hdw, 51″ W..500.00

Dry Sink

Ash/poplar, Co, cornice w/shelf/panel do/drw, rpl/rfn..........550.00
Pine, board/batten do, open well, thin top shelf, rpr/rpl.......435.00
Pine, brd/batten do, gallery well, rpl/rpr/rfn, 32x50″..........400.00
Pine, scalloped ends, old finish w/pnt traces, 42x60″..........350.00
Pine/poplar, 2 panel do/shallow well/gallery, rpl, 31x72″.......525.00
Poplar, Co, bracket ft/panel do/open top, rpt/rstr, 50x43″......475.00
Poplar, panel do/2 dvtl drw, hutch w/shelf, rpl/rfn, 47″ W.....450.00

Highboy

Cherry, QA, flat top/5 drw/4 in base, 1750/NE, 73x40″......6,600.00
Cherry, QA, swan necks/finials/fans/acorn pendants, 88″....25,000.00
Maple, QA, fan carving, 6 drws/4, rpl brasses/rfn, 71″.......5,000.00
Maple, QA, flat top, fan carved, 1765, married, rstr, 66″.....1,800.00
Maple/red grpt, Co QA, 5 drw/4 in base, orig hdw, 73x38½″..5,500.00

Lowboy

Cherry, QA, 1 long+3 short drw, fan carved, 32x35″........2,200.00
Curly maple, QA, rectangle top/1 long+2 short drw, 28x36″..4,675.00
Mahog, Chpndl, shell/acanthus carved legs/drw, c/b ft.......13,750.00
Walnut/inlay, QA, notched corner top/1 long+3 short drw...2,420.00

Loveseat, Art Nouveau, carved female bust in crest, 59″ long, $1,800.00.

Parlor Suite

Giltwood, Louis XVI style, settee, arm & side chair 2,200.00
Joseph Meeks, 66″ sofa, 2 arm chairs+4 side chairs 19,000.00
Rosewood, Rococo Revival, carved crests, 7-pc 4,500.00
Rosewood, vintage/foliage crest, att Meeks, sofa+5 chairs 7,900.00

Pie Safe

Pine, screen do/drw, yel, mortised/pegged, 1850s, 37x40″ 1,600.00
Poplar, punch tin panels, 2 dvtl drw, pnt layers, rpr, 51″ 520.00
Poplar, tin panel ends/4 do/compass stars/hearts, rfn, 65″ 640.00
Poplar, 12 tin panels w/stars, 2 dvtl drw, pnt, orig, 56″ 900.00
Walnut, sq corner posts/panel sides/do w/3 tin panels, 60″ 225.00

Secretary

Bookcase, maple, Chpndl, panel do/slant lid/4 drw, 66″, EX . . 7,700.00
Cherry, Co Sheraton, 2 panel do/fold-down/4 drw, 1784, 76″ . 2,300.00
Hplwht, diamond mullion do/2 drw/2 do, inlay, rst, 90x43″ . . . 1,100.00
Mahog/flame veneer, Emp, 2 do/4 dvtl drw, rpr, 2-pc, 67″ 1,350.00
Oak, side-by-side, curved glass 350.00
Pine, mold cornice/12-pane do/slant lid/4 drw, rfn, 81″ 1,600.00
Poplar, Co, 2 glaze do/slant lid/drw, orig red, as is, 85″ 1,400.00
Walnut, Co, applied moldings, fall front, fitted w/in, 60″ 1,400.00

Settee

Cherry fr/uphl, carved paw ft w/acanthus leaf/fluting, 58″ 550.00
Fr, 4-chair bk, lyre splats w/carvings, slip seat, 70″ L 700.00
Maple/pine, pnt/decor plank seat, 1840/PA, 75″ L 770.00
Oak, openwork sunbursts/trn spindles, Prairie School, 88″ 2,500.00
Pine, gr w/mc fruit, trn uprights/shaped crest, 1835, 74″ 2,700.00
Rosewood, Rococo, pierced foliate crestrail, 1855 . . . . 2,800.00
Walnut, Regency style, serpentine bk/cabriole legs, 48″ 400.00

Shelf

Cherry, scallop ends/center divider, 6 shelves, 50x55″, VG 740.00
Mahog, English, 2 w/X-ends, 2 drw, brass supports, 26x33″ 900.00
Mahog, 3 shelves over 3 base drw, brass hdw, 35½x38″ 900.00
Pine, mahog grpt, 5 w/beaded edge, molded cornice, 62x57″ . . . 230.00
Pine, old red finish, well made, G age, 30x33″ 350.00
Tiger maple, grad tier supports, scroll bk, 27″ W 250.00
Walnut, scalloped ends, holes for rope, 2 shelves, 37x28″ 135.00

Sideboard

Cherry/mahog front, Emp, high trn ft/free columns, 54″ W 400.00
Limbert, #1456, mirror, 2 sm drw/1 long/2 do, branded 700.00
Mahog, Fed, X-bands, shaped bkbrd, top w/drw/candle slides . . 2,750.00
Mahog/bellflower inlay, Fed, serpentine, 1790, 72″ W 9,625.00
Mahog/bellflower inlay, Fed, shaped top/conforming frieze 5,225.00
Mahog/inlay, Fed, serpentine, all orig, 42x71″ 4,125.00
Mahog/inlay, Fed, serpentine, 3 drw/2 do, 1795, rstr, 72″ 2,700.00
Mahog/inlay, Geo III, orig brass gallery, 65″ W 1,800.00
Pine/poplar, stout legs, 4 dvtl drw, top added, 32x48″ 575.00
Stickley, G; #814, plate rail, 2 cupbrd do/3 drw/drw, EX 850.00
Stickley, G; #817, plate rack, 2 do w/4 central drw, label 2,500.00
Stickley, L&JG; plate rack, arched apron, 48x54x24″ 500.00

Sofa

Duncan Phyfe, reeded mahog fr/carved crest, late 1800s, 83″ . . . 400.00
Mahog, acanthus/shell crest, scroll arms, lyre ft, 81″ 1,760.00
Mahog, Country Sheraton, rpr, re-uphl, 72″ 875.00
Mahog, Fed, satinwood panels in crest, uphl, rpr, 77″ 2,500.00
Mahog, Sheraton style, early 1900s, rpr/re-uphl, 48″ L 525.00
Mahog/aboina, acanthus crest, cornucopia/paw ft, 1825, 89″ 935.00
Mahog/bird's eye maple, Classical Revival, NE, 1820s 440.00
Mahog/inlay, Fed, shaped uphl bk/seat, reed legs, rpr, 73″ . . . 2,000.00

Stand

Adirondak, bent twigs, rustic, mc pnt, 18″ sq top 55.00
Adirondak, very lg heart, sm horseshoes, cloth top, 32″ 90.00
Birch, Co Hplwht, bird's eye drw w/reed rails, old red, sm 500.00
Birch, trn legs, dvtl drw, 9¾″ drop leaves, 15x20″ top 225.00
Butler's, curly maple, Sheraton, dvtl 20x32″ top tray, EX 1,600.00
Cherry, Co Emp, trn legs, dvtl drw, 2-brd 24″ sq top 175.00
Cherry, Co Emp, trn legs, 2 dvtl curve drw, 1-brd top 175.00
Cherry, Co Hplwht, 1-brd 17x22″ top, tripod w/reeded urn . . . 1,800.00
Cherry, EX trn legs, dvtl drw, rpl pull, 3-brd 18x20″ top 250.00
Cherry, trn maple legs/dvtl drw, 19x20″ poplar top, rfn 250.00
Cherry, 2 curly maple veneer curve front drw/trn legs, rfn 275.00
Cherry/inlay, Co Hplwht, 18″ sq top/gallery, minor rpr/rfn 525.00
Cherry/mahog, Emp, paw ft/shaped sq ped/10″ drop leaf, EX . . . 170.00
Crock, pyramid, 3-tier, late wire nails, gr pnt, 36x52″ 175.00
Crock, scallop fr/brackets, 4 grad rnd tiers, pnt/rpr, 52″ 450.00
Crock, 3-tier, pine, ½-circle ash shelves, rfn, 33x43″ 175.00
Curly maple, Co Sheraton, drop leaf, 2 dvtl drw, rpr/rpl 300.00
Curly maple, trn legs, dvtl drw, 1-brd 18x22″ top, rfn 375.00
Curly maple, trn legs, 2 dvtl drws, wood pulls, rfn/rpl 400.00
Curly maple/flame grain veneer, 1-brd top/1 drw, rfn 395.00
Mahog veneer on pine, Sheraton, 3 dvtl drw, rpl hdw, EX 600.00
Mahog/cherry, Co Emp, tripod/trn column/dvtl drw, rpl/rfn 175.00
Maple w/burl inlay/bird's eye veneer, Co Emp, drw, rpr/rfn 450.00
Pine, Co, maple grpt over red, arch apron, rpl 22x27″ top 425.00
Pine, early PA, trn legs, deep drw, 22x25″ 1-brd top 300.00
Pine/poplar, Co Hplwht, sq taper legs/drw/1-brd 19x24″ top 250.00
Poplar, Co Hplwht, 1-brd removable top has crack 200.00
Poplar top, maple trn legs, cherry apron, Co Sheraton, drw 325.00
Poplar w/red grpt on yel, Co Hplwht, 20x22″ 2-brd top 2,500.00
Stickley, G; #660, deep apron, rpl 18x14″ top, 20″ 425.00
Stickley, G; labeled & branded, 13″ dia, 18″ 125.00
Stickley, G; 3-drw drop leaf, decal sgn, 28x16¾x16″ 700.00
Stickley, L&JG; #587, drink stand, sq, base shelf, unsgn 375.00
Work, mahog, Sheraton, dvtl drw/panel do, 15″ fold top, 35″ . . 275.00

Stool

Cow horn feet, velvet crescent top, 1870s, 12x9x19″ 55.00
Limbert, leather top, sq w/single stretcher sides, 15x18″ 110.00
Mahog/ormolu, Classical Revival, 4 shaped supports, 1825 ..... 275.00
Piano, walnut, shell-form seat, Rococo, Italian, 1890 .... 950.00
Pine, primitive, late wire nail built, 12x11x13″ 45.00
Pine, yel rpt w/blk & gr striping, 7x7x16″ 65.00
Pine, 3-leg, primitive, 25x11″ dia 65.00
Pine/poplar, bl rpt, PA, 6⅝x7x15″ 65.00
Poplar, chip-carved top, wire nails, brn finish, 6x7x13″ 65.00
Stickley, G; #300, paper label/decal, 15x20x16″ 750.00
Stickley, G; #394, spring cushion, branded, 16x19x15″ 350.00
Windsor, Co, oval top, rfn, 8x9½x14″ 45.00
Windsor, splay legs, narrow trn ft, lg seat, 25x16″ 475.00

Table

Altar, Chinese, openwork apron, scrolled sides, 47″ W 60,000.00
Banquet, mahog, Geo, 3-part, 3-ped, extra leaves, 150″ W ... 5,100.00
Banquet, mahog/inlay, Hplwht, rpr/rpl, opens to 45x83″, pr 800.00
Breakfast, mahog, Geo III, 54x41″ tilt top, rst 1,000.00
Card, bird's eye maple/cherry inlay, Fed, bow front, 35″ W ... 2,420.00
Card, cherry/birch, Co Sheraton, bird's eye curved front 1,450.00
Card, mahog, acanthus uprights/hairy paws, ca 1820, 36″ W .. 1,540.00
Card, mahog, Classical, dolphin stds/ft, acanthus, 1820 ...... 1,900.00
Card, mahog, Sheraton, figured veneer apron/orig hdw, 36″ .. 1,300.00
Card, mahog/cherry inlay, serpentine/hinged leaf, 36″ W 1,320.00
Card, mahog/inlay, Fed, D-top w/hinged leaf, rstr, 36″ W 900.00
Card, mahog/inlay, Fed, serpentine, ca 1795, 29x36x18″ 1,430.00
Card, walnut, QA, rectangle top w/hinged leaf/drw, 34″ W 4,675.00
Center, cherry/pine, Fed, early 1800s, 27x50x35″ 465.00
Center, parcel gilt/walnut, Louis XV, marble top, 54″ 6,000.00
Cherry, Co Hplwht, 6-leg 16½″ drop leaf, rpr/rfn, 47″ W 450.00
Corner, walnut, QA, triangle top w/D-drop, ca 1750, 43x39″ .. 7,425.00
Curly maple, Co Sheraton, 6-leg, rnd corner 18″ drop leaf 750.00
Curly maple, 14″ sq drop leaf, trn legs, rfn, 39″ 825.00
Dressing, Louis XVI style, dore mts, 25x17″ lift lid, EX 700.00
Dressing, mahog, Fed, pineapple pilasters/lift lid, 35x36″ 450.00
Dressing, pine, curly maple grpt, drw/scallop crest, 30″ W 250.00
Dressing, pine, scallop crest, 2 curve step-bk drw/1, rpt 400.00
Dressing, pine/poplar, orig grpt/fruit decor, crest, 33″ W 625.00
Drum, mahog, Hplwht, 20″ top w/4 drw revolves, rpl hdw 650.00
Galleried 22″ W top pnt brn w/romantic landscape, oval, 24″ .. 475.00
Harvest, birch, 1-brd top, 9½″ drop leaves, rfn, 108″ W 3,000.00
Hutch, hardwood/pine seat, rnd 2-brd top, rpr/rpl/rfn, 43″ 425.00
Hutch, maple w/2-brd pine seat/breadbrd top, rpr/rfn, 45″ 750.00
Hutch, pine, carved/pnt, rnd tilt top/well, 1850s, 46″ 3,600.00
Hutch, pine, hinged, compartment, sq 3-brd 48x34″ top, rfn ... 850.00
Hutch, pine, lift lid, sq 3-brd top, partial worn graining 900.00
Hutch, 4-brd 44″ sq pine top, o/w orig red, mortise/pin 1,550.00
Library, mahog, Fed, drop leaf, brass paw ft/casters, 59″ 2,090.00
Low, gilt bronze pierced gallery, inlaid rosewood, 35″ dia 1,320.00
Mahog, Chpndl, D-form drop leaves, c/b ft, 1765, 33″ open 715.00
Mahog, drop leaf, 8 legs, 1-brd 25″ leaves, rpr/rfn, 52″ 450.00
Mahog, Fed, drop leaf, spade ft, 1785, rpr, 48″ 550.00
Mahog, QA, D-form drop leaves/cabriole legs, 42½″ open 1,870.00
Mahog, QA, wide rectangle drop leaves, 48x48″ open 4,400.00
Mahog, trn baluster legs, oval, extended: 237″ W 55,000.00
Majorelle, fruitwood/inlay, 63″ W, w/8 chairs 12,000.00
Maple, QA, rnd drop leaf, trn legs/duck ft, rpr/rfn, 49″ 1,700.00
Maple, tavern, trn legs, 'Nutting' copy w/label, 42″ W 900.00
Marjorelle, fruitwood w/inlay mistletoe, 2-tier, 31x34″ 1,650.00
Oak, Co English, scallop apron, 1 drw, 2-brd 15x25″ top 225.00
Oak, gate leg, mortised/pinned, G trn, drw, rfn/rst/rpl 300.00
Occasional, gilt bronze mt tulip/kingwood inlay, Louis XV 1,000.00
Occasional, Mission oak, base shelf over sq designs, 24″ W 500.00
Parlor, walnut, Eastlake, 20x30″ marble top/canted corners 175.00
Pembroke, birch, Co Sheraton, 9¾″ drop leaves, trn legs 600.00
Pembroke, cherry, Co Emp, trn/rope carve legs, rfn/rpl, 40″ ... 400.00
Pembroke, cherry, Co Hplwht, top: 21x41″ w/10″ leaves 200.00
Pembroke, walnut, Co Hplwht, 10″ drop leaves, rpl, 36″ 450.00
Pier, pine, pnt/gilt metal mt, Fed, ca 1815/MD, 35x45″ 990.00
Pine, Co Hplwht, dvtl drw, rpl top, 29x43″ 270.00
Pine, Co Hplwht, sq taper legs/4-brd tongue/groove 30″ top 300.00
Pine, sawbuck, 1-brd breadbrd 28x50″ top 395.00
Pool, Brunswick Balke, inlaid rosewood, 1880, 110″ 2,420.00
Pool, Brunswick Monarch, inlaid walnut/CI, lion base, 110″ .. 12,000.00
Rococo Revival, marble turtle top, floral/bird medallions 2,550.00
Rosewood, Rococo, turtle form marble top, 44″ W 1,980.00
Sewing, mahog, Hplwht style, fitted w/in, 17x24″ lift top 200.00
Side, fruitwood, kneeling African supports drape-carve top 5,000.00
Side, walnut, Chpndl, rectangular/drw, c/b ft, 31″ W, EX 5,500.00
Side, walnut, massive figural putti support 18″ marble top ... 3,025.00
Side, walnut/inlay, Geo II style, 3 drw/carved knees, 60″ 500.00
Stickley, G; #604, tea, arch X-stretcher, label, EX 500.00
Stickley, G; #605, telephone, paper label 225.00
Stickley, G; #607, tea, base shelf, X-stretcher 750.00
Stickley, G; #619, leather top, 3 drw, unsgn, 30x66″, EX 1,500.00
Stickley, G; #631, director's, trestle base, paper label 1,100.00
Stickley, G; #633, dining, 4 side+2 arm V-bk chairs 6,000.00
Stickley, G; #643, gaming, revolving/reversible top, EX 800.00
Stickley, G; #650, library, red decal, 36x30″ 485.00
Stickley, G; #655, spindle sides, lower shelf, unsgn, EX 1,500.00
Stickley, G; #657, spindle sides, Eastwood label, 36″ W 3,000.00
Stickley, G; #907, dressing, w/mirror, strap hdw 1,400.00
Stickley, G; library, 2 drw, mk w/gold seal, 29x54x32″ 600.00
Stickley, G; rnd, arch X-stretcher w/finial, decal, 48″ 900.00
Stickley, G; spindle sides, base shelf, red decal, 48″ W 2,200.00
Tavern, ash/maple/pine, Co QA, 1 drw, rpr/rpl 825.00
Tavern, birch, Co QA, 1-brd walnut 19x29″ top, drw, rfn 1,150.00
Tavern, curly maple/1-brd pine top, Co Hplwht, rpr/rpl/rfn 600.00
Tavern, maple, QA, pine 1-brd 24x26″ top, pnt base, sm rpr. 6,000.00
Tavern, pine/maple, Co QA, top scrubbed/red base, 36″ W ... 1,500.00

Tavern table, Federal, walnut, early 1800s, 29″ x 26″, $600.00.

Tea, cherry, Co Chpndl 36″ dia tilt top, tripod w/paw ft 600.00
Tea, curly maple, Fed, 31″ tilt top, cabriole legs, rstr 1,540.00
Tea, fruitwood facing w/marquetry, Regency style, 32″ dia 400.00

Tea, mahog, Chpndl, 32″ tilt top, acanthus legs, c/b ft......2,800.00
Tea, mahog, Geo style, 2nd period, 33″ lacquer decor top...1,700.00
Tea, mahog, Geo style, 30″ tilt top w/circle/fan carving........400.00
Tea, maple, Co, tilt top, tripod/snake ft, trn column, rfn.......575.00
Tea, tulipwood, Regency style, brass gallery, marble top.......200.00
Tea, walnut, Chpndl, tilt top/birdcage/3 c/b ft, 1790, 39″.....1,320.00
Trestle, pine, X-supports, early 1800s/PA, rstr, 92″ W.......3,025.00
Walnut, cabriole legs, 2 dvl apron drw, rfn, 45x38″...........775.00
Walnut, Chpndl, 2-part, hinged leaves, rstr, 101″...........2,600.00
Walnut, Co, 6-leg 22″ 1-brd drop leaf, rfn/rpr, 48″...........325.00
Walnut, drop leaf gate leg, bulb trn, mortised/pinned, rpl....1,200.00
Walnut, Hplwht, demilune, inlay/stringing, rfn, 22½″ W.......250.00
Walnut, Hplwht, demilune w/inlay, veneer front, rfn, 44″ W....500.00
Walnut, QA, D-form drop leaf, rstr/rpr, 58″ open............990.00
Walnut, QA, drop leaf w/drw, 1790/PA, rstr, 46″ W.........1,210.00
Walnut, QA drop leaf, sq 19″ leaves, top rpl/rfn.............600.00
Walnut, QA drop leaf swing leg/cut-out apron, rpr/rpl, 46″...1,300.00
Walnut, QA drop leaf/deep scallop aprons/3-toe ft, 16x45″...3,250.00
Walnut, Renaissance Revival, column+4 scroll legs, 30″ W....225.00
Walnut, Wm/Mary, gate leg, ½-ball ft, rstr, 52″ W..........3,575.00
Walnut, 25½″ dia tilt top, trn column/tripod, rpl.............275.00
Walnut/maple, W/M, gate leg, D-leaves/drw, rpr, 50″ open....4,620.00
Work, cherry/bird's eye maple, Fed, 1835/NE, 28x19″........605.00
Work, Co, trn cherry legs/pine apron, drw, 3-brd top, 42″......20.00
Work, mahog, Emp, 2 drw, lyre ped, 1825, EX..............200.00
Work, mahog, Emp, 2 drw/serpentine front/flip top/ped, EX....200.00
Work, mahog, Fed, 2 drw, 4 slim ring-trn legs, NE, ca 1820..1,100.00

Wardrobe

Amish, walnut, acorn ft, 2-panel do, 78x49″.................350.00
Cherry, trn ft/rnd corners/4-panel do removes, rpr/rpl, 78″.....675.00
Pine, 1-pc, panel do/ends, crown cornice, rfn/rpl, 70x64″......750.00
Poplar, well-scrolled apron, bracket ft, arch do, 86x51″.......725.00
Walnut, Emp, ebonized columns, stencil decor, paw/eagle ft..1,950.00

Washstand

Corner, mahog/inlay, Hplwht, bow front/bowl cut-out/drw......600.00
Mahog, Hplwht, base drw, sq 15″ cut-out top, rfn/damage.....150.00
Mahog, shaped splashbrd/2 drw frieze/acanthus supports.......415.00
Pine, orig red/blk grpt w/yel stencil, w/crest, rpr, 28″.........225.00
Pine/poplar w/orig grpt & foliage decor, base drw, cut-out......220.00

Galle

Emile Galle was one of the most important producers of cameo glass in France. His firm, founded in Nancy in 1874, produced beautiful cameo in the Art Nouveau style during the 1890s, using a variety of techniques. He also produced glassware with enameled decoration, as well as some fine pottery--animal figurines, table services, vases, and other objects d' art.

In the mid-1880s, he became interested in the various colors and texture of natural woods, and as a result began to create furniture which he used as yet another medium through which to express his art. Marquetry was the primary method Galle used in decorating his furniture--preferring landscapes, Nouveau floral and fruit arrangements, butterflies, squirrels, and other forms from nature. It is for his furniture and his cameo glass that he is best known today.

When no condition is indicated, the glass and pottery listed below are assumed to be in mint conditon; furniture is assumed excellent.

Cameo

Bottle, kneeling figure/bear, bk: equestrian, 4½″.............750.00
Bottle, poppies, floret stopper, lobed body, polished, 5″.......880.00
Bowl, sea grasses, mold-blown relief sea-shells, 12″ dia......3,500.00
Box, maple buds/leaves, gray/peach w/gr/wht, w/lid, 7″ dia.....550.00
Bud vase, flowering branches, gr on gray/peach, 6¾″.........385.00
Pitcher, bleeding hearts, pink/purple, 2 cuts, 3″..............795.00
Shade, lg blossom-form, amber/brn on ivory, polished, 10″...1,200.00
Vase, apple blossom branches, orange on yel, pyriform, 17″..2,000.00
Vase, apple branches, blown-out, bulbous, 12″, NM.........4,510.00
Vase, carnations, cherry red on lt yel, 8″...................800.00
Vase, clematis, bl/brn on yel, teardrop/slim neck, 19″........1,320.00
Vase, clematis, yel/gray/gr/brn, blown-out, bulbous, 9½″......3,500.00
Vase, cyclamen, red on yel, ovoid, 8″....................1,320.00
Vase, daffodils/bk: trees, flattened sphere/stepped ft, 8″......1,250.00
Vase, daisies, Chinese red/gr on gray, disk ft, 12″..........1,100.00
Vase, dill sprays, brn on yel/gr, dbl cone/rnd ft, 6″...........600.00
Vase, dragonflies/pond, ochre on gray/aqua, polished, 18″....2,600.00
Vase, dragonfly/lotus/pond, long neck/ball base, 23″.........2,900.00
Vase, elephants/palm trees, blown-out, bulbous, 15″........11,000.00
Vase, fir tree silhouette on mtn, expanded cylinder, 18″.....1,900.00
Vase, floral, platinum/brn, bulb w/stick neck, sgn, 18″.......1,275.00
Vase, floral, 21½″.......................................2,250.00
Vase, florals, 'windows,' gold/bl/lav/purple, 7½x7½″..........2,750.00
Vase, fuschia blossoms, enamel detail/gilt, 5½″.............1,800.00
Vase, hollyhocks allover, butterflies, 23″..................3,500.00
Vase, hyacinth, blown-out, purple/lav, 12½″................4,500.00
Vase, hyacinth, red on yel, rnd w/sm flared rim, 10½″.......1,430.00
Vase, hydrangea, purple on gray, shouldered cylinder, 10″.....770.00
Vase, iris/leafage, amber/lav on gray/amber, polished, 16″....2,000.00
Vase, iris/leafage, foil inclusions, slender w/bun ft, 13″.......1,800.00
Vase, ivy/berries, purple on bl/aqua, stick neck, 17½″.......1,320.00
Vase, landscape, purple/bl on gray, rnd w/flared lip, 8¾″.....1,210.00
Vase, leafage, gr on gray/rose, slightly waisted, 5″............330.00
Vase, leaves allover, red on gold, banjo form, sgn, 7″.........695.00
Vase, leaves/acorns, internal decor/gold inclusions, 9″.......2,000.00
Vase, leaves/berries, orange/brn, 6½″......................475.00
Vase, mushrooms, gray/wht w/brn, 2¼x3¼″..................550.00
Vase, nasturtiums, lav/plum on lav/gray, polished, 4¾″........660.00
Vase, nasturtiums, purple on gr/gray, 7¾″..................660.00
Vase, oak leaves, gold inclusions, etched w/in, polish, 9″.....2,250.00
Vase, orchid stalks, red on yel, bulbous w/flared lip, 7¾″......660.00
Vase, pine boughs & cones, brn on gray/yel, 16″...........1,500.00
Vase, pine boughs & cones, silver ft ring, flat ovoid, 9″......1,200.00
Vase, plums, purple on yel/wht, blown-out, ovoid, 15½″......4,500.00
Vase, poppies, gray/yel w/red, tiered ft, polished, 6″..........600.00

Vase, clematis, mold blown and cut, yellow and gray overlaid in green and brown, signed, 9½″, $3,500.00.

Vase, Queen's Lace/leaves, gray/bl w/lav/gr, baluster, 20″.....1,870.00
Vase, river scene w/birds, brn/orange, polished, 8x3″........1,000.00
Vase, rose branches, yel w/rose, ftd, 7″..................1,150.00
Vase, rose spray, red/burgundy on yel, 8″..................1,150.00
Vase, spider mums allover, shades of orange, sgn, 11″.......1,400.00
Vase, sycamore branches, gr on gray/salmon, 23″...........2,100.00
Vase, sycamore branches, lime on frost, str sides, 15″.......1,200.00
Vase, thistle, frosted, pink/yel/gr, 8″........................675.00
Vase, titled: Rio de Janeiro, 19″.........................4,000.00
Vase, trees/mtns, bl on yel, pyriform, 8″....................715.00
Vase, trees/mtns, shaded overlay, elongated ovoid, 17″.......2,200.00
Vase, upright branches w/buds, concave form, polished, 10″....650.00
Vase, vine/leaf, bulb base/stick neck, 23″..................1,850.00
Vase, wisteria, lav on frost to orange, sgn, 6″...............795.00
Vase, wisteria, violet on gray, tri-lobed, bulbous, 10½″.......1,500.00
Wall bracket, nasturtiums, ochre/salmon, gilt mts, 22″, pr....3,960.00

Enameled Glass

Bonbon, ribbons/bows/insects, 1800s, w/underplate, 5½″.......950.00
Bottle, scent; flowers/leaves, orig stopper, amber, 4½″.........500.00
Decanter, amber, thistles, rigaree on stopper, sgn, 9½″......1,500.00
Vase, fuchsia, rose/wht/pink/gr on gr, 12½″................1,500.00
Vase, 3 fish/seaweed/coral, ribbed crystal, sgn, gr, 9½″........575.00

Footed bowl, enameled thistle bloom on blown glass, engraved signature, 4½″, $550.00.

Furniture

Dressing table, tulip inlay on crest, 3 mirror panels, 50″.....3,000.00
Nest of 4 tables, inlaid w/tulips/irises/butterflies.............3,025.00
Sewing table, fruitwood marquetry, floral, shaped top, 20″....1,540.00
Table, inlaid w/squirrel, curving sides, 25″ L...............2,000.00

Pottery

Bowl, 2 figural ducks, lt/dk bl, red & gilt, sgn, 15″...........660.00
Compote, patriotic decor, reticulated, sgn Nancy St Ct........750.00
Ewer, figural, grasshopper in crown/regal attire, 16″.........1,800.00
Figurine, ducks, Imari colors, sgn EG/X-Lorraine, 7x15½″....1,450.00
Pitcher, peasants dance at farmhouse/musicians, 12″........1,200.00
Wall pocket, butterflies & bows, HP, tri-lobe, mc, 14″........850.00

Gambling Memorabilia

When no condition is indicated, the items listed below are assumed to be in excellent condition.

Bezique, dbl deck w/2 markers, instructions, 1879, in case......70.00
Book, Beyond the Mississippi..............................120.00
Book, Gaming Table, 1870..................................90.00
Book, It's All in the Draw, illus, US Cartridge Co, 1895.......125.00
Book, Sunshine & Shadows in New York, 1868.............100.00
Book, The Game of Draw Poker, Keller, 1887, 84 pg, sm tear...47.00
Book, The Gaming Table, Steinmetz, game history, 2 volumes...89.00
Book, The Open Book, JH Johnson, gambling tricks, 155 pg....91.00
Bottle, back bar; nude woman, frosted glass, 1880s, 14″.......295.00
Card press, holds 8 decks, brass thumbscrew, wood...........71.00
Card trimmer, brass, lever blade/wood hdl, 2 adjustments......535.00
Card trimmer, shear style, brass adjustable base, G Henry......868.00
Cardpress, early/crude, no hdl, wood hdld screw, 13x5x3″.....210.00
Cardpress, wood, slide lid/brass 'Mason' screw, 4-part.........292.00
Casino cage, Mason, brass/nickel plate, 16-lb, 18″ H..........485.00
Casino Chuck cage, dbl post, brass/nickel plate, 16″ H........295.00
Chip rack, w/175 chips/holds 700, leather covered, wood.......56.00
Cold Deck Machine, switches entire deck, cheat device........750.00
Corner rounder, cheat device, iron/brass/rosewood...........883.00
Dealing box, Faro, complete w/old cards, rare, 3x4x1½″.......250.00
Dice, HP blk pips, ivory, rare, ¾″, pr........................50.00
Dice cage, brass/nickel plate, w/dice, 12″ H.................165.00
Dice cage, wire, w/3 red dice, 9½x4½″......................50.00
Dice cage, wire w/felt interior, w/2 dice, 10x4½″..............72.00
Dice cup, Readem & Weep on lid, ca 1910...................65.00
Dice drop, octagonal, wood w/glass sides, 2 trips, 9x6″.........46.00
Dice wheel, Chuck A Luck & Red & Blk, wall mt, 23″ dia.....495.00
Faro casekeeper, suit of Diamonds.........................810.00
Faro layout, folding, walnut trim, Spades suit, unmkd, NM.....400.00
Game, Every Card a Winner, punchboard, folds, 35x13″........50.00
Game, Horse Derby, Germany, rare, 2″.......................69.00
Gaming wheel, flowers, HP, 36 numbers, many colors, 24″.....130.00
Hold-out, knee spread, complete, German silver thief, NM.....863.00
Hold-out, Wizard, for secreting cards, sleeve type...........250.00
Lottery ticket, colorful, 1930s, 6 for.......................25.00
Lottery ticket, 1894 Louisiana Lottery, gr/blk, set of 12........25.00
Match safe, SP, 3 dice inlay under glass w/brass rim, NM.......42.00
Playing cards, De La Rue, England, single deck, 1880.........41.00
Poker chip, emb swastika, 950 chips in wood case...........380.00
Poker chip, floral w/detail engraving, antique ivory............15.00
Poker chip, monogrammed MC, ivory, rare...................35.00
Poker chip, The Sunflower, antique ivory....................15.00
Poker chips, celluloid, mc swirl pattern, set of 5..............4.00
Poker dice, set of 5.......................................20.00
Roulette wheel, bakelite, 12″..............................38.00
Roulette wheel, wood, 6 eng ball deflectors/metal ball, 8″.......15.00
Sign, rvpt, El Dorado Hotel Casino, w/conquistador............75.00
Tray, roulette wheel rim, gambling items graphics, 13″, NM......73.00
Watch, #d horses on dial, pull stem to spin wheel, M.........239.00
Watch, dice on dial, wind stem & hands pick pr dice, NM.....262.00
Watch, roulette wheel spins around, suits instead of #s.........50.00
Wheel of Fortune, bunnies, 36 numbers, many colors, 30″......81.00
Wood engraving, Gambling Evil at Long Branch, July 1889.....34.00

Games and Puzzles

Among the most popular 19th century games attracting collectors today are the board games and their components which are hand carved and painted, often with great attention to detail. Near the last decade of the century, commercially marketed games were introduced, some by companies who are still working. As is true today, many Victorian games were instructional and educational as well as entertaining. Colorfully lithographed boxes and game parts add to their appeal, and subject matter often exhibits customs and attitudes of a bygone era.

Puzzles were invented in 1760 by an English map-maker whose intention was to facilitate the teaching of geography. By the mid-1850s, both America and Europe were producing children's puzzles. The earliest examples were made of wood, and were hand-cut. Die-cut cardboard puzzles were first manufactured in the 1890s, and 'adult' puzzles came into vogue. Although wood continued to be used, plywood replaced solid wood during the twenties and thirties, and interlocking pieces made them easier to construct.

Hand-colored, hand-cut, or special-interest 19th century puzzles are favorites of today's collectors; character-related and quality wooden puzzles are also very desirable.

When no condition is indicated, the items listed below are assumed to be in excellent condition.

50 Soldiers on Parade, Milton Bradley, in original box, $175.00.

Games

Around the World w/Nellie Bly, McLoughlin, sm, ca 1890......65.00
Authors, McLoughlin, #372, w/box........................20.00
Authors, Parker Bros, orig box..........................10.00
Blow Football, tin/paper/plastic, orig 10½x6″ box, EX..........20.00
Board, walnut, gr w/yel star; rvpt checkerboard on bk, 22″....185.00
Checkerboard, chamfered wood panel, pnt sqs/border, 20x14″..165.00
Checkerboard, inlaid walnut/maple, Drueke Mfg, 1900, 26″.....25.00
Checkerboard, pine, red/blk, gr border, late 1800s, 17x13″....150.00
Checkerboard, pine w/5″ walnut fr inlaid w/stars/diamonds.....245.00
Checkerboard, pnt wood, 2-sided, storage ea end, rpr/rpt......125.00
Checkerboard, walnut, yel stripe/gilt sqs, breadboard ends.....250.00
Checkerboard, wide poplar brd w/orig 3-color pnt, 15x19″.....220.00
Checkerboard, 2nd game on bk, old pnt, age cracks, 20x30″...195.00
Chess, ash/maple sqs w/walnut border, 24″; w/5″ figures.......570.00
Chester Gump in City of Gold, Milton Bradley................50.00
Fort Grant Target Game, litho paper on wood, 16″ W, VG....200.00
GHQ Battle, orig box, ca 1930s..........................30.00
India, Game of; 1920s, complete.........................20.00
Jolly Marble, Bliss, litho paper on wood, in 19½″ box, VG.....350.00
Les Contes de Fees, litho paper on cb, 10x13″ box, VG.......210.00
Library of Games, orig box..............................25.00
Lotto, McLoughlin Bros, orig box.........................15.00
Magic Fortune Teller, litho paper, 11″ box, McLoughlin, VG...200.00
Mail Coach, Whitman....................................40.00
Mail Express, Railroad on cover, 1890, McLoughlin..........125.00
Milton Bradley, w/Lulu & Tubby, playing board, box, 21x16″....75.00
Mosaic, marble games, 1920, orig box......................15.00
Motor Race, tin plate board w/spinners, Wolverine, 1925.......20.00
Peter Cottle, his trip to Chicago, orig box..................15.00
Pin the Tail on the Donkey, printed cloth, early 20th C.........35.00
Regeles du Sphynx, French, in wood box....................18.50
Sambo, dart board game, Wyandotte........................25.00
Skip Ball, Wyandotte....................................30.00
Snake Eyes, shows Blk man & woman on cover, in box, 1930s..35.00
Tabby Cat Party Muslin Game, 1917, Saalfield, 18x24″ cloth....25.00
Telegraph, tin/paper/wood, Bradley, orig 11x8″ box, VG........50.00
Touring, Parker Bros, ca 1937............................15.00
USA, Mystic Finger, litho paper, orig box, 9½″, EX...........30.00
Wonderful Game of Oz, Parker Bros, complete in box........120.00

Puzzles

Blocks, children/pet lithos, orig box, 6½x8½″, 20 for..........95.00
Blocks, For Dolly & Me, orig box, ca 1868..................280.00
Blocks, 6-sided wood, Victorian children playing, 24 for.......185.00
Breathless Moment, Goodwin, hunters/bears, Milton Bradley....200.00
Fighters for Victory, Marx, WWII, orig box..................20.00
Hopped Up Niggers, McLoughlin Bros, 1884................150.00
Huyler's Cocoa, 1800s...................................26.00
Locomotive, Bradley, orig box, 20x8½″, EX.................100.00
Our Battleship, The Oregon; McLoughlin, paper/cb, VG.......125.00
Our Gang, McKesson Drugs, mtd, 1932.......................60.00
Roosevelt & Rough Riders, c Maher, 1898, 18½x25″..........225.00
Smitty & Herby, fishing in boat, whale approaching, 1932......25.00
Train, Milton Bradley, makes 42″ train, 1882, orig box.......225.00
USA Pioneer Map, pcs shape of states, 1939, Platt & Munk.....25.00
Victor Talking Machine Co, record shape, 1908...............55.00

Gas Globes and Panels

Gas globes and panels, once a common sight, have vanished from the countryside, but are being sought by collectors as a unique form of advertising memorabilia. Early globes from the 1920s, now referred to as 'one-piece globes,' were made of molded milk glass, and were globular in shape. The gas company name was etched or painted on the glass. Few of these were ever produced, and this type is valued very highly by collectors today.

A new type of pump was introduced in the early 1930s, the old 'visible' pumps replaced by 'electric' models. Globes were changing at the same time. By the mid-thirties, a five-piece globe consisting of a pair of inserts, two retaining rings, and a metal body were being produced in both 15″ and 16½″ sizes. These were prone to damage and were made for only a few years. A third type, used in the thirties and forties, consisted of a glass frame retainer with two milk glass inserts. Occasionally, textured glass in red, yellow, or blue was used; these are rare today, and very valuable.

The most recently manufactured gas globes, used since the late 1940s, are made with a plastic body that contains two 13½″ glass lenses.

Note: Standard Crowns with raised letters were the one-piece globes that were made in the 1920s; those made in the 1950s (no raised letters), though one-piece, are not regarded as such by today's collectors. Both variations are listed below. When no condition is indicated, the items listed below are assumed to be in mint condition.

Type 1, Plastic Body, Glass Inserts—1940s-1950s

Champlin..100.00
Clark Brand, plastic bands w/glass insert....................85.00
Dixie, plastic band....................................125.00
DX Ethyl...85.00
DX Lubricating Gasoline, tan, plastic body.................100.00
Falcon, pictures falcon..................................300.00
Marathon...70.00
Mobil..50.00
Never Nox Ethyl..150.00

Shamrock, oval body....75.00
Spur....50.00
Texaco Sky Chief, plastic globe....80.00
Viking, pictures Viking ship....150.00

Type 2, Glass Frame, Glass Inserts—1930s-1940s

Atlantic Hi-Arc, glass gill body....175.00
Champlin Presto....150.00
Coltex Service Gasoline, unused....250.00
Derby....165.00
Dixie-Oils Gasoline Power to Pass....185.00
DX Ethyl....140.00
Gulf....175.00
Indian Gas....175.00
Koolmotor, clover shape....350.00
Marathon Ethyl, pictures runner....200.00
Metro, unused....125.00
Mobilgas....200.00
Penco Premium, 3-pc glass....150.00
Richfield Ethyl....175.00
Shell, clam shape....175.00
Silver Pep....175.00
Sinclair Ethyl....150.00
Skelly Anomarx w/Ethyl....250.00
Skelly Fortified Premium....140.00
Skelly Powermax....175.00
Skelly Regular....150.00
Standard Blue Crown....200.00
Standard Gold Crown....200.00
Standard Green Crown....300.00
Standard Red Crown....185.00
Standard White Crown....200.00
Texaco Diesel Chief....200.00
Texaco Star, blk outline on 'T'....200.00
Trophy, Our Premium Gasoline....185.00
White Rose Enarco, pictures little boy....300.00
WNAX....200.00

Type 3, Metal Frame, Glass Inserts—1920s-1930s

Amoco, metal body....225.00
Atlantic White Flash, orig box, M....250.00
Atlantic White Flash, 16½″....250.00
Essolene, metal fr....190.00
Mobil Ethyl, w/lg flying horse, metal band....225.00
Mobilfuel Diesel, lg horse, high profile, metal band....275.00
Mobilgas, stripes, 15″, rare....300.00
Multipower (Marathon), 15″....250.00
Puro-Pep, porcelain body, 15″....325.00
Red Crown, 15 or 16″....400.00
Rocor, w/eagle, metal fr....285.00
Sunland Ethyl, 15″....275.00
Sunoco, blue, 15″....225.00
Tydol, 16½″....250.00
Tydol & Tydex, metal band, 16½″....275.00

Type 4, One-Piece Glass Globes, No Inserts, Co. Name Etched, Raised or Enameled—1914-1931

Champlin Gasoline....900.00
Dixie, etched, 1-pc....750.00
Gargoyle....400.00
Gulf....350.00
Indian Gas, etched, Red Dot....850.00
Kanotex, etched....1,800.00
Musco....1,500.00
Shell, round, etched....350.00
Sinclair Aircraft, etched....2,000.00
Sinclair Aircraft, painted....1,400.00
Sinclair H-C, painted....600.00
Standard Blue Crown Solite, raised letters....500.00
Standard Red Crown, raised letters....450.00
Standard Red Crown Ethyl, raised letters....450.00
Texaco....350.00
Texaco Ethyl....550.00
White Eagle....650.00
White Rose, painted....1,600.00

Gaudy Dutch

Inspired by Oriental Imari wares, Gaudy Dutch was made in England from 1800 to 1820. It was hand decorated on a soft paste body with rich underglaze blues accented in orange, red, pink, green, and yellow. It differs from Gaudy Welsh in that there is no lustre (except on Water Lily). There are seventeen patterns, some of which are: War Bonnet, Grape, Dahlia, Oyster, Urn, Butterfly, Carnation, Single Rose, Double Rose, and Water Lily.

When no condition is indicated, the items listed below are assumed to be in mint condition.

Butterfly, tea bowl & saucer, EX....650.00
Carnation, tea bowl & saucer....500.00
Double Rose, coffee pot, domed lid, spout rpr, flakes, 11″....475.00
Double Rose, creamer....450.00
Double Rose, plate, minor scratches on enamel, 10″....325.00
Double Rose, soup plate, minor rim flake, enamel worn, 8¼″....80.00
Double Rose, sugar w/lid, worn, sm chips, 5½″....150.00
Double Rose, tea bowl & saucer....395.00
Double Rose, teapot, prof rpr on spout/lid/rim, stain, 6⅛″....250.00
Double Rose, waste bowl, minor enamel wear, 2¾x5⅜″....325.00
Dove, tea bowl & saucer, sm flakes/wear....175.00
Dove, waste bowl....570.00
Grape, plate, enamel touch up rpr, 8¼″....85.00
Grape, plate, 7″, M....325.00
Grape, soup plate, enamel wear/fading, rim flakes, 8¼″....75.00
Oyster, plate, 10″, minor scratches....325.00
Oyster, soup plate, underglaze bl floral border, 8½″, EX....450.00
Oyster, tea bowl & saucer....425.00
Primrose, toddy plate, 4¾″, G....350.00
Single Rose, creamer, wide mouth, stained....275.00
Single Rose, plate, dbl border, 10″, M....525.00
Single Rose, plate, stains/wear, 7¼″, pr....130.00
Single Rose, sugar bowl, w/lid....670.00
Single Rose, tea bowl & saucer....400.00
Sunflower, creamer, hairline in spout, stain/wear, 4½″....100.00
Sunflower, milk jug, 4½″, VG....550.00
Sunflower, plate, 8¼″, VG....460.00
Sunflower, tea bowl & saucer....650.00
Urn, sugar bowl, finial rpr....250.00
War Bonnet, creamer, w/spout, sm rim chip, 4½″....200.00
War Bonnet, plate, touched up gr enamel, 7¼″....120.00
War Bonnet, plate, 7″, M....570.00
War Bonnet, sugar, hairlines in bowl/enamel wear, 5¾″....250.00
War Bonnet, tea bowl & saucer, minor stains/flakes....285.00
War Bonnet, tea bowl & saucer, NM....475.00
War Bonnet, teapot, slight enamel wear, prof rpr, 6⅜″....225.00

Gaudy Ironstone

Gaudy Ironstone was produced in the mid-1800s in Staffordshire, England. Some of the ware was decorated in much the same colors and designs as Gaudy Welsh, while other pieces were painted in pink, orange, and red, with black and light blue accents. Lustre was used on some designs, omitted on others. The heavy ironstone body is its most distinguishing feature.

When no condition is indicated, the items listed below are assumed to be in mint condition.

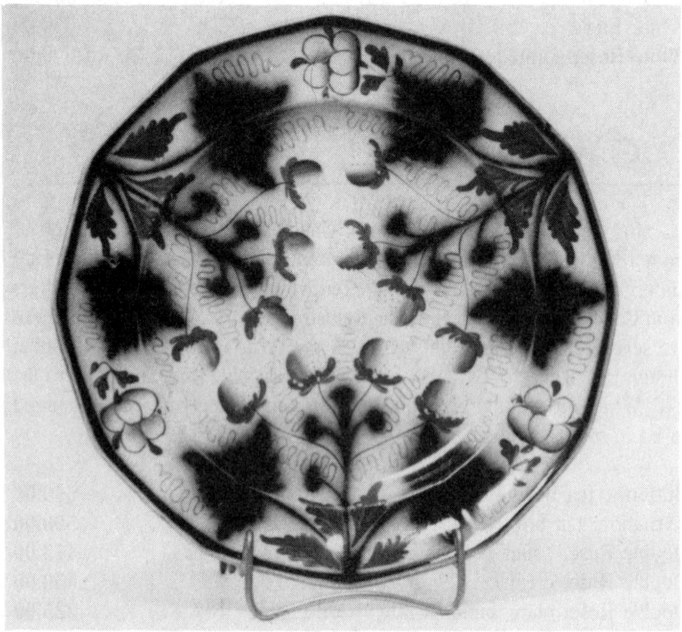

Plate, Strawberry pattern, signed Walker, 9¾", $125.00.

Bowl, serving; ped foot, open hdls....75.00
Cup & saucer, handleless; floral in red/bl/gr/blk, wear....50.00
Cup & saucer, leaf & berry, registry mk, minor ring chip....55.00
Pitcher, bl w/mc floral/birds/trees, registry mk, 6", NM....75.00
Pitcher, ogee sides, scroll hdl/ft/lip, rnd reserve, 6"....50.00
Plate, floral, gilt trim, Davenport, 10"....65.00
Plate, floral design, imp Pearl White, lustre trim, 8½"....30.00
Plate, red rose, 4-color motif, 9"....50.00
Plate, toddy; Seeing Eye, 5"....225.00
Waste bowl, floral in red/bl/gr/blk, 3⅛x6½"....50.00
Waste bowl, strawberry motif, edge chips, 3½x5¼"....40.00

Gaudy Welsh

Gaudy Welsh was an inexpensive hand-decorated ware made in both England and Wales from 1820 until 1860. It is characterized by its colors--principally underglaze blue, orange-rust, and copper lustre--and by its bold, uninhibited patterns. Accent colors may be yellow and green; pink lustre may be present, since lustre applied to the white areas appears pink. (The copper tone develops from painting lustre onto the dark colors.) The body of the ware may be heavy ironstone, creamware, earthenware, or porcelain; even style and shapes vary considerably. Patterns, while usually floral, are also sometimes geometric, and may have trees and birds.

When no condition is indicated, the items listed below are assumed to be in mint condition.

Bowl, Oyster, 6", EX....45.00
Creamer, Oyster....65.00
Creamer, Shanghai....90.00
Cup, Wagon Wheel....35.00
Cup & saucer, Oyster....65.00
Cup & saucer, Tulip....48.00
Mug, Tulip, miniature, 1⅞"....25.00
Pitcher, Oyster, 4½x4½"....85.00
Pitcher, Oyster, 5½"....95.00
Pitcher, Wagon Wheel, 8½"....175.00
Plate, dessert; Oyster....40.00
Plate, Flower Basket, 8½"....35.00
Plate, Tulip, 6"....22.50
Plate, Wagon Wheel, 7½"....50.00
Plate, Wagon Wheel, 8¾"....75.00
Platter, Morning Glory, copper lustre trim, 14½", EX....135.00
Sugar bowl, Daisy & Chain, w/lid....120.00
Sugar bowl, Tulip, hdls, w/lid....80.00
Teapot, Tulip, ca 1840....135.00

Geisha Girl

Geisha girl porcelains have only recently attracted a following in the collectibles market. They were made primarily for export in dinnerware, tea sets, and vases, in several patterns featuring Geisha girls in various daily pursuits. Some were entirely hand painted, others were hand decorated over decals or with stencils. Pieces were bordered in one of many bright colors--red, yellow, blue, green, or brown--and collectors generally prefer to match border colors when re-assembling a matching set.

When no condition is indicated, the items listed below are assumed to be in mint condition.

Bowl, berry; 5"....10.00
Bowl, fluted, 4½"....8.00
Bowl, nut; ftd, 5¾"....15.00
Chamberstick....28.00
Chocolate pot, red trim, 9½"....65.00
Chocolate set, fluted pot, 6 cups & saucers....95.00
Chocolate set, parasol pattern, 11-pc....125.00
Cookie jar....32.00
Creamer & sugar, cobalt w/gold leaf, w/lid, lg....30.00
Creamer & sugar, sm....14.00
Cup & saucer, bl w/gold, set of 4....35.00
Cup & saucer, Geisha girl inside cup....15.00
Egg cup....6.00
Jar, condensed milk; mc border, Satsuma style....35.00
Jar, ginger; lanterns, orange, rare, 4½"....35.00
Mayonnaise, Nippon, 3-pc....40.00
Mint dish, ftd, cobalt....25.00
Pitcher, milk; Satsuma style, 6"....55.00
Pitcher, 2⅛"....10.00
Plate, gold highlights, 6", set of 8....60.00
Plate, 2 life-size Geisha, gilt, scalloped/open edge, 11"....50.00
Plate, 7¼"....10.00
Shaker, mushroom, 3¼", pr....15.00
Shaker, octagon, 3", pr....15.00
Tea set, child's; 17-pc....95.00
Tea set, cobalt trim, pot, cr/sug, 6 c/s....125.00
Tea set, 3-pc....75.00
Teapot, pumpkin shape, w/lid, rust, 1-cup....25.00
Teapot, 4-cup....45.00
Toothpick holder....20.00
Tray, dresser; cobalt, 13x7½"....40.00
Tray, jewel; ftd....15.00

German Porcelain

The porcelain listed in this section is marked simply 'Germany.' Products of other German manufactures are listed in specific categories. When no condition is indicated, the items listed below are assumed to be in mint condition. See also Pink Pigs; Elfinware

Bathing Beauty, bisque, 3½"....55.00
Bottle, begging bulldog, bl....50.00
Bottle, goat figural, risque clothing, mc, 7½"....28.00
Bottle, Little Scotch: baby w/bottle figural, bisque....80.00
Bottle, man in striped pants, bisque....40.00
Bottle, scent; bluebird, removable head....40.00
Bottle, scent; child, blk hat, in yel bag, 4¼"....40.00
Bowl, blown-out floral rim w/floral center, Saxe, 2½x8x12"....100.00
Bowl, Georgia Rose, shell mold, gold flutes/ruffles, 9¾"....60.00
Bowl, yel roses/sprigs of lilac/leaves, fluted edge, 10"....45.00
Box, Jasper, Deco lady on lid, jeweled/irid, triangular....55.00
Box, snuff; commemorative, oval, hinged lid, 2½x2⅛"....170.00
Centerpiece, 3 people on boat, bisque, pastels, 12x6x13"....350.00
Cheese & cracker, tulips, 3-crown mk, 10"....30.00
Coffee pot, lady w/creamer/umbrella/purse figural, 11"....325.00
Coffee set, demitasse; roses on brn, CT mk, 1855, 19-pc....450.00
Cookie jar, wht w/pink/yel roses, gold trim, sgn, 6¾"....60.00
Creamer, blk dachshund head, orange w/in, mk MW Co, 4½x5".32.00
Creamer, crocodile figural, brns/blk/gold, 5x3½"....60.00
Cup & saucer, florals, gold trim, ornate, ca 1860....45.00
Egg cup, rooster driving car, whistle, mc, 2¼x1½x4"....30.00
Figurine, bathing baby in china tub, pnt features, 2¼x3"....250.00
Figurine, bride & groom, bisque, groom w/top hat, 3½", MIB...35.00
Figurine, bulldog, bl collar, sgn Metzler & Ortloff, 5"....165.00
Figurine, comic character 'Jeff,' bisque, 9"....50.00
Figurine, News Vendor, Schiebe Kister mk, 1834, 5¼"....95.00
Figurine, sleeping cat, wht/brn w/lt bl collar, 3¼x4½"....55.00
Figurine, sleeping Cupid, scarf on legs, X-swords mk, 3"....100.00
Figurine, wild boar, decorated bisque, 4½x7½"....115.00
Figurine, yel canary on branch, mk HR, 3"....35.00
Humidor, man figural, holds pipe & bail, imp mk, 8"....80.00
Mold, pudding; wht w/bl decor, 7x4½"....65.00
Place card holder, children figurals, set of 6....65.00
Plate, children in snow w/sm fire & birds, sgn RC w/crown....100.00
Plate, Evening at the Tontine Marshes, pierced, 9½"....22.00
Plate, fleur-de-lis, lg beige roses, clover border, 8½"....28.00
Plate, gold leaf border, fruit center, Frustenburg, 10"....50.00
Plate, tapestry finish w/Cupid & lovers, mk Germany, 9¾"....205.00
Plate, 2 little girls w/dolls, 7"....45.00
Plate, 2 maids & Cupid in woody glen, cobalt/gilt rim, 8"....45.00
Server, pnt flowers on ivory, dbl dish, center hdl....145.00
Sugar bowl, Silesia, La Touraine, Striegan, bellflowers....35.00
Teapot, pink roses on cream, lacy gold trim, 5¾x4⅜"....55.00
Toothbrush holder, Old Mother Hubbard figural....95.00
Toothbrush holder, Windmill figural....85.00
Vase, lady's portrait, 1: brn, 1: gr w/gold trim, 3", pr....75.00
Vase, man in panel, foliate/floral pendants/tulip top, 19"....300.00
Vase, tapestry, portraits of 3 ladies, 6"....165.00
Vase, 2 Greenaway-style girls' portraits, 6"....35.00

Gladding McBean and Company

In 1923, Gladding McBean purchased the Tropico plant in Glendale, California. While they are best known for their dinnerware, they also produced at least fifteen lines of art pottery, in a great many shapes and colors. (This section deals only with their artware; for dinnerware listings, see Franciscan.) For a short time, they stamped their wares with the Tropico Pottery mark; but the majority was signed 'GMcB' in an oval, 'Catalina Pottery,' or 'Franciscan.' Occasionally a paper label was used. The last catalog for art pottery was issued in 1942.

'Catalina Pottery' indicated wares produced on the mainland; Catalina Island wares were marked 'Catalina' (no 'Pottery'), or 'Catalina Island.' When no condition is indicated, the items listed below are assumed to be in mint condition.

Planter, figural lady, pink, 7", $20.00.

Bowl, ivory satin, oval, 15"....30.00
Bowl, ivory satin, turq gloss interior, 5½x7½" dia....25.00
Coffee pot, demitasse; Ruby....40.00
Pitcher, med bl glaze, Tropico mk, 5¾"....9.00
Vase, aqua w/pink interior, crimped cylinder, mk CP....30.00
Vase, coral & turq gloss, 5"....15.00
Vase, fish shape, ivory satin exterior....35.00
Vase, flat fan shape, ivory & turq satin....20.00
Vase, ivory satin, ftd, swirled base, Coronado, 10½"....18.00
Vase, Ox Blood, no mk, 8½"....40.00
Vase, shell, ivory & coral satin, 7¼"....25.00

Goebel

F.W. Goebel founded the Hummelwork Porcelain Manufactory in 1871, located in Rodental, West Germany. They produced porcelain figurines, plates, and novelties, the most famous of which are the Hummel figurines (these are listed in a separate section). There were many other series produced by Goebel--Disney characters, birds, animals, and the Friar Tuck Monks that are especially popular.

When no condition is indicated, the items listed below are assumed to be in mint condition. See also Collector Plates; Hummel

Bank, Friar Tuck Monks, mk W Germany....25.00
Bust, Elvis Presley....14.00
Condiment set, Friar Tuck Monks, full bee....65.00
Cookie jar, Cardinal in red robe....125.00
Creamer, clown w/blk face figural, crown mk....85.00

Salt and pepper shakers, Friar Tuck Monks, 2½″, $42.00.

Creamer, Friar Tuck Monks, stylized bee, 5½″ 36.00
Creamer & sugar, w/lid & 5″ tray, Friar Tuck Monks 65.00
Figurine, baby in wht crib 45.00
Figurine, Baby Robin 25.00
Figurine, Bambi, lying down, full bee, w/label, 2″ 110.00
Figurine, bird, CV-33 . . . . . 18.00
Figurine, blonde lady on sofa w/parrot, crown mk, #1764 . . . . . 150.00
Figurine, Blue Titmouse 20.00
Figurine, Colonial girl w/Russian wolfhound, 4⅜″ 28.00
Figurine, European Goldfinch 25.00
Figurine, Figaro, sitting, full bee, w/label, 2″ 95.00
Figurine, flamenco woman dancer, Art Deco, 10″ 150.00
Figurine, Grumpy, full bee 65.00
Figurine, Madonna, 10″ 70.00
Figurine, Madonna & Child, pastels, #106, full bee, 11″ 95.00
Figurine, Madonna & Child, wht, HM186, stylized bee, 8″ 40.00
Figurine, nude kneeling, terra cotta, 1953, 9½″ 45.00
Figurine, Pinocchio, sitting, full bee, w/label, 4″ 325.00
Figurine, rabbits 15.00
Figurine, Redstart 25.00
Figurine, swan, wht w/red beak, 6″ 16.00
Jar, cat figural, crown mk, w/lid 55.00
Jar, Friar Tuck Monks, stylized bee, 4½″ 30.00
Mug, child's; Humpty Dumpty 15.00
Mug, child's; wht parading elephants in relief, orange 60.00
Mug, Friar Tuck Monks, V & bee, sgn, 5″ 39.00
Night light, boy plays concertina/sings, glass eyes, 9½″ 95.00
Pitcher, brn/wht cow, full bee, 5½″ 24.00
Pitcher, Friar Tuck Monks, #747, 2/0, full bee 14.00
Pitcher, Mrs Gamp, full bee 39.00
Reamer, orange figural 50.00
Shakers, rooster & hen, wht w/red comb, full bee, 3″ 45.00
Vase, Bambi stands by hollow tree trunk, full bee, 5″ 325.00

Going-to-Bed Lamps

Going-to-Bed lamps, used for just that purpose, had a compartment for matches, a striker, and a socket to hold a burning match or a small taper. The match provided just enough illumination to enable one to find his way to bed after the oil lamp was extinguished.

When no condition is indicated, the items listed below are assumed to be in excellent condition.

Blk leatherized tin box w/brass trim, Berry's Pat, 2″ 25.00
Brass bear chained to post, cast brass/gilt, detailed, 3″ 210.00
Cylinder, brass, sm, 1¾″ 15.00
Emb brass w/red enamel/gilt, Royal Perfect Bougie Box, 3½″ 35.00
Filigree, brass, w/lt gr glass insert, scene on lid, 2″ 35.00
Lizard skin on tin, spring lid, mk Light, 1⅞″ 25.00
Owl figural, cast brass, glass eyes, 2¾″ 55.00
Wood canister w/ivory & brass trim, 3½″ 25.00

Goldscheider

The Goldscheider family operated a pottery in Vienna for many generations before seeking refuge in the United States following Hitler's invasion of their country. They settled in Trenton, New Jersey, in the early 1940s, where they established a new corporation, producing objects of art and tableware items. In 1946 Marcel Goldscheider established a pottery in Staffordshire, where he manufactured bone china figures, earthenware, etc., marked with a stamp of his signature.

When no condition is indicated, the items listed below are assumed to be in mint condition.

Bust, Chinese Boy & Girl, sgn, 8″, pr 140.00
Bust, Oriental, USA, pr 95.00
Figurine, Bachelor Carnation & Lady Violet, 7″, pr 97.00
Figurine, Blanche, artist sgn, 5″ 50.00
Figurine, Christmas Lady, w/Poinsettia, 1800s dress, 7½″ 75.00

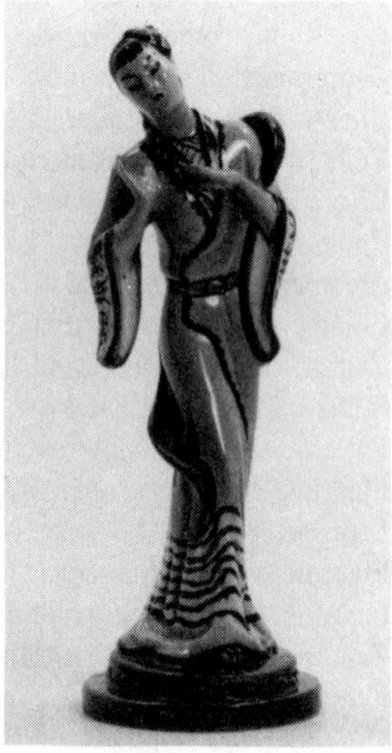

Figurine, Oriental in yellow robe, 10½″, $75.00.

Figurine, Colonial man bowing, USA, gray/pink, #79677, 8½″ 65.00
Figurine, Colonial woman, blk/bl dress, sgn, 7″ 50.00
Figurine, German Shepherd, recumbent, Vienna, 8″ L 65.00
Figurine, girl, short flowered skirt, Staffordshire, 8″ 175.00
Figurine, Japanese lady w/lantern, artist sgn 125.00
Figurine, Juliet w/Doves, USA, 12¼″ 225.00
Figurine, Lady Caller, 6″ 50.00
Figurine, lady in gr ruffled dress holds lg yel hat, 8½″ 65.00
Figurine, Madonna, sgn, pink, 5″ 22.00
Figurine, man holding cape & bouquet, 9½″ 75.00
Figurine, Nouveau nudes, artist sgn, dtd 1907, Austrian 1,250.00
Figurine, Quadrille, gold crest mk, Parker artist 38.00
Figurine, Siamese cat 40.00
Figurine, Southern Belle, pink, USA 62.00
Figurine, Yankee Doodle Dandy 60.00
Plaque, advertising; Goldscheider, Vienna 275.00
Smoker set, Dutch girl at well, holds cigarettes/ash tray 45.00

Gonder

Lawton Gonder grew up a ceramist. By the time he opened his own pottery in December, 1941, he had a solid background in both production and management. Gonder Ceramic Arts, Inc., purchased the old Peters and Reed-Zane Pottery in South Zanesville, Ohio. There they turned out quality commercial ware with graceful shapes in both Oriental and contemporary designs. Their greatest achievements were the development of their superior glazes: flambe; 24k gold crackle; and Chinese crackle glazes in celadon, ming yellow, and blue. Most of the ware is marked with 'Gonder' impressed in script, and a mold number.

When no condition is indicated, the items listed below are assumed to be in mint condition.

Cookie jar, maroon with white drip glaze, dog reclining on lid, $50.00.

Cornucopia, bl w/pink int, upright, 8½″ 8.50
Creamer & sugar, spatter decor, brn & cream, rare, lg 15.00
Figurine, leopard, sgn, jade gr, 18¼″ 50.00
Figurine, Mandarin lady, jade gr, 12″ 20.00
Figurine, South Seas Island girl, lime gr, 14″ 30.00
Ginger jar, Oriental dragons, 3-pc 30.00
Planter, swan, pink & gray, 9x8½″ 12.00
Vase, flower shape, pink-brn glaze, 8″ 9.00
Vase, H79, 8″, pr 12.00
Vase, tan swirl, 2-hdl, 9½″ 15.00

Goofus Glass

Goofus was an inexpensive type of lustre-painted pressed glassware made by many companies during the first two decades of the 20th century. Bowls and trays are most common, and red and gold combinations are found more often than blues and greens.

Authority Carolyn McKinley has compiled a lovely book *Goofus Glass, An Illustrated Value Guide*, available at your favorite bookstore. When no condition is indicated, the items listed below are assumed to be in mint condition.

Bowl, dahlia, scalloped, gold, ornate, 10x4″ 45.00
Bowl, grape, scalloped, orig pnt, sq, 10x5″ 60.00
Bowl, roses, 5-sided, rare, 9x3½″ 60.00
Compote, cherries, ruffled rim, 10″ 80.00
Compote & saucer, poppy, crackle glass, orig pnt, 4″, M 25.00
Decanter, amethyst, matching tray, w/stopper, 9″ 40.00
Jar, pickle; sailing ship & seagulls, 9½″, G pnt 25.00
Lamp, oil; cabbage rose, milk glass, miniature, 9″ 50.00
Lamp, poppy, Gone with the Wind base, 15″ 55.00
Plate, cake; acorn & leaf, amethyst, 12″ 20.00
Plate, cake; carnation w/elk center, orig pnt, rare, 13″ 45.00
Plate, holly, opal, orig pnt, 10½″, NM 45.00
Plate, rose & lattice, sm, orig pnt, 6″ 20.00
Plate, strawberries, 11″, M 40.00
Powder box, basketweave, milk glass, orig pnt, rare, M 50.00
Shakers, dogwood, orig pnt & tops, rare, 4″, pr 40.00
Syrup, cabbage rose, pnt scaled away, 5½″ 35.00
Tray, dresser; basketweave, roses, 7x10″ 25.00
Tray, dresser; roses, heart shaped, amethyst, rare, 6″ 50.00
Vase, bird sitting on grapevine, satin glass, 9″ 15.00
Vase, grapes, lg clusters, heavy bl glass, rare, 7″ 20.00
Vase, peacock, gold on clear, rare, 10½″ 75.00
Water bottle, basketweave, orig wht pnt, 10″ 40.00

Plate, monk and roses, original paint, 7″, $40.00., in mint condition.

Goss

The Goss Pottery was established in 1858 at Stoke-on-Trent in England. Their earliest products were quality porcelains, parian, and earthenware. Later, they also produced 'farings'--small souvenir items decorated with decals that were sometimes over-painted by hand. The decals represented English landmarks, coats of arms, or scenes of historical significance. Early wares were marked 'W.H.G.' or 'W.H. Goss.' After 1862, a falcon mark was used. The company was purchased in 1934 by Cauldon Potteries, Ltd.

When no condition is indicated, the items listed below are assumed to be in mint condition.

Aberdein Creamer & Sugar 12.00
Alnwick Celtic Urn 20.00
Antwerp Oolen Pot 30.00
Bideford Mortar 60.00
Boulogne Milk Can 20.00
Bristol Puzzle Cider Cup 60.00
Caerleon Lamp 30.00
Cambridge Sea Shell, #169 .... 32.00

Canary Earthen Jar....................................20.00
Canary Jarra..15.00
Channel Isle Lobster Trap.............................37.00
Cheshire Cat..20.00
Chichester Coronation Chair...........................20.00
Chichester Trinket Box, lg............................20.00
Colchester Famous Vase................................17.00
Eddystone Lighthouse..................................40.00
Egyptian Mocha Cup....................................20.00
Fleetwood Fish Basket, #106...........................28.00
Fraser's Cuach..30.00
Gilbraltar Alcaraza...................................18.00
Glastonbury Jack......................................20.00
Glastonbury Salt Cellar...............................40.00
Greenwich Cheese Dish w/lid...........................15.00
Highland Milk Grogan..................................28.00
Hitchin Possit Cup....................................20.00
Hornsea Roman Vase....................................20.00
Irish Bronze Pot......................................20.00
Itford British Urn....................................12.00
Jersey Milk Can, lg...................................28.00
Lanlawren Celtic Sepulchral Urn.......................20.00
Lazey Urn...20.00
Lincoln Vase..20.00
Litchfield Jug..20.00
Malmesbury Abbey Creamer & Sugar......................28.00
Manx Spirit Measure...................................48.00
Newbury Leather Bottle................................12.00
Newcastle Roman Jug...................................20.00
Ostend Tobacco Jar....................................10.00
Partick Shoe..20.00
Penmaenmawr Urn.......................................14.00
Ramsgate Candle Holder................................20.00
Reading Roman Urn.....................................20.00
Sandown Wall Pocket...................................20.00
Scarborough Jug.......................................18.00
Shrewbury Ewer..20.00
Staffordshire Tyg, hdl................................20.00
Tewkesbury Saxon Urn..................................15.00
Tony Panda Cottage....................................20.00
Tresvannacle Urn......................................13.00
Winchester Black Jack.................................40.00
Yarmouth Creamer, sm..................................15.00
50th Jubilee, bowl...................................100.00
50th Jubilee, pitcher................................100.00

Gouda

Since the 18th century the main center of the pottery industry in Holland was in Gouda. One of its earliest industries, the manufacture of clay pipes, continues to the present day. The artware so easily recognized by collectors today was first produced about 1885. It was decorated in the Art Nouveau manner. Stylized florals, birds, and geometrics were favored motifs; only rarely is the design naturalistic. The Nouveau influence was strong until about 1915. Art Deco was attempted, but with less success. Though most of the ware is finished in a matt glaze, glossy pieces in both pastels and dark colors are found on occasion, and command higher prices. Decoration on the glossy ware is usually very well executed. Most of the work shops failed during the depression, though earthenware is still being made in Gouda, and carries the Gouda mark. Until very recently, Regina was still making a limited amount of the old Gouda style pottery in a matt finish. Watch for the Gouda name, which is usually a part of the backstamp of the various manufacturers.

When no condition is indicated, the items listed below are assumed to be in mint condition.

Ash tray, gr/cobalt, house mk Anne Royal, 1¼x4⅛"..........38.00
Basket, frog, rope hdl, Regina, 8".......................120.00
Bowl, Art Nouveau, gr/brn, w/lid, 4x6"...................110.00
Bowl, floral, Anjer, w/lid, 6"............................60.00
Bowl, peacock motif, 5x18¼"..............................325.00
Candlestick, orange/bl/gr, Iottea, 4½x4½"................70.00
Candlestick, rust/yel/blk, Regina, 4½", pr...............150.00
Chamber stick, blk satin w/mc floral panels, 3x5⅝"........75.00
Creamer, rust/brn, 2½"....................................38.00
Cup & saucer, windmill scene, Royal.......................50.00
Ewer, gr/lav gloss w/Deco floral motif, schoolhouse mk, 8"......75.00
Figurine, girl, Plazuid, 11".............................165.00
Food warmer, pierced, solid yel, Plaziud House mk.........22.00
Humidor, house, sgn, matt tan/bl/gr, lg..................145.00
Inkwell, bl/gr/rust on wht, Schoonloven, 3" sq...........120.00
Jardiniere, 5-color, 5½".................................125.00
Jug, blk matt w/mc Deco motif, Emanuel, 11", +13x10" tray..275.00
Matchbox holder, Ivora, 2¾"...............................40.00
Pipe rack, 6-hole, mc on black, Regina, rare, 4x10"......200.00
Pitcher, blk w/gold design, 5"............................55.00
Pitcher, Metz Royal, mc, 5"...............................45.00
Pitcher, red dot decor, bl matt, house mk Z Waro, 2½"......22.00
Planter, sprouted seeds motif, 2-pc, 1½" bowl w/6x7" pot......250.00
Plaque, coat of arms, Koningen Wilhelmina, rare, 1893-1923...345.00
Plate, pastel floral/butterfly on wht, Jugenstill, 11"...190.00
Shoe, Regina, 25th Anniv Comm Wilhelmina, gr/blk on dark....75.00
Tea caddy, 7-color, glossy, no mk, 4".....................60.00
Vase, brn/gold/gr decor, schoolhouse mk, 2x1".............30.00
Vase, butterflies/poppies on wht, Zuid Holland, 5x13"....400.00
Vase, cobalt, blk matt finish, mk Blareth, 2-hdl, 5¼x6"...48.00
Vase, dahlia, sgn Royal Soedewahsen, 4"...................37.00
Vase, floral, mk, 2 ear hdls, 6½".........................58.00
Vase, floral, mk, 6¼".....................................50.00
Vase, floral, squat, 3"...................................30.00
Vase, glossy, Maasserma, 5½x6"...........................125.00
Vase, gourd shape, Lydia, Regina, 8"......................95.00
Vase, Ivora, mc pastel, Nouveau, 3x4"....................110.00
Vase, mc Deco motif, schoolhouse mk, 8"...................88.00
Vase, mc flowers, mk #2041/Crocus, 5¼"....................75.00
Vase, rust & bl daisies on tan, Janerio, 7x6½"............75.00
Vase, stylized florals, Regina Bochara, Crown mk, 10½".......125.00
Vase, 4-color, w/basket handle, Zuid Holland, 9x9"........425.00
Wall pocket, 11½"..145.00

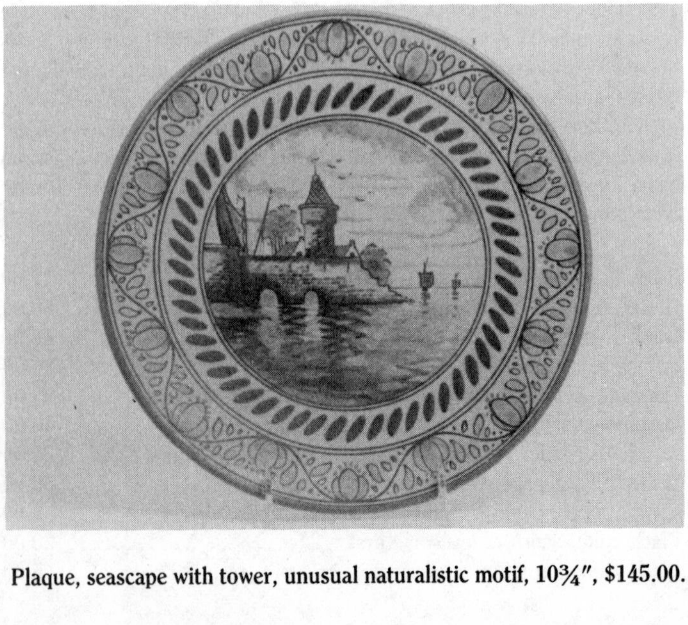

Plaque, seascape with tower, unusual naturalistic motif, 10¾", $145.00.

Graniteware

Graniteware, thin iron ware with an enamel coating, derives its name from its appearance. The speckled or mottled effect of the vari-colored enamels may look like granite--but there the resemblance stops. It wasn't especially durable! Expect at least minor chipping if you plan to collect.

Graniteware was featured in 1876 at Phily's Expo. It was mass-produced in quantity, and enough of it has survived to make at least the common items easily affordable. Color is an important consideration in evaluating an item; cobalt, brown, or green swirl is unusual, and thus are more expensive. Pieces of heavier weight, seam constructed, and those with wooden handles and tin lids are usually older.

In recent months, magazine articles featuring decorating ideas with an emphasis on the 'country look' have caused the price of graniteware to escalate--a trend which is likely to continue.

When no condition is indicated, the items listed below are assumed to be in excellent condition.

Baby bottle warmer, gray & wht speckled....65.00
Bucket, berry; bl, w/lid....58.00
Bucket, berry; child's, gray, tin lid, 5"....50.00
Bucket, berry; cobalt & wht swirl....55.00
Bucket, berry; cobalt diffused....58.00
Bucket, berry; dk bl & wht swirl, 6"....43.00
Bucket, berry; gray, w/lid, lg....45.00
Bucket, berry; gray, w/lid, 4"....46.00
Bucket, berry; wht, w/lid, sm....15.00
Bucket, dinner; gray, miner's....68.00
Bucket, water; brn & wht speckled....35.00
Bucket, water; cobalt & wht swirl....50.00
Bucket, water; gray....35.00
Bucket, water; med bl & wht swirl....50.00
Candle holder, bl w/blk trim....35.00
Candle holder, cream & gr....30.00
Candle holder, dk gr....30.00
Candle holder, gr....30.00
Candlestick, beehive, gray....95.00
Canister, 'Flour,' bl & wht speckled....65.00
Canister, 'Flour,' cream & gr....45.00
Canister, 'Flour,' wht, w/lid....25.00
Casserole, cobalt & wht swirl, w/lid....45.00
Cereal set, child's; bowl & milk pitcher, bl w/mc floral....35.00
Chamberstick, bl & wht swirl, no hdl....25.00
Chamberstick, wht, w/hdl....25.00
Coffee boiler, bl & wht mottled....60.00
Coffee boiler, bl & wht swirl....65.00
Coffee boiler, Chrysolite & wht swirl....75.00
Coffee boiler, chuckwagon, wht w/blk edge, bail hdl, 13"....38.00
Coffee boiler, cobalt & wht swirl....68.00
Coffee boiler, gray & blk, bail w/wood hdl, 11½"....50.00
Coffee boiler, gray mottle....28.00
Coffee pot, bl & wht, moss roses ea side, slant sides....65.00
Coffee pot, bl & wht swirl, gooseneck....65.00
Coffee pot, brn, gooseneck....42.50
Coffee pot, child's; bl....42.00
Coffee pot, Chrysolite & wht swirl, gooseneck, sm....85.00
Coffee pot, Chrysolite & wht swirl, str spout, sm....80.00
Coffee pot, cream w/red trim, gooseneck....25.00
Coffee pot, dk turq, gooseneck spout....45.00
Coffee pot, floral/birds, wht, brass/wood trim, pewter lid....180.00
Coffee pot, gr, wood hdl/SP bottom/rim/lid/spout cover, mk....125.00
Coffee pot, gray, CI hdl....75.00
Coffee pot, gray, gooseneck, 1-cup....55.00

Coffee flask, gray, 6½", $80.00.

Coffee pot, gray, w/tin lid, 10"....40.00
Coffee pot, red....21.00
Coffee pot, turq, tall....25.00
Coffee pot, turq & wht mottle, 8-cup....55.00
Coffee pot, turq honeycomb motif on wht & brn speckle, 10"....85.00
Coffee pot, wht w/gr trim, 6-cup....25.00
Coffee pot, yel w/gr trim, glass top....25.00
Coffee pot, 2-tone bl, lg....55.00
Colander, bl & wht marbleized....35.00
Colander, blk & wht speckled, ftd....17.00
Colander, brn & wht swirl....34.00
Colander, cobalt & wht swirl....38.00
Colander, gray mottled....14.00
Colander, wht w/cobalt trim, 3-corner....18.00
Cup, coffee; bl & wht swirl....12.00
Cup, gray, 4"....12.00
Cup, tea; bl & wht swirl....25.00
Cup & saucer, bl....22.00
Cuspidor, wht....25.00
Dbl boiler, bl speckled, w/lid....42.00
Dbl boiler, Chrysolite & wht swirl, lg....78.00
Dipper, bl & wht mottled....25.00
Dipper, cobalt & wht swirl, lg....60.00
Dipper, gray on gray speckle, 6⅝" dia....18.00
Dust pan, bl....75.00
Dust pan, gray....75.00
Egg cup, lt bl....20.00
Egg poacher, cobalt & wht, 6-hole....95.00
Egg poacher, gray....75.00
Feeding dish, infant's; wht....14.00
Fish boiler, gray....58.00
Flask, gray....60.00
Flowerpot, gray....90.00
Funnel, canning; lt bl & wht....48.00
Funnel, gray, hdls, 3½"....15.00
Hot plate, lt gr speckled, few chips....55.00
Jar, slop; bl & wht swirl....90.00
Kettle, bl & wht swirl, Berlin....38.00
Kettle, child's; gray w/bail, 3"....58.00
Kettle, cobalt & wht swirl, w/lid, NM....58.00
Kettle, robin's egg bl speckled, w/lid....35.00
Ladle, turq & wht swirl....20.00
Lunch pail, gray, 3-pc....75.00

Match box, rose decor, hanging.....65.00
Measure, gray, 1-cup.....30.00
Measure, mk Granite Iron Works, pat May 1876, 1-cup.....60.00
Measure, navy bl w/wht spatter, ½-gal.....35.00
Meat grinder, wht, Germany.....28.00
Meat grinder, wht agate, mk Harras.....45.00
Milk can, bl & wht mottled.....35.00
Mold, corn; gray.....70.00
Mold, wht, Cream City Ware Milwaukee, rnd.....12.00
Mug, child's; wht.....12.00
Napkin holder, wht & blk.....62.00
Pan, bake; gray, oval.....17.00
Pan, bl & wht swirl, rnd, 8″.....21.00
Pan, bl swirl, 8″.....24.00
Pan, bread; gray, 13″.....16.00
Pan, cake; bl & wht mottled, rectangular, w/hdls.....38.00
Pan, cake; bl & wht swirl, 9x13″.....52.00
Pan, cake; Chrysolite & wht swirl, rectangular.....25.00
Pan, cake; cobalt & wht swirl, 9x13″.....65.00
Pan, cake; dk bl, tube shape.....16.00
Pan, muffin; 12-hole, gray.....45.00
Pan, muffin; 6-hole, gray.....25.00
Pan, pie; bl & wht mottle.....16.00
Pan, pie; Chrysolite & wht swirl.....20.00
Pan, pie; cobalt & wht swirl.....14.00
Pan, pie; gray.....8.00
Pan, pie; gray & blk mottled.....16.00
Pan, pie; 2-tone bl.....12.00
Pan, pudding; bl & wht swirl, sm.....25.00
Pan, roasting; open, gray, 14½″.....9.00
Pan, sauce; aqua & wht swirl, hdls.....26.00
Pan, sauce; bl & wht mottled, tubular hdl, lg.....36.00
Pan, sauce; gray, hdls, 4½″.....28.00
Pan, speckled, gray, 4″.....15.00
Pitcher, bl, miniature.....40.00
Pitcher, bl, w/wash bowl.....75.00
Pitcher, syrup; aqua & wht swirl.....75.00
Pitcher, syrup; gray.....65.00
Pitcher, turq & wht mottle, 11″.....75.00
Pitcher, water; bl, lg.....58.00
Pitcher, water; gray.....38.00
Plate, child's; tan w/witch & rhyme.....15.00
Plate, cobalt.....14.00
Plate, wht w/underglaze flower.....15.00
Platter, gray, oval.....25.00
Platter, red & wht, 8-sided.....15.00
Platter, turkey; bl & wht mottled.....70.00
Platter, wht, oval.....7.00
Pot, chamber; gray & wht, w/lid.....22.00
Roaster, bl & wht mottled.....38.00
Roaster, brn & wht swirl.....50.00
Roaster, cobalt & wht swirl.....45.00
Roaster, gr w/wht spatter, rnd, w/lid.....35.00
Salt box, red.....95.00
Salt box, wht w/gold trim, hanging.....45.00
Saucer, cobalt & wht swirl.....7.00
Scoop, grocer's; gray, mk.....78.00
Skillet, aqua & wht swirl.....75.00
Soap dish, gray, w/tray.....25.00
Soap dish, gray, wall mt.....27.50
Soap dish, wht, oblong, Germany.....15.00
Soap dish, wht, sq.....10.00
Spittoon, bl & wht swirl, 2-pc.....45.00
Spoon, bl & wht swirl.....10.00
Spooner, floral on gray, pewter trim.....100.00
Steamer, bl & wht mottled, w/lid.....22.00
Stove, 'Home Comfort,' wood, towel bars, water reservoir.....1,800.00
Strainer, bl & wht swirl, rnd.....34.00
Strainer, brn & wht mottled.....26.00
Sugar bowl, no lid; gray.....50.00
Table, child's; ABCs.....75.00
Tea set, child's; wht & gr, snowflake, 8-pc.....150.00
Tea strainer, gray.....45.00
Tea strainer, wht.....13.00
Teakettle, bl speckled, EX.....60.00
Teakettle, blk.....35.00
Teakettle, gr, lg.....42.00
Teapot, gray, pewter trim, 11″.....175.00
Teapot, mc flowers/bird/foliage, metal top, wood hdl.....125.00
Teapot, speckled robin egg bl, Britannia metal, fancy hdl.....150.00
Teapot, turq, pewter top, Manning & Bowman.....85.00
Teapot, wht w/blk trim, 2-cup.....30.00
Tray, bl, 12x18″.....38.00
Tray, for highchair, wht.....12.00
Tray, meat server; wht, lg.....15.00
Tray, yel, rnd.....35.00
Tub, foot; gray.....55.00
Tumbler, bl.....30.00
Utensil rack, gray.....145.00
Utensil rack, scenic on bl-gr, wht w/bl trim, hanging.....125.00
Wash basin, bl, EX.....22.00
Wash basin, cobalt & wht swirl.....30.00
Wash basin, emerald & wht.....40.00
Wash basin, turq & wht swirl.....32.00
Washboard, bl.....65.00
Washboard, Enamel King, cobalt, wooden.....75.00

Green and Ivory

Green and ivory are the colors of a type of country pottery decorated with in-mold designs very similar to those of the more familiar blue and white wares. It is unmarked and was produced from about 1910 to 1935 by many manufacturers as part of their staple line of kitchenwares.

When no condition is indicated, the items listed below are assumed to be in near mint condition.

Bowl, Daisy & Waffle, 10″.....40.00
Bowl, Wedding Ring, 10″.....40.00
Butter crock, Daisy & Waffle.....90.00
Mug, Grape.....40.00
Pitcher, Basketweave & Morning Glory, rope hdl, 9″.....150.00
Pitcher, Cow, 6″.....85.00
Pitcher, Cow, 7½″.....110.00
Pitcher, Flying Birds, top & bottom gr.....150.00
Pitcher, Grape.....85.00
Pitcher, Grape Cluster in Shield, arrow bands, 9″.....95.00
Pitcher, Indian Head in War Bonnet, waffle body, 8½″, NM.....150.00
Pitcher, Pine Cone, 9″.....135.00
Pitcher, Rose on Trellis, lg.....95.00
Pitcher, Wild Rose, 9″.....110.00
Spittoon, Cosmos, 6″.....80.00

Greenaway, Kate

Kate Greenaway was an English artist who lived from 1846 to 1901. She gained world-wide fame as an illustrator of children's books, drawing children clothed in the styles worn by proper English and American boys and girls of the very early 1800s. Her book, *Under the Willow Tree*, published in 1878, was the first of many. Her sketches appeared in leading magazines, and her greeting cards were in great demand. Manufacturers of china, pottery, and metal products copied her characters to decorate children's dishes, tiles, salt and pepper shakers, as well as many other items.

When no condition is indicated, the items listed below are assumed to be in mint condition.

Almanac, 1883....80.00
Almanac, 1885....65.00
Almanac, 1887, Geo Routledge....65.00
Almanac, 1892....60.00
Book, Alphabet Book, 1885....50.00
Book, Chatterbox Hall, Greenaway illus, 1884....40.00
Book, Fancy Work, 1885....27.00
Book, Little Ann, illus....75.00
Book, Under the Window, pub Frederick Warne, London....45.00
Box, jewelry; Tufts SP, girl ea side of bottle on top....325.00
Cards, 4 Seasons, chromo litho, in fr, 1882, set....120.00
Catalog, Lady's Fancy Work, 1885....24.00
Christmas card....28.00
Comport, oval top, figural girl, Royal Worcester, ca 1885....265.00
Figurine, boy w/basket, 1893, Royal Worcester, 9x4¼″....550.00
Figurine, bread boy carries basket, sgn J Tufts, SP, 4½″....245.00
Figurine, girl w/tambourine, #1032, Royal Worcester, 9″....420.00
Figurine, girl: left hand in pocket, fan in right, bsk, 7½″....55.00
Hankie, silk, 16″....18.00
Lamp, children on fence, milk glass, bronze seashell base....300.00
Match holder, boy holding rabbit, w/striker....65.00
Match holder, girl holding teacup, bisque....65.00
Match holder, girl w/basket helps 2nd off fence, EX color....225.00
Match safe, SP....50.00
Shaker, girl in long fur trimmed coat & bonnet....50.00
Shakers, boy & girl, pr....100.00
Tablecloth, hand printed, Leacode Mills, +4 napkins....50.00
Tea set, girls w/carts, wht....265.00
Thimble holder, SP, seated figure, My Favorite Thimble....165.00
Toothpick holder, amberina, in ornate Tufts fr w/girl....550.00
Toothpick holder, SP, seated girl in coat, hat, lg....175.00

Greentown Glass

Greentown glass refers to the product of the Indiana Tumbler and Goblet Company of Greentown, Indiana, ca. 1894 to 1903. Their earlier pressed glass patterns were #1, a pseudo-cut glass design; #137, Pleat Band; and #200, Austrian. Another line, Dewey, was designed in 1898. Many lovely colors were produced, in addition to crystal. Jacob Rosenthal, who was later affiliated with Fenton, developed his famous Chocolate glass in 1900. The rich shaded opaque brown glass was an overnight success. Two new patterns, Leaf Bracket and Cactus, were designed to display the glass to its best advantage, but previously existing molds were also used. In only three years, Rosenthal developed yet another important color formula, Golden Agate. The Holly Amber pattern was designed especially for its production. The figural Dolphin dish and cover, with fish finial, is perhaps the most and easily recognized piece ever produced. Other animal dishes were also made; all are highly collectible. There have been many repros--not all are marked!

When no condition is indicated, the items listed below are assumed to be in mint condition.

#11, toothpick holder, clear w/EX gold....28.00
#11, vase, gr, 6″....30.00
Austrian, creamer, clear....30.00
Austrian, nappy, clear, hdld, w/lid....46.00
Austrian, punch cup, clear, ped ft....20.00
Austrian, punch cup, clear w/gold decor....22.00
Austrian, spooner, child's; clear....75.00
Austrian, spooner, clear, lg....30.00
Austrian, vase, clear, tall....65.00
Austrian, wine, canary....110.00
Austrian, wine, clear....25.00
Beehive, goblet, clear....66.00
Bowl, Mitted Hand, clear....40.00
Brazen Shield, bowl, berry; bl, sm....30.00
Brazen Shield, tumbler, bl....45.00
Brazen Shield, water set, bl, tankard+6 tumblers....425.00
Cactus, bowl, berry; chocolate, sm....45.00
Cactus, butter dish, flat base, chocolate....175.00
Cactus, butter dish, ped ft, chocolate....400.00
Cactus, cake stand, chocolate....850.00
Cactus, compote, chocolate, lg....220.00
Cactus, compote, chocolate, 5½″....135.00
Cactus, cracker jar, chocolate....250.00
Cactus, cruet, chocolate....165.00
Cactus, plate, chocolate, 7½″....110.00
Cactus, salt shaker, old lid, chocolate....65.00
Cactus, sauce dish, chocolate....40.00
Cactus, spooner, chocolate....100.00
Cactus, sugar bowl w/lid, chocolate....160.00
Cactus, toothpick holder, chocolate....65.00
Cactus, tumbler, chocolate....50.00
Cactus, tumbler, ice tea; chocolate....65.00
Cord Drapery, bowl, clear, 7½″....35.00
Cord Drapery, cake plate, clear, flat....30.00
Cord Drapery, cruet, amber....265.00
Cord Drapery, pitcher, water; gr, rare....185.00
Cord Drapery, syrup, chocolate....165.00
Cord Drapery, syrup, chocolate, no lid....105.00
Cord Drapery, tumbler, clear....45.00
Dewey, butter dish, amber....65.00
Dewey, creamer & sugar bowl w/lids, canary, breakfast sz....95.00
Dewey, cruet, amber....135.00
Dewey, cruet, clear, w/orig stopper....95.00
Dewey, mug, amber....32.00
Dewey, mug, gr....38.00
Dewey, mug, teal bl, NM....95.00
Dewey, pitcher, water; clear....75.00
Dewey, relish tray, canary, serpentine, lg....55.00
Dewey, relish tray, gr, serpentine, sm....45.00
Dewey, shaker, gr, old top....55.00
Dewey, water set, canary, 7-pc....395.00
Dolphin dish, chocolate, beaded rim, w/lid....195.00
Dolphin dish, chocolate, sawtooth rim, w/lid....175.00
Fleur-de-lis, celery, chocolate, rare....180.00
Geometric, bowl, chocolate, 6″....350.00
Herringbone, mug, chocolate....55.00
Herringbone Buttress, bowl, amber, 5″....150.00
Herringbone Buttress, sugar bowl w/lid, emerald gr....160.00
Holly, celery tray, clear....85.00
Holly, mug, clear, 4½″....90.00
Holly Amber, berry, ind; 4¾″....265.00
Holly Amber, butter dish....1,000.00
Holly Amber, compote, jelly; w/lid....850.00
Holly Amber, compote, 8″....1,500.00
Holly Amber, pitcher, water....1,750.00
Holly Amber, relish dish, oval, 2x4½x7½″....350.00

Holly Amber bowl, 8½″ diameter, $600.00.

Holly Amber, toothpick holder, 2½″; 1⅞″ base....465.00
Holly Amber, tumbler....500.00
Leaf Bracket, berry set, chocolate, 7-pc....275.00
Leaf Bracket, celery tray, chocolate....110.00
Leaf Bracket, creamer, chocolate, lg....65.00
Leaf Bracket, cruet, chocolate....145.00
Leaf Bracket, nappy, chocolate, triangular, hdld....50.00
Leaf Bracket, relish, chocolate, lg....75.00
Leaf Bracket, relish, chocolate, oval, sm....65.00
Leaf Bracket, spooner, chocolate....65.00
Leaf Bracket, table set, 4-pc, VG....375.00
Leaf Bracket, tumbler, chocolate....50.00
Mitted Hand, bowl, clear....40.00
Pitcher, Heron, chocolate....375.00
Pitcher, Ruffled Eye, amber....125.00
Pitcher, Ruffled Eye, chocolate....375.00
Pitcher, Running Deer, chocolate....400.00
Pitcher, Squirrel....400.00
Shuttle, creamer, chocolate, 6″....65.00
Shuttle, tumbler, chocolate....75.00
Shuttle, wine, clear....12.00
Stein, indoor drinking scene, chocolate....115.00
Stein, indoor drinking scene, Nile gr....90.00
Stein, outdoor drinking scene, chocolate....105.00
Teardrop & Tassel, butter dish, clear....50.00
Teardrop & Tassel, sauce dish, clear....12.00
Teardrop & Tassel, sugar bowl w/lid, clear....45.00
Teardrop & Tassel, tray, relish; gr, oval....75.00
Vase, Scalloped Flange, chocolate....70.00

Pitcher, Nile green, indoor drinking scene, 5″, $135.00.

Grueby

William Henry Grueby joined the firm of the Low Art Tile Works at the age of fifteen, and in 1894, after several years of experience in the production of architectural tiles, founded his own plant, the Grueby Faience Company, in Boston, Massachusetts. Grueby began experimenting with the idea of producing art pottery, and had soon perfected a fine glaze--soft and without gloss--in shades of blue, gray, yellow, brown, and his most successful, cucumber green. In 1900 his exhibit at the Paris Exposition Universelle won him three gold medals.

Grueby pottery was hand thrown and hand decorated in the Arts and Crafts style. Vertically thrust stylized leaves and flowers in relief were the most common decorative devices. Tiles continued to be an important product--unique (due to the matt glaze decoration) as well as durable. Grueby tiles were often a full inch thick. Obviously incompatible with the Art Nouveau style, the artware was discontinued soon after 1910.

The ware is always marked in one of several ways: 'Grueby Pottery, Boston, USA'; 'Grueby, Boston, Mass.'; or 'Grueby Faience.' The artware is often artist signed.

When no condition is indicated, the items listed below are assumed to be in mint condition.

Left, Vase, upright lotus leaves, thick blue glaze, original paper label, 5¼″, $550.00; Right, Vase, stalks and buds, green with patches of yellow, impressed factory mark, 7¾″, $500.00.

Bowl, gr matt, ruffled edge, sm chip, 2x5¼″....130.00
Bowl, gr-bl matt, lime gr w/in, imp circular mk, 4″....160.00
Paperweight, emb wht beetle on bl, 2½″ dia....140.00
Pot, deep bl, hand tooled, W Post, rpr+sm chip, 9½x4½″....350.00
Scarab, gr matt, imp Lotus mk, 3¼x2¼″....150.00
Tile, mc floral on red clay, EX mold, 4″ sq....150.00
Tile, mottled glaze, fully sgn, 2x6″....45.00
Tile, sailing ship, bl/tan/brn, sgn M Mc, 6″ sq....500.00
Tile, turtle & leaves, no mk, 1905, 6″....175.00
Vase, buds/leaves, yel on gr, Erickson, mk/dated, 7½″....1,200.00
Vase, gr, roll rim/3 tab hdls on tapering bulb, WP, 9″, EX....500.00
Vase, gr matt, 4⅝″....140.00
Vase, leaves relief, dk gr, sgn W Port, bottom flake, 8″....550.00
Vase, long overlapping leaves, textured gr, 7½″, EX....500.00
Vase, lotus leaves, gr w/cream, chalice form, lotus mk, 7″....550.00
Vase, mottled gr texture, (glaze misses), 5¾x5″....250.00
Vase, orange buds/gr leaves, bulbous, Erikson/dtd, 7x6½″....1,400.00
Vase, overlapped lotus leaves, bl, orig label, 5″....600.00

Vase, ribbed bands top & base, cylinder, gr, 7¾″............250.00
Vase, textured gr, narrow neck on bulbous body, 7½″.........250.00
Vase, thick lt bl matt, gourd form, flared, no mk, 3x3½″......125.00
Vase, tooled ribs, curdled butterscotch, rolled rim, 6¾″.......500.00
Vase, tooled/applied leaves, gr matt, 11½x5½″...............900.00
Vase, vertical leaves, deep gr, sgn WP, 10x5″...............800.00
Vase, yel flower buds on gr matt, paper label, 4″.............425.00

Gutta Percha

Gutta-percha is the plastic substance from the latex of several types of Malaysian trees. It resembles rubber but contains more resin. A patent for the use of this material in manufacturing an early type of plastic was issued in the 1850s, and it was used extensively for daguerreotype cases and picture frames.

When no condition is indicated, the items listed below are assumed to be in mint condition.

Box, shirt collar; X-cannons/flags, mk Wards 15½, '77.........55.00
Case, Beehive w/Grain Border, LP&Co, 6th plate, NM..........55.00
Case, Belt & Buckle, S Peck label, 6th plate..................65.00
Case, Bobby Shafto in sm boat w/flag/etc, 6 plate, LP&Co......85.00
Case, Chess Players, edge roughness, 9th plate...............35.00
Case, compote of fruit, brn, w/ambrotype, 5x6″, EX...........95.00
Case, deer, scroll edges, blk, w/tintype, 3½x4″, EX...........65.00
Case, Elizabethan knight & maiden, 9th plate................65.00
Case, Faithful Hound, dbl, 6th plate.......................115.00
Case, Falconer, 3¾x3⅛″....................................90.00
Case, farmer & maid, blk, w/tintype, edge chips, 2½x3″........45.00
Case, floral, blk, w/tintype, 2½x3″, EX.....................25.00
Case, floral, elaborate, brn, w/tintype, 3¼x3¾″, EX...........35.00
Case, foliage, brn, w/2 tintypes, 3¼x3¾″.....................50.00
Case, Fruits of Harvest, brn, 1⅞x2⅛″.......................50.00
Case, Habana, monument/trees/ships/etc, LP&Co, 4th plate....165.00
Case, haying scene & child chasing butterflies, brn, 5x6″......185.00
Case, Huntress, ruffled dress, jewelry, 4x3½″.................65.00
Case, Lady in Daguerreian Gallery, w/dag, 6th plate...........90.00
Case, Mary & Lamb, LP&Co, 9th plate.......................65.00
Case, Monitor, 9th plate, EX...............................60.00
Case, ribbon motif, LP&Co, 9th plate........................35.00
Case, sculptured scroll motif, w/2 dags, 6th plate.............65.00
Case, Shield & Shells, AP Critchlow & Co, 6th plate...........50.00
Case, Sickle & Sheaf, blk, w/2 tintypes, 2½x3″, EX............35.00
Drinking cup, expandable, Niles, 1860.......................22.00
Hand mirror, Leaf Scroll, basket of fruit, Art Deco............25.00
Match safe, Rosebery Cigars.................................34.00

Case, Habana, Littlefield, Parsons and Co., 4th plate, $165.00.

Haeger

In 1871 David Henry Haeger, a young son of German immigrants, purchased a brick factory at Dundee, Illinois, and began an association with the ceramic industry that his descendants have pursued to the present time. Soon their production was expanded to include drainage tile. By 1914 they had ventured into the field of commercial artware. Vases, figurines, lamp bases, and gift items in a pastel matt glaze carried the logo of the company name written over the bar of an 'H.' From 1929 to 1933, they produced a line of dinnerware in solid colors--blue, rose, green, and yellow-- which they marketed through Marshall Fields. Royal Haeger, their premium line designed in 1938 by Royal Hickman, and the Flower Ware line (1945 to 1950, marked 'RG' for Royal Garden), are especially desirable with collectors today. Ware produced before the mid-thirties sometimes is found with a paper label; these are also of special interest. A stylized script mark, Royal Haeger, was used during the forties; later a paper label in the shape of a crown was used.

The Macomb, Illinois plant, built in 1939, primarily made ware for the florist trade. A second plant, built there in 1969, produces lamp bases.

When no condition is indicated, the items listed below are assumed to be in mint condition.

Plaque, duck in relief, gray and white, 9″, $18.00.

Ash tray/box combo, turq w/bronze rosette, R1737, 10½″.......25.00
Compote, aqua w/brushings, Deco, 7½″.......................25.00
Console, w/10″ mermaid, Royal Haeger, 10″ dia...............60.00
Cornucopia, bl, #444A, 8x7½x4″.............................8.00
Figurine, tigress, amber, R314, Royal Haeger USA............40.00
Flower frog, nude on seal block, bl, 5x12½x5″................50.00
Planter, Colonial girl, yel, 3½x7x2½″........................8.00
Planter, deer head, amber, R115, Royal Haeger...............35.00
Planter, girl & buggy, #3282................................8.00
Planter, Madonna, wht, 5½x9x5″............................10.00
Planter, wicker baby buggy & Victorian lady..................10.00
Planter, young child figure in front..........................8.00
Shell bowl, R335, Royal Haeger, 14x3½x14″..................20.00
Vase, basket, #279, 9¼x21x9″.............................17.00
Vase, classic, #474, 7x9x7″.................................7.00
Vase, crackled glaze, 10½″.................................45.00
Vase, dancing girl, #3105...................................9.00
Vase, flying fish/bl agate, #3208/Royal Haeger, 5½x6x2½″......50.00
Vase, peacock, bl & gr on pink, Royal Haeger USA, 15″.......45.00

Vase, pillow shape on oval base, rabbit ea end 15.00
Vase, plume, blk high gloss, Royal Haeger, 6" 10.00
Vase, ribbed, ped ft, marbleized brn/cream, #3953, 6½" 22.00
Vase, rooster, mauve agate, Royal Haeger, 12" 35.00
Vase, shell, mauve agate, #483, Royal Haeger, 7" 35.00
Vase, swan, Royal Haeger, 8" 10.00
Vase, trout, mauve agate, R284, Royal Haeger, 9½x7¼x4½" 30.00
Vase, twin spout top, bulbous base, Aztec Gold, #4001 . . . . . 18.00
Wall pocket, girl's head, 4x10x3" 7.00

Hair Weaving

A rather unusual craft became popular during the mid-1800s. Human hair was used to make jewelry--rings, bracelets, lockets, etc. -- by braiding and interlacing fine strands of hair around hollow forms, with pearls and beads added for effect. Hair wreaths were also made, often using hair from deceased family members as well as the living. They were displayed in deep satin-lined frames along with mementos of the weaver or her departed kin. The fad was abandoned before the turn of the century.

When no condition is indicated, the items listed below are assumed to be in excellent condition.

Brooch, 15k, MOP plaque in floral hand-eng fr, 1½" 150.00
Brooch, 9k, glass panel w/twist of pearls/wire/hair, 1½" 125.00
Ring, gold, woven hair & 'Mother,' Victorian 450.00
Ring, 15k, 2 hearts w/mine-cut diamond/filigree, braid w/in 275.00
Watch chain, gold plated ends, 1890s 55.00
Wreath, shadow box fr, 20¾x24¾" 200.00

Necklace, hollow beads, cross pendant, ca 1840s, $85.00.

Hall

The Hall China Company of East Liverpool, Ohio, was established in 1903. Their earliest product was whiteware toilet seats, mugs, jugs, etc. By 1920, their restaurant-type dinnerware and cookingware had become so successful that Hall was assured of a solid future. They continue today to be one of the country's largest manufacturers of this type of product.

Hall introduced the first of their famous teapots in 1920; new shapes and colors were added each year until about 1948, making them the largest teapot manufacturer in the world. These and the dinnerware lines of the thirties through the fifties have become popular collectibles.

When no condition is indicated, the items listed below are assumed to be in mint condition. See also Autumn Leaf

Teapot, Basket, green with silver trim, 7", $75.00.

Banded, cookie jar, Indian red 45.00
Banded, jug, lettuce gr 14.00
Blue Blossom, casserole, w/lid 32.00
Blue Blossom, cookie jar, Banded 100.00
Blue Blossom, pitcher, jug 45.00
Blue Bouquet, baker, fluted, 7¾" 12.00
Blue Bouquet, bowl, salad; 9" 15.00
Blue Bouquet, creamer 6.00
Blue Bouquet, shakers, hdl, pr 16.00
Blue Bouquet, sugar bowl, w/lid 8.00
Blue Garden, bowl, batter 100.00
Bouquet, creamer, Zeisel 10.00
Bouquet, gravy boat, Zeisel 15.00
Bouquet, sugar bowl, Zeisel 12.00
Cameo Rose, bowl, fruit; 5¼" 4.00
Cameo Rose, bowl, soup; lg 10.00
Cameo Rose, bowl, vegetable; oval 18.00
Cameo Rose, creamer 8.00
Cameo Rose, plate, breakfast; 9¼" 5.00
Cameo Rose, plate, dinner 7.00
Cameo Rose, plate, 6¼" 4.00
Cameo Rose, platter, 15½" 18.00
Cameo Rose, shakers, pr 16.00
Cameo Rose, sugar bowl, open 10.00
Cameo Rose, sugar bowl, w/lid 15.00
Cameo Rose, teapot, 8-cup 46.00
Cameo Rose, tray, tidbit; 3-tier 40.00
Candle holder, teal, w/hdl, 2½" 12.00
Casserole, Trader Vic, red, Oriental decor in blk 17.50
Chinese Red, baker, fluted, lg 18.00
Chinese Red, bean pot, tab hdls, 2-qt 35.00
Chinese Red, bowl, grease; w/lid 15.00
Chinese Red, bowl, mixing; Straightside, set of 3 . . . . . 35.00
Chinese Red, canister, sugar 50.00
Chinese Red, canister, tea 50.00
Chinese Red, casserole, w/lid 22.00
Chinese Red, coffee pot 25.00
Chinese Red, creamer & sugar, w/lid 23.00
Chinese Red, jug, loop hdl 22.00
Chinese Red, jug, Sani-Grid, 5" 15.00
Chinese Red, jug, Sani-Grid, 6¼" 15.00
Chinese Red, jug, Sani-Grid, 7½" 32.00
Chinese Red, pitcher, ball jug; 2-qt, 7" 15.00

Chinese Red, pitcher, jug; Banded, 1½-pt, 5″ . . . 12.00
Chinese Red, shakers, Flute, pr . . . 25.00
Chinese Red, shakers, Sani-Grid, pr . . . 18.00
Chinese Red, syrup, Banded . . . 32.00
Chinese Red, teapot, 3-cup, creamer/sugar, Sani-Grid, set . . . 45.00
Coffee server, panel w/flowers in pots . . . 15.00
Colonial, jug, delphinium . . . 15.00
Colonial, jug, lettuce gr, no ice lip, #5, 6″ . . . 25.00
Crest, dripolator . . . 28.00
Crocus, bowl, mixing; 6″ . . . 12.00
Crocus, bowl, mixing; 7½″ . . . 13.50
Crocus, bowl, mixing; 9″ . . . 15.00
Crocus, bowl, salad; 9″ . . . 15.00
Crocus, casserole, Sunshine, w/lid . . . 25.00
Crocus, coffee dispenser, metal . . . 15.00
Crocus, coffee pot, dripolator, Colonial . . . 28.00
Crocus, coffee pot, step-down . . . 22.00
Crocus, creamer, Colonial . . . 14.00
Crocus, creamer & sugar, Art Deco, w/lid . . . 25.00
Crocus, cup & saucer . . . 9.00
Crocus, plate, 10″ . . . 8.00
Crocus, platter, 13¾″ . . . 18.00
Crocus, shakers, hdl, pr . . . 18.00
Crocus, soup tureen, Big Lip, w/lid . . . 85.00
Flareware, cookie jar/bean pot . . . 25.00
Flowerpot, syrup, w/lid . . . 28.00
Golden Squiggle, bowl . . . 7.00
Heather Rose, utility jug, 6½″ . . . 12.00
Matchbox holder, Palmer House, gold, #618, 5½″ . . . 20.00
Matchbox holder, teal, rectangular, 3¾″ . . . 12.00
Morning Glory, bowl, mixing; 7½″ . . . 12.00
Morning Glory, bowl, mixing; 9″ . . . 15.00
Morning Glory, casserole, w/lid . . . 27.50
Mt Vernon, bowl, fruit; 5″ . . . 4.50
Mt Vernon, coffee pot . . . 40.00
Mt Vernon, creamer . . . 6.50
Mt Vernon, flat soup . . . 8.50
Mt Vernon, gravy & underplate . . . 22.00
Mt Vernon, plate, 10″ . . . 7.50
Mt Vernon, platter, oval, 15½″ . . . 20.00
Mt Vernon, sugar bowl, open . . . 5.00
Mug, Ohio AAA Collection Gallery, 1910 Hupmobile, 1979 . . . 15.00
Mug, 1664 Official Tankard o/t Vorlo's Great Breweries . . . 25.00
Orange Poppy, baker, fluted, 3-pt . . . 18.00
Orange Poppy, ball jug . . . 24.00
Orange Poppy, bean pot, hdl . . . 60.00
Orange Poppy, bowl, cereal . . . 7.00
Orange Poppy, bowl, fruit . . . 6.00
Orange Poppy, bowl, mixing; deep, 10″ . . . 18.00
Orange Poppy, bowl, salad . . . 12.00
Orange Poppy, cake plate . . . 16.00
Orange Poppy, casserole, loop hdl . . . 30.00
Orange Poppy, casserole, oval, w/lid . . . 32.00
Orange Poppy, coffee pot, Golden Key . . . 35.00
Orange Poppy, coffee pot, S-Lid . . . 45.00
Orange Poppy, creamer & sugar, w/lid . . . 25.00
Orange Poppy, custard . . . 4.00
Orange Poppy, drip jar, w/lid . . . 18.00
Orange Poppy, flour dispenser, no wall bracket . . . 25.00
Orange Poppy, leftover, loop hdl . . . 32.00
Orange Poppy, plate, 7″ . . . 6.00
Orange Poppy, plate, 9″ . . . 8.00
Orange Poppy, platter, 11″ . . . 12.00
Orange Poppy, platter, 9½″ . . . 10.00
Orange Poppy, pretzel jar . . . 50.00
Orange Poppy, shakers, hdl, pr . . . 25.00
Orange Poppy, sugar bowl, w/lid . . . 16.00
Orange Poppy, teapot, Boston . . . 60.00
Poppy & Wheat, bowl, mixing; 10¼″ . . . 25.00
Poppy & Wheat, pitcher . . . 35.00
Radiant Ware, bowl, 4-pc . . . 75.00
Red Poppy, bowl, mixing; #4 . . . 12.00
Red Poppy, bowl, mixing; #5 . . . 15.00
Red Poppy, bowl, salad; 9″ . . . 12.00
Red Poppy, bowl, soup . . . 10.00
Red Poppy, bread box, slant front . . . 45.00
Red Poppy, canister set, red top . . . 35.00
Red Poppy, casserole, Sunshine . . . 20.00
Red Poppy, coffee pot, Rickson . . . 30.00
Red Poppy, coffee pot, w/metal insert . . . 38.00
Red Poppy, creamer & sugar, 4″ . . . 15.00
Red Poppy, cup . . . 5.00
Red Poppy, drip jar, Sunshine, w/lid . . . 12.00
Red Poppy, flour sifter, metal . . . 18.00
Red Poppy, paper dispenser . . . 10.00
Red Poppy, pitcher, jug; Sunshine, 7″ . . . 15.00
Red Poppy, pitcher, jug; 6¼″ . . . 14.00
Red Poppy, plate, cake . . . 12.00
Red Poppy, platter, oval, 13″ . . . 18.00
Red Poppy, platter, 11″ . . . 12.00
Red Poppy, range set, drip w/lid; hdld shakers . . . 32.00
Red Poppy, saucer . . . 3.00
Red Poppy, shakers, Egg Drop, pr . . . 12.00
Red Poppy, shakers, hdl, pr . . . 16.00
Red Poppy, sifter, metal grip . . . 20.00
Red Poppy, sugar bowl . . . 12.00
Red Poppy, teapot, Aladdin . . . 35.00
Red Poppy, teapot, New York . . . 30.00
Red Poppy, tray, rnd . . . 20.00
Red Poppy, tumbler, clear, 9-oz . . . 10.00
Red Poppy, tumbler, frosted, 5¼″ . . . 16.00
Refrigerator Ware, Aristocrat, pitcher, jug; w/lid, cobalt . . . 75.00
Refrigerator Ware, Dresden, water bottle, ceramic stopper . . . 40.00
Refrigerator Ware, Emperor, butter dish, gr . . . 20.00
Refrigerator Ware, Emperor, leftover, yel . . . 15.00
Refrigerator Ware, GE/Westinghouse, leftover, rectangular . . . 15.00
Refrigerator Ware, GE/Westinghouse, leftover, rnd, bl . . . 15.00
Refrigerator Ware, King, roaster, yel . . . 15.00
Refrigerator Ware, Patrician, leftover, lettuce gr . . . 18.00
Refrigerator Ware, Patrician, water server, bl . . . 30.00
Refrigerator Ware, Prince, water server . . . 30.00
Refrigerator Ware, Sears, leftover, cadet bl, 3-section . . . 40.00
Refrigerator Ware, Westinghouse, leftover, Aristocrat, gr . . . 12.00
Rose Parade, baker . . . 16.00
Rose Parade, bean pot . . . 40.00
Rose Parade, bowl, #5 . . . 15.00
Rose Parade, bowl, salad . . . 14.00
Rose Parade, casserole, w/lid, 1½-qt . . . 20.00
Rose Parade, drip jar, tab hdld . . . 16.00
Rose Parade, pitcher, lg . . . 18.00
Rose Parade, shaker, pepper . . . 7.50
Rose Parade, sugar bowl . . . 6.00
Rose White, casserole . . . 20.00
Rose White, drip jar, w/lid . . . 16.00
Rose White, pitcher, Sani-Grid, #658 . . . 8.00
Rose White, pitcher, 6½″ . . . 16.00
Rose White, sugar bowl . . . 8.00
Rose White, teapot, 3-cup . . . 25.00

Springtime, bowl, vegetable; 9″ 16.00
Springtime, cake plate 12.00
Springtime, coffee pot, all china 85.00
Springtime, creamer & sugar 16.00
Springtime, cup & saucer 8.00
Springtime, gravy boat 17.00
Springtime, plate, 9″ 7.00
Springtime, platter, 13″ 15.00
Springtime, shakers, hdld, pr 15.00
Springtime, teapot, French 45.00
Taverne, baker, French, fluted, $7\frac{3}{4}$″ 18.00
Taverne, bowl, Bobby; $7\frac{7}{8}$″ 20.00
Taverne, bowl, fruit 5.00
Taverne, bowl, salad; 9″ 15.00
Taverne, cake saver, wood bottom 18.00
Taverne, casserole, family size 22.00
Taverne, coaster 5.00
Taverne, coffee pot, all china 100.00
Taverne, coffee pot, Banded 30.00
Taverne, coffee pot, Colonial 33.50
Taverne, cookie jar, w/lid 60.00
Taverne, creamer, Colonial 8.00
Taverne, leftover, rectangular 22.00
Taverne, rolling pin 85.00
Taverne, shakers, Banded, pr 20.00
Taverne, shakers, Colonial, pr 28.00
Taverne, waffle iron 150.00
Teapot, Addison French, gold, 2-cup 30.00
Teapot, Addison French, yel w/gold, 4-cup 25.00
Teapot, Airflow, canary 22.00
Teapot, Airflow, Chinese red 38.00
Teapot, Airflow, cobalt 35.00
Teapot, Airflow, cobalt & gold, 6-cup 32.00
Teapot, Airflow, emerald 32.00
Teapot, Aladdin, bl turq, w/infuser 20.00
Teapot, Aladdin, blk w/gold 32.00
Teapot, Aladdin, chartreuse w/gold, w/infuser 25.00
Teapot, Aladdin, cobalt w/gold, oval opening 35.00
Teapot, Aladdin, delphite, mk Stephen Leeman Prod Co, NY 20.00
Teapot, Aladdin, gold swag 28.00
Teapot, Aladdin, maroon w/gold 25.00
Teapot, Aladdin, Morning Glory 38.00
Teapot, Aladdin, pink 25.00
Teapot, Albany, mahogany 28.00
Teapot, Albert, celadon 20.00
Teapot, Automobile, Chinese red 375.00
Teapot, Basketball, yel w/silver trim 300.00
Teapot, Boston, cobalt, 2-cup 30.00
Teapot, Boston, daffodil, 6-cup 20.00
Teapot, Boston, dresden 20.00
Teapot, Boston, maroon 20.00
Teapot, Boston, warm yel, 8-cup 20.00
Teapot, Disraeli, pink 20.00
Teapot, Doughnut, Chinese red 95.00
Teapot, Gladstone, pink 20.00
Teapot, Globe, cadet bl w/gold 42.00
Teapot, Hollywood, chartreuse, plain 22.00
Teapot, Hollywood, ivory, 8-cup 24.00
Teapot, Hollywood, marine, 4-cup 25.00
Teapot, Hook Cover, cadet bl w/gold stars 25.00
Teapot, Los Angeles, bl 22.00
Teapot, McCormick, lt bl 20.00
Teapot, McCormick, maroon 18.00
Teapot, McCormick, pink 20.00
Teapot, McCormick, turq, w/infuser 22.00
Teapot, McCormick, wht, w/infuser 35.00
Teapot, Moderne, bl 18.00
Teapot, Moderne, gold 25.00
Teapot, Nautilus, Canary 85.00
Teapot, New York, canary, 12-cup 22.00
Teapot, New York, cobalt, 4-cup 32.00
Teapot, New York, warm yel w/gold, 6-cup 25.00
Teapot, Parade, canary 18.00
Teapot, Parade, cobalt & gold 45.00
Teapot, Parade, emerald w/gold wear 25.00
Teapot, Parade, ivory 15.00
Teapot, Philadelphia, bl turq w/gold 25.00
Teapot, Philadelphia, cadet w/gold 22.00
Teapot, Philadelphia, pink w/gold 25.00
Teapot, Philadelphia, turq 22.00
Teapot, Rhythm, Chinese red 75.00
Teapot, Saf-handle, canary 40.00
Teapot, Star, turq w/gold 20.00
Teapot, Streamline, blk 38.00
Teapot, Streamline, dresden 35.00
Teapot, Streamline, red 45.00
Teapot, Surfside, canary w/gold 65.00
Teapot, Surfside, gr 60.00
Teapot, T-Ball, daffodil, sq 45.00
Teapot, T-Ball, maroon, rnd 38.00
Teapot, Twinspout, canary w/gold 40.00
Teapot, Twinspout, maroon 32.00
Teapot, Victoria, celadon 25.00
Teapot, Windshield, camellia w/gold dots 18.00
Teapot, Windshield, ivory/gold dots 18.00
Tom & Jerry, bowl, blk & gold, ftd, w/8 cups 75.00
Tom & Jerry, bowl, blk & gold, w/lid, 5-qt 45.00
Tulip, bowl, mixing; $7\frac{1}{2}$″ 14.00
Tulip, bowl, salad 15.00
Tulip, bowl, vegetable; oval 15.00
Tulip, cake plate, flat 12.00
Tulip, cup & saucer 10.00
Tulip, plate, 9″ 10.00
Vase, mortar type, wht, mk RX, sgn Owens, Ill 25.00
Wild Rose, baker, French, 3-pt 15.00
Wild Rose, bowl, mixing; #5 ....15.00
Wild Rose, casserole, w/lid 22.00
Wild Rose, creamer & sugar, w/lid 22.00
Wildfire, bowl, salad 8.00
Wildfire, bowl, vegetable; oval 18.00
Wildfire, casserole, w/lid 18.00
Wildfire, creamer & sugar, w/lid 20.00
Wildfire, grease jar 12.00
Wildfire, plate, 2-tier 25.00
Wildfire, platter, $13\frac{1}{2}$″ 12.00
Wildfire, shaker, egg shape 10.00
Wildfire, shakers, hdl, pr 18.00
Wildfire, teapot, Aladdin 40.00
Zeisel, bowl, cereal; Sunglow, 6″ 10.00
Zeisel, bowl, vegetable; Sunglow, $8\frac{1}{2}$″ 18.00
Zeisel, jug, seal brn, sm 15.00
Zeisel, plate, hdls, Sunglow, $10\frac{3}{4}$″ 12.50

Halloween

The origin of Halloween can be traced back to the ancient practices of the Druids of Great Britain who began their New Year on the 1st of

November. The Druids were pagans, and their New Year's celebrations involved pagan rites and superstitions. They believed that as the old year came to an end, the Devil would gather up all the demons and evil in the world and take them back to Hell with him. Witches were women who had sold their souls to the Devil, and with their black cat in attendance, flew up through their chimneys riding brooms. When the Roman Catholic Church came into power in 700 A.D., they changed the holiday into a religious event, called 'All Saints Day,' or 'Allhallows.' The evening before, October 31, became 'Allhallow's Eve,' or 'Halloween.'

Today Halloween is strictly a fun time, and Halloween items are fun to collect. Pumpkin head candy containers of papier mache or pressed cardboard, noisemakers, postcards with black cats and witches, costumes, and decorations--these are only a sampling of the variety available.

When no condition is indicated, the items listed below are assumed to be in excellent condition.

Candy container, box w/pumpkin-head kid in tux, 5″...........50.00
Candy container, cardboard cat w/bobbing head...............35.00
Candy container, pumpkin-head kid, 4″.......................20.00
Candy container, smiling jack-o'-lantern, 3½″...............50.00
Candy mold, devil holds club & chain, tin, 2-part, 1910, 6″....110.00
Cards, Gypsy Witch Fortune Telling..........................6.00
Clacker, frogs, molded tin, early...........................22.00
Clacker, pumpkin head, wood, Germany........................35.00
Clacker, spooky witch face, tin litho.......................5.00
Clacker, witch/fire/pumpkin, litho on tin, lg...............12.00
Costume, Chinaman, Halco Superb Brand, in box...............55.00
Decoration, blk cat, paper..................................18.00
Decoration, Full Size Skeleton, orig pkg....................20.00
Decoration, witch, paper, accordion style legs & arms, 29″.......8.00
Jack-o'-lantern, cat face...................................45.00
Jack-o'-lantern, papier mache, orig eyes, lg................20.00
Jack-o'-lantern, swivels open for candle, wire base, early.......300.00
Jack-o'-lantern, tin..18.00
Jack-o'-lantern, witch, w/candle, cb, orig, 1930s...........17.50
Lantern, candle; blk cat, screened, wire bail, 4x4x6″..........175.00
Lantern, orange tissue behind blk cb animal cut-outs.........12.00
Mask, Chinaman, Germany.....................................10.00
Mask, girl, wire..55.00
Mask, hooded ghost, wire....................................28.00
Whirligig, witch, broomstick arms, ca 1920..................130.00
Whirligig, witch w/cat on broomstick, ca 1920...............145.00
Witch hat, 1920s..25.00

Whirligig, folk art witch, orange, white and black, 16″, $750.00.

Hampshire

The Hampshire Pottery Company was established in 1871 in Keene, New Hampshire, by James Scollay Taft. Their earliest products were redware and stoneware utility items such as jugs, churns, crocks, and flowerpots. In 1878 they produced majolica ware which met with such success that they began to experiment with the idea of manufacturing art pottery. By 1883, they had developed a Royal Worcester type of finish which they applied to vases, tea sets, powder boxes, and cookie jars. It was also utilized for souvenir items that were decorated with transfer designs prepared from photographic plates.

Cadmon Robertson, brother-in-law of Taft, joined the company in 1904, and was responsible for developing their famous matt glazes. Colors included shades of green and brown, red and blue. Early examples were of earthenware, but eventually the body changed to semi-porcelain. Some of his designs were marked with an M in a circle as a tribute to his wife, Emoretta.

Robertson died in 1914, leaving a void impossible to fill. Taft sold the business in 1916 to George Morton, who continued to use the matt glazes that Robertson had developed. After a temporary halt in production during WWI, Morton returned to Keene and re-equipped the factory with the needed machinery to manufacture hotel china and floor tile. Because of the expense involved in transporting coal to fire the kilns, Morton found he could not compete with potteries of Ohio and New Jersey, who were able to utilize locally available natural gas. He was forced to close the plant in 1923.

When no condition is indicated, the items listed below are assumed to be in mint condition.

Ewer, hand-painted flowers, gold tri-lobe top, 6½″, $275.00.

Bowl, bl matt w/emb top rim, incurvate, sgn, 3x5½″...........50.00
Bowl, floral/leaves, dk matt, 2¼x6″..........................60.00
Bowl, Indian style line decor on shoulder, gr matt, 2x6″........45.00
Bowl vase, tulip/leaf, gr matt w/brn, drain holes, 6x11½″......325.00
Chocolate pot, emb florals, cobalt, 11″.....................120.00
Clock, bl matt, orig, rare..................................200.00
Ewer, gr, 9½″, flake..17.00
Ewer, gr matt, 10¾x10¼″.....................................100.00
Jar, cobalt, w/lid, 8″......................................85.00
Lamp, bedroom; bl glaze, shielded candle-holder shape........150.00
Lamp base, crocus relief, gr matt, 5½x10½″..................200.00
Lamp base, tulip/leaf relief, gr matt, 15″..................220.00
Mug, gr matt, sgn, 7x5″.....................................30.00
Paperweight, fish fossil relief, imp name & M, rnd, 3½″........85.00

Pitcher, gr matt, no mk, 5″ 65.00
Pitcher, Landing of Pilgrims, gilt base 100.00
Pitcher, raised leaves, snakeskin gr glaze, 8″ 85.00
Pot, leaves relief, gr matt, 7¼x5½″, NM 90.00
Stein, State Capitol, Albany, NY, Royal Worcester, 6″ 50.00
Teapot, Royal Worcester, butterfly finial 65.00
Vase, bl matt, cylindrical, 7½″ 145.00
Vase, bl matt, thick glaze, mk/#118, 5¼″ 100.00
Vase, bl matt, wht at top, dk bl at bottom, cylinder, 7″ 170.00
Vase, crocus relief, gr matt, 8½″ 165.00
Vase, gr matt, #183, 7″ 55.00
Vase, gr matt, #90, 9″ 65.00
Vase, gr matt, #95/M in circle, 7″ 75.00
Vase, gr matt, canister on compressed body/curled hdls, 5″ 60.00
Vase, gr matt, emb panels, 14¾″ 200.00
Vase, gr matt, 3¼″ 40.00
Vase, gr/brn matt, heavy glaze, 8″ 95.00
Vase, maroon over lt gr, 4½″ 45.00
Vase, molded leaf decor, gr matt, 2-hdl, ped ft, 5¾″ 100.00
Vase, textured bl matt, bulbous w/flared top, 9½x6¾″ 90.00
Vase, vertical grasses/buds, gr matt, 4¼″ 75.00
Vase, vertical spaced swirls, bl w/wht veining, 8x7½″ 250.00
Vase, vertical tulip & leaf, gr matt, #67/M in circle, 8½″ 245.00

Handel Lamps

Philip Handel was best known for the art glass lamps he produced at the turn of the century. His work is similar to the Tiffany lamps of the same era. Handel made gas and electric lamps, with both leaded glass and reverse painted shades. Chipped ice shades, with a texture similar to overshot glass were also produced. China and glassware decorated by Handel is rare and commands high prices on today's market. Teroma is a term used to describe glassware decorated on the obverse (outside) with paint that has a sandy finish. Many of the chinaware blanks were supplied by Limoges.

When no condition is indicated, the glass and china listed below are assumed to be in mint condition; lamp parts are assumed excellent.

Lamps

Base, 3-socket, copper finish, 24″ 250.00
Base, 4-branch, pond lily; bronze, gr/wht shade, 16″ 1,900.00
Chipped ice pnt shade, #6949DB, 23″ 1,650.00
Chipped ice/rvpt rose/dogwood 18″ shade; hdl/ft std 1,900.00
Copper flared shade w/tulip cut-out over gr glass, 24″ 1,250.00
Desk, floral, #6760 . . . . . 1,650.00
Desk, 6½″ ldgl gr shade, bronze base, sgn, 1895 . . . . . 1,400.00
Filigree over caramel glass panels, sgn base & shade, 26″ 2,800.00
Hanging, frosted amber globe w/pnt birds/floral, #7892, pr . . . 1,210.00
Hanging, frosted glass, bronze holder, wall mt, pr 295.00
Lava, Deco vines, bronze/marble/glass-ball std 1,400.00
Ldgl, 32-pc shade, bronze tripod std, Art Deco, dbl sgn 550.00
Ldgl 18½″ wisteria shade; tree trunk base, 29½″ 4,375.00
Ribbed shade, wht, leaves/branches/yel floral, sgn, 18x20″ 1,500.00
Rvpt yel floral, pnt metal std, sgn cloth label 1,320.00
Rvpt 17¾″ parrots/floral shade; orig cloth-tagged base 4,400.00
Rvpt/obverse pnt, parrots/flowers, crackle glass, 7½″ 800.00
Torche, rvpt Deco shade, sgn twice, 14″, pr 800.00

Miscellaneous

Cake plate, pink floral, gilt, reticulated, hdl, 10″ 85.00
Candle holder, Teroma, windmill scene, sgn, 8½″ 550.00
Humidor, brn w/2 dogs, sgn Bavry, glass, 6x5″ 350.00
Humidor, horse & dog, pipe on lid, artist sgn Kelsey 395.00
Humidor, owl on branch 325.00
Pitcher, tankard; fern leaf, bsk, artist sgn Parlow, 11″ 425.00
Tray, decorated porc, 14x14″ 350.00
Vase, Teroma, woodland scene, sgn Bedigie, #4209, 10″ 1,450.00

Vase, Teroma, #4207, $1,500.00.

Harker

The Harker Pottery was established in East Liverpool, Ohio, in 1840. Their earliest product was yellowware and Rockingham produced from local clay. After 1800, whiteware was made from imported materials. The plant eventually grew to be a large manufacturer of dinnerware and kitchenware, employing as many as three hundred people. It closed in 1972, after it was purchased by the Jeanette Glass Company.

Perhaps their best-known lines were their Cameo wares, decorated with white silhouettes in a cameo effect on contrasting solid colors. Floral silhouettes are standard, but other designs were also used. Blue and pink are the most often-found background hues; a few pieces are found in yellow.

When no condition is indicated, the items listed below are assumed to be in mint condition.

Bean pot/casserole, Amy, ind 5.00
Bowl, Cameo, 10″ 12.00
Bowl, Cameo, 7″ 8.00
Bowl, Cameo, 8″ 10.00
Bowl, cereal; Amy, tab hdl 5.00
Bowl, mixing; Red Apple, 8″ 10.00
Bowl, Red Apple, w/spout, 9½″ 15.00
Bowl, salad; Ivy Vine, w/spoon 18.00
Bowl, vegetable; Amy, rnd 10.00
Cake set, w/pastry server, Currier & Ives, 7-pc 30.00
Casserole, Red Apple, w/lid, 8½″ 20.00
Cup, Apple #2, 4¾″ 10.00
Cup, Cameo 5.00
Jug, Mallow & Pansy, w/lid, 6″ 13.00
Jug, utility; gr/yel/maroon flowers, 6″ 22.50
Mayonnaise, w/ladle, sm 18.00
Mug, beer; deer, brn/tan/gr, hound hdl, Rockingham, 5½″ 8.50

Mug, Cameo, pink........10.00
Mug, Cameo, toy soldier & elephant, pink & wht........15.00
Pie baker, Cameo, pink........10.00
Pie server, floral w/red border........10.00
Pie server, Mallow & Pansy........6.00
Pie server, Red Apple........12.50
Pie server & spoon, red rose w/yel & bl daisy........18.00
Pie server & spoon, Rose Bud, pr........18.00
Plate, Amy, 7″........5.00
Plate, cake; Amy, 10⅝″........12.00
Plate, cake; Apple & Pear, rnd........10.00
Plate, cake; Cameo........9.00
Plate, cake; Petit Point Rose, 2nd style........10.00
Plate, Cameo Rose, bl & wht, 11¾″........11.00
Plate, child's; Cameo, pink, 7¼″........10.00
Plate, Red Apple, 10″........5.00
Platter, Amy........12.00
Rolling pin, Amy........55.00
Rolling pin, Cameo, bl & wht, rare........80.00
Rolling pin, Cameo, pink........70.00
Rolling pin, Mallow & Pansy........65.00
Rolling pin, Petit Point Rose, 2nd style........60.00
Rolling pin, Poppy........55.00
Rolling pin, Red Apple........60.00
Rolling pin, Tulip........60.00
Shaker, Mallow & Pansy, w/blk lettering........4.00
Spoon, Amy........10.00
Sugar bowl, Cameo........6.00
Sugar scoop, Amy........38.00
Teapot, Cameo Rose, bl........20.00
Teapot, cat scene, 4-cup........23.00
Tray, utility; Amy........7.00
Tray, utility; Mexican........8.00

Harlequin

Harlequin dinnerware, produced by the Homer Laughlin China Company of Newell, West Virginia, was introduced in 1938. It was a light-weight ware, made in maroon, mauve blue, and spruce green, as well as all the Fiesta colors except ivory (see Fiesta). It was marketed exclusively by the Woolworth stores, who considered it to be their all-time best seller. For this reason, they contracted with Homer Laughlin to reissue Harlequin to commemorate their 100th anniversary in 1979. Although three of the original glazes were used in the reissue, the few serving pieces that were made have been restyled, and the new line offers no threat to the investment of collectors of old Harlequin.

The Harlequin animals, including a fish, lamb, cat, penguin, duck, and donkey, were made during the early 1940s, also for the dime-store trade. Today these are highly regarded by collectors of Homer Laughlin China.

When no condition is indicated, the items listed below are assumed to be in mint condition.

'36s bowl........9.00
'36s oatmeal, 6½″........5.50
Animals, maverics........22.00
Animals, regular colors........45.00
Ash tray, basketweave........20.00
Ash tray, regular........18.00
Baker, oval, 9″........8.50
Butter dish........35.00
Candle holder, pr........32.00
Casserole w/lid........35.00
Coffee cup & saucer, demitasse........20.00
Coffee cup & saucer, demitasse, '50s colors........29.00
Cream soup........7.00
Creamer, novelty........6.50
Creamer, regular........4.00
Creamer, w/high lip........20.00
Cup, large tankard........40.00
Cup & saucer, demitasse; '50s colors........29.00
Deep plate........10.00
Egg cup, ind........10.00
Fruit, 5½″........4.50
Jug, 22-oz........22.00
Marmalade........42.00
Nappy, 9″........9.00
Nut dish........6.00
Plate, 10″........7.50
Plate, 6″........2.50
Plate, 7″........3.00
Plate, 9″........4.50
Platter, 11″........6.50
Platter, 13″........9.00
Relish tray, 5-pc........45.00
Salad bowl, ind, 7″........7.50
Sauce boat........7.00
Saucer........1.50
Saucer/ash tray........25.00
Shakers, pr........7.00
Spoon rest, dk gr, red........135.00
Spoon rest, yel & turq........95.00
Sugar bowl........5.00
Syrup........85.00
Teacup........4.50
Teapot........23.00
Tumbler, w/car decal........22.00

Hatpin Holders

Most hatpin holders were made from 1860 to 1920 to coincide with the period during which hatpins were popularly in vogue. The taller types were required to house the long hatpins necessary to secure the large bonnets that were in style from 1890 to 1914. They were usually porcelain, either decorated by hand or by transfer with florals or scenics, although some were clever figurals. Glass examples are rare, and those of slag or carnival glass are especially valuable.

When no condition is indicated, the items listed below are assumed to be in mint condition.

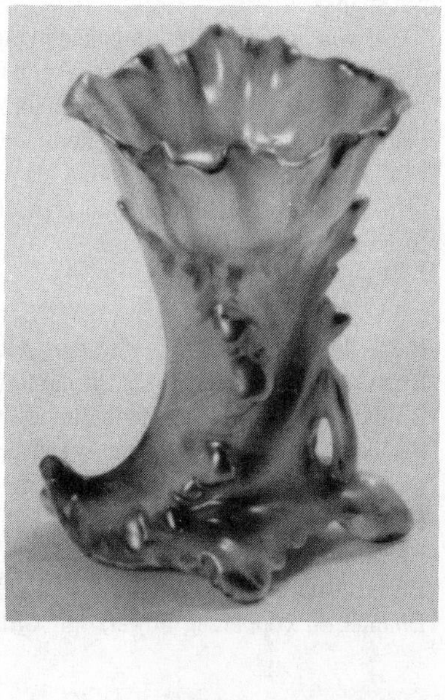

Poppy figural, satin finish, Royal Bayreuth, 4¼″, $350.00.

Airplane series, moriage trim, Nippon, 4¾" 165.00
Bl/wht Japanese export, windmill scene, HP, 4" 65.00
Cameo on bsk, urn form, Shafer & Vater, 5¼" 135.00
Carnival, Grape & Cable, gr 225.00
Carnival, Orange Tree, bl 195.00
Clover figural, 13-hole, Royal Bayreuth, bl mk, 4½" 350.00
Daisies & pink flowers reflected in water, octagon, RSP 145.00
Egyptian series, Schafer & Vater, rare 165.00
Geisha, seated w/fan, bsk figural, S&V, 4¾" 165.00
Gold moriage butterflies/top & base bands, Nippon, 5" 65.00
Gold top/base, HP violet, Pickard-Rosenthal mk, 4¾" 110.00
Gold top/stylized Nouveau motif, HP, Pickard, 4¾" 110.00
Gold/floral, HP, sgn O'Haver, Vienna Austria, 19-hole, 4¾" 65.00
Japan, desert scene 35.00
Jasper, sq w/dimensional strawberries, crown/sunburst mk 165.00
Lady & lily w/saucer base, Royal Bayreuth, bl mk, 4½" 450.00
Lady & peacock, decal, 7-hole, mk LP Limoges, 3⅝" 165.00
Man on horsebk, HP, Royal Doulton, Lambeth/Burslem, 4¾" . . . 125.00
Nouveau lady's head/jeweling, bsk/pearl, S&V, 5½" 195.00
Silver, cherub holds ring, velvet pincushion base, 4" 150.00
Silver, etched/eng cone w/wide ft, 16-hole, ca 1880, 5½" 150.00
Silver overlay on Bavarian china, 10-hole, ZS & Co, 4¾" 135.00
Souvenir, City of York crest, Goss, 3½" 85.00
Souvenir, portrait King Geo V, pearlized, ca 1910, 4½" 75.00

Hatpins

A hatpin was used to securely fasten a hat to the hair and head of the wearer. Hatpins, measuring from 4" to 12" in length, were worn from approximately 1850 to 1920. During the Art Deco period, hatpins became ornaments rather than the decorative functional jewels that they had been. The hatpin period reached its zenith in 1913 just prior to World War I, which brought about a radical change in women's headdress and fashion. About that time, women began to scorn the bonnet and adopt 'the hat' as a symbol of their equality.

The hatpin was made of every natural and manufactured element, in a myriad of designs that challenge the imagination. They were contrived to serve every fashion need and compliment the milliner's art. Collectors often concentrate on a specific type: hand-painted porcelains, sterling silver, commemoratives, sporting activities, carnival glass, Art Nouveau and/or Art Deco designs, Victorian gothics with mounted stones, exquisite rhinestones, escutcheon engraved and brass-mounted heads, gold and gems, or simply primitive types made in the Victorian parlor. Some collectors prefer the long pin-shanks while others select only those on tramblants or nodder-type pin-shanks.

If you are interested in collecting or dealing in hatpins, you will find that authority Lillian Baker has several fine books available on the subject, including her most recent publication, *Hatpins and Hatpin Holders*, complete with beautiful color illustrations and current market values. She is listed in the Directory under California, as well as 'Clubs and Newsletters.'

When no condition is indicated, the items listed below are assumed to be in mint condition.

Key: cab—cabachon

Brass, lg faux topaz w/in wire twist atop emb stem mt, 2¾" 55.00
Brass, triangle w/emb roses, lg faux amethyst atop, 1¼" 45.00
Brilliants, 4-color, 4 diamond shapes join, 1910, 3" W 65.00
Brilliants w/lg amethyst stone set in brass heart, 1¾" W 45.00
Cloisonne, oblong w/lily-o/t-valley, sgn, 2" L, 7¾" pin 75.00
Crystal, hand cut, blown teardrop w/in, 2½", 10½" pin 95.00
Egyptian motif, brass 45.00
Emerald glass bead, ¾", on 7⅞" steel pin 35.00
Enamel on copper, lg flower, sgn GED, 1", w/9½" brass pin . . . 45.00
Eternal Question, gilt on copper, Gibson girl, 2", 8" pin 95.00
Falcon's claw, SP set w/cairgorm, ¾", 9½" pin 95.00
Ivory openwork lattice ball, Japanese, ¾" bead on 8½" pin 125.00
Jet glass, riveted, sq w/heart at corners, bead fr, Czech 110.00
Peacock eye cab ea side in sterling collet mt, CH Horner 95.00
Pique on 1¼" tortoise ball w/½" tortoise ball dangle 150.00
Plastic, curling ram's horn, ca 1920, 2¼x2¼", 4" pin 18.00
Plastic, 5 grad rings, sm 1 in center, joined at base, 2" 15.00
Plique-a-jour lily ea side opal cab, sgn Depose/900, 1½" 350.00
Porcelain on brass, transfer of maiden/butterfly, 1¼" 85.00
Porcelain portrait w/gold overlay edge, 1½"x1", 9" pin 95.00
Satsuma, birds & leaves, HP, 1½" head on 10½" steel pin 125.00
Scarab w/in oval fr, German silver/enamel, 1½x1¼" 65.00
Sterling, heart w/Nouveau lady's head, 1", 7¼" steel pin 55.00
Sterling, lady's head, encompassed in flowing hair, 1" 45.00
Sterling, lady's head w/in clamshell, 1", 7¾" steel pin 55.00
Sterling, lady's head w/in floral-mtd Arts & Crafts fr, 1" 45.00
Sterling, rnd w/high-relief lady's head, Unger Bros, 1" 85.00
Sterling, stylized theatrical head, hollow/repousse, 1½" 85.00
Sunflower, brass 24.00
Turq matrix triangle atop brass openwork w/2 cabs, 1¾" 125.00
Vanity, brass filigree/rhinestones, mirror/puff, 1½x2" 250.00

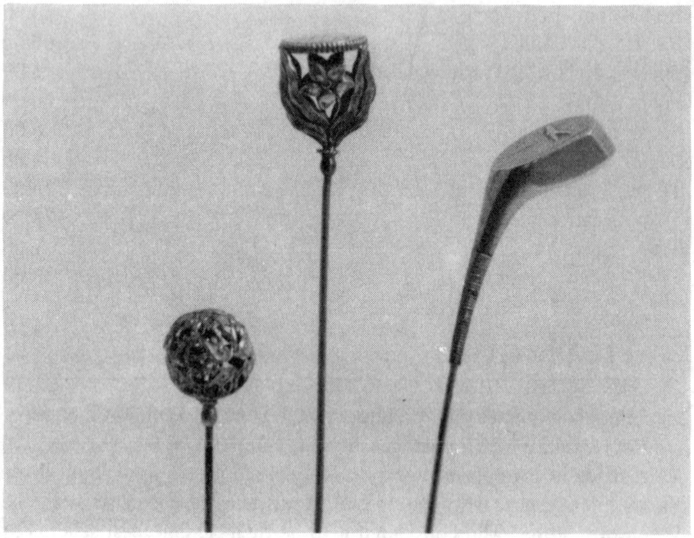

Left to right: Red and green enamel on gold filigree ball, 6½", $12.50; Monogrammed plate on floral mount, 9", $20.00; Golf club figural, 8", $30.00.

Haviland

The Haviland China Company was organized in 1840 by David Haviland, a New York china importer. His search for a pure white, non-porous porcelain led him to Limoges, France, where natural deposits of suitable clay had already attracted numerous china manufacturers. The fine hand-painted china he produced there was translucent and meticulously decorated, with each piece fired in an individual sagger.

It has been estimated that as many as 60,000 chinaware patterns were designed, each piece marked with one of several company backstamps. 'H. & Co.' was used until 1890, when a law was enacted making it necessary to include the country of origin. Various marks have been used since that time including 'Haviland, France'; 'Haviland & Co. Limoges'; and 'Decorated by Haviland & Co.'

Various associations with family members over the years have resulted in changes in management as well as company name. In 1892, Theodore Haviland left the firm to start his own business. Some of his ware was marked 'Mont Mery.' Later logos included a horseshoe, a shield, and various uses of his initials and name. In 1941, this branch moved to the United States. Wares produced here are marked 'Theodore Haviland, N.Y.' or 'Made In America.'

Though it is their dinnerware lines for which they are most famous, during the 1880s and 1890s they also made exquisite art pottery using a technique of underglaze slip decoration called 'Barbotine,' which had been invented by Ernest Chaplet. In 1885 Haviland bought the formula and hired Chaplet to oversee its production. The technique involved mixing heavy white clay slip with pigments to produce a compound of the same consistency as oil paints. The finished product actually resembled oil paintings of the period, the texture achieved through the application of the heavy medium to the clay body in much the same manner as an artist would apply paint to his canvas. Primarily the body used with this method was a low-fired 'faience,' though they also produced stoneware.

Authority Mary Frank Gaston has compiled a lovely book, *Haviland Collectibles and Objects of Art*, with full-color illustrations and current values; you will find her address in the Directory under Texas. Numbers in the listings below refer to pattern books by Arlene Schleiger. When no condition is indicated, items are assumed to be in mint condition.

Basket, flowers & butterflies, 6″ 45.00
Bone dish, bl florals, scalloped border, 6½″ 22.00
Bouillon cup, Albany, #107A 32.00
Bowl, Autumn Leaf, wht w/gold hdls, w/lid, 9″ dia 30.00
Bowl, Avalon, w/lid, rnd, 10″ 25.00
Bowl, Baltimore Rose, leaf shaped 40.00
Bowl, bird/floral border, Barbotine, BGR211, 11½″ 415.00
Bowl, dumpling; Dresden, shell shape, #679E 175.00
Bowl, lg pink roses on border, gold trim, pierced hdl, 8″ 20.00
Bowl, salad; roses/wildflower swags inside 95.00
Bowl, soup; Clover, flat, #98 .... 15.00
Bowl, vegetable; #386, w/lid 48.00
Bowl, vegetable; #64E 35.00
Bowl, vegetable; Albany, oval, w/lid, #107A 75.00
Bowl, vegetable; Princess, oval 35.00
Bowl, vegetable; Princess, rnd, w/lid 65.00
Bowl, vegetable; rnd, w/lid, #107A 75.00
Bowl, vegetable; rnd, w/lid, #58A 125.00
Box, dresser; violets, gold trim 55.00
Butter dish, w/drainer & lid 45.00
Butter pat, bl & pink florals, fluted edge 12.00
Butter pat, Plain Blank 10.00
Cake plate, sprays of violets 45.00
Candle holder, pink floral, pr 155.00
Charger, Art Nouveau florals, HP, American, 12″ 45.00
Charger, Princess on Star Blank, 1893, 12½″ 75.00
Chocolate pot, floral on cobalt/gold, Feu de Four, mk H&Co 275.00
Chocolate pot, florals, gilt decor, 8¾″ 95.00
Chocolate pot, lg mixed floral sprays, gold trim 175.00
Chocolate pot, pale yel flowers, 10″ 85.00
Chocolate pot, pink rose w/gold trim, +6 cups & saucers 525.00
Chocolate pot, rose sprays w/gold, #2 Blank, +4 c/s, 10½″ 250.00
Coffee set, pot/creamer/sugar, wide gold band 155.00
Compote, reticulated, plain 95.00
Cracker jar, cobalt decor w/gold trim 180.00
Cream soup & saucer, Silver Anniversary, gold trim 20.00
Creamer, Avalon, NY 15.00
Creamer & sugar, Garden Flower, ea w/lid 45.00
Creamer & sugar, pk rose spray w/gold, #540, Smooth Blank 55.00
Cup & saucer, Autumn Leaf 28.00
Cup & saucer, Avalon, NY 18.00
Cup & saucer, butterfly shaped hdl 100.00
Cup & saucer, chocolate; #22, Star Blank, w/gold, set of 6 .... 145.00
Cup & saucer, demitasse; Drop Rose 45.00
Cup & saucer, demitasse; Ranson, gold trim, set of 4 .... 92.50
Cup & saucer, demitasse; US Lighthouse Service/Gov't issue 30.00
Cup & saucer, Moss Rose 40.00
Ewer, enamel, pink floral sprays 65.00
Ferner, rare 175.00
Figurine, young girl, seated 350.00
Fish set, fish in center, gilt, platter & 6 plates 750.00
Gravy bowl, #486, sq 45.00
Hatpin holder, rosebud top, HP purple floral, gold trim 45.00
Luncheon set, Bridge game, red/gr clover, #113A, set for 4 .... 375.00
Mush set, turq border, gold trim 75.00
Pancake dish, pink flowers, gray foliage 95.00
Pitcher, floral on pink/gr, artist sgn, France, 8x6″ 110.00
Pitcher, gold/blk rim, Theo, 5¼″ 16.00
Pitcher, pink flowers HP on gr, scalloped base, ornate, 8″ 110.00
Pitcher, Sandoz, shaped like duck, 6″ 600.00
Plaque, HP grapes, American 95.00
Plaque, summer/winter, matt/ornate wood fr, H&Co, 16″, pr 260.00
Plate, bird & butterfly, 6″ 15.00
Plate, bird & roses, hdls, 10½″ 40.00
Plate, chop; roses, gold trim, 13″ 35.00
Plate, dinner; #133 .... 15.00
Plate, dinner; Albany, #107A 32.00
Plate, dinner; Autumn Leaf, #34911 .... 20.00
Plate, Field Flowers, ca 1800, 8″ 40.00
Plate, oyster; mk H&Co Depose, made for JE Caldwell, 7½″ 75.00
Plate, oyster; pink floral, gold decor, 5-shell 40.00
Plate, pheasants in field, H&C mk, artist sgn 95.00
Plate, salad; crescent shaped, pink flowers, gold trim 90.00
Plate, wht orchids on brn, 7½″ 18.00
Plate, wide cobalt border w/gold trim 45.00
Platter, Albany, #107A, 15½″ 65.00
Platter, poppy decor 85.00
Platter, Princess, 12″ 35.00
Ramekin, roses, w/underplate 20.00
Salt dip, Clover, scalloped border 15.00
Sherbet, peach flowers, ped ft 75.00
Soap dish, Moss Rose 40.00
Tea set, Moss Rose, pot/creamer/sugar 165.00
Tea set, scalloped base, fine design, pot, cr/sug 245.00
Teapot, bl/gold flowers, Limoges, 8″ 75.00
Tray, pen; roses, pink edge, gilt trim, 8½x3″ 20.00
Tureen, #133 .... 80.00
Tureen, Albany, #107, lg 125.00
Tureen, grn & wht florals, fancy hdls & finial 155.00
Vase, Barbotine, sgn w/initial of Midoux, 7¼″ 775.00
Vase, HP roses on gr, American, 12″ 95.00
Vase, Terra Cotta, sculpted florals, sgn Lindenher, 14″ 1,800.00

Baltimore Rose, covered dish, 10″ including handles, $125.00.

Hawkes

Thomas Hawkes established his factory in Corning, New York, in 1880. He developed many beautiful patterns of cut glass, two of which were awarded the Grand Prize at the Paris Exposition in 1889. By the end of the century, his company was renowned for the finest in cut glass production. The company logo was a trefoil form enclosing a hawk in each of the two bottom lobes, with a fleur-de-lis in the center.

When no condition is indicated, the items listed below are assumed to be in mint condtion.

Ash tray, cut glass, sgn....35.00
Ash tray, yel glass w/gilt silver overlay & rest, sgn, 3½″....95.00
Bonbon, Pillars & Diamonds, shell shape....95.00
Bottle, chili sauce; allover floral, hdl, ornate top, sgn....325.00
Bottle, scent; intricate polished intaglio, 14k stopper....300.00
Bottle, scent; verre de soie/acid etched, sterling stopper....125.00
Bottle, whiskey; strawberry, sterling jigger top, mk....165.00
Bowl, blown-out, sgn, 6″....285.00
Bowl, eng sailing vessel/cornucopia/bird of paradise, 10½″....95.00
Bowl, hobstar center/rim, feathered fan cuttings, 7″....80.00
Bowl, salad; Centauri pattern, rolled-in rim, sgn, 10″, NM....350.00
Carafe, water; Venetian....175.00
Celery dish, sharp hobstars, sgn....145.00
Compote, sterling-clad finial, eng wheel-spokes decor, 8″....95.00
Cordial, Delft Diamond, 3¾″....40.00
Cordial, Rock Crystal....37.00
Cruet, oil/vinegar, hobstars, bubble-cut stoppers, 8½″, pr....250.00
Cruet, vinegar; eng, sterling top....75.00
Decanter, hexagon panels, teardrop stopper, 13½″....195.00
Desk set, Gracia, sterling trim, sgn....385.00
Dish, Grecian, sq/shallow, 8¾″....350.00
Finger bowl, Chrysanthemum pattern....125.00
Goblet, Aquilla, 7″....42.00
Goblet, Aragon, 6½″....30.00
Goblet, Sierra, 7⅝″....75.00
Jug, wine; wheat etching, sgn....185.00
Lamp base, 3 eng fish, sgn, 12″....395.00
Napkin ring, 1¾″....95.00
Nappy, pinwheel, X-hatch, fan, sgn, no hdl, 5″....75.00
Pitcher, cocktail; block cut, SP top w/pour spout, sgn....245.00
Pitcher, Crocus, 7¾″....450.00
Pitcher, Gravic, tiger flower, notched hdl, bulbous, 7½″....285.00
Plate, cake; cut glass, sgn, center hdl....95.00
Plate, gr cut to clear, sgn Hawkes, 8″....80.00
Punch bowl, Albion, sgn, 20-lbs, 14″ dia....1,600.00
Punch bowl & base, hobstar & fan, swirled, 13½x15″....2,500.00
Rose bowl, apple gr, intaglio cut, sgn, 5¾″....100.00
Shakers, bl, intaglio floral, ped ft, gold base/top, pr....90.00
Shakers, ped ft, sq base, silver tops, pr....135.00
Shakers, swags/flowers, intaglio cut, gold rim, 4½″, pr....60.00
Sherbet, Cornwall, 5¾″....30.00
Sherbet, Foley, 4½″....30.00
Sherry, Louis, 5⅜″....30.00
Tray, dresser; medallion w/bird in flight, 1½″ gallery....245.00
Tray, Gravic Iris, sgn, 6½″....165.00
Tray, Mars, 1″ thick blank, 14x9″....650.00
Tumbler, juice; Doris, 3⅝″....40.00
Tumbler, juice; St George, 3¾″....25.00
Tumbler, juice; Wild Rose, 3½″....30.00
Tumbler, lemonade; Morning Glory, sgn, set of 6....295.00
Tumbler, old-fashioned; Vernacy, 3¾″....35.00
Vase, Albion, circular, sgn, 14″....700.00
Vase, floral swags & ribbons on gr, gold trim, sgn, 8¼″....125.00
Vase, flower garland/geometric etching, silver rim, 6¼″....275.00
Vase, Gravic Tulip, sterling rim, Jacobi & Jenkins, 10″....325.00
Vase, Gravic Tulip, sterling rim, Jacobi & Jenkins, 12″....350.00
Vase, long flared neck, compressed bulb body, 9½″....300.00
Vase, Navarre, trumpet form, sgn, 16½″....1,000.00
Vase, pirate ship, eng thick bl crystal, sgn, 10½″....185.00
Vase, Queen's, trumpet form, cut glass, sgn, 16″....800.00
Vase, stars & stripes, sgn, 10x3¾″....95.00
Vase, trumpet shape, clover mk, plain, 14″....175.00
Whipped cream set, sgn, 2-pc....250.00
Wine, Grapevines, 5⅝″....40.00
Wine, hobnail, rayed base, sgn, gr/clear, 6½″....150.00
Wine, Rock Crystal....37.00
Wine, Wheat, 5⅜″....30.00

Heisey

A.H. Heisey began his long career at the King Glass Company of Pittsburgh. He later joined the Ripley Glass Company which soon became Geo. Duncan and Sons. After Duncan's death, Heisey became half owner along with his brother-in-law, James Duncan. In 1895, he built his own factory in Newark, Ohio, starting production in 1896 and continuing until Christmas of 1957. At that time, Imperial Glass Corporation purchased some of the moulds. In 1968, they removed the old Diamond H from any moulds they put into use.

During their highly successful period of production, Heisey made fine hand-crafted tableware with simple yet graceful designs. Early pieces were not marked. After November 1901, the glassware was marked either with the 'Diamond H' or a paper label. Blown ware is often marked on the stem, never on the bowl or foot.

When no condition is indicated, the items listed below are assumed to be in mint condition.

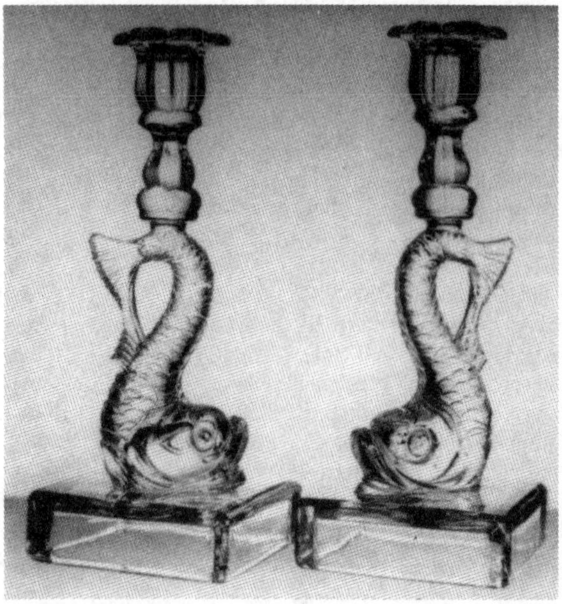

Dolphin candlesticks, pink, 10½″, $400.00 for the pair.

Animals

Clydesdale....400.00
Colts, set of 3....320.00
Dolphin, candlestick, pink, #110, pr....400.00
Donkey....275.00

Duck, ash tray........110.00
Elephant, lg........325.00
Elephants, 3 grad sizes in set........750.00
Fish, bookends, crystal, pr........200.00
Fish, candlestick........200.00
Fish, match holder........150.00
Gazelle........1,200.00
Geese, set of 3........450.00
Giraffe........170.00
Goose, cocktail........100.00
Goose, wings down........300.00
Goose, wings half........75.00
Goose, wings up........75.00
Hen........425.00
Horse head, bookends, frosted, pr........200.00
Horse head, cigarette box, crystal, #1489, 4¼x4″........65.00
Horse head, cocktail shaker........120.00
Kingfisher, flower block, moongleam........200.00
Mallards, set of 3........400.00
Plug horse........75.00
Pouter Pigeon........700.00
Rabbit, paperweight........165.00
Ringneck, pheasant........145.00
Rooster, Fighting; 8″........150.00
Rooster, vase, 6½″........95.00
Rooster, 5⅝″........425.00
Rooster head, cocktail shaker, 1-qt........95.00
Rooster stem, cocktail........60.00
Rooster stopper, cocktail shaker, Orchid........150.00
Scotty dog........120.00
Setter, ash tray, flamingo, #1286........40.00
Sparrow........65.00
Tropical Fish........1,000.00
Wood Duck........550.00

Dinnerware

Aristocrat, candlestick #21, 9″, pr........100.00
Athena, candy box, w/lid, #1541, sm, 5″........50.00
Banded Flute, toothpick, #150........35.00
Beaded Panel & Sunburst, toothpick holder, #1235........70.00
Beaded Panel & Sunburst, wine, #1235........40.00
Beaded Swag, opal; molasses, cornflower decor, #1295........180.00
Beaded Swag, opal; toothpick holder, rose decor, #1295........125.00
Beaded Swag, opal; tumbler, #1295........45.00
Beaded Swag, toothpick holder, #1295........45.00
Cherub, flamingo; candlestick #111, 11½″, pr........450.00
Classic, candlestick #16, 11″, pr........150.00
Clover Rope, sahara; beer mug, #1426........250.00
Coarse Rib, bowl, #406, 9″........20.00
Coarse Rib, jelly, 2-hdl, #407........15.00
Coarse Rib, mustard, w/lid, #407........27.50
Coarse Rib, plate, Hawthorne, #407, 8″........20.00
Coarse Rib Hotel, creamer & sugar, w/lid, #406........30.00
Cross Lined Flute, bowl, #451, 7″........30.00
Cross Lined Flute, goblet, #451........40.00
Cross Lined Flute, pitcher, #451, 1-pt........50.00
Cross Lined Flute, tumbler, #451........25.00
Crystolite, candleblock, #1503, pr........25.00
Crystolite, cordial, #5003........42.50
Crystolite, plate, #1503, 14″........22.50
Delaware, goblet, Checker Optic, Hawthorne, #3324, 9-oz........105.00
Diamond Optic, cobalt; vase, favor, #4229........90.00
Diamond Optic, moongleam; vase, favor, #4230........250.00
Diamond Optic, moongleam; wine, African, ftd/stem, 3-oz........40.00
Diamond Optic, sahara; vase, favor, #4231........100.00
Duquesne, tangerine; soda, Wide Optic, #3389........130.00
Empress, alexandrite; candlestick, toed, #1401, 6″, pr........450.00
Empress, alexandrite; plate, sq, #1401, 10½″........90.00
Empress, bowl, floral, lion, #1401, 10″........130.00
Empress, flamingo; candy box, w/lid, #1401, 6″........90.00
Empress, flamingo; nut dish, ind, #1401........20.00
Empress, flamingo; pitcher, dolphin ftd, #1401........120.00
Empress, flamingo; relish, triplex, #1401, 6″........25.00
Empress, moongleam; nut dish, Diamond Optic, ind, #1401........35.00
Empress, moongleam; oil, #1401, 4-oz........80.00
Empress, moongleam; relish, triplex, #1401, 7″........35.00
Empress, moongleam; shakers, #1401, pr........80.00
Empress, sahara; bowl, floral, #1401, 11″........75.00
Empress, sahara; candlestick, toed, #1401, 6″........85.00
Empress, sahara; compote, ftd, #1401, 6″........40.00
Empress, sahara; cream soup w/plate, #1401........30.00
Empress, sahara; mustard, w/lid, #1401........60.00
Fancy Loop, cake plate, ftd, #1205........75.00
Fancy Loop, emerald; toothpick holder, #1205........125.00
Fancy Loop, plaid; vase, Sherry, #1205, 6¾″........40.00
Fancy Loop, spooner, #1205........70.00
Fandango, compote, ftd, #1201, 9″........70.00
Fandango, cracker jar, #1201........120.00
Fandango, creamer & sugar, ind, #1201........50.00
Fandango, horseradish, w/lid, #1201........75.00
Fandango, molasses can, #1201........85.00
Fandango, nappy, crimped, #1201, 7″........40.00
Fandango, rose bowl, #1201, 4″........55.00
Fandango, toothpick, #1201........55.00
Fern, zircon; jelly, hdl, #1495, 6″........75.00
Flat Panel, horseradish, w/lid, #352........50.00
Grecian Border, goblet, #433, 9-oz........90.00
Half Circle, moongleam; creamer, ind, #1403........40.00
Heisey Rose, bowl, floral, 9½″........70.00
Heisey Rose, candlestick, 3-lite, pr........240.00
Heisey Rose, compote, 6½″........55.00
Heisey Rose, cordial........175.00
Heisey Rose, creamer & sugar........75.00
Heisey Rose, cruet........160.00
Heisey Rose, cup & saucer........60.00
Heisey Rose, decanter, 1-pt........190.00
Heisey Rose, dinner bell........175.00
Heisey Rose, goblet........40.00
Heisey Rose, ice bucket, dolphin ftd........225.00
Heisey Rose, lemon dish, w/lid........150.00
Heisey Rose, mayonnaise, 5½″........50.00
Heisey Rose, pitcher........300.00
Heisey Rose, plate, dinner; 10½″........125.00
Heisey Rose, plate, 8″........30.00
Heisey Rose, vase, fan shaped, 7″........115.00
Intercepted Flute, bowl, #470, 11″........55.00
Intercepted Flute, pitcher, #470, 3-pt........95.00
Intercepted Flute, tumbler, #470........40.00
Ipswich, cobalt; bowl, floral, #1405, 11″........200.00
Ipswich, flamingo; candy, w/lid, #1405, ½-lb........225.00
Ipswich, flamingo; creamer & sugar, #1405........80.00
Ipswich, flamingo; goblet, #1405, 10-oz........50.00
Ipswich, moongleam; plate, sq, #1405, 7″........22.00
Ipswich, plate, sq, #1405, 8″........15.00
Ipswich, sahara; cocktail shaker, #1405, 1-qt........275.00
Jack Be Nimble, candlestick, toy, #31, pr........60.00
Kalonyal, punch cup, #1776........27.50

Lariat, ash tray/nut dish, #1540, 4″ . . . 22.50
Lariat, cigarette box, w/lid, #1540 . . . 35.00
Lariat, coaster, #1540 . . . 6.00
Lariat, compote, ftd, #1540 . . . 22.50
Lariat, cruet, oval, #1540 . . . 45.00
Lariat, egg plate, #1540 . . . 125.00
Lariat, plate, buffet; #1540, 21″ . . . 50.00
Lariat, punch cup, #1540 . . . 8.00
Lariat, relish, moonglo cut, 3-part, #1540, 12″ . . . 35.00
Lariat, relish, 3-part, #1540, 10″ . . . 25.00
Lariat, sugar & creamer, #1540, pr . . . 30.00
Locket on Chain, bowl, #160, 8″ . . . 55.00
Locket on Chain, butter, w/lid, #160 . . . 110.00
Locket on Chain, punch cup, #160 . . . 25.00
Locket on Chain, wine, #160 . . . 65.00
Lodestar, dawn; ash tray, #1632 . . . 65.00
Lodestar, dawn; bowl, crimped, #1632, 11″ . . . 100.00
Lodestar, dawn; bowl, crimped, #1632, 6″ . . . 55.00
Lodestar, dawn; candy, w/lid, #1632 . . . 90.00
Lodestar, dawn; pitcher, #1632, 1-qt . . . 110.00
Lodestar, dawn; tray, celery; #1632 . . . 45.00
Mariette, cordial, unknown cutting, #3414 . . . 150.00
Mercury, candlestick, Hawthorne, #112, 3″, pr . . . 90.00
Mercury, moongleam; candlestick, #112, 3″ . . . 27.50
Morning Glory, flamingo; goblet, Diamond Optic, #3373 . . . 45.00
Nail, bowl, rnd, #462½, 4½″ . . . 30.00
Nail, bowl, sq, #462, 4½″ . . . 30.00
Narcissus cut, creamer & sugar . . . 45.00
Narcissus cut, goblet . . . 25.00
Narcissus cut, sherbet . . . 15.00
Narrow Flute, marmalade, #393 . . . 40.00
Narrow Flute, mustard, w/lid, #394 . . . 50.00
Narrow Flute, pitcher, #473, 3-pt . . . 55.00
Narrow Flute, punch bowl, Dr Johnson, #394 . . . 125.00
Narrow Flute, tray, biscuit; #393 . . . 75.00
Narrow Flute, tray, Domino Sugar, #394 . . . 40.00
Narrow Flute w/Rim, flamingo; bowl, oval, #473, 9″ . . . 40.00
Narrow Flute w/Rim, moongleam; relish, combination, #473 . . . 45.00
Narrow Flute w/Rim, nut dish, #1475, 3½″ . . . 20.00
Narrow Flute w/Rim, puff, w/lid, #473 . . . 40.00
Narrow Flute w/Rim, sardine dish, w/lid, #473 . . . 60.00
New Era, bottle, rye; #4044 . . . 90.00
New Era, bowl, floral, #4044, 11″ . . . 35.00
New Era, cordial, #4044 . . . 50.00
New Era, cup & saucer, demitasse; satin etched, #4044 . . . 30.00
New Era, goblet, #4044 . . . 25.00
New Era, pilsner, #4044 . . . 45.00
New Era, relish, #4044, 13″ . . . 25.00
New Era, wine, #4044 . . . 35.00
Octagon, bonbon, Hawthorne, #1229, 6″ . . . 25.00
Octagon, sahara; mayonnaise, #1229, 5½″ . . . 22.00
Old Sandwich, amber; beer mug, #1404, 12-oz . . . 350.00
Old Sandwich, cobalt; bar glass, #1404, 1½-oz . . . 95.00
Old Sandwich, creamer & sugar, rnd, #1404 . . . 50.00
Old Sandwich, cruet, #1404 . . . 40.00
Old Sandwich, flamingo; beer mug, #1404, 14-oz . . . 350.00
Old Sandwich, moongleam; beer mug, #1404, 18-oz . . . 275.00
Old Sandwich, moongleam; ice jug, #1404, ½-gal . . . 115.00
Old Sandwich, sahara; bowl, popcorn; #1404 . . . 125.00
Old Sandwich, sahara; plate, sq, #1404, 6″ . . . 15.00
Old Williamsburg, candelabra, 3-lite, #300, pr . . . 400.00
Old Williamsburg, candlestick, #2, 7″, pr . . . 85.00
Old Williamsburg, candlestick, #2, 9″ . . . 50.00
Orchid, basket, ftd, 8½″ . . . 300.00
Orchid, bottle, sherry; oval . . . 165.00
Orchid, bowl, crimped, 10″ . . . 50.00
Orchid, bowl, 8″ . . . 45.00
Orchid, candlestick, 1-lite, #112, pr . . . 65.00
Orchid, candlestick, 2-lite, #1615, pr . . . 225.00
Orchid, chocolate, w/lid . . . 120.00
Orchid, compote, oval, 7″ . . . 80.00
Orchid, compote, 6″ . . . 40.00
Orchid, cordial . . . 115.00
Orchid, cup & saucer . . . 50.00
Orchid, goblet . . . 40.00
Orchid, ice tankard, ½-gal . . . 325.00
Orchid, lemon dish, w/lid . . . 150.00
Orchid, mustard, w/lid . . . 125.00
Orchid, plate, cake; 12″ . . . 200.00
Orchid, plate, dinner . . . 100.00
Orchid, plate, salad; 8″ . . . 20.00
Orchid, plate, sandwich; 11″ . . . 55.00
Orchid, plate, torte; 14″ . . . 60.00
Orchid, relish, 3-compartment . . . 55.00
Orchid, saucer, champagne . . . 30.00
Orchid, shakers, pr . . . 70.00
Orchid, sherry . . . 80.00
Orchid, shot glass . . . 85.00
Orchid, soda, 7-oz . . . 50.00
Orchid, vase, ball shaped, 7″ . . . 300.00
Orchid, wine, 3-oz . . . 55.00
Peerless, toothpick, #300 . . . 25.00
Petticoat, moongleam; candlestick, dolphin, #109, 6″, pr . . . 450.00
Pillows, egg cup, #325 . . . 60.00
Pineapple & Fan, emerald; compote, jelly; ftd, #1255, 5″ . . . 155.00
Pineapple & Fan, toothpick holder, some gold, #1255 . . . 105.00
Pineapple & Fan, vase, #1255, 10″ . . . 22.50
Plantation, creamer & sugar, #1567 . . . 45.00
Plantation, cruet, #1567 . . . 75.00
Plantation, marmalade, w/lid, #1567 . . . 75.00
Plantation, pitcher, #1567, ½-gal . . . 110.00
Plantation, shakers, #1567, pr . . . 50.00
Pleat & Panel, amber; cruet, #1170 . . . 400.00
Pleat & Panel, flamingo; jelly, 2-hdl, #1170 . . . 20.00
Pleat & Panel, moongleam; cup & saucer, #1170 . . . 35.00
Pleat & Panel, moongleam; lemon dish, w/lid, #1170 . . . 40.00
Pleat & Panel, sahara; ice jug, #1170 . . . 130.00
Prince of Wales, bowl, #335, 8″ . . . 45.00
Prince of Wales, finger bowl, #335 . . . 20.00
Prince of Wales, punch cup, #335 . . . 15.00
Prince of Wales, rose bowl, ftd, #335 . . . 130.00
Priscilla, toothpick holder, #351 . . . 40.00
Prison Stripe, toothpick holder, #357 . . . 190.00
Provincial, limelight; plate, buffet; #1506, 17″ . . . 150.00
Provincial, limelight; tumbler, ftd, #1506, 9-oz . . . 40.00
Punty & Diamond Point, claret jug, #305 . . . 190.00
Punty & Diamond Point, toothpick holder, #305 . . . 185.00
Punty & Diamond Point, tumbler, #305, 8-oz . . . 55.00
Puritan, jug, squat, #341½, 3-qt . . . 60.00
Puritan, toothpick, #341 . . . 70.00
Queen Ann, creamer & sugar, Chateau cut, dolphin ft, #1509 . . . 60.00
Queen Ann, ice bucket, Chateau cut, #1509 . . . 60.00
Raised Loop, egg cup, #439 . . . 65.00
Recessed Panel, candy jar, #465, ½-lb . . . 30.00
Recessed Panel, candy jar, #465, 3-lb . . . 125.00
Recessed Panel, vaseline; candy jar, #465, 1-lb . . . 550.00
Revere, cordial, #1183, ¾-oz . . . 50.00
Revere, goblet, #1183 . . . 25.00

Revere, wine, #1183, 2-oz....30.00
Rib & Panel, preserve, ftd, w/lid, Hawthorne, #411, 6″....105.00
Ribbed Octagon, sahara; creamer & sugar, #1231....40.00
Ridgeleigh, ash tray, #1469, 4″....20.00
Ridgeleigh, ash tray, sq, #1469, 3″....7.00
Ridgeleigh, ash trays & cigarette holder, card suit, #1469....60.00
Ridgeleigh, cigarette box, oval, w/lid, #1469....55.00
Ridgeleigh, coaster, #1469, 3½″....10.00
Ridgeleigh, cruet, #1469....35.00
Ridgeleigh, goblet, #1469....25.00
Ridgeleigh, jelly, oval, ind, #1469....15.00
Ridgeleigh, mustard, w/lid, #1469....35.00
Ridgeleigh, perfume, #1469, 5-oz....60.00
Ridgeleigh, plate, sq, #1469, 8″....20.00
Ridgeleigh, puff box, #1469, 5″....35.00
Ridgeleigh, sahara; bowl, floral, oval, #1469, 12″....75.00
Ridgeleigh, vase, ball shaped, #1469, 7″....45.00
Ridgeleigh, zircon; cigarette holder, rnd, #1469....80.00
Rococo, compote, #1447, 6″....50.00
Rococo, creamer & sugar, #1447....50.00
Rococo, limelight; mayonnaise & relish, w/lid, #1447....250.00
Rococo, shakers, #1447, pr....65.00
Sandwich, flamingo; candlestick, dolphin, #110, 10″, pr....400.00
Sanitary, syrup, #360....50.00
Saturn, bowl, gardenia, limelight, #1485, 12″....130.00
Saturn, creamer & sugar, #1485....30.00
Saturn, goblet, #1485, 10-oz....12.00
Saturn, limelight; bowl, gardenia, #1485, 12″....130.00
Saturn, zircon; compote, #1485....125.00
Saturn, zircon; oil, w/stopper, #1485, 2-oz....125.00
Shasta, goblet, Wide Optic, daisy cut, #5013....65.00
Spanish, cobalt; goblet, 10-oz, #3404....100.00
Spanish, tangerine; goblet, #3404, 10-oz....200.00
Stanhope, mint, 2-hdl, #1483, 6″....18.00
Stanhope, plate, #1483, 15″....35.00
Stanhope, shakers, #1483, pr....35.00
Stanhope, vase, ball shaped, #1483, 7″....40.00
Stanhope, zircon; goblet, #1483, 9-oz....80.00
Steeplechase, flamingo; cocktail mixer, #4224....275.00
Sunburst, punch cup, #343....15.00
Sunburst, rose bowl, ftd, #343, 3″....125.00
Sussex, cobalt; goblet, #419....140.00
Sweed-Ad-O-Line, goblet, banquet, Wide Optic, #1423, 12-oz....160.00
Symphone, goblet, Minuet etched, #5010....55.00
Syrup, #371, 7-oz....35.00
Syrup, sahara; #372, 7-oz....75.00
Trident, sahara; candlestick, 2-lite, #134, pr....115.00
Tudor, cruet, #411, 6-oz....40.00
Tudor, jelly, ftd, Hawthorne, #411, 5″....45.00
Tudor, moongleam; cheese, 2-hdl, #411....20.00
Tudor, moongleam; preserve, w/lid, #411, 5″....40.00
Tudor, pickle, #411, 7″....15.00
Tudor Hotel, creamer & sugar, w/lid, Hawthorne, #411....90.00
Twentieth Century, dawn; pitcher, milk; #1415, 1-pt....90.00
Twentieth Century, flamingo; soda, ftd, #1415, 9-oz....40.00
Twentieth Century, sahara; bowl, cereal; underplate, #1415....55.00
Twist, alexandrite; bowl, floral, #1252, 9″....300.00
Twist, cup & saucer, #1252....20.00
Twist, flamingo; creamer & sugar, #1252....42.00
Twist, marigold; Kraft cheese plate, #1252....40.00
Twist, sahara; relish, 2-compartment, #1252, 8″....30.00
Urn/vase, #5012, 6″....20.00
Vase, alexandrite; ball shaped, #4045, 6″....200.00
Victorian, bottle, rye; w/stopper, #1425, 27-oz....70.00
Victorian, butter dish, w/lid, #1425, ½-lb....45.00
Victorian, cigarette box, w/lid, #1425, 6″....40.00
Victorian, cobalt; nappy, #1425, 8″....190.00
Victorian, compote, #1425, 5″....30.00
Victorian, moongleam; sherbet, #1425, 5-oz....50.00
Victorian, plate, buffet; #1425, 21″....75.00
Victorian, punch bowl, #1425....175.00
Warwick, bowl, horn of plenty type, #1428, 11″....225.00
Warwick, cigarette holder, #1428....17.00
Waverly, creamer & sugar, Orchid etched, ind, #1519....60.00
Whaley, mug, beer; club drinking scene, #4163....70.00
Whaley, mug, beer; golf scene, #4163....240.00
Wide Flat Panel, creamer & sugar, oval, Hawthorne/#354....125.00
Yeoman, candy box, w/lid, #1184....65.00
Yeoman, cobalt; salt, ind, #1184....150.00
Yeoman, goblet, #1184, 8-oz....25.00
Yeoman, marigold; egg cup, #1184....50.00
Yeoman, marmalade, w/lid, #1184....25.00
Yeoman, sahara; celery, #1184, 13″....20.00
Yeoman, vaseline; plate, oyster cocktail; #1184, 8″....45.00

Miscellaneous

Bar glass, #1205, Fancy Loop Variant, emerald, 2-oz....85.00
Bar glass, #2401, clowns, circus etched, 2-oz....150.00
Bar glass, #300½, flamingo, Colonial, 2-oz....45.00
Bar glass, #3380, Old Dominion, Diamond Optic, ftd, 1½-oz....90.00
Basket, #458, unknown floral cut, 8″....80.00
Basket, #459, bird & floral cut, 7″....170.00
Bottle, bitters; #335, Prince of Wales....125.00
Candelabra, #1469, Ridgeleigh, single, 10½″....120.00
Candelabra, #4044, New Era, 2-lite....80.00
Candlestick, #133, swan hdls, 6″, pr....250.00
Candlestick, #1455, Grape Cluster, 1-lite/bobeche/A prisms....55.00
Candlestick, #33, toy, Skirted Panel, 3½″....32.50
Cigarette jar & ash tray, #411, Tudor....90.00
Coaster, #1567, Plantation....12.00
Lamp, #21, electroportable, 9″ w/8″ cut shade....400.00
Marmalade, #1000, alexandrite, w/lid....375.00

Heubach

Gebruder Heubach is a German porcelain company that has been in operation since the 1800s producing quality figurines and novelty items. They are perhaps most famous for their doll heads and piano babies, most of which are marked with the circular rising sun device containing an 'H' superimposed over a 'C.'

When no condition is indicated, the items listed below are assumed to be in mint condition.

Baby, crawling, foot in air, wht bonnet w/gr trim, 7″....250.00
Baby, lying on back, hands touching raised left foot, 8½″....320.00
Baby, lying on bk, sgn, 6″ L....200.00
Baby, lying on stomach, thumb in mouth, 9″....320.00
Baby, nude, googly eyes/arms away/head cocked, imp mk, 4¾″....145.00
Baby, seated, arms up, in pink-trim nightie, 5½x4¾″....175.00
Baby, seated, gr ribbon through gown, incised mk, 8½″....370.00
Baby, seated, holding half of egg shell....300.00
Baby, seated, legs crossed, arms raised, wht gown, 10″....400.00
Baby, seated, nude, egg attached, 5x6″....175.00
Baby, seated, pink/wht gown/bonnet, sunburst mk, 7¾″....350.00
Baby, seated, touching toes, wht gown, aqua trim, 9½″....395.00

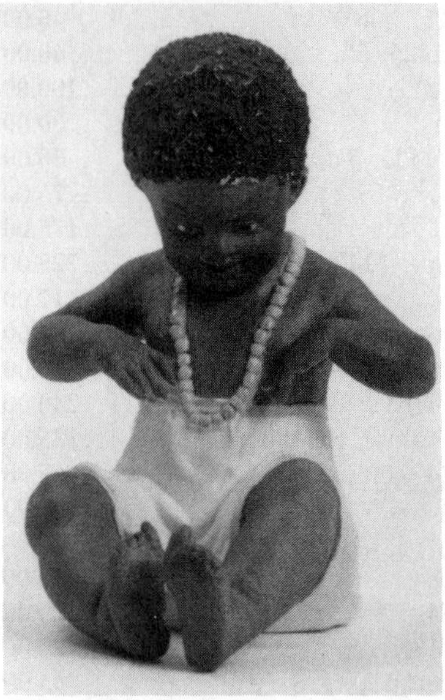

Black baby with necklace, in near mint condition, 5″, $550.00.

Baby, seated, wht pants, aqua trim, blk, sunburst mk, 6″......325.00
Baby boy, squats, nude, blonde hair, holds toes, sgn, 6″.......345.00
Baby girl, seated, pulling off pink socks, 6″................275.00
Baby girl, seated, ruffled nightie/floppy hat, sgn, 5″...........310.00
Black baby, seated, wht gown, holds ball/sunburst, rpr, 4″.....250.00
Boy, pouty, #6894....................................375.00
Card holder, 3x4″.....................................35.00
Choir girl, blonde, gold trim wht robe w/purple book, 8″......225.00
Dish, Jasper, Indian hatchet & shield, gr/wht, 4¼″.............58.00
Dog, brn/wht muzzled puppy sits on gr planks, 3x4″...........85.00
Dog, Collie; mk.......................................76.00
Dog, seated puppy w/floppy ears, sad face, imp mk, 5x7″......285.00
Dutch boy, bl shirt/tan pants, stands before sq vase, 6½″......200.00
Dutch boy, seated, shades of bl, mk, 4⅜x2⅜x3½″............150.00
Dutch girl, seated, gr/orange/wht dress, head to side, 6″.......200.00
Dutch girl, seated, red skirt/gr shirt, sgn, 4¼x2⅜x3½″.........150.00
Dutch girl, seated w/arms resting on baskets w/florals.........150.00
Girl, dancing, blonde, aqua dress, rose ribbon, sgn, 11½″......300.00
Girl, dancing, blonde, gr dress, lav ribbon, sgn, 6½x3½″.......150.00
Girl, on knees, 5″....................................125.00
Girl, standing before chair, mk, lg.........................450.00
Girl in bonnet, boy in sailor outfit, bl/wht/yel, 13″, pr.........400.00
Man & lady, intaglio eyes/pastel clothes, bisque, 15″, pr.......300.00
Peasant girl, gr/wht dress & apron, tan peanut basket, 9″......250.00
Peasant girl w/tambourine; boy w/mandolin, sgn, 9″, pr.......450.00
Toothpick holder, baby crawling, cracked egg shape, mk......150.00
Twin boy & girl, playing w/toes, finger rpr, 9″ L, pr..........450.00
Vase, Dutch girl, scenic, 4½″...............................38.00
Woman behind ship's wheel, decor bsk, imp mk, 11¼″........285.00

Historical Glass

Glassware commemorating particularly significant historical events became popular in the late 1800s. Bread trays were the most common form; but plates, mugs, pitchers, and other items were also pressed in clear as well as colored glass. It was sold in vast amounts at the 1876 Philadelphia Centennial Exposition by various manufacturers who exhibited their wares on the grounds. It remained popular well into the 20th century. Among the themes depicted were the Declaration of Independence, the Constitution, McKinley's 'It Is God's Way,' Remembrance of Three Presidents, the purchase of Alaska, and various presidential campaigns. These are to mention only a few.

In the listings below, when no condition is indicated, items are assumed to be in mint condition. Numbers are Lindsay numbers, referring to a standard reference guide used by many collectors. See also Pattern Glass

Bread Plates and Trays

American Flag w/38 stars, frosted center....................225.00
Angel Border..32.50
Be Industrious, deer & floral basket border.................50.00
Bible, L-200..55.00
Bishop's, L-201..65.00
Blaine & Logan, clear & frosted, L-315....................265.00
Bunker Hill...65.00
Bunker Hill, Prescott & Stark............................195.00
Cable, L-126..32.50
Columbia, L-54.......................................125.00
Columbus, 1892.......................................55.00
Columbus, 1892, milk glass..............................45.00
Constitution, L-43.....................................80.00
Continental, dtd, hand holding bar hdls.....................65.00
Currier & Ives, Donkey & Cart...........................85.00
Egyptian, Cleopatra....................................45.00
Faith, Hope, & Charity..................................55.00
Garden of Eden.......................................42.50
Geo Washington, frosted center, oval, 12″.................115.00
Geo Washington, 1732-1932, 8″..........................25.00
Golden Rule...70.00
Good Luck, Horseshoe..................................40.00
Grand Army o/t Republic, L-505.........................150.00
Grant, Patriot & Soldier, L-291...........................48.00
In Remembrance, Garfield, Washington, Lincoln.............60.00
Jefferson Davis, L-375..................................65.00
Let Us Have Peace, Grant, amber.........................45.00
Let Us Have Peace, Grant, bl............................45.00
Let Us Have Peace, Grant, clear..........................35.00
Liberty Bell, Signers...................................85.00
Liberty Bell, 8″..75.00
Lord's Supper...30.00
McKinley Memorial....................................37.50
Mormon Temple, L-238.................................350.00
Niagara Falls, L-489...................................150.00
Old State House, L-32..................................65.00
Old State House, Philadelphia...........................48.00

Bread tray, Give Us This Day Our Daily Bread, Horseshoe and Anchor, 13″, $38.00.

Pioneer Flour, tray, 90th Anniversary........40.00
Pleasant to Labor........30.00
Pleasure to Labor, Grape, rnd hdls, 10″........35.00
Polar Bear w/Seals........250.00
Railroad, L-134........70.00
Reaper, L-119........85.00
Remember the Maine, ship in center, 9½″........35.00
Remember the Maine, ship w/stars around edge, 9½″........35.00
Rock of Ages, L-236........48.00
Rock of Ages, milk glass center, pat Nov 1875........225.00
Royal Crying Baby........35.00
Spanish-American War, Dewey in wreath, Limoges, 7″........45.00
Symbolical, L-20........160.00
Teddy Roosevelt, dancing bears, oval, 10¼″........135.00
US Battleship Maine, egg & dart border, 5½″........35.00
Virginia Dare........40.00
Washington Centennial, w/Geo Washington, L-27........115.00
We Mourn Our Nation's Loss, Garfield........47.50

Butter dish, Frosted Eagle, Old Abe........250.00
Celery, Horn of Plenty........150.00
Compote, Jenny Lind........150.00
Covered dish, boat, Remember the Maine, clear........85.00
Covered dish, boat, Remember the Maine, gr........75.00
Covered dish, Cannon, L-147........65.00
Covered dish, Covered Wagon, L-128........200.00
Creamer, Classic, on log feet........225.00
Creamer, Log Cabin........225.00
Creamer, Westward-Ho, w/dog hdl........125.00
Cup, Bryan, w/lid, L-336........55.00
Cup, McKinley, w/lid........55.00
Goblet, Capitol Building........40.00
Goblet, Jumbo, 101 border........400.00
Goblet, Liberty Bell, L-35........37.50
Goblet, Liberty Bell, L-35, plain stem........85.00
Goblet, Lincoln Drape, flint........80.00
Goblet, Philadelphia Centennial........55.00
Hatchet, Washington, L-252........45.00
Jam jar, Log Cabin, vaseline, w/lid........675.00
Lamp, Emblem, 9 shields on font, burner dtd 1873, 7″........155.00
Liquor glass, Civil War, toast to union/inscription, L-480........125.00
Mug, Independence Hall on bottom........55.00
Mug, Tennessee, frosted, L-102........55.00
Mug, Washington bust, bk: Columbus bust, Columbian Expo...125.00
Paperweight, Plymouth Rock, L-17........85.00
Pickle dish, Emblem........69.00
Pickle dish, Flaming Sword, L-209........55.00
Pickle dish, L-58........65.00
Pitcher, water; Eden, L-207........75.00
Pitcher, water; Gibson Girl........350.00
Pitcher, water; Gridley........125.00
Pitcher, water; Spanish American War, Dewey, L-400........55.00
Plaque, Lincoln Log, milk glass, very rare........165.00
Salt cellar, ind; Liberty Bell, L-36........45.00
Sugar bowl, Jumbo & Barnum, elephant finial, Barnum heads..250.00
Toothpick holder, Just Out........110.00
Tumbler, Art Palace, World's Fair........55.00
Tumbler, Garfield, L-296........55.00
Tumbler, Grant, L-285........55.00
Tumbler, Logan, bust of Logan & name w/in wreath in base....65.00
Tumbler, Louisiana Purchase, clear........22.50
Tumbler, Louisiana Purchase, milk glass........17.50
Tumbler, McKinley & Hobart, Sound Currency........55.00
Tumbler, McKinley, Our President........55.00

Hobbs and Brockunier

Hobbs and Brockunier's South Wheeling Glass Works was in operation during the last quarter of the 19th century. They are most famous for their peachblow, amberina, Daisy and Button, and Hobnail pattern glass. The mainstay of the operation, however, was druggist items and plain glassware--bowls, mugs, and simple footed pitchers with shell handles.

When no condition is indicated, the items listed below are assumed to be in mint condition. See also Francisware

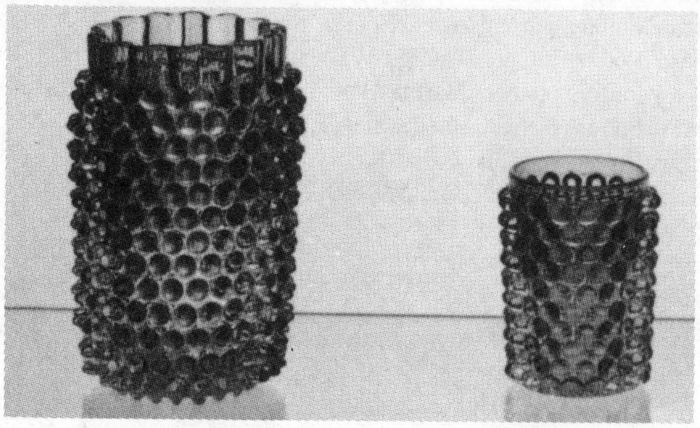

Left, Vase, rubena verde Hobnail, 6½″, $275.00; Right, Tumbler, rubena verde Hobnail, $160.00.

Bowl, rubena, ruffled/folded rim, 9½″ L........95.00
Cruet, Hobnail, clear opal........75.00
Cruet, Hobnail, vaseline opal........210.00
Pitcher, water; Optic, rubena........110.00
Pitcher, water; Raised Swirl, sq top w/polished pontil........75.00
Spooner, goat's head, rare, 1878........85.00
Syrup, Hobnail, clear opal........110.00

Hobnail

When no condition is indicated, the items listed below are assumed to be in mint condition. See also Hobbs and Brockunier; Fenton; Opalescent

Pitcher, amber, applied hdl, 7½″........65.00
Pitcher, amber, cased, ground pontil, water sz........150.00
Pitcher, amethyst, lav ruffled rim, clear hdl........60.00
Pitcher, cranberry, water sz........100.00
Pitcher, cranberry, 5¼″........65.00
Pitcher, ruby stained, milk sz........50.00
Vase, MOP hobs on clear frost to gold, sqd top, 6x5″........600.00

Homer Laughlin

The Homer Laughlin China Company of Newell, West Virginia, was founded in 1871. The superior dinnerware they displayed at the Centennial Exposition in Philadelphia in 1876 won the highest award of excellence. From that time to the present, they have continued to produce quality dinnerware and kitchenware, many lines of which are becoming very popular collectibles. Most of the dinnerware is marked with the name of the pattern, and occasionally with the shape name as well. The 'HLC' trademark is usually followed by a number series, the first two digits of which indicate the year of its manufacture.

When no condition is indicated, the items listed below are assumed to be in mint condition. See also Fiesta; Harlequin; Riviera

Amberstone, ash tray....16.50
Amberstone, bowl, vegetable....7.00
Amberstone, jam jar, w/lid....26.00
Amberstone, sandwich server, center hdl....10.00
Amberstone, sauce boat....14.00
Amberstone, shakers, pr....11.00
Amberstone, tea server....16.50
American Potter, ash tray....32.50
American Potter, candle holder, 2″....26.00
American Potter, creamer, ind....24.00
American Potter, cup & saucer, Zodiac, turq....42.00
American Potter, pitcher, George Washington....20.00
American Potter, pitcher, Martha Washington, 5″....29.00
American Potter, plate, Golden Gate Expo....32.50
American Potter, saucer, Zodiac....15.00
American Potter, toothpick holder....22.50
American Potter, vase, 7″....30.00
Casualstone, bowl, vegetable; rnd....7.00
Casualstone, casserole, w/lid....16.00
Casualstone, cup, coffee....4.50
Casualstone, marmalade....25.00
Casualstone, plate, dinner....5.00
Casualstone, shakers, pr....6.00
Century, platter, petitpoint motif, 11″....5.00
Century, platter, w/oval well, 10½″....7.00
Child's set, Tom Thumb, 3-pc....140.00
Debutante, teapot, red flower....12.00
Dogwood, plate, dessert; 6½″....3.00
Dogwood, plate, 9″....3.50
Epicure, bowl, gravy; 7½″....9.00
Epicure, bowl, vegetable....21.00
Epicure, casserole, ind, w/lid....16.50
Epicure, coffee pot, 10″....25.00
Epicure, platter, lg....7.00
Hacienda, bell, 5″....22.50
Hacienda, bowl, fruit; Fiesta shape, 5½″....13.50
Hacienda, bowl, vegetable; 8″....7.00
Hacienda, bowl, vegetable; 9″....8.00
Hacienda, butter dish....90.00
Hacienda, cup & saucer....8.00
Hacienda, nappy, Fiesta shape, 8½″....21.00
Hacienda, platter, w/oval well, 13½″....10.00
Hacienda, platter, w/sq well, 11″....8.00
Hacienda, teapot....26.00
Jubilee, coffee pot....11.00
Jubilee, plate, chop; 15″....5.00
Jubilee, plate, 10″....3.50
Jubilee, platter, 11″....3.00
Jubilee, teapot....11.00
Laughlin Art China, ewer, kittens play w/yarn, 15″....150.00
Laughlin Art China, pitcher, tankard; monk motif, 14″....190.00
Mexicana, bowl, fruit; 5½″....4.00
Mexicana, butter dish, ½-lb....38.50
Mexicana, candle holder, tri-pod, pr....65.00
Mexicana, casserole, 8½″....27.50
Mexicana, creamer....4.50
Mexicana, egg cup, rolled edge....14.00
Mexicana, nappy, 5″....4.50
Mexicana, plate, 9″....4.00
Mexicana, platter, 11½″....6.00
Mexicana, platter, 13″....8.50
Mexicana, sauce boat....7.50
New Century, bowl, cream soup; floral decal....12.00
New Century, cup & saucer, demitasse....30.00
Pitcher & bowl set, pink & yel roses on bl, gold trim....160.00
Priscilla, bowl, fruit; 9½″....12.00
Priscilla, bowl, mixing; 10¼″....18.00
Priscilla, bowl, mixing; 6½″....10.00
Priscilla, bowl, vegetable; oval, 9″....9.50
Priscilla, casserole, in metal holder, w/lid....19.50
Priscilla, coffee server....25.00
Priscilla, creamer....5.00
Priscilla, gravy boat....8.00
Priscilla, pie baker....15.00
Priscilla, pitcher, jug; open....12.00
Priscilla, plate, cake....10.00
Priscilla, plate, dinner; 9″....5.00
Priscilla, plate, soup; 8½″....6.50
Rhythm, bowl, fruit....4.00
Rhythm, casserole, rare, 3½x9″....32.50
Rhythm, nappy, 9″....7.00
Rhythm, plate, snack; 10¼″....10.00
Rhythm, plate, 10″....7.00
Rhythm, platter, 11½″....6.00
Rhythm, platter, 13½″....11.00
Rhythm, teapot, 5½″....20.00
Rhythm, tray, 3-tier....27.50
Rhythm Rose, bowl, nested, med....11.00
Rhythm Rose, cake server....8.50
Rhythm Rose, casserole, Kitchen Kraft, 8½″....14.00
Rhythm Rose, coffee pot, Kitchen Kraft....21.00
Rhythm Rose, creamer....5.00
Rhythm Rose, plate, cake; 10½″....8.00
Rhythm Rose, plate, deep, 8″....5.00
Rhythm Rose, plate, dinner; 9″....4.00
Rhythm Rose, plate, pie; Kitchen Kraft, 9½″....11.00
Rhythm Rose, platter, 13″....7.00
Serenade, casserole, w/lid....27.50
Serenade, coffee pot, 6-cup, 7½″....30.00
Serenade, plate, chop; 13″....16.50

Wash pitcher, pink with white raspberries, early 1900s, 12″, $100.00.

Serenade, plate, 10″ 7.00
Serenade, platter, 12½″ 11.00
Serenade, teapot 35.00
Skytone, teapot, bl w/gold trim 20.00
Tango, casserole, w/lid 13.50
Tango, nappy, 8¾″ 5.50
Tango, platter, 11¾″ 5.50
Tango, sugar bowl 5.50
Virginia Rose, bowl, nested, lg 13.50
Virginia Rose, bowl, vegetable; 8¾″ 10.00
Virginia Rose, casserole, w/lid, 10½″ 22.00
Virginia Rose, mug 9.00
Virginia Rose, pitcher, milk; 5″ 9.00
Virginia Rose, plate, cake; 10½″ 18.00
Virginia Rose, plate, dinner; 10½″ 5.50
Virginia Rose, plate, pie; 9½″ 12.00
Virginia Rose, platter, 11½″ 6.00
Virginia Rose, platter, 9½″ 6.00
Virginia Rose, sauce boat 11.00
Virginia Rose, shakers, pr 6.00

Hull

The A.E. Hull Pottery was formed in 1905 in Zanesville, Ohio, and in the early years produced stoneware specialities. They expanded in 1907, adding a second plant, and employing over two hundred workers. By 1920 they were manufacturing a full line of stoneware, art pottery with both airbrushed and blended glazes, florist pots, and gardenware. They also produced toiletware and kitchen items with a white semi-porcelain body. Although these continued to be staple products, after the stock market crash of 1929, emphasis was shifted to tile production. By the mid-thirties interest in art pottery production was growing, and over the next fifteen years, several lines of matt pastel floral decorated patterns were designed, consisting of vases, planters, baskets, ewers, and bowls in various sizes.

The Red Riding Hood cookie jar, patented in 1943, proved so successful that a whole line of figural kitchenware and novelty items were added. They continued to be produced well into the fifties.

Through the forties their floral artware lines flooded the market, due to the restriction of foreign imports. Although best known for their pastel matt glazed ware, some of the lines were high gloss. Rosella, glossy coral on pink clay body, was produced for a short time only, and Magnolia, although offered in a matt glaze, was produced in gloss as well.

The plant was destroyed in 1950 by a flood which resulted in a devastating fire when the floodwater caused the kilns to explode. The company rebuilt and equipped thier new factory with the most modern machinery. It was soon apparent that the matt glaze could not be duplicated through the more modern processes, however, and soon attention was concentrated on high gloss artware lines such as Parchment and Pine, and Ebb Tide. Figural planters and novelties, piggy banks, and dinnerware were produced in abundance in the late fifties and sixties. By the mid-seventies dinnerware and florist ware were the mainstay of their business. The firm continues to operate.

Authority Brenda Roberts has compiled a lovely book, *The Collectors Encyclopedia of Hull Pottery*, with full-color photos and current values; you will find her address in the Directory under Missouri. When no condition is indicated, the items listed below are assumed to be in mint condition.

Bank, Corky Pig, pastel yel/bl/rose 25.00
Blossomflite, basket, #2, pink & bl, 6″ 15.00
Blossomflite, basket, T-4, pink & blk, 9¼″ 25.00
Blossomflite, basket, T-9, pink, blk, & gold, lg 55.00
Blossomflite, candle holders, #11, pink & blk, pr 20.00
Blossomflite, console bowl, T-10, pink & blk 25.00

Vase, Bow Knot, B-4, 6½″, $45.00.

Bow Knot, candle holder, B-17, bl, pr 48.00
Bow Knot, cornucopia, B-5, bl & gr, 7½″ 45.00
Bow Knot, jardiniere, B-18, pink & bl, 5¾″ 42.00
Bow Knot, vase, B-2, pink & bl, 6″ 38.00
Bow Knot, vase, B-3, bl, 6½″ 40.00
Bow Knot, vase, B-4, bl, 6½″ 40.00
Bow Knot, vase, B-7, gr & bl, 8½″ 50.00
Bow Knot, vase, B-8, bl, 8½″ 45.00
Bow Knot, vase, B-9, pink & bl, 8½″ 48.00
Bow Knot, wall pocket, B-24, cup & saucer, bl, 6″ 42.00
Bow Knot, wall pocket, iron, no mk 40.00
Bow Knot, wall pocket, whisk broom, B-27, 8″ 40.00
Butterfly, ash tray, heart shape, 7″ 20.00
Butterfly, basket, B-13, wht matt 30.00
Butterfly, bowl, B-7, rectangular 20.00
Butterfly, creamer & sugar 40.00
Butterfly, jardiniere, B-5, wht, 5″ 12.00
Butterfly, lavabo set & hanger, B-24, B-25, wht 75.00
Butterfly, pitcher, 5″ 10.00
Butterfly, vase, B-14, 3-ft, 10½″ 35.00
Calla Lily, console bowl, #590, leaf shaped, pink & bl, 4″ 55.00
Calla Lily, vase, #504, 6″ 36.00
Calla Lily, vase, #530-33, pink & bl, 5″ 40.00
Calla Lily, vase, #550-33, pink & bl, 7½″ 48.00
Calla Lily, vase, brn & turq, slender neck, 8″ 48.00
Classic, vase, bl flower, ivory glaze, 5″ 12.00
Classic, vase, pink flower & glaze, 6″ 12.00
Dogwood, cornucopia, #522, pink & bl 55.00
Dogwood, ewer, #519, pink & bl, 13½″ 110.00
Dogwood, jardiniere, #514, 4″ 20.00
Dogwood, pitcher, #505, 8½″ 35.00
Dogwood, vase, #513, cream & turq, 6½″ 36.00
Dogwood, vase, #515, bl & peach, 8½″ 38.00
Dogwood, vase, #516, cream & turq, 4¾″ 18.00
Dogwood, vase, #530, 10½″ 40.00
Dogwood, vase, suspended; #502, bl & peach, 6½″ 40.00
Dogwood, window box planter, #508, pink & bl, 10½″ 55.00
Early Art, vase, #26, brush strokes, bl/turq/maroon, 8″ 22.00
Ebb Tide, basket, E-11, wine & chartreuse, 16½″ 55.00
Ebb Tide, basket, fish hdl, bl & gold, 7″ 30.00
Ebb Tide, candle holder, E-13, shrimp & turq, pr 12.50
Ebb Tide, creamer, E-15, pink & bl 20.00
Ebb Tide, ewer, E-10, shrimp & turq, 14½″, sm flake 30.00
Ebb Tide, sugar bowl, E-16, pink & bl, no lid 10.00
Ebb Tide, teapot, E-14, pink & bl, w/lid 65.00

Ebb Tide, vase, #1E, shell-shaped, pink & bl....20.00
Iris, basket, #408, pink & bl, 7″....65.00
Iris, bud vase, #410, peach, 7½″....35.00
Iris, console bowl, #409, pink & bl, 12″....75.00
Iris, ewer, #401, pink & bl, 8″....50.00
Iris, hanging basket, #412, rose & peach, 7″....40.00
Iris, hanging planter, #412, pink & bl, 4″....25.00
Iris, jardiniere, #413, pink & bl, 5½″....35.00
Iris, vase, #405, peach, 7″....35.00
Iris, vase, #405, pink & bl, 8½″....45.00
Iris, vase, #407, rose & cream, 7″....35.00
Iris, vase, bud; #410, pink & bl, 7½″....38.00
Lamp, pink matt, floral decor, 2-hdld, rare, 15″....150.00
Magnolia, glossy; cornucopia, H-10, pink floral, 8½″....22.50
Magnolia, glossy; cornucopia, H-15, dbl, 12″....40.00
Magnolia, glossy; creamer, H-21, pink floral....9.00
Magnolia, glossy; creamer & sugar, H-21 & H-22, bl floral....25.00
Magnolia, glossy; vase, H-13, pink, 10½″....30.00
Magnolia, glossy; vase, H-2, bl floral/gold trim, hdl, 5½″....16.00
Magnolia, glossy; vase, H-6, bl floral, 6½″....15.00
Magnolia, glossy; vase, H-7, pink floral, 6½″....12.50
Magnolia, glossy; vase, H-8, 8½″....26.00
Magnolia, matt; candle holder, #27, pink & bl, 4″, pr....26.00
Magnolia, matt; console bowl, #26, brn & yel, 12½″....40.00
Magnolia, matt; cornucopia, #19, pink & bl, 8½″....25.00
Magnolia, matt; cornucopia, #6, dbl, 12″....42.00
Magnolia, matt; creamer & sugar, #24 & 25, 3¾″....30.00
Magnolia, matt; ewer, #14, pink & bl, 4¾″....18.00
Magnolia, matt; ewer, #5, brn & yel, 7″....35.00
Magnolia, matt; pitcher, #14, pink & bl, 4¾″....18.00
Magnolia, matt; sugar bowl, #25, brn & yel, 3¾″....12.00
Magnolia, matt; tea set, #23, 24 & 25, 6½″, 3-pc....85.00
Magnolia, matt; vase, #1, brn & yel, 8½″....35.00
Magnolia, matt; vase, #11, brn & yel, 6¼″....20.00
Magnolia, matt; vase, #12, 2 wing-shaped hdls, 6¼″....20.00
Magnolia, matt; vase, #15, pink & bl, 6¼″....18.00
Magnolia, matt; vase, #2, brn & yel, 8½″....30.00
Magnolia, matt; vase, #20, pink & bl, 15″....150.00
Magnolia, matt; vase, #3, 8½″....27.50
Magnolia, matt; vase, #4, 6¼″....19.00
Magnolia, matt; vase, #7, pink & bl, 8½″....30.00
Magnolia, matt; vase, #9, brn & yel, 10½″....42.00
Mardi Gras/Granada, ewer, #66, rose & cream, 10″....40.00
Mardi Gras/Granada, fan vase, #47, wht, 9″....18.00
Mardi Gras/Granada, vase, #48, pink & bl, 9″....18.00
Mardi Gras/Granada, vase, #49, Deco, pink & bl, 9″....20.00
Old Spice, mug, Friendship decor....12.00
Old Spice, mug, Grand Turk decor....12.00
Open Rose, bowl, #113, wht, 3½″....30.00
Open Rose, candle holder, #117, bird shape, 6½″....25.00
Open Rose, cornucopia, #101, lg, pink, bl & wht, 8½″....38.00
Open Rose, cornucopia, #141, pink & bl, 8½″....40.00
Open Rose, creamer, #111, pink & bl, 5″....20.00
Open Rose, creamer, #111, wht, 5″....20.00
Open Rose, ewer, #106, wht, 13¼″....95.00
Open Rose, pitcher, #128, wht, 4¾″....12.00
Open Rose, sugar bowl, #112, wht, 5″....25.00
Open Rose, vase, #102, 8½″....40.00
Open Rose, vase, #108, fan shape, wht, 8½″....60.00
Open Rose, vase, #118, swan shape, pink & bl, 6½″....30.00
Open Rose, vase, #123, pink & bl, 6½″....30.00
Open Rose, vase, #130, 4¾″....18.00
Open Rose, vase, #136, 6¼″....32.00
Orchid, rose bowl, #317, bl, 4¾″....30.00
Orchid, vase, #303, pink & cream, 4¾″....25.00
Orchid, vase, #303, 8″....45.00
Orchid, vase, #304, pink & bl, 6″....35.00
Orchid, vase, #308, pink & bl, 6½″....35.00
Parchment & Pine, basket, S-3, brn & gr....42.00
Parchment & Pine, bowl or planter, oval, brn, 5½″....25.00
Parchment & Pine, candle holder, gr, 2¾x4½″, pr....30.00
Parchment & Pine, cornucopia, S-2-R, brn & gr....18.00
Parchment & Pine, ewer, S-7, tan & gray, 14″....75.00
Parchment & Pine, tea set....55.00
Parchment & Pine, vase, S-1, brn & gr....18.00

Tankard, #492 impressed on bottom, 'H in circle' mark, 9½″, $75.00.

Parchment & Pine, vase, S-4, brn & gr....30.00
Pine Cone, vase, #55, pink, 6½″....30.00
Planter, baby w/rattle, #92, pink & gold, 5½″....18.00
Planter, dbl swans, #81....20.00
Planter, dog w/ball of yarn, gr & brn, 6″....20.00
Planter, duck, lt gr....12.00
Planter, giraffe, #115, pink & gr, 8¼″....15.00
Planter, kitten in lg hat, #37, bl & wht matt, 6½″....25.00
Planter, love birds, #93, pink....16.00
Planter, madonna, #25, wht matt, 7″....12.00
Planter, parrot, #60, 9½″....20.00
Planter, poodle, #114, pink & gr, 8″....15.00
Poppy, vase, #606, pink & bl, 6½″....45.00
Poppy, vase, #607, pink & bl, 8½″....65.00
Poppy, wall pocket, #609, pink & bl, 9″....75.00
Red Riding Hood, bank, standing, 6¾″....235.00
Red Riding Hood, biscuit jar....190.00
Red Riding Hood, butter dish, 2-pc, 5½″....140.00
Red Riding Hood, canister, coffee....250.00
Red Riding Hood, canister, flour....250.00
Red Riding Hood, canister, salt....300.00
Red Riding Hood, canister, sugar....250.00
Red Riding Hood, canister, tea....250.00
Red Riding Hood, cookie jar....80.00
Red Riding Hood, creamer, side spout....75.00
Red Riding Hood, creamer, 5″....40.00
Red Riding Hood, jar, signed Hull Ware, #982, w/lid, 9″....90.00
Red Riding Hood, matchbox....400.00
Red Riding Hood, mustard jar, w/spoon....145.00
Red Riding Hood, pitcher, leaning, 7″....128.00

Red Riding Hood, pitcher, side pour....150.00
Red Riding Hood, pitcher, top pour, 8″....150.00
Red Riding Hood, shakers, 3½″, pr....18.00
Red Riding Hood, shakers, 5½″, pr....35.00
Red Riding Hood, sugar bowl....45.00
Red Riding Hood, teapot, w/lid, 8″....105.00
Red Riding Hood, wall pocket....200.00
Red Riding Hood, wolf dish....200.00
Rosella, cornucopia, R-13, coral w/wht & brn flowers, 8½″....30.00
Rosella, ewer, R-11-7R, ivory w/pink & gr flowers....35.00
Rosella, ewer, R-9, coral w/wht & gr flowers, 6½″....28.00
Rosella, vase, R-1, coral w/wht & gr flowers, 5″....20.00
Rosella, vase, R-2, coral w/wht & gr flowers, 5″....20.00
Rosella, vase, R-5, coral w/wht & brn flowers, 6½″....18.00
Rosella, vase, R-7, ivory w/pink & gr flowers, 6½″....20.00
Rosella, wall pocket, R-10, pink, trimmed in gold, 6¼″....35.00
Serenade, ash tray, S-23, bl, 13″....20.00
Serenade, basket, 7″....35.00
Serenade, bowl, fruit; lg pedestal, pink, 7″....55.00
Serenade, candle holder, S-16, pink, 6½″, pr....45.00
Serenade, casserole, w/lid, 9″....40.00
Serenade, creamer, pink, S-18....20.00
Serenade, mug, S-22, bl, 5½″....35.00
Serenade, pedestal dish, S-3, yel....15.00
Serenade, vase, S-4, hat shape, pink, 5½″....20.00
Serenade, window box, S-9, bl, 6x12″....29.00
Stoneware, beer mug, Alpine scene, H in circle....15.00
Stoneware, hanging jardiniere, 6½″....50.00
Stoneware, kitchen jar, ribbed, recessed top, #100, 5″....18.00
Stoneware, pretzel jar, Alpine scene, H in circle....100.00
Sunglow, basket, #84, yel, 6½″....22.00
Sunglow, grease jar, w/lid....7.00
Sunglow, hanging basket, #99, pink, 6″....20.00
Sunglow, pitcher, #52, pink, 24-oz....20.00
Sunglow, pitcher, #90, yel, 5½″....15.00
Sunglow, shakers, pink & yel, pr....15.00
Sunglow, vase, #100, pink, 6½″....20.00
Sunglow, vase, #94, pink, 8″....22.00
Sunglow, wall pocket, cup & saucer, pink....25.00
Sunglow, wall pocket, flatiron, pink....25.00
Sunglow, wall pocket, whisk broom, yel....24.00
Thistle, vase, #51, bl, 6½″....30.00
Thistle, vase, #52, bl, 6½″....30.00
Thistle, vase, #53, pink, 6½″....30.00
Tokay, basket, #11, moon shape, wht & gr, 10½″....30.00
Tokay, basket, #8, wht & gr, 8″....22.00
Tokay, basket, wht & gr, 11″....25.00
Tokay, bowl, fruit; #7, pink & gr w/gold trim, 6″....38.00
Tokay, candy on stem, w/lid, 8½″....25.00
Tokay, cornucopia, #10, pink & gr, 11″....22.00
Tokay, leaf dish, #19, 13″....15.00
Tokay, urn, #5, wht & gr, 5½″....14.00
Tulip, bud vase, #104-33, pink & bl, 6″....25.00
Tulip, jardiniere, #115-33, pink & bl, 7″....100.00
Tulip, jardiniere, #117-30, pink & bl, 5″....30.00
Tulip, vase, #100-33, pink & bl, 6½″....28.00
Tulip, vase, #102-33, 6″....26.00
Tulip, vase, #105-33, 8″....40.00
Tulip, vase, #107-33, 6″....32.50
Tulip, vase, #111-33, 6″....30.00
Wall pocket, flying goose, pink & bl, 6″....22.00
Wall pocket, picture fr, oval, #611, 8½″....22.00
Wall pocket, ribbon-tied package, #71, 6″....20.00
Wall pocket, violin, #85, 7″....20.00
Water Lily, candle holder, L-22, pink & bl, pr....35.00
Water Lily, cornucopia, L-7, w/label, 6½″....35.00
Water Lily, creamer, L-19, pink & bl, 5″....25.00
Water Lily, flowerpot w/saucer, L-25, brn & tan, 5¾″....45.00
Water Lily, jardiniere, L-23, brn & cream, 5½″....30.00
Water Lily, jardiniere, L-24, pink & bl, 8½″....100.00
Water Lily, sugar bowl, L-20, brn & cream, 5″....25.00
Water Lily, tea set, brn & cream....95.00
Water Lily, vase, L-1, pink & bl, 5½″....22.50
Water Lily, vase, L-10, 9½″....42.50
Water Lily, vase, L-13, 10½″....50.00
Water Lily, vase, L-5, pink & bl, 6½″....25.00
Water Lily, vase, L-6, pink & bl, 6½″....25.00
Wildflower, candle holder, W-22, pink & bl, pr....22.00
Wildflower, console bowl, W-21, pink & bl, 12″....45.00
Wildflower, cornucopia, W-10, pink & bl, 8½″....28.00
Wildflower, cornucopia, W-7, brn & yel, 7½″....25.00
Wildflower, ewer, W-2, brn & yel, 5½″....26.00
Wildflower, vase, W-12, brn & yel, 9½″....40.00
Wildflower, vase, W-13, 9½″....42.50
Wildflower, vase, W-14, 10½″....45.00
Wildflower, vase, W-15, pink & bl, fan shape, 10½″....55.00
Wildflower, vase, W-4, brn & yel, 6½″....25.00
Wildflower, vase, W-5, brn & yel, 6½″....20.00
Wildflower, vase, W-6, 7½″....27.50
Wildflower, vase, W-8, pink & bl, 7½″....26.00
Wildflower, vase, W-9, pink & bl, 8½″....35.00
Woodland, glossy; candle holder, W-30, rose & chartreuse, pr....22.00
Woodland, glossy; console bowl, W-29, rose & chartreuse, 14″....32.00
Woodland, glossy; cornucopia, W-10, rose & chartreuse, 11″....24.00
Woodland, glossy; cornucopia, W-2, rose & chartreuse, 5½″....12.50
Woodland, glossy; creamer, W-27, rose & chartreuse....9.00
Woodland, glossy; ewer, W-24, 13½″....65.00
Woodland, glossy; ewer, W-3, rose & chartreuse, 5½″....16.00
Woodland, glossy; jardiniere, W-7, rose & chartreuse, 5½″....28.00
Woodland, glossy; teapot, W-26, rose & chartreuse....45.00
Woodland, glossy; vase, W-4, bl & gr, 6½″....18.00
Woodland, glossy; vase, W-8, rose & chartreuse, 7½″....20.00
Woodland, glossy; wall pocket, pink/cream w/gr edge & hdl....24.00
Woodland, glossy; window box, W-14, rose & chartreuse, 10½″....18.00
Woodland, matt; candle holder, W-30, gr & yel, pr....32.00
Woodland, matt; cornucopia, W-2, gr & yel, 5½″....16.00
Woodland, matt; ewer, W-24, 13½″....45.00
Woodland, matt; jardiniere, W-7, rose & cream, 5½″....38.00
Woodland, matt; vase, W-16, gr & yel, 8½″....35.00
Woodland, matt; vase, W-4, rose & peach, 6½″....24.00
Woodland, matt; vase, W-8, yel & gr, 7½″....32.00
Woodland, matt; wall pocket, W-13, pink/cream/gr, 7½″....39.00

Hummel

Hummel figurines were created through the artistry of Berta Hummel, a Franciscan nun called Sister M. Innocentia. The first figures were made about 1935 by Franz Goebel of Goebel Art Inc., Rodental, West Germany. Plates, plaques, and candy dishes are also produced, and the older, discontinued editions are highly sought collectibles.

Generally speaking, an issue can be dated by the trademark. The first Hummels, from 1934-1950, were either incised or stamped with the 'Crown WG' mark. The 'full bee in V' mark was employed with minor variations until 1959. At that time the bee was stylized and represented by a solid disc with symmetrical angled wings completely contained within the confines of the 'V.' The three-line mark, 1964-1972, utilized the stylized bee, and included a three-line arrangement, 'c by W. Goebel, W. Germany.'

Another change in 1970 saw the 'stylized bee in V' suspended between the vertical bars of the 'b' and 'l' of a printed 'Goebel, West Germany.' Collectors refer to this mark as the 'last bee' or 'Goebel bee.' The current mark in use since 1979 omits the 'bee in V.'

When no condition is indicated, the items listed below are assumed to be in mint condition.

Key:
FB—full bee SB—stylized bee
GB—Goebel bee

A Fair Measure, #345, GB....95.00
A Letter to Santa Claus, #340, GB....115.00
Accordion Boy, #185, GB....60.00
Accordion Boy, #185, SB....85.00
Adoration, #23/1, SB, 6¼"....175.00
Adventure Bound, #347, GB, 7½x8½"....1,785.00
Angel Cloud Font, #206, SB....140.00
Angel Serenade, #214D, 3-line....35.00
Angel w/Accordion, #III/39/0, candle holder, SB....40.00
Angel w/Lute, #III/38/0, candle holder, SB....35.00
Angel w/Trumpet, #III/40/I, SB, 2¾"....90.00
Angel w/Trumpet, #III/40/0, candle holder, SB....35.00
Angelic Song, #144, SB....85.00
Apple Tree Boy, #142/3/0, SB....65.00
Apple Tree Girl, #141/3/0, FB....115.00
Artist, #304, GB....85.00
Auf Wiedersehen, #153, closed edition, FB, 7⅛"....470.00
Auf Wiedersehen, #153/0, no hat, FB....200.00
Autumn Harvest, #355, GB....75.00
Ba-Bee Ring, #30/0A&B, GB....70.00
Ba-Bee Ring, #30/0B, FB....60.00
Baker, #128, SB....85.00
Band Leader, FB....155.00
Barnyard Hero, #195/2/0, FB....130.00
Bashful, #377, GB....75.00
Be Patient, #197/2/0, SB....100.00
Begging His Share, #9., GB....70.00
Begging His Share, #9., SB....110.00
Begging His Share, #9., w/candle hole, SB....190.00
Big Housecleaning, #363, GB....100.00
Bird Duet, #169, old style, divided base, FB....135.00
Birdwatcher, #300, GB....110.00
Birthday Serenade, #218/2/0, 3-line....75.00
Blessed Event, #333, GB....140.00
Bookworm, #3/1, GB....115.00
Boots, #143/0, GB....85.00
Boots, #143/0, SB....75.00
Boy w/Bird, #34, ash tray, SB, 3½x6½"....95.00
Boy w/Horse, #117, SB....40.00
Boy w/Toothache, #217, SB....95.00
Brother, #95, SB....95.00
Builder, #305, 3-line....100.00
Busy Student, #367, GB....65.00
Candlelight, #192, old style, FB....485.00
Carnival, #328, 3-line....80.00
Celestial Musician, #188, 3-line, 7"....110.00
Chick Girl, #III/57, candy dish, old style, SB....185.00
Chick Girl, #57/0, FB....115.00
Chick Girl, #57/0, SB....85.00
Chicken Lickin, #385, GB, 4¾"....125.00
Chimney Sweep, #12/1, FB....110.00
Chimney Sweep, #12/2/0, SB....55.00
Cinderella, #337, GB....120.00
Close Harmony, #336, new style, 3-line....140.00
Confidentially, #344, GB....85.00
Congratulations, #17/0, no socks, SB....120.00
Coquettes, #179, SB....118.00
Crossroads, #331, GB....157.00
Culprits, #56A, eyes closed, SB....115.00
Culprits, #56A, eyes open, SB....125.00
Daisies Don't Tell, #380, GB, 5"....95.00
Display Plaque-Collector, #187, GB....65.00
Doctor, #127, GB....60.00
Doctor, #127, SB....95.00
Doll Bath, #319, 3-line....110.00
Doll Mother, #67, GB....95.00
Doll Mother, #67, old style, SB....125.00
Duet, #130, SB....130.00
Eventide, #99, SB....130.00
Farewell, #65/1, SB....130.00
Farm Boy, #66, SB....95.00
Feathered Friends, #344, GB....95.00
Feeding Time, #199/0, old style, FB....160.00
Feeding Time, #199/1, old style, SB....145.00
Festival Harmony, #173/0, 3-line....117.00
Flower Madonna, #10/III, bl robe, SB....325.00
Flower Vendor, #381, GB....90.00
Flying Angel, #366, GB....55.00
For Father, #87, SB....100.00
For Mother, #257, 3-line....65.00
Friends, #136/V, GB, 11"....500.00
Friends, #136/1, 3-line....90.00
Gay Adventure, #356, GB....65.00
Girl w/Fir Tree, #116, SB....40.00
Girl w/Nosegay, #115, FB....80.00
Globe Trotter, #79, old style, FB....200.00
Going to Grandma's, #52/0, old style, FB....180.00
Good Friends, #182, FB....175.00
Good Hunting, #307, old style, 3-line....140.00
Good Shepherd, #42/0, FB....125.00
Good Shepherd, #42/0, SB....90.00
Goose Girl, #47/3/0, FB....130.00
Goose Girl, #47/3/0, GB....66.00
Guiding Angel Set, #357-58-59, GB, 2¾"....120.00
Happiness, #86, SB....75.00
Happy Birthday, #176/0, SB....125.00
Happy Days, #150/2/0, SB....100.00
Happy Pastime, #62, ash tray, SB....95.00
Happy Traveler, #109/0, SB....85.00
Hear Ye, Hear Ye, #15/0, SB....105.00
Hear Ye, Hear Ye, #15/1, GB....83.00
Heavenly Angel, #21/0, FB....100.00
Heavenly Angel, #21/0, SB....55.00
Heavenly Lullaby, #262, 3-line, 3½x5"....280.00
Hello, #124/0, SB....115.00
Herald Angels, #37, candle holder, FB....150.00
Holy Child, #70, SB....85.00
Home From Market, #198/2/0, 3-line....60.00
Homeward Bound, #334, old style w/post, GB....185.00
Infant Jesus, #214A, SB....30.00
Infant of Krumbad, #78/1, GB....25.00
Joyful, #53, FB....80.00
Joyous News, #27/III, GB....70.00
Just Resting, #112 2/0, FB....115.00
King on One Knee, #214M, SB....90.00
Kiss Me!, #311, no socks, 3-line....95.00
Latest News, #184, Munchener Press, old style, sq base, FB....295.00
Let's Sing, #114, FB....185.00

Little Band, #392, 3-line....130.00
Little Bookkeeper, #306, 3-line....115.00
Little Cellist, #89/1, GB....75.00
Little Drummer, #240, GB....50.00
Little Fiddler, #2/0, brn hat, SB....100.00
Little Fiddler, #4, SB....95.00
Little Gabriel, #32/0, closed edition, FB, 5½″....110.00
Little Gardener, #74, oval base, SB....85.00
Little Goat Herder, #200/0, old style, FB....175.00
Little Guardian, #145, FB, 4″....110.00
Little Helper, #73, FB....110.00
Little Helper, #73, GB....55.00
Little Hiker, #16/1, SB....90.00
Little Hiker, #16/2/0, SB....55.00
Little Pharmacist, #322, 3-line....105.00
Little Scholar, #80, SB....95.00
Little Shopper, #96, SB....60.00
Little Sweeper, #171, SB....75.00
Little Tailor, #308, GB....90.00
Little Thrifty, #118, FB, 5½″....200.00
Little Tooter, #214/H, SB....60.00
Lost Sheep, #68, closed edition, SB, 5½″....135.00
Lost Sheep, #68/0, SB, 4½″....90.00
Lullaby, #24/3, Arabic number, SB, 6x8½″....345.00
Madonna w/Halo, #46/0, pink robe, SB....45.00
Mail Coach, #226, GB, 6x4½″....190.00
March Winds, #43, GB....55.00
March Winds, #43, SB....75.00
Max & Moritz, #123, FB....140.00
Max & Moritz, #123, SB....100.00
Meditation, #13/0, SB....90.00
Meditation, #13/2/0, GB....55.00
Merry Wanderer, #7/2, Arabic number, SB, 10″....695.00
Merry Wanderer, #7/2, GB, 9½″....475.00
Mischief Maker, #342, GB....93.00
Moorish King, #214L, SB....100.00
Mother's Darling, #175, GB....75.00
Mother's Helper, #133, FB....175.00
Mother's Helper, #133, SB....90.00
Mountaineer, #315, GB....85.00
Not for You, #317, GB....85.00
On Secret Path, #386, GB....95.00
Out of Danger, #56B, eyes closed, SB....115.00
Out of Danger, #56B, eyes open, SB....125.00
Photographer, #178, GB....110.00
Photographer, #178, 3-line....125.00
Playmates, #58/0, FB....115.00
Postman, #119, SB....120.00
Prayer Before Battle, #20, SB....115.00
Puppy Love, #1, SB....100.00
Retreat to Safety, #126, plaque, SB....120.00
Retreat to Safety, #201/2/0, old style, FB, 4″....135.00
Retreat to Safety, #201/2/0, old style, SB....95.00
Ride into Christmas, #396, GB....190.00
Ring Around Rosie, #348, GB....1,315.00
Run-A-Way, #327, GB....98.00
School Boy, #82/0, SB....80.00
Sensitive Hunter, #6/0, GB....63.00
Sensitive Hunter, #6/0, old style, FB....135.00
Sensitive Hunter, #6/0, old style, SB....100.00
Serenade, #85/II, SB....160.00
Serenade, #85/0, FB....110.00
She Loves Me, #174, eyes open, FB, 4½″....160.00
Shepherd Kneeling, #214/G, GB, 4⅞″....65.00

Umbrella Girl, 152/B/O, full bee mark, $265.00.

Shepherd w/Sheep, #214F, SB....100.00
Shepherd's Boy, #64, GB....75.00
Signs of Spring, #203/1, GB....85.00
Singing Lesson, #63, SB....80.00
Sister, #98, SB, 5¾″....95.00
Skier, #59, GB, 5″....95.00
Smart Little Sister, #346, GB....80.00
Smilin' Thru, #690, plaque, 4¾″....50.00
Soldier Boy, #332, 3-line....75.00
Soloist, #135, FB....100.00
Spring Cheer, #72, old style, FB, 5″....160.00
Spring Dance, #353/1, GB....240.00
School Girl, #81/2/0, FB....110.00
Star Gazer, #132, SB....90.00
Stitch in Time, #255, 3-line....95.00
Stormy Weather, #71, SB....225.00
Street Singer, #131, FB....110.00
Street Singer, #131, SB....80.00
Strolling Along, #5, GB....60.00
Strolling Along, #5, old style, FB....135.00
Surprise, #94/3/0, SB....95.00
Sweet Music, #186, SB, 4⅞″....80.00
Telling Her Secret, #196/0, SB....130.00
To Market, #49/0, FB....120.00
To Market, #49/3/0, GB....60.00
To Market, #49/3/0, SB....85.00
Trumpet Boy, #97, doughnut base, FB....100.00
Trumpet Boy, #97, SB....75.00
Umbrella Boy, #152A, SB, 8″....525.00
Umbrella Girl, #152B, SB, 8″....525.00
Vacation Time, #125, plaque, Crown mk, 4⅜x5¼″....350.00
Valentine Joy, #399....120.00
Village Boy, #51/2/0, 3-line....60.00
Visiting an Invalid, #382, GB....80.00
Volunteers, #50/2/0, SB....120.00
Waiter, #154/0, 'Rhein Wine' on bottle, FB....155.00
Waiter, #154/0, GB....70.00
Wash Day, #321, 3-line....105.00
Wayside Devotion, #28/II, GB, 7½″....165.00
Wayside Harmony, #111/1, FB....125.00
We Congratulate, #220, SB....85.00
Weary Wanderer, #204, GB, 6″....88.00
Which Hand?, #258, 3-line....70.00
Whitsuntide, #163, GB....110.00
Whitsuntide, #163, yel candle, SB....450.00
Worship, #84/0, FB....140.00

Hutschenreuther

Sources do not agree as to when the Carl Hutschenreuther factory was initially established in the Bavarian district of Germany. Most indicate a year near the middle of the 19th century. Carl's sons, Christian and Lorenz, later formed their own companies and operated independently until 1969. At that time Carl and Lorenz merged, and that firm is still in business today, producing limited edition plates, figurines, dinnerware, and other fine china.

When no condition is indicated, the items listed below are assumed to be in mint condition.

Cup & saucer, wht w/sm Africa map in blk, DAL, 2¾″.........15.00
Figurine, ballerina & male dancer, kissing, 9¼″..............250.00
Figurine, Columbine w/gold ball sits on stump, color, 13″......350.00
Figurine, horses & colts standing, mk, pr...................185.00
Figurine, King Arthur in regal robes, kneeling, 5¼″...........95.00
Figurine, Mephistopheles w/sword & scissors at hip, 6″........130.00
Figurine, mother bird feeds 2 babies, brn/wht, 6x8″...........75.00
Figurine, owl...55.00
Figurine, panda, mkd, bl eyes, artist sgn, 3½″................76.00
Figurine, Pantaloon, devilish figure, US Zone, 11½″..........150.00
Figurine, sparrow on branch, sgn K Tutter, 6½″.............120.00
Figurine, wht mouse sitting on hauches/tail in front, 2½″.......70.00
Figurine, 3 standing penguins, 5″.........................245.00
Plaque, peasant girl w/sheaf of wheat, 4x6″.................235.00
Plaque, Ruth, sgn Wagner, #107, ormolu fr, circle HR, 4x6″...750.00
Plate, Dice Throwers, 11¾″...............................85.00

Nude with two bears, 12″, $995.00.

Imari

Imari is a generic term which covers a broad family of wares. It was made in more than a dozen Japanese villages, but the name is that of the port from whence it was shipped to Europe. There are several types of Imari. The most common features a design with panels of birds, florals, or people, surrounding a central basket of flowers. The colors used in this type are underglaze blue, with overglaze red, gold, and green enamels. The Chinese also made Imari wares, which differ from the Japanese type in several ways--the absence of spur marks, a thinner type body, and a more consistent control of the blue. Imari type wares were copied on the continent by Meissen and by English potters, among them Worcester, Derby, and Bow.

When no condition is indicated, the items listed below are assumed to be in mint condition.

Plate, octagonal, ca 1835, $250.00.

Bottle, sake; on sq lacquered wood base, late, 10½″, pr.......250.00
Bowl, allover decor: people, wht/running bl, Japanese, 9½″.....175.00
Bowl, bamboo/birds, bl/yel/gray, ca 1820, 6″.................85.00
Bowl, butterflies & floral, scalloped, 7″......................40.00
Bowl, center flower, 6 panels, scalloped rim, 3½x9½″..........40.00
Bowl, floral, underglaze bl w/orange, oval, 9⅝x7⅝″...........135.00
Bowl, floral & butterflies, scalloped, 7x3″...................95.00
Bowl, floral medallions on brocade/scalloped, 1800s, 15″.....1,300.00
Bowl, foo dog in garden panels, medallions, mc/gold, 6″........75.00
Bowl, gold mums on orange border, scenic center, 1820, 6″....75.00
Bowl, man in garden reserves, bl/wht w/red/gold, lid, 4x5″.....175.00
Bowl, mc garden w/table/etc, inset lid, ca 1860s, 3½x4″........50.00
Bowl, mc house/mtn scene, ca 1830, 6″.......................80.00
Bowl, scenic border, bl/wht transfer, 1900, 6″.................15.00
Bowl, scenic w/lake/house/trees/mtns, red/gr/gold, 6″...........35.00
Charger, basket of flowers, cobalt/gr/red/yel, 12″.............165.00
Charger, basket of flowers/birds, 7-color, 1890s, 12″..........250.00
Charger, bird & flower, dk bl, octagonal, 17″................650.00
Charger, bird/mums/peonies, bl/wht, Greek Key rim, 18″.......350.00
Charger, blooming tree/rocks, bird rim, bl/wht, 1860, 16″......450.00
Charger, eagle on mtn overlooking landscape, bl/wht, 18½″....500.00
Charger, floral, mc, 16″...............................350.00
Charger, peony band, 3-Friends lozenges in jardiniere, 22″....650.00
Charger, scenic, bl/wht, late 1800s, 16″....................250.00
Charger, scenic w/people, bl/red/gr/purple on wht, 16″.......1,275.00
Charger, shishi bands/phoenix roundels, gilt, 1900, 18″.......500.00
Compote, bl dragon w/in bowl, scenic w/out, 1830s, 4x5½″....200.00
Compote, trees/bushes/rabbit, 3-color, 1860, 4¼x6″...........125.00
Cup, bl iris, gold traced, red seal, 3½″......................18.00
Dish, bl kirin center, 3 panels w/cranes, gilt, 1820, 6¼″........60.00
Dish, butterflies/mums in panels, bl/red/gold, 1830s, 5½″.......60.00
Dish, foo dog/vines, bl/red w/gold trim, ca 1860, 6½″..........70.00
Dish, mc floral/butterflies/clouds, red/gold accents, 5½″.........50.00
Dish, triangular, mc w/underglaze bl, 6½″ L..................50.00
Dish, vine/tendril border, plain center, bl/wht, 5″..............25.00
Plate, dragon, scalloped, bl/gr/gold on wht, 1860, 8½″........250.00
Plate, fish shape, bl & wht, caligraphy sgn in dbl ring..........36.00
Plate, floral & sm bird, mc, 1820s, 6″......................75.00
Plate, flowers & scenic panels, mc/gold, ca 1830, 8½″.........100.00
Plate, gold character, 3 panels w/birds, diapering, 6″.........125.00
Plate, scenic medallion, mc, ca 1850, 5¼″...................50.00
Plate, vase of flowers, orange/cobalt, scalloped, 10″............80.00

Soup plate, iron red/underglaze bl, 18th C, 9″...............250.00
Teapot, Arita Island, 1880s, +4 c/s........................295.00
Vase, birds/florals, bronze base/bird mtd hdls, 17″, pr.......1,540.00
Vase, birds/flowers, bronze lion hdls, crests, 30″............5,000.00
Vase, brocade panels w/phoenix, shishi finial, 1800s, 23″.....1,000.00

Imperial Glass

Although the Imperial Glass Company was organized in 1901, it was not until three years later that they began to manufacture glassware. Their early products were jelly glasses, hotel tumblers, etc., but by 1910 they were making a name for themselves by pressing quantities of Carnival Glass, the iridescent colored glassware that was popular during that time. From 1916 to 1920, they used the lustre process to make a line they called Imperial Jewels, now referred to as stretch glass. Opalescent glassware was introduced in the thirties and was made in Sea Foam, Harding Blue, Moss Green, and Burnt Almond. In contrast to these colored lines, Candlewick was a simple pattern in crystal glass, yet one for which the company is best known. All of these types are listed in specific sections of the book.

Free-Hand Ware, art glass made entirely by hand using no molds, was made for a short time only, from about 1923 to 1928. Nu-Cut was made to imitate cut glass; it was produced in crystal as well as color and was introduced in 1914.

The company closed in 1931, but soon reorganized and reopened as the Imperial Glass Corporation. In 1940 they bought the molds and assets of the Central Glass Works of Wheeling, West Virginia; and in 1958 they purchased molds from Cambridge and Heisey. Although Imperial later used these molds to reproduce the older pieces, they marked the reissues with the 'I' superimposed over a 'G' trademark used since 1951. The company sold out to Lenox in 1973, but continues today to make hand-pressed giftware items.

When no condition is indicated, the items listed below are assumed to be in mint condition. See also Candlewick; Carnival Glass; Opalescent Glass

Bookends, Cathay, Empress, blk onyx.......................125.00
Bookends, Cathay, LuFung, blk onyx........................125.00
Bookends, fish, verde gr..................................225.00
Bottle, scent; Cape Cod, #1601, w/stopper....................35.00
Bowl, Hobnail, blk ivy.......................................25.00
Bowl, Molly, lt bl opal, 8½″.................................22.00
Bowl, Old English, ftd, ruby, 9″.............................35.00
Box, Eagle, purple slag, w/lid...............................60.00
Box, Zodiac, azure bl, w/lid.................................45.00
Butter dish, #161, w/lid, ¼-lb...............................16.50
Butter dish, Holly, red slag satin...........................85.00
Candle holder, #100, dbl.....................................21.00
Candy dish, #1519/59, caramel slag, mk Heisey, w/lid.........150.00
Candy dish, Waverley, caramel slag, mk Heisey, w/lid.........100.00
Cocktail, Cape Cod, pineapple stem, set of 8.................45.00
Compote, Cape Cod, #160-45, ftd..............................26.00
Compote, crimped top, red slag, 6½″..........................50.00
Compote, Waverly, caramel slag, w/lid, mk Heisey.............80.00
Creamer & sugar, Cape Cod, #160-30...........................15.00
Cruet, oil; Cape Cod, #160-70................................20.00
Cup & saucer, #37...9.75
Decanter, whiskey; Cape Cod, #160-212, w/stopper, 24-oz.......35.00
Figurine, blk bull, mk Heisey...............................200.00
Figurine, bunnies, milk glass, pr............................14.00
Figurine, fighting rooster, pink, mk Heisey.................180.00
Figurine, flying mare, amber, mk NI.........................500.00
Figurine, kicking pony, mk Heisey............................20.00
Figurine, mallard, wings down, caramel slag.................200.00
Figurine, mallards, amber, mk Heisey, set of 3..............140.00

Bowl, amberina, grapes and leaf relief, signed, 3½″ x 9½″, $47.00.

Figurine, pig & 2 piglets, amber, mk Heisey, set............100.00
Figurine, rearing pony, ultra bl, mk Heisey..................20.00
Figurine, rooster, amber, mk IG.............................100.00
Figurine, rooster on nest, caramel...........................65.00
Figurine, show horse, amber, mk NI/Heisey...................180.00
Jar, Cape Cod, milk glass, wicker hdl, w/lid.................87.00
Junk boat, Cathay, crystal satin, sgn.......................150.00
Mayonnaise, Holly Band, wht milk glass w/bl trim, 3-pc.......55.00
Paperweight, bl ground w/wht logo...........................100.00
Paperweight, rabbit, milk glass..............................12.00
Pepper shaker, saloon; Johnny Bull, milk glass, IG mk........50.00
Pitcher, martini; Big Shot, gr...............................65.00
Pitcher, water; Cape Cod, #160-176, blown, 80-oz............110.00
Pitcher, water; Cape Cod, #160-24, pressed, 80-oz............80.00
Pitcher, water; Grape, milk glass............................55.00
Relish tray, #55, 8½″..16.00
Salad fork & spoon, Cape Cod, pr.............................45.00
Shakers, Cape Cod, #160-116, w/tray, pr......................15.00
Swan, caramel slag satin, 8″.................................75.00
Swan, gr slag, 4″..35.00
Swan, gr slag satin, 8″......................................85.00
Sweetmeat, Cathay, crystal satin, sgn.......................175.00
Tray, relish; Cape Cod, #160-55, 3-part, 9½″.................30.00
Tray, relish; Cape Cod, #160-56, 4-part, 9″..................25.00
Tray, relish; Ida Ruby, 3-part, 10½″.........................45.00
Tray, relish; rnd, 5 hdls, 6-part............................55.00
Tumbler, ftd, topaz, 12-oz...................................10.00
Tumbler, whiskey; Cape Cod, #160, 2½-oz......................20.00
Vase, Cape Cod, #160-22, ftd, 6¼″............................22.00
Vase, caramel slag, #133/1, 6″...............................75.00
Vase, Cathay, Fu Wedding, cranberry..........................75.00
Vase, Dancing Ladies, verde gr, 9″...........................45.00
Vase, fan; #87F, 8½″...21.00
Vase, flip; Hobnail, dk bl opal, 8″..........................25.00
Vase, free-hand, bl irid & cobalt loopings, 8½″, EX.........175.00
Vase, free-hand, bl/opal mosaic, allover irid, 8½″..........175.00
Vase, free-hand, bronze irid, bl irid w/in, 11½″............140.00
Vase, free-hand, cobalt, internal vines & leaves, 4½x5½″....150.00
Vase, free-hand, gold & wht loop/lustre throat, 9¾″, EX.....135.00
Vase, free-hand, gr/purple mirror irid, trumpet form, 10″...300.00
Vase, free-hand, red, verre de soie ft/brn irid throat, 8″..225.00

Vase, free-hand, yel, lustre throat, 10″, EX 65.00
Vase, free-hand, yel w/wht loops, orange irid w/in, 8¾″ 125.00
Vase, lt cranberry w/bl threading, fan form, 8½″ 90.00
Vase, rooster, red slag 50.00
Water set, Opaque Scroll, milk glass, 7-pc 150.00
Whiskey, Little Shot, red 20.00
Wine, Eagle, red slag satin 50.00

Imperial Porcelain

The Blue Ridge Mountain Boys were created by cartoonist Paul Webb and translated into three dimension by the Imperial Porcelain Corporation of Zanesville, Ohio in 1947. These figurines decorated ash trays, vases, mugs, bowls, pitchers, planters, and other items. The Mountain Boys series were numbered 92 through 108, each with a different and amusing portrayal of mountain life. Imperial also produced American Folklore miniatures--twenty-three tiny animals one inch or less in size-- and the All Capp Dogpatch series. Because of financial difficulties, the company closed in 1960.

When no condition is indicated, the items listed below are assumed to be in mint condition.

American Folklore Miniatures

Cat, 1½″ 40.00
Cow, 1¾″ 35.00
Hound dogs 35.00
Plaque, store ad, Am Folklore Porcelain Miniatures, 4½″ 300.00
Sow 30.00

Blue Ridge Mountain Boys by Paul Webb

Ash tray, #101, man with jug & snake 75.00
Ash tray, #103, hillbilly & skunk 75.00
Ash tray, #105, baby, hound dog & frog 110.00
Ash tray, pipe; #92, 2 men by tree stump 125.00
Box, cigarette; #98, dog atop, baby at door, sq 115.00
Decanter, #100, outhouse, man & bird 75.00
Decanter, man, jug, snake & tree stump, Hipsch Inc, 1946 ...... 75.00

Ash tray, baby knocking at outhouse, 8¼″, $125.00.

Figurine, man sitting, 3½″ 85.00
Figurine, man sitting w/chicken on knee, 3″ 95.00
Mug, #94, dbl baby hdl, 4¼″ 95.00
Mug, #94, ea w/different scene, set of 6 .... 360.00
Mug, #94, Ma hdl, 4¼″ 75.00
Mug, #94, man w/bl pants hdl, 4¼″ 65.00
Mug, #94, man w/yel beard & red pants hdl, 4¼″ 65.00
Pitcher, lemonade 15.00
Planter, #100, outhouse, man & bird 75.00
Planter, #104, Maw leaning over stump, w/baby & skunk 95.00
Planter, #104, Pa peeking around stump, w/baby & skunk 95.00
Planter, #105, man w/chicken on knee, wash tub 110.00
Planter, #110, man, snake, wht jug, 3″ 65.00
Planter, #110, man, snake, wht jug, 4½″ 65.00
Planter, #81, man drinking from jug, sitting by wash tub 75.00
Plaque, store ad, Handcrafted Paul Webb Mtn Boys, rare, 9″ ... 500.00
Shakers, Maw & Old Doc, pr 75.00

Miscellaneous

Items in this section that are designated 'IP' are miscellaneous novelties made by Imperial Porcelain; the remainder are of interest to Paul Webb collectors, though made by an unknown manufacturer. Prints on calendars and playing cards are signed 'Paul Webb.'

Calendar, 1954, 12 sgn scenes, Brown & Bigelow, complete 35.00
Hot pad, Dutch boy w/tulips, rnd, IP 30.00
Mug, #29, man hdl, sgn Paul Webb, 4¾″ 25.00
Planter, #106, dog sitting by tub, IP 75.00
Planter, #26, man & tree stump, sgn Paul Webb, bl 25.00
Planter, #27, man, jug & barrel, sgn Paul Webb 25.00
Playing cards, ad: Rafe Oiling Gun, Brown & Bigelow, MIB 35.00
Shakers, standing pigs, IP, 8″, pr 95.00

Indian Tree

Indian Tree was a popular dinnerware pattern produced by various potteries since the early 1800s to recent times. Although backgrounds and borders vary, the Oriental theme is carried out with the gnarled brown branch of a pink blossomed tree. Among the manufacturers marks, you may find represented such notable firms as Coalport, S. Hancock and Sons, Soho Pottery, and John Maddock and Sons.

When no condition is indicated, the items listed below are assumed to be in mint condition.

Bowl, cereal; Nasco 12.50
Bowl, ftd, Minton, 8½x11″ 45.00
Bowl, vegetable; Davison & Son, oval, 10″ 35.00
Bowl, vegetable; Maddock, oval, 9¾″ 35.00
Creamer, Maddock, 3″ 20.00

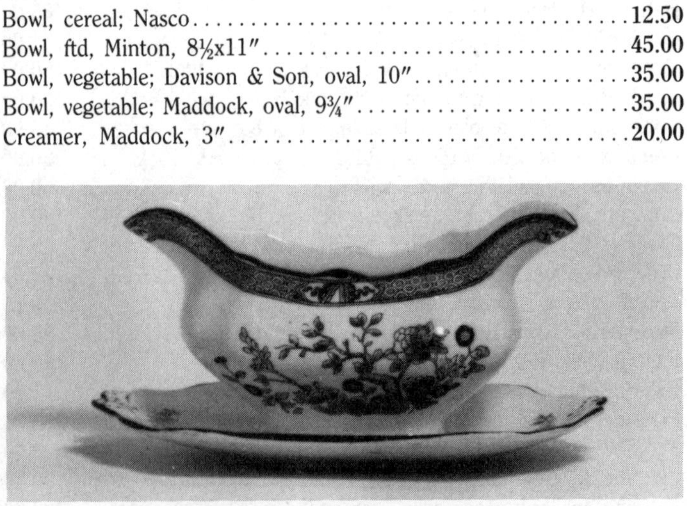

Faststand gravy boat, $30.00.

Cup & saucer, demitasse 20.00
Cup & saucer, gold key border, octagonal, 1890s, Coalport 40.00
Dish, Copeland Spode, 3½", pr 18.00
Plate, bread & butter; Johnson Bros 2.50
Plate, Burgess & Leigh, 9" 18.50
Plate, Maddock, 10" 16.00
Platter, Hancock, 11½" 30.00
Platter, Maddock, 11" 10.00
Platter, Maddock, 15" 20.00
Soup plate, Johnson Bros 9.00
Soup plate, Nasco 12.50
Teapot, Burgess & Leigh 45.00
Teapot, Coalport 45.00

Inkwells and Inkstands

Ink, the fluid form as we know it today, was not developed until 1836. The inkwell was a natural follow-up. They were made in many materials--glass the most common since it was non-porous and stain resistant. Pewter, silver, brass, and even gold was used, depending on the station and financial status of the owner. During the Victorian era, inkwells became more elaborate--some had two wells, others trays and pen holders, and a few had a well or shaker for fine sand or steel powder to sift onto wet ink to blot up the excess. Cut glass inserts and ornate brass frames were popular.

With the development of the fountain pen, the inkwell's usefulness began to decline.

When no condition is indicated, the items listed below are assumed to be in undamaged condition.

Angelica Kauffmann, HP scenes, gold work, sgn, 3½" 95.00
Baccarat type base, Nouveau SP top, 2x2" 50.00
Bear wearing neck tie, seated, metal, hinged lid, 4" 65.00
Beehive, relief Orientals, bird atop, bronze, 2x1⅞" 75.00
Beer bottle shape, brass, logo, Austria, 2⅞" 55.00
Bird & leaves, porc, hinged/attached plate, 3½x5⅞" 79.00
Block House, Ft Pitt, pnt red/blk metal 60.00
Blown, emerald, mushroom paperweight base, hat lid, 2¾" 135.00
Bonzo clown, glass figural, hinged, 3½" 35.00
Boot, amber glass, w/lid 65.00
Brass, hinged top, paw feet, pen rest, 5", 4x5½" base 85.00
Brass, malachite stone on cover/hinged/chain, rare, 5" dia 200.00
Brass, 2 faceted cut wells, Art Deco, holder/rest, 6x8½" 85.00
Bulldog & terrier by mailbox, brass plated, lid, 5½x5½" 75.00
Camel, brass, saddle lifts for well, orig pnt 75.00
Car, antique, hinged motor & for stamps, 2 wells/2 drivers 135.00
Car, antique, nickel plated, hinged lid, 5" 65.00
Cherubs/devils, emb bronze, marble insert, dbl 175.00
Cider barrel, crystal, dtd Mar 1, 1870 . . . . 30.00
Clown head, SP, ruffled tray, hinged, 4" 85.00
Cobalt glass, diamond shape 15.00
Colonial man w/bass fiddle, metal, w/2 cut glass wells 150.00
Copper lids on dbl glass wells; tray w/guns, bow & arrows 70.00
Coventry, blown 3-mold, olive gr, disk mouth, pontil, 1½" 90.00
Crystal, HP wht birds & flowers, blk, beaded, brass lid 165.00
Cut Block, azure bl, 2½" 95.00
Cut glass, bl, brass hinged glass lid 45.00
Cut glass, cranberry, gold swag, hinged brass lid, 5" 200.00
Cut glass, hobstar base/star ea side, SP lid, 1900, 3¾" 975.00
Cut glass, mushroom atop, brass hinged lid, 5" 200.00
Cut glass, silver overlay dome lid w/monogram, pewter neck 30.00
Diamond Point, pressed glass, SP serpentine tray 35.00
Dog, head lifts off, sgn Bonzo 125.00

Art Nouveau, bronze, with cherubs, musician, frog and salamander on lily pad, cobalt well under hinged lid, 5" x 11" x 5", $295.00.

Dog, Scotty, hinged, glass, 3" 150.00
Dog on stand, Rogers Quad plate, beveled glass well 195.00
Donkey, metal, natural colors, hinged saddle, 3½" 65.00
Eiffel Tower, pot metal, Paris scene in well cover 30.00
Fish, SP, hinged top, unusual, 5x5" 85.00
Flow blue, brass stand & top, 5¾x6" 195.00
Fount-O-Ink, porc, blk, rnd base w/4" rnd glass top 35.00
Frog, hinged lily pad & baby frog on bk, metal, 4" 95.00
Frog holding water lily, metal, hinged top 65.00
Hampshire, gr, rnd, 4" 85.00
Henriot Quimper, scalloped edge, rnd, France, 5" 50.00
Hercules fighting snake, brass w/rnd blk marble base, 5" 300.00
Horse's head, blk glass 30.00
Lady's head lid, SP, emb Nouveau florals, mk WB Mfg 38.00
Lantern shape, glass bottle/stopper, brassy tin fr, sq, 3" 35.00
Lion's head, bronze, paw ft, griffin pen rests, dtd 1887 . . . . 300.00
Lotus flower form, pewter, Chinese mk on base, 3-pc 75.00
Mailbox well, dogs/mailman, brass-plated iron, 7¼" 95.00
Marble, dbl pots, brass lids, 6" 35.00
Metal, emb, low flare ft, pen holders, swirl wells, 10" L 60.00
Nouveau, lady w/hands folded, pen rest, Made in France 75.00
Octopus & Art Nouveau girl, bronze, 8½x9" 400.00
Pitkin type, right swirl, sm cupped mouth, dk olive, 1½" 450.00
Puppy sucking baby bottle, dolphins, SP, 2½" sq, 3½" 95.00
Redware, helmet form w/ad: Helmet Rye, orig stopper, 4" 75.00
Revolving, blk amethyst, pear form, Deco styling, w/pen 75.00
Revolving, sapphire bl & milk glass wells, ca 1860s, 4½" 150.00
Rockingham, sleeping girl figural, 3¼" 120.00
Teakettle, ground mouth w/brass cap, gr-bl, 1⅝", EX 130.00
Teakettle, opal w/pnt floral, octagonal, ca 1830-80, 2½" 260.00
Teakettle, 10-sided, ground lip/silver cap, gold-yel, 2" 410.00
Teakettle, 6-sided, ground mouth/brass cap, yel-amber, 2" 200.00
Travel well, blk leather 30.00
Wood, brn sponging stencil hearts, S Silliman Co, 2¼" 125.00

Insulators

The telegraph was invented in 1844. The devices developed to hold the electrical transmission wires to the poles were called insulators. The telephone, invented in 1876, intensified their usefulness and by the turn of the century thousands of varieties were being produced in glass of various colors, pottery, and wood. Of the more than 3,000 types known to exist, today's collectors evaluate their worth by age and rarity of color. Aqua and green are the most common colors in glass, dark brown the most common in ceramic. Threadless insulators, made between 1850 and 1870, bring prices well into the hundreds.

In the listings that follow, the CD numbers are from an identification system developed in the late 1960s by N.R. Woodward. 'CD' refers to 'Consolidated Design.' When no condition is indicated, the items listed below are assumed to be in mint condition.

Diamond pony, purple, CA 102, 3½", $20.00.

Agee, CD 121, green-aqua 10.00
Agee, CD 124.6, smoke 12.00
Agee, CD 152.9, purple 20.00
AGM, CD 250.7, amber 100.00
AGM, CD 250.7, green 80.00
AGM, CD 250.7, yellow-green 40.00
Am Tel &Tel, CD 109/191, 2-pc transposition, aqua 10.00
Armstrong, CD 115, clear 1.00
Armstrong, CD 217, amber 6.00
Armstrong CSC, CD 128, smoke 5.00
Armstrong TS, CD 129, clear 4.00
Brookfield, CD 102, aqua 2.00
Brookfield, CD 104, aqua 5.00
Brookfield, CD 145, aqua 4.00
Brookfield, CD 150, aqua 70.00
Brookfield, CD 162, green 6.00
California, CD 133, aqua 4.00
California, CD 162, green 5.00
Canada, CD 121, purple 13.50
CCG, CD 124.7, lt straw 10.00
CCG, CD 124.7, straw 10.00
Chester, CD 123, aqua 500.00
Chicago, CD 135, blue 75.00
CNR, CD 143, aqua 4.00
Columbia, CD 262, green 70.00
Columbia, CD 263, aqua 65.00
Diamond, CD 102, amber olive 3.00
Dominion, CD 164, drip points, straw 6.00
FM Locke, Victor, NY, CD 287, aqua 10.00
Fred M Locke, Victor, NY, CD 297, green 10.00
Gayner, CD 153, drip points, aqua 5.00
GTP, CD 145, mauve 20.00
H&G Petticoat, CD 162, drip points, aqua 6.00
Hawley, CD 145, aqua 5.00
Hemingray, CD 102, aqua 10.00
Hemingray, CD 106, aqua 1.00
Hemingray, CD 121, aqua 5.00
Hemingray, CD 122, aqua 1.00
Hemingray, CD 122, opal 30.00
Hemingray, CD 154, aqua 2.00
Hemingray, CD 196, aqua 35.00
Hemingray, CD 202, green 24.00
Hemingray, CD 254, clear 125.00
Hemingray, CD 257, carnival 30.00
Hemingray, CD 302, aqua 20.00
Hemingray, CD 302/310, aqua 40.00
HG Co, CD 160, straw 18.00
Kerr, CD 128, clear 4.00
Knowles, CD 253, aqua 90.00
LGT Co, CD 131.4, aqua 50.00
Lynchburg, CD 112, drip points, aqua 5.00
Lynchburg, CD 164, drip points, aqua 4.00
Lynchburg, CD 164, lt green 10.00
Lynchburg, CD 205, aqua 15.00
Maydwell, CD 154, drip points, clear 5.00
McLaughlin, CD 164, emerald green 10.00
National, CD 110.5, aqua 110.00
NEGM, CD 145, green 15.00
NEGM, CD 267.5, emerald green 150.00
No Name, CD 121, aqua 10.00
No Name, CD 145, straw 10.00
No Name, CD 266, aqua 500.00
No Name, CD 267, emerald green 150.00
No Name, CD 270, green 150.00
No 2 Cable, CD 252, aqua 15.00
OVG Co, CD 112, aqua 5.00
Pyrex, CD 128, clear 3.00
Pyrex, CD 233, carnival 35.00
Pyrex, CD 320, clear 8.00
R Good Jr, CD 121, aqua 8.00
Standard, CD 143, purple 15.00
T-H, CD 245, aqua 65.00
THE Co, CD 134, aqua 12.00
Vertical Bar, CD 102, purple 8.00
Westinghouse, CD 162, clear 140.00
WFG Co, CD 121, aqua 10.00
WGM Co, CD 121, purple 12.00
Whital Tatum, CD 107, ice blue 5.00
Whital Tatum, CD 128, smoke 4.00
Whital Tatum, CD 154, pink 2.00
Whital Tatum, CD 162, clear 6.00
Whital Tatum, CD 197, smoke 10.00
WV 5, CD 125, aqua 5.00

Irons

Irons come in all shapes and sizes; there are sadirons, fluting irons, and tailor's irons, to name but the most common. Hooded sadirons, patented about 1870, supposedly shielded the ironer's hand from the heat. Box irons from the late 1800s had hinged rear doors to accomodate heated slugs. Charcoal irons worked on the same principal, but removing the ashes was a nuisance! Even the gas irons of the early 20th century had drawbacks. Pressure on the tank controlled the flame. Too little meant no heat, too much could result in an accident! Denatured alcohol and boiling water were also used as heat sources. Electric irons, though invented around the turn of the century, were not used to any great extent until electricity became a commonplace commodity several decades later.

When no condition is indicated, the items listed below are assumed to be in excellent condition.

Baby Betsy Ross, electric, in orig box....20.00
Charcoal, brass plate, removable hdl....70.00
Charcoal, CI, wood hdl, lady's head forms latch, 9x7½″....75.00
Charcoal, CI w/wood hdl, satyr-head latch, 7½″....25.00
Charcoal, combination smoothing & fluting....55.00
Child's, A-Best-O, miniature....30.00
Child's, clip-on hdl, dtd May 22, 1900, 4″ L....25.00
Child's, Dover, #602, 2-pc....30.00
Child's, Dover, Tuesday's Children, #247A, 1-pc....28.00
Child's, Dover Dolly....25.00
Child's, Dover USA, #271B, 2-pc....30.00
Child's, Ober #1, Chadrintall SC, 2½x3½″....20.00
Child's, Pearl, #257....35.00
Child's, Potts, #265D, 2-pc....40.00
Child's, WAPAK #2, 4″ L....25.00
Fluting, Geneva, 1866, 2-pc....65.00
Fluting, The Best....50.00
Gas, Coleman Self-Heating, Model 4-A, bl enamel....50.00
Gas, Comfort, metal logo in relief letters....32.50
Gas, Diamond, simple styling....22.50
Gas, Strause Gas Iron Co....45.00
Goffering iron stand, brass/iron, trn ped, arched ft....325.00
Sadiron, applied forged hdl, wafer-thin, 1700s....135.00
Sadiron, Colbrookdale, interchangable hdl....35.00
Sadiron, wrought iron w/scroll hdl, 6½″....85.00
Sadiron/fluter, combination, 1871....65.00
Sleeve, Sensible #1, detachable hdl....30.00
Slug, door opens to insert hot slug, wrought hdl, 1700s....125.00
Stuart, Iron Deficiency Anemia ad, mini....45.00
Tailor's, Cannon, twist hdl, 12-lb....38.00

Ironstone

During the last quarter of the 18th century, English potters began experimenting with a new type of body that contained calcinated flint and a higher china clay content, intent on producing a fine durable whiteware--heavy, yet with a texture that would resemble porcelain. To remove the last trace of yellow, a minute amount of cobalt was added, often resulting in a bluish-white tone. Wm. and John Turner of Caughley, and Josiah Spode II were the first to manufacture the ware successfully. Others, such as Davenport, Hicks and Meigh, and Ralph and Josiah Wedgwood, followed with their own versions. The latter coined the name 'Pearl' to refer to his product and incorporated the term into his trademark.

In 1813 a 14-year patent was issued to Charles James Mason, who called his ware Patented Ironstone. Francis Morley, G.L. Asworth, T.J. Mayer, and other Staffordshire potters continued to produce ironstone until the end of the century. While some of these patterns are simple to the extreme, many are decorated with in-mold designs of fruit, grains and foliage on ribbed or scalloped shapes. In the 1830s, transfer-printed designs in blue, mulberry, pink, green, and black became popular, and polychrome versions of Oriental wares were manufactured to compete with the Chinese trade.

When no condition is indicated, the items listed below are assumed to be in mint condition.

Baker, Atlantic, oval, no lid, Boote, 1858....31.00
Bowl, fruit; Bellflower, Edwards....30.00
Bowl, fruit; President, Edwards, 10½″....25.00
Bowl, ped ft, low, deep, Burgess....56.00
Bowl, soup; Ceres, flat, lg....22.00
Bowl, soup; Imari, Mason's, 1860s....50.00
Bowl, soup; 9⅞″....12.00
Bowl, Spring, sq, Grindley, 8½″....22.00
Bowl, syllabub; plain pattern, Meakin, 6x9″....145.00
Bowl, vegetable; Swirl, w/lid, Mayer & Elliot....115.00
Bowl, vegetable; Trent, w/lid, Alcock....75.00
Bowl, vegetable; w/lid, Wedgwood, sm....90.00
Bowl, vegetable; Wheat, w/lid, Baker....85.00
Bowl, vegetable; Wheat & Blackberry, w/lid, Meakin....95.00
Bowl & pitcher, Tracery, Johnson Bros....125.00
Bread plate, sheaf/eagles/Waste Not, 13¼″, EX....80.00
Cake stand, scalloped flange, JF....65.00
Coffee pot, Baltimore, Brougham & Mayer, 1850s....115.00
Coffee pot, Gothic, Edwards....165.00
Coffee server, figural goose spout, acorn finial....85.00
Coffee set, Ceres, copper lustre trim, Elsmore Forster....540.00
Compote, pk/brn floral, Pankhurst, sq, 5x8″....65.00
Compote, ribbed, Edward Clarke, 8¾″....65.00
Compote, scalloped rim & base, T&R Boote & Co, 8x10½″....80.00
Compote, stemmed, fluted, Edwards, miniature....77.00
Creamer, Gothic, 4½″....38.00
Creamer, Grenade, Boote....54.00
Creamer, Sydenham, Boote....70.00
Creamer, Wheat & Blackberry, Meakin....65.00
Cup, handleless; Corn & Oats, Davenport & Wedgwood....25.00
Cup, handleless; Trent....15.00
Cup & saucer, Ceres, Elsmore & Foster....35.00
Cup & saucer, Corn & Oats, Davenport & Wedgwood....35.00
Cup & saucer, handleless; Ceres, Meakin....45.00
Gravy boat, ribbed, Pankhurst....32.00
Gravy boat, Sharon Arch....30.00
Gravy boat, 8-sided, Shaw....34.00
Honey dish, Laurel, Wedgwood....20.00
Infant feeder, bl #s on side....30.00
Jug, puzzle; jester/cockfight, Elsmore & Forster, 8″....100.00
Mold, cauliflower, Alcock, lg....50.00
Mold, corn, med....45.00
Mold, crown, lg....54.00
Mold, grape, med....40.00
Mold, leaf, G Jones....54.00
Mold, poinsettia....52.00
Mold, rose, med....50.00
Mold, seafood....40.00
Pitcher, fully ribbed, Pankhurst, 9¾″....80.00
Pitcher, Hyacinth, Wedgwood, 9¼″....55.00
Pitcher, Lily, Burgess, milk sz....95.00
Pitcher, Sydenham, Barrow, 10½″....80.00

Sugar bowl, Johnson, 7″, $45.00.

Pitcher, Wheat, Wilkinson, 7½" 40.00
Plate, Corn & Oats, Davenport & Wedgwood, dessert sz 16.00
Plate, Corn & Oats, Davenport & Wedgwood, dinner sz 25.00
Plate, Meakin, 1870, 10" dia 25.00
Platter, Ceres, oval, 12" 35.00
Platter, Clementson, oval, 13½x10⅝" 25.00
Platter, Corn & Oats, Davenport & Wedgwood, med 30.00
Platter, oval, 12x8⅞" 15.00
Platter, Spring, Grindley, 14" 28.00
Platter, Wheat, Meakin, 20⅜x15⅜" 40.00
Punch bowl, Lily-of-the-Valley, Shaw 150.00
Relish, Pankhurst 22.00
Relish, Vineyard, Davenport, ca 1856 .... 35.00
Sauce tureen, emb, w/undertray, Clementson 88.00
Sauce tureen, Laurel Wreath, w/lid, Elsmore & Forster 150.00
Sauce tureen, Memmon, w/lid, Meir, 3-pc 88.00
Sauce tureen, Raspberry w/Bloom, ribbed, w/lid, Meakin 80.00
Sauce tureen, Ribbed Chain, w/lid, Pankhurst, 3-pc 85.00
Sauce tureen, Symington, w/ladle 125.00
Sauce tureen, 8-sided, Boote, 1851, 2-pc 90.00
Soup plate, Corn & Oats, Davenport & Wedgwood 16.00
Soup tureen, Ceres, w/undertray, Adams & Sons 450.00
Soup tureen, Twin Leaves, w/ladle, Edwards, 1851, 4-pc 350.00
Soup tureen, Wedgwood 130.00
Soup tureen, Wheat & Poppy, Canada shape, w/ladle, 1877 .... 350.00
Sugar bowl, Ceres, Elsmore & Forster 80.00
Sugar bowl, Cone w/Leaves, Edwards 65.00
Sugar bowl, Corn, w/lid, J Wedgwood 65.00
Sugar bowl, Gothic, Ridgway 60.00
Sugar bowl, Grenade 52.00
Syrup, plain, Meakin, w/pewter lid 85.00
Tea set, child's; ribbed design, 23-pc 175.00
Teapot, Cable & Ring, J&G Meakin, 8½" 75.00
Teapot, Gothic, Mayer 145.00
Teapot, St Louis, Edwards 95.00
Teapot, Wheat, mk Adams 65.00
Tureen, vegetable; Rosalind, brn, Meakin, w/lid, 11½x5½" 165.00
Vase, birds & flowers, cylinder, Mason's, rare, 1820, 10" 250.00
Wash pitcher, Prairie, Clementson 110.00

Ivory

Technically, true ivory is the substance composing the tusk of the elephant; the finest type comes from those of Africa. However, tusks and teeth of other animals--the walrus, for instance, the hippopotamus, and the sperm whale--are similar in composition and appearance and have also been used for carving. The Chinese have used this substance for centuries, preferring it over bone because of the natural oil contained in its pores, which not only renders it easier to carve, but also imparts a soft sheen to the finished product. Aged ivory usually takes on a soft caramel patina, but unscrupulous dealers sometimes treat new ivory to a tea bath to 'antique' it!

A bill passed in 1978 reinforced a ban on the importation of whale and walrus ivory.

When no condition is indicated, the items listed below are assumed to be in undamaged condition.

Beads, carved, w/7 elephants interspersed, 20" 75.00
Beads, 22½" 65.00
Cigarette holder, carved roses & leaves, 4" 35.00
Dog, guardian; EX carving, teakwood base, 6", pr 300.00
Dr's doll, fully carved, removable bracelet, 4" 65.00
Dr's doll, reclining, on wooden couch, 4" 75.00
Elephant, pagoda on bk, w/15 figures, jeweled, sgn, 3" 600.00
Fetish, carved, African, Gold Coast 85.00
Flower God w/staff; Goddess w/peony, sgn, 12½", pr 850.00
Foo lion, jeweled collar, coral eyes, head removes, 5" 140.00
God of Longevity, under pine tree, pomegranate in hand, 8" 280.00
God of Longevity, w/staff & sceptre, 12", pr 1,350.00
Goddess, multi-armed, stands on lotus base, 5" 175.00
Incense burner, foo dog/dragon panels/loose rings, 14" 1,050.00
Japanese basket vendor, Hong Kong, mc, 8" 250.00
Kwan Yin, w/magic wang & tassels, mc/sgn, 8" 275.00
Kwan Yin head, elaborate headdress w/Buddha, earrings, 6" 250.00
Kwan Yin on lotus base w/fly whisk & bottle, 12½" 650.00
Musicians, maids w/flute, lute, bells & pipes, 4", set of 4 .... 300.00
Oriental fisherman & wife in lg hats, w/equipment, 6", pr 200.00
Oriental fisherman w/staff & basket w/fish, ca 1820, 12" 650.00
Oriental fisherman w/8 lg fish, 2 children, 9½" 500.00
Oriental maid holds branch & sm bud, 10" 275.00
Oriental maid holds flower bud in vase, 8" 150.00
Oriental maid holds short hoe & branch, 12" 375.00
Oriental maid in kimono holds peony, rolled coiffure, 9" 250.00
Oriental maid playing lute, flowing robe/rolled hair, 5¼" 225.00
Oriental maid w/fan & peony in hands, coiled hair, 9½" 275.00
Oriental maid w/Pandean Pipes, 5" 175.00
Oriental man, boy & crane, holding staff & lilies, 8" 350.00
Oriental man & woman under pine tree, 9x4½x2" 600.00
Oriental man holds branch & knarled staff, 8" 165.00
Oriental man holds branch w/flowers & staff, 14" 600.00
Oriental man holds dragon head staff & branch, 10" 275.00
Oriental man w/peach branch, monkey, 9½x4¾" 625.00
Oriental nude stands in garden, 6x3½" 225.00
Peasant man w/baskets & mask, sgn, 5½" 175.00
Phoenix bird among flowers, coral eyes, 1880, 5½" 300.00
Phoenix bird on tree, blk on feathers, 10", pr 350.00
T'ang horse, polychrome, w/stand, 4¾x6½" 275.00
Tankard, battle scene, silver mtd, knight lid finial, 13" 1,800.00
Tankard, hunting scenes, 2-figure hdl, losses/rstr, 6" 1,650.00
Teapot, dragon-head spout, tail hdl, squirrels on lid, 5x4" 195.00
Tusk w/courtyard scene, dragon, phoenix, bamboo, pr 400.00

Triptych, Joan of Arc, Continental, early 19th century, 13¾", $4,500.00.

Jack-in-the-Pulpit Vases

Popular novelties at the turn of the century, Jack-in-the-Pulpit vases were made in every type of art glass produced. Some were simple--others elaborately appliqued and enameled. They were shaped to resemble the lily for which they were named.

When no condition is indicated, the items listed below are assumed to be in mint condition.

Bl w/wine hobnail ruffled edge, 6¾x6½″......................95.00
Burmese, flared pie-crust rim, Mt WA, 12½″................745.00
Cranberry, coil stem, clear petal ft, 9″.....................100.00
Cream overlay w/pink & wht applied flowers, ruffle, 7″........135.00
Gr opal stripe w/pink applied flower, gr leaf, 9x3″.............90.00
Gr overlay, clear petal ft, 6½″...............................95.00
Gr to yel opaque, ruffled top, emb pattern & ribs, 9x4½″.......90.00
Lav w/purple fluted edge, 7½x6″...........................100.00
Lt gr satin overlay, enamel flowers, camphor ft, 5½x7½″.......130.00
Opal, 5-petal flower top, bl & vaseline, 9⅛x5½″...............85.00
Rubena, applied vaseline ruffle, 11x5″......................125.00
Spatter, gr/wht, Dia Quilt base, ruffled, 9½x5¾″..............100.00
Yel opaque shaded to gr, dk gr ruffle, ribbed, 9x4½″..........90.00

Jackfield

Jackfield has come to be a generic term used to refer to wares with a red clay body and a high gloss black glaze. It originated at Jackfield, in Stropshire, England; however, it was also produced in the Staffordshire district as well. While some pieces are decorated with relief motifs or painted-on florals and gilding, many are unadorned. Teapots produced in the 18th century were known locally as 'black decanters.' These pots, and figural dogs and roosters, are the items most often found.

When no condition is indicated, the items listed below are assumed to be in mint condition.

Creamer, cow form, tail hdl, gilt trim, w/lid, 5″, NM...........35.00
Creamer, emb floral, 4″.....................................45.00
Dogs, Spaniels, old, 12x12″, pr...........................350.00
Pitcher, water; gr ivy leaves, heavy gold, 7½″................125.00

Jewelry

Jewelry as objects of adornment has always been regarded with special affection. Whether it be a trinket or a costly ornament of gold, silver, or enameled work, jewelry has personal significance to the wearer.

The art of the jeweler is valued as is any art object, and the names of Lalique or Faberge on collectible pieces bring prices demanded by the signed works of Picasso.

Once the province of kings and noblemen, jewelry now is a legacy of all strata of society. The creativity reflected in the jewelers' art has resulted in a myriad of decorative adornments for men and women, and the modern usage of 'lesser' gems and base metals has elevated the values and increased the demand for artistic merit on a par with intrinsic values. Luxuriously appointed pieces of Victorian splendor and Edwardian grandeur, now compete with the unique, imaginative renditions of jewelry produced in the exciting Art Nouveau period, as well as the adventurous translation of jewelry executed in man-made materials versus natural elements.

Today, prices for gems and gemstones crafted into antique and collectible jewelry, are based on artistic merit, personable appeal, pure sentimentality, and intrinsic values.

If you are interested in collecting or dealing in jewelry, you will find that authority Lillian Baker has several fine books available on the subject, complete with beautiful color illustrations and current market values. She is listed in the Directory under California.

When no condition is indicated, the items listed below are assumed to be in mint condition.

Key:
A/C—Arts and Crafts
AD—Art Deco
AN—Art Nouveau
cab—cabochon
comp—complementary
ct—carat
dia—diamond
gf—gold filled
grad—graduated
gp—gold plated
gw—gold washed
k—karat
plat—platinum
pw—penny weight
tw—total weight
wg—white gold
yg—yellow gold

Bracelet, garnet cluster, 1″ wide in front, $395.00.

Bracelet, bangle; AD style, rhinestones, safety chain...........12.00
Bracelet, bangle; celluloid, bl w/silver pnt/relief roses...........12.50
Bracelet, bangle; celluloid w/relief flower motif.................12.50
Bracelet, bangle; gf, eng scrolls & name, ⅜″ W...............30.00
Bracelet, bangle; pinchbeck, eng belt/buckle, ⅜″ W............60.00
Bracelet, bangle; pinchbeck, eng leaves w/2 hearts, ¼″ W.......45.00
Bracelet, bangle; silver, belt/buckle form, floral eng............65.00
Bracelet, bangle; 14k yg florentine finish, 10.3 grams.........150.00
Bracelet, bangle; 15k, sm pearl, twist trim, child's.............85.00
Bracelet, brass links w/enameled shields w/sodalite beads.......12.00
Bracelet, brass links w/3 glass stones, ½″ W.................22.50
Bracelet, charm; brass chain w/7 charms/ball separators........18.00
Bracelet, copper w/blk enameled swirls, ¾″ sq links.............8.00
Bracelet, expandable, 14 faceted blk horn plaques, 1″ W.......18.00
Bracelet, pinchbeck, 3 rows faux dia w/faux dia/onyx clasp......28.00
Bracelet, rolled gold ¾″ expansion, 19 pearls in horseshoe......65.00
Bracelet, sterling, 7-link/leaves w/abalone, Mexico-AM-925.......40.00
Bracelet, sterling, 9 lava cameos..........................110.00
Bracelet, 14k, 10 slides ea w/dia, ruby, opal, etc, 35 dwt......700.00
Bracelet, 14k chain link, 36 dwt...........................650.00
Bracelet, 14k w/62 matched cultured pearls..................450.00
Bracelet, 17 charms: $2½ gold pc, lg nugget, +15, 2+ oz...1,000.00
Bracelet, 18k, 54 semiprecious stones, 40+ dwt............1,200.00
Bracelet, 18k triple cable w/35 sm dia, 28 dwt.............1,850.00
Bracelet, 18k wide mesh by Tiffany & Co, 20+ oz..........1,300.00
Bracelet, 18k/enamel twists, Tiffany, 100+ dwt, set of 4.....2,100.00
Bracelet, 3 strands cultured pearls, 24-dia slide center.........325.00
Brooch, bl rhinestones, flower mt w/bl leaves, +earrings........25.00
Brooch, brass, faux turq center/4-leaf clover applique, 2″.......18.00
Brooch, brass, flowers/leaves, 10 ea set w/rhinestones, 3″.......17.50
Brooch, brass, lg gr stone w/4 rhinestones ea side, enamel......14.00
Brooch, brass, rose-cut ½″ crystal center w/beaded fr, 1″.......14.00
Brooch, brass, umbrella, bow on hdl, 5 sm red stones, 2¼″......8.50
Brooch, brass leaves/rose w/rhinestones, +earrings............15.00
Brooch, brass w/silver-colored applications, saiboat, 3″.........18.00
Brooch, cameo, lady's head, wht on bl, 14k fr w/pearls, 2″.....105.00
Brooch, celluloid bird, carved detail, 3 layers color, 3″..........15.00
Brooch, gw, bow w/tassel dangles, Kramer, 2¼″................15.00
Brooch, gw, cluster gold/blk glass stones, Selini, 2½″..........18.00
Brooch, gw leaf w/faux pearl flowers, Tortelane, +earrings......12.00
Brooch, gw/enamel, leaf, yel/bl glass sets/rhinestones, 3″........22.50
Brooch, HP porcelain, boy in gr hat/cape w/tamborine, 1¾″.....85.00

Brooch, marcasites, flower & leaves, ¾x1½" 24.00
Brooch, pewter/metal, teardrop/rnd dangle, Aurora Borealis 8.50
Brooch, pinchbeck, HP lady plaque, faux pearl surround, 2" 40.00
Brooch, plastic, dia shape, shell flower w/in, 3¾" 10.00
Brooch, plastic w/enamel flowers, rnd pewter-look fr, 1½" 8.00
Brooch, rolled gold, heart/faith/hope, w/pearl/etc, ⅞x1½" 25.00
Brooch, silver metal flower w/bl rhinestones, +earrings 12.00
Brooch, silver-look w/abalone, butterfly, Mexico, 1¾x1½" 8.50
Brooch, silver/gold horseshoe/scrolls/floral, mk 1893, 1½" 35.00
Brooch, sterling, bl/clear rhinestones, circular, 1¼" 14.00
Brooch, sterling, eng 'Best Wishes'/heart/flowers, ⅝x1¾" 22.00
Brooch, sterling, skate, sgn C&N, early 1900s, 2¼" 14.00
Brooch, sterling, 3 enamel-center flowers, Danish, 1½" 18.00
Brooch, sterling, 4 agate inlays/faux citrine, Scottish, 1½" 40.00
Brooch, sterling, ⅞" marquise blue-john on 2½" bar 18.00
Brooch, sterling anchor/eng wreath/enamel crown/marcasites 30.00
Brooch, sterling key set w/rhinestones in center sq, 3" L 12.00
Brooch, sterling spear dangle/agate heart, Scottish, 1x1¼" 30.00
Brooch, sterling/gw, gr stone in leaf/flower motif, 3" L 25.00
Brooch, 10k, flower spray, copper washed, 2¾x1½" 8.50
Brooch, 12k, mc glass stones in flower/leaf motif, 2¾" 20.00
Brooch, 12k gf, flower/leaf w/bl glass stone, 3½" 12.50
Brooch, 18k bird w/16 opals, ruby & sapphire eye, 17 dwt 475.00
Brooch, 18k bug w/coral body/head, ruby eyes+6 pearls, 1½" 275.00
Brooch, 18k 2-color Inca form w/5 sm sq dia, 7 dwt 140.00
Buckle, gw frame w/single row rhinestones, 2x1" 12.50
Chain, 14k multiple strands, 40+ dwt 800.00
Chain, 14k yg, herringbone, 17 grams, 19" 200.00
Charm, 14k automobile w/10 stones+6 sm pearls, 6 dwt 125.00
Chatelaine, silver filigree Nouveau head on holder+4 drops 265.00
Clip, brass, berries/leaves w/lg gold faux pearls 9.00
Clip, lg amethyst in silver fr set w/circles w/marcasites 18.00
Clip, pave-set rhinestones, oval & marquise stones, 2¼" 15.00
Clip, shoe; sq rhodium type bk w/2 rows rhinestones, pr 18.00
Crucifix, 18k/enamel, on 18k chain, 24 dwt 325.00
Cuff links, Siamese sterling, elephants 15.00
Earrings, dia clusters, tw .50 .... 300.00
Earrings, ea w/5mm & 7mm pearl, dangle style, 1900s 125.00
Earrings, flower w/.3½ dia surrounded by 6 2mm emeralds 225.00
Earrings, marcasites, sm cluster 10.00
Earrings, plat, 3 loops, ⅜ct central dia+36 sm dia 1,800.00
Earrings, rhinestone bug w/glass wings/eyes, Austria, 1¼" 18.00
Earrings, silver metal w/dangle & faux moonstones, 2" 22.50
Earrings, sterling, fan shape w/Siamese dancers, 1¼" W 12.00
Earrings, sterling, knotted twist, Chas Horner, 1907, 1½" 75.00
Earrings, sterling, pr leaves on oval mt 16.50
Earrings, sterling leaf, Heeber, 1" 12.00
Earrings, 14k, AD jade scalloped-top hoops w/.5 dia 90.00
Earrings, 14k scallop shells, 4 dwt 125.00
Earrings, 14k spirals w/⅜ct dia, tw ¾ct 400.00
Earrings, 18k cluster, ea w/6 semiprecious stones, 10 dwt 250.00
Earrings, 18k domes resembling tortoise bks, 10 dwt 450.00
Earrings, 18k lover's knots, 5 dwt 275.00
Earrings, 18k wg, pr ½" bars w/⅜" pear sapphire drop 275.00
Earrings, 3 hematite beads on silver wire, pink ball drop 15.00
Earrings, 3 sm dia on leaf 180.00
Earrings, 4mm emerald studs 90.00
Earrings, 5½mm sapphires studs 135.00
Earrings, 6mm pearl studs 40.00
Earrings, 7mm cab-cut amethyst studs 75.00
Locket, gf 1" heart eng w/ornate initials, Victorian 30.00
Locket, silver, blk enamel lace on wht, oval, 1½" 75.00
Locket, silver, English hallmarks, 2¾x1⅝" 85.00
Locket, 10k, heart shape w/red stone in star, w/chain, ¾" 85.00

Comb, tortoiseshell celluloid, 6¼", $47.50.

Necklace, AD plastic/blk jet beads, sqs/circles 18.00
Necklace, assorted colors/shapes pressed glass beads, 54" 25.00
Necklace, Aurora Borealis rhinestones, +earrings, 1950s 25.00
Necklace, blk jet w/clear faceted crystals, 28" 20.00
Necklace, brass chain, glass sets w/brass leaf loops/drop 18.50
Necklace, brass chain w/gr glass spacers/teardrop dangle 35.00
Necklace, brass chain/drop w/3 turq/rhinestone, +earrings 25.00
Necklace, chain w/faux topaz & clear stones in links 10.00
Necklace, cherry amber, faceted/grad, 35" 150.00
Necklace, gold color chain w/rhinestone drop, +earrings 25.00
Necklace, gold color on rnd glass beads w/brass spacers 15.00
Necklace, gold metal, gr rhinestones/opals, +earrings 18.00
Necklace, gr adventurine beads 25.00
Necklace, gw, sm scattered red stones, Trifari, +earrings 15.00
Necklace, honey amber, faceted/grad ovals, 29" 85.00
Necklace, red/gold beads/crystals/blk jets, Bohemian, 30" 30.00
Necklace, silver-look filigree chain w/lg bl glass pendant 15.00
Necklace, silver/enamel flowers, A/C, no mk, in case, 15½" 350.00
Necklace, topaz pressed crystal beads, 28" 17.00
Necklace, turq & crystal glass beads, W Germany, 18" 18.00
Necklace, wht beads w/3 rhinestone spacers, W Germany 18.00
Necklace, wht glass beads w/rhinestone clasp, +earrings 15.00
Necklace, wht glass rnd/sq beads w/clear glass separators 20.00
Necklace, yg beads, 14 dwt, 16" 200.00
Necklace, 18k, sm dia/rubies/sapphires, Gubelin, +earrings 2,000.00
Necklace, 18k Inca style, medallion & bracelet, 90 dwt 1,400.00
Necklace, 3-strand cultured pearls, 15" 300.00
Pendant, butterscotch amber, 2" 65.00
Pendant, pinchbeck fr, pietra dura floral, dia shape, 1" 105.00
Pendant, plique-a-jour, head of maiden set w/dia, Gautrait 14,300.00
Pendant, silver, pear-shaped wht paste w/in 16, 1" 35.00
Pendant, silver hand mirror, enamel decor, mk 1920, 2½" 45.00
Pendant, silver pierced tree, 5 turq/MOP cab & drop, case 900.00
Pendant, silver w/enamel flower, cross shape w/dangle, 1913 .... 65.00
Pendant, silver w/gr enamel shamrock, hallmk 1917, 1" dia 26.00
Pendant, silver/enamel, 2-part, Nouveau lady/MOP inlay, 2" 110.00
Pendant, sterling, jade leaf w/4 grad turq 40.00
Pendant, 10k w/dia chip, seed pearl drop, AN, 18" chain 85.00
Pendant, 10k 2-color gold, AD flower on leaf 90.00
Pendant, 14k, .19 dia 170.00
Pendant, 14k, dia center stone w/6 garnets, beaded mt 175.00
Pendant, 14k, HP bird on amethyst w/in sm pearls, 1900 .... 335.00
Pendant, 14k, jade, carved ea side, ca 1890, 1⅝x1¼" 400.00
Pendant, 14k, onyx w/5mm pearl center, gold edging 120.00
Pendant, 14k, 1½" carved carnelian 125.00

Pendant, 14k revolving world globe, 10 dwt 150.00
Pendant, 14k w/14mm synthetic alexandrite heart 165.00
Pendant, 14k wg filigree trim w/.5 dia+crystals, 1910 . . . . . 210.00
Pendant, 14k wg filigree w/opal+3 seed pearls, 1910 . . . . . 165.00
Pendant, 15k open circle w/amber bead suspension w/in, 1¼″ . . . 65.00
Pendant, 15k openwork w/3mm ruby, 1½x⅝″ 85.00
Pendant, 9k, ¾″ shell cameo w/in larger outer fr, 1⅛″ 75.00
Pin, bar; brass w/bl enamel, bird 12.50
Pin, bar; brass w/geometric cloisonne, 1¼″ W 7.00
Pin, bar; gf, rhinestone-set sword, Van Dell 15.00
Pin, bar; rhinestones w/base metal bk, 2″ 18.00
Pin, bar; silver metal fr w/lg gr cab stone, 1920 . . . . . 8.00
Pin, bar; sterling, blk onyx center, 2¼″ W 10.00
Pin, bar; 10k flower motif of 19 garnets, 1¾″ W 70.00
Pin, bar; 14k 2-color gold w/3mm center pearl, 2″ W 80.00
Pin, copper leaf w/bl enamel, Matisse Renoir, 3¼″ 20.00
Pin, gf open heart w/leaf spray, engraved, 1″ 8.00
Pin, gw bow w/flower & leaf dangle, pink stone in center 12.50
Pin, gw flower, Monet, 2″ 7.50
Pin, Siam sterling, etched boat, 1½x1¼″ 15.00
Pin, sterling, enamel leaves/scrolls, A/C, England, 1″ 110.00
Pin, sterling 4-leaf dogwood, Kalo, 2″ 160.00
Pin, sterling/gold overlay, tulips w/colored stones, '40s 10.00
Pin, 10k circle, seed pearls w/Eastern Star, ⅝″ 35.00
Pin, 14k, .6 pt dia+2½mm pearl & enameling, 1900 . . . . . 50.00
Pin, 14k wg filigree w/.3 dia & enameling, 1910 . . . . . 150.00
Pin, 14k yg w/6 rnd opals 250.00
Pin/clip combo, rhinestones in ribbon design, 2½″, pr 20.00
Pin/pendant, copper w/faux amethyst center, Hoffman, 1½″ 15.00
Pin/pendant, floral pietra dura in blk marble, 1¼x1″ 100.00
Pin/pendant, yg/plat chain, 44 tiny sq rubies+65 tiny dia 115.00
Pin/pendant, 15k, eng spheres, b/w enameling, ⅞x1⅛″ 75.00
Ring, gf, emerald-cut topaz 15.00
Ring, guard; plat w/6 dia, tw .48ct 275.00
Ring, man's; 10k, lg oval jade 80.00
Ring, man's; 14k brushed mt w/.8 dia 115.00
Ring, man's; 14k wax seal w/name & shield, ½x⅝″ 275.00
Ring, man's; 18k lion head w/.33 garnet 160.00
Ring, plat, 5ct dia w/2 sm .30ct baguettes 14,500.00
Ring, plat band set all around w/sm dia 185.00
Ring, rose gold, cameo bust on plaited hair ground 155.00
Ring, sterling, gray lava cameo, man w/medieval crown, ¾″ 65.00
Ring, sterling filigree w/abalone center, Mexico 15.00
Ring, wg, lg citrine ringed w/seed pearls, openwork bird 115.00
Ring, 10k, cameo w/2 sm dia 95.00
Ring, 10k, emerald-cut amethyst w/2 sm dia 40.00
Ring, 10k, flower/leaf mt w/.05 dia, eng shoulders 45.00
Ring, 10k, oval opal solitaire 25.00
Ring, 10k, oval opal w/4 sm dia 50.00
Ring, 10k, pr 2.50 topazes+2 sm wht sapphires 150.00
Ring, 10k, pr 5mm peridots in cross-over mt 80.00
Ring, 10k, 1.50 pear-shaped beryl, plain shank 95.00
Ring, 10k brushed yg, pear-shaped tiger eye 90.00
Ring, 10k w-yg filigree, crystal stone w/gold Eastern Star 50.00
Ring, 12k, devotional, IHS w/tau cross, blk enamel detail 165.00
Ring, 14k, .18 dia in Tiffany style mt, 1900 . . . . . 150.00
Ring, 14k, .25 emerald center+2 sm rubies+22 miner-cut dia . . 900.00
Ring, 14k, .28 dia in engraved Tiffany style mt, 1920 . . . . . 165.00
Ring, 14k, .30 emerald-cut citrine+3 .5 rubies ea side 325.00
Ring, 14k, .6 dia, claw set, 1890s 140.00
Ring, 14k, .8 dia in bar-top mt 75.00
Ring, 14k, amethyst, heart shape, 1920s 75.00
Ring, 14k, amethyst, lg oval cut, ca 1890 . . . . . 150.00
Ring, 14k, amethyst in ea of 4 clovers, sm dia in center 225.00
Ring, 14k, flower mt set w/13 sm+3½mm center pearl 170.00
Ring, 14k, lg aquamarine w/18 .3 dia+18 3½mm sapphires . . . 1,000.00
Ring, 14k, lg ruby star sapphire w/sm dia ea side 50.00
Ring, 14k, oval ¼x¾″ coral stone, plain mt 65.00
Ring, 14k, signet, engraved, scrollwork 55.00
Ring, 14k, ½x¾″ apple jade, 1920s 120.00
Ring, 14k, 18mm lt apple jade, gold wire trim 175.00
Ring, 14k, 2 rows pearls+1 row w/7½mm pearl+6 sm dia 495.00
Ring, 14k, 2 4½mm sapphires+2 sm pearls, Victorian 150.00
Ring, 14k, 3 sm dia in band style mt, 1890 . . . . . 170.00
Ring, 14k, 3½mm sapphire in filigree mt 80.00
Ring, 14k, 3mm center ruby w/7 .3 dia surround 240.00
Ring, 14k, 3mm sapphire+6 sm pearls in star mt 150.00
Ring, 14k, 4½mm ruby+8 .12 dia in flower mt 400.00
Ring, 14k, 40ct aquamarine w/10 sm dia ea side, 1930s 950.00
Ring, 14k, 5½mm bl star sapphire in love-knot mt 300.00
Ring, 14k, 5 2½mm rubies in starburst mt, wide band 130.00
Ring, 14k, 5ct emerald-cut kunzite+12 sm garnets, pierced 350.00
Ring, 14k, 5mm cab garnet in swirled bezel 85.00
Ring, 14k dome w/moonstones/etc, 12½ dwt 475.00
Ring, 14k w/wg face, row of 6 sm dia 95.00
Ring, 14k wg, .25 emerald, eng/open-bk mt, Masonic 125.00
Ring, 14k wg, 2 sm dia 55.00
Ring, 14k wg, 2.5 gr tourmaline w/8 sm dia on ea shoulder 145.00
Ring, 14k wg filigree w/.20 dia, 1920 . . . . . 145.00
Ring, 14k yg, amethyst quartz, 11¼ grams w/stones 150.00
Ring, 14k yg w/wg front, row of 4 .2 dia 30.00
Ring, 15k, .25 emerald, beaded bezel, 1920s 95.00
Ring, 15k, 2.50 beryl, eng mt, ornate shoulders, 1900 . . . . . 125.00
Ring, 15k, 2.50 rhodolite garnet, eng mt/pierced shoulders 135.00
Ring, 18k, marquise-cut jade 70.00
Ring, 18k, ornate rnd bezel w/lg garnet+4 sm emeralds 275.00
Ring, 18k, oval Siberian jade, ½x½x¼″ 140.00
Ring, 18k, 4ct marquise aquamarine, 4-strand twist bezel 175.00
Ring, 18k wg, bl sapphire in basket mt 100.00
Ring, 18k wg filigree AD style mt w/.15 dia+4 sm dia 200.00
Ring, 18k wg filigree w/.10 dia, 1910 . . . . . 115.00
Ring, 18k wg filigree w/2 dia+1 sapphire, ea 2½mm, 1910 . . . . 165.00
Ring, 22k, 1.50 ruby, plain shank, Victorian 400.00
Ring, 9k, .50 sapphire w/2 rose-cut garnets & 4 pearls 195.00
Ring, 9k, buckle form w/3 Persian turq, hallmk 1867 . . . . . 100.00
Ring, 9k, carnelian cherub cameo w/enamel detail, 1700s 250.00

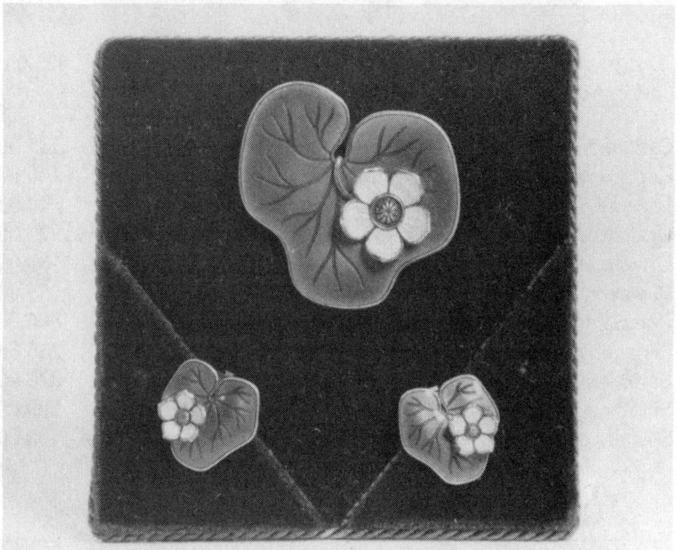

Set, enamel over sterling with gold wash, signed David Anderson, $145.00.

Ring, 9k, cluster: pearl & 7 sm Persian turq, Victorian 95.00
Ring, 9k, lg oval sardonyx cameo profile, plain shank 75.00
Ring, 9k, lt brn cameo w/Victorian gent, oval, ⅝″ 75.00
Ring, 9k, lt pk cameo, lady's portrait, ⅝″ 95.00
Ring, 9k, 2ct lt bl topaz, untreated, ornate mt 85.00
Ring, 9k, ¾ct emerald, sm wht spinel ea side, X-over mt 75.00
Ring, 9k, 3ct oval red tourmaline, scroll eng shoulders 150.00
Ring, 9k, 6 Persian turq cluster+sm rose-cut dia w/in star 110.00
Ring, 9k, 9.50 natural bl topaz, split shoulders, '30s 225.00
Stickpin, gw heart shape w/lt bl stone 8.00
Stickpin, lg pearl w/bow of brilliants+3 lg brilliants 6.00
Stickpin, pinchbeck, flower cameo+4 seed pearls, ⅜x½″ 45.00
Stickpin, pinchbeck, rvpt dog portrait, Essex crystal, ⅝″ 55.00
Stickpin, 18k/pinchbeck, faux ruby+10 sm jets in cluster 45.00
Tie bar & cuff links, Siamese sterling, Bali dancers 30.00
Watch chain, gf dbl link ⅜″ W w/2½″ eng links, w/fob 25.00
Watch chain, sterling curb links, hallmark 1884, 14″ 50.00
Watch chain, ¾x3″ gf mesh w/playing card dangle 35.00
Watch key, silver, knot in center, Victorian, 1½″ 30.00

Jewelry Boxes

Jewelry boxes have been made from metals of every type, wood, ivory, glass and china, some adorned with 'jewels' themselves, porcelain inserts, filigree work, or figural forms. Jewelry boxes of a long rectangular form, usually on legs and designed in the Art Nouveau style, are called jewelry caskets. Today, these have become popular collectibles.

When no condition is indicated, the items listed below are assumed to be in excellent condition.

Left to right; Art Nouveau casket with silver wash, 2½″ x 4″, $25.00; Casket with daisies on hinged lid, silver wash, 1¾″, $10.00.

Casket, SP heart shape w/repousse floral, Pairpoint 135.00
Copper, ball/claw ft, lion's heads, coins atop, ornate 100.00
Lacquer, blk w/MOP inlay, musical, rising drw & mirror, 8″ 40.00
Ormolu w/oval blk glass inserts w/HP birds, Moreau, 4x3x5″ . . . 275.00
Ormolu w/2¼″ HP portrait on ivory, eng, oval, 5¼x3¼″ 165.00
Poplar, blk pnt w/mc oval scene & floral spandrels, 3½x17″ 55.00
Porcelain, Rococo, HP figural landscape, Sevres, 8″ L 800.00
Serpentine, bird portrait, inlaid onyx stones, ftd, 2¾″ 255.00
Silver repousse w/Egyptian figures, Continental, 5″ L 325.00
Silver repousse w/tavern scene w/in, oval, Fr, 4½″ L 200.00
Spelter, gilt w/floral relief, scroll ring hdl, 5x5x4½″ 100.00

Judaica

The items listed below are representative of objects used in both the secular and religious life of the Jewish people. They are evident of a culture where silversmiths, painters, engravers, writers, and metal workers were highly gifted and skilled in their art. Most of the treasures shown in recently displayed exhibits of Judaica were confiscated by the Germans during the late 1930s up to 1945; by then eight Jewish synagogues and fifty warehouses had been filled with Hitler's plunder.

When no condition is indicated, the items listed below are assumed to be in excellent condition.

Amulet case, Italian silver-gilt, repousse cartouch, 4″ 1,800.00
Beaker, ceremonial, silver, repousse grapes, 3″; +6″ tray 335.00
Beaker, clear/gilt, eng vignette, German, 1750s, 4″ 900.00
Belt buckle, Polish silver, Day of Atonement, 1840, 2⅞″ 1,100.00
Candlestick, Sabbath; silver cylinder stem/sq base, 7″, pr 600.00
Circumcision knife, parcel-gilt German silver, 1806, 6″ 1,100.00
Esther scroll, eng Polish silver case, bird atop, 7″ 800.00
Esther scroll, Palestine silver, presentation, 5″ 1,200.00
Etrog container, Austrian silver, chased, emb w/lion, 6″ 600.00
Hanuka lamp, Moroccan brass, pierced birds & foliage, 11″ 350.00

Hanukah lamp, Austrian silver, marked AK, Vienna, 1841, 6½″, $1,500.00.

Marriage contract, Italian, parchment, 1880, 24x19″ 1,200.00
Marriage cup, German silver, tumbler w/inscription, 1800 . . . . . . 600.00
Menorah, silver w/acanthus repousse, branches, star, 5½″ 385.00
Noisemaker, pierced, whistle hdl, Am silver, 1878, 4″ 600.00
Seder plate, Geman pewter, order of seder chasing, 12″ 2,500.00
Seder plate, German silver, cast inscription & flowers, 16″ . . . 4,000.00
Spice box, can w/floral repousse, crimp ft, flag atop, 8″ 150.00
Spice tower, Polish silver filigree, eng presentation, 12″ 4,250.00
Torah mantle, embr silk, continental, 1700s, 29″ L 800.00
Torah pointer, Polish silver, tube w/3 knobs, inscription 1,100.00
Tray, bread; silver w/gold, verse, star & wheat, 15½x11″ 1,175.00

Jugtown

The Jugtown Pottery was started about 1920 by Juliana and Jacques Busbee, in Moore County, North Carolina. Ben Owen, a young descendant of a Staffordshire potter, was hired in 1923. He was the master potter, while the Busbees experimented with perfecting glazes and supervising design and modeling. Preferred shapes were those reminiscent of traditional country wares, and classic Oriental forms. Glazes were various: natural clay oranges, buffs, 'tobacco spit' brown, mirror black, white, 'frogskin' green, a lovely turquoise called Chinese blue, and the traditional cobalt decorated salt glaze. The pottery gained national recognition and as a result of their success, several other local potteries were established. Jugtown closed in 1959.

When no condition is indicated, the items listed below are assumed to be in mint condition.

Bowl, Chinese, bl, flared w/sm base, 4x8¾″ 180.00
Bowl, Chinese, red/bl, 4½x7″ 290.00
Creamer, gray w/bl lining, simple bl rim decor, 4″ 40.00
Creamer, redware, clear glaze w/brn speckles, sgn, 3¼″ 55.00
Jar, brn, hdls, w/lid, 9″ 50.00
Jardiniere, gr semi-gloss, 2 flat hdls, 5½x6¾″ 30.00
Plate, brn, 10″ 15.00
Plate, pumpkin color, 8⅝″ 45.00
Tea set, onionskin, cobalt design, 3-pc 100.00
Vase, Chinese, bl w/lg areas of red, 5x6½″ 200.00
Vase, Chinese, bl w/red, 7x7″ 225.00
Vase, Chinese, bl w/red veins, 4x2¾″ 140.00
Vase, Chinese, bl w/red veins, 5½x7″ 200.00
Vase, Chinese, gr drip on reddish bkground, bulbous, 6″ 255.00
Vase, Chinese, gr on upper body only, 5¾″ 150.00
Vase, Chinese, gr/brn/red, baluster w/sm rim hdls, 8″ 325.00
Vase, Chinese, gr/red thick gloss, 7½x3½″ 260.00
Vase, Chinese, much red, 4″ 250.00
Vase, Chinese, red/bl drip top half only, red clay, 5½″ 200.00
Vase, frogskin, sgn, 3x2½″ 60.00
Vase, gr-bl w/red & wht semi-gloss mottle, simple form, 5″ 225.00

Vase, Chinese blue with wine drip glaze, 6″ x 7″, $295.00.

K. P. M. Porcelain

Under the tutelage of Frederick the Great, King of Prussia, porcelain manufacture was instituted in Berlin in 1751 by William K. Wegeley. In jealous competition with Meissen, hard paste porcelain was produced--dinnerware, figurines, vases, etc.--some of which were undecorated while other pieces were hand painted in Watteau scenes, landscapes, or florals. It soon became evident that the factory was unable to offer serious competition. The King withdrew his support and the factory failed in 1757.

In 1761, Johann Ernst Gotzkowsky bought the rights and attempted a similar operation which soon failed due to financial difficulties. Still determined to gain the same recognition enjoyed by Meissen, the King bought the plant in 1763, and ruled the operation with an iron hand, often assuring his success by taking advantage of his position. The King died in 1786, but production has continued and quality tableware and decorative porcelains are still being made on a commercial basis.

Earliest marks were simply 'G' or 'W,' followed by the sceptre mark. After 1830, 'K.P.M.' with an orb or eagle was adopted.

When no condition is indicated, the items listed below are assumed to be in mint condition.

Female in flowing gown, marked KPM #1361, with crossed swords, 11½″, $600.00 in mint condition.

Bowl, floral, sgn, oval, 12″ 60.00
Chocolate pot, floral, 9½″ 47.50
Creamer, mc cherubs, orb & sceptre mks, 1870, 4½″ 290.00
Plaque, Assumption of the Virgin, sgn C Aut, 22x18″ 3,000.00
Plaque, Christ wearing crown of thorns, 12½x10″ 2,000.00
Plaque, Cupid & Psyche float in clouds, Walberg, 9x6⅜″ 1,760.00
Plaque, Daphne, ¾ pose/laurel wreath, after Kiesel, 12x10″ . . . 3,500.00
Plaque, lady w/7 children/husband, after Kaulbach, 11x8¾″ . . . 2,970.00
Plaque, landscape w/fir trees, Schmuz-Baudiss, 14x14″ 660.00
Plaque, nun sits in chair by arch window, Eckardt, 13x8″ 2,500.00
Plaque, Ruth, gray gown/holds wheat, after Landelle, 9x6½″ . . 1,800.00
Plate, Cupid at various pursits on bl, gilt rim, 9″, 6 for 990.00
Plate, fruit in center, HP, gold borders, 8⅝″, set of 8 . . . . 800.00
Plate, leaf form w/florals & gilt, orb & sceptre mk, 8½″ 185.00
Vase, jeweled trim, bl Caducaus mk, 8″ 1,100.00

Kayserzinn Pewter

J.P. Kayser Sohn produced pewter decorated in the Art Nouveau manner in Germany during the late 1800s and into the 20th century. Examples are marked with 'Kayserzinn' and the mould number within an elongated oval reserve.

When no condition is indicated, the items listed below are assumed to be in mint condition.

Card tray, nude, ocean waves relief, 8″, $165.00.

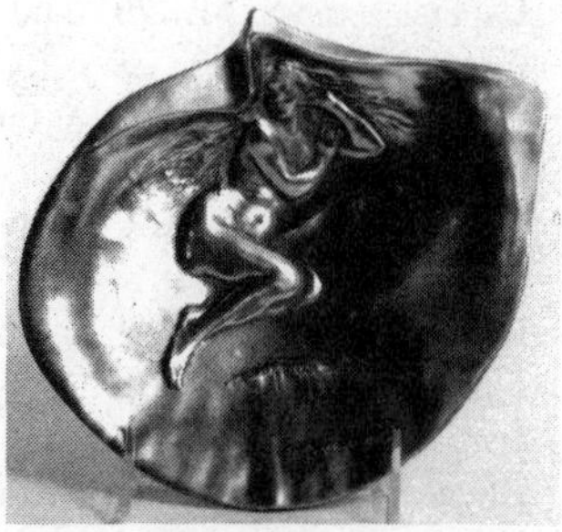

Bowl, #4065, ftd, 10″ 50.00
Bowl, floral, 4″ 38.00
Bowl, lg water lily in center, dragonflies, scalloped, 10″ 68.00
Bowl, tulips, leaves extend past fluted rim, sgn, 11x11″ 68.00
Cake plate, lilies, #4134, 11″ 80.00
Holy water font, sgn 79.00

Inkwell & pen tray, relief face on lid, #4333, 5½x7″ 500.00
Knife rest, dachshund 57.50
Lamp, oil; #4439, Aladdin, 10″ 160.00
Plate, shell scroll 1 side rim, rest lillies/insects, 11″ 68.00
Plate, 3 pods w/water lilies coming from ea, 11½″ 60.00
Stein, eagle-beak spout, wings on base, 13½″ 495.00
Vase, wheat & butterflies, #4310, 7¾″ 115.00

Keen Kutter

Keen Kutter was a brand name of E.C. Simmons Hardware, used from about 1870 until the mid-1930s. In 1923, Winchester merged with Simmons, but continued to produce Keen Kutter marked knives and tools. The merger dissolved and in 1940 the Simmons Company was purchased by Shapleigh Hardware. Older items are very collectible.

For further study, we recommend *Keen Kutter*, an illustrated price guide by Jerry and Elaine Heuring, available at your favorite bookstore or public library. When no condition is indicated, the items listed below are assumed to be in excellent condition.

Apple parer, pares and ejects, patent date May 24, 1898, $50.00.

Auger bits, set of 7 in roll-up case, from ¼″ to 1″ 40.00
Barrel hatchet, 3¼″ 22.00
Bit brace, hand-held ratchet type 45.00
Box tool, plated, 9″ 35.00
Broad axe, large logo 120.00
Butcher knives, #K160, pr, MIB 30.00
Butcher steel, w/brass logo for guard, 14″ 25.00
Cabinet scraper, #KK79, 2-hdl 35.00
Carpenter pinchers 10.00
Cutlery set, SP, 6 knives & forks, w/box 55.00
Dental snips, #K-11-D 10.00
Display case, for knives, 4-sided, mk on top & all glasses 110.00
Drain spade 15.00
Drawing knife, 8″ blade length, Keen Kutter written out 18.00
Food chopper, #KK10 .... 7.00
Garden trowel 10.00
Hammer, #KA7, rnd neck, curved claw, 7-oz 40.00
Hammer, ballpein; 24-oz 30.00
Hammer, straight claw, steel hdl w/rubber grip, 20-oz 20.00
Hammer, tack; magnetic, w/Keen Kutter on side 20.00
Hedge shears 15.00
Lapel pin, axe design, Simmons Keen Kutter 45.00
Lawn mower, push; rubber tires, Keen Kutter on wheels/hdl 25.00
Leather punch 8.00
Level, #KK3, adjustable, w/brass ends, 12″ 50.00
Level, #K69, CI, 9″ 75.00
Marking gauge 25.00
Meat & food cutter, #KK22, complete w/cookbook & box 25.00
Name plate, solid brass, from showcase 50.00
Oil stone, #K8, in orig cardboard box 30.00
Pipe vise, #KP200, ⅛″ to 2″ capacity 35.00
Plane, bench; #K8, iron, smooth bottom, 24″ 45.00
Plane, block; #KK103, iron, adjustable, 5⅜″ 20.00
Plane, rabbet; #KK190, 8″ 55.00
Pliers, 75-degree combination slip joint 25.00
Plumb bob, cone shape, screw top, 16-oz 20.00
Post-hole digger 15.00
Razor, junior safety; metal hdl, w/box 20.00
Razor, straight; #K15, folds into blk hdl w/logo 30.00
Razor hone, #K15, in pasteboard box 40.00
Razor strop, #K94, professional combo, dbl swing, 24x2½″ 35.00
Rip-saw blade, 8″, MIB 30.00
Ruler, folding; #K680, wooden, 24″ 20.00
Saw tool, for one-or two-man cross-cut saw 18.00
Scratch awl, red plastic hdl 8.00
Shears, curved blade, 9″ 10.00
Square, T-bevel, 10″ blade 20.00
Sweep, #KA14, 14″ 30.00
Tobacco cutter, mk EC Simmons/Keen Kutter/St Louis/USA 175.00
Tool cabinet, wall; oak, 27½x19x8″ 200.00
Upholster shears, 10″ 15.00
Waffle iron 125.00
Wrench, adjustable; chromium, 8″ 20.00
Wrench, pipe; 12″ 25.00
Wrench, screw; wood knife hdl, Black Jack under logo, 8″ 30.00

Kelva

Kelva was a trademark of the C.F. Monroe Company of Meriden, Connecticut, used on an opaque mold-blown glassware that was hand decorated with pastel florals and often set in ormolu holders. It was very similar to the company's other lines, Nakara and Wave Crest; only those pieces bearing the Kelva mark are listed here. All three types were in production from about 1900 until WWI.

When no condition is indicated, the items listed below are assumed to be in mint condition.

Box, bl w/apple blossoms, rnd ormolu collar, 4½″ 345.00
Box, gr w/beaded ribbon/pink floral, ormolu collar, 3½″ 425.00
Box, gr w/blown-out maple leaf on top, octagonal, 5″ 400.00
Box, jewel; olive gr, sgn, 8″ 875.00
Box, poppies on lid, ormolu base, rnd, ftd, 4″ 425.00
Humidor, 'Cigars,' str sides, 4¾″ 525.00
Pin dish, silver rim, hexagonal 165.00
Planter, lilies on pink, brass rim, 8″ 450.00
Vase, daisies on pink in bl reserve, 8″ 400.00

Bowl, pink with floral, ormolu collar, 2½″ x 8″, $175.00.

Kent

Kent was a small village in Ohio where several glasshouses were located in the very early 1800s. Experts are often able to attribute early examples to this area since it is felt that they exclusively used a particular number of swirls and diamonds in their molds.

When no condition is indicated, the items listed below are assumed to be undamaged.

Bottle, ½-post, 24-rib broken swirl, lt yel-gr, 4¾″............600.00
Bottle, 20 swirl ribs, globular, yel-amber, 6½″, NM..........200.00
Flask, chestnut; 24 swirl ribs, gold-olive, 6½″, EX...........450.00
Pan, 20-rib, folded-in rim, lt gr, 2½x8½″......................365.00
Pan, 20-rib broken swirl, folded rim, gr-aqua, 4½x1½″, NM....500.00
Pan, 24 vertical ribs, terminal ring, folded rim, aqua, 5″.......175.00
Tumbler, 20-rib broken swirl, EX mold, yel-amber, 4½″......2,000.00

Kenton Hills

Kenton Hills Porcelain was established in 1940 in Erlanger, Kentucky by Harold Bopp, former Rookwood superintendent, and David Seyler, noted artist and sculptor. Native clay was used; glazes were very similar to those that were currently being used at Rookwood. The work was of high quality, but because of the restrictions imposed on needed material due to the onset of the war, the operation failed in 1942. Much of the ware is artist signed and marked with the Kenton Hill name or cipher and shape number.

When no condition is indicated, the items listed below are assumed to be in mint condition.

Vase, turquoise glaze, 7¼″, $125.00.

Bookends, turtles, pr..165.00
Vase, bl bottle w/brn line decor, W Hentschel, 6½″..........175.00
Vase, bl leaves/berries on wht, Boop mk/sgn Hentschel, 12″....325.00
Vase, horse heads/line & ball band, sgn Hentschel, 5¾″.......170.00
Vase, relief decor, Arthur Conant, 6″...........................140.00
Vase, rust floral on bl gloss, sgn D Seyler, U-form, 9″........275.00

Kew Blas

Kew Blas was a trade name used by the Union Glass Company of Somerville, Massachusetts, for their iridescent art glass produced from 1890 until about 1920. The glass was made in imitation of Tiffany, and achieved notable success.

When no condition is indicated, the items listed below are assumed to be in mint condition.

Bowl, dk gr, bl w/in, ruffled, sgn, 8½″......................800.00
Finger bowl, gold, ruffled.......................................275.00
Salt cellar, gold..185.00
Sherbet, irid gold, sgn, 5″......................................200.00
Vase, zipper motif, gr & gold, sgn, 7¾″.......................850.00
Vase, zipper motif, tan, gr, gold, sgn, 4½″....................500.00

King's Rose

King's Rose is a soft paste ware that was made in Staffordshire, England, from about 1820 to 1830. It is closely related to Gaudy Dutch in body type as well as the colors used in its decoration. The pattern consists of a large full-blown orange-red rose with green, pink, and yellow leaves and accents.

When no condition is indicated, the items listed below are assumed to be in mint condition.

Coffee pot, oyster, pink band border, sm prof rpr, 11½″.......395.00
Cup & saucer, handleless; line border, set of 4..............340.00
Cup & saucer, handleless; stains/flaking/ring chips.............45.00
Cup & saucer, scalloped rim...................................145.00
Plate, oyster pattern, minor wear, 7″............................70.00
Plate, Queen's Rose, 6½″.......................................125.00
Plate, sectional border, 8″, EX..................................75.00
Plate, solid border, minor wear, 8″..............................85.00
Plate, vine border, 8½″ EX.......................................85.00
Platter, sectional border, 12½″.................................250.00
Saucer, vine border..30.00
Soup plate, sectional border, 9″...............................150.00
Toddy, vine border, 5¾″..70.00

Kitchen Collectibles

During the last half of the 1850s, mass-produced kitchen gadgets were patented at an astonishing rate. Most were ingeniously efficient. Apple peelers, egg beaters, cherry pitters, food choppers, and such were only the most common of hundreds of kitchen tools well designed to perform only specific tasks. Today all are very collectible.

When no condition is indicated, glassware and pottery items listed below are assumed to be mint; gadgets and patented tools are assumed excellent.

See also Appliances, Electric; Molds; Primitives; Tinware; Wooden Ware

Glassware

Bottle, water; gr, w/cap, 32-oz...................................17.00
Bowl, batter; gr..14.00
Bowl, mixing; crisscross, bl, 9½″................................25.00
Bowl, mixing; delphite, 9″..25.00
Bowl, mixing; gr, 16-oz...16.00
Bowl, mixing; wht glass, tulip decor, 9½″........................6.00
Bowl, refrigerator; red, w/lid, 6¼″..............................10.00
Bowl, utility; red, 4″..4.00
Butter dish, ribbed, transparent gr...............................34.75
Canister, coffee; emerald gr, Depression era, 7½″..............20.00
Canister, spice; peacock bl.......................................45.00
Canister, sugar; gr, 40-oz..35.00
Canister, tea; emerald gr, Depression era, 5½″.................16.00
Canister, tea; peacock bl...125.00

Cookie jar, ribbed, wire stand, tin lid.......................55.00
Dispenser, water; clambroth...............................37.50
Double boiler...15.00
Jar, pretzel; w/lid, gr.....................................35.00
Mayonnaise maker, Wesson..................................18.00
Measure, teaspoon...20.00
Measuring cup, w/beater insert, Depression, gr, 1-qt..........38.00
Measuring cup, 3-spout, 8-oz...............................12.00
Measuring cup, 4-pc, jadite.................................32.00
Pitcher, milk; delphite, Pyrex..............................30.00
Platter, meat; transparent bl, w/tree well, Pyrex..............14.00
Water dispenser, for refrigerator, w/spout, lt bl, 12x6″........185.00

Apple peeler, Goodell, dtd 1849...........................48.00
Apple peeler, Goodell, dtd 1899...........................42.00
Apple peeler, Goodell Turnable '98, 11″....................30.00
Apple peeler, Harbster Bros, CI, 1867......................50.00
Apple peeler, Hudson, CI, pat 1862.........................50.00
Apple peeler, Little Star...................................25.00
Apple peeler, Locky, late 1800s............................35.00
Apple peeler, Monroe Bros, Fitchburg, Massachusetts, 1856.....65.00
Apple peeler, Reading Hardware Co, CI......................65.00
Apple peeler, Sinclair Scott Co, Baltimore, 8-gear.............42.50
Apple peeler, White Mountain #3...........................35.00
Apple peeler, wood/wood fly wheel & crank, rpr/rpl, 32″........75.00
Baking rack, for potatoes, tin, 1909........................27.00
Beater, electric, w/gr bowl.................................18.00
Bottle opener, Rumford.....................................15.00
Bread maker, Universal #4..................................50.00
Cabbage cutter, Kraut Kutter, box type, Indianapolis #64.......38.00
Cabbage cutter, wood, Tucker & Dorsey, 16x6¼″.............18.00
Canning jar filler, tin, 1897................................12.00
Cherry seeder, Enterprise, iron, clamp type, 1883.............25.00
Cherry seeder, Enterprise #16, dbl.........................36.00
Cherry seeder, Holman, iron, clamp type.....................25.00
Cherry seeder, Home, dtd 1917.............................35.00
Cherry seeder, New Standard...............................20.00
Cherry seeder, Rollman #3.................................35.00
Chopper, Enterprise, clamp type............................25.00
Chopper, lg wrought steel crescent, curly maple hdl...........30.00
Chopper, wide sgn blade, trn wood hdls ea end, 10¾″.........25.00
Chopping board, maple, w/sides & juice grooves...............30.00
Churn, dk tin, crank hdl, 1-gal.............................65.00
Churn, glass, Dazey #40, pat 1922.........................50.00
Clothes dryer, Empire, Am Wringer Co, NY, hanger type........70.00
Clothes sprinkler, Chinaman figural, Sprinkle Plenty............20.00
Coffee measure, Dix coffee meter, dk tin, unusual.............38.00
Conservo canner & steam cooker, 1907, NM...................65.00
Cracker pricker/cutter, tin, scalloped edge, hdl................85.00
Cream whip, tin, Rumford, 1908............................15.00
Dipper, brass & wrought iron, FBS, pat Jan 26, '86, 14″......135.00
Dispenser, coffee; aluminum................................30.00
Egg beater, A&J, spiral hdl, wood knob, 1923..................8.00
Egg beater, CI, 1888.......................................27.50
Egg beater, Dover, 1891, 1½″ dia..........................21.00
Egg beater, Dover, 1904....................................18.00
Egg beater, Ladd #0, spiral hdl, pat 1908....................10.00
Flour sifter, Foley...8.00
Fly covers, screen wire, set of 5, 6½″ to 10½″..............165.00
Fly trap, screen wire, spherical, 1800s.......................50.00
Fly trap, tin w/screen slant sides, wire loop hdl, 9½″ H.........45.00
Food grinder, Enterprise #22................................20.00
Food grinder, Griswold #1110...............................35.00
Food grinder, Universal #1, w/attachments, orig box...........25.00
Food grinder, Universal #3, wood hdl, EX....................15.00
Fork/skimmer combination tool, CI, swivels, pat '09, 17″.......40.00
Fruit jar opener, Triumph, Forbes Chocolate, pat '03..........12.00
Fruit press, Wearever, aluminum, table model, 1920s..........12.00
Funnel, tin, ½-gal...12.00
Grater, cheese; hanging, wood & punched tin, w/drawer.......145.00
Grater, chocolate; Edgar, pat Nov 10, 1896.................185.00
Grater, Gilmore, hanging, tin, 1897.........................12.00
Grater, hand-punched dk tin ½-round, on pine board w/hdl....65.00
Grater, nutmeg; Bee Brand, dk tin, sm.......................18.00
Grater, nutmeg; Edgar, pat Aug 8, 1891-1896................65.00
Grater, nutmeg; iron cup on pierced disc, cranks, blk hdl.......65.00
Grater, nutmeg; The Boye, tin, narrow oblong w/sliding box.....60.00
Grater, pumpkin; pine, curved top & bottom, 24x6½″..........60.00
Grater, spice; Enterprise, mechanical iron clamp, 1890s........45.00
Grater, spice; Spong #0, wall mt, blk, EX....................35.00
Grater, wood & tin, wall hanging, 12″.......................27.50
Ice box, golden oak, rstr & rfn............................400.00
Ice box, mk Century Refrigerator/Beddey-Hall, not electric.....385.00
Ice box, oak, 2 glass & 2 wooden doors, 45x64″.............475.00
Ice cream freezer, dk tin, mk Kress, dtd 7/23/1912, 1-qt........32.00
Ice cream freezer, metal, Acme, pat 1910.....................38.00
Ice tongs, wood hdl, Ice & Fuel Co..........................15.00
Kraut chopper, 8½″ oval iron blade, long wood hdl, 22″.......48.00
Kraut masher, 1-pc wood, 27x2¾″...........................38.00
Lemon squeezer, maple, hinged, 2-part.......................55.00
Masher, potato; hand-carved wood..........................12.00
Masher, potato; wire twist, wood hdls.......................15.50
Measuring cup, 3-spout.....................................13.00
Meat cleaver, wolf head Evansville trademk..................35.00
Meat fork, Rumford...20.00
Meat tenderizer, dbl ended, iron, wood hdl, 1892, 10″ L.......20.00
Meat tenderizer, stoneware w/Albany slip, pat 1877, 9″, EX.....75.00
Meat tenderizer, wood..8.00
Meat/fruit press, Enterprise..................................48.00
Meat/fruit press, Wilders, pat 12/1906, dk tin, oblong..........45.00
Pan, popover; Griswold, 11-hole, EX........................30.00
Peach peeler, Sinclair Scott, Baltimore.......................45.00
Pestle, wood, trn hdl & ridges, 12″..........................25.00
Pie cover, tin, dtd 1899.....................................35.00
Pie wheel, brass, tooled, copper rivets, 4¼″..................75.00
Pie wheel, brass, 5⅝″......................................40.00
Pie wheel, brass w/serrated wheel, heart shaped end, 4″........45.00
Pie wheel, dbl, iron w/sm brass wheel, pat 18(?), 5¾″........150.00
Pie wheel, hand-forged iron, single wheel, curved hdl, 4″......150.00
Pie wheel, whalebone, trn wood hdl, 4¾″.....................80.00
Pie wheel, whalebone hdl/brass trim, copper wheel, 7½″.......225.00
Pot scrubber, wire rings.....................................18.00
Potato peeler, Hamlinite, 1920..............................33.00
Pudding steamer, dk tin, fluted, tube center, w/lid, lg..........35.00
Raisin seeder, Enterprise #36...............................35.00
Raisin seeder, Enterprise, iron, clamp-type, 1895..............25.00

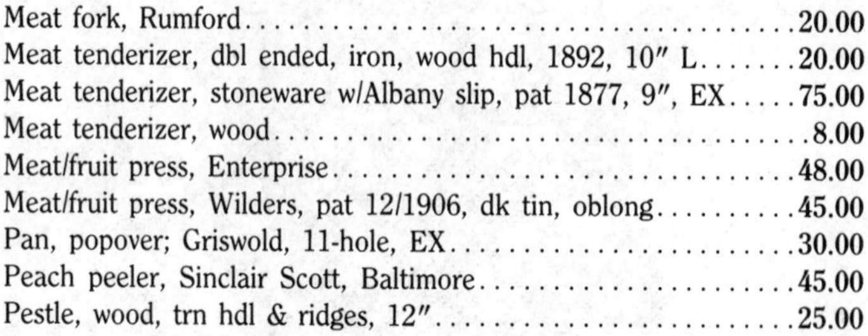

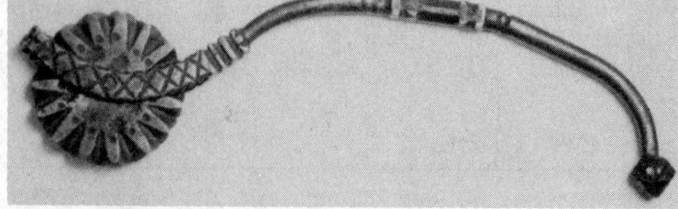

Pastry jagger, hand-wrought iron, late 18th century, 6¼″, $95.00.

Bean slicer, Alexanderwerk, 1078 (?), 11″, $45.00.

Raisin seeder, Gem, pat 1895....32.00
Raisin seeder, instructions on hdl: Scald Raisins, pat, 6″....80.00
Raisin seeder, Lightning #901....50.00
Rolling pin, amber, blown, Stoddard, New Hampshire....140.00
Rolling pin, amethyst, blown....150.00
Rolling pin, bottle gr, blown, 14″....125.00
Rolling pin, clear glass w/screw-on cap, 16″....25.00
Rolling pin, cobalt, blown, 14¼″....180.00
Rolling pin, dk amber, blown....105.00
Rolling pin, ebony, blown....140.00
Rolling pin, etched, crystal, blown, 15½″....75.00
Rolling pin, etched floral, crystal, blown, 14¼″....50.00
Rolling pin, milk glass, aluminum hdl....45.00
Rolling pin, milk glass, My True Love, 15″....185.00
Rolling pin, peacock bl....150.00
Rolling pin, stoneware w/maple hdls, blk eagle, 18½″....175.00
Sifter, Blood's pat 1861, wood: body/hdl/2 rollers....200.00
Sifter, Magic, oblong, dbl screen, instruction on ext....42.00
Sifter, sugar; dome screen bottom/wooden roller/crank hdl....175.00
Skillet, CI, Griswold #8, w/lid....35.00
Skimmer, brass & wrought iron, minor splits, 27″....125.00
Skimmer, brass w/flattened wrought iron hdl, loop end, 19″....105.00
Skimmer, brass w/well-shaped wrought iron hdl, 23½″, EX....145.00
Slicer, CI, mechanical, clamp-on, pat 1877....75.00
Slicer, potato; CI, clamp-on, mechanical, rnd disk, 1870....85.00
Spatula, Betty's Best Flour, heart shape....22.00
Spatula, brass & wrought iron, 15⅛″....75.00
Spatula, brass & wrought iron, 18¾″....105.00
Spoon, slotted, Rumford....15.00
Strawberry huller, brass, 1894....20.00
Toaster, for fireplace, maltese cross wire, wood hdl....37.00
Toaster, pyramid, wire racks....9.00
Waffle iron, CI w/wrought hdls, sq, 24½″....30.00
Waffle iron, Crusco #8, w/holder....35.00
Waffle iron, Griswold #8....50.00
Waffle iron, Griswold #9, pat 1880....75.00
Waffle iron, Wagner, pat Feb 22/1910, sq....50.00
Washboard, wood, w/redware scrub surface, regular sz, rare....225.00

Knives

Knife collecting as a hobby began in earnest during the 1960s when government regulations required for the first time that knife companies mark their product with the country of origin. The few collectors and dealers cognizant of this change at once began stockpiling the older knives made before this law was enacted. Another impetus to the growing interest in this area came with the Gun Control Act of 1968, which severely restricted gun trading. Frustrated gun dealers transferred their attention to knives. Today there are collectors clubs in many of the states.

The ones to look for are old bone handled knives in mint, unsharpened condition, pearl handles, Case doctor's knives, and large display models.

When no condition is indicated, the items listed below are assumed to be in mint condition.

Pocket Knives

Boker, Tree Brand, 5821, silver hdl, 4 blades, 3¼″....80.00
Boker, Tree Brand, 5856, pearl hdl, 3 blades, 3″....80.00
Boker, Tree Brand, 5949, stag hdl, 3 blades, 3⅞″....100.00
Boker, Tree Brand, 6189, hard rubber hdl, 4 blades, 3½″....28.00
Boker, Tree Brand, 6198, wht bone hdl, 2 blades, 3⅜″....60.00
Boker, Tree Brand, 6402, ebony hdl, 3 blades, 3⅜″....50.00
Boker, Tree Brand, 6514, nickel silver hdl, 2 blades, 3″....36.00
Boker, Tree Brand, 6608, celluloid hdl, 2 blades, 3⅞″....28.00
Boker, Tree Brand, 6999, gun metal hdl, 3 blades, 3″....50.00
Boker, Tree Brand, 9215, cocoa hdl, 1 blade, 4″....36.00
Boker, Tree Brand, 9302, silver hdl, 2 blades, 3½″....60.00
Boker, Tree Brand, 9633GB, gray buff hdl, 2 blades, 3¼″....36.00
Boker, Tree Brand, 9719, ebony hdl, 2 blades, 3¾″....40.00
Boker, Tree Brand, 9904, pearl hdl, 2 blades, 2⅞″....50.00
Boker, Tree Brand, 9974BW, compo hdl, 2 blades, 3¼″....28.00
Case, C61050 SAB, red bone hdl, 1 blade, tested....210.00
Case, Muskrat, gr bone hdl, 2 blades, tested, 3⅞″....210.00
Case, P197 L SS, blk pakkawood, dots, 4¾″....62.00
Case, P197L SS, blk pakkawood hdl, dots, 1 blade, 4¾″....62.00
Case, S2, XX, sterling silver hdl, 2 blades, 2¼″....75.00
Case, W1216, wire hdl, 1 blade, tested, 3⅛″....62.00
Case, 11011, walnut hdl, 1 blade, tested, 4″....55.00
Case, 310050, cream compo hdl, 1 blade, tested, 5⅛″....175.00
Case, 4200 SS, XX, wht compo hdl, 2 blades, 5½″....110.00
Case, 51215G, bone stag horn hdl, 1 blade, tested, 5″....320.00
Case, 52131, stag hdl, 2 blades, tested, 3⅝″....210.00
Case, 5214½, stag hdl, 2 blades, tested....150.00
Case, 53047, XX, stag hdl, 3 blades....60.00
Case, 5393, stag hdl, tested....240.00
Case, 54052, stag hdl, 4 blades, tested, 3½″....175.00
Case, 6100, gr bone hdl, 1 blade, tested....355.00
Case, 61013, gr bone hdl, 1 blade, tested, 4″....75.00
Case, 6104B, gr bone hdl, 1 blade, tested, 3⅜″....120.00
Case, 61048 SP, USA, Delrin hdl, 1 blade....22.00
Case, 6143, bone hdl, dots, 1 blade....18.00
Case, 6207, XX, gr bone hdl, 2 blades....90.00
Case, 62109X, XX, rough blk hdl, 2 blades, 3⅛″....46.00
Case, 6227, XX, bone hdl, 2 blades, 2¾″....24.00
Case, 6231½, XX, gr bone hdl, 2 blades....62.00
Case, 6235 EO, XX, bone hdl, 2 blades....105.00
Case, 6308, XX, rough blk hdl, 3 blades....97.00
Case, 6318, USA, bone hdl, 3 blades....45.00
Case, 6347 SH SP, gr bone hdl, 3 blades, tested....120.00
Case, 6383, XX, red bone hdl, 3 blades....72.00
Case, 6383 SAB, XX, bone hdl, 3 blades....150.00
Case, 6445R, rough blk hdl, 4 blades, tested....75.00
Case, 6488, bone hdl, 4 blades, transitions....25.00
Case, 6488, XX, rough blk hdl, 4 blades....125.00
Case, 83081, pearl hdl, 3 blades, tested, 3″....120.00
Case, 9229½, XX, imitation pearl hdl, 2 blades....62.00
Case, 9344, imitation hdl, 3 blades, tested....90.00
Case, 94047P, imitation pearl hdl, 4 blades, tested, 4″....175.00

Cattaraugus, 10851, French ivory hdl, 1 blade, 3⅛"...........38.00
Cattaraugus, 11057, cocobola hdl, 4⅛"......................34.00
Cattaraugus, 11704, celluloid hdl, 1 blade, 4"................90.00
Cattaraugus, 12099L, stag hdl w/lock, 1 blade, 4½"...........130.00
Cattaraugus, 12829, stag hdl, 1 blade, 5⅜"................510.00
Cattaraugus, 2013, mother of pearl hdl, 1 blade & file, 3"......55.00
Cattaraugus, 2022 OP, opal pearl hdl, 2 blades, 3⅜"..........55.00
Cattaraugus, 20232, French pearl hdl, 2 blades, 3"............32.00
Cattaraugus, 20701, wht fiberloid hdl, 2 blades, 3¾"..........45.00
Cattaraugus, 21259, stag hdl, 2 blades, 3½"..................80.00
Cattaraugus, 32794, fiberloid hdl, 3"........................90.00
Cattaraugus, 32976, ebony hdl, 3 blades, 3½"................95.00
Cattaraugus, 42172, French pearl hdl, 4 blades, 3⅞"..........95.00
Cattaraugus, 4509, stag hdl, 4 blades, 3"....................95.00
Remington, R191, redwood hdl, 2 blades......................80.00
Remington, R21, redwood hdl, 2 blades.......................45.00
Remington, R328, cocobola hdl, 2 blades.....................75.00
Remington, R392, blk hdl, 2 blades..........................90.00
Remington, R432, blk hdl, 2 blades, 3½"....................65.00
Remington, R475, pyremite hdl, 2 blades.....................80.00
Remington, R53, stag hdl, 2 blades..........................85.00
Remington, R590, buffalo horn hdl, 2 blades.................90.00
Remington, R609, nickel silver hdl, 2 blades, 3⅜"............70.00
Remington, R7026, stag hdl, 3 blades........................75.00
Remington, R75, pyremite hdl, 2 blades......................65.00
Russell, 0170, model stag hdl, 1 blade, 3⅞"................140.00
Russell, 0270, model stag hdl, 2 blades, 3⅞"...............196.00
Russell, 0277, model stag hdl, 2 blades, 3¾"...............220.00
Russell, 052, model stag hdl, 2 blades, 3⅜"................200.00
Russell, 1118, iron hdl, 1 blade, 3½"......................116.00
Russell, 2102, cocoa hdl, 1 blade, 3⅜".....................136.00
Russell, 215, cocobola hdl, 1 blade, 3"....................112.00
Russell, 2192, cocoa hdl, 1 blade, 4¼"......................72.00
Russell, 230, cocobola hdl, 1 blade, 3⅜"...................156.00
Russell, 252, ebony hdl, 2 blades, 3⅜".....................156.00
Russell, 322, ebony hdl, 2 blades, 3⅜".....................180.00
Russell, 430, wht bone, 1 blade, 3⅜".......................200.00
Russell, 450, wht bone hdl, 1 blade, 3⅜"...................200.00
Russell, 5102, buffalo horn hdl, 1 blade, 3⅜"..............156.00
Russell, 5202, buffalo horn hdl, 2 blades, 3⅜".............180.00
Russell, 623, genuine stag hdl, 2 blades, 3⅜"..............136.00
Winchester, 1050, celluloid hdl, 1 blade, 5"...............175.00
Winchester, 1201, nickel silver hdl, 1 blade, 3⅜"..........145.00
Winchester, 1621, ebony hdl, 1 blade, 4¾"..................115.00
Winchester, 1905, stag hdl, 1 blade, 4¼"...................210.00
Winchester, 2028, celluloid hdl, 2 blades, 3⅜".............175.00
Winchester, 2055, celluloid hdl, 2 blades, 3¼".............120.00
Winchester, 2079, celluloid hdl, 2 blades, 3⅜".............155.00
Winchester, 2201, nickel silver hdl, 2 blades, 3¼"..........115.00
Winchester, 2202, smooth fibre hdl, 2 blades, 3".............55.00
Winchester, 2215, nickel silver hdl, 2 blades, 3½"..........115.00
Winchester, 2337, pearl hdl, 2 blades, 2⅝".................145.00
Winchester, 2366, pearl hdl, 2 blades, 3¼".................155.00

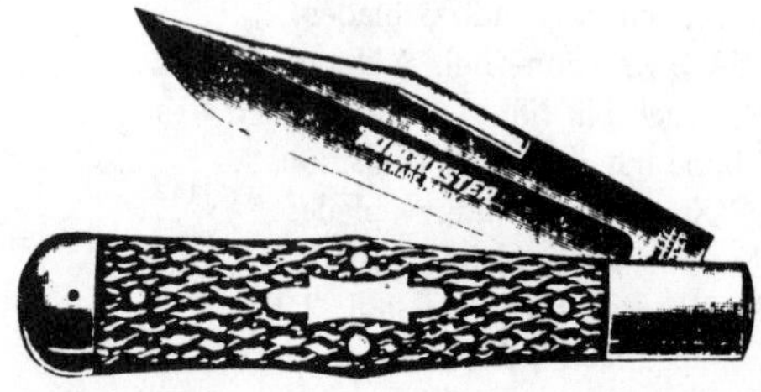

Winchester, #1920, stag handle, single blade, 5¼", $650.00.

Winchester, 2702, bone stag hdl, 2 blades, 3½".............165.00
Winchester, 2870, stag hdl, 2 blades, 3¾"..................140.00
Winchester, 2910, stag hdl, 2 blades, 3"...................140.00
Winchester, 2954, stag hdl, 2 blades, 3½"..................140.00
Winchester, 3006, celluloid hdl, 3 blades, 3⅞".............185.00
Winchester, 3350, pearl hdl, 3 blades, 3¼".................215.00
Winchester, 3902, stag hdl, 3 blades, 3½"..................245.00
Winchester, 3962, buffalo horn hdl, 3 blades, 4"............200.00

Miscellaneous

Bowie, brass guard, leather sheath, stag hdl, handmade........50.00
Bowie, WR Case, hunter's, tested, w/sheath, EX.............110.00
Dagger, Philippine crafted, leather scabbard, 1898, 16½".......45.00
Hunting, duck head shape bone hdl, scrimshawed horn sheath..150.00
Hunting, folding, curved blade, antler hdl, A Rouge, 6¾".......75.00
Hunting, Marbles, folding, stag hdls, compass, w/pouch........350.00
Hunting, Marbles, orig sheath, leather hdl...................35.00
Hunting, Marbles, tooled antler grip, leather sheath, 11"......175.00
Philippine crafted, leather scabbard, 1898, 23½"..............50.00
Skinning, Marbles, pat #1196, no sheath.....................25.00

Knowles, Taylor, Knowles

Isaac Knowles and Isaac Harvey operated a pottery in East Liverpool, Ohio, in 1853, where they produced both yellowware and Rockingham. In 1870, Knowles bought Harvey's interests and took as partners John Taylor and Homer Knowles. Their principal product was Ironstone china, but Knowles was confident that American potters could produce as fine a ware as the Europeans, and to prove his point hired Joshua Poole, an artist from the Belleek Works in Ireland. Poole quickly perfected a Belleek type china, but fire destroyed this portion of the company and before it could function again, their hotel china business had grown to the point that their full attention was required to meet market demands. By 1891 they were able to try again. They developed a bone china, as fine and thin as before, which they called Lotus. Henry Schmidt from the Meissen factory in Germany decorated the ware, often with lacy filigree applications, or with hand-formed leaves and flowers to which he added further decoration with liquid slip applied by means of a squeeze bag. Due to high production costs, with so much of the fragile ware damaged in firing, and because of changes in tastes and styles of decoration, the Lotus Ware line was dropped in 1896. Some of the early ware was marked 'KT&K China'; later marks have a star and a crescent, with 'Lotus Ware' added.

For further study, we recommend *American Belleek*, by Mary Frank Gaston; her address is listed in the Directory under Texas. When no condition is indicated, the items listed below are assumed to be in mint condition.

Lotus Ware

Biscuit jar, emb blackberry branches, mc, sgn, 7x6"..........675.00
Bowl, gr floral on pink & gr, gilt coral ftd, shell shape........395.00
Candy dish, seaweed design, coral ft, all wht, 7½x5½".........285.00
Creamer, shades of yel trim..................................95.00
Creamer, violets, artist sgn JH.............................125.00
Ewer, daisies & buttercups, gilt decor, twig hdl, sgn, 7½"......585.00
Pitcher, allover pansy decor, 7½x5½"........................365.00
Pitcher, yel & purple flowers, fishnet, twig hdl, wht, 3½"......295.00
Syrup, quadruple plate dispenser top, oldest mk..............190.00

Miscellaneous

Celery, floral, sceptor, gr mk...............................65.00
Punch bowl, aqua/wht shaded, gold: Tom & Jerry, +6 cups....250.00

Kutani

Kutani, named for the Japanese village where it originated, was first produced in the 17th century. The early ware, Ko Kutani, was produced for only about thirty years. Several types were produced before 1800, but these are rarely encounterd. In the 19th century, kilns located in several different villages began to copy the old Kutani wares. This later, more familiar type, has large areas of red with gold designs on a white ground decorated with warriors, birds, florals, etc., in controlled colors of red, gold, and black.

When no condition is indicated, the items listed below are assumed to be in mint condition.

Bowl, floral patterns, 1950s, 14″ 36.00
Bowl, women by lake on gr, gold/orange/gr border, 5″ 50.00
Creamer, Oriental people, red/gold brocade, mk 35.00
Creamer & sugar bowl, couple by lake w/birds, gilt, 3¾″ 140.00
Figurine, bird, gold, sgn, orig label, 6″, pr 65.00
Ginger jar, 3-color, foo dog finial, 5½″ 80.00
Koro, reserves front & bk w/florals, figural finial, 11½″ 750.00
Saki set, recent, 6-pc 10.00
Tea set, mother & daughter in reserve on cream, 19th C, 7″ . . . 185.00
Teapot, floral, gold, blown-out, 1890s, 5½″ 65.00
Teapot, gold floral on orange/wht, sgn, w/6 cups 65.00
Teapot/caddy, 4 c/s, children in reserves, diapering, 5″ 185.00
Vase, birds/flowers in fan reserves, stick neck, 7″ 125.00
Vase, florals in reserve, stick neck, 9¾″ 200.00
Vase, mc floral, sgn, 1920s, 12½″ 145.00

Teapot, multicolored, dragon spout, 7¾″, $145.00.

Labels

Before the advent of the cardboard box, wooden crates were used for transporting products. Paper labels were attached to the crates to identify the contents and the packer. These labels often had colorful lithographed illustrations, covering a broad range of subjects. Eventually the cardboard box replaced the crate, and the artwork was imprinted directly onto the carton. Today, these paper labels are becoming collectible, primarily for their art, but also for their advertising appeal.

When no condition is indicated, the items listed below are assumed to be in mint condition.

Apple, Best Strike, pitcher throws ball, Watsonville 25.00
Apple, Buffalo, buffalo surrounded by apples, Vernon 8.00

Hatchet Brand Sugar Corn, dated June 30, 1906, 10½″ x 9″, $15.00.

Apple, Deep Blue Sea, lg boat on open sea, Wapato 7.00
Apple, Diving Girl, girl dives into lake, Watsonville 9.00
Apple, En Avant, medieval battle scene, San Francisco 16.00
Apple, Lucky Strike, stone litho of man shooting buck 7.00
Apple, Old Gold, trunk of gold & pirate ship, Peachland 5.00
Apple, Our Pride, lg colorful parrot next to apple 7.50
Apple, Teacher's Pet, boy hands apple to teacher 6.50
Apple, 2 yel & 1 red apple, stock label, California 3.00
Cigar, Apollo, marble bust of Apollo, 6x9″ 14.00
Cigar, Barcelona, Spaniard w/men & horses, 4x4″ 14.00
Cigar, Big Wolf, wolf shows teeth, 6x9″ 4.00
Cigar, Butterfly, girl looks at parrot, 6x9″ 22.00
Cigar, College Maid, woman in cap & gown holds books, 4x4″ . . . 5.00
Cigar, Covered Wagon, cowboys & wagons cross desert, 6x9″ . . . 14.00
Cigar, Cuban Americans, keys & locks, emb & bronzed 5.00
Cigar, Elsa, bl & wht litho of woman, 4x4″ 7.00
Cigar, Fairy Wing, woman in wht robe w/wings, 6x9″ 32.00
Cigar, First Flag, eagle on Am emblem, emb & bronzed, 6x9″ 9.00
Cigar, General Sherman, Am Civil War portrait, 4x4″ 28.00
Cigar, Green Hat, Deco, man lights cigar, 1930, 6x9″ 18.00
Cigar, High Life, lions lean on crown, emb & bronzed, 6x9″ 4.00
Cigar, Indian, woman holds tobacco leaf, 4x4″ 5.00
Cigar, Jim Dandy, man dressed as Sherlock Holmes, 4x4″ 12.00
Cigar, Junius, bust of knight on shield, 6x9″ 5.00
Cigar, Miss Detroit, woman holds flag of Detroit, 4x4″ 28.00
Cigar, Negro, Blk man smokes cigar, 4x4″ 6.00
Cigar, Prize Rose, girl wears bonnet w/yel bow, 4x4″ 12.00
Cigar, Red Bird, bird on branch w/village bkground, 6x9″ 4.00
Cigar, Shamrock, horse head on gr bkground, 4x4″ 12.00
Cigar, Speckled Trout, trout jumps w/line in mouth, 4x4″ 12.00
Cigar, White Lily, bl & wht, hand holds lily, 4x4″ 8.00
Lemon, Basketball, 2 ladies play basketball, Claremont 35.00
Lemon, Diplomat, 4 lemons hang from banner, Corona 5.00
Lemon, Estero, coastal scene, gr bkground, Santa Barbara 3.00
Lemon, Index, hand points to name on crate of lemons 6.00
Lemon, Las Fuentes, fountain encircled by orchards 22.00
Lemon, Mariner, sailor holds on to helm at sea 6.00
Lemon, Meteor, bright meteor flies across label 4.00
Lemon, Ramona, Spanish senorita w/mission in bkground 4.00
Lemon, Santa, Santa w/bag over shoulder, Santa Paula 12.00
Orange, Airship, plane landing, Fillmore, California 15.00
Orange, Ana Co, kangaroo & ostrich, rising sun 10.00
Orange, Brownies, elves work with orange & juice 7.00

Orange, Co-ed, lady wears graduation cap & gown, Claremont....3.00
Orange, Cupid, blonde baby girl with wings..................18.00
Orange, Daisy, wht daisy blossom............................3.00
Orange, Exeter, lg orange w/map.............................3.00
Orange, Golden Circle, circle of oranges w/bl bkground.........3.00
Orange, Golden Trout, rainbow trout jumps out of water.......12.50
Orange, Have One, hand holds partly pealed orange............3.00
Orange, Legal Tender, $250 stack of $5 bills, Fillmore..........5.00
Orange, Lincoln, bust of Lincoln, oranges, Riverside............4.00
Orange, Old Mission, stone litho, 3 monks, mountains.........12.00
Orange, Orbit, orange as head of streaking comet, Exeter.......7.00
Orange, Rubaiyat, Arab couple by tent on oasis, Redlands.......4.00
Orange, Sierra Vista, stone litho, orange grove, Alps...........10.00
Orange, Stalwart, lg polar bear, red sunrise..................14.00
Pear, B Wise, owl shines from glow of moon, Sacramento......10.00
Pear, Bellboy, boy in red uniform holds tray of pears...........4.00
Pear, Grand Coulee, sm waterfall image, Coulee................5.00
Pear, Independent, Liberty Bell w/wht bkground, Yakima........4.00
Pear, Our Pick, wht chicken pecks at fruit, Loomis.............5.50
Pear, Placer, prospectors pan for gold, Auburn................6.00
Tobacco, Imperial Ruby, w/pretty girl, TD Wms Co, lg.........18.00
Tobacco, Long Distance.....................................5.00
Tobacco, Old Sport, personified animal w/highball.............28.00
Tobacco, Southdown, w/lg sheep, lg.........................18.00
Tobacco, Winner, horses jumping through stirrup.............28.00
Vegetable, Bronco, cowboy rides bronco, Castroville............5.00
Vegetable, Cheerio, man wears monocle & hat, Salinas..........3.00
Vegetable, Coin, 3 stacks of gold & silver coins................5.00
Vegetable, Conestoga, oxen pull wagon across prairie...........3.00
Vegetable, Grizzly Island, blk bear climbs rock.................5.00
Vegetable, Irish Beauty, woman's head, 4-leaf clovers............3.50
Vegetable, Lion, lg majestic lion, Watsonville..................3.00
Vegetable, Pride of the River, steamboat with passengers........4.00

Labino

Mr. Labino is currently producing glassware in Ohio. A ceramic engineer by trade, he was instrumental in developing the heat-resistant tiles used in space flights. His glassmaking shows his versatility in the art. While some of his designs are free-form and futuristic, others are reminiscent of the products of older glasshouses.

When no condition is indicated, the items listed below are assumed to be in mint condition.

Paperweight, red center in clear, sgn.......................275.00
Sculpture, free form, stalagmite w/in aqua film, 6¼″..........715.00
Vase, bl irid w/hdls, 1982, 4½″...........................245.00
Vase, gr opaque, pinched & crimped, 1965, 11″.............345.00

Pitcher, ruby, dated 1965, 5½″, $375.00.

Lace, Linens and Needlework

It has been recorded that lace was found in the tombs of ancient Egypt. Lace has always been a symbol of wealth and fashion. Italian laces are regarded as the finest ever produced, but the differences between them and the laces of France are nearly indistinguishable. In Munich a type of lace was woven, not by human fingers but by insects. Caterpillar lace was made by smearing a flat surface with an edible paste, over which the desired design was outlaid in oil. The caterpillars were repelled by the oiled areas, but ate the paste, all the while spinning their silken threads.

Needlework was revived during the middle of the 18th century, and became the favorite of feminine pastimes. Examples of many forms are readily available today--tatting, embroidery, needlepoint, and crochet--and although fragile in appearance have withstood the ravages of time with remarkable durability.

When no condition is indicated, the items listed below are assumed to be in excellent condition.

Key:

embr—embroidered	ms—machine sewn
hs—hand sewn	wc—watercolor

Bag, homespun linen, child's dress shape, embroidery, 15″......65.00
Bed tick, homespun, indigo/wht checks, hs, self lined, M......450.00
Bed tick, homespun, indigo/wht checks, hs, self lined, VG.....345.00
Bed tick, homespun cotton, bl/wht plaid, ms, self lined........275.00
Bed tick, homespun cotton, bl/wht/red, wht bk, loomed tape...450.00
Bed tick & bolster, homespun linen, onionskin dye, unused....600.00
Bed tick top, homespun, bl/onionskin gold, 41x76″............225.00
Bedspread, Battenburg, all lace, 90″ sq.....................350.00
Bedspread, crochet, ecru/pink, 82x105″......................95.00
Bedspread, crochet, geometrics, 66x72″......................70.00
Bedspread, crochet, Star & Popcorn, scalloped/fringed........195.00
Bedspread, crochet pink roses in wht blocks, 100x70″.........100.00
Bedspread, homespun, ecru/tan grid/embr, 70x90″, VG........400.00
Bedspread, lt weight wool, stripes/stars/etc, 88x102″, EX.......50.00
Chintz, polished, block stamped w/7 colors, 1820s, 65x17″.....45.00
Coverlet, bl/gold/natural plaid wool, 2-pc, 68x87″, VG.........175.00
Crib cover, crochet, sqs w/floral & misc animals, 30x50″......150.00
Doily, crochet, 'Bread,' 9x4″..............................12.00
Mattress cover, natural linen, stained, 54x80″, EX.............45.00
Napkin, red/wht linen, elaborate florals, fringed, 18x19″........10.00
Needlework, 3 birds on stylized tree, sgn/1832, 16x16½″.....425.00
Needlework on paper, cornucopia of mc flowers, fr, 4x6″.......30.00
Needlework on silk, lady at Shakespeare's grave, oval, 18″.....150.00
Needlework on silk, lady/cat/3 children in garden, 22x27″.....185.00
Needlework on silk, Moses/bullrushes, wc detail, 1819, 25″....240.00
Needlework on silk, mother/boy/pigs, elaborate, 24x19″.......250.00
Needlework on silk, shepherd/2 maids/sheep, English, lg.......200.00
Needlework/watercolor on silk, dog saves man, 112x15″.......385.00
Parlor cloth, blk silk w/pnt floral/embr/gold thread, 54″.......175.00
Parlor cloth, embr silk, exotic birds/butterflies/florals..........110.00
Parlor cloth, silk w/fruits & flowers, gold/silver embr..........200.00
Petit point, floral center & spandrels, 1839, 16x20″, EX.......80.00
Picture, crochet, Geo Washington bust in center, 20x23″.......45.00
Picture, filet crochet, Lord's Supper, 34x58″................100.00
Picture, tent-stitched canvas, Fishing Lady, 1750, 16x20″....3,850.00
Pillow sham, appliqued wreaths, calico, hm/ms, 23x29″, pr.....170.00
Pillowcase, homespun, wht w/bl copper-roller print, hs.........40.00
Pillowcase, homespun linen, crochet insert, lace trim, 20″......55.00
Quilt, linsey-woolsey, indigo/natural, vine quilting, VG.........800.00
Remnant, homespun cotton, wht/indigo plaid, 30x72″, EX.....150.00
Remnant, homespun linen, checkered/onionskin dye, 38x48″...200.00
Remnant, homespun linen, indigo/onionskin/wht, 40x72″, NM..300.00

Bone lace panels, attributed to Dagobert Peche for the Wiener Werkstatte, ca 1920, each approximately 7½″ wide, $250.00 each.

Sheet, coarse homespun, York Co/PA, 74x74″, EX...........105.00
Sheet, homespun, embroidered initials, 2-pc, minor wear........35.00
Sheet, red embroidered initials, 1836, 2-pc, 70x92″, NM.......65.00
Show towel, homespun, wht w/brn stripes, dtd 1838, 65″.......50.00
Show towel, homespun linen, drawnwork panel, fringe, 48″.....55.00
Show towel, homespun w/embroidered birds/tree/sgn, 15x47″...300.00
Show towel, wht homespun, bird embroidery, PA Dutch, 56″...150.00
Table cloth, Art Deco, damask, gold, +12 napkins............60.00
Table cloth, crochet, butterfly design, 52x74″, EX............185.00
Table cloth, crochet, medallions, 72x62″....................90.00
Table cloth, crochet, rosette design, 56x79″.................80.00
Table cloth, handmade linen cutwork, 68″ dia, +6 napkins.....95.00
Table cloth, homespun linen, natural/wht stripes, 104x64″.....125.00
Table cloth, Italian linen/cutwork, 103x68″, +12 napkins.......70.00
Table cloth, linen, Camellia pattern, 72″ sq, +6 napkins.......45.00
Table cloth, linen, lt bl/wht, 64x68″, +6 napkins.............35.00
Table cloth, linen, openwork/crochet flowers, +22 napkins.....275.00
Table cloth, linen, 1940s, 108″ L, +12 napkins...............60.00
Table cloth, linen/crochet trim, 48″ dia.....................20.00
Table cloth, Maderia Island, 12 dinner/12 tea napkins.........150.00
Table cloth, Portuguese wht linen.........................100.00
Table cloth, red, central medallion, foliage scrolls, 60″.........65.00
Table cloth, Venetian lace, medallion/floral/bird, 62x118″......175.00
Table cloth, wht satin-stitched flowers on linen, 26″ dia.........90.00
Table runner, Battenburg, 15x54″...........................55.00
Table runner, fringed, homespun linen, 12½x54″..............15.00
Table set, openwork/lace, 12 ea placemats/napkins, runner......50.00
Table set, organdy/linen, scrollwork, 12 mats/12 napkins.......110.00
Towel, coarsely woven homespun linen, ms hems, 16x39″.......10.00
Towel, homespun, wht w/bl border stripes & fringe, 24x43″.....20.00
Towel, homespun linen, red edge stripe/initials, ms hems.......30.00
Towel, linen, embr children at pump, worn fringe, 40″.........45.00
Wedding handkerchief, allover embroidery, 1784, 24″.........950.00

Lacy Glassware

Lacy glass became popular in the late 1820s after the development of the pressing machine. It was decorated with allover patterns--hearts, lyres, sheaves of wheat, etc.--and backgrounds were completely stippled. The designs were intricate and delicate, hence the term 'lacy.' Although Sandwich produced this type of glassware in abundance, it was also made by other eastern glassworks, as well as in the midwest. By 1840, its popularity on the wane and a depressed economy forcing manufacturers to seek less expensive modes of production, lacy glass began to be phased out in favor of pressed pattern glassware.

When no condition is indicated, the items listed below are assumed to be without obvious damage; minor roughness is normal.

Bowl, Beehive, 1⅜x9¼″................................85.00
Bowl, Oak Leaf, rim flakes, 6½″...........................30.00
Bowl, Oak Leaf, 1⅝x7¼″................................35.00
Bowl, Peacock Eye, 1⅝x9″, EX...........................70.00
Bowl, Plaid, minor flakes, 1¼x8″.........................60.00
Bowl, Scrolled Eye, shell & circle, minor flakes, 9½″.........200.00
Bowl, Star Medallion, 6-sided, sm.........................150.00
Creamer, heart shape....................................97.00
Dish, Beehive, octagonal, 9″, EX.........................25.00
Dish, Lyre, 7″, EX......................................25.00
Dish, Pineapple, cut rim, 6½x9″..........................80.00
Dish, Pipes of Pan, 6¼x8¼″.............................75.00
Dish, sapphire bl, miniature, 2¼″.........................55.00
Plate, Heart, 6¼″, EX...................................45.00
Plate, Plaid, 8″...37.00
Sauce dish, Roman Rosette, 4″...........................47.00
Sugar bowl, Gothic Arch, sm edge chips, 5⅜″...............52.50
Sugar bowl, Lyre & Acanthus leaf, 5¾″, EX.................75.00
Tray, Scroll & Fleur-de-Lis, Sandwich, 6″....................45.00

Left to right: Tureen, with lid and undertray, Sandwich, miniature, in excellent condition, $125.00; Creamer, Sandwich, miniature, in mint condition, $75.00.

Lalique

Beginning his lengthy career as a designer and maker of fine jewelry, Rene Lalique at first only daubled in glass, making small panels of pate-de-verre (paste on paste) and cire perdue (wax casting) to use in his jewelry. He also made small flacons of gold and silver with his glass inlays, which attracted the attention of M.F. Coty, who commissioned Lalique to design bottles for his perfume company. The success of this venture resulted in the opening of his own glassworks at Combs-la-Ville in 1909. In 1921, a larger factory was established at Wingen-sur-Moder, in Alasce-Lorraine. By the thirties, Lalique was world reknown as the most important designer of his time.

Lalique glass is lead based, either mold blown or pressed. Favored motifs during the Art Nouveau period were dancing nymphs, fish, dragonflies, and foliage. Characteristically the glass is crystal in combination with acid etched relief. Later, some items were made in as many as ten colors --red, amber, and green among them--and were occasionally accented with enameling. These colored pieces, especially those in black, are rare and highly prized by advanced collectors.

During the twenties and thirties, Lalique designed several vases and bowls reminiscent of American Indian art. He also developed a line in the Art Deco style decorated with stylized birds, florals, and geometrics. In addition to vases, clocks, automobile mascots, stemware and bottles, many other useful objects were produced.

Items made before his death in 1945 were marked 'R. Lalique'; later the 'R' was deleted even though some of the original molds were still used. Numbers found on the bases of some pieces are catalogue numbers.

When no condition is indicated, the items listed below are assumed to be in mint condition.

Key:

cl—clear	L—signed Lalique
cl/f—clear and frosted	RL—signed R. Lalique
fr—frosted	RLF—signed R. Lalique, France

Ash tray, Antheor, frosted mermaids, #293, RLF, 5½" 375.00
Ash tray, Medicis, nudes on rim, c/f, RLF, oblong, 5½" L 420.00
Ash tray, Naiade, sirene in panel, c/f, RLF 600.00
Ash tray, Zephyrs, center design, bl/yel opal, RL, 3" dia 375.00
Belt buckle, relief moths, bronze trim, ca 1920, RL 1,100.00
Bottle, atomizer; dancing nudes relief, gr, L, 6" 350.00
Bottle, pendant; acorn form/gilt plastic top, w/perfume, L 400.00
Bottle, scent; Bouquet de Faunes, emb masks, c/f, 4", pr 850.00
Bottle, scent; Cour Joie, for Nina Ricci, heart shape, 3¼" 200.00
Bottle, scent; cylinder, trailing wisteria, cl, RLF, 3" 300.00
Bottle, scent; dahlia blossom, w/blk enamel, RLF, 3½" 375.00
Bottle, scent; Dans la Nuit, emb stars/moon, cl, RL, 4½" 200.00
Bottle, scent; Lilas, floral, pear shape, c/f, Worth, 3" 250.00
Bottle, scent; lizard decor & stopper, blk glass, RL, 4" 825.00
Bottle, scent; Myosotis, nude stopper/floral, fr, RLF, 11" 1,675.00
Bottle, scent; nudes w/floral garlands, brass bulb, RL, 3" 275.00
Bottle, scent; ribbed can, cobalt, for Worth, RL, 2½" 300.00
Bottle, scent; Sirenes, opal, #2651, RLF, 6¾" 800.00
Bowl, hobnail, blk dot on tip of ea hob, RL, 9½" 225.00
Bowl, parakeets/florals, opal, RLF, 1925, 9" dia 1,200.00
Bowl, Vernon, opal sunflowers, sgn RL, 2x8" 325.00
Box, Cleones, lid: beetles/foliage; amber opal, RL, 6" dia 1,100.00
Box, Degas, lid: female form; cl, ca 1925, L, 3¼" dia 350.00
Box, Georgette, lid: dragonfly design; opal, RL, 8¼" dia 850.00
Box, Grande Muguets, lily o/t valley, bl opal, RL, 10" dia 1,700.00
Box, Orsay, floral, c/f, RLF, ca 1930, 3" dia 200.00
Box, 3 dancing nudes, peach stain, w/D'Orsay powder, RLF 325.00
Brandy glass, fish, bl stain on clear, ftd, RL, 2¾" 85.00
Brooch, convex, molded daisies, gold foil ground, L, 1¾" 825.00
Chandelier, allover blossoms, yel, silk cap/cords, RL, 12" 1,450.00
Clock, doves/floral, bl opal, orig, RL, not working, 9" 2,500.00
Clock, water nymphs w/pearly hair, opal, orig, RLF, 4½" 1,100.00
Cup & saucer, Cactus, blk, RL 85.00
Decanter, bird relief, bl stain, w/stopper, RL, 11" 220.00
Decanter, female nudes in panels, bud stopper, RL, 13¾" 605.00
Figurine, Guinea Hen, RL, 7" 700.00
Figurine, Joueuse do Flute, c/f, RL, 14½" 2,500.00
Finger bowl w/underplate, fish, dbl row, bl trim, RL 195.00
Hand mirror, 2 Oiseaux, firebirds/berry branch, RLF/L, 6" . . . 1,350.00
Hood ornament, Libellule, sm dragonfly, c/f, RLF, 6" 1,100.00
Hood ornament, Sirene, mermaid, opal, RL, 4" 925.00
Hood ornament, Tete de Belier, ram's head, amethyst, RLF . . 3,650.00
Hood ornament, Tete de Coq, rooster's head, c/f, LF, 7" 1,300.00
Menu holder, base w/grapes/grotesque mask, c/f, RLF, 5½" 265.00
Pendant, Fioret, nude, frosted, orig cloth chain, RL, 1½" 295.00
Pendant, frogs emb, pierced oval, cl w/gray-bl ground, RLF . . . 1,430.00
Pendant, mistletoe emb, azure bl, triangular, L, 1⅜" 550.00
Pendant, rows of wasps emb, emerald gr, oval, L, 2¼" 770.00
Pendant, woman & lovebirds emb, red, rectangular, RL, 1½" . . . 385.00
Pin, vultures & wreath emb, gr glass/gilt metal, L, 3⅓" 1,210.00
Platter, Assiette Dandelion, floral relief, c/f, RLF, 15" 750.00
Ring holder, 2 swans on 4" saucer 155.00
Scent burner, Sirenes, mermaids, opal w/gr enamel, RL, 7" . . . 1,900.00
Tumbler, heavy blown-out cherries, sgn, 4½" 135.00
Tumbler, Hesperides, cl w/frosted leaves, RL, 4" 95.00
Vase, Acanthus, emb leaves, butterscotch, RL, 11" 7,500.00
Vase, Acanthus, emb leaves, c/f, fr & polished, RL, 11" 1,200.00
Vase, Amiens, fern fronds as hdls, sq, topaz, RL, 5½" 950.00
Vase, Archers, emb archers/birds, cased amber, RL, 11" 3,250.00
Vase, Bacchantes, high relief nudes, opal, RL, 10" 4,950.00
Vase, Bleuets, cornflowers, c/f, RL, 6¼" 595.00
Vase, Brambles, bullet form, yel, RLF, 9½" 800.00
Vase, Brambles, molded brambles, bl w/wht enamel, RL, 8" . . 2,100.00
Vase, Enfants, loving cup, 2 emb cupids, c/f, RLF, 10½" 1,875.00
Vase, Esterel, allover Evergreen leafage, amber, RLF, 6" 1,350.00
Vase, Esterel, allover Evergreen leafage, cl, RLF, 6" 475.00
Vase, Eucalyptus, opal, RL, 6½", pr 950.00
Vase, Ferns, allover design, bl, RLF/#996, 7½" 2,150.00
Vase, Gui, opal w/bl wash, RL, 6½" 595.00
Vase, Montmorecy, cherries in relief, c/f, RL, 6½" 495.00
Vase, Nanking, geometric design, c/f, polished, RL, 13" 2,200.00
Vase, Oleron, allover fish in high relief, fr, RLF, 3½" 650.00
Vase, Penthievre, geometric fish design, bl, RL, 1925, 10" . . . 7,800.00
Vase, Perruches, emb parakeets, bl w/wht enamel, RLF, 10" . . 4,550.00
Vase, Poissons, grotesque fish, bl w/wht enamel, RL, 9½" 4,250.00
Vase, Rampillon, allover floral, emb diamonds, yel, RL, 5" . . . 1,050.00
Vase, Ronsard, crouching nude hdls, opal, RL, 8½" 1,975.00
Vase, Serpant, coiled snake, amber, RLF, 10½" 6,600.00
Vase, Tortues, allover turtles design, c/f, RL, 10¾" 2,500.00
Vase, Tourbillons, emb scrolls, cl w/blk enamel, RL, 8" 5,750.00

Perfume, Couer Joie, for Nine Ricci, 4", $350.00.

Lamps

The earliest known lamp was the primitive grease lamp, a small alabaster dish holding openly burning grease. An improved version, the Betty lamp introduced in the 18th century, made use of a lid and cloth wick. The development of the tubal wick by Swiss inventor Aime Argand in 1784 brought about a more sophisticated oil lamp, featuring a glass chimney. With the discovery of petroleum in 1859, new methods of producing artificial light were made possible, and bigger, heavier, more elaborate lamps came into vogue.

The most popular of the kerosene lamps were the Aladdins, introduced in 1908 by the Mantle Lamp Company of America. Aladdin lamps were made in over eighteen models and more than one hundred styles.

Banquet lamps were kerosene lighting devices with round glass globes, often with hand-painted decorations. They were quite similar to the Gone-with-the-Wind lamps of the 1870s.

Other types of early lamps were 'spark lamps,' small night-lights with limited illumination; and 'student lamps,' useful for late-night reading. Gas lamps were used, especially for outdoor lighting.

With the invention of the electric bulb in 1879, oil lamps slowly became obsolete. The light from the electric bulb was so bright, ornamental shades were necessary to reduce the glare. Glassmaker Louis C. Tiffany devoted most of his career in the latter 1800s to producing original and elaborate glass and bronze lamps for the electric bulb.

When no condition is indicated, the items listed below are assumed to be in excellent condition; glass parts are assumed mint. See also Bradley and Hubbard; Frankart; Handel Lamps; Tiffany

Aladdin Lamps

Alacite, G-211, candelabra.....105.00
Alacite, G-217, Leaf Spray.....24.00
Alacite, G-257, Oak Leaf.....26.00
Alacite, G-287C, w/metal.....63.00
Alacite, G-31, boudoir.....11.00
Alacite, G-34, boudoir.....11.00
Alacite, G-348, world.....253.00
Alacite, G-375, urn, Dancing Ladies.....475.00
Alacite, G-379, urn w/lid.....70.00
Alacite, night light, Hopalong Cassidy, gun in holster.....120.00
Beehive, B-80, clear crystal, w/burner.....38.00
Beehive, B-83, ruby crystal, w/burner.....230.00
Caboose, Model #23, w/shade.....45.00
Cathedral, Model B-111, gr moonstone, w/burner.....130.00
Colonial, Model B, #105, gr crystal, w/burner.....130.00
Corinthian, B-101, amber crystal, w/burner.....63.00
Corinthian, B-103, clear crystal, w/burner.....52.00
Corinthian, B-106, clear font, amber foot, w/burner.....47.00
Corinthian, B-114, wht moonstone, w/burner.....75.00
Corinthian, B-124, wht moonstone font, blk ft.....90.00
Floor lamp, Model B, no shade.....75.00
Hanging lamp, Model #1, w/#203 shade.....600.00
Hanging lamp, Model #10, w/shade, M.....335.00
Hanging lamp, Model #12, w/decorated shade.....370.00
Hanging lamp, Model #3, w/#203 shade, M.....555.00
Hanging lamp, Model #4, w/#205 shade.....515.00
Hanging lamp, Model #5, w/#215 shade.....245.00
Hanging lamp, Model #7, w/shade, M.....430.00
Hanging lamp, Model B, chain, w/parchment shade.....155.00
Hanging lamp, Model B, w/glass shade, M.....235.00
Hanging lamp, Practicus, w/shade, M.....560.00
Lincoln Drape, Short; B-61, amber crystal, w/burner, old.....1,300.00
Lincoln Drape, Short; B-62, ruby crystal, w/burner, old.....375.00
Lincoln Drape, Tall; B-74, clear, w/burner, old.....1,350.00
Lincoln Drape, Tall; B-75, alacite, scallop foot, w/burner.....225.00
Lincoln Drape, Tall; B-77, ruby crystal, w/burner, old.....410.00
Majestic, B-120, wht moonstone, w/burner, VG finish.....115.00
Night light, kneeling Arab woman, Fr porcelain, 7".....110.00
Opalique, G-130, figurine.....400.00
Opalique, G-163, figurine.....595.00
Opalique, G-77, figurine.....445.00
Orientale, B-130, ivory, w/burner, VG finish.....110.00
Orientale, B-132, rose gold.....130.00
Orientale, B-134, bronze, w/burner, VG finish.....93.00
Parlour lamp, Model #3, w/burner.....695.00
Powder dish lamp, G-50, w/shade.....215.00
Queen, B-95, wht moonstone, w/burner, VG metal finish.....135.00
Queen, B-98, rose moonstone, w/burner, VG metal finish.....155.00
Quilt, B-85, wht moonstone, w/burner.....95.00
Quilt, B-90, wht moonstone font/blk moonstone ft, w/burner.....105.00
Shade, #201, opal wht glass, fancy.....120.00
Shade, #203, hanging, opal.....78.00
Shade, #205, opal.....400.00
Shade, #215, hanging, opal.....73.00
Shade, #301, Chippendale, satin wht or enamel.....130.00
Shade, #516, hanging, opal glass.....127.00
Shade, #601F, for table lamp, roses.....405.00
Shade, #601F, roses.....400.00
Shade, #616F, hanging, poppies.....400.00
Shade, #620S, hanging, windmill.....315.00
Simplicity, B-26, w/decal.....210.00
Simplicity, B-29, gr, VG finish.....85.00
Solitaire, B-70, wht moonstone, w/burner.....1,110.00
Table lamp, G-16, electric.....250.00
Table lamp, G-234, golden pheasant, electric.....125.00
Table lamp, G-348, world, electric.....140.00
Table lamp, Model #1, w/burner, EX.....515.00
Table lamp, Model #10, w/burner.....245.00
Table lamp, Model #7, w/burner.....165.00
Treasure, B-136, chromium, w/burner, VG finish.....140.00
Treasure, B-137, bronze, w/burner, VG finish.....105.00
Venetian, Model A, #99, clear, w/burner, VG finish.....150.00
Vertique, B-87, rose moonstone, w/burner.....120.00
Vertique, B-93, wht moonstone, w/burner.....340.00
Victoria, B-25, decorated china, w/burner.....305.00
Vogue, E-200, ped ft.....140.00
Vogue, E-304, vase lamp.....153.00
Washington Drape, B-39, rnd base, clear, w/burner.....38.00
Washington Drape, B-41, rnd base, amber, w/burner.....62.00
Washington Drape, B-48, bell stem, gr, w/burner.....155.00
Washington Drape, B-50, filigree stem, clear, w/burner.....48.00
Washington Drape, B-51, filigree stem, gr, w/burner.....63.00
Washington Drape, B-54, plain stem, gr, w/burner.....51.00

Banquet Lamps

Amber w/cut t'prints, brass stem w/vintage, 15".....200.00
Amethyst cut to clear, brass w/emb rose stem, 15".....275.00
Bl opal w/diagonal stripes, 12¾".....450.00
Cupid stem, ball shade, ornate.....195.00
Cut overlay, brass base/fittings, 27".....300.00

Banquet lamp, green and white cameo shade, white metal and onyx stem, brass reservoir, 35", $1,000.00.

Chandeliers

Brass, baluster std, 3 scroll supports, 1700s, 11″ . . . 1,100.00
Copper/slag, sq lanterns on radiating arms, applied faces . . . 475.00
Frosted glass, pendant grapes over lights, Deco, 7-light . . . 700.00
Gilt bronze/etched glass, reed std, 9 panels in cone shade . . . 600.00
Strands of lg cut glass beads, bronze cap, 21x10″ . . . 295.00
Tin, center-joined punched cones, S-curve candle arms, 24″ . . . 500.00
Wrought iron fr, inverted glass dome, Stickley, 28″ dia . . . 3,500.00

Fairy Lamps

Burmese, bowl w/turned-down pleat skirt, sgn Webb, 5¾x5″ . . . 685.00
Burmese, cherries decor, Vict metal holder, on mirror, 8x4″ . . . 435.00
Burmese, fluted bowl w/3-ft base/pressed insert, Webb, 6½″ . . . 725.00
Burmese, lamp/menu holder, gold fr, 2 vases, 5x7″ . . . 785.00
Burmese, ped ft/dome top, ruffle/flare bowl, pnt fruit, 10″ . . . 1,250.00
Burmese, ruffled reversible base, Clarke cup, 5¾x7″ . . . 550.00
Burmese, Tunnecliffe base, Price's Sentinel candle, 4x4″ . . . 345.00
Cranberry, opal feathers, matching saucer, clear cup . . . 245.00
Cranberry verre moire, hat w/sides of base folded in, 8″ W . . . 545.00
Dia Quilt MOP, rose, crimp saucer base, 5¾x6¼″ . . . 635.00
Dia Quilt MOP, yel/chartreuse, crimp bowl base, 6x6″ . . . 785.00
Etched, 6 panels: portraits/females, lt bl/clear base, 4½″ . . . 335.00
Parian, wht/pink rose, 13 petals, 6 gr leaves, 4x3½″ . . . 285.00
Porcelain, Miss Muffet wht lithophane panels, 1-pc base/cup . . . 435.00
Satin, pink w/emb stars, crimp base, Clarke insert, 5x6″ . . . 435.00
Satin, pink/wht stripe/swirl dome & ruffle base, S&W, 6x5″ . . . 550.00
Swirl stripes: pink/wht/clear, crimped, sgn R 50725, 5½x7″ . . . 400.00
Threaded clear up/down crimp base, cased shade w/thorns, 5″ . . 235.00
Verre moire, lime/wht loops, ruffle base, Clarke cup, 6½″ . . . 450.00

Gone-with-the-Wind

Camels & riders . . . 250.00
Flowers, HP on frosted shade, sgn Climax, dtd 1890 . . . 475.00
Grapes on red satin glass, all orig, 25″ . . . 750.00
Roses, HP, Royal, all orig, 27″ . . . 595.00
Roses, HP, 25″ . . . 500.00
Roses, HP on gr, electrified, 19″ . . . 195.00
Water lilies on shade, New Rochester sgn brass font . . . 425.00

Hanging Lamps

Bluebirds, prism band, matching shade & font, 14″ . . . 795.00
Cranberry pull-down, brass mts, hall type . . . 170.00
Cranberry w/amber trim, 3 reeded applied hdls, 16x9¼″ . . . 395.00
Diamond Quilted MOP satin, melon sectioned, pink, 16½″ . . . 850.00
Gr to wht w/pink orchid, crescent moon, lovers in boat . . . 595.00
HP lilacs on shade, glass font, prisms . . . 325.00
Rose opal shade, bulbous, hall type . . . 310.00
Scenic shade, pull down, prisms . . . 300.00
Tin, kero, horizontal font, reflector, rpl chimney . . . 50.00
Whale oil, blown cone smoke bell/dome font/applied finial . . . 285.00

Lanterns

Archer & Pancoast, tin, kero burner, sq sides flare, 9″ . . . 125.00
Brass, kero, orig globe, pat 1874-1880, rpr, 11″, VG . . . 65.00
Brass, kero burner, pat Dec 24, 1867, 10″ . . . 105.00
Carbide, hand lantern, Justrite #12, NM . . . 110.00
Coach, brass, w/font & kero burner, beveled glass, 12″ . . . 52.00
Coach, tin, bevel glass, Weite Mfg, 1874, brass font, 12″ . . . 60.00
Deitz, farm, 4-panel/pierced tin cone/wire bail, 15″ . . . 150.00
Red & gold beaded sections, orig cover . . . 24.00
Ship's, kero, galvanized sheet metal, red/bl lens, 9″, pr . . . 80.00
Tin, candle, folds, orig japanning, Minor's Pat 1865, 5″ . . . 85.00
Tin, candle, glass 4 sides, pyramid top, rpt/rpr, 12″ . . . 45.00
Tin, candle, Paul Revere, allover pierced arch panels, 15″ . . . 250.00
Tin, candle, semi-circular, punched cone top w/hdl, 16″ . . . 145.00
Tin, punched circles/etc, cone-top cylinder, 12½″ . . . 150.00
Tin, whale oil, clear blown globe, base mk: pat/NE, 11″ . . . 190.00
Wood, candle, vented tin top, hinged door, 15″, VG . . . 125.00
Wood, candle, 4 red/clear glass sides, mortised, 12″, VG . . . 225.00

Lard Oil/Grease

Betty, swivel font lid, hook/chain, eng brass ornament, 3″ . . . 160.00
Betty, tin plate w/iron hanger, hinged front lid, 6″ . . . 85.00
Betty, wrought iron, G simple detail, w/pick & hanger, 4″ . . . 225.00
Betty, wrought iron, twist hanger, wire wick pick, pnt, 5″ . . . 105.00
Crusie, dbl; wrought iron, primitive, w/hanger, 5½″ . . . 120.00
Kinnear, Ufford, tin saucer, ring hdl, orig reflector . . . 495.00
Tin, copper tube, Swopes Pat, 11½″ . . . 350.00
Tin, emb D Kinnear's Pat, 1851, 7″ . . . 500.00
Tin hat shaped base, 4¾″ . . . 95.00
Wht clay/Albany slip, rnd base, finger hdl, 3¾″ . . . 400.00
Wrought iron, twist link hanger, 5¼″ . . . 45.00
Wrought iron, 4-spout, tooled center post, 7½″ . . . 75.00

Leaded Glass Lamps

Bigelow Kennard, geometric tiles w/scroll border, 26x19″ . . . 825.00
Cherry blossom, 24″ shade; simple tree trunk std, 22½″ . . . 2,475.00
Flowers w/in arch panels, irregular border; cast base, 23″ . . . 525.00
Hanging globe, lg butterflies, wht/red on gr, 13″, pr . . . 1,540.00
Magnolia, 24″ shade; tree trunk wht metal std, 28″ . . . 1,100.00
Ogee tiles/simple base band; std on disk w/4 pad ft, 28″ . . . 1,210.00
Wisteria, 24″ shade; tree trunk std w/open roots, 30½″ . . . 3,025.00

Miniature Lamps, Kerosene

Apple Blossom, orig base & shade . . . 135.00
Banquet, milk glass shade/HP flowers, brass base, P&A, 18″ . . . 550.00
Block & Dot, clear . . . 175.00
Blown, scalloped base, brass collar & burner, 3½″ . . . 100.00
Brass, w/brass shade . . . 125.00
Brownie, milk glass w/brass band, iron ring hdl . . . 85.00

Decorated Burmese, attributed to Thomas Webb, 9½″, $2,300.00.

Bulging Loop, pink gloss, banquet......125.00
Bull's Eye, clear......50.00
Bull's Eye, green......90.00
Buttercup......55.00
Clear, attached to brass saucer, pat Oct 28, 1873......55.00
Clear w/Iris shade & base......175.00
Delft bl & wht scene, orig chimney, sgn......45.00
Dia Quilt MOP, pink, brass ft, sq ruffled shade, 11½″......695.00
Flint, hexagonal w/Gothic arches, pewter collar, 8½″, EX......100.00
Glow lamp, clear base & shade......100.00
Greek Key, bl frost w/matching chimney, 8½″......87.50
Jr Rochester, pat Sept 14, 1886, 11″......275.00
Little Buttercup, clear......70.00
Little Harry......165.00
Little Jewel......90.00
Milk glass w/emb medallion, gilt decor......225.00
Mission, milk glass w/emb motif, gilt trim......125.00
Nutmeg, milk glass, brass band hdl......100.00
Our Drummer, clear glass stem, sq base......85.00
Panelled Cosmos, pink florals, NM......260.00
Pewter ped base, milk glass ribbed font & shade......200.00
Sparking, flow bl, w/china extinguisher, hdl, 3x5″......235.00
Spatter, gr w/brn, vertical pattern shade......210.00
Tiny Miller, brass, gr enamel rib shade, orig burner, 12″......90.00
Twinkle, gr, orig base & shade......145.00
Yel cased w/clear, shell ft, hdl, finger loop, 1800s......365.00

Pattern Glass Lamps

Aquarius, amber w/amber chimney, #1 burner......160.00
Aquarius, clear, #1 burner......65.00
Atterbury Swan, clambroth, pat 1868, 9″, EX......1,000.00
Atterbury Swan, opaque bl w/clear font, 1868, 17″......1,100.00
Ava, finger lamp, flat......60.00
Basketweave w/Flower Medallion, bl, finger lamp, ftd......95.00
Beaded Heart, gr stem, clear font w/frosted hearts, 10″......225.00
Beveled Blocks, stand lamp......145.00
Bolton, stand lamp......45.00
Bulging Waist, cobalt, finger lamp, flat......95.00
Bull's Eye, finger lamp, flat......35.00
Bull's Eye, gr, #2......200.00

Left to right: Lace maker's, pressed stem with blown globe atop, 9″, $190.00; Sandwich-type pressed glass fluid lamp with brass camphene burner, minor roughness, 9″, $110.00; Sandwich fluid lamp, square opaque pressed base, brass stem, Bull's Eye and Fleur-de-lis font, 9″, $100.00.

Bull's Eye font, wafer connector, 6″......85.00
Burne, stand lamp......160.00
Cable, whale oil, 8″......145.00
Circle & Ellipse, flint, 8½″......112.00
Coin Dot, opal, finger lamp, flat......140.00
Columbia Coin, milk glass, 10″......145.00
Coolidge Drape, finger lamp, flat......90.00
Corn in Shield, finger lamp, flat......125.00
Diamond Sunburst, finger lamp, flat......65.00
Dillaway, wavy shoulder, finger lamp, flat......65.00
Doric Column, milk glass w/bl & yel daisies, 9½″......185.00
Dorothy, finger lamp, flat......60.00
Dorothy, finger lamp, ftd......70.00
Elipse w/Thumbprint, finger lamp, flat......65.00
English Hobnail, amber, #1......125.00
Epaulet, stemmed......45.00
Erin Fan, finger lamp, ftd......50.00
Erin Fan, gr, #1......145.00
Eyebrow, finger lamp, flat......50.00
Eyewinker, stemmed, 8″......125.00
Fickle Block, bl, finger lamp, flat......110.00
Flattened Sawtooth, flint, 10″......120.00
Greek Key, finger lamp, ftd......50.00
Heart, gr, stand lamp......250.00
Heart, gr custard, finger lamp, flat......215.00
Herringbone Band, finger lamp, ftd......48.00
Illuminator, finger lamp, flat......50.00
King Comet, finger lamp, flat......50.00
King Comet, finger lamp, ftd......65.00
Lomax, #1......70.00
Lomax, finger lamp, flat......75.00
Lomax, finger lamp, ftd......50.00
Moon & Star, bl font, amber base, 12″, VG......275.00
Nosegay, finger lamp, flat......85.00
Octavia, stand lamp......45.00
Palmette, milk glass base, 10½″......88.00
Panelled Poppy, milk glass, 8½″......250.00
Panelled Wheat, rnd, 10″......165.00
Peacock Feather, bl, finger lamp, flat......95.00
Peacock Feather, bl, 10″......255.00
Peacock Feather, finger lamp, flat......55.00
Peacock Feather, 8½″......66.00
Peanut, finger lamp, ftd......50.00
Peanut, stand lamp......45.00
Pearl Panel w/sailboats & windmills, finger lamp, flat......85.00
Petal & Bulging Loops, bl, finger lamp, ftd......95.00
Picture Window, 9″......150.00
Post, oil burner, 11″......75.00
Prince Edward, gr, finger lamp, ftd......135.00
Prisms w/Plain Band, finger lamp, flat......65.00
Queen Heart, clear, #2......150.00
Queen Heart, gr, #2......350.00
Ring Punty, stand lamp......45.00
Ripley, finger lamp, ftd......150.00
Riven Ribs, stand lamp......145.00
Riverside Almond, finger lamp, ftd......85.00
Riverside Almond, stand lamp, squat......85.00
Riverside's Fern, gr & clear, finger lamp, ftd......175.00
Star Loop & Cable, stemmed......60.00
Sweetheart, whale oil, 9¾″......146.00
Swirl, cranberry wash, finger lamp, flat......95.00
Torpedo, oil burner, 3½″......70.00
Tulip, whale oil, flint, 9″......126.00
Turnip Prism, iron base, stand lamp......45.00

Waffle & Thumbprint, whale oil, dbl burner, 10″ 136.00
Washington, iron base, flint 126.00
Zipper & Rib, finger lamp, flat 65.00
Zipper Loop, marigold, #2 .... 300.00

Reverse Painted Lamps

Jefferson, scenic, w/glass base, sgn 1,450.00
Miller, florals, lt bl w/red, 12″ shade 325.00
Moe Bridges, boudoir, sgn base, rvpt scenic shade, 14″ 350.00
Pittsburgh, swans & pond scene; metal std, 16″ dia 850.00
PLB&G, boudoir, woodland scene, bronze swirl leaf base 325.00
Sunset scene, molded wht metal base, 14″ 155.00

Student Lamps, Kerosene

Brass w/coiled twists, rib peachblow shades, 20″ 500.00
Brass w/opaque wht shade, mk Berlin, 20″ 275.00
Knapp Mfg, NY, orig gr cased shade, pat 1877, brass, wired 475.00
Lincoln, nickel, dtd 1879, 7″ shade 595.00

Whale Oil/Burning Fluid

Blown eng font, serpentine base, wide knop stem, 11″ 275.00
Blown w/pressed ft, hollow stem/cone font/wafers, 10″ 135.00
Blown w/pressed step base, hollow stem/can font/cut panels 150.00
Brass, can font w/striped fire gilt, baluster stem, 4⅜″ 190.00
Brass, chamber lamp w/hinged snuffer cap, 3⅜″ 95.00
Cut overlay pear font, marble ft, att Sandwich, 10″ 175.00
Cut overlay pear font, wht/opal, Sandwich, 10″ 350.00
Dk bl w/bl-gr pear font, att Sandwich, 9½″ 200.00
Flint, sq base, 3-printie font, pewter collar, 9″ 85.00
Free-blown, ball font, multi-wafer connector, dome base 345.00
Gimbal, brass, saucer base, 7″ 65.00
Horn of Plenty, 9¾″ 177.00
Lg squat pear-cut overlay font, pink/wht/clear, 12″ 1,400.00
Onion font, ribbed std & wide ft, opaque wht, 13″ 700.00
Peg, brass, heavy flared base, sits upright, 5″ 95.00
Petticoat, floral cut decor, 5½″ 75.00
Prism base, plain font & stem 75.00
Squat cut font mt on dbl-cut overlay base, brass ft 300.00
Tin, saucer base, shade removes, orig japanning, 12″ 155.00
Waffle, reservoir removes, att Sandwich, 9¼″ 300.00

Miscellaneous

Alcohol, brass w/tin single spout burner, Dyott, 2¾″, VG 40.00
Argand, brass/marble base, blown/frost shade, prisms, 19″ 100.00
Argand, gilt metal/eng glass, single arm, J&I Cox, 20″, pr 1,980.00
Astral, etched shade, fancy prisms, not electric 275.00
Atterbury slag, pk marble gem base, cottage font, pat 1865 .... 450.00
Bicycle, Admiral Comb, w/bracket 50.00
Bicycle, English Dazzler 60.00
Bicycle, Globe, fork mt w/bracket 60.00
Bicycle, Silver King 75.00
Bracket, brass w/ornate wall mts, Adams & Westlake 95.00
Bracket, orig mercury reflectors, pr 125.00
Campaign torch, NP, well trn mahog hdl, 27½″ 75.00
Campaign torch, tin keg shaped font w/3 burners, tin shaft 95.00
Chicago Art Silver Shop, silver overlay on bronze, 10½x6″ 575.00
Chrome, dome shade/cylinder std, French, 1925, 19″, pr 1,870.00
Coleman, orig milk glass shade, 8″ base fuel tank, 20″ 55.00
Desk, gr 9″ shade, EM Roberts, 18″ 200.00
Dietz Beston, tin w/blown chimney, stovepipe burner, 12″ 55.00
Doughboys, Woodrow Wilson portrait/Liberty Bell shade, 16″ 115.00
Emeralite, #8734-B, w/base & shade, sgn 275.00
Emeralite, desk, pat May 11, 1909, all orig 265.00
Emeralite, table, stepped base/swivel arm/brn-figure shade 165.00
Figural, owl, satin glass ribbed half shade, EX detail, 18″ 575.00
Gas, wall fixture, triple swivel, opal chimney/shade 75.00
Grier Bros, miner's, tin, 3¾″ 45.00
Hitchcock, pottery base w/oak leaf bands, mechanical, 12″ 600.00
Islamic Mosque, mc glass, Austrian, late 1800s, 8¼″ 725.00
Motorcycle, Old Sol Hawthorne, brass 85.00
Peg, clear pressed panel font, applied base, 5″ 35.00
Peg, rose/pink, brass candlestick base, orig burner, 17¼″ 550.00
Peg, yel overlay swirl, satin glass, brass candle holder 1,100.00
Rembrandt, Nouveau, brass lady on base, caramel slag shade 175.00
Ripley, marriage, wht base/bl match holder/clambroth fonts 575.00
Skater's, copper, mk Perkins Marine Lamp Co, 6½″ 45.00
Triple-dolphin, wht base, bl/wht stripe font, 11½″ 7,200.00
Vasart, flower-form, ped ft, 5 spiked rims, 10¼″ 295.00
Wall, triple angle, emb brass, opal flame chimneys, in oil 895.00
Wanzer, hunting dog & rabbit on etched shade, mechanical 375.00
Wolfe Safety, heavy brass, 11″ 85.00

Law Related Collectibles

Law enforcement efforts in this country began as early as the 1700s. Since then various groups such as the Texas Rangers and U.S. Marshalls, now defunct, have left a colorful legacy, of interest not only to those now involved in law enforcement but to others as well.

Badges, old photos, wanted posters, handcuffs, and firearms are but a few of the relics that are included in this field of collecting.

When no condition is indicated, the items listed below are assumed to be in excellent condition. See also Badges

Billy club, trn wood, decor: yel hearts on graining, 17″ 55.00
Buckle, 'Police Dept' atop w/'City of NY' below, pre-1900 .... 75.00
Buckle, 'Police' in center, leaf edge design, rnd, w/belt 75.00
Handcuffs, Smith & Wesson, w/key 38.00
Magazine cover, Collier's; 2 police in car, cartoon, 1939 .... 10.00
Medal, Police Shooting, 10k gold, dtd 1929 .... 90.00
Pocket watch, eng w/Boston police badge & name, Waltham 500.00
Whistle, police; English 10.00

Le Verre Francais

Le Verre Francais was produced during the 1920s by Schneider, at Epinay-sur-Seine in France. It was a commercial art glass in the cameo style, composed of layered glass with the designs engraved by acid. Favored motifs were stylized leaves and flowers, or geometric patterns. It was marked with the name in script or with an inlaid filigrane.

When no condition is indicated, the items listed below are assumed to be in mint condition.

Bowl, 6 cameo-cut cats, rare, 2¾″ 985.00
Ewer, amethyst & pink floral, 12½″ 750.00
Night light, florals, globe shape, Art Nouveau base, 6″ 695.00
Vase, trees/fruit, undulating surface, ped ft, sgn, 6″ 550.00

Leeds

The Leeds Pottery was established in 1758 in Yorkshire, and under various managements produced fine creamware, often highly reticulated and transfer printed; shiny black glazed Jackfield wares; and figurines similar to those made in the Staffordshire area.

Little of the early wares were marked; after 1775, the impressed 'Leeds Pottery' mark was used. From 1781 to 1820, the name 'Hartley Greens & Co.' was added. The pottery closed in 1898.

When no condition is indicated, the items listed below are assumed to be in mint condition. See also Creamware

Charger, bl feather edge, 5-color urn w/floral, 14″............425.00
Charger, bl feather edge, 5-color urn w/floral, 15½″..........450.00
Coffee pot, dome lid, gaudy bl/wht, 10″....................400.00
Creamer & sugar, child's; bl/yel floral band, w/lid.............285.00
Cup plate, gaudy bl/wht floral, 3¾″, NM....................235.00
Mug, pearlware, engine trn, ca 1800.........................45.00
Plate, bl feather edge, bl/wht floral, 10″, EX................175.00
Plate, bl feather edge, gaudy bl/wht floral, 8½″, EX...........160.00
Plate, bl feather edge, gaudy 4-color floral, 8½″, NM..........325.00
Plate, bl feather edge, 5-color strawberry decor, 7½″..........300.00
Plate, toddy; peafowl in tree, 5-color, 5½″, EX..............265.00
Platter, bl feather edge w/gaudy bl/wht floral, 16″............250.00
Sugar bowl, shell hdls, mc decor, button finial...............250.00
Teapot, gaudy 4-color floral, soft paste, 7″, EX..............185.00

Legras

Legras and Cie was founded in St. Denis, France in 1864. Production continued until about 1914. In addition to their enameled wares, they made cameo art glass decorated with outdoor scenes and florals executed by acid cuttings through two to six layers of glass. Their work is signed 'Legras' in relief.

When no condition is indicated, the items listed below are assumed to be in mint condition.

Cameo

Rose bowl, relief snails, internal flecks, 6″..................750.00
Vase, grapevine, russet on peach, 16″.......................500.00
Vase, hydrangeas bloom at top, EX cutting, sgn, 9″..........850.00
Vase, swans in lake/trees, swollen cylinder, 11½″.............600.00
Vase, water lilies, gr w/gold highlights, bulbous, 5″...........280.00

Lenox

Walter Scott Lenox, former art director at Ott and Brewer, and Jonathan Coxon founded The Ceramic Art Company of Trenton, New Jersey, in 1889. By 1906, Cox had left the company, and to reflect the change in ownership, the name was changed to Lenox, Inc. Until 1930, when the production of American-made Belleek came to an end, they continued to produce the same type of high-quality ornamental wares that Lenox and Coxon had learned to master while in the employ of Ott and Brewer. Their superior dinnerware made the company famous, and since 1917 Lenox has been chosen the official White House China.

When no condition is indicated, the items listed below are assumed to be in mint condition. See also Collector Plates; Ceramic Art Company

Bowl, cabbage leaf, gr mk, 4½x7½″.........................135.00
Bowl, console; silver overlay, 11″............................95.00
Bowl, pink, shell shape, scalloped edge, gr wreath mk, 12″......45.00
Box, cigarette; gr w/wht relief sheaf, 3½x5″...................45.00
Box, gr & gold w/wht finial, 7″ L.............................95.00
Bust, Art Deco lady, head bowed, hair bobbed, wht, 4½″......125.00
Bust, male & female, gr mk, 9¼″, pr.......................650.00
Candy dish, bird finial, wht bottom, coral lid................115.00
Coaster, cobalt w/gold-wash sterling overlay...................50.00
Coffee set, silver iris overlay, ca 1910, 3-pc.................250.00
Compote, Art Deco shape, wht & gold, 6½x7½″..............85.00
Cream soup w/underplate, Rhodora..........................26.00
Creamer, cobalt w/silver overlay............................65.00
Creamer & sugar bowl, Washington's 200th birthday...........95.00
Cup & saucer, Black Royale.................................30.00
Cup & saucer, Cretan......................................35.00
Cup & saucer, demitasse; #448, burgundy, rare, set of 6.......200.00
Cup & saucer, demitasse; bird on branch, HP/mc, sgn Nosek....80.00
Cup & saucer, demitasse; in silver repousse mt, set of 6.......300.00
Cup & saucer, Forever.....................................30.00
Cup & saucer, Golden Wreath...............................40.00
Cup & saucer, Promise.....................................30.00
Cup & saucer, Rhodora.....................................30.00
Cup & saucer, Sachet......................................30.00
Ewer, mc stork in flight, gold, Worcester type................345.00
Figurine, bird, pink robin, 3½″.............................45.00
Figurine, bird, wht, 6½″...................................75.00

Toby jug, William Penn Treaty, white with pink Indian head handle, 7″, $200.00.

Figurine, lady w/fan, wht bisque, imp 1929, 8½″.............185.00
Figurine, Reader..395.00
Gravy boat, Rhodora.......................................99.00
Honey jar, beehive w/silver overlay, bees in relief............135.00
Humidor, flying geese, sgn Morley, NM......................295.00
Jar, tobacco; owl/pine cone, #328, 7½″.....................150.00
Lamp, celery w/wht swan hdls, 2-pc mk brass base, 22″........75.00
Mug, Crockery Board of Trade Meeting, 1896, 3-hdl, mini.....215.00
Mug, Indian chief wearing headdress, palette mk, lg..........200.00
Pen holder, gr w/wht ruffle, Sheaffer's, w/gold pen, 4″.........95.00
Plate, Beacon Hill, dinner..................................20.00
Plate, brook trout, emb gold border, Morley, Ovington, 9″.....100.00
Plate, Cretan, bread & butter...............................12.00
Plate, Cretan, dinner......................................25.00
Plate, Cretan, salad.......................................18.00
Plate, fruit; pear in center, sgn Morley......................135.00
Plate, Golden Wreath, dinner...............................31.00
Plate, Golden Wreath, salad................................22.00
Plate, McCall's Centennial, Art Nouveau head, 10½″...........90.00
Plate, Meadow Song, dinner.................................20.00
Plate, Melissa, dinner......................................20.00
Plate, Rhodora, dinner.....................................22.00
Plate, service; Canada Geese, acid etched gold rim, Morley.....250.00

Plate, Sonnett, bl wreath, 10½" 30.00
Plate, Tudor, dinner 35.00
Plate, Tudor, salad 25.00
Platter, Cretan, rnd chop 80.00
Service set, Starlight, china, set for 12+, 113-pc 2,300.00
Shade, floor lamp; ivory, ribbed 50.00
Shakers, Nipper, pr 32.50
Sugar bowl, Belvidere, S-314 .... 55.00
Tea set, pink roses on yel, 3-pc 275.00
Vase, birds/branches, artist sgn, gr/yel/bl, 15½" 300.00
Vase, cabbage roses, mc, Morley, 14" 595.00
Vase, cabbage roses on brn, sgn Geo Morley, 18" 695.00
Vase, cabbage roses on butterscotch, sgn Morley, 15" 650.00
Vase, floral panels/HP roses, silver overlay, cylindrical 575.00
Vase, gold/lav floral on rose, 8" 375.00
Vase, ivory w/red/wht roses, gold hdls/neck, ftd, 15" 400.00
Vase, Ming, design ea side, gilt trim, gr wreath mk, 7" 200.00
Vase, molded flowers, cone shape, pink base/cream top, 10" 75.00
Vase, pansies on brn, sgn W Morley, 10" 375.00
Vase, rose w/gold/violets, Worcester type, bulbous, 8" 235.00
Vase, scenic collar on cream/gold, palette mk, 4" 32.00
Vase, silver deposit, no mk, 4½" 75.00
Vase, woman's portrait, sgn Clayton, 12" 495.00
Vase, yel w/wht swan hdls, ped ft, shield shape, 10¼" 165.00

Letter Openers

Adolph Rupp, advertising 40.00
Art Nouveau, sterling, repousse floral, MOP blade 28.00
Art Nouveau semi-nude nymph, metal, dtd 1900, 9" 20.00
Arts & Crafts, hammered copper, lg strap hdl 20.00
Belmont Candy, bronze 18.00
Brass, inch & mm measurements, Lenscale, magnifying glass 25.00
Buffalo Env Co, copper, Roycroft, 8" 25.00
Detroit Stove Works, 'Jewel Stoves,' chrome 24.00
Dupont 30.00
Embalming fluid, bronze ad figural, Metal Arts 30.00
Gooch's Best Feed, lg red circle hdl 15.00
Jockey, full figure, heavy solid silver hdl, Tiffany 75.00
LA Surgical Supply, metal 6.00
Lighthouse 7.00
Lion Bonding & Surety Co, lion's head on hdl, brass 35.00
MOP w/sterling hdl 27.50
Oakland Cars 30.00
Owl, CI figural 10.00
Prudential Insurance 14.00
Railway Express Agency, logo in red, MOP hdl 12.00
Sailboat 7.00
Silver, repousse, sgn Kirk 50.00
Squibb & Sons, Chemists, nickel on brass, fancy 15.00
Stephey 20.00
Yale Locks, figural 65.00

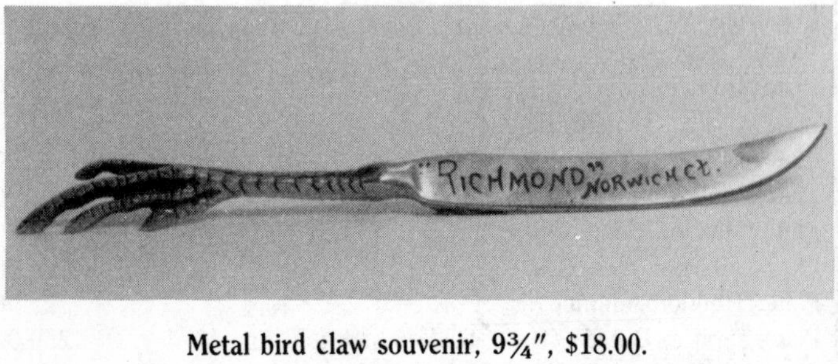

Metal bird claw souvenir, 9¾", $18.00.

Libbey

The New England Glass Company was established in 1818 in Boston, Massachusetts. In 1892, it became known as the Libbey Glass Company. At Chicago's Columbian Expo in 1893, Libbey set up a ten-pot furnace and made glass souvenirs. The display brought them world-wide fame. Between 1878 and 1918, Libbey made exquisite cut and faceted glass, considered today to be the best from the brilliant period. The company is credited for several innovations--the Owens bottle machine that made mass-production possible, and the Westlake machine which turned out both electric light bulbs and tumblers automatically. They developed a machine to polish the rims of their tumblers in such a way that chipping was unlikely to occur. Their glassware carried the patented Safedge guarantee.

Libbey also made glassware in numerous colors--cobalt, ruby, pink, green, and amber. In 1935, it was bought by Owens-Illinois, and remains a division of that company.

When no condition is indicated, the items listed below are assumed to be in mint condition.

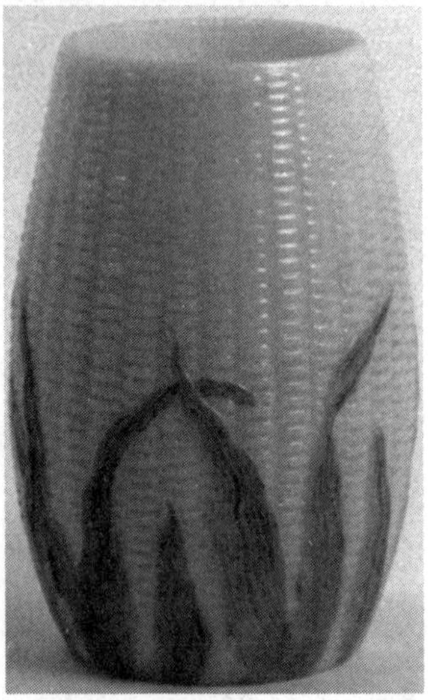

Maize celery vase, white with green leaves, 6½", $95.00.

Basket, amberina, amber hdl, sgn, 7½" 1,400.00
Bowl, brilliant cut, shallow, 9¾" 155.00
Bowl, hobstar/fern/notched prisms, low, 8" 90.00
Bowl, intaglio lilies & leaves, scalloped/3-ftd 150.00
Bowl, Kimberly pattern, deeply cut on heavy blank, 4x10" 270.00
Candlestick, cut panels/teardrop stem/facet knob, Sabre mk 85.00
Candlestick, opal camel stem 135.00
Celery, lovebirds, 11¼x4½x2" 1,095.00
Champagne, cut, hollow stem, sgn 85.00
Champagne, opal squirrel stem, sgn 70.00
Cocktail, opal kangaroo stem 135.00
Cream & sugar bowl, hobstars/diamonds/fans, set 135.00
Creamer & sugar, open; bl satin, World's Fair-1893, rare 500.00
Finger bowl, underplate; amberina, sgn w/1917 mk, 2½" 550.00
Goblet, eagle stem, 6½" 18.00
Goblet, etched bowl, bubble stems, mk, 5¼", set of 6 .... 295.00
Goblet, teardrop stem, blown pontil, sgn, 8 for 500.00
Maize, bowl, centerpiece; gr leaf decor, 4x8¾" 165.00
Maize, butter dish, gr leaves 650.00
Maize, celery vase, pearl w/gr leaves 150.00
Maize, salt shaker, bl leaves, pr 165.00
Maize, salt shaker, gold/bl leaves, brass top, pr 175.00
Maize, sugar shaker, pearl w/yel leaves, 5½" 200.00
Maize, vase, wht w/gr leaves, 6½" 75.00
Paperweight, Columbian Expo scene, Gov't Bldg, sgn Libbey 32.00

Pitcher, lemonade; Thistle, w/6 tumblers....................500.00
Pitcher, reverse amberina, thumbprint pattern, sgn, 7½″.......550.00
Plate, Santa Maria, sepia, Libbey Cut Glass, Toledo, 8″.......385.00
Shaker, flat-side egg shape, Columbian Expo, 1893...........95.00
Tumbler, brilliant cut, heavy, sgn..........................60.00
Tumbler, juice; Harvard.....................................35.00
Tumbler, Star & Feather, sgn................................30.00
Tumbler, strawberry diamond, early mk, set of 6............300.00
Vase, amberina, #3007 in 1917 catalog, w/hdls, 9½″..........445.00
Vase, amberina, mushroom flower form, orig label, 6x5″.......575.00
Vase, Colonna, waisted form, sabre mk, 7½″..................125.00
Vase, daisy/button cutting, stepped sq base, 1940, 16½″.......250.00
Vase, intaglio cut, ftd, 12″................................175.00
Vase, prunts, dk gr on clear, disk ft, sgn, 3″...............110.00
Vase, Radiant, orig label, sgn, 12″.........................295.00
Vase, spiral optic, sq base, cornucopia, 8″...................85.00
Wine, blk monkey stem, sgn, rare............................200.00

Limoges

From the mid-18th century, Limoges was the center of the porcelain industry of France, where at one time more than forty companies utilized the local kaolin to make a superior quality china, much of which was exported to the United States. Various marks were used; some included the name of the American export company rather than the manufacturer, and 'Limoges.' After 1891 'France' was added.

Pieces signed by factory artists are more valuable than those decorated outside the factory by amateurs.

For a more through study of the subject, we recommend you refer to *The Collector's Encyclopedia of Limoges Porcelain* by Mary Frank Gaston, with beautiful color illustrations and current market values. She is listed in the directory under Texas. When no condition is indicated, the items listed below are assumed to be in mint condition.

Ash tray, Grand Marnier Cognac, Union Limousine............22.00
Berry set, pink & wht flowers w/enamel, sgn Andre, LDBC.....225.00
Bowl, children at lake, sgn Villetelle, shallow, sq, 11″.........450.00
Bowl, parrots & fruit basket transfer, T&V, 10″...............65.00
Bowl, pastel florals w/bl scrolls, 3-ftd, Burroughs, 3x7″.........45.00
Bowl, pudding; mixed floral transfer, enamel, gold, Guerin.....145.00
Bowl, vegetable; removable drain tray, hdls, T&V, 9x12½″......85.00
Button, portrait decor, mk Limoges..........................20.00
Candle holder, rose & yel floral transfer, T&V, pr............125.00
Chamberstick, pink floral transfer, CF Haviland, 6″............65.00
Charger, HP fish decor, sgn Brisson, by LDBC, 13″..........175.00
Charger, HP pears, sgn Andre, LDBC, 13″...................155.00
Chocolate pot, much gold relief/roses on wht, w/tray+6 c/s....450.00
Coffee pot, gold trim on wht, Elite..........................50.00
Coffee set, Gold Wedding Band, CF Haviland, 3-pc...........275.00
Cracker jar, florals in 3 panels on cream, gilt, 7″............85.00
Creamer & sugar, open; lt bl w/gold ferns, T&V, 1888.........35.00
Cup & saucer, demitasse; wht w/gold trim, GDA..............30.00
Dresser set, Art Deco, HP geometric designs, Klingenberg.....175.00
Dresser set, tray w/3 boxes, gr/pink floral w/gold.............125.00
Fish set, gold paste floral on pink bkground, Elite, 14-pc......850.00
Fish set, seaweed decor, HP fish, Lanternier, 15-pc.........1,800.00
Hair receiver, sm bl flowers & butterflies, gold trim, wht........65.00
Humidor, Indian's peace pipe motif, yel/gold/orange, HP.......275.00
Ice cream set, floral sprays w/gold trim, Elite, 9-pc...........185.00
Ice cream set, purple thistles, HP, heavy gold, 13-pc..........275.00
Inkwell, mixed floral decor w/gold trim, T&V..................75.00
Mug, gooseberries, tankard style, 4½″........................70.00
Mug, grapes, Pouyat.......................................65.00
Pitcher, tankard; cavalier, sgn Baumy, mk B&H, 13½″........450.00
Pitcher, tankard; cherries, purple/red, sgn D&C, 13″..........145.00
Plaque, Napoleon battle scene, scalloped edge, 10½x11″......375.00
Plate, blackberries, sgn, 8″.................................55.00
Plate, boat scene, sgn Du Val, Coronet, 10″.................150.00
Plate, cavalier, sgn Luc, 10″...............................145.00
Plate, cobalt w/gold scrollwork, Pouyat, 10″..................45.00
Plate, floral, artist sgn, scalloped, 10¾″.....................50.00
Plate, flying game birds, gold Rococo trim, LRL, 12″.........125.00
Plate, game bird, sgn Felix, gold Rococo rim, 11½″..........225.00
Plate, mixed floral, gold trim, Guerin, 8″.....................12.00
Plate, Old Abbey, wht w/HP gold trim, 12″...................42.00
Plate, oyster; pink rose/leaves/ribbons, scalloped, 8½″..........50.00
Plate, pheasant, sgn Max, Coronet, 10″......................145.00
Plate, pheasants w/fruit & floral, gold Rococo rim, 13″........300.00
Plate, portrait, sgn Du Bois, 10″............................250.00
Plate, roses, pink/rose on pastel, gold Rococo rim, 13½″......175.00
Plate, wild duck, sgn Max, Coronet, 10″.....................120.00
Plate, winter scene w/wht/gold floral spray, G Tave, 11½″......350.00
Plate, winter/summer scenic, gold Rococo rim, 14″, pr........195.00
Plate, woman w/basket in snow scene w/windmill, no mk, 11″..125.00
Plate, yel floral/leaves, HP, scalloped, 8¼″, set of 12..........175.00
Platter, fish/lily pad, HP, sgn LePacot, 8x23½″...............125.00
Punch bowl, pink/wht dogwood blossoms on gr, T&V, 12″.....225.00
Punch bowl, pink/yel floral on dk gr, 9½″...................200.00
Punch bowl/stand, roses w/in & w/out, scalloped, T&V........675.00
Ramekin, pink floral w/gold..................................16.00
Ramekin, rose transfer, w/underplate, Ahrenfeldt.............15.00
Salt dip, pearlized interior/gold exterior, Bernardaud...........10.00
Sugar basket, bl floral transfer, Lanternier...................35.00
Tea set, dogwood, sgn JP, gold wishbone hdl, 3-pc...........185.00
Tea set, roses, mk WG&C, gilt, 3-pc........................165.00
Tray, cupid decor, Klingenberg, 11″..........................95.00
Tray, honeysuckle, artist sgn, gold trim, 12x8½″..............40.00
Tray, roses, artist sgn, Art Nouveau, hdls, T&V, 18x12″........58.00
Tureen, mixed floral, scalloped body, gold, Guerin, 7x12″.....145.00
Tureen, soup; quilted w/HP floral, cream w/gold trim..........85.00
Turkey set, 6 HP artist sgn designs, 20½″ platter, 13-pc.......600.00
Vase, floral, gr & gold borders, unusual shape, hdls, 12½″.....235.00
Vase, flying geese, Union Limousine, 12″.....................95.00
Vase, gold mum/gold legs/hdls, M Redon, 9″.................125.00
Vase, iris on pale pink bkground, Guerin.....................225.00
Vase, red & wht roses, Bernardaud, 9″......................135.00
Vase, roses, Rococo shape, Pouyat..........................145.00
Whiskey jug, HP red/pink/wht floral, T&V, 6″................225.00

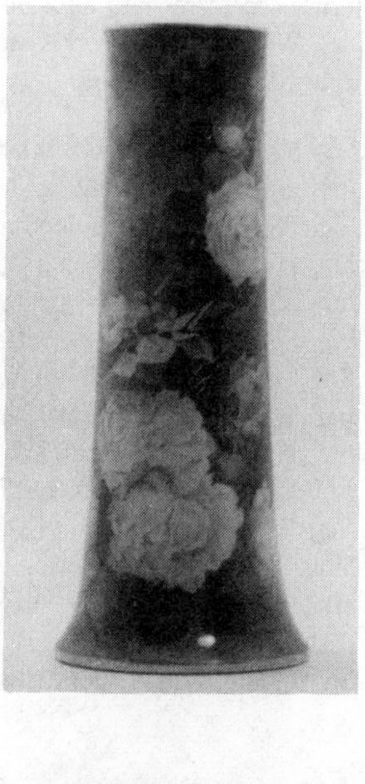

Floor vase, porcelain with allover pink and red roses, signed twice with 'Coronet' and green mark, signed by factory artist, 20″, $1,250.00.

Lithophanes

Lithophanes are porcelain panels with relief designs of varying degrees of thickness and density. Transmitted light brings out the pattern in graduated shadings, lighter where the procelain is thin, and shaded in the heavy areas. They were cast from wax models prepared by artists, and depict views of life from the 1800s, religious themes, or scenes of historical significance. First made in Berlin about 1825, they were used as lamp shade panels, window plaques, or candle shields. Later, steins, mugs, and cups were made with lithophanes in their bases. Japanese wares were sometimes made with dragons or Geisha lithophanes.

When no condition is indicated, the items listed below are assumed to be in mint condition. See also Steins

Key:
fr—framed   tz—trapezoid
rect—rectangular

Candle holder, Dancing Hours figure, Wedgwood 195.00
Lamp, fairy; 3 panels w/people, 4¾″ 495.00
Lamp, 5 rect panels, PPM/Germany; cut glass/brass std 750.00
Lamp, 5 tz panels w/children & scenes; glass/iron std, 21″ 750.00
Panel, Am historical view: Paterson Falls, PPM 165.00
Panel, lad plays flute, maid holds music in garden, 4½x5½″ 100.00
Panel, priest & acolyte at water's edge, PPM #113, 6x5″ 325.00
Panel, St Ann, PPM #337, 5¼x4⅜″; in stained glass fr 195.00
Panel in cast stand, girl in meadow w/collie, KPM, 17x12″ 375.00
Plaque, Le Seaux du Parc De Versailles, self fr, 6¾x8″ 140.00
Saki cup, faces appear when filled w/liquid 65.00
Shade, 5 tz panels, PPM, 6″ 675.00
Stein, brn/blk monk figural, lovely girl lithophane 325.00
Stein, dancing couple, transfer of deer, ½-L 135.00
Stein, man at table, lady standing; plowing transfer 175.00
Stein, nude in base, German porc, airplane finial, WWII 75.00
Stein, 2¼″ ruins of Hallenburg lithophane, w/lid, 8″ 120.00
Tea warmer, 4 scenic panels 265.00

Liverpool

In the late 1700s, Liverpool potters produced a creamy ivory ware, sometimes called Queen's Ware, which they decorated by means of the newly-perfected transfer print. Made specifically for the American market, patriotic inscriptions, political portraits, or other States themes were applied in black with colors sometimes added by hand. Before it lost favor in about 1825, other English potters made a similar product; today Liverpool is a generic term used to refer to all ware of this type.

When no condition is indicated, the items listed below are assumed to be in mint condition.

Jug, Boston Frigate, bk: Washington/Franklin, 10½″, EX 1,980.00
Jug, jolly man/verse/house, crack, 7″ 95.00
Jug, Montgomery/Washington, Frigate w/flag, eagle, EX 280.00
Jug, pig/verse/rider on horse, orange transfer, rpr 95.00
Jug, Salem shipyards w/poem, bk: Am ship, gilt rim, 8″ 550.00
Jug, Seal of US, Frigate w/British flag, hairline, 9¾″ 450.00
Jug, Telling Fortune in Coffee Grounds, 5¾″, VG 125.00
Jug, War of 1812, Brown/Decator, 5½″ 800.00
Jug, War of 1812, Pike/Perry, 7½″, NM 1,500.00
Jug, Washington Monument/Plan of Washington, rim chip, 9″ . . 600.00
Jug, Washington's Tomb/13 states, hairlines/prof rpr, 12″ 350.00
Mug, By Virtue We Have...a Great Empire, 3½″ 625.00
Mug, 2 angels w/banner, list of 15 states, 4⅞″, EX 2,800.00
Plate, 'Hope,' mc, 10″ 185.00
Soup plate, Let Wisdom Unite Us, sm edge flakes, 9⅞″ 80.00

Lladro

Lladro porcelains are currently being produced in Labernes Blanques, Spain. Their retired and limited edition figurines are popular collectibles.

When no condition is indicated, the items listed below are assumed to be in mint condition.

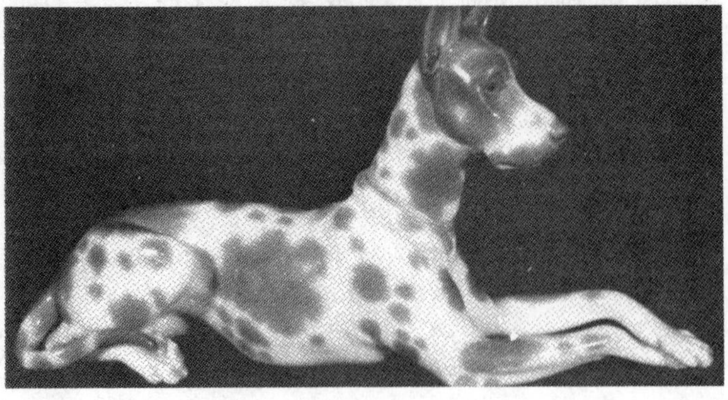

Great Dane, #1068, 6¾″ high, $200.00.

Boy soccer player, #5135 . . . . . 89.00
Girl feeding goose, 10″ 265.00
Girl picking flowers, #1287, 8½″ 200.00
Girl selling balloons, 10″ 180.00
Girl soccer player, #5134 . . . . . 89.00
Girl w/calla lilies, #4650, 9½″ 85.00
Girl w/ducks in basket, duck at her feet, 9¼″ 200.00
Girl w/umbrella & duck family, 11½″ 225.00
Hamlet, bisque, rare, 16″ 600.00
Harlequin w/guitar 495.00
Japanese peasant girl resting on basket of vegetables, 5½″ 165.00
Napping, #5070 . . . . . 155.00
Plate, Christmas, 1st edition, no box 20.00
Victorian lady w/dog, pearl hdl parasol, 14″ 100.00

Lobmeyer

J. and L. Lobmeyer, contemporaries of Moser, worked in Vienna, Austria during the last quadrant of the 1800s. Most of the work attributed to them is decorated with distinctive enameling; favored motifs are people in 18th century garb.

When no condition is indicated, the items listed below are assumed to be in mint condition.

Bowl, red/bl/gr/purple/yel floral w/curlique decor, 6¼″ 235.00
Mug, enamel poppies, gold rim, clear brn, 3½″ 40.00
Salt, 18th C man enameling, 2¼″ 70.00
Stem, allover floral, fishscale decor, 6¼″, set of 6 . . . . . 1,800.00
Tumbler, lemonade; 18th C lady enameling 150.00

Locke Art

In 1898 when he established the Locke Art Glassware Company in the Pittsburgh, Pennsylvania area, Joseph Locke already had proven himself many times over as a master glassmaker. After working in various leading English glasshouses for more than twenty-five years, he joined the Libbey Company where he invented processes for the manufacture of several types of art glass-- amberina, peachblow, pomona, and agata among them. Locke Art glassware was produced using an acid-etching process on imported crystal blanks of the highest quality. While the outlines of the designs were established through the use of a copper template, most of the work (including the trademark) was done by hand. The business closed in 1914.

When no condition is indicated, the items listed below are assumed to be in mint condition.

Brandy, flowers & leaves, sgn, paper sticker, 3¼″ 92.00
Goblet, poppies, sgn, 6½″ 75.00
Punch cup, poppies, sgn 75.00
Salt, vintage, ped ft, sgn, 1¼x2¼″ 55.00
Sherbet, turned-up base forms underplate, vintage, 3½″ 185.00
Tumbler, leaves & cherries, sgn, 5¼″ 85.00
Tumbler, rose nosegays, 5″, pr 145.00

Locks

The earliest type of lock in recorded history was the wooden cross-bar used by ancient Egyptians and their contemporaries. The early Romans are credited with making the first key-operated mechanical lock. The ward lock was invented during the Middle Ages by the Etruscans of Northern Italy; the lever tumbler and combination locks followed at various stages of history with varying degrees of effectiveness. In the 18th century, the first precision lock was constructed--it was a device that utilized a lever tumbler mechanism.

Two of the best-known of the early 19th century American lock manufacturers are Yale and Sargent and today's collectors value Winchester and Keen Kutter locks very highly. Factors to consider are rarity, condition, and construction. Brass and bronze locks are generally priced higher than those of steel or iron.

When no condition is indicated, the items listed below are assumed to be in mint condition.

Abloy Cutaway, w/key 30.00
Ames Sword, w/swivel for chain, 6-lever 30.00
Anchor, w/key 8.00
Barnes, Good Luck 65.00
Bear, w/key 9.50
Box, wrought iron/brass trim & lever hdls, w/keeper, 5½″ 90.00
Bruin, emb bear, no key 35.00
Bruno, iron, dog's face, w/key 12.00
Champion, 6-lever 200.00
Cincinnati Gas & Electric, emb on brass 12.00
Cleveland, 4-way, 8-lever, no key 17.50
Corbin, Excelsior, pancake push key type, no key 17.50
Corbin, iron, G&B, no key 7.50
Corbin, Iron Side, 6-lever, w/key 6.50
Corbin, Samson, 8-lever, no key 11.00
Corbin, USMC, pin tumbler, push key, no key 22.50
Cruso, brass, emb chicken, no key 40.00
Diamond Edge, brass, figural emblem 100.00
Door, bronze, winged lion decor, 1750s 175.00
Eagle, Hibbard, pin tumbler, push key, no key 22.50
Eagle, orig box, w/key, set of 7 .... 42.00
Eagle, Wm Enders Oak Leaf, 6-lever, w/key 10.00
Edwards, Safety Lever, 6-lever, w/key 6.50
Elbow, wrought iron, w/key & keeper, 4⅝x6″ 40.00
Fraim, DE Co, 4-lever, w/key 30.00
Fraim, DL&WRY, pin tumbler, swivel for chain, 4-lever, key 30.00
Fraim, Empire, pancake push key type, 6-lever, no key 17.50
Fraim, ICRR, pin tumbler, 4-lever, w/key 22.50
Fraim, power lever, no key 4.00
Geo Worthington Co, brass 30.00
Good Luck, w/key 65.00
Illinois Power Co, 3-lever, no key 30.00
Indian's head, emb, w/key 40.00
Keen Kutter, EC Simmons, w/key 110.00
Lion's head emb, dtd 1880 .... 30.00
Locking Chain Corp, Trio Chain Lock, no key 11.00
Miller, Protector, 3-lever, no key 6.50
Miller, Simmons Quality, 6-lever, w/key 6.50
Miller Internal Revenue 175.00
Miloco, w/key 8.00
Oneida, w/key 10.00
Rough Riders, emb rider on horse 45.00
Sargent, Greenleaf, 6-lever, no key 22.50
Sargent, Simmons, pin tumbler, push key, no key 22.50
Simmon's Victory 20.00
Simmon's Wireless CQD 85.00
Slaymaker, AT&SF, pin tumbler, 4-lever, w/key 22.50
Slaymaker, Pan Handle RR, pin tumbler, 4-lever, w/key 30.00
Tokheim, brass & iron, no key 7.50
Union, 6-lever 40.00
US Internal Revenue 100.00
US Mail, 2-lever, no key 11.00
Victory, w/key 10.00
Wilson Bohannon, 6-lever, w/key 22.50
Winchester, 6-lever, w/key 85.00
Yale, Belknap, 4-lever 30.00
Yale, Bi-Centric, 2 key holes, w/key 50.00
Yale, heart shape, 2-lever, no key 17.50
Yale, PCTRR, pin tumbler, 4-lever, w/key 30.00
Yale, pin tumbler, push key, no key 11.00
Yale, USN, pin tumbler, push key, swivel for chain, no key 22.50

Loetz

The Loetz Glassworks was established in Klostermule, Austria, in 1840. After Loetz's death, the firm was purchased by his grandson, Johann Loetz Witwe. Until WWII the operation continued to produce fine artware, some of which made in the early 1900s bears a striking resemblance to Tiffany's, with whom Loetz was associated at one time. In addition to the iridescent Tiffany-style glass, he also produced threaded glass and some cameo. Signed pieces bring premium prices.

When no condition is indicated, the items listed below are assumed to be in mint condition.

Vase, blue iridescent with silver overlay florals, signed, $1,100.00.

Bowl, rainbow spotted irid on gr, honeycomb, fluted, 4x10" 500.00
Bowl vase, bulbous, silver/bronze irid on gr, 6" 200.00
Bride's basket, gr fluted bowl/brass fr, unsgn, 11" 575.00
Centerpiece, oil spot vase+2 bowls in metal fr, unsgn, 18" 850.00
Inkwell, irid cranberry, brass lid & lily pad 295.00
Planter, damascene swirls, oil spots, pinched, 5x5x9" 450.00
Planter, gr, 3 twist ft, 4x8" 200.00
Sweetmeat, gr irid w/mc glass strands, SP lid, hdl 225.00
Sweetmeat, gr w/silver spider web, w/hdl, sgn 400.00
Sweetmeat, irid red, ornate shape, SP lid, unsgn, 6¼" 300.00
Vase, amber, allover thorns, 2 joined necks, unsgn, 9½" 700.00
Vase, amber/pk, bl irid pocks, pinched/fluted, unsgn, 3½" 155.00
Vase, amberina, irid w/gold flecks, floriform, flared, 8½" 375.00
Vase, amethyst & gr, heavily threaded, 10½" 250.00
Vase, amethyst irid, sgn, 8½" 395.00
Vase, amethyst/gold/turq irid, fan shape, ribbed, 13" 285.00
Vase, apricot w/wht feathering, wht w/in, sgn, 9" 750.00
Vase, bl irid, Art Nouveau silver overlay, unsgn, 4¾" 385.00
Vase, bl irid on gr, ftd/cylindrical/flared w/ribs, 5½" 185.00
Vase, bl irid w/wht pnt floral, unsgn, 4½" 75.00
Vase, bl irid w/yel threads, 4" 225.00
Vase, bl-blk w/gold leaves/berries, pinch sides, unsgn, 8" 285.00
Vase, bl/purple/brn irid on dk gr, quatrefoil top, 9" 115.00
Vase, blk/red pattern, silver collar, sgn/X-arrows, 2¼" 375.00
Vase, celadon, unsgn, 10" 75.50
Vase, gold irid on clear, gr threads, ruffled, 4x3¼" 235.00
Vase, gr & amethyst irid, ruffled top, sgn, 10" 600.00
Vase, gr irid, oil spots w/yel wavy lines, ruffled, 7¼" 450.00
Vase, gr irid, threaded, 14½" 285.00
Vase, gr irid base, gold shell top, unsgn, 12½x5¾x5" 450.00
Vase, gr irid spots on clear, optic ribs, pinched neck, 4" 135.00
Vase, gr oil spots, amethyst rim, flower form, 6½" 165.00
Vase, gr w/apricot waves & irid spots, twisted, unsgn, 4½" 665.00
Vase, gr w/lav irid, crimped top, threaded, 4x5" 120.00
Vase, gr w/mc irid, swirled/marbleized, 4-lobe top, 9" 300.00
Vase, gr/amethyst/gold/turq irid, fan shape, crimped, 8" 300.00
Vase, gr/bl irid w/veined gold design, twisted body, 13" 395.00
Vase, gr/turq swirls on amethyst, crimped base, 7" 145.00
Vase, irid, gold t'print indents, flared top, 3¼" 150.00
Vase, irid red & bl, encircled serpent, 10½x6½" 400.00
Vase, lt yel w/3 bl irid spotted lappets, unsgn, 7⅛" 600.00
Vase, mc, ball base w/tube top, unsgn, 8½" 475.00
Vase, mirror irid on gr, ruffled top, bulbous, 4½" 65.00
Vase, peach w/pulled feathering, sgn, 8" 750.00
Vase, pink top, bl oil spots on purple base, unsgn, 7½" 575.00
Vase, pink w/bl irid lappets, pinch sides, sgn, 6" 495.00
Vase, plat irid, ribbed, urn form, 4x3½" 265.00
Vase, plat irid, ribbed/flared, 8½" 325.00
Vase, plat irid w/turq threads, blown-out ft, 4-lobed, 4" 235.00
Vase, purple irid, threading, 11" 120.00
Vase, red irid, sgn sterling overlay, unsgn, 4¼" 450.00
Vase, red w/allover silver-bl irid, pinched, unsgn, 9" 700.00
Vase, red w/fine irid bl & navy waves, baluster, sgn, 7½" 750.00
Vase, red/opal on yel raindrops, feathers, unsgn, 12" 750.00
Vase, sapphire-bl w/amber irid spots, hdls, unsgn, 13½" 800.00
Vase, silver overlay, floral, waves & oil spots, unsgn, 6" 700.00
Vase, silver overlay on paperweight w/fronds, unsgn, 8½" 750.00

Longwy

The Longwy workshops were founded in 1798, and continue today to produce pottery in the north of France near the Luxembourgh-Belgian border. The ware for which they are best known was produced during the Art Deco period, decorated in bold color and geometric designs. Earlier wares made during the first quarter of the 19th century reflected the popularity of Oriental art, cloisonne enamels in particular. The designs were executed by impressing the pattern into the moist clay, and filling in the depressions with enamels. Examples are marked 'Longwy,' either impressed or painted under glaze.

When no condition is indicated, the items listed below are assumed to be in mint condition.

Bowl, mc floral on bl, bl w/out, 3¾" 38.00
Bowl, mc floral on burgundy, bl w/out, 5½" 55.00
Cup & saucer, wht w/bluebird/butterfly, floral bands 38.00
Dish, scalloped rim, Primavera, 5½" 55.00
Plate, centerpiece; floral/bird, in brass tripod fr, 12½" 325.00
Table lamp, red cylinder w/mc floral on 5½" blk base 135.00
Vase, bird on flowering branch, cylindrical, 6½x3" 160.00
Vase, floral, purple, cobalt w/in, cylindrical, mk, 4⅝" 125.00
Vase, floral on bl, top border, 7¼x3" 155.00
Vase, geometric on bl/blk/gold, crackle eggshell, sgn, 4" 95.00

Trivet, woman and exotic foliage, Primavera, after Mattise, 8", $850.00.

Lonhuda

William Long was a druggist by trade, who combined his knowledge of chemistry with his artistic ability, in an attempt to produce a type of brown glazed slip-decorated artware similar to that made by the Rookwood Pottery. He achieved his goal in 1889, after years of long and dedicated study. Three years later, he founded his firm, the Lonhuda Pottery Company. The name was coined from the first few letters of the last name of each of his partners, W.H. Hunter and Alfred Day. Laura Fry, formerly of the Rookwood company, joined the firm in 1892, bringing with her a license for Long to use her patented airbrush blending process. Other artists of note, Sarah McLaughlin, Helen Harper, and Jessie Spaulding joined the firm and decorated the ware with nature studies, animals, and portraits, often signing their work with their initials. Three types of marks were used on the Steubenville Lonhuda ware. The first was a linear composite of the letters 'LPCO' with the name 'Lonhuda' impressed above it. The second, adopted in 1893, was a die-stamp representing the solid profile of an Indian, used on ware patterned after pottery made by the American Indians. This mark was later replaced with an impressed outline of the Indian head, with 'Lonhuda' arching above it. Although the ware was successful, the business floundered due to poor management; in 1895, Long became a partner of Sam Weller and moved to Zanesville where the manufacture of the Lonhuda line continued. Less than a year later, Long left the Weller company.

When no condition is indicated, the items listed below are assumed to be in mint condition.

Pitcher, fish handle, rust and golden tan, 11″, $600.00.

Candlestick, floral, Stubenville & Indian head mk, 5¾″........165.00
Ewer, dogwood, trefoil lip, Helen M Harper, 10″, NM.........350.00
Loving cup, blossoms/buds, sgn SR McLaughlin, 1895 mk, 5″..350.00
Vase, fish & waves on gr, spherical, sgn, 6″.................600.00
Vase, floral, artist sgn, 2-hdl, glaze flaws, 5½″...............115.00
Vase, floral, 3 integral rim-to-width hdls, 3 ft, 6½″...........245.00
Vase, violet; yel violets, sgn HMH, Steubenville, 2x4″.........265.00

Lotton, Charles

Cologne, clear w/orange/wht poppies, sgn/1982, 5″...........350.00
Vase, floral, paperweight type, sgn Multi-flora, '77, 9x6″.......485.00
Vase, millefiori canes on bl, 3″...........................125.00

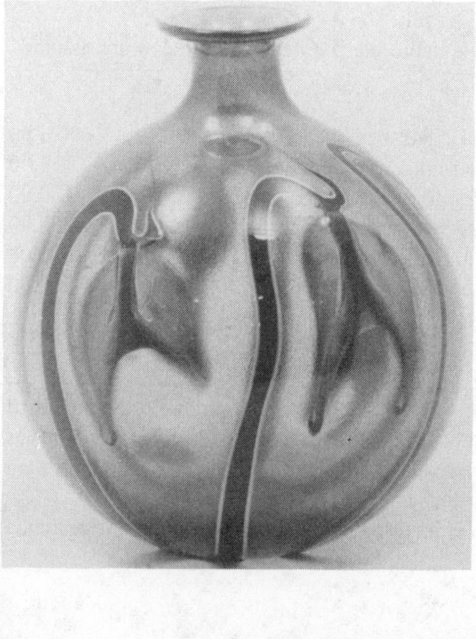

Bottle, green with yellow and black floral, signed and dated 1982, 5″, $150.00.

Lu Ray Pastels

Lu Ray Pastels dinnerware was introduced in the early 1940s by Taylor, Smith, and Taylor of East Liverpool, Ohio. It was offered in assorted colors--Persian Cream, Sharon Pink, Surf Green, Windsor Blue, and Gray--in complete place settings as well as many service pieces. It was a successful line in its day and is once again finding favor with collectors of American dinnerware.

When no condition is indicated, the items listed below are assumed to be in mint condition.

Bowl, fruit; 5½″...4.50
Bowl, mixing..30.00
Bowl, tab hdl, 6″..10.00
Bowl, vegetable; oval.....................................6.50
Bowl, 9″...7.50
Butter dish, w/lid, ¼-lb..................................18.00
Casserole, w/lid...20.00
Chop plate, 14″..13.50
Coffee pot, demitasse; ovoid, w/lid.......................25.00
Coffee pot, demitasse; w/lid..............................40.00
Creamer..5.00
Creamer, demitasse; ovoid................................10.00
Creamer, demitasse; straight sides........................15.00
Cup & saucer...6.50
Cup & saucer, demitasse..................................10.00
Egg cup...12.00
Epergne...35.00
Gravy w/attached underplate..............................12.50
Muffin cover, w/8″ underplate.............................45.00
Pickle dish...6.00
Pitcher, bulbous w/flat bottom............................25.00
Pitcher, ftd...25.00
Pitcher, juice; ovoid.....................................25.00
Pitcher, syrup...40.00
Plate, cake..15.00
Plate, Chatham Gray, rare color, 7″........................6.00
Plate, grill..11.00
Plate, serving; tab hdl....................................15.00
Plate, 10″..6.00
Plate, 7″...3.00
Plate, 9″...4.50
Platter, oval, 11½″..8.00
Shakers, pr...8.50
Soup plate..4.00
Sugar, w/lid, demitasse; ovoid............................10.00
Sugar, w/lid, demitasse; straight sides....................20.00
Teapot, w/lid..35.00
Tidbit, 2 tier..18.00
Tumbler, juice..10.00

Left to right: Demitasse pot, ovoid form, $25.00; Demitasse creamer, ovoid form, $10.00; Demitasse sugar bowl, ovoid form, $10.00.

Lunch Boxes

Early 20th century tobacco companies such as Union Leader, Tiger, and Dixie issued a series of square containers with flat metal carrying handles designed to be used for lunch boxes after the contents had been otherwise enjoyed. By 1930, oval lunch pails with colorful lithographed decorations on tin were being manufactured to appeal directly to children. These were made by Ohio Art, who in 1950 changed from the oval to the standard rectangular shape more often seen today. In 1950 the Aladdin Company issued the first of their character lunch boxes, decorated with pictures of Hopalong Cassidy, Trigger, Bozo, etc., fully fitted with matching thermos bottles.

Early boxes sometimes were die-pressed so that the shape of the character stood out in relief. Character decals were applied to the corresponding embossed designs. The thermos bottles, however, were lithographed and by the mid-fifties, so were the boxes.

Other companies--ADCO Liberty; Landers, Frary & Clark; and American Thermos--also produced character pails. Today's collectors often tend to specialize in those dealing with a particular subject. Western, space, TV series, Disney movies, or cartoon characters are among the most popular.

When no condition is indicated, the items listed below are assumed to be in excellent condition.

Adams Family, 1974 .... 5.00
Batman 10.00
Beatles, bl w/portrait, VG 45.00
Bedknobs & Broomsticks 4.50
Beverly Hillbillies 12.00
Blondie, 1969 .... 8.00
Bonanza, w/thermos 7.00
Cartoon Zoo Lunch Chest 10.00
Central Union Cut Plug Tobacco, EX 45.00
Central Union Cut Plug Tobacco, NM 75.00
Chuck Wagon, covered wagon shape 15.00
Cinco Tobacco 35.00
Cowboys & Indians 7.00
Daniel Boone 20.00
Dixie Queen, portrait, NM 110.00
Emergency, w/thermos 4.00
Fashion Cut Plug Tobacco, EX 100.00
Fat Albert 12.00
Fireball XL5, 1964 .... 12.00
Flintstones & Dino, 1962 .... 15.00
Gentle Ben, 1968 .... 4.50
Gunsmoke, Marshall Matt Dillon, 1959 .... 12.50
Harlem Globetrotters, 1971 .... 4.50
Hee Haw, w/thermos 8.00
Hiawatha Tobacco, rectangular 75.00
Hopalong Cassidy, w/thermos, EX 25.00
Jim Henson's Muppet Show, thermos 8.00
Just Suits Tobacco 60.00
Lassie & Black Beauty, 1962 .... 15.00
Mayo Tobacco Cut Plug 35.00
Osmonds, 1973 .... 3.50
Patterson's Seal Cut Plug Tobacco, basketweave 35.00
Peter Pan 8.00
Peter Rabbit 56.00
Pinocchio, tin, rectangular w/tray, WDP, 7" L 45.00
Planet of the Apes, w/thermos, 1974 .... 4.00
Plow Boy Tobacco, silver, NM 200.00
Plow Boy Tobacco, VG 115.00
Popeye, fishing scene, w/tin thermos, 1964, 8" L 25.00
Red Crest Tobacco, leather, w/rooster, JJ Bagley, 1890s 100.00
Roy Rogers & Dale Evans, Double R Bar Ranch, EX 20.00
Roy Rogers Chow Wagon, wagon shaped, w/thermos, M 50.00
Spaceship Moonbase 10.00
Star Trek, thermos only 12.00
Star Wars, 1977 .... 4.00
Steve Canyon, 1959 .... 12.00
Superman 8.00
Tom Corbett Space Cadet, Rockhill Radio, 1952 .... 25.00
Union Leader Cut Plug Tobacco, basketweave & paper bank 40.00
Vox Wagon, tin, rare, 1960 .... 35.00
Voyage to Bottom of Sea, w/thermos 8.00
Wagon Train, w/thermos, 1964 .... 5.50
Waltons, 1973 .... 3.00
Warnick & Brown Tobacco 65.00
Welcome Back Kotter, 1977 .... 4.00
Wild, Wild West, 1969 .... 8.00
Wild Fruit Tobacco 65.00
Winner Tobacco, superb color, EX 100.00
Woody Woodpecker, 1972 .... 6.50
Zorro 22.00

Green Turtle Cigars, green and chartreuse, 4½" x 7½" x 5½", $195.00.

Lustre Art Glass Co.

The Lustre Art Glass Company operated in Long Island, New York, from about 1920 until 1925, manufacturing iridescent lamp shades similar to those of Durand and Quezal.

When no condition is indicated, the items listed below are assumed to be in mint condition.

Gold bands on opal, gold lined, bell shape, sgn, 5" 375.00
Gold feather w/gr edge on opal, scalloped, sgn 125.00
Gold zipper, wht wavy design, ruffled edge, sgn, 5" 150.00
Gr border, brn/wht pulled feathers on gold, 5¼", pr 265.00
Opal leaves, gold base, threaded, sgn 245.00
Ruby, gold/wht/bl pnt flowers, crystal prisms, 13", pr 550.00

Maastricht

Maastricht, Holland, was the site of the De Sphinx Pottery, founded in 1836 by Petrus Regout. They made earthenware decorated with transfer prints, as well as dinnerware with gaudy hand-painted designs. Potteries are still working in this area today.

When no condition is indicated, the items listed below are assumed to be in mint condition.

Plate, George Washington, Mt. Vernon, signed Petrus Regout & Co., Maastricht, made in Holland, 9½″, $45.00.

Bowl, fruit; Oriental pattern, Timor, 9″....50.00
Compote, Oriental scene, 2″ gold trim, ftd, PaJong, 4½″....55.00
Cup & saucer, gaudy stick spatter floral....50.00
Pitcher, Timor, 4½″....65.00
Plaque, Royal Sphinx Holland, farm scene, bl/wht, 15½″....65.00
Plate, bl Delft scene, flowered border....20.00
Plate, gaudy stick spatter floral, 4-color, 9″....40.00
Plate, man on horsebk sells fruit, bl/wht, 8″....35.00
Plate, Roosevelt portrait, 10″....30.00

Magazines

Magazines are collected for their cover prints, and for the information pertaining to defunct companies and their products that can be gleaned from the old advertisements.

In the listings below, when no condition is indicated, items are assumed to be in very good condition. See also Prints

Key:
M—mint condition, in original wrapper
EX—excellent condition, spine intact, edges of pages clean and straight
VG—very good condition, the average as-found condition

American Detective, 1937, Feb, 96 pg, EX....7.00
Beauty Parade, 1941, Oct, Vol 1, #1, Earl Morgan cover, VG...20.00
Beauty Parade, 1944, Mar, 64 pg, 8½x11½″, EX....7.50
Burlesk, 1942, Aug, Vol 1, #1, Margie Hart/Gypsy Rose Lee....15.00
Certified Detective Cases #1, 1940, 10x13″....10.00
Collier's, 1902, Sept 22, Will Bradley cover....15.00
Confidential Confession, 1952, Feb & Mar....4.00
Cutie, 1944, May, #1....20.00
Esquire #1, 1933, Autumn....75.00
Eve #1, 1950, Oct....8.00
Fate, complete set from Spring 1949-May 1975, EX....133.00
First Military Conscription #1, 1940....5.00
Fortune, 1931, July, 6½-pg Coke article, VG....15.00
Fortune, 1940, Apr, EX....8.50
Glamour of Hollywood, 1939, Sept....5.00
Godey's Ladies Magazine, 1867, June, EX....12.00
Good Housekeeping, 1918, Kewpies ad, April Fool's Day....10.00
Harper's Weekly, M Parish, His Christmas Dinner....25.00
Harper's Weekly, 1862, Feb 15....7.00
Harper's Weekly, 1863, Jan 17, Homer engraving....50.00
Hearst's, 1922, Mar, Mucha cover, Parrish ad, VG....65.00
Hollywood, 1937, Oct, Dorothy Lamour....15.00
Hollywood Revue, 1931, May, Vol 1, #2, Joan Crawford....25.00
Keyhole Detective Cases, 1942, Mar....6.00
Ladies' Home Journal, 1898, Feb, My Valentine....8.00
Ladies' Home Journal, 1901, Aug, Alice in Wonderland ad....8.00
Ladies' Home Journal, 1911, Mar 15, Fisher cover, VG....18.50
Life, 1936, Nov 23, Vol 1, #1....35.00
Life, 1938, Oct 31, Abe Lincoln on Broadway, EX....3.00
Life, 1959, Apr 20, Monroe cover....10.00
Look, 1937, Dec 21, Shirley Temple entertains Santa....22.00
Look, 1938, Oct 11, Dionne Quints....15.00
Look, 1961, Sept 12, Kennedy One Year Later, VG....4.00
Look, 1963, Kennedy & His Family in Pictues....7.50
Magazine of Western History, 1886, Feb....5.00
McCall's, 1929, Oct, Zane Grey novel....5.00
Modern Screen, 1942, Jan, Judy Garland, M....18.00
Modern Screen, 1947, Mar, Clark Gable, M....16.00
Motion Picture, 1935, June, Dietrich cover, 82 pg, VG....15.00
Motion Picture, 1941, Aug, Veronica Lake....15.00
Motorsport, 1950, Oct....4.00
Movie Life, 1939, Dec, Shirley Temple cover, 66 pg, VG....29.00
Movie Life, 1941, July, Gene Autry cover, 66 pg, VG....22.00
Movie Life, 1941, Oct, Judy Garland cover, 66 pg, EX....18.00
National Geographic, 1902, July....35.00
National Geographic, 1909, Oct, Discovery of the Pole....35.00
National Geographic, 1911, July, Reptiles of All Lands....10.00
National Geographic, 1912, Oct, China....10.00
National Geographic, 1913, Nov, Philippines....10.00
National Geographic, 1914, Nov, Young Russia....7.50
National Geographic, 1916, May, Land of the Incas....7.50
National Geographic, 1919, Mar, special....7.50
National Geographic, 1922, Sept....5.00
National Geographic, 1932, Mar....5.00
National Geographic, 1945, May....5.00
National Geographic, 1968, Dec....5.00
People, Vol 1, #1, Mar 1974, EX....20.00
Photohistory, 1937, War in Spain....5.00
Photoplay, 1939, any month....25.00
Photoplay, 1945, Aug, Diana Lynn....20.00
Playboy, 1954, Apr....200.00
Playboy, 1954, Aug....100.00
Playboy, 1954, Dec....100.00
Playboy, 1954, Feb, EX....450.00
Playboy, 1954, Mar....300.00
Playboy, 1954, May....375.00
Playboy, 1955, Apr & May, VG....75.00
Playboy, 1955, Feb, EX....75.00
Playboy, 1955, Jan, EX....275.00
Playboy, 1956, Jan....30.00
Playboy, 1957, Jan-Dec, lot of 12, EX....350.00
Playboy, 1959, Jan-Dec, lot of 12, EX....225.00
Post, 1905, May 20, Wyeth....15.00
Saturday Evening Post, 1916, Aug 5, Rockwell cover, EX....150.00
Saturday Evening Post, 1920, Feb 7, Rockwell cover, EX....50.00
Saturday Evening Post, 1931, Nov 7, Rockwell cover....50.00
Saturday Evening Post, 1939, Feb 11, Rockwell cover....50.00
Saturday Evening Post, 1940, Aug 24, Rockwell cover....25.00
Saturday Evening Post, 1941, May 3, Rockwell cover....25.00
Saturday Evening Post, 1944, Apr 29, Rockwell cover, EX....25.00
Saturday Evening Post, 1946, Apr 6, Rockwell cover, EX....25.00

The Saturday Evening Post, May 3, 1941, Rockwell cover, $25.00.

Saturday Evening Post, 1948, Apr 3, Rockwell cover, EX.......25.00
Saturday Evening Post, 1948, Dec 25, Rockwell cover, EX......25.00
Saturday Evening Post, 1951, July 14, Rockwell cover, EX......15.00
Saturday Evening Post, 1955, Apr 16, Rockwell cover, EX......15.00
Saturday Evening Post, 1957, June 29, Rockwell cover, EX.....15.00
Saturday Evening Post, 1959, Oct 24, Rockwell cover, EX......15.00
Saturday Evening Post, 1960, Aug 27, Rockwell cover..........7.00
Saturday Evening Post, 1963, Jan 19, Rockwell cover, EX.......5.00
Saturday Evening Post, 1963, Mar 2, Rockwell cover...........6.00
Saturday Evening Post, 1976, Dec 25, Rockwell cover..........4.00
Screen Guide, 1941, Sept, Carole Landis....................17.00
Seventeen, 1948, Feb, EX.................................5.00
Sheer Folly, 1937, July, Vol 1, #1..........................20.00
Showgirls, 1943, Mar, Vol 1, #1............................20.00
Song Parade, 1941.......................................5.00
Strange Romances, 1939, Jan..............................5.00
Tidbits of Beauty, 1943, #1...............................15.00
Titter, 1943, Aug, Vol 1, #1...............................35.00
Town & Country, 1909, Jan................................5.00
TV Guide, 1960, May 7, Elvis Presley.......................10.00
US Camera #1, 1938, Autumn, Dietrich & Lombard portraits....35.00
Woman's Home Companion, 1909, Wyeth illus................5.00
Woman's Home Companion, 1917, Phillips cover, cut-outs, VG..25.00
Woman's Home Companion, 1934, July, Mickey Mouse article...10.00

Majolica

Majolica is a type of heavy earthenware, design-molded, and decorated in vivid colors with either a lead or tin type of glaze. It reached its height of popularity in the Victorian era; examples from this period are found in only the lead glazes. Nearly every potter of note, both here and abroad, produced large majolica jardinieres, umbrella stands, pitchers with animal themes, leaf shapes, vegetable forms, and nearly any other nature theme that came to mind. Few, however, marked their ware. Among those who did were Minton, Wedgwood, and George Jones in England; Griffin, Smith and Hill (Etruscan) in Phoenixville, Pennsylvania; and Chesapeake Pottery (Avalon and Clifton) in Baltimore.

When no condition is indicated, the items listed below are assumed to be in mint condition.

Basket, floral encrusted, 3 birds, 3 branch hdls, 18″..........250.00
Basket, twist rope hdl, bow at side, pink/brn, 6½x6″..........125.00
Bottle, barrel on twig base, branch on side, cat atop, 6″......100.00
Bowl, Begonia, vegetable, lg.............................100.00
Bowl, Begonia, 6″.......................................60.00
Bowl, Bird & Fan, Shorter & Boulton, 5″...................100.00
Bowl, Bird & Fan, Wardle, English registry mk, 10¾″........150.00
Bowl, cabbage leaf, luggage straps, turq, ftd................200.00
Bowl, Classical Series, Etruscan............................80.00
Bowl, emb cabbage leaves, mk Wedgwood, 2x6″, pr...........75.00
Bowl, fruit; seashell, Etruscan, sgn, 8″, VG................100.00
Bowl, mc leaves, attached flower frog, scalloped, 3½x5″........75.00
Bowl, pink/yel flowers, stippled gr ground, 5x11″, EX..........95.00
Bowl, Shell & Seaweed, Etruscan, 7″, EX....................150.00
Bowl, Shell & Seaweed, Etruscan, 8½″......................250.00
Bowl, yel daisies on turq, hdls, Germany, 11″...............100.00
Box, seated cow finial, leaves/fence on top, German...........70.00
Butter dish, Bamboo, Etruscan............................225.00
Butter dish, Shell & Seaweed, Etruscan, w/ice tray, rare.......950.00
Butter pat, Begonia Leaf..................................35.00
Butter pat, Pansy, Etruscan...............................35.00
Butter tub, mottled gr/yel, cow finial, sgn Royal, 3x4″.........110.00
Cake stand, Maple Leaves, tree trunk/leaf base, Etruscan.....165.00
Cake stand, pink w/gr leaves, tree base, Etruscan, 9½″, G......90.00
Cake stand, Pond Lily, George Jones........................250.00
Card holder, boy w/net, stork & cattails......................60.00
Charger, pink/lav tulips & daisies on gr, Steidlzairn, 14″.......150.00
Cheese keeper, Pond Lily, Holdcroft........................550.00
Coffee pot, brn mottled glaze, imp mk, lg...................125.00
Coffee pot, Shell & Seaweed, Etruscan, crack, lg.............250.00
Compote, Bellflower, cobalt, 5¼x9½″......................175.00
Compote, Bird & Fan, turq ground, Wedgwood...............250.00
Compote, Daisy, Etruscan, salad sz.........................130.00
Compote, Grape Leaf, Griffin, Smith & Hill, 9¼″.............175.00
Compote, Grape Leaf, pink, Etruscan, 9½″..................175.00
Compote, Maple Leaf, Griffin, Smith & Hill, 1879 mk.........175.00
Compote, molded cupid on flying lion, Etruscan, 4x9¾″.......200.00
Compote, Shell & Seaweed, Etruscan, rare, rstr..............750.00
Creamer, Bamboo, Etruscan, 4½″...........................85.00
Creamer, Coral, Etruscan, sm chip, rare.....................275.00
Creamer, emb grapes & leaves, mk Wedgwood, gr, 5x3½″......85.00
Creamer, Pineapple, no top................................40.00
Creamer, pink flower on yel/bl, English registry mk, 4″.........75.00
Creamer, Shell & Seaweed, albino, Etruscan.................125.00
Creamer, Shell & Seaweed, Etruscan, no mk.................275.00
Creamer, Wild Rose, Etruscan, 4¾″.........................75.00
Creamer & sugar, Blackberry on turq, lav w/in, England.......125.00
Creamer & sugar, Shell & Seaweed, Etruscan, sm chips.......475.00
Creamer & sugar, Water Lily..............................150.00
Cup, w/leaf & flower-form saucer...........................75.00
Cup & saucer, Bird & Fan, Shorter & Boulton, dia registry....125.00
Cup & saucer, Cobblestone, albino, Etruscan.................95.00
Cup & saucer, Shell & Seaweed, Etruscan, G.................225.00
Cuspidor, Basketweave w/Floral............................150.00
Dish, Begonia Leaf, England, 8″............................90.00
Dish, dessert; Fan & Bow, brn/yel/lav.......................100.00
Dish, standing squirrel, sgn, 10x9″........................130.00
Figurine, camel on rectangle base, brn/yel, 5½″..............150.00
Figurine, Psyche seated on rock, modeled after Falconette...1,150.00
Flowerpot, turq w/relief birds & flowers, England, 6″..........125.00
Goblet, sea monsters, sirens & centaurs, mc, English, 10″.....135.00
Humidor, cat holding ball, French..........................180.00
Humidor, duck head & shoulders w/pink shawl, gr/brn, 5½″....120.00
Humidor, Frenchman's head, 5″............................90.00
Humidor, man w/pipe, pipe finial, basketweave, bulbous.......100.00
Humidor, Shell & Seaweed, Etruscan, rare...................950.00
Inkwell, 5 cats riding unicycles, flower, 4-ftd, 8″ L...........125.00

Jardiniere, squirrels, gr.....95.00
Mug, Acorn, Etruscan, 3½″.....130.00
Mug, Lily, ftd, Etruscan, 4″.....125.00
Mug, Lily, on turq, Holdcroft, 3½″.....85.00
Mug, Trailing Ivy, on cobalt, 4″.....75.00
Mustache cup, Shell & Seaweed, Etruscan, no saucer, rare.....275.00
Pitcher, albino w/burgundy leaves & flowers, faience, 6″.....95.00
Pitcher, basketweave yel band w/pink peonies, Etruscan, 6″.....95.00
Pitcher, Begonia Leaf on Bark, 7½″.....95.00
Pitcher, Bent Trunk, tan/pink w/in, Wardle, England, 5¼″.....40.00
Pitcher, Bird & Fan, Wedgwood, 5½″.....325.00
Pitcher, Bird & Fan, Wedgwood, 6″.....350.00
Pitcher, Bow & Bamboo Stalks, bl bow, mc leaves/floral, 9″.....145.00
Pitcher, Commemorative of Edward & Alexandra, 5½″.....225.00
Pitcher, Corn, pink w/in, Etruscan, 8″.....145.00
Pitcher, fish, leaves around base, Morley & Co, 10½″.....178.00
Pitcher, Fish on Waves, Shorter, England, 6″.....110.00
Pitcher, flower & leaf spray ea side, Wedgwood, 6¾″, VG.....95.00
Pitcher, girl & dog, pewter lid, 8″.....200.00
Pitcher, Grant portraits, Am flag & eagle, English, 8½″.....225.00
Pitcher, Hawthorne, Etruscan, cobalt.....120.00
Pitcher, Honeysuckle & Hummingbirds, bright colors, 6¾″.....75.00
Pitcher, owl, Morley & Co, sm hairline, 8½″.....183.00
Pitcher, palm trees on bark ground, 6¾″.....75.00
Pitcher, Pineapple, 6½″.....175.00
Pitcher, purple flowers on gr/gold, rose w/in, France, 7½″.....145.00
Pitcher, Robin, 6½″.....95.00
Pitcher, Shell & Seaweed, Etruscan, sm.....190.00
Pitcher, Shell & Seaweed, Etruscan, water sz.....450.00
Pitcher, tankard; roses on olive, rose w/in, France, 7½″.....110.00
Pitcher, turq basketweave w/ferns, 2 butterflies.....135.00
Pitcher, Wild Rose, butterfly lip, Etruscan, 8″.....125.00
Pitcher, Wild Rose on Tree Bark, 9½″.....115.00
Pitcher, Wood Rose, tree bark mold, cream, 7½″.....75.00
Planter, allover Shell & Seaweed, England, 6″.....150.00
Plate, #1 of Classical Series, Etruscan, 9″.....60.00
Plate, basketweave w/berry clusters, Banks & Thorley, 7½″.....50.00
Plate, Begonia, Griffin, Hill & Smith, Etruscan, 9″.....95.00
Plate, Bird & Fan, Wedgwood, 9″.....95.00
Plate, Blackberry, bl.....38.00
Plate, Blackberry w/Basketweave, Etruscan, 8¼″.....75.00
Plate, blossoms & berries in center on cream, Wedgwood, 7″.....60.00
Plate, brewmaster on key, pink/brn, 10½″.....40.00
Plate, Cabbage Leaf, Etruscan, 8¾″.....95.00
Plate, cake; Maple Leaves, ped.....135.00
Plate, cake; Pineapple, brn/cream, ped ft, 2½x9½″.....145.00
Plate, Cauliflower, Etruscan, 9″.....125.00
Plate, cherries & butterflies on turq, German, 7″.....35.00
Plate, Classical, Cobblestone border, albino, Etruscan, 9″.....90.00
Plate, Fern & Bamboo, English registry mk, 7¾″.....75.00
Plate, Fern & Bow, Banks & Thorley, 8½″.....50.00
Plate, gr flower w/lily-of-the-valley on brn, #1132-2, 12″.....75.00
Plate, gr leaf on basketweave, Griffin, Smith & Hill, 9″.....95.00
Plate, Grape Leaf, fruit & flower, Wedgwood, 8½″.....95.00
Plate, Grape Leaf, pink edge, Etruscan, 9″.....85.00
Plate, Leaf, Etruscan, 8¾″.....110.00
Plate, Leaf, Wedgwood, 8″.....75.00
Plate, Lily Blossom, Holdcroft, 8″.....75.00
Plate, Maple Leaves, Etruscan.....95.00
Plate, Mercury w/woman, Griffin, Smith & Hill.....55.00
Plate, Oriental, Wedgwood, 8½″.....95.00
Plate, Overlapping Begonia Leaves.....95.00
Plate, oyster; red/bl, 6 shells open/6 reverse, E/Napoli.....110.00
Plate, oyster; 6-shell, burgundy/bl, 8½″, set of 8.....900.00

Match holder/ash tray, man in fez figural, 6″ x 5½″, $110.00.

Plate, Rose, Etruscan.....75.00
Plate, Shaggy Dog & Doghouse, 11″.....65.00
Plate, Spaniel Dog, beige border w/emb florals, GS&H.....75.00
Plate, Strawberry, Etruscan.....90.00
Plate, Strawberry, ribbed ground, Clifton Avalon, 10¾″.....100.00
Plate, Strawberry, wht, Etruscan, 9″.....75.00
Plate, Sunflower, German.....45.00
Plate, Waste Not, Want Not, pears in relief on brn, 12½″.....125.00
Plate, yel daisies on turq, German, 7″.....35.00
Platter, Begonia Leaf, mottled brn, yel/gr w/in, 12x8¼″.....150.00
Platter, cherries & butterflies on turq, German, 11″.....65.00
Platter, dog & doghouse, scalloped edge, 11″.....95.00
Platter, oak branch hdl, 3 acorns relief, 12″ L.....85.00
Platter, strawberries & leaves, +8 6″ plates, Wedgwood.....500.00
Platter, Wild Rose.....65.00
Shelf, tree trunk w/oak leaves, 9x8x6½″.....395.00
Smoke set, wht dog, doghouse for cigars, match bucket.....117.50
Smoking set, Happy Hooligan figural.....95.00
Spooner, Corn.....165.00
Spooner, Shell & Seaweed, shell hdls, Etruscan, rare.....350.00
Sugar bowl, Bamboo, Etruscan, 6″.....95.00
Sugar bowl, Wild Rose, w/lid, Etruscan, EX.....65.00
Syrup, bark w/relief twigs & daisies, twig hdl, pewter top.....140.00
Syrup, Coral, Etruscan, pewter top, rare.....375.00
Syrup, Maple Leaf.....130.00
Syrup, Pineapple.....115.00
Syrup, Shell & Seaweed, Etruscan, pewter top, 7″.....145.00
Syrup, Sunflower, Etruscan.....250.00
Teapot, Bamboo, Etruscan.....200.00
Teapot, Bamboo, Hampshire.....145.00
Teapot, Shell & Seaweed, Etruscan, sm.....295.00
Tile, fronds & flowers, aqua, 8x8″.....195.00
Toothpick holder, floral relief on gr to lt gr, scalloped.....58.00
Tray, ice cream; shells, snails, seaweed, Wedgwood, 15x9″.....550.00
Urn, raised flowers, 2 frogs on rim, cobalt w/gr w/in.....195.00
Vase, cream w/magenta leaves, Avalon Faience, 7″.....65.00
Vase, poppies & leaves, Shell & Scroll hdl, French, 12½″.....70.00
Vase, serpent hdls, imp #, rare, 8″.....75.00
Wall pocket, flowers & sea urchins, shoe shape, sgn, 4″.....100.00
Waste bowl, Blackberry, Clifton.....85.00

Malachite

Malachite is a type of art glass that exhibits strata-like layerings in shades of green--similar to the mineral in its natural form.

When no condition is indicated, the items listed below are assumed to be in mint condition.

Ash tray, floral, 4-ftd, Moser, 4¼x2¾″ 65.00
Ash tray, panther, lg 85.00
Lamp, floral & facets, eng floral chimney, att Moser, 9½″ 125.00
Vase, relief dancing nudes & grapes, 5¼″ 130.00

Box, relief nudes, with lid, 3½″ diameter, $175.00.

Mantua

A glasshouse was established in Mantua Township, Ohio, in 1821, for the purpose of manufacturing bottle-glass. Two years later, the proprietor, David Ladd, left Mantua, re-establishing and enlarging his glasshouse in Kent, Ohio.

Besides bottle-glass, flint glass items such as bowls, pitchers, decanters, etc., were also blown in green, aquamarine, amber, and amethyst shades. Preferred patterns were 16-rib, 32-rib, broken rib, swirled, corrugated, 15-diamond, and 3-mold.

When no condition is indicated, the items listed below are assumed to be undamaged.

Bottle, nursing; 15-diamond, bright aqua, 7⅞″, EX 375.00
Bottle, 16 vertical ribs, terminal ring, amethyst, 5¾″ 750.00
Bottle, 16-rib broken swirl, yel-amber, club shape, 9″, NM 675.00
Bottle, 26-rib broken swirl, club shape, aqua, 8″, NM 200.00
Bottle, 32-rib broken swirl, club shape, aqua, 8½″, NM 350.00
Flask, chestnut; 16 ribs, gr-aqua, 6″ 160.00
Flask, chestnut; 16 vertical ribs, terminal ring, amber, 4″ 300.00
Flask, chestnut; 16-rib broken swirl, gr-aqua, 5″, NM 215.00
Inkwell, 16-rib broken swirl, G impression, aqua, 1⅞″ 450.00
Pan, folded-in rim, violet, 1¾x5⅝″ 1,100.00
Pan, 15-diamond, folded-in rim, lt gr, 1¾x5¼″ 1,950.00
Pan, 16-rib broken swirl, folded rim, brilliant amber, 5″ 1,900.00
Pan, 16-rib broken swirl, folded-over rim, lt gr, 1¼x5″ 275.00
Salt cellar, 16 swirl ribs, 1⅜x3″ 115.00
Salt cellar, 16-rib, applied ft, amethyst, sm flake, 2½″ 325.00
Tumbler, 16 swirl ribs, honey-amber, 2⅞″ 135.00

Maps and Atlases

Maps are highly collectible, not only for historical value, but also for their sometimes elaborate artwork, legendary information, or data that has been proven erroneous. There are many types of maps, including geographical, military, celestial, road, and railroad. The most valuable are those made before the mid-1800s.

When no condition is indicated, the items listed below are assumed to be in excellent condition.

Key:
hc—hand colored

Atlases

Black's General of the World, Am Ed, Edinburgh, 1876 . . . . 125.00
Geographical/Historical/Commercial, Bradford, 1835, EX 385.00
Johnson's New Illustrated Family, 1868, full color/eng 285.00
Mitchell's New General, Philadelphia, 1872, eng borders 190.00
New Universal, by Taner, pub SA Mitchell, 1846 . . . . 675.00
Universal, Illustrated, Bradford/Goodricx, 1842, complete 825.00

Maps

Africa, Moll, pub 1740, 15x9″ 40.00
Alabama, Crams, litho-color, 1886, 11x13″ 10.00
Australia, 1840, coastal detail, charts, 12½x15½″ 35.00
Central America, Tallis, 3 vignettes, pub 1860, 14x11″ 30.00
Dutch, New England, inset of New Amsterdam/Indian tribes 295.00
Europe, Kitchin, no color, pub 1772, 10x8″, G 20.00
France, Tallis, 6 vignettes, pub 1860, 14x10½″ 30.00
Indiana, Colton, hc, rivers, decor border, 1855, 13x16″ 35.00
Kentucky & Tennessee, Johnson, hc, 1865, 16x22″ 30.00
Lake Superior, 1832, US & Canadian sides, 12x15 . . . . 45.00
London, plan of city, London Bridge, 1836, 15½x25″ 35.00
Military Map of the Battle of Waterloo, pub 1848, 9x7½″ 15.00
Naval Map of the Battle of Camperdown, pub 1848, 9x7½″ 20.00
Nebraska, Johnson, hc, eastern counties, 1873, 12x15″ 25.00
North & South Carolina, Johnson, hc, 2 vignettes, 16x22″ 30.00
North America, Hall, pub 1823, 10x8½″ 20.00
Northwest & Michigan Territories, 1833, 12½x15½″ 35.00
Ohio, Cowperthwaite, 1850, rare, 13x16″ 28.00
Polynesia, Tallis, vignettes w/islands, pub 1850, 14x10½″ 55.00

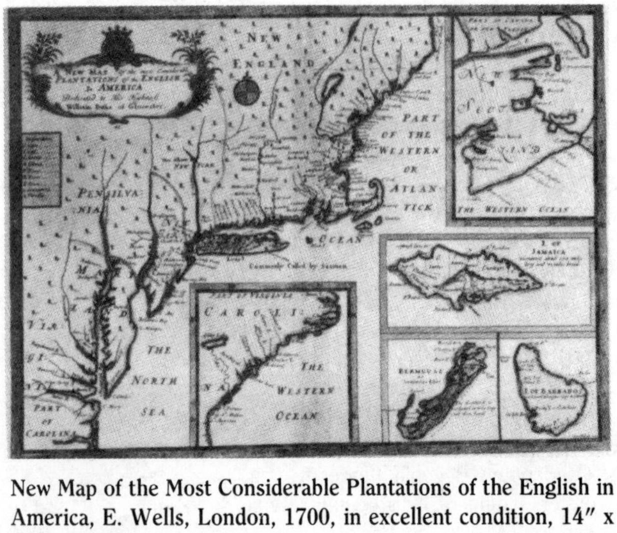

New Map of the Most Considerable Plantations of the English in America, E. Wells, London, 1700, in excellent condition, 14″ x 19″, $500.00.

Texas, Asher & Adams, hc, pub 1872, 24x17″ 35.00
United States, Russell, pub 1840, 10½x8½″ 25.00
Utah, unexplored regions, ca 1870, 12x15″ 25.00
Utah Territory, Johnson, hc, wagon routes, 1873, 12x15″ 25.00
World Map Showing Cook's Voyages, Tallis, pub 1860 .... 50.00

Marblehead

What began as therapy for patients in a sanitarium in Marblehead, Massachusetts, has become recognized as an important part of the Arts and Crafts movement in America. Results of the early experiments under the guidance of Arthur E. Baggs in 1904 met with such success that by 1908 the pottery had been converted to a solely commercial venture. Simple vase shapes were often incised with stylized animal and floral motifs or sailing ships; some were decorated in low relief; many were plain. Simple matt glazes in soft yellow, gray, wisteria, rose, tobacco brown, and their most popular, Marblehead blue, were used alone, or in combination. The Marblehead logo is distinctive--a boat with full sail, and the letters 'M' and 'P.' The pottery closed in 1936.

When no condition is indicated, the items listed below are assumed to be in mint condition.

Bowl, deep bl, w/flower frog, 2½x9″ 90.00
Bowl, floral & berry band at top, yel/bl/grn on bl, 3x6″ 610.00
Bowl, gr, 2x9″ 175.00
Bowl, gray, w/sm flower frog, 1¾x3½″ 125.00
Bowl vase, bl, 2¾x5¾″ 70.00
Bud vase, bl, cylindrical, 4⅞″ 110.00
Bud vase, brn, cylinder w/flared base, 5¾x2¾″ 80.00
Bud vase, gr, cylindrical, 4½″ 135.00
Bud vase, gray, cylindrical, 6″ 160.00
Candlestick, bl-gray, 3″ 40.00
Lamp, mustard yel, w/orig fittings, labels, 12″ 450.00
Pitcher, cream; dk bl gloss, lt bl w/in, 4¾″ 60.00
Pitcher, gr w/brn flecks, incised top band, Baggs, 8″ 395.00
Tile, sailing ship, HP, gr/brn shades, 5″ dia 420.00
Tile, sailing ship, lt bl, dk bl border, glossy, sgn, 4½″ 235.00
Vase, bl, V-shape, 6″ 110.00

Egyptian perfume bottle, glossy turquoise, paper label, ca 1922, one of 1,000 commissioned as souvenirs for King Tut Exhibition in New York, 5¼″, $525.00 at auction.

Vase, carved berries, bl w/red/orange/gr, bell form, 4″ 675.00
Vase, clover, incised, dk gr w/brn, artist sgn, 5¼″ 450.00
Vase, dk bl, concave cylinder, 7¾″ 175.00
Vase, dk bl, full body, 7¾″ 175.00
Vase, dk bl, 3½x3½″ 75.00
Vase, dk gr, waisted cylinder, 8½″ 180.00
Vase, dk gr, 3½″ 55.00
Vase, floral & leaves, gr to yel on bl, 5″ 565.00
Vase, geometrics, incised, mc on gray, Baggs, 4½x4½″ 675.00
Vase, gr, thrown, hdls, squat, 2¾x4½″ 190.00
Vase, gr, 4½″ 75.00
Vase, grapevine decor, bl/brn/gr on gr-yel, 3½″ 500.00
Vase, gray, top flares, 5½″ 145.00
Vase, gray w/bl flecks, bl w/in, 3½″ 70.00
Vase, gray w/bl flecks, slender flared cylinder, 5″ 120.00
Vase, gray w/brn flecks, cylindrical, 8½″ 225.00
Vase, leaf & berry relief, dk bl, 5¼″ 450.00
Vase, lg butterflies, bl on gray, artist sgn/label, 3¾″ 400.00
Vase, long stemmed florals & lg leaves, lt on dk gray, 7″ 725.00
Vase, wht w/gr/brn splotches, 3½″ 125.00
Wall pocket, bl, 6″ 55.00
Wall pocket, lav, horizontal ribs, 5″ 90.00
Wall pocket, pink, fan shape, 6″ 100.00

Marbles

Marbles have been popular with children since the mid-1800s. They've been made in many types from a variety of materials. Among some of the first glass items to be produced, the earliest marbles were made from a solid glass rod broken into sections of the proper length which were placed in a tray of sand and charcoal, and returned to the fire. As they were reheated, the trays were constantly agitated until the marbles were completely round. Other marbles were made of china, pottery, steel, and natural stones.

Below is a listing of the various types, along with a brief description of each. When size is not otherwise indicated, prices are listed for mint condition marbles of average size, ½″ to 1″.

Agates: stone marbles of many different colors, bands of color alternating with white usually encircle the marble, most are translucent.

Ballot Box: handmade (with pontils), opaque white or black, used in lodge elections.

Bloodstone: green chalcedony with red spots, a type of quartz.

China: with or without glaze, in a variety of hand-painted designs--parallel bands or bull's-eye designs most common.

Clambroth: opaque glass with outer evenly spaced swirls of one or alternating colors.

Clay: one of the most common older types, some are painted, while others are not.

Comic Strip: a series of machine-made marbles with faces of comic strip characters; Peltier Glass Factory, Illinois; twelve characters.

Crockery: sometimes referred to as Benningtons, most are either blue or brown, although some are speckled. The clay is shaped into a sphere, then coated with glaze and fired.

End of the Day: single-pontil glass marbles, the colored part often appears as a multicolored blob or mushroom cloud.

Goldstone: clear glass completely filled with copper flakes that have turned gold-colored from the heat of the manufacturing process.

Indian Swirls: usually black glass, with a colored swirl appearing on the outside next to the surface, usually irregular.

Latticinio Core Swirls: double-pontil marble, with an inner area with net-like effects of swirls coming up around the center.

Lutz Type: glass with colored or clear bands alternating with bands which contain copper flecks.

Micas: clear or colored glass with mica flecks which reflect as silver dots when marble is turned. Red is rare.

Onionskin: spiral type which are solidly colored instead of having individual ribbons or threads; multicolored.

Peppermint Swirls: made of white opaque glass with alternating blue and red outer swirls.

Ribbon Core Swirls: double-pontil marble, center shaped like a ribbon with swirls that come up around the middle.

Rose Quartz: stone marble, usually pink in color, often with fractures inside and on outer surface.

Solid Core Swirls: double-pontil marble, middle is solid with swirls coming up around the core.

Steelies: hollow steel spheres marked with a cross where the steel was bent together to form the ball.

Sulfides: generally made of clear glass with figures inside. Rarer types have colored figures or colored glass.

Tiger Eye: stone marble of golden quartz with inclusions of asbestos, dark brown with gold highlights.

Vaseline: machine-made of yellowish-green glass with small bubbles.

For a more thorough study of the subject, we recommend *Antique and Collectible Marbles*, an identification and value guide by Everett Grist; you will find his address in the Directory under Illinois.

Agate, contemporary, 1¾″ ... 50.00
Agate, gr & wht, ¾″ ... 20.00
Agate, 1¾″ ... 175.00
Banded Opaque, red & wht, 1¾″ ... 250.00
Banded Opaque, red & wht, ¾″ ... 50.00
Banded Opaque, 2″ ... 375.00
Banded Transparent Swirl, bl, ¾″ ... 5.00
Banded Transparent Swirl, lt gr, 1¾″ ... 150.00
Bennington, bl, 1¾″ ... 10.00
Bennington, bl, ¾″ ... 1.00
Bennington, brn, 1¾″ ... 5.00
Bennington, fancy, 1¾″ ... 15.00
Bennington, fancy, ¾″ ... 2.00
China, decorated, glazed, apple, 1¾″ ... 300.00
China, decorated, glazed, rose, 1¾″ ... 300.00
China, decorated, glazed, wht w/geometric designs, 1¾″ ... 45.00
China, decorated, unglazed, geometrics & flowers, ¾″ ... 75.00
Clambroth, opaque, bl & wht, 1¾″ ... 500.00
Clambroth, opaque, bl & wht, ¾″ ... 75.00
Clear Swirl Lutz-type, clear w/wht & gold swirls, ¾″ ... 65.00
Cloud, w/mica, red & wht, 1¼″ ... 150.00
Cloud, yel, rare, 1¾″ ... 150.00
Colored Transparent Swirl Lutz-type, ¾″ ... 75.00
Comic, Cotes Bakery, advertising ... 250.00
Comic, Kayo, rare ... 55.00
Comic, Little Orphan Annie ... 40.00
Comic, set of 12 ... 550.00
Comic, Skeezix, rare ... 55.00
Cork Screw, machine-made ... 1.00
End of Day, bl & wht, 1¾″ ... 200.00
Goldstone, ¾″ ... 35.00
Indian Swirl, 1¾″ ... 300.00
Indian Swirl, ¾″ ... 20.00
Indian Swirl Lutz-type, gold flakes, ¾″ ... 100.00
Line Crockery, clay, wht w/zigzag gr & bl lines, ¾″ ... 5.00
Mica, bl, ¾″ ... 15.00
Mica, gr, 1¾″ ... 250.00
Onionskin, w/mica, 1¾″ ... 350.00
Onionskin, w/mica, ¾″ ... 60.00
Onionskin, 1¼″ ... 85.00
Onionskin, 16-lobe, unusual, 2″ ... 500.00
Onionskin, 2″ ... 275.00
Onionskin, ¾″ ... 50.00
Onionskin, 4-lobe, 1¼″ ... 175.00
Onionskin Lutz-type, gold flakes, 1¾″ ... 375.00
Opaque Glass Swirl Lutz-type, bl, yel, gr, or vaseline, ¾″ ... 100.00
Opaque Swirl, gr, ¾″ ... 20.00
Peppermint Swirl, opaque, red, wht, & bl, ¾″ ... 25.00
Pottery, tan w/purple lines, 1¾″ ... 15.00
Ribbon Core Lutz-type, clear or transparent colors, 1¾″ ... 500.00
Slag, machine-made, sm ... 1.00
Slag, machine-made, 1¼″ ... 10.00
Solid Opaque, bl, ¾″ ... 10.00
Solid Opaque, gr, 1¾″ ... 200.00

Solid Core Swirl, 1¾″, $65.00.

Sulfide, American buffalo, 2″ ... 150.00
Sulfide, angel face w/wings, 1¼″ ... 200.00
Sulfide, baby in basket, 2″ ... 300.00
Sulfide, bird, 1¼″ ... 75.00
Sulfide, cat, 1¼″ ... 75.00
Sulfide, chicken, 1¼″ ... 75.00
Sulfide, child in crawling position, 1¼″ ... 200.00
Sulfide, child in dress, 2″ ... 275.00
Sulfide, child in long dress, 1¼″ ... 175.00
Sulfide, child sitting, 1¼″ ... 175.00
Sulfide, child w/hammer, 1¼″ ... 250.00
Sulfide, clown in peaked cap, 1¼″ ... 275.00
Sulfide, coin w/number 7, 2″ ... 275.00
Sulfide, dog, 1⅞″ ... 100.00
Sulfide, dog begging, 1¼″ ... 75.00
Sulfide, dog w/bird in mouth, 1¼″ ... 250.00
Sulfide, eagle, 1¼″ ... 100.00
Sulfide, elephant, 1¼″ ... 75.00
Sulfide, fish, 1¼″ ... 75.00
Sulfide, goat, 1¼″ ... 75.00
Sulfide, horse, 1¼″ ... 75.00
Sulfide, King of the Jungle, 2″ ... 150.00
Sulfide, Little Boy Blue, 2″ ... 275.00
Sulfide, Madonna, 2″ ... 300.00
Sulfide, number 4, 2″ ... 250.00
Sulfide, owl, 1¼″ ... 75.00
Sulfide, papoose, 2″ ... 275.00
Sulfide, papoose in cradle board, 1¼″ ... 275.00
Sulfide, pig, 1¼″ ... 60.00
Sulfide, President Garfield w/in heart, 2″ ... 500.00
Sulfide, raccoon, 2″ ... 150.00
Sulfide, Santa Claus, 2″ ... 300.00
Sulfide, sheep, 1¼″ ... 60.00
Sulfide, spread-winged owl, 1¼″ ... 150.00
Sulfide, squirrel, 2⅛″ ... 125.00

Sulfide, standing bear, 1¼″ 75.00
Sulfide, 2 doves or lovebirds in bl glass, 1¼″ 600.00

Marine Collectibles

When no condition is indicated, the items listed below are assumed to be in excellent condition. See also Ship Models; Scrimshaw

Bell, ship's; cast brass, 18″ 135.00
Bell, ship's; nickel, Chelsea 450.00
Bell, ship's; phenolic, Chelsea 375.00
Binnacle, brass on mahog pillar, A Lietz, 51½″ 660.00
Button, USN, ca 1812 . . . . .65.00
Chronometer, wood w/gimballs, up/down indicator, Waltham 350.00
Clock, ship's; brass, US Maritime #2100, Chelsea Clock Co 275.00
Diving helmet, copper/brass, 3 rnd glass plates, Schrader 450.00
Document, captain's handwritten protest, 2 pg, 1809 . . . . .38.00
Document, handwritten account of shipwreck, 12 pg, 1817 . . . . . .30.00
Document, insurance policy, Brig Juno, 1824 . . . . .35.00
Document, sale bill for whale ship, 4 pg, 1863, EX 70.00
Document, whale ship crew list, Honolulu, 1855, matted, VG . . .145.00
Drawing, Clipper Sunda, sgn DP Dorrian, 28x42″, EX 120.00
Fid, made from knarled sapling, 7¼″ 20.00
Figurehead, ¾ Jenny Lind, English, 1800s, rpt, 38″ 1,650.00
Lantern, ship's; brass, curved lens, Bakboord, kero, 21″ 50.00
Photo, Monongahela Under Studding Sails, matted/fr, 26x32″ . .300.00
Protractor, Wm Navigational School, Whipple, cb, 5½ 80.00
Sea chest, ship pnt w/in, compass stars on till, 15x42″ 2,200.00
Sextant, ebonized brass, lattice fr/w/box, Buff & Buff, 7″ 275.00

Sextant, 5″ x 10½″ x 11″, $450.00.

Martin Bros.

The Martin Bros. were studio potters who worked from 1873 until 1914, first at Fulham, and later at London and Southall. There were four brothers, each who excelled in their peculiar area. Robert, known as Wallace, was an experienced stonecarver. He modeled a series of grotesque bird and animal figural caricatures. Walter was the potter, responsible for throwing the larger vases on the wheel, firing the kiln, and mixing the clay. Edwin, an artist of stature, preferred more naturalistic forms of decoration. His work was often incised or with relief designs of seaweed, florals, fish, and birds. The fourth brother, Charles, was their business manager. Their work was incised with their name, place of production, and letters and numbers indicating month and year.

When no condition is indicated, the items listed below are assumed to be in mint condition.

Triple bird group, each with removable head, blues, greens and browns, incised details, signed R.W. Martin & Bros, Southhall, B-37, $1,100.00.

Chimpanzee on ped base, 5″ 210.00
Ewer, hummingbirds w/in arches, mc, sgn RWM/1882, 9″, EX . .350.00
Ewer, modeled troll's head, RWM/1890, firing crack, 4″ 500.00
Ewer, sq w/incised sea & shell fish, Martin Bros/1879, 11″ 800.00
Pitcher, brn/gr speckled, 10″ 175.00
Pitcher, incised birds, pinched spout, 10″ 235.00
Pitcher, incised foliage, 8″ 150.00
Pitcher, scallop shells, dragon spine hdl, 13″ 235.00
Spoonwarmer, modeled open-mouth reptile pitcher, sgn, 5″ 500.00
Stein, foliage, bl, monogram sgn, 5″ 125.00
Vase, amber-scaled fish on gr, incised, sq, 10-1901, 7″ 300.00
Vase, birds, insect, floral, incised, mc, bulbous, sgn, 9″ 250.00
Vase, comical grotesque fish, 4″ 165.00
Vase, demon masks in reserves, sgn, 8-1894, 13½″ 800.00
Vase, dragons & swallows, 14″ 300.00
Vase, fish, sea animals, incised, 2-hdl, 10½″, VG 650.00
Vase, fish & eels incised, brn, Southall, 4-1890, 5½″ 300.00
Vase, flying swallows, cylinder, 9″ 149.00
Vase, insects, floral, leaves on neck, incised, 1883, 10″ 250.00
Vase, red & brn streaked, 6″ 150.00
Vase, underwater fish relief, sgn Martin Bros/1906, 8″ 500.00

Mary Gregory

Mary Gregory glass, for reasons that remain obscure, is the namesake of a Boston and Sandwich Glass Company employee who worked for the company for only two years in the mid-1800s. Although no evidence actually exists to indicate that glass of this type was even produced there, the fine colored or crystal ware decorated with figures of children in white enamel is commonly referred to as Mary Gregory. The glass, in fact, originated in Europe, and was imported into this country where it was copied by several eastern glasshouses. It was popular from the mid-1800s until the turn of the century.

When no condition is indicated, the items listed below are assumed to be in mint condition.

Basket, pin; ruby, sm girl, ormolu hdl & ft, 3¼x3½″ 165.00
Bottle, barber; cobalt, boy & girl, pr 250.00
Bottle, wine; cranberry, girl w/flowers, clear stopper, 9″ 150.00

Box, amber, girl, heart border, brass mts, rnd, 4½″ 145.00
Box, amber, 2 girls, hinged, brass rings, rnd, 4¾x6″ 495.00
Box, amethyst, girl, foliage & dots, hinged lid, 4½x5½″ 200.00
Box, cobalt, boy & dots, hinged lid, 1⅛x2″ dia 165.00
Box, cobalt, girl w/bird, ormolu ft, w/lid, rnd, 5x5½″ 395.00
Box, cranberry, boy & garlands, rnd, 4¼x5¼″ 375.00
Box, gr, little girl, melon shape, enamel lid, 3x3¾″ 110.00
Box, jewelry; amethyst, boy, silver-ftd base & collar, sq 575.00
Box, jewelry; bl, boy & bird, ormolu ft, 5x3½x5½″ 450.00
Box, jewelry; blk, girl & swan, ornate Derby fr w/tall hdl 1,150.00

Jewel box, cobalt with white enamel girl and butterfly, 5½″ x 5″, $495.00.

Creamer, tankard; emerald gr, girl fishing w/lg hook, 6″ 135.00
Lamp, bristol bl, young boy, brass mt, 26″ 265.00
Perfume cylinder, amethyst, scene w/girl 60.00
Pitcher, amber, girl w/watering can, 12¾″ 195.00
Pitcher, cranberry, boy w/sailboat, tinted, 4-lobe top, 6½″ 195.00
Plate, cobalt, girl w/butterfly net, orig ormolu stand, 6″ 150.00
Stein, bl, boy w/butterfly, Inverted Thumbprint, 5½″ 175.00
Toothpick holder, cranberry, boy looking at bird 65.00
Tray, dresser; cranberry, boy & girl, 1¼x6½x9″ 225.00
Tray, dresser; emerald gr, 2 girls & boy, 1¼x8¾x10¾″ 225.00
Tumbler, amber, boy 50.00
Tumbler, aquamarine, girl & tree, 5″ 35.00
Tumbler, cranberry, girl, 4x2⅜″ 52.00
Vase, bl opaque, girl, scalloped/ftd, gilt, facing pr, 10″ 345.00
Vase, cobalt, boy, crystal shell trim at sides, 12½x5″ 165.00
Vase, cobalt, girl w/basket, dots at top & on lid, 14¼″ 265.00
Vase, cobalt, girl w/hat, 7¼x3″ 95.00
Vase, cranberry, boy w/hat, running, 9x3¾″ 165.00
Vase, cranberry, boy w/hat, 7¾x3½″ 125.00
Vase, cranberry, cherub & child, ruffled, ftd, 10x5″, pr 650.00
Vase, cranberry, girl sits w/garland, gold hdls, 13x7″ 495.00
Vase, emerald gr, girl & sailboat, reeded hdls, 11¾x5″ 275.00
Vase, emerald gr, girl w/stick, 12¼″ 160.00
Vase, emerald gr frost, girl w/flowers in apron, 9x4″ 175.00
Vase, sapphire bl, scalloped top, fancy metal base mt, 14″ 225.00

Massier

Clement Massier was a French artist-potter who established a workshop at Golfe Juan, France, in 1881, where he experimented with metallic lustre glazes. (One of his pupils was Jacques Sicardo, who brought the knowledge he had gained through his association with Massier to the Weller Pottery Company in Zanesville, Ohio.) The lustre lines developed by Massier incorporated nature themes with allover decorations of foliage or flowers on shapes modeled in the Art Nouveau style. The ware was usually incised with the Massier name, his initials, or the location of the pottery. Massier died in 1917.

When no condition is indicated, the items listed below are assumed to be in mint condition.

Jardiniere, vines w/fruit, gr/aqua/maroon/rose irid, 12″ 575.00
Jug, Persian design, Longwy-type, gilt, hdls, sgn, 12″ 350.00
Vase, floral, amber/gr irid on mottled brn, sgn, 1900, 8″ 750.00
Vase, purple irid/bl, pinched base, sgn, 4¾″ 400.00

Covered jar, light green with gold leaves, 5″, $295.00.

Match Holders

Before the invention of the safety match in 1855, matches were kept in match boxes and carried in pocket size match safes because they ignited so easily. John Walker, an English chemist, invented the match more than one hundred years ago, quite by accident. Walker was working with a mixture of potash and antimony, hoping to make a combustible that could be used to fire guns. The mixture adhered to the end of the wooden stick he had used for stirring. As he tried to remove it by scraping the stick on the stone floor, it burst into flames. The invention of the match was only a step away! From that time to the present, match holders have been made in amusing figural forms as well as simple utilitarian styles, in a wide range of materials. Most were wall-hanging; a few were table-top models––all designed to keep matches conveniently at hand.

When no condition is indicated, the items listed below are assumed to be in excellent condition.

Acorn in oak leaf & acorn fr on ped ft, CI, pat 1862, 5″ 40.00
Alligator, CI, w/striker, push down head, bk opens, 12″ 70.00
Amos 'n Andy, chalkware 75.00
Aunt Jemima, chalkware 20.00
Barrel shape, japanned tin, curved lift-lid, wall mt 38.00
Blk boy w/geese, bisque 48.00
Boot w/spurs, blk glass 30.00
Brumbach's Shoes 42.00
Chimney w/emb bricks, brass, 4¾″ 75.00
Coal hod, orange bail, milk glass 45.00
DeLaval 55.00

Twin urns on scrollwork backing, brass, patented 1867, 7½″, $58.00.

Des Moines Insurance....35.00
Dock Ash Stoves, wall mt....35.00
Dog w/hat & pipe, Bennington type....25.00
Dr Schoop's....100.00
Eagle & stars, 'Comb Case,' tin, lift-top compartment....56.00
EO Weber Lumber Co....52.00
Game pouch, metal, 2 birds & powder horn, 6¼″....95.00
Hanging game, hunting bag, horn, CI w/mc pnt, 8″....70.00
High-button boot on iron platform w/legs, CI....40.00
Horse, cast brass on ½-circle wood base, book holder....40.00
Horseshoe, wire nail construction, wall mt, 4½x6″....35.00
Judson Whiskey, child serving father, wall mt, 1907....55.00
Juicy Fruit, wall mt....65.00
Las Dos Nacinoes Cigar Co....76.00
Lax-Et....35.00
Maltese Cross, tin, dbl, wall mt....20.00
Man w/long nose & beard, chalk, adv NW Natn'l Ins Co, 6″....95.00
Milwaukee Harvesting....150.00
Mother's Worm Syrup....24.00
Redware, bull head pocket, mc acorns & leaves, 6¾″....110.00
Rockford Watch....195.00
Shoe, high-button type, pnt on CI....50.00
Solarine Metal Polish....75.00
Stonewear, emb surface, bl stripe top & base, cone, 3″....75.00
Tin, 'Matches' cut-out, openwork....25.00
Tublar Sharples Cream Separator, lady & cows....85.00
Vulcan Plows....200.00
Wood, chip-carved rim & front decor, high rnd bk, wall mt....95.00
Wood burnt decor: muzzled dog 'For...Safety,' '07, wall mt....45.00
Woodward & Hill, wood, oval, wall mt, 7½″....57.00

Match Safes

Match safes, aptly-named cases used to carry matches in the days before cigarette lighters, were used during the last half of the 19th century until about 1920. Some incorporated added features--hidden compartments, cigar cutters, etc.--some were figural, and others were used by retail companies as advertising give-aways. They were made from every type of material, but silverplated styles abound.

When no condition is indicated, the items listed below are assumed to be in excellent condition.

Anheuser Busch, brass....65.00
Art Nouveau, lady's head, floral, mk Sterling....55.00
Blk man's head, brass figural, 2⅛x1x1¾″....145.00
Boar's head 1 side, hooked fish on other, hallmk, sterling....60.00
Book, SP, ea end opens....38.00
Book figural, brass....35.00
Celluloid, pocket watch decor, Charles Granes Jewelers....24.00
Devil's head....295.00
Dog in center, chrome....44.00
Fist, brass figural, 2½x ¾x1¼″....95.00
Ivory, book shape....38.00
Ivory, cylindrical, X-hatched strike surface, w/lid, sm....130.00
Ivory, dbl sided, Berlin, 1887....110.00
John Traschl Wines, Cigars, Minneapolis, leather on metal....16.50
Mitchel & Mitchel Hahers, Chicago, heavy emb metal....17.50
Nude, full figure on both sides, scrolls, mk Sterling....75.00
Owl, SP figural, 1¾x ⅞x1¾″....85.00
Pig, SP figural, 1½x2½x1¼″....75.00
Pullman Automobiles, deer on bk, Art Nouveau....35.00
Sterling, kidney shape....35.00
Sterling, repousse floral border, rectangular, w/monogram....27.50
Tortoiseshell, both sides emb....65.00
Violin case, brass....125.00
Wolf's head, brass figural, 2x1¼″....110.00
World's Fair, monument relief ea side, nickel plate....40.00
Wylie Coal, brass, dtd 1890....20.00

Sterling with Art Nouveau lady's head, marked B2148, R, shield and anchor in circle, 2¼″ x 1½″, $95.00.

McCoy

The third generation McCoy potter in the Roseville, Ohio, area was Nelson, who with the aid of his father, J.W., established the Nelson McCoy Sanitary Stoneware Company in 1910. They manufactured churns, jars, jugs, poultry fountains, and footwarmers. By 1925, they had expanded their wares to include majolica jardinieres and pedestals, umbrella stands and cuspidors, and an embossed line of vases and small jardinieres in a blended brown and green matt glaze. From the late twenties through the mid-forties a utilitarian stoneware was produced, some of which was glazed in the soft blue and white so popular with collectors today. They also used a dark brown mahogany color, and a medium to dark green--both in a high gloss. In 1933, the company became known as the Nelson McCoy Pottery Company. They expanded their facilities in 1940, and began to make the novelty artwares, cookie jars, and dinnerware that today are synonomous with 'McCoy.' To date, more than two hundred cookie jars of every theme and description have been produced. Some are very common. Mammy, the Clown, and the Bear, although very old, are easy to find; while the Dalmations, Christmas Tree, and Kangaroo, for instance, though not so old are harder to locate.

The Indian and the Tepee, both made in the fifties, are two of the most popular and some of the most expensive!

More than a dozen different marks have been used by the company; nearly all incorporate the name 'McCoy,' although some of the older items were marked 'NM USA.'

When no condition is indicated, the items listed below are assumed to be in mint condition.

Cookie Jars

Animal Crackers....32.00
Apollo Age....140.00
Apple, 1950-64....22.00
Apple on Basketweave....25.00
Bananas....40.00
Barnum's Animals....35.00
Bear, cookie in vest....30.00
Bear, upside down, blk & wht....20.00
Bobby Baker....20.00
Caboose....35.00
Chef....35.00
Chiffoniere, Early American Chest....35.00
Chinese Lantern....25.00
Chipmunk....35.00
Christmas Tree....145.00
Circus Horse....60.00
Clown Bust....22.00
Clown in Barrel....30.00
Clyde Dog....22.00
Coalby Cat....30.00
Coffee Grinder....20.00
Coffee Mug....25.00
Colonial Fireplace....45.00
Cookie Barrel....25.00
Cookie Boy, aqua....75.00
Cookie Cabin....30.00
Cookie Jug, dbl loop, brn....15.00
Cookie Jug, single loop, 2-tone gr rope....18.00
Cookie Jug, w/cork stopper, brn & tan....12.00
Cookie Log....16.00
Cookie Safe....25.00
Cookstove....20.00
Corn....75.00
Covered Wagon....35.00
Cylinder, w/red flowers....15.00
Dalmations in Rocking Chair....85.00
Dog on Basketweave....25.00
Drum....30.00
Duck on Basketweave....30.00
Dutch Girl, boy on reverse....50.00
Dutch Treat Barn....30.00
Eagle, carved wood....15.00
Elephant....32.00
Elephant w/Split Trunk, rare....60.00
Engine....50.00
Forbidden Fruit....32.00
Friendship....45.00
Frontier Family....25.00
Fruit in Bushel Basket....30.00
Gingerbread Boy....28.00
Globe....50.00
Grandfather Clock....35.00
Granny....25.00
Hamm's Bear....35.00
Happy Face....20.00
Hen on Nest....35.00
Hillbilly Bear, rare....150.00
Hobby Horse....45.00
Honey Bear....30.00
Indian....125.00
Jack-O'-Lantern....175.00
Kissing Penguins....30.00
Kitten on Basketweave....30.00
Kittens on Ball of Yarn....30.00
Kookie Kettle, blk....18.00
Lamb on Basketweave....30.00
Liberty Bell....20.00
Little Clown....35.00
Lollipop....30.00
Mac Dog....30.00
Mammy....50.00
Mammy w/Cauliflower....165.00
Monk....30.00
Mother Goose....50.00
Mouse on Stump....17.00
Mr & Mrs Owl....35.00
Oaken Bucket....12.00
Old Churn....12.00
Pears on Basketweave....25.00
Pelican....60.00
Pepper, yel....18.00
Picnic Basket....35.00
Pineapple....30.00
Pirates Chest....22.00
Pot Belly Stove, blk....17.50
Pot Belly Stove, wht....20.00
Puppy, with sign....35.00
Quaker Oats....30.00
Red Barn, cow in door, rare....135.00
Rooster, wht....30.00
Rooster, yel....40.00
Snow Bear....40.00
Strawberry, 1955-57....25.00
Strawberry, 1971-75....15.00
Tepee....110.00
Tilt Pitcher, blk w/roses....26.00
Touring Car....40.00
Tudor Cookie House....50.00
Turkey....75.00
Upside Down Bear, panda....12.00
WC Fields....55.00
Wedding Jar....35.00
Windmill....40.00
Wishing Well....25.00
Woodsy Owl....50.00
Wren House....40.00
Yellow Bear....45.00
Yosemite Sam....20.00

Miscellaneous

Basket, pine cones, Rustic glaze, lt gr & tan....20.00
Bean pot, HP apple on yellowware....20.00
Bean pot, pods/leaves relief, brn gloss, #2, 1943....25.00
Bookends, lilies, pr....28.00
Bowl, yellowware w/pink & bl bands, lg....9.00
Coffee pot, Grecian, rare....60.00
Decanter, Apollo Series, astronaut....35.00

Calypso Line, banana boat, 6½" x 11", $30.00.

Decanter, Apollo Series, len....40.00
Decanter, Apollo Series, missile....20.00
Decanter, Jupiter 60 Locomotive, coal tender....40.00
Decanter, Pierce Arrow....35.00
Decanter, WC Fields....28.00
El Rancho Bar-B-Que, chuck wagon w/wheels....65.00
El Rancho Bar-B-Que, coffee server, warmer & 4 mugs....60.00
El Rancho Bar-B-Que, ice tub....25.00
El Rancho Bar-B-Que, iced tea server....45.00
El Rancho Bar-B-Que, salad bowl....22.00
El Rancho Bar-B-Que, sombrero serve-all....50.00
Hanging basket, basketweave w/ring 'hdls' relief, 7½"....20.00
Jardiniere, flying birds, matt turq, 7½"....15.00
Jardiniere, holly berries/leaves, turq gloss, med....15.00
Jardiniere & pedestal, quilted w/leaves, turq gloss, lg....90.00
Mug, souvenir, brn w/gold ink writing, imp mk, 4¼"....25.00
Pitcher, chicken figural, wht matt, 1943....15.00
Pitcher, water lily, fish hdl, gr gloss....25.00
Planter, anvil w/chain & hammer....10.00
Planter, Butterfly Line, figural butterfly, bl matt....10.00
Planter, duck w/detachable umbrella....40.00
Planter, hand w/cornucopia, pink gloss, 1942....12.00
Planter, Humpty Dumpty, USA....8.00
Planter, Mammy on scoop....28.00
Planter, Oriental & cart w/2 barrels, yel gloss....10.00
Planter, pup, sitting, cart behind....8.00
Planter, quail family, ivory, lt gr & brn....22.50
Planter, spinning wheel w/dog & cat....15.00
Planter, stork & basket, pink....10.00
Planter, stretch horse....8.00
Planter, turtle, lotus pads on bk, gr w/cold-yel detail....12.00
Planter, zebra mother & young....18.00
Planter/bookend, hunting dog, bird in mouth, pr....38.00
Planter/bookend, violin....16.00
Pretzel jar, 'Pretzels,' gr-bl gloss....45.00
Reamer, yel, old....65.00
Sand jar, sphinx head relief, tan & gr matt....125.00
Shakers, cucumber & red pepper, pr....12.00
Spoon rest, penguin figural, lime & dk gr....30.00
Sugar bowl, Suburbia, yel w/brn lid....5.00
Tea set, pine cones, 3-pc....38.00
Teapot, bl floral, 4-cup....18.00
Teapot, cherries & leaves relief, aqua gloss, ca 1926....40.00
Teapot, Grecian, rare....45.00
Vase, Arcature, 7"....15.00
Vase, Blossomtime, wht w/high relief flower, hdls, 6"....12.00
Vase, butterfly, gr, 9"....10.00
Vase, dbl row triangles at base, stepped neck, hdls, 7"....20.00
Vase, grape, 9¼"....10.00
Vase, hyacinth cluster figural, bl w/gr leaves, 1950....15.00
Vase, leaves & berries relief, bl matt, 7½"....10.00
Vase, magnolia figural, 1953....15.00
Vase, swan, wht, 9"....10.00
Wall pocket, anvil w/floral spray....15.00
Wall pocket, bird on sunflower....15.00
Wall pocket, bunch of grapes & leaves....15.00
Wall pocket, iron on trivet....15.00
Wall pocket, owls on trivet....18.00
Wall pocket, umbrella....12.00
Water sprinkler, turtle, twig hdl, gr gloss....22.00

McCoy, J. W.

The J.W. McCoy Pottery Company was incorporated in 1899. It operated under that name in Roseville, Ohio, until 1911, when McCoy entered into a partnership with George Brush, forming the Brush-McCoy Company.

During the early years, McCoy produced kitchenwares, majolica jardinieres and pedestals, umbrella stands and cuspidors. By 1903, they had begun to experiment in the field of art pottery, and though never involved to the extent of some of their contemporaries, nevertheless produced several art lines of merit.

Their first line was Mt. Pelee, examples of which are very rare today. Two types of glazes were used, matt green and an iridescent charcoal gray. Though the line was primarily mold formed, some pieces evidence the fact that while the clay remained wet and pliable, it was pulled and pinched with the fingers to form crests and peaks, in a style not unlike George Ohr.

The company rebuilt in 1904, after being destroyed by fire, and other artware was designed. Loy-Nel Art and Renaissance were standard brown lines, hand decorated under the glaze with colored slip. Shapes and artwork were usually simple but effective. Olympia and Rosewood were relief-molded brown-glaze lines, decorated in natural colors with wreaths of leaves and berries or simple floral sprays. Although much of this ware was not marked, you may find examples with the die-stamped 'Loy-Nel Art, McCoy' or an incised line identification.

When no condition is indicated, the items listed below are assumed to be in mint condition.

Left to right: Jardiniere with floral decor, 5", $40.00; Vase with floral decor, handles, 11", $90.00; Vase with roses, 6", $60.00.

Jardiniere, Loy-Nel Art, smoking cigars, rare study, 4"....200.00
Jardiniere, Loy-Nel Art, water lilies, 6½"....80.00
Jardiniere & pedestal, Loy-Nel Art, tulips, 28"....285.00
Mug, Olympia, leaf & berry band....85.00
Punch bowl, Olympia, grapes & vines....395.00
Tankard, Corn Line, no mk....95.00

Tray, Mt Pelee, divided w/hdl, blk metallic glaze, 7" L........180.00
Umbrella stand, Blended, emb wreaths & shells, #10, 19".....125.00
Umbrella stand, Loy-Nel Art, leaves & berries, 17½"..........200.00
Vase, Loy-Nel Art, leaves & berries, hdls, 10½"..............150.00
Vase, Loy-Nel Art, leaves & berries, sm hdls, 9".............135.00
Vase, Loy-Nel Art, lg daffodil, 9"...........................125.00
Vase, Loy-Nel Art, pansies, bulbous w/hdls, 8"...............110.00
Vase, Olympia, ears of corn, cylindrical, sgn S, 11"...........185.00
Vase, Olympia, jug form, 7"..................................150.00
Vase, Rosewood, floral relief, #41, 5".......................95.00
Vase, Rosewood, orange streaks on brn, 6".....................45.00

McKee

McKee Glass was founded in 1853 in Pittsburgh, Pennsylvania. Among their early products were tablewares of both the flint and non-flint variety. In 1888 the company relocated to avail themselves of a source of natural gas, thereby founding the town of Jeanette, Pennsylvania.

One of their most famous colored dinnerware lines, Rock Crystal, was manufactured in the 1920s. During the thirties and forties, colored opaque dinnerware, Sunkist reamers, and 'bottoms up' cocktail tumblers were popular, as well as a line of black glass vases, bowls, and novelty items. All are popular items with today's collectors.

The company was purchased in 1916 by Jeanette Glass, under which name it continues to operate.

When no condition is indicated, the items listed below are assumed to be in mint condition. See also Depression Glass.

Bird house, hanging; red, cone-shaped base, 6x5" dia..........45.00
Bowl, custard, w/spout, 7"...................................10.00
Bowl, mixing; custard, 6"....................................12.00
Bowl, mixing; Skokie gr, 9"..................................14.00
Bowl, yel, w/lid, 10-oz......................................16.00
Butter dish, w/lid, wht, 1-lb................................25.00
Candy dish, nude, ftd, blk, 8½".............................145.00
Candy dish, nude, ftd, jadite, 8½"..........................115.00
Canister, custard, Cereal, w/lid, 6".........................28.00
Coffee pot, custard, w/lid, 48-oz............................28.00
Egg cup, yel..9.00
Goblet, 8-oz, 6¾"..15.00
Ice bucket, Rainbow, 6"......................................20.00
Leftover, cobalt, 5x4".......................................22.00
Measuring cup, custard.......................................22.00
Measuring cup, yel, 16-oz....................................34.00
Measuring pitcher, hdl, custard, 2-cup.......................21.00
Measuring pitcher, Skokie gr, 4-cup..........................30.00
Punch set, Aztec, 15-pc.....................................110.00
Shaker, blk, 4¼", pr...19.00
Sherbet, ftd, 3½"..10.00
Table set, Queen, vaseline, 4-pc............................210.00
Tumbler, custard, 4"...14.00
Tumbler, lemonade; Rainbow, 4¾"..............................13.00
Tumbler, Sunbeam, gr...22.00
Vase, #1927, bl, M&StL RY, rare, 7½"........................275.00
Wine, Sunbeam..18.00

Medical Collectibles

The fields of medical-related items encompasses a wide area, from the primitive bleeding bowl, to the X-ray machines of the early 1900s. Other closely related collectibles include apothecary and dental items. Many tools that were originally intended for the pharmacist found their way to the doctor's office, and often dentists used surgical tools when no suitable dental instrument was available. A trend in the late 1700s toward self-medication brought a whole new wave of home-care manuals and 'patent' medical machines for home use. Commonly referred to as 'quack' medical gimmicks, these machines were usually ineffective, and occasionally dangerous.

When no condition is indicated, the items listed below are assumed to be in excellent condition.

Electraply, quack machine, battery operated, in box, $65.00.

Atomizer, St Regis, in box...................................10.00
Ball, pharmacist's; for crushing medication, 3"..............15.00
Bed pan, gray, Meinecke......................................10.00
Bleeder, brass, 16 blades...................................110.00
Bleeder, 12 blades in brass enclosure.......................125.00
Bleeder, 3 blades, brass keeper, mk Borwick...................70.00
Book, New Family Physician, King, 1860, 1127 pg..............20.00
Book, Science & Art of Surgery, Ericksen, 1885...............12.00
Bottle, IV; w/bail hdl, Abbott Laboratories..................35.00
Box, Father John's Medicine, dvtl, 12x12"....................24.00
Cabinet, dental, 19 paneled drawers, mirror, tiger oak.......1,100.00
Case, traveling; doctor's, pills, instruments, etc...........90.00
Chart, New Model Anatomical Manikin, cb layers lift, 36"......250.00
Dental instruments, ebony hdls, 1860s, set of 6.............160.00
Enema syringe, hard rubber, emb R Comb Co, 1851...............25.00
Hearing aid, silk tubing.....................................85.00
Jar, porcelain, Rexall, Latin inscriptions, set of 5........150.00
Lancet, triggered fleam type, brass & steel, w/box..........100.00
Microscope, brass, Martin drum type, ca 1890, 6¼"............75.00
Microscope, Leitz, 3-turrett, brass & blk, w/case...........240.00
Opthalmoscope, cased, Morton.................................95.00
Pin-back, Dr Le Gear Stock Remedies, giant horse, 1¼"........10.00
Post mortem set, 1870s, w/case..............................395.00
Puzzle, Jayne's Expectorant, tin litho bottle, 5½", VG.......28.00
Quack machine, chrome pads & grips, Burnley, 1890, w/box....45.00
Quack machine, Electro, Sears, oak case w/instructions......145.00
Quack machine, Master Violet Ray, in 12x9" case w/book......45.00
Quack machine, shock type, AA Potter, MC, Kansas City.......25.00
Retinoscope, ebony & brass hdl...............................75.00
Saw, amputation bow, ebony hdl..............................120.00
Sign, Cures Scalp Diseases, Dr Lyna's Hair Grower, 10x13"......5.00

Sign, Peptenzyme/Nephritin, Dr & skeleton fight over nude....285.00
Sign, Radcliffe's Great Remedy, bottle, tin, 1895..............85.00
Sign, WH Smith's Lung & Cough Syrup, cb, 11x14″............8.00
Sign, 8 Cures for 10¢, X-Ray headache tablets, cb, 5x13″........8.00
Spoon, pat 1879..60.00
Stethoscope, monaural, metal..............................95.00
Surgical kit, pocket size..................................275.00
Tooth key, wood hdl......................................155.00

Meissen

The Royal Saxon Porcelain Works was established in Meissen, Saxony, in 1710. Under the direction of Johann Friedrick Bottger, who in 1708 had developed the formula for the first true porcelain body, fine ceramic figurines with exquisite detail, and tableware of the highest quality were produced. Although every effort was made to insure the secrecy of Bottger's discovery, others soon began to copy his ware, and in 1731 Meissen adopted the famous crossed sword trademark to identify their own work. The term 'Dresden ware' is often used to refer to the Meissen porcelain, since Bottger's discovery and first potting efforts were in nearby Dresden.

When no condition is indicated, the items listed below are assumed to be in mint condition. See also Onion Pattern

Bottle topper, capped lady's head figural....................385.00
Bowl, basketweave/butterfly/florals, w/lid, X-swords, 8″.........250.00
Bowl, centerpiece; florals, ftd, reticulated, 8x12½″ L..........495.00
Bowl, florals/landscape, 1760s, w/lid, 4½″..................225.00
Bowl, florals/leaves relief, poultry decor, 1770, 4¾″...........110.00
Cake dish, grape leaves/grapes form, 19th C, 11½″ dia........150.00
Candelabra, 7-light, applied florals, 3 putti, 26″, pr, EX......1,980.00
Charger, cobalt w/gold relief, X-swords, 11″.................250.00
Cream jug, cherub molded design, relief floral, 1760..........110.00
Cup, 2-hdl, wht w/relief florals, att Bottger, 1715, EX.........250.00
Cup & saucer, landscape w/figures, ca 1740, set of 4..........950.00
Cup & saucer, reserves on cobalt, cup w/landscape...........450.00
Figurine, Apollo, arms up & to side/running, rstr, 15½″.......200.00
Figurine, Art, as nude maid w/emblematic objects, 19″, EX...1,210.00
Figurine, baby lying in bed plays w/brn/wht dog, 7½″.........800.00
Figurine, Bacchic celebration, nude/satyr+2 figures, 12″.....1,650.00
Figurine, beggar woman/hurdy-gurdy, basket w/child, 1700s...2,900.00
Figurine, blacksmith, lt gr vest/brn apron, 1750, 7½″, VG....1,100.00
Figurine, Ceres by flower-filled cornucopia w/cupids, 20″.....1,210.00
Figurine, child as 'night,' bl cloak, gilt globe, 7″............950.00
Figurine, Dutch fisherman, wife, X-swords, 1800s, 3″, pr......450.00
Figurine, farm girl w/basket, no mk, 1800s, 1¾″, EX.........225.00
Figurine, gallant w/basket of fruit, mc, 1870s, 10½″, NM......950.00
Figurine, grape picker, ca 1745, 7½″, EX.................2,000.00
Figurine, hound dog, close-cropped ears/head on paws, 5″ L...170.00
Figurine, laborer by stump, X-swords, 1700s, rpr, 4¼″, VG.....550.00
Figurine, lady, gallant, EX decor, X-swords, 1700, 2½″, pr...1,200.00
Figurine, lady, traveler, hands in muff, 1800, sgn, 2¼″........250.00
Figurine, lady w/chicken, ca 1745, 8″, EX..................1,600.00
Figurine, lovers w/instruments by tree, attendant, 10″, EX.....715.00
Figurine, nude Daphne pursued by Apollo in drape, 14″, EX...500.00
Figurine, oyster seller, mc, bl X-swords mk, 6x2½″..........550.00
Figurine, parakeet on stump, X-swords, 1700s, 2¼″...........350.00
Figurine, Provender for Monastery, X-swords, 1800s, 3″, VG...525.00
Figurine, Turkish soldier, sgn, 1740, rpr, 8″, EX...........1,200.00
Figurine, young girl w/wreath, 1760, 5⅝″...................350.00
Figurine, 1700s couple dances/strolls, scroll base, 7″, pr.....2,000.00
Mug, Aus Dankbarkeit, claw ft.............................110.00
Plaque, sorrowing Virgin Mary, X-swords, in fr, 12⅝x10½″.....550.00
Plate, floral/raised gold leaf/bl X-swords, wht, 11½″..........135.00
Plate, lace border, central bouquet, butterflies, 8″.............60.00
Plate, maiden w/cat portrait on wht, sgn/dtd 1868............400.00
Plate, man courts woman, cobalt rim, imp/Wolfsohn mk, 9½″..350.00
Plate, red w/wht & gold, X-swords, 7½″....................160.00
Plate, wht w/gold leaf emb, floral center, X-swords, 12″.......135.00
Platter, center rose/rosebud edge/scallop rim, wht, 10½″........93.00
Tea bowl & saucer, turq w/harbor view, sgn, 1770..........1,350.00
Tea set, gold emb/wht, tray, pot, cr/sug, 2 c/s, X-swords.......885.00
Teapot, birds in reserve on rose, sgn, 1750, rpr, 4″..........900.00
Vase, flowers/dragonflies, underglaze bl, w/lid, sgn, 9″.........525.00
Vase, HP panel/encrusted florals/Ceres figural finial, 53″.....7,000.00

Tete-a-Tete, floral bouquet medallions with a raised griffin and bust border on eggplant ground, in gilt wreath border, late 19th century, $1,600.00 for the 10-pc set.

Mercury Glass

Mercury glass was popular during the 1850s, and enjoyed a short revival at the turn of the century. It was made with two thin layers, either blown with a double wall or joined in sections, with the space between the walls of the vessel filled with a mixture of tin, lead, bismuth, and mercury. The opening was sealed to prevent air from dulling the bright silver color.

When no condition is indicated, the items listed below are assumed to be in mint condition.

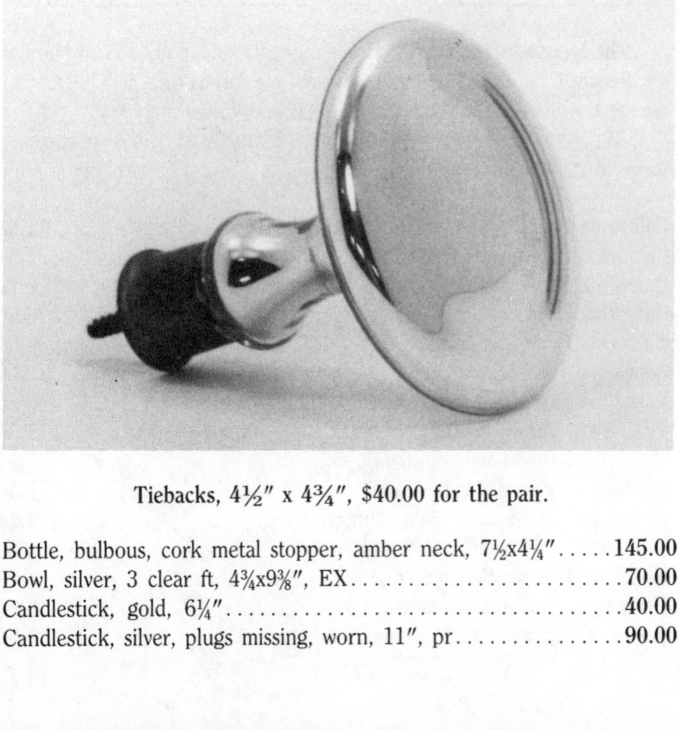

Tiebacks, 4½″ x 4¾″, $40.00 for the pair.

Bottle, bulbous, cork metal stopper, amber neck, 7½x4¼″.....145.00
Bowl, silver, 3 clear ft, 4¾x9⅜″, EX.......................70.00
Candlestick, gold, 6¼″......................................40.00
Candlestick, silver, plugs missing, worn, 11″, pr..............90.00

Candlestick, silver, tin liner, 4″....37.50
Candlestick, silver, 6½″, pr....60.00
Candlestick, silver w/wht floral, minor wear, 5″, pr....50.00
Candlestick, wheel eng flower, pewter socket, 9½″....45.00
Centerpiece, bl, baluster stem & base, worn transfer, 10½″....130.00
Centerpiece, silver ball & stand, 2 attached pcs, 11″....70.00
Compote, gold, 8¼″....85.00
Compote, silver w/wht floral, minor wear, 6⅜″....50.00
Figurine, mother & child, silver & gold, pnt features, 6″....40.00
Goblet, gold, enamel floral band, 5″....20.00
Mug, gold, applied hdl, minor wear, 2½″....20.00
Salt cellar, silver w/gold lining, enamel foliage, 2⅞″....25.00
Sugar bowl, silver w/wht enamel foliage, w/lid, 6¼″....30.00
Tiebacks, cobalt, tin fittings, 2½″, set of 8....425.00
Tiebacks, silver, emb flowers, pewter mts, 3⅝″, pr....40.00
Tiebacks, silver, eng vintage, pewter mts, 3½″, pr....20.00
Vase, gold, floral decor worn, 9½″, pr....50.00
Vase, gr w/mc floral & butterfly, 4⅝″....15.00
Vase, silver, spherical, 6¾″....45.00
Vase, silver w/bl pnt, resembling cut overlay, 7″, pr....75.00

Merrimac

Founded in 1897 in Newburyport, Mass., the Merrimac Pottery Company primarily produced tile and gardenware. In 1901, however, they introduced a line of artware that is attracting the interest of collectors. Marked examples carry an impressed die-stamp or a paper label, each with the firm name and the outline of a sturgeon, the Indian word for which was Merrimac.

When no condition is indicated, values are for examples in mint condition.

Bowl, blk metallic, red clay, ruffled, 3x8″....140.00
Bowl, gr feathered glaze, no mk, 4½x7½″....55.00
Fairy lamp base, dk gr feathered, no mk, pre-1900, 3x5½″....75.00
Vase, hand-modeled elephant heads, gr, cylinder, mk, 4½″....325.00
Vase, matt gr w/cream drip at top, closed cylinder, 4¾″....225.00
Vase, mottled yel-orange, unusual glaze, 12½x7″....475.00

Metlox

The Metlox Manufacturing Company was founded in 1927 in Manhattan Beach, California, but it was not until the forties that they began producing the dinnerware for which they have become famous.

When no condition is indicated, the items listed below are assumed to be in mint condition.

California Provincial, bowl, rnd vegetable, 10″....11.00
California Provincial, creamer....7.50
California Provincial, cup & saucer....7.00
California Provincial, plate, dinner....6.50
California Provincial, platter, 12″....13.00
California Provincial, soup....6.00
California Provincial, sugar bowl, w/lid....9.50
Cookie jar, clown, lg stand-out neck ruffle, Poppy Trail....15.00
Homestead Provincial, bowl, hdl, 8″....7.50
Homestead Provincial, bowl, 10″....7.50
Homestead Provincial, plate, dinner; 10″....4.25
Homestead Provincial, platter, oval, 14″....9.00
Homestead Provincial, server, 3-tier....12.00
Homestead Provincial, teapot....12.00
Poppy Trail, mustard....7.50
Poppy Trail, shakers, pineapple, pr....6.00
Poppy Trail, vase, floral, turq, bulbous, 5¾″....10.00
Poppy Trail, vase, incised flowers, antique gr, 7½″....10.00
Poppy Trail, wall pocket....10.00

Mettlach

In 1836, Nicholas Villeroy and Eugene Francis Boch, both of whom were already involved in the potting industry, formed a partnership and established a stoneware factory in an old restored abbey in Mettlach, Germany. Decorative stoneware with in-mold relief was their specialty, steins in particular. Through constant experimentation, they developed innovative methods of decoration. One process, called chromolith, involved inlaying colorful mosaic designs into the body of the ware. Later, underglaze printing from copper plates was used. Their stoneware was of high quality, and their steins won many medals at the St. Louis Expo and early world's fairs. Most examples are marked with an incised castle and the name 'Mettlach.' The numbering system indicates size, date, stock number, and decorator. Production was halted by a fire in 1921--the factory was not rebuilt.

When no condition is indicated, the items listed below are assumed to be in mint condition.

Key:
L—liter
PUG–painted underglaze

Ash tray, #2882, etched, Art Nouveau....141.00
Beaker, #1025, girl w/peacock, shepherd, boy musicians....65.00
Beaker, #2327/1200, PUG, Koln, ¼L....55.00
Beaker, #2368, glazed, shades of bl, ¼L....22.00
Beaker, #2368/1091, PUG, serving boy, rim chips, ¼L....49.00
Beaker, #2368/4242, PUG, Palm Springs, Florida, ¼L....54.00
Charger, #2443, maid w/attendants in relief, 18″....935.00
Coaster, #1032, PUG, dwarf....81.00
Gravy bowl, #270, silver trim....107.00
Humidor, #1231, etched cow & castle, eng SP lid, 9″....495.00
Jardiniere, #2170....265.00
Pitcher, #2210, bowling scene, wht on bl, bulbous, 3L....585.00
Pitcher, #2348, pewter lid, 13″....325.00
Plaque, #1044/1033, PUG, Alpine girl w/kids, sgn, 17″....583.00
Plaque, #1044/353, PUG, 2 Oriental women on boat, 14″....216.00
Plaque, #1044/357, PUG, 2 women pulled in rickshaw, 12″....162.00
Plaque, #1044/81, PUG, cavalier w/pipe, 17″....476.00
Plaque, #1044/92, PUG, Stadthaus in Berncastle, 14″....257.00
Plaque, #1044/93, PUG, building scene, 14″....194.00
Plaque, #1048/11, etched, men kneel for king, brn/blk, 16″....648.00
Plaque, #1418, bird & floral, sgn M Hein, 1896, 19¼″....995.00
Plaque, #1607, Autumn season, sgn Warth, 11″....300.00
Plaque, #2625, cavalier, 8″....200.00
Plaque, #3225/1290, PUG, elks heads & clock, purple on wht..270.00
Plate, #3096, octagonal, 9″....65.00
Punch bowl, #2602, relief, w/underplate....88.00
Punch bowl, #3334, relief, w/underplate....65.00
Stein, #1000, relief: 3 shields, gray, .3L....109.00
Stein, #1028, relief: couple w/harvest, ½L, M....140.00
Stein, #1028, relief: harvest scene, 3L, M....313.00
Stein, #1053, etched, 3 dwarfs drinking, pewter lid, 1L....675.00
Stein, #1174, etched, mosaic, brn w/bl/red/gold, 3L, M....335.00
Stein, #1266, relief: men drinking, ¼L....113.00
Stein, #1370, relief: couple & verse, ½L....135.00
Stein, #1395, etched, different playing card suits, ½L....357.00
Stein, #1475, etched, dwarfs working, 3-D dwarf inlay, ½L....875.00
Stein, #1526, fraternal crest, relief shield lid, HP, ½L....166.00

Stein, #1526/595, PUG, knight & verse, 1L....238.00
Stein, #1526/601, PUG, dwarfs at keg, ½L....195.00
Stein, #1526/604, PUG, occupational, fireman, ½L....292.00
Stein, #1527, etched, outdoor drinking scene, 1L....756.00
Stein, #1647, etched, tapestry, innkeeper w/stein, 1L....371.00
Stein, #1675, etched, scene of Heidelberg, ½L....567.00
Stein, #171, relief: dancing figures, ¼L....103.00
Stein, #1794, etched, Bismark in uniform, ½L....659.00
Stein, #1893, etched, star, 1L....486.00
Stein, #1909/1010, PUG, dwarfs drinking from keg, ½L....250.00
Stein, #1909/702, PUG, King of Hops, ½L....273.00
Stein, #1909/715, PUG, students & cavaliers w/Perkeo, ½L....243.00
Stein, #1909/943, PUG, knights & innkeeper, ½L....309.00
Stein, #1932, etched, 2 cavaliers toasting, sgn, ½L....437.00
Stein, #1997, etched, George Erhert Brewery, ½L....280.00
Stein, #2004, etched, fox & owl, pewter lid, ½L, NM....1,395.00
Stein, #2012, etched, shields, inlay w/VB on sail, ½L....437.00
Stein, #202, relief: men singing, 1L....310.00
Stein, #2024, etched, shields of Berlin w/city scenes, ½L....540.00
Stein, #2025, etched, many cherubs, bl, .3L....270.00
Stein, #2082, etched, boar hunt, orig pewter lid, ½L....707.00
Stein, #2086, relief: figures dance around stein, ¼L....190.00
Stein, #2090, etched, club stein, sgn Hein Schlitt, ½L....405.00
Stein, #2100, etched, Roman soldier & barbarian, sgn, ½L....900.00
Stein, #2104, etched, cavalier w/lance & stein, 1½L....1,134.00
Stein, #2140/884, PUG, skull & crossbones, ½L....1,070.00
Stein, #2176/1055, PUG, drunken cavalier, 2.7L....713.00
Stein, #2181/957, PUG, maiden, ¼L....178.00
Stein, #2182, relief: bowling scene, ½L....297.00
Stein, #2183/953, PUG, dwarfs drinking, 3L....405.00
Stein, #2184/966, PUG, dwarfs, .3L....265.00
Stein, #2192, etched, Etruscan scene, sgn H Schlitt, ½L....794.00
Stein, #2210, relief: man bowls as many watch, 3L....415.00
Stein, #2211, relief: man bowling/others watch, .3L....178.00
Stein, #2231, etched, cavaliers toasting, ½L....514.00
Stein, #2236, cavaliers, jester faces on 2 hdls, 6″....389.00
Stein, #2245, relief: monkeys & men, turtle on inlay, .3L....171.00
Stein, #2247, relief: 3 scenes of musicians & dancers, .3L....113.00
Stein, #2271-1055, PUG, drunken cavalier, ½L....225.00
Stein, #2324, etched, football game, music box in base, ½L....935.00
Stein, #2348/1022, PUG, boys play bagpipe/flute, 3.3L....432.00
Stein, #2394, etched, slaying of dragon, pewter lid, ½L....702.00
Stein, #2585, etched, Munich child on world/buildings, 1L....972.00
Stein, #2662, etched, hallucinating student sees mice, ½L....2,080.00
Stein, #2778, etched, carnival man, men drinking, sgn, 1L....1,724.00
Stein, #2780, etched, cavalier plays mandolin to lady, ½L....470.00
Stein, #2788/6133, PUG, Spanish cavalier, ½L....324.00
Stein, #2798, etched, 3 people from R Wagner's opera, ½L....621.00
Stein, #2800, etched, Art Nouveau, ½L....278.00
Stein, #2833-D, etched, Alpine couple, ½L....493.00
Stein, #2833-F, etched, fraternity students, sgn MC, ½L....540.00
Stein, #284, PUG, fraternal crest, ½L....148.00
Stein, #2869, relief: child & Bavarian lion, sgn....3,240.00
Stein, #2872, etched, Cornell University, 3 scenes, ½L....648.00
Stein, #2900, etched, version of Quilmes Brewery, 1L....327.00
Stein, #2900, factory & trains on track, Saar-Basin mk, 8″....650.00
Stein, #2957, etched, boy hurts foot while bowling, ½L....335.00
Stein, #3091, etched, drinking knight, sgn Schlitt, ½L....1,140.00
Stein, #3142, etched, shield, mug & Alpine dancer, sgn, 1L....756.00
Stein, #3143, etched, Alpine couple, shield, sgn, ½L....465.00
Stein, #3144, etched, blk clock w/Alpine couples, sgn, 1L....783.00
Stein, #32, relief: 3 archway scenes, ½L....370.00
Stein, #3200, etched, Heidelberg w/Perkeo at hdl, ½L....623.00
Stein, #3254, etched, Alpine couple & dog, ½L....406.00

Stein, #485, ½L, $395.00.

Stein, #328, relief: Gambrinus & walking steins, ½L....151.00
Stein, #71, relief work, mercury mk, 6¼″....195.00
Tumbler, #2327, rearing horse on shield, Stadt Stuttgart....65.00
Tumbler, #2334, florals, wht/brn on gr, incised....60.00
Vase, #1537, 4 seasons, incised, sgn C Gorig, 15″....275.00
Vase, #1749, maidens, incised, sgn C Gorig, 13″....385.00
Vase, #1844, floral, etched mc on gray, gold decor, 9½″....375.00
Vase, #2857, 11″....150.00
Vase, Nouveau female among poppies on dk bl, 11″....695.00
Wall charger, #354, 2 Japanese ladies in boat, mk, 14″....650.00

Midwestern Glass

As early as 1814, blown glass was made in Ohio. By 1835, glasshouses in Michigan were producing similar pattern-molded types that have long been highly regarded by collectors. During the latter part of the 19th century, all six of the states of the Northwest Territory were mass-producing the pressed glass tableware patterns that were then in vogue. Various types of art glass were produced in the area until after the turn of the century. Items listed here are attributed to the Midwest by certain physical characteristics known to be indigenous to that part of the country.

When no condition is indicated, the items listed below are assumed to be in mint condition.

See also Zanesville Glass; Findlay Onyx; Greentown Glass; Libbey Glass

Bottle, 18 vertical ribs in body, neck swirl, lt gr, 5½″....45.00
Bowl, 16 swirl ribs, folded rim, amethyst, 3¾″....450.00
Creamer, applied ft & hdl, bulbous body, sapphire bl, 3½″....600.00
Creamer, 15 vertical ribs, tooled rim, gr tint, 5″, VG....150.00
Cruet, 20 vertical ribs, applied hdls, minor wear/sickness....400.00
Flask, chestnut; 25 swirl rib, aqua, 6½″, NM....100.00
Jigger, 12 ribs swirl at flare lip, sapphire bl, 2⅜″....40.00
Sugar bowl, lacy, octagonal, w/dome lid, 6″, NM....85.00
Wine, cobalt, blown w/applied ft, 15-rib knop & bowl, 3½″....115.00

Militaria

Because of the wide and varied scope of items available to collectors of militaria, most tend to concentrate mainly on the area or areas that interest them most, or that they can afford to buy. Some items represent a major investment, and because of their value have been reproduced. Extreme caution should be used when purchasing Nazi items. Every badge, medal, cap, uniform, dagger, and sword that Nazi Germany issued is being reproduced today. Some repros are crude and easily identified as fakes, while others are very well done and difficult to recognize as reproductions.

Purchases from WWII veterans are usually your safest buys. Reputable dealers or collectors will normally offer a money-back guarantee on Nazi items purchased from them.

There are a number of excellent 3rd Reich reference books available in bookstores at very reasonable prices. Study them to avoid loosing a much larger sum spent on a reproduction!

When no condition is indicated, the items listed below are assumed to be in excellent condition.

Armband, Hitler Youth, red/wht cotton w/swastika....20.00
Armband, SS, red bkground w/blk swastika....40.00
Back pack, CW, blk oilcloth, leather straps/fittings, rare....50.00
Badge, Austria Republic Pilot, gr wreath w/shield & eagle....135.00
Badge, Austrian Glider instructor's, wreath w/wht gulls....55.00
Badge, beret; Special Air Service, embroidered silver wire....10.00
Badge, breast; Austrian, 50 Year Merit for Red Cross....50.00
Badge, cap; Army Pay Corps, King's crown, brass, 1902-1920...42.00
Badge, cap; Glider Pilot Regiment, King's crown, nickel....40.00
Badge, cap; King's Royal Rifle Corps, King's crown, brass....35.00
Badge, cap; Leicestershire Regiment, brass/metal, 1898....30.00
Badge, cap; Lincolnshire Regiment, brass/metal, 1898-1946....30.00
Badge, cap; Norfolk Regiment, brass/metal, 1898-1935....35.00
Badge, cap; Rifle Brigade, King's crown, nickel, 1937-1956....29.00
Badge, cap; Royal Air Force, King's crown, nickel, 1928....20.00
Badge, cap; Royal Army Pay Corps, King's crown, 1929-1953...30.00
Badge, cap; Royal Flying Corps, King's crown, bronze, 1912....75.00
Badge, cap; Royal Navy Chief Petty Officer's, embroidered....20.00
Badge, cap; WWII, Air Force Cadet, sterling, 2-pc, scarce....15.00
Badge, cap; WWII, US Navy, gilt/sterling, full size, 2-pc....12.00
Badge, GAR, red/wht/bl ribbon, 5-sided fort drop, 1897....10.00
Badge, Highland Regiment, nickel, 1942-1943....35.00
Badge, Italian Pilot's, eagle w/crown, sliding catch....75.00
Badge, Machine Gun Corps, King's crown, bronze, 1914-1918...50.00
Badge, Polish, 1st Class Balloon Observer's, wreath/eagle....300.00
Badge, Romanian Observer's, eagle w/shield, silver, rare....350.00
Badge, Romanian Pilot's, eagle on ball w/shield, rare....375.00
Badge, Royal Dragoons 1st, King's crown, brass/metal, 1902....30.00
Badge, Royal Irish Rifles, King's crown, brass, 1901-1913....35.00
Badge, Tank Assault, German WWII, given for 3 engagements...28.00
Badge, US Tomb of Unknown Soldier Honor Guard, hallmk....75.00
Badge, USAF Security Police, plastic hanger strap, frosted....28.00
Badge, Welsh Regiment, brass/metal, 1898-1920....35.00
Badge, WWI, Coastal Artillery, for shooting, X-cannons....35.00
Badge, WWII, Australasian Force, Kangaroo, brass....35.00
Badge, WWII, Croation Radio Operator's, wreath/bomb/shield..175.00
Badge, WWII, Dutch-East Indies Pilot's, eagle, scarce....130.00
Badge, WWII, Essex Regiment, plastic, scarce, 1942-1945....35.00
Badge, WWII, Glider Troops, frosted sterling, full sz....20.00
Badge, WWII, Polish Pilot's, wreath in eagle's mouth....85.00
Badge, WWII, Polish Squadron, arms mk PAPL, yel/gr cross....80.00
Badge, WWII, Russian, red velvet star, gold bullion, 2x2"....20.00
Badge, WWII, Russian Army Marksman, red flag/soldier, 1½"...23.00
Badge w/ribbon, GAR, red w/gold bullion fringe, 2½x9"....10.00
Badge w/ribbon, GAR, Veteran's Memoriam, silver print, blk....10.00
Bayonet, AK-47, wire cutter, blk scabbard, serial #057X....100.00
Bayonet, French Chassepot, brass grip, hook guard, 1871....25.00
Bayonet, WWI, w/scabbard, wood grips, mk on blade, EX....23.00
Bayonet, WWII, blade mk UFH, blk plastic grips/gr scabbard....20.00
Bayonet, WWII, mk AFH, blk plastic grip/gr fiber scabbard....15.00
Bayonet, WWII, mk AFH, nude under hand grips, some wear...15.00
Belt, ammunition; WWI, tan web w/brass snaps & fittings....7.00
Belt, Army officer's, blk leather, w/brass eagle buckle....50.00
Belt, officer's, web, w/bronze US buckle & tag, gr....35.00
Belt, Royal Navy, officer's, leather w/brass buckle, 1846....125.00
Belt, sword; officer's, blk leather, hanger straps, buckle....25.00
Belt, sword; Polish eagle, red leather w/straps & buckle....60.00
Belt, US Army officer's Sam Brown, leather w/brass buckle....5.00
Belt, US Marines, wht web, brass buckle w/USMC, NM....10.00
Belt, WWI, Army, Universal Pattern, leather w/brass buckle....95.00
Belt, WWI, w/shotgun shell loops, strap, nickel fr buckle....12.00
Beret, British 17/21, X-bar reads Glory Death Head....20.00
Beret, WWII, Royal Tank Regiment, w/King's crown badge....35.00
Binoculars, French made, hard case w/no lid or strap....10.00
Blazer crest, Parachute Regiment, embroidered gold/silver....15.00
Blazer crest, Royal Air Force Bomber Command, gold/silver....15.00
Blazer crest, Royal Military Police, embroidered....15.00
Blouse, Army, M1912, lt brn-gr wool, bronze buttons....20.00
Blouse, Army, WAC officer's, merit wreath & 2 bars, taupe....15.00
Blouse, WWI, Army officer's, whipcord, discharge chevron....25.00
Blouse, WWI, National Guard, MA state seal buttons, 1917....12.00
Blouse, WWII, Army officer's, label, no insignia....15.00
Book, CW, Battle of Gettysburg, Ltd Ed....40.00
Boots, CW officer's, sq toes, leather wing-tips/heels, M....80.00
Buckle, belt; cast brass H w/US in center oval....35.00
Buckle, German, DAF, silver aluminum w/emb swastika....30.00
Buckle, US in oval, brass, w/orig keeper, scarce, 1872....36.00
Buckle, WWI, German machinegunner, relief medallion, 2x4½"..28.00
Bugle, British Royal Army Ordinance military issue, 1917....65.00
Bullet mold, 20 rnd/34-cal, trn wood hdls, brass, 11", EX....98.00
Bullet mold, 20 rnds/25- & 30-cal, maple hdls, brass, EX....70.00
Button, cannon w/eagle & word Corp, cuff sz, scarce, 1800s....12.00
Button, CW Cavalry, eagle w/C in center shield, cuff sz....4.00
Button, discharge; WWI, bronze & silver, NM, set....5.00
Canteen, Cavalry, stenciled: US, mk RIA 1914, w/hanger, gr....18.00
Canteen, CW, bull's eye, camp scene, stopper/chain intact....75.00
Canteen, CW, bull's eye, w/stopper/chain/orig wood cover....55.00
Cap, field; Japanese Naval Landing Forces, gr, bill/strap....50.00
Cap, Imperial German, duck bill, chin strap, 'HANSA'/flags....50.00
Cap, visor; Irish Guards, bl w/gr band/piping, gold edge....50.00
Cap, visor; Royal Air Force, Air Marshall, gold braid....135.00
Cap, visor; Royal Artillery, officer's, khaki....45.00
Cap, visor; Spanish Am War, bl wool, EX....35.00
Cap, visor; WWI, Army officer's, whipcord body, chin strap....10.00
Cap, WWII, US Navy, Donald Duck, bl w/US Navy ribbon, M....5.00
Cap, WWII Coast Guard, duck bill, bl wool/gold ribbon, VG....20.00
Cape, US Infantry, bl wool w/lining, sm hook fasteners, EX....30.00
Cigarette case, steel/brass, emb Mussolini/Hitler/emblems....175.00
Compass, WWI, glass lens, nickel plated case, flips open....10.00
Compass, WWII, w/waterproof carrier....20.00
Cross, Iron; German, 2nd Class, w/ribbon, 1914....20.00
Cross, Italian, Armed Forces Service, 16-yr silver cross....16.00
Cross, Italian, War Valor, w/ribbon, bronze....18.00
Cross, US Army, distinguished service, WWII, bronze, cased....50.00
Dagger, WWI, German, Trench, scabbard, rare, 4¾" blade....75.00
Dog tag, WWI, name, serial #, mk USA....5.00
Drum, CW commemorative, 12 soldiers in fighting pose....400.00
Flag, Japanese, meatball, silk, sgn, 24x26"....30.00
Flag, Royal Navy, wht ensign, 24x36"....50.00
Flare gun, WWII, Air Force, plastic grip, sheet metal fr....40.00
Flight suit, Army-US Air Force, type K-2B, w/WWII hat, gr....25.00
Gas mask, WWI German, w/tin carrying can....20.00
Goggles, WWII, mountain ski troop, gr lenses w/fur trim....10.00
Hat, campaign; Army, felt/leather sweatband, chin strap....15.00

Hat, campaign; WWI, brn leather chin strap, brn felt 10.00
Hat, French officer's, beaver, silk/leather lining, w/case 40.00
Hat, Korean War USAF Officer's, peaked 20.00
Hat, Luftwaffe Pilot's, peaked 150.00
Helmet, camouflage; WWI, gr/yel/wht/blk w/red lines 25.00
Helmet, cavalry, yel horsehair plume/blk wool cover, rstr 60.00
Helmet, pith; German Army DAK Officer, felt, dated 1942 . . . . . . 60.00
Helmet, Royal Marines, brass ball top/chin chain, wht 125.00
Helmet, Swedish Tanker, ear & neck flaps/strap/blk leather 25.00
Helmet, trench; WWI M1916, camo steel, red/gr/blk bars 70.00
Helmet, Vietnam, Paratrooper's, chin strap 75.00
Helmet, WWI, sand finish, steel, EX liner/chin strap, VG 15.00
Helmet, WWI, 3rd Corps, bl/wht insignia, VG chin strap 35.00
Helmet, WWI, 30th Division, red/blk insignia, no strap 24.00
Helmet, WWI German, leather w/spike 100.00
Helmet, WWII, British RAF, type C, earphone sockets, brn 40.00
Helmet, WWII AAF, A-9, olive wool/leather, use w/headphones . . 70.00
Helmet, WWII flight, throat mike, sunglasses 50.00
Helmet, WWII Luftschutz combat, leather liner, pnt steel 35.00
Horn, CW, soldier/shield/heart/star/fox, carved, 10″ 250.00
Insignia, collar; WWII, VR, Officer's, brass, pr 10.00
Insignia, sleeve; US Eagle Squadron, 1940-1942 . . . . 50.00
Jacket, combat; WWII, US Marines, USMC buttons/pockets, NM . 20.00
Jacket, jump; WWII, sleeveless oversmock, unused 95.00
Jacket, shell; Cavalry, model 1861, eagle buttons, bl wool 375.00
Jacket, Vietnam, blk cotton w/slogan/maps, 1967 . . . . 40.00
Jacket, WWII, Paratrooper's, patch/jump wings/knife pocket 165.00
Jacket, WWII, US Eagle Squadron Pilot, w/insignia, bl wool 125.00
Kepi, CW, eagle buttons, brass-buckled chin strap, bl wool 195.00
Knap sack, CW, fold-up, 3 leather straps, oilcloth, rare 110.00
Knife, US Trench, brass knuckle type, US LF&C, w/scabbard . . . 125.00
Knife, US Trench, mk US LF&C, triangular blade, 1917 . . . . 45.00
Knife, WWII, mk EGW, leather grip & sheath, 7½″ blade 25.00
Knife, WWII, US Navy, brn leather grip/gray fiber scabbard 25.00
Knife, WWII, US Navy, leather grip/gray sheath, NM blade 25.00
Life jacket, WWI Mae West 25.00
Light, signal; US Navy, WWII, portable, w/case, 5x8″, M 50.00
Manual, WWII, sm arms/rifles/machine guns, etc, 234 pg 7.00
Medal, Am Indian Peace, Martin Van Buren bust, bronze, 3″ 48.00
Medal, British, silver, 1914-1918 . . . . 25.00
Medal, Canadian Volunteer, silver, 1939-1945 . . . . 35.00
Medal, Ethiopian War, king's bust/steam engine, bronze 25.00
Medal, German WWII, Close Combat, bronze, EX 65.00
Medal, Infantry, silver cross w/X-rifles, eng brooch 35.00
Medal, Royal Air Force, w/Malaya bar, silver 75.00
Medal, US Coast Guard Distinguished Service, satin gilt 125.00
Medal, US Navy Good Conduct, orig issue envelope 35.00
Medal, WWI, Veteran's Victory Honor, bronze eagle brooch 10.00
Medal, 50th Anniversary of Naval Aviation, bronze 15.00
Medal w/ribbon, Air Force Merit Achievement, silver 25.00
Medal w/ribbon, Coast Guard Good Conduct, bronze pendant . . . 25.00
Medal w/ribbon, GAR, Veteran's, eagle pin w/flag as ribbon 12.00
Medal w/ribbon, Italian, Military Valor, 2nd Class, silver 16.00
Medal w/ribbon, Italian, Naval Valor, 1st Class 16.00
Medal w/ribbon, Mexican Border Service, bronze pendant 40.00
Medal w/ribbon, Sons of Union Veteran's Post, bronze cross 12.00
Medal w/ribbon, US Army Meritorious Service 20.00
Medal w/ribbon, US Coast Guard Arctic Service, bronze 35.00
Medal w/ribbon, US Navy, Spanish Am War Veteran's, wht, 8″ . . 55.00
Medal w/ribbon, US Navy Medal of Honor, anchor/13-star pad . . 600.00
Medal w/ribbon, USMC Expeditionary, bronze pendant 25.00
Medal w/ribbon, USMC Good Conduct, eng, bronze, 1926 . . . . . . 30.00
Medal w/ribbon, USMC Yangtze Service, split brooch, bronze . . . 125.00
Medal w/ribbon, WWI, French Victory, w/US wrap brooch 20.00

Wall hanging, Nazi, heavy metal, 7½″ x 9″, $125.00.

Medal w/ribbon, WWII, Army Good Conduct, orig carton 10.00
Medal w/ribbon, WWII, Selective Service, w/lapel button 20.00
Mess kit, WWII, w/fork & spoon 5.00
Napkin, from Hitler's personal table service, initialed AH 150.00
Necklace, sweetheart; WWII, US Navy, 1″ cap badge on chain . . . 20.00
Patch, blazer; 325th Glider Infantry, silver bullion, wht 20.00
Patch, pocket; WWII, 505th A/B Infantry, embroidered, wht 25.00
Patch, pocket; 187th Airborn Infantry, Red Legs on twill 25.00
Patch, sleeve; WWI, German, Naval Petty Officer, Gunnery 7.00
Patch, sleeve; WWI, German, Petty Officer, Medical Cadet 7.00
Patch, sleeve; WWI, 28th Division, red felt keystone 10.00
Patch, WWI, 1st Corps, engineer's, red eng castle, 2¾x3″ 25.00
Patch, WWI, 76th Division, Liberty Bell on gr wool, scarce 20.00
Patch, WWII, US Marines, 1st MAC Artillery, embroidered 40.00
Patch, WWII, 7th Army, bl felt w/gold bullion center 8.00
Periscope, WWII, from tank, prismatic, 7x11″ 30.00
Picture, CW, Union soldier before US Capitol, 3¼x2¾″ 75.00
Pin, sweetheart; WWII, Coast Guard, gold stripe, sterling 18.00
Pin, sweetheart; 17th Airborn, w/sm jump wing, sterling 15.00
Pistol holster, WWII, .38, Webbing 22.50
Plaque, Special Air Service, SAS insignia, wood, mtd, 8x6″ 35.00
Poster, WWII, wrecked Japan building as Marine hospital 8.00
Pouch, Am Cavalry, 2 iron fr buckles, blk leather, 4x8″ 70.00
Pouch, ammo; CW, leather, emb: Rock Island Arsenal, VG 60.00
Pouch, WWII, US Marines, 2 snaps on flap, canvas web, 7x3″ . . . 10.00
Ring, WWII, US Marines, graduation style, MOP front 15.00
Saddle, CW, Confederate officer, EX 250.00
Saw, bone; CW, surgeon's, gutta percha checkered grip, 12″ 30.00
Scarf, WWII, Red Cross nurse's, wht w/RC patch on front 15.00
Shako, cadet's, Westpoint style, wht leather, brass plate 95.00
Shell, 37-85/PDPs 96/9.16, w/case, 6¾″ 14.00
Shell, 37mm, brass casing mk 1918 BF, iron shell 10.00
Shell, 37mm, eng scrolls: 1918-Onde Woods, brass case 15.00
Shell, 37mm, officer's desk ornament, w/case, 8½″ 11.00
Shell, 37mm-M54/1942/OWS, nose fuse, 4¾″ 5.00
Shirt, fatigue; officer's, US Army, SHAEF patch 5.00
Shirt, WWII, Army Sergeant's, stripes, 4 bars, patch 5.00
Spur, rowels detach, leather straps, brass, pre-1900, pr 10.00
Star, WWII, Air Crew Europe, British 65.00
Star, WWII, Pacific, British 20.00

Stove, WWII, portable, gas powered, w/cooking container.......10.00
Sword, British officer's, iron hilt, 26" curved blade, VG.......195.00
Sword, CW, staff & field officer's, no scabbard, 30" blade......46.00
Sword, War of 1812, brass hilt, 28" curved blade, EX.........55.00
Toggle rope, Paratrooper's, thick/heavy, w/wood hdl, 78".......35.00
Trench coat, WWII, full length, dbl breasted, cotton, belt.......15.00
Uniform, dress; British Royal Artillery, 1855, 3-pc............110.00
Uniform, Royal Artillery, khaki wool, complete, 1960s.........115.00
Uniform, Royal Highlanders Fusiliers, 3-pc..................110.00
Uniform, Royal Marines, captain's full-dress blues, EX.........350.00
Uniform, Royal Navy officer's, w/medal ribbons................95.00
Vest, survival; WWII, Air Force, type C-1, .45 holster, gr.......35.00
Vest, WWII, Viet Nam era, to carrying grenades/pockets, gr.....20.00
Walkie-talkie, Army, web carrying strap, antenna, aluminum.....40.00
Wings, Air Force Pilot, hallmk Amico, sterling, 2"............15.00
Wings, Balloon Pilot, orig, sterling, rare, 1-pc, 3"............145.00
Wings, Pilot/Observer, US in center of O, frosted sterling......200.00
Wings, Royal Navy Pilot's, embroidered gold wire.............20.00
Wings, Special Air Service, parachutist's, cloth, bl/wht..........12.00
Wings, WASP Pilot, reshaped AAF pilot wing, sterling, 3".....225.00
Wings, WWII, Air Force Air Crew, sterling, 1-pc, 3"...........20.00
Wings, WWII, Air Force Air Gunner, sterling, 1-pc, 3".........30.00
Wings, WWII, Air Force Navigator, silver w/bl globe, 3"........35.00
Wings, WWII, Air Force Service Pilot, hallmk Meyer, 3".......75.00
Wings, WWII, Army Paratrooper, hallmk Gemsco, sterling......20.00
Wings, WWII, Flight Surgeon, feather detail, gilt finish........100.00
Wings, WWII, Liason Pilot, shield w/L in center, frosted........75.00
Wings, WWII, Paratrooper, w/jump star, sterling, full sz........20.00
Wings, WWII, US Navy Pilot, sterling.......................40.00

G.I. Art

Ash tray, 105mm shell base w/pipe holder center, brass........25.00
Ash tray, 40mm shell base, 3 cigarette rests..................9.00
Bracelet, riveted central brass insignia/aircraft aluminum........15.00
Inkwell, P-38 plane on stand, 13".........................60.00
Lamp, walnut base, uses three 37mm cartridge casings.........22.50
Lighter, concealed in take-apart 37mm projectile.............10.00
Lighter, 20mm cartridge on sm walnut base, 7½".............18.00
Lighter, 50-cal, outside sparking mechanism..................10.00
Paperweight, inert WWII fragmentation grenade...............10.00
Paperweight, 50-cal cartridge on heavy rnd metal base..........6.00
Shell, WWI, French, 37mm, mk Verdun, 1918................15.00
Umbrella stand, cut-off 155mm shell case, lg................15.00

Milk Glass

Milk glass, so named because of its milky white color, has been produced since the 18th century. The early glass, made with cryolite, looks very much like true porcelain, and rings with a clear bell tone when tapped. It was made both here and in England.

When no condition is indicated, the items listed below are assumed to be in mint condition.

Candlesticks, Crucifix, attributed to New England Glass Co., 11⅜", $175.00 for the pair.

Bottle, Columbus Column, w/closure, 18¼"................500.00
Bottle, dresser; Crysanthemum, ball shape/matching stopper.....65.00
Bottle, dresser; scroll bottom, orig stopper, 9½"..............32.00
Bottle, duck, April 11, 1871, Atterbury, w/closure............525.00
Bottle, Elk's Tooth, gold pnt, w/metal stopper, 4"............85.00
Bottle, Grant's Tomb, w/dome closure......................200.00
Bottle, Joan of Arc, w/lid, 16½"..........................250.00
Bottle, Le Tsar Nicholas II, 13"..........................125.00
Bottle, scent; Beaded Diamond, bulbous bottom, long neck.....55.00
Bottle, Sitting Bear, orig labels, 11"......................115.00
Bottle, Statue of Liberty, w/lid, 15⅝"......................400.00
Bottle, 1939 World's Fair, 9"..........................10.00
Bowl, Beaded Jewels, w/lid, 3½", EX.......................25.00
Bowl, Down on the Farm, 9"..............................30.00
Bowl, Scroll, rnd, 8"...................................15.00
Bowl, sleigh form, oval, 5x10"...........................40.00
Bowl, 2 fish side by side, dtd, Atterbury, 11"................25.00
Box, dresser; Cherry Blossom & Lattice, HP, 9x4¼"..........85.00
Box, dresser; floral, emb dragonfly, oval, w/lid, 8x4"..........85.00
Butter dish, ribbed, beaded base, mk W over G...............20.00
Butter dish, Roman Cross...............................45.00
Butter dish, The Family, father, no eyes...................200.00
Cake stand, Blossom, 6x9"...............................25.00
Candle holder, w/metal hdl, 3½", pr.......................35.00
Candlestick, Dolphin, 9", pr.............................30.00
Candlestick, scroll on base, 6¾" tall, 3¾" base, pr...........45.00
Candy dish, Block & Fan, ftd, w/lid, EX....................35.00
Celery vase, Block & Fan Variant, EX......................35.00
Celery vase, Sawtooth, 9¾".............................30.00
Compote, Atlas, lacy edge, 8"............................50.00
Compote, Basketweave, w/lid, Atterbury, June 1874, rare......110.00
Compote, Blossom, lacy edge, 7½"........................30.00
Compote, Jenny Lind, 7½"..............................50.00
Compote, lattice edge, HP apple blossoms, w/lid, 7½x9".......135.00
Compote, Sawtooth, hexagonal lid finial, 8½x6"..............165.00
Compote, Sawtooth, open, 4x5¼".........................35.00
Compote, Scroll, round, 8x8"............................35.00
Cookie jar, Tree of Life, EX.............................46.00
Covered dish, Dewey, tile base...........................35.00
Creamer, Dahlia, 8-ftd, w/lid, 3¾".......................10.00
Creamer, Panelled Wheat...............................48.00
Creamer & sugar, ribbed, w/tin lid, 4¼"...................33.00
Donut stand, Floral Branch, w/candle attachment, 6x10⅜"......35.00
Egg cup, Birch Leaf...................................20.00
Flask, pocket; American eagle, banner, blown-out.............75.00
Goblet, Birch Leaf, 3⅞", pr.............................20.00
Goblet, Fruit Panels, 6"...............................15.00
Hair receiver, extruded floral metal top....................20.00
Hat, English Hobnail...................................30.00
Jar, dresser; Bison, oval...............................35.00
Jar, honey; Basketweave, w/lid, 5¼"......................20.00
Jar, Oriental, w/lid, 3¼"..............................15.00
Jar, powder; Bison, 3"................................25.00
Match holder, Panel & Rib, 2¾".........................20.00
Match holder, Straw Bundle, tied w/rope, 2⅛"...............20.00
Mug, Bar & Swirl, 3¾", pr.............................20.00
Mug, Bird & Wheat, lg, 3½"............................20.00
Mug, Leaf & Berry, 2"................................10.00
Mug, 3 panels w/different actors on ea, 5"..................15.00
Owl, glass eyes, orig pnt, solid, 5½"......................65.00
Paperweight, Washington Monument, 5½"...................50.00
Pitcher, Coreposis, decor, water sz.......................125.00
Pitcher, lady's head relief, 8"...........................50.00
Pitcher, Owl, w/glass eyes, water sz.......................150.00

Pitcher, Scroll, 9½″ .50.00
Pitcher, tankard; Scroll, 13¼″ .75.00
Pitcher, Windmill & Marigold, 6½″ .20.00
Plate, Beaded Edge, rnd, 8¼″ .20.00
Plate, Club & Fan, pnt lake scene, 9¼″ .15.00
Plate, Fan & Circle, 10½″ .28.00
Plate, Fleur-De-Lis w/Flag & Eagle, gold edge, 7¼″ .35.00
Plate, Niagara Falls, 7¼″ .15.00
Plate, Peg Border, Dewey bust in color, 7¼″ .20.00
Plate, Triangular Leaf & Chain, 8″ .30.00
Plate, Yacht & Anchor, decor, 7½″ .28.00
Plate, 2 Chicks, 7¼″ .20.00
Plate, 3 Bears, 7¼″ .30.00
Plate, 3 Kittens, gold pnt, 7″ .15.00
Platter, daisies, oak leaves/twisted branches, 14½x9½″ .125.00
Platter, Fish, pat '72, 13½x10″ .85.00
Platter, Retreiver, dog after bird, 13¼″ .125.00
Platter, Rock of Ages, oval, Atterbury, 12⅝″ .120.00
Ring tree, tree form, 3¼″ .20.00
Salt, master; Birch Leaf, flint .24.00
Salt, open; swan, Sandwich, 5″ .30.00
Salt, Sawtooth, w/lid, 5″ .25.00
Sauce dish, Blackberry, flat, 4″ .8.00
Shakers, Forget-Me-Not, pr .27.00
Shakers, HP floral, w/metal stand, pr .40.00
Spooner, Basketweave, pat June 1874, Atterbury, 4½″, EX .30.00
Spooner, Birch Leaf, flint .36.00
Spooner, Cameo, 4½″ .10.00
Spooner, Crossed Fern, 4½″ .15.00
Spooner, Melon w/Leaf & Net, April 23, 1878 .70.00
Spooner, Sandwich Loop, 5½″ .35.00
Spooner, Sunflower, 4½″ .15.00
Sugar bowl, Crown, w/lid, 5½″ .15.00
Sugar bowl, Princess Feather, goblet type, w/lid, 7⅜″ .30.00
Sugar bowl, Roman Cross, w/lid .35.00
Sugar bowl, The Family, mother, no eyes .80.00
Sugar shaker, Netted Oak .53.00
Syrup, Double Rib, decor .50.00
Syrup, Floral, 6⅜″ .30.00
Syrup, flowers between beaded dividing lines, 5¾″ .10.00
Syrup, hexagon, w/metal lid, 7″ .55.00
Syrup, Stippled Dahlia .56.00
Tray, dresser; 4 pinwheels, 9¼x6⅝″ .15.00
Tumbler, Diamonds & Beads, 3¾″, pr .15.00
Tumbler, red beaded line, 5″ .50.00
Vase, hand holding fluted horn, 8″ .25.00

Millefiori

Millefiori was a type of art glass popular during the late 1800s. Literally, the term means 'thousand flowers,' an accurate description of its appearance. Canes, fused bundles of multicolored glass threads such as are often used in paperweights, were cut into small cross sections, arranged in the desired pattern, refired and shaped into articles such as cruets, lamps, and novelty items.

It is still being produced, and many examples found on the market today are of fairly recent manufacture.

When no condition is indicated, the items listed below are assumed to be in mint condition. See also Paperweights

Bell, frosted hdl .25.00
Bowl, flaring free-form shape, 1½x5x6″ .15.00
Cruet, frosted hdl, clear faceted stopper .70.00
Figurine, dog, seated, 3½″ .65.00
Lamp, ball shade, on ped std, yel ground, 14x8″ .975.00
Paperweight, teapot form, solid, 3x5″ .35.00
Paperweight, turtle form, 5″ L .28.00
Slipper, camphor ruffle & heel, 5″ .135.00
Toothpick holder, hat shaped .45.00
Tumble-up, 7″ .75.00
Tumbler, paperweight base, 4″ .65.00
Vase, bulbous, hdls, 8″ .120.00
Vase, hdls, 5½x3½″ .45.00
Vase, stick neck, 11x4½″ .110.00
Vase, 7″ .75.00

Miniatures

There is some confusion as to what should be included in a listing of miniature collectibles. Some feel the only true miniature is the salesman's sample; other collectors consider certain small-scale children's toys to be appropriately referred to as miniatures, while yet others believe a miniature to be any small-scale item that gives evidence to the craftsmanship of its creator. For salesman's samples, see specific category; other types are listed below.

When no condition is indicated, the items listed below are assumed to be in excellent condition.

Bureau, cherry/poplar, 4 dvtl drw, cockbeading, 17x15″ .650.00
Bureau, Hplwht, 3 dvtl drw, veneered, 12″ .225.00
Bureau, pine w/red grpt, 4 drw/sq nails, 12x10x6″ .285.00
Bureau, poplar, trn ft, 3 dvtl drw, rpt, 18x16″, VG .250.00
Candlestick, pewter, 1⅜″ .12.00
Castor set, pewter fr, 3 bottles, mustard & lid .95.00
Chest, blanket; pine, dvtl/applied molding/trn ft, 14½x24″ .250.00
Chest, blanket; pine, orig red/yel hearts/stars, 24″ W, EX .850.00
Chest, blanket; pine, sponge pnt on ochre, NE, 1830, 9x24″ .880.00
Chest, blanket; rosemalling, late wire nails, 20″ W .225.00
Chest, Country Sheraton, cherry/poplar/4 cockbead drw, 23″ .775.00
Chest, Hplwht, mahog, Fr feet, 3 dvtl drw, 9½x7¾″ .245.00
Chest, mule; butternut/chestnut, trn ft/2 dvtl drw, 11x14″ .550.00
Chest, pine, bracket ft/dvtl, orig brn w/pnt panels, 19″ .90.00
Chestnut roaster, copper w/trn wood hdl, well made, 9″ .40.00
Coffee pot, tin, side spout, straight sloped sides, 3″ .45.00
Cupboard, hanging; oak, molded base/cornice, 1890s, 19″ .375.00
Cuspidor, brass, emb ad label on bottom: Ireland, 2x2¾″ .30.00
Dining set, German 800 silver, very ornate, 1900, 5-pc .350.00
Egg beater, A&J .10.00
Food grinder, Darling .25.00
Foot stool, fancy cut-out apron/ft, flame stitch top, 6x8″ .95.00

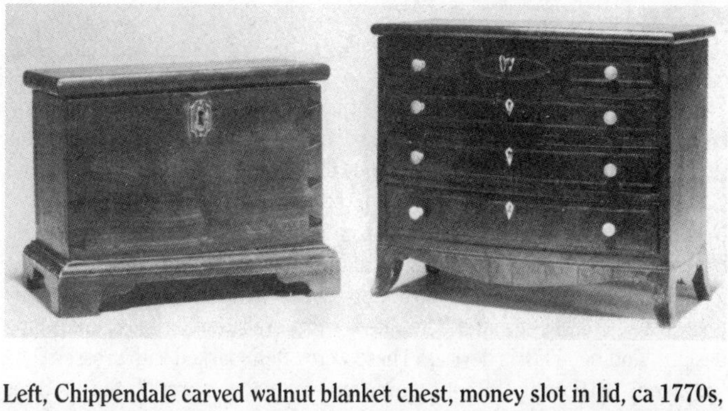

Left, Chippendale carved walnut blanket chest, money slot in lid, ca 1770s, 9″ tall, $650.00; Right, Chippendale carved walnut blanket chest, hinged lid, wrought iron strap hinges, original brass escutcheon, 1760-80, 17″ tall, $1,400.00.

Grater, tin, 2″ . . . 6.00
Kettle, CI, 3-ftd, Wagner . . . 18.00
Pan, cornstick; CI, Griswold . . . 45.00
Pan, cornstick; CI, Wagner . . . 40.00
Piano, baby grand; music box, open scroll, silver, 1½x2¾″ . . . 385.00
Pitcher & bowl, fiery blown opal, applied hdl, 3¼″ . . . 225.00
Shaving mirror, drw, tilt mirror, scroll fr, orig pnt, 9″ . . . 210.00
Skillet, CI, Wagner . . . 20.00
Teakettle, CI, Wagner . . . 100.00
Waffle iron, CI, pat 1910 . . . 25.00

Scaled 1:12″ Miniatures

Ranking at the top of today's leading collectibles, scaled miniatures represent the work of hundreds of artisans who supply local shops with highly prized one-of-a-kind articles and specialties, all scaled one inch to the foot. Many leading producers and distributors of collectibles have entered the field as well. Clubs for miniature enthusiasts have sprung up throughout the United States, Canada, and abroad.

Authority Lillian Baker has compiled a lovely book, *Creative and Collectible Miniatures*, with many full-color photos; you will find her address in the Directory under California.

Baby, Layette Set . . . 35.00
Baby's afghan, 1¾x2″ . . . 10.00
Bassinette, crochet cover . . . 20.00
Bathroom fixtures, porcelain . . . 17.50
Bell, cobalt, 1″ . . . 6.00
Birdcage . . . 15.00
Books, tooled leather . . . 75.00
Cat, Vienna bronze . . . 85.00
Christmas ornaments, 1″, set . . . 10.00
Christmas stocking, crochet . . . 7.00
Clock, wall; Victorian . . . 75.00
Dinnerware, porcelain . . . 45.00
Doll, Bye-Lo Baby, porcelain . . . 60.00
Doll, porcelain . . . 75.00
Lamp, hanging; Victorian . . . 75.00
Lamp, unlighted, ornate, lg . . . 35.00
Lamp, unlighted, sm . . . 12.00
Picture frame, lg . . . 9.00
Picture frame, sm . . . 6.00
Plant, lg . . . 16.00
Plant, sm . . . 8.00
Secretary, Queen Anne . . . 55.00
Towel rack, Victorian . . . 40.00
Violin, one-of-a-kind . . . 400.00

Minton

Thomas Minton established his firm in 1793 at Stoke on Trent, and within a few years began producing earthenware with blue printed patterns similar to the ware he had learned to decorate while employed by the Caughley Porcelain Factory. The Willow pattern was one of his most popular. Neither this nor the porcelain made from 1798 to 1805 was marked (except for an occasional number series), making identification often impossible.

After 1805 until about 1816, fine tea services, beehive-shaped honey pots, trays, etc., were hand decorated with florals, landscapes, Imari-type designs, and neo-classic devices. These were often marked with crossed 'Ls.'

From 1816 until 1823, no porcelain was made. Through the twenties and thirties the ornamental wares with colorful decoration of applied fruits and florals, and figurines in both bisque and enamel were usually left unmarked. As a result, they have been erroneously attributed to other potters. Some of the ware that was marked bears a deliberate imitation of Meissen's crossed swords.

From the late twenties through the forties, Minton made a molded stoneware line--mugs, jugs, teapots, etc.--with florals or figures in high relief. These were marked with an embossed scroll with an 'M' in the bottom curve. Fine parian ware was made in the late 1840s, and in the fifties Minton perfected and produced a line of quality majolica which gained them widespread recognition.

During the Victorian era, M.L. Solon decorated pieces in the pate-sur-pate style, often signing his work; these examples are considered to be the finest of their type. After 1862, all wares were marked 'Minton' or 'Mintons,' with an impressed year cypher.

When no condition is indicated, the items listed below are assumed to be in mint condition.

Tazza, cobalt with gold and silver enamel trees and birds, 2½″ x 9¼″, $185.00.

Bowl, HP flower bouquets, turq ribbons on turq, lg . . . 650.00
Box, florals, HP, gold trim, heart shape, 1½x2″ . . . 135.00
Bust, Evangeline, full color, 16″ . . . 600.00
Cabaret set, Willow, pot, cr/sug, 2 c/s, 15½″ tray, 1880 . . . 325.00
Cream soup w/stand, Hampshire . . . 45.00
Cup & saucer, chickens in 3 reserves on cobalt, gilt, 1867 . . . 350.00
Cup & saucer, Marouesa . . . 25.00
Cup & saucer, Porridge, birds, floral . . . 75.00
Oyster plate, majolica over scroddled ware . . . 250.00
Pilgrim flask, forest landscape in rnd gilt reserve, 9½″ . . . 500.00
Plate, cattle in stream, man on bridge fr by trees, matt . . . 300.00
Plate, cherub sits in tree, ormolu fr, sgn F Judd, 1880 . . . 400.00
Plate, Marouesa, dinner . . . 35.00
Plate, oyster . . . 125.00
Plate, roses in center, turq rim . . . 265.00
Tazza, red rose w/yel & wht buds on bl-gr, ca 1877, 3x9½″ . . . 75.00
Teapot, heads of dogs on wht, sgn Dean, +4⅞″ plate . . . 265.00
Tray, lg red HP roses, artist sgn, 12x9″ . . . 195.00
Vase, Cupid judge, maids' court, pate-sur-pate, Solon, 25″ . . . 5,000.00
Vase, emb flowers, #5, 4″ . . . 125.00
Vase, rosebuds, gilt jewels & swags, reserves of turq, 8″ . . . 175.00
Vase, Seccessionist, flambe & gr, 13″ . . . 165.00

Mirrors

The first mirrors were made in England in the 13th century of very thin glass backed with lead. Reverse painted glass mirrors were made in this country as early as the late 1700s, and remained popular throughout the next century. The simple hand-painted panel was separated from the mirrored section by a narrow slat, and the frame was either the dark-finished Federal style or the more elegant, often-gilded Sheraton.

Mirrors changed with the style of other furnishings, but whatever type you purchase, as long as the glass sections remain solid, even broken or flaking mirrors are more valued than replaced glass. Careful resilvering is acceptable if excessive deterioration has taken place.

When no condition is indicated, the items listed below are assumed to be in excellent condition.

Rococo style giltwood mirror, 59″ x 33″, $500.00.

Cheval, mahog, Classical, 1815, rstr, 80x44″ 2,530.00
Cheval, rosewood, Rococo, 70x36″ 880.00
Chip carved, worn blk/yel rpt, 21x25″ 75.00
Courting, rvpt fruit on wood fr, orig glass, 11x16″, VG 575.00
Curly maple, 14x18″ 115.00
Dressing, pine, carved/pnt, shaped crest, 1700s, 19″ 1,210.00
Empire, French, leaf/shell crest, leaf reserves, 51x31″ 175.00
Empire, gilt corner blocks/trns, brass rosettes, rvpt, 25″ 225.00
Empire, gilt gesso, over mantle, 3-part, foliage, 26x65″ 225.00
Empire, gilt rosettes/trn, blk rpt, rvpt boy/maid, 34x16″ 385.00
Flame grpt w/gold stencil X-trumpets & sunbursts, 13x17½″ 500.00
Giltwood, Fed, eagle atop/pendant w/3 candle supports, 44″ . .2,090.00
Giltwood, modeled as fruit garland on branch, w/drw, 26″ 385.00
Giltwood, Rococo style, ornate scroll/fruit crest, 59x33″ 550.00
Giltwood/gesso, Fed, eagle atop, convex, 43x26″ 1,000.00
Giltwood/gesso, Fed, eagle atop, shaped pendant, 41″ 1,320.00
Grpt, ca 1840s, 6x5″ 40.00
Grpt imitates curly maple, split trn/corner blocks, 13x11″ 190.00
Inlay, ogee, canted corners, gilt liner, wide fr, 25x32″ 85.00
Mahog, Fed, reeded colonettes, J Elliott & Sons, 1820, 38″ 600.00
Mahog veneer, beveled, 8½x10¾″ 20.00
Over mantel, oil painting w/3 mirror panels, gilt scrolls 650.00
Over mantel, papier mache/acid etched, Jennes & Bettridge 55.00
Pine, Co Queen Anne, simple crest, orig glass, 9x16″ 650.00
Pine, horseshoe shape, ca 1879s, rpl glass, 22x17x3″ 110.00
Pine, 2-part, rvpt house & trees, rpl glass/rfn, 12x19″ 175.00
Plateau, blown-out poppies, plain glass, SP, 16″ 165.00
Plateau, Sheffield, vintage base band/florals/paw ft, 18″ 300.00
Poplar, flame grain, natural finish turnings, 11x13″ 355.00
Poplar, trn columns & corner blocks, old blk pnt, 12x16″ 155.00
Scroll, Chpndl, mahog, orig glass, rpr/rpl, 12x24″ 225.00
Scroll, Chpndl, mahog veneer/pine, old glass, rpr/rpl, 36″ 800.00
Scroll, Co Chpndl, primitive, orig glass, rfn/rpr, 13x22″ 230.00
Scroll, mahog/inlay, gilt liner, eagle on crest, rpr, 35″ 235.00
Shaving, curly maple, rectangular/tilting, bowed case, 23″ 1,430.00
Shaving, inlaid mahog, on case w/6 sm drawers, ca 1830 . . . . . .275.00
Shaving, mahog, bow front, line inlay, 3 drw, 20x21x9″ 175.00
Walnut, gilt inner rim, branch-style carved edge, 34x26″ 90.00

Mocha

Mocha Ware is a utilitarian pottery made principally in England and to a lesser extent in France, between 1780 and 1839 on the then prevalent creamware and pearlware bodies. Initially only those pieces decorated in the seaweed pattern were called 'Mocha' while geometrically decorated pieces were referred to as 'Banded Creamware.' Other types of decorations were called 'Dipped Ware.' During the last thirty to forty years the term 'Mocha' has been applied to the entire realm of 'Industrialized Slipware'--pottery decorated by the turner on his lathe using coggle wheels and slip cups.

Mocha was made in numerous patterns--Tree, Seaweed or Dandelion, Rope (also called Worm or Loop), Cat's-eye, Tobacco Leaf, Lollypop or Balloon, Marbled and Marbled and Combed, Twig, Geometric or Checkered, Banded, and slip decorations of rings, dots, flags, tulips,wavy lines, etc. It came into its own as a collectible in the latter half of the 1940s and has become increasingly popular as more and more people are exposed to the rich colorings and artistic appeal of its varied forms of abstract decoration.

The collector should take care not to confuse the early pearlware and creamware Mocha with the later kitchen yellowware, graniteware, and ironstone sporting mocha-type decoration that was produced in America by such potters as J. Vodrey, George S. Harker, Edwin Bennett, and John Bell. This type was also produced in Scotland and Wales, and was marketed well into the 20th century.

When no condition is indicated, the items listed below are assumed to be in undamaged condition.

Staffordshire teapot, marbleized lollypop decoration, burnt-orange, brown and cream with dark brown bands and cream-colored spout, handle, and finial on pear-shaped ochre-yellow body, domed lid, ca 1790, very rare, old restoration to spout, hairline in body and lid, chip to lid, 10¼″, $1,500.00.

Bowl, earthworm, bl ground, sm 365.00
Bowl, earthworm in bl/brn on wht, 6½″, EX 260.00
Bowl, earthworm in brn/wht/tan, emb rim, 7½″, EX 425.00
Bowl, emb gr rim, bl stripes, cream band, hairline, 3x4¾″ 85.00
Bowl, marbled/combed decor below cogwheel band, sm 585.00
Bowl, seaweed, rust/brn bands, 4½″ 345.00
Creamer, bl stripes on wht & gray-bl, edge flakes, 3⅞″ 75.00
Creamer, cat's eye band, brn/putty stripes, 3¾″, EX 450.00
Creamer, 2 bl & 3 dbl brn bands, applied acanthus leaf hdl 195.00
Jug, cream; bl w/2 checkerboard bands, wht lip/hdl 460.00
Mug, blk seaweed resembles trees w/sm birds, orange, 3½″, EX . 525.00
Mug, brn seaweed on orange/emb border/3-color stripes, 5¾″ . . . 525.00
Mug, brn/tan/gr/wht stripes, rim chip w/in, 5″ 180.00
Mug, marbleized bl/brn/tan/zigzag rim band, 1830, rpr, 4½″ 400.00
Mug, seaweed & brn stripes on wide gray-gr band, 6″ 325.00
Mug, wht w/4 bl bands, applied acanthus leaf hdl, 5x5¼″ 175.00
Pepper castor, bl/blk w/cat's eye on ochre/wht, 4¼″, EX 300.00
Pepper castor, brn w/wht lines, bl on dome top, 4⅝″, VG 255.00
Pepper castor, circle band on rust/blk, wear/top chips, 4″ 225.00
Pepper castor, incised, brn/tan/gr, bulbous 250.00
Pepper castor, seaweed, bl on yel, chip 175.00
Pepper castor, stripes, bl/blk/wht, sm edge flakes, 4¾″ 125.00
Pepper castor, very fine bl/blk/wht stripes, 4⅛″ 150.00
Pepper castor, worm/cat's eye, pear shape, tan, 4⅝″, NM 450.00
Pitcher, blk stripes/bl/wht, edge wear/crow's ft, late, 5″ 40.00
Pitcher, cat's eye on brn w/bl/blk/wht stripes, 6″, NM 525.00
Pitcher, wht 'coral' branches, bl/tan/brn on wht, 6″, EX 300.00
Pitcher, worm band, cogwheel shoulder decor, tan w/mc, 8″ . . 1,225.00
Salt cellar, master; earthworm, ped base 250.00
Tankard, sprig swags, wht on tan/blk, gr rim, 4½″ 550.00
Tea bowl & saucer, handleless; blk seaweed on tan, EX 425.00

Molds

Food molds have become a popular collectible; not only for their value as antiques, but because they also revive childhood memories of elaborate ice cream Santas with candy trim, or barley sugar figurals adorning a Christmas tree. Ice cream molds were made of pewter and came in a wide variety of shapes and styles. Chocolate molds were made in fewer shapes, but were more detailed. They were usually made of tin, copper, and occasionally of pewter. Hard candy molds were usually metal, although the primitive maple sugar molds--often simple hearts, rabbits, and other animals--were carved from wood. Cake molds were made of cast iron or cast aluminum, and were most common in the shape of a lamb, a rabbit, or Santa Claus.

When no condition is indicated, the items listed below are assumed to be in mint condition.

Chocolate Molds

Basket, clamped, mk 'Made in USA, 6068,' 2-part, 3x9″ 45.00
Bears (3), 9½x12″ 125.00
Boy in tux & top hat, 2-part, 7½″ 50.00
Boy w/hands behind bk, mk, 2-part, 5½″, M 37.50
Bull dog, sm 40.00
Car, sedan, flat, 3x5″, M 7.50
Cat, seated, clamped, mk Made in USA, 2-part, #8230, 8″ 80.00
Chickens, pr on nest 58.00
Chicks in bonnets (2), Made in Germany, no bottom, 5″ 25.00
Christmas scene, flat, unmk, 4½x8″ 45.00
Clown w/concertina, 2-part, #15262, 9″ 72.50
Donkey, clamped, mk, 2-part, #15919, 7″ 50.00
Easter bunny, standing, 7½x4½x1¾″ 40.00
Egg, landscape/rabbit, pewter, clamped/hinged, 3x5x7″ 45.00
Egg w/grapes, lg 45.00
Elephant, standing, 2¼x4″ 25.00
Girl w/rabbit, both standing, no clamps, 2-part, #273, 7″ 50.00
Heart, clamped, Eppelsheimer trademk, mk, 2-part, 9x9″ 60.00
Heart, dbl, w/Cupid, hinged 58.00
Indian w/headdress, copper, 7½″ 50.00
Jack-O'-Lantern, clamped, no mk, 2-part, EX 30.00
Kewpie, mk Anton Reiche, Dresden, 8″ 75.00
Lamb, w/iron clip, 2-part, 4¾″ 45.00
Rabbit, copper, hinged, Eppelsheimer trademk, #8074, 4″ 30.00
Rabbit, flat lollipop mold w/8 rabbits, rare, 8x10″ 50.00
Rabbit, mk Griswold, CI, 2-part, 11x12″ 150.00
Rabbit, pulling wagon w/eggs 25.00
Rabbit, sitting, hinged, 10″ 75.00
Rabbit, standing, w/basket, 18″ 125.00
Rabbit, standing, 5″ 25.00
Rabbit, 2 standing around egg, w/indentations, 2-part, 9″ 52.00
Rabbit pulling cart, w/sign '5 miles to go,' flat, 5x7½″ 35.00
Rabbits in 2 cars, tin washed copper, hinged/clamped, 4x8″ 52.00
Rooster, indentations, no clamps, 2-part, #312, 9″ 110.00
Rooster, 10″ 135.00
Santa, standing, pewter, roller clamp, E-19-8146, 6¾x2¾″ 85.00
Santa w/pack & Christmas tree, mk Dresden, 6¼″ 65.00
Santas (4), mk Dresden, 4½x9″ 85.00
Snowman w/top hat, clamped, 2-part, rare, 4″ 47.50
Squirrel, sitting, 2-part w/clips, gray tin, 6x6″ 75.00
Squirrel w/acorn, lg bushy tail, 15″ 140.00
Stocking stuffed w/toys, mk, 2-part, rare, 8″ 110.00
Teddy Bear, rare clamps, 2-part, #2644, 11″ 150.00
Turkey, standing, 5½x4½x2½″ 65.00

Rabbits, chocolate mold, three-piece, 10½″, $67.50.

Ice Cream Molds

Ace of Clubs, E-903 . . . . 30.00
Airplane, E-1132 . . . . 65.00
Alligator, S-394 . . . . 50.00
American Beauty Rose, K-582 . . . . 35.00
American flag, #282 . . . . 45.00
American Legion emblem, E-1119 . . . . 20.00
Apples, cluster of 3, K-102 . . . . 25.00
Aster, K-236 . . . . 28.00

Automobile, early 1930s sedan, E-1223 .... 65.00
Baby bonnet, E-967 .... 44.00
Baby cradle, 3-pc 30.00
Baby lying down, E-1020 .... 35.00
Ball, E-936 .... 25.00
Basket, fancy, oval, #203 .... 30.00
Basketball, E-1150 .... 25.00
Battleship Monitor, S-512 .... 67.00
Bear, E-637 .... 45.00
Bell, S-404 .... 35.00
Bomb, S-318, lg 40.00
Book, open, E-957 .... 30.00
Bride & groom, E&Co, M-1201 .... 45.00
Bull, fighting, E-671 .... 54.00
Butterfly, E-679 .... 65.00
Calla lily, 3-part, S-210 .... 25.00
Candlestick, K-207 .... 34.00
Cannon, S-273 .... 45.00
Carnation, E-361 .... 26.00
Cat, E-644 .... 45.00
Cherries (4), E-340 .... 25.00
Chick, E-651 .... 45.00
Chick in egg, E-600 .... 34.00
Chicken, E-625 .... 58.00
Christmas candle in candlestick, E-932½ 65.00
Christmas star medallion, E-277 .... 58.00
Christmas stocking, K-590 .... 48.00
Christmas tree, E-1154 .... 60.00
Chrysanthemum, E-345 .... 30.00
Clown head, E-1035 .... 50.00
Coal tender, K-478 .... 75.00
Colonial lady's skirt, E-1185 .... 35.00
Cricket player (very rare), K-525 .... 73.00
Cucumber, E-226 .... 22.00
Cupid, K-492 .... 40.00
Cupid, seated, E-992 .... 55.00
Cupid on heart, E-1102 .... 45.00
Cupid on shell, #583 .... 40.00
Cupid w/bow, K-492 .... 32.00
Daisy, E-317 .... 34.00
Dice, S-199 .... 34.00
Dolphin, S-258 .... 54.00
Donkey, K-630 .... 44.00
Dove of Peace, K-342 .... 45.00
Eagle trophy, w/shield & cannons, K-517 .... 65.00
Eagle with US shield, S-239 .... 92.00
Easter lily, 3-pc, E-354 .... 30.00
Egg, E-907 .... 28.00
Egg, goose; K-298 .... 10.00
Fire engine, #497 .... 70.00
Football, 3-part, #381 .... 30.00
Gladiolus, #319 .... 40.00
Grape cluster, E-278 .... 30.00
Harp, K-361 .... 35.00
Headless Admiral, K-519 .... 33.00
Heart, S-475 .... 45.00
Heart w/hands, S-380 .... 35.00
Heart w/hump, E-956 .... 30.00
Hearts aflame, 'Love,' #300 .... 35.00
Hen, sitting, E-673 .... 45.00
High hat, #399 .... 30.00
Horn of Plenty, E-1004 .... 38.50
Horseshoe, #183 .... 32.00
Hyacinth, E-356 .... 30.00

Indian, #458, Des Cop'd 1896, Krauss, $75.00.

Kiwanis Club emblem, E-1111 .... 20.00
Lady riding bicycle, K-431 .... 65.00
Lily-of-the-Valley w/leaf, E-351 .... 55.00
Lincoln bust, K-597 .... 54.00
Lion's medallion, lion club emblem, E-1136 .... 22.00
Lobster, S-164 .... 53.00
Locomotive, K-477 .... 75.00
Log, E-987 .... 48.00
Magnolia, 3-part, #360 .... 35.00
Male golfer driving, K-463 .... 65.00
Maltese Cross, #296 .... 32.00
Man riding bicycle, S-551 .... 65.00
Martha Washington, K-461 .... 65.00
Masonic emblem, Shrine, E-1081 .... 20.00
Melon, #307 .... 30.00
Morning-glory, E-299 .... 50.00
Morning-glory (2), K-261 .... 36.00
New Year's bell, S-605 .... 33.00
Ocean liner, #612 .... 40.00
Odd Fellows links, #577 .... 20.00
Orange, E-307 .... 28.00
Orange blossom bouquet, E-360 .... 60.00
Orange medallion, K-410 .... 20.00
Owl, K-175 .... 56.00
Palmer Cox Brownie Chinaman, S-308 .... 75.00
Pansy, S-269 .... 28.00
Parrot, S-393 .... 45.00
Peach half w/stone out, CC 23.00
Pear, #151 .... 28.00
Piece of pie, E-1079 .... 32.00
Pig, sitting, #587 .... 50.00
Ping-pong racquet, K-591 .... 35.00
Pipe, S-374 .... 44.00
Poinsettia, E-1144 .... 42.00
Poppy, K-495 .... 34.00
Pork chop, S-139 .... 38.00
Potato, S-154 .... 20.00
Pug dog, S-390 .... 40.00
Pumpkin, E-309 .... 44.00
Rabbit, crouching, E-658 .... 45.00

Rabbit, K-189 .... 45.00
Race car & driver, E-1218 .... 50.00
Reindeer & sleigh, E-1172 .... 60.00
Ring, wedding; K-608 .... 20.00
Rose, S-334, sm 35.00
Rose bouquet, #194 .... 32.00
Rose leaves, E-336 .... 50.00
Santa Claus, dated 1890, E-991 .... 60.00
Santa Claus, K-427 .... 60.00
Shamrock, E-1039 .... 30.00
Shell, fancy, S-524 .... 44.00
Skull, E-1010 .... 50.00
Slipper, 3-part, E-899A 30.00
Squirrel, S-291 .... 66.00
Star, 'Mars,' S-352 .... 35.00
Stork, standing, E-1151 .... 45.00
Stork w/baby, flying, K-631 .... 45.00
Strawberry, K-112, sm 30.00
Swan, CC 40.00
Tomato, E-208 .... 25.00
Truck, E-1224 .... 40.00
Turkey, roasted, K-364 .... 18.00
Turtle, #S-184, sm 48.00
Uncle Sam, E-1073 .... 45.00
Uncle Sam, S-514 .... 65.00
Violin, S-544 .... 42.00
Washington as a boy, S-542 .... 78.00
Washington shield w/bust & flags, S-456 .... 50.00
Wedding bell w/Cupid, E-1019 .... 35.00
Whale, S-602 .... 56.00
Wheelbarrow, K-480 .... 30.00
Witch on broom, E-1153 .... 45.00
Yum-Yum, #201 .... 38.00
4-Leaf clover, #268 .... 30.00

Miscellaneous

Candy, lamb & donkey, carved beech, ½ of orig, 4x12" 130.00
CI, corn, Griswold, tea size 25.00
CI, corn, Wagoner, tea size 50.00
CI, lamb, dk bl enamel worn, 14½" L 75.00
CI, lamb, Griswold 85.00
CI, Santa, Hello Kiddies, Griswold Mfg Co, 12" 185.00
Copper, eagle relief, oval, heavy, 9½x7¼" 150.00
Copper, ear of corn, fluted skirt & rim, miniature 65.00
Copper, fish, curved, 9½" 45.00
Copper, scalloped & swirled, dvtl, tin w/in, 11" 125.00
Copper, swirled, 4" dia 60.00
Maple sugar, deeply carved heart w/tail, pine, 11x4x2" 60.00
Maple sugar, fluted heart shape, dk tin 7.00
Maple sugar, heart shape, carved birch, mk WH, 1½x4x8" 190.00
Maple sugar, paddle shape w/3 hand carved designs, 8x1¾" 50.00
Tin, cake, oblong, pewter top: pineapple, 3-pc 135.00
Tin, ear of corn, fluted skirt & rim, miniature 30.00
Tin, plum pudding, oval, 2-pc, lg 30.00
Tin, pudding, cone w/spiral, 8x6¾" 15.00
Tin, Turk's head, early 20th C, 3x6¾" 12.00
Tin/copper, bunch of grapes, fluted skirt, tin rim, 4¼x6" 125.00

Monmouth

The Monmouth Pottery Company was established in 1892 in Monmouth, Illinois. Their primary products were stoneware crocks, churns, and jugs, in salt glaze, Bristol, spongeware, and brown glaze. In 1906 they were absorbed by a conglomerate called the Western Stoneware Company. Monmouth became their #1 plant, and until 1930, continued to produce stoneware marked with their maple leaf logo.

Items marked 'Monmouth Pottery Co.' were made before 1906; after the merger, 'Co.' was dropped, and 'Ill.' was substituted.

When no condition is indicated, the items listed below are assumed to be in mint condition.

Sample crock, company name stenciled in cobalt on salt glaze, 2½", $100.00.

Bottle, water; w/cork stopper 20.00
Jardiniere, Brushware, Aztec pattern, 7" 45.00
Pitcher, bl, 1-pt 17.50
Vase, Egyptian motif, brn glaze w/in, 9" 42.50
Vase, gr feathered glaze, w/hdls, 9" 35.00
Vase, up & down design of bl moss, bl w/in, matt ext, 11½" 85.00
Wall pocket, Aztec pattern, 12½" 35.00

Mont Joye

Mont Joye was a type of acid-cut French cameo glass produced by Cristallerie de Pantin in Paris around the turn of the century. It is accented by enamels.

When no condition is indicated, the items listed below are assumed to be in mint condition.

Pitcher, amethyst, HP mc floral, sgn, 10" 350.00
Tumbler, frosted, HP iris/gold leaves, w/hdl, 5¾" 95.00
Vase, clear to cranberry, HP flowers/leaves, 11¾", pr 1,200.00
Vase, HP violets, elongated teardrop, 14" 600.00
Vase, opal, HP floral, 11" 500.00

Moorcroft

William Moorcroft was an English potter who worked for MacIntyre Potteries from 1897 to 1913, signing his pieces with his last name. In 1913 he established a workshop in Burslem, England, where he produced tablewares and a line of fine Art Nouveau vases, bowls, etc., which until 1919 were marked with the printed or impressed block lettered 'Moorcroft, Burslem.' After that, the patented 'W. Moorcroft' signature mark was used. Since 1921, 'Made in England' has been added.

Wm. Moorcroft died in 1945, and the work was continued by his son.

When no condition is indicated, the items listed below are assumed to be in mint condition.

Bowl, anemones, Queen mk, 4½" 50.00
Bowl, Aurelian Ware, 2-hdl/fancy silver lid, MacIntyre, 6" 200.00
Bowl, floral, mc on cobalt, w/lid, 7" 80.00

Left, Dish, Claremont, mushrooms on shaded green and blue ground, impressed marks and signed 'W.M.,' 8¾", $250.00; Left, Circular box and cover, Spanish Pattern, florals on blue-green ground, signed 'W. Moorcroft' and 'Made for Liberty & Co.,' ca 1920, 6½" diameter, $180.00.

Bowl, grapes, flambe, w/lid, 4" 175.00
Bowl, orchid on cobalt, orig label, 4" 45.00
Bowl, poppies, Florian Ware, 4" 100.00
Candlestick, Florian Ware, bl carnations on bl, 7½", pr 500.00
Canister, pomegranite, w/lid, 6½" 150.00
Coffee pot, poppies, MacIntyre 275.00
Coffee pot, Sicilian, MacIntyre 250.00
Creamer & sugar bowl, cobalt to gr w/mc floral, script sgn 130.00
Ewer, Florian Ware, yel tulips, jug hdl, 11¾" 550.00
Ginger jar, gr w/pink motif, label/incised mk, 8" 80.00
Goblet, gold trim, MacIntyre, 5¾" 550.00
Jam pot, bl flowers, attached stand, MacIntyre 150.00
Jar, leaves & berries, imp Wm Moorcroft, w/lid, 3½" 90.00
Lamp base, flambe, grapes & leaves, 13" 200.00
Pitcher, geometrics, pewter lid, MacIntyre, 8" 250.00
Pitcher, gesso faience, MacIntyre, pewter lid, 7" 250.00
Pitcher, jug; anemones, MacIntyre, 1-qt 175.00
Vase, Aurelian, Nouveau, cream bkground, MacIntyre, 8" 295.00
Vase, Florian Ware, bl & gr, MacIntyre, 11" 400.00
Vase, Florian Ware, bl & gr, wide ruffle, 4" 165.00
Vase, Florian Ware, bl cornflowers, 8" 275.00
Vase, Florian Ware, 3-color, 5" 235.00
Vase, Hazeldene, moonlight bl, 6½" 375.00
Vase, moonlight bl, 3½" 190.00
Vase, orange lustre, 5" 50.00
Vase, pansies, flambe, baluster form, 9" 300.00
Vase, pansies on cobalt, 5" 125.00
Vase, pink & red floral, sgn, 7¼" 65.00
Vase, pomegranate on cobalt, baluster form, 7" 100.00
Vase, pomegranate on cobalt, baluster form, 9½" 115.00
Vase, pomegranate on cobalt, globular, 8" 150.00
Vase, pomegranate on cobalt, ovoid, 6½" 90.00
Vase, pomegranate on cobalt, squat, 3" 50.00
Vase, roses, gilt, MacIntyre, 8" 165.00

Moravian Pottery & Tile Works

Dr. Henry Chapman Mercer was an author, anthropologist, historian, collector, and artist. One of his diversified interests was pottery. In 1898, he established the Moravian Pottery and Tile Works in Doylestown, Pennsylvania, the name inspired by his study and collection of decorative stove plates made by the early Moravians. Because the red clay he used there proved unfit for tableware, he turned to the production of handmade tile which he himself designed. Though never allowing it to become more than a studio operation, the tile works was nevertheless responsible for some important commercial installations, one of which was in the capitol building at Harrisburg.

Mercer died in 1930. Business continued in the established vein under the supervision of Mercer's assistant, Frank Swain, until his death in 1954. Since 1968, the studio has been operated by The Bucks County Commission, and tiles are still fashioned in the handmade tradition. They are marked 'Mercer,' and are dated.

When no condition is indicated, the items listed below are assumed to be in mint condition.

Tile, Bounty, bl & tan, 4x4" 65.00
Tile, emb tulip, incised mk, clear glaze, 5⅞x7⅛" 95.00
Tile, Pegasus, fr 85.00
Wall sconce, Mercer, 1900s, pr 200.00

Tile, Mayflower, green and tan, 4" sq., $65.00.

Morgan, Matt

From 1883 to 1885, the Matt Morgan Art Pottery of Cincinnati, Ohio, produced fine artware, some of which resembled the pottery of the Moores, with intense colors and gold accents. Some of the later wares were very similar to those of Rookwood, due to the fact that several Rookwood artists were also associated with the Morgan pottery.

Some examples were marked with a paper label; others with either a two- or three-line impression: 'Matt Morgan Art Pottery Co.,' with 'Cin. O.' sometimes added.

When no condition is indicated, the items listed below are assumed to be in mint condition.

Jug, relief corn stalks entwined in gold, liquor tag, 6½" 650.00
Vase, bamboo & butterfly, Limoges style, sgn MAD, 7¾" 550.00
Vase, bird & grasses on tan, gold trim, Daly, 1883, 14" 3,500.00
Vase, river scene, Limoges style, W McD, #231, 14x13", NM . 5,000.00

Moriage

The term 'moriage' refers to certain Japanese wares decorated with applied slipwork designs. There are several methods used to achieve the characteristic relief effect. The decorative devices may be designed separately and applied to the vessel, piped on in narrow ribbons of clay (slip-trailed), or built up by brushing on successive layers of liquified slip.

When no condition is indicated, the items listed below are assumed to be in mint condition. See also Nippon

Basket, marbleized medallions w/jeweling, 9" 275.00
Bowl, floral w/in & w/out, 2" enamel relief border, 3x11" 170.00
Bowl, nuts, diamond shape, jeweled hdls, 8" 45.00
Bowl, pods/leaves/nuts w/in, scallop rim, bead hdls, 11" 85.00
Box, dragon ware, scroll ft, 4¾x3⅝" 35.00
Box, powder; heavy wht design on dk gr 25.00
Candlestick, leaves/beads/gold bands, 7½", pr, EX 55.00

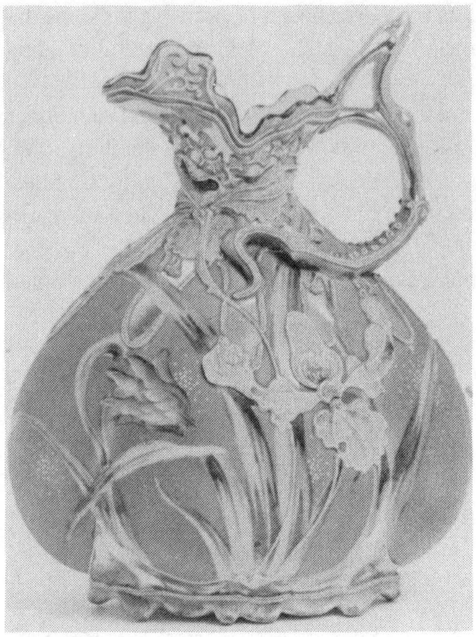

Ewer, orchids on green, gold handle and trim, 7½″, $265.00.

Chocolate pot, dragon ware	55.00
Creamer, dragon ware	25.00
Cup & saucer, demitasse; lithophane bottom, set of 6	135.00
Cup & saucer, dragon ware, set of 6	65.00
Ewer, bands of violets, bulbous, 10″	175.00
Ewer, floral, bulbous body, long slender neck, 12¼″	230.00
Ewer, mc floral & panels, 3½″	68.00
Manicure set, 3 tools, buffer & trinket box, rare, VG	150.00
Shakers, dragon ware, pr	12.00
Smoking set, rose medallions, 7½″ tray+2 urns	195.00
Sugar bowl, flowers in heavy slip, pagoda lid	65.00
Tea set, dragon ware, lithophane cups, 18-pc	115.00
Tea set, floral, wicker hdl, 3-pc	250.00
Vase, birds & pagoda, 12¼″	95.00
Vase, floral, pink/bl/wht/rust on bl, hdls, 2¾x1½″	35.00
Vase, floral medallions, gr w/wht slip, dbl hdls, ped, 9″	225.00
Vase, floral panels on gr, hdls, ped ft, 4¾″	65.00
Vase, violets, lt gr slipwork, low hdls, 9¼″	180.00
Vase, wheat over flowers, 6″	45.00

Mortar and Pestle

Mortars are bowl shaped vessels used for centuries for the purpose of grinding drugs to a powder or grain into meal. The masher or grinding device is called a pestle.

When no condition is indicated, the items listed below are assumed to be in excellent condition.

Brass, dbl ended, cylindrical, incised line decor, 16th C	75.00
Brass, early, w/pestle, 5″	55.00
Burl, hickory pestle, rpr/cracks, 7⅜″	95.00
Burl, lignum vitae pestle, age cracks, edge chips, 6½x7″	105.00
Cast iron, w/pestle, 5¾″	25.00
Cast iron, w/pestle, 7¾″	45.00

Morten Studio

Though background information on Morten Studios of Chicago, Illinois, is as yet impossible for us to locate, it is obvious from shows and tradepaper ads that their products are attracting the interest of today's collectors. Primarily they seem to have made figurines of all breeds of dogs, from less than 3″ in size up to about 6″. Occasionally you may find other animals and birds--horses, deer, lions, pumas, squirrels, and parrots have been reported. However, these are scarce and may command prices of as much as $70 to $80. Plaques such as the one illustrated are very rare, and are priced accordingly. The material used in their manufacture is a plaster-type composition with wires embedded to support its weight. Watch for flaking, cracks and separations--crazing seems to be present in some degree in nearly all examples.

When no condition is indicated, the items listed below are assumed to be in near mint condition, allowing for minor crazing.

Boxer, pup, 4″ L	30.00
Boxer, 7½″ L	50.00
Cocker Spaniel, blk & yel, 7½″	55.00
Cocker Spaniel, recumbent, buff, 5½″ L	35.00
Dachshund, sitting, 5″	35.00
Dalmation, 3″	30.00
Doberman Pinscher, 6¼″	45.00
French Poodle, blk, 5″	45.00
Horse, brn, 8″	65.00
Horse, Palomino, 7½″	70.00
Puppy, blk & tan, 3″	20.00
Shepherd pup, 3″	20.00

Wall plaque, dimensional Collie's head, 6½″ x 4½″, $65.00.

Morton Pottery

Six potteries operated in Morton, Illinois at various times from 1877 to 1976. Each traced its origin to six brothers who immigrated to America to avoid military service in Germany. The Rapp brothers established their first pottery near clay deposits on the south side of town where they made field tile and bricks. Within a few years, they branched out to include utility wares such as jugs, bowls, jars, pitchers, etc. During the ninety-nine years of pottery operations in Morton, the original factory was expanded by some of the sons and nephews of the Rapps. Other family members started their own potteries where artware, gift-store items, and special-order goods were produced. The Cliftwood Art Pottery, and the Morton Pottery Company had show rooms in Chicago and New York City during the 1930s. All of Morton's potteries were relatively short-lived operations with the Morton Pottery Company being the last to shut down on September 8, 1976.

For a more thorough study of the subject, we recommend *Morton's Potteries: 99 Years*, by Doris and Burdell Hall; their address can be found in the Directory under Illinois. When no condition is indicated, the items listed below are assumed to be in mint condition.

Mug, Drink What Is Pure, Speak What Is True, ca 1890-1910, 6″, $55.00 in Rockingham glaze; $65.00 in herbage green. Add 25% if marked 'Morton Pottery Works.'

Morton Pottery Works–Morton Earthenware Company (1877-1917)

Acorn bank, advertises Acorn Stoves, gr, 3″ ... 40.00
Bowl, yellowware w/wide center wht band, 10¼″ dia ... 32.00
Chamber pot, yellowware w/5 wht slip bands, 9″ dia ... 35.00
Cuspidor, cobalt, rare, 7″ ... 75.00
Food mold, Turk's hat design, brn Rockingham glaze ... 45.00
Milk jug, brn Rockingham glaze, 8-pt ... 80.00
Pie baker, yellowware, 7″ dia ... 22.00

Cliftwood Art Potteries, Inc. (1920-1940)

Beer set, pitcher w/6 steins, pink & gr drip glaze ... 130.00
Bookends, elephant figural, gray drip glaze, 4½x6½″ ... 95.00
Clock, octagonal, brn drip glaze, 7″ ... 100.00
Lamp, design #5, brn drip glaze, 10½″ ... 30.00
Lamp, lioness crouching on gr rocks w/blk pillar behind ... 45.00
Wine glass, emb Deco design, mulberry, 2½″ ... 12.00

Midwest Potteries, Inc. (1940-1944)

Ash tray, wht w/gold int, gold 3-D lady's hand in center ... 18.00
Figurine, female nude, gold decor, 12″ ... 75.00
Figurine, wild horse, rearing, gray spray glaze, 14½″ ... 35.00
Figurine, 2 canaries perched on stump, yel w/gold, 3½″ ... 20.00
Honey pitcher, gold ext, platinum interior, bulbous, 5″ ... 25.00
Masks, African Watusi male & female, blk glaze, pr ... 50.00
Miniature, bluebird, bl & yel ... 4.00
Miniature, colt, butterscotch color ... 8.00
Miniature, goose, wht w/gold beak ... 5.00
Miniature, hen & rooster, yel-brn drip glaze, pr ... 12.00
Miniature, polar bear, wht glaze ... 5.00

Morton Pottery Company (1922-1976)

Ash tray, Santa, red cap, pink cheeks, winking eye ... 3.00
Au gratin dish, gr glaze, hdld lid serves as hot plate ... 18.00
Casserole, royal bl, hdld, w/lid ... 15.00
Dresser tray, lady's pink lace collar w/HP brooch ... 6.00
Dresser tray, man's wht collar w/blk bow tie ... 7.00
Florence Nightengale lamp, wht glaze, lg size ... 10.00
Florence Nightengale lamp, wht glaze, sm size ... 6.00
Hair grower, Jiggs, red tile clay, grows grass 'hair' ... 24.00
Hair grower, Sunny Jim, wht bisque, grows grass 'hair' ... 12.00
Hanging basket, bisque, raised bird design, 7½″ dia ... 25.00
Jardiniere, emb basket decor, gr, 4″ ... 16.00
Sleigh, wht w/HP holly leaves & berries, 3¾″ ... 12.00
Wall pocket, duck in flight, bl, gr, yel & pink, 6″ ... 5.00
Wall pocket, long basket w/emb pink flower, 7¼″ ... 8.00
Wall pocket, parrot & grapes, bl, gr, yel & pink, 8½″ ... 10.00

American Art Potteries (1947-1963)

Bulb bowl, resembles open flower, pk & bl spray glaze, 2¾″ ... 12.00
Creamer & sugar, bulb hdls, deep bl & mauve spray glaze ... 18.00
Lamp, 8 gr sqs stacked atop 1 larger blk sq, 16″ ... 20.00
Nut cup, flower on 5-point leaf, pk/bl spray glaze, 1¾″ H ... 6.00
Planter, swan, purple spray glaze w/gold decor, 11″ ... 12.00
TV lamp, birds on limb w/curved planter, mauve spray glaze ... 14.00

Mosaic Tile Co.

The Mosaic Tile Company was organized in Zanesville, Ohio, in 1894 by Herman Mueller and Karl Langenbeck, both of whom had years of previous experience in the industry. They developed a faster, less-costly method of potting decorative tile, utilizing paper patterns rather than copper molds. By 1901 the company had grown and expanded, with offices in many major cities. Faience tile was introduced in 1918, greatly increasing their volume of sales. They also made novelty ash trays, figural boxes, bookends, etc., though not to any large extent. Until they closed during the 1960s, Mosaic used various marks that included the company name or their initials--'MT' superimposed over 'Co.' in a circle.

When no condition is indicated, the items listed below are assumed to be in mint condition.

Box, turtle, sm ... 45.00
Dish, pin; turtle, orange, many imp mks, w/lid, 1½x4½x3″ ... 75.00
Figure, bear, blk, 6x10¼″ ... 110.00
Figure, buffalo, 8″ ... 175.00
Figure, German Shepherd, 6x10¼″ ... 125.00
Figure, German Shepherd, 9x8″ ... 110.00
Ink blotter, bl gloss w/cherub portrait, 5x3″, NM ... 30.00
Tile, birds & flowers, bl & rose, 6″ ... 15.00

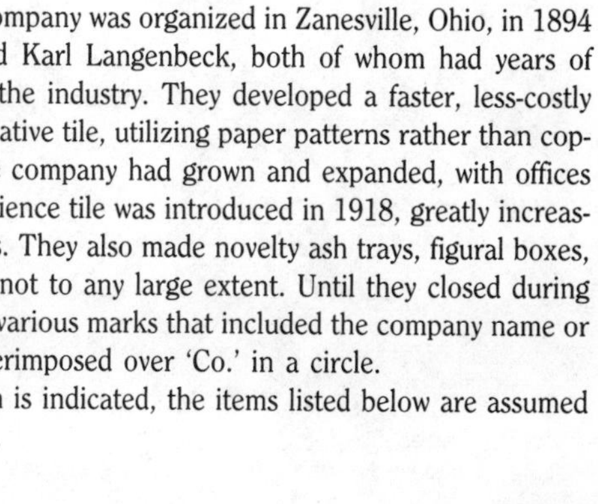

Tile, Oriental couple, verse border, 3-color, 6″, $35.00.

Tile, Lincoln profile, wht cameo on bl, hexagonal 25.00
Tile, map of Mt Desert Island, Maine, 6″ 12.00
Tile, monkeys & owls in tree, 6″ 25.00
Tile, Where are you going, my pretty maid?, 6″ sq 35.00
Tray, w/dog figurine, semi-gloss blk & gr, mk, 4″ 175.00

Moser

Ludwig Moser founded the Moser Glassworks in Czechoslovakia in 1857. He produced Art Nouveau style glass--cameo, intaglio cut, iridescent, and enameled ware. Most valued by collectors are items made between 1860 and 1920. The firm is still in operation.

Many items are attributed to Moser that are in fact French. Forged signatures are rampant.

When no condition is indicated, the items listed below are assumed to be in mint condition.

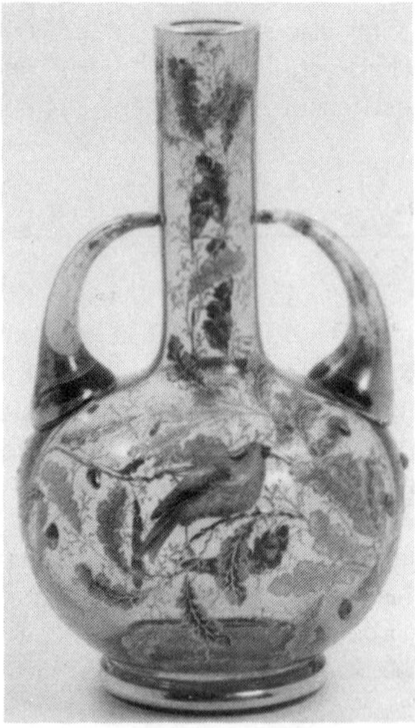

Vase, amber with applied bird and autumn foliage, 9″, $1,700.00.

Bowl, pink opaque, raised gold vines, shallow, 10″ 250.00
Box, dresser; gr floral w/enamel & gold, sgn, 6½″ dia 500.00
Box, pink opal, gold/wht/bl/red enamel, sgn, 2x3¼″ 350.00
Cordial, gr w/mc floral, gold trim, 2¼x1″, set of 4 . . . . 135.00
Cup & saucer, cranberry, pnt flowers, 'windows,' gold, sgn 325.00
Ewer, cranberry, band of flowers, gold scales ea side, 15″ 800.00
Goblet, amber, oak leaves & bugs, applied acorns, 5½″ 375.00
Goblet, cranberry, foliage, dragonfly & ladybug, 4″ 250.00
Goblet, gr cut to crystal, sgn 95.00
Lemonade set, amber w/gold/bl/pink enamel, sgn, 4-pc 695.00
Mug, gr w/oak leaves, pnt bee & acorns, unsgn, 3¼″ 295.00
Nightstand set, cranberry w/leaves & acorns, 6-pc 1,395.00
Pitcher, cranberry, insects, flowers, gold web, 8″ 395.00
Stemware, cranberry, floral w/insects, heavy enamel, 4¼″ 250.00
Tumbler, bl to clear, eng grouse, base cut, gold trim, 5″ 60.00
Tumbler, clear to fuschia, cut/eng pheasant/acid band/gold 60.00
Tumbler, cranberry, allover floral, much gold filigree, 4″ 180.00
Tumbler, cranberry w/mc leaves, 6 acorns, gold, 4″ 185.00
Tumbler, juice; cranberry, gold relief/mc, branches/leaves 185.00
Tumbler, juice; rubena, oak leaves, gold foliage & acorns 195.00
Tumbler, juice; yel, lace, red & gr jewels, ribbed, sgn 195.00
Vase, amber w/frieze, gold encrusted warriors, 6″ 400.00
Vase, amethyst, decor band, wide mouth, unsgn, 1920s, 6½″ . . . 100.00
Vase, amethyst to clear, gold flowers/border, sgn, 9½″ 200.00
Vase, bl w/amber ft, leaves, applied grapes, unsgn, 5¾″ 325.00
Vase, cabinet; gr & clear, Wood Lily, gold trim, 4½″ 85.00
Vase, cameo, jungle scene, purple, clear/frosted, sgn, 12″ 850.00
Vase, cranberry, heavy coralene & gold, sgn, w/lid, 13″ 1,250.00
Vase, cranberry, leaves, acorns, eagle & bird, ped ft, 24″ 6,500.00
Vase, parrot, mc/gold on opal pink to clear, 7x8x2½″ 2,500.00
Vase, pink opal, applied eagle/acorns, flat oval, sgn, 8″ 2,500.00
Vase, ruby w/gold & mc butterflies, dragons, flowers, 15″ 1,000.00
Vase, topaz, flamingo scene, optic quilted, 10¾x5½″ 500.00
Vase, w/7 mc enameled salamander ft, 6″ 375.00
Wine, Rhine; rubena verde, applied grapes, no mk, 4¼″ 595.00

Moss Rose

Moss Rose was a favorite dinnerware pattern of many Staffordshire and American potters from the mid-1800s. The Wheeling Pottery in West Virginia introduced their version in the 1800s, and it became one of their best sellers, remaining popular well into the nineties.

When no condition is indicated, the items listed below are assumed to be in mint condition.

Bowl, covered vegetable; Meakin, 12x7″ 60.00
Box, oval, no mk 14.00
Butter dish, lustre trim, sq, Grindley Ironstone 65.00
Child's set, KTK, 26-pc 200.00
Child's set, teapot, KTK, cr/sug, 6 c/s 150.00
Coffee pot 45.00
Coffee set, pot/sugar bowl/creamer, gold trim 175.00
Compote, 6½x11″, EX 150.00
Creamer & sugar bowl, no mk 20.00
Cup & saucer 15.00
Cup & saucer, Haviland 24.00
Gravy boat, Meakin 30.00
Gravy boat w/underplate, child's 25.00
Pitcher, 9″ 50.00
Plate, pink trim, mk Haviland, 8½″ 22.50
Plate, 10″, Meakin 20.00
Plate, 8″ 16.00
Platter, 12″ 25.00
Platter, 15x11″ 40.00
Soap dish, Haviland 40.00
Syrup pitcher, sgn Ironstone China, KT&K, dtd 1872 on lid . . . 165.00
Tea set, Haviland, 3-pc 165.00
Tea set, Japan, 16-pc+covers 58.00
Tea set, Meakin, 3-pc 185.00
Teapot, gooseneck spout, basketweave relief, T&V, 8½″ 75.00
Tureen, child's; w/lid 20.00

Mosser Glass Co.

Tom Mosser founded the Mosser Glass Co. in Cambridge, Ohio, during the late 1960s. Near-monthly issues are produced, each in a newly developed color or type of glass. Their Clown Series, each with a name that alphabetically follows the previous one, is perhaps their most popular.

Bear, Autumn Amber, 4″ 35.00
Bear, Fiesta, 4″ 35.00
Bear, Milk Glass, 4″ 35.00
Cat, Amethyst, 3″ 6.00
Cat, Cobalt, 3″ 6.00
Cat, Red, 3″ 7.00
Clown, Arty 75.00
Clown, Bags 30.00
Clown, Cleo 30.00

Clown, Daisy....40.00
Clown, Eros....30.00
Clown, Flip....10.00
Clown, Gabby....10.00
Clown, Iffy....10.00
Clown, Orie....10.00

Mother of Pearl

Mother-of-Pearl glass was a type of mold-blown satin art glass popular during the last half of the 19th century. A patent for its manufacture was issued in 1886 to Frederick S. Shirley, and one of the companies who produced it was the Mt. Washington Glass Company of New Bedford, Massachusetts. Another was the English firm of Stevens and Williams.

Its delicate patterns were developed by blowing the gather into a mold with inside projections that left an intaglio design on the surface of the glass, then sealing the first layer with a second, trapping air in the recesses. Most common are the Diamond Quilted, Raindrop, and Herringbone patterns. It was made in several soft colors, the most rare and valuable is rainbow--a blend of rose, light blue, yellow, and white. Occasionally it may be decorated with coralene, enameling, or gilt.

When no condition is indicated, the items listed below are assumed to be in mint condition.

Left to right: Vase, Herringbone, blue, 6″, $150.00; Vase, Raindrop, blue and white, 7¾″, $250.00; Ewer, Herringbone, blue, 8⅛″, $200.00; Cruet, Diamond Quilted, blue, no stopper, $260.00.

Basket, Herringbone, rose/pk, thorn hdl, 7½″....350.00
Bowl, Dia Quilt, bl, oblong w/4 ft, 5x8x7″, EX....285.00
Bowl, Dia Quilt, bl, tricorn, clear ft, mk Patent, 4½x5″....600.00
Bowl, Dia Quilt, wht, ruffled camphor edge, Mt WA, 8″....375.00
Bowl, Dia Quilt, wht w/gold & bronze flowers, 10½″....180.00
Bowl, fruit; Dia Quilt, pink, thorn hdl 1 end, 11″ L....545.00
Bowl, Herringbone, peach, thorn hdls/ft, rectangle top, 6″....550.00
Bud vase, Herringbone, bl, ruffled, 7″....195.00
Creamer, Raindrop, bl, reed hdl, rnd top, bulbous, 4½″....225.00
Ewer, Herringbone, apricot, flat oval body, ruffled, 7″....225.00
Ewer, Herringbone, bl, trilobed top, 8½x4″....200.00
Rose bowl, Dia Quilt, brn & tan shaded, att Webb, 2x2½″....275.00
Rose bowl, Ribbon, bl, 8-crimp top, 2¾x4″....210.00
Rose bowl, Ribbon, brn, frosted wafer ft, trilobe top, 2¾″....300.00
Rose bowl, Ribbon, lime/gold prunus, wafer ft/8-crimp, 2″....275.00
Rose bowl, Ribbon, wht, gold florals & trim, 2½x3″....495.00
Rose bowl, Swirl, brn to caramel, bl & gr between, 3x6½″....785.00
Sweetmeat, 6 ea yel/bl/pink rainbow bands, SP lid/bail, 6″....945.00
Tumbler, Dia Quilt, rose, enamel daisies, 4″....195.00
Tumbler, Herringbone, rubena cased....110.00
Vase, Coinspot, gr, pnt floral, ruffle, Webb prop mk, 12″....950.00
Vase, Dia Quilt, apricot, ruffled, thorn hdls, ftd, 8x4″....225.00
Vase, Dia Quilt, apricot to pink, ruffled, 8x3¾″....200.00
Vase, Dia Quilt, bl, bottle form, 7x3⅜″....110.00
Vase, Dia Quilt, butterscotch, sgn SP holder, 5″....400.00
Vase, Dia Quilt, butterscotch, sgn SP holder, 6½″....450.00
Vase, Dia Quilt, rose to lt rose, ruffled, 8x4¾″, pr....495.00
Vase, Dia Quilt, wht w/rainbow cameo, butterflies, 7x4½″....2,750.00
Vase, Feredzeichnung, caramel, gold traced, Pat 1959, 11″...1,750.00
Vase, Herringbone, bl, oval ruffle top, frost hdls, 7½x4″....225.00
Vase, Herringbone, peach, ruffled, 9¼x4″....175.00
Vase, Hobnail, butterscotch & pearl wht, rare, 6½″....475.00
Vase, Hobnail, clear to gold, sq folded-in top, 6x4½″....600.00
Vase, Swirl, amberina w/bl lining, bottle form, 11½″....795.00
Vase, Swirl, pink, deep ruffle top, hdls, ped ft, 11x4½″....275.00
Vase, Swirl, reverse amberina, enamel floral, 9¼x4½″....1,100.00
Vase, Swirl, rose to lt rose, 5x3¾″....225.00
Vase, Swirl, rose to pink, cone shape, 11x5″....245.00

Movie Memorabilia

Movie memorabilia covers a broad range of collectibles, from books and magazines dealing with the industry in general, to the various promotional materials which were distributed to arouse interest in a particular film. Many collectors specialize in a specific area--posters, pressbooks, stills, lobby cards, or souvenir programs (also referred to as premier booklets).

When no condition is indicated, the items listed below are assumed to be in excellent condition. See also Autographs; Personalities

Key:
cp—photo in center of sheet
D—director
P—producer

Lobby card, A Midsummer Night's Dream, James Cagney, 1935.150.00
Lobby card, A Ticket to Tomahawk, Marilyn Monroe, set....110.00
Lobby card, Bandolero!, Raquel Welch, 1968, set....20.00
Lobby card, Between Two Women, 1945, set....75.00
Lobby card, Botany Bay, James Mason, #4, 1953....5.00
Lobby card, Choo-Choo, Little Rascals, 1951, set of 4....20.00
Lobby card, Crossfire, Robert Young, cp, 1947....75.00
Lobby card, David Copperfield, Laurence Olivier, 1969, set....20.00
Lobby card, Escape from Alcatraz, Clint Eastwood, set....20.00
Lobby card, Flamingo Road, Joan Crawford, 27x41″, set....60.00
Lobby card, Free Eats, Little Rascals, 1952, set of 4....20.00
Lobby card, Holiday Affair, Robert Mitchum, #7, 1949....10.00
Lobby card, Isle of the Dead, Boris Karloff, 1945....50.00
Lobby card, June Bride, Robert Montgomery, #2, 1948....10.00
Lobby card, My Favorite Brunette, 1947, set....90.00
Lobby card, Once Upon a Honeymoon, Ginger Rogers, 1942....10.00
Lobby card, The Detective, Frank Sinatra, 1968, set....20.00
Lobby card, The Pink Panther, Peter Sellers, #8, 1964....5.00
Lobby card, The Tingler, Vincent Price, 1959, set....95.00
Lobby card, White Christmas, Bing Crosby, 1954, set....75.00
Magazine, Modern Screen, Errol Flynn, November 1943....7.00
Magazine, Motion Picture, Katheryn Hepburn, September 1944...9.00
Magazine, Motion Picture, Lena Horne, October 1944....7.00
Magazine, Movie Life, Elvis Presley, June 1960....6.00
Magazine, Movie Star Parade, Lauren Bacall, August 1941....8.00
Magazine, Movie Story, Bogart & Bergman, July 1944....8.00
Magazine, Screen Romances, Betty Grable, July 1943....8.00
Magazine, Stardom Annual, Elvis Presley & Dick Clark, 1959....4.50
Poster, A Southern Yankee, Red Skelton, 1948, 27x41″....35.00
Poster, A Star Is Born, Fredric March, cp, 1937, 22x28″....300.00
Poster, Air Raid Warden, Laurel & Hardy, 1943, 27x41″....225.00
Poster, Airport, Burt Lancaster, 1970, 27x41″....15.00

Poster, Babe Comes Home, Babe Ruth, 1927, 27x41″........900.00
Poster, Baby Face Nelson, Mickey Rooney, 1957, 14x22″.......20.00
Poster, Big Jake, John Wayne, 1971, 27x41″..................20.00
Poster, Boccaccio '70, Sophia Loren, 1962, 27x41″...........20.00
Poster, Bombers B-52, Natalie Wood, 1957, 27x41″...........20.00
Poster, Boy's Night Out, Kim Novak, 1962, 14x36″............15.00
Poster, Bullitt, Steve McQueen, 1969, 27x41″................25.00
Poster, Bye Bye Birdie, Ann-Margret, 1963, 27x41″...........20.00
Poster, Cabaret, Liza Minnelli, 1972, 27x41″.................35.00
Poster, Calcutta, Alan Ladd, 1946, 27x41″....................65.00
Poster, Carrie, Laurence Olivier, 1952, 27x41″...............30.00
Poster, Chisum, John Wayne, 1970, 27x41″....................20.00
Poster, Christmas Eve, George Raft, 1947, 27x41″............45.00
Poster, Clambake, Elvis Presley, 1967, 41x81″................35.00
Poster, Confidential Agent, Lauren Bacall, 14x36″.............50.00
Poster, Cool Hand Luke, Paul Newman, 1967, 27x41″.........25.00
Poster, Daddy Long Legs, Fred Astaire, 1955, 22x28″.........25.00
Poster, Death Wish, Charles Bronson, 1974, 27x41″...........15.00
Poster, Deep Valley, Ida Lupino, 1947, 27x41″...............40.00
Poster, Diary of a Madman, Vincent Price, 1963, 27x41″.......20.00
Poster, Girl Happy, Elvis Presley, 1965, 14x36″...............20.00
Poster, Have Rocket, Will Travel, 3 Stooges, cp, 27x41″.......25.00
Poster, Help!, Beatles, 1965, 40x60″.........................95.00
Poster, Hold That Kiss, Mickey Rooney, 1938, 27x41″.........75.00
Poster, Honkey Donkey, Little Rascals, 1952, 27x41″..........15.00
Poster, House on Haunted Hill, Vincent Price, 1959, 30x40″....65.00
Poster, It's in the Bag, Jack Benny, 1945, 27x41″.............35.00
Poster, Latin Lovers, Lana Turner, 1953, 27x41″..............25.00
Poster, Mirage, Laurence Olivier, 1965, 27x41″...............15.00
Poster, My Foolish Heart, Susan Hayward, 1950, 27x41″.......25.00
Poster, Psycho, Alfred Hitchcock/D, 1960, 27x41″............95.00
Poster, Riff-Raff, Pat O'Brien, 1947, 22x28″.................25.00
Poster, Slattery's Hurricane, Richard Widmark, 27x41″.........35.00
Poster, Son of Sinbad, Vincent Price, 1955, 27x41″...........25.00
Poster, Spinout, Elvis Presley, 1966, 30x40″.................30.00
Poster, Stagecoach, Norman Rockwell, 1966, 27x41″..........40.00
Poster, The Asphalt Jungle, Marilyn Monroe, 1950, 27x41″....125.00
Poster, The Birds, Alfred Hitchcock/D, 1963, 14x36″..........50.00
Poster, The Buccaneer, Yul Brynner, 1958, 27x41″...........30.00
Poster, The Farmer's Daughter, Loretta Young, 1947, 27x41″...65.00
Poster, The Happy Road, Gene Kelly, 1957, 22x28″...........15.00
Poster, The Hunchback of Notre Dame, Anthony Quinn, 14x36″.40.00
Poster, The Invisible Man, Claude Rains, 22x28″.............250.00
Poster, The Last Hurrah, Spencer Tracy, 1958, 27x41″........20.00
Poster, The Last Outpost, Ronald Reagan, 27x41″.............25.00
Poster, The Magic Sword, Basil Rathbone, 1961, 14x36″.......20.00
Poster, The Wayward Wife, Gina Lollobrigida, 1954, 22x28″....15.00
Poster, You're Never Too Young, Martin/Lewis, 1955, 14x22″...20.00
Pressbook, Anatomy of a Murder, James Stewart, 1959, 10 pg...15.00
Pressbook, Jack & the Beanstalk, Abbott & Costello, 1952......10.00
Pressbook, Moon Over Burma, Dorothy Lamour, 1940, 28 pg...35.00
Pressbook, Return of the Ape Man, Bela Lugosi, 1944, 8 pg....50.00
Pressbook, Rio Grande, John Wayne, 1955, 4 pg.............10.00
Pressbook, The Wonders of Aladdin, Donald O'Conner, 10 pg....5.00
Program, Ben Hur, EX...6.00
Program, King Kong, EX.......................................6.00
Program, Mutiny on the Bounty, EX...........................5.00
Still, Fort Apache, John Wayne, b/w, 1948, 8x10″.............4.00
Still, Gone With the Wind, Clark Gable, b/w, 8x10″............5.00
Still, Hello Dolly!, Barbra Streisand, b/w, set of 30.............30.00
Still, Murphy's War, Peter O'Toole, color, 1971, set of 12......15.00
Still, The Flim-Flam Man, George C Scott, color, set of 6.......10.00
Still, The Wizard of Oz, Judy Garland, b/w, 1939, 8x10″........3.50
Title card, Treasure of Sierra Madre, Humphrey Bogart.......200.00

Mt. Washington

The Mt. Washington Glass Works was founded in 1837 in South Boston, Massachusetts, but moved to New Bedford in 1869, after purchasing the facilities of the New Bedford Glass Company. Frederick S. Shirley became associated with the firm in 1874. Two years later the company reorganized and became known as the Mt. Washington Glass Company. In 1894, it merged with the Pairpoint Manufacturing Company, a small Brittania works nearby, but continued to conduct business under its own title until after the turn of the century. The combined plants were equipped with the most modern and varied machinery available, and boasted a working force with experience and expertise rival to none in the art of blowing and cutting glass.

In addition to their fine cut glass, they are recognized as the first American company to make cameo glass, an effect they achieved through acid-cutting methods. In 1885, Shirley was issued a patent to make Burmese, the yellow glassware tinged with a delicate pink blush. Another patent issued in 1886 allowed them the rights to produce Rose Amber, or amberina, a transparent ware shading from ruby to amber. Pearl Satin Ware and Peachblow, so named for its resemblance to a rosy peach skin, were patented the same year. One of their most famous lines, Crown Milano, was introduced in 1893. It was an opal glass either free blown or pattern molded, tinted a delicate color and decorated with enameling and gilt. Royal Flemish was patented in 1894, and is considered the most rare of the Mt. Washington art glass lines. It was decorated with raised gold enameled lines dividing the surface of the ware in much the same way as lead lines divide a stained glass window. The sections were filled in with one or several transparent colors, and further decorated in gold enamel with florals, foliage, beading, and medallions.

When no condition is indicated, the items listed below are assumed to be in mint condition. See also Salt Shakers and specific types such as Crown Milano, Burmese, Royal Flemish, etc.

Bowl, cameo, bird, pink/wht, gold-washed holder, sq, 4½x8″....845.00
Bowl, peppermint; cut glass star on base, 2⅝x8¾″............185.00
Bud vase, ruby overshot, bronze crane & dragonfly, 13½″.....385.00
Celery vase, Dia Quilt, amberina, 6½″......................250.00
Compote, Napoli w/oranges/blossoms on cranberry, sgn stand...950.00
Cracker jar, oak leaves & acorns..............................600.00
Creamer & sugar, cut bull's eye & notched prims, open.......300.00
Flower holder, bl & wht forget-me-nots, mushroom form.......150.00

Vase, Lava, 4½″ x 6″, $1,235.00.

Jewel box, lg portrait, blown-out mold, gilt, 5x10½" 950.00
Pitcher, clear w/gold, shrimp/seaweed/crabs, 1 on hdl, 9" 945.00
Pitcher, Verona, apple blossoms & leaves, gold traced 675.00
Pitcher, Verona, fish & seaweed, allover gold coral, 6½" 900.00
Rose bowl, pink Delft decor, egg shape, lg 575.00
Rose jar, peach w/florals, SP lid w/eng birds, 5" 230.00
Salt cellar, chicken head 275.00
Shaker, sitting hen form, SP head lid, w/label 365.00
Shakers, Palmer Cox Brownies motif, 2¾", pr 350.00
Sugar shaker, autumn leaves & berries, mc, egg form, 4½" 335.00
Sugar shaker, autumn leaves on wht, tomato form, SP top 325.00
Sugar shaker, daisies, mc on clear, very sm top, egg form 285.00
Sugar shaker, daisies, yel on orange to yel, egg form 215.00
Sugar shaker, florals of pink & wht dots, egg form 335.00
Sweetmeat, Napoli, PC Brownies, mc/crystal, turtle lid, 6" 1,085.00
Syrup, dusty rose-pink satin 295.00
Toothpick holder, autumn leaves on flat wht, hat form, 2⅛" 235.00
Vase, Ambero, couple on country lane, pnt w/in, sgn, 9" 645.00
Vase, Delft, village & castle, pnt decor, no mk, 12" 285.00
Vase, dragonflies & floral on lustreless wht, 10½" 550.00
Vase, Lava, 2 hdls, 4½x5" 1,235.00

Mulberry China

Mulberry china was made by many of the Staffordshire area potters from about 1830 until the 1850s. It is a transfer-printed earthenware or ironstone named for the color of its decorations, a purplish brown resembling the juice of the mulberry. Shades vary; some pieces look almost gray, with only a hint of purple. Some of the patterns, Corean, Jeddo, Pelew, and Formosa for instance, were also produced in Flow Blue ware. Others seem to have been used exclusively with the mulberry color.

When no condition is indicated, the items listed below are assumed to be in mint condition.

Plate, Dalguise, Wood & Sons, 9", $35.00.

Abbey, soap dish, w/lid & insert 95.00
Adelaide's Bower, plate, 10½" 35.00
Alleghany, basin, 13¾" 85.00
Athens, cup, handleless 50.00
Athens, plate, W Adams, 10½" 35.00
Athens, platter, 13½" 145.00
Balmoral Castle, mug, Wilkinson, 6¼" 38.00
Bochara, bowl, vegetable; w/lid, lg 150.00
Bochara, plate, 10½" 35.00
Bochara, platter, 14" 100.00
Bochara, sauce, w/lid, Edwards 120.00
Bosporus, plate, R Hall & Co, 9½" 45.00
Bread plate, railroad track border 35.00
Brush Stroke, plate, 8½" 30.00
Calcutta, plate, 8½" 28.00
Chariot, soup plate, 9¼" 35.00
Clyde Scenery, plate, 9" 45.00
Cologne, wash pitcher, Alcock, 13" 175.00
Corean, bowl, vegetable; w/lid 65.00
Corean, coffee pot, octagonal, 9½" 195.00
Corean, creamer 95.00
Corean, cup, handleless 50.00
Corean, cup, syllabub, EX 70.00
Corean, pitcher, water; lg 225.00
Corean, plate, PW & Co, 1830-1850, 8¾" 40.00
Corean, plate, PW & Co, 1830-1850, 9½" 65.00
Corean, platter, 12½" 150.00
Corean, platter, 15¾" 175.00
Corean, waste bowl, 5½" 65.00
Cyprus, coffee pot, Davenport 155.00
Cyprus, cup & saucer, Davenport 45.00
Cyprus, cup plate 35.00
Cyprus, plate, 10½" 50.00
Cyprus, plate, 7" 30.00
Cyprus, platter, 13¾x10½" 95.00
Eagle, cup & saucer, Podmore & Walker 75.00
Genoa, cup & saucer, Davenport, 1852 .... 40.00
Genoa, plate, 7" 20.00
Jeddo, creamer & sugar, Adams 90.00
Jeddo, cup plate 40.00
Jeddo, pitcher, 8" 125.00
Jeddo, plate, 9½" 50.00
Jeddo, sauce tureen, w/underplate, oval 150.00
Jeddo, sugar bowl w/lid, Wm Adams & Son 85.00
Kyber, cup & saucer, handleless 65.00
Kyber, plate, 10" 55.00
Marble, creamer, Wedgwood 75.00
Marble, soap dish, w/lid 58.00
Marble, wash pitcher 95.00
Ning Po, cup & saucer 40.00
Ning Po, pitcher, milk; R Hall 100.00
Ning Po, plate, 9½" 40.00
Panama, basin & pitcher 250.00
Pelew, bowl, vegetable 75.00
Pelew, cup & saucer, handleless 48.00
Pelew, gravy boat 85.00
Pelew, pitcher, milk; raised cherubs & grapes, 1-qt, EX 100.00
Pelew, plate, 9¾" 60.00
Pelew, platter, Ironstone, 16" 126.00
Pelew, relish, shell shape, E Challinor 50.00
Peruvian, plate, 9¾" 45.00
Peruvian, platter, 16" 125.00
Peruvian, teapot 150.00
Rhone Scenery, plate, TJ&J Mayer, 9½" 30.00
Rhone Scenery, platter, 15½" 145.00
Rhone Scenery, teapot 185.00
Rose, bowl, vegetable; open, 10" 66.00
Scinde, bowl, soup; 10½" 30.00
Tavoy, creamer 100.00
Tavoy, plate, 6¾" 30.00

Temple, bowl, open vegetable, 7x5½"....55.00
Temple, bowl, 12" dia....85.00
Temple, cup & saucer, Podmore Walker....40.00
Temple, gravy boat....95.00
Temple, pitcher, 7"....150.00
Temple, plate, Podmore & Walker, 10"....30.00
Temple, plate, 8"....25.00
The Sower, cup plate....55.00
Three Bouquets, plate, 8½"....30.00
Tonquin, plate, marbleized pattern, 10¼"....45.00
Tonquin, platter, Heath & Co, 1830s, 12½x9½"....125.00
Vincennes, cup & saucer, no hdls, Alcock, set of 12....445.00
Vincennes, pitcher, J Alcock, 9½"....135.00
Vincennes, plate, 10½"....45.00
Vincennes, plate, 7"....28.00
Vincennes, platter, 15½"....100.00
Vincennes, tureen, octagonal, w/lid....125.00
Washington Vase, creamer, 5½"....80.00
Washington Vase, cup & saucer....40.00
Washington Vase, plate, 8½"....30.00
Washington Vase, plate, 9¾"....50.00
Washington Vase, platter, 13¾"....90.00
Washington Vase, sauce, 5¼"....20.00

Muller Freres

Henri Muller established a factory in 1900 at Croismare, France. He produced fine cameo art glass decorated with florals, birds, and insects in the Art Nouveau style. The work was accomplished by acid engraving and hand finishing. Usual marks were 'Muller,' 'Muller Croismare,' or 'Croismare, Nancy.'

In 1910, Henri and his brother Deseri formed a glassworks at Luneville. The cameo art glass made there was nearly all produced by acid cuttings of up to four layers, with motifs similar to those favored at Croismare. A good range of colors were used, and some pieces were gold flecked. Handles and decorative devices were sometimes applied by hand. To commemorate Lindbergh's first flight, they designed a series of vases with cameo scenes featuring the monoplane. A second type of ware they produced was an acid-finished glass of bold mottled colors in the Deco style. Examples were signed 'Muller Freres' or 'Luneville.'

When no condition is indicated, the items listed below are assumed to be in mint condition.

Cameo

Lamp, stylized mums, 9¾" cone shade, cone base: 17"....2,200.00
Lamp, wisteria dome, openwork wisteria metal std, 26"....4,000.00
Vase, Deco parrots, gold mica encrusted & w/in, sgn, 10"....950.00
Vase, orchids, 3 cuts, gr, brn & red on wht, 8"....775.00
Vase, poppies, ivory on turq, polished, 10½"....1,200.00
Vase, poppies, 3 cuts, bulbous/flattened, 10x8½"....2,250.00
Vase, roses & foliage, 5 cuts, pear shape, 7½x5½"....1,500.00
Vase, roses on red & yel, pink w/bl mottle, 7¾"....1,500.00
Vase, shepherd & sheep, gold w/maroon, 6⅝"....1,100.00
Vase, storks, mtn scene w/chateau, 4 cuts, 8x4½"....1,500.00
Vase, trees & pond, plum on mottled wht, 5½"....700.00
Vase, trees & river, 3 cuts, wide mouth, taper body, 8½"....995.00
Vase, trees on shore, 3 cuts, frosted hdls, 10⅝"....1,895.00

Muncie

The parent of Muncie Clay Products was the Gill Clay Pot Company, who originally produced only pots and crucibles for the glass and metal refining industries. Located in Muncie, Indiana, the Gill Co. turned to the manufacture of decorative and utility pottery after WWI when trade with Germany, a primary pre-war source of industrial crucibles, was resumed. The company reorganized in 1931 under the title Muncie Potteries, Inc. Operations ceased in 1939.

Muncie Pottery is made of a heavier type of clay than that of most of its contemporaries; the style of its wares is sturdy and simple. The more collectible examples are reminiscent of Phoenix Glass vases, sculptured with lovebirds, grasshoppers and goldfish; and the Art Deco style vases that bear a striking resemblance to the Consolidated Glass Company's Ruba Rombic line. Glazes are varied; you will find subdued matt solids, mottled effects, and a drip glaze similar to Roseville's Carnelian. Examples are usually marked, some with 'Muncie' in impressed block letters; and/or 'A,' '1A,' '2A,' or '3A.'

In the listings that follow, when no condition is noted, items are assumed to be in mint condition.

Ash tray, w/matchbox holder, 5½"....15.00
Bud vase, gr over rose drip glaze, 9"....15.00
Bulb bowl, various colors, 8"....10.00
Candlestick, hand turned, 4", pr....25.00
Console set, pr candle holders #198, oval bowl, 12"....35.00
Ewer, rose over gr drip glaze, 8"....30.00
Flower holder, canoe, w/oval frog, orange & gr....45.00
Pitcher, tan w/blk streaks, base to hold music box, 7"....45.00
Vase, Art Deco, #301, 5"....35.00

Vase, modeled goldfish, green and gold, 8½", $75.00.

Vase, gr over lilac matt glaze, fan form, 8"....25.00
Vase, lav to bl, 4"....12.50
Vase, matt turq, 4"....11.50
Vase, matt turq, 4-lobed top, 4"....17.00
Vase, pink & aqua, sgn, 7"....24.00
Vase, sculptured, grasshoppers, gr or rose....75.00
Vase, violet; blk gloss, 4"....15.00
Wall pocket, rose....20.00
Water set, yel, 7-pc....75.00

Musical Instruments

The field of automatic musical instruments covers many different categories ranging from tiny dolls and trinkets concealing musical movements to huge organs and orchestrions which weigh many tons. Music boxes, first made in the late 18th century by Swiss watchmakers, were produced in both disc and cylinder models. The latter type employs a cylinder studded with tiny projections. As the cylinder turns, these projections lift the tuned teeth in the 'music comb' and the melody results. The value of the instrument depends upon the length of the cylinder and the quality of workmanship, though other factors must also be considered. Those in ornate cabinets or with extra features such as bells, mechanical birds, etc., often sell for much more. Units built into matching tables sell for about twice the amount they would bring otherwise. While small and medium size units are still being made today, most of the larger ones date from the 19th century.

Disc type music boxes utilize interchangeable steel discs with projecting studs, which by means of an intervening 'star wheel' cause a music comb to play. There are many different variations and mechanisms. Most were made in Germany, but some were produced in the United States. Among the most popular makes are Polyphon, Symphonion, and Regina. The latter was made in Rahway, New Jersey, from about 1894 through 1917.

Player pianos were made in a wide variety of styles. Early varieties consisted of a mechanism which pushed up to a piano and played on the keyboard by means of felt-tipped fingers. These use sixty-five note rolls. Later models have the playing mechanisms built in. At first these also used sixty-five note rolls, but those produced from about 1908 until 1940 use eighty-eight note rolls.

Coin-operated electric pianos are deluxe versions of player pianos. These incorporate expression mechanisms so that by using special-made rolls they can play the hand-recorded rolls of famous pianists. Popular makes include Ampico, Duo-Art, and Welte.

Roll-operated organs were made in many forms, ranging from table-top models to large foot-pumped versions. Of the latter, the Aeolian Orchestrelle is considered to be one of the best.

Unless noted, prices given are for instruments in fine condition, playing properly, with cabinets or cases in well-preserved or refinished condition. In all instances, unrestored instruments sell for much less, as do pieces with broken parts, damaged cases, and the like. On the other hand, particularly superb examples in especially ornate case designs, and pieces which have been particularly well restored often will command more.

Key:
c—cylinder
d—disc

Accordion, Tanzbar, roll operated....650.00
Band wagon, N Tonawanda/Wurlitzer type, w/125 rolls, rstr..15,000.00
Banjo, Howard #1....6,000.00
Banjo, ink-drawn flapper decor, sgn, 4-string, 1920s, 20"....85.00
Box, Abrahams Britannia, 11¾" d/single comb, upright case..1,540.00
Box, Bremond Mandoline, 15" 4-air c, walnut w/banding, 24".2,640.00
Box, Bruguier Musique Expessive, 13" 6-air c, brass inlay....825.00
Box, Ducommon Girod, 11" 6-air c, inlay case, rstr, 17½"...2,500.00
Box, Kalliope, 13¼" d/10 bells/zither, inlay, +9 d....2,200.00
Box, Kalliope, 9¼" d, etched floral on case, +20 d, 22x12"...800.00
Box, Lochmann Original #172 coin-op, 24⅜", walnut, 86"..10,120.00
Box, Mermod Freres, 13½" 8-air c/zither, crank, inlay, 28"....350.00
Box, Mermod Freres, 3½" 6-air c, foliate transfer, 14"....220.00
Box, Mermod Freres, 5½" 8-air c, crank, 17½"....300.00
Box, Mermod Freres, 6 c/8-air w/song sheet, winds, 6x17"....950.00
Box, Mermod Freres Guitare, 8¼" 6-air c/zither, inlay, 17"....715.00
Box, Mermod Freres Mira Console, 15¾" d, +25 d, 42"....4,000.00
Box, Mira, 9¼" d w/zither, mahog case, +13 d, 12½" L....800.00
Box, Otto & Sons Olympia, 8¾" d/single comb, w/4 d....415.00
Box, Paillard, Harpe Harmonique Piccolo, inlay case, 28"....1,870.00
Box, Paillard, 18" c/12-air w/song sheet, crank, 38x14"....2,500.00
Box, Paillard, 7½" 10-air c, wood w/transfer, 18"....525.00
Box, Regina #14 coin-op, 15½" d/single comb, 20½" L....2,000.00
Box, Regina #20, 11" d/single comb, mahog, +6 d, 14½"...1,210.00

Music box, Symphonian, made in Germany, 5¾" disc, $575.00.

Box, Regina #22, 8½" d/single comb, oak, +10 d, 12"....685.00
Box, Regina #31, changer....10,800.00
Box, Regina #51, oak table model, dbl comb, 1¢ play, orig...3,500.00
Box, Regina #6, 27" d/dbl comb, oak fold-top case, +20 d...4,500.00
Box, Regina Automatic, 15½" changer, orig clock/art glass..14,500.00
Box, Regina Automatic, 20¾" changer, bow-front, M rstr....12,500.00
Box, Stella, console, 17¼" d, +20 d, 25½x27½"....4,500.00
Box, Swiss, Bells in View, 11" 6-air c/rosewood/inlay, 21"....770.00
Box, Swiss, Bells in View, 13" 8-air c/rosewood/inlay, 22"....605.00
Box, Symphonion, 15" d/dbl comb, oak, +3 d, 24" L....1,200.00
Box, Victoria, 2 6-air 6" c/zither, walnut w/drw, 21½"....660.00
Concertina, hexagonal, mahog, 5-fold/21 bone buttons, case....125.00
Hammer dulcimer, 4 legs/35 chords/stand/2 hammers, 56"....895.00
Harmonica, Hohner, Pat 1926, Germany, orig box....40.00
Harp, giltwood, Neoclassical, Pl Browne & Co, 69"....2,200.00
Melodian, Mason & Hamlin, 1857, rfn/rstr....775.00
Nickelodeon, link style #2, w/accordion....10,000.00
Nickelodeon, Nelson-Wiggen, w/mandolin/xylophone, rstr....7,800.00
Nickelodeon, Seeburg A, oak, rfn/rstr....7,300.00
Nickelodeon, Seeburg K, w/pipes/eagle glass, EX rstr/rfn....9,500.00
Nickelodeon, Western Electric Mascot, oak/ldgl, rstr....7,800.00
Nickelodeon, Wurlitzer, oak, beveled oval glass, rstr....4,250.00
Orchestrion, Wurlitzer B, w/pipes/drums, rstr....18,500.00
Organ, dance; Arburo, many rolls, VG....14,000.00
Organ, dance; DeCap, 2 accordions/6 percussion, orig....9,500.00
Organ, military band; Artizan X-A-2, w/8 rolls, EX....12,500.00
Organ, military band; Wurlitzer #125....15,000.00
Organ, player; Aeolian #1250, M rstr....2,000.00
Organette, 6" d, winding hdl at side, +6 d, 9"....200.00
Piano, Apollophone player, w/phonograph, M rstr....6,800.00
Piano, automatic, 4 link rolls, from silent movie theater....9,800.00
Piano, baby grand; ebonized, Weber, ca 1920, 60" L....1,760.00
Piano, grand; Mason & Hamlin Ampico, player, rstr, 68"....12,000.00
Piano, grand; Steinway Duo-Art XR, player, rfn/rstr, 73"....7,500.00
Piano, grand; Steinway M, walnut, 1924, rfn/rst, 67"....6,000.00
Piano, Hupfeld Phonolitz player, golden oak w/lamps, rstr....4,500.00
Piano, John Osborn, mahog w/metal mt, 1840, 34x68"....1,540.00
Piano, Knabe Ampico, player, rstr w/roll collection....6,000.00
Piano, parlor; Chickering, rosewood veneer, 1865, EX....900.00
Piano, street; barrel operated, 10 tune, 1¢, 1900, M rstr....2,000.00
Piano, upright; Recordo, Cable Nelson, rstr/rfn....4,000.00
Piano, upright; Recordo, Kline, walnut, rstr....2,750.00
Piano, upright; Steinway, burl walnut, 56", EX rstr....2,200.00

Piano, rosewood, pierced candle stand either side of music stand, Collard & Collard of London, 54″ wide, $1,100.00.

Piano, upright; Steinway, rosewood, 1873, 48″, G orig........800.00
Piano, upright; Welte Farrand, rstr/rfn....................7,500.00
Pianolodeon, child's player; electric, plastic/wood, Chein.......300.00
Violano, Mills, dbl, M rstr..............................24,500.00
Violin, Amati, w/bow & fancy case.........................550.00
Violin, Stainer, w/bow & fancy case.........................750.00
Violin, Stradivarius copy, Grand Concert, restrung..........3,500.00

Mustache Cups

Mustache cups were popular items during the late Victorian period, designed specifically for the man with the mustache! They were made in silverplate as well as china and ironstone. Decorations ranged from simple transfers to elaborately applied and gilded florals. To properly position the 'mustache bar,' special cups were designed for the 'lefties'--these are the rare ones!

When no condition is indicated, the items listed below are assumed to be in mint condition.

Asters, pink & yel on wht, gilt, Germany....................32.00
Colonial couple, dog, red/yel/bl sponge decor, kettle form......125.00
Floral, gr, pink & wht, much gold, sgn RS Prussia............85.00
Floral, purple & red flowers, sgn Welmar, Germany............40.00
Floral, woman w/lilacs in hair, gold rim, pink lower ½..........28.00
Hunter, 3 deer running, raised deer head ea side, G color......50.00
Peacock feathers, bottom mk w/gold K......................30.00
SP, emb strawberry & floral band, gold wash w/in, Tufts.......100.00
SP, eng floral & monogram, gold wash w/in, Meriden.........125.00
Winter scene, birds fly over stream, trees, bl & gr.............20.00

Cobalt and gilt decoration on white, 3″, $40.00.

Nailsea

Nailsea is a term referring to clear or colored glass decorated in contrasting spatters, swirls, or loops. These are usually white, but may also be pink or blue. It was first produced in Nailsea, England, during the late 1700s, but was made in other parts of Britain and Scotland as well. Originally used for decorative novelties only, by 1845 pitchers, tumblers, and other practical items were being made from Nailsea-type glass.

When no condition is indicated, the items listed below are assumed to be in mint condition.

Basket, pink w/wht loops, 6x4″............................75.00
Bottle, scent; bl on opaque wht, 6½″......................125.00
Candy dish, gr w/swirls, applied rose finial & ft, 6x5″.........100.00
Flask, wht & red loops, minor wear, 10″...................100.00
Rolling pin, dk bl & blk w/wht flecks, 15″..................185.00
Rolling pin, pink & wht opal..............................200.00
Sugar shaker, peacock bl, diagonal wht-loop bands, ftd, 5″......95.00
Vase, bl w/wht loops, wht lining, clear applied flower, 9″.......95.00
Vase, pink & wht, cylindrical, 12″.........................165.00
Vase, red & wht w/blk amethyst ear hdls & base, 9″..........175.00

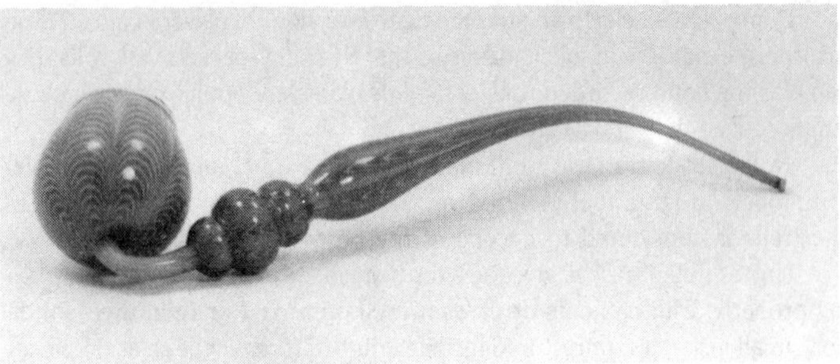

Pipe whimsey, cranberry with white loops, 22″, $450.00.

Nakara

Nakara was an opaque glassware made soon after the turn of the century by the C.F. Monroe Company. Though shapes were plainer and colors deeper, it was very similar to their famous Wave Crest line. Boxes of all sizes, pin trays, and dresser items of every sort were decorated with delicate hand-painted florals, and 'squeeze bag' lace reserves transfer printed with portraits of classical figures, birds, or Victorian ladies. Ormolu handles, bases, and collars, and scented satin box linings added opulence to the already elegant ware.

The C.F. Monroe Company closed in 1916.

When no condition is indicated, the items listed below are assumed to be in mint condition.

Box, bl w/pink florals, hinged lid, rnd, 4¾″.................265.00
Box, blown-out pansy on bl, 3¾″..........................350.00
Box, Burmese coloring w/daisies, sgn, mirror w/in, 6½″........575.00
Box, floral, crown mold, hinged lid, mirror w/in, 8½″.........695.00
Box, full length Queen Louise portrait, 8″ dia...............975.00
Box, gr w/wht enamel beading, pink floral, 3½x6″ dia.........400.00
Box, ring; floral on pink, hinged, sgn, scarce, 2¼″...........425.00
Box, watch; apple blossoms, lav/olive gr, lined, 3½″..........325.00
Card holder, pink w/flowers, 4x2½″.......................250.00
Hair receiver, bl/wht floral on pink, Bishop hat shape.........200.00
Humidor, frog reading paper, Nakara headlines, 6¾″..........700.00
Humidor, Indian chief's head.............................900.00
Vase, floral, beaded rim, 11½x6″.........................500.00
Whisk broom holder, bl w/pink floral, ormolu mt, sgn.........850.00

Napkin Rings

Napkin rings became popular during the late 1800s. They were made from various materials. Among the most popular were the silverplated figural types, many of which are listed below. For other types, see specific materials.

When no condition is indicated, the items listed below are assumed to be in good to very good condition.

Key:
gw—gold washed
SH & M—Simpson, Hall & Miller

Baby in cradle, rare....225.00
Barrel w/branches & leaves....45.00
Bird, spread wings, over nest w/eggs by ring, Webster....165.00
Bird, spread wings, 1 ea side ring....75.00
Bird & fan, ftd, exotic, Derby Silver Co....125.00
Black boy throws boomerang, near-nude, 3½″....160.00
Boy, in hat, rolled-up sleeves, pushes barrel ring....165.00
Boy, standing by fence, oval platform on 4 ft, Tufts....195.00
Branch, flowers/leaves on end, holds ring, Meriden....65.00
Butterflies, ea side of ring on lg fan base, Meriden....135.00
Butterfly, sits on ring, attached to bud vase & fan....155.00
Cat, atop ring, spits at dog w/paws on ring, Meriden....225.00
Cat, on hind legs, 1 paw on ring, Knickerbocker....150.00
Cat, w/arched bk in front of ring....150.00
Chair, ladderback; holds floral eng ring....110.00
Cherries & leaves, hanging from ring, leaf base, gw....135.00
Cherub, standing, quilted ring on bk, ornate, Middletown....125.00
Cherub leans on ring, shaped leaf base....125.00
Cherubs, dancing, holding ring, w/wings, lg....195.00
Cherubs, 1 ea side of ring on base, SH & M....115.00
Chick on wishbone, Derby....55.00
Chinaman, sits on sq base, emb bird on ring, SH & M....185.00
Condiment set, chariot on wheels, holds s&p/ring/butter pat....300.00
Condiment set, sm boy holds ring on head, w/salt/pepper....150.00
Cow, by ring, rnd base....185.00
Cow, rectangular platform....100.00
Cupid, atop ring, dog w/front paws on ring....150.00
Cupid peers around ring, heart base, wishbone ft, Wilcox....125.00
Cupid w/wings sits on ring, driving swan, Roger Smith....195.00
Dog, begging, by ring on oval....135.00
Dog, Boston Terrier, lg rnd fan, 1 ea side, Pairpoint....155.00
Dog, Bulldog, chained to doghouse, SH & M....275.00
Dog, Dachshund, ring on bk....125.00
Dog, French Poodle, standing, Tufts....155.00
Dog, full-bodied dog under ring, 3½″....95.00
Dog pulling cart, wheels revolve....225.00
Drummer boy, stands at attention, drumsticks in hand....235.00
Egyptian figures support ring, lion below, bud vase top....165.00
Fan, leans on ring on ball ft, Pairpoint....65.00
Floral brocade ring, fancy ball ftd, Derby Silver Co....45.00
Flower & leaf base, Meriden #162....65.00
Flowers on lily-pad base w/stem hdl, Middletown #96....85.00
Fox in harness, pulling ring on wheels....215.00
Goat, pulling ring on wheels, lg....275.00
Griffin, sitting atop ring, ornate base, Meriden....195.00
Horse prancing, pulling ring w/wheels, Rogers & Bro....245.00
Horses, artistic horse by etched horse, Pairpoint, rare....200.00
Horseshoe, leans against ring....65.00
Horseshoe on leaf, Good Luck, Bridgeport....55.00
Kangaroo & ostrich ea side of beaded-edge ring....125.00
Kate Greenaway, babies, condiment set/shakers/napkin ring....260.00
Kate Greenaway, boy, ring in right hand, Derby #182....185.00
Kate Greenaway, boy & girl ea side ring....225.00

Girl feeding begging dog, Rogers & Bro, Triple Plate, #199, $215.00.

Kate Greenaway, boy crawling, ornate ring on bk....165.00
Kate Greenaway, boy lies on tummy, hand under chin, lg hat....260.00
Kate Greenaway, boy on footstool, rope in hands, Meriden....225.00
Kate Greenaway, boy rolling ring....165.00
Kate Greenaway, girl in hat/long dress pushes ring, Rogers....195.00
Kate Greenaway, girl in long coat/muff+dog ea side ring....195.00
Kate Greenaway, girl sits w/ring on bk, JA Babcock....225.00
Kate Greenaway, girl w/rifle stands before ring, SH & M....195.00
Kate Greenaway, lady w/dog, ring in font, Wilcox....265.00
Lady watering flowers, barefoot, Eureka....275.00
Lady watering flowers, barefoot, Meriden #2209....125.00
Lion, lies on rectangular base, ring on bk, no mk....150.00
Owl, standing on book....145.00
Peacock on perch, ornate base, no mk....125.00
Rabbit, 2 lean on fancy ring, grassy base, sgn....245.00
Rip Van Winkle, w/dog & rifle, carries barrel on bk....500.00
Scissor-tail bird, leaf, Meriden....135.00
Soldiers in tunics hold bugles ea side of ring, RW & Co....95.00
Squirrel eats nut atop log ring, acorns alongside....130.00
Squirrel sits on hind legs by ring, lg tail, Wilcox....115.00
Squirrel w/nut sits by ring on rectangle base, Southington....115.00
Stag w/antlers, holds ring on bk, Rogers & Bro, lg....225.00
Stork, leans over decorated ring....125.00
Turtles, ring on bk, Meriden, #235....125.00
Wagon, on grassy oval, ring is lid for open salt, Wilcox....250.00
Wishbones, Best Wishes, atop triangular ring, Wilcox....55.00

Nash

A. Douglas Nash founded the Corona Art Glass Company in Long Island, New York. He produced tableware, vases, flasks, etc., using delicate artistic shapes and forms. After 1933, he worked for the Libbey Glass Company.

When no condition is indicated, the items listed below are assumed to be in mint condition.

Bowl, Chintz, silver gray on red, sgn, 3½x10″....485.00
Candlestick, Chintz, gr & bl stripes, wide flange & base....85.00
Candlestick, Chintz top, curved ball stem/bobeche, 4″, pr....450.00
Vase, Chintz, bl & gr, trumpet form, sgn, 10″, pr....395.00
Vase, Chintz, gray, rare color, ped ft, sgn, 5½″....625.00
Vase, Chintz rose, red w/yel pattern, sgn/RD85X, rare, 12″....725.00
Vase, gold irid, sgn, 5″....300.00

Bowl and undertray, opalescent with cranberry opalescent rims, 4¾″ diameter, $100.00.

Vase, gold irid, trumpet form, sgn/#529, 9½″ 325.00
Wine, Chintz, lav & gr, sgn, 6″ 60.00

Netsukes

Netsukes are miniature Japanese carvings made with holes called Himitoshi, either channeled or within the carved design, that allow it to be threaded onto a waist cord and worn with the kimono. Because the kimono had no pockets, the Japanese man hung his tools, his pipe and tobacco pouch, along with other daily necessities from his sash. The netsuke was the toggle that secured them all. Although most are of ivory, others were made of bone, wood, metal, porcelain, or semi-precious stones. Some were inlaid or lacquered. They are found in many forms, but figurals are the most common and desirable. They range in size from 1″ up to 3″, which was the maximum size allowed by law. Most netsukes represented the religion, mythology, and the habits of the average person; there was no written word, hence carvers depicted the daily life of the people.

Careful study is required to recognize the quality of the netsuke. Many have been made in Hong Kong in recent years, and even though some are very well carved, these are considered copies and avoided by the serious collector. There are many books that will help you learn to recognize quality netsukes, and most reputable dealers are glad to assist you. Use your magnifying glass to check for repairs.

When no condition is indicated, the items listed below are assumed to be in undamaged condition. Netsukes are ivory unless noted otherwise.

Key:
pch—polychrome

Arhat, holds alms bowl w/dragon, 1700s, Kyoto 445.00
Bird, stylized, inlaid eyes, wood, Mitsuyuki 185.00
Blind man atop elephant, balancing figure, 1700s, Kyoto 350.00
Boar, recumbent, snout aloft, legs Xd, wood, Masami 300.00
Bread seller, basket, on rock w/bush, EX art, pch, sgn 185.00
Cat, crouching, EX features/detail, Yukimasa 275.00
Cat & kitten, inlaid gr eyes, red/blk ladybug, Kenji 1,100.00
Children, 2 w/drum/ball/mask, monkey aside, pch, Hoshu 800.00
Daruma in lotus position, wrapped in cape, Sogyoku 125.00
Dragon, coiled tail, sgn, 2″ 50.00
Dutchman, dancing, long beard/hat, inlaid horn eyes, Kyoto 575.00
Elder fisherman, cormorant w/fish in beak aside, pch, sgn 185.00
Flounder, flat, smooth underside 125.00
Foo dog, recumbent, pup atop, fierce expression, sgn 85.00
Foo lion, standing, w/sm cub, 1½″ 40.00
Fukurokuju, seated, head low, knee raised, Yoshianga style 500.00
God of Wind, on bag etched w/2 beauties, sgn Koraku 1,125.00
Grape leaves/vines, figural carving, boxwood w/coral inlay 1,300.00
Hoju, dancing, fan in hand, engraved robes, wood, Hoju 400.00
Hokkei, sneezing, X-legged, wood, sgn Hokkei on ivory disk . . . 320.00
Horse, recumbent, head trn bk, rat on flank, sgn 110.00
Horse, recumbent, mouth open, looking back, Komei 150.00
Hotei, ivory, Victorian, EX 125.00
Ikaku Senin, woman of Benares on bk, blk hair, Hidemasa 350.00
Jurojin in patterned cape resembling tortoise, wood 300.00
Jurolin, lg figure, stag behind, EX detail, Tomomasa 250.00
Kakio digs pot of gold, wife/child alongside, Tomochika 500.00
Karako, 2 w/instruments, elaborate robes, worn, Hakuunsai 250.00
Kirin, sits/flaming tail meets head, EX work, 1700s, Kyoto 700.00
Man, seated/chanting, wood w/ivory baton, inlay sgn 450.00
Man w/pet monkey, jar for coins, textured/pch, sgn 185.00
Man's face, relief carved nose/beard, pop-eyed, sgn, 1¾″ 60.00
Monkey, eats sm peach, EX detail, wood, Masami, lg 250.00
Monkey God, eating lg peach, Sogyoku 125.00
Monkey rides gourd, EX detail, Meizan 275.00
Mums, rnd cluster, wht & brn w/brn leaves, Yuko 275.00
Mythical animal, recumbent, young atop, scaly body, sgn 95.00
Oni, crouching/frightened, Gyokuseki 350.00
Oni, sm 1 on bk of 2nd who reads scroll w/Shoki, Tomomasa . . 650.00
Oni, standing, holds gong/striker/proclamations, Matsuharu 500.00
Oni clings to overturned basket/2nd underneath, wood, sgn 350.00
Orientals, 2, w/tortoise, sgn, 1½″ 750.00
Puppy, paws on shell, inlaid horn eyes, fur detail, Kyoto 600.00
Ram, recumbent, looks at turtle on bk, sgn, 1½″ 45.00
Rat atop coil of rope, EX carving, sgn 115.00
Rat crouched on bag of rice, 1½x1″ 50.00
Rats, 7 in cluster, Kiku 225.00
Shishi scratches right ear w/left hind paw, sgn Garaku 700.00
Toad, chest puffed, sm toad atop, wood w/horn eyes, Masanao . . 400.00
Tortoise, young on bk, 1700s, sgn Garaku 300.00
Turtle, 3 young on bk, sgn, 2x1½″ 60.00
Water buffalo, lg spider on bk, carving only good 110.00
Water chestnut, jade 200.00
Woman holds baby, 2 sm children alongside, unsgn 200.00
Woman in kimono, bare breast, w/mask in front, 2″ 75.00

New England Glass Works

Founded in 1818 by Deming Jarves in Boston, Massachusetts, The New England Glass Company produced cut, blown-three-mold, free-blown, and pressed glass of the highest quality. They were recognized for their fine decorative accomplishments, using etching, gilding, and engraving to emphasize their wares. For more than fifty years, they produced prize-winning pressed glass dinnerware sets. Because they refused to compromise the quality of their product by using the cheaper lime-based glass that flooded the market in the 1860s, the company fell into financial trouble, and by 1877 was forced to close. However, William Libbey, who had been the sales manager there since 1870, leased the premises and resumed operations with his son, Edward Drummond Libbey, as full partner. In 1892, the firm became known as The Libbey Glass Company.

When no condition is indicated, the items listed below are assumed to be in mint condition. See also Libbey

Celery, amberina, Dia Quilt, 6¼″ 375.00
Celery, amberina, Venetian Diamond w/scalloped rim, 6½″ 425.00
Creamer, cobalt, crimped hdl, rough pontil, 1835, 3¾″ 395.00
Pitcher, amberina, Inverted T'print, water sz 200.00
Toothpick, fuchsia amberina, sq 150.00
Tumble up, amberina, Inverted T'print, 6″ 500.00
Vase, lily; amberina, w/label, 6¾″ 550.00

New Martinsville

The New Martinsville Glass Company took its name from the town in West Virginia where it began operations in 1901. In the beginning years, pressed tablewares were made in crystal as well as colored opalescent glass. Considered an innovator, the company was known for their imaginative applications of the medium in creating lamps made entirely of glass, vanity sets, figural decanters, and novelty figures. The company was purchased by Viking Glass in 1944. It is still in production; current wares are marked 'Viking' or 'Rainbow Art.'

When no condition is indicated, the items listed below are assumed to be in mint condition.

Ash tray, Janice, swan w/ruby neck, 4"....18.00
Bookends, Nautilus, pr....40.00
Bookends, rearing horses, pr....45.00
Bowl, Janice, flared, etched, 3-ftd, 11"....30.00
Bowl, Moondrops, oval, 2 hdls, jade, 8"....30.00
Bowl, Radiance, crimped, ruby, 9¾"....40.00
Cake stand, Princess, low, lace edge, ftd, 14"....15.00
Candelabra, 2-light, red, pr....50.00
Candelabra, 3-light, #425, pr....60.00
Celery, Janice, silver overlay, 11"....20.00
Compote, cheese; ruby, 2½"....20.00
Compote, Radiance, crimped, red, 6"....14.00
Cruet, Prelude etching, w/stopper....32.50
Cup & saucer, Radiance, red....12.00
Figurine, Baby Bear....40.00
Figurine, Baby Chicks, set of 6....225.00
Figurine, Bunny....45.00
Figurine, Drunk....85.00
Figurine, Elephant....85.00
Figurine, Fighting Duck, head down....35.00
Figurine, Fighting Duck, head up....35.00
Figurine, Gazelle....75.00
Figurine, Hen....45.00
Figurine, Mama Bear....175.00
Figurine, Papa Bear....275.00
Figurine, Police Dog....55.00
Figurine, Rearing Horse, head up....95.00
Figurine, Rooster....55.00
Figurine, Seal, w/ball....65.00
Figurine, Squirrel, no base....45.00
Figurine, Tiger, head down....195.00
Figurine, Wolfhound....70.00
Goblet, cordial; Hostmaster, ruby....15.00
Goblet, water; Prelude....18.50
Ice tub, Janice, 3-toe, gr....35.00
Marmalade, Janice, w/lid....20.00
Nautilus shell....25.00
Pitcher, Oscar, amber....20.00
Plate, ruby, 14"....30.00
Plate, torte; Janice, cupped, crystal w/sterling, 13½"....18.00
Swan, Janice, 10"....16.00
Tray, relish; Princess, oval, 3-part, 9¾"....11.00
Tumbler, water; ftd, ruby....12.00

Newcomb

The Newcomb College of New Orleans, Louisiana, established a pottery in 1895 to provide the students with first-hand experience in the fields of art and ceramics. Using locally dug clays--red and buff in the early years, white burning by the turn of the century--potters were employed to throw the ware which the ladies of the college decorated.

Until about 1910, a glossy glaze was used on ware decorated by slip painting or incising. After that, a matt glaze was favored. Soft blues and greens were used almost exclusively, and the decorative themes were chosen to reflect the beauty of the South. 1930 marked the end of the matt glaze period, and the art pottery era.

Various marks used by the pottery include an 'N' within a 'C,' sometimes with 'HB' added to indicate a 'hand-built' piece. The potter often incised his initials into the ware, and the artists were encouraged to sign their work. Among the most well-known artists were Sadie Irvine, Henrietta Bailey, and Fannie Simpson.

When no condition is indicated, the items listed below are assumed to be in mint condition.

Bowl, daffodils/leaves, H Bailey, H29/#246M/JM, 2¾x8½"....375.00
Bowl, floral, Simpson, 3x5"....350.00
Bowl, floral top border on bl matt, AF Simpson, 4x8"....400.00
Bowl, iris, deeply carved, pink on bl, AF Simpson, 6½x9"....700.00
Bowl, maroon & bl gloss, hand thrown, Meyer, 4½"....250.00
Bowl, yel buds & gr leaves, imp NC, 1915, 4½"....250.00
Bowl, 4-petal floral carved/pnt on bl, H Bailey, 3¾x6½"....350.00
Bowl vase, floral, pink on bl, H Bailey, 4x8"....485.00
Bud vase, closed crinum lily, Bailey, 8"....500.00
Creamer, daisies, incised on gr-bl, S Irvine, 1910, 4"....450.00
Inkwell, Irvine, 3-pc....575.00
Pitcher, concentric bl/gr rings, thrown, hdl, Irvine, 4½"....250.00
Plaque, cottage/grove of trees, bl/gray/pink, JH43, 10x6"....2,200.00
Vase, bl w/pink/gr top design, AF Simpson, 3⅝"....345.00
Vase, blk gloss, sgn Joseph Meyer/QB37 & #147, 6"....250.00
Vase, carved flowers on matt, 5½x5½"....450.00
Vase, daffodils, wht/pink on bl matt, H Bailey, 7"....750.00
Vase, daffodils w/long stems on bl matt, S Irvine, 8½"....1,100.00
Vase, floral & lg leaves, wht/gr on bl, AF Simpson, 6"....525.00
Vase, floral decor at top, EX art, Alma Mason, 5"....750.00
Vase, gr uneven semi-gloss over red clay, waisted, 4½x3½"....350.00
Vase, iris, transitional, wht on bl/gr matt, Irvine, 9⅛"....700.00
Vase, maroon matt glaze, 5½x5½"....350.00
Vase, med gr drip, hand trn w/visible rings, w/hdls, 5½"....310.00
Vase, med yel-gr, hand trn w/visible finger rings, 5"....250.00
Vase, morning-glories, carved/pnt on bl, AF Simpson, 8x5"....650.00
Vase, moss & moon, bl matt, Sadie Irvine, 5¼"....825.00
Vase, moss & moon, bl matt, sgn AA, 6¼"....800.00
Vase, moss & moon, EX art, bulbous, Sadie Irvine, 3½"....765.00
Vase, moss on trees, AF Simpson, 5"....650.00
Vase, scenic, bl matt, Sadie Irvine/#13/SW-35, 3¾"....400.00
Vase, thick brn gloss, sgn NC/J Hunt, 11", NM....125.00
Vase, wht floral on bl matt, sgn HB, 6"....450.00

Vase, floral band at shoulder, signed H. Bailey, 4¾", $575.00.

Newspapers

Newspapers are primarily collected for their news content. Those reporting important political or military events in the history of our country are usually of greater value.

When no condition is indicated, the items listed below are assumed to be in excellent condition.

Key:
lr—letter

American Traveller, Boston, Sir Walter Scott, Jan 19, 1830......4.00
American Traveller, Presidential message/Jackson, Dec 1829.....6.00
Asbury Park Evening Press, NJ, astronauts killed, Jan 1967......7.00
Asbury Park Evening Press, NJ, Ford sworn in, Aug 10, 1974....6.00
Asbury Park Evening Press, NJ, men on moon, July 21, 1969...14.00
Boston Daily American Statesman, Bunker Hill, June 1826.......4.00
Boston Daily Globe, death of Garfield, Sept 27, 1881..........12.00
Boston Evening Transcript, Will Rogers killed, Aug 1935.......28.00
Boston Gazette, Boston Massacre, reprint, March 12, 1770......6.00
Boston Investigator, Mormon despotism, May 27, 1857..........5.00
Boston Investigator, superstition, June 24, 1857................4.00
Boston Morning Post, lr on Texas independence, Feb 1837......8.00
Bucks County Intelligencer, crowning Queen Victoria, 1838.....15.00
Bulletin, sinking of the Titanic, April 16, 1912................9.00
Columbian Centinel, death of Napolean, Aug 18, 1821.........20.00
Columbian Centinel, death of Washington, Jan 1800...........15.00
Columbian Centinel, deposit 168,000 silver dollars, 1794.......15.00
Columbian Centinel, Plymouth Beach lottery, June 23, 1821.....6.00
Commercial Advertiser, NY, McKinley assassination, 1901.......14.00
Daily Alta California, California wine, Feb 26, 1866.............5.00
Daily Alta California, Civil Rights Act, Apr 14, 1866...........14.00
Daily Graphic, ladies' fashion swimwear, July 19, 1873.........12.00
Daily Union, Wash DC, Indians play lacrosse, Aug 21, 1853......7.00
Daily Union, yellow fever epidemic, Aug 31, 1853............10.00
Enquirer, Richmond, runaway slave ad, April 8, 1808..........12.00
Enquirer, Richmond, trial of Aaron Burr, Sept 19, 1807........15.00
Examiner, Spanish American War, Feb 26, 1898..............50.00
Frederick-Town Herald, Jefferson's policies, Jan 10, 1807.......15.00
Gallatin Union, Jewish custom, Oct 7, 1841...................12.00
Gazette of the US, M Washington in NY City, May 30, 1789....20.00
Harper's Weekly, Mr & Mrs Tom Thumb wedding, Feb 21, 1863.30.00
Hartford Times, R Fulton steamboat trip on Hudson, 1842......5.00
Honolulu Advertiser, Pearl Harbor attack, Dec 8, 1941.........65.00
Independent, NY, lr sgn by Santa Claus, Nov 21, 1867..........6.00
Landmark, Boston Tea Party, Oct 22, 1834...................4.00
Liberator, Boston, anti-slavery by W Garrison, July 1858........17.00
Marysville Daily Appeal, Civil War, Nov 20, 1861...............6.00
Massachusetts Centinel, US Constitution, Dec 17, 1788.........24.00
Nation Aegis, President Madison inauguration, March 1809.....15.00
National Advocate, Jackson's victory over British, 1815.........50.00
National Intelligencer, War of 1812, June 18, 1812.............9.00
New York Herald, Lincoln elected President, Nov 7, 1860......40.00
Niles' Weekly Register, Baltimore, G Washington, Sept 1817.....4.00
Niles' Weekly Register, Baltimore, War of 1812, Oct 1812.......9.00
NY Daily Mirror, Hitler's death, May 2, 1945.................57.00
NY Daily News, Nixon resigns, photos, Aug 9, 1974..........12.00
NY Daily Tribune, Mormon settlement at Salt Lake, 1848......12.00
NY Gazette & General Adviser, Ft George capture, Jan 1813.....6.00
NY Herald, Custer's Last Stand, July 15, 1876................14.00
NY Herald, KKK prisoners, Aug 13, 1872....................7.50
NY Magazine, cruelties of boxing, Nov 1794..................29.00
NY Times, April Fool's Day, April 1, 1870, 8 pg...............3.00
NY Times, bombing of Empire State Building, July 29, 1945.....9.00
Oakland Enquirer, California train wreck, Dec 1902, 8 pg.......7.00
Oakland Enquirer, T Roosevelt returns home, 1910, 20 pg.......6.00
Oakland Post Enquirer, D-Day, blimp photos, June 6, 1944.....22.00
Oakland Tribune, SF earthquake & fire, photo, Apr 20, 1906...32.00
Old Colony Memorial, death of Lafayette, Aug 28, 1824.........5.00
Old Colony Memorial, Lafayette visits US, Aug 7, 1824..........5.00
Providence Daily Journal, buried 166 years--alive, 1842.........12.00
Puritan Recorder, Dred Scott case, July 16, 1857..............7.00
Rhode Island American & Gazette, slave rebellion, Dec 1831....20.00
Riverside Daily Press, Al Capone, Aug 15, 1933..............14.00
Riverside Daily Press, Duke of Windsor marries, June 1937......9.00
Riverside Daily Press, Golden Gate Bridge, May 29, 1937........7.00
Riverside Daily Press, J Rockefeller Sr dies, May 24, 1937.......9.00
Sacramento Daily Union, how cannibals cook people, 1869......7.00
Sacramento Daily Union, Indian life & habits, July 9, 1874.......6.00
San Francisco Call, Alaska gold rush, May 11, 1899, 8 pg.......8.00
San Francisco Call, boxing at San Quentin Prison, Oct 1897.....5.00
San Francisco Call, wireless telegraph, May 7, 1899...........12.00
San Francisco Chronicle, death of FDR, Apr 15, 1945, 12 pg....9.00
San Francisco Chronicle, Shrine convention, June 1922.........6.00
San Francisco Chronicle, victims of cocaine, Dec 29, 1896......16.00
San Francisco Daily Evening Bulletin, gold rush, 1856.........15.00
San Jose Mercury & News, colored comics, 1945, 16 pg, M......4.00
Scientific American, horse-drawn fire engine, Sept 1867.........8.00
Scientific American, sewing machine, Sept 21, 1867...........10.00
Semi-Weekly Times, Jackson's last day, Mar 4, 1837............5.00
Spirit of the Times, Charles Dickens review, Dec 4, 1841.......11.00
Statesman, NY, Adams & Jefferson funeral, July 21, 1826........8.00
Statesman, NY, letter from Jefferson to Adams, Dec 1823........8.00
Stockton Daily Independent, FDR shooting attempt, 1933.......8.00
Stockton Daily Independent, fossils of giants, Dec 1865.........6.00
Stockton Daily Independent, ghosts & cannibalism, Feb 1880.....5.00
Stockton Daily Independent, how to catch highwaymen, 1865.....6.00
Stockton Daily Independent, Lincoln conspiracy, May 1867......9.00
Stockton Evening News, Ma Barker gang, Jan 16, 1935.........16.00
Stockton Evening Transcript, Stock Market crash, 1929........25.00
Stockton Weekly Independent, Big Foot, Oct 29, 1870..........6.00
Stockton Weekly Independent, Robert E Lee, Dec 3, 1870......8.00
Sun, NY, abolishing gambling houses, Mar 11, 1835............6.00
Sun, Philadelphia, biography of Daniel Boone, Oct 8, 1845....12.00
Sunday Call, Chinese coins & ghost towns, March 12, 1893......7.00
Truckee Republican, slang terms used today, Sept 24, 1884......6.00
Truckee Republican, stamp collecting history, Oct 4, 1884.......9.00
Weekly Examiner, hanging of murderer Durrant, Jan 13, 1898...27.00
Weekly Press, Atlantic cable, Aug 21, 1858..................12.00

Niloak

Benton, Arkansas, was an area rich with natural clay, high in quality and easily accessible. During the last half of the 1800s, a dozen potteries flourished there, but by 1898, the only one remaining was owned by Charles Dean Hyten. In 1909 he began to experiment, trying to preserve in his finished ware the many colors of the native clay. By 1912 he had perfected a method that produced the desired effect. He obtained a U.S. patent for his handcrafted Niloak Mission pottery, characterized by swirling layers of browns, blues, red, and buff clays. Only a few early pieces were glazed both inside and out; these are extremely rare. After the process was perfected, only the interior was glazed. The ware was marked 'Niloak,' the backward spelling of Kaolin, a type of fine porcelain clay. No sooner had production began than the pottery burned, but Hyten rebuilt, and added a stoneware line called Eagle Pottery. Hywood, an inexpensive novelty ware, was introduced in 1929--an attempt to boost sales during the onset of the depression years. Until 1934, when the management changed hands, the line was marked 'Hywood-Niloak.' After that, 'Hywood' no longer appeared on the ware.

Hyten left the pottery in 1941; in 1946 the operation closed.

Values listed below are average show prices. Our Niloak experts advise us, however, that in certain areas, prices may yet be from 20% to 30% under the norm.

When no condition is indicated, the items listed below are assumed to be in mint condition.

Ash tray, Mission Ware, 5″ 45.00
Bowl, bl, scalloped rim, squat, imp Block sgn, 3½x7″ 20.00
Bowl, gr, scalloped rim, squat, imp Block sgn, 3x5½″ 12.50
Bowl, Mission Ware, 2″ 35.00
Bud vase, Mission Ware, 6″ 75.00
Creamer, mauve w/gr tint overlay, raised sgn, 4¾″ 12.00
Ewer, mauve w/gr tint overlay, raised sgn, 6¾″ 15.00
Jug, blk gloss, w/stopper, 7″ 55.00
Pitcher, maroon, bulbous, 4″ 10.00
Planter, wht elephant 12.00
Toothpick, Mission Ware 35.00
Vase, bl, hdls, imp block sgn, 4½″ 10.00
Vase, bl, mottled, slender, orig label, 8″ 20.00
Vase, maroon, triple hdls, 5½″ 15.00
Vase, matt pink shading to bl at neck, twist hdls, 6″ 28.00
Vase, Mission Ware, bulbous, can top, brn/red/bl, 5½x3½″ 65.00
Vase, Mission Ware, bulbous w/12-hole top, 6″ 75.00
Vase, Mission Ware, dk reds/grays, 7x4½″ 90.00
Vase, Mission Ware, EX color, red/brn/bl, 8x5″ 100.00
Vase, Mission Ware, EX color w/reds, sandy texture, 9x4¾″ 130.00
Vase, Mission Ware, hourglass shape, 4½″ 45.00
Vase, Mission Ware, hourglass shape, 8″ 98.00
Vase, Mission Ware, lg swirls, dk colors, 6″ 45.00
Vase, Mission Ware, narrow base, wide top, 8x4½″ 95.00
Vase, Mission Ware, ogee shape, 9½″ 110.00
Vase, Mission Ware, ovoid w/flat flared rim, 6″ 65.00
Vase, Mission Ware, slim str body on disk ft, 7″ 70.00
Vase, Mission Ware, soda glass shape, 9¾″ 135.00
Vase, Mission Ware, swirls w/gr, 8″ 110.00
Vase, Mission Ware, turned over edge, narrows at base, 9″ 125.00
Vase, Mission Ware, waisted/lg to sm swirls/EX color, 6½″ 100.00
Vase, Mission Ware, wht/terra cotta/beige/bl, 3x3½″ 65.00
Vase, Mission Ware, wide lip, 8¼″ 95.00
Vase, Mission Ware, 10½″ 145.00
Vase, Mission Ware, 12″ 210.00
Vase, Mission Ware, 14″ 250.00

Squirrel planter, brown glaze, 5¾″, $45.00.

Nippon

Nippon generally refers to Japanese wares made during the period from 1891 to 1921, although the Nippon mark was also used to a limited extent on later wares. Nippon, meaning Japan, identified the country of origin to comply with American importation restrictions. After 1921, 'Japan' was an acceptable alternative. The term does not imply a specific type of product, and may be found on items other than porcelains. In the listings that follow, the numbers refer to these specific marks:

Key:
#1—China E-OH
#2—M in Wreath
#3—Cherry Blossom
#4—Double T Diamond in Circle
#5—Rising Sun
#6—Royal Kinran
#7—Maple Leaf
#8—Royal Nippon, Nishiki

Authority Joan Van Patten has compiled a lovely series, *The Collector's Encyclopedia of Nippon Porcelain*, with many full-color photos and current prices; you will find her address in the Directory under New York.

When no condition is indicated, the items listed below are assumed to be in mint condition. For items marked 'Noritake Nippon,' see Noritake Section.

Vase, scenic band on floral body, gold work and beading, signed Royal Nishiki, 16″, $150.00.

Ash tray, sailboats on bisque, moriage beaded trim 85.00
Ash tray, scenic on bisque, turq jeweling, 3 rests, gr #2 . . . . . 50.00
Asparagus set, 12½″ tray, six 7½″ plates, gr #2 . . . . . 350.00
Basket, violets, gold decor & hdl, 6½″ 85.00
Basket dish, floral, sgn, 10½″ L 65.00
Berry set, gold w/cobalt & lg roses, 9¾″ master+4 ind 285.00
Berry set, windmill scene, sgn, 5-pc 85.00
Bookends, Indian, pr 1,300.00
Bottle, scent; red rosebuds, gold trim, w/stopper, 6″ 65.00
Bowl, acorns/leaves/vines, clover shaped, 3-hdl, gr #2, 6″ 75.00
Bowl, blown-out sides w/heavy rose medallions, gaudy, lg 135.00
Bowl, center medallion, wht w/gold trim, bl #7, 8-sided 75.00
Bowl, floral medallions, raised gold beading, 10″ 75.00
Bowl, florals, gold tracing, on gr/rose shaded ground, 7½″ 50.00
Bowl, foliage, gr/purple, ftd, gold border, 5x11¾x8¼″ 160.00
Bowl, fruits/flowers/bird/branches/leaves, 2-hdl, gr #2 . . . . . 120.00
Bowl, grapes & daisies, gold border, oblong/ruffled, 7½″ L 50.00
Bowl, grapes w/gold & jeweled border, hdls, 11″ W 130.00
Bowl, lakeside scene on bisque, matt border, hdls, 6½″ 60.00
Bowl, lilacs w/gr leaves on gr, much gold, ftd, #7 mk, 9¼″ 110.00

Bowl, mc roses int & ext, 2 gold hdls, artist sgn, 8″...........60.00
Bowl, nut & pine cones, clover shape, 3-hdl, gr #2, 6½″........75.00
Bowl, nuts & gr forest, brn & wht w/brn matt trim, 9½″.......100.00
Bowl, orchids w/gr leaves, ftd, leaf mk, 8½″..................75.00
Bowl, roses, cobalt trim, gold rim, pierced gold hdls, 8″........85.00
Bowl, roses, pink/yel, gold rim, 3-ftd, 2¾x7½″................60.00
Bowl, roses, pink/yel on sepia, 2-hdl, sgn, gr #2, 5½″..........45.00
Bowl, roses, yel on brn w/in & w/out, 2 gold hdls, 7″..........45.00
Bowl, roses, yel/pk, aqua center, cobalt rim, Dow Sie mk, 9″....65.00
Bowl, scenic center, pink roses, much gold, scalloped, 9½″....300.00
Bowl, Washington DC scene, octagonal, much gold, 7″.........50.00
Bowl, 8 panels of pk roses on dk rose/gold medallions, 9½″....110.00
Box, trinket; woods & deer, moriage, ftd/oval, gr #2, 5x3″.....190.00
Butter dish, floral, w/drainer...............................55.00
Butter tub, sm pink roses, gold trim, 3-pc...................35.00
Cake plate, pink roses, blk/gold trim, open hdls, 10″..........35.00
Cake set, bluebirds & floral, gold trim, crown mk, 7-pc........110.00
Candle holder, blk w/gold on wht, 6″.......................50.00
Candlestick, gold floral, yel on flared rnd base, gr #2, 6″......110.00
Candlestick, sunset scene w/lake, house & trees, 5″, pr........220.00
Candy jar, water scenic w/church, #2, 4x5¾″...............135.00
Celery tray, canoe shape, w/6 salt dips, set...................85.00
Celery tray, celery stalk decor.............................45.00
Celery tray, floral w/gold border, open hdl, +6 salts...........85.00
Chamberstick, child's; floral & gold trim.....................40.00
Cheese & cracker, floral & gold decor......................40.00
Cheese dish, blk & gold, floral on wht, slant top, #7, 7½″.....145.00
Chocolate pot, bl forget-me-nots, sgn, +4 c/s................150.00
Chocolate pot, gold decor, +6 cups.......................325.00
Chocolate pot, gold traces, gold beaded, bl #7...............220.00
Chocolate pot, gray w/bl scenic, +6 c/s....................125.00
Chocolate pot, raised gold beading, much gold, bl #7.........219.00
Chocolate pot, roses, beading, turq/pink/gr, bl #2, +4 c/s......125.00
Chocolate pot, roses, gold & turq bands, bulbous, 10¾″.......290.00
Cigarette urn, birds in flight over enameled trees, bisque.......65.00
Coaster, Dutchman smoking pipe at edge of water.............25.00
Compote, int: forest scene, ped ft, HP, gr #2................325.00
Compote, jewels & floral, much gold, 2-part.................275.00
Compote, Nile scene, matt, jewel hdls, 8″....................65.00
Compote, sm pink roses, gold trim.........................45.00
Compote, swan scene, cobalt w/gold border, 9″..............175.00
Cookie jar, heavy beading, jewels, 7″.....................180.00
Cookie jar, melon rib, cream w/panels of flowers, ftd, 8″.......195.00
Creamer, flying bird, bl & wht............................16.00
Creamer & sugar bowl, child's; floral & gold trim.............40.00
Creamer & sugar bowl, scenic w/man in boat, bl..............90.00
Creamer & sugar bowl, wht w/pink/yel floral, heavy gold.......145.00
Dish, red floral w/gold trim, boat shape, gr #7, 7″ L...........45.00
Dish, riding scene, fluted.................................110.00
Dish, roses, gold trim, beaded edge, hdls, gr #7, 6½″..........45.00
Egg warmer, scenic.......................................125.00
Egg warmer, 6-egg, brn/gr/wht, #5........................185.00
Ewer, floral w/gold, 6½″..................................135.00
Ewer, gr w/roses & wht moriage lace, 7½″..................325.00
Ewer, portrait, gold/wht, gr #7, 6½″.......................350.00
Ewer, woodland scene, bl #7, 7″..........................225.00
Ferner, floral w/gold trim, 6-sided, gr #2, 7¾″...............180.00
Figurine, 3 monkeys, 'Speak no evil...Hear no evil,' brn.......145.00
Hair receiver, gold w/cobalt & lg roses......................55.00
Humidor, cigar on top w/cards, 3-hdl.......................450.00
Humidor, coach scene.....................................475.00
Humidor, crouching lion, blown-out, gr #2, 7¼″.............850.00
Humidor, floral, gold trim, 7″.............................150.00
Humidor, horse head decor, geometrics......................250.00
Humidor, Indian holds rearing horse, gr #2, 7″............1,000.00
Humidor, Indian on horseback, tortoiseshell finish, NM........325.00
Humidor, Johnny Appleseed, blown-out, gr #2, rare, 7″......1,500.00
Humidor, lamplighter, molded in relief, gr #2, 7¼″...........900.00
Humidor, moose head, brn/yel, oval form...................225.00
Humidor, Royal Flush in diamonds on brn bisque, 7½″.......380.00
Humidor, stylized mythological creature, gr #2, 5½″..........325.00
Humidor, windmill scene...................................300.00
Humidor, woodland & water on lt bl.........................225.00
Humidor, 3 horse heads, blown-out, gr #2, 7″..............800.00
Ice cream set, pink apple blossoms, 7-pc.....................60.00
Inkwell, beige/gold/blk flower, sgn, sq, 4″...................125.00
Inkwell, bl floral, gold trim, insert w/pen rest................150.00
Inkwell, palm trees, boat, 4″.............................125.00
Jam jar, scenic w/swan, gr #7..............................50.00
Ladle, mayonnaise; florals w/in, gold trim, #5, 5″..............20.00
Lamp, gold loops & flowers over mountain scene, 20″........250.00
Lazy Susan, pastels, heavy gold overlay, orig box, 10″........165.00
Lazy Susan, scenic, mk Nogoya, papier mache box, 10″........90.00
Match holder, Indian woman, gr mk, 2½″....................100.00
Match holder, red clown..................................100.00
Mayonnaise, w/ladle, simple floral..........................30.00
Muffineer, pink floral, gr leaves, gr #7, 4½″..................65.00
Mug, child's; girl & dog..................................75.00
Mug, dragons in gold relief on dk gr, 5½″...................235.00
Mug, house, lake & swan, 4½″............................100.00
Mug, Nile scene, moriage plants, enamel trim, gr #2, 4¾″.....100.00
Mug, scenic, gold beading, 4½″...........................165.00
Mustard, w/underplate, garden, trees & flowers, gold/beads......65.00
Nappy, woodland scene, open hdls, 7″......................40.00
Nut bowl, jeweled & beaded scenic..........................50.00
Nut bowl, jeweled w/moriage hdls, clover shape...............80.00
Nut bowl, pink/orchid floral, scalloped brn rim, 3-ftd, #1........45.00
Nut set, jeweled & beaded, master+6 ind....................120.00
Nut set, nut shell relief, 7″ master+6 cups..................225.00
Pitcher, flowers, much gold, sgn, 5″........................50.00
Pitcher, roses/leaves/scrolls, wht dots allover, unsgn, 9″........75.00
Pitcher, wht & pink flowers, gold, jewels, hexagonal, 6¾″......175.00
Pitcher, windmill scene, heavy enamel/jewel trim, 8″..........300.00
Planter, HP violets, fluted top, 9½x6x5″....................120.00
Planter, medallion decor, brn, w/flower holder, 5x10″...........85.00
Plaque, Arab on camel by campfire, 10″.....................230.00
Plaque, birds on branch, wide gold beaded rim, 9″............135.00
Plaque, bluebird, moriage, pnt pine cones, 7¾″...............90.00
Plaque, cow in meadow, gr #2, 10½″.......................180.00
Plaque, cows standing in water, gr #2, 10¼x8″...............400.00
Plaque, dog portrait, gr #2, 7¾″...........................300.00
Plaque, dog's head medallion center, moriage border, 10″.....350.00
Plaque, Dutch windmill scene, 9″...........................135.00
Plaque, Indian chief, moriage trim, cream/brn/gr, 10″.........750.00
Plaque, Indian w/turkey, sunset, blown-out, gr #2, 10½″.......800.00
Plaque, lav flowers on gr, gold trim, bisque, 10″.............185.00
Plaque, lav mtns & bridge, 1½″ gold jeweled border...........275.00
Plaque, lilacs on tan, moriage relief, sgn, 7½″................55.00
Plaque, man poling boat under bridge, 10″..................160.00
Plaque, moose, blown-out, gr #2, 10½″.....................725.00
Plaque, palm trees, boats & pyramids, moriage trim, 10″......160.00
Plaque, palm trees, lake, cottage & mountains, bl #7, 10″.....160.00
Plaque, palm trees by lake, sunset, brn matt trim, 10″.........160.00
Plaque, pineapple, peaches, grapes, Egyptian border, bl #7.....195.00
Plaque, pink flowers on gr, gold/red border, 11″.............180.00
Plaque, pink roses & gr leaves, 1″ gold swag border, 9″.......100.00
Plaque, scenic, bl floral border, 10″.......................145.00
Plaque, scenic, bl/pink/brn border, bl #7, 9″.................250.00

Plaque, blown-out Indian on horseback, 10½″, $800.00.

Plaque, scenic, light moriage trim, 7¾″......90.00
Plaque, scenic, ram & floral border, 10″......195.00
Plaque, scenic, vivid autumn colors, 10″......180.00
Plaque, scenic w/river & violet trees, 8¾″......100.00
Plaque, sm dog portrait, gr #2, 7¾″......300.00
Plaque, stag, blown-out, gr #2, 10½″......600.00
Plaque, stream, bridge & trees, 9½″......150.00
Plaque, stylized gr trees, 3″ pink rose band, 9″......110.00
Plaque, tree & berries, wht/red moriage......145.00
Plaque, windmill w/gold flowers, gr/wht/purple, bl mk, 9″......125.00
Plaque, 2 dogs, blown-out, gr #2, 10½″......950.00
Plaque, 2 Dutch sailors by ship, bisque, gr #2, 10¼″......150.00
Plaque, 2 riders on horses, wreath mk, 10″ dia......150.00
Plate, chop; coaching scene, 10″......275.00
Plate, cobalt w/heavy gold beading, 7¼″......125.00
Plate, Delft type, bl/wht, 10″......40.00
Plate, Egyptian hieroglyphic motif, octagon, 2-hdl, 9½″......85.00
Plate, full-blown roses, gold trim, gr #7, 10″......120.00
Plate, pink flowers/gr leaves/scenic, cobalt rim, 7¾″, pr......145.00
Plate, pink roses/gr leaves, tan w/gold border, bl #7, 9″......95.00
Plate, scenic, cobalt w/gold, 9″......85.00
Plate, trees/house/lake/boat/sunset, orange, crown mk, 8″......60.00
Ring tree, floral w/gold beading, gold hand, gr #2......55.00
Salt dip, floral band, gold trim, boat shape, purple #7......10.00
Sandwich luncheon set, bird/flowers, open hdl, gr mk, 7-pc....139.00
Sardine dish, w/underplate, scenic, gold fish finial......125.00
Saucer, pink & gr floral, crown mk......7.00
Shakers, gold w/turq beading & pink roses, pr......60.00
Shakers, wht crane on red, egg shape, pr......35.00
Smoke set, Arab & camel, tray/humidor/tray/etc, 7-pc......725.00
Spittoon, antique car scene, HP, sgn, miniature......125.00
Stein, 6 dogs, blown-out, gr #2......850.00
Sugar bowl, pink & red roses......15.00
Sugar bowl, rose garlands w/pale gr leaves......15.00
Syrup, w/underplate, violet decor on wht, gr #2......80.00
Tankard, burgundy/pink roses, cobalt beading, 12″......225.00
Tankard, elks, +4 mugs......600.00
Tankard, pink rose panels, moriage, bl/yel/gr, 10″......300.00
Tankard, red roses on cobalt, gilt, sgn, 13¼″......250.00
Tankard, stag, blown-out, gr #7, +6 mugs, 11½″......3,500.00
Tankard, yel/purple grapes over trees, gold rim, hdls, 11″.....195.00
Tea set, butterflies on bl, reg size cups, mk #5, 13-pc......195.00
Tea set, children pulling sled......139.00
Tea set, dragon, moriage slip-trail......150.00
Tea set, egrets, wht on bl, bl #7, 11-pc......150.00
Tea set, gold beads/hdls, HP scenic cameos, ftd, 15-pc......300.00
Tea set, lush flowers & jewels on blk, sgn......375.00
Tea set, oasis scene, jeweled hdls, bisque, gr #2......145.00
Tea set, rose border, red on wht......195.00
Tea set, roses, gold relief, ftd, gr #7, 3-pc......95.00
Tea set, swan scene, 13-pc......225.00
Tea strainer, pink floral w/gold tracery, bl/wht bands, 6″......60.00
Toothpick, 2 scenic panels, gold beading......35.00
Tray, pin; HP floral......20.00
Urn, 2-pc ped, 2-hdl, bl Royal Moriye Nippon mk, 10½″......300.00
Vase, coralene, bl/wht/lav geometric design, pat mk, 8¾″......225.00
Vase, coralene, lav roses, brn w/gold trim, 4¾″......160.00
Vase, coralene, scenic, 7″, EX......230.00
Vase, coralene flowers & branches, pat mk, ovoid, 10″......275.00
Vase, coronation, gr #7, 10″......85.00
Vase, cottage, floral branch in foreground, hdls, #8, 12″......175.00
Vase, Countess Anna Potocka portrait, bl #7, 7½″......345.00
Vase, cowboy on horse silhouette/sunset, 2-hdl, sq, 6½″......175.00
Vase, dragonfly, hydrangeas & spider web, 2 hdl, 10¼″......260.00
Vase, farmhouse, gr grass, Indian motif, gr #7, 11½″......150.00
Vase, floral, Deco, hexagonal, 10″......110.00
Vase, floral, pink w/gold accents, 3 gold hdls, 11½″......190.00
Vase, floral, pink/red, much gold, hdls, 9¼″......85.00
Vase, floral, rust/purple, gold/copper rim, hdls, 4½″......45.00
Vase, floral, wht on gray/gr w/gold, dbl hdls, 16″......195.00
Vase, floral, yel/wht, much gold/jewels, hdls, 10½″......195.00
Vase, floral & leaves, geometric traces, dbl hdls, gr #2, 9″.....100.00
Vase, floral w/panels of trees, lake, cottage, sunset, 12″......125.00
Vase, flower baskets on mauve, 13″......205.00
Vase, geometric, floral & thistles, bisque, bulbous, 10″......135.00
Vase, geometric floral on bisque, bulbous, gr #2, 7½″......115.00
Vase, house & trees, 2-hdl, Royal Nishiki, 12″......105.00
Vase, house/sunset/cherry branch, Royal Nishiki, hdls, 13″.....110.00
Vase, hunt scene w/stag & hounds, blown-out, 2-hdl, gr #2.....475.00
Vase, Indians at lake scenic, Imperial mk, 8½″, pr......350.00
Vase, marigold band, Deco X-stitch pattern, 11″......100.00
Vase, nasturtiums, yel/pink on dk gr, gold beaded base, 8″.....95.00
Vase, nasturtiums, yel/pink on gr, dragon hdls, gr #7, 8″......100.00
Vase, orchids, pink/purple on gr foliage, gold hdls, 15″......325.00
Vase, orchids, pink/wht w/mauve, leaves, gold hdls, 17″......350.00
Vase, pasture scene w/sheep, gold/jeweled trim, 13″......295.00
Vase, peonies & vines, Art Nouveau geometrics, 2-hdl, 12″.....125.00
Vase, pyramid & palm scene, gold trim, #7, 5″, pr......100.00
Vase, red panels around b/w panels, scenic center, 5½″......85.00
Vase, relief figure decor, Satsuma type, 2-hdl, 28″......425.00
Vase, roses, pastel bisque, enamel floral band, 10½″......185.00
Vase, roses, red/yel on wht, gold trim & hdls, 14½″......150.00
Vase, roses, red/yel/pink, moriage, 2-hdl, 8″......275.00
Vase, roses, yel/pink on brn, satin, bulbous, 7½″......110.00
Vase, roses, 4 panels, allover gold trim, sgn, 8¾″......95.00
Vase, roses & floral on tan, gold scroll, bulbous, 6½″......85.00
Vase, roses & gold leaf on gr, 12½″......165.00
Vase, roses on blended brn bisque, gr #2, 7¾″......85.00
Vase, roses on tan, fluted, hdls, Royal Nippon, 12″......100.00
Vase, sailboat in surging surf, cobalt, gr #2, 9″......350.00
Vase, scenic, bisque, hdls, gr #2, 6″......55.00
Vase, scenic, gold overlay, dragon hdls, 5½″......245.00
Vase, scenic, gold trim, dbl hdls, gr #7, 5½″......50.00
Vase, scenic & floral, bulbous, 10″, pr......350.00
Vase, scenic tapestry, bl #7, 6″......425.00

Vase, swan scene, rnd, 2-hdl, 14″ 160.00
Vase, tapestry, scenic, bl #7, 6″ 425.00
Vase, trees, lake, fields & hills, 2 gold hdls, bl #7, 9″ 200.00
Vase, trees, mountains w/snow, moriage, gr mk, 7″ 225.00
Vase, trees, yel, gold trace blk foreground/gold hdls, 14″ 225.00
Vase, Wedgwood style, gr #2, 9½″ 500.00
Vase, Wedgwood style, ring hdls, gr #2, 8″ 425.00
Vase, windmill, birds & trees, basket shape, gr #2, 6″ 157.00
Vase, windmill, jeweled hdls, gr #2, 4½″ 45.00
Vase, woodland scene, moriage trees & blossoms, 13″ 300.00
Vase, woodland scene, 9″ 200.00
Vase, 2 Indians: 1 sitting/1 by tree, Imperial mk, 8½″ 350.00
Whiskey jug, chickens/water, primitive, w/stopper, bl #2 . . . . . 400.00

Nodders

So called because of the nodding action of their head and hands, nodders originated in China where they were used in temple rituals to represent deity. Early in the 18th century, the idea was adapted by Meissen and by French manufacturers who produced not only china nodders but bisque as well. Most nodders are individual--couples are unusual. The idea remained popular until the end of the 19th century, and was used during the Victorian era by toy manufacturers.

When no condition is indicated, the items listed below are assumed to be in mint condition.

Blk man on fence holds rifle, pnt metal 120.00
Boy, bl/wht suit & cap, bisque, mk Germany, 3½″ 65.00
Buttercup, bisque, Germany, NM 175.00
Comical man, compo/wood/fur hair/glass eyes, Germany, 8″ 35.00
Comical man, wobble tongue, Occupied Japan, 3½″ 95.00
Comical man w/top hat, worn orig mc pnt, minor damage, 7½″ . . 35.00
English barrister, wht china w/gold trim, 6″ 150.00
Girl on pony holds puppy, bisque, EX detail/decor, 6½x5½″ 110.00
Group, family of 5, heads nod, w/dog, Siberian dress, 5½″ 350.00
Group, 3 ladies w/hats at tea party, fine bisque, 4x4″ 275.00
Indian w/fruit, seated, legs Xd in front, 5½″ 125.00

Female Pagoda figure, head, tongue, and hands 'nod,' Meissen crossed swords mark, #2888, minor repair, 12½″, $3,500.00.

Jester, seated, peach/wht outfit & hat, bisque, 3¾x2½″ 75.00
Lord Plushbottom, bisque, Germany, NM 125.00
Man, lady in sapling chairs, mc/compo, 6¾″, pr 110.00
Man sits beneath tree by fence, hat on tree, bisque, 5½″ 125.00
Oriental lady pulls cart, mc French bisque, 7x3x5″ 145.00
Oriental lady w/jar, robe, ornaments in blonde hair, 4⅞″ 75.00
Oriental man, bl/wht garb/hat, sits, w/dagger, bisque, 6″ 135.00
Oriental man, seated, hollow ceramic, gold w/in & w/out 150.00
Orphan Annie, bisque, Germany, NM 100.00
Peasant woman, stout, red nose, w/pitcher, mc/bisque, 7x3″ 125.00
Perry Winkle, bisque, Germany, NM 100.00
Poodle & bulldog, bisque, oval base, 4¾″ 135.00
Spanish couple, papier mache, old 20.00
Sultan, Sultaness, seated, bisque/pastels/gold, 3¾″, pr 175.00
Uncle Bim, bisque, Germany, NM 125.00
Uncle Walt, bisque, Germany, NM 100.00
Winnie Winkle, bisque, Germany, NM 100.00

Noritake

The Noritake Company was first registered in 1904 as Nippon Gomei Kaisha. In 1917, the name became Nippon Toki Kabushiki Toki. The 'M' in wreath mark is that of the Morimura Brothers, distributors with offices in New York. It was used until 1941. The tree crest mark is the crest of the Morimura family.

The Noritake Company has produced fine porcelain dinnerware sets and occasional pieces decorated in the delicate manner for which the Japanese are noted. Their Azalea pattern was produced exclusively for the Larkin Company, who gave the lovely ware away as premiums to club members and their home agents.

From 1916 through the thirties, Larkin distributed the fine china which was decorated in pink Azaleas on white with gold tracing along edges and handles. Early in the thirties, six pieces of crystal hand painted with the same design were offered: candle holders, a compote, a tray with handles, a scalloped fruit bowl, a cheese and cracker set, and a cake plate. All in all, seventy different pieces of Azalea were offered. Some, such as the fifteen-piece child's set, bulbous vase, china ash tray, and the pancake jug, are quite rare. Marks varied over the years; the earliest was the blue rising sun Nippon mark, followed by the Noritake M in wreath with variations. Later, the ware was marked 'Noritake, Azalea, hand painted, Japan.'

Authority Joan Van Patten has compiled a lovely book, *The Collector's Encyclopedia of Noritake*, with many full-color photos and current prices; you will find her address in the Directory under New York. When no condition is indicated, the items listed below are assumed to be in mint condition. Numbers refer to these specific marks:

Key:
#1—Cherry Blossom
#2—M in Wreath
#3—Maple Leaf mark

Azalea

Basket, mint; Dolly Varden, #193 . . . . . 90.00
Bonbon, #184, 6¼″ 35.00
Bowl, cream soup; 2-hdl, #363, 5″ 85.00
Bowl, deep, #310 . . . . . 45.00
Bowl, fruit; #9, 5¼″ 8.00
Bowl, oatmeal; #55, 5¾″ 12.00
Bowl, salad; hdls, #12, 10″ 36.00
Bowl, soup; #19, 7⅜″ 16.00
Bowl, vegetable; oval, hdls, #101, 10½″ 35.00
Bowl, vegetable; oval, hdls, #172, 9¼″ 35.00
Butter dish, w/lid, #314, 6¼″ 85.00
Butter pat, set of 6 . . . . . 250.00

Butter tub, #54, 5″ 35.00
Casserole, gold finial, w/lid, #372 .... 350.00
Casserole, w/lid, #16, 10¼″ 70.00
Celery, #444, rare, 10″ 235.00
Celery/roll tray, #99, 12½x6″ 45.00
Child's set, 15-pc 1,350.00
Coffee pot, #182 .... 450.00
Compote, #170 .... 65.00
Condiment set, #14, 5-pc 60.00
Creamer & sugar bowl, #123 .... 35.00
Creamer & sugar bowl, #449 .... 300.00
Creamer & sugar bowl, w/lid, #401 .... 65.00
Cruet, #190, 6¼″ 160.00
Cup, bouillon; 2-hdl, #124, 3¾″ 16.00
Cup & saucer, #2 .... 15.00
Cup & saucer, demitasse; #183 .... 85.00
Egg cup, #120, 3⅛″ 36.00
Glass ware, cake plate, 10½″ 50.00
Glass ware, candlestick, #114, pr 30.00
Glass ware, cheese & cracker set, 2-pc, 10″ 65.00
Glass ware, sandwich tray, 10″ 50.00
Grapefruit/candy bowl, #185, 3½x4½″ 95.00
Gravy boat, w/attached underplate, #40 .... 42.00
Jam jar, #125 .... 80.00
Jam jar & ladle, #125 .... 100.00
Jug, milk; #100, 1-qt, 5⅝″ 135.00
Lemon dish, hdl, #121 .... 22.00
Mayonnaise, w/underplate & ladle, #453 .... 36.00
Mustard, hdl, #191 .... 35.00
Plate, #13, 10″ 15.00
Plate, #4, 7½″ 9.00
Plate, #8, 6½″ 7.00
Plate, #98, 8½″ 16.00
Plate, cake; #10, 9¾″ 25.00
Plate, cake; hdl, #10, 9¾″ 30.00
Plate, grill; 3 sections, #338, 10¼″ 90.00
Plate, sq, #315, 7¾″ 38.00
Platter, #17, 14″ 45.00
Platter, #186, 16″ 300.00
Platter, #56, 12″ 34.00
Pot, demitasse; #183 .... 425.00
Refreshment set, 2-pc, #39 .... 35.00
Relish, #194, 8½″ 45.00
Relish, twin, loop hdls, rare, #450 .... 250.00
Relish, 2-part, #171, 8½x4¾″ 42.00
Relish, 4-part, #19, 10″ 95.00
Shakers, bulbous, #89, 3″, pr 22.00
Shakers, ind, #126, 2½″, pr 20.00
Shakers, tapered, #11, pr 18.00
Shell dish 200.00
Spoon holder, #189, 8″ 65.00
Syrup, #97 .... 50.00
Tea tile, #169, 6″ 44.00
Teapot, #15, 4½″ 70.00
Teapot, gold finial, #400 .... 360.00
Tray, #14 .... 10.00
Vase, bulbous, rare, #452, 6½″ 900.00
Vase, fan, dtd, #187 .... 120.00

Miscellaneous

Ash tray, flower medallions, cobalt trim 30.00
Ash tray, Indian in full headdress, raised tracing 100.00
Basket, Tree in Meadow, Dolly Varden #213 .... 65.00
Basket, 2 sections w/floral bouquet, gr sides, hdls, 4x8″ 35.00
Bottle, scent; Spanish dancer, flower finial, 6″ 125.00
Bowl, blk matt scene, gold lustre, gr #2, 11″ 110.00
Bowl, chestnut design, earth tones on bisque, gr #2, 6″ 42.00
Bowl, chestnut shaped, beaded hdls, gr #2, 4″ 35.00
Bowl, Deco, floral, purple, b/w striped border, 8½″ 30.00
Bowl, Deco medallion, yel/rust on wht, pierced hdls, 6½″ 30.00
Bowl, lav int w/cerise & yel flowers, 8-sided, #2 .... 57.00
Bowl, river/field/mountains/cottage, orange trim, hdls, 8″ 40.00
Bowl, scenic, floral motif, 2 pierced hdls, 8″ 25.00
Bowl, scenic, lake w/sunset, 3-ftd, 5½″ 20.00
Bowl, swans & ships, 3-ftd, w/9″ underplate, gr #2, 7″ 80.00
Bowl, walnut, blown-out, ball ftd, sgn, 7½″ 52.00
Bowl, 4 roses in oval medallions, Deco border, hdls, 8½″ 40.00
Box, dresser; doll figural, gold, 5½″ 175.00
Box, powder; full figure bird, 2-pc, red #2, 3¾″ 225.00
Cake plate, flower basket on orange, 2-hdl, red #2, 10″ 28.00
Cake plate, Madonna & child portrait, 2-hdl, gr #2, 11″ 120.00
Cake plate, Tree in Meadow, open hdls 25.00
Candle holder, birds & flowers on cream, red #2, pr 64.00
Celery dish+6 ind salts, bl/yel floral, gr wreath mk 55.00
Chalice, Spanish galleon/waves, gold/orange sails, gr #2, 6″ 145.00
Chocolate set, yel w/pink & wht flowers, +6 c/s, #1 .... 125.00
Cigarette jar, clown, w/lid, gr #2, 5″ 100.00
Compote, HP fruit, blk, 2-pc 200.00
Condiment set on tray, Tree in Meadow 27.00
Creamer & sugar, Chinese pheasant finial, floral band 65.00
Creamer & sugar, orange flowers, gr birds, gr #2 .... 58.00
Dealer's sign, gold #3, 3x6½″ 27.50
Demitasse set, b/w geometric design, gold lustre, 13-pc 175.00
Dinner set, Tree in Meadow, 86-pc 1,695.00
Dish, cheese; Occupied Japan, gold/wht, slanted, #175 .... 150.00
Dish, full figure nightengale, bl/pearl, oval, gr #2, 7″ 300.00
Figurine, fish, 8″ 45.00
Hatpin holder, lady figural, gr #2, 4½″ 145.00
Humidor, owl shape & mold, gr #2 .... 350.00
Humidor, Tree in Meadow 260.00
Jam jar, bl scenic bisque decor, fruit hdl, w/underplate 48.00
Jam jar, rose finial, lustre finish, w/underplate & ladle 45.00
Lemon dish, orange flower, bl lustre 18.00
Match holder & striker, floral w/gr trim on wht, 3¾″ 50.00
Napkin ring, clown design 20.00
Nappy, lav swan scene, clover shaped, gr #2, 4″ 25.00
Nut bowl, squirrel on front, blown-out 200.00
Nut set, chestnut decor, sq w/rolled-in sides, 7-pc 65.00
Nut set, gold/wht, lg master+4 sm bowls, #16034 .... 90.00
Plate, Art Deco, man & woman fishing, castle, 9½″ 75.00
Salt dip, gold/wht, #16034 .... 18.00
Salt dip, rose figural, 2¼″ base 20.00

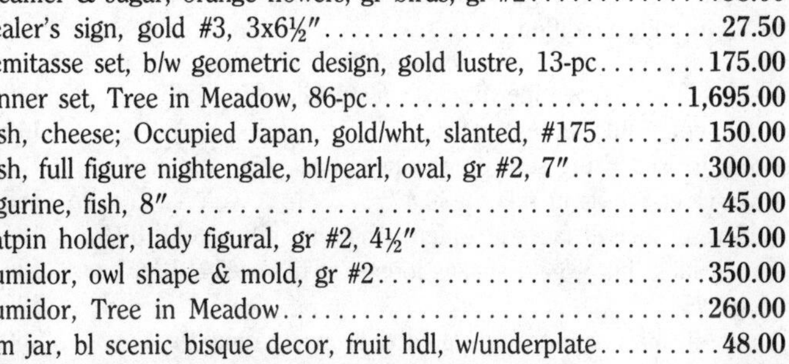

Night light, owl figural, green mark, 7½″, $800.00.

Spoon holder, floral decor, 2-hdl, red #2, 8″ 42.00
Sugar shaker, bird on swing, lustre 32.00
Tea set, basket of fruit design, bird finial, 6″ pot, 3-pc 125.00
Tea set, Tree in Meadow, 3-pc 70.00
Vase, autumn, ruffled top, gold hdls, 6½″ 45.00
Vase, basket; leaves, walnuts w/in, bl lustre, hdls, 6½″ 50.00
Vase, orange w/blk trim, gr #2, 4″ 37.00
Vase, pink/yel roses, gr leaves on wht, 2 gold hdls, 8″ 100.00
Vase, stream & fall trees, cobalt/much gold, spoke mk, 12″ 300.00
Vase, stylized gold outlined flowers, beige, gr #2, 7½″ 55.00
Vase, swan, lake, cottage, sunset, cobalt w/gold, 2-hdl, 5″ 95.00
Vase, yel roses on wht, gold trim & hdls, 8½″ 80.00
Wall pocket, figural bird perched on edge, gr #2, 9″ 175.00
Wall pocket, flowers, bee & butterfly, tan lustre, 5″ 45.00

Norse

The Norse Pottery was established in 1903 in Edgerton, Wisconsin, by Thorwald Sampson and Louis Ipson. A year later it was purchased by A.W. Wheelock and moved to Rockford, Illinois. The ware they produced was inspired by ancient bronze vessels of the Norsemen. Designs were often incised into the red clay body, dragon handles and feet were favored decorative devices, and they achieved a semblance of patina through the application of metallic glazes. The ware was marked with a stylized 'N' containing a vertical arrangement of the remaining letters of the name. Production ceased after 1913.

When no condition is indicated, the items listed below are assumed to be in mint condition.

Bowl, allover serpentine designs, gr on blk, #70, 4x7″ 120.00
Bowl, effigy ftd, serpent hdls 145.00
Bowl, incised rising sun, dragon head hdls, #50, rpr 125.00
Bowl vase, 8 owls in relief, #30-4″ 165.00
Bud vase, incised faces at widened bottom, blk w/gold, 6½″ 135.00
Candlestick, blk w/gold snakes looped at base, #54, 12″, pr 135.00
Mug, #51 . . . . 135.00
Tankard, mask spout, blk w/gold & bronze patina, 9x8″ 260.00
Vase, imp decor on bottom, gold rim/base, blk, 9¼″ 135.00
Vase, incised design, 9″ 150.00
Vase, lizard figural on side, metallic patina, 11½″ 450.00
Vase, zigzag pattern, gold on blk, #45, 4½″ 95.00

Bowl, effigy feet, serpent handles, incised, 4½″ x 7½″, $145.00.

North Dakota School of Mines

The School of Mines of the University of North Dakota was established in 1890, but due to a lack of funding, it was not until 1898 that Earle J. Babcock was appointed as Director and efforts were made to produce ware from the native clay he had discovered several years earlier. The first pieces were made by firms in the east from the clay Babcock sent them. Some of the ware was decorated by the manufacturer; some was shipped back to North Dakota to be decorated by native artists. By 1909, students at the University of North Dakota were producing utilitarian items--tile, brick, shingles, etc.--in conjunction with a ceramic course offered through the Chemistry Department. By 1910, a ceramic department had been established, supervised by Margaret Kelly Cable. Under her leadership, fine artware was produced. Native flowers, grains, buffaloes, cowboys, and other subjects indigenous to the state were incorporated into the decorations. Some pieces have an Art Nouveau--Art Deco style easily attributedto her association with Frederick H. Rhead, with whom she studied in 1911. During the twenties the pottery was marketed on a limited scale through gift and jewelry stores in the state. From 1927 until 1949, when Miss Cable announced her retirement, a more widespread distribution was maintained, with sales branching out into other states. The ware was marked in cobalt with the official seal--'Made at School of Mines, N.D. Clay, University of North Dakota, Grand Forks, N.D.'--in a circle. Very early ware was sometimes marked 'U.N.D.' in cobalt by hand.

When no condition is indicated, the items listed below are assumed to be in mint condition.

Bowl, blk Indian type design, Bentonite glaze, 3½x4½″ 325.00
Bowl, carved turkeys, gr/brn, #160, J Mattson, 3½x4″ 275.00
Bowl, gr & brn, EMK, Nov 25, 1926, sm 75.00
Bowl, gr w/bl drip, 3″ 60.00
Bowl, row of carved farm wives, gr/brn, Cable, Hovell, 4″ 350.00
Creamer & sugar, turq, #52 . . . . 63.00
Custard cup, 6 colored bands 60.00
Figurine, horse, terra cotta, sgn JTT, 6″ 125.00
Lamp, glossy brn, sgn, 3-pc 155.00
Paperweight, Parent's Day, 1940 . . . . 75.00
Pitcher, gr salt glaze, sgn JM & stamp, 22-oz, 5″ 60.00
Rose bowl, matt beige/carved, att Margaret Cable, 3x4½″ 350.00
Tile, carved scenic, 6-color, Mattson, 1928 . . . . 450.00
Tile, Norwegian girl, sgn JM & stamp, 4½″ 130.00
Tile, Parent's Day, dtd June, 1940, turq, 3½″ 90.00
Tray, Indian profile, sgn Laura Taylor & 'H,' orange, 5¼″ 95.00
Vase, bl gloss, 4½″ 45.00
Vase, brn & tan, Mattson, 8½″ 125.00
Vase, carved Indians on horsebk, Mattson, 9″ 525.00
Vase, dk bl, #264, 3″ 55.00
Vase, dk gr matt, 7″ 125.00
Vase, floral, lt gr gloss w/brn flecks, 4″ 160.00

Vase, oxen and covered wagon incised on celadon green, signed Huck, 3¾″ x 4½″, $95.00.

Vase, flowers & buds, incised, gr & bl glaze, R Allen, 7x7″....325.00
Vase, gingerbread men alternate w/flowers, Laign, 3¾″........140.00
Vase, gray w/bl & gr decor, ink mk/incised sgn, 6½″..........160.00
Vase, incised leaves, 6½x7″..........250.00
Vase, incised rings, gr, Cable, 7″..........115.00
Vase, incised wheat on glossy bl, sgn Huck, 4″..........165.00
Vase, leaves/vines on central band, gr matt, LM Barlow, 5″....165.00
Vase, line & dot incising, wht w/lt bl, Nouyum, 1950, 3″.......70.00
Vase, red to bl gloss, artist sgn, 3¾″..........45.00
Vase, shaded matt gr w/brn speckles, C22/1938, 6½″..........80.00
Vase, teardrops imp, orange gloss, EG, U-form, 2″..........45.00
Vase, yel matt, early UND mk, 3″..........60.00
Vase, 3 incised floral panels, dk bl/med bl, Huck, 3¾″........165.00

Northwood

The Northwood Company was founded in 1896 in Indiana, Pennsylvania, by Harry Northwood, whose father, John, was the art director for Stevens and Williams, an English glassworks. Harry Northwood joined the National Glass Company in 1899, but in 1901 again became an independent contractor, and formed the Harry Northwood Glass Company of Wheeling, West Virginia. He marketed his first carnival glass in 1908, and it became his most popular product. His company was also famous for its custard, goofus, and pressed glass. Northwood died in 1923, and the company closed.

When no condition is indicated, the items listed below are assumed to be in mint condition. See also Carnival; Custard; Goofus; Opalescent; Pattern Glass

Berry set, Cherry Lattice, 7-pc..........100.00
Bowl, Grape Frieze, emerald gr w/gold, 3-ftd, 10½″..........100.00
Bowl, Grape w/Thumbprints, clear w/stain, master berry........45.00
Bowl, Leaf & Beads, twig ftd, wht opal..........29.00
Bowl, Royal Ivy, rubena clear, sm berry..........32.00
Bowl, Royal Ivy, rubena clear, 8″..........95.00
Butter dish, Cherry Lattice..........100.00
Butter dish, Near Cut, clear, w/lid..........75.00
Butter dish, Peach, gr, G gold..........225.00
Butter dish, Royal Ivy, rubena clear..........280.00
Butter dish, Royal Oak, rubena clear..........190.00
Butter dish, Royal Oak, rubena frosted..........215.00
Celery, Ribbed Pillar, pink/wht satin spatter..........80.00
Creamer, Marigold, raspberry, N mk..........125.00
Creamer, Peach, gr, G gold..........145.00
Creamer, Royal Ivy, rubena frosted..........170.00
Creamer, Royal Oak, clear frosted..........90.00
Cruet, Royal Ivy, rubena clear..........275.00
Jar, Leaf Umbrella, mauve cased, no lid, 5x5″..........75.00
Mug, Fisherman's, custard w/gold & enamel decor..........95.00
Novelty, town pump & trough, vaseline opal..........195.00
Pickle castor, Royal Ivy, rainbow cased, ftd fr, w/tongs........350.00
Pickle castor, Royal Ivy, satin crackle, complete..........265.00
Pitcher, water; Cherry Thumbprint, clear, w/EX color, N mk....95.00
Pitcher, water; Leaf Umbrella, cranberry..........280.00
Pitcher, water; Leaf Umbrella, glossy yel..........340.00
Pitcher, water; Leaf Umbrella, mauve..........360.00
Pitcher, water; Peach, gr, G gold..........195.00
Pitcher, water; Royal Ivy, clear frosted..........130.00
Pitcher, water; Royal Ivy, rubena frosted..........235.00
Pitcher, water; Royal Oak, clear frosted..........100.00
Pitcher, water; Royal Oak, rubena clear..........250.00
Pitcher, water; Royal Oak, rubena frosted..........350.00
Rose bowl, Royal Ivy, cranberry..........95.00
Rose bowl, Royal Ivy, pink & yel spatter..........100.00
Rose bowl, Royal Ivy, rubena frosted..........95.00
Sauce dish, Royal Oak, clear frosted, 4″..........13.00
Sauce dish, Royal Oak, rainbow, 3¾″..........22.00
Spooner, Cherry & Plum..........55.00
Spooner, Royal Ivy, rubena frosted..........75.00
Sugar bowl, Peach, gr, G gold..........165.00
Sugar bowl, Royal Ivy, clear frosted, w/lid..........65.00
Sugar shaker, Royal Ivy, clear frosted..........75.00
Sugar shaker, Royal Ivy, rubena frosted..........175.00

Royal Oak salt and pepper shakers, rubena, 2¾″, $125.00 for the pair.

Syrup, Leaf Umbrella, cranberry..........325.00
Syrup, Leaf Umbrella, vaseline spatter..........345.00
Toothpick holder, Royal Ivy, rubena frosted..........126.00
Toothpick holder, Royal Oak, rubena clear..........100.00
Tumbler, Leaf Umbrella, pink spatter..........37.00
Tumbler, Royal Ivy, satin crackle..........50.00
Tumbler, Royal Oak, rubena frosted..........80.00
Vase, bl opal, ribbed, 11″..........40.00
Vase, corn motif, vaseline opal..........58.00
Water set, Apple Blossom, 7-pc..........285.00
Water set, Cherry & Lattice, gold decor, 7-pc..........325.00
Water set, gr w/enamel floral, pleated-top pitcher, 7-pc........250.00
Water set, Grape w/Gothic Arch, gr w/EX gold, 7-pc..........275.00
Water set, Oriental Poppy, gr w/gold decor, 7-pc..........325.00
Water set, purple flower w/gold leaves, 7-pc..........280.00
Whimsey, shoe, pull-up, red-brn/wht, rigaree/leaves, 3x5½″.....135.00

Nutcrackers

The nutcracker, though a strictly functional tool, is a good example of one to which man has applied ingenuity, imagination, and engineering skills. Though all were designed to accomplish the same end, hundreds of types exist in almost every material sturdy enough to withstand sufficient pressure to crack the nut. Figurals are popular collectibles, as are those with unusual design and construction.

When no condition is indicated, the items listed below are assumed to be in excellent condition.

Alligator, brass, China, 8½″..........32.00
Alligator, CI, much detail, 16″, EX..........100.00
Bird, brass, 5″ L..........9.00
Dog, cast steel, LA Althoff Mfg, 5¾″..........45.00
Dog, CI, made in Atlanta..........50.00
Dog, CI, wood base, no mk..........50.00
Dog on base, bronze, LA Althoff & Co, EX..........110.00
Dog's head, CI, G..........60.00
Elephant, CI, orig pnt, 1920s, 5x10″..........70.00

Lady's legs, brass, well modeled, 4½″ 35.00
Man's face, hand carved, EX detail, 9″ 65.00
Parrot, CI w/mc pnt, tail feather lever, 5¾″ 85.00
Punch & Judy, heavy brass 45.00
Rooster's head, brass, lg 15.00
Squirrel Cracker, CI, pat 1913, Tyler TX/Chicago 20.00
Squirrel on leaf, blk pnt CI 35.00
St Bernard, CI 60.00

Occupied Japan

Items marked 'Occupied Japan' have become popular collectibles in the last few years. They were produced during the period from the end of World War II until April 18, 1952, when the occupation ended. By no means was all of the ware exported during that time marked 'Occupied Japan'--some was marked 'Japan,' or 'Made In Japan.' It is thought that because of the natural resentment felt by the Japanese toward the occupation, only a fraction of these wares carried the 'Occupied' mark. Even though you may find identical 'Japan' marked items, because of its limited use, only those with the 'Occupied Japan' mark are being collected to any great extent.

This year we were assisted in our listings by the Occupied Japan Club, whose mailing address may be found in the Directory under 'Clubs, Newsletters, and Catalogues.'

When no condition is indicated, the items listed below are assumed to be in mint condition.

Ash tray, Blk boy & laundry 25.00
Ash tray, cowboy, silver 7.00
Ash tray, donkey, 3½″ 12.00
Ash tray, Indian paddling canoe, 4¼x2½″ 12.00
Basket, w/bunny, bl/yel 10.00
Bookends, boy & girl, miniature 35.00
Bowl, chocolate kiss shape, beige stripes, w/lid, 6x5¾″ 34.00
Bowl, Crown Derby-type decor, scalloped, Hokutosha, 8″ 50.00
Box, jewelry; grand piano, metal, silk lining, 5x3x2″ 19.00
Box, pin; heart shape, Niagara Falls 12.00
Bud vase, cherubs play tuba, 3½″, pr 22.50
Coaster, metal, red w/design 18.00
Coaster set, donkey pulling cart 18.00
Cornucopia, pink roses, bisque, 4x7″ 35.00
Cottage, for fish bowl 9.00
Creamer, cow 22.50
Creamer & sugar, metal, w/tray 15.00
Cup & saucer, demitasse; bl/yel leaves, gold traced, ftd 35.00
Cup & saucer, demitasse; floral on ea pc 15.00
Cup & saucer, demitasse; scenic 15.00
Cup & saucer, demitasse; violets 15.00
Cup & saucer, demitasse; yel lily, gr twig hdl 15.00

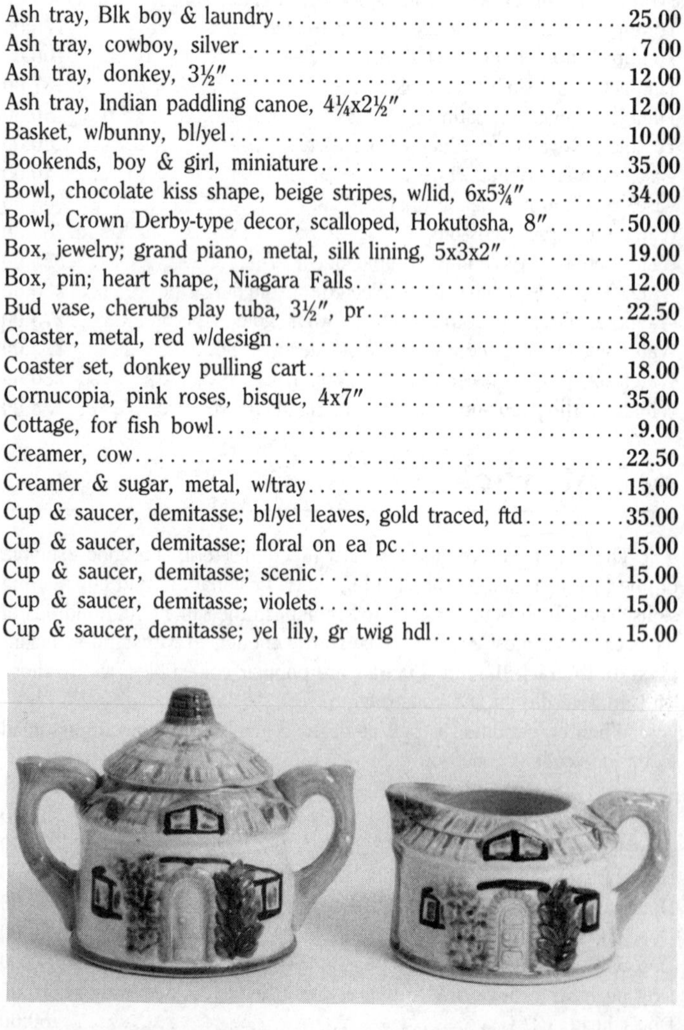

Creamer and sugar bowl, cottage figural, sugar bowl 4½″, $25.00.

Cup & saucer, dragon ware, orange lustre, gold trim 18.00
Dish, HP & gold decor on bl, Kusumoto, sq, 4″ 16.00
Doll, bisque baby, movable arms & legs, 3″ 30.00
Figurine, Am girl w/muff/coat/hat, sgn Maruyama, 8½″ 75.00
Figurine, angel w/star & violin, 2″ 7.50
Figurine, ballet dancer, applied lace tutu/flowers, 3⅝″ 9.00
Figurine, balloon man & seated woman, 3½″, pr 25.00
Figurine, bird, tan body, red head, blk tail, 2¼x3″ 8.00
Figurine, Blk accordion player, 5″ 15.00
Figurine, Blk boy w/shoeshine kit 22.00
Figurine, Blk horn player, 2¾″ 10.00
Figurine, boy in turban, platter of fish in hands, 4″ 10.00
Figurine, boy playing drum & cymbal, bisque, 4½″ 16.00
Figurine, boy seated w/dog & violin, 2½″ 7.50
Figurine, boy w/bird, girl w/fruit basket, bisque, 8″, pr 45.00
Figurine, boy w/broken watering can, EX quality 40.00
Figurine, boy w/concertina, 5″ 15.00
Figurine, boy w/trumpet, 6x7″ 55.00
Figurine, bust, applied lace collar, pnt face, 4⅜″ 14.00
Figurine, carnival doll, celluloid, 12″ 36.00
Figurine, chef holding wine bottle & glass, 3″ bell 22.00
Figurine, cherub w/wings playing flute, bisque, 6¼″ 40.00
Figurine, Colonial couple, he w/mandolin, oval base, 6″ 40.00
Figurine, Colonial man, 11″ 30.00
Figurine, Colonial man, 8″ 20.00
Figurine, Colonial man & lady, Orion China, 10″, pr 45.00
Figurine, Colonial man w/rose, 9½″ 35.00
Figurine, dog, terrier in gr cap, smoking pipe, 3½″ 8.00
Figurine, frog, gr leaf tie, sitting, 2¼x3¾″ 10.00
Figurine, gent, medieval outfit, red cape, 3½″ 7.50
Figurine, gent, w/red coat & flower in hand, 6″ 12.00
Figurine, Giesha girls, cobalt/red/wht clothes, 5¼″, pr 25.00
Figurine, girl feeding goose, 2½″ 7.50
Figurine, girl standing by fence, bisque, 9½″ 36.00
Figurine, Grandpa, whittled look, smokes pipe, cane, 4″ 15.00
Figurine, Hummel-style boy by planter playing violin, 5″ 14.00
Figurine, Hummel-style girl on fence w/banjo, 4″ 12.00
Figurine, Indian chief, 6″ 22.00
Figurine, lady, stands among flowers, bisque, 6″ 20.00
Figurine, lady, Victorian, bl, 4″ 8.00
Figurine, lady in summer dress w/2 Russian wolfhounds, 6½″ 68.00
Figurine, lady w/harpsichord, 2-pc, 3x2½″ 15.00
Figurine, lady w/parasol, Delft, 8″ 20.00
Figurine, man & lady hold bird & rabbit, gold trim, 9″, pr 50.00
Figurine, man in cape holding lute, 4″ 10.00
Figurine, Mary Poppins, holds edge of skirt up, mc, 4″ 10.00
Figurine, Mexican bandit, carrying shotgun, bisque, 6¼″ 22.00
Figurine, Oriental girl, holding yel flower, bisque, 4⅜″ 12.00
Figurine, parrot, 3″ 9.00
Figurine, shepherd, holds silver horn, bisque, 6¼″ 18.00
Figurine, squaw, headband, feathers, long braids, 4″ 8.50
Kaleidoscope 7.50
Lamp, Colonial couple, bisque, 10″ 45.00
Lamp, Colonial couple, 8″ 38.00
Lighter, camera on tripod 25.00
Match holder, dbl bisque figures, wall mt, sgn, 4x6″ 75.00
Mug, bulldog, 2¼″ 15.00
Planter, boy w/dog, 4½″ 12.00
Planter, donkey, dbl 18.00
Planter, Dutch children, 3¼x2½″ 10.00
Planter, gingham cat, 5¾″ 22.00
Planter, girl/boy w/schoolbook, bisque/pastel/gold, 6″, pr 45.00
Planter, Hummel-style girl playing accordion 14.00
Planter, zebra, 3″ 8.00

Plaque, shepherd couple, seated, in relief, oval, 14x11″........90.00
Plate, lovers in country, fancy borders, HP Andrea, 9″, pr......55.00
Shakers, Blk chef, 5″, pr........20.00
Shakers, boy & girl, seated, boy plays concertina, pr........15.00
Shakers, coffee pot set w/tray, metal/celluloid, pr........18.00
Shakers, ducks, orig box, mc, 2¼″, pr........9.00
Shakers, Indians, mc headdress, 3″, pr........11.00
Shakers, kitten & book, 3″, pr........18.00
Shakers, puppy, pr........6.50
Shakers, Senor & Senorita, colorful serape, 3¼″, pr........14.00
Shakers, tomato, w/tray, pr........14.00
Sheet & pr pillowcases, embroidered, w/label........35.00
Shelf sitter, sm Blk girl, w/wooden bench, 3½″........19.00
Stein, hdl, 6¼″........20.00
Sugar bowl, beehive, mk........20.00
Sugar bowl, windmill, bl roof, gr trees, w/lid, 4¼″........12.00
Tea set, demitasse; moriage slip-trail dragon, for 4........100.00
Teapot, brn w/pink flowers, sm........15.00
Teapot, demitasse; mc floral sprays, gold trim, 7¾″........20.00
Teapot, dk brn w/pink flower, ind........18.00
Teapot, floral, leaves, gold trim, w/lid, 4″........10.00
Toby mug, MacArthur, lg........65.00
Toby mug, man winking, 3½″........10.00
Toothpick holder, lady portrait medallion, Sevres type, 3″......10.00
Toothpick holder, nude girl, lustre colors, 3″........10.00
Toothpick holder, rabbits at base, bl, trumpet shape, pr........12.00
Tray, lacquer ware, blk, 10x16″........30.00
Tray, street vendor, holds doll, 7½″........50.00
Vase, Boy Scout, carrying umbrella, brn hat/knapsack, 4″.......10.00
Vase, cherubs w/flowers, flared, gold trim, 5″........15.00
Vase, cowgirl, gr hat, red vest, yel skirt, holster, 6″........11.00
Vase, floral w/gr background, 2½″........7.00
Vase, Hummel girl, holds basket & flower, bl dress, 3″........9.00
Vase, metal, ribs/scrolls/medallions, 6½″........32.00
Vase, moriage, 4½″, pr........16.00
Vase, triple log w/bluebirds........12.00
Wall pocket, Colonial lady in balcony, 4x2¾″........20.00
Wall pocket, mallard duck, dives in water, high relief........12.00

Ohr, George

George Ohr established his pottery around 1893 in Biloxi, Mississippi. The unusual style of the ware he produced, and his flamboyant personality earned him the dubious title of 'the mad potter of Biloxi.' Though acclaimed by some of the critics of his day to be perhaps the most accomplished thrower in the history of the industry, others overlooked the eggshell-thin walls of his vessels, each a different shape and contortion, and saw only that their 'tortured' appearance contradicted their own sedate preferences.

Ohr worked by himself with only minimal help from his son. His work was typically pinched and pulled, pleated, crumpled, dented, and folded. Lizards and worms were often applied to the ware, each with detailed, expressive features. He was well recognized, however, for his glazes, especially those with a metallic patina.

The ware was marked with his name, alone or with 'Biloxi' added. Ohr died in 1918.

When no condition is indicated, the items listed below are assumed to be in mint condition.

Bowl, purple/orange specks, pinched-top corset, sgn, 3½″......285.00
Candlestick, dk/lt gr mottle, ring-trn std, sgn, 3⅞″........160.00
Candlestick, gunmetal, pleated twist/2 odd hdls, unsgn, 5″.....420.00
Chamber pot, med gr to gunmetal, novelty, 2¼″........250.00
Cup, ash gray volcanic glaze, 3⅜″........150.00
Mug, brn metallic crystal/silver flecks, rust w/in, mk, 5″.......375.00
Mug, gr band on yel mottle, angle hdl, sgn, 4¾″........340.00
Mug, gr/gray splotched, hdl on concave bottom section, 4¾″...245.00
Mug, matt red/gr, crumpled angular hdl, GE Ohr, 4¼″........605.00
Pitcher, gray metallic, pinched, pointed hdl, imp mk, 4¾″.....375.00
Puzzle mug, gr/brn, leaf hdl, reticulated under lip, 3½″.......300.00
Vase, bl on pink, brn w/in, bulbous/crumpled lip, sgn, 4½″.....385.00
Vase, blk/brn, pinched, die stamp mk, 5½x4¼″........225.00
Vase, brn w/irregular red/blk dots, full bottom, 5½x2½″.......295.00
Vase, chocolate to blk, crimped, incised lines, 3½″........365.00
Vase, dk gr, lg lumps of crystals, crimped, sgn, 4¼″........295.00
Vase, dk red/lt red bk, sanded, twists/pleats/t'print, 4″........500.00
Vase, gr mottle, ruffled, swollen w/pinch sides, sgn, 5″........430.00
Vase, gr spotted, flared w/twist neck, incised center, 4¾″......725.00
Vase, lt brn speckled, pleated/twisted waist, sgn, 3⅝″........390.00
Vase, med/dk bl matt, bottle form, die-stamp mk, 5½x2″......125.00
Vase, metallic purple/bl, gr on gr dots w/in, 3-pinch, 3″.......325.00
Vase, metallic silver/blk, twist/crimp top, stamp mk, 4x4″......325.00
Vase, mottle red/turq/mustard, crimped, die-stamp, cabinet.....500.00
Vase, rust/gray gloss, rnd, sgn, 4x3″........295.00
Vase, speckled gloss, gr/brn/yel in glaze, 4½″........220.00
Vase, spotted rust to gr/brn to rust, slim ogee form, 5½″......335.00
Vase, yel w/gr lustre spatters, free-form, imp mk, 2¾″........210.00

Vase, high gloss green and yellow flambe, central twist, ribbed, footed base, signed, 4½″, $1,500.00.

Old Ivory

Old Ivory dinnerware was produced during the late 1800s in Selesia. The patterns are referred to by the numbers stamped on the bottom of each piece. The mark sometimes includes a crown, and the name 'Selesia.'

When no condition is indicated, the items listed below are assumed to be in mint condition.

Berry set, #83, 7-pc........340.00
Berry set, #84, 9½″ master; +six 5″ ind........185.00
Berry set, Englantine, 9½″ master+4 ind........140.00
Berry set, VII, 7-pc........175.00
Bonbon, #75, inside hdl, 6½″........95.00
Bouillon cup & saucer, #75........90.00
Bowl, #11, Chloron, master berry........65.00

Bowl, #16, 10″ 70.00
Bowl, #82, 9½″ 75.00
Bowl, #84, tab hdl, 6″ 55.00
Buffet server, ind; #200 .... 70.00
Cake plate, #11, open hdl, 10½″ 85.00
Cake plate, #16, pierced hdls, 10″ 60.00
Cake plate, #22 (Holly), pierced hdls, 10″ 225.00
Cake plate, #28, 10″ 65.00
Cake plate, #84 .... 80.00
Cake set, #84, pierced hdls, 10¼″; +six 6″ plates 175.00
Celery tray, #11, Clarion, 11¾x6″ 46.00
Celery tray, #16 .... 70.00
Celery tray, #75, 11½x5½″ 85.00
Chocolate pot, #75 .... 300.00
Creamer & sugar bowl, #28 .... 100.00
Creamer & sugar bowl, #84 .... 110.00
Cup & saucer, #15 .... 42.00
Cup & saucer, #16 .... 52.00
Cup & saucer, #200 .... 38.00
Cup & saucer, #202 .... 35.00
Cup & saucer, chocolate; #84 .... 45.00
Cup & saucer, demitasse; #15 .... 45.00
Pickle relish, #16, oval, 6½x4¾″ 32.00
Pickle relish, #200 .... 55.00
Pickle relish, #84, rectangular, 6½x4½″ 32.00
Pickle relish, #84, 7¾″ 65.00
Plate, #11, 7½″ 20.00
Plate, #11, 8½″ 30.00
Plate, #16, 6¼″ 18.00
Plate, #16, 6¾″, set of 6 .... 120.00
Plate, #16, 7½″ 23.00
Plate, #200, 6″ 16.00
Plate, #200, 8¼″ 28.00
Plate, #28, 7¾″ 23.00
Plate, #75, 6½″ 27.00
Plate, #84, 6″ 25.00
Plate, #84, 7¾″ 35.50
Plate, #84, 8¼″ 45.00
Platter, #84, 13½″ 150.00
Shakers, #15, pr 75.00
Shakers, #16, pr 75.00
Shakers, #75, pr 75.00

Plate, #22, Holly, 7¾″, $40.00.

Shakers, #84, pr 85.00
Sugar bowl, #28 .... 60.00
Toothpick, #16, barrel shape 195.00
Toothpick, #75 .... 150.00
Tray, dresser; #84, 12x7″ 130.00
Waste bowl, #84, interior decor, 3x5¾″ 75.00

Old Paris

Old Paris porcelains were made from the late 18th century until about 1900. Seldom marked, the term refers to the area of manufacture rather than a specific company. In general, the ware was of high quality, and characterized by classic shapes, colorful elegant decoration, and gold application.

When no condition is indicated, the items listed below are assumed to be in mint condition.

Cup & saucer, palace landscape on brn/gilt, ftd, 1850, 3½″ 325.00
Plate, birds, HP, gilt border, 1800s, 8¾″, set of 10″ 600.00
Teapot, mc floral on sides, much gold, 9½″ 250.00
Vase, floral spray, emb swag, ram head hdls, gilt, 19″, pr 500.00
Vase, French lady w/binoculars on pink, ped ft, 8¾″ 90.00

Vases, each with half portrait of rustic maiden on white ground, gilt trim, minor restoration, 18⅝″, $600.00 for the pair.

Old Sleepy Eye

Old Sleepy Eye was a Sioux Indian Chief who was born in Minnesota in 1780. His name was used for the name of a town, as well as a flour mill. The Sleepy Eye Milling Company, of Sleepy Eye, Minnesota, contracted the Weir Pottery Company of Monmouth, Illinois, to make steins, vases, salt crocks, and butter tubs which the company gave away to their customers in each bag of their flour. A bust profile of the old Indian and his name decorated each piece of the blue and gray stoneware. In addition to these four items, the Minnesota Stoneware Company of Red Wing made a mug with a verse which is very scarce today.

In 1906, Weir Pottery merged with six others to form the Western Stoneware Company in Monmouth. They produced a line of blue and white ware using a lighter body, but these pieces were never given as flour premiums. This line consisted of pitchers (five sizes), steins, mugs, sugar bowls, vases, trivets, and mustache cups. These pieces turn up only rarely in other colors and are highly sought by advanced collectors.

Advertising items, such as trade cards, pillow tops, thermometers, paperweights, letter openers, postcards, cookbooks, and thimbles are considered very valuable.

The original ware was made sporadically until 1937. Brown steins and mugs were produced in 1952.

When no condition is indicated, the items listed below are assumed to be in mint condition.

Calendar, 1904, $250.00.

Breadboard scraper, 5x6″ 450.00
Butter crock, Flemish 425.00
Calendar, 1903 .... 250.00
Cookbook, loaf of bread 250.00
Cookbook, sq 250.00
Fan, die-cut, portrait, wheat in headband 165.00
Flour sack, paper, 5-lb 175.00
Flour sack, yel cloth 275.00
Letter opener, bronze 900.00
Match holder, all wht 800.00
Match holder, pnt 1,500.00
Mirror, 1940s 15.00
Mug, verse, sgn Red Wing 1,250.00
Mug, wht & cobalt, 4¼″ 175.00
Paperweight, bronze plated 500.00
Pillow top, Monroe at Washington 650.00
Pillow top, trademark head in center 650.00
Pin-back button, recent 6.50
Pitcher, #1 .... 250.00
Pitcher, #2 .... 300.00
Pitcher, #3 .... 350.00
Pitcher, #4 .... 400.00
Pitcher, #5 .... 450.00
Pitcher, all gr, ½-gal 625.00
Pitcher, Indian & wigwams, flemish 1,200.00
Pitcher, yel & bl, 1-qt 990.00
Postcard 60.00
Salt crock 375.00
Sign, Chief Sleepy Eye in center oval, tin, 19¼x13½″ 1,200.00
Stein, bl & gray 450.00
Stein, bl & wht 500.00
Stein, brn, 1952 .... 360.00
Stein, cobalt 750.00
Stein, wht & brn 775.00
Stein, yel & brn 850.00
Sugar bowl, bl & wht 500.00
Teaspoon, demitasse; 3 roses in bowl 75.00
Teaspoon, Indian head hdl, snowshoe, sheaf of wheat 100.00

Vase, flemish blue and gray, $350.00.

Thimble 350.00
Vase, bl & gray, Indian head, 9″ 300.00
Vase, bl & wht 350.00

O'Neill, Rose

Rose O'Neill's Kewpies were introduced in 1909, when they were used to conclude a story in the December issue of *Ladies' Home Journal*. They were an immediate success, and soon Kewpie dolls were being produced world-wide. German manufacturers were among the earliest, and also used the Kewpie motif to decorate chinaware as well as other items. The Kewpie is still popular today, and can be found on products ranging from Christmas cards and cake ornaments to fabrics and wallpaper.

When no condition is indicated, the items listed below are assumed to be in mint condition.

Ash tray, standing Kewpie, marble, sgn, 5x4″ 75.00
Bell, brass Kewpie 45.00
Bell, crystal w/pink Kewpie doll hdl 28.00
Book, Kewpies, by Ruggles 45.00
Book, Lions o/t Lord, O'Neill illus, Wilson, Lothrop, 1903 .... 15.00
Book, Little Kewpie Book, sgn Rose O'Neill 10.00
Book, Needlework, w/several pg Kewpie needlework, ca 1914 .... 15.00
Book, Sing a Song of Safety, O'Neill illus 18.00
Booklet, Jell-O Girl Entertains, O'Neill illus 20.00
Bowl, 6 Kewpies, sgn, 7″ 110.00
Box, powder; Kewpie, celluloid, no lid, 5½″ 98.00
Box, powder; Kewpie, metal clip, sticker, mk France, 7½″ 185.00
Bud vase/placecard holder, bisque figural, sgn, 2½″ 300.00
Calendar, 1975, Kewpie 25.00
Candy container, glass figural, mk Germany, 3″ 45.00
Card holder, Kewpie 29.00
Christmas card, Kewpie, sgn & c, 2½x3½″ 12.00
Clock, Jasper, Kewpie, sgn Rose O'Neill, Germany, 3½″ 300.00
Creamer, Jasper, bl w/wht action Kewpie, Royal Rudolstadt 185.00
Cup & saucer, 8 action Kewpies, Rudolstadt 125.00
Display, Kewpie Garter, for Christmas 35.00
Door knocker, brass Kewpie figural 60.00
Fan, ice cream advertising, Kewpie, sgn 38.00
Flannel, butterflies, sgn 20.00
Flannel, seashore, 1914 .... 15.00
Jar, Jasper, bl/wht, sgn O'Neill, metal lid, 4″ 175.00

Kewpie, bisque, arms raised, Kewpie sticker on bk, 2" 95.00
Kewpie, bisque, fully jtd, orig sticker, mk, Bye-Lo, 4" 450.00
Kewpie, bisque, in tuxedo/high hat, stamped, orig, 1913 ....125.00
Kewpie, bisque, jtd arms, incised O'Neill, 6" 165.00
Kewpie, bisque, jtd arms, incised O'Neill on ft, 7" 175.00
Kewpie, bisque, jtd arms, sgn w/orig heart sticker, 10½" 595.00
Kewpie, bisque, jtd arms, sticker, mk on foot, 8½" 225.00
Kewpie, bisque, jtd arms, str legs, incised O'Neill, 5½" 145.00
Kewpie, bisque, jtd at hips, poseable, sgn, 6" 450.00
Kewpie, bisque, kneeling, sgn, 4" 375.00
Kewpie, bisque, molded shoes & socks, sgn on feet, 4¾" 275.00
Kewpie, bisque, orig label, dtd 1913, Japan, 4½" 85.00
Kewpie, bisque, sgn, 9", MIB 600.00
Kewpie, bisque, sitting, bug on ft, sgn, orig sticker, 3½" 400.00
Kewpie, bisque, sitting, holding pencil, 3½" 695.00
Kewpie, bisque, 2 reading book, 3½" 495.00
Kewpie, blk compo, heart decal, dressed, 1930, 11" 250.00
Kewpie, buttonhole; bisque, sgn, 2" 100.00
Kewpie, carnival chalkware 10.00
Kewpie, celluloid, arms out to side, 2¼" 20.00

Kewpie Musician, bisque, 4", $385.00.

Kewpie, celluloid, boy/girl in graduation outfit, 4½", pr 95.00
Kewpie, celluloid, movable arms, sticker, 5" 85.00
Kewpie, celluloid, Occupied Japan 75.00
Kewpie, celluloid, 2-pc knitted outfit, Irwin, 6½" 12.00
Kewpie, ceramic, w/wings, Japan 25.00
Kewpie, compo, bank, nude, sits w/arms around knees, 12" 48.00
Kewpie, compo, jtd arms, bl wings, label on chest, 11" 125.00
Kewpie, compo, movable arms, 9" 115.00
Kewpie, compo, no mk, 4½" 15.00
Kewpie, compo, on pedestal 155.00
Kewpie, compo, orig, 13" 175.00
Kewpie, compo, sgn, 11" 110.00
Kewpie, compo, 12", MIB 165.00
Kewpie, shoulder head, bsk head/shoulders, 9208/4, 3½" 375.00
Kewpie, silverplated, 5" 400.00
Kewpie Bride & Groom, celluloid, orig paper clothes, 4", EX 40.00
Kewpie Bride & Groom, compo, 10", pr 235.00
Kewpie Bride & Groom, dressed in crepe paper, Japan 110.00
Kewpie Bride & Groom w/Preacher, celluloid, 3½" 95.00
Kewpie Confederate Soldier, bisque, sgn, 3½" 275.00
Kewpie Governor, in chair, bisque, 3¾" 395.00
Kewpie Ho-Ho, sgn, sm 30.00
Kewpie Hot n' Tot, mk Kewpie, MIB 95.00
Kewpie Huggers, bisque, mk O'Neill on ft, 3¾" 175.00
Kewpie Kuddly, orig carrying case 70.00
Kewpie Negro, carved wood 45.00
Kewpie on stork, D in circle on base, sticker on bk, 4¼" 625.00
Kewpie Scholar, sitting, holding book, bisque, 4" 695.00
Kewpie Sweeper, bisque, w/trash can & broom, sgn, 5" 400.00
Kewpie Thinker, plaster, mk c 1914, 6½" 60.00
Kewpie Thinker, vinyl, mk on bk Kewpie, O'Neill, Cameo, 4" 25.00
Kewpie Traveler, w/umbrella & suitcase, bisque, 3½" 165.00
Letter opener, pewter, Kewpie figural, sgn Kewpie 59.00
Light bulb, Christmas tree; figural Kewpie 45.00
Match holder, brass figural 29.00
Match holder, pewter figural 50.00
Mug, action Kewpies, Royal Rudolstadt, 2½" 95.00
Mug, action Kewpies, Royal Rudolstadt, 3¾" 135.00
Mug, sterling, 4 Kewpies & bird, etched/chased, Mathews 390.00
Napkin ring, Kewpie, brass 39.00
Night light, bisque, sitting Kewpie, metal base, 4½" 125.00
Pamphlet, Kewpies & Little Mermaid, O'Neill, 1917, 3 pg 30.00
Paperweight, Kewpie 50.00
Perfume, Kewpie figural, clear glass w/pnt features, 3" 35.00
Planter, Kewpie boy wearing top hat, Lefton 25.00
Planter, Kewpie Thinker, bl glazed pottery, 6" 35.00
Plaque, Wedgwood Jasperware w/Kewpie, gr 65.00
Plate, Kewpie & frog transfer, Limoges 45.00
Plate, Kewpies, 1973, MIB 20.00
Plate, Wilson—Bavaria, 7", EX 95.00
Plate, 8 action Kewpies, fully mk, 9" 175.00
Plate, 9 action Kewpies, gr foliage, Rudolstadt, 7" 165.00
Plate, 9 action Kewpies, sgn O'Neill, Germany, 7¾" 90.00
Postcard, Kewpie mermaid, For Rainy Day, sgn O'Neill 25.00
Postcard, Kewpie w/frog & chick 25.00
Print, Jell-O ad, Dorothy's 5th Birthday, fr, 1920, 11x17" 35.00
Ragsy, bl, w/tag 30.00
Ring, pinky; Kewpie, 14k gold, mk 80.00
Sand pail, Kewpie & Scootles, tin, sgn, rare 150.00
Scootles, bisque, sgn on foot, rare, 4½" 400.00
Scootles, brass 95.00
Shakers, 2 Kewpies sitting w/rabbit between, china, 3", pr 750.00
Soap, Kewpie figural, MIB 65.00
Stickpin, Kewpie, celluloid, blk 65.00
Tea set, bl lustre china, Germany, miniature 90.00
Thimble, metal, mk Kewpie 35.00
Tie tac 18.50
Toothpick holder, Kewpie holding cornucopia, pewter 50.00
Tray, cloverleaf, gr Jasper w/pink Kewpies, Rudolstadt, 7" 300.00
Valentine, w/Kewpies 12.00
Wall plaque, Kewpie decor, Lefton 22.00
Wall plaque, sgn O'Neill, 8x11", set of 6 ....100.00
Whistle, Kewpie figural 18.00

Onion Pattern

The familiar pattern known to collectors as Onion acquired its name through a case of mistaken identity. Designed in the early 1700s by Johann Haroldt of the Meissen factory in Germany, the pattern was a mixture from earlier Oriental designs. One of its components was a stylized peach, which was mistaken to be an onion, causing the pattern to become known by that name. Usually found in blue, an occasional piece is also found in pink. The pattern is commonly associated with Meissen, but it has been reproduced by many others including Villeroy and Boch, and Royal Copenhagen.

When no condition is indicated, the items listed below are assumed to be in mint condition.

Bowl, Allerton, 8½" 45.00
Bowl, Blue Danube, on base, 6" 25.00

Bowl, leaf shape, hdl, Meissen, 7″ 85.00
Butter dish, Meissen 85.00
Butter pat, Meissen 20.00
Cache pot, w/underplate, X-swords, 7″ 350.00
Candle snuffer, SP hdl, Meissen, 10¼″ 60.00
Canister, Oatmeal, barrel shape, 6½″ 55.00
Canister, spice; set of 4 .... 120.00
Cheese board, no mk 35.00
Chop plate, high rim, X-swords, 11¾″ 160.00
Clothes sprinkler, flatiron shape, old 25.00
Creamer & sugar bowl, ftd, X-swords 165.00
Cup & saucer, demitasse; Meissen 35.00
Cup & saucer, X-swords 65.00
Cutting board, X-swords, 6x10″ 135.00
Dish, ftd; Blue Danube, 6″ 25.00
Feeder, baby; Meissen 45.00
Feeder, invalid 35.00
Funnel 75.00
Hot plate, Maastricht, Holland 45.00
Lemon dish, Meissen 35.00
Mustard pot w/underplate, rosebud finial, X-swords, 4¼″ 65.00
Nappy, leaf form, X-swords, 7″ 75.00

Rolling pin, marked Germany, 15″, $195.00.

Pitcher, water; X-swords, Rococo shape, Meissen, 1860s, 7″ 225.00
Plate, high rim, triangular, X-swords, 10″ 160.00
Plate, X-swords, 10½″ 70.00
Platter, Allerton, lg 65.00
Rolling pin 195.00
Sauce boat w/attached underplate, 2-hdl, X-swords 190.00
Server, shell shape, divided, w/hdl, X-swords, 12″ 300.00
Shakers, #99/83, pr 15.00
Shoe, Dutchman's, X-swords, 2¼x7″ 85.00
Soap dish, ftd, Vienna Woods 20.00
Stein, pewter lid, X-swords, 12″ 325.00
Strainer, all china 68.00
Strainer, wooden hdl 100.00
Sugar shaker, Blue Danube 20.00
Teapot, X-swords, 6-cup 325.00
Toothbrush holder, Vienna Woods, upright 20.00
Vase, ftd, X-swords, 5″ 85.00

Opalescent Glass

First made in England in 1870, opalescent glass became popular in America around the turn of the century. Its name comes from the milky white opalescent trim that defines the lines of the pattern. It was produced in table sets, novelties, toothpick holders, vases, and lamps.

When no condition is indicated, the items listed below are assumed to be in mint condition.

Alaska, bowl, berry; clear, sm 28.00
Alaska, butter dish, vaseline 250.00
Alaska, creamer, bl 65.00
Alaska, creamer, clear 32.00
Alaska, creamer, vaseline 55.00
Alaska, cruet, vaseline w/decor 200.00
Alaska, master salt, clear 25.00
Alaska, pitcher, water; vaseline 450.00
Alaska, sauce, clear 18.00
Alaska, sauce dish, vaseline 30.00
Alaska, spooner, bl 50.00
Alaska, table set, vaseline, 4-pc 495.00
Alaska, tray, celery; vaseline 110.00
Alaska, tumbler, vaseline 65.00
Arabian Nights, tumbler, bl, set of 6 .... 55.00
Argonaut Shell, bowl, berry; clear, 7″ 75.00
Argonaut Shell, bowl, bl, dome ftd, ruffled 35.00
Argonaut Shell, table set, bl, script sgn Northwood, 4-pc 895.00
Aurora Borealis, vase, bl, 6″ 30.00
Beaded Cable, rose bowl, bl, str sides 45.00
Beaded Fan, rose bowl, clear 35.00
Beaded Ovals & Holly, spooner, clear 65.00
Beads & Bark, vase, gr 55.00
Beatty Honeycomb, punch cup, clear, 3¼″ 30.00
Beatty Rib, berry set, clear, 7-pc 95.00
Beatty Rib, bowl, bl, 9″ 55.00
Beatty Rib, bowl, clear, shallow, 8″ 50.00
Beatty Rib, butter dish, clear 40.00
Beatty Rib, celery, bl 42.00
Beatty Rib, celery, clear 45.00
Beatty Rib, creamer, bl 45.00
Beatty Rib, finger/waste bowl, bl 30.00
Beatty Rib, mug, bl 38.00
Beatty Rib, toothpick holder, bl 34.00
Beatty Rib, toothpick holder, clear 23.00
Beatty Swirl, bowl, clear, shallow, 8″ 50.00
Beatty Swirl, bowl, master berry; clear 40.00
Beatty Swirl, butter dish, bl 150.00
Beatty Swirl, butter dish, clear 150.00
Beatty Swirl, creamer, clear, 5″ 40.00
Beatty Swirl, pitcher, water; bl 165.00
Beatty Swirl, syrup, bl, rare 200.00
Beatty Swirl, tray, water; clear 90.00
Beatty Swirl, tray, water; vaseline 55.00
Beatty Waffle, creamer, bl, 3¼″ 30.00
Beatty Waffle, creamer, clear, 3″ 20.00
Block & Flower Band, bowl, triangular, 5½″ 20.00
Blossom & Webb, bowl, clear, ruffled, collar base, 8½″ 20.00
Bowl, flashed rainbow opal w/enamel florals, fluted, 5″ 285.00
Bowl, peacock at fence, ruffled rim, bl, Northwood, 8½″ 75.00
Buttons & Braids, pitcher, water; clear 95.00
Buttons & Braids, pitcher, water; cranberry 235.00
Buttons & Braids, pitcher, water; gr 135.00
Carousel, bowl, bl, goofus center & ft 45.00
Christmas Snowflake, pitcher, water; cranberry, rope hdl 365.00
Chrysanthemum Base Swirl, toothpick, cranberry 90.00
Circled Scroll, bowl, berry; clear, 8¼″ 55.00
Circled Scroll, sauce, bl, ftd, 2½x4¼″ 20.00
Coin Spot, pitcher, bl, crimped edge, applied bl hdl, 8″ 120.00
Coin Spot, pitcher, water; clear 75.00
Coin Spot, pitcher, water; vaseline, ruffled top, hdl 135.00
Coin Spot, sugar shaker, bl, bulbous base, rare 85.00
Coin Spot, sugar shaker, bl, 9-Panel 85.00
Coin Spot, sugar shaker, cranberry satin, 5-panel 95.00
Coin Spot, syrup, clear 70.00
Coin Spot, syrup, cranberry, hinged SP lid 145.00
Coin Spot, tumbler, cranberry 45.00

Coin Spot, water set, clear, 7-pc....110.00
Coin Spot, water set, cranberry, rnd ruffled rim, 7-pc....300.00
Coin Spot & Swirl, syrup, bl....95.00
Daisy & Fern, cruet, bl, clear stopper....75.00
Daisy & Fern, cruet, clear....60.00
Daisy & Fern, finger bowl, bl....30.00
Daisy & Fern, pitcher, water; clear....125.00
Daisy & Fern, syrup, bl....115.00
Daisy & Fern, tumbler, cranberry....45.00
Delaware, bowl, master berry; cranberry....90.00
Diamond Spearhead, butter dish, vaseline....185.00
Diamond Spearhead, spooner, gr....65.00
Diamond Spearhead, sugar bowl, gr....115.00
Diamond Spearhead, toothpick, gr....50.00
Diamond Spearhead, toothpick, vaseline....85.00
Diamond Spearhead, tumbler, gr....65.00
Double Dahlia w/Lens, bowl, banana; gr & gold....45.00
Drapery, butter dish, bl, no gold....165.00
Drapery, celery vase, clear, blown, ruffled top....60.00
Drapery, spooner, bl w/gold....70.00
Drapery, sugar w/lid, bl, no gold....90.00
Drapery, tumbler, bl....25.00
Drapery, vase, bl, sgn N, 8"....65.00
Everglades, bowl, master berry; bl w/gold....119.00
Everglades, butter dish, bl w/gold....250.00
Everglades, compote, jelly; gr....40.00
Everglades, creamer & sugar, clear w/gold....90.00
Everglades, spooner, bl w/gold....65.00
Everglades, spooner, gr....55.00
Everglades, sugar bowl, bl w/gold, w/lid....135.00
Everglades, table set, bl, 4-pc, G gold....495.00
Fancy Fantails, rose bowl, clear w/cranberry trim, 4 legs....50.00
Feathers, celery vase, gr, flared top, scalloped....40.00
Fern, pitcher, water; tankard, cranberry, bl hdl, rare....325.00
Flora, butter dish, vaseline....245.00
Flora, spooner, gr....40.00
Fluted Scroll, bowl, bl, ftd, 6½"....25.00
Fluted Scroll, bowl, bl, 7½"....46.00
Fluted Scroll, bowl, vaseline, ftd, 6½"....30.00
Fluted Scroll, butter dish, bl w/enamel floral, lg....215.00
Fluted Scroll, butter dish, vaseline....165.00
Fluted Scroll, creamer, bl....40.00
Fluted Scroll, creamer, clear....36.00
Fluted Scroll, creamer, vaseline, enamel floral....65.00
Fluted Scroll, pitcher, clear, 5"....45.00
Fluted Scroll, pitcher, water; bl....197.00
Fluted Scroll, pitcher, water; clear....55.00
Fluted Scroll, pitcher, water; vaseline....225.00
Fluted Scroll, powder jar, bl, 5¼"....45.00
Fluted Scroll, puff box, vaseline....40.00
Fluted Scroll, shakers, clear, pr....30.00
Fluted Scroll, spooner, vaseline, enamel floral....75.00
Fluted Scroll, sugar bowl, enamel daisy decor, vaseline....125.00
Fluted Scroll, table set, bl, 4-pc....425.00
Fluted Scrolls, sauce dish, vaseline, 4-ftd....20.00
Frosted Leaf & Basketweave, spooner, vaseline....80.00
Gonterman Swirl, sugar bowl, bl....160.00
Gonterman Swirl, tumbler, amber....75.00
Grape & Cherry, bowl, bl, unusual shape....20.00
Greek Key & Scales, bowl, bl, ftd....35.00
Greek Key & Scales, bowl, bl, ruffled, 8"....30.00
Hobnail, basket, bl, ruffled, 8x7"....45.00
Hobnail, basket, cranberry....75.00
Hobnail, bowl, berry; vaseline, Hobbs....40.00
Hobnail, bowl, bl, ruffled, 10x4½"....59.00
Hobnail, bowl, clear, ruffled, 9½"....45.00
Hobnail, cruet, bl, Hobbs....245.00
Hobnail, goblet, clear....20.00
Hobnail, pitcher, water; rubena verde....325.00
Hobnail, tumbler, clear....20.00
Hobnail, tumbler, lav, 8-Row, 3¾"....100.00
Hobnail, vase, bl, lg....22.00
Hobnail & Paneled Thumbprint, butter dish, bl....145.00
Hobnail & Paneled Thumbprint, spooner, bl....70.00
Hobnail & Paneled Thumbprint, spooner, vaseline....65.00
Hobnail & Paneled Thumbprint, sugar bowl, vaseline....100.00
Hobnail & Paneled Thumbprint, table set, vaseline, 4-pc....365.00
Hobnail-in-Square, tumbler, clear....35.00
Honeycomb, celery vase, amber, blown....70.00
Honeycomb & Clover, bowl, master berry; bl....35.00
Idyll, creamer, clear....36.00
Idyll, creamer, gr....50.00
Idyll, spooner, gr....70.00
Intaglio, creamer, bl....50.00
Intaglio, creamer, clear....40.00
Intaglio, cruet, bl....125.00
Iris w/Meander, bowl, berry; bl....95.00
Iris w/Meander, butter dish, bl....265.00
Iris w/Meander, compote, jelly; bl....35.00
Iris w/Meander, compote, jelly; vaseline....35.00
Iris w/Meander, pitcher, water....300.00
Jackson, bowl, bl, 3 ft, 7½"....75.00
Jackson, cruet, vaseline....165.00
Jackson, pitcher, water; bl....195.00
Jackson, shakers, vaseline, pr....60.00
Jackson, sugar bowl, bl....110.00
Jefferson Spool, vase, clear....32.00
Jefferson Wheel, bowl, bl, fluted, 8½"....55.00
Jewel & Fan, bowl, gr, oval....19.00
Jewel w/Flower, bowl, bl, gold trim, 9"....65.00
Jewel w/Flower, bowl, bl, no gold, 9"....50.00
Jewel w/Flower, bowl, bl, 5"....30.00
Jewelled Heart, berry set, clear, 5-pc....88.00
Jewelled Heart, bowl, bl, ruffled, 10"....35.00
Jewelled Heart, pitcher, water; clear....136.00
Jewelled Heart, sauce dish, clear, ruffled....15.00
Jewelled Heart, spooner, gr....45.00
Leaf & Beads, bowl, gr, 3 ft, 3x8½" dia....40.00
Leaf Chalice, rose bowl, ped, gr....45.00
Lustre Flute, butter dish, bl....295.00
Many Loops, bowl, clear, 8¼"....25.00
Maple Leaf, compote, gr....30.00
Maple Leaf, compote, jelly; bl....46.00
Meander, bowl, bl, ruffled, tri-leg, 7"....35.00
Meander, bowl, gr, 3 spatula ft, ruffled edge, 9½"....25.00
Ocean Shell, bowl, bl, ftd....65.00
Palisades, vase, bl....36.00
Palm Beach, berry set, vaseline....350.00
Palm Beach, spooner, vaseline....75.00
Palm Beach, table set, vaseline, 4-pc....550.00
Palm Beach, tumbler, bl....85.00
Palm Beach, water set, vaseline, 7-pc....700.00
Poinsettia, bowl, clear, ruffled, 3-ftd....49.00
Poinsettia, bowl, cobalt fluted edge on wht, sq....145.00
Poinsettia, pitcher, water; tankard, bl....160.00
Poinsettia, tumbler, gr....20.00
Polka Dot, pitcher, water; clear, Burlington mk....110.00
Reflecting Diamonds, bowl, gr, 8"....20.00

Creamer and sugar bowl, Panelled Button and Daisy, vaseline, $45.00.

Regal, butter dish, gr....145.00
Regal, butter dish, gr w/G gold....175.00
Regal, creamer, bl....55.00
Regal, spooner, gr....55.00
Regal, sugar bowl, gr, w/lid....80.00
Reverse Swirl, bowl, berry; clear, 9″....46.00
Reverse Swirl, shot glass, clear....20.00
Reverse Swirl, sugar shaker, bl....125.00
Reverse Swirl, syrup, bl....125.00
Reverse Swirl, vase, bl, 8″....45.00
Ribbed Lattice, sugar shaker, bl....80.00
Ribbed Lattice, sugar shaker, cranberry, tall....90.00
Ribbed Lattice, syrup, clear....95.00
Ribbed Pillar, sugar shaker, cranberry satin, tall....110.00
Ribbed Spiral, bowl, bl, shallow....46.00
Ribbed Spiral, spooner, bl....60.00
Ribbed Spiral, tray, water; bl....55.00
Ruffles & Rings, bowl, aqua, ftd....30.00

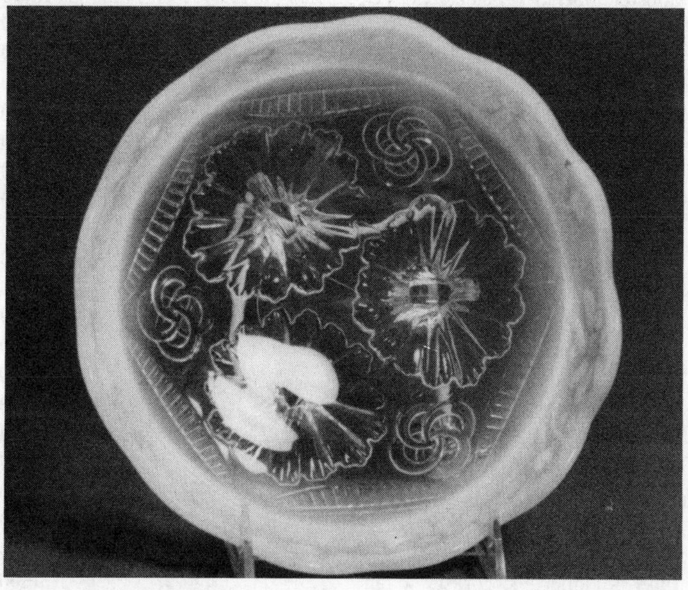

Bowl, Ruffles and Rings, clear with opal, 8″, $28.00.

Scroll w/Acanthus, cruet, bl....175.00
Scroll w/Acanthus, spooner, bl....60.00
Scroll w/Acanthus, spooner, vaseline....45.00
Sea Spray, bowl, gr, hdls....20.00
Seaweed, bottle, barber; bl....130.00
Shell, berry set, gr, 7-pc....285.00
Shell & Dots, bowl, bl, 9″....48.00
Shell & Wild Rose, bowl, gr, sgn N, 7½″....25.00
Snowflake & Plume, bowl, aqua, ftd....40.00
Spanish Lace, butter dish, bl....85.00
Spanish Lace, pitcher, water; bl....195.00
Spanish Lace, pitcher, water; clear....165.00
Spanish Lace, rose bowl, clear, 4″....40.00
Spanish Lace, sugar shaker, bl....110.00
Spanish Lace, sugar shaker, cranberry....145.00
Spanish Lace, sugar shaker, vaseline....110.00
Spanish Lace, tumbler, cranberry....45.00
Spool, compote, jelly; clear....50.00
Stars & Stripes, tumbler, clear....45.00
Sunburst-on-Shield, sugar bowl, bl, dbl-hdld....45.00
Swag w/Brackets, compote, jelly; gr....15.00
Swag w/Brackets, compote, jelly; vaseline....38.00
Swag w/Brackets, creamer, bl....65.00
Swag w/Brackets, pitcher, water; bl....285.00
Swag w/Brackets, spooner, bl....50.00
Swag w/Brackets, spooner, vaseline....40.00
Swastika, pitcher, water; clear....250.00
Swirl, cruet, cranberry....165.00
Swirl, pitcher, water; clear....95.00
Swirl, sugar shaker, bl....70.00
Swirl, sugar shaker, clear, 3x4″....48.00
Swirl, syrup, bl....110.00
Swirl, syrup, clear....65.00
Swirl, tumbler, clear....45.00
Swirled Windows, syrup, cranberry....225.00
Tokyo, bowl, master berry; bl....60.00
Tokyo, bowl, master berry; clear....52.00
Tokyo, bowl, master berry; gr....50.00
Tokyo, cake plate, clear, 8½″....30.00
Tokyo, compote, gr, 5″....20.00
Tokyo, creamer, bl, 5½″....85.00
Tokyo, creamer, gr....40.00
Tokyo, spooner, clear....45.00
Tokyo, sugar bowl, clear, w/lid....75.00
Tokyo, sugar bowl, gr, w/lid....80.00
Tokyo, table set: butter dish/creamer/sugar bowl, bl....375.00
Vintage, plate, bl, 7⅞″....22.00
Water Lily & Cattails, bowl, amethyst, ruffled, 9½″....22.00
Water Lily & Cattails, bowl, bl, 7″....25.00
Water Lily & Cattails, pitcher, water; amethyst....250.00
Water Lily & Cattails, plate, clear, 10″....25.00
Water Lily & Cattails, spooner, bl....50.00
Wheel & Block, bowl, clear....40.00
Wild Bouquet, spooner, clear....28.00
Wild Bouquet, sugar bowl w/lid, bl....150.00
Windows, pitcher, water; bl....125.00
Windows, sugar shaker, bl....135.00
Windows, sugar shaker, cranberry....165.00
Windows, syrup, bl....135.00
Wishbone & Drapery, plate, gr....18.00
Wooden Pail (Bucket), butter dish, bl....120.00
Wooden Pail (Bucket), spooner, bl....50.00
Wreath & Shell, berry set, bl....350.00
Wreath & Shell, bowl, berry; vaseline, sm....22.00
Wreath & Shell, celery vase, clear....88.00
Wreath & Shell, open salt, ind; vaseline....85.00
Wreath & Shell, sauce, vaseline....30.00

Opaline

A type of semi-opaque opal glass, opaline was made in white as well as pastel shades, and is often decorated with enamel work. It is similar in appearance to English bristol glass.

When no condition is indicated, the items listed below are assumed to be in mint condition.

Bottle, scent; bl w/gold & heavy floral enameling, 4¼" 80.00
Bottle, scent; lt bl w/gold trim, bulbous, 6¼" 80.00
Box, patch; bl w/gold prunus blossoms, lift-off top, 1½" 42.00
Ring tree, bl w/heavy gold & mc floral, 4¼x3¾" 65.00
Tumbler, bl, 2⅛" 22.00
Vase, pink w/heavy gold & mc floral, 12" 85.00

Openers

Around the turn of the century, manufacturers began to seal bottles with a metal cap that required a new type of bottle opener. Now the screw cap and the flip top are making bottle openers nearly obsolete.

There are many variations, some in combination with other tools. Many openers were used as means of advertising a product. Various materials were used, including silver and brass.

A figural bottle opener is defined as a figure designed for the sole purpose of lifting a bottle cap. The actual opener must be an integral part of the figure itself. The major producers of iron figurals were Wilton Products; John Wright, Inc.; Gadzik Sales; and L & L Favors. Openers may be freestanding three-dimensional, wall hung, or flat. They can be made of cast iron (often painted), brass, bronze, or aluminum.

When no condition is indicated, the items listed below are assumed to be in excellent condition.

African, kneeling, opener in base 15.00
Alligator, aluminum, EX 5.00
Anchor, w/corkscrew, VG 15.00
Bartender, composition material, VG 20.00
Bartender, wood, EX 10.00
Bass, VG 50.00
Bear, brass, wall mt, EX 15.00
Bear's head, CI 40.00
Beer drinker, blk, wall mt, Iron Art on bk, VG 25.00
Blk face, brass, wall mt, orig, EX 35.00
Blk face, gold, wall mt, rpt 10.00
Bull dog, wall mt 45.00
Clown, brass, wall mt, EX 20.00
Clown w/cigar in mouth, w/corkscrew 28.00
Clown's face, wall mt, G 35.00
Cowboy, aluminum, EX 5.00
Crab, brass, VG 15.00
Crab, red, EX 12.00
Dodo, aluminum, EX 5.00
Donkey, brass, VG 30.00
Donkey, brn, EX 20.00
Donkey, chrome, VG 20.00
Donkey, on shot glass 15.00
Drunk, at sign post, CI 12.00
Drunk, blk, wall mt, EX 25.00
Drunk, brass color, w/ash tray, G 8.00
Drunk, Lamp Post; CI 15.00
Drunk, no border on sign 20.00
Drunk, on palm tree, CI, EX 20.00
Drunk, on palm tree, hollow mold, EX 35.00
Drunk cowboy on cactus, pnt, hollow mold, G 90.00
Eagle, metal, EX 5.00
Elephant, brass, EX 17.00
Elephant, sitting on hind legs, blk, G 15.00
Elephant, standing on 4 legs, EX 8.00
Fish, abalone & brass, hinged, VG 25.00
Fish, brass, w/corkscrew, EX 25.00
Fish, pot metal, gold, VG 15.00
Flamingo, hollow mold, G 40.00
Foundryman, aluminum, EX 7.00
Goat, aluminum, EX 5.00
Goat, CI, G 22.00
Goose, CI, EX 25.00
Hammer, brass, EX 15.00
Handy Hans, EX 50.00
Hooker, w/sign, G 15.00
Horse's head, EX 5.00
Horse's hindquarters 20.00
Iroquois Brewery, Indian 30.00

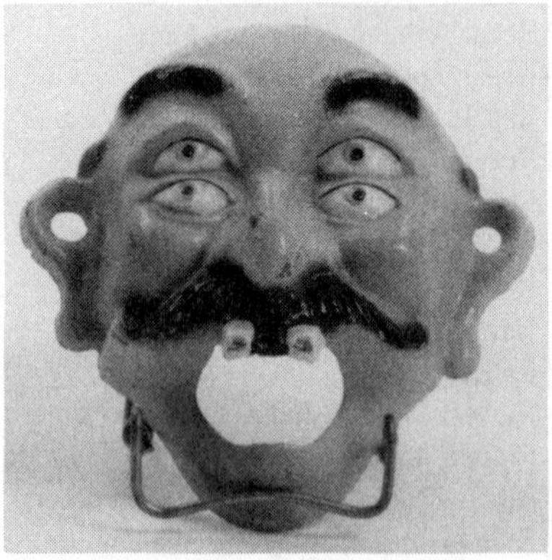

Four-Eyed Man, painted cast iron, marked Walton, 4", $37.50, in excellent condition.

Key, VG 3.00
Lobster, gold-coated pot metal, VG 5.00
Lobster, opener on front, CI, EX 15.00
Lobster, opener on sides, CI, VG 15.00
Mallard, CI, EX 22.00
Man, 4-eyed, bald, blk, wall mt, EX 10.00
Man, 4-eyed, bald, brass, wall mt, sm, EX 25.00
Man, 4-eyed, wall mt, VG 25.00
Monkey, aluminum, EX 5.00
Mr Snifter, chrome, EX 35.00
Nude, bronze, sgn Korbel 95.00
Nude, metal, England, 4" 20.00
Nude babies, 2 on top, 6" 38.00
Parrot, brass, w/can punch, EX 10.00
Parrot, chrome, w/corkscrew, VG 15.00
Parrot, metal, open mouth, yel perched on blk stand 20.00
Parrot, on bottle cap, gold pnt, EX 17.50
Parrot, on perch, EX 17.00
Pelican, chrome, Chase 15.00
Pelican, hollow mold, G 35.00
Pheasant, aluminum, EX 5.00
Pheasant's head, opener in base, Rubal Co, G 15.00
Pig, plastic, w/corkscrew, VG 12.00
Pig's hindquarters, corkscrew tail 30.00
Porcelain hdl, bl monogram Traek & Slip, metal chain 50.00
Pretzel, blk, EX 18.00
Pretzel, salted, VG 25.00
Ram, CI, horns open bottle, orig pnt 35.00
Rooster, CI, orig pnt 22.00
Sailor, VG 25.00
Seagull, CI, EX 25.00
Seahorse, brass 20.00
Seahorse, gold-coated pot metal, VG 5.00
Setter dog, aluminum, EX 5.00
Shark, brass, w/corkscrew 35.00

Spaniel, blk, EX....10.00
Squirrel, G....27.00
Teeth, brass, wall mt, EX....25.00
Tennis racket, brass, EX....15.00
Totem pole, brass, VG....10.00
Trout, G....20.00
White Rock Ginger Ale, figural....10.00
Woman, from India, bronze, EX....10.00
Woman, 4-eyed, brass, wall mt, EX....20.00
Woman, 4-eyed, w/curls, wall mt, brassy orig finish, EX....10.00

Opera Glasses

When no condition is indicated, the items listed below are assumed to be in excellent condition.

Brass & nickel, birds in relief, France....35.00
Leather covered, folding, Le Petit fabricant, Paris, 1923....35.00
MOP, Mermod-Jaccard, in case....60.00
MOP, Tiffany & Co, in velvet case....125.00

Mother-of-pearl and brass, LeMaire, Paris, in original case, $48.00.

Optical Items

Collectors of Americana are beginning to appreciate the charm of antique optical items, and those involved in the related trade find them particularly fascinating. Anyone, however, can appreciate the evolution of technology apparent when viewing a collection of old eye wear, and at the same time admire the primitive ingenuity involved in their construction.

When no condition is indicated, the items listed below are assumed to be in excellent condition.

Binoculars, brass/MOP, mk LeMaire F Paris, in case....40.00
Lorgnette, 'jet' celluloid w/paste stones, early 20th C....40.00
Lorgnette, folding, gold-washed sterling, in hdld case....75.00
Lorgnette, lg marcasite clip hdls....130.00
Lorgnette, papier mache, brass rings, silver inlay....50.00
Lorgnette, sterling vermeil, reticulated, 5¼"....135.00
Lorgnette, wht gold openwork, dtd 1917, snake skin case....130.00
Quizzing glass, eng pinchbeck/coral flower fr, Georgian....145.00
Spectacles, Ben Franklin, G....12.50
Spectacles, Ben Franklin type, aqua lens....16.00
Spectacles, sterling, Pince Nez, w/chain....45.00
Spyglass, brass, 4-part, collapsible, 9½" L....75.00

Orientalia

The art of the Orient is an area of collecting that has recently enjoyed a surge of interest, not only in those examples that are truly 'antique,' but in the 20th century items as well. Auction prices seem to well exceed their estimates with a regularity not apparent in many other collectible fields.

Because of the many aspects involved in a study of Orientalia, we can only try through brief comments to acquaint the reader with some of the more readily available examples and suggest specialized reference sources for detailed information.

Celadon, introduced during the Ching Dynasty, is a green-glazed ware developed in an attempt to imitate the color of jade. Designs are often incised or painted on over glaze in heavy enamel applications.

Chinese export ware was designed to appeal to Western tastes, and was often made to order. During the 18th century, vast amounts were shipped to Europe and on westward. Many of these dinnerwares were given specific pattern names--Rose Mandarin, Fitzhugh, Rose Medallion, Canton, and Armorial are but a few of the more familiar.

Cinnabar is carved lacquer work, often involving hundreds of layers built one at a time on a metal or wooden base. Later pieces are red; older examples tend to darken.

When no condition is indicated, items listed below are assumed to be mint with the exceptions of textiles and woodblock prints, which are assumed to be in excellent condition. See also Canton; Champleve; Cloisonne; Geisha Girl; Imari; Ivory; Kutani; Moriage; Netsuke; Nippon; Noritake; Peking Glass; Soapstone

Key:
ctp—contemporary
cvg—carving
E—export
FR—Famille Rose
FV—Famille Verte

Banko

Pitcher, 2 old men, 9"....125.00
Saki pot, monkeys, 8"....135.00
Teapot, duck, cattail finial, orig wire & rattan hdl, sgn....150.00
Teapot, 5 figures, wire hdl, 4"....175.00
Vase, man shooting another from cannon, 8"....125.00
Wall pocket, owl figural, enamel decor, 7½"....70.00

Blanc de Chine

Libation cup, rhinoceros horn form, emb deer/lion/tree, 3"....300.00
Vase, priest in landscape relief, chop mk, 7"....400.00

Lae Buddah, carved wood with gold wash, 10", $175.00.

Chinese Blue and White Porcelain sweetmeat dish, 5-pc, $195.00.

Blue and White Porcelain, Chinese

Dish, couple in courtyard scene, Kangxi mk, 10½" 600.00
Dish, foliate medallion, emblems at rim, Jiajing, 14" 700.00
Jardiniere, lg prunus sprays/scalloped floral rim, 15" W 700.00
Plate, central figure in landscape, diaper border 60.00
Vase, flowers, ruyi collar, 25" 600.00
Vessel, conch shell form, emb carp, red added later, 3¾" 180.00

Bronze

Aksobhya Buddha, gilt, ornate robes, 1500s, Tibet, 4½" 850.00
Bowl, alms; flared, high ft, gilt, Japanese/Moromachi, 8½" 500.00
Censer, lion head hdls, emb reserves, foo dog finial, 3½" 125.00
Censer, 3 legs w/gargoyle masks, open, early Tibet, 3" 85.00
Diety, 4-armed, w/mala/pustaka, ornate, 1100s, Khmer, 7" 500.00
Female, Xd legs/pierced robes, w/child, Indian, 1600s, 20" 580.00
Figures, old man/young girl, Japanese, 1890s, 8¾", VG 400.00
Ganesha, legs Xd on throne, holds Saivite attributes, 3½" 500.00
Guanyin, sits w/mirror/phoenix headdress, Korea, 1600, 12" 300.00
Incense burner, bulbous, lid: foo dog, Japanese, 4¼" 65.00
Incense burner, bulbous, lid: quail, Japanese, 1890, 22" 650.00
Jar, peacock carved on hinged lid, Tibet/Nepal, 5¼x3½" 145.00
Usabutu, separate top, Japanese, hdls, 3-legs, ca 1920, 9" 185.00
Vase, basketweave, porc liner, 1880s, 9" 175.00

Celadon

Charger, flowering branches in underglaze bl, 1900, 19" 375.00
Plate, exotic bird/flower enamel, 1850s, 7½", set of 4 .... 70.00
Saki pot, gr foliage w/pink flowers, ribbed, 5¼" 75.00
Shrimp dish, bird & butterfly decor, 1790-1820, 10¾x9" 275.00
Umbrella stand, wht flowers, ca 1850, 23½x13½" 250.00
Vase, carved peonies, crackle glaze, Ming, rstr, 18" 400.00

Chinese Porcelain

Basket w/stand, FR, armorial, reticulated, rpr, 9", pr 1,320.00
Bowl, E, hunting scenes medallions, diapered, 18th C, 5½" ... 1,600.00
Bowl, E, Judgement of Paris, ca 1750, rim hairline, 11" 650.00
Bowl, FR, dragons/waves/flaming pearl, 1850s, w/lid, 7x11" 135.00
Brush washer, sang de boeuf, magenta w/wht int, 5½x2" 175.00
Chamberstick, FV, bulb top, tapered middle, flare ft, 11" 125.00
Charger, FR, mandarins & ladies in court scene, 13" 695.00
Creamer, FR, mc diapering, floral & boat scene, no lid 50.00
Cup & saucer, E, basket of flowers, no hdl, mc, NM 185.00
Dog, E, standing, w/collar, wht, 1800s, 5", pr 450.00
Fitzugh, Blue; E, bottle, pine cone/beast medallion, 9¾" 700.00
Fitzugh, Blue; E, platter, pomegranates/panels/beasts, 20" 1,100.00
Fitzugh, Green; E, platter, beast/diaper medallion, 19" 1,000.00
Fitzugh, Orange; E, plate, birds & foliage, 9½" 225.00
Hotei, FR, rotund, 1890, 12" 75.00
Incense burner, FR, floral/3 elephant ft w/loose rings, 8" 175.00
Jug, milk; E, eagle/shield/banner: Don't Give Up Ship, 5" 550.00
Leaf dish, E, after Chelsea, ca 1770, rstr, 14", pr 2,640.00
Planter w/underplate, 1000-Flowers, court scene, 8½x11" 150.00
Plate, E, Am eagle/banner center, floral rim, 1815, 6", VG 800.00
Platter, well & tree, sm crest/floral/deer/insects, 18½" 600.00
Rose jar, FR, panels/flowers, pointed lid finial, 8½x9" 125.00
Salt cellar, demi-griffin crest, rectangular, 1731, rpr 990.00
Sauce boat, figures/water buffalo medallions, ribbed, 1780 ..... 800.00
Soup plate, FR, celadon w/pheasant on branch, 10", 14 for .. 1,045.00
Teapot, sepia flower basket, branch hdl, nut finial, 9", EX 60.00
Teapot, w/porcelain cozy, genre scene/foo dog mts/wire hdl 150.00
Vase, flambe, streaky purple to lt celadon, 1890s, 6½" 175.00
Vase, flambe w/milky & tan specks, Quialong mk, 14½" 825.00
Vase, FV, carp in ocean, dbl gourd form, 12" 515.00
Vase, FV, landscape panel on bl, brass base, 1850, 18" 675.00
Vase, peonies, deer, trees & poem, baluster form, 23" 400.00
Vase, red-orange foo lion motif & hdls, ca 1850, 23" 450.00
Vase, sang de boeuf dk red w/celadon int, bottle form, 14" 485.00

Furniture

Key:

Ch—Chinese	Ko—Korean
cvg—carving	lcq—lacquer
do—door	rswd—rosewood
drw—drawer	/—over
Jp—Japanese	

Altar table, Ch rswd w/MOP inlay, ca 1850, 19x38x35" 950.00
Cabinet, Ch rswd, shelves at top/2 do, EX cvg, 17C, 55x50". 12,000.00
Cabinet, Jp in Ch form, kinoki wood, EX cvg/lcq, 1900, 54" ... 750.00
Cabinet, Jp maple, 3 sections: 2 do/2 do/2 drw, 1920, 39" 375.00
Cabinet, Ko, mix woods, 2 sm do/2, lcq sides, 1920, 52x39" ... 450.00
Chair, Ch red-stain pine, minor cvg of dragons, 37x22x18" 750.00
Chair, Ch rswd, open cvg of incense burner/foo dogs, 1830 .... 525.00
Desk, Ch rswd, Ming style, 1800, 3-pc w/ft rest, 54x33x27" .. 4,000.00
Stool, Ch rswd, heavy, simple, ca 1850, 20x13x10" 175.00
Table, Ch rswd, detailed cvg, marble insert, 1900, 36" dia 375.00

Hardstones

Agate, 2-color, vase, carved dragon in cloud, w/lid, 4½" 150.00
Amber, cherry, elephant, trunk up, carved decor, 2½x4½" 125.00
Amethyst, beauty in long robe, holds peony, ctp, 5½" 235.00
Amethyst, incense burner, foo lion head/hdls/paw ft, 6x5" 275.00
Coral, red, girl in fancy kimono, hand to ear, 2½" 250.00
Jade, gray-gr, foo dog, recumbent, pre-1850, 3½" 150.00
Jade, lt gr, court lady w/fan & peony, flowing scarves, 6" 235.00
Jade, lt gr, phoenix on flowering branch+sm bird, 9x6½" 300.00
Jade, lt gr, vase, peony/leaf carving, w/lid, 6½x4" 250.00
Jade, lt gr w/wht, screen, agate flowers, turq insect, 11" 325.00
Jade, pendant, pear on leaf, pre-1850 .... 55.00
Lapis lazuli, musicians, 1 girl stands/1 sits, ctp, 3x3½" 500.00
Malachite, horse, recumbent, inlaid base, ctp, 2x4" 200.00

Quartz, red, Hotei, seated, 3x4x5″........................250.00
Tigereye, beauty w/peony, scarves/rolled hairdo, ctp, 5½″......350.00
Turq, kylin, reclining, ctp, 3x4″.............................350.00

Inro

Chinese cash, carved wood, gold lacquer on nashiji, 2-case.....900.00
Dragon fish/waves, lacquer/inlay, 3-case, 1700s, no mk........700.00
Flowering tree, bl underglazed porc, 4-case, sgn.............345.00
Gold lacquer, 5-case, bone ojime/netsuke....................400.00
Leather purse form/imp dragon/netsuke w/foo dog, 1900s, 9″...175.00
Wood, ink landscape, 4-case, ca 1920, 3¾″...................40.00

Jewelry

Beads, vegetable ivory carved as 18 Lohan, 1890, 9″..........65.00
Bracelet, rose quartz flower cvg in silver filgree, '30..........150.00
Bracelet, turq/coral children cvg/filigree silver, mk/1920........250.00
Buckle, gold wash brass set w/jade+2 type quartz, 1700, 3″...375.00
Hat top, gold wash brass filigree, 2″ bl Peking bead, 1830.....100.00
Kingfisher hairpin, flower form, 4″.........................50.00
Kingfisher headdress, dragons/figures/glass sets, 1820, VG......250.00
Necklace, jade, fine moss gr, ca 1920, 9″...................600.00
Necklace, Mandarin; Peking glass/various colors, 1900, 38″....225.00
Pin, carnelian flower form, gold wash SP filigree, '20, 1″.......65.00
Pin, jade, EX apple gr, in 14k mt, 2¼″.....................900.00
Pin, jade, mutton fat, in silver mt, 1½″.....................45.00
Ring, jade, EX apple gr, 14k Art Nouveau mt, 1900...........95.00

Lacquer

Box, cinnabar, berries/leaves/butterflies, oval, 11″ L..........150.00
Box, cinnabar, lid: Greek Key/florals/birds, 2x6x4″............70.00
Box, glove; HP geisha/child/birds/dragons, 11½″ L............55.00
Panel, gold on gr, arched top, 42″, pr......................150.00
Plaque, lady w/instrument, soapstone/ivory, 36″, set of 4.......550.00
Shop sign, ad: medicinal remedies, Japan/Meiji, 60x24″......1,100.00
Tray, cinnabar, pagodas/houses/bridge/people, 12x14″.........325.00
Tray, florals, red/gilt on blk, 19th C, 24″ L.................150.00
Tray, fly on bamboo, MOP inlay, canted corners, 9″...........30.00
Vase, ribbed panels w/florals, hexagon form, 18x9″............75.00

Mud Figures

Bearded man holding bundle, 3½″..........................25.00
Bearded man w/fan, 6″...................................60.00
Fisherman, seated, w/pole & fish, 5½″......................60.00
Man in cobalt robe holds book, 6″..........................45.00
Man in yel/turq robe w/fan, sits on stump, 5½″...............65.00

Rose Medallion

Rose Medallion is one of the patterns of Chinese export porcelain produced from the early 1800s until the first part of the 20th century. It is decorated in rose colors with panels of florals, birds, butterflies, and Chinese people. Earlier examples were decorated with gold tracery; some were heavily reticulated.

Bowl, bouillon; w/underplate & lid, late, sm..................65.00
Bowl, ca 1890, 6¾″.....................................75.00
Bowl, deep, 8″...125.00
Bowl, late, 10x1¾″.....................................75.00
Bowl, Made in China, 7″.................................75.00
Bowl, pedestal, oval, 3½x14½x12″.........................385.00
Bowl, rice; China..45.00
Bowl, somewhat sq, no mk, 8½x8¾″........................250.00
Bowl, soup; 1880s, 8½″...................................75.00
Bowl, vegetable; ca 1890, w/lid...........................175.00
Bowl, 1840s, w/lid, 8½x9½″...............................450.00
Bowl, 1840s, 10″..225.00
Butter pat, sq...40.00
Charger, late, 13½″......................................150.00
Compote, mk China, 3x6″.................................125.00
Compote, no mk, 4½x8¼″.................................245.00
Creamer, bulbous, mk China...............................45.00
Creamer & sugar bowl, wrapped hdls, w/lid, mk China, 3½″....165.00
Cup & saucer, ca 1890....................................75.00
Cup & saucer, China......................................35.00
Cup & saucer, demitasse; Made in China.....................30.00
Cup & saucer, hexagonal...................................30.00
Cup & saucer, wishbone hdl, no mk, early....................75.00
Ginger jar, ca 1890, 9″...................................175.00
Gravy boat, heavy, mk China, 1¾x8½″......................110.00
Gravy boat w/8″ underplate, heavy, wrapped hdl, mk China....145.00
Incense burner, figural top, ca 1900, 10″.....................95.00
Plate, ca 1893, 6″.......................................23.00
Plate, floral/butterflies/people, old, 5½″......................31.00
Plate, late, 5½″..17.00
Plate, mk China, 10″......................................65.00
Plate, mk Made in China, 7½″...............................28.00
Plate, mk Made in China, 8½″...............................35.00
Plate, no mk, 8½″...85.00
Plate, reticulated rim, 7¼″.................................55.00
Platter, ca 1890, 14x16″...................................285.00
Platter, ftd, early, 14″....................................440.00
Platter, oval, early, 19″...................................350.00
Platter, oval, early, 7½x10″................................140.00
Punch bowl, no mk, 5x11″..................................295.00
Sauce dish w/saucer, 19th C................................95.00
Saucer, deep; 6″..30.00
Sugar bowl, fruit finial, twist hdls, 4⅛″......................120.00
Sugar bowl, mk China......................................75.00
Tea set, 47-pc..425.00
Teapot, bulbous, dome lid, ca 1820s, 10″.....................950.00
Teapot, ca 1820s, 5″.......................................450.00
Teapot, ca 1890, 6″..75.00
Teapot, mk Made in China, dome lid, 6½″......................75.00
Teapot, straight sides, late, 4⅝″.............................70.00
Teapot, w/2 cups, in case...................................150.00
Tray, reticulated rim, orange peel glaze, 7¾x9″, NM............150.00
Vase, applied salamanders, foo dog hdls, early, 8″..............500.00
Vase, ca 1890, 12″...325.00
Vase, ca 1890, 4″..45.00
Vase, ca 1900, 7″, pr.......................................140.00
Vase, genre scenes, 1850, 10″...............................450.00
Vase, 1850, 3″...150.00

Satsuma

Satsuma is a type of fine cream crackle-glaze pottery or earthenware made in Japan as early as the 17th century. The earliest wares, made at the original kiln in the Satsuma province, were enameled with only simple florals. By the late 18th century a floral brocade, or nishikide, design was favored, and similar wares were being made at other kilns under the direction of the Lord of Satsuma. In the early part of the 19th century, a diaper pattern was added to the florals. Gold and silver enameling was used for accents by the latter years of the century.

During the 1850s, as the quantity of goods made for export to the Western world increased and the style of decoration began to evolve toward becoming more appealing to the Westerners, human forms such as Arhats, Kannon, Geisha girls, and Samurai warriors were added.

Today the most valuable pieces are those marked 'Kinkozan,' 'Shuzan,' 'Ryuzan,' and 'Kozan.' The genuine Satsuma 'mon' or mark is an 'X' within a circle--it may appear anywere on the ware.

Bottle, floral, much gold on wht, 5″....150.00
Bottle, scent; floral/butterfly/diapering, gourd form, 6″....250.00
Bowl, men w/balloons in parade, much gold, scalloped, 2x4″....250.00
Bowl, temple scene, Meiji Period, 1880s, 5½″....350.00
Bowl, 1000 Faces, 19th C, 12″....450.00
Box, genre scenes, sq legs, 2⅝x4⅜″....650.00
Candlestick, temple/floral, 6¾″, pr....250.00
Cracker jar, feudal lords/florals/butterflies on cobalt....350.00
Creamer & sugar bowl, giesha/lord, jeweling, scroll ft....250.00
Cup & saucer, floral/butterfly relief....125.00
Flask, med bl w/birds, sgn Nishiki, moon shape, 6¾″, pr....250.00
Incense burner, ladies/children on 2 sides, ca 1915, 2¼″....65.00
Incense burner, landscapes, foo dog face hdls, rpr, 1890s....200.00
Jar, chrysanthemum, Shi-Shi finial, ftd, hdls, 13½″....450.00
Mustard, Nishikide diapering/genre scenes, attached base....75.00
Pin, kimono; lady w/fan, 1-pc silver fr & bk, hallmk, 1¾″....250.00
Pitcher, Nishikide diapering/genre reserves, 5″....75.00
Pitcher, 6-sided, Nishikide diapering/genre reserves, 7″....125.00
Plate, figural patterns, 1940s....150.00
Plate, sq & rnd overlapping reserves w/genre scenes, 7½″....900.00
Plate, 2 feudal lords/diapering/gilt, Meiji period, 8½″....450.00
Saki pot, EX decor, dragon spout & hdl, 4¼″....600.00
Saki pot, squat, EX quality, 1⅝x3½″....450.00
Salt cellar, warrior in bowl, sgn....150.00
Salt cellar, 3 men in boat, sgn....250.00
Salt cellar, 3 warriors, sgn....150.00
Shakers, diapering, genre scenes, ca 1910, pr....75.00
Tea caddy, 6-sided, Nishikide diapering/genre reserves, 6″....125.00
Tea set, ribbed, Nishikide diapering/genre reserves, 9-pc....250.00
Tea set, wisteria....325.00
Teapot, children playing ball/floral on rim, sgn, 3x4¼″....650.00
Teapot, mums/diapering, gilt, Kinkozan mk/gold mon....250.00
Toothpick holder, ca 1890....125.00
Toothpick holder, rust leaves, Kinkozan/teakwood stand, pr....300.00
Vase, bridge/lake/village/Mt Fuji, baluster shape, 10″....250.00
Vase, butterflies/lily on bl, bamboo hdls, Awata, 10½″....250.00
Vase, chrysanthemums, 1920, 7″....125.00
Vase, dk bl, 2 panels: 15 women; 12 holy men/goddess, 9″....450.00
Vase, floral garden/pheasants, mc/gold on cobalt, 7x4″....550.00
Vase, florals, foo dog hdls, 15½″....250.00
Vase, foliage, gilt, Kinkozan, Meiji Period, 2″, pr....300.00
Vase, geese in flight, 1880, 7″....150.00
Vase, gold landscapes & pagodas, ca 1900, 5½″, pr....375.00
Vase, haloed Arhats & Kwannon, rolled rim, 1915, 12″....260.00
Vase, haloed Arhats & Kwannon, Taisho period, 9½″....175.00
Vase, lady on front, mc/gold, 3″, pr....45.00
Vase, Lords & Attendants, children playing, 1880, 24″....1,800.00
Vase, mc deco floral, decorated in CA, ca 1915, 2½″, pr....300.00
Vase, men fishing in pond, baluster shape, 9½″....250.00
Vase, millefleur decor, 2¼″, pr....150.00
Vase, Oriental children, gold lattice/clouds, 2½″....150.00
Vase, Oriental figures front/bk, mc/gold, 12″, pr....350.00
Vase, Oriental figures/flowers, much gold, 12″....250.00
Vase, pagoda & mountains, baluster shape, 8¾″....150.00
Vase, phoenix bird panels, tortoise ground, Awata, 15″....350.00
Vase, Samurai & Lords, artist sgn, 44″....3,000.00
Vase, scholars studying, fine work, ca 1880, 3¼″, pr....425.00
Vase, war lords & gods, mc w/gold tracings, 1920s, 15″....300.00
Vase, wht elephant, cobalt flowers, 6″....150.00
Vase, wisteria, gold tracing, rectangle base/top, 2¾″....125.00
Vase, wisteria, red reign mk, ca 1870, 6″....350.00
Vase, 15 women in garden, 12 men by Kwan Yin on bk, bl, 9″.245.00
Vase, 2 panels w/figures, heavy gold on cobalt, 3½″....125.00

Satsuma dish, cat and mouse scene, 1830s, 4⅞″ diameter, $650.00.

Snuff Bottles

The Chinese were introduced to snuff in the 17th century, and their carved and painted snuff bottles typify their exquisite taste and workmanship. These tiny bottles, seldom measuring over 2½″, were made of amber, jade, ivory, and cinnabar; and often had tiny spoons attached to their stoppers. By the 18th century, some were being made of porcelain, others were of glass with delicate designs tediously reverse painted with tiny brushes sometimes containing a single hair. Copper and brass were used, but to no large extent.

Agate, boys w/kites, 2-color cutting, jade top, 1890, 2¼″....175.00
Carnelian, floral carving, ca 1900, minor chips, 2½″....125.00
Glass, Peking, red w/cameo-carved birds, ca 1880, 2″....300.00
Glass, rvpt, beauty/scene on bk, EX work, no top, 1900, 2″....85.00
Glass, rvpt, scene, bird on rock on bk, ctp, 2½″....45.00
Ivory, lady figural, head is stopper, ca 1920, 2½″....120.00
Jade, apple gr, hollowed/flattened bottle form, 1880, 2″....900.00

Sumida

Bowl, orange crab/boy on brn/gray, boat form, 3¾x4¼x7¾″....110.00
Bowl, 2 women/2 men/boy climbing over edge, 4½x7½x8½″....198.00
Bowl, 3 applied figures on rim, seal sgn, 4½x7¾″....225.00
Humidor, child climbing lid....165.00
Mug, applied animals, bl seal sgn, lg....140.00
Pitcher, seated man, seal sgn....140.00
Tankard, 2 applied children, seal sgn, 4″ neck, 12½x5¾″....595.00
Vase, applied pigs/pinched body/glazed neck, seal sgn, 8¾″....160.00
Vase, boy w/hands outspread, brn/bl/gray mottled top, 6⅝″....85.00
Vase, children in relief on red, mottled top, bk mk, 12″....225.00
Vase, children in relief on red w/dk mottled top, 9½″....200.00
Vase, geisha in relief, bl on brn w/mottled top, 4½x4″....135.00
Vase, man in chair, bl/gray/brn top w/red bkground, 8¼″....88.00
Vase, man kneeling/dragon/man w/staff, flat/bulbous, 7¾″....110.00

Textiles

Altar cloth, turq silk/gold embr, dragons/bats/calligraphy.......350.00
Archway panel, silk w/embr, lined, velvet edging..............120.00
Dragon robe, bl silk w/gold couching, dragons/clouds/etc.....1,000.00
Dragon robe, EX embr on silk w/dragons/flowers, 1780, 54″..2,500.00
Dragon robe, silk, K'sou tapestry/dragons/baskets/bats, mc....2,500.00
Hat, red silk w/EX embr, open top, 9x9½″..................65.00
Lady's robe, silk, wide sleeves/EX embr/forbidden stitch.......975.00
Mandarin badge, silk K'sou, mc w/wht bird, 1850, 12x12″.....165.00
Obi cloth, embr, gold/silver threads, early 20th C, 3 for........175.00
Panel, red silk/EX embr lady w/flower basket, 1890, 60x24″....375.00
Sleeve panel, silk/embr ladies/forbidden stitch, 23x4″, pr......150.00
Sleeve panel, yel silk, forbidden stitch flower.................40.00

Woodblock Prints, Japanese

Choki, panel of triptych: children as attendants, 14½x9½″.....300.00
Eishi, Princess Sotoori..................................5,500.00
Harunobu, Client & Waitress at Teahouse.................6,500.00
Harunobu, Lady Regarding Sleeping Boy.................2,200.00
Hasui, Tokyo Street Scene...............................1,600.00
Kitao Masanobue, 2 bijin on promenade, 10x7½″, EX.........485.00
Kochiro Onchi, Woman Drying Her Hair..................1,600.00
Koryusai, Courtesan Dressing Her Kamuro................3,500.00
Kunisada, 2 ladies assist child climbing bridge at shrine.......600.00
Portfolio: Life of Kyoto, after Hasegawa......................50.00
Portfolio: 1 Yr of Kyoto, after Tokuriki........................90.00
Portfolio: 5 Courtesans, after Hasegawa......................50.00
Shinsui, Woman Applying Cosmetics.....................2,000.00
Shunei, assault on Imperial Palace in storm, 10x15″..........500.00
Shunko, Iyai Hanshiro IV in samurai role, 12½x5¾″..........400.00
Tanaka Masanobu, Ichimura Uzayemon VII as samurai, 12x5¾″.450.00
Toyokuni, Bijin & Man...................................2,600.00
Utamaro II, Two Women.................................1,900.00

Miscellaneous

Carving, man & child, bamboo root stem, 18th-19th C, 6½″....300.00
Hand mirror, silver metal w/enamel inlays+12 'jewels,' 9″......400.00
Mask, samurai, carved wood/pnt, Japanese, ca 1840...........135.00
Opium pipe, bamboo stem, jade bit & bowl, 6¾″..............189.00
Scandals, platform, Japanese, pr............................60.00
Scroll, ink landscape on silk, wood ends, Chinese, 24x62″.....300.00
Scroll, Mandarin portrait, mc, fr, ca 1880, 54x30″..........1,200.00
Scroll, rice paper w/HP woman w/fan, Japanese...............65.00

Orrefors

Orrefors Glassworks was founded in the early 1900s in the Swedish province of Smaaland. Utilizing the expertise of designers such as Lindquist and Gate, it produced art glass of the highest quality. Various techniques were used in achieving the decoration; some were wheel engraved, and others blown through a unique process that formed controlled bubbles or air pockets resulting in unusual patterns and shapes.

When no condition is indicated, the items listed below are assumed to be in mint condition.

Bowl, Ariel, scrolls, red/clear internal decor, ftd, 9½″.........385.00
Bowl, bl/clear, rose/pink bottom, sgn Edvard Hald, 5x2½″.....225.00
Bowl, Ravenna, geometric banding/gridwork, red/bl, sq, 10″....990.00
Champagne, ½ thumbprint, diamond point band, 5″, 8 for.....130.00
Tazza, 3-color internal decor, Expo 358-74/Johanson, 7″......595.00

Vase, Ariel Glass, oxblood and gray profiles, designed by Ingeborg Lundin, 1979, 6¾″, $2,000.00.

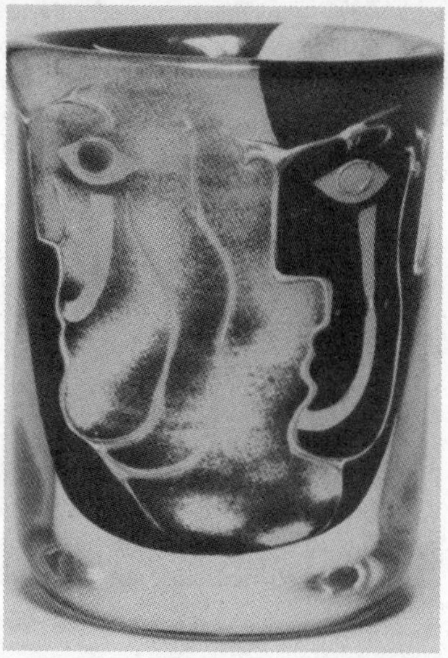

Vase, Ariel, air-trap geometrics, dk bl, Lundin, 6¾″..........800.00
Vase, Ariel, profiles, lime/olive, Lundin, 7½″.................700.00
Vase, Ariel, Venetian gondolier w/maid, bl in clear, 8″.......1,540.00
Vase, Fish-Graal, fish/seaweed w/in, E Hald, 5¾″.............465.00
Vase, Fish-Graal, fish/seaweed w/in, E Hald, 9″..............500.00
Vase, Graal, cylinder, banded cuttings, applied coil, 7″........275.00
Vase, nude lady on crescent moon shooting bow, Lindstrand...225.00
Vase, nude swimmer, Lindstrand, 1931, 8½″..................350.00
Vase, paneled, sgn/#1242 Yared, 8½″......................135.00
Vase, sm sq pyramidal forms relief, gr, flaring, Hald, 6½″......495.00

Ott and Brewer

The partnership of Ott and Brewer began in 1865 in Trenton, New Jersey. By 1876 they were making decorated graniteware, parian, and 'ivory porcelain'--similar to Irish belleek, though not as fine and of different composition. In 1883, however, experiments toward that end had reached a successful conclusion and a true belleek body was introduced. It came to be regarded as the finest china ever produced by an American firm. The ware was decorated by various means--hand painting, transfer printing, gilding, and lustre glazing. The company closed in 1893, one of many that failed during that depression.

In the listings below, the ware is belleek unless noted otherwise. When no condition is indicated, items are assumed to be in mint condition.

Chocolate pot, gold floral on gr & cream, dragon spout......1,095.00
Creamer, allover pansies, non-porcelain, sgn.................175.00
Creamer, lav/wht, gold trim, non-porcelain....................65.00
Creamer, Tridacna pattern, sgn, 2x3″.......................175.00
Ewer, thistles, melon ribbed, bulbous........................895.00
Jar, gold floral, 4¾″.......................................300.00
Sugar bowl, open; cactus, twig hdl..........................275.00
Sugar bowl, open; heavy gold leaves, twig hdl...............175.00
Teapot, cactus, gold trim, twig hdls.........................395.00
Tumbler, gold/turq trim at edge, pink w/in..................142.00
Vase, cobalt/gold, bulbous, gold curved hdls, rare, 4″.........300.00
Vase, yel pansies, 10″.....................................695.00

Overbeck

The Overbeck Studio was established in 1911 in Cambridge City, Indiana, by four Overbeck sisters. It survived until the last sister died in 1955.

Early wares were often decorated with carved designs of stylized animals, birds, or florals with the designs colored to contrast with the background. Others had tooled designs filled in with various colors for a mosaic effect. After 1937, Mary Frances, the last remaining sister, favored handmade figurines with somewhat bizarre features in fanciful combinations of color. Overbeck ware is signed 'OBK.'

Large vases from 8″ to 12″ usually command prices from $1,000 to $3,000 on today's market. When no condition is indicated, the items listed below are assumed to be in mint condition.

Figurine, bird on floral mound, 5-color, 3¾″ 160.00
Figurine, bride, hand modeled, mc, sgn, 5x3½″ 175.00
Figurine, bridesmaid, w/floral bouquet, sgn, 5x3½″ 200.00
Figurine, dog, brn/blk, well done, 4x4½″ 295.00
Figurine, elephant, yel/bl/blk/wht, glaze bubbles, 3x4″ 260.00
Vase, brn w/2″ incised mc band, sgn w/logo/EF, 4½x3″ 475.00
Vase, incised pastel flowers on pink, 3″ 400.00
Vase, incised stylized trees, brn/gr panels, sgn EH, 3¾″ 550.00

Figurine, girl in hoop skirt and hat, 5″, $325.00.

Overshot

Overshot glass is characterized by the beaded or craggy appearance of the surface. Earlier ware was irregularly textured, while 20th century examples tend to be more uniform.

When no condition is indicated, the items listed below are assumed to be in mint condition.

Finger bowl, cranberry 25.00
Pitcher, milk; bl w/amber hdl 60.00
Pitcher, pnk/wht spatter, trilobe & top, clear hdl, 8x5″ 150.00
Rose bowl, cranberry, 6x5″ 120.00
Tumbler, rubena, swirl 110.00
Vase, bl, ribbed, 8″ 85.00

Owens Pottery

J.B. Owens founded his company in Zanesville, Ohio, in 1891, and until 1907, when the company decided to exert most of its energies in the area of tile production, made several quality lines of art pottery. His first line, Utopian, was a standard brown ware with underglaze slip decoration of nature studies, animals and portraits. A similar line, Lotus, utilized lighter background colors. Henri Deux, introduced in 1900, featured incised Art Nouveau forms inlaid with color. Other important lines were Opalesce, Rustic, Feroza, Cyrano, and Mission, examples of which are rare today.

The factory burned in 1928, and the company closed shortly thereafter.

When no condition is indicated, the items listed below are assumed to be in mint condition. Values vary according to the quality of the artwork and subject matter. Examples signed by the artist bring higher prices than those that are not signed.

Bowl, Light, raspberries/branches, sgn Denny, 3½x7″ 55.00
Bowl, Lotus, floral, ruffled top, sgn Denny, 4x7″ 110.00
Bowl/vase, Utopian, floral, 3-ftd, sgn on foot, imp mk, 3″ 160.00
Ewer, Matt Utopian, brn/wht leaves, orange/gr, #1054, 10½″ . . . 155.00
Jug, Utopian, floral, artist sgn, 6¾″ 80.00
Jug, Utopian, mtn man portrait, 7x5″ 1,350.00
Lamp, Sudanese, floral/ribbon in gold on blk, 14½″ base 495.00
Lamp, Sudanese, mirror blk w/gold/red Nouveau design, 14″ . . . 400.00
Mug, Utopian, berries, Tot Steele, 5″ 85.00
Mug, Utopian, cherries, artist sgn, 5½″ 60.00
Mug, Utopian, floral, artist sgn, 5″ 70.00
Pitcher, Utopian, pansies, artist sgn, Owensart, 9¾″ 135.00
Tankard, Utopian, berries, sq hdl, 7¾″ 120.00
Tankard, Utopian, pansies, #1015, 12″ 150.00
Tile, grapes/leaves, cloisonne technique, sgn, 6″ 95.00
Tile, Matt Green, leaves in relief, 6x6″ 95.00
Vase, Aqua Verdi, bulbous w/narrow neck, imp/incised, 6x5″ 85.00
Vase, Feroza, violet-blk lustre, hdls, 6″ 165.00
Vase, Henri Deux, lady's head, 6″ 225.00
Vase, Henri Deux, lady's head/drapery hdls, gilt, 6¾x9″ 350.00
Vase, Henri Deux, leaves/roses/lady's head, 8¼″ 350.00
Vase, Lotus, emb mc florals, 8¾x4¾″ 195.00
Vase, Lotus, leaves, gr on gr to lav, cylindrical, 5″ 80.00
Vase, Matt Green, incised swirls, #219, 5½″ 35.00
Vase, Matt Green, pierced, 5″ 100.00
Vase, Matt Green, 2 integral rim-to-width hdls, #1139, 3″ 70.00
Vase, Matt Lotus, morning glories, pink/rose, Fouts, 11″ 145.00
Vase, Matt Utopian, blackberries, C Excel, twisted, 13x4″ 140.00
Vase, Matt Utopian, clover, artist sgn, stick neck, 11″ 175.00
Vase, Matt Utopian, floral, EX art, artist sgn, 13½″ 265.00
Vase, Matt Utopian, floral, 4½″ 70.00
Vase, Matt Utopian, lg flower/gr stems, artist sgn, 14½″ 120.00

Jardiniere and pedestal, Henri Deux, 22″, $600.00.

Vase, Matt Utopian, thistles, Chilcote, 10″ 95.00
Vase, Opalesce, gold w/red flower/purple stems, 12″ 295.00
Vase, Opalesce, gr w/allover floral, 13″ 395.00
Vase, Utopian, floral, #1032, bullet shape, sgn, 10″ 75.00
Vase, Utopian, floral, #1045, sgn, 10¾″ 75.00

Vase, Utopian, floral, wide compressed body, sgn SB, 3x5½″....60.00
Vase, Utopian, floral, 4″....50.00
Vase, Utopian, horse head, mouth foaming, sgn MT, 6½″....800.00
Vase, Utopian, Indian maiden portrait, sgn Williams....1,500.00
Vase, Utopian, leaves in orange/gr, twisted, 3½″....75.00
Vase, Utopian, pansies, artist sgn, 8″....90.00
Vase, Utopian, pansies, flaring sides, 10″....100.00
Vase, Utopian, pansies, inverted trumpet, sgn, 13¼″....125.00
Vase, Utopian, roses, flat spheroid, Timberlake, 5x10″....275.00
Vase, Utopian Light, floral, sgn, 6″....175.00

Pacific Clay Products

The Pacific Clay Products Company got its start as a consolidation of several smaller southern California potteries in the early 1920s. The main Los Angeles plant had been founded in 1890 to make kitchen stoneware, ollas and similar ware. Terra cotta and brick were later produced.

In 1932 Hostess Ware, a vividly-colored line of dinnerware, was introduced to compete with Bauer's Ring Ware. Coralitos, a lighter-weight, pastel-hued dinnerware line was first marketed in 1937, and a similar but less expensive line called Arcadia soon followed.

Artware including vases, figurines, candlesticks, etc., was produced from 1932 to 1942, at which time the company went into war-related work and pottery manufacture ceased. A limited amount of hand decorated dinnerware was also made.

When no condition is indicated, the items listed below are assumed to be in mint condition.

Bowl, cereal; Hostess Ware, orange, 5″....15.00
Bowl, mixing; stoneware, mc, #12....35.00
Bowl, salad; Hostess Ware, low ft, yel, 13″....25.00
Bowl, soup plate; Hostess Ware, gr, 6″....10.00
Carafe, cocktail; Hostess Ware, gr....50.00
Coffee server, Hostess Ware, gr, wood hdl, w/lid....20.00
Creamer, demitasse; wht....10.00
Cup & saucer, coffee; Hostess Ware, dk bl....25.00
Figurine, deer, Art Deco, HP, 6″....20.00
Pitcher, icebox; Hostess Ware, sq, upright, yel, w/lid....65.00
Planter, swan figural, blk, 13″ L....75.00
Plate, bread; Hostess Ware, gr, 6″....4.00
Plate, dinner; Hostess Ware, gr, 11″....10.00
Plate, lunch; Hostess Ware, gr, 9½″....8.00
Punch cup, Hostess Ware, gr....12.50
Shakers, Hostess Ware, lt bl, pr....8.50
Sugar bowl, open demitasse; Hostess Ware, brn....7.00
Teapot, Hostess Ware, lg ft, turq....75.00
Teapot, Hostess Ware, sm ft, long spout, yel....45.00
Tray, cheese board; Hostess Ware, orange, 11″ dia....35.00
Tray, Hostess Ware, tab hdl, orange, 15″ dia....50.00
Tray, relish; Hostess Ware, 3-sectioned, yel, 9″ dia....17.50
Vase, classic, plain, turq, 11½″....45.00
Vase, cornucopia, yel, 10″....30.00
Vase, stoneware, mc, 8″....25.00

Paden City

The Paden City Glass Company began operations in 1916, in Paden City, West Virginia. The company's early lines consisted largely of the usual pressed tablewares, but by the 1920s production had expanded to include colored wares, in translucent as well as opaque glass, and in a variety of patterns and styles. The company maintained its high standards of handmade perfection until 1949, when under new management, much of the work formerly done by hand was replaced by automation.

The Paden City Glass Company closed in 1951, and its earlier wares, the colored patterns in particular, are becoming very collectible.

When no condition is indicated, the items listed below are assumed to be in mint condition.

Bottle, cordial; Penny Line, w/stopper, ruby, rare, 9-oz....45.00
Bottle, water....20.00
Bowl, cream soup; Crow's Foot, ruby....12.00
Bowl, Spring Garden, 2-hdl, 8¾″....20.00
Box, candy; Crow's Foot, red....45.00
Cake stand, Crow's Foot, ftd, ruby, 12″....75.00
Candlestick, Crow's Foot, rnd, crystal, 7″, pr....50.00
Candlestick, Crow's Foot, sq, amethyst, pr....45.00
Candlestick, Crow's Foot, sq, ruby, pr....50.00
Candy dish, Crow's Foot, etched, 3-part, ruby....55.00
Candy dish, Crow's Foot, fancy, 3-ftd, gold....35.00
Candy dish, Gadroon-Wotta Line, ruby, w/lid, 3-part....55.00
Cheese & cracker, Crow's Foot, sq, sterling/ruby, 2-pc....75.00
Cocktail shaker, Aristocrat, +6 glasses....75.00
Compote, Crow's Foot, etched orchid, sq ft, ruby, 6¼″....60.00
Compote, Crow's Foot, ruby, 6″....22.50
Compote, Largo, stemmed, ruby, 7″....32.50
Compote, Penny Line, ftd, ruby, 7″....35.00
Cup & saucer, Crow's Foot, red....12.00
Figurine, Chinese pheasant....74.90
Figurine, pheasant, lt bl, 13½x6″....125.00
Figurine, pouter pigeon....69.90
Figurine, squirrel on log....30.00
Figurine, standing pony....50.00
Goblet, cordial; Diana & Cupid etched, 3⅝″....16.00
Ice tub....24.50
Mayonnaise, Aristocrat, crystal, 3-pc....25.00
Napkin holder....67.50
Plate, dinner; Maya, red, 9″....15.00
Plate, Spring Garden, 2-hdl, 11¼″....17.00
Shakers, Party Line, cobalt, pr....35.00
Syrup, w/glass lid, amber....30.00
Tray, sugar; swan head, gazebo etching, center hdl....38.00
Vase, Crow's Foot, flat, flared, ruby, 10″....29.00

Paintings on Ivory

Miniature works of art executed on ivory from the 1800s are assessed by the finesse of the artist, as is any fine painting. Signed examples and portraits with an identifiable subject are usually preferred.

Prices listed below are for undamaged examples.

Full-length figure of boy in black costume with white pantaloons, interior, attributed to Abraham Parsell, NY, 1840, 5½″ x 4″, $1,500.00.

Andrew Jackson, w/fr, 3½x4" 400.00
Gentleman in bl frock coat, Sir Billinghouse, Bath, 7x7" 150.00
Gentleman in military dress, rose gold/enamel fr, 4x2" 225.00
Gentleman w/whiskers, rose gold fr, braided hair bk, 2x1⅝" 325.00
Lady, elderly, British School, early 19th C, brass fr, 2¾" 75.00
Lady, identified, Continental, 19th C, brass fr, 3½x2½" 175.00
Lady in stylish dress, sgn Smart, brass/tortoise fr, 4x5" 235.00
Landscape, British, late 18th C, sgn Wilson, brass fr, 3¾" 200.00
Maid, seated, attentive winged male nude, sgn, ivory fr, 3" 275.00
Napoleon & Josephine, sgn, in fr, 4x5", pr 400.00
Nude standing in garden, ivory fr, 6¼x3½" 135.00
Young gentleman, identified as Gen Goodrich, oval, 2¾" 175.00
Young nobleman in armor vest & Maltese cross, fr, 4¼x5" 235.00

Pairpoint

The Pairpoint Manufacturing Company was built in 1880 in New Bedford, Massachusetts. It was primarily a metalworks, whose chief product was coffin fittings. Next door, the Mt. Washington Glassworks made quality glasswares of many varieties. (See Mt. Washington for more information concerning their artware lines.) By 1894 it became apparent to both companies that a merger would be to their best interest.

From the late 1890s until the 1930s, lamps and lamp accessories were an important part of Pairpoint's production. There were three main types of shades, all of which were blown: puffy--blown-out reverse painted shades (usually floral designs); ribbed--also reverse painted; and scenic--reverse painted with scenes of land or seascapes (usually executed on smooth surfaces, although ribbed scenics may be found occasionally). Cut glass lamps and those with metal overlay panels were also made.

Scenic shades were sometimes artist signed, and although many are unmarked, some are stamped 'Pairpoint Corp.' Blown-out shades may be marked 'Pat July 9, 1907.' Bases were made from bronze, copper, brass, silver, or wood, and are always signed.

Because they produced only fancy handmade artware, the company's sales lagged seriously during the depression, and as time and tastes changed, their style of product was less in demand. As a result, they never fully recovered and consequently part of the buildings and equipment were sold in 1938.

The company reorganized in 1939 under the direction of Robert Gunderson, and again specialized in quality hand-blown glassware. Isaac Babbit regained possession of the silver departments, and together they established Gunderson Glassworks, Inc. After WWII, because of a sharp decline in sales, it again became necessary to reorganize. The Gunderson-Pairpoint Glassworks was formed, and the old line of cut, engraved artware was reintroduced.

The company moved to East Wareham, Massachusetts, in 1957, but business continued to suffer, and the firm closed only one year later. In 1970, however, new facilities were constructed in Sagamore under the direction of Robert Bryden, sales manager for the company since the 1950s.

In 1974, the company began to produce lead glass cup plates which were made on commission as fund raisings for various churches and organizations. These are signed with a 'P' in diamond, and are becoming quite collectible.

When no condition is indicated, the items listed below are assumed to be in mint condition with the exception of lamp fittings which are assumed excellent.

Glassware

Basket, grapes, cherries & peaches, intaglio, 11x9x6" 165.00
Biscuit jar, blown-out base, burnt orange w/floral, 9½" 295.00
Bottle, scent; bubble-ball base & stopper, 5" 65.00
Bottle, scent; red flower top on clear, 8½" 165.00
Bottle, scent; ruby w/HP flowers, long clear stopper, 7" 95.00
Bowl, berry; peppermint stick, 7" 45.00
Box, handkerchief; intaglio flowers, hinged lid 325.00
Breakfast castor, wreath/cut dots, 3 bl bottles, SP holder 125.00
Candlestick, cut bl overlay, bubble-ball std, wide top/ft 400.00
Centerpiece, lt gr, bubble-ball connector, 7x11" 115.00
Cigarette holder, eng, cut, unsgn 65.00
Compote, amber, paperweight base, controlled bubble, 6½" 125.00
Compote, aurora, red amber, 4x6" 85.00
Compote, blk w/ornate silver overlay top/base, bubble ball 285.00
Compote, cobalt w/eng grape decor, 3¾x7" 80.00
Compote, Diamond Quilt, Rosaria, clear stem 125.00
Compote, gr w/bubble-ball connector, grape pattern 145.00
Compote, Mansfield, mint gr, w/lid, 10¼" 225.00
Cornucopia, ruby, clear bubble base, 8" 80.00
Cracker jar, amberina w/HP floral, SP lid & bail, sgn 350.00

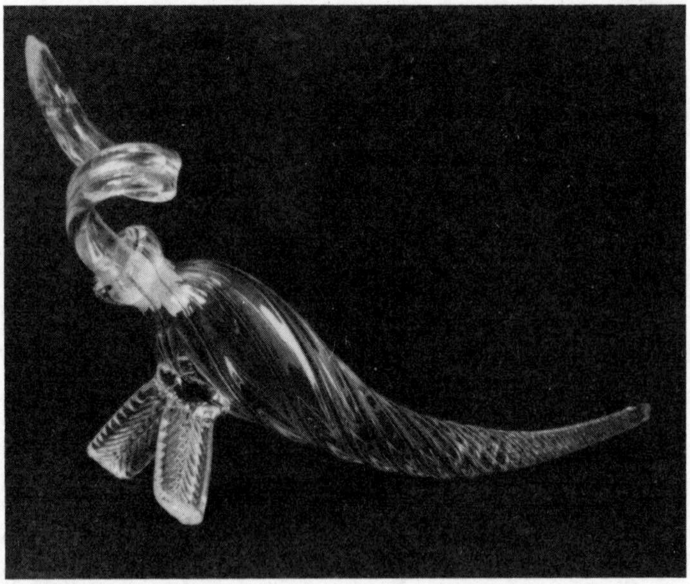

Perfume, footed cornucopia shape with curlique stopper, clear, 11½", $95.00.

Cup, peachblow, wht/decor w/in, pink to bl w/out, 1970s 75.00
Goblet, gr w/crystal bubble ball, 11½" 85.00
Goblet, wine; rouge flambe 32.00
Ice bucket, polar bear, clear 110.00
Paperweight, yel snake wrapped around bowl 75.00
Plaque, ad; 'Ambero'/grapes on yel, chipped ice exterior 750.00
Plate, salad; clear w/etched grapevine trim, 8", set of 6 . . . . 75.00
Swan, bl body, crystal neck & head, 6¾" 85.00
Tumbler, butterflies & daisies intaglio, heavy, 3¼" 30.00
Vase, canaria, grapes & leaf design, ball connector, 10" 110.00
Vase, cobalt swirls in crystal, cobalt ft, fluted, 11" 80.00
Vase, cranberry, controlled bubble-ball connector, 12" 175.00
Vase, gr, floral cutting, swirled ball stem, 12" 65.00
Vase, Nottingham cutting, #A1099, 10" 85.00
Vase, tavern glass, bulbous, #d pontil 85.00

Lamps

Brass shade w/red protruding jewels, chrome base, sgn 1,250.00
Brass 11" shade w/glass 'rocks'/emb copper floral std, 19" 800.00
Dresden, mc florals, P&A burner, 8" 435.00
Murano glass inserts, base etched w/water lilies, sgn, 12" 495.00
Puffy, 13" Oriental poppy, irreg dome shade; SP/brass base . . 2,400.00

Boudoir lamp, puffy shade with daisies and apple blossoms, on gilt-metal, vasiform standard, both signed, 6″ diameter, 11″ tall, $660.00.

Puffy, 6″ panels-w/floral-swags shade; vase std, 11″ 660.00
Puffy, 8″ apple blossom shade, Stratford, sgn twice 975.00
Rvpt w/wht floral, cameo scrolls, ribbed/irreg border, 23″ 2,600.00
Rvpt 15½″ Venetian boat scene shade; #3053 base, 20½″ 2,090.00
Rvpt 17″ rural roadside scene shade; sgn/#s urn std, 23″ 1,540.00
Rvpt 17½″ Exeter, farmer/children/house, W Macey, sgn base . 2,450.00
Rvpt 19½″ seagull shade, artist sgn, w/base, EX 2,950.00
Rvpt 8½″ Oriental pheasant shade; sgn bronzed 15″ base 650.00

Silverplate

Basket, cake; branch w/fruit hdl, emb fruit w/in, ftd 75.00
Basket, swan & cattails in bottom, grape border 45.00
Cigarette holder w/ash tray, floral 65.00
Coffee pot, fancy monogram, ebony finial & hdl, EX 85.00
Crumber, reticulated, beaded edge, blk hdl 15.00
Cup & saucer, bright-cut floral, sgn 50.00
Ladle, eng, 13″ 45.00
Nut bowl, figural squirrel on leaf shape bowl, ftd, 1890s 125.00
Nut bowl, leaves motif, on cherry/branch support, 8½″ 65.00
Set: tray, 9″ pitcher, 5″ goblet, 5″ ftd bowl 85.00
Shaving cup, emb florals, dtd 1899 .... 35.00
Sugar bowl spooner, eng & emb fr, clear bowl 125.00
Syrup, quadruple plate, 5″ claw ft 75.00
Tray, eng florals/leaves, ornate borders, hdls, 13x19½″ 95.00

Paper Dolls

No one knows quite how or when paper dolls originated. One belief is that they began in Europe as 'pantins' (jumping jacks) and were frequently worn as part of the costume. By the late 1790s, they were being mass-produced.

During the 19th century, most paper dolls portrayed famous dancers and opera stars such as Fanny Elssler and Jenny Lind. In the late 1800s, the Raphael Tuck Publishers of England produced many series of beautiful paper dolls. Also about this time, retail companies used them as advertisements to further the sale of their products. Around the turn of the century many popular women's magazines began featuring a page of paper dolls.

Most familiar to today's collectors are the books with dolls on cardboard covers, and clothes on the inside pages. These made their appearance in the late 1920s and early thirties. The most collectible of these, and the most valuable, are those representing celebrities, movie stars, and comic-strip characters of the thirties and forties.

Authority Mary Young has compiled an informative book, *Collector's Guide to Paper Dolls*, with current prices; you will find her address in the Directory under Ohio.

When no condition is indicated, the dolls listed below are assumed to be in mint, uncut original condition. Cut sets will be worth about half price, if all dolls and outfits are included and pieces are in very good condition. If dolls were produced in die-cut form, these prices reflect such a set in mint condition with all costumes and accessories.

American Family, Grinnell Lithographic #C1002, 1940 .... 25.00
American Miss Magic Doll, Parker Bros, 1957 .... 15.00
Animated Goldilocks, Milton Bradley #4101, w/3 bears 15.00
Baby Jane, Gertrude Breed, 1927 .... 17.50
Betsy Ballerina, DeJournette, w/stage & scenery changes 25.00
Betsy Ross, Platt & Monk #224B, 4 dolls, 1963 .... 6.00
Betty & Barbara, Milton Bradley #4382, 1934 .... 18.00
Betty Jane, Samuel Gabriel #D107, w/costumes & hats 20.00
Betty Marie, Londy Card #5F, 1932 .... 5.00
Big Girl, McLoughlin Bros #557, 1939 .... 15.00
Brenda Lee, Merry Manufacturing #4360, w/play phonograph 12.00
Bride, DeJournette #100 .... 8.00
Bronco Bess, Milton Bradley #4043, magnetic, 1950 .... 8.00
Brownie Scout, DeJournette, front & back style 12.00
Buster Brown & Tige, J Ottmann Lithograph 75.00
Caroline, Magic Wand #109, touch w/wand-clothes appear 18.00
Cheerleader Teen-Age Doll, Stephens Publishing #182 .... 8.00
Circus Day, Stephens Publishing #135, 1946 .... 6.00
Colonial Dolls, Platt & Munk #242, 8 dolls, 1960 .... 20.00
Costume Party, Samuel Gabriel #D137, w/dresses 40.00
Cuddly Dolls, Charles E Graham #0225 .... 25.00
Daniel Boone & Kit Carson, JV Sloan 12.00
Debby Doll, Jaymar Specialty–Great Lakes Press, 2 dolls 12.00
Debutantes, The; Samuel Gabriel #D135 .... 35.00
Deluxe Magic Mary, Milton Bradley #4900, 1959 .... 8.00
Dollies A' La Mode, Samuel Gabriel #896 .... 30.00
Dolls from the Land of Mother Goose, Platt & Monk #221 ...... 22.50
Dolly Darling, EP Dutton #2739 .... 40.00
Dollyland, Samuel Gabriel #D119, dresses & hats, set of 6 ...... 60.00
Dorothy Dimple & Her Friends, George W Jacobs, 1909 .... 8.00
Dotty Dress Doll, Carol Toys & Novelties, w/clothes 15.00
Fairy Favorite, MA Donohue #671, 1913 .... 30.00
Fashion Model, Samuel Gabriel #D116 .... 15.00
Filmland Fashions, Stephens Publishing #155 .... 10.00
Follies Girl, Jackie, Pla-Mor Toy, puzzle 17.50
Froggie Went a Courting, DeJournette #35 .... 8.00
Fun Farm Frolics, International Paper Goods #60, 1932 .... 35.00
Glitter Dolls, Playtime House #3152 .... 12.00
Hansel & Gretel, DeJournette #1440, gingerbread house 18.00
Heidi, DeJournette #200, pocketbook doll 8.00
I'm Growing Up Dolls, Platt & Munk #235A, 4 dolls, 1937 ...... 18.00
Ivy, Janex #2001, cardboard w/vinyl head, 1971 .... 5.00
Jack-o'-Lantern, George W Jacobs, 6 sheets 50.00
Jaunty Juniors, Reuben H Lilja #903, 6 pg, 1946 .... 17.00
Jet Airline Stewardess, Jaymar Specialty–Great Lakes Press 12.00
Johnny Jones, Goldsmith Publishing #2005, 1930 .... 16.00
Junior Shop, Samuel Gabriel #D106 .... 20.00
Katie, McLoughlin Bros 14.00
Lacey Daisy, Kits #1050, clothes lace on doll, 1949 .... 7.00
Let's Build Our Camp, Samuel Gabriel #D144, 1930 .... 20.00
Let's Play Eskimo, Rand McNally #211, 1937 .... 15.00
Lila Lee, Percy Reeves, 1920 .... 45.00

Little Audrey, Samuel Gabriel #250, w/4 outfits, 36"...........15.00
Little Bo Peep, DeJournette #903...........................10.00
Little Boy Blue, Platt & Munk #390, 1921...................30.00
Little Buntings, Platt & Munk #370, 1921...................30.00
Little Doctor, Reuben H Lilja #910.........................12.00
Little Laddie, Selchow & Righter...........................50.00
Little Orphan Annie, Samuel Gabriel #D113, w/dog Sandy......75.00
Little Pet's Play House, Samuel Gabriel #T147..............45.00
Lizzie, McLoughlin Bros....................................14.00
Lula-Bye-Bye, Charles E Graham #0237.......................25.00
Lynda-Lou, Lamp Studio.....................................15.00
Magic Mary, Milton Bradley #4132, first Magic Mary, 1946......10.00

The Bobbsey Twins Play Box, 1950, $22.50.

Magnetic Magic Mary, Milton Bradley #4010-1, 1958............7.00
Mamie, McLoughlin Bros.....................................14.00
Marguerite Clark, Percy Reeves, 1920.......................45.00
Mary & Madge the Round About Dolls, McLoughlin Bros #550..25.00
Merrie with the Go-Round Dresses, Milton Bradley #4847.......10.00
Miss Hollywood, Reuben H Lilja #902, 1942..................25.00
Mother & Daughter, Grinnell Lithographic #C1005, 1940.......25.00
Mr & Mrs Hawaii, Schattel's, 1955..........................10.00
My Doll Jill, Samuel Gabriel #D79..........................15.00
New Puss-in-Boots, EH Horsman..............................75.00
Paper Dolls of the World, George W Jacobs, Egyptian boy.......8.00
Party Dolls, Platt & Monk #225B, 2 dolls, 1942...............6.00
Patsy, Children's Press #3002, w/clothes & furniture, 1946......15.00
Peggy & Polly, Milton Bradley #4374, 1934..................18.00
Petticoat Junction, Avalon #301............................18.00
Polly Dolly, EM Leavens, 16½"..............................35.00
Princess Elizabeth Magic Doll, Parker Bros.................25.00
Princess Margaret Rose Magic Doll, Parker Bros.............25.00
Rag Doll Sue, Harter Publishing #H-100, 1931...............30.00
Sally Dimple, Burton Playthings #975, 1935.................22.50
School Mates, Samuel Gabriel #D100, w/wardrobe, set of 4.....18.00
Sew-Easy, Samuel Gabriel #D119.............................12.00
Shirley Temple, Samuel Gabriel #301, 1961..................20.00
Sisters, Samuel Gabriel #D135..............................25.00
Sleepy Time Girl, Milton Bradley #4785, w/dreamy eyes........12.00
Snuggly Dolls, Charles E Graham #0225, set of 5.............25.00
Stitch & Sew, J Pressman Toy Corp #1205......................6.00
Suzie Sweet, Samuel Gabriel #D94, w/dresses & hat...........10.00
Sweet Sue, Magic Wand #108...................................5.00
Sweetie-Pie Twins, Stephens Publishing #166, 1949............6.00
Teddy Bear & His Friends To Dress, Nourse, 1921............40.00
Teeny Weeny Pretty Dollies, Charles E Graham #02...........15.00
The Twinnies, Samuel Gabriel #D113, 1921, w/dresses & toys...35.00
Tina the Talking Paper Doll, Colorforms #5550, w/clothes......10.00
Tiny Twinkle, Charles E Graham #0221.......................18.00
Tommy Tom, Hubbell-Leavens.................................35.00
Triple-Joy-Book, Pinkham Press, dolls & game, 1927..........25.00
Twinkley Eyes, Milton Bradley #4792........................12.00
Wedding Party, Samuel Gabriel #D132........................30.00
Wide Awake & Fast Asleep Alice, Samuel Gabriel #D122.......30.00
Wild West Twins, National Paper Box #N11-29..................5.00
Winkle Family, Samuel Gabriel #D127........................40.00
Winnie & Her Wardrobe, McLoughlin Bros #555, 1939........25.00

Paperweights

The term 'paperweight' technically refers to any small, heavy object used to hold down loose papers. They have been made from a broad range of materials; many have been sold as souvenirs or given away by retail companies as advertising premiums. But today, those attracting the most interest are the glass collector weights.

During the mid-1800s the interest in these paperweights reached a high point, during which three major French factories were in close competition. The St. Louis, Baccarat, and Clichy companies were among the first to produce paperweights as a commercial venture, and their products are among the most valued. In the late 1860s, an unexplained decrease in their popularity caused the market for paperweights to diminish, and all three major companies eventually discontinued production.

The manufacture of paperweights in the United States, which began in the 1850s, did not experience this decline, and they have continued in production to the present time. The most valued antique American weights are from the New England, Sandwich, and Milleville companies. In 1954 a renewed surge of interest resulted in the organization of collectors clubs and an exciting new era of paperweight production. Because of this, the manufacture of weights by St. Louis and Baccarat was resumed, and contemporary artists such as Kaziun, Stankard, and Ysart are bringing their own ingenuity to this rediscovered art form.

When no condition is indicated, the items listed below are assumed to be in mint condition.

Key:

cl—clear	latt—latticinio
con—concentric	mc—multicolor
fct—faceted	mill—millefiori
gar—garland	NE—New England
grd—ground	o/l—overlay
jsp—jasper	sil—silhouette

Ayotte, Rick

Butterflies, 4 on wht grd, compound, 1983..................450.00
Hawaiian Honeycreeper, w/berries, wht grd, compound, '83....500.00
House Wren, on branch w/tree trunk & sun, lt bl grd, 1982....350.00
Ovenbird, on ground in foliage, 1983.......................400.00
Parula Warbler, 1983.......................................400.00
Scarlet Tanager, on branch w/leaves & caterpillar, cl grd......250.00
Yellow Thoated Warblers, pr, fct, 1980.....................325.00

Baccarat, Antique

Butterfly, w/mill gar, star-cut base, 2½", VG...............1,500.00
Clematis, amethyst w/stardust center cane, mill gar, 1⅞".......950.00
Close mill, mushroom, cable torsade w/in bands, cut base......770.00
Close mill, rooster/squirrel/monkey/pelicans sil, 1847, 3".....1,100.00
Con mill, variety of red/wht/bl/gr/yel canes, 2½"..............350.00
Dogrose, 5 bl/wht petals, stalk/leaves, star base, 2⅞"........1,210.00

Left to right, Clichy, twenty multicolor canes on strips of white filigree, 2¾" diameter, $775.00; Baccarat, green and white looped millefiori canes surrounding a rose, 2½", $600.00; New England, millefiori with three concentric rings surrounding a red and white cane, all on latticinio ground, 2¾", $325.00.

Pansy, w/wht stardust-center cane, star-cut base, 2¼" 550.00
Spaced mill, rooster & flower sil canes, lace grd, 1⅞" 625.00
Strawberries, 1 lg/2 sm, on stalk w/leaves, star-cut base 4,200.00

Baccarat, Modern

Bellflowers, orange, on cl purple grd, 1983, 3⅛" 375.00
Butterfly, cobalt grd, 1971 .... 175.00
Fruit, in brn wicker basket, wht opaque grd, fct, '76, 2½" 325.00
Lizard, gr jsp grd, 1973 .... 150.00
Peony w/buds, foliage & bug, cl purple grd, 1983, 3⅛" 400.00
Seahorse, bl grd, 1975, 3⅛" 390.00
Sulfide, Gridel, butterfly, 1979 .... 325.00
Sulfide, Gridel, dog, 1978 .... 275.00
Sulfide, Gridel, lovebirds, 1977 .... 200.00
Sulfide, Gridel, rooster, 1971, 3⅛" 150.00
Sulfide, Harry Truman, overlay 175.00
Sulfide, James Monroe 60.00
Sulfide, Martin Luther King gilded cameo 125.00
Sulfide, Napoleon Bonapart Memorial 150.00
Sulfide, Robert E Lee, cl, fan cut base 210.00
Sulfide, Sam Rayburn, overlay 250.00
Sulfide, Will Rogers, overlay 225.00
Sulfide, Woodrow Wilson, overlay 125.00

Caithness

Crocus 195.00
Floral Fountain, red 175.00
Lunar III 130.00
Stormy Petral, 1977 .... 95.00
Three Wise Men, 1978 .... 150.00

Clichy, Antique

Close-pack, in gr & wht stave basket w/mc canes, 2⅝", VG 675.00
Scattered mill, 2 roses, opaque turq grd, 3" 1,500.00
Spaced mill, complex pastry-mold cane, 2 rows+gar, 2⅜" 450.00
Spaced mill, roses in 5 complex canes, bl over wht grd, 2" 650.00
Swirl, turq/wht, cobalt/wht central setup, 2⅞", EX 935.00

J Glass

Dahlia, 1980 .... 125.00
Patterned mill, 7 complex canes, 1980 .... 125.00
Primrose, 1980 .... 125.00
Ruffle Edge Primrose, 1981 .... 145.00
Wild Rose, 1981 .... 175.00

Kaziun, Charles

Con mill, center shamrock, adventurine grd, fct/ped, 3¼" H 1,100.00
Morning Glory, pk/wht/cl, stalk/leaves/bud, foil bee, 2⅛" 1,100.00
Rose, 15 yel/pk petals, 4 leaves, ped, 3" H 2,200.00
Rose, 3 w/gold foil bee, gr leaves, purple grd, 2" 742.00
Spider Lily, 4 leaves, red w/gold specks grd, ped, 2" H 330.00

Manson/Scotia

Copper snake, 1979 .... 255.00
Cruxiform, w/complex cane, 1980 .... 168.00
Manta Ray, 1979 .... 280.00
Snake, gr adventurine w/yel markings, sandy grd 252.00
Sulfide, Royal Wedding, Charles & Lady Di, mill gar, fct 110.00

Perthshire

Crown, ribbons & lat twists from central cane, 1969, 2½" 325.00
Flower, red w/gr stem, mill canes form basket, 1972, 2" 250.00
Mill gar, w/center colored flower sil, 1974 .... 110.00
Pattern mill, cane twists & torsade, 1977 .... 65.00
Pattern mill garland, w/sil canes, 1979 .... 245.00
Primrose, bl & wht, w/stem & leaves, triple o/l, 1977 .... 325.00
Spaced mill, on latt, w/sil canes, miniature, 1982 .... 75.00
Stylized bl & wht flower, w/gar, fct, 1976 .... 95.00

St. Louis, Antique

Macedoine, w/dog sil, 1⅞" 450.00
Nosegay, 4 florets & leaves in cl glass, 6/7/1 fct, 3¼" 650.00
Spaced mill, wht/red/gr/bl, in clear glass, 3" 390.00

St. Louis, Modern

Cherries, yel stems/gr leaves, latt basket, fct, '75, 3" 350.00
Close mill of complex canes, 1981 .... 420.00
Cross, latt twist-border canes divide mill canes, 1981 .... 480.00
Flower on latt, 1982 .... 430.00
Hostage, fct, 1981 .... 380.00
Mill 'flowers,' latt & torsades form basket, 1981 .... 840.00
Red 'Clichy' roses, on wht grd, 1976 .... 300.00
Strawberries, 1982 .... 430.00
Sulfide, G Washington, gold on bl grd, dbl overlay, 1976 .... 350.00
Valentine Bouquet, 1983 .... 440.00
White flower, w/eleven petals, bl grd, 1963 .... 300.00

Stankard, Paul

Apple Blossoms, 6 w/many buds, 2 stalks w/leaves, '80, 3½" 2,200.00
Blackberries, 3 w/blossoms & buds, gr leaves, cl, 1979, 3" 1,045.00
Bouquet, 4 varieties of flowers, cl glass, 1979, 3" 1,210.00
Dogwood, cobalt grd, 1975, 2⅞" 700.00
Lady Slipper Orchid/2 buds in crystal, sgn w/S cane, '82 .... 1,000.00
Spider Orchid, w/roots & seed pod, cl glass, 3" 825.00
Wht blossoms, 3 w/stalks/leaves/roots, cobalt grd, 1980 .... 682.00

Trabucco, Victor

Butterfly, w/2 daisies & bud, Ice Block, 1981, 3x3½" 450.00
Convulvous, 2 w/bud & foliage, 1983 .... 400.00

Crab Apple, w/open flower & 2 buds, 1983................400.00
Sweet Peas, 1981.......................................250.00
Yellow Bellflower, w/foliage, 1982.......................275.00

Whittemore, Francis D.

Acorns & Oak Leaves, on cobalt grd, 2⅛″..................320.00
Rose, 15 pk petals/gr leaves, ped base, sgn W, 2¾″..........220.00
Wild Rose, w/bud, gr grd, 2¼″...........................350.00

Ysart, Paul

Cluster mill, w/circle of ribbons, gr grd, script sgn............400.00
Cluster mill, w/mill cane gar, cl grd, 1940s, cane sgn.........425.00
Coiled snake, brn adventurine w/pk & yel dots, gr grd, 2¾″....600.00
Dragonfly, adventurine wings, lt bl grd w/mill, 3″.............625.00
Flower, violet & wht on gr stem & leaves, pk/wht jsp grd......450.00
Scattered mill, on muslin, 1940s, 2½″......................600.00

Miscellaneous

Antique Bacchus, close mill, bl/wht/red basket, 3⅛″, VG.......715.00
Antique Bohemian, mushroom, 4 roses, complex center cane...750.00
Antique Bohemian, spaced mill on latt, horse sil cane, 2¾″....450.00
Antique NE, apple, set on cl glass foot, 2⅝″................935.00
Antique NE, crown, mc floret, twisted ribbons, 2¼″...........660.00
Antique NE, nosegay, hollow pastry-mold cane gar, ray grd....490.00
Antique NE, 5 pears & 4 cherries in latt basket, 2⅞″.........625.00
Antique Sandwich, buttercup, w/bud/leaves/stalk, jsp grd.......825.00
Antique Sandwich, poinsettia, bl/wht jsp grd, 2¾″............495.00
Antique Stourbridge, con mill, 5 rows, central cluster, VG.....110.00
Concentric, 5 & 1 fct, dated 1969, 3″......................150.00
Crystal, pyramid form, 5″...................................35.00
D'Albret, Churchill & Union Jack, Pinchbeck................150.00
Deer, reclining, CI, old gold pnt, late 19th C, 3½x3″..........35.00
Hansen, Robert; bl flower w/buds, pk grd, fct, early, 2¼″......150.00
Hansen, Robert; pk flower w/buds, honeycomb fct, 2¼″.......165.00
LaBelle, Wm Davis; wht rose/gr leaves, ftd, 1888, 3″, NM......50.00
Lewis, Pete; Primrose, red & wht, w/butterfly, 1975, 2⅜″......175.00
National Surety Co, eagle on globe, bronze..................30.00
Ravenna, 5-petal wht lily, 3¼″.............................15.00
Snake, coiled in knot, wrought iron, 7″ L..................135.00
Tarsitano, Del; 3 cherries, stalks/branches/leaves, 2¾″.........467.00
Whitefriars, concentric mill, Mayflower sil cane, fct, '70........200.00
Whitefriars, concentric mill, mc fish central motif, fct.........200.00

Papier Mache

The art of papier mache was mainly European. It originated in Paris around the middle of the 18th century, and became popular in America during Victorian times. Small items, such as boxes, trays, inkwells, frames, etc., as well as extensive ceiling moldings and larger articles of furniture were made. The process involved building layer upon layer of paper soaked in glue, coaxed into shape over a wood or wire form. When dry, it was painted or decorated with gilt or inlays. Inexpensive 20th century 'notions' were machine processed and mold-pressed.

When no condition is indicated, the items listed below are assumed to be in excellent condition.

Box, MOP inlaid rose branch, gold trim, 1x4¾x3½″..........195.00
Cat, mouse in mouth, orange/wht stripe, head nods, 9½″ L....195.00
Dachshund, orig pnt, 20th C, 28″ L, VG....................175.00
Dish, japanned, 2 ladies in garden, 6½″......................45.00
Dog, brn/wht, sgn Sell, Columbus, 22x20½″ L, VG...........135.00

Tea tray painted with a fox hunting scene, ca 19th century, 32″, $3,000.00, auction estimate.

Letter box, wall mt w/figures/pagodas in gold, Japan, 9″........65.00
Nodder, German character w/pipe, window display, 11″........150.00
Plaque, snow scene, dtd 1800, 6″ dia........................45.00
Store display, lg man's shoe, pnt brn, 25″ L................350.00
Tiger, HP, 1900s, 12″, EX...............................65.00
Toy, policeman, press chest/mouth moves, 12″...............115.00
Tray, blk lacquer, gilt floral, bamboo stand, 1850, 31x25″.....750.00
Tray, pearl inlay, mc floral, scalloped, brass hdl, 8″, EX........42.50

Parian Ware

Parian is hard paste unglazed porcelain made to resemble marble. First made in the mid-1800s by Staffordshire potters, it was soon after produced in the United States by the U.S. Pottery at Bennington, Vermont. Busts and statuary were favored, but plaques, vases, mugs, and pitchers were also made.

When no condition is indicated, the items listed below are assumed to be in mint condition.

Maiden dipping amphora into stream, softly tinted, after W.B. Kirk, dated 1857, 14″ long, $900.00.

Bust, Charles Sumner, politician for Civil Rights, 11¾″.........70.00
Bust, Geo Washington, ped base, 11″........................65.00
Bust, Longfellow, bk: name/verse, 10¾″.....................85.00
Bust, Queen Victoria, on blk wood stand, 1897, 6½″..........75.00
Doll, sitting in 1800s parian bathtub, tinted, mk #6, 2½″.......65.00
Ewer, snake hdl, floral relief, 6¾″...........................40.00
Figurine, Colonade, warrior & horses, Germany, 7½″ L........65.00
Figurine, ear of corn w/husks peeled bk, cherubs, 7½″.........40.00
Figurine, girl w/basket of flowers, mk R/L, tinted, 16x6″.......295.00
Figurine, man on rock holds birds above, dog by side, 9½″....135.00
Figurine, man w/cloak & beret, no mk, 13½x4⅛″............115.00
Figurine, Match Making, pr owls on branch, 1871 reg mk, 7″..265.00
Figurine, Net Mender, lady w/fishing net, no mk, 11½x4¼″....145.00
Figurine, nude boy by tree petting bird, sgn J&TB, 8x4¾″.....135.00
Figurine, Ruth, oval base, 13″............................175.00
Figurine, seated Psyche has Cupid's quiver, he afloat, 9″......165.00
Loving cup, Bacchus/women, bl/wht, award mk, Meigh, 7″.....295.00
Pitcher, Arabian scenes in relief, twig hdl, 7″................175.00
Pitcher, Babe in the Woods, lav, sgn, water sz...............250.00
Pitcher, boys climb tree, bird's nest on bk, Mayer, 6¾″.......225.00
Pitcher, children relief, lav, Alcock, 9″......................285.00
Pitcher, man on 1 side/lady on other, masque face, 9½″.......145.00
Pitcher, Naomi & daughters-in-law, lav/wht, dtd 1847..........225.00
Pitcher, witches stirring cauldron, Alcock, 1840s..............200.00
Plaque, North Carolina Tobacco, ladies/cornucopia, 12x12″....175.00
Vase, Grecian lady bust, laurel leaf crown ea side, 5½″.........35.00
Vase, spill; Babes in the Woods, sage gr, TJ Mayer, 1850.......85.00

Pate-Sur-Pate

Pate-sur-pate, literally paste on paste, is a technique where relief decorations are built up on a ceramic body by layering several applications of slip, one on the other until the desired result is achieved. Usually only two colors are used, and the value of a piece is greatly enhanced as more color is added.

When no condition is indicated, the items listed below are assumed to be in mint condition.

Pilgrim flask, Night and Day emblematic figures in white on dark green, decorated by Schenck, George Jones Mfg., repaired, 14″, $950.00.

Basket, birds & thistles, 4-color, crowned circle mk, 7½″......600.00
Box, cobalt, cherubs/lion/chariot, gold trim, Limoges, 3¾″.....120.00
Box, mythical lovers, wht on bl, Limoges, 5″ sq.............160.00
Plaque, nymph & waves, wht on cobalt, Limoges, 1900, 7x4″..400.00
Vase, cupid frieze, 2 neck panels, ornate hdls, w/lid, 27″.....2,500.00
Vase, Cupid judge/lg court, Solon, Minton, hdls, rstr, 25″....1,800.00
Vase, manacled couple/putti, 7-color, Solon, Minton, 20″.....5,000.00
Vase, medallion of Diane, wht/lav on celadon, Schultz, 9½″....575.00
Vase, 2 putti over sea, 5-color, gilt, Meissen, 8¾″...........1,000.00

Pattern Glass

Pattern Glass was the first mass-produced fancy tableware in America, and was much prized by our ancestors. From the 1840s to the Civil War, it contained a high lead content and is known as 'Flint Glass.' It is exceptionally clear and resonant. Later glass was made with soda lime, and is known as non-flint.

By the 1890s this pattern glass was produced in great volume in thousands of patterns, and colored glass came into vogue. Today, the highest prices are often paid for these later patterns flashed with rose, amber, canary, and vaseline; stained ruby; or made in colors of cobalt, green, yellow, amethyst, etc. Demand for Pattern Glass declined by 1915, and glass fanciers were collecting it by 1930. No other field of antiques offers more diversity in patterns, prices, or pieces than this unique and historical glass that represents the Victorian era in America.

For a more thorough study on the subject, we recommend *The Collector's Encyclopedia of Pattern Glass*, by Mollie Helen McCain, available from Collector Books. In the listings that follow, if color is not noted, the glass is clear. When no condition is indicated, the items are assumed to be in mint condition.

Actress, butter dish, 6″..................................32.00
Actress, cheese dish, Lone Fisherman.......................225.00
Actress, cheese dish, The Two Dromios......................200.00
Actress, compote, open; 7¼x7¼″...........................45.00
Actress, creamer, frosted foot & stem.......................76.00
Actress, jam jar w/lid.....................................80.00
Actress, pickle jar, Love's Request..........................40.00
Actress, platter, Miss Nielsen.............................100.00
Actress, platter, Pinafore..................................60.00
Actress, sauce dish, flat, 4½″.............................18.00
Actress, sauce dish, ftd, 4″...............................22.00
Actress, spooner...72.00
Admiral Dewey, see Greentown, Dewey
Adonis, see Washboard
Alabama, celery vase......................................30.00
Alabama, creamer...30.00
Alabama, cruet...55.00
Alabama, relish dish......................................15.00
Alabama, syrup...65.00
Alabama, toothpick holder.................................60.00
Alligator Scales, goblet, flint..............................28.50
Almond Thumbprint, master salt............................14.00
Amazon, bowl, flat, flared, 5½″............................12.00
Amazon, butter dish.......................................34.00
Amazon, champagne.......................................20.00
Amazon, creamer, miniature................................28.00
Amazon, goblet, etched....................................30.00
Amazon, salt cellar, master................................12.00
Amazon, shaker, salt.......................................10.00
Amazon, tumbler, etched...................................26.00
American Beauty, tumbler, gr, gilt trim......................23.00
Andes, see Beaded Tulip

Anthemion, pitcher, water, 8¼″ 35.00
Apollo, bowl, plain, 8″ 19.00
Apollo, celery vase, frosted 35.00
Apollo, creamer, etched 35.00
Apollo, plate, etched 30.00
Apollo, plate, plain 25.00
Apollo, sauce dish, plain, 4″ 6.00
Apollo, sauce dish, w/stand 12.00
Apollo, sugar bowl, etched, w/lid 40.00
Apollo, tray, water; plain 45.00
Apollo, tumbler, etched or frosted 25.00
Aquarium, pitcher, water 150.00
Aquarium, pitcher, water, gr 290.00
Arched Grape, celery vase 40.00
Arched Grape, champagne 50.00
Arched Grape, creamer 60.00
Arched Grape, goblet 25.00
Argus, champagne 40.00
Argus, egg cup 25.00
Argus, goblet 45.00
Argus, spill 43.00
Argus, sugar bowl 40.00
Argus, tumbler, ftd, 4¼″ 58.00
Argus, tumbler, whiskey 47.00
Arrowsheaf, pitcher, water 42.00
Art, cake stand, 7¾″ 52.00
Art, celery vase 35.00
Art, sauce dish, flat, 4″ 16.00
Art, sugar bowl, open 30.00
Art Novo, goblet, plain 32.00
Art Novo, sauce dish, flat, gilt trim or ruby stained 23.00
Ashburton, bottle, bar; canary, qt 610.00
Ashburton, bottle, bitters; flint 56.00
Ashburton, celery vase, ftd 70.00
Ashburton, celery vase, ftd, low gauffered rim 110.00
Ashburton, champagne 53.00
Ashburton, champagne, cut, gilt decor 78.00
Ashburton, claret, low stem 38.00
Ashburton, claret, tall stem 58.00
Ashburton, compote, open, low standard, 7½″ 64.00
Ashburton, cordial 68.00
Ashburton, egg cup 40.00
Ashburton, egg cup, dbl 90.00
Ashburton, egg cup, flint, clambroth 126.00
Ashburton, goblet 30.00
Ashburton, mug, 4¾″ 70.00
Ashburton, mug, 7″ 120.00
Ashburton, tumbler, ale; flint 63.00
Ashburton, tumbler, bar 57.00
Ashburton, tumbler, ftd 80.00
Ashburton, tumbler, ships 70.00
Ashburton, wine 35.00
Ashman, see Etched Fern
Atlanta, see Clear Lion Head
Atlas, cake stand, 8½″ 24.00
Atlas, champagne 27.00
Atlas, cordial, 3½″ 30.00
Atlas, creamer, flat base 17.00
Atlas, goblet 27.00
Atlas, pitcher, milk; tankard, 10″ 28.00
Atlas, salt cellar, ind 9.00
Atlas, toothpick holder 14.00
Atlas, tumbler, water 30.00
Atlas, wine, etched 30.00

Aurora, decanter, orig stopper 30.00
Aurora, decanter, ruby stained, orig stopper 140.00
Aurora, goblet, etched 25.00
Aurora, wine 20.00
Aurora, wine, etched 27.00
Austrian, butter dish 85.00
Austrian, creamer, gilt trim 30.00
Austrian, creamer, toy 24.00
Austrian, goblet 46.00
Austrian, salt shaker, pr 27.00
Austrian, wine, vaseline 125.00
Baby Thumbprint, see Dakota
Bakewell Block, decanter, w/stopper, qt 75.00
Bakewell Block, wine, flint 57.00
Balder, see Pennsylvania
Ball & Swirl, creamer 23.00
Ball & Swirl, goblet 24.00
Ball & Swirl, pitcher, water 35.00
Baltimore Pear, butter dish 35.00
Baltimore Pear, celery vase, ftd 35.00
Baltimore Pear, pitcher, water 75.00
Banded Buckle, spooner 30.00
Banded Buckle, sugar bowl, open 22.00
Banded Buckle, tumbler, bar 57.00
Banded Portland, see Virginia
Bar & Diamond, celery vase, flat base 15.00
Bar & Diamond, cruet, orig stopper, 3½″ 23.00
Bar & Diamond, cruet, tankard 20.00
Bar & Diamond, goblet 25.00
Bar & Diamond, jug, orig stopper, 10″ 37.00
Bar & Diamond, pitcher, tankard; 10½″ 40.00
Bar & Diamond, sauce dish, flat or ftd 8.00
Bar & Diamond, shaker, salt 12.00
Bar & Diamond, shakers, w/holder, pr 47.00
Bar & Diamond, sugar bowl, etched, w/lid 47.00
Bar & Diamond, tray, water; 10¼″ 30.00
Bar & Diamond, wine 27.00
Barberry, bread plate 23.00
Barberry, celery vase 36.00
Barberry, goblet 30.00

Barberry, pitcher, water; bulbous 80.00
Barberry, plate, 6″ 17.00
Barberry, spooner 36.00
Barley, butter dish 30.00
Barley, goblet 25.00
Barley, jar, jam; no lid 23.00
Barley, pitcher, water 40.00
Barley, plate, rare, 6″ 37.00
Barley, platter, 9½x11½″ 20.00

Barley, sauce dish, ftd, 4¼″....7.00
Barley, spooner....22.00
Barley, tray, relish; 10¾x5½″....12.00
Barred Forget-Me-Not, celery vase, ftd, hdl....34.00
Barred Forget-Me-Not, creamer....30.00
Barred Forget-Me-Not, goblet....30.00
Barred Forget-Me-Not, spooner....20.00
Barred Forget-Me-Not, sugar bowl, w/lid....40.00
Barred Oval, creamer....20.00
Barred Oval, pitcher, water; ruby stained, etched....250.00
Barrel Huber, see Huber
Basketweave, cup & saucer, amber....34.00
Basketweave, cup & saucer, yel....30.00
Basketweave, goblet, yel....30.00
Basketweave, mug, 3″....13.00
Basketweave, pitcher, water; bl....50.00
Basketweave, plate, rnd hdl, 8¾″....12.00
Basketweave, sauce dish, milk glass, flat, 4″....9.00
Basketweave, tray, rural scene, bl or yel, 12″....47.00
Beaded Bull's Eye & Drape, see Alabama
Beaded Dewdrop, see Wisconsin
Beaded Grape, bowl, shallow, sq, gr, 5¼″....20.00
Beaded Grape, creamer, gr....38.00
Beaded Grape, cruet, gr....75.00
Beaded Grape, cruet, plain....15.00
Beaded Grape, platter, 10¼x7¼″....18.00
Beaded Grape, tumbler, water; gilt trim....22.00
Beaded Grape, wine....36.00
Beaded Grape, wine, gr....65.00
Beaded Grape Medallion, creamer, banded....52.00
Beaded Grape Medallion, goblet, banded....25.00

Beaded Grape Medallion, goblet, pattern ft....30.00
Beaded Grape Medallion, spooner, banded....30.00
Beaded Loop, see Oregon
Beaded Medallion, bottle, castor; mustard....17.00
Beaded Medallion, bottle, castor; oil, orig stopper....26.00
Beaded Medallion, egg cup....20.00
Beaded Medallion, spooner....18.00
Beaded Medallion, sugar bowl, open; flint....20.00
Beaded Panel & Sunburst, creamer....33.00
Beaded Panel & Sunburst, cruet, faceted stopper....33.00
Beaded Swirl, see Swirled Column
Beaded Tulip, goblet....32.00
Beaded Tulip, sauce dish, ftd, 4½″....10.00
Bearded Head, compote, w/lid....70.00
Bearded Head, egg cup....36.00
Bearded Head, pitcher, water....100.00
Bearded Head, salt cellar, master....46.00
Bearded Head, sauce dish, ftd, 4″....17.00
Bearded Head, sugar, w/lid....45.00
Bellflower, celery vase....162.00
Bellflower, compote, low, flint, 7″....58.50
Bellflower, egg cup....33.00
Bellflower, goblet, coarse rib....33.00
Bellflower, spooner....35.00
Bellflower, sugar bowl, w/lid....40.00
Bent Buckle, see New Hampshire
Bethlehem Star, compote, open....25.00
Bethlehem Star, creamer....25.00
Bethlehem Star, cruet....20.00
Bethlehem Star, sugar bowl....30.00
Bethlehem Star, tumbler....18.00
Bevelled Diamond & Star, cheese dish....40.00
Bevelled Diamond & Star, creamer....22.00
Bevelled Diamond & Star, decanter, ruby stained....88.00
Bevelled Diamond & Star, decanter, w/orig stopper....34.00
Bevelled Diamond & Star, dish, oblong, 5x8″....10.00

Bevelled Diamond & Star, pitcher, milk; 7″....20.00
Bevelled Diamond & Star, plate, 10″....18.00
Bevelled Diamond & Star, sauce dish, collared base, 4″....10.00
Bevelled Diamond & Star, shaker, salt, pr....12.00
Bevelled Diamond & Star, tray, wine; 9″....18.00
Bevelled Diamond & Star, wine....18.00
Bird & Fern, see Hummingbird
Bird & Strawberry, bowl, oval, ftd, 9¼″....32.00
Bird & Strawberry, cake stand, 8¾″....66.00
Bird & Strawberry, compote, open....110.00
Bird & Strawberry, creamer....45.00
Bird & Strawberry, cup, punch....20.00
Bird & Strawberry, sauce dish, ftd....18.00
Bird & Strawberry, sugar bowl, open....35.00
Blackberry, goblet....35.00
Blackberry, spooner....50.00
Blaze, bottle, oil; orig stopper, 6″....40.00
Blaze, champagne....70.00
Blaze, creamer, molded hdl....46.00
Blaze, egg cup....40.00
Blaze, sugar bowl, flint, w/lid....56.00
Bleeding Heart, butter dish....60.00
Bleeding Heart, compote, open....25.00
Bleeding Heart, egg cup....40.00
Bleeding Heart, goblet....40.00
Block & Fan, bowl, ftd, collared, 8″....20.00
Block & Fan, cake stand, 8½″....20.00
Block & Fan, celery vase....32.00
Block & Fan, celery vase, flat base....17.00
Block & Fan, plate, 6″ or 7″....22.00
Block & Fan, sauce dish, ftd, 3¾″....8.00
Block & Fan, sauce dish, ruby stained, ftd, 4″....27.00
Block & Fan, sugar bowl, w/lid....32.00
Block & Fan, sugar shaker....36.00

Block & Star, see Valencia Waffle
Block w/Thumbprint, goblet....18.00
Block w/Thumbprint, salt cellar, flint....23.00
Block w/Thumbprint, tumbler, ftd....18.00
Block w/Thumbprint, tumbler, ftd, flint....25.00
Blue Jay, see Cardinal Bird
Bosworth, see Star Band
Bow Tie, bowl, shallow....15.00
Bow Tie, cake stand, 9"....47.00
Bow Tie, compote, 5½x10½"....65.00
Bow Tie, creamer....40.00
Bow Tie, goblet....40.00
Bow Tie, jar, marmalade; w/lid....45.00
Bow Tie, spooner....35.00
Bradford Grape, champagne....58.00
Bradford Grape, goblet....23.00
Bradford Grape, goblet, flint....50.00
Brittanic, berry, master; gold....32.00
Brittanic, bottle, castor....27.00
Brittanic, syrup....50.00
Broken Column, bowl, shallow, 7x2¼"....25.00
Broken Column, compote, jelly; red dots....112.00
Broken Column, compote, open; 6¾x5½"....40.00
Broken Column, creamer....28.00
Broken Column, cruet, orig stopper....55.00
Broken Column, cup, punch; bl....57.00
Broken Column, dish, oval, 11x5"....17.00
Broken Column, pitcher, water....55.00
Broken Column, shakers, salt, pr....30.00
Broken Column, spooner....35.00
Broken Column, tray, relish; 7¾x5"....14.00
Broken Column, tumbler, water....37.00
Bryce, cake stand, 10"....23.00
Bryce, compote, jelly....25.00
Bryce, creamer....18.00
Bryce, cruet....50.00
Bryce, plate, 8¼"....18.00
Buckle, egg cup....28.00
Buckle, goblet....23.00
Buckle, goblet, flint....36.00
Buckle, salt cellar, master; oval....37.00
Buckle, sauce dish, shallow....12.00
Buckle, sugar bowl, open; non-flint....24.00
Buckle, sugar bowl, w/lid; flint....57.00
Buckle, tumbler, bar....55.00
Buckle, wine, non-flint....78.00
Buckle & Diamond, pitcher, water....57.00
Buckle w/Star, celery vase, ftd....25.00
Buckle w/Star, sugar bowl, open....18.00
Buckle w/Star, sugar bowl, w/lid....43.00
Buckle w/Star, tumbler, bar....55.00
Buckle w/Star, wine....25.00
Bull's Eye, goblet, low, flint....33.00
Bull's Eye, goblet, tall stem....62.00
Bull's Eye, spooner....37.00
Bull's Eye, wine, flint....55.00
Bull's Eye & Daisy, champagne, gilt trim....15.00
Bull's Eye & Daisy, goblet, gr eyes....20.00
Bull's Eye & Daisy, tumbler, water; gilt trim....12.00
Bull's Eye & Fan, bowl, shallow, bl, gilt trim, 8⅜"....30.00
Bull's Eye & Fan, celery vase, lg....34.00
Bull's Eye & Fan, creamer, 3¼"....15.00
Bull's Eye & Fan, goblet....25.00
Bull's Eye & Fan, pitcher, water....45.00
Bull's Eye & Fan, sauce dish, flat, 5¼"....7.00
Bull's Eye & Fan, tumbler, water; bl, gilt trim....30.00
Bull's Eye & Wishbone, goblet, flint....152.00
Bull's Eye Band, see Reverse Torpedo
Bull's Eye in Heart, see Heart w/Thumbprint
Bull's Eye w/Diamond Points, goblet, flint....97.00
Bull's Eye w/Diamond Points, honey dish, 3½"....14.00

Bull's Eye w/Diamond Points, sauce dish, flat, 4¼"....8.00
Bull's Eye w/Diamond Points, tumbler, bar....112.00
Bull's Eye w/Fleur-de-Lis, bottle, bar; qt....77.00
Bull's Eye w/Fleur-de-Lis, goblet....77.00
Bull's Eye w/Fleur-de-Lis, salt cellar, master....56.00
Bull's Eye w/Fleur-de-Lis, sugar bowl, open; flint....57.00
Button Arches, cup, punch; ruby stained, etched....18.00
Button Arches, tumbler, water; ruby stained....25.00
Button Arches, wine, clambroth....27.00
Button Arches, wine, ruby stained, etched....33.00
Button Band, cake stand....65.00
Button Band, castor bottle....30.00
Button Band, goblet, etched....30.00
Button Band, sugar bowl, open....15.00
Cabbage Rose, creamer....55.00
Cabbage Rose, goblet....35.00
Cabbage Rose, salt cellar, master....27.00
Cabbage Rose, tumbler....45.00
Cable, goblet, flint....75.00
Cable, honey dish, flint, 3½"....12.00
Canadian, butter dish, w/lid....85.00
Canadian, creamer....60.00
Canadian, pitcher, water....90.00
Canadian, wine....56.00
Cane, goblet....20.00
Cane, goblet, bl....36.00
Cane, kettle, amber, 2½"....19.00
Cane, kettle, bl....17.00
Cane, plate, apple gr or bl, 4½"....13.00
Cane, waste bowl, amber....30.00
Cane & Rosette, compote, open....17.00
Cane Horseshoe, cruet....35.00
Cape Cod, goblet....40.00
Capitol Building, champagne or goblet....33.00
Cardinal, see Cardinal Bird
Cardinal Bird, creamer....35.00
Cardinal Bird, goblet....33.00
Cardinal Bird, sugar bowl, w/lid....47.00
Carnation, berry set, gold, New Martinsburg, 7-pc....160.00
Cathedral, bowl, relish; fish shape, ruby stained....56.00
Cathedral, cake stand, bl....66.00
Cathedral, sauce dish, flat, 4"....7.00
Cathedral, sugar bowl, open....16.00
Cathedral, wine....30.00

Centennial, see Liberty Bell
Chain, butter dish....14.00
Chain, goblet....19.00
Chain, plate, 7"....15.00
Chain, wine....17.00
Chain & Shield, creamer....16.00
Chain & Shield, goblet....22.00
Chain & Shield, pitcher, water....41.00
Chain w/Diamonds, see Washington Centennial
Champion, pitcher, water....52.00
Champion, tumbler....16.00
Chandelier, cake stand....85.00
Chandelier, celery vase....37.00
Chandelier, creamer....30.00
Chandelier, sauce dish, flat, 3¼"....18.00
Checkerboard, cup, punch....5.00
Checkerboard, goblet....17.00
Checkerboard, sauce dish, ruby stained, gilt trim, 4½"....15.00
Checkerboard, tumbler, 4½"....20.00
Checkerboard, wine....20.00
Cherry & Cable, creamer....25.00
Cherry & Cable, goblet....20.00
Cherry & Cable, pitcher, water....62.00
Classic, butter dish, w/lid....155.00
Classic, celery vase....155.00
Classic, goblet....196.00
Classic, pitcher, water....275.00
Clear Lion Head, compote, open....65.00
Clear Lion Head, salt shaker....16.00
Coin, US; cake stand....230.00
Coin, US; celery vase, flat base, dimes....136.00
Coin, US; compote, open; quarters & half dollars, 7"....325.00
Coin, US; goblet, dimes....150.00
Coin, US; spooner, quarters....200.00
Coin Glass, see Coin, US
Colonial, champagne....28.00
Colonial, champagne, flint....53.00
Colonial, goblet, knob stem....57.00
Colonial, salt cellar, master....18.00
Colonial w/Garland, see Fern Garland
Colorado, bowl, ftd, gr, 9½"....30.00
Colorado, butter dish, w/lid, bl....225.00

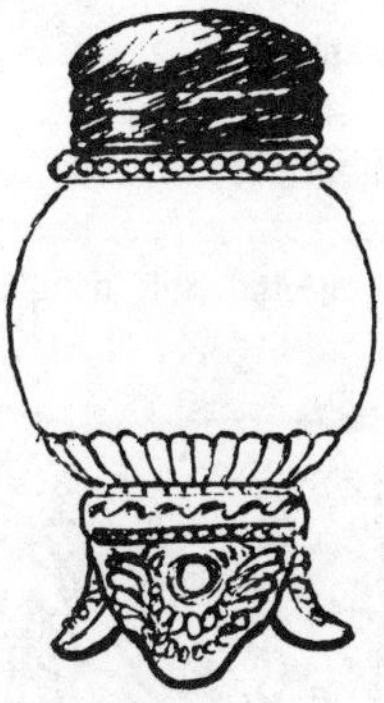

Colorado, pitcher, water; gr....175.00
Colorado, sauce dish, ftd, gr, 4¾"....17.00
Colorado, sugar bowl, open; bl or gr....27.00
Colorado, tricorn dish....6.00
Colorado, tumbler, water; ruby stained....20.00
Columbian Coin, berry set, gilded, 7-pc....295.00
Columbian Coin, claret, clear & frosted....145.00
Columbian Coin, creamer....240.00
Columbian Coin, pitcher, milk....170.00
Columbian Coin, spooner....40.00
Columbian Coin, syrup....130.00
Columbian Coin, table set, clear w/EX gold, 4-pc....350.00
Compact, see Snail
Coral, see Fishscale
Cord Drapery, see Greentown
Cottage, champagne....50.00
Cottage, compote, jelly; gr....47.00
Cottage, creamer....20.00
Crescent & Fan, see Starred Scroll
Croesus, bowl, ftd, gr, gilt trim....66.00
Croesus, butter dish, gr, gilt trim....96.00
Croesus, creamer, gr....56.00
Croesus, cruet, gr, gilt trim....200.00
Croesus, sauce dish, ftd, gr, gilt trim, 3¾"....34.00
Croesus, spooner, gr....62.00
Croesus, spooner, purple....86.00
Croesus, tumbler, gr, gilt trim....40.00
Crossed Block, goblet....18.00
Crowfoot, see Yale
Crown Jewels, see Chandelier
Crystal Ball, see Atlas
Crystal Wedding, banana stand....75.00
Crystal Wedding, bowl, berry; scalloped top....35.00
Crystal Wedding, bowl, relish; frosted....25.00
Crystal Wedding, butter dish....40.00
Crystal Wedding, cake stand....65.00
Crystal Wedding, creamer....75.00
Crystal Wedding, creamer, etched....56.00

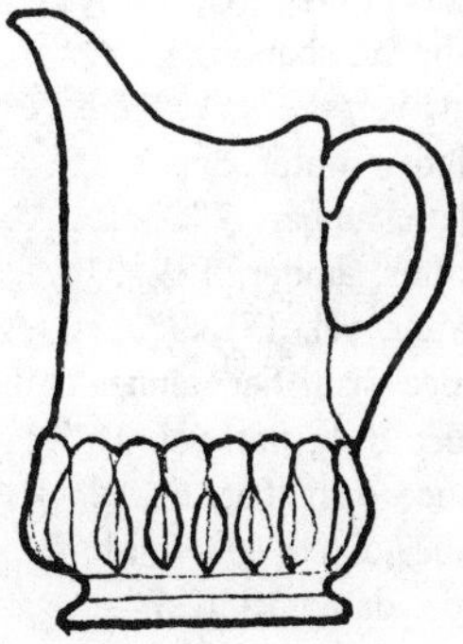

Crystal Wedding, creamer, ruby flashed....40.00
Crystal Wedding, goblet, etched band or flower etched....35.00
Crystal Wedding, goblet, ruby flashed....40.00
Crystal Wedding, sauce dish....10.00
Crystal Wedding, spooner....70.00
Crystal Wedding, sugar bowl, frosted....65.00
Crystal Wedding, sugar bowl, w/lid....50.00
Crystal Wedding, tumbler, ruby flashed....42.00
Cube & Diamond, see Log & Star
Cube w/Fan, see Pineapple & Fan
Cupid & Venus, butter dish, w/lid....65.00
Cupid & Venus, champagne....110.00
Cupid & Venus, goblet....50.00
Cupid & Venus, mug....20.00
Cupid & Venus, pitcher, water....65.00
Cupid & Venus, plate, amber, 10"....110.00
Cupid & Venus, plate, 10¼"....25.00
Cupid & Venus, wine....94.00
Curled Leaf, celery vase, gilt trim....30.00
Curled Leaf, creamer, applied hdl....26.00
Currant, creamer....60.00
Currant, sauce dish, flat, 4"....7.00

Currier & Ives, goblet....26.00
Currier & Ives, sauce dish, flat, 4½″....5.00
Currier & Ives, syrup....60.00
Currier & Ives, tray, wine; balky mule, 9½″....68.00
Currier & Ives, wine....18.00
Cut Log, bowl, relish....13.00
Cut Log, celery vase....15.00
Cut Log, compote, open; 5x3½″....55.00
Cut Log, compote, open; 8¼x6½″....65.00
Cut Log, creamer, 5½″....30.00
Cut Log, mug....15.00
Cut Log, pitcher, tankard....90.00
Cut Log, pitcher, water....75.00
Cut Log, shakers, salt, pr....40.00
Cut Log, sugar bowl, open; ind....20.00
Cut Log, sugar bowl, w/lid....26.00
Cut Log, wine....24.00
Dahlia, bowl, oval, 6x8¾″....17.00
Dahlia, bread tray, oval, hdld....36.00
Dahlia, cake stand, 9½″....28.00
Dahlia, egg cup....57.00
Dahlia, pitcher, water; amber....68.00
Dahlia, plate, hdl, amber, 9″....25.00
Dahlia, plate, 7″....43.00
Dahlia, tray, relish....14.00
Dahlia, wine....40.00
Daisy & Button, bowl, tricorn, yel, 8″....25.00
Daisy & Button, bread plate, amber, hdls, 9x13″....30.00
Daisy & Button, butter pat, fan shape....10.00
Daisy & Button, cake basket, yel, 7x5½″....126.00
Daisy & Button, dish, fan shape....12.00
Daisy & Button, hat, yel, 3⅞″....26.00
Daisy & Button, pitcher, water....85.00
Daisy & Button, plate, amber, 7″....15.00
Daisy & Button, platter, amber, 13½x9″....35.00
Daisy & Button, platter, yel, 13½x9″....40.00
Daisy & Button, sauce dish, flat, amber or bl, 4½″....15.00
Daisy & Button, sauce dish, flat, yel, 4¾″....10.00
Daisy & Button, sauce dish, flat, 5″....7.00
Daisy & Button, shoe, dated, gilt finish, 7″....58.00
Daisy & Button, shoe, dated 1886, 7″....33.00
Daisy & Button, shoe on Fishscale tray....90.00
Daisy & Button, sitz bath tub, 9″....100.00
Daisy & Button, sleigh, amber, 7¾x4½″....116.00
Daisy & Button, sugar bowl, bl....45.00
Daisy & Button, toothpick holder, amber....26.00
Daisy & Button, toothpick holder, amberina....225.00
Daisy & Button, toothpick holder, yel....35.00
Daisy & Button, tumbler, water....14.00
Daisy & Button, waste bowl....23.00
Daisy & Button 'V,' mug....18.00
Daisy & Button 'V,' pitcher, vaseline, 7½″....60.00
Daisy & Button 'V,' sauce dish, flat, amber, 4½″....13.00
Daisy & Button 'V,' tumbler, water; amber....23.00
Daisy & Button 'V', waste bowl, amber....30.00
Daisy & Button w/Crossbar, celery vase, vaseline....52.00
Daisy & Button w/Crossbar, cruet....25.00
Daisy & Button w/Crossbar, cruet, vaseline, lg....135.00
Daisy & Button w/Crossbar, goblet, amber....33.00
Daisy & Button w/Crossbar, mug, yel, 2⅞″....23.00
Daisy & Button w/Crossbar, mug, 3″....13.00
Daisy & Button w/Crossbar, pitcher, water; amber, 8″....48.00
Daisy & Button w/Crossbar, sauce dish, flat, amber, 4″....13.00
Daisy & Button w/Crossbar, sauce dish, ftd, yel, 3¾″....15.00

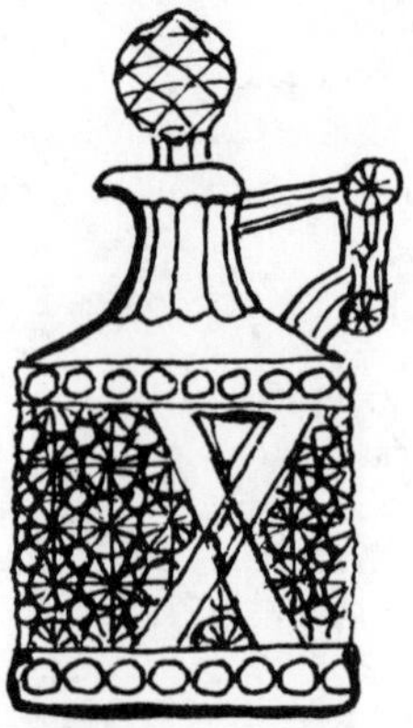

Daisy & Button w/Crossbar, tumbler, water....16.00
Daisy & Button w/Crossbar, waste bowl, yel....23.00
Daisy & Button w/Crossbar, water set, amber, 9-pc....188.00
Daisy & Button w/Thumbprint, goblet....29.00
Daisy & Button w/Thumbprint, sauce dish, sq, amber, 4″....16.00
Daisy & Button w/Thumbprint, syrup, amber, rare....145.00
Daisy & Scroll, cruet, gr, NM....325.00
Dakota, butter dish, etched....57.00
Dakota, cake stand, etched....60.00
Dakota, celery vase, ped ft, etched....40.00
Dakota, compote, etched, w/lid, 6″....68.00
Dakota, compote, jelly; etched....38.00
Dakota, compote, jelly; etched, w/lid....73.00
Dakota, creamer, etched....66.00
Dakota, goblet....20.00
Dakota, goblet, etched....35.00
Dakota, mug, ruby stained, hdld....36.00
Dakota, pitcher, tankard; etched, 11¾″....190.00
Dakota, sauce dish, ftd, 3¼″....8.00
Dakota, spooner, etched....25.00
Dakota, spooner, ped ft....18.00
Dakota, spooner, ped ft, etched....36.00
Dakota, sugar bowl, etched, w/lid....60.00
Dakota, sugar bowl, w/lid....28.00
Dakota, tray, wine; 10½″....78.00
Dakota, tumbler, etched w/birds....57.00
Dakota, tumbler, water; ruby stained....35.00
Dakota, wine....20.00
Dakota, wine, etched....35.00
Deer & Pine Tree, bread plate....48.00
Deer & Pine Tree, butter dish....65.00
Deer & Pine Tree, tray, amber, 13x7¾″....64.00
Delaware, bowl, amethyst....125.00
Delaware, bowl, shallow, octagonal, gilt trim, 9″....25.00
Delaware, butter dish, gr....42.00

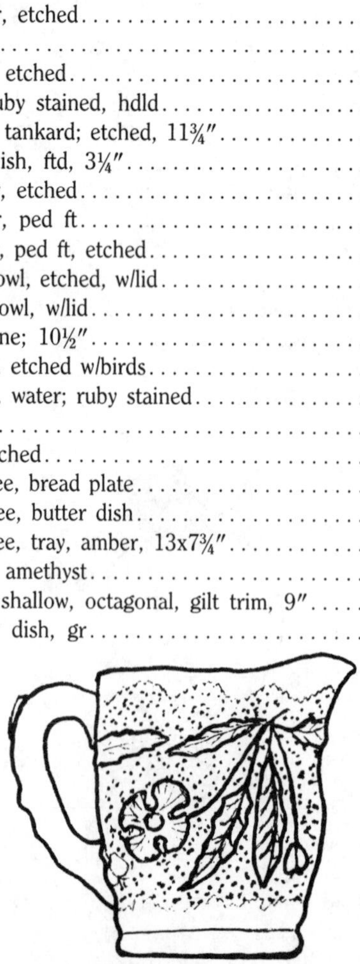

Delaware, celery vase, gr, gilt trim....66.00
Delaware, creamer, gr....26.00
Delaware, creamer, gr, gilt trim, 3¾″....45.00
Delaware, finger bowl, gilt trim....22.00

Delaware, pitcher, tankard; gr, gilt trim, 9½″ . . . 110.00
Delaware, pitcher, water; decorated . . . 110.00
Delaware, sauce dish, pink, gilt trim, 5x3¼″ . . . 37.00
Delaware, spooner, gr . . . 44.00
Delaware, sugar bowl, open . . . 44.00
Delaware, tray, pin; 7x3½″ . . . 15.00
Delaware, tray, pin; 9x4¾″ . . . 18.00
Delaware, vase, gr, gilt trim, 5¾″ . . . 40.00
Dew & Raindrop, cordial . . . 19.00
Dew & Raindrop, goblet . . . 38.00
Dew & Raindrop, wine . . . 15.00
Dewdrop in Points, pitcher, water . . . 35.00
Dewdrop in Points, tumbler, ftd . . . 17.00
Diamond Cut w/Leaf, creamer . . . 23.00
Diamond Cut w/Leaf, goblet . . . 20.00
Diamond Cut w/Leaf, plate, 7¼″ . . . 13.00
Diamond Cut w/Leaf, wine . . . 25.00
Diamond Horseshoe, see Aurora
Diamond Medallion, see Grand

Diamond Point, celery vase . . . 66.00
Diamond Point, champagne . . . 70.00
Diamond Point, claret . . . 70.00
Diamond Point, creamer, flint . . . 128.00
Diamond Point, egg cup, flint, clambroth . . . 116.00
Diamond Point, goblet . . . 40.00
Diamond Point, salt cellar, master . . . 30.00
Diamond Point, sauce dish, flat, 4″ . . . 7.00
Diamond Point, sauce dish, 5¼″ . . . 13.00
Diamond Point, spill . . . 28.00
Diamond Point, sugar bowl, w/lid . . . 66.00
Diamond Point, wine . . . 48.00
Diamond Quilted, bowl, shallow, amber, 7″ . . . 18.00
Diamond Quilted, bowl, shallow, yel, 9″ . . . 23.00
Diamond Quilted, sauce dish, flat, bl, 4″ . . . 10.00
Diamond Quilted, sauce dish, ftd, amethyst, 4″ . . . 12.00
Diamond Quilted, sauce dish, ftd, yel, 3¾″ . . . 12.00
Diamond Quilted, sauce dish, ftd, 4″ . . . 10.00
Diamond Quilted, wine . . . 12.00
Diamond Rosettes, sugar bowl, flint, w/lid . . . 50.00
Diamond Thumbprint, cake stand, flint, 3x8⅜″ . . . 175.00
Diamond Thumbprint, stopper, flint, qt . . . 26.00
Diamond Thumbprint, tumbler, bar . . . 62.00
Dinner Bell, see Cottage
Divided Diamonds, goblet, flint . . . 58.00
Divided Hearts, celery vase, ped ft . . . 57.00
Divided Hearts, egg cup, flint . . . 86.00
Dogwood, see Art Novo
Doric, see Feather
Dot & Dash, compote, w/lid . . . 50.00
Dot & Dash, spooner . . . 30.00
Dot & Dash, sugar bowl . . . 40.00
Double Leaf & Dart, see Leaf & Dart
Double Red Block, see Hexagonal Bull's Eye
Double Wedding Ring, see Wedding Ring
Dragon, compote, open; 8¼x4¾″ . . . 66.00
Draped Red Block, see Loop & Block
Drapery, egg cup . . . 20.00
Drapery, goblet . . . 22.00
Drapery, plate, 6″ . . . 15.00
Drapery, spooner . . . 30.00
Egg in Sand, goblet . . . 26.00
Egg in Sand, goblet, amber . . . 46.00
Egg in Sand, pitcher, water . . . 40.00
Egg in Sand, tray, swan & flowers in base, 7¾x5″ . . . 30.00
Egg in Sand, tray, 12½x8″ . . . 23.00
Egyptian, bread plate, Cleopatra . . . 55.00
Egyptian, bread plate, tab hdls . . . 45.00
Egyptian, goblet, ruins of Parthenon . . . 40.00
Egyptian, sauce dish, flat, 4″ . . . 8.00
Egyptian, spooner . . . 30.00
Elephant, see Jumbo
Emerald Green Herringbone, see Green Herringbone
Empress, butter dish, gold . . . 96.00
Empress, compote, stemmed . . . 56.00
Empress, sugar bowl, etched . . . 46.00
English Hobnail Cross, see Klondike
Etched Dakota, see Dakota
Etched Fern, celery vase . . . 30.00
Etched Fern, goblet . . . 35.00
Eugenie, champagne, flint . . . 78.00
Eureka, creamer, flint . . . 45.00
Eureka, cruet, flint . . . 180.00
Eureka, goblet, flint . . . 30.00
Eureka, goblet, non-flint . . . 20.00
Eureka, salt cellar, master . . . 25.00
Excelsior, Early; bar bottle, flint, pewter stopper, qt . . . 80.00
Excelsior, Early; bar bottle, pt . . . 35.00
Excelsior, Early; syrup, applied hdl . . . 110.00
Excelsior, Early; syrup, gr, rare . . . 752.00
Eyewinker, cake stand . . . 55.00
Fairfax Strawberry, see Strawberry
Fan w/Crossbars, see Champion
Fan w/Diamond, bowl, shallow, 6x8″ . . . 12.00
Fan w/Diamond, creamer . . . 25.00
Fan w/Diamond, egg cup . . . 22.00
Fan w/Diamond, goblet . . . 25.00
Fan w/Diamond, pitcher, water . . . 52.00
Fan w/Diamond, sugar bowl, open . . . 18.00
Fancy Loop, bottle, water . . . 65.00
Fancy Loop, cruet . . . 70.00
Fancy Loop, goblet . . . 60.00
Fancy Loop, jar, mustard; w/lid . . . 45.00
Fancy Loop, toothpick holder . . . 37.00
Fancy Loop, tumbler, water . . . 28.00

Feather, bowl, ftd, 4⅞″ 17.00
Feather, bowl, shallow, oval 12.00
Feather, cake stand, 9″ 35.00
Feather, goblet, low flint 25.00
Feather, honey dish, 3½″ 10.00
Feather, pitcher, water 38.00
Feather, plate, 10″ 35.00
Feather, sauce dish, flat, 4″ 8.00
Feather, sugar bowl, w/lid 30.00
Feather, syrup 110.00
Feather, tumbler, water 48.00
Feather, wine 37.00
Feather Duster, compote, jelly 13.00
Feather Duster, pitcher, water 34.00
Feather Duster, pitcher, water; gr 53.00
Feather Duster, spooner, gr 25.00
Feather Duster, tumbler, gr 12.00
Feeding Swan, goblet, etched 53.00
Feeding Swan, pitcher, etched, 7¾″ 66.00
Feeding Swan, tumbler, water; etched 20.00
Fern Garland, wine 12.00
Festoon, creamer 23.00
Festoon, pitcher, water 55.00
Festoon, sauce dish, flat, 4″ 6.00
Festoon, tray, water; 10″ 25.00
Figure Eight, see Bryce
Filley, see Texas Bull's Eye
Fine Cut & Block, compote, open; bl, 7¾″ 68.00
Fine Cut & Block, creamer, bl blocks 65.00
Fine Cut & Block, creamer, yel blocks 75.00
Fine Cut & Block, goblet, buttermilk 25.00

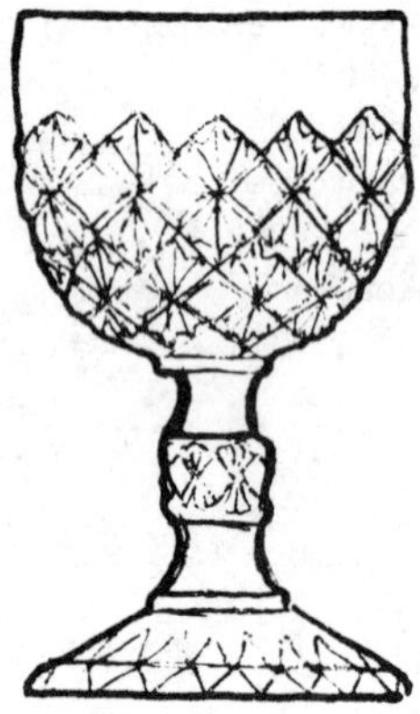

Fine Cut & Block, spooner 44.00
Fine Cut & Block, spooner, bl blocks 57.00
Fine Cut & Block, tumbler, water 18.00
Fine Cut & Block, waste bowl, amber 46.00
Fine Cut & Diamond, see Grand
Fine Cut & Feather, see Feather
Fine Cut & Panel, bread plate 32.00
Fine Cut & Panel, goblet 22.00
Fine Cut & Panel, plate, yel, 6″ 12.00
Fine Cut & Panel, plate, 7″ 15.00
Fine Cut & Panel, sauce dish, ftd, yel, 3¾″ 15.00
Fine Cut & Panel, wine, amber 34.00
Fine Rib, celery vase, ftd, flint 40.00
Fine Rib, egg cup 20.00
Fine Rib, salt cellar, ind 12.00
Fine Rib, salt cellar, master 23.00
Fine Rib, sugar bowl 48.00
Finecut Medallion, see Austrian
Fingerprint, see Almond Thumbprint

Fishscale, cake stand 30.00
Fishscale, celery vase 25.00
Fishscale, goblet 30.00
Fishscale, pitcher, milk 26.00
Fishscale, slipper on tray, bl 20.00
Flamingo Habitat, creamer 40.00
Flamingo Habitat, goblet 25.00
Flamingo Habitat, sherbet, ftd, 3¾x4¼″ 12.00
Flamingo Habitat, spooner 25.00
Flamingo Habitat, sugar bowl 40.00
Flat Diamond, egg cup 18.00
Flat Diamond, goblet 26.00
Flat Diamond, spooner 27.00
Flat Diamond & Panel, bottle, bar; qt 62.00
Flat Diamond & Panel, decanter, w/stopper 50.00
Flat Diamond & Panel, egg cup 22.00
Flat Diamond & Panel, goblet 78.00
Flat Diamond & Panel, honey dish, 3¼″ 10.00
Flat Diamond & Panel, sauce dish, flat, 3½″ 10.00
Flat Panel, see Pleating
Fleur-de-Lis & Drape, pitcher, water 30.00
Fleur-de-Lis & Drape, sugar bowl, w/lid 20.00
Fleur-de-Lis & Drape, tray, relish; gr, 8x5¼″ 17.00
Fleur-de-Lis & Drape, tray, water; 11½″ 20.00
Fleur-de-Lis & Tassel, see Fleur-de-Lis & Drape
Flora, see Opposing Pyramids
Flower & Pleat, sugar shaker 65.00
Flower & Pleat, tumbler, frosted 15.00
Flower Pot, bread plate, L-202 .... 30.00
Flower Pot, creamer 30.00
Flower Pot, sauce dish, ftd, 3¾″ 10.00
Flying Robin, see Hummingbird
Flying Stork, goblet 56.00
Forest Ware, see Ivy in Snow
Four Petal, sugar bowl, pagoda, flint, dome top, w/lid 52.00
Four Petal Flower, see Delaware
Frost Crystal, creamer, ruby stained 50.00
Frosted Circle, bowl, shallow, 7″ 23.00
Frosted Circle, butter dish 36.00
Frosted Circle, compote, open, 9x6″ 27.00
Frosted Circle, creamer 27.00
Frosted Circle, cruet 65.00
Frosted Circle, goblet 25.00
Frosted Circle, sauce dish, flat, 4″ 8.00
Frosted Circle, spooner 30.00
Frosted Circle, sugar bowl, open 13.00
Frosted Circle, sugar bowl, w/lid 40.00
Frosted Leaf, goblet, flint 50.00
Frosted Leaf, ladies' goblet, rim smooth 52.00
Frosted Leaf, sauce dish, 4¼″ 18.00
Frosted Leaf, sugar bowl, open; flint 49.00
Frosted Ribbon w/Double Bars, pitcher, water; bulbous 67.00
Frosted Roman Key w/Ribs, see Roman Key
Frosted Stork, bread plate, 11¾x8″ 45.00
Frosted Stork, celery vase 60.00
Frosted Stork, pitcher, water; applied hdl 127.00
Galloway, bowl, shallow, 10x4″ 23.00
Galloway, compote, jelly 35.00
Galloway, creamer 26.00
Galloway, cup, punch 7.00
Galloway, finger bowl 40.00
Galloway, mug 40.00
Galloway, pitcher, water; rose flashed 125.00
Galloway, plate, 8″ 25.00

Galloway, sauce dish, ftd....15.00
Galloway, sauce dish, shallow, flared, 4″....7.00
Galloway, shakers, pr....14.00
Galloway, spooner....23.00
Galloway, sugar shaker....40.00
Galloway, syrup....65.00
Galloway, toothpick holder....30.00
Galloway, tumbler, water; gilt trim....23.00
Galloway, wine....57.00
Garden Fruits, champagne....20.00
Garden Fruits, creamer, applied hdl....24.00
Garden Fruits, goblet....13.00
Garden Fruits, pitcher, water; applied hdl, 10″....47.00
Garden of Eden, bread plate....45.00
Garden of Eden, platter....20.00
Garden of Eden, sauce dish, flat, hdl, lg....13.00
Garden of Eden, sauce dish, flat, hdl, sm....9.00
Garden of Eden, sauce dish, ftd, 4⅛″....8.00
Garfield Drape, compote, low ft, w/lid, 6″ dia....60.00
Garfield Drape, creamer....27.00
Garfield Drape, goblet....40.00
Garfield Drape, pitcher, milk....56.00
Garfield Drape, pitcher, water....60.00
Garfield Drape, plate, 11″....52.00
Garfield Drape, sauce dish, ftd, 4″....9.00
Garfield Drape, spooner....30.00
Gem, see Nailhead
Giant Sawtooth, goblet, flint....85.00
Gold Band, bowl, berry; vaseline....45.00
Gold Band, creamer, vaseline....45.00
Gold Band, spooner, vaseline....45.00
Gold Band, sugar bowl, vaseline....95.00
Gothic, bowl, shallow, 7″....70.00
Gothic, egg cup....38.00
Gothic, goblet, flint....57.00
Gothic, wine....137.00
Grand, bread plate....22.00
Grand, compote, open; 7x6″....20.00
Grand, goblet....27.00
Grand, plate, 10″....18.00
Grand, sauce dish, flat, 4″....7.00
Grand, wine....36.00
Grape & Festoon, goblet....25.00
Grape & Festoon, plate, 6″....19.00
Grape & Festoon, salt cellar, master....24.00
Grape & Festoon, sauce dish, flat, 4″....8.00
Grape & Festoon, sauce dish, flat, 5″....13.00
Grape & Festoon, spooner, stippled leaf....23.00
Grape Band, goblet....20.00
Grape Band, plate, 6″....14.00
Grape Band, tumbler, bar....25.00
Grapes, tray, bread; w/motto, 10″....18.00
Grasshopper w/Insect, celery tray....35.00
Grasshopper w/Insect, celery vase....60.00
Grasshopper w/Insect, creamer....30.00
Grasshopper w/Insect, pitcher, water....62.00
Grasshopper w/Insect, plate, ftd, 8½″....15.00
Grasshopper w/Insect, sauce dish, ftd, etched, 4″....9.00
Grasshopper w/Insect, spooner....45.00
Grasshopper Without Insect, creamer....20.00
Green Herringbone, cruet, gr....90.00
Green Herringbone, pitcher, water; gr....65.00
Guardian Angel, see Cupid & Venus
Hairpin, celery vase....40.00
Hairpin, creamer, flint, 1″....18.00
Hairpin, egg cup....18.00
Hairpin, egg cup, opaque wht....75.00
Hairpin, goblet, flint....40.00
Hairpin, goblet, non-flint....23.00
Hairpin, salt cellar, master....20.00
Hairpin, sauce dish, flat, 4″....8.00
Hairpin, spooner, flint, w/rayed base....38.00
Hairpin, tumbler, whiskey; applied hdl....47.00
Hairpin w/Thumbprint, creamer, flint....87.00
Hairpin w/Thumbprint, goblet, flint....46.00
Hand, compote, open, 9x5″....20.00
Hand, cordial....86.00
Hand, goblet....42.00
Hand, syrup....30.00
Hanover, goblet....22.00
Hanover, pitcher, water; amber....92.00
Hanover, plate, 10″....18.00
Hartley, creamer....25.00
Hartley, goblet....22.00
Hartley, pitcher, water; yel....77.00
Hartley, plate, 10¾″....20.00
Hartley, sauce dish, ftd, amber, 4″....14.00
Hartley, sauce dish, ftd, 4″....8.00
Harvard Yard, wine....15.00
Hawaiian Lei, bowl, relish; dbl....30.00
Hawaiian Lei, bowl, shallow, 5x4″....18.00
Hawaiian Lei, bowl, shallow, 8x3″....15.00
Hawaiian Lei, cake stand, 9¾″....30.00
Hawaiian Lei, compote, open; 8x6½″....23.00
Hawaiian Lei, plate, 10¾″....15.00
Hawaiian Lei, wine....30.00
Heart w/Thumbprint, bowl, shallow, gilt trim....27.00
Heart w/Thumbprint, cup, punch....17.00
Heart w/Thumbprint, goblet....50.00
Heart w/Thumbprint, nappy, gr....36.00
Heart w/Thumbprint, plate, 6″....25.00
Heart w/Thumbprint, sauce dish, flat, gilt trim....17.00
Heart w/Thumbprint, tray, card; folded edge....18.00
Heart w/Thumbprint, tumbler, water....22.00
Heart w/Thumbprint, vase, 6″....37.00
Heart w/Thumbprint, wine....32.00
Hearts & Spades, see Medallion
Heavy Panelled Finecut, creamer, 6″....20.00
Heavy Panelled Finecut, hat, yel....22.00
Heavy Panelled Finecut, plate, amber, 5¼″....10.00
Heavy Panelled Finecut, salt cellar, ind; yel....16.00
Heavy Panelled Finecut, shaker, salt....10.00
Heavy Panelled Finecut, tray, rectangle, 12x7½″....18.00
Heavy Panelled Finecut, tumbler, bar....18.00
Heavy Panelled Finecut, tumbler, water....13.00
Herringbone Band, see Ripple
Hexagon Block, pitcher, tankard; 12″....78.00
Hexagon Block, sauce dish, flat, amber, etched, 4¼″....12.00
Hexagon Block, tumbler, water....33.00
Hexagonal Bull's Eye, goblet....38.00
Hexagonal Bull's Eye, tumbler, water....38.00
Hexagonal Bull's Eye, wine....40.00
Hickman, bowl, shallow, 5″....10.00
Hickman, champagne....18.00
Hickman, compote, open....20.00
Hickman, creamer, ind; gr....18.00
Hickman, cup, punch....8.00
Hickman, cup, punch; gr....13.00

Hickman, Jack-in-Pulpit dish, 6x8″ 12.00
Hickman, shaker, salt 10.00
Hidalgo, celery vase, flat base, amber stained 33.00
Hidalgo, celery vase, flat base, etched 22.00
Hidalgo, cruet, clear & frosted 65.00
Hidalgo, goblet, etched 14.00
Hidalgo, sauce dish, flat, hdl, 4½″ 10.00
Hidalgo, syrup, clear & frosted 75.00
Hinoto, goblet, flint 62.00
Hinoto, salt cellar, master 14.00
Hinoto, tumbler, whiskey; hdld 46.00
Holbrook, see Pineapple & Fan
Holly, see Greentown, Holly
Holly Amber, see Greentown, Holly Amber
Honeycomb w/Flower Rim, bowl, berry; gr 46.00
Honeycomb w/Flower Rim, creamer, gr, 4″ 40.00
Honeycomb w/Flower Rim, goblet, gr, gilt trim 60.00
Honeycomb w/Flower Rim, sauce dish, ftd, gr, 4″ 17.00
Honeycomb w/Flower Rim, tray, celery; 11½x5½″ 15.00
Honeycomb w/Flower Rim, vase 17.00
Hops & Barley, see Wheat & Barley
Horn of Plenty, bottle, bar; qt 115.00
Horn of Plenty, celery vase, ftd 170.00
Horn of Plenty, compote, open; 10¼x9½″ 147.00
Horn of Plenty, compote, open; 8″ 50.00
Horn of Plenty, decanter, orig stopper, qt 178.00
Horn of Plenty, decanter, w/faceted stopper, flint, qt 96.00
Horn of Plenty, egg cup 37.00

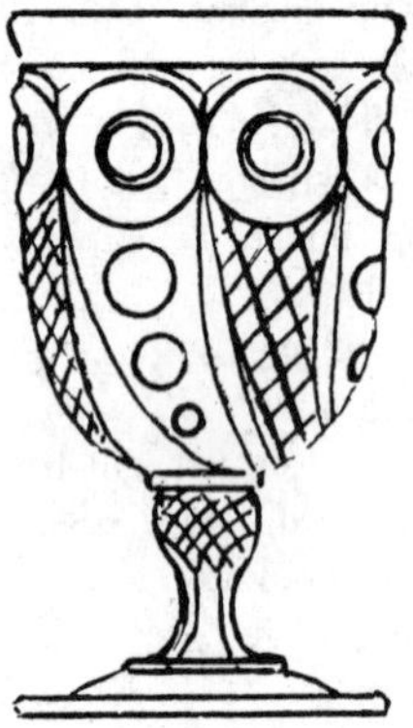

Horn of Plenty, goblet 70.00
Horn of Plenty, plate, 6″ 66.00
Horn of Plenty, sauce dish, flat, 4½″ 13.00
Horn of Plenty, sauce dish, flat, 5″ 23.00
Horn of Plenty, spill 47.00
Horn of Plenty, sugar bowl 78.00
Horn of Plenty, sugar bowl, pagoda lid 88.00
Horn of Plenty, tumbler, bar; flint 62.00
Horn of Plenty, wine 125.00
Horseshoe, cake stand, 7¼″ 50.00
Horseshoe, creamer, hotel type, 6½″ 97.00
Horseshoe, goblet 27.00
Horseshoe, sauce dish, ftd, 4″ 9.00
Horseshoe, spooner 25.00
Horseshoe, sugar bowl, open 15.00
Horseshoe, tray, bread 40.00
Horseshoe, waste bowl 40.00
Huber, egg cup, flint 17.00
Huber, egg cup, non-flint 12.00
Huber, goblet, flint 17.00
Huber, goblet, ladies' size 17.00
Huber, goblet, non-flint 12.00
Huber, salt cellar, master 18.00
Huber, tumbler, bar; flint, 4¼″ 23.00
Huber, tumbler, bar; 10-panel, non-flint 20.00
Huber, tumbler, bar; 8-panel 20.00
Huber, vase, non-flint 20.00
Huber, wine, non-flint 8.00
Huber, wine, 8-panel 20.00
Huckle, see Feather Duster
Hummingbird, pitcher, milk 50.00
Hummingbird, pitcher, water 85.00
Hummingbird, pitcher, water; bl 126.00
Hummingbird, tumbler, bar; amber 47.00
Hummingbird, water set, amber, 7-pc 355.00
Iceburg, see Polar Bear
Idaho, see Snail
Illinois, basket, 11½x7″ 100.00
Illinois, compote, jelly; 5x4″ 20.00
Illinois, plate, sq, 7″ 18.00
Illinois, tray, relish; 8½x3″ 10.00
Illinois, tumbler, water 20.00
Indian Tree, see Barley
Indiana, see Greentown, Cord Drapery
Indiana Swirl, see Feather
Inverted Fern, butter dish, flint 50.00
Inverted Fern, egg cup 30.00
Inverted Fern, goblet 40.00
Inverted Fern, salt cellar, master 22.00
Inverted Thistle, see Late Thistle
Inverted Thumbprint, cup, punch; gr w/amber hdl 20.00
Inverted Thumbprint, finger bowl, amber 17.00
Inverted Thumbprint, pitcher, water; bl 97.00
Inverted Thumbprint, sugar shaker, amethyst 52.00
Inverted Thumbprint, syrup, bl, tapered/pinched base, hdl 125.00
Inverted Thumbprint, syrup, rubena, ring neck, tapered 150.00
Inverted Thumbprint & Star, goblet 17.00
Inverted Thumbprint & Star, goblet, bl 30.00
Iowa, sauce dish, 4½″ 7.00
Irish Column, see Broken Column
Ivy in Snow, goblet 27.00
Ivy in Snow, sugar bowl, open 30.00
Ivy in Snow, syrup 70.00
Jacob's Ladder, butter dish 56.00
Jacob's Ladder, cake stand 56.00
Jacob's Ladder, creamer 35.00
Jacob's Ladder, pitcher, water; bulbous 157.00
Jacob's Ladder, plate, 6″ 30.00
Jacob's Ladder, salt cellar, master 30.00
Jacob's Ladder, sauce dish, 4½″ 9.00
Jacob's Ladder, spooner 30.00
Jersey Swirl, bread plate, sapphire bl, 8″ 25.00
Jersey Swirl, compote, flint, w/lid, 11¾″ 75.00
Jersey Swirl, plate, amber, 8″ 18.00
Jersey Swirl, plate, 10″ 22.00
Jersey Swirl, plate, 6″ 10.00
Jersey Swirl, tumbler, water; amber 30.00
Jewel Band, see Scalloped Tape
Jewel w/Dewdrop, bread plate, Our Daily Bread 45.00
Jewelled Moon & Star, bowl, shallow, 6¾″ 15.00
Jewelled Moon & Star, cake stand, 8½″ 30.00
Jewelled Moon & Star, carafe 25.00
Jewelled Moon & Star, celery vase 36.00
Jewelled Moon & Star, cruet 20.00
Jewelled Moon & Star, goblet, gilt trim 47.00

Jewelled Moon & Star, pitcher, cider; ½-gal....136.00
Jewelled Moon & Star, tumbler, water; gilt trim....25.00
Job's Tears, see Art
Jumbo, butter dish, oblong, no hdl....465.00
Jumbo, castor set w/bottles, no hdl....150.00
Jumbo, creamer....150.00
Jumbo, jar, powder; frosted, w/lid....77.00
Jumbo, jar; marmalade, w/lid....155.00
Jumbo, shakers, pr....80.00
Jumbo, spoon rack....580.00
Jumbo, table set, 4-pc....950.00
Kentucky, cake stand, 9½"....40.00
Kentucky, cup, punch; gr....15.00
Kentucky, sauce dish, ftd, 3¼"....6.00
Kentucky, toothpick holder....27.00
Kentucky, wine....30.00
King's Crown, bowl, berry; boat shape, ruby stained....112.00
King's Crown, butter dish, ruby stained....125.00
King's Crown, celery vase....75.00
King's Crown, celery vase, ruby stained, 6"....85.00
King's Crown, creamer, ind; etched, ruby stained....25.00
King's Crown, creamer, ruby stained, 4¾"....65.00
King's Crown, creamer & sugar....150.00
King's Crown, goblet....15.00
King's Crown, goblet, ruby stained....35.00
King's Crown, pitcher, bulbous, ruby stained, 8"....175.00
King's Crown, pitcher, tankard; 11½"....46.00
King's Crown, shakers, ind; ruby stained, pr....95.00
King's Crown, shakers, pr....25.00
King's Crown, spooner, 4½"....75.00
King's Crown, toothpick holder....17.00
King's Crown, toothpick holder, etched, ruby stained....30.00
King's Crown, toothpick holder, ruby stained....25.00
King's Crown, tumbler, etched, ruby stained....40.00
King's Crown, water set, 11" tankard+6 tumblers, ruby stain...350.00
King's Crown, wine, etched, ruby stained....40.00
King's Crown, wine, ruby stained....33.00
Klondike, butter, Dalzell/Gilmore/Yeighton, w/lid, ca 1885....300.00
Klondike, pitcher, water; amber stain....545.00
Klondike, sugar bowl, frosted & gold, w/lid....250.00
Lace, see Drapery
LaClede, see Hickman
Lacy Daisy, bowl, shallow....23.00
Lacy Daisy, butter dish....33.00
Lacy Daisy, sauce dish, flat, 2⅛"....10.00
Lacy Daisy, sauce dish, flat, 4"....9.00
Lacy Daisy, sugar bowl, w/lid....22.00
Ladder w/Diamonds, butter dish, gilt trim....40.00
Ladder w/Diamonds, creamer, ind; gilt trim....13.00
Ladder w/Diamonds, cup, punch....8.00
Ladder w/Diamonds, goblet, ice-water....20.00
Ladder w/Diamonds, shakers, pr....20.00
Ladder w/Diamonds, sugar bowl, open; ind....10.00
Ladder w/Diamonds, toothpick holder....23.00
Ladder w/Diamonds, tumbler, water; gilt trim....13.00
Ladder w/Diamonds, tumbler, water; ruby stained, gilt trim....27.00
Lady Hamilton, champagne....36.00
Lady Hamilton, egg cup, saucer base....18.00
Lady Hamilton, goblet....20.00
Lady Hamilton, platter, frosted, 13x9"....30.00
Lady Hamilton, sauce dish, flat, 4"....6.00
Lady Hamilton, sugar bowl, open....10.00
Lady Hamilton, wine....22.00
Late Block, butter dish, ruby stained....60.00
Late Block, creamer, ruby stained....50.00
Late Block, goblet....36.00
Late Block, goblet, ruby stained....44.00
Late Block, pitcher, water; ruby stained....146.00
Late Block, rose bowl, ruby stained, 4"....57.00
Late Block, spooner, ruby stained....30.00
Late Block, sugar bowl, w/lid....46.00
Late Block, tumbler, ruby stained....33.00
Late Block, tumbler, water; ruby stained....30.00
Late Block, wine, ruby stained....36.00
Late Buckle, see Buckle w/Star
Late Washington, table set, decor, 4-pc....78.00
Lattice & Oval Panels, see Flat Diamond & Panel
Lawrence, see Bull's Eye
Leaf, see Maple Leaf
Leaf & Dart, goblet....26.00
Leaf & Dart, sugar bowl, open....20.00
Leaf & Dart, wine....28.00
Leaf & Flower, syrup, amber stained....145.00
Leaf Bracket, see Greentown, Leaf Bracket
Leaf Medallion, tumbler, gr, gilt trim....50.00
Lee, sugar bowl, flint, w/lid....97.00
Lee, wine....127.00
Liberty Bell, butter dish, miniature....152.00
Liberty Bell, compote, open....18.00
Liberty Bell, goblet....33.00
Liberty Bell, platter, states, 13x8¼"....56.00
Liberty Bell, sauce dish, flat, 4"....20.00
Liberty Bell, sugar bowl, w/lid....65.00
Liberty Bell, tray, relish; states....36.00
Lily-of-the-Valley, cruet....110.00
Lily-of-the-Valley, goblet, etched....45.00
Lily-of-the-Valley, pitcher, water....195.00
Lincoln Drape, goblet....60.00
Lion, bowl, clear/frosted, oblong, w/lid, 8⅞x5½"....126.00
Lion, bowl, relish; lion hdls....40.00
Lion, bread plate, lion w/mate....75.00
Lion, butter dish, frosted, etched Lily-of-the-Valley....100.00
Lion, compote, frosted rampant lion finial, w/lid, 7⅛"....112.00
Lion, goblet....60.00
Lion, sauce dish, 4"....32.00
Lion, table set, 4-pc....230.00
Lippman, see Flat Diamond
Locket-on-Chain, wine....88.00
Log & Star, cruet, amber, orig stopper....70.00
Log & Star, goblet....20.00
Log Cabin, butter dish, w/lid....285.00
Log Cabin, creamer....130.00
Log Cabin, jam jar, w/lid....300.00
Log Cabin, spooner....95.00
Log Cabin, sugar bowl....300.00
Loganberry & Grape, sauce dish, ftd, 4"....7.00
Long Spear, see Grasshopper (with or without Insect)
Loop, egg cup....18.00
Loop, wine....17.00
Loop & Block, goblet....47.00
Loop & Block, sugar bowl, clear, w/lid....25.00
Loop & Block, water set, 7-pc....355.00
Loop & Dart, bowl, shallow, 8x5"....17.00
Loop & Dart, celery vase....42.00
Loop & Dart, creamer, applied hdl....36.00
Loop & Dart, goblet, flint....37.00
Loop & Dart, goblet, non-flint....20.00
Loop & Dart, sauce dish, flat, 3¾"....7.00

Loop & Dart, spooner, flint...30.00
Loop & Dart, spooner, non-flint...25.00
Loop & Dart, sugar bowl, w/lid...36.00
Loop & Fan, see Maryland
Loop & Moose Eye, compote, open; 7x3½″...33.00
Loop & Moose Eye, egg cup, flint...30.00
Loop & Moose Eye, egg cup, non-flint...18.00
Loop & Moose Eye, spooner...25.00
Loop & Moose Eye, sugar bowl, w/lid...57.00
Loop & Moose Eye, tumbler, bar...47.00
Loop & Petal, sugar bowl, flint...88.00
Loop w/Dewdrop, pitcher, water...66.00
Loop w/Stippled Panels, see Texas
Lotus, see Garden of Eden
Magnet & Grape (Frosted Leaf), egg cup...77.00
Magnet & Grape (Frosted Leaf), goblet...60.00
Magnet & Grape (Frosted Leaf), sauce dish, flat, 4⅛″...19.00
Magnet & Grape (Frosted Leaf), spooner...60.00
Magnet & Grape (Frosted Leaf), sugar bowl, open...44.00
Magnet & Grape (Frosted Leaf), tumbler, ftd...77.00
Maine, butter dish...23.00
Maine, pitcher, water...52.00
Maine, sauce dish, flat, 4″...13.00
Maltese, see Jacob's Ladder
Manting, champagne, flint...45.00
Manting, goblet, flint...37.00
Manting, tumbler, bar; flint...47.00
Manting, wine, flint...37.00
Maple Leaf, finger bowl, yel...46.00
Maple Leaf, plate, bl, 11″...46.00
Maple Leaf, plate, sq, 8½″...18.00
Maple Leaf, platter, yel, 13x9″...36.00
Maple Leaf, tumbler, frosted...25.00
Marquisette, celery vase...35.00
Marquisette, goblet...25.00
Marsh Pink (sq Fuchsia), creamer...34.00
Maryland, cake stand, 9½″...30.00
Maryland, goblet...30.00
Maryland, pitcher, milk; 7″...27.00
Maryland, sauce dish, flat, gr, 3¾″...17.00
Maryland, sauce dish, flat, 3¾″...7.00
Maryland, tray, relish; 4½x8½″...12.00
Mascotte, basket, hdld, 9½″...30.00
Mascotte, bowl, shallow, etched, 9x2¾″...35.00
Mascotte, butter pats...12.00
Mascotte, cake stand, 8″...36.00
Mascotte, carafe...36.00
Mascotte, celery vase, etched...36.00
Mascotte, celery vase, ftd...19.00
Mascotte, creamer...18.00
Mascotte, sauce dish, ftd, 4″...9.00
Mascotte, shaker, salt...9.00
Mascotte, spooner, etched...25.00
Mascotte, sugar bowl, etched, w/lid...30.00
Mascotte, tumbler, water; etched...35.00
Massachusetts, cruet...40.00
Massachusetts, cup, punch...15.00
Massachusetts, decanter...70.00
Massachusetts, goblet...47.00
Massachusetts, mug...18.00
Massachusetts, olive dish, 3½x5″...9.00
Massachusetts, plate, 8″...25.00
Massachusetts, rum jug, lg...125.00
Massachusetts, shot glass...16.00
Massachusetts, tumbler, juice; gilt trim...20.00
Massachusetts, tumbler, whiskey...15.00
Massachusetts, vase, gr, 10″...35.00
Massachusetts, vase, 7″...13.00
Massachusetts, wine...47.00
Medallion, bread plate, open rim...25.00
Medallion, cake stand, 9¼″...23.00
Medallion, goblet...25.00
Medallion, pitcher, water; yel...70.00
Medallion, sauce dish, flat, amber, 4¼x3¾″...8.00
Melrose, compote, jelly; 5⅛″...13.00
Melrose, goblet...20.00
Melrose, pitcher, tankard; 10″...40.00
Melrose, wine, etched...22.00
Memphis, master punch bowl & base, tulip top, sgn N...395.00
Memphis, pitcher, water...50.00
Michigan, celery vase, pink blush...85.00
Michigan, finger bowl, 4¾″...16.00
Michigan, goblet, gilt trim...30.00
Michigan, olive dish, 6x4¾″...7.00
Michigan, sauce dish, flat, 5″...6.00
Michigan, syrup...75.00
Michigan, tumbler, water...22.00
Millard, creamer, amber stain...40.00
Millard, goblet, amber stain, etched...77.00
Millard, spooner, ruby stain...40.00
Millard, sugar bowl, open; ruby stain...28.00
Milton, see Log & Star
Minerva, bowl, relish...30.00
Minerva, bread plate...60.00
Minerva, jam jar...45.00
Minerva, sauce dish, ftd, 4″...12.00
Minerva, spooner...35.00
Minnesota, carafe, water...36.00
Minnesota, creamer, 3¼″...23.00
Minnesota, cruet, orig stopper...33.00
Minnesota, flower frog, gr, 2-pc...47.00
Minnesota, goblet, gilt trim...19.00
Minnesota, sugar bowl...30.00
Minnesota, toothpick holder...22.00
Minnesota, tumbler, water...14.00
Minnesota, wine...25.00
Minor Block, see Mascotte
Mirror, goblet, flint...30.00
Mirror, tumbler, bar; flint...28.00
Mirror, wine, flint...40.00
Missouri, mug, gr...40.00
Missouri, pitcher, water; gr...70.00
Missouri, spooner, gr...50.00
Missouri, sugar bowl, gr...60.00
Mitered Diamond, bowl, shallow, sq, amber, 7½″...23.00
Mitered Diamond, tray, relish; bl, 8½x5″...8.00
Mitered Diamond, wine, amber...33.00
Mitered Diamond Point, see Zig Zag
Moesser, see Overall Lattice
Monkey, bowl, scalloped, 4½x8″...400.00
Monkey, pitcher, water...425.00
Moon & Star, bottle, bitters; pewter top, flint...86.00
Moon & Star, goblet...38.00
Moon & Star, sauce dish, flat, 4″...5.00
Moon & Star, sauce dish, ftd, 4″...12.00
Moon & Star, spill, flint...46.00
Moon & Star, tray, relish; 8x4¾″...10.00
Moon & Star, tumbler, bar; flint...66.00

Moon & Star w/Waffle Stem, see Jewelled Moon & Star
Moon & Stork, goblet....96.00
Morning Glory, sauce dish, flat, flint, 4″....46.00
Morning Glory, wine, rare....175.00
Nail, bowl, shallow, ruby stained, etched, 6″....46.00
Nail, butter dish, etched, w/lid....35.00
Nail, cake stand....52.00
Nail, pitcher, water....66.00
Nail, sauce dish, ftd, 3½″....10.00
Nailhead, bowl, shallow, 6″....17.00
Nailhead, cake stand....25.00
Nailhead, compote, w/lid, 6¼x6¼″....40.00
Nailhead, goblet....23.00
Nailhead, pitcher, water....50.00
Nailhead, plate, sq, 7″....18.00
Nailhead, plate, 9″....15.00
Nailhead, sugar bowl, open....13.00
Nailhead, tray, relish; 8¾x5¼″....12.00
Nailhead, tumbler, water....43.00
Nailhead, wine....20.00
New England Pineapple, champagne, flint....167.00
New England Pineapple, egg cup, flint....40.00
New England Pineapple, goblet, flint....57.00
New England Pineapple, ladies' goblet....77.00
New England Pineapple, salt cellar, master; flint....43.00
New England Pineapple, tumbler, bar; flint....97.00
New England Pineapple, wine....137.00
New Hampshire, goblet, gilt trim....25.00
New Hampshire, mug, gilt trim....13.00

New Hampshire, pitcher, water....50.00
New Hampshire, toothpick holder, gilt trim....30.00
New Jersey, berry set, 7-pc....170.00
New Jersey, compote, jelly....20.00
New Jersey, cruet, orig stopper....49.00
New Jersey, pitcher, water....75.00
New Jersey, plate, 10½″....20.00
New Jersey, plate, 8¾″....15.00
New Jersey, sauce dish, flat, 4¼″....9.00
New Jersey, water set, gilt trim, 7-pc....167.00
New Jersey, wine, flared, gilt trim....30.00
North Pole, see Polar Bear
Notched Rib, see Broken Column
O'Hara Diamond, compote, jelly; ruby stained....47.00
O'Hara Diamond, plate, gr, 10″....17.00
O'Hara Diamond, tumbler, water; ruby stained....23.00
Oaken Bucket, see Wooden Pail
Oats & Barley, see Wheat & Barley
Old Man of the Mountain, see Bearded Head
One Hundred & One, pitcher, water; bulbous....120.00
One Hundred & One, plate, 8″....15.00
One Hundred & One, spooner....17.00
One-O-One, see One Hundred & One
Open Basketweave, goblet....13.00
Open Plaid, see Open Basketweave
Open Rose, compote, open; 7¾x4″....33.00
Open Rose, egg cup....18.00
Open Rose, sugar bowl, open....22.00
Opposing Pyramids, celery vase....36.00
Opposing Pyramids, pitcher, tankard....46.00
Oregon, bowl, shallow, 7¾x2½″....13.00
Oregon, butter dish....60.00
Oregon, cake stand, 9½″....18.00
Oregon, carafe, whiskey....18.00
Oregon, compote, open; 8¼″....20.00
Oregon, cruet....65.00
Oregon, goblet....30.00
Oregon, pitcher, water....45.00
Oregon, shakers, salt, pr....20.00
Oregon, sugar bowl, gr....75.00
Oregon, sugar bowl, gr, w/lid....75.00
Oregon, syrup....70.00
Oregon, tray, relish; 7½x3¾″....10.00
Oriental, creamer, ftd....40.00
Oriental, spooner....45.00
Oriental, sugar....65.00
Oriental, tumbler, water....17.00
Orion, see Cathedral
Orion Thumbprint, sauce dish, ftd, bl....9.00
Orion Thumbprint, sugar bowl, yel, w/lid....35.00
Ostrich Looking at Moon, see Moon & Stork
Oval Loop, see Question Mark
Oval Mitre, compote, open; 6¾x5¾″....40.00
Oval Mitre, creamer, applied hdl, flint....47.00
Oval Mitre, goblet, flint....40.00
Oval Mitre, spooner, flint....37.00
Overall Lattice, wine....15.00
Owl & Possum, goblet....50.00
Paisley, bowl, shallow, amethyst dots, 6″....18.00
Paisley, creamer, gr dots....30.00
Palmette, bowl, oval, 6x9″....15.00
Palmette, creamer, applied hdl....47.00
Palmette, plate, variant, amber....20.00
Palmette, plate, variant, 10¼″....13.00
Palmette, salt cellar, master....23.00
Palmette, tumbler, ftd....40.00
Panelled Acorn Band, creamer, applied hdl....40.00
Panelled Acorn Band, goblet....30.00
Panelled Acorn Band, spooner....33.00
Panelled Acorn Band, sugar bowl, open....25.00
Panelled Cherry, see Cherry & Cable
Panelled Daisy, goblet....26.00
Panelled Daisy, pitcher, water....40.00
Panelled Daisy, plate, sq, 9″....23.00
Panelled Daisy, sauce dish, sq, flat, 4″....6.00
Panelled Daisy, tumbler, water....32.00
Panelled Daisy & Button, see Queen
Panelled Dewdrop, creamer....25.00
Panelled Dewdrop, goblet....30.00
Panelled Dewdrop, mug, applied hdl....36.00
Panelled Dewdrop, plate, 7″....16.00
Panelled Dewdrop, wine....20.00
Panelled Diamond Cross, goblet....15.00
Panelled Diamond Cross, goblet, amber....20.00
Panelled Diamond Cross, goblet, bl....40.00
Panelled Diamond Cut & Fan, see Hartley
Panelled Dogwood, see Art Novo
Panelled Forget-Me-Not, compote, w/lid, 6x8½″....50.00
Panelled Forget-Me-Not, goblet....40.00
Panelled Grape Band, creamer, applied hdl....40.00

Panelled Grape Band, goblet 20.00
Panelled Herringbone, goblet 15.00
Panelled Herringbone, plate, sq, gr 22.00
Panelled Herringbone, sauce dish, flat, gr, 4½″ 5.00
Panelled Herringbone, tray, relish; gr, 8x4½″ 15.00
Panelled Herringbone, tumbler, water; gr 16.00
Panelled Nightshade, goblet 22.00
Panelled Nightshade, goblet, amber 46.00
Panelled Nightshade, goblet, bl 66.00
Panelled Nightshade, wine 15.00
Panelled Oval, champagne, flint 52.00
Panelled Oval, egg cup 35.00
Panelled Stippled Bowl, see Stippled Band
Panelled Sunflower, bowl, w/lid 40.00
Panelled Sunflower, goblet 30.00
Panelled Sunflower, sugar bowl 25.00
Panelled Thistle, compote, 5″ 20.00
Panelled Thistle, cruet 35.00
Panelled Thistle, doughnut stand, 6½″ 25.00
Panelled Thistle, pitcher, 7½″ 36.00
Panelled Thistle, plate, 10¼″ 18.00
Panelled Thistle, rose bowl, w/bee, lg, ftd, 5½″ 52.00
Panelled Thistle, shaker, salt 35.00
Panelled Thistle, tumbler, water 40.00
Panelled Thistle, wine, w/bee 30.00
Panelled Zipper, see Iowa
Panelled 44, butter dish, ruby stained, w/lid 85.00
Panelled 44, creamer 20.00
Pangyric, see Prism & Crescent
Parachute, goblet 18.00
Pavonia, goblet 30.00
Pavonia, pitcher, water; etched, 9½″ 85.00
Pavonia, sauce dish, ftd, 4″ 8.00
Pavonia, tumbler 20.00
Pavonia, waste bowl, etched 35.00
Pavonia, water set, ruby stained, etched, 5-pc 255.00
Pavonia, wine, etched 35.00
Peerless, see Lady Hamilton
Pennsylvania, bowl, shallow, 2½x9″ 30.00
Pennsylvania, carafe 37.00
Pennsylvania, creamer, lg size 40.00

Pennsylvania, cup, punch 9.00
Pennsylvania, decanter, hdl, orig stopper 90.00
Pennsylvania, goblet 18.00
Pennsylvania, plate, 8″ 30.00
Pennsylvania, sauce dish, flat, 5¼″ 8.00
Pennsylvania, shot glass 9.00
Pennsylvania, spooner 25.00
Pennsylvania, sugar bowl, open 14.00
Pennsylvania, sugar bowl, w/lid 40.00
Pennsylvania, syrup 42.00
Pennsylvania, tumbler, juice 9.00
Pennsylvania, tumbler, water; gilt trim 25.00
Pennsylvania, wine, gilt trim 17.00
Pentagon, decanter, ruby stained, not orig stopper 60.00
Pentagon, wine 16.00
Pentagon, wine, ruby stained, etched 40.00
Pillar, bottle, bitters 40.00
Pillar, claret, flint, 6⅛″ 56.00
Pillar, goblet, flint 44.00
Pillar, tumbler, ale; flint 43.00
Pillar Bull's Eye, wine, flint 50.00
Pillow & Sunburst, creamer & sugar, ruby & yel stain 33.00
Pillow & Sunburst, pitcher, water 35.00
Pillow Encircled, celery vase, flat base 13.00
Pillow Encircled, spooner, ruby stained, etched 30.00
Pillow Encircled, tray, gr, 9½x5½″ 20.00
Pillow Encircled, tumbler, etched 15.00
Pillow Encircled, tumbler, ruby stained, etched 25.00
Pineapple & Fan, cruet, gr, gilt trim 235.00
Pineapple & Fan, pitcher, water; amber 68.00
Pineapple & Fan, sugar shaker 30.00
Pineapple & Fan, tumbler, amber 30.00
Pineapple & Fan, tumbler, gr, gilt trim 45.00
Pineapple Stem, see Pavonia
Pioneer, see Westward Ho
Pioneer's Victoria, bowl, shallow, ruby stained 40.00
Pioneer's Victoria, tray, wine 13.00
Pioneer's Victoria, wine, etched 22.00
Pioneer's Victoria, wine, ruby stained 40.00
Pitcairn, see Sunk Prism
Pleat & Panel, bread plate 18.00
Pleat & Panel, celery vase 36.00
Pleat & Panel, compote, w/lid 46.00
Pleat & Panel, creamer 30.00
Pleat & Panel, plate, sq, 6″ 20.00
Pleat & Panel, plate, sq, 7″ 20.00
Pleating, pitcher, water; ruby stained 95.00
Pleating, toothpick holder, ruby stained 36.00
Plume, bowl, shallow, sq, 8¼″ 17.00
Plume, celery vase 30.00
Plume, goblet 25.00
Plume, spooner 30.00
Pogo Stick, plate, 7″ 9.00
Pogo Stick, syrup 50.00
Pointed Jewel, compote, jelly; 4½x4½″ 15.00
Pointed Jewel, cup & saucer 15.00
Pointed Jewel, goblet 25.00
Pointed Jewel, sugar bowl, w/lid 30.00
Pointed Panelled Daisy & Button, see Queen
Pointed Thumbprint, see Almond Thumbprint
Polar Bear, goblet, frosted 110.00
Polar Bear, tray, clear, 15½x11″ 100.00
Popcorn, goblet, lined ears 30.00
Popcorn, pitcher, w/ears 75.00
Popcorn, sugar bowl, w/ears 17.00
Portland, bowl, shallow, sm, w/lid 20.00
Portland, celery vase, flat base 20.00
Portland, cracker jar 45.00
Portland, creamer, 4″ 20.00
Portland, goblet, gilt trim 30.00
Portland, lamp, 9″ 60.00
Portland, wine, gilt trim 30.00
Portland w/Diamond Point Band, see Virginia
Powder & Shot, creamer, flint 96.00
Powder & Shot, egg cup 46.00

Powder & Shot, goblet....56.00
Powder & Shot, spooner....33.00
Powder & Shot, sugar bowl, open....30.00
Prayer Rug, see Horseshoe
Pressed Diamond, creamer, canary....20.00
Pressed Diamond, pitcher, water; amber....75.00
Pressed Diamond, salt cellar, ind; bl....12.00
Pressed Diamond, salt shaker, amber....20.00
Pressed Leaf, champagne....22.00
Pressed Leaf, egg cup, flint....20.00
Pressed Leaf, goblet....22.00
Pressed Leaf, salt cellar, master....16.00
Pressed Leaf, sauce dish, flat, flint, 4"....10.00
Pressed Leaf, tray, relish; 7x5"....13.00
Primrose, pitcher, water....40.00
Primrose, plate, amber, 7"....17.00
Primrose, plate, bl, 4½"....15.00
Primrose, platter, amber, 12x8"....23.00
Primrose, sauce dish, flat, bl, 4"....9.00
Primrose, tray, bl, 10"....30.00
Primrose, tray, relish; amber, 9¼x5"....20.00
Primrose, tray, relish; 8x5¼"....12.00
Princess Feather, goblet....35.00
Princess Feather, honey dish....13.00
Princess Feather, plate, 9"....30.00
Princess Feather, sugar bowl, open....30.00
Printed Hobnail, bowl, shallow, 6¾"....10.00
Printed Hobnail, goblet....20.00
Printed Hobnail, tumbler....12.00
Priscilla, butter dish, w/lid....40.00
Priscilla, sauce dish, flat, gr, gilt trim, 4½"....15.00
Priscilla, spooner....18.00
Priscilla, tumbler, gr....18.00
Prism, compote, open....22.00
Prism, egg cup, dbl, flint....25.00
Prism, egg cup, flint....22.00
Prism, spooner, flint....37.00
Prism, tumbler, bar; low flint....23.00
Prism & Crescent, tumbler, bar; flint....40.00
Prism & Daisy Bars, see Panelled Diamond Cross
Prism Arc, see, X-Logs
Prism w/Diamond Points, goblet....20.00
Prism w/Diamond Points, salt cellar, master....18.00
Prism w/Diamond Points, spooner....25.00
Psyche & Cupid, bread plate....32.00
Psyche & Cupid, goblet....52.00
Punty & Diamond Point, bottle, scent....45.00
Punty & Diamond Point, cup, punch....16.00
Punty & Diamond Point, sugar shaker....38.00
Pygmy, see Torpedo
Queen, bowl, oval, 7¾x5¼"....12.00
Queen, compote, w/lid, 12"....46.00
Queen, goblet....20.00
Queen, goblet, amber....33.00
Queen, goblet, bl....40.00
Queen, wine....23.00
Question Mark, goblet....25.00
Question Mark, shaker, salt; no top....15.00
R&H Swirl Band, see Bar & Diamond
Rabbit Tracks, see Parachute
Raindrop, creamer, amber, 4½"....20.00
Raindrop, creamer, bl....30.00
Raindrop, pitcher, water; amber....50.00
Raindrop, sauce dish, ftd, bl, 4¼"....12.00
Ray, plate, flint, 6"....15.00
Ray, spooner....25.00
Rayed Flower, tumbler, gilt trim....13.00
Rayed Flower, water set, gilt trim, color, 5-pc....88.00
Rayed Flower, wine....10.00
Recessed Pillar Thumbprint Band, see Nail
Recessed Pillared Red Top, see Nail
Red Block, see Late Block
Red Top, see Button Arches
Regal Block, tray, wine; 9¼"....16.00
Regal Block, wine....12.00
Regent, see Leaf Medallion
Reverse Torpedo, bowl, shallow, ruffled, 10½"....86.00
Reverse Torpedo, celery vase, flat base....42.00
Reverse Torpedo, compote, open; 6x4¼"....46.00
Reverse Torpedo, goblet....66.00
Reverse Torpedo, nappy, 5"....16.00
Reverse Torpedo, sauce dish, cobalt....18.00
Reverse Torpedo, wine, ruby stained....25.00
Reverse Torpedo, wine, ruby stained, vintage etched....33.00
Ribbed Droplet Band, butter dish, amber stain....85.00
Ribbed Droplet Band, spooner, amber stain....45.00
Ribbed Droplet Band, water set, frosted, amber stain, 7-pc....255.00
Ribbed Grape, goblet, flint....40.00
Ribbed Ivy, bowl, shallow, flint, 8"....68.00
Ribbed Ivy, compote, open; 7"....56.00
Ribbed Ivy, goblet....40.00
Ribbed Ivy, sauce dish, flat, 4"....12.00
Ribbed Ivy, tumbler, whiskey; applied hdl....96.00
Ribbed Palm, creamer, flint....40.00
Ribbed Palm, egg cup....12.00
Ribbed Palm, egg cup, flint....25.00
Ribbed Palm, plate, 6"....22.00
Ribbed Palm, salt cellar, master....25.00
Ribbed Palm, sauce dish, flat, 4"....8.00
Ribbed Palm, sugar bowl, open....30.00
Ribbed Palm, wine....40.00
Ribbed Thumbprint, cruet, bl, enameled floral....175.00
Ribbon, creamer....25.00
Ribbon, goblet....30.00
Ribbon, sauce dish, hdld, sq, 3¾"....12.00
Ribbon, spooner....22.00
Ribbon, sugar bowl, w/lid....35.00
Ribbon Candy, see Bryce
Ripple, bowl, oval, 6x9"....4.00
Ripple, creamer, applied hdl....40.00
Ripple, cup & saucer....18.00
Ripple, egg cup....18.00
Ripple, goblet....25.00
Ripple, spooner....17.00
Ripple, sugar bowl, open....18.00
Ripple Band, see Ripple
Rising Sun, goblet, gilt trim....16.00
Rising Sun, tumbler, gilt trim....14.00
Rising Sun, wine, purple trim....30.00
Roanoke, bowl, shallow, ruby stained....26.00
Roanoke, cake stand, 10"....40.00
Roanoke, compote, jelly; 5x4½"....20.00
Roanoke, creamer, gr....20.00
Roanoke, sauce dish, flat, ruby stained, 4¾"....12.00
Roanoke, waste bowl, ruby stained, etched, 4"....33.00
Rochelle, see Princess Feather
Roman Cross, see Crossed Block
Roman Key, celery vase, frosted....70.00

Roman Key, champagne, frosted....78.00
Roman Key, egg cup, flint, frosted....37.00
Roman Key, goblet, flint, frosted....48.00
Roman Key, goblet, frosted....35.00
Roman Key, sauce dish, flat, frosted, 4¼"....12.00
Roman Key, spooner, frosted....27.00
Roman Key, sugar bowl, frosted, w/lid....40.00
Roman Key, sugar bowl, open; frosted....30.00
Roman Key, tumbler, bar; frosted....78.00
Roman Key, tumbler, frosted, ftd....46.00
Roman Key, wine, frosted....57.00
Roman Rosette, bowl, berry; 7¼"....23.00
Roman Rosette, cake stand, 9⅜"....46.00
Roman Rosette, compote, jelly; 4¾x4¾"....18.00
Roman Rosette, creamer....25.00
Roman Rosette, goblet....35.00
Roman Rosette, mug, 3½"....16.00
Roman Rosette, platter, 11x9"....23.00
Roman Rosette, sauce dish, flat, 4"....8.00
Roman Rosette, shakers, pr....30.00
Rope Bands, goblet....28.00
Rope Bands, sugar, w/lid....28.00
Rope Bands, wine....19.00
Rose & Sunbursts, see American Beauty
Rose in Snow, bread plate....40.00
Rose in Snow, compote, open; yel, 5¾"....56.00
Rose in Snow, plate, 7"....16.00
Rose in Snow, plate, 9¼"....18.00
Rose in Snow, sauce dish, ftd, 4"....13.00

Rose in Snow, tumbler....36.00
Rose Sprig, bowl, ftd, 9x4"....18.00
Rose Sprig, cake stand, bl....50.00
Rose Sprig, celery vase....35.00
Rose Sprig, compote, oval, amber, 8x7½"....36.00
Rose Sprig, mug, applied hdl....46.00
Rose Sprig, tray, rectangle, yel....30.00
Rose Sprig, tray, relish; boat shape....20.00
Rose Sprig, tray, relish; boat shape, bl....36.00
Rosepoint Band, goblet....30.00
Rosette & Palms, banana stand, sm....33.00
Rosette & Palms, celery vase....25.00
Rosette & Palms, compote, open....22.00
Rosette & Palms, compote, w/lid....42.00
Rosette & Palms, goblet....25.00
Rosette & Palms, plate, 10"....11.00
Rosette & Palms, spooner....25.00
Rosette & Palms, sugar bowl, w/lid....43.00
Rosette & Palms, wine....20.00
Rosette Medallion, see Feather Duster
Royal Crystal, see Tarantum's Atlanta
Royal Ivy, see Northwood
Royal Oak, see Northwood
Sandwich Star, spill, clear....35.00
Sandwich Star, spill, flint, clambroth....426.00
Sawtooth, cake stand, non-flint, 10"....56.00
Sawtooth, celery vase, flint, knob stem....56.00
Sawtooth, celery vase, non-flint, knob stem....18.00
Sawtooth, champagne, flint, knob stem....56.00
Sawtooth, creamer, applied hdl, non-flint....30.00
Sawtooth, egg cup....50.00
Sawtooth, goblet, non-flint, knob stem....18.00
Sawtooth, salt cellar, master....15.00
Sawtooth, salt cellar, master; flint, milk glass....20.00
Sawtooth, salt cellar, master; milk glass, w/lid....33.00
Sawtooth, salt cellar, master; non-flint, w/lid....18.00
Sawtooth, spill, flint....36.00
Sawtooth, spooner, non-flint....20.00
Sawtooth, wine, ruby stained top, non-flint....25.00
Sawtooth Band, see Amazon
Scalloped Band, see Scalloped Lines
Scalloped Daisy Red Top, see Button Arches
Scalloped Lines, egg cup....15.00
Scalloped Lines, goblet....25.00
Scalloped Loop, see Yoked Loop
Scalloped Tape, creamer....30.00
Scalloped Tape, wine....12.00
Scroll, egg cup....18.00
Scroll, goblet....17.00
Scroll, shaker, salt; ftd, gr milk glass....17.00
Scroll, tumbler, bl milk glass....33.00
Scroll w/Flowers, bread plate....30.00
Scroll w/Flowers, egg cup, hdld....18.00
Scroll w/Flowers, goblet....23.00
Scroll w/Flowers, wine, amber....35.00
Seneca Loop, see Loop
Sequoia, see Heavy Panelled Finecut
Sheaf & Block, goblet....16.00
Sheaf & Block, wine, gilt trim....7.00
Shell & Jewel, pitcher, water; cobalt....100.00
Shell & Jewel, tumbler....20.00
Shell & Spike, see Shell & Tassel
Shell & Tassel, bowl, shallow, 9¼x5½"....13.00
Shell & Tassel, butter dish, w/dog....100.00
Shell & Tassel, butter pat, shell shape....10.00
Shell & Tassel, creamer....46.00
Shell & Tassel, sauce dish, sq, hdld, 4"....12.00
Shell & Tassel, spooner....35.00
Shell & Tassel, sugar bowl, w/lid, dog finial....85.00
Shell & Tassel, tray, ice cream....46.00
Sheraton, bread plate, bl, 10½x8"....25.00
Shoshone, bowl, shallow, gr, 7"....12.00
Shoshone, compote, jelly, 5"....18.00
Shoshone, creamer, amber stain....46.00
Shoshone, cruet, gr....75.00
Shoshone, shakers, pr....25.00
Shoshone, spooner, amber stain....46.00
Shoshone, sugar bowl, breakfast; w/lid....16.00
Shoshone, tray, relish; gilt trim, 7¾x4"....10.00
Shrine, butter dish, w/lid....42.00
Shrine, compote, jelly....15.00

Shrine, creamer....30.00
Shrine, pitcher, water....47.00
Shrine, relish....15.00
Shrine, salt shaker....22.00
Single Rose, creamer....20.00
Single Rose, sugar bowl, w/lid....23.00
Skilton, compote, ruby flashed....55.00
Skilton, pitcher, water....39.00
Smocking, goblet, medium flint....36.00
Smocking, jar, w/lid....30.00
Smocking, spill, flint....40.00
Smocking, sugar bowl, flint, w/lid....46.00
Smocking, sugar bowl, open; flint....26.00
Snail, bowl, shallow, oval, 8¾x5″....18.00
Snail, butter dish....76.00
Snail, cruet, w/stopper, rare....125.00
Snail, plate, 7¼″....38.00
Snail, shaker, salt; ruby stained....50.00
Snail, spooner....33.00
Snakeskin, goblet....25.00
Snakeskin, sauce dish, flat....7.00
Snakeskin w/Dot, plate, amber, 4½″....10.00
Snakeskin w/Dot, plate, milk glass, 7″....16.00
Spades, see Medallion
Spirea Band, bowl, oval, amber, 7x4½″....10.00
Spirea Band, bowl, oval, amber, 9x5¼″....13.00
Spirea Band, creamer, bl....33.00
Spirea Band, sauce dish, flat, amber, 4″....7.00
Spirea Band, shakers, amber, pr....30.00
Spirea Band, spooner, amber....27.00
Sprig, cake stand, 10″....46.00
Sprig, compote, open; 8x7″....20.00
Sprig, creamer....30.00
Sprig, cruet, cranberry....155.00
Sprig, goblet....27.00
Sprig, pitcher, water....50.00
Sprig, sauce dish, flat, 3¾″....8.00
Sprig, wine....45.00
Squirrel, butter dish....130.00
Squirrel, goblet, rare....426.00
Squirrel, pitcher, water....200.00
Squirrel, sauce dish, flat, 4¼″....18.00
Star Band, butter dish....17.00
Star Band, creamer....16.00
Star Band, pitcher, water, 9″....32.00
Star Band, spooner....16.00
Star Rosetted, bread plate, A Good Mother....45.00
Star Rosetted, goblet....18.00
Star Rosetted, sauce dish, ftd, 4¼″....5.00
Starred Scroll, champagne....15.00
Starred Scroll, decanter....43.00
Stars & Bars, creamer....18.00
Stars & Bars, cruet, amber....65.00
Stars & Bars, cruet, bl....135.00
Stayman, see Tidy
Stedman, champagne, flint....30.00
Stedman, egg cup, flint....20.00
Stedman, goblet, flint....30.00
Stedman, syrup, applied hdl, 8¼″....100.00
Stippled Band, goblet, flint....25.00
Stippled Band, salt cellar, master; flint....20.00
Stippled Chain, goblet, flint....23.00
Stippled Chain, salt cellar, master....20.00
Stippled Chain, sauce dish, 4½″....5.00
Stippled Chain, spooner....22.00
Stippled Cherry, bowl, shallow, 8¼″....16.00
Stippled Cherry, creamer....23.00
Stippled Cherry, sauce dish, flat, 4″....7.00
Stippled Daisy, creamer....16.00
Stippled Daisy, tray, water; 10″....18.00
Stippled Medallion, egg cup, flint....30.00
Stippled Medallion, goblet....30.00
Stippled Panelled Flower, see Maine
Stippled Scroll, see Scroll
Stippled Star, creamer....55.00
Stippled Star, plate, bread....40.00
Stippled Star, spooner....25.00
Strawberry, creamer, applied hdl....66.00
Strawberry, goblet....40.00
Strawberry, relish, scoop form, 8½x4¾″....16.00
Strawberry, sauce dish, flat, milk glass, 4″....12.00
Strawberry, sugar bowl, milk glass, w/lid....40.00
Strawberry, sugar bowl, open; milk glass, flint....25.00
Strawberry, tray, relish; milk glass, 8½x4¾″....26.00
Strawberry, tumbler, bar....46.00
Sunburst, goblet....20.00
Sunburst, pitcher, milk....33.00
Sunburst, plate, 10¾″....17.00
Sunburst, plate, 8″....12.00
Sunburst, sauce dish, ftd, 4¼″....7.00
Sunburst, sauce dish, hdld, 5″....7.00
Sunburst, tray, relish; w/lid, 8¾x3½″....20.00
Sunk Honeycomb, creamer, ruby stained, 4½″....25.00
Sunk Honeycomb, cup, punch....7.00
Sunk Honeycomb, shaker, salt....7.00
Sunk Honeycomb, shaker, salt; ruby stained....20.00
Sunk Honeycomb, wine, etched....17.00
Sunk Honeycomb, wine, ruby stained....33.00
Sunk Honeycomb, wine, ruby stained, etched....40.00
Sunk Prism, cake stand....22.00
Sunken Buttons, cake stand....28.00
Sunken Buttons, wine, amber....45.00
Swan, creamer....45.00
Swirl, see Jersey Swirl
Swirled Column, butter dish, gr, w/lid....45.00
Swirled Column, creamer....15.00
Swirled Column, cup, punch; gilt trim, gr....10.00
Swirled Column, egg cup....12.00
Swirled Column, egg cup, milk glass....14.00
Swirled Column, sauce dish, flat, 4½″....5.00
Swirled Column, sauce dish, ftd, gr, 4″....12.00
Swirled Column, shaker, salt, gr....46.00
Tackle Block, goblet, rnd, flint....33.00
Tarantum's Atlanta, cruet....20.00
Tarantum's Atlanta, powder jar, w/lid....25.00
Tarantum's Atlanta, tumbler....19.00
Tarantum's Atlanta, tumbler, ruby stained....40.00
Teardrop & Diamond Block, see Art
Teardrop & Tassel, see Greentown, Teardrop & Tassel
Teardrop & Thumbprint, goblet, etched....25.00
Texas, creamer....10.00
Texas, pitcher, water....175.00
Texas, toothpick holder....24.00
Texas Bull's Eye, goblet....22.00
The Prize, cup, punch, gr....13.00
The Prize, table set, gr, gilt trim....100.00
The Prize, tumbler, water....19.00
The States, compote, low stem....46.00

The States, creamer, gr, gilt trim, 2½″ 20.00
The States, dish, flat, 4¾″ 8.00
The States, pitcher, water 35.00
The Summit, toothpick holder, ruby stained 50.00
Theatrical, see Actress
Thousand Eye, cake stand, amber, 8½″ 50.00
Thousand Eye, compote, open; amber, 8¼″ 35.00
Thousand Eye, compote, open; vaseline 35.00
Thousand Eye, cruet, amber 175.00
Thousand Eye, cruet, 3-knob, vaseline 325.00
Thousand Eye, goblet, amber 30.00
Thousand Eye, mug, amber, 2½″ 18.00
Thousand Eye, mug, apple gr or yel, 2″ 23.00
Thousand Eye, plate, apple gr, 5¾″ 18.00
Thousand Eye, plate, sq, amber, 8″ 20.00
Thousand Eye, sauce dish, flat, bl, 4″ 12.00
Thousand Eye, shakers, bl, pr 82.00
Thousand Eye, tumbler, water; lt amber 23.00
Thousand Eye Band, goblet 20.00
Thousand Eye Band, wine, etched 12.00
Three Face, butter dish, w/lid 120.00
Three Face, cake stand 95.00
Three Face, celery vase 75.00
Three Face, claret 145.00
Three Face, compote, open; 9″ 175.00
Three Face, creamer 125.00
Three Face, goblet 125.00
Three Face, saucer, champagne 150.00
Three Panel, compote, open; amber, 7½″ 22.00
Three Panel, goblet, bl 43.00
Three Panel, goblet, yel 40.00
Three Panel, sauce dish, ftd, amber 12.00
Thumbprint, celery vase 92.00
Thumbprint, champagne, flint 90.00
Thumbprint, honey dish, 3¼″ 5.00
Thumbprint, salt cellar, master 20.00
Thumbprint, sauce dish, 4¼″ 10.00
Thumbprint, spooner, flint 50.00
Thumbprint, tumbler, ftd 30.00
Thumbprint, wine 28.00
Thumbprint Band, see Dakota
Thunderbird, see Hummingbird
Tidy, goblet 20.00
Tidy, pitcher, water; bulbous 50.00
Tidy, spooner 25.00
Tiny Fine Cut, decanter, orig stopper 72.00
Tiny Fine Cut, wine 12.00
Tiny Lion, spooner, etched 30.00
Tong, sugar bowl, flint, w/lid 50.00
Torpedo, bowl, flared top, 9½″ 35.00
Torpedo, bowl, shallow, 8½x2¾″ 16.00
Torpedo, bowl, 8″ 25.00
Torpedo, bowl, 9″ 35.00
Torpedo, celery vase 45.00
Torpedo, compote, open; 8⅜x7¾″ 56.00
Torpedo, creamer 40.00
Torpedo, cruet 45.00
Torpedo, goblet, etched 55.00
Torpedo, goblet, plain 50.00
Torpedo, pitcher, buttermilk; 7¾″ 55.00
Torpedo, pitcher, etched, 11¾″ 100.00
Torpedo, pitcher, milk; 9″ 66.00
Torpedo, salt dip 33.00
Torpedo, spooner 30.00
Torpedo, sugar bowl, w/lid 50.00
Torpedo, syrup, ruby stained 165.00
Torpedo, tumbler, water; ruby stained 38.00
Tree of Life, bowl, shallow, 6¾″ 18.00
Tree of Life, butter dish, sgn, flint 56.00
Tree of Life, compote, open; hand stem 66.00
Tree of Life, compote, open; sgn Davis, 7½x11″ 176.00
Tree of Life, creamer, applied hdl 43.00
Tree of Life, creamer, applied hdl, sgn 66.00
Tree of Life, epergne, child Samuel stem, sgn Davis 196.00
Tree of Life, goblet, Portland, flint 50.00
Tree of Life, goblet, Portland, sgn, flint 60.00
Tree of Life, goblet, Sandwich 50.00
Tree of Life, sauce dish, flat, 3¼″ 8.00
Tree of Life, sauce dish, leaf shape, 5⅞x4¼″ 10.00
Tree of Life, tray, ice cream, 14x7½″ 25.00
Tree of Life, tumbler, 4½x3⅜″ 30.00
Triangular Prism, goblet 18.00
Triangular Prism, goblet, ladies' size 16.00
Triangular Prism, spooner, flint 30.00
Triangular Prism, tumbler, bar 13.00
Triangular Prism, wine 16.00
Triple Triangle, creamer, ruby stained 43.00
Triple Triangle, goblet, ruby stained 40.00
Triple Triangle, pitcher, water; ruby stained 100.00
Triple Triangle, spooner, ruby stained 35.00
Triple Triangle, sugar bowl, ruby stained, w/lid 43.00
Triple Triangle, tumbler, ruby stained 40.00
Triple Triangle, wine, ruby stained 40.00
Truncated Cube, creamer, ruby stained, 3″ 25.00
Truncated Cube, shaker, salt; ruby stained 20.00
Truncated Cube, tumbler, water 12.00
Truncated Cube, wine 13.00
Tulip, compote, jelly; variant, flint 25.00
Tulip, syrup, applied hdl 56.00
Tulip, tumbler, ale; flint 56.00
Tulip, tumbler, whiskey; hdld, 3″ 32.00
Tulip w/Sawtooth, bottle, bar; pt 62.00
Tulip w/Sawtooth, celery vase, ftd, non-flint 23.00
Tulip w/Sawtooth, champagne, non-flint 33.00
Tulip w/Sawtooth, goblet, flint 66.00
Tulip w/Sawtooth, salt cellar, master 30.00

Tulip w/Sawtooth, salt cellar, master; non-flint 15.00
Tulip w/Sawtooth, tumbler, bar; flint 86.00
Tulip w/Sawtooth, tumbler, bar; non-flint 30.00
Tulip w/Sawtooth, wine, non-flint 20.00
Two Panel, compote, oval, amber, 6½x8″ 19.00
Two Panel, creamer, bl 35.00
Two Panel, goblet, amber 33.00

Two Panel, sauce dish, flat, oval, amber or bl....10.00
Two Panel, sauce dish, ftd, oval, amber....13.00
Two Panel, tray, relish; yel, 9x4¼″....17.00
Two Panel, tray, water; amber, 10x15″....50.00
Valencia Waffle, compote, open; bl....30.00
Valencia Waffle, goblet....20.00
Valencia Waffle, goblet, amber....40.00
Valencia Waffle, pitcher, water; amber....66.00
Valencia Waffle, sauce dish, flat, sq, bl, 4″....12.00
Valencia Waffle, sauce dish, sq, ftd, 4″....15.00
Valencia Waffle, tray, amber, 13¼x9½″....46.00
Victor, see Shell & Jewell
Viking, see Bearded Head
Virginia, butter dish, rose-flashed....150.00
Virginia, creamer, gilt trim, ind....14.00
Virginia, goblet....40.00
Virginia, jar, pomade....33.00
Virginia, tray, relish; 8¾x4″....10.00
Virginia, vase, gilt trim, 6″....18.00
Virginia, wine....22.00
Waffle, bottle, bar; qt....32.00
Waffle, celery vase, ftd, flint....40.00
Waffle, compote, open; flint, 9½x8″....36.00
Waffle, creamer, flint....136.00
Waffle, egg cup....27.00
Waffle, goblet, flint....70.00
Waffle, plate, 6″....14.00
Waffle, salt cellar, master; flint....30.00
Waffle, sugar bowl, lg, flint, w/lid....62.00
Waffle, syrup, applied hdl, flint....86.00
Waffle, waste bowl, ruffled top, flint....76.00
Waffle & Thumbprint, bowl, rectangle, 9¼x7¼″....27.00
Waffle & Thumbprint, decanter, orig stopper, pt....77.00
Waffle & Thumbprint, goblet....58.00
Waffle & Thumbprint, spill, lamp base type....116.00
Waffle & Thumbprint, tumbler, bar; flint....58.00
Washboard, butter dish, w/lid....50.00
Washboard, compote, yel, w/lid, 8¼″....88.00
Washington, Early; bowl, shallow, flint, 6x9¼″....12.00
Washington, Early; claret, flint....136.00
Washington, Early; egg cup, flint....66.00
Washington, Early; salt cellar, ind; flint....13.00
Washington, Early; salt cellar, master; flat, rnd....30.00
Washington Centennial, bowl, shallow, 9x6″....22.00
Washington Centennial, bread plate....100.00
Washington Centennial, bread plate, frosted bust....110.00
Washington Centennial, cake stand, 8¼″....46.00

Washington Centennial, celery vase, ftd....38.00
Washington Centennial, compote, open....40.00
Washington Centennial, compote, w/lid....60.00
Washington Centennial, creamer....88.00
Washington Centennial, goblet....42.00
Washington Centennial, pitcher, milk....80.00
Washington Centennial, plate, 7″....76.00
Washington Centennial, salt cellar, master; oval....30.00
Washington Centennial, sauce dish, flat....10.00
Washington Centennial, sugar bowl, open....30.00
Washington Centennial, tray, relish; bear paw, dated....23.00
Waterlily, see Rosepoint Band
Waterlily & Cattails, sauce dish, flat, 4½″....7.00
Waterlily & Cattails, tray, water....18.00
Waterlily & Cattails, tumbler, bl opal....30.00
Wedding Ring, champagne....76.00
Wedding Ring, sauce dish, flint, 4″....9.00
Westmoreland, cracker jar, w/lid....35.00
Westmoreland, creamer, ind....13.00
Westmoreland, cruet, orig stopper....23.00
Westmoreland, egg cup....22.00
Westward Ho, compote, oblong, w/lid, 8x10″....275.00
Westward Ho, compote, oval, low ped, w/lid, 6¾x4¼″....152.00
Westward Ho, creamer....86.00
Westward Ho, creamer, dog hdl....135.00
Westward Ho, goblet....96.00
Westward Ho, jar, jam....145.00
Westward Ho, pitcher, water....112.00
Westward Ho, platter, 13x8¾″....76.00
Westward Ho, sugar bowl, w/lid....150.00
Wheat & Barley, goblet....27.00
Wheat & Barley, goblet, amber....40.00
Wheat & Barley, mug, amber, 3¾″....33.00
Wheat & Barley, plate, hdld, amber, 11″....25.00
Wheat & Barley, plate, 7″....18.00
Wheat & Barley, sauce dish, ftd, amber, 4″....15.00
Wheat & Barley, shaker, salt; bl....40.00
Wheat & Barley, tumbler, water, amber....33.00
Wildflower, butter dish....36.00
Wildflower, cake basket, ped, no hdl, gr....96.00
Wildflower, compote, open; amber, 7″....23.00
Wildflower, creamer, amber....30.00
Wildflower, goblet, apple gr....46.00
Wildflower, pitcher, water; amber....56.00
Wildflower, pitcher, water; apple gr....66.00
Wildflower, salt cellar, turtle form, apple gr....32.00
Wildflower, sauce dish, flat, apple gr, 4″....12.00
Wildflower, sugar bowl, w/lid....20.00
Wildflower, tray, oval, amber, 11x13″....43.00
Wildflower, tray, oval, apple gr, 11x13″....56.00
Wildflower, tray, relish; amber, 9¼x4″....18.00
Wildflower, tray, relish; apple gr, 9¼x4¼″....20.00
Wildflower, tumbler, water; amber or yel....30.00
Willow Oak, bowl, shallow, 7″....13.00
Willow Oak, cake stand, amber, 8¾″....40.00
Willow Oak, compote, w/lid, 10½x6¼″....46.00
Willow Oak, goblet....33.00
Willow Oak, pitcher, milk....32.00
Willow Oak, tumbler, water....40.00
Windflower, compote, w/lid....60.00
Windflower, tumbler, bar....36.00
Wisconsin, celery vase....38.00
Wisconsin, cup & saucer....45.00
Wisconsin, pitcher, water....60.00
Wisconsin, plate....15.00
Wisconsin, salt shakers, pr....45.00
Wooden Pail, creamer, amethyst....46.00
Wooden Pail, match holder, amber, hdld....20.00

Wooden Pail, toothpick holder, yel....30.00
X-Logs, goblet....20.00
Yale, pitcher, water; w/6 goblets....195.00
Yoked Loop, compote, open; flint, 7"....20.00
Yoked Loop, goblet, flint....22.00
Yoked Loop, goblet, gr, flint....18.00
Yoked Loop, sugar bowl, open....20.00
Yoked Loop, tumbler, whiskey; hdld....26.00
Zig Zag, goblet....20.00
Zig Zag, shaker, salt....8.00
Zig Zag, wine....18.00
Zipper Slash, cordial....20.00
Zipper Slash, egg cup....22.00
Zipper Slash, salt cellar, master....8.00
Zipper Slash, wine....20.00
Zippered Block, compote, open; 7¼x7¼"....23.00
Zippered Block, goblet....36.00
Zippered Block, shaker, salt; ruby stained....36.00

Paul Revere Pottery

The Saturday Evening Girls were a social group of young Boston ladies who met to pursue various activities, among them pottery making. Their first kiln was bought in 1906, and within a few years it became necessary to move to a larger location. Because their new quarters were near the historical Old North Church, they chose the name Paul Revere Pottery. With very little training the girls produced only simple ware. Until 1915, the pottery operated at a deficit. Then a new building with four kilns was constructed on Nottingham Road. Vases, miniature jugs, children's tea sets, tiles dinnerware, and lamps were produced, usually in soft matt glazes with simple stylized nature decorations often incised on the ware. Occasional examples in a dark high gloss may also be found.

Several marks were used: 'P.R.P.'; 'S.E.G.'; or the circular device, 'Boston, Paul Revere Pottery' with the horse and rider.

The pottery continued to operate, and even though their product sold well, the high production costs of the handmade ware caused the pottery to fail in 1946.

When no condition is indicated, the items listed below are assumed to be in mint condition.

Jar, bulbous form with insects on yellow band, white ground, dated 1-12-14, 5¼", $800.00.

Bowl, bl w/blk line at top, 1¾" H....100.00
Bowl, brn mottle w/repetitive goose decor, 5x11½"....350.00
Bowl, goose & initials on wht w/bands, SEG/1920, 6½"....160.00
Bowl, Greek Key band, tan/bl on gr, S Galner, SEG/1914, 6"..290.00
Bowl, lt bl drip over bl, no mk, 4x5"....40.00
Bowl, scene w/3 chicks in center, wht w/bl band, 1½x6"....300.00
Candlestick, bl, SEG/artist sgn/#d/labels, 8", pr....50.00
Flowerpot, bl, SEG, 4"....40.00
Jar, chicks on rust band on gr/brn, SEG, 4½"....350.00
Jar, insects on yel band on wht, 2nd on lid, SEG/1914, 5¼"...800.00
Paperweight, goose, 8-sided, SEG....125.00
Plate, hills/trees at rim, monogram in center, SEG, 8"....150.00
Plate, simple floral border, bl w/brn, sgn EG, 6½"....125.00
Tile, landscape relief border, Edith Brown, 1926, 5½" dia....160.00
Tile, Paul Revere/horse/title, R Bucchini, SEG/1911, 6x4"....450.00
Trivet, Paul Revere on horsebk, 5-color, SEG, 4¼" dia....400.00
Trivet, stylized crocus-incised corners, Mangini/SEG, 5½"....300.00
Vase, banded 6-color scenic, Edith Brown/2-1923, 4½x4"....450.00
Vase, blk gloss, w/label, 10"....75.00
Vase, cobalt speckled, sgn Eva Geneco/1920, SEG, 10"....60.00
Vase, copper overlay, waisted neck, 8½"....160.00
Vase, gr tree band on lt bl, bulbous, SEG/FL, 4¾"....450.00
Vase, yel matt, artist sgn, 4½x3½"....60.00
Wall pocket, dk gr, plain....50.00

Pauline Pottery

Pauline Pottery was made from 1883 to 1888 in Chicago, Ill., from clay imported from the Ohio area. Its founder was Mrs. Pauline Jacobus, who had learned the trade at the Rookwood Pottery. Mrs. Jacobus moved to Edgerton, Wisconsin, to be near a source of suitable clay, thus eliminating shipping expenses. Until 1905, she produced high quality wares, able to imitate with ease designs and styles of such masters as Wedgwood and Meissen. Her products were sold through leading department stores, and the names of some of these firms may appear on the ware. Not all were marked, and unless signed by a noted local artist, positive identification is often impossible. Marked examples carried a variety of stamps and signatures: Trade Mark with a crown, Pauline Pottery, and Edgerton Art Pottery are but a few.

When no condition is indicated, the items listed below are assumed to be in mint condition.

Box, powder; violets on yel/gr ground, no mk....245.00
Jar, cream w/bl stippling, pink/bl flowers, 6x4"....600.00
Teapot, floral, pastels, gold trim, strainer, sgn, 9"....725.00
Vase, rose, sgn, 4x5"....450.00

Vase, dark gray-green stoneware with cut-away band of leaves on stippled background, signed Pauline Pottery, 5", $550.00.

Peachblow

Peachblow, made to imitate the colors of the Chinese Peachbloom porcelain, was made by several glasshouses in the late 1800s. Among them were New England Glass, Mt. Washington, Webb, and Hobbs Brockunier and Company. Its pink shading was achieved through action of the heat on the gold content of the glass. While New England Peachblow shades from pink to cool white, Mt. Washington's tends to shade from peach to ivory. Although usually glossy, a satin finish was also produced, and many pieces were enameled and gilded.

When no condition is indicated, the items listed below are assumed to be in mint condition; the finish is glossy unless noted.

Dish, ruffled rim, New Martinsville, 5½″ diameter, $135.00.

Bowl, berries decor, melon rib, crimped top, oval, 9x10″......350.00
Bowl, flared, scalloped, NE, 2¾x5½″......745.00
Bowl, porridge; NE, 3⅔x4½″......435.00
Cruet, EX color, amber faceted stopper/hdl, Wheeling, 6¾″...1,250.00
Cup, punch; NE......325.00
Cup & saucer, wht reed hdl, Gunderson......200.00
Decanter, ped ft, Gunderson, w/stopper, 9½″......250.00
Ewer, Gunderson, 6″......135.00
Jar, honeycomb, SP lid & bail, Webb, 3″......325.00
Pitcher, amber hdl, 4-sided top, Wheeling, 7x7½″......1,250.00
Pitcher, sq top, amber hdl, 4⅝″......500.00
Pitcher, water; applied amber hdl, Wheeling, rare, lg......1,250.00
Plate, Gunderson, 8″......65.00
Rose bowl, pinched/ruffled, Gunderson, 3½x4½″......50.00
Shade, gas light; NE, fitter: 2¼″, 4½x6¼″......385.00
Sugar bowl, fancy hdls, no lid, Mt WA, 2½″......1,600.00
Sugar bowl, 2 hdls, World's Fair, 1893, NE......450.00
Sugar shaker, SP top, Wheeling, 5x3″......550.00
Tumbler, bl floral, English......165.00
Tumbler, Wheeling, 3½″......250.00
Tumbler, Wheeling, 4x2¾″......300.00
Vase, applied flowers on satin, 5x1½″......395.00
Vase, cameo, passion flower, butterfly on bk, English, 6″......2,750.00
Vase, elongated gourd form, Wheeling, 9″......650.00
Vase, floral enamel, sgn TW & Sons, 6″......350.00
Vase, floral/butterfly/bands in gold, Webb, 7½x4½″......895.00
Vase, gold floral & butterfly, slim neck/bulbous, Webb, 8″......495.00
Vase, gold prunus, Webb, 3¼x2⅜″......325.00
Vase, gold prunus & bird, bottle form, Webb, 9″......550.00
Vase, lily; EX color, NE, 9¾″......785.00
Vase, lily; Mt WA, 6¼x2½″......1,750.00
Vase, lily; satin, NE paper label, 8¼″......845.00
Vase, Morgan, Wheeling, 7¾″......945.00
Vase, squirrels/grapes, gold/silver relief, hdls, 10½″, pr......485.00

Peking Glass

The first glasshouse was established in Peking in 1680. It produced glassware made in imitation of porcelain, a more desirable medium to the Chinese. By 1725, multi-layered carving with a cameo effect resulted in a wider range of shapes and colors. The factory was closed from 1736 to 1795, but glass made in Po-shan and shipped to Peking for finishing continued to be called Peking glass.

Twentieth century ware is usually decorated in soft frosted colors on relief-molded designs.

When no condition is indicated, the items listed below are assumed to be in mint condition.

Goblet, amethyst, thick stem, mk China, 6¼″......85.00
Vase, bird on branch cameo, bl to wht, 10″......280.00
Vase, birds cameo, yel to wht, bottle form, 9″, pr......500.00
Vase, butterflies/narcissus cameo, yel to wht, 9¾″, pr......475.00
Vase, clambroth, polished pontil, reeded hdls......90.00
Vase, crane on limb of pine tree cameo, gr to wht, 12″......425.00
Vase, ducks & water lilies cameo, red cut to wht, 5x10″......210.00
Vase, monkeys in pomegranate tree cameo, red/wht, 9″, pr......485.00
Vase, peony cameo, gr to wht, Ching dynasty mk, 14″......600.00

Left to right: Vase, bright yellow, 8-sided, signed, 5½″, $375.00; Vase, blue cut to white, 6¼″, $350.00; Pair of vases, brown-red cut to white, 7″, $475.00.

Peloton

Peloton glass was first made by Wilhelm Kralik in Bohemia in 1880. This unusual art glass was produced by rolling colored threads onto the transparent or opaque glass gather as it was removed from the furnace. Usually, more than one color of threading was used, and some items were further decorated with enameling. It was made with both shiny and acid finishes.

When no condition is indicated, the items listed below are assumed to be in mint condition.

Pitcher, clear with well executed yellow enameled flowers and large green leaves, 7½″, $375.00.

Cracker jar, ribbed w/yel/bl/red threads on satin, SP lid.......475.00
Cruet, amber w/wht threads, 3-petal top, stopper, 6¼″........325.00
Pitcher, water; amber w/pink/wht/bl/gr threads, 12x5″.........550.00
Rose bowl, pastels on wht, 6-crimp top, 2¼x2½″.............265.00
Vase, cranberry threads, Kralik, Bohemia, 7½″..............150.00
Vase, lav-gray w/pastel threads, bulbous, crimped, 3¼″........215.00
Vase, pastel threads, fan form, ruffled, 4¾x4⅜″..............295.00
Vase, pastel threads, ribbed, clear wafer ft, 5¾x3½″..........275.00
Vase, pastel threads, squat w/folded 3-lobe top, 4x4½″........300.00
Vase, pink/bl/wht/yel threads, emb/tricorn, 7x5¾″............325.00

Pennsbury

New in the collectibles market, Pennsbury Pottery is drawing quite a following! Established in the 1950s in Morrisville, Pennsylvania, by Henry Below, the company produced dinnerware and novelty items, much of which was sold in gift shops along the Pennsylvania Turnpike. Some of their ware was hand painted in blue on white, some in multicolors on a light orange-brown. Pennsylvania Dutch motifs, Amish couples, and barbershop singers were among their most popular decorative themes. Sgraffito, or hand incising, was used extensively.

The company marked their wares 'Pennsbury Pottery' or 'Pennsbury Pottery, Morrisville, PA.' They closed during the early 1970s.

When no condition is indicated, the items listed below are assumed to be in mint condition.

Ash tray, advertising, 1935...............................25.00
Ash tray, emb dog in center, oval, 7½″.....................30.00
Butter dish, tulip, 4x5½″................................25.00
Butter dish, 2 birds.....................................50.00
Cigarette box, incised/HP rooster on lid, brn, 2¼x3¾x4¾″......25.00
Figurine, bird, Magnolia Warbler, #112.....................38.00
Figurine, rooster, 12″...................................125.00
Figurine, rooster & chicken, brn/beige, pr, lg...............225.00
Hot plate, Amish people, 6″..............................25.00
Mug, Amish couple, 4¾″.................................25.00
Mug, Sweet Adeline......................................22.50
Pitcher, hex, 4½″.......................................12.50
Pitcher, hex & heart, 3″.................................10.00
Pitcher, milk; rooster decor...............................36.00
Pitcher, water; eagle decor...............................42.00
Plaque, open book, stand-up..............................20.00

Vinegar and oil jugs, figural head stoppers, 7″, $75.00 for the pair.

Plate, angel..18.00
Plate, Christmas, 1970.................................30.00
Plate, gr eagle w/banner: E Pluribus Unum, shield, 8″.........25.00
Tray, NEA Centennial, 1957..............................20.00
Wall plaque, skunk decor................................18.00

Pens and Pencils

The first metallic writing pen was patented in 1809 and soon machine-produced pens with steel nibs gradually began replacing the quill. The first fountain pen was invented in 1830, but due to the fact that a suitable metal for the tips had not yet been developed, they were not manufactured commercially until the 1880s. The first commercial producers were Waterman in 1884, and Parker with the Lucky Curve in 1888.

The self-filling pen, in 1890, featured the soft interior sack which filled with ink as the metal bar on the outside of the pen was raised and lowered. Variations of the pumping mechanism were tried until 1932 when Parker introduced the Vacumatic, a sackless pen with an internal pump.

When no condition is indicated, the items listed below are assumed to be in excellent condition.

Key:

AF—aeromatic filler	GPT—gold plated trim
BF—button filler	I—initialed
cartr—cartridge	LF—lever filler
CPT—chrome plated trim	NPT—nickel plated trim
ED—eyedropper filler	TD—touchdown filler
GFM—gold filled metal	VF—vacumatic filler

Fountain Pens

Conklin, #2NL, 1912, blk chased hard rubber, EX............69.00
Conklin, #20, 1920, blk chased hard rubber, M...............85.00
Conklin, #30P, 1920, blk chased hard rubber, EX.............59.00
Conklin, #40, 1918, red hard rubber, EX...................250.00
Conklin, S, 1903, red mottled hard rubber, EX..............195.00
Dunhill, 1929, blk w/Oriental decor, EX....................95.00
Gold Medal, 1926, red mottled hard rubber, EX..............69.00
Moore, #94A, 1941, bronze & silver striped, EX..............39.00
Moore, 1904, non-leakable, blk chased hard rubber, ED, EX....25.00
Moore, 1948, blk w/gold-tone cap, EX......................20.00
Parker, #23, 1905, red mottled hard rubber, ED, EX.........195.00
Parker, #45, 1959, blk, stainless cap, cartridge, VG............8.00
Parker, #51, 1956, blk, gold filled cap, AF, EX..............45.00
Parker, Black Giant, 1912, blk hard rubber, NPT, ED, NM...1,400.00
Parker, Blue Diamond Vacumatic, 1942, VF, EX...............29.00
Parker, Duofold, 1930, blk hard rubber, BF, EX..............45.00
Parker, Duofold, 1939, gold, blk geometric pattern, BF, EX.....39.00
Parker, Duofold Jr, 1927, mandarin yel, EX..................95.00
Parker, Duofold Jr, 1928, mandarin yel, BF, EX..............95.00
Parker, Lady Duofold, 1929, red hard rubber, BF, EX.........69.00
Parker, Lucky Curve, 1932, blk, BF, EX....................25.00
Parker, Maxima Vacumatic, 1939, emerald striped, VF, EX....275.00
Parker, Pastel, 1929, coral Moire, BF, M...................49.00
Parker, Super 21, 1956, gray, stainless cap, CPT, AF, EX......20.00
Parker, Super 21, 1957, gray, stainless cap, CPT, AF, VG......10.00
Parker, True Blue, 1931, BF, VG..........................39.00
Parker, Vacumatic, 1935, burgundy pearl, VF, EX.............59.00
Parker, Vacumatic, 1936, gold streaked marble, VF, EX........29.00
Parker, Vacumatic, 1940, silver pearl, VF, EX...............25.00
Parker, VS, 1947, gray, stainless cap, CPT, BF, M...........65.00
Sheaffer's, #3, 1935, gold striped, VG.....................12.00
Sheaffer's, #3-25, 1923, blk, EX.........................20.00
Sheaffer's, #3-25, 1932, blk, VG.........................15.00

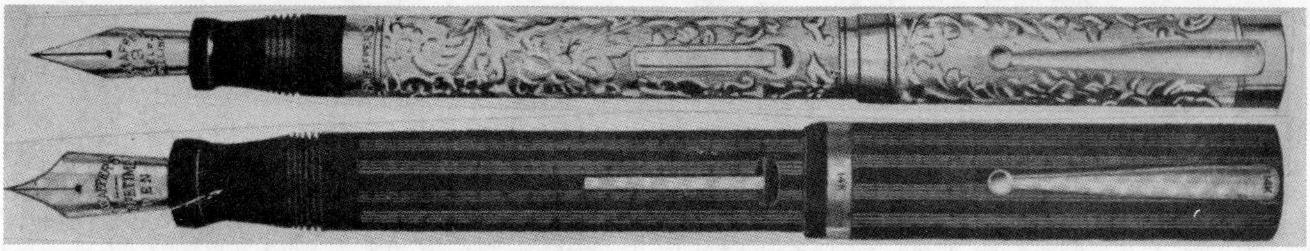

Top to bottom: 1923 Sheaffer No. 3, self-filing pen in chased sterling silver, lever filler, $175.00; 1923 Sheaffer Lifetime in lined black hard rubber with solid gold trim, lever filler, $200.00.

Sheaffer's, #5-30, 1927, gr jade, VG....22.00
Sheaffer's, #5-30, 1928, gr jade, VG....24.00
Sheaffer's, Junior, 1935, silver striped, NPT, VG....15.00
Sheaffer's, Lady Lifetime, 1926, gr jade marbled, EX....39.00
Sheaffer's, Lifetime, 1938, gold striped, M....175.00
Sheaffer's, Lifetime, 1939, emerald striped, EX....39.00
Sheaffer's, Snorkel, 1954, pink, TD, EX....18.00
Sheaffer's, TM Triumph, 1951, blk, TD, EX....29.00
Sheaffer's, Triumph Lifetime, 1946, gold striped, EX....39.00
Sheaffer's, Wasp Clipper, 1939, emerald, EX....29.00
Swan, Eternal, 1927, red hard rubber, EX....95.00
Swan, Eternal 48 ETN, 1923, blk, EX....195.00
Swan, Swallow, 1928, bl marbled, EX....29.00
Swan, 1924, GFM, EX....29.00
Swan, 1939, webbed silver & blk marbled, NPT, EX....19.00
Wahl-Eversharp, Bantam, 1932, pink pearl spiral, AF, EX....25.00
Wahl-Eversharp, Bantam Doric in Morocco, 1932, AF, EX....30.00
Wahl-Eversharp, Doric, 1932, burgundy marbled, EX....125.00
Wahl-Eversharp, Pacemaker, 1938, bl marbled, rare, EX....49.00
Wahl-Eversharp, Silver Seal Doric in Cathay, 1933, M....175.00
Wahl-Eversharp, Skyline, 1946, maroon, VG....18.00
Wahl-Eversharp, Tempoint, 1918, blk chased hard rubber, EX....35.00
Wahl-Eversharp, 1920, blk chased hard rubber, EX....29.00
Wahl-Eversharp, 1925, red mottled, EX....79.00
Wahl-Eversharp, 1927, pearl & blk, VG....39.00
Wahl-Eversharp, 1953, bl, EX....19.00
Waterman's, Ideal, 1929, Persian (gr & red marbled), VG....35.00
Waterman's, Ideal #0552, 1924, Gothic, GFM, EX....140.00
Waterman's, Ideal #16, 1907, blk hard rubber, ED, EX....85.00
Waterman's, Ideal #452, 1925, pansy panel sterling, I, EX....175.00
Waterman's, Ideal #52, 1924, blk chased hard rubber, NPT....19.00
Waterman's, Ideal #52V, 1920, blk chased hard rubber, NPT....32.00
Waterman's, Ideal #58, 1925, rose ripple, marbled, EX....795.00
Waterman's, Ideal #7, 1925, red ripple hard rubber, EX....125.00
Waterman's, Ideal #92V, 1933, turq, EX....32.00
Waterman's, Ideal #994, 1928, olive ripple, EX....225.00

Mechanical Pencils

Conklin, Endura, 1927, sapphire, EX....39.00
Conklin, 1920, blk chased hard rubber, EX....39.00
Conklin, 1931, gr marbled, VG....25.00
Conklin, 1932, gr & blk striped, NPT, EX....35.00
Moore, 1922, blk chased hard rubber, M....29.00
Parker, Duofold, 1930, red, with sticker, M....65.00
Parker, Duofold Jr, 1927, blk hard rubber, EX....85.00
Parker, Duofold Sr, 1928, red hard rubber, EX....185.00
Parker, Pastel, 1928, beige-gray, M....39.00
Parker, Vacumatic, 1939, bl striped, EX....79.00
Parker, Vacumatic Repeater, 1939, silver pearl, NPT, VG....39.00
Parker, 1932, gold pearl marbled, EX....15.00
Parker, 1932, silver pearl marbled, NPT, EX....10.00
Wahl-Eversharp, Bantam, 1932, pink pearl marbled, EX....20.00
Wahl-Eversharp, Doric, 1933, gr marbled, M....29.00
Wahl-Eversharp, Doric, 1934, gr & gold marbled, EX....25.00
Wahl-Eversharp, Repeater, 1950, bl, chrome-gold top, M....25.00
Wahl-Eversharp, Repeater, 1955, red, M....20.00
Wahl-Eversharp, Skyline Repeater, 1942, bl striped, EX....20.00

Sets

Chilton, 1930, burgundy marbled, TD....195.00
Conklin, Endura, 1930, gr pearl marbled, EX....295.00
Conklin, 1930, gold marbled, rare, EX....195.00
Gold Medal, 1939, emerald striped, BF, M....29.00
Moore, 1930, gold pearl marbled, EX....39.00
Moore, 1935, emerald pearl marbled, EX....42.00
Parker, #51, 1951, pink, Lustraloy cap, CPT, I, AF, EX....39.00
Parker, Duofold, 1931, gr & pearl, BF, M....165.00
Parker, Vacumatic, 1940, gold, blk web pattern, VF, EX....39.00
Parker, 1931, cream & gold pearl, BF, rare, M....295.00
Swan, Swallow, 1930, gr jade, M....95.00
Swan, 1934, lav pearl marbled, EX....29.00
Wahl-Eversharp, Airlite, 1938, silver pearl, CPT, EX....35.00
Wahl-Eversharp, Gold Seal Doric, 1940, blk, EX....295.00
Wahl-Eversharp, 1952, blk, M....25.00
Waterman's, Ideal, 1945, gold marbled, M....32.00

Personalities, Fact and Fiction

One of the largest and most popular areas of collecting today, if tradepaper ads and articles be any indication, is character-related memorabilia. Everyone has a favorite or favorites, whether they be comic-strip personalities or true-life heroes.

The earliest comic strip dealt with the adventures of the Yellow Kid, the smiling, bald-headed Oriental boy always in a nightshirt. He was introduced in 1895, a product of the imagination of Richard Fenton Outcault. Today, though very hard to come by, items relating to the Yellow Kid bring premium prices.

In 1902, Buster Brown and Tige, his dog and constant companion, another of Outcault's progenies, made it big in the comics as well as in the world of advertising. Shoe stores appealed to the younger set through merchandising displays that featured them both; today, the items from their earlier years are very collectible.

Though her 1923 introduction was unobtrusively made through only one newspaper, New York's *Daily News*, Little Orphan Annie, the vacant-eyed redhead in the inevitable red dress, was quickly adopted by hordes of readers nationwide; and before the demise of her creator, Harold Gray, in 1968, she starred in her own radio show. She made two feature films, and in 1977 'Annie' was launched on Broadway.

Other early comic figures were Moon Mullins, created in 1923 by Frank Willard; Buck Rogers by Philip Nowlan in 1928; and Betty Boop, the round-faced, innocent-eyed, chubby-cheeked Boop-Boop-a-Doop girl of the early

1930s. Bimbo was her dog, and KoKo her clown friend.

Popeye made his debut in 1929, as the spinach-eating sailor with the spindly-limbed girlfriend, Olive Oyl, in the comic strip, *Thimble Theatre*, created by Elzie Segar. He became a film star in 1933, and had his own radio show that during 1936 played three times a week on CBS. He obligingly modeled for scores of toys, dolls, and figurines, and especially those from the thirties are today very collectible.

Tarzan, created around 1930 by Edgar Rice Burroughs; and Captain Midnight, by Robert Burtt and Willfred G. Moore are popular heroes with today's collectors. During the days of radio, Sky King of the Flying Crown Ranch (also created by Burtt and Moore) thrilled boys and girls of the mid-1940s. Hopalong Cassidy, Red Rider, Tom Mix, and the Lone Ranger were only a few of the other 'good guys' always on the side of law and order.

But of all the fictional heroes and comic characters collected today, probably the best loved and well known is Mickey Mouse. Created in the late 1920s by Walt Disney, Micky (as his name was first spelled) became an instant success with his film debut, Steamboat Willie. His popularity was parlayed through windup toys, watches, figurines, cookie jars, puppets, clothing, and numerous other salables. Items from the 1930s are usually copyrighted 'Walt Disney Enterprises'; thereafter, 'Walt Disney Productions' was used.

Authority David Longest has compiled a fine book, *Character Toys and Collectibles*, with full-color photos and current market values; you will find his address in the Directory under Indiana. When no condition is indicated, the items listed below are assumed to be in excellent condition.

Related areas include Autographs and Movie Memorabilia. See also specific items, such as: Banks; Big Little Books; Cartoon Books; Children's Books; Comic Books; Cookie Jars; Dolls; Lunchboxes; Paper Dolls; Pinback Buttons; Posters; Toys

Beatles plastic figures, (missing one guitar), set of four, $175.00.

Amos & Andy, ash tray, cast metal, 5" 225.00
Amos & Andy, book, All About A & A, hard cover, 126 pg 50.00
Amos & Andy, candy bar box, authority of Correll/Gosden 275.00
Amos & Andy, card party score pads & tallies, in box, NM 35.00
Amos & Andy, chalkware Andy, 11" 120.00
Amos & Andy, chalkware figures, Art Statuary Co, 7½", pr 175.00
Amos & Andy, puzzle, Pepsodent premium, 8x10", w/mailer 70.00
Amos & Andy, stand-up figures, 7½" & 8½", pr 45.00
Amos & Andy, tablet 15.00
Amos & Andy, walkers, movable eyes, orig box 1,500.00
Amos & Andy, wood jtd dolls, pr 350.00
Amos & Andy, 1¢ candy wrapper, w/NRA Eagle 85.00
Andy & Minn, toothbrush holder 65.00
Andy Gump, mirror & brush, celluloid, EX 35.00
Andy Gump, smoking stand, pnt EX, 30" 75.00
Babe Ruth, baseball score pad, Quaker Oats, rare 45.00
Bambi, book, Walt Disney's Bambi, Grosset & Dunlap, VG 30.00
Bambi, clock, animated, Bambi/Thumper/Flower, Bayard, MIB .. 110.00
Bambi, picture, Bambi & mother, framed, 1940s, M 110.00
Bambi, planter, by tree stump w/Thumper, 1949, 7x7", EX 18.00
Barbie, wrist watch, 1963 .... 25.00
Barney Google, board game 65.00
Barry Goldwater, doll, Remco, 1964, 5½", MIB 25.00
Bashful (dwarf), figurine, ceramic, Evan Shaw, 6¼", EX 75.00
Beatles, bank, pictures & signatures 30.00
Beatles, book, A Hard Day's Night, paperback, 1964 .... 18.00
Beatles, book, Paul McCartney & Wings, hard cover, 1978 .... 10.00
Beatles, book, The Beatles Forever, hard cover, 1978 .... 18.00
Beatles, book, Yellow Submarine, paperback, 1968 .... 9.50
Beatles, car mascot, bobbing heads, set of 4, MIB 800.00
Beatles, gum machine plastic rings, set of 4 .... 8.50
Beatles, hair spray 110.00
Beatles, jigsaw puzzle, b/w, still in package, 8½x11" 14.00
Beatles, keyring, guitar shape, 1966, 3½" 5.50
Beatles, magazine, Vol 1, #1, VG 50.00
Beatles, medallion, shiny gold metal, 1964 .... 5.50
Beatles, metal faces on orig display card, ca 1964 .... 35.00
Beatles, minted copper plated coin, visit to US, 1964 .... 25.00
Beatles, music box, Play Guitar Like the Beatles 15.00
Beatles, Paul doll, Remco 36.00
Beatles, pencil set, set of 4 .... 9.50
Beatles, playing cards, full deck, b/w, 1964 .... 15.00
Beatles, pocket mirror, 1964, 3x2" 5.50
Beatles, portrait, oilcloth, EX 10.00
Beatles, Quiz Book, 1975 .... 8.50
Beatles, Ringo model, Revell, boxed 66.00
Beatles, talcum powder 250.00
Beatles, tennis shoes 100.00
Beatles, thermos, Yellow Submarine 25.00
Beatles, tie tack, gold & blk, 1964 .... 12.00
Beatles, tray, metal w/4 color pictures, autographed, EX 55.00
Beatles, whistle, police type, from movie Help, 1966 .... 4.00
Beatles, wig, authentic, cut-out Beatle faces at top 28.00
Betty Boop, ash tray, lusterware, 1930s 95.00
Betty Boop, bisque, playing drum, EX orig pnt 85.00
Betty Boop, buckle, celluloid, lg 50.00
Betty Boop, buckle, celluloid, sm 35.00
Betty Boop, celluloid figure, playing violin, 3" 60.00
Betty Boop, chalkware figure, 18" 60.00
Betty Boop, doll, Cameo, orig dress, 11½" 550.00
Betty Boop, pocket watch 150.00
Betty Boop, valentine, mechanical 18.00
Betty Boop, wall pocket, Fleischer Studios, Japan 95.00
Betty Boop & Bimbo, ash tray 165.00
Bozo the Clown, hand puppet, polka dot outfit, wool hair 16.00
Buck Rogers, atomic pistol 75.00
Buck Rogers, book, pop-up; Dangerous Mission 120.00
Buck Rogers, display, liquid helium water pistol, 1936, NM 150.00
Buck Rogers, paint book, 1935, 11x18" 95.00
Buck Rogers, pop gun 47.00
Buck Rogers, solar map, orig mailing tube, rpr tear, rare 265.00
Buck Rogers, Strato kite, 1947 .... 20.00
Bugs Bunny, bank, cast metal 60.00
Bugs Bunny, bank, next to barrel, rect base, pot metal, 5" 35.00
Buster Brown, cloth patch, 1930s 5.00
Buster Brown, iron figure in cart pulled by iron dog, 1900 .... 395.00
Buster Brown, whistle, tin, cylindrical 20.00
Buttercup & Spare Ribs, tin platform toy, 1920s 750.00
Captain Marvel, Magic Eyes, in envelope 16.00
Captain Marvel, sm kite figure, kit in envelope 20.00
Captain Marvel, wrist watch 150.00
Captain Midnight, decoder, 1947 .... 35.00

Captain Midnight, decoder, 1949..........................20.00
Captain Midnight, Secret Squadron manual, color, 16 pg, NM...50.00
Charlie Chaplin, doll, compo, Louis Amberg, 1915, 26″.......625.00
Charlie Chaplin, squeeze toy, compo head, Japan, 1920s......225.00
Charlie Chaplin, whistle, tin litho figural....................45.00
Charlie Chaplin, windup, Spain, MIB..........................25.00
Charlie Chaplin, windup, walks, compo/metal, 1920s, 11″......575.00
Charlie McCarthy, book, CM Meets Snow White, Whitman, EX..45.00
Charlie McCarthy, figure, cb, 21″..........................35.00
Charlie McCarthy, game, Radio Party, Chase & Sanborn, '38....48.00
Charlie McCarthy, soap figural, in orig cylinder box, 5½″.......35.00

Charlie McCarthy radio, bakelite, Majestic, 6″ x 7″ x 5″, $500.00

Chester Gump, in cart pulled by horse, CI, 1905.............425.00
Cinderella, doll, WDP, in orig rnd case.......................25.00
Cinderella, tumbler, w/Godmother, from series, 1960s, 4″.......12.00
Cinderella, wrist watch/orig slipper, '40s, US Time, ½ box......65.00
Cisco Kid, cap pistol, MIB...................................35.00
Cisco Kid, face mask...12.00
Cisco Kid, tray puzzle, 1951..................................12.00
Daffy Duck, bank, leans against tree, rect base, pot metal.......35.00
Dale Evans, hat..15.00
Davy Crockett, Ballad of; record, w/jacket.....................20.00
Davy Crockett, model kit flintlock pistol, MIB..................16.00
Davy Crockett, wall clock, Davy on face & pendulum.........100.00
Dennis the Menace, creamer..................................16.00
Dick Tracy, book, Night Crawler, hard cover w/dust jacket......20.00
Dick Tracy, book, pop-up; Capture of Boris Arson, 1935.......65.00
Dick Tracy, camera w/case...................................42.00
Dick Tracy, squad car, tin, 1949.............................66.00
Dick Tracy, target game, tin, Marx, 1941, w/box...............40.00
Dick Tracy, tie clasp..15.00
Dick Tracy, wrist watch, 1947, MIB.........................180.00
Dionne Quints, bowl, chrome.................................28.00
Dionne Quints, calendar, 1938................................25.00
Dionne Quints, doll, cloth body, straight hair, 23″, EX........850.00
Dionne Quints, doll, orig dress & hat, 7½″, M...............200.00
Dionne Quints, dolls, all orig, w/pin, 14″, M................550.00
Dionne Quints, dolls, compo, sleep eyes, orig, Matrix, 11″....1,600.00
Dionne Quints, dolls, orig bed w/names, orig clothes, 7½″....1,350.00
Dionne Quints, fan, 1936....................................12.00
Dionne Quints, playing cards, MIB............................85.00
Dionne Quints, spoons, set of 5.............................100.00
Disney, Fantasia Unicorn, carousel toy, 1940, 25″............150.00
Disney, game, Electric Quiz, Jaymar, MIB.....................35.00
Disney, Greeting Cards to Color, Transogram, 1950s...........10.00
Disney, penny book, Brave Little Tailor, scarce, 4x4¾″, EX.....20.00
Disney, Silly Symphony Lights, scarce, set of 8 in box, EX.....155.00
Dolly Parton, doll, EG-Goldberger, 1977, 12″, MIB............19.00
Donald Duck, ash tray, glass, DD pnt in base, 1950s, 4″.......12.00
Donald Duck, bank, compo as sailor by lifesaver, 1938........125.00
Donald Duck, bank, plaster nodder, Donald in boat, VG........22.50
Donald Duck, bisque, hands on hip, Japan, 1¾″...............50.00
Donald Duck, bisque, on scooter, 3½″.......................65.00
Donald Duck, bisque, w/bugle, late '30s, Japan, 3″............45.00
Donald Duck, book, DD & His Nephews, 1940, EX...............8.00
Donald Duck, book, DD in Bringing Up Boys, 4¾x6¾″, VG.....12.00
Donald Duck, book, linen, 1935, VG.........................125.00
Donald Duck, calendar picture, DD's Golf Game, 8¼x10″, VG...35.00
Donald Duck, candy container, Seiberling.....................70.00
Donald Duck, celluloid figure, long billed, 3″, 1930s...........95.00
Donald Duck, ceramic, holds apple, 4″........................7.50
Donald Duck, charm, molded plastic/pnt, Japan, 1″............10.00
Donald Duck, charm, sterling, ¾″...........................45.00
Donald Duck, costume, 1930s................................165.00
Donald Duck, dinner plate, as ice cream/nut vendor, 8″, VG....65.00
Donald Duck, doll, oilcloth, French, in box, 9″, EX..........175.00
Donald Duck, doll, Sea Captain, pnt rubber, Dell, 10″.........35.00
Donald Duck, felt figure, Italy, 10″, NM......................40.00
Donald Duck, floating toy, w/Nephews, Sun Rubber, MIB.......30.00
Donald Duck, game, Bean Bag, Parker, WDP, 1939, MIB......85.00
Donald Duck, game, For Young Folks, 1938, w/box............45.00
Donald Duck, Jack-in-Box, wood box, compo head, VG........90.00
Donald Duck, napkin ring, Plastic Novelties, die-cut, EX........36.00
Donald Duck, paint box, 1933.................................20.00
Donald Duck, pencil sharpener, DD/house, plastic, 1″ dia.......35.00
Donald Duck, planter, cowboy, ceramic, 1940s, 6″.............32.00
Donald Duck, popcorn, tin container w/contents, 5″............20.00
Donald Duck, projector, Stephens Prod, MIB...................42.00
Donald Duck, soap figure, 1930s.............................45.00
Donald Duck, Sun Camera, plastic, Herbert George, w/box......50.00
Donald Duck, toothbrush holder, bisque, long bill, 5″.........150.00
Donald Duck, tumbler, chocolate milk; w/poem, WDP, 4″.......8.00
Donald Duck, wallpaper trim, in box..........................20.00
Donald Duck, watering can, 1938.............................45.00
Dopey, book, He Don't Talk None, linen, Whitman, scarce, G...65.00
Dopey, papier mache/glitter candy container, WDP, '38, 5½″....55.00
Dorothy Hamill, doll, Ideal, 1977, w/ice rink, 11½″, MIB.......35.00
Dumbo, book, Dumbo of the Circus, scarce, 1948, VG..........45.00
Dumbo, pitcher, ceramic, mk Walt Disney......................25.00
Elsie Cow, cookie jar..50.00
Elsie Cow, creamer, full figure...............................30.00
Elsie Cow, soap figural, MIB.................................85.00
Elvis Presley, dog tag bracelet, orig card dtd 1956............15.00
Elvis Presley, doll, World Doll, Supergold, #1, 21″, MIB.......80.00
Felix, cloth windup, Pat Sullivan, orig card, 1922, 11″........750.00
Felix, dinnerware, English china, minor damage, 10-pc.........75.00
Felix, doll, wood jtd, Pat Sullivan, 1925, 8½″...............200.00
Felix, dressed in cowboy outfit, 1920s, 14″..................375.00
Felix, iron figure, 1920s, 2¾″..............................175.00
Felix, sparkler, 1930s, EX...................................85.00
Felix, stuffed jointed doll, 1930s, English version, 12″........125.00
Felix, tin target..10.00
Felix & Poindexter, metal figure, 1½″........................45.00
Ferdinand, bisque, sits in grass, smells flower, '30s, 3″........35.00
Ferdinand, bracelet, WDE.....................................40.00
Ferdinand, doll, compo, Ideal, 1940s.........................110.00
Ferdinand, hand puppet, compo/cloth, Crown, 1938, 9″........45.00

Flash Gordon, book, Caverns of Mongo, hard bk/jacket, 1936...50.00
Flash Gordon, space pistol, pop gun...75.00
Flash Gordon, water pistol...95.00
Flintstones, camera, Sun Pix, in box, 1964...15.00
Gene Autry, bicycle horn, pistol shape...50.00
Gene Autry, cap gun, belt & holster...55.00
Gene Autry, cap gun, CI...35.00
Gene Autry, club badge, M...17.00
Gene Autry, guitar, Emenee, MIB...130.00
Gene Autry, gun & holster set, dbl...76.00
Gene Autry, record album, 78 rpm...22.00
Gene Autry, thermos...20.00
Goldilocks, book, pop-up, 1934...75.00
Goofy, bisque, hand on behind, 1 gesturing, 1940, 3″...50.00
Groucho Marx, necktie...26.00
Happy Hooligan, tin crank toy, dances on drum, 1930s...595.00
Hopalong Cassidy, cap pistol, MIB...95.00
Hopalong Cassidy, cereal bowl, pottery, WS George...10.00
Hopalong Cassidy, Good Luck coin...10.00
Hopalong Cassidy, Good Luck horseshoe...5.00
Hopalong Cassidy, ice cream container, qt...15.00
Hopalong Cassidy, milk glass set: plate, bowl, mug & glass...75.00
Hopalong Cassidy, newspaper comic strip from '50s...5.00
Hopalong Cassidy, plate, milk glass, 7″...18.00
Hopalong Cassidy, pocket knife, G picture...30.00
Hopalong Cassidy, puzzle, 1950s, 9x12″...25.00
Hopalong Cassidy, radio, Arvin, 1946...95.00
Hopalong Cassidy, tie clasp, Bar-20 Ranch, on card...12.50
Hopalong Cassidy, tie slide...15.00
Hopalong Cassidy, tumbler, milk glass, 4¼″...15.00
Hopalong Cassidy, wrist watch, EX...75.00
Hopalong Cassidy, wrist watch, MIB...120.00
Howdy Doody, bubble bath set...45.00
Howdy Doody, Flub-A-Dub Flip-A-Ring, orig package, ca 1955...25.00
Howdy Doody, night light, figural...60.00
Howdy Doody, paint set, in box, 1950s...25.00
Howdy Doody, puppet, composition...75.00
Howdy Doody, puppet show figures on orig card...50.00
Howdy Doody, rocking chair, musical...85.00
Howdy Doody, straw holder, MIB...36.00
Huckleberry Hound, camera, Sun Pix, in box, 1964...15.00
Ignatz Mouse, wood jtd figure, orig pnt...55.00
Jack Armstrong, cereal bowl, 1939...35.00
Jack Armstrong, Hike-O-Meter...12.50
Jack Armstrong, pedometer...20.00
Jack Armstrong, Shooting Plane, radio premium, orig box...65.00
Jack Armstrong, talisman, brass, 1936, NM...50.00
Jack Armstrong, torpedo light...15.00
Jackie Robinson, doll, outfit/bat/comic/etc, in box, 1940s...325.00
James Bond, Gilbert Action Figure, scuba outfit, MIB...85.00
James Bond, pillowcase, unused...15.00
Jiggs, chalk figure, 1920s, 8½″...55.00
Jiggs & Maggie, jigsaw puzzles, 1932, set of 4 in orig box...35.00
Jimmy Allen Flying Club, flying lessons, in envelope...75.00
John Drake, Secret Agent Game, 1966, MIB...15.00
John Travolta, doll, Chemtoy, 1977, 12″, MIB...18.00
Katzenjammer Mama, compo mechanical doll, 1920s, 9″...225.00
Lady, Disney dog, clock, MIB...45.00
Lady & Tramp, rug, 22x36″...35.00
Lassie, coloring book set, Whitman, 12 in orig box...20.00
Little Black Sambo, board game, in box, 1934...75.00
Little Lulu, doll, molded face, string hair, cloth stuffed...100.00
Lone Ranger, chalk figure, 1940s, 15″...55.00
Lone Ranger, deputy badge...18.00
Lone Ranger, guitar, instrument quality, 1940s...110.00
Lone Ranger, Hi-Yo Silver badge, tin litho pin-back, 1938, NM...25.00
Lone Ranger, marionette, full body/stringless, orig box...60.00
Lone Ranger, paint book, Whitman, 1940...25.00
Lone Ranger, pedometer...32.00
Lone Ranger, radio...225.00
Lone Ranger, ring, 6-gun...20.00
Lone Ranger, Target Game, Marx, MIB...90.00
Lone Ranger, Target Game, 1939, EX...35.00
Margaret O'Brien, coloring book, unused...15.00
Marie Osmond, doll, Mattel, 1976, 11½″, MIB...18.00
Marilyn Monroe, doll, World Doll, ltd, 7 Yr Itch, MIB...110.00
Marilyn Monroe, doll, World Doll, 1983, red gown, 18″, MIB...60.00
Marilyn Monroe, necktie, rare...175.00
Marilyn Monroe, tip tray, nude...16.00
Mary Marvel, wrist watch, EX...62.00
Melvin Purvis, Secret Operator Manual, color, 28 pg, NM...45.00
Mickey, Minnie & Pluto, wrapper, Toasted Nut Chocolate...40.00
Mickey & Donald, crayons, tin box, unused...22.00
Mickey & Donald, in Duck Car, celluloid, 4″...200.00
Mickey & Donald, telephone set, orig box, 1930s...45.00
Mickey & Donald, weather forecaster, box, 1950...25.00
Mickey & Globe Trotters, blank map/no labels, M...75.00
Mickey & Globe Trotters, map w/all bread labels, M...125.00
Mickey & Minnie, bisque, w/cane/umbrella, Japan, 4½″, pr...145.00
Mickey & Minnie, bisque, 1930s, 2¾″, pr...95.00
Mickey & Minnie, marionettes, pressed wood & wood, 13″, pr...150.00
Mickey & Minnie, napkin holders, 3-D celluloid, 2″, pr...290.00
Mickey & Minnie, paper dolls, w/clothes, 1930s...100.00
Mickey & Minnie, pillow cover, M&M w/umbrella, 17″ sq...45.00
Mickey & Minnie, toothbrush holder, arm-in-arm, bisque...150.00
Mickey & Pluto, child's plate, 3-part, WDE, Patriot China...70.00
Mickey Mouse, alarm clock, windup, Ingersoll, 5″, MIB...250.00
Mickey Mouse, Auto Magic Picture Gun, MIB...55.00
Mickey Mouse, baby rattle, celluloid, WDE, EX...100.00
Mickey Mouse, baby spoon, Silver Craft, WDP, MIB...60.00
Mickey Mouse, bank, Clubhouse Treasury, Mattel, w/MM key...50.00
Mickey Mouse, bank, dime registering, tin, 1939, 2″ sq...225.00
Mickey Mouse, bank, figural, hands on hips, aluminum, 8¾″...325.00
Mickey Mouse, bank, MM bandleader, plastic, Knickerbocker...35.00
Mickey Mouse, bank, Post Office, tin, Happynack, 5″...65.00
Mickey Mouse, bisque, in nightgown, 1930s, 4″...65.00
Mickey Mouse, bisque, sits holding Pluto's ears, 1930s, 2″...65.00
Mickey Mouse, bisque, w/cane, 1930s, 4½″...75.00
Mickey Mouse, book, Adventures of MM, McKay, 1931, VG...53.00
Mickey Mouse, book, Big Big Book, EX...95.00
Mickey Mouse, book, Illustrated Movie Stories, 190 pg, VG...135.00
Mickey Mouse, book, MM & the Beanstalk, 1947, VG...35.00
Mickey Mouse, book, MM in Giant Land, McKay, 1934...40.00
Mickey Mouse, book, MM Nursery Stories, 1937, VG...55.00
Mickey Mouse, book, MM Story Book, McKay, 1931...55.00
Mickey Mouse, book, MM Summer Vacation, 4¾x6¾″, VG...12.00
Mickey Mouse, book, pop-up; c 1933, Bl Ribbon Books...150.00
Mickey Mouse, bowl, plastic, Beetleware, 5″ dia...12.00
Mickey Mouse, brush, sterling...65.00
Mickey Mouse, bubble gum card, MM w/movie stars, scarce...40.00
Mickey Mouse, bubble gum picture card album, ca 1933, EX...45.00
Mickey Mouse, celluloid, as hiker w/alpenstock, w/5 spoons...110.00
Mickey Mouse, celluloid, strung arms/head, WDE/Japan, 4″...275.00
Mickey Mouse, charm, molded/pnt plastic, Japan, 1″...15.00
Mickey Mouse, club bandleader outfit, MIB...35.00
Mickey Mouse, coloring book, set of 11 w/20 pg, 5¾x6¾″...40.00
Mickey Mouse, cup, MM playing banjo, silver, rare...115.00
Mickey Mouse, doctor kit, plastic, Japan, MIB...30.00

Mickey Mouse, doll, paper label, Steiff, 4½", EX.............275.00
Mickey Mouse, doll, Sun Rubber, 10"........................40.00
Mickey Mouse, doll, velvet/cloth, odd pose, 1930s, 12", EX....135.00
Mickey Mouse, doll, wood w/compo head, jtd, 1930s, 10"......550.00
Mickey Mouse, dominoes, in box............................68.00
Mickey Mouse, door plate, brass, Disneyland opening, 1950.....48.00
Mickey Mouse, drum, MM playing drum on face, WDE, 1936....70.00
Mickey Mouse, fire engine, w/Pluto on back, Sun Rubber.......35.00
Mickey Mouse, fountain pen, plastic, Inkograph, WDE, 5"......75.00
Mickey Mouse, game, MM Coming Home, dice/16-pc, scarce.....60.00
Mickey Mouse, garden ornament, 1930s.....................45.00
Mickey Mouse, greeting cards, w/crayons, unused.............10.00
Mickey Mouse, hanky, waters flowers w/Pluto, 8½", EX.........20.00
Mickey Mouse, house, cardboard, w/orig envelope, 30", M.....250.00
Mickey Mouse, lantern slide, Mickey Crusoe, set of 2, VG.......15.00
Mickey Mouse, milk pump, plastic w/straw, Morris, on card......10.00
Mickey Mouse, MM Band, bisque, 1½", 4-pc.................75.00
Mickey Mouse, Mousekartooner, MIB........................15.00
Mickey Mouse, pencil box, cb die-cut MM, Dixon, 8".........185.00
Mickey Mouse, pin-back, Globe Trotter.......................20.00
Mickey Mouse, plate, Happy Birthday MM, limited ed/1928-78...50.00
Mickey Mouse, playing cards, complete, orig box, 1¾x2½"......35.00
Mickey Mouse, playing cards, MM juggles, 2", MIB.............40.00
Mickey Mouse, postcard, MM holds box, w/Pluto, 1940s, EX....20.00
Mickey Mouse, projector, MM Club, Stephens Prod, MIB.......42.00
Mickey Mouse, radio, Emerson, 1930s......................800.00
Mickey Mouse, ring, enamel.................................45.00
Mickey Mouse, ring, gold-metal, relief profile.................65.00
Mickey Mouse, soap, pnt figure, Castille, 4"..................45.00
Mickey Mouse, soda straws, orig box, 1950s....................9.00
Mickey Mouse, sparkler, 1930s.............................225.00
Mickey Mouse, tea set, china, tan lustre, 1933, 17-pc, EX.....127.00
Mickey Mouse, toy chest, padded seat top, early 1930s........145.00
Mickey Mouse, tractor, Sun Rubber..........................35.00
Mickey Mouse, tumbler, blk pnt/glass, name to side, '30s.......18.00
Mickey Mouse, washing machine, child's/tin litho, Ohio Art.....110.00
Mickey Mouse, watch, lapel; MM decal on bk, w/strap, NM.....390.00
Mickey Mouse, watch, pocket; bicentennial, Bradley, MIB......125.00
Mickey Mouse, watch, wrist; rnd face, Ingersoll, 1930s........250.00
Mickey Mouse, watch, wrist; sq, Ingersoll/US Time, 1948......150.00
Minnie Mouse, celluloid figure, Borgfeldt....................195.00
Minnie Mouse, cereal bowl, Salem China, 1934...............45.00
Minnie Mouse, doll, Dean's Rag Book Co, 1930s, 7".........350.00
Minnie Mouse, doll, Sun Rubber, 10"........................25.00
Minnie Mouse, doll, wood, WDE, 5½", NM.................100.00
Minnie Mouse, knitting in rocking chair, Marx, MIB...........350.00
Minnie Mouse, wrist watch, stainless case, Ingersoll, MIB......225.00
Moon Mullins, wood jtd figure w/cigar, 6"...................95.00
Mork, doll, talking, poseable, plastic, Mattel, 9", MIB..........10.00
Mr Magoo, tumbler, 1962...................................10.00
Olive Oyl, hand puppet, rubber/cloth, 14"....................40.00
Orphan Annie, ash tray, lusterware, 1930s...................76.00
Orphan Annie, clothespin set w/washline & pulleys, on card....100.00
Orphan Annie, dog whistle, 3-way, w/Sandy's head, NM.........45.00
Orphan Annie, doll, w/Sandy doll, wood, 6", pr...............90.00
Orphan Annie, mug, ceramic................................25.00
Orphan Annie, Ovalentine mug..............................35.00
Orphan Annie, shake-up mug................................18.00
Orphan Annie, song sheet, 1930-1931........................18.00
Orphan Annie, Treasure Hunt Game Board, 1933..............22.00
Orphan Annie, Tucker County Race Puzzle, 1933..............60.00
Orphan Annie, wall pocket..................................95.00
Orphan Annie, wrist watch, rnd, New Haven, MIB............125.00
Our Gang, coloring book, Saalfield, 1938....................35.00
Our Gang, pencil box, from silent movies....................25.00
Paul Stanley, Kiss rock group, doll, plastic, Mego, 12½"........12.00
Peter Rabbit, jigsaw puzzle, orig box, set of 5................25.00
Peter Rabbit, sand pail......................................25.00
Pinocchio, bank, compo, Pinocchio leans on tree, WDE, 5"....125.00
Pinocchio, centerfold, Why I Picked Pinocchio, 1939, VG......10.00
Pinocchio, clock, animated, Jiminy on head, Bayard, MIB......175.00
Pinocchio, pencil sharpener, imp Walt Disney.................32.00
Pinocchio, pin-back, Hi Diddle Dee Dee, 1" dia...............15.00
Pinocchio, postcard, Italy, set of 12 in folder, EX.............20.00
Pinocchio, soap, dimensional, Castille, 1939, in box, 3"........40.00
Pinocchio, statue, pnt Sirocco, 2"...........................48.00
Pinocchio, tumbler, poem on bk, 1940s, 4¾"..................16.00
Pinocchio, wood, jtd, old, 8", EX............................75.00
Pinocchio, wood & compo doll, Ideal, 11", VG...............135.00
Pluto, animated clock, molded plastic bowl face/bone hands....225.00
Pluto, book, Mother Pluto, Whitman, 64 pg, 5½x4¾", VG......20.00
Pluto, ceramic figurine, Laguna Pottery......................65.00
Pluto, charm, gf/sterling, dimensional, Wells Co, on card.......30.00
Pluto, planter, w/wheelbarrow, ceramic, 1940s, 6".............45.00
Pluto, rubber figure, 3"......................................18.00
Pluto, rug, Pluto pulls friends in wagon, 20x40"...............55.00
Popeye, ash tray, plaster figure sits on stump, 6".............100.00
Popeye, ash tray, wood die-cut/hands on hips, 12"............175.00
Popeye, bank, dime registering, flat metal, 1929..............48.00
Popeye, bank, dime registering, 1956........................15.00
Popeye, book, animated; w/the Pirates, Sagendorf/Duenewald....75.00
Popeye, book, Big Big Book, Thimble Theater, 1935...........55.00
Popeye, celluloid figure, wood ft, 1939, 5"..................70.00
Popeye, clothes brush, decal on wood, Monarch, 1929, 5"......45.00
Popeye, crayon set, in tin box, lg sz crayons, Am Crayon.......20.00
Popeye, fountain pen, plastic/eng metal clip, Penco, 1935.......90.00

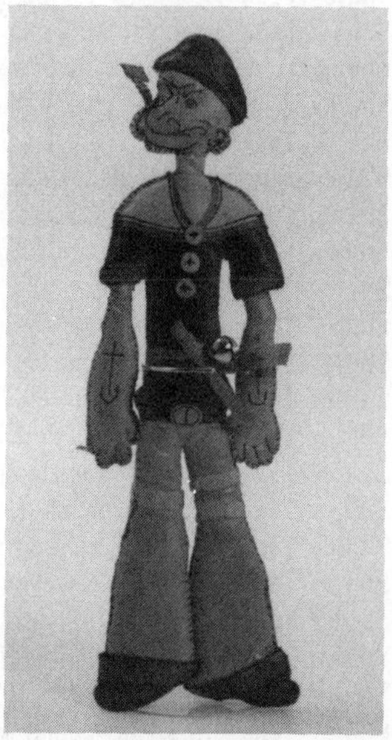

Popeye, oilcloth doll, 11½", $95.00.

Popeye, game, Pipe Toss game, 1935, in box..................30.00
Popeye, guitar music box, MIB..............................60.00
Popeye, mechanical pencil, 10"..............................37.00
Popeye, napkin holder, plastic w/decal, early, 3".............50.00
Popeye, night light, iron boat, filament light works, 1935......400.00
Popeye, paint book, Whitman/#2081, 1937, NM...............75.00
Popeye, paint box, 1933....................................15.00
Popeye, pencil sharpener....................................22.00
Popeye, picture puzzles, 4 in orig box, 1932..................65.00
Popeye, Pin the Tail game, P at ship's wheel, Whitman, '37.....45.00

Popeye, pin-back, NY Evening Journal, full figure, punching.....30.00
Popeye, playing cards, head w/pipe on bl box, Whitman, MIB...30.00
Popeye, song book, Famous Music Corp, 1936...............65.00
Popeye, wood figure, jointed, 1930s, 5½"....................65.00
Porky Pig, chalkware figure.................................20.00
Porky Pig, costume, in box, 1950............................30.00
Porky Pig, pencil holder, cast metal........................15.00
Red Riding Hood, book, pop-up; 1934.........................20.00
Red Riding Hood, cereal bowl, Staffordshire.................30.00
Red Ryder, coloring book, unused, 1952......................12.00
Rin Tin Tin, rifle pen, orig mailer.........................40.00
Robin Hood, lunch box, 1956.................................15.00
Roy Rogers, bank, boot shape................................35.00
Roy Rogers, cap pistol, repeating, MIB......................42.00
Roy Rogers, game, horseshoe, Ohio Art.......................22.00
Roy Rogers, gloves, children's..............................48.00
Roy Rogers, harmonica, in orig package......................20.00
Roy Rogers, horseshoe game #30, no box, complete, EX.......30.00
Roy Rogers, jigsaw puzzle, boxed............................10.00
Roy Rogers, lantern, tin w/glass globe, battery operated........36.00
Roy Rogers, mug, Quaker Cereal..............................18.00
Roy Rogers, mug & bowl, china, pr...........................30.00
Roy Rogers, spurs, leather w/jewels.........................22.00
Roy Rogers, thermos...10.00
Seven Dwarfs, perfume bottles, Russian, MIB................120.00
Sgt Preston, Big Inch Land Deed.............................12.00
Shirley Temple, barret & bow, w/cameo face, 1930s...........45.00
Shirley Temple, beauty bar, Gabriel, #341, in box, 1950s.......45.00
Shirley Temple, book, Dimples, Saalfield Pub, #1760, 1936.....25.00
Shirley Temple, book, Little Colonel, w/dust jacket...........30.00
Shirley Temple, book, ST at Play, Saalfield, 1935.............35.00
Shirley Temple, book, ST's Favorite Poems, #1720, 1936, EX...22.00
Shirley Temple, book, ST's Treasury Book, dust jacket, M......25.00
Shirley Temple, book, Sussanah of the Mounties, #1785, M.....24.00
Shirley Temple, book, This is My Crayon Book, #1771.........30.00
Shirley Temple, book, Wee Willie Winkle, #1769, M...........25.00
Shirley Temple, bowl, cobalt w/wht transfer.................45.00
Shirley Temple, campaign card, political....................15.00
Shirley Temple, child's dress, tagged.......................40.00
Shirley Temple, creamer, cobalt w/wht transfer..............38.00
Shirley Temple, doll buggy, blk wood w/color decals, mk......600.00
Shirley Temple, fan, ST w/RC Cola, I'll Be Seeing You.........22.00
Shirley Temple, fountain pen................................75.00
Shirley Temple, hair styler set, orig box...................35.00
Shirley Temple, magazine, Popular Songs, 'Curly Top,' 1935....18.00
Shirley Temple, movie star stamps...........................12.00
Shirley Temple, photo, head resting on hands, 8x10"..........13.00
Shirley Temple, photo, holding Cocker Spaniel, old, 6x9"......13.00
Shirley Temple, photo, New York Sunday News, June 12, 1938..25.00
Shirley Temple, photo, orig gray frame w/ped stand, 6x8"......22.00
Shirley Temple, pin, ST fan club, beige w/bl...................3.50
Shirley Temple, pin, The World's Darling, ST & doll...........3.50
Shirley Temple, pitcher, cobalt w/wht transfer..............35.00
Shirley Temple, playing cards, new deck.....................12.00
Shirley Temple, playing cards, orig box, EX.................50.00
Shirley Temple, poster, Captain January, 1936..............750.00
Shirley Temple, poster, The Littlest Rebel, 1935...........750.00
Shirley Temple, punchboard, Little Miss Charming............12.00
Shirley Temple, purse mirror, 1930s, 2x2½"..................20.00
Shirley Temple, sailor outfit, boxed set, 1974..............18.00
Shirley Temple, see Dolls, Shirley Temple
Shirley Temple, sheet music, Animal Crackers in My Soup......12.00
Shirley Temple, sheet music, Goodnight My Love, 1936........12.00
Shirley Temple, sheet music, Polly-Wolly-Doodle.............12.00
Shirley Temple, sheet music, When I Grow Up.................12.00
Shirley Temple, soap, orig box & packing, red & bl bows......135.00
Shirley Temple, souvenir book, Tournament of Roses, 1939.....20.00
Shirley Temple, tea set, pink w/wht cameo of ST head........120.00
Sky King, stamping kit......................................45.00
Snow White, alarm clock, animated, Bayard, EX..............150.00
Snow White, book, Charlie McCarthy Meets SW, 9½x11½", VG..45.00
Snow White, ceramic figure, Am Pottery, 9".................165.00
Snow White, film, feature length, 4 film strips, color, VG.......19.00
Snow White, papier mache/glitter candy container, WDP, 5½"...85.00
Snow White, Tap-A-Way Set, 8 foil pictures w/tool, Naylor.....175.00
Snow White & 7 Dwarfs, bisques, SW: 5½", dwarfs: 4"........175.00
Snow White & 7 Dwarfs, board game, Milton Bradley, 1937.....68.00
Snow White & 7 Dwarfs, handkerchief, WDP, 8"................12.00
Snow White & 7 Dwarfs, mask, Whitman #990, book of 8, EX..78.00
Snow White & 7 Dwarfs, recipe book..........................20.00
Sparkle Plenty, soap figural, MIB...........................24.00
Star Trek, pinball game, colorful box, 1976.................12.50
Straight Arrow, finger puppets, cb, sheet of 10, M...........25.00
Superman, alarm clock, animated, 1940, scarce..............550.00
Superman, bank, dime registering, EX........................90.00
Superman, chalkware figure..................................50.00
Superman, swim goggles, 1940s, MIB..........................40.00
Superman, toothbrush, battery operated, in box, 1974.........15.00
Superman, valentine, 1940s..................................15.00
Tarzan, book, Big Big Book, VG..............................48.00
Three Bears, handkerchief set, 1950s........................22.00
Three Pigs, ash tray, lusterware, Japan, 1930s, 3"............65.00
Three Pigs, bank, tin.......................................40.00
Three Pigs, book, 3 Pig's Picnic & Other Stories, VG..........12.00
Three Pigs, divided dish, Disney, Patriot China, 1930s.........75.00
Three Pigs, jigsaw puzzle, Jay Mar, 400+ pcs, MIB............15.00
Three Pigs, playing cards, in box, 3¾x2½"...................40.00
Three Pigs, toothbrush holder, fiddle/flute/trowel, bisque........90.00
Three Pigs, Valentines Day card, Hall Bros, EX...............21.00
Tom Corbett, arcade card....................................10.00
Tom Corbett, record, w/jacket, 1951.........................20.00
Tom Corbett, Space Academy Certificate, M...................50.00
Tom Mix, arrowhead..35.00
Tom Mix, bandana..60.00
Tom Mix, bird call, musical.................................15.00
Tom Mix, book, Big Big Book, Scourge of Paradise Valley......40.00
Tom Mix, book, Draw & Paint, Whitman, 1935..................35.00
Tom Mix, Christmas card, 1926...............................30.00
Tom Mix, periscope, w/instruction booklet...................52.00
Tom Mix, photo, silver fr, NM...............................65.00
Tom Mix, Ralston Str Shooter Newspsper, Life of TM, 4 pg.....28.00
Tom Mix, ring, tigereye, rare..............................125.00
Tom Mix, rocker parachute, 1948.............................56.00
Tom Mix, telescope..45.00
Tom Mix, writing manual.....................................18.00
Uncle Remus, game, Zip, Parker Bros.........................20.00
Uncle Sam & English John Bull, bell ringer toy, CI...........750.00
Uncle Walt & Skeezix, toothbrush holder, bisque, 1930s.......75.00
Uncle Willie & Emmie, toothbrush holder, bisque, 1930s.......65.00
Wild Bill Hickock, cap pistol/spurs/jail keys/etc, in box.........50.00
Wild Bill Hickock & Jingles, badge & card, in leather case......15.00
Will Rogers, thermometer, bronzed metal, EX.................40.00
Willy Post & Will Rogers, lamp..............................45.00
Wimpy, tie clip, enameled decor on metal, 1930s.............65.00
Wizard of Oz, 10 Aurora figures, in package, 1967............25.00
Woody Woodpecker, alarm clock, WW at the Cafe, animated...100.00
Wyatt Earp, gun, Buntline Hubley, in package, 1959............35.00
Yellow Kid, cap bomb, CI, Ives.............................150.00

Yellow Kid, movie flip book, rare, 1895....................126.00
Yellow Kid, paperweight, CI................................375.00
Yellow Kid, pin-back button, #34............................24.00
Yellow Kid, pin-back button, #36............................15.00
Yellow Kid, pin-back button, #7.............................15.00
Zero, nodder, of Beetle Bailey strip, pnt compo, 7½", EX......35.00
Zorro, wrist watch, orig strap, WDP.........................45.00

Peters and Reed

John Peters and Adam Reed founded their pottery in Zanesville, Ohio, just before the turn of the century, using the local red clay to produce a variety of wares.

Moss Aztec, introduced about 1912, has an unglazed exterior with designs molded in high relief, and the recesses highlighted with a green wash. Only the interior is glazed to hold water. Pereco, named for Peters, Reed and Company, is glazed in semi-matt blue, maroon, or cream. Orange was also used very early, but such examples are rare. Shapes are simple with in-mold decoration, sometimes borrowed from the Moss Aztec line.

Wilse Blue is a line of high gloss medium blue with dark specks on simple shapes. Landsun, characterized by its soft matt multicolor or blue and gray combinations, is decorated either by dripping or by hand brushing, in an effect sometimes called Flame or Herringbone. Chromal, in much the same colors as Landsun, may be decorated with a realistic scenic, or the swirling application of colors may merely suggest one.

Shadow ware is a glossy, multicolor drip over a harmonious base color. When the base is black, the effect is often iridescent.

Perhaps the most familiar line is the brown high glaze artware with the 'sprigged' type designs. Although research has uncovered no positive proof, it is generally accepted as having been made by Peters and Reed. It is interesting to note that many of the artistic shapes in this line are recognizable as those made by Weller, Roseville, and other Zanesville area companies.

Other lines include Mirror Black, Persian, and an unidentified line which collectors call Mottled Colors. In this high gloss line, the red clay body often shows through the splashed-on multicolors.

In 1922, the company became known as the Zane Pottery. Peters and Reed retired, and Harry McClelland became president. Charles Chilcote designed new lines, and production of many of the old lines continued. The body of the ware after 1922 was light in color.

Marks include the impressed logo or ink stamp 'Zaneware' in a rectangle.

When no condition is indicated, the items listed below are assumed to be in mint condition.

High Glaze Brown Ware tankard with grapes and leaves, 10½", $125.00.

Chromal

Vase, lg trees in foreground, bulbous, 6¾"...................195.00
Vase, road/house/trees, indistinct scenic, w/label, 8¾".........200.00
Vase, stylized scenic, 7½x4¼"............................170.00

High Glaze Brown Ware

Jug, ear of corn on front & reverse, 5½x5½"................125.00
Jug, grapes/leaves relief, bulbous, 6¼x5"....................70.00
Pitcher, tankard; grape & vine decor, sm rpr, 12"............150.00
Vase, floral garlands, ped ftd, flat shoulders, 2-hdl, 8½"........50.00
Vase, floral relief, squat, 4 ftd............................35.00
Vase, floral swag, Aladdin lamp form w/loop hdls, 4½x8"......100.00
Vase, wreath front & bk, 13½"..............................75.00
Vase, wreath w/cherubs, 12½"...............................95.00

Landsun

Bowl, brushed bl/gray on beige, 2x6"........................35.00
Box, powder; rnd...30.00
Pitcher, mottled brn/gray, 7¾".............................50.00
Vase, #40C...38.00
Vase, bulbous, mk, 6½".....................................45.00
Vase, cylinder neck, bulbous base, 5"........................35.00

Moss Aztec

Bowl, dragonfly, low, 6"....................................25.00
Bowl, pine cones, sgn Ferrell, 3x6¼"........................50.00
Bowl, vines & berries, 3x8"..................................35.00
Hanging basket, basketweave.................................40.00
Hanging basket, flowers.....................................28.00
Vase, nasturtiums, no mk, 10"...............................35.00
Wall pocket, floral, cone shape, sgn Ferrell, 10".............65.00
Wall pocket, grapes, 8½"....................................50.00
Window box, musician w/reclining couple, mk Ferrell, 13" L...125.00

Pereco

Bowl, beaded recessed band, #605, 2x4¾"....................30.00
Bowl, butterfly, gr, 15"....................................20.00
Bowl, lattice w/flower band, 2¼x4¾"........................25.00
Bowl, laurel branches/berries, 9"............................65.00
Vase, emb flowers, corset, 11¾"............................45.00
Wall pocket, emb Egyptian w/asp, 8".........................65.00

Shadow Ware

Vase, blown-out top on cylindrical body, 9"...................75.00
Vase, cream w/bl/blk/orange/brn drip, bulbous, 9".............95.00
Vase, dk gr w/lt gr drip, 4¾"...............................45.00
Vase, ivory w/brn to bl drip, 9"..............................85.00

Pewabic

The Pewabic Pottery was formally established in Detroit, Michigan, in 1907, by Mary Chase Perry Stratton and Horace James Caulkins. The two had worked together since 1903, firing their ware in a small kiln Caulkins had designed especially for use by the dental trade. Always a small operation which relied upon basic equipment and the skill of the workers, they took pride in being commissioned for several important architectural tile installations.

Some of the early artware was glazed a simple matt green; occasionally other colors were added, sometimes in combination, one over the other in a drip effect. Later, Stratton developed a lustrous crystalline glaze.

The body of the ware was highly fired and extremely hard. Shapes were basic, and decorative modeling, if used at all, was in low relief. Mary Stratton kept the pottery open until her death in 1961. In 1968, it was purchased and reopened by the Michigan State University.

Several marks were used over the years: a triangle with 'Revelation Pottery' (for a short time only), 'Pewabic' with five maple leaves, and the impressed circle mark.

When no condition is indicated, the items listed below are assumed to be in mint condition.

Ash tray, irid, 5″....100.00
Bowl, bl to red w/HP border, rnd die mk, 4x7½″....325.00
Bowl, gr drip glaze, 4½″....135.00
Bowl, turq on lime gr, irid glaze, scalloped rim....125.00
Bowl vase, inscription, gr matt, mk Comstock, 1908, 5″ W....185.00
Cup & saucer, Tiffany-type irid....150.00
Plate, zodiac, yel crackle & bl irid....165.00
Tile, bl lustre floral on matt wht, 2¾″ sq....60.00
Tile, wht flower on turq lustre, 5″ sq....110.00
Vase, beige gloss, globe form, incised mk, 8x8″....125.00
Vase, bl drip on blk matt, circle mk, 3½x2½″....275.00
Vase, bl irid w/pastel highlights, hand thrown, 8½x6″....750.00
Vase, bl matt, backwards imp mk, strong shoulder, 3¾″....225.00
Vase, bl streaked, fold-over lip, incised mk, 6″....130.00
Vase, corn/husks, wht on brn, hand carved, dtd '08, 5½x4″....475.00
Vase, gold, silver & bl irid glaze, 4x3″....350.00
Vase, lt gr & yel lustre w/gr lustre drip, 2½″....295.00
Vase, pink irid w/bl, gr & yel highlights, 4″....185.00

Pewter

Pewter is a metal alloy of tin combined with small amounts of lead, copper, or brass. It has been used since the days of Ancient Rome, and was imported to this country from England by the American Colonists. Much of the Colonial pewter was melted during the American Revolution to make bullets, which accounts to some extent for the scarcity of examples from this period. Production of pewter in the United States reached its peak after the Revolution.

When no condition is indicated, the items listed below are assumed to be in excellent condition.

Basin, Compton, Thomas & Townsend, 2½x10½″, VG....175.00
Basin, Continental, angel touch mk, worn, 2½x11¾″....105.00
Basin, eagle touch mk w/BB, 1¾x6½″....450.00
Basin, no mk, dents in bottom, 2⅜x10¾″....85.00
Basin, no mk, worn/sm metal breaks, 3x10¼″....105.00
Basin, traces of touch mk, sm rim break, 8″....125.00
Bed pan, London touch mk, Evans & Matthews, w/hdl, 11¼″....50.00
Bowl, German touch mk w/angel, 1¼x8″....40.00
Bowl, lovebird mk, Phila, last half 18th C, 6½″....495.00
Bowl, no mk, ftd, polished, 3½x6″....65.00
Bowl, Orivit, lg poppies, 9x12″....48.00
Bowl, Thos Danforth, ca 1800, deep, 11½″....330.00
Bowl, unmk American, 2x6″....150.00
Candlestick, att Homan & Co, push-ups, 9¾″, pr....290.00
Candlestick, no mk, w/push-ups, 8″, pr....185.00
Candlestick, w/removable bobeche, unsgn, 18½″, pr....210.00
Candlestick, w/removable bobeche, 7⅜″....95.00
Chalice, English, mk 'Willm S Burton, 69 Oxford St,' 6¼″....95.00
Champagne bucket, Orivit, 6 molded sections/florals, 8x11″....175.00
Charger, Graham & Wardrop, 14¾″, EX....165.00

Inkwell, American, mid-1700s, 8″ diameter base, $125.00.

Charger, incomplete touch mk Jacobs #95, worn, 12⅛″....325.00
Charger, J Mettery, Hand Made in Belgium, 9″....49.00
Charger, London, indistinct mk, rpr/polished, 14½″....150.00
Charger, Thos Boardman touch mks, minor dents, 13″....400.00
Charger, touch mk incomplete, rim stamped AS, 15″, VG....150.00
Charger, unmk American, 13⅜″....250.00
Coffee pot, copper bottom, R Strickland, Albany, NY, 9¾″....85.00
Compote, no mk, minor surface wear, 4¾x7¾″....200.00
Creamer & sugar bowl on tray, Flagg & Homan, oval panels....225.00
Cup, ear hdl, worn w/rim split on hdl, 3″....40.00
Dish, Continental, 3 shield shape touch mk w/lions, 4½″....25.00
Egg cup, 2⅝″....300.00
Flagon, communion; no mk, flared ft, minor dent, 10½″....90.00
Flagon, no mk, worn spout & surface, 10½″....175.00
Flagon, unmk European, engraved crest/1810, 11½″, EX....105.00
Hot plate, English, touch mk w/lg lion, worn, 9½″....35.00
Lamp, Capen & Molineux, rnd base, whale oil burner, 8″....255.00
Lamp, dbl bull's eye, 8″....350.00
Lamp, E Capen, acorn font, brass whale oil burner, 5″, pr....400.00
Lamp, H Hopper, fluid burner, rejoined stem, 5½″....150.00
Lamp, time; brass wick support, clear font w/#s, 13″....325.00
Lamp, unmk, American, stripped threads on burner, 7¼″....60.00
Lamp, unmk, American, whale oil, no burner, 9″....140.00
Measure, English, bellied, wear, sm hole in rim, 2¼″....20.00
Measure, John Warne, qt, 6⅝″....65.00
Measure, Sheffield, England, bellied, 4⅝″....15.00
Measure, tankard; English, 'Pint'/pub name on base, 5″, EX....45.00
Measure, tankard; Geradin & Watson touch mk, 1-qt, 6″....65.00
Measure, tankard; hinged lid & simple thumbpc, dents, 4¼″....35.00
Measure, tankard; hinged lid w/thumbpc, Imperial Gill, 4¼″....185.00
Measure, tankard; WR Loftus, ½-pt, 3⅝″....30.00
Measure, tankard; Yates & Birch, 1-pt, minor hdl rpr, 4½″....70.00
Measure, XY in triangle, bellied, 1¾″....35.00
Measure, Yates, English, 1-qt....75.00
Measure, Yates, tulip shape, mk V, w/hdl, ½-pt....58.00
Pitcher, cream; unmk American, w/lid, 6⅛″....200.00
Pitcher, F Porter, WE-TE Rook #1, bulbous, 6¾″....275.00
Pitcher, Homan & Co, scroll hdl, w/lid, 11½″....150.00
Pitcher, tavern; side spout, English....110.00
Pitcher, unmk American, hinged lid, ear hdl, rpr, 6⅛″....125.00
Pitcher, unmk American, hinged lid, ear hdl, 5¼″, VG....95.00
Pitcher, X w/2 lines, 9″....650.00

Plate, BB&B Barns, Phila, scratches/battered, 8″ . . . 175.00
Plate, Compton, minor wear, 7¾″ . . . 55.00
Plate, crown touch mk & London, 8½″ . . . 65.00
Plate, dbl eagle touch mk: Geo Lightner, 8¾″, EX . . . 225.00
Plate, engraved monogram 'MDC,' surface wear, 6⅝″, pr . . . 30.00
Plate, George Grenfell, London touch mk, minor wear, 8″ . . . 85.00
Plate, Hard Metal, London, knife scratches, 9¼″, pr . . . 100.00
Plate, Henry Maxted, London, minor battering, 9″ . . . 80.00
Plate, Leonard Reed & Barton, 10¼″ . . . 150.00
Plate, Merwin Wilson Co, 10¾″ . . . 40.00
Plate, no mk, scalloped, 9¼″ . . . 55.00
Plate, no mk, sm dents & scratches, 8¼″ . . . 65.00
Plate, no mk, worn, 9¼″ . . . 75.00
Plate, partial mk: Robert–, London, 9″ . . . 60.00
Plate, Richard Yates, minor wear/corrosion, 9″ . . . 65.00
Plate, Sheldon & Feltman, battered, 10⅜″ . . . 155.00
Plate, sm indistinct touch mk, knife scratches, 10⅞″ . . . 135.00
Plate, TC, English, scratches/wear, 8⅛″ . . . 55.00
Plate, Thos & Townsend, minor wear, 7½″ . . . 60.00
Plate, Thos Boardman, 8½″ . . . 265.00
Plate, TW, parital griffin touch mk, minor wear/dents, 8″ . . . 55.00
Plate, W Scott, worn, 9¾″ . . . 70.00
Porringer, no mk, sm rim splits, 5½″, VG . . . 230.00
Porringer, no mk, sm trefoil hdl w/heart cut-out, 3⅞″ . . . 85.00
Porringer, Stede, pierced hdl, 4″ . . . 50.00
Salt cellar, ftd, pitted surface, 2⅛x2¾″ . . . 20.00
Soup plate, B Barns, 2 eagle touch mks, 12″, NM . . . 400.00
Soup plate, Reed & Barton, minor dents, 10⅛″ . . . 85.00
Soup plate, Townsend & Compton, minor wear, 12″ . . . 100.00
Spoon, Hall's Patent, shell on back of bowl, 7½″ . . . 75.00
Spoon, tablespoon, James A Conn, Sheffield, wear, 8⅜″ . . . 7.50
Tall pot, J Danforth, lid rpr, Jacobs #100, 10¼″ . . . 375.00
Tall pot, J Munson, split under hdl, soldered, 10½″ . . . 285.00
Tall pot, Sellew & Co, Cincinnati, 9½″ . . . 175.00
Tall pot, unmk American, 10½″ . . . 225.00
Tankard, castle touch mk, crest, dolphin thumbpc, 7″, VG . . . 85.00
Tea set, James Dixon & Sons, 3-pc, 9¼″ . . . 250.00
Teapot, Atkin Bros, English, Sheffield, worn hdl, 5¼″ . . . 18.00
Teapot, DWK, squat, concave footing, dome lid, rpr, 7¾″ . . . 250.00
Teapot, flying insect touch mk, hdl & ring damage, 6½″ . . . 155.00
Teapot, J Dixon & Sons, England, melon sections, 7¼″ . . . 110.00
Teapot, Japanese, foo dog finial, seal on bottom, 1800, 9″ . . . 150.00
Teapot, Sellew & Co, wood hdl/finial, minor dents, 7″ . . . 325.00
Teapot, unmk American, minor damage/pitting, 6¾″ . . . 135.00
Teapot, unmk American, minor resoldering, 8¼″ . . . 245.00
Teapot, Wm McQuilkin, dent in lid, 9½″ . . . 200.00
Tray, Silberzinn, leaf figural/stem hdl/emb floral, 11x9″ . . . 65.00
Wine server, German, 6-sided, panel w/pendant grapes, 12½″ . . . 85.00

Phoenix Bird

Blue and white Phoenix Bird china has been produced by various Japanese potteries from the early 1900s. With slight variations the design features the Japanese bird of paradise and scroll-like vines of Kara-Kusa, or Chinese grass. Although some of their earlier ware is unmarked, the majority is marked in some fashion. More than forty different stamps have been reported, with 'Made in Japan' the one most often found. Newer items if marked at all, carry a paper label. Compared to the older ware, the coloring of the new is whiter and the blue more harsh; the design is sparse, with more ground area showing. Although collectors buy even 'new' pieces, the older is of course more highly prized and valued.

For further reading, we recommend *Phoenix Bird China*, A Pictorial Reference Guide, by Debra Kneal Hadley, available from your favorite bookstore. When no condition is indicated, the items listed below are assumed to be in mint condition.

Bouillon, 2-hdl, 2x4″; w/5½″ underplate . . . 17.00
Bowl, berry; 1¼x4¾″ . . . 8.00
Bowl, cream soup; 1½x7¼″ . . . 25.00
Bowl, rice; inside design, 2x5″ . . . 15.00
Bowl, rice; 2-hdl, 3-ft, w/lid, 4¾x7¼″ . . . 55.00
Bowl, sauce; oval, 1¼x7¾″ . . . 17.00
Bowl, serving; oval, 1½x8½″ . . . 28.00
Butter, 7¼″ dia plate, straight-sided lid . . . 65.00
Chocolate pot, crown border, scalloped base, w/lid, 9″ . . . 75.00
Creamer, bulbous, long spout, 2¾″ . . . 14.00
Cup, demitasse; straight sided, 2¼″ . . . 12.00
Cup, straight sided, 2¾x3″ . . . 15.00
Cup, tea; 2x4″ . . . 8.00
Cup & saucer, Occupied Japan . . . 15.00
Dish, sauce; leaf shape, pierced hdl, w/leaf underplate . . . 40.00
Egg cup . . . 11.00
Egg cup, dbl, 3⅛″ . . . 12.00
Gravy, 2-hdl, w/lid & attached 8¼″ underplate . . . 50.00
Ladle, 6¼″ . . . 22.00
Marmalade, 2-hdl, w/lid, 5½″ . . . 20.00
Mustard pot, scalloped base, w/hdl & lid . . . 40.00
Pitcher, bell shape, 7″ . . . 50.00
Plate, cake; pierced hdls, 9¾″ . . . 18.00
Plate, dinner; 9¾″ . . . 30.00
Plate, luncheon; 8½″ . . . 15.00
Plate, salad; 7¼″ . . . 10.00
Platter, oval, 10″ . . . 18.00
Platter, oval, 14″ . . . 32.00
Saucer, 5½″ . . . 3.00
Shaker, 6-sided, 3¼″ . . . 22.00
Sugar, bulbous, 2-hdl, 4″ . . . 18.00
Teapot, bell shape, pattern covers spout, w/lid, 5″ . . . 40.00
Tumbler, crown border, 2⅝″ . . . 12.00
Tureen, oval, 2-hdl, w/lid, 4⅞x12″ . . . 68.00

Tea strainer, 5½″, $40.00.

Phoenix Glass

Founded in 1880 in Monaca, PA, the Phoenix Glass Company became one of the country's foremost manufacturers of lighting glass by the early 1900s. Today, however, collectors are primarily interested in the Sculptured Artware produced from the 1930s to the mid-1950s. These beautiful mold-blown pieces are most often found in white milk glass (called 'opal') or crystal with various satin finishes or fired-on color treatments.

Quite often, however, glassware made by the Consolidated Lamp and Glass Company of Coraopolis, PA, only about fifteen miles from Monaca, is mistaken for Phoenix wares. Compounding the confusion is the fact that one of Consolidated's major designers also developed several designs for Phoenix. In some cases the pieces are almost identical in size and shape, but the patterns differ in certain details. For example, the Phoenix 'Dancing Girl' vase has only six ladies, while the Consolidated version has seven, plus the figure of Pan playing his flutes. Another distinguishing characteristic is that perhaps 80% of the time Phoenix applied color to the background, while Consolidated generally applied color to the raised design itself. The glassware of both firms is of equal quality.

When no condition is indicated, the items listed below are assumed to be in mint condition.

Bowl, Diving Girl, crystal w/satin, 14x6x4" 110.00
Bowl, Tiger Lily, trn-bk edge, wht, 12" 85.00
Bowl, Tiger Lily, wht, 11½" 85.00
Bowl, Water Lily, wht, 14¼" 100.00
Candy box, Violets, wht w/bl, 6¾" 45.00
Shade, #4529, Stalactite, rich cut, prism/beaded, crystal 25.00
Shade, #5204 Ball, flint opal twist, 8" dia 20.00
Vase, Bluebells, wht w/red & MOP, 7" 65.00
Vase, Cosmos, wht w/brn, 7½" 65.00
Vase, Daisy, cream w/yel & wht frost, ball shape, 9¼" 95.00
Vase, Dancing Girl, 6 nudes, wht w/tan, 11½" 185.00
Vase, Fern, wht w/gray & MOP, 7" 40.00
Vase, Fern, wht w/pink & gr, 7" 55.00
Vase, Madonna, wht w/bl, 10" 140.00
Vase, Star Flower, wht w/red & MOP, ball shape, 7" 55.00
Vase, Thistle, wht, orig box, 1976, 18" 75.00
Vase, Thistle, wht w/bl, 18" 250.00
Vase, Wild Geese, wht satin w/MOP, oval, 9¼" 95.00
Vase, Wild Geese, wht w/brn & ivory, oval, 9¼" 150.00
Vase, Zodiac, 4-panel, wht w/tan, 10" 175.00

Phonographs

The phonograph, invented by Thomas Edison in 1877, was later manufactured by various companies who incorporated their own variations with the original Edison model. Those with the large morning-glory horns are expecially desirable.

When no condition is indicated, the items listed below are assumed to be in excellent condition.

Key:
mg—morning glory
rpd—reproducer

Busy Bee, grand disk player, rfn/gold leaf horn, EX orig 350.00
Carilon, metal case, sound-reflecting lid 125.00
Columbia AB Concert McDonald 1,200.00
Columbia AF Concert 1,000.00
Columbia AT, mg horn & crane 300.00
Columbia AU 350.00
Columbia BC 850.00
Columbia BE, oak case, 30" mg horn, ca 1906, +60 cylinders 450.00
Columbia BF, 6" mandrel 465.00
Columbia BI, disk player, lg ornate oak horn/case, EX 1,600.00
Columbia BI, nickel horn 650.00
Columbia BKT, nickel horn 850.00
Columbia Regent, desk model 450.00
Edison Alva, wood cygnet 4,800.00
Edison Amberola #30 .... 325.00
Edison Amberola #50, mahog, EX 450.00
Edison Amberola #75, oak case 450.00
Edison Amberola DX 330.00
Edison B Triumph, 2 min, no horn 495.00
Edison C-4, radio phonograph 700.00
Edison Concert, w/crane & orig blk/brass horn, +5 records 2,000.00
Edison Concert, 1906, Model J rpd 2,100.00
Edison Fireside, Diamond B rpd, signet horn & crane 535.00
Edison Gem, cylinder, G orig 495.00
Edison Gem A, banner decal, key wind 350.00
Edison Home, banner decal, lg red mg horn, 2/4-min 500.00
Edison Home, 2-min cylinder, 14" horn 295.00
Edison Home, 2/4-min, bl mg horn, signature case 350.00
Edison Home, 2/4-min, brass bell horn w/crane 400.00
Edison Home, 2/4-min, cygnet horn 450.00
Edison Opera, oak case, orig 2,200.00
Edison Spring Motor, all brass mandrel, record shaver 1,100.00
Edison Standard, Diamond B rpd, cygnet horn & crane 525.00
Edison Standard, mg horn 425.00
Edison Standard, Suitcase model, 2-min 400.00
Edison Standard, 2-min, banner decal, 14" brass bell horn 365.00
Edison Standard, 2/4-min, 14" brass bell horn 375.00
Edison Standard C, mg horn, VG 275.00
Edison Standard H, 4-min rpd, 2/4-min gear, 30" metal horn 435.00
Edison Triumph, metal cygnet horn, EX 950.00
Edison Triumph, oak horn, EX 1,600.00
Edison Triumph, triple spring motor, 2-min cylinder 750.00
Edison Windsor, coin operated, cylinder floor model 7,500.00
Harmony Talking Machine 350.00
Jay-O-Phone, disk player, mahog w/glass window 595.00
Lamp-O-phone, no shade 750.00
Mikiphone, pocket phonograph 150.00
Multiphone, 10¢ coin op, w/24 cylinders, all orig 4,800.00
Pathe COQ, 3" mandrel, open works 525.00
Peter Pan, camera type 195.00
Regina Princess #551 .... 450.00
Reginaphone #240, serpentine floor model w/dragons, G orig 5,000.00
Standard Phonograph Co, Model A, mg horn 375.00
Standard Phonograph Co, Model H 450.00
Standard Phonograph Co, Model X 325.00
Thorenn's Excelda, camera type 160.00
Victor, credenza record cabinet 600.00
Victor D, brass bell horn 900.00
Victor E, front mt 600.00
Victor I, sm oak horn, M orig 1,200.00
Victor II, humpback w/blk horn 650.00
Victor III, lg oak horn, EX 1,300.00
Victor III, 22" blk horn, orig, M 600.00
Victor IV, Exhibition soundbox, 21" blk horn w/brass bell 650.00
Victor IV, mahog horn, M orig 1,200.00
Victor M, rear mt 700.00
Victor MS, front mt 1,000.00
Victor O, rear mt, 15" petal mg horn, 8" turntable 650.00
Victor R Royal, front mt, brass bell horn, 7" turntable 600.00
Victor V, lg petal horn, EX 1,200.00
Victor VE #940, art case 1,200.00
Victor VI, orig 14k gold plated trim 2,000.00
Victor VV, 1050 X, coin op, auto changer 700.00
Victor VV-I-70, table model 125.00
Victor XVI, oak upright, M 300.00
Zonophone C, 30" all brass horn, rfn/rstr 725.00

Photographica

Photographic collectibles include not only the cameras and equipment used to 'freeze' special moments in time, but also the photographic images produced by a great variety of processes that have evolved since the daguerrean era of the mid-1800s.

Among the earliest cameras was the sliding box on a box camera. It was focused by sliding one box in and out of the other, thus adjusting the distance of the lens to the ground glass. This was replaced on later models with leather bellows. These were the forerunners of the multi-lens cameras developed in the late 1870s, which were capable of recording many small portraits on a single plate. Double lens cameras produced stereo images which, when viewed through a device called a stereoscope, achieved a 3-dimensional effect. In 1888, George Eastmann introduced his box camera, the first to utilize roll film. This greatly simplified the process, making it possible for the amateur to enjoy photography as a hobby. Detective cameras, those disquised as books, handbags, etc., are among the most sought after by today's collectors.

Many processes have been used to produce photographic images: daguerreotypes--the most-valued examples being the full-plate which measures 6½" x 8½"; ambrotypes, produced by an early wet-plate process whereby a faint negative image on glass is seen as positive when held against a dark background; and tintypes, contemporaries to ambrotypes, but produced on japanned iron, and not as easily damaged.

Other collectible images include carte de visites, known as CDVs, which are portraits printed on paper, and produced in quantity. The CDV fad of the 1800s enticed the famous and the unknown alike to pose for these cards, which were circulated among the public to the extent that they became known as 'publics.' When the popularity of CDVs began to wane, a new fascination developed for the cabinet photo, a larger version measuring about 4½" x 6½".

Stereo cards, photos viewed through a device called a stereoscope, are another popular collectible. The glass stereo plates of the mid-1800s and photo prints produced in the darkroom are among the most valuable.

When no condition is indicated, the items listed below are assumed to be in excellent condition; cameras are in cases unless noted otherwise.
See also Gutta Percha

Albums

Celluloid, lg scene of Romeo & Juliet, EX....70.00
Cloth cover, 2 cabinets & 11 CDVs, 19 pg, 7x8½"....15.00
Leather cover, 18 CDVs, 23 gold-edge pg....26.00
Leather cover, 8 cabinet photos, 17 pg, 9x12"....10.00
Musical, girl & horse in holly/poinsettia reserve, 12x9"....150.00
Musical, keywound, single comb, w/4½" disks, 1900, 15"....300.00
Velvet, cover w/drw & bell-shaped mirror, w/stand....85.00
Velvet, heart mirror in ornate fr on front, w/stand....85.00
Velvet, oval mirror in ornate 'brass' fr on front, 1890s....65.00
Velvet w/nickel motto, lock, 37 cabinet views & CDVs, 11"....75.00

Ambrotype

4th plate, Civil War Union band, oval vignette, cased....750.00
4th plate, man playing drums, cased....275.00
6th plate, boy w/lg horn w/gilded ends, ruby glass, ½ case....65.00
6th plate, boy w/suit & tie, wooden fr: 7½x8½"....175.00
6th plate, family at beach, sailboat, cased....85.00
6th plate, girl in gown w/arm around Cocker Spaniel, cased....55.00
6th plate, little girl afraid of camera, cased....35.00
6th plate, occupational, carpenter, formal clothes, tools....160.00
6th plate, schooner w/2 masts/rigging, dockside, in case....350.00
6th plate, soldier seated w/pistol in belt....80.00
6th plate, woman sidesaddle on horse, cased....125.00
6th plate, 2 bearded gents in red/wht/bl suits, w/case....225.00
9th plate, floppy-eared hound dog, cased....55.00

Cabinet Photo

Alexander, strong circus man bending iron w/hands, Wendt....35.00
Che-Mah!, The Only Chinese Dwarf, albumen, Wendt....15.00
Clara Bert, lady w/hair 66" long, Eisenmann....35.00
Indian aid, 7 girls being sold by a society, Lacey, 1890s....5.00
Kiowa Warrior, Indian child stands on chair, crying, Irwin....30.00
M'lle Prospetto & Pets, Hephzibah/Don Quixote, Eisenmann....35.00
Millie Betra, Serpent Queen, Ringling Bros imp, JV Brown....12.00
Sandow, strong man w/bare chest flexing biceps, Newsboy....35.00
Snake Lady, lady performing contortionist move, Eisenmann....45.00
Tattooed Man, man w/completely tattooed body, Eisenmann....40.00
Texas Giants, Shield Brothers, 4 men over 7 ft 8", Wilkes....40.00
Tradesmen, 3 craftsmen w/aprons & hats, 1800s, Van De Wall..35.00
Wild Men of Borneo, Waino & Plutaino, albumen, Wendt, VG...15.00

Cameras

Akarex, range-finder, 35mm, Germany, 1950s....125.00
Ansco Memo, focusing model, w/2 cassettes, ½ fr, NM....140.00
Ansco Speedex 4.5, Germany, speed to 200, w/case....24.00
Baby Brownie Special, plastic, set of 3, EX....12.00
Beau Brownie, box, pastel pebble-grain cover, rare, EX....63.00
Beirette, Compur Rapid shutter, 35mm, rare, 1930s....100.00
Bilora (Bella), Germany, plastic, 127 film, w/case, NM....12.00
Brownie #2, model E, box, 120 film, 1903-1916....8.00
Brownie #2-A, model C, box, gr, scarce, EX....18.00
Brownie Turret, movie, f1.9, 3 lens, in color carton, M....10.00
Bullet, #4, box, 4" wood spool, 1898, EX....36.00
Bullseye #2, box....8.50
Bullseye #2, model D, box, VG....13.00
Bullseye 98, #2, box, opens from top....16.00
Buster Brown #2A, Ansco, 118 film, 2½x4½" prints....45.00
Charlie Tuna, Star-Kist, 126 instant, color or b/w, bl, M....85.00
Coronet #020, English, box, no strap, 4½", EX....9.00
CP Stirn, concealed vest, w/walnut case, 1886, EX....2,250.00
DeMoulin Bros, trick: shoots water stream, wood, 7½x7½"....400.00
Detrola 127, model KW, Anast 3.5, shutter perfect....14.00
Eastman Kodak Co, glass beaker, 4", NM....7.00
Ensign E29, Houghton-Butcher, orig carton, roll film, bl....50.00
Hawkeye #1-A, brass plate/shutter mt, pat 1898-1910, case....30.00
Hawkeye Dectective, natural wood, rare, 1890s....193.00
Hawkeye Rainbow #2, model C, box, maroon, EX....14.00
Houghton's Ltd, pocket watch detective, 25 exposure, rare...2,000.00
Kodak #3, model C, fold pocket, rotary shutter, 1885-1893....45.00
Kodak #3, model H, fold pocket, pat 1894-1908, 7½x4½"....30.00
Kodak #4, model F, cartridge, pat 1890-1902, 5" spool, EX....70.00
Kodak #5, folding, satchel style, red bellows, rare....595.00
Kodak Brownie, 127, plastic, w/cord....4.00
Kodak Jr, #1-A, 116 film, 1898-1915, EX....10.00
Kodak Original, G Eastman, 100 exposure, w/film, 1888, VG..2,500.00
Kodak Retina 11, Stuttgart #142.F2, 10 speeds to 500, NM....80.00
Kodak 6.3, #2-C, model A, auto, A-130 film, scarce, w/case....75.00
Mackenstein, pinhole, ¼ plate, brass lens, rare, EX....750.00
Pathex, blk steel, w/3-ft tripod, NM....11.00
Perfex de Lux f2.8, speed to 1250, w/locking device, case....24.00
Photo Jumelle, J Carpentier, binocular style, 1890s, EX....285.00
Pixie, sub-mini, plastic, 16mm, rare, w/case....50.00
Plate, brass Gundlach lens mt, wood drop-board, 5x6"....45.00
Polaroid, 95-A, no sports finder....8.00
Premo Pony, Rochester Optical, ¼ plate, tripod, blk, NM....145.00
Rapitake, 35 mm, w/2 cartridges, mfg La Rose, rare, M....295.00
Regal, mini, plastic, color, 35 mm, scarce, in carton, EX....12.00
Retina 1, non-rangefinder 126, VG....47.00
Revere 8, model #88, movie, crackle finish, EX....10.00
Ruberg 127, Germany, blk tin, scarce, VG....27.00
Samoca 35111, Japan, chrome & blk leatherette, 4x3", EX....27.00
Shalco, Japan, w/film, carton & instruction sheet, 2", NM....15.00

Shure Shot, single exposure, glass plate, wood, 3x3x3¾"......250.00
Standard, plastic, w/roll of 127 film, orig carton, NM............3.00
Tropical Una, J Sinclair, 3 plate holders, w/case, rare, M.....1,600.00
Universal Minute 16, no cassettes, w/case, EX................36.00
Waterbury Detective, Scovill, leather, 1888, 4x5" plates.......350.00
Weno Hawkeye #7, box, EX..............................25.00
Whittaker, micro sub-mini, 16mm, w/leather case, 2¾", M......55.00

Carte De Visite

Boy seated w/wooden fife, mk NY............................8.00
Cat, Glosser, horizontal view of sleeping tabby, VG............20.00
Confederate soldier, in uniform, full-length view...............45.00
Fingals Cave, Island of Staffa..............................6.00
Fireman, red shirt w/gold badge, hat says '3 ADM'............45.00
Fort Fisher Memorial, Cargo, sailor amputee & orphan boy.....45.00
Henry Longfellow, author, wht hair & beard, Warren, VG.......15.00
James Garfield, intense profile.............................9.00
Maharajah & Maharana, he in jeweled robes & headgear, VG....15.00
Maryland officer, w/sash & sword, wht gloves, mk Baltimore.....25.00
NY officer, armed w/sword, eagle buckle, mk Hopper, NY.......25.00
Pig, 1 w/smiling face & 1 w/rear-end view, pr.................12.00
Queen Midget, German Rose, sm woman in gown, Eisenmann...12.00
Queen Victoria & Prince Albert, Notman, rare, VG............25.00
Soldier, full-length view of Samuel Yaple, no kepi, Webb.......12.00
Union soldier, holds pistol across chest, vignette, VG..........18.00

Cases

Leather, ambrotype, multi-image, 9th plate, rare, VG..........145.00
Mother of pearl, memento inscription, ¾ plate...............200.00
Mother of pearl floral-spray inlay on leather, ¼ plate..........110.00
Velvet, color-tinted decorative brass corners, 6th plate..........75.00

Daguerreotypes

4th plate, A Lincoln, fr..............................17,600.00
4th plate, American Indian in white man's clothes, ½ case......41.00
4th plate, brother & sister portrait, cased...................40.00
6th plate, Blk man in 3-pc suit w/gold pinky ring, cased.......365.00
6th plate, boy's arm around spaniel, girl w/flowers, cased......150.00
6th plate, man & wife posed in a loving manner, cased.........24.00
6th plate, man in suit, sgn McElroy, cased...................30.00
6th plate, man w/3-pc suit, vignette, ½ case.................45.00
6th plate, occupational, appears to be a cab driver, cased.......35.00
6th plate, Pirate or the Maid's Trial, cased, engraving..........125.00
6th plate, post mortem of man w/freckles, w/cover, cased.......90.00
6th plate, scruffy man in jazzy vest, Babbit, cased.............60.00
6th plate, The Businessman, sits in Victorian chair, cased.......20.00
6th plate, woman w/lace gloves, cased........................25.00
9th plate, man w/lg bow tie, Beard, w/blk leather case..........75.00
9th plate, occupational, carpenter w/hammer & nails, cased....225.00
9th plate, woman w/earrings, vignette, Phipps, ½ case..........35.00

Photos

Albumen, Fly's Gallery, 15 cavalry soldiers, 5¼x8½"...........68.00
Albumen, portrait of WB Kinne, 4th Sgt Gainesville Rifles......25.00
Albumen, Salt Lake City from Prospect Hill, sgn Savage........40.00
Albumen, Stebbins, mountains in New Hampshire, 45x32", VG..85.00
Albumen, western logging group in undershirts & suspenders....10.00
Albumen, western scenes, 19th century, set of 4..............60.00
Albumen, 2 harem girls sitting on bed, 2 views, 4¼x6", EX......9.00
Clipper Ship Panay, Stebbins, blind stamp, 7½x9½"...........65.00
Edward Curtis, A Koskimo House, Van Gelder paper, 9x12"....40.00
Edward Curtis, Acoma Water Girls, lg folio, on tissue..........90.00
Edward Curtis, Flathead Dance, lg folio, on Japan paper.......100.00
Edward Curtis, Gossiping–San Juan, #598, lg folio, tissue......115.00
Edward Curtis, His Fights–Oglala, on Japan paper, 1908.......55.00
Edward Curtis, Klamath Hunter, #573, lg folio, on tissue......175.00
Edward Curtis, Laguna Architecture, lg folio, on tissue.........72.00
Edward Curtis, Tolowa Woman, #461, lg folio, on tissue.......115.00
Edward Curtis, Yakima Man & Woman, orotone on glass....1,300.00
Edward Curtis, Zuni Pottery, Japan paper, 9x12"..............40.00
Grand Canyon from Brink of Fall, Haynes, 16¼x 21½".........95.00
Midget, sm lady sits on stool w/man kneeling, 5¾x6¾", M......20.00
Occupational, Yorkville Ice, sgn, 19th century, set of 3.........20.00
Old Wolf, Indian warrior wears feather & choker, DF Barry.....42.00
San Francisco Fire, Blumberg, 1906, 4½x7¼"................43.00
Sepia, Girl Hunter, Indian w/bow, DF Barry, 10x8"............60.00
Sepia, White Clover, Indian maiden, DF Barry, 7x5"...........50.00
Silver print, Billy Buckskin, sgn, Carl Moon, 9x6"............80.00
Silver print, collection of 1920s trucks, 8x10", set of 20.......200.00
Silver print, Deadwood Cigar Shop, interior view, 6½x8"........60.00

Stereoscopic Views

In evaluating stereo views, the date and condition are all-important. Some views were printed over a thirty to forty year period--'first generation' prices are far higher than later copies.

Airplane, 1st air rail trip, July 8, 1929, Keystone #32372.......15.00
Albumen, Mayors of Kansas City, MO, DI Thomson, 1886......20.00
Alpine Lake, view of lake & mountains, Wheeler #47, VG......28.00
Among the Winnebago Indians, HH Bennett #276, VG..........55.00
Apache Lake, view of lake & mountains, Wheeler #30, VG......26.00
Balancing Rock, yel mt, VG...............................3.00
Bath, The; Kanab, WA; campsite near stream, Wheeler #54.....25.00
Boaters at Windermere, 3 people in rowboat, Ogle & Edge......7.00
Boom Lake, Brainerd, cream mt, FJ Haynes #126, VG.........12.00
Butterfly Collection, butterflies/moths mt, Kilburn #89..........15.00
Central Park, girls at boat landing, children on stairs..........12.00
Clear Creek, view of mining town below Idaho, Chamberlain....12.00
Col Lindbergh, Spirit of St Louis, Keystone #32062, EX........15.00
Colorado, tracks along Creek Wall Bend, Chamberlain #290....14.00
Confederate Monument & Church, New Orleans, Lilienthal.......8.00
Connecticut Disaster, tornado destruction, D French............8.00
Contemplation, striped tabby cat curled up on book...........15.00
Cooley's Ranch, view of ranch, Wheeler #32.................28.00
Court of the Hercules Mill, Queretara, WH Jackson #5182......15.00
Crystal Falls, Bear Canyon, yel mt, Gurnsey...................3.00
Dead Giant, giant tree w/tunnel, Watkins #3089, VG...........16.00
Deer, 4 deer in Zoological Gardens, VG.......................10.00
Deer Hunting, men w/fallen deer, deer strung up, Bennett......12.00
Denver, buildings & Rocky Mountains, Chamberlain #389........14.00
Departure, The; mother prays as son leaves w/soldier...........7.00
Diego & His Burro, cream mt, WH Jackson #2050.............30.00
Echo Canyon, Looking Down, pink mt, WH Jackson.............3.00
Eclipse of the Sun, 4 phases, Alfred Bros, 1867, EX...........85.00
Engineers Camp Bozeman Tunnel, cream mt, FJ Haynes.......18.00
Factory interior, Pacific Cotton Mills, cab mt, Hamor, VG........8.00
Fast Day–A Horrible Intrusion, priest hides turkey, 1850s.......12.00
Florida, interior of Spanish fort, St Augustine..................4.00
Fortune Teller, woman in cape reads young girl's palm, VG......8.00
Fourth of July Parade, T Sweeny, Ryder's Gallery, 1873, VG....35.00
French Cathedral in Quebec, w/12 carriages, Vallee #47........12.00
Gold Miners, gold miners along shute, Anthony #474..........17.00
Grand Canyon of Colorado, walls of canyon, Wheeler #61......28.00

Grand Canyon of the Arkansas River, A Martin, VG............3.50
Grand Central Station, train & depot, Anthony #8069, VG.......9.00
Grand Teton, 2 men on horseback, FJ Haynes #1776, VG.......9.00
Great Falls of Yellowstone, cream mt, FJ Haynes...............3.00
Grotto Spring, Grand Canyon, Wheeler #136, EX.............40.00
Hawaii, View of Government Building, 1870s...................7.00
Hermit of Quidnit, bearded old man in rustic setting, VG.......12.00
Hero's Wife, woman cries on man's shoulder, Silvester, VG......9.00
Houseworth Celebrities, L&H Clark are circus performers.......30.00
Hunting Series, 2 old men w/killing of ducks, Bennett..........15.00
Hydraulic Mining, close-up of main pipe w/tank, #803, VG......55.00
Ice Views, frozen Thornton Ferry Depot, Lawrence.............5.00
Indian Pueblo of Zuni, interior view, Wheeler #16, VG.........30.00
Instantaneous, people at Ramsgate beach, Blanchard #319.......5.00
Iona, 2 views of St Martin's Cross, Wilson #39 & #258, VG......9.00
Little Bo Peep, Bo sleeping & Bo carries staff w/sheep, VG.....18.00
London Zoo, camel, lion, wht pelican, F York................12.00
Mammoth Anvil Rock, yel mt, Gurnsey........................3.00
Martha's Vineyard, view of camp ground from Highlands, VG.....6.00
Miss Love, close-up of lady w/fine outfit, London Stereo.........6.00
Miss Ward, lady plunges through mid-air, 1889, VG............9.00
Mountain Lion, cabinet size mount, WH Jackson, VG..........10.00
Mt Kearsage, view of men at Summit House, Sherburne, EX.....7.00
Natural Monument in Monument Park, yel mt, Gurnsey.........3.00
Oil Regions, Dunham's Rollway, PA, derrick/men/oil barrels.....18.00
Old Abe, Wisconsin War Eagle, Bennett #304.................15.00
Oyster Day, 2 women shuck as man gulps oysters & ale, VG.....6.00
Pioneers' Cabin, hollowed redwood house, Watkins #3516, VG..14.00
President Lincoln & Thad, view of Lincoln & his son...........5.00
President Wilson, cabinet seated w/Wilson at head of table......10.00
Product Exhibit, pickles, ketchups, sauces, Gilman, 1870s......28.00
Red River Train, Indian portraits, Indian w/wagons, Martin......55.00
Rock Island, IL; people under bridge, residence, Newberry.......9.00
Roman Coliseum, donkey & cart, Guerard, VG.................5.00
Rome, Forum, Colosseo, 2 other views of city, E Behles........18.00
Russia, statue/boats by St Petersburg wall, 1860s, Felisch.......22.00
Salem, MA; street scene of stores & flags, Whipple, VG.........10.00
San Francisco, Jewish Synagogue, T Houseworth #235, EX.....50.00
Santa Claus, tree & lots of toys, American Stereo, EX.........18.00
Savannah, GA; view from top of Presbyterian Church, Ryan......6.00
Scenery of Union Pacific RR, 3 views, Jackson, VG............19.00
School Kids, class portrait on school steps, Alden, VG...........5.00
Sconset Bank, workers w/tools in street, J Freeman, EX........22.00
Shooting Wen-Ga-Rah, Indians w/rifles, HH Bennett #275......55.00
Shoshone Falls, view of falls, Wheller #48, VG................35.00
Soda Springs, ID; sm town w/houses in rural setting............18.00
Southern Steamer, Steamboat Rosa being loaded...............35.00
Strictly Confidential, girl on tiptoes whispers to mother..........9.00
Tabernacle, The; Salt Lake City, Weitfle #434................12.00
Tower Creek, Yellowstone Park, stereo effect, Marshall, VG......5.00
Une Maison De Campagne, 9 people on picnic in the woods.....9.00
Union Pacific RR, Tower Rock, Savage & Ottinger #171, EX....17.00
Utah, Morman family posed in front of log cabin..............15.00
Vermont, Memphremagog House, Steamer & Lake, Webster, VG..8.00
View Across Black Canyon, man near river bank, Wheeler #3...16.00
View Down Black Canyon, Wheeler #2.........................9.00
Watkins Pacific RR, Summit of Castle Peak, #190, VG.........10.00
Wisconsin River, 2 men in canoes, Bennett #176, EX..........20.00
Yellowstone Salmon Trout, lt bl mt, FJ Haynes #1284, EX.......9.00

Tintypes

Horse & wagon, man in horse-drawn wagon, 2½x3½", EX......20.00
Mormons, child on horse w/2 men, CDV size..................11.00
Rural house & barn, w/3 figures at fence, walnut fr, 5x7".......80.00
Whole plate, occupational, men hold woodenware, oval fr......125.00
4th plate, Civil War soldier from 3rd NJ Cavalry.............120.00
4th plate, Civil War soldiers in mock fist fight................40.00
4th plate, The Miller, early Mason, Bartlett, gilt wood fr........80.00
4th plate, 2 western cowhands playing poker.................165.00
6th plate, Cavalry corporal in uniform w/sword, cased..........55.00
6th plate, Cavalry soldier holding drawn saber, ½ case.........85.00
6th plate, swashbuckler w/caped uniform/#11 on kepi, cased....145.00
6th plate, Texas CSA Soldier, w/mortuary record, matted......220.00
6th plate, Union Cavalry soldier, revolver/knife, cased..........60.00
6th plate, Virginia rebel w/flintlock pistol, cased..............250.00
6th plate, Zouave, w/ammunition pouch, in case, M...........200.00
6th plate, 3 carpenters: 1 w/sq, 1 w/saw, 1 w/level, VG.........30.00
6th plate, 4 soldiers in musician-type uniforms.................35.00

Viewers and Slides

Brewster, focusing & leather-bound lenses, mirrored flap.......225.00
Brewster, French, non-focusing, emb SG & Co, EX...........145.00
Carte de visite, wooden box, holds 1 CDV, NM................75.00
Ferrier, 12 glass stereo views of Paris, in box, set, EX........150.00
Glass slides, scenes of WWI, bakelite tray w/22 slides..........50.00
Lantern slide, kaleidoscope, crank operated, 4½x7"...........45.00
Stereo viewer, wooden, fold-up eye pc, brass support card......47.50
Vautier, cigarette ad, tin litho, w/47 views, 3", EX..............55.00
View Master, w/200 reels & orig envelope, Sawyer, 1940s......115.00

Miscellaneous

Bank, Kodak, box Brownie shape, CI, w/hdl & orig key, 1903..325.00
Bottle stopper, pnt man w/camera, mt on cork, 1930s, EX......30.00
Brooch, ambrotype of grinning boy w/dog, center swivels.......95.00
Candle lamp, uses single candle, red ruby glass, 8½"...........45.00
Cigarette lighter–camera, KKW, cable release, w/tripod.........16.00
Cuff links, w/photos of young man, gold, EX, pr..............45.00
Fan, Foust Studio, bamboo look, cardboard, wood hdl, 1910....25.00
Flash pistol gun, Chelsea, gun stock shape hdl, rare..........200.00
Perfume bottle, Victorian, ambrotype of man, rare............225.00
Photo pop gun, Universal Pictures, makes loud bang, 1914.....30.00
Poster, Grande Journee Cinematographique, sgn, 28x36"......200.00
Print roller, rubber/iron, 5½" trn hdl.......................15.00
Stanhope, binoculars, brass, Universal Exhibition/Chicago.......45.00
Stanhope, cross, 8 diamond-like stones, Lord's prayer..........25.00
Stanhope, radio, sterling silver charm, note & number dial......70.00
Stanhope, watch fob, 6 views of Niagara falls, 18 stones........65.00
Tripod, brass w/aluminum top, leg swivel action, 4-feet.........17.00

Stanhope, Eiffel Tower, cast metal, 4", $47.50.

Piano Babies

A familiar sight in Victorian parlors, piano babies languished atop shawl covered pianos in a variety of poses: crawling, sitting, on their tummies, or on their backs playing with their toes. Some babies were nude and some wore gowns. Sizes ranged from about 3″ up to 12″. The most famous manufacturer of these bisque darlings was the Heubach Brothers of Germany who nearly always marked their product; see Heubach for more listings. Watch for reproductions.

When no condition is indicated, the items listed below are assumed to be in mint condition.

Girl, reclining, rattle in hand, plays w/dog, 9″ 195.00
Girl holds puppy w/pacifier in mouth, 11″ 250.00
Laying on side, nude, bisque/pnt features, Japan, 4¾″ 35.00
Laying on side, wearing feathered cap, bl/wht shift, 9x5″ 195.00
Reclining on elbow, kicking legs, in gown, Hertwig, 2½″ 195.00
Sitting, lacy dress, jeweled moth on skirt, Germany, 10″ 225.00

Pickard

Founded in 1897 in Chicago, Illinois, the Pickard China Company was originally a decorating studio, importing china blanks from European manufacturers. Some of these early pieces bear the name of those companies as well as Pickard's. Trained artists decorated the wares with hand-painted studies of fruit, florals, birds, and scenics, and often signed their work. In 1915, Pickard introduced a line of 23k gold over a dainty floral-etched ground design.

In the 1930s, they began to experiment with the idea of making their own ware, and by 1938 had succeeded in developing a formula for fine translucent china. Since 1976 they have issued an annual limited edition Christmas plate. They are now located in Antioch, Illinois.

The company has used various marks: 'Pickard' with double circles; the crown mark; 'Pickard' on a gold maple leaf; and the current mark, the lion and shield. Work signed by Challinor, Marker, and Yeschek is especially valued by today's collectors.

When no condition is indicated, the items listed below are assumed to be in mint condition.

Bonbon, garden scene w/roses, scalloped, ovoid, 1912, 7″ 60.00
Bowl, all gold w/fruits at center, sgn Yeschek, 10½″ 175.00

Mug, Dutch fishing boats and windmills, artist signed, J.P. over L, France, 5″, $395.00.

Bowl, gold w/in, continuous scene w/out, Challinor, 6¾″ 295.00
Bowl, red Nouveau poppies on gold, 10″ 160.00
Bowl, red poppies, gold border, sgn Breidel, Rosenthal, 6″ 95.00
Bowl, Roman garden scene, sgn Challinor, sq, hdls, 8x6″ 150.00
Bowl, strawberries/gooseberries, Challinor, Bavarian, 8″ 125.00
Candle holder, allover gold etched floral, 2½″, pr 25.00
Candy, divided; allover gold etched floral, hdl, 6¼″ 50.00
Celery tray, allover gold etched floral, open hdls, 11½″ 45.00
Chocolate pot, pink clover, gold hdls, sgn Reuny 225.00
Coffee pot, cobalt w/encrusted gold, Chinese enamel, ftd 275.00
Creamer & sugar, Aura Argenta Linear, sgn Hess 110.00
Creamer & sugar, exotic birds/floral/butterfly, Klein 135.00
Creamer & sugar, flower decor, sgn Challinor 45.00
Creamer & sugar, open; gold hdls/wide band w/ivy, Limoges 75.00
Cup & saucer, demitasse; floral/band of fruit, set of 6 . . . . 185.00
Jug, golden pheasant, Italian garden band, 6 panels, gold 270.00
Pitcher, cider; Italian garden, Challinor 350.00
Pitcher, floral, blk/beige/gold bands, Hessler, 8″ 250.00
Pitcher, fruit/blossoms, gilt top/base/hdl, 7⅜″ 225.00
Pitcher, tankard; red currants, wide gold border, sgn, 9½″ 275.00
Plate, cake; strawberries/fruit, gold center, sgn, 12″ 130.00
Plate, dainty fruit on 2″ border, lav/bl/gold, sgn, 8″ 65.00
Plate, floral, artist sgn, Haviland, 8″ 65.00
Plate, floral, sgn James, 8½″ 75.00
Plate, garden scene w/wall, Challinor, pierced hdls, 7″ 225.00
Plate, iris, much gold, sgn Brazek, Haviland, 7½″ 65.00
Plate, mc violets/swirl stems, gold border, Limoges, 6″ 50.00
Plate, moon/trees on bl matt, sgn James, 8¾″ 195.00
Plate, Oriental poppies, much gold, sgn Gasper, 9″ 145.00
Plate, scenic, thick gold etched border, sgn Marker, 10″ 150.00
Plate, shamrocks, gold band decor, 10″ 90.00
Plate, strawberries, 1″ gold border, Fuchs, Limoges, 8″ 85.00
Sugar shaker, long-stemmed violets, gold top, sgn, 1910 . . . . 195.00
Tea set, stylized design, artist sgn on hdl 300.00
Urn, gold filigree w/peacock, artist sgn Marker, 10″ 475.00
Vase, dandelions on turq to bl, gilt bands, sgn, 1905, 8½″ 150.00
Vase, lake/2 trees, sgn E Challinor, maple leaf mk, 5¼″ 320.00
Vase, lav flowers/trailing leaves, cream/gold trim, 6½″ 90.00
Vase, palm trees & water, sgn E Challinor, 1912-1919 . . . . 300.00
Vase, 3 lilies, heavy gold neck, sgn HR, 8¾″ 90.00
Vase/lamp, peacock, bk: floral, hdls, sgn Challinor, 18½″ 500.00

Pickle Castors

The pickle castor is a novel item made popular during the Victorian period. It consists of a glass insert, usually a type of colored art glass, contained in a decorative metal frame. A pickle fork or tongs are usually hung from the frame.

In the listings below, the description prior to the semi-colon (;) refers to the jar (insert), and the remainder of the line describes the frame. Where no condition is indicated, the silverplate is assumed to be in very good to excellent condition; glass jars are assumed mint.

Albertine, floral decor; Pairpoint fr w/tongs 475.00
Amber T'print; Hartford fr w/birds/flowers, tongs 195.00
Amber w/floral; Meriden SP ftd fr w/fancy tongs 250.00
Amberina w/bird, NE; ftd saucer base w/side bail, Queen 450.00
Amethyst/clear insert; James Tufts Quadruple ped stand 225.00
Apple Blossom mold, milk glass; Colonial fr w/lacy hdl 250.00
Beatty Rib, bl opal; SP fr 185.00
Bl satin Reverse Swirl; 'C' bail on ornate Tufts fr, tongs 300.00
Block; Reed & Barton fr w/fork 95.00
Cane, amber; sgn Webster fr w/tongs 175.00
Cane & Fans; Meriden openwork top fr w/tongs, 10¼″ 95.00

Cranberry Baby Thumbprint with enamel floral and leaves, in ornate frame with tongs, 11¼", $295.00.

Clear/textured jar; fancy hdl, side ornamentation, tongs.........95.00
Cranberry, Diamond Quilted, pnt floral; w/lid & tongs.........295.00
Cranberry, pnt floral/bands, gold trim; SP fr w/tongs, 10"......300.00
Cranberry opal Ch'mum Base Rev Swirl, Tufts fr w/elephant....295.00
Cranberry Reverse T'print; SP lid, fr & tongs................275.00
Cranberry spatter Ribbed Pillar; simple Tufts fr w/tongs.......250.00
Cranberry swirl opal; emb leaves/floral fr, tongs ea side........300.00
Cranberry T'print w/daisies; ornate Middletown fr w/tongs......350.00
Cranberry T'print w/floral; ftd ornate Wilcox fr w/tongs........335.00
Cranberry vertical optic; Greenaway girl skips rope on fr.......295.00
Cut velvet; twist rope fr w/fancy hdl by Middletown...........500.00
Daisy & Button, amber, daisies/foliage/birds; SP fr, tongs......275.00
Daisy & Button w/V Ornament, vaseline; ornate Hartford fr....275.00
Dbl, cranberry T'print; Pelton fr w/peacock figure, 16"........500.00
Dbl, Elk Medallion jars; floral finials/fern trimmed bail........235.00
Dbl, panel w/wreath cutting; sgn Wilcox fr w/tongs...........250.00
Dbl, satin barrel jars; leaf-trimmed, sq-ftd base...............300.00
Dbl, vaseline, Dia Quilt; SH&M fr, dome lids, fretwork hdl.....325.00
Emerald Baby Ivt T'print, much gold/pnt; fancy fr w/tongs.....450.00
Floral relief sq insert; Webster & Son quadruple plate ft.......250.00
Frosted/textured jar; simple fr, lg pickle on lid................85.00
Hobnail, 11-Row, pink; ornate tall fr w/tongs................475.00
Honeycomb, bl opal; simple ball-ftd Reed-Barton fr, tongs.....185.00
MOP Herringbone, bl; ornate Rogers fr....................595.00
Overshot sq insert; Meriden pat 1872 w/Egyptian figures fr.....325.00
Panelled Zipper; Meriden ftd stand w/fork & tongs............85.00
Panels w/emb birds/butterflies; fancy ftd fr, ea pc mk R&B.....285.00
Panels w/eng florals; Assyrian head tongs, Launton fr.........125.00
Pigeon blood T'print bulbous jar; ftd fr w/leaves & tongs......400.00
Pink Pine Cone, satin; ftd fr, shells on rnd bail, w/tongs.......325.00
Pumpkin jar on SP wheeled cart, cherub figural, SH&M, 11"...600.00
Reverse Swirl, opal; ftd Tufts fr w/applied flowers, tongs.......200.00
Rubena, bark textured; chick finial, saucer base w/fork........450.00
Rubena Optic Rib; Pairpoint fr w/loops & top trim, tongs......195.00
Rubena T'print w/floral; tongs on boar-head hook, Tufts.......400.00
Stippled jar; floral emb Pairpoint fr w/top trim, tongs.........125.00
Verona, ribbed lav/clear, HP daisies; Pairpoint fr w/tongs......350.00
Yel w/dogwood, bulbous Mt WA jar; claw/ball-ftd ornate fr.....400.00

Pie Birds

Pie birds or vents were used around 1930 to prevent pies from boiling over in the oven. When the juices began to bubble and expand, they were contained within the hollow form; as the pie cooled, the juices drained back into the pie.

When no condition is indicated, the items listed below are assumed to be in mint condition.

Bird, cream w/pink & bl trim.............................10.00
Bird, lt & dk gray w/yel, 4½"............................10.00
Bird, lt brn, 4¼"..8.50
Blackbird...10.00
Blk chef w/spoon, underglaze color, 4¼"...................30.00
Brass, unusual, 3" L....................................55.00
Elephant, seated, pink, 4"...............................45.00

Baker man, maroon and black on ivory, 5¼", $25.00.

Pigeon Blood

Pigeon blood glass, produced in the late 1800s, may be distinguished from other dark red glass by its distinctive orange tint.

When no condition is indicated, the items listed below are assumed to be in mint condition.

Butter dish, Venecia, enamel decor, orig base, rare...........350.00
Creamer, Venecia, enamel decor.........................125.00
Darning egg, blown, ground end.........................105.00
Lamp, hall, hanging, paneled, orig brass fr.................260.00
Pitcher, w/adventurine, pulled feather, water sz..............230.00
Pitcher, water; Venecia.................................150.00
Plate, 7½"..20.00
Shakers, Bulging Loop, orig tops, pr.......................65.00
Sugar bowl, Torquay, w/orig lid..........................250.00

Pin-back Buttons

Most of the advertising buttons made until the 1920s were top-quality full-color celluloid (plastic) covered buttons termed 'cellos.' Many were issued in sets on related topics featuring historical people and events, animals and birds, and other themes. Several cigarette, gum, and candy companies used buttons as inserts in their products. Usually the name of the company or product was printed on a paper placed in the back of the button and held securely by the pin. Most of the back papers are still in place today, aiding in the identification of the button. Beginning in the 1920s, a large number of buttons were lithographed (printed on metal); these buttons are referred to as 'lithos.' Nearly all advertising buttons are collected today with perhaps these exceptions: common buttons picturing flags of various nations, general labor union buttons denoting the payment of dues, and similar buttons with clever sayings.

Following is a listing of some of the most popular non-political buttons. Values reflect buttons which have designs centered, colors aligned, no fading or yellowing, no spots or stains, and no cracks, splits, or dents. See also Political Entourage

Avery Tractors, die-cut....50.00
Blondie....5.00
Bond Bread, airplanes, set of 6....60.00
Brooklyn Dodgers, ribboned souvenir, w/ball & bat....18.00
Buster Brown Bread, 1¼"....16.00
California, Vote Dry....15.00
Ceresota Kid, 1¼"....15.00
Chevy 6....9.00
Civil War Memorial, Vets at gravesite....10.00
Clown on button & hanging horseshoe....10.00
Coronation, George VI & Elizabeth....15.00
Dagwood....5.00
Dead Shot....45.00
Don Winslow....6.00
Effanbee Dolls....8.00
Electric Horseless Carriages, 1¼"....40.00
Foxy Grandpa, NY Journal premium, 1¼"....11.00
GAR Veteran, w/bow....10.00
GAR 30th Encampment, St Paul....10.00
Gen MacArthur....10.00
Globe Trotter, Mickey Mouse....30.00
Gold Dust Washing Powder....32.50
Huber Tractors....35.00
Maltex Health Club, w/locomotive....18.00
Mickey Mouse, advertising Emerson radio, 1934....50.00
Nabisco Golden Anniversary....10.00
New Idea Manure Spreader....35.00
Quiz Kids....7.00
REO, sm....12.00
South Bend Watch Company....20.00
Winchester, Wonderful Topperweins Who...Cartridges....45.00

Pink Lustre Ware

Pink lustre was produced by nearly every potter in the Staffordshire district in the 18th and 19th centuries. The application of gold lustre on white or light colored backgrounds produced pinks, while the same over dark colors developed copper. The wares ranged from hand-painted plaques to transfer-printed dinnerware.

When no condition is indicated, the items listed below are assumed to be in mint condition.

Jug, stylized strawberry vine resist, Leeds, ca 1812, 7½", $180.00.

Bowl, bird & flower medallion, floral band w/in, 3x6"....65.00
Bowl, house, target center, pk trim, shallow, 7½"....85.00
Bowl, house, 2-story, 2½x6"....55.00
Bowl, mother playing w/son on Empire sofa, 5½"....22.00
Cup, house....25.00
Cup & saucer, floral, Dixon & Co....35.00
Cup & saucer, handleless; blk transfer decor....30.00
Cup & saucer, house, 2-story....40.00
Cup & saucer, mother & daughter in garden, 1825....50.00
Cup & saucer, raised gold leaves/flowers, MIG....37.50
Jug, 3 children w/names, Masonic devices, dtd 1828, 9½"....770.00
Mug, child's; Faith & Hope, blk transfer, 2¼"....45.00
Pitcher, mk HP, Gray's Pottery, 3¼"....15.00
Plate, Jolly Drover, sq, Lancaster, 6", set of 6....100.00
Plate, scroll & flowers, 7¼"....20.00
Saucer, church, deep, 5½"....38.00

Pink Pigs

Pink Pigs on cabbage green were made in Germany around the turn of the century. They were sold as souvenirs in train depots, amusement parks, and gift shops. 'Action Pigs' (those involved in some amusing activity) are the most valuable, and prices increase with the number of pigs. Though a similar type of figurine was made in white bisque, most serious collectors perfer only the pink ones. They are marked in two ways: 'Germany' in incised letters, and a black ink-stamped 'Made in Germany' in a circle.

Action pig playing piano, second with mandolin, Home Sweet Home, $115.00.

1 by purse....65.00
1 climbing out of sq scalloped bowl....65.00
1 coming out of cup....65.00
1 in bathtub....90.00
1 in case looking through binoculars....85.00
1 lg pig sitting behind 3" trough....55.00
1 on binoculars, gold trim....95.00
1 reclining on horseshoe ash tray....70.00
1 sitting on log, mk Germany....65.00
1 standing by toothpick holder w/camera on neck....75.00
1 wearing chef's costume, holds frypan, w/basket....80.00
2, mother at pump bathing baby in tub....115.00
2 by eggshell....80.00
2 in car, 4½" L....115.00
2 in purse....75.00
2 in top hat, tux & cane, dancing....95.00
2 on binoculars, gold trim....115.00
2 on cotton bale, 1 peers out of hole, 1 over top....90.00
2 on see-saw on top of pouch bank....75.00
2 on top hat....95.00

Pisgah Forest

The Pisgah Forest Pottery was established near Mount Pisgah in Arden, North Carolina, by Walter B. Stephen in 1914. Stephen is best known for his Cameo Ware which he decorated by hand in the pate-sur-pate style with scenes portraying covered wagons and other subjects related to the pioneer days. He also produced a turquoise crackled ware, and developed a fine crystalline glaze, examples of which are highly prized by today's collectors. The ware was marked 'Pisgah Forest,' often with a potter at the wheel. Stephen died in 1961, but the work was continued by his associates.

When no condition is indicated, the items listed below are assumed to be in mint condition.

Bowl, semi-gloss, gr/red, low, 3″..........30.00
Bowl, turq, sgn Stephen/1946, 4″..........55.00
Bowl vase, gr matt, pink w/in, sgn, 4¾x4¼″..........35.00
Bowl vase, turq, 1937, 4½″..........36.00
Creamer, Cameo, dk gr w/wht wagon/etc, Stephen/1960, 3″....175.00
Pitcher, aqua, 1938, 5″..........23.00
Pitcher, bl gloss, w/lid, 5¼″..........25.00
Pitcher, Cameo, gr w/wht covered wagon, Stephen/1953, 2¾″..140.00
Pitcher, Cameo, gr/bl, band w/wagons, pink w/in, 5″..........250.00
Pitcher, Cameo, pink/gr, Indian/buffalo, 1930, 6″..........280.00
Pitcher, Cameo, western scene, sgn Stephen/1941, 5½x6″.....280.00
Vase, aqua, pink w/in, 1942, 3″..........16.00
Vase, Cameo, bl/brn, wagons/etc, sgn Stephen/1940, 6¾″......465.00
Vase, cream, pink w/in, 1940, 3¼″..........20.00
Vase, crystalline, EX bl w/wht, Stephen/1941, 7x4½″..........195.00
Vase, crystalline, wht/cream w/bl & pink, 6¼″..........165.00
Vase, forest gr, pink w/in, 3-hdl, 13½x10½″..........95.00
Vase, gr gloss, pink w/in, mk Stephen/1948, 4¾″..........40.00
Vase, gr gloss, 3-hdl, 5¼″..........25.00
Vase, gr matt, touches of red in glaze, 6¼″..........40.00
Vase, gr-bl, pink w/in, 1938, 3″..........23.00
Vase, maroon, 1950s, 6″..........23.00

Left to right: Mug, pate-sur-pate buffaloes and Indian on horseback, white on green, signed Stephen, 1961, 2¾″, $200.00; Mug, experimental Wedgwood-type cameo, wagon and oxen, green on white, 3¼″, $150.00.

Pittsburgh

As early as 1797, utility window glass and hollowware were being produced in the Pittsburgh area. Coal had been found in abundance, and it was there that it was first used instead of wood to fuel the glass furnaces. Because of this, as many as 150 glass companies operated there at one time. However, most failed due to the economically disasterous effects of the War of 1812. By the mid-1850s, those that remained were producing a wide range of flint glass items including pattern-molded and free-blown glass, cut and engraved wares, and pressed tableware patterns.

When no condition is indicated, the items listed below are assumed to be in undamaged condition.

Bottle, bar; 8 panels, bulbous lip, sapphire bl, 11″..........495.00
Bottle, bar; 8 ribs w/applied cobalt, 12½″, NM..........550.00
Bottle, gemel; free blown, red & wht loopings, 10″..........265.00
Bowl, folded rim, cobalt, 3x7″..........450.00
Candlestick, pillar mold, flint, wide ft, bulb stem, 10″..........635.00
Carafe, pillar mold, 3 applied neck rings, opaque wht..........265.00
Compote, cut & frosted swags w/bellflower tassels, 7x8″....275.00
Compote, cut panels, strawberry diamonds & fans, 7x9″, EX...245.00
Compote, cut strawberry diamonds/fans/circles, 7x10½″..........400.00
Compote, hollow baluster stem, folded rim, 7½x9″, VG..........135.00
Compote, pillar mold, flint, ribbed, folded rim, 6x8″..........165.00
Compote, pillar mold, flint, wide ft, flared, 9x11½″..........435.00
Compote, Princess Feather, hairpin base, 3x7½″..........275.00
Compote, 12 swirl rib, wafer & baluster stem, w/lid, 6x6″......275.00
Cordial, 6 cut panels, wafer stem, flared, canary, 3⅜″..........250.00
Creamer, eng florals, tooled threading, rib hdl, 5″, NM......1,450.00
Cruet, lt vertical ribs in base, disk stopper, cobalt, 7″..........200.00
Decanter, pillar mold, hollow hdl, collar, cobalt, 10¾″..........550.00
Decanter, pillar mold, 8 ribs, canary, pewter top, 11″..........600.00
Flask, chestnut; 19 ribs broken swirl, sapphire bl, 4⅛″..........625.00
Hat, blown, amber, 5½x7″..........75.00
Jar, pickle; flared folded rim, cylindrical, 10½x12″..........155.00
Jigger, 15 arched ribs, sapphire bl, 2¼″..........55.00
Jigger, 8 arched panels, sapphire bl, 2¼″..........40.00
Lantern chimney, eng banner w/RH Sawer & swags, 5″, EX.....75.00
Pan, applied cobalt rim on clear, 2⅜x5⅞″..........175.00
Pitcher, cut panels, strawberry diamonds & fans, 6½″, EX.....400.00
Pitcher, pillar mold, applied hdl, amethyst tint, 6½″..........275.00
Pitcher, pillar mold, flint, applied hdl, pontil, 9″..........200.00
Pitcher, pillar mold/8 swirl ribs, hollow hdl, violet, 8½″......7,200.00
Pitcher, 12 rib swirl, solid hdl, 9¾″..........425.00
Salt cellar, 6 panels, cobalt, 3″, EX..........45.00
Spill holder, punty & bull's eye, fiery opal, EX..........525.00
Sugar bowl, flanged, knob finial, cobalt, wht w/in, 7″..........1,400.00
Sugar bowl, flat knop stem, eng leaves, applied finial, 8″.....1,000.00
Sugar bowl, wafer stem, domed lid w/folded rim, 8½″..........400.00
Sugar bowl, 12 vertical ribs, dome lid, 7½″..........400.00
Syrup, 8 ribs, ftd, hollow hdl, pewter bird finial, 11″..........450.00
Tumbler, cut panel w/strawberry diamonds & fans, 3½″..........65.00
Tumbler, 6 panel, bl-aqua, 3½″, NM..........65.00
Tumbler, 7 panels & arches, sapphire, 3⅜″..........65.00
Tumbler, 8 panel, fiery opal, 3¼″..........95.00
Vase, cut & eng florals, swirl base, wafer stem, ftd, 8½″.......600.00
Vase, lg bowl w/folded rim, wide applied ft, 11″, NM..........140.00
Vase, pillar mold, flint, baluster stem, scalloped, 9″..........105.00
Vase, wafer stem, imp diamond diapering, eng florals, 8⅜″.....735.00
Whiskey, clear w/applied bl rim, 2″..........65.00
Whiskey, cut strawberry diamonds & fans, 2⅜″..........40.00

Playing Cards

Playing cards can be an enjoyable way to trace the course of history. The art, literature, and politics of an era can be gleaned from a study of its playing cards. When royalty lost favor with the people, Kings and Queens were replaced by common people. During the periods of w , generals, officers, and soldiers were favored. In the United States, early examples had portraits of Washington and Adams as opposed to Kings, Indian chiefs instead of Jacks, and goddesses for Queens.

Tarot cards were used in Europe during the 1300s as a game of chance, but in the 18th century they were used to predict the future, and were regarded with great reverence.

The backs of cards were of no particular consequence until the 1890s. The marble design used by the French during the late 1800s and the colored wood-cut patterns of the Italians in the 19th century are among the first attempts at decoration. Later, the English used cards printed with portraits of royalty. Eventually cards were decorated with a broad range of subjects from reproductions of fine art to advertising.

Although playing cards are becoming a popular collectible, prices are still relatively low. Complete decks of cards printed earlier than the first postage stamp can still be purchased for less than $100.

Periodic auction catalogs are available from 'Full House' Antique Playing Cards and Gambling Memorabilia. See the Directory under 'Clubs, Newsletters and Catalogs' for their address.

When no condition is indicated, the items listed below are assumed to be in excellent condition.

Key:

C—complete	J—Joker
cts—courts	OB—original box
hc—hand colored	sz—size

Advertising

Bovril, English, wide, ad on ea Ace, 1925, no J, 52, VG........18.00
Cutty Sark Whiskey, sailing ship bks, 1920s, OB..............12.00
Nash 50th Anniv, Great Cars for 50 yrs, 1902-52, sealed.......25.00
Old Saratoga, Perfection PCC, ca 1890, 52+J, OB, VG........50.00
Van Camp Pork & Beans, gold edges, special Aces/Spades, OB...6.00
Whannis Ginger Ale, J: man on wall fishing in bucket, 1895....25.00

France and Belgium

Aluette, Dieudonne, Angers, 1890 tax stamp/gold corners, C....75.00
Fluorescent, by Heron, blk w/yel suits, ca 1960, 52+JJ, OB......8.00
Melbourne Olympics, track & rings, orange/navy, sealed OB.....16.00
Salvador Dali, Fourn #450, ca 1969, 52+J..................55.00
Tennis Brand, Beirman, early tennis scene, 1926, 52+J, OB....10.00
1900 Paris Expo, Geuens-Willaert, sq corners/no indices, C.....25.00

Games

Hoods' War Game, US/Spain, CL Wood, 1900, 45-star flag bk...25.00
Old Maid, McLoughlin Bros, NY, orig box...................15.00
Smiler, Cow & Gate Milk Co, English, ca 1900, 48 C, VG......12.00
Touring, Wallie Dow Co, ca 1920, 100C, OB, VG.............15.00
Trolley, by Snyder, 1904, C w/booklet, orig long box, VG.......20.00
Votes for Women, Panko, by Gurney, 1918, 48C, OB, EX......60.00

Germany, Austria, and Czechoslovakia

Czech Trappola, M Severa/Ant Kratchovil, Prag, 1890 stamp...125.00
Dondorft #145, 1908 Italian tax stamp, 52C, OB, EX.........450.00
Paitnik, lg crown pattern, 1920 tax stamp, 32C, EX...........20.00
Patience, WUST, hc, dbl deck, ca 1860, in needlepoint case...225.00
Piquet Karten #54, CL Wust, sq corners/no indices, C, OB.....50.00

Great Britain

Barribal Guitarrista, narrow named, gold bk ground, 52, VG....25.00
Goodall, Royalty: Geo V, Prince of Wales/Princess Mary, VG...175.00
Goodall Bezique, sq corners, no indices, 1870, 32C, VG.........8.00
Our Prince, in Army uniform, waves: Hello Canada, 1920, VG...36.00
Queen Victoria Dia Jubilee, gray ground, historic cts, EX......110.00
Shakesperian, Original by Waddington, ca 1914, 52+J, OB.....95.00
Stopforth & Sons, sq corner, no indices, 1-way cts, 32C.......100.00
Worshipful, Royal Visit to S Africa, red border, 1947, VG......40.00

Italy, Spain, and Latin America

Bullfight, Guerrero for Uruguay, ca 1940, 52+J, OB, EX.......16.00
Giuoco D'Arme, ltd ed reprint of DiBrianville Heraldic.........18.00
Naipes Nacionales, by Jaques, ca 1940, 40C, orig wrapper......50.00
Panguingue, by Roura, Barcelona, 1940, 112+2 extra, C.......35.00
100th Anniv of death of Manzoni, plastic, lt ed, C/in case.......17.00

Miniatures and Patience

Czech Patience, by Casino, film: Baker Emperor cts, 52+JJ.....10.00
Dondoft #163, dbl deck, red tax stamp, ca 1900, VG/in case....15.00
Dondorf #27, 4 Corners o/t Earth, sq corners, 1880, OB, VG...40.00
Tom Thumb, by Woolley, sq corners/no indices, 1890, OB, EX..20.00

Souvenir and Expositions

Chicago Views, radium finish, for AC McClury, 1900, OB, EX...80.00
Columbia River Highway, Multinomah Falls, tax dtd 1917, OB...65.00
Columbian Expo, by Clark, 1893, 52+J+blank, VG...........50.00
Hopi Boy, scenic souvenir, 43 of 52, scarce..................75.00
San Diego Zoo, 54 photos of animals, C, OB.................11.00
WA State, gold edges, 1899, 52+J & map card, EX..........40.00
Yellowstone Park, wide, scenic, orange/wht bks, C, OB, VG.....18.00

Tarot and Fortune Telling

Astrological Fate, USPC, ca 1909, 52+3 extra+12 zodiac, OB..40.00
Etteilla, sq corner/dbl border, 1890 tax stamp, VG............60.00
Gumppenberg Tarot, hc copper engraved, ca 1835, 75 of 78...350.00
Gypsy Lore, 1918..10.00
Livre du Destin, Grimaud, sq corners/1890 tax stamp, C, VG....65.00
Witches of Fortune, #62, ca 1898.........................25.00
Wizard, fortune on ea card, England, ca 1900, 52+, OB, VG...60.00

Transformations

Kinney, full sz, ca 1899, bks damaged from mounting, 52+J...120.00
Samuel Hart, US, ca 1860, extremely rare, C, worn & soiled...400.00
Ye Witches #62, USPC, ca 1896, 1 damaged card, C, OB, VG..45.00

Transportation: Airline, Steamship, Railroad

Aberdeen SS Line, London to Australia, 1910, 52, OB, VG.....30.00
Am Airlines, eagle w/AA in circle on gray, ca 1948............10.00
Am Airlines Collector Series, DH-4/Ford Tri Motor, pr..........8.00
Columbus Line, B&B, 52+JJ..............................5.00
LLoyd-Trestino Line, by Piatnik, Jubilee Whist, '20, VG........50.00
NYK Line, Goodall, special Aces/Spades, 1935, OB, VG........12.00
P&O, pink/wht bks, DeLaRue Pneumatic, ca 1910, 52+J, OB...30.00
Phillipine Airlines, by Maesmakers, silver bks, 1965............10.00

United States

A Dougherty, 26 Beekman, bl Aces/Spades, no indices, 1865....65.00
American PCC, gold edges, ca 1875, 52C, NM...............50.00
Bannister Babies II, Card Quips by B&B, 52+J, OB..........20.00
BonBons, wide name, USPC, monotone, no border, bl, C, OB...20.00
Boxer brand PC by USPC, dragon J, gold edge, 52+J.........45.00
Bridge HQ Contest Hands, deals 12 hands, 1932, 52+3, C/OB..40.00
Buster Brown PC, comic strip faces, patience sz, 1906, OB.....55.00

Car-D-Ice, dice playing, ca 1930, 52+J, rare, OB, VG..........25.00
Caterson & Brotz, ca 1880, unusual J, 52+J, VG.............40.00
Faro, Samuel Hart NY, sq corner, no indices, 1-way cts, C......75.00
Kennedy Kards, 1963, 52+J, OB.........................20.00
Laugh In, ea w/quip from TV show, Rowan/Martin cts, OB......20.00
NY Athletic Club, USPC, special Aces/Spades/bks, 52+J, OB.....6.00
Poetry, by Congress, wide name/gold edge, dbl pinochle, OB....25.00
Queen High Equality, Emjay, 1971, 52+JJ+title card..........22.00
Russell's Regents, Willis Russell, Romeo/Juliet, 52+J, OB......50.00
Sportsman's, Russell & Morgan Ptg, 1886, 52, no J, VG........25.00
Squeezers #220, NYCC, steamboat box, tax stamp: 1899.......35.00
Stage 65X, USPC, different star on ea, 1908, 52+J, OB........65.00
Transparent, by Transparent PCC, NY, ca 1860, rare, 52+J...250.00
Twin-Dex, narrow name, Russell Regents–390, Hunting/Spring...50.00
1932 Olympic Games, Wenger, 52+J (Joe E Brown), OB......100.00

Political Entourage

The most valuable political items are those from any period which relate to a political figure whose term was especially significant or marked by an important event, or one whose personality was particularly colorful. Posters, ribbons, badges, photographs, and pin-back buttons are but a few examples of the items popular with collectors of political memorabilia.

Political campaign pin-back buttons were first mass-produced and widely distributed in 1896 for the president-to-be William McKinley and for the first of three unsuccessful attempts by William Jennings Bryan. Pin-back buttons have been used during each presidential campaign ever since and are collected by many people. The scarcest ones are those used in the presidential campaigns for James Davis in 1924 and for James Cox in 1920.

When no condition is indicated, the items listed below are assumed to be in excellent condition. See also Autographs.

Badge, Cox/Roosevelt, cb Cox picture, buckeye drop, 1920....325.00
Badge, Hughes, bronze, bl ribbon: Chief Aide 1916, M........125.00
Badge, McKinley Honest Dollar..........................85.00
Badge, Republican '96 Convention/Citizens Committee header...45.00
Badge, shield w/eagle, US Police, Carter inauguration, '77.....175.00
Book, song; Garfield/Arthur campaign, 1880.................18.00
Bookmark, For Pres...Bryan/photo, bl/wht celluloid, tassel.....125.00
Bookmark, silk, Wilson pin-back attached, 1912 Convention....35.00
Bottle stopper, Eisenhower figural.......................75.00
Box, Rumform Flour, wood, 'Vote for Dewey' stencil..........50.00
Button, Alf Landon, sunflower/picture, 1¼"..................9.00
Button, Bryan/Keaton, jugate, sepia, 1908.................350.00
Button, Bryan/Stevenson, shield design, 1¼"................30.00
Button, Cleveland/Hendrix, brass........................32.00
Button, clothing; Henry Clay, bust faces left, name, NM.......100.00
Button, clothing; Seymour ferro, bead border, 21mm, NM.....175.00
Button, clothing; Taylor, Rough & Ready/Hero..., brass, NM....45.00
Button, Debs/Hanford, Socialist Party, 1904.................85.00
Button, Gen MacArthur, portrait.........................10.00
Button, Hoover, inaugural, w/picture, 1929, 1¼"..............22.00
Button, John Davis, ⅞"..................................65.00
Button, Lafayette, presentation brass, 1844..................68.00
Button, LaFolette/Wheeler, bronze.......................30.00
Button, Pres Wilson portrait............................10.00
Button, Roosevelt, A Gallant Leader, w/picture...............7.00
Button, Roosevelt/Fairbanks, jugate......................15.00
Button, Teddy Roosevelt, celluloid.......................22.00
Button, Wilson/Marshall jugate.........................15.00
Button, Wm H Harrison, brass, 1840......................58.00
Button, Wm Taft, w/photo, 1¾"..........................85.00
Card game, Teddy Bear, 22 cards show Roosevelt, mc, M.......50.00
Cigar label, Taft portrait, mc, 2½", M.......................20.00
Compact, lady's; I Like Ike...............................35.00
Ferrotype, Stephen Douglas & Herschel Johnson, 1860.........72.00
Hat, I Like Ike..10.00
Invitation, Eisenhower inaugural ball, w/envelope..............25.00
Knife, pocket; etched picture of President Warren Harding......65.00
Lapel stud, Harrison....................................15.00
Locket, tortoiseshell w/pinchbeck rim, Lincoln photo, 1"......160.00
Magazine, Life, John F Kennedy memorial ed................15.00
Magazine rack, Washington & Lincoln busts, metal, 21x16"....195.00
Medal, Cleveland emb signature on brass bar, cb photo drop....80.00
Medal, Grant bust/tomb, 1897, Numismatic Society, bronze.....95.00
Medal, Nixon/Agnew, bronze, Franklin Mint, 1973............40.00
Medal, Washington, Indian Peace, 1789, bronze, 2½", NM.....160.00
Medal, Washington, Roman bust, Voltaire/1778, bronze, 41mm.190.00
Medal, Wilson 1913 official inaugural, bronze, 2¾", EX.......225.00
Medallion, Abraham Lincoln, bk: wreath w/dates, bronze, 3"....50.00
Mirror, Wallace bust/FDR shadow behind, b/w celluloid, 2".....45.00
Mug, Gen Eisenhower toby, mk Barrington, 1950s, 7".........85.00
Mug, mc Taft/Sherman portrait, porcelain, 5", EX.............50.00
Pail, glass; McKinley, Full Dinner Pail, Pick & Co, no lid......195.00
Paperweight, Eisenhower, profile molded w/in.................35.00
Paperweight, McKinley...................................30.00
Parade torch, Grant campaign, wood staff, tin, rare, 1868.......95.00
Pencil, Roosevelt/Garner jugate, mc celluloid, 1936............65.00
Photo, Al Smith, autograph, in orig fr......................45.00
Photo, Senator Mondale, autograph, orig senator's envelope.....20.00
Pin, eagle, Cleveland/Hendricks jugate, 1885 inauguration......250.00
Plaque, Grant bust in horseshoe, gilt iron, Let Us...Peace.......80.00
Plaque, Grant/Colfax, relief busts Washington & Lincoln.....2,090.00
Plate, Garfield, clear glass...............................45.00
Plate, McKinley/Roosevelt, brn transfer, milk glass, 5½"........30.00
Playbill, Ford's Theatre, night of Lincoln's Assassination.....1,800.00
Poster, Charles E Hughes for President, 1916, 17x21".........60.00
Poster, Cox/Roosevelt, w/sepia photos, 16x20"...............45.00
Poster, Herbert Hoover for Pres, w/portrait, 1928.............15.00
Program, Roosevelt/Fairbanks inaugural, 1905................30.00
Program, Roosevelt/Garner inaugural, Mar/1933..............20.00
Program, Truman inaugural, 1949..........................16.00
Puzzle, Roosevelt, 3-D, Technocrat, 2¼x4"..................25.00
Shakers, JFK in rocking chair, dtd 1962, pr..................25.00
Snuff box, Washington medallion/burlwood, 1790s, 2⅞x1¾", M.995.00
Spoon, Cleveland/wife busts, baby (Ruth) in bowl, sterling.......40.00

Plaque, bust profile of Lincoln, bronze, 10½" x 8½", $125.00.

Textiles

Andrew Jackson's Farewell Address, silk, portrait/eagle........215.00
Armband, FDR campaign, red felt w/bl Repeal & Roosevelt.....50.00
Bandana, B Harrison/L Morton, stars/stripes border, 1888.....250.00
Bandana, Cleveland & Thurman, eagle/flag, 22x26", EX.......160.00
Bandana, FDR Carry On, 1940 w/1932 retoric, rare, 21".......55.00
Bandana, Garfield/Arthur jugate, canal boat scene, eagle.......165.00
Bandana, Hancock & English, wht/red/blk, minor stains, 22"...145.00
Bandana, Harrison/Morton, bl w/portraits & flags, 22", NM....165.00
Bandana, I Like Ike, w/elephant, red/bl/blk on wht, 13"........55.00
Bandana, McKinley/Hobart, silk w/photographic images, sm.....40.00
Bandana, Phila Intn'l Exhibition 1876, Washington/Grant......100.00
Bandana, Protection for Am Industries, red/wht/bl, 27".........75.00
Bandana, Roosevelt Battle Flag 1912, Progressive, portrait......55.00
Bandana, Roosevelt caricature, TR in cowboy hat in center.....75.00
Bandana, Wilkie, stars/stripes, red/bl on wht, 1940, 22"........45.00
Bandana, Win w/Ike for President, swag/stars/portrait, 28"......45.00
Banner, McKinley, bl/wht stars, Patriotism/etc, silk, 23".......125.00
Banner, mourning; Franklin D Roosevelt, woven silk, 12x16"....40.00
Banner, Wm Penn bust, Bi-Centennial 1682-1882, Phila, 37"...50.00
Flag, Benjamin Harrison, 1892, bust portrait, 10x14".........235.00
Flag, Grover Cleveland in oval, red/bl/brn on wht, 25x18".....300.00
Flag, Lincoln/Hamlin.................................2,090.00
Flag, Lincoln/Johnson, cotton............................2,200.00
Flag, US Grant for President, S Colfax for Vice, 5x7"..........30.00
Flag banner, Lincoln/Hamlin, 1860.......................8,250.00
Flag banner, Stephen A Douglas/Herschal Johnson, 1860....4,070.00
Greeley/Brown: Reform & Liberty; Grant/Wilson: Victory.....2,625.00
Pennant, Elect Thos Dewey Pres, w/picture, lg................12.00
Pennant, Garfield/Arthur, red/bl cotton, 10x28", EX..........105.00
Pennant, Truman bust, 35th Division Reunion, 26"............65.00
Pillow, pictures Wilson & Pershing, WWI, fringe, slogans.......45.00
Ribbon, BF Butler, The People's Choice 1884, b/w, rare......225.00
Ribbon, Blaine Logan & Victory, portrait JGB, gold/purple......50.00
Ribbon, Fisk/Brooks jugate, 1888.........................225.00
Ribbon, Harrison & Morton, 1888..........................90.00
Ribbon, Harrison/Reid jugate, woven silk, eagle/shield, M......100.00
Ribbon, Henry Clay......................................95.00
Ribbon, McKinley/Hobart portraits, slogan, Oct 31, '96, 7"......35.00
Ribbon, Republican National Convention 1892/Press, M........25.00
Ribbon, Washington, eagle, Centennial, silk, 3x18"............50.00
Ribbon, Washington/eagle/flags, silk, JB Champromy, 6x10".....55.00
Ribbon, WH Harrison memorial, NY 4/10/41, elaborate, M......50.00
Scarf, Win with Ike for President, w/portrait, 26".............35.00
Umbrella, flags/stars, red/bl, Sprague Co, 38" dia, VG..........50.00
Washington, Effect of Principle, Behold the Man, 14", VG......75.00

Tie tack, Ike...20.00
Toby mug, Taft..70.00
Watch fob, Taft in large letters on suitcase shape.............25.00
Watch fob, Taft portrait in blk/gold brass shield, NM..........40.00
Watch fob, Taft/Sherman, Good Luck, 1908, w/strap...........20.00
Watch fob, Wilson on 1½" dia celluloid, mk Moffet, 5½".......35.00
Watch fob, Wm Jennings Bryan, no strap....................95.00
Wheaton bottle, JF Kennedy..............................25.00
Wheaton bottle, Nixon/Agnew, amber.......................20.00

Pomona

Pomona glass was patented in 1885 by the New England Glass Works. Its characteristics are an etched background of crystal lead glass often decorated with simple designs painted with metallic stains of amber or blue. The etching was first achieved by hand cutting through an acid resist. This method, called first grind, resulted in an uneven feather-like frost effect. Later, to cut production costs, the hand-cut process was discontinued in favor of an acid bath, which effected an even frosting. This method is called second grind.

When no condition is indicated, the items listed below are assumed to be in mint condition.

Bowl, 2nd grind, bl cornflowers, ruffled, 2½x5½".............175.00
Bowl, 2nd grind, cornflowers, crimped rim, 8"................260.00
Carafe, 2nd grind, cornflowers............................190.00
Creamer, 2nd grind, blueberries..........................250.00
Cruet, 2nd grind, Inverted T'print, toed base...............250.00
Cup, punch; 1st grind, Baby T'print w/cornflower decor.......160.00
Cup, punch; 1st grind, bl cornflowers+6-Row hobnail, 2½"....165.00
Cup, punch; 1st grind, plain..............................65.00
Finger bowl, 2nd grind, ruffled, amber edge, w/underplate.....100.00
Finger bowl, 2nd grind, ruffled, amber edge, 6"...............75.00
Pitcher, lemonade; 1st grind, 2 rows bl cornflowers, 12".......985.00
Pitcher, 1st grind, sq top, plain, 4½"......................150.00
Pitcher, 2nd grind, butterfly & wheat, 9½"..................945.00
Toothpick holder, Dia Optic amber rim, incurvate/scalloped....145.00
Toothpick holder, 2nd grind, tricorn top...................145.00
Tumbler, 1st grind, hobnail, tapered, 3¾"..................100.00
Tumbler, 2nd grind, acanthus leaves in amber, 3¾"..........115.00
Tumbler, 2nd grind, cornflowers..........................150.00
Tumbler, 2nd grind, pansy & butterfly......................175.00
Vase, 1st grind, cornflowers.............................195.00
Water set, 1st grind, Inverted Dia Quilt w/in, 7-pc............750.00

Pitcher, 2nd grind, acorn and oak leaf decor, 8", $385.00.

Popcorn and Peanut Machines

The popcorn and peanut machines that were a popular sight a century ago were often elaborately decorated. Some were designed with special attention-getting features, such as a small clown to turn the peanut roaster, or a fascinating steam engine placed where curious onlookers could watch it power the rotating corn popper. The vendor hoped that should the enticing aroma of his wares go unnoticed, the appeal of his machine would capture the attention of those passing by!

Peanut roaster, electric/belt pulley, Holcomb & Hoke, rstr.....350.00
Peanut roaster, sidewalk-type, Bartholomew, rstr, 1900s......1,500.00
Popcorn machine & peanut roaster, Holcomb/Hoke, unrstr...3,500.00

Post Cards

A German by the name of Von Stephan is credited for inventing the postcard, first printed in Austria in 1869. They were eagerly accepted by the Continentals and the English alike, who saw them as a more economical way to send written messages. Three years later post cards were introduced in America.

The first to be printed in the United States were plain U.S. postal cards. Photo cards, first sold here in the 1880s, were made in Germany by order of the Leighton Company of Portland, Maine. But the Columbian Exposition of 1892-93 was the spark that ignited the post card phenomenon. Souvenir cards by the thousands were sent to folks back home--Expo scenes, transportation themes, animals, birds, and advertising messages became popular. There were patriotic themes, Black themes, and cards for every occasion.

In 1907, the Payne-Aldrich Bill placed such a high tariff on imported cards that dealers began to turn to American printers and lithographers. Some of the earliest post card publishers were Raphael Tuck, and Nister and Gabriel. Early 20th century illustrators such as Brundage, Rose O'Neill, and Clapsaddle designed cards that are especially valued today.

Though the post card rage waned at the onset of WWI, they rank today among the most sought-after paper collectibles.

When no condition is indicated, the items listed below are assumed to be in excellent condition, whether used or unused.

A Quiet Game, 3 Black boys shoot craps......................5.00
Advertising, Coca-Cola, Pause That Refreshes, pre-1920........10.00
Advertising, litho interior, ship Oceana, Hamburg line, pr.......10.00
Advertising, Metropolitan Insurance, employees, set of 10.......25.00
Advertising, Red Star Line, officers on deck, sgn Cassiers.......15.00
Advertising, Walkover Shoes, Pilgrim scenes, set of 8..........35.00
Alligator border, The Plaza/St Augustine, Langsdorf..........25.00
American Girl series, The Henry Hutt Girl, Amrour & Co........7.50
Atwell, Mabel Lucie; Do Please Write, girl at desk, #490........7.00
Atwell, Mabel Lucie; Got a Cigawette Picture, rompered boy......7.00
Atwell, Mabel Lucie; Hush!, girl/sleeping child/golliwog.........12.00
Atwell, Mabel Lucie; Nobody Loves Me, puppy/girl/new baby......7.00
Auto, Bluebird race car, Sir Malcolm Campbell, on linen........6.00
Baseball comic, Safe, players kisses lady catcher, sepia..........5.00
Billy Possum, Good Eating Here, eats Teddy Bear, sgn Crite....14.00
Boileau, Phillip; Lullabye, young mom w/sleeping baby.........16.00
Boileau, Phillip; The Flirt, boy & girl in skating hats...........16.00
Brown, Tom; Out Paced, auto comic, car passes buggy..........8.00
Brundage, Frances; Little Miss Muffett, girl/spider, Tuck........25.00
Bunnel, Thanksgiving, King for a Day, Lounsbury..............9.00
Busy Bears, Days of the Week/Friday, mopping floor, Austin.....7.50
Campaign, I'm for Dick Nixon/How About You?, 1960..........7.00
Canal scene, Aqueduct, Delaware Canal......................4.00
Carmichael, I Love My Wife but Oh You Kid series, milkmaid....6.50
Carr, Gene; Pals, rough-looking boy holds lg firecracker.........8.00
Carr, Gene; St Patrick's, After the Parade, Rotograph...........9.00
Cat, Now You Stop, female w/tassels at neck, A Thiele.........12.00
Charming Children, riding cockhorse, etc; Ill PC Co, 6 for......25.00
Christy, F Earl; Tommie, flirty girl's hair forms '?'............12.00
Christy, F Earl; woman w/gr hat, wht feathers, gr gown.........10.00
Clapsaddle, Easter, boy paints eggs/barrel/chicks, VG............6.50
Clapsaddle, July 4th, Liberty & Union..., girl sews flag..........10.00
Clapsaddle, July 4th, We Will Stand, Uncle Sam-type boy.......10.00
Clapsaddle, New Year's, gold key/bl ribbon/gold '1912'.........10.00
Clapsaddle, St Patrick's, family in speeding car.................7.50
Clapsaddle, Valentine, Indian boy & girl, lg heart, VG...........8.50
Clapsaddle, Valentine, King/Queen of Hearts holding hands.....15.00
Clipper Ship Dreadnought, metallic luminous finish.............7.00
Coin card, Portugal, 11 coins, highly emb, Walter Erhard.......14.00
Comic, Funny Man Series, #3/Man of Leisure & Optimist, PFB..10.00
Comic, Mother-In-Law Series, #3/I Always Did Maintain, PFB....10.00
Cracker Jack Bears, on ship at Jamestown Expo, Moreland.....18.00
Decoration Day, series #1, set of 6, gold border, Nash.........42.00
Die-cut country scene, cottage, moon, windows light up........17.00
Dirigible, Departure of Patrie, French, very close shot..........18.00
Donald Duck, as cowboy, w/nephews, Coming My Way, 1950s...15.00
Donald Duck, dancing, #2, Meco, Lisbon, Portugal, 1946.......15.00
Donald Duck & Daisy w/rolling pin, late 1940s, Paletti.........10.00
Dutch Children series, boy w/fishing pole & pail, PFB...........7.50
DWIG, Smiles series #169, red border, set of 12, VG-EX.......75.00
Early airship, The Famous Stobel, St Louis, 1907..............10.00
Early stagecoach, in front of New Hampshire post office.........7.50
Early views, Livingston's Picturesque America, White House......6.00
Ebner, P; Son Anniversaire, little girl reads letter, VG..........14.00
Ebner, P; The Scolding, girl w/elegant dolls & furniture.........14.00
Ebner, Pauli; children in doorway, child-angels with sled........14.00
Fantasy, semi-nudes in smoke from cigarette, 2 on matchbox....17.00
Fire engine, early motorized, Flying Squadron, Manchester.......9.00
Fire engine, horse-drawn/by station, Camp Custer, Michigan......7.00
Fisher, Harrison; King of Hearts, mom & dad w/baby, VG......15.00
Fisher, Harrison; Sketching, woman w/pad & pencil, #616......15.00
Gibson, CD; Bertha, Sepia series #1, #52, Henderson...........9.00
Gibson, CD; Irene, woman's head against lt gr ground...........9.00
Gibson, CD; Last Day of Summer, couple on beach, b/w.........9.00
Golf comic, Disaster on the Links, Scotsman w/broken club......6.00
Golliwog, full size photo, Oh, Golly!, Davidson Bros...........20.00
Golliwog, full view w/blk felt face, publisher: Valentine..........25.00
Griggs, HB; black devil with jack-o'-lantern, VG...............12.00
Griggs, HB; Miss Columbia speaking to small G Washington....10.00
Halloween, owl on pumpkin, witch rides owl, Winsch, EX.......35.00
Halloween, 2 owls on branch, moon in bkground, Whitney.......9.00
HM Queen Alexandra, bas relief, b/w, 'jewels' & glitter..........8.50
Hold-to-light, belle in ermine, snake appears, EX..............15.00
Hold-to-light, Gruss Aus Koln, center city, pre-1920, VG.........25.00
Hold-to-light, Santa die-cut, brn robe, kids on balcony..........95.00
Hold-to-light, woman sitting/stork brings twins, VG...........15.00
Horoscope, April, tulip & diamond, Nouveau, Southwick.........8.00
Humanized cats, The Governess, teacher w/4 kittens, b/w........8.00
Innis, John; Indians in a Snow Storm, VG......................8.50
Innis, John; Northwest Mounted Policeman, VG...............20.00
Installment set, Fish Story, fish/surprised man, Wildwood.......20.00
Interior scene, Dental Parlor, Dr Richan, shows equipment......12.00
Jamestown Exposition, 1907, Bird's Eye View, Bosselman Co.....5.00
Kewpies, Think of Me, bride/groom, Klever Kard #293.........30.00
King, H; Coney Island Girl, bathing beauty....................9.00
Kirchner, R; A Peep/lady w/mirror, Bruton Gallery, unsgn......25.00
Kirchner, R; Geisha, 2 under parasol, man behind, VG.........60.00
Leap Year, woman chooses 1 of 3 men, 1912, 2 cards for......12.00
Lord's Prayer, set of 8 cards, emb, series #264, ASB..........60.00
Marsallus, Irene; Valentine, girl's face inside a daisy...........10.00
Mechanical, Christmas, children inside house, Clapsaddle.......35.00
Mechanical, Doing the Charleston, couple dances, Dennis Co....35.00
Mechanical, horseshoe of pansies/3 disks for calendar, PFB.....15.00
Mechanical, Valentine, sailor boy holds flowers, lifts hat........30.00
Night Before Christmas, gold trim, Nash, complete set of 6.....40.00
Novelty, Bathing Beauties, red & bl silk suits, VG............14.00
Novelty, bear in mountains, attached fur, sgn Linke.............9.00

Kewpie post cards, clockwise: seen through window, Kewpies chopping down Christmas tree; Christmas message--two Kewpies peek around door; New Year message, Kewpies ringing bell in tower; Kewpies helping Santa in window; $25.00 to $35.00 each.

Novelty, made from soil of Ireland, Limerick street scene.......15.00
Novelty, Magic Moving Picture, move tab & see cockfight.......25.00
Novelty, Young Lady Named Mabel, girl w/buttons for face......22.00
O'Neill, Rose; Valentine, It's Such a Dear, Kewpie wedding.....28.00
Outcault, Buster Brown & Tige/Blk boy eats melon, Tammen....10.00
PFB Co, Tea for One, comic old maid, #6742-1..............12.00
PFB Co, 2 girls in field of pink flowers, heavy emb, #7046.......7.00
Political, T Roosevelt, Good Motto series, Sheahan............10.00
Railroad station, Perkasie, PA, shows train, elegant.............5.00
Real photo, crowd greet Pres Taft at RR station in NH........10.00
Real photo, destructive storm at Winthrop Beach, MA..........7.00
Real photo, early touring car & riders, close view..............7.00
Real photo, horse & buggy w/passengers, close view............7.00
Real photo, Pope Benedict in Vatican corridor, very close.......4.50
Remington, F; Calling the Moose, c 1905, Detroit #14183......30.00
Russel, Chas; Antelope Hunting, Ridgely Calendar Co..........16.00
Sager, Xavier; man in formal attire views women..............20.00
Sager, Xavier; risque women w/WWI soldiers, 3 cards..........50.00
Santa, bl robe, seen through window, pull tab/boy appears......80.00
Santa, brn robe, pulls sled, heavy emb, glossy, United Art......12.00
Santa, gr suit, puts letter on mantle w/attached knit sock.......15.00
Santa, in snowstorm, icicle border, heavy emb, Davidson.......17.00
Santa, red silk suit, girl w/blue silk blanket, VG...............30.00
Santa, w/Turkish fez, dips dolls in dyepot, German, VG........18.00
Schultz, FW; Roping the Bull, western action scene............7.00
Smith, Jessie Wilcox; Among Poppies/3 kids in field, VG.......15.00
Snow Babies, children in fuzzy suits, sgn MEP, Stecher........12.00
Sowerby, M; elf sitting on dandelion watches mouse............8.00
Sowerby, M; Fairy Frolic, fairies & elves around campfire.......10.00
Sowerby, M; Peter Pan series, Wendy flying to Peter...........10.00
Sporty Bears, A Dip in the Surf, sgn MDS, Ulmann...........10.00
Stamp card, England, #40, 17 stamps, emb, Ottmar-Zieher.....12.00
Suffrage First, Votes for Women series, Campbell Art Co........45.00
Suffragettes attack policeman, National #641, Millar/Lang.......15.00
Tambourine Children, girl on pony, Anglo-American of NYC.....6.00
Tarrant, M; Toy Shop, boy/girl look in window, Medici Soc......6.00
Ten Commandments, I am the Lord, angels, PFB #8554-1......15.00
Thiele, A; How I Love You, poodle in straw hat, GANA Co.....14.00
Thiele, Arth; dachshund in tux greets female dog at door.......18.00
Thiele, Arth; Easter, rabbit family on stagecoach, VG..........16.00
Thiele, Arth; hunters ride horses attached to dirigibles.........20.00
Tuck, Breakfast In Bed, geese eating frogs, VG...............10.00
Tuck, Brown Paper series, Gossips & Under Control, pr.........8.00
Tuck, Connoisseur series, Rosalind, sgn Asti...................8.00
Tuck, Horse Heads, 2 steeds in harness, #9692, sgn Walker.....7.00
Tuck, Kris Kringle series, Santa at window/kids in bed, #5......12.00
Tuck, Lincoln's Birthday series #155, set of 6................50.00
Tuck, Military series #405, US Navy Captain, heavy emb, VG....16.00
Tuck, Queen's Doll's House/series I #4500, Wine Cellar.........5.00
Tuck, St Albans Pageant, Set #1, #9510, 6 cards, M...........50.00
Tuck, State Capitols series, Utah, building w/people, seal........5.00
Tuck, The Gordon Highlanders, military, sgn H Payne, 6 for....48.00
Tuck, Vignettes of London series, #s 1/5/7, litho, early.........30.00
Underwood, Clarence; Pleasant Reflections, lady w/mirror.......12.00
Upton, Florence; Golliwog in Prison, w/stick dolls, Tuck........28.00
US Navy Zepplin, over Akron Municipal Airport, linen, '40s......6.00
Valentine, embroidered silk, 2 bluebirds fly to red heart.........8.00
Wain, Louis; portrait of long-haired silver cat, G..............35.00
Wain, Louis; We Could Put Up..., 3 owls in tree, VG..........30.00
White House, Washington, copper windows, luminous...........5.00
Woven-in-silk, Marriage, b/w turns to color, Neyret Freres......40.00

Posters

Advertising posters by such French artists as Monet and Toulouse-Lautrec were used as early as the mid-1800s. Color lithography spurred their popularity. The circus, movies, and patriotic causes are popular categories with poster collectors today. Works of noted artists such as Fox, Parrish, and Herrick bring high prices. Other considerations are good color, interesting subject matter, and of course, condition.

When no condition is indicated, the items listed below are assumed to be in excellent condition. See also Circus Collectibles; Movie Memorabilia; Political Entourage

Key: lm—linen mounted

Advertising

Anheuser-Busch, Indians attack stagecoach, fr, 7x16"..........40.00
Burpee Seeds, Nasturtiums, 1934..........................135.00
DuPont, various game birds, 1920.........................165.00
Ferry's Seeds, flower vase/moon in window, '16, 28", NM......175.00
Galakton Infant Food, nanny w/baby, Penfield, 1890s, fr, M....575.00
Hercules Powder, A Double on Quail, 1922.................160.00
Hercules Powder, Right in the Blind, 1922..................150.00
Merchand's Golden Hair Wash, blonde in swimsuit, 1934, M....95.00
Michelin, To Your Health, Bibenbum/banquet table, '05, M....425.00
Murphy Bros Tailors, man in suit w/lady, fr, 14½x20", VG......30.00
Rocket Cycles, French officer on bicycle, ca 1900, lm, 51".....200.00
Schroeder & Sons Coach Works, 9 scenes, blk, 1879, 13x20"...40.00
Stutz, New Safety, sedan/lake scene, ca 1926, 28x37", M......500.00

Magic

Carter Beats the Devil, playing poker, ca '20, 14x22", M.......80.00
Kno, Russian magician w/match, girl in flame, 1959, 23x33"...125.00
Kuo the Magician/Soviet Circus, face w/spectacles, '53, lm.....300.00
Laurant, Man of Many Mysteries, man/rabbits, 1915, lm, M....275.00
Servais Leroy/Decapitation Mystery, 1905, Friedlander, lm.....450.00
Solanis, hat w/flowers/birds/etc, Conte, 1945, 26x39", M.......135.00

Minstrel

Baird's Famous, Midget 4/Zouave Cadets, 1880, lm, 54", M....285.00
Original White Star, 4 in military attire, 1880s, lm, NM.......300.00
Stock, man w/long pointed boots, 1899, Friedlander, 32"......300.00
2 Coons o/t Sunny South, portraits/vignettes, 1885, 20x24"....750.00

Theatrical

Agatha Christie Cafe Noir, woman w/cup, 1930s, 25x33", M....325.00
Aladdin, British local production, girl in cave, '20s, M..........50.00
Autobanditen Opera, 2 men in car, Friedlander, '13, M.......450.00
Cinderella, runs down steps, J Hassall, 1896, lm, 13x30"......300.00
Donskoi Ventrilique, man w/dog, 1906, Friedlander, 28x38"....425.00
In Old Kentucky, Blk marching band, 1893, Strobridge, 29"...350.00
Little Peggy O'Moore, man talks to girl, 1890s, 20x28", NM....75.00
Moscow Theater Festival, pianist/opera house, 1935, 28x40"...200.00
Sidonias Laugh Factory, couple on globe, 1913, Friedlander...400.00
The Stowaway, Dickie to the Rescue, ship, 1890s, 40", NM....225.00
Uncle Tom's Cabin, Lincoln w/kneeling slave, 1890s, 10x27"....75.00

Transportation

Int'l Boat Show/Paris, male mermaid, Dec 1928, 45x60", NM..675.00
Italian Air Armada/1933 Chicago Expo, planes over sea, 25"....40.00
Red Star Line, old sailor looks at ship, Cassiers, 26x27"......350.00
Schnebergbahn/Bei Wein, winged male, Alfred Roller, 34x45"..350.00
Speed to Winter Playgrounds/Pullman, woman/dogs, 1935, NM.300.00
SS France/Luxury for All, lg ship, Bob Peak, '62, 45", NM....225.00
Summer...Riviera, Blue Train/trestle, ca '25, lm, 26x40".......575.00
1912 Paris Airshow, pilot over Grand Palais, Dorival, NM......675.00

Travel

Australia, kangaroo, man w/boomerang, ca 1931, 26x40", M...165.00
Austria Invites You, young woman, Atelier, '30s, 26x38", M....275.00
Budapest, 2 men in steamy water, ca 1938, lm, 23x34", M.....300.00
Come to Ulster, Anchor Line, couple hiking, ca '30, 25x40"...125.00
Connemara (Ireland), LMS Rail, P Henry scene, 26x40", NM...150.00
Deauville (France), girl/car/ship/plane, '30s, 31x41", M........225.00
Deutschland, city street scene, Jupp Wiertz, 25x40", NM......475.00
Israel/Land of Bible, Jonah/whale, MJ David, '54, 27", M.......95.00
Mexico, Paricutan Volcano erupting, 1943, 29x40", M........200.00
Vichy (France), people/hotel, Tauzin, 1910s, lm, 26x39", M....350.00

War

A Careless Word/Another Cross, cross on beach, Atherton......65.00
America Calls/Navy, soldier & Columbia, Lyendecker, NM......425.00
Americans All, Columbia holds wreath/flag, Christy, 40x27"....125.00
And They Said We Couldn't Fight, soldier/helmets, mc litho.....50.00
Answer the Red Cross, buffalo in bl/red/gr on wht, 30x20"......50.00
At the Service of All Mankind, Red Cross savior, mc...........45.00
Avenge Dec 7th, angry man, Arizona exploding, B Perlin, M...100.00
Blood or Bread, man helping buddy from building, 30x20"....110.00
Books Wanted, Marine w/books, blk bkground, CB Falls, EX...200.00
Boys & Girls, Uncle Sam w/boy & girl, Flagg, 30x20"..........75.00
Britains & Canadians, red/bl/wht, ragged edges, 40x30"........20.00
Buy War Bonds, Uncle Sam leads soldiers/planes, Wyeth, EX..150.00
Careless Matches..., Japanese soldier/forest fire, 24", M.........50.00
Clear the Way, naval action w/sailors manning guns, 30x20"....90.00
Columbia Calls, Columbia on globe w/banner, Halstead, VG.....85.00
Come On, soldier w/rifle, mc, Whitehead, 30x20"............96.00
Do Your Duty/Join Marines, gun crew loading on deck, M......50.00
Eat Less...Be Thankful..., harvest scene, Hendee, EX, 30".....100.00
Every Girl Pulling for Victory, girl rowing boat, 22x28"........75.00
First...for Democracy, Marines, zeppelin, Schaefer, lm, EX.....165.00
For Home & Country, American GI w/wife & child, 40x30".....40.00
Gee! If I Were a Man/Navy, sailor girl, Christy, 1918, EX......475.00
Girl on the Land Serves the Nation's Need, 25x30"...........120.00
Girl Reserves of the YWCA, bl/blk/yel, 30x20"...............40.00

Britain's Day poster, illustrated by James Montgomery Flagg, very good condition, 30", $80.00.

Go Over the Top/Marines, Marine w/machine gun, mc, 30", EX.100.00
Have You Answered the Red Cross Christmas Roll Call, Fisher..25.00
He's Home Over There, nightime scene, Herter, 40x28"........30.00
Hun-His Mark-Blot It Out, bloody hand, St John, 40x30"......56.00
Hunger, hungry family, for Belgium, W Releigh, EX, 30".......75.00
I Want You for US Army, Uncle Sam pointing finger, Flagg....450.00
If You Want to Fight, Join the Marines, lady Marine, Christy...175.00
Invest, bl/red on wht, huge bl V, 20x20"....................20.00
Joan of Arc Saved France, brandishing sword, Coffin, EX.......60.00
Keep Him Free, American Bald Eagle, Bull, 30x20"...........76.00
Keep It Coming, Army food trucks, mc, 30x20"...............50.00
Lend 10% of Your Pay, falling paratrooper, 18x23", M.........75.00
Lest We Perish, promoting relief in Near East, 30x20", EX.....50.00
Let Santa Bring WSS to All Patriots, EX....................25.00
Look Who's Listening, Big 3 as rats, Seagram's, 18x24".........50.00
Make Our American Red Cross in Peace As in War, 30x20"....30.00
Must Children Die & Mothers Plead in Vain, 40x30", EX.......40.00
Not at Home to Autocracy, Anti-militarism theme, 22x30"......35.00
Our Carelessness/Their Secret Weapon, Hitler & Tojo, M.......75.00
Pro Patria/Join Army, Cavalrymen w/lg banners, Welsh, EX....150.00
Remember Argonne, Liberty Loan campaign, brn tones........45.00
Remember Belgium, Hun dragging girl, mc, Young............50.00
Ships Are Coming, American Bald Eagle/ships, 30x20".........70.00
Sights Set for Victory, female worker/lg gun sight, 40", M.....100.00
Sir Don't Waste While Your Wife Saves, bl/red/wht, 30x20".....45.00
Someone Talked, drowning man's hand points to viewer, 40"...125.00
Sow Seeds of Victory, Columbia w/basket, Flagg, EX, 20x30"..115.00
Spirit of America, Red Cross worker, mc, Christy..............60.00
Sword is Drawn, Columbia w/ships in bkground, lm, 40", EX...250.00
That Liberty Shall Not Perish from the Earth, Pennell, EX....135.00
The Drive, political cartoon poster, 1918, 22x30".............20.00
They Asked for It..., soldiers in truck, General Motors.........95.00
They Fight for You, Protect Them, wounded soldier...........80.00
Third Red Cross Roll Call, worker w/outstretched arms.........80.00
To Arms/Enlist in Navy, bugler, battleship bkground, EX......150.00

US Marine, Be a Sea Soldier, marine seated, mc, 40x30″.......70.00
US Marines, marine in uniform, ship in background..........120.00
US Marines, 2 Marines in uniform, 40x30″...................40.00
Victory Is a Question of Stamina, soldiers....................85.00
Victory Loan Flyer, 4 biplanes flying over locomotive..........90.00
Women! Help America's Sons..., woman, ships bkground, EX...100.00
Workers Lend Your Strength, United War Workers, 27x20″....30.00
World Fellowship, graduating student, Treidler, 40x30″........40.00

Miscellaneous

Anti-Vietnam, See Nation Destined to Save the World, M.......35.00
Auto Race in the Air, racers jump off slide, Friedlander.......425.00
Hans & Fritz, the Katzen Jammer Kids, cartoon, 28x41″.......50.00
Monoplane image, cowboy pilot, Am frontier, Friedlander......350.00
Yale, Till Life's Sun..., bulldog, Yale seal at bottom, M.........85.00

Pot Lids

Pot lids were pottery covers for containers that were used for hair dressing, potted meats, etc. The most desirable were decorated with colorful transfer prints under the glaze in a variety of themes, animal and scenic. The first and probably the largest company to manufacture these lids was F and R Pratt of Fenton, Staffordshire, established in the early 1800s. The name or initials of Jesse Austin, their designer, may sometimes be found on exceptional designs. Although few pot lids were made after the 1880s, the firm continued into the 20th century.

When no condition is indicated, the items listed below are assumed to be in mint condition.

Albert Memorial, w/carriage, Pratt type, minor crazing, 4″.....100.00
Holborn Viaduct, Pratt type, 4″...........................150.00
Landing the Catch, Pratt type, 4⅛″........................100.00
Pegwell Bay, lobster fishing, Pratt type, 4″..................375.00
Phila Exhibition, 1876, drawn by Austin, Pratt type, 4¼″......400.00
Residence of Anne Hathaway, Shakespear's wife, etc, 4″.......100.00
Royal couple portrait, minor hairline, 4⅛″...................90.00
Tam-O'-Shanter, Pratt type, 4¼″, EX.......................275.00
Thames Embankment, Pratt type, 3¾″.......................300.00
Trafalgar Sq, drawn by Austin, Pratt type, 4¼″..............500.00
Transplanting Rice, Pratt type, 4⅛″........................375.00
Village Wedding, edge chips under rim, 4″....................75.00
Village Wedding, Pratt, in fr..............................120.00
Walmer Castle Kent, w/sentry, mk Tatnell & Son, 4½″........200.00
Windsor Castle, cows grazing on castle lawn, 6″..............95.00
7 Ages of Man, drawn by Austin, Pratt type, age crack, 4⅛″...225.00

Left to right: 'War,' battle scene after Wouvermann, signed by Jesse Austin, Fenton, 5½″ long; 'Dangerous,' skating scene, from a drawing by Jesse Austin, Pratt, 2⅞″ diameter, $325.00.

Powder Horns and Flasks

Though powder horns had already been in use for hundreds of years, collectors usually focus on those made after the expansion of the United States westward in the very early 1800s.While some are basic and very simple, others were scrimshawed and highly polished. Especially nice carvings can quickly escalate the value of a horn that has survived intact to $300 to $400. Those with detailed maps, historical scenes, etc. bring even higher prices.

Metal flasks were introduced in the 1830s; and by the middle of the century they were produced in quantity and at prices low enough that they became a viable alternative to the powder horn. Today's collector regards the smaller flasks as the more desirable and valuable, and those made for specific companies bring preminum prices.

Examples listed below are assumed to be in excellent condition.

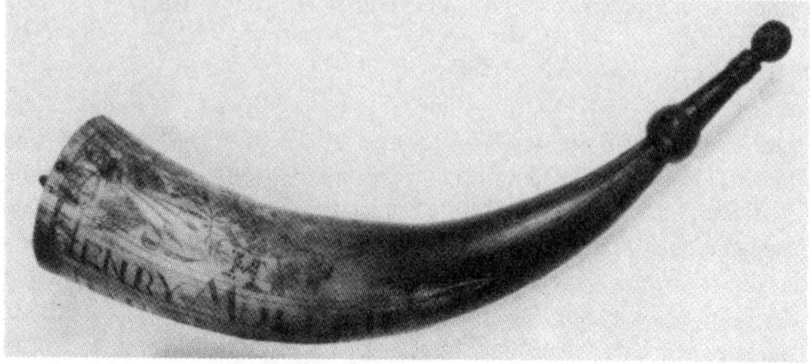

Engraved regimental powder horn, townscape of village Fredrickstown,Pennsylvania, signed and dated Jan. 19, 1781, turned throat and wood plug, 10½″, $350.00.

Flask, brass, shell relief, 8⅜″, EX..........................65.00
Flask, brass, 2-tone, emb, 2 base compartments, 4½″..........35.00
Flask, copper, emb dog & tree, brass fittings, 7¾″............65.00
Flask, copper, emb dog/pheasants, brass fittings, 6¼″..........50.00
Flask, copper, emb shells, brass fittings, 4½″.................35.00
Flask, copper, emb X-flags w/arm aiming gun, MA Arms, 4¼″...95.00
Flask, copper w/copper fittings, 4¾″........................45.00
Flask, SP traces, emb stags/fox/foliage, 8½″.................135.00
Horn, brass trim, measure on end w/spring latch, 14″..........55.00
Horn, carved end, eng ship w/Am flag/ladies/Indian, 8″, VG....200.00
Horn, chip carved wood end, trn spout, 12¼″..................155.00
Horn, chip carved wood end, 8″.............................45.00
Horn, cow's, 19th C, 8½″..................................28.00
Horn, eng Am eagle/PA State House, 11″.....................495.00
Horn, eng early Boston map, chip carved spout, 13¾″........800.00
Horn, eng map of North & Mohawk Rivers w/forts, 1761, 11″..400.00
Horn, eng ships/fish/flags/rifle/birds/name, worn, 12½″.........175.00
Horn, hunter/dogs/deer/birds/sgn/1804, losses/rpr, 16½″.......325.00
Horn, regimental, legend/1781/townscape/tulips/bird, 10½″.....450.00
Horn, simple compass-circle engraving, 10″...................50.00
Horn, trn wooden end & threaded tip, 17″....................90.00

Pratt

Prattware is a type of relief molded earthenware with polychrome decoration. Scenic motifs with figures were popular; sometimes captions were added. Jugs are most common, but teapots, tableware, even figurines were made. The term 'Pratt' refers to Wm. Pratt of Lane Delph, who is credited with making the first of this type, though similar wares were made later by other Staffordshire potters.

When no condition is indicated, the items listed below are assumed to be in mint condition.

Bowl, Dr Syntax Drawing After Nature, mc on brn, 3½x10″, VG.95.00
Cottage, wht bricks, bl/yel trim, 2 chimneys, 3½″, EX.........260.00

Four Seasons, ca 1780-90, in excellent condition, 8½", $2,800.00.

Creamer, peacocks in relief, 4-color, EX....135.00
Cup, satyr face relief, frog w/in, 4⅞"....210.00
Figurine, cradle w/hood, child w/in, yel w/bl mottle....300.00
Figurine, lady w/fan, 5-color, rpr on base, 5"....100.00
Figurine, recumbent deer, hollow, ca 1820, 4½"....525.00
Mug, satyr, 3½"....175.00
Mustard jar, bl w/hunt scene, reg mk 1856, Fenton....55.00
Pitcher, blk w/classical Greek figures, 5½"....150.00
Plaque, blacksmith/horse/lady/2 men, 6-color, 8x9", EX....250.00
Plaque, house, lady reads to children, Webster, 1834, 8"....185.00
Plate, Long Live the Queen....45.00
Plate, snow owl w/2 chicks, bl/gold rim, Fenton mk, 8½"....110.00
Platter, emb fish, 5-color, miniature, 4" L, VG....125.00
Tea caddy, 2 men/lady in 18th C dress, 5-color, no lid, 5"....325.00

Precious Moments

Figurines and bells created by Samuel Butcher and produced by Enesco Co. of Chicago, a division of Stanhome Products, are becoming some of the most sought-after collectibles on today's market. Often referred to as 'America's Hummels,' these pieces endear themselves to many through the inspirational messages that they portray. The first twenty-one pieces were made in 1979. These were unmarked, and today are the most valuable. Since then, they have been marked with a different mark for each year of production--older marks bring higher prices. Retired figures, especially those from 1981, are also highly valued. A newsletter edited by Rosie Wells is available if you want more information. She is listed in the Directory under Clubs, Newsletters, and catalogs.

Items listed below are assumed to be in mint condition, and without the box.

Bell, #5211....39.00
Boy Jogging....40.00
Boy w/Black Eye, no mk....80.00
Boy w/Black Eye, retired....50.00
Boy w/Ice Cream Cone, retired....70.00
Bride & Groom, doll, pr....600.00
Call Club to Order, #0103....35.00
Come, Let Us Adore Him, E-2011, retired....245.00
Eggs Over Easy, no mk....90.00
Eggs Over Easy, retired....50.00
Girl w/Puppies, #1378, retired....550.00
God's Ray, #841, club pc....35.00
God's Speed, D-3112, recent....45.00
Hello, Lord, It's Me, #811, retired....275.00
In Dawn's Early Light, retired....40.00
Indian Boy, #1380, retired....25.00
Indian Girl, #1380, retired....25.00
Jogger, no mk....75.00
Plate, Music for Queen & Fantasy Festival, pr....115.00
Plate, Twinkle Twinkle....15.00
Praise the Lord Anyhow, #1374B....50.00
Put on a Happy Face, #822....95.00
Smile, God Loves You, #821....120.00
We Have Seen a Star....30.00

Pre-Columbian Artifacts

The term 'pre-Columbian' loosely refers to some time prior to 1492, when Columbus arrived in America. In particular, it indicates pre-1492 artifacts of Central and South America, some of which can be dated as early as 4000 B.C. Artifacts representing the cultures of the Inca, Maya, and Aztec Indians are avidly sought by the collector. These may be made of precious metals and hardstones, or of pottery. Some were used in rituals and religious rites; some such as bowls and other utensils, though strictly utilitarian, nevertheless convey through form and decoration the craftsmanship of these early tribes.

When no condition is indicated, the items listed below are assumed to be in excellent condition.

Key:
tc—terra cotta

Axe-God, jade, Costa Rica, deep gr, 4⅛"....800.00
Bird, squatting w/arms on legs, eyes bulge, tc, Lenca, 4½"....125.00
Bowl, figure/deities heads, orange/blk, Mayan, AD 550-950...1,320.00
Bowl, Xipetotec w/teardrop eyes, tc, Mayan, AD 750-1250, 4½".585.00
Colima dog, standing, brn pnt, Protoclassic, 100 BC-AD 250.1,000.00
Duck, flaring spout tail, squat, 1150-550 BC, 4½"....1,500.00
Female, lg hollow body/loop arms, tc, Lenca, chip, 4¼x4½"....140.00
Figure, schematic arms up, stone, Mezcala, 300-100 BC, 4⅞"..660.00
Figure, seated, calling, legs crossed, red clay, Mayan, 2"....60.00
Head, appliqued features, grotesque, hollow, tc, Mayan, 3½"....65.00
Head, ceremonial, hollow, headdress, hole, tc, Mayan, 3¼"....75.00
Head, sacrificial, headdress, slant eyes, clay, Olmec, 3½"....40.00
Hunchback, red-brn w/cream, Chinesco, 100 BC-AD 250, 6"..1,000.00
Pendant, alligator; jade, Costa Rica, 300 BC-AD 300, 3¼"...1,210.00
Pendant, jade, human form, pale gr, 2 holes for eyes, 2½"....95.00
Queen, seated, headdress/earplugs/hollow, tc, Mayan, 4¾"....200.00
Queen, seated, hollow, headdress, tc, Mayan, rstr base, 6"....195.00
Rattle, seated female w/male, Jaina, AD 550-950, 7½"....1,500.00
Whistle, animal head w/snout, eyes bulge, tc, Lenca, 2"....45.00
Whistle, seated dwarf w/headdress, Mayan, AD 550-950, 4"....330.00
Whistle, turkey head, bold lines, tc, Mayan, 3½x3½", VG....95.00

Primitives

Like the mouse that ate the grindstone, so has collectible interest in primitives increased, a little bit at a time, until demand is taking bites instead of nibbles into their availability. Although the term 'primitives' once referred to those survival essentials contrived by our American settlers, it has recently been expanded to include objects needed or desired by succeeding generations--items representing the cabin-n'-cornpatch existence as well as examples of life on larger farms and in towns. Through popular usage, it also respectfully covers what are actually 'country collectibles.'

From the 1600s into the latter 1800s, factories employed carvers, blacksmiths, and other artisans, whose hand work contributed to turning out quality items. When buying, 'touchmarks'--a company's name and/or location, and maker's or owner's initials--are exciting discoveries.

Primitives are uniquely individual. Following identical forms, results more often than not show typically personal ideas. Using this as a guide, combined with circumstances of age, condition, desire to own, etc., should lead to a reasonably accurate evaluation. For items not listed, consult comparable examples.

In business for profit, a dealer cannot reach the buying level of emotional evaluations which a seller of inherited artifacts might expect, nor can he pay retail prices, but may instead be able to offer only 50% of the retail due to his considerable expenses. To continue to read and visit exhibits is the best approach toward knowledgeable purchasing.

Authority Kathyrn McNerney has compiled several lovely books on primitives and related topics: *Primitives, Our American Heritage; Collectible Blue and White Stoneware*; and *Antique Tools, Our American Heritage*. You will find her address in the Directory under Florida. When no condition is indicated, the items listed below are assumed to be in excellent condition. See also Butter Molds and Stamps; Copper; Farm Collectibles; Fireplace Implements; Kitchen Collectibles; Molds; Tinware; Woodenware

Barrel, oak staved, iron side hdls/bands, hinged lid, 17″........95.00
Bed warmer, brass, eng florals, trn hdl, 44″ L...............245.00
Bed warmer, brass, eng florals, trn wood grpt hdl, 43″........375.00
Bed warmer, copper, eng floral & bird, trn wood hdl, 42″.....160.00
Bed warmer, copper, punched-out flowers, maple hdl, 1700s....295.00
Box, apple; curly poplar, traces of old red, 3¼x9½x11″.........85.00
Box, knife scouring & pumice; pine, hanging................130.00
Box, knife; ash, dvtl, cut-out hdl in arch divider, 10x17″.......65.00
Box, knife; cherry, dvtl, lid flaps, 8½x13½″.................295.00
Box, knife; maple w/some curl, 2-section, rfn, 7¾x11″..........95.00
Box, knife; pine, varnished, 2¾x12x8¾″....................35.00
Box, salt; pine, hanging, 2-section, slant top, 15″.............75.00
Box, tinder; brass, hdl & candle socket on lid, 4½″ W........180.00
Box, tinder; tin, drum form, candle socket on lid, 3″.........205.00
Box, tinder; tinned sheet iron, iron striker, 1¼x3x4½″........265.00
Broom, birch splint, hearth cleaning, 36″ L..................95.00
Broom, birch splint, sm...................................65.00
Broom, splintered birch, stub hdl, 1800s, 4½″................90.00
Broom, splintered birch, stub hdl, 1800s, 9″................115.00
Brush, hearth; sq paddle, bristles 3 sides, trn hdl, 45″........145.00
Bucket, pickle; tin bands, old mustard pnt, bail hdl, 13″......110.00
Bucket, well; oak staved, iron bands & bail hdl, heavy.........75.00
Candle box, pine, sliding lid, orig blk pnt, 10¾″ L............55.00
Candle box, poplar, bevel lid slides, orig red, 5¾x9x14″.......145.00

Candle mold, 49-tube (odd numbers very unusual), 12½″ x 8½″, $685.00.

Candle mold, 1-tube, tin, crimped rnd top & base, 10½″......135.00
Candle mold, 1-tube, tin, sq base & top, 21½″...............125.00
Candle mold, 12-tube, tin w/traces of gr pnt, 10¾″............65.00
Candle mold, 18-tube, pewter in pine fr, Francis, 16x22″......700.00
Candle mold, 18-tube, tin in wood fr, 16x9x19″..............150.00
Candle mold, 2-tube, tin, 10½″............................75.00
Candle mold, 24-tube, pewter in pine fr, 16½x7x19½″.........625.00
Candle mold, 3-tube, crimped oval top & bottom, 11″, EX......65.00
Candle mold, 4-tube, in row, oval crimped top, side hdl........55.00
Candle mold, 6-tube, tin, 10¼″............................60.00
Candle mold, 8-tube, tin, good hdl, 10¾″....................65.00
Candle mold, 8-tube, tin, sq base/hdl, tubes pointed atop.......75.00
Carpet beater & bed smoother, wire/brass/wood hdls, pr........75.00
Carriage step, wrought iron, twisted brace, 8x10″.............15.00
Carrier, pine, canted sides, divider w/hdl, rpt, 4x16″...........30.00
Cheese drain, spindled, half-moon shape, 15x24″.............235.00
Chestnut roaster, brass w/oval sheet brass pan/hdl, 18½″.......50.00
Chopping board, pine, 8-sided, many old chop mks, 14x14x1″...50.00
Churn, bentwood, orig blk pnt, red/gold stencil, 10-gal........300.00
Churn, Elmers Double Ace #2/pat '80, bentwood/old pnt, 33″..295.00
Churn, floor standing, pine w/tin liner, CI crank, 32x13″......190.00
Churn, staved barrel/iron bands, center crank hdl, 18″ dia.....165.00

Butter churn, Hall Bro. Mfg., 13″, $185.00.

Coal sieve, bentwood w/heavy wire bottom, 14″...............45.00
Coffee roaster, sheet iron, 20″ hdl, 8½x10½″.................20.00
Cranberry scoop, root hdl, iron teeth, wrought nails, 15″......115.00
Curry comb, sq w/CI horse, trn wood hdl, 5x7½″.............70.00
Dough box, pine, dvtl, trn/splay poplar legs, 21x38″, VG......350.00
Dough box, pine, mortised/pinned, breadboard top, bl pnt.....500.00
Dutch oven, tin w/wrought iron spit, rpt, 22½x24″............125.00
Foot warmer, carpeted tin, for buggy.......................48.00
Foot warmer, pewter, oval, brass cap, ring hdl...............95.00
Foot warmer, skater's; wood box, 7 rows of holes, 14x9x7″....110.00
Foot warmer, tin w/punched circles & hearts, 5¾x7¾x9″......150.00
Foot warmer, tin/mortised fr/trn posts, factory made, 6x9″......65.00
Knife rack, pine, handmade, rnd corners, oblong, 19x11″......110.00
Lamp, canting; tin, flat lard-type wick, 7″...................375.00
Medicine cabinet, pine, bevelled mirror, drawer below..........65.00
Muddler/toddy stick, birch, 1-pc............................15.00
Pegboard, wood w/8 cut-out hooks, orig gray pnt, 81″ L......145.00
Powder keg, wooden, 4 rows hickory lap banding top/bottom...135.00
Quilt rack, pine, 3 heavy bars, shoe ftd.....................85.00

Rack, baker's; 6 removable slat shelves, old red, 63x23" 250.00
Rack, drying, floor standing, pat date/label, 17 arms..........135.00
Rack, drying, pine, folding, mortised, three 42x57" parts......135.00
Rack, drying; pine, shoe ft, 34x49".......................150.00
Rack, drying; pine, three 63x32" parts folds, cloth hinges.....125.00
Rack, drying; woven splint, mortised pine fr, rpr, 38x46"......165.00
Rack, drying; 4 arms, tripod base w/center post, 44"..........175.00
Rack, hanging; pine, scalloped w/12 wrought hooks, 72"......170.00
Rack, hanging; 2 trays, slat bk, simple stencil, 10x15".........85.00
Rack, plate drying; dvtl pine, scalloped ends, rpr, 37x44"......275.00
Rack, plate drying; pine, English, mortised, 48x43"...........200.00
Rug beater, wood hdl, wire...............................15.00
Sap skimmer, dk tin/punched designs, trn wood hdl, 1800s....125.00
Scissor wick trimmer, brass, in ring hdl stand, 1800s, 7"......225.00
Scissor wick trimmer & tray, brass, Colonial style, 9½".........85.00
Scissors, forged iron, late 1700s, 6½"......................125.00
Shoulder yoke, hand hewn, for carrying sap, 1-pc.............75.00
Sorting board, poplar, cut-out zigzag ends, no finish, 35".......65.00
Spoon rack, carved oak w/flying angel/flowerpot/etc, 23x9".....450.00
Strike steel, hand-forged iron, for tinder boxes, 1700s..........95.00
Sweat scraper, for horses, wood, 1-pc.......................45.00
Sweater stretcher, old pine, movable arms, adult size..........65.00
Washboard, all wooden, w/soap pocket, 14x22"...............50.00
Washboard, bentwood frame, old dk tin scrub surface..........65.00
Washboard, Handi, aluminum surface, curved hdl atop, mini....25.00
Washboard, Mother Hubbard, pnt VG/movable grooved rollers...98.00
Washboard, The Arlington, wood, 10 twist-shaped rollers......110.00
Washboard, The Naiad, Top Notch Soap Saver, metal ridges....17.50
Washboard, wood, bright bl glass scrub surface, rare..........125.00
Washboard, wood, handmade, w/driven wires as scrub surface...90.00
Washboard, wood w/glass scrubbing surface, 23x12½"..........15.00
Washboard, wringer at top, wood fold-up stand at bk.........135.00
Washboard, 1-pc walnut, hand cut, 1⅜" thick, 18x8".........165.00
Washtub clothes stomper, wood hdl on rnd copper base, 43"...27.50
Whetstone carrier, hewn w/belt clip, red pnt, 1-pc............95.00
Whetstone carrier, wood, pointed bottom, old leather strap.....48.00
Wick pick, whalebone hdl, trn base w/blk pnt, 5½", EX.......175.00
Wrench, fruit jar; adjustable, pat 1906, 2-pc..................12.50
Wringer, wood, corrugated roller on plank, hand crank, 26"....55.00

Prints

The term 'print' may be defined today as almost any image printed on paper by any available method. Examples of collectible old 'prints' are Norman Rockwell magazine covers and Maxfield Parrish posters and calendars. 'Original print' refers to one achieved through the efforts of the artist, or under his direct supervision. A 'reproduction' is a print produced by an accomplished print maker, who reproduces another artist's print or original work.

Thorough study is required on the part of the collector to recognize and appreciate the many variable factors to be considered in evaluating a print. Prices vary from one area of the country to another, and are dependent upon new findings regarding the scarcity or abundance of prints as such information may arise. Although each collector of old prints may have their own varying criteria by which to judge condition, for those who deal only rarely in this area, or newer collectors, a few guidelines may prove helpful. Staining, though unquestionably detrimental, is nearly always present in some degree, and should be weighed against the rarity of the print. Professional cleaning should improve its appearance and at the same time help preserve it. Avoid tears that affect the image; minor margin tears are another matter, especially if the print is a rare one. Moderate 'foxing' (brown spots caused by mold or the fermentation of the rag content of old paper) and light stains from the old frames are not serious unless present in excess. Margin trimming was a common practice, but look for at least ¾" to 1½" margins, depending on print size.

When no condition is indicated, the items listed below are assumed to be in very good to excellent condition.

Audubon, John J.

Audubon is the best known of American and European wildlife artists. His first series of prints, 'Birds of America,' was produced by Robert Havell of London. They were printed on Whitman watermarked paper, bearing dates of 1826 to 1838. The Octavo Edition of the same series was printed in three editions, the first by J.T. Bowen under Audubon's direction. There were seven volumes of prints, each 11" x 7", the first five bearing the J.J. Audubon and J.B. Chevalier mark, the last two, J.J. Audubon. They were produced from 1840 through 1871. The Bien Edition prints were full size, made under the direction of Audubon's son and daughter in the late 1850s. Due to the onset of the Civil War, only 105 plates were finished. These are considered to be the most valuable of the reprints of the 'Birds of America' series.

In the 1950s New York Graphics reproduced the full-color prints through photolithography; and in 1971 the complete set was reprinted by Johnson Reprint Corp. of New York, and Theaturm Orbis Terrarum of Amsterdam. Examples of the latter bear the watermark G. Schut and Zonen.

Although Audubon is best known for his portrayal of birds, one of his less-familiar series, 'Viviparous Quadrupeds of North America,' portrayed various species of animals. Assembled in corroboration with John Bachman from 1839 until 1851, these prints are 28x22" in size.

Audubon, John J.

American Badger, XLVII, Bowen, 1844......................330.00
American Beaver, XLVI, Bowen, 1844.......................495.00
American Crossbill, CXCVII, Havell, 1837.................1,650.00
American Elk–Wapiti Deer, LXII, Bowen, 1845..............495.00
American White Pelican, CCCXI, Havell, 1836............22,000.00
Baltimore Oriole, #217, Bien, 1860.........................825.00
Baltimore Oriole, XII, Havell............................6,820.00
Barn Owl, #34, Bien, 1860..................................550.00
Barn Swallow, CLXXIII, Havell, 1833......................1,210.00
Belted Kingfisher, #77, Havell, Jr, 1830..................3,300.00
Black & White Creeper, #90, Havell, Jr, 1830...............550.00
Black American Wolf, LXVII, Bowen, 1845...................550.00
Black Warrier, LXXXVI, Havell, 1833......................2,310.00
Black-Billed Cuckoo, XXXII, Havell.......................3,960.00
Bonapartian Gull, CCCXXIV, Havell, 1836...................660.00
Brant Goose, CCCXCI, Havell, 1837........................1,540.00
Brewer's Blackbird, #492, Bowen, 10x7"......................25.00
Canada Lynx, XVI, Bowen, 1845............................1,100.00
Canvas-Backed Duck, Amsterdam, plate #301...............1,400.00
Cardinal Grosbeak, CLIX, Havell, 1833....................3,300.00
Caribou or American Reindeer, CXXVI, Bowen, 1847.........550.00
Chesnut-Sided Warbler, LIX, Havell.........................550.00
Cinnamon Bear, #127, Bowen..................................50.00
Cock of the Plains, CCCLXXI, Havell, 1837................2,860.00
Common American Wildcat, #1, Bowen, 1842................2,090.00
Cougar, XCVII, Bowen, 1846.................................660.00
Downy Woodpecker, CXII, Havell, 1831.....................3,190.00
Dwarf Thrush, #147, Bowen, 10x7"...........................25.00
Female Wild Turkey, Amsterdam, plate #6.................1,200.00
Forked-Tailed Flycatcher, CLXVIII, Havell, 1833...........4,620.00
Gadwall Duck, #388, Bien, 1860.............................605.00
Glossy Ibis, CCCLXXXVII, Havell, 1837....................4,070.00
Gold Crown Wagtail, #148, Bowen, 10x7"......................15.00

Harris' Buzzard, #5, Bowen, 10x7" 25.00
Hooded Merganser, CCXXXII, Havell, 1834 ..... 1,870.00
Iceland or Jer Falcon, CCCLXVI, Havell, 1837 ..... 8,800.00
Indigo-Bird, #74, Havell, 1829 ..... 770.00
Lazuli Finch, Crimson-Necked Bull-Finch, CCCCXXIV, Havell ..330.00
Mockingbird, #138, Bien, 1860 ..... 990.00
Musk Ox, CXI, Bowen, 1847 ..... 385.00
Night Hawk, CXLVII, Havell, 1832 ..... 1,760.00
Nine-Banded Armadillo, #146, Bowen 110.00
Plumed-Partridge, CCCCXXIII, Havell, 1838 ..... 1,540.00
Polar Bear, #91, Bowen 80.00
Prong-Horned Antelope, LXXVII, Bowen, 1845 ..... 715.00
Purple Martin, XXII, Havell, 1833 ..... 2,420.00
Red-Headed Duck, CCCXXII, Havell, 1836 ..... 1,980.00
Red-Shouldered Hawk, LVI, Havell 5,500.00
Reddish Egret, #371, Bien, 1860 ..... 1,650.00
Rocky Mountain Sheep, LXXIII, Bowen, 1845 ..... 605.00
Ruby-Throated Hummingbird, XLVII, Havell 6,325.00
Snow Bird, XIII, Havell 660.00
Snowy Owl, CXXI, Havell 20,350.00
Stanley Goldfinch, #185, Bowen, 10x7" 35.00
Swallow-Tailed Hawk, #72, Havell, 1829 ..... 1,760.00
Swift Fox, LII, Bowen, 1844 ..... 495.00
Traill's Fly-Catcher, #45, Havell, 1828 ..... 605.00
Trumpeter Swan, CCCLXXVI, Havell, 1837 ..... 7,425.00
Virginia Partridge, Amsterdam, plate, #76 ..... 900.00
White Heron, CCCLXXXVI, Havell, 1837 ..... 9,350.00
White-Legged Oyster Catcher, CCCCXVII, Havell, 1838 ..... 880.00
Wood Duck, Amsterdam, plate, #206 ..... 1,100.00
Wood Thrush, #73, Havell 770.00
Yellow-Breasted Chat, #244, Bien, 1860 ..... 330.00
Yellow-Crowned Heron, CCCXXXVI, Havell, 1836 ..... 5,775.00
Yellow-Winged Sparrow, CXXX, Havell 880.00

Black Cupid Awake and Asleep, matted and framed, 7½" x 5½", $250.00 for the pair.

Baillie, Coronation of the Virgin, VG 30.00
Baillie, Eliza, VG 50.00
Bartlett, Wm Henry; Centre Harbor, sm folio, 1838 ..... 20.00
Bartlett, Wm Henry; Saratoga Lake, sm folio, 1838 ..... 18.00
Bartlett, Wm Henry; Trenton Falls, sm folio, 1839, VG 18.00
Bartlett, Wm Henry; View From Hyde Park, 1837, 4¾x7¼" 18.00
Bartlett, Wm Henry; View From Mt Ida, Near Troy, sm, 1839 ... 20.00
Bartlett, Wm Henry; Village of Catskill, sm folio, 1839 ..... 22.00
Bartlett, Wm Henry; Village of Little Falls, 4¾x7¼", VG 18.00
Bierstadt, Albert; The Rocky Mountains, 1866, 26x35¾" 1,430.00
Bingham, George; Jolly Flat Boat Men, fr, 22½x26¼" 2,310.00
Cameron, Trotters on the Snow 195.00
Catlin, George; Catching the Wild Horse, fr, 1844 ..... 1,320.00
Couse, EI; The Chief, RR map on bk, dbl glass, 1927 ..... 100.00
Creswick, The Cooling Stream, fr, VG 320.00
Cupid Asleep, MBP Keason, c 1897, in fr, 14½x19" 80.00
Cupid Asleep, tin fr, 5x7" 22.00
Cupid at Rest, matted in fr, 5x7" 65.00
Cupid Awake, Asleep, Madonna & Child, 3 sm attached ovals ... 55.00
Cupid Awake, Asleep, Parkinson, 1897, no fr, 6x8", pr 25.00
Cupid Watching, brn leather grain oval fr, 12x18", EX 150.00

Currier and Ives

Nathaniel Currier was in business by himself until the late 1850s when he formed a partnership with James Merrit Ives. Currier is given credit for being the first to use the medium to portray newsworthy subjects; and the Currier and Ives views of 19th century American culture are familiar to us all. Values are given for prints that are in very good condition.

Abbey of Clare-Galway, sm folio 40.00
Abraham Lincoln, The Nation's Martyr, b/w, sm folio 60.00
Abraham Lincoln, The Nation's Martyr, sm folio 95.00
Adelaide, N Currier, sm folio 60.00
Agnes, N Currier, sm folio 60.00
Alice, sm folio 60.00
Amelia, N Currier, sm folio 60.00
American Beauty, sm folio 50.00
American Forest Game, lg folio, 1866 ..... 1,600.00
American Game, lg folio, 1866 ..... 1,600.00
American Homestead, Autumn, sm folio 350.00
American Homestead, Summer, sm folio 300.00
American Homestead, Winter, sm folio 625.00
American Mountain Scenery, med folio 425.00
American Prize Fruit, N Currier, 1862, lg folio 1,550.00
American Railroad Scene, Snowbound, sm folio, 1872 ..... 1,600.00
Andrew Jackson, 7th President of US, N Currier, sm folio 95.00
Autumn on Lake George, sm folio 150.00
Base Hit, sm folio 225.00
Battle of Anteitam, MD, Sept 17, 1862, sm folio 150.00
Battle of Buena Vista, Feb 23, 1847, sm folio 150.00
Battle of Cedar Creek, VA, Oct 19, 1864, sm folio 150.00
Battle of Chancellorsville, VA, May 3, 1863, sm folio 150.00
Battle of Chattanooga, TN, Nov 24 & 25, 1863, sm folio 150.00
Battle of Fair Oaks, VA, May 31, 1862, lg folio 700.00
Bear Hunting, Close Quarters, sm folio 450.00
Beautiful Empress, sm folio 50.00
Beauty of the Atlantic, sm folio 50.00
Between Two Fires, sm folio 225.00
Blackfish Nibble, sm folio 225.00
Bombardment & Capture of Fort Henry, sm folio 250.00
Bombardment of Island #10, sm folio 225.00
Bouquet of Roses, sm folio 80.00
Brave Boy of the Waxhaws, sm folio, 1876 ..... 200.00
Bridge at the Outlet, Lake Memphremagog, sm folio 160.00
Brook Trout, Just Caught, med folio 250.00
Burning of the Ocean Monarch of Boston, N Currier, sm folio ..250.00
Butt of the Jokers, sm folio 150.00
Byron & Marianna, sm folio 45.00
Capture of Andre, 1790, N Currier, sm folio 125.00
Cares of a Family, sm folio 300.00
Caroline, sm folio 60.00

American Farm Scenes No. 2, N. Currier, large folio, in excellent condition, $1,200.00.

Carrier Dove, sm folio........50.00
Celebrated Trotting Stallion Patron, sm folio........300.00
Central Park, The Bridge, sm folio........325.00
Champions of the Union, med folio........175.00
Charles, N Currier, sm folio........125.00
Children's Pic-Nic, sm folio........95.00
City of New York & Environs, sm folio, 1875........500.00
Clipper Ship Red Jacket, N Currier, lg folio, 1855........3,500.00
Clipper Ship Sweepstakes, N Currier, lg folio, 1853........3,500.00
Col Elmer Ellsworth, 1st Regiment, sm folio........80.00
Col Frank P Blair, sm folio........80.00
Constitution & Java, N Currier, sm folio, 1846........395.00
Cooling Stream, med folio........350.00
Copped at a Cock Fight, sm folio........225.00
Cornwallis Is Taken, sm folio........350.00
Darktown Fire Brigade, A Prize Squirt, sm folio........250.00
De Boss Rooster, sm folio........225.00
Dead Game, Quail, sm folio........200.00
Dead Game, Woodcock, sm folio........250.00
Death of Napolean, N Currier, sm folio........80.00
Death of President Lincoln, b/w, sm folio........80.00
Death of Stonewall Jackson, sm folio........80.00
Death Shot, sm folio........170.00
Declaration Committee, sm folio........230.00
Deer in the Woods, sm folio........150.00
Deer Shooting in the Northern Woods, sm folio........425.00
Don't You Want Another Baby?, sm folio........80.00
Dotty Dimple, sm folio........60.00
Draw Poker, Getting 'Em Lively, sm folio........225.00
Eastern Beauty, sm folio........50.00
Echo Lake, White Mountains, oval, med folio........450.00
Eliza, N Currier, sm folio........60.00
Emeline, N Currier, sm folio........60.00
Emma, sm folio, VG........60.00
English Winter Scene, sm folio........230.00
Evening Star, sm folio........50.00
Express Train, sm folio........1,200.00
Fall of Richmond, VA, April 2, 1865, sm folio........170.00
Falls 'Des Chats,' Ottawa River Canada, sm folio........175.00
Famous Trotting Mare Goldsmith Maid, Record 2:14, sm folio........300.00
Fanny, N Currier, sm folio........50.00
Farmer's Friends, sm folio........150.00
First Under the Wire, sm folio........300.00
Flower Girl, N Currier, sm folio........50.00
Flowers, sm folio........70.00
Fording the River, N Currier, med folio........320.00
Foul Tip, sm folio........250.00
Four Seasons of Life, Middle Age, lg folio........1,200.00
Francis R Shunk, Governor of PA, N Currier, sm folio........60.00
Franklin Pierce, 14th President of US, N Currier, sm folio........95.00
Friedr Hecker, Germany 1848, N Currier, sm folio........30.00
Frontier Lake, sm folio........150.00
Fruit & Flower Piece, med folio........250.00
Fruit & Flowers, Grapes, Peaches, Roses, sm folio........110.00
Fruit Vase, sm folio........110.00
Fruits, Autumn Varieties, sm folio........110.00
Fruits of Temperance, sm folio........150.00
Fruits of the Seasons, sm folio........110.00
Garfield Family, b/w, sm folio........60.00
Gems of American Scenery, sm folio........295.00
Gen Andrew Jackson, N Currier, sm folio........75.00
Gen Franz Sigel at Battle of Pea Ridge, sm folio........95.00
Gen Grant & Family, b/w, sm folio........60.00
Gen Israel Putnam, Iron Son of '76, N Currier, sm folio........125.00
Gen Joseph E Johnston, b/w, sm folio........80.00
Gen US Grant, Nation's Choice for President, sm folio........65.00
George Washington, 1st Pres of US, N Currier, sm folio........95.00
Georgianna, N Currier, sm folio........60.00
Getting a Hoist, A Bad Case of the Heaves, sm folio........200.00
Grand Horse St Julien, sm folio........300.00
Grand National Whig Banner Onward, N Currier, sm folio........125.00
Grand US Centennial Exhibition 1876, sm folio........175.00
Grandma's 'Specs,' sm folio........60.00
Grant & His Generals, b/w, med folio........150.00
Great Fire at Boston, Nov 9, 1878, sm folio........250.00
Great Victory in Shenandoah Valley, Sept 19, 1864, sm folio........150.00
Grottoes of the Sea, sm folio........75.00
Halt by the Wayside, sm folio........150.00
Happy Home, N Currier, sm folio........75.00
Harbor for the Night, sm folio........275.00
Harriet, N Currier, sm folio........60.00
Harvest, sm folio........190.00
Harvesting, The Last Load, sm folio........190.00
Haunted Castle, sm folio........70.00
He Is Saved, b/w, sm folio........50.00
Henry, N Currier, sm folio........125.00
Henry Clay of KY, N Currier, sm folio........125.00
Hiawatha's Departure, lg folio........370.00
High Bridge at Harlem, NY, N Currier, sm folio........300.00
Home in the Wilderness, sm folio........595.00
Home of the Deer, Morning in the Adirondacks, lg folio........3,000.00
Home of Washington, Mt Vernon, VA, med folio........195.00
Home on the Mississippi, sm folio........395.00
Home Sweet Home, sm folio........150.00
Home to Thanksgiving, 1867, lg folio........9,000.00
Hopeful, sm folio........300.00
Hot Race to the Wire, sm folio........300.00
Household Pets, N Currier, sm folio........50.00
Hudson Near Cold Spring, sm folio........190.00
Hundred Leaf Rose, sm folio........110.00
Hung Up with the Starch Out, sm folio........190.00
In Full Bloom, sm folio........50.00
In the Mountains, sm folio........200.00
Interior of Fort Sumter During the Bombardment, sm folio........250.00
Inundation, The; sm folio........90.00
Irish Beauty, sm folio........50.00
Ivy Bridge, sm folio........125.00

James Madison, 4th President of US, N Currier, sm folio.......95.00
John Quincy Adams, 6th President of US, N Currier, sm folio...95.00
John Tyler, 10th President of US, N Currier, sm folio..........95.00
Josephine, N Currier, sm folio..........................60.00
Julia, sm folio...60.00
Kiss Me Quick, sm folio.................................90.00
Knitting Lesson, med folio.............................375.00
Lady Suffolk, med folio..............................1,200.00
Lady Thorn, sm folio...................................300.00
Lafayette at the Tomb of Washington, N Currier, sm folio......75.00
Lake Memphremagog, sm folio............................160.00
Lake of the Dismal Swamp, sm folio.....................130.00
Lakes of Killarney, sm folio............................70.00
Landscape & Cattle, med folio..........................325.00
Lapped on the Last Quarter, sm folio...................300.00
Last War-Whoop, The; N Currier, 1856, lg folio.........3,500.00
Laying Back Stiff for a Brush, sm folio................190.00
Lexington of 1861, sm folio............................195.00
Life & Age of Woman, sm folio..........................125.00
Life of a Fireman, The Night Alarm, N Currier, lg folio......2,000.00
Life of a Fireman, The Ruins, N Currier, 1854, lg folio......2,000.00
Life of a Sportsman, Coming into Camp, sm folio............300.00
Lincoln Family, b/w, sm folio...........................60.00
Little Beauty, med folio................................90.00
Little Blossom, sm folio................................50.00
Little Brother, sm folio................................60.00
Little Brother & Sister, sm folio.......................60.00
Little Brothers, sm folio...............................60.00
Little Caroline, sm folio...............................60.00
Little Daisy, sm folio..................................50.00
Little Favorite, N Currier, sm folio....................50.00
Little Flora, sm folio..................................50.00
Little Jennie, sm folio.................................60.00
Little Lily, b/w, sm folio..............................40.00
Little Manly, sm folio..................................55.00
Little Playfellow, N Currier, sm folio..................50.00
Little Protector, N Currier, sm folio...................50.00
Little Red Riding Hood, sm folio........................90.00
Little Sisters, sm folio................................60.00
Little Snowbird, sm folio..............................225.00
Little Sunbeam, sm folio................................60.00
Little Thoughtful, sm folio.............................50.00
Loss of Steamer Cimbria, sm folio......................250.00
Lottie, sm folio..60.00
Low Water in the Mississippi, 1868, lg folio...........3,500.00
Lucky Escape, N Currier, med folio.....................250.00
Lydia, N Currier, sm folio..............................60.00
Magic Lake, med folio..................................120.00
Maiden Rock, sm folio..................................350.00
Main Building, Grand US Centennial Exhibition 1876/sm folio..180.00
Maj Gen Benjamin F Butler, sm folio.....................95.00
Maj Gen George B McClellan, sm folio....................95.00
Maj Gen John C Fremont, sm folio........................95.00
Maj Gen Nathaniel P Banks, sm folio.....................95.00
Maj Gen Philip H Sheridan, sm folio.....................95.00
Maj Gen US Grant at Seige of Vicksburg, sm folio............95.00
Maj Gen William Rosecrans/Battle of Murphreesboro, sm folio...95.00
Maj Gen Winfield Hancock/Battle near Spottslvania, sm folio....95.00
Mammoth Iron Steamship Leviathan, sm folio.............250.00
Marriage Evening, sm folio..............................80.00
Martha Washington, b/w, sm folio........................50.00
Meeting of the Waters in the Vale of Avoca, sm folio..........70.00
Mischievous Little Kittie, sm folio.....................90.00
Moonlight, The Ruins, sm folio..........................60.00
Moonlight in the Tropics, sm folio......................95.00
Moonlight Promenade, sm folio...........................60.00
Morning in the Woods, 1865, lg folio.................2,000.00
Morning Star, sm folio..................................50.00
Mountain Ramble, sm folio..............................150.00
Mountain Spring, West Point Near Cozzen's Dock, med folio...550.00
Mule Train on an Upgrade, sm folio.....................225.00
My Love & I, sm folio...................................60.00
My Sweetheart, sm folio.................................50.00
Nettie, sm folio..60.00
New England Home, sm folio.............................175.00
New England Homestead, N Currier, sm folio.............175.00
Niagara Falls from Goat Island, med folio..............270.00
Niagara Falls from the Canada Side, sm folio...........175.00
Nip & Tuck, sm folio...................................200.00
Noontide, A Shady Spot, sm folio.......................150.00
Nova Scotia Scenery, med folio.........................325.00
O Dat Watermillon, sm folio............................225.00
Old Barn Floor, 1868, lg folio.......................2,000.00
Old Blandford Church, sm folio.........................150.00
Old Ford Bridge, sm folio..............................150.00
Old Oaken Bucket, sm folio.............................150.00
Old Ruins, sm folio.....................................95.00
Old Windmill, med folio................................300.00
On the Owago, sm folio.................................150.00
On the St Lawrence, sm folio...........................295.00
Pacing Wonder, Little Brown Jug of Chicago, sm folio.......300.00
Pacing Wonder Sleepy Tom, sm folio.....................300.00
Partridge Shooting, sm folio...........................325.00
Patriot of 1776 Defending His Homestead, sm folio...........195.00
Peerless Goldsmith Maid, sm folio......................300.00
Phebe, N Currier, sm folio..............................60.00
Pilot Boat in a Storm, sm folio........................400.00
Playful Family, sm folio................................75.00
Playmates, N Currier, sm folio..........................70.00
Prairie Fires of the Great West, sm folio..............800.00
Prairie Hens, sm folio.................................250.00
Presidents of the US, Washington to Polk, N Currier, sm......150.00
Presidents of the US From 1789-1861, N Currier, sm folio.....150.00
Pride of the South, sm folio............................50.00
Prize Trotter, sm folio................................300.00
Quails, N Currier, sm folio............................250.00
Queen Elizabeth, sm folio...............................50.00
Queen of Beauty, sm folio...............................50.00
Rarus, sm folio..300.00
Record for Birth & Baptism, sm folio....................60.00
Rival Roses, sm folio...................................85.00
River Side, sm folio...................................150.00
Roadside Cottage, med folio............................300.00
Roadside Mill, sm folio................................150.00
Robert Burns & His Highland Mary, sm folio..............45.00
Rose, The; sm folio.....................................80.00
Rose of Beauty, sm folio................................50.00
Rubber, The; sm folio..................................230.00
Rural Lake, med folio..................................300.00
Rush for the Pole, sm folio............................200.00
Rysdyk's Hambletonian, Great Sire of Trotters, sm folio.......300.00
Sacred Tomb of the Blessed Redeemer, sm folio...........30.00
Sale of the Pet Lamb, N Currier, 1852, lg folio........400.00
Saratoga Lake, sm folio................................175.00
Saratoga Springs, sm folio.............................175.00
Scene on the Susquehanna, sm folio.....................250.00
Siege & Capture of Vicksburg, Miss July 4, 1863, sm folio.....150.00
Sinking of the Steamship Ville Du Havre, sm folio..........225.00

Snipe Shooting, N Currier, 1852, lg folio....3,000.00
Snow Storm, med folio....1,300.00
Soldier's Adieu, N Currier, 1847, sm folio....115.00
Soldier's Grave, In Memory of George Bradbury, sm folio....90.00
Soldier's Return, N Currier, 1847, sm folio....115.00
Son & Daughter of Temperance, N Currier, sm folio....90.00
Son of Temperance, N Currier, 1848, sm folio....90.00
Squirrel Shooting, sm folio....450.00
Stanch Pointer, sm folio....195.00
Star of the East, sm folio....50.00
Stopping Place on the Road, 1868, lg folio....2,500.00
Storming of Fort Donelson TN, sm folio....160.00
Storming the Heights at Monterey by American Army, sm folio....130.00
Summer in the Country, sm folio....150.00
Summer Landscape, sm folio....150.00
Summer Morning, med folio....250.00
Summer Night, sm folio....150.00
Summer Ramble, med folio....250.00
Sunnyside on the Hudson, sm folio....160.00
Surrender of Cornwallis at Yorktown, N Currier, sm folio....275.00
Surrender of Gen Johnston near Greensboro, NC, 1865, sm....150.00
Surrender of Gen Lee at Appomatox, April 9, 1865, sm folio....175.00
Surrender of Port Hudson, LA, July 8, 1863, sm folio....150.00
Susanna, N Currier, sm folio....60.00
Susie, sm folio....60.00
Sylvan Lake, sm folio....150.00
Take Care!, sm folio....50.00
Taking a Smash, sm folio....180.00
Team Fast on the Snow, sm folio....250.00
Team Fast to the Pole, sm folio....250.00
Thatched Cottage, sm folio....150.00
To the Rescue, b/w, sm folio....45.00
Tomb of Washington, Mt Vernon, VA, med folio....170.00
Tree of Life, N Currier, sm folio....75.00
Tree of Temperance, N Currier, 1849, sm folio....90.00
Trotting Stallion Mambrino Gift, sm folio....300.00
Trying It On, sm folio....175.00
Tumbled to It, sm folio....200.00
United American, N Currier, sm folio....80.00
US Mail Steamship Arctic, N Currier, 1850, med folio....400.00
Valley Falls, VA, sm folio....175.00
Vase of Flowers, N Currier, 1847, sm folio....95.00
View on Long Island, NY, 1857, lg folio....2,000.00
Village Blacksmith, N Currier, med folio....550.00
Washington, 1st in War, 1st in Peace, N Currier, sm folio....65.00
Washington at Princeton, Jan 30, 1777, N Currier, sm folio....350.00
Western Farmers Home, sm folio....270.00
Who Will Love Me?, sm folio....50.00
Wild Duck Shooting, On the Wing, sm folio....425.00
William Harrison, 9th President of US, N Currier, sm folio....95.00
William Johnston, Governor of PA, N Currier, sm folio....50.00
William Penn's Treaty w/the Indians, sm folio....175.00
Winter Evening, N Currier, 1854, med folio....1,600.00
Woodcock Shooting, N Currier, 1855, sm folio....425.00
Woodlands in Winter, sm folio....395.00
Wreck of the Atlantic, sm folio....195.00
Yankee Doodle on His Muscle, sm folio....190.00
Young Cavalier, N Currier, sm folio....50.00

Fisher, Harrison

Harrison Fisher (1875-1934) was America's most highly-paid illustrator circa 1910 when he earned $50,000 a year. He did nearly one hundred covers for *The Saturday Evening Post*, over two hundred covers for *Cosmopolitan*, as well as covers for many other magazines. He also did postcards, prints, and other illustrations, among them several large books including *The Harrison Fisher Book, A Dream of Fair Women, Maidens Fair, American Belles*, and *A Girl's Life and Other Pictures*. Many of the 'prints' seen today are pages removed from these books. These have value, but not as much as individual prints issued as such.

American Bells, orig bookplate, unmatted, 1908....15.00
Greatest Moments of a Girl's Life, 6 scenes, 28x10" fr....95.00
Soldier kissing girl, in fr, 11x9"....30.00

Fox, R. Atkinson

Dreamland, sgn, orig fr, 9x13"....35.00
English Gardens, #57....35.00
Forest Primeval....45.00
Glorious Vista, lg....65.00
Indian Summer, ornate gold scalloped fr, lg....90.00
Love's Paradise, 8x14"....40.00
Old Fashioned Garden, EX fr, 18x30"....75.00
Perfect Day, sgn, orig fr, 21½x15½"....70.00
Spring Beauties, sgn, 25½x11½"....55.00
Stately Sentinals, fr, 16x24½"....45.00

Gould, John

Crex Pratensis, hc, unmatted, 14½x21½"....170.00
Great Northern Diver....560.00
Pink-Footed Goose....500.00
Pintail....660.00
Red-Breasted Merganser....665.00
Surf Scoter....415.00
Syrrhaptes Paracloxus, quail, hc, unmatted, 21"....150.00
Trochalopteron Variegatum, hc, 1870....160.00
Tufted Duck....685.00

Gutmann, Bessie Pease

Awaking, 14x21"....18.00
Baby w/puppy in his arms, 15x10¾"....55.00
Bit of Heaven, 14x21"....18.00
Bride, 19½x15½"....60.00
Chuckles....65.00
Chums, 1st edition....23.00
First Step....23.00
Friendly Enemies, 11x14"....20.00
Home Builders, fr....40.00
In Slumberland, 14x21"....22.00
Love Is Blind, 1st edition....23.00
Loves Blossom, 11x14"....18.00
Lullaby, 14x21"....23.00
Mighty Like a Rose, 11x15"....40.00
Miss Flint, 11x14"....18.00
On Dreamland's Border, 20x15½"....60.00
On the Up & Up, 14x21"....20.00
Reward, The; in orig fr....50.00
Snowbird, 1st edition....23.00
Sonny Boy, 14x21"....18.00
Sunkist, 14x21"....18.00
Television, 14x21"....20.00
Thank You God....23.00
Trio, Cupid That's Me/Contentment/Excuse my Back, tin fr....88.00
Waiting For Daddy....23.00

Homer, Winslow

All in the Gay & Golden Weather, June 12, 1969............30.00
Bathing at Long Branch, Aug 26, 1971.....................37.00
Country Store–Getting Weighed, March 25, 1971.............50.00
Dad's Coming, wood eng, full sheet, Harper's, Nov 1, 1873.....90.00
Gathering Berries, wood eng, full sheet, July 11, 1874........105.00
Last Days of Harvest, Dec 6, 1973.........................40.00
Noon Recess, wood eng, full sheet, Harper's, June 28, 1873.....75.00
On the Road to Lake George, Appleton's Journey, July 1969....30.00
Spring in the City, Harper's Weekly, April 17, 1958...........40.00

Icart, Louis

Louis Icart was a French artist who immortalized the French woman through his etchings, which were widely produced during the 1920s. Most of his post-1920 etchings carry a U.S. copyright notice in the margin, as well as Icart's personal intaglio seal.

After the Raid, sgn, blindstamp, fr.......................1,795.00
After the Walk, sgn, blindstamp, G color...................995.00
Bewilderment, sgn, blindstamp, fr........................1,150.00
Black Shawl, sgn, c 1925/Les Graveurs Modernes, fr, 12x9"....300.00
Blue Bandana, sgn, blindstamp, fr..........................850.00
Book, Destin De Femme.....................................850.00
Broken Blue Jug...650.00
Casanova, sgn/stamp, c 1928/Icart, Paris, in fr, 20x13"........385.00
Cinderella, sgn/stamp, c 1927/Icart, Paris, in fr, 14x18".......400.00
Conchita, sgn, blindstamp, fr............................1,695.00
Coursing II, sgn/stamp, c 1929/Icart, Paris, stain, 16x26"......880.00
Don Juan, sgn, blindstamp, fr............................1,250.00

Le Poeme, etching and drypoint in colors, Louis Icart, signed in pencil in margin and with blind stamp, 18" x 22", $500.00.

Fall, sgn, blindstamp, fr..................................495.00
Flower Seller, sgn, blindstamp, fr, G color..................975.00
Girl in Crinoline, sgn, blindstamp, fr.....................1,095.00
Homeage to Gwenmeyer, sgn, blindstamp, fr..............4,075.00
In the Trenches, sgn, blindstamp, fr......................2,350.00
Kiss of the Motherland, sgn, blindstamp, fr...............2,195.00
Kittens (Petits Chats).....................................950.00
La Nuit et le Moment, edited by Guillot, '46, set of 23......3,300.00
Laughing, sgn, blindstamp, fr..............................925.00
Laziness, sgn, blindstamp, fr............................1,925.00
Love Letters, sgn, blindstamp, fr..........................950.00
Masks (Les Masques)....................................1,400.00
Miss America, sgn, blindstamp, fr........................2,495.00
Morning Cup, sgn, blindstamp, fr.........................1,975.00
Muff, sgn, blindstamp, fr................................1,150.00
Nurse, sgn, blindstamp, fr...............................1,075.00
Peacocks, sgn, blindstamp, fr............................1,350.00
Pink Alcove, sgn, blindstamp, fr...........................745.00
Symphony in White, sgn, blindstamp, fr...................2,350.00
Tea, sgn/stamp, c 1926/Les Graveurs Modernes, fr, 18x14½"...250.00
Thoroughbreds, sgn, blindstamp, fr.......................4,950.00
Two Women Before a Coach, sgn/stamp, in fr, 1925, 12x9"....385.00
Untitled, seated lady w/cat................................675.00
Venus...600.00
Waltz Echoes, sgn, blindstamp, fr........................1,795.00
Wisteria, sgn, blindstamp, fr............................1,450.00
Woman in Bonnet...725.00
Woman in Shawl, sgn, c 1924/Les Graveurs Modernes, 12x9"..300.00
Wounded Dove, no fr.......................................800.00
Wounded Dove, sgn, blindstamp, fr........................1,250.00

Kellogg, American Scenery, View on the Connecticut, med.....130.00
Kellogg, Battle of Champion Hills, MS, May 16, 1863, VG.....120.00
Kellogg, Rural Sweets......................................60.00
Koehler, Darktown Fire Brigade, Investigating a Smoke, sm....170.00
Koehler, Darktown Fire Brigade, Slightly Demoralized, sm.....140.00
Koehler, Darktown Fire Brigade, The Last Shake, sm, EX.....190.00
Koehler, Darktown Hook & Ladder Corps, sm folio...........190.00

Kurz and Allison

Louis Kurz founded the Chicago Lithograph Company in 1833. Among his most notable works were a series of thirty-six Civil War scenes and one hundred illustrations of Chicago architecture. His company was destroyed in the Great Fire of 1871, and in 1880 Kurz formed a partnership with Alexander Allison, an engraver. Until both retired in 1903, they produced hundreds of lithographs, in color as well as black and white.

Battle of Champion Hills, MS, lg folio, EX.................150.00
Battle of Corinth, lg folio, VG............................150.00
Battle of Lexington, b/w, med folio, 14½x21", EX............30.00
Battle of Opequan or Winchester, VA, lg folio, EX...........170.00
Battle of Pea Ridge, AR, lg folio, EX......................350.00
Battle of Princeton, lg folio, EX..........................190.00
Battle of Savannah, b/w, med folio, EX......................30.00
Battle of Tippecanoe, lg folio, VG.........................150.00
Battle of Wilson's Creek, MO, lg folio, EX.................170.00
Capture of El Caney, lg folio, VG..........................170.00
Capture of Fort Fisher, lg folio, VG.......................150.00
Charge of the 24th & 25th Colored Infantry, lg folio, VG......150.00
Col Theodore Roosevelt, b/w, lg folio, VG...................60.00
Columbus Return to Barcelona & Reception, lg folio, VG......130.00
De Soto's Discovery of the Mississippi, lg folio, VG...........130.00
Entrance of Fernando Cortez into Mexico, lg folio, VG........150.00
Gen John C Breckenridge, b/w, lg folio, VG..................55.00
Gen US Grant & Family, b/w, lg folio, VG....................55.00
Great Connemaugh Valley Disaster–Johnstown Flood, lg folio...170.00
Surrender of Adm Cervera July 3, 1898, b/w, lg folio, VG......125.00

McKenney and Hall

Chippeway Widow, 14x20"...................................85.00
Chitte Yoholo, Seminole Chief, Greenough, 1836, 14x20", EX..155.00

Choncape, An Otto Second Chief, Bowen, 10x7″ . . . 25.00
Foke Luste Hajo, Seminole Chief, Bowen, 1842, 14x20″, EX . . . 155.00
Itcho Tustinnuggee, Seminole Chief, Rice & Clark, 1843, EX . . . 155.00
John Ross, A Cherokee Chief, Bowen, 10x7″ . . . 45.00
Julcee Mathla, Seminole Chief, Rice & Clark, 1843, 14x20″ . . . 155.00
Kishkekosh, A Fox Brave, Bowen, 10x7″ . . . 55.00
Me-Te-A, Pottawatomi Chief, 14x20″, EX . . . 150.00
Micanopy, Seminole Chief, Greenough, 1836, 14x20″, EX . . . 170.00
Mistippee, Son of Yoholo Micco, Creek Chief, 1836, 14x20″ . . . 150.00
Mo Hon Go, Biddle, 1834, 14x20″, EX . . . 155.00
Nahet-Luc-Hopi, Muskogee Chief, Rice & Clark, 1842, 14x20″ . . . 150.00
Neamathla, Seminole Chief, Greenough, 1836, 14x20″, EX . . . 155.00
Opothle Yoholo, Creek Chief, Biddle 1837, 14x20″, EX . . . 170.00
Red Bird, A Winnebago, Bowen, 10x7″ . . . 45.00
Se-Loc-Ta, Creek Chief, Greenough, 14x20″, EX . . . 170.00
Tahtohon, An Ioway Warrior, Bowen, 10x7″ . . . 35.00
Tukoseemathla, A Seminole Chief, Bowen, 10x7″ . . . 75.00
Tustennuggee Emathla, Creek Chief, Rice & Clark, 14x20″ . . . 170.00
Wa Bish Kee Pe Nas (White Pigeon) Chippewa, 14x20″, EX . . . 130.00

Nutting, Wallace

Born in 1862, Nutting pursued many careers. His hand-tinted photographs of landscapes and interior scenes are prized by collectors today. He was also a writer, minister, farmer, and a furniture maker, designing reproductions of early American pieces. Collectors of his prints should be aware of rosy-hued, inconsistently bright or dark examples--especially large prints of *An Elaborate Dinner* and *A Chair for John*. These have been reproduced.

Among the Beeches, w/mat, 18¼x16″ . . . 34.00
An Elaborate Dinner, c 1919, sgn, on mat, 15x12″ . . . 67.00
An Old Colony Parlor, c 1913, 12¾x10½″ . . . 78.00
Apple Over the Brook, c 1908, sgn, gilt fr, 16½x11½″ . . . 45.00
Berkshire Mountain Brook, c 1922, sgn, 19¼x14¾″ . . . 45.00
Birch Grove, in fr, 13x10″ . . . 33.00
Bit of Sewing, interior, sgn, 11x13½″ . . . 80.00
Bit of Tea, interior, sgn, 15x18″ . . . 85.00
Blooms at the Bend, 21x12″ . . . 25.00
Book Settle, c 1909, sgn, 16½x10½″ . . . 70.00
Delicate Stitch, 13x11″ . . . 73.00
Embroidery, c 1916, 15x12″ . . . 70.00
Her Old Trundle Bed, sgn, 17x13″ . . . 95.00
Hollyhock Cottage, fr, 4x6″ . . . 23.00
Honeymoon Stroll, 5x7″ . . . 23.00
House surrounded by lovely scenery, 14¾x11½″ . . . 67.50
Lady leans in front of blazing hearth, 7½x5½″ . . . 50.00
Lady sets out dishes, re-matted, 9½x7½″ . . . 45.00
Larkspur, 5x7″ . . . 25.00
Little River with Mt Washington, in fr, 6x9¼″, VG . . . 35.00
Main Surf, in fr, scarce, 21½x13½″ . . . 47.00
Maple Sugar Cupboard, in fr, 15″ . . . 65.00
Mexican Zinnias, in fr, rare, 17x14″ . . . 85.00
Monument Between the Blossoms, scarce, fr: 15x12″ . . . 55.00
New Hampshire October, in fr, 17x14″ . . . 37.00
Pergola Amalfi, scarce, 12x15″ . . . 46.00
Petals Above & Below, gilt fr, 14½x11½″ . . . 30.00
Scenic, sheep grazing, old fr, 8x9″ . . . 60.00
Seascapes/cliffs/caves of LaJolla, rare, 23½x19½″ . . . 115.00
Sheffield Heirloom, sgn, 18½x15½″ . . . 95.00
Stepping Stones at Bolton Abbey, gilt fr: 18x15″ . . . 70.00
Stitch in Time, 11½″ . . . 75.00
Swimming Pool, 5x7″ . . . 28.00
Undulating Reflections, 14¾x11½″ . . . 59.00

Parrish, Maxfield

Maxfield Parrish was a painter and illustrator who began his career in the last decade of the 19th century. His work remained prominent until the early 1940s. His most famous painting, *Daybreak*, was published in print form and sold nearly two thousand copies between 1910 and 1930. Prices are for unsigned prints, unframed unless noted.

Advertising, Edison Mazda, Jan 1919 . . . 40.00
Advertising, Fisk Tire, Fit for a King, b/w, 8¾x12½″ . . . 8.50
Advertising, Hires, gnome w/glass, orig, 8x11″ . . . 45.00
Advertising, Jell-O, Polly & kettle, orig fr, 1924, 14″ . . . 45.00
Advertising, Old King Cole, cigar box label, 6x10″, M . . . 35.00
Advertising, Pipe Night at the Players, 6x9½″ . . . 15.00
Air Castles, nude nymph blows bubbles, orig fr, 12x16″ . . . 105.00
Bank check, hand written, personal, orig fr, rare, 1962 . . . 85.00
Bellerophon at Fountain of Pyrene, ca 1906, 9x11½″, VG . . . 75.00
Benign Dragon, London News, Dec 1910 . . . 92.00
Book, Arabian Nights, Scribner, 1st ed, 1909 . . . 85.00
Book, Edison Mazda, Wonder Book & Tanglewood Tales, 1910 . 85.00
Book, Eugene Field's Poems of Childhood, Scribner/1904, VG . . . 50.00

Garden of Allah, Maxfield Parrish, published by House of Art for Reinthal & Newman, in original frame, 16″ x 30″, $175.00.

Book, Knave of Hearts, hard bound, M . . . 600.00
Book, Knave of Hearts, soft bound, G . . . 150.00
Book, Maxfield Parrish, Ludwig, M . . . 50.00
Book, The Early Years, Skeeters, M . . . 150.00
Bookplate, Decorations for Curtis Dining Hall, 2 pg, M . . . 25.00
Bookplate, Knave of Hearts, man in pile of books, orig fr . . . 75.00
Bookplate, Little Peach, 6½x9″, M . . . 12.00
Bookplate, Such Sights as Youthful Poets Dream, 6½x9″, M . . . 12.00
Box, Crane's Chocolate, The Hope Chest, rare, 1915, EX . . . 150.00
Calendar, waterfall, complete, lg, M . . . 500.00
Calendar of Cheer, w/52 week sheets, sgn, 1929 . . . 30.00
Canyon, sealed, orig fr, M . . . 135.00
Centaur, The; orig ornate fr, scarce, 1910, 11x13″ . . . 95.00
Chiron the Centaur, 2 nudes & Centaur standing, orig fr . . . 90.00
Christmas card, A New Day or Afterglow, 6x8¼″ . . . 9.00
Christmas card, Silent Night, 1950s, 5¼x7½″, M . . . 9.00
Christmas card, Twilight Hour, Brown & Bigelow, 6x7¼″ . . . 9.00
Christmas card, When Christmas Comes, 5¼x7½″ . . . 9.00
Circes Palace . . . 55.00
Contentment, orig ornate fr, 1928, 9½x13″ . . . 90.00
Daybreak, orig fr, ca 1954, 10x18″ . . . 85.00
Daybreak, orig ornate fr, 1923, 13x21″ . . . 110.00
Dinkey Bird . . . 110.00
Djer Kiss w/Elves . . . 95.00
Djer Kiss w/Maiden . . . 85.00
Dreaming, sealed, orig fr, 18x30″, M . . . 450.00
Dreamlight, orig fr, 15x20″, M . . . 300.00
Dreamlight, orig ornate fr, 1925, 8½x11½″ . . . 90.00
Ecstasy, Edison Mazda, orig fr, scarce, 1930, 16½x22½″ . . . 450.00

Enchantment, sm......115.00
Evening, nude nymph in lake, orig ornate fr, 1922, 7x11"......85.00
Everybody in the Brave Country, London News, Dec 1910......25.00
Farmer, The; Collier's, June 23, 1906......37.00
Fisherman & Geni, Arab on beach, orig fr, 1909, 10x13"......65.00
Friendly Man in the Moon, London News, Dec 1922......35.00
Garden of Allah, 3 maidens by pool, orig fr, 17½x32½"......175.00
Golden Hours, orig ornate fr, 1929, 9x12"......90.00
Greeting card, Twilight Hour, 1950s, 6x7¼", M......9.00
Hilltop, med......225.00
Ink blotter, VT Assoc for Billboard Restriction, M......50.00
Interlude......165.00
Jason & His Teacher......100.00
Lady Ursula, orig ornate fr, 1925, 12x14"......56.00
Lady Violetta, orig fr, 1925, 12x14"......70.00
Lampseller of Bagdad, orig ornate fr, 9½x13"......125.00
Land of Make Believe, orig ornate fr, rare, 1912, 11x13"......125.00
Light bulb tester, Edison Mazda, lg, G......850.00
Lute Players, sm......50.00
Lute Players, 1924, 18x30", M......250.00
Magazine, Scribner, Oct 1899, G......165.00
Magazine cover, Sleeping Beauty, G......275.00
Manager, The; comical man in cape, orig fr, 1925, 10x11"......45.00
Morning, maiden on rock looks up, orig fr, 1922, 13x16"......110.00
Night Has Fled, sm......150.00
Old Romance, nude maiden in Grecian garden, orig fr, 7x10"...45.00
Opalescent Dream, London News, Dec 1913......45.00
Page, The; knave sitting on wall, orig fr, 1925, 12x14"......95.00
Peace at Twilight, winter scene, scarce, orig fr, 10½x13"......90.00
Pierrot's Serenade, plays mandolin, orig fr, 11½x13½"......95.00
Playing cards, Egypt, Mazda, in box, 1922......200.00
Postcard, Pied Piper......65.00
Poster, The Idiot, 13x21½", M......65.00
Poster, The Reluctant Dragon, Nash, ca 1973, 17x14"......30.00
Primitive Man, orig ornate fr, 1921, 10x13"......140.00
Prometheus, Edison Mazda, orig fr, rare, 1920, 10x13"......195.00
Prometheus, sealed, orig fr, rare, lg, M......900.00
Prospector, The; Collier's, Feb 4, 1911......35.00
Queen Gulnare, orig ornate fr, 1906, 11x13½"......85.00
Reveries, orig ornate fr, 1927, 17x25"......325.00
Reveries, 1960s, 7x11", M......25.00
Romance, maiden & knave standing, orig fr, 1925, 15x27"......425.00
Rubaiyat, lg......275.00
Seein' Things, 6¾x9¼", M......15.00
Sign, metal, 2-sided, Edison Mazda, G......300.00
Six Ingredients, orig fr, 1925, 12x14"......65.00
Solitude, Edison Mazda, maiden on rock, orig fr, 9x11", VG....65.00
Song of Sixpence, comical, King & Queen at table, orig fr......45.00
Spirit of the Night, orig ornate fr, 1919, 10x14"......135.00
Spirit of Transportation, sealed, orig fr, M......250.00
Spring, orig ornate fr, rare, 1905, 11½x13½"......125.00
Sunrise, orig ornate fr, 1933, 10x12½"......120.00
Tranquility, 1950s, 22x28", M......80.00
Triplicate, sealed, orig fr, rare, M......425.00
Twilight, Brown & Bigelow, scarce, fr, 1937, lg......100.00
Venetian Lamplighter, orig ornate fr, 1924, 10x13½"......125.00
Violetta & the Knave, orig ornate fr, 1925, 12x14"......75.00
Waterfall, The; orig ornate fr, 1931, 9½x12"......95.00
Wild Geese......135.00

Prang, Louis

Apple Blossoms & Bees, 1885, 7½x10¾"......20.00
Battle of Antietam, Prang's American Litho Co, EX......90.00
Battle of Spottsylvania, VG......190.00
Cowslips, 1886, 7½x10½"......18.00
Dogwood, 1886, 7½x10½"......18.00
Elder, 1886, 7½x10½"......18.00
Home of Abraham Lincoln, 14x16", VG......65.00
Magnolia, 1886, 7½x10½"......18.00
Partridge, L Prang & Co, w/mat, 4¾x7¾"......20.00
Sunset, California Scenery, walnut fr w/ gold liner, 1868......75.00
Trillium, 1886, 7½x10½"......20.00

Remington, Frederic

Ambushed Picket, Harper's Weekly, July 8, 1889......20.00
At the Waterhole, sgn, 20x14"......60.00
Evening on a Canadian Lake, orig label & fr, 12x18", EX......65.00
Evening on a Canadian Lake, sgn, 20x14"......85.00
Quarrel Over Cards, Harper's Weekly, April 23, 1887......30.00
Questionable Companionship, wood engraving, Harper's......25.00
Soldiering in the SW–Rescue of Corp Scott, Harper's, 1886......25.00

Don Jose Sepulvida and Bucking Bob, Frederic Remington, 1861, from *A Knight Errant of the Foot Hills*, Vol. 1, signed in pencil, $425.00.

Yard long, Bridal Flowers, Mary E Hart......65.00
Yard long, Carnation Symphony, no fr......25.00
Yard long, Cats, in old fr......85.00
Yard long, Chickens, Ben Austrian......140.00
Yard long, Chicks, 16 play in flowers, Cambric, fr......115.00
Yard long, Fall Leaves, in gold flower/leaf fr......50.00
Yard long, Field of Poppies, Clarkson, no fr......35.00
Yard long, Fruit, sgn Guy Bedford......35.00
Yard long, Lady w/Brooch, advertising Selz shoes, fr......115.00
Yard long, Pansies......50.00
Yard long, Puppies, fr, 1905......115.00
Yard long, Shower of Lilacs, Muller, sgn, orig fr, 1897......100.00
Yard long, Study of Roses, Paul DeLongpre, no fr......35.00
Zogbaum, Rufus; A Picket Post in the Indian Country, 1889......8.00
Zogbaum, Rufus; Beef Issue in the Indian Territory, 1890......18.00
Zogbaum, Rufus; Hunting Wild Turkey by Moonlight, Apr 1889..10.00

Purinton

Purinton Pottery was made in Wellsville, Ohio as early as 1936. But in 1941, the company relocated in Shippenville, Pennsylvania, and began making the hand-painted dinnerware that is today gaining in popularity with collectors. Bold brush strokes of color were used create simple, yet appealing patterns such as their popular Apple, Pensylvania Dutch, Fruit, and Tea Rose. Each design was made in full sets of tableware as well as accessory pieces. The company closed in 1959.

Values are given for examples in mint condition.

Bowl, berry; apple, sm....5.00
Bowl, cereal; apple....6.00
Coffee pot, apple, 8-cup....20.00
Creamer, apple....7.00
Jug, apple, 5-pt....15.00
Jug, Dutch, apple, 2-pt....12.00
Jug, Kent, apple, 1-pt....9.00
Pitcher, apple, 3-qt....18.00
Pitcher, red/bl/gr floral, odd shape, hdl atop, 7″....7.00
Plate, chop; apple, dotted edge, 12″....12.00
Shakers, apple, lg, pr....8.00
Shakers, brn/chartreuse floral, jug shape, sm, pr....9.00
Shakers, fruit, in wire holder, set....8.00
Sugar bowl, apple....8.00
Teapot, apple, 2-cup....10.00
Teapot, apple, 6-cup....18.00
Teapot, apple & pear, 1-cup....7.00
Tumbler, apple, 12-oz....8.00

Purses

A popular new collectible, one that seems to have captured the attention of many, is metal mesh and beaded bags. They are found in floral-beaded velvets that represent the tastes of the turn of the century, or in styles recalling the flapper era. Deco styling is also represented, and these are usually made from metal mesh in a gold or silver finish. Some of the mesh bags are enameled with florals or birds, and some are fitted inside with mirrors and compacts. All are very collectible, and prices reflect their popularity.

When no condition is indicated, the items listed below are assumed to be in excellent condition.

Alligator, suede lined....20.00
Beaded, beige faille, embroidery trim/drawstrings, relined....15.00
Beaded, blk carnival, rectangular, 7x5x4½″....25.00
Beaded, clutch, gray/silver Deco design, mk Czech, zipper....12.00
Beaded, clutch, shell pink bugles, snaps, mirror, in box....20.00
Beaded, copper on knitted yarn, dk celluloid top/clasp....45.00
Beaded, diamond shape, red w/bead fringe, brass fr/chain....50.00
Beaded, drawstring pouch, allover glass beads....25.00
Beaded, drawstring pouch, bl w/mc beads....40.00
Beaded, drawstring pouch, wht crochet w/tassles....18.00
Beaded, emb pastel leaves/flowers w/clear beads, 9½x5½″....18.00
Beaded, envelope, seed pearls & sequins on wht, 5x8″....14.00
Beaded, floral, tapestry, EX....65.00
Beaded, geometrics on bl/blk, fringe, tortoise chain hdl....35.00
Beaded, marcasite 1″ diamonds on pink, fringe, SP fr, 9x6″....48.00
Beaded, mc flowers on wht, mirror, snaps/fringe, chain hdl....45.00
Beaded, over-the-wrist pouch type, red....50.00
Beaded, peacock in beading, velvet/satin, w/belt, in box....60.00
Beaded, people design, name & year 1832 in beading....100.00
Beaded, roses/morning-glories on wht, fringe, SP fr, 6x10″....45.00
Beaded, seed pearls/mc muted leaf/floral forms emb overall....30.00
Beaded, vertical beads, lined, SP fr, gr....27.50
Beaded, 5 blk & 1 bl rows, pouch w/beaded tassel....18.00
Brocade, blk, pearl & rhinestone fr, chain hdl, French....10.00
Celluloid, orange/amber, X motif on lid, w/hdls, 4x8″....110.00
Coin, leather, wht lily form w/advertising....25.00
Coin, velvet w/crochet drawstring top, gold thread/sequins....55.00
Crochet, navy bl....18.00
Crochet flowers/metal beads, ornate fr, France....125.00
Elginite, red & chrome, Deco style, w/chain....50.00
Embroidered Nouveau mc design on satin/jeweled brass clasp....40.00
Leather, hand tooled, Arts & Crafts....25.00
Lucite, etched floral on bottom, cylinder shape, gray hdls....12.50
Mesh, Art Deco, Whiting & Davis....40.00
Mesh, Art Nouveau style, SP, w/chain, 4½″....38.00
Mesh, basket of flowers, fringe, mk El Sah, Whiting Davis....95.00
Mesh, brass, mc jewels on reticulated fr, chain hdl, 5x6″....35.00
Mesh, clutch, Whiting & Davis....19.00
Mesh, cockatoo on perch, enamel....65.00
Mesh, German, silver, fancy, w/chain, 5x6″....25.00
Mesh, silver, hallmk, 1890s....95.00
Mesh, sterling, child's head & fish, repousse, 5¼″....180.00
Mesh, sterling, Whiting & Davis, 8½x6″....125.00
Mesh, wht, Whiting & Davis, 1950s....18.00
Metal frame, red rose on blk, leaf design, silk lined, hdl....35.00
Petit point, roses on silk, ornate fr w/48 stones....125.00
Sequins, blk flowers, gold clasp, chain hdl....20.00
Silver metal disks/tortoise hdls, Whiting Davis, in mk bag....75.00
Suede, brass clasp & pull w/clear beads/pearls/rhinestones....150.00
Velvet, w/drawstring, Victorian....18.00

Beaded with Venetian canal and boat scene; clasp, knob and frame studded with blue beads, 13¼″ x 8″, $175.00.

Quezal

The Quezal Art Glass and Decorating Company of Brooklyn, New York, was founded in 1901 by Martin Bach. A former Tiffany employee, Bach's glass closely resembled that of his former employer. Most pieces were signed 'Quezal,' a name taken from a Central American bird. After Bach's death in 1920, his son-in-law, Conrad Vohlsing, continued to produce a Quezal-type glass in Elmhurst, New York, which he marked 'Lustre Art Glass.'

When no condition is indicated, the items listed below are assumed to be in mint condition.

Bowl, brilliant gold, flared rim, sgn, 3x6¼″....275.00
Bowl, feathering, gold/gr to wht/gr, gold w/in, 3½x7″....1,350.00
Bowl vase, gold w/purple highlights, sgn, 2¾″ W....155.00
Candle vase, gold irid, sgn, 11″....195.00
Nut bowl, wine irid, self rimmed, sgn, set of 4....650.00

Rose bowl, leaves & vines, gold on opal, 4¾″ 1,400.00
Salt, gold, ribbed, sgn, 1x2¾″ 155.00
Salt, gold, sgn, 1x2¾″ 150.00
Shade, fish net, gold w/bl irid/gold int/optic ribs, 4 for 785.00
Shade, gold, bell form, sgn, 5½″ 175.00
Shade, gold, calcite w/in, bulbous, 7″ 375.00
Shade, King Tut, heavy ribs, 6½″ 200.00
Shade, lime w/gr-bordered orange drape, gold w/in, sgn, pr 300.00
Shade, opal bonnet w/gold trellis, gold w/in, 7″ dia 700.00
Shade, opal snakeskin on gold, gr border, boudoir shape 125.00
Shade, wht pulled feathers on gr irid, 5½″ 225.00
Vase, agate, everted lip on bulb, ca 1905-1925, sgn, 4¼″ 550.00
Vase, bl irid, baluster form, flared rim, sgn, 8″ 425.00
Vase, bl irid, dimpled, sgn, 3″ 325.00
Vase, bl irid w/pearlized vine & leaf, sgn, 10″ 875.00
Vase, brn tracing at top, gold shades on opal, sgn, 6½″ 1,450.00
Vase, feathering at base, gold/brn/wht, gold w/in, 7x3½″ 1,250.00
Vase, floriform, amber irid w/gr/bl feathers, label, 5″ 500.00
Vase, gold w/pink highlights, flared w/bulb base, 10″ 525.00
Vase, gold w/pink highlights, trumpet form, 10″ 495.00
Vase, gold w/violet highlights, 8″ 445.00
Vase, opal w/gold-edged gr feathers, gold w/in, 5½″ 750.00
Vase, opal w/gold-edged gr feathers, gold w/in, 6½x5″ 985.00
Vase, random damascene decor, wht & gold, disk ft, sgn, 8″ . . 2,250.00
Vase, sweet pea; pulled gr lustre threads, gold w/in 990.00
Vase, wht/gr swirls, gold hooked feathers, 4¼″ 775.00

Quilts

Quilts, while made out of necessity, nevertheless represent an art form which expresses the character and the personality of the designer. During the 17th and 18th centuries, quilts were considered a necessary part of a bride's hope chest--the traditional number required to be properly endowed for marriage was a 'baker's dozen'! Quilts were used not only for bed coverings, but for curtains, extra insulation, and mattresses as well. The early quilts were made from pieces salvaged from cloth items that had outlived their original usefulness, and from bits left over from sewing projects. Regardless of shape, these scraps were fitted together following no organized lines. The resulting hodge-podge design was called a crazy quilt.

In 1793, Eli Whitney developed the cotton gin, and as a result, textile production in America became industrialized. Soon inexpensive fabrics were readily available, and ladies were able to choose from colorful prints and solids to add contrast to their work. Both pieced and appliqued work became popular--pieced quilts were considered utilitarian, while appliqued work was shown with pride of accomplishment at the fair. Today many collectors prize pieced quilts and their intricate geometric patterns above all other types. Many of these designs were given names: Daisy and Oak Leaf, Grandmother's Flower Garden, Log Cabin, and Ocean Wave are only a few. Appliqued quilts involved stitching one piece, carefully cut into a specific form such as a leaf, a flower, or a stylized device, onto either a large one-piece ground fabric or an individual block. Often the background fabric was quilted in a decorative pattern.

Amish women scorned printed calicos as 'worldly,' and instead used colorful blocks set with black ground fabrics to produce a stunning pieced effect.

During the Victorian era, the crazy quilt was revived, but the ladies of the 1870s used plush velvets, brocades, silks, and linen patches and embroidered along the seams with feather or chain stitches.

Another type of quilting, highly prized and rare today is trapunto. These quilts were made by first stitching the outline of the design onto a solid sheet of fabric which was backed with a second having a much looser weave. White was often favored, but color was sometimes used for accent. The design (grapes, flowers, leaves, etc.) was padded through openings made by separating the loose weave of the underneath fabric; a backing was added and the three layers quilted as one.

Besides condition, value is judged on intricacy of pattern, color effect, and craftsmanship.

When no condition is indicated, the items listed below are assumed to be in excellent condition.

Key:

dia—diamond	hs—hand sewn
embr—embroidered	ms—machine sewn

Amish

Goose flight w/9-Patch sqs down center, OH, 58x79″ 425.00
Lg simple dia in maroon/gr/gray/bl/purple, Lancaster Co 600.00
Log Cabin, rich dk colors, 60x80″ 575.00
Lone Star, contemporary, 43″ 135.00
Lone Star, lt pastels w/dk bl/purple/blk, mc star, 1925 . . . . 700.00
Oversize sq contains sq w/lg diamond, pattern quilting, EX 200.00
25-Patch sq in pink/blk alternate w/blk sqs, ms binding 275.00
9-Patch in center, blues on blk sateen, worn, 35x38″ 225.00

Appliqued

Bear's paws, ice cream cone border, 1800s, minor wear 325.00
Birds & heart center, bird/flower spandrels, PA, top only 150.00
Floral, lg/stylized, EX pattern quilting, 72″ sq 350.00
Floral, stylized on wht w/dk grid, feather stitch border 950.00
Floral bouquets, scalloped, rpr/worn/faded, 74x86″ 275.00
Floral lattice, scalloped border, ms applique, hs quilting 275.00

Appliqued, stylized floral with swag border, 87″ x 88″, $725.00

Floral medallions, stylized w/meandering border, calicos 405.00
Floral medallions, vine border, G quilting, worn/faded 250.00
Floral w/drooped buds, floral swag border, EX quilting, EX 725.00
Floral w/fan-like blossoms, pattern quilted, worn/stains 250.00
Floral/vine border, red/goldenrod/yel-gr, EX quilting, EX 450.00
Flowering tree, corner spandrels, contemporary, 74x94″ 350.00
Heart & leaf, 3-color, PA, ca 1870, crib sz 2,200.00

Leaves, stylized; vining border, on homespun, EX quilting.....550.00
Oak leaf, 3 various devices, sgn in embr, 80x94", EX work...1,000.00
Optical 4-blade pinwheels, striped border, calicos, EX.........500.00
Starflowers, stylized, wht w/goldenrod/red/gr calico, worn......105.00
4 tulip medallions, lg/stylized, worn binding, 78x78"..........250.00
9 floral & leaf stylized devices, red/gr, stains, 74x80".........375.00
9 floral pinwheels & dots, vine border, homespun, EX........450.00
9 medallions w/potted vine border, EX quilting, minor wear....450.00
9-Patch, calicos, 82x78"....................................225.00
9-Patch Variant, 68x76", EX.................................125.00

Pieced

Album, 9-Patch sqs w/ink names, minor wear & stains........350.00
Around the World, olive-brn/wht homespun, EX quilting.......470.00
Blazing Star, 9 lg mc stars on on wht, 1900, king sz.........400.00
Bow Tie, mc prints on wht, well quilted, unused, 72x74"......200.00
Brunswick Star, bl/brn, 1920................................100.00
Cluster of Stars, star quilted, 1880, fading/losses, 40".........415.00
Crazy, EX embr on silk/velvet/etc, flag-like bk, 1890, EX......275.00
Crazy, wool/flannel, abstract, shell quilting, 1900, EX.........770.00
Crib, lightning bolt bars, red/gr calico, 38x47"...............275.00
Crib, lt sqs w/dk bars, reversible, 38x47"...................375.00
Cross pattern, gr calico on wht homespun, stains, 66x78".....225.00
Diamonds of dk strips w/pieced sq intersections, 60x71".......220.00
Floral, stylized; sawtooth/vine border, on homespun, worn.....525.00
Flower Garden, prints on wht, yel border, 68x90"............175.00
Flying Geese variation, mc vertical rows, bl sashing...........250.00

Pieced, Pinwheel Block, blue and white polka-dot patches, diagonal line and diamond quilting, 76" square, $750.00.

Friendship, snowflakes/EX quilting, calico, 1870, crib sz.......825.00
Geometric flower-like triangles, blk/wht/red, minor stain.......125.00
Goose Tracks, EX quilting, 1900, unused....................310.00
Grandma's Fan, red/bl, minor stain.........................110.00
Hexagonal blocks w/stars, calicos, G quilting, 74x94".........335.00
Hovering Hawk, calicos, top only, 72x80"...................110.00
Irish Chain, unused, 84"...................................200.00
Irish Chain, 72x80"..160.00
Jacob's Steps, calicos on wht, bl border, 1880s, 105x96"......265.00
Laurel Wreath, red/gr/bl on wht, 1920......................150.00
Le Moyne Star, sawtooth border, cube/diagonal quilted, 40"..2,475.00
Log Cabin, mc prints w/red sqs & dia, 88x92"...............195.00
Log Cabin, Straight Furrow, sheer wools, PA, late 1800s......300.00
Log Cabin, velvet on blk, doll size, worn, 18x21"............105.00
Lone Star, G quilting, minor wear, 90x92"..................225.00
Lone Star, line/feather/floral quilted, fading, 1890, crib........770.00
Lone Star, pastels to dk colors, minor wear, 86x88"..........150.00
Lone Star, VG quilting, minor wear/fading, 66x67"...........325.00
Orange Peel, sgn in ink/1854, EX quilting, EX..............400.00
Pinwheel, sm pattern, calicos, minor stains, 1800s, 84x88".....385.00
Pinwheel Block, diagonal line/dia quilted, 1800s, fading.......825.00
Rob Peter to Pay Paul, pastels, heart quilting, EX............155.00
Rolling Star, red/gr on wht, EX quilting, 1880, 90x94", VG....245.00
Rose Blossom & Bud, calico/chintz, sgn/1855, 88x100", EX..1,430.00
Snowflakes, EX pattern quilting, calico/homespun, 77x78".....795.00
Snowflakes in dia, wht on red, feather quilting, unwashed......750.00
Sqs w/sqs in center alternate w/solid sqs, calico, 87x88".......275.00
Starflowers alternate w/quilted designs of hearts/etc, VG.......170.00
Stars, red on wht ground, worn/fading, 70x80"..............185.00
Stars, 4 rows of 4, w/crowned corners, calico, 70x72", EX.....300.00
Trees, stylized; calicos, unwashed, stains....................500.00
Triple Irish Chain, 72x80".................................400.00
Tulips, stylized/geometric, feather/ocean wave stitch, VG.......285.00
Wedding Ring, scalloped border, 66x82"....................200.00
Wild Goose Chase, linsey-woolsey, late 18th C, fading.........935.00
Wreaths, embr feather quilted, scalloped, minor wear, 96".....175.00
12 wheels on mc calico on wht sq in lt gr grid, ms/hs, 89"....250.00
16 stars in mc stripes on red w/brn-gray grid, 76x78".........240.00
20 color wheels, mc print on wht, unwashed, 74x90".........180.00
30 pinwheels, unused, 76x88"..............................200.00
4-point star w/diamond center, 30 sqs, early 1900s, NM.......235.00
7 Sisters, calicos, flowerhead quilting, 1930, 100x80".........880.00
9 stars, calico, sawtooth border, pattern quilted, stains........350.00
9-Patch w/red bow ties, red/gr calico on homespun, stains.....400.00

Trapunto

Appliqued floral medallions, padded birds/urns, EX work.....2,800.00
Chintz, floral border/central wreath padded, sgn/1846, NM...3,000.00
Floral w/central spray/birds/fans/etc, 1858, EX quilting.......1,700.00
Wht on wht, vine/floral edge & 10" border padded, homespun..600.00
13 wreaths of gr calico leaves & red padded berries, EX.......700.00

Miscellaneous

Mennonite, stars, reversible quilting, EX colors, 82x100"......275.00
Pieced/applied, sampler-type motif, dia quilted, 1800s, EX.....770.00
Pieced/applied chintz, roses/birds, tester, early 18th C.......2,475.00
Whole cloth, copper-plate print, Indians kidnap child, 92"....1,100.00

Quimper

Quimper is a type of pottery produced in Quimper, France. A tin enamel-glazed earthenware pottery with hand-painted decoration, it was first produced in the 1600s by the Bousquet and Caussy Factories. Little of this early ware was marked.

By the late 1700s, three factories were operating in the area, manufacturing the same type of pottery. The Grande Maison de HB, a company formed because of a marriage joining the Hubaudiere and Bousquet families, was a major producer of Quimper pottery. They marked their wares with various forms of the 'HB' logo, but of the pottery they produced, collectors value examples marked with the 'HB' within a triangle most highly.

Francois Eloury established another pottery in Quimper in the late 1700s. Under the direction of Charles Porquier, the ware was marked simply

'P.' Adolph Porquier replaced Charles in the 1850s, marking the ware produced during that period with an 'AP' logo.

Jule HenRiot began operations in 1886, using molds he had purchased from Porquier. His mark was 'HR,' and until the 20th century he was in competition with The Grande Maison de HB. In 1926 he began to mark his wares 'HenRiot Quimper.'

In 1968, the two factories merged. They are still in operation under the name Les Faenceries de Quimper.

The factory sold in the fall of 1983 to Sarah and Paul Janssens, from the United States, making it the first time the owners are not French.

When no condition is indicated, the items listed below are assumed to be in mint condition.

Bookend, seated children, artist Berthe Savigny, HB, pr.......450.00
Bowl, peasant lady, floral rim, HenRiot, 10" dia..............65.00
Butter pat, geometric pattern, HenRiot, 2" dia................20.00
Candlestick, figural man holding pot on head, HR, 8½".......285.00
Candlestick, horse figural, yel w/brn sponge.................175.00
Coffee set, Croisille pattern, pot/cr/rstr sug, 4 c/s.............475.00
Coffee set, hexagon, peasants, pot/cr/sug+6 c/s, HenRiot......495.00
Cup & saucer, heart shape, lady w/floral, HR.................70.00
Cup & saucer, hexagonal, man w/floral, HenRiot..............30.00
Cup & saucer, trefoil, fleur-de-lis w/ermines, 19th C, HB........95.00
Figurine, Bebe au Mouchoir, artist Berthe Savigny, HB........250.00
Figurine, Fillette, artist Porson, HB........................275.00
Figurine, Les Deux Vieux, artist Brion, 15"..................850.00
Figurine, Perrik & Marik, HenRiot, 6", pr...................300.00
Figurine, Ste Vierge w/Christ Child, HenRiot, 7¼"............145.00
Ginger jar, Rouen pattern, bird finial, 19th C, HR mk, 11"....350.00
Hors d'oeurve dish, couple/goose/bagpipe, 3-part, '30s, HB.....245.00
Inkwell, dbl; imp flower, man & lady, insets/lids, HR..........215.00
Inkwell, sq, cut corners, seated lady, inset/lid, HenRiot........165.00
Knife rest, figural sailor, artist Maillard.....................85.00
Picture frame, detailed man & lady, late 1800s, HB...........550.00
Pitcher, figural man w/bagpipe, miniature, HenRiot............65.00
Pitcher, lady w/florals, unsgn, mid-19th C, 6½"...............85.00
Pitcher, pinch lip, man, HenRiot, 1940s, 8"..................45.00

Left to right: water pitcher, signed HN206, peasant lady in panel, 8", $310.00; Double cruet, four figures of peasants in panels, blue rope handles, restored, 6½", $150.00.

Planter, man & lady w/florals, ftd, hdld, rect, HR Quimper.....375.00
Plaque, retic border, relief man w/horn, 19th C, PB mk.......450.00
Plate, asparagus; detailed lady, late 19th C, HB..............185.00
Plate, basket of flowers, 19th C, HB, 8½" dia................85.00
Plate, basket of flowers, 1940s, HenRiot, 8½" dia.............45.00
Plate, Botanical w/seahorse, 19th C, imp & sgn PB...........350.00
Plate, concentric yel/bl bands, lady, 1940s, 10" dia...........45.00
Plate, concentric yel/bl bands, man, 1940s, 9¼" dia...........25.00
Plate, geometric, HR Quimper, 9" dia.........................75.00
Platter, oval w/scalloped rim, lady, unsgn, att AP, 19th C......225.00
Platter, oval/scallop, men bowling/decor riche, PB Quimper....550.00
Porringer, crowing rooster, HR Quimper.......................45.00
Porringer, yel, florals, HB Quimper..........................25.00
Porringer, yel/bl concentric bands, lady, HenRiot, 1940s........20.00
Powder box, figural lady, artist Maillard, HenRiot............250.00
Salt, dbl bagpipe, lady/man, bow hdl, HR....................85.00
Salt, oval, floral wreath, HB Quimper........................25.00
Snuff bottle, book shape, man, unsgn.......................150.00
Teapot, rnd w/dolphin hdl & spout, lady & man, HR Quimper..400.00
Vase, dolphin feet, tulip shape, decor riche, HenRiot..........375.00
Vase, dragon hdls, urn shape, decor riche, HR, 17"..........575.00
Wall piece, retic, relief peasants at spring, 1800s, PB mk......850.00
Wall pocket, bagpipe, lady w/distaff, HR.....................185.00
Wall pocket, cone w/ruffled rim, lady, HR....................185.00

Radford

The Jasperware listed below was made in Zanesville, Ohio, at the A. Radford Pottery Company incorporated there in 1903. This type of ware was first designed and produced in 1896 when Albert Radford worked in Tiffin, Ohio. The Zanesville Jasper, in contrast to the original line, was decorated with Wedgwood-type cameos in relief that were not applied, but were formed within the general mold. The only mark found on the ware is a two-digit shape number. The Tiffin Jasper, though not always marked, is sometimes impressed 'Radford Jasper.'

After only a few months Radford sold the plant to Arc-En-Ciel and moved his works to West Virginia. In addition to the regular line of utility wares, several artware lines were also produced there. Among them were Ruko, a standard brown underglaze decorated line; Thera, matt glazed with slip decoration; and Radura, usually done in matt green glazes.

When no condition is indicated, the items listed below are assumed to be in mint condition.

Jasper

Letter holder, lady w/bow & target scene, #61...............500.00
Mug, lt bl w/grapes/florals in wht, #25, 5"..................225.00
Pitcher, grapes, Old Man Winter on hdl, #17, 9"............600.00
Vase, bust of Lincoln, bk: eagle, #12, 7"...................300.00
Vase, Grecian lady & man, cone shape, #21, 9".............600.00
Vase, kneeling lady w/arms up, bird in hand, #24, 9".........600.00
Vase, lady w/dog, bk: Roman, man kneeling, #18, 7".........300.00
Vase, lady w/flowers, bk: grapes, #59, 4"..................150.00
Vase, man's head both sides, twisted, 3"....................100.00
Vase, seated lady, trees & dog, #22, 9"....................600.00
Vase, 2 Cupids w/instruments, column on 1 side, #14, 7"......300.00

Miscellaneous

Candlestick, Ruko, floral, #1457, 7"........................190.00
Jardiniere, Ruko, floral, fluted, 10"........................200.00
Vase, Ruko, floral, 16".....................................500.00
Vase, Thera, 12½"..215.00

Radios

Vintage radios represent a field of collecting that is becoming very popular. There were thousands of styles and types produced, the most popular of which today are the breadboard and the cathedral. Consoles are usually considered less saleable since their size makes them hard to display and store.

When no condition is indicated, the items listed below are assumed to be in excellent condition.

Aeriola SR #864 . . . 210.00
Amberola DX . . . 425.00
Amberola X . . . 425.00
Andrews Type II, battery op, Deco panel . . . 325.00
Apex, metal cabinet, external speaker . . . 150.00
Arline #54K, wood case . . . 25.00
Atwater Kent, Model #10, breadboard, VG . . . 650.00
Atwater Kent, Model #12, breadboard . . . 950.00
Atwater Kent, Model #20, lg . . . 100.00
Atwater Kent, Model #40 . . . 100.00
Atwater Kent, Model #44, w/speaker . . . 145.00
Bendex, marbleized bakelite, gr/blk . . . 185.00
Clarion, semi-round top . . . 285.00
Crosley Bandbox #601, external speaker . . . 110.00
Crosley Magic Chef, Deco style, w/timer . . . 25.00
Crosley Musicone, metal cabinet, external speaker . . . 130.00
Crosley RFL #75, w/case . . . 175.00
Crosley WLW, 37 tubes, public address, misc features, 60" . . . 3,900.00
Emerson, Snow White, cream-colored cottage w/emb figures . . . 800.00
Emerson, table top, 1940s . . . 45.00
Fada, bakelite, bullet shape, all butterscotch . . . 235.00
Fada, bakelite, bullet shape, yel w/red trim . . . 275.00
Fada, floor model, Deco, 2 bk-to-bk nudes . . . 2,200.00
Freed-Eisemann NR . . . 200.00
Freshman Masterpiece, floor model . . . 300.00
General Electric SX22 . . . 350.00
Holster Calbot, w/speaker . . . 85.00
International Katte, plastic, 1933 . . . 175.00
Jewett Super, w/speakers . . . 100.00
Kodel C13, cloth-covered case . . . 225.00
Kodel C13, wooden case . . . 150.00
Mantel #30, w/speakers . . . 110.00
Marshall, silver, cathedral . . . 275.00
Perless #2, w/speakers . . . 100.00
Philco #37-61, cathedral . . . 75.00
Philco #51, clock-radio, mantel, rare, lg . . . 425.00
Philco #60, rfn . . . 175.00
Philco #70, rfn . . . 425.00
Philco #71 . . . 325.00
Philco #89, rfn . . . 265.00
Philco #90 . . . 375.00
Philco #90, w/case . . . 425.00
Philco #91, cathedral, scarce, EX . . . 210.00
Radiola #111, no tubes . . . 100.00
Radiola #111A, no tubes . . . 110.00
Radiola #18 . . . 55.00
Radiola #20 . . . 285.00
Radiola #3A . . . 190.00
RCA, 4-band, brn bakelite, 1948 . . . 80.00
RCA Radiola #33, w/speakers . . . 75.00
RCA T8-14 . . . 150.00
Scott, 23 tubes, Tasman cabinet . . . 370.00
Scott Acousticraft, console . . . 310.00
Scott Phantom, Louis XV style cabinet . . . 725.00
Scott Philharmonic, Chippendale cabinet, record changer . . . 600.00
Scott Philharmonic, Chippendale Grand cabinet . . . 700.00
Silvertone case, oak case, new springs, VG . . . 360.00
Steinite AC-1, EX orig . . . 165.00
Universal, rnd top, orig finish . . . 310.00

Garod, orange and yellow bakelite, 6" x 11", $250.00.

Victor VVVI, VG . . . 150.00
Wings, cathedral . . . 200.00
Zenith #6G 601M, Wavemagnet, battery operated . . . 52.00
Zenith #6S128 . . . 225.00
Zenith Stratosphere, 25 tubes, 3 speakers, 5 wave bands . . . 3,800.00

Railroadiana

As evidenced by the growing number of ads in the trade papers today, collecting railroad-related memorabilia is fast becoming one of America's most popular hobbies. The range of collectible items available is almost endless, considering the fact that there are more than 175 different railroad lines represented.

Some collectors prefer to specialize in one railroad in particular, while others attempt to collect at least one item from every railway line that is known to have existed. For the advanced collector, there is the challenge of locating rarities from short-lived railroads; for the novice there are abundant keys, buttons, passes, and playing cards. Among the most popular specializations are dining-car collectibles--flatware, glassware, dinnerware, etc., in a wide variety of patterns and styles.

For a more thorough study we recommend *Railroad Collectibles*, Third Revised Edition, by Stanley L. Baker, available at your local library or bookstore. When no condition is indicated, the items listed below are assumed to be in excellent condition except dinnerware and glassware which are considered mint.

Key:
BS—bottom stamp
RR—railroad
SM—side mark
TM—top mark

Dinnerware

Ash tray, C&O, Chessie, top logo . . . 70.00
Ash tray, GN, Mountains & Flowers, BS . . . 53.00
Bowl, baked apple; ATSF, Adobe, BS, EX . . . 60.00
Bowl, berry; GN . . . 35.00
Bowl, berry; UP, Harriman Blue . . . 15.00
Bowl, CB&Q, Violets & Daisies, w/lip, 6½" . . . 30.00
Bowl, cereal; ATSF, Adobe, BS, EX . . . 40.00
Bowl, cereal; UP, Challenger, TM . . . 12.00
Bowl, cereal; UP, Desert Flower, BS . . . 12.00
Bowl, cereal; UP, Harriman Blue . . . 20.00
Bowl, FEC, Peninsular, 4x5" . . . 15.00
Bowl, grapefruit; UP, Desert Flower . . . 20.00

Bowl, MP Lines, Eagle, 6″ . . . 50.00
Bowl, oatmeal; B&O, Capitol, top logo . . . 35.00
Bowl, salad; MP Lines, Eagle, 3x8½″ . . . 50.00
Bowl, serving; CB&Q, Violets & Daisies, 7″ tapered to 2¾″ . . . 185.00
Bowl, serving; UP, Streamliner, 9″ . . . 25.00
Bowl, soup; B&O, Centennial, w/Potomac Valley, 9″ . . . 45.00
Bowl, soup; D&RG, Exposition, w/lip, ca 1939, 8″ . . . 32.00
Bowl, soup; D&RG, Prospector, w/lip, 7″ . . . 32.00
Bowl, soup; N&W, Yellowbird, wide rim, 9″ . . . 45.00
Bowl, soup; NYC, Mercury, w/o stripe, TM & BS . . . 8.00
Bowl, soup; SOO Line, Logan, BS . . . 100.00
Bowl, sugar; R&B, Salt Lake route, lid w/spoon hole, BS . . . 400.00
Bowl, UP, w/lip, no BS, 6½″ . . . 15.00
Bowl, vegetable; GN, w/GNR monogram, Hill, TM, 6½″ . . . 60.00
Butter pat, ATSF, Black Chain, 3½″ . . . 15.00
Butter pat, ATSF, California Poppy, BS, 1924, 3½″ . . . 40.00
Butter pat, CMStP&P, Traveler, BM . . . 38.00
Butter pat, PRR, Purple Laurel, BM . . . 35.00
Butter pat, SP, Prairie Mountain, BM . . . 51.00
Butter pat, UP, Harriman Blue . . . 22.00
Butter pat, UP, Winged Streamliner, top logo, EX . . . 12.00
Celery dish, D&RGW, Rio Grande . . . 80.00
Celery dish, Milwaukee, Galatea . . . 45.00
Celery dish, UP, Blue & Gold . . . 10.00
Chocolate pot, ATSF, Membreno, BM . . . 135.00
Chocolate pot, ATSF, Poppy . . . 85.00
Creamer, ind; ATSF, Membreno, hdl, BM . . . 165.00
Creamer, ind; Pullman, Indian Tree, SM . . . 24.00
Creamer, ind; SP, Sunset, SM . . . 65.00
Creamer, ind; UP, Streamliner . . . 32.00
Creamer, R&B, Salt Lake route, hinged lid, BS, 8-oz . . . 400.00
Creamer, WKP, Ft Wayne, logo on side . . . 150.00
Cup, bouillon; CMStP&P, Traveler . . . 20.00
Cup, bouillon; GN, Oriental . . . 40.00
Cup, bouillon; PRR, Purple Laurel . . . 12.00
Cup, bouillon; Wabash, Banner, top logo . . . 75.00
Cup, bouillon; WP, Feather River, SM . . . 30.00
Cup, C&O, Chessie . . . 76.00
Cup, CB&Q, Violets & Daisies, BM . . . 55.00
Cup, demitasse; GN . . . 90.00
Cup, demitasse; UP, Desert Flower . . . 35.00
Cup, UP, no BS . . . 15.00
Cup & saucer, ATSF, no BS, EX . . . 40.00
Cup & saucer, bouillon; UP, Blue & Gold . . . 30.00
Cup & saucer, CB&Q, Violets & Daisies, mug style . . . 85.00
Cup & saucer, CM&StP, The Olympian, TM . . . 110.00
Cup & saucer, coffee; UP, Harriman Blue . . . 55.00
Cup & saucer, coffee; UP, Streamliner . . . 38.00
Cup & saucer, demitasse; Alaska RR, McKinley, SM . . . 185.00
Cup & saucer, demitasse; Blue & Gold . . . 30.00
Cup & saucer, demitasse; D&RGW, Prospector . . . 99.00
Cup & saucer, demitasse; Erie, Starucca, top logo . . . 165.00
Cup & saucer, demitasse; UP, Streamliner, BM . . . 42.00
Cup & saucer, demitasse; WP, Feather River, SM . . . 88.50
Cup & saucer, MP Lines, squat style, Eagle, no BS . . . 85.00
Cup & saucer, NP, Monad, TM . . . 125.00
Cup & saucer, PRR, Mountain Laurel . . . 22.00
Cup & saucer, SRY, Piedmont, BM . . . 65.00
Cup & saucer, UP, Desert Flower, BM . . . 65.00
Cup & saucer, UP, Historical, EX . . . 250.00
Egg cup, double; GN . . . 40.00
Egg cup, single; UP, Harriman Blue . . . 40.00
Gravy boat, ATSF, Membreno, BM . . . 83.50
Gravy boat, B&O, Centenary, Shenange BS . . . 40.00
Gravy boat, SP, Prairie Mountain . . . 78.50
Gravy boat, SP, Sunset, SM . . . 99.50
Ice cream shell, ATSF, Membreno . . . 70.00
Ice cream shell, SL&SF, Denmark . . . 33.00
Ice cream shell, UP, Streamliner . . . 28.50
Milk bottle, MP Lines, Sunnymeade Farm, buzzsaw logo, 1946 . . 15.00
Mustard stand, ATSF, Poppy . . . 40.00
Plate, ACL, Carolina, BM, 9″ . . . 25.00
Plate, ATSF, Adobe, BS, dinner sz . . . 90.00
Plate, ATSF, Adobe, BS, salad sz . . . 50.00
Plate, ATSF, California Poppy, 7¾″ . . . 28.00
Plate, ATSF, Membreno, BM, 7½″ . . . 68.50
Plate, ATSF, Poppy, 7″ . . . 19.50
Plate, ATSF, Poppy, 9¾″, BM . . . 52.00
Plate, B&O, Centenary, Scammell, BM, 6½″ . . . 40.00
Plate, B&O, Centenary, Scammell, BM, 8″ . . . 42.50
Plate, C&O, George Washington, TM, 10½″ . . . 490.00
Plate, C&O, George Washington, TM, 9″ . . . 135.00
Plate, CB&Q, BR, Onadaga, Aristocrat, BS, 1926, 7¼″ . . . 100.00
Plate, CB&Q, Violets & Daisies, dinner sz . . . 60.00
Plate, CB&Q, Violets & Daisies, 7″ . . . 40.00
Plate, CM&StP&P, Galatea, BM, 9″ . . . 175.00
Plate, CNW, Wild Rose, dinner sz . . . 80.00
Plate, CP, Bows & Leaves, 9½″ . . . 50.00
Plate, CPR, Brown Maple Leaf, TM, 9″ . . . 40.00
Plate, CRI&P, Golden State, BM, 7¾″ . . . 99.50
Plate, D&RGW, Rio Grande, dinner sz, EX . . . 100.00
Plate, GN, Hill, TM, luncheon sz . . . 90.00
Plate, GN, Mountains & Flowers, BM, 7″ . . . 30.00
Plate, Key Route, TM, 8½″ . . . 175.00
Plate, L&N, Green Leaf, divided, dinner sz . . . 45.00
Plate, Milwaukee, Galatea, dinner sz . . . 110.00
Plate, Milwaukee, Galatea, 8″ . . . 85.00
Plate, MP, State Capitols, diesel service, BM . . . 325.00
Plate, MP, State Flowers, steam service, BM . . . 225.00
Plate, MP Lines, Eagle, BS, 6½″ . . . 40.00
Plate, N&W, Centennial, bk stamp, 1938, service sz . . . 650.00
Plate, NP, TM, bread sz . . . 24.00
Plate, NYC, Country Gardens, 10½″ . . . 50.00
Plate, NYC, DeWitt Clinton, BS, 7¾″ . . . 40.00
Plate, PRR, Mountain Laurel, BM, 9½″ . . . 30.00
Plate, PRR, Purple Laurel, BM, 9½″ . . . 40.00
Plate, Pullman, Indian Tree, TM, 7½″ . . . 55.00
Plate, Pullman, Indian Tree, TM, 9″ . . . 75.00
Plate, Rio Grande, TM, bread sz . . . 4.00
Plate, SL&SF, Denmark, 7¾″ . . . 16.50
Plate, SL&SF, Denmark, 9½″ . . . 25.00
Plate, SOO Line, BS, salad sz . . . 50.00
Plate, SRY, Peach Blossom, BS, luncheon sz . . . 50.00
Plate, UP, Challenger, TM, 10″ . . . 60.00
Plate, UP, Challenger, TM, 6″ . . . 20.00
Plate, UP, circus theme, children's sz . . . 185.00
Plate, UP, Harriman Blue, dinner sz . . . 40.00
Plate, UP, Harriman Blue, salad sz . . . 25.00
Plate, UP, Historical, BS, 7¼″ . . . 100.00
Plate, UP, Portland Rose, salad sz . . . 120.00
Plate, UP, Streamliner, oval, 9″ . . . 20.00
Plate, UP, Streamliner, 10½″ . . . 55.00
Plate, Wabash, Banner, TM, 5″ . . . 75.00
Plate, Wabash, Banner, TM, 7½″ . . . 90.00
Plate, Wabash, Banner, TM, 9½″ . . . 200.00
Plate, WP, Feather River, TM, 5½″ . . . 27.50
Plate, WP, Feather River, TM, 7¼″ . . . 40.00
Platter, ACL, BS, 1948, 12″ . . . 28.00

Platter, ATSF, Poppy, 7½″ 30.00
Platter, ATSF, Poppy, 9″ 30.00
Platter, B&O, Centenary, Scammell, BM, 11½″ 110.00
Platter, CMStP&P, Peacock, oval, 8″ 16.00
Platter, CMStP&P, Traveler, BS, 8¼″ 20.00
Platter, CNW, Wild Rose, 6″ 35.00
Platter, D&RG, Prospector, oval, 7″ 35.00
Platter, D&RGW, Prospector, TM, 9x11½″ 125.00
Platter, Erie, Chataqua, TM, 10½″ 310.00
Platter, GM&O, Rose, 7″ 10.00
Platter, GN, Mountains & Flowers, BM, 9″ 48.00
Platter, Milwaukee, Galatea, 12″ 85.00
Platter, Milwaukee, Galatea, 8″ 65.00
Platter, Milwaukee, Galatea, 9″ 70.00
Platter, Monon logo, oval, 7″ 125.00
Platter, MP, Eagle, BM, 10″ 65.00
Platter, MStP&SStM, Logan, BM, 11″ 96.50
Platter, NP, Yellowstone, oval, TM, 7″ 46.50
Platter, NP, Yellowstone, TM, 9x11″ 90.00
Platter, PRR, Keystone, TM, 9½″ 49.50
Platter, Pullman, Calumet, TM, 12½″ 88.00
Platter, Pullman, Indian Tree, oval, TM, 8½″ 52.50
Platter, UP, Challenger, TM, 9¾″ 30.00
Platter, UP, Challenger, 8″ 40.00
Platter, UP, Desert Flower, 10″ 30.00
Platter, UP, Desert Flower, 8″ 25.00
Platter, UP, Harriman Blue, 12″ 40.00
Platter, UP, Harriman Blue, 14″ 55.00
Platter, UP, Harriman Blue, 7″ 20.00
Platter, UP, Harriman Blue, 9″ 30.00
Platter, UP, Historical, TM & BM, 6x8″ 155.00
Platter, UP, Historical, 9″ 125.00
Platter, UP, Overland, 11″ 17.00
Platter, UP, Streamliner, 8″ 21.00
Platter, WP, Feather River, TM, 5x7½″ 47.50
Sauce boat, UP, Winged Streamliner, BS 15.00
Sauce dish, ATSF, Poppy, 5″ 11.50
Sauce dish, CB&Q, Violets & Daisies, 5½″ 17.50
Sauce dish, CMStP&P, Peacock, 5½″ 17.50
Sauce dish, CMStP&P, Traveler, 5½″ 21.00
Sauce dish, GN, Glory of the West, BM, 5″ 29.50
Sauce dish, IC, Coral, 5½″ 13.00
Sauce dish, PRR, Broadway, TM, 5½″ 21.00
Sauce dish, PRR, Mountain Laurel, 5½″ 7.00
Saucer, coffee; Burlington Route, CA Zephyr, violets/daisy 8.00
Saucer, coffee; UP, Portland Rose 70.00
Saucer, demitasse; Milwaukee, Galatea 35.00
Sherbet, ATSF, Membreno, BM 80.00
Sherbet, B&O, Derby 38.00
Sherbet, CNW, Wild Rose, ftd, w/lid 35.00
Sherbet, D&RGW, Prospector, SM 32.00
Sherbet, UP, Streamliner 22.00
Sugar bowl, ATSF, Poppy 55.00
Sugar bowl, Milwaukee, Galatea 85.00
Teapot, ATSF, Membreno, BM 235.00
Teapot, B&O, Capitol, SM 225.00
Teapot, UP, Streamliner, 32-oz 75.00
Tray, celery; UP, Blue & Gold, no BS, 10½″ 15.00
Tray, relish; NYC, Mercury, w/stripe, TM & BS 33.00

Glassware

Ash tray, ATSF, Santa Fe in script, 3x4″ 14.00
Cordial, ATSF in script 22.50
Ice cream dish, UP, red & bl stripes 10.00
Shot glass, Pullman cast in bottom 24.50
Shot glass, UP, SM 12.00
Tumbler, iced tea; B&O, from dining car, set of 4 . . . . 35.00
Tumbler, MP Lines, Eagle & logo, w/gold rim, 5″ 22.00
Tumbler, Sante Fe, etched w/8 stripes, scarce, 4″ 18.00
Water glass, B&O, script, SM 7.00
Water glass, NP, red/blk Monad SM 24.00
Water glass, PRR, 4½″ 13.50

Linens

Blanket, Pullman, w/logo, tan, 48x72″ 55.00
Blanket, UP, w/logo, gray on blk, 84x60″ 155.00
Headrest, AT&SF, wht w/red stripe 8.00
Headrest cover, GM&O, wht w/red logo 9.00
Headrest cover, L&N, red on cream 9.00
Headrest cover, UP, red/gray streamliner on yel 9.50
Hot pad, C&O, tan w/gray tiger Chessie, 5″, set of 8 . . . . 25.00
Napkin, ATSF, Santa Fe in script, wht on wht 25.00
Napkin, CRI&P, Rock Island, wht on wht, 20x20″ 18.00
Napkin, FW&DC, emb oak leaf, wht on wht w/red letters 15.00
Napkin, L&N, center logo, wht on wht, 20x20″ 18.50
Napkin, Santa Fe in corners, emb floral/fern, wht, 19x19″ 8.00
Napkin, UP, pink woven logo on pink, 20x20″ 10.00
Napkin, UP, The Overland Route, wht on wht 21.00
Pillowcase, Pullman, California Zephyr, pink 9.00
Pillowcase, SP, bl woven logo on wht 12.00
Pillowcase, UP 2.00
Pillowcase, WU, pr 4.00
Sheet, Pullman 5.00
Table cloth, C&NW, yel on yel, 54x54″ 12.00
Table cloth, California Zephyr 3.00
Table cloth, GM&O, center logo, wht on wht, 48x35″ 22.00
Table cloth, Pullman, California Zephyr, pink 9.00
Table cloth, RG, Bouquet Floral, wht on wht, 36x34″ 20.00
Table cloth, UP, peach woven logo on peach 16.00
Towel, ATSF, bl stripe on wht, hand sz, 17x24″ 7.00
Towel, ATSF, red on wht, hand sz, 14x17″ 7.00
Towel, Burlington Route stamped on square, 31x16″ 5.00
Towel, C&O, bl stripe on wht, bath sz 22.50
Towel, Pullman, bl stripe on wht, hand sz, 17x24″ 9.00
Towel, SP, bl stripe on wht, hand sz, 17x31″ 9.00
Towel, UP, bl on wht, hand sz 6.00

Silver, Flatware

Fork, dinner; B&O, TM 15.00
Fork, dinner; BR, Century, TM 8.00
Fork, dinner; CB&Q, Belmont 10.00
Fork, dinner; CB&Q, California Zephyr, Century 10.00
Fork, dinner; CMStP&P, Ambassador 8.00
Fork, dinner; PRR, #133 . . . . 8.00
Fork, dinner; R&B, Belmont, TM reverse BR logo 12.00
Fork, dinner; Rock Island, Wallace, #60, TM & BS 12.00
Fork, oyster; UP, Savoy 5.00
Fork, salad; R&B, Belmont, TM reverse BR logo 12.00
Knife, butter; CB&Q BR, Modern 10.00
Knife, butter; GN, Hutton 10.00
Knife, dinner; CB&Q, California Zephyr, Century 8.00
Knife, dinner; CB&Q BR, Modern 8.00
Knife, dinner; CMStP&P, Ambassador 8.00
Knife, dinner; GM&O, Broadway 10.00
Knife, dinner; NP, Silhouette 10.00

Knife, dinner; Pere Marquette....15.00
Knife, dinner; SR, #1 Century, International....10.00
Knife, dinner; SR, Sierra or Vassar, Reed & Barton....15.00
Knife, table; CB&Q, Belmont....10.00
Spoon, bouillon; CB&Q, Modern....10.00
Spoon, bouillon; CMStP&P, Ambassador....10.00
Spoon, bouillon; UP, Savoy....4.00
Spoon, demitasse; UP, Savoy....12.00
Spoon, grapefruit; NP, TM....10.00
Spoon, iced tea; Erie, top logo....12.00
Spoon, iced tea; R&B, Belmont, TM reverse BR logo....12.00
Spoon, serving; CB&Q, California Zephyr, Century....8.00
Spoon, serving; CB&Q, Modern, BR....8.00
Spoon, serving; UP, Savoy....6.00
Spoon, soup; BR, Century, TM....8.00
Spoon, soup; CMStP&P, BS....7.00
Spoon, table; ATSF, Cromwell....8.00
Spoon, table; CB&Q, Belmont....10.00
Spoon, table; CMStP&P, Ambassador....8.00
Spoon, table; SCL, Zephyr....8.00
Spoon, table; Seaboard, Zephyr....8.00
Spoon, table; UP, Sierra....8.00
Spoon, tea; CMStP&P, Ambassador....10.00
Spoon, tea; UP, Savoy....8.00
Spoon, teaspoon; PRR, Keystone, Int'l Silver, King, 1888....20.00
Spoon, teaspoon; R&B, Belmont, TM reverse BR logo....12.00
Spoon, teaspoon; UP, Savoy, BS....8.00

Silver, Hollow Ware

Bouillon cup, N&W, TM Cavalier....22.00
Butter icer, R&B, Rio Grande Commissary, 1928....4.00
Butter pat, L&N, top logo....45.00
Butter pat, NYC, top logo....45.00
Butter pat, Santa Fe, BS in gold letters, 1948, 2x2"....20.00
Coaster, CB&Q, Zephyr, rare, TM....25.00
Coffee pot, MP, BS, 14-oz....25.00
Coffee pot, R&B, Art Deco, SM & BS, 1941, 14-oz....85.00
Coffee pot, R&B, Salt Lake route in diamond, BM, 10-oz....400.00
Creamer, CN, BS....20.00
Creamer, Pullman, Art Deco, w/hinged lid, BM, 1930, 5-oz....100.00
Crumber, Sante Fe, Albany, BS....70.00
Finger bowl, Rio Grande, BS, 1941, 3⅛"....15.00
Gravy boat, NP, w/lid, BS....40.00
Menu holder, R&B, Art Deco, SM & BS, sq....95.00
Money tray, Sante Fe, fluted edge, BM in English script....45.00
Pitcher, syrup; CN, BM....48.00
Salt shaker, PRR, monogram, BS....50.00
Sauce boat, CN, BS....45.00
Sauce boat, UP....19.00
Sugar bowl, ACL, SM & BS, no lid....15.00
Sugar bowl, GN, Oriental....80.00
Sugar bowl, Pullman, BS, 1933, 7-oz....100.00
Sugar tongs, CP, TM....19.00
Syrup, Pullman, w/hinged lid, BM: PP Car Co, scarce, 1895....225.00
Teapot, NP, BS....65.00
Teapot, Queen & Crescent, mfg Wallace....25.00
Tongs, sugar; UP, SM....25.00
Tray, tip; NYC, rnd, TM, 6½", VG....35.00

Wax Sealers and Accessories

American RY Express Co-2154, blk wood hdl, Messenger....35.00
AT&SF, agent, brass toadstool hdl, Lyons, KS....75.00
CB&Q, fancy 2-tone wood hdl, Bussey, IA....125.00
Commercial Wax Sealers, Web, brass hdl....45.00
KCM&B, iron bulb hdl, Sullicent, AL....115.00
National Express, varnished, wood bulb hdl, Willshire, OH....95.00
NYC RR-B 184, blk lacquer wood hdl, Albany, NY....65.00
RY Express Agency, public, blk hdl, Hastings, MN....30.00
SE Co-4797, tall iron hdl, Whitakers, NC....55.00
TSL&KC RR-144, tall fancy wood hdl, walnut....150.00
Utensil, for melting wax, torch type, hook hdl, tin, 2½"....37.50
WC, Ore Docks, fancy wood hdl, Ashland, WI....135.00
Wells Fargo, tall wood bulb hdl, Hampton, MN....150.00
Y&MV, nickel plated brass, toadstool hdl....115.00

Miscellaneous

Badge, cap; CTA Line Instructor #4581....16.00
Badge, cap; GN Brakeman....31.00
Badge, cap; Milwaukee Road over Trainman, mc, w/cap....65.00
Badge, cap; MStP&SSM Brakeman....50.00
Badge, cap; MStP&SSM RY Brakeman....65.00
Badge, cap; NYC Conductor, cut-out metal, 1¼x3"....15.00
Badge, cap; NYC Flagman, skeleton letters....40.00
Badge, cap; NYC Pullman Porter....50.00
Badge, cap; Pullman Porter....50.00
Badge, cap; RY Express, enamel logo, red on silver....55.00
Badge, cap; Santa Fe Brakeman, porcelain w/silver....95.00
Badge, cap; Santa Fe Conductor, nickel plated over brass....70.00
Badge, cap; Santa Fe Conductor, porcelain w/gold....95.00
Badge, cap; Santa Fe Courier Nurse, silver/bl, rare....125.00
Badge, cap; Sante Fe Conductor....23.00
Badge, cap; SOO Line Brakeman....70.00
Badge, cap; St Louis Depot #2976 Baggage Agent....5.00
Badge, cap; Trainman....7.00
Badge, cap; UP Brakeman, silver letters on blk, ¾x4"....15.00
Badge, cap; Vandalia Line Baggagemaster, silver/blk, rare....115.00
Badge, service; RY mail, #43790....40.00
Bell, steam loco; TC, w/history of bell, brass, 17"....1,250.00
Bell, trolley; outside clapper, old....30.00
Belt buckle, mainline through Rockies, brass, oval, 3x4"....17.00
Blotter, MP, Sunshine Special, wht & red, M....4.00
Book, Commuter Railroads, Dorin, Bonanza Co, 192 pg, M....7.50
Book, Highliners, Beebe, Bonanza Co, M....7.50
Book, Locomotive Catechism, 1978 reprint of 1908 edition....5.00
Book, Locomotive Dictionary Cyclopdia, 1919....100.00
Book, Pictorial History of Trains, Hamilton, 192 pg, lg....8.00
Book, Rulebook for Employees, SP&S RY Co, set....15.00
Booklet, New Employees, 16 pg, 8½x5½"....3.00
Booklet, Rocky Mountain Honeymoon, ca 1887, 16 pg, 5¼x3½"..50.00
Brochure, GN, set of 5, VG....30.00
Brochure, Illinois Terminal, Know Your Illinois, fold-out....6.00
Brochure, NP, Redwood Empire Tour, steam cover, 12 pg....5.00
Brochure, UP, Western Wonderland, 1966....5.00
Bulletin board, N&W, shop/safety, w/safety posters, old....95.00
Bulletin board, wooden train, 36x72"....70.00
Button, brakeman's; MRR, 3 lg & 4 sm, set....15.00
Button, lapel; dbl screw on bk, blk & red logo, 1x1¾"....15.00
Button, uniform; PPC CO, mk HV Allen, wreath, gold, dome....45.00
Button cover, CM&StP, Fox, lg dome, gold, pat 1886....4.00
Calendar, C&O, Chessie, 6 views, 1963, wall sz, EX....20.00
Calendar, wall; MP, diesel version, M....175.00
Cap, conductor's; NP....18.00
Clock, UP, battery operated, oak, 26x20"....100.00
Clock, wall; Postal Telegraph Electric Bichronous, case....95.00
Clock, Western Union Naval, battery operated, w/steel case....400.00

Coin tray, D&RG, California Zephyr, 5 compartments, 17x4½" . . . 40.00
Cuff links, from uniform button, silver, pr . . . 5.00
Envelope, money parcel, C&O, unused, 1931, M . . . 4.00
Envelope, to hold money, orig seal imp on bk, letter sz . . . 40.00
Fire extinquisher, AT&SF, w/brass hand pump, 14", VG . . . 50.00
Gauge, water; Gits Bros, Chicago, early, diesel, M . . . 8.00
Globe, CNR, clear, etched w/sm letters, 3¼", M . . . 15.00
Globe, L&N, red cast, 3¼", M . . . 23.00
Globe, N&W, clear cast in rnd panel, Corning, 5⅜", M . . . 35.00
Globe, SAL, clear etched, lg letters, 3¼", M . . . 23.00
Hat, conductor's; Pullman, gold braid, w/badge, VG . . . 60.00
Hat, porter's; Pullman, wht braid, w/badge . . . 60.00
Headlight, Pyle-National Steam Loco, #313, wired for 110 v . . . 425.00
Inkwell, N&W, N&W & Capitol Pat cast on base, glass . . . 125.00
Key, switch; Adlake, brass, sm cut, old . . . 12.00
Key, switch; AT&SF, Adlake, hollow barrel, brass . . . 14.00
Key, switch; B&O, lg head, mk . . . 15.00
Key, switch; brass, unmk, old . . . 5.00
Key, switch; C&W, Adlake, brass, rare . . . 40.00
Key, switch; D&H, Slaymaker, hollow barrel/brass, serial # . . . 28.00
Key, switch; D&RG, Adlake, #F5735, A&W football logo . . . 35.00
Key, switch; ERR, brass heart, cast across bk, w/worn key . . . 75.00
Key, switch; IC, Adlake, hollow barrel, brass, serial # . . . 12.00
Key, switch; L&N, Adlake, hollow barrel, brass, worn . . . 14.00
Key, switch; L&N, Dayton, hollow barrel/brass, serial # . . . 28.00
Key, switch; MoPac, Adlake, #6123, dk brass . . . 12.00
Key, switch; MoPac, Adlake, hollow barrel, brass, serial # . . . 12.00
Key, switch; N&W, F-S Hardware, hollow barrel, brass . . . 20.00
Key, switch; NC&StL, Fraim, hollow barrel, brass, mk . . . 55.00
Key, switch; NS, Adlake, hollow barrel/brass, last issue . . . 25.00
Key, switch; NYCS-TH, brass, house key, pocket worn . . . 15.00
Key, switch; P&N, Adlake, hollow barrel, brass, last issue . . . 45.00
Key, switch; SO, worn . . . 12.00
Key, switch; SRY, ES Fraim, hollow barrel, brass, mk . . . 24.00
Key, switch; SRY-SR, hollow barrel, brass, pocket worn . . . 16.00
Lamp, caboose; C&O, Handlan, dbl mk, orig yel pnt, M . . . 150.00
Lamp, caboose; N&W, Handlan, model #50, emb shade, rstr . . . 95.00
Lamp, gauge; Dietz Backhead, before WWII, blk w/silver int . . . 35.00
Lamp, PRR, Trainman's Flagging, single red 5" lens, rstr . . . 105.00
Lamp, semaphore; IC, Adlake, rnd top, emb lid, rpt, mk . . . 45.00
Lamp, semaphore; NYC&StL, full oil int/single lens . . . 125.00
Lamp, semaphore; RI Lines, Adlake, full oil int, mk, rstr . . . 125.00
Lamp, switch; Adlake, electric, rewired for 110 v current . . . 65.00
Lamp, switch; Adlake Standard, full oil int, 4½" lens . . . 105.00
Lamp, switch; Armspear, steel, full oil int, 5½" lens, rpt . . . 65.00
Lamp, switch; C&O, Handlan, full oil int, dbl mk, rstr . . . 150.00
Lamp, switch; Frisco, Handlan, full oil int/mk plate, rstr . . . 125.00
Lamp, switch; Handlan, electric, cast metal, hinged, M . . . 55.00
Lamp, switch; Handlan, mk Mopac, red/gr lens, full oil int . . . 100.00
Lamp, switch; PRR, Adlake, Keystone SM, 4½" wht lens . . . 145.00
Lamp, switch; Wabash, mk on door, very old, rstr . . . 95.00
Lantern, ACL, Aklake Kero, red globe, EX . . . 35.00
Lantern, Adams & Westlake, Pullman on bell, brass, SM, EX . . 650.00
Lantern, Adams Exp Co, clear globe, drop fount, pat 1897 . . . 385.00
Lantern, B&O, A&W, drop fount, dbl guard, clear globe . . . 175.00
Lantern, B&O, A&W Reliable, dbl guard, clear globe, mk . . . 155.00
Lantern, B&O, Casey, red B&O globe, pat 1903, EX . . . 75.00
Lantern, BR&P, Dietz #39, bell bottom, cast globe, M . . . 300.00
Lantern, C&C, Armspear, clear globe, rstr, rare, 1913 . . . 275.00
Lantern, C&O, Adlake #250, clear etched globe/dome top, EX . . . 35.00
Lantern, CCC&StL, Handlan, clear globe, lg mk, 1913 . . . 115.00
Lantern, CM, cobalt bl, 5⅜" globe, TM, scarce . . . 350.00
Lantern, CM&StP, Adlake Reliable, Corning globe, 1923 . . . 75.00
Lantern, CMStP&P, Adlake Kero, clear globe, cleaned . . . 30.00
Lantern, CStPM&O, A&W, Safety First globe, EX fr . . . 485.00
Lantern, Dietz XLCR, squat bell bottom, N&W Corning globe . . . 45.00
Lantern, ERR, A&W Co, clear Corning globe, cleaned . . . 85.00
Lantern, Frisco System, National Brass Mfg, Corning globe . . . 285.00
Lantern, GRR, Armspear, drop fount, wire fr, clear globe . . . 255.00
Lantern, GT, A&W Reliable, bell bottom, clear globe, M . . . 125.00
Lantern, hand; KIT, A&W Kero, short/bl globe, M . . . 75.00
Lantern, hand; N&W, A&W Kero, short/clear/rnd globe, NM . . . 55.00
Lantern, hand; PE, A&W Kero, short/red/etched globe, M . . . 85.00
Lantern, hand; VGN, A&W Kero, bl globe, never fired, M . . . 145.00
Lantern, HV, Adlake Reliable, clear globe, 1923, M . . . 115.00
Lantern, HV, Keystone Casey, red Corning globe, NM fr . . . 175.00
Lantern, I-U, Handlan, single fr, lid mk, clear globe . . . 175.00
Lantern, IC, Dietz #39, Vulcan wire bottom, dbl Corning . . . 95.00
Lantern, IHB, Adlake Kero, post-WWII, clear globe, NM . . . 30.00
Lantern, K&M, Dietz Tall Vesta, NYCS globe, mk, rare . . . 100.00
Lantern, L&N, Adlake Reliable, clear Corning globe, EX . . . 75.00
Lantern, L&N, Adlake Reliable, clear globe, 1913 . . . 55.00
Lantern, LI, Armspear, clear Corning globe, 1913 . . . 165.00
Lantern, LS&MS, A&W Reliable, clear globe, 1-pc lid, M . . . 225.00
Lantern, MK&T, Handlan, lid mk, flat top, barrel globe . . . 85.00
Lantern, N&W, Adlake Kero, clear globe, M . . . 35.00
Lantern, N&W, Armspear Kero, clear globe, cleaned, M . . . 25.00
Lantern, N&W, clear globe, never used, M . . . 35.00
Lantern, NP, Adams & Westlake, 3¼" clear glass globe . . . 25.00
Lantern, NYC, A&W Reliable, clear Corning globe, 1913 . . . 115.00
Lantern, NYC, Dietz #6, burner assembly, 6" clear globe, M . . . 150.00
Lantern, NYNH&H, Adlake Reliable, dbl clear globe, M . . . 115.00
Lantern, NYNH&H, Vesta, red etched globe, 1940, NM . . . 35.00
Lantern, NYO&W, A&W, clear globe, lg 6" bell bottom . . . 325.00
Lantern, P&R, A&W, Corning cast globe, pat 1897, NM fr . . . 185.00
Lantern, P&R, Armspear, drop fount, clear globe, 1913 . . . 85.00
Lantern, Pere Marquette, clear globe, mk, NM fr . . . 375.00
Lantern, PRR, A&W, drop fount, red cast globe, pat 1897 . . . 165.00
Lantern, PRR, A&W Reliable, clear globe, 3-pc lid, rare . . . 225.00
Lantern, PRR, Adlake, 5⅜" clear globe, TM . . . 65.00
Lantern, PRR, dome, Keystone, Armspear/Adlake Kero, M . . . 35.00
Lantern, RI Lines, Handlan, dbl guard fr, Corning globe . . . 165.00
Lantern, Santa Fe, A&W, dbl guard, clear globe, pat 1895 . . . 185.00
Lantern, Seaboard, clear globe, pat 1903, M . . . 250.00
Lantern, Seaboard Casey, clear cast globe, pat 1903, M . . . 250.00
Lantern, SRY, Adlake Kero, clear globe, January 1933, EX . . . 30.00
Lantern, SRY, Adlake Kero, clear globe, M . . . 28.00
Lantern, SRY, Adlake Kero, post-WWII, red fresnel globe . . . 30.00
Lantern, SRY, Armspear, drop fount, clear Corning globe . . . 85.00
Lantern, SRY, Armspear, sm insert pot, clear globe, 1925 . . . 45.00
Lantern, SRY, dome, Adlake Reliable, clear globe, 1913 . . . 85.00
Lantern, SRY in M, clear cast globe, 3-pc lid, 1913, M . . . 325.00
Lantern, T&P, Adlake, red unmk globe, cleaned, 1913, EX . . . 75.00
Lantern, TC, Adlake Kero, red globe, rare, cleaned, EX . . . 75.00
Lantern, V&SW, A&W, dbl guard, clear etched globe, rare . . . 350.00
Lantern, VGN, Adlake Kero, pre-WWII, bl globe, 1945, M . . . 125.00
Lantern, VRY, A&W, dbl guard, clear etched Corning globe . . . 375.00
Lantern, VRY, A&W Reliable, dbl guard, extra clear globe . . . 495.00
Lantern, Wabash, Adlake, clear Flag Logo globe/3-pc lid . . . 225.00
Lantern, WT Co, Adlake Kero, red globe, M . . . 30.00
Letter opener, NP, baked potato, bronze, lg . . . 45.00
Letter opener, VRY, eng, brass, mk Whitehead & Hoag . . . 95.00
Lock, general; C&NW, Adlake . . . 10.00
Lock, general; C&NW, Slaymaker, brass . . . 51.00
Lock, general; CStP&P, Adlake, steel . . . 7.00
Lock, general; FEC, brass heart, Edwards, w/chain & key . . . 125.00
Lock, general; N&W, XLCR, brass padlock, w/flat key . . . 15.00
Lock, general; NC&StL, Yale & Towne, w/dust cover, rare . . . 45.00

Lock, general; PRR, Slaymaker....10.00
Lock, general; SP Lines, brass heart, flat, cleaned....75.00
Lock, signal; CB&Q, brass heart, cleaned & polished, sm....18.00
Lock, signal; Erie, Corbin, brass, mk, M....14.00
Lock, signal; IC, brass....6.00
Lock, signal; IC, brass semi-heart, cleaned....18.00
Lock, signal; NC&StL, brass semi-heart, scarce....45.00
Lock, signal; NKP, Yale, brass, stamp on rim, w/flat key....17.00
Lock, signal; NYCS, brass, uses flat key (not included), M....12.00
Lock, signal; NYCS, Corbin, brass padlock, M....12.00
Lock, signal; RF&P, semi-heart, steel hollow barrel key....20.00
Lock, switch; B&O, F-S Hardware Co, brass heart, M....35.00
Lock, switch; B&O, Slaymaker, w/worn key, NM....55.00
Lock, switch; B&S, Slaymaker, brass heart, key/chain....165.00
Lock, switch; BT, Bohannon, brass heart, pat 1885....150.00
Lock, switch; C&WM, brass heart, upside down M, w/key....75.00
Lock, switch; CR, on hasp, Slaight, brass heart, w/chain....175.00
Lock, switch; FEC, Edwards, brass heart, w/brass chain....85.00
Lock, switch; K&IT, Adlake, steel, pat 1912....8.00
Lock, switch; N&W, cast back, standard, M....35.00
Lock, switch; N&W, cast heart, 1957 on shackle, w/key....75.00
Lock, switch; N&W, Slaymaker, cast across bk, w/key....75.00
Lock, switch; NC&StL, brass heart/cast across bk, w/key....145.00
Lock, switch; NYC, Bohannon, mk on hasp, w/mk key, 1916....55.00
Lock, switch; P&R cast across bk, Fraim, brass heart, M....150.00
Lock, switch; SR, Arrow logo, cast across bk, w/E-S key....85.00
Lock, switch; T&B, pat Jones, brass heart, w/chain....225.00
Lock, switch; T&SE, Miller, steel, figure 8, mk hasp....25.00
Lock, switch; T&W, Dayton, brass heart, w/chain, lg....245.00
Lock, switch; TEP Co, brass heart, cast up bk, w/unmk key....20.00
Lock, switch; UP, brass heart, cast up center of bk, EX....40.00
Lock, switch; VGN, brass heart, 1941 on shackle, rare....275.00
Lock, switch; VGN over RY cast on bk, brass heart, rare, M....245.00
Lock, switch; VGN stamped on hasp, Yale, brass heart....175.00
Lock, switch; VRY, Edwards & Co, brass heart, mk, w/key....155.00
Match striker, wall mt....4.00
Medallion, service; SRY, eng, 34 years, w/box, rare, M....85.00
Menu, luncheon; SRY, Crescent, 1978, M....3.00
Menu, N&W, 1960s, M, set of 6....5.00
Menu, SOO Line, Camp Wanaki Party, July 1, 1944....9.00
Office forms, Burlington Line, for depot....5.00
Oil can, PRR, Keystone, Heavy Car Journal, EX....25.00
Oil can, stores Journal oil, 3-gal, cleaned....8.00
Oiler, engineer's; N&W, longspout, SM, cleaned/rpt, old....30.00
Paperweight, ERY, trolley, cast brass or bronze....45.00
Paperweight, IC, Centennial medallion, 1851-1951, desk sz....30.00
Paperweight, Milwaukee Road Walking Bear, Yellowstone logo..100.00
Pass, AT&SF, annual, 1943-1944....5.00
Pass, C&NW, annual, 1909....5.00
Pass, C&O, annual, 1911, M....5.00
Pass, C&O, annual, 1911, old English printing, M....10.00
Pass, C&O, annual, 1930, M....4.00
Pass, CB&Q, annual, 1904....40.00
Pass, GC&SF, annual, 1904....40.00
Pass, H&CW, annual, 1886....40.00
Pass, L&N, annual, 1917, M....6.00
Pass, MK&T, annual, 1904....40.00
Pass, NC&StL, annual, 1922, w/logo....9.00
Pass, RF&P, Washington Southern, annual, 1914....10.00
Pass, SW RR of G, annual, 1878, M....30.00
Pass, T&P, annual, 1880, lg 1½" intertwined letters....40.00
Pass, V&SW, annual, 1914, M....25.00
Pass, W&W, annual, 1878, sm card sz, M....25.00
Pass, WF&S, annual, 1926....5.00
Pin, celluloid & brass 4-4-0 loco, w/scrollwork, 1900....30.00
Pin, lapel; MRR....19.00
Pin, lapel; Santa Fe, conductor's, quarter sz, bl....30.00
Pin, lapel; scenic line of the world, screw-on bk, 1"....7.00
Pin, lapel; 42 yrs service, bl & wht, 10k gold....10.00
Pin, MP Booster Club, screw bk post, red/blk on silver, M....15.00
Pin, N&W Veteran, steam loco, 14k gold, hallmk on bk, M....45.00
Pin, service; 33 yr....15.00
Pin-bk button, ACL, 100% Safety, wht on purple, 1931, ⅞"....6.00
Pin-bk button, BCR&N, red diamond logo, wht, scarce, ⅞"....25.00
Pin-bk button, BR, Silver Zephyr, dk bl, 1¼"....5.00
Pin-bk button, C&O, Chessie kitten, wht, 1½"....15.00
Pin-bk button, GN, American flag/house, bl, scarce, 1¾"....30.00
Pin-bk button, LV, Blk Diamond Express, red flag, ⅞"....12.50
Playing cards, Amtrak, red/wht/bl, in wrapped case, M....4.00
Playing cards, BN, wht on gr, clear plastic box, dbl deck....12.50
Playing cards, D&RG, steam train, state seals, single deck....35.00
Playing cards, MR, pinochle, Indian/legend, single deck, M....15.00
Playing cards, PRR, steam engines, 1946 Centennial, single....38.00
Playing cards, SP, gold Sunset logo, 52 scenes/single deck....15.00
Playing cards, SRY, gold logo on case, dbl deck, MIB....25.00
Playing cards, UP, Joker is map, single deck, w/case, MIB....20.00
Playing cards, WP&Y, train/red bk, orig 2-pc case, single....110.00
Pocket watch, Seth Thomas, train on bk, worn, lg....20.00
Postcard, CH&N, postmk Arcadia, FL, color litho, 1922....3.00
Postcard, PRR, The Broad Limited, art litho, unused, 1927....4.00
Postcard, Texas Zephyr, set of 15....6.00
Radio, from old steam engine....8.00
Ruler, system map & main line logo, T-square, plastic, 12"....4.00
Score pad, gin rummy; California Zephyr, red/wht/bl, set....7.00
Shaving mug, occupational, C Dunson, 1900, rare, M....300.00
Sign, Baggage Room, gold leaf, wood, blk, 11x84", VG....375.00
Sign, cardboard; Helm's Snuff, store ad, w/fr, EX....45.00
Sign, Monon, depot, tin, 30x144"....12.00
Sign, REA, metal, 72x12"....50.00
Sign, RGS, Dining Room, wood, blk w/gold letters, 11x84"....400.00
Sign, RGS, No Shaving Allowed, blk w/gold letters, 24x8"....300.00
Sign, Santa Fe, bl & wht, 36x36", VG....100.00
Sign, station; Western Union, dbl sided, porcelain, 24x48"....150.00
Sign, WUT & CO, porcelain, 24x12"....20.00
Spittoon, Cotton Belt, graniteware, wht w/bl lettering....55.00
Spittoon, CPR, nickel plated, emb ⅝" letters....55.00
Spittoon, N&W, lg N&W on outside rim, CI, reconditioned....95.00
Stapler, D&RG, Swingline, uses Tot staples, TM....4.00
Stepbox, SRY, aluminum, silver pnt, SM....125.00

Passenger car stepstool, Northern Pacific, $150.00.

Stickpin, lapel; N&W, mk Whitehead & Hoag Newark..........45.00
Stickpin, N&W, safety first logo, mc enamel, late 1930s........25.00
Stock certificate, CB&N, 1886.............................6.00
Stove, caboose; L&N, CI, 450-lb, prof cleaned/rpt, orig........475.00
Suitcase, conductor's.....................................5.00
Telegraph key, Vibroplex, Model #3011....................40.00
Telegraph relay, JH Bunnell, type 2-2.....................45.00
Telegraph sounder, JH Bunnell Co, mk/sounder arm stamp, EX..20.00
Telegraph sounder, Western Union..........................20.00
Telegraph switchboard, CNW depot, 12 lines, oak, 26x21"......50.00
Telephone, candlestick...................................15.00
Thermos, Pullman, chrome, SM, VG.........................55.00
Ticket punch, half fare..................................10.00
Ticket validator, Hills Model A Centennial Machine...........225.00
Timetable, ACL, public, full system, June 1915...............16.00
Timetable, ACL Northern, May 1983..........................9.00
Timetable, ATSF, Missouri, April 1913......................20.00
Timetable, ATSF, Panhandle, Dec 1917......................20.00
Timetable, B&O, employee, Cincinnati Division, Sept 1940.......7.50
Timetable, B&O, public, full system, w/map, 84-pg, 1924.......18.00
Timetable, BN, employees, Omaha region, #6, May 19, 1974.....3.00
Timetable, CB&Q, employee, Ottumwa Division, Apr 1962.......5.00
Timetable, CB&Q, employee, Ottumwa Division, Sept 1931......14.50
Timetable, CB&Q, employees, Lincoln division, Apr 27, 1969.....3.00
Timetable, CB&Q, public, w/10 RRs of Burlington, 1892.......42.00
Timetable, CM&StP, public, Milwaukee Road, Feb 1931........12.00
Timetable, Colorado & Southern, employee, July 1952..........7.00
Timetable, D&RG, Pueblo division, #161, Feb 1, 1951..........5.00
Timetable, Erie, employee, Oct 1956.........................6.00
Timetable, Florida East Coast, Oct 15, 1936, M...............10.00
Timetable, Florida East Coast RY, public, Feb 1932...........11.00
Timetable, GM&O, employee, Eastern Division, Apr 1962........5.00
Timetable, GN, Minot Division, ETT #115, Nov 30, 1966........7.00
Timetable, L&N, public, 1950..............................5.00
Timetable, MK&T, public, The Katy, 1955....................4.00
Timetable, MP, employee, Palestine Division, June 1926.........9.00
Timetable, PRR, employee, Chicago Terminal, Sept 1937.......10.00
Timetable, SRY, employee, Birmingham Division, Jan 1950......6.00
Timetable, UP, Feb 1, 1919, M............................15.00
Timetable, UP, Nebraska division, #3, Sept 13, 1948...........5.00
Timetable, Wabash, employee, Montpelier Division, Apr 1951.....7.00
Timetable, Wabash, public, 1935............................8.00
Tin snips, C&O, SM.......................................20.00
Token, UP, World's Fair, 1939..............................4.00
Torch, PRR, Dayton Malleable Iron, evenly pitted, CI, EX......24.00
Towel rack, brass, sm.....................................35.00
Tray, tin, passenger steamer, Cunard Steamers, 28x39", EX....110.00
Uniform, conductor's; B&O, 2-pc suit, bl....................45.00
Validating machine, Centennial, w/die, complete...............35.00
Waste puller, Seaboard, steel, SM Journal, cleaned............10.00
Watch fob, N&W Veteran, front of N&W steam loco, M........25.00
Whistle, back-up; Sherburne Co, brass, cleaned, EX...........30.00
Wrench, caboose; SCL, shop-made multi-purpose, cleaned/rpt...15.00
Wrench, dbl open-end; L&N, shop mk, cleaned...............12.00

Razors

As straight razors gain in popularity, prices increase. And with the lure of investment appreciation, the novice or the speculator sometimes find themselves making purchases that later prove to be unwise. It is important to be able to recognize the material the handle is made of. This has a great bearing on value, and imitations abound.

Learn to distinguish between celluloid and genuine ivory. Razors with plain celluloid handles are practically worthless unless the blade carries a desirable trademark. Those with decorations of scrollwork, leaves and vines, and those with decorative metal on each end fall into the $8 to $12 price range. Even plain ivory handles are not especially valuable unless paired with a well-marked blade from a good manufacturer. On a more positive note, celluloid-handled razors with designs such as castles, windmills, nudes, deer, alligators, automobiles, horses, cowboys, peacocks, and various kinds of birds, etc., are very desirable--some more than others--and are usually worth from $25 to $50 to collectors. Those with a figural handle such as a fish, shotgun, eagle or a barber pole might be worth in excess of $100 for an especially nice example. Ivory, on the other hand, is rarely found, and if the carvings are well done, clean, undamaged specimens should start at about $100 and escalate according to the intricacy of the design.

Buffalo horn is sometimes mistakenly called bone. It is usually black, translucent tan, or gray. Though plain handles are worth very little, the early heat-molded examples with a motif such as mentioned above often sell for more than $100. In the same range are mother-of-pearl and stag (deer horn) handles; very elaborate designs go even higher, but watch for imitations.

There is one imitation, however, that is highly desirable. That is jigged bone made to look like stag. This material is rough textured, dyed a handsome tan or brown, and usually examples with these handles sell in the $40 to $75 range. Razors with wooden handles are very rare, but even those from the 1800s are worth only about $35, since they are usually very plain. Twentieth century examples are only valued at around $15. Don't be fooled by buffalo horn colored in imitation of tortoise--and you'll find celluloid imitations, too. Genuine tortoise handles are worth from $25 to $100 depending on age, condition and workmanship. Sterling razors are valued at $75 and up, but make sure they are marked 'sterling.' Even if you were to mistake aluminum for silver, those with relief-cast designs are worth $50 to $75--only $20 or so if the design is incised.

Corn razors were made to pare troublesome corns on the feet. They are a bit smaller and if plain worth a little more than full-size razors. Fancy examples are generally not worth as much as their full-size counterparts.

The older blades are wedge-shaped (flat-sided) in cross-section; hollow-ground blades (made after 1880) are concave. Generally speaking, those etched with words only are worth little more than a plain, common blade. Try to find those with people, places, and things--the more famous, the better.

When no condition is indicated, the items listed below are assumed to be in excellent condition.

Key:
bd—blade
cell—celluloid
pt—point

Alexander Coppel, hollow ground bd, glossy hdl..............13.00
Ambercrombie & Fitch, France, hollow ground bd, ivory hdl....37.00
American Knife & Razor, etched bd: Primo Grade, blk hdl.......9.00
Bengall, England, hollow ground bd, rnd silver hdl............85.00
Bert & Co, Sheffield, etched: flowers/leaves/scroll..............68.00
Bohler Extra Stahl, etched bd w/city of Koln, blk cell hdl.......16.00
Boker & Co, pictures SS St Louis on bd, horn hdl, box, EX....55.00
C Crookes Improved Razor, hollow ground bd/coded hdl, rare...17.00
Case, Temperite, made in USA, hollow ground bd, blk hdl......22.00
Case's Ace, hollow ground bd, imitation pearl hdl, M..........44.00
Century, Made in Japan, gr hdl: Otto Deutsch & Sohne........14.00
Clark Warranted, wedge bd, straight blk horn hdl, rare.........60.00
Clauss Fremont, etched bd w/spread eagle, blk hdl, rare........30.00
Clauss Fremont, imitation ivory hdl, nude lady on man's bk.....60.00
Collede, in cardboard box, pat 1913, complete.................30.00
Cosmo Manufacturing, hollow ground bd, tight hdl, pink........55.00
Cottrell Hardware, etched bd w/scroll, blk celluloid hdl.........40.00
Dovo, imitation pearl & German silver hdl, trademark..........15.00
Eagle Brand, magnetized, etched spread eagle on bd..........12.00

Orange striped celluloid handle, etched blade with eagle and 'Improved Eagle Razor, Garland Cutlery Co., Germany,' $35.00.

Edson, 1-pc head, mk, lined case 20.00
EL & Co, Sheffield, etched bd w/Masonic symbols, blk hdl 120.00
Ern, hollow ground bd, imitation ivory hdl, raised deer 80.00
F Fenney, Sheffield, running fox trademark & Tally-Ho 15.00
F Reynolds, Sheffield, semi-hollow ground bd, horn hdl, G 30.00
G Johnson, wedge bd, horn hdl pressed w/rib & shell 50.00
G Wostenholm & Sons, imitation ivory hdl, castle/sailboat 17.00
Garland Cutlery, etched bd: eagle faces right/blk cell hdl 16.00
Geneva Cutlery, Warranted, etched w/spread eagle, blk hdl 37.00
Geo Butler, Sheffield, etched bd w/picture of Shakespeare 17.00
Geo Savage, XXX Pat, horn hdl w/NY & cornucopia on 1 side . . . 80.00
Geo Wostenholm, Sheffield, etched bd, blk horn hdl 13.00
German, etched in gold w/jouster on horse & World Master 36.00
Germania, nude lady picking grapes on hdl, grapes on top 34.00
Gilbert Brothers, Sheffield, wedge bd, pressed horn hdl 30.00
Gillette, Milaby Decollete, gold/imitation ivory hdl, case 30.00
H Boker, etched bd: Good as Gold, imitation ivory hdl 16.00
H Boker, etched gold bd: King Cutter, imitation ivory hdl 12.00
H Boker, etched/steel/hollow ground bd, blk hdl 18.00
H Sears & Son, etched bd, hdl mk Queen, 1865 . . . . . 10.00
Imperial Razor Co, old car etched on bd, horn hdls, EX 45.00
Imperial Razor Warranted, etched Maltese Cross, 4-part hdl 53.00
Imperial Razor Warranted, hollow ground etched bd, blk hdl 44.00
Indian doing war dance, emb on celluloid hdl 28.00
J Elliot, bd stamped Silver Steel, hollow ground, blk hdl 16.00
J Elliot, deep thumb groove, sm notched pt, silver steel 37.00
J Elliot, wedge bd w/notched pt, silver & blk horn hdl 20.00
J Heiffor, Sheffield, etched wedge bd, clear horn hdl 50.00
K Engels & Son, etched bd, imitation ivory hdl w/eagle 100.00
Lund & Cornhill, flat/straight scales, tortoiseshell hdl 36.00
Marlow, etched bd: Plymouth Rock, EX 40.00
Marshes & Shepherd, Sheffield, deep thumb groove, 1830s 40.00
N Shapleigh Hardware, hollow ground bd, windmill on hdl 105.00
Ontario Cuttlery, Indian chief, hollow ground bd, blk hdl 10.00
Othello, etched hollow ground bd, imitation ivory hdl, VG 40.00
Oxford Razor Warranted, hollow ground bd, deer on blk hdl 40.00
Oxford Razor Warranted, hollow ground bd, nude on hdl 35.00
Oxford Razor Warranted, nude lady eats grapes on lower ½ 30.00
Rich Cuttlery, hollow ground bd, imitation ivory hdl, rare 27.00
Rogers Cutlery, imitation ivory hdl, narrow bd, horse head 35.00
Rogers Cutlery, nude w/robe, imitation hdl, hollow ground 28.00
Rolls, lined metal case, w/instruction sheet, M 10.00
S Worth & Sons, Sheffield, wedge bd, bone hdl 16.00
Sheffield, etched/hollow ground bd, blk horn hdl 27.00
Sheffield Steel, hollow ground bd w/Geo Washington, rare 95.00
Shepherd Warranted, Sheffield, hollow ground bd, horn hdl 37.00
Slack & Grimold, Sheffield, etched bd: The Favorite 15.00
Sperry & Alexander, hollow ground bd, raised teardrop hdl 27.00
Steinbruck & Drucks Solingen, eng bust of Mozart, rare 20.00
Superior Razor, Sheffield, wedge bd, eagle on horn hdl 55.00
Superior Temper, flat bone hdl w/wavy lines, 1810, VG 75.00
T Bingham, bd stamped Silver Steel, dbl thumb grip, VG 22.00
Vulcan Thomas Ellin, hollow ground bd, stamped Army Razor . . . 70.00
W Greaves & Sons, wide hollow ground bl, cow horn hdl 10.00
Wade & Butcher, etched bd: stagecoach, brass spine, 1840 . . . . . 45.00
Wade & Butcher, etched semi-wedge bd, rnd blk horn scales . . . 100.00
Wade & Butcher, Sheffield, etched steel wedge bd w/pt 40.00
Wade & Butcher, Sheffield, ivory hdl monogrammed HRW 25.00
Wade & Butcher, Sheffield, wedge etched bd/eagle, wood hdl 15.00
Wade & Butcher, wedge bd, 3-pc MOP hdl, German silver ends . 365.00
Wade & Butcher Special, hollow ground bd, real pearl hdl 100.00
Wadsworth Razor Co, hollow ground bd, imitation ivory hdl 50.00
Warranted, Sheffield, etched: The Prince's Own/crown on bd 14.00
Weldon Furnace, Sheffield, refined steel, blk horn scales 80.00
Wester Bros, monkey eating fruit w/dog on other side, rare 20.00
WH Morley & Sons, etched bd: Hamburg Ground, bamboo hdl . . 10.00
Wilinson Sword, 1 day on ea bd, velvet-lined case, 7 bd 60.00
Williams Razors, etched bd: The Williams, blk hdl 12.00
Wostenholm, hollow ground bd, flat/straight blk horn hdl 60.00

Reamers

Reamers have been made in hundreds of styles and colors, and by as many manufacturers. Their purpose is to extract the juices from lemons, oranges, and grapefruits. The largest producer of glass reamers was McKee, who pressed their products from many types of glass--custard, delphite and Chalaine blue, opaque white, Skokie green, black, caramel and white opalescent, Seville yellow, and transparent pink, green, and clear. Among these, the black and the caramel opalescents are the most valuable.

The Fry Glass Company also made reamers that are today very collectible. Their vaseline glass juicers with embossed lettering, both the straight-sided and ruffled-top models, are valued at well over $200. The Hazel Atlas Crisscross orange reamer in pink often brings in excess of $175; the same in blue, $150. Hocking produced a light blue orange reamer and, in the same soft blue, a 2-pc. reamer and measuring cup combination. Both are considered rare and very valuable, with $350 and up for the 1-pc. and $400 and up for the 2-pc. currently quoted estimates. The Federal reamer bottom beaded 'Pat Jan. 6, 1909' are one-of-a-kind examples, so market values are very difficult to establish. In addition to the colors mentioned, red glass examples¢¢transparent or slag--are rare and costly.

Among the most valuable ceramic reamers are those of American potteries. The Spongeband reamer by Red Wing is valued in excess of $300; Coorsite reamers with gold or silver trim are worth $200 and up. Figurals are popular--Mickey Mouse and John Bull may bring $200 to $300. Others range from $45 to $150. Fine china 1- and 2-pc. reamers are also very desirable and command very respectable prices.

When no condition is indicated, the items listed below are assumed to be in mint condition.

Ceramic, camel 90.00
Ceramic, chick, Goebel 80.00
Ceramic, child's; baby/crescent moon, 2-hdl cup/reamer lid 55.00
Ceramic, child's; emb chicks, 2-hdl cup/reamer lid 45.00
Ceramic, child's; Noah's Ark, ribbed 2-hdl cup/reamer lid 50.00
Ceramic, child's; orange figural, 1-hdl cup/reamer lid 45.00
Ceramic, Chinaman 90.00
Ceramic, cottage, w/tumblers 55.00
Ceramic, dog face 60.00

Ceramic, floral decor, 2-pc, Germany....55.00
Ceramic, floral lustre, 2-pc, Japan....35.00
Ceramic, John Bull....250.00
Ceramic, lemon (figural), Germany....28.00
Ceramic, Mickey Mouse....250.00
Ceramic, monkey....75.00
Ceramic, pelican....60.00
Ceramic, turtle, Japan....80.00
Coorsite, Ade-O-Matic, various colors....80.00
Coorsite, w/gold or silver trim....200.00
Easley's, improved patent, March 6, 1900, crystal....10.00
Federal, loop hdl, amber....18.00
Federal, pink....22.00
Federal, ribbed, loop hdl, amber....15.00
Federal, seed dam, tab hdl, gr....9.00
Federal, seed dam, tab hdl, ribbed, amber....20.00
Federal, tab hdl, pink, 5¼"....75.00
Fleur-de-lis, not emb, wht milk glass....45.00
Fry, ruffled top, emb, loop hdl, emerald gr....162.00
Fry, ruffled top, loop hdl, vaseline....162.00
Fry, straight side, emerald gr....40.00
Fry, straight side, milk wht....212.00
Fry, straight side, pink....40.00
Fry, tab hdl, amber....187.00
Hazel Atlas, Crisscross, lemon reamer, tab hdl, cobalt bl....137.00
Hazel Atlas, Crisscross, loop hdl, pink, 6⅛"....240.00
Hazel Atlas, lemon reamer, tab hdl, wht w/red trim ring....20.00
Hazel Atlas, pink, 32-oz pitcher & reamer....132.00
Hazel Atlas, tab hdl, clambroth, emb....65.00
Hazel Atlas, tab hdl, pink....23.00
Hazel Atlas, tab hdl, wht....17.00
Hazel Atlas, yel, 2-cup....325.00
Hocking, fruit juice reamer, gr, 2-qt....20.00
Hocking, fruit juice reamer, w/decal, bl, 1-qt....425.00
Hocking, gr, F2-73-4-1....11.00
Hocking, orange reamer, ribbed, loop hdl, gr....13.00
Hocking, paneled, loop hdl, gr....15.00
Hocking, tab hdl, gr clambroth....80.00
Jeannette, gr....11.00
Jeannette, jadite....15.00
Jeannette, Jennyware, loop hdl, pink....50.00
Jeannette, pitcher & reamer, transparent gr, emb sunflower....75.00
Jeannette, seed dam, tab hdl, gr, sm....27.00
Jeannette, sm loop hdl, dk jadite....25.00
Jeannette, tab hdl, pink, lg....23.00
Jenkins, loop hdl, gr....77.00
Limoges, 2-pc, old....120.00
Mac-Beth Evans, loop hdl, clambroth....325.00
McCoy, boat-shaped, yel....60.00
McKee, ftd, emb McK, wht, sm....26.00
McKee, grapefruit reamer, gr....237.00
McKee, grapefruit reamer, gr milk glass....140.00
McKee, grapefruit reamer, pink, rare....400.00
McKee, grapefruit reamer, transparent gr....300.00
McKee, grapefruit reamer, yel....187.00
McKee, Sunkist, blk....475.00
McKee, Sunkist, caramel opalescent....600.00
McKee, Sunkist, dk jade....225.00
McKee, Sunkist, dk tan....235.00
McKee, Sunkist, loop hdl, Crown Tuscan....137.00
McKee, Sunkist, loop hdl, dk gr....200.00
McKee, Sunkist, loop hdl, French ivory....33.00
Morton Pottery, Cliftwood....60.00
Nippon, 2-pc....85.00

Ceramic 'Puddin'head,' brown and black striped shirt, blue pants, yellow and green lid 'hat,' 6", $120.00.

Paden City, pitcher & reamer, amber....225.00
Paden City, shaker type/metal insert, pink-amber, complete....55.00
Royal Bayreuth, scenic....150.00
Royal Rudolstadt, 2-pc....110.00
Sunkist, caramel....200.00
Sunkist, gr opal....120.00
Sunkist, jadite....20.00
Sunkist, pink....40.00
Sunkist, wht....10.00
Sunkist, yel opaque....40.00
US Glass, etched, loop hdl, pink, 2-cup....38.00
US Glass, loop hdl, pink w/fruit....33.00
US Glass, loop hdl, wht....92.00
US Glass, pitcher & reamer, loop hdl, pink, 2-pc....137.00
US Glass, pitcher & reamer, slick hdl, gr....27.00
US Glass, reamer pitcher, lt gr....175.00
US Glass, slick hdl, frosted gr....30.00
US Glass, slick hdl, gr....137.00
US Glass, slick hdl, pink....32.00
US Glass, 4-cup pitcher w/reamer, snowflake design, 2-pc....43.00
Valencia, emb, crystal....137.00
Valencia, not emb, loop hdl, amber-pink....175.00
Vidrio, pitcher & reamer, gr, 2-pc....137.00
Westmoreland, amber, 2-pc....137.00
Westmoreland, flattened loop hdl, crystal w/flowers....50.00
Westmoreland, pitcher, emb w/lemon & orange, loop hdl, gr....175.00
Westmoreland Specialty Co, gr....210.00

Records

Records of interest to collectors are generally not the million-selling hits by 'superstars'; very few records by Bing Crosby, for example, are of any more than nominal value, and those that are valuable usually don't even have his name on the label! Collectors today are most interested in records that were made in limited quantities, early works of a performer who later became famous, and those issued in special series or aimed at a limited market. These are bringing prices well in excess of their original cost. The most widely collected categories are Jazz, Dance Bands, Celebrity, Blues,

Rhythm and Blues, Country and Western, Hillbilly, Rockabilly, and Rock and Roll.

Note: LPs and EPs (Extended Play 45 rpm) must be in their original jackets, without which they are often unsaleable at any price.

This year we were assisted in our listings by L.R. Docks, author of *American Premium Record Guide*, which lists 50,000 records by over 6,000 artists; you will find his address in the Directory under Texas.

When no condition is indicated, the items listed below are assumed to be in excellent condition.

Key:

Bro—Broadway	Me—Meritt
Bru—Brunswick	Orch—Orchestra
Ch—Champion	Para—Paramount
Col—Columbia	Va—Variety
Edi—Edison	Vi—Victor
Ha—Harmony	Vo—Vocation

Alabama Four, Looking This Way, Bro 8209, 78 rpm....6.00
Alabama Washboard Stompers, I Need Lovin', 78 rpm, Vo 1635....20.00
Allen, Ronnie; High School Love, San 209, 45 rpm....10.00
Armstrong, Louis; Lyin' To Myself, 78 rpm, Decca 835....7.00
Asparagus Joe, Boston Burglar, Ch 15752, 78 rpm....8.00
Atkins, Chet; Finger-Style Guitar, RCA Vi 1383, LP....17.00
Baby Doo, The Death of Walter Barnes, Decca 7763, 78 rpm....10.00
Baldwin, Luke; I Love the Jailer's Daughter, Ch 15945....12.00
Barrow, Raymond; Walking Blues, Para 12803, 78 rpm....75.00
Beach Boys, The; Surfin', X 301, 45 rpm....87.00
Berry, Chuck; Johnny B Goode, Chess 1691, 78 rpm....10.00
Billy Boy, I Ain't Got You, Vee Jay 171, 45 rpm....7.00
Birmingham Jug Band, Kickin' Mule Blues, Okeh 8866, 78 rpm....87.00
Birmingham Sam, Landing Blues, Savoy 5558....9.00
Blake, Charley; Daddy & Home, Supertone 9476, 78 rpm....10.00
Bogan, Lucille; Coffee Grindin' Blues, Bru 7083....25.00
Booker Orchestra, Salty Dog, Gennett 6375, 78 rpm....25.00
Boone, Jimmy; Crazy Blues, Superior 2661, 78 rpm....32.00
Brenston, Jackie; Leo the Louse, Chess 1496, 45 rpm....15.00
Brooks, Bob; Red River Valley, Col 15689-D, 78 rpm....7.00
Brown, Freddie; Whip It to a Jelly, Para 12910, 78 rpm....60.00
Buck, Peter; That's Enough, Drew-Blan 1005, 45 rpm....7.00
Buck & Bubbles, Rhythm for Sale, Col 2873-D, 78 rpm....12.00
Burns, Daphne; Weeping Willow Tree, Para 3032, 78 rpm....9.00
Busby, Frank; Prisoner Bound, Decca 7295, 78 rpm....8.00
Byrd, Robert; Bippin' & Boppin', Jamie 1039, 45 rpm....7.00
Campbell, Bob; Starvation Farm Blues, Vo 02798, 78 rpm....62.00
Campbell, Gene; Lazy Woman Blues, Bru 7184, 78 rpm....42.00
Carolina Cotton Pickers, Western Swing, Vo 03539, 78 rpm....10.00
Carolina Twins, One Dark & Rainy Night, Vi 21575, 78 rpm....8.00
Carter, Harry; Hoo Doo Blues, Bluebird 6095, 78 rpm....15.00
Carter Family, Wildwood Flower, Bluebird 5356, 78 rpm....7.00
Cartwright Brothers, Utah Carroll, Col 15410-D, 78 rpm....10.00
Carver Boys, The Brave Engineer, Para 3198, 78 rpm....17.00
Cash, Johnny; I Walk the Line, Sun 241, 78 rpm....8.00
Cassanovas, The; Please Be Mine, Apollo 519, 45 rpm....14.00
Chantels, The; Every Night, End 1015, 45 rpm....6.00
Charles, Ray; Rockhouse, Atlantic 2006, 78 rpm....12.00
Chicago Footwarmers, The; Goin' to Town, Okeh 8675, 78 rpm....30.00
Clark, Duke; 11:29 Blues, Ch 16624, 78 rpm....40.00
Clovers, The; Lovey Dovey, Atlantic 1022, 45 rpm....10.00
Commodores, The; Hello Baby, RPM 488, 45 rpm....12.00
Cookie's Gingersnaps, Messin' Around, Okeh 8390, 78 rpm....40.00
Corn Cob Crushers, Dill Pickle Rag, Ch 16373, 78 rpm....17.00
Country Paul, Side Walk Boogie, King 4573, 45 rpm....12.00
Craddock, Billy 'Crash'; Birddoggin', Colonial 721, 45 rpm....8.00
Crosby, Bing; Lazy Day, Bru 6306, 78 rpm....8.00
Davis, Jimmie; She's a Hum-Dinger, Vi 23587, 78 rpm....25.00
Davis, Link; Mama Say No, Okeh 7046, 45 rpm....9.00
Deejays, The; Love Me Baby, SRC, 45 rpm....87.00
Delaney, Tom; Bow-Legged Mama, Col 14122-D, 78 rpm....10.00
Delmore Brothers, The Farmers Girl, Bluebird 7383, 78 rpm....8.00
Derksen, Arnie; She Wanna Rock, Decca 30906, 45 rpm....10.00
Dixie Jazz Band, Makin' Friends, Challenge 999, 78 rpm....10.00
Dixie String Band, Atlanta Special, Para 3316, 78 rpm....12.00
Domino, Fats; Rose Marie, Imperial 5251, 45 rpm....10.00
Down Home Boys, It's All Gone Now, Vi 38567, 78 rpm....50.00
Dreams, The; I'll Be Faithful, Savoy 1157, 45 rpm....8.00
Dunbar, Frank; Nobody's Darling on Earth, Superior 2538....25.00
Dusky Dailey, Misunderstandin' Man, Vo 05110, 78 rpm....10.00
Dynamics, The; This Love of Ours, Emjay 1928, 45 rpm....6.00
Edwards, Carrie; Dirty Mistreater, Co 14652-D, 78 rpm....17.00
Edwards, Tibby; Flip Flop & Fly, Mercury 70591, 45 rpm....7.00
Ellington, Duke; Old Man Blues, Bluebird 6450, 78 rpm....13.00
Ellis, Seger; Cheerful Little Earful, Co 2362-D....6.50
Everetts, Dorothy; Macon Blues, Co 14444-D, 78 rpm....17.00
Fabian, Rockin' Hot, Chancellor 5019, LP....21.00
Ferguson, John; Railroad Daddy, Challenge 159, 78 rpm....7.00
Fisher, Sonny; Rockin' & Rollin', Starday 207, 45 rpm....35.00
Five Jinks, Cushion Foot, Bluebird 6905, 78 rpm....9.00
Five Satins, Can I Come Over Tonight, Cub 9090, 45 rpm....6.00
Flamingos, That's My Desire, Chance 1140, 45 rpm....100.00
Foley, David; I'll Never Be Yours, Ch 393, 78 rpm....10.00
Foster, Owen; Wilkes County Blues, Vi 20934, 78 rpm....12.00
Four Chickadees, Teenage Blues, Checker 849, 45 rpm....9.00
France, Steve; Dream Boy, Renown 110, 45 rpm....10.00
Frenchy's String Band, Sunshine Special, Co 14387-D....20.00
Garner, Cora; Wouldn't Stop Doing It, Col 14659-D, 78 rpm....15.00
Georgia Cotton Pickers, Diddle-Da-Diddle, Col 14577-D....40.00
Georgia Melodians, Red Hot Mama, Edi 51394, 78 rpm....10.00
Gladiola, The; Little Darlin', Excello 2101, 45 rpm....8.00
Goldrush, All My Money Is Gone, Jaxyson 6, 78 rpm....13.00
Goodman, Benny; Night Wind, Col 3015-D, 78 rpm....12.00
Gray, Billy; Tennessee Toddy, Decca 29800, 45 rpm....6.00
Gray, Geneva; Fortune Teller Blues, Okeh 8449, 78 rpm....13.00
Gregory, Bobby; Hoopee Scoopee, Okeh 45473, 78 rpm....12.00
Gunter, Arthur; Honey Babe, Excello 2058, 45 rpm....6.00
Hackberry Ramblers, Cajun Crawl, Bluebird 2013, 78 rpm....10.00
Halton Brothers, Hook & Line, Ch 16628, 78 rpm....17.00
Hamp, Charles W; Sweetheart's Holiday, Okeh 41308, 78 rpm....7.00
Harmonica Bill, The Prisoner's Radio, Ch 16393, 78 rpm....17.00
Harptones, I Depend on You, Bruce 104, 45 rpm....8.00
Harris, Sim; Pass Around the Bottle, Oriole 916, 78 rpm....9.00
Hawkins, Buddy Boy; Awful Fix Blues, Para 12539, 78 rpm....50.00
Hayes, Nap; Somethin' Doin', Okeh 45231, 78 rpm....17.00
Heartbreakers, My Love, Vik 0299, 45 rpm....27.00
Helton, Ernest; Royal Clog, Okeh 45010, 78 rpm....10.00
Henderson, Fletcher, & Orchestra; Just Blues, Ajax 17029....25.00
Highlanders, Flop-Eared Mule, Para 3171, 78 rpm....40.00
Hightower's Night Hawks, Boar Hog Blues, Black Patti 8045....250.00
Hill, Bob; He Was a Good Man, Vi 23718, 78 rpm....35.00
Holly, Buddy; Reminiscing, Coral (LP) 57426....25.00
Honey Swamp Stompers, Wipin' the Pan, Ha 856-H, 78 rpm....6.00
Hooker, Earl; Race Track, King 4600, 45 rpm....10.00
Horton, Johnny; Lover's Rock, Col 41043, 45 rpm....8.00
Hot Shot Love, Wolf Call Boogie, Sun 196, 45 rpm....40.00
Hound Head Henry, My Silver Dollar Mama, Vo 1288, 78 rpm....50.00
Hughey, Dan; Froggie Went A-Courtin', Ch 15466, 78 rpm....8.00
Hunter, Slim; Big Bill Blues, Superior 2837, 78 rpm....50.00
Hutchens Brothers, I'm Free Again, Ch 15588, 78 rpm....6.00
Ink Spots, Melody of Love, King 1336, 45 rpm....8.00

Irvin, Kitty; Copenhagen, Gennett 5592, 78 rpm..............20.00
James, Sonny; Young Love, Capitol 3602, 78 rpm..............7.00
Jenkins, Hazekiah; The Panic Is On, Col 14585-D, 78 rpm.....17.00
Jennings, Waylon; The Stage, Trend '63 106, 45 rpm...........9.00
Johns, Whitey; The Prisoner's Rosary, Ch 895, 78 rpm..........8.00
Johnson, Gene; Jimmie the Kid, Timely Tunes 1551, 78 rpm....17.00
Johnson, Ki Ki; Lady Your Clock Ain't Right, QRS 7003.......62.00
Johnson, Lonnie; Bull Frog Moan, Okeh 8695, 78 rpm.........14.00
Johnson, Tommy; Alcohol & Jake Blues, Para 12950, 78 rpm..150.00
Jolson, Al; You Are Too Beautiful, Bru 6500, 78 rpm..........13.00
Jones, Sonny; I'm Pretty Good at It, Vo 05124, 78 rpm........15.00
Jungle Band, The; Wang Wang Blues, Bru 6003, 78 rpm.......10.00
Justice, Dick; Cocaine, Bru 395, 78 rpm......................17.00
Kelly Brothers, Always Remember, Vi 23833, 78 rpm..........13.00
Kennedy, Tiny; Blues Disease, Trumpet 188, 45 rpm...........7.00
Kentuckians, Jack Davies'; Sick O' Licks, Ch 16607...........25.00
King, BB; The Blues, Crown 5063, LP.......................13.00
Kinks, Long Tall Sally, Cameo 345, 45 rpm..................17.00
Kirby's Kings of Jazz, Green River Blues, Bell 591, 78 rpm.....15.00
Lamplighters, Five Minutes Longer, Federal 12192, 45 rpm.....10.00
Landon, Lee; Lullaby Yodel, Ch 15767, 78 rpm...............12.00
Lee, Jerry; Smiling Blues, Herwin 93014, 78 rpm.............42.00
Leroy's Dallas Band, Tampa Shout, Col 14402-D, 78 rpm.......17.00
Lewis, Earnest; West Coast Blues, Parrot 791, 45 rpm.........10.00
Lewis, Smiley; Play Girl, Imperial 5234, 45 rpm..............25.00
Lewis, Ted, & His Band; Farewell Blues, Col 2029-D..........10.00
Lillie Mae, Mama Don't Want It, Okeh 8920, 78 rpm...........18.00
Little Richard, Heeby-Jeebies, Specialty 584, 78 rpm............8.00
Locke, Rusty; Milk Cow Blues, TNT 1012, 78 rpm..............7.00
Logics, One Love, Everlast 5015, 45 rpm......................8.00
Louisiana Lou, Go 'Long Mule, Vi 23858, 78 rpm..............13.00
Lullaby Larkers, Shine on Harvest Moon, Ch 16257, 78 rpm....20.00
Magic Sam, Mr Charlie, Chief 7013, 45 rpm....................8.00
Martin Brothers, Whistling Rufus, Para 3217, 78 rpm..........20.00
Martindale, Wink; Deck of Cards, Dot (LP) 3245...............15.00
Marvin, Johnny; Go Along Bum, Vi 23728, 78 rpm..............8.00
McBooker, Connie; Short Baby Boogie, Eddie's 1928, 78 rpm...25.00
McCoy, William; How Long Baby, Col 14393-D, 78 rpm.........17.00
McHugh's, Jimmy, Bostonians; The Whoopee Stomp, Ha 836-H..15.00
McKinney Brothers, Old Uncle Joe, Ch 16830, 78 rpm.........12.00
Mello-Kings, Valerie, Herald 518, 45 rpm.......................7.00
Memphis Bob, Little Marion McLean, Col 15735-D, 78 rpm......8.00
Midnight Ramblers, Down in the Alley, Vo 03517, 78 rpm.......8.00
Miller, Bobby; Little Bo Peep, Band Box 322, 45 rpm...........6.00
Miller, Lillian; Kitchen Blues, Okeh 8381, 78 rpm.............35.00
Miller, Stanley; Lost Train Blues, Ch 15315, 78 rpm............8.00
Mills Brothers, The; Diga Diga Doo, Bru 6519, 78 rpm.........13.00
Mills' Merry Makers, Moanin' Low, Perfect 15208, 78 rpm.......8.00
Mitchell, Lee; Rootie Tootie Baby, Sharp 0862, 45 rpm........12.00
Monkey Joe, Tailor Made Woman, Vo 04814, 78 rpm............8.00
Montana Slim, Yodeling Cowgirl, Bluebird 6827, 78 rpm.........6.00
Moonshiners, Midnight Waltz, Vi 40284, 78 rpm...............8.00
Morse, Lee; Walkin' My Baby Back Home, Col 2417-D, 78 rpm.10.00
Moss, Teddy; Ocean Wave Blues, Gennett 7055, 78 rpm.......50.00
Murphy, Chuck; Rhythm Hall, Col 21305, 45 rpm..............10.00
New Orleans Bootblacks, Flat Foot, Col 14337-D, 78 rpm......35.00
New Yorkers, The; Parkin' in the Moonlight, Bru 6164.........10.00
Nite Riders, Doctor Velvet, Apollo 466, 45 rpm................12.00
Noles, Flora; Little Mohee, Okeh 45037, 78 rpm................6.00
Norris, Land; Groundhog, Okeh 40096, 78 rpm.................10.00
North-West Melody Boys, Rain, Ch 15365, 78 rpm............10.00
O'Diamonds, Jack; The Ducks Yas Yas, Para 12786, 78 rpm....50.00
Oakdale, Slim; No Hard Times, Crown 3461, 78 rpm............8.00
Oaks, Charlie; Boll Weevil, Vo 15342, 78 rpm..................8.00
Oliver, Joe 'King'; Farewell Blues, Bru 3741, 78 rpm..........25.00
Owen, Kenny; I Got the Bug, Poplar 106, 45 rpm...............8.00
Palmer, Sylvester; Lonesome Man Blues, Col 14492-D, 78 rpm..35.00
Patrick, Luther; Cornbread, Gennett 6448, 78 rpm.............12.00
Paul, Jerry; Step Out, Holiday 1001, 45 rpm..................12.00
Perkins, Gertrude; Gold Daddy Blues, Col 14313-D, 78 rpm.....10.00
Petway, Robert; My Baby Left Me, Bluebird 9008, 78 rpm......13.00
Piano Red, Pay It No Mind, Groove 0101, 45 rpm..............7.00
Pork Chop Green, She Walks Like a Maltese Cat/Gennett 7116..40.00
Pork Chop Jackson, Lonesome Man Blues, Supertone 9510.....50.00
Presley, Elvis; Blue Moon, RCA Vic 6640, w/cover, 78 rpm.....25.00
Presley, Elvis; Love Me Tender, RCA Vic 4006, 45 rpm (EP)....10.00
Price, Ray; Jealous Lies, Bullet 701, 78 rpm.................25.00
Queen City Blowers, Stomp Off, Let's Go, Ch 15030, 78 rpm....10.00
Quinn, Frank; Pop Goes the Weasel, Okeh 45030, 78 rpm......7.00
Radio Mac, Ain't We Crazy, Vi 40101, 78 rpm..................7.00
Rainbow, Mary Lee, Pilgrim 703, 45 rpm.....................18.00
Ramblin' Bob, Big Apple Blues, Bluebird 7987, 78 rpm........15.00
Rector Trio, Skyland Rag, Col 15658, 78 rpm.................18.00
Red Hotters, The; Hot Mustard, Silverton 3560, 78 rpm.......100.00
Reed, Jerry; Bessie Baby, Capital 3882, 45 rpm................7.00
Rhythm Kings, The; Please Tell Me, Vi 23283, 78 rpm.........25.00
Rice, Edd; Cricket on the Hearth, Vo 5220, 78 rpm............10.00
Ritter, Tex; Bill the Bar Fly, Decca 5305, 78 rpm..............7.00
Robbins, Marty; Maybelline, Col 21446, 45 rpm...............10.00
Robinson, Elzadie; Wicked Daddy, Para 12689, 78 rpm........60.00
Rodgers, Jessie; Back in Jail Again, Bluebird 7042, 78 rpm......7.00
Rogers, Buck; Little Rock Rock, Starday 245, 45 rpm..........18.00
Rose, Lucy; Papa, You're Too Slow, Ch 15471, 78 rpm........25.00
Royals, Moonrise, Federal 12088, 45 rpm.....................80.00
Savannah Syncopators, The; Wa Wa Wa, Bru 3373, 78 rpm....13.00
Sedaka, Neil; Laura Lee, Decca 30520, 45 rpm................12.00
Seven Little Clouds of Joy, You Rascal, You, Bru 7180........35.00
Shines, Johnny; Brutal Hearted Woman, JOB 1010, 45 rpm.....50.00
Slim Smith, Bread Line Blues, Crown 3118, 78 rpm............10.00
Smith, Bessie; Eavesdropper's Blues, Col 14010-D, 78 rpm......12.00
Smith, Bessie; Pickpocket Blues, Col 14304-D, 78 rpm.........17.00
Smith, Kate; One Sweet Letter from You, Col 911-D, 78 rpm...10.00
Smith, Susie; Sore Bunion Blues, Ajax 17064, 78 rpm..........20.00
Son Becky, Cryin' Shame Blues, Vo 04081, 78 rpm............17.00
Speckled Red, You Got to Fix It, Bluebird 7985, 78 rpm.......15.00
Stanton, Frank; Creole Girl, Superior 2521, 78 rpm...........25.00
State Street Swingers, Swing Cat Swing, Vo 03364, 78 rpm......8.00
Stewart, Priscilla; Biscuit Roller, Para 12402, 78 rpm..........32.00
Sullivan, Joe; Little Rock Getaway, Decca 600, 78 rpm..........8.00
Tampa Red, Nutty & Buggy Blues, Bluebird 6425, 78 rpm......14.00
Taylor, Sallie; Seven Men Blues, Supertone 9365, 78 rpm.......32.00
Tennessee Drifters, Boogie Beat Rag, Dot 1001, 78 rpm.........8.00
Texas Alexander, Farm Hand Blues, Okeh 8526, 78 rpm.......20.00
Thomas, Al, 'Fats'; Dog Days, Checker 759, 45 rpm.............8.00
Thompson, Bud; Five Cent Cotton, Crown 3418, 78 rpm.......10.00
Three Jolly Miners, Freakish Blues, Vo 15009, 78 rpm..........13.00
Tom & Jerry, Hey, Schoolgirl, Big 613, 45 rpm...............10.00
Tremer, George H; Spirit of '49 Rag, Gennett 6242, 78 rpm....50.00
Uncle Dave Macon, Bake That Chicken Pie, Vo 5148, 78 rpm...30.00
Valentines, I Love You Darling, Rama 181, 45 rpm.............12.00
Vicksburg Ten, Clarinet Marmalade, Ch 15477, 78 rpm........17.00
Virginia Four, The; Dig My Jelly Roll, Decca 7662, 78 rpm.....10.00
Wallace, Minnie; Field Mouse Stomp, Vo 03106, 78 rpm.......20.00
Walter Family, Patty on the Turn Pike, Ch 16643, 78 rpm.....20.00
Washboard Rhythm Band, Going, Going, Gone, Col 14680......42.00
Washboard Wonders, It Ain't Right, Bluebird 6464, 78 rpm......8.00
Washington, Louis; Run, Sinner, Run, Vo 02634, 78 rpm......20.00
Watson, El; Bay Rum Blues, Vi 21585, 78 rpm................15.00

Whidby, Lulu; Home Again Blues, Black Swan 2005, 78 rpm....12.00
White, John; Strawberry Roan, Romeo 5066, 78 rpm...........8.00
White Way Players, Ev'rybody Dance, Van Dyke 71816.........8.00
Whitman, Slim; China Doll, Imperial 8156, 45 rpm.............8.00
Wiley, Lee; As Though You Were There, Gala 4, 78 rpm........8.00
Williams, Fess, & His Joy Boys; Dixie Stomp, Vo 15690........40.00
Williams, Mary Lou; Clean Pickin', Decca 115, 78 rpm..........9.00
Williams' Washboard Band, Move Turtle, Bluebird 5230.........9.00
Wilson, Garland; Rockin' Chair, Okeh 41556, 78 rpm..........10.00
Winston, Edna; Peepin' Jim, Vi 20407, 78 rpm...............20.00
Wisconsin U Skyrockets, Postage Stomp, Para 12642, 78 rpm...87.00
Yale Collegians, Blue Again, Okeh 41474, 78 rpm.............15.00
Young, Clarence; That's a Plenty, Ch 15991, 78 rpm..........12.00

Red Wing

The Red Wing Stoneware Company, founded in 1878, took its name from its location in Red Wing, Minnesota. In the 1920s, the name was changed to the Red Wing Union Stoneware Company after a merger with several of the other local potteries. For the most part, they produced utilitarian wares such as flowerpots, crocks, and jugs. In about 1930, their catalogues offered a line of art pottery vases in colored glazes, some of which featured handles modeled after swan's necks, snakes, or female nudes. Other examples were quite simple, often with classic styling. After the addition of their dinnerware lines in the early thirties, 'Stoneware' was dropped from the name, and the company became known as Red Wing Potteries, Inc. They closed in 1967.

For further study we recommend *Red Wing Stoneware*, An Identification and Value Guide by Dan and Gail DePasquale and Larry Peterson, available at your local library or bookstore. When no condition is indicated, the items listed below are assumed to be in mint condition with the exception of stoneware which is assumed exellent.

Brushware

Birdhouse...125.00
Bowl, bulb, lg....................................22.50
Bowl, bulb, sm....................................10.00
Flowerpot, w/storks...............................18.00
Mug, w/monk, gr, VG...............................22.00
Vase, bulbous, 2-hdl, Union Stoneware, 9½"................40.00
Vase, flowers, mk RW Union Stoneware, gr, 10½"...........40.00
Vase, w/storks, mk RW Union Stoneware, 12"...............50.00

Commercial Artware

Ash tray, 75th anniversary..............................32.50
Bowl, console; brn stoneware w/1½" turq band, 11½"..........35.00
Box, gr, Art Pottery stamp, 4x6½"........................45.00
Bud vase, triple; gr gloss, 7¾"............................13.00
Candlestick, ivory, #397, pr..............................15.00
Candlestick, ivory w/grapes, #622, pr....................22.50
Figurine, dog...50.00
Figurine, donkey, sitting, braying, brn, 5"...................60.00
Figurine, flamenco dancers, 10", pr......................130.00
Flower frog, 2 angel fish, cream, 9"........................55.00
Pitcher, King Neptune & griffins, ivory w/purple, 10"..........35.00
Planter, dachshund, gr, 7"...............................24.00
Planter, giraffe, #896....................................20.00
Planter, ivory, M1486.....................................10.00
Planter, maroon w/gray int, B2016.......................10.00
Toothpick holder, 'Gopher State,' gopher & log, rare, 1932....100.00
Vase, bird & flower, bl....................................15.00

Figurine, cowgirl, 11¾", $75.00.

Vase, Deco, fan shape, dk red-orange, B1418A, 6½"...........35.00
Vase, dk gr w/yel int, M1457..............................10.00
Vase, Egyptian motif & figures, urn form, #159.............125.00
Vase, Egyptian style, gr glaze, trailing vine relief, 9"..........40.00
Vase, gardenia, wht w/brn, 10½"...........................25.00
Vase, gray w/maroon leaves, tall, #1204.....................15.00
Vase, gray w/pink int, B2103, 8"...........................25.00
Vase, high-button shoe, 9"................................28.00
Vase, ivory w/green int, #1174............................12.50
Vase, lady between pillars, #1175, 10½"....................45.00
Vase, matt, ivory, #1028..................................25.00
Vase, pink speckled, tall.................................15.00
Vase, pink w/gray int, B2100..............................12.50
Vase, Roman design, #159.................................125.00
Vase, turq, w/hdls, Art Pottery stamp, 12"...................20.00
Vase, 75th Anniversary, brn, 8"...........................45.00

Cookie Jars

Chef, yel..35.00
Katrina, bl..40.00
Monk, bl..40.00
Pineapple, aqua..28.00
Rooster, #249..18.00

Dinnerware

Bob White, bowl, pouring spout, hdl, & lid..................45.00
Bob White, bowl, salad; 10"..............................50.00
Bob White, bowl, vegetable; divided, 14"...................20.00
Bob White, casserole, w/lid, in fr, 4-qt....................45.00
Bob White, cookie jar.....................................25.00
Bob White, cup & saucer..................................12.50
Bob White, gravy boat, w/blk stand.........................45.00
Bob White, gravy boat, w/lid..............................24.00
Bob White, hors d'oeuvre bird.............................39.00
Bob White, mug..22.00
Bob White, pitcher, 60-oz, 14½"............................28.00
Bob White, plate, bread & butter, 6½"......................5.00
Bob White, plate, 11"....................................12.00
Bob White, platter, oval, 13½"............................15.00
Bob White, sauce dish....................................5.00
Bob White, shakers, bird form, pr..........................25.00
Bob White, shakers, tall, pr...............................18.00

Bob White, teapot....37.50
Bob White, tray, French bread....24.00
Brittany, plate, chop; 14″....10.00
Capistrano, bowl, vegetable; divided....10.00
Capistrano, platter, 13″....12.00
Chevron, cup & saucer, demitasse....45.00
Iris, French casserole....25.00
Iris, pitcher, water; purple....20.00
Iris, plate, dinner; sgn, dated Jan 15, 1951....15.00
Iris, platter, 13″....14.00
Lexington Rose, bowl, vegetable....8.00
Lexington Rose, bowl, w/lid, 4½″....5.00
Lexington Rose, creamer & sugar, w/lid....20.00
Lexington Rose, cup & saucer....10.00
Lexington Rose, plate, center hdl, metal 7½″....7.00
Lexington Rose, plate, chop....7.50
Lexington Rose, plate, dinner; 10″....6.00
Lexington Rose, platter, oval....10.00
Lexington Rose, relish, 3-part....15.00
Lexington Rose, teapot....30.00
Lotus, plate, 10½″....6.00
Plum Blossom, creamer & sugar, w/lid....16.00
Plum Blossom, cup & saucer....7.50
Plum Blossom, platter....8.00
Provencial Oomph, beverage server, w/lid....25.00
Provencial Oomph, bowl, rare, 6″....17.50
Smart Set, sugar & creamer....20.00
Smart Set, vegetable, divided....10.00
Tampico, casserole....18.00
Tampico, creamer & sugar, w/lid....20.00
Tampico, cup & saucer....9.00
Tampico, platter, 15″....14.00
Tampico, teapot....32.50
Town & Country, bowl, salad; metallic, 13″....10.00
Town & Country, cup, chartreuse....5.00

Stoneware

Baking dish, ribbed, mc sponge....50.00
Bean pot, brn/wht, bailed, bottom sgn, w/lid, 1-qt....60.00
Bean pot, brn/wht, bailed, bottom sgn, w/lid, ½-gal....50.00
Bean pot, brn/wht, bailed, bottom sgn, 1-gal....50.00
Bean pot, spongeware, red & bl on Saffron, orig lid, 1-gal....175.00
Beater jar, Gray Line....125.00
Beater jar, plain....25.00
Beater jar, w/advertising....75.00
Beater jar, Western, Wesson Oil....80.00
Bottle, hot water; leaf design, brn....75.00
Bowl, batter; Gray Line....300.00
Bowl, fruit; gr....15.00
Bowl, Gray Line, IA ad, 5x8″....145.00
Bowl, Gray Line, 10″....75.00
Bowl, Gray Line, 12″....125.00
Bowl, Gray Line, 5″....90.00
Bowl, Gray Line, 6″....50.00
Bowl, Greek Key, IA ad, #8....70.00
Bowl, Greek Key, 10″....65.00
Bowl, Greek Key, 12″....85.00
Bowl, Greek Key, 6″....45.00
Bowl, mixing; dk bl, #9....75.00
Bowl, mixing; sponge, bl band, 6″....27.00
Bowl, Saffron, grape decor, yel....60.00
Bowl, spongeware w/panels, 11″....80.00
Bowl, spongeware w/panels, 5″....60.00
Bowl, spongeware w/panels, 6″....40.00
Butter churn, salt glaze, mk w/red wing & #5, 5-gal....115.00
Butter jar, elephant ear leaves, 2-gal cut in half, 20-lb....125.00
Butter jar, Gray Line, bailed, w/lid, 3-lb....225.00
Butter jar, Gray Line, bailed, w/lid, 5-lb....275.00
Butter jar, w/advertising, bl band, w/lid....175.00
Cake stand, Gray Line....600.00
Casserole, Gray Line, w/lid, any size other than sm....150.00
Casserole, Gray Line, w/lid, sm....250.00
Casserole, Saffron, w/lid....60.00
Christmas tree holder, top holes for screws, 1912....250.00
Churn, lg wing, 3-gal....98.00
Churn, lg wing, 5-gal....150.00
Churn, sm wing, bail hdls, dtd 1915, 3-gal....150.00
Churn, sm wing, 5-gal....195.00
Cookie jar, Gray Line, w/lid....350.00
Crock, salt glaze, dbl P mk, unsgn, 3-gal....62.00
Crock, sm wing, 5-gal....75.00
Custard cup, Gray Line, sm....75.00
Flowerpot, Albany slip, brn, 7″....175.00
Fruit jar, Mason, ½-gal....115.00
Funnel, mk Acid Proof Measure, rare, 1907....275.00
Jar, ball-lock, blown top, lg red wing, 2-gal....87.00
Jar, ball-lock, sm wing, 5-gal....95.00
Jar, beater; no wing, 20-lbs butter....95.00
Jar, Mason's, 1-qt or 2-qt....120.00
Jug, ball-lock; sm wing, 5-gal....145.00
Jug, beehive, elephant ear leaves, oval, wht glaze, 5-gal....200.00
Jug, brn top shoulder, wing & oval, 5-gal....225.00
Jug, foil wing stamped on bottom, ⅛-pt....180.00
Jug, pat 1915, 15-gal....25.00
Jug, shoulder; sm wing, 5-gal....125.00
Jug, wht shoulder, wing & circle, 5-gal....50.00
Juleps dispenser, cattails, sgn, rare....85.00
Kover-Weight, 10-lb, rare....80.00
Meat roaster, bisque, w/hdl & lid....112.00
Milk pan, bottom sgn, bl....125.00
Milk pan, North Star, brn, lg....70.00
Mug, Gray Line....300.00
Nappy, notches on rim, bl glaze, unsgn....62.00
Pipkin, brn bottom/wht top, 4-pt....225.00
Pitcher, barrel shaped, hand-drawn lines, bottom mk, brn....100.00
Pitcher, Cherry Band, plain, 8″....100.00
Pitcher, Cherry Band, plain, 9″....125.00
Pitcher, Cherry Band, w/advertising, 6″....200.00
Pitcher, Cherry Band, w/advertising, 8″....135.00
Pitcher, Cherry Band, w/advertising, 9″....165.00
Pitcher, grapes, brn, 9½″....135.00
Pitcher, Gray Line, w/advertising & date, tall....200.00
Pitcher, Western Cattail, bulbous, 1-gal, 9″....225.00
Pitcher, Western Cattail, bulbous, 6″....200.00
Pitcher, Western Cattail, bulbous, 7″....100.00
Pitcher, Western Cattail, bulbous, 8″....150.00
Poultry fount, ½-gal....35.00
Preserve jar, salt glaze, cylindrical, sgn, orig stone lid....175.00
Preserve/snuff jar, North Star, dk gr glaze, 1-gal....137.00
Reamer, Gray Line....400.00
Refrigerator jar, Gray Line, w/lid, lg....300.00
Refrigerator jar, Gray Line, w/lid, med....275.00
Refrigerator jar, Gray Line, w/lid, sm....250.00
Refrigerator jar, w/lid, stenciled label, 3-lb....125.00
Refrigerator jar, w/lid, stenciled label, 5-lb....150.00
Salt crock, hanging; Gray Line, w/lid....500.00
Salt shaker, Gray Line....225.00

Spittoon, wht bottom/brn top, lg.....250.00
Umbrella stand, sponge, red & bl.....450.00
Water cooler, Red Wing Union trademk, 3-gal.....262.00
Water cooler, sm wing, w/lid, 5-gal.....200.00

Redware

The term redware refers to a type of simple earthenware produced by the Colonists as early as the 1600s. The red clay used in its production was abundant throughout the country, and during the 18th and 19th centuries redware was made in great quantities. Intended for utilitarian purposes such as everyday tableware, or use in the dairy, redware was simple in design and decoration. Glazes of various colors were used, and a liquid clay referred to as 'slip' was sometimes applied in patterns such as zigzag lines, daisies, or stars.

When no condition is indicated, the items listed below are assumed to be in excellent condition.

Left to right: Pie plate, signed John Bell, ca 1840-60, undamaged, 7½", $130.00; Pot, brown glazed interior, signed John Bell, one very small chip, 7½" x 6" diameter, $70.00.

Bear, hand molded, clear glaze on brn, 7½".....65.00
Bird fountain, jug form w/half dish at base, glaze w/in, 5".....30.00
Bottle, doughnut; running brn/clear/gr glaze, 7¼".....90.00
Bottle, flask; dk brn, worn/flakes, 6".....55.00
Bottle, imp JS Henne, clear glaze w/brn dots, flakes, 9".....135.00
Bottle, incised wavy lines, blk glaze, 5¼".....35.00
Bottle, squat shape w/pinched center, gray-gr glaze, 3½".....500.00
Bowl, clear glaze w/daubs of brn, flakes, 3¼x9⅞".....315.00
Bowl, clear w/brn spots, applied hdls, 4½x8", EX.....155.00
Bowl, finger-crimped rim, blk glaze, edge wear, 2⅛x3¼".....35.00
Bowl, gr int glaze, flared sides, 5x8¼".....45.00
Bowl, marbleized wht/dk brn, high dome lid, 12x11", VG.....570.00
Bowl, milk; finger-crimped ring, 2¼x7½", EX.....125.00
Bowl, milk; wht w/in, gr rim stripe, 8x18" dia.....55.00
Bowl, milk; yel slip wavy lines, glaze wear/flakes, 3x9½".....50.00
Bowl, miniature, clear & brn running glaze, 1⅜".....105.00
Bowl, orange & gr, orange dots w/in rim, sponged, 4x9", EX...255.00
Bowl, 3 wavy lines yel slip, coggled, oval, 3¾x12x18".....700.00
Charger, coggled edge, 3-line yel slip decor, wear, 2x12¼".....750.00
Charger, coggled edge, 4-line yel slip decor, 1⅝x11½".....825.00
Charger, yel slip monogram 'MA' in center, rim chips, 12¼"...400.00
Charger, 3-line yel slip decor, rim & surface chips, 12".....225.00
Charger, 4 puddles of yel slip, coggled edge, chips, 13".....325.00
Churn, imp Gordy's Pottery, edge chips, redware lid, 16".....105.00
Creamer, dk brn glaze, 4".....50.00
Creamer, mottled dk brn & amber glaze, 3⅛".....85.00
Creamer, pinched spout, Albany slip, wht clay, flakes, 3⅝".....45.00
Crock, ovoid, gr-gray glaze, 4¾x6¼".....25.00
Cup, dk brn glaze, edge chips, 2½".....30.00
Cup, dk brn shiny glaze, rim wear, 7½".....45.00
Cup, incised lines/partial incised name on bottom, brn.....145.00
Cup, pouring spout, dk brn glaze, flakes, 1½x2¾".....55.00
Cuspidor, miniature, octagonal w/emb eagles & hdl, 4½".....75.00
Cuspidor, wht slip w/gr/brn runs, Shenandoah, 7", EX.....275.00
Cuspidor, wht w/gr & brn, S Bell & Son, 6½", VG.....225.00
Dish, brn sponging & speckles, old edge flakes, 1½x6¼".....65.00
Dish, divided, wht slip decor on rim, 9x11½".....65.00
Dish, serving; oblong, brn metallic glaze, 11x13½".....55.00
Dog's head, hand tooled & molded, olive amber w/brn, 4".....75.00
Flowerpot, crimped rim, 1-pc w/saucer, brn, 6x10", EX.....20.00
Flowerpot, saucer base, gr/clear w/wht slip, tooled, 5".....150.00
Frame, C Brown, oval, gr-amber glaze, 11¾x13".....300.00
Inkwell, house shape w/glass insert, edge wear, 1¾".....135.00
Jar, brn mottled glaze, w/side hdl, rim flake, 6".....85.00
Jar, canning; Solomon Bell, gr w/orange/gr mottle, 8", EX.....235.00
Jar, clear glaze on dk brn, rim chips, 5⅛".....55.00
Jar, clear glaze w/brn splotches, w/hdl, rim chips, 5⅞".....235.00
Jar, cup-type hdl, wht slip, gr glaze, minor wear, 3½".....265.00
Jar, dk brn sponging, ovoid, wear/chips, 5".....110.00
Jar, emb foliage trim, brn running glaze, wear/flakes, 9".....33.00
Jar, gr mottle int, w/hdls, 8½", EX.....65.00
Jar, jelly; wht clay, amber glaze w/brn int, wear, 4¼".....13.00
Jar, ovoid, brn mottled glaze, sm rim flakes, 4⅝".....45.00
Jar, ovoid, clear glaze on dk brn, glaze wear on rim, 4¼".....85.00
Jar, ovoid, clear glaze w/brn splotches, w/hdl, 5½".....145.00
Jar, ovoid, clear glaze w/dk brn splotches, 5⅝".....125.00
Jar, ovoid, int glaze, 5½".....25.00
Jar, ovoid, miniature, clear glaze w/1 brn dot, wear, 1⅝".....95.00
Jar, ovoid, miniature, clear glaze/blk spots, flakes, 2½".....95.00
Jar, ovoid, 2-tone clear gr glaze, minor rim flakes, 5⅛".....115.00
Jar, scalloped, tooled wavy band, ovoid, dk brn, 9½", EX.....90.00
Jar, tooled rim, stripes/swags/tassels, gr/brn, 14x16".....450.00
Jug, blk speckled metallic, applied hdl, ovoid, 7", EX.....110.00
Jug, dk brn (blk), ft chip, sm edge flakes on hdl, 4".....75.00
Jug, gr speckled, imp John Bell, Waynesboro, 8".....450.00
Jug, gr w/brn speckles, ovoid, edge chips, 7½".....75.00
Jug, gr-amber glaze w/brn flecks, flakes/hairline, 5¼".....155.00
Jug, grotesque, gr ash glaze, Lanier Meaders, 9¾".....125.00
Jug, incised band, strap hdl, spotted, 2⅞", EX.....35.00
Jug, ovoid, dk brn shiny glaze, ribbed hdl, flakes, 8¾".....55.00
Jug, ovoid, dk gr-brn glaze, strap hdl, wear/lip chips, 8".....110.00
Jug, ovoid, gr glaze, lg strap hdl, 5⅝".....220.00
Jug, ovoid, miniature, clear glaze, brn flecks, chips, 2¼".....95.00
Jug, ovoid, miniature, pumpkin w/brn slip, w/strap hdl, 4".....455.00
Jug, ovoid, miniature, tooled band, clear glaze, hdl, 2⅞".....275.00
Lamp, C Brown, Pennsylvania, 3 openings for wicks, 4¼".....300.00
Loaf pan, oval, 3-line yel slip, coggled edge, 12¼x15½".....500.00
Milk bottle cooler, unglazed, flake/hairline, 12¾".....85.00
Milk pan, amber glaze w/crows ft/wavy lines of red, 2¾x8½"....135.00
Milk pan, clear glaze w/dk brn splotches, chips, 3¼x10".....55.00
Milk pan, gr olive glaze, surface flake, 2½x12½".....75.00
Mold, chocolate; standing rabbit, mottled red-amber, 5¾".....175.00
Mold, curved fish, glazed int, minor flakes, 12".....65.00
Mold, fish shape, clear glaze w/brn spots & drips, 11½".....350.00
Mold, Turk's head, brn sponged rim, 3¾x9¾".....90.00
Mold, Turk's head, clear glaze w/brn flecks, 2½x 8¼".....40.00
Mold, Turk's head, creamy amber w/brn splotches, 8¾".....115.00
Mold, Turk's head, gr glaze w/red highlights, 3x9", EX.....45.00
Mold, Turk's head, swirled design, imp John Bell, 4x8½".....255.00
Mug, clear glaze w/brn splotches, wear/hairlines, 3".....75.00
Mug, clear gr glaze w/brn flecks, edge wear/flakes, 4¼".....70.00

Mug, incised lines, strap hdl, gr glaze, 4⅛" 410.00
Mug, ovoid, brn fleck glaze, strap hdl, base hairline, 3¾" 105.00
Mug, ovoid w/hdl, clear w/brn highlights, glaze wear, 4" 50.00
Mug, speckled cream glaze, sm flakes, 4¾" 85.00
Pie plate, clear glaze w/yel slip, label on bk, 2x8⅞", EX 280.00
Pie plate, dbl crossed wavy lines in yel slip, wear, 7⅜" 145.00
Pie plate, slight coggled edge, 2-line slip/dots, 7½" 90.00
Pie plate, wht & brn slip decor, worn int/chips, 8¼" 65.00
Pie plate, yel slip decor w/zigzags, flakes, 1¼x9¼" 250.00
Pie plate, 3 wavy lines yel slip, minor wear, 8¾" 175.00
Pitcher, amber w/brn running flecks, minor wear, 4⅛" 115.00
Pitcher, clear glaze w/good red-orange color, flakes, 8" 65.00
Pitcher, good shape, brn speckled glaze, strap hdl, 6⅝" 120.00
Pitcher, miniature, clear glaze, rim & foot chips, 2¼" 95.00
Pitcher, miniature, dk metallic glaze, minor flakes, 2" 65.00
Pitcher, ovoid, clear gr glaze w/brn splotches, wear, 6¼" 115.00
Pitcher, squat; thin coat of yel slip w/clear glaze, 3¾" 105.00
Pitcher, strap hdl, pinch spout, clear glaze, 8", EX 70.00
Plate, coggled edge, yel slip initials, 8½", EX 280.00
Rooster, hand molded, gr glaze, mk JCC, 7⅜" 140.00
Salt cellar, clear gr glaze, rim & foot chips, 1¼x3¼" 115.00
Salt cellar, some wht slip under clear w/running gr, 3½" 175.00
Salt cellar, tooled band, clear w/brn splotches, 1⅜x2⅞" 100.00
Spittoon, lady's; scroll relief, lead glaze, 2½x5" 110.00
Teapot, edge wear/minor chips, 3" 50.00
Tile, emb tulip, bl & wht glaze, edge flakes, 5⅞x7⅛" 55.00
Tile, roof; JB Hamilton, dtd 1871, 13x9x1½" 24.00
Tumbler mold, ribbed, edge chips, 4¼" 85.00

Religious Items

When no condition is indicated, the items listed below are assumed to be in excellent condition.

Crucifix, MOP w/bronze figure of Jesus, bk: 14 stages, 10" 170.00
Hymnal, leather bound, watercolor fraktur bookplate, 1790 .... 350.00
Icon, virgin, brass/pnt, Byzantine-form, 1750, Russian, 7" 385.00
Icon, 3 saints, brass/pnt, sgn NI-KA w/cross, Russian, 2½" 175.00
Icon, 3 saints, enamel/brass, Russian, 1875, 2½x2¼" 110.00
Last rites accouterments in oak box w/brass trim, pat 1897 .... 165.00
Shrine, hanging, pine, scroll crest, trn crosses, pnt, 26" 125.00

Reverse Painting on Glass

Verre eglomise is the technique of painting on the underside of glass. Dating back to the early 1700s, this art became popular in the 19th century when German immigrants chose historical figures and beautiful women as subjects for their reverse glass paintings. Advertising mirrors of this type came into vogue at the turn of the century.

When no condition is indicated, the items listed below are assumed to be in excellent condition.

Bonbon box w/brass band, Napoleon bust on lid, 5" dia 200.00
Country scene w/people/ducks, sgn, shadowbox fr, 6x12", pr 150.00
European bridge scene w/gold foil, 19x29" 50.00
Landscape w/lake & trees, tinsel bk, gilt fr, 22½x28½" 150.00
Mirror, cottage on hill w/tree, gilded wood, 9x4¼", EX 195.00
Mother holds baby in christening gown, 1890s, oval, 45" 705.00
Scenic w/MOP Goddess of Liberty, NY, oval fr 35.00
Sign, Watches Repaired, silver leaf 45.00
Statue of Liberty, dtd 1917, in oval fr 65.00
Strawberries, in old gilt fr, 7x9", EX 95.00

Richard

Richard, who at one time worked for Galle, made cameo art glass in France during the 1920s. His work was often multi-layered and acid cut with florals and scenics in lovely colors. The ware was marked with his name in relief.

When no condition is indicated, the items listed below are assumed to be in mint condition.

Cameo

Vase, floral, tan & gr on gray, 13" 565.00
Vase, house, mtn scene, 2 cuts, 8x5" 650.00
Vase, lake/boats, 2 cuts, 4" 350.00
Vase, mtns/trees/river/castle on orange, bl ft, sgn, 10¼" 750.00

Ridgway

As early as 1792, the Ridgway brothers, Job and George, produced fine quality earthenwares in Shelton, Staffordshire, marking their product 'Ridgway, Smith & Ridgway,' and later, 'Job & George Ridgway.' About 1800 the brothers split and each had his own firm, both in Shelton. They were joined in the business by various members of the Ridgway family, and in fact their descendants still operate there today.

The two firms created by the split were the Bell Works and the Cauldon Pottery. Bell produced stone china and earthenware decorated with blue transfer printing. Their mark was 'J. & W. Ridgway' or 'J. & W.R.,' until 1848 when 'William Ridgway' was used.

The Cauldon Pottery made earthenware, stone china, and high-quality porcelains fine enough to win them the distinction of being appointed potters to the Queen. From 1830, their wares attest to this fact, bearing the Royal Arms mark with 'J.R.' within the crest. In 1840, '& Co.' was added.

Most examples of Ridgway's wares found today are transfer-printed historical scenes.

When no condition is indicated, the items listed below are assumed to be in mint condition.

See also Staffordshire, Historical; Flow Blue

Bowl, Coaching Days, 7½", $50.00.

Ash tray, Coaching Days, Fresh Teams....28.00
Ash tray, Coaching Days, w/metal matchbox stand....500.00
Bowl, Coaching Days, Eloped, 9″....75.00
Bowl, vegetable; gr, Grecian, w/lid, 8x8″....35.00
Box, Coaching Days, brn, 5 scenes, w/lid....85.00
Cheese dish, floral/leaves, mk Lahore, bl hdl, w/lid, 6½″....135.00
Creamer, Coaching Days....40.00
Cup & saucer, Royal Vistas Ware, famous paintings....20.00
Jug, Mr Pickwick, silver lustre trim/hdl, 8⅛″....65.00
Mug, Coaching Days, brn, silver lustre top/hdl, 5x4¾″....45.00
Mug, Coaching Days, brn, 4″....40.00
Pitcher, jug; Coaching Days, brn, 7″....75.00
Pitcher, tankard; Coaching Days, brn, 12¼″....145.00
Pitcher, tankard; Congressional Library scene, tan/lustre....70.00
Pitcher, tavern scene, mustard yel, 1835, 6″....65.00
Plaque, Coaching Days, Taking Up the Mails, yel, 12″ dia....100.00
Plate, Coaching Days, Falstaff Inn West Gate, 9″....30.00
Plate, Coaching Days, Journey's End, brn, 9″....45.00
Plate, Coaching Days, Racing the Mail, gr, 6¾″....25.00
Platter, country scene, red transfer, sgn, 15″ L....47.50
Teapot, Coaching Days, brn, silver lustre trim, 4½″....95.00
Tray, Coaching Days, Christmas Visitor, brn, 12½″....100.00
Tray, Mr Pickwick, scalloped, 12½″....90.00
Tumbler, Coaching Days, 4″....35.00
Vase, bud; gr w/etched garlands, gilt, 10″....95.00

Riviera

Riviera was a line of dinnerware introduced by the Homer Laughlin China Company in 1938. It was sold exclusively by the Murphy Company through their nationwide chain of dime stores. Riviera was unmarked, lightweight, and inexpensive. It was discontinued sometime prior to 1950. Colors are mauve blue, red, yellow, light green, and ivory. On rare occasions dark blue pieces are found, but this was not a standard color.

When no condition is indicated, the items listed below are assumed to be in mint condition.

Baker, oval, 9″....6.50
Batter set, complete....110.00
Butter dish....45.00
Casserole w/lid....42.00
Creamer, regular....5.00
Cup & saucer....6.50
Fruit, 5½″....4.00
Jug, juice; yellow....45.00
Jug w/lid....45.00
Nappy, 8¼″....8.50
Plate, deep, 8″....6.50
Plate, red, 9″....5.75
Plate, 10″....6.50
Plate, 6″....2.50
Plate, 7″....3.50
Plate, 9″....4.50
Platter, 11″....9.00
Platter, 12″....10.50
Sauce boat....8.00
Shakers, pr....6.00
Sugar bowl....6.50
Syrup w/lid....50.00
Teapot....35.00
Tumbler, hdld....38.00
Tumbler, juice....28.00

Robertson

Fred H. Robertson, clay expert for the Los Angeles Brick Company, and son of Alexander Robertson of the Roblin Pottery, experimented with crystalline glazes as early as 1906. In 1934, Fred and his son George established their own works in Los Angeles, but by 1943 they had moved operations to Hollywood. Though most of their early wares were turned by hand, some were also molded in low relief. Fine crackle glazes and crystallines were developed. The ware was marked with 'Robertson,' 'F.H.R.,' or 'R.,' with the particular location of its manufacture noted. The small pottery closed in 1952.

When no condition is indicated, the items listed below are assumed to be in mint condition.

Bowl, lav/gray flambe w/some crystals, LA, incurvate, 7″....250.00
Box, powder; turq glaze w/HP orange rose, Hollywood....65.00
Vase, bl crackle, miniature....60.00
Vase, Chinese bl crackle w/hdls, 3x1½″....65.00
Vase, red, 3x1½″....65.00

Robinson Clay Products

In the early 1900s, Whitemore, Robinson and Company merged with the E.H. Merrill Company to form Robinson Clay Products of Akron, Ohio. They produced stoneware, fine glazed Rockingham, and yellowware until 1915, when the emphasis was shifted to bricks, tile, etc. In 1920 the company merged with the Ransbottom Brothers Pottery Company of Roseville, and was thereafter known as the Robinson Ransbottom Company. (See Robinson Ransbottom)

When no condition is indicated, the items listed below are assumed to be in mint condition.

Jug, Harry O Wolff Wholesale Liquor Dealer ad, ½-gal....125.00
Mug, bl & gray, Windy City, sgn Akron Clay Products, rare....135.00
Mug, golfer, bl/wht stoneware....125.00
Pitcher, Windy City....235.00

Robinson Ransbottom

In 1900 the four Ransbottom brothers founded the Ransbottom Bros. Pottery company in Ironspot, Ohio, very close to Roseville. They produced utilitarian stoneware products until 1920, when they merged with the Robinson Clay Products Company of Akron. Production was broadened to include kitchenwares, and 'Early American' accessories. Cookie jars were an important line from the 1930s until recent times. The company is still in operation in Roseville, Ohio. Items made after the merger were marked 'RRPCO (for Robinson Ransbottom Pottery Company) Roseville.' The green and brown streaky glazed flowerpots, jardinieres, and pedestals which they produce today are often mistaken for older products of the Roseville Pottery Company, which operated there until the 1950s.

When no condition is indicated, the items listed below are assumed to be in mint condition.

Butter crock, emb bl/wht vintage, sgn, 5x8″, EX....135.00
Cookie jar, Cow Jumped Over the Moon....35.00
Cookie jar, Dutch Boy....35.00
Cookie jar, Dutch Girl....35.00
Cookie jar, Fat Policeman, G....30.00
Cookie jar, Peter Pumpkin Eater....40.00
Cookie jar, Rooster....35.00
Cookie jar, Sheriff Pig, yel hat....35.00

Cookie jar, whale, rare, $150.00.

Cookie jar, Wise Bird, EX....35.00
Planter, strawberry, 5″....13.50
Vase, Cocker Spaniel, gr & brn, 6″....20.00

Roblin

In the late 1800s, Alexander W. Robertson and Linna Irelan established a pottery in San Francisco, combining parts of their respective names to coin the name Roblin. Robertson was responsible for potting and firing the ware, which often reflected his taste for classic styling. Mrs. Irelan did much of the decorating, utilizing almost every method, but favoring relief modeling. Mushrooms and lizards were her favorite subjects. Vases were a large part of their production, all of which were made from native California red, buff, and white clays. The ware was well marked with the firm name or the outline of a bear. Roblin Pottery was destroyed in the earthquake of 1906.

When no condition is indicated, the items listed below are assumed to be in mint condition.

Disk, wht flowers on red clay, clear glaze, dtd/sgn, 2″....90.00
Vase, bisque, rnd sides, 3¼″....135.00
Vase, elephant's foot form, lava-like brn/cream, 2x3″....125.00
Vase, incised top line, bisque, brn, 3¾″....140.00

Rockingham

In the early part of the 19th century, American potters began to favor brown-and buff-burning clays over red because of their durability. The glaze favored by many was Rockingham, which varied from a dark brown mottle to a sponged effect sometimes called tortoiseshell. It consisted in part of manganese and various metallic salts, and was used by many potters until well into the 20th century.

When no condition is indicated, the items listed below are assumed to be in mint condition.

Baker, EX color & mottle, 1850s, oval, 12½x9½″....175.00
Bank, acorn, 2¾″....60.00
Bottle, building shape, flakes/hairline, 7½″....25.00
Bottle, fish, sm chips, 11″....250.00
Bottle, pepper-shot revolver shape, some roughness, 7¾″....155.00
Bottle, shoe, old lip flake, 6¼″....70.00
Bottle, shoe, sm flake, 9¼″....85.00
Bowl, oval, minor wear, 8¼″....65.00
Bowl, oval, 1⅞x7¼x9¾″....75.00
Bowl, oval, 12½″....110.00
Bowl, rnd, rim flakes, 3⅜x10½″....110.00
Bowl, rnd, 2⅝x5¼″ dia....55.00
Bowl, rnd, 3¼x6⅝″....95.00
Creamer, cow w/milkmaid, w/out lid, sm flake, 5⅜″....115.00
Creamer, ogee sides, paneled, 5″....35.00
Cuspidor, paneled w/Gothic arches, edge chips, 4½x7½″....50.00
Cuspidor, shell shape, 8¾″....75.00
Cuspidor, 4½x8″....35.00
Figurine, dog, seated, shell designs on base, 10½″....75.00
Figurine, lion, British Jack shield on oval base, 5½″....45.00
Figurine, spaniel, seated, Ohio area, 1860, 4″....250.00
Flask, att CC Thompson Pottery, 7¼″....85.00
Inkwell, figural masks, 4″....75.00
Inkwell, sleeping youth, hairline on bottom/flake, 5¾″....55.00
Jar, close-fitting mismatched lid, sm edge flakes, 6⅛″....45.00
Jug, sq, minor rim flake, 10¼″....75.00
Mold, vintage decor, oval, rim hairline/flake, 5½x7¾″....105.00
Mug, concave sides, 3″....100.00
Mug, emb band, VG color, 3½″....90.00
Mug, 3½″....75.00
Mug, 4″....65.00
Pie plate, glazed-over rim crack, 1⅜x11¾″....125.00
Pie plate, minor scratches, 1⅜x10″....100.00
Pie plate, minor wear, 1⅝x10⅜″....100.00
Pitcher, emb acanthus leaf, lt brn w/bl splashes, 12″....250.00
Pitcher, emb American eagle on Liberty Bell, minor wear....210.00
Pitcher, emb animal scenes, hound hdl, flakes, w/lid, 10¾″....225.00
Pitcher, emb arm/hammer, Protection to Am Industry, 9″, EX..200.00
Pitcher, emb ear of corn, minor edge wear, 9½″....75.00
Pitcher, emb ear of corn, 6¾″....50.00
Pitcher, emb fouled anchor, Mayer Trenton, 8″....250.00
Pitcher, emb hanging game, yel clay, E Liverpool, 9½″....225.00
Pitcher, emb hunt scene w/foliage, trunk hdl, 8″....150.00
Pitcher, emb hunter & dog, hairline in base/hdl chips, 9″....100.00

Pitcher, acanthus leaf relief, honey-colored glaze, East Liverpool, ca 1850-60, in excellent condition, 12″, $250.00.

Pitcher, emb hunter & game, minor base crack, 6⅜″....90.00
Pitcher, emb lady's head medallion, 7″....125.00
Pitcher, emb lady's head medallion & mask on hdl, 8¼″....100.00
Pitcher, hound hdl, emb hanging game, 8″....250.00
Pitcher, hound hdl, sgn Harker Taylor, ca 1850s, 10″....600.00
Pitcher, man's face figural, edge flakes, 8″....100.00
Pitcher, Toby, 5⅞″....55.00
Plate, rayed center, scalloped rim, 7⅞″....225.00

Plate, 8½", EX....150.00
Platter, octagonal, minor wear/chips, 12¾" L....150.00
Platter, oval, 13½"....125.00
Pot, w/side hdl, emb leaf on lid, stains/rim flakes, 6"....65.00
Shaving mug, emb Toby, imp label E&W Bennett, 4⅛"....175.00
Soap dish, oval, 3½x4¾"....85.00
Stirrup cup, fox head, minor edge flakes, 4¾"....65.00
Teapot, Toby, glued rpr on spout, 9¼"....85.00
Wash board, wood w/pottery scrub panel, 1890, 24x12"....200.00

Rockingham, English

Though first established in 1745 in Swinton in Yorkshire, it was not until 1826 that the company, backed by Earl Fitzwilliam of the Rockingham estate, began to mark their wares with the Earl's crest, and the name Rockingham. While the earlier products were strictly earthenwares, at this point porcelain was introduced. Due to losses incurred in the firing, and the high costs of their decorations, the firm became insolvent in 1842.

Their porcelain was very soft, and signed with the griffin mark. Pattern numbers are 1559 or below, or in the series from 2/1 to 2/78. This will help the buyer to reject imitations that also carry the griffin mark.

Values are for undamaged specimens unless noted otherwise.

Bottle, Landlord figural, head is stopper, 1820, 5¾"....800.00
Castle, mauve w/wht encrustations, gold trim, 4⅛"....525.00
Cottage, hexagon, red/gold arch door, lambs on steps, 4½"....425.00
Cottage, mauve, pagoda roof, spiral columns, 1815, 5½"....500.00
Cottage, twin turrets, cobalt roof/portico, red door, 5⅜"....450.00
Lion on rectangular plinth, incised detail, 8½x11"....500.00
Mug, grapevine border, 6½"....100.00
Pastille burner, cottage, rain barrel, doghouse w/dog, 6"....325.00
Pastille burner, cottage, twin towers, peaked roof, 5", EX....425.00
Swan, preening position, wht w/gold trim, 3¾"....350.00
Toll house, dovecote under eaves, 1820, 12¾"....575.00

Lion figure, 2nd quarter of 19th century, minor crack, 11", $350.00.

Rockwell, Norman

Norman Rockwell began his career in 1911 at the age of seventeen doing illustrations for a children's book entitled *Tell Me Why Stories*. A few short years later in 1916, he produced the *Saturday Evening Post* cover that made him one of America's most-beloved artists. Though not well accepted by the professional critics of his day who did not consider his work to be art but 'merely' commercial illustration, Rockwell's popularity grew to the extent that today there is an overwhelming abundance of examples of his work, or those related to the theme of one of his illustrations.

When no condition is indicated, the figurines listed below are assumed to be mint and the paper items are assumed excellent.

See also Collector Plates; Magazines

Book, Norman Rockwell Illustrator, A Guptill, 1946, 1st ed....28.00
Display card, Pepsi Santa, 24"....50.00
Figurine, Artist's Daughter....27.50
Figurine, Baby's First Step....225.00
Figurine, Back from Camp....100.00
Figurine, Back to School....35.00
Figurine, Barbershop Quartet....850.00
Figurine, Baseball, Grossman, MIB....250.00
Figurine, Bride & Groom, Rockwell Museum, musical....50.00
Figurine, Carrolers....32.00
Figurine, Country Boy, Grossman....150.00
Figurine, Cradle of Love....27.50
Figurine, Daydreamer, Grossman, 1973-'74....50.00
Figurine, Discovery, Grossman....100.00
Figurine, Dreaming in the Attic....20.00
Figurine, First Haircut....110.00
Figurine, Grandpa's Ballerina....100.00
Figurine, Happy Birthday Dear Mother....175.00
Figurine, Jolly Coachman....75.00
Figurine, Lazybones, Grossman....250.00
Figurine, Little Veterinarian, Goebel, 1961....375.00
Figurine, Love Letters, Grossman....400.00
Figurine, Magic Potion....98.00
Figurine, Marriage License, Gorham....95.00
Figurine, Missed, Gorham, retired....110.00
Figurine, Quartet, Grossman....900.00
Figurine, Redhead, Grossman....170.00
Figurine, Schoolmaster, Grossman....220.00
Figurine, See America First, Grossman, MIB....250.00
Figurine, Summertime 1933, Grossman, 1973-'74....50.00
Figurine, Sweet 16, Rockwell Museum....40.00
Figurine, Take Your Medicine....90.00
Figurine, Vintage Time....45.00
Figurine, Waiting for Santa....100.00
Figurine, Wrapping Christmas Presents....110.00
Figurine, 4 Seasons, boy & dog....320.00
Poster, Let's Give Him Enough, WWI, sgn....1,000.00
Poster, Schmidt's Beer, by Rivershore, limited edition....25.00
Print, Audubon Paints Passenger Pigeon, sgn, 20x25"....275.00
Print, Eddie Arcaro Weighing In, pen & ink, sgn, 19x25"....300.00
Print, Firehouse, pen & ink, sgn, 24x24"....300.00
Print, GI Homecoming, sgn, 20x24"....250.00
Print, Horseshoe Forging Contest, Ettinger ed, sgn/#d....2,500.00
Print, Kennedy portrait, Ettinger ed, sgn/#d....1,500.00
Print, Shuffleton Barber Shop, sgn, 20x24"....250.00
Print, Truth About Santa, litho, sgn, 18x24"....250.00
Print, 3 Boys Fishing, litho, sgn, 18x24"....250.00
Print, 4 Seasons, Spring Flowers, sgn, 10x12"....375.00
Tray, tin, Who's Having More Fun?, kids eating corn, orig....35.00

Rogers, John

John Rogers (1829-1904) was a machinist from Manchester, New Jersey, who turned his hobby of sculpting into a financially successful venture. From the originals he meticulously fashioned of red clay, he had bronze master molds made from which plaster copies were cast. He specialized in five different categories: theatrical, Shakespeare, Civil War, everyday life, and horses. His large detailed groupings portrayed the life and times of the period between 1859 and 1892.

When no condition is indicated, the items listed below are assumed to be in very good to excellent condition.

Charity Patient....650.00
Checkers at the Farm....425.00
Chess....1,200.00
Council of War....850.00

Coming to the Parson, $375.00.

Elder's Daughter....800.00
Favored Scholar....400.00
Fetching the Doctor....750.00
Going for the Cows....450.00
Nominated in the Band....350.00
One More Shot....500.00
Playing Doctor....700.00
Returned Volunteer....600.00
Rip Van Winkle at Home....400.00
Rip Van Winkle on the Mountain....450.00
School Days....550.00
Taking the Oath & Drawing Rations....475.00
Tap on the Window....400.00
The Balcony....1,200.00
Traveling Magician....750.00
Uncle Ned's School....750.00
We Boys....425.00

Rookwood

The Rookwood Pottery Company was established in 1879, in Cincinnati, Ohio. Its founder was Maria Longworth Nichols Storer, daughter of a wealthy family who provided the backing necessary to make such an enterprise possible. Mrs. Storer hired competent ceramic workers who through constant experimentation developed many lines of superior art pottery. While in her employ, Laura Fry invented the airbrush blending process for which she was issued a patent in 1884. From this, several lines were designed that utilized blended backgrounds.

One of their earlier lines, Standard, was a brown ware decorated with underglaze slip-painted nature studies, animals, portraits, etc. Iris and Sea Green were introduced in 1894, and Vellum, a transparent mat glaze line, in 1904. Other lines followed: Ombroso in 1910, and Soft Porcelain in 1915. Many of the early artware lines were signed by the artist.

Soon after the turn of the 20th century, Rookwood manufactured 'production' pieces that relied mainly on molded designs and forms, rather than freehand decoration, for their esthetic appeal.

The Depression brought on financial difficulties from which the pottery never recovered. Though it continued to operate, the quality of the ware deteriorated, and the pottery was forced to close in 1967.

Unmarked Rookwood is only rarely encountered. Many marks may be found, but the most familiar is the reverse 'RP' monogram. First used in 1886, a flame point was added above it for each succeeding year until 1900. After that, a Roman numeral added below indicated the year of manufacture. Impressed letters that related to the type of clay utilized for the body were also used--G for ginger, O for olive, R for red, S for sage green, W for white, and Y for yellow.

Artware must be judged on an individual basis. Quality of the artwork is the prime factor to consider. Portraits, animals, and birds are worth more than florals; and pieces signed by a particularly reknowned artist are highly prized.

When no condition is indicated, the items listed below are assumed to be in mint condition.

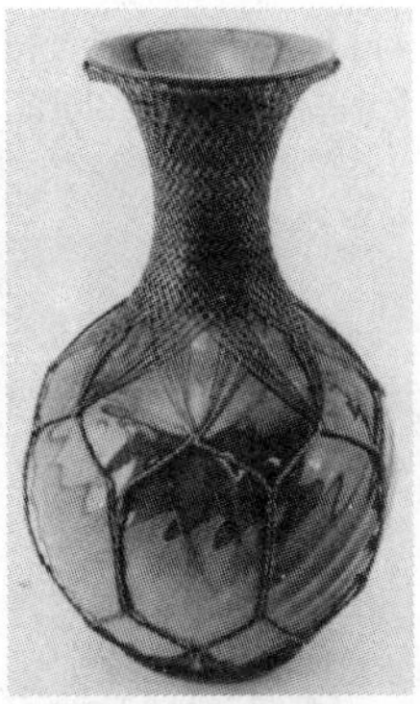

Sterling silver mesh over floral on green shaded to amber glossy ground, mesh marked sterling, initialed ARV (Albert Robert Valentien), 11¾", $1,500.00.

Bisque

Jar, Oriental tree/birds, M Daly, 1885, w/lid, 7½"....825.00
Sugar bowl, florals, incised/pnt, cream clay, #21, 1884....100.00
Vase, cherry blossoms, gilt, Laura Fry, 1886, 8¼"....650.00
Vase, floral/dragonflies, AR Valentien, 1883, 10¾"....1,950.00
Vase, sm flowers, gr to peach, Ed Abel, #498E, 1891, 5¾"....445.00

Iris

Bud vase, cherry blossoms, Coyne, 1906, 8½"....300.00
Mug, frog in water/floral, 3-hdl, JD Wareham, S1337, 1897...1,900.00
Pitcher, 3 ducks/water, Shirayamadani, 1897, 9", Xd but M....700.00
Pot, sm floral on wht to pink, L Asbury, #956, 1906, 2x5"....450.00
Vase, berries/flowers, yel/rust on yel, R Fechheimer, 6½"....485.00
Vase, bl berry/leaves/vines, gr/gray, Bishop, 1904, 7½"....675.00
Vase, bl berry/pink leaves, gray, Xd, Rothenbush, 8¼"....575.00
Vase, cherry blossoms, gr to peach & lav, S Coyne, 8½"....650.00
Vase, clover blossoms, Ed Diers, 1902, 6¼"....500.00
Vase, clover/blossoms, CC Lindeman, 1906, 7"....365.00
Vase, crocus front/bk, Clara Lindeman, #925E, 1903, 6¼"....310.00
Vase, daisies, lt yel/gr, Van Horn, 6½"....575.00
Vase, daisies/grasses, K Van Horn, 1908, 8"....645.00
Vase, dogwood at top, Constance Baker, #840D, 1903, 9½"....650.00
Vase, dogwood branch, Lenore Asbury, 1905, 8¾"....625.00
Vase, dogwood branches, Coyne, 1906, 8½"....695.00
Vase, fish in waves, pink/gr, S Coyne, 1911, 6"....460.00
Vase, floral, gray w/lt purple, Bishop, EX art, 1903, 4½"....500.00
Vase, floral, purple/pink on wht/bl, Baker, 1901, 9"....875.00
Vase, floral branches, gray/wht/peach, I Bishop, 1904, 4"....275.00
Vase, floral on brn to yel, J Zettel, 1901, 5¾"....385.00
Vase, floral on wht, slim form, JD Wareham, 1897, 6½"....395.00
Vase, floral spray, heavy slip, Sara Sax, 1899, 7"....435.00
Vase, floral/leaves on lt gr/pink, Diers, 1901, 5½"....525.00
Vase, gray/wht pansies, gr/wht/gray, Lincoln, 1904, 7"....850.00
Vase, lg thistles/leaves, C Schmidt, 1907, 11"....3,000.00
Vase, mistletoe, pink/gr/lav, Asbury, 1910, 8¾"....700.00
Vase, orchids, C Schmidt, 1903, 10½"....1,750.00
Vase, pansies, cream/peach ground w/bl/gr, S Sax, 1901, 6"....365.00
Vase, poppies/pods, Irene Bishop, EX art, 1908, 8¼"....950.00
Vase, scenic, gr/purple/pink/yel/bl, Hurley, 1920, 7¾"....900.00
Vase, sweet peas, lav/pink/gr, C Steinle, #1358E, 1911, 7"....895.00
Vase, tulip, Sara Sax, EX art, 1906, 5½"....450.00
Vase, wisteria, dk gray/lav, Ed Diers, #901C, 1902, 9"....720.00
Vase, 3 lg fish, underwater, ET Hurley, EX art, 1905, 10"...3,200.00

Vase, 3-petal floral at top, G color, Fechheimer, 1902, 9″.....850.00
Vase, 5 lg gr fish, ET Hurley, 1904, hairline, 6¾″............535.00
Vase, 7 daisies, cream/lt bl at top, C Steinle, 1906, 7½″.......650.00

Jewel Porcelain

Bowl, quilted relief, turq, #6681, 1937, 3x12″................70.00
Vase, bl/gr w/bl floral, Epply, 1922, #1667-11″..............575.00
Vase, blackberry on wht, stick neck, LEY, 1945, 5″..........160.00

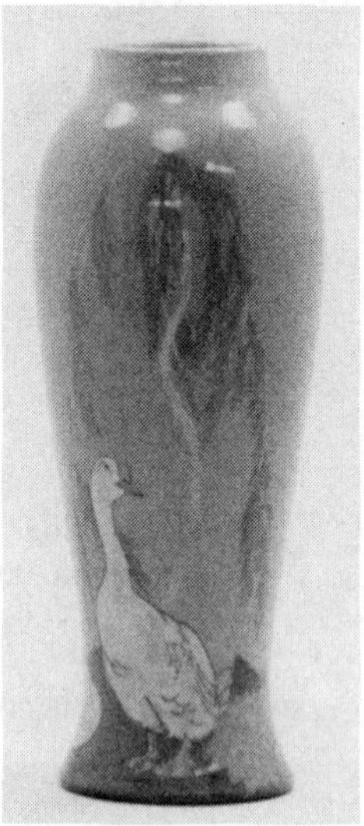

Jewel Porcelain, scenic with Japanese geese, signed Arthur Conant, 1920, 11″, $3,500.00.

Limoges

Dish, reeds/butterfly, red clay, 1884, 1½x5½″................145.00
Honey jug, bats/reeds, gold trim, #61, 1883, 4½″............300.00
Honey jug, bl berries on wht, gold trim, L Fry, 1882, 4¾″.....435.00
Honey jug, butterfly, tan clay/gold trim, Daly, 1883, 4¾″......245.00
Honey jug, reeds/bamboo shoots, blk/beige/gold, 1883, 4¾″....200.00
Honey jug, reeds/butterfly, brn clay/gold trim, Rettig, 5″.......265.00
Pitcher, bees, Humphreys, EX art, anchor mk, 1882, 7″.......525.00
Pitcher, blk birds/reeds/wht cloud, McDonald, 1882, 6½″......425.00
Pitcher, yel flowers, gr/brn/wht, artist sgn, 1882, 7½″.........375.00
Porridge saucer, Uncle Remus, EP Cranch, 1885, 6½″........290.00

Mat

Ash tray, owl on side, bl, 1915, 4¼x7″.....................110.00
Ash tray, seal on side on rnd dish, gr, 1924, 4¼x7″..........145.00
Bowl, berries, modeled, red/gr, CA Duell, 1909, 2½x4¾″......110.00
Bowl, flower, Arts & Crafts line decor, 1920, 2¾x6″...........35.00
Bowl, molded duck design, bl, 1919, 2x4½″..................50.00
Bowl, panel relief, red/gr, #1188, 1911, 2x5″.................35.00
Flower frog, man w/3 horses, wht, 1923, 6¼″, Xd but M.......90.00
Inkwell, 4 lappets, dk gr, #1076, 3¼x5½″..................165.00
Mug, grapes, blk on gr, Coyne, 1905, 6½″..................120.00
Mug, owl mold, oak leaves/acorns hdl, red/gr, 1909, 5⅝″......150.00
Vase, allover florals, Shirayamadani, ftd U-form, 1930, 9″......850.00
Vase, berry/holly relief, yel, 1922, 6¾″......................45.00
Vase, bl buds w/curved vines on gr, Hentschel, 1910, 10″.....250.00
Vase, bl w/brn touches, #2108, 1928, 6″....................40.00
Vase, bl w/red touches at top, 1926, 6¾″....................45.00
Vase, bright bl, #1356, 1917, 8½″........................125.00
Vase, dogwood/vine incised, A Pons, #9350, 1907, 8″.........350.00
Vase, female figures relief, dk bl, L Abel, 1925, 13″..........150.00
Vase, fish relief at bottom, #2323, 1920, 7¾″.................95.00
Vase, floral, emb yel w/purple dripping, CS Todd, 1917, 7″....200.00
Vase, floral, incised top, brn/bl, WE Hentschel, 1911, 14″.....185.00
Vase, floral incised, blk, CS Todd, 1913, 8¾″...............300.00
Vase, floral incised, gr w/bl/red, Fechheimer, 1904, 10″.......345.00
Vase, floral incised, McPherson, 1905, 4″..................375.00
Vase, floral relief, bl, 1930, 5″.............................40.00
Vase, floral relief, bl w/red, #2141, 1916, 6″.................60.00
Vase, floral relief, red w/gr at top, #2114, 1915, 6½″..........75.00
Vase, floral relief at top, gr/brn, #1370, 1914, 7″............150.00
Vase, leaf relief, gr, 1903, 5½″............................55.00
Vase, leaf/circular devices relief, bl, 1927, 4¾″...............45.00
Vase, line/leaf relief, bl, #291, 1925, 8¾″....................70.00
Vase, nude figure around top, gr Z glaze, AM Valentien, 4″....210.00
Vase, seahorse relief, pink/gray, #814, 1916, 5¾″.............75.00
Vase, unicorns/vines incised, hand thrown, Hentschel, 8″......395.00
Wall plaque/candle holder, Arts & Crafts design, lt gr, 9″......130.00
Wall pocket, iris relief, brn/gr, 1924, 12½x9″................225.00

Porcelain

Jardiniere, royal bl gloss w/yel int, #2465, 1921, 8x11″.........90.00
Vase, bl birds/flowers/gr leaves, wht, Ley, 1945, 6″...........375.00
Vase, blooming branches, Shirayamadani, #1697C, 1936, 8x6″..775.00
Vase, cherry blossoms, Shirayamadani, #2724, 1944, 5¾″......325.00
Vase, chevron-like stripes, mc, L Holcamp, 1951, 7″..........110.00
Vase, fish, butter-fat glaze, Jens Jenson, 1934, 5¼″...........500.00
Vase, floral, artist sgn, mc, 1946, 4″.......................210.00
Vase, floral, butter-fat glaze, Shirayamadani, 1925, 5½″.......550.00
Vase, gr leaf/vine, bl floral/2 bl birds, Ley, 1945, 13⅜″........475.00
Vase, gr-bl w/dk bl floral, Sax, 1931, 5½″..................200.00
Vase, lg flowers/buds, G color, LN Lincoln, 1924, 11″........425.00
Vase, lg leaves/flowers, wht on brn, E Barrett, 1944, 6¾″......145.00
Vase, pendant florals, Shirayamadani, #6621, 1936, 8¼″.......525.00
Vase, relief mermaids, bl gloss int, wht/brn drip, 7¾″.........160.00
Vase, rust w/butter-fat wht, Rueben Menzel, 1949, S mk, 7″...350.00
Vase, shells at base, lines, JD Wareham, 1952, 6¾″...........300.00
Vase, sm birds/flowers at shoulder, Epply, 1937, 4″...........210.00
Vase, stylized flowers, clear glaze, W Rhem, 1943, #6197F....250.00
Vase, swirling leaves, butter-fat, J Jensen, 1943, 6½″..........165.00
Vase, wht band w/red floral on gr, HE Wilcox, 1922, 6½″.....245.00
Vase, wht/red floral, bl branches, Sax, 1920, 6¾″............400.00
Vase, 4 lg peacock feathers, 4 neck hdls, S Sax, 1917, 17″...2,200.00

Sea Green

Mug, grapes, Baker, 1889, 6″, EX color....................750.00
Vase, flying rooks, slim neck/ball body, Hurley, 1898, 7″.....1,350.00
Vase, lilies, wht/shaded gr, S Toohey, ogee form, 1900, 8″...2,000.00
Vase, tiny floral, wht on gr w/bl at base, LN Lincoln, 7″.......850.00
Vase, very lg speckled fish, ET Hurley, '03, 10″, Xd but M...2,000.00

Standard

Basket, floral, strap hdl, 1889, 5″.........................180.00
Chocolate pot, daisies, C Steinle, str sides/lg hdl, 9½″.........600.00
Coffee pot, floral, flower on lid, OG, 1892, 9″...............465.00
Coffee pot, holly leaves/berries, E Felton, 1900, 8½″..........425.00
Creamer, floral, C Steinle, crimped sides, 1894, 2¾″..........110.00
Creamer & sugar bowl, autumn leaves, CC Lindeman, #331....550.00
Dish, leaves, sgn SS, quatralobe form, 1901, 5¾″.............95.00
Ewer, carnation, AM Valentien, 1889, 9½″...................750.00
Ewer, clover, S Toohey, trefoil lip, 1890, 5″................285.00
Ewer, daisies, silver on hdl/ruffled top/body mk CTW, 4″....3,650.00
Ewer, floral, ET Hurley, crimped top, 1899, 6¾″.............285.00
Ewer, floral, J Swing, EX art, 1902, 5¾″, Xd but M..........365.00

Ewer, fruit, ruffled top, ER Felton, 1897, 5½"...............425.00
Ewer, leaves/berries/partial silver overlay, Matchette, 7"......2,700.00
Ewer, orange poppy, K Hickman, 1898, 7½"................450.00
Ewer, sm floral, J Zettel, simple form, 1893, 5½"............225.00
Ewer, sm floral, ruffled edge, SL, 1893, 8"..................245.00
Ewer, sweet peas, ED Diers, trefoil top, #868, 1900, 9x4¼"....750.00
Humidor, lg iris, OG Reed, 1898, 8"........................795.00
Jug, monk plays trombone, silver 'wicker,' MA Daly, 9½".....4,400.00
Mug, bearded man in hat, Sturgis Laurence, 1896, 4¾", NM...550.00
Mug, portrait of old man, Wilcox, 1891, 4½"..............1,000.00
Mug, wheat, L Van Briggle, 1901, 5¼"....................325.00
Mug, 2 doves w/nest, lt brn, E Cranch, 1891, 4½"...........850.00
Pitcher, blossoming branch, #769, 3½".....................275.00
Pitcher, daffodil, tiny spout, S-hdl, 1901, 6"................315.00
Pitcher, spider mum on yel to amber, hand thrown, 1886, 8"..265.00
Vase, berries, red/brn, AR Valentien, full pear form, 7½"......550.00
Vase, berries, silver floral overlay, OG Reed, 1893, 9½"......3,700.00
Vase, berries/holly, str neck/compressed body, Felton, 6½".....185.00
Vase, carnations, ED Foertmeyer, EX art, #614E, 1893, 8½"...550.00
Vase, cavalier portrait, Van Briggle, 1897, 6¾"..............575.00
Vase, chestnut/leaves, bulbous, Coyne, 1900, 5½"............250.00
Vase, clover, F Rothenbush, EX art, 1900, 5¼"..............375.00
Vase, clover, Lindeman, EX art, 1901, 7"....................395.00
Vase, clover, orange on brn, Lincoln, 1901, 7½".............225.00
Vase, collie dog portrait, ET Hurley, 1900, 8".............1,150.00
Vase, crocus, yel on brn, S Toohey, 1899, 7"................495.00
Vase, daisies, C Schmidt, 1897, 4¼"........................325.00
Vase, daisies, vertical decor, C Steinle, 1909, 7".............375.00
Vase, floral, floral & ribbon silver overlay, Nourse, 5".......3,400.00
Vase, floral, Fortmeyer, 1899, 7"...........................275.00
Vase, floral, lg flat leaves, L Asbury, EX art, 1902, 7".........475.00
Vase, floral, lg wht/yel, C Lindeman, 1907, 6½"..............395.00
Vase, floral, OG Reed, EX art, hdls, 1889, 4"...............275.00
Vase, floral, orange, JD Wareham, 1902, 14¼"...............825.00
Vase, floral, Sally Coyne, 1903, 10", Xd but M..............395.00
Vase, floral, w/allover silver overlay, Dubowski, 1892, 7".....3,600.00
Vase, floral w/floral silver overlay, A Sprague, 1893, 5"......2,700.00
Vase, floral/Nouveau style, silver rim, Hurley, 1899, 10".......400.00
Vase, fruit, L Van Briggle, 1900, 4¼"......................295.00
Vase, gr leaves, monkey arm behind leaf, sgn, #464, 9"......1,200.00
Vase, Indian portrait, 3-hdl, Harriet Wilcox, 1898, 7".......3,500.00
Vase, leaves, hdls, CC Lindeman, 1902, 4¾"................395.00
Vase, leaves/berries, Lindeman, 1902, 5"...................350.00
Vase, lion portrait, ET Hurley, 1899, 7"....................925.00
Vase, man w/beard portrait, H Strafer, #707BB, 5¾".........700.00
Vase, mushroom, 2-hdl, Diers, 1900, 6".....................700.00
Vase, nasturtiums, LN Lincoln, 1904, 5"....................325.00
Vase, poppies, E Noonan, 1905, 6½".......................325.00
Vase, poppies, John D Wareham, EX art, 1895, 7"............695.00
Vase, poppies/pods, Mary Nourse, EX art, #907C, 14".......1,765.00
Vase, rose, yel on brn, ET Hurley, 1899, 3¼"...............325.00
Vase, silver overlay w/flowers, holly, 2-hdl, Strafer, 5".......3,050.00
Vase, wisteria, Rothenbush, EX art, 1897, 9"................300.00

Vellum

Bowl, roses at top, K Van Horn, 4 tab ft, 1912, 3½".........175.00
Mug, clover, sterling hdl/top band, Sara Sax, 1905, 5"........850.00
Plaque, birch trees, pink/bl/wht, Hurley, 1948, 9½x11⅞".....2,550.00
Plaque, Cluster of Pines, Sally Coyne, 8½x6½"..............825.00
Plaque, dawn scenic, sgn CJM, 1919, 5x9"...................700.00
Plaque, Italian Sailing, C Schmidt, 1915, in fr, 6x8".........1,550.00
Plaque, lakeshore scene, Loridna Epply, 1918, 9½x7".......1,650.00
Plaque, landscape w/house/trees/road, Rothenbush, fr, 6x8"...1,650.00
Plaque, pond w/birch trees, ET Hurley, 1948, 11¾x9¾".....2,500.00
Plaque, Quiet Waters, Lenore Asbury, 1919, 8x10½"........1,325.00
Plaque, river scenes, L Asbury, 1920s, 13x10".............2,000.00
Plaque, Ships Anchored in Lagoon, C Schmidt, 6x8"........1,600.00
Plaque, snow scene, Sally Coyne, 8x10"..................1,950.00
Vase, berries/branches, Ed Diers, 1925, 3¾".................300.00
Vase, cherry blossoms, E Diers, full body, 1914, 5¼".........200.00
Vase, dogwood, pink on bl, sgn SC, 1910, 7¼"..............250.00
Vase, floral, pink/bl, McLaughlin, 1915, 7"...................190.00
Vase, floral at shoulder, L Asbury, EX art, 1930, 5½".........290.00
Vase, floral at top, MH McDonald, 1914, 5¾"................175.00
Vase, floral/buds in band, L Asbury, 1908, 8½"..............200.00
Vase, grapes/leaves, wht band at top, Epply, 7¼".............350.00
Vase, gulls over waves, ET Hurley, 1908, 13", Xd but M.....1,050.00
Vase, leaf/floral incised, EX art, Coyne, '08, 10".............650.00
Vase, night, trees/men's silhouettes, ET Hurley, 1909, 11"...1,450.00
Vase, night scene, bl/lav/pink, Asbury, 1918, 7¾"............675.00
Vase, rose decor on top, plain bottom, Ed Diers, 1921, 8".....450.00
Vase, roses, Ed Diers, EX art, U-form, 1931, 6¼"............575.00
Vase, roses, ET Hurley, #6184G, 1942, 5"...................250.00
Vase, sailing ship/pink sail, gr, Rothenbush, 1907, 7½"........750.00
Vase, scenic, bl/gr/cream, Asbury, 1919, 7½"................565.00
Vase, scenic, brn/orange/gr, F Rothenbush, 1910, 9½"........725.00
Vase, scenic, Ed Diers, EX art, waisted top & ft, 1916, 8"...1,250.00
Vase, scenic, ET Hurley, #614E, 1939, 7¾"................1,045.00
Vase, scenic, Fred Rothenbush, 1920, 6"....................625.00
Vase, scenic, harbor w/boat, C Schmidt, 1924, 7½"........3,000.00
Vase, scenic, lake/trees, ET Hurley, 1939, 10¼"............1,350.00
Vase, scenic, snow, Sally Coyne, 1923, 7½"................1,100.00
Vase, scenic, soft colors, Ed Diers, 1921, 7¾"...............765.00
Vase, scenic, trees, Asbury, EX art/detail, 1924, 15¼".......2,150.00
Vase, scenic, trees, deep color, CJ McLaughlin, 1915, 9"......900.00
Vase, scenic, water at dusk, ET Hurley, 1911, 5¾"..........650.00
Vase, seascape/rocks, ET Hurley, 1906, 7½"................1,050.00
Vase, 3 carved peacock feathers, Sara Sax, 1913, 10".......1,750.00
Vase, 3 lg fish, ET Hurley, EX art, full sgn, 1904, 6¾".......750.00
Vase, 6 sailing ships/people/trees, SE Coyne, GV, 1909, 7"....865.00

Wax Mat

Bowl, emb floral, pink/gray, 4 molded ft, 1921, 3x6"...........25.00
Bud vase, floral, LN Lincoln, 3-color, 7¼"....................85.00
Bud vase, stylized floral, J Pullman, #2309, 1930, 7"..........160.00
Candlestick, gr/bl, long twisted hdls, 1921, 7", pr............165.00
Vase, basketball players relief, gr/brn, Rehm, 1934, 6½".......425.00
Vase, berries/leaves at shoulder, LN Lincoln, 1924, 7"........225.00
Vase, bl w/red & purple decor, CS Todd, 1921, 3¾"...........130.00
Vase, cherries incised, 3-color, CJ McLaughlin, 1918, 8½".....175.00
Vase, floral, bl w/yel/blk runs, CS Todd, 1921, 5¾"..........125.00
Vase, floral, C Klinger, trumpet shape/#2734, 1925, 8"..........70.00
Vase, floral, L Abel, 1927, 12¼"..........................675.00
Vase, floral, pink/red/purple/gr, Epply, 1931, 5⅛"............170.00
Vase, floral, red/wht/gr w/wht, Shirayamadani, 1933, 7"........575.00
Vase, floral, red/yel on bl w/drips/runs, CS Todd, '21, 6"......270.00
Vase, floral, simple, Shirayamadani, 1932, 5½"...............500.00
Vase, floral on red circle, red/bl, McLaughlin, 1918, 8¼".....150.00
Vase, floral rim, hourglass form, gr-bl, K Jones, 1926, 6"......275.00
Vase, grapes, carved at neck, CS Todd, 1915, 8½x6"..........475.00
Vase, grapes, SE Coyne, 1925, 8"...........................200.00
Vase, leaf relief, pink/gr, #6454, 1934, 3¾"...................55.00
Vase, leaves/acorns, LN Lincoln, 2-color, 1928, 9"...........400.00
Vase, magnolias, Sally Coyne, full body, #2782, 1925, 9½".....400.00
Vase, panel relief, pink/gray, #2420, 9"........................85.00
Vase, panel/berry relief, pink/gr, #2088, 1926, 5½"............65.00

Vase, rooks relief band at neck, bl/gr, #2314, 1921, 7" 150.00
Vase, 3 peacock feathers in relief, pink/gr, 1921, 6" 75.00
Wall pocket, floral, pink/gr, fan form, 1927, 6½" 65.00

Miscellaneous

Ash tray, 1924, spade shape, bl gloss 17.50
Ash tray, 1941, frog on side, gr gloss 110.00
Ash tray, 1947, rook, dk pink gloss, 4x7" 95.00
Ash tray, 1948, nude on side, gr gloss 65.00
Ash tray, 1949, twin electric bulb, maroon, dbl logo 95.00
Ash tray, 1952, owl, gr gloss, 4¼x6½" 60.00
Ash tray, 1955, gray, #7018 ....25.00
Ash tray, 1956, 'Cincinnati,' blk letters on gr, 8¾" 25.00
Ash tray, 1957, blk, free form, #7143 ....40.00
Basket, satin bl, 1-hdl, 3½x4" 45.00
Bookends, 1921, elephant, wht, #2444 ....180.00
Bookends, 1922, rooks, gr, #2274 ....185.00
Bookends, 1927, rooks, brn gloss, #2776, W McD, 5½" 250.00
Bookends, 1929, trees, gr mat, WP McDonald imp, 5½" 120.00
Bookends, 1950, horse head, cream 150.00
Bookends, 1951, panther, gr gloss 185.00
Bowl, Cameo, Toohey, #460, EX art, 4½", pr 175.00
Bowl, 1929, fish in 6-panel relief, gr/blk, #6086, 3x6" 55.00
Bowl, 1945, lily relief, bl gloss, 4¼x6" 65.00
Bowl, 1945, yel gloss, #7201, 3½x7" 25.00
Box, 1944, floral relief, cream glaze, 1½x4¾" 125.00
Box, 1946, sm horses on lid, lt bl/wht beehive, L Abel, 5" 110.00
Box, 1963, dragon relief on lid, bl gloss, 1¾x5" 65.00
Bud vase, 1919, floral relief, bl, #2478, 7" 85.00
Bud vase, 1943, gray/brn/wht gloss, #2545, 7" 35.00
Bud vase, 1949, gr gloss, mk 1st Scientific Assembly, 6½" 35.00
Bud vase, 1952, speckled gray, #3375 ....40.00
Bud vase, 1958, dragon relief, dk pink gloss, 7" 120.00
Candle holder, 1927, lily design, ivory, #2292, pr 50.00
Candlestick, 1928, elephant, yel gloss, 4", M 35.00
Coffee pot, RP mk, wht gloss w/bl ships, 5½" 60.00
Creamer & sugar bowl, wht gloss w/bl ships, pr 65.00
Cup & saucer, 1935, wht gloss w/bl flower & fleur-de-lis 20.00
Dish, 1916, verde gr, flat, #1383 ....20.00
Dish, 1938, relief flowers, gr, #6393 ....35.00
Figurine, 1943, cockatoo, dk pink to brn/yel, 9" 135.00
Figurine, 1945, deer, Louise Abel, #6170, wht, 6" 75.00
Figurine, 1946, cat, wht mat, L Abel imp, 7" 245.00
Figurine, 1948, 3 male singers w/songbook, pink 175.00
Figurine, 1950s-60s, wht head, gray/brn bottom, 9" 165.00
Figurine, 1951, bird, gray/brn gloss, unusual, 9" 180.00
Flower frog, 1921, Pan & turtle, blk gloss, #2336, 7" 150.00
Jar, 1911, Egyptian style, bl mat, #249, 5" 55.00
Lamp base, 1946, wisteria relief, bl mat, 13½" 45.00
Match holder/ash tray, 1934, bat figural, slate bl, #2939 ....110.00
Paperweight, 1930, dog, wht mat, #277, 4¾" 135.00
Paperweight, 1934, rose, 3½", Xd but M 45.00
Paperweight, 1964, duck, orange gloss, 2¼" 90.00
Paperweight, 1965, duck, wht mat, 2¼" 0.00
Planter, #1954, aqua/gray, #7049 ....65.00
Plaque, architectural; Roman warrior bust, faience, 18" 500.00
Tankard, boys drink from mugs relief, C'ti Co-op Co, 9" 500.00
Tile, faience, geometric, 3-color, 4x4" 75.00
Tile, old Masters' works, faience, gold fr, set of 4, 7" 750.00
Tile, sailing ship, faience, 4-color, in fr, 12" sq 550.00
Tray, 1933, owl on side, acorn/leaves emb, wht, #6396, 4½" 70.00
Trivet, wht w/ships, mk RP & M-28 ....40.00
Trivet, 1927, butterflies/flower basket, bl/yel/wht, 5¾" 100.00
Trivet, 1930, bird/branches, 4-color, 6¼" dia 110.00
Trivet, 1943, Dutch woman/children/boat/etc, 4-color, 5¾" 110.00
Urn, 1922, high gloss, reticulated outer lid, #2581, 13½" 575.00
Vase, gray/wht raised design on blk, majolica type, 8¼" 265.00
Vase, 1921, Art Deco loopings on gr-bl, Hentschel, 6" 600.00
Vase, 1930, poppies relief, gr, #1710, 10¾" 150.00
Vase, 1931, crystalline glaze, brn/gold, 4" 60.00
Vase, 1932, brn w/bl drip, yel w/in, 6¾" 120.00
Vase, 1935, deer/leaves relief, bl gloss, #6053, 7½" 45.00
Vase, 1936, nude, fish/line design, gr, Abel, 9½" 225.00
Vase, 1939, bamboo molding, bl gloss, #6588, 6½" 75.00
Vase, 1940, molded circle/leaf/line decor, bl, 5½", pr 55.00
Vase, 1945, mistletoe relief, bl gloss, #6545, 3¾" 55.00
Vase, 1945, wht bisque, #6144, 3" 45.00
Vase, 1946, floral relief, gr, #2989, 7" 55.00
Vase, 1946, fruit relief, dk pink gloss, #2122, 4½" 40.00
Vase, 1946, leaf/pod relief, bl gloss, #2592, 5" 45.00
Vase, 1946, wht bisque, #2545F, 7" 45.00
Vase, 1948, butterflies in relief, gr gloss, #6509, 4¼" 65.00
Vase, 1949, leaf/floral relief, yel gloss, #2090, 4½" 45.00
Vase, 1950s, dk brn w/gray drip, 10" 50.00
Vase, 1951, Mexican figures relief, gr gloss, #6792, 5½" 95.00

Rosemeade

Rosemeade was the name chosen by Whapeton Pottery Company of Whapeton, North Dakota, to represent their product. The founders of the company were Laura Meade Taylor and R.J. Hughes, who organized the firm in 1940. It is most noted for small bird and animal figural designs, either in high gloss or a Van Briggle-like matt glaze. The ware was marked 'Rosemeade' with an ink stamp, or carried a 'Prairie Rose' sticker. The pottery closed in 1961.

When no condition is indicated, the items listed below are assumed to be in mint condition.

Ash tray, ND 1st National Bank, Bismark, 75th Anniv, gr 20.00
Ash tray, pheasant, Bismark, ND souvenir 32.00
Creamer, lt bl, 3" 18.00
Figurine, boot, blk, 5¼" 27.00
Figurine, elephant, pink, solid, 3" 22.00
Figurine, fawn, standing, decorated/glossy, 8" 35.00
Figurine, frog, sgn 25.00

Stork flower frog within black bowl, with label, stork: 7½", $45.00.

Figurine, swan, bl bisque, 5″ 25.00
Pie bird, elephant, seated, pink, 4″ 45.00
Pitcher, incised rearing horse, high-gloss tan, 5¾″ 30.00
Planter, squirrel decor 18.50
Plaque, gopher decor 20.00
Plaque, state commemorative, gr 18.00
Shakers, blk bears, pr 15.00
Shakers, bobwhite male & female, pr 10.00
Shakers, buffaloes, pr 15.00
Shakers, cats, pr 15.00
Shakers, dalmation heads, pr 8.00
Shakers, flamingos, pr 18.00
Shakers, pheasants, pr 16.00
Shoe, bl, Victorian 10.00
Vase, violet; pink satin, 3″ 14.00

Rosenthal

In 1879, Phillip Rosenthal established the Rosenthal Porcelain Factory in Selb, Bavaria. Its earliest products were figurines and fine tablewares. The company has continued to operate to the present decade, manufacturing limited edition plates.

When no condition is indicated, the items listed below are assumed to be in mint condition.

See also Collector Plates

Bowl, bl decor, scroll blank, mk Delft Savoy, oval, 13x8¾″ 150.00
Charger, Delft scenic, rich bl, 15″ 150.00
Figurine, bear, standing on hind legs, brn, 5¼″ 130.00
Figurine, Boston bulldog, sitting puppy, legs askew, 7″ 285.00
Figurine, Boston terrier, b/w, 7½x3½″ 115.00
Figurine, bulldog, wht w/blk spots, 6x4″ 100.00
Figurine, child w/flowers over shoulder, w/fawn, Lote, 6½″ 200.00
Figurine, Cupid kneels on bed of red roses, #8, 7½″ 135.00
Figurine, dachshund, sitting on haunches, 7¼″ 150.00
Figurine, English Springer Spaniel, bird in mouth, 9x5½″ 135.00
Figurine, fairy, riding on snail, 3½x3½″ 185.00
Figurine, lizard, ½x2½″ 40.00
Figurine, moth on pine cone, 1½x2¾″ 30.00
Figurine, pelican on diamond-form tray w/water lilies, 3½″ 115.00
Figurine, pointer, b/w, 8x6″ 125.00
Figurine, poodle, standing, wht w/gr collar, sgn, 8½x9″ 235.00
Figurine, princess bends over frog, from fable, 8½″ 225.00
Figurine, seagull, flies over rolling waves, sgn, 7x9″ 95.00

Vase, 2-tone gray with floral, 10″, $170.00.

Mug, purple grapes at top, trailing vines, 5″ 40.00
Mustard, Botticello 20.00
Plaque, St Jerome reading Scriptures, 10x8″ 550.00
Plate, lady's portrait, gilt, mk Malmaison, 10″ 70.00
Plate, Masonic, Benton portrait, cobalt border, 10¼″ 49.00
Plate, strawberries, sgn, 1908, 8″ 50.00
Tray, pink roses, bl/gold border, 11¾″ 25.00
Urn, portrait, dbl hdl, w/lid, 10½″ 185.00
Vase, floral, 11″ 85.00
Vase, HP by Mutual Studios, 7″ 20.00

Roseville

The Roseville Pottery Company was established in 1892 by George F. Young in Roseville, Ohio. Finding their facilities inadequate, the company moved to Zanesville in 1898, erected a new building and installed the most modern equipment available. By 1900 Young felt ready to enter into the stiffly competitive art pottery market.

Roseville's first art line was called Rozane. Similar to Rookwood's Standard, Rozane featured dark blended backgrounds with slip-painted underglaze artwork of nature studies, portraits, birds, and animals.

Azurean, developed in 1902, was a blue and white underglaze art line on a blue blended background. Egypto (1904) featured a matt glaze in a soft shade of old green and was modeled in low relief after examples of ancient Egyptian pottery. Mongol (1904) was a high gloss oxblood red line after the fashion of the Chinese Sang de Boeuf. Mara (1904), an iridescent lustre line of magenta and rose with intricate patterns developed on the surface or in low relief, successfully duplicated Sicardo's work.

These early lines were followed by many others of highest quality: Fudjiyama and Woodland (1905-06) reflected an Oriental theme; Crystalis (1906) was covered with beautiful frost-like crystals.

Della Robbia, their most famous line introduced in 1906, was decorated with designs ranging from florals, animals, and birds, to scenes of Viking warriors and Roman gladiators. These designs were accomplished by sgraffito with slip-painted details.

Very limited but of great importance to collectors today, Rozane Olympic (1905) was decorated with scenes of Greek mythology on a red ground.

Pauleo (1914) was the last of the artware lines. It was varied--over two hundred glazes were recorded--and some pieces were decorated by hand, usually with florals.

During the second decade of the century until the plant closed forty years later, new lines were added regularly, each reflecting the tastes of its time. Some of the more popular of the middle period lines were Donatello, 1915; Futura, 1928; Pinecone, 1931; and Blackberry, 1933. The floral lines of the later years have become highly collectible. Pottery from every era of Roseville production--even its utility ware--attest to an unwavering dedication to quality and artistic merit.

Examples of the fine art pottery lines present the greatest challenge to evaluate. Scarcity is a prime consideration. The quality of artwork varied from one artist to another. Some pieces show fine detail and good color, and naturally this influences their value. Studies of animals and portraits bring higher prices than the floral designs. Artist's signatures often increase the value of any item, especially if the artist is one who is well recognized.

When no condition is indicated, the items listed below are assumed to be in mint condition.

Apple Blossom, basket, #309-8″ 60.00
Apple Blossom, basket, 10″ 86.00
Apple Blossom, bookends, #359 . . . . 75.00
Apple Blossom, bowl, #328-8″, gr 30.00
Apple Blossom, candle holders, #351, pr 40.00
Apple Blossom, console bowl, #331-12″, pink 45.00
Apple Blossom, console bowl, boat shape, bl, 10″ 36.00

Apple Blossom, cornucopia, #321-6″, pink, pr.....70.00
Apple Blossom, ewer, #316, pink, 8″.....50.00
Apple Blossom, hanging basket.....85.00
Apple Blossom, jardiniere, bl, 6″.....50.00
Apple Blossom, pitcher, pink, 8″.....55.00
Apple Blossom, vase, #373-7″, bl.....44.00
Apple Blossom, vase, #381, chartreuse gr, 6″.....24.00
Apple Blossom, vase, bud.....15.00
Artwood, planter set, #1050, gray, 3-pc, 4″.....40.00
Artwood, vase, #1053-8″.....32.50
Autumn, jar w/lid, 10″.....135.00
Aztec, vase, bl w/single wht stylized floral, 9″.....225.00
Aztec, vase, lt bl w/wht stylized floral, 8″.....225.00
Azurean, tankard, berries/leaves, ornate hdl, 12¼″.....1,250.00
Azurean, vase, holly leaves & berries, C Leffler, 10¾″.....1,100.00
Baneda, console bowl, 10″.....50.00
Baneda, jardiniere, detailed band, pink, 7″.....135.00
Baneda, vase, gr, 4″.....48.00
Baneda, vase, gr, 9″.....125.00
Baneda, vase, ovoid, 6″.....55.00
Baneda, vase, red, tall U-form w/base hdls, 12″.....200.00
Baneda, vase, str neck/ball shape, hdls, gr, 6″.....65.00
Baneda, vase, 8½″.....125.00
Baneda, wall pocket, pink.....185.00
Bank, apple.....100.00
Bank, buffalo.....150.00
Bank, cat.....175.00
Bank, dog.....150.00
Bank, lion.....125.00
Bank, monkey.....150.00
Bittersweet, bookends, #859, yel, pr.....75.00
Bittersweet, cornucopia, gray, 8″.....42.00
Bittersweet, ewer, #816-8″, yel.....52.00
Bittersweet, vase, #886-12″, yel.....140.00
Bittersweet, vase, #887-14″, gr.....165.00
Bittersweet, vase, #888-16″.....190.00
Bittersweet, wall pocket.....60.00
Blackberry, candlestick, #1086-5″, pr.....175.00
Blackberry, hanging basket.....295.00
Blackberry, jardiniere, 4″.....85.00
Blackberry, jardiniere, 6″.....175.00
Blackberry, jug, 5″.....145.00
Blackberry, vase, beehive shape, 4″.....105.00
Blackberry, vase, bulbous w/ear hdls, 5″.....125.00
Blackberry, vase, compressed body w/hdls, 4¼″.....110.00
Blackberry, vase, wide mouth, sm hdls, 4″.....115.00
Blackberry, vase, 12½″.....450.00
Blackberry, vase, 8″.....150.00
Blackberry, wall pocket.....325.00
Bleeding Heart, basket, #361-12″, bl.....100.00
Bleeding Heart, bowl, 6-sided, bl.....45.00
Bleeding Heart, candlestick, #1139-4½″, pink.....25.00
Bleeding Heart, ewer, bl, 6½″.....45.00
Bleeding Heart, vase, hexagonal opening, hdld, 6½″.....50.00
Bleeding Heart, vase, paper label, hdls, 7½x5½″.....55.00
Bleeding Heart, wall pocket, pink.....85.00
Blended, fern dish, 7″.....75.00
Bottle, pig.....100.00
Burmese, bookends, wht figural.....95.00
Burmese, candle holder, woman's face, blk, 7¾″, pr.....140.00
Burmese, candlesticks, gr, pr.....30.00
Burmese, plaque, #82-B, blk.....145.00
Burmese, wall pocket, #72-B, blk.....145.00
Burmese, wall pocket, #82-B, wht.....145.00
Bushberry, basket, gr, 6½″.....42.00
Bushberry, bookends, pr.....100.00
Bushberry, bud vase.....45.00
Bushberry, candle holder, bl, pr.....26.00
Bushberry, cider set: pitcher/6 mugs, #1325 & #1, brn.....325.00
Bushberry, cornucopia, #115-8″, bl.....40.00
Bushberry, ewer, 10″.....80.00
Bushberry, ewer, 15″.....200.00
Bushberry, hanging basket.....100.00
Bushberry, jardiniere & pedestal, 10″.....750.00
Bushberry, mug, #1-3½″.....50.00
Bushberry, planter, #383-6″, brn.....30.00
Bushberry, teapot.....90.00
Bushberry, vase, #156-6″.....35.00
Bushberry, vase, #29-6″, bl.....35.00
Bushberry, vase, #31-7″, bl.....37.50
Bushberry, vase, #33-9″, hdls, bl.....40.00
Bushberry, vase, #38-12″, bl.....100.00
Bushberry, vase, #39-14″, bl, flared twig hdls.....165.00
Bushberry, vase, bud; dbl, bl.....45.00
Bushberry, wall pocket, bl.....85.00
Capri, basket, tan, 10″.....60.00
Capri, cornucopia, blk/wht/pink glaze.....40.00
Capri, leaf dish, bl/wht.....30.00
Capri, planter, #558, red mottle.....40.00
Capri, vase, red mottle, mauve & turq hdls.....45.00
Carnelian I, bud vase, dbl, gr.....32.00
Carnelian I, candle holders, pr.....25.00
Carnelian I, jardiniere, gr on gr, 5x7″.....30.00
Carnelian I, vase, fan shape, bl, hdls, 8″.....35.00
Carnelian I, vase, 18″.....210.00
Carnelian I, wall pocket, bl drip over bl, 8″.....55.00
Carnelian I, wall pocket, 9½″.....65.00
Carnelian II, bowl, gr, w/hdls, 3x9″.....30.00
Carnelian II, candle holders, pink, pr.....30.00
Carnelian II, vase, bulbous, hdls, bl/turq, 7½″.....42.00
Carnelian II, vase, pink/gr, 14½″.....125.00
Carnelian II, wall pocket, mottled red/gr, soft colors, 8″.....65.00
Cherry Blossom, flowerpot, pink.....130.00
Cherry Blossom, vase, ftd, 8″.....146.00
Cherry Blossom, vase, hdls, 7″.....90.00
Cherry Blossom, vase, pink, 10½″.....185.00
Cherry Blossom, vase, str sides, sm rim hdls, 12½″.....240.00
Cherry Blossom, wall pocket, brn.....300.00
Cherry Blossom, wall pocket, pink.....295.00
Chloron, candle sconce, warrior, 17″.....400.00
Chloron, jug, swirl leaf design, gr matt, sm chip, 8½″.....120.00

Chloron, relief-molded lilies, 8¾″, $350.00.

Chloron, mug....90.00
Chloron, vase, ftd, 4½x5″....90.00
Chloron, vase, gourd; emb cherries/leaves, sgn, 8½″....300.00
Chloron, vase, 7″....140.00
Clemana, vase, sm angle hdls, 6½″....85.00
Clemana, vase, 8″....195.00
Clematis, basket, 10″....60.00
Clematis, bookends, pr....88.00
Clematis, bowl, #455-4″, brn....25.00
Clematis, candle holder, #1158-2″, gr....20.00
Clematis, cornucopia, #193-6″, gr....35.00
Clematis, ewer, bl, 15″....115.00
Clematis, ewer, gr, 10″....70.00
Clematis, jardiniere & pedestal, gr, 25″....385.00
Clematis, pedestal, bl....100.00
Clematis, tea set....145.00
Clematis, urn, #107-8″, bl....55.00
Clematis, vase, #105-7″, bl....35.00
Clematis, vase, #114-15″, brn....195.00
Clematis, vase, #187-7″, bl....27.00
Clematis, vase, bud....15.00
Clematis, vase, gr, 12″....125.00
Clematis, wall pocket, bl....52.00
Colonial, shaving mug....55.00
Colonial, toothbrush holder....65.00
Columbine, bookends, #8-5″, w/pocket, bl, pr....95.00
Columbine, bowl, #404, w/frog, bl....80.00
Columbine, candle holders, #15, 7″, pr....55.00
Columbine, ewer, #18-7″, bl....75.00
Columbine, rose bowl, 3″....42.00
Columbine, urn vase, #400-6″, bl....40.00
Columbine, vase, #13-6″....30.00
Columbine, vase, #27-14″....150.00
Columbine, vase, #27-16″, bl....175.00
Columbine, vase, rose, 7″....42.00
Columbine, vase, 8″....46.00
Columbine, wall pocket, pink....80.00
Corinthian, bowl, ivory/gr, 6½″....52.00
Corinthian, bowl, ivory/gr, 8″....66.00
Corinthian, bowl, no mk, 3″....40.00
Corinthian, bud vase, dbl....28.00
Corinthian, planter, dbl....35.00
Corinthian, vase, 10½″....65.00
Corinthian, vase, 8″....50.00
Corinthian, wall pocket, 12″....85.00
Corinthian, wall pocket, 8″....65.00
Cornelian, bowl, 15½″....85.00
Cornelian, pitcher, emb corn, 6″....75.00
Cosmos, basket, #357-10″....75.00
Cosmos, console bowl, 12″....45.00
Cosmos, ewer, bl/gr, 10″....80.00
Cosmos, vase, #946-6″, bl....32.00
Cosmos, vase, tan, hdls, 6½″....37.50
Cosmos, vase, 18″....150.00
Cosmos, wall pocket, #1285, brn, 6½″....50.00
Cosmos, wall pocket, #1286, tan, 8″....65.00
Cosmos, window box, #381-9″, gr....40.00
Creamware, mug, FOE....80.00
Creamware, mug, masonic motif, HP, sgn Osman, rare....95.00
Cremona, vase, hdls at flat top, cylinder, pink, 12½″....125.00
Cremona, vase, slender shape, gr, 12″....100.00
Cremona, vase, vine/leaf, gr, 4x7″....45.00
Crystalis, futuristic shape w/3 hdls at top, 8½″....1,050.00
Crystalis, vase, Rozane wafer, 5½″....750.00
Crystalis, vase, 3 faces around top, seal, rare, 14½″, EX....950.00
Dahlrose, bud vase, triple....55.00
Dahlrose, candlestick, 3½″, pr....70.00
Dahlrose, jardiniere, 10″, w/pedestal....550.00
Dahlrose, jardiniere, 8″, w/pedestal....425.00
Dahlrose, vase, 2-hdl, 8¼″....45.00
Dahlrose, vase, 6″....25.00
Dahlrose, vase, 8″....40.00
Dahlrose, wall pocket, 10″....85.00
Dahlrose, wall pocket, 8″....70.00
Dawn, bookends, yel, pr....100.00
Dawn, ewer, #834, yel, 15″....325.00
Dawn, vase, 8″....52.00
Decorated Matt, jardiniere, lilies-of-the-valley, lg....475.00
Della Robbia, ewer, inscription, 5½″....950.00
Della Robbia, teapot, Rozane wafer, bell shape, 6½″....1,275.00
Della Robbia, vase, path through trees, Smith, 10¼″....2,700.00
Dogwood I, umbrella stand....300.00
Dogwood I, wall pocket, rare....85.00
Dogwood II, jardiniere, 8½x8″....65.00
Dogwood II, wall pocket, 10″....65.00
Donatello, bowl, 2¾″....22.00
Donatello, bowl, 5″....40.00
Donatello, bowl, 9½″....60.00
Donatello, bud vase, dbl....45.00
Donatello, bud vase, 10″....46.00
Donatello, compote, 5″....60.00
Donatello, console bowl, 7″....50.00
Donatello, frog....20.00
Donatello, hanging basket....140.00
Donatello, jardiniere & ped, 28″....480.00
Donatello, pitcher, 6½″....140.00
Donatello, powder jar....120.00
Donatello, vase, trumpet shape, 10″....62.00
Donatello, vase, 12″....125.00
Donatello, wall pocket, 10″....85.00
Donatello, wall pocket, 11½″....95.00
Dutch, humidor....100.00
Dutch, mug....65.00
Dutch, pitcher, tankard; w/6 mugs....495.00
Dutch, tankard....185.00
Earlam, jardiniere, bl, 4″....25.00
Earlam, vase, #521-7″....60.00
Earlam, vase, 8″....75.00
Earlam, wall pocket....200.00
Early pitcher, Bridge, NM....40.00
Early pitcher, Grapes, NM....65.00
Early pitcher, Landscape, NM....45.00
Early pitcher, Tulip, NM....45.00
Early pitcher, Wild Rose....65.00
Egypto, console bowl, 3-hdls, 3x8½″....100.00
Egypto, pitcher, 3-way, seal, 3½″....235.00
Egypto, vase, raised medallion, 5½″....235.00
Falline, vase, bl, 6″....145.00
Falline, vase, bottom ribbed, long hdls, brn, 9″....235.00
Falline, vase, brn/gr, 7½x6¼″....160.00
Falline, 11″ console bowl w/pr 4½″ sticks....225.00
Ferella, bowl, 5″....125.00
Ferella, bowl w/flower frog, 1-pc, 4¼x9½″....195.00
Ferella, vase, brn, hdls, 4½″....140.00
Ferella, vase, brn, hdls, 5¼″....150.00
Ferella, vase, brn, U-form w/long side hdls, 5x4″....165.00
Ferella, vase, brn, wide U-form on disk ft, 4x5″....145.00
Ferella, vase, red, 12″....230.00

Ferella, vase, red, 2-hdl, 10½" 210.00
Ferella, vase, red, 5" 150.00
Ferella, vase, red, 8¼" 190.00
Ferella, vase, 2-hdl, red, 9" 200.00
Ferella, wall pocket, red 350.00
Florane, bud vase, gr, #79-7" 38.00
Florane, underplate, for flowerpot, 4" 20.00
Florane, vase, tan, 7" 41.00
Florane, vase, 6" 30.00
Florane, window box, 10" 26.00
Florentine, ash tray 35.00
Florentine, basket, #231-7", RV ink stamp 100.00
Florentine, basket, #322, 8½" 125.00
Florentine, hanging basket, 9" 105.00
Florentine, jardiniere, #602, blonde, 6½" 65.00
Florentine, jardiniere, 10", w/pedestal 500.00
Florentine, vase, 7" 45.00
Florentine, wall pocket, brn, 8½" 65.00
Florentine, wall pocket, 12½" 85.00
Forget-Me-Not, pitcher, 3½" 30.00
Foxglove, bookends, pr 88.00
Foxglove, bowl, #418-4" 25.00
Foxglove, cornucopia, #166-6", bl 40.00
Foxglove, ewer, #11-6½", bl 50.00
Foxglove, ewer, #5-10", bl 85.00
Foxglove, hanging basket, bl, 5½" 90.00
Foxglove, jardiniere, #659, bl, sm 19.00
Foxglove, vase, #42-4", hdls, bl 25.00
Foxglove, vase, bl, 18" 250.00
Foxglove, wall pocket, pink 68.00
Freesia, basket, #390-7" 50.00
Freesia, basket, #391-8" 60.00
Freesia, basket, #392-10" 70.00
Freesia, bookends, brn, pr 75.00
Freesia, bowl, #464-6", bl 28.00
Freesia, bowl, gr, 2 hdls, 10" 52.00
Freesia, bud vase, bl 40.00
Freesia, candle holder, bl, 2" 25.00
Freesia, candle holder, bl, 4½" 32.00
Freesia, console bowl, #469-14", hdls 60.00
Freesia, cornucopia, #197-6" 27.50
Freesia, creamer, brn 32.00
Freesia, ewer, #19-6" 42.50
Freesia, jardiniere & pedestal, bl, 24" 365.00
Freesia, pitcher, gr, 10" 62.00
Freesia, sugar, brn 32.00
Freesia, tea set, brn 145.00
Freesia, vase, #118-6", bl 36.00
Freesia, vase, #121-8", bl 49.00
Freesia, vase, #123-9", gr 55.00
Freesia, vase, #127-12", gr 190.00
Freesia, vase, #128-15", bl 205.00
Freesia, vase, #139-18", brn 300.00
Freesia, vase, #200-7" 40.00
Freesia, vase, #463-5", ftd, brn 40.00
Freesia, wall pocket, bl 55.00
Freesia, window box, #1392-8, 10½" 32.00
Fuchsia, cornucopia 65.00
Fuchsia, vase, #895-7", bl 54.00
Fuchsia, vase, #905-18" 175.00
Fuchsia, wall pocket, brn 110.00
Fudji, stylized design, blown-out top, flared body, 8¾" 850.00
Fudji, stylized florals, scalloped top, unsgn, 8½" 700.00
Fudji, vase, 8x5", EX glaze 1,450.00
Fujiyama, Nouveau florals on bisque, sgn, 11½" 750.00
Fuschia, bowl, brn, hdld, 5" 52.00
Fuschia, bowl vase, #346-4" 35.00
Fuschia, candlesticks, brn, pr 75.00
Fuschia, cornucopia, #129-6", brn 65.00
Fuschia, pitcher, w/ice lip 90.00
Fuschia, vase, #347-6" 55.00
Fuschia, vase, #348-5" 45.00
Fuschia, vase, #645-3" 35.00
Fuschia, vase, #892-6" 50.00
Fuschia, vase, #896-8", brn 65.00
Fuschia, vase, #901-10", brn 70.00
Fuschia, vase, 12" 140.00
Futura, hanging basket, terra cotta, orig chains 170.00
Futura, vase, ball on rhomboid platform, lt/med bl, 7½" 165.00
Futura, vase, beehive w/leaves at top, pink/orange, 8¾" 325.00
Futura, vase, bottle w/stacked neck, pink/gr, 8¼" 110.00
Futura, vase, cone form, #397, 6" 130.00
Futura, vase, cone w/stepped side devices, disk ft, 8" 175.00
Futura, vase, cylinder w/stepped top/base, sq hdls, 6" 125.00
Futura, vase, flat sided fan w/rectangle rim, bl/gr, 6x9¼" 72.50

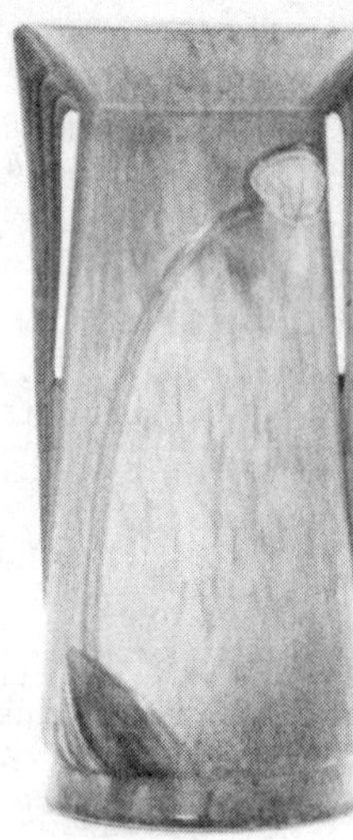

Futura, blue and white with floral decor, 13", $300.00.

Futura, vase, gr gloss w/gray leaves, #391, /2" 260.00
Futura, vase, sq on flat base, floral sprig, 6" 85.00
Futura, vase, stepped rings on full body, #394, 12" 565.00
Futura, vase, twisted hexagon, pink/rose, 8¼" 180.00
Futura, vase, twisted sq, honey brn/gr, unsgn, 6¾" 110.00
Futura, wall pocket 175.00
Gardenia, basket, gr, 10" 75.00
Gardenia, basket, gray, 8" 62.00
Gardenia, bookends, pr 85.00
Gardenia, bowl, #600-4", gr 25.00
Gardenia, cornucopia, gr, #521-6" 25.00
Gardenia, ewer, #618-15" 165.00
Gardenia, ewer, gr, 10" 60.00
Gardenia, ewer, gray, 6" 30.00
Gardenia, hanging basket 95.00
Gardenia, vase, brn, 10" 65.00
Gardenia, vase, 15" 175.00
Gardenia, wall pocket, gray 75.00
Gardenia, window box, 12" 30.00
Gold Traced, candlesticks, tall, pr 120.00
Hexagon, bowl, RV ink stamp, brn, 2¼x7" 75.00
Hexagon, vase, RV ink stamp, #272-10" 155.00
Hexagon, vase, RV ink stamp, slender, brn, 8¼" 135.00
Holland, mug, 4" 40.00

Holland, pitcher & bowl set....345.00
Hyde Park, ash tray, #1970....15.00
Imperial I, basket, elegant shape, brn, 12½″....120.00
Imperial I, sand jar, 11x12″....180.00
Imperial I, vase, 14″....100.00
Imperial I, vase, 9x8½″....75.00
Imperial II, ash tray, bl/gold, 2x6½″....95.00
Imperial II, bowl, #205-8″, bl w/streaks of gold....175.00
Imperial II, candleholder, orange/mottled gr....75.00
Imperial II, vase, rose mottle, incised rings on neck, 7″....160.00
Imperial II, vase, spattered pink, line neck decor, 8½″....285.00
Imperial II, vase, 4½″....75.00
Imperial II, wall pocket, triple, orange/gr....200.00
Iris, bookends, bl, pr....95.00
Iris, bowl, #357-4″, pink....30.00
Iris, bowl, #359-5″, bl....35.00
Iris, hanging basket, #305-5″, bl....145.00
Iris, jardiniere, bl, 3½″....32.50
Iris, vase, hdls, pink, 4½″....20.00
Iris, wall pocket, brn....120.00
Iris, wall shelf, bl....125.00
Ivory, flower holder, nude, silver sticker, 9″....285.00
Ivory Tint, jardiniere, w/liner, 9″....165.00
Ivory Tint, tankard, rose highlights, 13½″....195.00
Ixia, basket, #346-10″, yel/brn....55.00
Ixia, candle holders, dbl, tan, pr....60.00
Ixia, console bowl....50.00

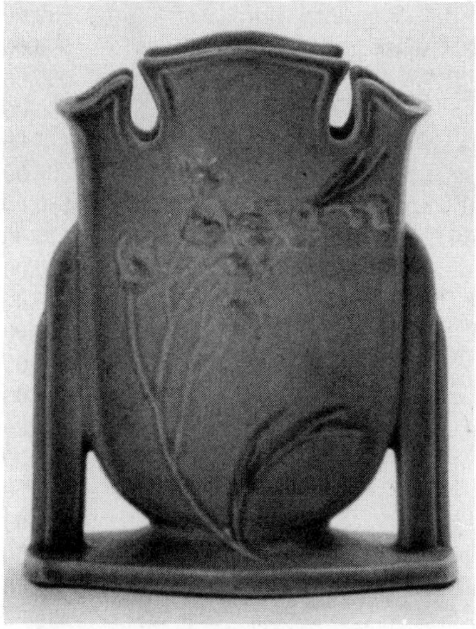

Ixia, #858-8″, $50.00.

Jardiniere & pedestal, lion masks, HP roses, 33x20″....750.00
Jonquil, basket, 9″....130.00
Jonquil, bowl, w/frog attached, 10″....115.00
Jonquil, candlestick, #1082-4″, pr....75.00
Jonquil, hanging basket....225.00
Jonquil, jardiniere, hdls, 5″....65.00
Jonquil, vase, bulbous, broad hdls, 6¾″....125.00
Jonquil, vase, ftd, 4″....35.00
Jonquil, vase, hdls, 4½″....37.50
Jonquil, vase, 7″....75.00
Jonquil, wall pocket....225.00
Juvenile, bowl, lamb, sm....30.00
Juvenile, bowl, Little Bo Peep, rolled edge....40.00
Juvenile, bowl, rabbits, rolled edge....40.00
Juvenile, creamer, chicks on gr band....35.00
Juvenile, creamer, dog, RV stamp, 3½″....50.00
Juvenile, cup, bowl & plate, rabbit....135.00
Juvenile, mug, Sunbonnet Girl, RV stamp....65.00
Juvenile, plate, duck in hat....45.00
Juvenile, plate, rabbit, rolled edge....45.00
Juvenile, plate, Sunbonnet Girl, flat....40.00
Knights of Pythias, mug, 5″....80.00
La Rose, candle holder....15.00
La Rose, wall pocket....65.00
Landscape, sugar bowl....45.00
Landscape, tea set, 3-pc....250.00
Laurel, vase, brn, 6¼″....50.00
Laurel, vase, gr, 10″....70.00
Laurel, vase, orange, cone shape w/angle hdls, 7″....75.00
Lombardy, bowl, turq, 2x5½″....60.00
Lombardy, vase, mottled bl, 6″....95.00
Lombardy, wall pocket, glossy turq....200.00
Lotus, pillow vase, yel w/bl, 10½x8½″....125.00
Lotus, planter, L9-4″....65.00
Lotus, wall pocket, brn....135.00
Luffa, floor vase/sand jar, 15½″....325.00
Luffa, jardiniere & pedestal, w/sticker, scarce, gr, 24½″....590.00
Luffa, vase, bulbous, gold sticker, brn, 9″....95.00
Luffa, vase, top hdls, disk ft, 12⅜″....125.00
Luffa, vase, 13″....135.00
Luffa, vase, 6″....42.00
Luffa, vase, 7″....55.00
Luffa, wall pocket....200.00
Lustre, candlestick, coral, 11″, pr....65.00
Lustre, vase, coral, 9″....50.00
Lustre, vase, orange, cylindrical, 10¼″....55.00
Magnolia, basket, #383-7″....50.00
Magnolia, bookends, pr....35.00
Magnolia, bowl, #655-3″....18.00
Magnolia, bowl, brn, 10″....52.00
Magnolia, bowl, brn, 12″....80.00
Magnolia, bowl, gr, 5″....30.00
Magnolia, cookie jar....125.00
Magnolia, cornucopia, brn, 6″....35.00
Magnolia, ewer, #14-10″, bl....65.00
Magnolia, ewer, brn, 15″....145.00
Magnolia, flower frog, brn, elongated hdl, 4x6″....50.00
Magnolia, hanging basket....50.00
Magnolia, pitcher, cider; brn....100.00
Magnolia, planter, #186-6″, gr....27.00
Magnolia, tea set....140.00
Magnolia, vase, #97-14″, bl....220.00
Magnolia, vase, gr, 5″....42.00
Magnolia, wall pocket, gr....55.00
Matt Color, hanging basket, pink satin....5.00
Mayfair, vase, #1004-9″, leaf hdl....65.00
Mayfair, vase, #1016-10″, scalloped top, gr....55.00
Mayfair, wall pocket, corner, grayish-beige....52.00
Medallion, dresser set....290.00
Ming Tree, basket, #508-8″, wht....55.00
Ming Tree, basket, #510-14″, gr....95.00
Ming Tree, bookends, pr....85.00
Ming Tree, candlestick, #551, wht, pr....45.00
Ming Tree, conch, turq....46.00
Ming Tree, ewer, #516-10″, wht....55.00
Ming Tree, vase, #568-8″, wht....45.00
Ming Tree, window box, #509-10″, bl....55.00
Ming Tree, window box, #568-8″, wht....35.00
Mock Orange, basket, #909-8″, pink....50.00

Mock Orange, bowl, gr, 12″ . . . 66.00
Mock Orange, candle holder, gr, 2″ . . . 25.00
Mock Orange, ewer, 6″ . . . 40.00
Mock Orange, pillow vase, #972-7″ . . . 32.00
Moderne, vase, disk ft, hdls, 7½″ . . . 55.00
Moderne, vase, lav, Deco shape, 12″ . . . 88.00
Moderne, vase, wht/rust highlights, 7½″ . . . 50.00
Mongol, vase, 14″ . . . 600.00
Monticello, basket, 4″ . . . 165.00
Monticello, basket, 6″ . . . 200.00
Monticello, vase, brn, volcano shape, 5″ . . . 38.00
Monticello, vase, bulbous body w/rim to shoulder hdl, 7″ . . . 80.00
Monticello, vase, jug form, 7″ . . . 62.00
Monticello, vase, waist-to-base hdls, 5″ . . . 55.00
Monticello, vase, waisted top w/hdls, orange, 4″ . . . 55.00
Monticello, vase, 10½″ . . . 165.00
Monticello, vase, 2-hdl, bl, 8″ . . . 80.00
Morning Glory, bowl, wht, 6″ . . . 86.00
Morning Glory, pillow shape, w/low hdls, gr, 7″ . . . 145.00
Morning Glory, vase, #724-6″, wht . . . 125.00
Morning Glory, vase, U-shape on disk ft, side hdls, gr, 5″ . . . 150.00
Morning Glory, vase, wht, full body, w/hdls, 10¼″ . . . 265.00
Morning Glory, vase, wht, 8″ . . . 150.00
Morning Glory, wall pocket, wht . . . 350.00
Moss, candle holder, pink, low, pr . . . 40.00
Moss, console bowl, 12″ . . . 42.00
Moss, vase, #779-8″, 2-hdl, bl . . . 57.50
Moss, wall pocket, gr, 10″ . . . 125.00
Moss, wall pocket, gr, 8″ . . . 92.00
Mostique, bowl, stylized iris design, 5½″ . . . 30.00
Mostique, centerpiece bowl, high glaze, rare, 3x9½″ . . . 75.00
Mostique, jardiniere, stylized iris decor, 8¼″ . . . 70.00
Mostique, planter, 2¾″ . . . 30.00
Mostique, spittoon . . . 90.00
Mostique, vase, tan, 8″ . . . 50.00
Mostique, wall pocket, 10½″ . . . 75.00
Olympic, pitcher, Ulysses at Table of Circle, 7″ . . . 800.00
Orange Blossom, candle holder, #351, brn, pr . . . 30.00
Orian, candle holder, bl . . . 25.00
Orian, rose bowl vase, #274-6″, tan/bl . . . 75.00
Orian, vase, slim neck w/hdls, yel w/turq w/in, 12½″ . . . 100.00
Orian, vase, str neck w/rings on bulb, red w/gr hdls, 7″ . . . 85.00
Orian, wall pocket, bl . . . 325.00
Panel, bud vase, dbl, RV ink stamp, brn . . . 45.00
Panel, pillow vase, pods, dk gr, 6x7″ . . . 60.00
Panel, vase, brn, 6″ . . . 40.00
Panel, vase, gr w/leaves, 7x4″ . . . 65.00
Panel, vase, unpaneled, gr, 10″ . . . 165.00
Panel, wall pocket, daisies, RV ink stamp, gr, 9½″ . . . 95.00
Panel, wall pocket, nude . . . 250.00
Pasadena, planter, brass support, triangular, pk, 7½x3½″ . . . 32.00
Pauleo, lamp . . . 750.00
Pauleo, lg nasturtium/vine on bl lustre, 13″, NM . . . 300.00
Pauleo, vase, blk/bl/violet glaze, 16½″ . . . 650.00
Peony, basket, #376-7″ . . . 45.00
Peony, basket, #378-10″ . . . 55.00
Peony, basket, #379-12″, pink-gr . . . 77.00
Peony, bud vase, hdls, pink, #173-7″ . . . 30.00
Peony, console bowl, #433-14″ . . . 65.00
Peony, hanging basket . . . 110.00
Peony, jardiniere, 5″ . . . 20.00
Peony, planter, #661-3″, hdls, gr . . . 23.50
Peony, planter, #662-5″, yel . . . 29.50
Peony, tea set, pink . . . 90.00
Peony, vase, #57-4″, pink . . . 26.50
Peony, vase, #61-7″ . . . 38.00
Peony, vase, #70-18″, gold . . . 165.00
Peony, vase, side hdls, disk ft, 18½″ . . . 200.00
Persian, bowl, 3½″ . . . 66.00
Persian, pitcher, 7″ . . . 95.00
Persian, sugar & creamer, stylized shoulder band . . . 95.00
Pinecone, ash tray, #499 . . . 46.00
Pinecone, ash tray, brn, leaf shape, #497, 1½x7″ . . . 65.00
Pinecone, banana boat, #445-6″, gr . . . 40.00
Pinecone, basket, #352-8″, w/flower frog, brn . . . 200.00
Pinecone, basket, #408-6″, brn . . . 75.00
Pinecone, basket, #441-10″, 3-legged, brn . . . 175.00
Pinecone, bookend/planter, brn, pr . . . 150.00
Pinecone, bowl, #276, oval, orig paper label/2-hdl, 11x5″ . . . 89.00
Pinecone, bowl, #345-6″, brn . . . 40.00
Pinecone, bowl, #632-3″, brn . . . 30.00
Pinecone, bud vase, triple, brn . . . 65.00
Pinecone, candle holder, #451, bl, 4″, pr . . . 36.00
Pinecone, candlestick, #1099-5″, brn, pr . . . 100.00
Pinecone, candlesticks, triple; #1106-5½″, gr, pr . . . 145.00
Pinecone, console bowl, #322-12″, brn . . . 60.00
Pinecone, console bowl, gr, 9″ . . . 50.00
Pinecone, cornucopia on base, brn, #126, 6¼″ . . . 45.00
Pinecone, dish, brn, needle hdl, #427, 5½″ . . . 65.00
Pinecone, dish, candy; #497, gr . . . 26.00
Pinecone, ewer, bl, 15½″ . . . 245.00
Pinecone, hanging basket, brn . . . 150.00
Pinecone, jardiniere, #632-10″, & pedestal, brn . . . 850.00
Pinecone, jardiniere, #632-8″, & pedestal, brn . . . 500.00
Pinecone, jardiniere, brn, 3¼″ . . . 30.00
Pinecone, jardiniere, brn, 5″ . . . 65.00
Pinecone, mug, #960-4″ . . . 75.00
Pinecone, pitcher, #415, gr . . . 200.00
Pinecone, pitcher, #485-10″ . . . 150.00
Pinecone, pitcher, ice lip, bl . . . 175.00
Pinecone, pitcher, 6″ . . . 150.00
Pinecone, planter, #455-6″, brn . . . 35.00
Pinecone, planter, #633-5″, hdls, gr . . . 33.00
Pinecone, sand jar, brn . . . 500.00
Pinecone, tumbler, brn . . . 100.00
Pinecone, tumbler, gr . . . 75.00
Pinecone, vase, #704-7″, brn . . . 45.00
Pinecone, vase, #712-12″, brn . . . 125.00
Pinecone, vase, #747-10″, brn . . . 95.00
Pinecone, vase, #839-6″, brn . . . 35.00
Pinecone, vase, #842-8″, gr . . . 65.00
Pinecone, vase, #850-14″, brn . . . 250.00
Pinecone, vase, #908-8″, twig hdls, gr . . . 85.00
Pinecone, wall pocket, dbl, gr . . . 110.00
Pinecone, wall shelf, brn, #1, 8½″ . . . 195.00
Pinecone, window box, #431, bl, 15″ . . . 75.00
Poppy, bowl, #642-3″, pink . . . 35.00
Poppy, ewer, pink, 10″ . . . 78.00
Poppy, rose bowl . . . 25.00
Poppy, wall pocket, gray . . . 145.00
Primrose, candlestick, #1105-4½″, pr . . . 125.00
Primrose, pedestal, brn . . . 125.00
Primrose, vase, shoulder hdls, 10½″ . . . 60.00
Quaker, dresser tray, girl w/hat w/in red center . . . 75.00
Raymor, bowl, vegetable . . . 25.00
Raymor, coffee pot, swinging; metal stand, brn . . . 165.00
Raymor, pitcher, slant top, avacado mottle, 10½″ . . . 40.00
Raymor, platter, 14″ . . . 15.00

Raymor, ramekin w/lid....15.00
Raymor, relish tray....25.00
Raymor, shakers, wht, pr....20.00
Rosecraft, bowl, royal bl, 2x8½″....32.00
Rosecraft, bud vase, bl....45.00
Rosecraft, candlestick, 10″, pr....65.00
Rosecraft, vase, bl lustre, 11½″....88.00
Rosecraft Black, bowl, 2x8½″....30.00
Rosecraft Black, bowl, 9½″....40.00
Rosecraft Black, ginger jar, 10″....150.00
Rosecraft Black, vase, #318-8″....155.00
Rosecraft Black, vase, 5½″....75.00
Rosecraft Black, wall pocket, 9″....125.00
Rosecraft Blended, jardiniere, brn, 6″....55.00
Rosecraft Blended, vase, 6″....28.00
Rosecraft Blended, window box....32.00
Rosecraft Hexagon, vase, brn w/orange, orange int, 6¼″....70.00
Rosecraft Hexagon, wall pocket....120.00
Rosecraft Vintage, bowl, 9″....35.00
Rosecraft Vintage, bowl vase, RV ink stamp, 3″....45.00
Rosecraft Vintage, bowl w/frog, 3x9½″....55.00
Rosecraft Vintage, vase, 8″....60.00
Rosecraft Vintage, wall pocket, no hdl, brn....110.00
Rosecraft Vintage, window box....250.00
Royal Capri, bud vase, 7″....210.00
Royal Capri, planter, #558-7″....210.00
Royal Capri, vase, #79-7″....225.00
Rozane, bud vase, yel/orange floral, 8¼″....90.00
Rozane, card holder, wild roses, G Neff....210.00
Rozane, compote, floral, 6½″....85.00
Rozane, ewer, floral, artist sgn, dbl hdl, 9½″....340.00
Rozane, flower/vine, same in silver overlay, #923/4, 5″....1,200.00
Rozane, mug, no decor, 4″....55.00
Rozane, vase, acorn/leaf, 7¼″....120.00
Rozane, vase, ferns, rim to base hdls form circle, 6″....235.00
Rozane, vase, floral, pillow form, 7″....245.00
Rozane, vase, floral, waisted neck, 4″....80.00
Rozane, vase, holly/berry, slim neck/compressed body, 5½″....125.00
Rozane, vase, poppies, bulbous, wafer mk, 8½″....180.00
Rozane, vase, roses, flange/compressed body/disk base, 7″....165.00
Rozane, vase, yel berry, wafer mk, artist sgn, 6½″....140.00
Rozane Light, vase, pine cones/leaves, lt brn/wht, 7¼″....185.00
Rozane Light, vase, sweet peas, sgn Myers, 13″....395.00
Rozane 1917, basket, ivory, 9″....52.00
Rozane 1917, bowl, ivory, hdl, 8″....35.00
Rozane 1917, candle holder, ivory, 7″....25.00
Rozane 1917, compote, wht, 6″....70.00
Rozane 1917, lamp base, wht, 6½″....32.00
Rozane 1917, pitcher, wht....86.00
Rozane 1917, wall pocket, grn....85.00
Rozane 1940s, vase, bl, hdld, 8″....30.00
Russco, candle holder, gr/tan, 4½″, pr....36.00
Russco, cornucopia, gold label, 8⅜″....26.00
Russco, vase, gr/cream crystalline, ped ft, 8½″....65.00
Savona, console bowl, salmon....60.00
Savona, vase, lime gr, 12½″....225.00
Savona, wall pocket, bl....225.00
Silhouette, basket, #708-6″....30.00
Silhouette, bowl, wht-gr, 4″....15.00
Silhouette, cigarette box, bl....50.00
Silhouette, console bowl, wht & gr....35.00
Silhouette, cornucopia, #722, aqua....31.00
Silhouette, ewer, #717-10″, bl & gr....62.00
Silhouette, ewer, red, 6″....40.00
Silhouette, planter, #728-10″....23.00
Silhouette, vase, #763-8″, nude....155.00
Silhouette, vase, #787-10″, nude, rose....185.00
Silhouette, wall pocket, #766, red....75.00
Silhouette, window box, 10″....25.00
Snowberry, ash tray....32.00
Snowberry, basket, bl, 8″....65.00
Snowberry, basket, gr, 7″....55.00
Snowberry, bookends, #1, pink, pr....65.00
Snowberry, bowl, pink, 6″....30.00
Snowberry, bowl, 13″....45.00
Snowberry, bud vase, #1BV-7″, bl....29.50
Snowberry, candlestick, gr, 2½″, pr....55.00
Snowberry, flowerpot, w/saucer, bl....45.00
Snowberry, jardiniere, bl, 6″....35.00
Snowberry, pedestal, bl....135.00
Snowberry, planter, rectangle....22.00
Snowberry, tea set, bl....95.00
Snowberry, vase, floor type, 18″....165.00
Snowberry, vase, 15″....100.00
Snowberry, wall pocket, bl....45.00
Sunflower, jardinere, 8″....62.00
Sunflower, jardiniere, vase hdld, 5½″....40.00
Sunflower, vase, hdls, 5″....45.00
Sunflower, vase, 12″....165.00
Sunflower, vase, 2-hdl, 4½″....40.00
Sunflower, vase, 2-hdl, 6¼″....70.00
Sunflower, vase, 6″....50.00
Sunflower, vase, 7x5″....80.00
Sunflower, wall pocket....225.00
Teasel, candle holder, rose....15.00
Teasel, ewer, #890-18″....195.00
Teasel, vase, lt bl, reticulated top, ftd, 12″....85.00
Teasel, vase, 15″....150.00
Thornapple, basket, #365-7″....50.00
Thornapple, candle holder, gr, 2½″, pr....60.00
Thornapple, vase, 6″....46.00
Thornapple, vase, 9″....60.00
Thornapple, wall pocket, #1280-8″, bl....110.00
Topeo, vase, red, full-bodied cylinder w/tab hdls, 8″....125.00
Topeo, vase, red, 7¼″....100.00
Tourist, bowl, 3½x7″....750.00
Tourist, jardiniere, 10x12″....850.00
Tourmaline, bowl, turq, paper label, 3x9″....36.00
Tourmaline, candlesticks, 5″, pr....75.00
Tourmaline, vase, #332-8″, bl....45.00
Tourmaline, vase, #517-6″, bl....30.00
Tourmaline, vase, ball shape, bl, 5″....35.00
Tourmaline, vase, 7″....40.00
Tuscany, bowl, gray, 2½x6¾″....22.00
Tuscany, bowl, w/frog, pink, 7″....40.00
Tuscany, bowl, 10″....40.00
Tuscany, flower arranger vase....30.00
Tuscany, planter....42.00
Tuscany, vase, gray, 8¼″....50.00
Tuscany, vase, pink, 7¼″....35.00
Velmoss, vase, gr, 6″....35.00
Velmoss, wall pocket, pink....275.00
Velmoss Scroll, vase, bulbous, 5″....60.00
Velmoss Scroll, wall pocket, wide body, 11″....145.00
Victorian, vase, lt gr w/yel-gr floral shoulder band, 8″....225.00
Vista, vase, sm hdls, 15″....100.00
Vista, vase, 18″....150.00
Vista, wall pocket....225.00

Volpato, bowl, ped ft, 12″ 65.00
Volpato, bud vase 45.00
Volpato, jar w/lid 175.00
Volpato, jardiniere, 6x6″ 70.00
Volpato, vase, wht, 7x3½″ 135.00
Volpato, vase, 6″ 85.00
Water Lily, basket, pink, 12″ 85.00
Water Lily, candlestick, brn, 2″, pr 32.00
Water Lily, conch shell, #438-8″, rare, brn 55.00
Water Lily, console bowl, #443-12″, pink 52.00
Water Lily, cookie jar, brn 100.00
Water Lily, ewer, #11-10″ 85.00
Water Lily, ewer, #12, 15″ 130.00
Water Lily, vase, #175-8″ 50.00
Water Lily, vase, #71-4″, bl 25.00
Water Lily, vase, #72-6″ 32.00
Water Lily, vase, #78-9″ 55.00
White Rose, basket, #364-12″ 75.00
White Rose, bookends, pr 68.00
White Rose, cornucopia, brn-gr, 6″ 30.00
White Rose, ewer, #981-6″, bl 45.00
White Rose, frog w/hdl 19.00
White Rose, tea set, gr 125.00
White Rose, vase, #146-6″, pink-gr 40.00
White Rose, vase, #992-15″, bl 140.00
White Rose, wall pocket, pink 62.00
Wincraft, bookends, pr 60.00
Wincraft, bowl, #226-8″, gr 29.50
Wincraft, candle holder, brn 25.00
Wincraft, console bowl, grapes, gr, 12″ 35.00
Wincraft, creamer, bl, #271C 10.00
Wincraft, vase, #281-6″, brn 30.00
Wincraft, vase, bl, 8″ 52.00
Wincraft, vase, brn, 12″ 80.00
Wincraft, wall pocket, #266-4″ 76.00
Wincraft, wall pocket, #267, rnd 65.00
Wincraft, window box, #286-12″ 55.00
Windsor, vase, #547-6″, geometrics, bl 75.00
Windsor, vase, bl w/geometrics, 8x4″ 70.00
Windsor, vase, ferns, bulbous, 7x6″ 135.00
Wisteria, bowl, bl, 12″ 80.00
Wisteria, candle holder, bl, gold sticker, 4½″ 95.00
Wisteria, hanging basket 250.00
Wisteria, vase, #634-7″ 85.00
Wisteria, vase, bl, 6″ 80.00
Wisteria, vase, cylindrical w/rim hdls, 10″ 150.00
Wisteria, vase, flared, concave sides, waist hdls, 10″ 145.00
Wisteria, vase, 9″ 115.00
Wisteria, wall pocket, brn 250.00
Woodland, bud vase, floral on stem, flared sides, 8″ 450.00
Woodland, vase, naturalistic floral, 8″ 500.00
Zephyr Lily, basket, #393-7″ 45.00
Zephyr Lily, basket, #394-8″, gr 55.00
Zephyr Lily, basket, bl, 10″ 65.00
Zephyr Lily, bookends, pr 75.00
Zephyr Lily, bowl, brn, 10″ 40.00
Zephyr Lily, bud vase, #918-7″ 23.00
Zephyr Lily, candlestick, brn, 4″ 15.00
Zephyr Lily, creamer & sugar, #7-C&S, gr 45.00
Zephyr Lily, ewer, #23-10″, bl 70.00
Zephyr Lily, ewer, 6½″ 36.00
Zephyr Lily, flowerpot w/dish, brn 45.00
Zephyr Lily, hanging basket 60.00
Zephyr Lily, planter, #470-5″, gr 40.00
Zephyr Lily, vase, #130-6″, hdls, tan 33.00
Zephyr Lily, vase, #131-7″, hdls, bl 35.00
Zephyr Lily, vase, #141-15″, bl 200.00
Zephyr Lily, vase, #205-6″ 28.00
Zephyr Lily, vase, bl, 12″ 60.00
Zephyr Lily, wall pocket, brn 50.00

Rowland and Marcellus

Though the impressive back stamp seems to insist otherwise, Rowland and Marsellus Company were not Staffordshire potters, but American importers who commissioned various English companies to supply them with the blue-printed historical ware that had been a popular import item since the early 1800s. Plates, cups and saucers, pitchers, and platters were sold as souvenirs from 1890 to 1920. The mark may be in full or 'R. & M.' in a diamond.

When no condition is indicated, the items listed below are assumed to be in mint condition.

Jug, Discovery of America, 8″ 165.00
Plate, Allentown, PA, rolled edge, 10″ 48.00
Plate, Asbury Park, New Jersey, flat style, 8½″ 28.00
Plate, Capt John Smith, portrait, rolled edge, 10½″ 45.00
Plate, Chas Dickens, rolled edge 45.00
Plate, Landing at Hendricks, Hudson, rolled edge, 10½″ 45.00
Plate, Lewis & Clark Centennial, Portland, OR, 1905, 10″ 45.00
Plate, Miles Standish Monument, rolled edge 45.00
Plate, Minneapolis, falls, library, boathouse, etc, 10″ 45.00
Plate, Niagara Falls, rolled edge, 10½″ 36.00
Plate, Plymouth Rock, rolled edge 30.00

Plate, inscribed: Ride of Paul Revere, blue and white, 10″, $75.00.

Plate, Portland, OR, flat style 30.00
Plate, Providence 35.00
Plate, Robert Burns 48.00
Plate, Statue of Liberty, 6 scenes in border 48.00
Plate, Theodore Roosevelt, 26th Pres, rolled edge, bl, 10″ 60.00
Plate, Thos Jefferson, Florida souvenir, rolled edge, 10½″ 60.00
Plate, Valley Forge 45.00

Royal Bayreuth

Founded in 1794 in Tettau, Bavaria, the Royal Bayreuth firm originally manufactured fine dinnerwares of superior quality. In more recent times, they have produced lines of dinnerware and accessory items such as humidors, vases, ash trays, and boxes in patterns called Rose Tapestry, Sunbonnet Babies, Beach Babies, and Devil and Cards. These are highly sought by today's collectors. Figural creamers, sugar bowls, and shakers in the shape of tomatoes, grapes, shells, and animals were made in abundance, and it is these figurals that command the higher prices today.

When no condition is indicated, the items listed below are assumed to be in mint condition.

Ash tray, cows, cigar rests....55.00
Ash tray, equestrian scene, bl mk....45.00
Ash tray, girl/basket/farm scene, spade form, hdl, bl rim....55.00
Ash tray, hunter w/dog, heart shape....55.00
Ash tray, man w/lyre courts lady, heart shape, 5¼"....55.00
Ash tray, pastoral scene w/cows, cigarette rests....50.00
Basket, dbl, girl/dog, intertwining hdls, unmk....225.00
Basket, Rose Tapestry, 5x5"....300.00
Basket, wht/yel roses, bl mk, 5¼"....115.00
Bell, girl & dog, bl mk....125.00
Bowl, cereal; Sunbonnet Babies, sweeping, bl mk....150.00
Bowl, grape cluster, pearl w/lav leaves, hdl, no mk, 9½x6"....250.00
Bowl, poppy, 10"....165.00
Bowl, Sunbonnet Babies, cleaning, 7½"....325.00
Bowl, Sunbonnet Babies, fishing, barn/trees bkground, 5¾"....175.00
Bowl, Sunbonnet Babies, mending on porch/orange bottom, 6"....175.00
Box, boy & girl sailing, bl mk....69.00
Box, Brittany woman, kidney shape, bl mk....8.00
Box, children on sled....60.00
Box, cigarette; musicians....70.00
Box, pin; cows in pasture scene, w/lid, gr/brn, bl mk....42.00
Box, pin; floral w/much gold tracery, bl mk, 2½" sq....48.00
Box, pin; Lilac Tapestry, 2x3½"....150.00
Box, pin; yel roses on lid & sides, bl mk, M....42.00
Box, riders & dogs, pie-cut shape, bl mk....68.00
Box, Rose Tapestry, 3" dia....165.00
Box, stamp; Devil & Cards....200.00
Cake plate, Rose Tapestry, pink, open hdl, 10¼"....365.00
Cake plate, Rose Tapestry, 3-color, open hdl, 10¼"....425.00
Cake plate, Sunbonnet Babies, washing/hanging out, 10½"....250.00
Cake set, Sunbonnet Babies, 7-pc....650.00
Candlestick, Devil & Cards, 3½x6"....260.00
Candlestick, elk, 3x7"....90.00
Candlestick, Little Bo Peep, bl mk....75.00
Candlestick, Murex shell, mk DEP, 6½"....145.00
Candlestick, riders & dogs, bl mk....65.00
Candlestick, Sand Babies, shield bk....165.00
Candlestick, Sunbonnet Babies, shield bk, bl mk....395.00
Candy dish, Devil & Cards....250.00
Candy dish, Sunbonnet Babies, fishing, 2-hdl, ftd, 9½x4¼"....195.00
Chamberstick, Japanese chrysanthemum, tapestry, hdl, BM....325.00
Chamberstick, roses/pansies/forget-me-nots, BM....95.00
Chocolate pot, boy & 3 donkeys, +4 matching cups....275.00
Chocolate pot, boy w/donkey scenic, bl mk....185.00
Chocolate pot, Rose Tapestry, pink, bl mk....950.00
Chocolate pot, Rose Tapestry, 3-color....1,050.00
Creamer, apple....70.00
Creamer, bellringer....175.00
Creamer, bull, blk w/cerise details....155.00
Creamer, clown, red....180.00

Rose Tapestry basket, 3-color roses, 5½", $325.00.

Creamer, coachman, bl mk....165.00
Creamer, cockatoo, bl mk....140.00
Creamer, conch shell, long ruffled spout, satin....65.00
Creamer, conch shell, tall w/diagonal ribs, red twig hdl....75.00
Creamer, cow pasture scene, bl mk, 3½"....43.00
Creamer, crow, blk w/red beak & brn eyes....130.00
Creamer, Devil & Cards, bl mk, 3¾"....125.00
Creamer, duck....75.00
Creamer, elk, bl mk....68.00
Creamer, fish head, EX color....98.00
Creamer, frog, dk gr, EX color....92.00
Creamer, goat head, orange jacket, gr pants, shoes, 6"....75.00
Creamer, lemon, bl mk....75.00
Creamer, lettuce leaf....75.00
Creamer, lobster, red....47.00
Creamer, lobster & lettuce leaf....77.00
Creamer, melon....135.00
Creamer, milkmaid....200.00
Creamer, moose head....35.00
Creamer, mountain goat....145.00
Creamer, Murex shell, scuttle shape, bl mk....42.00
Creamer, oak leaf....80.00
Creamer, Old Man of the Mountain, unmk....40.00
Creamer, orange....105.00
Creamer, oyster & pearl, cerise top & bottom, bl mk....65.00
Creamer, pansy, bl mk....140.00
Creamer, parakeet, gr, bl mk....155.00
Creamer, pelican, no mk....55.00
Creamer, poodle, shaded gray to wht, salmon int....185.00
Creamer, poppy, red, stem hdl, 3-color center pod....100.00
Creamer, Rose Tapestry, 3-color, str sides, bl mk, 3"....115.00
Creamer, Rose Tapestry, 4¾"....225.00
Creamer, Sand Babies, bl mk....62.00
Creamer, seal, shaded gray & pink....225.00
Creamer, Sunbonnet Babies, mending, boat shape, 4¼" L....250.00
Creamer, Sunbonnet Babies, scrubbing/washing windows, 2¾"....150.00
Creamer, Sunbonnet Babies, washing & ironing, bl mk....125.00
Creamer, water buffalo, blk....135.00
Creamer, 3 men & sailboat, blk bkground, 3¼"....150.00
Creamer & sugar, lemon, bl mk....150.00
Creamer & sugar, rose, w/lid, pink/yel, bl mk....395.00

Creamer & sugar, Rose Tapestry, w/lid....................340.00
Creamer & sugar, Snow Babies, bl mk....................185.00
Creamer & sugar, strawberry....................135.00
Creamer & sugar, Sunbonnet Babies....................250.00
Creamer & sugar, tomato, red w/gr leaf, lg....................90.00
Cup, demitasse; Devil & Cards....................67.00
Cup & saucer, red rose, sgn, rare, lg....................195.00
Cup & saucer, Sunbonnet Babies, cleaning, bl mk....................175.00
Demitasse pot, Brittany woman, lg hdl, bl/wht, 7½″....................115.00
Desk set, inkwell/blotter/letter holder/pen dish....................285.00
Dish, child's; Dutch skating scene, bl mk....................88.00
Dish, child's; girl & dog, bl mk....................88.00
Dish, child's; Jack & the Beanstock, bl mk, VG....................68.00
Dish, child's; Sunbonnet Babies, scrubbing/washing, bl mk....................250.00
Dish, clover-leaf; Rose Tapestry, 3-color, bl mk, 5x4½″....................130.00
Dish, clover-leaf; Sunbonnet Babies, sewing....................125.00
Dish, clover-leaf; tapestry w/Arab & horse, hdl, bl mk, 4″....................165.00
Hair receiver, lady & ducks, lt yel, 4¼x2½″....................95.00
Hair receiver, Rose Tapestry, pink, gold ft, bl mk....................145.00
Hair receiver, Rose Tapestry, pink/yel, 3 gold ft, bl mk....................165.00
Hair receiver, Rose Tapestry, 3-color, 3 gold ft, 4″ dia....................185.00
Hair receiver, Sunbonnet Babies, ruffled, bl mk....................295.00
Hair receiver, wht w/heavy gold trim, bl mk....................39.00
Hatpin holder, penguin, 5″....................300.00
Hatpin holder, riders & dogs, mk DEP....................195.00
Hatpin holder, Rose Tapestry, fancy scroll base....................295.00
Hatpin holder, Sunbonnet Babies, w/pin dish, 2-pc....................200.00
Humidor, Devil & Cards, bl mk....................450.00
Humidor, hunting scene, fancy lid, bl mk....................195.00
Humidor, troubadours, sgn Dixon....................250.00
Match holder, clown....................185.00
Match holder, Devil & Cards....................350.00
Match holder, enamel storks, yel high glaze, bl mk....................295.00
Match holder, shell, wall mt, mk Deponiert....................60.00
Mug, beer; Devil & Cards....................200.00
Mug, Nursery Rhyme, w/hdl, bl mk, 2″....................55.00
Mug, Sunbonnet Babies, ironing, bl mk, 3¼″....................150.00
Mug, Sunbonnet Babies, sweeping....................110.00
Mustard, irid wht w/orange irid hdl, w/lid & spoon....................110.00
Mustard, lobster, red, w/lid....................47.00
Mustard, poppy, pink MOP....................175.00
Mustard, shell, irid, ftd, w/ladle, sgn Bavaria only....................35.00
Nappy, Jack & Jill scene, verse border, heart shape, 5½″....................57.00
Nappy, lg roses, reticulated edges, lg ring hdl, bl mk....................63.00
Nappy, Rose Tapestry, 3-color, wishbone hdl, scalloped....................135.00
Nut bowl, master; poppy, yel to MOP, 4-ft, bl mk, 6″....................145.00
Nut set, Rose Tapestry, 3-color, gold ft, master+4 ind....................00.00
Pitcher, apple, milk, bl mk....................95.00
Pitcher, castle in mountains, tapestry, 4″....................145.00
Pitcher, clam-digger girl, barn bkground, bl mk, 4¼″....................125.00
Pitcher, coachman, water....................375.00
Pitcher, cockatoo, bl mk, milk....................175.00
Pitcher, cows in pond, gr at top & bottom, bl mk, 5″....................95.00
Pitcher, cows/trees, pinched gr bottom & hdl, bl mk, 4¼″....................125.00
Pitcher, Devil & Cards, milk....................175.00
Pitcher, Devil & Cards, water, gr mk....................380.00
Pitcher, duck, registery mk, milk....................145.00
Pitcher, Dutch scene, 5″....................85.00
Pitcher, Dutch waterboy scene, ring hdl, bl mk, 7″....................145.00
Pitcher, fish, bl mk, 5½″....................197.00
Pitcher, fish head, lemonade, 8″....................250.00
Pitcher, grape, water....................275.00
Pitcher, Little Miss Muffet, bl mk, 4½″....................75.00
Pitcher, man w/rearing horses, bl mk, 3½″....................150.00
Pitcher, musicians, bl mk, 7″....................160.00
Pitcher, oxen/pond, 2 hdls on same side, bl mk, 4″....................150.00
Pitcher, parakeet, milk....................215.00
Pitcher, robin, milk....................175.00
Pitcher, rooster/turkey/chickens, wall bkground, bl mk, 4″....................150.00
Pitcher, Rose Tapestry, pinch spout, milk....................145.00
Pitcher, sheep grazing, pinched spout, 4″....................115.00
Pitcher, shell, water....................300.00
Pitcher, Snow Babies, milk....................95.00
Pitcher, St Bernard, milk....................185.00
Pitcher, storks, milk, yel & wht, bl mk, 6½″....................92.00
Pitcher, Sunbonnet Babies, cleaning floor & window, 3½″....................250.00
Pitcher, Sunbonnet Babies, fishing, pinch spout, bl mk, 4″....................165.00
Pitcher, Sunbonnet Babies, scrubbing/washing windows, 4½″....................210.00
Pitcher, Sunbonnet Babies, sweeping, bulbous, bl mk, 4½″....................195.00
Pitcher, Sunbonnet Babies, sweeping, pinch spout, 3¾″....................185.00
Pitcher, Sunbonnet Babies, w/broom/dustpan, bulbous, 4″....................275.00
Pitcher, Sunbonnet Babies, washing/hanging clothes, 3½″....................250.00
Pitcher, Sunbonnet Babies, washing/ironing, pinch spout, 4″....................210.00
Pitcher, tapestry, dogs & moose, pinch spout, bl mk 4″....................200.00
Pitcher, tomato, water....................200.00
Pitcher, trout, water....................275.00
Planter, Arab/horses, ring hdls/ruffled top, w/insert, 3½″....................125.00
Planter, Rose Tapestry, pink, 2 gold hdls, fluted, 2¾″....................150.00
Planter, Rose Tapestry, 3-color, gold hdls, liner, 2¾″....................185.00
Planter, 2 musicians, bl mk, M....................58.00
Plaque, Rose Tapestry, pink, gold scroll edge, 9½″....................375.00
Plate, Goose Girl, 6″....................55.00
Plate, man w/rearing horses, gabled house, bl mk, 6″....................150.00
Plate, oak leaf; satin, bl mk, 6¾″....................35.00
Plate, Rose Tapestry, molded edge, 6″....................100.00
Plate, Rose Tapestry, 7½″....................195.00
Plate, Snow Babies on sled, bl mk, 8″....................110.00
Plate, Sunbonnet Babies, cleaning floor/window, 6″....................200.00
Plate, Sunbonnet Babies, ironing, 7½″....................135.00
Plate, Sunbonnet Babies, washing/hanging clothes, 7½″....................135.00
Powder jar, elk scene on lid....................85.00
Powder jar, poppy, MOP, bl mk....................175.00
Relish, Murex shell, bl mk....................85.00
Relish, 2 musicians, bl mk....................58.00
Ring tree, ivory w/yel roses, bl mk....................78.00
Rose bowl, Sunbonnet Babies, washing/ironing, bl mk, 3″....................190.00
Salt, master; Devil & Cards, Devil hdl, bl mk, scarce....................195.00

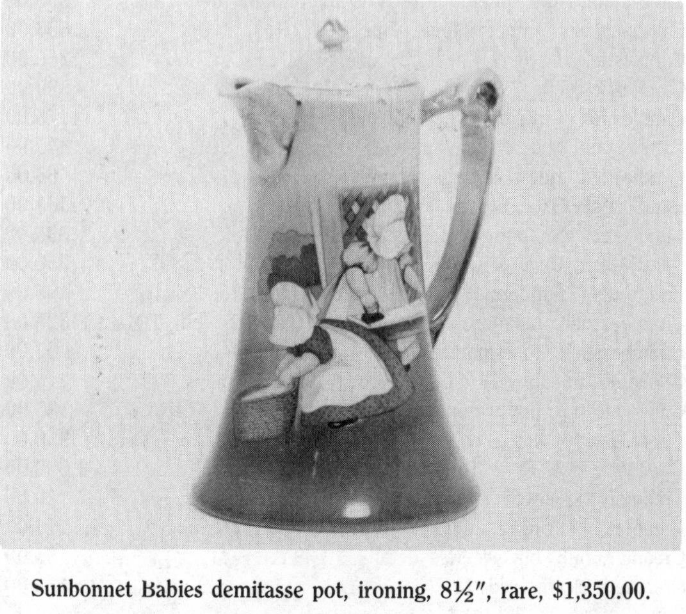

Sunbonnet Babies demitasse pot, ironing, 8½″, rare, $1,350.00.

Shaker, Sand Babies, 3½″ 37.00
Shakers, Arab & horse in desert scene, pr 55.00
Shakers, grapes, pr 85.00
Shakers, Murex shells, mk Germany, pr 50.00
Shakers, Sunbonnet Babies, mending/washing/hanging, pr 225.00
Shoe, blk 75.00
Shoe, lady's high-lace, blk; bl mk 65.00
Shoe, man's oxford, EX details, cinnamon to tan, unmk 85.00
Shoe, Rose Tapestry, bl mk 270.00
Shoe, Rose Tapestry, gr mk 185.00
String holder, rooster, bl mk 165.00
Sugar bowl, Devil & Cards, w/lid 175.00
Sugar bowl, grape 55.00
Sugar bowl, man fishing, full scene, bl mk 62.00
Sugar bowl, Murex shell, bl mk 55.00
Sugar bowl, open; gr matt w/wht roses, bl mk 24.00
Sugar bowl, open; lobster 50.00
Sugar bowl, open; wht, heavy gold trim, bl mk 24.00
Sugar bowl, poppy 125.00
Sugar bowl, rose, yel/pink, bl mk 175.00
Sugar bowl, Rose Tapestry, 3-color 225.00
Sugar bowl, Sunbonnet Babies, broom & dust pan, boat shape . 250.00
Teapot, boy & donkeys by pond, bl mk, 5½″ 250.00
Teapot, Dutch boy w/kite/dog, gold hdl/rim, bl mk, 4x3½″ 95.00
Teapot, man w/donkey, bulbous, 3-cup, bl mk 145.00
Teapot, orange 85.00
Teapot, sunset/river, gold/rose, bl mk, 4⅛x3¼″ 55.00
Toothpick, Little Bo Peep, pot shape, ftd, hdl 135.00
Toothpick, riders & dogs, scuttle 75.00
Toothpick, riders & dogs, 3-hdl, bl mk 80.00
Tray, celery; wht w/heavy gold trim, gold mk, 12½″ 24.00
Tray, dresser, chrysanthemums, tapestry, 7½x10″, rare 275.00
Tray, dresser; Devil & Cards 475.00
Tray, elk, mk, 6½″ 80.00
Tray, pin; Arab & horse, club shape, beaded edge, bl mk 42.00
Tray, pin; Jack & the Beanstalk, bl mk 62.00
Tray, pin; Rose Tapestry, maple leaf/center rose, bl mk 125.00
Tray, Rose Tapestry, bl mk, 7½x10″ 185.00
Vase, castle, scenic, 2-hdl, bl mk, 9″ 175.00
Vase, Dutch boy w/kite & dog, gray/brn, bl mk, 4¼″ 55.00
Vase, fighting cocks, 4½″ 75.00
Vase, lady's portrait, sgn Bouck, wine w/relief gold, 6″ 195.00
Vase, man & turkeys, bulbous, bl mk, 6¼x3½″ dia 150.00
Vase, man & woman on jumping horses, 5 dogs, bl mk, 6″ 95.00
Vase, Sand Babies, 3-hdl, bl mk, 3⅝″ 90.00

Royal Bonn

Royal Bonn is a fine paste porcelain, ornately decorated with scenes, portraits, or florals. The factory was established in the mid-1800s in Bonn, Germany; however most pieces found today are from the latter part of the century.

When no condition is indicated, the items listed below are assumed to be in mint condition.

Cheese dish, floral, rnd 30.00
Ewer, parrot on tree, HP, 12″ 85.00
Plate, chrysanthemums, HP, gilt, sq, 8½″ 35.00
Urn, cows/farm in reserve, gold neck/hdls/sq ped base, 12″ 175.00
Vase, floral tapestry, serpent climbs neck, HP, sgn, 12½″ 175.00
Vase, flowers, brn/yel w/gold/orange, wide body, 8x5″ 95.00
Vase, full length lady & child, ornate hdls, urn form, 16″ 795.00
Vase, girl's portrait, gold neck hdls/bulbous, sgn, 7½″ 450.00

Vase, green with yellow hand-painted florals, #2627, 12½″, $110.00.

Vase, orchids, gr w/pink/wht, gold trim, teardrop shape, 8″ 110.00
Vase, roses, HP, 7″ 82.00
Vase, roses, yel/wht/pink on shaded pastels, 8x3″ 88.00
Vase, ¾ portrait of lady w/stole, sgn, 9½″ 550.00

Royal Copenhagen

The Royal Copenhagen Manufactory was established in Denmark in about 1775 by Frantz Henrich Muller. When bankruptcy threatened in 1779, the Crown took charge, and the fine dinnerware and objects of art produced after that time carry the familiar logo, the crown over three wavy lines.

When no condition is indicated, the items listed below are assumed to be in mint condition.

Bust, young girl w/pnt scarf, Johannes Kedezoorf, 14″ 150.00
Cup & saucer, #910/1870, floral on beige 30.00
Decanter, Rosenborg Castle 60.00
Figurine, Blk-Headed Gull, #1468 . . . . . 55.00
Figurine, blue jay, 3″ 25.00
Figurine, bluebirds, pr side by side, 4″ L 75.00

Tray, lobster in relief, 10″, $100.00.

Figurine, boy in pointed hat/long coat, w/umbrella, #1145.....135.00
Figurine, boy w/ball, #3542.....125.00
Figurine, boy w/lunchbox, #865.....145.00
Figurine, collie lies on stomach, paws outstretched, 5x11".....190.00
Figurine, cow on stomach w/legs underneath, gray/wht, 4x6"...180.00
Figurine, drummer boy, #3647.....75.00
Figurine, Lhasa Apso, seated, #1006, 4½x5½".....135.00
Figurine, lovebirds, #402.....95.00
Figurine, mermaid w/dolphin, #2348.....75.00
Figurine, mouse sits on chestnut, preening, #511, 2½".....65.00
Figurine, Pan rides atop turtle, #858, 3¾".....150.00
Figurine, penguin, 2¾".....125.00
Figurine, penguins, pr standing, 4".....200.00
Figurine, rabbit, #375.....140.00
Figurine, rabbit eating, #1019.....45.00
Figurine, robin, 2½".....60.00
Figurine, seal, nose upturned, 4⅞".....200.00
Figurine, seated Dutch girl knitting/wearing hat, #1314-6".....185.00
Figurine, shepherd dog, begging, 8".....450.00
Figurine, Siamese cat, #3281, 8".....110.00
Figurine, sparrow, 4" L.....45.00
Figurine, turtle doves on branch w/leaves & florals, #402.....75.00
Figurine, young girl cradling doll, #1938.....115.00
Platter, Flora Danica, botancial specimen, 13".....715.00
Tureen, Flora Danica, botanical specimens, 13" W.....2,200.00
Urn, cigarette; #2688A.....22.00

Royal Copley

Royal Copley is a decorative type of pottery made by the Spaulding China Company in Sebring, Ohio, from 1939 to 1960. In addition to the Royal Copley mark, some pieces were also marked with the company's name.

When no condition is indicated, the items listed below are assumed to be in mint condition.

Bird figurine, 7½", $15.00.

Bank, piggy; bl, 6½".....25.00
Bank, piggy; brn, 5½".....22.00
Boot, wht w/gold trim top & base, florals, Spaulding, 6½".....8.00
Figurine, goldfinch on stump, 6½".....10.00
Figurine, mallard on stump, 8".....15.00
Figurine, Oriental boy w/lantern.....8.00
Pitcher, pears on beige, 8".....23.00
Planter, Balinese girl, paper label, 8½".....22.50
Planter, barefoot girl & boy, red outfit w/bl hat, 7½".....12.00
Planter, Blackamoor figure, paper label, 8½".....20.00
Planter, cat, 8".....14.00
Planter, deer & fawn, paper label, rectangular.....15.00
Planter, duck, game birds of America, 9½".....10.00
Planter, Oriental girl.....12.00
Planter, rooster, sgn.....15.00
Planter, running horse, horse on 1 side, paper label, 6".....12.50
Planter, teddy bear, 6½".....16.00
Shakers, hen & rooster, pr.....12.00
Vase, ivy, ftd, 8".....8.00
Vase, rooster, 7".....14.00
Wall pocket, Oriental girl w/hat.....15.00
Wall pocket, rooster.....12.50
Wall pocket, yel hat, lg.....12.00

Royal Crown Derby

In the latter years of the 1870s, a new firm, the Derby Crown Porcelain Company Ltd. began operations in Derby, England. Since 1890, when they were appointed Manufacturers of Porcelain to Her Majesty, their fine porcelain wares have been known as Royal Crown Derby. Their earliest wares were marked with a crown over 'Derby'; often a complicated dating code indicated the year of manufacture. After 1890, the 'Royal Crown Derby, England' mark was employed; in 1921, 'Made In England' was substituted in the wording. 'Bone China' was added after 1945.

When no condition is indicated, the items listed below are assumed to be in mint condition.

Bud vase, Imari, gourd shape, red mk, 3½".....75.00
Coffee pot, Imari, 2-pt.....400.00
Creamer & sugar bowl, Imari, Dublin shape, w/lid.....295.00
Creamer & sugar bowl, Imari, simple shape.....140.00
Cup & saucer, Imari.....80.00
Ewer, iris, dk bl/gold on wht, gilt twist hdl, 1890, 8½".....275.00
Pilgrim flask, red w/gilt lion masks, HP reserve, 1878, 8".....900.00
Pitcher, mc floral outlined in gold, cobalt bl, 1881, 6½".....225.00
Plate, Imari, 8¼".....69.00
Vase, orange/cobalt/much gold, bulbous, #1128, 4x2¾".....138.00
Vase, pink roses on wht, 2 gold hdls, 7½".....250.00

Royal Dux

The Duxer Porzellan Manufactur was established by E. Eichler in 1860. Located in what is now Duchcov, Czechoslovakia, the area was known as Dux, Bohemia, until WWI. The war brought about changes in both the style of the ware as well as the mark. Pre-war pieces were modeled in the Art Nouveau or Greek Classical manner, and marked with 'Bohemia' and a pink triangle containing the letter 'E.' They were usually matt glazed in green, brown, and gold. Better pieces were made of porcelain while the larger items were of pottery. After the war the ware was marked with the small pink triange, but without the Bohemia designation; 'Made in Czechslovakia' was added. The style became Art Deco, with cobalt blue a dominant color.

When no condition is indicated, the items listed below are assumed to be in mint condition.

Centerpiece, girl w/basket & goose, flower bowl base, 7x9".....125.00
Centerpiece, 2 entwined Nouveau maids standing, 20x18".....600.00
Figurine, boy & girl at well, pink triangle mk, 24", pr.....1,000.00
Figurine, Boy Harvester, pink triangle mk, 13".....175.00
Figurine, classical lady, Cupid on shoulder, 1900, 14".....400.00
Figurine, classical lady w/jug & bowl, satin, sgn, 20x6½".....475.00

Figurine, dancer, semi-nude, Art Deco, cobalt/gold, 9¾" 150.00
Figurine, dancing couple, floral dress, gilt, 1920s, 9" 150.00
Figurine, dancing lady/man w/violin, 1700s dress, 15", pr......800.00
Figurine, fawn, oak foliage, 8x11½" 110.00
Figurine, flamenco dancer, 1925, 11" 150.00
Figurine, girl in gold sailor suit, 1915, 7" 130.00
Figurine, girl w/shell at sides, pink triangle mk, 15x14" 350.00
Figurine, Greek potter, seated, 1900, 8" 195.00
Figurine, lady, bl/gold satin dress, 9¾" 275.00
Figurine, lady w/basket, sgn, 10¾" 325.00
Figurine, lady w/water jar & cup, 18" 300.00
Figurine, Nouveau maid w/lamp, gent w/hourglass, 15", pr.....750.00
Figurine, nude, pink triangle mk, 1940s, 8" 140.00
Figurine, peasant boy/girl, ca 1900, 13", pr 375.00
Figurine, shepherdess w/toga & sheepskin robe, goats, 14¾" ...300.00
Figurine, stallions, 1 galloping/1 rearing, 1900s, 11½x15" 250.00
Figurine, Tea Time, couple/table/dogs, bl/gold, 1940, 12x15" ...300.00
Figurine, Venus lies on seashell, pink triangle mk, 1900s 350.00
Jar, Art Nouveau maid character face, 9" 400.00
Vase, applied flowers/fruit, rose, 2-hdls, matt colors, 5" 85.00
Vase, beige/yel w/floral, hdls, 10½x7" 95.00
Vase, blown-out lady's face, hair forms hdls, gr swirl, 9" 225.00
Vase, Dutch girl by tree figural, pink triangle mk, 17" 375.00
Vase, flowers in high relief, ca 1900, 14" 130.00
Vase, full figure maid w/bow & arrow in relief, 14" 390.00
Vase, lady w/water jug at seaside, cream/tan/gr, 12", pr 595.00
Vase, sirens on waves, Nouveau, 17", pr 600.00
Vase, 2 maidens on rim, gray, pink triangle mk, 11½" 285.00

Royal Flemish

Royal Flemish was made from the late 1880s, and was patented in 1894 by the Mt. Washington Glass Company. Transparent glass was enameled with one or several colors, and the surface divided by a network of raised lines suggesting leaded glass work. Some pieces were further decorated with enameled florals, birds, or Roman coins.

When no condition is indicated, the items listed below are assumed to be in mint condition.

Cracker jar, coins front & bk, pink/mauve/maroon 1,500.00
Cracker jar, leaves/thistles, pink w/gold tracing, sq, 7½" 2,200.00
Cracker jar, lg roses decor 1,475.00
Lamp (drilled vase), 10 Guba ducks fly by sun, 11x7" vase...1,285.00
Pitcher, silver floral w/berry centers, clear hdl, 7x7¼" 1,950.00
Vase, floral, lav/gr/gold on opaque, #0583, 6" 1,600.00
Vase, jewels form florals in gold, no mk, lug hdls, EX 985.00
Vase, pansies w/gold border, gold fern bkground, 5¾x7" 1,750.00
Vase, serpent, falcon on bk, gold on red/tan, 10½" 3,500.00

Vase, pansies with gold border, gold fern background, 5¾" x 7", $1,750.00.

Royal Rudolstadt

The hard paste porcelain that has come to be known as Royal Rudolstadt was produced in Thuringia, Germany, in the early 18th century. Various names and marks have been associated with this pottery--one of the earliest was a hay fork symbol associated with Johann Frederich von Schwarzburg-Rudolstadt, one of the first founders. Variations, some that included an 'R,' were also used.

In 1854, Earnst Bohne produced wares that were marked with an anchor and the letters 'EB.' Wares commonly found today are those made during the late 1800s and early 20th century. These are usually marked with an 'RW' within a shield under a crown, and the words 'Crown Rudolstadt.' Items marked 'Germany' were made after 1890.

When no condition is indicated, the items listed below are assumed to be in mint condition.

Dresser set, violets, gold trim, 3-pc 125.00
Hair receiver, yel roses on yel, gold trim, crown mk, 4" 55.00
Lamp/vase, wht w/emb top/base trim, pink clover, hdls, 20" 95.00
Pitcher, bird/leaves, cream w/pastels, relief sgn, 8x5" 75.00
Plate, HP violets, wide gold border, LHS Germany, 8" 32.00
Plate, pastel roses, 8½" 30.00
Plate, roses, artist sgn, 6" 20.00
Plate, winter scene/ice man/sleigh, Prussia, steeple mk 52.50
Relish, HP floral, artist sgn, Prussia mk, 8¾" 20.00
Vase, HP pink roses, baluster shape, gold rim, 12" 75.00
Vase, tapestry, bl flowers on wht ground, low base, 7½x6" 250.00

Vase, Satsuma-style decoration, ca late 1880s, 9½", $325.00.

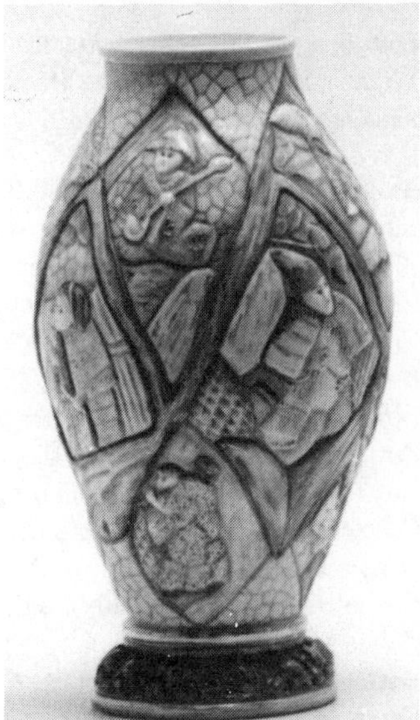

Royal Worcester

The Worcester Porcelain Company was deeded in 1751. During the first, or Dr. Wall period (so called for one of its proprietors), porcelain reflecting an Oriental influence was decorated in underglaze blue. Useful tablewares represented the largest portion of production, but figurines and decorative items were also made. Very little of the earliest wares were marked, and can only be identified by a study of forms, glazes, and the porcelain body which tends to transmit a greenish cast when held to light. Late in the fifties a crescent mark was in general use, and rare examples bare a facsimile of the Meissen crossed swords. The first period ended in 1783 and the company went through several changes in ownership during the next eighty years. The years from 1783-1792 are referred to as the Flight period. Marks were a small crescent, a crown with 'Royal,' or an impressed 'Flight.' From 1792-1807 the company was known as Flight and Barr, and used the trademark 'F&B' or 'B,' with or without a small cross. From 1807-1813 the company was under the Barr, Flight, and Barr management; this era is recognized as having produced porcelain of the highest quality of artistic decoration. Their mark was 'B.F.B.'

From 1813-1840 many marks were used, but the most usual was 'F.B.B.' under a crown, to indicate Flight, Barr and Barr. In 1840 the firm merged with Chamberlain; and in 1852 they were succeeded by Kerr and Binns. The firm became known as Royal Worcester in 1862.

Since 1930, Royal Worcester has been considered one of the leaders in the field of limited edition plates and figurines.

When no condition is indicated, the items listed below are assumed to be in mint condition.

Left to right: November, modeled by F.G. Doughty, 7¾″, $135.00; Goat Woman, modeled by Phoebe Stabler 6½″, $225.00; Grandmother's Dress, modeled by F.G. Doughty, 6½″, $135.00.

Basket, floral, gold trim, gr mk, 3½″ 120.00
Biscuit jar, beige/aqua w/relief pattern, gold, 1897, 6x5″ 195.00
Biscuit jar, daisies, emb swirls on beige, #1380, 1899, 7″ 240.00
Biscuit jar, daisies/fuchsias/sm flowers, SP top/lid, 1899 .... 240.00
Biscuit jar, floral, yel/lav on beige, SP fittings, 6x5″ 240.00
Bottle, scent; pansies on beige, gold, ball form, 1887, 4″ 225.00
Bowl, basketweave, figural girl & tree stump aside, 6″ 475.00
Bowl, Bengal tiger, scalloped/diapered, Tall-Davies, 11″ 1,000.00
Box, shell design, silver hdl/lid, sgn, 6x5½″ 375.00
Cake plate, baskets of roses/garlands, 1″ silver band, 11″ 125.00
Candle snuffer, Cook, pink w/wht apron, purple mk 75.00
Chocolate pot, floral, 4-ftd, 4 sides, 13″ 600.00
Coffee pot, floral, purple mk 225.00
Cornucopia, scroll base, florals, #1975, 1898, 7x5x6″ 325.00
Creamer, turq bands/floral garland/branch hdl, 18th C, 4⅝″ 200.00
Cup, flowers, beige, 3-hdl, 1891, 1¾″ 90.00
Cup & saucer, demitasse; bl/wht floral, ca 1884 .... 35.00
Cup & saucer, demitasse; florals, gold tracery 45.00
Cup & saucer, handleless; exotic bird/branch, 1700 .... 250.00
Cup & saucer, handleless; garden courting scenes, 1770, pr 600.00
Cup & saucer, Willow, B750, ca 1902 .... 25.00
Ewer, flowers & butterflies, beige, slim neck w/ring, 17½″ 750.00
Ewer, gold poppies/leaves/hdl/ft, vines/buds, 1887, 13″ 325.00
Ewer, purple floral on tan, gold trim, sgn, 9″ 275.00
Fairy light, water carrier, gilded, made for Clarke, 17″ 990.00
Figurine, bl Titmouse, base w/flowers & fruit, 3″ 60.00
Figurine, Bullfinch, on rock w/floral spray, 2¼″ 55.00
Figurine, Eastern Water Carrier, 20″, pr 1,900.00
Figurine, Friday's Child, boy w/bird, Nightengale 125.00
Figurine, girl/boy w/instruments, Egyptian dress, 15″, pr 1,200.00
Figurine, Goosie, Goosie, Gander, 5½″ 225.00
Figurine, Greenaway boy w/basket, 1893, 9x4¼″ 550.00
Figurine, John Bull, gold trim, 1903, 6¾x2½″ 425.00
Figurine, Joy, Sorrow, ea w/bird, satin, 1886, 9″, pr 895.00
Figurine, lady w/fishing basket, mc clothes, #1202, 8″ 400.00
Figurine, Little Boy Blue, lying by sheep 100.00
Figurine, London Cry, cucumbers, purple mk, Parnell, #3227 .... 225.00
Figurine, Merry New Song, purple mk, Parnell, 1938, #3252 .... 225.00
Figurine, Mischief, F Doughty 100.00
Figurine, Peter Pan w/rabbit, seated, 8″ 250.00
Figurine, rabbit w/basket on back, #2514, 1911, 4¾x2¼″ 450.00
Figurine, robin, base w/flowers & fruit, 3″ 60.00
Figurine, Scotsman, gold trim, 1903, 6x2⅝″ 425.00
Figurine, Sorrow, mc glaze, 9″ 200.00
Figurine, Thursday's Child, girl, Doughty, #3260 .... 125.00
Figurine, Two Babies, F Doughty 105.00
Figurine, Wednesday's Child 115.00
Figurine, Wind Girl, red hair, b/w costume, gr mk, 5½″ 250.00
Figurine, Yankee, gold trim, 1906, 6¾x2¼″ 425.00
Figurine, 1st Cuckoo, FG Doughty, 6½″ 185.00
Figurine, 3 hounds, Doris Lindner, #3132, 1930, rare 500.00
Jar, spice; floral medallions on cobalt scale, 18th C, 6½″ 550.00
Leaf dish, florals, ca 1760, 10½″ L 550.00
Mansion house, encrusted roof, 3 chimneys, 6″ dia base, 5″ 4,700.00
Mug, holly on tan, 1892, 3¼″ 75.00
Pilgrim flask, Japanese style/geese/ornate hdls, 1878, 20″ 1,200.00
Pilgrim flask, stork/bamboo relief, lt bl/wht, 1890, 8½″ 550.00
Pitcher, florals, elephant head hdl, #418, 6½″ 275.00
Pitcher, florals, gold trim, #1587, 1902, 6x2⅛″ 135.00
Pitcher, leaf mold, leaf hdl, tan/gr w/gold trim, 1903, 7″ 225.00
Pitcher, red bird on ivory, high glaze, sgn, 1911, 3¼″ 200.00
Pitcher, red/gold mums front/bk, ornate hdl, 1886, 6¼″ 175.00
Plate, rabbit/flying geese, cobalt foliage, 1882, 10″ 150.00
Plate, tiger & hounds, 3 rim reserves, ca 1815, EX 650.00
Platter, Blue Willow, oval, 10½″ 30.00
Salt dip, pheasants, artist sgn 150.00
Sauce boat, leaf form, branch hdls, florals, Dr Wall, 9″ 350.00
Soup plate, cobalt scalloped border/floral center, Dr Wall 245.00
Sugar shaker, girl w/hat figural, #1103, 7½x2¾″ 450.00
Teapot, fruit on rust & tan, gilt spout/finial, sgn, 4½″ 180.00
Teapot & stand, Lord Henry Thynne Service, 1770, 5½″ 1,000.00
Thimble, bird on ivory ground 125.00
Toothpick, floral, 3 hdls 95.00
Vase, dbl retic top, reserves: gold birds/butterflies, 7½″ 950.00
Vase, floral, basket shape w/rope hdl, 1893, 5½″ 225.00

Vase, floral, four claw feet, #206862/1639, 8¾″, $750.00.

Vase, floral, gold dragon hdl, 8″ 345.00
Vase, floral, gold trim, ped ft, 1913, 4x2x5½″ 160.00
Vase, floral, 7″ globe body, ftd, fluted/flared, 1880, 16″ 600.00
Vase, fruit in reserve on cobalt, gilt, Chivers, 1903, 3½″ 450.00
Vase, gold relief mums/bees, masks front/bk, dog hdls, 14″ 750.00
Vase, wicker, bl w/pink floral, ftd, 1873, 8¼″ 450.00
Waste bowl, Lord Henry Thynne Service, 1700, 6½″ 1,600.00

Roycroft

Near the turn of the century, Elbert Hubbard established the Roycroft Printing Shop in East Aurora, New York. Named in honor of two 17th century printer-bookbinders, the print shop was just the beginning of a community called Roycroft, which came to be known world-wide. Hubbard became a popular personality of the early 1900s, known for his talents in a variety of areas, from writing and lecturing to manufacturing. The Roycroft community became a meeting place for people of various capabilities, and included shops for the production of furniture, copper, leather items, and a multitude of other wares which were marked with the Roycroft symbol, an 'R' within a circle below a stylized cross. Hubbard lost his life on the Lucitania in 1915; production in the community continued until the Depression.

When no condition is indicated, the items listed below are asssumed to be in mint condition.

Ash tray, hammered copper, bowl shape, crimped rim, 6½″ W 65.00
Book, Book of Roycrofter, autographed, 1907 .... 35.00
Book, Last Ride, Robert Browning, vellum w/silk straps 200.00
Book, Little Journeys, +guide, hard cover, set of 14 .... 95.00
Book, No Enemy But Himself, E Hubbard, 1934 .... 14.00
Book, Philosophy, 1930 .... 25.00
Book, Sesame & Lilies, J Ruskin, cloth spine, sgn Hubbard 165.00
Book, Wm Morris, by Elbert Hubbard, emb suede, 8¾x5½″ 35.00
Bookends, copper, triangles w/incurvate sides, 4½″ 55.00
Bookends, hammered copper, open frame style w/decor, 8½″ 60.00
Bookmark, suede leather, fringed, Build Strong/sgn, 11″ 35.00
Box, hammered copper, brass/stud detail, rectangle, lid, 8″ 225.00
Bud vase, glass flower tube, brass finish, 8¼″ 85.00
Candlestick, hammered brass, disk ft, slim std, 8″, pr 220.00
Candlestick, hammered brass, 2-lite, 8-side base, 9″ W, pr 150.00
Chamberstick, brass finish, ftd, open scroll hdl, 2¼″, pr 50.00
Desk set, hammered brass, blotter/inkwell/letter holder/fr 190.00
Frame, brass finish, standing, 5x3″ 55.00
Humidor, copper, flange holds 6 pipes, 6x8″ 80.00
Lamp, hammered copper, dome shade, slim std, 18″ 435.00

Lamp, copper with Steuben gold iridescent glass shade, ca 1910, 16″ diameter, 10″ high, $1,400.00.

Notebook, hard cover, 1927 .... 25.00
Notebook, soft cover, 1927 .... 15.00
Plate, logo center front, 8″ 85.00
Poster, Philistine, sgn Dwight Collins, 18½x10½″ 150.00
Sconce, wall mt, arrowhead form, brass washed, no mk, 8″ 80.00
Scrapbook, 1921 .... 25.00
Tray, card; #1107, 2x8¾″ 85.00
Tray, copper, octagonal, dbl hdls, logo sgn, 15″ W 140.00
Tray, hammered brass over copper, octagonal w/hdls, 9¾″ dia 85.00
Vase, Am Beauty, hammered copper, stick neck, 12¼″ 350.00
Vase, Am Beauty, hammered copper, strap/stud detail, 12″ 225.00
Vase, Am Beauty, 19″ 775.00
Vase, hammered brass, 4⅝″ 85.00
Vase, hammered copper, bulbous, 5″ 115.00
Vase, hammered copper, compressed body, waisted neck, 4″ 85.00
Vase, hammered copper, emb band, cylindrical, 5″ 120.00
Vase, hammered copper, scalloped flared rim, 5½″ 85.00
Vase, hammered copper/silvered band, cylindrical, #203, 6″ 485.00
Wall sconce, hammered copper, #402, 8¾″, pr 185.00

Rozenburg

Some of the most innovative and original of Art Nouveau ceramics were created by the Rozenberg factory at The Hague in The Netherlands, between 1885 and 1916. Some pieces are similar to Gouda. Rozenburg also made highly-prized, very thin eggshell pieces, eagerly sought after by collectors. T.A.C. Colenbrander was their artistic leader, with J. Schelling and J. Kok designing many of the eggshell pieces.

Bud vase, pastel spring flowers, Van Rossum/Schelling, 3½″ 350.00
Cup, chickens & florals, sgn Schelling, 2¼″ 400.00
Cup & saucer, floral on white eggshell 800.00
Ginger jar, floral, polychrome, w/lid, 20″ 850.00
Vase, bombe; lav/gr floral, eggshell, 2-hdl, 1900, 11″ 2,600.00
Vase, bud & flowers, eggshell, sq baluster, 14″ 1,650.00
Vase, dancing Dutch boy designs, 4 sm hdls, 12″ 700.00
Vase, ear hdls, Colenbrander, 10x9½″, pr 750.00
Vase, flower & parrot, eggshell, sq baluster, 9½″ 1,450.00
Vase, mc flowers, Schelling, 2-hdl, 10½″ 650.00
Vase, yel iris on ogee panel baluster form, Schelling, 10″ 1,600.00

Rubena

Rubena glass was made by several firms in the late 1800s. It is a blown art glass that shades from clear to red.

When no condition is indicated, the items listed below are assumed to be in mint condition.

Bottle, scent; clear panels & faceted stopper, 5⅜x1¾″ 75.00
Bottle, scent; stippled, gold trim, faceted stopper, 6⅝″ 95.00
Condiment set, cut panels, 3 bottles, SP holder, 5¾″ 170.00
Ewer, frosted, eng floral/bow, gold-washed pewter mts, 13″ 140.00
Jelly dish, crimped edge, threaded, triangular, SP holder 165.00
Muffineer, cut diagonal stripes, SP top, sq, 6½″ 135.00
Pitcher, Inverted T'print, ground pontil, water sz 250.00
Pitcher, optic, HP flowers, applied clear hdl, water sz 185.00
Sugar shaker, cut panels, 5¾″ 70.00
Tumbler, Herringbone, satin/cased 135.00
Tumbler, Inverted T'print w/enamel decor, 5″ 65.00
Vase, pnt w/in & w/out, deep scalloped top, 7x9½″ 225.00
Vase, 2″ dia at rim, 10″ 48.00

Rubena Verte

Rubena Verte glass was introduced in the late 1800s by Hobbs, Brockunier and Company, of Wheeling, West Virginia. Its transparent colors shade from red to green.

When no condition is indicated, the items listed below are assumed to be in mint condition.

Finger bowl, threaded....80.00
Pitcher, pnt apple blossoms & butterfly, gr hdl, 6″....325.00
Pitcher, ground pontil, verde hdl....250.00
Pitcher, pnt floral, reed hdl, bulbous, Mt WA, 6″....325.00
Tumbler, 10-Row Hobnail, 4″....225.00
Vase, enameled lady decor, goblet form, 6¾″....225.00

Ruby Stained Souvenirs

Ruby flashed or stained glass was made by the application of a thin layer of color over clear. It was used in the manufacture of some early pressed tableware and from the Victorian era well into the 20th century for souvenir items which were often engraved on the spot with the date, location, and buyer's name.

When no condition is indicated, the items listed below are assumed to be in mint condition.

Berry set, Thumbprint, boat shape, 7-pc....195.00
Butter dish, Fleur-de-lis, no gold....110.00
Castor set, Thumbprint, 4-bottles....300.00
Celery, Co-op Block....45.00
Creamer, Button Arches, 4″....32.00
Creamer, Sunk Honeycomb, name/1908, 4½″....27.00
Goblet, Ruby Thumbprint....30.00
Mug, Button Arches....30.00
Mug, Lacy Medallion....22.50
Mug, Sunken Honeycomb, 1907....22.00
Pitcher, Button Arches, 2½″....18.50
Pitcher, Ivy in Snow, 5½″....65.00
Pitcher, Lacy Medallion, 2¼″....17.50
Pitcher, tankard; Thumbprint, 8½″....85.00
Pitcher, water; Pleating....95.00
Shakers, Bull's Eye, pr....35.00
Spooner, Spearpoint Band, frosted, gold....50.00
Sugar bowl, Loop & Drop....65.00
Toothpick, Heart Band....25.00
Toothpick, King's Crown....35.00
Tumbler, Arched Oval....27.50
Tumbler, Diamond w/Peg....30.00
Tumbler, Heart Band....20.00
Tumbler, Loop & Drop....30.00
Water set, Button Arches, gold & frosted band, 7-pc....195.00

Rugs

When no condition is indicated, the items listed below are assumed to be in excellent condition.

Key:
comp—complimentary
dia—diamond
gb—guard border
med—medallion
s/a—semi-antique

Hooked

Hooked rugs are treasured today for their folk art appeal. It was a craft that was introduced to this county in about 1830 and flourished its best in the New England states. The prime consideration is not age, but artistic appeal. Scenes with animals, buildings, and people; patriotic designs; or whimsical themes are preferred. Condition is, of course, also a factor. Marked examples bearing the stamps of 'Frost and Co.,' 'Abenakee,' 'C.R.,' and 'Ouia' are highly prized.

Hooked rag rug, folk art design with running horse, scalloped and polka-dot border, very good color, minor repair and wear, 25″ x 42″, $1,250.00.

Rag, bl/red snowflake & flowers on wht ground, stain, 26x36″..225.00
Rag, cat, blk/orange on salmon/gr ottoman, rpr, 28½x45″....220.00
Rag, cat & 3 kittens w/ball of yarn, dia border, 24x35½″....725.00
Rag, checkerboard, blk w/mc stripes, braided edge, 30x42″....85.00
Rag, checkerboard of mc stripes, braided edge, 34x69″....95.00
Rag, deer leaps over waves, stylized, 25x47″, VG....275.00
Rag, dog, gr/brn, olive border w/stripes, 17½x38½″....150.00
Rag, dog, stylized, abstract bkground, wear/fading, 28x44″...1,000.00
Rag, floral, colors good, primitive, mid-1800s, 22x34″....110.00
Rag, floral, mc bkground, mc zigzag border, 31x40″....375.00
Rag, floral w/in scroll reserve, mc on bl, 24x43″....115.00
Rag, floral w/mc roses, stylized foliage border, 36x79″....165.00
Rag, floral w/red & gold circles, mc border, 32x37″....195.00
Rag, geometric, gr/red/wht floral, fringed ends, 19x44″....35.00
Rag, geometric, very colorful, unused, 25x36″....140.00
Rag, geometric leaf in all colors, lt bl bkground, 24½x73″....80.00
Rag, geometric w/many colors, wear, 27x42″....55.00
Rag, girl w/bonnet, b/w bkground w/orange flowers, 23x37″....230.00
Rag, girl w/umbrella, gray/brn/orange bkground, 23x44″....235.00
Rag, grid of 4-lobe medallions/cherries, mc on tan, 70x36″....115.00
Rag, intricate interlocking medallions, mc, 28x46″....165.00
Rag, kittens in basket, mc, 40x25″....250.00
Rag, lg farmhouse/barn/gr lawn/flowers, ca 1930, 40x61″....1,430.00
Rag, limb w/oak leaves & 8 butterflies, bl & brn, 26x36″....165.00
Rag, lion & serpent, scrolled reserve, late 1800s, 29x68″....660.00
Rag, owl on limb, yel bkground, red/blk/wht border, 30x56″...600.00
Rag, reindeer w/antlers, stars/moon, early 1900s, 23x23″....330.00
Rag, rooster, yel & bl w/red comb, faded/wear, 25½x44″....800.00
Rag, roses & lilies, gold/brn leaf scrolls, wear, 25x39″....50.00
Rag, running horse, floral border, beige bkground, 42x46″...1,700.00
Rag, running horse, scalloped border, 25x42½″....1,250.00
Rag, scottie, blk, buff w/red collar, fence/floral, 40x27″....165.00
Rag, stylized scene w/palm trees in all colors, 28½x38½″....165.00
Rag, stylized sheep, mc zigzag border, 24½x35½″....115.00
Rag, 2 deer & swans in stream, cabin & trees, 1923, 43x30″...285.00
Rag, 2 wht geese, scalloped border, worn/rpr, 27½x50″....325.00
Rag/yarn, lion on cliff above water, wood fr, 28x42″....325.00

Rag/yarn, stylized floral center w/4 lg gr leaves, 21x35″........85.00
Rag/yarn, stylized flowering trees, scallop border, 26x36″.......90.00
Runner, rag, geometric floral in many colors, 20x140″........175.00
Runner, rag, striped squares w/herringbone zigzag, 36x120″...400.00
Yarn, checkerboard, beige & cream w/designs, 72x108″.......700.00
Yarn, stylized floral, red/blk/bl/brn/beige, 47x72″.............135.00

Oriental

The Oriental and Eastern rug market has enjoyed a renewal of interest in recent years, as collectors have become aware of the fact that some of the semi-antique rugs (those sixty to one hundred years old) may be had at a price within the range of the average buyer.

Akstafa, star med w/in link-crab border, rpr, 116x46″.......3,750.00
Belouchistan, lobed med in bird/flower motif, 67x36″.........800.00
Belouchistan, red/brn hooked med on ivory, 47x32″........1,500.00
Bijar, turtle-shaped medallion w/spandrels, 41x70″..........1,300.00
Caucasian, mat, red & bl w/camel hair, wear/rpr, 22x33″......230.00
Caucasian, mc, 36x50″..................................290.00
Chi Chi, sm dk bl cartouches w/mc flowerheads, 58x51″.....3,600.00
Chinese, peony/meandering vines, bl border, 93x61″........1,300.00
Esari, bl w/lg S-panel+2 on ivory, flat mc skirts, 41x37″.....2,000.00
Gendje, gold w/mc palmettes, flower/vine gb, 102x41″.......2,750.00
Gorovan, trimmed & rebound borders, wear & rpr, 75x144″...300.00
Iranian, serebend center, VG color, 53x83″..................900.00
Iranian, serebend center, 25x31″..........................135.00
Kashmir, medallions on red, comtemporary, 42x108″.........325.00
Kazak, red/bl on bl, minor wear, 50x81″....................900.00
Khotan, persimmon w/dl bl/gr rosettes, wave border, 60x37″..1,100.00
Kirman, floral in pink/wht/brn on bl, 24x37″................225.00
Kuba, floral motifs in mc barberpole border, gbs, 52x46″....4,000.00
Kuba, florals w/human & animals, dragon border, 94x43″....3,000.00
Lesghi, bl w/4-color stars/med border in gr/red gb, 58x47″...3,000.00
Lillihan, floral on wine, minor wear, 37x50″...................700.00
Mahal, geometric floral w/deer in ea corner, 24x41″..........350.00
Pakistan Bokhara, modern, handmade, wool, 24x37″.........145.00
Perpedil, ram's horns in leaf/flowerhead border, 45x34″......2,800.00
Persian, mc floral in red/bl/gr on ivory bkground, 24x50″......100.00
Persian, medallion on red, minor wear, 48x67″..............175.00
Persian, pictorial in bl/wht/camel/brn/gr, 55x76″............475.00
Pillar, Chinese, 2 Tibetan monks, wave end panel, 94x57″...2,000.00

Sarouk Oriental rug, deep red ground with allover floral design of sprays, three borders have flowers and two border stripes have dogtooth pattern, 41″ x 57″, excellent condition, $600.00.

Prayer, Afgan, brn arch, wine mihrab w/mc responds, 84x39″.1,800.00
Prayer, Akstafa, hooked motif trellis, 66x34″...............1,600.00
Prayer, Bordjalou Kazak, dia med, running dog gb, 46x41″..1,500.00
Prayer, Melas, 3 dia latchook motifs in arch, 48x42″.........4,500.00
Qashqa'i, serrated dia medallion, palm/leaf border, 82x51″...5,800.00
Sarouk, floral medallion on dk bl, 24x240″................1,200.00
Sarouk, floral on deep salmon red, 70x140″.................800.00
Sarouk, red/gold/bl/blk, some wear/replaced fringe, 51x77″.....350.00
Serab, runner, medallions/horsemen/birds, 144x44″.........1,600.00
Shirvan, exotic animals/men, silk highlights, 60x50″.........3,000.00
Shirvan, floral rosettes, dragon border, floral gb, 62x50″.....2,500.00
Shirvan, trellis of serrated cartouches, 53x42″.............2,500.00
Shirvan Marasali pictorial, ¾ female portrait, 61x50″........7,000.00
Throne, Chinese, brn w/dragons w/in symbol border, 25x27″..1,250.00
Turkoman Bokhara, worn, 84x108″.........................175.00
Veramin, floral spray lattice, flat woven skirt, 143x50″.......2,000.00

Miscellaneous

Amana Colonies, earth tones, cotton, early 1800s, 57x26″......50.00
Amana Colonies, mc bands, cotton, early 1900s, 81x32″.......75.00
Amish, wool rags, blk/gray/rust/wine/gr/tan, '20s, 48x38″........55.00
Carpet, rag, PA, stripes, unused, 3 pcs make 9x12 ft.........435.00
Felt, hand woven, blk/mc strips, early 20th C, 58x25″..........70.00
Loomed, cotton rags, narrow & thick bands, 1930s, 73x27″.....80.00
Penny, wool/felt w/yarn fringe, wear/faded, 23x38″............165.00

Rumrill

During the early 1930s, the Red Wing Union Stoneware Company of Red Wing, Minnesota, produced pottery for George Rumrill of Little Rock, Arkansas. Rumrill not only designed the ware, but marketed it as well. In 1938 when the Shawnee Pottery Company of Zanesville, Ohio, submitted a lower bid, he awarded the contract to them, and they continued to manufacture decorative pottery for Rumrill until the early forties. His designs can be identified by the 'RumRill' mark or label.

When no condition is indicated, the items listed below are assumed to be in mint condition.

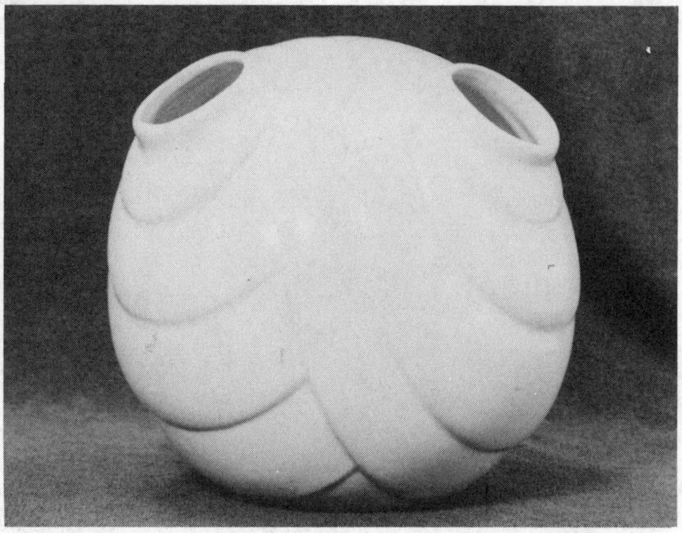

Vase, Art Deco draping, white with three openings, 5¾″, $45.00.

Bookends, polar bear, blk matt, 1930s.......................55.00
Ewer/vase, hdl, #195.....................................20.00
Pitcher, bl spatter, tilt ball, ice lip, 7″........................18.00
Planter, wishing well figural, wall hanging....................30.00

Vase, dk rose, 4½″ 10.00
Vase, fan shape, mottled bl, #522, 6¼″ 12.00
Vase, gr, ribbed, hdls, 7½″ 18.50
Vase, incised Grecian figures, wht slip/gr, hdl, mk/#d, 8″ 50.00
Vase, ribbed, gr, hdls, 7½″ 18.50

Russel Wright Dinnerware

Russel Wright, one of America's foremost industrial engineers, also designed several lines of ceramic dinnerware which are today becoming popular collectibles. His first line, American Modern, was manufactured by Steubenville Pottery Company from 1939 until 1959. It was produced in a variety of solid colors, in assortments chosen to stay attune with the times.

In 1944, he designed his Iroquois line. Due in part to its thick and heavy styling, it is more easily found today than American Modern which was prone to damage easily. The earlier examples of Iroquois were heavily mottled, while later pieces were smoothly glazed. The ware was marked with Wright's signature and 'China by Iroquois.' It was marketed in fine department stores throughout the country. After 1950, the line was restyled and marked 'Iroquois China by Russel Wright.'

When no condition is indicated, the items listed below are assumed to be in mint condition.

American Modern

Bowl, salad 25.00
Bowl, vegetable; divided 25.00
Bowl, vegetable; oval 15.00
Bowl, vegetable; 11½″ 15.00
Bowl, vegetable; 9¾″ 10.00
Butter dish 65.00
Casserole w/hdl 25.00
Celery dish 12.50
Chop plate, 13″ 15.00
Creamer & sugar 17.50
Cup & saucer, demitasse 35.00
Gravy boat 12.00
Lug fruit 7.50
Lug soup 5.00
Mug 35.00
Pitcher, water; 11″ 25.00
Plate, 10″ 6.00
Plate, 6″ 2.00
Plate, 8″ 4.00
Saucer 1.50
Shakers, pr 10.00
Sherbet, stemmed 17.00
Sugar bowl, w/lid 7.00
Teapot, demitasse 30.00
Teapot, w/lid 38.00
Tumbler, juice 25.00
Wine 16.50

Iroquois

Bowl, cereal, w/lid 8.00
Bowl, fruit; 5½″ 5.00
Bowl, soup; flat 9.50
Bowl, vegetable; divided, bl, 10″ 10.00
Bowl, vegetable; 8″ 14.00
Butter dish 50.00
Casserole, divided, w/lid, lg 24.00
Casserole, w/lid, lg 20.00
Coffee server, individual, w/lid, 4½″ 35.00

Ash tray, gray, $55.00.

Creamer, stacking 5.00
Creamer & sugar, lipped, w/lid 14.50
Cup & saucer 6.00
Pitcher, juice; 1½-qt 25.00
Plate, bread & butter, 6″ 3.00
Plate, dinner; 10″ 6.00
Plate, salad, 7″ 4.00
Platter, 12¾″ 15.00
Platter, 14½″ 20.00
Sugar bowl, stacking 7.50
Wine carafe 40.00

Russian Art

Before the Revolution in 1917, many jewelers and craftsmen created exquisite marvels of their arts, distinctive in the extravagent detail of their enamel work, jeweled inlays, and use of precious metals. These treasures aptly symbolized the glitter and the romance of the glorious days under the reign of the Tsars of Imperial Russia.

The most famous of these master jewelers was Peter Carl Faberge. Following the tradition of his father, he took over the Faberge workshop in 1870 at the age of twenty-four. His specialties were enamel work, clockwork automated figures, carved animal and human figures of precious or semiprecious stone, and his best-known creations, the Imperial Easter Eggs, each with an entirely different design.

By the turn of the century, his influence had spread to other countries, and his work was revered by royalty and the very wealthy. The onset of the war marked the end of the era.

When no condition is indicated, the items listed below are assumed to be in mint condition.

Belt buckle, neillo, dagger closure on chain, 84 mk, 1890 .... 165.00
Box, horse-drawn sleigh/figures, 84 silver assay mk, 4″ 325.00
Box, lacquerware w/HP scenic lid, 3x7x11″ 450.00
Bronze, lady pirate, A Gratcheff, Woerffell casting, 9½″ 2,500.00
Chamberstick, copper, hallmarked, 4¼″ 125.00
Chess set, porc, Communists/Capitalists, 1934, 32-pc 660.00
Cup, dessert; porc, gr/bl, w/underliner, 2-hdl, ca 1893 .... 50.00
Napkin ring, lacquerware w/HP scene 125.00
Pendant, dagger & sheath, neillo silver, 84 mk, 2-pc, 3x2″ 30.00
Pitcher, hammered brass w/copper rivets, mk FN, 6¼x2½″ 45.00
Print, Cavalier & Young Girl, Kossak, mat, 1857, 19″ 25.00
Print, Portrait of Prince AM Golitzin, heliogravure, 20″ 20.00

Samovar, brass, hallmarked, 7¼" 175.00
Spoon, silver w/enamel, sgn Sazikov 250.00
Spoon, silver-gilt, opaque & translucent enamel, intricate 185.00
Teacup, thin porc w/bl/gr geometric, Kornilow Bros 45.00
Teapot, porc, bl/red decor, Russian crest mk/Kornilow Bros 25.00
Tray, brass, hallmarked, w/hdls, 9" 90.00
Trav. copper, hammered, hallmarked, w/hdls, 16" 125.00

Bowl, multicolored enameling on silver, signed Ohcunnikov, 3½", $1,000.00.

Sabino

Sabino art glass was produced by Marius-Ernest Sabino in France during the 1920s and thirties. It was made in opalescent, frosted, and colored glass, and was designed to reflect the Art Deco style of that era. In 1960, using molds he modeled by hand, Sabino once again began to produce art glass using a special formula he himself developed that was characterized by a golden opalescence. Although the family continued to produce glassware for export after his death in 1971, they were never able to duplicate Sabino's formula.

When no condition is indicated, the items listed below are assumed to be in mint condition.

Box, ring; lg 225.00
Butterfly, wings open, sm 26.00
Chick, drinking 45.00
Chick, jumping 45.00
Dog, Pekingese, sm 19.00
Dove, head down, sm 19.00
Dove: Le Boulant, lg 295.00
Dove: Palombe, lg 295.00
Dove: Ramier, lg 295.00
Fish, #3, sm 19.50
Hen 27.00
Knife rest, butterfly 45.00
Lady & doves 315.00
Madonna, rnd base, sm, 3" 30.00
Madonna w/halo, lg 210.00
Mockingbird, lg, 6x4¼" 79.00
Nude silhouette 160.00
Owl, 4½" 65.00
Panthers group 465.00
Right hand 195.00
Snail, open top, sgn 65.00
Stork 150.00
Tray, sm butterfly, rnd 69.00
Tray, thistle, 4" dia 32.00
Turkey 27.00
Vase, beehive 210.00
Venus de Milo, sm, 2¾" 25.00

Salesman's Samples and Patent Models

Salesman's samples and patent models are often mistaken for toys or homemade folk art pieces. They are instead actual working models made by very skilled craftsmen who worked as model makers. Patent models were made until the early 1900s. After that, the patent office no longer required a model to grant a patent. Often the name of the inventor or the model maker and the date it was built is noted on the patent model. Salesman's samples were occasionally made by model makers, but more often by an employee of the company. These usually carry advertising messages to boost the sale of the product. Though they are still in use today, the most desirable examples date from the 1800s to about 1945.

When no condition is indicated, the items listed below are assumed to be in excellent condition.

Baby bottle, Evenflo, 2½" 12.00
Bowl, crockery, 3½" dia 22.00
Burial vault, self-sealing, wht porc, 3x6½x2½" 125.00
Calling card folio, Victorian 25.00
Chest, oak, 2 over 3 drawer, orig hdw, English, 14x12x9½" 325.00
Clothes wringer, wood & iron 60.00
Coffee grinder, Daisy 60.00
Coffee grinder, red pnt on CI, works, 4" 95.00
Corn planter, 2-row, patent model 610.00
Corn silo 110.00
Cultivator, 1-row, riding, M 250.00
Disc, riding, single 275.00
Domino set, wood & bone, in mahog violin case, 6" 185.00
Gaming wheel on stand, early, sgn, rare, 12" 330.00
Harrow, riding, w/carry case 210.00
Harrow, spike-tooth; patent model 55.00
Hatchet, early shield logo 200.00
Hay baler, horse powered, patent model 450.00
Hay loader, patent model 125.00
Hay mower, riding, Buckeye 725.00
Hay rake, riding, dumper, w/carry case 550.00
Horseshoe, brass snowcleat, miniature 36.00
Ice cream freezer, Wht Mountain Jr 195.00
Ice tongs 25.00
Neon light, bl star, in carrying case 70.00
Plow, sulky; riding, patent model 275.00
Plow, walking; patent model 75.00
Pole building, US Steel, orig wood box 225.00
Reaper, Buckeye, needs repair 925.00
Road grader, Adams 450.00
Safe, tin, combination dial/thick walls, 1901, 18x15" 700.00
Seltzer bottle, crystal, 4" 36.00
Skillet, CI w/blk enamel, 4" 20.00
Stove, Bucks #2 Junior, 42-lb, 24x12x18" 750.00
Stove, Spark, potbelly, orig grates/poker/lid/hdl, 14x8" 395.00
Stove w/griddle, skillet, 2 buckets, CI, Gem, 5" 75.00
Trunk, leather, hand-wrought hdw, John Clement's label, 8" 65.00
Tub, ftd, CI, Wolff 30.00
Weathervane, horse, molded tin/brass rod, Alby Co, 8½" 155.00
Windmill, Mast & Foos 325.00

Ladder, wood and metal, marked FLMACo Mfg. Corp., patent #2743049, 12", $185.00.

Windmill, Toleado, 1875 . . . . 200.00
Window lock 32.00
Wood roller, horse-drawn, patent model 45.00
Work bench w/vise, saw/plane/etc, wood 150.00
Work gloves, rubber 20.00

Saloon Memorabilia

The period between the Civil War and the onset of the prohibition era in 1919 furnishes the most charming and collectible examples of early saloon memorabilia. Photographs of early establishments, beer steins, advertising signs, and 'bar room nude' portraits are only a few of the varied items from the Golden Age of saloons that are popular with today's collectors.

When no condition is indicated, the items listed below are assumed to be in excellent condition.

Bottle, back bar; Brandy, leaf design, bevelled glass, 10" 90.00
Bottle, back bar; cut Irish Colbreth Whiskey, w/stopper 108.00
Bottle, back bar; cut/gold Briar Grove Whiskey, cylinder 80.00
Bottle, back bar; etched Cedarhurst Whiskey, fluted neck 90.00
Bottle, back bar; etched Gin, w/stopper, EX 90.00
Bottle, back bar; etched Rum, leaf design, cylinder, 11" 62.00
Bottle, back bar; etched/gold Mt Vernon Whiskey, cylinder 90.00
Bottle, back bar; gold Royal Arms, coat of arms/shield 90.00
Bottle, back bar; IW Harper 55.00
Bottle, back bar; Lewis, #66 . . . . 65.00
Bottle, back bar; wht enamel/script Fortuna, cylinder, EX 80.00
Bottle, back bar; wht enamel/script Michelson's Brandy 90.00
Bottle, back bar; wht enamel/script Rye, cylinder, 11", EX 80.00
Bottle, whiskey; decanter style, silver, w/stopper, 10" 79.00
Clock, Old Mr Boston, shape of whiskey bottle, b/w, 23x10" 75.00
Corkscrew, bar mt, Saratoga Victoria Natural Water 165.00
Dice cup, Hotel International, leather, old, 4x2½" 15.00
Dispenser, Dry Sherry, barrel shape, mc bird/foilage, 13" 350.00
Ice shaver, Clawson, early 700.00
Ice shaver, Worth Bros, w/brass blade, CI, 7x2x2" 7.00
Painting, dogs cheating at cards, wood fr, 19½x14½" 62.00
Photo, 3 men drinking w/bartender, 8x10" 79.00
Plate, bar scene, gold/brn Art Nouveau edge, Vienna, 10" 55.00
Print, Beer Saloon in Bottle Alley, Harpers, ½ pg, 1880 . . . . 5.00
Print, skeleton serves man, woodcut, Harper's, March 1874 . . . . . 92.00
Sign, Gents Shaving & Saloon, 2-sided, wood, wht, 30" 138.00

Salt Glaze

As early as the 1600s, potters used common salt to glaze their stoneware. This was accomplished by heating the salt, and introducing it into the kiln at maximum temperature. The resulting gray-white glaze was a thin, pitted surface that resembled the peel of an orange.

When no condition is indicated, the items listed below are assumed to be in mint condition.

Creamer, flowers & eagle emb, bl striping, Castleford, 4½" 60.00
Pitcher, Argyle, bl/gray, raised registry mk, 7⅞x3¾" 75.00
Pitcher, Gothic lattice w/ivy emb, wht, registry mk, 9¾" 35.00
Pitcher, Gypsy, Jones & Wally, dtd 1842, 9¾" 115.00
Pitcher, leaves & grain emb, rope hdl, wht, Cobridge, 10" 75.00
Pitcher, lg flower emb on each side, bl, Victorian, 9½" 95.00
Pitcher, robed lady w/sword, 2nd w/bowl, lt bl, 1899, 9" 125.00
Pitcher, Scottish tavern scene, man on horse, Ridgway, 7¾" 70.00
Pitcher, soldiers/hawks emb, gray, Ridgway/Abington, 7" 118.00
Pitcher, storks feed on acorns in cattails, emb, 7" 75.00
Pitcher, tankard; acorn/maidens emb, wht/bl, Dudson, 6¾" 65.00
Teapot, oval w/leaf & vine decor, slide-on lid, #22, 6x10" 100.00
Vase, Opening Leaves, emb, 5¾" 45.00

Salts

Before salt became refined, processed, and 'free-flowing' as we know it today, it was necessary to serve it in a 'cellar.' An innovation of the early 1800s, the master salt cellar was placed by the host and passed from person to person. Smaller 'individual' salts were a part of each place setting. A small silver spoon was used to sprinkle it onto the food.

The screw top salt shaker was invented by John Mason in 1858. In 1871, when salt became more refined, some ceramic shakers were molded with pierced tops. 'Christmas' shakers, so called because of their December 25, 1877, patent date, were fitted with a rotary agitator designed to break up any lumps in the salt. They were produced by the Boston and Sandwich Glass Company in various colors. Today much of the interest in collecting is concentrated on art glass, Wavecrest, and custard glass examples. (See also specific categories.)

If you would like to learn more about the subject of salts, there are several fine books available. *5,000 Open Salts*, written by William Heacock and Patricia Johnson, has many full-color illustrations and current values; you will find Patricia Johnson's address in the Directory under California. Mildred and Ralph Lechner have compiled a full-color value guide, *The World of Salt Shakers*; their address can be found in the Directory under Virginia. When no condition is indicated, the items listed below are assumed to be in mint condition.

Key: HM—hallmarked

Open Salts

In the listings below, the numbers refer to *5,000 Open Salts* by Johnson and Heacock, and *Pressed Glass Salt Dishes*, by L.W. and D.B. Neal. Lines with 'repro' within the description reflect values for reproduced salts.

Austria, #1272, HP, rnd, sgn, ind 12.00
Belleek, #1310, HP, rnd, ruffled top, sgn, ind 35.00
Burmese, #75, Webb, ca 1890, 1¾" dia 400.00
Celery salt, #1720, HP, EX quality, ind 10.00
Cut glass, #123, cranberry, etched, ped, ca 1890 . . . . 85.00
Cut glass, #2919, faceted 10.00
Cut glass, #3009, ped, sgn Clark 25.00

Amber squirrel on stump, #4671, $85.00.

Cut glass, #3034-3035, heart/club/diamond/spade, set of 4.....100.00
Cut glass, #3064, sgn Hawkes..........40.00
Cut glass, #3088, zippered..........10.00
Cut glass, #3101, Diamond Point..........10.00
Cut glass, #3166, sgn J Hoare..........35.00
Cut glass, #3698, sgn Waterford, ped, ca 1970..........25.00
Cut glass, #3699, Waterford type, ped, ca 1860..........75.00
Cut glass, #601, Waterford type, gr, ped, ca 1860..........125.00
Daum Nancy, #10, windmill scene..........500.00
Doulton, #1851, HM sterling rim, Lambeth, sgn, ca 1900..........65.00
Dresden, #1689, w/attached flowers, ind..........35.00
Elfinware, #1222, sgn Japan, ind..........10.00
Elfinware, #1244, wheelbarrow, sgn Germany, ind..........85.00
Elfinware, #1258, sgn Germany, tub shape, ind..........18.00
Elfinware, #1270, heavily decorated, sgn Germany, ind..........30.00
German, #1150, HP, dbl..........35.00
Haviland, #1400, ind..........27.00
Intaglio, #159, butterfly, pnt, sgn..........45.00
Intaglio, #215, bl, gr, etc, unsgn..........15.00
KPM, #1135, wht w/gold border, dbl..........35.00
KPM, #1155-1156, figural, mk, pnt, dbl, ca 1860..........275.00
Lacy, American, non-flint, repro, ca 1920-1940, VG..........45.00
Lacy, Avon, repro..........5.00
Lacy, French, amber, non-flint, repro, ca 1920-1940, VG..........65.00
Lacy, Metro Museum of Art, vaseline, bl, sgn, repro, VG..........15.00
Lacy, Neal-BF-1, basket of flowers, VG..........75.00
Lacy, Neal-BF-1B, basket of flowers, opal, chip on leg..........125.00
Lacy, Neal-BT-8, Lafayette boat, cobalt, sgn Sandwich, VG.....950.00
Lacy, Neal-DI-8, dbl, roughage on bottom..........140.00
Lacy, Neal-EE-3B, eagles on 4 corners, VG..........150.00
Lacy, Neal-EE-8, eagle, rnd, M..........280.00
Lacy, Neal-GA-2, cathedral windows, cobalt, leg chip..........125.00
Lacy, Neal-HN-18A, opaline, ftd, VG..........250.00
Lacy, Neal-NE-1A, opaque wht, sgn NE Glass Co Boston, EX..225.00
Limoges, #1275, HP, rnd, sgn, ind..........12.00
Meissen, #1169, w/hdl, dbl..........95.00
Meissen, #1595, sq, ind..........60.00
Millefiore, #609, European, ca 1900, 2″ dia..........250.00
Monet Stump, #19, ca 1900, ind..........85.00
Moorcroft, #1762, sterling London HM rim, sgn, ca 1920..........55.00
Mt Washington, #35-44, unsgn..........85.00
Nippon, #1365, HP..........10.00
Nippon, #1454, HP floral, tub shape, ind..........12.00
Nippon, #1495, HP, ped, ind..........16.00
Nippon, #1714, celery salt, ind..........4.00
Pickard, #1569, sq, ind..........45.00
Plique-de-jour, #83, Viking boat, Norway 930-S, 2½″..........650.00
Pressed glass, #2087, French, cobalt, dbl..........40.00
Pressed glass, #2548, bow tie, ind..........25.00
Pressed glass, #2572, Brazillian, ind..........10.00
Pressed glass, #2656, snail, ind..........28.00
Pressed glass, #2673, Fandango, Heisey, ind..........18.00
Pressed glass, #2674, Fancy Loop, Heisey, ind..........20.00
Pressed glass, #2680, English Hobnail, ind..........8.00
Pressed glass, #2689, Liberty Bell, 1776-1876, ind..........55.00
Pressed glass, #2850, tub shape, Heisey, sgn, ind..........12.00
Pressed glass, #2910, faceted, ind..........6.00
Pressed glass, #3018-3021, Euchre, ind..........12.00
Pressed glass, #3044, Moon & Star, old, ind..........40.00
Pressed glass, #3510, Washington Centennial, master..........45.00
Pressed glass, #3516, Panelled Grape Band, master..........25.00
Pressed glass, #3539, butterfly, master..........35.00
Pressed glass, #3540, Sawtooth Circle, master..........18.00
Pressed glass, #3567, Open Plaid, master..........15.00
Pressed glass, #3581, Tree of Life, 'salt' on side, master..........65.00
Pressed glass, #3582, Roman Key, master..........25.00
Pressed glass, #3589, Stippled Bowl, master..........27.00
Pressed glass, #3609, Beaded Acorn Leaf Band, master..........35.00
Pressed glass, #3621, Tulip w/Sawtooth, master..........35.00
Pressed glass, #3636, Bearded Head, master..........30.00
Pressed glass, #3741, horseshoe, ind..........27.00
Pressed glass, #3758, turtle, ind..........35.00
Pressed glass, #3764, automobile, sgn Pontieux, dbl..........55.00
Pressed glass, #3777, child figural hdl, France, dbl..........35.00
Pressed glass, #3796-3798, plain, European, dbl..........22.00
Pressed glass, #426, Jersey Swirl, bl, ind..........25.00
Pressed glass, #442, Daisy & Button Triangle, bl, ind, old..........25.00
Pressed glass, #506, Wildflower, turtle base, amber, master....125.00
Pressed glass, #564, Two Panel, bl, vaseline or gr, master..........25.00
Pressed glass, #870, Moon & Star, any color, repro, ind..........5.00
Pressed glass, #958-960, chicken/lid, sgn Vallerystahl, ind..........55.00
Pressed glass, #998, Bird & Berry, Degenhart, unsgn, ind..........12.00
Quimper, #1135, sgn, dbl, old..........45.00
Royal Bayreuth, #1666, animals, ped, ind..........55.00
Royal Bayreuth, #1667, figural claw form, ind..........65.00
Royal Copenhagen, #1332, ind..........45.00
Royal Doulton, #1870, sterling HM rim, ca 1873..........95.00
Royal Worcester, #1861, dbl wall, ind, ca 1862..........120.00
Satsuma, #1931, ca 1940-1960, ind..........20.00
Scalloped feet, #1390, artist HP, ind..........16.00
Sowerby, #139, #385, #2090, sgn & #d..........55.00
SP, #319, American, ruby liner, mk Derby..........55.00
SP, #3994, American, ruffled, rnd, ind..........12.00
SP, #653, American, cobalt liner, mk W&S..........12.00
SP, English, paw ft, ruby liner, ca 1900..........55.00
SP, English, w/spoons, set of 4, ca 1880, MIB..........100.00
SP, European, vaseline, ruffled, SP holder, ca 1880..........125.00
Sterling, #3034, American, ped, ca 1930..........30.00
Sterling, #323, ruby liner, Gorham, ca 1890..........125.00
Sterling, #379, English, gr liner, ind..........75.00
Sterling, #3937, French, w/matching spoon, liner, ind..........100.00
Sterling, #3976, medallion, ped, Gorham, ca 1860..........145.00
Sterling, #3983, German 800..........45.00
Sterling, #3992, plain, Gorham, ca 1920..........20.00
Sterling, #4166, English, ornate, HM, ca 1899..........65.00
Sterling, #4208, medallion, Albert Cole, ca 1860..........160.00

Sterling, #4260, Viking boat 900, Norway....................35.00
Sterling, #4260, Viking boat 900, Norway, w/pepper...........75.00
Sterling, #4286, German, ca 1800, master, pr...............400.00
Sterling, #4735, Russian salt chair, HM, ca 1890.............450.00
Sterling, #713, 2 salts/pepper/mustard, cobalt liners, HM.......300.00
Sterling, #720, French, cobalt liner, HM, ca 1845, master.....175.00
Sterling, #761, French, cobalt, HM, dbl, ca 1845.............140.00
Sterling, Austria Hungary, w/mustard, HM, dbl, ca 1850.......275.00
Sterling 800, #2062, figural/cobalt inserts, European, dbl......125.00
Steuben Calcite, #34, ped................................200.00
Stevens & Williams, #72, opal, vaseline ruffles................95.00
Tiffany, #1, witches pot, sgn.............................250.00
Tiffany, #3, pulled ears, sgn.............................250.00
Tiffany, #30, bl, ruffled top, sgn.........................300.00
Webb, #84, 2-color, sgn.................................700.00
Wedgwood, #1850, sterling HM rim, sgn, ca 1897............125.00

Shakers

In the following listing, prices are for single shakers unless noted 'pair.' Values are for old original shakers. Some of these have been reproduced, and this will be noted in the description.

Acorn, blk, Hobbs Brockunier, rare........................55.00
Acorn, shaded pink to wht, Hobbs Brockunier................40.00
Annie, ftd base..35.00
Apricot Band, HP brn w/8 apricots around base, pr...........30.00
Ball fruit jar, (reproduced), pr, MIB........................20.00
Bark Translucent, (Royal Flemish), HP decor, Mt Washington..425.00
Beaded Bottom, milk glass, Dithridge, ca 1898, pr............40.00
Beaded Dahlia, bl opaque, pr..............................55.00
Beaded Dahlia, gr, pr....................................70.00
Beaded Dahlia, pink......................................33.00
Beaded Loop, (Oregon), (reproduced by Imperial), pr...........20.00
Bevelled Diamond & Star..................................25.00
Broken Column, red staining, rare, pr.......................30.00
Buldging 3-Petal, pink cased, part of condiment set, pr.........50.00
Button Arches, ruby flashed, ca 1897-1906...................20.00
Cameo, frosted w/bl leaves & gooseberries in relief..........125.00
Cane Woven, opaque bl, (reproduced), pr....................38.00
Cat, metal head, glass eyes, cased glass, gr/purple, pr..........85.00
Cattail, early china......................................28.00
Chick head, HP decor, milk glass, Mt Washington............250.00
Christmas, aqua, sgn lid dated 1877, 2⅝″....................50.00
Christmas, cobalt, dbl breaker, Britannia top, 3¾″............175.00
Clover Leaf...26.00
Cockle Shell, in orig fr, Mt Washington, pr.................800.00
Cockle Shell, satin w/floral decor, Mt Washington............225.00
Cone, gr opaque, Consolidated Lamp & Glass................20.00
Cone, wht milk glass, Consolidated Lamp & Glass.............22.00
Cord & Tassel, gr..20.00
Cord & Tassel Double, bl/gr, pr............................65.00
Corn w/Husk, milk glass, pr...............................55.00
Cosmos, (Apple Blossom), bl opaque, tall, pr.................65.00
Cotton Bale, bl opaque, ca 1894, pr.........................45.00
Cotton Bale, wht opaque, Consolidated Lamp, ca 1894.........20.00
Creased Bale, pink cased, Dithridge, ca 1894-1905, pr.........60.00
Creased Neck, HP floral, milk glass, pr......................40.00
Creased Waist, wht w/decor, New Martinsville, pr.............50.00
Curlicue, no lid..10.00
Currier & Ives, bl, rare...................................55.00
Currier & Ives, vaseline, rare.............................55.00
Cut Log, (Cat's Eye & Block), pr...........................40.00
Dog, sitting, vaseline w/chromed pewter head, glass eyes........55.00
Double Crossroads, amber.................................19.00
Double Leaf, gr opaque...................................25.00
Double Leaf, pink cased...................................35.00
Draped Column, HP opalware, Wavecrest, pr................100.00
Egg, milk glass, flat side, Columbia Expo, pewter top..........50.00
Elephant, pewter/SP head, glass body, pr....................64.00
Erie Twist, enamel flowers, pink, CF Monroe, 1890s...........30.00
Eyewinker, (reproduced)..................................20.00
Fan Beaded, milk glass, pr.................................30.00
Fancy Arch, no lid..10.00
Feather Panel, clear opal..................................28.00
Fig, satin w/HP flowers on bl, Mt Washington...............105.00
Fish, decorated milk glass..................................30.00
Fish, pink cased, pr......................................75.00
Flower Band, red frosted, pr...............................75.00
Flower Band, vaseline, pr..................................35.00
Fluted Scrolls, bl opal w/enamel, pr.........................95.00
Foggy Bottom, vaseline....................................40.00
Forget-Me-Not, (Challinor #20), milk glass, ca 1891, pr.........27.00
Forget-Me-Not, milk glass, tall, pr..........................45.00
Forget-Me-Not, Pewee & companion w/tray, bl milk glass.......65.00
Foursquare, (Billow), HP w/pink decor, Wavecrest.............65.00
Galloway, (Virginia)......................................14.00
Guttate, cranberry, pr.....................................77.00
Guttate, pink satin, (reproduced), pr........................66.00
Half Cone, satin, Consolidated Lamp & Glass, 1890s...........48.00
Hand & Fishscale, frosted, (reproduced).....................45.00
Harvard, (Quihote), custard.................................60.00
Hickman, (La Clede)......................................10.00
Hobnail w/Thumbprint, sapphire bl..........................18.00
Horseshoe, amber, rough lid................................25.00
Intaglio, emerald gr w/gold, Northwood, rare, pr.............250.00
Inverted Baby Thumbprint, reverse amberina, pewter top, rare..165.00
Inverted Fan & Feather, pink slag, Northwood, 1900s.........400.00
Inverted Thumbprint, amberina, tall.........................95.00
Inverted Thumbprint, enamel flowers, cased, gr, 2-part lid......30.00
Iris w/Meander, amethyst, rare, pr.........................175.00
Iris w/Meander, gr w/gold decor, pr.........................75.00
Jackson, custard, Northwood, pr...........................110.00
King's Crown, (Thumbprint), ruby, pr........................40.00
Kokomo...12.00
Kokomo, w/holder, pr.....................................47.00
Lacy Scrolls, bl opaque, pr.................................50.00
Ladder w/Diamonds, Duncan & Miller, ca 1904, pr.............20.00
Leaf, palm, wht opaque....................................20.00
Leaf & Spear, HP satin opalware, Wavecrest, pr..............155.00
Leaf Base, ca 1910-1913, pr................................30.00
Leaf Mold, cased cranberry, pr............................140.00
Leaf Mold, vaseline spatter, frosted, brass tops, pr...........125.00
Leaf Overlap, pink cased, pr...............................60.00
Longwy, turq w/pnt floral, French Pottery, ca 1870-1880.......30.00
Mardi Gras, thin neck.....................................15.00
Mascotte...9.00
Melon, HP satin, Gillinder, ca 1888-1892.....................30.00
Melonette, milk glass.....................................12.00
Mitered Diamond Point, (Zigzag), wht milk glass..............15.00
Optic, custard, souvenir, Jefferson..........................35.00
Oval Bulging, gr...25.00
Owl Little, crystal w/amber glass eyes, HP pears.............100.00
Owl Little, frosted w/amber glass eyes, HP pears.............135.00
Panel & Star, vaseline....................................23.00
Panelled Rib Bulbous, HP opalware, Wavecrest, pr............85.00
Peachblow New England, (Wild Rose), pink to wht...........500.00
Peachblow Wheeling, pink to yel cased, Hobbs Brockunier.....350.00

S-Repeat, ca 1901-1910, amethyst, $85.00 each.

Periwinkle, (Many Petals), pink satin, New Martinsville..........55.00
Pillar, burmese satin, Mt Washington, pr..................225.00
Pillar Ribbed, bl, Mt Washington..........................50.00
Pillar Ribbed, burmese glossy, Mt Washington, pr............800.00
Pillar Ribbed, burmese satin, Mt WA, ca 1888-90, pr.........450.00
Pillar Ribbed, HP decor, Mt Washington....................48.00
Pineapple & Fan, clear, w/sterling lid, pr..................30.00
Pineapple Figure, pink cased...............................30.00
Pineapple Figure, pink cased, pr...........................65.00
Pleated Skirt, bl opaque...................................22.00
Pleated Skirt, gr opaque...................................22.00
Pressed Diamond, amber....................................20.00
Quilted Phlox, gr cased, Northwood.........................30.00
Rib Base Twenty One, HP opalware, Wavecrest, pr..............75.00
Richardson, w/agitator, ca 1867-1877........................25.00
Roman Rosette, pr..20.00
Roman Rosette, ruby flashed, orig glass stand..............110.00
Royal Ivy, cranberry & clear...............................60.00
Sawtooth, bulbous, dk bl, pr...............................30.00
Sawtooth & Thinline, pr....................................45.00
Sawtooth & Thinline, wht satin w/enamel decor................45.00
Scroll, gr opaque, ftd......................................17.00
Scroll, Low; pink cased....................................20.00
Scroll, Twisted; milk glass, pr.............................30.00
Scroll & Leaf Hexagon, HP opalware, Wavecrest...............40.00
Scroll Wave, bl & wht opalware w/HP flowers, Wavecrest.......90.00
Sequoia...10.00
Shell Overlapping, bl, pr...................................35.00
Shell Overlapping, milk glass, pr...........................30.00
Shoshone, pr...25.00
Shrine, clear, very scarce.................................25.00
Snail, pr..75.00
Snail, ruby stained..50.00
Spider Web, (Alba), pink opaque, Dithridge, pr...............50.00
Spider Web, wht milk glass.................................20.00
Spirea Band, amber, pr.....................................30.00
States, glass lids, pr......................................45.00
Sunk Honeycomb..7.00
Sunk Honeycomb, ruby stained..............................20.00
Sunset, custard, ca 1894-1900, pr...........................60.00
Sunset, milk glass, pr.....................................30.00
Swirl, HP, frosted, short...................................32.50
Swirl & Bulge, w/transfer decor, Wavecrest...................35.00
Teepee, thin neck..18.00
Thumbprint Wavecrest, wht opalware w/HP decor, Wavecrest....30.00
Tomato, off wht, w/enamel decor, Mt Washington, 1890s.......65.00
Tomato, undeveloped burmese w/special holder, Mt WA, set....350.00
Triple Rib, milk glass......................................15.00
Triple Rib, pink opaque....................................18.00
Truncated Cube, ruby stained...............................20.00
Tulip, wht opalware w/HP decor, Wavecrest....................40.00
Vine Border, bl..25.00
Wheat & Barley, bl...40.00
Woven Neck, HP opalware w/floral decor, Wavecrest...........90.00
X-Ray, gr w/gold decor, Riverside Glass, ca 1896-99, pr.......110.00
Zippered Block, ruby stained...............................36.00

Samplers

American samplers were made as early as the colonial days; even earlier examples from 17th century England still exist today. Changes in style and decorative motif are evident down through the years. Verses were not added until the late 17th century. By the 18th century, samplers were used not only for sewing experience but as an educational tool. Young ladies who often signed and dated their work embroidered numbers and characters of the alphabet, as well as fancy stitches. Fruits and flowers were added for borders; birds, animals, and Adam and Eve were popular subjects. Later, houses and other buildings were included. By the 19th century, the American Eagle and the little red schoolhouse had made their appearance.

When no condition is indicated, the items listed below are assumed to be in excellent condition.

Finely stitched floral border with house, trees, birds, hearts, flower baskets, and two verses, signed and dated 1824, 22″ x 26″, $3,800.00.

Adam & Eve/serpent/tree/angels/etc, losses, 16″..............350.00
Adam & Eve/serpent/tree/verse, 1843, worn/faded, 20x14″.....460.00
Alphabets, birds, flowering trees, mahog veneer fr, 13x17″.....275.00
Alphabets & name, X-stitch, red/wht, unfr, 5¾x8″.............65.00
Alphabets & name, 1819, in gr on linen, 12x17″, VG..........265.00
Alphabets/long verse, EX work, 1799, G color, 18½x22″.......675.00
Alphabets/verse, bird/tree border, 1825, 15x18″..............450.00
Alphabets/verse, lists vowels, 1819, 12x16″, VG..............270.00
Alphabets/verse, vine border/flowers/trees, 13x18″, EX........300.00
Alphamumerics, sgn, faded/stained, 9x18″....................125.00

Alphanumerics, sgn/1852, rpr/stains, 9x28" . . . 420.00
Alphanumerics/verse, sgn, stitched to cardboard, 12x14" . . . 200.00
Alphanumerics/verse, sgn/1796, minor stains, 16x17" . . . 450.00
Bird, stylized flowering trees, verse, 1837, 13x18" . . . 400.00
Birth & baptism, flower basket border, linen, 1831, 19x21" . . . 500.00
Building/trees/alphabets/verse, sgn/1835, G fr, 20x20" . . . 775.00
Family record, 1813-1900, floral border, 25x28" . . . 375.00
Family record/alphabets/monument/sm house, 1830, 17", EX . . . 1,430.00
Flowering trees/flowerpots/sm animals/birds, 13" . . . 165.00
House/cows/trees/landscape/admonition, 1836, 19", EX . . . 600.00
House/fence/trees/verse/alphanumerics, 1813, 18x15" . . . 1,325.00
House/trees/ladies/alphabets, 1799, in fr, 8x9½" . . . 1,225.00
House/trees/monument/verse/alphanumerics, sgn/1833, 17" . . . 1,100.00
House/trees/record: 1750-1800, faded/sm holes, 22x23" . . . 450.00
Landscape w/house w/in alphabet/vine bands, sgn/1820, 16" . . 3,300.00
Memorial, parrots/flower baskets/hearts, ca 1810, 11x11" . . . 375.00
Memorial, simple verse, 1794, sq, 5¾" . . . 275.00
Miniature, alphanumerics, Forget Me Not in gold, 3x3½" . . . 285.00
Miniature, alphanumerics, homespun, 1879, 5x6" . . . 110.00
Tree/cats/crowns/people/lions/verse/etc, sgn/1827, 15x18" . . . 1,200.00
2 girls, real hair/pnt faces, settee, legend/1823, 15x19" . . . 1,210.00

Sandwich Glass

The Boston and Sandwich Glass Company was founded in 1820 by Deming Jarves in Sandwich, Massachusetts. Their first products were simple cruets, salts, half-pint jugs, and lamps. They were attributed as being one of the first to perfect a method for pressing glass, a step toward the manufacture of the 'lacy' glass, which they made until about 1840. Many other types of glass were made there--cut, colored, snakeskin, hobnail, and opalescent among them.

After the Civil War, profits began to dwindle due to the keen competition of the Western factories who were situated in areas rich in natural gas and more suitable coal and sand resources. The end came with an unreconcilable wage dispute between the workers and the company, and the factory closed in 1888.

When no condition is indicated, the items listed below are assumed to be in undamaged condition.

See also specific types of glass.

Candlesticks, dolphin stems, 10", $550.00 for the pair.

Bird drinking font, blown, loop hanger, 6¼" . . . 225.00
Bottle, vinegar; blown 3-mold, cobalt, w/stopper, 6½" . . . 275.00
Bottle, vinegar; mold-blown, tam-o'-shanter stopper . . . 350.00
Bowl, dbl Horn of Plenty w/Princess Feather, oval, 8" . . . 210.00
Bowl, Diamond & Plume, brilliant lt bl, 5" . . . 295.00
Bowl, Industry, 6¼" . . . 245.00
Bowl, lacy, oval, miniature, NM . . . 70.00
Bowl, Pipes of Pan, oblong, 8" . . . 525.00
Candlestick, acanthus leaf, bl top on clambroth, 9½", pr . . . 1,100.00
Candlestick, acanthus leaf, 1840s, 9½", pr . . . 300.00
Candlestick, column, bl/wht petal top on bl, 1840s, 9" . . . 350.00
Candlestick, column w/petal top, clambroth, 9¼" . . . 125.00
Candlestick, dolphin, bl top on wht, 1840s, 9⅝" . . . 650.00
Candlestick, dolphin, jade gr on wht, 1840, rare, 10¼" . . . 1,150.00
Candlestick, dolphin, petal top, opal, late, 9¼", pr . . . 300.00
Candlestick, dolphin, sq base, canary yel, 9¾" . . . 375.00
Candlestick, dolphin, 1-step base, canary yel, 10½", pr . . . 875.00
Candlestick, lady in drape figural, 1840, 9⅝" . . . 550.00
Candlestick, Loop & Petal, canary yel, 6⅝", pr, VG . . . 250.00
Candlestick, Loop & Petal, opaque bl, 6¾", pr, NM . . . 850.00
Christmas salt, amethyst, w/agitator, dtd . . . 110.00
Compote, Diamond T'print, flint, 9¼x11⅜" . . . 400.00
Compote, free-blown, folded lip, pressed dbl paw ft, 5x6" . . . 250.00
Compote, Loop, flint, 8x10½" . . . 150.00
Compote, Loop, opaque wht, 3½x8½" . . . 150.00
Compote, Waffle & T'print, flint, 7x11" . . . 350.00
Creamer, blown 3-mold, applied hdl, folded rim, cobalt, 4" . . . 525.00
Cup & saucer, lacy, miniature . . . 175.00
Decanter, blown 3-mold, flared mouth, violet bl, ½-pt, EX . . . 200.00
Dish, open ribbon sides, yel-gr, very rare, 2½x5¾" . . . 1,200.00
Goblet, ripple pattern, pr . . . 50.00
Honey dish, Roman Rosette, opal . . . 65.00
Jar, preserve, out-folded rim/free-blown, olive gr, 11¾" . . . 355.00
Lamp, overlay, wht/clear, ball font, brass shaft, 8¾" . . . 365.00
Pitcher, crackle glass, w/ice bladder . . . 200.00
Pitcher, lacy, miniature . . . 70.00
Salt cellar, lacy, miniature, EX . . . 80.00
Sauce dish, Crossed Swords, cobalt, NM . . . 150.00
Sauce dish, Princess Feather . . . 145.00
Sauce dish, Prism w/Diamond Point border, ca 1840-50 . . . 50.00
Spill, Star, canary . . . 400.00
Spooner, Hairpin, opal/opaque . . . 175.00
Sugar bowl, Gothic Arch, dome lid, clambroth, EX . . . 225.00
Sugar bowl, 3-mold, folded rim on lid, applied ft, 6" . . . 3,150.00
Tureen w/lid & undertray, lacy, miniature, EX . . . 125.00
Twine holder, cobalt rim, wheel engraved, free-blown . . . 295.00
Vase, mustard cased w/orange, ribbed, turned-down rim, 2½" . . . 145.00
Whiskey taster, paneled, canary, rough pontil . . . 120.00
Whiskey taster, paneled, lt opal gr, rough pontil . . . 135.00
Wine, clambroth ft & stem, opaque med bl bowl, blown, 3½" . . 185.00

Sarreguemines

Sarreguemines, France, is the location of Utzschneider and Company, founded in 1770, producers of transfer-printed dinnerware, figurines, and novelty ware, usually marked 'Sarreguemines.'

When no condition is indicated, the items listed below are assumed to be in mint condition.

Bowl, woven basket w/wht egg finial, sgn, 6x8½" . . . 175.00
Box, pin; Greenaway kids on lid, rnd, 1x6" . . . 40.00
Pitcher, allover relief: children climbing trees . . . 85.00
Pitcher, character, Scotsman, 7¾" . . . 75.00

Pitcher, character, scowling man/stand-up collar, 7½″ 85.00
Pitcher, character, smiling man, bulbous, 8½″ 98.00
Pitcher, character head, bulbous, 5x3½″ 65.00
Pitcher, figural, barking hound sits & glares 110.00
Pitcher, rooster family/hawk relief, majolica, 8″ 48.00
Plate, apples on leaf, majolica, 7½″ 30.00
Plate, boy & girl in doorway, 8½″ 35.00
Plate, castles/floral border, artist sgn, 6½″, set of 8 .... 60.00
Plate, clowns & music motif, 8″ 24.00
Plate, ea w/different Napoleonic battle, 8″, set of 6 .... 165.00
Plate, humorous French military scenes 20.00
Plate, strawberries on bl, majolica, 8″ 35.00

Satin Glass

Satin glass is simply glassware with a velvety matt finish achieved through the application of an acid bath. This procedure has been used by many companies since the 19th century both here and abroad, on many types of colored and art glass.

When no condition is indicated, the items listed below are assumed to be in mint condition.

Bud vase, bl w/orange floral, 8″ 55.00
Cookie jar, pink, emb snowflakes, SP rim/lid/bail 275.00
Cracker jar, Diamond Quilted, pink, SP lid/hdl 295.00
Creamer & sugar, open; bl, World's Fair–1893, Libbey, rare ... 500.00
Ewer, peach overlay, floral enamel, trilobed top, 7¾x3″ 95.00
Ewer, pink overlay, enamel floral, trilobed top, 9x3¾″ 100.00
Ewer, yel overlay w/wht flowers/scrolls, ruffled, 9x3x5″ 135.00
Jam dish, pink w/blk birds, shell ruffle, SP holder, 4½″ 175.00
Pitcher, bl w/pink & yel floral, overlay, 6x4½″ 245.00
Pitcher, Florette, pink, w/6 tumblers 425.00
Powder box, lovebirds finial 35.00
Rose bowl, bl, butterfly/floral, 4-pinch top/petal ft, 5½″ 135.00
Rose bowl, bl/wht/gold floral, frosted ft, crimped, 7x4″ 135.00
Rose bowl, clear studs/ft, pnt floral, 8-crimp, cased, 4¾″ 135.00
Rose bowl, lt bl, 5x5″ 55.00
Rose bowl, rose shaded, petal mold, 4x5″ 70.00
Tumbler, Florette, pink overlay 35.00
Vase, aqua, gold/bl enamel, camphor hdls, ped ft, 9″ 100.00
Vase, bl, Diamond Quilted, ped base, narrow neck, 9½″, pr 250.00
Vase, Florette, pink overlay, wht lining, German mks, 5¾″ 195.00
Vase, pale gr, owl resting on branch, HP, 6¾″ 90.00
Vase, pink ribbed, bulbous, w/frosted ruffle, 10¼″ 115.00
Vase, yel w/bl ft, trumpet shape, 10½″ 35.00
Water set, Cone, yel, 7-pc 265.00

Scales

In today's world of pre-measured and pre-packaged goods, it is hard to imagine the days when such products as sugar, flour, soap, and candy first had to be weighed by the grocer. The variety of scales used at the turn of the century was highly diverse; at the Philadelphia Exposition in 1876, one company alone displayed over three hundred different weighing devices. Among those found today, brass and iron models are the most common.

When no condition is indicated, the items listed below are assumed to be in excellent condition.

Key:
bal—balance   lb—pound
g—gram

Bismar, measuring ladle, 0-200 g, 0-7 oz, aluminum, Fr 4.00
Brass, hanging, w/hook, 0-24 lb 20.00
Brass, platform spring, trn ped/disk base, sgn Brown, 1878 .... 150.00
Brass, 2-tray balance w/10 weights up to 50 g, bl case 50.00
Brower Mfg, egg weighing 15.00
Buffalo, person, CI, brass beam, height gauge 175.00
Buffalo, unequal arm, candy, red & gold, brass scoop 50.00
Charles Forschner, hanging, w/hook, 0-50 lb 20.00
Charles Forschner, New York, hanging, w/hook, 0-200 lb 35.00
Chatillon, hanging, w/hook, 0-24 lb 25.00
Chatillon, Improved Spring Balance, 145 lb, hanging, 16½″ 25.00
Chatillon, Spring Balance, 20 lb, hanging, w/pan & chains 50.00
Chatillon, straight spring, brass face, 0-100 lb 35.00
Chatillon, trip, CI, brass side beam 55.00
Chinese Dotchin, ivory beam, wood violin-shaped case 100.00
Computing Scale Co, postal, fan type, emb brass trim 125.00
Computing Scale Co #146, butcher, lights up, 34″ 425.00
Computing Scale Co #85, fan type, emb trim, 10 lb cap 125.00
Detecto, hanging, w/galvanized basket 35.00
Dodge Mfg Co, Micrometer, with pan 250.00
Dodge Mfg Co, Micrometer, with scoop 250.00
Dollydale by Robson, hand-held weighing scoop, 0-5 lb 40.00
Eastman-Kodak, w/weights, sgn, orig box, M 65.00
Excelsior by Sargent, hanging, w/hook, 0-25 lb 25.00
Excelsior Improved, hanging, brass 25.00
Fairbanks, store, brass scoop, dtd 1877 .... 55.00
Forschner, brass-face spring, 60 lb, 4¼x13″ 45.00
Forschner, Improved Circular Spring Balance, 30 lb/hanging 45.00
Franklin, copper hopper, pnt iron base, 3 lb 60.00
Gifford Wood Co, ice, spring, hanging w/hook, 200 lb 30.00
Gold, brass w/3 brass weights, orig velevet-lined box 55.00
Gold, decorated steel beam, brass pans, 18th C 75.00
H Troemner, apothecary, brn marble top, Roberval pr 225.00
Hanson, hanging, w/hook, 0-50 lb 18.00
Howe, postal, 0-16 oz, CI, brass platform, beam, weight 35.00
IBM #166, candy, 0-2 lb 125.00
IBM #167, candy, 0-5 lb 150.00
IDL Deluxe, postal, 3¢ 1st class letter 20.00
Imperial, confectioners, 2 lb 10.00
Jones Bimington, CI, brass beam, cloverleaf feet & wts 90.00
Koch Butcher's Supply, hanging, ornate 70.00
Kodak, photographic, 6 weights, no pans 25.00
Kohlbusch, Herman, gold assay bal, glass case: 28x23x12″ 350.00
Mancur, hide, hanging w/hook, 2 ranges 0-40/20-350 lb 60.00
Mills Novelty Co, beam, penny weighing 900.00
National Poultry, egg weighing, metal 18.00
National Store Specialty, fancy base, 10″ 295.00
Oakes, egg weighing 10.00
Ohaus, pharmacy, w/brass weights 90.00
Peerless Aristocrat Deluxe, 'Lollipop,' 1¢ coin-op 850.00
Pelouze, kitchen 14.00
Pelouze Crescent, postage, bl, tin, 1903, 3″ 22.00
Pennsylvania Scale Co, hanging, w/galvanized basket 40.00
Platform, counter type, CI, brass beam, w/weights 75.00
Platform, counter type, CI, brass beam & scoop 45.00
PS&W, steelyard, hanging, w/2 hooks, 0-25 lb 25.00
Salter & Co, steel, spring, cylindrical, 1800s, 0-21 lb 35.00
Sargent & Co, 300 lb ice, cylindrical 45.00
Steelyard, 2 ranges, 2 single/1 dbl hooks, 19″ L 25.00
Toledo, fan, candy, all nickel 135.00
Toledo, fan, candy, brass trim & scoop, 1903 .... 125.00
Toledo, fan, candy, 0-3 lb 85.00
Toledo, fan, grocery, brass trim, orig platter 135.00
Toledo, fan, 0-500 g, brass scoop 55.00
Torison Balance Co, apothecary 45.00
Torison Balance Co, laboratory, glass sides 100.00
Triner Ideal, postal, 0-2 lb, 3¢ first class 20.00

Schafer and Vater

Schafer and Vater operated in Volkstadt, Germany, from the last decade of the 1800s until about 1920. They produced novelties such as figural bottles, flasks, vases, etc., marked with an 'R' within a star device.

When no condition is indicated, the items listed below are assumed to be in mint condition.

Bottle, fireman w/hose, Fire Water....70.00
Bottle, Indian head in colorful headdress, 5″....70.00
Box, Cupid & nymph, bl jasper, oval, 5″....45.00
Box, Priscilla & John Alden, bl jasper, 3¼″ sq....38.00
Clock, lady playing 2 lutes, gr & wht, 7″....75.00
Creamer, bear w/overcoat & muff, 3½″....50.00
Creamer, Blk man, comical, 3½″....95.00
Creamer, Chinaman holds goose by feet, long hair forms hdl....68.00
Creamer, clown w/lute....85.00
Creamer, cow in dress, bl, #6517, 3¾″....90.00
Creamer, Cupids w/garlands, ram head spout, gr jasper....55.00
Creamer, Dutch maid w/basket on bk holding pitcher....55.00
Creamer, goose in bonnet & shawl, #6452, 5½″....126.00
Creamer, lady clown kneeling, w/cape & fan....50.00
Creamer, maid w/jug & keys, 3½″....90.00
Creamer, seated goat w/boutonnieres, 5½″....112.00
Creamer, witch flying/holding fan, floral, bl, 3¼″....78.00
Creamer, witch kneeling, bl & wht, 4″....50.00
Creamer, woman w/fan, bl/wht, 4″....70.00
Figurine, comical bald lady, sitting, bl dress, feet move....135.00
Figurine, comical man, blk coat, blk cat, yel hat, nodder....95.00
Figurine, dog, eye bandaged, 'Why Be Unhappy'....135.00
Hatpin holder, Egyptian series....135.00
Match holder, laughing man, #8013....90.00
Match holder, portly dancing Blk couple, hands joined, 4½″....225.00
Shakers, smiling apple/pear, pr....95.00
Teapot, smiling apple, 1-cup....125.00
Tray, pin; emb pink Grecian girls' heads on corners, 4x5″....38.00
Urn, Grecian lady in wht ship in center, sage gr, 6″....110.00
Vase, bud; boy facing wall, 'I'm so discouraged,' 4⅛″....130.00

Tea Party, each head nods, 1¾″ x 5″ x 3¾″, $260.00.

Schlegelmilch Porcelain

Authority Mary Frank Gaston has compiled a lovely book, *R.S. Prussia*, with full-color illustrations and current values; you will find her address in the Directory under Texas. When no condition is indicated, the items listed below are assumed to be in mint condition.

Key:
BM—blue mark
RM—red mark
GM—green mark
SM—steeple mark

E.S. Germany

Fine chinaware marked 'E.S. Germany' or 'E.S. Prov. Saxe' was produced by E.S. Schlegelmilch at his Suhl Factory in Thuringia region of Prussia from the turn of the century until about 1925.

Ash tray, horse & colt decor, Prov Saxe....48.00
Bowl, lady's portrait on gr lustre, 9½″....225.00
Bowl, pheasants & roses, oval, w/hdls, Prov Saxe, 10½″....65.00
Bowl, roses, Prov Saxe, 5½″....45.00
Box, trinket; Indian portrait, violin shaped, Royal Saxe....125.00
Cake plate, Indian portrait & bear, Royal Saxe, 9¾″....400.00
Chocolate pot, roses, Royal Saxe....110.00
Cup, Indian portrait on irid gr....85.00
Dish, divided; yel roses, center hdl, Royal Saxe....90.00
Lobster dish, floral w/Tiffany finish, Royal Saxe....300.00
Match holder, portrait on irid gr....185.00
Pitcher, lemonade; roses, Royal Saxe, 8″....125.00
Plate, Indian transfer on wht, silver trim, Royal Saxe, 7″....95.00
Plate, Sitting Bull portrait, 8½″....350.00
Relish, flowers/foliage, orange/cream, leaf shape, hdls....20.00
Rose jar, floral, irid, Prov Saxe, 7½″....135.00
Sugar bowl, roses on yel, w/lid....55.00
Toothpick holder, Indian chief, relief scrolls....95.00
Tray, celery; bird decor, Prov Saxe....65.00
Tray, dresser; mixed floral decor, ES Crown....75.00
Tray, pin; floral, gold trim, Prov Saxe....16.00
Vase, floral, gold tracery, Aladdin lamp shape, 4½x9″....130.00
Vase, lady seated w/dog, Prov Saxe, 13″....575.00
Vase, lady w/doves, Art Nouveau shape, Prov Saxe, 12″....425.00
Vase, lady w/doves, pearl finish, 3 hdls, Prov Saxe, 7″....250.00
Vase, lady's portrait, beading, pearl, Royal Saxe, 9″....175.00
Vase, lady's portrait, bl neck/base, Royal Saxe, 11″....250.00
Vase, lady's portrait, irid w/turq jewels, dbl hdls, 11″....245.00
Vase, lady's portrait, medallions, gold hdls/trim, 9″....225.00

E.S. Prussia

E.S. Prussia was a mark used by the Erdmann Schlegelmilch porcelain manufactory established in 1861 in the Prussian province in Saxony, Germany. Most examples seen today date from the early 1900s until the factory closed in the 1920s.

Bowl, roses, 2-hdl, 5½″....30.00
Sugar bowl, primroses, blown-out bottom, yel, rare color....45.00

R.S. Germany

In 1869, Reinhold Schlegelmilch began to manufacture porcelain in Tillowitz, in upper Silesia. He had formerly worked with his brother, Erdmann, in his factory in Suhl, in the German province of Thuringia. Both areas were rich in resources necessary for the production of hard paste porcelain. Wares marked with the name 'Tillowitz' and the accompanying 'R.S. Germany' phrase, are attributed to Reinhold. The most common mark is a wreath and star in a solid color, under the glaze. Items marked 'R.S. Germany' are usually more simply decorated than R.S. Prussia. Some reflect the Art Deco trend of the 1920s. Certain hand-painted floral decorations and hand-painted themes such as 'Sheepherder,' 'Man with Horses,' and

'Cottage' are especially valued by collectors--those with a high gloss finish or on Art Deco shapes in particular.

Not all hand-painted items were painted at the factory. Those with an artist's signature, but no 'Hand Painted' mark, indicate that the blank was decorated outside the factory.

Baby reamer, bl w/pink roses, much gold....65.00
Berry set, pink roses, 7-pc....90.00
Bonbon, daisies on gr, 6″....25.00
Bowl, blown-out floral on deep rose, gold trim, 2½x8x12½″....110.00
Bowl, iris, red SM, 10″....65.00
Bowl, lav floral, gold trim, 9¾″....35.00
Bowl, orange/orchid/wht floral on cream/gr/bl, GM, 10″....80.00
Bowl, wht w/gold trim, hdl, BM....22.00
Bowl, 4 lilies of the valley, 4 ft, ruffled rim, 2½x6¼″....42.00
Box, powder; pink roses, dainty....25.00
Cake plate, lg wht poppies, Nouveau border, gold trim, 10″....40.00
Cake set, roses/multifloral on shaded ground, 7-pc....90.00
Candy dish, lg poppies, beige/gold, ball ft, 2-hdl....45.00
Celery, bird of paradise, 11″....275.00
Celery, wht/pink roses on pink, gold tracings, BM, 5x10½″....59.00
Chocolate pot, baskets of wht violets, BM....110.00
Chocolate pot, gilt/pink roses/leaf border, GM, +6 c/s....350.00
Chocolate pot, lg roses on gr, GM, +6 c/s....325.00
Chocolate pot, roses, HP, BM, +4 c/s....200.00

Dessert set, each piece with different lady, pink roses between yellow circles, R.S. Germany, $370.00 for the 5-pc. set.

Compote, scenic: mill, boat & windmills, lg....275.00
Creamer & sugar, chickadee & bluebirds....90.00
Cup & saucer, chocolate; BM....25.00
Cup & saucer, dogwood blossoms, blown-out, lt brn....38.00
Hair receiver, roses & gold relief leaves, GM....65.00
Hatpin holder, calla lily w/gr leaf, gold trim, 4½″....45.00
Hatpin holder, pink & yel roses, 4 molded feet....48.00
Hatpin holder, pink w/2 bands of roses & gold....50.00
Hatpin holder, wht roses on pastel gr, lg....60.00
Jar, cracker; pink roses, hdls....90.00
Mayonnaise, floral, w/underplate & ladle....50.00
Mustard, dogwood on gr & wht, no spoon, 3″....65.00
Nappy, hydrangeas, lt gr, triangular....45.00
Nut set, magnolias on satin, gold trim, ftd, 5-pc....75.00
Pencil holder, roses, mk Compliments Omaha Crockery, flat....67.50
Pitcher, pastel roses, scalloped rim, gold hdl, 3¾″....65.00
Pitcher, tankard; poppies/pansies, gr/yel, blown-out, 12″....250.00
Plate, carnations, open hdl, GM....55.00
Plate, Christmas Rose, dozen wht roses, BM, 9″....35.00
Plate, Crown Crane, rare, 7″....500.00
Plate, game birds/pheasants, landscape w/house/tower, 8¼″....55.00
Plate, irises, 6¼″....40.00
Plate, lg pink/orange nasturtiums, 9½″....42.00
Plate, orange poppies, 10″....42.00
Plate, pink/yel carnations on shaded ground, 8½″....35.00
Plate, poppies, 8″....30.00
Plate, roses, gr/wht/gold, 8″....35.00
Plate, tulips on cream/brn, gr star, 6¼″....17.50
Plate, wht tulips, HP, 6¼″....20.00
Relish, daisies on gr, 13″ L....39.00
Relish, w/creamer & sugar, poinsettia decor, set....240.00
Shaving mug, floral, SM....60.00
Sugar bowl, gr & yel mottle....15.00
Syrup, floral, w/underplate....150.00
Tray, dresser; flowers/vine on bl border, cream, 7½x4¼″....55.00
Tray, pin; yel/pink long stemmed roses in center, oblong....23.00
Tray, relish; mc floral on ivory....25.00
Tray, wht floral/leaves on cream/gr, open hdls, GM, 5x15″....39.00
Trivet, wht/pink floral/gr leaves on cream/bl, BM, 6¼″....34.00
Wall pocket, parrot, GM....85.00

R.S. Poland

'R.S. Poland' is a mark attributed to Reinhold Schlegelmilch's Tillowitz, Silesia Factory.

Hatpin holder, pink rose buds on rust....85.00
Vase, pink roses/gold garlands & hdls on wht satin, 9x4½″....140.00
Vase, portrait: 4 full-length females, sgn, 8″....250.00

R.S. Prussia

Art porcelain bearing the mark 'R.S. Prussia' was manufactured by Erdmann and Reinhold Schlegelmilch from the late 1870s to the early 1900s in a Germanic area known until the end of WWI as Prussia. The vast array of mold shapes in combination with a wide variety of decorations is the basis for R.S. Prussia's appeal. Themes can be categorized as figural (usually based on a famous artist's work), birds, florals, portraits, scenics, and animals.

Berry set, cabbage roses, blown-out lilies, pearl, 7-pc....400.00
Biscuit jar, bow tie mold, gold trim, no mk....180.00
Bowl, barnyard scene, rare orange coloring, RM, 10½″....750.00
Bowl, bluebirds, floral center, RM, 10½″....425.00
Bowl, church scene, scalloped edge, gr, no mk, 6″....40.00
Bowl, dogwood, gold beading, pearl finish, ftd, 6″....75.00
Bowl, fleur-de-lis, int/ext: roses, gold/bl, ftd, RM, 7¾″....140.00
Bowl, floral, gr/wht, satin finish, scalloped, 5¼″....45.00
Bowl, floral, lav/pink, iris mold, ftd, RM, 6½″....165.00
Bowl, floral, RM, 10½″....210.00
Bowl, floral, sawtooth mold, gr/gold border, no mk, 10½″....130.00
Bowl, flowers in water scenic, RM, 11″....225.00
Bowl, lady feeds chickens, bronze irid, no mk, 10″....595.00
Bowl, Lebrun Girls portrait, cobalt border....850.00
Bowl, lilacs, lav/gr/bl/yel, scalloped rim, RM, 2″....185.00
Bowl, master schooner, pearl finish, brn/wht, RM, 11″....700.00
Bowl, Melon Boys, keyhole, wht w/gr opal jewels, RM, 10″....1,200.00
Bowl, mill scene, brn, sawtooth, RM, 10¼″....750.00
Bowl, mill scene, brn, 3-ftd, 7″....275.00
Bowl, Old Man of Mountains, icicle mold, RM, 11″....700.00
Bowl, ostrich....2,300.00
Bowl, pheasant w/trees, lily pad mold, RM, 10¾″....600.00
Bowl, poinsettias, iris mold, Wheelock, 10″....190.00
Bowl, poppies, lime w/shadow floral, iris mold, RM, 10½″....275.00
Bowl, poppies in center, dk pink/wht w/in, RM, 9¼″....185.00
Bowl, poppy, blown-out, 15″....700.00

Bowl, Quiet Cove, Old Man of Mtn, circle mold, RM, 8½x11" . . 650.00
Bowl, roses, carnation mold, gold center, RM, 9½" 195.00
Bowl, roses, fleur-de-lis ft, 5x2⅞" 115.00
Bowl, roses, gold beading on wht, RM, 10" 200.00
Bowl, roses, pk/wht on pearl, gold, scalloped, shallow, 7" 40.00
Bowl, roses, scallop/beaded petal mold rim, no mk, 10" 85.00
Bowl, snowbird, icicle mold, 3-ftd 650.00
Bowl, Summer Season, bowl-in-bowl, 10½" 795.00
Bowl, swans, icicle mold, gold border, berry sz 500.00
Bowl, swans on lake, temple, RM, 8½" 500.00
Bowl, swans/pines/canal, sawtooth edge, gr/bl, RM, 10¾" 600.00
Bowl, Winter Season, iris mold, satin, 10½" 895.00
Bowl, 4 portraits, Seasons, RM 1,350.00
Butter dish, pink roses on cream, gold traced, insert, RM 695.00
Cake plate, Old Man of Mountains, open hdl, RM, 10½" 475.00
Cake plate, peacock, icicle mold 725.00
Cake plate, pink floral, gold traces at edge, open hdl 155.00
Cake plate, swans w/gazebo, open hdls, 11¼" 545.00
Celery, pheasant & pine trees, RM, 12x6" 275.00
Celery, swans, icicle mold, pierced hdls, RM, 12" 375.00
Celery tray, roses, stippled floral mold, pink/red, no mk 145.00
Celery tray, roses, stippled floral mold, tan/gr, RM, 12" 175.00
Chocolate pot, Flossie portrait, molded leaf ft, no mk 425.00
Chocolate pot, Melon Eaters, jeweled 1,800.00
Chocolate pot, orchids emb, allover roses, hourglass shape 195.00
Chocolate pot, pink roses, point & clover mold, 10¼" 395.00
Chocolate pot, pink/yel/violet flowers, ball/ft mold, 9¼" 375.00
Chocolate pot, roses, gold beading on wht, RM 395.00
Chocolate pot, roses & snowballs, 6 molded ft, RM, 9" 349.00
Coffee pot, much gold, pie crust ruffle base, ped ft 110.00
Cracker jar, allover mc flowers, ornate hdls, RM 225.00
Cracker jar, blown-out irises & red floral on bl, RM 150.00
Cracker jar, Colonial figures, floral, no mk 380.00
Cracker jar, leaf mold, leaf hdls, 10-pointed ft, no mk 275.00
Cracker jar, pink/wht roses, satin finish, 4-scallop mold 350.00
Cracker jar, pk/wht roses, cream/bl/pk, hdls, 5x7¾" 135.00
Cracker jar, snowball, satin finish 190.00
Cracker jar, snowball & roses, gr/yel, RM 350.00
Creamer, church, ftd, gr tint, RM 150.00
Creamer, mill scene, gr 130.00
Creamer, Queen Louise portrait, molded leaf ft, no mk 265.00
Creamer, water lilies reflection, lt bl, icicle mold, RM 250.00
Creamer & sugar, mill & cottage scene, gr/wht, RM 300.00
Creamer & sugar, pink/wht/yel roses on bl, 4-ftd, emb ribs 250.00
Creamer & sugar, pk poppies on yel-gr, ped ft, sq base, RM . . . 195.00
Creamer & sugar, red roses on cream, ped ft 175.00
Creamer & sugar, sheepherders/bluebird, jeweled, ped ft 575.00
Creamer & sugar, snowbird 500.00
Creamer & sugar, Winter, gr/gold/wht satin, ftd, RM 450.00
Creamer & sugar, 3 swans on lake, icicle mold, bl, RM 650.00
Cup, coffee; Melon Eater, RM 200.00
Cup, coffee; swan/temple/urn/pine trees, satin, RM 150.00
Cup & saucer, demitasse; wht floral, gr/yel/cream, ped ft 62.00
Egg dish, floral, hdls 300.00
Ewer, Summer Season, 9" 1,325.00
Gravy boat, Melon Eaters, 2-hdl 475.00
Hair receiver, lid w/4 jewels, yel & wht roses, wht base 100.00
Hair receiver, roses, cream/yel/pk, scalloped, 4½x2½" 100.00
Hatpin holder, Midst Snow and Ice, Admiral Perry, sgn 800.00
Humidor, roses, octagonal, RM, 6x5¼" 650.00
Jam jar, castle scene, w/orig saucer & lid, RM 600.00
Loving cup, Melon Eaters, jeweled, 9" 1,150.00
Mustache cup, floral, sgn, w/saucer 120.00
Mustache cup, floral, Tiffany/blown-out, LeBrun, RM 500.00
Mustard jar, cottage scene on brn, w/spoon 150.00
Mustard jar, girl w/ribbon in hair, blown-out floral, RM 150.00
Mustard jar, snowbird 300.00
Pitcher, lemonade; wht/pink roses, dk gr/wht, RM, 8½" 590.00
Plate, bluebirds, RM, 10½" 450.00
Plate, carnations, pink/wht on lt gr, shell edge, RM, 11" 215.00
Plate, Dice Players, mk Wurfelspieler & Murillia, RM, 9" 395.00
Plate, farmyard, swag & tassel, RM, 7¾" 350.00
Plate, floral, pink on bl carnation mold, RM, 7¾" 135.00
Plate, floral, satin finish, 8½" 105.00
Plate, hydrangeas, gr/lav/orange, satin finish, RM, 7¾" 95.00
Plate, mill scene, gr/yel, #90, RM 650.00
Plate, pear, peach & raspberries, brn/cream, 10½" 275.00
Plate, poppies & daisies, 6-medallion mold, RM, 11" 155.00
Plate, Quiet Cove, 5-circle, bl-gray, RM, 10¼" 450.00
Plate, rose clusters, gold tracings, satin, 8¾" 115.00
Plate, roses, pink on cream, RM, 7½" 48.00
Plate, roses/hydrangeas, ribbon/jewel mold, RM, 10½" 185.00
Plate, sheepherder & bluebirds, RM, 11" 450.00
Plate, snowbird, RM 850.00
Plate, Winter Season, blown-out iris mold, satin, RM 650.00

Plate, icicle mold, lady with flowers, red star mark, Gesentzlich Geschutzt, 1¼" x 8½", $875.00.

Plate, 2 swans, temple & pine trees, satin, RM, 8¾" 300.00
Plate, 3 lg peaches in center, open hdl, RM, 10" 150.00
Plate, 3 swans on lake, icicle mold, lt bl, RM, 8½" 400.00
Plate, 4 blown-out irises on yel/gr/coupe shape/hdls, 10¼" 225.00
Relish, pink roses/ivy, gold trim, scalloped hdl, RM, 9½" 50.00
Relish, scenic w/duck & trees 400.00
Relish, swan & gazebo, RM, 8" 150.00
Schooner, tankard; rare, 11½" 1,650.00
Shaving mug/drain, carnation mold/shadow flowers/roses, RM . . . 175.00
Sugar bowl, dogwood, much gold, RM 62.00
Sugar bowl, pink & wht poppies on bl/yel, icicle mold, RM 135.00
Sugar bowl, pink/wht/yel roses on bl, 4-ftd, emb ribs, RM 250.00
Sugar sifter, red roses, curved/pleated bottom, RM 110.00
Syrup, floral, scalloped, satin finish, w/underplate, RM 150.00
Syrup, orchids, cream/gold/orchid/bl, w/underplate, 4½" 100.00
Syrup, pink roses, gold border/ruby jewels, w/underplate 210.00
Syrup, pink roses & hydrangeas, flat base, RM 168.00
Syrup, swan, satin finish, no mk, w/underplate 150.00

Tankard, bluebirds & swans 475.00
Tankard, floral, carnation mold, 11½" 950.00
Tankard, lady/flowers, bk: lady/dogs, Tiffany, no mk, 14" 2,200.00
Tankard, pink roses on gr, gold jewels, RM, 9½" 400.00
Tankard, roses, ball/ft mold, RM, 14½" 750.00
Teapot, castle scene, #623, RM 550.00
Toothpick holder, Melon Eaters, jeweled, 2-hdl 800.00
Tray, bread; 2 swans/temple/pines, satin, RM, 12½x6½" 300.00
Tray, bun; swans, icicle mold 425.00
Tray, dresser; Fall Season, blown-out poppy, satin finish 1,650.00
Tray, dresser; pink/wht roses, pierced hdls, mk, 12x7½" 145.00
Tray, dresser; roses, point/clover mold, gilt, RM, 8x12" 240.00
Tray, pheasants/oval beaded medallions, w/hdls, RM, 7x14" 525.00
Vase, church, gr tint, RM, 4" 175.00
Vase, Dice Throwers, gr/yel/lav, ped ft, opal jewels, 8" 550.00
Vase, floral, jeweled, loving cup form, RM, 10" 250.00
Vase, floral on satin, dbl hdl, 11¾" 375.00
Vase, lilies/sm floral, gilt, 3-part top/hdls, RM, 9" 245.00
Vase, Melon Eaters, jeweled, fancy hdls, RM, 10½" 1,075.00
Vase, mill scene, brn/yel, bottle shape, RM, 6½" 400.00
Vase, ostrich, 2-hdl, rare 600.00
Vase, roses, hdls, 10½" 290.00
Vase, roses/pearl jewels, satin w/lav shade, hdls, RM, 6" 385.00

R.S. Suhl, E.S. Suhl

Porcelains marked with this designation are attributed to Schlegelmilch's Suhl factory.

Incense burner, floral, Tiffany maroon 135.00
Vase, daisies on gray, 12" 125.00
Vase, Nightwatch, 6½" 600.00

R.S. Tillowitz

R.S. Tillowitz marked porcelains are attributed to Reinhold Schlegelmilch's Tillowitz, Silesia factory.

Dish, pheasants on black ground with gold rising sun, 8", $200.00.

Bowl, ruffled, 4 molded ft, HP lilies, gold, 2½x6" 48.00
Creamer & sugar, shaded gr w/wht lilies 175.00
Mustard pot, forget-me-nots, gold hdl/finial, HP, w/ladle 55.00
Plate, cherries decor, 11" 23.00
Vase, floral, 7", pr 85.00

Schneider

The Schneider Glass Company was founded in 1914 at Epinay-sur-seine, France. They made many types of art glass, some of which sandwiched designs between layers. Other decorative devices were applique and carved work. These were marked 'Charder,' or 'Schneider.'

During the twenties, commercial artware was produced with Deco motifs, cut by acid through two or three layers, and signed 'LeVerre Francais' in script or with a section of inlayed filigrane.

When no condition is indicated, the items listed below are assumed to be in mint condition.

See also Le Verre Francais

Bowl, centerpiece; 3 cherries, bl/yel swirl stem, sgn, 7" 300.00
Bowl, orange mottled, flared, 9" 75.00
Bowl, red rim/mottled yel ftd center, iron fr w/roses, 10" 225.00
Compote, amethyst stem & ft, red-orange bowl, sgn, 12" 270.00
Ewer, France, sgn, mottled amethyst/red, applied hdl, 6½" 175.00
Vase, air bubbles, abstract shape, heavy crystal, 5" 125.00
Vase, bl satin w/gold rim/HP flowers, ca 1914, 14", pr 895.00
Vase, bl/blk/clear, orange int, wrought iron ftd base, 5½" 250.00
Vase, gray/amber, applied lav opal top band, bulbous, 8½" 375.00
Vase, yel/orange/amethyst, 8" 250.00

Left to right: Vase, mottled rose shading to white, purple and gray blue, on purple glass foot, acid stamped, 11", $700.00; Right, Vase, applied pine cone decoration, intaglio carved at the shoulder with leaves, opaque mustard ground, 14½", $1,600.00.

Schoolhouse Collectibles

Schoolhouse collectibles bring to mind memories of a bygone era when the teacher rang her bell to call the youngsters to class in a one-room schoolhouse--where often both the 'hickory stick' and an apple occupied a prominent position on her desk.

When no condition is indicated, the items listed below are assumed to be in excellent condition.

Bell, bell metal, trn wood hdl, 8" 32.00
Book, exercises in pen in ink, blk/red ink decor, 8x12" 40.00

Book, Introduction to Algebra, J Day, leather bound, 1839.....12.00
Book, mathematics exercises, pen/ink, 1858, 8½x13".........175.00
Book, McGuffey's 5th Reader, 1857..........................14.00
Book, Monroe's 6th Reader, 1872............................10.00
Book, Wilson's 4th Reader, 1860.............................8.00
Desk, teacher's; walnut, trn legs, dvtl drw/top, lift lid..........275.00
Desk, teachers; pine/poplar/cherry, lift lid, 37x36"............175.00
Pencil box, cherry, swivel lid, old patina, rnd, 11"............125.00
Pencil box, early auto racing scene, wood fr...................25.00
Pencil box, Jack & Jill, complete litho, wood fr, 8"............12.00
Pencil box, Little Red Riding Hood, litho scenes, wood fr......18.00
Pencil box, Niagara Falls, scene on top, 2 levels..............40.00
Pencil box, papier mache, birds, hinged lid, France............20.00
Pencil box, Scholar's Companion, slide top, tin, pat 1874.......45.00
Pencil box, school slate shape, full contents, wood fr..........80.00
Pencil box, WWII, tanks & warships on top, fabric............19.00
Pencil sharpener, desk; CI, Victorian.........................35.00
Pencil sharpener, hand crank, 'Automatic,' pat 1906/07, 5".....45.00
Printer's set, letters/#s/animals/etc, in wood case, 1932.........90.00
Slate, dbl, hinged, 14x10", EX binding.......................40.00
Slate, wood fr, 7½"..12.00

Scouting Collectibles

Scouting was founded in England in 1907 by a retired Major General, Lord Robert Baden-Powell. Its purpose is the same today as it was then--to help develop physically strong, mentally alert boys who are taught basic fundamentals of survival and leadership. The movement soon spread to the United States, and in 1910 a Chicago publisher, William Boyce set out to establish Scouting in America. The first World Scout Jamboree was held in 1911 in England. Baden-Powell was honored as the Chief Scout of the World. In 1926, he was awarded the Silver Buffalo Award in the United States. He was knighted in 1929 for distinguished military service, and for his scouting efforts. Baden-Powell died in 1941.

For further reading on the subject, we recommend *Scouting Collectibles* by R.J. Sayers; you will find his address in the Directory under Texas. When no condition is indicated, the items listed below are assumed to be in excellent condition.

Beadcraft outfit, loom/beads/thread, official, '35, in box.........20.00
Board, 40 Knots, Learn to Tie Them, Nabisco premium, '50.....8.00
Book, Boy Scouts Year Book, 1923........................10.00
Book, Golden Anniv Book of Scouting, Rockwell illus, 1959....12.00
Book, Handbook for Boys, Rockwell cover, 1940s..............8.50
Book, Handbook for Boys, 2nd Ed, 1927....................15.00
Book, Handbook for Scoutmasters, 16th printing, 1932........15.00
Book, Handbook for Scoutmasters, 2nd Ed/2nd printing, '20....20.00
Book, Scout Naturalists in Rocky Mtns, dust jacket, '32.........6.00
Bookends, emblem motif, iron, lg..........................16.00
Booklet, National Jamboree, 1953............................8.00
Bracelet & barrett, Girl Scout, gold plated...................12.00
Camp set: knife, fork & spoon, logo on case, 1940s...........10.00
Compass, octagonal, brn plastic, '50s-'60s, VG.................5.00
Cup, folding; eagle on top..................................5.00
Doll, cloth/compo, uniform/overseas cap, '50s, 14", VG.........40.00
Flannel, Honor Unit, purple/yel w/beard, 1857-1957, 9x7"......15.00
Flashlight, brass..12.50
Fork, Brownie..4.00
Game, Troop of Boy Scouts, 40 stand-ups, in box, pat 1914....60.00
Lapel pin, Eagle Scout, sterling, mkd, '60s...................8.00
Manual, membership; celluloid, 1914.........................10.00
Medal, Japanese, Memory of Tokyo Tower, dtd 1958, w/box.....10.00
Medal, Trail, Lincoln bust, silvered, w/ribbon..................8.00
Neckerchief, staff; embroidered bust of Baden-Powell, VG.......13.00
Neckerchief, 1967 World Jamboree 'Fisherman,' yel, printed.....11.00
Neckerchief slide, Liberty bust/insignia, brass, '50s era..........5.00
Patch, Eagle Scout, oval, embroidered, '50s..................12.00
Patch, pocket; 1967 World Jamboree, Jamboree design, VG......7.00
Patch, 1964 National Jamboree, Jamboree design, 6" dia, VG....9.00
Pencil tin, Girl Scouts, Wallace Pencil Co, rare...............30.00
Photo, boy, early uniform w/sleeve insignias, b/w, 5x7"..........6.00
Photo on card mt, troop in peaked hats, 1920s, 7x9½".........6.00
Plate, Regout, Dutch, 1937, 8¾"..........................35.00
Sash, gr cotton, w/28 type D badges, 4 type E, '50s, VG.......45.00
Sash, Order o/t Arrow, red embroidered arrow, '50s, VG.......10.00
Sewing kit, Girl Scout, gold plated, leatherette case............6.00
Signaler, radio/blinker/telegraph, official, VG box.............20.00
Tie pull, brass...2.00
Uniform, Indian; Campfire Girls............................12.00
Vest, w/orig 1935 Jamboree patch+18 other patches...........85.00
Whistle, nickeled brass, Lanyard loop, mk Gotham, '50s.........6.00

Left to right: Every Boy's Library Edition of the Handbook, 1919, excellent condition, $22.00; 2nd Edition Handbook, 1922, fair condition, $20.00.

Scrimshaw

The most desirable examples of the art of scrimshaw can be traced back to the first half of the 19th century, to the heyday of the whaling industry. Some voyages lasted for several years, and conditions on board were often dismal. Sailors filled the long hours by carving or engraving designs in whale or walrus ivory. Using the tools of their trade, they created animal figures, boxes, pie crimpers, etc., often emphasizing the lines of their carvings with ink or berry stain.

Eskimos also make scrimshaw, sometimes borrowing designs from the sailors who traded with them.

When no condition is indicated, the items listed below are assumed to be in excellent condition.

Basket, picket fence, all whalebone, brass tacks, 4½x5x6"....1,100.00
Busk, Am eagle/flowers/verse, 1845, 11", VG................465.00
Busk, baleen, verse/geometrics bk: Am flags/trees, 14", EX....330.00
Busk, eagle/shield/1882/whalers/whaleboaters, 7½"............300.00
Clothespin, whalebone, 1800s, 5", 8 for......................350.00
Dolphin jaw, Napoleon III on horsebk, bk: ship, 20"..........770.00
Netsuke, whale tooth, Victorian lady/ship, 1800s, 3"..........605.00
Pan bone, whaling bark/whales/men/longboats, 1850, 9x15"..3,025.00
Spoon, salt; bone...10.00

Engraved pan bone, fully-rigged whaling bark with school of whales, some captured, some pursued by men in longboats, minor warping, ca 1850, 8″ x 14″, $2,750.00.

Whale tooth, Am eagle over US shield/flags/etc, 4″, pr........550.00
Whale tooth, Am eagle/X-flags/banner, bk carved, 5″, EX......880.00
Whale tooth, Arabian princess/fawn, bk bust of lady, 7″.......660.00
Whale tooth, captain lecturing cabin boy, 4″..................80.00
Whale tooth, Legend of Caractacus, stippled, 1800s, 5″, pr....660.00

Seals and Sealing Wax

A seal is used to affix a stamp or embossment either on an official paper or on wax such as was once used on correspondence. The sealing wax was first melted, then allowed to drip on the seam of the envelope or the writing paper. The imprint of the seal on the wax was an easily identifiable device, or the writers monogram.

When no condition is indicated, the items listed below are assumed to be in undamaged condition.

Bone, twisted stem w/carved fist atop, 2¾″..................15.00
Brass, Artful Dodger, 2⅛″..................55.00
Brass, bust, w/letter G, 2⅜″..................45.00
Brass, bust of George Washington, 2½″..................135.00
Brass, bust of Shakespeare, 2⅜″..................55.00
Brass, bust of Sir Walter Raleigh, 2½″..................55.00
Brass, bust of William IV, 3″..................55.00
Brass, classical lady & child, 2⅜″..................25.00
Brass, comical figure in military uniform, 2⅝″..................55.00

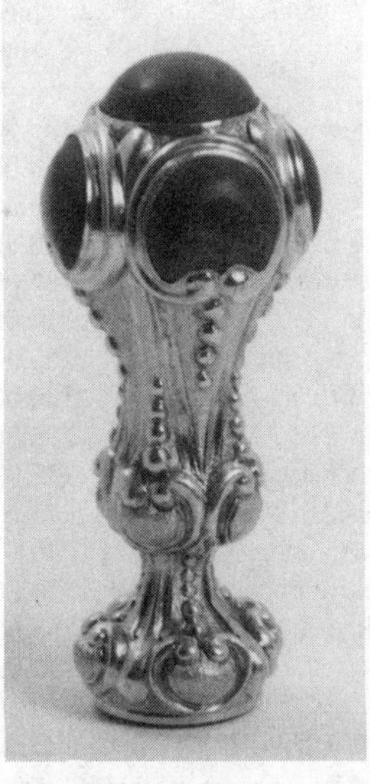

Gold-washed sterling Rococo scrollwork set with malachite stones, carnelian bloodstone intaglio seal, 4″, $400.00.

Brass, flint lock musket, 4″..................135.00
Brass, hand clutches foliage scrolls & bird, orig gilding.........45.00
Brass, horse head, 2⅜″..................145.00
Brass, lady's leg w/shoe & garter, 2⅜″..................155.00
Brass, man, 2⅝″..................45.00
Brass, Napolean on globe, 2⅝″..................55.00
Brass, phoenix head, 2¼″..................55.00
Brass, portly man w/bent pipe, 2⅛″..................55.00
Brass, thumb screw w/eng, seal w/bird, 1⅞″..................35.00
Fob, chalcedony engraved w/initials/scrolls, 18k, 1¼″..........185.00
Girl-in-a-swing, Cupid on lion, porcelain, 1760, EX...........200.00
Girl-in-a-swing, Cupid on tree trunk, porcelain, 1760, EX......200.00
Girl-in-a-swing, 2 wht doves in arbor, porcelain, 1760, EX.....150.00
Ivory, lg knob hdl, trn stem..................65.00
Ring, bloodstone w/bust of animal on crown & letters, 18k.....250.00
Silver, Blk boy & alligator in palm tree, sterling, 2¼″..........60.00
Silver, chased floral design, 1⅞″..................20.00
Silver, man bending at waist, EPNS, 1½″..................13.00
Silver, screw-out pick, 2¾″..................205.00
Spy glass hdl, gilt metal w/cut glass disk: cupid/lady............35.00
Watch fob, carnelian w/coat-of-arms engraving, hdl, ⅞″........275.00
Whalebone, turned, w/brass tip, sm chips, 2⅞″..................95.00
Wood, carved horse leg w/silver shoe & tip, IC mk, 3⅞″.......145.00
Wood, carved shoe w/brass trim, 2¾″..................115.00

Sebastians

Sebastian miniatures were first produced in 1938 by Prescott W. Baston, in Marblehead, Massachusetts. Since then, he has modeled more than four hundred. These figurines have been sold through gift shops all over the country, primarily in the New England states. In 1976, Baston withdrew his 'Sebastians' from production. Under an agreement with the Lance Corporation of Hudson, Massachusetts, one hundred designs were selected to be produced by that company under Baston's supervision. Those remaining were discontinued. In the short time since then, the older figurines have become very collectible.

When no condition is indicated, the items listed below are assumed to be in mint condition.

Abraham Lincoln, looking ahead, 1947..................95.00
American Bank, Nashville, c 1966..................150.00
Aunt Polly, 1948..................52.00
Becky Thatcher..................135.00
Benjamin Franklin..................95.00
Boy & Girl Skaters, sgn 1st Edition, pr..................75.00
Building Days, sgn, pr..................69.00
Catherine Laffite..................225.00
Charles Dickens, 1952..................35.00
Cleopatra..................375.00
Clown, gr label..................85.00
Colonial Kitchen, 1952..................35.00
Concord Minuteman, Marblehead..................100.00
Corner Drugstore, Marblehead..................65.00
Countess Oliva..................260.00
David Copperfield & Wife..................60.00
Dutchman's Pipe..................300.00
Evangeline..................225.00
Family Picnic, sgn..................50.00
Family Sing, MIB..................112.50
Grand Canyon, plate, sgn..................60.00
Grandma at Cookstove, sgn/dtd 1947..................35.00
Hannah Penn..................95.00
House of Seven Gables..................140.00

In the Candy Store (Necco) 180.00
James & Elizabeth Monroe, pr 195.00
Jesse Buffman 00.00
John Smith & Pocahontas, pr 215.00
Jordan Marsh Observer 260.00
Lepenseur, Auguste Rodin (The Thinker) 300.00
Lincoln 40.00
Lobster man, sgn, c 1947, VG 45.00
Malvolio 260.00
Mark Anthony 330.00
Masonic Bible 600.00
Motif #1, sgn 60.00
Mr Obocell, gr & silver Marblehead label 135.00
Neighboring Pews 450.00
Nurse, VG 25.00
Parade Rest, sgn PW Baston 55.00
Patrick & Sarah Henry, pr 195.00
Paul Bunyan 150.00
Plaque, Marblehead, PW Baston Bellringer, 1951, copy 200.00
Princess Elizabeth & Lt Philip Mountbatten, 1947, pr 275.00
Priscilla Alden 150.00
Priscilla Fortescue 450.00
RH Stearns, Chestnut Hill Mall 410.00
Rip Van Winkle 50.00
Sampling the Stew 135.00
Santa, music box 3,000.00
Savin Sandy 180.00
Scrooge 120.00
Shawmut Indian, color 165.00
Sidewalk Days, Boy & Girl, pr 75.00
Spirit of '76, Marblehead label 65.00
Swan Boat 150.00
Thomas Jefferson 75.00
Toll House, Pilgrims, 1947 .... 75.00
Tom Sawyer 135.00
Uncle Sam 10.00
Victorian Couple 180.00
Weighing the Baby 375.00
Williamsburg Governor & Lady, pr 120.00

Sevres

Fine quality porcelains have been made in Sevres, France, since the early 1700s. Rich ground colors were decorated with hand-painted portraits, scenics and florals, transfer printing or decalcomania, and were often embellished with heavy gold. These wares are the most respected of all French porcelain. Their style and designs have been widely copied; some of the items listed below are Sevres-type wares.

Unless noted otherwise, values are for examples in mint condition.

Bowl, courting couple, sgn Leune, ftd, oval, gilt mt, 12" 550.00
Bowl, HP reserves on bl, gilt bronze mt, w/lid, 15¼" 880.00
Box, reserve w/2 maids/gent w/caged dove on bl, sgn, 13" L 1,000.00
Bust, Peter the Great, on waisted socle, late 19th C, 18" 700.00
Casket, figural panels top/sides, serpentine, 14" L 1,540.00
Center bowl, bronze fr: base w/3 satyr supports+3 mermaids 1,500.00
Center bowl, putti/clouds, pierced gilt mts, 4 ft, 19" 2,420.00
Cup & saucer, dbl walled, reticulated band, gilt, 1½" 350.00
Jardiniere, serpentine/pierced brass mt, HP panel, 27" L 2,200.00
Jewel casket, Cupid/putti in landscape, gilt mts, 11" L 660.00
Pedestal, Pascault HP central band, onyx top/base, 40½" 3,300.00
Plate, lady's portrait, sgn Chateau des Tuileres, 9" 175.00
Plate, Mme De Lamballe, sgn Moreau, ivory/gr/gilt, 1800s 225.00

Portrait plate, 'La Bourbon,' signed Delaeruix, cobalt and gold, 1700s, 10", $550.00.

Plate, vines/leaves, gilt on wht, HP, 1811 .... 150.00
Tazza, floral, HP, bronze ormolu, ca 1875 .... 150.00
Urn, ftd, artist sgn, lion's head hdls, w/lid, 14" 800.00
Urn, spiral lid/neck, can body w/scenic, sgn/dtd 1758, 19" 1,250.00
Vase, frieze w/Cupid/bridge/maid, sgn Demonceaux, 27" 1,500.00
Vase, Napoleonic battles, Desprez, gilt mts, 53" 5,500.00
Vase, Napoleonic battles, L Vernet, w/lid, 40" 5,225.00
Vase, parian, encrusted florals, lg hdls, sq base, 6" 600.00
Vase, portrait/HP, gilt hdls/base, sgn Wagner, 9½x3½" 660.00
Vase, pottery, 3 gilt lion masks on crystalline, 1907, 5½" 600.00
Vase, reserve w/lovers in woods, E Grisard, w/lid, 18", pr 1,500.00
Vase, shepherd lovers, after Boucher by Aly, w/lid, 37" 5,500.00
Vase, soldiers/battleground, H Desprez, gilt mts, 34", pr 12,650.00
Vase, 2 maids/gent/fountain, sgn, gilt mts, 46" 7,425.00
Vase, 3 maids at loom/suitor, Bellanger, gilt mt, lid, 36" 3,080.00

Sewer Tile

Whimsies, advertising novelties, and other ornamental items were sometimes made in potteries where the primary product was simply tile.

When no condition is indicated, the items listed below are assumed to be in undamaged condition.

Bank, head: smiling boy, tooled hair, ears low on head, 5" 130.00
Bird, primitive, hand formed, 2½" 50.00
Dish, hexagonal, incised birds/etc, primitive, 2¼" 15.00
Dog, G detail, tooled coat/collar/face, 11", EX 210.00
Dog, open legs, rectangle base, tooled features, sgn, 4¾" 135.00
Dog, seated, G tooling, brn-gray mottle, 9" 210.00
Dog, seated on oval base, G detail, brn glaze, sgn, 13" 305.00
Dog, simple tooled features, Empire Clay Co, 7" L 105.00
Eagle, upright, wings folded, glazed, 7" 235.00
Frog, tooled features/heart on bk, inset necklace/eyes, 6" 115.00
Humidor, tree stump/dog finial w/2 open legs, Whatcher, 7" 275.00
Inkwell, dk brn, edge chips, 3⅜" 30.00
Lion, recumbent, rectangle plinth, G primitive detail, 9½" 70.00
Lion, tooled detail/rhinestone eyes, flat bk, Lee Co, 12" 265.00
Pitcher, bark surface, tooled knots, applied stars, 8½" 70.00
Planter, stump form, old edge chips, 7½" 30.00
Planter, stump w/3 open branches, mk not legible, 24" 125.00

Sewing Items

In the early colonial days, the teaching of needlework skills was considered an important part of a young girl's education. The Victorians developed many curious yet functional sewing accessories. One of these is the sewing bird. Made of brass, wood, or iron, these figural tools were designed to be clamped onto the top of the worktable. Through the lever action of the tail, the beak would open and close to hold the fabric in the proper position for hand sewing. A velvet pincushion often topped it off.

The first mechanical sewing machine was invented by Thomas Paint, an Englishman, in 1790. The first American patent went to Elias Howe in 1840--but Howe took his invention to England! Not until 1846, when the Wheeler Wilson Mfg. Company was founded, were there any truly functional home sewing machines. The first electric machine was developed by Isaac Singer in 1889.

Thimbles have long been collectible. Some were made of silver--a few in gold. Many were embossed with scrolls, engraved, and occasionally jeweled! Hallmarked examples are especially valuable.

When no condition is indicated, the items listed below are assumed to be in excellent condition.

Basket, fine weave, curlique grass bands, 3x8x8½″ 65.00
Basket, splint, cloth lined, 3 pincushions, 4½x6½″ 60.00
Basket, wicker, ornate weaving, hinged lid, 11x7x4″ 20.00
Book, instruction; Merrow Sewing Machines 22.00
Box, cherry, lift top/cushion/drw, holds 6 spools, 5x7x6″ 50.00
Box, compartment in base, Pease, varnished, 7″ 175.00
Box, curly maple/intricate inlay & trn, 8x6x5½″ 1,500.00
Box, inlaid mahog, bun ft/mirror/5 lift-out parts, 10x8x6″ 150.00
Box, PA folk art, pine, drw/thread caddy top, 15″ 95.00
Box, sewing machine attachment; oak, dtd 1889 . . . . 25.00
Box, spool; walnut, drw/8 ivory eyelets, lift top, 7x5½″ 55.00
Box, trn 'tree' w/wire rods for spools, drw, 13½″ 105.00
Box, vinegar sponged, 1 drw, trn support, 1860s, 11x8x8″ 140.00
Box, walnut, cabinet top w/sliding doors, base drw, 12x8″ 90.00
Button, brass, lot of 18 . . . . 10.00
Button, fancy metal, lady & floral motif, Victorian, lg 28.00
Button, red/wht morning glory, openwork, French, 1¼″ 18.50
Button, sterling w/emb putto, sgn JS, French, 1899, 1⅛″ 25.00
Buttonhole maker, Will & Finck 150.00
Case, sewing machine tool; folding oak, 1889 . . . . 12.00
Case, thimble/needle; enamel scenic, Halcyon Bilston 75.00
Catalogue, Sinsmore Sewing Machine Sales, 1954, 32 pg 12.00
Darning egg, celluloid 6.00
Darning egg, cobalt glass 48.00
Darning egg, wood 5.00

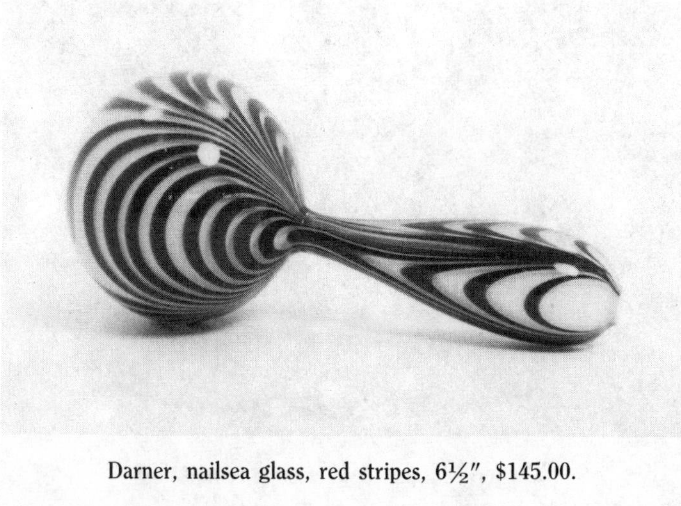

Darner, nailsea glass, red stripes, 6½″, $145.00.

Drawer, from oak sewing machine, applied side trim, 6 for 30.00
Eyelet punch, sterling, adjustable gauge 22.00
Needle case, ash, 1 drw, orig pulls, Watson's Needles, sm 45.00
Needle case, book, beaded, roses/lyre, 1839, silk w/in, sm 95.00
Needle case, book, paper cover, beaded front 10.00
Needle case, boxwood barrel, Accept...Best Wishes, Germany 25.00
Needle case, emb floral/eng, 6 hinged compartments, mk Gem . . 135.00
Needle case, eng people, sterling, Mexican 22.00
Needle case, parasol figural, ivory, rare, 4¼″ 135.00
Needle case, pea pod figural, ivory, rare, 4″ 150.00
Needle case, sheaf of wheat figural, ormolu, hinged, 3½″ 135.00
Needle case, sterling, Art Nouveau 65.00
Needle case, umbrella figural, ivory, 3½″ 20.00
Needle case, vegetable ivory, intricate carving, 4¾x1″ 65.00
Pin casket, emb butterfly/leaf, ormolu, hinged lid, 2¾″ 95.00
Pin casket, sliding leaf lid w/butterfly, ftd, English 135.00
Pincushion, bird on olive branch, beaded, 7x9x4″ 50.00
Pincushion, boot, half laced, SP, Meriden, 2½″ 25.00
Pincushion, canoe, silver, 1905, 1x4x1″ 50.00
Pincushion, cat, bisque 14.00
Pincushion, clown, wax, 6″ 30.00
Pincushion, girl by ball, porcelain basket of ribbon roses 65.00
Pincushion, Montreal & maple leaf, beaded, star shape, 6″ 28.00
Pincushion, Pug dog lying by 6-sided cushion, mk JB, 1920s 40.00
Pincushion, rabbit, copper metal, sgn 35.00
Pincushion, treen, free ring trn in base, rpl cover, 3¼″ 35.00
Pincushion, wood bucket, lift lid w/mirror w/in, decor, 2″ 45.00
Pincushion/tape measure, charcoal iron, metal/wood, 3¼″ 20.00
Punch, eng relief, w/gauge, mkd, 5½″ 28.00
Scissors, buttonhole; measuring blade 12.00
Scissors, buttonhole; plain blade 8.00
Scissors, embroidery; fancy sterling hdl 28.00
Scissors, wrought iron, 11″ L 10.00
Seam ripper, gr mottled celluloid 8.50
Sewing bird, brass, cast/emb, pincushion on bk, 5¼″ 125.00
Sewing bird, brass, vertical pincushion, unusual form, 4″ 200.00
Sewing bird, iron, wings close to body, heart thumbscrew 195.00
Sewing bird, silver gilding, 2 plush pincushions, 3⅜″ 125.00
Sewing bird, SP, 1 cushion, dtd 1893 . . . . 135.00

Sewing bird, bronze with two red velvet pincushions, dated 1853, in near mint condition, $195.00.

Sewing clamp, ornate brass hand holds table screw, 1859 . . . . 65.00
Sewing kit, cone shape, Sealtest Ice Cream 20.00
Sewing kit, emb tin, yel tassel, Calvert Whiskey 15.00
Smoothing board, arched open hdl, 38″ L 85.00
Tape measure, book, leather, Austria 28.00
Tape measure, clam, SP 37.00
Tape measure, coronation coach, brass, red windows, 2½″ 35.00

Tape measure, dog seated on rnd base, celluloid 35.00
Tape measure, doghouse w/bulldog tape, metal, Germany 50.00
Tape measure, Fab soap, celluloid, NM 6.00
Tape measure, flask: I Made Kentucky Famous in a Measure 37.00
Tape measure, German helmet, brass/blk Maltese Cross, 1914 . . . 65.00
Tape measure, girl w/mandolin, porcelain 35.00
Tape measure, holly design on sterling 65.00
Tape measure, Mammy, lady bug tape, blk celluloid 75.00
Tape measure, owl, brass w/glass eyes, 1½" dia 18.00
Tape measure, pig, celluloid, wht w/HP flowers, 2" 25.00
Tape measure, pig, plastic w/advertising 27.50
Tape measure, pig, SP 35.00
Tape measure, pig on oval base, pink celluloid 35.00
Tape measure, rooster, celluloid 35.00
Tape measure, sailing ship, celluloid 35.00
Tape measure, shoe, silver, emb: 3 Ft in 1 Shoe 55.00
Tape measure, straw hat, Victorian, tin 49.00
Tape measure, teakettle, brass 50.00
Tape measure, windmill, brass 45.00
Tape measure, 2 bees on top, bee tape pull 40.00
Tatting shuttle, metal, Boyle 6.00
Thimble, brass, child's 6.00
Thimble, brass, emb rim 12.00
Thimble, daisies, Dorcas 55.00
Thimble, egg shape MOP holder 15.00
Thimble, gold filled, leaf band, Thos Brogan 75.00
Thimble, metal, For a Good Girl 20.00
Thimble, sterling, anchor mk, pat May 28, 1889 . . . . 25.00
Thimble, sterling, bright-cut/eng border 20.00
Thimble, sterling, daisy band, agate top, 1899 . . . . 125.00
Thimble, sterling, emb rim 22.00
Thimble, sterling, incised gold band 22.00
Thimble, sterling, palm trees, Royal Spa, 1933 . . . . 69.00
Thimble, sterling, plain 12.00
Thimble, sterling, star band, Simon 30.00
Thimble, yel enamel on sterling, moonstone top, Norwegian 195.00
Thimble, 10k, dbl row bright-cut rim, mk 80.00
Thimble, 10k, scenic band 85.00
Thimble, 14k, beaded, eng bell shape rim 85.00
Thimble, 14k, engraved monogram/1897, floral border 85.00
Thimble, 14k, narrow bright-cut rim, monogram 90.00
Thimble, 18k pink/yel gold, border of leaves in relief 95.00
Thimble holder, acorn, wood 35.00
Thimble holder, Alpine boy/6 thimbles, brass, rnd base, 4" 85.00
Thimble holder, cats thread holder, SP, 3" base 55.00
Thimble holder, lady, Art Nouveau, SP, 6 holders, Austria 35.00
Thread cutter, knife edge under spring, gilt iron, 1874, 3" 25.00
Thread holder, bird/post, Victorian, rnd ftd base, holds 3 . . . . 95.00
Thread holder, ivory, barrel shape, int spool, 2" 80.00
Thread holder, thimble on top, Eastern Star emblem 8.00
Thread/thimble holder, wht metal baby figural, ftd base 85.00
Water lens, lace maker's 120.00
Yard stick, dressmaker's; Richardson's Tailor System 35.00

Sewing Machines

Beckwith, hand crank, attach to table, CI, 1871-72 . . . . 125.00
Brunonia, leaf type, hand crank, 1885 . . . . 135.00
Burh Rotary, ft pedal, oak case, drw at sides 50.00
CI Singer, hand crank/wood base, orig, 1880s, 12½x6x6½" 75.00
DW Clark, patent model, cast brass, orig, 3½x6¼x1¾", NM 295.00
Fristen–Rossman, hand crank, inlaid hardwood case 125.00
GI Jones, claw feet, orig box, VG 150.00
Singer, foot-powered, early 1900s 65.00
Singer, hand crank, wood base, CI, orig, 1887, 14½x7½x9" 65.00
Stitchwell, hand crank/clamp-on, box, HP decor, 5½x6x3¼" 98.00
Wilcox & Gibbs, CI, 1st pat 1871, w/crest, 1883, 10x7¾x5½" . . . 95.00
Wilcox & Gibbs, hand crank, SM Co (Deposee), 10¾x6x8¼" 80.00

Shaker Items

The Shaker community was founded in America in 1776 at Niskeyuna, New York, by a small group of English 'Shaking Quakers.' The name referred to a group dance which was part of their religious rites. Their leader was Mother Ann Lee.

By 1815 their membership had grown to more than one thousand in eighteen communities as far west as Indiana and Kentucky. But in less than a decade, their numbers began to decline, until today only a handful remain.

Their furniture is prized for its originality, simplicity, workmanship, and practicality. Few pieces were signed. Some were carefully finished to enhance the natural wood; a few were painted.

Although other methods were used earlier, most Shaker boxes were of oval construction with overlapping 'fingers' at the seams to prevent buckling as the wood aged. Boxes with original paint fetch double the price of an unpainted box; size and number of fingers should also be considered.

Although the Shakers were responsible for weaving a great number of baskets, their methods are not easily distinguished from those of their outside neighbors, and it is nearly impossible without first-hand knowledge to specifically attribute one to their manufacture. They were involved in various commercial efforts other than cabinetmaking--among them sheep and dairy farming, sawmills, and pipe and brick making. They were the first to raise crops specifically for seed, and to market their product commercially. They perfected a method to recycle paper, and were able to produce wrinkle-free fabrics.

When no condition is indicated, the items listed below are assumed to be in excellent condition.

Almanac, 1886, edge wear, 6x7¾" 75.00
Basket, ash splint, dbl hinged lid, hoop hdl, 10x12x8¼" 150.00
Basket, berry, splint, 2½x4" 105.00
Basket, gathering; oblong/dbl wrap rim/hoop hdl, 13x17x11" . . . 175.00
Basket, gathering; woven splint, G color, 10¾x14¾" 85.00
Basket, laundry; single wrap rim, sq, dbl hdl, 31x23" 725.00
Basket, laundry; splint w/bentwood rim hdls, 13½x19x31" 100.00
Basket, maple splint, for draining cheese, 1850, 8½x20½" 300.00
Basket, miniature, cheese draining, natural finish, 1x1¾" 400.00
Basket, miniature, weathered splint, 4x5" 125.00

Berry basket, 3½" x 5", $100.00.

Basket, sewing; 3-finger, copper tacks, oval, EX..............250.00
Basket, storage; rnd top/sq bottom, no hdl, 11¾x13"..........120.00
Bed, infant's, pine, dvtl, mk NF, orig bl/lt mauve, 48x39"......400.00
Bonnet, miniature, silk, in paper box, blk & gray, 2".........200.00
Bonnet, split poplar, tight weave, brn bands, silk tie, EX......425.00
Booklet, Story of, Favorite Recipes, 1882 calendar, 6x8".......30.00
Box, apple; simple, no hdl, att Canterbury, 2⅝x7½" sq.........75.00
Box, blanket; pine, red finish, fitted w/till, 2 drw.............575.00
Box, knife; cherry, natural finish, blind dvtl, carved hdl........175.00
Box, knitting needle; poplar/crackle varnish, mk Mary Page....150.00
Box, seed; outer label NM, traces of 1 w/in, Mt L, 11½x24"....550.00
Box, sewing; pine/butternut, ivory eyelets, drw, stained........325.00
Box, sewing; veneer, mahog w/flame grain, 1890, 3x8x11"......45.00
Box, sewing; 4-finger, oval, maple base, silk lining, 3x7".......200.00
Box, spice; 1-finger, copper tacks, brn finish, 3¼x4½".........135.00
Box, spit; maple/pine, orig yel pnt, Enfield, NH, 3x4¾".......450.00
Box, spit; pine/oak, orig mustard pnt, Meader, 4½x14½"......300.00
Box, 1-finger, copper tacks, natural, oval, 3⅜x4⅝"..........200.00
Box, 1-finger, iron tacks, natural, sm crack, 1½x2¾"...........55.00
Box, 1-finger, iron tacks, natural, 1⅝x3¼x4¼"...............65.00
Box, 1-finger, iron tacks/wood pins, natural, 7⅜x9", VG.......125.00
Box, 2-finger, copper tacks, natural, 3⅞x5¼", EX............300.00
Box, 2-finger, copper tacks, orig gr pnt worn, 5¼x8".........400.00
Box, 2-finger, copper tacks, rfn/gr traces, 4¼x6⅜"............175.00
Box, 2-finger, copper tacks, 2 layers yel finish, 4⅜x6".........400.00
Box, 3-finger, copper tacks, old brn stain traces, 6x8¾".......435.00
Box, 3-finger, copper tacks, orig dk gray-gr pnt, 8⅜x11"......735.00
Box, 3-finger, maple/pine, oval, orig bl-gray pnt, 2¼x6".......425.00
Box, 3-finger, maple/pine, oval, orig mustard pnt, 2½x6½".....350.00
Box, 4-finger, cedar top, maple/pine base, oval, orig red.....1,800.00
Box, 4-finger, copper tacks, maple/pine, rfn, 5½x9½x14"......500.00
Box, 5-finger, hickory/pine, oval, 19th C, red, 8½x17x14"....2,500.00
Broom, orig label, 37"...................................115.00
Bucket, berry; pine, mk Good Boy in gr, wht wash, wood hdl..250.00
Bucket, cherry/walnut/oak, trn wood/wire hdl, 9½x12".........250.00
Bucket, staves, wire bail, wood hdl, Enfield label, 6¾"........250.00
Cabinet, label; red pnt, Mt Lebanon, NY, 14½x8x26" L.......825.00
Candlestand, birch, tripod base, column threaded, 15" dia.....400.00
Cape, wool, shawl collar/hood, red w/bl/wht neck, ½ length......80.00
Carrier, 4-finger, cherry/pine/maple, natural finish, oval........400.00
Carrier, 4-finger, copper tacks, natural, 3x7x9", EX..........150.00
Carrier, 4-finger, maple/pine, red finish, hickory hdl.........1,800.00
Carrier, 5-finger, copper tacks, hdl, 'Sage,' 11x15", EX........325.00
Chair, child's arm; #1, simple, mushroom cap arms, label......400.00
Chair, revolving; hickory/pine/maple, blk finish, 26½".........600.00
Chair, side; birch, orig finish, cane seat, tilters, 41".........2,000.00

Child's ladderback chair, labeled #1 Mt. Lebanon, 3-slat, tape seat, original finish, 28", $550.00; Side chair, tilters, 3-slat, splint seat, figured maple, Mt. Lebanon, 37", $550.00.

Chair, side; ladderbk, #4, old varnish stain & rush seat........125.00
Chair, side; ladderbk, 3-slat, splint seat, old red, Ohio.........275.00
Chair, side; maple, orig finish, taper seat, tilters, 36".........650.00
Chest, pine, 4 dvtl drw, cut-out ends, 35½x30x10½"........1,100.00
Chest, pine/poplar, varnish, taper ft, 3 dvtl drw, sgn.........3,750.00
Cloak, wool, shawl collar/hood/full length, violet, 46".........300.00
Clothes hanger, birch/tiger birch, orig finish, 46x15¼"........125.00
Clothes hanger, wood, simple, Mt Lebanon, 16½", 6 for........40.00
Clothespins, oak, hand carved from 1 pc, 6", set of 4.........150.00
Cupboard, hanging; cherry/pine, natural, 24x16x7¼"........1,000.00
Cupboard, kitchen; poplar, 6 shelves, gr/gray, 67x29½x11½"...950.00
Darner, ball-in-socket, late 1800s..........................80.00
Darner, wood, 7" L..30.00
Desk, pine, natural finish, slant top/turn leg, 30x41x19¼".....450.00
Desk, school; pine, slant front/taper leg, bl, 31¼x44¼x19"...2,000.00
Dipper, maple, carved from heartwood, chrome yel, sm rpr...1,000.00
Dipper, oak/pine, single wrap, trn maple hdl, 7x12½x6".......200.00
Door, pine, oak grain finish, raised panel, 78"x30"............90.00
Dough box, dvtl poplar, taper legs, rnf/rpr, 31x33"...........325.00
Dust pan, maple/tin, flared pan, trn hdl, 8x6½".............200.00
Fabric, bolt of woven gray horsehair, 19th C, 312x24"........225.00
Footstool, cherry, orig varnish, bootjack ends, 5½x8x14"......175.00
Footstool, pine, Shaker brackets, brn, 8½x13½x8½"..........175.00
Footstool, slant top, old finish, trn legs, Mt L, 7x12".........225.00
Gloves, Brethren's, sheepskin, brn leather palms, 1870s........50.00
Grooming kit, comb/shoe hook/knife/thimble/bottle/case, 3".....85.00
Hat form, for wide-brimmed straw hats, wood/pnt, 12¾x15"....400.00
Jar filler, tin, removable strainer, 4¾" w/4" hdl...............45.00
Land deed, purchased by Enfield Society in 1854, in fr.........85.00
Lap board, pine, orig finish, cut-out for waist/yardstick........100.00
Map, Enfield, NH township, litho by WH Reese, 1855.........145.00
Mirror, hand; dbl string inlay fr, MOP inlay hdl, 12"..........175.00
Mortar & pestle, maple, brn finish, turned/scribed, 11x6".......60.00
Peg rail, pine/maple, natural finish, 12 pegs, 63".............275.00
Pegboard, poplar w/5 walnut hooks, old finish, 40" L.........135.00
Rack, drying; pine, mortised/shoe ft, red rpt on gr, EX........225.00
Reel, maple X-base, mortised pine top w/orig pnt, 31"........230.00
Rocker, #3, 3-slat, trn finials, label: Mt L, worn seat..........350.00
Rocker, #5, 4-slat, shaped mushroom arms, gr tape seat.......500.00
Rocker, #6, ladderbk, orig label/finish, rpl parts.............400.00
Rocker, #6, maple, dk stain, decal, orig 16½" H seat, 41".....700.00
Rocker, #7, mushroom arms, shawl bar, Mt Lebanon, seat rpl..775.00
Rocker, eldress's, birch/maple, scroll arms, 4 slats, rfn.......3,200.00
Rocker, maple, 3-slat, mk FW, yel, 14" H seat............1,400.00
Rocker, sister's, natural maple, 15½" H seat, 39"............375.00
Rug, woven cotton, diagonals w/orange/blk/red/gray, 32x54".....50.00
Ruler, wood, att Shakers, 6"..............................50.00
Scarf, homespun w/center embroidered initials, 34" sq.........15.00
Scoop, cherry, natural finish, carved, 6½x2¼"...............300.00
Sheet, homespun wool, hand sewn/embroidered '2,' 2-pc, KY...155.00
Shelf, cherry, dvtl case construction, 30x24x6¾", set of 4......750.00
Shovel, ash, ball-top, wrought iron, 35½"...................100.00
Sieve, horsehair, bentwood fr, 5⅞"........................125.00
Sieve, horsehair, 2-color, copper nails, 12½"..................95.00
Spinning wheel, natural finish, mk FW, 1820-1830...........550.00
Stand, cherry top & drw front, tiger/bird's eye maple legs....3,300.00
Stand, pine w/hardwood posts, 1-brd 20" sq shelf/top, rfn......400.00
Stool, milking; maple, natural finish, hdl, 13x16x11"..........250.00
Stool, poplar, mortised, bootjack ends, nailed, brn pnt........200.00
Stool, 2-step, pine, hinged top step for storage, 11x14½"......200.00
Stove, CI, penny ft, Enfield, NH..........................400.00
Stove, CI, str legs, Canterbury, NH, 19x26"................300.00
Sun hat, tight weave, cotton tape head fr, Enfield, 16" L......145.00
Swift, maple, on clamp, orig mustard pnt...................200.00

Table, harvest; pine, red stain, trn leg, 27x60x24"............550.00
Table, sewing; walnut, 2 dvtl drw/1-brd 20x29" top, rfn.......700.00
Table, work; cherry, rpl 41x53" top removes, 2 drw, EX.....1,750.00
Table, work; maple/birch, natural, cleated, 32x24" top........900.00
Table, work; pine/figured birch, drw/trn leg/9" leaf, 35".......850.00
Tool, basket maker's, walnut, 2 sets of knives, 22"...........200.00
Towel bar w/bracket, wood/salmon pnt, Enfield, 20" L........190.00
Utensils, pie lifter, fork, hand wrought skimmer, bowl.........400.00
Warming shelf, three 9½" tin disks clamp to stove pipe.......205.00
Yarn winder, table clamp, 3 arms, 4 posts..................235.00

Shaving Mugs

In the 1860s it became a popular practice for every shaving man to have his own shaving mug. Mugs belonging to men who frequented the barber shop for their tonsorial services were often personalized with their owner's name, and kept on display on the barber's shelf. Occupational shaving mugs became the high point of individualism during this period. China mugs, mostly made in France, Germany, and Austria, were imported, by American barber supply companies where artists hand painted the occupation, fraternal or sports affiliation of its customer on the mug, and added the name, usually in gold. The mug was then fired in a kiln for later use and displayed in the local barber shop. Because of sanitary rules and restrictions imposed around 1915, they were eventually taken off the barbers' shelves.

Today, occupational shaving mugs are the most valuable of all the decorated mugs. Although some are valued by the excellence of the artist, most are priced by the rarity of the subject matter.

The John Hudson Moore Company produced a line of Sportsman mugs in 1953 and 1954.

When no condition is indicated, the items listed below are assumed to be in mint condition.

Aluminum, eng The Model, fancy hdl.......................20.00
Bird & flowers, hold to light: see 3 people toasting, rare........70.00
Birds, spread eagle & Chinese Pagodas, mk Ironstone, bl.......75.00
Copper, dbl compartment, Civil War era....................125.00
Doulton Burslem, floral, w/scroll...........................20.00
EC Starkey, floral, bl/red/yel/pink..........................28.00
England, bl iris on both sides, rim/hdl decor................20.00
Floral, bird w/ribbon, pink flowers/gr leaves.................35.00
Floral, red w/gold leaves, wide gold band, fancy hdl............51.00
Floral, upper ⅓: pink, lower ⅔: wht w/red flowers............27.00
Flying eagle, scrolls/roses/2 flags/shield, polychrome..........195.00
Fraternal, Bauscher Weiden, USAF in Europe, wht, gold trim...20.00
Fraternal, BPOE, elk's head & owner's name, Limoges.........75.00
Fraternal, Forester of America, gold bands on bottom..........76.00
Fraternal, Gillespy, X-flags w/stag in center, bottom mk H.....103.00
Fraternal, JM Alexander, Masonic, floral, wht w/gold trim.......95.00
Fraternal, Knights of Columbus, shield, gold trim.............60.00
Fraternal, LG Seager, Knights of Pythias, shield & swords......80.00
Germany, Feida China, 4 pink flowers/gr leaves, gold bands.....25.00
Germany, NJ Pottery Co, lg home w/man in yard, pink rim......30.00
Germany 64, monk playing violin, brn bkground..............15.00
Glass, opaque pink w/emb songbird, sq hdl, 3⅜"..............35.00
Hall China 600, gr flowers & leaves on both sides............14.00
Indian face motif...68.00
Kids sitting under umbrella inside house, gold trim, EX........45.00
Limoges, Lady Liberty, eagle shield holds banner & name......95.00
Metal openwork, wht glass liner, brush rest, fancy hdl..........40.00
Oak openwork, floral & diamonds, milk glass liner, eng hdl.....35.00
Occupational, autoist, w/early car & driver, trees/house........200.00
Occupational, banjo player, w/instrument & full name.........325.00
Occupational, bearded man by peddler's wagon, poem, bl/yel....50.00
Occupational, boxer, bottom mk Bavaria, rare, G color.........72.00
Occupational, butcher, steer w/4 tools, mk DY Ryan..........112.00
Occupational, butcher tools/steer's head, Limoges/BS Co.......185.00
Occupational, courtroom scene w/lawyer/judge/policeman.......375.00
Occupational, engineer..................................100.00
Occupational, express wagon driver........................265.00
Occupational, exterminator, w/rodent in reserve............1,200.00
Occupational, farmer plowing w/2 horses, name in gold........450.00
Occupational, fireman, horse-drawn pumper/4 men, bl w/band..210.00
Occupational, florist or decorator, w/hanging planter...........60.00
Occupational, grocery scene.............................100.00
Occupational, horse breeder, WL Gray, bottom mk P Germany.208.00

Occupational, blacksmith scene, gold name and trim, marked T&V, $435.00.

Occupational, hunter, H Hunt, dog sniffing/rabbit/flowers......255.00
Occupational, hunter, 2 dogs w/fire in gold of base, gr........200.00
Occupational, lady w/Scales of Justice, wht w/gold trim.........50.00
Occupational, man fixing bell on wall......................300.00
Occupational, musician, marching drummer, bottom mk, rare...525.00
Occupational, piano player, w/upright piano & full name.......325.00
Occupational, policeman, Charlie of the Gay '90s, brn.........126.00
Occupational, pool hustler, 2 men at table, name, CT mk......200.00
Occupational, printer, holds printer's stick, gold scroll.........275.00
Occupational, printer, w/printing press & full name...........300.00
Occupational, RR worker, coal tender & loco, name in gold....150.00
Occupational, saloon keeper..............................250.00
Occupational, sulky driver, driving time: 2-11¼ on mug........395.00
Occupational, telegrapher, w/name........................135.00
Occupational, telephone lineman at work, HP...............330.00
Occupational, trolley car operator, 5 passengers, 1913........342.00
Occupational, tugboat captain, lg tugboat & full name.........700.00
Organ grinder, w/monkey, fence, tree, mk 8938...............55.00
Outdoor scene, house/boat/trees/water/mountains/flowers.......250.00
Scuttle, elephant head, gray w/cream tusks, 4½x5⅞"..........125.00
Silver, floral, eng front, holder w/insert & brush, Buck.........80.00
Silverplate, Apollo Silver, base design, brush rest, wide.........35.00
Silverplate, Derby, flowers, ebony finish/milk glass liner.........40.00
Silverplate, eng, monogrammed w/C & 1853-1903, w/brush.....133.00
Silverplate, JS Co, milk glass liner.........................45.00
Silverplate, Marion Plate, brush rest, quad plate, short.........40.00
Silverplate, Van Bergh, raised floral, brush rest, short..........45.00
Stone China Warranted, roses/leaves, gold rim, gr.............25.00
Turnabout, before/after, Staffordshire.......................65.00
V&D Austria, Isaac Hetrich emb in gold on wht...............47.00
Victoria Silver, eng Fred, lift-out center, w/holder/brush.......110.00

Shawnee

The Shawnee Pottery Company operated in Zanesville, Ohio, from 1937 to 1961. They produced inexpensive novelty ware--vases, flowerpots, and figurines--as well as a very successful line of figural cookie jars. These cookie jars and their dinnerware, the Corn Line, are very popular with today's collector's.

When no condition is indicated, the items listed below are assumed to be in mint condition.

Ash tray/coaster set, #411, USA....22.00
Candle holder, #3026, w/hdl....12.00
Candle holder, cornucopia, wht, pr....10.00
Candle holder, platinum trim, #3026....22.00
Cookie jar, drummer boy....75.00
Cookie jar, Dutch boy, bl pants....35.00
Cookie jar, Dutch boy, w/floral decals & gold trim....75.00
Cookie jar, Dutch boy, w/patches & gold trim....125.00
Cookie jar, Dutch boy, w/stripes....55.00
Cookie jar, Dutch boy, yel pants....30.00
Cookie jar, Dutch girl, gold trim, decals & label....87.50
Cookie jar, Dutch girl, w/tulip....55.00
Cookie jar, Mugsey, gold trim....85.00
Cookie jar, owl, gold trim....72.50
Cookie jar, pink elephant, wht or blk collar....40.00
Cookie jar, Puss 'N Boots....45.00
Cookie jar, Puss 'N Boots, gold trim....75.00
Cookie jar, Puss 'N Boots, gold trim & flower decals....75.00
Cookie jar, Smiley Pig, (bank/cookie) dk base....100.00
Cookie jar, Smiley Pig, plain....45.00
Cookie jar, Smiley Pig, w/bl bandana....50.00
Cookie jar, Smiley Pig, w/gr bandana, gold trim & decal....100.00
Cookie jar, Smiley Pig, w/shamrocks under glaze....55.00
Cookie jar, Winnie Pig, (bank/cookie) heavy gold trim....150.00
Cookie jar, Winnie Pig, gr collar....55.00
Corn, bowl, #5....13.00
Corn, bowl, #6....17.00
Corn, bowl, fruit; #92....14.00
Corn, butter dish, #72....30.00
Corn, casserole, #74....40.50
Corn, cookie jar....65.00
Corn, creamer, #70....15.00
Corn, creamer & sugar, w/lid....35.00
Corn, cup, #90....16.00
Corn, mug, #69....25.00
Corn, plate, #68, 10"....18.00
Corn, platter, #96....25.00
Corn, relish, #79....16.50
Corn, salad bowl, #93....21.00
Corn, shakers, lg, pr....15.00
Corn, shakers, sm, pr....10.00
Corn, sugar bowl, #78....18.00
Corn, teapot, #75, 30-oz....42.00
Creamer, elephant....16.50
Creamer, lobster, paper label....18.00
Creamer, Puss 'N Boots....16.50
Creamer, Smiley Pig....18.00
Pitcher, Bo Peep....35.00
Pitcher, Bo Peep, gr trim, lg....35.00
Pitcher, Chanticleer....35.00
Pitcher, emb rose spray, gold trim, #40....20.00
Pitcher, Little Boy Blue....30.00
Pitcher, Smiley Pig, allover gold....95.00
Pitcher, Smiley Pig, lg....30.00
Pitcher, Smiley Pig, red flower, lg....30.00
Planter, baby shoes....3.00
Planter, basket, #640....14.00
Planter, bird, neck outstretched, beak open....6.00
Planter, bird on planter, #767....12.00
Planter, boot....6.00
Planter, bow knot, gold trim, #518....12.00
Planter, bow knot, saucer base....4.00
Planter, boy at wall....7.50
Planter, butterfly....3.00
Planter, car, #506....10.00
Planter, cart, #775....12.00
Planter, clock, #1262....10.00
Planter, coal bucket, J541P....12.00
Planter, covered wagon....7.00
Planter, crib....12.00
Planter, dog, nose to ground....5.00
Planter, elephant, blk figural....25.00
Planter, frog on lily pad....16.00
Planter, giraffe....10.00
Planter, girl at basket....5.00
Planter, goose, USA, sm....3.00
Planter, high heel shoe....7.00
Planter, horse, #506....30.00
Planter, hound & jug....7.00
Planter, hound & pekingese....4.00
Planter, house, J543P....16.00
Planter, kids in shoe....9.00
Planter, leather grain, #885....4.00
Planter, mouse, #705....16.00
Planter, Oriental w/umbrella....4.00
Planter, Polynesian girl, #896....12.00
Planter, rabbit, #703....15.00
Planter, ram, #515....12.00
Planter, rickshaw, #539....3.00
Planter, rocking horse....10.00
Planter, rooster, #503....14.00
Planter, skunk, #512....14.00
Planter, squirrel, #664....5.00
Planter, stagecoach, J545P....18.00
Planter, Three Pigs....5.00

Planter, fawn figural, $15.00.

Planter, Uncle Sam hat....5.00
Planter, water trough....12.00
Planter, watering can, red or pink....8.00
Planter, windmill, #715....14.00
Planter, world....15.00
Shakers, Chanticleer, sm, pr....12.00
Shakers, Dutch boy & girl, 5", pr....20.00
Shakers, Dutch children, pr....14.00
Shakers, Farmer Pig, sm, pr....10.00
Shakers, flowerpot, gold trim, pr....15.00
Shakers, flowerpot, plain, pr....8.00
Shakers, Little Chef, gold trim, S or P base, pr....16.00
Shakers, milk pail, pr....8.00
Shakers, Mugsey, lg, pr....28.00
Shakers, owl, gr eyes, mk USA, pr....15.00
Shakers, Smiley Pig, gold trim, 2½", pr....25.00
Shakers, Smiley Pig, gr, 5", pr....20.00
Shakers, Swiss children, pr....14.00
Shakers, wheelbarrow, pr....12.00
Shakers, Winnie & Smiley, 2½", pr....15.00
Shakers, Winnie Pig, 2½", pr....12.00
Teapot, Granny Anne, gr apron....41.00
Teapot, Granny Anne, peach apron....41.00
Teapot, rose in relief, allover gold....35.00
Teapot, Tom Tom, bl base....44.00
Teapot, 6-petal flower on wht, USA....20.00
Vase, bud, #1125....5.00
Vase, flowered, #1225....12.00
Vase, frog playing guitar....8.00
Vase, girl at cornucopia....8.00
Vase, leaf, #823....20.00
Vase, philodendron leaf, #805....10.00
Vase, ribbed, gold trim, #809....18.00
Vase, tulip, #1115, gold trim....12.00
Vase, twin doves....15.00
Vase, yel ivy, #805....10.00
Vase, 2-hdl, ped ft, sm....3.00
Vase, hand w/lily, lg....20.00
Wall pocket, clock, #530....12.00
Wall pocket, grandfather clock....14.00
Wall pocket, Little Bo Peep....12.00
Wall pocket, Little Jack Horner....12.00

Shearwater Pottery

Since 1928, generations of the Peter and Walter Anderson families have been producing figurines and artwares in their Ocean Springs, Mississippi, studio.

When no condition is indicated, the items listed below are assumed to be in mint condition.

Bowl, bl, subtle rings, 3½" opening, 3½"....60.00
Bowl, gr w/gray highlights, 2¾x8½"....35.00
Bowl, warrior/horse/Indian motif, underglaze, Anderson, 9½"...150.00
Cup & saucer, demitasse; bl/brn, woodpecker hdl....20.00
Figurine, Blk man fiddling/Chicken Thief, recent, 5½ , pr....80.00
Pitcher, gr w/gray drip, 4"....30.00
Pitcher, turq, 5½"....20.00
Vase, bulbous, imp circular mk, gr semi-gloss glaze, 5¼"....135.00
Vase, gr semi-gloss, hdls, imp circular mk, 5¼"....135.00
Vase, gr/gun metal gray, ribbed/bulbous w/narrow neck, 7"....45.00
Vase, impressed ducks, bl neck/gr body, 5¾x6"....160.00

Figurine, drinking pirate, blue glaze, 6", $140.00.

Sheet Music

Sheet music is often collected more for the colorful lithographed covers rather than for the music itself. Transportation songs which have pictures or illustrations of trains, ships, and planes; ragtime tunes which feature popular entertainers such as Al Jolson; or those with Disney characters are among the most valuable.

When no condition is indicated, the items listed below are assumed to be in near mint condition.

Alsacian Railroad Gallops, Guignard, 1845....50.00
America First, picture of Uncle Sam/Miss Liberty, Brockman....8.00
American Patrol, Meecham, Statue of Liberty/soldier/flag....5.00
Ballad of John & Yoko, by Lennon/McCartney, w/Beatles....10.00
Beatles Dance, Presser Halt, photos of beatles dancing....5.00
Bonne Nuit, Here Comes the Groom, Bing Crosby/Jane Wyman...6.00
Born to Be Kissed, from movie same name, J Harlow, 1934....8.00
Break the News to Mother, 1897....15.00
Burning Sands, from movie same name, Paramount, 1922....6.00
Can't Help Lovin' Dat Man, from Show Boat....10.00
Chico, Chico, from Doll Face, Carmen Miranda....5.50
Choreography, from White Christmas, B Crosby, 1953, M....7.00
Clam Bake, Elvis Presley, VG....35.00
Daughter of Rosie O'Grady, Gladys Leslie....15.00
Did I Remember, from Suzy, J Harlow/C Grant/F Tone....8.00
Dig You Later, from Doll Face, Miranda, Robins Music Corp....5.50
Don't Mention Love to Me, from In Person, G Rogers, 1935....6.00
Embraceable You, from Girl Crazy, Mickey Rooney/J Garland....10.00
Flirtation Walk, from movie same name, D Powell, R Keeler....4.00
For Old Glory, picture Washington crossing Delaware, VG....6.00
Friendly Mountains, from Emperor Waltz, Crosby/J Fontaine....7.00
Friendly Persuasion, from movie same name, Cooper/McGuire....4.00
Gasoline Gus & His Jitney Bus, Gay, 1915....16.00
God Bless America, Irving Berlin, Kate Smith, 1938....5.00
Golden Years, The; from Houdini, Tony Curtis, Janet Leigh....3.00
Harnden's Express Line Gallopade & Trio, Firth/Hall, 1841....35.00
Hiram Green Good-Bye, pictures Hiram leaving, inset, 1905....6.00
His Rocking Horse Ran Away, from And the Angels Sing....5.00
Hold Your Man, from movie same name, J Harlow, 1933....8.00
Honey! You'se Ma Lady Love, Blk kids on fence, Mann, 1897....8.00
Honeychile, from movie same name, Judy Garland....3.00
Hot Stuff, The Monkees, by M Jaggar/K Richards, 1976....5.50
How'd You Like to Be My Wife?, couple on ring, Dempsey, VG...6.00
Huckleberry Pie, pictures man in pie, Hanlon/Conrad, 1918....6.00
I Concentrate on You, Broadway Melody of 1940, F Astaire....6.00

I'll Be Home, Pat Boone....................................3.00
I'll Walk Alone, Dinah Shore................................3.00
I'm at Your Service, Girls, picture of J Eltinge, 1915, EX.........6.00
I'm Crying Just for You, lady weeping, McCarthy/Monaco, VG....6.00
I'm Not Your Steppin' Stone, The Monkees, w/photos, 1966.....6.00
I've Got to Sing a Torch Song, from Gold Diggers, Powell.......8.00
In the Park, from Gold Diggers, D Powell, 1933................8.00
Into My Heart, from In Gay Madrid, by Turk/Ahlert, 1930.......8.75
Keep Away from...Who Owns An Automobile, Berlin, 1912.....22.00
King of the Air, plane over NY City, Glenn Curtis.............12.00
Kiss Me Goodnight, lady holds roses, Brown/Goodwin, EX.......6.00
LeVoyage Aerien, Louis, 1845..............................40.00
Liberty Bell, Mohr, 1917..................................15.00
Little Kiss at Twilight, from Give Me a Sailor, B Grable.........8.00
Lonely, from Call of the Flesh, R Navarro, Robins graphics......8.75
Long Ago & Far Away, from Cover Girl, R Hayworth/L Brooks...6.00
Love Is Here to Stay, from An American in Paris, G Kellyan.....5.00
Love Somebody, Doris Day & Buddy Clark......................4.00
Lovely Lady, King of Burlesque, A Faye/W Baxter/J Oakie.......7.00
Melody Farm, from Everybody Sing, J Garland, by Kahn/Kaper...9.00
Mid the Blue Grass of Kentucky, Harris, 1909.................9.00
Mona Lisa, from Captain Carey, USA, Alan Ladd/W Hendrix.....4.00
Moonlight & Shadows, from Jungle Princess, D Lamour........10.00
Mop Rag, Remick, Eaton, wash bucket & mop, 1909, VG.......7.00
My Country 'Tis of Thee, Stern, strollers by water, 1917.........5.00
My Dog Loves Your Dog, from Scandals, A Faye, by Geo White.11.00
My Little Congo Maid, Gordon, Mohr, jungle hut & scene.......7.00
Napoleon's Last Charge, ET Paull, battle scene, 1932, VG.......7.00
Oceana Roll, pictures steamer/nautical scenes, Lewis/Denni.......8.00
Of All Things, from Duchess of Idaho, E Williams, 1950........6.00
Oh By Jingo, from Linger Longer Letty, C Greenwood..........8.00
Oh the Pity of It All, from My Gal Sal, R Hayworth/Mature......6.00
Oh! How I Hate to Get Up in the Morning, Berlin, 1918, VG....15.00
Old Playmate, Kate Smith.................................3.00
On the Good Ship Lollipop, Shirley Temple....................8.00
One I Love, from Everybody Sing, J Garland, by Kahn/Kaper.....9.00
Orchids in the Moonlight, Flying Down to Rio, F Astaire........3.00
Over the Rainbow, from Wizard of Oz, J Garland, rare.........20.00
Over There, Cohan, 1917...................................13.00
Pale Hands, from Hers to Hold, D Durpin, by Hope/Finden.....12.50
Pass That Peace Pipe, from Good News, Allyson & Lawford......4.00
Peg o' My Heart, from movie same name, Laurette............10.00
Peter Pan, I Love You, from Peter Pan, Marilyn Miller..........7.00
Peter Pan, Stern, J Crook, sgn on top cover, 16 pg............7.00
Polar Bear Polka, Albert Berg, 1865, 13x10", EX.............40.00
Pretty Girl is Like a Melody, from Ziegfeld Follies, 1919........6.00
Put the Blame on Mame, from Gilda, Rita Hayworth............7.00
Rail-Road, Meineke, 1828................................135.00
Road is Open Again, Warner Bros & Vitaphone, D Powell.......8.00
Road That Leads to Love, Irving Berlin, 1917, lg size, VG.......8.00
Runaway June, 1915, Norma Phillips, 1915...................15.00
Same Sort of Girl, from Girl From Utah......................8.00
Santa Claus is Coming to Town, F Langford, 1934.............6.00
School Where Lincoln Went, cabin/eagle/pennants, Hardy, VG....6.00
Shoo-Shoo Baby, Andrew Sisters, 1900s.......................4.00
Silver Heels, Indian girl, O'Dea/Moret, 1905, VG...............6.00
Singin' in the Rain, from Hollywood Revue of 1929.............6.00
Smile! Smile! Smile!, from musical In Panama, bull fight........6.00
Smoke Dreams, from After the Thin Man, by Freed/Brown, MGM.6.00
Smoky Mokes, 4 Blk kids, Holzmann, 1899, VG...............10.00
So Long Mary, from play 45 Minutes from Broadway, 1905......6.00
Soliloquy, from Carousel, G MacRae/S Jones/C Mitchell..........4.00
Somebody's Coming to my House, Berlin, rpr, lg sz, 1913.......6.00
Stars & Stripes Forever March, The; Sousa, 1897.............14.00
Sweet & Simple, from Scandals, Alice Faye, by George White....6.00
Take Me to the Midnight Cake Walk Ball, D Pollard, 1915.....10.00
Tell That to the Marines, from Sinbad, Al Jolson..............10.00
That Red Cross Girl of Mine, picture of RC nurse, 1917, VG.....6.00
That's How I Need You, from 2 Weeks With Love, D Reynolds...5.50
There'll be Sunshine for You, sepia close-up of Leslie..........15.00
There's the One for Me, from Bulldog Drummond, Yellen/Akst...8.75
Till the Swanee River Runs Dry, Freidman, Mahoney, 1919......7.00
True Blue Lou, from The Dance of Life, N Carroll/H Skelly......7.00
Two Lost Souls, from Damn Yankees, Gwen Verdon.............3.00
Valleri, The Monkees, by T Boyce/B Hart, cover w/Monkees......6.00
We're in the Money, from Gold Diggers, by Dubin/Warren.......8.00
What Makes the Sunset?, from Anchors Aweigh, Sinatra/Kelly....5.00
When Alexander Takes His Ragtime Band to France, 1918, VG..7.50
When I Sing, from It Started With Eve, D Durpin, 1941.......12.50
When the Major Plays Those Minor Keys, DeCosts, 1916.......12.50
When You Wish upon a Star, 1940, from Pinocchio movie.....12.00
Whispers in the Dark, from Artists & Models, Jack Benny.......4.00

Shelley

In 1872 Joseph Shelley became a partner with James Wileman, owner of Foley China Works, thus creating Wileman & Co., in Stoke-on-Trent. Twelve years later James Wileman withdrew from the company, though the firm continued to use his name until 1925 when it became known as Shelley Potteries, Ltd.

Like many successful 19th century English potteries, they produced useful household wares as well as dinnerware of considerable note. In 1896 the beautiful Dainty White shape was introduced, and it is regarded by many as synonymous with the name of Shelley. In addition to the original Dainty 6-Flute design, other lovely and dainty shapes were produced: 14-Flute, Shell, Queen Anne, and the more modern shapes of Mode, Regent, and Eve.

Though often overlooked, striking earthenware was produced under the direction of Frederick Rhead and later Walter Slater and his son Eric. Many notable artists contributed their talents in designing unusual, attractive wares: Rowland Morris, Mabel Lucie Attwell, and Hilda Cowham, to name but a few.

In 1966 Allied English Potteries acquired control of the Shelley Company, and by 1967 the last of the exquisite Shelley China had been produced to honor the last of the overseas orders. In 1971 Allied English Potteries merged with the Doulton group. The name Shelley China Ltd. still exists, and it has been reported that Royal Doulton has produced trial wares bearing the Shelley backstamp.

In the listings below, when no condition is noted, items are assumed to be in mint condition.

Ash tray, Blue Rock, straight edge..........................35.00
Ash tray, Dainty Blue, 6 flutes, 5"..........................32.50
Ash tray, White Shell, 3½"..................................18.50
Bowl, vegetable; Harebell, bl hdls & finial, w/lid, 9"...........74.00
Box, trinket; Dainty Blue, w/lid, 4½" dia.....................58.00
Butter dish, Blue Rock, 6 flutes.............................85.00
Butter dish, Bridal Rose, 6 flutes...........................50.00
Butter dish, Rose Pansy FMN, 6 flutes.......................85.00
Butter pat, Blue Rock.......................................21.00
Butter pat, Dainty Green....................................22.50
Butter pat, floral border.....................................11.00
Butter pat, Regency...18.00
Butter pat, Rose Spray......................................20.00
Candy dish, Dainty Blue, 6 flutes, 4¼"......................38.00
Candy dish, Dainty White, 6 flutes, 6" dia....................29.50
Candy dish, Pansy, rnd, 4"..................................30.00
Candy dish, Rose & Red Daisy, 10 flutes.....................31.50

Chamber pot, Attwell, 7″ 68.50
Chamberstick, Dainty Pink, brass holder, 6 flutes, 6″ 29.50
Chamberstick, Wild Anenome, brass center holder, 6″ 28.00
Chocolate pot, Dainty Mauve, 6 flutes, 8″ 165.00
Chocolate pot, Regency, 6 flutes, 8″ 140.00
Cigarette holder, Dainty Pink, 6 flutes, 2″ 32.00
Cigarette holder, Rose Spray FMN, 3″ 32.00
Cigarette holder, Rosebud, 3″ 25.00
Coffee pot, Dainty Pink, 6 flutes, 6½″ 150.00
Coffee pot, Regency, 6 flutes, 8″ 125.00
Creamer, Rose & Red Daisy, 6 flutes 25.00
Creamer, Stocks, 6 flutes 20.00
Creamer & sugar, Dainty Blue, w/tray, 6 flutes 86.00
Creamer & sugar, Indian Peony, ftd 42.00
Creamer & sugar, Rose & Red Daisy, 6 flutes 59.00
Creamer & sugar, Rose Pansy FMN, 6 flutes 66.50
Creamer & sugar, Rose Spray, gr trim 45.00
Creamer & sugar, Thistle, 6 flutes 45.00
Creamer & sugar, Violets, 6 flutes 46.50
Cup & saucer, Archway of Roses, Queen Anne shape 42.00
Cup & saucer, Begonia, 6 flutes 38.00
Cup & saucer, Blue Rock, 14 flutes 40.00
Cup & saucer, Blue Rock, 6 flutes 42.00
Cup & saucer, Celandine, 14 flutes 38.00
Cup & saucer, Celandine, 6 flutes 42.00
Cup & saucer, Charm, bl 25.00
Cup & saucer, Daffodil 40.00
Cup & saucer, Dainty Blue, 6 flutes 42.00
Cup & saucer, Dainty Mauve, 6 flutes 45.00
Cup & saucer, demitasse; Blue Rock, 16 flutes 38.00
Cup & saucer, demitasse; Campanula, 16 flutes 38.00
Cup & saucer, demitasse; Daffodil, 6 flutes 38.00
Cup & saucer, demitasse; Dainty Green, 6 flutes 40.00
Cup & saucer, demitasse; Harebell, 6 flutes 39.50
Cup & saucer, demitasse; Pansy, 16 flutes 38.00
Cup & saucer, demitasse; Rose & Red Daisy, 6 flutes 36.00
Cup & saucer, demitasse; Rose Pansy FMN, 6 flutes 35.00
Cup & saucer, demitasse; Rosebud, 6 flutes 38.00
Cup & saucer, demitasse; Summer Glory, pink 36.00
Cup & saucer, Harebell, shell shape 38.00
Cup & saucer, Heraldic ware, Coronation of Edward VIII 65.00
Cup & saucer, Indian Peony, ftd 35.00
Cup & saucer, Melody, floral int, peach ext, shell shape 35.00
Cup & saucer, mini; Campanula 55.00
Cup & saucer, mini; Dainty Blue 65.00
Cup & saucer, mini; Dainty Green 60.00
Cup & saucer, mini; Rose Pansy FMN 60.00
Cup & saucer, mini; Shamrock 60.00
Cup & saucer, Pansy 35.00
Cup & saucer, Primrose, 6 flutes 38.50
Cup & saucer, Rock Garden, shell shape, yel 42.00
Cup & saucer, Rose Pansy FMN, 6 flutes 42.00
Cup & saucer, Rosebud, shell shape, pink 40.00

Cups and saucers, left to right: Harebell, $38.00; 6-Flutes, $38.00.

Cup & saucer, shell shape, floral int, yel ext 38.00
Cup & saucer, shell shape, peach int, floral ext, ftd 35.00
Cup & saucer, Stocks, shell shape, pink trim 39.50
Cup & saucer, Stocks, 6 flutes 38.00
Cup & saucer, Summer Glory, straight edge 35.00
Cup & saucer, Tapestry Rose, notched edge, gold trim 39.50
Cup & saucer, Thistle, 6 flutes 40.00
Egg cup, Dainty Green, 6 flutes, sm 40.00
Egg cup, Rose & Red Daisy, 6 flutes, sm 40.00
Egg cup, Stocks, 2½″ 38.00
Jam jar, Blue Rock, w/lid 36.50
Jam jar, Campanula, 6 flutes, w/lid 42.00
Jam jar, Dainty Pink, 6 flutes, w/lid & underplate 60.00
Loving cup, Heraldic ware, Coronation Geo VI, princess 72.50
Mustard jar, Rosebud, w/lid & underplate 58.00
Pitcher, Melody, gr hdl & trim, 7½″ 85.00
Pitcher, Rose Pansy FMN, 6 flutes, w/lid, 5″ 55.00
Place card, Attwell, for shopping list 50.00
Plate, Begonia, 6 flutes, 10″ 50.00
Plate, Blue Rock, 6 flutes, 11″ 55.00
Plate, Blue Rock, 6 flutes, 6″ 22.00
Plate, Blue Rock, 6 flutes, 8″ 35.00
Plate, Bluebell Wood, 8″ 35.00
Plate, cake; Blue Rock, ftd, 6 flutes, 8″ dia 85.00
Plate, cake; Hollyhocks, 8″ 46.00
Plate, cake; Rosebud, ftd, 6 flutes, 8″ dia 83.50
Plate, cake; Violets, 8″ 45.00
Plate, Campanula, 6 flutes, 8″ 28.00
Plate, Crochet, wht, 8″ 25.00
Plate, Dainty Mauve, 6 flutes, 8″ 30.00
Plate, Dainty Pink, 6 flutes, 8″ 31.50
Plate, Heather, 8″ 30.00
Plate, Heraldic ware, Coronation of Geo VI, shell shape 65.00
Plate, Lily of the Valley, 6 flutes, 8″ 25.00
Plate, Old Sevres, 1″ sterling fr, 7″ 99.50
Plate, Old Sevres, 1½″ sterling fr, 11″ 185.00
Plate, Primrose Chintz, 8″ 25.00
Plate, Regency, 6 flutes, 10¾″ 55.00
Plate, Regency, 6 flutes, 8″ 25.00
Plate, Rose & Red Pansy, 8x9½″ 30.00
Plate, Rose Pansy FMN, w/bl hdls, 8½″ 45.00
Plate, Rose Pansy FMN, 6 flutes, 10½″ 30.00
Plate, Rose Pansy FMN, 6 flutes, 6″ 20.00
Plate, Rosebud, 6 flutes, 10¾″ 50.00
Plate, Rosebud, 6 flutes, 8″ 35.00
Plate, Spring Bouquet, gold trim, 8″ 25.00
Plate, Tapestry Rose, gray flowers & peach, 8″ 30.00
Plate, Wild Anemone, 6 flutes, 8″ 25.00
Set, 3-pc; Archway of Roses, Queen Anne shape, 8″ 68.00
Set, 3-pc; Begonia, 6 flutes, 6″ plate 60.00
Set, 3-pc; Begonia, 6 flutes, 8″ plate 70.00
Set, 3-pc; Blue Daisy, 8″ plate 67.00
Set, 3-pc; Blue Rock, 14 flutes, 8″ plate 72.50
Set, 3-pc; Blue Rock, 6 flutes, 8″ plate 70.00
Set, 3-pc; Dainty Blue, 6 flutes, 8″ plate 72.00
Set, 3-pc; Dainty Mauve, 6 flutes, 8″ plate 70.00
Set, 3-pc; Dainty Pink, 6 flutes, 7″ plate 65.00
Set, 3-pc; Green Daisy, 8″ plate 72.00
Set, 3-pc; Harebell, 6 flutes, 8″ plate 72.00
Set, 3-pc; Hedgerow, 6 flutes, 8″ plate 65.00
Set, 3-pc; Lily of the Valley, 6 flutes, 8″ plate 65.00
Set, 3-pc; Maytime, gold trim, 8″ plate 72.00
Set, 3-pc; Regency, 6 flutes, 10″ plate 72.50
Set, 3-pc; Regency, 6 flutes, 8″ plate 65.00

Set, 3-pc; Rose Pansy FMN, 6 flutes, 8″ plate................70.00
Set, 3-pc; Rose Spray, 14 flutes, 8″ plate....................71.00
Set, 3-pc; Rose Spray, 6 flutes, 8″ plate.....................72.00
Set, 3-pc; Rosebud, 6 flutes, 8″ plate........................70.00
Set, 3-pc; Sunray, 8″ sq plate................................50.00
Set, 3-pc; Thistle, 6 flutes, 8″ plate........................72.00
Set, 3-pc; Violets, 6 flutes, 8″ plate........................72.50
Set, 3-pc; Wild Anemone, 14 flutes, 8″ plate..................67.50
Set, 3-pc; Wildflower, 6 flutes, 8″ plate.....................65.00
Smoke set, Rosebud, cigar holder/2 ash trays, 4″ dia..........72.50
Snack set, Blue Rock, 6 flutes, cup/indented 8″ plate.........55.00
Snack set, Dainty Blue, 6 flutes, cup/indented 8″ plate.......52.00
Tea & toast, Dainty Pink, cup & indented 6x9″ tray............58.50
Tea & toast, Rose & Red Daisy, cup & indented 6x9″ tray.....59.00
Teapot, Indian Peony, ftd, 7″.................................95.00
Teapot, Mushroom, Attwell, 4″.................................98.50
Teapot, Regent shape, bl dots w/shadow effect.................89.50
Teapot, Rosebud, 6 flutes, 4″................................110.00
Teapot, Stocks, 6 flutes, 6″.................................125.00
Teapot, Wildflowers, pink trim, 5½″..........................130.00
Vase, deco enamel birds/floral, blk, 7″.......................65.00
Vase, Indian Peony, 7″..58.00

Silhouettes

Silhouette portraits were made by positioning the subject between a bright light and a sheet of white drawing paper, the resulting shadow traced and cut out. The paper was mounted over a contrasting color and framed. The process was simplified by an invention called the Physiog-notrace, a device that allowed tracing and cutting to be done in one operation.

Experienced silhouette artists could do full-length figures, scenics, ships, or trains. Some of the most famous of these artists were Charles Peale Polk, Charles Wilson Peale, James Elsworth, and William King.

When no condition is indicated, the items listed below are assumed to be in excellent condition.

Boxers, cut cloth (stained), May 19, 1867, fr, 12½x14½″.......225.00
Family, hollow cut, watercolor costumes, old blk fr, 8x9¾″.....375.00
Lady, hollow cut, fancy hair, pine fr, 3⅝x4⅝″.................115.00
Lady, hollow cut, pen/ink/pencil, blk cloth bk, orig fr, 5x6″....185.00
Lady, hollow cut, sgn, rpl back, gilded fr, 4⅝″ sq.............50.00
Lady, primitive watercolor, rosewood veneer fr, 5⅝x6⅝″.......105.00
Lady, sgn CL Barber, 1820s, fr, 4½x5⅛″........................50.00
Lady in chair, WH Brown, old blk fr, 16¼x18½″.................300.00
Man, Capitol view, sgn WH Brown, gilded fr, 10⅝x15⅝″.......225.00
Man, J Pyle by M Hubbard, old blk fr, 4½x5⅝″..................90.00
Man, pen & ink, matted & fr, 5⅝x6¼″..........................100.00
Man, rvpt, orig gilded pine fr, flakes in bkground, 5x5¾″.......95.00
Man, wax relief bust, orig fr, sgn, Home, 1791, 5¼x6⅜″.......135.00

George Washington, watercolor silhouette, signed S. Folwell, Pinxt, 1791, small tear, in frame, 3½″ x 2½″, $700.00.

Old woman, primitive cut, oval wood fr, 4x4⅞″..................45.00
Page w/9 cut-outs by Edouart, old gilded fr, 10¾x13½″.......525.00
Peale's Museum, hollow cut, gilded fr, 14¾x17¾″..............250.00
Pr, cupids w/arrows, old gilded fr, 1900s, 4⅝x5⅝″..............25.00
Pr, Mr & Mrs, hollow cut, pencil mk, orig fr, 4⅛x5⅛″........240.00
Pr, Mr & Mrs Judge, sgn in pencil, mat/fr, 19¾x24″..........275.00
Sea captain, sgn Sam'l Metford, fr, 8¼x11½″...............2,300.00
Soldier, hollow cut, stained paper, old blk fr, 4⅛x4¾″..........35.00

Silver

Silver flatware is being collected today, either to replace missing pieces of heirloom sets, or in lieu of buying new patterns, by those who admire and appreciate the style and quality of the older ware. Prices vary from dealer to dealer; some pieces are harder to find and are therefore more expensive. Items such as olive spoons, cream ladles, lemon forks, etc., once thought a necessary part of a silver service, may today be slow to sell, and as a result dealers may price them low and make up the difference on items that sell more readily. Many factors enter into evaluation--popular patterns may be high due to demand, even though easily found, while scarce patterns may be passed over by collectors who find them difficult to reassemble.

When no condition is indicated, the items listed below are assumed to be in mint condition.

Key: FH—flat handle HH—hollow handle

Coin Silver

Bailey & Parker, dessert spoon, fiddle tip.....................23.00
Ball, Black & Co, dinner fork, French Thread, 7¾″...........35.00
BC Frobisher, teaspoon, Basket of Flowers, pr.................80.00
BC Frobisher, tongs, spoon ends, 6″...........................60.00
CAW Crosby, dessert spoon, fiddle tip.........................18.00
Collingwood & V, serving spoon, oval tip w/rattails, pr.........45.00
DS & Co, master salt spoon, beaded hdl........................18.00
E Mead & Co, teaspoon, 5⅝″....................................15.00
E Whitney, condiment ladle....................................32.00
GG Clark, serving spoon, 2-part, 9″...........................40.00
GS & GE Rogers, serving spoon, fiddle top, lg.................26.00
GS & GE Rogers, teaspoon, fiddle tip, set of 12..............180.00
H&S Ballard & Fuller, condiment ladle, ribbed, plain tip.......32.00
H&S/anchor, sugar shell, ribbed bowl dtd May 21, 1860........30.00
IS Porter, tongs, spoon ends, scalloped, 5⅝″..................55.00
JB Jones, master salt spoon, plain, pr........................32.00
JH Hollister, teaspoon, fiddle top, mk Pure Coin, set of 6......90.00
John Stevenson, ladle, monogram, 5¼″..........................50.00
John Stevenson, spoon, salt; monogram, 4″.....................40.00
Jones, Ball & Co, fish slice, cut-out fish, 1850, 12″..........300.00
Julep cup, ear hdl, Bigelow Bros, Kennard Boston, 1845, 4″...160.00
L Kimbal & Co, master salt spoon, fiddle tip..................20.00
N Harding & Co, serving fork, 5-tine, engraved, 9x2¾″........140.00
Osgood, serving spoon, eng bowl, scalloped, cut hdl, 8″........80.00
P Dickenson & Co, dessert spoon, plain........................20.00
Pap boat, engraved, dtd 1854.................................125.00
RH Bailey, teaspoon, slightly battered, monogram, 5¾″.........10.00
ST Crosby, fish slice, figural, emb scroll hdl, 11½″...........50.00
WF Horn, serving spoon, ribbed bowl, bright-cut hdl, 8″.......80.00
Whitney & Osgood, preserve spoon, eng/scallops/cut hdl, 7″....65.00
Wilson, Philadelphia, teaspoon, bright-cut....................30.00
Wm Gale & Son, egg spoon, 1840, set of 4.....................120.00

Flatware

Afterglow, cocktail fork......................................20.00
Afterglow, place fork...35.00

Afterglow, serving spoon ... 50.00
Agean Weave, dinner fork ... 35.00
American Victorian, cold meat fork ... 40.00
American Victorian, cream soup spoon ... 25.00
American Victorian, salad fork ... 25.00
American Victorian, sugar shell ... 25.00
Andante, cream soup spoon ... 25.00
Andante, dinner fork ... 35.00
Andante, gravy ladle ... 50.00
Andante, serving spoon ... 50.00
Angelique, cold meat fork ... 56.00
Angelique, sugar shell ... 30.00
Angelique, teaspoon ... 25.00
Aspen, dinner fork ... 35.00
Aspen, salad fork ... 30.00
Ballet, cream soup spoon ... 30.00
Ballet, dinner fork ... 35.00
Ballet, salad fork ... 30.00
Beauvior, cold meat fork ... 68.00
Beauvior, dessert spoon ... 41.00
Beauvior, knife, 9¾″ ... 25.00
Beauvior, serving spoon ... 78.00
Belle Rose, dinner fork ... 35.00
Belle Rose, salad fork ... 30.00
Belle Rose, teaspoon ... 25.00
Belvedere, cream soup spoon ... 30.00
Belvedere, dinner fork ... 36.00
Betsy Patterson, dinner fork ... 35.00
Betsy Patterson, serving spoon ... 47.50
Bridal Bouquet, cream soup spoon ... 30.00
Bridal Bouquet, dinner fork ... 35.00
Bridal Bouquet, gravy ladle ... 41.50
Bridal Rose, beef fork, Alvin, sm, EX ... 75.00
Bridal Rose, berry spoon, Alvin, EX ... 175.00
Bridal Rose, salad fork, Alvin, EX ... 65.00
Bridal Rose, sardine server, Alvin, EX ... 85.00
Bridal Rose, teaspoon, flower in bowl, Alvin, EX ... 45.00
Brocade, dinner fork ... 35.00
Burgundy, cream soup spoon, oval ... 35.00
Burgundy, dessert spoon ... 40.00
Buttercup, dinner fork, 7½″ ... 39.00
Buttercup, salad fork ... 30.00
Buttercup, sugar shell ... 30.00
Buttercup, teaspoon ... 20.00
Buttercup, 5 o'clock spoon ... 20.00
Camellia, cake server ... 32.00
Camellia, cold meat fork ... 52.00
Camellia, cream soup spoon ... 30.00
Camellia, dinner fork ... 35.00
Camellia, gravy ladle ... 40.00
Camellia, salad fork ... 30.00
Cameo, cold meat fork ... 48.00
Cameo, cream soup spoon ... 25.00
Candle Light, cheese knife ... 25.00
Candle Light, dinner fork, 7¼″ ... 35.00
Candle Light, iced tea spoon ... 25.00
Canterbury, dinner fork ... 40.00
Carpenter Hall, cream soup spoon ... 32.00
Carpenter Hall, dinner fork, 8⅞″ ... 37.50
Casa Grande, cake server ... 30.00
Casa Grande, dinner fork ... 37.50
Casa Grande, gravy ladle ... 45.00
Casa Grande, sugar shell ... 30.00
Celeste, dinner fork ... 35.00
Celeste, knife ... 25.00
Celeste, olive fork ... 27.50
Celeste, salad fork ... 30.00
Chantilly, cocktail fork ... 17.50
Chantilly, cream soup spoon ... 30.00
Chantilly, dinner knife, 9¾″ ... 25.00
Chantilly, melon spoon ... 30.00
Chantilly, pie fork, 6″ ... 30.00
Chantilly, salad fork ... 30.00
Chantilly, sauce ladle ... 35.00
Chantilly, serving spoon ... 45.00
Chateau Rose, cream soup spoon ... 30.00
Chateau Rose, dinner fork, 7⅞″ ... 37.50
Chateau Rose, gravy ladle ... 47.50
Chateau Rose, iced tea spoon ... 30.00
Chippendale, cream soup spoon, oval ... 30.00
Chippendale, dinner fork, 7⅝″ ... 37.50
Chippendale, jelly server ... 30.00
Chippendale, salad fork ... 30.00
Classique, gravy ladle ... 45.00
Classique, salad fork ... 30.00
Contessina, cold meat fork ... 57.00
Contessina, iced tea spoon ... 30.00
Contessina, salad fork ... 30.00
Contessina, serving spoon, perforated ... 51.00
Contessina, sugar shell ... 30.00
D'Orlean, gravy ladle ... 46.00
D'Orlean, sugar shell ... 25.00
Damask Rose, cold meat fork ... 36.00
Damask Rose, dessert spoon ... 30.00
Damask Rose, dinner fork ... 30.00
Damask Rose, iced tea spoon ... 25.00
Damask Rose, knife, 9½″ ... 25.00
Damask Rose, place spoon ... 35.00
Damask Rose, salad fork ... 30.00
Danish Baroque, carving set, sm ... 45.00
Danish Baroque, dinner fork ... 35.00
Debutante, cold meat fork ... 40.00
Debutante, teaspoon ... 25.00
Della Robbia, bonbon ... 27.50
Della Robbia, chowder ... 35.00
Dolly Madison, butter knife, FH ... 30.00
Dolly Madison, salad fork ... 30.00
Dresden Scroll, cold meat fork ... 50.00
Dresden Scroll, gravy ladle ... 62.00
Duke of Windsor, dinner fork, 7″ ... 30.00
Duke of Windsor, master butter, FH ... 35.00
Duke of Windsor, sugar shell ... 35.00
El Grande, cold meat fork ... 72.00
El Grande, dinner fork, 8″ ... 40.00
El Grande, knife, 9¼″ ... 25.00
El Grande, salad fork ... 35.00
El Grande, serving spoon ... 64.00
Eloquence, butter knife, FH ... 35.00
Eloquence, dinner fork, 7⅜″ ... 40.00
Eloquence, salad fork ... 35.00
Eloquence, serving salad fork ... 85.00
Eloquence, sugar shell ... 35.00
Eloquence, teaspoon ... 30.00
Enchanting Orchard, cream soup spoon ... 30.00
Enchanting Orchard, salad serving spoon ... 65.00
Enchanting Orchard, serving spoon ... 50.00
English Provincial, salad fork ... 35.00
English Shell, cream soup spoon ... 30.00

English Shell, dinner fork, 7½″ 35.00
English Shell, lemon fork 17.50
English Shell, sugar shell 30.00
English Shell, teaspoon 25.00
Esplanade, cream soup spoon 31.00
Esplanade, iced tea spoon 27.50
Esplanade, jam server 30.00
Esplanade, salad fork 30.00
Esplanade, serving spoon 57.00
Etruscan, butter knife, FH 35.00
Etruscan, cream ladle, Gorham, EX 42.50
Etruscan, cream soup spoon 30.00
Etruscan, iced teaspoon, Gorham, EX 35.00
Etruscan, master butter 35.00
Etruscan, pickle fork, Gorham, EX 29.50
Etruscan, ramekin fork, Gorham, EX 30.00
Etruscan, sugar shell 35.00
Etruscan, sugar tongs, Gorham, EX 37.50
Etruscan, tablespoon, Gorham, EX 60.00
Evening Rose, salad fork 30.00
Evening Rose, sugar shell 30.00
Fairfax, dinner fork 37.50
Fairfax, salad serving set, all sterling 175.00
Feather Edge, cold meat fork 75.00
Feather Edge, sauce ladle 40.00
Feather Edge, serving spoon 57.50
Festival, cream soup spoon 30.00
Festival, dinner fork 37.50
Festival, master butter 30.00
Festival, salad fork 30.00
Florentine Lace, gravy ladle 49.00
Florentine Lace, iced tea spoon 30.00
Florentine Lace, salad fork 30.00
Florentine Lace, sauce ladle 35.00
Florentine Lace, serving spoon 57.00
Florentine Lace, sugar scoop 30.00
Flower Lane, cream soup spoon, oval 30.00
Flower Lane, salad fork 30.00
Flower Lane, sugar spoon 30.00
Fontana, cream soup spoon 30.00
Fontana, dinner fork, 7¼″ 35.00
Fontana, salad fork 30.00
Fragrance, jelly server 27.50
Fragrance, salad fork 30.00
Fragrance, serving spoon 45.00
Francis, cheese server 30.00
Francis, gravy ladle 62.00
French Provincial, dinner fork, 7⅞″ 37.50
French Provincial, sugar shell 30.00
French Renaissance, cream soup spoon 30.00
Frontenac, cream ladle, Simpson Hall & Miller, EX 75.00
Frontenac, demitasse spoon, EX 20.00
Frontenac, pickle fork, Simpson Hall & Miller, EX 40.00
Frontenac, sugar spoon, Simpson Hall & Miller, EX 35.00
Frontenac, sugar tongs, Simpson Hall & Miller, sm, EX 75.00
George & Martha, cold meat fork 54.00
George & Martha, cream soup spoon 30.00
George & Martha, dessert spoon 30.00
George & Martha, gravy ladle 54.00
George & Martha, master butter, FH 35.00
George & Martha, salad fork 30.00
George & Martha, serving spoon 50.00
George & Martha, sugar shell 30.00
George & Martha, tablespoon 40.00
Grand Baroque, cake server 37.50
Grand Baroque, dinner fork, 7⅞″ 48.00
Grand Baroque, gravy ladle 66.00
Grand Baroque, sugar shell 30.00
Grand Renaissance, dinner fork, 8″ 40.00
Grand Renaissance, knife, 9″ 25.00
Grand Renaissance, salad fork 27.00
Grand Renaissance, serving spoon, perforated 59.00
Grand Renaissance, teaspoon 30.00
Greenbrier, cream soup spoon 25.00
Greenbrier, dinner fork, 8″ 35.00
Greenbrier, gravy ladle 38.00
Greenbrier, iced tea spoon 20.00
Greenbrier, serving spoon 45.00
Heiress, salad fork 25.00
Horizon, cream soup spoon, oval 25.00
Horizon, gravy ladle 38.00
Horizon, serving spoon 40.00
Hunt Club, serving spoon 42.00
Inaugral, cream soup spoon 30.00
Inaugral, jelly server 25.00
Intermezzo, dinner fork, 7″ 27.00
Joan of Arc, dinner fork 35.00
John & Priscilla, dinner fork 35.00
John & Priscilla, master butter 30.00
John & Priscilla, salad fork 30.00
Julianna, serving spoon 34.00
King Christian, butter knife, FH 30.00
King Christian, cake cutter 35.00
King Christian, cream soup spoon 30.00
King Edward, cream soup spoon, Gorham 23.00
King Edward, dinner fork, Gorham, 7⅞″ 37.00
King Edward, pie fork, Gorham, 6¼″ 26.00
King Edward, pie server, Gorham 31.00
King Edward, place spoon, Gorham 32.00
King Edward, serving spoon, Gorham 55.00
King Richard, dinner fork 42.00
King Richard, knife, 9¾″ 26.00
King Richard, serving spoon 48.00
King Richard, teaspoon 26.00
Lace Point, dessert spoon 23.00
Lace Point, dinner fork, 7½″ 32.00
Lancaster, berry spoon, shell bowl, Gorham, EX 135.00
Lancaster, dinner fork, Gorham, EX 50.00
Lancaster, lettuce fork, Gorham, EX 75.00
Lancaster, luncheon fork, Gorham, EX 37.50
Lancaster, pie server, all silver, Gorham, VG 157.50
Lancaster, salad fork, Gorham, EX 55.00
Lancaster, tomato server, flat, Gorham, EX 145.00
Lily, butter pick, 2-tine, Whiting/Div of Gorham, EX 75.00
Lily, cocktail/seafood fork, Whiting/Div of Gorham, EX 40.00
Lily, cold meat fork, Whiting/Div of Gorham, EX 149.00
Lily, lettuce fork, Whiting/Div of Gorham, EX 150.00
Lily, mustard ladle, Whiting/Div of Gorham, EX 137.50
Lily, salad serving spoon & fork, Whiting/Div of Gorham, EX 395.00
Lily, teaspoon, Whiting/Div of Gorham, EX 40.00
Madam Jumel, cold meat fork 57.00
Madam Jumel, cream soup spoon 30.00
Madam Jumel, serving spoon 50.00
Madam Jumel, stuffing spoon 75.00
Madeira, dinner fork 30.00
Marlborough, salad fork 30.00
Marlborough, serving spoon 55.00
May Melody, salad serving spoon 62.00

Meadow Rose, dinner fork, 7¼″ 29.00
Meadow Rose, knife, 9⅝″ 20.00
Meadow Rose, master butter, FH 33.00
Meadow Rose, master butter, HH 20.00
Meadow Rose, nut server 24.00
Meadow Rose, perforated serving spoon 58.00
Meadow Rose, pie fork, 5⅞″ 30.00
Medici, dinner fork, new, 7⅞″ 46.00
Medici, honey/jam server, new 28.00
Medici, knife, new, 9¾″ 22.00
Melrose, cold meat fork 52.00
Melrose, cream soup spoon 30.00
Melrose, dinner fork, 7½″ 36.00
Melrose, master butter, HH 29.00
Melrose, salad fork 30.00
Melrose, soup spoon 30.00
Melrose, sugar shell 26.00
Milburn Rose, gravy ladle 42.00
Milburn Rose, master butter 24.00
Modern Victorian, dinner fork, 7⅜″ 25.00
Mt Vernon, gravy ladle 33.00
Mt Vernon, horseradish spoon 35.00
Nocturne, salad fork 26.00
Nocturne, sugar shell 26.00
Old English, sauce ladle 26.00
Old Master, cream soup spoon 23.00
Old Master, dinner fork, 7¾″ 39.00
Old Master, gravy ladle 40.00
Old Master, knife, 9¾″ 20.00
Old Master, salad fork, 6⅜″ 25.00
Old Master, serving spoon 51.00
Old Newberry, butter knife, FH 30.00
Old Newberry, dinner fork, 7⅛″ 35.00
Panetheon, serving spoon 42.00
Park Avenue, dinner fork, 7″ 28.00
Park Avenue, gravy ladle 28.00
Prince Eugene, iced tea spoon 25.00
Princess Patricia, gravy ladle 42.00
Processional, dinner fork, 7¼″ 30.00
Queen Lace, dinner fork, 7¼″ 35.00
Queen Lace, jelly server 30.00
Queen Lace, serving spoon 50.00
Rambler Rose, cream soup spoon 27.50
Rambler Rose, gravy ladle 46.00
Repousse, dinner fork, 7¼″ 30.00
Repousse, jelly server 28.00
Richelieu, master butter 35.00
Richelieu, serving spoon 60.00
Rondo, cream soup spoon 25.00
Rondo, dinner fork, 8″ 33.00
Rondo, gravy ladle 39.00
Rose Cascade, knife, 9¼″ 25.00
Rose Cascade, salad fork 30.00
Rose Cascade, serving spoon 52.00
Rose Cascade, sugar shell 26.00
Rose Point, dinner fork, 7″ 31.00
Rosepoint, cake server 26.00
Rosepoint, steak knife 26.00
Royal Danish, cocktail fork 20.00
Royal Danish, dessert spoon 35.00
Royal Danish, dinner fork, 7⅛″ 36.00
Royal Danish, dinner fork, 7⅝″ 48.00
Royal Danish, iced tea spoon 25.00
Royal Danish, knife, 9″ 25.00
Royal Danish, pie server 31.00
Royal Danish, sugar shell 30.00
Royal Satir, dessert spoon 29.00
Royal Satir, dinner fork, 7¾″ 35.00
Royal Windsor, salad fork 30.00
Silver Melody, dessert spoon 35.00
Silver Melody, dinner fork, 7¼″ 36.00
Silver Melody, serving spoon, perforated 55.00
Silver Melody, sugar shell 30.00
Silver Rhythm, cold meat fork 62.00
Silver Rhythm, dinner fork, 7¼″ 34.00
Silver Surf, gravy ladle 42.00
Soliloquy, dinner fork, 7½″ 30.00
Soliloquy, gravy ladle 45.00
Soliloquy, serving spoon 51.00
Southern Charm, cold meat fork 40.00
Southern Charm, cream soup spoon 27.50
Southern Charm, iced tea spoon 20.00
Southern Colonial, salad fork 30.00
Southern Colonial, serving spoon 56.00
Southern Grandeur, knife, 8¾″ 25.00
Southern Grandeur, master butter, FH 30.00
Southern Grandeur, salad fork 30.00
Southern Grandeur, teaspoon 25.00
Southern Rose, cream soup spoon 27.00
Southern Rose, dinner fork 32.00
Southern Rose, gravy ladle 48.00
Southern Rose, knife 25.00
Southern Rose, salad fork 27.50
Spanish Lace, cold meat fork 50.00
Spanish Lace, dessert spoon 30.00
Spanish Lace, dinner fork, 7⅝″ 35.00
Spanish Lace, knife, 9¼″ 25.00
Spanish Lace, pie server 29.00
Spanish Lace, serving spoon 46.00
Spanish Lace, teaspoon 25.00
Spanish Provincial, iced tea spoon 25.00
Spanish Provincial, perforated serving spoon 50.00
Spanish Provincial, salad fork 30.00
Spring Glory, cream soup spoon 30.00
Spring Glory, dinner fork, 7¼″ 35.00
Spring Glory, salad fork 30.00
Spring Glory, teaspoon 25.00
Stately, iced tea spoon 20.00
Stately, master butter 24.00
Strasbourg, dinner fork, 7⅝″ 41.00
Strasbourg, honey/jam server 27.00
Strasbourg, serving spoon 58.00
Tara, dinner fork, 7⅜″ 31.00
Tara, iced tea spoon 25.00
Tara, knife, 9″ 25.00
Tara, salad fork 25.00
Tara, serving spoon 56.00
Tranquility, cream soup spoon 20.00
Twilight, cold meat fork 45.00
Twilight, dinner fork, 7½″ 35.00
Twilight, iced tea spoon 25.00
Twilight, salad fork 30.00
Twilight, serving spoon 50.00
Versailles, coffee spoon 27.50
Versailles, dessert fork, 6″ 55.00
Versailles, salad fork 55.00
Versailles, salad server set 350.00
Vespera, dinner fork, 7½″ 35.00

Victorian, master butter....26.00
Virginia, gravy ladle....46.00
Virginian, cream soup spoon....25.00
Virginian, dinner fork, 7¼"....30.00
Virginian, salad fork....27.50
Wild Rose, cold meat fork....56.00
Wild Rose, cream soup spoon....30.00
Wild Rose, dinner fork, 7⅝"....35.00
Wild Rose, pie server....30.00
Wild Rose, serving spoon, perforated....39.00
Willow, cold meat fork....42.00
Windslow, iced tea spoon....25.00
Windslow, salad fork....30.00
Young Love, cream soup spoon....30.00
Young Love, dinner fork, 7½"....35.00
Young Love, gravy ladle....55.00
Young Love, soup spoon, oval....35.00
1810, serving spoon....50.00

Flatware, Antique

Gorham, bonbon spoon, shell bowl, nude w/seashell, 1890....75.00
Gorham, claret ladle, pierced/eng bowl, child w/bird, 12"....195.00
Hester Bateman, gravy ladle, Geo III, floral pendants, pr....250.00
Hester Bateman, serving spoon, beaded border, eagle crest....90.00
Hester Bateman, serving spoon, castle/serpent crest, 1782....120.00
Hester Bateman, serving spoon, Geo III, rnd top/buck crest....110.00
Hester Bateman, teaspoon, date/essay 1761-62 London....150.00
John Keens, gravy ladle, unicorn crest, monogram, 1796, pr....110.00
John Round & Son, soup ladle, shell tip, 1900....95.00
JS, Dublin, serving spoon, Geo III, rnd tip....40.00
Lewis Kimball, dessert spoon, rattail tip, set of 4....40.00
Michael Keating, berry spoon, fruit emb/diamond eng, 4 for....275.00
ML, London, stuffing spoon, rnd tip, 1800....55.00
Paul Storr, serving spoon, Geo III, shell decor tip/lions....125.00
PR, marrow spoon, Geo III, shell bk bowl, scoop shaft....65.00
Robert Gray & Son, serving spoon, Wm IV, fiddle tip, pr....80.00
Starling Wilford, stuffing spoon, Geo II, plain top, 4-oz....200.00
Teaspoon, applied 14k Oriental lily pad/peonies, Sheibler....95.00
Thos Watson, serving spoon, Geo IV, fiddle tip, pr....70.00
TKB, stuffing spoon, Ed VII, plain rnd tip w/mono, 5-oz....70.00
Walker & Hall, salt spoon, spiral stem, 1896, set of 4....35.00
Wm Chawner, stuffing spoon, ribbed border/fiddle tip, 1823....85.00

Hollow Ware

Until the middle of the 19th century, the silverware produced in America was custom made on order of the buyer directly from the silversmith. With the rise of industrialization, factories sprung up that manufactured silverware for retailers who often added their trademark to the ware. Silver ore was mined in abundance, and demand spurred production. Changes in style occurred at the whim of fashion. Repousse decoration (relief work) became popular about 1885, reflecting the ostentatious taste of the Victorian era. Later in the century, Greek, Etruscan, and several classic styles found favor. Today, the Art Deco styles of this century are very popular with collectors.

In the listing that follows, manufacturer's name or trademark is noted first; in lieu of that information, listings are by item. Weight is given in troy ounces.

A Michelsen, cup, fluted, gold washed w/gr enamel, 6½-oz....300.00
AE Warner, julep cup, cast ear hdl, monogram, 3½"....275.00
Backruch, candelabra, 7-light, acanthus/masks, 22", pr....3,850.00
Bailey, Banks & Biddle, butter pat, Kirk style, 3x3"....75.00
Bailey, Banks & Biddle, platter, scroll rim/cartouch, 15"....715.00
BB, London, mug, 1883, 7-oz....125.00
Birmingham, vase, Art Nouveau, corset shape, hdls, 4½"....58.00
Black, Starr & Frost, tray, 23½-oz, 12½" dia....300.00
Burrage Davenport, dish cross, Geo III, swivel arms, 11" L....825.00
Cartier, platter, Art Deco, 20th C, 18"....2,000.00
Chester Billings & Son, tea set, #550, 26-oz, 3-pc....250.00
Creamer, cow, long horns, insect eng on lid, 2½x4½"....180.00
Crichton, candlestick, Geo III style, 1916, 12", set of 4....1,320.00
Dominick & Haff, centerpc bowl, on ped w/4 paw ft, 13"....660.00
Dutch, basket, cobalt liner, openwork scene, 4x3½"....160.00
Edward Wood, salt, rnd w/3 hoof ft, ca 1743, set of 4....475.00
English, candlestick, columns/sq festoon ft, 1800, 13", pr....275.00
English, candlestick, Rococo style, weighted, 8½", 4 for....1,300.00
English, cream pitcher, repousse, 11-oz, late, 4"....225.00
Ensko, candlesticks, Colonial style, sq base, 10½", pr....2,200.00
F Hingelberg Aarhus, ewer, Deco, coil at neck, 6½"....45.00
Froment-Meurice, coffee set, raffia chased bands, 3-pc....1,100.00
FW Cooper, kettle on lampstand, twig spout/florals, 20"....880.00
Georg Jensen, beaker, #211, Jensen design, 1919, 3⅜"....495.00
Georg Jensen, bowl, C-scroll strap hdls, ftd, 11"....1,100.00
Georg Jensen, bowl, foliate/berries stem, rnd ft, 8"....1,320.00
Georg Jensen, box, oval w/foliage wreath, 5" L....525.00
Georg Jensen, candlestick, fluted columms, rnd ft, 9¾", pr....1,870.00
Georg Jensen, coasters w/lid, Bernadotte design, 3" dia....1,210.00
Georg Jensen, dresser set, Art Deco, Pyramid, 5-pc....935.00
Georg Jensen, goblet, cup-like support w/lg beads, w/lid....990.00
Georg Jensen, gravy boat, underplate & ladle, #177A, 1925....1,540.00
Georg Jensen, plate, grid eng centers, 10½", set of 6....2,640.00
Georg Jensen, salt, foliate/berried stems, rnd ft, 8 for....660.00
Georg Jensen, sugar tongs, acorns & scrolls....55.00
Georg Jensen, tea kettle on lampstand, #150, 14½"....3,500.00
Georg Jensen, tray, rnd w/scalloped edge, hammered, 12"....990.00
Georg Jensen, tray, scalloped edge oval, 23"....2,000.00
German, tankard, emb medieval battle, mask t'pc, 10½"....660.00
GF, English, smoke tray w/lighter/box, 1892, 6¾"....70.00
Gorham, after-dinner coffee set, Etruscan, pot: 9¾", 3-pc....720.00
Gorham, bread tray, Chantilly, ftd, 12" L....320.00
Gorham, centerpc bowl, Martele, iris/primrose, 18½"....550.00
Gorham, inkwell, Martele, repousse, pad ft, glass well, 5"....1,980.00
Gorham, master salt, mussel shell, sand on base, ftd, 1890....95.00
Gorham, pitcher, paneled, floral/leaf swag/pendants, 9¾"....200.00
Gorham, pitcher, water; dolphin head spout, 1859, 9"....385.00
Gorham, plate, 6⅜", set of 10....1,200.00
Gorham, platter, quad-reeded border, 61-oz, monogram, 21"....750.00
Gorham, tazza, Martele, Art Nouveau, 10½", pr....2,750.00
Gorham, tazza, Martele, Art Nouveau, 8"....935.00

Austrian, figural mermaid centerpiece, ca 1900, 15 dwts., 48 oz., 9", $1,200.00.

Gorham, tea & coffee service, foliage/shells/scrolls, 7-pc......4,950.00
Gorham, tea & coffee set, masks/strapwork, 1865, 6-pc......2,000.00
Gorham, teakettle on lampstand, strapwork reserves, 14"......825.00
Gorham, tray, Japanese style, bright-cut/eng bird, 8x6"........195.00
Gorham, vase, elongated pear w/emb iris, ftd, 1900, 18".......825.00
Gorham, vase, Martele, lobed pear form, emb grapes, 19"....8,250.00
Gorham, water pitcher, repousse scrolls, 7¼"................440.00
Heimerdinger, bowl, lion mask ring hdls, paw/ball ft, 15"......500.00
Howard, compote, foliage/flowers, gilt, 1903/4, 13", 3 for....1,800.00
Int'nl, tea & coffee service, Royal Danish, 5-pc.............1,320.00
Intn'l, salt & pepper set, cobalt liners, 4-pc.................225.00
IR in rectangle, goblet, ribbons/swags emb/chased, 7", pr....2,090.00
Italian, candlestick, grape borders/column stems, 10", pr......770.00
IW, att John West, sauce boat, Geo III, shell/hoof ft, 6½".....467.00
JE Caldwell, plate, openwork rim, emb/chased vines, 13¾".....550.00
Jean-Baptiste Harleux, dish, semi-nude/cupid/Bacchus, 10"....1,320.00
John Edwards, entree dish, Geo III, w/lid, 12¾", pr.........1,430.00
John Langlands, cup, 2 scroll hdls, Geo III, 1760, 5".........357.00
John Roberts, candlestick, Geo III, tulip sconce, 8", pr........605.00
Joseph Willmore, cigar case, raffia chased, 1835, 4¾" L.......275.00
Kirk, sauce boat, repousse florals, 6¼" L..................180.00
Knife rest, squirrel eating nut figural.........................30.00
Konoike, tea set, iris/reeds, repousse/chased, 1900, 4-pc.......880.00
L Sawyer, julep cup, strap hdl, 1834 inscription, 4"..........165.00
London, salt cellar, hoof ft, mks for 1770-71, 2½", pr.........150.00
Lunt Silversmiths, tea & coffee service, Geo style, 5-pc.......2,310.00
Messrs Barnard, vase, masks on lion pelt ground, 18½"......4,935.00
Monell & Wms, tea set, urn form, chased floral, 1830, 3-pc....990.00
Mt Vernon Co, cake basket, openwork/foliage border, 11".....415.00

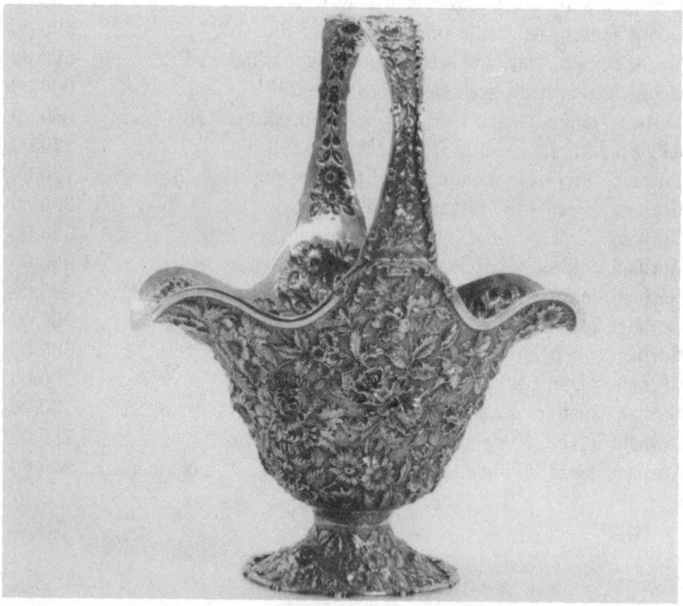

Basket, attributed to Kirk & Son, allover floral repousse, 13" x 11", $1,800.00.

Paul Storr, muffin basket, acanthus hdl/pierced rim, 10".....4,750.00
Peter & Anne Bateman, chocolate pot, acanthus hdls, 13¾"..1,600.00
Peter & Anne Bateman, sugar basket/pr salts, foliage/swags....605.00
Philip Rundell, tea set, fluted band/arrows/acanthus, 4-pc.....6,000.00
Philip Rundell, tea tray, shell/foliage/winged horses, 25".....3,500.00
R Wallace & Sons, bowl, scrolls/shells/gilt, 1900, 15" L.......415.00
Reed & Barton, centerpiece, applied iris on ped ft, 13" W.....660.00
Reed & Barton, platter, well/tree, ribbon/oak leaves, 23".....1,100.00
Richard Rugg, salver, Geo II, foliage/scrolls, 1755, 12".......1,210.00
Robert & David Hennell, condiment set, 4 cut glass bottles....225.00
Robert Hennell, goblet, eng crests/gilt w/in, 1785, 6", pr.....1,200.00
Robert Hennell, salt, bright-cut/pierced, ftd, 1788, 4 for.......467.00
S Kirk & Son, candlesticks, repousse, 11½", pr............2,000.00
S Kirk & Son, centerpiece bowl, floral emb/chased, 13".......935.00
S Kirk & Son, sauce boat, repousse, ftd, 6¼"...............225.00
Sam Whitford, inkstand, Geo III, 3 glass containers, 1801.....605.00
Samuel Massey, creamer, Geo III, emb/chased foliage, 6"......330.00
Samuel Roberts Jr & Geo Cadman, toast rack, Geo III, 8-oz..2,000.00
Steiff, shakers, repousse vintage, pear shape, ftd, 6", pr.......280.00
Tea ball, figural teapot, chain & ring........................45.00
Theo B Starr, tray, monogrammed, 38-oz, 14" dia...........400.00
Thos Daniels, salt, pierce/eng foliage/ribbons, 3", 4 for........770.00
Towle, bowl, Lady Diana, 10-oz, 8½"......................100.00
Towle, bread basket, Lady Diana, 16-oz, 12½"..............140.00
Turin, chalice, paterae chasing w/in strapwork, 9½"..........660.00
W Adams, teakettle on lampstand, 1840, 18-oz, 17½".........880.00
Wm Cripps, teapot, can form, eng foliage/scrolls, 1750, 4".....350.00
Wm Robertson, sauce boat, Geo III, leaf cap hdl/ft, 7½" L.....500.00
Woodside Sterling, 3-pc coffee service w/tray, Art Deco......1,540.00

Silver Lustre Ware

Silver lustre is a type of earthenware with a metallic surface, produced in the early 1800s in Staffordshire, England. These wares were most popular prior to 1840, when the technique of electroplating was developed, and silverplated wares came into vogue.

Compote, 5" dia..80.00
Creamer, 6"..58.00
Loving cup, copper lustre w/in, 4½x5"......................60.00
Shaker, horizontal ribs, ftd, minor wear, 3⅝"................35.00
Teapot, Queen Anne, 5½x9½"............................175.00
Toby shaker, full-figure man w/cone hat, 5"..................75.00

Silver Overlay

The silver overlay glass made during the 1800s was decorated with a cut-out pattern of sterling silver applied to the surface of the ware.

When no condition is indicated, the items listed below are assumed to be in mint condition.

Bottle, cobalt, leaf overlay, 9¼"..........................110.00
Bottle, scent; clear, medallion overlay, mk Fine, 3¾"..........75.00
Bottle, scent; clear, scroll/flower silver, flare base, 8".........135.00
Bottle, scent; cranberry, heavy overlay, 4½x3"...............300.00
Parfait glass & underplate, clear, set.......................65.00
Pitcher, clear, flower & branches overlay, 8¼"...............275.00
Pitcher, gr, bowling man overlay ea side....................245.00
Vase, amethyst, Deco geometric emb overlay sgn twice, 9½"....135.00
Vase, crystal, iris lip overlay, 8½".........................125.00
Vase, gr, heavy floral overlay, ped ft, 10¾"..................350.00
Vase, rubena w/eng; silver top band & disk, 12".............225.00

Silverplate

Silverplated flatware is fast becoming the focus of attention for many of today's collectors. In the listings that follow, prices are for pieces in like-new condition with no monogram. Worn pieces or those with monograms will be substantially less. It is generally not profitable to restore worn pieces, except those from the very valuable patterns.

When no condition is indicated, the items listed below are assumed to be in mint condition.

Flatware

Aldine (1895), sugar spoon....16.00
Alhambra (1907), grapefruit spoon....14.00
Ambassador (1847), cold meat fork....17.50
Arbutus (1883), pickle fork, long hdl....15.00
Ashland (1914), cake serving fork....13.00
Assyrian Head (1847), cocktail fork....13.00
Assyrian Head (1847), mustard ladle....35.00
Assyrian Head (1847), soup ladle....82.00
Assyrian Head (1847), sugar tongs....30.00
Avon (1847), demitasse spoon....11.00
Ballad (1953), gravy ladle....15.00
Berkshire (1847), grapefruit spoon....15.00
Berkshire (1847), soup spoon, rnd....13.00
Berkshire (1847), sugar spoon....13.00
Bird of Paradise (1923), cream ladle....18.00
Bridal Wreath I (1915), sugar tong....12.00
Bridal Wreath II (1950), pie server, pierced....13.00
Century (1923), ice cream fork....13.00
Charter Oak (1847), bouillon spoon....20.00
Charter Oak (1847), cold meat fork....23.00
Charter Oak (1847), grapefruit spoon....20.00
Columbia (1847), cake serving fork....35.00
Crown (1885), pie knife, ornate blade....32.00
Croyden (1887), tomato server....15.00
Daffodil (1847), cold meat fork....20.00
Daffodil (1950), berry spoon....30.00
Daffodil (1950), pickle fork....12.50
Daisy (1892), cold meat fork....10.00
Del Mar (1939), cold meat fork....13.00
Dresden (1911), fish server....32.00
Elmore (1905), sugar spoon....12.00
Ermine (1910), cream/sauce ladle....10.00
Esperanto (1967), gravy ladle....12.00
Evening Star (1950), cold meat fork....17.50
Flemish (1900), punch ladle, hdl 11½″....60.00
Floral (1835), butter spreader, ind....20.00
Floral (1835), pastry server, HH....22.00
Floral (1938), cold meat fork....23.00
Floral (1938), youth knife....13.00
Flower (1906), gravy ladle....14.00
Flower De Luce (1904), soup spoon, rnd....12.00
Grosvenor (1921), relish spoon, pierced....12.50
Guest of Honor (1935), cake server....12.00
Hanover (1901), cold meat fork....20.00
Hanover (1901), grapefruit spoon....12.50
Hardwick (1908), ice cream fork....12.00
Heritage (1847), pie server, pierced....13.00
Invitation (1940), butter spreader, ind....10.00
Isabella (1913), tablespoon....12.00
Jamestown (1916), pastry server....18.00
Jewell (1916), cream/sauce ladle....12.00
Kings (1980), sugar tong, claw ends, 5¼″....22.00
La Vigne (1881), butter knife....13.00
La Vigne (1881), cold meat fork....29.00
La Vigne (1881), fish fork, 6½″....35.00
La Vigne (1881), pastry fork....25.00
Lakewood (1914), salad serving fork....18.00
Laurel Mist (1966), dessert server....15.00
Leonora (1905), berry spoon....16.00
Leota (1912), berry spoon....18.00
Lilyta (1909), cold meat fork....23.00
Lorne (1847), gravy ladle....20.00
Louis XVI (1900), carving fork....12.00
Louisiana (1924), tomato server....18.00
Louvain (1918), tomato server....25.00
Magic Rose (1847), tablespoon, pierced....12.00
Masterpiece (1932), pastry server....12.00
Masterpiece (1932), sugar tong....12.00
May Queen (1951), sugar tong....12.50
Melrose (1898), cold meat fork....13.00
Melrose (1898), cream/sauce ladle....13.00
Milady (1940), bonbon server....10.00
Moselle (1906), cream/sauce ladle....66.00
Moselle (1906), teaspoon....15.00
Moss Rose (1949), tomato server....18.00
Mystic (1903), cold meat fork....22.00
Mystic (1903), oyster ladle....50.00
Narcissus (1908), berry spoon....20.00
Navarre (1847), cold meat fork....12.00
New Century (1898), tomato server....23.00
Newport (1847), salt spoon, master....15.00
Norfolk (1847), butter knife....10.00
Old Colony (1847), olive spoon/fork....30.00
Orange Blossom (1910), cake server....30.00
Orange Blossom (1910), salad fork....16.00
Oregon (1900), pie server....22.00
Orient (1879), cocktail fork....10.00
Orient (1879), cream/sauce ladle....22.50
Oxford (1907), pickle fork, long hdl....16.00
Pansy (1914), oyster fork, twisted hdl....13.00
Patrician (1914), jelly server....10.00
Paul Revere (1927), cake fork....22.50
Princess (1847), butter knife....12.00
Proposal (1954), tablespoon, pierced....12.00
Puritan (1910), sugar tong....10.00
Queen Bess II (1946), gravy ladle....15.00
Remembrance (1847), cold meat fork....19.50
Remembrance (1847), gravy ladle....27.50
Renaissance (1886), tablespoon....13.00
Rex (1902), fish serving knife....23.00
Rhythmic (1957), tablespoon....10.00
Richmond (1897), tablespoon....10.00
Rose & Leaf (1937), nut spoon....8.00
Rose Song (1964), cold meat fork....12.00
Royal (1890), mustard ladle....16.00
Royal Lace (1973), tablespoon, pierced....10.00
San Diego (1889), orange spoon, M....13.00
Shakespear (1924), gravy ladle....12.00
Sharon (1847), dinner fork, HH....10.00
Sharon (1847), salad serving fork....27.50
Sharon (1847), sugar tong....22.00
Shelburne (1914), jelly server....12.50
Sheraton (1910), cold meat fork....17.50
Sierra (1914), sugar tongs, claw ends....16.00
Silver Bouquet (1960), butter spreader....10.00
Siren (1847), cocktail fork....16.00
Siren (1847), pie server....30.00
South Seas (1955), cold meat fork....17.50
South Seas (1955), salad serving fork....17.50
St Paul (1896), cream ladle....13.00
Thistle (1906), berry spoon....30.00
Thistle (1906), gravy ladle....25.00
Tours (1801), fish serving knife....23.00
Triumph (1968), berry spoon....16.00
Triumph (1968), cold meat fork....15.00
Twilight (1956), dessert server....12.00

Unique (1879), pie server....22.00
Victor (1882), sugar spoon....10.00
Vineyard (1906), cream/sauce ladle....15.00
Vineyard (1906), pie server....18.00
Vintage (1847), butter knife, twisted hdl....15.00
Vintage (1847), cream ladle....36.00
Vintage (1847), jelly trowel....76.00
Vintage (1847), salad fork....32.00
Vintage (1847), tablespoon....12.00
Vista (1940), gravy ladle....12.00
Waldorf (1894), cold meat fork....16.00
Webster I (1915), sugar tongs, floral ends....22.00
White Orchid (1953), jelly server....12.50
Whittier (1915), cold meat fork....12.00
Wildwood (1908), fruit spoon....10.00
Windsor (1847), salt spoon, master....12.00
Yale I (1894), butter knife, twisted hdl....13.00
Yale I (1894), oyster ladle, hdl 9″....66.00
Yale I (1894), salad fork....16.00

Hollow Ware

Basket, bride's; pierced diamonds, eagle at ft, florals....110.00
Basket, bun; lattice, dancing people, ball ft, sgn/#d, 12″....45.00
Basket, cake; birds/flowers, ped ft, mk, Victorian, 9″....55.00
Basket, glass insert, Nouveau, w/lid, German, 1920, 9x9½″....145.00
Basket, repousse, swing hdl, ball ft, openwork, Derby, 4½″....22.00
Bowl, Sheffield, hdl removes, eng spider/web, w/lid, 12x9″....175.00
Box, Sheffield, rectangular, gadroon borders, hinged lid....55.00
Bud vase, eng floral, ornate hdls, ftd, Tufts, 6″....25.00
Butter dish, cow finial, w/knife, Meriden, 5½x8″....125.00
Can, chased Rococo designs, 5″....55.00
Candelabra, Sheffield, ornate floral/leaf decor, 15″, pr....350.00

Spoon-holder sugar bowl, signed Derby frame, cranberry flashed insert, 8½″, $475.00.

Candle snuffer & tray, scroll/shell/eng florals, sgn....115.00
Candlestick, Geo III style, w/hurricane shade, 19″, 4 for....770.00
Candlestick, Sheffield, oval vase form, fluted/reeded, 10″....250.00
Candlestick, Sheffield, 4½″, 4 for....100.00
Casserole, Sheffield, gadroon dbl hdls w/ivory grips, open....45.00
Chafing tray, 3-burner, electroplate nickel, DNA, 29″....100.00
Champagne bucket, ped ft, ornate hdls, no mk, 10″....75.00
Coffee pot, ind; Sheffield, gadroon rims/wood hdl, 7½″....70.00
Coffee service, pear-shaped pot, rnd tray, Rogers, 4-pc....70.00
Coffee urn, repousse, tall legs, ivory hdl, Derby, 13½″....145.00
Cologne stand, Victorian lady's arms hold bottle, Tufts....200.00
Compote, repousse, Victorian, 9″....35.00
Cracker jar, eng 'Crackers,' flower finial, Columbia, 8″....110.00
Cup & saucer, bright-cut, Tufts....35.00
Cup & saucer, scroll/florals/strawberries, Tufts, lg....75.00
Decanter caddy, w/3 crystal ribbed decanters....225.00
Egg caddy, relief lions on ft, heart bail, 6-cup, SH & M....165.00
Entree dish, Sheffield, oval, scroll decor, w/lid, 12½″....165.00
Jigger, chick leans against thimble, Acme....35.00
Knife rest, dogs sitting ea end....75.00
Lamp, cigar; emb windmills/duck/girl/etc, sgn Apollo....15.00
Mustache cup & saucer, bright-cut floral, Barbour Bros....95.00
Pitcher, applied acorns, beaded/scalloped top, lg....48.00
Pitcher, bear finial on hinged lid, Gorham & Co, 12¼″....175.00
Pitcher, cocktail; inlaid pnt rooster, Meriden, 12½″....50.00
Platter, Sheffield, pierced drip tray, shell/scroll, 22½″....200.00
Salver, Sheffield, bird crest eng, beaded border, ftd, 9″....100.00
Spoon warmer, nautilus form, w/lid, English....150.00
Syrup, scroll decor, Poole Silver, w/tray, 5″....45.00
Tea service, Sheffield, melon rib, gold wash w/in, 3-pc....200.00
Teapot, eng rose/scroll, ivory heat resistors on leaf hdl....70.00
Toast rack, 6-slice, center ring hdl, ball ft....55.00
Toothpick, chicken, wishbone, cracked egg, Best Wishes....75.00
Toothpick, owl by side, Barbour, 2x2½″....65.00
Tray, pierced rim, gadroon edge, shell/leaf hdls, 26″....175.00
Tray, repousse border w/fencing/cows/birds/etc, Derby, 13″....125.00
Tray, Sheffield, gadroon border, shell/leaf corners, 24″....105.00
Tureen, applied petal floral/woodman/cook, quadruple plate....67.00
Tureen, reticulated ft, bright-cut, hdls, bulbous, 10½″....60.00
Tureen, Sheffield, w/hdls, ball ft, ca 1815, 8½″ L, pr....495.00
Vase, floral eng diapering, gold branches, Tufts, 10″....68.00
Vase, scroll/floral/people emb, trumpet shape, Derby, 12″....55.00
Waiter, Chippendale style, 29½″ L....300.00
Waiter, reticulated/reeded rim, oval, 30″....300.00
Wine cooler, Sheffield, campana form, ca 1820, 9⅝″, pr....770.00

Silver Resist

The process for decorating pottery with the silver resist method involved first coating the design, or that portion of the pattern that was to be left unsilvered, with a water soluble solution. The lustre was applied to the entire surface of the vessel, and allowed to dry. Before the final firing the surface was washed, removing only the silver from the coated areas. This type of ware was produced early in the 1800s, by many English potteries, Wedgwood included.

When no condition is indicated, the items listed below are assumed to be in undamaged condition.

Bowl, simple floral on ivory, 6″....70.00
Jug, robin on branch in oval, mc, silver florals, 6½″, EX....715.00
Mug, bird & foliage, Leeds, 3¾″....85.00
Pitcher, wht w/lustre decor, ca 1890, 5¾″....45.00

Sinclaire

In 1904, H.P. Sinclaire and Company was founded in Corning, New York. For the first sixteen years of production, Sinclaire used blanks from other glassworks for his cut and engraved designs. In 1920, he established his own glass blowing factory in Bath, New York. His most popular designs utilize fruits, flowers, and other forms from nature. Most of Sinclaire's glass is unmarked.

When no condition is indicated, the items listed below are assumed to be in mint condition.

Bowl, eng floral, rolled rim, opaque yel, +pr sticks, 13″.......275.00
Bread tray, Fuchsia & Russian, 7x11″.......................375.00
Candlestick, swirl ribbed stem, sgn, lt gr, 10¼″...............65.00
Card tray, Assyrian, 7x6″...............................1,050.00
Celery, Adam, eng, 10½″.................................195.00
Cheese & cracker, Flute & Panel, pat Apr 5, 1910, 9½″ dia...250.00
Compote, Flutes & Panel border, gr, 7″.....................85.00
Compote, Silver Threads, hollow coned-out ft/sgn, 8x8″, pr....850.00
Decanter, Rock Crystal Daisies, mushroom stopper...........275.00
Jardiniere, #1023, sgn, 6½x7½″...........................450.00
Pitcher, water; Stratford.................................295.00
Plate, Adam, patented, 8½″...............................675.00
Platter, Diamonds & Silver Threads, rare, 14½x11½″........2,500.00
Tray, card; Diamonds & Silver Threads, rare................950.00
Vase, acid cut-bk, 4-griffin border, ivory trim, 9½″............225.00
Vase, eng floral, sgn, 12″...............................185.00
Wine, heavy flute pattern, S in wreath, sgn...................30.00

Sitzendorf

When no condition is indicated, the items listed below are assumed to be in mint condition.

Candelabra, boy & girl on ea base, 5-branch, ca 1850, pr....2,000.00
Figurine, allegorical, swans pull lady in chariot, 15x14″......2,000.00
Figurine, cupids/3 ladies/gent/sheep/etc, 9½x13½″............825.00
Figurine, lady in sedan chair, 4½″.........................250.00
Figurine, lovers, he points to girl w/doves, Voigt, 6½x3″.......250.00
Figurine, musical, 2 ladies/gent/girl, gilt, 18x12″............1,500.00

Slag Glass

Slag glass is a marbleized opaque glassware made by several companies from about 1870 until the turn of the century. It is usually found in purple, or in caramel, though other colors were also made. Pink is rare and very expensive.

When no condition is indicated, the items listed below are assumed to be in mint condition.

Caramel, butter dish, Button & Arches........................55.00
Caramel, creamer, Arched Swans.............................75.00
Caramel, match holder......................................35.00
Caramel, spooner, Arched Swans.............................55.00
Green, creamer, lacy edge, variegated, lg......................45.00
Green, sugar bowl, w/lid....................................92.00
Pink, cruet, Inverted Fan & Feather, rare...................950.00
Pink, pitcher, applied clear hdl, rare, 5¼″..................125.00
Pink, sauce dish, Inverted Fan & Feather, ftd, 2½x4½″........225.00
Pink, shaker, salt; Inverted Fern & Feather, orig lid..........175.00
Pink, tumbler, water; Inverted Fan & Feather, 3⅞″...........260.00
Purple, bowl, Dart Bar, 8″....................................45.00
Purple, cake stand, Plain Ring, ftd.........................125.00
Purple, celery dish, fluted, 8″................................45.00
Purple, celery vase, Jewel, 8¼″...............................35.00
Purple, chalice, Maple Leaf..................................35.00
Purple, compote, jelly; threaded...............................55.00
Purple, compote, Majestic Crown, w/lid......................200.00
Purple, creamer, Scroll w/Acanthus...........................55.00

Fruit bowl, Inverted Fan & Feather, light pink and white, 5″ x 9 ″, $650.00.

Purple, match holder, Daisy & Button, 3x5″....................25.00
Purple, pitcher, water; Dart Bar...............................85.00
Purple, pitcher, windmill scene & house......................200.00
Purple, plate, lattice edge, 10½″..............................75.00
Purple, spooner, Flower & Panel...............................45.00
Purple, vase, Beads & Bark....................................35.00
Purple, vase, Maple Leaf, chalice form.........................35.00
Red, ash tray, Imperial, orig label, 8″.........................22.00
Red, bowl, basket shape, raised ovals, 2 knobs, hdl, 11x6″......85.00

Smith Bros.

Alfred and Harry Smith founded their glassmaking firm in New Bedford, Massachusetts. They had been formerly associated with the Mt. Washington Glass Works, working there from 1871 to 1875 to aid in establishing a decorating department.

Smith Bros. glass is valued for its excellent enameled decoration on satin or opalescent glass. Pieces were often marked with a lion in a red shield.

When no condition is indicated, the items listed below are assumed to be in mint condition.

Plate, Santa Maria, on lustreless white, 7″, $225.00.

Biscuit jar, roses, melon rib, SP lid/bail, sgn, 8½" 600.00
Bowl, bl scroll w/orange flowers, melon ribbed, sgn, 2½x4" 295.00
Bowl, pansies & beaded rim on wht, melon shape, 2½x4" 225.00
Bowl, raised gold floral, melon rib, beaded rim, 2½x4½" 225.00
Creamer & sugar, apple blossoms/leaves, rampant lion mk 585.00
Humidor, pansies on cream, SP lid w/molded pipe, 7x5" 485.00
Pin holder, florals, glossy, no mk, 3¾" 165.00
Planter, ribs, floral on cream satin, SP insert, 4x8" 260.00
Planter, ribs, violets on gloss, SP collar/insert, 10½" 575.00
Rose bowl, orange daisies & bl scrolls on ribbing, 4½" dia 245.00
Salt cellar, gold/beaded rim, floral/beading, 1½x3" 65.00
Shaker, pansies, melon rib, 1¼x2⅛" 85.00
Sugar shaker, floral, melon rib, SP top 175.00
Toothpick holder, Columned Ribs, cream w/bl floral, sgn 175.00
Vase, herons in rushes, pink, 4½" 45.00
Vase, rose branches/insects, wht/yel shaded, 10½" 450.00
Vase, swirls w/pnt florals, gilt, 6¾" 350.00
Vase, water lily on marbleized ground, ball shape, 4¼" 230.00
Vase, wisteria front/side, oval w/sq top, no mk, 10x6x3" 485.00

Snow Babies

Early in the 1800s, snow babies--little figurals in white snowsuits--originated in Germany. They were made of sugar candy and were often used as decorations for Christmas trees. Later on, they were made of marzipan, a confection of crushed almonds, sugar, and egg whites. Eventually, porcelain manufacturers began making them in bisque. They were popular until WWII. Some reproductions are now found on the market.

When no condition is indicated, the items listed below are assumed to be in mint condition.

Angel, sitting, arms outstretched, 1¾" 200.00
Babies, 3 on sled, no mk, 3" 55.00
Baby, holding baton 110.00
Baby, on snowball, Japan, 2¼" 38.00
Baby, riding bear, Japan, 2¾" 38.00
Baby, sitting, Japan, 1" 12.00
Baby, sitting in shell, WPA wooden dollhouse, 1½" 95.00
Baby, sitting on red sled, mk Germany, 1⅜" 40.00
Baby, sitting on sled, Japan, 2½" 38.00
Baby, sleeping in igloo, Santa climbing chimney 95.00
Baby, standing, Germany, 2½" 55.00
Baby, standing, out-stretched arms, 1⅜" 30.00
Baby, standing, wearing back pack & hat, 4½" 195.00
Baby, w/seal & ball, Japan 45.00
Baby bear, mk Germany, 1½" 40.00
Bear, German, 1" 18.00
Bear, w/2 babies in red snowsuits, German 165.00
Igloo, baby inside, Santa on roof, German 185.00

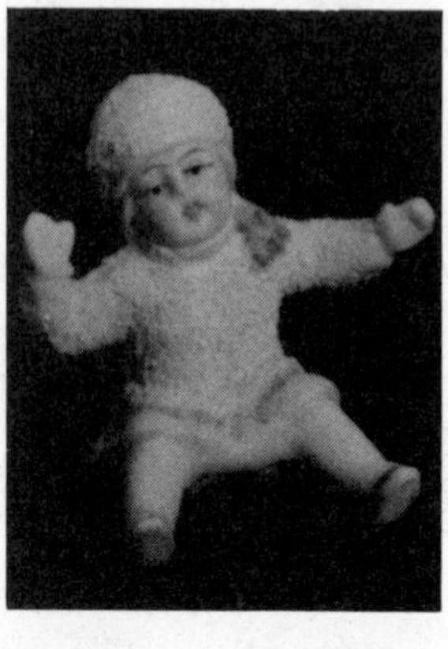

Little girl sitter, ruffled skirt, 2", $70.00.

Planter, girl on sled, 4" 275.00
Santa, sits forward in boat 110.00
Seal, on ball, Japan, 2" 32.00
Snow pup, on skis, sgn 110.00

Snuff Boxes

As early as the 17th century, the Chinese began using snuff. By the early 19th century, the practice had spread to Europe and America. It was used by both the gentlemen and the ladies alike, and expensive snuff boxes and bottles were the earmark of the genteel. Some were of silver or gold set with precious stones or pearls, while others contained music boxes.

When no condition is indicated, the items listed below are assumed to be in excellent condition. See also Orientalia, Snuff Bottles

Box, agate, brass bound, 1½" sq 90.00
Box, blk lacquer, man w/wht beard & money bag, HP, 4", EX . . . 45.00
Box, blk lacquer, monk & Sister kissing, HP, 3¾", EX 95.00
Box, brass, horseshoe shape, 2½x3¼" 45.00
Box, horn, handmade, ca 1810 . . . . 85.00
Box, horn, inlaid w/tortoise & ivory, 1¾x3¾" 50.00
Box, horn, oval w/capped ends, hand-shaped closure, 2¾x4" . . . 105.00
Box, leather w/silver crest, George the 3rd, rare 295.00
Box, Limoges, floral on pink porcelain, gilt design on top 200.00
Box, papier mache, girl w/flower transfer, 2¾" dia 65.00
Box, papier mache, MOP inlay, sm 36.00
Box, papier mache, reverse litho, Napoleon w/gold bezel 465.00
Box, pewter, US, 1810, EX 85.00
Box, silver, floral & Oriental decor, repousse, oval, 1893 . . . . 80.00
Box, silver, Geo III, repousse hunting scene in scroll 175.00
Box, sterling, engine trn, enamel florals, French, 1800 . . . . 195.00
Box, tin w/emb Blk boy, My Massa sells tobacco, 2¾" 95.00
Box, tole, orig pnt w/landscape & fishing boy, 1¾x2½" 60.00
Box, 14k gold padlock form, enamel Egyptian head, 10 dwt 200.00

Soapstone

Soapstone is a soft talc in rock form with a smooth, greasy feel, from whence comes its name. In colonial times, it was extracted from out-croppings in large sections with hand saws, carted by oxen to mills, and fashioned into useful domestic articles such as footwarmers, cooking utensils, inkwells, etc. During the early 1800s it was used to make heating stoves and kitchen sinks. Most familiar today are the carved vases, bookends, and boxes made in China during the Victorian era.

When no condition is indicated, the items listed below are assumed to be in mint condition.

Ariadne & panther, after Daeneker, 24½" 1,540.00
Ash tray, leaf form, scalloped, floral relief, 3x4" 125.00
Basket of various fruits, mc, w/grasshopper, 4½x5x8" 60.00
Box, MOP inlay, sgn, 3x5" 40.00
Budda, on lotus throne, flame behind, gr/yel flecks, 10½" 50.00
Busts of Cupid & Psyche in embrace, 1880s, 30" 2,000.00
Foo lion, in clouds, flames at front, fancy plinth, 8½x9" 80.00
Foo lion, male w/ball, female w/young, 6½x5½", pr 80.00
Geisha kneeling, ca 1880, 3¼x3½" 75.00
Girl holds tray of mc fruit aloft, 13" 80.00
Incense burner, 3 ogre head ft/lion hdls/loose rings, 8½" 90.00
Inkwell, dome-shaped building, blk, 4 quill holders 150.00
Lion, recumbent, fitted teak base, 6" 50.00
Man & woman, 8", pr 125.00

Monkeys standing on each other's heads, 4½″ 50.00
Rooster on rock, high plumed tail feathers, 9″ 60.00
Screen, reticulated disk w/bird & flowers, 6½″ dia 35.00
Vase, dbl, figural monkeys, 7x5″ 80.00

Rooster and roses, 6″, $145.00.

Soda Fountain Collectibles

As the neighborhood ice cream parlor becomes a thing of the past, soda fountain memorabilia, from fancy backbars to ice cream advertising, is becoming a popular field of collecting. One area of interest is the glassware used to serve the more elaborate ice cream concoctions. A sundae glass is familiar to us all, but there was also a 'mondae' glass, narrow at the bottom and flaring to a top dimension equal to one scoop! And a 'tuesday' glass with a rim wide enough to accommodate two scoops of ice cream side by side! At least part of their appeal is due to the mouth-watering memories they revive.

When no condition is indicated, the items listed below are assumed to be in excellent condition with the exception of glassware items which are mint.

Carton, Bing Crosby Ice Cream, ½-gal 4.00
Chair, sgn, Thonet Bentwood, ca 1889, set of 3 .... 100.00
Child's set, aluminum soda fountain, Mirro, complete/boxed 65.00
Cone holder, crystal, no insert, w/cover 75.00
Cone holder, porc top, 1917 .... 325.00
Scoop, Dover, old style, 2-way action 140.00
Scoop, Fry Ice Cream Sandwich 145.00
Scoop, Gilchrist #31 .... 50.00
Scoop, Hamilton Beach, hard rubber hdl 12.00
Scoop, ICYPI 110.00
Scoop, Indestructo, 1923, size 40 .... 32.00
Scoop, Kinger Ice Cream, 1894, EX 125.00
Scoop, Medco, nickel over brass, wood hdl, 2½″ bowl 35.00
Scoop, Quick & Easy 65.00
Scoop, Trojan, EX 50.00
Sign, Ice Cream Parlor w/pointing finger, pnt canvas 125.00
Sign, mc, glass, 10x10″ 65.00
Sign, neon; Fountain Service, Franceformer, 38″ 110.00
Soda glass, Diamond mk, tall 15.00
Straw holder, amber 295.00
Straw holder, crystal, 12″, EX 90.00
Straw holder, crystal, 9½″ 60.00
Straw holder, gr 275.00
Straw holder, King Research, Canada 30.00

Soft Paste

Soft paste refers to a low fired, granular type of porcelain that must be glazed to retain water.

When no condition is indicated, the items listed below are assumed to be in mint condition.

Bowl, barber's; Oriental scene, bl transfer, 2¼x8x11″ 130.00
Bowl, gaudy bl/wht, 4⅜x10″, VG 200.00
Bowl, gaudy 3-color floral, short hairline/flakes, 3½x7½″ 285.00
Charger, bl feather edge, bl floral, Leed's type, 14″, EX 140.00
Coffee pot, gaudy bl/wht, dome top, 12″, EX 400.00
Cup & saucer, handleless; gaudy bl/wht, EX 95.00
Cup & saucer, miniature; gaudy 3-color floral swags 115.00
Cup plate, med dk bl transfer of hyena, 4″, EX 195.00
Figurine, tiger, yel-ochre w/blk stripes, 3¼″, EX 130.00
Pitcher, Farmer's Arms decor, 6-color, 8½″, VG 800.00
Pitcher, gaudy bl/wht, 7½″, EX 195.00
Plate, Gen LaFayette, Welcome to Land of Liberty, 6¾″, VG 500.00
Platter, gaudy bl/wht, emb feather edge, 17″, EX 175.00
Shaker, bl stripes, collar pierced on side, 4½″, EX 60.00
Shaker, med bl w/fishing scenes transfer, 3½″, EX 45.00
Sugar bowl, gaudy bl/wht, emb lion head hdls, 4½″, EX 80.00

Urns, cobalt ground, elephant head handles, French, 18th century, 14″, $800.00 for the pair.

South Jersey Glass

As early as 1739, Caspar Wistar established a factory in Salem County, taking advantage of the large beds of sand suitable for glass blowing, and abundant forests available for fueling his furnaces. Scores of glassworks followed, many of which were short-lived. It is generally conceded that aside from the early works of Wistar and the Harmony Glass Works, which emerged from the Glassboro factory originally founded by the Strangers, the finest quality glassware was blown after 1800. In the 1850s, coal was substituted for the wood as fuel. Though a more efficient source of heat, the added cost of transporting the coal inland proved to be the downfall of many of the smaller factories. By the 1880s, many had failed.

Glassware can be attributed to this area through the study of colors, shapes, and decorative devices that were favored there; but because techniques were passed down through generations of South Jersey glass blowers, without specific documentation it is usually impossible to identify the specific factory that produced it.

When no condition is indicated, the items listed below are assumed to be in undamaged condition.

Bowl & pitcher, wht opal looping, 7½" pitcher, EX...........550.00
Creamer, applied hdl, cobalt, early 19th C, 3¾"..............150.00
Creamer, knop stem, applied swirl 2nd gather, turq, 6", EX....650.00
Cuspidor, lt gr w/wht opal looping, 5¼"....................300.00
Decanter, cobalt w/opaque spiral, 8¾"......................420.00
Mug, lily pad, applied hdl, aqua, 4¼".......................65.00
Pitcher, clear w/cobalt hdl & rim, 7½"....................225.00
Pitcher, crimped ft, applied hdl/lip collar, aqua, 7", NM.......850.00
Pitcher, dbl rib hdl, long neck, flared, sapphire bl, 6½".......650.00
Pitcher, lily pad, crimp ft, rib hdl, lt gr, 7", EX............1,650.00
Pitcher, lily pad, crimp ft, 2-rib hdl, lt gr, 7½", M..........2,250.00
Pitcher, tooled ft, flared/tooled lip, bl-gr, 6", NM.............375.00
Salt cellar, flared, wide applied ft, dk violet-bl, 2x3"..........425.00
Vase w/witch ball, cobalt w/wht loopings, folded rim, 7¾"....1,275.00
Wig stand, mc tree-like center, 8¼".......................400.00

Water pitcher, pale green with lily pad decoration, crimped foot and 2-rib handle, in flawless condition, 7½", $2,250.00.

Spangle Glass

Spangle glass, also known as Vasa Murrhina, is cased art glass characterized by the metallic flakes embedded in its top layer. It was made both abroad and in the United States during the latter years of the 19th century, and it was reproduced in the 1960s by the Fenton Art Glass Company.

Vasa Murrhina was a New England distributor who sold glassware of this type manufactured by a Dr. Flower of Sandwich, Massachusetts. Flower had purchased the defunct Cape Cod Glassworks in 1885 and used the facilities to operate his own company. Since none of the ware was marked, it is very difficult to attribute specific examples to his manufacture.

When no condition is indicated, the items listed below are assumed to be in mint condition.

Carafe, dk bl w/gold flakes, melon rib, 8x5"..................60.00
Ewer vase, bl over wht w/mica 'coral,' ruffled, 8".............110.00
Pitcher, pink/yel/bl/burgundy spatter/gold mica, w/tumbler......200.00
Rose bowl, bl to wht w/silver flecks, cased, 5x5¼"............115.00
Rose bowl, pink/bl, pontil, 4½"............................35.00
Vase, cobalt w/mica, wht cased, urn form, 5½"..............100.00
Vase, orange over wht, gold spangles, crystal applique, 8"......95.00
Vase, pink w/mica over wht, vaseline hdls/shell trim, 10"......110.00
Vase, pink/bl w/maroon spatter & mica, wht lining, 9x4½".....100.00
Vase, red/yel w/wht lining, scalloped, 9x4"....................45.00

Vase, applied cherries and leaves, 7½", $95.00.

Spatter Glass

Spatter glass, characterized by its multicolor 'spatters,' has been made from the late 19th century to the present by American glass houses as well as those abroad. Although it was once thought to have been made entirely by workers at the 'end of the day' from bits and pieces of left-over scrap, it is now known that it was a standard line of production.

When no condition is indicated, the items listed below are assumed to be in mint condition.

Pitcher, red and white spatter on clear, clear reeded handle, 8", $225.00.

Basket, applied thorn hdl, 4 applied feet, old, 7x5" 60.00
Bottle, liquor; swirl, hexagonal, cork stopper, 11½" 75.00
Bottle, scent; Rick Secker Sweet Cologne, clear hdls, 8½" 60.00
Celery vase, cranberry/wht 85.00
Ewer vase, pink cased w/HP pansies, 9" 65.00
Ewer vase, salmon, shaded tones, 12½" 135.00
Pitcher, brn/wht, ground pontil, 8½" 145.00
Pitcher, ruby/wht, clear reed hdl, sq mouth, 8" 135.00
Pitcher, yel/maroon/wht, yel w/in, metal top, bulbous, 5" 85.00
Ring tree, yel w/gold band, mc florals, 3¼x3½" 58.00
Tumbler, water; royal bl/wht, 3¾x2⅝" 35.00
Vase, pink/yel/orange w/clear case, ribbed swirl, 7¾" 80.00
Vase, rigaree trim, hobnail mold, ftd, 9" 85.00
Vase, yel/red/orange, 11" 65.00

Spatterware

Spatterware is a general term referring to a type of decoration used by English potters beginning in the late 1700s. Using a brush or a stick, brightly colored paint was 'dabbed' onto the soft paste earthenware items, achieving a 'spattered' effect which was often used as a border. Because much of this type of ware was made for export to the United States, some of the subjects in the central design, the schoolhouse and the eagle patterns, for instance, reflect American tastes. Yellow, green, and black spatterware is scarce and highly valued by collectors.

When no condition is indicated, the items listed below are assumed to be in mint condition.

Key: PR—professional repair

Bowl, bl/red/gr/blk w/foliage, flower & fruit, 4x13" 65.00
Bowl, purple, bull's eye center, flakes/stains, 7½" 45.00
Bowl, rainbow, gr/red, 4x12" dia 495.00
Creamer, bl, flake on spout, 4" 85.00
Creamer, bl, rose in red/gr, sm flakes, 3½", VG 95.00
Creamer, brn, 4-petal flower in 3 colors, paneled, PR, 5⅝" 325.00
Creamer, rainbow, blk/purple, 5¾" 450.00
Creamer, rainbow, gr/red/bl, minor wear & flakes, 3¾" 150.00
Creamer, red, dahlia in red/bl/gr/blk, PR, 4¼" 110.00
Cup, handleless; red, peafowl in red/bl/ochre/blk, 1¼", VG 75.00
Mug, bl, sq hdl, 4", VG 150.00
Pitcher, bl, fort pattern, 3-color, prof rpr, 5½" 425.00
Pitcher, bl, paneled, fort pattern, stains/hairlines, 6¼" 400.00
Pitcher, bl, red transfer of man & horses, 9½" 285.00
Pitcher, peafowl on leafy branch, 3-color, 6" 375.00
Pitcher, purple, PR on spout 155.00
Plate, bl, acorn in 4 colors, 8⅜", EX 375.00
Plate, bl, dahlia in red/gr/blk, sm edge flakes, 8¾" 145.00
Plate, bl, fort pattern, stains/hairlines in rim, 7⅝" 155.00
Plate, bl, peafowl, 3-color, 8¼" 250.00
Plate, bl, peafowl in red/gr/bl/blk, flakes/hairline, 8½" 150.00
Plate, bl, rose in red/gr/blk, minor wear, 9¾" 215.00
Plate, bl, schoolhouse in red/brn/gr, ring flake, 9¾", EX 550.00
Plate, bl, tulip in red/bl/gr/blk, 8⅜", EX 250.00
Plate, gr, peafowl in red/yel/bl/blk, edge flakes, 10 ", EX 410.00
Plate, gr, schoolhouse in red/blk/gr, 8¼", EX 625.00
Plate, purple, acorn in gr/ochre/blk, 8½", EX 375.00
Plate, purple, dahlia in red/bl/gr/blk, 8⅜", EX 275.00
Plate, rainbow, bl/lav, rose in 4 colors, flake, 10¾" 150.00
Plate, rainbow, bl/purple, 10" 275.00
Plate, rainbow, blk/purple, 4-color tulip, 8½", EX 475.00
Plate, rainbow, red/gr bars, bull's eye center, 9½" 250.00
Plate, rainbow, red/purple, bull's eye, 9½" 225.00
Plate, rainbow, yel/red, bull's eye, 8¼", EX 525.00
Plate, red, primrose in purple/gr/blk/ochre, wear, 8⅝" 210.00
Plate, red, tulip in red/bl/gr/blk, ring flake, 10⅝", VG 400.00
Plate, toddy; purple, acorn in 4 colors, stained, 5" 400.00
Plate, tulip in red/gr/yel, imp Cotton & Barlow, 8¾" 265.00
Platter, rainbow, red/gr, canted corners, stains, 15¾" 625.00
Saucer, red, parrot, 6" 225.00
Saucer, red, peafowl in red/bl/gr/blk, minor flakes, 5" 125.00
Sugar bowl, bars of purple/bl alternate, w/lid, 4½" 245.00
Sugar bowl, bl, peafowl in bl/ochre/red/blk, flake, 4⅜" 252.00
Sugar bowl, rainbow, bl/purple, 3¾x4½" 225.00
Sugar bowl, red, parrot in red/gr/blk, 4⅜", EX 575.00
Sugar bowl, red, tulip in red/bl/gr/blk, paneled, 6⅞" 225.00
Tall pot, bl, octagonal w/grape finial, sm flakes, 10" 225.00
Tea bowl & saucer, bl, beehive in gr/yel/blk, EX 950.00
Tea bowl & saucer, bl, bud & berries in 4 colors, hairlines 165.00
Tea bowl & saucer, bl, peafowl, 3-color 235.00
Tea bowl & saucer, bl, rooster in 3 colors, flake 475.00

Waste bowl, 3-color peafowl on red spatter, 5½", in excellent condition, 350.00.

Tea bowl & saucer, gr, peafowl in 4 colors, flakes 300.00
Tea bowl & saucer, gr, schoolhouse in red/brn/gr 495.00
Tea bowl & saucer, pink, rooster 475.00
Tea bowl & saucer, rainbow, brn/blk, 4-color tulip 300.00
Tea bowl & saucer, rainbow, red/bl 245.00
Tea bowl & saucer, rainbow, red/gr, miniature, EX 135.00
Tea bowl & saucer, rainbow, red/gr, w/rose 325.00
Tea bowl & saucer, rainbow, red/gr bars 185.00
Tea bowl & saucer, red, thistle 235.00
Tea bowl & saucer, red, tulip in 3 colors, hairline 175.00
Tea bowl & saucer, red/yel, thistle in red/gr 500.00
Tea bowl & saucer, yel, thistle in red/gr, flake 600.00
Teapot, bl, peafowl in 4 colors, lid too big, flakes, 8¾" 300.00
Teapot, rainbow, red/bl, octagonal, bl hdl/rim/spout, 9" 395.00
Teapot, rainbow, red/purple, paneled, stains/chips, 7½" 210.00
Teapot, rainbow, yel/red, minor roughness/flakes, 5¼", EX 750.00
Teapot, red, acorn in gr/blk/ochre, paneled, PR, 8⅜" 575.00
Teapot, yel, thistle in red/gr, flakes/hairline, PR, 7¼" 750.00
Wash bowl, bl, 4½x13⅝" 90.00
Waste bowl, bl, fort pattern, stains/hairline, 3⅜x6½" 195.00

Spelter

Spelter figurines are cast from commercial zinc and coated with a metallic patina. The result is a product very similar to bronze in appearance, yet much less expensive.

When no condition is indicated, the items listed below are assumed to be in excellent condition.

Bookends, Indian w/bow kneels on rocks, teepee, 8x7½" 195.00
Girl feeds cat, marble base, sgn Pilet, 11½" 225.00
Hunting dog, Setter, no mk, 6½x13" 165.00
Incense burner, Egyptian nude holding duck lies on stomach ... 110.00
Lamp, male/female musician, orig gr shade, base: 11x3" 115.00
Lion, sgn Coinchon, 8¾x6½" 125.00
Peasant girl & fisherman, 1890, 12", pr 140.00
Roman soldiers, gilded, sgn, lg, pr 200.00
Young woman, kneels w/berries/bird in hands, Chiparus, 14" . 2,000.00

'Can't You Talk,' child and dog, Victorian, 5" x 7½", excellent condition, $45.00.

Spode-Copeland

The Spode Works were established in 1770 and continued to operate under that title until 1843. Their earliest products were typical underglaze blue printed patterns, though basalt was also made. After 1790 a translucent porcelain body was the basis for a line of fine enamel decorated dinnerware. Stone china was introduced in 1805, often in patterns reflecting an Oriental influence.

In 1833 Wm. Taylor Copeland purchased the company, continuing business in much the same tradition. During the last half of the 19th century, Copeland produced excellent parian figures and groups with such success that many other companies attempted to reproduce his work. He employed famous painters to decorate plaques, vases, and tablewares, many examples of which were signed by the artist. Most of the Copeland wares are marked with one of several variations that incorporate the firm name.

When no condition is indicated, the items listed below are assumed to be in mint condition.

Bowl, bl scenic, Italian, Copeland, 7x12" 50.00
Bust, Ophelia, 11" 375.00
Cheese keeper, wht relief angels/puppy on gr, acorn finial 140.00
Coffee can & saucer, Imari, #963, 1804 ...... 235.00
Coffee pot, jasper, bl/wht, dancing maidens, 8½" 85.00
Coffee pot, jasper, bl/wht, hunting scene, 10½" 135.00
Cup & saucer, Auld Lang Syne, red, EX lg, 5½" 45.00
Cup & saucer, Brompton 14.00
Cup & saucer, Italian, Copeland 38.00
Cup & saucer, Rose Spray, mini 20.00
Dessert service, 4" ftd cake dishes+6 plates, early 20th C 125.00
Figurine, Clown, Royal Jade, Art Deco, 3½" 30.00
Figurine, pelican, Royal Jade, Art Deco 22.00
Figurine, Spring, parian, Copeland, 1850, 10" 125.00
Gravy boat, Italian 36.00
Pitcher, Chicago scenes, bl/wht parian, #81, 8" 350.00
Pitcher, Fortuna, gray/wht 150.00
Pitcher, women relief, bl/wht, pewter lid, Copeland, 6½" 75.00
Plate, dinner; Fleur-de-Lis, brn 20.00
Plate, landscape in jeweled reserve, cobalt, 1885 ...... 175.00
Plate, luncheon; Brompton 8.00
Plate, Queen's Ware, bl/ochre floral, sgn, 10", EX 65.00
Teapot, Dancing Hours, bl/cream, 4½x4⅛" 89.00
Teapot, Tower, flow blue, 6-sided, Spode 290.00
Teapot/tea tile, ladies dancing, garlands on cream/bl, 5½" 135.00
Tureen w/ladle & underplate, blk transfer grape, Copeland 65.00

Cottage, Gothic mansion with brick walls and clock, in near mint condition, ca 1820, 4", $1,350.00.

Spongeware

Spongeware is a type of factory-made earthenware that was popular during the last quarter of the 19th century. It was decorated by dabbing color onto the drying ware with a sponge, leaving a splotched design at random or in simple patterns. Sometimes a solid band of color was added. The vessel was then covered with a clear glaze and fired at a high temperature. Blue on white is the most preferred combination, but green on ivory, orange on white, or those colors in combination may also occasionally be found.

When no condition is indicated, the items listed below are assumed to be in excellent condition.

Baking dish, brn/gr on yel, lid makes pie plate, 8¼" 45.00
Baking dish, red/brn/bl on cream, stain/crazed, w/lid, 8½" 105.00
Bottle, bl/wht, potato form, 7" L, EX 345.00
Bowl, brn on yel, rim spout & rim ears, wear, 4⅜x7½" 35.00
Bowl, bl/tan on wht, 6x11½" 185.00
Bowl, bl/wht, deep, oval, 5½" 140.00
Bowl, bl/wht, plain rim, deep, 10¼" 225.00
Bowl, bl/wht, scalloped edge, 8½" 230.00
Bowl, bl/wht, shallow, oval, 8½x11" 175.00
Bowl, bl/wht, sq, 7¼" 210.00
Bowl, bl/wht, wide top rim, sponge band inside, 3x7¼" 125.00

Bowl, brn on yel, 2⅛x7"; 2x5½"; 1¾x4"; set of 3 .... 95.00
Bowl, brn/gr on yel, hairline in base, w/lid, 8" 65.00
Bowl, gr on cream, brn bands, 5" ft ring, 5x10" 100.00
Bowl, mixing; brn on yel, 4½x9" 70.00
Creamer, brn/gr on yel, stains, 4½" 75.00
Cup & saucer, handleless; bl/wht 130.00
Cuspidor, bl sponge rim/base/bl band, emb grapes, 5x7" 125.00
Dish, lt bl/wht, saucer shape, 8¼" 45.00
Mug, bl/wht, good color, 3½" 155.00
Mush cup w/saucer, bl/wht, gold edge 245.00
Pitcher, bl on yel, edge gilt, 12", VG 165.00
Pitcher, bl/rust on wht, fish figural, 10" 165.00
Pitcher, bl/rust on yel, tapered, wavy top, 7" 125.00

Pitcher, multicolored sponging, 7 x 9½", 275.00.

Pitcher, bl/wht, scalloped lip, bl band, 11¾" 200.00
Pitcher, bl/wht, 6½" 175.00
Pitcher, bl/wht, 7x3" 175.00
Pitcher, bl/wht, 8¾" 275.00
Pitcher, brn/bl on yel, gilt trim, emb pattern, 9" 95.00
Pitcher, gr/brn, advertising on relief panel, ribbed, 4½" 145.00
Pitcher, gr/brn, barrel staves, 7½" 110.00
Pitcher, gr/brn on yel, 5¼" 45.00
Pitcher, tankard; bl/wht, 7¼" 275.00
Plate, bl/wht, scalloped rim, 10¼" 130.00
Plate, bl/wht, 9¼" 70.00
Platter, bl/wht, scalloped rim, 6½x9¼" 190.00
Platter, bl/wht, 9x13" 225.00
Soap dish, w/gr stick spatter rim 105.00
Spittoon, gr/gray/brn on yel, rectangle, convex rib 135.00
Tray, bl/wht, 9½" 145.00
Vase, bl/wht, late, 4⅝" 90.00
Water cooler, bl/wht, w/lid & advertising 425.00
Water cooler, bl/wht, w/wooden lid, 2-gal 225.00
Water cooler, bl/wht, 3-pc, NM 500.00

Spoons

Souvenir spoons have been popular remembrances since the 1890s. The early hand-wrought examples of the silversmith's art are especially sought and appreciated for their fine craftsmanship. Commemorative, personality related, advertising, those with Indian busts, and those with floral designs are only a few of the many types of collectible spoons.

In the following listing, spoons are entered by state, character, or occasion.

When no condition is indicated, the items listed below are assumed to be in mint condition.

Key:

B—bowl	FF—full figure
BR—bowl reverse	GW—gold wash
emb—embossed	H—handle
eng—engraved	HR—handle reverse

Alaska, B: view of mountain; H: miner, 3⅜", demi 14.50
Alaska, H: polar bears/dog team, B: plain w/Fairbanks, 5½" 49.00
Arkansas, B: eng name Hot Springs, H: state seal/eagle, 5" 17.00
Atlantic City, B: emb lighthouse, H: scroll, demi 15.00
Atlantic City, H: bathing beauty, B: emb beach view, 4⅛" 45.00
August, birth month, Warren Mansfield, ... 25.00
Bear & Berne on BR; B: plain; H: twisted w/animal hoof 45.00
Bonbon, B: flower form; H: emb flower, Art Nouveau 45.00
Boston, B: Old South Meeting House/H: Bunker Hill Monument. 16.00
Buffalo, B: McKinley Monument 50.00
California, San Francisco, B: enamel/flower/name, heavy 32.00
California, San Francisco fire, detailed front & bk 125.00
Canada, Quebec, B: emb bridge/turrets, H: maple leaf/beaver 9.00
Canada, Toronto, City Hall bldg in B; H: Champlain figure 75.00
Canal Street, New Orleans, LA scene emb in B; H: Blk boy 175.00
Capitol Bldg emb in B; H: word Washington, demi 11.00
Capitol Bldg in B; H: Geo Washington bust w/emb name, 5⅝" 18.00
Carnegie Library in bowl, H: relief iron worker on tip 60.00
Chicago, B: emb Art Institute; H: emb name/flowers/motto 29.00
Chicago, eng in GW B; twist H w/acorn & oak leaves, 4⅜" 13.00
Child's head w/weight/name/birth on H 30.00
Church steeple emb B; H: cannon form/Princeton tiger head 60.00
Cincinnati, B: Suspension Bridge; H: water lily, demi 14.50
Cluster of grapes & Los Angeles in B; H: fruit picker, tsp 80.00
Colorado, B: plain; H: Indian/burro/tools; HR: scene, 5⅛" 26.50
Colorado, Denver, B: plain; H: capitol, 3⅞", demi 11.00
Columbus ship in B; H: globe & Columbus' head; HR: decor 35.00
Cuba, B: plain; BR: much history, French hdl 22.00
Delaware Water Gap, sterling, demi 14.00
Detroit, B: eng name; H: fancy w/grapes & leaves, 5½" 17.00
Dutch monkey, B: emb figures at forge; rooster on hdl tip 125.00
Easter & enamel flowers in B; H: floral, demi 45.00
Eastern Star, B: eng Lady Garfield 1891-1920; H: lady/star 26.00
Egg, B: plain; H: 2 relief chicks hatch from shell, demi 35.00
England, London, plain B, H: man kills dragon, demi 10.00
Fish Creek eng in B; H: fish figural 28.00
Florida, B: Augustine City Gate, H: Blk boy/alligator 60.00
Florida, B: Augustine City Gate, H: eagle, demi 10.00
Florida, B: eng name; H: state seal/eagle, Watson, 5" 16.50
Fort Concho eng in B; H: rifle shape, tsp 100.00
Garden of Gods scene & rock emb in B; H: prospector, tsp 85.00
Geisha girl, parasol is bowl, 6¼" 200.00
Illinois, Rockford; GW B: enamel Am flag 60.00
Indian figural H; B: plain, breastplate, tsp 200.00
Indians emb in B; twisted H w/Pike's Peak, HR: Pike's Peak 45.00
Iowa, Casey, high school 16.00
John Harvard, B: plain; H: statue/autograph, demi 12.00
Juneau Park & Lake Front view in B; H: emb floral 30.00
Kansas, Howard, courthouse, tsp 16.00
Kansas, Wichita eng in B; H: college girl figure, tsp 65.00
Landing of the Pilgrims, 1620, coffee 27.50
Louisiana, B: New Orleans/statue/pelican; H: fruit, tsp 45.00
Maine, Biddeford, B: eng leaf & name; H: leaf, demi 9.00

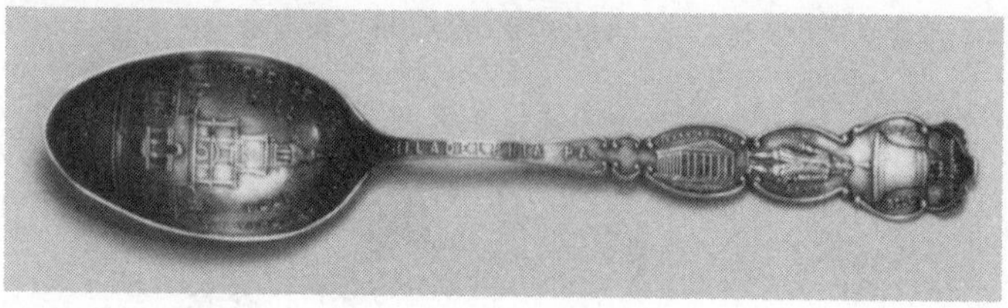

Souvenir, Independence Hall, Water Street Front, sterling, 5½″, $18.00.

Massachusettes, B: plain; H: paddle shape w/lg FF fish 35.00
Michigan, Lansing, B: plain; H: side view of capitol, 5½″ 16.00
Michigan, Muskegon, B: emb view Hackley School, H: floral 19.00
Miner, B: emb miner pans for gold; H: miner, 4⅛″ 56.00
Mining scene in bowl, FF miner H 55.00
Mississippi, B: plain; H: eagle & boat, 3⅜″ 11.00
Missouri, B: emb mule/motto; H: state seal/corn/wheat, 5″ 23.00
Missouri, B: plain; H: state seal; HR: flag/eagle, 5¼″ 14.00
Missouri, St Louis eng in B; H: flying stork w/baby, tsp 25.00
Montana, B: plain; H: mountains & tools, 4⅛″ 13.00
Montana, Butte, Anaconda Mine, tsp 16.00
Mt Ranier scene eng in GW B, H: cattails, by Towle, 4½″ 10.00
Mt Tacoma, B: emb view; H: floral, 4⅛″ 10.00
Mt Vernon, B: emb view; H: bust of Geo & Martha, demi 15.50
Mt Vernon, B: GW capitol; H: Geo chopping tree, demi 30.00
New Mexico, B: plain; H: Chinese Temple, 4¼″ 11.00
New Rice Hotel, B: emb view; H: Sam Houston/star, demi 14.00
New York, B: emb New York; H: flame motif, 3⅞″ 15.00
New York, B: New York eng; Gorham, fleur-de-lis, demi 17.00
New York, Brooklyn & man's profile on H; B: plain, demi 30.00
New York, Hoosick Falls, B: eng name; H: scroll, demi 11.00
New York, Saratoga Spring, B: emb name; H: Indian on globe . . 65.00
New York, Troy, B: heart shape; H: arrow shape, demi 30.00
Niagara Falls, B: emb view; H: Indian head/corn, demi 19.00
Niagara Falls, B: GW w/emb view of falls; H: cattails, 5⅜″ 19.00
Nigara Falls & Indian figure H; B: plain, tsp 110.00
November Zodiac H; B: plain, Watson 35.00
Old Fort Marion scene emb in B; H: Juan Ponce De Leon, tsp . 135.00
Old Mission, San Diego view in B; H: Indian warrior shape 75.00
Omaha, B: eng name; H: lily-of-the-valley, Watson, 5½″ 14.00
Omaha, B: name; H: FF girl graduate, 5¾″ 46.00
Oregon, Eugene, B: 4 emb buildings; H: apples, 5¾″ 19.00
Owl hdl, world globe, X-oars, football, silver 78.00
Palm tree emb in B; H: shape of monk, Junipero Serra, demi . . . 45.00
Pennsylvania, Franklin, B: GW w/eng oil wells; H: floral 26.00
Pennsylvania, Pittsburg, B: Carnegie Library/Fort Pitt, 5¼″ 45.00
Philadelphia, B: heart shape; H: arrow shape; HR: 1892 . . . . 45.00
Philadelphia, B: plain; H: emb name & Wm Penn, demi 17.00
Plain B; H: pedestal form w/Buffalo, NY & buffalo on tip 45.00
Planter's Hotel emb in bowl; H: Planter's St Louis, demi 20.00
Plymouth, demitasse, B: plain; H: side view of landing 19.50
Plymouth, side view of ship, Durgin, 5¾″ 21.00
Pres McKinley, tsp 18.00
Purdue University, B: eng Electrical Bldg; H: PU pennant 24.00
Rhode Island, B: emb Stone Mill, H: anchor, Gorham, 5¾″ 35.00
Roosevelt, Teddy; H: FF on horse; BR: name Rhoda, demi 65.00
Roulette wheel on B; H: Monte Carlo & 3 enamel cards 75.00
Salem Witch, coffee 47.50
San Francisco emb in B; H: shape of sword & feather 60.00
San Gabriel Mission emb in B; H: state seal/capitol, 3⅞″ 12.00
Ships in harbor, H: emb miner & word California 35.00
St Augustine, B: plain; H: bldg in shield/leaves, 6″ 22.00
St Louis bridge emb in B; H: bust at tip, tsp 35.00
Statue of Liberty eng in B; H: NY World's Fair 1939 . . . . 30.00
Sword form w/bird at hilt on H; B: plain, tsp 45.00
Texas, El Paso, swastika hdl, sterling w/eng GW B 18.00
Tulsa, B: eng name & JT; H: Indian head w/artifacts, 5⅛″ 25.00
Union Square & St Francis Hotel view in B; H: floral 35.00
US Capitol emb in B; H: Washington Monument shape, demi . . . 30.00
US Signal Station & Pike's Pead emb B; H: train, demi 45.00
Utah, Mormon Temple, lightweight, 3″ 10.00
Utah, Salt Lake City, temple, tsp 16.00
Vermont, B: GW w/eng word Windsor; H: state seal/Vermont 19.00
Vermont, Bennington, B: view of monument; 3⅞″ 13.00
Vermont, Rutland, B: plain; H: emb letters, 5⅝″ 12.00
Washington, Spokane, courthouse, tsp 16.00
West Point cadet, B: plain; H: FF cadet, 4¼″ 32.00
William McKinley, B: eng word Canton; H: bust/autograph 19.00
Wisconsin, LaCrosse, B: plain; H: emb State Normal School 16.00
WWI, B: plain; H: form of Doughboy, tsp 125.00
Yale, B: eng Vanderbilt Hall; H: Indian head, demi 19.00
1000 Islands, B: GW w/name; H: Indian in canoe, 5⅞″ 65.00

Sporting Goods

When no condition is indicated, the items listed below are assumed to be in excellent condition.

Baseball, Jo DiMaggio autograph 40.00
Baseball, Ted Williams autograph 30.00
Baseball blanket, B-18, Casey Stengel, 1914, 5x5″ 35.00
Batting glove, Mike Schmidt, autographed 20.00
Bicycle, Cresent, 1893, NM 1,250.00
Book, Baseball Guide, Spaulding, 1918 . . . . 47.00
Book, Fishing & Shooting Sketches, G Cleveland, 1907 . . . . 30.00
Book, pressbook, Packers, 1946 . . . . 15.00
Book, When the Dogs Bark 'Treed,' E Barker, 1946, 1st ed 40.00
Booklet, Famous Sluggers, Louisville Slugger Bats, 1931 . . . . 5.00
Calendar, memory; Honus Wagner, signs ball for boy, 1955 . . . . . 25.00
Catalog, Spring & Summer Athletic Sports, Spaulding & Bros . . . 45.00
Cigar box label, picture of Honus Wagner, 1911 . . . . 800.00
Film cartrige, Lou Brock in Base Running, autographed 70.00
Float ball, olive gr, mk Fales, 5″ 10.00
Ice skates, Connecticut 70.00
Ice skates, wood, hand-forged runners, 19th C 65.00
Ice skates, wood platform/curl blades w/brass acorn finial 220.00
Medal, bronze, Mother's Day, NY Yankees, 1967 . . . . 15.00
Pennant, Yankee, color picture of entire team, rare, 1964 . . . . . . 45.00
Photo, Gary Carter & Pete Rose, autographed, color, 8x10″ 15.00
Pitcher, cocktail; golf scenes, sterling, Deco, open hdl 24.00
Print, Pete Rose, sgn by subject, JM Everett, ltd ed 50.00
Program, Globetrotters, Chamberlain autograph+9, 1958 . . . . 20.00
Program, Joe Frazier/Muhammed Ali World Heavyweight fight . . . 50.00
Salada Tea coin, Duke Snider, 1963 . . . . 25.00
Salada Tea coin, Frank Robinson, 1963 . . . . 12.00
Salada Tea coin, Sandy Koufax, 1963 . . . . 17.00
Scorer, Babe Ruth, Quaker Oats premium 45.00
Sled, wood, mortised/pinned, red/blk/gold stripes, 27″ 285.00
Sled, wood, red w/yel/blk stag/dog/ship, rpr/splits, 34″ 300.00
Stamp, duck, strip of 4 . . . . 600.00
Stamp, Federal, rare, 1935 . . . . 125.00
Statue, Babe Ruth w/bat, Hartland 65.00
Statue, Cleveland Indian, gold tooth, 8″ 65.00
Target ball, Perth NB Glassworks 85.00
Target ball, sapphire bl, quilted, E Jones Gunmaker, 2⅝″ 75.00
Uniform jersey, Chet Lemon, Chicago White Sox 250.00
Yearbook, Mets, 1968 . . . . 12.00

Staffordshire

Scores of potteries sprang up in England's Staffordshire district in the early 18th century; several remain to the present time. Some of the larger companies as well as specific types of ware are listed in other sections of this book.

Figurines and groups were made in great numbers; dogs were favorite subjects. Often they were made in pairs, each a mirror image of the other. They varied in heights from 3″ or 4″ to the largest, measuring 16″ to 18″.

The Historical ware listed here was made throughout the district; some collectors refer to it as Staffordshire Blue Ware. It was produced as early as 1820, and because much was exported to America, it was very often decorated with transfers depicting scenic views of well-known American landmarks. Early examples were printed in a deep cobalt. By 1830, a softer blue was favored, and within the next decade, black, pink, red, and green prints were used. Although sometimes careless about adding their trademark, many companies used their own border designs that were as individual as their names.

When no condition is indicated, the items listed below are assumed to be in mint condition.

Key:

blk—black	l/b—light blue
d/b—dark blue	m/b—medium blue
gr—green	m-d/b—medium dark blue

Plate, Capitol at Washington, dark blue, 10″, $265.00.

Historical

Bowl, Battery, NY, d/b, shallow, 6½″........................950.00
Bowl, Castle of Lavenza, d/b, Wood, 12½″.................150.00
Bowl, Catskill Mtns, Hudson River, d/b, Wood, 9¾″..........500.00
Bowl, East View of LaGrange, d/b, Wood, 8″................375.00
Bowl, Lake, Regents Park, d/b, beaded rim, Wood, 10½″......350.00
Bowl, Landing of Columbus, purple, Adams, 7¾″............125.00
Bowl & pitcher, LaFayette at Franklin's Tomb, d/b, 9x12″...1,500.00
Coffee pot, Commodore McDonough's Victory, hi-dome, rstr..1,100.00
Coffee pot, Fruit & Floral, d/b, high dome................550.00
Coffee pot, LaFayette at Franklin's Tomb, d/b, Wood, 11″...1,500.00
Creamer, Wadsworth Tower, d/b, Wood....................400.00
Cup & saucer, Baltimore Hospital/Univ of Maryland, d/b.....1,600.00
Cup & saucer, Chancellor Livingston, d/b, Wood.............375.00
Cup & saucer, Floral & Urn, d/b, Clews......................75.00
Cup & saucer, Floral & Urn, d/b, Stubbs....................75.00
Cup & saucer, LaFayette at Franklin's Tomb, d/b............275.00
Cup plate, Arched Stone Bridge, d/b, Wood, 3¾″............480.00
Cup plate, Battery, d/b, Wood's trefoil border, 3⅝″..........245.00
Cup plate, Fruit & Birds, d/b, 4¼″.........................75.00
Cup plate, Gen Jackson, Hero of New Orleans, carmine.......650.00
Cup plate, LaFayette/Washington, carmine, VG..............325.00
Cup plate, Letter of Introduction, d/b......................300.00
Cup plate, Oriental Scenery, Fakeer's Rock, d/b, 4¼″, VG.....40.00
Cup plate, Residence o/t Late R Jordan, lt bl...............285.00
Cup plate, Ship Anchored, 3¾″............................325.00
Cup plate, View Near Sandy Hill, brn, Clews, 4″..............75.00
Mug, child's; Cornwallis Surrenders Sword, blk/pink lustre.....725.00
Pepper pot, Landscape View, m/b..........................135.00
Pitcher, Albany, l/b, Meigh, 8¾″..........................165.00
Pitcher, City Hall, NY; Hospital, NY; d/b, 6″...............650.00
Pitcher, Erie Canal Inscription, Utica Tribute, d/b, 6″.........800.00
Pitcher, Harbor Scene, m-d/b, Rogers, 9″...................345.00
Pitcher, Lake Scenery, pink, EW&S, 11″....................85.00
Pitcher, milk; LaFayette at Franklin's Tomb, d/b, 4½″........450.00
Pitcher, Mount Vernon, d/b, 8″...........................750.00
Pitcher, Newburgh, pink, Clews, 9″........................225.00
Pitcher, NY City Hall/Hospital, d/b, Stevenson, 6″............500.00
Pitcher, States, d/b, Clews, 7½″...........................900.00
Plate, Aqueduct Bridge at Rochester, d/b, Wood, 7½″........600.00
Plate, Armitage Park, d/b, Wood's grapevine border, 5½″.......70.00
Plate, Arms of Rhode Island, d/b, Mayer, 8¾″...............450.00
Plate, Baltimore & Ohio RR, level, d/b, Wood, 10¼″, NM.....550.00
Plate, Bamborough Castle, d/b, Adams, 10″..................70.00
Plate, Bank o/t United States, d/b, Stubbs, 10″..............375.00
Plate, Boston State House, d/b, Rogers, 7¼″................145.00
Plate, British View, d/b, Henshall, 9¾″.....................60.00
Plate, Building on Cliff, d/b, Davenport, 7″..................70.00
Plate, Capitol in Washington, d/b, 10¼″....................425.00
Plate, Castle of Furstenfeld, d/b, Henshall, 9″................65.00
Plate, Cathedral at York, d/b, Wood, 6½″....................50.00
Plate, Catholic Cathedral, NY, d/b, 5¾″..................1,000.00
Plate, Cave Castle, Yorkshire, m/b, 8⅝″.....................45.00
Plate, Chief Justice Marshall, Troy Line, d/b, 10″............375.00
Plate, City of Albany, State of NY, d/b, shell border, 10″......375.00
Plate, Commodore MacDonnough's Victory, d/b, 10″..........345.00
Plate, Commodore MacDonnough's Victory, d/b, 7½″.........235.00
Plate, Constitution & Guerriere, d/b, 10″...................900.00
Plate, Cupid Imprisoned, d/b, Wood, minor scratches, 9″.......85.00
Plate, Cupid Imprisoned, d/b, Wood, 10″....................100.00
Plate, Cupid Imprisoned, d/b, Wood, 6½″.....................75.00
Plate, Dartmouth, d/b, Wood's irregular shell border, 9¼″.....220.00
Plate, Dog, d/b, Quadruped series, 8½″.....................95.00
Plate, Erie Canal at Buffalo, red, 9¾″.......................65.00
Plate, Erie Canal Inscription, Governor, d/b, 10″.............300.00
Plate, Escape o/t Mouse, d/b, Clews, 10″...................175.00
Plate, Fairmount, Near Philadelphia, d/b, 10″................175.00
Plate, Falls of Montmorenci Near Quebec, 9″.................245.00
Plate, Faulkbourn Hall, d/b, 8¾″..........................80.00
Plate, Finsbury Chapel, d/b, 5½″...........................75.00
Plate, Franklin's Birthplace, d/b, Wood, 10″.................120.00
Plate, Fruits, d/b, Stubbs, 6½″............................50.00
Plate, Fruits, d/b, 10″....................................80.00
Plate, Fulham Church, d/b, Hall, 8½″.......................70.00
Plate, Ghaut of Cutwa, d/b, Hall, 8¾″......................60.00
Plate, Gilpin's Mill o/t Brandywine, d/b, Wood & Sons, 9″.....325.00
Plate, Harvard College, d/b, RS&W, 10″.....................285.00
Plate, Hawthornden, d/b, Adams, 8¾″.......................70.00
Plate, Hoboken in New Jersey, d/b, Stubbs, 7″...............225.00

Plate, Hospital Boston, d/b, Stevenson, 9″ 250.00
Plate, Ibex, d/b, Wood's Zoological series, 6½″ 70.00
Plate, Insane Hospital, Boston, d/b, Ridgway, 7¼″ 195.00
Plate, Junction o/t Sacandaga & Hudson, l/b, Clews, 7″ 70.00
Plate, Landing o/t Fathers at Plymouth, m/b, Wood, 5½″ 120.00
Plate, Landing o/t Fathers at Plymouth, m/b, Wood, 8½″ 130.00
Plate, Landing o/t Fathers at Plymouth, m/b, 10″ 150.00
Plate, Landing of LaFayette, d/b, Clews, 10″ 325.00
Plate, Landing of LaFayette, d/b, 8½″ 225.00
Plate, Library, Philadelphia, d/b, Ridgway, 8¼″ 200.00
Plate, Llanarth Court, d/b, Hall, 10″ 75.00
Plate, Maison de Raphael, d/b, Wood, 6½″ 120.00
Plate, Man in Chariot, m-d/b, 10″ 50.00
Plate, Mohamedan Mosque & Tomb, d/b, Hall, 9″ 70.00
Plate, Moulin Sur La Marne a Charenton, d/b, 9¼″ 150.00
Plate, Near Fishkill, d/b, Clews, 7¾″ 250.00
Plate, New Haven, pink, 10″ 85.00
Plate, Niagara Falls, d/b, Wood, 10″ 335.00
Plate, NY City Hall, blk, Jackson, 10″ 80.00
Plate, NY City Hall, d/b, 10″ 190.00
Plate, Oriental pagoda by river, d/b, Clews, 10½″ 80.00
Plate, Pagoda, d/b, Clews, 8¾″ 65.00
Plate, Pagoda & Fountain, d/b, 10″ 70.00
Plate, Pains Hill, Surrey, d/b, 10″ 70.00
Plate, Park Theatre, d/b, RS&W, 10″ 245.00
Plate, Pass in the Catskills, d/b, Wood, 7½″ 300.00
Plate, Pittsburgh, brn, Clews, 10″ 225.00
Plate, Pittsfield Elm, d/b, Clews, 10½″ 275.00
Plate, Pittsfield Elm, d/b, Clews, 8¾″ 250.00
Plate, Quadrupeds, I Hall, m/b, 9¾″ 85.00
Plate, Sailboats & High River Bank, d/b, Clews, 5½″ 75.00
Plate, Shell, d/b, Stubbs, 8½″ 70.00
Plate, St Catherine's Hill, d/b, 7¾″ 65.00
Plate, States, d/b, 10″ 275.00
Plate, Table Rock, Niagara, d/b, 10¼″ 350.00
Plate, Trenton Falls, 3 people, d/b, Wood, 7¾″ 250.00
Plate, Union Line, d/b, 9⅛″ 375.00
Plate, Upper Ferry Bridge Over Schuylkill River, d/b, 9¾″ 175.00
Plate, Utica Tribute, Erie Canal Inscription, d/b, 7½″ 350.00
Plate, View Near Fishkill, l/b, Clews, 10″ 80.00
Plate, Villa in Regents Park, d/b, Adams, 10″ 80.00
Plate, Vue du Chauteau Ermenoville, d/b, 10″ 150.00
Plate, Washington, Cities series, d/b, 7¾″ 250.00
Plate, West Point, Hudson River, blk, Clews, 8″ 75.00
Plate, Wm Penn's Treaty, l/b, 10¾″ 40.00
Plate, Young Philosopher, d/b, Wood, 10″ 130.00
Platter, America & Independence, d/b, Clews, 15″, VG 550.00
Platter, Andulusia, pink, Adams, 11″ 75.00
Platter, Castle Gardens, d/b, Wood's, 18½″ L 1,200.00
Platter, Christianburg, Africa, d/b, E Wood, 18½″ 1,150.00
Platter, East View of LaGrange, d/b, Wood, 9¾″ 395.00
Platter, Kidbrook Sussex, d/b, Stevenson, 10½″ 160.00
Platter, Landing of LaFayette, d/b, Clews, 17″ 750.00
Platter, Landing of LaFayette, d/b, 11″ 575.00
Platter, Little Falls at Luzerne, blk, 18″ 245.00
Platter, Newburgh, blk, Jackson, 16″ 200.00
Platter, Niagara Falls from American Side, d/b, 14½″ 1,150.00
Platter, Residence o/t Late Richard Jordan, JH&Co, 16″ 390.00
Platter, Residence o/t Late Richard Jordan, 9¾″ 295.00
Platter, Skenectady on Mohawk River, pink, 10″ 150.00
Platter, States, d/b, Clews, 13″ 525.00
Platter, Theatre Printing House, d/b, 18¾″ 475.00
Platter, Upper Ferry Bridge over Schuylkill, d/b, 18″ 700.00
Platter, West Acre House Norfolk, d/b, Hall, 9¾″ 235.00
Sauce boat, Boston State House, d/b, Ridgway 345.00
Sauce boat, Picturesque Scenery, d/b, Hall 165.00
Sauce boat, Yanguesian Conflict, d/b 300.00
Sauce tureen, undertray, Charleston Exchange, d/b, Ridgway 650.00
Saucer, LaFayette at Franklin's Tomb, d/b, 6¾″ 150.00
Saucer, New York City Hall, d/b, Stubbs 110.00
Saucer, Virginia Church, m-d/b 85.00
Saucer, Wadsworth Tower, d/b, Wood, 6¾″ 145.00
Soup, Albany, Cities series, d/b, Clews, 9¾″ 325.00
Soup, Baltimore & Ohio RR, level, d/b, Wood, 10″ 550.00
Soup, Dilston Tower, d/b, Adams, 10″ 70.00
Soup, Goggerddan Cardisanshire, d/b, Riley, 10″ 85.00
Soup, Octagon Church, Boston, d/b, 10″ 245.00
Soup, Palestine, d/b, Stevenson, 10″ 90.00
Soup, Penns Treaty, pink, 9¼″ 75.00
Soup, Sancho Panza at the Boar Hunt, d/b, 9¾″ 175.00
Soup, Staughton's Church, d/b, Ridgway, 8″ 250.00
Soup, Vue du Chateau Ermenoville, d/b, 10″ 150.00
Soup, Writtle Lodge, d/b, Stevenson, 10″ 90.00
Sugar bowl, American Eagle on Urn, d/b, Clews, lg 750.00
Sugar bowl, LaFayette at Franklin's Tomb, d/b, 4¾″, VG 475.00
Sugar bowl, Wadsworth Tower, d/b 425.00
Sugar bowl, Washington w/Scroll in Hand, d/b 475.00
Sugar bowl, Water Girl, d/b 175.00
Teapot, Chancellor Livingston, d/b, Wood 750.00
Teapot, LaFayette at Franklin's Tomb, d/b, apple shape, VG 750.00
Teapot, LaFayette at Franklin's Tomb, d/b, Wood 550.00
Teapot, Washington w/Scroll in Hand, d/b, Wood 525.00
Toddy plate, Don Quixote, Repose in the Woods, d/b, 5½″ 145.00
Toddy plate, Kenilworth Castle, m-d/b, Wood, 5⅛″ 95.00
Tray, Mosaic Tracery, d/b, w/hdl, 12″ 200.00
Tray, Planetarium, d/b, prof rpr, 8″ L 135.00
Tureen, country scene w/cows, l/b, w/lid, 10x14″, EX 125.00
Wash bowl, Baltimore, l/b, Meigh 325.00
Waste bowl, Christmas Eve, d/b, Clews, 10″ 250.00

Miscellaneous

Baby feeder, 1700s, 6¾″ 250.00
Bank, spaniel head, blk/wht, wear & sm flakes, 3¾″ 55.00
Bottle, scent; flask w/landscape, gilt bird atop, 3″ 500.00
Box, cow on lid, blk/mc, rpr/minor flake, 8¼″ 115.00
Box, money; cottage figural, salt glazed, ca 1820s, 4x3½″ 325.00
Chamber pot, floral swags, pink/gr on cream, 9″ dia 65.00
Chamber pot, miniature, rose design in red/gr, 1½″, EX 125.00
Chamber pot, Queen's Hotel, Eastbourne, wht, 9″ dia 45.00
Chamber pot, Shah, gr/yel, 9½″ dia 65.00
Cottage, high peaked roof, 3 grillwork shutters, steps, 8″ 400.00
Cottage, pastille burner, lift-off roof, ca 1825, 4½″ 375.00
Cottage, pastille burner, w/2 chimneys, dbl door, 5″ 325.00
Cottage, Tudor, octagonal, roof detaches, 1820, 4¾″ 625.00
Creamer, cow, lav lustre/iron red decor, Swansea, 5½x7″ 425.00
Creamer, cow, rust/wht, on base, w/lid, stains/wear, 4¾″ 90.00
Creamer, cow, tail hdl, rust/wht/gilt, w/lid, 4″, NM 80.00
Creamer, gaudy red/gr florals, blk stripe, 2½″, EX 40.00
Figurine, basketweave cradle, molded baby, spatter, 1½x5″ 500.00
Figurine, Battle for the Breeches, sgn Haggar, no base 500.00
Figurine, boy w/dog, hollow, Walton School, 5½″ 275.00
Figurine, boy/cockerel & girl/chicks, John Walton, 6½″, EX 900.00
Figurine, cat, seated, rust/wht w/gr base, late, 7¼″, pr 45.00
Figurine, cat, sitting on haunches, ribbons, mc, 8″, pr 110.00
Figurine, Charity w/3 children, ca 1810 ....200.00
Figurine, Charlotte at Tomb of Werther, ca 1800, 9″ 190.00
Figurine, couple, clock & deer between, 11″, NM 175.00

Row 1: Red squirrel, ca 1800, 3¼″, $550.00; Pug, pearlware with brown spots and brown eyes, repair to tail, ca 1790, 3¼″, $800.00; Row 2: Inkstand, small dog on footstool, ca 1800, near mint condition, 1¾″, $400.00; Swan, blue with yellow markings, ca 1800, near mint condition, 3⅜″, $210.00.

Figurine, cows: w/milkmaid; w/youth, mc/gilt, 5¾″, pr, EX.....210.00
Figurine, Dandies, 2 mc figures on base, 6¾″...............350.00
Figurine, Diane w/bow, Neale, 12″.........................165.00
Figurine, dog, blk/wht, sitting, 7½″, pr, VG..................100.00
Figurine, dog, pnt face, gilt trim, facing pr, 15½″............150.00
Figurine, dog, rust/wht w/lustre trim, late, 7″, pr..............90.00
Figurine, dog, wht, copper lustre markings, 11″, pr...........275.00
Figurine, Dr Becker & Prince, Alpha Factory................150.00
Figurine, Duke of Connaught on horse, 1850, 13″...........110.00
Figurine, eagle, octagonal base, 7¾x3″.....................300.00
Figurine, Edward & Alexandra, blush color, 1900, 13″, pr.....450.00
Figurine, Elijah & Raven, Wood, 1790, 10″.................225.00
Figurine, Four Seasons, by Dixon & Austin, ca 1820, 8″.....1,200.00
Figurine, gazelle, recumbent; bocage, Walton School, 4″......395.00
Figurine, Gen Wolseley, on horse, 13″......................90.00
Figurine, girl w/flowers, 1830s, 6″..........................50.00
Figurine, girl w/2 mice, yel mouse house, 5½″...............150.00
Figurine, Grace Darling & sailor, overturned boat, 7¾″........225.00
Figurine, grayhound w/dead rabbits on base, mc, 8½″, pr......260.00
Figurine, Hope w/Anchor, ca 1810........................135.00
Figurine, horse, on base, 5x4¾″..........................425.00
Figurine, hound chasing hare, mc, 10½″...................125.00
Figurine, hunting dog, wht w/gray patches, ca 1850, 3½″......150.00
Figurine, Lady Lytteton & Princess, 1848...................150.00
Figurine, lady w/tambourine, bisque, turq/gold trim, 12″........45.00
Figurine, lamb, recumbent, coleslaw coat, gilt, 3½″, pr........150.00
Figurine, lion, recumbent, softpaste w/mc pnt, 2¾″, EX.......100.00
Figurine, lion, tan glaze, late, 11¼″, pr....................300.00
Figurine, lion standing, glass eyes, no base, 11x13″..........200.00
Figurine, musician on recumbent deer, rpr flags, 10½″, pr.....275.00
Figurine, New Marriage Act, att O Sherrat, ca 1825, 6x6″.....600.00
Figurine, Patrick Sarsfield Earl of Lucan on horse, 14″.......110.00
Figurine, Prince Albert, standing, ca 1840, 12″..............165.00
Figurine, Prince Albert on horse, 1840, 8″..................145.00
Figurine, Queen Alexandria, 12″............................75.00
Figurine, Queen Victoria/King of Sardinia & dog, 1855, 14″...140.00
Figurine, rabbit, recumbent, ears bk, mc, minor wear, 3″ L....220.00
Figurine, sailor's wife & son, marbleized base, 9½″...........500.00
Figurine, Scotsman w/bagpipes & dog, gold trim, 1850s, 17″...325.00
Figurine, Scottish couple sit above clock, ca 1850, 14″........150.00
Figurine, Scottish couple w/drum/flags, facing pr, 11″, EX.....275.00
Figurine, Scottsman, dancing lass, mc, 20th C, 6″, pr.........100.00
Figurine, seahorse, ca 1830, 2¼x2½″......................275.00
Figurine, shepherd w/sheep & harp, wht, 12½″..............110.00
Figurine, squirrel on base, 6¼″, pr........................600.00
Figurine, Tailor of Gloucester, His Wife, 5″, pr, NM..........900.00
Figurine, Tam O'Shanter, seated, 1830s, 5″.................100.00
Figurine, The Widow, Walton School, 1810, 11″..............175.00
Figurine, Thos Smith/Wm Collier, Mortal Combat, 1860, 13″...170.00
Figurine, Tithe Pig, Walton School, ca 1815, 6x9″...........800.00
Figurine, Uncle Tom & Little Eva, 10″......................450.00
Figurine, Victoria & Albert, ca 1850, 11″, pr................500.00
Figurine, Victoria/Albert/baby on throne, 1840, 8″............150.00
Figurine, Village Group, hollow, Walton School, 1800, 7″.....585.00
Figurine, Wesley, White Robe, 1850, 8″....................100.00
Figurine, Wesley in the Pulpit, 1850, 11″...................125.00
Figurine, whippet, full color, 1850s, 6″.....................175.00
Figurine, whippet, rabbit at ft, 7½″ L......................100.00
Figurine, whippet, recumbent on oval base, mc, 4⅜″, pr, EX...170.00
Figurine, witch riding swan, 1850, 8″.......................135.00
Figurine, 2 musicians, doves on clock between, 9″............135.00
Inkstand, Greek lady w/caduceus sits on stool, 7x12″.........350.00
Jug, camels/elephants, bl transfer w/mc, mask spout, 5″........65.00
Jug, Chinese scene, wht w/mc enameling, 7″...................75.00
Jug, flying Cupid in wreath, wht w/mc, 7″....................75.00
Jug, rabbits, blk transfer on putty, gold trim, 5½″.............65.00
Mug, British lion/eagle/Crimea poem, blk/mc, 1858, 4″, EX.....60.00
Mug, children play in lake, red transfer, 'Martha,' 2⅜″.........40.00
Mug, Chinese Flute, 2 children/dog, red transfer, 2½″..........36.00
Mug, Partridge Shooting, mc, sm rim flakes, 2½″..............45.00
Plate, Eastern Empire scene, blk transfer w/mc, 8″............60.00
Plate, English country scene w/church & cottage, l/b, 10″......35.00
Plate, Favourite, girl w/cat, daisy border, 7½″...............70.00
Plate, floral rim emb/mc, center transfer: Amusement, 8″.......85.00
Plate, floral/leaf molded edge, rustic scene, 1830, 6½″.........25.00
Plate, Vincennes, gray-purple, Alcock, 10½″..................55.00
Platter, emb bl feather edge, em florals/eagles, 17″, EX.......215.00
Platter, English fishermen, m/b, 17½″.......................85.00
Salt cellar, sheep figural, 5x4″...........................500.00
Spill, boy & girl, lamb & dog, 2 birds on tree, 10x9″.........750.00
Spill, huntsman & dog, 14″...............................110.00
Spill, man & lady, ca 1840, 5″.............................60.00
Spill, man & woman by tree w/dog & lamb, 7″...............175.00
Spill, milkmaid & cows, 5½″, pr..........................450.00
Spill, 2 children, 1840s, 5″...............................65.00
Spill, 2 swans, bl coleslaw, orange w/in, 4½″................225.00
Whistle, bird form, ochre w/biscuit interior, 1800, 3″, EX......275.00
Whistle, hound's head form, ca 1825, rpr, 1¾″ L.............250.00
Whistle, rabbit form, gr w/brn & gr mottle, sm rpr, 2⅝″.......750.00

Stained Glass

There are many factors to consider in evaluating a window or panel of stained glass art. Besides the obvious factor of condition, intricacy, jeweling, beveling, and the amount of selenium (red, orange, and yellow) present should all be taken into account. Remember, repair work is itself an art, and can be very expensive.

Globe, band of lg butterflies w/in brickwork, 13", pr........1,650.00
Panel, waterfall/hillside, pnt details, in fr, 43x29".............825.00
Shade, ceiling; caramel w/gr/gold sqs at bottom, Deco, 23"....425.00
Shade, 12 curved panels, blown-out fruit in border, 24".......800.00
Window, enamel detail, lady in robe before cross, 60x48"....2,200.00
Window, Gothic arch panels, bl scroll at base, 29x43½", pr....600.00
Window, hollyhocks/iris/lotus, Bigelow Kennard, 20x18".....4,950.00
Window, HP reserves, scrollwork, ca 1902, 38x31", pr........350.00

Stanford

The Stanford Company produced a Corn Line very similar to that of the Shawnee Company, that is today becoming very collectible.

When no condition is indicated, the items listed below are assumed to be in mint condition.

Corn Line, cookie jar, 9⅓", $40.00.

Corn line, cookie jar.....................................40.00
Corn line, creamer & sugar..............................15.00
Corn line, shakers, pr....................................12.00
Corn line, spoon holder..................................30.00
Corn line, teapot..38.00

Stangl

In 1913 the Fulper Pottery was acquired by J. Martin Stangl, who had previously been employed there as a superintendent of the technical division. Under Stangl's direction, the production of dinnerware was initiated. In addition to the artwares already being made, figurines--most notably the Audubon birds modeled after the *Birds of America* series--became a large part of their output. These birds have become very popular with collectors in recent years. They are easily identified by the 'Stangl' mark on the base. Stangl pottery was produced until Martin Stangl's death in 1972.

When no condition is indicated, the items listed below are assumed to be in mint condition.

Birds

Bird of Paradise, #3408...................................85.00
Blackpoll Warbler, #3810................................110.00
Blue Headed Vireo, #3448.................................55.00
Bluebird, #3276..60.00
Bluebirds, #3276D..125.00
Broadbill Hummingbird, #3629, 4½x6½"..................95.00
Broadtail Hummingbird, #3626...........................105.00
Cardinal, #3444, matt red finish.........................85.00
Cardinal, #3444, pink.....................................68.00
Chestnut-Backed Chickadee, #3811......................65.00
Chestnut-Sided Warbler, #3812..........................70.00
Chickadees, #3581..155.00
Cliff Swallow, #3852.......................................50.00
Cockatoo, #3405..48.00
Cockatoo, #3580, med......................................90.00
Cockatoo, #3584, 12"......................................200.00
Cockatoos, #3405D...85.00
Duck, #3250B..40.00
Duck, #3431, blk/wht.......................................80.00
Evening Grosbeak, #3813..................................120.00
Flying Duck, #3443..250.00
Goldfinches, #3635..185.00
Gray Cardinal, #3596......................................48.00
Hen, #3446, gray..88.00
Hen Pheasant, #3491.......................................165.00
Hummingbirds, #3599D....................................325.00
Kentucky Warbler, #3598..................................45.00
Key West Quail Dove, #3454..............................235.00
Kingfisher, #3406...45.00
Kingfishers, #3406D.......................................125.00
Lovebird, #3400...40.00
Nuthatch, #3593..46.00
Oriole, #3402..55.00
Orioles, #3402D..100.00
Painted Bunting, #3452....................................75.00
Parakeets, #3582D, bl.....................................150.00
Parrot, #3449...140.00
Parula Warbler, #3583.....................................40.00
Penguin, #3274...275.00
Prothonatary Warbler, #3447, yel........................50.00
Redstarts, #3490D...185.00
Rieffers Hummingbird, #3628..............................95.00
Rivoli Hummingbird, #3627...............................160.00
Rooster, #3445, yel...95.00
Rufous Hummingbird, #3585...............................34.00
Shoveler Duck, #3455......................................245.00
Titmouse, #3592...30.00
Turkey, #3275...275.00

Western Blue Bird, #3815, 7", $250.00.

Wilson Warbler, #3597........45.00
Wren, #4301........40.00
Wrens, #3401D........90.00

Miscellaneous

Americana, teapot, #2000, yel........15.00
Apple Delight, server, center hdl........15.00
Ash tray, Canada goose........25.00
Ash tray, pheasant, #2926C, 11x7¾"........30.00
Ash tray, Sportsman, jumping deer........20.00
Baby plate & cup, ABCs........55.00
Bella Rosa, cup & saucer........12.00
Bella Rosa, plate, dinner........15.00
Bowl, ocean view/sailboat/seagulls, Kate Field, 9¼"........98.00
Caribbean, ewer, 8"........15.00
Colonial, cup & saucer, bl........6.00
Colonial, plate, dinner; bl........9.00
Colonial, platter, bl........9.00

Steins

Steins have been made from pottery, pewter, glass, stoneware, and porcelain, from very small up to the four-liter size. They are decorated by etching, in-mold relief, decals--and occasionally they are even hand painted. Some porcelain steins have lithophane bases. Collectors often specialize in a particular type--faience, regimental, or figural--while others limit themselves to the products of only one manufacturer.

When no condition is indicated, the items listed below are assumed to be in mint condition. See also Mettlach

Key:
L—liter   tl—thumb lift

Brass, barrel shape, ¼L........75.00
Character, barbell, pottery, 1L, M........240.00
Character, barrel, porcelain, yel w/brn bands, .3L, M........130.00
Character, bowling pin, pottery, ½L, M........190.00
Character, Dooley, pottery, made for Utica Brewery, ½L, M........55.00
Character, Happy Radish, Musterschutz, ½L, M........460.00
Character, Indian, bisque porcelain, E Bohn, ¼L, M........400.00
Character, iron maiden, stoneware, ½L, M........380.00
Character, lawn tennis, pottery, 1L, M........295.00
Character, monk w/skullcap/robe, salt glaze stoneware, 7½"........175.00
Character, nun, litho of monk/nun/cross, 6¾x4½"........345.00
Character, nun, lithophane base, porcelain, 6¾"........345.00
Character, skull, inlay lid, bisque, 2½", M........275.00
Character, Uncle Sam, porcelain, Musterschutz, ½L, M........1,950.00
Character, well-dressed German, stoneware, ½L, M........245.00
Character, 4 men under umbrella, porcelain, pewter lid, ½L..1,000.00
Faience, boy fishing, postwar, ½L, M........70.00
Faience, deer scene, postwar, 1L, M........100.00
Faience, 1900 copy of Nurnberg, ½L........110.00
Glass, applied hdl, cut t'prints, pewter lid, eng: O, 4L........35.00
Glass, blown, diagonal groove, amber, 14", M........140.00
Glass, blown, enamel branches & leaves, amber, 16", M........175.00
Glass, blown, enamel elk in snow, amber, 15", M........175.00
Glass, blown, enamel guitar player, ½L, M........135.00
Glass, blown, enamel harvest, cobalt, brass hdl, 15", M........190.00
Glass, blown, enamel verse & seal, ½L, M........120.00
Glass, blown, enamel woman in panel, opaline, base line........160.00
Glass, blown, fluted w/2 bands, amber, 15½", M........160.00
Glass, blown, ground/polished circle design, eng lid, .4L........95.00
Glass, blown, 50th anniversary, cut panels, pink on clear, 5"...485.00
Glass, pressed, enamel Munich Maid on ribbed body, ½L, M....95.00
Glass, pressed, relief Munich Maid on base, 8-sided, ½L, M.....70.00
Glass & pewter, detailed pewter overlay/glass body, 12½"......455.00
Lithophane, Alpine couple, porcelain, ½L, M........125.00
Lithophane, floral scene w/irid color, porcelain, ½L, M........85.00
Lithophane, Gruss aus Rothenberg photo, M Wossner, 9"........110.00
Pewter, Art Nouveau design, 8-sided, ½L........110.00
Pewter, athletics, 2nd place, glass bottom, 1861, ½L........140.00
Pewter, bullet shape, eng w/soldier behind machine gun, ½L...215.00
Pewter, hand hammered, geometric design, ½L, M........190.00
Pewter, hand hammered, shield & floral, 3 ball ft, 10", M.....215.00
Pewter, Pilsner shape, ¼L........80.00
Pewter, plain design w/strap hdl, ½L........55.00
Pewter, relief: Art Nouveau floral, ½L........160.00
Pewter, relief: cavalier/maiden, William Tell finial, 21"........655.00
Pewter, relief: Falstaff, ½L........200.00
Pewter, relief: Hershey Park, 2¼", M........15.00
Pewter, relief: scenes of Nurnberg, mk F&M, .2L, NM........80.00
Pewter, relief: stag/fox/pheasant, ½L, M........220.00
Pewter, relief: tavern scene, tang rpr, ½L........85.00
Pewter, screw jug, 6-sided w/eng design & 1831, 7"........160.00
Porcelain, Blue Onion w/matching lid, dwarf tl, ½L, M........480.00
Porcelain, floral scene, litho, ½L, M........115.00
Porcelain, transfer, George Washington, 3", M........25.00
Porcelain, transfer, innkeeper filling steins, ½L, M........100.00
Pottery, monkey atop, bear hdl, cats on sides, mc, 8¾"........200.00
Pottery, Oriental scenes, heavy enamel, set on lid, ½L, M......290.00
Pottery, relief: Alpine man, ½L, M........50.00
Pottery, relief: Biblical scenes, pewter lid, 14½"........55.00
Pottery, relief: boar hunt, animal heads on base, ½L, M........185.00
Pottery, relief: children w/photo in inlay, 4", M........40.00
Pottery, relief: comical scene of man under water, ½L, M........80.00
Pottery, relief: drinking cavaliers, Perkeo on inlay, ½L........135.00
Pottery, relief: dwarf & girl, 5½", M........25.00
Pottery, relief: man & 2 women, ½L, M........40.00
Pottery, relief: mandolin players & cavalier, inlay lid, ½L.....110.00
Pottery, relief: many people in wine cellar, 1L, M........90.00
Pottery, relief: mason, occupational, ½L, M........140.00
Pottery, relief: outdoor drinking scene, Viking lid, 14½"........300.00
Pottery, relief: space shuttle scenes, Ceramarte, 1981, ½L........60.00
Pottery, relief: trumpeter & horse, 1L, M........60.00
Pottery, relief: zither player & 2 women, ½L, M........40.00
Pottery, relief: 2 Alpine couples, ½L, M........50.00
Pottery, relief: 2 men at table give flowers to maiden, ½L........65.00
Pottery, relief: 3 panels of cherubs, 2L, M........80.00

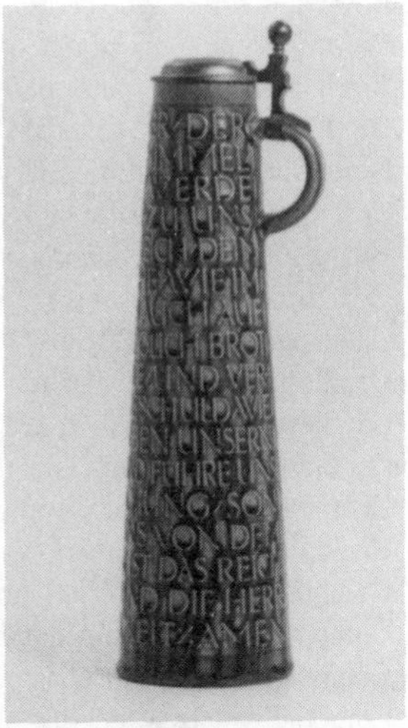

Pottery stein with Lord's Prayer in German, 14¾", $145.00.

Pottery, transfer, scene of Mainz, ½L, M....................110.00
Pottery, transfer, swan & lyre, rpr tang, ½L..................70.00
Puzzle, pottery, emb hunting scene/animals, thorn hdl, 6″......85.00
Regimental, Gen Regt Ulm, 1910-1912, 4 maneuver scenes, ½L.297.00
Regimental, 2 maneuver scenes w/royal figure, porcelain, ½L...325.00
Regimental, 4 maneuver scenes, Stuttgart, porcelain, ½L, M....445.00
Regimental, 4 maneuver scenes, 11 Field Art Cassel, ½L, M....430.00
Regimental, 5 Garde Du Corps, 3 parade scenes, ½L, M.....1,135.00
Silverplate, relief: creature plays music to nude women.......1,200.00
Silverplate, relief: outdoor feast, postwar, .3L, M.............135.00
Stoneware, barmaid on barrel, porcelain inlay, ½L, M..........45.00
Stoneware, relief: cavalier & maiden, cobalt, 1L, M............85.00
Stoneware, relief: hunter w/kill, cobalt, 1L, M.................55.00
Stoneware, relief: indoor scene, cobalt, ½L, M................35.00
Stoneware, relief: monkey/bat/coat of arms, pewter lid, 7″.......35.00
Stoneware, relief: outdoor feast, cobalt, ½L, M................40.00
Stoneware, relief: 3 men & maiden, cobalt, ½L, M.............50.00
Stoneware, transfer, floral & verse, bl, ½L, M.................50.00
Tin, transfer, Munich Maid, some wear, 2½″.....................25.00
Wood, burned-in floral, 4″...................................25.00
Yellowware, tan band, pewter lid eng: FDU 1760, 9½″, EX....140.00

Steuben

The Steuben Glass Works of Corning, New York, was founded in 1903 by Frederick Carder and Thomas Hawkes. They made art glass of high quality similar to some of Tiffany's work. One of their earliest types of art glass was aurene, a lustrous metallic gold or blue. They also made verre de soie, rosaline, and silverene. In 1918, Steuben became a branch of Corning Glass Works.

When no condition is indicated, the items listed below are assumed to be in mint condition. See also Aurene; Verre de Soie

Ash tray, topaz w/bl leaf hdl...............................125.00
Bottle, scent; pomona gr, ribbed, sgn/#6887, 5½″............125.00
Bottle, scent; verre de soie, jade gr stopper, #6233, 4¼″......150.00
Bottle, scent; yel jade, slender, #1988, 7¾″.................450.00
Bowl, acid cut-back, jade, 8″ dia........................1,650.00
Bowl, amethyst, silverina, air-trap/mica flecks/ftd, 5x11″.......700.00
Bowl, aurene/calcite, ruffle top, yel, #3080, 8½″..............395.00
Bowl, centerpiece; aurene & calcite, lg......................350.00
Bowl, centerpiece; ivorene, lotus leaf, ped base, 6x14″........350.00
Bowl, cranberry, 6½x12″....................................275.00
Bowl, crystal w/bl threads, sgn fleur-de-lis, 12″...............190.00
Bowl, gr jade, sgn F Carder & Steuben, 2x12½″.............350.00
Bowl, inverted bell w/8 globs forming ft, sgn, 10″ dia.........385.00
Bowl, lotus, ftd, sgn, bristol yel, +9″ plate w/lotus rim........125.00
Bowl, Mariner's, allegoric/compass, by Waugh, in case, 16″...7,425.00
Bowl, pomona gr, puffy base w/4 supporting tubes, #3080.....125.00
Bowl, topaz, swirl, sgn/#6118, 9½″..........................75.00
Bowl, verre de soie, ped ft, 4x14″...........................75.00
Box, puff; Oriental Poppy, glossy, flower finial, 3⅝x5″.........900.00
Box, puff; rosaline, alabaster knob, 5½x5″ dia...............300.00
Box, trinket; Victorian, 4 scrolled brass ft, hinged lid.........135.00
Cake pan, sgn/#6220, 16″..................................125.00
Candlestick, amber, 10″....................................135.00
Candlestick, amethyst & gold, #2596, 10″.....................175.00
Candlestick, clear twist stem/canary base, sgn/#5194, 10″......110.00
Champagne, Oriental Poppy, sgn, 6¼″........................325.00
Cocktail, bl w/clear stem, silver rim, sgn/#3107, 7″...........135.00
Compote, aurene, calcite, unsgn, 5¼x8″......................345.00
Compote, calcite, pink highlights, orig label, 5x8″............450.00
Compote, jade gr w/alabaster stem & base, 8x10″.............140.00
Compote, topaz & celeste bl, 7x7″..........................175.00
Compote, yel silverina, air trap/mica flecks, 5x7″.............650.00
Cordial, celeste bl..50.00
Cruet, verre de soie, eng floral, sgn/#3061...................185.00
Figurine, koala bear, in fitted leather case, 5¾″............1,250.00
Figurine, porpoise, upright, sgn, 5½″........................450.00
Finger bowl w/underplate, millefiori, heart/vines.............1,750.00
Flower block, Buddha, alabaster, dbl-row celadon base........250.00
Flower bowl, topaz swirl-rib top on pomona gr ped ft, 4x5″.....95.00
Goblet, celeste bl, rosa stem, sgn/#3551, 8″..................75.00
Goblet, clear top, amethyst twist stem, #6563, rare, 9″.........90.00
Goblet, cobalt, #6792, 5″...................................20.00
Goblet, gold ruby w/clear twist stem, swirl, #6474, 9″..........30.00
Goblet, Lust, Sidney Waugh, sgn, 7½″.......................880.00
Goblet, pomona gr, sgn/#2882, 6″............................30.00
Goblet, selenium red, etched grapevine, 6″..................650.00
Goblet, topaz, sgn/#2882, 6″...............................25.00
Goblet, verre de soie, 6″...................................50.00
Jar, woman/child eng, L Kroll, w/lid, 18″..................2,090.00
Lamp, dbl acid cut-back, gr/blk Chinese decor, 35½″.........945.00
Lamp, moss agate shade, kneeling nudes ea side on marble..1,850.00

Dresser jars, acid cut-back rosaline to alabaster, each with its original label, 6¼″, $1,900.00 for the pair.

Lamp base, plum jade, acid cut-back, 14x6″................1,400.00
Mug, Mat-su-no-ke, ftd, applied gr decor, rim & hdl, 6″.......225.00
Pilgrim flask, lake w/trees on shore, autumn shades, 9″......1,850.00
Pitcher, cocktail; clear w/blk reeding, +8 glasses.............600.00
Pitcher, gr, swirl, w/lid, #6435, +6 tumblers.................225.00
Plate, clear w/blk reeding, sgn, 8″..........................40.00
Plate, verre de soie..25.00
Plate, verre de soie, sgn F Carder, 8½″.....................45.00
Shade, dk gr w/melon stripes, platinum border, sgn, 10″.....2,250.00
Shade, gold irid, unusual shape, sgn, 6″.....................50.00
Shade, gr feathers on calcite, gold aurene w/in, sgn..........185.00
Shaker, bristol yel, bubbles, self-threading, sgn, 1½x2¼″........95.00
Sherbet, amethyst, sgn, w/underplate........................55.00
Sherbet, calcite w/platinum lining, ribbed, 4x4″..............115.00
Sherbet, gr jade w/alabaster stem, #1526, w/underplate........150.00
Sherbet, lt bl jade w/alabaster ft & stem, w/underplate.........400.00
Sherbet, rosaline w/alabaster ft & stem, w/underplate..........250.00
Sherbet, verre de soie, w/underplate........................50.00
Stocking darner, bl aurene.................................625.00
Stocking darner, gold aurene...............................465.00
Tumbler, lemonade; pomona gr w/topaz wafer, #6518, 5″.......20.00
Tumbler, red, 6″...60.00
Urn, aquamarine, ftd, 9″...................................190.00
Vase, acid cut-back clear/frosted, cameo sgn, 8½x8″..........595.00

Vase, acid cut-back gr jade/alabaster, butterfly, 12″ 1,800.00
Vase, acid cut-back gr jade/alabaster, Chinese, 4½″ 800.00
Vase, acid cut-back gr jade/alabaster, florals, 7½x8″ 1,450.00
Vase, acid cut-back rosaline, bird, urn shape, lg 1,250.00
Vase, amber, swirled & ribbed, #6031, 7″ 95.00
Vase, bud; clear, controlled air bubble, sgn, 8″ 180.00
Vase, calcite, gold aurene w/in, flared, w/label, 6x7½″ 265.00
Vase, calcite, gold aurene w/in, ruffled top, Carder, 7″ 285.00
Vase, cintra, bl-gr, Compton pattern, 14¾″ 2,000.00
Vase, dk bl jade, melon sections, sgn/#7429, 4½x7″ 1,100.00
Vase, French bl, bubbly, 5½x4½″ 85.00
Vase, gr, controlled bubbles, threading, fan shape, 8″ 115.00
Vase, gr, flared top, ped ft, 4″ opening, 6″ 55.00
Vase, gr jade, swirl, sgn/#6031, 7″ 175.00
Vase, gr jade w/upright alabaster hdls, bulbous, 10″ 900.00
Vase, gr w/controlled bubbles, threading, fan shape, 8″ 110.00
Vase, gr w/eng ship, fan form, #6287, 8½″ 185.00
Vase, gr/gold stripes w/purple tones, ftd, 12″ 795.00
Vase, ivorene w/blk base, fan form, 8½″ 375.00
Vase, ivory, #2683, 8″ 265.00
Vase, ivory/blk, floriform, 12″ 795.00
Vase, lt amber w/celeste bl rim, unsgn/#938, 5″ 70.00
Vase, lt bl silverina, flared cylinder shape, rare, 10″ 475.00
Vase, Oriental Poppy, #378 figural Tiffany base, 19″ 1,900.00
Vase, plum jade, stick neck, sgn/#2256 ....145.00
Vase, rosaline, eng garlands, alabaster footing, 9x7½″ 775.00
Vase, topaz ribbed, top & base rims trn over, 8″ 95.00
Vase, Tyrian, flat fan w/4 openings, heart leaves, 6½″ 1,600.00
Vase, verre de soie, ribbed, scalloped, #1980, 4″ 30.00
Vase, verre de soie/gr reeded upper body, ftd, #3143, 6″ 95.00
Vase, wisteria, ribbed, unusual color, 4¾″ 150.00
Wine, French bl, sgn, 6½″ 45.00
Wine, gr jade w/alabaster twist stem, sgn/#5154, 9″ 140.00
Wine, jade, #7160 ....75.00
Wine, rosaline, twisted alabaster stem 245.00
Wine, topaz 85.00
Wine, topaz w/clear stems, mica throughout top, 7″ 225.00
Wine, verre de soie, 3½″ 50.00

Stevengraph

A Stevengraph is a small picture made of woven silk, resembling an elaborate ribbon, created by Thomas Stevens in England in the latter half of the 1800s. They were matted and framed by Stevens, usually with his name appearing on the mat, or more commonly the trade announcement on the back of the mat. He also produced silk bookmarks, all of which have 'Stevens' woven in silk on one of the mitered corners.

When no condition is indicated, the items listed below are assumed to be in excellent condition.

Bookmark, A Blessing 30.00
Bookmark, Geo Washington Centennial 110.00
Bookmark, Greetings of the Season, Christmas colors, EX 65.00
Bookmark, Happy Birthday, lyrics & music 70.00
Bookmark, Happy May Thy Birthday Be, sgn 70.00
Bookmark, Many Happy Returns 60.00
Bookmark, Remember Me 45.00
Bookmark, To Mother 65.00
Bookmark, Wish You a Merry Christmas & a Happy New Year ..65.00
Bookmark, 1893 Columbian Expo, Last Rose of Summer 110.00
Boxers, orig fr & mat, TS Coventry, G color 225.00
Called to Rescue, Heroism at Sea 235.00
Columbian Expo, Landing of Columbus 275.00
Death, The; orig gold leaf fr, sgn mat, 8½x 11¼″ 250.00
Death of McKinley 215.00
Finish, The; fr, EX 185.00
For Life or Death, Heroism on Land 350.00
Full Cry, orig gold leaf fr, sgn mat, 8½x11¼″ 200.00
Good Old Days, orig mat, in fr 250.00
Last Lap, orig mat 295.00
Meet, The; in fr 165.00
Parkin Coventry 165.00
Present Time, orig mat, titles on bk of 2-way fr 425.00
Robert Burns, orig mat, titles on bk, in fr 365.00
Start, The; fr, EX 185.00
Water Jump, The; fr, EX 185.00

Stevens and Williams

Stevens and Williams glass was produced at the Brierly Hill Glassworks in Stourbridge, England, for nearly a century, beginning in the 1830s. They were credited with being among the first to develop a method of manufacturing a more affordable type of cameo glass. Other lines were also made--silver deposit, alexandrite, and engraved rock crystal to name but a few.

When no condition is indicated, the items listed below are assumed to be in mint condition.

Finger bowl, Dia Quilt, rose w/citron threads, trilobed 135.00
Lamp, Swirl, cased peppermint stripe, clear ruffle ft, 10″ 135.00
Pitcher, bl flower/gr leaves, scissor-cut top, hdl, 2⅞″ 175.00
Rose bowl, bl satin opal stripes, box pleated, 4½x4″ 135.00
Rose bowl, MOP, rose/pink, attached gr leaf tray, 4x5¾″ 450.00
Rose bowl, raised bl thorns, blown-out, clear rim, 3¾x2½″ 125.00
Rose bowl, Zipper, honey amber, reg mk, 2¼x2¾″ 125.00

Rose bowl, green Jewel glass, 2¾″, $125.00.

Tumbler, amber, applied amber pear & apple, gr leaves, 3¾″ ...225.00
Vase, amber w/lg applied red strawberry, 4x3⅝″ 300.00
Vase, cameo, floral, chipped bkground, multi-layered, 11½″ ...2,250.00
Vase, clear w/twisted gr trailing lily pads, 8½″ 200.00
Vase, clear/gr/pink, intaglio, swans/lilies, 7½x4½″ 650.00
Vase, cranberry, melon ribbed, 5 clear ft, 4½″ 105.00
Vase, cream, pink w/in, 2 applied leaves, 3 ball ft, 7¼″ 300.00
Vase, dk brn w/gold/silver blossoms, moonstones, 6¾″, EX 385.00
Vase, gr/amber ruffled applied leaf, crimped top, 6¾″ 145.00
Vase, opal/ruby lined, applied leaves, 3 amber loop ft, 7″ 250.00
Vase, pink, wht casing, ruffled rim, applied hdls, 5½″, pr 99.00
Vase, pink w/applique plums, wht lining, 7x4″ 325.00
Vase, rose color, MOP satin glass, Pompeiian Swirl, 9¾x5″ 600.00
Vase, wht, oak leaves/amber acorn, urn shape/ped base, 10″ ...400.00
Vase, wht w/amber & rose flowers, amber ruffled edge, 6″ 250.00
Vase, wht w/amber applied fruit, rose top ruffle, 8″ 350.00

Stiegel

Baron Henry Stiegel produced glassware in Pennsylvania as early as 1760, very similar to glass being made concurrently in Germany and England. Without substantiating evidence, it is impossible to positively attribute a specific article to his manufacture. Although he made other types of glass, today the term Stiegel generally refers to any very early ware made in shapes and colors similar to those he is known to have produced--especially that with etched or enameled decoration. It is generally conceded however, that most glass of this type is of European origin.

When no condition is indicated, the items listed below are assumed to be in undamaged condition.

Left to right: Stiegel-type flip glass with etched top band, 6″, $50.00; Stiegel-type flip glass with fine overall engraved foliage, 6″, $100.00; Stiegel-type flip glass engraved with a large tulip, minor rim bruise, 6″, $70.00.

Bottle, eng pot of flowers, threaded glass cap, 6½″ 180.00
Chalice, heart/flower/German script, air trap in stem, 7¾″ 225.00
Creamer, 20-diamond, applied ft/hdl, deep cobalt, 3⅞″, NM 450.00
Flask, chestnut; checkered diamonds, flakes/sick/worn, 6″ 675.00
Flask, Diamond Quilted, blown, amethyst 3,000.00
Flip, eng birds & foliage, 5⅝″ 150.00
Flip, eng tulip, 5½″ 65.00
Flip, etched top band, 6″ 50.00
Flip, lg eng tulip, free-blown, 7¼″ 350.00
Flip, polychrome bird & flowers, 4¾″ 475.00
Flip, wheel eng band of vesicas & dots, 1700s, 6¼″ 195.00
Flip, 10-panel w/eng band at top, 5″ 75.00
Flip, 12-panel base, simple eng rim, 6″ 75.00
Flip, 24-panel, wheel eng vesica & dot, late 1700s, 6¼″ 225.00
Mug, tree w/2 birdcages & birds, etched, strap hdl, 5″ 175.00
Pitcher, 19 vertical ribs, rim swirl, 5″, EX 235.00
Salt, master; 15-rib swirl, petal ft, lt gr 450.00
Salt, ogee w/18 vertical ribs, petal ft, 2¾″ 55.00
Salt, 11-diamond, applied ft, deep violet-bl, 3″, NM 300.00
Salt, 18-diamond, applied ft, cobalt, 3″ 105.00
Salt, 24-diamond, ftd, opal rim on deep violet-bl, 3⅛″ 225.00
Sugar bowl, applied ft, flame finial, cobalt, w/lid, 6¾″ 475.00
Wine, eagle in rnd frame w/German script, engraved, 6¼″ 150.00
Wine, ribbed bowl, peacock gr, 2⅞″ 175.00

Stocks and Bonds

Scripophily (scrip-awfully)--the collecting of 'worthless' old stocks and bonds--gained recognition as a serious collectible around the mid-1970s. Today, there are an estimated 5,000 collectors in the United States and 15,000 world-wide. Collectors who come from numerous business fields mainly enjoy the hobby aspect, though there are those who consider scripophily an investment.

Some collectors like the historical significance that certain certificates have. Others prefer the beauty of older stocks and bonds that were printed in beautiful colors with fancy artwork and ornate engravings. Even autograph collectors are found in this field, on the lookout for signed certificates.

Many factors help determine the collector value: autograph value, age of the certificate, the industry represented, whether it is issued or not, its attractiveness, condition, and collector demand.

Certificates from the mining, energy, and railroad industries are the most popular with collectors. Other industries or special collecting fields include banking, automobiles, aircraft, and territorials.

When no condition is indicated, the items listed below are assumed to be in near mint condition. In many descriptions, two-letter state abbreviations immediately follow company name.

Key:

cp—coupon
I/C—issued/cancelled
I/U—issued/uncancelled
U—unissued
vgn—vignette

Alleghany Mining, CO, I/C, Leadville issue, town/RR vgn 40.00
Arvilla Tunnel & Mining, CO, I/U, eagle/shield vgn, 1906 . . . . . 19.00
Atlantic/St Lawrence RR, sterling certificate, 1890s, vgn 25.00
Automatic Gas Lamp Co, NB, U, goddess vgn/seal/stamps, '99 . . . 22.00
Azripe Gold & Copper, AZ Terr, I/U, vgn/seal 17.00
Bonanza Chief Gold Mine, MT Terr, miner/mule vgn, I/U, '81 . . . 45.00
Bond, Confederate $1000, Archer/Daly, w/Jackson, sgn Tyler 40.00
Bond, Confederate $1000, payable in specie or cotton, 1863 . . . . 40.00
Bond, Confederate $500, Evans/Cogswell, w/7 coupons 35.00
Bond, Ft Wayne Airport, I/C, airplane/1 pg cp, '29, 10x15″ 16.00
Bond, Idaho Territory, 12%, sgn Sec/Treas, 1866, issued 110.00
Burlingame Telegraph/Typewriter, I/U, w/typewriter/founder 50.00
Chance Silver Mine, CA, U, 'C'/lg vgn, on onionskin, 1874 . . . . . 17.00
Chicago, Rock Island, Pacific RR, I/C, locomotive vgn, '15 . . . . . 18.00
Chicago, Rock Island, TX RR, I/U, artwork/illus, 1903 . . . . . 25.00
City of NY Ins Co, gr certificate, city skyline illus, '29 . . . . . 5.00
Consolidated Water Utica NY, I/C, waterfall vgn, '04, NM 15.00
Denver & Rio Grande Western RR, specimen, 1947 . . . . . 11.00
Diamond Coal/Coke, Utah Terr, I/C, coal car vgn/seal, 1895 . . . . . 35.00
Ely Gibralter Mining, UT, I/U, 3 mining vgn/seal, 1915 . . . . . 15.00
February Premier Mining/Leasing, NV, I/U, eagle vgn, '09 . . . . . 16.00
Franklin Mining, WI, I/U, title on lg banner, 1906 . . . . . 19.00
Grace Oil, TX, I/U, Spindletop boom, gold seal/border, '01 . . . . . 18.00
Graham Mercantile, NM Terr, I/U, eagle vgn, 1 of 5 issued 55.00
Hidden Treasure Gold Mine/Milling, SD, I/U, 3 vgn, 1902 . . . . . 19.00
Hopkins Mail Receptacle Co, VA, I/U, goddess vgn, 1915 . . . . . 16.00
IL Mining & Reduction, UT, I/U, 3 portrait vgn, 1901 . . . . . 20.00
Iron Springs Outing Club, AZ Terr, I/U, goddess vgn, '03 . . . . . 22.00
Judge Mining & Smelting, NJ, I/C, Miss Liberty vgn, 1917 . . . . . 16.00

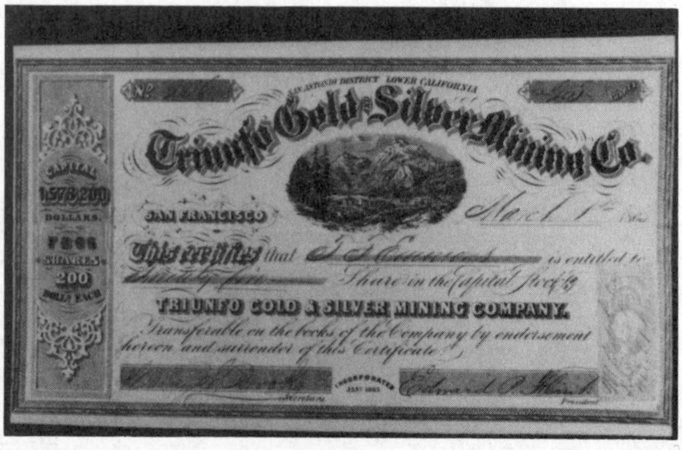

1865 California mining stock, attractive title, excellent illustration of mining camp in mountains, 25¢ revenue stamp, uncancelled, original cost $5,000, collector value $85.00 to $100.00.

Kimberly Gold Star Mine, NV, I/U, eagle/shield vgn, gr/blk......22.00
N Star Mining, AZ Terr, I/U, 3 mine vgn/gold border, 1911.....17.00
New Era Electric Storage & Power, I/U, artwork, 1893.........24.00
NV Prince Gold Mine, SD, I/U, Miss Liberty vgn, orange/gr.....20.00
Ohio Copper Co, ME, I/U, 3 miners & drill vgn, ABNCo, '10....18.00
Ohio-Keating Gold Mining, Butte MT, I/U, sm train vgn, '12....15.00
Orion Gold & Copper, AZ Terr, I/U, miners vgn/border, '18.....13.00
Oro Grande Exploration/Developemnt, AZ Terr, I/U, 3 vgn......23.00
Portland & Boothbay Steamboat Co, stock, U.................10.00
Roxanna Gold Mining/Tunneling, WV, miners vgn/border, '98...19.00
S Pacific Mine, NY, I/U, 3-in-1 mine vgn, HLBNCo, 1882.......45.00
Squaw Mtn Tunnel Gold Mine, CO, I/U, seal/miners vgn, '96....23.00
Summit Petroleum, TX, I/U, gusher/train vgn, 1919............16.00
Tacoma Eastern RR, U, train in mtn vgn, 1900s, 10x12".......20.00
Transcontinental Transport & Mining, U, train vgn, 1900s......14.00
United Chino Oil & Refining, AZ, I/U, oil derrick vgn, '18......17.00
US Oil, TX, I/U, Miss Liberty/eagle vgn, Spindletop era........23.00
WA Meteor Mining, WA, I/U, Geo WA vgn/gold seal, '05.......23.00
Zephyr Mining, CO, I/C, mine vgn, copper underprint, 1881.....50.00
1st Natn'l Bank, Bisbee, AZ Terr, I/C, vgt w/buggies, '06.......17.00

Stoneware

There are three broad periods of time that collectors of American pottery can look to in evaluating and dating the stoneware and earthenware in their collections.

Among the first permanent settlers in America were English and German potters who found a great demand for their individually turned wares. The early pottery was produced from red and yellow clays scraped from the ground at surface levels. The earthenware made in these potteries was fragile and coated with lead glazes that periodically created health problems for the people who ate or drank from it.

There was little stoneware available for sale until the early 1800s because the clays used in its production were not readily available in many areas and transportation was prohibitively expensive. The opening of the Erie Canal and improved roads brought about a dramatic increase in the accessibility of stoneware clay, and many new potteries began to open in New York and New England.

Collectors have difficulty today locating earthenware and stoneware jugs produced prior to 1840, because few have survived intact. These ovoid or pear-shaped jugs were designed to be used on a daily basis. When cracked or severely chipped, they were quickly discarded.

The value of hand-crafted pottery is often determined by the cobalt decoration it carries. Pieces with elaborate scenes (a chicken pecking corn, a bluebird on a branch, a stag standing near a pine tree, a sailing ship, or people) may easily bring $600-$3,000 at auction.

After the Civil War, there was a need and a national demand for stoneware jugs, crocks, canning jars, churns, spittoons, and a wide variety of other pottery items. The competition among the many potteries reached the point where only the largest could survive. To cut costs, most potteries did away with all but the simplest kinds of decoration on their wares. Time-consuming brush-painted birds or flowers quickly gave way to more simply executed swirls or numbers and stenciled designs. The coming of home refrigeration and Prohibition in 1919 effectively destroyed the American stoneware industry.

Investment possibilities:

Early nineteenth century stoneware with elaborate decorations and a potter's mark is expensive and will continue to rise in price, though not as rapidly as in the past few years.

Late nineteenth century hand-thrown stoneware with simple cobalt swirls or numbers is still reasonably priced and a good investment.

Mass produced stoneware (ca 1890-1920) is available in large quantities, inexpensive, and will slowly increase in price over the decade of the 1980s.

At this point, reproductions of 'fakes' are not a major concern. Much of the reproduction stoneware is dated on the bottom of the piece. The Beaumont Pottery of York, Maine, which produced the 'finest reproduction stoneware of the twentieth century,' scratched the date into each piece.

In the following listing, 'c/s' means 'cobalt on salt glaze'; all decoration described before this abbreviation is in cobalt.

When no condition is indicated, the items listed below are assumed to be in excellent condition. See also Bennington

Bottle, JC, brushed initials, c/s, 10½".......................75.00
Bottle, pig figural, Albany slip, 7¼", EX.....................85.00
Bottle, pig figural, hand molded, BB Pottery, 8", VG.........650.00
Bowl, top band, emb fern leaves on sides, c/s, 4x7½"..........45.00
Chicken fountain, emb birds over well, brn/tan glaze, 7½"......30.00
Churn, bird on stump, c/s, Ottman Bros, 4-gal, EX...........880.00
Churn, daisies/leaves, c/s, Hart & Son, Sherburne, 20", EX....395.00
Churn, floral, G detail, c/s, rpl lid/dasher, 16", EX...........155.00
Churn, floral & 2, c/s, 16", VG.............................145.00
Churn, hearts/stars/X, c/s, JP Parker, chip/hairline, 19"........250.00
Churn, incised 5, brn glaze w/blk, edge chips, 18".............80.00
Churn, splashes, c/s, P Rodenbaugh, ovoid, 15¾", EX........160.00
Churn, splashes at hdls, c/s, imp 4, ovoid, rpl lid/dasher.......130.00
Churn, X w/5-flower surround, c/s, N Clark, 5-gal, 19"........450.00
Cooler, emb staves, brush/quill decor, c/s, #4, keg shape......775.00
Cooler, flower, 12 & 1872, c/s, WJ & EG Schrop, hdls, 26"...475.00
Crock, anchor, lg; c/s, imp #3, bad crack/chips, 10"..........270.00
Crock, apple butter; abstract flower, c/s, JB Caire, 7".........225.00
Crock, basket of multiflora, c/s, Whites Utica, 11", VG........485.00
Crock, bird, longtail, on branch; c/s, Whites Utica, 9½".......425.00
Crock, bird on branch, c/s, Haxtun & Co, 1½-gal............300.00
Crock, bird on branch, c/s, imp #4, 11½"..................375.00
Crock, bird on lg leaf, brushed c/s, FB Norton, 11"...........475.00
Crock, bird on stump, c/s, imp #4, hairline under hdl, 11".....450.00
Crock, bird on stump, lg tail; c/s, Reidinger-Caire, 12"........500.00
Crock, bird on twig, slip c/s, Haxtun/Ottman, 10", EX........400.00
Crock, bird w/polka dots & 2, c/s, S Hart, 9"...............215.00
Crock, birds crossed, c/s, S Hart, Fulton, NY................465.00
Crock, cabbage rose, full-blown w/ribbon; lg, c/s, NY, 1-gal.....185.00
Crock, chicken pecking corn, c/s, imp #2, 9"................360.00
Crock, chicken pecking corn, c/s, P Sweet, 10¼"............550.00
Crock, chicken pecking corn, c/s, rim/hdl chips, 10⅝".........425.00
Crock, chicken pecking corn, fat; c/s, imp #4, 11½"..........700.00
Crock, daisy on field of dots, c/s, Somerset, 7"..............190.00
Crock, daisy/leaves, naturalistic; c/s, Farrington, 10"..........300.00
Crock, deer, leaping; w/tree & 5, c/s, J Burger, 12", EX.....2,000.00
Crock, dog, lg/spotted; c/s, Brady & Ryan, 1½-gal, VG........550.00
Crock, feather & 5, c/s, J Fisher, rim hairline, 12½"...........95.00
Crock, floral, brushed c/s, EE Hall & Co, 9x12", EX.........125.00
Crock, floral, c/s, hdl crack, 7x8"..........................85.00
Crock, floral, c/s, NA White & Son, Utica, minor chips, 9"....165.00
Crock, floral, c/s, Ottman Bros, 1-gal, 7½"..................150.00
Crock, floral, lg; c/s, Roberts, Binghamton, 3-gal, EX.........165.00
Crock, floral spray w/ribbon tie, c/s, Whites, 1-gal............165.00
Crock, goblet motif, c/s, Whites Utica, stains/chips, 10½"......150.00
Crock, leaf, notched/veined; c/s, HM Whitman, 1-gal, EX......185.00
Crock, orchid, slip c/s, NA White & Son, 10", NM...........240.00
Crock, orchid, slip c/s, White & Son, 8¾"..................225.00
Crock, parrot on branch, c/s, imp #4, 11¾", EX.............350.00
Crock, parrot on branch, c/s, JA & CW Underwood, 7½", EX..395.00
Crock, peafowl on leafy nest, c/s, Hart Bros, 10", EX.........500.00
Crock, rooster & 4, stencil c/s, hairlines, 12"................125.00
Crock, stripes/wavy lines/flowers, c/s, E Fowler, 13¾",VG......250.00

Crock, sunflower w/3 in face, c/s, J Berger, 10", EX..........300.00
Crock, 4 looped motifs, c/s w/lid, sm rim flakes, 7½" W.......205.00
Flask, gray, flattened ovoid, ca 1840, 7¾"..................70.00
Flask, Seagram's, 9"..................................140.00
Flask, tan, 7¾"......................................60.00
Jar, applied ivy, blues on salt glaze, w/lid, 8x7½", VG..........75.00
Jar, bird, lg tail/dots; c/s, Cowden & Wilcox, ovoid, 10".......500.00
Jar, bird, lg; '2,' c/s, Albany, NY, 2-gal, VG.................265.00
Jar, bird on branch & 6, c/s, 1½-gal........................235.00
Jar, bird w/polka dots, c/s, hairlines/lip/hdl chips, 11".........275.00
Jar, canning; brush strokes, c/s, curved shoulders, 8½".........95.00
Jar, canning; cam-lever seal, J Sexton ad, Western, ½-gal.......60.00
Jar, canning; stenciled AP Donaghho, c/s, minor chips, 8"......50.00
Jar, canning; stenciled AP Donaghho, rare size, 5½"..........225.00
Jar, canning; stenciled Conner & Snederer, c/s, 8", NM.......100.00
Jar, canning; stenciled LB Dilliner/roses, c/s, 10".............105.00
Jar, canning; stenciled New Geneva/wavy lines, c/s, 9".........175.00
Jar, canning; stenciled NF Behrens, c/s, 10", NM.............75.00
Jar, canning; stenciled Palatine Pottery/pear, c/s, 8½".........155.00
Jar, canning; stripes/wavy lines, c/s, 8"......................55.00
Jar, canning; tulip & rim stripe, c/s, minor flakes, 8".........135.00
Jar, canning; 3 brushed stripes, c/s, tumbler form, 6"..........95.00
Jar, dandelion/scrolls, c/s, Nichols/Boynton, 10½", EX.........225.00
Jar, Federal shield, c/s, Haxton, Ottman & Co, 2-gal..........770.00
Jar, floral, c/s, N White, Utica, ovoid, 11", NM..............155.00
Jar, floral, c/s, open hdls, European, hairlines, 7".............50.00
Jar, floral, c/s, ovoid, edge flakes, 12½"....................140.00
Jar, floral, dbl, stripes, c/s, imp #2, rim flake, 11"............175.00
Jar, floral, good/stylized; c/s, Fort Edward/4, 14", EX.........225.00
Jar, floral, simple, brushed c/s, imp Olean, NY, 2-gal..........140.00
Jar, floral, simple, c/s, S Purdy, ovoid, 9½", NM.............195.00
Jar, floral, simple; brushed c/s, 1-qt........................100.00
Jar, floral, sm, & 2, c/s, N White, Utica, ovoid, 11", NM......155.00

Jar, marked Lyons, cobalt flower, #2, 14½", $325.00.

Jar, floral & bar, brushed c/s, 10"..........................225.00
Jar, floral flourish, elaborate, c/s, Ballard Bros, 12½"........300.00
Jar, floral spray, c/s, Connelly & Palmer, 2-gal, NM...........235.00
Jar, floral spray, lg/fancy, c/s, Vaughan & Mott, 4-gal..........300.00
Jar, floral sprays, elaborate; c/s, Whites Utica, 13½", EX......325.00
Jar, horse, simple/stylized/incised; c/s, 11"..................700.00
Jar, imp L Seymour/5 stars, highlighted in c/s, ovoid, 9"........95.00
Jar, imp Warton & Fenton, highlighted in c/s, ovoid, 10".......95.00
Jar, leaf & 3, c/s, ovoid, minor rim flakes, 13¼".............150.00
Jar, poppy, lg/sweeping/dot detail; c/s, W Roberts, 13¼".......250.00
Jar, primitive brushed decor & 2, c/s, Havens, ovoid, 12"......195.00
Jar, stenciled Hamilton & Jones, c/s, 11¾", NM..............115.00
Jar, stenciled Hamilton & Jones, c/s, 13¾", EX..............180.00
Jar, stenciled Hamilton & Jones/roses/stripes, c/s, 14".........205.00
Jar, stenciled HH Mallory, stripes/waves, c/s, 17", EX.........120.00
Jar, stenciled TF Reppert, c/s, hairlines, 14"................105.00
Jar, stenciled TF Reppert & wavy lines, c/s, 11½"............130.00
Jar, stripes/foliage scrolls, c/s, Excelsior Works, 9½"..........350.00
Jar, stripes/vines/tulips/2 in dotted oval, c/s, 13", EX..........525.00
Jar, stripes/wavy lines/foliage scrolls, c/s, 12"...............200.00
Jar, tooled hearts, open hdls, Charleston, ovoid, 3"...........450.00
Jar, tulip, dbl; c/s, F Stetzenmeyer & Geotzman, 11", EX......150.00
Jar, tulip/imp Dillon Henry, c/s, ovoid, 12¾", VG.............165.00
Jar, 2 & simple brushed 'leaves,' c/s, 11½", EX...............55.00
Jar, 4 & hdl decor in c/s, P Rodenbaugh, ovoid, 13½", EX....265.00
Jug, Albany slip, ovoid, 9", VG............................30.00
Jug, batter; leaves under spout, c/s, 1-gal, NM...............250.00
Jug, bird, road runner; c/s, DI Lazier.......................880.00
Jug, bird, stylized; 1835, c/s, Clark & Fox, 12"..............300.00
Jug, bird on branch, blurred; c/s, Evan B Jones, 13½", EX....245.00
Jug, bird on branch, c/s, #3, 15", EX.......................345.00
Jug, bird on branch, c/s, NY Stoneware Co, 18½"............450.00
Jug, bird on branch, c/s, Whites Utica, 1-gal................435.00
Jug, bird on branch & 'Pea Soup,' c/s, ME Vail, 15½", VG....750.00
Jug, bird on twig, c/s (tan), Lewis & Cady, Fairfax, 2-gal.......400.00
Jug, bird w/top knot, c/s, Haxton & Co, 14", EX.............325.00
Jug, bl lettering: Wedderburn's, Pure Wines, 1906, ½-pt........65.00
Jug, brn, imp Little Brown Jug, Old 1869 Rye Whiskey, qt......75.00
Jug, brn, scratched Compliments, Sl Gerock, TX, miniature....100.00
Jug, brn beehive top, Neat-Richardson Drug Co, KY, 1-gal.....140.00
Jug, brn cone top, Adolph Goldhammer, Denver, CO, 1-gal....135.00
Jug, brn cone top, Banner Liquor Store, Winona, MN, 2-gal...110.00
Jug, brn cone top, Finn & Laskey, Detroit, MI, 1-gal..........110.00
Jug, brn cone top, Griesel Bros, Winona, MN, ½-gal..........125.00
Jug, brn dome top, Simon & Lewis, Rock Island, IL, 1-gal.....140.00
Jug, brn top, Drink Plezee, best...on earth, IN, 1-gal..........110.00
Jug, brn/cream, Hoffman House, Blended Whiskey, miniature....50.00
Jug, brn/cream, JW Harper, Nelson Co, KY, miniature.........40.00
Jug, Compliments, Farmers Co, White, SD, miniature..........90.00
Jug, cream w/blk letters/picture, RH Parker on banner, qt......65.00
Jug, dog w/polka dots, fence, EX art, J&E Norton, 16¾".....6,100.00
Jug, flat sided, emb apples/branches, pat 8/11/1891, 12".......150.00
Jug, floral, brushed c/s, CA&E Harrington w/address, 12"......150.00
Jug, floral, c/s, NY Stoneware Co, 13½"....................145.00
Jug, floral, c/s, Ottman Bros, minor flakes, 12"...............125.00
Jug, floral, c/s, SS Perry, ovoid, stains/rpr, 14"..............150.00
Jug, floral, c/s, T Harrington, Lyons, semi-ovoid, 2-gal.........165.00
Jug, floral, c/s, Whites Utica/2, lip flakes, 13"...............145.00
Jug, floral, child-like; hdl decor & 2, c/s, ovoid, 12¾"..........90.00
Jug, floral, geometric/dbl; c/s, AS Bigalow, lg hdls, 20"........225.00
Jug, floral, lg/stylized; c/s, Fort Edward, 13¾"...............250.00
Jug, floral, simple; c/s, H Weston, hairline, 11"...............130.00
Jug, floral, stylized; c/s, S Hart, ovoid, 10", EX..............155.00
Jug, floral, 3 on stem; c/s, CE Pharis, ovoid, 15¾", EX.......200.00
Jug, floral & 3, well done, c/s, 16"........................145.00
Jug, floral nosegay, c/s, Wm Warner, beehive type, 1-gal.......185.00
Jug, floral spray, c/s, Pratt Wheeler & Co, Battleboro.........575.00
Jug, floral/leaves w/dots, c/s, Penn-Yan, ovoid, 11", EX.........325.00
Jug, floral/leaves/squiggle/dot detail, c/s, Selby, 13"...........300.00
Jug, floral/lg leaves/dot detail, c/s, Cooperative, 17"..........300.00
Jug, flower basket, quillwork c/s, WA Lewis, 2 hdls, 18".......625.00
Jug, foliage, c/s, Edmands & Co, hairlines/chips, 11¾"........145.00
Jug, foliage, feathery; c/s, Edmands & Co, hairlines, 11¾".....115.00

Hot water bottle, 'Sta Hot' in circle in cobalt, 12", $350.00.

Jug, foliage, 3 sprigs; c/s, SW Braun, 13½" 135.00
Jug, foliage scrolls & 2, c/s, AC Morton, RR Grocer, 15" 250.00
Jug, G Martin, 1825, imp mk, lip flakes, 11" 105.00
Jug, grapes & leaves, hdl ring, c/s, Cowden & Wilcox, 17" 510.00
Jug, HA Schunk, Pure Family Liquors, Iowa, ½-gal 68.00
Jug, imp M Meade, Albany slip, ovoid, 7" 130.00
Jug, incised bird, highlighted in c/s, ovoid, 12", EX 450.00
Jug, incised vintage allover, c/s, ovoid, G Baird, 18", EX 2,300.00
Jug, John H Donley...NY, script, c/s, Geddes, 11½" 155.00
Jug, leaf, simple; c/s, Ottman Bros, 11¼" 115.00
Jug, leaf, 3-lobe; c/s, T Harrington, semi-ovoid, 2 gal 175.00
Jug, lg 2 in lyre form, brushed c/s, S Hart Fulton, 12½" 185.00
Jug, Lobby Liquor House, SD, ½-gal 120.00
Jug, Old Joe, Oldest Distillery in Anderson, 1818, ½-gal 88.00
Jug, poppy, c/s, N White & Co, 1-gal, NM 190.00
Jug, simple brushed decor, c/s, C Hart & Co, 13½", EX 200.00
Jug, stag w/wings, c/s, OL&AK Ballard, ovoid, 13½", EX 1,100.00
Jug, stenciled Jas Benjamin Stoneware Depot, c/s, 13¾", EX 70.00
Jug, stenciled Shaefer & Driehorst, Liquors, c/s, 14", EX 145.00
Jug, Try Me Once, You Will Try Again, Detrick, ½-pt 30.00
Jug, tulip, brushed c/s, Pfaltzgraff, 2-gal, 13½" 285.00
Jug, tulip in low bowl, brushed c/s, M Woodruff, 14", EX 240.00
Jug, Warner & Ray Druggists, imp/highlight in c/s, 9" 55.00
Jug, wht cone top, KY Liquor House, Springfield, MO, 1-gal 105.00
Jug, Xs/tornado, c/s, Haxtun & Co, Ft Edward, 2-gal, EX 245.00
Jug, zigzag squiggle, c/s, NA White & Son, Utica, 10½", NM 105.00

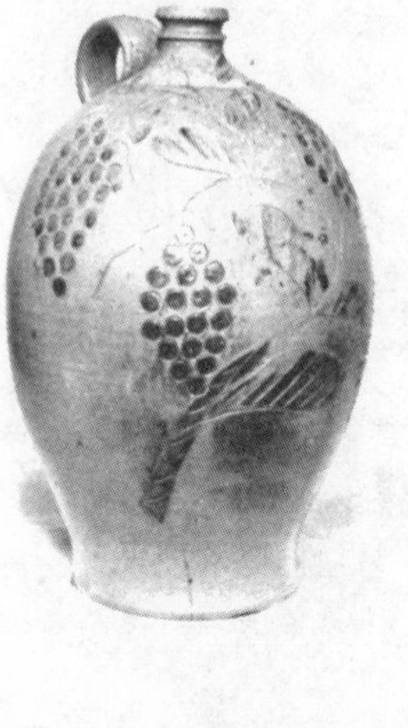

Jug, incised vintage filled in with cobalt, attributed to G Baird, Huron County, Ohio, minor flakes, 18", $2,300.00.

Pitcher, Am Beauty Rose, brn, 9" 150.00
Pitcher, batter; floral/foliage, c/s, spout flake, 9" 450.00
Pitcher, Columbian Expo, tri-color relief, rare, 1893, 8" 330.00
Pitcher, Egyptian Sphinx spout, 10" 65.00
Pitcher, floral, blk/wht brushed decor on brn, 7½", EX 45.00
Pitcher, floral, brushed/quillwork c/s, ovoid, 11" 475.00
Pitcher, Flying Bird, brn & gr 275.00
Pitcher, grapes w/rickrack on waffle ground, brn, 7½" 140.00
Pitcher, grapes w/rickrack on waffle ground, Star Co, 9" 90.00
Pitcher, tan mottle w/applied motif on dk brn, German, 9" 50.00
Rolling pin, w/dept store ad 135.00
Spittoon, ferns, brushed c/s, 3¾x7¼" 250.00
Spittoon, flower petals at spill hole/leaves, c/s, 3¾" 275.00
Stein, imp circles, c/s, pewter lid, mk 0.5L/triangle, 5" 40.00
Stein, stripes, c/s, straight sides, 6¼" 40.00
Tankard, coggles w/bl wash on Albany, hand thrown, 6½" 85.00

Store

Perhaps more than any other yester-year establishment, the country store evokes the most nostalgic feelings for folks old enough to remember its charms--barrels for coffee, crackers, and big green pickles; candy in a jar for the grocer to weigh on shiny brass scales; beheaded chickens in the meat case outwardly devoid of nothing but feathers. Today, mementos from this segment of Americana are being collected by those who 'lived it' as well as those less fortunate.

When no condition is indicated, the items listed below are assumed to be in excellent condition. See also Advertising

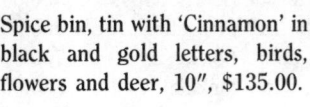

Spice bin, tin with 'Cinnamon' in black and gold letters, birds, flowers and deer, 10", $135.00.

Account book, dtd 1826, worn marbleized paper binding, 12" 40.00
Bag holder, wood, floor model 175.00
Barrel, coffee; wood, Hitchcock-Hill stenciling, w/lid 32.50
Barrel, cracker; PW Crackers, pre-1900, wood, NM 135.00
Bill spike, metal, wall mt, ornate 12.50
Bin, spice; gold spice name below bevelled mirror 100.00
Book, account; calligraphy, 1890 .... 46.00
Box, biscuit shipping & display, tole-type tin, w/lid 37.50
Box, cracker; wood w/label: Robinson Bros, 9x14x24", VG 100.00
Broom rack, iron, rnd, revolving, hanging type 65.00
Broom rack, KY Cardinal Cigars, w/2 emb tin signs, holds 5 .... 250.00
Buggy whip holder 75.00
Cabinet, Diamond Dye, poster front: lady/cherubs, 30½" 550.00
Cabinet, Dy-O-La, wood w/mc tin front insert, labeled, 17" 250.00

Cabinet, roll front, advertisments, French, Jacquot's..........225.00
Cabinet, screw; 72 drw, rfn..............................850.00
Case, cigar; golden oak, 8 drw, orig locks/hdw, 17½x12"......350.00
Case, counter top, Am Candy & Nut, walnut................175.00
Case, counter top, chewing gum; oak, pre-1900, NM..........100.00
Case, counter top, Remington knives, glass slant front........125.00
Case, seed; Rice's Seed, collapsible, wood/tin, 18½"...........70.00
Cash register/receipt machine, wood, lg.....................225.00
Cheese cutter, counter top, +cleaver, iron/wood/orig decor....250.00
Cheese cutter, wht porc, Corcoran Manufacturing Co..........35.00
Cheese dome, blown glass, applied knob, ca 1870, 15x17".....175.00
Dispenser, coffee; brass, oval, 23x9½" dia..................295.00
Dispenser, coffee; gold leaf letters on tin, 7x24x12½".........300.00
Dispenser, orangeade; 'Pony-Brand,' 3 glass globes...........300.00
Dispenser, ribbon; Emmons & Dobson, Trunks, Bags, Gloves....65.00
Hand truck, oak w/wood wheels, adv Comfort Soap, dtd 1904..135.00
Lamp, hanging; waffle pattern, brass & copper...............180.00
Papper holder w/cutter, counter top........................15.00
Scales, tobacco; adv: Speckled Beauty & Early Bird............37.50
Sign, 'Pork,' gold leaf wood letters on red, oval, 31x20".......400.00
Sign, wood w/pnt name, beveled edges, weathered, 20x48".....400.00
String holder, counter top, tin canister, brass bars/blade.......130.00

Stoves

Parlor stoves range from the simple to the very ornate. Many were obviously relative to a specific style of furnishing--Rococo, Gothic, or Greek, for instance. This is due to the fact that they were first designed in wood, carved and constructed by cabinetmakers who transferred to them the decorative devices they routinely used on furniture. The wooden stove that resulted was then used as a basis for the mold.

When no condition is indicated, the items listed below are assumed to be in excellent condition.

A Belanger, Barge #14, parlor box, scrollwork trim, sm.......150.00
Albany #2, CI column parlor, 2 door+1 on side, urn atop.....200.00
B&M #5, CI potbelly RR, 1910s, 48x32x32"................300.00
C Newcomb, CI fireplace, sunburst motif, 1800, 28x24x30"...1,250.00
C&EL Granger, 2-column parlor, front & side door, 1830s.....300.00
Fuller, Warren & Morrison, Floral Parlor #2, CI heater......1,000.00
Glenwood Baseburner #6, coal burner, 1909, 68x25x25"......700.00
Glenwood C-280, CI kitchen cookstove, water tank/dbl shelf....850.00
Golden Globe #180, potbelly, isenglass door, urn finial........800.00
Imperial Clarion 8-20, CI cookstove, chrome base/trim.......1,500.00
Newberry, Filley & Co #4, CI parlor, 10" urn atop, 26".......300.00
Portland Stove Foundry, Ideal Atlantic #8-20, CI cookstove.....12.50
Regal Universal, base burner............................900.00

Morison and Manning, column parlor stove, ca 1830, 42", $2,150.00.

Rnd oak, #16-T-31, complete.............................285.00
Sard & Co, emb acorn on dbl doors, scrollwork, CI, 39" W....110.00
SH Bansom, CI parlor, ornate, rnd air intake/side door/urn....220.00
Sunny Hearth #2, CI coal-burning fireplace, 1850s, 35x30"....250.00
Sunshine Franklin #16, CI fireplace, 2 storks decor, 1850s.....250.00
Sylvan Red Cross #31, CI parlor, ornate, tiles/6" urn, 37".....225.00
Walker & Pratt, Good Cheer #22, fireplace, nickel trim.......225.00
Wood & Bishop, Popular Clarion, CI cookstove, chrome trim...850.00

Strawberry Lustre Ware

Strawberry lustre is a general term for creamware decorated with hand-painted strawberries, vines and tendrils, and pink lustre trim. It was made by many manufactures in England in the 19th century, most of whom never marked their ware.

When no condition is indicated, the items listed below are assumed to be in undamaged condition.

Cup & saucer, handleless; very early, lg...................190.00
Plate, 10½"..130.00
Platter, 11"..135.00
Sauce boat, 5"..175.00
Sugar bowl, S-shape, w/lid, very early.....................180.00
Teapot, vine border, red line border, ftd, 11"...............375.00
Waste bowl, early, 6½"..................................120.00

Stretch Glass

Stretch glass, produced from the early 1900s until after 1930, was made in an effort to emulate the fine art glass of Tiffany and Carder. The glassware was sprayed with a special finish while still hot, and a reheating process caused the coating to contract, leaving a striated, crepe-like iridescence. Northwood, Imperial, Fenton, and the United States Glass Company were the largest manufacturers of this type of glass.

When no condition is indicated, the items listed below are assumed to be in mint condition.

Bowl, bl, treebark ft, 2¾x9½"...........................22.00
Bowl, bl, 3x10".......................................24.00
Bowl, console; red, 14"................................175.00

Vase, blue, 8", $24.50.

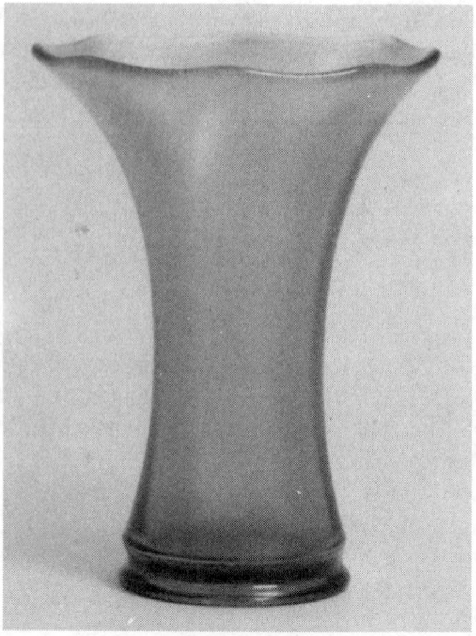

Bowl, gold, fluted edge, 10″ ... 35.00
Bowl, gr, ftd, 3x7½″ ... 22.50
Bowl, orange, Imperial, 3½x7½″ sq ... 48.00
Bowl, purple, 3½x9″ ... 35.00
Bud vase, bl, 11¾″ ... 22.00
Candle holders, bl, Imperial, 8″, pr ... 67.50
Candlesticks, pink, 2¾″, pr ... 24.00
Candy dish, pink, w/lid, 9½″ ... 30.00
Compote, bl, twig base, Northwood, 6″ ... 40.00
Compote, bl, 4x5½″ ... 18.00
Compote, pink, 5¼x6¼″ ... 25.00
Compote, purple, 7x6″ ... 45.00
Jar, candy; vaseline ... 25.00
Plate, brn/orange, 10″ ... 16.00
Sherbet w/underplate, vaseline ... 22.00
Vase, gr, vertical cuttings, 8″ ... 35.00
Vase, red, 8½″ ... 60.00
Vase, vaseline, fan form, 7″ ... 25.00

String Holders

Today, if you want to wrap and secure a package, you have a variety of products to choose from: cellophane tape, staples, etc. But in the 1800s, string was about the only available binder; thus the string holder--either the hanging or counter type--was a common and practical item found in most homes and businesses.

When no condition is indicated, the items listed below are assumed to be in excellent to near mint condition.

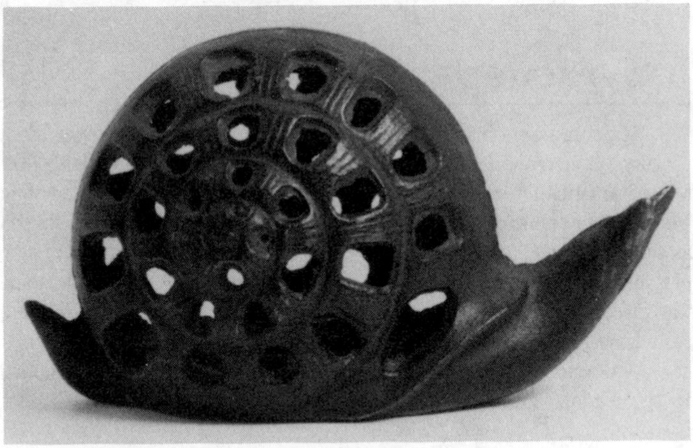

Cast metal snail figural, 4½″ x 7″, $55.00.

Apple, chalkware ... 20.00
Baker boy, chalkware ... 18.00
Ball shape, CI, 2-pc, 4″ ... 30.00
Beehive, CI, #7 ... 20.00
Beehive, CI, pat dates at top, worn bl/yel pnt, 6½″ ... 25.00
Bird, stoneware ... 28.00
Black bellhop ... 75.00
Boy & pipe ... 20.00
Cat, red bowtie, ceramic ... 35.00
Cat w/ball of twine, chalkware ... 20.00
Dutch girl, CI ... 62.50
Girl, wearing flowing skirt & muff, Japan ... 17.50
Iron, wall mt, pierced cup, #1154, pat Oct 27, 1908 ... 18.00
Jaxoli Soap, gypsy kettle ... 65.00
Lady, full-figure blonde, ceramic ... 45.00
Mammy, ceramic, Japan ... 45.00
Pear, chalkware ... 18.50
Puppy, ceramic ... 25.00
Red Goose Shoes, CI ... 750.00
Red Goose Shoes, tin ceiling mt ... 750.00
Soldier, chalkware ... 20.00
Spanish man, Deco, chalkware ... 22.00
SSS for the Blood, kettle shape ... 125.00
Stoneware, dome shape w/hole in finial, Albany slip, 6x8½″ ... 65.00
Strawberry w/face, chalkware ... 25.00
Sunbonnet baby ... 45.00

Sugar Shakers

Sugar shakers, or muffineers as they were also called, were used during the Victorian era to sprinkle sugar and spice onto breakfast muffins, toast, etc. They were made of art glass, in pressed patterns, and in china.

When no condition is indicated, the items listed below are assumed to be in mint condition.

Apple Blossom, opaque wht w/EX enamel decor, Northwood ... 125.00
Baby Thumbprint, amberina ... 200.00
Beaded Swirl, milk glass ... 32.00
Cone, pink satin ... 100.00
Daisies & Leaves, cut glass, 5¾″ ... 16.00
Daisy & Fern, bl, wide waist ... 80.00
Egg, lt yel w/russet shading, daisy decor, Mt WA ... 245.00
Erie Twist, satin, orig lid ... 250.00
Fan, milk glass, Windemere ... 55.00
Forget-Me-Not, opaque bl ... 115.00
Forget-Me-Not, opaque gr ... 125.00
Forget-Me-Not, opaque pink ... 95.00
Gargoyle, milk glass, Gillinder ... 65.00
Leaf Mold, bl satin ... 125.00
Leaf Umbrella, cased glossy bl ... 136.00
Little Shrimp, ivory ... 68.00
Melligo, milk glass w/enamel decor ... 25.00
Melon, Gillinder ... 115.00
Melon, Smith Bros ... 175.00
Netted Oak, milk glass w/decor ... 70.00
Nine Panel, pink satin ... 55.00
Peachblow, SP top, Wheeling, 5x3″ ... 550.00
Quilted Phlox, apple gr ... 85.00
Rubena ... 80.00
Sawtooth Band, milk glass ... 20.00
Spatter, pink w/clear neck ring ... 65.00
Ten Panels, clambroth, mk AG Co, 4½″ ... 14.00
Venetian Diamonds, cranberry ... 80.00
Windows, bl opal ... 150.00

Coin Spot, cranberry, 4½″, $70.00.

Summit Art Glass

Summit Art Glass Company, owned by Russell and Joanne Voglesong of Mogadore, Ohio, are producers of a line of Contemporary limited edition figurines, as well as quality reproductions of antique glass toothpicks, tumblers, salt dips, etc., made from molds once used by such companies as Northwood, U.S. Glass, and Gillinder and Sons. Their glass is marked with a 'V in circle.'

Values are given for examples in mint condition.

Chessie cat on hamper, cobalt....20.00
Creamer, Holly Band, Strawberry Tangerine....20.00
Dish, dolphin, cobalt, w/lid....20.00
Dish, pony, cobalt, w/lid....20.00
Melanie doll, Canyon Whisper....15.00
Melanie doll, Emerald Swirl....20.00
Melanie doll, Oriental Splendor....20.00
Melanie doll, Paradise Orchid....15.00
Melanie doll, Tom's Surprise....45.00
Mug, Holly Band, Strawberry Tangerine....15.00
Owl, cobalt....10.00
Owl, gr....10.00
Sugar, Holly Band, Strawberry Tangerine....30.00
Toothpick holder, elephant, amber....10.00
Toothpick holder, elephant, cobalt....10.00
Toothpick holder, elephant, gr....10.00
Toothpick holder, Owl-N-Stump, amber....10.00
Toothpick holder, Owl-N-Stump, sapphire bl....10.00

Sunderland Lustre

Sunderland lustre was made by various potters in the Sunderland district of England during the 18th and 19th centuries. It is characterized by a splashed-on application of the pink lustre, which results in an effect sometimes referred to as the 'cloud' pattern. Some pieces are transfer printed with scenes, ships, florals, or portraits.

When no condition is indicated, the items listed below are assumed to be in undamaged condition.

Bowl, house pattern, 6" dia....80.00
Bowl, soup; Moses in Bullrushes, 7¾"....32.00
Creamer, scenic, 2½"....45.00
Cup & saucer, Moses in Bullrushes, bl clouds, wishbone hdl....55.00
Goblet, cloud pattern....125.00
Mug, cloud pattern, 3"....65.00
Mug, pink w/sea shells, 2 hdls....62.50
Pitcher, Mariner's Compass/Sailor's Tear, 6"....190.00
Pitcher, Masonic motif, blk transfer w/mc, hairlines, 7"....200.00
Pitcher, motto/poem, 'Success...Volunteers, Choice'....185.00
Plaque, Express, RR transfer, 8x9"....225.00
Plaque, Rev John Wesley, Best of All God is With Us, 7"....225.00
Plate, cloud pattern, 7"....25.00
Plate, Dickens' Days, rope trim, 8"....35.00
Salt cellar, ftd, minor wear/scratches, 2x3"....65.00

Swastika Keramos

Swastika Keramos was a line of artware made by the Owens China Co., of Minerva, Ohio, around 1902-1904. It is characterized either by a 'coralene' type of decoration, similar to the Opalesce line made by the J.B. Owens Pottery Company of Zanesville, or by the application of metallic lusters, usually in simple designs. Shapes are often plain, and handles squarish and rather thick, suggestive of the Arts and Crafts style.

When no condition is indicated, the items listed below are assumed to be in mint condition.

Vase, coralene decor, bullet form w/4 sq hdls, 7½"....125.00
Vase, gold w/lg red lustre flower, 7½"....180.00
Vase, gr matt, 4"....40.00

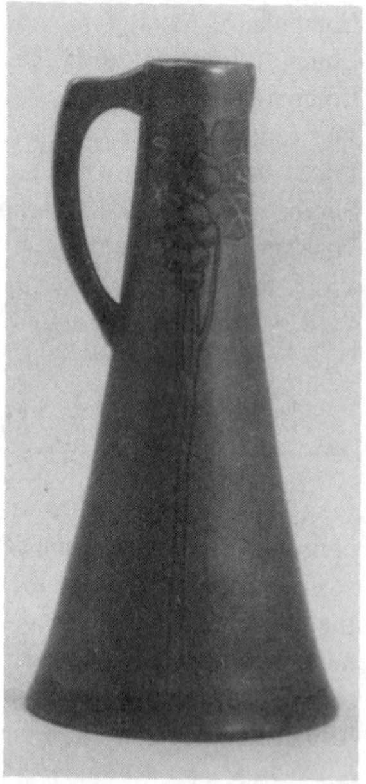

Ewer vase, gold with olive green grapes and copper leaves, 10¾", $195.00.

Syracuse

Syracuse was a line of fine dinnerware which was made for nearly a century by the Onondaga Pottery Company of Syracuse, New York. Collectors of American dinnerware are focusing their attention on reassembling some of their many lovely patterns. In 1966, the firm became officially known as the Syracuse China Company in order to better identify with the name of their popular chinaware. By 1971, dinnerware geared for use in the home was discontinued, and the company turned to the manufacture of hotel, restaurant, and other types of commercial tableware.

When no condition is indicated, the items listed below are assumed to be in mint condition.

Plate, gentleman with table, 8¼", $35.00.

Bowl, salmon to gr, cream w/in, dtd, old mk, 4x9"....30.00
Clover, bowl, vegetable; rnd....15.00
Clover, creamer & sugar....18.00
Clover, plate, dinner....9.00
Clover, sauce dish....4.00
Coralbel, bowl, vegetable; rnd, 9"....35.00
Coralbel, pickle dish....23.00
Coralbel, plate, 9¾"....16.00
Plate, American Songbird, set of 8....100.00

Plate, Indian carrying canoe, Portage, Akron, O, 8″ 24.00
Plate, ship, wht, sgn The Viking, Meleor, pat 1908, 10⅛″ 38.00
Rose Marie, bowl, cereal 10.00
Rose Marie, cup & saucer 20.00
Rose Marie, plate, dinner 15.00

Syrups

When no condition is indicated, the items listed below are assumed to be in mint condition.

Alba, milk glass w/decor 52.00
Apollo, pink, pewter top, McKee 68.00
Artichoke, clear frosted, orig lid 70.00
Barbarry, applied hdl 85.00
Beaded Hexagon, plain, milk glass 45.00
Bellflower, orig tin top, very rare 550.00
Block, gold top, pewter neck ring, dtd Apr 1867 inside lid 110.00
Block, ruby 140.00
Block & Bull's Eye, pat March 20, 1883, 7″ 45.00
Catherine Anne, milk glass, orig lid 45.00
Coin Spot, bl opal 100.00
Columbian Coin, frosted, pat date in lid 160.00
Cordova, w/rare bulbous lid 60.00
Crystal, pewter lid/hdl/base 150.00
Daisy & Button, amber, dbl panel, pewter top 45.00
Daisy & Fern, bl opal, orig lid 120.00
Diamond & Sunburst, applied hdl 45.00
Fern, clear opal 85.00
Fern etching, amber hdl, dolphin lid support, Pat 1872 .... 70.00
Forget-Me-Not, milk glass, Challinor 75.00
Guttate, pink cased, 7x4¼″ 145.00
Hercules Pillar, amber 115.00
Hercules Pillar, bl, w/orig lid 145.00
Hercules Pillar, sapphire bl 135.00
Hobnail, clear opal, Hobb's 110.00
Interlocking Hearts 42.50
Lacy Floral, milk glass 50.00
Leaf Mold, glossy vaseline spatter 295.00
Leaf Umbrella, bl satin 325.00
Leaning Pillars, amber 85.00

Rubena, optic panel, brass top, 6″, $225.00.

Medallion Sprig, amethyst to clear 225.00
Midwest Pomona 80.00
Netted Oak, milk glass, decor 70.00
Pansy, milk glass, bulge bottom 65.00
Pennsylvania, clear 35.00
Pine Cone 295.00
Polka Dot, bl 180.00
Ribbed, opaque bl, applied hdl, pewter top, 6¾″ 205.00
Rubena, threaded, Northwood 250.00
Silverplate, eng/emb birds/flowers, tankard type/Meriden, 4″ 45.00
Silverplate, ladies' heads, engravings, Meriden, 8″ 75.00
Stippled Dahlia, milk glass 56.00
Thompson's 77, Truncated Cube, ruby-flashed top 50.00
Torquay, milk glass w/yel decor 95.00
Valencia Waffle, amber 125.00

Taylor, Smith and Taylor

The firm of Taylor, Smith & Taylor operated in Newell, West Virginia, from 1899 until 1981. Some of their most popular products with today's collectors are their dinnerware lines from the '30s and '40s. See also Lu Ray Pastels and Vistosa

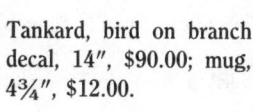

Tankard, bird on branch decal, 14″, $90.00; mug, 4¾″, $12.00.

Pitcher, portrait of red-garbed monk, Latona China, ½-gal 95.00
Pitcher, tankard; dog decals, +4 matching mugs 150.00

Tea Caddies

Because tea was once regarded as a precious commodity, special boxes called caddies were used to store the tea leaves. They were made from various materials: porcelain, carved and inlaid woods, and metals ranging from painted tin or tole to engraved silver.

When no condition is indicated, the items listed below are assumed to be in excellent condition.

Fruitwood, apple form, early Geo III, 7″ 950.00
Lacquer, red & gold floral on blk, Russian, 8″ dia 50.00
Mahog on pine, line inlay/ball ft/brass escutcheon, 5x6x8″ 200.00
Mahog veneer on oak, brass bail/escutcheon, rst, 5x9½″ 155.00
Paris porcelain, La Courtille factory, ca 1800 .... 200.00
Peking porcelain, turq w/pink flowers, 4½x6″ 55.00
Sheffield, canister w/ribbed lid, sgn Mappin & Webb 85.00

Gilded quillwork panels and lid with inlaid wooden dividers, cobalt blue glass almond-shaped insert under escutcheon, minor wear and damage, 6½", $325.00.

Silver, chased acanthus leaves base, London/1904, 4", EX......65.00
Silverplate, emb leaves/scrolls, knob finial, mk Wilcox..........45.00
Walnut, 2 compartments/beveled knob covers, lid/key, 4½".....150.00

Tea Leaf Ironstone

Tea Leaf Ironstone became popular in the 1880s, when the American middle class housewives became bored with the plain white Stone china that English potters had been exporting to this country for nearly a century. The original design has been credited to Anthony Shaw of Longport, who decorated the plain Ironstone with a hand-painted copper lustre design of bands and leaves. Originally known as Lustre Band and Sprig, the pattern has since come to be known as Tea Leaf Lustre. It was produced with minor variations by many different firms, both in England and the United States. By the early 1900s, it had become so commonplace that it had lost much of its appeal.

When no condition is indicated, the items listed below are assumed to be in mint condition.

Baker, no lid, Furnival....30.00
Bone dish....55.00
Bowl, ind vegetable; rectangular....22.00
Bowl, mush; Meakin....45.00
Bowl, oblong, 5¼x7½"....35.00
Bowl, soup; Burgess, 9"....26.00
Bowl, soup; pink lustre, Davenport....30.00
Bowl, sq, Meakin, 6½"....18.00
Bowl, sq, Meakin, 8⅜"....24.00
Bowl, vegetable; sq, w/lid, Bamboo....75.00
Bowl, vegetable; w/lid, Meakin....75.00
Bowl, vegetable; w/lid, Wedgwood....85.00
Butter dish, dbl groove, w/insert, w/lid, Meakin....125.00
Butter dish, Mellor Taylor....145.00
Butter dish, sq, w/lid, Wedgwood....125.00
Butter dish, w/drain, w/lid, Shaw....125.00
Butter pat, Mellor Taylor....14.00
Butter pat, rnd....14.00
Butter pat, sq, Meakin....14.00
Chamber pot, Fish Hook, Meakin, w/lid....150.00
Coffee pot, Fish Hook....125.00
Coffee pot, Wilkinson....125.00
Coffee pot, Wilkinson Hulme....130.00
Compote, ftd, Shaw....300.00
Creamer, Alcock....125.00
Creamer, Bamboo, Alfred Meakin....125.00
Creamer, bulbous, Wedgwood....95.00
Creamer, rectangular, 5"....125.00
Creamer & sugar, Wilkinson....195.00
Cup & saucer, Bamboo, Meakin....65.00
Cup & saucer, handleless....75.00
Cup & saucer, Lily-of-the-Valley, Meakin....100.00
Cup & saucer, Mellor-Taylor....65.00
Cup & saucer, Wedgwood....60.00
Doughnut stand, Shaw....325.00
Gravy boat, gold lustre, w/undertray, Bishop & Stonier....75.00
Pitcher, Alcock, 8⅜"....125.00
Pitcher, Bamboo, 7⅛"....150.00
Pitcher, Bamboo, 8"....185.00
Pitcher, Bamboo, 9"....195.00
Pitcher, Bishop & Stonier, 12"....75.00
Pitcher, Burgess, 7"....125.00
Pitcher, Johnson Bros, water sz, lg....185.00
Pitcher, Meakin, Chelsea, milk sz, sm....135.00
Pitcher, rectangular, 7"....115.00
Pitcher, w/bowl, wash set, Wilkinson....325.00
Plate, cake; Fish Hook, Meakin....55.00
Plate, dbl band, Davenport, 6½"....26.00
Plate, Meakin, 7¾"....12.00
Plate, Pepper Leaf, Elsmore-Forster, 7½"....20.00
Plate, 10"....26.00
Plate, 7¾"....15.00
Platter, Chinese shape, oval, Shaw, 14"....50.00
Platter, Meakin, 12⅞x9⅜"....35.00
Platter, Mellor, 14x11"....55.00
Platter, 15⅝x11⅜"....65.00
Platter, 17¾x13¾"....65.00
Sauce, Meakin, sq....18.00
Sauce, sq, Bishop Powell, 4½"....12.00
Shaving mug, Chinese shape, Shaw....145.00
Shaving mug, Meakin....125.00
Shaving mug, w/berries, Shaw....125.00
Soap dish, lustre, w/insert & lid, Meakin....125.00
Soap dish, no drain, w/lid, Powell & Bishop....60.00
Sugar bowl, Bamboo....55.00
Sugar bowl, bulbous, Wilkinson....55.00
Sugar bowl, Dbl Groove, Meakin, w/lid....60.00
Sugar bowl, Lily-of-the-Valley....175.00
Sugar bowl, Powell-Bishop....35.00
Tea waste bowl....75.00
Tea waste bowl, Lily-of-the-Valley....95.00
Teapot, Alfred Meakin....85.00
Teapot, Davenport, 9"....125.00
Teapot, Empress, Adams....110.00
Teapot, Meakin....145.00
Teapot, Morning Glory, Elsmore-Forster....195.00
Toothbrush holder....125.00
Toothbrush holder, Wedgwood....125.00
Tray, bread; open hdls, Shaw....75.00
Tureen, sauce; Bamboo, w/lid & ladle, Meakin, 3-pc....300.00

Tureen with lid, ladle and undertray, 4" x 6" x 4½", $350.00.

Tureen, sauce; Cable, w/lid, Shaw, 3-pc 195.00
Tureen, sauce; Grindley, 4-pc 350.00
Tureen, sauce; H Burgess, lt crazing, 13½x9" 295.00
Tureen, sauce; w/ladle, Alfred Meakin, 4-pc 375.00
Tureen, sauce; w/lid, Meakin 95.00
Tureen, soup; w/lid, underplate & ladle, Bamboo, Meakin 795.00
Wash basin & pitcher, Meakin, 2-pc, 15½" 350.00

Teco

Teco artware was made by the American Terra Cotta and Ceramic Company, located near Chicago, Illinois. The firm was established in 1886 and until 1901 produced only brick, sewer tile, and other redware. Their early glaze was inspired by the matt green made popular by Grueby. 'Teco green' was made for nearly ten years. It was similar to Grueby's, yet with a subtle silver-gray cast.

The company was one of the first in the United States to perfect a true crystalline glaze. The only decoration used was through the modeling and glazing techniques; no hand painting was attempted. Favored motifs were naturalistic leaves and flowers.

The company broadened their lines to include garden pottery, faience tiles and panels. New matt glazes--browns, yellows, blue, and rose--were added to the green in 1910. By 1922, the artware lines were discontinued; the company closed in 1920.

Values are dictated by size and glaze color--colors other than green bring the higher prices. High glaze is seldom seen and expensive.

Teco is usually marked with a vertical impressed device comprised of a large 'T' to the left of the remaining three letters.

When no condition is indicated, the items listed below are assumed to be in mint condition.

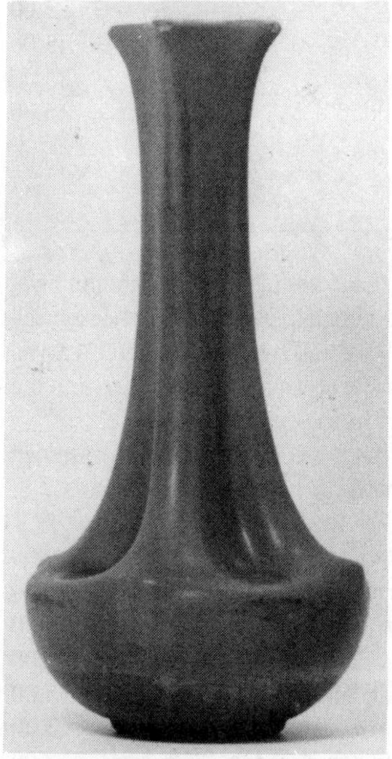

Vase, quatralobed body, matt green glaze, 17", $275.00.

Ash tray, eagle 125.00
Bowl, holly relief, matt gr, 2½x9" 100.00
Candlestick, matt gr, 2½", pr 175.00
Candlestick, mustard, curved hdl 55.00
Ewer, matt gr, 4" 60.00
Mug, leaves relief, matt gr, 5¾" 200.00
Pitcher, matt gr, 4½" 30.00
Pitcher, speckled gray, serpentine base-divided hdl, 9" 160.00
Vase, angle ear hdls on tall cylinder, sgn, 11" 175.00
Vase, blk w/gr highlights, 12" 575.00
Vase, bud; matt gr, 5½" 75.00
Vase, dk matt gr, bulbous, ring collar, 4" 95.00
Vase, matt bl w/silver 'sparkle,' swelled cylinder, 8" 265.00
Vase, matt gr, bulbous, incurvate, 5" 125.00
Vase, matt gr, bulbous, 4-corner base, 7½x8" 375.00
Vase, matt gr, buttressed, dbl gourd, sgn, 6½x5½" 250.00
Vase, matt gr, hdls, 10¾" 150.00
Vase, matt gr, waisted neck w/flat sq hdls, 8½" 165.00
Vase, matt gr, 4 rim-to-base conforming angle hdls, 7" 210.00
Vase, matt gr, 5" 65.00
Vase, matt gr, 8½x5¼" 100.00
Vase, matt gr w/gray, 4 long S-hdls on slim neck, 12" 385.00
Vase, matt gr w/yel flecks, sq rim/base projections, 5½" 120.00
Vase, med matt gr, shouldered form, sm opening, 2" 80.00
Wall pocket, emb flowers, matt gr 195.00

Teddy Bear Collectibles

The story of Teddy Roosevelt's encounter with the bear cub has been oft recounted--with varying degrees of accuracy--so it will suffice to say that it was as a result of this incident in 1902 that the Teddy Bear got his name.

These appealing little creatures are enjoying renewed popularity with collectors today. To one who has not yet succumbed to their obvious charms, one bear seems to look very much like another. How to tell the older ones? Look for long snouts, jointed limbs, large feet and felt paws, long curving arms, and glass or shoe-button eyes. Most old bears have a humped back and are made of mohair stuffed with straw or excelsior. Cute expressions, original clothes, a nice personality, and, of course, good condition add to their value.

When no condition is indicated, the items listed below are assumed to be in excellent condition.

Fully jointed Teddy, glass eyes, plush coat, hand-sewn nose and mouth, felt paws, early 1900s, 23½", $450.00.

Bears

BMC Bruins, orig label, 1907, EX, pr 1,500.00
Celluloid head, straw stuffed, 3" 45.00
Celluloid head, straw stuffed, 5" 65.00
Clown, fully jtd, straw stuffed, ca 1929, 14" 150.00

Cosy, w/tag & button, 8″ 85.00
Fully jtd, bl plush/straw stuffed/glass eyes, 1920s, 15″ 185.00
Fully jtd, curly mohair, glass eyes, 39″, VG 200.00
Fully jtd, lamb's wool, stitched features, expressive, 10″ 125.00
Fully jtd, Merrythought label, 15″ 125.00
Fully jtd, mohair, button eyes, orig felt pads, 12″, G 185.00
Fully jtd, mohair, glass eyes, 6″ 45.00
Fully jtd, mohair, rpl felt pads, early, 30″, EX 380.00
Fully jtd, mohair, stick pin eyes/felt paws, 1910, 28″, EX 425.00
Fully jtd, mohair, straw stuffed, ca 1915, 36″ 950.00
Fully jtd, mohair, straw stuffed, lg ears/G hump, 30″, EX 410.00
Fully jtd, mohair, straw stuffed, orig pads, 22″ 265.00
Fully jtd, mohair, straw stuffed, very long arms, 20″, EX 160.00
Fully jtd, mohair, straw stuffed, 1900s, 14″, EX 225.00
Fully jtd, mohair, straw stuffed, 1940s, 12½″ 85.00
Fully jtd, mohair, wht, straw stuffed, 1920s, 12″, VG 120.00
Fully jtd, plush, straw stuffed, bk hump, early, 18″, EX 300.00
Fully jtd, plush, straw stuffed, early, 24″, EX 270.00
Fully jtd, plush, 1940s, 22″ 85.00
Fully jtd, sheepskin, 14″ 90.00
Fully jtd, straw stuffed, lt gr novelty type, 1920s, loved 75.00
Fully jtd, w/tag 'Character,' 1930, 13″ 95.00
Fully jtd, wool w/brn felt paws/ft, shank eyes, 14″ 85.00
Fully jtd, yel mohair, 1920s, 22″, EX 225.00
Growler, fully jtd, gold mohair, hump bk, button eyes, 20″ 500.00
Growler, fully jtd, mohair, felt paws, lg, 36″, EX 650.00
Lead, 1″ 18.00
Mechanical, head/paws/mouth moves, 9″, VG 220.00
Mohair, cinnamon color, 1930, 16″ 225.00
Mohair, pointed nose/head center seam, English, 1930s, 18″ . . . 175.00
Schuco, bl knit suit, gray, 12″ 78.00
Schuco, tumbling, sm 195.00
Traveling Roosevelt Bears, Seymour Eton, set of 8 . . . . 325.00
Velvet, 3″ 35.00
World's Fair, 1903 . . . . 2,000.00

Miscellaneous

Bank, Teddy figural, CI 125.00
Blocks, paper covered, Three Bears motif 500.00
Book, Betty & Teddy, mc 18.00
Book, Busy Bears, 8 lg color prints, Schoonmaker, worn 65.00
Book, Little Johnny & the Teddy Bears, comic, color, 1907 . . . . 85.00
Book, Mother Goose's Teddy Bears, 1907 . . . . 85.00
Book, Mr Cinnamon Bear, 1909 . . . . 30.00
Book, Roosevelt Bears Abroad, 16 color prints, 1907 . . . . 90.00
Book, Teddy Bear Book, 16 color illus+b/w, 1916 . . . . 27.00
Book, Teddy Bears Come to Life, 1907 . . . . 28.00
Book, The Teddy Bear That Prowled at Night, 1924 . . . . 24.00
Bottle, baby's; clear w/emb Teddy bear 20.00
Buttonhook, sterling, full figure Teddy atop, 8½″, VG 80.00
Dish, child's; Teddy bear decor, china 100.00
Egg cup, Teddy decals, 3 views, 2½″ 15.00
Flour sack, Bewley's Milk, Teddy bear doll shape 45.00
Game, cloth Teddy bears, 1906 . . . . 50.00
Game, Who Can Kill Teddy Bear, uncut 175.00
Hankie, w/bear, embroidery 10.00
Label, Lanz Products, w/bears 22.00
Muff, pink, w/teddy, 1930s, 9″ 75.00
Mug, Roosevelt Bear & Buddy Tucker, china 20.00
Mug, SP, ftd 25.00
Ornament, Teddy bear, straw stuffed, celluloid head, 5″ 22.00
Paper doll, Horseman Teddy Bear, 10½″ 75.00
Paper doll, w/5 outfits & hats, Selchow & Righter 250.00

Toboggan Teddies, white Castile molded soaps, red flannel scarves, in cardboard toboggan sleigh, 7″ long, $95.00.

Photo, standing girl, Teddy alongside, studio sgn, 20x16″ 75.00
Pin, figural Teddy, pearl tummy/rhinestone eyes, '50s, 1½″ 22.00
Plate, bears digging Panama Canal, verse, Roosevelt, 6¼″ 48.00
Plate, bears reading & smoking pipe, emb milk glass 90.00
Plate, bears under umbrella, wht metal, orig pnt, 2¾″ 60.00
Plate, dancing bears, Molly Coddles verse, Roosevelt, 7″ 48.00
Plate, Roosevelt Bears play tennis, advertising 60.00
Plate, wall hanging; milk glass, Roosevelt bears 30.00
Postcard, Busy Bears, color, Ullman Co, M, set of 12 . . . . 75.00
Postcard, 7 days of week, w/Teddy bears, set of 7 . . . . 120.00
Sand pail, Teddy bear, tin, Chein 22.00
Tape measure, stuffed Teddy bear, 3″ 45.00
Toothbrush holder, Teddy bear, German 35.00
Trade card, figural Teddy, 1908 calendar 15.00

Telephones

Since Alexander Graham Bell's first successful telephone communication, the phone itself has undergone a complete evolution in style as well as efficiency. Early models, especially those wall types with ornately carved oak boxes, are of special interest to collectors. Also of value are the candlestick phones from the early part of the century.

When no condition is indicated, the items listed below are assumed to be in excellent condition, all original with no reproduction parts.

American Bell, candlestick, 1915 . . . . 100.00
AT&T, candlestick, pat 1892 on transmitter cup, 1904 . . . . 125.00
Automatic Electric, pay phone, 3 slot, 1940s 75.00
Coach Co, oak, brass bells 95.00
Danish, French horn desk-type, orig gr silk cords, 1913 . . . . 55.00
Desk-type, crank on side, 1920s 45.00
Green Telephone & Electric, oak wall/cathedral top, 25″ 250.00
Kellogg, candlestick, oak Magneto box 125.00
Kellogg, wall phone 175.00
Monarch, fiddle back wall phone, oak 200.00
North Electric, wall phone, oak, Cleveland, OH 200.00
Railroad, candlestick, w/headset 50.00
Stromberg Carlson, candlestick, bell box, nickel trim, 1909 . . . . 125.00
Stromberg Carlson, wall phone, 2-box, oak 285.00
Sumpter Telephone Co, wall phone w/receiver, oak 195.00
Wall, metal, hand-held ear pc, dial, mouthpc above 75.00

Western Electric, cradle phone, oval base, 1920s-1930s........45.00
Western Electric, dial candlestick, 1919....................150.00
Western Electric, intercom wall phone, oak, 1912.............55.00
Western Electric, wall phone, oak.........................225.00

Teplitz

Teplitz, in Czechoslovakia, was an active art pottery center at the turn of the century. The Amphora Pottery Works was only one of the firms that operated there. (See Amphora.) Art Nouveau and Art Deco styling was favored, and much of the ware was hand decorated, with the primary emphasis on vases and figurines. Items listed here are marked 'Teplitz' or 'Turn,' a nearby city.

When no condition is indicated, the items listed below are assumed to be in mint condition.

Bust of lady, marked Made in Austria, 11½″, $395.00.

Ewer, yel flowers/leaves on wht, gold band/trim/hdl, 11¼″......195.00
Figurine, lady, gold/bronze skin, Nouveau, Doebrieh, 15″......650.00
Figurine, Nouveau lady holds grapes, ¾-figure, 15″..........595.00
Humidor, portrait decor...............................125.00
Pitcher, warrior on horseback, 4″..........................95.00
Vase, bl poppy, 4-hdl, red crown mk, Turn, 7½″, pr.........175.00
Vase, blown-out, Colonial lady w/parasol, 9½″...............185.00
Vase, floral/leaves on tan/gold, EW mk, 2-hdl, 1880s, 16″.....450.00
Vase, grapes on bl irid, 12″..............................190.00
Vase, lady's head/pansies, Art Nouveau/Crown Oakware, 12½″...60.00
Vase, mermaid in relief, mc florals, brn/gold, sgn, 19x6″.......595.00
Vase, nude maiden emerges from lilies, 17″.................500.00
Vase, pate-sur-pate seaweed/orange leaves on bl, hdls, 5″.......65.00
Vase, pendant wisteria, gr/bl/rose, sgn, 19″.................600.00
Vase, reticulated, mushroom decor, 11″....................450.00
Vase, roses w/gold tracing on yel-gr, HP, hdls, 10½″..........175.00
Vase, wht floral on cobalt, narrow neck, rnd, hdl, 10″........135.00
Vase, woman carrying water, HP on bronze, 5½″...............65.00

Terra Cotta

Terra cotta is a type of earthenware or clay used for statuary, architectural facings, or domestic articles. It is unglazed, baked to durable hardness, and is characterized by the color of the body, which may range from brick red to buff.

When no condition is indicated, the items listed below are assumed to be in mint condition.

Bust, crying child w/fly on nose, GD Paris Depose, 6″.........80.00
Bust, Diana, Samson Bros, Am Art Clay Works, 1892, 11″....550.00
Figure, cherub, floral apron, gilt wood base, 8″, pr...........110.00
Figure, Colonial girl w/fan, sgraffito lace/etc, 11″.............135.00
Figure, gypsy musician, 11″, pr...........................250.00
Figure, owl, detailed, Evans & Howard, St Louis, 28″, EX.....350.00
Garden eagle, Italian, 20th C, 29″, pr......................400.00
Sculpture, represents oil industry, Waylande Gregory, 27″.....500.00
Stein, applied iris, Cane Ware, rare, 1800-1810...............75.00

Thermometers

Though the collecting of advertising thermometers has been popular for years, only recently have decorative thermometers come into their own as bona fide items of interest and value.

Indoor and outdoor decorative models have been manufactured for hundreds of years, yet their relative scarcity enhances their value and interest for the collector. Most American thermometers manufactured early in the 20th century were produced by Taylor (Tycos), and today their thermometers remain the most plentiful on the market. They also serve as the price standards for most historical thermometers.

Insofar as sheer beauty, uniqueness, and scientific accuracy, decorative thermometers are far superior to the ordinary and inexpensive versions which carry advertising. Decorative thermometers run the gamut from plain tin household varieties to the highly ornate creations of Tiffany and Bradley and Hubbard. They have been manufactured from nearly every conceivable material--oak, sterling, brass, and glass being the favorites--and have tested the artistry and technical skills of some of America's finest craftsmen. Ornamental models can be found in free-hanging, wall-mounted, or desk/mantle versions.

Thermometer prices, for the most part, have hovered around the $25 level for the last five years, although those with mercury tubes, figural designs, or in short supply have fetched somewhat higher prices. Some price changes showed dramatic shifts downward as a number of thermometers considered to be quite rare appeared on the market in surprising numbers. Items with damaged or missing parts bring greatly reduced prices.

Virtually all American-made thermometers available today as collector items were made between 1875 and 1940. The Golden Age of decoratives ended in the early 1940s as modern manufacturing processes and materials robbed them of their natural distinctiveness. European thermometers, while of comparable beauty and craftsmanship, have not yet migrated to this country in any great numbers; those produced in America still dominate the buy/sell market.

When no condition is indicated, the items listed below are assumed to be in mint condition.

Key:

mrc—mercury	sc—scales
pmc—permacolor	stl—stainless

A Heiligman, rosewood bk, wht emb sc, mrc, 10x1⅜″..........37.00
AB Co, pot metal Greek child, brass sc, pmc, 4½″............35.00
Alexander, folding; Fahrenheit & Reamur scales, mrc, 1850s....54.00
American Thermometer, outdoor; steel & porc, mrc...........25.00
Bargess Reversible Box, brass sc, oak case, mrc, 5½″..........30.00
Bradley & Hubbard, bronze Colonial figure/scale, mrc, 11″.....30.00
Bradley & Hubbard, eng gold plate, gunflint, mrc, 15″.........60.00
Bradley & Hubbard, scroll bk, steel/cb, Mensh, mrc, 8″.......225.00
Brannan, brass case, F&C stl scales, mrc, 1932...............38.00
C Wilder Co, bear & billboard figural brass, mrc, 6½″.........45.00

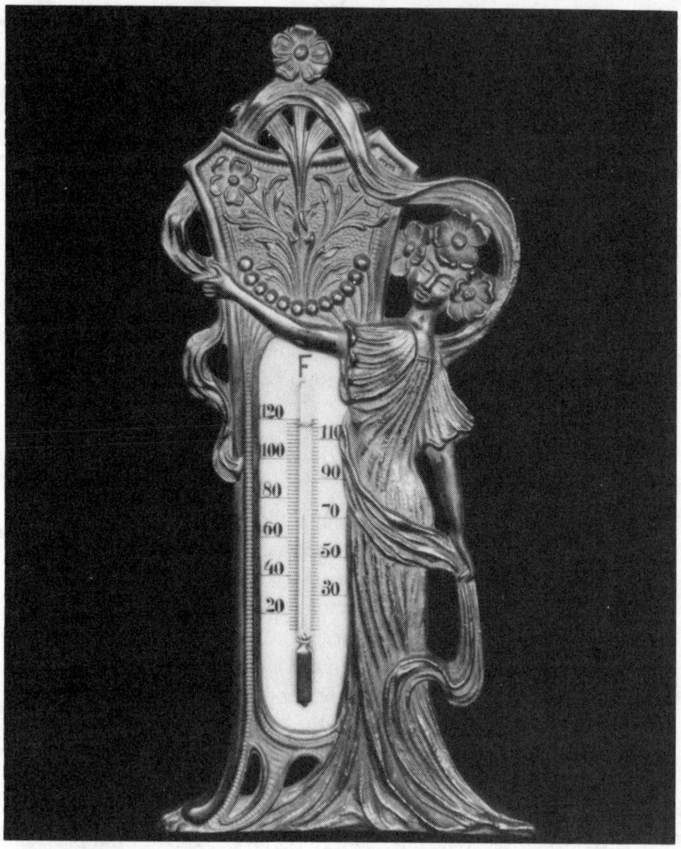

Westminster desk model, bronze Art Nouveau goddess, mercury in bulb, ivory scale, ca 1910, 10″ x 4″, $70.00.

C Wilder Co, Buffalo Incubator Co, mrc, hanging model........85.00
CE Large, hanging; Cottage Barometer, 2-tube, 1918..........26.00
CE Large, kitchen; The Modern Thermometer, tin, pmc.......150.00
Chester, desk; stl scale, sterling bezel, mrc, 2x6″..............95.00
Clark, desk; ivory ped, crown, mrc, 1904, 7″.................48.00
Cloister, inkwell, stl bk & base w/side angels, 1901..........1,050.00
Compton, SP flowers/butterflies, on ped, mrc, 4½″............24.00
Desk-type, carved walrus tusk, 2-tier disc base, 1860, 9″.......220.00
E Berman Co, desk; brass/filigree/top scrollwork, mrc, 8″.......55.00
Fahrenheit, indoor, oak w/brass sc, pmc, 1889, 7″............45.00
Freeborn, desk; bronze w/lead decor/brass scale, mrc, 8″.......39.00
G Barnes, oak fold-out box, plastic scale, mrc, 2½″............75.00
G Cooper, desk; bell shape w/cupola, sterling, dial, 2x3″.......40.00
Golub, hanging; mahog/brass bulb cap/lg sc/red spirit, 9x2″.....50.00
H Lauramark, hanging; gold stipple on boxwood, 0-120, mrc....60.00
Helmut, desk; scroll edge, stl & plastic, easel ped, 6″..........30.00
Hiergelsell Bros, cabinet/oak bk, bl liquid, indoor, #159........40.00
Hiergelsell Bros, spiral tube cabinet, red liquid, #160..........70.00
Hineberg, hanging; curved ivory sc, thin bulb, mrc, 1923.......22.00
Hohmann Maurer Co, steel F&C scales & bk, mrc, 12″........27.00
Hygro Autometer, 2 magnifying tubes w/stand, mrc, #T5558.....45.00
Jeseth Ltd, desk; Mercury figure w/base filigree, mrc, 7″........63.00
LC Tower, Weather Prognosticator, cherry/brass sc, mrc........18.00
Moeller Instrument Co, metal w/brass sc, pmc, 12″............30.00
Negretti & Zambra, desk; wht bakelite/mahog/blk spirit, 8x3½″..68.00
Orchard, iron case, brass face, w/glass intact, 14″.............35.00
Pace Mfg Co, cottage barometer, storm glass, pmc, 8½″........25.00
Phila Therm Co, hygrometer; brass sc, rotating bezel, 1928.....40.00
Reau, desk; ornate blk bronze, wood sc, C&F, mrc............57.00
Reaumar, hanging; French, 2-bulb, wood, ca 1795, 14x2″......95.00
S Mitzutani, alabaster ped, top candle figural, mrc, 15″.......120.00
Samuel Sloan & Co, boiler, blk steel Deco top, pmc..........650.00
Short & Mason, recording drum; copper case, 1910...........78.00
Souche, desk; alabaster ped, paper sc inset, mrc, 8x2½″........75.00
Standard Co, for Fairbanks & Co, rnd, brass case, 1886, 7″....70.00
Standard Co, hanging; ivory scale, flower pattern, mrc, 9″......25.00
Standard Co, hanging; rnd, brass rim, -40 to 150, dial.........35.00
Taylor, Comfortmeter, brass sc on gr bk, pmc, 7″.............23.00
Taylor, hanging; pnt wood, red spirit, 6x24″.................20.00
Taylor Bros, hanging; ornate wood bk, brass sc, 10x7″.........21.00
Tiffany, desk; horoscope, bronze, mrc, 1907, 4x7″............86.00
Tycos, incubator hygrometer; glass reservoir, 4x4″.............16.00
Tycos, maxi/minimum, japanned tin/brass, mrc, #T5452, 8″.....25.00
Vogue, desk; Victorian, dial, gr, 1931.......................12.00
W Pratt, desk; wood inlays, ivory sc, mrc, 1900, 6″...........63.00
Wilder, desk; ped, wood, brass sc, mrc, 1923.................38.00

Threaded Glass

Threaded glass has been made both here and abroad since the 1870s. The procedure was done entirely by hand until about 1876 when a machine was developed to apply the fine threads to the glass automatically.

Bowl, vaseline, ruffled, ground pontil, 5½″...................28.00
Compote, clear w/cranberry, att Sandwich, 6½x9″............500.00
Cracker jar, clear, silver bail & collar.......................45.00
Plate, cranberry, ground pontil, Victorian, 8¾″...............45.00
Sweetmeat, emerald gr w/random irid threading, SP top/hdl.....70.00
Sweetmeat, vaseline trim, ruffled, SP basket fr, 6¼″..........115.00
Tumbler, clear rigaree, gr random threading..................60.00

Tiffany

Louis Comfort Tiffany was born in 1848, to Charles Lewis and Harriet Young Tiffany of New York. By the time he was eighteen, his father's small dry goods and stationery store had grown and developed into the world-reknowned Tiffany and Company.

Preferring the study of art to joining his father in the family business, Louis spent the next six years under the tutelage of noted artists. He returned to America in 1870, and until 1875 painted canvases that focused on European and North African scenes. Deciding the more lucrative approach was in the application of industrial arts and crafts, he opened a decorating studio called Louis C. Tiffany and Co., Associated Artists. He began seriously experimenting with glass, and eschewing traditionally painted-on details, he instead learned to produce glass with qualities that could suggest natural textures and effects. His experiments broadened and he soon concentrated his efforts on vases, bowls, etc., that came to be considered the highest achievements of the art. Peacock feathers, leaves and vines, flowers and abstracts were developed within the plane of the glass as it was blown. Opalescent and metallic lustres were combined with transparent color to produce stunning effects. Tiffany called his glass Favrile, meaning handmade.

In 1900 he established Tiffany Studios and turned his attention full time to producing art glass, leaded glass lamp shades, and household wares with metal components. He also designed a complete line of jewelry which was sold through his father's store. He became proficiently accomplished in silver work and produced such articles as hand mirrors embellished with peacock feather designs set with gems, and candlesticks with Favrile glass inserts.

Tiffany's work exemplified the Art Nouveau style of design and decoration, and through his own flamboyant personality and business acumen he perpetrated his tastes onto the American market to the extent that his name became a household word. Tiffany Studios continued to prosper until the second decade of this century when due to changing tastes his influence began to diminish. By 1920 the company had closed.

Serial numbers were assigned to much of Tiffany's work, and letter prefixes indicated the year of manufacture: A-N for 1896-1900; P-Z for 1901-1905. After that the letter followed the numbers with A-N in use from 1906-1912; P-Z from 1913-1920. O-marked pieces were made especially for friends of relatives; X indicated pieces not made for sale.

When no condition is indicated, the items listed below are assumed to be in mint condition.

Glassware

Bowl, gold irid w/swirl rib, flared, 9½" 650.00
Bowl, gold w/purple highlights, ruffled, sgn, 9⅞" 650.00
Bowl, paperweight, petals, yel/brn-purple on pumpkin, 5½" ... 7,150.00
Bowl, peacock bl, paper label, sgn/#d, 7" 385.00
Bowl, uncarved agate, allover lozenges, bl on wht, 5" 4,000.00
Candlestick, gold Merovingian, lily pad base, #d, 20" 725.00
Candy dish, lav w/opal rays, scalloped rim, sgn, 1x8" dia 385.00
Champagne, Manhattan, gold irid, hollow stem, sgn, 7" 325.00
Compote, amber irid w/gr leaves/vines, dimpled stem, 9" 1,450.00
Compote, aqua irid, stretched rim, sgn, 5" 475.00
Compote, turq pastel, delicate shape, sgn/#d, 4½" 435.00
Compote, yel rim, feather in bowl/ft, twist stem, sgn, 7½" 725.00
Decanter, amber irid, pinch body/stick neck, w/12 liqueurs ... 2,750.00
Finger bowl, clear w/rose/gr lotus center, 7" underplate 2,000.00
Finger bowl, gold irid stretch, ruffled, sgn, w/7" plate 375.00
Liqueur, amber w/etched Vintage band, 4½", set of 12 .... 1,430.00
Mushroom, wht blossoms/gr stems w/in, bronze stand, 8½" ... 9,350.00
Pitcher, bl irid, corset shape, sgn, 4¼" 750.00
Plate, nut; amber irid, shallow center, scalloped, 3½" 55.00
Punch glass, gold, spreading hollow stem, sgn, 3½" 140.00
Salt, gold, ribbed, ped ft, sgn, 1½" 200.00
Salt, gold irid, bean pot shape, 2 hdls, sgn 185.00
Screen, table; yel w/bl & amber leaves, 4-panel, 9¾x17" 2,100.00
Sherbet, gold, Vintage, intaglio cut, sgn, 3½" 295.00
Sherbet, lt gr, opal top band, sgn #115, 3½" 275.00
Toothpick holder, gold, bulbous ½" base, flares, #1300 .... 350.00
Toothpick holder, gold, paper label, sgn, 2½" 325.00
Toothpick holder, gold, teardrops throughout, waisted 425.00
Toothpick holder, stripes in shades of gr/orange, sgn, 2" 300.00
Vase, amber irid, lobed form, 1910, 2½" 235.00
Vase, amber irid, silver-bl lappet band on feathering, 5" 1,000.00
Vase, amber irid w/amber/gr irid drapes, lobed body, 9½" 900.00
Vase, amber irid w/gr vines, leaves, intaglio, ovoid, 9" 1,760.00
Vase, amber irid w/zigzag bands in ochre/gr/purple, 5½" 1,150.00
Vase, bud; amber irid, fluted, lobed everted rim, ftd, 8" 650.00
Vase, cameo, iris on tooled orange, bk: scales, sgn Ex, 3" ... 5,500.00
Vase, cameo, leaves/vines at shoulder, green on yel, 6" 4,950.00
Vase, cameo, morning glory, med gr/purple on frost, 8¾" 4,125.00
Vase, cameo, spider mums, amber/wht/gr, #6532E, 9¾" 1,870.00
Vase, cameo, wht w/red/gr nasturtiums, 5¼" 3,000.00
Vase, cased yel w/amber/bl irid lappets on dk bl, 3¼" 1,600.00
Vase, cut w/narcissus/X-hatched, etched silver lip mt, 12" 1,375.00
Vase, Cypriote, amber irid w/gold trailings, dbl cone, 8" 935.00
Vase, Cypriote, pitted amber irid, sgn Ex 42, 3½" 2,860.00
Vase, Cypriote, swirled scrolls, silver-bl/brn on gr, 8½" 2,200.00
Vase, Cypriote, 3 panels on amber/bl irid scrolls, 7½" 4,000.00
Vase, dk bl irid w/band of silver-bl loops/bands, 2¾" 1,300.00
Vase, dk to silver bl, paneled, sgn, 6" 550.00
Vase, emerald w/waves in silver-bl, baluster, 4½" 1,500.00
Vase, feathers, amber on translucent ivory, baluster, 19" 1,500.00
Vase, feathers, gold on ribbed gr, opal neck, sgn, 7" 2,500.00
Vase, feathers, gold/gr on opal, sgn/#d, 2½" 950.00
Vase, feathers, gr/gold irid, teardrop w/rnd dome ft, 18" 1,200.00
Vase, feathers, silver-bl on brn/ochre, sgn, 5¾" 1,500.00

Vase, pulled feathers, green and gold, J1285, L.C. Tiffany, Favrile, 5¼", $895.00.

Vase, feathers, silver-bl on deep turq, blk rim, 1919, 11" 7,150.00
Vase, floriform, bl irid, sgn/#1017Q, 10½" 1,500.00
Vase, floriform, bl w/leaves/flowers, sgn/#d, 11" 1,350.00
Vase, floriform, feathers/gr on amber, ruffled, U4023, 14" 2,200.00
Vase, floriform, gold, ruffled, sgn, 11½" 1,650.00
Vase, floriform, gold, sgn, 9¾" 1,000.00
Vase, floriform, gold, short stem, sgn/#d, 3¾" 395.00
Vase, floriform, leafage, gr on opal ribbing, 15" 4,950.00
Vase, floriform, pearl/opal/thin gr leaves/deep U-form, 9" 1,500.00
Vase, floriform, transparent yel w/opal feathers, 11" 2,800.00
Vase, foliate devices w/in panels, clear, intaglio, 8¼" 1,320.00
Vase, gold irid, 6-sided, ped ft, sgn/#d, 8" 385.00
Vase, gold irid cylinder in bronze/enameled base, 16" 1,150.00
Vase, gold w/grn leaves at base, inverted trumpet, 8½" 750.00
Vase, gr to cobalt, flared, sgn/#d, 6¼x7" 550.00
Vase, gray/gr shades to tan/brn, upright tan/yel ribs, 2¾" 1,600.00
Vase, irid cylinder in silver bronze mt w/emb waves, 11" 725.00
Vase, ivory neck, silver-bl lappets & scrolls, bulbous, 4" 800.00
Vase, Lava, free-form, irregular blk/bl/mauve ground, 4¾" 3,850.00
Vase, leaves, wht on gr w/clear casing, irid w/in, '27, 9" 2,860.00
Vase, leaves & tendrils, gr & gold on opal, 8½" 2,500.00
Vase, lotus, intaglio carved, amber w/internal decor, 5½" 3,410.00
Vase, lt bl w/gr blossoms/red berries/mc confetti, 4¼" 3,200.00
Vase, lt gr base, pulled gold swirl decor top, sgn, 4¼" 950.00
Vase, lt pink, crystal ft, sgn, #d, 6" 385.00
Vase, maple leaf/vine, gold w/pink highlights, 9" 1,500.00
Vase, medial band of irid bl lappets/amber neck, #5226, 7" ... 4,800.00
Vase, millefiori leaves/blossoms, irid on bl-gr, sgn, 14" 4,400.00
Vase, millefiori leaves/vines, baluster shape, sgn, 6" 2,750.00
Vase, millefiori relief leaves, florettes throughout, 4¾" 2,750.00
Vase, millefiori/gr leaves on tan irid, dbl gourd, 11" 2,200.00
Vase, millefiori/hearts/vines, aqua, bulbous, sgn/#d, 5½" 2,750.00
Vase, paperweight, gr vines w/in clear, millefiori, 2½" 1,430.00
Vase, paperweight, leaves, olive/yel w/in amber, sgn, 5¾" 2,860.00
Vase, paperweight, poppies w/millefiori centers, 8⅜" 8,800.00
Vase, paperweight, reactive, sgn/#d, 5¼" 4,750.00
Vase, peacock feathers on dk red, bulbous, sgn, 3¼" 2,650.00
Vase, pearlized w/internal quilting, experimental, 3½" 1,100.00
Vase, pumpkin irid, yel w/in, baluster, 1892, sgn, 7¾" 3,300.00
Vase, red cased in yel, amber irid wash, ovoid, sgn, 2¾" 1,650.00
Vase, Tel el Amarna, silver scrolls, red w/blk neck, 6" 11,000.00
Vase, thin zipper bands of ochre/brn on gr/brn opaque, 3" ... 1,650.00
Vase, tomato-red irid, yel irid w/in, ovoid, 2¼" 1,760.00
Vase, trailings, amber irid on clear, opal w/in, Nash, 4" 1,430.00
Vase, trumpet; feather motif, Dore mt, artichoke knop, 14" ... 1,100.00

Vase, trumpet; gold irid, flared ft, 12″ 750.00
Vase, yel w/gr lappets thin neck, base w/irid scrolls, 12″ 800.00
Vase, zigzag band/feathering, yel w/opal stripes, 9″ 2,530.00
Wine, gold decorated, cut stem, 3½″ 750.00

Jewelry

Earrings, 18k bird wings, 8½ dwt 300.00
Pin, 18k maple leaf 140.00
Ring, man's, scarab, sterling 275.00

Lamps

Aladdin, cone on slim std, yel w/rows of gr scallops, 14″ 2,000.00
Arabian, dk bl lustre, 3 prunts atop & on stem, sgn, 14½″ 3,400.00
Base, bronze, coiled stringing, rnd leaf molded base, #358 .... 2,090.00
Base, bronze, paneled, swelling cylinder, domed base, #532 .... 1,760.00
Base, bronze, putto/bird finial, tripod w/paw ft, #576 .... 770.00
Base, glass/bronze, feathers/palmettes on gr-blk irid, 17″ 2,475.00
Bridge, feather bands, cased caramel; harp std w/3 ft, 54″ 2,090.00
Candle, gr/gold shade; gr base, correct insert, rare color 2,250.00
Candle, ruffle/stretched red/bl 5½″ shade; bronze std, 18″ 900.00
Candle, ruffled gold shade, insert & base, sgn, 14″ 1,500.00
Chandelier, brickwork, sharply conical, pierced cap, 23½″ 4,675.00
Chandelier, ldgl 25″ nasturtium trellis, irregular border 13,200.00
Chandelier, 3-row turtle-bk tile & ldgl, sgn, 18″ dia 11,000.00
Desk, dk patina, bronze harp base, sgn shade/base, 17″ 1,250.00
Desk, irid waves on cased ribbed caramel, 3-arm/5-ftd, 15″ 1,870.00
Desk, opal amber w/gr feathers bell shade; #499/S924 std 2,090.00
Floor, base only, cylindrical bamboo stalk w/roots, #10195 .... 6,600.00
Floor, ldgl 22″ brickwork shade; #379 std w/leafy base 8,800.00
Floor, ldgl 22½″ tulips shade; 4-ftd leaf mold std, 64″ 23,100.00
Lantern, 6-sided dbl cone w/tiles, jewels, sq std, 25″ 2,100.00
Lily, 18-light, amber irid; bronze lily-pad base, 20″ 21,000.00
Lily, 3 sm inverted shades, 1 upright, sgn, 30″ 625.00
Lily, 7-light, amber irid; base #385 w/lily pads, 21″ 9,350.00
Lily, 7-light, feathered opal shades; lily-pad base, 22″ 5,775.00
Shade, blk w/wht lining, no mk 400.00
Shade, ldgl dome w/acorn band, 24″ dia 4,500.00

Leaded glass tulip motif shade, pierced base blown with green glass, both pieces signed, shade diameter: 16½″, $6,600.00.

Shade, lt gr random feathers, flowerpot shape, 5″ 260.00
Shade, yel dome w/8 gr feathers, bronze fitting, 12″ 2,100.00
Table, caramel/irid waves, 14½″ shade; #30123 base, 19″ 2,200.00
Table, counter-balance, irid cased glass w/feathers, 15″ 1,980.00
Table, gold base/opal-clear std w/gr flame, Damascus shade 1,850.00
Table, ldgl #1162 dragonfly shade; simple #533 std, 23″ 7,150.00
Table, ldgl 12″ apple blossom shade; #9908 tiled base, 19″ 12,650.00
Table, ldgl 14″ brickwork dome; sgn/#1420 std, 19″ 3,700.00
Table, ldgl 14″ sgn bl turtle-bk tiles shade, sgn base 8,500.00
Table, ldgl 15″ cherry blossom shade; sgn/#507 std, 20″ 4,500.00
Table, ldgl 16″ acorn band shade; 4 strap ft/urn std, 21″ 2,750.00
Table, ldgl 16″ apple blossom sgn shade; sgn dore/base 10,500.00
Table, ldgl 16″ dragonfly shade; bulbous sgn/#2128 base 7,000.00
Table, ldgl 16″ rambling rose shade; openwork #28610 std 19,800.00
Table, ldgl 16″ tile band/brickwork shade; tiled std, 22″ 7,800.00
Table, ldgl 17″ poppy w/filigree shade; 3-prong #444 std 12,100.00
Table, ldgl 17″ woodbine shade; bulbous root-ft base, 19″ 6,325.00
Table, ldgl 18½″ clematis shade; 3-leg #440 std, 22″ 7,700.00
Table, ldgl 20″ black-eyed Susan shade; urn std w/leaves 16,500.00
Table, ldgl 20″ dragonfly shade; 4-ftd #538 std, 25″ 9,900.00
Table, ldgl 20″ Greek Key border shade; #D803 std, 25″ 6,875.00
Table, ldgl 20″ nasturtium shade; gradoon bun base std 16,500.00
Table, ldgl 20½″ poppy/filigree shade; #584 std, 25¼″ 23,100.00
Table, ldgl 21″ pendant laburnum shade; #529 Roman std 22,000.00
Table, ldgl 29″ peony shade; tree-trunk #355 std, 39″ 46,200.00
Table, lt gr 19″ favrile base w/peacock eyes, cloth shade 3,000.00

Metal Work

Ash tray, jewel enamel on rim, brn patina, sgn 135.00
Blotter ends, Zodiac, dk patina, pr 185.00
Box, bronze flowers & trellis over gr glass 195.00
Candlestick, bronze bamboo reed w/8-segment base, 10″, pr 1,650.00
Candlestick, bronze cup w/blown-out glass on slim std, 20″ 350.00
Candlestick, Queen Anne's Lace cup, bronze w/SP/gilt, 18″ 2,200.00

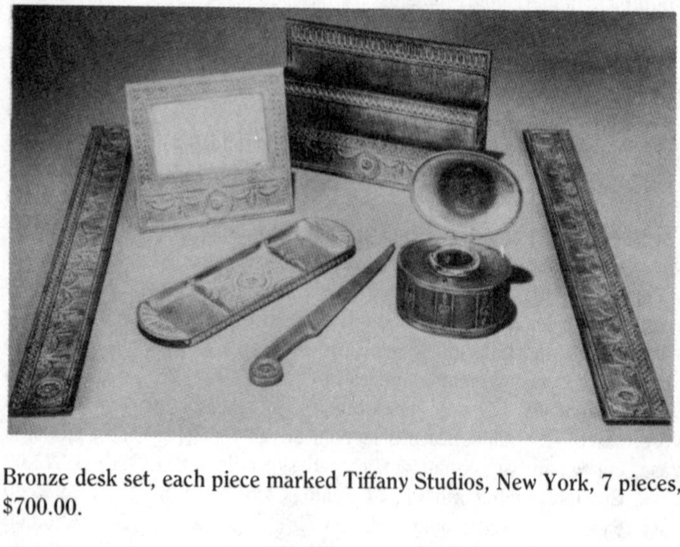

Bronze desk set, each piece marked Tiffany Studios, New York, 7 pieces, $700.00.

Clock, bronze, Deco figural, 8-day & chimes, sgn, 17″ 750.00
Clock, mantel; 8-sided face, emb swags, gilt-bronze, 11″ L 2,000.00
Desk set, Adams, bronze, sgn/#d, 7-pc 600.00
Desk set, enamel/silver-bronze, leather-look/crests, 6-pc 1,210.00
Desk set, Grape, bronze w/abalone, ink/tray/blotter ends 475.00
Desk set, Grape, bronze w/abalone, 5 blotters/box 350.00
Desk set, Indian, gilt-bronze, clock/rack/box, 3-pc 1,300.00
Desk set, Nautical, gilt-bronze, inkwell/pen knife+3 pcs 800.00
Desk set, Spanish, gilt-bronze, inkwell/rack+2 pcs 1,000.00

Desk set, Venetian, gilt-bronze, clock+10-pc...............2,200.00
Desk set, Venetian, gilt-bronze, dbl inkwell+7 pcs..........1,400.00
Desk set, Zodiac, sgn/#d, 8-pc...........................715.00
Desk set, Zodiac, 13½" lamp/ash tray/calendar+8 pcs.......1,760.00
Ink stand, octagon, dore-bronze, sgn/#d....................300.00
Inkwell, Chinese, bronze, hinged lid, #1753, 4¾"............440.00
Inkwell, crab, bronze w/shell mount, bucket in claws, 8½"....2,090.00
Inkwell, Zodiac, dk patina.................................225.00
Letter opener, brass, sgn...................................38.00
Letter rack, Am Indian, bronze, lg.........................225.00
Letter rack, Zodiac, dk patina.............................275.00
Paperweight, Ardvark, bronze...............................225.00
Paperweight, Hippo, bronze.................................225.00
Pen tray, Zodiac, dk patina..................................95.00
Pen wiper, Zodiac, dk patina...............................135.00
Plaque, copper/silver, sq w/silver fish/dragonfly, 11".........1,045.00
Tray, bronze, nesting set of 4: 4x5" to 2x3½"...............325.00
Tray, bronze w/gold dore finish, sgn, set of 3: 3½to 5"........275.00

Pottery

Vase, butterscotch w/brn-tone streaks, 6x7"..................475.00
Vase, fuschia emb, cylinder, bronze patina, #288, 10".........495.00
Vase, gunmetal w/red/gr, yel shows through, sgn, 4½", VG.....270.00
Vase, peach branch emb, pinched lip, unglazed ext, 10".......440.00
Vase, reticulated leafage/pendant pods, blk, 6¼", EX..........660.00
Vase, SP bronze floral overlay, #BP313, 8½"..............1,250.00
Vase, sq w/incised lip, lower body abstract incised, 9½".......495.00
Vase, yel/rust gloss, line motif top & base, 6½x7"............695.00

Bowl vase, hand sculptured, dore bronze glaze, marked BP219, L.C.T., 3" x 6½", $1,600.00.

Silver

Ash tray, cherub...140.00
Bowl, emb/chased w/roses/etc, grapes at rim, oval, 16".......1,100.00
Bowl, etched bird/foliage, shallow, 1915, 13½"...............770.00
Cake basket, 4 foliate lion paw ft, floral chased, 15¾"........990.00
Candlesticks, 12" pr; +10" bowl, tulip sconces/strapwork....1,320.00
Centerpiece, floral emb/chased rim, 4 paw ft, 16½" L........1,760.00
Cigar box, Art Deco, cedar lined, 9½" L....................660.00
Cocktail shaker, etched/eng w/putti & grapevine, 7⅜".........660.00
Creamer & sugar, w/sifter spoon, Japanese style, 3".........1,760.00
Desk set, relief thistles of copper & zinc, in case, 7-pc.......1,430.00
Dessert dish, shell shape w/foliate scrolls, 11¼" L, pr........1,100.00
Dresser set, hammered Crafts design, 10-pc..................425.00
Flatware service, Lap Over Edge, 48-pc....................4,070.00
Flatware service, Olympian, in box, 156-pc................5,500.00
Inkwell, fan-crested lion mts, glass snail insert, 5½".........1,430.00
Tazza, Japanese, applied grapes/fronds, ca 1878, 5⅜", pr....4,400.00
Tazza, wavy rim, floral emb/chased, paw ft, 10" L, pr.......1,210.00
Tea & coffee service, Indo-Persian, ca 1875, 10" pot, 5-pc...2,420.00
Toilet set, Art Deco, gilded, 11-pc..........................800.00
Trophy cup, RR wheels/station/presentation, paw ft, 10".....2,200.00
Vase, amphora form w/silver mt: female masks/urns, 12½"....1,210.00
Water set w/15" tray, etched laurel/swag bands, 1924, 7-pc...3,500.00

Miscellaneous

Cocktail stirrer, 14k, 5 dwt................................110.00
Evening bag, brocade w/birds, lighter/2 cases/comb, 7½".......350.00
Ldgl window, angel/2 Marys/landscape/inscription, 60x48"....4,400.00
Ldgl window, woman/children/landscape/inscription, 60x48"...6,875.00
Ldgl window, 2 trees centering lake/rocks/mtns, 36x23"......4,675.00
Watercolor on paper morning glories, sgn LCT/1913, 22x22....10,175.00

Tiffin Glass

The Tiffin Glass Company was founded in 1887 in Tiffin, Ohio, one of the many factories composing the U.S. Glass Company. Its early wares consisted of tablewares and decorative items such as lamps and globes. Among the most popular of all Tiffin products was the black satin glass produced there during the 1940s. In 1959 U.S. Glass was sold, and in 1962 the factories closed. The plant was re-opened in 1963 as the Tiffin Art Glass Company. Products from this period were tableware, hand-blown stemware, and other decorative items.

When no condition is indicated, the items listed below are assumed to be in mint condition.

Bookends, Lady Legs, vanilla opaque.........................50.00
Bottle, scent; HP floral, blk satin, tong applicator.............65.00
Bulldog, blk satin..25.00
Candlestick, etched Cosmos, twisted, flared base, 8½"..........75.00
Cocktail, June Night...18.50
Cocktail, Persian Pheasant...................................20.00
Console set, blk w/gold bands, Deco styling, 4-pc............225.00
Console set, bowl & pr 2½" candlesticks, bl satin, 4-pc.........85.00
Finger bowl, June Night, w/underliner, 4¼"..................22.50
Goblet, Cherokee Rose, 9-oz.................................18.00

Wall vase, gold satin glass in wrought iron basket with vining flowers, 15", $68.00.

Goblet, Fuchsia, tall . . . 15.00
Goblet, wine; June Night . . . 22.50
Goblet, wine; Princess, #643 . . . 15.00
Lamp, parrot . . . 200.00
Marmalade, lt gr, 3-ftd, #310½, 6½″ . . . 10.00
Pitcher, satin glass, 10″ . . . 55.00
Plate, Flanders, yel, 8″ . . . 15.00
Plate, luncheon; Fuchsia . . . 10.00
Rose bowl, blk satin, poppies, 6″ . . . 38.00
Sherbet, Persian Pheasant, tall . . . 16.00
Tumbler, iced tea; La Fleur, yel . . . 16.50
Tumbler, juice; June Night, ftd, 5″ . . . 16.00
Tumbler, Persian Pheasant, etched, ftd, pink, rare, #037 . . . 35.00
Tumbler, Persian Pheasant, ftd juice, 5-oz . . . 18.00
Tumbler, Persian Pheasant, ftd water . . . 16.00
Tumbler, Thistle, flat, 2½-oz . . . 6.50
Vase, blk satin w/coralene poppies, 9x8″ . . . 95.00
Vase, bud; Cherokee Rose, crystal, 8″ . . . 15.00
Vase, poppies, vaseline, bulbous . . . 25.00
Vase, poppies on blk satin, bulbous, 5″ . . . 35.00

Tiles

Though originally strictly functional, tiles were being produced in various colors and used as architectural highlights as early as the Ancient Roman Empire. By the 18th century, Dutch tiles were decorated with polychrome landscapes and figures. During the 19th century, there were over a hundred companies in England involved in the manufacture of tile. By the Victorian era, the use of decorative tiles had reached its peak. Special souvenir editions, campaign and portrait tiles, and Art Nouveau motifs with lovely ladies and stylized examples from nature were popular. Today, all of these are very collectible.

When no condition is indicated, the items listed below are assumed to be in mint condition.

Beaver Falls, floral relief, four VG 6x6″ tiles for . . . 20.00
Boston Light, the first lighthouse in America, 1918 . . . 60.00
California Art, mottled bl/gr/gray semi-gloss, 6x6″ . . . 10.00
California Art, terra cotta w/floral relief, 4-color, 4x4″ . . . 25.00
Cathedral Church of St Paul, erected 1820, 1922 . . . 55.00
Claycraft, border type, 1¾x3¾″ . . . 10.00
Claycraft, scenic, 4x4″ . . . 50.00
Franciscan, Anniv Ceramic Tile Institute, dk gr, 1980, 4″ . . . 20.00
GF Brunt, Christopher Columbus, gray/wht, hexagonal, 3½″ . . . 10.00
House of Seven Gables, Salem, 1929 . . . 55.00
Indianapolis, Ind; emb Indian head, amber glaze, 6″ . . . 75.00
Intn'l, heads in relief, honey brn, sgn, 6″, pr . . . 165.00
Low, child's head, dk brn, 6″ sq . . . 85.00
Low, floral, brn/amber, 7x7¾″ . . . 65.00
Low, Four Seasons, bl gloss, minor crazing, 6x4″, set . . . 310.00
Low, head of lady in bonnet, 4¼″ dia . . . 90.00
Low, nude children drag lg bird's carcass, 2-part, 10x16″ . . . 500.00
Low, Parthenia portrait, honey brn, EX detail, 13x10″, EX . . . 170.00
Low, Queen Elizabeth portrait, tan, 8x8″, NM . . . 160.00
McDuffie, calendar, 1916 . . . 65.00
Minton, acorns/leaves relief, brn, sgn, 6x6″, NM . . . 25.00
Minton, stylized floral, 4-color, 6x6″ . . . 45.00
Moresque, floral/peacocks, unglazed w/bl wash, sgn, 8x12″ . . . 175.00
Moresque, ship, 6x6″ . . . 60.00
Mount Vernon, Home of Washington, 1892 . . . 65.00
Old North Church, Boston, 1902 . . . 60.00
Pardee, wht rabbit on lt gr, sgn/mk, 4½″, EX . . . 100.00
Pomona, bl w/wht sailing ships, cloisonne technique, 6″ . . . 35.00

Wheeling, Oriental figures, 5-color, 6″, $90.00.

S&S, border tiles, cloisonne technique, 2x6″, 6 for . . . 50.00
S&S, geometric, 6x6″ . . . 25.00
S&S, stylized dolphin, cloisonne technique, 3-color, 3x6″ . . . 55.00
S&S, 4 tiles form medallion, cloisonne technique, 5-color . . . 45.00
Trent, boy w/sheep, Gallimore, 6x18″ . . . 235.00
Tropico, landscape, 4x4″ . . . 75.00
Washington Elm, Cambridge, 1899 . . . 65.00
Wedgwood, calendar, 1906 . . . 65.00
Wedgwood, calendar, 1910 . . . 58.00
Wedgwood, calendar, 1916 . . . 58.00
Wheeling, drawing of people/park, mk Washington Sq, 6″ . . . 60.00
Wheeling, Moorish floral, bl/brn on wht, sgn, 6″, EX . . . 27.50

Tinware

In the American household of the 17th and 18th centuries, tinware items could be found in abundance, from food containers to footwarmers and mirror frames. Althouth the first settlers brought much of their tinware with them from Europe, by 1798 sheets of tin plate were being imported from England for use by the growing number of American tinsmiths.

Tinwares were often decorated, either by piercing or painted designs, which were both free-hand and stenciled. (See Toleware.) By the early 1900s, many homes had replaced their old tinware with the more attractive aluminum and graniteware.

When no condition is indicated, the items listed below are assumed to be in near mint condition.

Bank, can shape, emb flowers/hearts/etc, dk tin . . . 40.00
Basket, rigid dbl curve hdl, crimp tin ribbon decor, 9″ . . . 165.00
Bath tub, old pnt, arched wide rim, seat . . . 160.00
Boiler, sheet tin, w/lid, 2 side hdls, 14x11½x16½″ . . . 45.00
Cabinet, spice; 8-drawer, pediment top, 13½″ . . . 125.00
Candlestick, hogscraper, w/push-up, 6⅝″ . . . 95.00
Canister, country store or apothecary, gr pnt, 9⅜″, pr . . . 50.00
Chamber stick, w/push-up, 3¾″, pr . . . 90.00
Cheese drainer, w/hdls, 5¾x19″ dia . . . 60.00
Coffee pot, tinsmith made, cone-on-cone shape, PA, 11″ . . . 285.00
Cookie cutter, birds, 2¾″, pr . . . 22.00
Cookie cutter, Christmas tree, early 20th C, 7x3½″ . . . 26.00
Cookie cutter, dancing Dutchman, minor resoldering, 9¼″ . . . 155.00
Cookie cutter, deer leaping, 4½″ . . . 55.00
Cookie cutter, dog primitive, 4″, pr . . . 10.00
Cookie cutter, dove, highly detailed, wood back, 5x3″ . . . 35.00
Cookie cutter, Dutch lady, hdl missing, 5¼″ . . . 20.00
Cookie cutter, fish, wood back, 3″ L . . . 65.00

Cookie cutter, giraffe, hdl missing, 5¾" 105.00
Cookie cutter, heart, lg cylindrical hdl, 3" 38.00
Cookie cutter, heart, 19th C, 4x4x1½" 24.00
Cookie cutter, hollow ball, cuts 6 different animals 110.00
Cookie cutter, horse, primitive, 5¾" 60.00
Cookie cutter, pig, 6" L 65.00
Cookie cutter, pipe, slightly corroded, 6¼" 23.00
Cookie cutter, rooster, slightly corroded, 5" 35.00
Cookie cutter, tulips, stylized, w/stem & leaf, 4¼" 55.00
Cookie cutter, turkey, primitive, 5½" 95.00
Cookie cutter, 4 card suits, heavy, late 1800s, 5x4x1¼" 46.00
Cookie cutter, 8 open-bk cutters soldered to form circle 55.00
Creamer, cylinder, sm cylinder top, long spout, w/lid, 6" 30.00
Grater, punched, well-made mortised/trn wood fr, 14" 85.00
Hot plate, compass star punching, 6¾" dia 160.00
Jug, milk; unusual form, raw tin, 1800s, 9½" 55.00
Lamp, conical, single spout, 4½" 22.50
Lamp, skater's, 6¾" 23.00
Milk can, set of 3, bail hdls, w/lids, dk tin, qt/2-qt/gal 75.00
Mold, floral design, 6" & 7½", pr 60.00
Pan, cake; heart shape, 9½x11", pr 80.00
Pastry sheet, dk, curved bottom/ribbed bk, w/rolling pin 285.00
Pitcher, wide flange spout, 9" 60.00
Rolling pin, dk tin w/wooden hdls 90.00
Rolling pin, wood hdls, 17" L 90.00
Sander, asphaltum, yel brush decor, 1800s 215.00
Sconce, dbl; dbl curve pans, dbl crimp crests, 11¾" 400.00
Sconce, rnd crimp reflector & edge pan, sm mirror, 9", pr 650.00
Sconce, sm crimped circular crest, 13½" 75.00
Sconce, 2 brass burners/tube spouts/snuffers/reflector, 9" 100.00
Sifter, sq dvtl pine fr, punched tin bottom, 15x20" 105.00
Toddy warmer, dk tin, rare 145.00

Tobacciana

Tobacciana is the generally accepted term used to cover that field of collecting that includes smoking pipes, cigar molds, cigarette lighters, humidors--in short, any article having to do with the practice of using tobacco in any form.

Tobacco tin-tags, strips of metal attached to a plug of tobacco for means of brand identification, are becoming popular collectibles, especially those featuring animals of political and patriotic themes. It is estimated that over 12,000 brands were produced.

Perhaps the most valuable variety of pipes is the meerschaum--hand carved from a clay-like medium formed by the action of the water on disintegrating seashells on the ocean floor. These figural bowls often portray an elaborately carved mythological character, an animal, or a historical scene. Amber is often used for the stem. Other collectible pipes are corncob (Missouri Meerschaum) and Indian peace pipes of clay or catlinite. (See American Indian Artifacts.)

Chosen because it was the Indians who first introduced the white man to smoking, the cigar store Indian was a symbol used to identify tobacco stores in the 19th century. The majority of them were hand carved between 1830 and 1900, and are today recognized as some of the finest examples of early wood sculptures. When found, they command very high prices.

When no condition is indicated, the items listed below are assumed to be in excellent condition.

Ash tray, Indian head, gold bee, cigarette rest in mouth 20.00
Ash tray, rabbit in brush, gold-bronze, Barbedienne, 6" 225.00
Box, brass, oval w/chased decor, 18th C, 5¾" 135.00
Box, brass, 8-sided, Dutch, 1830, 5½x2¾x1" 180.00
Box, brass/copper, 8-sided, Dutch, 1800, 5x3x1¼" 190.00
Box, cigar; porc lining, brass plate/key, holds 100, 13½" 40.00
Box, copper, oval, Dutch, 1880, 3½x2x1½" 85.00
Box, silver w/gold int, scrolls/florals/portrait, 4" 175.00
Box, top revolves, wood w/silver mt w/smoking scenes, 3½" 200.00
Card, cigarette; Helmar Turkish, 38 states for 100.00
Card, cigarette; Helmar Turkish, 63 coats of arms for 175.00
Card, cigarette; Taryeton, Henry cartoons, 1936, 5 for 15.00
Card, cigarette; Will's Coronation series, set of 47 .... 30.00
Card, tobacco; Honest Long Cut, actresses, 2x4", set of 12 .... 90.00
Card, tobacco; New's Boy, scantily clothed 1890s star 5.00
Case, holds pipe/tobacco/flint, floral/checkerboard, 5" 185.00
Chopper, CI, cylindrical, 13 blades, 10x5¼" 72.50
Cigar dispenser, Elm City, coin-op 1,200.00
Cigar holder, carved ivory, floral 40.00
Cigar holder, meerschaum, dog in relief, w/case 50.00
Cigar holder, meerschaum, lounge w/lady, amber tip, 3¾" 65.00
Cigar holder, meerschaum, 3 dogs 68.00
Cigar holder, MOP, 3" 45.00
Cigar press, leafy base, dog on hdl, CI, 9½" L 30.00
Cigar press box, 10-tray, 8x6x18" 30.00
Cigar store Indian, headdress/tobacco leaf/pipe, 1860, 67" 2,475.00
Cigar store Indian Princess, sgn W DeMuth Co 4,900.00
Cigarette dispenser, bronze donkey, lift tail to release 175.00
Cigarette dispenser, elephant w/howdah, CI, 9x5x3" 90.00
Cigarette holder, carved ivory, 4½" 28.00
Cigarette holder, cranberry glass w/sterling overlay, sgn 95.00
Cigarette holder, ebony & silver, no mk 10.00
Cigarette holder, meerschaum, dog carving, orig case 38.00
Cigarette roller, mk R&H Vougue Sr, 16" 7.00
Cigarette roller, red metal, Brown & Williamson, 1930s 25.00
Cigarette silk, Old Mill, lady busts w/signatures, 6 for 30.00
Cigarette urn/scalloped underplate, Argenta, Gustavsberg 30.00
Cutter, cigar, desk; blk hdl, w/cigar box opener, 6" 95.00
Cutter, cigar, desk; emb sterling, w/pipe packer & opener 100.00
Cutter, cigar, desk; eng/monogrammed, sterling, 4½" 65.00
Cutter, cigar, desk; silver w/MOP hdl, , 6½" 130.00
Cutter, cigar, desk; w/opener, niello, 5" 130.00
Cutter, cigar, pocket; barrel & funnel, silver 125.00
Cutter, cigar, pocket; bottle w/advertising, ivory 105.00
Cutter, cigar, pocket; boy using potty, chrome 130.00
Cutter, cigar, pocket; Geo Washington in relief, brass 130.00
Cutter, cigar, pocket; guillotine, w/monogram, 14k gold 95.00
Cutter, cigar, pocket; gun, w/onyx hdl, chrome 155.00
Cutter, cigar, pocket; heart shape, 14k gold, 1¼x1" 85.00
Cutter, cigar, pocket; horse collar, chrome 100.00
Cutter, cigar, pocket; Johnnie Walker bottle, brass 105.00
Cutter, cigar, pocket; pocket knife, brass 30.00
Cutter, cigar, pocket; razor blade w/pencil, gold plated 130.00
Cutter, cigar, pocket; revolver w/blk onyx hdl, chrome, 3" 230.00
Cutter, cigar, pocket; scissors, w/etching, silver 35.00
Cutter, cigar, table; bird, mk Gladenbeck, metal, 9x4" 180.00
Cutter, cigar, table; boy astride barrel, miniature 120.00
Cutter, cigar, table; dog & match holder, brass, 10½x3½" 135.00
Cutter, cigar, table; knight's helmet, miniature 70.00
Cutter, cigar, table; man bowing w/top hat, bronze, 8" 610.00
Cutter, cigar, table; mariners' wheel, brass, 4½" 130.00
Cutter, cigar, table; monkey leans in pot, w/match holder 100.00
Cutter, cigar, table; pig, spring action, sterling 120.00
Cutter, cigar, table; seltzer bottle attached to ash tray 150.00
Cutter, cigar, table; ship's wheel, inscription, brass 70.00
Cutter, cigar, table; Victorian lady w/lg bust, miniature 150.00
Cutter, cigar; Krank Cigars, cart shape 295.00
Cutter, cigar; semi-mechanical, mk Royal Perfectos, Hubble 235.00
Cutter, plug; Brown's Mule, RJ Ryenolds, Enterprise #5837 .... 72.50

Cigar store Indian, carved from single pine plank, in full headdress and yellow-fringed green costume, holding tobacco leaf and pipe, ca 1850-1870, 67″, $2,200.00.

Cutter, plug; Champion Knife Improved, orig pnt, NM..........62.50
Cutter, plug; Good Luck, Good Cheer, Thank You, Call Again...90.00
Cutter, plug; ornate side plates, Johnson Co, 1914, VG pnt.....55.00
Cutter, plug; Spearhead, PJ Sorg, scrollwork on bk, 16″.......100.00
Cutter, plug; Standard Cutter, Reading Hardware Co...........47.50
Cutter, plug; Triumph, SCWW Co..........................45.00
Cutter, plug; 5 Bros Tobacco Works, orig pin striping.........65.00
Figure, Wm Penn by tree w/box of cigars, papier mache, 63″..660.00
Humidor, baby head w/bonnet & pacifier, porc, 5½″...........95.00
Humidor, Blk boy smoking pipe atop, pottery................85.00
Humidor, Blk man's head w/pipe, colored bisque, 4½x3¾″......85.00
Humidor, brn skinned lady's head w/bandana, bisque, 5x4″.....85.00
Humidor, head of blonde w/cigar, wears fez, majolica, 5½″......55.00
Humidor, lg Russian boy w/cossack hat & fur collar, bisque....245.00
Humidor, man, mk JWR, German, 1900s, 9″.................95.00
Humidor, man w/beard in turban, bl smeared pottery, Dudson...95.00
Humidor, sm Victorian girl knits in red chair, porc, 8″........135.00
Humidor, 6 faces in relief, lid w/figural head, Oriental..........85.00
Lighter, cigar; country store, Rosa, kerosene, orig globe.......290.00
Lighter, cigar; country store, running Grecian lady............650.00
Lighter, cigar; pistol, Hance-Parker Mfg, Meriden..............75.00
Lighter, cigar; Salty Sailor, eyes light up/pipe w/element.......295.00
Lighter, cigarette; Bully, revolver shape, brass, 1914...........30.00
Lighter, cigarette; Dunhill Tinder Pistol, England, 20th C.......55.00
Lighter, cigarette; pictures Little Abner, Dogpatch USA........40.00
Pipe, Am Colonist's, pottery, 17th C........................15.00
Pipe, briar, carved bust of Geo Washington, amber bit........475.00
Pipe, briar, gutta percha lady's leg stem, CW era..............30.00
Pipe, briar, head of bearded man w/tasseled hat & pipe, 7″.....50.00
Pipe, briar, Queen Victoria head, silver trim, w/case, EX........65.00
Pipe, clay, bearded man w/tooled hair, primitive, 2½″..........30.00
Pipe, clay, cannon-form bowl w/woman at neck, French, 1861...50.00
Pipe, clay, inscribed 'Cork' on stem, Irish, 5″..................10.00
Pipe, maple, Am eagle on flag carving, brass fittings, 6″.......100.00
Pipe, meerschaum, bearded sultan head, 5½″.................90.00
Pipe, meerschaum, clown..................................75.00
Pipe, meerschaum, eagle's claw figural, in box................69.00
Pipe, meerschaum, Elizabethan lady w/hat..................150.00
Pipe, meerschaum, hand holds torch bowl..................225.00
Pipe, meerschaum, hand w/amber ball, no stem.............120.00
Pipe, meerschaum, head of Blk man, EX detail, in case, 6″....200.00
Pipe, meerschaum, lady w/hat.............................200.00
Pipe, meerschaum, lady: long curls/lacy hat/amber parasol.....350.00
Pipe, meerschaum, lady's hand w/stylus writes on egg shape....180.00
Pipe, meerschaum, lion head, amber stem, 3½x6½″...........115.00
Pipe, meerschaum, lion's head bowl, amber stem, 3½x6½″......95.00
Pipe, meerschaum, mermaid, amber stem, ca 1940, 12″ L.....150.00
Pipe, meerschaum, nude, 8½″ L...........................150.00
Pipe, meerschaum, running dog scene, SP/wood/pearl stem, 8″..35.00
Pipe, meerschaum, Shakespeare...........................175.00
Pipe, meerschaum, Sherlock Holmes type, tuba shape..........35.00
Pipe, meerschaum, sm fox on top, orig leather case, 3″........32.00
Pipe, meerschaum, Turk's head, amber stem................130.00
Pipe, meerschaum, 16 amber jewels & stem, curved, sm cased...45.00
Pipe, meerschaum, 2 horses, stem separated from bowl, case...125.00
Pipe, pine, man's head figural bowl, 1½x4½″................30.00
Pipe, porcelain, HP man & dog, Germany...................80.00
Pipe, rosewood, carved stag on bowl, Victorian, lg............100.00
Pipe, wooden bowl, sterling overlay, dogs & trees.............40.00
Pipe holder, pine/oak, primitive, 3 tiers of holes, 10½″.........75.00
Pipe rest, copper plated, recumbent Scottie, Ronson, 5½″......28.00
Pipe tamp, ball & chain, brass, 2¾″........................15.00
Pipe tamp, boot, carved wood, 1½″..........................30.00
Pipe tamp, bust of Sir Walter Drake, brass, 2⅜″..............15.00
Pipe tamp, carved column, ivory, 2¾″.......................15.00
Pipe tamp, hand w/long clay pipe, brass, 2⅛″................35.00
Pipe tamp, horn shape, bone w/silver trim, 2¾″...............25.00
Pipe tamp, Indian w/enamel Panama coat of arms, sterling......25.00
Pipe tamp, leg w/boot, brass, 2″...........................20.00
Pipe tamp, man bending at waist, SP, sgn EPNS, 1⅝″.........20.00
Pipe tamp, medallion w/Mater Jesu Christie, brass, 2½″........20.00
Pipe tamp, Robin Hood, brass, mk England, 2¼″..............30.00
Pipe tamp, silver, w/folding spoon & pick, mk Tiffany, 2¼″.....20.00

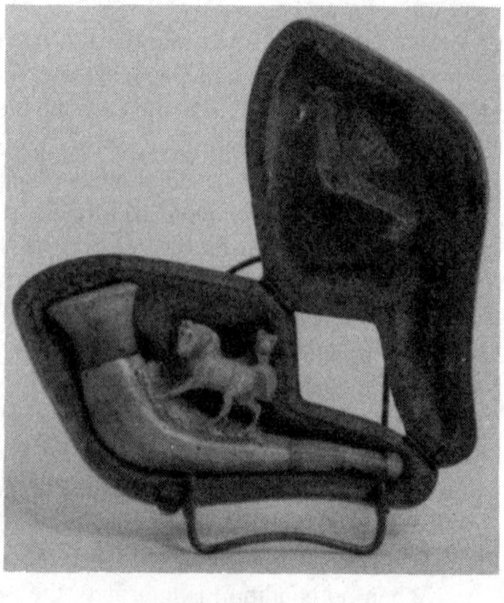

Meerschaum pipe, two carved horses in curve, marked Genuine Meerschaum, 4½″, $50.00.

Toby Jugs and Mugs

The delightful drinking mug known as the Toby dates back to the 18th century, when factories in England produced them for export to the American colonies. Named for the character Toby Philpot in the song *The Little Brown Jug*, the Toby was fashioned in the form of a jolly fellow, usually holding a jug of beer and a glass. Some were seated, while others were full-bodied figurals. The earlier examples were made with strict attention to details such as fingernails and teeth. Originally representing only a non-entity, a trend developed to portray well-known individuals such as George II, Napoleon, and Ben Franklin. Among the most valued Tobies are those produced by Ralph Wood I in the late 1700s. By the mid-1830s, Tobies were being made in America.

When no condition is indicated, the items listed below are assumed to be in mint condition.

Man in tricorn hat, holding pitcher, blue coat, yellow pants, 11″, $400.00.

Jug, Captain Hook, Burlington Ware, 6¾″ 35.00
Jug, Country Squire, Ralph Wood, 1780 .... 850.00
Jug, Drunken Sal, Davenport, 1815 .... 1,200.00
Jug, Duke of Wellington, Stephen Green, Lambeth, 7½″, VG 85.00
Jug, Duke of Wellington (?), salt glazed, English, 6¾″ 25.00
Jug, Elihu Yale, 1933, Wedgwood, 6″ 65.00
Jug, Guardsman, Shorter 50.00
Jug, Hearty Good Feller, mc, Staffordshire, 11″ 200.00
Jug, Lord Nelson, stoneware, cream w/olive-brn hat, 10″, VG 40.00
Jug, man w/pipe & dogs, Wedgwood, 5″ 75.00
Jug, Martha Gunn, Wood, 1790 .... 700.00
Jug, Mid-Shipman, Beswick, 5½″ 40.00
Jug, Napoleon, mk Stephen Green, Lambeth, hairline, 9″ 95.00
Jug, Officer, in tricorner hat/medals, mc, France, 7″, EX 55.00
Jug, Old King Cole, Shorter & Sons, 5½″ 70.00
Jug, Pickwick, mk Beswick 15.00
Jug, Policeman, Shorter 36.00
Jug, Punch holding dog, full figure, sgn, English, 6½″ 90.00
Jug, Rockingham, Scotsman's head, 8⅛″ 60.00
Jug, Rockingham, tricorn hat, arms on rotund stomach, 9¾″ 85.00
Jug, Sailor, sitting/holding jug, Staffordshire, 1770 .... 900.00
Jug, Silly Billy, Staffordshire, 1810 .... 300.00
Jug, sitting man, mkd Japan, colorful, 3¾″ 20.00
Jug, Snuff-Taker, Wheildon, 1790 .... 750.00
Jug, Tony Weller, Beswick, 7″ 135.00
Jug, yellowware, hand molded, English, 5½″, VG 50.00

Toleware

The term 'toleware' originally came from a French term meaning 'sheet iron.' Today it is used to refer to paint-decorated tin items. The earliest toleware was hand painted; by the 1820s, much of it was decorated by means of a stencil. Among the most collectible today are those items painted by the Pennsylvania Dutch in the 1800s.

When no condition is indicated, the items listed below are assumed to be in excellent condition.

Box, dome top, orig mc brush stroke decor, 8″ L 125.00
Box, snuff; orig landscape w/fishing boy, 1¾x2½″ 60.00
Box, spice; w/6 rnd canisters, stripes/stencil, wear, 9½″ 55.00
Box, tobacco; Famous Cake Box Mixture, yel stencil/brn, 5″ 45.00
Canister, blk/red/yel striping/'Mace,' Mfd HF Heacock, 10″ 145.00
Canister, spice; 7 sm w/in, grater in lid, stencil, 8″ dia 75.00
Coal hod, chickens/ducks in panel, paw ft, English, 21″ 245.00
Coffee pot, florals, worn but G color, resoldered, 8½″ 450.00
Coffee pot, stylized floral worn, gooseneck, G hdl, 10¾″ 525.00
Creel, fish/'Leuree,' orig pnt/stencil, miniature, 3x3¾″ 40.00
Cup, pink w/stenciled decor/My Girl, faded, 1¾x3″ 35.00
Lamp, candle; dbl socket on boat shape, shallow shade, rpt 325.00
Needle case, blk w/red/yel worn decor, 9½″ L 60.00
Pitcher, molasses; stenciled gilt flower/yel band, sgn 175.00
Shaker, cup type, orig decor worn, 4¼″ 80.00
Tea caddy, florals, mc on brn, worn, early, 4⅛″ 200.00
Tray, bun; flower center, open hdls, boat shape, 1830, 12″ 325.00
Tray, florals, mc on blk, octagonal, touch-up, 9x12½″ 165.00
Tray, fox hunt w/floral border, blk lacquer stand, 29x21″ 650.00
Wall pocket, red/pink pnt flowers on blk, 6¾x3x7″ 40.00

Tools

Before the Civil War, tools for the most part were handmade. Some were primitive to the point of crudeness, while others reflected the skill of those who took pride in their trade. Increasing demand for quality tools and the dawning of the age of industrialization resulted in tools that were mass-produced.

Factors important in evaluating antique tools are scarcity, usefulness, and portability. Those with a manufacturer's mark are worth more than unmarked items.

When no condition is indicated, the items listed below are assumed to be in excellent condition.

Adze, bowl; sgn Ream, 7″ curved blade 115.00
Adze, cooper's; DR Barton, 1892, 9″ blade 35.00
Adze, cooper's; stamped DR Bart, 7¼″ 27.50
Adze, ship; White, laminated, w/lip, hdl, 5¼″ 65.00
Adze, shipbuilder's; 5″ blade 40.00
Auger, Stearns & Co, hollow, 6¾″ blade 26.00
Axe, broad; S Simmons & Co, NY, Cast Steel, rpl hdl, 11″ 25.00
Axe, broad; short off-set wood hdl, 11½″ blade 30.00
Axe, broad; steel edge, 13½″ blade 55.00
Axe, broad; w/wood hdl, 10″ blade, 26″ L 25.00
Axe, fireman's; Warren Axe, orig red hdl, 10″ head, 34″ 35.00
Axe, hand; wrought iron, 5″ head, 14″ overall 28.00
Axe, side; cooper's, 9½″ blade, 19½″ 45.00
Bench, cobbler's; rstr/rpl drw, pine, primitive, rfn, 44″ 300.00
Bevel, emb Marshall-Wells, adjustable, iron, blade pitted 7.00
Bevel, Stanley, adjustable, iron, pat 1908, w/10″ blade 14.50
Bevel, Stanley, rosewood/brass, 10″ blade 9.50
Bevel, Stanley #18, adjustable ends, nickel 14.50
Blacksmith's carry-all, pine/poplar w/worn pnt, 12x12½″ 75.00
Blacksmith's mandrel, iron cone, for making rings/hoops 250.00
Blacksmith's tongs, flat jaw, 19″ hdls 8.50
Blow torch, brass ferrule, trn wood hdl, 3x2½″ 35.00
Book press, CI w/red/blk pnt, 12x18½″ 100.00
Brace, boring; CI, 12½″ 10.00

Brace, corner; Miller Falls #502 .... 25.00
Brace, corner; Stanley #80, VG wood 35.00
Brace, lignum vitae head, no thumbscrew/wrought iron, 10″ 39.00
Brace, mk #2W, wimble, rosewood hdl, brass ferrule, scarce 49.00
Buck saw, mortised wood fr, 15½″ L 25.00
Calipers, boxwood, w/brass screw & wing nut, delicate 35.00
Calipers, brass, shaped like pr legs, old patina, 3″ 70.00
Calipers, unmk, old, brass, 11″ 39.00
Calipers, wrought, 10x14″ 15.00
Carpet stretcher, The Cody, iron/wood, pat 1892 .... 18.00
Carpet stretcher, The Star, wood/iron, ratchet/rope 18.00
Chisel, Buck Bros, name on blade & hdl, ¼″ blade 8.50
Chisel, Greenlee, 1″ blade, 14″ overall 15.00
Chisel, lathe sizing; Buck Bros, 21″ 42.00
Chisel, mortise; Buck, swan-neck lock, boxwood hdl, ½x22″ 35.00
Clamp, wood, 15x12″ 20.00
Clapboard marker, Stanley, pat July 6, 1886, minor rust 12.00
Cutter, glass; France, brass, 4″ 4.00
Digger, post hole; clamshell shovels, split hdl 25.00
Divider, nickel plated, points telescope from 13″ to 19″ 35.00
Drill, breast; brass, 15″, EX 250.00
Drill, breast; North Bros #1555, EX 55.00
Drill, chain; Goodell-Pratt 10.00
Drill, hand; Goodel Bros, w/brass bit dispenser, pat 1891 .... 21.00
Drill, hand; Miller Falls #2A, hollow hdl, red wheel, 14½″ 25.00
Drill, hand; steel/brass, drills mortise pins, 17″ 45.00
Drill, push; Johnson & Tainter's, w/9 orig bits & tin case 65.00
Gauge, butt; Stanley #92, brass shaft/thumbscrew, rare 75.00
Gauge, marking; DM Lyon & Co, brass plated fence, boxwood 40.00
Gauge, marking; Stanley #77, rosewood, brass trim 27.00
Gauge, mortise; Stanley #98, steel, VG 16.00
Gauge, panel; wood screw, 6″ fence, 18″ 14.00
Gauge, steam; iron bk, glass front, brass, 6″ 29.00
Hammer, broom maker's; brass ferrule, 9″ 30.00
Hammer, dbl claw, rpl hdl, minor surface rust 150.00
Hammer, napping; used in road building 10.00
Hammer, stone working; flat edge surface, 4-lb head 16.00
Hammer pin, wagon; w/pulling claw, dbl tree pin/hammer 15.00
Hatchet, hewing; Keen Kutter, orig hdl, worn logo 15.00
Hatchet, hewing; Kelly Axe, mk True Temper on bk, orig hdl 15.00
Hatchet, no mk, steel, 6½″ 5.00
Hoof trimmer, Western Cutlery, bone hdl 8.50
Iron, soldering; handmade, primitive, 2-lbs, 13″ 11.50
Iron, soldering; swivel type, copper/wrought iron hdl, 14″ 14.00
Knife, hay; 8″ blade, 34″ overall 25.00
Level, Mayes, wood, 24″ 15.00
Level, pocket; Stanley #31, pat 1896, 3″, EX 25.00
Level, Stanley #00, mk SW in heart, cherry, 20″, EX 20.00
Level, Stratton Bros, mahog, pat 1888, 30″ 45.00
Mallet, bench; wooden, lg 6.00
Mallet, carpenter's; burl, 12¾″ 30.00
Mallet, carpenter's; maple burl, trn hickory hdl, 10½″ 30.00
Mallet, wood; 1½″ iron band at ea end of head 14.00
Mallet, 1 side flat, 1 side curved, burl, rare, 1800s 125.00
Mold, brick; wood w/iron, Calvert impression, makes 10 .... 60.00
Nail header, rnd, wrought iron, 10″ 10.00
Plane, bench; carpenter's, 16″ 30.00
Plane, block; Sargent #5206, carpenter's, low angle, EX 20.00
Plane, block; Stanley #118, low angle, steel, EX 28.00
Plane, block; Stanley #60½, low angle, adjustable throat 23.50
Plane, block; wood w/simple carved detail, 12¼″ 30.00
Plane, brass, instrument maker's 125.00
Plane, bull-nose; mk ICS, gunmetal, walnut wedge, 1x3½″ 125.00
Plane, chamfer; walnut, 2x7¼″ 85.00
Plane, chip carved/tooled detail, 2 trn hdl, dtd 1831, 11″ 200.00
Plane, circular; Stanley #113, no lateral, most orig pnt 75.00
Plane, combination; Stanley #50, WWII type, 1 cutter, EX 40.00
Plane, cooper's; makes inside groove on barrel edge, 15″ 30.00
Plane, dado; Stanley #39½, VG 45.00
Plane, DR Barton & Co NY, 22″, VG 26.00
Plane, edge block; Stanley #95 .... 95.00
Plane, for cutting 2″ crown molding, wood, 11″ 52.00
Plane, fore; Casey & Co, dk patina, wood, 18″ L, 3x3″ 27.00
Plane, fore; Stanley #29, wood bottom, EX 30.00
Plane, horn; mk Austria, wood, EX 16.00
Plane, jack; Bailey #5¼, mk SW in heart on blade, EX 42.00
Plane, jack; Bed Rock #605, pat 1895, EX 30.00
Plane, jack; Stanley #S5, no rivets in bed, scarce, EX 95.00
Plane, jointer; Stanley #7, rosewood knob/hdl, 1910, EX 49.00
Plane, Ohio Tool, dbl blade, brass joining pins, wood, 9½″ 35.00
Plane, rabbet; iron, 1¾″ cut, 9″ overall 95.00
Plane, Scoito Works, 22″, VG 23.00
Plane, scrub; Stanley #40½, mk SW in heart on blade, EX 65.00
Plane, ship; mk DR Barton, 1883, 25″ 25.00
Plane, side bead; beech, in box, Woodrow & Co 25.00
Plane, smooth; Bailey #3C, rosewood hdl & knob, EX 40.00
Plane, smooth; Owasco Tool Co #19, deer on blade, 8″ 19.00
Plane, Stanley #1, EX 650.00
Plane, Stanley #2 .... 150.00
Plane, Stanley #29, metal/wood, 20″, VG 22.00
Plane, Stanley #4, iron, pat 1910, rosewood hdl, rust/rpr 16.00
Plane, Stanley #4C, corrugated bottom, rosewood knob/hdl 37.00
Plane, Stanley #85, NM 825.00
Plane, tongue & groove; Stanley #49, cast w/B, 75% plating 40.00
Plane, Traut's #46, mk, japanned, w/guard plate, 1 blade 50.00
Pliers, dbl hammer/cutters/wire grippers, 1903 .... 12.00
Pliers, Mills Hog Ringer, pat 1865-1872, EX 8.00
Pulley, barn; CI, openwork iron fr, 7″ 8.50
Pulley, 2 iron wheels & hook, oval, wood, 12″, VG 5.00
Router, 'D'; metal clad bottom, light maple, 4x7″ 35.00
Router, beech w/full brass sole, 12″ 40.00
Router, coach maker's; dbl, all orig, fruitwood, 18″ 125.00
Router, coach maker's; orig hdl, wrought iron, rust, 22″ 28.00
Router, WWII type, japanned, orig box 30.00
Rule, architect's; J Dobie & Co, 4-fold, ivory, 24″ 335.00
Rule, folding, bone w/NP trim, minor cracks, 12″ L 30.00
Rule, Jordan, Germany, folding, ½″ W, 48″, EX 8.00
Rule, Stephens #70, 4-fold, boxwood, 12″ 17.00
Rule, 4-fold, German silver fittings, delicate, ivory, 18″ 225.00
Saw, back; cabinetmaker's, 12″ blade, VG 12.00
Saw, back; Henry Disston & Sons, 10″ blade, EX 16.00
Saw, bow; boxwood hdls, beech, 9x15″ 89.00
Saw, cabinetmaker's; Hill & Howel, brass bk, 14″ blade 26.00
Saw, fret; wood fr, brass trim, iron fittings, 13″ L 75.00
Saw, hack; Jackson, cast steel, wood hdl, EX 17.00
Saw, hack; Old Miller Falls, brass ferrule, adjusts, EX 12.50
Saw, ice; factory made, steel blade, 60″ 45.00
Saw, jeweler's; sq fr, wood hdl, brass ferrule, EX 7.50
Saw, lg fret, w/cam blade adjustment, beech hdl, 13x18″ 65.00
Saw, pad; H Disston & Son, brass ferrule, beech hdl 25.00
Saw, stair; Geo Bishop & Co, high gloss finish, 11″, M 35.00
Scorp, closed, long hdl, wrought iron, 4¼″ blade, 34″ 65.00
Scraper, floor; flat type, wood, 5″ blade 7.00
Scraper, Stanley #112, blade rpl, EX 85.00
Scraper, Stanley #81, rosewood sole, EX 18.00
Scraper, Stanley #82, hanging hole in hdl, EX 12.00
Screwdriver, 4-in-1, 3 in hdl of other, knurled, brass 7.25
Shears, hand forged, loop hdl, iron, some rust, 4″ blades 19.00

Shoe last, iron, dbl 14.00
Shoe last, laminated wood, in form of high heeled boot, 13" 30.00
Spokeshave, Goodell-Pratt #36, pattern maker's, EX 25.00
Spokeshave, Stanley #54, adjustable throat, EX 25.00
Spokeshave, Stanley #84, boxwood, SW in heart, scarce, EX 35.00
Sprayer, garden; w/3 nozzles, trn wood hdl, brass, 1½x20" 45.00
Square, barn; hand forged, scarce, 2" W, ¼" thick, 20x30" 23.00
Square, cherry wood hdl, brass 25.00
Square, Stanley, 4" blade, 3" brass studded rosewood hdl 18.00
Square, Wm Marples & Son, rosewood/brass, no measure marks . . 9.00
Tester, hay; wrought, for checking hay condition, 38" 32.00
Toolbox, 2 trays, 1-board top, poplar, 14x27x17" 175.00
Toolbox, 3 trays, dvtl corners, walnut, 16x26x14" 75.00
Trammel, wrought iron, sawtooth, G detail, from 40½" 50.00
Vise, leather worker's; wood, block base w/4 legs, 25" 35.00
Vise, pin; for fine handwork, 4¼" 20.00
Vise, Stanley #700, woodworker's; heavy, EX 35.00
Wheel measure, CI, Wiley/Russell Mfg, Greenfield, MS, 12" 35.00
Wheel measure, wrought iron, initials, 11" 20.00
Wrench, adjustable, pat June 14, 1887, Boynton's, 13" 45.00
Wrench, American Beauty, 8" 11.00
Wrench, Billings & Spencer Co, 1879, 7" 13.00
Wrench, Crescent Tool Co, 8" to 10" 10.00
Wrench, monkey; inset hdl, wood, 6½" 5.50
Wrench, Neverslip, 9" 11.00
Wrench, Tokyo Tatag, 4½" 8.00
Wrench, Trojan, 11" 21.00
Wrench, Wakefield #19, 1922, 8" 7.00

Toothpick Holders

Toothpick holders have been popular table accessories since the Victorian era. They were made in pressed glass patterns as well as in all types of art glass and china.

When no condition is indicated, the items listed below are assumed to be in excellent condition. Beware of reproductions.

Croesus, green with gold trim, Riverside Glass Co., 2¼", $85.00. Watch for reproductions which are thicker, poorly gilded; these are worth $10.00.

Alabama 45.00
Amberina, fuschia, sq, New England 150.00
Arched Ovals, gr w/gold 36.00
Art glass, amber optic w/floral, blown, orig holder 110.00
Art glass, pink satin/wht int, enamel floral, ruffled rim 125.00
Atlanta, frosted 35.00
Barrel, camphor, metal top & base rim 35.00
Basketweave, amethyst w/gold, Bellair 35.00
Beaded Grape, gr 40.00
Beaded Swag, ruby stained 30.00
Beatty Honeycomb, clear opal 35.00
Beatty Rib, bl opal 35.00
Beatty Rib, clear opal 25.00
Beatty Waffle, bl opal 45.00
Beatty Waffle, clear opal 40.00
Bees on a Basket, blk 38.00
Bent Buckle, clear w/gold 30.00
Blk boy, milk glass, #372, orange/blk 55.00
Blocked Thumbprint Band, ruby souvenir 28.00
Boy taking off shoes, SP, Derby 140.00
Bundle of Sticks 20.00
Burmese, blossom decor, Webb 435.00
Button & Star Panel 15.00
Button Arches, gold band 25.00
Button Arches, plain 25.00
Button Arches, ruby stained 30.00
Cactus, chocolate (beware of repros) 65.00
Cadmus 40.00
Carnival glass, Kitten, marigold 125.00
Champion 19.00
Champion, clear w/gold 30.00
Chinaman holding umbrella, SP 135.00
Chrysanthemum Base Swirl, clear opal 40.00
Chrysanthemum Leaf 30.00
Church Windows, maiden's blush 20.00
Colorado, clear w/gold 25.00
Cordova 16.00
Croesus, gr w/gold (beware of repros) 95.00
Daisy & Button, amber 26.00
Daisy & Button, amber, barrel, metal rim top & bottom 40.00
Daisy & Button, amber, w/flared rim 35.00
Daisy & Button, amberina, tri-leg 175.00
Daisy & Button, yel 35.00
Daisy & Button w/V Ornament 40.00
Delaware, gr w/gold 68.00
Diamond Spearhead, bl opal 45.00
Dog & Hat, amber (beware of repros) 40.00
Double Eye Hobnail, amber 25.00
Duncan Teepee 30.00
Fan, amber 18.00
Fancy Loop 37.00
Findlay Onyx, custard 400.00
Fleur-De-Lis 15.00
Floradora, gr w/gold 60.00
Florette, shiny 55.00
Flower & Pleat, clear & frosted 40.00
Francesware Swirl, frosted, amber trim 75.00
Gaelic 15.00
Galloway 25.00
Girl holding basket, bisque, pastels, 6¾" 125.00
Grapes 25.00
Harvard, custard, no decor 45.00
Harvard, custard, souvenir 25.00
Harvard, ruby flashed, etched Sault St Marie 30.00
Heart Band, ruby 36.00
Holly Amber, 2½", 1⅞" base, rare 465.00
Horseshoe & Clover, milk glass 30.00
Illinois 25.00
Inverted Eye 30.00
Iowa 22.00
Iris w/Meander, bl opal 85.00
Iris w/Meander, clear opal 35.00
Iris w/Meander, sapphire bl 55.00
Jefferson Colonial, gr w/gold 40.00
Jefferson Optic, custard, souvenir 36.00
Jersey Swirl, spittoon shape, ruby stained 30.00

Kansas....40.00
Kentucky....35.00
King's Crown....19.00
Lacy Medallion, gr, plain or beaded top....16.00
Lacy Medallion, gr w/gold, plain or beaded top....22.00
Ladder w/Diamonds....23.00
Leafy base holds wicker basket, SP, Tufts, 7¼" L....45.00
Little Gem, custard, souvenir....45.00
Man, lg sack on shoulder, by tree trunk, porcelain, 3½"....155.00
Milk glass, bulbous, str neck, bl/pink decor....16.00
Minnesota, 3-hdl....20.00
National's Eureka, ruby stained....45.00
New Hampshire....26.00
Oaken Bucket, yel....30.00
One-O-One, lime gr....50.00
Oval Arches, w/gold, souvenir....30.00
Overall Hobnail, bl opal....40.00
Overall Hobnail, clear opal....35.00
Owl, SP figural, branch by side, 2x2⅛"....65.00
Pairpoint, SP w/eng flowers, lattice work....45.00
Panelled Thistle (beware of repros)....46.00
Pansy, gr opaque....35.00
Pansy, pink satin....55.00
Parrot on perch by holder w/openwork top edge, SP, Tufts....85.00
Peacock w/spread wings, SP....85.00
Pennsylvania....30.00
Pineapple, bl milk glass....65.00
Pineapple & Fan....50.00
Pleat & Bow, wht opaque w/pink flowers....20.00
Pleating, ruby stained....36.00
Pomona, 1st grind, 2¼"....145.00
Porcupine figural, SP, Rogers Smith Co....36.00
Portland, maiden's blush....35.00
Queen's Necklace, ped ft....30.00
Ranson, vaseline, Riverside....40.00
Reeding....20.00
Reverse Swirl, frosted cranberry speckled, rare....110.00
Rexford....15.00
Ribbed Barrel....30.00
Ribbed Base, lt gr opaque....16.00
Ribbed Thumbprint, ruby stained, souvenir....25.00
Ring & Beads, custard....60.00
Rising Sun....25.00
Romona....30.00
Rooster, eng 'Picks' on holder, SP, 2x2x3"....125.00
Rooster figural by wicker basket, SP, 5¾"....75.00
Royal Ivy, rainbow frosted craquelle....125.00
Royal King, ruby & clear....35.00
Royal Oak, rubena....75.00
Ruby Thumbprint....25.00
Ruby Thumbprint, souvenir, World's Fair 1893....36.00
Saxon, clear & ruby....25.00
Scalloped Skirt, amethyst....35.00
Scroll, fan ft, milk glass....20.00
Scroll Shell, milk glass....30.00
Serrated Prism....36.00
Shamrock, ruby stained w/gold....40.00
Shell & Seaweed, milk glass....35.00
Shrine....56.00
Star in Bull's Eye, maiden's blush w/gold....31.50
Star of Bethlehem....25.00
Stippled Dewdrop & Raindrop, amber....76.00
Summit, ruby stained....50.00
Tacoma....22.00
Tarentum's Ladder w/Diamonds....26.00
Teepee....30.00
Texas....22.00
Texas Star....16.00
Thompson's #77, clear & ruby....35.00
Thousand Eye, bl....30.00
Thousand Eye, vaseline....30.00
Tiny Optic, bl....30.00
Trophy....19.00
Trophy, ruby, souvenir....20.00
Truncated Cube....22.00
Truncated Cube, ruby stained....25.00
US Rib, clear w/gold....25.00
US Rib, gr w/gold....30.00
Valencia, cranberry, tall collar....80.00
Vermont, clear w/gold....30.00
Wedding Bells, clear/gilt alternating....28.00
Zipper Slash, ruby, souvenir....25.00

Torquay 'Devon Motto' Ware

Torquay is a unique type of pottery made in the South Devon area of England from 1876. At the height of productivity, at least a dozen companies flourished there, producing simple folk pottery from the area's natural red clay. The ware was both wheel-turned and molded, and decorated under the glaze with heavy slip resulting in low-relief nature subjects or simple scrollwork.

Three of the best-known of these potteries were: Watcombe (1876-1962); Aller Vale (in operation from the mid-1800s, producing domestic ware and architectural products); and Longpark (1890 until 1957). Watcombe and Aller Vale merged in 1901 and operated until 1962 under the name of Royal Aller Vale and Watcombe Art Pottery.

Perhaps the most famous type of ware potted in this area was Motto Ware, so called because of the verses, proverbs, and quotations that decorated it. This decor was achieved by the sgraffito technique--scratching the letters through the slip to expose the red clay underneath. The most popular decorative devices were cottages, black cockerel, multi-cockerel, and a scrollwork pattern called Scandy. Other popular patterns were Kerswell Daisy, ships, kingfishers on blue ground, and many different birds, also on blue grounds.

Aller Vale ware may sometimes be found marked 'H.H. and Company,' a firm who assumed ownership from 1897 to 1901. 'Watcombe Torquay' was an impressed mark used from 1884 to 1927.

When no condition is indicated, the items listed below are assumed to be in mint condition.

Basket, Cockerel, oval, 'Homemade Preserves,' 5"....35.00
Biscuit barrel, Ship, w/lid, 5½x6"....65.00
Bowl, band of flowers on gr, rose bowl shape, w/motto, 3¾"....18.00
Butter, Scandy, clover shape, Watcombe, 'Take a little...'....30.00
Butter dish, Pixie, motto....35.00
Candlestick, Cockerel, Longpark, motto, 4¼"....35.00
Chamberstick, Scandy, Aller Vale, w/motto, 5" saucer base....35.00
Cheese dish, Cottage, rectangular top, motto, 5¼x6½"....50.00
Coffee pot, Scandy, Aller Vale, 'May we be kind'....40.00
Condiment holder, w/salt/pepper/egg cup/mustard, 3½"....80.00
Creamer, Cockerel, 'Help yerzel ter cream,' 2¼"....25.00
Creamer, Cottage, Watcombe, tadpoles/motto/str collar, 4¼"....22.00
Creamer, Scandy, tadpoles & motto, Longpark, 3¼"....18.00
Cup & saucer, Cottage, Dartmouth, motto, 5½" cup, 8½"....40.00
Curling iron tile, forget-me-not pattern, 4⅝x7"....45.00
Dish, Scandy, 3-compartment, 'Cheese, Biscuits, Butter'....50.00
Egg cup, Cockerel, 'Fresh Laid,' ped ft, 2¾"....18.00

Egg cup, kingfisher, sgn England, ped ft, deep saucer..........20.00
Hair receiver, Scandy, Tormohun ware, 3″..................30.00
Ink pot, Scandy, 'Dip Deep,' 2½″ W.........................35.00
Jam dish w/hdl, Cockerel, 'Be aisy w/the jam'................32.00
Jar, tobacco; Kerswell Daisy, 'Pipe, Cigar, Cigarette,' 6″........65.00
Jug, Cottage, Aller Vale, barrel shape w/motto, 4x4″..........35.00
Jug, puzzle; sunset & sailboats, 'More haste, less speed'........35.00
Jug, Ship, hdl thru pierced rim, Hastings, 'Make hay'..........35.00
Jug, Toby; 6¾x3″...75.00
Match striker, Scandy, motto, 3½″ base.....................45.00
Mug, Cottage, Dartmouth, 'Kind words are music,' 3¾″........16.00
Mug, shaving; Multi-Cockerel, 4x5½″ hdl to spout............75.00
Pepper pot, Cockerel, 'Padstow, Hot & Strong,' acorn shape....12.50
Pitcher, Cockerel, 'Better do one thing,' 4¼″.................35.00
Pitcher, Scandy/motto, hdl thru pierce rim, Aller Vale, 4″......35.00
Platter, Multi-Cockerel, oval, 'A place for,' 7⅜x10½″...........70.00
Statue, figure, terre cotta classical, Watcombe, 11½″..........300.00
Sugar bowl, Cockerel, Longpark, 'Be aisy w/the sugar'.........25.00
Sugar bowl, Cottage, crimp rim, Longpark, w/motto, 3¼″.......30.00
Sugar bowl, Cottage, Dartmouth, 'Do you take sugar?'..........18.00
Sugar bowl, seagull, Dartmouth, 4″.........................18.00
Sugar bowl, Thistle, lg ped bowl, ruffled rim, Longpark.........35.00
Tea tile, Multi-Cockerel, heavily potted, 'Place pot...me'........38.00
Teapot, Cockerel, motto, 6″..................................50.00
Teapot, dbl Cottages, 'Av a cup of tay,' EX art, 9x11″........350.00

Teapot, Cottage, 'Remembered joys are never past,' Watcombe Devon Motto Ware, brown, $45.00.

Toast rack, Scandy, 5 rail, 'Help yerself to toast,' 3x5″.........55.00
Tobacco jar, Kerswell Daisy, 'Pipe, cigar, cigarette,' 6″.........65.00
Tray, Scandy, long verse, imp Watcombe Torquay, 7¼x11″.....70.00
Tumbler, sailboats, 'Dinna let yer modesty...,' flared, 4″........18.00
Vase, boat at sea, Watcombe, 'Lands End,' 4″.................18.50
Vase, dolphin, 3-ftd, Watcombe Torquay, 3½x2¾″, pr..........65.00
Vase, faience, Cottage, wood fence/gate, hdls, early, 4″.........40.00
Vase, Kingfisher, 2-hdl, Longpark, 12½″......................95.00
Vase, sailboat & people, motto, 5½″..........................50.00
Vase, Scandy, ovoid w/2 dimples, 'pound of pluck,' 6″.........38.00
Vase, sunset & sailboats, 2 dimples, motto, 6½″..............35.00

Tortoiseshell Glass

By combining several shades of glass--brown, clear, and yellow--glass manufacturers of the 19th century were able to produce an art glass that closely resembled the shell of the tortoise. Some of this type of glassware was manufactured in Germany. In America it was made by several firms, the most prominent of which was the Boston and Sandwich Glass Works.

When no condition is indicated, the items listed below are assumed to be in mint condition.

Bowl, 3½x7¾″..85.00
Card holder, flattened U-form, disk ft, 2¾″...................58.00
Pitcher, applied amber hdl, 8½″............................125.00
Pitcher, sq lip, fine swirl ribs, lg areas of cream, 8″..........275.00
Vase, bottle shape, no mk, 12″...............................75.00
Vase, bulbous, ruffled, 9″..................................145.00
Vase, enamel flowers, bulbous, 6x4″..........................65.00
Vase, English, ca 1910, 8″....................................85.00

Toys

Toys, obviously, are fun to collect. But especially those made before WWII also have sound investment potential. Lithograph-printed mechanical toys, for instance, are especially popular with today's collectors, and steadily continue to increase in value year after year. Condition of any type of toy is critical--they were made for children to play with, and many that have survived to the present are in a well-played-with state, which only serves to enhance the value of those that remain in excellent condition. In the listings below, toys are listed by manufacturer's name when at all possible, otherwise by type.

When no condition is indicated, the items listed below are assumed to be in excellent condition.

Key:
b/o—battery operated
w/up—windup
NP—nickel plated

Cast Iron

Cast iron toys were made from shortly before the Civil War until the beginning of the 20th century. They are evaluated to a large extent by scarcity, complexity, design, and detail.

Boat, steam wheeler, on wheels, 5″ L.......................50.00
Chester Gump, in cart pulled by horse, 1905................350.00
Columbus, landing, bell ringer, 1893........................350.00
Contractors Dump Wagon, w/Blk man driver, 16″ L...........60.00
Fire hose reel wagon, horse drawn, 17″ L...................260.00
Fire pumper, pulled by 3 horses & driver, 18″ L.............150.00
Fire wagon, Fire Patrol, 16″ L..............................160.00
Fire wagon, w/ladder, pulled by 3 horses, 18″ L.............130.00
Fire wagon, w/ladder, pulled by 3 horses, 25″ L.............150.00
Fire wagon, w/ladders/2 horses/2 separate men, 1900, 27″.....385.00
Hay wagon, horse & driver..................................110.00
Ice wagon, pulled by 2 horses, 14″ L........................175.00
Locomotive & tender, orig blk pnt, late 1800s, 12″ L..........90.00
Merry-go-round, children on horses, orig pnt, 5″.............250.00
Overland Circus Wagon, w/driver, 17″ L.....................235.00
Paddle-wheeler, The Puritan, 5x10″.........................200.00
Plane, Lindy, 4″ L...75.00
Pony cart, 4″, VG..35.00
River boat, City of NY, 15″ L...............................640.00
Speedboat, w/driver, 1930, 5½″.............................110.00
Steam shovel, mounted on Mack truck, 'General,' '30, 10½″...450.00
Stove, kitchen; 'American,' 1910, 9″, w/pots & pans...........65.00
Tractor, wood roller on front end, worn NP bk wheels, 4″ L....50.00
Uncle Sam & English John Bull, bell ringer...................750.00
Wild Mule Jack, bell ringer, figure riding mule................475.00

Company or Country of Manufacturer

Althoff Berman, rocking horse, w/bell, tin, 1870s, EX.........250.00
Arcade, Chester Gump Cart, pnt CI, 7½″, EX...............350.00
Arcade, Grayhound People Mover, Great Lakes Expo 1936, iron.65.00
Arcade, Tow Truck, 4½″, VG.............................60.00
Arcade, truck cab/trailer, w/2 cars/2 trucks, CI, '38, 15″.......475.00

Arcade, International Harvester truck, cast iron with red paint, original labels, 11″ long, $275.00.

B&R, Kid Flyer, boy pushes soap-box scooter, w/up, 1920s....250.00
B&R, Kids Special, boy riding tricycle, w/up, 1920s...........250.00
Baldwin, hen, tin, crank, clucks & lays eggs, 5⅜″, EX.........22.50
Barclay, cannon car, w/movable gun, 4″.....................30.00
Barclay, Renault Tank..................................22.00
Barclay, truck, anti-aircraft, wht tires......................27.00
Bing, Gunboat, pnt tin w/up, rpl masts, 11″ L, EX...........500.00
Bing, Touring Car, 2-seater/driver, clockwork, 12½″, VG......825.00
Bing, 2-Car Garage, tin litho, 2 sgn clockwork cars...........250.00
Britains, Farm General Purpose Plow, orig box, #6F, EX......170.00
Britains, farm w/carriage/horses/log/orig box, Rike-Kumler......140.00
Britains, Fordson Major Tractor, rubber tires, #128F, EX......130.00
Britains, Home Farm Series, horse rake, orig box/tag, #8F.....100.00
Britains, Home Farm Series, horse roller w/man, orig box......75.00
Britains, Home Farm Series, trumbrel cart, orig box, #4F......110.00
Brower, automatic dancer, Blk man, clockwork, 1873, 9″....2,530.00
Buddy L, Aerial Truck, orig decals, 30″ L, NM.............650.00
Buddy L, Hook & Ladder, orig decals, EX rstr.............400.00
Buddy L, Water Tank Sprinkler Truck, orig decals, EX rstr....450.00
Carette, car, 1910 model, w/driver, w/up, crank, 6″...........650.00
Carette, Landaulette, tin litho clockwork, ca 1910, 9″, EX...1,540.00
Carette, Steam Launch, pnt tin, canopy/3-blade prop, 14″.....990.00
Carpenter, pumper, horizontal, #14 boiler, 18½″, VG........1,000.00
Chad Valley, car, remote control, MIB.....................65.00
Chein, Aquaplane #59, mechanical, tin, orig box, EX..........55.00
Chein, Barnacle Bill the Sailor, walks, w/up, 1930s...........185.00
Chein, Blk dancer, key w/up, tin, 5″.......................25.00
Chein, Blk native on mechanical alligator, w/up, '40s, M........95.00
Chein, Blk native on mechanical alligator, w/up, '40s, MIB.....125.00
Chein, clown walking on hands, w/up, tin, 4½″, EX............30.00
Chein, Crank Church Organ, tin, 9x7″, EX..................25.00
Chein, Disney Musical Top, tin w/wood hdl, 6″, MIB...........30.00
Chein, Disneyland Tea Set, tin, service for 2, MIB.............45.00
Chein, Disneyland Wind-Up Ferris Wheel, 1950s.............225.00
Chein, Felix-type cat on scooter, w/up, 1930s................175.00
Chein, ferris wheel, tin, 18″............................100.00
Chein, Happy Hooligan, tin w/up, EX......................180.00
Chein, horse w/tin litho wagon, 'Dispatch,' CI, 11″, VG.........75.00
Chein, Mickey Mouse pail, tin w/beach scene, 7″..............60.00
Chein, native on turtle's bk.............................75.00
Chein, Popeye hits punching bag, w/up, 1930s, w/orig box...1,250.00
Chein, Popeye in barrel, walks, w/up, 1930s.................250.00
Chein, Popeye jointed wood figure, 1930s, 11″..............325.00
Chein, Streetcar 270, Broadway 270, tin litho, 8″, EX........130.00
Chein, Walking Popeye, tin w/up.........................225.00
China, chick, tin w/up.................................19.00
CK, Jolly Mouse, w/up, orig box, EX......................35.00
Clauss, farm scene, carved/pnt wood, orig box, 21-pc.........65.00
Corgi, Popeye Paddle Wagon, moving figures, 1967, 6″, MIB...150.00
Corgi, Popeye Paddle Wagon, 1969, 3″, MIB.................95.00
CR, Nazi camouflage wrecker w/crane, 3 men, w/up, '30, 16″...450.00
Cragstan, Sparkling Tank, #10459, tin, orig box, EX..........15.00
Dinky, armored car, #630...............................15.00
Distler, firehouse w/ladder truck, tin litho, 12″ house.........715.00
Doepke, Adams Grader, #2006...........................100.00
Doepke, dwarf, Grumpy, bsk.............................65.00
Doepke, dwarf, Sneezy, bsk.............................65.00
Doepke, Euclid earth hauler truck, #2009..................150.00
Doepke, Unit Mobil Crane, #2007........................100.00
DRGM, seal, clockwork, 60% pnt, 7¼″......................40.00
English, auto, long front, w/driver, w/up, 1920s.............195.00
English, Meccano race car, w/up, 12″ L....................500.00
Fisher Price, Mickey Mouse playing xylophone, 1939...........75.00
Fisher Price, Pluto w/basket, 1930s.........................45.00
Fleischmann, ocean liner, pnt tin, clockwork prop, 13½″......770.00
FMB, Le 500G, Marque Deposie Francus, circus bear, 8½″....210.00
French, Aventures De Coquenano, paper/wood horse/rider, EX.350.00
French, bear on wheels turns head, real fur, w/up, 1900.......325.00
French, dump truck w/driver, side dumper, w/up, 1910........475.00
French, Les Plaisirs Du Jardin d'Acclimatation, in box, EX.....550.00
French, Omnibus, tin litho clockwork, orig box, 1930, 10″.....550.00
French, street lamp, stained lead/glass/tin, in box, 6″, EX.....100.00
French, Theatre Des Marionettes, litho paper/cb, 11″, EX......60.00
G&K, dump truck w/driver, crank dumps load, Germany, 1915..350.00
Gama, tank, w/tools, #65, 4″, EX..........................50.00
Gely, mallard duck, tin, friction, Germany, 5″ L...............28.00
Geo Brown, lady & horse, counter-weighted, 1870, 15″......5,830.00
German, alligator, w/up, 8″..............................40.00
German, battleship w/3 ships, attendant flotilla, 8″, EX........650.00
German, Busy Lizzie, sweeps carpet, w/up, 1920s............650.00
German, cat chases mouse back & forth, w/up, 1920s.........250.00
German, cat: wheels/spark eyes; chases mouse, HP w/up, '10...325.00
German, chicken in suit, mechanical, unmk, rare, 8″...........35.00
German, coupe, tin litho w/up, electric lights, 15″, VG........700.00
German, cowboy on horse twirls lasso, w/up, 1930s, MIB......195.00
German, Felix the Cat, walks, w/up, 1924, Pat Sullivan........250.00
German, ferris wheel/power plant, tin w/up, 4x8″ base, EX.....110.00
German, Indian holds bow & arrow, HP, w/up, 1900..........375.00
German, monkey, clothed, plays snare drum, w/up, '20s.......350.00
German, monkey in car, tin.............................100.00
German, peacock, walks/moves neck, w/up, Ebo Pao-Pao, 1920.275.00
German, Q-Boats, hull w/3 interchangeable superstructures.....600.00
German, rams butting, tin litho w/up, 5½″, EX..............125.00
German, rocking horse w/clown, wood/papier mache w/up, EX..400.00
German, streetcar, pulled by horse, tin litho, 12½″, EX.......800.00
German, sulky, driver, tin/compo w/up, 6½″, EX.............125.00
German, Traffic Cop, tin litho, mechanical, 5″, EX............60.00
Gibbs, lead horse w/tin carriage, 4¾″ L, EX..................35.00
Gong Bell Mfg, clown, dog jumps through hoop, w/bells, 12″.3,025.00
Gong Bell Mfg, Wild Mule Jack, rpl bell, 8″ L..............385.00
Gong Bell Mfg, 2 Coons, Blk man/log/raccoon, ca 1800s, 9″..3,300.00
Gunthermann, Bonzo on Tricycle, tin litho, 6¾″, VG.........385.00
Hercules, Rumble Seat Coupe, tin litho, 17½″ L, EX.........200.00
Hubley, Auto Transport Trailer, 7¾″.......................65.00
Hubley, Bell Telephone truck/pole trailer/shovel, #478, EX.....500.00
Hubley, Ferris Wheel, clockwork, w/people, 1893, 17″.......1,250.00
Hubley, Motor Express trailer............................35.00

Hubley, Mr Magoo, in car, tin plated, 1961 .... 65.00
Hubley, Streamlined Racer, CI, wht rubber tires, 5½" L 50.00
Hubley, wrecker, rpt, 6" L 50.00
Ideal, Mickey & Donald Speedway, MIB 50.00
Ideal, Roy Rogers horse trailer & jeep, MIB 55.00
Irwin, Dancing Cinderella & Prince, plastic, in box, NM 50.00
Italy, Charlie Chaplin mechanical figure, plastic, 1950s 65.00
Italy, Happy Hooligan in Goat Cart, tin w/up, 7", EX 350.00
Ives, bear, sets on haunches, clockwork, fur covered, 8½" 500.00
Ives, Cosner Trotter, clockwork, pat Mar 7, 1871, 11", EX 3,500.00
Ives, horse, ea leg articulated, orig straw tail, 3 wheels 1,100.00
Ives, Smoking Gen Grant, CI chair, redressed, 14" 1,870.00
Ives, trotter w/rider, pnt tin clockwork, 1871, 10", NM 3,300.00
Japan, boy on tricycle, tin/celluloid/cloth w/up, 8½", VG 125.00
Japan, Cadet, tin litho w/up, working, orig box, 6", EX 40.00
Japan, car, pulling motor boat, friction, tin 35.00
Japan, cat wheels mouse in stroller, clockwork, 1910, box 825.00
Japan, dog standing w/book, tail turns, celluloid, 6", EX 28.00
Japan, elephant, walking on tin barrel, plush covered tin 25.00
Japan, Frankie the Roller Skating Monkey, b/o, in box, VG 60.00
Japan, gorilla, b/o remote, in box, 9", VG 150.00
Japan, Grand-Pa Car, puffs smoke/noise, b/o 45.00
Japan, High Speed Racer, tin friction, in box, 11", EX 100.00
Japan, Horse Race, tin litho/celluloid w/up, 6½", EX 80.00
Japan, Mickey Mouse, walks, celluloid w/up, working, 7", EX 1,000.00
Japan, Mickey Mouse on Horse, wood/celluloid w/up, 7", EX 750.00
Japan, Native Warrior, tin litho w/up, working, 6", EX 70.00
Japan, Snake Charmer, tin litho b/o, 6½", VG 110.00
Japan, squirrel w/nut, w/up, gray, EX 35.00
Japan, Tarzan, tin/plastic b/o remote, orig box, NM 125.00
Japan, Tobe Toy, wood, figure pops out, 3½x1½", EX 150.00
Jaymar, Make Your Own Funnies, 10 wood figures, in box, EX 450.00
Jaymar, Mickey Mouse, pnt wood, bird on perch w/bell, 6" 45.00
Kenton, Bakery Wagon, pulled by horse, 1910, 13" 395.00
Kenton, Buckeye ditcher, orig pnt, 12", EX 375.00
Kenton, cannon, firecracker; Admiral Dewey, CI 175.00
Kenton, chariot, 3 horses & lady driver, CI, 1915, 10" L 440.00
Kenton, double-decker bus, pnt CI, 10", EX 450.00
Keystone, Express Truck, orig decals, EX rstr 300.00
Kingsbury, sedan, tin litho w/up, rubber tires, 12½", VG 900.00
Leeway, horse on wheels, all orig, 16" L 110.00
Lehmann, Alabama Coon Jigger, tin w/up, 1914 .... 325.00
Lehmann, Anxious Bride Nanni, tin litho clockwork, 9" 1,430.00
Lehmann, Autobus, tin litho w/up, working, 8", EX 1,100.00
Lehmann, balking mule pulls clown in cart, w/up, 1910 .... 195.00
Lehmann, Beetle, w/up, 1905 .... 95.00
Lehmann, Berolina Touring Car, tin litho, all orig, 6½" 1,540.00
Lehmann, Bucking Broncho #625, pnt tin clockwork, 7" L 450.00
Lehmann, cat chases mouse on rod, clockwork, 10½" 525.00
Lehmann, Century Cycle, 3-wheel car, man holds hat, w/up 350.00
Lehmann, Dancing Sailor #535, pnt tin, all orig w/box, 7½" 770.00
Lehmann, Dare Devil, tin litho w/up, 7", EX 375.00
Lehmann, Duo, rabbit/rooster, tin w/up, losses, 6½", EX 350.00
Lehmann, EPL-1, tin w/up, props missing, 7", VG 275.00
Lehmann, Hanson Cab, tin litho w/up, arm missing, EX 550.00
Lehmann, Kadi, 2 Chinamen carrying tea chest, w/up 550.00
Lehmann, Limousine, tin/electric lights, 12½", VG 1,000.00
Lehmann, Nu-Nu, tin litho w/up, in box, 5½", EX 600.00
Lehmann, Paddy's Dancing Pig, pnt tin w/up, in box, 6", NM 850.00
Lehmann, Quack-Quack, goose pulls goslings in cart, w/up 250.00
Lehmann, seal, w/up 100.00
Lehmann, ToTo auto, tin w/up, 1914 .... 245.00
Lehmann, Tut Tut, man drives auto while playing horn, w/up 850.00
Lehmann, UHU, litho/pnt tin w/up, in box, 9" L, VG 1,200.00
Lehmann, Zig Zag, pnt/litho tin w/up, 4½" wheel, EX 850.00
Lehmann, Zulu, ostrich cart w/driver, tin w/up, 7", EX 350.00
Limoge, France, clown acrobat, bisque head, lever op, 13" 660.00
Linemar, Casper the Ghost mechanical tank, w/up 145.00
Linemar, Donald Duck Acrobat, tin/celluloid w/up, 6½", EX 150.00
Linemar, Jungle Trio, tin/plastic b/o, rpl, EX 200.00
Linemar, Mickey Mouse Acrobat, tin/celluloid w/up, 6½", EX 175.00
Linemar, Playful Pluto, tin litho w/up, orig box, 4½", NM 150.00
Linemar, Pluto Acrobat, tin/celluloid w/up, 6½", EX 100.00
Linemar, Pluto Lantern, tin/rubber/glass, in box, 6", EX 125.00
Linemar, Popeye balances Olive Oyl in chair 850.00
Linemar, Popeye Lantern, figural, tin w/glass stomach, MIB 135.00
Linemar, Popeye on skates, w/up 450.00
Linemar, Popeye on unicycle, MIB 450.00
Linemar, Popeye throws basketball, w/up 850.00
Lionel, Peter Rabbit Chick Mobile, w/up handcar, 1930s 475.00
Martin, man plays piano, musical, w/up, France, 1900 .... 750.00
Marx, Amos & Andy, walking w/up, fixed eyes, 1930s, pr 1,100.00
Marx, Amos & Andy Fresh Air Taxi, w/up, complete, 1930s 650.00
Marx, Balky Mule 50.00
Marx, Blondie's Jalopy, tin w/up, orig box, 16", EX 1,250.00
Marx, BO Plenty walks w/Baby Sparkle, w/up, 1930s, MIB 150.00
Marx, Boy's Camp 150.00
Marx, Bunny Express train, tin litho, O ga, in box, NM 300.00
Marx, Crazy Car, 4 Wheels/No Brakes, man & dog, w/up, '20s 160.00
Marx, dairy truck w/2 wht milk glass bottles, sheet iron 100.00
Marx, Disney Carry-All Dollhouse, MIB 85.00
Marx, Disney TV Playhouse, tin litho stage, litho box, MIB 150.00
Marx, Donald Duck Duet, tin litho w/up, 10", EX 350.00
Marx, Dopey, tin w/up, 1938, 9", EX 125.00
Marx, Electric Convertible, tin/plastic, in box, 20", EX 110.00
Marx, fire engine w/siren, sheet iron, 1927, 5x9", EX 45.00
Marx, fire truck, ride-on, orig box, NM 160.00
Marx, fireman climbs ladder, w/up, 1930s 175.00
Marx, Fort Apache Stockade 95.00
Marx, Funny Firefighters/Crazy Firetruck, w/up, 1930s 350.00
Marx, Hey, Hey, Chicken Snatcher, 1926 .... 650.00
Marx, Honeymoon Express, MIB 120.00
Marx, Hootin' Hollow Haunted House, partially working, EX 225.00
Marx, Joe Penner, man w/duck, mechanical, tin 185.00
Marx, Joy Rider, key w/up, tin, 5x8" 160.00
Marx, Little Orphan Annie jumps rope, 1930s 450.00
Marx, Lone Ranger Hi-Yo Silver, printed tin, c 1938, 7" 125.00
Marx, Lone Ranger Ranch 85.00
Marx, Medieval Castle Fort 125.00
Marx, Merry Makers Band, 4 musical mice, marque, 1920s 750.00
Marx, Merry Makers Band, 4 musical mice, 1920s 650.00
Marx, Milton Berle car, w/up, MIB 145.00
Marx, Mortimer Snerd, tin w/up, 1939, 9", VG 150.00
Marx, Mortimer Snerd drives Crazy Car, w/up, 1930s 375.00
Marx, motorcycle cop 65.00
Marx, Mysterious Pluto, metal w/up w/wheels, orig box, '40s 150.00
Marx, Officer 666, walks & changes expression, w/up, 1930s 395.00
Marx, Orphan Annie skips rope, w/Sandy, w/up, H Gray, pr 895.00
Marx, PD on motorcycle, pat #2001625, w/up 45.00
Marx, Peter Pan tea set, china, 23-pc, MIB 300.00
Marx, Pinocchio, c Walt Disney, 1939, 8½", EX 140.00
Marx, policeman on motorcycle w/sidecar, w/up, 8", EX 120.00
Marx, Popeye & Olive Oyl on roof 650.00
Marx, Popeye Flip-Over Tank, tin, 3x4" 225.00
Marx, Popeye in Airplane, orange & yel, tin w/up, crank 350.00
Marx, Popeye Pirate Pistol, tin litho clicker, NM in box 165.00
Marx, Popeye w/parrots, tin litho w/up, working, 8½", EX 150.00
Marx, Porky Pig doll, w/up, MIB 185.00

Marx, Race Car #12, tin litho w/up, working, 16″, EX........100.00
Marx, Rex Racer, tin litho w/up, orig box, 8½″ L, NM........300.00
Marx, Ring-a-Ling, circus, tin, 8x8″........................275.00
Marx, Roy Rogers Ranch.................................85.00
Marx, Sandy (Orphan Annie's dog) chases ball, w/up, 1930s....250.00
Marx, Skybird Flyer, tin litho w/up, in box, 9″ pylon, EX......150.00
Marx, Solo Flight, Dagwood in airplane, w/up, 1935..........350.00
Marx, Sparkling Doughboy Tank, orig box, 10″..............150.00
Marx, Superman, flat metal figure pushes tank over, 1940.....250.00
Marx, Tidy Tim the Clean-Up Man, pushing cart, w/up, '30s....225.00
Marx, Tow Truck, ride-on, orig box VG, NM................110.00
Marx, Tricky Taxi, car, tin w/up, 1½x4½″....................50.00
Marx, Uncle Wiggily, tin, orig box, EX.....................350.00
Marx, Whistling, Spooky, Kooky Tree, tin/plastic b/o, VG......800.00
Marx, Whoopee Car, cowboy drives Crazy Car, w/up, 1930s....160.00
Marx, WWII Tank, man w/rifle pops up, w/up, 10″...........125.00
Marx, Zorro, horse/accessories, plastic, Walt Disney, MIB.......45.00
Mattel, Popeye Pop-Up Spinach Can, jack-in-box, 1957.........45.00
Minic, Break Down Lorry Motor Service, tin, orig, 2x6″, EX....80.00
Minic, limousine w/chauffeur, tin w/up, English, 1¼x5″.........65.00
Minic, roadster w/4 seats, tin w/up, 1x4″, EX.................65.00
Minic, steam roller.....................................20.00
Minic, taxi, tin w/up, bl w/blk top, 4″.......................55.00
Minic, wrecker truck, tin w/up, 1½x5″, EX...................50.00
Nifty, Barney Google rides Spark Plug, w/up, 1924..........1,250.00
Nifty, Skidoodle, tin litho w/up, working, 19½″, VG..........550.00
Norah Wellings, penguin, mohair, 7½″........................48.00
Ny Lint, Howdy Doody steers '20s cart, w/up, 1950s..........165.00
Occupied Japan, bear, fabric, mechanical....................45.00
Occupied Japan, bird hops & sings, celluloid, w/up, 5″ L.......45.00
Occupied Japan, boy on sled, tin & celluloid, MIB.............55.00
Occupied Japan, Chevrolet, bk motion, tin...................68.00
Occupied Japan, dog playing, MIB..........................47.00
Occupied Japan, dog sits up & begs, 5½″.....................50.00
Occupied Japan, traveling boy, w/suitcase, MIB...............58.00
Occupied Japan, turtle, mechanical, tin, orig box, 5x2″, M......15.00
Occupied Japan, Zoot-Suit Jigger, Blk by sign, w/up, 1945.....225.00
Ohio Art, shooting gallery, tin litho........................30.00
Ohio Art, tea set, fairy scenes on bl ground, 4-place set........25.00
Ohio Art, tea set, Little Red Riding Hood, 14-pc w/box........22.00
Ohio Art, tea set, Pinocchio scenes, 4-place set...............30.00
Playskool, Pullman, pnt pressed steel, 9½x11½″, EX..........180.00
Plaything, HoHo Hoop & Monkey, tin, 10″, EX................40.00
Pratt & Letchworth, Hansom cab w/horse, pnt CI, 12″........365.00
QRS DeVry Corp, Playasax, tune on punched paper roll, 10½″.125.00
Remco, Wizard of Oz, robot, tin, unused, in box, 1969, lg.....150.00
Schieble, hook & ladder, pressed steel, box, 21¼″, L, VG.....550.00
Schuco, Boy Mouse, dressed, mohair, 1950s, 10″, EX..........65.00
Schuco, boy playing violin, w/key & certificate, 4½″, EX.......150.00
Schuco, Charlie Chaplin twirls cane, w/up, 1920s, 6½″........450.00
Schuco, Comic Cat, mohair, squeaks, 1950s, 11″.............65.00
Schuco, drummer, tin w/up...............................55.00
Schuco, elephant, mohair, 1950s, 9x12″.....................65.00
Schuco, Examico car, #4001, MIB..........................90.00
Schuco, Foxi, dressed, mohair, 1950s, 9″, MIB................65.00
Schuco, Girl Mouse, dressed, mohair, 1950s, 10″, EX..........65.00
Schuco, Patsy, dressed, mohair, 1950s, 10″, MIB.............75.00
Schuco, Pit, dressed, mohair, 1950s, 10″, MIB................75.00
Schuco, race car, wrench, #1050, EX........................60.00
Schuco, standing cat, mohair, blk, 1950s, 8″..................65.00
Sear's Roebuck, Uncle Sam Nodder Phaeton, 1960s, EX......200.00
Seymore, Dick Tracy camera, EX...........................25.00
Spain, Kalin Circus, pnt wood/cloth, engine/6 cars/etc, EX.....100.00
Steelcraft, Mack dump truck, open cab, decals, sheet iron......75.00
Stock, Acrobat in Hoop, tin litho w/up, 6″ figure, EX.......2,200.00
Strauss, Interstate double-decker bus, w/driver, w/up, 11″......375.00
Strauss, Lux-A-Cab, tin litho w/up, 8″ L, EX................300.00
Strauss, Tip Top, Blk man pushes cart, w/up, 1920s..........225.00
Strauss, Tom Twist the Clown, walks & stands on head, '20s...450.00
Strauss, Travel Chicks, tin litho w/up, 7½″, EX..............160.00
Structo, garbage truck, 21″...............................26.00
Technofix, motorcycle, w/driver, w/up......................80.00
Tootsie Toy, Coupe, #4636...............................18.00
Tootsie Toy, Ford coupe, w/rumble seat, tin, 1928, 8″, VG.....45.00
Tootsie Toy, Ford tractor & disc, G graphics on box, MIB......75.00
Tootsie Toy, Graham wrecker.............................45.00
Tootsie Toy, Smitty & Herby on motorcycle.................195.00
Tootsie Toy, Smitty on delivery cycle......................160.00
TPS Japan, skating rabbit, MIB...........................175.00
Unique Art, Howdy Doody Band, w/up, 1950s, w/orig box.....550.00
Unique Art, Jazzbo Jim, Blk w/banjo on roof, w/up, 1921......250.00
Unique Art, Kiddy Cyclist, boy rides tricycle, w/up............145.00
Unique Art, Li'l Abner Dog Patch Band, w/up, 1940s.........350.00
Unique Art, Rodeo Joe car, MIB..........................155.00
US Gas Co, gas pump, tin, red...........................95.00
US Zone Germany, motorcycle & driver, w/up, tin, 7½x6″, M...320.00
USA, Calculating Hen, cb chicken on noisemaker, 1936, 8″.....65.00
USA, Magic Wheel Optical Toy, litho paper, in box, VG.......850.00
USA, Silver Bullet Race Car, tin litho, 25″, VG..............190.00
USA, Thimble-Drome Prop-Rod, cast plastic, gas engine, NM....80.00
Watrous Mfg Co, boys sawing watermelon, w/bell, CI, 8½″....3,625.00
Winter Associates, Blk banjo player, plays Old Susannah......465.00
Winter Associates, sand toy w/lady dancer..................330.00
Wolverine, battleship, litho, 14¾″, EX.....................20.00
Wolverine, refrigerator, brn, newer model, 15x7½″............18.00
Wolverine, refrigerator, 13½x8″...........................25.00
Wolverine, washing machine, wringer/agitator work, 12″.......100.00
Woods Mechanical Toys, man pushing cart, tin, 6x6″..........45.00
Wyandotte, H Pennyworth in car, Popeye comic, w/up, 1940s..275.00
Wyandotte, hen, press & she lays marbles, tin, 8″, EX.........30.00
Wyandotte, sedan, tin/pnt pressed steel, 15″ L, EX...........100.00
Wyandotte, shooting gallery..............................65.00
Wyandotte, Woody, car, tin, 7x18″.........................30.00
Yone, fire engine w/ladder that slides, w/up, 4″...............25.00

Cranks and Windups

Armored car, tin litho w/up, 9½″ L, EX....................500.00
Barnum & Bailey wagon w/3-part cage, tin clown/animals......600.00
Bear, playing snare drum, musical, HP, w/up, 1900...........495.00
Bear, reading book, turns pages, w/up, 7″..................125.00
Bear, stuffed cloth, 5½″, rides w/up metal scooter, '30s........250.00
Bear, walking, celluloid, w/up, 4½x5″......................25.00
Boat, The Liberator, on wheels, wood, w/up, 25″ L............35.00
Bullfighter, walks, w/cape & sword, compo/wood, w/up, '20s....195.00
Chicken pecking, HP tin, squeaks, 1870s, 8x6″, EX..........210.00
Clock, tin/brass, clockwork clown & bear atop, 3¾″..........175.00
Clown on wheels pushes umbrella w/stick, HP, w/up, 1900.....385.00
Clown w/flute, music on cat's tail, musical w/up, HP, '90s......750.00
Dog bites Black boy w/watermelon, celluloid/cloth, 6″, EX.....250.00
Dove, HP tin on pewter wheels, keywound, head nods, 8″, VG.195.00
Elf, w/up, 6″, VG......................................35.00
Ham & Sam Minstrel Team, tin w/up, 1921.................450.00
Happy Boy, plays cymbal, compo/metal/cloth, w/up, '20s, 9″....175.00
Horse, compo w/wood legs/felt body, rearing, legs move, 9″.....95.00
Horse, felt over wood, keywound, tail spins, 5″...............55.00
Men playing pool, w/up, 1930s, 14″.......................160.00
Monkey, eats banana/tail spins, cloth body/tin face, w/up........15.00

Mortimer Snerd band, tin w/up....485.00
Mother bear, pulling 2 baby bears, blk, w/up, EX....95.00
Mule, bucking, tin w/up, 6x5″....20.00
Parrot, rocks on swing, tin w/up, 9″ L....80.00
Race Car #25, tin litho w/up, working, 14½″, VG....120.00
Ranger Motor Express, semi w/driver, w/up, '40, 6″, MIB....75.00
Roadster, metal, w/CI driver, w/up, 1920s, 10½″....225.00
Rocking R Ranch, 2 boys on see-saw, mechanical w/up, 6x18″..40.00
Soldier, WWI German, crawls w/rifle, HP, w/up, 1915....475.00
Woman at sewing machine, tin w/up, mc pnt worn, rpr, 5¾″...500.00
3 mice do somersaults & pull wheeled device, w/up, 1930s....175.00

Farm Toys

Allis Chalmers, tractor, AC-4, blk tires, G&B, EX....175.00
Allis Chalmers, tractor, AC-6, Arcade decal, EX....400.00
Allis Chalmers, tractor, Model C, 1950....80.00
Allis Chalmers, tractor/wagon, Arcade, 12¾″....135.00
Allis Chalmers, tractor/wagon, wht rubber tires, Arcade, 9″....24.00
Arcade, corn cutter & binder....37.00
Arcade, corn planter, rubber wheels....25.00
Arcade, dump hay rake, 5″....33.00
Arcade, dump hay rake, 7″....60.00
Arcade, farm mower....22.00
Avery, tractor, 1920s, Arcade, 4¾″....90.00
Farmall, tractor, Cultivision A, Arcade....240.00
Ford, tractor, Arcade, 4″....60.00
Ford, tractor, Hubley 6000....16.00
Fordson, tractor, Arcade, 4″....45.00
Fordson, tractor, 1920s, Arcade, 3½″....39.00
Fordson, tractor w/driver, CI, Arcade, 5¾″....87.00
Hubley, tractor, steam boiler in front, early 1920s, 4¾″....60.00
John Deere, thresher, mid-1930s, Vindex....425.00
John Deere, tractor, cast aluminum, 7″....40.00
John Deere, tractor, CI, rubber tires, Arcade, 7″....125.00
Kingsbury, tractor, mechanical, 8″, w/driver....120.00
McCormick-Deering, spreader, steel/blk rubber, '50s, 10½″....37.00
McCormick-Deering, spreader w/shaft, Arcade....90.00
McCormick-Deering, thresher, CI, Arcade, 10″....165.00
McCormick-Deering, thresher, Model 450x, 1932, Arcade, 9½″.150.00
McCormick-Deering, tractor, Model 10-20, Arcade....150.00
Monarch, tractor, Hubley, 5½″....120.00
Oliver, tractor, blk rubber wheels, Arcade, 7″....125.00

John Deere combine, cast iron with driver, made by Vindex, $1,125.00.

Friction

Car, tin w/CI driver....80.00
Car, tin w/CI driver & 2 lady passengers, 9x11″....230.00
Delivery truck, w/driver, 8x12″....180.00
Japan, World Circus truck, animal's heads move....25.00
Limousine, tin w/CI driver, 14″ L....270.00

Guns

Though toy guns were patented as early as the 1850s, the cap pistol was not invented until 1870, when paper caps that were primarily developed to detonate muzzleloaders became available. Some of the earlier models were very ornate, and were occasionally decorated with figural heads. Most are marked with the name of their manufacturer--Ace, Daisy, Bulldog, Victor, and Excelsior are the most common.

Aim To Save, ca 1909, VG....125.00
Best C19, cowboy type....30.00
Big Buster, cap automatic, CI, 2-pc trigger, 1915, Kilgore....40.00
Billy the Kid, cap pistol, CI, 1930, Kilgore, 6¾″....25.00
Bulldozer, cap pistol, six-shooter, CI, July 1874....145.00
Butting Match Mechanical Pistol, CI....250.00
Cap gun on stick, 28″ L....15.00
Chieftain, cap pistol, CI, 1920, National, 11″....35.00
Clip Jr, cap pistol, CI, 1935, Stevens, 5¼″....17.00
Colt 45, die-cast, Hubley....15.00
Daisy, BB gun, single-shot, model 38, 30″ L....18.00
Daisy Buzz Barton Special, BB gun, #195....35.00
Daisy Cinematic Picture Pistol, mid-1940s....35.00

Me & My Buddy Pistol, marked Pat Pending, Wyandotte Toys, 7¾″, $85.00.

Flintlock Jr, cap pistol, 7″....18.50
G-Man Automatic, sparkles when wound, 1930s, Marx....25.00
Gene Autry, cap pistol, CI, 1939, Kenton, 8⅜″....30.00
H-Bar-Q, cap pistol, CI, 1925, Kilgore, Made in USA, 7½″....25.00
Invincible, CI, 50-shot cap pistol, Kilgore....25.00
Jack Armstrong Airplane Gun, 1936, Daisy....45.00
Jr Police Chief, cap automatic, CI, 1938, Kenton, USA, 3⅞″....15.00
Kilgore, cap cannon, CI....69.00
Klotz, cap gun, fireless, torpedo cane paper roll, 1911....60.00
Lightning Express, animated cap pistol....300.00
National #380, cap pistol, CI, 1930s, 7″....31.00
Oh Boy, cap pistol, CI, 1922, National, 5½″....15.00
Peacemaker, cap pistol, CI, 1940, Stevens, Made in USA, 8″....20.00
Red Ryder Air Rifle, 1940, w/CI lever, Daisy....50.00
Roy Rogers, cap pistol, CI, 11″....45.00
Sambo figural....225.00
Snappy Jack, ca 1935, English....30.00
Super-Numatic Pistol....15.00
Texan, cap pistol, CI, 1940, Hubley, Made in USA, 9¼″....25.00
Wild West, cap pistol, CI, '30, National, Made in USA, 6½″....23.00
Yellow Kid, cap gun....50.00

Pedal Cars and Ride-On Toys

Blue Streak, sheet metal/wood, orig pnt, Gendron, 40″......1,050.00
Cadillac, Steelcraft, sheet metal, orig pnt, 36″, EX..........225.00
Car, Flyer, tin/wood, some orig pnt, tool box/crank, 36″.......675.00
Car, Gendron, sheet metal/wood, orig pnt, wire wheels, 42″....295.00
Car, Jalopy, no windshield, minor rust, 30″ L...............125.00
Car, Stearns, tin/CI/wood/hard rubber tires, 30″ L, VG........700.00
Casey Jones, Cannon Ball Express, Carton Mfg, 40″, VG......115.00
Dump truck, Mack....................................550.00
Fire truck ladder wagon, Gendron, worn pnt, 60″, VG........350.00
Flyer, Toledo, sheet metal/wood, orig pnt, 40″ L, VG.........325.00
Tricycle, horse, leather saddle, wood, 1880s................380.00
Tricycle, horse, pnt cast metal/wood, ca 1900, rstr............350.00
Tricycle, horse, wood/iron, fretwork guards, 31″ L..........1,450.00
Tricycle, McKee & Harrington, 14″ rear wheels, 1875, VG...2,000.00

Penny Toys

Car, tin, German, 3″.....................................75.00
Chinaman, tin litho, EX.................................125.00
Elves sawing log, tin litho, mechanical, VG..................125.00
Horse w/carriage, gilded, #130, sm.........................85.00
Mother pushing child in chair, tin litho, EX.................150.00
Negro dancer on roof, tin litho, mechanical, EX.............175.00
Polo player, animated, tin, 4″ L..........................200.00
Pool player, tin litho, VG.................................75.00
Squirrel in cage, mechanical...............................95.00
Zeppelin in hanger, tin litho, mechanical, NM...............475.00

Pipsqueaks

Pipsqueak toys were popular among the Pennsylvania Germans. The earliest had bellows made from sheepskin. Later, cloth replaced the sheepskin, and finally paper bellows were used.

Bird, compo, minor wear & rpr, working, 8″................185.00
Bird, compo, rpr/rpt, silent, 5½″...........................85.00
Bird on perch, red, rpr bellows, 7½″.......................130.00
Dog, standing, blk/wht, rpr bellows, silent, 6″...............170.00
Duck on basket, blk/wht/orange/yel/brn, silent, 4½″...........120.00
Parrot, looking backward, compo, damage/rpt, silent, 3½″......75.00
Rooster on spring legs, rpr bellows, 8½″, VG.................185.00
Sheep, compo/wood/wooly coat, minor rpr/rpl, working, 5″.....185.00
Swan, rpr base, top good, silent, 5″.......................200.00

Pull Toys

Boy w/oversize dog, tin w/worn orig pnt, 2 wheels gone, 7″....185.00
Bull dog, fierce, fanged mouth opens, growler, glass eyes......350.00
Cow, hide covered, moos when head is trn, 4 wheels, 11″.....275.00
Dog on wheels, papier mache, brn/wht.....................350.00
Donkey, compo/wood, nodding head, leather ears/mane, 6½″....95.00
Draft horse, bob-tail, wheels are checkers, nail-top mane.......230.00
Duck, waddles, orig, 9x9″...............................35.00
Elephant, molded tin w/worn orig pnt, 6½″, EX...............65.00
Elephant, pnt compo, wood base, tin wheels, 1890s, 6x5x4″....90.00
Elephant, pressed papier mache/compo, tin wheels, 5½x4″.....110.00
Elephant, straw-stuffed cotton, iron wheels, wire hoop, 8″......125.00
Horse, compo/pnt wood, applied mane/tail, German, 7½x9″....130.00
Horse, prancing; tin w/orig pnt, imp 'Chester,' 6″ L, VG.......185.00
Horse, primitive cut-out head/neck on stick w/wheels, 37″.....205.00
Horse, wood/old blk haircloth, horsehair mane/tail, 16x15″.....450.00

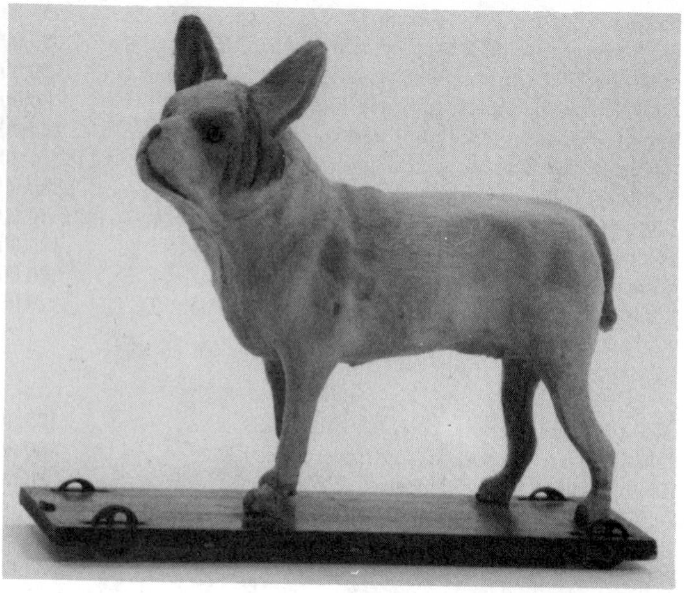

Dog, glass eyes, very early pull toy, 12″ long, $295.00.

Horse & rider w/cart, tin w/orig mc pnt, 5½″, VG............125.00
Horse w/jockey, pnt tin, American, ca 1890, 14″...........1,870.00
Rabbit, cast zinc on tin base, zinc wheels, pnt, 4½″..........165.00

Schoenhut

Acrobat, bisque face....................................190.00
Alligator, glass eyes....................................350.00
Bare Back Rider, 8½″...................................150.00
Barney Google & Spark Plug, 1922 King Features tag, 8″, M..750.00
Billy goat, leather beard & tail, orig pnt....................220.00
Bread Truck Driver......................................175.00
Buffalo, pnt eyes, reg size, EX...........................150.00
Camel, 2 humps, NM.....................................295.00
Circus horse, wht...75.00
Circus tent, Humpty Dumpty, VG..........................785.00
Circus tent, w/pnt audience, rare, 30x20″...................550.00

Schoenut child's table, with paper label, in excellent condition, top measures 15″ x 21″, $350.00.

Circus wagon...95.00
Clown, orig clothes, minor wear, reg size....................75.00
Clown, reduced size..40.00
Clown, w/ladder & chair, orig clothes.........................175.00
Clown, 7″, NM..95.00
Clown on box..175.00
Delvan Cowboy...110.00
Dollhouse, bungalow, 16x16″, EX...............................275.00
Donkey, glass eyes..65.00
Donkey, pnt eyes, 9½″...55.00
Elephant, glass eyes, reg size, VG..............................150.00
Elephant, pnt eyes, rpl tail, reg size...........................75.00
Felix, 4″...135.00
Goat, glass eyes, NM...250.00
Goat, pnt eyes...95.00
Golfer, male, club cracked, G orig pnt, 36″...................205.00
Golfer, male, orig finish & props, 33″ L........................190.00
Golfer, 36″ on rod..295.00
Horse, w/leather saddle, orig, 5½″...............................75.00
Jolly Jigger Girl...425.00
Kangaroo, pnt eyes..395.00
Lady bareback rider, bisque head.................................250.00
Maggie..175.00
Monkey, orig clothes...210.00
Mule, leather ears & tail, 9x6″....................................175.00
Piano, iron cabriole legs, w/candelabra..........................147.50
Piano, nudes & nymphs, 1900, 16″................................98.00
Piano, 12-key, Cupid scene..75.00
Piano, 18-key...65.00
Piano, 20-key, upright, mahog w/orig cherub litho, 21″ L......100.00
Pig, NM...375.00
Playblocks in wagon, 11″ L..70.00
Polar bear, VG...350.00
Poodle, pnt eyes..185.00
Rabbit, pnt eyes...375.00
Ringmaster, bisque head...225.00
Ringmaster, w/lion tamer, 2-pc.....................................70.00
Saddle horse, blk mane & tail, pnt eyes, 5x7″..................110.00
Seal, leather ears & flippers, orig pnt............................350.00

Steiff

Margaret Steiff began making her felt stuffed toys in 1800, in Germany. The animals she made were tagged with an elephant in a circle. Her first Teddy bear, made in 1903, became such a popular seller that she changed her tag to a bear. Felt stuffing was replaced with excelsior and wool, and when it became available, foam was used. In addition to the tag, look for the 'Steiff' ribbon, and the button inside the ear. For further information we recommend *Teddy Bears and Steiff Animals*, a full-color identification and value guide by Margaret Fox Mandel, available at your local book store or public library.

Baboon, Coco, beige mohair, jtd head, 1957-1968, 5½″........45.00
Badger, Diggy, mohair, straw stuffed, rare, ca 1964, 4″.........65.00
Bat, Eric the Bat, mohair, straw stuffed, rare, 1960s, 8″.......250.00
Bear, Dr O'Bear, mohair, fully jtd, 1920, 14″....................350.00
Bear, Emerson, mohair, fully jtd, w/button, 1907, 20″..........750.00
Bear, Fillmore, mohair, fully jtd, big ears, ca 1918, 23″.......400.00
Bear, inset shoebutton eyes/lg hump/long curved arms, 17″....525.00
Bear, Jackie, miniature, mohair, fully jtd, 6½″..................450.00
Bear, Lucky, mohair, straw stuffed, fully jtd, 1908, 10″........450.00
Bear, Madonna, mohair, straw stuffed, fully jtd, 16″.............450.00
Bear, miniature, mohair, fully jtd, ca 1915, 3¾″..................225.00
Bear, Panda, cotton, fully jtd, w/button, rare, 13″...............225.00
Bear, Petsy, dralon, fully jtd, 1971-1977, 12″......................95.00
Bear, Poker Face, mohair, straw stuffed, fully jtd, 21″.........400.00
Bear, Rosie, pink rayon, fully jtd, 1930s, 16″.....................150.00
Bear, Shirley O'Bear, plush, Shirley Temple curls, 12″...........75.00
Bear, Teddy, miniature, mohair, fully jtd, 1957, 6″...............125.00
Bear, Tuxedo, mohair, fully jtd, Snoopy clothes, 15″.............100.00
Bear, Yes/No, mohair, fully jtd, w/button, 1920-1930, 13″......350.00
Beaver, Nagy, mohair, straw stuffed, jtd head, 1964, 10″......175.00
Bison, brn mohair, felt horns, 1960s, 11x15″......................175.00
Boar, Wild Boar, mohair, straw stuffed, jtd head, 8″.............175.00
Cat, Fluffy, mohair, sitting, w/button, 1930s, 4½″................65.00
Cat, Susi, mohair, sitting, w/tag & button, 4″.......................55.00
Cat, Tabby, mohair, w/tag & button, ca 1945-1952, 5½″..........65.00
Chimpanzee, brn mohair, fully jtd, wht, 1960, 4″...................35.00
Colt, cotton plush, standing, w/button, 1957, 11″.................125.00
Cow, mohair, Hereford markings, 6½″................................75.00
Crab, Crabby, 8 mohair legs, w/button, rare, 11″ long..........175.00
Deer, Bambi, brn spotted velvet, standing, w/button, 5½″.......35.00
Deer, Bocky, yel & brn mohair, ca 1973, 9″..........................65.00
Dog, Chow-Chow Brownie, mohair, w/tag & button, 7″ long.....95.00
Dog, Dachshund, mohair, on wheels, orange felt, 8″..............175.00
Dog, Floppy Beagle, mohair, w/tag, 1960s, 6½″.....................75.00
Dog, Mopsy, mohair, straw stuffed, ca 1969, 8½″...................75.00
Dog, Snobby, Poodle, mohair, straw stuffed, 5½″...................45.00
Dog, Tessie, Schnauzer, mohair, standing, 1950s, 11″............125.00

Steiff poodle, 10″, $90.00.

Doll, German man, mohair wig, fully jtd, w/button, 22″..........900.00
Doll, Ginny, walks puppy, Foxy, 1955-1960, 3¼″..................125.00
Doll, Ichabod, school teacher, w/button, ca 1905-1911, 18″....875.00
Doll, Inspection Sergeant, fully jtd, w/button, 21″.................900.00
Doll, Monkey Man, comical policeman, fully jtd, 17″..............900.00
Dromedary, brn plush, straw stuffed, rare, ca 1957, 13″.........225.00
Dwarf, Lucki, fully jtd, pnt eyes, ca 1957, 22″.....................200.00
Elephant, Cosy Trampy, dralon, foam rubber stuffed, 8″...........75.00
Fox, Caught in the Act, mohair, straw stuffed, 1950s, 25″.......450.00
Fox, Xorry, mohair, straw stuffed, w/button, ca 1964, 4½″........55.00
Giraffe, yel mohair w/orange spots, ca 1968, 31″..................225.00
Goat, Baby Goat, wht & brn mohair, straw stuffed, 1950, 9″....75.00
Goldfish, yel & orange mohair, straw & cotton stuffed, 26″....195.00
Goose, wht & gray mohair, straw stuffed, ca 1957, 5″..............45.00
Groundhog, Murmy, wht & tan mohair, straw stuffed, 4½″.........55.00
Hedgehog, mohair, straw stuffed, jtd head, 1957-1970, 5″........55.00
Kangaroo, Kangoo, mohair, baby in pouch, velvet Joey, 20″....250.00

Lamb, Lamby, wht plush, straw stuffed, 1950s, 8½" 75.00
Lamb, Lamby, wool plush, bl ribbon, w/tag, 1950s, 4" 45.00
Leopard, dralon, yel glass eyes, w/button, ca 1972, 20" 95.00
Lion, Leo, mohair, on wheels, 1920s, 12x14" 400.00
Lion, Leo, mohair, straw stuffed, 12" high, 20" long 275.00
Lioness, Lea, yel & brn mohair, w/tag, ca 1957-1969, 4½" 55.00
Llama, wht mohair, straw stuffed, w/tag & button, 6½" 65.00
Mickey Mouse, blk velvet, pnt mouth, rare, 1930s, 7" 600.00
Monkey, gold mohair, pnt eyes, w/tag, 13" 65.00
Moose, Moosy, brn mohair, straw stuffed, ca 1964, 10" 175.00
Owl, Wittie, mohair, straw stuffed, felt beak & wings, 4" 35.00
Panther, blk dralon fur, yel glass eyes, 1973-1980, 20" 150.00
Penguin, wht mohair, orange felt feet, blk flippers, 8½" 75.00
Pig, pk mohair, curled tail, felt mouth, 3" 55.00
Pony, mohair, straw stuffed, pnt mouth, standing, 5" 55.00
Rabbit, Hopping Rabbit, wht mohair, straw stuffed, 5½" 65.00
Rabbit, Manni, wht mohair w/brn & gray, straw stuffed, 8" 125.00
Racoon, Raccy, mohair, straw stuffed, w/button, 4" 45.00
Rhinoceros, Nosy, gray mohair, straw stuffed, 4" 45.00
Seal, beige mohair, straw stuffed, 1950s, 14" 95.00
Spider, Spidy, mohair, straw stuffed, w/tag, 1960s, 2½" 200.00
Turtle, Slo, brn mohair w/yel underside, 1957-1977, 5½" 35.00
Walrus, Paddy, beige mohair w/spots, nylon tusks, 5½" 65.00
Zebra, mohair, straw stuffed, w/tag, 1957, 8½" 75.00
Zebra, wooden pull toy, on wheels, 8x6½" 45.00

Toy Soldiers

Toy soldiers were popular playthings with children of the 19th century. They were made by many European manufacturers in various sizes until 1848, when a standard size of approximately 1⅓" was established. The most collectible of all toy soldiers were made in England by Britains Ltd. from 1893 to 1966. In America, some of the important manufacturers were Barclay, Manoil, Grey, and All-Nu.

Barclay, Soldier, #799, sits & fires anti-aircraft gun, NM 20.00
Bellum, German Soldier Firing, cap firer, EX 60.00
Britains, African Warrior, Zulus, #147, orig box, NM 90.00
Britains, American Civil War 1862 Union Cavalry, #2056, EX ... 65.00
Britains, Arab Display, #2046, orig box, EX 150.00
Britains, Arab Display, #2046, 4 mtd/8 on foot, set, VG 165.00
Britains, Australian Army Infantry, Battle Dress, #2031, NM 95.00
Britains, Band Drums, Bugles o/t Line, #9137, in box, NM 65.00
Britains, Band o/t 2nd Dragoons, #1720, orig box, set, EX 260.00
Britains, Bedouin Arabs, #187, marching, Wisstock box, NM 88.00
Britains, Canada, Fort Henry Guards, #9158, orig box, EX 55.00
Britains, Coldstream Guard, #120, 8 kneeling, set of 8, NM 80.00
Britains, Danish Army Danskehaer, #2018, orig box, EX 260.00
Britains, Egyptian Camel Corps, #48, lt coats, in box, NM 95.00
Britains, Egyptian Cavalry, #115, set of 5, MIB 110.00
Britains, Egyptian Cavalry, #9264, G box, EX 65.00
Britains, Esercito Italiano Army, Carabinieri, in box, NM 150.00
Britains, Fort Henry Guard Canada, #2148, orig box, EX 65.00
Britains, France, Zouaves, #9166, charging, orig box, EX 55.00
Britains, French Army, L'armee Francais, Cuirassiers, EX 60.00
Britains, French Foreign Legion, #2137, in box, EX 55.00
Britains, German Infantry, #432, gray uniforms, in box, NM 85.00
Britains, Gloucestershire Regiment, marching at slope, NM 125.00
Britains, Governor-General's Foot Guards, #1634, in box, NM ... 70.00
Britains, Grenadier Guards, #1283, set of 8, MIB 77.00
Britains, Grenadier Guards, #9121, marching at slope, EX 110.00
Britains, GS Limbered Wagon, #1330, in box, EX 220.00
Britains, Gurkha Rifles, #197, Whisstock box/set of 8, MIB 88.00
Britains, Home Guard, #1918, marching w/slung arms, EX 30.00
Britains, India, 13th Duke of Connaught's Lancers, #9262 ...... 65.00
Britains, India Skinner's Horse, #9161, mounted/turbans, NM 70.00
Britains, Indian Army Service Corps, #1893, gr uniform, EX 95.00
Britains, Irish Guards, #2078, officer/6 at present arms 100.00
Britains, Kings Royal Rifle Corps, #2072, G box, EX 90.00
Britains, Life Guards, #2019, full dress, G box, EX 70.00
Britains, Naval Officers, #1911, set of 7, MIB 121.00
Britains, Papal State, Swiss Guards, #9371, orig box, EX 135.00
Britains, Princess Patricia's Canadian Light Infantry, NM 60.00
Britains, Red Army Cavalry Parade Uniform, #2028, orig box ... 100.00
Britains, Red Army Infantry, #2032, steel helmets, EX 80.00
Britains, Royal Army Gun, #1201, EX 30.00
Britains, Royal Army Medical Corps Unit, #1723, orig box 75.00
Britains, Royal Artillery Gun & Detachment, #9420, box, EX ... 175.00
Britains, Royal Canadian Mounted Police, #2134, in box, EX 55.00
Britains, Royal Fusiliers, marching at slope, #7, EX 130.00
Britains, Royal Fusiliers & 9th Royal Lancers, #9345, EX 165.00
Britains, Royal Marines, #1284, running at the trail, EX 16.00
Britains, Royal Marines, #1353B, officer w/sword, EX 20.00
Britains, Royal Marines, #1357B, standing at attention, EX 20.00
Britains, Royal Marines, #1365B, standing at ease, EX 20.00
Britains, Royal Marines, #35, at the slope, EX 120.00
Britains, Royal Marines, #35, officer/7 marching, set, NM 88.00
Britains, Royal Marines, #9140, marching, orig box, EX 80.00
Britains, Royal Scots Greys, #9210, EX 120.00
Britains, Scots Guard, #75, officer/piper/5 marching, NM 93.00
Britains, Skinner's Horse, #47, orig box, EX 75.00
Britains, Somerset Light Infantry, #9143, EX 105.00
Britains, Soviet Cavalry, mounted on horses, set of 5, VG 120.00
Britains, Union Cavalry, #2056, orig box, EX 60.00
Britains, Union Infantry, #2059, orig box, EX 75.00
Britains, US Army Cavalry, #229, orig box, EX 80.00
Britains, W Africa Togaland Warriors, #202, orig box, NM 75.00
Britains, 1st Kings Dragoon Guards, #2074, orig box, EX 70.00
Britains, 12th Royal Lancers (Prince of Wales), #2076, EX 85.00
Britains, 12th Royal Lancers Mounted, #9217, orig box, EX 60.00
Britains, 16th/15th Lancers, #33, G orig box, EX 85.00
Britains, 7th Queen's Own Hussars, #2075, EX 65.00
Elastolin, British Artillery man w/Ramrod, VG 20.00
Elastolin, Colonial soldiers w/Geo Washington, 13-pc, EX 260.00
Elastolin, flagbearer marching w/tin flag, EX 118.00
Elastolin, German general saluting, VG 65.00
Elastolin, infantryman, #63, marching w/slung rifle, EX 15.00
Elastolin, kneeling & firing guns, 13-pc, NM 70.00
Elastolin, marching riflemen/leader/flagman, 7-pc, EX 100.00
Elastolin, national war flag, EX 115.00
Elastolin, officer marching w/sword, sword missing, NM 25.00
Elastolin, riflemen lying down, 7-pc, EX 50.00
Elastolin, Schellenbaum, 7½", VG 165.00
Elastolin, Scottish Guards, 15-pc, NM 160.00
Elastolin, soldier typing w/typewriter & table, EX 115.00
Elastolin, stretchers/barriers/soldier/RC tent, 7-pc, NM 60.00
Elastolin, Swiss Alpine skier, VG 55.00
Elastolin, w/grenades, 6-pc, EX 55.00
German, gun emplacement, papier mache/wood, 9x6", NM 55.00
German, trench section, wood/papier mache, 7x4", NM 45.00
Hill, knights, w/horse-drawn carriage, lead, 70-pc, EX 10.00
Lead, Italian, w/rifles/machine guns/flagman, 15-pc, 1¾" 25.00
Lead, Prussian Band, 2", NM 40.00
Lead, Regiment of Lancers, #S120, Cherilea Products, EX 65.00
Lineol, charging standard bearer, tin flag, EX 75.00
Lineol, foreign, 12-pc, EX 135.00
Lineol, MacKesson, VG 50.00
Lineol, marching, red & bl uniforms, 12-pc, EX 125.00

Lineol, marching, w/plumes on helmets, 12-pc, EX 175.00
Lineol, Naval standard bearer, tin flag, EX .70.00
Lineol, radio operator, VG 45.00
Lineol, soldier holding Nazi Swastikafoil, NM 90.00
Lineol, soldier marching w/Schellenbaum, 4¾″, VG 50.00
Manoil, aviator, #525, holds lg missile, NM 20.00
Manoil, general, #4515, at attention, saluting, NM 50.00
Manoil, soldier, #45, marching w/flag, NM 12.00
Mignot, French Artillery Caisson, in box, NM 80.00
Mignot, French Artillery Gun Team, in box, NM 90.00

Trains

Electric trains were produced as early as the late 19th century. Names to look for are Lionel, Ives, and American Flyer.

The following listings were prepared by Bruce C. Greenberg and are taken from his comprehensive publications on Lionel, American Flyer, and Ives trains. The prices presented are the most common versions of each item. In many cases, there are several other variations often having a substantially higher value. Identification numbers given in the listings below actually appear on the item.

Key:

Std Gauge—Standard Gauge

American Flyer 283, S Gauge engine w/tender, EX 35.00
American Flyer 332DC, S Gauge engine w/tender, EX 300.00
American Flyer 332DC, S Gauge engine w/tender, G 100.00
American Flyer 360, 361 S Gauge diesels, EX 120.00
American Flyer 360, 361 S Gauge diesels, G 50.00
Ives 11, 0 Gauge steam engine w/tender, EX 125.00
Ives 11, 0 Gauge steam engine w/tender, G 75.00
Ives 1118, 0 Gauge steam engine w/tender, EX 125.00
Ives 1118, 0 Gauge steam engine w/tender, G 65.00
Ives 1132, Wide Gauge steam engine & tender, 1921-26, EX . . .750.00
Ives 1132, Wide Gauge steam engine & tender, 1921-26, G 300.00
Ives 3240, 1 Gauge electric engine, 1912-20, EX 600.00
Ives 3240, 1 Gauge electric engine, 1912-20, G 300.00
Ives 3241, Wide Gauge electric engine, 1921-25, EX 175.00
Ives 3241, Wide Gauge electric engine, 1921-25, G 80.00
Ives 3243, Wide Gauge electric engine, 1921-28, EX 400.00
Ives 3243, Wide Gauge electric engine, 1921-28, G 175.00
Lionel 1668, 0 Gauge steam engine & tender, 1937-41, EX 55.00
Lionel 1668, 0 Gauge steam engine & tender, 1937-41, G 30.00
Lionel 2037, 0 Gauge steam engine/tender, 1954-55, 57-58, EX . .45.00
Lionel 2037, 0 Gauge steam engine/tender, 1954-55, 57-58, G . . .25.00
Lionel 224, 0 Gauge steam engine & tender, 1938-42, EX 75.00
Lionel 224, 0 Gauge steam engine & tender, 1938-42, G 45.00
Lionel 2343, 0 Gauge diesels, two units, EX 150.00
Lionel 2343, 0 Gauge diesels, two units, G 100.00
Lionel 252, 0 Gauge electric engine, 1926-32, EX 125.00
Lionel 252, 0 Gauge electric engine, 1926-32, G 90.00
Lionel 380, Std Gauge electric engine, 1923-27, EX 250.00
Lionel 380, Std Gauge electric engine, 1923-27, G 120.00
Lionel 408E, Std Gauge electric engine, 1927-36, EX 450.00
Lionel 408E, Std Gauge electric engine, 1927-36, G 225.00
Lionel 42, Std Gauge electric engine, 1913-23, rnd hood, EX . .450.00
Lionel 42, Std Gauge electric engine, 1913-23, rnd hood, G 200.00
Lionel 50, 027 Gauge gang car, 1955-64, EX 45.00
Lionel 50, 027 Gauge gang car, 1955-64, G 15.00
Lionel 58, 027 Gauge rotary snowplow, 1959-61, EX 400.00
Lionel 58, 027 Gauge rotary snowplow, 1959-61, G 160.00
Lionel 60, 0 Gauge trolley, 1955-58, EX 80.00
Lionel 60, 0 Gauge trolley, 1955-58, G 40.00
Lionel 675, 0 Gauge steam engine & tender, 1947, EX 100.00
Lionel 700E, 0 Gauge steam engine & tender, 1937-42, G . . .1,700.00
Lionel 726, 0 Gauge steam engine & tender, 1946-49, EX 300.00
Lionel 726, 0 Gauge steam engine & tender, 1946-49, G 150.00
Lionel 773, 0 Gauge steam engine/tender, 1950, 1964-66, EX . .750.00
Lionel 773, 0 Gauge steam engine/tender, 1950, 1964-66, G . . .475.00
Lionel 8, Std Gauge electric engine, 1925-32, EX 125.00
Lionel 8, Std Gauge electric engine, 1925-32, G 60.00

Miscellaneous

Airplane, pnt pressed steel/wood, 18″ wingspan, EX 150.00
Airplane Panorama, paper/wood, mechanical, 13x9¼″, EX 160.00
Altweiber-Muhle, paper/wood, hot-air powered, 16x13″, EX 700.00
Arabian sulkie, tin, orig box, EX 65.00
Bear, nodder on wheels, papier mache, 1900, 9x13″ 300.00
Bear, plush, on rnd wood base, balance toy, 8″, VG 350.00
Blocks, ABC/animals, pressed stamped wood, ea 2¼″ 65.00
Blocks, The Dolls; litho paper/wood, in 7¾″x6¾″ box, VG 150.00
Blocks, 16 that together make complete Victorian litho 75.00
Buttercup & Spare Ribs, tin platform toy, 1920s 750.00
Cannon, brass & iron, orig pnt, early, 4½x12″ 45.00
Circus vendor, eyes move, mechanical, tin, early, 6½″ 210.00
Crazy Cat, w/hump, 1930s, 12″ 150.00
Drummer, boy on wood base, celluloid, mechanical 40.00
Electric range, tin/chrome, blk/lt bl, 7x6x10″ 45.00
Horse, leather cover, 24x28″ 75.00
Mess wagon, w/cart, unmk, tin, 2x9″ 83.00
Monkey, blows bubbles, battery operated, tin 10.00
Pretty Village, hotel+7 bldgs, McLoughlin, 1897, in box 175.00
Punch Jack-in-the-Box, paper/wood, plaster head, 3¾″, EX 225.00
Rooster, stands on cylinder, crows, tin litho, 9½″, EX 35.00
Sailboat, wood, 6x8″ 80.00
Sleigh on rockers, horse head & reins, orig striping, 30″ 400.00
Stuffed, blk mohair cat w/bushy fur tail/glass eyes, 11x9″ 85.00
Stuffed, cow, velvet, glass eyes, early 1900s, 16x9x5½″ 125.00
Stuffed, elephant, button eyes, flanel/calico blanket, 12″ 100.00
Stuffed, Felix the Cat, straw in velvet, arms move, 11″ 155.00
Stuffed, mouse, handmade, cotton, sewn details, '30s, 11″ 85.00
Wood keg w/pull-out cloth alphabet scroll, 3¼″ 195.00
Zilotone, #48, plays by record, mechanical, tin 250.00

Rocking horse, hair cloth, original glass eyes and mane, turn of the century, 34″ rockers, 25″ tall, $795.00.

Trade Signs

Trade signs were popular during the 1800s. They were usually made in an easily recognizable shape that one could mentally associate with the particular type of business it was to represent, especially appropriate in the days when many customers could not read!

When no condition is indicated, the items listed below are assumed to be in excellent condition.

Apple, from apple farm, cut-out tin in steel fr, 26″............65.00
Blacksmith, horseshoe, laminated wood w/iron hanger, 32x39″...75.00
Boats for Charter, wood, cut-out fish, rpt/rpr, 35″............155.00
Boot, high heeled, 1-pc pnt wood, 1850s, 23x11x4″..........485.00
Boot, pieced wood w/tin edging, wrought iron hangers, 27″....375.00
Butcher's, steer atop 3 butchering tools, CI, 20″.............770.00
Butcher's knife & cleaver, wood, from butcher shop, pr.......145.00
Castor set in ped fr, carved pine, glass merchant's, 8x13″......140.00
Dentist, Dr Dennert, Dentist Upstairs, wood, early.............65.00
Dentist, tooth shape, wht pnt wood w/blk name, 22x11½″.....275.00
Dry Goods, Cloaks, Suits, Shoes, curved brass/enamel, 30″.....200.00
Fish, carved pnt wood, fins/scales relief, 1800s, 58″ L.......2,200.00
Game dealer, applied hanging game, wood/mc, 1900, 42x33″...200.00
Hardware, pnt wood, owl, 38x12″.........................115.00
Inn, owl w/stein, carved wood, age cracks, 20th C, 22x26″.....180.00
Key, cast aluminum w/orig pnt, 30″, EX....................150.00
Pocket watch, CI, dbl-sided, pnt only VG, 23″...............285.00
Shoe shop, leather spectator shoe w/wood eyelets, 3-D, 26″..2,800.00
Stationery, rvpt/beveled glass/copper on wood fr, pre-1900.....195.00
Tavern, drummer, carved relief, mc pnt, contemporary, 41″....250.00
Top hat, w/scrolled sign bracket, wrought iron, 1900, 34″.....350.00
Undertaker, gold leaf on tin, ea side pnt, 1 w/coffin..........150.00

Tramp Art

Today considered a type of American folk art, tramp art was made from the late 1800s until after the turn of the century. Often produced by 'tramps' and 'hobos' from wooden materials which could be scavenged--crates and cigar boxes for instance--articles such as jewelry boxes and picture frames were usually decorated by chip-carving and then stained.

When no condition is indicated, the items listed below are assumed to be in excellent condition.

Box, allover applied chip carving, cigar label w/in, 9½″.........70.00
Box, applied rosettes & edge trim, cigar box label, 6½″........45.00
Box, applied triangles, 7½x11″..........................40.00
Box, chip-carved heart/circles, 2 hanging strips, 8″ W..........85.00
Box, ped base, diamond shape, early 1900s, 6x5″.............38.00
Box, pincushion top, 9½x6½″..........................40.00
Comb case, hanging, cut-outs/leaf/star/etc, 11x9x4″...........110.00
Frame, X-corners, G bold detail, 4″ W; 24x28″, pr............90.00
Frame, X-corners, 10x11″..............................20.00
Frame, X-corners w/gold leaf on ea, rpr, 11x12½″.............30.00
Frame, 6¾x7¾″.....................................25.00
Magazine rack, wall mt.................................90.00
Matchbox, hanging, allover chip carving, 7″..................40.00
Secretary/bookcase, CE Littlefield, dtd 1896, 85x51″........3,850.00
Shaving mirror, ball ft, looped outer edge, 15x13″............45.00
Shaving mirror, drw in base, allover chip carving, 33x15″......300.00

Traps

Though of interest to collectors for many years, trap collecting has gained in popularity over the past ten years in particular, causing prices to appreciate rapidly. Traps are usually marked on the pan as to manufacturer, and the condition of these trademarks are important when determining their value. Grading is as follows:

Good: ½ of pan legible
Very Good: legible in entirety, but light
Fine: legible in entirety, with strong lettering
Mint: in like-new, shiny condition
Prices listed here are for traps in fine condition.

Alligator #1 Killer......................................125.00
Allsteel #4 Double Long Spring...........................40.00
Arrow #1 Jump..35.00
Austin Humane Killer #1.................................18.00
Bear, Oneida Community #5, dbl long spring w/teeth, 1900....285.00
Blake & Lamb #23 Sod Pan...............................35.00
Blake & Lamb #40 Double Under Spring....................45.00
California Gopher #44, wood.............................10.00
Catch 'Em Alive, mousetrap, wood & tin, early...............52.00
Champion Multi Trigger..................................185.00
Cinch Mole Trap..15.00
Crago Clutch #4 Missoula Montana........................285.00
Crescent #3 Double Long Spring..........................110.00
Cush-In-Grip #1 Rubber Lined Jaws........................22.00
Cyclone Metal Mouse Trap...............................20.00
Davenport Half Circles Killer.............................100.00
Diamond #11 Coil Spring.................................15.00
Diamond #31 Coil Spring.................................15.00
Diamond #31½ Coil Spring...............................20.00
Duncan Rabbit Trap, England.............................50.00
Eclipse #1...45.00
Economy #2 Double Long Spring..........................65.00
Elgin Mouse Trap..8.00
Erie, rattrap, wood, iron hinges...........................30.00
Flotrap, Cazenovia NY...................................210.00
Fly, tin & wire, w/instructions, Columbia....................45.00
Fly, tin & wire screen, hanging, 9″........................22.50
Fut Set Metal Mouse.....................................15.00
Gibbs Two Trigger.......................................8.00
Goshen Killer...180.00
Hand wrought, dbl spring, 17″ L..........................35.00
Harmons Live Bait, with teeth & bait cage..................235.00
Hawley Norton #1½......................................8.00

Helfrich 'Eliminator' #750 .... 23.00
Herters Bear Trap 250.00
Holdfast #1 Long Spring 8.00
Ideal Mole Trap 20.00
It Mouse Trap 20.00
Jullsons Mole Trap Brass 225.00
JVJ Gopher Trap 25.00
Ketchall Mouse 4.00
Kriket #1 Jump Trap 8.00
Last Word Mouse Trap 15.00
Lomar #3 Coil Spring 12.00
Macabee Gopher 4.00
Museum Special Mouse Trap 3.50
Nelson Boode #2 .... 65.00
Newhouse, gopher trap 6.00
Newhouse #0 .... 45.00
Newhouse #1 Oneida Community, single spring 25.00
Newhouse #15, bear trap, jaws open 11¾″, overall 34½″ 250.00
Newhouse #150 .... 275.00
Newhouse #2 Oneida Community, dbl spring 30.00
Newhouse #2½ 38.00
Newhouse #21½ 45.00
Newhouse #3 Oneida Community, dbl spring 40.00
Newhouse #4½, Kenwood NY 140.00
Newhouse #5 Bear 275.00
Newhouse #81 .... 24.00
Niagara Special #1 Long Spring 10.00
Oneida #3, w/teeth 40.00
Oneida Jump #4 .... 15.00
Onieda Killem #1 .... 35.00
Phillips Gopher 30.00
Prott #1¼, Madison WI 15.00
Renkens Gopher 15.00
Rev-o-Noc #101 .... 45.00
Rival Mouse Trap 12.00
Sabo Killer Den Trap 75.00
Sargent #0 .... 15.00
Sargent #11, 2-hole pan 12.00
Sargent #71½ Double Under Spring 200.00
Save-A-Leg #210 .... 45.00
Shur Katch, fly trap, wire, dome shape 39.00
Snappy Mouse, Harvard IL 10.00
Snappy Rat, Harvard, IL 10.00
Stop Thief #3½ Killer 22.00
Sure Catch, rattrap, w/Anchor Brand Clothes Wringer ad 12.00
Sure Catch Mouse Orange 6.00
Taylor 'Sure Kill' Mole Trap 22.00
Taylor Special #1 .... 10.00
Teeter Mole 45.00
Trip Trap Mouse 15.00
Triumph #1¼ Super Grip 10.00
Triumph #315X 65.00
Triumph #415X Bear Trap, w/teeth 100.00
Triumph Jump #3, easy set sq grip 30.00
Verbail Chain Trap 95.00
Victor #10 Rabbit Trap 65.00
Victor #13 Jump, w/teeth 25.00
Victor #3, dbl spring 8.00
Victor #41 Double Trap 65.00
Victor #91 Shoulder Catch 12.00
Webley Cam Spring #3 .... 15.00
Webley Cam Spring #4 .... 15.00
Wolf, Newhouse #4½, dbl long spring, rusty, EX 85.00
Wolf, timber; ATC Newhouse #114, dbl spring, EX 110.00

Trivets

Although strictly a decorative item today, the original purpose of the trivet was much more practical. They were used to protect table tops from hot serving dishes; and irons, heated on the kitchen range, were placed on trivets during the pressing process to protect work surfaces. The first patent date was 1869, and many of the earliest trivets bore portraits of famous people or patriotic designs. Florals, birds, animals, and fruit were other favored motifs.

When no condition is indicated, the items listed below are assumed to be in near mint condition.

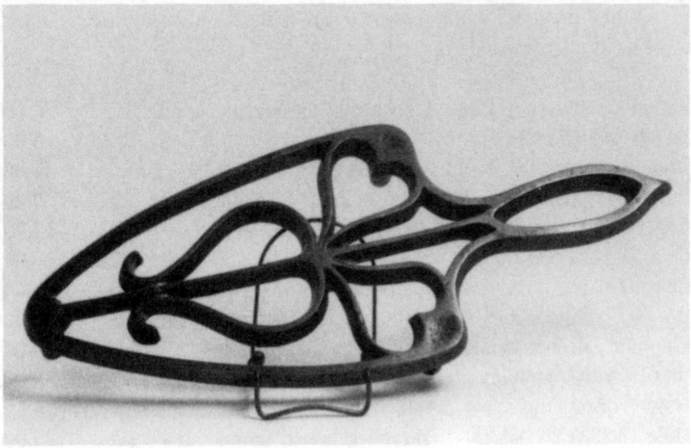

Cast brass, openwork with hearts, footed, 10″, $55.00.

Brass

#2167, 7″ 40.00
Foliage, 10½″ 20.00
Heart, scrolled detail, 8″ 45.00
Heart, w/iron ft, polished, 5¾″ 85.00
Heart & foliage, 7½″ 80.00
Lyre shape, trn ft, 6″ 65.00
Spade form w/heart cut-out, w/copper ft, 7⅝″ 65.00

Cast Iron

Brooms, canes ea side, pnt, 8″ 12.50
Cut-out urn, pinwheel tooling, heavy, 11″ 25.00
Geo Washington 145.00
God Bless Our Home, on horseshoe, dtd 1886 .... 45.00
Good Luck to All Who Use This Stand, horseshoe 40.00
Heart in center & ea end of hdl, rnd, 3 legs, 10¾″ 25.00
Jenny Lind on bar, 10¼″ 20.00
Kettle, beavers & leaves, 'Good Luck,' horseshoe shape 75.00
Oak leaf 37.50
Pinwheel & compass star, pnt, triangular w/hdl, 10¾″ 30.00
Stove top, rays filled w/circles & stars, 18x18″ 125.00
Vintage, S scroll sides, sq, pnt, 7¾″ 15.00

Wrought Iron

Penny ft, 3 zigzag rods, walnut hdl, 11″ 65.00
Rectangular w/4 bars, 7x12″ 25.00
Scrolled detail, well-formed hdl, 12½″, EX 75.00
Stylized foliage, tooled sides & hdls, 12″ L 95.00

Trolls

The modern day version of the troll was designed in 1952 by Helena and Marti Kuuskoski, of Tampere, Finland. Those made by DAM and those marked with a horseshoe are among the most valuable, since both are made from the original Kuuskoski design. Many copies have been produced, the best of which are the Wishniks, made by the Uneeda Doll Company. These were first marketed in 1979 and are currently still available.

Troll animals are scarce, and values are rising rapidly.

Authority Susan Miller has compiled an amusing and informative book, *The Troll Book*, with many photos and current prices; you will find her address in the Directory under Indiana.

When no condition is indicated, the items listed below are assumed to be in excellent condition.

Batman, red suit, yel bat at neck, blk mask/cape, unmk, 3″.....20.00
Boy bank, Dam...15.00
Bride & groom, Wish Nik, Uneeda, pat D-190 & 918, pr.......35.00
Burlap outfit, furry tail, detailed nails, Dam Things, 7″.........50.00
Cheerleader, molded-on clothes/mohair hair, wht gloves, 3″.....15.00
Cow, well-formed udder, horns, Dam Things, 1964, 3″.........25.00
Cowgirl bank, paste-on hair, molded clothes, 8½″.............25.00
Donkey, sitting, vinyl, mohair hair, Dam Things, 1964, 3″......25.00
Elephant, sitting, wrinkled skin, Dam Things, 1964, 3″.........25.00
Giraffe, vinyl, mohair, plastic eyes, unmk, Dam Things.........85.00
Horse, vinyl, long mane & tail, Dam, 1964, 3″................35.00
Hula Girl, Wish Nik, skirt rooted at waist, mohair, 5½″........25.00
Leprechaun, rubber, wht hair/beard, yel pants/shoes, unmk......55.00
Lion, unmk, Dam Things, lg..............................85.00
Rain Coat banks, girl/boy, orange hair, Thomas Dam, 7″, pr....40.00
Sailer, wht cloth outfit, wht to dk hair, w/tag, Dam, 11″........95.00
Santa bank, wht beard & hair, Thomas Dam, 7″..............65.00

Girl bank, marked Dam in blue raincoat, 8″, $15.00.

Trunks

In the the days of steamboat voyages, stage coach journeys, and railroad travel, trunks were used to transport clothing and personal belongings. Some, called 'dome top' or 'turtle backs' were rounded on top to better accommodate milady's finery. Today, some of the more interesting examples are used in various ways in home decorating. For instance, a flat topped trunk may become a coffee table, while a smaller dome style may be 'home' for antique dolls or a Teddy bear collection.

When no condition is indicated, the items listed below are assumed to be in excellent condition.

Dome top, dvtl pine/poplar, worn grpt, rpl lock/hasp, 24″.......65.00
Dome top, leather w/studs, iron hdw, 26x21x39″, VG.........135.00
Dome top, pine, carved eagle on lid, rpl/rfn, 30″ L...........325.00
Dome top, pine, orig red pnt w/blk grpt, 13x36x15″, VG......125.00
Dome top, tooled leather, wrought bail, 1771 paper, 13″ L....125.00
Leather on wood, brass studs, iron hdls/lock, 11½x13x22″......95.00
Louis Vuitton, divided tray w/sm lift-out trays, 22x40″.........635.00
Louis Vuitton, rust/bl/wht, fitted for shoes, 35″ L............330.00
Pine, dvtl, iron banding/braces/hinges, rpt/losses, 15x32″.......95.00
Pine, iron bound, iron lock, orig bl pnt worn, 14x15x20″......100.00
Pine, vinegar grain, dvtl, iron hasp/hdls, 16x18x20″..........195.00
Wood/leather cover, cylindrical, brass studs, 30″ L............55.00

Typewriters

The first commercially successful typewriter was the Sholes and Glidden, introduced in 1874. By 1882 other models appeared, and by the 1890s dozens were on the market. At the time of the First World War, the ranks of typewriter makers thinned, and by the 1920s only a few survived.

Collectors informally divide typewriter history into the pioneering period, up to about 1890; the classic period, from 1890 to 1920; and the modern period, since 1920.

There are two broad classifications of early typewriters: (1) Keyboard machines, in which depression of a key prints a character, and, via a shift key, prints up to three different characters per key. (2) Index machines, in which a chart of all the characters appears on the typewriter, the character is selected by a pointer or dial, and is printed by operation of a lever or other device. Even though index typewriters were simpler and more primitive than keyboard machines, they were none-the-less a later development, designed to provide a cheaper alternative to the standard keyboard models that were selling for upwards of $100. Eventually second-hand keyboard typewriters supplied the low-price customer and index typewriters vanished except as toys. Both classes of typewriters appeared in a great many designs.

It is difficult, if not impossible, to assign standard market prices to early typewriters. Unlike collectors of postage stamps, carnival glass, etc., few people collect typewriters--so there is no active marketplace from which to establish prices. Also, condition is a very important factor, and typewriters can vary infinitely in condition. A third factor to consider is that an early typewriter achieves its value mainly through the skill, effort, and time of the collector who restores it to its original condition, in which case its purchase price is insignificant. Some unusual looking early typewriters are not at all rare or valuable, while some very ordinary looking ones are scarce and could be quite valuable. No general rules apply.

When no condition is indicated, the items listed below are assumed to be in excellent condition.

American Flyer, orig box................................45.00
Automatic...500.00
Brooks..500.00
Cash..500.00
Crandall..500.00
Crown...600.00
Fitch...500.00
Ford..500.00
Fox...200.00
Franklin, early..175.00
Hall, 1886, EX..275.00
Hammond Multiplex, swinging sector, ribbon, 3-row, w/case....200.00
Lambert...200.00

McCool....200.00
McLoughlin....300.00
Merritt, linear index, plunger selector, 1900, w/case, 12″....135.00
Niagara....500.00
O'Dell, last pat date 1890, no case, G....200.00
Oliver #5, w/dust cover....35.00
Peoples....150.00
Pocket....300.00
Postal, type-wheel, ribbon inked, 3-row, 1905, w/case, 15″....200.00
Remington, portable, 1929....25.00
World, last pat date 1886, orig case....200.00

Uhl Pottery

Founded in Evansville, Indiana, in 1854 by German immigrants, the Uhl Pottery was moved to Huntingburg, Indiana, in 1908 because of the more suitable clay available there. They produced stoneware--Acorn Ware jugs, crocks, and bowls--which were marked with the acorn logo and 'Uhl Pottery.' They also made mugs, pitchers, and vases in simple shapes and solid glazes marked with a circular ink stamp containing the name of the pottery and 'Huntingburg, Indiana.' The pottery closed in the mid-1940s.

When no condition is indicated, the items listed below are assumed to be in mint condition.

Casserole, rose, w/lid....37.50
Mug, Grape w/Leaf Band, med bl, 5¼″....38.00
Pitcher, head of Lincoln, deep bl, 10″....400.00
Pitcher, head of Lincoln, deep bl, 4¾″....135.00
Pitcher, head of Lincoln, deep bl, 6″....225.00
Pitcher, head of Lincoln, deep bl, 7″....235.00
Pitcher, head of Lincoln, deep bl, 8″....250.00
Pitcher, pink, 8″....35.00

Unger Brothers

The Art Nouveau silver produced by the Unger Brothers, who operated in Newark, New Jersey, from the early 1880s until 1909, is fast becoming very popular on today's collectibles market. In addition to tableware, they also made brushes, mirrors, powder boxes and the like for milady's dressing table, as well as jewelry and small personal accessories such as match safes and flasks. They often marked their products with a circle seal containing an intertwined 'UB.' When no condition is indicated, the items listed below are assumed to be in mint condition.

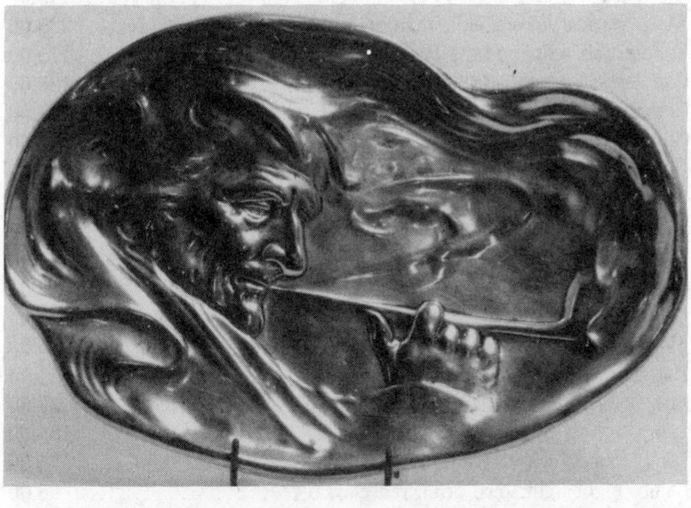

Tray, man smoking pipe, marked sterling 925 fine #0395, $350.00.

Flask, Gibson Girl's head, smoking cigarette, mk....265.00
Food pusher, floral repousse....45.00
Handbag, velvet, leather w/in, cupids/scrolls on hdl, 8x6″....195.00
Hatpin, English bulldog head w/ruby eyes, mk, 7¾″....125.00
Jar, powder; cut glass, w/floral emb sterling top....135.00
Jar, powder; notched prism/'Love's Dream' sterling lid....175.00
Napkin ring, w/Art Nouveau ladies....65.00
Pin, owl head w/glass eyes, 1⅝″ W....300.00
Pot, demitasse; 8 panels, ped ftd/insulated ivory hdls, mk....245.00
Tray, bonbon; iris, 5½″....165.00
Vase, eng floral, 8 panels, flared top, ped ft, 14x4½″....255.00
Violet, figural, sterling, 1″ dia....60.00

Universal

Universal Potteries Incorporated operated in Cambridge, Ohio, from 1934 to 1956. Many lines of dinnerware and kitchen items were produced, in both earthenware and semi-porcelain. In 1956 the emphasis was shifted to the manufacture of floor and wall tiles, and the name was changed to the Oxford Tile Company, Division of Universal Potteries. The plant closed in 1976.

When no condition is indicated, the items listed below are assumed to be in mint condition.

Ballerina, casserole, dk gr, w/lid....10.00
Ballerina, gravy boat, yel....5.00
Ballerina, plate, 2-hdl, 12″....12.00
Ballerina, sugar bowl, dk gr....3.50
Bittersweet, drip jar....15.00
Calico Fruit, creamer & sugar....17.50
Calico Fruit, cup & saucer....6.00
Calico Fruit, custard....4.50
Calico Fruit, jug, w/lid, 5″....27.00
Calico Fruit, jug, w/lid, 7¾″....35.00
Calico Fruit, platter, 13¾″....15.00
Cattail, bowl, refrigerator; w/lid....6.00
Cattail, bowl, rnd, 9″....11.50
Cattail, bowl, salad; 9¾″....15.00
Cattail, bowl, soup; flat....7.00
Cattail, butter dish....30.00
Cattail, creamer....6.00
Cattail, cup & saucer....7.00
Cattail, gravy boat....10.00
Cattail, jug, w/stopper, 2-qt....20.00
Cattail, pitcher, glass....65.00
Cattail, plate, utility; 11½″....7.00
Cattail, plate, 10″....8.00
Cattail, platter, 13½″....11.00
Cattail, scales....25.00
Cattail, shakers, pr....12.50
Cattail, sugar bowl....9.00
Cattail, tumbler, 4¾″....11.00
Tom & Jerry, bowl, hunt scene, w/8 cups....50.00

Val St. Lambert

Since its inception in Belgium at the turn of the 19th century, the Val St. Lambert Cristalleries has been involved in the production of high quality glass, specializing in cameo.

When no condition is indicated, the items listed below are assumed to be in mint condition.

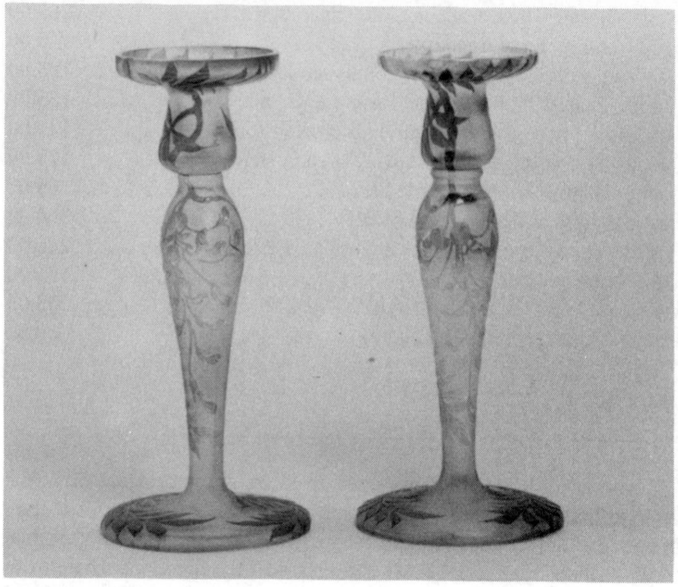

Candlesticks, purple cameo florals on lavender, 9″, $750.00 for the pair.

Bottle, scent; rubena verte cameo cut w/flowers, 8½″ 475.00
Jar, cranberry & clear cameo, faceted ball finial, 5½″ 145.00
Pitcher, sm pink floral emb on frost, 13″ 245.00
Plate, Old Masters, sgn, orig paper stickers, limited ed.........55.00
Rose bowl, bats, castle, & moon cameo, 6″ 850.00
Tray, gr, Art Deco, sgn, 16¼″ dia 175.00
Vase, floral cameo/bronze overlay leaves, cobalt w/in, 12″ 495.00

Valentines

Pagan ritual once held that on Valentine's Day the birds of the air elected to choose their mates; and as this premise was eagerly adopted by the homo sapien species, romantic poems became a familiar expression of one's intentions. By the mid-1800s, comical hand-colored lithographic and wood block prints were mass-produced both here and abroad. At the turn of the century, the more-romantic, often-mechanical German imports forced many American companies out of business. Today's collectors often specialize in: Comic, postcards, mechanical, Victorian, Kewpies, Greenaway characters, or those signed by a specific artist are among many well-established categories.

When no condition is indicated, the items listed below are assumed to be in near mint condition.

Broadside, comic, English.................................26.00
Buster Brown & Tige, sgn Outcault, Tuck.....................8.00
Child, roses/dove/hearts, fold-out, Germany, G................15.00
Dog, dressed as doctor w/heart & bag, orig envelope............5.00
Figural, cb, Raphael Tuck..................................19.00
Fold-out, boy, holds valentine, eyes move, Stecher litho........12.00
Fold-out, boy & girl, heart & trellis, G......................10.00
Fold-out, boy in bl checked suit, red roses, Germany...........10.00
Fold-out, child, dressed as angel, emb flowers................15.00
Fold-out, heart, boy & girl, flowers, Germany.................15.00
Fold-out, honeycomb, 11″...................................9.50
Fold-out, puppies, bowl & hearts, Germany....................12.00
Girl, hearts on suit, spins wheel w/animals, '29 postmark.......15.00
Kewpies Bring Violets, bl..................................25.00
Pencil sketch, 1882.......................................14.00
Punch & Judy, 1900, 6x8″...................................30.00
Woodblock, hand colored, English, 1840......................24.00

Van Briggle

The Van Briggle Pottery of Colorado Springs, Colorado, was established in 1901 by Artus Van Briggle, whose early career had been shaped by such notables as Karl Langenbeck and Maria Nichols Storer. His quest for several years had been to perfect a completely flat matt glaze, and upon accomplishing his goal, he opened his pottery. His wife, Anne, worked with him, and they, along with George Young, were responsible for the modeling of the wares. Their work typified the flow and form of the Art Nouveau movement, and the shapes they designed played as important a part in their success as their glazes. Some of their most famous pieces were Despondency, Lorelei, and Toast Cup.

Increasing demand for their work soon made it necessary to add to their quarters as well as their staff. Although much of the ware was eventually made from molds, each piece was carefully trimmed and refined before the glaze was sprayed on. Their most popular colors were rose, blue, green, and gray.

Van Briggle died in 1904, but the work was continued by his wife. New facilities were built and by 1908, in addition to their artware, tiles, garden ware, and commercial lines were added.

By the twenties, the emphasis had shifted from art pottery to novelties and commercial wares. As late as 1970, reproductions of some of the early designs continued to be made.

Until about 1920, most pieces were marked with the date and shape number. Before Van Briggle's death, Roman numerals identified the artist: 'I' for Anne, 'II' for Harry Bangs, and 'III' for Van Briggle. The 'AA' mark was the earliest mark; 'Colorado Springs, Colorado' was used after 1920; and 'USA' was added from 1922 to 1930

When no condition is indicated, the items listed below are assumed to be in mint condition.

Ash tray, Ming bl, 4½″.....................................16.00
Bookends, bears by tree trunk, dk bl-gr, pre-1920, 7″, pr......200.00
Bookends, owl, Persian rose, pr............................135.00
Bookends, ship, pr..125.00
Boot, bl, 2½″..25.00
Bowl, acorns, burgundy, old mk..............................65.00
Bowl, dk gr, #270D, 1906..................................200.00
Bowl, dragonflies, dk plum, 1917, sm.........................85.00
Bowl, floral panels, lt bl on buff clay, 1906, 2x5¾″...........225.00
Bowl, leaves, gr, #858, pre-1920, 6½″.......................110.00
Bowl, leaves, gr-bl matt, #511, 1908-11, 2x5″..................95.00
Bowl, leaves, Persian rose, #733, 5½″........................55.00
Bowl, open petal tulip top, Persian rose, 3¾″ H...............25.00
Bowl, purple, #230, 1907..................................195.00
Bowl, vertical leaves/buds, maroon w/gr, #228, 1904, 3″ H.....225.00
Candlestick, bl/gr, #445, 1906.............................175.00
Candlestick, Cupid, ornate, sgn LB, pr......................125.00
Chamberstick, Persian rose, w/hdl, 1915, 8″, pr...............175.00
Conch shell, maroon, 12″...................................65.00
Conch shell, turq, 9″......................................40.00
Creamer, Persian rose, standard mk, paper label, 2½″.........45.00
Figurine, donkey, '20s, sm..................................36.00
Figurine, elephant, bl, mk Van Briggle, 5x7½″.................55.00
Figurine, owl on stump, turq, 9″............................40.00
Flower frog, 2 lg acorns, turq, 3¼x6½″.......................25.00
Flower frog, 3 frogs in center, dk maroon/bl, 2½x4¾″..........25.00
Hat, bl, 2″..25.00
Jar, dk bl top shades to turq base, w/lid.....................37.50
Lamp, bl, all orig, 1950s, 10″.............................135.00
Lamp, good luck emblem, orig shade, 10″....................475.00
Lamp, night light, owl, gr/bl, red clay, 6¼″...................95.00
Lamp, puppy; Persian rose, orig shade, 8″...................125.00

Vase, rustic rose, dated 1904, signed with the 'AA' mark, #93, 12", $900.00.

Lamp, Rebecca at Well, Persian rose, no shade, pr. 320.00
Lamp base, yucca pods/leaves, Persian rose, #157, USA, 18" . . .275.00
Mug, Kappa Sigma letters in gold on gr, pink w/in, 4¾" 165.00
Paperweight, elephant, bl, solid 75.00
Paperweight, rabbit, bl, solid 75.00
Plaque, Indian Brave, Big Buffalo, Ming turq 45.00
Plaque, poppies, maroon/bl, 1920, 8½" .300.00
Vase, bats at bottom, red/bl, 1916, cylinder, 11" 500.00
Vase, bl matt, #119, 1908-11, 4¾" 175.00
Vase, bud; rose/bl matt, 8¼" 30.00
Vase, buds swirl to ft, bl/lav, dbl gourd, ca 1915, 8¼" 110.00
Vase, buds/stems, bl-gr, dk brn clay, 1908-11, 4¾" 160.00
Vase, butterfly, bl, #688, 1913 . . . . .165.00
Vase, caramel matt, #684, 1908-11, 1½x4" 50.00
Vase, daffodils, gr matt w/red touches, 1906, 9" 750.00
Vase, dappled gr/bl matt, wide flat hdls, CS, 1921, 7½" 150.00
Vase, day lilies, dk chocolate brn w/olive, USA, 11" 110.00
Vase, dragonfly hdl, Persian rose, #668, 9¾" 75.00
Vase, emb decor, robin's egg bl on buff, 1908-11, 3¾" 115.00
Vase, floral, burgundy/bl glaze, 1920s, 9x8" 125.00
Vase, floral, maroon w/dk bl, #194, 2½" 65.00
Vase, floral, vertical, maroon/bl, 1920s, 6¾" 65.00
Vase, floral, vertical, yel-brn matt, #381, 1907, 9" 600.00
Vase, floral/stems, bl, 3 hdls, 1914, 8½" 195.00
Vase, gr, #277, 1905, 13½" 1,200.00
Vase, gr, 1908-1911, 5" 195.00
Vase, gr/brn/blk glaze, 1907-1912, 5¼x6¾" 225.00
Vase, gr/pink matt beaded glaze, #649½, 1905, 4¼" 225.00
Vase, gray-bl & plum, #362, 1908-11, 5½" 110.00
Vase, leaf/berries at wide shoulder, imp 502X, 1915, 9" 265.00
Vase, leaf/bud design, gr matt/red at bottom, #693, 7" 120.00
Vase, leaf/flower, rose w/bl, rose bowl shape, 4½x7" 60.00
Vase, leaves, bl on maroon, hdls, 1920s, 8¾" 90.00
Vase, leaves, cylinder top w/hdls/bulbous, #49, '03, 10" 1,200.00
Vase, leaves, dk brn body w/dk gr matt, #509, 4¾" 125.00
Vase, leaves, lt gr to bl, #851, 4¾" 110.00
Vase, leaves, maroon on design & at base, #698, 1910, 2½" . . .135.00
Vase, leaves, mulberry, #9, 1919, 5" 85.00
Vase, leaves, pointed, maroon/bl, 1915, 5¾" 85.00
Vase, leaves, rose/bl, 1918, 6¾" 100.00
Vase, leaves, vertical, gr matt/brn clay, #409, 1906, 5x5" 475.00
Vase, leaves, vertical, gr-bl to dk bl, #859, 1926, 5¼" 55.00
Vase, leaves, vertical, lt gr matt, #406, 1906, 5" 575.00
Vase, leaves, vertical, maroon/bl, 1920s, 4½" 27.50
Vase, leaves allover, maroon w/bl & gr, 2-hdl, 13" 175.00
Vase, leaves at shoulder, bl on maroon, #847, 1917, 4¼" 90.00
Vase, lotus leaves, squat, Persian rose, 2" 45.00
Vase, lt brn matt w/bl at top & dripping on brn, #476, 5" 200.00
Vase, mistletoe, dk gr over dk brn clay, 1908-11, 4" 120.00
Vase, mistletoe, lt bl, dtd 190 (?), #179, 3" 335.00
Vase, mistletoe/berry, slate bl w/brn, #179, 1908-11, 2½" 90.00
Vase, moths, dk to lt bl, 6¼" 37.50
Vase, mustard/bl glaze, #135, 1907-1912, 9¼" 325.00
Vase, narcissus, turq shaded, 1" top, 6¼" .25.00
Vase, olive w/rose brushed design, 1907, 4¼" 225.00
Vase, Persian rose, #786, 11¼" 195.00
Vase, poppies, dk maroon/dk bl matt, #21, 4" 75.00
Vase, poppy pods/leaves, dk bl on lt bl, EX mold, 10" 150.00
Vase, red to gr, #671, 1908-11, 7½" 395.00
Vase, ribbed, relief band at neck, med gr, #147, 1903, 3½" 550.00
Vase, rust bisque, #109, 1908-11 . . . . .125.00
Vase, stems curl up to violets, bl base to turq top, 4½" 27.50
Vase, thistle blooms, med bl, 1918, 7½" .145.00
Vase, tulips/leaves, EX mold, bl/gr/red, #751, 1908-11, 12" 435.00
Vase, vertical foliage, lt bl/gr, #179, 1908-11, 2¾" 140.00
Vase, vertical relief, gr matt, rnd top, 1907, 8" 295.00
Vase, violets on long stems, turq/bl blend, 4½" 27.50
Vase, violets/leaves, turq/bl, 1919-20, 3½" 60.00
Vase, widened base, dk maroon w/touches of bl, #496, 5¼" 165.00
Vase, yucca, bl, #700, 1908-11, 6¼" 265.00
Vase, 3 leaves, purple matt, imp AP/Van Briggle/1906, 1¾" 285.00
Vase, 3-Indian, brn/gr, 11" 175.00
Vase, 3-Indian, rose, 11½" 195.00

Vance Avon

Although pottery had been made in Tiltonville, Ohio, since about 1880, the ware manufactured there was of little significance until after the turn of the century, when the Vance Faience Company was organized for the purpose of producing quality artware. By 1902 the name had been changed to the Avon Faience Company, and late in the same year it and three other West Virginia potteries incorporated to form the Wheeling Potteries Company. The Avon branch operated in Tiltonville until 1905, when production was moved to Wheeling. Art pottery was discontinued.

From the beginning, only skilled craftsmen and trained engineers were hired. Wm. P. Jervis and Frederick Hurten Rhead were among the notable artists responsible for designing some of the early artware. Some of the ware was slip decorated under glaze, while other pieces were molded with high relief designs. Examples with squeeze bag decoration by Rhead are obviously forerunners of the Jap Birdimal line he later developed for Weller. Ware was marked 'Vance F. Co.'; 'Avon F. Co., Tiltonville'; or 'Avon W. Pts. Co.'

When no condition is indicated, the items listed below are assumed to be in mint condition.

Bowl vase, cats in relief, brown glaze, signed Vance F. Co., 7½" x 8½", $500.00.

Pitcher, hound hdl, emb vintage/hunt motif, brn/yel, mk, 12″ . . . 70.00
Pitcher, monkey figural, shaded brn, no mk, 5x6″ . . . 60.00
Pitcher, squeeze bag, Birdimal type, sgn/#1257, 5″ . . . 580.00
Vase, allover mermaid/waves relief, ball shape, 12½″, NM . . . 485.00
Vase, chains of ivory in relief, 5 holes, rare, 11½″ . . . 195.00
Vase, squeeze bag scene, bulbous, mk WPT Co, 6x5½″, NM . . . 140.00

Vaseline

Vaseline, a greenish-yellow colored glass produced by adding uranium oxide to the batch, was made in large quantities during the Victorian era. It was used for pressed glass tablewares, vases, and souvenir items.

When no condition is indicated, the items listed below are assumed to be in mint condition.

Figural hat matchholder–toothpick, Petticoat pattern, 3½″, $85.00.

Butter dish, Daisy & Button, sadiron shape . . . 125.00
Candlestick, hexagonal, 2 sections, wafer connectors, 7″ . . . 125.00
Candlestick, loop base, petal socket, 7″, pr, VG . . . 200.00
Candy dish, HP w/flowers, ftd, w/lid, 7″ . . . 85.00
Canoe, Daisy & Button, 8″ L . . . 30.00
Celery vase, allover design, scalloped top, pressed, 7⅞″ . . . 68.00
Compote, Two Panel, 11″ . . . 85.00
Cruet, applied clear hdl, cut crystal stopper . . . 65.00
Decanter, floral/butterfly, applied ribbon ft/hdl, stopper . . . 65.00
Lamp, hexagonal, loop font, brass collar, 9½″, NM . . . 150.00
Loving cup, mold-blown, heavy, 8½″ . . . 60.00
Mug, Daisy & Button . . . 23.00
Mug, paneled design, 5¼x3½″ . . . 60.00
Perfume, pillar mold, cut panels/flare lip w/ring, stopper . . . 225.00
Pitcher, gold leaves/pink & wht floral, 7½x5″ . . . 145.00
Relish, whisk broom, Pat Apl For . . . 38.00
Sugar bowl, loop & petal, scallop rim, 6″, EX . . . 225.00
Vase, hex bowl w/looping, scalloped, marble base, 11″, pr . . . 400.00
Vase, ruffled top, 9″ . . . 45.00
Wine server, grape etch, silver base/spigot/hdls, 15½″ . . . 750.00

Venetian Glass

Venetian glass is a thin, fragile ware, usually made in colors, often with internal gold or silver flecks. It was produced on the island of Murano, near Venice, from the 13th century to the early 1900s.

When no condition is indicated, the items listed below are assumed to be in mint condition.

Ash tray, dk gr w/enamel & gold, 5″ . . . 15.00
Basket, crown tuscan, curled hdl . . . 45.00
Basket, lav/pink, ribbing w/bubbles, goldstone hdl, 8x6½″ . . . 45.00
Basket, purple/clear, notched rim, gold flecked hdl, 6½″ . . . 55.00
Bud vase, gold top/base border, cloverleaf motif, 12″ . . . 95.00
Candlesticks, yel dragon stems, 10″, pr . . . 250.00
Compote, leaf-form bowl, griffin on stem, dolphin std, 13″ . . . 150.00
Compote, topaz, dragon shape stem, scalloped, 8″ . . . 80.00
Cup & saucer, demitasse; latticinio, wht/yel, 1895, 2¼″ . . . 135.00
Decanter, ruby w/much gold, HP violets, +4 shot glasses . . . 165.00
Ewer, gr/yel swirl loops on wht opaline, VB Florence, 12″ . . . 85.00
Figurine, fish, mc stripes, goldstone lips, Murano, 4¾x4″ . . . 19.00
Figurine, pheasants, bl w/lav tails, gold flecks, 17″, pr . . . 100.00
Jar, pink, clear w/gold flecks bubble stem/finial, 7″ . . . 80.00
Obelisk, clear w/stalagmites of wht/bl, sgn, 16¼″, pr . . . 1,000.00
Plate, wht & goldstone swirls, broken pontil, 7″ . . . 35.00
Sculpture, yel, rnd red/line devices, amphorus, Ferro, 26″ . . . 1,800.00
Vase, pink, gold dust, bottle shape, blown, bulbous, 4½″ . . . 30.00
Vase, pink, silver speckles, 10″ . . . 35.00
Vase, red/mauve, gold flecks w/in, handkerchief form, 11″ . . . 1,650.00

Jar, blue and white swirls on clear with gold-flecked flower finial, $150.00.

Verlys

Verlys art glass, produced in France after 1931 by the Holophane Company of Verlys, was made in crystal with acid-finished relief work in the Art Deco style. Colored and opalescent glass were also used.

In 1935 an American branch was opened in Newark, Ohio. Wares manufactured there were very similar, but less expensive.

Both factories signed their wares 'Verlys'--the American branch by etching, the French with a molded signature.

When no condition is indicated, the items listed below are assumed to be in mint condition.

Ash tray, lovebirds, directorie bl . . . 85.00
Ash tray, rearing horse, sgn Carl Schming . . . 40.00
Bowl, birds & bees, American, sgn, 12″ . . . 169.00
Bowl, Cupid w/bow & hearts, 6″ . . . 85.00

Bowl, frosted, thistles, 3-toe, sgn, 8½" 75.00
Bowl, pine cone, bl, ftd, 6" 85.00
Bowl, pine cone, 6¾" 55.00
Bowl, roses, 5½" 50.00
Bowl, tassel, bl, 12" 190.00
Bowl, waves, frosted & clear, France, rare, 11¼x3½" 325.00
Bowl, wild duck, crystal, 13¼" 95.00
Box, bubble design, rnd, France 125.00
Box, chrysanthemum on lid, topaz, 2-pc, 5½" dia 315.00
Centerpiece, doves, frosted, oval, 12¼" L 130.00
Charger, birds & bees, American, 12" 170.00
Charger, water lilies & pods, frosted, sgn, 13¾" 195.00
Figurine, elephant, topaz, rare 325.00
Figurine, pigeon, frosted, rare, 4¼" 285.00
Planter, water lilies, 7x11" 110.00
Plate rest, shell pattern, opal, rnd, 4⅞" 145.00
Vase, frosted maidens: 1 dancing, 1 kneeling, crystal, 8½" 95.00
Vase, icicle, script sgn, 8" 100.00
Vase, laurel, sgn, 10½x8½" 125.00
Vase, lovebirds, fan shape, 5" 125.00
Vase, mandarin, 9" 195.00
Vase, wheat, bl, 9½" 295.00

Vase, fan form, clear frosted glass with lovebirds in relief, 5" x 6½, $125.00.

Vernon Kilns

Vernon Potteries Ltd. was established by Faye G. Bennison in Vernon, California, in 1931. The name was later changed to Vernon Kilns, and until it closed in 1958, dinnerware and figurines were their primary products. Among its wares most sought by collectors today are items designed by such famous artists as Rockwell Kent and Walt Disney.

Authority Maxine Nelson has compiled a lovely book, *Versatile Vernon Kilns*, with full-color photos and current prices; you will find her address in the Directory under California.

When no condition is indicated, the items listed below are assumed to be in mint condition.

Ash tray, Detroit, Hudson Co 8.00
Bel Air, chop plate, lg 6.00
Brown-Eyed Susan, carafe 20.00
Casa California, plate, G Turnbull, 6" 3.00
Coral Reef, creamer 16.00
Coral Reef, plate, 9½" 18.00
Dolores, cup & saucer 10.50
Dolores, fruit, sm 4.00
Dolores, plate, bread & butter 3.50
Dolores, plate, dinner 8.00
Early California, bowl, lug chowder 8.00
Early California, bowl, mixing 15.00
Early California, bowl, vegetable; oval, 9" 10.00
Early California, creamer, demitasse 10.00
Early California, creamer & sugar 18.00
Early California, egg cup 10.00
Early California, jug, 1-pt 10.00
Early California, plate, grill 18.00
Early California, plate, 10½" 7.50
Early California, plate, 9½" 6.00
Early California, platter, 12" 12.00
Early California, sugar bowl 9.00
Early California, sugar bowl, demitasse; open 15.00
Fantasia, bowl, pink mushrooms, #120 .... 120.00
Fantasia, bowl, satyrs in relief, wht w/pink int, 7" 185.00
Fantasia, figurine, Baby Weems, #37, 6" 95.00
Fantasia, figurine, Centaurette, #18, 7½" 200.00
Fantasia, figurine, elephant, Walt Disney, #41 .... 100.00
Fantasia, figurine, satyr, aqua, #124 .... 145.00
Fantasia, vase, fairies, mc floral on wht, #122, 2¾x12¼" 175.00
Fruitdale, gravy boat 17.50
Fruitdale, plate, dinner 8.00
Gingham, flowerpot w/saucer, 5" 25.00
Gingham, jug/carafe, w/stopper 16.00
Hawaiian Flowers, bowl, fruit 8.00
Hawaiian Flowers, plate, 10½" 18.00
Hawaiian Flowers, plate, 9½" 16.00
Homespun, carafe, w/stopper, 48-oz 16.00
Homespun, casserole, w/lid, 8" 12.00
Homespun, chop plate 10.00
Homespun, creamer & sugar 15.00
Homespun, cup & saucer 7.00
Homespun, pitcher, ½-pt 10.00
Homespun, shakers, pr 7.00
Mayflower, bowl, coupe soup 5.00
Mayflower, platter, oval, 12" 12.00
Moby Dick, chowder, open; bl, 6" 27.00
Moby Dick, creamer, Rockwell Kent, 5" 48.00
Moby Dick, place setting, Rockwell Kent, 5-pc 65.00
Moby Dick, plate, luncheon; brn, 9½" 25.00
Modern California, bowl, vegetable, 9" 10.00
Modern California, teapot, lilac 25.00
Mojave, gravy boat 10.00
Native California, bowl, fruit 4.00
Native California, plate, 10½" 8.00
Native California, soup, rim 7.00
Organdie, ash tray, coaster 10.00
Organdie, bowl, vegetable, 7" 10.00
Organdie, butter dish, ¼-lb 22.50
Organdie, carafe, w/lid 35.00
Organdie, casserole, w/lid 30.00
Organdie, creamer 7.50
Organdie, creamer, ind 8.00
Organdie, creamer, w/lid 12.00
Organdie, cup & saucer 10.00
Organdie, cup & saucer, demitasse 15.00
Organdie, flowerpot w/saucer, 5" 25.00
Organdie, lug chowder 8.00
Organdie, mug 20.00
Organdie, plate, chop; 14" 20.00
Organdie, plate, dinner; 10½" 9.00

Figurine, Disney Copyright 1940, 6″, $150.00.

Organdie, plate, tidbit; 2-tier 15.00
Organdie, platter, oval 10.00
Organdie, sugar bowl, w/lid 10.00
Organdie, teapot, 8 cup 30.00
Organdie, tumbler, convex sides, 5″ 16.00
Our America, bowl, salad; bl, Rockwell Kent, 11″ 62.00
Our America, coffee pot, ind 45.00
Our America, egg cup, Rockwell Kent 30.00
Our America, plate, Rockwell Kent, 9⅜″ 25.00
Plate, Bits of Old England, #8 . . . . . 20.00
Plate, Bits of the Old West, Horse Thieves 20.00
Plate, General MacArthur, 10½″ 15.00
Plate, Marine Hymn 12.00
Plate, Presidential #2 . . . . . 18.00
Plate, Roosevelt, war scene, red, 1942, 10½″ 30.00
Plate, Rosalie Brown 12.00
Plate, South Dakota, bl 8.00
Plate, Will Rogers 25.00
Plate, Williamsburg, VA, historic 10.00
Santa Barbara, cup & saucer, demitasse 9.00
Tam-O'-Shanter, platter, oval, 14″ 14.00
Tickled Pink, coffee server, w/lid, 10¾″ 16.00
Tickled Pink, creamer & sugar, open; mk 4.25
Tickled Pink, platter, oval, 9½″ 5.00
Tradewinds, casserole, w/lid 15.00
Tradewinds, pitcher, 2-qt 15.00
Tradewinds, plate, dinner 6.00
Ultra California, creamer 10.00
Ultra California, cup & saucer, demitasse 12.00
Ultra California, egg cup 10.00
Ultra California, platter, 12″ 12.00

Verre de Soie

Literally meaning glass of silk, this type of glass is named for its lovely, almost pearl-like lustre.

When no condition is indicated, the items listed below are assumed to be in mint condition.

Centerpiece, 4-petal top, melon ribbed/swirled, 7¾x11″ 150.00
Cracker jar, pnt flowers, SP lid 110.00
Shade, bell shape, sgn Steuben 75.00
Vase, bulbous, ruffled, 7″ 110.00

Vienna

In 1719, Claude Innocentius de Paquier established a hard paste porcelain factory in Vienna where he produced highly ornamental wares similar to the type produced at Meissen. Early wares were usually unmarked, but after 1744, when the factory was purchased by the Empress, the Austrian shield (often called 'beehive') was stamped on underglaze.

When no condition is indicated, the items listed below are assumed to be in mint condition. Values are for hand painted items; decal decorated items would be considerably lower.

Vase, scene with nude and cherubs, gold overlay leaves and flowers, 13″, $1,295.00.

Clock, mantle; maids/cupids on base/dome top, 1900, 15″ 715.00
Creamer & sugar, portraits, pink & gold 185.00
Cup & saucer, Alpine village w/in, beehive/#7777, 2″ 165.00
Cup & saucer, flowers, bl/much gold, ped ft, 4½″ 125.00
Cup & saucer, girl's portrait, bl jeweling, lg 295.00
Figurine, Venus in shell-chariot w/2 nymphs, 12½″ 990.00
Figurine, young boy, 'onyx' base, beehive/#837, RV, 7″ 285.00
Plaque, Ein Traum, sgn Ullmar, beehive mk, gold fr, 12″ 975.00
Plaque, Jupiter & Juno, sgn Richter, 19″ dia 1,200.00
Plate, Echo, sgn Wagner, 10″ 500.00
Plate, female portrait, gold emb rim, sgn Wagner, 9½″ 550.00
Plate, Little Captive, portrait, sgn, beehive mk, 10″ 250.00
Plate, Paris & Helena, cobalt w/gold border, 10″ 550.00
Plate, peasants comraderie, beehive mk, cobalt/gold, 9½″ 400.00
Plate, Rinaldo/Armida, sgn Wildner 550.00
Tray, wine; male & female center, gold border, hdls, 15″ 500.00
Urn, classical scene, pink/bl/gold, beehive, hdls/lid, 25″ 1,200.00
Urn, figures on medallion, w/lid, beehive mk, Carlsbad 550.00
Vase, classic figure, maroon/gold, pierced lid, RV, ″ 450.00
Vase, cupids, cobalt bl, reticulated top, hdls, 5¼″ 450.00
Vase, lady's portrait in base, floral in neck, Wagner, 15″ 1,100.00

Viennese Enameled Ware

When no condition is indicated, the items listed below are assumed to be in excellent condition.

Coin purse, on chain & belt hook, pnt ea side, 1800s 550.00
Ewer, courting couple in garden, 1870s, 5½″ 750.00
Suite, Watteau scenes, settee, 4 chairs, table, secretary 1,850.00

Villeroy and Boch

The firm of Villeroy and Boch, located in Mettlach, Germany, was brought about by the 1841 merger of three German factories--the Wallerfangen factory, founded by Nicholas Villeroy in 1787; the Mettlach factory, founded by Jean Francis Boch in 1809; and his father's factory in Septfontaines, established in 1767. Villeroy and Boch produced many varieties of wares, including earthenware with printed underglaze designs, and the famous the castle mark with the name 'Mettlach.'

When no condition is indicated, the items listed below are assumed to be in mint condition.

See also Mettlach

Baker, 4 cameo vignettes, dbl eagle lozenge mk, gray..........95.00
Chamber pot, child's; children & floral decals, 4¼"............75.00
Coffee pot, cut sponge, Virginia pattern.....................85.00
Jar, bearded heads relief, brn/cream, 5x4½"..................28.00
Pitcher, bl w/cherry & leaves decor, 5"......................45.00
Pitcher, child's; wht w/children decals, bulbous, 7¾"..........95.00
Platter, Alphina, mtn castle scene in blk, 14½"...............25.00
Platter, Yorkshire, 14"....................................28.00
Slop jar, child's; children decals, wicker hdl, w/lid, 7"..........95.00
Stein, wht figures on bl, tan/wht trim, pewter lid, 6", VG.......85.00
Vase, sgraffito geometrics, bottle form, 12"..................80.00

Platter, snow scene on tapestry ground, #467, 9¾" x 6", $175.00.

Vistosa

Vistosa was produced from about 1938 through the early-forties. It was Taylor, Smith and Taylor's answer to the very successful Fiesta line of their nearby competitor, Homer Laughlin. Vistosa was made in four solid colors--mango red, cobalt blue, light green, and deep yellow. 'Pie crust' edges and a dainty five-petal flower on handles and lid finials made for a very attractive yet never-the-less commercially unsuccessful product.

When no condition is indicated, the items listed below are assumed to be in mint condition.

Bowl, salad...95.00
Creamer...7.50
Cup & saucer, demitasse...................................20.00
Egg cup...18.00
Gravy...55.00
Pitcher, ball shape.......................................35.00

Creamer and covered sugar bowl, $20.00.

Plate, chop; 11"..12.50
Plate, 9"..5.00
Shakers, pr...12.50
Sugar, w/lid..12.50
Teapot..75.00

Volkmar

Charles Volkmar established a workshop in Tremont, New York, in 1882. He produced artware decorated under the glaze in the manner of the early barbotine work done at the Haviland factory in Limoges, France. He relocated in 1888 in Menlo Park, New Jersey, and together with J.T. Smith established the Menlo Park Ceramic Company for the production of art tile. The partnership was dissolved in 1893.

From 1895 until 1902, Volkmar located in Corona, New York, first under the name Volkmar Ceramic Company, later as Volkmar and Cory, and for the final six years as Crown Point. During the latter period he made art tile, blue underglaze Delft-type wares, and colorful polychrome vases, etc. The Volkmar Kilns were established in 1903 in Metuchen, New Jersey, by Volkmar and his son.

Wares were marked with various devices consisting of the Volkmar name, initials, or 'Crown Point Ware.'

When no condition is indicated, the items listed below are assumed to be in mint condition.

Vase, dk gr veined glaze, hand thrown, 2¾x4"...............250.00
Vase, gr matt, bulbous, sq mouth, 6".......................125.00
Vase, gr on gr, flaring sides, 8½"..........................290.00

Volkstadt

The Volkstadt Porcelain Factory was established in Thuringia, Germany about 1760. They continue to operate to the present, often marking their wares with a 'crossed hayfork' device used since the late 1700s.

When no condition is indicated, the items listed below are assumed to be in mint condition.

The Introduction, shield mark, 29" wide, repaired, $800.00.

Figurine, exotic bird w/long tail, wht Rococo base, 6¾" 150.00
Figurine, Greek mythological subject, 12" 375.00
Figurine, table w/mirror, maid does lady's hair, 1910, 13" 800.00

Wade

George Wade and Son, Ltd., of England, makes inexpensive ceramic character figures and giftware that is becoming popular with collectors. Several lines have been produced: Little Creatures, Nursery Favorites and mini-Nursery Rhyme Characters.

Little Creatures

Angel Fish 5.00
Butterfly 5.00
Kangaroo 5.00
Poodle, wht 10.00
Walrus 5.00
Zebra 5.00

Nursery Favorites

Goosey Gander 8.00
Humpty Dumpty 8.00

Nursery Rhyme and Fairy Tale Figurines

Gingerbread Man 15.00
Goosey Gander 5.00
King Cole 5.00
Queen of Hearts 5.00
Three Bears 15.00

Walley

The Walley Pottery operated in West Sterling, Massachusetts, from 1898 to 1919. Never more than a one-man operation, Walley himself hand crafted all his wares from local clay. The majority of his pottery was simple and unadorned, and usually glazed in matt green. On occasion, however, you may find high- and semi-gloss green, as well as matt glazes in blue, cream, brown, and red. The most rare and desirable examples of his work are those with applied or relief-carved decorations.

Some pieces are marked 'WJW.'

When no condition is indicated, the items listed below are assumed to be in mint condition.

Bowl, brn w/textured lt gr overglaze, 1⅝x4½" 75.00
Bud vase, gr/oxblood, 5" 200.00
Vase, gr & brn matt, applied leaves, sgn WJW, 6½x6" 600.00
Vase, gr matt, applied leaves, sgn WJW, 8x4½" 500.00
Vase, gr matt, bulbous w/sm collar, squat, 3" 120.00
Vase, gr w/brn flecks, flare top on bulb, sgn WJW, 3½" 165.00
Vase, ribbed, gr/brn, hand thrown, ped ft, 7x4¼" 195.00

Walrath

Frederick Walrath was a studio potter who worked from around the turn of the century until his death in 1920. He was located in Rochester, New York, until 1918, when he became associated with the Newcomb Pottery in New Orleans, Louisiana.

When no condition is indicated, the items listed below are assumed to be in mint condition.

Bowl, attached nude in center, gr, rare, 10½x10" 495.00
Flower frog, swan figural, lt gr, 3¾x4½" 225.00
Tankard, chestnuts/leaves, brn/lt gr on dk beige, 1911, 10" 185.00
Vase, bl-gray matt, hand thrown, 7¾x6", NM 70.00
Vase, 5-color matt, stylized clovers, mk, 5½x3½" 1,000.00

Walter, A.

Almaric Walter was employed from 1904 through 1914 at Verreries Artistiques des Freres Daum in Nancy, France. After 1919 he opened his own business where he continued to make the same type of quality objects d'art in pate-de-verre glass as he had earlier. His pieces are signed A. Walter, Nancy H. Berge Sc.

Ash receiver, sq w/bumblebee in corner, turq/bl, 1925, 3½" 660.00
Bird, long beak to chest, shaped socle, lt/dk bl, 8" 715.00
Bookend, fox & trellis w/grapes relief, yel/gr, 1925, 5¾" 770.00
Bowl, flared, gr walls w/gr & bl relief rays, 6" dia 770.00
Box, pine cone finial, yel/gr, 3½" dia 715.00
Buddha, seated, elaborated headdress, deep yel, 6¾" 660.00
Buddha, seated, lt gr, unsgn, ca 1925, 3¼" 330.00
Dish, foliage w/3 shells at rim, gr/rust/mustard, 6" dia 550.00
Fox, sleeping, on sq base, lt gr w/rust & bl, 4½" L 770.00
Paperweight, bird upon waves, aqua/gr, 3⅜" L 440.00
Paperweight, snail munches on berried branch, 3¼" L 1,980.00
Paperweight w/scrolling snakes/leaves, gr/yel, 4½" dia 465.00
Pendant, beetle in relief, rust/blk on ochre/yel, 2¾" L 550.00
Pendant, dragonfly on leaf, turq/gr on bl, 1⅞" dia 715.00
Sea lion, seated, dk to lt gr, ca 1925, 6½" 550.00

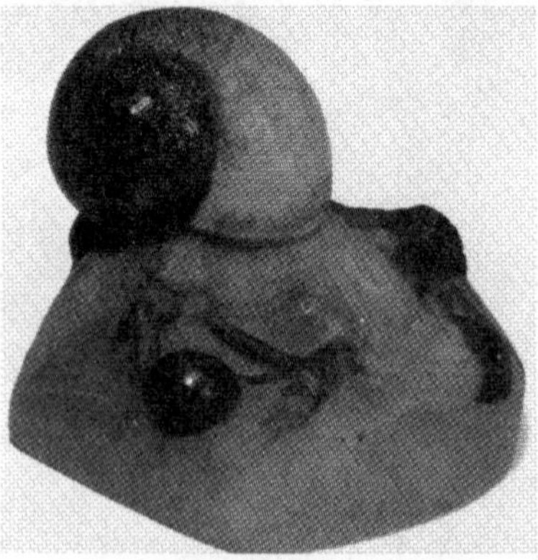

Snail figural paperweight, orange, yellow and green, signed, 3" long, $1,800.00.

Tray, beetles at hdls, oval, gr/yel, 6½" L 1,320.00
Vase, rnd leaves at base, vertical stems, lime w/gr, 4½" 1,500.00
Vase, 3 beetles in relief, sienna/gr, coupe form, 6½" 1,500.00
Veilleuse, bird floating on waves, bl/gr, 7½" L 1,650.00
Veilleuse, domed coffer form, relief floral, ball ft, 4" 605.00
Veilleuse, dove, head on chest, bl/gr, 7" L 1,320.00
Vide poche, fan form w/ruffled edge, ivy relief, 9" dia 2,640.00

Wannopee

The Wannopee Pottery, established in 1892, developed from the reorganization of the financially insecure New Milford Pottery Company of New Milford, Connecticut. They produced a line of mottled glaze pottery called 'Dutchess,' and a similar line in porcelain. Both were marked with the impressed sunburst 'W,' with 'Porcelain' added to indicate that particular body type.

In 1895, semi-porcelain pitchers in three sizes were decorated with relief medallion cameos of Beethoven, Mozart, and Napoleon. Lettuce-Leaf Ware was first produced in 1901, and used actual leaves in the modeling. Scarabronze, made in 1895, was their finest artware. It featured simple Egyptian shapes with a coppery glaze. It was marked with a scarab, either impressed or applied.

Production ceased in 1903.

When no condition is indicated, the items listed below are assumed to be in mint condition.

Chamberstick, brn/dk brn/blk, w/hdl, 13″ 50.00
Ewer, brn/moss gr gloss, squat body, 4¾″ 25.00
Lamp base, mc majolica streaky glaze, 11¾x7½″ 85.00
Teapot, dk drip glaze 55.00
Vase, brn/gr/blk majolica, w/hdls, 13¾″ 100.00
Vase, gold/bl/pink/brn irid, S-hdls, 6″ 65.00

Warwick

The Warwick China Company operated in Wheeling, West Virginia, from 1887 until 1951. They produced both hand-painted and decaled plates, vases, tea and coffee pots, pitchers, bowls, and jardinieres featuring lovely florals or portraits of beautiful ladies done in luscious colors. Backgrounds were usually blendings of brown and beige, but ivory was also used.

Various marks were employed, all of which incorporate the Warwick name.

For a more thorough study of the subject, we recommend *Why Not Warwick* and *Warwick China Guide* both by Donald C. Hoffmann; his address can be found in the Directory under Illinois.

When no condition is indicated, the items listed below are assumed to be in mint condition.

Bowl, gr w/rose decor, 3-ftd, 3½″ tall 85.00
Humidor, brn w/fisherman, bulbous, matching lid, 5¼″ 125.00
Jardiniere, brn w/Beck dog scene, flat top, 12¼″ 300.00
Jardiniere, brn w/monk, flat top, 12¼″ 200.00
Marmalade jar, brn to yel, poppies, ornate hdls, w/lid, 4″ 55.00
Mug, brn w/eagle, sq hdl, imp VP, 4½″ 55.00
Mug, brn w/Gibson Girl, sq hdl, imp VP, 4½″ 95.00
Mug, matt, w/fisherman, sq hdl, imp VP, 4½″ 75.00
Mug, pedestal; brn w/opera scenes, rnd hdl, 5½″ 90.00
Pitcher, beer; Tobio, brn w/bulldogs, 7″ 110.00
Pitcher, beer; Tobio, brn w/fruit, 7″ 75.00
Pitcher, beer; Tobio, charcoal w/floral, 7″ 125.00
Pitcher, beer; Tobio, red w/monk, 7″ 90.00
Pitcher, brn w/poinsettias, hdls, 12″ 95.00
Pitcher, bulbous/fluted/ornate hdl, red w/floral, 10″ 120.00
Pitcher, bulbous/fluted/ornate hdl, wht to gr/floral, 10″ 125.00
Pitcher, cider; brn w/fruit decor, rnd hdl, 6¼″ 150.00
Pitcher, lemonade; brn w/portrait, fluted, ornate hdl, 6½″ 150.00
Pitcher, lemonade; pink/portrait, fluted, ornate hdl, 6½″ 285.00
Plate, brn w/eagle, 9½″ 100.00
Plate, brn w/Indian, 9½″ 130.00
Plate, calendar; 1910, girl w/horse, 8″ 85.00
Plate, children's nursery rhyme, 7¼″ 30.00
Plate, flow blue w/maple leaf pattern, 10½″ 65.00
Plate, fraternal, Masons, wht w/dbl gold rim, 8″ 35.00
Plate, Lincoln's picture on wht bkground, 9″ 120.00
Plate, monk on red, 9½″ 120.00
Plate, portrait, wht bkground, fluted gold rim, 12″ 135.00
Rose bowl, Pansy, brn w/floral, 4″ 55.00
Spittoon, lady's; lt brn w/wht center, floral decor, 7¼″ 150.00
Spittoon, man's; brn tones, no decal, emb on body, 6¾″ 150.00
Stein, curved hdl, brn w/Gibson Girl, 13″ 225.00
Stein, curved hdl, bust portrait of monk, 13″ 165.00
Stein, sq hdl, brn w/Dickens character, 10½″ 160.00
Stein, sq hdl, brn w/fisherman, 10½″ 150.00
Stein, sq hdl, brn w/nude, 10½″ 260.00
Stein, sq hdl, charcoal w/monk, 10½″ 200.00
Stein, sq hdl w/support bar, brn w/FOE, 10½″ 148.00
Stein, sq hdl w/support bar, brn w/monk, 10½″ 145.00
Vase, Bouquet, brn w/floral, twig hdl, 10½″ 95.00
Vase, Bouquet, brn w/nude, twig hdl, 10½″ 160.00
Vase, Bouquet, charcoal w/floral, twig hdl, 10½″ 115.00
Vase, Bouquet, gr, lg red/wht/pink roses, twig hdl, 10½″ 280.00
Vase, Bouquet, pink w/portrait, twig hdl, 10½″ 325.00
Vase, Bouquet, red w/floral, twig hdl, 10½″ 105.00
Vase, Bouquet, rose color w/floral, twig hdl, 10½″ 295.00
Vase, Carnation, brn w/floral, bulbous w/narrow neck, 10½″ 80.00
Vase, Carnation, pink w/portrait, narrow neck, 10½″ 280.00
Vase, Carol, matt w/pine cones, bulbous top & bottom, 8½″ 195.00
Vase, Flower, trumpet shape, flat top, brn w/floral, 10″ 80.00
Vase, Flower, trumpet shape, flat top, matt brn, beechnuts 95.00
Vase, Flower, trumpet shape, flat top, matt gr w/beechnuts 100.00
Vase, Flower, trumpet shape, flat top, pink/portrait, 10″ 250.00
Vase, Maria, brn/floral, narrow/bulbous top/sq hdls, 10″ 200.00
Vase, Maria, red/portrait, narrow/bulbous top/sq hdls, 10″ 275.00
Vase, Narcis, pillow-shaped, brn w/beechnut, 6¾″ 135.00
Vase, Narcis, pillow-shaped, brn w/pine cone, 7″ 115.00
Vase, Narcis, pillow-shaped, brn w/portrait, 8½″ 115.00
Vase, Narcis, pillow-shaped, charcoal w/floral, 6¾″ 185.00
Vase, Narcis, pillow-shaped, charcoal w/nude, 8½″ 300.00
Vase, Narcis, pillow-shaped, matt w/portrait, 7″ 190.00
Vase, Narcis, pillow-shaped, red w/portrait, 8½″ 240.00
Vase, Narcis, pillow-shaped, wht w/birds, 7″ 220.00
Vase, Senator, stick neck/fluted, brn w/floral, 11½″ 130.00
Vase, Senator, stick neck/fluted, matt grn to tan/pine cone 145.00
Vase, Senator, stick neck/fluted, matt tan to gr, portrait 185.00
Vase, Senator, stick neck/fluted, red w/floral, 13¼″ 140.00
Vase, Senator, stick neck/fluted, red w/portrait, 11½″ 180.00
Vase, trumpet shape, fluted top, brn w/floral, 13½″ 100.00
Vase, trumpet shape, fluted top, matt w/beechnuts, 13½″ 130.00
Vase, trumpet shape, fluted top, red w/floral, 15¼″ 110.00
Vase, trumpet shape, fluted top, yel to gr w/floral, 15¼″ 195.00
Vase, Verona, red w/floral, ring hdl, 11¼″ 125.00

Wash Sets

Before the days of running water, bedrooms were standardly equipped with a wash bowl and pitcher as a matter of necessity. A 'toilet set' was comprised of the pitcher and bowl, toothbrush holder, covered commode, soap dish, shaving dish and mug. Some sets were even more elaborate. Through everyday usage, the smaller items were often broken, and today it is unusual to find a complete set.

Porcelain sets decorated with florals, fruits, or scenics were produced abroad by Limoges in France, and some were imported from Germany and England. During the last quarter of the 1800s and until after the turn of the century, American-made toilet sets were manufactured in abundance. Tin and graniteware sets were also made.

When no condition is indicated, the items listed below are assumed to be in excellent condition.

Empire, bl/wht windmills, 12″ pitcher+bowl+chamber pot 235.00
Flow blue, floral w/gold trim, English, 12″ pitcher+bowl 395.00

Homer Laughlin, pink & yel roses on bl, gold trim, 2-pc.......160.00
Losol Ware, ironstone, bird/flowers, gaudy colors, 2-pc........425.00
Mason's Ironstone, mc Oriental decor, 1840s, pitcher+bowl....590.00
Villeroy & Boch, child's; wht w/children decals, 3-pc..........200.00

Watch Fobs

Watch fobs have been popular since the last quarter of the 19th century. They were often made by retail companies to advertise their products. Souvenir, commemorative, and political fobs were also produced——all are popular collectibles today.

When no condition is indicated, the items listed below are assumed to be in excellent condition.

Allis Chalmers, colored porc, 3-pc equipment.................65.00
Allis Chalmers, Model L-10...................................35.00
American Crawler Cranes.......................................5.00
American Legion, Paul Revere's Ride, Boston, 1930...........10.00
American Legion Convention...................................10.00
Armour Co, steer's head......................................29.00
Atkins Saws, saws entwined, AAA in circle, writing on bk.......35.00
Autocar, radiator, cut-out...................................10.00
Avery, bulldog...75.00
Babe Ruth, keep score w/base discs..........................135.00
Barker-Wheeler, Peoria; Art Nouveau lady.....................40.00
Blatz, beer barrel...67.50
Bucyrus Erie, railroad shovel, cut-out......................120.00
Budweiser, w/strap...26.00
Bull Dog Tobacco, Won't Bite, red bulldog....................65.00
Bull Durham Tobacco, 14k gold plated.........................23.00
Case, steel lug farm tractor.................................50.00
Case Plow Works, hand holding plow, rnd......................39.00
Caterpillar, truck..3.00
Caterpillar Holt, 2-ton model, brass, EX....................200.00
Caterpillar Tractor, Peterson Tractor Company................75.00
Clark, loader...5.00
Cleveland Rock Drills..15.00
Columbian Expo...12.00
Cyrus McCormick, centennial..................................25.00
Diamond Edge...75.00
Euclid Tractor, TC-12...4.00
Evening Gazette, baseball, score keeping on bk, 1912..........75.00
Ford, farm tractor...10.00
Fordson Tractor, cut-out.....................................75.00
Frampton Foster Lumber Co, Pittsburg.........................22.50
Garland Stove..35.00
Gipps Amberlin Beer, porc...................................100.00
Godair-Crowley Cattle Commission Co..........................25.00
Gooch's Macaroni...30.00
Green River Whiskey, horseshoe outline.......................27.00
Hanson Clutch & Machinery, track-type crane..................15.00
Heinz, girl holding catsup bottle............................28.00
Honer Little Lady, harmonica, 1⅜".............................14.00
Horseshoe around horse head..................................12.00
Hunter shooting lion, brass..................................12.00
Illinois Tractor Co, tractor figural, bronze/leather strap.........25.00
Independent Harvester Co, wheat shock........................18.00
Ingersoll-Rand, construction worker/jackhammer, metal, rnd.....10.00
Interlocking Cement Stave Silo Co, silo & cows feeding........40.00
International Harvester, dbl globe, corn stalks/wheat..........65.00
International Harvester, rnd, bucking bronco on front.........110.00
J Wm Jennings Bryan, 1908....................................40.00
Jamestown Expo...10.00
Jesse James, fiber, w/attached button........................35.00
John Deere, Hoover #197, dk bl porc, oval...................120.00
John Deere, Hoover #204, dozer................................4.00
Joy Rock Drills, Hoover #355..................................8.00
Kellogg's Toasted Corn Flakes, brass & enameled..............35.00
King Oscar 5¢ cigars, emb King Oscar.........................60.00
Lee, broom...40.00
Leisey Brewery, porc...75.00
Marion, steam shovel, brass, oval............................45.00
Masonic, brass & porc..12.00

Left to right: Indian with bow and arrow, enamel work, 5¼", $25.00; Thomas Wildey Founder, I.O.O.F. 100th Anniversary, 1819-1919, $15.00.

Masonic, lady riding horse, Louisville, KY, 1909..............12.00
Masonic Local Interest.......................................20.00
Massey-Ferguson, key chain type...............................4.00
Master Photo Finishers of America............................26.00
Mexican Border Service, 1916.................................50.00
Michigan State Auto School, solid brass, 2 tires/#32 racer......20.00
National Cash Register.......................................85.00
National Motorcycle Gypsy Tour, 1922.........................25.00
National Sportsman, deer in relief...........................30.00
National Sportsman, w/accompanying pin, set..................50.00
NY State Fair, 1921...2.00
Oakland Car, bl/wht, porc....................................75.00
Old Reliable Coffee, brass...................................34.00
Order of RR Conductors, emb RR car, passengers, conductor...65.00
Panhandle Old Settlers' Association, shape of Texas...........12.00
Peters' Weatherbird Shoes, enameled..........................30.00
Pettibone, brass...20.00
Plymouth, locomotive...20.00
Princeton University, brass, 1908.............................5.00
Racine, WI, Homecoming, 1909..................................5.00
Red Diamond Overalls, w/RR man...............................35.00
Red Face Pulleys...40.00
Red Goose Shoes, enameled....................................30.00
Reo car..45.00
Runner jumping hurdles..5.00
Santa Fe Trails, emb covered wagon & oxen, Missouri, 1913....37.50
Savage Rifles, Indian w/rifle................................85.00
Saxon, pop-out...85.00
Shapleigh Hardware Co..35.00
Shield & Seal, University of Iowa.............................5.00
Spread eagle, bronze..5.00
State Farm Mutual Auto Ins Co, enameled car, 1920s...........20.00
Statue of Liberty, bronze....................................35.00
Stewart Clipper, #9, w/strap.................................55.00
Strauss Bros...25.00
Studebaker...90.00

Studebaker, wagon...60.00
Thew Lorian Cranes...10.00
Turkey Coffee...60.00
US Seal, 14k gold plated...8.00
Valparaiso College, 1904...5.00
Victorian, curved figural, fern trim, emb base, SP, 3″...68.00
Wabco, truck...12.00
Western Electric Co...42.00
Wm J Bryant...60.00
World's Championship Rodeo Contest, Chicago...10.00

Watch Stands

Watch stands were decorative articles designed with a hook from which to hang a watch. Some displayed the watch as the face of a grandfather clock, or as part of an interior scene with figures in period costumes and contemporary furnishings. They were popular products of Staffordshire potters and silver companies as well.

When no condition is indicated, the items listed below are assumed to be in mint condition.

Brass/copper street light/rnd fr/wood box, battery op...45.00
Cherub holds bird aloft, SP, Meriden, 6″...95.00
Couple ea side of deer, antlers frame, Staffordshire, 7″...150.00
Cupid on plinth, gold bronze, w/19th C watch, 9½″...275.00
Greenaway girl behind disk holds hook for watch, Poole SP...145.00
Mahog w/cut-out applied heart, scratch carving, late, 6″...35.00
Semi-nude, spaniel at side, porcelain, 8″...125.00

Bisque, figural girls each side, 8″, $165.00.

Watches

First made in the 1500s in Germany, early watches were actually small clocks, suspended from the wrist or belt. By 1700 they had become the approximate shape and size we find today. The first watches produced in America were made in 1810. The well-known Waltham Watch Company was established in 1850, and their inexpensive 'Waterbury' models were produced by the thousands.

Open face and hunting case watches of the 1890s were solid gold or gold-filled and were often elaborately decorated in several colors of gold. Gold watches became a status symbol in this decade, and were worn by both men and women on chains with fobs or jeweled slides. Ladies sometimes fastened them to their clothing with pins often set with jewels. The chatelaine watch was worn at the waist, only one of several items such as scissors, coin purses, or needle cases, each attached to small chains. During this period, movements and cases could be purchased separately, so inexpensive cases may sometimes be found containing well-jeweled movements, or the contrary may be true.

Most turn of the century watch cases were gold filled, and these are plenitful today. 18k cases are rare, and 22k cases are very valuable! Sterling cases, though interest in them is on the increase, are not in great demand.

When no condition is indicated, the items listed below are assumed to be in mint condition.

Key:
adj—adjusted
brg—bridge plate design movement
d/s—double sunk dial
fbd—finger bridge design
g/f—gold filled
g/j/s—gold jewel setting
h/c—hunter case
HCI#P—heat, cold, isochronism & position adjusted
j—jewel
k—karat
mvt—movement
o/f—open face
r/g/p—rolled gold plate
s—size
s/s—single sunk dial
w/g/f—white gold filled
y/g/f—yellow gold filled

Adams & Perry, 20s, 20j, 18k, key wind, rare...5,000.00
Am Watch Co, #1857, stem wind...150.00
Am Watch Co, 0s, y/g/f, h/c...125.00
Am Watch Co, 0s, 13j, 14k, h/c, s/s, 1907...325.00
Am Watch Co, 10s, 23j, 14k, Maximus A, rare...750.00
Am Watch Co, 12s, 15j, 14k, h/c, #1894, Colonial...325.00
Am Watch Co, 12s, 17j, g/f, h/c, s/s, model 1894...175.00
Am Watch Co, 12s, 17j, Masonic symbols on dial...175.00
Am Watch Co, 12s, 17j, 14k, o/f, #1894, Colonial...225.00
Am Watch Co, 12s, 21j, g/j/s, gold train, Maximus...325.00
Am Watch Co, 12s, 7j, 14k, o/f, #1894...175.00
Am Watch Co, 14s, 13j, #1884, 14k, h/c...1,150.00
Am Watch Co, 14s, 15j, #1874, 14k, split second, scarce...1,600.00
Am Watch Co, 14s, 16j, #1874, 14k, dbl dial...3,300.00
Am Watch Co, 16s, 11j, h/c, stem wind, #1872, rare...350.00
Am Watch Co, 16s, 15j, #1868, ¾ movement, key wind...675.00
Am Watch Co, 16s, 17j, #1899, dbl roller, lever set...115.00
Am Watch Co, 16s, 17j, y/g/f, h/c, 1899, PS Bartlett...160.00
Am Watch Co, 16s, 19j, #1872, ¾ movement, stem wind...600.00
Am Watch Co, 16s, 19j, maltese cross stopwork, scarce...1,600.00
Am Watch Co, 16s, 19j, ¾ movement, stem wind, rare...900.00
Am Watch Co, 16s, 21j, #1899, adj...170.00
Am Watch Co, 16s, 21j, #1899, dbl roller, lever set...150.00
Am Watch Co, 16s, 21j, r/g/p, o/f, lever set RR, 1899...135.00
Am Watch Co, 16s, 21j, w/g/f, o/f, lever set RR, 1908...140.00
Am Watch Co, 16s, 21j, y/g/f, 5 position, #645...165.00
Am Watch Co, 16s, 23j, silver case, orig dial, 1908...650.00
Am Watch Co, 18s, 11j, #18, ¾ motion, key wind, pat 1858...1,750.00
Am Watch Co, 18s, 11j, #1857, eagle on case, key wind...300.00
Am Watch Co, 18s, 11j, #1857, key wind, scarce...675.00
Am Watch Co, 18s, 11j, #1883, Broadway model, key wind...100.00
Am Watch Co, 18s, 11j, thin model, key wind...475.00
Am Watch Co, 18s, 11j, 14k, h/c...850.00
Am Watch Co, 18s, 13j, #1883...225.00
Am Watch Co, 18s, 15j, #1857, stem wind, Ellery...450.00
Am Watch Co, 18s, 15j, #1870, key wind...400.00
Am Watch Co, 18s, 15j, h/c, y/g/f, lever set...225.00
Am Watch Co, 18s, 15j, 14k mc box hinge case...1,800.00

Am Watch Co, 18s, 17j, g/f, s/s, Canadian RR Time Service....265.00
Am Watch Co, 18s, 17j, h/c, #1892, g/j/s, rare...............580.00
Am Watch Co, 18s, 19j, #1892, stem wind..................130.00
Am Watch Co, 18s, 19j, #1892, stem wind, EX..............115.00
Am Watch Co, 18s, 21j, #1883, g/j/s, adj, o/f................200.00
Am Watch Co, 18s, 21j, #1892, lever set, o/f................160.00
Am Watch Co, 18s, 21j, #1892, stem wind, 2-tone...........150.00
Am Watch Co, 18s, 21j, #1892, wind indicator, Crescent St..1,400.00
Am Watch Co, 18s, 7-11j, #1857, key wind.................200.00
Am Watch Co, 18s, 7j, y/g/f, h/c..........................135.00
Am Watch Co, 20s, 19j, ¾ plate, key wind, adj, rare........3,000.00
Am Watch Co, 6s, 11-15j, 10k, h/c........................275.00
Am Watch Co, 6s, 19j, 14k, mc gold case..................600.00
Am Watch Co, 6s, 7j, y/g/f, h/c, 1899, EX..................175.00
Ball, 12s, 19j, 14k w/g/f, h/c, Illinois.......................325.00
Ball, 18s, 18k, h/c, E Howard & Co VII, orig case, EX......4,500.00
Ball (Hamilton), 18s, 17j, g/f, o/f, lever set RR, #999..........375.00
Ball (Hamilton), 18s, 21j, g/f, o/f, lever set RR, #999..........450.00
Ball (Waltham), 16s, 17j, g/f, Official Standard, RR...........275.00
Cheshire Watch Co, 18s, 11j, h/c, stem wind................350.00
Cheshire Watch Co, 18s, 21j, h/c, coin silver, stem wind.......600.00
Chicago Watch Co, 18s, 11j, key wind.....................450.00
Chicago Watch Co, 18s, 7j, o/f...........................200.00
Columbia, 6s, 7j, fancy g/f, h/c, lever set, 1896...............165.00
Columbus Watch Co, 18s, 11j, coin silver...................135.00
Columbus Watch Co, 18s, 11j, h/c, lever set.................200.00
Columbus Watch Co, 18s, 15j, mc 14k case................2,600.00
Columbus Watch Co, 18s, 15j, 18k, key wind & set.........1,300.00
Columbus Watch Co, 18s, 16j, key wind & set, rare..........700.00
Cornell, 18s, 11j, key wind..............................500.00
Cornell, 18s, 15j, key wind..............................425.00
Cutout Independence, 18s, silver, key wind, rare.............425.00
Dennison, Howard, Davis, 18s, 15j, #1857, key wind........1,450.00
Dudley, Masonic, 1st model, 12s, 19j, 14k, flip-open bk......2,800.00
Dudley, Masonic, 3rd model, Masonic dial/mvt..............2,000.00
Elgin, 0s, 15j, g/f, mc h/c...............................200.00
Elgin, 0s, 15j, 14k, h/c..................................350.00
Elgin, 0s, 15j, 14k, mc case w/10 point diamond.............450.00
Elgin, 0s, 15j, 20-yr y/g/f, h/c, fancy dial, EX...............225.00
Elgin, 0s, 7j, g/f, h/c, s/s.................................140.00
Elgin, 0s, 7j, y/g/f, h/c, gold/pink dial.....................175.00
Elgin, 0s, 7j, 14k g/f, h/c, matching g/f chain.................225.00
Elgin, 12s, 15j, 14k, h/c.................................425.00
Elgin, 12s, 15j, 14k, mc case..............................500.00
Elgin, 12s, 17j, g/f, h/c, s/s, grade #321....................175.00
Elgin, 12s, 17j, 14k, GM Wheeler..........................350.00
Elgin, 12s, 19j, h/c, Lord Elgin............................225.00
Elgin, 12s, 19j, nickel plate, h/c, ¾ movement...............175.00
Elgin, 12s, 19j, 14k, h/c.................................400.00
Elgin, 12s, 21j, 14k, o/f, Lord Elgin........................500.00
Elgin, 12s, 7j, y/g/f, h/c..................................160.00
Elgin, 16s, 15j, doctor's, 4th model, 14k, 2nd sweep hand.....650.00
Elgin, 16s, 15j, 3 fbd, h/c, lever set Convertible..............200.00
Elgin, 16s, 17j, g/f, mc h/c, lever set......................375.00
Elgin, 16s, 17j, 14k, h/c.................................600.00
Elgin, 16s, 17j, 14k, mc h/c.............................1,100.00
Elgin, 16s, 21j, BW Raymond, 5 positions...................165.00
Elgin, 16s, 21j, Father Time, silveroid......................110.00
Elgin, 16s, 21j, Veritas, 3-finger bridge model...............300.00
Elgin, 16s, 21j, y/g/f, h/c, Ferguson dial....................450.00
Elgin, 16s, 21j, 14k, o/f, BW Raymond......................575.00
Elgin, 16s, 23j, y/g/f, o/f, HCI5P, BW Raymond..............250.00
Elgin, 16s, 23j, y/g/f, o/f, HCI5P, Veritas...................525.00
Elgin, 16s, 23j, 14k, 6 j/s, HCI5P, Lord Elgin.............2,200.00
Elgin, 16s, 7j, h/c, mc dial................................325.00
Elgin, 18s, 11j, lever set, key wind..........................90.00
Elgin, 18s, 15j, BW Raymond, stem wind...................100.00
Elgin, 18s, 15j, y/g/f, lever set, stem wind, box hinge case.....425.00
Elgin, 18s, 15j, 14k, BW Raymond, box hinge case.........1,150.00
Elgin, 18s, 15j, 18k, BW Raymond, 46 penny weight........1,500.00
Elgin, 18s, 17j, lever set, stem wind......................125.00
Elgin, 18s, 17j, o/f, stem wind, silveroid, Father Time.........100.00
Elgin, 18s, 17j, silveroid, o/f, s/s, lever set, rstr..............100.00
Elgin, 18s, 17j, 14k, mc h/c, stem wind...................1,800.00
Elgin, 18s, 19j, o/f, 6 j/s, ¾ plate, BW Raymond.............225.00
Elgin, 18s, 21j, silveroid, stem wind, BW Raymond...........125.00
Elgin, 18s, 21j, silveroid, stem wind, Veritas.................135.00
Elgin, 18s, 21j, wind indicator, free sprung, Father Time.....1,300.00
Elgin, 18s, 23j, 14k, o/f, stem wind, Veritas.................950.00
Elgin, 18s, 7j, coin silver, h/c, s/s, lever set.................125.00
Elgin, 18s, 7j, Fahys #1 h/c, s/s, fancy hands, mc dial.........300.00
Elgin, 6s, 11j, h/c..225.00
Elgin, 6s, 11j, 14k, h/c, s/s, lady's pendant.................425.00
Elgin, 6s, 15j, 14k, mc h/c.................................600.00
Elgin, 6s, 15j, 18k, enamel h/c, stem wind................1,400.00
Elgin, 6s, 15j, 18k, h/c, ¾ movement......................525.00
Elgin, 6s, 7j, g/f, h/c, s/s..................................150.00
Fellows & Schell, 18s, 15j, key wind & set, rare............4,200.00
Hamilton, #3342418, 17j, metal dial, case mk CB 1941.......245.00
Hamilton, #904, 12s, 21j, ¾ movement, adj...................150.00
Hamilton, #914, 12s, 17j, 14k..............................275.00
Hamilton, #918, 12s, 19j, w/g/f, adj.........................150.00
Hamilton, #923, 10s, 23j, 14k, 5 position...................550.00
Hamilton, #926, 18s, 17j, g/f, o/f, lever set..................130.00
Hamilton, #929, 18s, 15j, nickel plate, h/c..................325.00
Hamilton, #930, 18s, 16j, nickel plate, silveroid, o/f..........150.00
Hamilton, #931, 18s, 16j, nickel plate, h/c..................425.00
Hamilton, #932, nickel plate, o/f, scarce....................850.00
Hamilton, #933, 18s, 16j, h/c...............................900.00
Hamilton, #946, 23j, 'Loaner' on case.......................625.00
Hamilton, #947, 23j, h/c, orig/sgn, EX.....................5,500.00
Hamilton, #950B, 16s, 23j, y/g/f, o/f, brg...................475.00
Hamilton, #951, 16s, 23j, 14k, HCI5P, pendant set.........3,500.00
Hamilton, #962, 16s, 17j, o/f, bridge plate, pendant set........800.00
Hamilton, #966, 16s, 17j, o/f, ¾ movement, pendant set.......850.00
Hamilton, #968, 16s, 17j, o/f, ¾ movement, pendant set.......650.00
Hamilton, #971, 16s, 21j, h/c, ¾ movement, pendant set......275.00
Hamilton, #972, 16s, 17j, w/g/f, o/f, d/s, HCI5P/lever set.......175.00
Hamilton, #976, 16j, y/g/f, o/f, ¾ plate, pendant set...........250.00
Hamilton, #981, 0s, 17j, 18k, h/c...........................350.00
Hamilton, #992, 16s, 21j, y/g/f, HCI5P......................175.00
Hamilton, #992B, 16s, 21j, silver, o/f, ¾ movement...........175.00
Hamilton, #992B, 16s, 21j, 10k y/g/f, RR, fancy case.........250.00
Hamilton, #992E, 16s, 21j, y/g/f, o/f........................175.00
Hamilton, #994, 16s, orig case............................1,250.00
Hamilton, #995, 16s, 19j, h/c, g/j/s, bridge................1,650.00
Hamilton, 16s, 17j, o/f, Official Standard...................450.00
Hamilton, 18s, 7j, o/f, full movement, lever set, scarce.......1,400.00
Hampden, 12s, 17j, 14k, mc h/c...........................1,200.00
Hampden, 12s, 17j, 14k, o/f, thin model, Paul Revere.........375.00
Hampden, 16s, 15j, y/g/f, h/c, lever set....................185.00
Hampden, 16s, 17j, h/c, stem wind........................200.00
Hampden, 16s, 17j, 14k, h/c, mc.........................1,500.00
Hampden, 16s, 23j, ¾ movement, g/j/s, adj..................275.00
Hampden, 18s, 11j, h/c, stem wind........................165.00
Hampden, 18s, 11j, lever set, silver case...................100.00
Hampden, 18s, 15j, h/c, stem wind........................225.00
Hampden, 18s, 15j, nickel plate, Lafayette..................150.00

Hampden, 18s, 15j, o/f, key wind . . . 125.00
Hampden, 18s, 15j, 14k, mc h/c . . . 2,200.00
Hampden, 18s, 17j, h/c, damaskeened, adj, Dueber . . . 165.00
Hampden, 18s, 17j, h/c, stem wind . . . 235.00
Hampden, 18s, 17j, o/f, damaskeened, adj, Dueber . . . 125.00
Hampden, 18s, 17j, 14k, h/c, lever set . . . 750.00
Hampden, 18s, 19j, h/c, g/j/s, adj, Dueber . . . 475.00
Hampden, 18s, 21j, 6 j/s, 2-tone, Special Railway . . . 150.00
Hampden, 18s, 23j, John Hancock, g/j/s, adj . . . 225.00
Hampden, 18s, 23j, 14k, h/c, Special Railway . . . 775.00
Hampden, 7j, g/f, h/c, Molly Stark . . . 135.00
Howard, 12s, 17j, w/g/f, o/f, s/s, adj, 3 position, Series 7 . . . 125.00
Illinois, 12s, 21j, 14k, h/c, brg, HCI5P, Illini model . . . 425.00
Illinois, 16s, 15j, ¾ movement, adj . . . 115.00
Illinois, 16s, 17j, g/j/s, gold train, 2-tone, IL Central . . . 175.00
Illinois, 16s, 17j, nickel, 3 fbd, 6 j/s . . . 140.00
Illinois, 16s, 17j, y/g/f, brg, adj, Great Northern Special . . . 350.00
Illinois, 16s, 17j, 14k, h/c . . . 650.00
Illinois, 16s, 19j, Bunn, mk Jewel Barrel . . . 300.00
Illinois, 16s, 21j, Bunn Special . . . 175.00
Illinois, 16s, 21j, h/c, g/j/s . . . 175.00
Illinois, 16s, 21j, HCI5P, ¾ plate, Santa Fe Special . . . 425.00
Illinois, 16s, 21j, nickel, C&O Special, ¾ movement, adj . . . 1,100.00
Illinois, 16s, 21j, y/g/f, o/f, 60-hour, Bunn Special 161A . . . 350.00
Illinois, 16s, 21j, 14k, o/f, 60-hour, Bunn Special . . . 600.00
Illinois, 18s, 11j, h/c, key wind, model #3 . . . 125.00
Illinois, 18s, 11j, silveroid, Alleghany, key wind . . . 120.00
Illinois, 18s, 15j, key wind & set, #1, adj, Stuart . . . 900.00
Illinois, 18s, 15j, transition . . . 100.00
Illinois, 18s, 15j, 9k, h/c, stem wind . . . 500.00
Illinois, 18s, 16j, o/f, key wind, Bunn . . . 800.00
Illinois, 18s, 17j, #3, 5th pinion . . . 275.00
Illinois, 18s, 17j, adj, stem wind . . . 125.00
Illinois, 18s, 17j, adj, 5th pinion, #3, Stuart, scarce . . . 950.00
Illinois, 18s, 17j, h/c, stem wind, #1, Bunn . . . 475.00
Illinois, 18s, 17j, silveroid, stem wind, Bunn Special . . . 150.00
Illinois, 18s, 21j, coin silver, stem wind, Bunn Special . . . 175.00
Illinois, 18s, 24j, Ben Franklin, orig case . . . 3,000.00
Illinois, 18s, 26j, Ben Franklin . . . 7,500.00
Illinois, 18s, 26j, Penn Special, orig case . . . 7,000.00
Illinois, 23j, 60-hour/Sangamo Special/solid bow/orig case . . . 950.00
Illinois, 6s, 7j, 10k, h/c, lever set, safety pinion, 1887 . . . 225.00
Jules Jurgensen, 17j, sterling pendant . . . 165.00
Keystone, 18s, 15j, y/g/f, h/c, colored dial . . . 225.00
Longines, 16s, 8-day, up & down indicator . . . 350.00
Longines, 18s, 21j, base metal, o/f, s/s, US Arms AC . . . 450.00
Montandon, 10s, 13j, 14k, h/c, lever set . . . 250.00
New Haven, Dick Tracy, oblong face, orig box, rare, 1937 . . . 200.00
New York, 15j, wolf's teeth wind . . . 1,500.00
New York Std, y/g/f, sports timer, Dan Patch, orig . . . 350.00
New York Std, 0s, 7j, h/c, 1895 . . . 125.00
New York Std, 16s, 7j, y/g/f, h/c . . . 150.00
Newark, 18s, 15j, silver, h/c, key wind, rare . . . 450.00
Rockford, 18s, 15j, coin silver, exposed wheel . . . 400.00
Rockford, 18s, 15j, full plate, mc dial, key wind . . . 325.00
Rockford, 18s, 17j, silver, h/c . . . 145.00
Rockford, 18s, 19j, h/c, g/j/s, transition . . . 700.00
Rockford, 18s, 24j, mk RG, orig case . . . 1,400.00
Rockford, 18s, 26j, orig case . . . 16,000.00
Rockford, 18s, 9j, #1, full movement, key wind . . . 175.00
Rolex, 25j, w/g trim . . . 595.00
Seth Thomas, 0s, 7j, #1, o/f, h/c . . . 165.00
Seth Thomas, 18s, 17j, nickel plate, ¾ movement, o/f . . . 160.00
Seth Thomas, 18s, 17j, ¾ movement, 2-tone, mk . . . 250.00
Seth Thomas, 18s, 17j, 6 j/s, HCI5P, Maiden Lane, rare . . . 1,200.00
Seth Thomas, 18s, 21j, model #260, HCI5P, full plate, RR . . . 425.00
Seth Thomas, 18s, 23j, g/j/s, HCI5P, dbl roller, rare . . . 1,850.00
Seth Thomas, 18s, 7j, #36 o/f, #37 h/c, Eagle Series . . . 110.00
Seth Thomas, 18s, 7j, ¾ movement, bk: eagle/Liberty model . . . 125.00
Seth Thomas, 18s, 7j, ¾ movement, mc dial . . . 225.00
Seth Thomas, 21j, Maiden Lane, mk, rare . . . 2,200.00
Seth Thomas, 25j, Maiden Lane, mk, rare . . . 3,600.00
Seth Thomas, 6s, 7j, 14k, h/c, nickel plate, ¾ movement . . . 350.00
South Bend, 12s, 21j, o/f, Studebaker . . . 175.00
South Bend, 16s, 15j, g/f, h/c, lever set . . . 150.00
South Bend, 16s, 15j, g/f, o/f, s/s, #207 . . . 90.00
South Bend, 16s, 19j, g/j/s, brg, Grade 245 . . . 1,200.00
South Bend, 18s, 21j, h/c, g/j/s, full plate, Grade 328 . . . 425.00
Suffolk, 0s, 7j, g/f, h/c, lever set . . . 175.00
Swiss, Goliath, o/f, 8-day, ¼-hour, repeater, 4″ . . . 650.00
Swiss, h/c, 5-minute, repeater . . . 375.00
Swiss, 8/0s, 8j, 14k h/c, s/s, EX dial . . . 155.00
US Watch Co of Waltham, 18s, 21j, The President . . . 1,000.00
Washington, 18s, 17j, nickel silver, o/f, lever set Senate . . . 175.00
Washington, 18s, 17j, silver, o/f, lever set, Liberty Bell . . . 185.00
Wrist, Argus, gold dial, leather strap, Quartz, no winding . . . 100.00
Wrist, Elgin, man's, Official Boy Scout on case, ca 1934 . . . 200.00
Wrist, Hamilton, doctor's, 17j, g/f, duo dial . . . 235.00
Wrist, Hamilton, lady's, diamonds on case/bezel/bracelet . . . 695.00
Wrist, Hamilton, man's, 14k, #500, Electric . . . 225.00
Wrist, Hamilton, man's, 25j, g/f, self wind, rnd . . . 125.00
Wrist, Lord Elgin, 21j, 14k, rectangular . . . 175.00

Waterford

The Waterford Glass Company operated in Ireland from the late 1700s until 1851 when the factory closed. One hundred years later, in 1951, another Waterford glassworks was instituted that produced glass similar to the 18th century wares--crystal glass, usually with cut decoration. Today, Waterford is a generic term referring to the type of glass first produced there.

When no condition is indicated, the items listed below are assumed to be in mint condition.

Pair of Waterford sweetmeats, 12″, $350.00 each; Bowl with lid and undertray, cut crystal, Waterford type, $75.00.

Bottle, scent; notched body & stopper, 4½″ . . . 60.00
Bowl, basketweave, hdls, oval boat shape, 1850s, 4x8¾″ . . . 200.00
Candlestick, star-cut base, 6″, pr . . . 50.00
Creamer & sugar bowl, cut diamond pattern, sgn . . . 45.00
Decanter, paneled neck & stopper, star-cut base, 12″ . . . 70.00

Decanter, Sawtooth Rib, dbl rope ring neck, qt, EX..........200.00
Jam jar, ped ft, 5½″..........40.00
Rose bowl, spike diamond band, laurel border, 5½″..........40.00
Salt cellar, cut, 3″..........30.00
Sweetmeat, dbl dome lid, disk atop, scallop rim, ftd, 12″..........350.00
Vase, bud; sgn, 7″..........50.00
Wine glass, Alana, sgn, set of 6..........150.00

Watt Pottery

The Watt Pottery Company was incorporated on July 5, 1922, in Perry County, Crooksville, Ohio. Their products were stoneware jars, jugs, milk pans, Dutch pots, mixing bowls (white with blue bands), churns, preserve jars, and chicken waterers, all marked in cobalt with their trademark, 'Acorn.' In 1935, these items were discontinued, and the company began to make free-hand decorated kitchen and ovenware items such as 'Banded' and 'Decorated' mixing bowls, 'Spaghetti' bowls, canister sets, covered casseroles, nappies, cookie jars, ice buckets, pitchers, handled French casseroles, bean pots, salad sets, and dog dishes. Bold brush strokes of red and green contrasted with the natural buff color of the glazed body; several patterns were produced: 'Red Apple,' 'Star Flower,' 'Rooster,' 'Autumn Foliage,' 'Morning Glory,' and 'Tulip.' Other lines were 'Basket Weave' (made in solid colors), 'Wood Grain' (a brown glazed line), and 'Royal Danish' dinnerware.

Fire destroyed the entire manufacturing plant on October 4, 1965.

Because of the country flavor of the hand-decorated yellowware pieces, Watt Pottery is fast becoming a favorite collectible. Much of the ware was made for advertising premiums and is often found stenciled with the name of a retail company.

When no condition is indicated, the items listed below are assumed to be in mint condition.

Bean pot, Ovenware, w/4 individual servers..........45.00
Bowl, Apple, w/lid, 8″..........40.00
Bowl, flower, #39..........35.00
Bowl, Star Flower, red, 6¼″..........15.00
Casserole, Star Flower, w/lid, 8⅝″..........35.00
Pitcher, Apple, 4″..........20.00
Pitcher, Apple, 7″..........30.00
Pitcher, Rooster, 5½″..........35.00
Pitcher, Star Flower, 8″..........35.00
Pitcher, Tulip, #62..........25.00
Platter, bl/wht flower, 12″..........35.00
Shakers, Star Flower, pr..........30.00
Sugar bowl, Red Apple, hdls, 4½″..........25.00
Vase, Apple, hdls, 4″..........30.00

Wave Crest

Wave Crest is the trademark used on a line of creamy opaque glassware manufactured by the C.F. Monroe Company of New York, who operated there from 1892 until 1916. Vases, boxes, tablewares, and humidors in swirled and blown-out shapes were either hand painted or transfer printed with florals, scenics, or portraits. Many pieces were enhanced with ornately scrolled ormolu handles, feet, or rims. Several marks were used: the black mark, 'Trade Mark Wave Crest'; the Red Banner mark; and the paper label, 'Wave Crest Ware, Patented Oct. 4, 1892.'

When no condition is indicated, the items listed below are assumed to be in mint condition.

Atomizer, lav to gr w/floral enameling, bulbous..........425.00
Bowl, pansies on side, sgn, ormolu hdls, 2½x9½″..........225.00
Box, Baroque Shell, floral, lt gr, sgn, 3″ dia..........195.00
Box, Baroque Shell, floral, red banner mk, hinged lid, 5½″..........350.00
Box, Baroque Shell, floral, red banner mk, 4x7″ dia..........600.00
Box, Baroque Shell, sgn, bl, 6″ across hdls, open..........145.00
Box, cherubs, lt bl, oblong, 5½″..........450.00
Box, cupids & flowers, 4″..........315.00
Box, floral in cartouch on brn, ormolu lion ft, 5x4x8½″ dia..........995.00
Box, hexagon, 2 shells relief on lid, gr shaded, 2¾″ H..........275.00
Box, Puffy, Collars & Cuffs, no mk, 7″ dia..........760.00
Box, Puffy, ladies/trees, ormolu collar/corner mts, 3x5″ dia..........650.00
Box, Rococo, floral, hinged, sgn, 3¼″ dia..........450.00
Box, Swirl, bl flowers/wht beading on lt yel, 3¼″ dia..........450.00
Box, Swirl, bl forget-me-nots & woodland scene, 4x7″ dia..........500.00
Box, Swirl, clear frosted, w/gold traced & jeweled floral..........950.00
Box, Swirl, Collar & Cuff; orig lining..........700.00
Box, Swirl, daisies, pink/gr, sgn, 3¾x7½″ dia..........535.00
Box, Swirl, florals/buds/sprigs, ormolu ft, 6½x7½″ dia..........750.00
Box, Swirl, pink/purple floral, brass collar, no lid, 3″ W..........95.00
Box, Swirl, red floral, 5½″ dia..........425.00
Box, Swirl, woodland scene, bl floral, no mk, 4x7″ dia..........500.00
Box, tobacco; pink & gold lettering..........575.00
Broom holder, emb blank, ormolu mt/sgn, w/wisk broom, rare..........875.00
Card holder, floral on bl, emb, sgn, 4½x2½″..........265.00
Cracker jar, emb pink & bl pansies on yel, barrel shape..........350.00
Cracker jar, moon & stars, unsgn..........500.00
Cracker jar, pink floral w/cupids on bl, 7″..........550.00
Cracker jar, pink w/mc floral, SP lid, no mk..........450.00
Cracker jar, Puffy, florals on bl, cut-out hdl, sgn..........700.00
Creamer, Swirl, floral, SP rim, hdl, 3½″..........500.00
Cruet, pink floral, lt gr on wht, sgn, no stopper, rare..........425.00
Ferner, Puffy, bl violets on wht, gold tracery, 7″..........265.00
Humidor, Cigars, sgn..........500.00
Lamp, boats & swans decor, electrified..........600.00
Letter holder, Puffy, bl floral, wht beading, ormolu rim..........265.00
Paperweight, lav floral, ormolu cherub on top, ftd, rare..........400.00
Photo receiver, floral..........300.00
Pin dish, Swirl, floral, brass rim & hdl, 4″..........95.00
Plaque, full-length portrait..........1,575.00
Salt cellar, pr..........70.00
Shakers, Scroll, chrysanthemums, unsgn, 4½″, pr..........235.00
Shakers, Swirl, bl/wht florals w/in swirls, sq, pr..........150.00
Smoke set, cigarette holder+2 match holders, ftd ormolu fr..........450.00
Sugar bowl, Swirl, pink daisies/wht dots, SP lid/bail..........300.00
Sugar sifter, Swirl, floral & bl shadow scroll panels..........350.00
Sweetmeat jar, pansy decor, dbl twisted hdl, red banner mk..........395.00
Toothpick, cat & branches transfer, ormolu base & rim..........185.00
Toothpick, floral, straight sides, ormolu trim..........135.00
Tray, pin; pink floral on wht, dbl shell, sgn, 3″ dia..........75.00
Tray, pin; Swirl, floral on wht, ormolu hdls, 5½″..........100.00
Vase, robin-bl w/floral medallions, ormolu fr, 6¾″..........650.00
Vase, 2 views w/ducks, rest blown-out, ormolu hdls/ft, 16″..........945.00

Weapons

Among the varied areas of specialization within the broad category of weapons, guns are by far the most popular. Muskets are among the earliest firearms; they were large-bore shoulder arms, usually firing black powder, with separate loading of powder and shot. Some ignited the charge by flintlock or caplock, while later types used a firing pin with a metallic cartridge. Side arms, referred to as such because they were worn at the side, include pistols and revolvers. Pistols range from early single-shot and multiple barrels to modern types with cartridges held in the handle. Revolvers were supplied with a cylinder that turned to feed a fresh round in front of the barrel breech. Other firearms include shotguns, which fired round or conical bullets and had a smooth inner barrel surface, and rifles, so named because the interior of the barrel contained spiral grooves (rifling) which increased accuracy.

When no condition is indicated, the items listed below are assumed to be in excellent condition.

Key:

bbl—barrel	hdw—hardware
cal—caliber	h/s—half stock
conv—conversion	mag—magazine
cyl—cylinder	oct—octagon
f/l—flintlock	p/b—patch box
f/s—full stock	perc—percussion
ga—gauge	

Bayonet

British, for Snyder Enfield, iron mts/scabbard, 1800 .... 55.00
Foot artillery type, bronze hdl/brass mts w/scabbard, 1850 .... 150.00
French sabre, ca 1885, w/scabbard 135.00
Sawback, 19″ blade mk Waffenfabrik Neuhauser, w/scabbard 50.00

Carbine

Evans, lever action 44 cal, 22″ bbl, New Model, 1879 .... 225.00
Gwyn & Campbell Union type II, 52 cal, 20″ bbl, VG 350.00
Joslyn 1862, 54 cal, 22″ bbl, inspector's mks, VG 400.00
Spencer, 52 cal, Civil War, EX 425.00
US M1, 30 cal military, Underwood, flash muzzle barrel tip 300.00
Werndl, Austrian breechloader, 1870 .... 125.00
Winchester 1894 saddle ring, 30-30 cal, 75% bl, 1921 .... 325.00

Musket

Miguelet-Flint, Turkish type, 60 cal 55″ bbl, EX decor 210.00
Miguelet-Flint Arabian, 50 cal 44½″ bbl, copper mts 110.00
Springfield, 1846 69 cal 42″ bbl 250.00
Springfield, 1884 ramrod bayonet, 45-70, EX 375.00

Pistol

Arabic style f/l, banana lock dtd 1700s, eng/script 275.00
Asa Waters, Dragoon horse, conv flint to perc, 1843 .... 225.00
Bedford county, perc, sgn Amos Border, G 650.00
CG Haenel Suhl, semi-automatic 22 cal, Schmeisser's Pat 150.00
Colt, mk Russel Waddell & Majors, holster, 1849 .... 650.00
DA Starr, perc, Civil War soldier's name & regiment 385.00
Derringer, perc, wood & silver trim, 3″ bbl, 7″ 270.00
Dueling, Robinson, h/s perc 45 cal spur trigger+case, pr 3,250.00
Dutch, Revolutionary War type, orig flint/curled trigger 240.00
English, f/l, sword combination, rare, 1760, G 850.00
GW Bates, Ipswich, single shot, 22 cal, 8½″ oct bbl 195.00

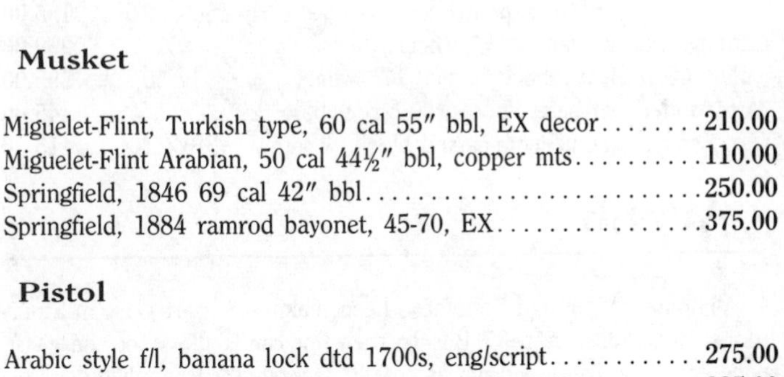

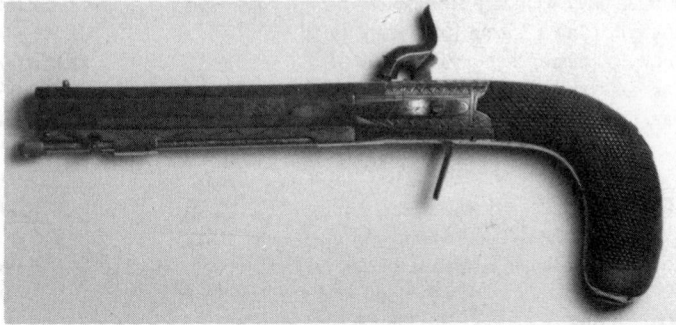

Boot pistol, military naval officer's, 1857, 11″, $425.00.

Ketland & Co, officer's, silver mtd, 1770s, G 775.00
Muff, pop-out trigger, screw-on bbl, Belgium, 1840 .... 195.00
Smith & Wesson #1, 2nd issue 22 rim fire cal, 7″ 185.00
Union Fireams Co, automatic 32 S&W cal 4″ bbl, Riefgraber 600.00
Waters, orig flint, mk N Carolina on bbl, 1836, G 525.00

Revolver

Austrian, military WWI, 54 cal 10″ bbl, hand eject 100.00
Belgian, pin fire, 7mm 3½″ bbl 35.00
Colt Patterson Belt, 34 cal/5½″ bbl +11½″ bbl & cyl 11,000.00
Colt 1849, 31 cal, 6″ bbl, partial scene, EX 235.00
Colt 1875, single action, 45 cal, 7½″ bbl 1,750.00
Eagle Arms pocket, 30 cal 50 shot, w/orig box/cleaning rod 625.00
Russian type, cartridge 32 cal w/flip trigger, 1918, 5″ 40.00
S&W Model 2, 32 cal, 5″ bbl, EX 175.00
Savage, 6-shot 36 cal 7″ oct bbl, walnut grips, 1860 .... 1,400.00
Smith & Wesson, 45 cal Colt 6¾″ bbl, nickel plated 350.00
Union Firearms, automatic 32 cal 6-shot, 3″ bbl, nickeled 800.00

Rifle

AM Hagadorn, perc 32″ dbl bbl w/starter, 58 cal, walnut 1,100.00
Bell-Wingert Hawkin-style, 45 cal 34″ oct bbl, p/b, eng 550.00
Curly maple f/s, perc lock mk Robbins, Keefer bbl 200.00
Curly maple h/s, silver inlay, Jas Golcher, 50″ 450.00
Evans New Model sporting, 44 cal, 30″ bbl, VG 175.00
Golcher Hawkin, perc h/s w/p/b, 50 cal 29″ bbl, brass mts 175.00
Goulcher-Bowlby, Hawkin-style perc, brass/silver inlay 275.00
Hagdorn-Cole, side-by-side perc 58 cal 12 ga, fancy/walnut 750.00
Harper Ferry, orig flint, 1816, VG 1,250.00
KY, curly maple f/s w/perc lock, eng 43″ bbl, 46″ 250.00
KY, curly maple h/s w/damage, 31″ bbl, 46″ 175.00
KY, maple f/s f/l, brass p/b/inlay, Angstadt, 61″ 1,025.00
KY-Jaeger, deer carving, f/l, brass trim, 1760, VG 900.00
Mauser, Model 71, 11mm cal 33½″ bbl single shot 120.00
Perc f/s, lock mk Henry Parker, 41½″ bbl, 57″ 110.00
Perc h/s, lock mk ICK, 18½″ bbl, worn, 34½″ 200.00
Perc h/s, lock mk TC Mortimer, 20″ bbl, 34¾″ 225.00
Remington #1½ sport, 32 cal 26″ oct bbl ⅞″ muzzle 300.00
Sliding breech action, 50 cal rimfire, KY conv, eng 225.00
Tennessee perc, long f/s, sgn, 48″ octagon bbl, VG 925.00
Winchester 1886, 26″ oct bbl, 44-40 cal, VG 205.00
Winchester 1892, 20-25 cal lever action, VG 625.00
Winchester 1894, 25-35 cal, NM 600.00
Winchester-Lee, straight pull 6mm M1895 USN issue 300.00
Wingert, Hawkin-style 40 cal 36″ oct bbl, eng deer 400.00
Wingert, side-by-side perc 45 cal 30″ oct bbl, eng/walnut 1,100.00

Shotgun

English, 30 ga dbl bbl, Sharpe lockplates, eng 225.00
Hagdorn-Cole, perc 44″ dbl bbl 16 ga, steel furniture 550.00
Parker Bros, dbl bbl 16 ga, VG 525.00
Perc, p/b in stock/rnd bbl, whittled ramrod, 53″ 275.00
Stevens 940A, 410 ga, NM 75.00
Syracuse New Baker, dbl bbl 12 ga, pat 1887, EX 175.00
Winchester Model 12 Featherweight, 12 ga 400.00
WW Greener, eng 32″ dbl bbl 10 ga, checkered wood, 1880s 1,000.00

Sword

Ames, artillery short 1833 model w/scabbard 200.00
British officer's, etched blade, reign of Wm IV, scabbard 165.00

European style, iron hilted, broad, 40″ blade, 16th C.........175.00
French Artillery, short, model 1822, Napoleonic mk..........145.00

Weathervanes

The earliest weathervanes were of handmade wrought iron and were generally simple angular silhouettes with a small hole suggesting an eye. Later, copper, zinc, and polychromed wood with features in relief were fashioned into more realistic forms. Ships, horses, fish, Indians, roosters, and angels were popular motifs.

In the 19th century, silhouettes were often made from sheet metal. Wooden figures became highly carved and were painted in vivid colors. E.G. Washburne and Company in New York was one of the most prominent manufacturers of weathervanes during the last half of the century.

Two-dimensional sheet metal weathervanes are increasing in value due to the already heady prices of the full-bodied variety. Originality, strength of line, and patination help to determine value.

Key:
fb—full-bodied f/fb—flattened full-bodied

Cow, fb Jersey w/horns, cast zinc head, CI arrows, 33x46″...2,640.00
Cow, molded/hammered copper/G gilt, f/fb, Cushing, 16x28″..5,500.00
Cow, tin, on decorative CI 21″ arrow, 9x7″.................120.00
Deer, copper/gilt, molded antlers/ears/fur, Cushing, 28″.....13,200.00
Eagle, fb, outstretched wings, on orb/arrow, gilt, 23″ W.....1,210.00
Fish, fb copper w/sheet copper fins/tail, gilt pnt, 18x36″.....1,210.00
Goddess of Liberty, molded copper/emb details, Jones, 36″..28,600.00
Horse, Index, copper/zinc, f/fb, J Howard, rare sz, 18″ L....12,100.00
Horse, Index, copper/zinc, f/fb, J Howard, 19x25″.........10,175.00
Horse, jumps over fence, copper/zinc/gilt, Waltham, 31″....37,400.00
Horse, rearing, copper/zinc, f/fb, emb detail, Jewell, 18″.....4,950.00
Horse, running, copper w/iron head & arrow, G patina, 16½″..425.00
Horse, running, copper w/tooled detail, G patina, 32″ L.......590.00
Horse, running, cut from 2 pcs sheet iron, 1890s, 20″, EX....275.00
Horse, running, fb copper w/zinc head, rod std, 12¾″.......1,540.00
Horse, running, galvanized sheet tin, on iron bar, 43″ L......230.00
Horse, running, tin/CI, lightning rod/directional, 14x10″.......160.00
Horse, sheet/CI, f/fb/pnt traces, Rochester Works, 19x24″....2,750.00
Horse, trotting; copper/zinc/G gilt, f/fb, Waltham, 32″ L.....3,850.00
Horse/rider, copper/zinc/pnt/emb detail, f/fb, Jewell, 27″......7,700.00
Horse/rider, molded copper/gilt traces, f/fb, 1880, 19″ L.....5,500.00
Pig, molded copper/cast zinc, f/fb, Cushing, 13x21″.........6,875.00
Pig, tin/iron/CI directional, lightning rod, 9x5″...............115.00
Ram, copper, f/fb w/repousse detail, rod std, 14x18″........6,050.00
Ram, copper/zinc, f/fb, EX patina, 1850s, 22x28½″.........7,700.00
Ram, copper/zinc/EX patina, f/fb, 1850s, 22x28″...........7,700.00
Ram, molded/sheet copper, f/fb, repousse detail, 14x18″.....6,050.00
Rooster, CI/sheet metal tail, f/fb, relief feathering, 24″.......2,310.00
Rooster, handmade galvanized tin, 9″, on arrow w/pyramid.....95.00
Rooster, sheet metal, directionals/trn post/rpt, 45½″..........300.00

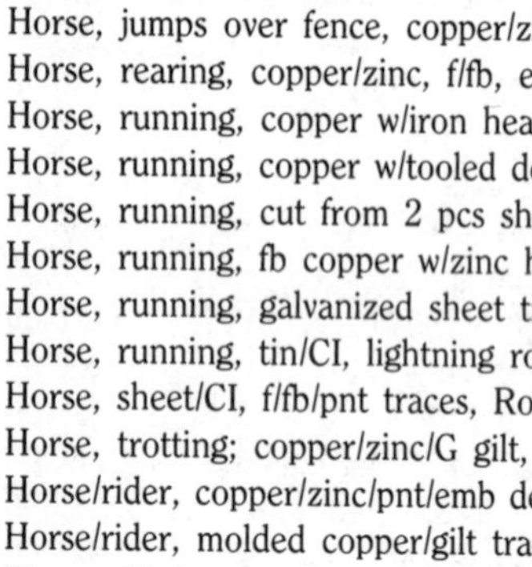

Rearing horse, flattened, full-bodied form from sheet zinc with applied repousse mane and tail, A.L. Jewell & Co., Waltham, MA 17″ x 18″, $4,950.00.

Weaving

Early Americans used a variety of tools and a great amount of time to produce the material from which their clothing was made. Soaked and dried flax was broken on a flax brake to remove waste material. It was then tapped and stroked with a scutching knife. Hackles further removed waste and separated the short fibers from the longer ones. Unspun fibers were placed on the distaff of the spinning wheel for processing into yarn. The yarn was then wound around a reel for measuring. Three tools used for this purpose were the niddy-noddy, the reel yarnwinder, and the click reel. After it was washed and dyed, the yarn was transferred to a barrel-cage or squirrel-cage swift and fed onto a bobbin winder.

Today, flax wheels are more plentiful than the large wool wheels, since they were small and could be more easily stored and preserved. The distaff, an often discarded or misplaced part of the wheel, is very scarce. French spinners from the Quebec area painted their wheels. Many have been stripped and refinished by those unaware of this fact. Wheels may be very simple or have a great amount of detail, depending upon the owner's ethnic background and the maker's skill.

When no condition is indicated, the items listed below are assumed to be in excellent condition.

Flax wheel, old bl pnt, NY State..........................495.00
Hatchel, board w/2 scratch-carved hearts, 1793, 5½x22″........25.00
Hatchel, rosehead nails, w/cover............................35.00
Niddy-noddy, maple, chip carved w/iron tack initials, 18½″......55.00
Niddy-noddy, maple, mortised/pinned, rfn, 18″................35.00
Niddy-noddy, maple/chestnut, G detail, worn finish, 18″........45.00
Niddy-noddy, wood pegs/mortised w/wedges, early 1800s, 10″...155.00
Spinning wheel, maple, 17″ wheel, rfn......................250.00
Spinning wheel, scrubbed maple, 17″ wheel..................295.00
Yarn winder, trn base, spool w/X top & base, 29½″...........45.00
Yarn winder, walnut, chip-carved block, w/counter, 38x27″.....115.00

Webb

Thomas Webb and Sons have been making fine art glass in Stourbridge, England, since 1837. Besides their fine cameo glass, they have also made enameled ware, and pieces heavily decorated with applied glass ornaments. The butterfly is a motif that has been so often featured that it tends to suggest Webb as the manufacturer.

When no condition is indicated, the items listed below are assumed to be in mint condition.

Biscuit jar, cameo, lime/wht w/allover berries, 6½″..........2,195.00
Bowl, bird/floral, wht opal/pink lined, 3 ft, 6x8″..............350.00
Bowl, butterscotch, raised gold enamel......................225.00
Bud vase, cameo, 3-color, chrysanthemums/butterfly, 6¼″....1,870.00
Creamer, cameo, yel/wht, floral/butterfly, sgn, 3½″............975.00
Finger bowl w/underplate, cameo, 3-color, both sgn.........2,250.00
Inkwell, cameo, citron frost w/wht floral, sq, 4½″...........1,500.00
Inkwell, cameo, 2-color, roses/butterflies, bell form..........1,250.00
Jar, amberina, honeycomb, w/SP lid & bail, 5″..............295.00
Jar, florals & gold on ivory satin, ormolu ft/rim/lid, 6½″.......595.00
Perfume, cameo, bl w/wht floral in reserves, sq, unsgn, 6″....1,395.00
Perfume, cameo, bl w/wht leaves, lay-down, unsgn, 3¾″.......595.00
Perfume, cameo, yel w/wht leaves, unsgn, 2¼x1⅜″............375.00
Perfume, cameo, 3-color floral, flattened bulb, 3½x2½″........750.00
Rose bowl, cameo, wht/pink flowers on lime, unsgn, 2½x2¾″...995.00
Vase, apricot satin, bulbous, long neck, crimped rim, 12″......225.00
Vase, birds/floral/dragonflies, enameled, prop mk, 12″, pr......725.00
Vase, brn shaded satin, gold branches/prunus, cased, 5x3½″...495.00

Vase, cameo, bl w/wht crocus & bands, unsgn, 5½x3¼" 1,395.00
Vase, cameo, citron w/wht roses & butterfly, 7" 1,600.00
Vase, cameo, dk red w/wht ivy, unsgn, 3⅝x1½" 795.00
Vase, cameo, olive/wht, rosebush/butterflies, flared, 8" 1,350.00
Vase, cameo, red w/wht floral & border, unsgn, 4½x3¼" 1,175.00
Vase, cameo, red w/wht floral & butterfly, unsgn, 9" 1,750.00
Vase, cameo, red w/wht floral & leaves, 10½x3¼" 2,250.00
Vase, cameo, red w/wht rosebush & butterfly, unsgn, 8" 1,850.00
Vase, cameo, tan, lg fruit/stems/leaves/bands, GEM, 10½" 2,500.00
Vase, cameo, 3-color, floral/butterfly, sgn, 6¼" 1,500.00
Vase, cameo, 3-color floral, unsgn, 4¼x1¾" 1,150.00
Vase, floral & bird on ivory, gold rim, prop mk, 9⅜" 325.00
Vase, floral & butterfly, gold on bl satin, 8" 150.00
Vase, gr decor on cream/red/bl/orange, Petit Point, #d, 7" 225.00
Vase, MOP Coinspot, lime w/mc floral, prop mk, 12x6½" 950.00
Vase, orange w/gold foil spangle, pnt bird on front, 9½" 385.00

Perfume vial, 2-color cameo, allover blossoms and leaves on red ground, in original fitted Mappin & Webb case, 10", $1,100.00.

Wedgwood

Josiah Wedgwood established his pottery in Burslem, England, in 1759. He produced only molded utilitarian earthenwares until 1770, when new facilities were opened at Etruria. It was there he introduced his famous Basalt and Jasperware. Jasperware, an unglazed fine stoneware decorated with classic figures in white relief, was usually produced in blues, but it was also made in ground colors of green, lilac, yellow, black, or white. Occasionally, three or more colors were used in combination. It has been in continuous production to the present day, and is the most easily recognized of all the Wedgwood lines. (Jasper is a body of solid color; the term 'Jasper-Dip' refers to ware with a white body that has been dipped in an overlay color. This type, introduced in the late 1700s, is the type most often encountered on today's market.)

Though his Jasperware was highly acclaimed, on a more practical basis his Creamware was his greatest success. Due to the ease with which it could be potted, and because its lighter weight significantly reduced transportation expenses, Wedgwood was able to offer 'china' ware at affordable prices. Queen Charlotte was so pleased with the ware that she allowed it to be called 'Queen's Ware.' Most creamware was marked simply 'Wedgwood.' ('Wedgwood & Co.' and 'Wedgwood' are marks of other potters.)

From 1769 to 1780, Wedgwood was in partnership with Thomas Bently; artwares of the highest quality bear the mark indicating this partnership.

Moonlight Lustre, an allover splashed-on effect of pink intermingling with gray, brown, or yellow, was made from 1805 to 1815. Porcelain was made, though not to any great extent, from 1812 to 1822. Both of these types of wares were marked 'Wedgwood.'

Stone china and Pearlware were made from about 1820 to 1875. Examples of either may be found with a mark to indicate their body type.

During the late 1800s, Wedgwood produced some fine Parian and Majolica. Creamware, hand painted by Emile Lessore, was sold from about 1860 to 1875.

From the 20th century, several lines of lustre wares--Butterfly, Dragon, and Fairyland (the latter designed by Miss Makeig-Jones) have attracted the collector, and as their prices suggest, are highly sought after and admired.

Nearly all of Wedgwood's wares are clearly marked. 'Wedgwood' was used before 1891, after which time 'England' was added. Most examples marked 'Made In England' were made after 1921. A detailed study of all marks is recommended for accurate dating.

When no condition is indicated, the items listed below are assumed to be in mint condition.

Key:
WW—Wedgwood　　WWE—Wedgwood England

Basket, Creamware, woven lattice, oval, w/stand, WWE, 8x9" ... 195.00
Biscuit jar, Jasper, dk bl, melon base, WW, 6x6" 200.00
Biscuit jar, Jasper, dk bl, SP fittings, WW, 6¾x5" 155.00
Biscuit jar, Jasper, dk bl, WWE, 5½x5" 125.00
Biscuit jar, Jasper, lav, hunt scenes, England, 6½" 150.00
Biscuit jar, Jasper, lav/gr/wht, WW, 5½x4¾" 600.00
Biscuit jar, Jasper, yel w/blk lions' heads/etc, WW, 6½" 300.00
Bottle, water; enameled flowers, Rosso Antico, 11" 250.00
Bowl, Butterfly Lustre, MOP, flame int, vase mk, 4" 150.00
Bowl, Butterfly Lustre, orange & MOP, 2½x5" 100.00
Bowl, Dragon Lustre, MOP int, WWE, 7¼x3¼" 200.00
Bowl, Dragon Lustre, 8-sided, fruit w/in, WWE Z 4829, 6½" ... 175.00
Bowl, Fairyland Lustre, Daventry, 9½" 800.00
Bowl, Jasper, dk bl, ca 1874, WW, 4x3" 90.00
Bowl, Jasper, sage gr, ca 1958, WWE, 8x3¾" 75.00
Box, gr, heart shaped, WWE, w/lid, 3½x4¼x2" 50.00
Bust, Milton, Parian, EW Wyon, WW, 14¼" 300.00
Cache pot, Majolica, bl/brn/turq/wht, rim to base hdls, 9" 350.00
Cameo, Jasper, Apollo, lt bl, WW, 1⅝x2" 50.00
Candlestick, Jasper, lt bl, WW, 7¼" 125.00
Candlestick, Jasper, med bl, ca 1955, WWE, 1½", pr 100.00
Cheese dish, Jasper, lt bl, WWE, 7½x11" 100.00
Cigarette lighter, Jasper, lt gr, Ceasar, WWE 40.00
Compote, Queen's Ware, reticulated, rope rim hdls, 4¾x8" 175.00
Creamer, Basalt, glazed int/Battlement lip, WW, 4x4" 50.00
Creamer, Basalt, silver rim, ca 1850 .... 55.00
Creamer, Drabware, lt brn, 1830s, WW, 5x2½" 195.00
Creamer, Jasper, lt bl, WWE, 2" 20.00
Cup & saucer, Basalt, cameo decor, WWE 35.00
Cup & saucer, Basalt, Husk & Berry, glazed int, WW 135.00
Cup & saucer, Canadian Coat of Arms/Niagara Falls, WWE 55.00
Cup & saucer, handleless; Basalt, WW, cup: 3x2¼" 95.00
Ewer, water; Basalt, gilded, ca 1860, 15" 400.00
Figurine, bulldog, Basalt, wht glass eyes, WW, 2¾x2x5" 200.00
Figurine, cat, Basalt, yel glass eyes, WW, 4¾x1½x3⅜" 250.00
Figurine, Cupid & Psyche, Basalt, rnd plinths, WW, 8½" 500.00
Figurine, elephant, Basalt, wht tusks, WWE 400.00
Figurine, Eros & Euphrosyne, Basalt, WW, 16½" 600.00
Figurine, Pug, Basalt, amber eyes, early, 4⅞" 250.00
Figurine, raven, Basalt, WW, 4¼x5¾" 200.00
Flowerpot, Jasper, dk bl, w/underliner, ca 1850, 5" 150.00
Jar, Jasper, dk bl, figures & lions' masks, 1850, 7" 175.00
Jardiniere, Jasper, band of flowers/drainage hole, WW, 2⅝" 75.00
Jardiniere, Stoneware, olive gr, flared top, 7½x8¼" 200.00
Jug, agate swirl, brn, satyr's head, Doric, WW, 8½" 400.00
Jug, Jasper, dk bl, trefoil spout, WW, 6½" 125.00
Jug, Jasper, lt bl, WWE, 4x4½" 40.00
Jug, Jasper, sage gr, WWE, 8" 90.00
Matchstrike, Majolica, turq/brn/cream, ca 1885, WW, 5x4" 175.00
Medallion, Basalt, Valerious Maximiniani, WW, 2¼x1½" 85.00
Medallion, Jasper, bl, wood plaque w/brass rim, WW, 7½x10" .. 175.00
Monteith, Jasper, blk/gold, replica for club, '53, 12" 175.00
Mug, Jasper, dk bl, made for Elkington, WW, 5x4" 145.00
Plate, Creamware, Little Red Riding Hood, HP, WW, 10¼" 100.00
Plate, Creamware, Russian, HP, Thomas Allen, WWE, 9" 100.00
Plate, dinner; Creamware, ribbon edge w/gilt, WW, 1790s 65.00

Plate, Fairyland Lustre, pixies on bridge, bl, 10¾" 500.00
Plate, Moonlight Lustre, shell form, early, 10¼" 300.00
Plate, shell; Majolica, gr & brn, ca 1868, WW, 8" 95.00
Platter, Creamware, HP, ca 1871, WW 125.00
Platter, Pearlware, HP, 1870s, WW 150.00
Salad set, Majolica, silver mtd, 2 servers, 9½" bowl 375.00
Salt cellar, Dragon Lustre, bl/orange, dog head decor, 2¼" 130.00
Sauce bowl, Creamware, early, w/lid, 7" 175.00
Shakers, Jasper, lt gr, ca 1955, WWE, 4", pr 50.00
Sugar bowl, Basalt, Greek mythology cameos, WW, 3¾x2⅛" . . . 125.00
Sweetmeat, Jasper, gr/lav/wht, SP fittings, WW, 4½x3½" 300.00
Tea caddy, Jasper, lt gr, 7" 200.00
Tea set, Jasper, sage gr, 3-pc, WW 175.00
Teapot, Basalt, Widow knop on cover, WW, 4¾x7¼" 225.00
Teapot, Caneware, basketweave, acanthus hdl/spout, WW, 4½" . 225.00
Teapot, Drabware, Gothic decor, bearded faces, WW, 8½x6¼" . . 225.00
Teapot, Jasper, dk bl, trees & figures, 1850 . . . . 150.00
Teapot, Jasper, dk bl, WWE, 6¼x4½" 75.00
Teapot, Jasper, lt bl, WW, 6x3½" 125.00
Teapot, Jasper, lt bl, WWE, 5x4" 75.00
Teapot, Rosso Antico, blk anthemia border, WW, 9x4½" 400.00
Teapot, terra cotta, enamel flowers, lg 300.00
Teapot, terra cotta, enamel flowers, sm 200.00
Tray, Jasper, lt bl, JF Kennedy, ca 1968, WWE, 4⅜" 35.00
Urn, Basalt, gilt trim, w/lid, 1860, 11" 450.00
Urn, Jasper, dk bl, maidens as 4 Seasons, w/hdls, WW, 12" 425.00
Vase, Basalt, Canadian Coat of Arms/imp Etruria, WWE, 4" 50.00
Vase, Dragon Lustre, bl w/gold decor, 9¾x4¾" 300.00
Vase, Fairyland Lustre, Candlemass, 9" 800.00
Vase, Hummingbird Lustre, bl, flame inside top, 12x5¾" 300.00
Vase, Hummingbird Lustre, bl, flame inside top, 5x2⅜" 150.00
Vase, Jasper, bl/lav/wht, Lincoln, ca 1820-40, 5" 400.00
Vase, Jasper, blk, Portland, ca 1840, full size, 10½" 750.00
Vase, Jasper, dk bl, urn form, 10" 325.00
Vase, Jasper, lt bl, bolted base, CDT 1865, WW, 12x5" 300.00
Vase, Jasper, lt bl, Portland, WW, 7x5" 225.00
Vase, terra cotta, enamel flowers, hdls, WW, 2⅛" 100.00

Biscuit barrel, high glaze dark blue with wheel-cut floral, silver lid and handle, signed Wedgwood, 6½", $335.00.

Weller

The Weller Pottery Company was established in Zanesville, Ohio, in 1882, the outgrowth of a small one-kiln log cabin works Sam Weller had operated in Fultonham. Through an association with Wm. Long, he entered the art pottery field in 1895, producing the Lonhuda ware Long had perfected in Steubenville, six years earlier. His famous Louwelsa line was merely a continuation of Lonhuda, and was made in at least five hundred different shapes until 1924.

Many fine lines of artware followed under the direction of Charles Babcock Upjohn, art director from 1895 to 1904: Dickens Ware (1st line), underglaze slip decorations on dark backgrounds; Turada, featuring applied ivory bands of delicate openwork on solid dark brown backgrounds; and Aurelian, similar to Louwelsa, but with a brushed-on rather than blended ground.

One of their most famous lines was 2nd Line Dickens, introduced in 1900. Backgrounds, characteristically caramel shading to turquoise matt, were decorated by sgraffito with animals, golfers, monks, Indians, and scenes from Dickens novels. The work is often artist signed.

Sicardo, 1903, was a metallic lustre line in tones of flame, rose, blue, green, or purple, with flowing Art Nouveau patterns developed within the glaze.

Frederick Hurten Rhead, who worked for Weller in 1903 to 1904, created the prestigious Jap Birdimal line, decorated with geisha girls, landscapes, storks, etc., accomplished through application of heavy slip forced through the tiny nozzle of a squeeze bag. Other lines to his credit are L'Art Nouveau, produced both in high gloss brown and matt pastels, and 3rd Line Dickens, often decorated with Cruikshank's illustrations in relief.

Other early artware lines were Eocean, Floretta, Hunter, Perfecto, Dresden, Etched Matt, and Etna.

In 1920 John Lessel was hired as Art Director, and under his supervision several new lines were created. LaSa, LaMar, Marengo, and Besline attest to his expertise with metallic lustres.

The last of the artware lines and one of the most sought after by collectors today is Hudson, first made during the early 1920s. Hudson, a semimatt glazed ware, was beautifully artist decorated on shaded backgrounds with florals, animals, birds, and scenics. Notable artists often signed their work, among them Hester Pillsbury, Dorothy England Laughead, Ruth Axline, Claude Leffler, Sarah Reid McLaughlin, E.L. Pickens, and Mae Timberlake.

During the thirties, Weller produced a line of garden ware and naturalistic life-sized figures of dogs, cats, swans, geese, and playful gnomes.

The depression brought a slow steady decline in sales, and by 1948, the pottery was closed.

When no condition is indicated, the items listed below are assumed to be in mint condition.

Arcadia, vase, rose; 8½" 30.00
Ardsley, umbrella stand, 19" 335.00
Ardsley, vase, gr w/cattails, 9" 35.00
Atlas, bowl, triangular, cream w/gr leaves, #23-10" 55.00
Atlas, vase, star shape, 5½" 40.00
Aurelian, vase, blackberries, sgn L McGrath, 11" 400.00
Auroro, vase, clover, brn w/bl stems on bl/wht, sgn, 9" 350.00
Baldin, vase, slim neck, apples at base, 7" 28.00
Barcelona, candle holders, pr 65.00
Barcelona, pitcher, 6" 135.00
Blossom, basket, bl, 6" 25.00
Blossom, vase, 7½" 18.00
Blue & Decorated, pendant floral band, EX art, 10¼" 220.00
Blue & Decorated, vase, sm top floral band, cylinder, 7" 100.00
Blue Drapery, hanging basket 60.00
Blue Drapery, wall pocket, 8" 60.00
Bonito, bowl, sgn Cecil Exline, 7" 65.00
Bonito, flowerpot, w/saucer, 5" 150.00
Bonito, vase, bl daisies, 6" 65.00
Bonito, vase, 9" 95.00

Breton, planter, brn, emb floral band, 4½″ 35.00
Breton, vase, brn, 9″ 45.00
Brighton, figurine, woodpecker, 6½″ 125.00
Brighton, flower frog, swan, 5″ 100.00
Burntwood, jardiniere, chickens, 8″ 250.00
Burntwood, vase, grapes & vines, 7½″ 80.00
Cactus, boy w/bag, bl/gr, 5″ 80.00
Cactus, monkey, bl/gr, 4″ 80.00
Camelot, vase, incised wht decor on yel matt, 5¼″ 60.00
Cameo, hanging basket 45.00
Candis (Regal), fan vase, floral motif 60.00
Chase, vase, bulbous, 5½″ 150.00
Chase, vase, cylindrical, 10″ 225.00
Chengtu, vase, hexagonal, orange, 11″ 100.00
Chengtu, vase, 6½″ 45.00
Classic, hanging basket, fancy openwork, cream, 4x7½″ 70.00
Claywood, vase, butterflies, squat, 3½″ 40.00
Claywood, vase, Egyptian pharoahs/beetles, 10x4½″ 80.00
Claywood, vase, mice motif, 2″ 35.00
Cloudburst, vase, 5″ 85.00
Coppertone, bowl w/frog on side & lily pad, 10¼″ 165.00
Coppertone, candle holder, turtle 100.00
Coppertone, pitcher, fish hdl, 7½″ 220.00
Coppertone, turtle, 1¾x5″ 85.00
Coppertone, vase, 4¾″ 25.00
Copra, bowl, HP poppies, closed ring hdls, 10¼″ 120.00
Darsie, vase, 3″ 25.00
Darsie, wallpocket, wht, 8¾″ 48.00
Dickens I, jardiniere, fence/pigs/trough, 7x11″, NM 325.00
Dickens I, vase, berries/holly on dk gr, lg loop hdls, 6″ 175.00
Dickens I, vase, spider mum, pillow form, sgn, 7½″ 295.00
Dickens II, jug, monk, head/shoulders, 5½″ 235.00
Dickens II, mug, monk, full figure, sgn 350.00
Dickens II, pillow vase, leaping stag, sgn 400.00
Dickens II, pillow vase, mallard duck & baby, 5¼″ 275.00
Dickens II, tankard, Indian w/feathers, Pickens, 12″ 925.00
Dickens II, vase, Bo Peep/sheep, sgn HF, wide body, 9¾″ 665.00
Dickens II, vase, lady golfer, flask shape, 7½″ 375.00
Dickens III, mug, boy wipes face, bl seal, 5″ 500.00
Dickens III, tankard, bl/wht Art Nouveau floral, sgn 495.00
Dickens III, vase, full-figure gentleman, 9″ 450.00
Eocean, jardiniere, carnations around rim, 7x10″ 145.00
Eocean, jardiniere, mushrooms, shoulder hdls, 5½x6½″ 175.00
Eocean, kitten portrait on gray, Elizabeth Blake, 5½″ 900.00
Eocean, loving cup, floral, 2-hdl, 4″ 130.00
Eocean, vase, floral, 4″ 90.00
Eocean, vase, flower & bud, lt gr w/pink, 11¼″ 145.00
Eocean Late, bud vase, flowers, 5″ 40.00
Eocean Late, vase, cherries, cylindrical, 8¾″ 120.00
Eocean Rose, vase, dk top w/lg floral on lt body, CLL, 9″ 285.00
Etched Matt, blonde lady w/wht lilies in hair, 7½″ 235.00
Etched Matt, floral, orange, 6½″ 80.00
Etched Matt, vase, berries/leaves, concave shape, 10½″ 165.00
Ethel, vase, fan shape, mk, 6¾″ 65.00
Etna, vase, cherries, gray & blk, 8½″ 95.00
Etna, vase, floral, flat, 6½″ 80.00
Etna, vase, orange dandelions in relief, 9″ 100.00
Flask, All's Well, 4″ 140.00
Flask, FOE 85.00
Flask, Never Dry, 6″ 135.00
Flask, Take a Plunge, 6″ 140.00
Flemish, jardiniere & pedestal, cream w/rust, 40″ 625.00
Flemish, tub, 3½″ 45.00
Flemish, wall pocket, pink dogwood 55.00
Florenzo, basket, lobed, loop hdl, full kiln ink stamp, 7″ 150.00
Florenzo, jar, reticulated top w/lily finial, gr/wht, 7½″ 155.00
Floretta, mug, grapes, 5½″ 95.00
Floretta, vase, grapes, purple on wht/gr, ruffled, 14″ 235.00
Floretta, vase, strawberries, ruffled top, w/hdls, 5¾″ 65.00
Forest, hanging basket 135.00
Forest, jardinere, 7½″ 100.00
Forest, vase, fan form, 8″ 40.00
Frosted Matt, vase, inverted trumpet, gr crystalline, 12½″ 85.00
Fruitone, jardiniere, lg 95.00
Fruitone, vase, 6″ 50.00
Geode, vase, bl, bulbous 75.00
Glendale, vase, bird & nest, 6¼″ 165.00
Glendale, vase, 4″ 100.00
Glendale, wall pocket, birds on branch, 7x7″ 140.00
Glendale, wall pocket, mother bird w/birds in nest, 12½″ 165.00
Greenbriar, vase, 10″ 135.00
Hobart, candle holder, girl kneeling 95.00
Hobart, console set, girl & duck 125.00
Hobart, figurine, girl, 7½″ 75.00
Hobart, flower frog, swan, matt ivory 28.00
Hobart, wall pocket, semi-nude, aqua 85.00
Hudson, bowl vase, clover/leaves at shoulder, sgn, 3x7″ 175.00
Hudson, vase, bird in grape arbor, on wht, 9½″ 595.00
Hudson, vase, crocus, yel/wht on bl, H Pillsbury, 6″ 200.00
Hudson, vase, daffodil, lav/cream, 12¼″ 180.00
Hudson, vase, daisies, blk/wht on rose, floral trim, 7¼″ 125.00
Hudson, vase, dogwood, bulbous, 5½x5½″ 110.00
Hudson, vase, dogwood, Morris, full neck/body w/hdls, 6½″ 185.00
Hudson, vase, floral, bl w/pink & wht, Morris, 7½″ 170.00
Hudson, vase, floral, rose/lav on pink/gr, Pillsbury, 6″ 175.00
Hudson, vase, house/trees/mtns/sheep, Pillsbury, 8¾″ 1,300.00
Hudson, vase, lg floral/flat leaves, McLaughlin, 9½″ 365.00
Hudson, vase, lilies o/t valley, Pillsbury, 6¼″ 165.00
Hudson, vase, morning glories, pink/yel, sgn N Walch, 9¾″ 265.00
Hudson, vase, roses, bulbous, sgn, hdls, Pillsbury, 7″ 350.00
Hudson, vase, sailing ship/trees, Pillsbury, 8½″ 900.00
Hudson, vase, 2 swans in pond/garden in bkground, 10″ 650.00
Hudson Perfecto, pansies, blk outlined, bulbous, 5¾″ 135.00
Hudson Perfecto, vase, full-blown poppies, Leffler, 9x8″ 465.00
Hunter, vase, butterflies, pillow form, sgn Upjohn, 5½″ 425.00
Hunter, vase, duck flies over water, sgn, 5¼x5¼″ 425.00
Ivory, jardiniere, swan motif, Knifewood type, 5½″ 45.00
Ivory, wall pocket, 7½″ 35.00
Jap Birdimal, back of Japanese man, sgn Rhead/CMM, 6½x6½″ 900.00
Jap Birdimal, humidor, Dutch landscape, sgn Rhead, 7½″ 450.00
Jap Birdimal, mug, Chirping Cup My Matin' Song, 5¼″ 170.00
Jap Birdimal, standing geese, lav, 4″ 250.00
Jap Birdimal, vase, peacock feathers, wht/bl on gray, 7″ 365.00
Jewel, vase, home/floral/jewels, 16½″, VG 550.00
Kenova, vase, applied turtle, army gr, 5¼″ 295.00
Kenova, vase, flower/branches/leaves relief, imp mk, 8¾″ 110.00
Klyro, vase, fan shape, 6″ 22.00
L'Art Nouveau, ewer, lady/floral/ bisque, 9½″ 80.00
Lamar, vase, red w/blk landscape, T Dunlavy, 14½″ 350.00
Lamar, vase, red w/blk landscape, 7″ 150.00
LaSa, vase, landscape, 10½″ 240.00
LaSa, vase, landscape w/palm trees, 6″ 150.00
Lorbeek, bud vase, 3 openings 65.00
Louella, jar w/lid, 9½″ 110.00
Louella, vase, cabinet, 5½″ 65.00
Louwelsa, Blue; pillow vase, blackberries, 5¼″ 600.00
Louwelsa, Blue; vase, cherries, cylinder, 7″ 450.00
Louwelsa, Blue; vase, floral/leaf, sgn J, 4½x4″ 300.00

Louwelsa, pillow vase with cat portrait, signed Blake, 7" x 8½", $1,800.00.

Louwelsa, Blue; vase, raspberries, 11" 860.00
Louwelsa, bowl vase, floral, 3 ft, crimped top, 4½" 60.00
Louwelsa, candlestick, orange flower/brn, artist sgn, 4¾" 70.00
Louwelsa, clock, floral, fan-shape top, 7" 390.00
Louwelsa, clock, floral, w/top 'hdl,' 6x4¾" 450.00
Louwelsa, ewer, 2 orange roses, sgn, 6" 125.00
Louwelsa, jardiniere, iris, 8½x7½" 185.00
Louwelsa, jug, berries/leaves, sgn ER, ball shape, 6" 125.00
Louwelsa, jug, dbl; berries/leaves, artist sgn, 6¼" 165.00
Louwelsa, pitcher, fish, shell-molded top & spout, 11¼" 435.00
Louwelsa, planter, daisy decor, sq, 3x4" 85.00
Louwelsa, stein, beer; cherries/leaves, silver overlay, 6" 675.00
Louwelsa, tankard, Indian portrait, sgn Dunlavy 12" 1,250.00
Louwelsa, vase, Indian portrait entire side, E Suleer, 11" 1,400.00
Louwelsa, vase, pansy, 8" 90.00
Louwelsa, vase, roses, 3-hdl, Albert Haubrich, 7x8" 230.00
Louwelsa, vase, yel crocus, 4¼" 60.00
Luxor, bud vase, 7½" 25.00
Malvern, basket, 8" 30.00
Malvern, circle vase, 8" 55.00
Malvern, vase, 7" 40.00
Mammy, cookie jar 250.00
Mammy, creamer 140.00
Manhattan, vase, vertical lotus leaves, tan, 6½" 35.00
Marbleized, vase, 9x4½" 70.00
Marvo, candleholders, pr 35.00
Marvo, planter, 2-part log 30.00
Marvo, wall pocket, gr 35.00
Melrose, candlestick, 13", pr 165.00
Melrose, vase, 5" 30.00
Modeled Etched Matt, vase, gr w/yel roses, 8½" 120.00
Monochrome, compote, beige, 9" 45.00
Muskota, crab 52.00
Muskota, flower frog, boy fishing 95.00
Muskota, flower frog, sm salamander atop, imp mk 45.00
Muskota, kneeling woman 140.00
Muskota, starfish 50.00
Muskota, swan 65.00
Muskota, washer woman 280.00
Neiska, vase, yel, 6½" 25.00
Nile, vase, hdls, 9" 85.00
Noval, vase, 8" 60.00
Oakleaf, bud vase, dbl; V-shape w/leaf in center, 7" 18.00
Panella, ginger jar, in-mold script, cream & beige 35.00
Paragon, candlestick, yel, pr 40.00
Paragon, vase, maroon, 7½" 60.00
Parian, vase, 12" 50.00
Pearl, vase, 7¾" 85.00
Roma, wall pocket, Dupont motif, 10½" 60.00
Roma, window box, floral relief, imp mk, ivory/bl, 13x5x6" 115.00
Rosemont, bowl, late line, 2½x9½" 25.00
Sabrinian, ash tray, lg 150.00
Sabrinian, ash tray, sm 95.00
Sabrinian, flower frog, seahorse, ½ kiln ink stamp, 5" 110.00
Sabrinian, planter, seashell 85.00
Selma, vase, cylindrical, daisies, 5x3" 50.00
Sicardo, vase, allover star design, bl/gr, 4¾" 260.00
Sicardo, vase, mums, blown-out top, sgn, 11½", NM 1,100.00
Silvertone, console bowl, 12½" 90.00
Silvertone, vase, apple blossoms, w/hdls, 9" 115.00
Silvertone, vase, flowers & butterflies, hdls, 12" 150.00
Silvertone, vase, grapes, w/hdls, 6½" 60.00
Silvertone, wall pocket, 11" 75.00
Softone, planter, pink, oval, 3-ftd, 10" 15.00
Softone, vase, curved rim, yel, 8¼" 25.00
Souevo, vase, pear form w/hdls at width, 10" 125.00
Souevo, vase, 7" 75.00
Souevo, wall pocket, 9" 60.00
Souvenir, 1904 Expo, Geo Washington on tan disk, blk coat 95.00
Stellar, vase, sgn Pillsbury 185.00
Sydonia, cornucopia, 6½" 25.00
Sydonia, vase, lav, 9" 30.00
Turada, humidor 275.00
Turada, jardiniere, 8" 250.00
Turkis, vase, 8" 75.00
Tutone, basket, 7½" 60.00
Tutone, vase, tri-corner shape, 8" 35.00
Warwick, basket, artist sgn 110.00
Warwick, circle vase, 7" 65.00
Warwick, wall pocket, 11½" 60.00
Wild Rose, basket, 5½" 25.00
Wild Rose, candle holder, triple 35.00
Wild Rose, hanging basket 35.00
Wild Rose, tankard, 12" 45.00
Wild Rose, vase, bulbous body, ornate hdls, 9½" 35.00
Wild Rose, vase, 2-hdl, 6½" 20.00
Woodcraft, bowl, plums, 3½x8" 60.00
Woodcraft, bowl, squirrel figural 55.00
Woodcraft, bud vase, 6½" 36.00
Woodcraft, fan vase, 8" 30.00
Woodcraft, hanging basket, fox 165.00
Woodcraft, log planter, oak leaf 50.00
Woodcraft, smoking set, tree stump, 5" 150.00
Woodcraft, vase, apples on bark, 12" 150.00
Woodcraft, wall pocket, owl, 10" 125.00
Zona, cup & saucer, cherry decor, w/8" plate 55.00
Zona, pitcher, Kingfisher, full color, 8" 150.00
Zona, pitcher, wobbly duck 85.00

Western Americana

Relics from the era of the Western Frontier to the age of the cowboys hold a fascination for many. Leather items, such as holsters, saddles, and chaps, are often elaborately hand tooled and sometimes bear the mark of their makers. 'California' spurs were ornate, sometimes inlaid with silver work, and are considered very desirable among today's collectors. So are those stamped 'McChestney,' 'Kelly,' 'G.A. Bischoff and Co.,' and 'J.O. Bass.'

Sheriff's badges, old photographs, Express memorabilia, and barbed wire--in short, anything from the Old West is being collected.

When no condition is indicated, the items listed below are assumed to be in excellent condition.

See also Badges

Bit, silver overlay sides, German, Crockett Hackamore 125.00
Book, Dalton Gang, Bandits o/t Far West, dime novel, Ward 15.00
Book, Rube Burrow, King of Train Robbers, dime novel, Ward . . 15.00

Bosal, rawhide w/mohair rein rope....60.00
Branding iron, 'P'....30.00
Bridle bit, gal leg, Crockett....200.00
Bucket, grease; for Conestoga wagon....85.00
Canteen, water, round, no cap....10.00
Chaps, bat wing, brass studs on leather....450.00
Chaps, bat wing leather w/pockets, 3 conchas ea leg, 1900....165.00
Chaps, blk angora, shotgun type, ca 1800s, VG....350.00
Chaps, blk/wht angora, Power, Pendleton....550.00
Chaps, shotgun, by Furstnow, Miles City, MT, w/provenance....500.00
Coat, buffalo fur, handmade, pre-1900, med length....250.00
Cowboy hat, Tom Mix style, wht, 1920s....140.00
Gauntlets, silver & brass studs, sgn....125.00
Hobbles, rawhide....25.00
Holster, pistol; leather, emb: Fort Collins, tooled, 1880s....150.00
Leg iron, chrome plated, SF Sheriff on iron, key/chain....50.00
Photo, Buffalo Bill profile in hat, silverprint, 1890, VG....75.00
Program, Buffalo Bill's Wild West Show, 1909....35.00
Scabbard, saddle type, basketweave design, Lawrence, EX....50.00
Scabbard, saddle type, solid butt, pre-1900....50.00
Show bill, Buffalo Bill's, Cody on cover/buffalo, 1895....125.00
Spittoon, brass, Wells Fargo....350.00
Spurs, aluminum, leather straps, no mk....35.00
Spurs, brass, eng, short shank-metal, sm....30.00
Spurs, bronco-riding; metal straps, heavy, sm rowels....40.00
Spurs, chrome, handmade rowels, buttons made in body....25.00
Spurs, chrome, some silver on side/shank/bottom, Crockett....145.00
Spurs, emb aluminum, chap guard, mk under button: Crockett..35.00
Spurs, emb iron, chap guard, spoke rowel, Buerman....125.00
Spurs, emb iron, spoke rowel, chap guard, early CA style....75.00
Spurs, emb iron w/some silver, chap guard/star rowel, N&J....80.00
Spurs, emb stainless steel, Rodeo, Kelly....50.00
Spurs, iron, leather straps, sm....15.00
Spurs, iron, Paddy Ryan, some silver/chap guards, Crockett....150.00
Spurs, silver mtd, pierced, iron rowels, early 19th C, 7"....130.00
Tapaderos, emb braid design, 20"....55.00
Wagon jack, Conestoga, wrought fittings, tooling, 1802....165.00
Western saddle, hand tooled, FE Burris, 1930-40s, VG....525.00
Western saddle, hand tooled, w/silver conchos, Keyston....1,500.00

Western Stoneware Co.

The Western Stoneware Co. was formed in 1906, a merger of seven companies: Monmouth Pottery, Weir Pottery, Macomb Pottery, Macomb Stoneware, D. Culbertson Stoneware, Clinton Stoneware, and Fort Dodge Stoneware. Besides their stoneware products, they also manufactured garden ware, and some artware. One by one each branch of the corporation closed and today only one plant remains, located in Monmouth, Ill., on the site of the old Weir Pottery.

Bottle, water; rare....450.00
Butter crock, 5-lb....175.00
Crock, cobalt fruit, 8-gal....45.00
Humidor, cobalt: Yale Mixture, lid chips....90.00
Jar, leaf, 2-gal....25.00
Jug, wht w/brn top, leaf, ½-gal....20.00
Jug, wht w/brn top, leaf, 2-gal....27.00
Mug, bl & wht, barrel shape....55.00
Mug, Seattle, w/bands....65.00
Pitcher, cattails, 7"....110.00
Syrup pitcher, wht w/brn top....20.00

Wheatley, T. J.

In 1880, after a brief association with the Coultry Works, Thomas J. Wheatley opened his own studio in Cincinnati, Ohio, claiming to have been the first to discover the secret of underglaze slip decoration on an unbaked clay vessel. He applied for and was granted a patent toward that end. Demand for his ware increased to the point that several artists were hired to decorate the ware. The company incorporated in 1880 as the Cincinnati Art Pottery, but until 1882, it continued to operate under Wheatley's name. Ware from this period is marked 'T.J. Wheatley,' or 'T.J.W. and Co.,' and it may be dated.

When no condition is indicated, the items listed below are assumed to be in mint condition.

Bowl, leaf relief, gr textured glaze, 2¾x11½"....200.00
Lamp, thick gr glaze, pottery cap, wood base, rewired, 19"....750.00
Vase, daisies on bl, pillow shape, sgn EC Carpenter, 8½"....185.00
Vase, leaf & bud relief, matt gr, ovoid, sgn/#d, 6¾"....425.00
Vase, leaves & berries relief, matt gr, unsgn, 11½x4"....485.00
Vase, leaves & berries relief, matt gr, unsgn, 13¾"....525.00
Vase, mums, yel/wht on gr, sgn/1880, 10"....450.00

Whieldon

Thomas Whieldon was regarded as the finest of the Staffordshire potters of the mid-1700s. He produced marbled and black Egyptian wares, as well as tortoiseshell, a mottled brown glazed earthenware accented with touches of blue. In 1754 he became a partner of Josiah Wedgwood.

When no condition is indicated, the items listed below are assumed to be in mint condition.

Left to right: Whieldon-type tea caddy and cover, with Apollo and floral sprigs, dated 1779, repaired, 6", $700.00; Coffee pot, green, yellow and brown streaky glaze, 1760-65, restored, 9", $800.00.

Cup & saucer, sprigged florals....1,200.00
Flask, birds & floral, gr/brn mottled glaze, rare, 4"....410.00
Pitcher, Toby, 8"....110.00
Plate, mottled gr/sepia/tan, 9¾"....325.00
Teapot, brn mottled glaze, ftd, bird finial/twig hdl, 4¼"....565.00
Teapot, cauliflower, dk gr, ca 1760....1,000.00

Wicker

Wicker is the basket-like material used in many types of furniture and accessories; it may be made from bamboo cane, rattan, reed, or artificial fibers. It is airy and lightweight, and very popular in hot regions.

Imported from the Orient in the 18th century, it was first manufactured in the United States in about 1850. The elaborate, closely woven Victorian designs belong to the mid-to-late 1800s, and the simple styles with coarse reedings usually indicate a post-1900 production. Art Deco styles followed in the twenties and thirties.

The most important consideration in buying wicker is condition--it can be restored, but only by a professional. Age is an important factor, but be aware that 'Victorian-look' furniture is being manufactured today.

When no condition is indicated, the items listed below are assumed to be in excellent condition.

Basinette, decorated in white and pink, ca 1900, $250.00.

Basket, sewing; tufted lining, brass/enamel thread holder........20.00
Birdcage, natural, fancy wall bracket mt....................140.00
Chair, breakfast; heavy, dtd 1917, rstr, set of 4..............700.00
Chair, tight weave, w/diamond design, sq cushioned seat.......270.00
Chaise, wicker legs, open weave apron, simple design.........385.00
Conversation bench, early 1900s..........................425.00
Davenport, tight weave, wing-bk, cushioned seat..............280.00
Footstool, sq base, rnd top w/uphl insert, 9½x12″............100.00
Kneeling bench, w/ram's horn at top edge, late 1800s.........450.00
Lamp, table; vase-shaped base, dome shade, 22″.............150.00
Lamp base, bentwood shade holder, Heywood-Wakefield, 17″....35.00
Lounge, tight weave, bk & arm rest, cushioned..............390.00
Plant stand, Victorian, orig tin planter, 30x12x12″...........95.00
Rocker, high-bk, arms & apron very elaborate, 1890s, 38″.....675.00
Rocker, loose weave, sq bk w/high arm rest.................240.00
Rocker, tight weave, low sides & seat, design on bk..........300.00
Set, couch, rocker & chair, 1930s, 3-pc...................1,175.00
Settee, loose weave, ½ cushioned bk & cushioned seat........280.00
Stroller, doll; Victorian, high wheel, orig pnt/upholstery........495.00
Swing, tight weave seat & trim rnd bk, curved bk............250.00
Table, tight weave, rnd, w/2 shelves.......................180.00
Tea cart, tight weave, bottom shelf/front wheels, top tray......260.00
Tea cart, 2-tier, simple weave, wood fr, 30x36″ L............350.00
Tray, serving, 19″..25.00

Willets

The Willets Manufacturing Company of Trenton, New Jersey, produced a type of belleek porcelain during the late 1880s and 1890s. Examples were often marked with a coiled snake that formed a 'W,' with 'Willets' below, and 'Belleek' above.

Not all Willets is factory decorated. Items painted by amateurs outside the factory are worth considerably less.

In the listings below, all items are belleek unless noted otherwise. When no condition is indicated, the items listed below are assumed to be in mint condition.

Bowl, floral, ruffled/hdls, sgn HB, brn mk, 1½x8″............145.00
Bowl, portrait reserve, lattice/florals, sgn SA Rowe, 4x9″......325.00
Bowl, roses, gilt, crimped rim w/hdls, 6″....................125.00
Chocolate pot, gold paste floral on cream, dragon hdl.........395.00
Creamer & sugar bowl, gold swags/baskets, roses, ftd.........150.00
Creamer & sugar bowl, gold w/mc flowers, dragon hdls, #210...150.00
Cup & saucer, twig hdl.....................................67.00
Hatpin holder, silver decor, sgn, 5″..........................75.00
Mug, berries & leaves on coral to cream, sgn, 4½″............85.00
Mug, friendship; gold dragonfly/floral w/bl dots, 3-hdl.........325.00
Mug, HP berries/leaves on coral & cream, artist sgn, 4½″.......85.00
Pitcher, tankard; dog portrait/artist sgn, dragon hdl, 16″......695.00
Pitcher, tankard; HP grapes, sgn, 7″.........................55.00
Plate, allover sm roses, gilt, 8″............................95.00
Plate, gold paste leaf spray, scalloped, 5½″...................45.00
Plate, gold sprays, brushed scallop & emb edge, pk mk, 5½″....45.00
Plate, red snapper/water, dbl trim w/gold medallions, 9″........65.00
Plate, sm red roses, Worcester type........................120.00
Vase, lg pink cabbage roses on gr, 12″......................420.00
Vase, lion portrait on chocolate, Houghton, rare.............395.00
Vase, portrait of woman, floral on cream, paste work, lg.......795.00
Vase, red/cream roses, Rococo design, scalloped lip, 16″......195.00
Vase, yel roses & gr leaves on lt yel/tan, sgn, 8¼″............195.00

Willow Ware

Willow Ware, inspired no doubt by the numerous patterns of the blue and white Nanking imports, has been popular since the late 18th century, and has been made in as many variations as there were manufacturers. English transfer wares by such notable firms as Allerton and Ridgway are the most sought after and the most expensive. Japanese potters have been producing Willow patterned dinnerware since the late 1800s and American manufacturers have followed suit. Although blue is the color most commonly used, mauve, black, and even multicolor Willow Ware may be found. Complimentary glassware, tinware, and linens have also been made.

In addition to 'Allerton' and 'Ridgway,' both companies used the possessive from of their names in marking their wares (i.e. Allerton's, Ridgway's).

For further study, we recommend the book *Blue Willow*, with full-color photos and current prices, written by Mary Frank Gaston. You will find her address in the Directory under Texas.

When no condition is indicated, the items listed below are assumed to be in mint condition.

Key:
pc—polychrome

Bank, 3 stacked pigs, modern Japan, 7″......................25.00
Bone dish, Wood & Sons, 7½x4½″..........................17.00
Bottle, scent; Copeland, English, w/stopper, 6″..............140.00
Bowl, Allerton's, flared edge, rnd, 1930s, 2½x10″.............65.00
Bowl, Booth's, bow knot border, 10″........................55.00
Bowl, Booth's, open, oval, 10″............................45.00
Bowl, border pattern w/gold line, porcelain, 8¼x10¼″..........35.00
Bowl, Clews Warranted, Staffordshire, #919, flat, 10x1¼″.......40.00
Bowl, Johnson Bros, w/hdl, 6¼x2¼″........................10.00
Bowl, Mason's, Canton, 6½″..............................15.00
Bowl, soup; Allerton's, imp crown, mk #868, flat, 9″...........17.50
Bowl, Steventon & Sons, oval, 8½″..........................25.00

Bowl, vegetable; Thos Dimmock, sq w/lid, 10″ . . . 145.00
Butter dish, pattern on 4 sides, rnd lid . . . 45.00
Butter pat, England, 3½″ . . . 13.00
Butter pat, Made in Japan, 3″ . . . 14.00
Cake plate, Steventon & Sons, 10″ . . . 33.00
Cake stand, N&B, 3x12″ . . . 140.00
Candle holder, Doulton & Co, Flow Blue, 7½″ . . . 300.00
Chamber pot, Doulton & Co, Flow Blue, 5½x9¼″ . . . 175.00
Chamber pot, English, tin, unmk . . . 75.00
Charger, Allerton's, 13″ . . . 50.00
Child's dinner service, Made in Japan, 18-pc set . . . 225.00
Child's set, tin, 23-pc . . . 45.00
Clock, German, 8-day, tin . . . 75.00
Coffee pot, birds/bridge/temple, electric, Japan, 1940, 8″ . . . 72.00
Coffee pot, modern, Wedgwood, 8″ . . . 75.00
Compote, Doulton & Co, Flow Blue, 3x9″ . . . 150.00
Compote, simple line border, unmk, polychrome, 3x9½″ . . . 65.00
Creamer, Buffalo China, 2½″ . . . 16.00
Creamer, Occupied Japan, flared spout/pinched base, 4″ . . . 23.00
Creamer, Shenango, 1½″ . . . 16.00
Creamer, Walker China, 2″ . . . 16.00
Creamer & sugar, Johnson Bros . . . 60.00
Cup, Auld Lang Syne, Copeland China . . . 28.00
Cup, chili; unmk, 4x4¼″ . . . 17.00
Cup, demitasse; Grainger, butterfly border/14k gold bands . . . 45.00
Cup, Homer Laughlin . . . 5.00
Cup, unmk, red, 1900s . . . 25.00
Cup & saucer, demitasse; Burgess & Leigh . . . 18.00
Cup & saucer, demitasse; butterfly border, 2 Temples II . . . 15.00
Cup & saucer, demitasse; Copeland, Dagger/Mandarin II . . . 25.00
Cup & saucer, demitasse; Mandarin II center, Dagger border . . . 20.00
Cup & saucer, Johnson Bros . . . 12.00
Cup & saucer, Sebring Pottery, 2 Temples II center . . . 12.00
Decanter, whiskey; modern, 8″ . . . 25.00
Dinner bell, egg shape/fluted base, porcelain, ring hdl, 4″ . . . 15.00
Drainer, meat; Dagger border, 16″ . . . 100.00
Drainer, meat; English, Turner center, unmk, 14¼x10¼″ . . . 80.00
Egg cup, English, single, unmk . . . 18.00
Gravy boat, Allerton's, underplate: 9x5″, boat: 8x4″ . . . 60.00
Gravy boat, Copeland, Dagger border/Mandarin II, 3½x8″ . . . 70.00
Infant feeder, English, unmk, 4″ . . . 125.00

Platter, English, Corona Ware, Stoke-On-Trent, 11″ x 8″, $85.00.

Jar, ginger; Mason's, Scroll & Flower border, Turner, 7½″ . . . 70.00
Lamp, Japan, kerosene, 11½″ . . . 50.00
Match holder, Willow medallion, 'Matches,' 1950s, 6½″ . . . 45.00
Mold, pudding; Booth's, 3″ . . . 30.00
Mold, pudding; England, incised mk, 4½″ . . . 35.00
Pitcher, milk; Gater, Hall & Co, HP, polychrome, lid, 7½″ . . . 160.00
Pitcher, milk; Green & Co, polychrome, 4″ . . . 100.00
Pitcher, milk; Keele Pottery, 2 Temples II, polychrome . . . 75.00
Pitcher, milk; men/bridge/temple, stoneware, wht, 7″, M . . . 36.00
Plaque, wall; English, brass plate, oak fr, 7″ . . . 70.00
Plate, Adderly's, Daisy, floral border, 8½″ . . . 60.00
Plate, Allerton's, butterfly border/2 Temples II center, 9″ . . . 25.00
Plate, Allerton's, mk A in wreath, ca 1929, 10¼″ . . . 22.00
Plate, Britannia Pottery, mulberry, 1920s, 6½″, M . . . 36.00
Plate, Canton, Chinese, HP, 10″ . . . 70.00
Plate, chop; Canton, w/Nanking border, porcelain, 9¾x11¼″ . . . 45.00
Plate, Clarence Pottery, dbl border, 1895, 9⅞″, M . . . 23.00
Plate, Copeland, Dagger border/Mandarin II, 8½″ . . . 25.00
Plate, Copeland, Mandarin II, ribbed edge, imp mk, 10″ . . . 17.50
Plate, Crown Staffordshire, 2 Temples II center, pc, 9″ . . . 50.00
Plate, Doulton, Flow Blue, traditional border & center, 9½″ . . . 60.00
Plate, fish; Alcock's, Mandarin II center, 10x7″ . . . 100.00
Plate, Globe Pottery, 9″ . . . 7.50
Plate, grill; Carr China, NY Grill, 10″ . . . 10.00
Plate, grill; Made in Japan, 9¾″ . . . 10.00
Plate, grill; Shenango China, Scroll & Flower/Turner, 10″ . . . 15.00
Plate, grill; Wellsville China, pink w/cream bkground, 9¾″ . . . 10.00
Plate, Homer Laughlin, 9″ . . . 7.50
Plate, Johnson Bros, 8″ . . . 7.50
Plate, Kemple, milk glass, no border, 1½″ . . . 25.00
Plate, Maddock, traditional border/center, polychrome, 10″ . . . 25.00
Plate, Mason's, Flower & Scroll border/Turner center, 10″ . . . 18.00
Plate, napkin; Bridgewood, butterfly/2 Temples II, 6½″ . . . 55.00
Plate, Old York Willow, Castle Museum commemorative, 9″ . . . 25.00
Plate, Pountney, Flow Blue, Mandarin/Flower & Scroll, 7¼″ . . . 40.00
Plate, Ridgway's, 10″ . . . 15.00
Plate, Royal, Bridal Gold Floral border, 6¼″ . . . 10.00
Plate, simple line border/simple center, milk glass, 10″ . . . 20.00
Plate, Wallace, traditional border & center, brn, 10″ . . . 20.00
Platter, Andrew Stevenson, ca 1818, 16¾x13½″ . . . 175.00
Platter, Bell, traditional, mulberry, 11½x9½″ . . . 100.00
Platter, Bell, traditional border & center, 12x10″ . . . 70.00
Platter, Blakewell Bros, 1900s, 12½″, M . . . 122.00
Platter, Burgess & Leigh, Scroll & Flower, 11¼x8½″ . . . 75.00
Platter, ironstone, minor wear/scratches, 15½″ . . . 75.00
Platter, Made in Japan, pre WWII, oval, 8½x11″ . . . 15.00
Platter, Ridgway's, traditional, polychrome, HP, 6½x5″ . . . 55.00
Platter, Staffordshire, 20½″, EX . . . 185.00
Platter, Villeroy & Boch, Germany, crazing on bk, 9x12″ . . . 17.50
Platter, well & tree, 15x19″ . . . 175.00
Platter, Willow Ware by Royal China, rnd, 10½″ . . . 15.00
Pot, demitasse; Burleigh, Scroll & Flower border, 7½″ . . . 90.00
Punch bowl, unmk, inside border, 6x9¼″ . . . 130.00
Salt box, Japan, 5x5″ . . . 60.00
Shakers, Japan, 3″, pr . . . 25.00
Spoon, soup; Japan, 5½″ . . . 6.00
Spoon rest, Japan, 9″ . . . 25.00
Syrup, frosted glass, 5″ . . . 30.00
Tea caddy, Rington . . . 175.00
Tea set, Copeland, sold by Tiffany, ca 1800, 3-pc . . . 395.00
Teapot, Booth's, 7″ . . . 100.00
Teapot, Maling, Mandarin II . . . 80.00
Teapot, Worcester Royal, 1886 . . . 125.00
Toaster, Pan Electrical Mfg, 7x7″ . . . 200.00

Toothpick holder, Buffalo China, 2¼" 30.00
Tray, bread; Booth's, 12" 85.00
Tray, red/blk on fabric, brass hdls, glass top, 14x18" 25.00
Trivet, Japan, sq 25.00
Tumbler, clear glass, wht w/bl, gold rim, 5¼x1⅞" 10.00
Tumbler, juice; Japan, unmk, 3½" 10.00
Tureen, English, mk Semi-China in sq 400.00
Tureen, ironstone, English, unmk, 15x11" 550.00
Tureen, soup; w/lid, ladle & underplate, Burleigh 295.00
Vase, Japan, unmk, 5" 45.00
Wash set, Wedgwood, bowl: 16", pitcher: 10" 600.00
Waste bowl, English, 3x6" 40.00

Winchester

The Winchester Repeating Arms Company lost their important government contract after WWI, and of necessity turned to the manufacture of sporting goods, hardware items, tools, etc., to augment their gun production. Between 1920 and 1931, over 7,500 different items, each marked 'Winchester Trademark U.S.A.,' were offered for sale by thousands of Winchester Hardware stores throughout the country. After 1931 the firm became Winchester-Western.

When no condition is indicated, the items listed below are assumed to be in excellent condition.

Axe, boy's 32.00
Axe, camp; 11½" hdl, VG 42.00
Battery, flashlight; #1511 .... 14.00
Belt, canvas shell; German silver bear head buckle, 1891 .... 90.00
Booklet, The Winchester Idea, guns/tools etc, 1920s 35.00
Booklet, Western Ammo, 1934, pocket sz 45.00
Bullet mold, 32-165 caliber 34.00
Bullet mold, 38 caliber 50.00
Calendar, 1930, Indian guide & hunter in canoe, fr, M 350.00
Calendar, 1933, 5 duck hunters play poker, complete pads 350.00
Case, shipping; wood, holds twelve 1897 riot guns 75.00
Casting rod, #5090, telescoping, steel, VG 85.00
Casting rod, #6390, 1-pc, EX 85.00
Casting rod, steel, 4-pc 65.00
Catalog, 1891, Snively Hardware, March, Wyoming, EX 175.00
Catalog, 1892, October, 84 pg 205.00

Cartridge board, in frame, 46"x36", $2,000.00.

Catalog, 1919, March, EX 175.00
Catalog, 1925, guns, w/envelope 135.00
Catalog, 1925, orig envelope, 205 pg, 3x12" 145.00
Catalog, 1930, pocket sz 25.00
Catalog, 1931, tools/fishing tackle/knives/flashlights, EX 150.00
Catalog, 1932, cartridges & shells, 44 pg 35.00
Catalog, 1949, w/price list 35.00
Catalog, 1951, gun & ammo 20.00
Catalog, 1954, pocket sz 20.00
Catalog, 1955 .... 20.00
Change mat, W brand, red felt w/wht reverse print, 12x15" 105.00
Cigar box opener 15.00
Comic book, 1950 .... 28.00
Countersink bit 26.00
Drill bit, wood, EX 20.00
Envelope, frontiersman w/73 rifle 28.00
Envelope, hunter & guide shooting over rock, color 22.50
Envelope, mk Big Red W, post mk 1919, EX 20.00
Envelope, model 12, 2 hunters & dog, post mk, EX 22.00
Fishing reel 80.00
Flashlight, 2-cell, chrome w/copper cap & head, EX 16.00
Golf club, mashie, wood hdl, EX 115.00
Invoice, 1858, EX 20.00
Knife, butcher; #1025, sharpened, 7½" blade, VG 22.50
Level, VG 48.00
Oil can, red & yel, EX 10.00
Padlock, w/key, EX 75.00
Paperweight, blk, 1910, EX 80.00
Pencil box, fabric, scarce 45.00
Pin-back button, picture of shotgun 95.00
Plane, block 40.00
Plane, wood; #3045 .... 75.00
Pliers, snap ring 35.00
Poster, cowboy holding rifle w/foot on ram, orig, 1904 .... 675.00
Poster, Duck Hunter in Camp at Breakfast, paper, 18x30" 27.00
Poster, rifles, sexy blonde, 1970s 12.00
Poster, Toperwins, fr, 1920s, 18x30" 295.00
Poster, World's Greatest Shooting Team, rare, fr, 18x24" 865.00
Poster, WWII, b/w w/red trademk, soldiers, fr, 19x24", EX 35.00
Rifle, air; lead shot filled 18.00
Roller skates, MIB 65.00
Roller skates, pr, EX 20.00
Screwdriver, brass ferrule, 9", VG 23.00
Screwdriver, wood hdl, 3", VG 18.00
Shears, VG 25.00
Shell, dummy shot, salesman's sample 95.00
Shell, 1-lb, 1918, EX 25.00
Sign, Authorized Dealer, gold print on red, fr, 12x20", EX 137.50
Sign, felt, Ammunition for Sale, in fr, 13x11" 95.00
Sign, Super-X, banner & rifle 15.00
Stickpin, New Rival, shot shell, bl, EX 50.00
Tie pin 15.00
Tin container, after shave, hunter w/gun & dog 55.00
Trap, hand; for skeet birds, mk on clamp, pat June 1919 .... 23.00
Wood bit, #6 .... 10.00
Wrench, open-end, ⅞" & ¾", EX 30.00

Windmill Weights

Windmill weights were used to protect the windmill's plunger rod from damage during high winds by adding weight that slowed down the speed of the blades.

When no condition is indicated, the items listed below are assumed to be in excellent condition.

Buffalo, flat/detailed, wood base, 16½"....................700.00
Bull, Fairbury, CI, model #17, 38-lb.......................650.00
Chicken, Hummer Model L, 8-lb, 10x9"...................375.00
Crescent moon, Fairbanks Morse Mfg, 19-lb, 10x7x2".........125.00
Crescent moon, Fairbanks Morse Mfg, 22-lb, 10½"..........125.00
Horse, Dempster, CI, 13-lb, 16½x17"......................350.00
Horse, tooled mane & cropped tail, open legs, CI, 16½x17"....475.00
Letter W, CI, Althouse & Wheeler, late 19th C, 16½x9½".....265.00
Rooster, CI, G detail, 18¾"..............................475.00
Rooster, CI, Hummer E #184, worn rpt, wood base, 13"......350.00
Rooster, CI, 15½"..325.00
Rooster, CI, 9½"...142.00

Wire Ware

Two thousand years B.C, wire was made by cutting sheet metal into strips which were shaped with mallet and file. By the late 13th century, craftsmen in Europe had developed a method of pulling these strips through progressively smaller holes until the desired gauge was obtained. During the Industrial Revolution of the late 1800s, machinery was developed that could produce wire cheaply and easily, and it became a popular commercial commodity. It was used to produce large items such as garden benches and fencing, as well as innumerable small pieces for use in the kitchen or on the farm.

When no condition is indicated, the items listed below are assumed to be in excellent condition.

Basket, egg; early 20th C, 4x10½"..........................25.00
Basket, egg; folding, ftd, very lg.............................60.00
Basket, egg-gathering style, bail hdl, 3¾x6" dia top...........35.00
Basket, folding; tulip shape, decorative design.................35.00
Basket, hanging; heavy looped wire, sm.......................30.00
Basket, hanging; twisted wire, Victorian, 5½x8x6"............45.00
Bun basket, sm diamond design, oval, 2 end hdls..............55.00
Clothes hanger for puffy-shoulder Vict dress, coiled, 20"........40.00
Comb holder, hanging; twisted wire.............................65.00
Compote, disk ft, 7x9"......................................150.00
Compote, twisted wire, looped wire top, ftd, 4½x4½" dia......100.00
Dictionary stand...50.00
Floral armature, anchor shape, early 20th C, 17x12x1½".......65.00
Fruit holder, concentric ovals in base, scallops, 17x11x2".......85.00
Garden bench, G detail, 3 scroll ft, 52", EX..................500.00
Hat/coat rack, hanging, 5 hooks, fancy bk, 24x5½"...........150.00
Letter holder, heart design & curlicue, twisted wire............45.00
Lid holder, half wagon wheel shape, loop to hang, 13¼x6".....35.00
Lid holder, ornate w/loops & circles, heavy wire...............45.00
Pie rack, holds 2 pies, side & top hdls, old dark wire..........48.00
Plant stand, Victorian..175.00
Potato boiler, spherical, low ftd base, early 19th C..........175.00
Towel holder, hanging, holds 5 towels, fancy designs..........95.00
Trivet, for iron, ornate/twisted, loop hdl, ftd, lg...............65.00
Trivet, for iron, triangular, ornate back, loop hdl, ftd..........38.00
Trivet, ornate center design, ftd, 8" dia.......................32.00
Wastebasket, early 1900s......................................24.00

Witch Balls

Witch balls were a Victorian fad touted to be meritorious toward ridding the house of evil spirits and thus warding off sickness and bad luck. Folklore would have it that by wiping the dust and soot from the ball the spirits were exorcised. It is much more probable, however, considering the fact that such beautiful art glass was used in their making, that the ostensus Victorians perpetrated the myth rather tonge-in-cheek while enjoying them as lovely decorations for their homes.

When no condition is indicated, the items listed below are assumed to be in mint condition.

Clear w/opal looping, minor wear, 6"......................125.00
Clear w/red, bl & wht loops, 4"...........................275.00
Cobalt to sapphire bl, blown in mold, 2½"...................100.00
Gr w/opal swirls, 5"...95.00
Jar, amber, 4"; w/matching 2¾" ball cover, S Jersey..........300.00
Pitcher, blown, opal blue, applied hdl, 5; w/4" ball cover......225.00
Vase, clear w/wht opal looping, 8½"; matching 7½" ball.......450.00
Vase, cobalt w/wht loops, flare/fold lip, 7¾"; w/ball..........1,275.00
Vase, opaque wht urn shape, 14"; ball: wht w/bl loops, pr.....450.00
Vase, red/wht/bl looping, 10½"; matching 7" ball...........1,700.00

Wood Carvings

Wood sculptures represent an important section of American folk art. Wood carvings were made not only by skilled woodworkers, such as cabinetmakers, carpenters, etc., but by amateur 'whittlers' as well. They take the form of circus-wagon figures, carousel animals, decoys, busts, figurines, and cigar store Indians. Oriental artists show themselves to have been as proficient with the medium of wood as they were with ivory or hardstone.

When no condition is indicated, the items listed below are assumed to be in excellent condition.

Bust, Ben Franklin, oak, G detail, alligatored finish, 15"......700.00
Comb box, eagle & serpent atop, gr/bl/natural, 1900, 9x8".....125.00
Couple, mid-19th C dress, pnt, early 1900s, 8", pr...........125.00
Eagle, laminated walnut, G detail, 35" wing span.............300.00
Goat, standing on rectangular plinth, orig mc, 7"............325.00
Horse, laminated, sm legs/ft, lg head, glass eyes, 36", EX....2,650.00
Man in coffin, pornographic, Bernhard Vasanaja, 5"..........350.00
Mannequin, articulated, carved hands/ft/face/hair, 33".........300.00
Plaque, A Lincoln relief, pine, Paulenske, '20s, 11x9x1"........65.00
Plaque, NW Coast Indian clan figure, 3-tiered hat, 31x15".....785.00

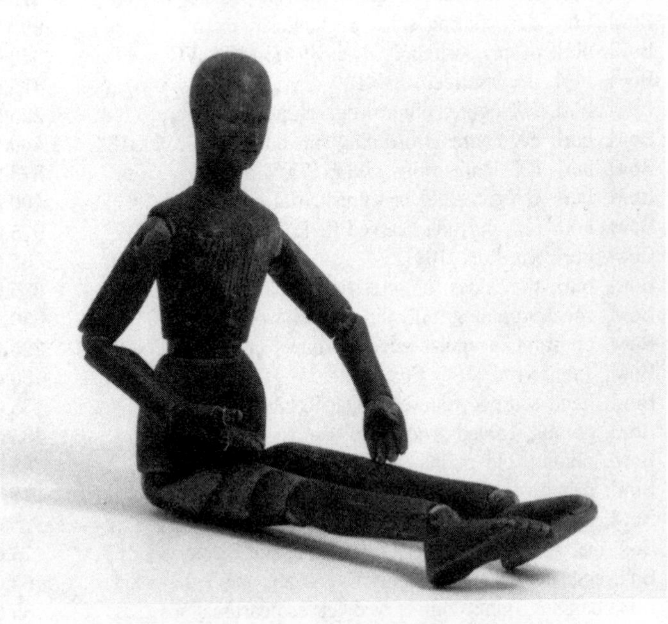

Artist's model, early to mid-19th century, 16", $595.00.

Squirrel eats nut, on mound w/sm mushrooms, fur effect, 9″....75.00
Toy, sea monster w/fish tail, paw ft, teeth, mc pnt, 9″..........550.00
Wall bracket, eagle/snake on rock base support, 1800s, 18″....780.00

Wood, Enoch and Sons

Enoch Wood began his own business in Burslem, England, about 1784. By 1790 he was in partnership with James Caldwell, and until 1818 he was best known for his busts and plaques.

From 1818 to 1846, the firm was known as Enoch Wood and Sons. They produced the underglaze blue transfer-printed dinnerware, much of which was specifically designed for export to America.

When no condition is indicated, the items listed below are assumed to be in mint condition.

Bust, Virgin Mary, ca 1810, 16½″........................2,000.00
Figurine, Equestrian General, on mount, 18th C, 9¾″..........750.00
Pitcher, Sylvan, ironstone w/floral transfer, 8½″................55.00
Plaque, Judgement of Paris, 9″............................425.00
Plate, acanthus relief/transfer, yel glaze earthenware, 8½″......275.00
Plate, English scenery, bl/wht transfer, 10″....................28.00
Plate, turkey in landscape transfer, mc floral, 7½″..............85.00

Woodenware

Woodenware, or treenware as it is sometimes called, generally refers to those wooden items used in the preparation of food, such as spoons, bowls, food molds, etc. Common during the 18th and 19th centuries, these wares were designed from a strictly functional viewpoint, and were used on a day-to-day basis. With the advent of the Industrial Revolution bringing new materials and products, many of the old woodenwares were simply discarded. Today, original hand-crafted American woodewnwares are extremely difficult to find.

When no condition is indicated, the items listed below are assumed to be in excellent condition.

Apple butter stirrer, paddle w/holes/carved leaf, 46″ hdl........48.00
Bowl, bird's eye, oval, 5x24x14″..........................325.00
Bowl, burl, ash w/G figure, scrubbed, knothole, 4½x11½″......225.00
Bowl, burl, ash w/scrubbed finish, well-shaped lip, 6x13½″.....475.00
Bowl, burl, deep flaring sides, rectangular, 6x16″............990.00
Bowl, burl, deeply scalloped, oval, 3½x7½x10″, VG...........350.00
Bowl, burl, dry speckled, 3½x13″ dia......................475.00
Bowl, burl, EX figure, minor edge chips, 3¼x11″............225.00
Bowl, burl, EX figure, protruding rim hdls, oval, 5x11x18″...1,400.00
Bowl, burl, EX figure, worn, 5x17x17½″....................875.00
Bowl, burl, G figure, old brn finish, rim cracks, 4x8″.........400.00
Bowl, burl, rim end hdls, carved ft, EX figure, 5½x12x17″.....975.00
Bowl, burl, rim hdls, 10x12½″............................805.00
Bowl, burl, thin sides, oblong, rim crack, 10x15″............625.00
Bowl, cheese-draining; burl, linen cloth/wood pegs, 20″........850.00
Bowl, chestnut, irregular edge & shape, cracks, 6x17x18″.....225.00
Bowl, eating; rnd, 18th C................................50.00
Bowl, hand scorped, uneven edge, 5x17x16½″...............135.00
Bowl, oblong, carved grooves to use as scrub surface, 28″.....185.00
Bowl, oblong, old patina, age cracks, 4½x11x19″.............65.00
Bowl, primitive, old bl pnt, oblong, 9x25″...................75.00
Bowl, salt; cherry, trn ped base...........................28.00
Box, egg shape, ped base, acorn finial, pnt maple, 8″..........75.00
Box, egg; oblong, Boss-Handy Egg Crate, pat 1910, w/lid.......60.00
Box, hanging; pine, chip-carved leaves/heart/scallops...........85.00
Box, pantry; 2-finger, oval, 2½x6″ L.......................150.00

Bread board, maple, carved leaf edge, octagonal, 11½x11½″....75.00
Bucket, bentwood swing hdl, ca 1900, 5x4½″ top dia.........110.00
Bucket, oak staved, piggin hdl, iron bands, 14½x14″ dia......165.00
Bucket, staves, metal bands, old pnt, 7x10″, NM.............185.00
Bucket, staves, metal bands, wood hdl, orig red, 3½x4½″.......75.00
Bucket, sugar; staves, copper tacks, gr pnt, 15″..............135.00
Bucket, sugar; staves, finger bands/copper tacks, sgn, 14″......75.00
Bucket, sugar; staves, worn bl rpt, 10x9½″, EX...............70.00
Bucket, sugar; staves, worn yel-brn grpt, 9¾″................125.00
Bucket, water; staves, wood-pinned bail, buttonhole hoops.....145.00
Butter curler, tiger maple, hand carved, EX form.............175.00
Butter ladle, maple, short nub hdl, 1800s.....................25.00
Butter ladle, tiger maple, lg smooth hook end, 1700s.........120.00
Butter paddle, chestnut, 8″..............................20.00
Butter paddle, maple, minor edge wear, 12″..................45.00
Butter paddle, maple w/little curl, 7½″......................25.00
Butter paddle, maple w/some curl, age cracks, 10″............55.00
Butter roller, chip-carved yoke, fish-tail hdl, 7″..............295.00
Butter scoop, burl, EX figure, unusual shape hdl, 8½″........400.00
Butter scoop, primitive, 10¼″ L............................45.00
Butter scoop, wide hdl, hook for edge of bowl, 8¾″...........45.00
Butter tamper, right angle hdl.............................85.00
Butter worker, rnd wood center hdl w/2 wood ribbed rollers.....55.00
Cheese curd breaker, hopper w/crank, roller w/wood teeth.....130.00
Cheese drainer, arrow-form spindles, NE, 1700s, sq, 26½″.....900.00
Cheese drainer, solid slanted sides, slat bottom..............120.00
Cheese ladder, pine, 3 rungs, mortised/pegged, sq nails.........70.00
Cheese press, w/pulleys, wood tooth gear, red pnt, 46x19″.....375.00
Churn, staves w/metal bands, pnt traces, 20½″...............105.00
Churn, staves w/wood bands, minor damage, worn finish, 25″..145.00
Clothes line winders, hickory, hand hewn, 1700s..............55.00
Cookie board, Am eagle/shield; flower basket/horn, 8x14″....1,400.00
Cookie board, bunch of grapes w/tin edge, G detail, 5x8″......175.00
Cookie board, cherry, heart/floral; deer/dog/1771, 10x14″......775.00
Cookie board, man on horse/flowers/swags in circle, 12x11″....600.00
Cookie board, man w/ladder, oblong, 4¼x2½x5/8″.............65.00
Cookie board, poplar disk w/fish-tail crest, 14¾″ dia...........75.00
Cookie board, pr of parrots; bk: young girl, 4½x12″..........135.00
Cookie board, walnut, flower basket; Am flag/shield, 7x12″.....800.00
Cookie board, 2 flowers, bk: polka-dot rectangle, 5x9″.........70.00
Cookie board, 2 full figures ea side, primitive, 5x23″..........180.00
Cookie board, 3 coiled snakes w/tin edges, 7x10″............275.00
Cookie board, 3 part: rooster/men & grapes/equestrian, 16″....150.00
Cookie board, 4 part: churning, sweeping, etc, 4x25″.........175.00
Cookie board, 5 scenes w/people/birds/animals ea side, 4x20″..285.00

Cookie press, rooster, 4″ diameter, $295.00.

Curd knife, ornate carved hdl.....65.00
Cutting board, maple, horse-head form, early 1900s, 21x18″.....65.00
Doughnut cutter, all wood w/elongated knob hdl.....85.00
Egg stand, pine, 2 tier: ea holds 1 dozen.....48.00
Flour scoop, long oval bowl, curved shaped hdl, 1700s, 12″.....85.00
Funnel, maple, 1-pc.....140.00
Grease dipper, hand scorped, deep bowl, primitive.....50.00
Herb grinder, ped base, wheel on axle, NE, 1700s, 13″ L.....550.00
Jar, ball shape, elaborated trn finial, old red, 3¾″, EX.....70.00
Jar, burl, G figure, lathe trn, late, 5¼″.....85.00
Jar, maple w/little bird's eye, trn ft & lid, 5¾″.....105.00
Jar, Pease, bulbous, w/lid, 4⅛″, NM.....190.00
Jar, Pease, ftd, orig worn finish, minor crack, 4″.....110.00
Jar, poplar, yel sponged decor on red, G trn, worn, 9″.....500.00
Jug, syrup; staved, lip carved from stave, w/lid, 1700s.....465.00
Knife, dough; pistol-grip hdl, 25″ L.....75.00
Lemon squeezer on fr, hinged w/indent/drains/3 legs, 1850s.....200.00
Maple sugar dipper, long hdl.....235.00
Measure, staves, for peck, other end ½ peck, mk RCW, 12″.....75.00
Mortar, burl, w/lignum vitae pestle, worn/cracks, 5¾″.....145.00
Noggin, all wood, stave constructed, hinged lid, 11″.....200.00
Noggin, maple, 1-pc, 7″.....220.00
Pastry roller, carved heart/stars, tin cutting edges, 6½″.....115.00
Pastry roller, chip carved/foliage, trn hdl, 13¾″.....125.00
Peel, pine, 6″ hdl, 1800s, 16″ dia.....55.00
Peel, short hdl, tapered to edge, 1-pc.....85.00
Pestle, curly maple, trn, 11½″.....40.00
Pestle, curly maple, trn, 18½″.....65.00
Potato masher, maple, mid-19th C, 12½x5″.....18.00
Reamer, lemon; hand hewn, bulbous, 1-pc.....175.00
Reamer, lemon; mushroom knob on end of hdl.....85.00
Reamer, wooden, tube shape, carved wheel design, bulb hdl.....85.00
Rolling pin, bird's eye maple, 17″.....55.00
Rolling pin, curly maple, 16½″, EX.....85.00
Rolling pin, dbl roller, early 1800s, 13½″.....250.00
Rolling pin, maple, button-knob hdls, 1-pc wood, lg.....45.00
Rolling pin, tiger maple, well-shaped knob hdls, 16¾″.....75.00
Rum cask, charred oak, 6 iron bands, wood stopper, 11x7½″.....45.00
Salt, trn, yel varnish, 3⅞x4″.....40.00
Salt box, curved bk w/hole for hanging, w/lid, old pine.....65.00
Sander, boxwood, rnd, 3½″.....45.00
Sander, saucer top, bulbous bottom, 3⅜″.....40.00
Scoop, hand scorped, long rounded oval bowl, 15½″.....110.00
Scrub stick, corrugated, hdld, 1-pc.....150.00
Sieve, horsehair, mc plaid.....175.00
Sieve, winnowing; hickory hdls, rosehead nails, 46″ dia.....285.00
Sieve, winnowing; splint bottom, 22″ dia.....295.00
Skimmer, clamshell shaped, 7½″.....175.00
Smoothing board, birch w/4 compass stars, horse hdl, 29″ L.....800.00
Smoothing board, stylized/EX form, horse hdl, 1817, 26½″.....775.00
Spoon, cherry, 1 end stirrer/other end scoop, 6½″.....95.00
Spoon, deep bowl, fanned coffin-end hdl w/incising, 4¼″.....250.00
Spoon, egg-shape bowl, pot-edge hook on hdl end, 13″.....85.00
Spoon, hand carved, flat rounded bowl, 19″.....25.00
Spoon, maple w/some curl, good patina, worn, 12¾″.....55.00
Stocking stretcher, curly maple, some worm holes, 17½″.....32.50
Sugar bowl, lid/wire bail, Painesville, O, bulbous, 4½″.....350.00
Swigler, birch, inset ends, 1-pc, for rum.....60.00
Tankard, staved, hdl, 2 buttonhole hoops, 1700s, 8x8″.....575.00
Tankard, staved ft & lid closing, 7″.....350.00
Tub, staved, tin banded/wood hdls, brn-red pnt, 7x13x18″.....115.00
Tub, sugar; staved, fingered lid, buttonhole hoops, 1700s.....175.00
Wash board, dbl faced, tusk tenon mortised, cut nails.....50.00
Water keg, field; staved, finger-lap, rosehead nails, pegs.....285.00

World's Fairs and Expos

Since 1851 and the Crystal Palace Exhibition in London, World's Fairs and Expositions have taken place at a steady pace, except during wartime. These events have been the source of tens of thousands of souvenirs, and collectors today find the possibility of locating representative examples an exciting challenge.

When no condition is indicated, the items listed below are assumed to be in excellent to mint condition.

Key: T/P—Trylon & Perisphere

St. Louis World's Fair, enameled tin cup, $125.00.

1876 Centennial, Philadelphia

Book, Centennial Diary, 32 pgs of general info, 3x5″.....22.50
Handkerchief, 23x28″.....75.00
Magazine, souvenir.....35.00
Medallion, president of expo: J Hawley, wood, 2½″.....90.00
Medallion, wood, shows main building, 3″.....48.00
Plate, ironstone w/mc transfer: Phila Exhibition, 8½″.....25.00
Towel, Geo Washington, shield, woven design, wht, 17x29″.....75.00

1893 Columbian, Chicago

Book, Columbian Gallery, portfolio of photos, b/w, 250 pg.....25.00
Book, Columbian World's Fair Atlas, general, 194 pg.....25.00
Book, Dream City, photos, Thompson, over 200 pg, 11x14″.....25.00
Book, Graphic History of the Fair, Engelhard, illus/240 pg.....27.50
Book, Magic City, 300 photos, b/w, Buel, 11x13″.....25.00
Book, Story of Columbus & World's Columbian Expo.....35.00
Book, World's Fair Thru a Camera, over 80 pg, 5¼x6½″.....12.00
Coin, Columbian/1893/Exposition, silver metal.....15.00
Coin, half dollar, US Commemorative, silver.....15.00
Creamer & sugar bowl, hdls & shells w/gold, Coalport, sm.....150.00
Folder, photo of The Old Mill, cb, 4½x5½″.....5.00
Handkerchief, silk, Administration Bldg.....28.00
Hatchet, Geo Washington, Libbey Glass, 8″ hdl, 4″ blade.....37.50
Match safe, building, lithographed tin, mc.....80.00
Medal, design of Machinery Hall, high relief, wood.....90.00
Medal, St-Gaudens/reverse: Barber, presentation case, sgn.....100.00
Paperweight, Am Wine Co.....45.00
Paperweight, Utah State Bldg, Libbey Glass Co.....50.00
Pitcher, milk; amber optic, bulbous, applied hdl, 6¾″.....110.00

Plate, Lagoon Looking South/World's Fair, wht china, 8″.......32.50
Plate, lusterless wht w/transfer of fair, Mt WA, 7¾″............75.00
Playing cards, different scenes on ea, complete................75.00
Postcard, Agricultural Building, goldsmith, trimmed edges........5.00
Postcards, various scenes, official, Goldsmith.................15.00
Spoon, Art Palace in bowl, SP, minor wear...................10.00
Spoon, demitasse; bust of Columbus at top, plain bowl.........10.00
Stick pin, face of Columbus.............................35.00
Stone litho, ferris wheel, under glass, 20x24″.................65.00
Straight razor, fair building etched on blade..................65.00
Tablecloth, wht linen, dtd, 48x76″.........................55.00
Tickets, admission, 10 different, set......................100.00
Tray, emb Machinery Hall, border decor, dk metal, 3x3″.......15.00
Tumbler, Administration Bldg, wht frost design, glass, 3½″......25.00
Tumbler, Art Palace, wht frost design, glass, 3½x2½″..........25.00
Tumbler, cranberry border...............................45.00
Watch fob, w/keystone case opener, silver colored metal........42.50

1898 Omaha

Sheet music, Sod Shanty................................25.00
Teaspoon, etched bowl..................................28.00

1901 Pan American

Booklet, Official Views of Pan Am Expo, Arnold, 50 pg, EX....15.00
Booklet, Souvenir of the Great Pan-Am Expo, illus, 48 pg......10.00
Mug, pottery, w/eagle..................................40.00
Playing cards, different view of expo on each card.............40.00

1904 St. Louis

Award medal, bronze, orig case..........................50.00
Match safe, Lewis & Clark...............................45.00
Mirror, pocket; mc fair scene, celluloid.....................60.00
Paperweight, mc scene, glass............................30.00
Picture fr, cardboard w/florals/Exhibition Hall, 9½x7″..........25.00
Plate, lace edge, glass, Festival Hall & Cascades, 7″...........20.00
Playing cards, different scene on ea card, complete............85.00
Postcard, hold-to-light, various scenes, Cupples...............30.00
Postcard, silver bkground, various scenes, Cupples..............7.50
Purse, leather, braided hdl, Cascades/date on front, 9x5″.......35.00
Ribbon, Geo Washington, woven silk.......................100.00
Souvenir coin of admission, brass, #d.......................30.00
Spoon, demitasse; sterling...............................25.00
Spoon, emb building in bowl, sterling.......................50.00
Watch fob, emb scenes, nickel, 3-part......................60.00
Watch fob, Jefferson & Napoleon, emb, aluminum, 4-part.......60.00

1915 Panama Pacific

Bell, brass, eagle base..................................75.00
Book, Official Souvenir View Book, 40 pg, 9½x12½″..........20.00
Book, The Exposition, color centerfold, illus Reid, 9x12″.......17.50
Book, The Jewel City, Macamber/Williams illus, 204 pg, EX.....20.00
Booklet, #1, Hercules cover, color studies...................25.00
Booklet, 'Snapshots'....................................10.00
Booklet, Views of the Panama Pacific Expo, photos, 24 pg......12.00
Folder, #11, bird's-eye view of fair, color, 4x6″.............12.50
Folder, Painted Desert Exhibit, minor edge wear...............5.00
Medal, Liberty Bell on yel & bl ribbon, metal, 3¾″...........15.00
Medal, male & female nudes/building/wreath, gilded bronze.....50.00
Mirror, pocket; Independent Order Foresters.................37.50
Pin-back button, bl & wht bull's eye on gold bk, ¾″............5.00
Pin-back button, red/wht/bl lettering, celluloid................15.00
Postcard, Oregon State building, mc, not mailed...............3.00
Spoon, Palace of Horticulture/Tower of Jewels, 5½″...........22.50
Tie clip, gold globes on wht/red, enamel bk/elliptical, 1⅛″......10.00
Tip tray, Buffalo Brewing Co............................70.00
Tray, emb design of 5 fair buildings, metal, rnd, 5″............15.00
Tray, emb Palace of Horticulture, wht metal, 9x3½″...........12.00

1933 Chicago

Ash tray, Chrysler building, copper..........................6.00
Book, La Belgique Pictoresque, on Belgium village, 60 pg......12.00
Book, Official Pictures, Donnelley, over 60 pgs, 7x10″.........12.00
Booklet, Pullman's Diamond Jubilee, illus, 10 pg, M............7.00
Bracelet, Century of Progress comet w/6 scenes, copper........17.50
Bracelet, Century of Progress design, silver colored metal.......15.00
Brochure, map of fair, Ed Price Co, opens to 11x9″............3.00
Catalog, Exhibition of Paintings & Sculpture, 120 pg..........10.00
Cigarette lighter, Match King, strike on side, blk, 1x1½″.......20.00
Cocktail shaker, recipes for drinks on side, 11x4″.............50.00
Folder, postcard; 16 color scenes of fair, unused...............8.00
Lucky penny, Indian head/Fort Dearborn, copper, 2¼″.........10.00
Needle folder, fair buildings, mc, 6½x4½″...................15.00
Newspaper, Big News, Sinclair Oil, Dinosaur Exhibit photo.......5.00
Penny, souvenir, skyride scene, elongated.....................4.00
Plate, Blk Forest, raised border, octagonal, Pickard, 7½″.......25.00
Shaker, Carillon Tower/Travel Building, metal, 3″, pr..........10.00
Shot glass, false bottom w/pr of dice, clear plastic top..........15.00
Sign, shaped like German beer stein, cb, 14″..................15.00
Spoon, Administration Building in bowl, hdl designs...........12.50
Spoon, Court of States Building in bowl, Indian on hdl.........15.00
Spoon, Science Court in bowl, Wm Rogers..................12.50
Ticket stub, admission....................................8.00
Tray, center design/4 edge designs, oblong, metal, 6½x3½″.....10.00
Tray, crumb; emb designs, various scenes, 2-part..............12.50
Tray, mc scene of Lama Temple, round, tin, 4″...............20.00
Tray, Travel & Transportation Bldg/Belguim Village, 5x3½″.....10.00
Umbrella, Japanese style, paper w/wood hdl, EX..............15.00

1939 New York

Ash tray, T/P design, brass, 4½″..........................12.50
Book, Official Souvenir Book, over 100 pg, 10½x14″, EX......22.50
Book, Railroads on Parade, many photos, 20 pg, 10x13″.......12.00
Book, Your World of Tomorrow, mc cover/illus, 24 pg, 9x12″...10.00
Cake server, silverplate, Geo Washington on hdl.............30.00
Cane...20.00
Cigarette tin, rare.......................................110.00
Clock, travel type, folds into own metal case, red/bl face.......100.00
Coaster, Federal Building, mc fair scenes, 3″................10.00
Coaster, Hall of Communication, mc fair scenes, tin, 3″........10.00
Coaster, US Steel Building, mc fair scenes, tin, 3″............10.00
Fish knife, mc, 5″.......................................28.00
Knife, mk made in USA, T/P design, glass, orig cb box, 8½″....30.00
Letter, on NY World's Fair stationery.......................15.00
Matchbook cover, mk Visit the Wrigley Exhibit, T/P design......5.00
Mirror, T/P design in bl, bl letters, 2½x3½″.................12.50
Newspaper, NY Herald Tribune, color & b/w ads, 64 pg.........7.00
Pin, T/P design, imp New York World's Fair 1939, w/chain.....12.50
Plate, Geo Washington, T/P design, 8 scenes, bl/wht, 11″......50.00
Pocket knife, Boy Scout type, multi-purpose blades, mk........20.00
Spoon, Borden Bldg in bowl, T/P design on hdl, bk mk, 6″......7.50
Spoon, mk on bk Wallace Al, NYWF, T/P design on hdl, 6″.....6.00
Tray, Administration Building scene, dull metal, 7½x4″.........12.50

Wrought Iron

Until the middle of the 19th century, almost all the metal hand forged in America was made from a material called wrought iron. When wrought iron rusts, it appears grainy, while the mild steel that was used later shows no grain, but pits to an orange peel surface. This is an important aid in determining the age of an ironwork piece.

When no condition is indicated, the items listed below are assumed to be in near mint condition.

Andiron, crook neck w/heart finial, G detail, 18½", pr........475.00
Broiler, primitive, trivet size, 7x14¼"........................40.00
Broiler, rotary, sq rack, 20½" L..............................50.00
Broiler, w/hdl, 10x18"..65.00
Caliper, dbl, w/twisted hdl, pitted, 17"......................70.00
Candlestick, spiral, old wood base & push-up, 8½"............115.00
Dipper, long hdl, 22¼"..18.00
Dough scraper, tooled hdl/initials/1774, 5½", VG.............165.00
Fork, brass inlay lines/foliage/heart/1824 in hdl, 17".......250.00
Fork, elongated diamond hdl, 16¼".............................90.00
Fork, tooled flower on hdl, 9½"...............................35.00
Fork, well-shape hdl, pitted, 19½"............................65.00
Fork, 2-tine, well-shaped hdl, 15¾"...........................30.00
Hinge, strap; carved bird's head end, 38½", pr................90.00
Hinge, strap; primitive tulip-like ends, 44½", pr.............80.00
Hinge, strap; w/rattail pintels, 4 mtd on brd, ea 5" L.......125.00
Hook, S-form, 13" L...15.00
Kettle shelf, penny ft, blk pnt, 12½x11x13¾"..................30.00
Lighting device, socket on adjustable spring-clip rod, 33"...245.00
Loom light, rush holder w/candle socket counterweight, 18"...215.00
Meat hook, 4¼" & 5", pr.......................................40.00
Ornament, ceiling; primitive, flower & pine cone, 9½x13½".....85.00
Pan, spider base, 12" hdl, 7½" W..............................70.00
Peel, flattened area in hdl, faceted finial, 40½" L...........80.00
Peel, ram's horn finial, 49".................................115.00
Rack, utensil; arch brackets/scroll crest, G detail, 13½"....250.00
Rush light, knob counterbalance, 9½"..........................60.00
Rush light, tripod, candle socket counterweight, 15½"........185.00
Sconce, candle; primitive, w/scrolled detail, 20", pr........100.00
Sconce, 12 prickets for candles, scrolled arms, 30", pr......130.00
Skewer, twist/tooled hdl, 30" L...............................10.00
Skimmer, primitive, 18" & 18½", pr............................30.00
Spatula, fancy hdl, 19¾"......................................75.00
Spatula, tapered hdl, good scrolled hanger, 20¾"..............45.00
Spatula, twist hdl, sm blade, 14".............................15.00
Spatula, well-shaped, 17½"....................................40.00
Taster, European, primitive, sm w/tooled hdl, 8" & 9½", pr....80.00
Thumb latch, 9½"..10.00
Tongs, ember; 7¾"...55.00
Trammel, sawtooth, 34"..85.00
Utensil rack, 2 pine tree-like finials, edge tooling, 12¾"....95.00
Utensil rack, 3 scrolled devices in ornate crest, 30" W......250.00
Utensil rack, 5 hooks, stylized floral, pnt, 16" L...........325.00

Yellowware

Yellowware is an inexpensive, plain type of earthenware, so called because of the color of the clay used in its manufacture. Pieces may vary from buff to yellow to nearly brown; the glaze itself is clear. Some yellowware was decorated with blue, white, brown, or black bands; only seldom was it relief molded.

Yellowware was made to a large extent in East Liverpool, Ohio, but other Ohio potteries, as well as some in Pennsylvania and Vermont also produced it. English yellowware has a harder body composition. Because it was not often marked, it is almost impossible to identify the manufacturer.

There is a growing interest in this type of pottery, and consequently, prices are continually increasing.

When no condition is indicated, the items listed below are assumed to be in excellent condition.

Set of five nested bowls, floral sprig decoration, marked Jefford's Pottery, Philad. PA, largest: 8" diameter, $250.00 for the set.

Bank, pig, brn mottle...55.00
Bank, spaniel dog, brn splashed/gr base rim, 5¼".............195.00
Bedpan, w/flying turtle.......................................50.00
Bowl, batter; emb leaf, wht slip w/in, ca 1860s, 6x13"........90.00
Bowl, brn bands, 15½x7".......................................45.00
Bowl, cottage scene, 7".......................................18.00
Bowl, emb design, ft ring, 3x5¾", NM..........................25.00
Bowl, lg rim spout, wht band w/brn stripes/bl seaweed, 8"....180.00
Bowl, mixing; gr & wht bands, deep yel, 5½x10¾"...............48.00
Bowl, nested; bl bands/wht stripes, 5⅜" to 7½", set of 3......55.00
Bowl, serving; slant sides, mk Sharpe Warranted, 3x9½"........85.00
Bowl, w/advertising, 7".......................................20.00
Bowl, wht stripes, 5½"..12.00
Bowl, wht stripes, 8½"..20.00
Bowl, wide wht band w/brn borders, 3⅜x7", EX..................50.00
Chamber pot, wht band, 2".....................................50.00
Chamber pot, wht band w/brn stripes, bl seaweed, 5¾x8"........60.00
Chamber pot, wht line decor, w/hdl, 4¾x7".....................50.00
Crock, butter; wht bands......................................58.00
Crock, butter; wht/brn stripes, no lid, ½-gal.................42.50
Crock, pantry; Sugar..85.00
Crock, salt; emb peacocks, hanging crest, amber runs, 4x6"....85.00
Custard cup, 2 bl bands, 2½x3"................................14.00
Jar, beater; wht stripes, Johnson Bros, Franklin, MN..........50.00
Jar, wht band w/brn stripes & gr seaweed, w/lid, 6½x8"........95.00
Mold, pineapple in scalloped oval, 4⅞"........................65.00
Mug, checkerboard in bl, stains, 3"...........................35.00
Mug, cobalt bands, straight sides, late 1800s, Peoria.........50.00
Mug, wht slip bands, no mk, late 1800s........................55.00
Pan, emb flowers on bottom, 3x10".............................58.00
Pie plate, finger crimped edge, purple glaze, 10".............55.00
Pitcher, bl sponge top/base bands, good luck sgn emb, 6½"....125.00
Pitcher, brn stripe, Red Wing, 7".............................75.00
Pitcher, buttermilk; rust/bl sponge, emb diamond/acorn, 9"...145.00
Rolling pin, 15"...150.00

Zanesville Glass

Glassware was produced in Zanesville, Ohio from as early as 1815 until 1851. Two companies produced clear and colored holloware pieces in five characteristic patterns: (1) diamond faceted, (2) broken swirls, (3) vertical swirls, (4) perpendicular fluting, (5) un-patterned with scalloped or fluted rims and strap handles. The most readily identified product is perhaps the whiskey bottles made in the vertical swirl pattern, often called globular swirls because of their full round body. Their necks vary in width--some have a ringed rim and some are collared. They were made in several colors: amber, light green, and light aquamarine the most common.

When no condition is indicated, the items listed below are assumed to be in mint condition.

Beaker, amber, 2¾"....150.00
Bottle, club; 24 slightly swirled ribs, dk yel-olive, 8"....1,250.00
Bottle, globular, amber, 5¼"....375.00
Bottle, globular, applied hdl, dk amber, 5", NM....1,550.00
Bottle, globular, dk to gold-amber, 11¾"....800.00
Bottle, 16-rib left-hand swirl, amethyst, 5⅝"....750.00
Bottle, 24 swirl ribs, globular, amber, good imp, 9"....600.00
Bottle, 24 swirl ribs, globular, aqua, 7⅞"....450.00
Bottle, 24 swirl ribs, globular, dk red-amber, 7¾"....550.00
Bottle, 24 swirl ribs, globular, grass gr, 8½"....1,100.00
Bottle, 24 vertical melon ribs, dk amber, 7", NM....550.00
Bottle, 24-rib broken swirl, globular, gold-amber, 5", NM....2,700.00
Bowl, milk; folded rim, amber, 3¾x8½", EX....450.00
Compote, applied ft, knop stem, amber, 3½x5½"....2,000.00
Creamer, 10-diamond, applied hdl, brilliant lt gr, 4", NM....1,750.00
Flask, chestnut, 10-diamond, dk amber, 5", NM....750.00
Flask, chestnut, 10-diamond, gold-amber, 4½", EX....600.00
Flask, chestnut, 24 vertical ribs, aqua, ½-pt, 5½"....115.00
Flask, chestnut; G'father, 24 vertical rib, gold-amber, 8"....1,000.00
Flask, chestnut; G'father, 24-rib broken swirl, amber, 8½"....2,700.00
Flask, chestnut; 10-diamond, brilliant lt gr, 5"....800.00
Flask, chestnut; 10-diamond, brilliant yel-amber, 5⅜"....1,300.00
Flask, chestnut; 24 swirl ribs, amber, 5", NM....350.00
Flask, chestnut; 24 swirl ribs, aqua, pint, 6½"....150.00
Flask, chestnut; 24 swirl ribs, dk red-amber, 6", EX....300.00
Flask, chestnut; 24 swirl ribs, EX imp, gr, 6¼", NM....800.00
Flask, chestnut; 24 vertical ribs, gold-amber, 5", NM....300.00
Flask, chestnut; 24 vertical ribs, gold-amber, 7", NM....625.00
Flask, chestnut; 24 vertical ribs, yel-gr, 5¾"....550.00
Flask, chestnut; 24-rib broken swirl, gold-amber, 5", NM....350.00
Flip, 24 swirl ribs, lt gr, rim flake, 5¾"....375.00
Inkwell, 10-diamond, brilliant lt gr, 2¼"....5,750.00
Inkwell, 24 vertical ribs, gold-amber, 1⅞"....800.00
Inkwell, 24 vertical ribs, straight sides, aqua, 2⅝"....140.00
Pan, gr, expanded 24-rib, out-folded rim, 9½"....550.00
Pan, 10-diamond, folded rim, aqua, 1⅝x4¾"....725.00
Pan, 10-diamond, folded-in rim, brilliant lt gr, 1⅜x5½"....2,000.00
Pan, 24 ribs, folded rim, gold-amber, 1½x5⅜"....650.00
Pan, 24 ribs, folded-in rim, amber, 1½x6"....2,000.00
Pan, 24 ribs, straight in bottom, swirl at rim, aqua, 6½"....375.00

Left to right: Pitcher, 24 swirled ribs and applied ribbed handle, light green, near mint condition, 6", $450.00; Sugar bowl, double dome lid with folded rim and ball finial, bluish-aqua, near mint, 7", $2,600.00; Flip glass, 24-rib broken swirl, pale green, small rim flake, 5¾", $375.00.

Pitcher, 24 swirl ribs, rib hdl, lt gr, 6", NM....450.00
Salt cellar, urn shape, flared rim, ftd, dk amber, 3½", NM....1,400.00
Sugar bowl, dbl dome lid w/ball finial, bl-aqua, 6¾", NM....2,600.00
Sugar bowl, open, amber, pontil flake, 2¾x5"....85.00
Sugar bowl, 24 vertical ribs, dbl dome lid, amber, 5½x7"....8,100.00

Zsolnay

Zsolnay pottery has been made in Hungary since the mid-1800s. Early wares were highly ornamental--some with high relief Art Nouveau motifs, others depending on surface decoration for their appeal. Today, the firm produces figurines with an iridescent glaze which are becoming very collectible.

When no condition is indicated, the items listed below are assumed to be in mint condition.

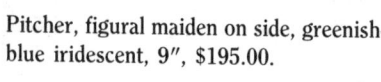

Pitcher, figural maiden on side, greenish-blue iridescent, 9", $195.00.

Bowl, boat form, allover mc on cream, reticulated, 3½x13½"....495.00
Bowl, dbl horn, reticulated, florals, gold lined, 7½x12"....475.00
Bowl, rose Persian motif, bl steeple castle mk, sq, 6"....175.00
Box, gold/gr irid, w/lid, 4x5"....70.00
Ewer, gold/gr irid, Art Nouveau molded designs, old mk....230.00
Figurine, boxer dog, 5"....60.00
Figurine, buffalo, 6x9¾"....130.00
Figurine, eagle, gold/gr irid, 6½"....75.00
Figurine, fox, gold/gr irid, 4½"....50.00
Figurine, French poodle, gold/gr irid, 3½x4"....45.00
Figurine, giraffe, gold/gr irid, 7½"....60.00
Figurine, nude on plinth, 11x4½"....265.00
Figurine, pr bears, 5x7½"....220.00
Figurine, pr polar bears on plinth, gold/gr irid, 4½x7½"....150.00
Figurine, reclining fawns, 3½x6¼"....125.00
Figurine, retriever, gold/gr irid, 7x9"....85.00
Figurine, spaniel, seated, gold/gr irid, sgn, 5"....80.00
Jar, petal; reticulated, enamel, EX....225.00
Plate, tan shell w/red/gold flowers, reticulated, 8½"....180.00
Tray, celery; floral, pastel, pierced band, lustre, 13x7½"....175.00
Vase, allover decor, reticulated, mc on cream, 8"....495.00
Vase, allover reticulated, dbl wall, bl/gold/tan, 6½"....360.00
Vase, climbing nude, irid, rare, 14"....150.00
Vase, flagstone decor on red, gold mk, ovoid, 5½"....95.00
Vase, irid, 4½"....75.00
Wall bracket, pierced funnel form, foliate devices, 8", pr....500.00

We take this opportunity to express our sincere gratitude and appreciation to each person who contributed to the preparation of this guide. It was our goal this year to increase the number of categories and thanks to the cooperation of those listed, that goal was attained. We believe the credibility of our book is greatly enhanced through their efforts. Thank you all.

Charles & Barbara Adams
Middleboro, Massachusetts

Geneva D. Addy
Winterset, Iowa

American Graniteware Association
Downers Grove, Illinois

James Anderson
New Brighton, Minnesota

Tim Anderson
Provo, Utah

Warren R. Anderson
Provo, Utah

The Antiquarian Old Book Store
Portsmouth, New Hampshire

Linda Antonation
Bellevue, Washington

Dick & Ellie Archer
Yardley, Pennsylvania

Lillian Baker
Gardena, California

Michael Baker
Moundsville, West Virginia

Roger Baker
Woodside, California

Kit Barry
Brattleboro, Vermont

Scott Benjamin
Los Angeles, California

Phyllis & Tom Bess
Tulsa, Oklahoma

Ed Beth
Williamsburg, Missouri

John E. Bilane
Union, New Jersey

Sandra V. Bondhus
Watertown, Connecticut

Dick & Wauneta Bosworth
Kansas City, Missouri

Rick Botts
Des Moines, Iowa

Don & Irma Brewer
Battle Creek, Michigan

Wm. J. Brinkley
McLeansboro, Illinois

Jim Broom
Effingham, Illinois

LeRoy F. Bruggink
Cedar Grove, Wisconsin

Robert Glenn Bumbera
Port Clinton, Ohio

Phyllis Mills Burton
Midlothian, Virginia

Jim Calison
Walden, New York

Tod Carley
Int'l Society of Antique Scale Collectors
Deerfield, Illinois

Sally S. Carver
Chestnut Hill, Massachusetts

Jackie Chamberlain
La Canada, California

Jack Chipman
Redondo Beach, California

Angelana Clark
Moundsville, West Virginia

Joe R. & Wilma Clark
Reynoldsburg, Ohio

Bea Cohen
Easton, Pennsylvania

Mary E. Collier
San Jose, California

Robert & Deloris Cowan
Appleton, Wisconsin

Robert L. Daly
Flint, Michigan

John Danis
Rockford, Illinois

Gael deCourtivron
Sarasota, Florida

Jack Dempsey
Redondo Beach, California

Dennis Dillon
Williamsburg, Missouri

DLK Collectables & Nostalgia
Johnstown, Pennsylvania

L.R. 'Les' Docks
San Antonio, Texas

Ron Donnelly
Panama City Beach, Florida

Robert A. Doyle
Fishkill, New York

Louise Dumont
Coventry, Rhode Island

Ken & Jackie Durham
Washington, DC

William Durham
Belvidere, Illinois

William Edgerton
Darien, Connecticut

Bill Edwards
Rushville, Indiana

Delleen Enge
Ojai, California

Louella Epstein
Washington, DC

Zaney Erchul
San Diego, California

Roberta Etter
Oradell, New Jersey

Joseph Ferrara
Newburgh, New York

Gene Florence
Lexington, Kentucky

Tobin Fraley
Oakwood, California

Terry Friend
Galax, Virginia

Ruth Forsythe
Galena, Ohio

Daniel Fortney
Milwaukee, Wisconsin

Ron Fox
North Babylon, New York

William Galaway
Belvidere, Illinois

Mary Frank Gaston
Bryan, Texas

Tony George
El Toro, California

Steve Geppi
Baltimore, Maryland

Walter Glenn
Atlanta, Georgia

Belle Godwin
Atlanta, Georgia

Bruce C. Greenberg
Sykesville, Maryland

Jeff Greenberg
Brooklyn, New York

Woody Griffith
Crystal Lake, Illinois

Everett Grist
Charleston, Illinois

Norman Haas
Quincy, Michigan

Doris & Burdell Hall
Morton, Illinois

Dave Harris
Kokomo, Indiana

Warren D. Harris
Carmichael, California

The Harrison Fisher Society
San Diego, California

John Hathaway
Bryant Pond, Maine

Ted Haun
Kokomo, Indiana

Richard A. Haussmann
Montgomery, Illinois

Ron Heberlee
Scottsdale, Arizona

Carl Heetderks
Zeeland, Michigan 49464

Randy Hilst
Pekin, Illinois

Gene Hochman
Livingston, New Jersey

Pat & Don Hoffmann
Aurora, Illinois

Dee Hooks
Lawrenceville, Illinois

Lar Hothem
Lancaster, Ohio

Hardy Hudson
Longwood, Florida

Marje Hunsaker
White Salmon, Washington

Ralph Jaarsma
Pella, Iowa

Patricia A. Johnson
Torrance, California

Wes Johnson
Louisville, Kentucky

Jim & Kathy Kelly
Pittsburgh, Pennsylvania

Lorrie Kitchen & Dan Tucker
Toledo, Ohio

Mr. & Mrs. Jerry & Gerry Kline
Maumee, Ohio

Bob Laroski
Louisville, Kentucky

Eloise LaVigne
Charleston, South Carolina

Mildred & Ralph Lechner
Mechanicsville, Virginia

Gerard Leduc
Newburgh, New York

Len Linscott
Titusville, Florida

Jeffrey Lipschutz
Maitland, FLorida

Gloria List
Santa Monica, California

Dee Long
Lacon, Illinois

Jennie D. Long
Kingsburg, California

David Longest
Clarksville, Indiana

Paul J. Longo
South Orleans, Massachusetts

Carl F. Luckey
Killen, Alabama

Clarence & Betty Maier
Montgomeryville, Pennsylvania

Cork Marcheschi
Minneapolis, Minnesota

Richard G. Marden
Wolfeboro, New Hampshire

Mollie Helen McCain
Jackson, Michigan

Louis K. & Susan P. Meisel
New York City

Patty Messenger
Bowling Green, Ohio

Carolyn Moore
Bowling Green, Ohio

National Cambridge Collectors Inc.
Cambridge, Ohio

Boyd W. Nedry
Comstock Park, Michigan

Betty Newbound
Union Lake, Michigan

The Occupied Japan Club
Louisville, Kentucky

Old World Antiques
Kansas City, Missouri

Steve Oliphant
Van Nuys, California

Ruth Osborne
Higginsport, Ohio

Pat & Laurie O'Shea
Holyoke, Massachusetts

Lowell Owens
New Hartford, New York

Marge Pappin
Camillus, New York

Dick Pardini
Stockton, California

Pen Fancier's Club
Dunedin, Florida

Louis Picek
West Branch, Iowa

Gene Price
Erwin, Tennessee

Frank W. Rachubinski
Montreal, Canada

Ferill J. Rice
Kaukauna, Wisconsin 54130

Debbie & Bill Rees
Zanesville, Ohio

Brenda Roberts
Marshall, Missouri

Joleen A. Robison
Lawrence, Kansas

Barbara Rosen
Wayne, New Jersey

John & Barbara Rudisill
Medfield, Massachusetts

R.J. Sayers
Andrews, Texas

Marianne Schneider
Hallowell, Maine

Fred & Lila Shrader
Crescent City, California

Allan Smith
Sherman, Texas

Pat Smith
Independence, Missouri

Wm. H. Smith
Madison, California

Denny Stapp
Georgetown, Indiana

Gwendolyn L. Stebbins
Davison, Michigan

Lois & Milt Steinfeld
Westfield, New Jersey

The Sterling Shop
Silverton, Oregon

Marvin & Jeanette Stofft
Tell City, Indiana

Rosella Tinsley
Osawatomie, Kansas

Bob Toke
Boston, Massachusetts

Ruth Van Kuren
Clarence Center, New York

Joan F. Van Patten
Rexford, New York

Peter Warns
Emerson, New Jersey

Margaret & Kenn Whitmyer
Gahanna, Ohio

Doug Wiesehan
St. Charles, Missouri

Don Williams
Ottumwa, Iowa

Robert F. Willis
Grand Rapids, Michigan

Ron L. Willis
Moore, Oklahoma

Roy M. Willis
Lebanon Junction, Kentucky

Roger Wilson
Boston, Massachusetts

D.D. Woollard, Jr.
Bridgeton, Missouri

Alabama

Carl F. Luckey Communications
Rt. 4, Box 301, Lingerlost Tr., Killen, 35645
Freelance writer specializing in art antiques & collectibles

Arizona

Heberlee, Ron
8011 E. Roosevelt, Scottsdale, 85257
Specializing in English pottery

California

Baker, Lillian
15237 Chanera Ave., Gardena, 90249
Author Collector Books on jewelry, hatpins & hatpin holders, miniatures

Baker's Lady Luck Emporium
Baker, Roger
Box 4117, Woodside, 94062; 415-851-7188
Specializing in Saloon Americana - advertising, gambling, bar bottles, cigar lighters

Benjamin, Scott
7250 Franklin Ave. #216, Los Angeles, 90046; 213-876-2056
Specializing in gasoline pump globes

Bettinger, Robert
Box 376, Moffett Field, 95132; 408-946-5972
Specializing in American art pottery

Chamberlain, Jackie
1520 Foothill Blvd., La Canada, 91011; 818-790-5416
Specializing in holiday collectibles, antique reference books, Teddy bears, pewter ice cream molds

California Spectrum
Chipman, Jack
Box 1429, Redondo Beach, 90278
Specializing in California & other American ceramics

Collier, Mary E.
5311 Prune Blossom Dr., San Jose
Specializing in Cordey porcelain

Enge, Delleen
912 N. Signal, Ojai, 93023
Author of *Franciscan Ware*, specializing in Catalina Island pottery, Franciscan pottery, matching service by mail

Joezane Antiques
Erchul, Zaney
715 Avalon Court, San Diego, 92109
Specializing in old hatpins & hatpin holders

George, Tony
El Toro, 92630; 714-951-1310
Specializing in watch fobs

Harris, Warren D.
6130 Rampart Dr., Carmichael, 95608
Specializing in thermometers

Johnson, Patricia A.
Box 1221, Torrance, 90505
Specializing in open salts

Nelson, Maxine
Box 1686, Huntington Beach, 92647
Author Collector Books on *Vernon Kiln* pottery

Nonesuch Gallery
List, Gloria
1211 Montana Ave., Santa Monica, 90403
Specializing in American Indian artifacts, cowboy relics, American folk art, Southwest textiles, Santos & Retablos, Mexican Colonial

Long, Jennie D.
Box 522, Kingsburg, 93631; 209-897-5077
Author of *An Album of Candy Containers Volumes I & II*, privately published

Oliphant, Steve
5255 Alott Ave., Van Nuys, 91401; 818-789-2339
Specializing in phonographs

Pardini, Dick
3107 N. El Dorado St., Stockton, 95204; 209-466-5550
Specializing in California Perfume Company items: buyer & information center

Shrader Antiques
Shrader, Fred & Lila
2025 Highway 199, Crescent City, 95531; 707-458-3525
Specializing in railroad, steamship & other transportation memorabilia; Shelley & select Americana

The Glass House
Smith, Wm. H.
Box 65, 143 Main St., Madison, 95653
Specializing in Historical glass

Tobin Fraley Studios
295 4th St., Oakland, 94607; 415-654-3031

Shirley Vickers Antiques
Vickers, Shirley
Box 3428, San Diego, 92103; 619-296-4751
Specializing in china repair & general antiques

Canada

Rachubinski, Frank W., 'Chinaman'
12564 Aime Leonard, Montreal N., Quebec, H1G4H7; 514-676-2391
Specializing in fine decorative English & Continental antique porcelains, both selling & buying

Thuro, Catherine M.V.
Specializing in kerosene lamps & lighting

Connecticut

Bondhus, Sandra V.
Box 203, Watertown, 06795; 203-274-1064
Author of *Quimper: A French Folk Art Faience*
Specializing in Quimper Pottery

Mechanical Music Center, Inc.
Edgerton, William
25 Kings Highway N., Box 88, Darien, 06820; 203-655-9510
Specializing in mechanical musical instruments, illustrated catalogs

Florida

Coburn's Antiques & Things
Coburn, Tony & Linda
22405 S. Dixie Highway, Miami, 33170

Cocaholics
deCourtivron, Gael
4811 Remington Dr., Sarasota, 33580; 813-351-1560
Specializing in Coca-Cola memorabilia

Saturday Matinee
Donnelly, Ron
Box 7047, Panama City Beach, 32407
Specializing in Big Little books, movie posters, antique advertising

Hudson, Hardy
340 Feather Place, Longwood, 32779
Specializing in Majolica, American art pottery

Line Jewels
Linscott, Len
3557 Nicklaus Dr., Titusville, 32780
Specializing in glass insulators

McNerney, Kathryn
502 Kettering Way, Orange Park, 32073
Author Collector Books on Blue & White, primitives, tools

Georgia

Geode Ltd.
Glenn, Walter
3393 Peachtree Rd., Atlanta, 30326; 404-261-9346
Specializing in contemporary jewelry & Frankart

Godwin Antiques
Godwin, Belle
205 Hilderbrand Dr., Atlanta, 30328
Specializing in Majolica, Chinese export porcelain, Staffordshire figures, decorative accessories—mostly Continental

Illinois

Briggerman's Antiques
Briggerman, Lawrence
1309 E. St., Charleston, 61920; 217-345-2543
Specializing in china, glass, pottery

Brinkley Interiors & Galleries
Brinkley, Wm. J., Owner
401 S. Washington Ave., McLeansboro, 62859
Specializing in Meissen, Dresden, European porcelains

Broom, Jim
Box 65, Effingham, 62401
Specializing in opalescent pattern glassware

Carley, Tod
VP - Int. Society of Antique Scale Collectors
407 Kingston Terrace, Deerfield, 60015
Specializing in scales

Danis, John
2929 Sunnyside Dr. B327, Rockford, 61111; 815-877-6098
Specializing in R. Lalique

Hospice House Antiques
Durham, William; Galaway, William
9633 Beaver Valley Rd., Belvidere, 61008; 815-547-5128
Specializing in Tea Leaf ironstone & white ironstone

Griffith, Woody
4107 White Ash Rd., Crystal Lake, 60014; 815-459-7808
Specializing in Jewel-T, Noritake, Hall

The Old Chenoa Co.
Grinnell, Millicent H.
Rt. 24; 815-945-5621
Specializing in Flow Blue china

Grist, Everett
734 12th St., Charleston, 61920
Specializing in marbles

B&B Antiques
Hall, Doris & Burdell
210 W. Sassafras Dr., Morton, 61550
Authors of *Morton's Potteries: 99 Years.*
Specializing in Morton pottery, American dinnerware, early American pattern glass, historical items, small primitives

Haussmann, Richard A.
Past President, Aurora Historical Society
Aurora, 60506

Hilst, Randy
1221 Florence #4, Pekin, 61554; 309-346-2710
Specializing in old fishing tackle

Hoffmann, Pat & Don, Sr.
1291 N. Elmwood Dr., Aurora, 60506; 312-859-3435
Authors of *Why Not Warwick; China Collectors Guide*
Specializing in Warwick china

Dee's China Shop
Hooks, Dee
Box 142, Lawrenceville, 62439
Specializing in R.S. Prussia, Royal Bayreuth, Haviland, other fine china

Larry's Antiques
Lafary, Larry & Jane
2316 N. Knoxville Ave., Peoria, 61604; 309-686-0100
Specializing in tools, advertising and pottery

Long, Dee
112 S. Center, Lacon, 61540
Specializing in reamers

Yester-Daze, The;
Pekin, 61554
Specializing in pottery & Depression Glass

Indiana

Bond's Antiques & Collectables
Bond, Helen
7012 Hawks Hill Rd., Indianapolis, 46236; 317-823-4685
General line, antiques

Mary Jane Antiques
Burton, Mary Jane
105 W. 91st St., Indianapolis; 848-9439
Specializing in porcelain, glass, jewelry

Van's Old Fashion Shop
Collins, Vanice
6252 E. Southport Rd., Indianapolis; 317-783-2004
Specializing in glassware, vintage clothes, jewelry

Beth's Antique
Conrad, Beth
Box 654, Monticello; 219-583-5133
Specializing in cut glass, art glass, fine china

Edwards, Bill
423 N. Main, Rushville, 46173
Author Collector Books on carnival glass

Hoosier Peddler
Harris, Dave
5400 S. Webster St., Kokomo, 46902; 317-453-6172
Specializing in advertising, toys

Ted's Treasures
Haun, Ted
2426 N. 700 East, Kokomo, 46901; 317-628-3640
Specializing in American dinnerware, ceramic arts

Longest, David K.
Box 2183, Clarksville, 47131-2183
Author Collector Books *Character Toys & Collectibles*. Specializing in Disneyana, comic character toys, early children's toys (1900 to 1950), encourages questions & correspondence

Mary's Antiques
Indianapolis; 317-862-4609

Miller, Susan
1103 Waynetown Rd., Crawfordsville, 47933
Tea Leaf, Autumn Leaf, author of book on Trolls

Prince, Irwin & Eileen
Indianapolis, 46260; 317-255-1913
Specializing in sealing wax seals

Roush, J.L.
739 W. 5th St., Marion, 46953; 317-662-6126
Specializing in art glass, fine china, art pottery, arts & crafts

Scowden, Virgil
303 Lincoln, Williamsport, 47993; 317-762-3408
Antiques musueum, general line, tours

Mary Spoerle Antiques
Spoerle, Mary
1100 N. Eleanor; 317-241-0362

Stapp, Denny
Rt. 3, Box 111, Georgetown, 47122
Specializing in knives, straight razors

Marnette Antiques
Stofft, Marvin & Jeanette
Tell City, 47586; 812-547-5707
Specializing in Ohio art pottery, cut glass, R.S. Prussia - buy & sell

Iowa

Addy, Geneva D.
Winterset, 50273; 515-462-3027

Botts, Rick
2545 S.E. 60th Court, Des Moines, 50317-5099
Publisher -- Jukebox Collectors Newsletter
Collector of Wurlitzer jukeboxes, sales of jukebox books, service manuals, etc.

De Pelikaan Antieks
Jaarsma, Ralph
627 Franklin St., Pella, 50219
Specializing in Dutch antiques

Larson's Antiques
Larson, Gaylord & Betty
RR #2, Fort Dodge, 50501; 515-573-3557
Specializing in American art pottery

Main Street Antiques
110 W. Main St., Box 340, West Branch, 52358
Specializing in folk art, country Americana, the unusual

Nichols Art Pottery
Nichols, Harold J.
632 Agg Ave., Ames, 50010; 515-292-9167
Specializing in American art pottery, Roseville, Weller

Williams, Don
Ottumwa, 52501
Specializing in art glass

Kansas

Robison, Joleen A.
502 Lindley Dr., Lawrence, 66044
Collector Books author on advertising dolls

Tinsley's Antiques
Tinsley, Rosella
105 15th St., Osawatomie, 66064
Specializing in primitives, kitchen, farm, graniteware, textiles, miscellaneous

Kentucky

American Crown Antiques
Louisville, 40200

Florence, Gene
Box 7186H, Lexington, 40522
Author Collector Books on Depression Glass, Occupied Japan

The Occupied Japan Club
c/o Sissie Jackson
4908 Old Heady Rd,, Louisville, 40299

Johnson, Wes
1725 Dixie Hwy., Box 10247, Louisville, 40210
Specializing in Cracker Jack: toys, point of sale, packages, etc.; Checkers Confection, Schoenhut toys

Willis, Roy M. - Ceramic Decanters
Box 428, Lebanon Jct., 40150; 502-833-2827 after 6 p.m. EST
Specializing in Wild Turkey, Ski Country, McCormick, Lionstone, Hoffman, Old Bardstown, Old Commonwealth, others

Louisiana

Bettinger, Lewis; Jr.
2229 Centenary Blvd., Shreveport; 318-222-2020
Specializing in American art pottery

Maine

Hathaway's Antiques
Hathaway, John
Upper Main St., Bryant Pond, 04219; 207-665-2124
Specializing in fruit jars -- mail order a specialty

Schneider's Antiques
Schneider, Marianne
Box 310, 130 Water St., Hallowell, 04347; 207-662-0002
Specializing in fine toys, banks, child-related items

Maryland

Geppi's Comic World, Inc. (contact Bob Cook)
7019/20 Security Blvd., Baltimore, 21207; (or) 1718 Belmont Ave. Bay G, Baltimore 21207
Specializing in comic books, original art, & related items

Greenberg, Bruce C.
7543 Main St., Sykesville, 21784
Specializing in toy trains; author

Humphrey, George C.
4392 Prince George Ave., Beltsville, 20705; 301-937-7899
Specializing in John Rogers groups

Massachusetts

Adams, Charles & Barbara
Middleboro, 02346; 617-947-7277
Specializing in Bennington (brown only)

Carver, Sally S.
179 South St., Chestnut Hill, 02167
Author of *The American Postcard Guide to Tuck*; columnist for *Hobbies; Collector's News; Postcard Collector; Antique Trader Price Guide*
Specializing in all better quality antique pre-1930 postcards

Paul Longo Americana
Longo, Paul J.
Box 490, Chatham Rd., South Orleans, Cape Cod, 02662; 617-255-5482
Specializing in political pins, ribbons, banners, autographs, old stocks & bonds, baseball memorabilia

That's Interesting
O'Shea, Pat & Laurie
Box 4968, Holyoke, 01040
Specializing in Sebastians

Rudisill's Alt Print Haus
Rudisill, John & Barbara
3 Lakewood, Medfield, 02052; 617-359-2261
Specializing in Currier & Ives

Toke, Bob; Wilson, Roger
41 Park Dr. Penthouse, Boston, 02215
Specializing in S.E.G., decorated Marblehead, Grueby, W.J. Walley, Merrimac, Hampshire

Michigan

Daly, Robert L.
Box 3236, Flint, 48502
Collector of early American bottles & flasks, specializing in bitters bottles & historical whiskey flasks

Haas, Barbara & Norman
264 Clizbe Rd., Quincy, 49082; 517-639-8537
Specializing in American art pottery

The Limited, Ltd.
Heetderks, Carl
2508 68th Ave. #97, Zeeland, 49464
Specializing in old mark Hummels

Modern Times
Lopez, Andrew
Box 1294, Jackson, 49204; 517-782-9910
Specializing in pottery

McCain, Mollie Helen
400-J Peppertree Circle, Jackson, 49203
Author of *The Collector's Encyclopedia of Pattern Glass*
Specializing in pattern glass

Nedry, Boyd W.
728 Buth Dr., Comstock Park, 49321; 616-784-1513
Specializing in traps & trap-related items

Newbound, Betty
4567 Chadsworth, Union Lake, 48085
Author Collector Books on Blue Ridge Dinnerware
Specializing in collectible china & glass

Oswald, Bob & Bernie
5596 Ridge Dr., Reading, 49274; 517-283-2763
General line

Grandma's Antiques
Robinson, Lucille
RR #2, Camden; 517-368-5822
Specializing in china, glass, primitives

Stebbins, Gwendolyn L.
7167 Kessling, Davison, 48423
Specializing in Handel lamps, glassware & related items, figural cookie jars

R.F. Willis Gallery
Willis, Robert F.
Grand Rapids; 616-456-8400
Specializing in Orientalia, antique jewelry, textiles, Oriental rugs

Minnesota

Anderson, James
Box 12704, New Brighton, 55112; 612-484-3198
Specializing in old fishing lures & reels, also tackle catalogs, posters, calendars

St. Elmos - I.O.F.A.
Marcheschi, Cork
2418 Stevens Ave. S., Minneapolis, 55404
Specializing in neon lighting of all types & Deco period lighting, advanced Art Deco

Missouri

Whetstone Antiques
Beth, Ed; & Dillon, Dennis
Box 26, Williamsburg, 63388; 314-254-3597 or 3162
General line

Kansas City Trade Winds
Bosworth, Dick & Wauneta
73073 N.W. 75th St., Kansas City, 64152
Specializing in Fenton glass, American art pottery, Parrish prints

Antique Corner
Dodds, Paul & Rosemary
West Plains; 417-256-2193
General antiques

Silver Flute Antiques
Dodds, Rebecca
Box 4955, Springfield, 65808
Specializing in jewelry, silver collectibles

Miller, John D.
RR 2, Box 127A, DeSoto, 63020; 314-586-6914
Specializing in pottery, glassware, antiques, collectibles

Old World Antiques
1812 W. 45th St., Kansas City, 64111
Specializing in Sabino, furniture, clocks, jewelry, 18th & 19th century paintings, chandeliers, decoratives

The Ozark Peddler
203 N. 3rd St., Ozark; 417-485-3442
Specializing in country store, advertising items, Blue & White stoneware, country furniture

Potters Wheel Antiques
RR 2, Box 76, Mt. Vernon, 65712; 417-466-3396
Specializing in cookie jars, pottery

Country Side Antiques
Roberts, Brenda
Rt. 2, Marshall, 65340
Specializing in Hull pottery & general line
Author Collector Books on Hull Pottery

Smith, Pat
Independence
Author Collector Books doll book series

D&R Farm Antiques
Wiesehan, Doug
RR 3, Box 202, St. Charles, 63301
Specializing in salesman's samples & patent models, antique toys, farm toys, metal farm signs

Incurable Collectors
Wilson, Beverly
Box 301, Diamond, 64840
Woollard, D.D., Jr.
11614 Old St. Charles Rd., Bridgeton, 63044
Specializing in World's Fair & Exposition memorabilia

New Hampshire

The Antiquarian Old Book Store
1070 Lafayette Rd., Portsmouth, 03801; 603-436-7280
New Hampshire's largest used/rare book store
Specializing in erotica, illustrated books, magazines

Marden, Richard G.
Box 524, Elm Street, Wolfeboro, 03894; 603-569-3209

New Jersey

Bilane, John E.
2065 Morris Ave., Apt. 109, Union, 07083
Specializing in antique glass cup plates

Etter, Roberta
Box 22, Oradell, 07649; 201-261-5467
Specializing in fine antique photographica: cameras, images, stereo views & viewing devices, related ephemera; $3.00 for sample catalog

Full House
Hochman, Gene
29 Hampton Terrace, Livingston, 07039; 201-992-0084
Mail auctions; specializing in antique playing cards, gambling memorabilia

Rago, David
Box 3592, Station E, Trenton, 08629; 609-585-2546
Specializing in Arts & Crafts, American art pottery

Rosen, Barbara
6 Shoshone Trail, Wayne, 07470
Specializing in figural bottle openers

Spellman, Richard W.
610 Monticello Dr., Brick Township, 08723
Specializing in newspapers

Steinfeld, Lois & Milt
633 Westfield Ave, Box 457, Westfield, 07091
Specializing in collectible glass & china, Victorian silverplate & other small collectibles

Warns, Peter
59 Ross Ave., Emerson, 07630
Specializing in antique cash registers

New Mexico

Jantiques
Berryman, Jan
203 Country Rd, Hobbs, 88240; 505-392-3301
Specializing in American made dinnerware

New York

Tools of Distinction
Calison, Jim
Walden; 914-778-5058
Specializing in antique & collectible tools

Doyle Auctioneers & Appraisers
Doyle, Robert A.
98 Main St., Fishkill, 12524; 914-896-9492
Specializing in liquidations of specialized collections through illustrated catalog-backed auctions

Fehner's Antiques
2611 Ave. S., Brooklyn, 11229
SASE for lists: jewelry, glass, European china, books, porcelain, pottery

Fer-Duc Antiques
Ferrara, Joseph; & Leduc, Gerard
Box 1303, Newburgh, 12550 Specializing in American art pottery (Ohr, Rookwood, Zanesville), 19th & 20th century American paintings

F.T.S. Inc.
Fox, Ron
416 Throop St., North Babylon, 11704;
516-669-7232
Specializing in steins; Auctions with illustrated catalogs & video tapes

Elan
Greenberg, Jeff
9949 Shore Rd. #103, Brooklyn, 11209;
Specializing in 20th century decorative arts, art glass, designer furniture, lighting & objects 1900-1960

Juliana, Chuck
304 Straub Rd., Rochester, 14626;
716-227-2260
Specializing in Rookwood

Susan P. Meisel Objet D'Art Gallery
Meisel, Louis K. & Susan P.
141 Prince St., New York City, 10012
Specializing in Clarice Cliff, Bugatti furniture, 20th century decorative arts

Owens' Collectables
Owens, Lowell
12 Bonnie Ave., New Hartford, 13413
Specializing in beer advertising

Yellow Barn Antiques & Collectibles
Pappin, Marge
532 Hinsdale Rd., Camillus, 13031;
315-487-5349
Specializing in old & new glass, furniture

Mood Indigo
Petipas, Diane
172 Prince St., New York, 10012;
212-925-7591
Specializing in Fiesta, Hall, Art Deco

Ruth & Dale Van Kuren Antiques
Van Kuren, Ruth
5990 Goodrich Rd., Clarence Center, 14032;
716-741-2606
Specializing in Buffalo pottery, general line

Van Patten, Joan F.
Box 102, Rexford, 12148
Author Collector Books on Nippon & Noritake

Ohio

Adams, Betty
419-886-3926
Specializing in Ohio pottery

Barbara Jean Antiques
Toledo; 419-476-2681
Specializing in glassware, jewelry, furniture

Barnett's Antiques
Barnett, Nadine
419-352-5194
Shows & mail order or appointment, specializing in china & glass

Bettinger, Lewis & Alice
Canton, 44708; 216-478-5475
Specializing in American art pottery

Golden Apple Antiques
Blair, Betty
403 Chillicothe St., Jackson, 45640;
614-286-4817
Specializing in art pottery, general line

Bumbera's Antiques
Bumbera, Robert Glenn
400 W. 3rd St., Port Clinton, 43452;
419-734-2901
Specializing in Art Deco, decoys, general line

Town & Country Antiques
Clark, Joe R. & Wilma
7770 Rodebaugh Rd., Reynoldsburg, 43068;
614-863-2637
Specializing in clocks & watches

Cousino, Carol
5414-302nd St., Toledo, 43611; 419-726-4513
Specializing in antique jewelry

Red Barn Antiques
De Luca, Mary A.
5510 W. Lakeshore Dr., Port Clinton, 43452;
635-2045
General line

Wayside Antiques
Ferguson, Maxine
2290 E. Pike, Zanesville, 43701
General line, furniture, dolls, pottery, glass

Forsythe, Ruth A.
Box 327, Galena, 43021
Author of *Made in Czechoslovakia*

Garen, David R.
308 Melody Lane, Defiance, 43512;
419-784-2816

Phone-Tiques
Guenin, Tom
Box 454, Chardon, 44024
Specializing in antique telephones & antique telephone restoration

Shinn House of Antiques
Heffelfinger, Don & Carol
419-289-1201
Specializing in art glass, hand painted china, vintage clothing, general line

Hothem House
Hothem, Lar
Box 458, Lancaster, 43130
Specializing in books for collectors

Lustre Pitcher Antiques
Kao, Fern
Box 312, Bowling Green, 43402; 419-352-5928
Specializing in Shelly China, small antiques

Kara-Tiques—Antiques & Collectibles
Kimple, Joan
419-726-5290
Appointment & shows only
Specializing in Wedgwood, glassware, collectibles

Kitchen, Lorrie; & Tucker, Dan
Toledo, 43612; 419-478-3815
Specializing in depression era glass, Hall china, Fiesta, Blue Ridge, Shawnee

Kline, Mr. & Mrs. Jerry & Gerry
604 Orchard View Dr., Maumee, 43537;
419-893-1226
Specializing in collecting Torquay pottery; coordinators of Torquay Pottery Collectors' Society

The Hitching Post
McDaniel, Doris
7467 SR 88, Ravenna, 44266; 296-3686
Specializing in Heisey, Cambridge, general line

Messenger, Patty
Bowling Green, 43402

Wooden Squirrel Antiques
Moore, Carolyn
445 N. Prospect, Bowling Green, 43402;
419-352-7879
Specializing in primitives, yellowware, graniteware

National Cambridge Collectors Inc.
Box 416, Cambridge, 43725
Specializing in Cambridge glass

Osborne, Ruth
Box 85, Higginsport, 45131; 513-375-6605
Specializing in vintage clothing, lamps

The Pottery Place
Powell, Betty
8111 Olentangy River Rd., Worthington, 43085; 614-885-1962
Specializing in American art pottery, Deco

Rees, Debbie & Bill
631 Dryden Rd., Zanesville, 43701;
614-454-2788
Buying & selling: Watt, Blue & White stoneware, Steiff, cookie jars, Roseville pottery

Rouppas, William
Box 822, Toledo, 43601
Specializing in early fishing items, old medical & dental

Stagecoach Antique Mall
Rt. 40½ mile west of I-70, Norwich Exit 16, 7527 E. Pike, Norwich, 43767

Market Square Antiques
Strehle, Ed & Joyce
212 Market St., Portsmouth, 45662;
614-354-4796
Specializing in pottery, furniture, lamps, general line antiques

C&M Antiques
Van Aman, Mildred E.
254 Newark Rd., Mt. Vernon, 43050;
614-392-7708
Specializing in fine glass & china

Walker, Bunny
Box 502, Bucyrus, 44820; 419-562-8355
Specializing in dolls, teddy bears, cookie jars, art pottery

Whitmyer, Margaret & Kenn
Box 30806, Gahanna, 43230
Author Collector Books on children's dishes
Specializing in depression era collectibles

Susan-Tiques
Willhauck, Colleen
4349 Burnham Ave., Toledo, 43612;
419-476-5921
Specializing in glassware & jewelry

Wood, Mildred
419-726-3161
Shows & appointments only

Willow House Antiques
Wunderle, Cheryl & Steve
Columbus
General line

Young, Mary
1040 Greenridge Dr., Kettering 45429
Author Collector Books *Collector's Guide to Paper Dolls.*

Oklahoma

Bess, Phyllis & Tom
Authors of *Frankoma Treasures*
14535 E. 13th St., Tulsa, 74108; 918-437-7776
Specializing in Frankoma pottery

Willis, Ron L.
2110 Fox Ave., Moore, 73160
Specializing in militaria

Oregon

The Sterling Shop
Box 595, Silverton, 97381; 503-873-6315
Specializing in silver

Pennsylvania

Artiques
Archer, Dick & Ellie
Box 152, Yardley, 19067
Specializing in Victorian silverplate: figurals, fancy holloware & collectibles

Atkinson, Phil & Karol
903 Apache Trail, Mercer, 16137;
412-475-2490
Specializing in antique advertising & country store collectibles

Cohen, Bea
Box 825, Easton, 18044-0825; 215-252-1098
Specializing in spatterware, Gaudy Dutch, mocha, chalkware, Dedham, spongeware, Canton

DLK Collectables & Nostalgia
2778 Richland St., Johnstown, 15904
Specializing in animated clocks & watches, space toys, pre-prohibition breweriana

Krause, Gail
994 Jefferson Ave., Washington, 15301
Author book on Duncan Glass

The Kelly Collection
Kelly, Jim & Kathy
1621 Princess Ave., Pittsburgh, 15216;
412-561-3379
Buying Phoenix glass & glass company catalogs; selling Depression glass, American pottery & china, & small antiques

Maier, Clarence & Betty
Mail order: The Burmese Cruet
Box 432, Montgomeryville, 18936;
215-855-5388
Specializing in Victorian art glass

Rhode Island

Louise's Collectibles
Dumont, Louise
591 Old Main St., Coventry, 02816;
401-828-2799
Specializing in cookie jars, pottery: Hull, Gonder, Abingdon, Shawnee, W McCoy, Black Americana

Leaward Antiques
Box 3181, Newport, 02840
Buy, sell, appraise American art pottery

South Carolina

Yesterday's Girl
LaVigne, Eloise & Roy
1080 Morrison Dr., Charleston, 29403;
803-577-3541
Specializing in antique & vintage clothing, jewelry, accessories & related items

Texas

Shellac Shack
Docks, L.R. 'Les'
Box 32924, San Antonio, 78216;
512-492-6021
Author of *American Premium Record Guide*
Specializing in vintage records

Gaston, Mary Frank
Box 342, Bryan, 77806
Author Collector Books on china & metals

Southeastern Antiques & Appraisers
Sayers, R.J.
Box 246, Andrews, 79714
Specializing in Boy Scout collectibles, English furniture, 30 years experience

Smith, Allan
1806 Shields Dr., Sherman, 75090; 214-893-3626
Specializing in advertising, especially Coke, Pepsi, RC, Dr. Pepper; western stars' items, tin windup toys, Red Goose shoes

Utah

Anderson, Tim
Box 461, Provo, 84603; 801-374-1888
Specializing in autographs: buys single items or collections - historical, movie stars, Mormons, sports figures, etc.

Distinctive Documents
Anderson, Warren R.
Box 1475, Orem, 84057; 801-373-6790
Old stock certificates & bonds, western documents & books, financial ephemera, autographs, maps, prints

Vermont

Barry, Kit
86 High St., Brattleboro, 05301
Author of *The Advertising Trade Card*
Specializing in advertising trade cards & ephemera in general

Virginia

Burton, Phyllis Mills
9620 Morley Rd., Midlothian, 23113
Specializes in Blue Bird china

Friend, Terry
Rt 4, Galax, 42333; 703-236-9027 after 9:30 p.m. EST
Specializing in coffee mills

Lechner, Mildred & Ralph
Box 554, Mechanicsville, 23111
Author Collector Books on sale shakers.
Specializing in art and pattern glass salt shakers, circa 1870-1940

Washington

Antonation, Linda
Box 1551, Bellevue, 98009; 206-822-0678
Specializing in Black Americana, quarterly catalogs of items for sale

Harry & Marje Hunsaker Antiques
Box 685, White Salmon, 98672
Specializing in Irish Belleek, old Indian baskets & beadwork, Majolica

Washington, DC

Durham, Ken & Jackie
By appointment
909 26 St. N.W., 20037; 202-338-1342
Specializing in countertop arcade machines, trade stimulators, & vending machines

Courtney Gallery
Epstein, Louella
2500 Calvert St. N.W., 20008; 202-387-8818
Member of International Appraisers Assoc. & Netsuke Kenkyukai Club

West Virginia

Baker, Michael; Clark, Angelana
Box 826, Moundsville, 26041
Specializing in Fostoria glass

Wisconsin

Bruggink, LeRoy F.
313 Ramaker Ave., Cedar Grove, 53013
Specializing in Tea Leaf ironstone, kerosene lamps

Cowan, Robert & Deloris
Box 843, Appleton, 54912; 414-734-0847
Specializing in Cowan pottery

Fortney, Daniel
Suite 713 Chalet at the River, 823 N. 2nd St., Milwaukee, 53203
Specializing in china & glass

Rice, Ferill J.
302 Pheasant Run, Kaukauna, 54130
Specializing in Fenton art glass

Lejon Antiques
Thompson, John O.
3013 Irene Dr., Eau Claire, 54701; 715-832-3618
Specializing in Staffordshire, Leeds, Sunderland, American primitives

Photos on the following pages have been reproduced by the kind permission of Sotheby Parke Bernet, Inc., from auction catalogues copyright 1985: 24, 26, 28, 29, 32, 92, 109, 116, 131, 135, 136, 145, 164, 170, 191, 193, 194, 197, 199, 202, 217, 218, 226, 232, 240, 245, 255, 267, 299, 308, 340, 342, 369, 380, 382, 384, 387, 388, 425, 433, 434, 498, 500, 552, 575, 583, 588.

INDEX

Books on Antiques and Collectibles

Most of the following books are available from your local book seller or antique dealer, or on loan from your public library. If you are unable to locate certain titles in your area you may order by mail from COLLECTOR BOOKS, P.O. Box 3009, Paducah, KY 42001. Add $1.00 for postage for the first book ordered and $.65 for each additional book. Include item number, title and price when ordering. Allow 14 to 21 days for delivery. All books are well illustrated and contain current values.

Books On Glass and Pottery

1444	Coll. Ency of Depression Glass, 7th Ed., Florence	$19.95
1542	Depression Glass Pocket Guide, 4th Ed., Florence	$9.95
1443	Kitchen Glassware of the Depression, 2nd Ed., Florence	$19.95
1368	Standard Ency. of Carnival Glass, Edwards	$24.95
1365	World of Salt Shakers, Lechner	$9.95
1396	Elegant Glassware of the Depression, 2nd, Florence	$19.95
1379	Coll. Ency. of Glass Candlesticks, Archer	$19.95
1443	Children's Glass Dishes, China & Furniture, Lechler	$17.95
1627	Children's Glass Dishes, China & Furniture, 2nd	$19.95
1435	Children's Dishes, Whitmyer	$9.95
1438	Oil Lamps II, Thuro	$19.95
1311	Coll. Ency. of R.S. Prussia, Gaston	$24.95
1033	Coll. Ency. of Weller Pottery, Huxford	$24.95
1034	Coll. Ency. of Roseville Pottery, Huxford	$19.95
1035	Coll. Ency. of Roseville Pottery II	$19.95
1039	Coll. Ency. of Nippon Porcelain, Van Patten	$19.95
1350	Coll. Ency. of Nippon Porcelain II	$19.95
1665	Coll. Ency. of Nippon Porcelain III	$24.95
1358	Coll. Ency. of McCoy Pottery, Huxford	$19.95
1276	Coll. Ency. of Hull Pottery, Roberts	$19.95
1210	Coll. Ency. of Limoges Porcelain, Gaston	$19.95
1512	Coll. Ency. of Fiesta, Fifth Ed., Huxford	$9.95
1312	Coll. Blue & White Stoneware, McNerney	$9.95
1373	Coll. Ency. of Am. Dinnerware, Cunningham	$24.95
1425	Cookie Jars, Westfall	$9.95
1440	Red Wing Stoneware, DePasquale	$9.95
1432	Blue Willow, Gaston	$9.95
1439	Coll. Ency. of Flow Blue China, Gaston	$19.95
1447	Coll. Ency. of Noritake, Van Patten	$19.95
1538	Hall China, Whitmyer	$9.95
1633	Russel Wright Dinnerware, Kerr	$9.95
1664	Coll. Ency. of Heisey Glass, 1925-1938, Bredehoft	$24.95
1669	Majolica Pottery, 2nd Ed., Katz-Marks	$9.95

Books On Dolls

1066	Coll. Ency. of Half-Dolls, Marion & Werner	$29.95
1067	Madame Alexander Coll. Dolls, Smith	$19.95
1068	Madame Alexander Coll. Dolls II	$19.95
1069	Price Guide only for Madame Alexander	$3.95
1076	Antique Coll. Dolls, Smith	$17.95
1077	Antique Coll. Dolls II, Smith	$17.95
1079	Modern Coll. Dolls, Smith	$17.95
1080	Modern Coll. Dolls II, Smith	$17.95
1081	Modern Coll. Dolls III, Smith	$17.95
1082	Modern Coll. Dolls IV, Smith	$17.95
1516	Modern Coll. Dolls V, Smith	$19.95
1375	Effanbee Dolls, Smith	$19.95
1089	Patricia Smith's Doll Values	$9.95
1090	Patricia Smith's Doll Values, Series II	$9.95
1446	Patricia Smith's Doll Values, Series III	$9.95
1430	World of Barbie Dolls, Manos	$9.95
1630	Vogue Ginny Dolls, Smith	$19.95
1631	German Dolls, Smith	$9.95
1635	Horsman Dolls, 1950-1970, Gibbs	$19.95
1648	World of Alexander-Kins, Smith	$19.95

Other Collectibles

1212	Marketplace Guide to Oak Furniture	$17.95
1283	Marketplace Guide to Victorian Furniture	$17.95
1279	Victorian Furniture, McNerney	$8.95
1118	Antique Oak Furniture, Hill	$7.95
1124	Primitives, Our American Heritage, McNerney	$8.95
1437	Coll. Guide to Country Furniture, Raycraft	$8.95
1457	American Oak Furniture, McNerney	$9.95
1278	Art Nouveau & Art Deco Jewelry, Baker	$9.95
1128	Bottle Pricing Guide, 3rd Ed., Cleveland	$7.95
1427	American Beer Can Enecy., 1983-1984 Ed.	$9.95
1154	Antique Tools, Our American Heritage	$8.95
1539	Modern Guns, Rev. 5th Ed., Quertermous	$11.95
1277	Silverplated Flatware, Hagan	$14.95
1181	100 Years of Collectible Jewelry, Baker	$9.95
1374	Antique Purses, Holiner	$9.95
1377	Elvis Collectibles, Cranor	$12.95
1524	Collectible & Antique Marbles, Grist	$9.95
1514	Character Toys & Collectibles, Longest	$19.95
1513	Teddy Bears & Steiff Animals, Mandel	$9.95
1442	Creative & Collectible Miniatures, Baker	$9.95
1426	Indian Arrowheads & Projectile Points, Hothem	$7.95
1441	Collectors Guide to Post Cards, Wood	$9.95
1436	Antique Iron, McNerney	$7.95
1465	Haviland Collectibles & Art Objects	$19.95
1537	Coll. Guide to Country Baskets, Raycraft	$9.95
1540	Modern Toys, 1930-1980, Baker	$19.95
1623	Country Stoneware & Pottery, Raycraft	$9.95
1624	Antique Brass, Gaston	$9.95
1628	Antique Copper, Gaston	$9.95
1638	Flea Market Trader, 5th Ed.	$8.95
1662	American Pictorial Quilts, Mosey	$19.95
1666	The Book of Country, Raycraft	$19.95
1668	Flint Blades & Proj. Points of N.A. Indian, Tully	$24.95
1670	Red Wing Collectibles, DePasquale	$9.95